The Grove Dictionary of

American Music

Volume Four

The Grove Dictionary of

American Music

Second Edition

Volume Four

Haas, Jonathan – Kyser, Kay

Edited by

Charles Hiroshi Garrett

OXFORD
UNIVERSITY PRESS

OXFORD
UNIVERSITY PRESS

Oxford University Press is a department of the
University of Oxford. It furthers the University's objective
of excellence in research, scholarship, and education
by publishing worldwide.

Oxford   New York
Auckland   Cape Town   Dar es Salaam   Hong Kong   Karachi
Kuala Lumpur   Madrid   Melbourne   Mexico City   Nairobi
New Delhi   Shanghai   Taipei   Toronto

With offices in
Argentina   Austria   Brazil   Chile   Czech   Republic   France   Greece
Guatemala   Hungary   Italy   Japan   Poland   Portugal   Singapore
South Korea   Switzerland   Thailand   Turkey   Ukraine   Vietnam

Oxford is a registered trade mark of Oxford University Press
in the UK and certain other countries.

Published in the United States of America by
Oxford University Press
198 Madison Avenue, New York, NY 10016

The first edition was published as *The New Grove Dictionary of American Music*
Edited by H. Wiley Hitchcock and Stanley Sadie (Macmillan, 1986)

The Library of Congress Cataloging-in-Publication Data

The New Grove Dictionary of American Music
The Grove dictionary of American music / edited by Charles Hiroshi Garrett. -Second edition.
volumes ; cm.
Revision of *The New Grove dictionary of American music*, originally published in 1986.
Includes bibliographical references.
ISBN 978-0-19-531428-1 (print set : alk. paper)—978-0-19-999059-7 (v.1 : alk. paper)—978-0-19-999060-3
(v.2 : alk. paper)—978-0-19-999061-0 (v.3 : alk. paper)—978-0-19-999062-7 (v.4 : alk. paper)—978-0-19-999063-4
(v.5 : alk. paper)—978-0-19-999064-1 (v.6 : alk. paper)—978-0-19-999065-8 (v.7 : alk. paper)—978-0-19-999066-5
(v.8 : alk. paper)—ISBN (invalid) 978-0-19-973925-7 (e-book)   1. Music—United States—Encyclopedias.
2. Music—United States—Bio-bibliography.   I. Garrett, Charles Hiroshi, 1966–   II. Title.
ML101.U6N48 2013
780.973'03—dc23   2012002055

1 3 5 7 9 8 6 4 2

Printed in the United States of America
on acid-free paper

Contents

General Abbreviations

A	alto, contralto [voice]		ASOL	American Symphony Orchestra League
a	alto [instrument]		Assn	Association
AA	Associate of the Arts		attrib(s).	attribution(s), attributed to; ascription(s), as-cribed to
AAS	Associates in Arts and Sciences			
AB	Alberta; Bachelor of Arts		Aug	August
ABC	American Broadcasting Company; Australian Broadcasting Commission		aut.	autumn
			AZ	Arizona
Abt.	Abteilung [section]		aztl	*azione teatrale*
ACA	American Composers Alliance			
acc.	accompaniment, accompanied by		B	bass [voice], bassus
accdn	accordion		B	Brainard catalogue [Tartini], Benton catalogue [Pleyel]
addl	additional			
addn(s)	addition(s)		b	bass [instrument]
ad lib	ad libitum		*b*	born
AFM	American Federation of Musicians		BA	Bachelor of Arts
AFRS	Armed Forces Radio Service		bal(s)	ballad opera(s)
AFR&TS	Armed Forces Radio & Television Service		bap.	baptized
aft(s)	afterpiece(s)		Bar	baritone [voice]
Ag	Agnus Dei		bar	baritone [instrument]
AGMA	American Guild of Musical Artists		B-Bar	bass-baritone
AIDS	Acquired Immune Deficiency Syndrome		BBC	British Broadcasting Corporation
AK	Alaska		BC	British Columbia
AL	Alabama		bc	basso continuo
all(s)	alleluia(s)		BCE	before Common Era [BC]
AM	Master of Arts		Bd.	Band [volume]
a.m.	ante meridiem [before noon]		BEd	Bachelor of Education
AMC	American Music Center		Beds.	Bedfordshire
Amer.	American		Berks.	Berkshire
amp	amplified		Berwicks.	Berwickshire
AMS	American Musicological Society		BFA	Bachelor of Fine Arts
Anh.	Anhang [appendix]		BFE	British Forum for Ethnomusicology
anon.	anonymous(ly)		bk(s)	book(s)
ant(s)	antiphon(s)		BLitt	Bachelor of Letters/Literature
appx(s)	appendix(es)		blq(s)	burlesque(s)
AR	Arkansas		blt(s)	burletta(s)
arr(s).	arrangement(s), arranged by/for		BM	Bachelor of Music
ARSC	Association for Recorded Sound Collections		BME,	
a-s	all-sung		BMEd	Bachelor of Music Education
AS	American Samoa		BMI	Broadcast Music Inc.
ASCAP	American Society of Composers, Authors and Publishers		BMus	Bachelor of Music

bn	bassoon
BRD	Federal Republic of Germany (Bundesrepublik Deutschland [West Germany])
Bros.	Brothers
BRTN	Belgische Radio en Televisie Nederlands
Bs	Benedictus
BS, BSc	Bachelor of Science
BSM	Bachelor of Sacred Music
Bte	Benedicite
Bucks.	Buckinghamshire
Bulg.	Bulgarian
bur.	buried
BVM	Blessed Virgin Mary
BWV	Bach-Werke-Verzeichnis [Schmieder, catalogue of J.S. Bach's works]
C	contralto
c	circa [about]
c	cent(s)
CA	California
Cambs.	Cambridgeshire
Can.	Canadian
CanD	Cantate Domino
cant(s).	cantata(s)
cap.	capacity
carn.	Carnival
cb	contrabass [instrument]
CBC	Canadian Broadcasting Corporation
CBE	Commander of the Order of the British Empire
CBS	Columbia Broadcasting System
CBSO	City of Birmingham Symphony Orchestra
CCNY	City College of New York
CD(s)	compact disc(s)
CE	Common Era [AD]
CeBeDeM	Centre Belge de Documentation Musicale
cel	celesta
CEMA	Council for the Encouragement of Music and the Arts
cf	confer [compare]
c.f.	cantus firmus
CFE	Composers Facsimile Edition
CG	Covent Garden, London
CH	Companion of Honour
chap(s).	chapter(s)
chbr	chamber
Chin.	Chinese
chit	chitarrone
cho- reog(s).	choreography, choreographer(s), choreographed by
Cie	Compagnie
cimb	cimbalom
cl	clarinet
clvd	clavichord
cm	centimetre(s); *comédie en musique*
CM	Northern Mariana Islands (US Trust Territory of the Pacific)
cmda	*comédie mêlée d'ariettes*
CNRS	Centre National de la Recherche Scientifique
c/o	care of
CO	Colorado
Co.	Company; County
Cod.	Codex
coll.	collected by
collab.	in collaboration with
colln	collection
col(s).	column(s)
com	*componimento*
comm(s)	communion(s)
comp.	compiler, compiled by
comp(s).	composer(s), composed (by)
conc(s).	concerto(s)
cond(s).	conductor(s), conducted by
cont	continuo
contrib(s).	contribution(s)
Corp.	Corporation
c.p.s.	cycles per second
cptr(s)	computer(s)
Cr	Credo, Creed
CRI	Composers Recordings, Inc.
CSc	Candidate of Historical Sciences
CT	Connecticut
Ct	Contratenor, countertenor
CUNY	City University of New York
CVO	Commander of the Royal Victorian Order
Cz.	Czech
D	Deutsch catalogue [Schubert]; Dounias catalogue [Tartini]
d.	denarius, denarii [penny, pence]
d	died
DA	Doctor of Arts
Dan.	Danish
db	double bass
DBE	Dame Commander of the Order of the British Empire
dbn	double bassoon
DC	District of Columbia
Dc	Discantus
DD	Doctor of Divinity
DDR	German Democratic Republic (Deutsche Demokratische Republik [East Germany])
DE	Delaware
Dec	December
ded(s).	dedication(s), dedicated to
DeM	Deus misereatur
Den.	Denmark
Dept(s)	Department(s)
Derbys.	Derbyshire
DFA	Doctor of Fine Arts
dg	*dramma giocoso*
dir(s).	director(s), directed by
diss.	dissertation
dl	*drame lyrique*
DLitt	Doctor of Letters/Literature
DM	Doctor of Music
dm	*dramma per musica*
DMA	Doctor of Musical Arts
DME, DMEd	Doctor of Musical Education

DMus	Doctor of Music
DMusEd	Doctor of Music Education
DPhil	Doctor of Philosophy
Dr	Doctor
DSc	Doctor of Science/Historical Sciences
DSM	Doctor of Sacred Music
Dut.	Dutch
E.	East, Eastern
EBU	European Broadcasting Union
EdD	Doctor of Education
edn(s)	edition(s)
ed(s).	editor(s), edited (by)
EdS	Education Specialist
EEC	European Economic Community
e.g.	exempli gratia [for example]
el-ac	electro-acoustic
elec	electric, electronic
EMI	Electrical and Musical Industries
Eng.	English
eng hn	english horn
ENO	English National Opera
ens	ensemble
ENSA	Entertainments National Service Association
EP	extended-play (record)
esp.	especially
etc.	et cetera
EU	European Union
ex., exx.	example, examples
f	forte
facs.	facsimile(s)
fa(s)	farsa(s)
fasc(s).	fascicle(s)
Feb	February
ff	fortissimo
f, ff	following page, following pages
f., ff.	folio, folios
fff	fortississimo
fig(s).	figure(s) [illustration(s)]
FL	Florida
fl	flute
fl	floruit [he/she flourished]
Flem.	Flemish
fp	fortepiano [dynamic marking]
Fr.	French
frag(s).	fragment(s)
FRAM	Fellow of the Royal Academy of Music, London
FRCM	Fellow of the Royal College of Music, London
FRCO	Fellow of the Royal College of Organists, London
FRS	Fellow of the Royal Society, London
fs	full score
GA	Georgia
Gael.	Gaelic
GEDOK	Gemeinschaft Deutscher Organisationen von Künstlerinnen und Kunstfreundinnen

GEMA	Gesellschaft für Musikalische Aufführungs- und Mechanische Vervielfaltingungsrechte
Ger.	German
Gk.	Greek
Gl	Gloria
Glam.	Glamorgan
glock	glockenspiel
Glos.	Gloucestershire
GmbH,	Gesellschaft mit Beschränkter Haftung [limited-liability company]
grad(s)	gradual(s)
GSM	Guildhall School of Music, London (to 1934)
GSMD	Guildhall School of Music and Drama, London (1935–)
GU	Guam
gui	guitar
H	Hoboken catalogue [Haydn]; Helm catalogue [C.P.E. Bach]
Hants.	Hampshire
Heb.	Hebrew
Herts.	Hertfordshire
HI	Hawaii
hmn	harmonium
HMS	His/Her Majesty's Ship
HMV	His Master's Voice
hn	horn
Hon.	Honorary; Honourable
hp	harp
hpd	harpsichord
HRH	His/Her Royal Highness
Hung.	Hungarian
Hunts.	Huntingdonshire
Hz	Hertz [c.p.s.]
IA	Iowa
IAML	International Association of Music Libraries
IAWM	International Alliance for Women in Music
ibid.	ibidem [in the same place]
ICTM	International Council for Traditional Music
ID	Idaho
i.e.	id est [that is]
IFMC	International Folk Music Council
IL	Illinois
ILWC	International League of Women Composers
IMC	International Music Council
IMS	International Musicological Society
IN	Indiana
Inc.	Incorporated
inc.	incomplete
incid	incidental
incl.	includes, including
inst(s)	instrument(s), instrumental
intl	international
int(s)	intermezzo(s), introit(s)
IPEM	Instituut voor Psychoakoestiek en Elektronische Muziek, Ghent
IRCAM	Institut de Recherche et Coordination Acoustique/Musique

ISAM	Institute for Studies in American Music
ISCM	International Society for Contemporary Music
ISDN	Integrated Services Digital Network
ISM	Incorporated Society of Musicians
ISME	International Society for Music Education
It.	Italian
Jan	January
Jap.	Japanese
Jb	Jahrbuch [yearbook]
JD	Doctor of Jurisprudence
Jg.	Jahrgang [year of publication/volume]
Jr.	Junior
jr	junior
Jub	Jubilate
K	Kirkpatrick catalogue [D. Scarlatti]; Köchel catalogue [Mozart: no. after '/' is from 6th edn; also Fux]
kbd	keyboard
KBE	Knight Commander of the Order of the British Empire
KCVO	Knight Commander of the Royal Victorian Order
kg	kilogram(s)
Kgl	Königlich(e, er, es) [Royal]
kHz	kilohertz [1000 c.p.s.]
km	kilometre(s)
KS	Kansas
KY	Kentucky
Ky	Kyrie
L.	no. of song in R.W. Linker: *A Bibliography of Old French Lyrics* (University, MS, 1979)
L	Longo catalogue [A. Scarlatti]
LA	Louisiana
Lanarks.	Lanarkshire
Lancs.	Lancashire
Lat.	Latin
Leics.	Leicestershire
LH	left hand
lib(s)	libretto(s)
Lincs.	Lincolnshire
Lith.	Lithuanian
lit(s)	litany (litanies)
LittD	Doctor of Letters/Literature
LLB	Bachelor of Laws
LLD	Doctor of Laws
loc. cit.	loco citato [in the place cited]
LP	long-playing record
LPO	London Philharmonic Orchestra
LSO	London Symphony Orchestra
Ltd	Limited
Ltée	Limitée
m	metre(s)
MA	Massachusetts; Master of Arts

Mag	Magnificat
MALS	Master of Arts in Library Sciences
mand	mandolin
mar	marimba
MAT	Master of Arts and Teaching
MB	Bachelor of Music; Manitoba
MBE	Member of the Order of the British Empire
MD	Maryland
ME	Maine
MEd	Master of Education
mel	*melodramma, mélodrame*
mels	*melodramma serio*
melss	*melodramma semiserio*
Met	Metropolitan Opera House, New York
Mez	mezzo-soprano
mf	mezzo-forte
MFA	Master of Fine Arts
MGM	Metro-Goldwyn-Mayer
MHz	megahertz [megacycles]
MI	Michigan
mic	microphone
Middx	Middlesex
MIDI	Musical Instrument Digital Interface
MIT	Massachusetts Institute of Technology
MLA	Music Library Association
MLitt	Master of Letters/Literature
Mlle, Mlles	Mademoiselle, Mesdemoiselles
MM	Master of Music
M.M.	Metronome Maelzel
mm	millimetre(s)
MMA	Master of Musical Arts
MME, MMEd	Master of Music Education
Mme, Mmes	Madame, Mesdames
M, MM.	Monsieur, Messieurs
MMT	Master of Music in Teaching
MMus	Master of Music
MN	Minnesota
MO	Missouri
mod	modulator
Mon.	Monmouthshire
movt(s)	movement(s)
mp	mezzo-piano
MPhil	Master of Philosophy
MP(s)	Member(s) of Parliament
Mr	Mister
Mrs	Mistress; Messieurs
MS	Master of Science(s); Mississippi
MSc	Master of Science(s)
MSLS	Master of Science in Library and Information Science
MSM	Master of Sacred Music
MS(S)	manuscript(s)
MT	Montana
Mt	Mount
MTNA	Music Teachers National Association
mt(s)	music-theatre piece(s)
MusB, MusBac	Bachelor of Music

muscm(s)	musical comedy (comedies)
MusD,	
MusDoc	Doctor of Music
musl(s)	musical(s)
MusM	Master of Music
N.	North, Northern
nar(s)	narrator(s)
NB	New Brunswick
NBC	National Broadcasting Company
NC	North Carolina
ND	North Dakota
n.d.	no date of publication
NDR	Norddeutscher Rundfunk
NE	Nebraska
NEA	National Endowment for the Arts
NEH	National Endowment for the Humanities
NET	National Educational Television
NF	Newfoundland and Labrador
NH	New Hampshire
NHK	Nippon Hōsō Kyōkai [Japanese broadcasting system]
NJ	New Jersey
NM	New Mexico
n(n).	footnote(s)
Nor.	Norwegian
Northants.	Northamptonshire
no(s).	number(s)
Notts.	Nottinghamshire
Nov	November
n.p.	no place of publication
NPR	National Public Radio
n.pub.	no publisher
nr	near
NRK	Norsk Rikskringkasting [Norwegian broadcasting system]
NS	Nova Scotia
NSW	New South Wales
NT	North West Territories
Nunc	Nunc dimittis
NV	Nevada
NY	New York [State]
NZ	New Zealand
ob	*opera buffa*; oboe
obbl	obbligato
OBE	Officer of the Order of the British Empire
obl	*opéra-ballet*
OC	Opéra-Comique, Paris [the company]
oc	*opéra comique* [genre]
Oct	October
off(s)	offertory (offertories)
OH	Ohio
OK	Oklahoma
OM	Order of Merit
ON	Ontario
op. cit.	opere citato [in the work cited]
op., opp.	opus, opera [plural of opus]

op(s)	opera(s)
opt.	optional
OR	Oregon
orat(s)	oratorio(s)
orch	orchestra(tion), orchestral
orchd	orchestrated (by)
org	organ
orig.	original(ly)
ORTF	Office de Radiodiffusion-Télévision Française
os	*opera seria*
oss	*opera semiseria*
OUP	Oxford University Press
ov(s).	overture(s)
Oxon.	Oxfordshire
P	Pincherle catalogue [Vivaldi]
p.	*pars*
p	piano [dynamic marking]
PA	Pennsylvania
p.a.	per annum [annually]
pan(s)	pantomime(s)
PBS	Public Broadcasting System
PC	no. of chanson in A. Pillet and H. Carstens: *Bibliographie der Troubadours* (Halle, 1933)
PE	Prince Edward Island
perc	percussion
perf(s).	performance(s), performed (by)
pf	piano [instrument]
pfmr(s)	performer(s)
PhB	Bachelor of Philosophy
PhD	Doctor of Philosophy
PhDEd	Doctor of Philosophy in Education
pic	piccolo
pl(s).	plate(s); plural
p.m.	post meridiem [after noon]
PO	Philharmonic Orchestra
Pol.	Polish
pop.	population
Port.	Portuguese
posth.	posthumous(ly)
POW(s)	prisoner(s) of war
pp	pianissimo
p., pp.	page, pages
ppp	pianississimo
PQ	Province of Quebec
PR	Puerto Rico
pr.	printed
prep pf	prepared piano
PRO	Public Record Office, London
prol(s)	prologue(s)
PRS	Performing Right Society
pseud(s).	pseudonym(s)
Ps(s)	Psalm(s)
ps(s)	psalm(s)
ptbk(s)	partbook(s)
pt(s)	part(s)
pubd	published
pubn(s)	publication(s)
PWM	Polskie Wydawnictwo Muzyczne

QC	Queen's Counsel
qnt(s)	quintet(s)
qt(s)	quartet(s)
R	[in signature] editorial revision
R	photographic reprint [edn of score or early printed source]
R.	no. of chanson in G. Raynaud, *Bibliographie des chansonniers français des XIIIe et XIVe siècles* (Paris, 1884)
R	Ryom catalogue [Vivaldi]
r	recto
R	response
RAAF	Royal Australian Air Force
RAF	Royal Air Force
RAI	Radio Audizioni Italiane
RAM	Royal Academy of Music, London
RCA	Radio Corporation of America
RCM	Royal College of Music, London
rec	recorder
rec.	recorded [in discographic context]
recit(s)	recitative(s)
red(s).	reduction(s), reduced for
reorchd	reorchestrated (by)
repr.	reprinted
re(s)	response(s) [type of piece]
resp(s)	respond(s)
Rev.	Reverend
rev(s).	revision(s); revised (by/for)
RH	right hand
RI	Rhode Island
RIAS	Radio im Amerikanischen Sektor
RIdIM	Répertoire International d'Iconographie Musicale
RILM	Répertoire International de Littérature Musicale
RIPM	Répertoire International de la Presse Musicale
RISM	Répertoire International des Sources Musicales
RKO	Radio-Keith-Orpheum
RMCM	Royal Manchester College of Music
rms	root mean square
RNCM	Royal Northern College of Music, Manchester
RO	Radio Orchestra
Rom.	Romanian
r.p.m.	revolutions per minute
RPO	Royal Philharmonic Orchestra
RSFSR	Russian Soviet Federated Socialist Republic
RSO	Radio Symphony Orchestra
RTÉ	Radio Telefís Éireann
RTF	Radiodiffusion-Télévision Française
Rt Hon.	Right Honourable
RTVB	Radio-Télévision Belge de la Communauté Française
Russ.	Russian
RV	Ryom catalogue [Vivaldi]
S	San, Santa, Santo, São [Saint]; soprano [voice]
S	sound recording

S.	South, Southern
s	soprano [instrument]
s.	solidus, solidi [shilling, shillings]
SACEM	Société d'Auteurs, Compositeurs et Editeurs de Musique
San	Sanctus
sax	saxophone
SC	South Carolina
SD	South Dakota
sd	*scherzo drammatico*
SDR	Süddeutscher Rundfunk
SEM	Society for Ethnomusicology
Sept	September
seq(s)	sequence(s)
ser.	series
Serb.	Serbian
ser(s)	serenata(s)
sf, *sfz*	sforzando, sforzato
SFSR	Soviet Federated Socialist Republic
sing.	singular
SJ	Societas Jesu [Society of Jesus]
SK	Saskatchewan
SMT	Society for Music Theory
SO	Symphony Orchestra
SOCAN	Society of Composers, Authors and Music Publishers of Canada
Sp.	Spanish
spkr(s)	speaker(s)
Spl	Singspiel
SPNM	Society for the Promotion of New Music
spr.	spring
sq	square
Sr.	Senior
sr	senior
SS	Saints (It., Sp.); Santissima, Santissimo [Most Holy]
SS	steamship
SSR	Soviet Socialist Republic
Staffs.	Staffordshire
STB	Bachelor of Sacred Theology
Ste	Sainte
str	string(s)
St(s)	Saint(s)/Holy, Sankt, Sint, Szent
sum.	summer
SUNY	State University of New York
Sup	superius
suppl(s).	supplement(s), supplementary
Swed.	Swedish
SWF	Südwestfunk
sym(s).	symphony (symphonies), symphonic
synth	synthesizer, synthesized
T	tenor [voice]
t	tenor [instrument]
tc	*tragicommedia*
td(s)	*tonadilla(s)*
TeD	Te Deum
ThM	Master of Theology
timp	timpani
tm	*tragédie en musique*

TN	Tennessee		VHF	very high frequency
tpt	trumpet		VI	Virgin Islands
Tr	treble [voice]		vib	vibraphone
trad.	traditional		viz	videlicet [namely]
trans.	translation, translated by		vle	violone
transcr(s).	transcription(s), transcribed by/for		vn	violin
trbn	trombone		vol(s).	volume(s)
tr(s)	tract(s); treble [instrument]		vs	vocal score, piano-vocal score
TV	television		VT	Vermont
TWV	Menke catalogue [Telemann]		v, vv	voice, voices
TX	Texas		v., vv.	verse, verses
U.	University		W.	West, Western
UCLA	University of California at Los Angeles		WA	Washington [State]
UHF	ultra-high frequency		Warwicks.	Warwickshire
UK	United Kingdom of Great Britain and Northern Ireland		WDR	Westdeutscher Rundfunk
			WI	Wisconsin
Ukr.	Ukrainian		Wilts.	Wiltshire
unacc.	unaccompanied		wint.	winter
unattrib.	unattributed		WNO	Welsh National Opera
UNESCO	United Nations Educational, Scientific and Cultural Organization		WOO	Werke ohne Opuszahl
			Worcs.	Worcestershire
UNICEF	United Nations International Children's Emergency Fund		WPA	Works Progress Administration
			WQ	Wotquenne catalogue [C.P.E. Bach]
unorchd	unorchestrated		WV	West Virginia
unperf.	unperformed		ww	woodwind
unpubd	unpublished		WY	Wyoming
UP	University Press			
US	United States [adjective]			
USA	United States of America		xyl	xylophone
USO	United Service Organisations			
USSR	Union of Soviet Socialist Republics			
UT	Utah		YMCA	Young Men's Christian Association
			Yorks.	Yorkshire
			YT	Yukon Territory
v	verso		YWCA	Young Women's Christian Association
v.	versus		YYS	(Zhongguo yishu yanjiuyuan) Yinyue yanjiusuo and variants [Music Research Institute (of the Chinese Academy of Arts)]
V	versicle			
VA	Virginia			
va	viola			
vc	cello			
vcle(s)	versicle(s)		Z	Zimmermann catalogue [Purcell]
VEB	Volkseigener Betrieb [people's own industry]		zargc	*zarzuela género chico*
Ven	Venite		zar(s)	zarzuela(s)

Discographical Abbreviations

The abbreviations used in this dictionary for the names of record labels are listed below. In recording lists the label on which each recording was originally issued is cited, and no attempt is made here to indicate the affiliations of labels to companies. The names of a number of record labels consist of series of capital letters; although these may be abbreviated forms of company names they are not generally listed here as they constitute the full names of the labels concerned.

AAFS	Archive of American Folksong (Library of Congress)	Ev.	Everest	OK	Okeh
		EW	East Wind	Omni.	Omnisound
		Ewd	Eastworld	PAct	Pathé Actuelle
A&M Hor.	A&M Horizon	Fan.	Fantasy	PAlt	Palo Alto
ABC-Para.	ABC-Paramount	FaD	Famous Door	Para.	Paramount
AH	Artists House	FD	Flying Dutchman	Parl.	Parlophone
Ala.	Aladdin	FDisk	Flying Disk	Per.	Perfect
AM	American Music	Fel.	Felsted	Phi.	Philips
Amer.	America	Fon.	Fontana	Phon.	Phontastic
AN	Arista Novus	Fre.	Freedom	PJ	Pacific Jazz
Ant.	Antilles	FW	Folkways	PL	Pablo Live
Ari.	Arista	Gal.	Galaxy	Pol.	Polydor
Asy.	Asylum	Gen.	Gennett	Prog.	Progressive
Atl.	Atlantic	GrM	Groove Merchant	Prst.	Prestige
Aut.	Autograph	Gram.	Gramavision	PT	Pablo Today
Bak.	Bakton	GTJ	Good Time Jazz	PW	Paddle Wheel
Ban.	Banner	HA	Hat Art	Qual.	Qualiton
Bay.	Baystate	Hal.	Halcyon	Reg.	Regent
BB	Black and Blue	Har.	Harmony	Rep.	Reprise
Bb	Bluebird	Harl.	Harlequin	Rev.	Revelation
Beth.	Bethlehem	HH	Hat Hut	Riv.	Riverside
BH	Bee Hive	Hick.	Hickory	Roul.	Roulette
BL	Black Lion	Hor.	Horizon	RR	Red Records
BN	Blue Note	IC	Inner City	RT	Real Time
Bruns.	Brunswick	IH	Indian House	Sack.	Sackville
BS	Black Saint	ImA	Improvising Artists	Sat.	Saturn
BStar	Blue Star	Imp.	Impulse!	SE	Strata-East
Cad.	Cadence	Imper.	Imperial	Sig.	Signature
Can.	Canyon	IndN	India Navigation	Slnd	Southland
Cand.	Candid	Isl.	Island	SN	Soul Note
Cap.	Capitol	JAM	Jazz America Marketing	SolS	Solid State
Car.	Caroline	Jlgy	Jazzology	Son.	Sonora
Cas.	Casablanca	Jlnd	Jazzland	Spot.	Spotlite
Cat.	Catalyst	Jub.	Jubilee	Ste.	Steeplechase
Cen.	Century	Jwl	Jewell	Sto.	Storyville
Chi.	Chiaroscurro	Jzt.	Jazztone	Sup.	Supraphon
Cir.	Circle	Key.	Keynote	Tak.	Takoma
CJ	Classical Jazz	Kt.	Keytone	Tei.	Teichiku
Cob.	Cobblestone	Lib.	Liberty	Tel.	Telefunken
Col.	Columbia	Lml.	Limelight	The.	Theresa
Com.	Commodore	Lon.	London	Tim.	Timeless
Conc.	Concord	Mdsv.	Moodsville	TL	Time-Life
Cont.	Contemporary	Mel.	Melodiya	Tran.	Transition
Contl	Continental	Mer.	Mercury	20C	20th Century
Cot.	Cotillion	Met.	Metronome	20CF	20th CenturyFox
CP	Charlie Parker	Metro.	Metrojazz	UA	United Artists
CW	Creative World	MJR	Master Jazz Recordings	Upt.	Uptown
Del.	Delmark	Mlst.	Milestone	Van.	Vanguard
Dis.	Discovery	Mlt.	Melotone	Var.	Variety
Dra.	Dragon	Moers	Moers Music	Vars.	Varsity
EB	Electric Bird	MonE	Monmouth-Evergreen	Vic.	Victor
Elec.	Electrola	Mstr.	Mainstream	VJ	Vee-Jay
Elek.	Elektra	Musi.	Musicraft	Voc.	Vocalion
Elek. Mus.	Elektra Musician	Nat.	National	WB	Warner Bros.
EmA	EmArcy	NewJ	New Jazz	WP	World Pacific
ES	Elite Special	Norg.	Norgan	Xan.	Xanad
Eso.	Esoteric	NW	New World		

Bibliographical Abbreviations

The bibliographical abbreviations used in this dictionary are listed below. Full bibliographical information is not normally supplied for nonmusical sources (national biographical dictionaries) or if it may be found elsewhere in this dictionary (in the lists following the articles ("Dictionaries and encyclopedias," "Histories," and "Periodicals") or in *Grove Music Online* (in the lists that form parts of the articles "Dictionaries & encyclopedias of music," "Editions, historical," and "Periodicals"). The typographical conventions used throughout the dictionary are followed here: broadly, italic type is used for periodicals and reference works, and roman type for anthologies, series, etc.

19CM	*19th Century Music*
20CM	*20th Century Music* [retitled in 2000; see 21CM]
21CM	*21th Century Music* [see also 20CM]
ACAB	*American Composers Alliance Bulletin*
AcM	*Acta musicological*
AM	*American Music*
AMw	*Archiv für Musikwissenschaft*
AMZ	*Allgemeine musikalische Zeitung*
Anderson 2	E.R. Anderson: *Contemporary American Composers: a Biographical Dictionary* (Boston, 2/1982)
AnM	*Anuario musical*
AnMc	*Analecta musicological*
AnnM	*Annales musicoloques*
ANB	*American National Biography Online*
ARJS	*Annual Review of Jazz Studies*
ARSCJ	*Association for Recorded Sound Collections Journal*
AsM	*Asian Music*
Baker 5[–9]	*Baker's Biographical Dictionary of Musicians, 1958–2001*
Baker 20thC.	*Baker's Biographical Dictionary of 20th-Century Musicians*
BAMS	*Bulletin of the American Musicological Society*
BMw	*Beiträge zur Musikwissenschaft*
BPiM	*The Black Perspective in Music*
BWQ	*Brass and Woodwind Quarterly*
Campbell GC	M. Campbell: *The Great Cellists*
Campbell GV	M. Campbell: *The Great Violinists*
CBY	*Current Biography Yearbook*
CC	B. Morton and P. Collins, eds.: *Contemporary Composers*
CMc	*Current Musicology*
CMR	*Contemporary Music Review*
CohenE	A.I. Cohen: *International Encyclopedia of Women Composers*
COJ	*Cambridge Opera Journal*
DAB	*Dictionary of American Biography* (New York, 1928–37, suppls., 1944–81)
DB	*Down Beat*
DBL	*Dansk biografisk leksikon* (Copenhagen, 1887–1905)
DBL2	*Dansk biografisk leksikon* (Copenhagen, 2/1933–45)

DBL3	*Dansk biografisk leksikon* (Copenhagen, 3/1979–84)
DCB	*Dictionary of Canadian Biography*
Dichter-ShapiroSM	H. Dichter and E. Shapiro: *Early American Sheet Music*
DBY	*Down Beat Yearbook*
DNB	*Dictionary of National Biography* (Oxford, 1885–1901, suppls., 1901–96)
EDM	*Das Erbe deutscher Musik* (Berlin and elsewhere)
EitnerQ	R. Eitner: *Biographisch-bibliographisches Quellen-Lexikon*
EMC1	*Encyclopedia of Music in Canada* (Toronto, 1981)
EMC2	*Encyclopedia of Music in Canada* (Toronto, 2/1992)
ES	F. D'Amico: *Enciclopedia dello spettacolo*
EthM	*Ethnomusicology*
EthM News letter	*Ethno[-]musicology Newsletter*
EwenD	D. Ewen: *American Composers: a Biographical Dictionary* (New York, 1982)
FAM	*Fontes artis musicae*
Feather-Gitler BEJ	L. Feather and I. Gitler: The Biographical *Encyclopedia of Jazz* (New York, and Oxford, England, 1999)
FétisB	F.-J. Fétis: *Biographie universelle des musiciens*
FisherMP	W.A. Fisher: *One Hundred and Fifty Years of Music Publishing in the United States* (Boston, 1933)
FriedwaldB	W. Friedwald: *A Biographical Guide to the Great Jazz and Pop Singers* (New York, 2010)
GEWM	*The Garland Encyclopedia of World Music*
GMO	*Grove Music Online*
Grove 1[–5]	G. Grove, ed.: *A Dictionary of Music and Musicians*
Grove6	*The New Grove Dictionary of Music and Musicians*
Grove7	S. Sadie and J. Tyrell, eds.: *The New Grove Dictionary of Music and Musicians* (2/London, 2001)
GroveA	*The New Grove Dictionary of American Music*
GroveAS	W.S. Pratt, ed.: *Grove's Dictionary of Music and Musicians: American Supplement* (New York, 1920, 2/1928, many reprs.)

GroveI	*The New Grove Dictionary of Musical Instruments*
GroveJ	*The New Grove Dictionary of Jazz*
Grove J2	*The New Grove Dictionary of Jazz (2/2002)*
GroveO	*The New Grove Dictionary of Opera*
GroveW	*The New Grove Dictionary of Women Composers*
GSJ	*The Galpin Society Journal*
GV	R. Celletti: *Le grandi voci: dizionario critico-biografico dei cantanti*
HDM4	*Harvard Dictionary, 4th ed.*
HiFi	*High Fidelity*
HiFi/ MusAm	*High Fidelity/Musical America*
HMYB	*Hinrichsen's Musical Year Book*
IAJRCJ	*International Association of Jazz Record Collectors Journal*
IMSCR	*International Musicological Society Congress Report*
IRASM	*International Review of the Aesthetics and Sociology of Music*
ISAMm	*Institute for Studies in American Music* (New York)
ITO	*In Theory Only*
JAMIS	*Journal of the America Musical Instrument Society*
JAMS	*Journal of the American Musicological Society*
JazzM	*Jazz Monthly*
JbMP	*Jahrbuch der Musikbibliothek Peters*
JEFDSS	*The Journal of the English Folk Dance and Song Society*
JEMF	*J[ohn] E[dwards] M[emorial] F[oundation] Quarterly*
JFSS	*The Journal of the Folk-song Society*
JIFMC	*Journal of the International Folk Music Council*
JJI	*Jazz Journal International*
Jm	*Jazz magazine* (Paris)
JMT	*Journal of Music Theory*
JRBM	*Journal of Renaissance and Baroque Music*
JRME	*Journal of Research in Music Education*
JSAM	*Journal of the Society for American Music*
JT	*Jazz Times*
JVdGSA	*Journal of the Viola da Gamba Society of America*
KdG	*Komponisten der Gegenwart*, ed. H.-W. Heister and W.-W. Sparrer
LAMR	*Latin American Music Review*
LaMusicaD	G.M. Gatti and A. Basso: *La musica: dizionario*
MB	*Musica britannica* (London)
MEJ	*Music Educators Journal*
MF	*Die Musickforschung*
MGG	F. Blume, ed.: *Die Musik in Geschichte und Gegenwart*
MJ	*Music Journal*
ML	*Music and Letters*
MM	*Modern Music*
MMR	*The Monthly Musical Record*
MO	*Musical Opinion*
MQ	*The Musical Quarterly*
MR	*The Music Review*

MSD	*Musicological Studies and Documents* (Rome)
MT	*The Musical Times*
MTNAP	*Music Teachers National Association: Proceedings*
MusAm	*Musical America*
NAW	E.T. James, J.W. James, and P.S. Boyer, eds.: *Notable American Women* (Cambridge, MA, 1971; suppl., 1980)
NOHM	*The New Oxford History of Music*, ed. E. Wellesz, J.A. Westrup, and G. Abraham (London, 1954–)
NRMI	*Nuova rivista musicale italiana*
NZM	*Neue Zeitschrift für Musik* [retitled 1920, see ZfM]
ÖMz	*Österreichische Musikzeitschrift*
ON	*Opera News*
OQ	*Opera Quarterly*
PAMS	*Papers of the American Musicological Society*
PASUC	*Proceedings of the American Society of University Composers*
PMA	*Proceedings of the Musical Association* [retitled 1944, see PRMA]
PNM	*Perspectives of New Music*
PRMA	*Proceedings of the Royal Music Association* [see *PMA*]
RaM	*La rassegna musicale*
RBM	*Revue belge de musicologie*
RdM	*Revue de musicology*
ReM	*La revue musicale*
RiemannL	*Riemann Musik Lexicon*, rev. W. Gurlitt (Mainz, Germany, 12/1959–75)
RISM	*Répertoire international des sources musicales*
RN	*Renaissance News*
RRAM	*Recent Researches in American Music* (Madison, WI)
RS	*Rolling Stone*
Schuller-EJ	G. Schuller: *Early Jazz* (New York, 1968/R)
Schuller-SE	G. Schuller: *The Swing Era* (New York, 1989)
Schwarz GM	B. Schwarz: *Great Masters of the Violin*
SIMG	*Sammelbände der Internationalen Musik-Gesellschaft*
SMA	*Studies in Music*
SMz	*Schweizerische Musikzeitung/Revue musicale suisse*
SouthernB	E. Southern: *Biographical Dictionary of Afro-American and African Musicians*
Thompson	O. Thompson: *The International Cyclopedia of Music and Musicians*
VintonD	J. Vinton, ed.: *Dictionary of Contemporary Music* (New York, 1974)
VMw	*Vierteljahrsschrift für Musikwissenschaft*
Waterhouse-LangwillI	W. Waterhouse: *The New Langwill Index: a Dictionary of Musical Wind-Instrument Makers and Inventors*
YIFMC	*Yearbook of the International Folk Music Council*
ZfM	*Zeitschrift für Musik* [see NZM]
ZIMG	*Zeitschrift der Internationalen Musik-Gesellschaft*

Library Abbreviations

AAu	Ann Arbor, University of Michigan, Music Library
AB	Albany (NY), New York State Library
AKu	Akron (OH), University of Akron, Bierce Library
AtaT	Talladega (AL) Talladega College
ATS	Athens (GA), University of Georgia Libraries
ATet	Atlanta (GA), Emory University, Pitts Theology Library
ATu	Atlanta (GA), Emory University Library
AU	Aurora (NY), Wells College Library
AUS	Austin, University of Texas at Austin, The Harry Ransom Humanities Research Center
AUSm	Austin, University of Texas at Austin, Fine Arts Library
BAR	Baraboo (WI), Circus World Museum Library
BAep	Baltimore, Enoch Pratt Free Library
BAhs	Baltimore, Maryland Historical Society Library
BApi	Baltimore, Arthur Friedheim Library, Johns Hopkins University
BAu	Baltimore, Johns Hopkins University Libraries
BAue	Baltimore, Milton S. Eisenhower Library, Johns Hopkins University
BAw	Baltimore, Walters Art Gallery Library
BER	Berea (OH), Riemenschneider Bach Institute Library
BETm	Bethlehem (PA), Moravian Archives
BEm	Berkeley, University of California at Berkeley, Music Library
BL	Bloomington (IN), Indiana University Library
BLl	Bloomington (IN), Indiana University, Lilly Library
BLu	Bloomington (IN), Indiana University, Cook Music Library
BO	Boulder (CO), University of Colorado at Boulder, Music Library
BU	Buffalo (NY), Buffalo and Erie County Public Library
Ba	Boston, Athenaeum Library
Bc	Boston, New England Conservatory of Music, Harriet M. Spaulding Library
Bfa	Boston, Museum of Fine Arts
Bgm	Boston, Isabella Stewart Gardner Museum, Library
Bh	Boston, Harvard Musical Association, Library
Bhs	Boston, Massachusetts Historical Society Library
Bp	Boston, Public Library, Music Department
Bu	Boston, Boston University, Mugar Memorial Library, Department of Special Collections
CA	Cambridge (MA), Harvard University, Harvard College Library
CAe	Cambridge (MA), Harvard University, Eda Kuhn Loeb Music Library
CAh	Cambridge (MA), Harvard University, Houghton Library
CAt	Cambridge (MA), Harvard University Library, Theatre Collection
CAward	Cambridge (MA), John Milton Ward, private collection [on loan to CA]
CF	Cedar Falls (IA), University of Northern Iowa, Library
CHAhs	Charleston (SC), The South Carolina Historical Society
CHH	Chapel Hill (NC), University of North Carolina at Chapel Hill
CHua	Charlottesville (VA), University of Virginia, Alderman Library
CHum	Charlottesville (VA), University of Virginia, Music Library
CIhc	Cincinnati, Hebrew Union College Library: Jewish Institute of Religion, Klau Library
CIp	Cincinnati, Public Library
CIu	Cincinnati, University of Cincinnati College - Conservatory of Music, Music Library
CLAc	Claremont (CA), Claremont College Libraries
CLU	USA, Los Angeles, CA, University of California, Los Angeles

CLp	Cleveland, Public Library, Fine Arts Department
CLwr	Cleveland, Western Reserve University, Freiberger Library and Music House Library
COhs	Columbus (OH), Ohio Historical Society Library
COu	Columbus (OH), Ohio State University, Music Library
CP	College Park (MD), University of Maryland, McKeldin Library
CR	Cedar Rapids (IA), Iowa Masonic Library
Cn	Chicago, Newberry Library
Cp	Chicago, Chicago Public Library, Music Information Center
CtY	USA, New Haven, CT, Yale University
Cu	Chicago, University, Joseph Regenstein Library, Music Collection
Cum	Chicago, University of Chicago, Music Collection
DAVu	Davis (CA), University of California at Davis, Peter J. Shields Library
DAu	Dallas, Southern Methodist University, Music Library
DLC	USA, Washington, DC, Library of Congress
DMu	Durham (NC), Duke University Libraries
DN	Denton (TX), University of North Texas, Music Library
DO	Dover (NH), Public Library
DSI *(JOHP)*	USA, Washington, DC, Smithsonian Institution: Jazz Oral History Program
Dp	Detroit, Public Library, Main Library, Music and Performing Arts Department
E	Evanston (IL), Garrett Biblical Institute
EDu	Edwardsville (IL), Southern Illinois University
EU	Eugene (OR), University of Oregon
Eu	Evanston (IL), Northwestern University
FAy	Farmington (CT), Yale University, Lewis Walpole Library
FW	Fort Worth (TX), Southwestern Baptist Theological Seminary
G	Gainesville (FL), University of Florida Library, Music Library
GB	Gettysburg (PA), Lutheran Theological Seminary
GR	Granville (OH), Denison University Library
GRB	Greensboro (NC), University of North Carolina at Greensboro, Walter C. Jackson Library
HA	Hanover (NH), Dartmouth College, Baker Library
HG	Harrisburg (PA), Pennsylvania State Library
HO	Hopkinton (NH), New Hampshire Antiquarian Society

Hhc	Hartford (CT), Hartt College of Music Library, The University of Hartford
Hm	Hartford (CT), Case Memorial Library, Hartford Seminary Foundation [in ATet]
Hs	Hartford (CT), Connecticut State Library
Hw	Hartford (CT), Trinity College, Watkinson Library
I	Ithaca (NY), Cornell University
ICJic	USA, Chicago, IL, Jazz Institute of Chicago
ICU	USA, Chicago, IL, University of Chicago
IDt	Independence (MO), Harry S. Truman Library
IO	Iowa City (IA), University of Iowa, Rita Benton Music Library
InUAtm	USA, Bloomington, IN, Indiana University Archives of Traditional Music
K	Kent (OH), Kent State University, Music Library
KC	Kansas City (MO), University of Missouri: Kansas City, Miller Nichols Library
KCm	Kansas City (MO), Kansas City Museum, Library and Archives
KN	Knoxville (TN), University of Tennessee, Knoxville, Music Library
LAcs	Los Angeles, California State University, John F. Kennedy Memorial Library
LApiatigorsky	Los Angeles, Gregor Piatigorsky, private collection [in STEdrachman]
LAs	Los Angeles, The Arnold Schoenberg Institute Archives
LAuc	Los Angeles, University of California at Los Angeles, William Andrews Clark Memorial Library
LAum	Los Angeles, University of California at Los Angeles, Music Library
LAur	Los Angeles, University of California at Los Angeles, Special Collections Dept, University Research Library
LAusc	Los Angeles, University of Southern California, School of Music Library
LBH	Long Beach (CA), California State University
LEX	Lexington (KY), University of Kentucky, Margaret I. King Library
LNT	USA, New Orleans, LA, Tulane University [transcripts of interviews held at LNT were published on microfilm as New York Times Oral History Program: New Orleans Jazz Oral History Collection (1978–9)]
LOu	Louisville, University of Louisville, Dwight Anderson Music Library
LT	Latrobe (PA), St Vincent College Library
Lu	Lawrence (KS), University of Kansas Libraries
M	Milwaukee, Public Library, Art and Music Department
MAhs	Madison (WI), Wisconsin Historical Society

MAu	Madison (WI), University of Wisconsin
MB	Middlebury (VT), Middlebury College, Christian A. Johnson Memorial Music Library
MED	Medford (MA), Tufts University Library
MG	Montgomery (AL), Alabama State Department of Archives and History Library
MT	Morristown (NJ), National Historical Park Museum
Mc	Milwaukee, Wisconsin Conservatory of Music Library
MoKmb	Kansas City, MO, Kansas City Museum of History
MoUSt	USA, St. Louis, MO, University of Missouri
NA	Nashville (TN), Fisk University Library
NAu	Nashville (TN), Vanderbilt University Library
NBu	New Brunswick (NJ), Rutgers - The State University of New Jersey, Music Library, Mabel Smith Douglass Library
NCH (HCJA)	USA, Clinton, NY, Hamilton College: Hamilton College Jazz Archive
NEij	Newark (NJ), Rutgers - The State University of New Jersey, Rutgers Institute of Jazz Studies Library
NH	New Haven (CT), Yale University, Irving S. Gilmore Music Library
NHob	New Haven (CT), Yale University, Oral History Archive
NHub	New Haven (CT), Yale University, Beinecke Rare Book and Manuscript Library
NNC	USA, New York, NY, Columbia University
NNSc	USA, New York, NY, Schomburg Collection, New York Public Library
NNSc (HBC)	USA, New York, NY, Schomburg Collection, New York Public Library, Hatch-Billops Collection
NNSc (LAJOHP)	USA, New York, NY, Schomburg Collection, New York Public Library, Louis Armstrong Jazz Oral History Project
NO	Normal (IL), Illinois State University, Milner Library, Humanities/Fine Arts Division
NORsm	New Orleans, Louisiana State Museum Library
NORtu	New Orleans, Tulane University, Howard Tilton Memorial Library
NYamc	New York, American Music Center Library
NYbroude	New York, Broude private collection
NYcc	New York, City College Library, Music Library
NYcu	New York, Columbia University, Gabe M. Wiener Music & Arts Library
NYcub	New York, Columbia University, Rare Book and Manuscript Library of Butler Memorial Library
NYgo	New York, University, Gould Memorial Library [in NYu]
NYgr	New York, The Grolier Club Library
NYgs	New York, G. Schirmer, Inc.
NYhs	New York, New York Historical Society Library
NYhsa	New York, Hispanic Society of America, Library

NYj	New York, The Juilliard School, Lila Acheson Wallace Library
NYkallir	New York, Rudolf F. Kallir, private collection
NYlehman	New York, Robert O. Lehman, private collection [in NYpm]
NYlibin	New York, Laurence Libin, private collection
NYma	New York, Mannes College of Music, Clara Damrosch Mannes Memorial Library
NYp	New York, Public Library at Lincoln Center, Music Division
NYpl	New York, Public Library, Center for the Humanities
NYpm	New York, Pierpont Morgan Library
NYpsc	New York, New York Public Library, Schomburg Center for Research in Black Culture in Harlem
NYq	New York, Queens College of the City University, Paul Klapper Library, Music Library
NYu	New York, University Bobst Library
NYw	New York, Wildenstein Collection
NYyellin	New York, Victor Yellin, private collection
Nf	Northampton (MA), Forbes Library
NjR	USA, Newark, NJ, Rutgers, the State University of New Jersey
NjR (JOHP)	USA, Newark, NJ, Rutgers, the State University of New Jersey: Jazz Oral History Project
Nsc	Northampton (MA), Smith College, Werner Josten Library
OAm	Oakland (CA), Mills College, Margaret Prall Music Library
OB	Oberlin (OH), Oberlin College Conservatory of Music, Conservatory Library
OX	Oxford (OH), Miami University, Amos Music Library
PHci	Philadelphia, Curtis Institute of Music, Library
PHf	Philadelphia, Free Library of Philadelphia, Music Dept
PHff	Philadelphia, Free Library of Philadelphia, Edwin A. Fleisher Collection of Orchestral Music
PHgc	Philadelphia, Gratz College
PHhs	Philadelphia, Historical Society of Pennsylvania Library
PHlc	Philadelphia, Library Company of Philadelphia
PHmf	Philadelphia, Musical Fund Society [on loan to PHf]
PHphs	Philadelphia, The Presbyterian Historical Society Library [in PHlc]
PHps	Philadelphia, American Philosophical Society Library
PHu	Philadelphia, University of Pennsylvania, Van Pelt-Dietrich Library Center
PO	Poughkeepsie (NY), Vassar College, George Sherman Dickinson Music Library

PRObs	Providence (RI), Rhode Island Historical Society Library
PROu	Providence (RI), Brown University
PRV	Provo (UT), Brigham Young University
PRs	Princeton (NJ), Theological Seminary, Speer Library
PRu	Princeton (NJ), Princeton University, Firestone Memorial Library
PRw	Princeton (NJ), Westminster Choir College
Pc	Pittsburgh, Carnegie Library, Music and Art Dept
Ps	Pittsburgh, Theological Seminary, Clifford E. Barbour Library
Pu	Pittsburgh, University of Pittsburgh
Puf	Pittsburgh, University of Pittsburgh, Foster Hall Collection, Stephen Foster Memorial
R	Rochester (NY), Sibley Music Library, University of Rochester, Eastman School of Music
SA	Salem (MA), Peabody and Essex Museums, James Duncan Phillips Library
SBm	Santa Barbara (CA), Mission Santa Barbara
SFp	San Francisco, Public Library, Fine Arts Department, Music Division
SFs	San Francisco, Sutro Library
SFsc	San Francisco, San Francisco State University, Frank V. de Bellis Collection
SJb	San Jose (CA), Ira F. Brilliant Center for Beethoven Studies, San José State University
SL	St Louis, St Louis University, Pius XII Memorial Library
SLC	Salt Lake City, University of Utah Library
SLug	St Louis, Washington University, Gaylord Music Library
SM	San Marino (CA), Huntington Library
SPma	Spokane (WA), Moldenhauer Archives
SR	San Rafael (CA), American Music Research Center, Dominican College
STEdrachmann	Stevenson (MD), Mrs Jephta Drachman, private collection; Mrs P.C. Drachman, private collection
STO	Stony Brook (NY), State University of New York at Stony Brook, Frank Melville jr Memorial Library
STu	Palo Alto (CA), University, Memorial Library of Music, Department of Special Collections of the Cecil H. Green Library
SY	Syracuse (NY), University Music Library
SYkrasner	Syracuse (NY), Louis Krasner, private collection [in CAh and SY]
Su	Seattle, University of Washington, Music Library
TA	Tallahassee (FL), Florida State University, Robert Manning Strozier Library
TNF	Nashville (TN) Fisk University
TxU	Austin (TX) University of Texas
U	Urbana (IL), University of Illinois, Music Library
Uplamenac	Urbana (IL), Dragan Plamenac, private collection [in NH]
V	Villanova (PA), Villanova University, Falvey Memorial Library
WB	Wilkes-Barre (PA), Wilkes College Library
WC	Waco (TX), Baylor University, Music Library
WGc	Williamsburg (VA), College of William and Mary, Earl Gregg Swenn Library
WI	Williamstown (MA), Williams College Library
WOa	Worcester (MA), American Antiquarian Society Library
WS	Winston-Salem (NC), Moravian Music Foundation, Peter Memorial Library
Wc	Washington, DC, Library of Congress, Music Division
Wca	Washington, Cathedral Library
Wcf	Washington, Library of Congress, American Folklife Center and the Archive of Folk Culture
Wcg	Washington, General Collections, Library of Congress
Wcm	Washington, Library of Congress, Motion Picture, Broadcasting and Recorded Sound Division
Wcu	Washington, Catholic University of America, Music Library
Wdo	Washington, Dumbarton Oaks
Wgu	Washington, Georgetown University Libraries
Whu	Washington, Howard University, College of Fine Arts Library
Ws	Washington, Folger Shakespeare Library
Y	York (PA), Historical Society of York County, Library and Archives

Volume Four

Haas, Jonathan – Kyser, Kay

A Note on the Use of the Dictionary

This note is intended as a short guide to the basic procedures and organization of the dictionary. A fuller account will be found in "About the Dictionary," pp. xxi–xxiv, vol. one.

Alphabetization of headings is based on the principle that words are read continuously, ignoring spaces, hyphens, accents, parenthesized and bracketed matter, etc., up to the first punctuation mark, then again thereafter if that mark is a comma. "Mc" and "Mac" are alphabetized as "Mac," "St." as "Saint."

Cross-references are shown in small capitals, with a large capital at the beginning of the first word of the entry referred to. Thus "The UNIVERSITY OF MICHIGAN was founded in Detroit in 1817" means that the entry referred is not "University of Michigan" but "Michigan, University of."

Abbreviations used in the dictionary are listed on pp. vii–xx, in the order General (beginning on p. vii), Discographical (p. xiv), Bibliographical (p. xv), and Library (p. xvii).

Work-lists are normally arranged chronologically (within section, where divided), in order of year of composition or first publication (in the latter case dates are given in parentheses). Italicized abbreviations (such as *DLC*) stand for libraries holding sources and are explained on p. xvii.

Recording-lists are arranged chronologically (within section, where divided), typically in order of date of issue. Abbreviations standing for record labels are explained on p. xiv.

Bibliographies are arranged chronologically (within section, where divided), in order of year of first publication, and alphabetically by author within years. Abbreviations standing for periodicals and reference works are explained on p. xv.

H

Haas, Jonathan (*b* Chicago, IL, 6 Sept 1954). Timpanist. After studying at Washington University, St. Louis, and at the Juilliard School under Saul Goodman, he was nominated "Young Artist of 1982" by *Musical America.* He gave the first-ever solo timpani recital in the Carnegie Hall recital room in 1980. Haas was appointed principal timpanist with the New York Chamber SO in 1980 and the Aspen Chamber Orchestra in 1984, and became principal percussionist with the American SO in 1990. He also plays "hot jazz" timpani with his band, Johnny H. and the Prisoners of Swing; that group's self-titled album includes Duke Ellington's composition for jazz timpani, *Tympaturbably Blue.* Haas plays "rock" kettledrum with the band Clozshave, and has recorded a solo mallet book (keyboard percussion instruments) for the album *Zappa's Universe.* He has also recorded with Aerosmith, Emerson, Lake, and Palmer, Michael Bolton, and Black Sabbath. Various classical composers, including Karlheinz Stockhausen, Philip Glass, Irwin Bazelon, Marius Constant, Stephen Albert, Eric Ewazen, Thomas Hamilton, Robert Hall Lewis, Jean Piche, and Andrew Thomas, have written works for him. Haas has recorded many 20th-century works, including Sergei Prokofiev's *Peter and the Wolf,* Aaron Copland's *Three Latin American Sketches,* and George Crumb's *A Haunted Landscape.* He is director of New York University's Department of Music and Performing Arts Professions' Percussion Studies Department, and has given over 200 concert demonstrations as part of his "Drumfire" educational program. He is also the originator of the Aspen Percussion Ensemble at the Aspen Music School, which he has directed since 1974.

JAMES HOLLAND/MEGAN E. HILL

Hackett, Bobby [Robert Leo] (*b* Providence, RI, 31 Jan 1915; *d* Chatham, MA, 7 June 1976). Jazz cornetist, guitarist, and bandleader. He was originally a ukulele player, and graduated to guitar before specializing on cornet. During the early 1940s he worked briefly in Glenn Miller's orchestra playing guitar and cornet; he was a member of the Casa Loma Orchestra from 1944 to 1946 and thereafter was often the featured cornetist in groups led by Eddie Condon. He worked with Benny Goodman (1962–3), and made tours of Europe with the singer Tony Bennett (1965, 1966) and of Japan with George Wein (1971).

Hackett was a supremely melodic jazz improviser whose cornet tone was glorious in all registers. Because much of his life was spent playing in clubs with small bands he was too readily described as a Dixieland stylist; in fact, his sophisticated phrasing and subtle use of harmonies enabled him to fit into many types of jazz ensemble. He was an individualist whose inspiration came from the work of two dissimilar players, Armstrong and Beiderbecke. His skill at improvising attractive melodies is apparent on his solo in "String of Pearls," recorded with Glenn Miller in 1941.

BIBLIOGRAPHY
P. Harris: "Bouquets to the Living: All Schools Dig Bobby Hackett," *Down Beat,* xviii/3 (1951), 1
A. Napoleon: "A Conversation with Bobby Hackett," *JJ,* xxvi/1 (1973), 2
W. Balliett: "More Ingredients," *Alec Wilder and his Friends* (Boston, 1974), 67; repr. in *BalliettA (1996),* 143
S. Holzer: "Bobby Hackett: Records under other Leaders," *Record Research* (1978), nos.159–60, p.14; (1979), nos.161–2, p.10; nos.165–6, p.15 [discography]

JOHN CHILTON/R

Hackett, Charles (*b* Worcester, MA, 4 Nov 1889; *d* New York, NY, 1 Jan 1942). Tenor. On the recommendation of LILLIAN NORDICA he studied at the New England Conservatory with Arthur J. Hubbard, and later with Vincenzo Lombardi in Florence. In 1914 he made his debut in Genoa as Wilhelm Meister, which also served for his La Scala debut (1916). He appeared at the Paris Opéra as a servant in *Maria di Rohan* in 1917, returning as the Duke and Romeo in 1922. After a season in Buenos Aires (1917–18) he made his Metropolitan debut in 1919 as Almaviva; there he later sang Lindoro (*L'italiana in Algeri*), Rodolfo, Pinkerton, Romeo, and Alfredo. At Monte Carlo (1922–3) he sang Cavaradossi and Des Grieux (*Manon*). He was closely identified with the Chicago Opera (1922–35) and took part in the premiere of Charles Wakefield Cadman's *A Witch of Salem* (1926) and Hamilton Forrest's *Camille* (1930). In the same year, he appeared at Covent Garden as Almaviva, Fenton, and Romeo in Nellie Melba's farewell performance. He continued to sing until 1939. Hackett made a number of records, including duets with Maria Barrientos and Rosa Ponselle; they document a secure technique and a certain elegance, though there is also a sense of routine about them. That sense is completely dispelled by the sweep and finesse of his style in a recording of a Metropolitan Opera broadcast of Gounod's *Roméo et Juliette* from 1935.

BIBLIOGRAPHY

L.F. Holdridge: "Charles Hackett," *Record Collector*, xxii (1974–5), 173–214

RICHARD DYER, ELIZABETH FORBES/R

Hackleman, Martin (Marty) (*b* 7 Jan 1952). Horn player. Hackleman began studying horn in Houston with Caesar LaMonaca. Other teachers included Barry Tuckwell and Roland Berger. At nineteen, while at the University of Houston, he was appointed principal horn of the Calgary Philharmonic and accepted the same position two years later with the Vancouver Symphony. He was a member of THE CANADIAN BRASS from 1983 to 1986 and left the group to join the EMPIRE BRASS QUINTET in 1986. In 1989 he discontinued his association with Empire Brass and returned to his position in Vancouver. In 2000 he moved to the National Symphony Orchestra. In addition to his current position with the National Symphony, he is also a member of Summit Brass and serves as principal horn of the Washington Symphonic Brass. He has taught at the University of Maryland, Boston University, the University of British Columbia, the University of Missouri–Kansas City Conservatory, and the Chamber Music Sessions at the Banff Centre in Alberta, Canada. Hackleman can be heard on many recordings with the Vancouver Symphony, Montreal Symphony, National Symphony, Washington Symphonic Brass, Canadian Brass, Summit Brass, Tidewater Brass, and Empire Brass. He has released one solo recording, *Romanza* (2000). His publications include two etude books, *21 Characteristic Etudes for High Horn Playing* and *34 Characteristic Etudes for Low Horn Playing*, published in 1990 by the Swiss company, Editions Bim International Music Publishing.

PATRICK RICHARDS

Hackley [née Smith], **E(mma) Azalia** (*b* Murfreesboro, TN, 29 June 1867; *d* Detroit, MI, 13 Dec 1922). Soprano. She studied voice, violin and piano in 1870 in Detroit and performed with the Detroit Musical Society. In 1894 she married in Denver where she was the first African American to graduate (University of Denver, BA, 1900). She then started her career as a singer, while writing articles for *The Statesman*, including, "Influence of Music in the Negro Home and on Youth." In 1901 she moved to Philadelphia, became music director of the Episcopal Church of the Crucifixion in 1904, and founded the 100-voice People's Chorus, later called the Hackley Choral Society. In 1905 she organized recitals for talented musicians including Marian Anderson and Roland Hayes. In 1906 she studied in Paris with Jean de Reszke.

In 1908 Hackley founded a scholarship to help young African American artists to go to study in Europe. Clarence Cameron White, Nathaniel Dett, and Kemper Harreld were among the beneficiaries. In 1909 she moved to Chicago and founded the Hackley Music Publishing Company and the Vocal Normal School for underprivileged African American students. In 1911 she sang her last concert at the Chicago Orchestra Hall. The year after she self-published *A Guide in Voice Culture*, and in 1914 and 1915 she wrote about issues relevant to African American classical musicians in *The New York Age*. In 1916 she toured in the United States to lecture about being an African American musician, educator, and woman. She composed *Carola (A Serenade)* in 1918 and conducted African American choral folk songs in Tokyo and in 1920 in California. The year after, she collapsed in Oakland during a concert and retired to Detroit. She died of brain hemorrhage in 1922.

Established in 1943 at the Detroit Public Library, the E. Azalia Hackley Collection documents music, drama, dance, broadcasts, and films by African American artists. The music collection consists of over 600 pieces composed and published between 1799 and 1922.

BIBLIOGRAPHY

"Song Festivals among Negroes," *MusAm*, xxix/22 (1919), 16

M.M. Davenport: *Azalia: The Life of Madame E. Azalia Hackley* (Boston, 1947)

L.P. Brevard: *A Biography of E. Azalia Smith Hackley, 1867–1922, African-American Singer and Social Activist* (Lewiston, NY, 2001)

D.G. Nettles: *African-American Concert Singers Before 1950* (Jefferson, NC, 2003)

DOMINIQUE-RENÉ DE LERMA/VALERIA WENDEROTH

Haden, Charlie [Charles Edward] (*b* Shenandoah, IA, 6 Aug 1937). Double bass player, bandleader, and composer. His signature style as a jazz bass player—improvising harmonies to melodic lines by ear—is rooted in his role as Cowboy Charlie in his family's country-music band. He sang with the group professionally between the ages of two and 15, when a bout of polio damaged his vocal cords. An avid fan of classical music and jazz, he learned the latter on his brother's double bass by playing along with records. After high school and a stint as the house bass player for the TV show *Ozark Jubilee*, he was drawn to Los Angeles in 1956 by the then-rare jazz-inclusive music department at the Westlake College of Modern Music (chosen over a scholarship offer from Oberlin Conservatory) and by his hope of meeting his favorite pianist, Hampton Hawes. He soon became a regular on the jazz club scene, working with artists such as Hawes, Art Pepper, Paul Bley, and Dexter Gordon.

Haden is best known for his role in the saxophonist-composer Ornette Coleman's groundbreaking quartet and early recordings (1959–61). Although Coleman was an outsider to the LA scene with his raw sound, rough intonation, and disregard of the conventions followed by jazz players, the insider Haden felt drawn to those qualities. The two clicked immediately and forged their mutually intuitive style of improvising by working up renditions of Coleman's conventionally scored tunes with chord changes; these they used to provide loose guidelines for performance rather than the more formal constraints on improvisation offered by conventional lead sheets. With the trumpeter Don Cherry and the drummer Billy Higgins, Coleman's quartet ushered in the revolutionary FREE JAZZ style. Although he has worked on other projects, Haden's association with Coleman has continued through performances at occasional gigs and award ceremonies. In 1976, he formed the band Old and New Dreams with fellow former Coleman sidemen to perform primarily Coleman's compositions.

Haden worked in the late 1960s and early 1970s with other free-jazz musicians, recording with the trombonist Roswell Rudd, the saxophonist Archie Shepp, the keyboard player and harpist Alice Coltrane, and the pianist Keith Jarrett, the last of which he has had an enduring professional relationship with. In 1969 he recorded the big-band album *Liberation Music Orchestra* with the arranger Carla Bley. Its material had left-wing political themes, mostly drawn from Spanish Civil War songs and contemporary events in South Africa and South America. He subsequently recorded two more albums with Bley in 1982 and 1990. Haden has also worked on projects involving non-Western musics, notably from Mexico, Cuba, Brazil, Argentina, Scandinavia, and Portugal, and pop musicians including Rickie Lee Jones, Elvis Costello, Beck, and Ringo Starr. With the pianist Hank Jones, the guitarist Pat Metheney, and his wife and children, he has mined the black church spirituals and the white hymns and country-music roots of his own family background. From 1986 he has led a quartet based in Los Angeles, with the saxophonist Ernie Watts, the pianist Allen Broadbent, and the drummer Larance Marable, which has specialized in the film music of late 1940s Hollywood and the American songbook.

In 1982 Haden was hired by the California Institute of the Arts to launch and direct its jazz studies program. His stated emphasis there has been to cultivate the personal and spiritual core of the creative process in his students. "I tell [my students] that if they want to become a great musician," he has said, "they should strive to become…a good human being with humility and appreciation and givingness." In 1997 the Los Angeles Jazz Society named him Jazz Educator of the Year.

Haden can be seen as maintaining the tradition of such jazz bass players as Jimmy Blanton, Walter Page, and (his own favorite) Wellman Broad, for what he called their "sound of the rainforest, the wood" on the instrument. His white, country roots infused the free-jazz revolution, which was dominated by African Americans, with a musical integration that outlived its moments of exclusively black-identity expressions. Similarly, his international and left-wing politics and rural populism provided an alternative to the African American political expressions associated with the music. His early and ongoing openness to collaborations outside the United

States put him at the vanguard of the now widespread genre of world jazz, which was also pioneered by Cherry. His contributions to the traditional American songbook repertoire have increased that strain's sophistication and elegance while defusing its identity as elitist, precious, and detached from the grassroots.

SELECTED RECORDINGS
As leader: *Liberation Music Orchestra* (1969, Imp.); *Old and New Dreams* (1976, Black Saint); *The Survivors' Suite* (1977, ECM); *Folk Songs* (1979, ECM); *Silence* (1987, SN); *Steal Away* (1995, Polygram); *Land of the Sun* (2004, Verve); *Private Collection* (2007, Naim/Premiere); *Rambling Boy* (2008, Decca)
As sideman with O. Coleman: *The Shape of Jazz to Come* (1959, Atl.); *This is our Music* (1960, Atl.)

BIBLIOGRAPHY
GroveJ
E. Charry: "Freedom and Form in Ornette Coleman's Early Atlantic Recordings," *ARJS*, ix (1997–8), 261–94
F. Davis: "Charlie Haden: Bass," *Atlantic Monthly* (2000), Aug, 78–83
A. Goodman: "Jazz Legend Charlie Haden on his Life, his Music, and his Politics," <http://www.democracynow.org/2006/9/1/jazz_legend_charlie_haden_on_his> (2006)
MIKE HEFFLEY

Hadley, Henry (Kimball) (*b* Somerville, MA, 20 Dec 1871; *d* New York, NY, 6 Sept 1937). Composer and conductor. His father taught him the piano, the violin, and conducting, and he studied harmony with STEPHEN ALBERT EMERY and counterpoint and composition with GEORGE WHITEFIELD CHADWICK in Somerville and at the New England Conservatory (to 1894). He also studied counterpoint with Eusebius Mandyczewski in Vienna (1894–5) and composition with Ludwig Thuille in Munich (1905–7). Hadley was especially influenced by Chadwick, who was a good friend and mentor, and by Richard Strauss, whom he met in London in 1905. Hadley taught at St. Paul's School in Garden City, New York (1895–1902, succeeding Horatio Parker), and he pursued a highly successful conducting career in the United States and, from 1904, in Europe. He was conductor of the Mainz Stadttheater (1907–9) and of the Seattle SO (1909–11), and he formed and conducted the San Francisco SO (1911–15). He was associate conductor of the New York PO (1920–27) and founder and conductor of the semi-educational Manhattan SO (1929–32), an orchestra formed to promote the works of American composers. He also conducted in Japan and South America. Hadley was a tireless and effective advocate of American music, both in performance and as a lecturer. In 1933 he founded the NATIONAL ASSOCIATION FOR AMERICAN COMPOSERS AND CONDUCTORS (NAACC), which endowed the Henry Hadley Memorial Library (the Americana Collection), now housed at the New York Public Library. He also founded the Berkshire Music Festival (1934) and conducted the orchestra there for the first two seasons. He was elected to the American Academy of Arts and Letters in 1924. Hadley's abundant compositions were written in a conventional, late-Romantic and expressive style; they were popular in his lifetime, and received repeated performances but mixed critical reaction, though their fluency and technical excellence was universally praised. He was awarded the Paderewski Prize in 1901 for his Second Symphony. Hadley wrote several works for his brother Arthur (1874–1936), a cellist, including the *Konzertstück* op.61. His opera *Cleopatra's Night* was given by the Metropolitan Opera and was the first work to be conducted there by its composer (though not in its first performances). Hadley was commissioned by the Vitaphone Company to compose and conduct what may have been "the first musical score to be recorded and played in synchronism with an entire motion picture" (Canfield) for *When a Man Loves* (released November 1926).

In 1933 the *Musical Courier* could call Hadley "probably the most important composer in the contemporary American musical scene," but his standing as a composer has since declined and it is perhaps first as a conductor and promoter of American music that he deserves recognition. The Henry Hadley Foundation was established in 1938 in New York to promote cooperation among American musicians and to provide scholarships and financial aid for the training and encouragement of American composers.

See also NATIONAL ASSOCIATION OF COMPOSERS, USA.

WORKS

DRAMATIC

Happy Jack (operetta, S.F. Batchelder), 1897
Nancy Brown (operetta, F. Ranken), op.63, 1903, New York, 1903
Safié (op, 1, E. Oxenford, after a Persian legend), op.63, Mainz, Stadt, 4 April 1909
The Atonement of Pan (music drama, J. Redding), 1912, Sonoma County, CA, 10 Aug 1912
The Pearl Girl (operetta, W.J. Hurlburt), op.73
Azora, the Daughter of Montezuma (op, 3, D. Stevens), op.80, 1914, Chicago, Auditorium, 26 Dec 1917
The Masque of Newark (pageant, T. Stevens), 1916, Newark, 1916
Bianca (op, 1, G. Stewart, after C. Goldoni: *La locandiera*), op.79, 1917, New York, Park, 18 Oct 1918
Cleopatra's Night (op, 2, A.L. Pollock, after T. Gautier), op.90, 1918, New York, Met, 31 Jan 1920
Semper virens (music-drama, Redding), op.97, 1923, Sonoma County, 1923
The Fire Prince (operetta, Stevens), Schenectady, NY, 1924
A Night in Old Paris (op, 1, F. Truesdell, after G. McDonough), 1924, private perf. New York, Dec 1924; NBC Radio, 20 Jan 1930
The Legend of Hani (music drama, J. Cravens), 1933, Sonoma County, 29 July 1933
The Red Flame (musl, L. Anderson)

ORCH

Ballet Suite, op.16, 1895; Festival March, op.5, orch, band, 1897; Sym. no.1 "Youth and Life," d, op.25, 1897; Sym. no.2 "The Four Seasons," f, op.30, 1901; Herod, ov., F, op.31, 1901; In Bohemia, ov., Eb, op.28, 1902; Oriental Suite, op.32, 1903; Sym. Fantasia, Eb, op.46, 1904; Salome, tone poem, E, op.55, 1905–6; Sym. no.3, b, op.60, 1906; Konzertstück, e, op.61, vc, orch, 1907; The Culprit Fay, rhapsody, e, op.62, 1908; Lucifer, tone poem, C, op.66, 1910; Sym. no.4 "North, East, South, and West," d, op.64, 1911; The Atonement of Pan, suite, 1912 [from op]; Silhouettes, suite, Eb, op.77, 1918; Othello, ov., f#, op.96, 1919; The Ocean, tone poem, Eb, op.99, 1920–21; Suite ancienne, F, op.108, 1924 [orig. vc, pf]; Streets of Pekin, suite, A, 1930; San Francisco, suite, C, op.121, 1931; Youth Triumphant, ov., band, 1931; Alma mater, ov., Ab, op.122, Boston, 1932; The Legend of Hani, suite, 1933 [from op]; Scherzo diabolique, D, op.135, 1934; Sym. no.5 "Connecticut," c, op.140, 1935; other works

VOCAL

The Fairies (W. Allingham), op.3, S, SATB, orch/pf, 1894; Lelawala (ballade, G.F.R. Anderson), op.13, SATB, orch, 1898; In Music's Praise (cant., Anderson), op.21, S, T, B, SATB, orch, 1898; The Princess of Ys (cant., E.W. Mumford), op.34, women's vv/mixed vv, orch, 1903; A Legend of Granada (cant., Mumford), op.45, S, Bar, SSAA, New York, 1904; Merlin and Vivian (lyric drama, Mumford), op.52, solo vv, SATB, orch, 1906; The Fate of Princess Kiyo (cant., Oxenford), op.58, S, S, SSAA, orch, New York, 1907; The Nightingale and the Rose (cant., E.W. Grant), op.54, S, SSAA, orch, New York, 1911; The Golden Prince (cant., D. Stevens, after O. Wilde), S, Bar, SSAA, orch, New York, 1914; Music, an Ode (H. Van Dyke), op.75, solo vv, SATB, orch, 1915; The Fairy Thorn (cant., C.B. Fenno), op.76, S, Mez, female vv, pf/orch, New York, 1917; In Arcady (idyll, E.F. Weatherly), op.83, SATB, orch; The New Earth (ode, L.A. Garnett), op.85, S, A, T, B, SATB, orch, 1919; Prophecy and Fulfillment (Pss., hymns), Christmas ant., op.91, S, A, T, SATB, orch, 1922; Resurgam (orat, Garnett), op.98, S, A, T, B, SATB, orch, 1922; Mirtil in Arcadia (pastoral, Garnett), op.100, solo vv, nar, children's chorus, orch, 1926; The Admiral of the Seas (cant., Fenno), T, SATB, orch, 1928; Belshazzar (cant., Garnett), op.112, solo vv, SATB, orch, 1932
Anthems and other choral pieces; over 200 songs

OTHER WORKS

Sonata, op.23, vn, pf, 1895; Str Qt no.1, op.24, c1896; Pf Trio no.1, op.26, c1896; Pf Qnt, op.50, New York, 1919; When a Man Loves, film score, 1926; Pf Trio no.2, 1933; Str Qt no.2, op.132, 1934; pf pieces

MSS in *NYp (American Collection)*
Principal publishers: Ditson, G. Schirmer, Schmidt

BIBLIOGRAPHY

EwenD
H. Boardman: *Henry Hadley, Ambassador of Harmony* (Atlanta, GA, 1932)
P. Berthoud, ed.: *The Musical Works of Dr. Henry Hadley* (New York, 1942)
J. Canfield: *Henry Kimball Hadley (1871–1937): his Life and Works* (diss., Florida State U., 1960)
S. Feder: "Making American Music: Henry Hadley and the Manhattan Symphony Orchestra," *A Celebration of American Music: Works and Music in Honor of H. Wiley Hitchcock*, ed. R.A. Crawford, R.A. Lott, and C.J. Oja (Ann Arbor, MI, 1990), 356–82
N.E. Tawa: *Mainstream Music of Early Twentieth-Century America* (Westport, CT, 1992)

RICHARD JACKSON/R

Hadley, Jerry (*b* Princeton, IL, 16 June 1952; *d* Poughkeepsie, NY, 18 July 2007). Tenor. After vocal studies at the University of Illinois and with Thomas LoMonaco in New York, he made his debut as Lyonel in *Martha* (1978, Sarasota). Several seasons at the New York City Opera, beginning in 1979 (as Arturo in *Lucia di Lammermoor*), established him as a leading lyric tenor: his roles included Des Grieux (*Manon*), Pinkerton, Tom Rakewell, Werther, and Gounod's Faust. His European debut in Vienna as Nemorino in 1982 was followed by appearances in Berlin, Geneva, Glyndebourne, Hamburg, London, and Munich. He made his Metropolitan Opera debut as Des Grieux in 1987. His lyrical, italianate voice and dramatic immediacy made him a fine interpreter of the Mozart, French lyric, and Italian repertories. He was an equally accomplished artist in the concert hall in works such as *Messiah, Elijah,* and Britten's *War Requiem,* all of which he recorded. Among his many operatic recordings are *Faust, Werther, La bohème,* and *The Rake's Progress,* in all of which his firm line and ardent manner are in evidence. He received three Grammy awards for his vocal performances in the recordings of *Candide* (1992), *Susannah* (1995), and *Jenůfa* (2004).

BIBLIOGRAPHY
M. Kimmelman: "A Singer Finds His Creative Range," *The New York Times* (14 Aug 1987)

CORI ELLISON/ALAN BLYTH/MARIDA RIZZUTI

Hagan, Helen Eugenia (*b* Portsmouth, NH, 10 Jan 1893; *d* New York, NY, 6 March 1964). Composer and pianist. She attended the Yale University School of Music (1906–12), studying composition with HORATIO PARKER. After graduation (BMus), she performed her Piano Concerto with the New Haven SO. A Yale fellowship enabled her to study with Vincent d'Indy and Blanche Selva at the Schola Cantorum in Paris. Having briefly pursued a performing career, she turned to education and became head of the music department at the George Peabody College for Teachers. Her one-movement concerto in C minor, one of the earliest extant works in the genre by an African American woman composer, adheres to the Lisztian tradition, featuring a virtuoso solo part and fluid chromatic harmonies (an arrangement for two pianos is held at Yale University). Hagan's other works included piano pieces and a violin sonata (before 1912), all lost. (*GroveW*, D. Metzer [incl. bibliography]; *SouthernB*)

DAVID METZER

Hageman, Richard (*b* Leeuwarden, Netherlands, 9 July 1882; *d* Beverly Hills, CA, 6 March 1966). Composer and conductor of Dutch birth. He studied with his father at the Amsterdam New Music Institute and at the Brussels Conservatory. When he was 16 he was appointed coach to the Nederlandse Opera, of which he was later conductor. For a short time he was accompanist to Mathilde Marchesi in Paris, and in 1906 he traveled to New York in the same capacity with Yvette Guilbert. He conducted at the Metropolitan Opera (1908–22), the Chicago Civic Opera (1922–3), and the Los Angeles Grand Opera (1923). He was also conductor of the Fairmount SO in Philadelphia and head of the opera department at the Curtis Institute. In later years he worked at the Paramount studios in Hollywood, writing scores for a number of John Ford's films, including *Stagecoach* (1939) and *Fort Apache* (1948). His opera, *Caponsacchi*, first performed at Freiburg as *Tragödie in Arezzo* in 1932, was staged at the Metropolitan in 1937.

WORKS
(selective list)

Stage: Caponsacchi (op, 3, R. Browning), 1931; I Hear America Call (orat, R.V. Grossman), Bar, SATB, orch, 1942; The Crucible (orat, B.C. Kennedy), 1943

Film scores: Stagecoach, 1939; The Long Voyage Home, 1940; Fort Apache, 1948; Three Godfathers, 1948; She Wore a Yellow Ribbon, 1949; Wagon Master, 1950

Orch: Ov. "In a Nutshell"; Suite, str

Chbr: October Musings, vn, pf, 1937; Recit and Romance, vc, pf, 1961

Songs, 1v, pf: Do not go, my love (R. Tagore), 1917; May Night (Tagore), 1917; At the Well (Tagore), 1919; Happiness (J. Ingelow), 1920; Charity (E. Dickinson), 1921; Nature's Holiday (T. Nash), 1921; Animal Crackers (C. Morley), 1922; Christ went up into the Hills (K. Adams), 1924; Me Company Along (J. Stephens), 1925; The Night has a Thousand Eyes (F.W. Bourdillon), 1935; Christmas Eve (J. Kilmer), 1936; Music I Heard with you (C. Aiken), 1938; Miranda (H. Belloc), 1940; Lift thou the Burdens, Father (K.C. Simonds), 1944;

The Fiddler of Dooney (W.B. Yeats), 1946; over 50 other songs, many arr. for chorus

Principal publisher: G. Schirmer

PHILIP L. MILLER/MICHAEL MECKNA

Hagen, Daron Aric (*b* Milwaukee, WI, 4 Nov 1961). Composer and pianist. He studied composition with Homer Lambrecht and Les Thimmig at the University of Wisconsin, Madison (1979–81), and with NED ROREM at the Curtis Institute (BM 1984). He entered the Juilliard School in 1984 (MM 1987), where his teachers included DAVID DIAMOND, JOSEPH SCHWANTNER, and BERNARD RANDS. He also studied with Witold Lutosławski (Evian Music Festival, 1983) and LEON KIRCHNER (Tanglewood, 1986). He was founding director of the Perpetuum Mobile Concerts (1982) and served as composer-in-residence of the Long Beach SO (1994). He has held academic affiliations with Bard College (1988–97), New York University (1988–90), the City College of New York (1993–4, 1997), and the Curtis Institute of Music (1996–8). In addition, he has been composer in residence at Princeton University Atelier (1998, 2005), Miami University of Ohio (1999–2000), and the University of Pittsburgh (2007) and artist in residence at Baylor University (1998–9) and the University of Nevada Las Vegas (2000–2002). Among his honors are a Bearns Prize (1985), the Barlow International Composition Prize for Chamber Music (1985), and a Friedheim Award (1994). His commissions include works for the New York PO, Buffalo PO, Albany SO, the King's Singers, Texas Opera Theatre, and the Seattle Opera, which premiered *Amelia* in 2010.

With several hundred songs dating back to his teenage years, the art song is the cornerstone of Hagen's compositional output, even though he has produced four symphonies, several concertos, and has had considerable success writing for brass and wind ensembles. His earliest published song cycle, *Echo's Songs* (1983) is strongly influenced by his first teacher, Rorem. In *Dear Youth* (1991), a cycle setting American Civil War texts, Hagen's compositional style shows a range of influences from jazz to Lutheran hymns. His first opera, *Shining Brow* (1990–92), features a similarly broad stylistic palette and an uncommon theatrical instinct which his subsequent operas continue to exploit.

WORKS
STAGE

Shining Brow (op, 2, P. Muldoon), 1990–92; Vera of Las Vegas (cabaret, 1, Muldoon), 1995; Bandanna (op, 2, Muldoon), 1999; The Antient Concert: a Dramatic Recital for Four Singers (Muldoon), Bar, T, Mez, S, str qt or pf, 2007; New York Stories: an Opera in Three Slices (B. Grecki/D. Hagen), 2010; Amelia (op, 2, G. McFall/S. Wadsworth), 2010; Little Nemo in Slumberland (op, 2, J.D. McClatchy, based on comic strips by W. McCay), S, T, B, children's vv, orch, 2012; A Woman in Morocco (op, 2, B. Grecki/D. Hagen), S, S, S, Mez, T, Bar, B-Bar, orch, 2013

INSTRUMENTAL

Orch: Prayer for Peace, str, 1981; A Stillness at Appomattox, 1982; Conc., vn, chbr orch, 1983; Andersonville Ov., 1983; Prayer for Peace, str orch, 1983; Sym. no.1: "Short Symphony," 1985–8; Grand Line: a Tribute to Leonard Bernstein, 1986; Sym. no.2: "Common Ground," 1987–90; Adagietto, str, 1990 [from Sym. no.1]; Heliotrope, chbr orch, 1989, rev. 1996; Fire Music, 1991; Philharmonia, 1992;

Conc., flugelhorn, str, 1992 [arr. flugelhorn, wind, 1994]; Conc., hn, wind, str, 1993; Built Up Dark, chbr orch, 1995; Night Again, chbr orch, 1995 [arr. wind, 1997]; Conc., vc, orch, 1996 [arr. wind ens, 1997]; Postcards from America, 1996; Sym. no.3: "Liturgical," 1997; Emmanuel Fugue, 1998 [from Sym. no.3]; Suddenly, 1999 [arr. band, 2000]; Much Ado, ov., 2000; Angels, str orch, 2000; Advance, 2000; Conc., ob, str orch, 2000 [arr. ob, str qt, 2001]; Seven Last Words, pf LH, orch, 2001; Susurrus, 2003; Romeo and Juliet, fl, vc, orch, 2004; Gesture Drawings, 2006; Orpheus and Eurydice, conc., vn, vc, pf, orch, 2006; Masquerade, conc., vn, vc, orch, 2007; Sym. no.4: "River Music" (W. Whitman/M. Twain), SATB, orch, 2008; Northern Lights, 2009; Genji, conc., koto, orch, 2011 [arr. koto, str qt, 2011]; Songbook, conc., vn, str orch, hp, perc, 2011

Chbr and solo inst: Wind Songs, ob, bn, hn, 1982; Divertimento, va, hp, vib, 1983; Suite, vn, 1984; Pf Trio no.1: Trio Concertante, 1984; Occasional Notes, org, 1985; Occasional Notes, 11 pfmrs, 1985; Sonata no.1, fl, pf, 1985; Str Qt no.1, 1985; Suite, vc, 1985; Pf Trio no.2: J'entends, 1986; Suite, va, 1986; Love Songs, vc, pf, 1987; Higher, Louder, Faster!, vc, 1987; Qualities of Light, pf, 1987; Interior, chbr ens, 1988; Fl Qnt: The Presence Absence Makes, fl, str qt, 1988; Jot!, cl, mar, pf, 1989; Sennets, Cortege, and Tuckets, wind, perc, 1989; Trio, fl, va, hp, 1989; Vocalise: Homage to Bud Powell, tpt/flugelhorn, pf, 1991; Everything Must Go!, brass qnt, 1992; Music from Shining Brow, brass qnt, 1993; Built up Dark, pf, 1995; Conc., brass qnt, 1995; Ov. to Vera, chbr ens, 1995; Sussex Carol, vc, 1996 [part of Silent Night, Music for the Christmas Season suite]; Duo, vn, vc, 1997; Night, Again, wind ens, 1997; Forward!, brass, perc, 1998; Bandanna Ov., band, 1999; Serenade, chbr ens, 1999; Wedding Dances from Bandanna, band, 1999; Nocturne, pf, str qnt, 2000; Qnt, ob, str qt, 2000; Pf Variations, 2002; Snapshot no.1: Wedding Day, str qt, 2003; Sonata no.2, fl, pf, 2003; Chbr Sym., chbr ens, 2003; Pf Trio no.3: Wayfaring Stranger, 2006; Snapshot no.2: Virginia Countryside, str qt, 2006; Pf Trio no.4: Angel Band, 2007; Agincourt Fanfare, brass ens, perc, 2007; Suite for Pf, 2009; Book of Days, cl, va, pf, 2010

VOCAL

Choral: A Walt Whitman Requiem (W. Whitman), S, SATB, str, 1984; Little Prayers (T. Mann, S. Kierkegaard), SATB, 1986; Little Prayers (St Thomas Aquinas, T. Mann, S. Kierkegaard), SATB, 1989; Joyful Music (Laudate deum, Alleluia), Mez, SATB, tpt, orch, 1993 [arr. Mez, SATB, brass, perc, 1994]; The Voice Within (D. Hammarskjöld), SATB, pf, 1993; The Elephant's Child (R. Kipling), 6 male vv/SATTBB, 1994; 4 Poems (W. Blake), SATB, pf, 1994; The Waking Father (P. Muldoon), 6 male vv/SATTBB, 1994; Taliesin "Choruses from Shining Brow" (Muldoon), SATB, orch/pf, 1995; Hope (E. Dickinson), SATB, pf, 1996; Hosanna, SATB, 1996; Litany of Reconciliation (Coventry Cathedral tesserae), SATB, 1996; Stewards of your Bounty (S.C. Lowry), SATB, tpt, orch/pf, 1996; Silent Night (Music for the Christmas Season suite), SATB, vc, synth/vib, 1996; Once in Royal David's City, SA, vc, 1996 [arr. str orch, 2006]; At Bethlehem Proper, TB, vc, 1996; What Child Is This? (W.C. Dix), SATB, 1996; God Rest Ye / Emmanuel, SATB, 2 vc, 1996; Lullay, SATB, 1996; O Come, Emmanuel, SATB, 1996; Litany of Reconciliation (text from Coventry Cathedral), SATB, 1996; Gandhi's Children (M.M. Gandhi), children's chorus, chimes, 1997; Light Fantastic (cant., W. Shakespeare, Whitman, M. Harrison, Gordon, Byron, T. Schneebaum), T, children's chorus, orch, 1999 [rev. T, SA, chbr ens, pf, 2004]; We're All Here, SATB, chbr ens, 2002 [arr. SATB, pf, 2008]; I Had Rather (G. Washington), SATB, 2004; Flight Music (A. Earhart), SSAA, str qt, 2005; Vertue (G. Herbert), SATB, pf, 2005; Song of Gabriel, SATB, str orch, 2010

Solo: Echo's Songs (W. Blake, S. Teasdale, E.A. Poe, B. Johnson, G. Stein, C. Sandburg, Shu Ch'isiang, W. Whitman), 1v, pf, 1983; 3 Silent Things (Whitman, R. Graves, C. Rosetti, J. Larson, R. Jeffers, A. Crapsey, P. Goodman, W. Stevens), S, vn, va, vc, pf, 1984; Love Songs (G. Hagen, R. Hauser, Blake, Z. Dunei, S. Gorham, G. McFall), 1v, pf, 1986; Rapture and Regret (V. Woolf, I. Dinesen), 1v, vc, pf, 1987 [rev. 2005]; Dear Youth (A.C. Ketchum, H. Ropes, A. Smith, M. Ingram, M.B. Chestnut), S, fl, pf, 1990 [Smith's O, For Such a Dream, arr. S, SATB, pf, 2006]; Muldoon Songs (P. Muldoon), 1v, pf, 1992; Lost in Translation (R. Kelley, R.M. Rilke, G. Seferis, W.H. Auden, D. Campana), 1v, ob, vc, hpd, 1994; Merrill Songs (J. Merrill), 1v, pf, 1995; Love Scene from Romeo and Juliet (W. Shakespeare), S, Bar, fl, pf

trio, 1996; Songs of Madness and Sorrow (H. Garland, Hagen, Wisconsin State Journal, Mendota State Mental Hospital records, advertisements), T, chbr ens, 1996; Prelude and Prayer (P. Muldoon), S, wind ens, 1999; Love in a Life (R. Browning, N. Alsadir, E. Dickinson, G. Gordon, L. Byron, T. Roethke, W. Whitman, T. Lodge), 1v, pf, 1981–99; Heart of the Stranger (A. Codrescu, C. Baudelaire, P. Verlaine, W. Blake, J. Keats, K. Roberts, A.E. Houseman, G. Hagen, W. Whitman, T. Roethke), 1v, pf, 1983–99; Larkin Songs (P. Larkin), 1v, pf, 2000; Figments (A.W. Gray), 1v, pf, 2000; Phantoms of Myself (S. Griffin), 1v, pf, 2000; Letting Go (M. Strand, C. Rosetti, R. McCann, G. Hagen, M. Skinner, S. Sandy), 1v, pf, 1983–2002; Alive in a Moment (W.H. Auden), Bar, str qt, 2003; Sappho Songs (trans. M. Barnard), S, Mez, vc, 2004; Banner of My Purpose (letter of Major Sullivan Bailou to his wife), Bar, band, 2006; We Two (Whitman), 2v, pf, 2006; Songs of Experience (Whitman, G. McFall, S. Teasdale, S. Dunn, E. Lawless, E. Dickinson), 1v, pf, 2007; We Happy Few, B/T, pf, 2010

MSS in *PHf*

Principal publishers: ECS, *Carl Fischer, Burning Sled*

JAMES CHUTE

Hagen, Earle (Harry) (*b* Chicago, IL, 9 July 1919; *d* Rancho Mirage, CA, 26 May 2008). Composer for film and television, arranger, and trombonist. His family relocated to Los Angeles when he was still a boy; at Hollywood High School he picked up the trombone and baritone. He left home at 16 to pursue a career as a trombonist in big bands, ultimately playing with Ray Noble, Benny Goodman, and Tommy Dorsey. While with Noble, he wrote the jazz standard "Harlem Nocturne" in 1939, which he would later use as the theme for *Mike Hammer* (1984–7). Largely self-taught as a composer, Hagen studied with ERNST TOCH in 1944. During the war, he arranged for the orchestra of the Army Air Corps Radio Production Unit, subsequently arranging and orchestrating (under Alfred Newman) for 20th Century Fox during the late 1940s into the 1950s. Hagen orchestrated such films as *Kiss of Death* (1947), *Gentlemen Prefer Blondes* (1953), *Carousel* (1956), and *Compulsion* (1959). In the meantime, he composed uncredited extra music for Fox releases (including *Love Me Tender*) and began to work in television, initially as composer (with Herbert Spencer) for the Danny Thomas series *Make Room for Daddy* (1953–60). Thomas and producer Sheldon Leonard consistently worked with Hagen on television shows beginning with *The Andy Griffith Show* (1960–8), the memorable whistling theme of which established his career as television composer. Other important series themes included those for *The Dick Van Dyke Show* (1961–6), *Gomer Pyle U.S.M.C.* (1964–9), *I Spy* (1965–8), *That Girl* (1966–71), *The Mod Squad* (1968–72), and *The Dukes of Hazzard* (1983–5). His autobiography suggests that he composed and conducted 3,000 television episodes in all. He possessed the ability to create an appropriate and memorable theme through effective melodic writing, colorful scoring, and stylistic deftness, regardless of the show's genre. Hagen won an Emmy in 1968 for his compositional work on *I Spy*. He retired from film and television composition in 1986. In his later years, he informally taught at UCLA and USC, and authored two textbooks about film scoring and an autobiography. His manuscript scores for television music are preserved at UCLA.

WRITINGS

Scoring for Films: a complete Text (Los Angeles, 1971)

Advanced Techniques for Film Scoring: a complete Text (Los Angeles, 1990)

Memoirs of a famous Composer Nobody Ever Heard Of (Philadelphia, 2000)

WORKS

DRAMATIC

The Love Offering (musical), 1982; unperformed

INSTRUMENTAL

Harlem Nocturne, 1939

FILM SCORES

The Girl Rush, 1955; Spring Reunion, 1957; Let's Make Love, 1960 (uncredited); The new Interns, 1964

TELEVISION MOVIES

The Monk, 1969; The Runaways, 1975; Having Babies, 1976; Killer on Board, 1977; True Grit, 1978; Ebony, Ivory and Jade, 1979; Alex and the Doberman Gang, 1980; The Hustler of Muscle Beach, 1980; Farewell to the Planet of the Apes, 1981; Stand by your Man, 1981; Muggable Mary, Street Cop, 1982; I Take these Men, 1983; Murder Me, Murder You, 1983; More than Murder, 1984; North Beach and Rawhide, 1985; Return to Mayberry, 1986; The Return of Mickey Spillane's Mike Hammer, 1986

TELEVISION SERIES

Where's Raymond?, 1953; Make Room for Daddy, 1953–60; The Barbara Stanwyck Show, 1960–61; The Andy Griffith Show, 1960–68; The Dick Van Dyke Show, 1961–6; Gomer Pyle, U.S.M.C., 1964–9; I Spy, 1965–8; That Girl, 1966–71; Accidental Family, 1967; Rango, 1967; The Danny Thomas Hour, 1967–8; The Guns of Will Sonnett, 1967–9; The mod Squad, 1968–72; The new People, 1969; Mayberry R.F.D., 1968–71; The new Andy Griffith Show, 1971; The Don Rickles Show, 1972; M*A*S*H, 1972–83; Planet of the Apes, 1974; Mary Hartman, Mary Hartman, 1976–7; Eight is Enough, 1977–81; The Dukes of Hazzard, 1983–5; Mickey Spillane's Mike Hammer, 1984–5

BIBLIOGRAPHY

J. Burlingame: *TV's Biggest Hits: the Story of television Themes from Dragnet to Friends* (New York, 1996)

B. Babcock: "Memoirs of a famous film Composer: an Interview with Earle Hagen," *Score*, xviii/4 (2003), 12–17

E. Frankel: "A Eulogy for Earle Hagen," *The Cue Sheet*, xxiii/3 (2008), 22–31

JAMES DEAVILLE

Hagen, Francis Florentine (*b* Salem (now Winston-Salem), NC, 30 Oct 1815; *d* Lititz, PA, 7 July 1907). Composer and Moravian pastor. He received theological training at the Moravian Seminary in Pennsylvania. Though he was always devoted to music, he, like many other Moravian composers, spent his professional life first as a teacher and then as pastor of several congregations in Pennsylvania, North Carolina, and Staten Island, New York. His compositions include choral anthems with orchestra; solo songs with piano; an extended Overture for full orchestra; and a significant number of organ preludes, included in *Church and Home Organist's Companion*, edited by Hagen and published in 1880 and 1881.

Hagen's organ preludes, based upon hymn tunes known both within and beyond the American Moravian Church, reflect the influence of the 19th-century gospel music movement. They also carry tonal colors that are characteristic of the piano works of the much younger

Edward MacDowell (1860–1908), who was still a student in Europe at the time Hagen's works were being published in Philadelphia. His vocal works retain the clarity of text setting characteristic of his Moravian heritage, while incorporating harmonies and colors characteristic of 19th-century romanticism.

BIBLIOGRAPHY

J. Boeringer: *Morning Star: the Life and Works of Francis Florentine Hagen (1815–1907)* (Winston-Salem, NC, 1986)

N.R. Knouse: *The Music of the Moravian Church in America* (Rochester, NY, 2008)

NOLA REED KNOUSE

Hagen, Theodore (*b* Hamburg, Germany, 15 April 1823; *d* New York, NY, 27 Dec 1871). German-born musician and critic. He immigrated to America in 1854. He studied piano and theory in Hamburg and, in 1841–2, Paris. Hagen soon made his name as a music critic, contributing to journals in France and Germany, including Schumann's *Neue Zeitschrift für Musik*, and publishing two books in German as well, *Civilisation und Musik* (Leipzig, 1846) and *Musikalische Novellen* (Leipzig, 1848). After his arrival in the United States he settled in New York and assumed the editorship of the *New-York Musical Review and Choral Advocate*, published by the brothers Lowell Mason, Jr., and Daniel Gregory Mason, in early 1855. Later that year the Mason brothers consolidated the journal with another publication, the *Musical Gazette*; the resultant *New-York Musical Review and Gazette* was edited by Hagen until 1862, at which time he also became its proprietor.

Hagen's frequent contributions to music criticism were colored by his German heritage. An avid Wagnerite, Hagen disparaged the performances of popular artists such as Louis Moreau Gottschalk, often exhorting him to play more Beethoven, Mendelssohn, or Schumann. Furthermore, he formed the Haydn Quartet in 1858, playing violin, and enthusiastically championed the increasingly fashionable Steinway pianos.

BIBLIOGRAPHY

J.T. White: *The National Cyclopaedia of American Biography*, vi (New York, 1896)

V.B. Lawrence, ed.: *Strong on Music: The New York Music Scene in the Days of George Templeton Strong*, ii–iii (Chicago, 1995 and 1999)

LAURA MOORE PRUETT

Hagen, von [van]. Family of Dutch American musicians. Composer Peter Albrecht von Hagen, Sr. (*b* The Netherlands, 1755; *d* Boston, MA, 20 Aug 1803) and his wife Elizabeth Joanetta Catherine von Hagen (*b* ?Amsterdam, The Netherlands, 1750; *d* Suffolk Co., MA, 1809–10), also a composer, immigrated to the United States in 1774. They settled first in Charleston, South Carolina, but by 1789 were in New York, where they were active as performers, teachers, and concert managers, promoting themselves and others in a series called "Old City Concerts." At first they were rivals of Henri Capron, James Hewitt, and G.E. Saliment, who were also presenting subscription concerts, but the two groups amalgamated in 1794 to present grander concerts than either had previously. In 1796 the family moved to Boston (where they changed their name from van to von) and from 1798 P.A. von Hagen Jun. & Co. became one of the most important music dealers and publishing establishments, which advertised a "Musical Magazine and Warehouse" for the sale of instruments and sheet music. The firm's repertoire consisted of patriotic songs, selections from ballad operas, and von Hagen's own compositions. He became musical director of the Federal Theater (1797–1800) and was organist at King's Chapel from 1798 until his death in 1803. After his death, Elizabeth succeeded him as organist at King's Chapel and continued to teach piano in Salem and at Mrs. Rowson's Academy in Boston.

Peter Albrecht von Hagen, Jr. (*b* ?Charleston, SC, *c*1779–81; *d* Boston, MA, 12 Sept 1837) was a child prodigy on the violin. Like his father, he performed on several instruments and also composed. He became organist at Trinity Church, Boston, in 1800, and after 1810 led bands in South Boston and Fort Eustis, Virginia. He was active with his father in the family publishing firm, but owing either to his lack of interest or incompetence, the firm's fortunes deteriorated and its stock was sold in 1804 to Gottlieb Graupner. After his father's death, von Hagen's reputation declined and he became an alcoholic, but in 1833 he was a member of the viola section in the orchestra at the Tremont Theatre, Boston.

The individual authorship of music by von Hagen and his father is often uncertain; the known published works up to 1825 include at least 12 songs (including *Monody* and *Kiss the Brim and Bid it Pass*), four marches for piano, and one overture. Elizabeth von Hagen is known to have composed a piano sonata and two piano concertos; her only piece to have been published, however, is a set of keyboard variations entitled *The Country Maid, or, L'amour est un enfant trompeur* (*c*1809).

BIBLIOGRAPHY

C. Burney: *The present State of Music in Germany, the Netherlands, and the United Provinces* ii (London, 1773), 314

"A Unique Letter," *Dwight's Journal of Music*, xviii (1860), 232

O.G.T. Sonneck: *A Bibliography of early secular American Music* (Washington, DC, 1905; rev. and enlarged by W.T. Upton, 2/1945/R1964)

O.G.T. Sonneck: *Early Concert-life in America (1731–1800)* (Leipzig, 1907/R1978)

H.E. Johnson: *Musical Interludes in Boston, 1795–1830* (New York, 1943/R1967)

H.E. Johnson: "The Musical von Hagens," *The New England Quarterly* xvi/1 (1943), 110–17

R.J. Wolfe: *Secular Music in America, 1801–1825: a Bibliography* (New York, 1964)

R.J. Wolfe: *Early American Music Engraving and Printing* (Urbana, IL, 1980)

J. Tick: *American Women Composers before 1870* (Ann Arbor, MI, 1983), 65–66

BARTON CANTRELL/LORETTA GOLDBERG,
H. EARLE JOHNSON/R

Haggard, Merle (Ronald) (*b* Bakersfield, CA, 6 April 1937). Country singer-songwriter. The son of farmers who fled Oklahoma for California during the Depression, Haggard has produced chart-topping and critically acclaimed songs for more than four decades. At the time of Haggard's birth, the family lived in a converted railroad car just outside Bakersfield. His father, by then a railroad yardman, died of a stroke before Haggard reached ten. His mother, a bookkeeper, raised Merle and two siblings on her own. As a teenager, he ran away from home and had run-ins with the law. As his hit song "Mama Tried" (Capitol, 1968) would later retell, he "turned 21 in prison" while serving a three-year sentence at San Quentin after trying to burglarize a liquor store.

Upon parole, Haggard took farming and blue collar jobs and spent his free time in Bakersfield's honkytonks. Haggard played guitar for Bakersfield house bands before joining Wynn Stewart's outfit in Las Vegas. Encouraged by fellow musicians to record his own songs, he cut his first single, "Skid Row," on Bakersfield's Tally label in 1962. By 1965 Haggard had scored his first top-ten *Billboard* country hit and signed with Capitol Records. Haggard's early singles were characterized by frank portraits of prison life, historical allusions, and a rich lyricism that offered moving portraits of migrant poverty and recalled the songwriting of Woody Guthrie. His compositions were also intimately tied to working-class experiences of Southern California's white working class and, in songs such as "Hungry Eyes" (Capitol, 1968) and "California Cottonfields" (Capitol, 1969), Haggard's own family experiences. Although left-leaning listeners praised Haggard's early compositions, his biggest commercial breakthrough came in 1969 with the release of the seemingly jingoistic and anti-hippie "Okie from Muskogee." Used by the organizers of the "National Week of Unity" to promote a hawkish message in support of the Vietnam War on country radio, it was also interpreted as a paean to the Dust Bowl migrants and was embraced by countercultural antiwar rock musicians who performed it ironically. Haggard went on to record tribute albums to country pioneer Jimmie Rodgers and western swing bandleader Bob Wills. He also penned and recorded critically- and popularly-acclaimed numbers such as "If We Make It Through December" (Capitol, 1973). Since the 1980s Haggard has proved a versatile songwriter and musician, experimenting with blues, honky-tonk, western swing, jazz, Dixieland, and bluegrass. During interviews, he has repeatedly criticized what he sees as the bland country-pop approach of Nashville. In 2000 and 2001, he recorded two albums on the punk label Anti. His political views remain difficult to categorize, but he has been critical of the Iraq War.

See also BAKERSFIELD SOUND.

BIBLIOGRAPHY

M. Haggard: *Sing Me Back Home* (New York, 1981)

M. Haggard and T. Carter: *Merle Haggard's My House of Memories: For the Record* (New York, 1999)

P. LaChapelle: *Proud to Be an Okie: Cultural Politics, Country Music, and Migration to Southern California* (Berkeley, 2007)

PETER LACHAPELLE

Haggin, B(ernard) H. (*b* New York, NY, 29 Dec 1900; *d* New York, NY, 29 May 1987). Music critic. Based in New York throughout his career, Haggin graduated from the Juilliard School in 1920. He wrote for the *Brooklyn*

Daily Eagle (1934–7) and *The Nation* (1939–57), and contributed a regular column about music on the radio to *The New York Herald Tribune* (1946–9). Following his tenure at *The Nation*, Haggin continued to write frequently for American literary reviews, including *The Hudson Review*, *The New Republic*, *Musical America*, and *The Yale Review*. As a critic, Haggin typically assessed the quality of concerts, as compared to previous performances, more than he engaged in evaluating repertoire? The new media of musical reproduction afforded him the opportunity to do so with authority, and for many years Haggin supplied record reviews to the *Yale Quarterly*. Throughout his career he insisted on the value of phonograph records as educational documents of performance. In his detail-oriented writings on records, Haggin often drew attention to the proper audio equipment for the enjoyment of classical music. He authored an early guide to recorded music, *Music on Records* (1938), and continued to cultivate a canon of performances for his listeners with revisions and new publications (*The Listener's Musical Companion*, 1956). Haggin focused his attention on European works from 1700 to 1900, frequently dismissing music of his own century (*A Book of the Symphony*, 1937). One notable exception is ballet; amongst American critics he was an early champion of Balanchine as a choreographer. A central figure in music criticism in the United States, particularly during the 1930s and 1940s, he was forceful in the articulation of his opinions and reluctant to compromise his artistic standards. Though he lost his charismatic presence in the musical community toward the end of his career, he remained iconoclastic in his writings. Haggin publicly disparaged his colleagues and frequently earned their scorn, for example, following a roll call of poor critics in *Music Observed* (1964). Performances' fidelity to the score and technical precision were of utmost importance to Haggin; they served as one basis for the critic's vocal advocacy of Toscanini throughout his career (*Conversations with Toscanini*, 1959). Through his many books, one of which is a collection of his essays (*Music in* The Nation, 1949), Haggin sought to influence the tastes of a generation of music lovers and to educate an intellectual and literary audience unfamiliar with music (*Music for the Man who Enjoys* Hamlet, 1944).

PATRICK J. SMITH/ANDREA F. BOHLMAN

Hagopian, Richard Avedis (*b* Fowler, CA, 3 April 1937). Oud player. Born to Armenian parents, Hagopian played both the violin and the clarinet as a child. At age 11, he began playing the oud, a short-necked plucked instrument that is an ancestor of the European lute. In addition to studying the oud with Kanuni Garbis Bakirgian, Hagopian sought to master both classical and folk repertoires of Armenia, to learn the dumbeg and the kanoun (traditional Armenian instruments), and to explore Armenian culture, religion, and dance. Highly esteemed for his performance skills, he was granted the title "Oudi" in 1969 by the virtuoso player Udi Hrant Kenkulian, symbolizing Hagopian's mastery of the instrument. He has released numerous albums featuring

Armenian music for various ensembles—with the Kef Time Band, under his own name, and with collaborators such as Yuri Yunakov and Omar Faruk Tekbilek. His playing on *Gypsy Fire* (1995) prompted *Rhythm Music Magazine* to reaffirm his reputation as "one of the best oud players on the planet." In 1989 the NEA named him a National Heritage Fellow. In 2011 he participated with his grandson Andrew Hagopian in an apprenticeship program for the Alliance for California Traditional Arts, passing on his knowledge of Armenian music to a new generation.

CATHERINE WOJTANOWSKI

Hague, Eleanor (*b* San Francisco, CA, 7 Nov 1875; *d* Flintridge, CA, 25 Dec 1954). Folklorist, writer, lecturer, music patron, and singer. Born into a wealthy family (her father James Hague was a prominent geologist and mining engineer), she used her inheritance to support her research into Latin American music, particularly Mexican American and Mexican folksong. Prior to moving to Pasadena, California, in 1920, she lived in New York and Stockbridge, Massachusetts. She studied music privately in France and Italy, was a member of the New York Oratorio Society, and directed church choirs in New York before she began work as a folklorist and folksinger by the early 1910s (she gave guitar-accompanied folksong recitals in that decade). Hague published numerous collections and studies of Mexican American, Mexican, and other Latin American folksongs; translated (with Marion Leffingwell) Julián Ribera y Tarragó's *Historia de la música árabe medieval y su influencia en la española*; transcribed traditional New Mexican alabados for Juan B. Rael's *The New Mexican Alabado* (1951); and translated folksongs for Luisa Espinel's *Canciones de mi padre: Spanish Folksongs from Southern Arizona* (1946). Hague directed and funded the Jarabe Club of Pasadena, a folk-dance club for Mexican American youth. She was a generous patron of the Southwest Museum in Los Angeles, sponsoring Harry Partch in 1933 to transcribe Charles Lummis's cylinders of Native American music; she also sponsored three of Frances Densmore's studies of Native American music (of Santo Domingo Pueblo, the Maidu, and the Cheyenne and Arapaho). Her book *Latin American Music* was one of the first such works in any language. The Eleanor Hague Manuscript (Southwest Museum) is one of the most important collections of 18th-century dance music performed in Latin America.

WRITINGS
(selected list)

"Spanish-American Folk-Songs," *Journal of American Folklore*, xxiv/93 (1911), 323–31
"Spanish Songs from Southern California," *Journal of American Folklore*, xxvii/105 (1914), 331–32
Folk Songs from Mexico and South America, arr. E. Kilenyi (New York, 1914)
"Spanish-American Folk Songs," *Memoirs of the American Folklore Society*, x (1917), entire issue
Early Spanish-Californian Folk-Songs, arr. G. Ross (New York, 1922)
Music in ancient Arabia and Spain (London, 1929), translation and abridgement by E. Hague and M. Leffingwell of J. Ribera y Tarragó,

Historia de la música árabe medieval y su influencia en la española (Madrid, 1927)

Latin American Music: Past and Present (Santa Ana, CA, 1934)

"Some California Songs," *Masterkey*, viii (1934), 15–18, 115–17

"California Songs—III," *Masterkey*, xi (1937), 89–93

"La música en California," *Anuario de la Sociedad Folklórica de México*, vi (1945), 83–86

BIBLIOGRAPHY

E. Waldo: "Eleanor Hague (1875–1954)," *Western Folklore*, xiv/4 (1955), 279–80

R. Stevenson: "Eleanor Hague (1875–1954): Pioneer Latin Americanist," *Inter-American Music Review*, xiv/1 (1994), 57–66

C.H. Russell: "The Eleanor Hague Manuscript: a Sampler of musical Life in Eighteenth-Century Mexico," *Inter-American Music Review*, xiv/2 (1995), 39–62

J. Koegel: "Preserving the Sounds of the 'Old' Southwest: Charles Lummis and his Cylinder Collection of Mexican-American and Indian Music," *Association for Recorded Sound Collections Journal*, xxix/1 (1998), 1–29

JOHN KOEGEL

Hahn, Hilary (*b* Lexington, VA, 27 Nov 1979). Violinist. A child prodigy, she took up the violin at the age of three and studied first in Baltimore with Klara Berkovich and then, from the age of ten, with JASCHA BRODSKY. Later, she attended the Curtis Institute, Philadelphia, where she studied violin with JAIME LAREDO and chamber music with FELIX GALIMIR and GARY GRAFFMAN. Hahn made her major concerto debut with the Baltimore SO at the age of 12, and her debut with the Philadelphia Orchestra in 1993, quickly followed by debuts with the Cleveland Orchestra, the New York PO, and the Pittsburgh SO. In 1995, at 15, she made her European debut, playing the Beethoven Violin Concerto with Maazel and the Bavarian RSO. The following year she gave her first concert at Carnegie Hall and signed an exclusive contract with Sony Classical, with whom she has recorded an award-winning disc of Bach sonatas and partitas, and concertos by Beethoven, Brahms, Barber, Stravinsky, Shostakovich, Mendelssohn, and Edgar Meyer. In 2000 Hahn played in the Last Night of the Proms (her Proms debut), and during the 2000–01 season made her first tour of Japan, as soloist with the Berlin PO. In 2002 she signed an exclusive recording contract with Deutsche Grammophon. She has since recorded concertos of Bach, Elgar, Vaughan Williams, Paganini, and Spohr, and an album of the concertos of Schoenberg and Sibelius for which Hahn won a Grammy.

In 2009 Hahn performed the world premiere of Jennifer Higdon's Violin Concerto. She has also developed her early interest in chamber music, appearing regularly with the Marlboro Music Festival in Vermont, the Chamber Music Society of Lincoln Center, and Skaneateles Festival, and touring in partnership with the pianist Garrick Ohlsson, and later, pianist Natalie Zhu, with whom she recorded an album of Mozart violin sonatas in 2005. She made her feature film soundtrack debut in 2004 for *The Village*, playing solos in the Academy Award–nominated score by James Newton Howard. She has also performed in nonclassical spheres, recording a solo for the art rock band And You Will Know Us by the Trail of Dead in 2005, and performing with folk-rock artist Josh Ritter. In 2007 Deutsche Grammophon produced the DVD *Hilary Hahn: a Portrait*.

BIBLIOGRAPHY

Violin Virtuosos (San Anselmo, CA, 2000)

RICHARD WIGMORE/MEGAN E. HILL

Haieff, Alexei (Vasilievich) (*b* Blagoveshchensk, Siberia, 25 Aug 1914; *d* Rome, Italy, 1 March 1994). Composer of Russian birth. When he was six his family moved to China, and in 1932 he came to the United States; he became an American citizen in 1939. Haieff studied at the Juilliard School with FREDERICK JACOBI and RUBIN GOLDMARK (1934–8), and in 1938–9 he was a pupil of NADIA BOULANGER in Cambridge, Massachusetts, and in Paris. In 1942 he received the Lili Boulanger Memorial Award and a medal from the American Academy in Rome. Other honors include an award from the American Academy of Arts and Letters (1945), Guggenheim Fellowships (1946, 1949), the Rome Prize (1947), the New York Music Critics' Circle Award for the Piano Concerto no.1 (1952), and the American International Music Fund Award for his Second Symphony (1960). He was composer-in-residence at the American Academy in Rome in 1952–3 and 1958–9, visiting professor at SUNY, Buffalo (1962, 1964–5), Andrew Mellon Professor at the Carnegie Institute of Technology (1962–3), visiting professor at Brandeis University (1965–6), and composer-in-residence at the University of Utah (1967–70). He then divided his time between Europe and the United States before settling in Rome for the remainder of his life. In 1947 choreographer George Balanchine created the ballet *Divertimento*, composed solely of Haieff's music; the New York City Ballet revived *Divertimento* in 1993 to honor the tenth anniversary of Balanchine's death. Haieff's music is neo-Classical, moving with vitality and clean crispness.

BIBLIOGRAPHY

EwenD

Obituary, *New York Times* (3 March 1994)

WORKS

(selective list)

Ballets: Zondilda and her Entourage (M. Cunningham), 1946; Beauty and the Beast, 1947, rev. as 2 separate works, Ballet in B♭, 1953, Ballet in E, 1955

Orch: Sym. no.1, 1942; Divertimento, small orch, 1944, choreog. Balanchine, 1947; Vn Conc., 1948; Pf Conc. no.1, 1949–50; Eclogue (La nouvelle Heloïse), hp, str, 1953; Sym. no.2, 1957; Sym. no.3, 1961; Caligula (R. Lowell), Bar, orch, 1971; Pf Conc. no.2, 1976 [based on Sonata, 2 pf, 1945]

Chbr and solo inst: Sonatina, str qt, 1937; Bagatelles, ob, bn, 1940–55; Suite, vn, pf, 1941, lost; Serenade, ob, cl, bn, pf, 1942; Eclogue, vc, pf, 1945; Sonata, 2 pf, 1945; Str Qt, 1951; Pf Sonata, 1955; Saints' Wheel, pf, 1960; Sonata, vc, pf, 1963; Eloge, 9 insts, 1967; Rhapsodies, gui, hpd, 1980; Duet, 2 fl, 1982; Wind Qnt, 1983

Chorus: Orthodox Holy Week Music, 1969

Incid music

Principal publisher: EMI

PEGGY GLANVILLE-HICKS/OLIVER DANIEL/

ELIZABETH PERTEN

Haig, Al(an) [Allan] **(Warren)** (*b* Newark, NJ, 19/22 July 1922; *d* New York, NY, 16 Nov 1982). Jazz pianist. Haig's year of birth has appeared incorrectly as 1924 in all known reference sources. He studied classical piano at Oberlin College, Ohio, from 1940 but left in 1942 to serve in the Coast Guard. Stationed in the New York area, he was able to pursue his blossoming interest in jazz. After working with Tiny Grimes in 1944, he joined the quintet of Dizzy Gillespie and Charlie Parker, contributing outstanding solos to what are widely regarded as the first full-blown bop recordings, including "Salt Peanuts" (1945, Guild). After joining Charlie Barnet's big band, he worked with Gillespie in Los Angeles and made further important recordings with the trumpeter in New York (1946). He toured with Jimmy Dorsey and continued recording bop as a freelance pianist before joining Parker's quintet (1948–50), which performed in Paris in 1949; Parker's rhythm section also worked as accompanists to Stan Getz, with whom Haig continued in 1951. His career then quickly declined. He worked in obscurity in Puerto Rico, Miami, and the greater New York area until he was rediscovered; he then toured widely and recorded as an unaccompanied soloist and the leader of a trio during the 1970s and early 80s. Haig's early bop recordings are remarkable for his ability to improvise single-note lines with clarity at blistering tempos. During his second, revived career, he sometimes played in a more rhapsodic and contrapuntal manner, but without any loss of his characteristic dexterity.

BIBLIOGRAPHY

A. Morgan: "Al Haig: an Introduction and Discography," *JazzM*, ii (1956–7), no.8, 26–8; no.9, 24–6

M. Harrison: "Al Haig," *Jazz Review*, iii/5 (1960), 22

M. Harrison: "Al Haig," *Jazz Era: the Forties*, ed. S. Dance (London, 1961), 119

G. Hoefer: "Al Haig," *DB*, xxxii/22 (1965), 17, 38 only

I. Gitler: *Jazz Masters of the Forties* (New York, 1966), 132

M. Gardner: "Al Haig," *JazzM*, no.186 (1970), 4–7 [interview]

J. Shaw: "The Reminiscences of Al Haig," *JJI*, xxxii (1979), no.3, 4–5, 9 only; no.4, 17–19 [incl. discography]

Obituary: *New York Times* (17 Nov 1982)

Obituary: *DB*, l/2 (1983), 13

"Al Haig," *Swing Journal* [Japan], xxxvii/1 (1983), 200 [discography]

R. Horricks: "Al Haig," *Profiles in Jazz: from Sidney Bechet to John Coltrane* (New Brunswick, NJ, 1991), 107–17

BARRY KERNFELD/R

Hailstork, Adolphus (Cunningham) (*b* Rochester, NY, 17 April 1941). Composer. He studied composition with Mark Fax at Howard University, Washington, DC (BMus 1963), with NADIA BOULANGER at the American Conservatory, Fontainebleau, France (summer 1963), at the Manhattan School (BMus 1965, MMus 1966), and at Michigan State University, East Lansing (PhD 1971). He has taught at Michigan State (1969–71) and Youngstown (Ohio) State University (1971–6), Norfolk (Virginia) State University (1977–2000), and Old Dominion University since 2000 as Eminent Scholar. As well as commissions for orchestral, choral, and brass ensemble works, his opera *Paul Laurence Dunbar* was commissioned by the Dayton Opera Association. His honors include the Ernest Bloch award for choral composition (1970–1), the Belwin-Mills/Max Winkler band composition award (1977), and commissions from the J.C. Penney Corporation, the Edward Tarr Brass Ensemble,

Virginia SO, Massachusetts Council of the Arts, National Association of Negro Musicians, Williams College, Louisville Orchestra, Cincinnati Musical Festival Association, Baltimore SO, St. Louis Opera, Lyric Opera of Kansas City, Dayton Opera Company, Cincinnati Opera, Boys Choir of Harlem, Detroit SO, American Guild of Organists, and others. He was named Cultural Laureate of Virginia in 1992 and received honorary doctorates from the College of William and Mary (2001) and Michigan State University (2004). His musical language is postmodern and pluralistic, embracing a variety of contemporary techniques as well as references to ethnic idioms. His works have been performed in Europe as well as in the United States.

WORKS

Stage: The Race for Space (muscm, D.R. Moore, Hailstork), 2 S, 2 T, chorus, spkrs, dancers, pf, 1963; Paul Laurence Dunbar: Common Ground (op, 1, Martin), 1992; Joshua's Boots (S. Kander), 3 S, Mez, 2 T, 1 Bar, SATB, children's chorus, orch, 1998; Rise for Freedom (D. Gonzalez), 22 singers, chbr orch (2007)

Orch: Phaedra, tone poem, 1966; Statement, Variations and Fugue, 1966; Capriccio for a Departed Brother: Scott Joplin, str, 1969; From the Dark Side of the Sun, s sax, 3 fl, mar, vib, glock, cel, perc, str, 1971; Bellevue, 1974; Celebration, 1974; Out of the Depths, sym. band, 1974; Conc., vn, hn, orch, 1975; American Landscape no.1, band, 1977; Epitaph in memoriam MLK, Jr, 1979; Sport of Strings, str, 1981; American Guernica, band, 1982; American Landscape no.3, 1982; American Landscape no.4, 1984; An American Port of Call, ov., 1985; Sym. no.1, 1988; My Lord What a Morning, chbr orch, 1989; Intrada, 1990; Sonata da chiesa, str, 1990; Pf Conc., 1992; Festival of Music, 1993, Sym. no.2, 1998; Sym. no.3, 2003; Vn Conc., 2004

Chbr: Sonata, hn, pf, 1966; SA-1, jazz ens, 1971; Sextet, str, 1971; Sonata, vn, pf, 1972; Bagatelles, brass qt, 1973; Pulse, perc ens, 1974; Spiritual, brass octet, 1975; Scherzo, solo perc, 2 fl, 2 cl, 2 tpt, 2 trbn, 1975; Processional and Recessional, 2 tpt, trbn, hn, 1977; American Landscape no.2, vn, vc, 1978; Pf Sonata, 1978–81; Pf Trio, 1987; Consort Piece, fl, cl + sax, tpt, vn, vc, 1995; Sanctum, rhapsody, vn, pf, 1995; Sonata, tpt, pf, 1996; As Falling Leaves, fl, va, harp, 2002; Str Qt, 2003; inst duos, other pf and org works

SATB unacc.: In memoriam Langston Hughes, 1967; Set me as a Seal upon thy Heart, 1979; A Carol for all Children, 1983; 5 Short Choral Works, 1984; Songs of Isaiah, 1987; The Song of Deborah, 1993; Let the Heavens be Glad, 1996; several other unacc. choruses

Other vocal: A Charm at Parting, song cycle, Mez, pf, 1969; Lament for the Children of Biafra, 1v, nar, jazz ens, perc, 1969; Spartacus Speaks, TTBB, brass, perc, 1970; Serenade, S, SSA, vn, pf, 1971; My Name is Toil, SATB, brass, perc, 1972; Oracle, T, female vv, 3 fl, 2 perc, tape, 1977; Ps lxiii, SATB, brass, org, 1981; Done Made my Vow (orat), S, T, Tr, nar, SATB, orch, 1985; Songs of Love and Justice, S, pf, 1992; 4 Love Songs, T, pf, 1994; Slave Song, B, chbr orch, 1996; Summer Life: Song Cycle on Poems of Emily Dickinson, S, str qt, pf, 2004; other songs

MSS in *Whu*

Principal publishers: Fema, Hinshaw, Marks, MMB, Piedmont

BIBLIOGRAPHY

SouthernB

A. Tischler: *Fifteen Black American Composers: a Bibliography of their Works* (Detroit, 1981)

W. Banfield: "Hailstork, Adolphus Cunningham," *International Dictionary of Black Composers* (Chicago, 1999)

W. Banfield: *Musical Landscapes in Color: Conversations with Black American Composers* (Lanham, MD, 2003)

DORIS EVANS MCGINTY/DOMINIQUE-RENÉ DE LERMA

Hair, Harriet I(nez) (*b* Spartanburg, SC, 28 June 1935). Music educator and scholar. She graduated from Mount Holyoke College (BA 1957), Harvard Graduate School of Education (MAT 1958), Converse College (MM

1962), and Teachers College, Columbia University (EDD 1971), and studied music theory with NADIA BOULANGER (1955–6). She taught music in the public schools of Waltham and Weston, Massachusetts (1958–61), and at Converse College (1961–9) and the University of Georgia (1971–2000). At Georgia she was a Senior Teaching Fellow (1991–2), General Sandy Beaver Teaching Professor (1988–91), and chair of Music Education (1993–2000). Her research, which focused on children's responses to music stimuli, appears in prominent journals and in *Applications of Research in Music Behavior* (ed. Madsen and Prickett, 1987). She also presented papers at numerous conferences of the Research Commission of the International Society for Music Education, National Symposia on Research in Music Behavior, and Music Educators National Conference (MENC). Hair was chair (1994–6) and a member of the Executive Committee of the MENC Society for Research in Music Education (1990–6), National Chair of the MENC Council of Student Members (1982–4), secretary of the National Consortium of Computer-Based Music Instruction (1982–6), and on the editorial committee of the *Journal of Research in Music Education* (1982–8).

JERE T. HUMPHREYS

Hairston, Jester (Joseph) (*b* Belews Creek, NC, 9 July 1901; *d* Los Angeles, CA, 18 Jan 2000). Arranger, choral conductor, and actor. He grew up in Homestead, Pennsylvania, where he sang in school and church choirs. After two years of study at Massachusetts Agricultural College he transferred to Tufts University where he graduated with a music degree in 1929. In search of opportunities to sing professionally, he went to New York where he joined the Hall Johnson Choir in 1931. From that point forward, his career progressed with remarkable consistency in three streams. By the mid-1930s, he had established himself as a skillful arranger and conductor of choral music. In the latter capacity he travelled extensively in the United States and abroad until well into his nineties. His published arrangements are characterized by lively, repetitive, and often syncopated rhythms, fundamental harmonies with well-spaced modulations, and colorful melodies that are always true to their ethnic origins. Among the best known of more than ninety such works are *Amen, Deep River, Elijah Rock, Poor Man Lazrus,* and *Mary's Little Boy Chile.* The acting stream of his career began with his portrayal of Ko-Ko in the San Francisco production of *The Swing Mikado* in 1939, included the role of Jethro in *The Alamo,* and ended in 1991 after four years as Rolly Forbes in the TV sitcom *Amen.* He gained a high profile through his involvement with the popular entertainment media, but his career seems defined mainly through his work as a choral conductor and clinician and as an arranger of African American folk songs and spirituals.

BIBLIOGRAPHY
A. Collier: "Jester Hairston," *Ebony,* xliii/5 (1988), 126–30
H. Wiencek: *The Hairstons: An American Family in Black and White* (New York, 1999)
H.L. Caldwell: "Hairston, Jester Joseph," *International Dictionary of Black Composers,* ed. S.A. Floyd (Chicago, 1999), i, 524–7
Jester Hairston: a Celebration of His Life in Music and Pictures (New York, 2000)

WARREN FIELDS

Haitian American music. *See* LATINO MUSIC.

Hajos, Karl (T.) (*b* Budapest, Hungary, 28 Jan 1889; *d* Hollywood, CA, 1 Feb 1950). Composer and conductor of Hungarian birth; naturalized American in 1930. He was educated at the Academy of Music in Budapest and studied piano with Emil Saur in Vienna. In 1921 and 1922, he composed operettas in Berlin, Germany, before immigrating in 1924 to New York, where he continued writing operettas through 1928. Moving to Hollywood, he scored films at Paramount as a staff composer from 1928 to 1934. He spent a year at Universal in 1935, then two at Republic, where his music made its way into Westerns and serials. Seeking other work he became the conductor of the short-lived California Symphony Orchestra in 1937, provided commentary for California Opera radio broadcasts in 1938, and served as musical director for a Los Angeles Civic Light Opera production in 1942. Returning to film scoring in 1943, it took him two years before he landed at Producers Releasing Corp. (PRC). In 1945 he scored a half dozen PRC films before being named musical director for the company the following year. He was charged with supervising the composing, orchestrating, and recording for company productions and continued to provide his own original scores for a dozen films over the next two years. Around 1947 he founded Karl Hajos Music Service and scored films until his death in 1950.

WORKS
(selective list)

FILM SCORES
Loves of an Actress, 1928; Morocco, 1930; Dishonored, 1931; The Song of Songs, 1933; Four Frightened People, 1934; Hitler's Madmen, 1943; Summer Storm, 1944; Kill or Be Killed, 1950

FILM SONGS
Sunbeams Bring Dreams of You, 1928 [from *Loves of an Actress*]; Adoration, 1928 [title song from the film]; Beggars of Life, 1928 [title song from the film]; Lonely Little Senorita, 1933 [from *Cradle Song*]; Manhattan Moon, 1935 [title song from the film]; My Other Me, 1935 [from *Manhattan Moon*]; Waitin' for the Sun, 1937 [from *Rainbow on the River*]; Summer Storm, 1944 [title song from the film]

OPERETTAS
The Red Cat, Berlin, 1923; The Waltz King, New York, 1925; Her Majesty, New York, 1927

STAGE MUSICALS
White Lilacs, New York, 1928 [based on the life of Frederic Chopin]; America Sings, New York, 1934 [based on the life of Stephen Foster]

ORCHESTRAL
Two symphonic poems for orchestra; Phantasy for Piano and Orchestra
Numerous works published in Berlin, Budapest, and Vienna in the 1920s
MSS in USC Department of Special Collections

WARREN M. SHERK

Hakim, Omar (*b* New York, NY, 12 Feb 1959). Drummer. He took up drums at an early age and first played professionally at the age of nine in a jazz band led by his father, Hasaan Hakim, who was a trombonist. He left that band at the age of 11 to play funk. After working with Weather Report (1982–5), he played with Sting and from time to time with Miles Davis (1986–8). From the late 1970s Hakim has been busy in the studio and on tour supporting a string of high-profile performers in rock, pop, jazz, fusion, and soul; these include Roy Ayers, Anita Baker, George Benson, David Bowie, Mariah Carey, Dire Straits, Gil Evans, Brian Ferry, Astrud Gilberto, Herbie Hancock, Madonna, Miriam Makeba, David Sanborn, John Scofield, Carly Simon, Bruce Springsteen, and the Urban Knights. Alongside other highly regarded drummers, Hakim played on a tribute album to the drummer Buddy Rich, *Burning for Buddy* (1997, Atlantic). He is a versatile player, at home in diverse musical styles, and has also worked as a drum clinician. He has been noted for his facility as a programmer since the advent of drum machines, for his association with electronic drums, and for his bolt-upright, "praying mantis" posture. Hakim has made two educational videos, *Express yourself* (1993, Alfred Publishing Company) and *Let it Flow* (1993, Alfred Publishing Company), and his own albums, *Rhythm Deep* (1990, GRP Records), *The Groovesmith* (2000, Oh Zone Entertainment), and *We Are One* (2008, Oh Zone Entertainment), on which he composes, sings, and plays guitar and piano.

BIBLIOGRAPHY

GroveJ

W.F. Miller: "Omar Hakim," *Modern Drummer*, xiii/7 (1989), 8–23, 52–55

A. Budofsky, ed.: *The Drummer: 100 Years of Rhythmic Power and Invention* (Cedar Grove, NJ, 2006)

B. Keefe: "Switched on Interview: Omar Hakim," *Drummer*, lxxii/October (2009), p. 64

G. Nicholls: "Complete…Omar Hakim," *Rhythm* (2010), July, p. 21

GARETH DYLAN SMITH

Hakim, Talib-Rasul [Chambers, Stephen Alexander] (*b* Asheville, NC, 8 Feb 1940; *d* New Haven, CT, 31 March 1988). Composer. He studied at the Manhattan School of Music (1958–9), the New York College of Music (1959–63), and the New School for Social Research, New York (1963–5). His major teachers and advisors included HALL OVERTON, WILLIAM SYDEMAN, HALE SMITH, CHARLES WHITTENBERG, MORTON FELDMAN, MARGARET BONDS, and ORNETTE COLEMAN. He taught at Pace College (1970–72), Adelphi University (1972–9), Nassau Community College (1971–81), and Morgan State University. He also coordinated the Brooklyn Philharmonic Community Concert Series and was active as a radio and television producer. He was the recipient of awards from the Bennington Composers Conference (1964–9) and the Connecticut Commission on the Arts (1981–2), among others. In 1973, on his conversion to Sufism, he changed his name.

Hakim's compositions, frequently scored for unusual instrumental combinations, feature rich harmonies and often incorporate extended performance techniques.

Birmingham Reflections (1985), in honor of Martin Luther King, was commissioned by the New Haven SO. *Ramadhān-Meditations* for winds and piano (1986), a work written for the Woodhill Players, creates a meditative feeling using free improvisation on a set of given pitches accompanied by a repetitive piano drone.

WORKS

Orch: Shapes, 1965; Visions of Ishwara, 1970; Reflections of the 5th Ray, nar, orch, 1972; Sketchy Blue-Bop, jazz band, 1973; Re/currences, 1974; Concepts, 1976; Rhu-barb, jazz band, 1976; Arkan-5, orch, tape, 1980; Az-Zaahir/Al Baatin, 1981; Bir-ming-ham Reflections, nar, orch, 1985

Vocal: Ode to Silence, S, pf, 1964; Sound-Image, S, A, brass, str, perc, 1969; Set-Three, S, vc, pf, 1970; Tone Prayers, mixed chorus, pf, perc, 1973; Music, S, 9 players, 1977; Psalm of Akhnaton, *c*1365–1348 BC, Mez, fl, pf, 1978; Quote-Unquote, Bar, ob, tpt, perc, 1983; Spiritual and Other Fragments from Another Time and Other Places, SATB, ww, brass, pf, str, 1983

Chbr and solo inst: Mutations, b cl, tpt, hn, va, vc, 1964; Peace-Mobile, ww qnt, 1964; 4, cl, tpt, trbn, pf, 1965; A Pf Piece, 1965; Encounter, ww qnt, tpt, trbn, 1965; Portraits, fl, cl, bn, pf, perc, 1965; Titles, ww qt, 1965; Contours, ob, bn, hn, tpt, vc, db, 1966; Currents, str qt, 1967; Inner-Sections, fl, cl, trbn, pf, perc, 1967; Roots and Other-Things, fl, ob, cl, hn, tpt, trbn, va, vc, db, 1967; Sound-Gone, pf, 1967; Placements, pf, perc, 1970; on BEing still…on the 8th, ww, vc, db, pf, perc, 1978; Fragments from Other Places—Other Times, perc, 1982; "Ramadhān-Meditations" (9-Ramazān 1406 AD—May 1986 AD), ww qnt, pf, 1986

Principal publishers: Bote & Bock, G. Schirmer

BIBLIOGRAPHY

E. Southern: "America's Black Composers of Classical Music," *MEJ*, lxii/3 (1975–6), 46–59

T. Johnson: "Talib-Rasul Hakim has found his music," *Village Voice* (20 Feb 1978)

C.E. Oliver: Selected Orchestral Works of Thomas J. Anderson, Arthur Cunningham, Talib-Rasul Hakim and Olly Wilson (diss., Florida State U., 1978)

ALISON DEBORAH JONES

Halau o Kekuhi. Hawaiian hula school in Hilo, Hawaii. Founded in 1953 by Edith Kanaka'ole, the school has been instrumental in the preservation and dissemination of hula and chant practices associated with Pele, the goddess of fire. Knowledge about these traditions was passed down to Kanaka'ole through matrilineal descent for at least seven generations, and she in turn instructed her own daughters, Pualani Kanaka'ole Kanahele and Nalani Kanaka'ole, who inherited the school in 1979 upon their mother's death.

The style of hula taught and performed by the school, 'aiha'a, is characterized by a bent-knee posture and vigorous movements, a reflection of the energy and power of the volcano goddess. In addition to learning hula, dancers at the school become fully immersed in the culture of Hawaii and hula. They learn the Hawaiian language and how to play the ipu (gourd) and pahu (sharkskin drum), and create their own costumes and props using the traditional materials and practices.

The school's most ambitious production, *Holo Mai Pele*, incorporates hula and chant with narrative and theatrical stagecraft. The three-hour production, which premiered on Maui in 1995, presents ancient chants about Pele and Hi'iaka, the patron goddess of hula. In 2001 the troupe presented it at Wolf Trap (Virginia) for the "Faces of America" series. A television production of this hula drama was created for the Public Broadcasting Service's *Great Performances: Dance in America* series. The Hawaiian Academy of Recording Arts awarded the school the Na Hoku Hanohano Award for Best Hawaiian Language Performance for their album *Uwolani* in 1999.

BIBLIOGRAPHY
P. Kanahele: *Holo Mai Pele*, trans. K. Higashi, ed. D.M. Dudoit (Honolulu, 2001)

PAULA J. BISHOP

Hale, Joseph P. (*b* Bernardston, MA, 24 Oct 1819; *d* New York, NY, 15 Oct 1883). Piano manufacturer. As a young adult in Worcester, Massachusetts, Hale worked as a builder and sold shoes, crockery, and other domestic goods. He came to New York in 1860 to invest his capital (reported as $30,000–$35,000) in piano manufacturing. He first went into partnership with James H. Grovesteen, but formed his own company in 1863, situated in lower Manhattan and, from 1866, at locations near Tenth Avenue and 36th Street. Hale built three factories in succession in the block between 35th and 36th Streets, west of Tenth Avenue. The first collapsed during construction in December 1870; the second, built in 1871 and augmented in 1875 and 1877, burned down in September 1877; the third and largest, erected in 1878, was used by Hale until his death, and later by his son-in-law, who ran a revived company until 1894.

Hale employed the stencil system, supplying agents, dealers, and other purchasers with instruments marked with whatever names they desired. Although there is little evidence that Hale's known stencils and registered trade-marks were deceptive, he was accused repeatedly by John Christian Freund, in the *Music Trade Review*, of manufacturing "bogus" pianos that were passed off to gullible buyers as high-quality instruments. The feud between Freund and Hale also involved a trade protective society formed in early 1876, which pitted Hale against William Steinway, who was allied with Freund. Hale, for his part, was associated with Albert Weber, Steinway's chief competitor in the Centennial Exposition in Philadelphia later that year. The destruction of Hale's factory in 1877 emboldened Freund to accuse him of criminal negligence. Early in 1878, Hale sued Freund for libel, although he later withdrew his suit when Freund apologized; in desperate financial straits, Freund received a loan from Hale, who was also an active money-lender, as well as an investor in railroads in the Midwest.

Hale produced pianos in great volume at the cheapest possible cost and sold them at low prices, mostly in the Midwest and South. In 1869 he was listed as the seventh largest piano manufacturer in America in terms of gross annual sales. At first Hale made only square pianos, but his production of uprights began in 1877, and by 1879 they outnumbered squares by two to one. Hale bought most of his piano parts in bulk, ready-made from suppliers. His factories, heated by stoves, had no boilers and consequently no steam engines, as power machinery was not necessary for the hand

assembly, varnishing, and finishing done there. The work in his factories was supervised by foremen with whom he made financial arrangements according to the contract system. After his death, estimates of Hale's wealth ranged from $5,000,000 to over $10,000,000. Hale's business methods earned him a posthumous reputation as "the father of the 'commercial' piano of America" (Alfred Dolge) and "the founder of the present day piano business" (Henry Z. Steinway).

BIBLIOGRAPHY
Music Trade Review, i/3 (1875) to x/9 (1879)
M.H. Smith: *Successful Folks. How They Win. Illustrated in the Career of Eight Hundred Eminent Men* (Hartford, CT, 1878), 368–78
A. Dolge: *Pianos and Their Makers*, i (Covina, CA, 1911/*R*), 179–81
N. Groce: *Musical Instrument Makers of New York* (Stuyvesant, NY, 1991), 65–6, 69–70
H.Z. Steinway: personal communication, 14 December 2005

WILLIAM E. HETTRICK

Hale, Philip (*b* Norwich, VT, 5 March 1854; *d* Boston, MA, 30 Nov 1934). Music critic. After graduating from Yale (1876), he studied in Europe with Carl Haupt, Woldemar Bargiel, JOSEPH RHEINBERGER, and Alexandre Guilmant (1882–7), and then settled in Boston in 1889. He was music critic for the *Boston Post* (1890–91) and *Boston Journal* (1891–1903), correspondent for the *Musical Courier* (1892–8), music and drama critic for the *Boston Herald* (1903–33), and editor of the *Musical Record* (1897–1901), the *Musical World* (1901–2), and the two-volume collection *Modern French Songs* (1904).

Hale is best known for his program notes for the Boston SO, written between 1901 and 1934. These are scholarly, witty, and ample, and became the model for American program annotators. He insisted on evaluating each work as it appeared to him and became known for the quotability of his negative opinions (he once said of Ludwig van Beethoven's Fifth Piano Concerto that "the finale, with the endless repetitions of a Kangaroo theme, leads one to long for the end"). Though his shrewd evaluation of modern music caused him to be represented as a crabbed reactionary, even cringing at Johannes Brahms, he was, in reality, a fair-minded and forward-looking critic. He was one of the earliest American champions of Debussy and other contemporary French composers, while also showing an evenhanded approach to modern works from other European and American composers. Subsequently, the respect he attained as both a program notes writer and a Boston-area critic redefined him as a major arbiter of musical taste in Boston at the turn of the century.

WRITINGS
ed., with L.C. Elson: *Famous Composers and Their Works* (Boston, 1900)
ed. J.N. Burk: *Philip Hale's Boston Symphony Programme Notes* (Garden City, NY, 1935, 2/1939/*R*1971)
MSS in *MB*

BIBLIOGRAPHY
E.F. Edgett: "Hale, Philip," *DAB*
J.A. Boyd: *Philip Hale, American Music Critic, Boston, 1889–1933* (diss., U. of Texas, Austin, 1985)

WAYNE D. SHIRLEY/BRENDAN HIGGINS

Hale, Robert (*b* San Antonio, TX, 22 Aug 1943). Bass-baritone. He studied at Boston University and the New England Conservatory, and debuted in 1966 singing W.A. Mozart's *Figaro* with the Goldovsky Opera. In 1967 he joined New York City Opera, where he sang Mozart's Figaro, Count Almaviva, Don Giovanni, Raimondo, Henry VIII (*Anna Bolena*), Oroveso, Giorgio (*I puritani*), and the Father (*Louise*). He sang Claudius (*Hamlet*) at San Diego in 1978 and the four *Contes d'Hoffmann* villains at Buenos Aires in 1980. For his European debut he sang the Dutchman in *Der fliegende Holländer* in Stuttgart in 1978 and soon began to take on heavier roles such as Pizarro, Iago, Mephistopheles (Gounod and Boito), Scarpia, and Escamillo, which he sang in Germany and at Zürich, Lisbon, and San Francisco. He debuted in Covent Garden as John the Baptist in 1988 and returned as Orestes (*Elektra*) in 1994. During the 1990s he earned a reputation for Wagnerian roles, especially as Wotan (Deutsche Oper, Berlin 1990, Vienna Staatsoper 1992–3, the Théâtre du Châtelet in Paris 1994, and elsewhere) and as the Dutchman (La Scala 1989 and the Metropolitan 1990). At Salzburg he has sung Pizarro and Barak (*Die Frau ohne Schatten*).

A selection of his videos and audio recordings include performances in *Der Ring des Nibelungen* (Wolfgang Sawallisch, Munich) and *Die Frau ohne Schatten* (EMI) as well as Richard Strauss's *Salome* (Chandos), Joseph Haydn's *Die Schöpfung*, and Robert Schumann's *Das Paradies und die Peri* (Deutsche Grammophon). In the meantime, Hale has also maintained an active career as a recitalist. While performing with the duo Hale and Wilder for more than two decades, he concertized throughout the world and released 21 recordings. He performed frequently with the soprano Inga Nielsen, to whom he was married for many years, and now is often seen in concert with his new wife, soprano Julie Davis.

ELIZABETH FORBES/JOSEPH E. MORGAN

Haley, Bill [William John Clifton] (*b* Highland Park, MI, 6 July 1925; *d* Harlingen, TX, 9 Feb 1981). Rock and roll singer and bandleader. Featured in the film *The Blackboard Jungle* (1955), Haley's 1954 version of Max Freedman and Jimmy DeKnight's "Rock around the Clock" was the first internationally known rock and roll recording. Haley sang in the clear, clipped manner of a square-dance caller, while his backing group, the Comets, included the raucous saxophone of Rudy Pompilli, guitar, double bass (played in a slap-bass style by Al Rex), and drums. During the group's concerts, Pompilli and bassist Rex often would lie on the stage to play their instruments. Their musical style had been fashioned mainly from the heavily rhythmic western swing of Haley's earlier group the Saddlemen and the jump-blues style associated with Louis Jordan. In 1951, the Saddlemen had recorded a cover version of "Rocket 88," whose original version by Jackie Brenston is sometimes cited as the first rock and roll record. Other hits added current hipster and jive-talk phrases in the titles of such songs as "Crazy Man Crazy," "Razzle Dazzle," and "See you later alligator." Bill Haley and his Comets appeared in the film *Rock around the Clock* (1956) and toured Europe and Australia, but, compared with the teenage Elvis Presley, the avuncular Haley was an unlikely rock and roll star. He moved away from rock and played country music in the 1960s, occasionally returning to his hits at rock and roll revival concerts in later years.

BIBLIOGRAPHY

J. Swenson: *Bill Haley* (London, 1982)

J.W. Haley and J. von Hoëlle: *Sound and Glory* (Wilmington, DE, 1990)

J. Dawson: *Rock around the Clock: the Record that Started the Rock Revolution!* (San Francisco, 2005)

DAVE LAING/R

Haley, (James) Ed(ward) (*b* Logan Co., WV, *c*1883–5; *d* Ashland, KY, 3 Feb 1951). Fiddler. Born in southern West Virginia, he was blinded by a childhood bout of measles. He was drawn to the fiddle early and eventually came to depend on it for his livelihood. His wife Ella (born Martha Ella Trumbo, date unknown–1954), was also a blind musician, and they busked together at county fairs and court days throughout eastern Kentucky and southern West Virginia. Their home was in Ashland and elsewhere in northeast Kentucky. In 1946–7 Haley's son Ralph supplied a disc recording machine for a family project to record their father. These home recordings were distributed to various Haley children, and in the early 1970s Lawrence Haley brought some to the Library of Congress to be copied. Out of that project came a documentary LP recording presenting a selection of the materials. The release of the LP had an impact among fiddlers of the American instrumental folk music revival. A generation later, performer John Hartford, who had adopted Ed Haley's recordings as a mission, produced a nearly complete edition of the Haley recordings on two double-CD sets. Haley had a large repertory drawn from many sources, ranging from old British and American breakdowns to rags and slow airs. His mixed style also reflected multiple sources: he performed many tunes in the separate-stroke style of the Ohio River Valley of West Virginia and Kentucky, but other tunes in the mixed "long-bow" style of the Upland South.

RECORDINGS
(selective list)

Ed Haley: *Parkersburg Landing* (1975, Rounder 1010); *Ed Haley: Forked Deer* (1997, Rounder 1131/1132); *Ed Haley: Grey Eagle* (1998, Rounder 1133/1134)

ALAN JABBOUR

Haley, Jack [John Joseph, Jr.] (*b* Boston, MA, 10 Aug 1898; *d* Los Angeles, CA, 6 June 1979). Actor and performer. Haley initially became an electrician in the Boston area. However, he soon left that career to pursue vaudeville and toured in the team Krafts and Haley. He began his Broadway career in the 1924 original musical revue *Round the Town*. In 1929 Haley starred as Jack Martin in the musical comedy *Follow Thru* with lyrics by DeSylva and Brown and music by Henderson. He and his costar, Zelma O'Neal, performed the hit number "Button up your Overcoat." Haley was later cast in the 1932 musical comedy *Take a Chance* by DeSylva and Schwab.

In the 1948 musical revue *Inside USA*, Haley's character displayed effective physical comedy while portraying a weary traveler booked in a room with a trick bed. Haley served as the radio host of *Wonder Show* (1938–9), a show sponsored by Wonder Bread, which featured Gale Gordon as the announcer and regular appearances by Lucille Ball. Haley replaced Buddy Ebsen as the Tin Man in the film *The Wizard of Oz*. Haley's warm lyric baritone captured the sentimentality of the character while his dancing included both physical comedy and graceful movement. His Hollywood career totaled over thirty films.

BIBLIOGRAPHY
J. Lahr: *Notes on a Cowardly Lion* (New York, 1969)
M. Cohen: *Heart of the Tin Man: the Collected Writings of Jack Haley* (Beverly Hills, CA, 2000)

SYLVIA STONER-HAWKINS

Hall, David (*b* New Rochelle, NY, 16 Dec 1916). Discographer, editor, and writer on music. A self-taught musician, he studied psychology at Yale University (BA 1939) and Columbia University (1939–40). He has held a wide variety of positions, including classical music program annotator for NBC (1942–8); music director of the classical division of Mercury Records (1948–56), where he oversaw the "Living Presence" recordings; director of the American-Scandinavian Foundation's music center (1950–57); music editor of *Hi-Fi Review* (1957–63) and contributor to its successor, *Stereo Review*, until it ceased publication in 1998; and president of CRI (1963–7). A Fulbright Teaching Fellowship in 1956 allowed him to teach advanced recording techniques at the University of Copenhagen. A champion of contemporary music, he published the first discography of Charles Ives in 1964. In 1967 he became head of the Rodgers and Hammerstein Archives of Recorded Sound at the New York Public Library. After his retirement in 1983, he was a classical music consultant to the National Academy of Recording Arts and Sciences through 2000. He was a founding member of the Association for Recorded Sound Collections and the first editor of its *Journal* (1968–71). He also served as its president (1979–83) and was given the first ARSC Distinguished Service Award in 2003. In addition to his many articles and reviews, Hall compiled *The Record Book* (1940 and suppls.; international edn 1948), which incorporated discographic information about living American composers, and *The Disc Book* (1955), one of the first buyer's guides of the LP era.

PAULA MORGAN/JIM FARRINGTON

Hall, D(avid) C. (*b* Lyme, NH, 16 May 1822; *d* Boston, MA, 11 Feb 1900). Bandleader, keyed bugle soloist, and brass instrument manufacturer. He began his playing and band-leading career in Hartford, Connecticut (1844–5), then New Haven, Connecticut (1845–6) and Lowell, Massachusetts (1847–53). He was presented with a solid gold keyed bugle on 15 April 1850 by the Lowell band. In 1853 Hall succeeded Patrick Gilmore as leader of the Boston Brass Band and retained this position for many years. In 1861 Hall joined with J. Lathrop Allen and mechanics George W. and Benjamin F. Quinby to form Allen & Hall, a new brass instrument firm at 334 Washington Street, Boston. In 1862, following Allen's departure, the firm continued under the name of D.C. Hall, and in 1866 it became Hall & Quinby. A year later the company moved to 62 Sudbury, and from this time through 1875 Hall & Quinby were the leading producers of brasses in Boston.

In 1876 D.C. Hall established his own company again at 126 Court Street, and the shop at 62 Sudbury was continued as Quinby Bros. Hall evidently sought to take advantage of European advances in instrument design and the increasing use of woodwinds, by entering into arrangements with Parisian makers A. Lecomte & Co., Gautrot, and Buffett, Crampton & Co., as well as C. Mahillon & Co., to import their products. He also attempted to broaden his business even more by offering stringed instruments, guitars, and percussion.

The business does not seem to have gone well, and by 1878 Hall had given up the new shop. He continued his playing and band-leading career until late in the century, but began spending winters in California near San Diego.

Examples of Allen & Hall, D.C. Hall, and Hall & Quinby instruments are found in the John H. Elrod Memorial Collection, Germantown, Maryland; The Musical Instrument Museum, Tempe, Arizona; The Henry Ford, Dearborn, Michigan; the Museum of Fine Arts, Boston; and the National Music Museum at the University of South Dakota. Hall family papers are located at The Henry Ford, Dearborn, Michigan. A privately published collection of these materials is available electronically from The Henry Ford and from R.E. Eliason.

BIBLIOGRAPHY
W. Waterhouse: *The New Langwill Index* (London, 1993), 157–58
R.E. Eliason: "D. C. Hall and the Quinby Brothers," *JAMIS*, xxxiii (2007)

ROBERT E. ELIASON

Hall, Edmond (*b* New Orleans, LA, 15 May 1901; *d* Boston, MA, 11 Feb 1967). Jazz clarinetist. Son of a clarinetist, he was the second of five brothers to become a musician. He began performing with various bands in New Orleans by 1919. He toured the Gulf Coast with Buddy Petit (1921–3), and spent the mid-1920s with lesser known groups in Florida and Georgia. Moving to New York in 1928, he played in Claude Hopkins's swing orchestra from 1929 to 1935. In the late 1930s he returned to small groups, recording with Mildred Bailey and Billie Holiday, and working at the Café Society with Henry "Red" Allen, Teddy Wilson, and as a leader (1944–6). During the mid-1940s he also recorded with Eddie Condon. Hall soon became one of the most highly regarded dixieland clarinetists, although he considered himself more of a swing player in the mold of Benny Goodman, and his driving sense of rhythm and phrasing shows that influence. After leading groups in Boston (1946–50), he joined the band at Condon's club. In 1955 he succeeded Barney Bigard in Louis Armstrong's All Stars, touring and recording for three years. He freelanced from 1958 until his death. Hall's playing is marked by soaring high register solos with a throaty, vocalized tone and wide terminal vibrato.

BIBLIOGRAPHY
B. McRae: "Edmond Hall," *JJ*, xxiii/12 (1970), 24
M. Selchow: *Profoundly Blue: a Bio-discographical Scrapbook on Edmond Hall* (Lübbecke, Germany, 1988)

CHARLES E. KINZER

Hall, Frederick Douglass (*b* Atlanta, GA, 14 Dec 1898; *d* Atlanta, GA, 28 Dec 1982). Composer and arranger. He studied at Morehouse College (BA 1921), Chicago Musical College (BMus 1924), the RAM (Licentiate Degree 1933–5), and Columbia University Teachers College (MA 1929, DMusEd 1952). His teaching appointments included positions at Dillard University (1936–41, 1960–74), Alabama State University, Montgomery (1941–55), and Southern University (1955–9). A prolific composer and arranger of works for chorus, he was known both for his unique compositions and his arrangements of spirituals. He also wrote music for the piano and, as a result of his study of West African folksong, made many arrangements of African songs. Internationally known as a lecturer, choral workshop director, and choral conductor, he was the recipient of numerous honors, including the Julius Rosenwald Fellowship, the Phelps-Stokes Fund Research Fellowship, and the General Education Board Fellowship. (*SouthernB*)

JAMES STANDIFER

Hall, Jim [James Stanley] (*b* Buffalo, NY, 4 Dec 1930). Jazz guitarist. He began playing guitar professionally as a teenager in Cleveland. After attending the Cleveland Institute of Music (BM 1955), where he studied piano and composition, he moved to Los Angeles and took classical guitar lessons with VICENTE GÓMEZ. From 1956 to 1959 he was a member of the Jimmy Giuffre Three. In the early 1960s Hall moved to New York and made his name as a leading jazz guitarist, working with figures such as Ben Webster, Paul Desmond, Lee Konitz, Sonny Rollins, Tommy Flanagan, Bob Brookmeyer, and Art Farmer. After joining the band on *The Merv Griffin* in 1965, he returned to jazz full time and recorded with Gil Evans, Ron Carter, Pat Metheny, and Joe Lovano, among others. He has remained active as a jazz guitarist since that time working in various ensembles, proving especially effective in small groups. One of the most influential jazz guitarists since Charlie Christian and Django Reinhart, Hall is known for his warm, soft, natural tone, legato articulation, motivic sensibility, reserved dynamics, lyricism, rhythmic flexibility, introspection, and careful taste.

Over the course of his career, he has occasionally collaborated with such classical artists as the violinist Itzhak Perlman and the Kronos Quartet. He has also composed works such as *Peace Movement*, for guitar and symphony orchestra, which he premiered with the Baltimore SO in 2004. In the same year he was awarded a Jazz Masters Fellowship by the NEA. In 2006 he was awarded the Chevalier dans l'ordre des arts et des lettres by the French government.

BIBLIOGRAPHY
GroveJ; *MGG2* (J. Schwab)
J. Schwab: "Jim Hall: Analytische Betrachtungen zum Vater der modernen Jazzgitarre," *Jf*, xxxiv (2002), 115–31
M. Fagien, ed.: *Jazziz Chronicles: the Guitarists* (New York, 2003)
B. Milkowski: "Undercurrents: Guitarist Jim Hall Duologues through the Years," *JT*, xxxv/10 (2005), 54–8
M.A. Woelfle: "Jim Hall," *Jazz-Klassiker*, ed. P.N. Wilson (Stuttgart, 2005), 528–33

JÖRG JEWANSKI

Hall, Rhodolph (*b* Lyme, NH, 22 July 1824; *d* New Haven, CT, 10 Dec 1878). Keyed bugle, cornet, and clarinet soloist. He played with brass bands, dance bands, circuses, minstrel shows, bell ringers, and other concert ensembles, and toured widely, including trips throughout the eastern and mid-western states, California, Cuba, Canada, and England. In 1853 he became "second leader" of the Boston Brass Band under his brother, D. C. HALL. A unique feature of his performances after 1860 was the use of a cornet with an echo attachment. In 1867 he was given an elaborately decorated, solid-gold cornet by his friends and admirers. He claimed to have "a written contract for the largest salary of any American instrumentalist of my kind that has yet lived" while touring as cornet and clarinet soloist with the Peak Family Bell Ringers in 1870. The Hall Family Papers are held at the Henry Ford Centennial Library in Dearborn, Michigan.

BIBLIOGRAPHY
R.E. Eliason: "Rhodolph Hall, Nineteenth-Century Keyed Bugle, Cornet and Clarinet Soloist," *JAMIS*, xxix (2003)

ROBERT E. ELIASON

Hall, Robert Browne (*b* Bowdoinham, ME, 30 June 1858; *d* Portland, ME, 8 June 1907). Cornetist, bandmaster, and composer. He came from a musical family and studied cornet at an early age. When he was 16 his family moved to Richmond, Maine. At 19 he was solo cornetist with a summer band at Old Orchard Beach, Maine, and at 20 he played with J.T. Baldwin's First Corps of Cadets Band of Boston, alternating as cornet soloist with Alessandro Liberati. In 1882 he became director of the Bangor (Maine) Band. He also led a number of other bands for brief periods, among them that of the Tenth Regiment NY National Guard at Albany, and Chandler's Military Band of Portland, Maine. Around 1890 he moved to Waterville, Maine, to direct the Waterville Military Band (also known as Hall's Military Band). As a cornet soloist, Hall was rated one of the finest in the Northeast. He wrote 112 compositions, of which the best-known are the marches *Independentia, Officer of the Day, New Colonial, W.M.B.* (Waterville Military Band), *S.I.B.A.* (Southern Illinois Band Association), *De Molay Commandery, Funebre, Gardes du corps* and *Tenth Regiment* (published in England as *Death or Glory*). Because of the success of his marches, Hall came to be known as the "New England March King." Manuscripts, concert programs, photographs, and memorabilia relating to Hall are held at the Maine State Library, Augusta, the Reddington Museum of the Waterville Historical Society, and the R.B. Hall Memorial Tape Anthology,

Vineyard Haven, Massachusetts. Many of his compositions are included in the *Heritage of the March* recordings compiled by Robert Hoe (1, C, E, H, P, T, MM, OO, and WW).

BIBLIOGRAPHY

W.C. White: *A History of Military Music in America* (New York, 1944), 139–41 [photograph]

G.D. Bridges: *Pioneers in Brass* (Detroit, 1965); CD-ROM (Coupeville, WA, 2000)

T.C. Bardwell: "Robert Browne Hall (the New England March King)," *Music Journal Anthology 1968*, ed. R. Cumming (New York, 1968), 33

T.C. Bardwell: "The New England March King," *Fanfare*, i/10 (1977), 28

R.F. Swift: "Credit Overdue: R. B. Hall," *Woodwind, Brass & Percussion*, xxi/7 (1982), 20

W.H. Rehrig: *The Heritage Encyclopedia of Band Music* (Westerville, OH, 1991, suppl. 1996); CD-ROM (Oskaloosa, IA, 2005)

G.W. Bowie: *R.B. Hall and the Community Bands of Maine* (Ph.D. diss., U. of Maine, 1993)

N.E. Smith: *Program Notes for Band* (Lake Charles, LA, 2000), 264–6

RAOUL F. CAMUS

Hall, Thomas S. (*b* Philadelphia, PA, 1791; *d* New York, NY, 23 May 1874). Organ builder. After an apprenticeship with English-trained John Lowe of Philadelphia, he began building organs there following Lowe's death in 1811. He moved to New York around 1816, and took young HENRY ERBEN as an apprentice; two years later he married Erben's older sister Maria. Some substantial organs were built in this early period, including those for the Unitarian Church of Baltimore (1818), St. George's Episcopal Church, New York (1822), and the Catholic Cathedral in Baltimore (1824). In 1824 he took his former apprentice, Erben, into a partnership that lasted until 1827, when Erben left to establish his own business, and which resulted in several organs for churches in New York and elsewhere. Hall continued to obtain significant contracts from churches such as St. Thomas's Episcopal in New York (1832), and in 1846 he formed a partnership with John Labagh (1810–92) under the name of Hall & Labagh. An important organ from this period was the large three-manual instrument of 1855 in St. Joseph's Catholic Church of Troy, New York. James L. Kemp (1827–91) became a partner in 1868, and in 1870 the firm built a replacement for Hall's earlier organ in St. Thomas's Church. Hall retired in 1872, and the firm continued under the name of Labagh & Kemp until 1891, when it was sold to the short-lived partnership of Chapman & Symmes.

BIBLIOGRAPHY

P.T. Cameron: "Business Records of Hall, Labagh & Co.," *The Tracker*, xiv/4 (1969–70), 5–6; xv/1 (1970–71), 1–3; xv/2, 6–8; xv/3, 6–10; xv/4, 14–18; xvi/1 (1971–2), 11–15

J. Ogasapian: *Organ Building in New York City: 1700–1900* (Braintree, MA, 1977)

S. Pinel: "Thomas S. Hall, 19th Century New York Organbuilder," *The Diapason*, lxxxi/2 (1990), 14–16

S. Pinel: "Thomas S. Hall, Founder of the New York School of Organbuilders," *De Mixtuur*, lxv (1990), 246–63

BARBARA OWEN

Hall, Tom T. (*b* Olive Hill, KY, 25 May 1936). Country music singer-songwriter and guitarist. After preparing for a career in journalism at Roanoke (Virginia) College,

he worked with a bluegrass band, the Kentucky Travelers, as a DJ on radio station WMOR, and as a songwriter. In the US Army from 1957 to 1961, he was a DJ for the Armed Forces Network while stationed in Germany and later worked at radio stations in Kentucky, Virginia, and West Virginia. In 1963, Jimmy C. Newman's record of Hall's "DJ for a Day" (Decca) reached the top ten on *Billboard*'s "Hot Country Singles" chart. Hall moved to Nashville in 1964; working at first as a salaried songwriter, he began writing for Dave Dudley ("Mad," Mercury, 1964), Johnny Wright ("Hello Vietnam," Decca, 1965), Roy Drusky, Stonewall Jackson, Flatt and Scruggs, and others. Although not interested in a performing career at first, Hall released "I Washed My Face in the Morning Dew," Mercury, 1967), the first of many singles. In 1968, Jeannie C. Riley's recording of Hall's "Harper Valley P.T.A." (Plantation) topped *Billboard*'s country and pop charts, and in 1970, "A Week in a Country Jail" (Mercury) became the first of Hall's own recordings to do the same.

Hall's repertory includes story songs based on his own early life, cheating songs, homespun philosophy, love-songs, silly songs, children's songs, and reworkings of traditional favorites. Hall hosted the syndicated television show *Pop Goes the Country* and has authored a novel, a book on songwriting, and an autobiography. Since Alan Jackson's 1996 hit with Hall's song "Little Bitty" (Arista Nashville), Hall and his wife Dixie (an English-born performer and songwriter in her own right) have focused their efforts on the subgenre of bluegrass, encouraging younger artists and writing songs for Larry Sparks, Don Rigsby, and others. Dixie Hall's *Daughters of Bluegrass* projects and *Tom T Hall Sings Miss Dixie & Tom T* were released on the Halls' own Blue Circle Records label.

BIBLIOGRAPHY

T. Adler: "The Unplotted Narratives of Tom T. Hall," *Journal of Country Music*, iv/2 (1973), 52

T.T. Hall: *How I Write Songs: Why you Can* (New York, 1976)

T.T. Hall: *The Storyteller's Nashville* (Garden City, NY, 1979)

B. Allen: "Tom T. Hall's Struggle for Balance," *Journal of Country Music*, ix/3 (1983), 4

G. Himes: "Who needs Country radio? Not Tom T. Hall," *New York Times* (13 Jan 2008)

RONNIE PUGH/LEE BIDGOOD

Hall (Ward), (Adele) Vera (*b* Payneville, AL, 6 April 1902; *d* Livingston, AL, 29 Jan 1964). Folk singer. From Sumter County, Alabama, Hall knew a vast repertoire of African American folk songs and spirituals and was well-known for singing among her community. During the Great Depression, the Works Progress Administration sent agents into the field to record American vernacular musical traditions. The foremost of these was John Lomax (with his son Alan). Another local Alabama WPA employee, Ruby Pickens Tartt, suggested Hall to the Lomaxes as someone they should record; they did so in July 1937. Hall's recordings were broadcast over the BBC, where British listeners were exposed to her version of "Another Man Done Gone" as an example of American folk music. In 1948 she traveled with Alan Lomax to New York to perform at the American Music

Festival. She was also recorded by Harold Courlander in the early 1950s. Courlander's recordings were released by Folkways Records and were popular with folk music enthusiasts in the late 1950s and early 60s. Her song "Wild Ox Moan," one closely identified with her, was performed by numerous other folk singers in subsequent years. Even though she lived until 1964, by which time the folk revival was in full swing, she was not one of the Southern performers brought by folklorists to any of the large northern folk festivals.

BIBLIOGRAPHY

J. McGregory: "The Significance of Vera Ward Hall," *Tributaries: Journal of the Alabama Folklife Association*, v (2002), 72–91

JEFF PLACE

Hall & Oates. Musical duo. Formed by Daryl (Franklin) Hall [Hohl] (*b* Pottstown, PA, 1946; singer, songwriter, keyboardist, guitarist) and John (William) Oates (*b* North Wales, PA, 1949; guitarist, songwriter), the duo is known primarily for BLUE-EYED SOUL recordings made between 1975 and 1984. Both were musically active in their teens and early twenties, during the flowering of Philadelphia's soul music scene. While neither is intimately connected to the emergence of Philly Soul, both recorded with Kenneth Gamble before the founding of Philadelphia International.

The two musicians met in 1967 while studying at Temple University, in North Philadelphia, and by 1972 had formed their musical partnership. They recorded regularly between 1972 and 1990, but their most popular work started with the song "Sara Smile" (1975) and ended with "Out of Touch," from *Big Bam Boom* (1984). ("She's Gone," recorded in 1972, reached the *Billboard* Top 10 only after it was reissued in 1976).

Most of Hall and Oates's music is clearly single-based pop, much of it conceived within the framework of the Philly Soul sound—coupling funk rhythms, string and horn arrangements, and "sweet" or "smooth," crooning vocals. Their albums each have some measure of sonic cohesion—*Private Eyes* (1981) nods towards new wave, and H_2O (1982) incorporates harder funk and rock elements, in what they called "Rock and Soul"—but they are principally collections of singles, not reaching for conceptual or programmatic integration.

Race is the most compelling issue surrounding the critical reception of their work. The epithet "blue-eyed soul" marks them not only as individually white, but ultimately as part of a generic white appropriation of black music. Regarding this Hall has stressed that the R&B scene in which he and Oates grew up was racially mixed, and that there was musical exchange—and at times exploitation—in every possible direction.

Their work has achieved a steady presence and longevity both as an emblematic sound and as a classic look—Hall's feathered hair, and Oates's mullet and magnificent mustache—of the early 1980s. Their recordings have been widely sampled in hip hop, particularly in the 2000s, and the duo saw a significant resurgence of popularity in the early 2010s.

GABRIEL SOLIS

Halpern, Steven (*b* United States). New Age pianist and producer. He played jazz trumpet and guitar during the 1960s in New York, and has credited John Coltrane as an early influence. He became interested in sonic healing and Eastern religions, both of which became fundamental to the transformation of his musical style. After undergoing a spiritual awakening in 1969 in the Santa Cruz mountains, Halpern developed what he called "anti-frantic alternative" music, releasing his first album, *Spectrum Suite*, in 1975. It became one of the foundational, and most influential, albums of NEW AGE music. To create what was labeled music for "meditation and inner peace," Halpern performed slowly unfolding, almost arrhythmic melodies on keyboards and synthesizers. Often using choral backdrops for his minimalist, meandering, and warm sonic environments, he weaves together spiritual growth and musical freedom with the goal of bringing self-actualization and wellness to the listener. He has released over 70 recordings featuring instrumental music as well as guided meditation. These include recordings targeted for specific purposes, such as *Enhancing Self-Esteem* (1991), *The Art of Sexual Ecstasy* (1994), *Overcoming Substance Abuse* (1994), and *Achieving your Ideal Weight* (1997). Halpern also writes books on the subject of sound healing.

JONAS WESTOVER

Hamblen, (Carl) Stuart (*b* Kellyville, TX, 20 Oct 1908; *d* Santa Monica, CA, 8 March 1989). Singing cowboy, radio personality, and songwriter. Hamblen attended high school in Clarendon, Texas, and college in Lubbock and Abilene, where he studied to become a teacher. As early as 1925, he was singing on radio in Dallas and Fort Worth, going by the moniker "Cowboy Joe." In 1929 he journeyed to Camden, New Jersey, aiming to record for Victor, the label that had signed Jimmie Rodgers. According to some claims, now known to be apocryphal, when the Victor executives brushed him off, he camped out with his dog in their lobby until finally wearing them down. Hamblen then headed for Los Angeles, where he auditioned for KFI and was hired for their *Saturday Night Jamboree*. He briefly joined the Beverly Hill Billies, then formed his own band, the Lucky Stars, which included a young Patsy Montana. In 1934 he began recording for the upstart Decca label, for whom he cut his classic "Texas Plains." Hamblen soon became immensely popular on radio in southern California, and a friendly rivalry with the Sons of the Pioneers led to more than a few rather rough practical jokes.

He found work in films as well, where his tough good looks typecast him in roles as bad guy, sheriff, or Indian. He continued to record for smaller labels before signing with Columbia Records in 1949, an association that produced several classic songs such as "Remember Me (I'm the one who Loves You)" and "It Is No Secret (What God Can Do)." He converted to Christianity after attending a Billy Graham appearance, and he devoted much of the rest of his career to religious pursuits; he even ran for president on the Prohibition Party ticket in 1952.

Hamblen returned in 1954 to RCA Victor, where he scored his biggest success as a recording artist and songwriter with "This Old House," though Rosemary Clooney's number-one pop version outsold his by far. After the coming of rock and roll, he spent the next three decades in semiretirement, picking and choosing his appearances, radio shows, and recordings.

DOUGLAS B. GREEN

Hamblin, Thomas S(owerby) (*b* London, England, 14 May 1800; *d* New York, NY, 8 Jan 1853). Actor and manager. He began his acting career as a utility player in regional theaters in England, gradually learning the profession, and eventually finding bookings in London. He worked in London theaters from 1819 until he left for the United States in 1825. His first American appearance was in the role of Hamlet at the Park Theater in New York, and he continued to tour widely in the United States until 1830, when he took on the management of the Bowery Theater in New York. From 1830 until his death in 1853, Hamblin was one of the leading New York managers, and under his management the Bowery emerged as a popular and highly successful theater. Hamblin challenged the primacy of the Park Theater, and won by appealing to the local nativist male audience, the "Bowery B'hoys." Hamblin staged a diverse range of entertainment for these men, ranging from blackface minstrel performances and circus acts to melodrama and Shakespeare performed by audience favorites such as Edwin Forrest and Junius Brutus Booth. He also opened his theater for local voluntary fire companies to hold their balls, and staged benefit performances for organizations that served his audience. In his position at the Bowery, Hamblin was instrumental in shaping a local American drama that contrasted sharply with the imported plays and stars preferred by the social elite.

BIBLIOGRAPHY

T.A. Brown: *History of the American Stage* (New York, 1870/*R*1969)

M.C. Henderson: "Bowery Theatre," *Cambridge Guide to American Theatre*, ed. M. Banham (Cambridge, UK, 1995), 121

GILLIAN M. RODGER

Hambone. African American dance-song. It is accompanied by an elaborate form of handclapping and slapping of thighs, knees, and buttocks. The song consists of a rhymed chant, generally made up of children's rhymes or "floating verses" (lyrics that fit different songs equally well). It was practiced first by slaves and was later adopted by entertainers. The charleston, a popular dance of the 1920s, and a rock-and-roll dance known as the Charley-bop utilized a minor detail of the hambone, the act of crossing and uncrossing the hands on the knees as they fan back and forth. In the 1950s the hambone attracted widespread popular attention as the result of a recording, "Hambone" (1952, reissued 1982), by the Chicago drummer Red Saunders. Saunders had seen 11-year-old Sammy McGrier of Evanston, Illinois, performing the hambone at an amateur show, and decided to record his performance using a backup vocal and instrumental group. The number was one of the hits of 1952, and spawned several cover versions; its lyrics, though credited to Saunders and Leon Washington, are in fact taken from the traditional hambone.

BIBLIOGRAPHY

D. Gilbert: *American Vaudeville* (New York, 1940/*R*1968)

M. and J. Stearns: *Jazz Dance: the Story of American Vernacular Dance* (New York, 1968/*R*1979)

L.F. Emery: *Black Dance in the United States from 1619 to 1970* (Palo Alto, CA, 1972, 2/1980/*R*1988)

R.M. Nolen: *Hoecakes, Hambone, and All That Jazz: African American Traditions in Missouri* (Columbia, MO, 2003)

B.S. Glass: *African American Dance: An Illustrated History* (Jefferson, NC, 2007)

W.K. MCNEIL/R

Hamburg, Jeff (*b* Philadelphia, PA, 12 Nov 1956). Composer. He studied acoustics and composition at the University of Illinois (1975–8), continuing his studies at the Royal Conservatory in The Hague with Louis Andriessen (1978–84). He is currently president of the Dutch Composer's Guild (het Genootschap Nederlandse Componisten), and serves on the board of Buma/Stemra, the performance rights society of the Netherlands. In 2002 he received the Visser-Neerlandia Music Prize.

Hamburg's music is steeped in Jewish culture and does not follow in the footsteps of his traditional musical education. Its fluent and vigorous idiom, whether lyrical or terse, may be inspired by multifarious Jewish musical dialects from the diaspora, yet it manifests a profoundly personal texture in the way its harmonies move between tonality and modality, and in the use of an abundance of musical gestures with precision and of a lush, coloristic palette. Voices and language predominate, and melodic lines, particularly those for the solo voice, are often characterized by the inflections of folk music. Yiddish history and poetry also inform much of his work. His chamber opera *Esther* is based on the biblical story, and the moving song cycle *Zey…* traces events in modern Jewish history. Another song cycle, *Wine, Love and Death*, is set to texts by the medieval Jewish poets Samuel Ha-Nagid and Moses Ibn Ezra. His works *Kumi, Ori* and *The Song of Songs* are based upon biblical texts from the books of Jeremiah, Isaiah, and the Songs of Songs. The texts of *The Song of Songs* are further intertwined with medieval Hebrew love poetry. Some of Hamburg's recent works comment upon his own family history. His orchestral work *Americana* (2011) is a musical essay on immigration from Eastern Europe to America, and *Podolian Dances* (2009) incorporates klezmer melodies from Podolia, Ukraine, a region connected to Hamburg's family history. His search for his family's roots was featured in a 2008 documentary, *Terpe, kind mains, terpe* [Persevere, my child, persevere]. Other recent works include *Finf Yiddish Lider* for mezzo-soprano and harp, and *The Dream of Existence*, a violin concerto accompanied by symphonic winds. Hamburg has also published a translation of *The Apollonian Clockwork: on Stravinsky*, by Elmer Schönberger and Louis Andriessen (1989).

WORKS
(selective list)

Stage: Esther (chbr op, 4, Hamburg, after Bible: *Esther*), 1992

Song cycles: Zey…[They…] (Z. Landau, M. Leib, J. Ha-Levy), S, fl, cl, b cl, hn, hp, str, 1994; Wine, Love and Death (S. Ha-Nagid, M. Ibn Ezra), S, accdn, vc, 1996

Orch: Sym. in Es, 1982, rev. 1994; Partus, 1989; Schuylkill, str, 1995; Klezmer Sym., chbr orch, 1998, rev. 2000; David, 5 psalms for wind orch, 1999; Conc., fl, orch, 2000; Kumi, Ori, T, orch, 2003; Podolian Dances, str, 2009; Vn Conc. no.1 "The Dream of Existence," vn, sym. winds, 2010; Americana, orch, 2011

Chbr and solo inst: Passacaglia, 3 rec (amp), 1983; Yod, sax, sax/pic, trb, vn, db, pf, perc, 1986; The Golem, 5 sax, 5 tpt, 4 trbn, db, pf, drum kit, 1994; Rapide, vn, 1995; The Song of Songs, T, fl, 2 actors, 2005; Four Langston Hughes Songs, SATB, 2006; Finf Yiddish Lider, Mez, hp, 2009

Principal publisher: Future Classics Music

BIBLIOGRAPHY

S. Levy: "Joodse inspiratie in moderne composities," *Levend joods geloof*, xliii/6 (1997), 20–21

J. van der Heide: "Het Kol Nidrei in composities van Beethoven, Bruch, Schoenberg en Hamburg," *Mens en Melodie*, liii/9 (1998), 340–44

FRANS VAN ROSSUM/SARAH EYERLY

Hamelin, Marc-André (*b* Montreal, Canada, 5 Sept 1961). Canadian pianist and composer. His father was an accomplished amateur pianist who taught his son from the age of five and introduced him to the music of Charles-Valentin Alkan, Leopold Godowsky, and Kaikhosru Sorabji, whose works would figure prominently in Hamelin's career. At age nine he enrolled at the École Vincent d'Indy in Montreal, where he studied piano with Yvonne Hubert. Hamelin received additional training at Temple University in Philadelphia (BMus, 1983; MMus, 1985), where his teachers included Harvey Wedeen and RUSSELL SHERMAN.

Hamelin earned critical acclaim in the 1980s for his prodigious technique and his progressive programming of pianist-composers from the 19th and 20th centuries. In 1982 he won first prize in the International Stepping Stones category of the Canadian Music Competitions, and also won the International Piano Competition in Praetoria, South Africa. His fame grew in 1985 when he took top honors in Carnegie Hall's International American Music Competition, which awarded him a recording contract with New World Records and concert appearances throughout the United States. Hyperion Records has since released his numerous recordings of avant-garde music. His concerts also feature solo and ensemble works from the standard repertory, including Beethoven's works for cello and piano, which he performed in 1991 with cellist Sophie Rolland.

Most of Hamelin's compositions are for solo piano and probe the instrument's technical possibilities, including a set of etudes in every minor key (1984), cadenzas, and transcriptions. Other scoring combinations include three pieces for pianola and *Fanfares* for three trumpets (2003), both of which are distributed by the Sorabji Archive.

Accolades include the Sylvia Gelber Foundation Award (1987) and the Virginia P. Moore Prize (1989), both of which were bestowed by the Canada Council. He has received nine Grammy nominations, and his recording of Godowsky's *Complete Studies on the Chopin Études* won Gramophone Magazine's Instrumental Award in 2000. In 2003 Hamelin became an Officer of the Order of Canada, and he was made a Chevalier de l'Ordre du Québec in 2004. He has won the Juno Award six times (1996–8, 2003, 2006, 2008).

BIBLIOGRAPHY

J. Eichler: "A Virtuoso who Favors the Fringe," *New York Times* (24 March 2002), A29

R. Rimm: *The Composer-Pianists: Hamelin and the Eight* (Portland, OR, 2002)

F. Child: "Marc Andre Hamelin: the Praiseworthy Pianist," *National Public Radio* (20 Aug 2009)

LINCOLN BALLARD

Hamerik [Hammerich], **Asger** (*b* Frederiksborg, Denmark, 8 April 1843; *d* Frederiksborg, Denmark, 13 July 1923). Danish composer, conductor, and educator. He received help in composition from Niels Gade and Johan Peter Emilius Hartmann (1859–62) and studied piano and conducting with HANS FREIHERR VON BÜLOW in Berlin; in 1864 he moved to Paris, changed the spelling of his name to Hamerik, and became a pupil of Hector Berlioz. Performances of his music were well received, and his conducting abilities also attracted attention. After Berlioz's death in 1869, Hamerik went first to Italy and then, early in 1871, to Baltimore to take up an appointment as director of the Peabody Conservatory. During his 27 years in that post he exerted an important influence on American musical life. W.S.B. Mathews included him in a short list of European immigrants "who represented the best culture of European musical circles, and who adapted themselves to America and American ideas without impairing their loyalty to artistic ideals, and who found in new environs invigorating inspirations." As a conductor of the Peabody SO he was noted as an exponent of Scandinavian Romanticism. He composed many of his major works in the United States, and his five *Nordische Suiten* (1872–80), six of his symphonies, and the Requiem op.34 were first performed in Baltimore. His last important work, and the culmination of his spiritual and symphonic development, was the Choral Symphony op.40 (1898); it also marked his farewell to the United States. After a conducting tour of Europe he settled in Copenhagen in May 1900. During the latter part of his life he composed little. Despite his association with Berlioz and his stay in the United States, his Danishness remained evident in his works, and his symphonies form an important chapter of the genre in Denmark between those of Gade and Carl Nielsen. His compositions include four operas, six large choral works, eight symphonies, other orchestral works, and a piano quintet.

BIBLIOGRAPHY

DBL; *GMO*

"Asger Hamerik," *Brainard's Musical World* (Aug 1878); repr. in *Brainard's Biographies of American Musicians*, ed. E.D. Bomberger (Westport, CT, 1999)

W.S.B. Mathews, ed.: *A Hundred Years of Music in America* (Chicago, 1889/*R*1970)

R. Hove: "Asger Hamerik, en dansk symphoniker," *Nordisk musikkultur*, vi (1957), 105–11

R. Robinson: *A History of the Peabody Conservatory of Music* (thesis, Indiana U., 1969)

JOHN BERGSAGEL/RUTH B. HILTON/
E. DOUGLAS BOMBERGER

Hamilton, Chico [Foreststorn] (*b* Los Angeles, CA, 21 Sept 1921). Jazz drummer, bandleader, and commercial composer. He toured with Lionel Hampton and Lester

Young, among others (1940–41), before serving in the US Army. From 1948 to 1955 he regularly accompanied Lena Horne and in 1952 he played in Gerry Mulligan's original pianoless quartet. In 1955 Hamilton founded the first of a series of quintets which introduced such emerging jazz musicians as Eric Dolphy, Ron Carter, Jim Hall, and Charles Lloyd. The groups' innovative instrumentation—winds, cello, guitar, double bass, and drums—and soft, controlled sounds became, by jazz standards, extremely popular; their performances were captured on film in *The Sweet Smell of Success* (1957) and *Jazz on a Summer's Day* (1958). From 1960 Hamilton's quintet adopted a gutsy blues and swing style, and Hamilton subsequently replaced the cello with a trumpet and then a trombone. In 1966 he embarked on a second career as a composer for radio and television advertisements with the establishment of Chico Hamilton Productions in New York. In the 1970s he occasionally led fusion and experimental jazz combos. Hamilton has continued to record and perform and has taught for many years at the New School. In 2004 he was awarded an NEA Jazz Master Fellowship.

BIBLIOGRAPHY

J. Tynan: "Chico Hamilton," *DB*, xxiii/6 (1956), 12
D. Morgenstern: "Flexible Chico," *DB*, xxxiv/12 (1967), 18
J. Shaw: "Chico's Changes," *J&B*, ii/6 (1972), 6
W. Enstice and P. Rubin: *Jazz Spoken Here: Conversations with Twenty-two Musicians* (Baton Rouge, LA 1992)
B. Milkowski: "The Sweet Smell of Success: Chico Hamilton," *JT*, xxxi/9 (2001), 52–7
Oral history material in *NNSc* (LAJOHP)

BARRY KERNFELD/R

Hamilton, Clarence G(rant) (*b* Providence, RI, 9 June 1865; *d* Wellesley Hills, MA, 14 Feb 1935). Organist and teacher. He graduated from Brown University in 1888 and then studied with Arthur Foote, George Whitefield Chadwick, Tobias Matthay, and Edward Dannreuther. From 1889 until 1904 he worked in Providence as a church organist and private teacher, receiving an MA from Brown in 1900. He then joined the faculty of Wellesley College, where he taught until 1933, serving as chairman of the department from 1927. He was also organist and choirmaster of the Congregational Church in Wellesley. From 1913 he directed a summer music school in Boothbay Harbor, Maine, and lectured sporadically at Boston University (1918–30) and at Columbia University (1926). He was a departmental editor of *Etude* from 1922 until his death. Hamilton wrote several textbooks on music history, music appreciation, and piano playing, and composed some songs and partsongs, piano music, and choruses for interpolation in *Electra* (1912) and *Medea* (1914). His principal publisher was O. Ditson.

WILLIAM OSBORNE

Hamilton, David (Peter) (*b* New York, NY, 18 Jan 1935). Music journalist and critic. He studied at Princeton University (BA 1956, MFA 1960) and at Harvard (MA 1960). At Princeton he worked with Milton Babbitt, Edward Cone, W. Oliver Strunk, and Arthur Mendel; at Harvard his teachers included Walter Piston and Gustave Reese.

He was music and record librarian at Princeton from 1960 to 1965, and music editor at W.W. Norton & Co from 1968 to 1974. He worked as music critic of *The Nation* (1968 to 1994), as contributing editor to *High Fidelity* (1969–84), and as New York music correspondent for the *Financial Times* of London (1969–74). In 1981 he was elected vice-president of the Music Critics Association and became coproducer (with Dorle J. Soria) of the Metropolitan Opera Historic Broadcast Recording series. He was program annotator for the Metropolitan Orchestra's Carnegie Hall concerts, and was also a contributing editor to *Opera Quarterly*. He taught at the Manhattan School of Music and the Juilliard School. His writings have appeared in *Opus*, *Opera News*, the *New Yorker*, *High Fidelity*, the *New York Times*, and the *Financial Times*, and he was the editor of *The Metropolitan Opera Encyclopedia*. As a critic and writer Hamilton is particularly concerned with 19th- and 20th-century music, and his broad knowledge of the recorded literature has led to a special interest in discography.

WRITINGS

"Arnold Schoenberg: a Discography," *Perspectives on Schoenberg and Stravinsky*, ed. B. Boretz and E.T. Cone (Princeton, NJ, 1968), 255–67
"A Synoptic View of the New Music," *HiFi/MusAm*, xviii/9 (1968), 44–61
"The Recordings of Copland's Music," *HiFi/MusAm*, xx/11 (1970), 64–72, 116 only
"Igor Stravinsky: a Discography of the Composer's Performances," *PNM*, ix/2–x/1 (1971), 163–79
The Listener's Guide to Great Instrumentalists (New York, 1982)
"The Mapleson Huguenots Cylinder Again," *OQ*, v/1 (1987–8), 11–21
ed.: *The Metropolitan Opera Encyclopedia* (New York and London, 1987)
"Schoenberg's First Opera," *OQ*, vi/3 (1988–9), 48–58
"Early Puccini Performance: a Condition of Transition," *The Puccini Companion*, ed. W. Weaver and S. Puccini (New York, 1994), 303–14

PAULA MORGAN/HANNAH LEWIS

Hamilton, Jimmy [James] (*b* Dillon, SC, 25 May 1917; *d* Christiansted, St. Croix, Virgin Islands, 20 Sept 1994). Jazz clarinetist, tenor and alto saxophonist, pianist, flutist, composer, arranger, and bandleader. He played trumpet alongside Dizzy Gillespie and Charlie Shavers in Frank Fairfax's band in 1935. In the late 1930s he abandoned baritone horn, trumpet, tuba, and trombone to switch exclusively to reed instruments. Hamilton played clarinet and tenor saxophone with Lucky Millinder, Jimmy Mundy, Bill Doggett, Teddy Wilson, Benny Carter, Eddie Heywood, and Yank Porter and recorded with Billie Holiday (1939–42). Billy Strayhorn heard him with Wilson at Café Society Downtown and invited him to sit in with the Ellington band, where he became principal clarinetist, doubling on tenor saxophone, and a major Ducal arranger (1943–68). In 1959 Hamilton appeared with Ellington and was heard on Ellington's soundtrack of *Anatomy of a Murder*. In 1968 he moved to the Virgin Islands, where he performed with his wife, the pianist Vivian Smith, at various venues, led a quartet at Hotel Buccaneer, and made weekly broadcasts from the Holger Danske Hotel on WSTX-AM. He also taught brass and reed instruments at Christiansted Central High School and acted as a sales representative for several musical instrument manufacturers. In the 1980s Hamilton joined Clark Terry's Ellington Spacemen at Carlos I in New York, played briefly with Mercer Ellington, toured Europe as a soloist, and performed and recorded alongside Alvin Batiste and David Murray as a member of John Carter's Clarinet Summit. His outstanding musicianship, pure tone, and soaring range on the clarinet inspired compositions by Ellington and Billy Strayhorn such as "The Tattooed Bride," "Air Conditioned Jungle," "Flippant Flurry," "Ad Lib on Nippon," and "Bluebird of Delhi," which were played only by Hamilton. As a leader he recorded 11 albums, five after leaving Ellington.

BIBLIOGRAPHY

S. Dance: *The World of Duke Ellington* (New York, 1970)
E. Ellington: *Music is my Mistress* (New York, 1973)
E. Lambert: *Duke Ellington: a Listener's Guide* (Lanham, 1999)

PATRICIA WILLARD

Hamilton, Scott (*b* Providence, RI, 12 Sept 1954). Tenor saxophonist. Between the ages of five and six he played drums, piano, and harmonica. His only formal music training occurred at the age of eight when he took lessons on the clarinet. By the age of 14 he was performing on harmonica regularly with a local blues band (1968–70). When Hamilton was 16, he took up tenor saxophone and began performing on the instrument a month later. After playing in an organ and saxophone group, he toured around New York and New England with the Hamilton–Bates Blue Flames (1971–6). In 1976, at the age of 22, he moved to New York, where he worked with Roy Eldridge, Hank Jones, Anita O'Day, Illinois Jacquet, Jo Jones, Vic Dickenson, Tiny Grimes, and occasionally with the house band at Eddie Condon's club. The pianist John Bunch helped Hamilton get his first recording date in late 1976 and enabled him to perform with Benny Goodman intermittently until the mid-1980s. Hamilton formed his own group in 1977 and began recording for the Concord label. He has subsequently recorded with Dave McKenna, Jake Hanna, Rosemary Clooney, Woody Herman, Tony Bennett, Gerry Mulligan, Flip Phillips, Maxine Sullivan, Ruby Braff, Warren Vache, Bucky Pizzarelli, Cal Collins, and Maxine Sullivan. He moved to London in 1998 and to near Florence in Italy in 2007.

BIBLIOGRAPHY

L. Feather and I. Gitler: *The Biographical Encyclopedia of Jazz* (New York, 1999/R)
D. Gelly: "The New Swing," *Masters of Jazz Saxophone: The Story of the Players and Their Music*, ed. T. Bacon and D. Gelly (London, 2000), 188–91

CHIP HENDERSON

Hamlisch, Marvin (Frederick) (*b* New York, NY, 2 June 1944; *d* Los Angeles, CA, 6 Aug 2012). Composer. After demonstrating precocious talent, he became the youngest student to attend the Juilliard School of Music, where he studied piano reluctantly from 1951 to 1965; while still there, he worked as a rehearsal pianist for *Funny Girl* (1964). In 1965 he attained early success as a popular songwriter when two songs he composed

with a high school friend, Howard Liebling, "Sunshine, Lollipops, and Rainbows" and "California Nights," were recorded by Lesley Gore; one other song he composed as a teenager, "Travelin' Life," was recorded years later by Liza Minnelli, another high school friend, on her first album. Concurrently with his studies in music at Queens College, from which he graduated in 1967, Hamlisch was employed for two seasons as a vocal arranger and rehearsal pianist for a wide variety of acclaimed performers on *The Bell Telephone Hour*. An engagement as a pianist at a private party for the producer Sam Spiegel led to *The Swimmer* (1968), the first of more than three dozen film scores over the next 30 years. A prominent early film success was an Academy Award nomination for "Life Is What you Make It" (lyrics by Johnny Mercer) from *Kotch* (1971). Three years later Hamlisch gained national celebrity when he became the first film composer to win three Oscars in one year, for both the score and title tune from *The Way We Were*, and for the adaptation of Scott Joplin's music in *The Sting* (the year's Best Picture). Among Hamlisch's later film scores, several received nominations for Best Song. These included two songs with the lyricist Carol Bayer Sager, "Nobody Does It Better" from *The Spy Who Loved Me* (1977) and "Through the Eyes of Love" from *Ice Castles* (1978); two songs with Alan and Marilyn Bergman, "The Last Time I Felt Like This" from *Same Time, Next Year* (1978) and "The Girl Who Used to Be Me" from *Shirley Valentine* (1989); and "Surprise, Surprise" with the lyricist Edward Kleban, newly composed for the 1985 film version of *A Chorus Line*. He also received another Best Score nomination for *Sophie's Choice* (1982).

Hamlisch's first Broadway musical, *A Chorus Line* (1975), a show about the inner lives, dreams, and fears of 17 dancers desperately auditioning for eight spots on a chorus line, was a triumph for the director and choreographer Michael Bennett and a major hit, running for over 6,000 performances. In addition to winning the Tony and New York Drama Critics' Circle Awards for best musical and Tony Awards for Hamlisch's music and Kleban's lyrics, *A Chorus Line* was also the first musical in 15 years to be awarded a Pulitzer Prize for Drama. A second international success followed four years later: *They're Playing Our Song*, with a book by Neil Simon and a pervasive disco score. The show, which featured only two stars, each however frequently backed by a trio of alter egos, was loosely based on a real-life romance between Hamlisch and Sager. Future musicals achieved neither commercial nor, with isolated exceptions, critical success. *Jean Seberg* (1983), which depicted the stormy and politically sensitive life of the actress, quickly opened and closed in London. The next musical, *Smile* (1986), an adaptation of a cult movie about a teenage beauty pageant, with the lyricist Howard Ashman also serving as both the librettist and the director, was quickly deemed a failure and closed after 48 Broadway performances, although it was later praised as "perhaps the most underappreciated musical of the eighties" by Mandelbaum (1991). Hamlisch's second collaboration with Neil Simon, an adaptation of Simon's successful film *The Goodbye Girl* (1977), also closed after a short Broadway run in 1993 and, after extensive revisions and new lyrics by Don Black, fared even less well in London. Hamlisch's later Broadway work includes the scores to two shows that opened for short runs in 2002, *Sweet Smell of Success: the Musical*, a musical version of the dark 1957 film classic with lyrics by Craig Carnelia and a book by John Guare, and Nora Ephron's *Imaginary Friends*, a play with music, also with lyrics by Carnelia. His death occurred during a tryout at the Tennessee Performing Arts Center in Nashville of a musical directed by Jerry Lewis based on the 1963 film *The Nutty Professor.*

In a style with pronounced, albeit generally scaled-down, rock features, Hamlisch produced both memorable lyrical ballads ("The Way We Were," "What I Did for Love") as well as rhythmically driving numbers ("I Hope I Get it," "They're Playing Our Song"). *Chorus Line* in particular demonstrates Hamlisch's ability to evoke a wide variety of dance styles ranging from soft shoe ("I Can Do That") to the waltz ("At the Ballet"), with musical numbers that present formally complex musical biographical stories and dramas in a varied mixture of song, recitative, speech, and intricate ensembles.

WORKS

MUSICALS
(unless otherwise stated, dates are those of first New York performances; librettists and lyricists are listed in that order in parentheses)

A Chorus Line (J. Kirkwood and N. Dante, E. Kleban), orchd B. Byers, H. Kay, and J. Tunick, Public Theatre, 15 April 1975 [incl. One, What I Did for Love]; film, 1985

They're Playing Our Song (N. Simon, C. Bayer Sager), orchd R. Burns, R. Hazard, and G. Page, Imperial, 11 Feb 1979 [incl. Fallin', They're Playing Our Song]

Jean Seberg (J. Barry, C. Adler), London, National, 15 Nov 1983

Smile (H. Ashman), orchd S. Ramin, Byers, Hazard, and T. Zito, Lunt-Fontanne, 24 Nov 1986 [after film, 1975; incl. Smile, In Our Hands]

The Goodbye Girl (N. Simon, D. Zippel), orchd Byers and Zito, Marquis, 4 March 1993 [after film, 1977; incl. No More]; rev. London, Albery, 1997

FILMS
(selective list)

The Swimmer, 1968; The April Fools, 1969; Take the Money and Run, 1969; Flap, 1970; Move, 1970; Bananas, 1971; Kotch, 1971; Something Big, 1971; Fat City, 1972; The War between Men and Women, 1972; Save the Tiger, 1973; The Sting, 1973; The Way We Were, 1973; The Prisoner of Second Avenue, 1975; The Spy Who Loved Me, 1977; The Champ, 1979; Chapter Two, 1979; Same Time, Next Year, 1978; Starting Over, 1979; Ordinary People, 1980; Seems Like Old Times, 1980; The Fan, 1981; Pennies from Heaven, 1981; I Ought to Be in Pictures, 1982; Sophie's Choice, 1982; Romantic Comedy, 1983; A Chorus Line, 1985; Three Men and a Baby, 1987; Little Nikita, 1988; The Experts, 1989; The January Man, 1989; Shirley Valentine, 1989; Frankie and Johnny, 1991; Missing Pieces, 1992; The Mirror Has Two Faces, 1996

OTHER WORKS
Orch: Anatomy of Peace, 1991

Individual songs, incl. Sunshine, Lollipops, and Rainbows, 1965; Break It to Me Gently, 1977; One Song, 1992 [for Olympics, Barcelona]; Good Morning, America [theme song]

BIBLIOGRAPHY
A. Kasha and J. Hirschhorn: *Notes on Broadway: Conversations with the great Songwriters* (Chicago, 1985)

D.M. Flinn: *What they Did for Love: the untold Story behind the Making of "A Chorus Line"* (New York, 1989)

K. Mandelbaum: A Chorus Line *and the Musicals of Michael Bennett* (New York, 1989)

K. Kelly: *One Singular Sensation: the Michael Bennett Story* (New York, 1990)

J.P. Swain: *The Broadway Musical: a critical and musical Survey* (New York, 1990)

K. Mandelbaum: *Not since Carrie: 40 Years of Broadway musical Flops* (New York, 1991)

M. Hamlisch (with G. Gardner): *The Way I Was* (New York, 1992) [autobiography]

G. Stevens: *The Longest Line: Broadway's Most Singular Sensation* (New York, 1995)

R. Viagas: *On the Line: The Creation of "A Chorus Line," with the Entire Original Cast* (Pompton Plains, NJ, 2006)

GEOFFREY BLOCK

Hamm, Charles (Edward) (*b* Charlottesville, VA, 21 April 1925; *d* Lebanon, NH, 16 Oct 2011). Musicologist. He received his PhD in 1960 from Princeton University. He taught at Princeton, the Cincinnati Conservatory of Music, Tulane University, the University of Illinois at Urbana-Champaign, and Dartmouth College before retiring in 1989; after retiring, he served as Professor Emeritus at Dartmouth College. His earliest work focused on the notation and stylistic musical traits of the Renaissance, particularly those of Dufay and Power, and includes the revision of his dissertation, *A Chronology of the Works of Guillaume Dufay* (1964); "The Motets of Lionel Power," which appeared in *Studies in Music History: Essays for Oliver Strunk* (1968); and an edition of Power's complete works (1969). Hamm maintained a lifelong interest in these areas, as well as in opera and ballet, publishing his article "Interrelationships between Manuscript and Printed Sources of Polyphonic Music in the Early Sixteenth Century: an Overview" in 1980, just three years before *Music in the New World*. His book *Opera* appeared in 1966, and the following year he published *Stravinsky: Petrushka*, which included the first English translation of the ballet's stage directions, along with a detailed analysis of the work.

Today, however, Hamm is perhaps best known for his work on music of the 20th century, American music, and popular music. His first foray into these areas was *Contemporary Music and Music Cultures*, written in 1975 with ethnomusicologist Bruno Nettl and popular-music specialist Ronald Byrnside, followed by his study *Yesterdays: Popular Song in America* (1979) and *Music in the New World* (1983), long used as a textbook for American music courses. Hamm's work in popular American music was among some of the earliest serious scholarship on the topic and was highly influential on the burgeoning field as it emerged as a legitimate area of study during the 1980s and 1990s. Hamm edited the early songs of Irving Berlin and discovered and worked extensively with a previously unknown 1935 manuscript edition of George Gershwin's *Porgy and Bess*, which was premiered in 2006 by the Nashville Symphony. His interests in the field also focused on the heritage and influence of popular song: he traveled to South Africa to study Zulu influences on American song and to China to explore the availability and dissemination of, and influences on, popular music there. Also a composer, Hamm wrote a number of short operas to his own libretti, including

The Secret Life of Walter Mitty (1956), based on the work by James Thurber, before deciding that "musical judgment outstripped my ability as a composer and I began seeing my own music as not very good"; his works also include the novelty "Round," written for the University of Illinois Contemporary Chamber Players. He served as the President of the American Musicological Society from 1972 to 1974, and was a founder of the International Association for the Study of Popular Music (IASPM). In 2002 Hamm was given the Society for American Music's lifetime achievement award.

WRITINGS

"Rock and the Facts of Life," *Anuario Interamericano de Investigacion Musical*, vii (1971), 5–15

"The Theatre Guild Production of *Porgy and Bess*," *JAMS,* xl/3 (1987), 495–532

"Irving Berlin's Early Songs as Biographical Documents," *MQ*, lxxvii/1 (1993), 10–34

Putting Popular Music in its Place (Cambridge, 1995)

"Alexander and His Band," *American Music*, xiv/1 (1996), 65–102

Irving Berlin: Songs from the Melting Pot; the Formative Years, 1907–1914 (New York, 1997)

"The Firebrand of New York: Kurt Weill and his 'Broadway Operetta,'" *ML*, lxxxv/2 (2004), 239–54

EDITION

Irving Berlin: Early Songs, 1907–1914 (Madison, WI, 1994–5)

BIBLIOGRAPHY

GMO

F.J. Oteri, "A Tribute to Charles Hamm—Composer, Historian, Educator," *NewMusicBox*, 30 May 2007, <http://www.newmusicbox.org/articles/a-tribute-to-charles-hamm/>

The Center for Black Music Research, Charles Hamm Papers, <http://www.colum.edu/CBMR/library/archives/research/Charles_Hamm_papers.php>

KENDRA PRESTON LEONARD

Hammer, Jan (*b* Prague, Czechoslovakia, 17 April 1948). Jazz keyboard player, composer, producer, drummer, and bandleader of Czech birth; naturalized American. His mother, Vlasta Pruchova, was a jazz singer in Prague and his father played bass and vibraphone. He attended the Academy of Musical Arts in Prague and formed the Junior Trio with the bass player Miroslav Vitous and the drummer Alan Vitous, which lasted from 1962 to 1966. After the invasion of Czechoslovakia by the USSR in 1968, he moved to the USA to accept a scholarship to study at the Berklee College of Music. However, he abandoned his studies after a year and a half to work with Sarah Vaughan.

As a member of John McLaughlin's group the Mahavishnu Orchestra (1971–3), Hammer played electric and acoustic pianos and began using the Minimoog synthesizer (on the album *Birds of Fire*), quickly becoming a major influence on other keyboard players. Hammer is often cited as having developed a synthesizer style that mimics that of an electric guitar, but he instead credits the influence of Indian and Eastern European music. Several albums on which Hammer performed with Elvin Jones during the early 1970s helped to introduce the synthesizer to more mainstream jazz. *Timeless* (1974, ECM) with John Abercrombie and Jack DeJohnette is another notable album.

Hammer's recordings as a leader feature his compositions and employ extensive overdubbing to create complex synthesizer orchestrations. His album *The First Seven Days* (1975, Nemperor) shows the influences of Western classical, Indian, and African music with little conventional jazz to be heard. In the 1970s and 80s Hammer performed and recorded, notably with Jeff Beck, Al Di Meola, and Neal Schon. In the mid-1980s his soundtrack for the television series *Miami Vice* earned him two Grammy awards (1985) and its theme was a number one on the *Billboard* singles chart. In the early 2010s he was performing in public infrequently and concentrating on film and television scoring instead.

BIBLIOGRAPHY

J. Solothurnmann: "If You are an Improviser, you Compose!" *JF* [intl edn], no.30 (1974), 34–39

H. Nolan: "Jan Hammer: Saved by the Synthesizer," *DB*, xliii/5 (1976), 17–18, 39

J. Coryell and L. Friedman: *Jazz-Rock Fusion: the People, the Music* (New York, 1978)

D. Milano: "Jan Hammer," *CK*, iv/10 (1978), 20–22

D. Milano: "Jan Hammer Scores Big with *Miami Vice*," *Keyboard* (1985), 38–40, 44, 46, 48, 52, 54

A. Taylor and M. Small: *Masters of Music: Conversations with Berklee Greats* (Boston, 1999)

MICHAEL FITZGERALD

Hammer, Stephen (*b* Rochester, NY, 14 April 1951). Oboist and maker of historical oboes; cofounder of BOSWORTH AND HAMMER.

Hammered [hammer] **dulcimer**. A multi-string board zither played with small hand-held mallets. North American hammered dulcimers are shallow trapezoidal boxes with strings arranged in courses of two to six strings each. North American performers often place the instrument on an angled stand to play it. During the 19th century, a "parlor model" developed through the addition of legs, hinged lids, and other refinements. Traditionally called dulcimers, the prefix "hammer" or "hammered" has been used increasingly to distinguish this instrument from the unrelated APPALACHIAN DULCIMER.

Although the claim that a dulcimer was imported to Jamestown, Virginia, in 1609 has yet to be substantiated, dulcimers were almost certainly introduced to North America by English colonists before 1700. In 1717 Judge Samuel Sewall wrote of hearing one in Salem, Massachusetts; later in the 18th century, dulcimer players advertised public performances in several American cities. During the 19th century, dulcimers were built both by folk craftsmen and commercial makers. Dulcimer shops flourished in New England and western New York from the 1840s through the 1870s, notably those of John Low in Clinton, Massachusetts (*c*1860); Ezra Durand, Norwich, Connecticut (*c*1867); Morgan and Hiram Sackett, Irving, New York (1850s); Harrison and Lewis Wade, Stedman, New York (*c*1855); and Henry Ransom, Sherman, New York, and Newport, Kentucky (1856 to *c*1863). In 1860 John Low, who had published *The Dulcimer Instructor* (1858), was the first of several shop owners to receive a patent for improvements to the instrument.

James A. MacKenzie (1845–1905), a dulcimer manufacturer in Minneapolis, Minnesota, during the last quarter of the 19th century, also received several patents for his experimental dulcimers, which he called "piano harps," and for which he published an instruction manual (c1891). It is more difficult to document the instrument-building activities of folk craftsmen, but distinctive regional styles of construction developed in western New York and the Great Lakes region, West Virginia, and the Piedmont region of North Carolina.

In North America, dulcimers were used primarily to play dance music and were often included in string bands. Despite the publication of several instructional books (the earliest was C. Haight's *A Complete System for the Dulcimer*, 1848) the dulcimer remained a folk instrument. Musically, the dulcimer's role of providing arpeggiated chords and bass lines in the jigs, reels, and waltzes that feature prominently in the repertoire of traditional string bands was increasingly supplanted by the proliferation of inexpensive and more prestigious keyboard instruments such as the upright piano and the parlor organ. In spite of attempts to revive interest in it, most notably the establishment in 1924 of Henry Ford's Early American Orchestra, which played for country dances in Dearborn, Michigan, and on radio, the construction and playing of dulcimers had largely died out before a revival began in the 1960s. In 1963 The Original Dulcimer Players Club was organized in central Michigan; the following year dulcimerists Elgia Hickok and Chet Parker appeared at the Newport Folk Festival. Increased interest was sparked by the seminal 1966 recording *The Hammered Dulcimer Played by Chet Parker* (Folkways) and the appearance of new makers such as Sam Rizzetta of Kalamazoo, Michigan; Denis Dorogi of Brocton, New York; and Howard Mitchell of Washington, DC. Commercial recordings by traditional players, such as West Virginians Russell Fluharty and Worley Gardner, and New York dulcimer virtuoso Paul Van Arsdale, as well as releases by talented revival performers such as Bill Spence, Ed Trickett, Walt Michael, Mitzie Collins, Guy Carawan, and John McCutcheon, brought awareness of the hammered dulcimer to new audiences. Sam Rizzetta's group *Trapezoid*, which featured a quartet of hammered dulcimers, was particularly influential. In 1975 *The Dulcimer Players News*, a magazine encompassing the interests of both hammered and Appalachian dulcimers, began publication. In the early 21st century, there are scores of North American dulcimer makers, including several large-scale operations. Players abound, as do annual dulcimer festivals, gatherings, competitions, and instructional programs.

Less widespread than the Anglo-American tradition has been the use of other types of dulcimer among North American immigrant groups. These include the *Hackbrett* played by German Americans, the *yangqin* played by Chinese Americans, the *santur* played by immigrants from North Africa and the Middle East, the *santouri* played by Greek Americans, and the *cimbalom* played by Hungarian Americans and other groups from Eastern Europe. Variant colloquial names for the Anglo-American dulcimer, such as "whamdiddle" and "lumberjack's piano," have been commonly used.

BIBLIOGRAPHY

H.W. Mitchell: *The Hammered Dulcimer: How to Make it and Play it* (Washington, DC, 1968)

D. Kettlewell: *The Dulcimer* (Tisbury, England, 1976)

S. Rizzetta: "The Hammer Dulcimer–History and Playing," *The Hammer Dulcimer Compendium*, ed. M. Holmes (Silver Spring, MD, 1977)

N. Groce: *The Hammered Dulcimer in America* (Washington, DC, 1983)

P. Gifford: *The Hammered Dulcimer: a History* (Lanham, MD, 2001)

NANCY GROCE

Hammerstein, Oscar, I (*b* Stettin [now Szczecin, Poland], 8 May 1846; *d* New York, NY, 1 Aug 1919). Impresario. He studied harmony and counterpoint, and also learned to play the piano, flute, and violin. While still in his teens he ran away to Hamburg, and later to New York, where he worked in a cigar factory. He began to speculate in real estate and, as his fortunes increased, built theaters in which he presented a variety of productions. He composed intermezzos, a ballet, and the operettas *The Kohinoor* (1893) and *Santa Maria* (1896), none of which achieved any success. In 1906 he founded the Manhattan Opera Company, which opened with Vincenzo Bellini's *I puritani* on 3 December in the newly built Manhattan Opera House. The company challenged the entrenched Metropolitan Opera in presenting the standard Italian repertory as well as contemporary works, and gave the American premieres of four operas by Jules Massenet, Umberto Giordano's *Siberia*, Gustave Charpentier's *Louise*, and *Elektra* and *Pelléas et Mélisande*. Singers who performed with the company included Nellie Melba, Alessandro Bonci, Lillian Nordica, Luisa Tetrazzini, Mary Garden, Emma Calvé, John McCormack, Giovanni Zenatello, and Maurice Renaud. In April 1910 Hammerstein sold his interests in the company to the Metropolitan for $1,200,000 and promised not to produce opera in New York, Boston, Philadelphia, or Chicago for the next decade. Two seasons at the newly built London Opera House (later the Stoll Theatre) in 1911–12 were financial failures.

BIBLIOGRAPHY

V. Sheean: *Oscar Hammerstein I: the Life and Exploits of an Impresario* (New York, 1956)

J.F. Cone: *Oscar Hammerstein's Manhattan Opera Company* (Norman, OK, 1966)

JOHN FREDERICK CONE

Hammerstein, Oscar (Greeley Clendenning), II (*b* New York, NY, 12 July 1895; *d* Doylestown, PA, 23 Aug 1960). Lyricist, librettist, producer, and publisher. Born into a notable theatrical family, his grandfather and namesake was the flamboyant opera impresario OSCAR HAMMERSTEIN I (1847–1919), who created and lost a handful of opera houses and companies around the turn of the century. Hammerstein studied law at Columbia, where he became involved in the Varsity shows and, after graduation, continued to write songs. By 1919 Hammerstein had left the legal profession and begun to write plays and lyrics full time. His first Broadway musical was *Always You* (1920) with composer Herbert Stothart and,

Richard Rodgers, Irving Berlin, Oscar Hammerstein II, and Helen Tamiris auditioning performers, 1948. (Library of Congress, Prints & Photographs Division, NYWT&S Collection, LC-USZ62-126707)

as would be the pattern throughout his career, Hammerstein wrote both the libretto and lyrics. During the 1920s he contributed to a handful of operettas, most notably *Rose-Marie* (1924), with composer Rudolf Friml, and *The Desert Song* (1926), with Sigmund Romberg. After some experimenting, he and composer Jerome Kern created the landmark *Show Boat* (1927), the first musical play of the American theater. With the demise of operetta and the emphasis on frivolous musical comedies and revues during the Depression, Hammerstein's career faltered and his Hollywood efforts were failures except for his song "The Last Time I Saw Paris" with Kern, which won the Academy Award for Best Song in 1941.

Hammerstein's second and equally productive career began with his collaboration with composer RICHARD RODGERS. The team consistently presented the finest musical plays of the 1940s and 1950s, including *Oklahoma!* (1943), *Carousel* (1945), *South Pacific* (1949), *The King and I* (1951), and *The Sound of Music* (1959). The team also produced Broadway shows by others, most memorably Irving Berlin's *Annie Get Your Gun* (1946); they wrote scores for Hollywood, such as *State Fair* (1945 and 1962); and for television they provided *Cinderella* (1957). Hammerstein had a solo hit with *Carmen Jones* (1943), his updating of *Carmen* using Bizet's music. Hammerstein's heartfelt lyrics are distinguished by their simplicity and sincerity, often eschewing the clever rhymes and dazzling wordplay that were characteristic of his contemporaries. He brought an honesty to libretto and lyric writing that influenced all the major theater songwriters of the postwar American theater, and his works, particularly *Show Boat* and those with Rodgers, remain in the popular musical theater repertory.

WRITINGS

Six Plays by Rodgers and Hammerstein (New York, 1959)
The Songs of Oscar Hammerstein II (New York, 1975)
Lyrics (Milwaukee, rev. 1985)
Rodgers and Hammerstein Revisited (Winona, MN, 1986)
Rodgers & Hammerstein: the Illustrated Songbook (New York, 2005)
The Complete Lyrics of Oscar Hammerstein (New York, 2008)

WORKS

STAGE
*(Unless otherwise indicated, librettos and lyrics are by Hammerstein; composers are in brackets, co-librettists in parentheses. *Directed by Hammerstein.)*

Always You [H. Stothart], 5 Jan 1920
Tickle Me [Stothart] (O. Harbach, F. Mandel), 17 Aug 1920
Jimmie [Stothart] (Harbach, Mandel), 17 Nov 1920
Daffy Dill [Stothart] (G. Bolton), 22 Aug 1922
Queen o' Hearts [L. Gensler, D. Wilkinson] (Mandel, S. Mitchell), 10 Oct 1922
Wildflower [V. Youmans, Stothart] (Harbach), 7 Feb 1923
Mary Jane McKane [Youmans, Stothart] (W.C. Duncan), 25 Dec 1923
Rose-Marie [R. Friml, Stothart] (Harbach), 2 Sept 1924 [incl. Indian Love Call, Rose-Marie], films, 1936, 1954
Sunny [J. Kern] (Harbach), 22 Sept 1925 [incl. Sunny, Who?], films, 1930, 1941
Song of the Flame [G. Gershwin, Stothart] (Harbach), 30 Dec 1925; film, 1930
The Wild Rose [Friml] (Harbach), 20 Oct 1926
The Desert Song [S. Romberg] (Harbach, Mandel), 30 Nov 1926 [incl. The Desert Song, One Alone], films, 1929, 1943, 1953
Golden Dawn [E. Kálmán, Stothart] (Harbach), 30 Nov 1927; film, 1930
*Show Boat, [Kern], 27 Dec 1927 [incl. Can't Help Lovin' Dat Man, Make Believe, Ol' Man River, Why Do I Love You?], films, 1929, 1936, 1951
Good Boy [B. Kalmar, H. Ruby, Stothart] (Harbach, H. Myers, B. Kalmar), 25 Sept 1928
*The New Moon [Romberg] (Mandel, L. Schwab) 19 Sept 1928 [incl. Lover, Come Back to Me; One Kiss; Stouthearted Men], films, 1930, 1940
*Rainbow [Youmans] (L. Stallings), 21 Nov 1928; film, as *Song of the West*, 1930

Sweet Adeline [Kern], 3 Sept 1929 [incl. Don't Ever Leave Me, Why Was I Born?], film, 1935
Ballyhoo [L. Alter] (H. Ruskin, L.K. Brill), 22 Dec 1930
*The Gang's All Here [L. Gensler, R. Whiting] (R. Crouse, M. Ryskind, O. Murphy, R.A. Simon), 18 Feb 1931
*Free for All [R. Whiting] (Schwab), 8 Sept 1931
*East Wind [Romberg] (Mandel), 27 Oct 1931
*Music in the Air [Kern], 8 Nov 1932 [incl. I've Told Every Little Star, The Song Is You], film, 1934
May Wine [Romberg] (Mandel), 5 Dec 1935
Gentlemen Unafraid [Kern] St. Louis, 3 June 1938
*Very Warm for May [Kern], 17 Nov 1939 [incl. All the Things You Are]
*Sunny River [Romberg], 4 Dec 1941
Oklahoma! [R. Rodgers], 31 March 1943 [incl. Oh, What a Beautiful Mornin', People Will Say (We're in Love), The Surrey with the Fringe on Top, Oklahoma!], film, 1955
Carmen Jones [G. Bizet], 2 Dec 1943; film, 1954
Carousel [Rodgers], 19 April 1945 [incl. If I Loved You, June is Bustin' Out All Over, You'll Never Walk Alone, Soliloquy], film, 1956
Allegro [Rodgers], 10 Oct 1947 [incl. The Gentleman Is a Dope]
South Pacific [Rodgers] (J. Logan), 7 April 1949 [incl. Bali Ha'i, Some Enchanted Evening, There is Nothin' Like a Dame, I'm in Love With a Wonderful Guy], film, 1958; TV, 2001
The King and I [Rodgers], 29 March 1951 [incl. Getting to Know You; Hello, Young Lovers; I Have Dreamed; Shall We Dance?; Something Wonderful], films, 1956, 1999 (animated)
Me and Juliet [Rodgers], 28 May 1953 [incl. No Other Love]
Pipe Dream [Rodgers], 30 Nov 1955
Flower Drum Song [Rodgers] (J. Fields), 1 Dec 1958 [incl. Love, Look Away; You Are Beautiful; I Enjoy Being a Girl], film, 1961
The Sound of Music [Rodgers] (H. Lindsay, Crouse), 16 Nov 1959 [incl. Climb Every Mountain, Do-Re-Mi, My Favorite Things, The Sound of Music, Edelweiss], film, 1965
A Grand Night for Singing [Rodgers] (musical revue), 17 Nov 1993
State Fair [Rodgers] (T. Briggs, L. Mattioli), 27 March 1996

FILMS

Viennese Nights [Romberg], 1930
Children of Dreams [Romberg], 1930
The Night is Young [Romberg], 1935 [incl. When I Grow Too Old to Dream]
Give Us This Night [E.W. Korngold], 1936
High, Wide, and Handsome [Kern], 1937 [incl. The Folks Who Live on the Hill]
The Great Waltz [J. Strauss], 1938
The Lady Objects [B. Oakland], 1938
State Fair [Rodgers], 1945 [incl. It's a Grand Night for Singing, It Might as Well Be Spring]; remake, 1962

TELEVISION

Cinderella [Rodgers], 1957 [incl. In My Own Little Corner, Do I Love You Because You're Beautiful?]; remakes, 1965, 1997

BIBLIOGRAPHY

D. Taylor: *Some Enchanted Evenings* (New York, 1952)
S. Green: *The Rodgers and Hammerstein Fact Book* (Milwaukee, 1963)
S. Green: *The Story of Rodgers and Hammerstein* (New York, 1963)
H. Fordin: *Getting to Know Him: a Biography of Oscar Hammerstein II* (New York, 1977)
E. Mordden: *Rodgers and Hammerstein* (New York, 1992)
S. Citron: *The Wordsmiths: Oscar Hammerstein II and Alan Jay Lerner* (New York, 1995)
F. Nolan: *The Sound of their Music: the Story of Rodgers and Hammerstein* [revised] (New York, 2002)
T. Hischak: *The Rodgers and Hammerstein Encyclopedia* (Westport, CT, 2007)
O. Hammerstein III: *The Hammersteins: a Musical Theatre Family* (New York, 2010)

THOMAS S. HISCHAK

Hammond, John (Henry, Jr.) (*b* New York, NY, 15 Dec 1910; *d* New York, NY, 10 July 1987). Record producer and critic. He was born into a wealthy family and attended Yale University. Family connections and affluence later gave him the resources to advocate for and fund controversial projects, including racially integrated music performances. As a teenager, he became fascinated by African American music and was drawn to the clubs and theaters of Harlem. He produced a live jazz radio show in the early 1930s and his first records, some of which were released on Columbia's race record division, OKeh. In 1933 he recorded an important series of sessions for UK Columbia featuring Fletcher Henderson, Benny Carter, and Benny Goodman, whose orchestra he helped to form in 1934. In the same year he supervised Bessie Smith's last recorded sessions, and he heard the 17-year old Billie Holiday singing at the Moore's Club in Harlem. His advocacy helped lead to Holiday's first recordings in 1933 with Benny Goodman, and, from 1935 to 1937, as a soloist with Teddy Wilson. Hammond was also an early advocate of Count Basie, and was influential in bringing his orchestra to national prominence in 1936. In 1938 and 1939 he organized the two historic "From Spirituals to Swing" concerts in Carnegie Hall.

A tireless talent scout, he advanced the careers of artists as varied as Charlie Christian (whom he teamed with Goodman in 1939), George Benson, Aretha Franklin, Leonard Cohen, and Pete Seeger. His 1961 rerelease of recordings by Robert Johnson sparked a revival of interest in the blues artist's work. He signed Bob Dylan and Bruce Springsteen to Columbia Records, leading to their first commercial recordings. Although best known for his association with Columbia (1937, 1939–43, 1959–75), Hammond also served in executive positions with Brunswick/Vocalion, Keynote, Majestic, Mercury, and Vanguard. From 1931 he wrote widely on jazz, popular music, and issues of racial equality for music periodicals and the general press, including an influential column for the British jazz magazine *Melody Maker*; he also published an autobiography, *John Hammond on Record* (New York, 1977/R). In 1986 Hammond was inducted into the Rock and Roll Hall of Fame. Yale University hosts a collection of his papers.

BIBLIOGRAPHY

I. Kolodin: "Number One Swing Man," *Harper's*, clxxix (1939), 431–40
C. Graham: "Meet the A&R Man: John Hammond," *Down Beat*, xxviii/21 (1961), 23–24
P.J. Sullivan: "John Hammond," *Jazz Journal*, xxi/9 (1968), 6–8
J. McDonough: "John Hammond: Man for All Seasons," *Down Beat*, xxxviii/5 (1971), 13–15, 32
J. Hammond, with I. Townsend: *John Hammond on Record* (New York, 1977)
"Hammond, John (Henry, Jr.)," *CBY* 1979
L. Feather: "John Hammond," *The Passion for Jazz* (New York, 1980/R), 176–88
D. Chamberlain and R. Wilson, eds.: *The Otis Ferguson Reader* (Highland Park, IL, 1982), 97
D. Prial: *The Producer: John Hammond and the Soul of American Music* (New York, 2006)

EDWARD BERGER/JOANNA R. SMOLKO

Hammond, Richard (Pindell) (*b* Kent, England, 26 Aug 1896; *d* New York, NY, Dec 1980). Composer. He was educated in the United States, graduating from the Yale

University School of Music. After naval service in World War I, he continued musical studies with EMERSON WHITHORNE, MORTIMER WILSON, and NADIA BOULANGER. Together with Whithorne he founded the Composers' Music Corporation, a publishing house for contemporary music, and he served on the executive boards of the League of Composers, the Franco-American Music Society, and the Hollywood Bowl Association. He also wrote on new music for *Modern Music* and other journals. His compositions are essentially neo-romantic in style; they have received most performances from societies for modern music, and all remain unpublished.

WORKS
(selective list)

Orch: 5 Chinese Fairy Tales, 1921; West Indian Dances, 1930; Suite after Reading "The Woman of Andros," 1930; Sinfonietta, 1931; 2 suites: Dance Music, 1933, 1937; Suite: Unto the Hills, 1939; Suite: Excursion, 1940

Vocal: Voyage to the East, Mez/Bar, orch, 1926; 5 chansons grecques, Mez/Bar, 15 insts, 1928; 5 Madrigals, 1v, insts, 1930; songs

Other works: Sonata, ob, pf, 1928; ballets, choral music, pf pieces

PEGGY GLANVILLE-HICKS/BARBARA A. RENTON/R

Hammond organ. An electronic organ developed in 1933–4 by engineers Laurens Hammond (*b* Evanston, IL, 11 Jan 1895; *d* Cornwall, CT, 3 July 1973) and John M. Hanert (1909–62). Hammond founded the Hammond Clock Co. in Chicago in 1928 to manufacture clocks incorporating a synchronous motor that he had patented. From 1933 he and Hanert developed the Hammond organ, patenting it in 1934 and demonstrating it in April 1935. The instrument was an immediate success—Henry Ford and George Gershwin were early purchasers. By the end of the 1930s the company (renamed the Hammond Organ Co.) was making about 200 instruments a month. The original Hammond organ Model A (introduced in 1935) had two 61-note manuals and a 25-note pedal board. Also familiar to organists was the "swell" pedal, a foot-operated volume control. The stops of a pipe organ were replicated with the electronic equivalent "drawbars," which controlled the relative volume of the different tone wheels. This was soon followed by other improved models, the most famous of which was the B-3. The company pioneered several features of electronic organ design that remain common. In 1949 it produced its first spinet organ, with two staggered manuals overlapping by an octave. A one-manual chord organ was first marketed in the early 1950s. A familiar addition to most Hammond organs is the LESLIE loudspeaker, which affects the sound like a tremulant stop on a pipe organ.

Jazz and popular musicians, including Ethel Smith, Fats Waller, Jimmy Smith, and Wild Bill Davis, helped to gain a wide audience for the Hammond, and developed a distinctive style of "swinging" staccato playing. After World War II, demand grew for the Hammond organ as an instrument for use at home. On the popular music front, it saw a huge surge in popularity in rock, R&B, and soul music. Groups like Booker T. & the MGs, Steppenwolf, and Procol Harum made the Hammond organ an integral part of their sound. Hammond organs became mainstay instruments both on stage and in studios.

Hammond also made purely vacuum tube–based instruments like the Novachord (1938), the Solovox (1940), and the S6 chord organ (1950). In the 1970s the company switched over to solid state transistor technology and eventually to integrated circuits. Hammond ceased operations in 1985, and the rights were sold to Suzuki, who as Hammond Suzuki USA continued producing instruments under the Hammond brand using modern digital technology. In recent decades more "virtual" tone-wheel organs like the Roland VK-8, Hammond/ Suzuki KX-3, and Nord Electro have become popular Hammond organ substitutes. Such developments became even more virtual when computer software emulations like Native Instruments' B4 were introduced.

See also ELECTRONIC INSTRUMENTS.

BIBLIOGRAPHY

W. Baggally: "The Hammond Organ: a New Electro-Acoustic Musical Instrument," *Wireless World*, xli (1937), 134–36

N.H. Crowhurst: *Electronic Organs* (Indianapolis, 1960; 3/1975)

T.L.M. Rhea: *The Evolution of Electronic Musical Instruments in the United States* (diss., George Peabody College, Nashville, TN, 1972); rev. as "The History of Electronic Musical Instruments" in T. Darter, ed.: *The Art of Electronic Music* (New York, 1984), 1–63

D. Crombie: "The Hammond Story," *Sound International*, xxix (1980); rev. in T. Bacon, ed.: *Rock Hardware: the Instruments, Equipment, and Technology of Rock* (Poole, England, 1981), 88–91

M. Vail: *The Hammond Organ: Beauty in the B* (Milwaukee, 1997, 2/2002)

HUGH DAVIES/BRANDON SMITH

Hammons, Thomas (*b* Shawnee, OK, 24 Dec 1951). Bass-baritone. He studied at Cincinnati College-Conservatory with Italo Tajo and made his professional operatic debut with Santa Fe Opera, as the Doctor in Stephen Oliver's *The Duchess of Malfi*, in 1978. He has subsequently been acclaimed for his roles in two important world premieres: as Henry Kissinger in John Adams's *Nixon in China* (1987, Houston) and as both the first officer and the terrorist "Rambo" in the same composer's *The Death of Klinghoffer* (La Monnaie, 1991). Since his Metropolitan debut in 1996, as the Sacristan in *Tosca*, he has sung for the house each season in buffo roles, including Bartolo (*Il barbiere di Siviglia*). Hammons has also appeared at many of the other major US and Canadian opera houses, in roles including Peter Quince, Don Alfonso, the Bosun (*Billy Budd*), and Dulcamara (*L'elisir d'amore*), which he sang at the Opéra de Montréal in 2002.

RICHARD WIGMORE/R

Hammons Family. The music of the Hammons family of Pocahontas County, West Virginia, has commanded attention for a century or more. In the late 1960s Dwight Diller, a young local musician, began visiting to learn their music. Brothers Sherman (1903–88) and Burl Hammons (1908–93) played fiddle and banjo; sister Maggie Hammons Parker (1899–1987) sang traditional ballads and songs; all three were storytellers; and the entire family represented a way of life Diller admired. Through Diller, other young musicians drawn to older Appalachian traditions came to visit, then West Virginia University professor Patrick Gainer and Library of

Congress folklorist Alan Jabbour arrived to document the family. From these impulses emerged *The Hammons Family* (1973), a recorded box set with illustrated booklet.

Several years later a 1947 collection of discs recorded by folklorist Louis Chappell of West Virginia University was unearthed. In 1984, *The Edden Hammons Collection*, an album featuring the music of Edden Hammons (1876–1955), an uncle and legendary fiddler of the previous generation, joined the earlier box set in sharing the family's traditions. Both albums have been rereleased in updated form on CD.

The fiddling, banjo-playing, and singing of the Hammonses have enriched the folksong and instrumental folk music revival, and other branches of the Hammons family have been discovered whose music and memories amplify the family's contribution to a wider appreciation of Appalachian traditions.

ALAN JABBOUR

Hampson, (Walter) Thomas (*b* Elkhart, IN, 28 June 1955). American baritone. He studied in Spokane and Los Angeles, making his debut in 1978 at Spokane in *Hänsel und Gretel*. In 1981 he won first prize at the Metropolitan Opera Auditions. Engaged at Düsseldorf (1981–4), he performed the roles of Herald (*Lohengrin*), Harlequin (*Ariadne auf Naxos*), Belcore, and Nanni (Haydn's *L'infedeltà delusa*). He sang Henze's *Prince of Homburg* at Darmstadt, Guglielmo at St. Louis (1982), Malatesta at Santa Fe (1983), and Count Almaviva at Aix-en-Provence (1985). In 1984 he was engaged at Zurich, where over the next decade his roles included Massenet's Lescaut, Handel's Julius Caesar, Marcello, Don Giovanni, Rossini's Figaro (also the role of his Covent Garden debut in 1993), Posa (*Don Carlos*), and the Prince of Homburg. In 1986 he made his Vienna Staatsoper debut as Guglielmo, and his Metropolitan debut as Count Almaviva, which he also sang at his Salzburg debut (1988). Other roles at the Metropolitan have included Billy Budd and Coroebus (*Les Troyens*). At San Francisco he has sung Monteverdi's Ulysses (1990) and created Valmont in Conrad Susa's *Dangerous Liaisons* (1994). In 1998 he sang the title role in *Guillaume Tell* at the Vienna Staatsoper and the following year performed the title role in *Werther*, in Massenet's downward transposition, at the Metropolitan. His movement towards heavier repertory is exemplified by two recent roles: the title role in Busoni's *Doktor Faust*, which he sang at the Metropolitan in the 2000–01 season, and Amfortas, which he performed at the Opéra National, Paris, in 2001. In 2009 he added the role of Scarpia and made his debut as Iago (2011), both at the Zurich Opera House. A charismatic actor, Hampson has a grainy, flexible voice and is also an outstanding recitalist with a broad repertory: in addition to his lieder recordings, he has performed and recorded little known songs by American composers, including Bowles, Griffes, and MacDowell, performed music by Stephen Foster, George Crumb, and John Adams, recorded an important collection of songs from Whitman poems, *To the Soul* (EMI 1997,

2006), and created *Night Speech*, a song cycle by Stephen Paulus (1989). He has premiered works from Wolfgang Rihm, Friedrich Cerha, Michael Daugherty, and Matthias Pintscher. He has been particularly closely associated with the songs of Mahler, singing and recording all the Mahler song cycles in both piano-vocal and orchestral versions under the batons of Leonard Bernstein, Klaus Tennstedt, Luciano Berio, Simon Rattle, and Michael Tilson Thomas, including singing the low part of *Das Lied von der Erde*. Hampson has also contributed important scholarly research; he has co-edited the *Knaben Wunderhorn* songs for the critical edition of the Gustav Mahler Gesellschaft (Universal Edition, Vienna) and recorded the music with the conductor-less Wiener Virtuosen, emphasizing Mahler's original intent to use a solo singer and using the composer's original orchestration and order of the songs. In 2008 Hampson created the Hampsong Foundation, the goal of which is to provide multifaceted support for performances of existing songs, particularly American art songs, and the creation of new works. The foundation works with musicians, musicologists, and institutions to foster a performance practice that connects the historical, cultural, and poetic context of songs to the music itself and grew out of Hampson's collaboration with the Library of Congress (2005–06) on his first Song of America project, a performance he subsequently brought to Tanglewood and Ravinia, and recorded for his own Thomas Hampson Media imprint (2009). During 2009–10, he served as the New York Philharmonic's first Artist-in-Residence as well as its Leonard Bernstein Scholar.

BIBLIOGRAPHY

R.V. Lucano: "A Conversation and then Some with Thomas Hampson," *Fanfare*, xv/2 (1991–2), 225–33

E. Seckerson: "Hit and Myth," *Gramophone*, lxix/April (1992), 38–41

T. Voigt: "Das Interview," *OW*, xxxiii/7 (1992), 12–15

M. Parouty: "Le roi baryton," *Diapason*, 397 (1993), 34–7

ELIZABETH FORBES/GEORGE J. GRELLA JR.

Hampton, (George) Calvin (*b* Kittanning, PA, 31 Dec 1938; *d* Port Charlotte, FL, 5 Aug 1984). Organist and composer. He studied organ and composition at Oberlin College with Fenner Douglass and Joseph Wood (BM 1960) and at Syracuse University with ARTHUR WILLIAM POISTER and EARL GEORGE (MM 1962). He was Director of Music at Calvary Episcopal Church (later including Holy Communion and St George's parishes), Gramercy Park, New York, from 1963 to 1983. He was famous for "Fridays at Midnight" organ recital series at Calvary Church from 1974 to 1983. His hymn tunes and harmonizations are found in many hymnals in America today. In addition to his organ works and choral anthems, he wrote important orchestral and chamber works. His *Concerto for Saxophone Quartet and Chamber Orchestra* was given its première by the New York PO in June 1977. Hampton's numerous recital appearances and distinguished recordings, including that of his own transcription of Mussorgsky's *Pictures at an Exhibition,* confirmed his reputation as a performer and inventive composer and arranger for organ.

WORKS

Org: Prelude and Variations on Old 100th, 1970; Transformation of Despair, 1971; God Plays Hide and Seek, org, tape, 1973; Music for an Important Occasion, 1975; Organ Concerto, 1981; 2 Suites, 1981; In Praise of Humanity, 1981; 5 Dances, 1982; 3 Pieces, 1982; Fanfare for the New Year, 1983; The Alexander Variations, 2 org, 1984

Stage: Candlelight Carol Service, solo vv, chorus, orch, org, pantomime, dancers, 1978; It Happened in Jerusalem (music drama), solo vv, chorus, org, tape, perc, actors, speakers, dancers, 1982

Large ens: Conc., sax qt, perc, str, 1973; Conc., org, str, 1980

Vocal: Labyrinth (M. Abreu), S, sax qt, 1974; Cant. for Palm Sunday (Fortunatus), T, chorus, org, 1981; other songs and choral works, incl. c20 anthems

Inst: Triple Play, 2 pf, ondes martenot, 1967; Catch-up, 2 pf, tape; other works

Principal publishers: Wayne Leupold, McAfee Music Corp, Peters

VERNON GOTWALS/SARAH L. MARTIN

hampton, dream (*b* Detroit, MI, 13 Sept 1970). Writer, filmmaker, and cultural critic. She received undergraduate and graduate degrees in film from NYU's Tisch School of the Arts. Her short film, *I Am Ali*, won Best Short Film at the Newport International Film Festival in 2002. Her 2010 documentary, *Black August: A Hip-Hop Documentary Concert*, grew out of her work with the Malcolm X Grassroots Movement, and integrates footage from the Black August Hip Hop Benefit Concert series and interviews with musicians, academics, and activists on political prisoners and the injustices of the prison system.

As a journalist hampton has published on hip hop and popular culture in magazines such as *The Village Voice*, *Harper's Bazaar*, *Vibe*, and *The Source*. She was an editor for *The Source* in the 1990s, and a contributing writer at *Vibe*. She has profiled or interviewed the most successful figures in hip hop of the 1990s, including Jay-Z, Nas, Tupac, and Biggie Smalls, who after being the subject of a college documentary film assignment later became a friend and the godfather of hampton's daughter. As familiar as she is with the most commercially successful side of commercial hip hop, hampton has also written critically and personally about the often problematic relationship between young black women and popular hip hop. She cowrote an unreleased autobiography of Sean "Jay-Z" Carter, and later collaborated with him on *Decoded* (New York, 2010). hampton spells her name in lower case as a tribute to author bell hooks.

BEAU BOTHWELL

Hampton, Lionel (Leo) [Hamp] (*b* Louisville, KY, 20 April 1908; *d* New York, NY, 31 Aug 2002). Vibraphonist, drummer, and bandleader. He was brought up in Birmingham, Alabama, where his first musical experiences involved playing drums in the local church. Around 1919 his family moved to Chicago, and Hampton became a member of the *Chicago Defender* youth band. He received music lessons from Major N. Clark Smith, who also taught him to play the xylophone and the marimba. He was soon working as a drummer with local bands including Les Hite's orchestra, with which he toured the West Coast in 1927. In Los Angeles he played with Reb Spikes, among others. He also worked with Hite's New Sebastian Cotton Club Orchestra. In 1930 Hampton recorded with Louis Armstrong, and it was during this recording session that he began playing the vibraphone, which soon became his main instrument. Armstrong's "Memories of You" was Hampton's first recorded performance on the instrument.

In the early 1930s Hampton took theory lessons at the University of Southern California. At the same time he performed with his own bands, which featured such musicians as Don Byas, Tyree Glenn, and Herschel Evans. In 1936 he joined Benny Goodman's quartet with Teddy Wilson and Gene Krupa. Hampton's vibrant technique offered a counterpart to Goodman's clarinet playing, bringing a vitality and energy to the stage where Goodman shone with technical precision. "Dizzy Spells," from Goodman's concert at Carnegie Hall in January 1938, provides an excellent example of the spontaneity of their dialogues even in a piece heavily dependent on arrangement. Hampton also made recordings under his own name during these years, featuring some of the most prominent musicians of the swing era.

Hampton performed with Goodman's quartet and sextet until 1940, when he decided to form his own big band. He hired mostly young musicians, many of whom later made a name for themselves; they include Cat Anderson, Dexter Gordon, Johnny Griffin, Milt Buckner, and Charles Mingus, as well as such singers as Dinah Washington, Joe Williams, and Betty Carter. In 1942 Hampton had a popular hit with "Flyin' Home," which featured a tenor saxophone solo by Illinois Jacquet; in 1945 he had another hit with "Hey Ba-ba-re-bop," a catchy vocal feature with call-and-response phrases between Hampton and his band or the audience. In performances Hampton increasingly featured his showmanship along with the music. He danced and sang, and his flashy interludes on piano—which he usually played with two fingers while his regular pianist played boogie-woogie bass lines—and drums were a popular concert highlight. His frequent riff arrangements were crowd-pleasers, although his strongest pieces tended to be ballads.

Throughout the 1950s and 60s Hampton led big bands which included such modern musicians as Clifford Brown, Gigi Gryce, and Quincy Jones. He toured internationally as a goodwill ambassador for the US State Department and recorded in small band settings, notably with Art Tatum and Oscar Peterson. In the 1970s Hampton often reduced the instrumentation of his traveling bands to between eight and 12 musicians, but from the mid-1980s he employed a big orchestra again. He received many honors and performed at the inauguration of several presidents. In 1985 the jazz festival at the University of Idaho was named after him; two years later the same university changed the name of its music school to the Lionel Hampton School of Music.

Lionel Hampton was a virtuoso vibraphonist whose solos exude a seemingly inexhaustible energy, yet his lyrical melodic and harmonic qualities should not be underestimated. One of the first musicians to give the vibraphone a distinctive personal sound, Hampton adjusted his instrument's vibrato, used a vigorous mallet technique, and played swinging single-note lines with a driving rhythmic power, often accompanied by his own vocal shouts. Subsequent vibraphonists have revered him as the father of the vibraphone in jazz. Hampton is the author of *Method for Vibraharp, Xylophone and Marimba* (New York, 1967) and, with J.-C. Forestier, *The New Lionel Hampton Vibraphone Method* (Zurich, c1981).

SELECTED RECORDINGS

As leader: I Can't Get Started (1939, Vic. 26453); Flyin' Home (1942, Decca 18394); Hey Ba-ba-re-bop (1945, Decca 18754); *Lionel Hampton's Jazz Giants* (1955, Norgran 1080); *Newport Uproar* (1967, RCA LSP3891)

As sideman: L. Armstrong: Memories of You (1930, OK 41463); B. Goodman: Moonglow/Dinah (1936, Vic. 25398); Stompin' at the Savoy (1936, Vic. 25521); Dizzy Spells (1938, Col. SL16)

BIBLIOGRAPHY

B. Ulanov: "Again Lionel Hampton Steps Ahead with a New Program for his Great Band," *Metronome*, lxii/12 (1946), 9, 42

R. Gehman: "Lionel Hampton," *Treasury of Jazz*, ed. E. Condon and R. Gehman (New York, 1956/R1975 as *Eddie Condon's Treasury of Jazz*), 299–308

D. Morgenstern: "Lionel Hampton: the Band the Critics Forgot," *DB*, xxxii/9 (1965), 17 only

L.K. McMillan: "Good Vibes from Hampton," *DB*, xxxix/8 (1972), 12–13, 26

S. Dance: "Lionel Hampton," *The World of Swing* (New York, 1974, rev. 2/2001 as *The World of Swing: an Oral History of Big Band Jazz*), 265–78

O. Flückiger: *Lionel Hampton: Selected Discography, 1966–1978* (Reinach, Switzerland, 1978, enlarged 2/1980 as *Lionel Hampton: Porträt mit Discography, 1966–79*)

A.J. Smith: "Lionel Hampton: Half a Century Strong," *DB*, xlv/14 (1978), 20–21, 53–4, 56, 62

L. Hampton and J. Haskins: *Hamp: an Autobiography* (New York, 1989)

WOLFRAM KNAUER

Hampton, Slide [Locksley Wellington] (*b* Jeanette, PA, 21 April 1932). Trombonist, composer, arranger, and educator. A rare left-handed trombonist, Hampton was already touring with his father's band at age 12, was performing with Lionel Hampton at Carnegie Hall at age 20, and joined Maynard Ferguson's band thereafter, penning memorable charts such as "Three Little Foxes" and "Slide's Derangement." His dual talents as performer and writer led to subsequent work with Art Blakey, Thad Jones-Mel Lewis, Max Roach, Dizzy Gillespie, and Woody Herman. Self-led groups over the years include the Slide Hampton Octet (which included Booker Little, Freddie Hubbard, and George Coleman), the nine trombone and rhythm section World of Trombones, and more recently his own quartet, quintet, and Slide Hampton Ultra Big Band. He spent much of the 1970s working in Europe with expatriates Benny Bailey, Dexter Gordon, and Art Farmer; the 1990s included a world tour with the Dizzy Gillespie Alumni All-Stars, and a post as arranger and special adviser for the Carnegie Hall Jazz Band. He commands a fluid, precise, and harmonically posed playing style, while his writing is a lexicon of arranging tapestries that excel in making mid-sized ensembles sound larger than numbered, and

giving like-sounding instruments distinctive musical voices. A contributor to numerous recordings, concerts, and tours by major artists over six decades, he has been honored with two Grammy Awards for arranging (1998, 2005) and with a Jazz Masters Fellowship from the NEA in 2005.

JEFFREY HOLMES

Hanby, Benjamin R(ussel) (*b* Rushville, OH, 22 July 1833; *d* Chicago, IL, 16 March 1867). Composer. He was educated at Otterbein College, Westerville, Ohio, and in 1858 became a minister. He later left the ministry and taught in singing-schools; he also worked for the John Church publishing company in Cincinnati and, from 1865, for Root & Cady of Chicago. He wrote children's songs for school and Sunday school and edited books of such pieces for Root & Cady, one of which, *Our Song Birds* (1866), contained his popular Christmas songs "Who is he in yonder stall?" and "Santa Claus, or Up on the House Top." Of his nearly 80 songs only two others have secured him lasting fame, and both are minstrel songs that manifest his sympathy for the abolitionist cause: the immensely popular "Darling Nelly Gray" (1856), with its simple, accessible, hymn-like melody, actually helped to turn the emotions of the North against slavery, and "Ole Shady" (1861) hoped to encourage the escape of the slaves.

BIBLIOGRAPHY

ANB (D. Cockrell)

D.C. Shoemaker: *Choose You This Day: The Legacy of the Hanbys*, ed. Harold B. Hancock and Millard J. Miller (Westerville, OH, 1983)

J.B. Gross: *Benjamin Russel Hanby, Ohio Composer-Educator* (diss., Ohio State University, 1987)

DALE COCKRELL/R

Hance, James F. (*fl* New York, NY, c1818–33). Composer and music teacher. He apparently gave up music in about 1833 to become a carpenter. His piano music, including variations, rondo arrangements, and divertimentos on tunes from Rossini's operas, are of high quality. His writing occasionally harks back to late 18th-century style, as in the use of the Alberti bass in *The Cossack Rondo* (1927), but the rondo *Le songe celeste!* (n.d. [1818–21]) shows more imagination in its thematic manipulation and tonal diversions. His best work is to be found in the *Russian Dance* variations (n.d. [1823–6]), which include a long sequential passage modulating to distantly related keys and several cadenza sections.

WORKS

(selective list)

(all for pf; all were published in New York, n.d., unless otherwise indicated; estimated dates of publication are given in brackets)

Hungarian Air, variations ([1818–20]); Le songe celeste!, rondo ([1818–21]); Non mi ricordo, waltz (Philadelphia, n.d. [?1821]); Two Admired Waltzes (Philadelphia, n.d. [?1821]); Will you come to the bower, variations (after T. Moore) (Boston, n.d. [1823–4]); Russian Dance, variations ([1823–6]), ed. in RRAM, ii (1977); Au clair de la lune, variations ([1824]); The Constellation (1826); Fragments from the opera Il barbiere di Siviglia, divertimento [after Rossini] (1826); First Grand Fantasie, variations (n.p., n.d. [1826–7]); The Cossack Rondo (1827); The Marion, impromptu with variations (n.p., 1827)

Polish Military Waltz (1827); The Amaranth, waltz ([1829–35]); Fragments from Cinderella, divertimento [after Rossini] (n.p., 1831); Presentation Quick Step (n.p., 1850)

Principal publishers: Dubois, Dubois & Stodart, Pond

BIBLIOGRAPHY

R.J. Wolfe: *Secular Music in America 1801–1825: a Bibliography* (New York, 1964)

B.A. Wolverton: *Keyboard Music and Musicians in the Colonies and United States of America before 1830* (diss., Indiana U., 1966)

J.B. Clark: *The Dawning of American Keyboard Music* (New York, Westport, CT, and London, 1988)

J. BUNKER CLARK/R

Hanchett, Henry Granger (*b* Syracuse, NY, 29 Aug 1853; *d* Siasconset, MA, 19 Aug 1918). Pianist, organist, lecturer, teacher, and physician. He studied music as a child with Ernst Held in Syracuse, and later with leading teachers in New York and Berlin. He studied medicine at Syracuse University and in 1884 graduated from the New York Homoeopathic Medical College. He practiced medicine for several years, but retired from practice to devote his entire attention to music. He gave many lectures and recitals at the Brooklyn Institute in 1893–1901, and presented at least 150 lectures and recitals in the popular New York Board of Education Free Courses in 1889–1910. Hanchett made extensive lecture-recital tours around the United States, and held music positions in several colleges. He was organist and music director at several New York churches in 1884–98, and was a founder of the American Guild of Organists in 1897. He was the American inventor of the sostenuto pedal on pianos in 1873. In addition to several books on medical topics, he wrote *Teaching as a Science; An Address Read Before the Music Teachers National Assoc. at Buffalo, NY, July 1880, and Other Essays* (1882); *The Art of the Musician: A Guide to the Intelligent Appreciation of Music* (1905); and *An Introduction to the Theory of Music* (1916). His compositions include a Te Deum, a Benedictus, and an Easter anthem.

SARAH L. MARTIN

Hancock, Gerre (*b* Lubbock, TX, 21 Feb 1934; *d* Austin, TX, 21 Jan 2012). Organist. He took a BMus in organ at the University of Texas at Austin in 1955 and subsequently studied at the Sorbonne and Union Theological Seminary, New York. His organ teachers included E. William Doty, Jean Langlais, and ROBERT S. BAKER, and he studied composition and improvisation with NADIA BOULANGER, KENT KENNAN, and M. Searle Wright. He held church appointments at St. Bartholomew's, New York (1960), Christ Church Cathedral, Cincinnati (1962), and St. Thomas's, Fifth Avenue, New York, where as organist and master of choristers (1971–2004) he achieved international acclaim. In 1971 he joined the faculty at the Juilliard School, where he taught through 2004; additionally he served from 1974 as visiting faculty both at Yale University and at the Eastman School. Hancock was also active as guest conductor with Concert Royal and the Orchestra of St. Luke's in New York. After 1963 he gave recitals throughout the world, performed at many national conventions of the American Guild of Organists (AGO) and at the centenary celebrations of

the Royal College of Organists in London (1963), and he made many appearances with the St. Thomas Choir in concert and on television. He was particularly well regarded as a master of improvisation. He was a Fellow of the AGO, the Royal School of Church Music, and the Royal College of Organists; he held honorary degrees from Nashotah House Episcopal Seminary (MusD 1985), the University of the South (MusD 1998), General Theological Seminary (DivD 2004), and Westminster Choir College of Rider University (MusD 2009). He received the Medal of the Cross of St. Augustine from the Archbishop of Canterbury in 2004. His extensive list of compositions includes choral works, hymns, and organ music. His textbook, *Improvising: How to Master the Art*, was published in Oxford in 1994, and he is the subject of a DVD published in 2006 in the AGO Masters Series.

CHARLES KRIGBAUM/JAMES H. COOK

Hancock, Herbie [Herbert Jeffrey] (*b* Chicago, IL, 12 April 1940). Jazz pianist, keyboard player, and composer. He was born into a musical family and began studying piano at the age of seven. Four years later he performed the first movement of Mozart's Piano Concerto no.5 with the Chicago SO in a young people's concert. He formed his own jazz band while attending Hyde Park High School; his early influences were from Oscar Peterson, Bill Evans, and the harmonies of Clare Fischer, Gil Evans, and Ravel. Hancock began studies at Grinnell College with a double major in music and engineering, the latter an early interest that later was manifested in his groundbreaking synthesizer work. He switched to composition in his junior year, and by the time he left Grinnell in 1960 he was already working in jazz clubs in Chicago with Coleman Hawkins. The trumpeter Donald Byrd invited him to join his quintet and move to New York, where during Hancock's first recording session with the group, Blue Note was sufficiently impressed to offer him his first date as a leader, in May 1962. The resulting album, *Takin' Off*, drew considerable public attention through an original tune, "Watermelon Man," which had a strong gospel influence and charted on jazz and R&B radio. Hancock also worked briefly in Eric Dolphy's group and recorded with Hank Mobley, Jimmy Heath, Oliver Nelson, and Kenny Dorham.

In May 1963 Hancock joined Miles Davis's group, which became known as the trumpeter's second great quintet. Hancock's piano style had by this time evolved into a highly personal blend of blues and bop with sophisticated harmony and exquisite tone. With Davis's sidemen Ron Carter and Tony Williams, Hancock helped revolutionize traditional jazz concepts of the rhythm section and its relation to the soloists, and established a musical rapport with an extraordinary degree of freedom and interaction. During his five years with the quintet Hancock also led his own groups, recording several albums for Blue Note including *Maiden Voyage* (1965), *Speak Like a Child* (1968), and *The Prisoner* (1969). These featured compositions that have since become jazz standards: "Maiden Voyage," "Dolphin

Dance," "Cantaloupe Island," and "Speak Like a Child." Hancock also composed the score for Michelangelo Antonioni's film *Blow-Up* (1966) and worked as a sideman with Blue Mitchell, Lee Morgan, Bob Brookmeyer, Sonny Rollins, Jackie McLean, Sam Rivers, and Woody Shaw, as well as with his fellow sidemen in Davis's band Williams and Wayne Shorter. Although he officially left Davis's group in 1968, Hancock continued to record with him until 1970 and played electric piano and organ on many of Davis's important jazz-rock albums including *In a Silent Way*, *Bitches Brew* (both 1969, Col.), and *A Tribute to Jack Johnson* (1970, Col.).

From 1970 to 1973 Hancock led a sextet that combined elements of jazz, rock, and African and Indian music with electronic devices and instruments. He also used the name Mwandishi during this period. Influenced by Davis's fusion recordings the sextet, which included Joe Henderson, Johnny Coles, and Billy Hart, was notable for its colorful doubling of instruments, tasteful blend of acoustic and electronic sounds, and mastery of compound meters (*Mwandishi*, 1970, WB, and *Sextant*, 1972, Col.). Thereafter Hancock began to use electric and electronic instruments more extensively, including the Fender-Rhodes piano which he played through a variety of signal processors such as wah-wah and fuzz pedals. Later he turned to the Mellotron and the Hohner Clavinet and finally to various synthesizers, sequencers, and electronic percussion units. Hancock's album *Head Hunters* (1973, Col.) with his ensemble of the same name, was the first by a jazz artist to go platinum and marked the beginning of a commitment to more commercial types of music, particularly rock, funk, and disco, and contained the Sly Stone–influenced hit single "Chameleon." Although Hancock returned occasionally to jazz projects in the late 1970s, particularly with his Davis-alumni band V.S.O.P and his piano duos with Chick Corea, his focus during this period was on crossover music that achieved considerable commercial success. In 1983 the single "Rockit" reached the top of the pop charts, and its promotional video received widespread critical acclaim; it demonstrated Hancock's ability to use the most complex innovations in electronic technology to produce fascinating music.

After this success Hancock turned his attention almost exclusively to jazz for the next two years. He acted and played in the film *Round Midnight* (1986) and won an Oscar for his score. From 1987 he recorded and toured internationally with all-star groups that included Carter, Williams, Gil Scott-Heron, Michael Brecker, Jack DeJohnette, Dave Holland, Pat Metheny, Vernon Reid (of Living Colour), and Shorter. Hancock's album *Dis is da Drum* (1994, Verve) included material in a hip hop style, and on *The New Standard* (1996, Verve) he recorded versions of pop songs by the Beatles, Prince, Simon and Garfunkel, and Steely Dan, among others. During the late 1990s Hancock worked with a reunited Headhunters band and recorded an album of works by Gershwin (*Gershwin's World*, 1998, Verve) which won multiple Grammy awards. Hancock's music also began to reappear on the charts through the sampling of his earlier material, notably the use of "Cantaloupe Island" by the British hip hop group Us3 on "Cantaloop (Flip Fantasia)" (BN, 1993). Since then his projects have continued to explore crossover influences and collaborators. His recording *River: the Joni Letters* (2007, Verve) featured compositions by Joni Mitchell and became only the second jazz album to win the Grammy Award for Album of the Year, and his tribute to John Lennon, *The Imagine Project* (2010, Hancock), included such varied artists as John Legend, Dave Matthews, and The Chieftains.

WORKS
(selective list)

Inst: Driftin', Watermelon Man (from Takin' Off; 1962, BN); Cantaloupe Island, One Finger Snap (from Empyrean Isles; 1964, BN); Dolphin Dance, Little One, Maiden Voyage (from Maiden Voyage; 1965, BN); Riot, Speak Like a Child, The Sorcerer (from Speak Like a Child; 1968, BN); Chameleon, Watermelon Man (from Head Hunters; 1973, Col.); I Thought it was You (from Sunlight; 1978, Col.); Rockit (from Future Shock; 1983, Col.)

Film scores: Blow-Up (dir. M. Antonioni, 1966); Death Wish (dir. M. Winner, 1974); A Soldier's Story (dir. N. Jewison, 1984); Round Midnight (dir. B. Tavernier, 1985); Colors (dir. D. Hopper, 1988); Harlem Nights (dir. E. Murphy, 1989)

BIBLIOGRAPHY

B. Johnson: "Herbie Hancock: into his own Thing," *DB*, xxxviii/2 (1971), 14 only

R. Townley: "Hancock Plugs In," *DB*, xli/17 (1974), 13

D. Milano and others: "Herbie Hancock," *Contemporary Keyboard*, iii/11 (1977), 26

C. Silvert: "Herbie Hancock: Revamping the Past, Creating the Future," *DB*, xliv/15 (1977), 16

D.N. Baker, L.M. Belt, and H.C. Hudson, eds.: "Herbie Hancock," *The Black Composer Speaks* (Metuchen, NJ, 1978), 108–38 [incl. list of compositions]

B. Primack: "Herbie Hancock: Chameleon in his Disco Phase," *DB*, xlvi/10 (1979), 12

J. Balleras: "Herbie Hancock's Current Choice," *DB*, xlix/9 (1982), 15–17

L. Lyons: "Herbie Hancock," *The Great Jazz Pianists: Speaking of their Lives and Music* (New York, 1983/R), 269–84

H. Mandel: "Herbie Hancock: of Films, Fairlights, Funk…and all that other Jazz," *DB*, liii/7 (1986), 16–19 [incl. discography]

N. Suzuki: *Herbie Hancock: 1961–1969* (Shizuoka, Japan, 1988) [discography]

J. Tamarkin: "Herbie Hancock: Energy in the Environment," *JT* (Sept 2010), also available at <http://jazztimes.com/articles/26370-herbie-hancock-energy-in-the-environment>

Oral history material in *Neij*

BILL DOBBINS/BARRY LONG

Handbell. A bell with a handle (shaft or loop), held in the hand for ringing; *see* BELLRINGING.

Handel and Haydn Society. One of the oldest continuing concert societies in the United States. It was founded in Boston in 1815, with the original purpose to improve the performance level of sacred music. Thomas Webb, Gottlieb Graupner, and Asa Peabody issued the original invitation for a meeting in which the society was formed, with 46 original members. Webb was elected its first president. The society gave its first public concert on 25 December 1815. It quickly evolved into a major choral concert organization, presenting the first complete performances in America of Handel's *Messiah* (1818), Haydn's *The Creation* (1819), Verdi's Requiem

(1878), and Bach's St. Matthew Passion (1879). The society has performed *Messiah* annually since 1854.

The society nearly foundered soon after its creation because of financial difficulties. It was rescued, however, through the publication of a collection of church music by an obscure bank teller in Savannah, Georgia, Lowell Mason. The *Handel and Haydn Society Collection of Church Music*, originally published in 1822, went through at least 18 editions and remained in print until 1839. The success of the publication placed the society on sound fiscal footing and led to Mason being elected President and Conductor in 1827. He remained in that position until 1832. In 1847 the society split the positions of President and Conductor, later Artistic Director. Charles F. Horn served as conductor from 1847–9, J.E. Goodson, 1851–2, and Carl Bergmann, 1852–4. A series of long-tenured conductors followed: Carl Zerrahn, 1854–98, Emil Mollenhauer, 1899–1927, Thompson Stone, 1927–59, Edward F. Gilday, 1959–67, Thomas Dunn, 1967–86, Christopher Hogwood, 1986–2001, and Grant Llewellyn, 2001–6. After a shared leadership of Roger Norrington, Llewellyn, and Harwood, Harry Christophers became Artistic Director in 2009.

Throughout the 19th and much of the 20th century the society consisted of an amateur chorus and professional instrumentalists hired for the occasion. When Symphony Hall was built in 1900, the Handel and Haydn Society developed a close rapport with the Boston Symphony Orchestra, using the BSO's instrumentalists, providing a chorus for the BSO, and gaining access to the hall for their concerts.

Gender issues arose as early as Mason's tenure when the society suffered from the lack of female voices. Women were sought as singers, but were not allowed membership in the H&H. They were referred to as "Ladies of the Chorus" until 19 June 1967, when they attained full membership and voting rights.

Beginning with Dunn the society moved from a primarily choral organization to one balanced between choral and orchestral. The chorus was transformed from a large amateur group into a small, professional ensemble. Under the leadership of Hogwood, the society began to emphasize historically informed performance, stressing period instruments. Today the H&H claims to have the largest audience of any period performing group in North America. It also frequently performs in Europe, has issued numerous recordings, and has an Educational Outreach Program providing vocal instruction in Boston Public schools.

BIBLIOGRAPHY

J.S. Dwight: "Music in Boston," in *The Memorial History of Boston*, ed. Justin Winsor (Boston, 1881), iv, 415–64

C.C. Perkins and J.S. Dwight, *History of the Handel and Haydn Society*, i (Boston, 1883)

M.D. Herter Norton "Haydn in America (before 1820)," *MQ*, xviii/2 (April 1932), 309–37

H.E. Johnson, *Hallelujah, Amen! the Story of the Handel and Haydn Society of Boston* (Boston, 1965)

M. Broyles, *"Music of the Highest Class": Elitism and Populism in Antebellum Boston* (New Haven, CT, 1992)

MICHAEL BROYLES

Handt, Herbert (*b* Philadelphia, PA, 26 May 1926). American tenor and conductor. His cousin was the Romanian conductor Otto Ackermann (1909–60). While studying at the Juilliard School he sang in the NBC chorus under Toscanini, and continued his studies at the Vienna Academy with Julius Patzak and Hans Swarowsky. He also studied in Rome, at Accademia di S. Cecilia. His debut as a tenor was at the Vienna Staatsoper as Rinuccio in *Gianni Schicchi* (1949), and he soon acquired a reputation as a specialist in contemporary music; he created roles in Malipiero's *Venere prigioniera* (1957, Florence) and Menotti's *Maria Golovin* (1958, Brussels), and appeared in the first Italian or French productions (sometimes both) of works by Berg (*Wozzeck*), Busoni (*Turandot*), Britten (*Midsummer Night's Dream*), Menotti (*Martin's Lie*), and Henze. He also performed in concert, in particular as an oratorio soloist. He made his conducting debut at Rome in 1960, and devoted time to conducting performances of little-known Italian works by Francesco Barsanti, Luigi Boccherini, Francesco Geminiani, and Gioachino Rossini, often preparing the performing editions; he was associated with the Rossini Foundation in Pesaro for many years. He subsequently made his home in Lucca, where he formed the Associazione Musicale Lucchese, the Lucca Chamber Orchestra, and the Marlia International Festival. He also directed the Opera School of Chicago and instituted the first spring season of the Chicago Opera Theatre (1974). His early recordings include *Idomeneo* (1950), for which he was much praised as Arbaces, Haydn's Orpheus in *Orfeo ed Euridice* with Swarowsky (also 1950), Sextus in the first complete *Giulio Cesare* (Handel) also with Swarowsky (1952), and the original-cast recording of *Maria Golovin*.

WILLIAM WEAVER, NÖEL GOODWIN/NICOLA BADOLATO

Handy, John (Richard) (Dallas, TX, 3 Feb 1933). Alto saxophonist and music educator. He was raised in California, where he studied clarinet before switching to alto saxophone. He has also played tenor and baritone saxophones, flute, piano, oboe, and percussion. Handy started his career performing in San Francisco with the blues musicians Lowell Fulson and Pee Wee Crayton and the jazz musicians Freddie Redd, Pat Martino, and Bobby Hutcherson. He then moved in 1958 to New York, where he formed his own group and worked with the pianist Randy Weston and the bass player and composer Charles Mingus (including the album *Mingus Ah Um*, 1959, Col.). In 1959 he recorded his first album, for Roulette. After studying music at San Francisco State College (BA 1963), he had a parallel career as a teacher, working at San Francisco State University and Conservatory, the University of California at Berkeley, and Stanford University, among other institutions. He rejoined Mingus in 1964 and then formed his own combo, an acclaimed group that performed at the Monterey Jazz Festival in 1965. After 1970 he played with musicians from India, performed with orchestras and jazz-rock ensembles, and led his own groups. He later helped revive Mingus's music with the ensemble Mingus Dynasty and with Gunther Schuller (*Epitaph*, 1989,

Col.). In 1999 the John Handy Jazz Festival was started in San Francisco.

BIBLIOGRAPHY
G. Hoefer: "Search for Self: John Handy," *DB*, xxviii/6 (1961), 15
E. Kolb: "John Handy: Interview," *Cadence*, x/6 (1984), 15
P. Elwood: "John Handy Revisited," *DB*, lxiii/10 (1996), 32

LUCA CERCHIARI

Handy, W(illiam) C(hristopher) (*b* Florence, AL, 16 Nov 1873; *d* New York, NY, 28 March 1958). Composer and bandleader. His main claim to fame is summarized by the controversial appellation of "Father of the Blues" that he assiduously cultivated, that others applied to him, and that became the title of his autobiography (1941). Whether or not he deserved this lofty status, there can be no doubt that Handy played a major role in the early popularization of the blues form and in the arrangement and adaptation of what was essentially a type of folk music into something that was acceptable and accessible to mainstream American and international tastes.

There are two main problems in cutting through the hagiography and arriving at an objective assessment of Handy's role and importance in the blues and in American music. One is the fact that he viewed and treated the blues primarily as a musical form, whereas throughout most of its history it has existed also as a performance art and an evolving set of musical styles. The other is the fact that most of what we know about his life comes directly or indirectly from Handy himself. In different accounts details have varied and been altered, reinterpreted, and polished to support his status as a central figure in blues music and an icon in 20th-century American music.

Handy's life and career in music can be divided into several distinct phases. Up to 1903 there was a period of formal training in music, absorption and observation of various types of music ranging from folksongs and spirituals to popular ragtime and light classics, and an itinerant life with participation in late 19th-century currents in popular music, including quartet singing, leading a minstrel show band, and college music teaching. From 1903 to 1911 Handy underwent a period of intensive exposure to African American folk music, especially the newly emerging blues, in the Mississippi Delta and Memphis, and this music influenced his repertory as a bandleader, arranger, and performer. The year 1912 saw him launch a successful career as a composer, arranger, and publisher of blues music, in which he drew inspiration and material from what he had been exposed to earlier. His success lasted into the early 1920s. The remainder of his life was spent in consolidating his business position and reputation through high-profile performances and through his writings, in exploring other types of music with somewhat less success, in receiving many honors, and in serving as a spokesman and advocate for blues and African American folk music in general.

Handy was the son and grandson of Methodist ministers in Florence and his family expected him to follow in their footsteps. However, he showed an early interest in a musical career and eventually became proficient on organ, piano, guitar, and especially cornet and trumpet. He studied vocal music for 11 years in the Florence District School with Professor Y.A. Wallace, a graduate of Fisk University, also studying popular music with the violinist Jim Turner. He left Florence in 1892 and organized a brass band in Bessemer, Alabama, and later a vocal quartet in Birmingham, Alabama. The quartet went on the road but was stranded in St. Louis in 1893 without work. Handy drifted to Evansville, Indiana, and worked with local brass bands there and in Henderson, Kentucky. In 1896 he joined the band of Mahara's Minstrels, where he became a lead cornetist, arranger, and eventually bandleader. For the next several years he toured throughout the United States, Canada, Mexico, and Cuba, taking two years off (1900–02) to teach at the Agricultural and Mechanical College in Normal, Alabama.

In 1903 Handy took over the leadership of the Knights of Pythias band in Clarksdale, Mississippi. During his travels through the state's Delta region he frequently heard performances of folk blues and was impressed by their popularity with both black and white audiences. He began arranging these songs and other folktunes for his band. By 1907 Handy was resident in Memphis, leading the Knights of Pythias band there. His band was hired to play for the 1909 mayoral campaign of E.H. Crump, for which Handy arranged an instrumental version of a folksong that had been critical of Crump's reform pledges. The tune was successful and helped Crump to win the election.

In 1912 Handy published "Mister Crump" as "The Memphis Blues," combining it with typical 12-bar, three-line blues strains to create a medley along the lines of a ragtime instrumental tune. Although it was not the first published blues, as Handy would later claim, it was certainly the most popular to date, especially after the publication the following year of lyrics by George A. Norton that prominently linked Handy and his band with the blues and Memphis. With Harry Pace, Handy established a publishing company, Pace and Handy (known as "The Home of the Blues"), later to become Handy Brothers, and had successes for the next several years with "Jogo Blues" (1913), "St. Louis Blues" (1914), "Yellow Dog Blues" (1914), "Joe Turner Blues" (1915), "Hesitating Blues" (1915), "Ole Miss" (1916), "Beale Street Blues" (1917), "Loveless Love" (1921), "Aunt Hagar's Children Blues" (1921), "Harlem Blues" (1923), and "Atlanta Blues" (1924). He recorded with his band for Columbia Records in 1917 and for Paramount and Okeh Records in 1922 and 1923. In 1918 he shifted his base of operations from Memphis to New York.

From 1924 onward, Handy turned his attention increasingly to the arrangement and publication of traditional spirituals and to songs and tunes on broader African American themes, including collaborations with a variety of lyricists. He consolidated his position in the blues with the publication in 1926 of an anthology of his works and those of other composers, and his autobiography in 1941. He produced concerts of African American music and was a leading figure in the Harlem Renaissance of the 1920s. A park on Beale Street in

Memphis was dedicated in his honor in 1931 and a statue erected there in 1960. In his later years Handy frequently appeared at civic and charity events and spoke on behalf of the dignity of blues and folk music. A film based on his life, *St. Louis Blues*, starring Nat "King" Cole, was released in 1958, and in 1969 the United States honored Handy with a postage stamp. The major annual awards for accomplishment in blues music were for many years known as Handys in his honor.

WORKS
(selective list)
(dates are those of copyright; first published in Memphis until 1918, thereafter in New York)

EDITIONS

Blues: an Anthology (New York, 1926, rev. 1972/R and 1990 by J. Silverman and 2012 by E. Hurwitt)
W.C. Handy's Collection of Negro Spirituals (New York, 1938)
A Treasury of the Blues (New York, 1949) [with an historical and critical text by Abbe Niles]
Vocal: Over 150 blues, popular songs, stage songs, art songs, and spiritual arrs., incl. Mister Crump, perf. 1909 (1926), rev. as Memphis Blues, pf (1912), repr. with lyrics (G.A. Norton), 1913; St. Louis Blues, 1914; Yellow Dog Blues, 1914; The Hesitating Blues, 1915; Joe Turner Blues, 1915; Beale Street Blues, 1916; The Kaiser's Got the Blues (D. Browne), 1918; Darktown Reveille (W. Hirsch), collab. C. Smith, 1923; Golden Brown Blues (L. Hughes), 1927; Opportunity (W. Malone), 1932
Inst: Jogo Blues, pf, 1913; Ole Miss, military band, 1916; Aframerican Hymn, military band, chorus, 1916; Aunt Hagar's Children Blues, pf, 1921, repd with lyrics (J.T. Brymn), 1922; Go down, Moses, org, band, 2 pf, 1930; other works

BIBLIOGRAPHY

GroveA (E. Southern); *SouthernB*
D. Scarborough: "The 'Blues' as Folk-Songs," *Publications of the Texas Folklore Society*, ii (1923), 52–66
W.C. Handy: *Father of the Blues: an Autobiography* (New York, 1941/R)
A. Morrison: "W.C. Handy: Broadway's Grand Old Man of Music," *Ebony*, ix/11 (1953), 59–62
"Evening Sun Goes Down," *Ebony*, xiii/6 (1958), 96–8
E.R. Montgomery: *William C. Handy, Father of the Blues* (Champaign, IL, 1968)
G.W. Kay: "William Christopher Handy," *JJ*, xxiv/3 (1971), 10–12
E. Southern: *The Music of Black Americans: a History* (New York, 1971, 3/1997)
E. Southern: *Readings in Black American Music* (New York, 1971, 2/1983)
E. Southern: "In Retrospect: Letters from W.C. Handy to William Grant Still," *BPM*, vii (1979), 199–234; viii (1980), 65–119
L. Abbott and D. Seroff: "'They cert'ly sound good to me': Sheet Music, Southern Vaudeville, and the Commercial Ascendancy of the Blues," *AM*, xiv/4 (1996), 402–54
D.A. Jasen and G. Jones: *Spreadin' Rhythm around: Black Popular Songwriters, 1880–1930* (New York, 1998)
E.S. Hurwitt: "W(illiam) C(hristopher) Handy," *International Dictionary of Black Composers*, ed. S.A. Floyd Jr. (Chicago, 1999), 549–58
E.S. Hurwitt: *W.C. Handy as Music Publisher: Career and Reputation* (diss., CUNY, 2000)
E.S. Hurwitt: "Abbe Niles, Blues Advocate," *Ramblin' on my Mind: New Perspectives on the Blues*, ed. D. Evans (Urbana, IL, 2008), 105–51
D. Robertson: *W.C. Handy: the Life and Times of the Man who Made the Blues* (New York, 2009)
P.C. Muir: *Long Lost Blues: Popular Blues in America, 1850–1920* (Urbana, IL, 2010)

DAVID EVANS

Hanks, Nancy (*b* Miami Beach, FL, 31 Dec 1927; *d* New York, NY, 7 Jan 1983). Arts administrator, consultant, and public official. In 1949 she graduated magna cum laude from Duke University with a major in political science. She also attended summer sessions at the University of Colorado and Oxford University. From 1951 to 1953 she was secretary to the Director of the Office of Defense Mobilization. Hanks was appointed to the President's Advisory Committee on Government Organization and became Assistant to the Under Secretary of Health, Education, and Welfare. She was named Special Assistant to the President on Foreign Affairs (1955–6) and served as assistant to Nelson A. Rockefeller (1956–9). For the next ten years, she was an Associate of Laurance Rockefeller at the Rockefeller Brothers Fund. Her most renowned contribution to American musical culture came once she was appointed in 1969 as the second chairperson of the National Endowment for the Arts (NEA), becoming the first female to occupy that post. In her eight-year tenure she dramatically increased NEA funding and US government support for music and the arts; the budget rose from $8 million to $114 million. She returned to the Rockefeller Brothers Fund in 1977 until her untimely death at the age of 56. The American Associations of Museums established an award in her honor, and she received many awards and honorary degrees. Hanks also served as a trustee at Duke University and the Jackson Hole, Wyoming, Preserve.

BIBLIOGRAPHY
M.W. Straight, *Nancy Hanks, an Intimate Portrait: The Creation of a National Commitment to the Arts* (Durham, NC, 1988)

ANYA LAURENCE

Hanlon, Kevin (Francis) (*b* South Bend, IN, 1 Jan 1953). Composer and guitarist. He studied composition at Indiana University, South Bend (BA 1976), the Eastman School of Music (MM 1978), and the University of Texas, Austin (DMA 1983). His principal teachers included Barton McLean, SAMUEL ADLER, WARREN BENSON, and MARIO DAVIDOVSKY (at the Berkshire Music Center). He has taught at the University of Kentucky (1982–3), the University of Arizona (1983–8), and Southern Methodist University (from 1988). As a guitarist he has performed with, directed, and helped to found a variety of ensembles, ranging from those focused on contemporary concert music to those exploring rock and inter-arts improvisation. He is the music director and cofounder of the Quintet for the End of Time and has been instrumental in developing other musical groups that focus on contemporary music, such as Some Things Happening and the New Arts Collective. In 2010 he held an extensive residency at the Banff Center. He has also appeared as a singer and conductor. His honors include a Koussevitzky award (1981) and fellowships from the Fromm Foundation (1981) and the AMC (1982).

Hanlon's musical career began as a guitarist in rock bands; he had the opportunity to open for such acts as Alice Cooper and Ted Nugent. As his musical experience widened, he remained committed to the creative and expressive roots of progressive, improvisatory vernacular music. His experiences range from playing in Irish music sessions to performing major operatic roles. As a result,

Hanlon has produced a broad spectrum of works, usually tonally focused and rhythmically charged, and has created compelling unity from diverse styles. His orchestral music has been performed by the Chicago SO and other prominent American orchestras. Because of its radically different styles, Hanlon's music calls for a diverse range of groups to perform it. Much of his music, both as a performer and as a composer, has been released on disc, and he continues to regularly perform live.

WORKS

Orch: Cumulus nimbus, 1977; Lullaby of my Sorrows, chbr orch, 1982; Sym. no.1, 1982; Stratae, 1983; Relentless Time, small orch, 1984; Kaleidoscopic Image, 1986; On an Expanding Universe, 1986; Chronological Variations, str, 1987; Nuit d'etoiles, 1987; The Lark of Avignon, wind ens, pf, 1993; Clarion, 1997

Chbr and solo inst: Second Childhood, s rec, a rec, ukulele, elec gui, pf, bells, toys, 1976; Variations, a sax, tape delay, 1977, rev. 1981; Toccata, pf, 1980; Str Trio, 1981; Clarion, trbn choir, 1982; Centered, chbr ens, tape, 1983; Prelude, org, 1990; Cripples, chbr ens, 1991, The Lullaby, va qt, 2010

Vocal: Through to the End of the Tunnel, 1v, tape delay, 1975–6, rev. 1980; An die ferne Geliebte (A. Jeitteles), 1v, pf, 1980; A.E. Housman Song Cycle, 1v, chbr ens, 1982; 5 Choral Introits, chorus, ens, 1982

Principal publishers: Broude, Doubting Scholar Press

LANCE W. BRUNNER/JONAS WESTOVER

Hanna, Sir Roland (Pembroke) (*b* Detroit, MI, 10 Feb 1932; *d* Hackensack, NJ, 13 Nov 2002). Jazz pianist. He learned music from his father in early childhood and studied classical piano from the age of 11. Later he was influenced by the jazz pianists Tommy Flanagan, Hank Jones, Art Tatum, and Teddy Wilson. After serving in the army (early 1950s) he studied music at the Eastman (1953–4) and the Juilliard (BM 1960) schools of music. Hanna worked briefly with Charles Mingus, joined Sarah Vaughan (1960), and later worked freelance and led a trio at such clubs as the Five Spot in New York (1963–6). In 1970 he was knighted by the Liberian government in honor of a series of benefit performances that he organized to raise funds for education in Liberia. His performances and recordings with the Thad Jones–Mel Lewis Orchestra from 1966 to 1974 brought him considerable critical acclaim but, unfortunately, scant public attention and few opportunities for further work. Hanna supported himself in part through teaching at Eastman, the Manhattan School of Music, the New School, and Queens College. From around 1971 into the 1980s, he was the pianist of the New York Jazz Quartet, in which he worked with Hubert Laws, Ron Carter, and Billy Cobham; later members included Ben Riley and George Mraz. During the last decades of his career, he composed chamber and orchestral works, recorded with the group Mingus Dynasty, and toured with the Lincoln Center Jazz Orchestra. His improvisational dexterity, lush harmonic language, and wide-ranging compositions indicated that Hanna had a rare grasp of piano history in all styles of music, giving him an eloquence rarely matched by his peers.

BIBLIOGRAPHY

J. Hasse: "Roland Hanna: Inside Insight," *DB*, xxxvii/20 (1970), 16
R. Townley and E. Nemeyer: "The Two-fisted Rubato of Sir Roland Hanna," *DB*, xlii/7 (1975), 15
L. Tompkins: "The Magic of the Piano: Roland Hanna," *CI*, xviii/11 (1980), 20
L. Tompkins: "Roland Hanna on his Piano Preferences," *CI*, xviii/12 (1980), 23
M. Tucker: "Seven Steps to Piano Heaven: the Artistry of Sir Roland Hanna," *ISAM Newsletter*, xxx/1 (2000), 4–5, 13
Obituary, *New York Times* (15 Nov 2002)

BILL DOBBINS/R

Hannay, Roger (Durham) (*b* Plattsburgh, NY, 22 Sept 1930; *d* Chapel Hill, NC, 27 Jan 2006). Composer and teacher. He studied composition at Syracuse University, Boston University, and the Eastman School of Music (PhD 1956); his teachers included Dika Newlin, HOWARD HANSON, and LUKAS FOSS. In 1966 he became head of the department of theory and composition at the University of North Carolina, Chapel Hill, where he founded and directed the New Music Ensemble and the electronic music studio. He served as a professor of music there from 1966 until his retirement in 1995. After retirement, he continued his work as a composer, penning many new works, as well as revising several earlier ones. He received grants and commissions from the American Music Center, the North Carolina Symphony, ASCAP, the Keenan Foundation, the Pogue Foundation, and the NEA (1975), as well as residencies at the MacDowell Colony (1982) and Yaddo (1992).

Hannay's compositions can be parsed into three early phases, before he settled into what might be called his mature style. His earliest works (1952–4) employ dissonant tonality and expand rapidly to an extensive use of the 12-tone system. His music from 1955 to 1964 exhibits an individual alternation and mixture of serial techniques with free atonality and tonal elements. From 1966 to 1969, like many other composers of the time, he was deeply involved with experimental electronic and percussion music and with mixed-media theater works containing social and political commentary (*Marshall's Medium Message, Live and in Color!*). After 1970 his music reflects a new lyricism, often involving reinterpretations of music of the past (*Listen, Tuonelan Joutsen, Scarlatti on Tour*). His Third and Fourth Symphonies, subtitled "The Great American Novel" and "American Classic," respectively, are collage works based on recompositions of American symphonic music of the 19th and early 20th centuries. In 1983 he completed the opera *The Journey of Edith Wharton*, a large "dramatic-musical exploration" from which he later extracted a one-act chamber opera, as well as a suite. In 2003 he finished his Symphony no.8. His last work, *Farewell, be Well* (2005) for orchestra, was premiered in a chamber arrangement at a memorial concert for Hannay at UNC, Chapel Hill, with Hannay's daughter Dawn (violist for the New York Philharmonic) serving as one of the performers. His papers, including a typescript for his unpublished collection of autobiographical essays, *My Book of Life*, are held by UNC Library.

WORKS

Stage and mixed media: Two Tickets to Omaha (The Swindlers) (chbr op, 1, J. Lamb), 1960; The Fortune of Saint Macabre (op, 1), 1963; America Sing!, tape, opt. visuals, 1967, collab. D. Evans; Live and in Color! (R. Hannay), announcer, painter, perc, tape, visuals, 1967; The

Interplanetary Aleatoric Serial Factory, ens, tape, audience, visuals, 1969; Squeeze Me, ens, visuals, 1969; Glass and Steel, tape, opt. film, 1970; Cabaret Voltaire, tape, female reciter, S, sax, perc, visuals, 1971, rev. 1978; Tuonelan Joutsen [after J. Sibelius], eng hn, 4-track tape, opt. film, 1971; Arp-Dances, film, dance, 1977; Fantasy, tape, film, 1980; The Journey of Edith Wharton (op, 2, R. Graves), 1983; Scenes from a Literary Life (op, 1, adapted from The Journey of Edith Wharton), 1990

Vocal: Cantata (Bible), 1952, rev. 1994; Requiem (W.Whitman), S, chorus, orch, 1961; Shakespeare Songs, TTBB, 1961; The Fruit of Love (E. St. V. Millay), S, pf, 1964, arr. S, chbr ens, 1969; Marshall's Medium Message (Hannay), girl announcer, 4 perc, 1967; Sayings for our Time (Hannay), chorus, orch, 1968; Choral Fantasias I, II, III (Hannay), chorus, orch, 1970; The Prophecy of Despair (Hannay), TTBB, perc, 1972; Vocalise, S, tape, opt. brass, 1972; Phantom of the Opera (G. Leroux), S, org, 1975; Songs from Walden (H. Thoreau), T, pf, 1980; Emerging Voices (Hannay), SATB, 1984; Hold the Fort, SATB, pf, 1990; others

Orch: Sym. no.1, 1953, rev. 1973; Dramatic Ov. (Homage to Arnold Schoenberg), 1955, rev. 1981; Sym. no.2, 1956; Sym. no.3 "The Great American Novel," large orch, opt. chorus, 1976; Sonorous Image, 1968; Fragmentation II, orch, 1969, rev. 1995; Listen, 1971; Celebration, 1975, rev. 1993; Suite "Billings" [after W. Billings], youth orch, 1975, arr. band as American Colonial, 1979; Sym. no.4 "American Classic," orch, solo vv, opt. tape, 1977; Introduction and Allegro, sym. band, 1981; Pastorale—from Olana, hn, str, 1982; The Age of Innocence [suite from The Journey of Edith Wharton], 1983; Sic transit spiritus, wind ens, 1984, rev. 1992; Sym. no.5 in 5 mvts., 1987; Sym. no.6 for str orch, 1992; Sym. no.7 in 1 mvt., 1996; Sym. no.8, 2003; others

Chbr and inst: Rhapsody, fl, pf, 1952; Divertimento, wind qnt, 1958; Designs (Str Qt no.3), 1963; Structure, perc ens, 1965, rev. 1975; Fantôme, cl, va, pf, 1967; Confrontation, perc solo, tape, 1969, arr. tape as Mutation, 1969; Elegy (Peace for Dawn), va, tape, 1970; Time Remembered, cl, pf, 1970; Chanson sombre, fl, va, hp, 1972; Grande concerte, vn, 1972; Sphinx, tpt, tape, 1973; Four for Five, brass qnt, 1973; O Solo Viola, 1974; Str Qt no.4, 1974; Pied Piper, cl, tape, 1975; Festival of Trumpets, 10 tpt, 1978; Nocturnes, ww qnt, 1979; Sonata, tpt, 1980; Suite, fl, cl, vc, pf, 1981; Epode, fl, pf, 1982; Addendum, ob, pf, 1982; Posthaste, cl, 1982; Souvenir, fl, cl, vn, vc, perc, pf, cond., 1984; Trio-Rhapsody, fl, vc, pf, 1984; Souvenir II, fl, cl, vn, vc, pf, 1986; Modes of Discourse, fl, vn, vc, 1988; Scarlatti on Tour, hpd, 1991; others

Pf: Abstractions, 1962; Sonata, 1964; Sonorities, 1966, rev. 1991; The Episodic Refraction, pf, tape, 1971; Mere Bagatelle, pf 4 hands, synth, 1978; Serenade, pf, synth, 1979; Dream Sequence, pf, tape, 1980; Luminere, 1991; others

Principal publishers: Galaxy, Media Press, Peters, Seesaw

BIBLIOGRAPHY

D. Chittum: "Current Chronicle: Philadelphia," MQ, lv (1969), 401–3
D. Gillespie: "The Electronic Music-Plus Festival, 1977," HiFi/MusAm, xxviii/3 (1978), 20
E. Schwartz: "Electronic Plus," HiFi/MusAm, xxx/5 (1980), 36
R. Hannay: "Composer, Interrupted," NewMusicBox, 14 June 2005, <http://www.newmusicbox.org/article.nmbx?id=4271>

DON C. GILLESPIE/ALAN SHOCKLEY

Hanson. Pop band. It was formed by three brothers of the same last name: Isaac (b Tulsa, OK, 17 Nov 1980; guitar), Taylor (b Tulsa, OK, 14 March 1983; keyboards), and Zac (b Zachary, Tulsa, OK, 22 Oct 1985; drums) Hanson. All three brothers have shared singing and songwriting responsibilities. Their first professional appearance as a singing group took place in Tulsa in 1992.

Before they were signed to a major recording label, the brothers recorded and performed a variety of a cappella covers and original material, leading to two independently released albums they sold at festival performances in their hometown. Their first commercial album, Middle of Nowhere (1997), featuring the single

"MMMBop," sold over 10 million copies worldwide. In 1998 Hanson was nominated for three Grammy awards, including Best New Artist. The band capitalized on the popularity of pop music and boy bands in the 1990s, and their catchy sound and lyrics, together with their prepubescent vocal ranges, were well received by young audiences. They released several more albums with growing critical acclaim but less commercial success than their major label debut.

As the brothers grew, their sound matured and became more rock-oriented, while a dispute with their record label led them to record and release their music independently with their label 3CG Records, reaching a smaller audience. The group continues to record albums and tour through smaller venues in North America. Their 2010 album Shout it Out was celebrated with a free concert in New York that had to be shut down due to the unexpectedly large crowds, resulting in highly publicized rioting.

JESSICA L. BROWN

Hanson, Howard (Harold) (b Wahoo, NE, 28 Oct 1896; d Rochester, NY, 26 Feb 1981). Composer, educator, and conductor. He studied at Luther College, Wahoo (diploma 1911), with PERCY GOETSCHIUS at the Institute of Musical Art (1914), and at Northwestern University (BA 1916), where he was an assistant teacher in 1915–16. Subsequently he was a theory and composition teacher at the College of the Pacific in California (1916–19) and became dean of the Conservatory of Fine Arts in 1919. During his time in California, Hanson wrote his first important compositions, including the Concerto da camera, a Grieg-influenced work, and California Forest Play of 1920, which won the Rome Prize in 1921. Hanson became the first American winner of the prize to take up residence in Rome, and during his three years in Italy he studied orchestration with Ottorino Respighi and the work of the great Italian visual artists. These experiences were to play a crucial role in Hanson's later compositions; his post-1921 compositions frequently feature lush Respighi-like orchestrations, and his variation-form work Mosaics was acknowledged by the composer as having been directly influenced by his study of Italian mosaics over 35 years before.

Back in the United States in 1924, Hanson was appointed director of the Eastman School of Music, Rochester, a post he held until 1964. He built the institution into one of the finest university schools of music in the Americas, broadening its curriculum, improving its orchestras, and attracting outstanding faculty members. Among Hanson's composition students were JACK BEESON, WILLIAM BERGSMA, and PETER MENNIN. In 1964 Hanson founded the Institute of American Music at the Eastman School, making a substantial financial contribution to help the Institute in meeting its goal of publishing and disseminating American music and providing for research in the history of 20th-century styles. Hanson was also deeply involved with national music organizations, such as the National Association of Schools of Music, the Music Teachers National Association (president, 1930–31), and the Music Educators National Conference.

He was also a founder and president of the National Music Council. His addresses at conferences of these organizations frequently dealt with advocacy issues in the performing arts. Among Hanson's numerous awards were 36 American honorary degrees, membership of the Swedish Royal Academy of Music, a Pulitzer Prize for Symphony no.4, the Ditson Award, and the George Foster Peabody Award. He was elected to the National Institute of Arts and Letters in 1935 and to the Academy of the American Academy and Institute of Arts and Letters in 1979.

Hanson was also active for five decades as a conductor, making his American debut in 1924, directing the New York SO in the premiere of his symphonic poem *North and West*, at the invitation of Walter Damrosch. He subsequently conducted widely in both the United States and Europe, his association particularly strong with the Boston SO, for which he wrote the *Elegy* and the Symphony no.2. As a conductor, Hanson especially featured American compositions, and was an early champion of William Grant Still and John Alden Carpenter.

Hanson has generally been considered a neo-romantic composer, influenced by Edvard Grieg and Jean Sibelius, due in part to the success of the Second Symphony. However, he also took at times a more abstract approach to musical structure, as in the *Mosaics* and in the Concerto for Piano and Orchestra in G op.36, notable for its prevalence of short thematic fragments and traces of jazz and Tin Pan Alley. His multi-movement works also tend to be thematically cyclical. Hanson's combination of quotations from Gregorian chant and little-known chorales, sometimes biting bitonal harmonies, and driving motor rhythms proved highly applicable to the concert band—a medium he explored from the mid-1950s to the 1970s, in such works as *Chorale and Alleluia* and *Dies natalis II*. His frequently performed *Serenade* for flute, harp, and strings op.35 and the *Fantasy* for clarinet and chamber orchestra (the second movement of the ballet suite *Nymph and Satyr*) of 1978 combine transparent textures with melodic and harmonic touches of Impressionism. All Hanson's works display rhythmic vitality, frequently using tonally based ostinatos and sensitity towards timbral combination.

Hanson was the author of articles in professional journals, particularly related to music education and support for the performing arts in America. He contributed regularly to the *Rochester Times-Union* until the mid-1970s and wrote *Music in Contemporary American Civilization* (Lincoln, NE, 1951). His most important publication, however, was *Harmonic Materials of Modern Music: Resources of the Tempered Scale* (New York, 1960), a seminal work in what would later be termed pitch-class set theory.

WORKS
(selective list)

STAGE AND CHORAL
Stage: California Forest Play of 1920 (ballet, D. Richards), op.16, California State Redwood Park, 1920; Merry Mount, op.31 (op, 3, R.L. Stokes, after N. Hawthorne), op.31, 1933, New York, Met, 10 Feb

1934; Nymph and Satyr (ballet suite), lost, 2nd movt pubd as Fantasy, cl, chbr orch, 3rd movt pubd as Scherzo, bn, orch
Choral: North and West (sym. poem, textless), op.22, chorus obbl, orch, 1923; The Lament for Beowulf (trans. W. Morris and A. Wyatt), op.25, chorus, orch, 1925; 3 Songs from Drum Taps (W. Whitman), op.32, Bar, chorus, orch, 1935; The Cherubic Hymn (Gk liturgy, trans. S. Hurlbut), op.37, chorus, orch, 1949; How Excellent Thy Name (Ps viii), op.41, female vv, pf, 1952; Song of Democracy (Whitman), op.44, chorus, orch, 1957; Song of Human Rights, op.49, chorus, orch, 1963; Ps cl, male chorus, 1965; Ps cxxi, Bar, chorus, orch, 1968, arr. mixed chorus, 1969; Streams in the Desert (Bible: *Isaiah*), chorus, orch, 1969; The Mystic Trumpeter (Whitman), nar, chorus, orch, 1970; New Land, New Covenant (orat., I. Watts, J. Newton, Bible, T.S. Eliot, Declaration of Independence); Sym. no.7 "The Sea" (Whitman), chorus, orch, 1977

ORCHESTRAL
Sym. Prelude, op.6, 1916; Sym. Legend, op.8, 1917; Sym. Rhapsody, op.14, 1918; Before the Dawn, sym. poem, op.17, 1919; Exaltation, sym. poem, op.20, with pf obbl, 1920, arr. 2 pf, small ens; Sym. no.1 "Nordic," e, op.21, 1922; Lux aeterna, sym. poem, op.24, with va obbl, 1923, arr. vc, pf; Pan and the Priest, sym. poem, op.26, with pf obbl, 1926; Org Conc., op.27, 1926, rev. as Conc. for Org, Hp, and Str, op.22 no.3, 1941; Sym. no.2 "Romantic," op.30, 1930; Sym. no.3, op.33, 1937–8, rev. with wordless choral finale; Merry Mount, suite, 1938; Fantasy, str, 1939 [based on Str. Qt, op.23]; Sym. no.4 "The Requiem," op.34, 1943; Serenade, op.35, fl, hp, str, 1945, arr. fl, pf; Pf Conc., G, op.36, 1948; Pastorale, op.38, ob, hp, str, 1949; Fantasy-Variations on a Theme of Youth, pf, str, op.40, 1951; Sym. no.5 "Sinfonia sacra," op.43, 1954; Elegy, op.44, 1956; Mosaics, 1957; Summer Seascape, 1958; Bold Island Suite, op.46, 1961 [incl. Summer Seascape]; For the First Time, 1963; Summer Seascape II, va, str qt, str, 1966; Dies natalis I, 1967; Sym. no.6, 1968; Rhythmic Variations on 2 Ancient Hymns, str, lost; see also Choral

OTHER WORKS
Wind ens: Chorale and Alleluia, op.42, band, 1954; Centennial March, band, 1967; Dies natalis II, band, 1972; Young Person's Guide to the Six-Tone Scale, pf, wind, perc, 1972; Laude: Chorale, Variations and Metamorphoses, band, 1976; Variations on an Ancient Hymn, 1977
Chbr: Conc. da camera, op.7, pf, str qt, 1917; 3 Miniatures, op.12, pf, 1918–19; Scandinavian Suite, op.13, 1918–19; Str Qt, op.23, 1923; Vermeland, pf, 1926, arr. org; Dance of the Warriors, pf, 1935; Enchantment, pf, 1935; Pastorale, op.38, ob, pf, 1949, arr. ob, hp, str, 1949; Elegy, va, str qt, 1966
Songs, pf pieces, arrs.

Principal publisher: Fischer

BIBLIOGRAPHY
EwenD; *VintonD* (N. Slonimsky)
B.C. Tuthill: "Howard Hanson," *MQ*, xxii (1936), 140–51
M. Alter: "Howard Hanson," *MM*, xviii (1940–41), 84–9
R.T. Watanabe: "Howard Hanson's Manuscript Scores," *University of Rochester Library Bulletin*, v/2 (1950), 21–4
R.T. Watanabe: *Music of Howard Hanson* (Rochester, NY, 1966)
R.T. Watanabe: *American Composers' Concerts and Festivals of American Music* (Rochester, NY, 1972), 1925–71
H. Gleason and W. Becker: "Howard Hanson," *20th-Century American Composers* (Bloomington, IN, rev. 2/1980), 78–91 [incl. further bibliography]
R. Sutton: "Howard Hanson: Set Theory Pioneer," *Sonus*, viii/1 (1987), 17–39
D.R. Williams: *Conversations with Howard Hanson* (Arkadelphia, AR, 1988)
W.M. Skoog: *The Late Choral Music of Howard Hanson and Samuel Barber* (diss., U. of Northern Colorado, 1992)
J.E. Perone: *Howard Hanson: a Bio-Bibliography* (Westport, CT, 1993)
M.V. Plain: *Howard Hanson: a Comprehensive Catalog of the Manuscripts* (Rochester, NY, 1997)
A.S. Kalyn: *Constructing a Nation's Music: Howard Hanson's American Composers' Concerts and Festivals of American Music, 1925–1971* (diss., U. of Rochester, 2001)

W. Simmons: *Voices in the Wilderness: Six American Neo-Romantic Composers* (Lanham, MD, 2004)

A. Cohen: *Howard Hanson in Theory and Practice* (Westport, CT, 2004)

RUTH T. WATANABE/JAMES PERONE/R

Hapa. Hawaiian slack key guitar duo. It was formed in 1983 by New Jersey native Barry Flanagan, who relocated to Maui, and Honolulu native Keli'i Kaneali'i. Their distinctive blend of Hawaiian traditionalism with world beat eclecticism has significantly impacted the sound of today's Hawaiian music. The group's eponymous CD debut in 1993 broke sales records and won both "Contemporary Hawaiian Album of the Year" and "Album of the Year" at the 1994 Na Hoku Hanohano (Hawaiian Grammy) Awards. Despite several personnel swaps (bassist/vocalist Nathan Aweau for Kaneali'i in 2002; singer/songwriter Ron Kuala'au for Aweau in 2010), it remains one of Hawaii's most in-demand and recognizable music acts. The 2005 album *Maui* (Finn) peaked at number seven on Billboard Magazine's World Music charts.

If themes of serenity and natural beauty have long been integral to Hawaiian music, Hapa's key contribution has been to add nuance in terms of musical and social composition. On the musical end, Hapa has enjoyed success by alloying Hawaiian *oli* (chant), *mele* (song), *hula* (dance), and slack key guitar traditions with a diverse range of influences, including Paul Simon, Ry Cooder, The Chieftains, the Gipsy Kings, jazz, surf music, and U2. On the social front, the group's appropriation of the Hawaiian term *hapa* ("half-half," or "ethnically mixed")—and its concomitant musical category *hapa-haole* ("half-white")—presents a symbolic if not actual challenge to racialized understandings of Hawaiian culture, including those present in the Contemporary Hawaiian music genre. Whereas Hawaiian Renaissance musicians used the genre to fashion a connection to Hawaiian tradition and distance new musical productions from implication in the webs of tourism, mainland borrowing, and exploitation that characterized older *hapa-haole* songs, Hapa effectively turned the tables by embracing aspects of *hapa-haole* as Hawaiian tradition, with far-reaching consequences for the Hawaiian music scene.

BIBLIOGRAPHY

M.D. Moss: "Hapa," *Sing Out! The Folk Song Magazine*, xliii/1 (1998), 74–77

WILLIAM BARES

Happening. The term "Happening" refers to an artistic event that combines elements of theater, performance art, music, and the plastic arts; these events tend to be bounded by either a series of actions or a preset duration, though their structure is sometimes looser. Happenings are typically nonnarrative, forgoing plot and character in favor of the associative potential of static objects and human action. Happenings frequently emphasize interaction between performers and spectators and often take place outside of conventional gallery or concert spaces. The American artist Allan Kaprow is generally credited with coining the term in his 1958 essay "The Legacy of Jackson Pollock," in which he called for a new "concrete art," comprised of quotidian objects and framed moments from everyday life. Kaprow later published a series of instructions for a Happening in the Rutgers literary review, *The Anthologist*. John Cage's writing and teaching were also foundational to the idea of the Happening. In 1952 Cage staged an untitled event at Black Mountain College that presaged the Happenings of the 1950s and 60s. At this event, Cage read from his own writing and the American Constitution while ascending and descending a ladder, the painter Robert Rauschenberg propped several of his "White Paintings" around the performance space, the pianist David Tudor played the prepared piano and changed the station on a small radio, and Merce Cunningham danced among the spectators' chairs, all while sped-up Édith Piaf records played from a gramophone in the corner. The Black Mountain event contained a number of features that would come to characterize later Happenings: an indeterminate structure, flexible spatial delineation between audience and performers, and a fluid boundary between different media. Other notable practitioners of the Happening include Carolee Schneemann, Jim Dine, and Claes Oldenburg.

BIBLIOGRAPHY

M. Sanford, ed.: *Happenings and Other Acts* (London, 1995) [a reissue of the 1965 "Happenings" issue of *The Drama Review*]

M. Kirby: *Happenings* (New York, 1965)

A. Kaprow: *Some Recent Happenings* (New York, 1966)

R. Kostelanetz: *Metamorphosis in the Arts: a Critical History of the 1960s* (New York, 1980)

S. Banes: *Greenwich Village 1963: Avant-Garde Performance and the Effervescent Body* (Durham, NC, 1993)

A. Kaprow: *Essays on the Blurring of Art and Life* (Berkeley, 2003)

KELSEY COWGER

Harbach [Hauerbach], **Otto (Abels)** (*b* Salt Lake City, UT, 18 Aug 1873; *d* New York, NY, 24 Jan 1963). Librettist and lyricist. He was educated at Knox College, then taught English for six years at Whitman College before going to New York for further study at Columbia University. In 1902 he became a newspaper journalist and the following year a copywriter for an advertising agency. His friendship with the composer Karl Hoschna led him to try his hand at writing musicals, and their collaboration *Three Twins* (1908, including the song "Cuddle Up a Little Closer, Lovey Mine") was a great success. Harbach soon became a prolific writer; he produced over 40 works for Broadway and also wrote occasionally for films. After Hoschna's death in 1911 he entered into a successful partnership with Rudolf Friml. Many of his best lyrics and librettos, however, were written after 1920 in collaboration with his younger protégé Oscar Hammerstein II. Among his best-known songs are "Rose-Marie" and "Indian Love Call" (*Rose-Marie*, 1924; written in collaboration with Hammerstein), "The Night Was Made for Love" (*The Cat and the Fiddle*, 1931), and "Smoke Gets in Your Eyes" (*Roberta*, 1932). Harbach was a founding member of ASCAP and served with it in numerous roles, including president.

WORKS

(Unless otherwise indicated, all are musicals and librettos and lyrics are by Harbach (H); collaborating librettists and lyricists are listed in that order in parentheses. Dates are those of first New York performance.)

Three Twins (C. Dickson; H), music by K. Hoschna, 15 June 1908 [incl. Cuddle Up a Little Closer, Lovey Mine]

Bright Eyes (Dickson; H), music by Hoschna, 28 Feb 1910

Madame Sherry, music by Hoschna, 30 Aug 1910 [incl. Every Little Movement]

Dr. De Luxe, music by Hoschna, 17 April 1911

The Girl of my Dreams, music by Hoschna, 7 Aug 1911

The Fascinating Widow, music by Hoschna, 11 Sept 1911

The Firefly, music by Friml, 2 Dec 1912 [incl. Giannina (Mia), Love Is Like a Firefly, Sympathy]

High Jinks, music by Friml, 10 Dec 1913 [incl. Something Seems Tingleingleing]

The Crinoline Girl (H; J. Eltinge), music by P. Wenrich, 16 March 1914

Suzi, music by A. Renyi, 3 Nov 1914

Katinka, music by Friml, 23 Dec 1915 [incl. Allah's Holiday]

You're in Love (collab. E. Clark), music by Friml, 6 Feb 1917

Kitty Darlin' (H; collab. P.G. Wodehouse), music by Friml, 7 Nov 1917

Going Up, music by L. Hirsch, 25 Dec 1917 [incl. Going Up, The Tickle Toe]

Tumble In, music by Friml, 24 March 1919

The Little Whopper (H; collab. B. Dudley), music by Friml, 13 Oct 1919

Tickle Me (collab. O. Hammerstein, F. Mandel; collab. Hammerstein), music by H. Stothart, 17 Aug 1920

Mary (collab. Mandel; H), music by Hirsch, 18 Oct 1920 [incl. The Love Nest]

Jimmie (collab. Hammerstein, Mandel; collab. Hammerstein), music by Stothart, 17 Nov 1920

June Love (collab. W.H. Post; B. Hooker), music by Friml, 25 April 1921

The O'Brien Girl (collab. Mandel; H), music by Hirsch, 3 Oct 1921

The Blue Kitten (collab. W.C. Duncan), music by Friml, 13 Jan 1922

Molly Darling (collab. Duncan; P. Cook), music by T. Johnstone, 1 Sept 1922

Wildflower (collab. Hammerstein), music by V. Youmans, Stothart, 7 Feb 1923 [incl. Bambalina, Wildflower]

Jack and Jill (F. Isham; collab. others), music by various composers, 22 March 1923

Kid Boots (collab. W.A. McGuire; J. McCarthy), music by H. Tierney, 31 Dec 1923

Rose-Marie (operetta, collab. Hammerstein), music by Friml, Stothart, 2 Sept 1924 [incl. Indian Love Call, The Mounties, Rose-Marie]

Betty Lee (H; collab. I. Caesar), music by Hirsch, C. Conrad, 25 Dec 1924

No, No, Nanette (collab. Mandel; collab. Caesar), music by Youmans, 16 Sept 1925

Sunny (collab. Hammerstein), music by J. Kern, 22 Sept 1925 [incl. Sunny, Who?]

Song of the Flame (operetta, collab. Hammerstein), music by G. Gershwin, Stothart, 30 Dec 1925 [incl. Song of the Flame]

Kitty's Kisses (collab. P. Bartholomae; G. Kahn), music by Conrad, 6 May 1926

Criss Cross (collab. A. Caldwell), music by Kern, 12 Oct 1926

The Wild Rose (collab. Hammerstein), music by Friml, 20 Oct 1926

The Desert Song (operetta, collab. Hammerstein, Mandel; collab. Hammerstein), music by S. Romberg, 30 Nov 1926 [incl. The Desert Song, One Alone, The Riff Song, Romance]

Oh, Please! (collab. Caldwell; Caldwell), music by Youmans, 17 Dec 1926

Lucky (collab. B. Kalmar, H. Ruby), music by Kalmar, Ruby, Kern, 22 March 1927

Golden Dawn (collab. Hammerstein), music by E. Kálmán, Stothart, 30 Nov 1927

Good Boy (collab. Hammerstein, H. Myers; Kalmar), music by Kalmar, Ruby, Stothart, 5 Sept 1928

Nina Rosa (H; Caesar), music by Romberg, 20 Sept 1930

The Cat and the Fiddle, music by Kern, 15 Oct 1931 [incl. The Night Was Made for Love, She Didn't Say Yes, Try to Forget]

Roberta, music by Kern, 18 Nov 1933 [incl. Smoke Gets in Your Eyes, The Touch of Your Hand, Yesterdays, You're Devastating]

Forbidden Melody, music by Romberg, 2 Nov 1936

BIBLIOGRAPHY

T.S. Hischak, "Otto Harbach," *American Song Lyricists, 1920–1960*, ed. P. Furia (Detroit, 2002), 210–18

D.A. Jasen: *Tin Pan Alley: an Encyclopedia of the Golden Age of American Song* (New York, 2003)

GERALD BORDMAN/JONAS WESTOVER

Harbert, Wilhelmina K(eniston) (*b* Plymouth, NH, 27 Dec 1888; *d* Stockton, CA, 23 Sept 1970). Music therapist. After studying music at Boston University, Harbert opened the Oaks Home Music School for adults and children in Stockton, California (1933). She used her formidable talents as a pianist and vocalist to entertain American troops hospitalized in France during World War I. Her experiences with physically and emotionally injured soldiers, and later as a volunteer in New England settlement houses, hospitals, and institutions, solidified her desire to pursue a career in music therapy well before the formal establishment of the profession in 1950. Though she lacked formal training in music therapy, Harbert began teaching courses in the same at the College (now University) of the Pacific in 1942, and served as director of the campus clinic there until her retirement in 1959. She received many accolades for her work in music therapy and music education, including honorary life membership in the National Association for Music Therapy (1961) and the California Music Educators Association's Mancini Award for Excellence (1966).

WRITINGS

Some Principles, Practices and Techniques in Music Therapy (Stockton, CA, 1947)

Opening Doors Through Music: a Practical Guide for Teachers, Therapists, Students, Parents (Springfield, IL, 1974)

WILLIAM B. DAVIS

Harbison, John (*b* Orange, NJ, 20 Dec 1938). Composer. He was born into an intellectually and culturally vigorous environment; his earliest significant musical impressions were of jazz (he was the pianist in his own jazz band by the age of 11) and Bach. Together with Stravinsky they were to remain his chief musical influences. Harbison has written that the Bach cantatas were formative for him in the way that the Beethoven quartets are for many musicians. He studied with WALTER PISTON at Harvard, winning honors in both composition and poetry (BA 1960). Later studies were with Blacher at the Berlin Musikhochschule (1961) and ROGER SESSIONS and EARL KIM at Princeton (MFA 1963). Very decisive for Harbison was a summer (1963) spent at the Santa Fe Opera at the invitation of Sessions, where the complete operas of Stravinsky were being rehearsed and performed in the presence of the composer. He has been composer-in-residence with the Pittsburgh SO (1981–3) and the Los Angeles PO (1985–8), and was the recipient of the 1987 Pulitzer Prize for *The Flight into Egypt*, a MacArthur Fellowship (1989), and the Heinz Award (1997). In 1969 he became a professor at the

Massachusetts Institute of Technology, receiving the honorific position of Institute Professor in 1996. Harbison is Acting Artistic Director of Boston's Emmanuel Music, co-Artistic Director of the Token Creek Chamber Music Festival, and President of the Aaron Copland Fund for Music.

The works from his earliest period show the dual influences of serialism and Stravinskian neo-classicism. Jazz, too, is apparent in such early works as the Duo for flute and piano. From a conflict between serial segmentation and a concern for pitch centers at the opening, the work moves towards a more defined tonality in the uninhibited jazz impulses of the neo-classical final movement. Harbison went through a period of intense engagement with serialism before finding his own distinctive voice. *Confinement*, for large chamber ensemble, is structured so that the pervasive serial procedures themselves become restraints against which the emotional thrust of the music must pit itself. Jazz elements, as typified by the saxophone, are present throughout. In the operas *Winter's Tale* and *Full Moon in March*, with librettos adapted by the composer from Shakespeare and W.B. Yeats, the element of ritual, implicit in Harbison's earlier work, becomes overt in the hieratic nature of scene construction. The operas are psychological in the sense that archetypal situations are explored, but the focus is on using the music to reveal the universal rather than the personal utterance of the texts. An abhorrence of the notion of composition as an emotional diary informs Harbison's music, making it all the more striking when a deeply personal note sounds, as in the darkly turbulent Symphony no.2 or the harrowing lament of the final movement of the Piano Quintet.

Exceptional in Harbison's prolific output are his many song cycles, and the most significant of these is the work with which he consolidated his mature style, *Mottetti di Montale*, an engagement with Eugenio Montale's love poems that recalls the Müller cycles of Schubert. He establishes tonal centers by various means, employs jazz-derived chords without imparting the flavor of jazz, and unifies the cycle with linear planning. Magical effects are accomplished with an economy of means reminiscent of Stravinsky or Britten. The music achieves its effect in part through a subtle allusion to stylistic elements which remain suggestively or provocatively in the background. His conducting commitments have included the Cantata Singers and the new music group Collage, and his active involvement with Emmanuel Music in Boston has prompted the composition of a body of choral works that includes the remarkable motets *Ave verum corpus* and *Concerning Them which are Asleep*. Unconnected with Emmanuel but of great significance is *Emerson* for double chorus, an intense, radiant meditation on two excerpts from Emerson's *Essays*, almost Schütz-like in its text specificity and in the remarkable way that Harbison carves a powerful dramatic structure out of meaning and syntax in Emerson's prose.

Central to his extensive chamber music output are the three string quartets, which are studies in contrast: the first austere and determinedly self-referential, the second spacious and refulgent, and the third warmly mysterious. Among the most frequently played of Harbison's chamber works are the Piano Quintet and the Wind Quintet. Of the concertos, which figure prominently in Harbison's work, the most important is that for violin; it was written for his wife, the violinist Rose Mary Harbison, who has been the inspiration for many of his important works. In 1995 the Metropolitan Opera commissioned him to write a full-scale opera, enabling Harbison to fulfill an ambition to set F. Scott Fitzgerald's novel *The Great Gatsby* as a stage work. Jazz accents inform the music at all levels, ranging from freshly composed pop songs to the darker inflections of Gatsby's monologues. Jointly commissioned by the Pontifical Council for the Promotion of Christian Unity and the Pontifical Council for Inter-religious Dialogue for the historic "Papal Concert of Reconciliation," Harbison's *Abraham*, a sacred motet for brass and antiphonal choirs, premiered in 2004 at the Vatican, with Pope John Paul II in attendance.

Harbison has defined his artistic credo as an attempt to "make each piece different from the others, to find clear, fresh, large designs, to reinvent traditions." His work is eclectic, ever open to fresh sources of development in the music of any style or period, and always rigorously self-disciplined. Reveling in ambiguities of all kinds, it reveals further levels of meaning upon repeated listening.

WORKS
(selective list)

DRAMATIC

The Merchant of Venice (incid. music, W. Shakespeare), str qnt, 1971; Winter's Tale (op, Harbison, after Shakespeare), 1974, San Francisco, 20 Aug 1979, rev. 1991; Full Moon in March (op, 1, Harbison, after W.B. Yeats), 1977, Cambridge, MA, 30 April 1979; Ulysses (ballet, 2), 1983; The Great Gatsby (op, 2, Harbison and M. Horwitz, after F. Scott Fitzgerald), 1999, New York, Met, 20 Dec 1999

INSTRUMENTAL

Orch: Sinfonia, vn, orch, 1963; Diotima, 1976; Pf Conc., 1978; Vn Conc., 1980, rev. 1987; Sym. no.1, 1981; Conc., ob, cl, str, 1985; Remembering Gatsby: Foxtrot for Orch, 1985; Fanfare for Foley's, brass, perc, 1986; Sym. no.2, 1987; Conc., double brass choir, orch, 1988; Va Conc., 1989; David's Fascinating Rhythm Method, 1991; Ob Conc., 1991; Sym. no.3, 1991; Fl Conc., 1993; Vc Conc., 1993; The Most Often Used Chords (Gli accordi più usati), 1993; I, II, III, IV, V: Fantasia on a Ground, str, 1993; Waltz-Passacaglia, 1996; Partita, 2001; Sym. no. 4, 2003; Darkbloom: Overture for an Imagined Opera, 2004; Canonical American Songbook, 2005; Conc. for Bass Viol, 2005; Milosz Songs, S, orch, 2006; The Great Gatsby—Suite, 2007; Sym. no.5, Mez, Bar, orch, 2007; Double Conc., vn, vc, 2009

Band: Music for 18 Winds, 1986; Three City Blocks, 1991; Olympic Dances, 1996

4–12 insts: Confinement, 12 insts, 1965; Serenade, 6 players, 1968; Die Kürze, fl, cl, vn, vc, pf, 1970; Snow Country, ob, str qt, 1979; Wind Qnt, 1979; Pf Qnt, 1981; Organum for Paul Fromm, pf, mar, vib, hp, vc, 1981; Exequien for Calvin Simmons, a fl, b cl, 2 va, vc, vib, pf, 1982; Str Qt no.1, 1985; Magnum mysterium, brass qnt, 1987; Str Qt no.2, 1987; Christmas Vespers, spkr, brass qnt, 1988; Little Fantasy, brass qnt, 1988; 19 Nov 1828, pf qt, 1988; Str Qt no.3, 1993; Six American Painters, fl, vn, va, vc, 2000, also vers. for ob, vn, va, vc, 2000; Str Qt no.4, 2002; Cucaraccia and Fugue, 4 va, 2003; French Horn Suite, 4 hn, 2006; Cortège, 6 perc, 2008

1–3 insts: Duo, fl, pf, 1961; Parody Fantasia, pf, 1968; Pf Trio, 1969; Bermuda Triangle, amp vc, t sax, elec org, 1970; Amazing Grace, ob, 1972; 3 Occasional Pieces, pf, 1978; Variations, cl, vn, pf, 1982;

Twilight Music, hn, vn, pf, 1985; Pf Sonata no.1, 1987; 4 More Occasional Pieces, pf, 1987–90; Fantasy Duo, vn, pf, 1988; Fanfares and Reflection, 2 vn, 1990; 14 Fabled Folksongs, vn, mar, 1992; Inventions for a Young Percussionist, perc, 1992, also vers. for Young Pianist; Suite, vc, 1993; San Antonio, a sax, pf, 1994; Trio Sonata, (str trio)/(cl, cl, b cl)/(ob, eng hn, bn)/(s sax, a sax, bar sax)/kbd, 1994; On an Unwritten Letter, pf, 2000; Sonata no.2, pf, 2003; Trio II, vn, vc, pf, 2003; Ten Micro-Waltzes, pf, 2004; Abu Ghraib, vc, pf, 2006; Leonard Stein Anagrams, pf, 2009; Diamond Watch, 2 pf, 2010

VOCAL

Choral: Ave Maria, female chorus, 1959; Music when Soft Voices Die, chorus, hpd/org, 1966; 5 Songs of Experience on Poems of William Blake, SATB, 2 perc, str qt, 1971; Nunc Dimittis, male chorus, 1975; The Flower-Fed Buffaloes, Bar, chorus, fl, cl, t sax, vn, vc, db, perc, 1976; The Flight into Egypt (sacred ricercar), S, Bar, chorus, org, orch, 1986; 2 Emmanuel Motets, chorus, 1990; O Magnum Mysterium, chorus, 1992; Concerning Them which are Asleep (Bible: I Thessalonians), SSATBB, 1994; Juste judex, Bar, A, chorus, orch, 1994 [movt 5 of Requiem der Versöhnung, collab. Berio, Cerha, Dittrich and others]; Recordare, S, A, T, B, orch, 1995 [from Requiem der Versöhnung]; Emerson (R.W. Emerson), double chorus, 1995; Veni creator spiritus, male chorus, 1996; 4 Psalms, S, Mez, T, B, chorus, orch, 1999; Abraham, double chorus, 2 brass choirs, 2004; But Mary Stood, S, chorus, str orch, 2005; A Clear Midnight, TTBB, 5 str, 2007; Madrigal, SATBB, 2007

Solo vocal: Elegiac Songs (E. Dickinson), Mez, chbr orch, 1974; Book of Hours and Seasons (Goethe), Mez/T, fl, vc, pf, 1975; Moments of Vision (T. Hardy), S, T, Renaissance ens, 1975; Samuel Chapter, S/T, fl, cl, vc, pf, perc, 1978; Mottetti di Montale, Mez, pf/ens, 1980, 1998, 1990; Mirabai Songs, S, pf/ens, 1982; The Natural World, S/Mez, fl, cl, vn, vc, pf, 1987; Rot und Weiss, 1v, fl, vn, vc, pf, 1987; Simple Daylight (M. Fried), S, pf, 1988; Words from Paterson (W.C. Williams), Bar, fl, ob, va, vc, hp, pf, 1989; Between Two Worlds (R. Bly, J. Boehme), S, 2 vc, 2 pf, 1991; The Rewaking (Williams), S, str qt, 1991; The Flute of Interior Time, Bar/Mez, pf, 1992; Chorale Cant. (M. Luther, Fried), S, ob, str qt, db, 1995; Flashes and Illuminations, Bar, pf, 1995; Il saliscendi bianco (E. Montale), Mez, chbr orch, org, 1999 [orch vers. of Motetti di Montale, book 2]; North and South (E. Bishop), S, eng hn, cl, bn, vn, va, vc, db, 2001; Ain't Goin' to Study War No More, Bar, 2 tpt, snare drum, str orch, 2003; Milosz Songs, S, pf, 2006; The Seven Ages, Mez, fl, clar, vn, vc, perc, pf, 2008

Recorded interviews in NHoh
Principal publisher: Associated

BIBLIOGRAPHY

J. Peyser: "Harbison's Continuing Ascent," New York Times (16 Aug 1981)

J. Tassel: "A Homecoming for John Harbison," Boston Globe (26 Feb 1984)

J. Harbison: "Six Tanglewood Talks," PNM, xxiii/2 (1984–5), 12–22; xxiv/1, (1985–6), 46–60

J.R. Spittal: "Three City Blocks" by John Harbison (diss., U. of Cincinnati, 1995)

C.O. Vangelisti: John Harbison's "Mirabai Songs": a Poetic and Musical Analysis (diss., U. of Texas, 1997)

B.M. Ciechowski: "John Harbison: Streichquartett Nr. 3," Untersuchungen zum Streichquartettschaffen amerikanischer Komponisten nach dem Zweiten Weltkrieg (diss., Mainz U., 1998), 87–106

M. Brody: "'Haunted by Envisioned Romance': John Harbison's Gatsby," MQ, lxxxv/3 (2001), 413–55

DAVID ST GEORGE/ELIZABETH PERTEN

Harburg, E(dgar) Y(ipsel) [Yip] [Hochberg, Isidore] (*b* New York, NY, 8 April 1896; *d* Brentwood, CA, 5 March 1981). Lyricist and librettist. Born of poor Russian immigrant parents on the East Side of Manhattan, he started writing light verse in high school and attended City College, where he worked on the campus newspaper and submitted comic pieces to the city's newspaper columnists. After graduation Harburg went into business,

but his family's electrical supply firm failed with the Wall Street crash of 1929, so he started writing full-time. His first of many collaborators was composer Jay Gorney, and some of their songs were seen in Broadway revues as early as 1929. In *Americana* (1932) their song "Brother, Can You Spare a Dime?" was featured and it subsequently swept the nation, becoming a theme song of the Depression. Throughout the 1930s and 40s Harburg contributed to several Broadway musicals, most memorably *Finian's Rainbow* (1947) with composer Burton Lane, and films, in particular *The Wizard of Oz* (1939) with composer Harold Arlen. His other composer-collaborators include Lewis Gensler, George Gershwin, Johnny Green, Jule Styne, and Sammy Fain. During the 1950s Harburg was blacklisted from Hollywood because of his political ideas, but he did write a handful of Broadway musicals, most of them satirical and provocative but few of them successful.

Harburg was one of the very few American lyricists with a political agenda. Although his works are musical comedies and fantasies, he tackled such subjects as racial prejudice, government corruption, the atom bomb, women's rights, and the ravages of war. Ironically, his book musicals, for which he usually wrote the librettos as well as the lyrics, were unusually sprightly and his satire was often light-footed. Harburg's lyrics are known for their sly wit, clever wordplay, and short, terse phrasing.

WORKS
(*Also wrote the libretto. Composers in brackets; co-librettists in parentheses.)

STAGE

Earl Carroll's Sketch Book [J. Gorney] 1 July 1929
Earl Carroll's Vanities [Gorney] 1 July 1930
Ballyhoo of 1932 [L. Gensler] 6 Sept 1932
Americana [Gorney] 5 Oct 1932 [incl. Brother, Can You Spare a Dime?]
Walk a Little Faster [V. Duke] 7 Dec 1932 [incl. April in Paris]
Ziegfeld Follies [Duke] 4 Jan 1934 [incl. I Like the Likes of You]
Life Begins at 8:40 [H. Arlen] 27 Aug 1934 [incl. Let's Take a Walk around the Block, You're a Builder-Upper]
Hooray for What! [Arlen] 1 Dec 1937 [incl. Down With Love, Moanin' in the Mornin']
Hold on to Your Hats [B. Lane] 11 Sept 1940 [incl. Don't Let It Get You Down]
Bloomer Girl [Arlen] 5 Oct 1944 [incl. The Eagle and Me, Right as the Rain, I Got a Song]
Finian's Rainbow* [B. Lane] (F. Saidy) 10 Jan 1947 [incl. Old Devil Moon, How Are Things in Glocca Morra?, Look to the Rainbow, If This Isn't Love, When I'm Not Near the Girl I Love], film 1968
Flahooley* [S. Fain] (Saidy) 14 May 1951 [Here's to Your Illusions, He's Only Wonderful]
Jamaica* [Arlen] (Saidy) 31 Oct 1957 [incl. Cocoanut Sweet, Ain't It de Truth?, Push de Button]
The Happiest Girl in the World* [J. Offenbach] (Saidy, H. Myers) 3 April 1961
Darling of the Day [J. Styne] 27 Jan 1968

FILMS

The Sap from Syracuse [J. Green], 1930
Moonlight and Pretzels [Gorney], 1933
The Singing Kid [Arlen], 1936 [incl. I Love to Sing-a]
Gold Diggers of 1937 [Arlen], 1936
The Wizard of Oz [Arlen], 1939 [incl. Over the Rainbow, We're Off to See the Wizard, Follow the Yellow Brick Road, If I Only Had a Brain]

At the Circus [Arlen], 1939 [inc. Lydia the Tattooed Lady]
Ship Ahoy [Lane], 1942 [incl. Poor You]
Cairo [A. Schwartz], 1942 [incl. Buds Won't Bud]
Cabin in the Sky [Arlen], 1943 [incl. Happiness Is a Thing Called Joe]
Meet the People [Fain, Arlen, Lane], 1944
Can't Help Singing [J. Kern], 1944 [incl. Californ-i-ay, Can't Help Singing]
California [E. Robinson], 1946
Gay Purr-ee [Arlen], 1962 [incl. Paris Is a Lonely Town]

TELEVISION
The Great Man's Whiskers [Robinson], 1973

BIBLIOGRAPHY
L. Engel: *Their Words Are Music: the Great Theatre Lyricists and Their Lyrics* (New York, 1975)
P. Furia: *The Poets of Tin Pan Alley: a History of America's Great Lyricists* (New York, 1990)
T. Hischak: *Word Crazy: Broadway Lyricists from Cohan to Sondheim* (New York, 1991)
H. Meyerson and E. Harburg: *Who Put the Rainbow in The Wizard of Oz? Yip Harburg, Lyricist* (Ann Arbor, MI, 1993)
                                THOMAS S. HISCHAK

Hard bop. A term applied to the earthier music that developed from bebop in the 1950s. Although not a precisely delineated genre, the music is characterized by an elemental, driving urgency inherited from blues, gospel, and rhythm and blues, combined with the harmonic and rhythmic complexity of bebop.

Its practitioners were largely African American, and it thrived in the urban and industrial centers of New York, Chicago, Pittsburgh, Detroit, and Philadelphia. Initially it formed an integrated part of the culture, heard on juke boxes and in clubs as part of the popular music of the day. It is sometimes described as a reaction to cool or West Coast jazz, but is more accurately seen as a parallel development from common roots.

Hard bop had a heavier, earthier feel than bebop and generally relied on a fairly rigid theme-solos-theme structure and a close adherence to the underlying chord progressions in creating melodic improvisations. The standard instrumentation featured trumpet, tenor saxophone, and a piano-led rhythm trio, although larger line-ups often added trombone or guitar, and the related soul-jazz phenomenon centered on a trio format of Hammond organ, guitar, and drums.

Hard bop made less use of standard show tunes than earlier genres had done. Many compositions still employed a notable degree of complexity, often drawing on nonstandard forms and fast-moving chord progressions, but the music was most widely known for its march- and blues-based tunes, which featured simpler harmonic structures, repetitive ear-catching themes, and little in the way of developed ensemble writing. Many became popular hits, notably Horace Silver's "The Preacher" (1955, Blue Note), Nat Adderley's "Work Song" (1960, Riverside), Bobby Timmons's "Moanin'" (1958, Blue Note) and "Dis Here" (1959, Riverside), Benny Golson's "Blues March" (1958, Blue Note), and Herbie Hancock's "Watermelon Man" (1962, Blue Note).

Perhaps the most fundamental constituent of hard bop lay in the more nebulous area of "feel." That reliance on the primal sounds and tonalities of blues, rhythm and blues, folk, and gospel idioms created an emphasis that generated the soulful and funky characteristics associated with the form.

Hard bop's central practitioners included Art Blakey, Silver, Cannonball and Nat Adderley, the Heath Brothers, the Jones Brothers, the trumpeters Lee Morgan and Kenny Dorham, the saxophonists Hank Mobley, Jackie McLean, and Lou Donaldson, the pianists Sonny Clark and Bobby Timmons, the guitarists Kenny Burrell, Grant Green, and Wes Montgomery, and the organ players Jimmy Smith, Richard Holmes, and Les McCann. Some of the work of John Coltrane, Miles Davis, Sonny Rollins, and the Max Roach–Clifford Brown group can also been described as hard bop.

BIBLIOGRAPHY
J. Goldberg: *Jazz Masters of the Fifties* (New York, 1965/*R*)
D.H. Rosenthal: *Hard Bop: Jazz and Black Music, 1955–1965* (New York, 1992/*R*)
T. Owens: *Bebop: the Music and its Players* (New York, 1995/*R*)
K. Mathieson: *Cookin': Hard Bop and Soul Jazz, 1954–65* (Edinburgh, 2002)
                                KENNY MATHIESON

Hardcore. Hardcore, a subgenre of punk rock, developed in the late 1970s, striving to be "harder, faster, louder" than earlier iterations of the genre. Many devotees believe Black Flag of Hermosa Beach, California, pioneered the subgenre, although others, including D.O.A. (Vancouver), Dead Kennedys (San Francisco), and Bad Brains (Washington, DC), also contributed to hardcore's early development. Frequently these bands ignored typical song structures such as verse-chorus-verse or AABA, and instead created very short, fast, simple songs with barked or shouted rapid-fire vocals. Hardcore shows tended to be hypermasculine environments, involving highly athletic stage performances as well as slamdancing and stagediving by fans.

Taking punk's do-it-yourself ethos further than many of their predecessors, hardcore bands were instrumental in creating DIY punk institutions. Members of the Dead Kennedys, Black Flag, and Minor Threat founded the still-operating Alternative Tentacles, SST, and Dischord labels respectively. Black Flag played a particularly important role in forging punk touring contacts.

By the early 1980s, hardcore had become the public face of punk. The media sensationalized violence at hardcore shows, which—to the dismay of many existing fans—seemed to exacerbate what had been a small problem by attracting an element that enjoyed fighting more than the music. Hardcore remains influential in punk today.

BIBLIOGRAPHY
M. Azerrad: *Our Band Could Be Your Life: Scenes from the American Indie Underground 1981–1991* (Boston, 2001)
D. MacLeod: *Kids of the Black Hole: Punk Rock in Postsuburban California* (Norman, OK, 2010)
                                M. MONTGOMERY WOLF

Hard country. The hard country style foregrounds country music's regional, working-class, and rural accents and subject matter. Thematically, hard country emphasizes struggle, loss, and the authenticity of the song as an expression of the personal experience of the artist. In instrumentation, honky-tonk arrangements of guitar, steel guitar, fiddle, drums, and bass predominate, though the gothic elements of traditional bluegrass may also qualify it as a "hardcore" music. Together, these elements constitute an oppositional pose to what many hard country artists and fans see as the perennial "pop" drift of mainstream country production. As such, hard country can be as much an argument about the genre's history and proper form as it is a musicological descriptor. Hard country artists and fans also espouse a loyalty to the traditional core of country music, though this has not precluded hard country performers from borrowing liberally from the blues and rock. Indeed, borrowings from the blues may well provide one of the defining qualities of hard country music, as this was what set apart the patron saints of hard country, Jimmie Rodgers and Hank Williams, from many of their contemporaries. Geographically, hard country has often imagined itself to be outside of Nashville's orbit, with its headquarters in Texas (Houston, Austin) and California (Bakersfield). Practitioners of hard country include David Allan Coe, Merle Haggard, Waylon Jennings, Jamey Johnson, George Jones, Loretta Lynn, Johnny Paycheck, Billy Joe Shaver, Ernest Tubb, and Dale Watson.

See also COUNTRY MUSIC.

BIBLIOGRAPHY

R. Peterson: *Creating Country Music: Fabricating Authenticity* (Chicago, 1997)

B. Ching: *Wrong's What I Do Best: Hard Country Music and Contemporary Culture* (New York, 2001)

A. Fox: *Real Country: Music and Language in Working-Class Culture* (Durham, NC, 2004)

JASON MELLARD

Harding, Albert Austin (*b* Georgetown, IL, 10 Feb 1880; *d* Champaign, IL, 3 Dec 1958). Bandmaster, educator, and arranger. At 14 he acquired a cornet, and taught himself to play. During his high school years he played bugle for a cadet organization, learned fife, piccolo, baritone horn, trombone, and drums, and joined the Paris (Illinois) Concert Band, which he led in his senior year. From 1899 to 1902 he directed and played in bands and orchestras in Paris, Champaign, and Urbana (Illinois), and Terre Haute (Indiana); he then entered the University of Illinois, where he played cornet in the band and bassoon in the orchestra. He was assistant director of the band from 1905 to 1907, then director until 1948. He soon changed its instrumentation, obtaining a symphonic, less brassy sound by making greater use of oboes, bassoons, alto and bass clarinets, tenor and baritone saxophones, and horns in place of alto horns; he also added alto and bass flutes, soprano and alto flugelhorns, soprano and bass saxophones, a double bassoon, and experimented with such unusual instruments as the ophicleide, heckelphone, basset-horn, A♭ clarinet, alto trumpet, bass trumpet, and the full family of seven sarrusophones, from soprano through contrabass. He made almost 150 of his own arrangements of works by such composers as Kodály,

Prokofiev, Shostakovich, Richard Strauss, Dohnányi, and Ibert. His marching band's performances at football games prefigured opening and half-time ceremonies.

Harding became a professor at Illinois in 1921, and taught conducting, instrumentation, and arranging. From 1930 to 1933 he directed the college band of the National Music Camp at Interlochen. He organized a series of "clinics" for band directors, the first of which was held at the University of Illinois in 1930; these were so successful that the Mid-West International Band and Orchestra Clinic (now the Midwest Clinic) was established. Harding was held in high esteem by Sousa and many other prominent bandmasters; he is a charter member of the American Bandmasters Association, which he served as president in 1937. He was instrumental in the formation of the College Band Directors National Association, and was elected its first honorary life president in 1941. Sousa called the Illinois band "the world's greatest college band," bequeathed his library of over 3,000 scores and parts and other memorabilia to Harding, and would accept any performer recommended by him without an audition. Among Harding's many students who achieved outstanding reputations of their own may be mentioned Glenn Cliffe Bainum, Raymond F. Dvorak, Clarence Sawhill, George Wilson, Keith Wilson, Neil A. Kjos, Allen Britton, Guy Duker, Russell Howland, Milburn Carey, and his successor at Illinois, Mark Hindsley. Harding's personal papers, scores, manuscripts, and memorabilia are held at the University of Illinois.

BIBLIOGRAPHY

C.E. Weber: *The Contribution of Albert Austin Harding and his Influence on the Development of School and College Bands* (diss., U. of Illinois, 1963)

C.E. Weber: "Albert Austin Harding: Pioneer College Bandmaster," *Journal of Band Research*, iii/1 (1966), 5–12

G.A. Brozak: "Revelli and Fennell: The Albert Austin Harding Influence," *Journal of Band Research*, xxxviii/1 (2002), 1–24

RAOUL F. CAMUS

Harding, Walter N(ewton) H(enry) (*b* London, England, ?1883; *d* Chicago, IL, 12 or 13 Dec 1973). Pianist and music collector of English birth. Having immigrated to the United States with his parents when he was about four years of age, he spent the remainder of his life in Chicago as a ragtime and vaudeville pianist and an organist in churches and theaters. Around the turn of the century he began to amass one of the largest private music collections in the United States, laying particular emphasis on opera and on English and American song imprints. Few scholars were granted access to the collection during Harding's lifetime, and on his death the entire collection was transferred to the Bodleian Library in Oxford, England. Harding's American music holdings consisted largely of 60,000 to 70,000 items of sheet music, with particular strengths in the areas of ragtime, comic opera, minstrel-show music, war songs, and Chicago imprints.

BIBLIOGRAPHY

D.W. Krummel: "A Musical Bibliomaniac," *MT*, cxv (1974), 301–2

J. Geil: "American Sheet Music in the Walter N. H. Harding Collection at the Bodleian Library, Oxford University," *Notes*, xxxiv (1978), 805–13

H.E. Solheim: *Walter N.H. Harding and the Harding drama collection at the Bodleian Library, Oxford* (diss., U. of Washington, 1985)

JEAN GEIL/R

Hard rock. A term emerging in the mid-1960s, alongside and in contrast to "soft rock," to designate a subgenre of rock characterized by aggressive electric guitar riffs, pumping rhythm, and swaggering machismo. The roots of hard rock can be located amongst groups extending the urban blues tradition following British blues rock groups. The Rolling Stones, for instance, laid the groundwork for the hard rock genre with several key stylistic features—a thick, dark texture produced by the musicians' fondness for the lower register of the guitars and bass, Charlie Watts's loose-skinned drums, and Mick Jagger's voice placed decidedly in a lower register. Representative hard rock groups from the 1960s through the 1990s include Steppenwolf, Grand Funk Railroad, Aerosmith, Van Halen, and the Black Crowes.

In the early 1970s hard rock groups were indistinguishable from HEAVY METAL groups, the latter term having arisen from media descriptions of Steppenwolf, Jimi Hendrix, and Led Zeppelin. Thus the heaviness of hard rock and heavy metal are shared, but hard rock rarely duplicates heavy metal's fondness for madness or mysticism. Instead, hard rock can be understood as a genre pushing forward the agenda of the sexual revolution: it is both liberal (in terms of its anthemic proclamations for sexual freedom and sovereignty from commitment), yet oppressive in its unapologetic misogyny and themes of heteronormative sexual conquest.

BIBLIOGRAPHY

S. Fast: *In the Houses of the Holy: Led Zeppelin and the Power of Rock Music* (New York, 2001)

T. Harrison: "'Empire': Chart Performance of Hard Rock and Heavy Metal Groups, 1990–1992," *Popular Music & Society*, xxx/2 (2007), 197–225

T. Harrison: "Decoding Van Halen: Sexual Coding Devices of a Hard Rock Group, 1978–1984," *International Journal of the Humanities*, v/4 (2007), 115–22

MICKEY VALLEE

Hare, Maud Cuney (*b* Galveston, TX 16 Feb 1874; *d* Boston, MA 13 Feb 1936). Music historian, concert pianist, and playwright. She studied piano at the New England Conservatory of Music (1890–95) and privately with Emil Ludwig and Edwin Klabre. After teaching at the Texas Deaf, Dumb, and Blind Institute for Colored Youths at Austin (1897–8), the settlement house of the Institutional Church of Chicago (1900–01), and Prairie View (Texas) State Normal and Industrial College for Negroes (1903–4), she married lawyer William Hare and resettled in Boston by 1906.

Hare enjoyed a reputation as the leading authority on African American music during her era. A product of the Harlem Renaissance, she was music critic of *The Crisis* (ca. 1910–19) and contributed articles to the *Musical Observer, The Musical Quarterly,* and *Christian Science Monitor.* For about two decades, Hare toured the United States with African Canadian baritone William Richardson, giving lecture-recitals. She also traveled extensively throughout Louisiana, Mexico, and the Caribbean, collecting folk songs and musical instruments. This data provided the foundation for her book *Negro Musicians and Their Music* (1936), the first major survey of black music since James Monroe Trotter's *Music and Some Highly Musical People* (1878). In 1927 she established the Boston-based Allied Arts Center and produced her own play *Antar of Araby* (1929), with incidental music by Clarence Cameron White and Montague Ring (pseudonym for Amanda Ira Aldridge). Besides *Six Creole Folk Songs* (New York, 1921), several unpublished songs by Hare are held at the Clark-Atlanta University archives.

WORKS

ed., Six Creole Songs, with original Creole and translated English text (New York, 1921)

Antar of Araby, four-act play [with suggested incidental music by Clarence Cameron White and Montague Ring (aka Amanda Ira Aldridge) (Boston, 1929) (published in Plays and Pageants from the Life of the Negro, Willis Robinson, ed. (Washington, DC, 1930), 27–76; electronic reprint, New York: Alexander Street Press, 2009 [<http://www.aspresolver.com/aspresolver.asp?BLDR;PL000332>] (Requires subscription.)

WRITINGS

"Afro-American Folk-Song Contribution," *Musical Observer* xv (Feb. 1917), 13, 21, 51.

"Folk Music of the Creoles: Parts 1 & 2," *Musical Observer*, xix (Sept–Oct , 1920), (Nov 1920), 12–14 [reprint, *Negro: Anthology*, ed. Nancy Conrad. New York, *c*1934], 241–6]

"George Polgreen Bridgetower," *The Crisis*, xxxiv (1927), 122, 137–9

"Portuguese Folk-Songs, from Provincetown [sic], Cape Cod, Mass." *Musical Quarterly*, xiv (1928), 35–53

Negro Musicians and Their Music (Washington, DC, 1936) [repr. New York, 1974; with introduction by J.H. Love, New York, 1996]

BIBLIOGRAPHY

Maud Cuney-Hare Collection. Wood Library Archives, Clark-Atlanta University, Atlanta, GA (<http://www.auctr.edu/rwwl/FindingAids%5CCUNHARE.pdf>)

"Maud Cuney Hare Develops Library for Music Research," *Norfolk New Journal and Guide*, 6 April 1935, p. 4, col. 4

D. Hales: *Southern Family in Black and White: The Cuneys of Texas* (College Station, TX, 2000), 94–137

JOSEPHINE WRIGHT

Hare Krishna. A Vaishnava Hindu devotional movement dedicated to the worship of Krishna and known for the ecstatic singing of *kirtan*. The movement, formally known as the International Society for Krishna Consciousness (ISKCON), was established in New York by Bengali guru A.C. Bhaktivedanta Swami Prabhupada in 1966 and has since attained international popularity. The Hare Krishna movement traces its spiritual lineage to the 15th-century Indian saint Chaitanya Mahaprabhu, who began the performance of kirtan as it was later practiced in ISKCON.

Kirtan is a process of singing scriptural texts and mantras as a form of congregational call-and-response music. Hare Krishnas emphasize chanting the Maha Mantra, a petition to Hari, or Vishnu, and his avatars Krishna and Rama. Krishna devotees also interpret the name "Hare" as a name for Krishna's beloved Radha. Because the mantra is composed of names for Krishna it serves as the predominant form of worship and means of salvation: "Hare Krishna Hare Krishna Krishna Krishna

Hare Hare Hare Rama Hare Rama Rama Rama Hare Hare." According to ISKCON belief, the presence of Krishna is contained in the sound of his name, and the process of chanting brings the singer into the presence of the divine. Because the holy names are believed to carry Krishna's presence, special emphasis is placed on chanting loudly so that those within earshot may also benefit. The singing of the mantra as kirtan is extremely prevalent in Hare Krishna practice, both as an act of worship unto itself and as an accompaniment to other ritual and festival activities.

Traditionally kirtan is performed in a style loosely based on Indian folk music models. A kirtan leader draws on a pool of stock melodies to sing verses of scripture or mantras that are repeated by the congregation. Common accompanying instruments include the harmonium, drums (especially the *mridanga*), and hand cymbals. Flutes, violins, guitars, and other instruments may also be involved. Kirtan often stimulates spontaneous, ecstatic dancing among members of the congregation. By the early 2010s kirtan performances based on rock, reggae, and other popular music forms had become increasingly common.

BIBLIOGRAPHY

A.C.B.S. Prabhupada: *Chant and Be Happy: the Power of Mantra Meditation* (Los Angeles, 1983)

G.L. Beck: "Hare Krishna Mahamantra: Gaudiya Vaishnava Practice and the Hindu Tradition of Sacred Sound," *The Hare Krishna Movement: the Post-Charismatic Fate of a Religious Transplant*, ed. E. Bryant and M. Ekstrand (New York, 2004), 35–44

N. Delmonico: "Chaitanya Vaishnavism and the Holy Names," *Krishna: A Sourcebook*, ed. E.F. Bryant (New York, 2007), 549–75

S. Rosen: *The Yoga of Kirtan: Conversations on the Sacred Art of Chanting* (Nyack, New York, 2008)

SARA BLACK BROWN

Hargail Music. Firm of music publishers and dealers in musical instruments. It was founded in New York in 1941 by Harold Newman, then president of the American Recorder Society. The firm's first publication was Gail Kubik's Suite for Three Recorders, and Newman used his own and Kubik's forenames to form that of the company. Hargail specialized in recorder music, and though its early output was for the adult amateur, much of its later music was intended for schools; it also published music for Orff instruments and contemporary American music. In addition to its publishing activities, the firm dealt in recorders (it manufactured the plastic Harvard model) and sold guitar kits. Newman remained president of Hargail until his death in 1989. In 1991 CPP/Belwin acquired the catalog of Hargail Music Press. CPP/Belwin itself became a subsidiary of Warner/Chappell in 1994; the company's publications have been distributed by Alfred Music Publishing.

BIBLIOGRAPHY

K. Wollitz: "An Interview with Harold Newman, Music Publisher," *American Recorder*, xiii (1972), 3

FRANCES BARULICH/LEAH BARNSTETTER

Hargrove, Roy (Anthony) (*b* Waco, TX, 16 Oct 1969). Jazz trumpeter. He attended Arts Magnet High School in Dallas, where Wynton Marsalis heard him play at a jazz clinic in 1987 and subsequently invited him to sit in with his band. Hargrove then attended the Berklee College of Music (1988–9) before leaving to pursue a studio career in New York. In 1995 he won the *Down Beat* reader's poll for outstanding trumpeter. After making five albums with Novus, he recorded extensively for Verve; for the first of these albums (*With the Tenors of our Time*, 1994, Verve) he teamed up with Joe Henderson, Stanley Turrentine, Johnny Griffin, and Joshua Redman. The inspired lyricism often heard in his improvisations invites comparison to Clifford Brown. An outstanding example of his melodic gift can be heard in his rendition of "The Nearness of You" (1995). Attending jam sessions in Cuba prompted Hargrove to form a ten-piece band called Crisol in 1996; the resulting album *Habana* (1997, Verve) won a Grammy award for Best Latin Jazz Performance in 1997. From the late 1990s Hargrove's albums have increasingly integrated the grooves and timbres of funk and hip hop. In 2003 he founded a hip-hop jazz collective called the RH Factor. He has also collaborated with such artists as Erykah Badu, D'Angelo, Common, and Method Man. In his music Hargrove emphasizes influences that encourage a broader view of the jazz tradition. For example, "Camaraderie" (2006) draws inspiration from Lester Bowie, who encouraged him to depart from the comforts of bebop. Although Hargrove has expressed a desire to erase the boundaries between jazz and hip hop, he continues to affirm his jazz heritage in albums recorded by his quintet.

SELECTED RECORDINGS

Diamond in the Rough (1989, Novus); *Public Eye* (1990, Novus); *Tokyo Sessions* (1991, Novus); *The Vibe* (1992, Novus); *Of Kindred Souls* (1993, Novus); *With the Tenors of our Time* (1994, Verve); *Family* (1995, Verve), incl. The Nearness of You; *Parker's Mood* (1995, Verve); *Moment to Moment* (2000, Verve); *Hard Groove* (2003, Verve); *Strength* (2004, Verve); *Distraction* (2006, Verve); *Nothing Serious* (2006, Verve), incl. Camaraderie; *Food* (2008, EmA); *Emergence* (2009, EmA)

BIBLIOGRAPHY

N. Chinen: "Roy Hargrove: Groovin' Hard," *JT*, xxxiii/5 (2003), 70–80

J. Murph: "Can't Stop Won't Stop," *JT*, xxxviii/10 (2008), 50–54

MATTHEW ALAN THOMAS

Harlem Renaissance, the [New Negro movement]. Typically thought of as a literary movement of the 1920s and early 30s, it encompassed music and other arts, and it extended beyond New York to other urban centers. Cultural, social, and music historians disagree as to what marks the exact beginning of the Harlem Renaissance, but they generally concur that by the end of World War I the Renaissance was under way. Markers of significant cultural change in the face of persistent racism against African Americans had appeared before and during the war. In 1909 a group of black and white intellectuals, jurists, and others formed the National Association for the Advancement of Colored People to fight segregation, discrimination, and racism. US industrialization and mobilization for World War I prompted African Americans from Southern states to move to

Northern urban centers in search of opportunity and to escape the oppressive racial violence and segregated Jim Crow practices of the American South. By the 1920s nearly one million blacks lived in Harlem, which displaced Washington, DC, as the capital of black America. Chicago, Detroit, and Los Angeles were among other cities that saw a sharp increase in their African American population. All these developments helped set the stage for a black cultural Renaissance.

Jazz and blues, which had thrived during the 1910s in Southern black communities, spread to Northern urban centers and internationally during the 1920s. In the wake of the popularity of Mamie Smith's "Crazy Blues" (1920) and the subsequent craze for recorded blues, the music industry marketed race records to recent black migrants (*see* RACE RECORD). Such records marked the country's continuing social and legal segregation at the same time that they helped to popularize blues queens such as Bessie Smith and Clara Smith and jazz performers including Duke Ellington and Louis Armstrong. The musical *Shuffle Along* (1921) is often viewed as a watershed event that helped create a vogue for African American music. With a book by Flournoy Miller and Aubry Miles, lyrics and music by Noble Sissle and Eubie Blake, and leading actress Florence Mills, the show moved from Harlem to Broadway in May 1921 and toured US cities. Its hit, "I'm Just Wild about Harry," was later used as a campaign song for President Harry S. Truman.

A post-war increase in leisure time and the emergence of cabarets and nightclubs—in response to the start of Prohibition in 1919—expanded opportunities and the audience for African American performers during the Harlem Renaissance. White audiences became increasingly interested in black musical culture, often drawn to venues that featured black performers but were open only to white audiences; other theaters staged performances with segregated seating. Though its log-cabin exterior and jungle interior reflected racist stereotypes of the era, the Cotton Club featured top black musicians such as Ellington, whose band provided music for house productions and social dancing from 1927 to 1931. Pianist Thomas "Fats" Waller likewise provided music for the rival Connie's Inn.

On 21 March 1924, a group of writers (including Jean Toomer, Jessie Fauset, Countee Cullen, Langston Hughes, and Howard University Professor Alain Locke) were invited by sociologist Charles S. Johnson to dine at New York's Civic Club. Locke later edited an issue of *Survey Graphic,* the forerunner of his *The New Negro* (1925), an anthology of essays, poetry, short stories, and art reproductions. Locke included several essays on music that complemented W.E.B. Du Bois's classic essay on "the sorrow songs" (1906). Writers Hughes, who drew on the 12-bar blues form in his poetry, and Zora Neale Hurston wrote extensively on African American music. White observers also participated in spurring interest in African American culture: Carl Van Vechten wrote extensively about jazz and blues and photographed numerous musical and literary figures, while heiress Nancy Cunard published an anthology, *Negro* (1933). African American publications—including the

Crisis, Opportunity, the Chicago *Defender,* and New York's *Amsterdam News* and *Age*—also featured regular coverage of African American music during this period, generally focusing on the world of art music and themes involving "racial uplift."

Some art music activities in the Harlem Renaissance featured interactions among black musical and literary artists and intellectuals. William Grant Still's ballet *Sahdji* began as a short story by Richard Bruce (Nugent) that appeared in *The New Negro,* and Locke wrote the ballet scenario for Still. The intellectual impact of the movement also resonated. Still went on to compose his *Afro-American Symphony,* which drew upon jazz, blues, and spirituals, thereby realizing Du Bois's and Locke's aesthetic vision that African American vernacular music be used in symphonies and other concert works. Other composers such as Florence Price and jazz pianist James P. Johnson followed suit. Performance practices also changed during this period. In 1921 tenor Roland Hayes included spirituals on his London Aeolian Hall recital, thereby inaugurating the tradition of African American singers performing spirituals on their concert and recital programs.

From an aesthetic and political standpoint, Locke, Du Bois, and others envisioned that familiarizing white Americans with African American art and culture would formidably aid in the fight against racism, thus promoting civil rights and battling discrimination. With the onset of the Great Depression, the immediate impact of the Harlem Renaissance declined as white patronage dwindled. Some cultural historians have deemed the movement unsuccessful, for it took another generation to reach the major milestones of the Civil Rights movement. Nonetheless, Harlem Renaissance-era music—jazz, blues, and, to a lesser extent, art music—left an indelible stamp on American culture.

BIBLIOGRAPHY

A. Locke: *The New Negro* (1925/R 1999)

N. Cunard: *Negro* (1933/R New York 1996)

N. Huggins: *The Harlem Renaissance* (New York, 1971)

D.L. Lewis: *When Harlem Was in Vogue* (New York, 1981)

S. Floyd Jr.: *Black Music in the Harlem Renaissance: a Collection of Essays* (New York, 1990)

P. A. Anderson: *Deep River: Music and Memory in Harlem Renaissance Thought* (Durham, NC, 2001)

L. Schenbeck: *Racial Uplift and American Music, 1878–1943* (Jackson, MS, 2012)

GAYLE MURCHISON

Harlem stride. *See* STRIDE.

Harley, Rufus (*b* Raleigh, NC, 20 May 1936; *d* Philadelphia, PA, 1 Aug 2006). Jazz bagpiper, saxophonist, and flutist. In his early teens he worked odd jobs to pay for his first instrument, a C-melody saxophone. He left school at 16 to seek work while playing gigs in various Philadelphia night spots; his first steady job was playing for Mickey Collins's big band. In the late 1950s he began taking music lessons with Dennis Sandole who was his mentor for much of his career.

Inspired after watching television coverage of John F. Kennedy's funeral procession, which included the

Canadian Black Watch ensemble playing the bagpipes, Harley decided to take up the instrument. He found his first set at a pawnshop in New York and spent six months practicing. He was brought to the attention of Joel Dorn, a DJ at Philadelphia's radio station WHAT, who at the time was working as an assistant to the Atlantic Jazz producer Nesuhi Ertegun. Dorn produced all of Harley's albums for Atlantic. The first, *Bagpipe Blues*, received a great deal of notice, especially in Detroit. This early attention resulted in high-profile appearances, including a set at the Newport Jazz Festival in 1968, performances on numerous television shows, and a minor role in Francis Ford Coppola's film *You're a Big Boy Now* (1966). Harley recorded three more albums for Atlantic until his contract was terminated in 1970. His first album with an independent label, *Re-Creation of the Gods*, was released in 1972. After appearing at a concert at Carnegie Hall in May 1974 that also included Sonny Rollins, Dizzy Gillespie, and Charles Mingus, Harley joined Rollins's European tour later that year, which included the Montreaux Jazz Festival; a recording of his performance at the festival was released as *The Cutting Edge*, 1974). For the rest of his life he continued to play and make occasional albums as a leader; he also appeared as a guest artist on albums for a diverse group of artists, ranging from Laurie Anderson to The Roots.

SELECTED RECORDINGS

As leader: *Bagpipe Blues* (1965, Atl.); *Scotch and Soul* (1966, Atl.); *A Tribute to Courage* (1967, Atl.), *King/Queens* (1969, Atl.); *Re-creation of the Gods* (1972, Ankh); *Brotherly Love* (1998, Tartan Pride); *Sustain* (2005, Isma'a/Discograph)

BIBLIOGRAPHY

B. Houston: "Jazz Bagpipes are No Laughing Matter," *Melody Maker*, xli/8 (1966), 8

J. Cody: "The Pipes, the Pipes are Calling, but Get an Unexpected Answer," *Wall Street Journal* (26 Aug 1993), suppl.B, p.1

P. Relic: "It's Piping Hot," *Mojo*, no.81 (2000), 18–19

C. Powell: *The Jazzish Bagpiper: Rufus Harley Jr. in Conversation with Charles A. Powell* (Stuart, FL, 2007)

DANIEL GOLDMARK

Harline, Leigh (*b* Salt Lake City, UT, 26 March 1907; *d* Long Beach, CA, 10 Dec 1969). Composer and conductor. He studied music at the University of Utah and took private piano and organ lessons with the conductor of the Mormon Tabernacle Choir, J. Spencer Cornwall. After working for radio stations in his native city, he moved to California (1928), where he arranged music and conducted for radio stations in Los Angeles and San Francisco. From 1932 to 1941 he worked for Walt Disney, writing for the Silly Symphony series and many other short films. He also composed for Disney's first two animated feature films: *Snow White and the Seven Dwarfs* and *Pinocchio*; for the latter he won Academy Awards for best original score and best song ("When you Wish upon a Star"). After leaving Disney he worked at various studios (mainly RKO and 20th Century-Fox), composing, conducting, and arranging for more than 120 feature films and several television programs. Although sometimes typecast as a scorer of comedies,

Harline was a skillful, imaginative, and often original craftsman, whose best work reveals a genuine dramatic flair. Two of his Disney scores, *The Pied Piper* (1933), a miniature operetta, and *The Old Mill* (1937), in its lyrical expression, musical unity, use of "symphonic" scoring, and textless female chorus, must be considered among his most agreeable and imaginative works.

WORKS
(selective list)

Film scores: Silly Symphonies, 1932–9 [incl. The Pied Piper, 1933, Music Land, 1935, The Country Cousin, 1936]; The Old Mill, 1937; Snow White and the Seven Dwarfs, 1937, collab. P.J. Smith, F. Churchill; Pinocchio, 1940; Mr. Bug Goes to Town, 1941; The Pride of the Yankees, 1942; Tender Comrade, 1943; China Sky, 1945; Isle of the Dead, 1945; Johnny Angel, 1945; Man Alive, 1945; A Likely Story, 1947; The Farmer's Daughter, 1947; The Boy with Green Hair, 1948; They Live by Night, 1949; Perfect Strangers, 1950; The Happy Years, 1950; Broken Lance, 1954; Good Morning, Miss Dove, 1955; The Enemy Below, 1957; The Wayward Bus, 1957; Ten North Frederick, 1958; The Wonderful World of the Brothers Grimm, 1962; 7 Faces of Dr. Lao, 1964

Orch: Civic Center Suite, 1941; Centennial Suite, 1947

BIBLIOGRAPHY

R.V. Steele: "Fairyland Goes Hollywood," *Pacific Coast Musician*, xxvi/22 (1937), 10 only [interview]

R. Care: "The Film Music of Leigh Harline," *Film Music Notebook*, iii/2 (1977), 32–48 [incl. complete list of film scores]; repr. in *Film Music Notebook: a Complete Collection of the Quarterly Journal, 1974–1978*, ed. E. Bernstein (Sherman Oaks, CA, 2004), 406–22

FRED STEINER/R

Harlow, Larry [Kahn, Lawrence Ira] (*b* Brooklyn, NY, 20 March 1939). Salsa pianist, bandleader, and producer. He developed an interest in both jazz and Latin music as a teenager, while he attended the New York High School of Music and Art in Harlem. A multi-instrumentalist most widely recognized for his talent as a pianist, he has been known for combining traditional Cuban sounds with innovative arrangements. He debuted as bandleader in 1965 with *Heavy Smoking*, the second album released by the newly formed Fania Records. Affectionately nicknamed "*El judío maravilloso*" (the marvelous Jew) by fellow musicians, he became a member and producer of the original Fania All-Stars, an ensemble band that achieved international acclaim for its live concerts. In 1973 Harlow brought Latin music to Carnegie Hall with the opera *Hommy* (inspired by the Who's rock opera *Tommy*), and in 1974 he released *Salsa*, considered one of his best recordings. In addition, *La Raza Latina: a Salsa Suite* (1977), which narrated the diasporic histories of salsa through music, was nominated for Best Latin Recording Grammy. Harlow returned to explore jazz with a live performance in New York that was released as *Live at Birdland* (2002).

Harlow has produced approximately 50 albums for other artists and has production credits for more than 200 others. As of the early 2010s he continued to tour internationally, both individually and with the "Latin Legends," an ensemble brought together by Harlow that included some of Latin music's most talented veterans, including Ismael Miranda, Adalberto Santiago, and Bobby Sanabria. In 2000 Harlow was inducted into the International Latin Music Hall of Fame, and in 2008 he received the Latin Recording Academy Trustees Grammy for his contributions to the field of recording.

BIBLIOGRAPHY
J.S. Roberts: *The Latin Tinge: the Impact of Latin American Music on the United States* (New York, 1979)
C.M. Rondón: *The Book of Salsa: a Chronicle of Urban Music from the Caribbean to New York City* (Chapel Hill, NC, 2008)
                                                                MARISOL NEGRÓN

Harman, Carter (*b* Brooklyn, NY, 14 June 1918; *d* Stowe, VT, 23 Jan 2007). Critic and composer. He studied composition with ROGER SESSIONS at Princeton University (BA 1940) and with OTTO LUENING at Columbia (MA 1949), having taught at Princeton from 1940 to 1942. Milton Babbitt introduced him to the possibilities of film soundtrack manipulation, and in 1954 he made his first experiments in tape composition. He held positions as a music critic with the *New York Times* (1947–52) and *Time* (1952–7), and wrote many journal articles as well as *A Popular History of Music* (New York, 1956, 2/1969). Later in life, he worked as a recording engineer as well as a location sound engineer for such films as *Lord of the Flies*. He served as president of the West Indies Recording Corporation in Puerto Rico (1960–69); in 1967 he became executive vice president and producer for CRI and from 1976 to 1984 its executive director. His compositions are lyrical and expressive, and his vocal works demonstrate an ability to set words naturally and attractively. He saw himself principally as an advocate for contemporary music, both as a writer and as a producer of recordings, for which services he received in 1981 both the Commendation of Excellence from BMI and the Laurel Leaf Award of the ACA.

WORKS
Stage: Blackface (ballet), 1947, arr. orch suite, 1948; The Tansy Patch (musical fantasy, N. Hallanan), 1949, renamed The Food of Love, 1951; Circus at the Opera (children's op, D. Molarsky), 1951
Orch: 3 Episodes, 1949; Music for Orch, 1949
Vocal: From Dusk to Dawn (E.E. Cummings), S, str qt, 1951; A Hymn to the Virgin (anon.), vv, 1952; You and I and Amyas (anon., *Oxford Book of English Verse*), round, 3 vv, 1952; Castles in the Sand (Molarsky), song cycle, female v, 1952; many children's songs, 1947–52
Other: several ens works, incl. Variations, str qt, 1950; pf pieces; Alex and the Singing Synthesizer, elec, 1974–7
                                                           BARBARA A. RENTON/R

Harmati, Sandor (*b* Budapest, Hungary, 9 July 1892). Violinist, conductor, and composer of Hungarian birth. After graduating from the National Hungarian Royal Academy of Music, he served briefly as concertmaster of the Budapest State SO. He settled in New York in 1914, where he became second violinist in the Letz Quartet (1917–21), conductor of various local ensembles (1922–3), and co-founder in 1922 of the Lenox String Quartet, with which he played until 1925. He then conducted the Omaha SO until 1930, spending the 1927–8 season as an American delegate to the ISCM in Frankfurt am Main and as a guest conductor with European orchestras. He assumed permanent directorship of the Musicians' SO for the Unemployed in New York City in the early 1930s, and in the two years before his death was professor of music at Bard College in Annandale, New York. An ardent champion of American music, Harmati was also a founding member of the American Music Guild in 1920 (the year he became an American citizen). Many of his compositions were celebrated in his time, though few seem to have gained any lasting popularity. His best-known work was the song "The Bluebird of Happiness" (1934, with words by E. Heyman), which in numerous recorded versions sold well over a million discs. He was awarded the Pulitzer Traveling Scholarship in Music for his symphonic poem *Folio* in 1922 and the Philadelphia Chamber Music Prize for a string quartet in 1925; for his one-act opera *Prelude to a Melodrama* (première under Stowkowski in 1928), he received the Juilliard Foundation Prize. Others of his published works include incidental music to *The Jeweled Tree* (1926, authorship unknown), pieces for violin solo, and numerous songs.

BIBLIOGRAPHY
I. Weil: "The American Complex," *MusAm*, xlix/11 (1929), 30 only
D. Ewen: *Composers of Today* (New York, 1934), 106 only
                                                     WILLIAM GEOFFREY SHAMAN

Harmonica [mouth organ]. A free reed instrument consisting of a small casing containing chambers of multiple pre-tuned reeds secured at one end. It is placed between the lips and played by inhalation (drawing) and exhalation (blowing), unwanted holes being masked by the tongue.

Shortly after German clockmaker Matthias Hohner established his harmonica firm in 1857, he shipped some to American relatives. Hohner pioneered the use of machine-punched reed covers and mass-produced wooden combs, and harmonicas became popular on both sides of the Atlantic. President Abraham Lincoln carried a harmonica in his pocket, and the instrument was played by Civil War soldiers and by frontiersmen such as Wyatt Earp and Billy the Kid.

W.C. Handy recalled hearing train imitations played on the harmonica in the 1870s, and the Hohner Marine Band diatonic (in multiple keys) became one of the defining sounds of early blues style. It was usually played in second position, a fifth above the normal tuning (also called "cross harp" due to the dominant seventh chords generated). Wood-combed harmonicas were often dipped in water to improve the tone and "bendability" of notes in this style.

By the 1920s, the German harmonica industry produced more than 50 million instruments a year, exporting them to many countries, including some 22 million each year to the United States. Following the success of Mamie Smith's "Crazy Blues" (1920), "race records" intended for African American audiences, like those by the Memphis Jug Band, began to feature the harmonica. Humphrey Bate was the first to play old-time music on the harmonica on Nashville radio (1925), and DeFord Bailey was the first on the *Grand Ole Opry* (1926). The 1925 White House Christmas tree was decorated with fifty harmonicas, and the *Hohner Harmony Hour* radio show debuted on Friday nights at 8:30 p.m. John Philip Sousa composed his

Harmonica Wizard March after conducting the 52 member Philadelphia Harmonica Band at the 1926 Sesqui-Centennial Exposition.

Four giants of blues harmonica rose to prominence in 1930s Chicago: LITTLE WALTER (Marion Jacobs), Big Walter Horton, SONNY BOY WILLIAMSON, and SONNY BOY WILLIAMSON II (Alec Rice Miller). Miller played with a full blues band on daily *King Biscuit Time* broadcasts and helped to popularize cross harp technique and the use of hand effects to imitate the human voice. Jacobs revolutionized the instrument by cupping his hands around a "bullet" microphone marketed to radio dispatchers: this gave him a powerful, distorted, mid-range timbre that could compete with the electric guitar. Harmonica bands, pioneered by Borrah Minnevitch and the Harmonica Rascals, became popular on the vaudeville circuit and reached a peak during the AFM recording ban from 1942 to 1944. "Peg O' My Heart" (1947) by Jerry Murad's Harmonicats reached number one on the *Billboard* charts, and the harmonica was officially recognized by the AFM in 1956.

JUNIOR WELLS, JAMES COTTON, Paul Butterfield, and John Popper popularized the harmonica as an R&B and rock instrument. They used a variety of bends and overdraws (stalling one reed, introduced in the early 1970s by Howard Levy) to achieve a chromatic scale. "Juke," recorded by Little Walter in 1952, was the first harmonica instrumental to make the *Billboard* R&B charts. Bass harmonicas were developed for ensemble playing, and groups such as the Harmonica Rascals and the Harmonica Gentlemen (who backed up The Andrews Sisters and Danny Kaye), featured the bass. A miniature diatonic harmonica was the first instrument in space: Astronaut Wally Schirra Jr. played "Jingle Bells" on a Hohner "Little Lady" during the 1965 Gemini 6 mission. The 1965 Newport Folk Festival featured harmonicists such as the newly-electrified Bob Dylan, followed by Melvin Lyman, who played a twenty-minute improvisation on "Amazing Grace."

The chromatic harmonica has two reed plates in keys a semitone apart, with a metal slide enabling the player to change plates. Notable American jazz/pop chromatic players include TOOTS THIELEMANS, Norton Buffalo, and STEVIE WONDER. Many Chicago blues musicians played stock chromatics in third position (one full tone higher, also called "slant harp"). Classical virtuosos LARRY ADLER and Tommy Reilly adapted violin concertos by Bach and Vivaldi and commissioned over fifty concert works by composers such as Milhaud and Vaughan Williams. Contemporary master Robert Bonfiglio has revived concertos by Henry Cowell and Villa Lobos and commissioned new concertos from Lowell Liebermann and Pulitzer-prize winner Paul Moravec.

American design innovations have made the instrument more versatile: reeds were usually riveted, bolted, or screwed in place, but All-American models from the 1940s were held in place by tension. The United States experienced a harmonica shortage during World War II since most manufacturers were based in Germany and Japan. Wood and metal were in short supply due to military demand, so Finn Magnus, a Dutch American

entrepreneur, developed the molded-plastic harmonica. American engineer CHAM-BER HUANG's Hohner 2016 CBH (introduced in 1975) replaced the slides and resonating chambers with Delrin plastic resins.

The Deutsches Harmonikamuseum (Trossingen) and the Alan G. Bates Collection at the National Music Museum (Vermillion, ND), hold the world's largest harmonica collections. The Bates archive contains over 2,500 instruments and 2,000 pieces of trade literature and ephemera, including antique sheet music.

BIBLIOGRAPHY

G. Weiser: *Blues & Rock Harmonica* (Anaheim, 1990)
P. van der Merwe: *Origins of the Popular Style: the Antecedents of Twentieth-Century Popular Music* (Oxford, 1992)
K. Field: *Harmonicas, Harps and Heavy Breathers: the Evolution of the People's Instrument* (New York, 1993; revised ed. 2000)
M. Häffner and C. Wagner: *Made in Germany, played in the USA: die Geschichte der Mundharmonika in den USA* (Trossingen, 1993)
A. Smith: *Confessions of Harmonica Addicts: a History of American Harmonica Ensembles* (Richfield, OH, 2008)

LAURA PRICHARD

Harmoniemusik. Musical wind ensemble, usually five to eight instruments, of pairs of oboes and/or clarinets, horns, and one or two bassoons, without drums, popular during the 18th century.

See BAND §1.

Harmonium. A small instrument of the REED ORGAN family. The term is commonly used in Europe to refer to all reed organs, of whatever size or construction. Such instruments were widely disseminated, especially by the colonial powers in Africa and India. Though upright models are found, the most common is a small portable instrument set in a box. Models are made in various sizes with a range of stops and couplers. The instrument is usually played while sitting on the floor, the player fingering the keyboard with one hand and pumping a bellows at the back with the other. It is often used to provide a heterophonic contrapuntal texture for vocal music.

BIBLIOGRAPHY

GMO

BARBARA OWEN/ALASTAIR DICK/N. LEE ORR

Harmony. Manufacturer of fretted stringed instruments. The Harmony Musical Instrument Company was started by Wilhelm J.F. Schultz (*b* Hamburg; *d* Chicago, IL, 1925) in 1892 in Chicago, Illinois. Harmony manufactured low- to middle-grade flattop guitars, mandolins, and banjos, providing many generations of musicians with inexpensive, but well made, instruments.

By about 1897 Harmony was supplying the catalog retailer Sears, Roebuck, & Co., of Chicago. Capitalizing on the popularity of Hawaiian music in 1915, Harmony began producing ukuleles and in 1916 became a subsidiary of Sears, offering Supertone brand instruments. Celebrity Harmony endorsers included Roy Smeck (1928) and Bradley "Houn' Dog" Kincaid (1929).

In 1925 Jay Kraus (or Krause; *d* Chicago, IL, 1968) joined Harmony and then succeeded Schultz to the presidency in 1926. In 1932 Harmony introduced its first archtop guitars and in 1936 debuted its first electric guitars and amps. In 1938 Harmony purchased the Stella and Sovereign brand names from the remains of its former rival, Oscar Schmidt. In 1940 Jay Kraus left Harmony and then purchased the company, renaming it the Harmony Company. Harmony continued to supply Sears with instruments now called Silvertone.

During the 1950s Harmony introduced bright new colors for its Colorama guitars. Harmony's first solid-body electric guitar line, the Stratotones, were offered from 1953–7, after which Harmony abandoned solid-bodies until the Silhouette line in 1964. Following the death of Kraus, Charles A. Rubovits became president with a trust in control. However, growing imports from Japan and a sudden drop in demand combined to doom American mass manufacturing of guitars. Harmony's main competitors, Kay and Valco, went out of business in 1968. Harmony struggled on into the 1970s with guitars little changed from the 1960s. In one last ditch effort, Harmony introduced a line of high quality acoustic flattops called the Harmony Opus in 1975, but these were unsuccessful. The Harmony name was sold to a conglomerate called Global in 1976. Thereafter, the brand occasionally appeared on instruments imported from Korea into the early 1980s. In 2000 MBT International made an unsuccessful attempt to revive the brand. In 2008, Charles Subecz formed the Original Harmony Guitar Company, Inc., in Barrington, Illinois, to reproduce original Harmony designs. In 2009 Jack Westheimer (*b* Mannheim, Germany, 27 Feb 1930; *d* 13 Aug 2012) and former Harmony executive Larry Goldstein (*b* Minneapolis, MN, 4 April 1943) purchased the name to use on a new line of Asian-made replicas which debuted in 2011.

BIBLIOGRAPHY
T. Wheeler: *American Guitars* (Revised and updated edition, New York, 1992)
M. Wright: *Electric Guitars: the Illustrated Encyclopedia* (San Diego, 2000)
M. Wright: *Acoustic Guitars: the Illustrated Encyclopedia* (San Diego, 2003)

MICHAEL WRIGHT

Harmony Society [Harmonie Gesellschaft]. Separatist group founded by Johann Georg Rapp (*b* Germany, 1 Nov 1757; *d* Economy [now Ambridge], PA, 7 Aug 1847) from Iptingen, a village in Württemberg. A millenarian preacher, Rapp formed a communal society with several hundred followers and immigrated to the United States in 1804. They built a village north of Pittsburgh they called Harmony; by 1810 the community consisted of 140 families (about 700 persons) and cultivated 3000 acres. The name Harmony was chosen to reflect the religious spirit that bound them together. In 1814, they sold the village and built the town of NEW HARMONY, Indiana. In 1825, they sold that site to the industrialist Robert Owen and moved to a 3000-acre tract near Pittsburgh that they called Economy. They grew wealthy through agriculture, industry, and investments, but the practice of celibacy gradually reduced their membership.

Harmonist musical activities were extensive at all three locations and were encouraged by Rapp, who was perhaps a flutist. They were under the direction of the society's physician, Johann Christoph Mueller (1777–1845), a violinist, pianist, and flutist, who gradually expanded the orchestra to a Classical-era instrumentation and assembled a repertory that between 1825 and 1831 comprised some 300 pieces. Concerts at Economy were open to the public and typically offered marches, dances, overtures, and symphonies by Johann Baptist Vanhal, Johann Sterkel, Ignace Pleyel, Niccolò Jommelli, Gioachino Rossini, W.A. Mozart, Joseph Haydn, and other 18th-century composers. The Harmonist orchestra and choirs performed excerpts from cantatas and oratorios by Haydn, Luigi Cherubini, G.F. Handel, Mozart, and J.G. Schade, as well as sectarian pieces by Mueller and other Harmonist composers. Most were arranged by Mueller to accommodate Harmonist vocal and instrumental resources. Charles von Bonnhorst (*b* 1776), a Pittsburgh attorney and amateur violinist, wrote about 30 quadrilles and waltzes for the Harmonist musicians during the 1820s. Mueller and Harmonist composer Jacob Henrici (1804–92) wrote short keyboard pieces, odes for voices and instruments, and hymns. Five compilations of hymn texts with tune names were published, the largest being the *Harmonisches Gesangbuch* of 1827, printed by Mueller on the Harmonists' own press.

Around 1827, the English-born clarinetist, pianist, and composer William Cumming Peters (1805–66) was hired to teach the society's musicians. Peters was then operating a music store in Pittsburgh in partnership with John H. Mellor and William Smith. While employed by the Harmonists, he composed a Symphony in D (1831) for their orchestra, arranged works for various instrumental combinations, and composed an ode, *O schöne Harmonie*, for the Harmonist choir. He later established a music-publishing dynasty in the Midwest—which became one of the leading American firms—with various partners, including his brother Henry J. Peters, Joel D. Field, Frederick J. Webster, and later with his sons William, Alfred, and John.

The Harmony Society suffered a schism in 1832 and Mueller left with the dissenters. Orchestral music declined and the musical emphasis after 1835 was on singing classes and brass bands. Alsatian-born musician Jacob Rohr (1827–1906), a noted Pittsburgh bandmaster, was hired by the Harmonists around 1878. Under his direction the Economy Cornet Band gained regional distinction. Meanwhile, through manufacturing and investments, the society became extremely wealthy, even as the aging membership declined.

Musical activities culminated with John S. Duss (1860–1951), a cornetist and admirer of Patrick Gilmore, who diverted Harmonist funds to organize professional bands that he rehearsed at Economy. Regional tours began in 1895 and included appearances in Louisville, St. Paul, and Buffalo. In 1897 the band was named Duss's Economy Band (soon thereafter, "Duss's Band"), and concerts included his own compositions, among them *Liberty Chimes March, Life's Voyage Waltz, The*

Limited Express March, and *March G.A.R. in Dixie*. His own publishing firm, W.C. Ott and Company of Beaver Falls, Pennsylvania, published most of these works.

In 1902, Duss hired the New York Metropolitan Orchestra, its concertmaster Nahan Franko, and two of its star singers, soprano Lillian Nordica and baritone Edouard de Reszke, with whom he toured the United States and Canada between 1903 and 1907. Concerts were also given at the Metropolitan Opera House and St. Nicholas and Madison Square Gardens. The final appearance of Duss's Band was at the Toronto Exhibition in 1907. After prolonged lawsuits, the Harmony Society was dissolved in 1906 and portions of the community were subsequently designated a historic site and museum by the state of Pennsylvania. The vast Harmonist library comprising hundreds of books, many dating from as early as the 17th century, business documents, music—printed and in manuscript—were cataloged as a WPA project. Some items remain in an archive at Economy Village, but most have been moved to the Pennsylvania Historical and Museum Commission building in Harrisburg.

BIBLIOGRAPHY
K.J.R. Arndt: *George Rapp's Harmony Society 1785–1847* (Philadelphia, 1965)
R.D. Wetzel: *The Music of George Rapp's Harmony Society, 1805–1906* (diss., U. of Pittsburgh, 1970)
K.J.R. Arndt: *George Rapp's Successors and Material Heirs* (Cranbury, NJ, 1971)
K.J.R. Arndt and R.D. Wetzel: "Harmonist Music and Pittsburgh Musicians in Early Economy," *Western Pennsylvania Historical Magazine*, liv/2–4 (1971)
K.J.R. Arndt: *A Documentary History of the Indiana Decade of the Harmony Society 1814–1824* (Indianapolis, IN, 1975)
R.D. Wetzel: *Frontier Musicians on the Connoquenessing, Wabash, and Ohio: a History of the Music and Musicians of George Rapp's Harmony Society, 1805–1906* (Athens, OH, 1976) [with cat. of the Harmonist music library, Economy Village, Ambridge, PA]
R.D. Wetzel: *"Oh! Sing no more that gentle song": the Musical Life and Times of William Cumming Peters (1805–66)* (Warren, MI, 2000)
RICHARD D. WETZEL

Harms. Firm of music publishers. It was founded in New York in 1875 by the brothers Alexander T. Harms (*b* New York, NY, 20 Feb 1856; *d* New York, NY, 23 Oct 1901) and Thomas B. Harms (*b* New York, NY, 5 Jan 1860; *d* New York, NY, 28 March 1906). T.B. Harms & Co. issued contemporary popular music, and the success of such early publications as "When the Robins Nest Again" (1883) and "The Letter that Never Came" (1886) led other Tin Pan Alley publishers to emulate the firm's promotional activities. In 1901 Max Dreyfus (*b* Kuppenheim, Germany, 1 April 1874; *d* Brewster, NY, 12 May 1964), who had been working for Harms as an arranger, bought a 25% interest in the firm, and though over the next few years he achieved complete managerial and financial control, he retained the Harms name for the firm, making it the leading publisher of musical stage songs. In 1903 he employed Jerome Kern as a composer; Kern subsequently became a partner. The firm also issued the works of George Gershwin, who was engaged in 1918 as a songwriter, and in the 1920s it began to publish the music of Richard Rodgers. Dreyfus sold his interest in the company to Warner Bros. in 1929 when it became part of the Music Publishers Holding Corporation; he stayed on as a consultant until he set up in 1935 the American branch of Chappell, a company affiliated with Chappell of London, owned by his brother Louis Dreyfus (1877–1967). In 1969 that part of Harms connected with the estates of Louis Dreyfus (who had been a director of Harms) and Kern was bought by Lawrence Welk and became part of the Welk Music Group.

BIBLIOGRAPHY
S.N. Behrman: "Profiles," *New Yorker* (6 Feb 1932), 20–24
D.A. Jasen: *Tin Pan Alley* (New York, 1988)
FRANCES BARULICH

Harney, Ben(jamin) R(obertson) (*b* Middletown [now in Louisville], KY, 6 March 1871; *d* Philadelphia, PA, 11 March 1938). Ragtime songwriter, pianist, and singer. Despite statements to the contrary by Eubie Blake, Harney came from an established white Kentucky family. He apparently received formal training on the piano, for, in later years, he played classical compositions as written and then repeated them in ragtime. At the age of 14 he entered a military academy in Kentucky, where he remained for four years. During this period he probably visited saloons where black pianists played, because, one year before leaving school, he composed what is now considered the earliest ragtime song, "You've been a good old wagon but you've done broke down." From 1889 he was active in Louisville, playing in a saloon at the corner of Eighth and Green Streets. In 1895 a Louisville businessman financed the publication of "You've been a good old wagon" and it became an immediate hit. On the strength of this success Harney moved to New York, where, in 1896, he achieved popularity playing and singing in the new musical style. From this time until 1923, when he suffered a heart attack, Harney pursued a successful career in show business, touring throughout the United States, England, Europe, and East Asia. Thereafter he seldom performed, and with the eclipse of ragtime by jazz he was soon forgotten. By 1930 he was living in poverty in Philadelphia.

Harney produced a large number of ragtime songs, but three stand out from the others: "You've been a good old wagon" (1895), "Mr. Johnson turn me loose" (1896), perhaps his most popular song, and "The Cakewalk in the Sky" (1899). The syncopated rhythm in these songs, and Harney's own renditions of them, were described by contemporaries as being black in character. Harney's *Ragtime Instructor* (1897) was the first method book to teach the new syncopated piano style.

WORKS
(selective list)

Songs (lyrics by Harney unless otherwise stated): You've been a good old wagon but you've done broke down, 1895; Mr. Johnson turn me loose, 1896; I love my honey, 1897; There's a knocker layin' around, 1897; Draw that color line, 1898; If you got any sense you'll go, 1898; You may go but this will bring you back, 1898; The Black Man's Kissing Bug, 1899; The Cakewalk in the Sky, 1899; The hat he never ate (H.S. Taylor), 1899; Tell it to me, 1899; The only way to keep her is in a cage, 1901; T.T.T., 1903

Principal publisher: Witmark

BIBLIOGRAPHY
DAB (R. Blesh)

R. Blesh and H. Janis: *They all played ragtime* (New York, 1950, 4/1971), 93–7, 210–4, 216–8, 225–30

W.H. Tallmadge: "Ben Harney: White? Black? Mulatto?," *Sonneck Society Bulletin*, v/3 (1979), 16–17

W.H. Tallmadge: "Ben Harney: the Middlesborough Years, 1890–93," *AM*, xiii/2 (1995), 167–94

E.A. Berlin: "Reflections on the Ben Harney Mystery," *The Mississippi Rag* (1997), 17–18

Unpublished material on Harney in library of the Kentucky Historical Society in Frankfort, KY

WILLIAM H. TALLMADGE/R

Harnick, Sheldon (*b* Chicago, IL, 30 April 1924). Lyricist. After serving in the Army, he attended Northwestern University, where he studied violin and received a Bachelor of Music degree. His first song on Broadway, for which he wrote both the music and the lyrics, appeared in *New Faces of 1952*. After teaming with composer Jerry Bock on *The Body Beautiful* (1958), Harnick concentrated on lyrics only for a string of highly successful Broadway musicals featuring Bock's tuneful music and Harnick's character-driven lyrics. The pair gained acclaim when *Fiorello* (1959), about the charismatic titular mayor of New York, won the Pulitzer Prize for Drama. Their most acclaimed collaboration, *Fiddler on the Roof* (1964), often considered the last of the "Golden Age" musicals, for a time became the longest running musical on Broadway before it closed in 1972. Other works include *Tenderloin* (1960), *She Loves Me* (1963), *The Apple Tree* (1966), and *The Rothschilds* (1970). After this last work the team severed their working relationship, but they reunited to write one last song, "Topsy Turvy" for the Broadway revival of *Fiddler on the Roof* (2004). After his partnership with Bock disintegrated, Harnick worked with several different composers, including Michael Legrand and Richard Rodgers, with whom he wrote *Rex* (1976). He has worked as a translator, an opera librettist, and an occasional composer, writing the theme songs for two films and the musical *Dragons*, for which he created the book, music, and lyrics. He has received three Antoinette Perry (Tony) awards.

BIBLIOGRAPHY
R. Altman and M. Kaufman: *The Making of a Musical* (New York, 1971)

P. Lambert: *To Broadway, To Life!: the Musical Theater of Bock and Harnick* (New York, 2011)

JESSICA HILLMAN

Harold Melvin and the Blue Notes. One of the most popular purveyors of Philly soul during the 1970s, the group originated in Philadelphia, Pennsylvania, as the Charlamagnes before it changed its name in 1954. Led by Harold Melvin (1939–97), the group performed and recorded throughout the 1950s and 60s with limited success. Its first charting recordings included "My Hero" in 1960, released on the Val-ue label, and "Get out (and let me cry)," released on Landa in 1965. The group's fortunes changed when TEDDY PENDERGRASS joined the ensemble as lead vocalist in 1970. The group signed with Kenny Gamble and Leon Huff's Philadelphia International Records in 1972 and finally broke into the charts that same year with "If you Don't Know me by Now." A number of equally successful releases followed: "I miss you" (1972), "The Love I Lost" (1973), "Don't leave me this way" (1975), and "Bad Luck" (1975). This trajectory came to a sudden end when, following disagreements over wages and billing, Pendergrass left the group to establish an equally if not more successful presence as a soloist. The group left Philadelphia International in 1977 and signed with ABC Records, though only one release, "Reaching for the World," broke into the charts that same year. Subsequently, the group experienced some of their former glory in England, where their material has been covered with great frequency by artists such as Simply Red and Jimmy Somerville. In fact, Harold Melvin and the Blue Notes were one of the most covered of all acts on Philadelphia International. The group performed until Melvin's death in 1997, after which they continued as the Legendary Blue Notes.

DAVID SANJEK

Harp guitar [harp-guitar]. The term "harp guitar" most commonly refers to guitars with extra floating bass strings developed in America from the 1890s to the 1930s. The exact number of extra bass strings is immaterial, numbering anywhere from one to 12, as is the method of attaching the extra strings, which include such configurations as a second neck, a hollow arm extension protruding from the upper bass side bout, a "theorboed" extension off the main headstock, a harp-like frame, or any amalgamation of these elements. Occasionally, mid-range or treble "harp" string banks are used. The common defining element is that the extra strings are plucked with the thumb or fingers, but not fretted as the neck strings are. The term has grown to include visually and/or functionally similar instruments introduced in other countries over the past three-and-a-half centuries.

The first instrument to be specifically named a harp guitar was built and patented by Hans J. Hansen of Chicago in 1891. The most numerous early American harp guitars were the large archtop instruments made by the Gibson Company (1903–30s), the Larson brothers' hollow-arm model built for W.J. Dyer & Bro. (*c*1901–20), and Chris Knutsen's original patented hollow-arm instruments built in a variety of forms (*c*1895–1930). During this period, nearly every important guitar builder or company offered harp guitars, considered a staple of the better "BMG" (Banjo, Mandolin, and Guitar) groups—everything from small guitar trios to large mandolin orchestras. The harp guitar's role and popularity could be likened to the piano's, as it supplied both bass and accompaniment, with significantly louder and fuller tone along with its expanded range. Music written specifically for the harp guitar was extremely rare, as it was (and has remained) largely unnecessary—the players simply transpose the desired chord's root note or bass line down an octave.

Other players included numerous vaudeville performers who were naturally drawn to both the enhanced visual aspects and increased volume of the more spectacular instruments. The advent of resonator guitars, and shortly after, electric guitars, along with the decline and demise of the BMG community, spelled the end for these important and popular instruments in America. Long forgotten and unfairly judged as a novelty, harp guitars have since been re-evaluated and re-popularized by historians and players alike. As of the early 2010s, there were hundreds of musicians the world over dedicating themselves to new music for the instrument, along with harp guitar builders, and even Chinese production factories, creating updated instruments to accommodate them.

GREGG MINER

Harreld, Kemper (*b* Muncie, IN, 31 Jan 1884; *d* Detroit, MI, 23 Feb 1972). Violinist and music educator. He studied at the Chicago Musical College with FELIX BOROWSKI, at the Sherwood Music School, and at the Fredericksen Violin School. While in Chicago he was conductor of the Choral Study Club's orchestra. In 1911 he joined the faculty of the Atlanta Baptist College (now Morehouse College), and established its music department; he spent his free time studying folk music in the southern states. During the summer of 1914 he studied violin with Siegfried Eberhardt in Berlin. In 1927 Harreld became chairman of the music department at Spelman College and later founded the Atlanta University-Morehouse-Spelman Chorus and Orchestra, whose concerts were given before unsegregated audiences; the Morehouse College Quartet, which he directed, sang twice for President Roosevelt. By 1937 he had organized his own string quartet, and from 1937 to 1939 he served as president of the National Association of Negro Musicians, which he had helped organize in 1919. Harreld's pupils included Fletcher Henderson, Mattiwilda Dobbs, Edmund Jenkins, Willis Laurence James, Herbert F. Mells, G. Johnson Hubert, and Frederick D. Hall.

BIBLIOGRAPHY
J.P. Green: *Edmund Thornton Jenkins: the Life and Times of an American Black Composer, 1894–1926* (Westport, CT, 1982)
DOMINIQUE-RENÉ DE LERMA

Harrell, Lynn (Morris) (*b* New York, NY, 30 Jan 1944). Cellist and teacher. He is the son of baritone MACK HARRELL and violinist Marjorie Fulton. After lessons with Heinrich Joachim in New York and Lev Aronson in Dallas, Harrell studied at the Juilliard School with LEONARD ROSE and at the Curtis Institute of Music with ORLANDO COLE. He also attended master classes with Gregor Piatigorsky and Pablo Casals. In 1960 Harrell debuted at Carnegie Hall with the New York Philharmonic. From 1965 to 1971 he was principal cellist in the Cleveland Orchestra; he was the only player to solo under George Szell in New York. 1971 marked Harrell's New York solo recital debut; in 1974 he debuted in Europe. In addition to sharing the first Avery Fisher Prize with Murray Perahia (1975), he took part in the Ford Foundation's Concert Artists program, which allowed him to commission and perform Donald Erb's Cello Concerto. Harrell has given master classes at the Aspen, Ravinia, and Vienna Music Festivals, among others. In 1994 he played in the Vatican Concert commemorating the Holocaust, and in 1999 he performed in the three-week "Lynn Harrell Cello Festival" with the Hong Kong Philharmonic. He has performed all over the world, in particular with leading orchestras in the United States, Europe, Japan, Korea, Malaysia, Taiwan, Hong Kong, Australia, and New Zealand. Conductors with whom he has regularly worked include James Levine, André Previn, Leonard Slatkin, Yuri Temirkanov, and Michael Tilson Thomas. In 2010 Harrell and his wife, violinist Helen Nightengale, started the HEARTbeats Foundation, a charity based in Los Angeles devoted to helping children overcome the challenges of poverty and conflict through music. He serves as Artist Ambassador and as a board member of the foundation. Along with Itzhak Perlman and Vladimir Ashkenazy, Harrell received two Grammy Awards, one for Pyotr Tchaikovsky's Trio in A Minor, Op. 50 (1981), and the other for Ludwig van Beethoven's complete Trios (1987).

Harrell began his pedagogical career at the Cincinnati College-Conservatory (1971–6), and then moved to the Juilliard School (1976–86). He held the Gregor Piatigorsky Chair at USC (1986–92) before taking the International Chair for Cello Studies at the Royal Academy of Music in London (1986–93), where he became Principal (1993–5). He took over the Artistic directorship of the LA Philharmonic Institute (1988–91), and then taught at Rice University's Shepherd School Music (2002–8).

Harrell's playing is distinguished by its rich lyricism, the deep, soulful sounds he creates with the instrument, his superb technique, and the deft execution of his musical ideas. He plays a 1721 Montagnana cello.

BIBLIOGRAPHY
"Lynn Harrell," *Current Biography Yearbook* (1983), 169–72
M. Campbell: *The Great Cellists* (North Pomfret, VT, 1988), 312–5
RICHARD BERNAS/DENNIS K. MCINTIRE/
REBECCA SCHWARTZ-BISHIR

Harrell, Mack (*b* Celeste, TX, 8 Oct 1909; *d* Dallas, TX, 29 Jan 1960). Baritone, father of LYNN HARRELL. He studied at the Juilliard School and in 1939 won the Metropolitan Opera Auditions of the Air and made his debut with the company as Biterolf in *Tannhäuser*. He created Samson in Bernard Rogers's *The Warrior* (1947) and continued to appear at the Metropolitan until 1958, singing a wide repertory that included Masetto, Papageno, Kothner, Amfortas, John the Baptist, Captain Balstrode (*Peter Grimes*), and Nick Shadow, his best-known role, which he sang in the American premiere of *The Rake's Progress* in 1953. He appeared with New York City Opera, making his debut in 1944 as Germont, and in Chicago and San Francisco. His repertory also included Escamillo, Marcello, Valentin, Luna, Golaud, and Wozzeck, which he recorded, and he took part in the US premieres of Darius Milhaud's *Christophe Colomb* (1952, Carnegie Hall) and his *David* (1956, Hollywood Bowl). He taught at the Juilliard School from 1945 to 1956. Harrell possessed a sturdy lyric baritone of remarkable beauty and was a considerable musician and artist, but perhaps the most notable aspect of his singing was the directness of its human appeal.

RICHARD DYER, ELIZABETH FORBES

Harrell, Tom [Thomas Strong] (*b* Urbana, IL, 16 June 1946). Jazz trumpeter, flugelhorn player, composer, and arranger. After graduating from Stanford University in 1969 with a music composition degree, he toured with Stan Kenton's and Woody Herman's big bands. Harrell worked with Horace Silver's quintet in the 1970s and Phil Woods's quintet in the 1980s, while playing with an astonishing array of artists, ranging from the Mel Lewis Orchestra to Lee Konitz to Cold Blood. He has participated in more than 260 recordings, including 26 albums as a leader, and has been a perennial winner of critics' and readers' polls in *Down Beat* and *Jazz Times*, a nominee for Jazz Journalists Association Awards Trumpeter of the Year (2010 and 2011), a Grammy nominee, and a recipient of multiple SESAC awards. His current quintet has recorded four albums to date, beginning with *Light On* (2007, High Note), and he continues to perform, tour, and record. He is also an arranger and composer and earned a grant from Chamber Music America in 2006; his music has been performed and recorded by the Danish Radio and WDR big bands, and the Metropole and Brussels Jazz orchestras. His album *Wise Children* (2003; RCA Bluebird) combined orchestral instrumentation with guitars, a quintet, and voices, while the acclaimed album *The Art of Rhythm* (1998, RCA) utilized a chamber group and strings. During a career of more than four decades, Harrell has successfully managed schizophrenia and has moved with facility from small combo to big band to orchestral settings. As a trumpeter he possesses a warm, accessible tone and an improvisational vocabulary that offers fresh rhythmic, harmonic, and melodic innovation.

JEFFREY HOLMES

Harrigan, Edward Green (*b* Corlears Hook, NY, 26 Oct 1844; *d* New York, NY, 5 June 1911). Performer and playwright. Born in the predominantly Irish community of Corlears Hook on Manhattan's Lower East Side to a ship-building tradesman father and a minstrel song-singing and dancing mother, he apprenticed as a shipyard caulker after he left school at age 14. He also snuck away to minstrel shows and learned singing and banjo playing from his mother. When his parents divorced in the early 1860s, he signed on as a deckhand on a ship and worked as a sailor until 1867, when he settled in San Francisco and resumed work as a caulker.

Harrigan supplemented his income by performing as an Irish singer and minstrel. He was successful enough that within a year he left his work on the waterfront and moved full-time into theatrical entertainment. After the 1869 theatrical season, he returned to New York

before becoming an itinerant variety performer. During a stopover in Chicago he met a young falsetto singer, Anthony Cannon, who performed as "Master Antonio," and the pair teamed up as Harrigan and Hart. Under this name they performed songs and sketches in Irish character and in blackface.

During the early 1870s Harrigan and Hart were among a small number of highly popular variety performers. They frequently worked for the manager John Stetson at his New York theater, the Theatre Comique. There they developed an act that fleshed out their topical sketches into one-act pieces and eventually longer dramas. It was also here that Harrigan met composer David Braham, who provided music for Harrigan's Mulligan Guard plays during the late 1870s and 80s. Harrigan married Braham's daughter Annie in 1876.

Harrigan and Hart's partnership dissolved in 1885 due to increasing interpersonal conflict. Harrigan moved into the Park Theater, where he continued to stage his own urban topical dramas. In four seasons he earned enough money to build his own theater on West 35th Street near Sixth Avenue. By 1895 Harrigan had reached a peak and was considering taking a troupe on an international tour when his oldest son, a member of the company, suddenly fell ill and died. Unable to continue with his plans, he shut his theater and withdrew from performance.

In the late 1890s Harrigan returned to the stage, performing in vaudeville, with plans to return to writing and performing in his own large-scale works. He opened *The Mulligans* in 1901, and he continued to work in New York until 1908. When he died three years later, Harrigan left a note for his wife indicating that he had met all of his theatrical ambitions.

BIBLIOGRAPHY

E.J. Kahn Jr.: *The Merry Partners: the Age and State of Harrigan & Hart* (New York, 1955)

R. Moody: *Ned Harrigan: From Corlear's Hook to Herald Square* (Chicago, 1980)

J. Franceschina: *David Braham: the American Offenbach* (New York, 2003)

GILLIAN M. RODGER

Harris, Barry (Doyle) (*b* Detroit, MI, 15 Dec 1929). Jazz pianist, composer, and educator. He first encountered music through the church where his mother worked as a pianist and he first performed. After starting piano lessons at the age of four, he taught himself the boogie-woogie style of Albert Ammons before hearing bebop at a performance by Charlie Parker at Club El Sino in 1947. Having played some of his first professional engagements with Frank Rosolino, Harris became the house pianist at the Blue Bird Inn in Detroit, where he accompanied Lester Young, Sonny Stitt, Miles Davis, and Parker, among others. After travelling to New York in 1956 to record with Thad Jones and Hank Mobley, Harris remained in Detroit until 1960, when he moved to New York to join Cannonball Adderley's group. Harris made his first recording as a leader in 1958 for the Argo label. Throughout the 1960s, he enjoyed working relationships with Coleman

Hawkins and the A&R man Don Schlitten, for whom Harris recorded for Riverside and Xanadu. Although an active performer and recording artist, he solidified his place as an important jazz educator through his codification of passing-note scales, his employment of moving diminished chords, and his ability to demystify bebop's complexities. Harris created the Jazz Cultural Center as a hub for his educational initiatives in 1982 and was awarded an honorary doctorate from Northwestern. He has continued to teach, perform, and live in Weehawken in the home of Baroness Pannonica de Koenigswarter that he shared with Thelonious Monk from the 1970s. Harris can be seen in the film *Thelonious Monk: Straight no Chaser* (1989).

BIBLIOGRAPHY

M. Gardner: "Barry Harris," *JazzM*, no.151 (1967), 28

M. Bourne: "Barry Harris: Keeper of the Bebop Flame," *DB* lii/9 (1985), 26 [incl. discography]

A. Scott: "'Sittin' In': Barry Harris' use of the Jam Session as a Jazz Pedagogical Device," *Journal of Popular Music Studies*, xvi/3 (2004), 283–90

ANDREW SCOTT

Harris, Charles K(assel) (*b* Poughkeepsie, NY, 1 May 1865/7; *d* New York, NY, 22 Dec 1930). Songwriter and music publisher. Although he never learned to read or write music, he taught himself to play the banjo as a child, and at the age of 18 he became a banjo teacher and songwriter in Milwaukee. He performed his songs at amateur entertainments and attended performances of professional companies appearing in Milwaukee; he also became local correspondent for the New York *Dramatic News*.

After he had received royalties of only 85 cents for one of his songs, Harris established his own publishing company and almost immediately brought out his most successful work, "After the Ball" (1892), which was first interpolated by James Aldrich Libbey in a Milwaukee production of Hoyt's musical *A Trip to Chinatown*. After advance orders for 75,000 copies of the song, sales eventually reached some five million, and the royalties enabled him to open offices in New York and Chicago. He published his own songs and the works of other writers, including several shows produced by Joe Weber and Lew Fields, such as Victor Herbert's *Dream City* and *The Magic Knight* (both 1906) and A. Baldwin Sloane's *Tillie's Nightmare* (1910). His ability to judge which songs would sell rapidly made him one of the most successful publishers of popular music in the United States. In order to promote his publications he persuaded singers with ability and reputation to perform them in their shows.

Harris was reportedly the first publisher to print a singer's picture on a song cover; a photograph of Libbey appeared on the cover of *After the Ball*. He also claimed to be the first promoter to make and use slides to illustrate a song. These were hand-colored photographs mounted on glass and projected onto a screen, either to illustrate the story or to provide the words so that the audience could sing along; Harris often appeared as one of the song's characters.

Although none of Harris's later songs had as great a success as "After the Ball," many were among the most popular of the period and sold more than a million copies each, including "Just Behind the Times" (1896), "Break the news to mother" (1897), "'Mid the Green Fields of Virginia" (1898), "Hello Central, give me heaven" (1901), and "Always in the Way" (1903). When Adelina Patti made her farewell tour of the United States in 1903 she commissioned a song from Harris, the ballad "The Last Farewell."

Harris was an active member of the Music Publishers' Association. With Herbert, John Philip Sousa, and Reginald De Koven he fought to ensure the successful passage of the American copyright bill in 1909. Harris also served as the first secretary of ASCAP on its formation in 1914. He wrote the manual *How to Write a Popular Song* (New York, 1906/R) and an autobiography, *After the Ball: 40 Years of Melody* (New York, 1926/R), which includes a list of 111 of his songs.

WORKS
(selective list)
(all works published in New York unless otherwise stated)

c300 songs, incl. Kiss and let's make up, 1891; After the Ball, Chicago, 1892; While the Dance Goes On, 1894; Better than Gold, 1895; Cast Aside, 1895; Just Behind the Times, Milwaukee, 1896; Break the news to mother, 1897; 'Mid the Green Fields of Virginia, 1898; Is life worth living?, 1899; For Old Times Sake, 1900; I've a longing in my heart for you, Louise, 1900; Hello Central, give me heaven, 1901; I'm wearing my heart away for you, 1902; Always in the Way, 1903; The Best Thing in Life, 1907; Songs of Yesterday, 1916

Principal publisher: Harris

BIBLIOGRAPHY

W. Craig: *Sweet and Lowdown: America's Popular Song Writers* (Metuchen, NJ, 1978), 45 only

C. Hamm: *Yesterdays: Popular Song in America* (New York, 1979), 284–88, 290–1, 297–302

K.A. Kanter: *The Jews on Tin Pan Alley: the Jewish Contribution to American Popular Music, 1830–1940* (Cincinnati, 1982)

JOAN MORRIS

Harris, Cyril M(anton) (*b* Detroit, MI, 20 June 1917; *d* New York, NY, 4 Jan 2011). Acoustician. At UCLA he studied mathematics and physics (BA 1938, MA 1940), then went to the Massachusetts Institute of Technology to study acoustics under Philip McCord Morse (PhD 1945). In posts at Bell Telephone Laboratories (1945–51) and Columbia University (from 1952), where he taught in the engineering school as well as the graduate school of architecture and planning, he researched the acoustical properties of building materials, airborne sound, and musical instruments. He was acoustical consultant for more than 100 halls, including the Metropolitan Opera House (1966); Powell Symphony Hall, St. Louis (renovation 1968); Great Hall, Krannert Center for the Performing Arts, University of Illinois (1969); the concert hall and opera house at the John F. Kennedy Center (1971); Orchestra Hall, Minneapolis (1974); National Center for the Performing Arts, Bombay, India 1980); Avery Fisher Hall (renovation 1976); Symphony Hall, Salt Lake City (1979); and the New York State Theater (renovation 1982). He used traditional building materials and shapes: rectangular auditoriums, wooden walls

Harris, John   59

and floors, plaster ceilings, and uneven surfaces to help diffuse sound. Harris also wrote numerous books on acoustics and architecture.

BIBLIOGRAPHY
CBY 1977 (Harris, Cyril M(anton))
B. Bliven Jr.: "Quiet Man," *New Yorker*, xlviii (17 June 1972), 39
B. Bliven Jr.: "Annals of Architecture: a Better Sound," *New Yorker*, lii (8 Nov 1976), 51
W. Grimes: Obituary, *New York Time* (8 Jan 2011)

Harris, Eddie (*b* Chicago, IL, 20 Oct 1934; *d* Los Angeles, CA, 5 Nov 1996). Saxophonist, composer, and pianist. His inclusive and wide-ranging musical approach made him one of the pioneers of jazz fusion, a crossover artist with popular appeal, and a proponent of electronics and experimental instruments. A great deal of Harris's musical development can be traced back to his roots in Chicago. He first began to learn music during church services there, picking up the basic rudiments of piano. It was as a pianist that he made his professional debut, accompanying such greats as Charlie Parker and Lester Young, as well as recording with fellow Chicagoan Gene Ammons. As a teenager Harris attended DuSable High School, a Chicago institution known for contributing to the development of several notable jazz musicians, including Nat "King" Cole and Johnny Griffin. After attending Roosevelt College, he left Chicago to join the army. In 1959 he performed one of his first gigs as a bandleader at the Archway Supper Club in Chicago. In 1960 he recorded the theme from the movie *Exodus* which became a hit single and sold more than a million copies. Harris retained this high level of mass appeal and commercial success as he established himself as a leading jazz-fusion crossover artist. In 1967 he released another popular single, "Listen Here" (from the album *The Electrifying Eddie Harris*, 1967, Atl.) followed in 1969 by "Cold Duck Time" (*Swiss Movememt*, 1969, Atl.) with Les McCann, with whom he collaborated frequently. For jazz purists Harris's most important and highly regarded work is his composition "Freedom Jazz Dance," which was recorded by Miles Davis on the album *Miles Smiles* (1966, Col.).In 1974 Harris began touring extensively throughout the United States, Africa, and Europe. He wrote a number of books on jazz improvisation and composition, including *The Eddie Harris Interverlistic Concept for all Single Line Wind Instruments* (Chicago, 1971/*R*1984 as *The Intervallistic Concept: Saxophone*), *Modern Jazz Licks for Sight Reading*, and *The Eddie Harris Fakebook*.

E. RON HORTON

Harris, Emmylou (*b* Birmingham, AL, 12 April 1949). American Country-folk singer-songwriter. Emmylou Harris came late to music. While studying drama at the University of North Carolina at Greensboro, she found her musical inspiration in the folk music of Bob Dylan, Pete Seeger, Joan Baez, and Judy Collins. Harris left school and moved to Greenwich Village, where she submerged herself in the folk scene and recorded her first album, *Gliding Bird* (Jubilee Records, 1969). After a divorce and an unsuccessful stint in Nashville, Harris

moved to Washington, DC, where, in 1971, she met Gram Parsons. She sang backup vocals on Parsons's albums *GP* (Reprise 1973) and *Grievous Angel* (Reprise 1974), and became increasingly interested in country and country-rock.

Like Parsons, who died tragically in 1973, Harris also signed with Reprise. Her first albums revealed the influence of Parsons's artistic vision, fusing old and new country styles with a variety of rock, folk, bluegrass, and Cajun influences. Her debut album, *Pieces of the Sky* (Reprise, 1975), brought together an eclectic gathering of songs, ranging from Merle Haggard and the Louvin Brothers to the Beatles. It also featured Harris's touching tribute to Parsons, "Boulder to Birmingham." Harris made steady progress in the country music industry; a neo-traditionalist, she continued to draw on traditional country, overlooked artists, and up-and-comers. On her Grammy Award-winning fifth album, *Blue Kentucky Girl* (Reprise, 1979), Harris moved away from the country-rock sound of *Elite Hotel* (Reprise, 1975) and *Luxury Liner* (Reprise, 1977) towards a more traditional approach. Her output from the 1980s didn't fare as well on the charts, but she returned to prominence with her critically-acclaimed *Wrecking Ball* (Elektra) in 1995.

Known for her expressive, high-lonesome voice and her instinct for harmonizing, Harris is a much sought-after duet partner and backup vocalist. She has worked with numerous artists, including Bob Dylan, Dolly Parton, Linda Ronstadt, Neil Young, and Patty Griffin. She also appeared on the Grammy Award-winning soundtrack of *O Brother, Where Art Thou?* (Mercury, 2000). In 2008, she was inducted into the Country Music Hall of Fame.

BIBLIOGRAPHY
J. Brown: *Emmylou Harris: Angel in Disguise* (Kingston, ON, 2004)

JADA WATSON

Harris, John (*fl* London, England, and Boston, MA, *c*1730–69). Spinet and harpsichord maker of English birth. By 1730 he was working in Red Lion Street, London. That year he was granted a patent for "a new [!] invented harpsichord"; its description implies a type of instrument with only unison stringing but fitted with some octave coupler device. Harris immigrated to the United States, settling in Boston in 1768; the *Boston Gazette* (18 September 1768) contains the following notice:

> It is with pleasure that we inform the Public, that a few days since was shipped for Newport, a very curious Spinnet, being the first ever made in America, the performance of the ingenious Mr. John Harris, of Boston, (son of the late Mr. Joseph Harris of London, Harpsichord and Spinnet Maker), and in every respect does Honour to that Artist, who now carries on Business at his House, a few Doors Northward of Dr. Clark's, North End of Boston.

A spinet by John Harris of Boston, dated 1769, is in the Metropolitan Museum of Art, New York.

BIBLIOGRAPHY
D. Boalch: *Makers of the Harpsichord and Clavichord* (London, 1956, 2/1974)
R. Russell: *The Harpsichord and Clavichord* (London, 1959, rev. 2/1973)/REF>

HOWARD SCHOTT

Harris [Harris-Schofield], **Margaret R(osezarian)** (*b* Chicago, IL, 15 Sept 1943; *d* New York, NY, 7 March 2000) Conductor, pianist, and composer. After her first piano recital, given in 1947 at the Cary Temple Auditorium of Chicago, her teachers Mildred Hall and Leo Salkin supported her tour through the United States. In 1953 she performed one of Wolfgang Amadeus Mozart's concertos with the Chicago SO and won a scholarship to attend the Curtis Institute in Philadelphia. She earned bachelor's and master's degrees from the Juilliard School. She later achieved prominence as an African American female conductor of symphony orchestras and several ballet companies. She took over as musical director of Opera Ebony, which she had co-founded in 1973, and of Broadway musicals such as *Hair, Raisin, Two Gentlemen of Verona, Guys and Dolls,* and *Amen Corner.* In 1972 she received a National Association of Negro Musicians Award, and in 1987 she became a Dame of Honour and Merit, Order of St. John Knights of Malta. Some months before her death, Harris had been appointed associate dean of the Pennsylvania Academy of Music in Lancaster. Her compositions include two ballets, an operatic work (*King David*), *Israel Suite,* and two piano concertos.

BIBLIOGRAPHY
A.I. Cohen: *International Encyclopedia of Women Composers* (New York, 1987)
H. Walker-Hill: *Piano Music by Black Women Composers* (Westport, CT, 1992)
D.A. Handy: *Black Conductors* (Metuchen, NJ, 1995)
                                             DANIELE BUCCIO

Harris, Murray M. (*b* Illinois, 1866; *d* Phoenix, AZ, 26 June 1922). Organ builder. In 1883, his family moved to Los Angeles, and he briefly worked for Samuel Symonds, an organ installer for George S. Hutchings of Boston. Encouraged by Symonds, in 1888 he went to Boston, where he spent six years learning the trade with the Hutchings firm. He returned to Los Angeles in 1894, when he formed a partnership with Henry C. Fletcher, and in the same year built a small organ for the Church of the Ascension in Sierra Madre. This partnership dissolved in 1897, shortly after the completion of an organ for B'nai B'rith Synagogue in Los Angeles. In 1898, after a short-lived partnership with George L. Maxfield, Harris began building organs under his own name and soon was getting contracts for significant organs, including those for First Methodist Church, Los Angeles (1899), and the chapel of Stanford University (1901). In this period he was experimenting with pneumatic and electric actions and by 1902 is said to have had a staff of about 50. By 1903 he had contracted to build a large organ for the St. Louis Exposition but was encountering financial difficulties, and the following year he left the company, which reorganized as the Los Angeles Art Organ Co. In 1906 Harris incorporated under the name of Murray M. Harris Co. in a new factory and soon was again building substantial organs with electro-pneumatic action, including those for Pasadena Presbyterian Church (1908) and St. Paul's Cathedral, Los Angeles (1911). By 1913 he was again in financial distress; his assets were sold to the Johnson Piano & Organ Co. and he retired. Harris is regarded as a pioneer of the organ industry in California, as well as an innovator. The St. Louis organ, designed and begun by Harris but completed by the Los Angeles Art firm, later became the core of the celebrated concert organ in Wanamaker's Philadelphia department store.

BIBLIOGRAPHY
"Organ Building on the Pacific Coast," *Music,* xv (Nov 1898), 89–91
E.C. Hopkins: "Organ Building in the Southwest," *American Organist,* ix (March 1926), 62
J. Lewis: "The History of the Murray M. Harris Co.," *The Bicentennial Tracker,* ed. A.F. Robinson (Richmond, VA, 1976), 110–14
D.L. Smith: *Murray M. Harris and Organ Building in Los Angeles, 1894–1913* (Richmond, VA, 2005)
J. Lewis: *Forgotten Organ Builders of Old California 1855–1900* (Exeter, NH, 2012)
                                             BARBARA OWEN

Harris, Rebert H. (*b* Trinity, TX, 23 March 1916; *d* Chicago, IL, 3 Sept 2000). Gospel singer. He began singing in the Harris Christian Methodist Church, Trinity (named after his father who was pastor there), and when he was ten formed a family group, the Friendly Five, with his brothers and cousins; their repertory included a song Harris wrote at the age of eight, "Everybody ought to love his soul." He attended Mary Allen Seminary in Crockett, Texas, for two years, but he left in 1936 to join the SOUL STIRRERS. The membership of the group at that time was Harris (lead), Ernest D. Roundless (tenor), Silas Roy Crain (second tenor), Mozelle Franklin (baritone), and Jesse J. Farley (bass). Harris soon gained a reputation as a "sweet" singer, his clear tenor-baritone voice leading the group in even-tempered renditions of gospel ballads and jubilee songs. The Soul Stirrers moved to Houston in the late 1930s and settled in Chicago in the early 1940s, where they became one of the leading gospel groups. Harris's style greatly influenced other gospel performers, including Sam Cooke (who assumed the leadership of the Soul Stirrers when Harris retired in 1955), the soul singer Johnnie Taylor (a member of the Highway QC's, a gospel group formed by former members of the Soul Stirrers), Archie Brownlee, and Kylo Turner, a member of the Pilgrim Travelers. In 1944 Harris formed the National Quartet Convention of America (subsequently called the National Singing Quartet Convention). Harris continued to sing in other capacities, both as a member of the Gospel Paraders (in 1960) and later with the Masonic Quintet. His final professional recording, the album *Because He Lives* (1978), contained several gospel favorites and brought him more accolades. He was inducted into the Rock and Roll Hall of Fame in 1989 as part of the Soul Stirrers.

BIBLIOGRAPHY
T. Heilbut: *The Gospel Sound: Good News and Bad Times* (New York, 1971/*R*1975)
D. Seroff: "On the Battlefield: Gospel Quartets in Jefferson County, Alabama," *Repercussions: a Celebration of African-American Music,* ed. G. Haydon and D. Marks (London, 1985)
Obituary: *New York Times,* 9 Sept 2000
                          HORACE CLARENCE BOYER/JONAS WESTOVER

Harris, Roy [LeRoy] **(Ellsworth)** (*b* nr Chandler, OK, 12 Feb 1898; *d* Santa Monica, CA, 1 Oct 1979). Composer. He was one of the most important figures in the establishment of an American symphonic music. His works reflect a broad historical and international frame of reference while also conveying a strongly nationalist stance through the influence of Anglo-American folk tunes and other materials relating to the American ethos.

1. Life. 2. Works. 3. Style.

1. LIFE. Harris was reared on a homestead claimed during one of the Oklahoma land rushes. In 1903 the family moved to the San Gabriel Valley, where Harris farmed with his father, eventually earning his own land. During his teens he shortened his given name to Roy. While also active in a variety of sports, he received his first music instruction, on the piano, from his mother; later he took up the clarinet. Harris recalled being profoundly affected by the sounds of nature, by train whistles echoing in the valley, and by the changing light of the countryside's sunrises and sunsets, which affected his ideas about fine gradations in harmonic color. He repeatedly referred to his agricultural background when explaining his ideas about musical form, melodic development, and the creative process more generally.

After graduating from high school in 1916, Harris studied at what is now UCLA (1917) and the University of California, Berkeley (1918, 1921), where he first attempted large-scale composition. During 1924–5 he studied with ARTHUR FARWELL, who encouraged him and introduced him to Walt Whitman's poetry, of which he later made numerous settings. Among his other early teachers and advisers were Clifford Demorest, Ernest Douglas, Alec Anderson, FANNIE CHARLES DILLON, HENRY SCHOENEFELD, Modest Altschuler, and Arthur Bliss. In 1926 he traveled east for the premiere of his orchestral Andante, staying at the MacDowell Colony, where he met Aaron Copland, who encouraged him to study with NADIA BOULANGER. He did so from 1926 to 1929, with financial assistance from Alma Wertheim and, in 1927 and 1929, from Guggenheim Fellowships (he received a third in 1975). Under Boulanger's tutelage, he wrote his Concerto for Piano, Clarinet and String Quartet, whose premiere in Paris established him as one of the more promising young American composers. Though he distanced himself from many aspects of neo-classicism, preferring to consider himself a "contemporary classicist," he shared with other Boulanger students an interest in form, counterpoint, and melodic line. The figures to whom he acknowledged the greatest debt during these years were Bach, Beethoven, Josquin, Lassus, and other Renaissance polyphonists.

In 1929 he injured his spine in a fall and returned to the United States. Immobilized following surgery, he learned to compose away from the piano, refining his concepts of melody, harmony, and texture. After convalescing he taught at Mills College and received a creative fellowship from the Pasadena Music and Art Association (both 1931–2). His first national recognition

came through Koussevitzky, for whom he wrote his first symphony, the *Symphony 1933,* and in 1935 he was the first composer to be featured in the Composers' Forum-Laboratory concerts. In 1934 he joined the Juilliard summer faculty and met Beula Duffey, a young Canadian pianist and faculty colleague. They were married in October 1936 (Harris had had three previous marriages, the first producing a daughter, and an extramarital liaison resulting in a son). The composer renamed his bride Johana, after J.S. Bach. The couple had five children between 1943 and 1957.

In addition to managing household tasks and keeping up a substantial teaching and performing career, Johana often served as technical consultant on her husband's piano writing, assisting in rendering it more idiomatic and, in the case of a very few works, even suggesting keyboard textures or expanding on designs established by the composer (e.g. in the *American Ballads* and the Fantasy for Organ, Brass, and Timpani). She also contributed valuable help in revisions of piano parts; however, claims that Johana's contributions went much further, to the point of composing under her husband's name (Spizizen, 1993) remain justifiably contested.

After teaching briefly at Mills College (1933), Harris held positions at the Westminster Choir School (later College; 1934–8) and Juilliard (summers only, 1934–8). He also taught at Cornell University (1941–3), Colorado College (1943–8), Utah State Agricultural College (1948–9), Peabody College for Teachers (1949–50), Pennsylvania College for Women [Chatham College] (1951–6), Southern Illinois University (1956–7), Indiana University (1957–60), Universidad Interamericana de Puerto Rico (San Germán, 1960–61), UCLA (1961–70), University of the Pacific (1963–4), and California State University, Los Angeles (1970–76). Among his best known pupils were WILLIAM SCHUMAN and PETER SCHICKELE. His teaching was idiosyncratic, involving adaptations of the church modes and examinations of individual compositions, including his own work in progress.

Besides teaching, he organized numerous music festivals, the most ambitious being the 1952 Pittsburgh International Festival of Contemporary Music. He also founded the International Congress of Strings in 1959, served as chief of music programming for the overseas branch of the Office of War Information (1945–8), and visited the USSR in a delegation of American composers sponsored by the US State Department (1958).

Harris was assertive to the point of egocentrism, bold and earthy in temperament, capable of both great anger and robust humor. His behavior was also sometimes erratic and some who knew him saw marked mood swings. This has led a few observers to suggest that he suffered from some form of bipolar disorder, though he was never officially examined or diagnosed. Whatever the case may be, the force of Harris's personality won him both friends and detractors over the course of his long career.

Although Harris's popularity declined during the 1950s and 1960s, interest in him revived during his last years, particularly during the run-up to the US Bicentennial in 1976. In 1973, the Roy Harris Archive (now

Roy Harris. (Lebrecht Music & Arts)

the Roy Harris Collection) was established at California State University, Los Angeles, and in 1979 a Roy Harris Society was formed to promote performances, recordings, publications, and research, achieving success in some of these areas during its short life. More recently, Harris's daughter, Patricia, has donated important documents to the Library of Congress.

2. WORKS. Harris composed over two hundred works in a wide variety of genres, but his symphonies and chamber music have earned the highest regard. Characterized by broad, at times rhetorical, gestures and visionary aspiration, these works contain some of his most striking music as well as characteristic flaws. Early in his career, he determined to write only on commission. Many of his published and unpublished scores are interrelated through shared material (Stehman 1973, 1984, 1991).

Possibly Harris's most significant contribution to the symphonic literature was his exploration of the single-movement form. Four of his roughly thirteen symphonies (nos. 3, 7, 8, and 11) employ this design, most containing recurring melodic ideas that help create unity. In his multi-movement symphonies the tempos and characters of the individual movements sometimes correspond with classical models, though the forms often differ and vocal parts or narration are occasionally incorporated. The Third Symphony (1938) is the best known and most often performed, but nos. 4, 5, 6, 7, and 8 are worthy of more detailed investigation and

more frequent performance. Many of Harris's Symphonies refer to elements of American music and culture, including the choral *Folksong Symphony* (no.4), the "Gettysburg" Symphony (no.6), the "San Francisco" Symphony (no.8), the "Abraham Lincoln" Symphony (no.10), the "Pere Marquette Symphony" (no.12), and the "Bicentennial" Symphony 1976 (no.13). In similar fashion, nearly all the shorter orchestral and band works bear descriptive titles. They are uneven in quality, but the finest, such as *Cimarron, Chorale for Strings, Epilogue to Profiles in Courage–JFK, Kentucky Spring, Memories of a Child's Sunday, Ode to Friendship, Symphonic Epigram, Time Suite,* and *When Johnny Comes Marching Home,* contain many felicities and much skillful craftsmanship.

Harris's chamber compositions tend to be more intensively polyphonic than the orchestral works, with greater independence in the individual parts. Most are for strings, from which the composer sometimes demanded an almost orchestral sonority. The most substantial works include the Piano Quintet, the String Quartets nos. 2 and 3, the Violin and Violoncello Sonatas, and *Soliloquy and Dance* for viola and piano. The Third Quartet, a set of preludes and fugues on modal subjects, exemplifies Harris's individual approaches to modality and counterpoint. The Quintet, in three interconnected movements based largely on a single theme, has an expansive breadth of architecture and great intensity of expression. For this score, Harris chose thematic material that contained all twelve pitches of the chromatic scale but emphasized tonality and "autogenetic" unfolding; in so doing, he sought to set himself apart from both Schoenbergian serialism and Stravinskian neo-classicism.

In his concerted works Harris did not always fully exploit the idiomatic resources of the solo instruments; nevertheless, he created works of depth and polish, such as the Fantasy for Piano and Orchestra, and the Two-Piano Concerto, sometimes using a one-movement form incorporating variation procedures. His small number of solo piano works includes a group of folksong arrangements, *American Ballads.* The Piano Sonata (1928) exhibits the lean textures, angular lines, rhythmic complexity, and grandeur that mark his early works.

Choral compositions form an important part of Harris's output. His early efforts are somewhat instrumental in nature, with occasionally awkward prosody, but many of the pieces written as he matured reveal sensitivity and practicality gained from experience in writing for both amateur and professional groups. Notable are the Symphony for Voices and the *Folksong Symphony* (no.4); the former features some affecting onomatopoetic writing and one of the great 20th-century choral fugues, while the latter reveals a high level of technical skill and demonstrates colorful variety in its symphonic treatment of ethnically diverse folksong materials. In addition to works for choir and band and a mass setting for men's voices and organ (based on folk songs of the American southwest), Harris's vocal scores also include a few exquisitely crafted and deeply expressive songs (notably a setting of Sandburg's *Fog*) and some substantial solo cantatas. Of these, *Abraham Lincoln Walks at Midnight* and *Give Me the Splendid Silent Sun* represent a peak in his creativity, craftsmanship (especially in the integration of contrasts within gradually unfolding large structures), and handling of prosody.

Apart from some dance collaborations with Hanya Holm during his years at Colorado College, Harris showed little interest in collaborative works for the theater or for film, finding it difficult to reconcile his autogenetic technique with sudden changes of scene and character or the musical depiction of specific actions. Nevertheless, the ballet *From this Earth* and the film score *One-Tenth of a Nation* contain many distinctive ideas and textures that effectively amplify the emotional resonance of the underlying drama.

3. STYLE. Harris's melodies, in their contours, modality, and flexibility of phrase structure, owe a debt to monophonic chant, Renaissance choral polyphony, Anglo-American folk music, African American spirituals, and early Protestant hymnody. He employed a "polytonal" adaptation of the church modes, in which melodic phrases are often based on a combination of different modes built on the same tonic, this making available pleasantly varied inflections of particular scale degrees.

Harris based his mature harmonic idiom on the overtone series, considering it his mission to explore "modern consonance" as so many others had explored dissonance. The most important intervals were for him the perfect fourth and fifth (his "organum" sonorities). His earliest surviving compositions, however, at times suggest the influence of Franck and Skryabin, possibly owing to his studies in France. During the 1930s he pared his vocabulary to the major and minor triads, and from the mid-1940s these were generally used in polychords for which he developed a classification within a harmonic spectrum ranging from "savage dark" to "savage bright" (Evett 1946). On this spectrum, he ranked both polychords and the three positions of a triad based on the degree to which the upper notes of the chord are reinforced by the overtones of the lowest note. His chord movement is founded on an extended set of relationships derived from the dominant and subdominant areas of a given tonal center by means of common-tone connections. Root movement is often by thirds, though fourths, fifths, and seconds also appear, particularly at cadences. Harris believed that "harmony should represent what is in the melody, without being enslaved by the tonality in which the melody lies." Thus one sometimes experiences a tension between the harmonic implications of the melody, with its prevailing modal mixtures, and the supporting chords. Nonetheless, he considered harmony an important tool not just for supporting melodies or giving a piece architectural form but also for creating and controlling overall resonance.

The fundamental formal principle in Harris's music is autogenesis, through which a melody is generated by a seed motif out of which the first phrase grows, each succeeding phrase either germinating in like fashion or launching itself from a figure in the last bars of the preceding phrase. His aim was to produce an effect of gradual organic growth, and thus the music often unfolds additively in blocks of gradually differing textures. In terms of rhythm, this often means that phrase length is exceptionally fluid. In many instances, passages begin with slow, lyrical long notes and gradually introduce smaller values, which eventually prevail; fast music usually features a more even distribution of note-values within phrases and sometimes employs asymmetrical meters. Though some of this livelier music contains sharp contrasts, these are difficult to manage within the organic principles of Harris's formal aesthetics. Other forms and procedures Harris used are theme and variations, fugue (often a hybrid fugue-variation type), and ternary form (either ABA or ABC), in many cases modified to reconcile these designs with his autogenetic precepts.

In the treatment of polyphony, Harris's early works are deeply indebted to traditional practice, sometimes producing awkward harmonic results but with careful attention to the unfolding of individual lines. In his mature idiom, the counterpoint emerges from a clearer harmonic background, though occasionally at the expense of melodic variety or rhythmic independence among the parts.

Harris's orchestration is clear, even lean in his early scores, with little doubling of parts. Motifs and figurations are idiomatically conceived for the instruments. His layout is generally conventional, but in some scores from the 1940s on he used saxophones, baritone horn, and a grouping of piano, harp, chimes, and vibraphone that provided bell-like, chordal punctuation. In addition to his orchestral achievements, Harris was a pioneer in exploring the resources of the concert band. Overall, he preferred to score in discrete choirs. He treated the strings especially flexibly, allotting them both extensive melodic and accompanimental functions, usually with a complete harmonic texture. An increasing use of *divisi* during the 1940s and 1950s imparts a growing lushness to the sound. In his brass writing, he often liked to play the "sharp-tone" instruments (trumpets and trombones) against the "round-tone" ones (horns, baritone horn, tuba).

In addition to using folk tunes in arrangements and as thematic materials, Harris employed other strategies for evoking the American scene, including allusions to popular dance rhythms and elements of jazz, and texts drawn from Whitman and Lincoln. Many of his compositions are programmatic or based on folk figures, incorporating traits that Harris believed to be particularly "American," or celebrating patriotic occasions. For much of his career he tended to depict in such music an idealized vision of America, but later he tempered this with a great awareness of contemporary problems, sometimes engaging in biting social commentary to express his commitment to racial equality and justice as, for example, in his score for chorus and band, *Whether This Nation*.

Harris was a prodigious reviser and self-borrower, reworking themes, and even entire compositions, in creating new pieces. This resulted from a sometimes wavering technique and a lack of firm self-criticism when composing (though he could be ruthless once a work was finished). His music reveals a dual nature: in addition to the miniaturist represented by his unaccompanied choral pieces and short piano compositions, there is the extrovert, "civic" composer whose music suggests, especially through its steady, organic growth, a visionary aspiration marked by large gestures and great thematic expanses.

Widely acclaimed in the 1930s and 1940s, Harris's stature is still a matter for debate. Many of his works remain unpublished and unrecorded, though an increase in recording activity in recent years has begun to remedy this. Some observers believe he failed to fulfil his early promise, suffering an arrested technical and stylistic development, while others perceive an increasing mastery of technique and a growing sophistication (sometimes at the expense of raw originality and vitality of the earlier works) as his career unfolded. Whatever the verdict, the musicality, breadth of vision, and generosity of impulse that form Harris's best music stand as testament to mid-century optimism, and the longer course of his career reflects a courageous engagement with every aspect of American musical life.

WORKS
DRAMATIC
One-Tenth of a Nation (film score), A, chbr ens, 1940; rec. New York, cAug 1940

From this Earth (ballet, 5 scenes), chbr en, 1941; Colorado Springs, 7 Aug 1941

Namesake (A Theatre Dance) (ballet, 9 scenes), vn, pf, 1942; Colorado Springs, 8 Aug 1942, 4 movts pubd as 4 Charming Little Pieces, vn, pf

What so Proudly we Hail (Dance Suite Based on American Folk Songs) (ballet, 5 scenes), wordless vv, str, pf, 1942, scene 4 lost; Colorado Springs, 8 Aug 1942

Ballet on the Subject of War [? = Walt Whitman Suite]

Turn on the Night (Crocodile Smile) (incid music, J. Lawrence, R.E. Lee), chbr ens, 1961; Philadelphia, 7 Aug 1961

ORCHESTRAL WITHOUT SOLOISTS
Andante 1925, rev. 1926 [for projected sym. "Our Heritage"]; American Portrait 1929, sym., 1929, rev. 1931; Concert Piece, 1930 or 1932; Andantino, 1931, rev. 1932; Toccata 1931; Ov. "From the Gayety and Sadness of the American Scene," 1932; Sym. 1933 (Sym. no.1), 1933; Sym. no.2, 1934; When Johnny Comes Marching Home (An American Ov.), 1934, rev.; Farewell to Pioneers: a Sym. Elegy, 1935; Prelude and Fugue, 1936, rev.; Time Suite, 1937, movts 2–4 extracted as 3 Sym. Essays; Sym. no.3, 1938, rev. 1938; American Sym., 1938, inc.; Prelude and Fugue, 4 tpt, 1939 [arr. of Prelude and Fugue no.1 from Str Qt no.3]

American Creed, 1940; Acceleration, 1941, rev. 1941; Ode to Truth, 1941; 3 Pieces, 1941 [nos. 1 and 3 from Folksong Sym.], no.2 extracted as Evening Piece; Work, 1941; Fanfare for the Forces, c1942; Folk Rhythms of Today, 1942, rev.; Sym. no.5, 1942, rev.; March in Time of War, 1943; Sym. no.6 "Gettysburg," 1944

Chorale, 1944; Ode to Friendship, 1944, rev. c1945; Memories of a Child's Sunday, 1945, rev.; Mirage, 1945; Variation on a Theme by Goossens, 1945 [Variation 7 of 10, each by a different composer]; Children's Hour, 1946; Celebration Variations on a Timp Theme from Howard Hanson's Third Sym., 1946; Melody, 1946; Radio Piece, pf, orch, 1946; The Quest, 1947; Kentucky Spring, 1949; Cumberland Conc. for Orch, 1951; Sym. no.7, 1952, rev. 1955; Sym. Epigram, 1954; Sym. Fantasy, 1954; Ode to Consonance, 1956; Elegy and

Dance, 1958, rev.; Sym. no.8 "San Francisco," 1962; Sym. no.9, 1962; These Times, pf, small orch, 1963; Epilogue to Profiles in Courage–JFK, 1964, rev. 1964

Horn of Plenty, 1964; Salute to Youth, 1964; Rhythms and Spaces, 1965 [arr. of 3 Vars. on a Theme (Str Qt no.2)]; Sym. no.11, 1967

BAND
Sad Song, jazz band [mvt 2 of inc. American Sym., perf. independently], 1938; Cimarron, sym. ov., 1941; When Johnny Comes Marching Home, 1941; Rhythms of Today, 1942, rev., (arr. L. Intravaia), c1946; Conflict (War Piece), 1944; Sun and Stars, 1944; Fruit of Gold, 1949; Dark Devotion, 1950; Kentucky Jazz Piece, 1950; Sym. "West Point," 1952; Ad majorem gloriam Universitatis Illinorum, tone poem, 1958; Bicentennial Aspirations, 1976, inc.

CONCERTED WORKS
Conc., pf, str, 1936 [arr. of Pf Qnt]; Conc. V, 1938, scoring inc., withdrawn; Conc., pf, band, 1942; Chorale, org, brass, 1943; Fantasia, band, pf, 1943; Conc. no.1, pf, 1944; Toccata, org, brass, 1944; Conc., 2 pf, orch, 1946; Theme and Vars., acc., orch, 1947; Elegy and Paean, va, orch, 1948; Vn Conc., 1949; Fantasy, pf, "Pops" orch, c1951; Conc. no.2, pf, 1953; Fantasy, orch, pf, 1954; Fantasy, org, brass, timp, 1964; Conc. amp pf, brass, db per 1968; movt 1 lost, movts 2–3 released as Concert Piece

CHORAL
With orch/band: Challenge 1940 (Harris, US Constitution), Bar, SATB, orch, 1940; Folksong Sym. (Sym. no.4) (US trad., P.S. Gilmore [L. Lambert]), 1940, 1942; Railroad Man's Ballad (T.L. Siebert, after ragtime ballad Casey Jones), SATB, orch, 1941; Freedom's Land (A. MacLeish), Bar, SATB, orch, 1941, also for male vv, band, 2 versions, 1942; Sammy's Fighting Sons (Harris), unison vv, orch, 1942, pubd as Sons of Uncle Sam, unison vv, pf; Rock of Ages (trad.), SATB, orch, 1944; Take the Sun and Keep the Stars (Harris), unison vv, band, 1944, arr. band, 1944, fs lost [Official Battle Anthem of the Second Army Air Force]

Blow the Man Down (US trad., A. Tennyson), Ct, Bar, SATB, orch, 1946; Red Cross Hymn (Harris), chorus, band, c1951; The Hustle with the Muscle (Harris), male vv, band, 1957; Sym. no.10 "Abraham Lincoln" (Harris, Lincoln), speaker, SATB, brass, 2 pf, perc, 1965, movts 1–3 rev. unison vv, pf, 1965, rev., SATB, orch, 1967, lost; The Brotherhood of Man (Declaration of Independence, Lincoln), SATB, orch, 1966; Whether this Nation (Harris, S. Harris, MacLeish), SATB, band, 1971; America, We Love Your People (Harris), SATB, band, 1975; Bicentennial Sym. 1976 (Sym. no.13) (US Constitution, Harris, Lincoln), SATB, orch, 1975–6

With insts: Fantasy (Sp.-Amer. trad.), SATB, str trio, c1925, lost; Song Cycle (W. Whitman), female vv, 2 pf, 1927; Freedom's Land (MacLeish), unison vv/1v, pf, 1941; Our Fighting Sons (Harris), unison vv, brass, pf, org, timp, c1943–4; Walt Whitman Suite, SATB, str qt, 1944; Alleluia (Motet for Easter), SATB, brass, org, 1945, rev. SATB, org, 1946, rev. SATB, str, org, 1947; Mi chomocho (Moshe uvnay Yisroel) (Bible), T/Bar, SATB, org, 1946

They say that Susan has no heart for learning (Harris), SSA, pf, 1947, rev. Bar, SSA, pf, 1953; Mass (Ordinarium Missum) male vv, org, 1948; Remember November (Election Day is Action Day) (F. Shorring), unison vv, pf 4 hands, 1952, rev. Bar/spkr, male vv, pf, 1952; Pep Song (R. Zetler), unison vv, pf, 1955, lost; Each Hand Has Need (?Harris), SATB/SATB, org, c1956

Folk Fantasy for Festivals (Bible, Ainsworth Psalter, US trad., Harris), folk singers, solo vv, spkrs, SSAATTBB, pf, 1956; Our Tense and Wintry Minds (H. Carruth), unison vv, org, 1956; Read, Sweet, how Others Strove (E. Dickinson), SATB, org, 1956; Jubilate for Worship (Alleluia, single-word text) SATB, brass, pf, perc, 1964; Peace and Goodwill to All (Peace and Goodwill to All: single-phrase text), SATB, brass, org, perc, 1970

Unacc.: A Song for Occasions (Whitman), 1934; Sym. for Voices (Whitman), 1935; Sanctus, 1937; When Johnny Comes Marching Home (Gilmore [Lambert]), 1937; He's gone away (US trad.), 1938; Whitman Triptych, 1938; A Red-Bird in a Green Tree (trad.), 1940; Choral Fanfare (G. Taggard), 1939; Ps xxxii, harmonized late 1930s, rev. G. Lynn as Gethsemane (W. Wilcox), 1933; To Thee, Old Cause (Whitman), 1941; Year that Trembled (Whitman), 1941; Freedom's Land (MacLeish), male vv/female vv, pf/org ad lib/SATB, 1941

Freedom, Toleration (The Open Air I Sing) (Whitman), 1941; The Bird's Courting Song (US trad.), 1942; Work Song (railroad work song), B-Bar, SATB, 1943; A War Song of Democracy (Harris), unison vv, c1942, lost; Li'l boy named David (spiritual), 1943; Cindy (US trad.), 1949; If I had a ribbon bow (US trad.), 1949; Ps cl, 1957

CHAMBER

Impressions of a Rainy Day, str qt, 1925, lost; Conc., pf, cl, str qt, 1926; str qt no.1, 1929; Conc., 2 vn, 2 va, 2 vc, 1932; Fantasy, wind int, pf, 1932; Three Vars. on a Theme (Str Qt no.2), 1933; 4 Minutes–20 Seconds, fl, str qt, 1934; Pf Trio, 1934; Poem, vn, pf, 1935, lost
Pf Qnt 1936; Str qt no.3 (4 Preludes and Fugues), 1937; Soliloquy and Dance, va, pf, 1938; Str Qnt, 1940; 4 Charming Little Pieces, vn, pf 1942 [from ballet Namesake]; Sonata, vn, pf, 1941; Lyric Studies, solo ww, pf, 1950; Sonata vc, 1964, rev. 1968, rev. as Duo, 1975; Childhood Memories of Ocean Moods, pf, str qt, db, 1966, rev. 1967

SOLO VOCAL

Evening Song (Tennyson), 1v, pf, 1940; La Primavera (Sp.-Amer. trad.), 1v, pf, 1940; Freedom's Land (MacLeish), 1v/unison vv, pf, 1941, [also choral]; Waitin' (Harris), 1v, pf, 1941; Lamentation (textless), S, va, pf, 1944; Take the Sun and the Stars (Official Battle Anthem of the Second Army Air Force) (Harris), 1v, pf, 1944; Fog (Sandburg), 1v pf, 1945; Wedding Song (K. Gibran), B, str trio, org, 1947
Abraham Lincoln Walks at Midnight (cant., V. Lindsay), Mez, pf trio, 1954; Give me the Splendid Silent Sun (cant., Whitman), Bar, orch, 1955, rev. 1956; Canticle of the Sun (cant., St Francis), S, 11 insts, 1961; Sweet and Low (Tennyson), 1v, pf, 1962; Sym. no.12 "Pere Marquette" (Lat. mass, Bible), T/spkr, orch, 1968, rev. 1969; Cantata to Life (K. Gibran), S, wind, perc, db, 1973; Rejoice and Sing (Bible, Whitman), B, str qt, pf, 1976, arr. Mez, str qt, pf, 1977

KEYBOARD

Pf: Sonata, 1928, rev.; Little Suite, 1938; Suite in 3 Movts, 1939–c1942; American Ballads, 2 sets, 1942–5; True Love Don't Weep (Vars. on an Amer. Folk Song), c1944; Toccata, 1949 [based on withdrawn 1939 Toccata]
Org: Chorale, 1946 [arr. G. Lynn from Conc., str sextet, 1938; F. Tulon, 1964; ?J. Kirkpatrick, pf 4 hands]; Alleluia (Motet for Easter), arr. 1946; Etudes for Pedals, 1964, rev. 1972

ARRANGEMENTS AND TRANSCRIPTIONS

J.S. Bach: The Art of the Fugue, str qt, 1934, collab. M.D.H. Norton [omits canons and 2 fugues]
J.S. Bach: 5 Chorales: 1 Bestir Thyself, 2 In dulci jubilo, 3 Joyful Sing, 4 O God, Thou Holy God, 5 O God Enthroned, chorus, band, early 1940s
J.S. Bach: Organ Preludes: 1 Komm, Gott, Schöpfer, heiliger Geist, 2 Christ lag in Todesbanden, 3 Das alte Jahr vergangen ist, 4 Liebster Jesu, wir sind hier, 5 In dulci jubilo, pf, collab. J. Harris, c1946
J.S. Bach: Prelude and Fugue S. 532, pf, collab. J. Harris
J.S. Bach: Fl Sonata no.1: Largo, wind qnt, 1932, lost
J.S. Bach: "48," i: Prelude and Fugue no.16, small orch 1932
F. Couperin: 4 Pieces, wind qnt, 1932, lost
S. Foster: Old Black Joe, SATB, c1938
J.B. Lully: 2 operatic numbers, S, str orch, pf, 1934
J.J. Niles: The Story of Norah, SATB, 1933
J.S. Smith: The Star-Spangled Banner, str qt, 1941–2
M.J. Hill: Happy Birthday, 1951 [for Mary Zimbalist]
J. Sweelinck: Fantasia, d, orch, mid-1930s
4 songs orchd for Shaun Harris Record Album, 1973

EDITIONS

R. Harris and J. Evanson, eds.: Singing Through the Ages (New York, 1940) [anthology]
Various edns of choral works by P. Dumonte, H. Hassler, R. Lahmer, C. LeJeune, A. Lotti, G. Lynn, G. Pitoni, I. Strom, J. Sweelinck, G. Verdi, c1935–45, some lost

MSS in LAcs, Wc, NYpl
Principal publishers: Associated, Belwin-Mills, C. Fischer, Golden, T. Presser, G. Schirmer, Shawnee, Warner, EMI

BIBLIOGRAPHY

P. Rosenfeld: An Hour with American Music (Philadelphia, 1929), 117–25
A. Farwell: "Roy Harris," MQ xviii (1932), 18–32
H. Cowell: "Roy Harris," American Composers on American Music: A Symposium (New York, 1933/R), 64–9
W. Piston: "Roy Harris," MM xii (1934–5), 73–83
P.H. Reed: "Roy Harris: American Composer," American Music Lover, iii (1938), 406–10
A. Mendel: "The Quintet of Roy Harris," MM xii/1 (1939), 25–28
R. Harris: "Perspective at Forty," Magazine of Art, xxxii (1939), 638–9, 667–71
R. Harris: "Folksong: American Big Business," MM xviii (1940–41), 8–11; repr. in E. Schwartz and B. Childs, eds.: Contemporary Composers on Contemporary Music (New York, 1967), 160–64
A. Copland: The New Music (New York, 1941, rev. 2/1968 as Our New Music), 118–26
R. Evett: "The Harmonic Idiom of Roy Harris," MM xiii (1946), 100–7
N. Slonimsky: "Roy Harris," MQ xxxiii (1947), 17–37
N. Slonimsky: Roy Harris: Cimarron Composer (MS, CLU-MUS, 1951)
R. Harris: "Composing: an Art and a Living," Music Journal, xi/1 (1953), 31, 78
G. Chase: America's Music: from the Pilgrims to the Present (New York, 1955, rev. 3/1987), 570–71, 574–8
R. Sabin: "Roy Harris: Still Buoyant as Composer and Teacher," Musical America lxxvii/2 (1957), 17, 24–5
M. Evans: Dialogues I and II (MS, CLU, c1968) [interviews]
P. Ashley: "Roy Harris," Stereo Review xxi/6 (1968), 63–73
D. Stehman: The Symphonies of Roy Harris: an Analysis of the Linear Materials and of Related Works (diss., U. of Southern California, 1973)
L.C. Gibbs and D. Stehman: "The Roy Harris Revival," American Record Guide, xlii (1979), no.7, p.8; no.8, p.4
R. Stevenson: "Roy Harris at UCLA: Neglected Documentation," Inter-American Music Review ii/1 (1979), 59–73
Roy Harris: A Life in Music, BBC documentary, dir. P. Bartlett (1980)
B. Zuck: A History of Musical Americanism (Ann Arbor, 1980)
M. Bialosky: "Roy Harris: In Memoriam (But Keep Your Hats On)," CMS xxii (1982), 7–19
R. Harris: Composer of American Music. Oral History Program, University of California, Los Angeles (1983), interviewed by D.J. Schippers (1962) and A.G. Tusler (1966, 1968, and 1969)
W.D. Curtis: "Roy Harris (1898–1979): a Discography," Journal [Association for Recorded Sound Collections], xiii/3 (1982), 60–79; repr. and rev. in D. Stehman: Roy Harris: a Bio-Bibliography (New York, 1991)
N. Strimple: "An Introduction to the Choral Music of Roy Harris," Choral Journal xxii/9 (1982), 16–19
D. Stehman: Roy Harris: An American Musical Pioneer (Boston, 1984)
D. Stehman and L.C. Gibbs: "Roy Harris," Ovation v/6 (1984–5), 14–19
D. Stehman: Roy Harris: a Bio-bibliography (New York, 1991)
L. Spizizen: "Johana and Roy Harris: Marrying a Real Composer," MQ xxvii (1993), 579–606; see also response by D. Stehman, MQ lxxviii (1994), 637–9
M.D. Robertson: "Roy Harris's Symphonies: an Introduction," part I Tempo ccvii (1998), 9–14
American Creed: The Art of Roy Harris, radio documentary, produced E. Blair (Washington DC, 1998)
D. von Glahn: The Sounds of Place: Music and the American Cultural Landscape (Boston, 2004)
E. Paquin: Johana Harris: a Biography (Lanham, MD, 2011)
B. Levy: Frontier Figures: American Music and the Mythology of the American West (Berkeley, 2012)

DAN STEHMAN/BETH E. LEVY

Harris, (William) Victor (b New York, NY, 27 April 1869; d New York, NY, 15 Feb 1943). Conductor, composer, and pianist. As a child, he sang boy soprano in several churches, singing solos in many oratorios and cantatas. He studied piano with Charles Blum, singing with

William Courtney, composition with Frederick Schilling, and conducting with ANTON SEIDL, and he began his career as an organist at various churches in the New York area. He was a rehearsal pianist and coach at the Metropolitan Opera (1892–5), conductor of the Utica Choral Union (1893–4), and assistant conductor to Seidl at the Brighton Beach Summer Concerts (1895–6); after 1899 he devoted himself primarily to teaching and composing. He also enjoyed a strong reputation as an accompanist, appearing frequently with major concert artists. He was particularly supportive of new music of his era, championing Arthur Foote and others. From 1902 to 1936 Harris gained considerable fame as the conductor (and founder) of New York City's St. Cecilia Club, which boasted one of the finest ensembles of women's voices in the country, and under his leadership its concerts became major musical events. As a composer he is best remembered for his many solo songs, such as "Just as it Used to Do" (1906), though his published works also include several quartets for male and female voices and a cantata; a suite for piano and several orchestral works survive in manuscript. Clearly inspired by the popular Romanticism of his day, his part-writing was especially skillful, prompting a commission by the widow of Ethelbert Nevin for choral arrangements of her husband's songs.

BIBLIOGRAPHY
"Victor Harris," *MusAm*, xxx/5 (1919), 25
                    WILLIAM GEOFFREY SHAMAN/JONAS WESTOVER

Harris, Wynonie [Mr. Blues] (*b* Omaha, NE, 24 Aug 1913; *d* Oakland, CA, 14 June 1969). Rhythm-and-blues singer. The son of Mallie Hood Anderson and, it appears, a Native American known as "Blue Jay," he gained his surname from his stepfather, Luther Harris. A high-school dropout, he began dancing and singing professionally in the 1930s in Omaha clubs before moving to Los Angeles. There he became a local sensation in the early 1940s, performing frequently at Club Alabam and becoming known as "Mr. Blues." He joined Lucky Millinder's band, with whom he performed in New York, toured, and made his recording debut with "Who Threw the Whiskey in the Well" (Decca, 1944); the song was released in 1945, after Harris and Millinder had parted ways, and hit number one on the rhythm-and-blues chart. He also worked with Lionel Hampton, Johnny Otis, and Oscar Pettiford. From 1947 to 1954 he recorded an extended series of rhythm-and-blues tracks on the King label, for which he has remained best known. Tracks such as his cover of Roy Brown's "Good Rockin' Tonight" (1948) and "All she Wants to Do is Rock" (1949) offer Harris' characteristically risqué tales, with his raspy, belting voice supported by a joyously honking jump-blues band and a heavy backbeat; their titles, lyrics, and sensibility also pointed the way toward rock-and-roll. After his King contract ended, Harris recorded for another decade but never transitioned from his earlier style into one that proved as appealing for newer audiences.

BIBLIOGRAPHY
N. Tosches: "Wynonie Harris: the Man who Shook Down the Devil," *Creem,* xi (Aug 1979), 48
T. Collins: *Rock Mr. Blues: the Life and Music of Wynonie Harris* (Milford, NH, 1995) [incl. discography]
                    CHARLES HIROSHI GARRETT

Harrison, G[eorge] **Donald** (*b* Huddersfield, England, 21 April 1889; *d* New York, NY, 14 June 1956). Organ builder of English birth. He was a graduate of Dulwich College who began his career as a patent attorney before entering the Henry Willis firm of London as an engineer, eventually becoming a director of the firm. In 1927 he immigrated to the United States to work as an engineer for the Skinner Organ Company, then one of the leading firms in the country. In 1931 this growing firm acquired the assets of one of its major rivals, the Aeolian Company, and changed its name to Aeolian-Skinner, and two years later Harrison was appointed technical director. His more eclectic and classically oriented tonal concepts, as exemplified in organs built under his direction, including those for Church of the Advent in Boston (1934) and the Chapel of the Groton School (1935), attracted the attention and support of influential organists such as Ernest White, Carl Weinrich, and E. Power Biggs, with the result that clients increasingly preferred Harrison over Skinner in the tonal design of their organs. Harrison's investigation into neo-Baroque tonal ideas resulted in an "experimental" organ installed in Harvard University's Germanic Museum in 1937 and made famous by Biggs in his weekly organ recital broadcasts. In 1940, a few years after the departure of Skinner from the firm, Harrison became the president of Aeolian-Skinner, and among his significant projects immediately following World War II were the rebuilding of the large organs in Methuen Memorial Music Hall (1946) and the Mormon Tabernacle in Salt Lake City (1947). A number of notable organs followed, including those for Symphony Hall (1949), St. Paul's Cathedral (1950), and the Christian Science Mother Church (1952) in Boston, as well as Riverside Church (1955) in New York. Harrison was engaged in the tonal finishing of another major New York organ in St. Thomas's Church when he succumbed to a fatal heart attack in 1956.

BIBLIOGRAPHY
W.E. Zeuch: "An Appreciation of the Work of G. Donald Harrison," *American Organist,* xvi/9 (1933)
W.K. Covell: "G. Donald Harrison," *MO 79* (1956)
A.L. Vivian: "G. Donald Harrison: a Study of Several of his Organ Designs," *Diapason,* lxix/2 (1978)
J. Ambrosino: "G. Donald Harrison," *American Organist,* xxii/12 (1988)
C. Callahan: *Aeolian-Skinner Remembered* (Minneapolis, 1996)
A. Kinzey& S. Lawn: *E.M. Skinner/Aeolian-Skinner Opus List* (Richmond, VA, 1997)
C.R. Whitney: *All the Stops* (New York, 2003)
                    BARBARA OWEN

Harrison, Guy Fraser (*b* Guildford, England, 6 Nov 1894; *d* San Miguel de Allende, Mexico, 20 Feb 1986). Conductor and organist of English birth. A scholarship to the Royal College of Music in London, won when he was only 16, enabled him to study organ with Walter Parrott, piano with Herbert Sharp, and conducting with Walford Davies. For six years he worked in Manila as a church organist before immigrating to the United States in 1920. He was organist and choirmaster at St. Paul's Cathedral in Rochester, New York (1920–4), and a faculty member of the Eastman School (1922–5, 1944–5). With the encouragement of Albert Coates (director of the Rochester PO, 1923–5), he turned to conducting, first leading the Eastman Theater Orchestra (1924–9). He then conducted the Rochester Civic Orchestra (1929–49), became music director of the Rochester Civic Opera, and from 1930 was associate director of the Rochester PO. In 1951 Harrison was appointed conductor of the Oklahoma City SO; four years later he became its music director, a post he occupied until his retirement in 1972. Active in radio as early as 1929, he broadcast regularly with the Rochester Civic Orchestra and later gave weekly performances with the Oklahoma City SO over the Mutual Broadcasting System. In the latter part of his tenure with this orchestra, he recorded prize-winning compositions by John La Montaine, Spencer Norton, John Pozdro, and Edmund Haines on the CRI label. These exhibit the same broad understanding and careful attention to detail that characterized his earlier mastery of the standard repertory.

BIBLIOGRAPHY
H. Stoddard: "Guy Fraser Harrison," *Symphony Conductors of the U.S.A.* (New York, 1957), 74

WILLIAM GEOFFREY SHAMAN

Harrison, Hazel (Lucile) (*b* La Porte, IN, 12 May 1883; *d* Washington, DC, 28 April 1969). Pianist. She studied as a child with Victor Heinze and played for Ferruccio Busoni during his American tour. She was the first American-trained soloist to appear with a European orchestra (Berlin PO, 22 October 1904, with concertos of Edvard Grieg and Fryderyk Chopin op.11, conducted by August Sharrer). She returned to Germany in 1911 and studied with Hugo von Dalan. Busoni, hearing her again, placed her with his student EGON PETRI. She appeared in recitals in Chicago and several other American cities before making her formal New York debut at Aeolian Hall in May 1922. While teaching at the Tuskegee Institute (1931–6), Howard University (1936–55), Alabama State A & M College (1958–63), and Jackson College, she continued her performing career: she made appearances with the Minneapolis SO under Eugene Ormandy (1932) and with the Hollywood Bowl SO under Izler Solomon (1949), and toured regularly until her retirement in the 1960s.

BIBLIOGRAPHY
J.E. Cazort and C.T. Hobson: *Born to Play: the Life and Career of Hazel Harrison* (Westport, CT, 1983)
D.A. Richardson: "Harrison, Hazel," *Black Women in America: an Historical Encyclopedia*, i, ed. D.C. Hine (New York, 1993), 540–41

DOMINIQUE-RENÉ DE LERMA

Harrison, Jimmy [James Henry] (*b* Louisville, KY, 17 Oct 1900; *d* New York, NY, 23 July 1931). Jazz trombonist and singer. He toured with minstrel shows before moving to New York in 1922. There he played in groups with June Cook, Elmer Snowden, Duke Ellington, and, notably, Fletcher Henderson, with whom he recorded his best work (1927–30). An operation for stomach cancer incapacitated him in 1930, and after attempted comebacks with Henderson and Chick Webb he died while at the height of his powers.

Harrison's sonorous tone, bold ideas, and flexible technique led to his being called the Father of Swing Trombone, and his influence on other jazz trombonists has been lasting. Harrison's outgoing personality enabled him to give successful imitations of the comedian Bert Williams, an example being his performance on Henderson's "Somebody Loves me" (1930). At the time of his death he was developing a more advanced harmonic approach.

BIBLIOGRAPHY
R. Stewart: "The Father of Swing Trombone (Jimmy Harrison)," *Jazz Masters of the Thirties* (New York, 1972/R1980), 51

JOHN CHILTON/R

Harrison, Lou (Silver) (*b* Portland, OR, 14 May 1917; *d* Lafayette, IN, 2 Feb 2003). Composer. He became recognized particularly in three broad areas: music for percussion ensemble, experiments with just intonation, and syntheses of Asian and Western styles. His works at times call for Chinese, Korean, and Indonesian instruments along with Western ones, and many pieces feature instruments of Harrison's own construction. His style is marked by a notable melodicism: even his percussion and 12-tone compositions have a decidedly lyrical flavor.

Harrison spent his formative years in northern California, where his family settled in 1926. Before graduating from Burlingame High School in December 1934, he had studied the piano and violin, sung as a treble soloist, and composed keyboard and chamber works, including several quarter-tone pieces. In 1935 he entered San Francisco State College (now University), and in his three semesters there studied the horn and clarinet, took up the harpsichord and recorder in an early music consort, sang in several vocal ensembles, and composed a number of works for early instruments, including a set of six harpsichord sonatas inspired by the works of Domenico Scarlatti.

In spring 1935 Harrison enrolled in Henry Cowell's course "Music of the Peoples of the World" at the University of California Extension in San Francisco. There he first heard recordings of the Indonesian gamelan, an ensemble for which he would ultimately compose extensively. His fascination with the gamelan was reinforced four years later when he saw a Balinese group at the Golden Gate Exposition on Treasure Island. In 1935 Harrison began private composition lessons with Cowell, with whom he developed an enduring friendship. The following year, at Cowell's suggestion, he wrote to Charles Ives requesting music for performance; after an exchange of correspondence, Harrison received a crate of photostat scores including Ives's songs, most of his chamber music, and some of his orchestral works.

Lou Harrison with his transfer harp, Aptos, California, 1977. (Betty Freeman/Lebrecht Music & Arts)

During the next ten years Harrison studied these compositions avidly, editing several for performance and/or publication. Through Cowell, Harrison also developed a fascination with American Indian and early Californian culture, reflected in works throughout his career, among them the Mass to St. Anthony for voices accompanied by percussion ensemble (rescored in 1952 for voices, strings, trumpet, and harp). The Mass's vocal lines suggest indigenous melodic types that had been incorporated into 18th-century Californian mission services. The work's opening motif—a "cry of anguish" occasioned by Hitler's invasion of Poland in 1939—is also one of Harrison's earliest political statements.

While in San Francisco, Harrison collaborated with several West Coast choreographers: among them, Bonnie Bird, Carol Beals, Tina Flade, Marian van Tuyl, and Lester Horton. In 1937 he was engaged by Mills College as a dance accompanist; he also taught courses in composition for the dance at its summer sessions. Cage sought him out in 1938 on the recommendation of Cowell, and it was through Harrison that Cage was hired by Bird at the Cornish School in Seattle. At the Mills College summer sessions in 1939 and 1940, and in San Francisco in 1941, Harrison and Cage staged high-profile percussion concerts, which Harrison continued in 1942 after Cage had moved to Chicago. For a 1941 performance they jointly composed *Double Music* for four percussionists, each writing two of the parts. Consultation between the two composers was minimal: they predetermined an overall length for the work, as well as instrumentation and salient rhythmic motives. Thereafter, they worked with complete independence. Here and in works wholly his own, notably *Canticles*

nos.1 and 3, *Song of Queztalcóatl,* and the Suite for Percussion, the traditional battery is expanded to encompass "found" instruments, such as brake drums, flowerpots, and metal pipes, as well as instruments from other cultures, such as the clay ocarina and the *teponaztli*, a wooden slit-drum from Mexico traditionally made from a hollow log.

In August 1942 Harrison moved to Los Angeles, where he was engaged by UCLA to teach Labanotation as well as musical form and history for dancers. He enrolled in Arnold Schoenberg's weekly composition seminar, which, he later noted, taught him the "importance of simplicity and method" to complement the "license for freedom" he had learned from Ives. The most notable work from his Los Angeles period is the Suite for Piano, composed for Frances Mullen Yates.

The following year Harrison moved to New York, where he became one of Virgil Thomson's "stringers" at the *New York Herald Tribune* (1944–7). He also wrote for *Modern Music, Listen,* and *View* (including studies on Ives, Edgard Varèse, and Schoenberg) and published an extended essay "About Carl Ruggles." On 5 April 1946 he conducted the premiere of Ives's Third Symphony, which he had edited from the original manuscript. For this work Ives received the Pulitzer Prize of 1947, which he insisted on splitting with Harrison. Harrison continued to compose in a Ruggles-inspired dissonant contrapuntal language; among his most successful compositions from this period is the organ work *Praises for Michael the Archangel*, which he later orchestrated for use in his *Elegiac Symphony*. In spite of his successes, however, Harrison adjusted poorly to the stress and noise of New York, first developing an ulcer and then in 1947 suffering a nervous breakdown for which he was hospitalized for nine months. He used the experience as a catalyst for change in his compositional style, eschewing the dense counterpoint of his early New York years. The period immediately after his hospitalization was one of his most productive, with the composition of *The Perilous Chapel* and *Solstice* (for the dancer and choreographer Jean Erdman), two suites for string orchestra, the Suite for Cello and Harp, and the Suite for Violin, Piano, and Small Orchestra (which contains, in two of its movements, evocations of gamelan music). Summer residencies at Reed College, Oregon, in 1949 and 1950 led to the stage pieces *Marriage at the Eiffel Tower* and *The Only Jealousy of Emer*.

In 1951 Harrison accepted a position at Black Mountain College, North Carolina, which he held for two years. There he completed several earlier works and wrote a host of new ones, including the chamber opera *Rapunzel*, a 12-tone work with a melodic language that is at once rugged and lyrical. The opera's third act won a 20th-Century Masterpiece Award at the 1954 International Conference of Contemporary Music. Meanwhile the publication of Harry Partch's *Genesis of a Music* in 1949 stimulated Harrison's exploration of just intonation. His study bore fruit in *Seven Pastorales* (1949–51) and in *Strict Songs* (1955), which was composed for the Louisville Orchestra shortly after Harrison had returned to California and settled in the (then) rural town of

Aptos. *Strict Songs* makes use of Harrison's own poetry, inspired by Navajo ritual songs, and it calls for the retuning of the fixed-pitch instruments in the orchestra to create intervals with vibration ratios in superparticular proportions (4:3, 8:7, etc.). Its four movements also explore different pentatonic divisions of the octave. Harrison called for similar retunings in many later compositions as well. In addition he developed a radical system called "Free Style," in which individual pitches are determined purely by their proportional relationship to preceding and following pitches without adhering to a fixed tonal center. His *Simfony in Free Style* (1955), a four-minute composition including viols with movable or independently placed frets and specially constructed flutes, has never been performed live with the specified instrumentation, but it has been recorded in a digital realization by David Doty (which can be heard on the disc accompanying Miller and Lieberman, *Composing a World*). After Harrison returned to California in 1953, he for the most part abandoned 12-tone serialism, which he used thereafter primarily for antiwar statements (often in the context of equal temperament) to symbolize the mechanization of Western industrial society.

During these early years in Aptos, Harrison composed two concertos for violin accompanied by percussion ensemble and completed a Suite for Symphonic Strings. He also began to develop closer ties with Asia, which he visited for the first time in 1961 as a delegate to the East-West Music Encounter in Tokyo. In 1961 and 1962 Harrison spent several months in Korea and Taiwan studying, among other instruments, the double-reed Korean *p'iri* and the Chinese psaltery, *zheng*. A number of subsequent works, such as *Nova Odo* (1961–8), *Pacifika Rondo* (1963), and *Music for Violin and Various Instruments* (1967), call for ensembles of mixed Western and Asian instruments. A Phebe Ketchem Thorne award in 1966 allowed Harrison to spend six months in Mexico, where he wrote his *Music Primer* and composed a new finale for his first symphony, the Symphony on G.

In 1967 Harrison met William Colvig (1917–2000), an electrician and amateur musician, who became his partner as well as a dedicated collaborator on instrument building and tuning experiments. In 1971 they constructed a set of metallophones tuned to a pure D major scale and built from materials easy to procure (e.g., steel conduit tubing, aluminum slabs, and stacked tin cans as resonators). Noting the instruments' superficial resemblance to a gamelan, they called the ensemble "An American Gamelan." To these instruments Harrison and Colvig added galvanized garbage cans and cut-off oxygen tanks struck with baseball bats, thus integrating Indonesian sounds, junk materials, the percussion ensemble, and just intonation (*see* GAMELAN). Harrison composed three works for this novel ensemble: the puppet opera *Young Caesar* (1971, rewritten as a standard opera with Western instrumentation in 1988); *La Koro Sutro* (1972, a setting of the Buddhist *Heart Sutra* in Esperanto, a language in which Harrison was fluent); and the Suite for Violin and American Gamelan (1974),

composed jointly with his student Richard Dee. Harrison and Colvig later built two additional gamelan for San Jose State University and Mills College, both modeled on traditional Javanese instruments but tuned in just intonation.

After studies with the renowned performer and teacher K.R.T. Wasitodiningrat (Pak Cokro) in 1975, Harrison began to compose for traditional gamelan ensembles. He ultimately wrote more than three dozen gamelan works, at times combining the ensemble with vocalists and/or Western solo instruments. These works exhibit typical features of gamelan music, including a texture of polyphonic stratification (in which higher-pitched instruments perform elaborations over a basic structural melody called the balungan), characteristic figuration patterns, and changes in irama (in which the length of the balungan notes changes without simultaneous alteration in the speed of the ornamental figuration). Among the most impressive works combining gamelan with Western instruments is the Concerto for Piano with Javanese Gamelan of 1987. Here the piano is retuned to match the gamelan instruments. The concerto serves at once as an expression of cross-cultural linkage and as evidence of Harrison's marvelous feel for timbral coloration, a trait also well in evidence in his four symphonies. At times Harrison brought Western concepts to bear on his gamelan works, such as the *Threnody for Carlos Chávez* for viola and gamelan, which features eight levels of triple meter in a structure inspired by the European Ars Nova notation system.

At the same time Harrison increasingly returned to composing for Western instruments, his later works including three more symphonies, several concertos, and a host of chamber compositions (e.g., the *String Quartet Set*, the *Varied Trio,* and the Piano Trio). In many of these works, he explored cross-cultural applications of compositional techniques, often using gamelan textures, embellishment styles, and metric structures in works for Western instruments (e.g., Fourth Symphony and Piano Trio). He often set for himself rigorous compositional strictures such as permitting the use of only a limited number of melodic intervals (a process he called "interval control") or constructing thematic material from a restricted set of melodic or rhythmic cells. Interval control figured in his works as early as the 1930s and continued to be a useful tool into the 1980s, for instance in his monumental *Grand Duo* for violin and piano from 1988. This major work also shows Harrison's long-term fascination with the music of the Middle Ages by including an estampie, a medieval dance that features paired sections (A A' B B' C C', etc.). Harrison loved the estampie, which he used in about a dozen works.

From his earliest years in San Francisco, Harrison articulated political views of multiculturalism, ecological responsibility, and pacifism in both writings and musical compositions. Many of his early works have political overtones (*Waterfront—1934, Conquest, France 1917—Spain 1937*), as do *Pacifika Rondo, Nova Odo*, the three *Peace Pieces,* and *Homage to Pacifica*. Harrison was also politically active in the gay rights movement: his opera *Young Caesar* deals with homosexuality and cross-cultural partnership by describing an affair between Caesar (representing the West) and Nicomedes, King of Bithynia (the East).

In addition to his musical compositions and prose writings, Harrison was a published poet and a painter. He was renowned for his calligraphic script and designed several computer fonts. He taught courses in composition and world musics at San Jose State University, Stanford University, Cabrillo College, the University of Southern California, and Mills College. Harrison was elected to the National Institute of Arts and Letters in 1973 and received numerous awards including a Creative Grant from the Institute (1948), two Guggenheim awards (1952 and 1954), Rockefeller grants funding two trips to Asia (1961–2), a Fulbright scholarship supporting a residency in New Zealand (1983), and the Edward MacDowell Medal (2000). He died suddenly of heart failure on 2 February 2003 in Lafayette, Indiana, on his way to a major festival of his music at the Ohio State University.

WORKS
(selective list)
(for fuller list including juvenilia and lost works see Miller and Lieberman, 1998)

DRAMATIC

Ops: Rapunzel (chbr op, 6 scenes, W. Morris), 1952–3, New York, YMYWHA Kaufmann Auditorium, 14 May 1959; Young Caesar (puppet op, 2, R. Gordon and Harrison), 5 solo vv, Amer. gamelan, Western and Asian insts, 1971, Pasadena, California Institute of Technology, 5 Nov 1971, rev. as standard op, solo vv, male chorus, chbr orch, 1988, Portland, OR, Portland Center for the Performing Arts, 9/10 April 1988, rev. 2000, incl 7 new arias and duets

Dance scores: Waterfront—1934, perc, c1935–6; Green Mansions, (pf, perc, rec)/2 pf, 1941; Jephtha's Daughter, fl, perc, other insts ad lib, 1941, rev. 1963; In Praise of Johnny Appleseed, 3 perc, 1942; Gigue and Musette, pf, 1943; Changing Moment, pf, 1946; Western Dance (The Open Road), pf/(fl, bn, tpt, vn, vc, pf), 1947; The Perilous Chapel, fl, vc, hp, perc, 1948–9, rev. 1989; Solstice, fl, ob, tpt, 2 vc, db, tack pf, cel, 1949–50; Chorales for Spring, pf, 1951

Io and Prometheus (Prometheus Bound), pf, 1951, arr. vv, insts, 1985; The Glyph, prep pf, perc, 1951; Little Gamelon for Katherine Litz to Teach with, pf, 1952; Praises for Hummingbirds and Hawks, chbr orch, 1952, withdrawn; Jephtha's Daughter, fl, perc, other insts ad lib, 1941, rev. 1963; Reflections in Motion, tape, 1966; New Moon, fl, cl, tpt, trbn, vn, db, perc, 1986, rev. 1989; Ariadne, fl, perc, 1987; Tandy's Tango, pf, 1992; Rhymes with Silver, pf qt, perc, 1996

Incid music: The Winter's Tale (W. Shakespeare), fl, tpt, 2 vn, va, vc, perc, 1937; Electra (Euripides), chbr orch, 1938; The Trojan Women (Euripides), orch, 1939, part lost; The Beautiful People (W. Saroyan), tpt, pf, 1942; Marriage at the Eiffel Tower (J. Cocteau), fl, cl, tpt, vn, vc, db, pf, perc, 1949; The Only Jealousy of Emer (W.B. Yeats), fl, vc, db, tack pf, perc, 1949; Cinna (P. Corneille), tack pf, 1955–7; The Rainbow Boy and the Corn Maiden (E. Gridlow), solo vv, unison vv, rec, fl, va, hp, perc, 1970s; Lazarus Laughed (E. O'Neill), fl, ob, trbn, hp, perc, str, 1994

Film scores: Nuptiae (dir. J. Broughton), chorus 2vv, Filipino kulintang, 1968; Discovering the Art of Korea (dir. D. Myers), Asian-Western ens, 1979; Beyond the Far Blue Mountains (dir. M. Davies), gamelan, 1982; Devotions (dir. Broughton), gamelan, 1983; The Scattered Remains of James Broughton (dir. Broughton, J. Singer), metallophone, drum, 1987

ORCHESTRAL

Full orch: Sym. on G, 1947–64, rev. with new finale, 1966; Marriage at the Eiffel Tower, suite, 1961 [from incid music]; Elegiac Sym., 1975; Third Sym., 1982, rev. 1985; Pf Conc., 1985; Air for the Poet, 1987; Fourth Sym. (Last Sym.), 1990, rev. 1991–5; A Parade for M.T.T., 1995; Pi-pa Conc., 1997

Chbr orch: Alleluia, 1945; Motet for the Day of Ascension, 1945, withdrawn; 7 Pastorales, 1949–51; Suite, vn, pf, small orch, 1951; At the Tomb of Charles Ives, 1963; Elegy, to the Memory of Calvin Simmons, 1982

Str: First Suite for Str, 1948, withdrawn, rev. as New First Suite, 1995; Suite no.2, 1948; Nocturne, 1951; Suite for Sym. Str, 1960; Suite, arr. K. Lewis, vn, str, 1977 [from Suite, vn, Amer. gamelan]; Suite, arr. R. Hughes, vc, str, 1997 [from Suite, vc, hp, and Suite, vc, pf]; Suite, arr. D.R. Davies, vn, pf, str, 1997 [from Suite, vn, Amer. gamelan]

VOCAL

Choral: Mass to St Anthony, unison vv, tpt, hp, str, 1939–52, Kyrie, Gloria rev. vv, pic, perc, 2001; Easter Cant., A, SATB, chbr orch, 1943–66; Onward Christian Soldiers, unison vv, tpt, org, c1945, withdrawn; Strict Songs, 8 Bar/male vv, chbr orch, 1955, arr. Bar, SATB, chbr orch, 1992; Nak Yang Chun [Spring in Nak Yang], vv, chbr orch, 1961, collab. Lee Hye-Ku; Nova Odo, male vv, speaking vv, orch, 1961–8; A Joyous Procession and a Solemn Procession, 2vv, 2 trbn, 5 perc, 1962

Haiku, unison vv, shiao, hp, wind chimes, gong, 1967; Peace Piece 1, unison vv, chbr orch, 1968; Orpheus, T, SATB, 15 perc, 1969; La Koro Sutro, SATB, org, hp, Amer. gamelan, 1972, arr. K. Lewis, vv, orch, c1977; Scenes from Cavafy, Bar, male vv, hp, Javanese gamelan, 1980; Gending in Honor of Aphrodite, vv, hp, Javanese gamelan, 1982, rev. 1986; Mass for St Cecilia's Day, unison vv, hp and org ad lib, 1983–6

3 Songs, male vv, chbr orch, 1985; Faust, S, T, B, vv, chbr orch, Sundanese gamelan degung, 1985; A Soedjatmoko Set, 1v, unison vv, Javanese gamelan, 1989; Homage to Pacifica, 1v, vv, spkr, bn, perc, hp, psaltery, Javanese gamelan, 1991; Now Sleep the Mountains, All, vv, perc, 2 pf, 1992, withdrawn; White Ashes (Gobunsho), vv, kbd, 1992

Solo vocal: Pied Beauty, Bar, vc, perc, 1940; Sanctus, A, pf, 1940; King David's Lament, T, pf, 1941; May Rain, 1v, pf, perc, 1941; Fragment from Calamus, Bar, pf/str qt, 1946; Alma Redemptoris Mater, Bar, vn, trbn, tack pf, 1949–51; Holly and Ivy, T, hp, 2 vn, vc, db, 1951–62; Vestiunt Silve, Mez, fl, 2 va, hp, 1951–94

Peace Piece 3, A/Bar, 2 vn, va, hp, 1953, rev. 1968; Air from Rapunzel, S, fl, str trio, hp, pf, 1954; Political Primer, Bar, perc, orch, 1958, inc.; Peace Piece 2, T, chbr orch, 1968; Ketawang Wellington, 1v, Javanese gamelan, 1983; Foreman's Song Tune (Coyote Stories), 1v, Javanese gamelan, 1983–7; Gending Moon, male v, Javanese gamelan, 1994

WESTERN INSTRUMENTAL ENSEMBLE

5 or more insts: Renaissance ens: Binary Variations on "O Sinner Man," 1934–77, withdrawn; France 1917—Spain 1937, str qt, 2 perc, 1937, rev. 1968; Simfony in Free Style, plastic fls, trbns, viols, hps, tack pf, 1955; Praise(s) for the Beauty of Hummingbirds, fl, 2 vn, cel, perc, 1952; Conc. in slendro, 3 kbd, vn, 2 perc, 1961, rev. 1972; Majestic Fanfare, 3 tpt, 2 perc, 1963; Festive Movt, fl, cl, vn, vc, pf, 1972, withdrawn; The Clays' Qnt, tpt, hn, mand, hp, perc, 1987; An Old Times Tune for Merce Cunningham's 75th Birthday, pf qnt, 1993; see also dramatic (Dance scores) [Western Dance, 1947; Solstice, 1949–50; New Moon, 1986; Rhymes with Silver, 1996], (Incid music) [The Only Jealousy of Emer, 1949; Marriage at the Eiffel Tower, 1949]

3–4 insts: Serenade, 3 rec, 1943; Str Trio, 1946; Suite no.2, str qt, 1948 [alternative version for str orch]; Nocturne, 2 vn, tack pf, 1951, withdrawn; Songs in the Forest, fl, vn, pf, vib, 1951–92; Str Qt Set, 1979; Air for the Poet, 1 inst, 2 ostinatos, 1987; Varied Trio, vn, pf, perc, 1987; Pf Trio, 1990; Small Set from Lazarus Laughed, fl, vc, cel, 1999 [from incid music]; see also dramatic (Dance scores) [The Perilous Chapel, 1948–9]

1–2 insts other than kbd: Sonata, vn, 1936, withdrawn; Air, g, fl, drone, 1947; Suite, vc, hp, 1949; Serenade, gui/hp, 1952; Avalokiteshvara, hp/grand psaltery/gui, perc, 1964; Beverly's Troubadour Piece, hp/gui, perc, 1967; In Memory of Victor Jowers, cl/eng hn, pf/hp, 1967; Music for Bill and Me, hp/gui, 1967; Solo to Anthony Cirone, perc, 1972; Jahla in the Form of a Ductia to Pleasure Leopold Stokowski on his 90th Birthday, hp/gui, perc, 1972; Sonata in Ishartum, hp/gui, 1974; Serenade, gui, perc ad lib, 1978; Grand Duo, vn, pf, 1988; Threnody for Oliver Daniel, hp, 1990; Suite, vc, pf, 1995; Music for Remy, ob, perc, 1998; see also dramatic (Dance scores) [Waterfront-1934; c1935–6; Ariadne, 1987]

Arrs. by R. Hughes: Schoenbergiana, fl, wind qnt, 1944, arr. 1962 [from str qt]; Serenade, C, wind qnt, 1944, arr. 1962 [from pf piece]; Party Pieces, 4 wind, pf, 1963 [from Sonorous and Exquisite Corpses, collab. Cage, Thomson, Cowell, 1944–5]

PERCUSSION ENSEMBLE

Large ens: Conc., vn, 5 perc, 1940–59, rev. 1974; Labyrinth no.3, 11 players, 1941; Conc., org, 8 perc, pf, cel, 1973; Double Fanfare, 12 players, 1980, collab. A. Cirone, withdrawn; Canticle no.3, ocarina, gui, 5 perc, 1942, rev. 1989

For 2–5 players: First Conc., fl, 2 perc, 1939; Fifth Simfony, 1939; Bomba, 1939; Tributes to Charon, 1939–82; Canticle no.1, 1940; Song of Quetzalcoatl, 1941; Simfony no.13, 1941; Double Music, 1941, collab. Cage; Canticle and Round in Honor of Gerhard Samuel's Birthday, 1942–93; Suite, 1942; Canticle no.5, 1942; Fugue, 1942; Recording Piece, 1955; see also dramatic (Dance scores) [In Praise of Johnny Appleseed, 1942]

GAMELAN

Javanese: Lagu Sociseknum, 1976; Lancaran Daniel, 1976; Music for Kyai Hudan Mas, 1976, rev. with pic tpt ad lib, 1981; Gending Jody, 1977; Gending Paul, 1977; Music for the Turning of a Sculpture by Pamela Boden, 1977; Gending Alexander, 1981; Gending Hephaestus, 1981; Gending Hermes, 1981; Gending Demeter, 1981, rev. 1983; Gending in Honor of the Poet Virgil, 1981, rev. 1985; Ladrang Epikuros, 1981; Double Conc., vn, vc, gamelan, 1982; Gending Claude, 1982; Gending Dennis, 1982; Gending in Honor of Herakles, 1982

Gending Pindar, 1982; Lancaran Molly, 1982; Gending in Honor of Palladio, 1982–3; Foreman's Song Tune, 1983, rev. with 1v, 1987; For the Pleasure of Ovid's Changes, 1983, rev. 1986; Gending in Honor of James and Joel, 1983; Gending Max Beckmann, 1984, rev. 1991; Gending Vincent, 1984; Ladrang in Honor of Pak Daliyo, 1984–6; Philemon and Baukis, vn, gamelan, 1985–7; Cornish Lancaran, s sax, gamelan, 1986, rev. 1989; Conc., pf, gamelan, 1987; In Honor of Munakata Shiko, 1997; A Dentdale Ladrang, 1999; Ladrang Carter Scholz, 1999; Orchard, 1999; see also dramatic (Film scores) [Beyond the Far Blue Mountains; Devotions], VOCAL (Choral) [Scenes from Cavafy; Gending in Honor of Ahprodite; A Soedjatmako Set; Homage to Pacifica], VOCAL (Solo vocal) [Ketawang Wellington, Foreman's Song Tune, Gending Moon]

Amer.: Suite, vn, Amer. gamelan, collab. R. Dee, 1974; see also dramatic (Ops) [Young Caesar], VOCAL (Choral) [La Koro Sutro]

Balinese: A Round for Jafran Jones, 1991

Cirebonese: Lagu Cirebon, 1983; Lagu Lagu Thomasan, 1983; Lagu Victoria, 1983; Lagu Elang Yusuf, 1984

Sundanese: Main Bersama-sama [Playing Together], hn, gamelan degung, 1978; Serenade for Betty Freeman and Franco Assetto, 1978; Threnody for Carlos Chávez, va, gamelan degung, 1978; Lagu Pa Undang, 1985; Ibu Trish, 1989; see also vocal (Choral) [Faust]

GENERAL: BOOK MUSIC, SELECTED INSTS, 1994

Other works with non-western instruments

Asian ens: Moogunkwha, Se Tang Ak [Sharon Rose, a New Song in the Old Style, or a New Tang Melody], Korean court orch, 1961; Quintal Taryung, (2 Korean fl, changgo ad lib)/(2 rec, drum ad lib), 1961–2; Suite, 4 haisho, perc, spkr, 1992

Asian, African and Western insts: Air, vn, ya zheng, gender, 1940, rev. 1970s; Prelude, p'iri, reed org, 1961; Pacifika Rondo, 1963; At the Tomb of Charles Ives, 1963; Music for Vn with Various Insts, vn, reed org, 1 perc, psaltery, 4 mbiras, 1967, rev. 1969; A Phrase for Arion's Leap, 3 ya zheng, 2 hp, perc, 1974

Asian solo inst: Psalter Sonato, great psaltery/zheng, 1961, rev. 1962; Wesak Sonata, cheng, 1964; The Garden at One and a Quarter Moons, great psaltery/zheng, 1964, rev. 1966; Suite for Sangen, shamisen, 1996

KEYBOARD

Pf: Ground, e, 1936, rev. 1970; Largo ostinato, 1937, rev. 1970; Saraband, 1937; Prelude, 1937; Third Pf Sonata, 1938; Reel (Homage to Henry Cowell), 1939; Suite, 1943; New York Waltzes, 1944–51; A 12-Tone Morning After to Amuse Henry, c1944–5; Triphony, 1945; 2 Unused Pieces for José Limón, 1945; Homage to Milhaud, 1948; Little Suite, 1949; Double Canon for Carl Ruggles, 1951; Festival Dance, 2 pf, 1951, rev. 1996

Fugue for David Tudor, 1952; Waltz for Evelyn Hinrichsen, 1977; A Summerfield Set, 1988; An Old Times Tune for Merce Cunningham's 75th Birthday, arr. M. Boriskin, 1993; see also dramatic (Dance scores) [Gigue and Musette, 1943; Changing Moment, 1946; Western Dance, 1947; Chorales for Spring, 1951; Io and Prometheus, 1951; Tandy's Tango, 1992]

Other: 6 Cembalo Sonatas, 1934–43; Praises for Michael the Archangel, org, 1947; Estampie for Susan Summerfield, org, 1981; Pedal Sonata, org, 1989; Sonata for Hpd, 1999; see also dramatic (Incid music) [Cinna]

MSS in U. of California, Santa Cruz, OAm; recorded interviews in NHoh

Principal publishers: Peters, Peer International, American Gamelan Institute, A-R Editions, Associated, Music for Percussion, Warner

WRITINGS

About Carl Ruggles (Yonkers, NY, 1946); repr. in *The Score*, no.12 (1955), 15–26, and in Garland (1987), 39–45

"Refreshing the Auditory Perception," *Music East and West: Tokyo 1961*, 141–3

"Creative Ideas in Classical Korean Music," *Korea Journal*, ii/11 (1962), 34–6

Korean Music (MS, c1962, LAuc)

"Some Notes on the Music of Mouth-Organs," *Umakhak ronch'ong: Yi Hye-Gu paksa song'su kinyom* [Essays in ethnomusicology: a birthday offering for Lee Hye-Ku] (Seoul, 1969)

Music Primer: Various Items about Music to 1970 (New York, 1971, 2/1993)

"Thoughts about 'Slippery Slendro'," *Selected Reports in Ethnomusicology*, vi (1985), 111–17

"Cloverleaf: a Little Narrative with Several 'Off-Ramps'," *1/1: the Quarterly Journal of the Just Intonation Network*, v/2 (1989), 1–2, 14–15; repr. in *Companion to Contemporary Musical Thought*, i, ed. J. Paynter and others (London, 1992), 248–55

Joys and Perplexities: Selected Poems of Lou Harrison (Winston-Salem, NC, 1992)

"Lou Harrison's Political Primer," *Frog Peak Anthology*, ed. C. Scholz and L. Wendt (Hanover, NH, 1992), 77–83

Articles in *ACA Bulletin, Dance Observer, Ear, Impulse, Listen: the Guide to Good Music, Modern Music, View,* and *Xenharmonikon*

For fuller list of writings see Miller and Lieberman (1998).

BIBLIOGRAPHY

P. Yates: "Lou Harrison," *Arts and Architecture*, lxi/2 (1944), 26, 37

P. Yates: "A Trip up the Coast," *Arts and Architecture*, lxxiv/12 (1957), 4ff

P. Yates: "A Collage of American Composers," *Arts and Architecture*, lxxv/12 (1958) and lxxvi/2 (1959) [complete issues]

P. Yates: "Lou Harrison," *American Composers' Alliance Bulletin*, ix/2 (1960), 2–7

V.M. Rathbun: *Lou Harrison and his Music* (thesis, San Jose State U., 1976)

W. Leyland: "Lou Harrison," *Gay Sunshine Interviews* [San Francisco], no.1 (1978)

L.V. Celso: *A Study and Catalogue of Lou Harrison's Utilization of Keyboard Instruments in his Solo and Ensemble Works* (thesis, San Jose State U., 1979)

P.G. Gardner: *"La Koro Sutro" by Lou Harrison: Historical Perspective, Analysis and Performance Considerations* (DMA diss., U. of Texas, Austin, 1981)

D. Baker: *The Percussion Ensemble Music of Lou Harrison, 1939–1942* (DMA diss., U. of Illinois, 1985)

V. McDermott: "Gamelans and New Music," *MQ*, lxxii (1986), 16–27

P. Garland, ed.: *A Lou Harrison Reader* (Santa Fe, NM, 1987)

D.L. Brunner: *The Choral Music of Lou Harrison* (DMA diss., U. of Illinois, 1989)

D. Keislar: "Six American Composers on Nonstandard Tunings," *PNM*, xxix/1 (1991), 176–211

D.L. Brunner: "Cultural Diversity in the Choral Music of Lou Harrison," *Choral Journal*, xxxii/10 (1992), 17–28

D. Burwasser: *A Study of Lou Harrison's Concerto for Violin and Percussion Orchestra and Concerto for Organ and Percussion Orchestra* (diss., CUNY, 1993)

H. Von Gunden: *The Music of Lou Harrison* (Metuchen, NJ, 1995)

D. Nicholls: "Transethnicism and the American Experimental Tradition," *MQ*, lxxx (1996), 569–94

D. Nicholls, ed.: *The Whole World of Music: a Henry Cowell Symposium* (Amsterdam, 1997)

L.E. Miller and F. Lieberman: *Lou Harrison: Composing a World* (New York and London, 1998, rev. 2004 as *Composing a World: Lou Harrison, Musical Wayfarer*, Urbana, IL)

L.E. Miller and F. Lieberman: "Lou Harrison and the American Gamelan," *AM*, xvii/2 (1999), 145–77

L.E. Miller: "The Art of Noise: John Cage, Lou Harrison and the West Coast Percussion Ensemble," *Perspectives on American Music, 1900–1950*, ed. M. Saffle (New York, 2000), 215–63

B. Ravenscroft: "Working Out the 'Is-Tos and As-Tos': Lou Harrison's Fugue for Percussion," *PNM*, xxxviii/1 (2000), 25–43

L.E. Miller: "Method and Madness in Lou Harrison's *Rapunzel*," *Journal of Musicology*, xix/1 (2002), 85–124.

L.E. Miller: "Lou Harrison and the Aesthetics of Revision, Alteration, and Self-Borrowing," *21CM*, ii/1 (2005), 1–29

S. Neff: "An Unlikely Synergy: Lou Harrison and Arnold Schoenberg," *JSAM*, iii/2 (2009), 155–93

L.E. Miller and F. Lieberman: *Lou Harrison* (Urbana, IL, 2006)

LETA E. MILLER (work list with CHARLES HANSON)

Harry, Debbie [Deborah] (*b* Miami, FL, 1 July 1945). Singer and performer. Adopted at three months of age, she was raised in Hawthorne, New Jersey. After college graduation in 1965 she moved to New York, where she worked as a waitress at Max's Kansas City and also as a Playboy Bunny. In 1967 she began her professional singing career with the folk-rock band Wind in the Willows, which released a self-titled album with Capitol Records before disbanding a year later. In 1974 Harry joined the Stilettos, which performed regularly at CBGB, a New York club. Guitarist Chris Stein and Harry, who dated from the late 1970s to the early 90s, left the Stilettos to form a new band, resulting in the creation of Blondie in 1975. Though their music is not audibly representative of the punk style as it is widely recognized, Blondie's appearances at CBGB were a precursor to New York's punk scene. Harry was the lead singer and also a songwriter, responsible for co-writing most of Blondie's biggest hits. Blondie initially experienced moderate success in North America but had a much greater following overseas, until the single "Heart of Glass" from their sophomore album *Parallel Lines* became a number one hit in the United States in 1978.

Harry has worked hard to establish her identity as an individual, as the band name has often been mistaken as her own. The common misconception led the band to adopt a promotional campaign featuring the slogan "Blondie is the name of the band." Blondie's popularity established Harry's image as a seductive platinum blonde, but her consciously dark, exposed roots played with the established and iconic bombshell look. In 1981 Harry released her first solo album, *Koo Koo*, just before Blondie disbanded in 1982; a second solo album, *Def, Dumb and Blonde* appeared in 1989 and she began working under the name Deborah Harry. While in between solo records, Harry took time away from recording and performing to help Stein as he battled an autoimmune disease, from which he eventually recovered. She also began acting, taking a lead role in John Waters's *Hairspray* (1988) among other movie and television roles. In 1997 Harry began performing and recording with the group the Jazz Passengers before

reuniting with Blondie in 1998. The band recorded the album *No Exit* and embarked on a tour to promote that release and their reunion. In 2006 Blondie was inducted into the Rock and Roll Hall of Fame. Harry has been a longtime advocate for AIDS research, using her fame to bring attention to a number of awareness efforts like MAC Cosmetics' Viva Glam campaign and to promote medical research with organizations like Geoffrey Beene's Rock Stars of Science effort.

BIBLIOGRAPHY

L. Bangs: *Blondie* (New York, 1980)

D. Harry, C. Stein, and V. Bockris: *Making Tracks: the Rise of Blondie* (New York, 1998)

G. Valentine: *New York Rocker: My Life in the Blank Generation, with Blondie, Iggy Pop, and Others, 1974–1981* (London, 2002)

A. Metz, ed.: *Blondie, From Punk to the Present: a Pictorial History* (Springfield, MO, 2002)

JESSICA L. BROWN

Harsanyi [née Morris], **Janice** (*b* Arlington, MA, 15 July 1929; *d* Tallahassee, FL, 22 March 2007). Soprano and teacher. After studies at the Westminster Choir College, Princeton (BMus 1951), and the Philadelphia Academy of Vocal Arts, she made her debut in Britten's song cycle *Les illuminations* with the Philadelphia Orchestra in 1958. She made her Carnegie Hall debut singing Berlioz's *La Damnation de Faust* in 1959. In 1965 she appeared in recital at Wigmore Hall, London, and sang in Europe with the Philadelphia String Quartet. She performed with orchestras throughout the United States and toured with the Bach Aria Group (1966–7), the Princeton Chamber Orchestra (1966–70), and the Piedmont Chamber Orchestra (1974–6). She worked with such noted composers as Toscanini, Stokowski, and Robert Shaw. Although Harsanyi sang more than a dozen operatic roles including the American premieres of Handel's *Imeneo* and *Amadigi di Gaula*, she was known best as a recitalist and soloist. The clarity and accuracy of her voice made her an especially fine interpreter of many 20th-century works, including a number that were dedicated to her by Roger Sessions, John Harbison, Charles Schwartz, Alan Stout, Harold Schiffman, and Robert Ward, of which she gave the first performances. She also gave the American premieres of works by Wolfgang Fortner, Krenek, and Ahmet Adnan Saygun. Among her recordings are Orff's *Carmina Burana* with the Philadelphia Orchestra under the Baton of Eugene Ormandy (1960) and George Rochberg's Quartet no.2 (1962). Harsanyi taught at various institutions, including Westminster Choir College, Princeton Theological Seminary, North Carolina School of the Arts, and Florida State University. She was married to conductor Nicholas Harsanyi.

BIBLIOGRAPHY

J. Harbison: "Singer on a Mission," *Presbyterian Life*, xiv/8 (1961), 11

M. Hinson: "TSO's 'First Lady' Dies," *Tallahassee Democrat* (23 March 2007), A1

ANNE MINKO/MICHAEL HIX

Harshaw, Margaret (*b* Philadelphia, PA, 12 May 1909; *d* Libertyville, IL, 7 Nov 1997). Mezzo-soprano, later soprano. In the early 1930s she won a series of competitions leading to performances in Philadelphia, Washington, and New York. In 1936 she enrolled at the Juilliard School and studied with Anna Schoen-René. After winning the Metropolitan Opera Auditions of the Air in 1942, she made her Metropolitan debut as the Second Norn in *Götterdämmerung* and in subsequent seasons sang such roles as Azucena, Amneris, and Mistress Quickly. At San Francisco (1944–7) her roles included Ulrica, Brangäne, and Debussy's Geneviéve. During the 1950–51 season she changed to soprano parts, succeeding Helen Traubel in the heroic Wagnerian repertory (Isolde, Senta, Kundry, and Brünnhilde) and remained with the Metropolitan until the close of the 1963–4 season. She sang 375 performances of 39 roles in 25 works with the company. During this period she also fulfilled engagements at Covent Garden (1953–6), where she excelled as Brünnhilde in Kempe's *Ring* cycles, at Glyndebourne (appearing as Donna Anna in 1954), and in Paris and San Francisco. She toured South America several times and appeared with most of the major orchestras in the United States. She was a convincing actress and possessed a good, though by no means great, Wagnerian voice; her tone was evenly produced over a wide range. She taught at the Curtis Institute and Indiana University (1962–93), and became one of the finest singing teachers in the United States. Among her many students were Sharon Sweet, Benita Valente, and Michael Sylvester.

BIBLIOGRAPHY
H. Rosenthal: *Great Singers of Today* (London, 1966)
P. Jackson: *Saturday Afternoons at the Old Met* (New York, 1992)
Obituary, *New York Times* (11 Nov 1997)
MAX DE SCHAUENSEE/KAREN M. BRYAN

Hart, Clyde (*b* Baltimore, MD, 1910; *d* New York, NY, 19 March 1945). Jazz pianist. He first gained recognition in New York during the late 1930s while playing with Stuff Smith, Roy Eldridge, Lionel Hampton, John Kirby, and Oscar Pettiford. He played regularly at Minton's Playhouse and clubs on 52nd Street during the early 1940s when the bop style was being formulated. Hart was one of the first swing pianists to adapt his music to the new style of Charlie Parker and Dizzy Gillespie, both of whom he accompanied in several important early bop recordings. Abandoning the left-hand patterns of the stride style, he began to state the harmonic progressions in a spare, rhythmic manner, leaving the pulse to the bass player and drummer. Unfortunately, his early death from tuberculosis occurred before he had fully incorporated the new vocabulary into his solo style.

BIBLIOGRAPHY
G. Hoefer: "Clyde Hart: Forgotten Pianist," *DB*, xxxi/3 (1964), 21
D. Salemann: *Clyde Hart 1931–1945* (Berlin, 2003)
BILL DOBBINS/R

Hart, Lorenz (*b* New York, NY, 2 May 1895; *d* New York, NY, 22 Nov 1943). Lyricist. He was the elder child of German-born businessman Max Hart and Frieda Isenberg. His career as one of Broadway's most celebrated lyricists is dominated by his collaboration with Richard Rodgers, whom he met in 1919. They began writing songs for revues and musical comedies that were produced on college campuses and at summer camps. Occasionally producers picked up material and inserted it into a Broadway production, as Lew Fields did with "Any Old Place with You," which appeared in *A Lonely Romeo* (1919). Fields's son Herbert, a Columbia University alumnus like Rodgers and Hart, choreographed their early shows and soon became their librettist. In the early 1920s, though, they took day-jobs, Hart translating Viennese operettas for United Plays. It was not until 1925 that the Rodgers and Hart song "Manhattan" became the hit of a Theatre Guild fundraiser, *The Garrick Gaieties*, an ambitious one-night revue which received rave notices and landed the pair on Broadway with a string of experimental book shows, beginning with *Dearest Enemy* (1925). A series of seldom-revived shows followed, including *Present Arms* (1928) and *Ever Green* (1930), that began to develop the idea of integrating song with scene. An adaptation of Mark Twain's novel *A Connecticut Yankee* (1927) was their first overwhelming success, with Hart's pithy lyrics pitting contemporary New York dialog against an older English idiom. With a strong reputation on both sides of the Atlantic, Rodgers and Hart were enticed to Hollywood in 1932. Their experiences there were short lived, and they were disappointed to find their creativity governed by studio bosses. With few achievements and unexplained production delays stalling work, they returned to Broadway in 1935. During the last half of the 1930s they created the most celebrated shows of their careers, including *On your Toes* (1936), *Babes in Arms* (1937), *The Boys from Syracuse*, which starred Lorenz's brother Teddy as one of the twins, (1938), and *Pal Joey*, which introduced Gene Kelly as Joey (1940). It is their song hits that have remained, including: "Ever Green," "Manhattan," "Blue Moon," "I can't give you anything but love," "My Funny Valentine," "The lady is a tramp," "Bewitched," and many more. Hart's lyrics tingle with wit and energy, sometimes risqué, always erudite. But his worsening depression and alcoholism, alongside his less than reliable working attitude meant that Rodgers increasingly carried the burden of their productivity. By the early 1940s Rodgers was looking elsewhere—with Hart's approval—for another collaborator, ending almost a quarter of a century of this partnership. Finally, with Rodgers now teamed up with veteran lyricist Oscar Hammerstein II and enjoying the impact of their new show *Oklahoma!*, the Rodgers and Hart collaboration came to an end with a revival of *A Connecticut Yankee* (1943). The revival was a success, and the newly written material evidence of a still brilliant lyricist at work. However, Hart had no chance to enjoy his success. Rushed to the hospital with complications caused by pneumonia, he quickly deteriorated. Even an attempt by first lady Eleanor Roosevelt to release the new miracle-drug penicillin from its exclusive military use was not enough. Surrounded by doting friends, his collaborator, and his brother Teddy, he died during the evening of 22 November 1943.

WORKS
(selective list)

THEATER

Fly with Me (1920); Poor Little Ritz Girl (1920); You'll Never Know (1921); The Melody Man (1924); The Garrick Gaieties (1925, rev. 1926); Dearest Enemy (1925); The Fifth Avenue Follies (1926); The Girl Friend (1926); Lido Lady (1926) (London); Peggy-Ann (1926); Betsy (1926); One Dam Thing after Another (1927) (London); A Connecticut Yankee (1927); She's my Baby (1928); Present Arms (1928); Chee-Chee (1928); Spring is here (1929); Heads Up! (1929); Simple Simon (1930); Ever Green (1930) (London); America's Sweetheart (1931); Jumbo (1935); On your Toes (1936); The show is on (1936); Babes in Arms (1937); I'd rather be right (1937); I married an angel (1938); The Boys from Syracuse (1938); Too Many Girls (1939); Higher and Higher (1940); Pal Joey (1940); By Jupiter (1942); Miss Underground (1942) (with music by Emmerich Kalman); A Connecticut Yankee (revival) (1943)

FILM

The Hot Heiress (1931); Love me tonight (1932); The Phantom President (1932); Hallelujah, I'm a bum! (1933); Hollywood Party (1934); The Merry Widow (1935); Mississippi (1935); Dancing Pirate (1936); Fools for Scandal (1938); They Met in Argentina (1941)

BIBLIOGRAPHY

S. Marx and J. Clayton: *Rodgers and Hart: Bewitched, Bothered, and Bedevilled* (London, 1977)

D. Hart and R. Kimball, eds.: *The Complete Lyrics of Lorenz Hart* (New York, 1986)

F. Nolan: *Lorenz Hart: a Poet on Broadway* (New York and Oxford, 1994)

G. Block: *The Richard Rodgers Reader* (New York, 2002)

G. Marmorstein: *A Ship without a Sail: the Life of Lorenz Hart* (New York, 2012)

DOMINIC SYMONDS

Hart, Moss (*b* New York, NY, 24 Oct 1904; *d* Palm Springs, CA, 20 Dec 1961). Librettist and director. As a young man he worked as an office boy for theatrical producer Augustus Pitou and started to write plays in the early 1920s. His first musical, *Jonica* (1930, written in collaboration with Dorothy Heyward), was a failure, but he made an impact with *Once in a Lifetime* (1930). His next offerings, *Face the Music* (1932, music by Irving Berlin) and a revue, *As Thousands Cheer* (1933, Berlin), won great acclaim. He is perhaps best known for the comedies he wrote in collaboration with GEORGE S. KAUFMAN, but the two also produced librettos for musicals, including *I'd rather be right* (1937, music by Richard Rodgers). Other major Broadway shows were *The Great Waltz* (1934, music by J. Strauss), *Jubilee* (1935, lyrics and music by Cole Porter), and *Lady in the Dark* (1941, lyrics by Ira Gershwin, music by Kurt Weill). Hart also provided sketches for revues and, in later years, served as director of *Miss Liberty* (1949), *My Fair Lady* (1956), and *Camelot* (1960). He also wrote several screenplays, including one for *Gentlemen's Agreement* (1947). His writing, always literate and witty, ranges from the whimsical trivialities of his early successes to the more thoughtful observations of his later works. He wrote an autobiography, *Act One* (1959), which was turned into a movie in 1963.

BIBLIOGRAPHY

CBY 1960 ("Hart, Moss")

S. Bach: *Dazzler: the Life and Times of Moss Hart* (New York, 2001)

b.d. mcclung: *Lady in the Dark: Biography of a Musical* (New York, 2007)

GERALD BORDMAN/JONAS WESTOVER

Hart, Tony [Cannon, Anthony J.] (*b* Worcester, MA, 25 July 1855; *d* Worcester, MA, 4 Nov 1891). Actor and singer. A mischievous child, he was placed at age 11 by his parents in the Lyman School, a reform school, in an effort to control him. He rebelled and ran away to Boston, where he worked odd jobs until a publican who employed him noticed his singing skills. He subsequently worked on the periphery of the theatrical world for a number of years as a boy soprano, billed as "Master Antonio." In 1870 Hart was in Chicago where, by chance, he met EDWARD HARRIGAN, a minstrel performer ten years his senior. Harrigan was impressed by Hart's falsetto singing voice and the two teamed up as Harrigan and Hart.

Hart made the most of his ability to sing falsetto in the duo's sketches and songs, frequently appearing as a female character. He made both a convincing and attractive female partner for Harrigan, although he was also capable of playing the more grotesque comic female types. Female impersonation was common in minstrelsy, although after the Civil War the character type emphasized beauty and fashion to a greater extent than before the conflict. Hart portrayed a range of characters, both male and female.

Beginning in 1879 Hart was featured in a series of topical musical comedies written by Harrigan and the composer David Braham. This series catapulted the pair to success and they assembled a small dramatic company to assist them. In 1882 Hart married the actress Gertie Granville, who had joined the company the previous season. The marriage contributed to disagreements between the partners, for Harrigan's wife did not get along with Granville and Granville believed that Hart was due more credit than he was being given. By the mid-1880s these differences were publicly known and elicited comments in the trade newspapers. Harrigan and Hart finally split in 1885. Hart was unable to maintain success on his own and also began to show signs of increasing mental instability, most likely due to syphilis. He was committed to the State Lunatic Hospital at Worcester, Massachusetts, in 1888, where he died three years later.

BIBLIOGRAPHY

E.J. Kahn Jr.: *The Merry Partners: the Age and State of Harrigan & Hart* (New York, 1955)

R. Moody: *Ned Harrigan: From Corlear's Hook to Herald Square* (Chicago, 1980)

GILLIAN M. RODGER

Hart, Weldon (*b* Bear-Place Spring, TN, 19 Sept 1911; *d* East Lansing, MI, 20 Nov 1957). Composer, teacher, and violinist. After studying in Nashville at George Peabody College (BS 1933) and Ward-Belmont Conservatory (Violin Diploma 1933), in 1934 he became professor at Western Kentucky State College, a position he held until 1938, when he was made director of the orchestra and theory division. He received an MM degree at the University of Michigan (1939), where he studied violin with Vasily Bezekirsky, and the PhD in composition at the Eastman School (1946), where he was a pupil of HOWARD HANSON (composition) and BERNARD ROGERS (orchestration). While at Eastman he was a teaching fellow (1943–6) and a member of the first violin section of the Rochester PO (1944–6); he also served as chairman of the National Composers Congress (1945). He was director of the music department at Western Kentucky State College from 1946 to 1949, when he became director of the school of music at West Virginia University, a position he kept for eight years. In 1957 he was engaged as head of the music department at Michigan State University, but shortly after his arrival he committed suicide.

A composer primarily of orchestral and choral works, Hart was particularly interested in American folk music and used folksongs as settings for several of his orchestral pieces. In 1945 he was awarded first prize in the category of orchestral composition for *A Symphonic Movement* by ABC through the National Fellowship of American Composers.

WORKS

Orch: Tone Poem, 1933; Sinfonietta, 1936; The Dark Hills, sym. poem, 1939; Darling Cory, 1944; A Sym. Movt, 1945; Sym. no.1, 1946; Pennyrile Ov., 1947; John Jacob Niles Suite, 1948; Vn Conc., 1951; Irish Legend, band, 1953; Stately Music for Str, 1955; Piece for Brass Choir, Perc, 1957; Suite for Small Orch: Pavan; Song and Celebration, band

Chbr: Sonatina, d, fl, vn, 1931; Fugue, ob, cl, bn, 1939; Str Qt no.1, 1939; Interlude, fl, bn, 1945; Piece for 2 vn, va, vc; Nocturne, vn, pf; Piece for Three, tpt, cl, bn; Fugue, vn, va, vc; Str Qt no.2; 9 pf pieces, several solo vn works

Vocal: 3 West Virginia Folk Songs, chorus, orch, 1954; O Sing unto the Lord, SATB, orch; 6 choral partsongs, several songs

MSS in *NRU-Mus*
Principal publishers: Birchard, C. Fischer

BIBLIOGRAPHY

C. Reis: *Composers in America: Biographical Sketches* (New York, 4/1947/R 1977, rev. and enlarged edn of *American Composers*)
Obituary, *State Journal* (Lansing, MI, 21 Nov 1957)
R. Watanabe: "Music Manuscripts of Weldon Hart," *University of Rochester Library Bulletin*, ix (1964), 27

KATHERINE K. PRESTON

Hartford. Capital city of Connecticut (pop. 124,775; metropolitan area 894,014; 2010 US Census). The city was settled in 1635 and incorporated in 1784. The spread of musical literacy began in Hartford around 1725 with the arrival of singing master George Beale, who taught in the city's first singing-schools. In 1727 Reverend Timothy Woodbridge of the First Ecclesiastical Society and founder of Center Church, the first church in Hartford, encouraged the teaching of psalms by note rather than by lining-out, the common practice of the time; in 1733 the society formally advocated for this newer practice of "Regular Singing" or singing by note or rule. In 1769 a society of singing masters gathered in the South Meeting House to perform new vocal compositions with instrumental accompaniment. Important singing masters in Hartford during the Revolutionary era included Amos Bull, Timothy Olmstead, and Andrew Law; Law was granted the first copyright in Connecticut in 1781 for tunes in his publications. The diaries of lexicographer Noah Webster, who lived in Hartford in the 1780s, further describe local contemporary musical life.

Following self-imposed exile to London after accusations of Loyalist leanings, Rev. Samuel Peters wrote his "false" blue laws in *A General History of Connecticut* (1781), stating that playing any instrument except drum, trumpet, and jaw harp was forbidden; no such law existed. Violins were owned by Hartford residents before 1708. By the mid-century the fife had been introduced into the British Army, whose regimental bands influenced local musical life; New England later became a center for manufacture and trade of fifes and drums. The wealthy owned spinets, virginals, and pianos; after the war English pianos were imported extensively. The first organ in Hartford, built by George Catlin, was installed in Christ Church around 1800. Previously only pitch pipes or tuning forks had been permitted in church.

Hartford's strategic position between New York and Boston made it a stop for many touring musicians, from singers (Jenny Lind, 1851; Carlotta Patti, 1869; Clara Louise Kellogg, 1871) and pianists (Louis Gottschalk, early 1860s; Anton Rubinstein, 1873; Ignacy Jan Paderewski, 1892) to leading international orchestras under conductors such as Theodore Thomas (1868), Carl Zerrahn (Germania Orchestra, 1869), and Hans von Bülow (1875). From 1794 to 1799 Hallam and Hodgkinson's New York theatrical troupe presented comic operas by English composers Samuel Arnold, William Shield, Thomas Arne, and Stephen Storace, and concerts of music by Joseph Haydn, Stamitz, and Ignace Joseph Pleyel.

Although theater was temporarily banned in 1800, public musical performances flourished during the 19th century. Center Church (1807) was home to the city's first concert hall, and it has remained active as a venue. After 1807, when 100 singers gave an unaccompanied performance of George Frideric Handel's "Hallelujah" chorus at the dedication of Center Church, every church in the city formed its own choir. Hartford's first organized musical society, the Euterpian Society (1816–8), presented concerts of vocal and instrumental music. In 1818 English tenor Charles Incledon offered a song recital, possibly Hartford's first. The Jubal Society (1822–4), the city's first significant chorus, was succeeded by the Choral Society (1827–30), which gave the first complete performance of *Messiah* with organ accompaniment in 1828.

According to Hartford composer Dudley Buck, the city's first large choral concert with orchestra took place in 1858, when Henry Wilson conducted Felix Mendelssohn's 42nd Psalm and "Inflammatus" from Gioachino Rossini's *Stabat mater*. Other choral groups were the Beethoven Society (1858–74), Hartford Sängerbund (1858), Hosmer Hall Choral Union (1881–1903), all-female Treble Clef Club, out of which grew the Hartford Oratorio Society (1920–49), Hartford Chorale (1972), CitySingers of Hartford (1982), and Hartford's oldest surviving choral group, the all-male Choral Club of Hartford (1907). In 1934 Friends and Enemies of Modern Music sponsored the premiere of *Four Saints in Three Acts*, a controversial opera by Virgil Thomson with a libretto by Gertrude Stein. This group, founded in 1929 by the museum's director, A. Everett "Chick" Austin, and Francis Goodwin II, for several years presented concerts of 20th-century music at a time when little contemporary music was performed in Hartford. CONCORA/Connecticut Choral Artists, Inc., was founded in 1974 by conductor and artistic director Richard Coffey. It has been billed as Connecticut's premier professional choir, and it received the Governor's Arts Award in 2003.

The First Company, Governor's Foot Guard Band, began in 1809 with 14 musicians, six fifers, and four drummers. The first music written specifically for the company, *Foot Guard Quick Step* by Claudio S. Grafulla, was published in 1845 in Hartford, a major publishing center of the time. In 1887 the present-day Armory on High Street was built as a home for the Foot Guard and became an essential element of the Hartford social scene. The first Hartford appearance of the Boston SO occurred at the Armory; the John Philip Sousa band played an annual concert for nine years, beginning in 1892; and other appearances included Paderewski, the Strauss Orchestra, and Gilmore's Band. In 1904 the Foot Guard Band was revived, having hired Colt's Band as their musical ensemble for 28 years; members came from Hartford-area bands, namely Hatch's Military Band, Pope's Band, Colt's Band, and the American Band in Providence. In 1915 band members became enlisted members of the First Company, Governor's Foot Guard, following a dispute with the musicians' union regarding participation in the Memorial Day parade. Laura Lovich was the first female bandmaster, appointed in 1995. Band members provide music for the Governor's Inaugural Ball, parades, and other ceremonial activities.

The city's first significant orchestra was the Hartford PO (1899–1924). Hartford's principal concert hall has been the Horace Bushnell Memorial Hall (built 1930; capacity 3277), home to the Connecticut Opera Association (1942–2009) and the Hartford SO (1934–). The Hartford SO, under the name the Civic Symphony Orchestra of Hartford, was created as a public service under the Federal Emergency Relief Corporation, giving two free weekly concerts. In 1935 the Federal Music Project, part of the WPA, provided a salary increase to the players. The Hartford SO hired its first female music director, Carolyn Kuan, in 2011.

Chamber music moved from private homes to music halls with the advent of such groups as the original Memnon Club (1885–1900). Local chamber music organizations have included the Musical Club of Hartford (1891), Chamber Music Plus (1980), and the Connecticut Guitar Society (1985). The Wadsworth Atheneum (1934; capacity 308), the first U.S. public museum and one of the first museums to have an auditorium suitable for theatrical presentations, has routinely hosted chamber performances. The smaller Belding Theater was built adjoining the Bushnell in 2008. The XL Center, formerly the Hartford Civic Center (1975/2007; capacity 16,500) has been used primarily for rock and folk concerts.

As of 2012 the Greater Hartford Arts Council (1971) was the ninth largest United Arts fund in the United States, and it supported more than 150 area organizations and 2000 cultural events in the Greater Hartford area each year. The annual New England Fiddling Contest (1974–84) experienced a rebirth, returning to Bushnell Park in 1999 and relocating to Manchester, Connecticut, in 2008. The Celtic festival Pipes in the Valley held its first event in 2002, and was later partnered with Riverfront Recapture. Attendance had grown from 2000 to 25,000 in 2010. Sponsored by the Olde Burnside Brewing Company, Pipes in the Valley has hosted groups such as Clann an Drumma (now Albannach), 7 Nations, the Red Hot Chilli Pipers, and the local Manchester (Connecticut) Regional Police & Fire Pipe Band.

Jazz was heard in Hartford as early as 1919 and has remained an integral part of the city's cultural activities. As of 2012 the Hartford Jazz Society (1960) was thought to be the oldest jazz society in existence in the United States. The Garden Area Neighborhood Council's Summer Jazz Festival (1966) has been a free outdoor concert series. Since 1967 the Greater Hartford Festival of Jazz, a non-profit organization conceived by Hartford jazz bassist Paul Brown, has presented free summer concerts in Hartford's Bushnell Park; in 1991 the name was changed to the Monday Night Jazz Series to accommodate a new weekend jazz festival, which retained the former name. The annual August Jazz Festival (attendance 45,000 in 2010) has been the largest free jazz festival in New England; since 1977 it has been sponsored by Real Art Ways, an alternative arts and cultural center. The Artists Collective, Inc., (1965) was founded by saxophonist and NEA Jazz Master Award recipient Jackie McLean (1931–2006) and his wife, Dollie. The Collective presented jazz and gospel concerts and other artistic endeavors at rented venues throughout Hartford; its new facility on Albany Avenue has been an important component of the economic development of Hartford. It has been the only multi-arts and cultural organization in Connecticut focused on cultural and artistic contributions of African and Caribbean influences.

The Hartford Conservatory was founded in 1890 under the auspices of the Hartford Theological Foundation as the Hartford School of Music, and it closed its doors in May 2011. The Hartt School of Music, Dance, and Theatre, in West Hartford, was established in 1920 by Julius Hartt, Moshe Paranov, and associated teachers. Highlights of the school's early history include the first complete opera performance on television (*Hansel and Gretel*, 1943, WRGB in Schenectady, New York), directed by Paranov. In 1957 the Hartt School merged with the Hartford Art School and Hillyer College to form the University of Hartford. The growth of the Hartt School was furthered by the philanthropic efforts of Alfred C. Fuller, founder of the famous Fuller Brush Company and namesake of the Alfred C. Fuller Music Center, where the Hartt School has been housed. In 1997 his wife Mary Primrose Fuller bequeathed nearly $20 million to the school to ensure continuing support for Hartt programs.

The school expanded to the new Mort and Irma Handel Performing Arts Center in 2008. As of 2012 the

Hartt School encompassed the Jackie McLean Institute of Jazz, the Community Division and its more than 2200 students; in collaboration with the university's Maurice Greenberg Center for Judaic Studies, it was the first NASM-accredited school to offer a Bachelor of Music in pre-cantorial studies. In 2010 and 2011, there were roughly 705 undergraduate students and 175 graduate students, instructed by 54 full-time and 120 part-time collegiate faculty and majoring in composition, instrumental and vocal performance, jazz studies, music education, music history and theory, music and performing arts management, music production and technology, dance, and theater, including both actor training and music theater.

The nine-time Grammy-winning Emerson String Quartet was the quartet-in-residence from 1982 to 2002, and the Quartet's many awards included being honored by the Governor of Connecticut for outstanding cultural contributions to the state, the University of Hartford Medal for Distinguished Service (1994), and honorary doctorates from the University of Hartford (2011). In the early 2010s faculty additions included Grammy and Pulitzer Prize-winner Jennifer Higdon as a composer-in-residence in 2010, and Edward Cummings (2011), formerly of the Hartford Symphony. Notable 21st-century Hartt School alumni include Jonathan Lee Iverson (the youngest and first African American ringmaster for Ringling Bros. and Barnum & Bailey Circus), Tony-nominee (2009) Marin Ireland, Javier Colon (inaugural winner of NBC's *The Voice* in 2011), and Ryan Speedo Green (2011 Metropolitan Opera National Council winner). 16 October 2010 was proclaimed Hartt School Day by Governor M. Jodi Rell, citing the school's community involvement and pursuit of excellence.

BIBLIOGRAPHY

J.H. Trumbull and S. Peters: *The true-blue laws of Connecticut and New Haven and the false blue-laws invented by the Rev. Samuel Peters, to which are added specimens of the laws and judicial proceedings of other colonies and some blue-laws of England in the reign of James I* (Hartford, 1876)

N.H. Allen: "Old Time Music and Musicians," *Connecticut Quarterly*, i (1895), 274, 368; ii (1896), 54, 153; iii (1897), 66, 286; iv (1898), 319

N.H. Allen: *Music in a New England State: from Psalmody to Symphony in Connecticut* (Connecticut Historical Society, 1925), MS 35251

First Congregational Church: *The First Congregational Church, East Hartford, Connecticut, 1702–1902* (Hartford, 1902)

F.H. Johnson: *Musical Memories of Hartford* (Hartford, 1931/R 1970)

A.W. Coote: *Four Vintage Decades: the Performing Arts in Hartford, 1930–1970* (Hartford, 1970)

L.W. Fowles: *An Honor to the State: the Bicentennial History of the First Company, Governor's Foot Guard* (Hartford, 1971)

R.M. Wilson: *Connecticut's Music in the Revolutionary Era* (Hartford, 1979)

M.F. Sax: *In Meeting House, Parlor and Concert Hall: Three Centuries of Music in Hartford* (Hartford, 1986)

F.G. Way: *Scarlet Coat and Busby Hat: the 225th Anniversary of the First Company, Governor's Foot Guard* (Connecticut, 1998–1999)

S.A. Marini: "The New England Singing School: Sacred Music and Ritual Community in Revolutionary America," *Prism*, xiv/8 (2005), 1–2, 4

VICTOR T. CARDELL (with NINA DAVIS-MILLIS)/
TABITHA W. HEAVNER

Hartford [Harford], **John** (*b* New York, NY, 30 Dec 1937; *d* Nashville, TN, 4 June 2001). Country and bluegrass songwriter, multi-instrumentalist, and singer. Raised in St. Louis, he began playing fiddle, banjo, guitar, and other instruments as an adolescent, inspired by his parents' love of square dance music and by bluegrass radio broadcasts and performances. He learned from and often performed with traditional musicians from surrounding rural regions. Moving to Nashville in 1965, he secured a recording contract with RCA (and added the "t" to his surname). His compositions reflected influences ranging from the traditional and bluegrass music of his youth to Brill Building-style pop, Bob Dylan, and The Beatles, situating him among Nashville's most progressive young songwriters. His "Gentle on My Mind," a hit for Glen Campbell in 1967–8, remains one of the most recorded songs in history.

The commercial success of "Gentle on My Mind" gave Hartford considerable economic—and, thus, artistic—freedom. *Aereo-Plain* (1971), his first Warner Brothers album, combines bluegrass ensemble style with his eclectic compositional vocabulary and rock-influenced, semi-improvisational arrangements. His recorded output from *Mark Twang* (Flying Fish, 1976) forward, released mostly on independent labels, is stylistically diverse and includes collaborations with leading musicians in various genres. Its instrumentation ranges from unaccompanied fiddling and singing to elaborate arrangements featuring renowned session instrumentalists. In the 1990s, he researched the career of Appalachian fiddler Ed Haley and recorded two albums of Haley's repertoire. Shortly before his death from lymphoma, he recorded *Hamilton Ironworks* (Rounder, 2001), a tribute to his early mentors. Acclaimed as much for his colorful live performances as for his compositions and recordings, Hartford appeared prominently in several television programs and documentary films, including *Down from the Mountain* (Mike Zoss Productions, 2000). Hartford's complex artistic identity embraced both the traditional antecedents of country music and the hippy counterculture. A steamboat pilot, he incorporated his knowledge of riverine folklife into his songs and performances. He is remembered as an inventive instrumentalist, composer, lyricist, raconteur, and humorist.

BIBLIOGRAPHY

B. Silver: "John Hartford," *Bluegrass Unlimited*, xiv, 4 (1979), 12–16

J. Cohen: "An Interview with John Hartford," *Sing Out*, 28 (1980), 2–5

A. Menius: "John Hartford: Living His Dreams," *Bluegrass Unlimited*, 19 (1985), 14–18

N. Strauss: "Fiddling and Picking His Way to Perfection," *New York Times* (6 Oct 1999), reprinted in *The Bluegrass Reader*, ed. Thomas Goldsmith (Urbana, 2004), 316–18

MATT MEACHAM

Harth, Sidney (*b* Cleveland, OH, 5 Oct 1929). Violinist, conductor, and teacher. He studied at the Cleveland Institute (1945–9), and with MISHEL PIASTRO and George Enescu (1949–51). After winning the Naumburg Award he made his New York debut in 1949, his Paris debut in 1952, and won second prize in the Wieniawski Competition in 1957. In 1961 and 1966 he toured the USSR. He has appeared with most of the major symphony orchestras around the world. He has also performed often with his own string quartet and as part of a two-violin team with his wife, Teresa Testa (1927–2010). He was leader and assistant conductor of the Louisville Orchestra (1953–9) and leader of the Chicago SO (1959–62). He also led the Casals Festival Orchestra in Puerto Rico from 1959 to 1965 and again in 1972. He was leader and associate conductor of the Los Angeles PO (1973–9) and music director of the Puerto Rico SO (1977–9), in addition to leading other groups. His distinguished career as a teacher has included positions at the University of Louisville, the Hartt School, De Paul University, Carnegie-Mellon University, Mannes College, Yale University, and Duquesne University, where he currently teaches violin and serves as orchestral director.

The policy of the Louisville Orchestra to commission contemporary composers led to Harth's giving first performances of such works as Wallingford Riegger's Theme and Variations and Edmund Rubbra's *Improvisation*, and he himself commissioned and gave the first performance of *Colloquies* by Norman Dello Joio. However, he also plays the Classical repertory and has recorded sonatas and quartets by Johannes Brahms, Franz Schubert, W.A. Mozart, and Gabriel Fauré, revealing technical mastery and musical insight. His beautiful tone is enhanced by his "Comte d'Armaille" Stradivari of 1737.

BIBLIOGRAPHY
SchwarzGM
J. Creighton: *Discopaedia of the Violin, 1889–1971* (Toronto, 1974)
H. Hanani: "Multi-Purpose Man on the Run," *The Strad*, civ (1993), 1074–7

BORIS SCHWARZ/MARGARET CAMPBELL/R

Hartke, Stephen (Paul) (*b* Orange, NJ, 6 July 1952). Composer. He began his musical career as a professional boy chorister before composition lessons with Leonardo Balada at the United Nations International School. He then studied at Yale University, the University of Pennsylvania, where he was strongly influenced by George Rochberg's break with postwar serialism, and the University of California, Santa Barbara. After a year as a visiting professor at the University of São Paulo, Hartke joined the composition department at the University of Southern California in 1987.

Hartke came of age with the American neo-romantics, but his music tends to avoid the lush textures and cinematic gestures common to many composers of that school. Instead, he leans toward a cheerful eclecticism, demonstrating his indebtedness to Charles Ives's and Rochberg's aesthetic positions. His orchestration shows the influence of Igor Stravinsky's middle-period, and his highly variegated rhythms have a nervous energy that draws variously on bebop jazz, the spiky minimalism of Louis Andriessen, and Balinese gamelan music. His harmony, poised on the outskirts of tonality, is often marked by his careful study of Franco-Flemish polyphony. His restless inspirations are from sources as varied as Joan Miro's paintings, cartoons from Looney Tunes and R. Crumb, and Indonesian puppet theater. Deeply

affecting, hard-won, lyrical "breakthroughs" occur at the close of two important works of the 1990s, the Symphony no.2 (1990) and the Violin Concerto (1992). His opera *The Greater Good* (2006), based on Guy de Maupassant's tragic short story "Boule de Suif," is perhaps his greatest achievement, an excursion into Barber-like harmonic vocal lyricism and penetrating orchestral characterization.

WORKS
(selective list)
Orch: Alvorada, str, 1983; Maltese Cat Blues, 1986; Pacific Rim, 1988; Sym. no.2, 1990; Vn Conc. "Auld swaara," (1992); The Ascent of the Equestrian in a Balloon, 1995; Sym. no.3, 2003
Vocal: 4 Madrigals (old Port.) SATB/(2 S, A, T, B), 1981; 2 Songs for an Uncertain Age (W.H. Auden, G. Leopardi), S, orch, 1981; Cançoes modernistas (M. de Andrade), 1v, cl, b cl, va, 1982; Iglesia abandonada (F. García Lorca), S, vn, 1982; Sons of Noah (P. Littell), S, 4 fl, 4 bn, 4 gui, 1996; Tituli, 5 male voices, per, 1999; Precepts, SATB, ob, org, str orch, 2007
Opera: The Greater Good, 2006
Chbr and solo inst: Caoine, vn, 1980; Post-Modern Homages, pf, 1984–92; Sonata-Variations, vn, pf, 1984; Oh Them Rats is Mean in My Kitchen, 2 vn, 1985; Precession, 13 insts, 1986; The King of the Sun, tableaux, pf qt, 1988; The Pf Dreams of Empire, pf, 1994; Wulfstan at the Millenium, 10 insts, 1995; The Horse with the Lavender Eye, cl, vn, pf, 1997; Percolative Processes, per, 2005; Meanwhile, fl, cl, va, vc, per, pf, 2007; Night Songs for a Desert Flower, str qt, 2009

Principal publisher: Keiser Classical (BMI)

ALEX ROSS/S. ANDREW GRANADE

Hartman, Johnny [John Maurice] (*b* Houma, LA, 3 July 1923; *d* New York, NY, 15 Sept 1983). Singer. Hartman studied at Chicago Music College and recorded in the 1950s with pianists Earl Hines and Erroll Garner and trumpeter Dizzy Gillespie. He developed a crooning vocal approach that drew on Nat "King" Cole, from whom he adopted the inclination to sing pop and country tunes, and on Frank Sinatra, similarly becoming a specialist in performing love songs and slow-tempo interpretations of standards. Hartman's vocal style has also been appreciated for its timbre, cool rhythmic approach and almost theatrical delivery. His discography is limited to fewer than 20 albums but includes a masterpiece recorded with saxophone player John Coltrane (*John Coltrane and Johnny Hartman*, 1963, Impulse!). After playing with other saxophonists, including George Coleman and Jimmy Heath, he turned toward a trio format with, among others, Roland Hanna at the piano and George Mraz at the bass. He also toured Japan and Australia, where he hosted his own television show in 1968.

BIBLIOGRAPHY
D. Cerulli: "Johnny Hartman," *Down Beat*, xxiv/10 (1957), 34
W. Friedwald: *A Biographical Guide to the Great Jazz and Pop Singers* (New York, 2010), 201
G. Akkerman: *The Last Balladeer: the Johnny Hartman Story* (Lanham, MD, 2012)

LUCA CERCHIARI

Hartmann, Arthur (Martinus) (*b* Philadelphia, PA, 22 July 1881; *d* New York, NY, 30 March 1956). Violinist, teacher, and composer. He pretended to be Hungarian-born and adopted a mythical birthplace (Maté Szalka) but in fact he was born in Philadelphia, his impoverished parents having arrived from Hungary in 1879. He made his debut at the age of six in Philadelphia, where wealthy sponsors supported his violin lessons for six years with Martinus Van Gelder. Further studies followed in Boston with Loeffler (violin) and Homer Norris (composition). By the time he was 12 he had mastered a large repertory and begun to give concerts. In 1900 he moved to Europe, where he won Ysaÿe's approval in London and lived for a number of years in Berlin. After sensational appearances with the Philadelphia Orchestra (1906) and the New York PO (1908), he settled in Paris in 1908, becoming a friend of Debussy, whose music he transcribed and with whom he performed in 1913. He left Paris for the United States at the outbreak of World War I and made a successful transcontinental tour in 1916–17. In 1919 he moved to Rochester, where he led a private string quartet for George Eastman; he served on the faculty of the new Eastman School in 1921–2. In the late 1920s he settled in New York, dividing his time between solo and quartet concerts, teaching and composing, and editing and transcribing; he was active until his retirement in 1954. He contributed numerous articles to music journals (including *Musical America* and *Musical Courier*), wrote an instructional method for the violin (1926), and was an editor of *Who's Who in Music* in 1941.

At the height of his career, Hartmann was undoubtedly a highly accomplished violinist, both technically and intellectually; Joachim praised his playing of Bach, and Debussy also expressed his admiration. Yet, in spite of critical acclaim in the United States and Europe (particularly in Scandinavia), he never achieved great international fame. He had a strong affinity for teaching, and he was a skillful transcriber. His writings reveal self-confidence and intelligence.

WRITINGS

S. Hsu, S. Grolnic, and M.A. Peters, eds.: *"Claude Debussy as I knew him" and other writings of Arthur Hartmann* (Rochester, NY, 2003)

BIBLIOGRAPHY

W. Armstrong: "Arthur Hartmann, Violinist and Thinker," *The Musician*, xx (1915), 153 only
A.W. Kramer: "Enigma of Hartmann's Nationality," *MusAm*, xxii/9 (1915), 36 only
Obituary, *New York Times* (31 March 1956)

BORIS SCHWARZ/R

Hartt School of Music. Music school established in 1920 in West HARTFORD.

Harvard Musical Association [HMA]. Private charitable corporation in Boston, MA. The General Association of Past and Present Members of the Pierian Sodality (a student organization formed in 1808 at Harvard University) was founded in 1837 and changed its name to the Harvard Musical Association in 1840. The Association soon realized that it could not effect one of its original purposes, "to have regular musical instruction introduced in the College." Under the leadership of John Sullivan Dwight (1873–93), the HMA then concentrated on its other two original goals, directed toward Boston

rather than Harvard: to create a library for the musical public and to foster higher standards of musical taste. From 1844 to 1849 the Association presented Boston's first public series of chamber music concerts. In 1850 members raised $100,000 in 60 days to build Boston's Music Hall; in 1863, they raised an additional $60,000 for the installation there of what was then the largest organ in the United States. From 1865 to 1882 the HMA sponsored the Harvard Orchestra, conducted by Carl Zerrahn.

Currently the HMA hosts a sight-reading orchestra, provides free rehearsal and recital space, and offers prizes to music students and performers, awards to community organizations, and commissions to composers. Privately it continues to present annual concert seasons by prominent chamber musicians.

BIBLIOGRAPHY

A.W. Hepner: *Pro bono artium musicarum: the Harvard Musical Association 1837–1987* (Boston, 1987)
The Harvard Musical Association, <http://www.hmaboston.org/>

MARY WALLACE DAVIDSON

Harvard University. Private university in Cambridge, Massachusetts. *See* BOSTON (I); *see also* LIBRARIES AND COLLECTIONS. For details of the Harvard Musical Association *see* BOSTON (I).

Harwood, C(harles) William (III) (*b* Richmond, VA, 14 March 1948; *d* Little Rock, AR, 26 April 1984). Conductor. After studying piano and conducting as a youth he attended Yale University (BA 1970, MM 1973, MMA 1974), where his conducting teachers were FENNO HEATH and GUSTAV MEIER. After a year of study at the Hochschule für Musik in Berlin on a fellowship (1973), he returned to Yale in 1974 and became music director of various organizations, including the Yale SO and the Eastern Opera Theater of New York. In 1975 he made his opera debut at Yale in Mozart's *Idomeneo* and conducted the American premieres of Niccolò Piccinni's *La buona figliuola maritata* and Offenbach's *Robinson Crusoé*, and in 1977 conducted at Yale the world premiere of Debussy's *La chute de la maison d'Usher*. Harwood became director of the Texas Opera Theater and assistant conductor of the Houston SO in 1977; he was named associate conductor of that orchestra in 1980, when he also served as music director of the Arkansas SO. In 1981 he received the Stokowski Conducting Prize and as a result made his New York debut in Carnegie Hall with the American SO. In 1982 he was appointed music director of the Arkansas Opera Theater. He died unexpectedly at the age of 36, and Eduard Qualls dedicated his Symphony no.1, "An Arkansas Childhood," to Harwood's memory.

Harwood was an ardent champion of contemporary opera and symphonic music. He gave the premiere of Rochberg's *The Confidence Man* (1982) with the Santa Fe Opera Company and of Paulus's *The Village Singer* (1979) and *The Postman Always Rings Twice* (1982) with the Opera Theatre of St. Louis. With the latter company he took *The Postman* to the Edinburgh International Festival in 1983, in what was the first appearance of an American opera company at that event; in the same year he conducted Gershwin's *Porgy and Bess* in its original version at Carnegie Hall and on tour. To promote new symphonic music he initiated Contemporary Trends, a series of concerts by the Houston SO devoted solely to new American music, in 1982.

SORAB MODI/JONAS WESTOVER

Hassell, Jon (*b* Memphis, TN, 22 March 1937). Composer and trumpeter. After studying the trumpet, he received a DAAD grant to study composition in Cologne with Karlheinz Stockhausen and Henri Pousseur (1965–7) and pursued further study at the Eastman School of Music (BM 1969, MM 1970), where his teachers included BERNARD ROGERS. During the late 1960s he performed with ensembles led by Terry Riley and La Monte Young and composed works reflecting the influences of electronic music and minimalism. He has described *Solid State* (1969) as surrounding the audience with "vibrational forms evoking the…shift of sand dunes." In 1972 he began to study Indian music with Pandit Pran Nath, developing a quasi-vocal style of trumpet playing that has enabled him to "curve" melodic lines—manipulating pitches with his lips, or by loosening or removing the mouthpiece—which are often unrecognizable as being played by a trumpet. He has combined this technique with elements from electronic and free jazz to create syntheses of African, Asian, and Western musics. This he calls "Fourth World" music, suggesting a combination of Third World musics and First World electronic experimentation. The dense, muted timbres, complex repetitive rhythms, and sophisticated heterophony of Hassell's output after 1977 have been influential to musicians working in genres that cross between popular and art styles. His compositions include dance scores for Merce Cunningham, MOMIX, Dai Rakuda Kan, and Alvin Ailey, and collaborations with Brian Eno, Peter Gabriel, Talking Heads, David Sylvian, and the West African ensemble Farafina; his stage works often involve generously political attitudes. The Jon Hassell Concert Group has performed at major venues and festivals internationally; he began touring with a new ensemble, Maarifa Street, in 2005.

WORKS

Stage: Sulla astrada (music theater, after J. Kerouac: *On the Road*), 1982, Venice, May 1982, collab. M. Criminali; Zangezi, 1983–4; In Tseghi, choir, chamber group, 2008; Conversation Piece (with B. Eno), 2009

Other works: Music for Vibs, 1965; Blackboard Piece with Girls and Loops, 2 girls, 2 pitch-producing blackboards, 1968; Landscape Series, mixed media, 1969–72; Map nos.1–2, hand-held magnetic playback heads, 1969; Solid State, 2 synth, 1969; Superball, 4 players with hand-held magnetic tape heads, 1969; Pano da costa, str qt, 1987; Rainforest, installation, 1989

RECORDINGS
(selective list)

Vernal Equinox (1978/90); *Earthquake Island* (1979); *Fourth World Vol.1: Possible Musics* (1980); *Fourth World Vol.2: Dream Theory in Malaya* (1981); *Aka-Dabari-Java:/Magic Realism* (1983); *Power Spot* (1986); *The Surgeon of the Nightsky Restores Dead Things by the Power of Sound* (1986); *Flash of the Spirit* (1989); *City: Works of Fiction* (1990); *Dressing for Pleasure* (1994); *Fascinoma* (1999);

Maarifa Street: Magic Realism, Vol. 2 (2005); *Last Night the Moon Came Dropping Its Clothes in the Street* (2009)

BIBLIOGRAPHY

GroveA (C. Passy) [incl. further bibliography]
R. Palmer: "An Explorer on Music's Borderlands," *New York Times* (20 Nov 1981)
D. Toop: "Jon Hassell: the Pleasure Principle," *The Wire* [UK] no.126 (1994), 36–4

PAUL ATTINELLO

Hassler, Simon (*b* Germany, 25 July 1832; *d* Philadelphia, PA, 24 Jan 1901). Conductor and composer of German birth. He came to Philadelphia in 1842. His father, Henry Hassler, who became an American citizen in 1844, conducted at the Arch Street Theatre (1844), the Chestnut Street Theatre (1845), and the Walnut Street Theatre (1846–55), and was a member of the Musical Fund Society from 1847. Simon directed orchestras at the Walnut Street Theatre (1865–72), the Chestnut Street Theatre (1872–82), and the Chestnut Street Opera House (1882–99). He composed popular dance pieces, such as marches, galops, and quadrilles, as well as music for many of Shakespeare's plays, and a Festival March, which was performed at the opening of the Permanent Exhibition at Philadelphia in 1876. In 1854 he became a member of the Musical Fund Society, and he conducted the concert celebrating the remodeling of the society's concert hall in 1891. John Philip Sousa played under Hassler at the Chestnut Street Theatre during the late 1870s and produced some of his first transcriptions for its orchestra. An unsigned portrait of Hassler hangs in the Music Department of the Philadelphia Free Library.

Hassler's brother and sister were also musicians. Mark Hassler (*b* Germany, 1834; *d* Philadelphia, PA, 30 Nov 1906) directed the music at society balls in Philadelphia, Baltimore, and Washington, DC, and was reputedly the first to introduce Johann Strauss's waltzes into dances in America. He was music director at the Arch Street Theatre for a time, and conducted numerous "hops" at Congress Hall in Cape May, New Jersey. Rosalie Hassler Rau was an accomplished pianist. Three of Mark's children were also musicians: Herbert directed the orchestra at the Chestnut Street Opera House for a while; Harriet became a singing teacher in New York; and Arthur managed dance and concert orchestras in Philadelphia.

THOMAS E. WARNER/R

Hastings, Francis H(enry) (*b* Weston, MA, 13 July 1836; *d* Kendall Green, MA, 23 Feb 1916). Organbuilder. Raised as a farmer, Hastings entered the renowned organ firm of E. & G.G. Hook in Roxbury, Massachusetts, as an apprentice in 1855. He showed leadership and rose through the company's ranks, becoming a partner with Elias and George G. Hook in 1871. Nameplates that year began to read E. & G.G. Hook & Hastings. Following the deaths of the founders, he assumed control of the firm in 1881. In 1889, he moved the firm to Kendall Green, MA, built a new factory, and in 1893 it was incorporated as HOOK & HASTINGS (although the firm began using this name on organs as early as 1881). Hastings was known for his artistic and mechanical skills and showed excellent business judgment. The firm he led dominated the church organ industry around Boston for much of the late 19th and early 20th centuries. Following Hastings's death, the firm was led by Arthur L. Coburn (1860–1932). The firm closed in 1936 during the Great Depression.

BIBLIOGRAPHY

"Francis H. Hastings, Pioneer Builder, Dead," *Diapason*, vii/5 (1916), 1 only

P.W. Fox: *Farm Town to Suburb: the History and Architecture of Weston, Massachusetts, 1830–1980* (Portsmouth, NH, 2002)

STEPHEN L. PINEL

Hastings, Thomas (*b* Washington, Litchfield Co., CT, 15 Oct 1784; *d* New York, NY, 15 May 1872). Composer, tunebook compiler, hymn writer, and writer on music. His early musical education came largely from independent study and family encouragement. In 1797 the family moved from New England to Clinton, New York, where Thomas led a village choir and began teaching singing schools. He became active in the Oneida County Musical Society (later named the Handel and Burney Society), formed around 1814. In 1815 he began his career as a tune book compiler. He taught singing schools in Utica and the surrounding area, and from 1819 to 1823 in the region of Troy and Albany.

In 1823 Hastings settled in Utica, where he edited the *Western Recorder*, a religious weekly. His regular column on church music helped to establish his reputation, and he made occasional trips from Utica to lecture and advise religious groups on the subject. In 1832 he moved to New York City, where he organized a program of collective music instruction for the choirs and congregations of more than a dozen churches. He remained in New York until the end of his life as a teacher and choirmaster, a compiler of sacred tune books and other publications, a participant in musical and religious associations, and a leader in musical "conventions" and "normal institutes" for the training of music teachers.

Hastings is estimated to have composed some 1000 sacred pieces—many published anonymously or under pseudonyms—and written about 600 hymn texts. His tunes "Toplady," "Ortonville," "Retreat," and "Zion" were popular in American hymnals during the 19th and 20th centuries, and are still found in some collections. He assisted in the compiling of about 35 collections of music, produced several books and articles on music, and founded and edited a monthly periodical, the *Musical Magazine* (1835–7).

Hastings exemplified the concern for "taste" that dominated the ideology of American sacred music from the second decade of the 19th century. He was critical of the unorthodox harmonic style of the Yankee psalmodists, the use of shape-note notation, and particularly opposed the contrafacting of secular melodies into hymn tunes. He believed that the chordal texture and orthodox thoroughbass harmonies of contemporary Anglo-European hymnody—the idiom in which he cast his own compositions and arrangements—were founded upon established principles of musical "science." In his view the "state of infancy" of music in America meant that an elaborate musical style could not effectively express religious emotions to most American worshippers. In an 1837 letter, he claimed particular virtue for the cautious, straightforward hymn tune style that he and Lowell Mason had helped to establish, noting that "Europe has no style strictly devotional that compares at all with what we are cultivating in this country."

Hastings's first and perhaps foremost tune book, *Musica sacra* (1815, 2/1816), "compiled at the request, and published under the patronage of the Oneida County Musical Society," was combined with Solomon Warriner's *The Springfield Collection* (1813), and as *Musica sacra*, or *Springfield and Utica Collections United* went through 10 editions and many reprints over two decades (1818–38). Other tune books were published under the sponsorship of the New York Academy of Sacred Music (*The Manhattan Collection*, 1836, *The Sacred Lyre*, 1840); the American Tract Society (*Sacred Songs for Family and Social Worship*, 1842, rev. and enlarged 2/1855, *Songs of Zion*, 1851); the Methodist Episcopal Church (*Indian Melodies*, 1845, a book of tunes by Thomas Commuck, harmonized by Hastings); and the Presbyterian Church's Board of Publications (*The Presbyterian Psalmodist*, 1852, *The Presbyterian Juvenile Psalmodist*, 1856). Hastings collaborated with Lowell Mason in *Spiritual Songs for Social Worship* (1832), a collection of less formal songs that was intended to undo the "damage" caused to "correct" church music by Joshua Leavitt's *The Christian Lyre* (1831). He also worked with a number of other compilers, including W.B. Bradbury, I. B. Woodbury, G.F. Root, and P. Phillips. His *Dissertation on Musical Taste* (1822/R, 2/1853/R), the first full-length musical treatise by an American-born author, was an important landmark, and his *The History of Forty Choirs* (1854/R) provides evidence of the state of church music in America during the mid-19th century and further commentary by Hastings on his philosophy of church music.

BIBLIOGRAPHY

DAB (W.T. Utter)

J.E. Dooley: "Introduction," in T. Hastings: *Dissertation on Musical Taste* (Albany, NY, 1822/R), v–xv

J. Julian: *Dictionary of Hymnology* (London, 1892, 2/1907), 494–495, 1569

F.J. Metcalf: *American Writers and Compilers of Sacred Music* (New York, 1925/R)

M.B. Scanlon: "Thomas Hastings," *MQ*, xxxii (1946), 265–77

J.E. Dooley: *Thomas Hastings: American Church Musician* (diss., Florida State U., 1963)

R. Stevenson: *Protestant Church Music in America* (New York, 1966), 81–2

M.D. Teal: "Letters of Thomas Hastings," *Notes*, xxxiv (1977–8), 303–18

L.M. Roth: *Heaven, Harmony, and Home: Thomas Hastings's and Joshua Leavitt's Dueling Tunebooks* (diss., U. of Wisconsin-Madison, 1996)

J.M. Jordan: *Sacred Praise: Thomas Hastings on Church Music in Nineteenth-Century America* (diss., Southwestern Baptist Theological Seminary, 1999)

H.W. Williams: *Thomas Hastings: an Introduction to His Life and Music* (New York, 2005)

RICHARD CRAWFORD/DAVID W. MUSIC

Hathaway, Donny (Edward) (*b* Chicago, IL, 1 Oct 1935; *d* New York, NY, 13 Jan 1979). Rhythm-and-blues vocalist, pianist, songwriter, and arranger. He attended Howard University in Washington, DC, and worked as a writer and producer in Chicago before signing in 1969 with Atlantic Records and releasing the albums *Everything Is Everything* (1970), *Donny Hathaway* (1971), and *Extension of a Man* (1973). Hathaway's best-known single as a solo artist was "The Ghetto" (1970), which romanticized inner-city life; later solo recordings often featured his soulful, melismatic vocals, and intricate keyboard work. Hathaway found his greatest commercial success with duet partner Roberta Flack, with whom he recorded "You've Got a Friend" (1971), "Where is the Love" (1972), and "The Closer I Get to You" (1978). *Roberta Flack & Donny Hathaway* (1972) was the most successful album of his career. Hathaway battled mental illness, which caused a decrease in output during the late 1970s and contributed to his suicide in 1979.

BIBLIOGRAPHY

Obituary, *New York Times* (15 Jan 1979)

ANDREW FLORY

Haubiel [Pratt], Charles (Trowbridge) (*b* Delta, OH, 30 Jan 1892; *d* Los Angeles, CA, 26 Aug 1978). Composer and pianist. He made his recital debut at the age of 14 at the New York College of Music. From 1909 to 1913 he studied in Europe with RUDOLF GANZ (piano) and Alexander von Fielitz (theory); he returned to the United States in 1913 to tour with the Czech violinist Jaroslav Kocian. After teaching in Oklahoma City at Kingfisher College and the Musical Arts Institute (1913–17), he served in France during World War I, and returned to New York in 1919 to study with ROSARIO SCALERO (composition) and Modest Altschuler (orchestration). From 1920 to 1930 he taught piano at the Institute of Musical Art, continuing his own piano studies with JOSEF LHÉVINNE and ROSINA LHÉVINNE (1928–31), and from 1923 to 1947 taught composition and theory at New York University. In 1935 he founded the Composer's Press, serving as president until 1966 when the firm was taken over by Southern Music. He moved to California in the 1960s.

Haubiel won first prize in the Schubert Centennial Contest in 1928 with his symphonic variations *Karma*; other of his numerous awards are the Swift Symphonic Award (for *Portraits*, 1935), the New York Philharmonic Symphony Contest award (for the Passacaglia from *Solari*, 1938), and the Harvey Gaul Prize (for Five Etudes for Two Harps, 1953). A prolific composer, Haubiel was an avowed classicist and a skillful contrapuntist; his music is characterized by a synthesis of Romantic, Classical, and Impressionistic elements, combining a diatonic vocabulary with flowing and graceful melodic lines and coloristic 20th-century harmonies. Some 20 of his works have been recorded.

WORKS

Stage: Brigands Preferred (comic op, M. Leonard), 1929–46; Passionate Pilgrim (incid music, M.C. Munn), *c*1937; The Witch's Curse (fairy tale op), 1940; The Birthday Cake (operetta, H. Flexner), *c*1942;

Sunday Costs 5 Pesos (Mexican folk op, J. Niggli), 1947, rev. as Berta, 1954; The Enchanted Princess, *c*1955; Adventure on Sunbonnet Hill (children's operetta, K.H. Bratton), *c*1971

Orch: Mars Ascending, 1923; Karma, sym. variations, 1928, rev. as Of Human Destiny, 1968; Vox cathedralis, 1934; Portraits (3 ritratti caratteristici), 1935; Solari, 1935–6; Suite passacaille, 1936; Sym. in Variation Form, 1937; Miniatures, str, 1938–9; Passacaglia Triptych, 1939–40; 1865 AD, 1945; Pioneers: a Sym. Saga of Ohio, 1946, rev. 1956; American Rhapsody, 1948; A Kennedy Memorial, 1965; Heroic Elegy, 1970; several other orch works, many orch transcrs. of chbr or inst pieces

Chbr ens, 3 or more insts: Duoforms, pf trio, 1929–13; Lodando la danza, ob, pf trio, 1932; Romanza, pf trio, 1932; Pf Trio, 1932; Gay Dances, pf trio, 1932; Echi classici, str qt, 1936; In the French Manner, fl, vc, pf, 1942; Trio, fl, vc, pf, 1942; Str Trio, 1943; Trio, cl, vc, pf, 1969; numerous other works for a variety of inst ens, incl. 5 pf trios, 5 trbn qts

1–2 insts: Cryptics, bn, pf, 1932; En saga, vn, pf, 1938; Gothic Variations, vc, pf, 1943; Portraits, pf, *c*1944; Sonata, vc, 1944; Ariel, pf, *c*1945; Nuances, fl, pf, 1947; Shadows, vn/vc, pf, 1947; Sonata, vc, pf, 1951; 5 Etudes, 2 hp, 1953; Epochs, vn, pf, 1954; Toccata, pf, 1956; American Rhapsody, pf, *c*1964; Cryptics, vc, pf, 1973; Capriccio diabolico, pf; many others, incl. 8 vn, pf works, *c*30 pf works, children's pf pieces, works for 2 pf, solo org, hp, vn, fl

Vocal: 3 cants, incl. Father Abraham (E.N. Hatch), solo vv, SATB, nar, orch, *c*1945; Portals (sym. song cycle, M. Mason), high v, orch, 1963; Threnody for Love (F. Blankner), A, fl, cl, vn, vc, pf, 1965; works for chorus, orch; 1 motet; *c*10 choral partsongs; 1 choral song cycle; *c*25 songs

MSS in *Wc, CAh*, University of Wyoming, Laramie

Principal publishers: Composer's Press, Elkan-Vogel, Southern

BIBLIOGRAPHY

EwenD; *GroveO*

J.T. Howard: *Our Contemporary Composers* (New York, 1941)

D. Ewen: *American Composers Today* (New York, 1949)

G.A. Ryder: *Melodic and Rhythmic Elements of American Negro Folk Songs as Employed in Cantatas by Selected American Composers between 1932 and 1967* (diss., New York U., 1970)

Obituary, *Billboard* (9 Sept 1978)

KATHERINE K. PRESTON/MICHAEL MECKNA

Haugen, Marty (*b* Wanamingo, MN, 30 Dec 1950). Liturgical music composer, workshop presenter, and recording artist. After earning degrees in psychology (BA, Luther College) and Pastoral Studies (MA, University of St. Thomas), Haugen began writing songs for Catholic and Protestant congregations. Initially influenced by the St. Louis Jesuits, Haugen writes music in a contemporary style that is accessible to the average parishioner. Of his several Mass settings, his *Mass of Creation* has been sung throughout the entire English-speaking world. The same is true for his Lutheran liturgies, *Holden Evening Prayer* and *Now the Feast and Celebration*.

The texts of Haugen's songs rely heavily on Scripture, especially the Psalms, and are set in simple refrain-verse or strophic forms; they also feature attractive melodies and accompaniments that can be performed by flexible combinations of instruments. His songs' harmonic schemes range from simple ("This is the Day," "With Joy You Shall Draw Water") to relatively sophisticated ("As A Tree By Streams of Water," "Taste and See"), and he is one of the few current liturgical composers who composes successfully in the minor mode ("Shepherd Me, O God," "Wind Upon the Waters," and "Burn Bright," which also employs changing meters). Haugen has also made successful arrangements of plainchant (*Easter Alleluia, Creator of the Stars of Night*) and hymns (*We Walk by Faith, The King of Love My Shepherd Is*).

Haugen has recorded more than 30 collections of his music; many of these compositions have been included in modern hymnals. Among his best-known songs are "All Are Welcome," "Canticle of the Sun," "Gather Us In," and "We Are Many Parts."

KATHLEEN SEWRIGHT

Hauk, Minnie [Hauck, Amalia Mignon] (*b* New York, NY, 16 Nov 1851; *d* Villa Triebschen, nr Lucerne, 6 Feb 1929). Soprano, later mezzo-soprano. She first studied with Gregorio Curto of New Orleans. Shortly after 1860 her family returned to New York, where she studied with ACHILLE ERRANI at the suggestion of Max Maretzek, who subsequently signed her to a contract with his company. Her operatic debut, when she was 14, was in Brooklyn, as Amina in *La sonnambula* (13 October 1866); her New York debut was as Prascovia in Meyerbeer's *L'étoile du nord* (3 November 1866). She toured with Maretzek's company (1866–7) and sang Juliet in the American premiere of Gounod's *Roméo et Juliette* at the New York Academy of Music (15 November 1867). On her first trip to Europe in 1868, financed by the publisher Gustav Schirmer, she was accompanied by her mother, a constant companion and close adviser throughout her career.

In Paris, Hauk studied with MAURICE STRAKOSCH and made her debut in the spring of 1869. Her London debut, at Covent Garden, was the following October with J.H. Mapleson's company, with which she was associated for many years. After appearances in Italian operas in Paris, Moscow, and St. Petersburg (1869–70), she sang in German operas in Vienna (1870–73) and Berlin (1874–7); in the latter she was a principal during the first season of the Komische Oper (1874). In 1878 Hauk had engagements in Brussels and London, during which she first sang the title role of *Carmen*. Later that year she toured the United States with Mapleson's troupe; she performed in both London and the United States until 1881. That year she married Baron Ernst von Hesse-Wartegg, an Austrian nobleman, journalist, and author; they mounted a worldwide concert tour that lasted three years. She sang the title roles in the first American performances of *Carmen* (23 October 1878) and *Manon* (23 December 1885). Her only season at the Met was 1890–91. She subsequently organized her own (short-lived) opera company, which presented the first Chicago performance of *Cavalleria rusticana* (28 September 1891). Her last operatic appearance in America was as Selika in Meyerbeer's *L'Africaine* (Philadelphia, 4 November 1893); her final London performance was as Santuzza in *Cavalleria rusticana* (8 February 1895). Hauk subsequently lived mainly in Switzerland with her husband; after his death in 1918 she lived in Berlin.

Hauk's voice was a mezzo-soprano of great force and richness; she was also an accomplished actress who is credited with infusing Italian opera with powerful dramatic realism. She was a quick study and had an enormous repertory (about 100 parts). She sang fluently in four languages and was best known for her performances of *Carmen* (which she sang some 500 times), although *L'Africaine* became a popular vehicle late in her career.

BIBLIOGRAPHY

DAB (F.H. Martens)
NAW (F.D. Perkins)
M. Hauk: *Memories of a Singer*, ed. E.G. Hitchcock (London, 1925)
Obituary, *New York Sun* (6 Feb 1929)
Obituary, *New York Herald Tribune* (7 Feb 1929)
Obituary, *Musical Courier* (14 Feb 1929)
O. Thompson: *The American Singer* (New York, 1937/*R*), 93ff
J.S. Kendall: "The Friend of Chopin, and Some Other New Orleans Musical Celebrities," *Louisiana Historical Quarterly*, xxxii (1948), 856–76
H.D. Rosenthal, ed.: *The Mapleson Memoirs* (London, 1966)
J.F. Cone: *First Rival of the Metropolitan Opera* (New York, 1983)

H. WILEY HITCHCOCK/KATHERINE K. PRESTON

Haunani [Kahalewai, Kahalewai] (*b* Hilo, HI, 19 Feb 1929; *d* San Carlos, CA, 2 March 1982). Hawaiian singer. She received most of her formal training in high school. She began her professional career singing with a band in a small club outside of Honolulu. In later years, she formed her own group, the Rainbow Serenaders, and performed throughout the islands. She caught the attention of Don the Beachcomber, who invited her to join the show at his restaurant in Waikiki. Webley Edwards then gave her a regular spot on his radio show *Hawaii Calls*. She was known for her distinct contralto voice but was capable of reaching well into the mezzo-soprano range.

In 1959, Haunani signed her first record deal with Capitol Records. She recorded three albums with that label before moving to Decca Records in 1965 where she recorded four more. Her repertoire included *hapa haole* songs (songs with Hawaiian themes and English lyrics), songs in the Hawaiian language, pop standards such as "Some Enchanted Evening," and other songs associated with the Pacific islands. She was accompanied by a typical Hawaiian band consisting of the steel guitar, acoustic guitars, 'ukulele, and double bass, and was often backed by a mixed chorus. Haunani regularly performed at the Monarch Room at the Royal Hawaiian Hotel and at the Kahala Hilton in Honolulu, and toured mainland United States, Canada, Japan, Australia, and Europe. Haunani also composed, arranged, and produced. In 1996, she was posthumously inducted into the Hawaiian Music Hall of Fame, and the Hawaiian Academy of Recording Arts awarded her a Lifetime Achievement Award in 2002.

RECORDINGS
(selective list)
Trade Wind Islands (Capitol T1203, 1959); *Moon of the Southern Seas* (Capitol T1381, 1960); *Haunani* (Capitol T1700, 1962); *Haunani: The Voice of Hawaii* (Decca DL74561, 1965); *Aloha from Haunani* (Decca DL74705, 1966); *Island Spotlight on Haunani* (Decca DL74895, 1967); *From Hawaii with Love* (Decca DL75013, 1968)

PAULA J. BISHOP

Hauser [Houser], **William** (*b* Bethania, NC, 23 Dec 1812; *d* Wadley, GA, 15 Sept 1880). Composer and tune book compiler. He was a Methodist minister and also worked as a physician. In 1841 he moved to Georgia, settling eventually in Wadley. He compiled *The Hesperian Harp* (Philadelphia, 1848), which, with 552 pages, was the largest shape-note tune book in common use in the South. In four-shape notation, it contains 36 of Hauser's own compositions as well as many original arrangements of tunes from earlier publications. With Benjamin Turner, Hauser issued a second tune book, *The Olive Leaf* (Philadelphia, 1878), in seven-shape notation, which included 48 of his own works. Much of the music reflects the northern influence of gospel hymns.

See also SHAPE-NOTE HYMNODY.

BIBLIOGRAPHY

G.P. Jackson: *White Spirituals in the Southern Uplands* (Chapel Hill, NC, 1933/R), 70, 336

J.D. Scott: *The Tunebooks of William Hauser* (diss., New Orleans Baptist Theological Seminary, 1987)

D.W. Patterson: "William Hauser's Hesperian Harp and Olive Leaf: Shape-note Tunebooks as Emblems of Change and Progress," *Journal of American Folklore*, ci/1 (Jan–March 1988), 23–36

JOHN F. GARST/R

Haussermann, John (William, Jr.) (*b* Manila, Philippines, 21 Aug 1909; *d* Denver, CO, 5 May 1986). Composer and organist. His father was the attorney general of the first American civil government in the Philippines and wrote the city charter for Manila before moving with his family to New Richmond, Ohio, in 1915. Afflicted with cerebral palsy from childhood, Haussermann studied music at the Cincinnati Conservatory (1924–7) and at Colorado College, before going to Paris in 1930 to study organ with Marcel Dupré. While in Paris he became friends with Ravel and began serious study of composition with Le Flem. In 1934 Haussermann moved to Cincinnati, where he founded a contemporary concert series. That year, Goossens led the Cincinnati SO in the first performance of Haussermann's *Nocturne*; he subsequently performed many of Haussermann's orchestral works, including his best-known composition, the *Voice Concerto* (1942). One of his more unusual compositions is his *Serenade for Theremin and Piano*.

After moving to Briarcliff, New York, Haussermann had an organ built jointly by Aeolian-Skinner and Holtkamp, and loaned it to the 1939 New York World's Fair, for which he established an organ committee that sponsored recitals and compositions. He occasionally made public appearances as an organist, performing his own compositions and improvisations. In 1940 he was a founder of the American Colorlight Music Society, which promoted the theories of Skryabin and László. With the exception of a period in Mallorca (1953–7), he lived again in Cincinnati from 1947 to 1967 and was an active supporter of the Cincinnati College-Conservatory. He dictated his compositions painstakingly by playing a single note at a piano; an assistant confirmed the pitch at a second instrument. Haussermann's works have a Chopinesque fluency and are rhythmically propulsive (though regular) and metrically fluid, with a French sensibility in their whole-tone harmonies. They are deft reminiscences of music

of a bygone era, whose freshness and fluency belie the difficulty of their inception.

Haussermann's manuscripts, memorabilia, and papers are held at the Music Division of the Library of Congress and at the University of Illinois Archives.

WORKS

Orch: Nocturne and Danse, op.8, 1933; After Christmas, suite, op.10, 1934; Sym. no.1, op.16, 1937–8; Rhapsodic Ov., op.17, pf, chbr orch, 1939–40; Sym. no.2, op.22, 1941; Voice Conc., op.25, 1942; Ronde carnavalesque, op.29 no.1, 1943; Ecologue romanesque, op.29 no.2, 1943; Sym. no.3, op.34, 1947; Stanza, op.37, vn, orch, 1949; Conc., op.48, org, str, 1985

Pf: 24 preludes symphoniques, op.2, 1932–3; 2 Sonatines, opp.3, 7, 1932–3; Ballade, burlesque, et legende, op.14, 1936; 2 Waltzes, op.33, 1946–7; 7 Bagatelles, op.35, 1948; Fantasy, op.42, 1955; 9 Impromptus, op.43, 1959; 5 Harmonic Etudes, op.45, 1968; 2 pf duos

Org: 7 Chorals, op.6, 1933; Suite gothique, op.9, 1933–4; 2 Sonatas, op.19, 1939; Nuptial suite, op.26, 1943

Chbr: Pf Qnt, op.11, 1934; Qnt (Conc. da camera), op.1, fl, ob, cl, bn, hpd, 1935; Suite rustique, op.13, fl, vc, pf, 1935–6; Str Qt, op.15, 1936; Poeme et Clair de lune, op.20, vn, pf, 1939–40; Serenade, op.23 no.3, theremin, pf, 1940; Divertissements, op.21, str qt, 1941; Sonata, op.24, vn, pf, 1941; Improvisata, op.39, theremin, str, 1950; En-revant, op.40, vn, pf, 1954

Vocal: 5 Singing Miniatures (various), op.12, S, pf, 1933–4; 3 Moods (Haussermann), op.18, 1v, pf, 1939; On the River (Chin.), 5 songs, op.30, v, pf, 1945; Sacred Cant., op.31, Bar, orch, 1946–55; 2 Vocalises, op.38 no.1, Bar, pf, no.2, S, pf, 1955; 3 Pss (xxiii, xci, c), op.44, T, pf, 1959; St Francis' Prayer, chorus, op.46, 1968; 4 Haiku for Nelga, S, pf, op.47, 1982; a few other songs

Many other works inc. or withdrawn

Principal publishers: Boosey & Hawkes, Composer's Press, Kenyon, Senart, G. Schirmer

SUSAN FEDER/JONAS WESTOVER

Hautboys. Musical wind ensemble usually consisting of three oboes and a bass oboe or bassoon with snare drums, popular in military units from the end of the 17th century until the rise of HARMONIEMUSIK. The term denoted the military band as well as the instrumental combination, a practice that continued in some countries into the 19th century.

See BAND §1.

Havasupai. Native American tribe whose members live in a verdant, isolated region near and in the Grand Canyon of Arizona. Havasupai culture has been influenced by other proximate Native American cultures, but retains its unique character; while assimilating a large number of song types from many sources. They have a lively tradition of song types not reported elsewhere in North America. The language of the Havasupai belongs to the Yuman family, but their music differs sufficiently from other Yuman types to be considered distinct from the California-Yuman musical tradition. Havasupai music does, however, owe something to the California-Yuman and Great Plains Indians, whose relaxed vocal delivery resembles their own, and from whom some (though not all) of their songs are borrowed. Members of the tribe use frame drums to accompany some songs and gourd rattles for others; no other musical instruments are used. The typical Havasupai song has a short, strophic melody, with two to six short phrases, and a form such as AB, AAB, AABC, ABCA, or AABBCA. Often the penultimate or last phrase of a strophe has slightly higher melodic material than the rest, but in all cases the range is small—rarely greater than a 5th or 6th. The text in most native Havasupai songs is through composed, consisting principally of real words rarely vocables, altered slightly by adding extra syllables and changing some vowels and consonants into a "song language." The song often ends abruptly, sometimes in the middle of a strophe. Havasupai song genres can be divided into those which originated with them and those they borrowed from other cultures. Original Havasupai genres include medicine, weather, and circle dance songs. Medicine songs traditionally were sung by a shaman during healing ceremonies, using a gourd rattle as accompaniment. Many Havasupai also had personal medicine songs that they sang without instrumental accompaniment. No singing shamans remain today among the Havasupai, but some of their songs are remembered, and a few people still sing their personal medicine songs. Medicine songs are believed to have been revealed by spirits to members of the tribe while they slept. Weather songs were used to try to alter the climate and like medicine songs they were acquired via dreams. Some weather songs are remembered, but the Havasupai consider it to be dangerous to sing them except within a ceremony.

Circle Dance songs accompany the popular social dance. Although the Havasupai have had this dance for centuries, most of the present-day songs were inspired by the GHOST DANCE of 1890, when the Havasupai were converted by the Paiute (bridging the connection between original and borrowed songs). Recently some Havasupai have begun to dream and compose new songs. In the Circle Dance the singer sits in the middle of a circle and plays a drum for accompaniment while the dancers hold hands and move clockwise with a sidestep. Each Circle Dance song has only one or two words, mostly in the Havasupai language (a few are in English or Paiute); the rest of their texts consist of vocables. The songs are still widely sung and are the most popular type of traditional song today. They are sung at most social occasions, especially at night during the Peach Festival.

Borrowed song genres include sweathouse, hunting, kachina, horse, bird, tomant (mourning), and salt; more recent generations have shown interest in genres such as rock and country. Sweathouse songs are mostly old with a few new ones being composed. It is said that these songs were learned from the southern Piute, from whom the Havasupai acquired the tradition of the sweathouse (a communal bath, much like a sauna, used mainly for curative purposes). The songs have the typical paired-phrase patterning of the Great Basin musical style (AA BB CC etc.), and they are sung inside of the sweathouse without accompaniment. Unlike other songs they consist principally of vocables without text. Hunting songs belong to families, each of which has its own set of such songs. They are sung quietly, without instrumental accompaniment, often in the sweathouse during purification of the body in preparation for hunting, or around the fire at night in a hunting camp. Hunting songs are intended to tame deer, and to make easier

the task of finding and killing them. Kachina songs, pertaining to ancestral spirits, are remembered by only a few, and are no longer performed publicly. They were borrowed from the neighboring Hopi, and were sung at social gatherings, especially the Peach Festival (an annual gathering of the Havasupai to which other tribes are invited). The rhythm and form of the songs are considerably simpler than those of their Hopi counterparts. (The Hopi sing many Havasupai songs also in substantially altered form.) A member of the tribe who had been raised by the Navajo brought horse songs, originally from the Navajo Beauty Way, to the Havasupai. They are now sung to tame horses and to keep them moving steadily when they are herded or driven. Bird, tomant, and salt songs are cyclical songs in the Yuman style many learned in the 20th century from the Mohave and Chemehuevi. They are sung at social gatherings, but more often at funerals and memorial ceremonies, which were once conducted among the Havasupai without singing or dancing. While there are Havasupai who know and perform the song cycles, and have dreamed some (a singer's having dreamed a cycle validates his right to perform it), Mojave singers, who are often invited to attend memorial ceremonies, are deferred to in such instances to be the lead singers.

Lullabies are not considered by the Havasupai to be "true songs." They are merely ditties, some in the old traditional style, others improvised. Most of them have no real words. The *cante fable* is a long, traditional myth with one or more songs interpolated therein. The tales are told in the third person, while all emotions are expressed, and all characters quoted, in song form using the first person. There is no instrumental accompaniment and these stories are told only in winter. This use of songs within stories is prevalent in the Great Basin, Yuman, and O'odham cultures. The Walapai and the Yavapai, who speak dialects closely related to that of the Havasupai, also have these songs.

Narrative songs are stories told entirely in song form, and may be 15 to 20 minutes long. Like the *cantes fables* they are sung only in winter. Women's songs and men's songs are secular pieces that can be sung anywhere at any time as a form of self-expression. Most commonly they are love-songs made up by young women describing the subject of their affections; others are women's complaints against relatives, including husbands. Some are work songs, such as the popular Piñon Nut songs are sung while gathering the nuts that are used for food. Less often men compose the music; one well-known example is the Farewell Song, composed generations ago by an old man too weak to travel, who sang farewell to the lands he used to wander. These songs have no instrumental accompaniment; they are often comic or poignant, and always very poetic.

Traditional songs are still sung and listened to among the Havasupai, but they are not as popular as some newer genres brought in from outside. Hymns (some of which have been translated into Havasupai), rock, country music, and reggae are all heard in the canyon. Thus the Havasupai hold true to their old tradition of welcoming music of all forms into their community.

DISCOGRAPHY
American Indian Music of the Southwest (Folkways, 1951)

BIBLIOGRAPHY
L. Spier: "Havasupai Ethnography," *Anthropological Papers of the American Museum of Natural history*, xxix/3 (1928), 83–292
C.L. Smithson: *The Havasupai Women* (Salt Lake City, 1959)
C.L. Smithson and R. Euler: *Havasupai Religion and Mythology* (Salt Lake City, 1964)
L. Hinton: *Havasupai Music: a Linguistic Perspective* (Tübingen, Germany, 1984)
L. Hinton and L. Watahomigie, eds.: *Spirit Mountain: an Anthology of Yuman Story and Song* (Tucson, 1984)
J. Martin: *The Havasupai* (Flagstaff, 1986)
C.L. Smithson: *Havasupai Legends: Religion and Mythology of the Havasupai Indians of the Grand Canyon* (Salt Lake City, 1994)

LEANNE HINTON/J. RICHARD HAEFER

Haverly, J.H. [Jack] (*b* Bellefonte, PA, 30 June 1837; *d* Salt Lake City, UT, 28 Sept 1901). Minstrel show manager. He began his career in 1864 in Michigan and Ohio, and by the late 1860s and early 1870s he was managing his own and others' minstrel troupes. From about 1873 he concentrated his talents on his own company, Haverly's Minstrels, and began to buy interests in other companies and theaters in several cities. The trend toward huge companies began with Haverly's Mastodon Minstrels in 1878, with its "40, count 'em, 40" performers; by 1880 he had a company of 100. After 1883 minstrelsy was dominated by the type of large, profitable company, traveling nationwide, that Haverly had pioneered; such companies replaced the raucous shows of the early troupes with lavishly produced variety entertainments. Haverly's Mastodon Minstrels disbanded in 1896, and Haverly retired from active management shortly after. He was probably minstrelsy's most successful organizer and promoter, having a good sense of the public's taste and a flair for advertising and producing.

BIBLIOGRAPHY
E.L. Rice: *Monarchs of Minstrelsy* (New York, 1911)
C. Wittke: *Tambo and Bones: a History of the American Minstrel Stage* (Durham, NC, 1930)
R.C. Toll: *Blacking up: the Minstrel Show in Nineteenth-century America* (New York, 1974)

ROBERT B. WINANS/R

Hawaii [Hawai'i]. Lying in the North Pacific Ocean just a few degrees south of the Tropic of Cancer, approximately 2550 miles southwest of Los Angeles, the Hawaiian islands archipelago comprises over 130 islands stretching over 1500 miles. The southernmost high volcanic islands are inhabited, while the lower islands and shoals to the north are a wildlife preserve. The 2010 US Census reported a statewide population of 1.36 million.

The first settlers arrived some 2000 years ago from islands to the south, and in ensuing centuries their language and culture developed distinct from ancestral relations. The arrival of British explorer Capt. James Cook in 1778 drew the islands into the global system of European and eventually American capitalism and imperialism. The archipelago's indigenous people embraced Christianity and literacy, introduced by missionaries of the Boston-based American Board of Commissioners for Foreign Missions (ABCFM), along with the constitutional government of the kingdom that was unified under one ruler by 1810. Capitalists who developed sugar cultivation drew their labor workforce from China, Japan, the Philippines, and elsewhere. A coup led by American businessmen in 1893 was followed by formal annexation to the United States in 1898, and statehood in 1959. By the late 1880s, Hawai'i was already developing as a tourist destination; and tourism promotion was augmented by the circulation of exoticist stereotypes. Contemporary Hawai'i sustains a multicultural melange of peoples and lifeways, and a history of over two centuries of global interaction. (Note: Hawaiian-language spellings, including the name Hawai'i, follow official State of Hawai'i usage.)

All of these factors inform any consideration of Hawaiian music in the 21st century. The indigenous performance traditions of the Native Hawaiian people have remained at the core of "Hawaiian music," even as that core has been transformed by musical incorporations and appropriations by Hawaiians and non-Hawaiians alike, both inside and outside Hawai'i. The multicultural milieu in Hawai'i, moreover, has blurred boundaries between ethnicity and culture. Since the 1970s, the vibrant movement for Native Hawaiian sovereignty and self-determination has added yet more layers of musical expression that are meaningful to Generation-X youth.

1. Indigenous native Hawaiian performance. 2. Indigenous performance expanded.

1. INDIGENOUS NATIVE HAWAIIAN PERFORMANCE. Mele—poetic text—is the basis for Native Hawaiian performance. All performance is classified in one of two general modes. Poetic recitation that is accompanied by interpretive choreographed dances is called HULA. Poetic recitation without dance is called oli. The primary distinction between oli and hula is the presence, in hula, of rhythmic pulse and meter. The absence of dance in oli performance eliminated any need for meter, allowing the performer more latitude for expression.

Oli embraces at least five named styles whose musical characteristics span a spectrum from conversational patter of indeterminate pitch, to patterns of prolonged pitch: 1) *kepakepa*, rapid conversation patter used to deliver lengthy enumerations of prayer or genealogical detail; 2) *kāwele*, a relatively unpitched but dramatically heightened delivery useful for presenting myths and legends; 3) *olioli*, recitation with sustained pitch, primarily on one tone, varied by the use of named articulatory techniques and pitch embellishments; 4) *hō'aeae*, which uses patterns of prolonged pitches with even greater use of vocal embellishments; and 5) *ho'ouweuwē*, lamenting, with the range and prolongation of pitch most dramatically expanded by wailing.

Hula classifications recognized distinctions in the sacredness of the subject matter in texts. *Hula pahu* were the most sacred dances, dedicated to the most powerful

Hula dancers with pahu and ipu drummer. (Hawaiian Historical Society)

within the pantheon of divinities. Dancers were accompanied by one or more musicians who recited the mele to the accompaniment of a *pahu* sharkskin-covered log drum, played either solo, in groups, or in combination with a smaller drum called *pūniu*, a fishskin-covered bowl-shaped vessel, most often of coconut. The next class of sacred dances, *hula ʻalaʻapapa*, honored powerful ruling chiefs who, in the Hawaiian worldview, were direct descendants of divine gods and goddesses. Dancers were accompanied by one or more musicians seated on the ground, who recited the mele to the accompaniment of *ipu heke*, a gourd idiophone of Hawaiian invention found nowhere else in the Pacific. The ipu heke is constructed of two gourds glued together at their necks, with a soundhole cut in the top. The instrument is held with the left hand, and played by thumping it on the ground and slapping it on its side. Basic rhythmic patterns are combinations of the two tones produced.

A range of percussive handheld implements may be incorporated into choreographed dances. These implements are manipulated by dancers, and enhance the sonic dimension of hula performance. They include *ʻulīʻulī* feather decorated rattle, *ʻūlili* triple-gourd string-pulled rattle, *pūʻili* split bamboo rattle, *kālaʻau* sticks, *ʻiliʻili* waterworn pebbles, and *papa hehi* wooded treadle board. When dances are choreographed as seated dances, the dancers also intone the mele as they execute the choreography.

In addition to the percussive instruments and handheld implements used in hula performance, indigenous sound-producing instruments also included *ʻohe hano ihu* nose-blown flute used in courtship as a substitution for voice, *ʻūkēkē* one-stringed mouth harp, *pū* conch shell trumpet used for signalling, *oeoe* bull-roarer, and *niʻau kani* leaf whistle used for amusement.

2. INDIGENOUS PERFORMANCE EXPANDED. During the early decades of European and American presence in the islands, Hawaiian musical horizons were expanded by ship bands entertaining their Hawaiian hosts as well as by the experiences of Hawaiians who signed onto ship crews. Accounts by visitors increased interest in the islands among traders, governments with military might and imperial designs, and eventually, Christian missionaries. Over the 19th century, the expansion of indigenous Hawaiian performance drew from two main sources—the acquisition of knowledge and practice of western music taught by missionaries, and a distinctly Hawaiian incorporation of musical instruments and instrumental traditions of European and American origin.

The American Protestant missionaries who arrived in 1820 worked strategically to learn the Hawaiian language. The first printed product from the missionary press in 1822, a primer that associated spoken Hawaiian with roman alphabets, was followed in 1823 by a collection of 47 hymn texts translated from English. Its title, *Na Himeni Hawaii…* used the term *hīmeni* Hawaiianized from "hymn." Missionary efforts included systematic instruction in the rudiments of western music practice, through singing schools, and use of the system of western staff notation. In 1834, a Hawaiian-language music primer was published as an introduction to the first printed tunebook which contained 194 hymns. Needless to say, the indigenous performance traditions and their tributes to the panoply of deities became the target of missionary-inspired censure and attempted extermination.

Despite eventual denominational diversity in Hawaiʻi, Protestant hymnody and hymn-singing have enjoyed predominance among Hawaiians. The earliest repertoire of metric psalm tunes, consolidated in the tunebook *Ka Lira Hawaii* (1842/R), was eclipsed in popularity by American Sunday School gospel hymnody, which has prevailed in printed hymnals through the 20th century. Congregational singing is the foundation of harmonized choral singing as maintained in the annual Song Contest among the secondary-level classes at the privately-endowed Kamehameha Schools.

HYMNODY and hymn-singing practice is at the root of secular song composition. By the 1860s, Hawaiian songwriters emerged among missionary-educated students who were capable of notating their work in musical scores. They used the alternating verse-chorus format of gospel hymnody as models, and drew on sentimental Victorian parlor songs as their thematic inspiration. Prominent among the first generation of Hawaiian songwriters were four royal siblings—collectively called "Nā Lani 'Ehā"—King David Kalākaua (r. 1874–1891), LILI'UOKALANI, QUEEN OF HAWAI'I (r. 1891–1893), Miriam Likelike, and Willian Pitt Leleiohoku. Several hundred songs were published as sheet music and in notated songbooks between 1869 and the 1960s. The term *mele Hawai'i* appears in these publications to distinguish these songs from Christian hīmeni and older forms of mele used in hula. Songbook publishers included Honolulu's Bergstrom Music Co.; Wall, Nichols, Co.; and The Hawaiian News Co., and co-publication agreements ensued, especially with San Francisco's Sherman, Clay & Co. In the 20th century, publication of mele Hawai'i repertoire was dominated by songwriter Charles E. King. Two of his volumes, *Book of Hawaiian Melodies* and *Songs of Hawaii* went through many printings between 1916 and 1948.

The adoption of musical instruments began with the guitar. Tradition has it that the guitar was brought by cowboys from Mexico, and its use flourished in rural locales. By the turn of the 20th century a distinctly Hawaiian melodic finger-picking style had materialized, named *kī hō'alu* after the practice of slackening strings to altered tunings; this style did not come to popular attention through commercial recordings until the late 1940s. A wind band was started by King Kamehameha III (r. 1824–1854). Under the direction of Prussian bandmaster Henry Berger from 1872–1915, the Royal Hawaiian Band achieved international renown, winning a band competition in San Francisco in 1884, and touring the United States and Europe. Berger composed several marches which incorporated tunes of mele Hawai'i into the trio sections, one of the most famous being "Hilo March." In the early 1880s, the instrument modelled on the Portugese machete came to be called 'ukulele and gained widespread popularity (*see* UKULELE).

By the 1880s, amidst concerted efforts by non-Hawaiian capitalists to usurp land and political power, the reigning King David Kalākaua promoted a renaissance of indigenous Hawaiian traditions. Performances of oli and hula flourished under royal patronage. Practitioners who had safeguarded the traditions against Christian suppression began to create anew, and a modern form of hula and accompanying song emerged, called *hula ku'i* (*ku'i* literally meaning "hula which joins old and new"). Instruments of non-Hawaiian origin—in particular guitar and 'ukulele—melodies using western musical elements and harmonization, innovative hula movements, and a new strophic template for poetic format were fused with Hawaiian poetic idioms, vocal articulatory techniques, and pre-existing hula movements. Hundreds of new mele compositions were published in Hawaiian-language newspapers. In the political turmoil of the 1890s, the format of hula ku'i was the favored expression of Queen Lili'uokalani's supporters. The distinct poetic format was also presented with accompaniment of indigenous ipu heke, in a performance stream that became known in the early 20th century as *hula 'ōlapa*, distinguishing this performance style from the guitar-accompanied hula ku'i.

By the turn of the 20th century, Hawaiian music and hula had moved to the forefront of entertainment as well as the marketing of Hawai'i as a tourist destination. Scheduled steamship transportation to Hawai'i facilitated burgeoning numbers of visitors. Hawaiian entertainers toured on vaudeville and chautauqua circuits across the continental United States. Hawaiian songwriter and music publisher A.R. "Sonny" Cunha composed a series of songs using English lyrics that marked the birth of "hapa haole song"—songs considered "half Hawaiian." In 1915, the debut of the song "On the Beach at Waikiki" in the Hawaiian Pavilion at the Panama-Pacific Exposition in San Francisco was one of the sparks to the ensuing national craze for Hawaiian music. While the earliest hapa haole songs were in the strophic format of hula ku'i, songwriters in

Don Ho. (Photofest/Lebrecht Music & Arts)

New York's Tin Pan Alley music publishing industry instantly began churning out Hawai'i-themed songs in English, using the 32-bar AABA popular song form that became convention among subsequent Hawai'i-based composers of hapa haole song such as R. Alex Anderson, Harry Owens, Jack Pitman, and Tony Todaro.

A parallel development was the emergence of a new guitar technique, attributed to Hawaiian schoolboy Joseph Kekuku, of using a piece of steel rather than fingers on the guitar neck to stop the strings. This melodic style came to the attention of US recording company executives, who began recording Hawaiian music as early as 1891. Following the publicity given to Hawaiian musicians at the 1915 Panama-Pacific Exposition, Hawaiian records outsold all other categories, according to the Victor Records catalog. Hawaiian music recordings were also produced by Columbia, Edison, Okeh, and Brunswick, and touring performers also made studio recordings globally in cities such as New York, Paris, Sydney, Shanghai, and Delhi. (An award-winning discography by T. Malcolm Rockwell documents the production of 78-rpm discs up to 1960.) Marketed as HAWAIIAN GUITAR, the popularity of records spurred music publishers such as William Smith (New York), Oahu Publishing (Cleveland), and Bronson (Detroit) to flood a crowded market with sheet music and instruction manuals. (Note that the Hawaiian guitar playing style is distinct from the rural-based style that gained public popularity in the 1940s as SLACK KEY GUITAR.)

The Hawaiian music being offered in Waikiki hotel showrooms and night spots, quickly imitated and exported by touring musicians, was presented by medium-sized instrumental ensembles whose arrangements reflected various trends in American popular music. These orchestras presented floor shows followed by music or after-dinner dancing. Headlining bandleaders, whose name graced recordings and songbooks, include Johnny Noble, Harry Owens, Andy Iona, Dick McIntire, Ray Kinney, and Pua Almeida.

The popularity of Hawaiian music extended into Hollywood musical films, which in turn spawned showrooms across the continent that offered musicians lucrative and extended employment opportunities. The cadre of musicians who enjoyed film studio and recording contracts (especially on the Decca Records label) include Andy Iona, Ray Kinney, Sam Koki, Dick McIntire, Lani McIntire, and Danny Stewart. In 1935, the *Hawaii Calls* radio show began weekly live broadcasts from Waikiki. Hawaiian music's popularity was further bolstered during World War II as thousands of US soldiers deployed to the Pacific passed through Hawai'i, taking away fond memories and thoughts of returning as visitors.

In addition to the ubiquity of Hawaiian music and hula entertainment in the tourist industry—which emphasized the more accessible hula ku'i, hapa haole songs, and Hawaiian guitar rather than the more esoteric chanted hula 'ōlapa fare—Hawaiian music was also cultivated as a central element in community-based commemorations as well as in family celebrations marking rites of passage such as birthdays, graduations, and weddings. Privately-run studios offering hula instruction proliferated after the 1920s, supporting demand for live and recorded music. To meet that demand, Honolulu-based record labels started up in the 1940s, of which Bell, 49th State (named prior to Alaska being admitted to the Union ahead of Hawai'i), and Waikiki Records dominated the supply of hula ku'i and hapa haole songs through the 1960s. Subsequent Hawaiian record labels devoted to Hawaiian music include Tradewinds, Hula, Sounds of Hawaii, Mahalo, Makaha, Lehua, and Poki. The extensive catalogs built up by these record labels capture continuity in Hawaiian-language songwriting, among whom Lena Machado, Bill Ali'iloa Lincoln, John K. Almeida, Alice Namakelua, and Mary Kawena Pukui were particularly prolific.

While musicians freely incorporated a wide range of stringed and wind instruments and even drumsets, the core instrumentation established for hula ku'i songs is what is referred to as a "'ukulele trio"—'ukulele, rhythm guitar, and bass. Instruments that provide fill-in embellishment include the steel guitar and a distinctly Hawaiian semi-improvised piano style. Vocal styles included judicious use of named ornamental techniques carried over from oli chanting, such as *'i'i* vibrato, *aeae* glide, and *he'u* laryngealization. A distinctive feature of Hawaiian singing is located in emphasizing the timbral contrasts between lower and upper voice registers. While male vocalists have developed virtuosic technique in singing extensively in the falsetto register, both male and female vocalists embellish melodic movement from one register to the other with a yodel-like break called *ha'i*. Prominent falsetto singers in the early to mid-20th century include Mike Ho'omanawanui, Andy Cummings, George Kainapau, Joe Keawe, and Benny Kalama. After a brief period where falsetto singing fell out of favor among singers, a new generation emerged that included Ledward and Nedward Ka'apana and cousin Dennis Pavao, Clyde Sproat, and Rick and Sol Ho'opi'i; the members of the Hawaiian Isle Serenaders—Kekua Fernandez, Sam Bernard, Keali'i Joy, and Darrell Lupenui, Tony Conjugacion; and most recently the original trio Nā Palapalai—Keao Costa, Kehau Tamure, and Kuana Torres. Falsetto singing contests organized in the 1990s have encouraged young singers to learn the technique, and both the contests and the contestants have spawned numerous recordings. In the succession of women ha'i singers, four singers have loomed large: Lena Machado, Genoa Keawe, Amy Hanaiali'i Gilliom, and Raiatea Helm.

In the 1960s, as Hawaiian youth were being drawn to American popular and rock music, a new generation of Hawai'i-based songwriters writing in English reclaimed Hawai'i from the overly romanticized and exoticized imagery in hapa haole songs. The songwriter Kui Lee valorized themes of home and homecoming, and broke from the Tin Pan Alley legacy of the

32-bar AABA popular song format. Lee's songs were championed by singer Don Ho.

The tide turned dramatically in the 1970s with a vigorous resurgence of interest in Hawaiian culture that reversed several decades of waning interest in Hawaiian music and hula among Hawaiian youth. Recording activity shifted away from groups contracted by venue operators (such as hotels, boat excursions, and revues) toward artists addressing and expressing quests for identity. Eddie Kamae and The Sons of Hawaii exemplified the approach of combining choral harmonization and rhythm guitar; subsequent groups embracing this strategy include the Makaha Sons and Ho'okena. A different approach, of pursuing innovative fusions of Hawaiian repertoire with idioms from popular, rock and jazz musics, had as its leader Peter Moon and his group the Sunday Mānoa. After the Sunday Mānoa split up in the late 1970s, Peter Moon continued to headline his own band, while Robert and Roland Cazimero became the Brothers Cazimero. New songwriters emerged to generate new repertoire that coexisted with songs passed from the past, including Kihei de Silva, Dennis Kamakahi, Kenneth Makuakane, Keli'i Tau'a, and Palani Vaughan. The iconic steel guitar associated with Hollywood and tourist stereotypes fell from favor among Hawaiians, but its popularity continues across the United States and Europe, especially among fans who discovered Hawaiian music before the 1970s resurgence. The Nā Hōkū Hanohano "Stars of Distinction" awards were established in 1979 to recognize artistic and technical achievement in recording; they are often referred to as Hawai'i's version of the Grammy Awards.

Renewed interest in the hula led to a revival of chanted hula, now called *hula kahiko*, as well as continued performance of hula ku'i and hapa haole songs, now called *hula 'auana*. Hula students affiliate with privately-run hālau schools directed by kumu hula master instructors. Many kumu hula are also accomplished musicians in both ancient chant and modern hula ku'i performance, and have enjoyed success as recording artists as well. Serious hula acolytes comb for historical repertoire in the archival collections at Honolulu's Bishop Museum, which holds 19th-century manuscripts as well as field recordings from the 1920s and 30s collected by anthropologists Helen Roberts, Kenneth Emory, and Theodore Kelsey. Ethnomusicologist Elizabeth Tatar completed an important study of Helen Roberts's materials and other archival resources. The publication of Tatar's monograph *Nineteenth Century Hawaiian Chant* in 1982 supported the efforts of students of oli to revive nearly-defunct techniques.

The Hawaiian guitar playing technique called kī hō'alu or slack key enjoyed a great surge in popularity in the 1970s. The older generation of guitarists, including Gabby Pahinui, Sonny Chillingworth, Ray Kane, and Leonard Kwan, were lionized as exponents of a continuous orally-transmitted tradition. Keola Beamer authored the first instructional book in 1973, and has since been one of the leading champions of making

instruction accessible through workshops and even online. The Ka'apana family from the remote southeastern Kalapana region of Hawai'i island incorporated slack key into ensemble vocal performance. New age pianist George Winston was drawn to the style, and conceived of a comprehensive documentation effort. Several dozen CDs were issued on his Dancing Cat record label, and extensive national touring by the artists since the late 1990s expanded appreciation of Hawaiian slack key. This forms the backdrop for the dominanation of slack key compilation albums in five of the seven years of the existence of a dedicated category for Hawaiian music in the Grammy Awards, from 2004–2011.

Two developments brought about renewed popularity of the 'ukulele in the 1990s, in both ensemble and solo playing. Although the instrument had maintained a continuous presence in accompaniment for hula, it had been eclipsed by youth preference for guitar instead. In ensemble playing, strumming patterns suddenly became the focus of accelerating speed and variety. The playing of Kehau Tamure, a member of the group Nā Palapalai, is widely admired. In solo playing, charismatic performers began to push the boundaries of technique to unprecedented levels of virtuosity. Soloists who have successful performance and recording profiles that are grounded in Hawaiian repertoire include Troy Fernandez, Brittni Paiva, Daniel Ho, Bryan Tolentino, and Jake Shimabukuro.

A successful movement to revitalize the Hawaiian language through immersion education has yielded a new generation of bilingual songwriters. Prominent among them are Kainani Kahaunaele, Kaumaka'iwa Kanaka'ole, and Keali'i Reichel.

While Hawaiian music is a distinct ethnic culture with a deep heritage, contemporary musicians and audiences move fluidly between the ancestral traditions, their present-day expressions, and music genres popular nationally and globally. Jamaican reggae music has been successfully transplanted into the Hawai'i context, where artists tailor the music around lyrics relevant to Hawai'i themes and concerns. African American hip-hop music and culture also enjoys a more modest presence; the group Sudden Rush produced three albums between 1994 and 2002 that combined Hawaiian-language rapping on Hawaiian nationalist perspectives.

Hawai'i's capital city of Honolulu has long hosted a cosmopolitan musical life. Throughout the early and mid-1800s, touring troupes enroute between North America, Australia and Asia gave performances of theater and opera. Music instruction in Hawai'i schools followed American and European conventions, as did the establishment of professional companies in symphony orchestra, opera, theater, and ballet. The opening of Maui Arts & Cultural Center in 1994 dramatically expanded state-of-the-art facilities to host performances, exhibitions, and gatherings beyond Honolulu.

The Music Department at University of Hawai'i at Mānoa, established in 1947, has provided tertiary-level music instruction, and has produced many K-12 music educators for Hawai'i schools. In the 1950s the Music Department drew upon master artists in Hawai'i's Pacific and Asian communities as a central component of an internationally respected program in ethnomusicology. The Music Department began offering graduate-level study towards the masters degree in 1960, and PhD-level study in 1992.

Other campuses in the University of Hawai'i system also offer programs devoted to Hawaiian music. The University of Hawai'i Hilo incorporates Hawaiian mele and hula in its Hawaiian language degree programs, and the Hawa'i Lifestyles Program at Hawai'i Community College offers a dedicated track in hula. On O'ahu, the Windward Community College launched the Hawaii Music Institute in 2001 to offer classes and community programming. In 2007 Honolulu Community College began a partnership with Belmont University in Nashville, to offer courses in the Music and Entertainment Learning Experience (M.E.L.E.), where students can earn associate degrees in music business or audio engineering. In 2011 University of Hawai'i Maui College launched its Institute of Hawaiian Music, directed by Grammy Award-winning producer and slack key guitarist George Kahumoku, Jr.

BIBLIOGRAPHY

N.B. Emerson: *Unwritten Literature of Hawaii; the Sacred Songs of the Hula* (Washington, DC, 1909/R)

H.H. Roberts: *Ancient Hawaiian Music* (Honolulu, 1926/R)

D. Kahananui: *Music of Ancient Hawaii* (Honolulu, 1962)

G. Daws: *Shoal of Time* (Honolulu, 1974)

D. Barrère, M.K. Pukui and M. Kelly: *Hula: Historical Perspectives* (Honolulu, 1979)

G.S. Kanahele, ed.: *Hawaiian Music and Musicians: an Illustrated History* (Honolulu, 1979)

E. Tatar: "Toward a Description of Precontact Music in Hawai'i," *Ethnomusicology*, xxv/3 (1981), 481–92

J.H. Hopkins: *The Hula* (Hong Kong, 1982, 2/2012)

E. Tatar: *Nineteenth-Century Hawaiian Chant* (Honolulu, 1982)

G.H. Lewis: "'Da kine' Sounds: the Function of Music as Social Protest in the New Hawaiian Renaissance," *American Music*, ii/2 (1984), 38–52

A.K. Stillman: "Published Hawaiian Songbooks," *Notes*, xliv/2 (1987), 221–39

D.W. Bandy: *The History of the Royal Hawaiian Band 1836–1980* (thesis, U. of Hawaii at Mānoa, 1980)

L. Ruymar: *The Hawaiian Steel Guitar* (Anaheim Hills, CA, 1996)

A.K. Stillman: "Hawaiian Hula Competitions: Event, Repertoire, Performance, Tradition," *Journal of American Folklore*, cix (1996), 357–80

A.K. Stillman: "Beyond Bibliography: Interpreting Hawaiian-Language Protestant Hymn Imprints," *EthM*, xl/3 (1996), 469–88

J. Beloff: *The Ukulele: a Visual History* (San Francisco, 1997, 2/2003)

D.E. Hall: "Opera in 19th-Century Hawai'i," *Hawaiian Journal of History*, xxxi (1997), 71–96

J.K. Osorio and K.G.T. Young: *Lei Mele No Pauahi: Music, Past and Present, at Kamehameha Schools* (Honolulu, 1997)

P. Hayward, ed.: *Sound Alliances: Indigenous Peoples, Cultural Politics and Popular Music in the Pacific* London, 1998 [incl. A. N. Weintraub, "Jawaiian Music and Local Cultural Identity in Hawai'I"; A. K. Stillman: "Hula Hits, Local Music and Local Charts: Some Dynamics of Popular Hawaiian Music"]

F.Y. Akindes: "Sudden Rush: *Na Mele Paleoleo* (Hawaiian Rap) as Liberatory Discourse," *Discourse*, xxiii/1 (2001), 82–98

P. Hennessey: "Launching a Classic: *Aloha 'Oe* and the Royal Hawaiian Band Tour of 1883," *Journal of Band Research*, xxxvii/1 (2001), 29–44

D.E. Hall: *The Honolulu Symphony: A Century of Music* (Honolulu, 2002)

A.K. Stillman: "Of the People Who Love the Land: Vernacular History in the Poetry of Modern Hawaiian Hula," *Amerasia Journal*, xxviii/3 (2002), 85–108

J.R. Carr: *In the Wake of John Kanaka: Musical Interactions between Euro-American Sailors and Pacific Islanders, 1600–1900* (diss., U. of California, Santa Barbara, 2006)

T.M. Rockwell: *Hawaiian & Hawaiian Guitar Records 1891–1960* (Kula, HI, 2007), <http://78data.com>

C.H. Garrett: *Struggling to Define a Nation: American Music and the Twentieth Century* (Berkeley, 2008), 165–213

A. Sala: *Claiming the Colonial and Domesticating the Foreign: A Native Hawaiian Aesthetic for the Piano in Hula Ku'i Music* (thesis, U. of Hawai'i at Mānoa, 2011)

I. Stagner: *Kumu Hula: Roots and Branches* (Honolulu, 2011)

J. Tranquada and J. King: *The 'Ukulele: A History* (Honolulu, 2012)

Dancing Cat Records: *Hawaiian Slack Key Book* (Santa Cruz, n.d.), <http://www.dancingcat.com/skbook-tableofcontents.php>

A.K. Stillman: *Hawaiian Music and Hula: Bibliography of Printed Sources*, <http://sitemaker.umich.edu/hawn.music/>

A.K. Stillman: *Hawaiian Music for Listening Pleasure: Recordings, Recommendations and Remarks*, <http://amykstillman.wordpress.com>

AMY KU'ULEIALOHA STILLMAN

Hawaiian guitar [lap steel guitar; lap steel; steel guitar]. Hawaiian guitar is a performance practice in which the strings of a Guitar are stopped with a smooth object, usually a cylindrical steel bar, rather than the fingers. The instrument is laid across the player's lap with the string plane parallel to the ground, and the strings are plucked with metal or plastic plectra. The use of the bar produces a highly characteristic tone and allows for expressive vibrato and a smooth portamento. As the bar is laid across the string plane, players are largely restricted to the intervals of the instrument's tuning, which is based upon an open chord (for example, E-A-e-a-c#-e').

The genesis of the tradition is generally traced to Joseph Kekuku (1874–1932), who claimed to have invented the style in the 1880s. Other possible sources include an immigrant named Gabriel Davion, who is thought to have played the steel guitar in imitation of the South Indian *gottuvadhyam*. Further analogues of this technique include European zithers such as the *scheitholt*, the *hummel*, and the *épinette des Vosges*—each of which can be played with a wooden stick—and the Japanese *ichigenkin* and *nigenkin*, which are played with an ivory cylinder.

In the early 1900s, the style was brought to the United States mainland, where it was featured in the 1915 Panama-Pacific International Exhibition and the musical revue *Bird of Paradise*. Hawaiian guitarists such as Sol Ho'opi'i, Frank Ferera, and Pale K. Lua became popular recording artists in this period. The style's foundation in Hawaiian vocal music was slowly eroded as it was assimilated into new musical contexts. On the one hand, notated instruction manuals for amateur players featured Hawaiian tunes alongside works by Wagner, Brahms, and Foster. On the other hand, performers such as Jimmie Rodgers and the Dixon Brothers combined the technique with Southern vernacular vocal styles. Virtuosos such as Roy Smeck also incorporated elements of classical technique, jazz, and blues.

In the 1920s and 30s, attempts to increase the guitar's volume resulted in the RESONATOR GUITAR, the introduction of electrical amplification, and the advent of the solidbody lap steel guitar. The sustain and glissando produced by the new electric instruments produced the iconic sound now associated with Hawaiian steel guitar music. Amplified steel guitars became a mainstay of country music styles such as western swing and honky tonk, and an important signifier of country music in other genres. The lap steel is also featured in the African American sacred steel tradition, where it is valued for its ability to imitate the voice. Outside of the United States, the steel guitar has been used in African pop music as well as classical music of North India.

See also HAWAII.

BIBLIOGRAPHY
H. Roberts: *Ancient Hawaiian Music* (Honolulu, 1926)
G. Kanahele, ed.: *Hawaiian Music and Musician: an Illustrated History* (Honolulu, 1979)
M. Hood: "Musical Ornamentation as History: the Hawaiian Steel Guitar," *Yearbook for Traditional Music*, xv (1983), 141–48
S. Phillips: *Mel Bay Presents the Art of the Hawaiian Steel Guitar: Over 50 Great Solos with Detailed Analyses and Historical Background.* Vol. 1 (Pacific, MO, 1991)
L. Ruymar, ed.: *The Hawaiian Guitar and its Great Hawaiian Musicians* (Anaheim Hills, CA, 1996)
G.T. Noe and D.L. Most: *Chris Knutsen: From Harp Guitars to the New Hawaiian Family: History and Development of the Hawaiian Steel Guitar* (Everett, WA, 1999)
A. Volk: *Lap Steel Guitar* (Anaheim, CA, 2003)
T. Miller: "The Origins and Development of the Pedal Steel Guitar" (M.M. Thesis, University of South Dakota, 2007)
C.H. Garrett: *Struggling to Define a Nation: American Music and the Twentieth Century* (Berkeley, 2008)

TIMOTHY D. MILLER

Hawaiian music. *See* HAWAII; HAWAIIAN GUITAR; *and* UKULELE.

Hawaii Music Curriculum Program [HMCP]. Curriculum project inspired by the Contemporary Music Project, sponsored by state and Title III federal funds. The HMCP began in 1968 as a comprehensive K-12 "spiral" music curriculum in which students participated as listeners, performers, composers, and scholars.

BIBLIOGRAPHY
B. Hanley and J. Montgomery: "Contemporary Curriculum Practices and their Theoretical Bases," *The New Handbook of Research on Music Teaching and Learning*, ed. R. Colwell and C. Richardson (New York, 2002), 125–6
M.L. Mark: *Contemporary Music Education* (New York, 3/1996), 166–8

CAROLYN LIVINGSTON

Hawes, Bess Lomax. *See* LOMAX.

Hawes, Hampton (Bennett) (*b* Los Angeles, CA, 13 Nov 1928; *d* Los Angeles, CA, 22 May 1977). Jazz pianist, bandleader, and composer. Hawes grew up in Los Angeles where his father was a minister and his older sister studied classical piano. In 1947, after high school, he joined Howard McGhee's quartet in which he played with Charlie Parker. Hawes visited New York City and toured the South before returning to California and joining Red Norvo's group. He was an active partici-

pant in the Central Avenue scene in Los Angeles, working with Dexter Gordon, Teddy Edwards, and Wardell Gray. Early recordings were made with well-known players including Shorty Rogers, Art Pepper, and Howard Rumsey.

His first recordings as a leader were made for the Discovery label shortly before he was drafted into the US Army in 1952, serving in Korea. Back in California, Hawes made a series of LPs for Contemporary Records between 1955 and 1958, when he was convicted of drug possession. Sentenced to ten years at Fort Worth, he was pardoned in 1963 by President Kennedy.

He made four more records for Contemporary before departing for Europe and Asia where he spent most of the remainder of the 1960s. In the early 1970s he began experimenting with more commercial styles and electric instruments, but later returned to acoustic piano. His final recordings were duets with bassist Charlie Haden, issued after Hawes's death from a massive stroke.

BIBLIOGRAPHY
H. Hawes: *Rise Up Off of Me* (New York, 1974)
A. Taylor: *Notes and Tones: Musician-to-Musician Interviews* (New York, 1982)

MICHAEL FITZGERALD

Hawkins, Coleman (Randolph) [Bean, Hawk] (*b* St. Joseph, MO, 21 Nov 1904; *d* New York, NY, 19 May 1969). Jazz tenor saxophonist.

1. Life. 2. Musical style.

1. LIFE. He was taught piano from the age of five by his mother, a schoolteacher who played organ. He took up the cello at about the age of seven, then requested a tenor saxophone, which he received on his ninth birthday. By the time he was 12 he was performing professionally at school dances. He went to high school in Chicago, then (by his own account) attended Washburn College in Topeka, Kansas, for about two years, during which time he studied harmony and composition.

Hawkins's first regular job, beginning in the spring of 1921, was playing in the orchestra of the 12th Street Theater in Kansas City. That summer the blues singer Mamie Smith performed at the theater and offered Hawkins a position touring with her group, the Jazz Hounds. By March 1922 Hawkins was working with Smith at the Garden of Joy in New York. He made his first recordings with her shortly afterward, but his contributions are frequently indiscernible, a notable exception being on "I'm gonna get you." Early in 1923 he toured with the Jazz Hounds as far as California, where the group performed in the revue *Struttin' Along*, but he left after the band returned to New York in June.

Hawkins then worked as a freelance player with various bandleaders including Wilbur Sweatman, whose group opened at the new club Connie's Inn in June. Fletcher Henderson heard Hawkins with Sweatman and employed him to record with his group the following August. During this period Hawkins also joined the pianist Ginger Jones and the trumpeter Charlie Gaines at the Garden of Joy, and played with Cecil Smith and Louis Hooper at the Renaissance Casino. Both Hawkins and Henderson appear to have played under the violinist Ralph "Shrimp" Jones at the Bamville Club near the end of that year. The association with Henderson proved decisive for Hawkins, as Henderson engaged him when he formed a band to play at the Club Alabam in early January 1924. Hawkins remained with the group until March 1934, making numerous recordings and attracting worldwide notice. In his first substantial recorded solo, on Henderson's "Dicty Blues" (1923), he reveals an authoritative style, big sound, and fast vibrato.

Until the end of 1930 Henderson's band spent most of each year at the Roseland Ballroom, although it played occasionally at other venues in the New York area, particularly the Savoy Ballroom. It also traveled widely, visiting New England, the East Coast, and the Midwest, and making a tour of the South during the first two weeks of 1933. Finally, when a tour of Great Britain fell through in 1934, Hawkins contacted the English bandleader and impresario Jack Hylton and arranged to tour the country on his own with local groups. As the acknowledged star of the Henderson group, Hawkins clearly felt it was time to move on.

Hawkins arrived in England on 30 March 1934 and toured as the guest of Jack Hylton's band and Mrs. Jack Hylton's band. His success was such that he decided to stay in Europe, performing with the Ramblers early in 1935 in The Hague and then playing freelance in Paris, Laren, Zürich (with the Berries), and elsewhere; he also made numerous recordings with the Ramblers, the Berries, and other groups assembled for studio sessions. Perhaps the most famous of these sessions was one in Paris on 28 April 1937 including Django Reinhardt and Benny Carter, where Hawkins played with fervor and rhythmic drive, even beginning his solo on "Crazy Rhythm" with repeated riffs. Hawkins returned to England on 11 March 1939, commencing a tour sponsored by the Selmer instrument company. Local musicians accompanied him at each performance. He finally returned to New York in July 1939.

American musicians, generally unaware of Hawkins's European recordings, anxiously awaited his return. He formed a nine-piece band and opened at Kelly's Stables on 5 October. At the end of a recording session a few days later he improvised two choruses on "Body and Soul" that reestablished his importance to musicians while introducing him to a mass audience. The recording was a commercial and musical success, notable for its harmonic ingenuity and clarity, consistent use of double time, warmth of sound, and relaxed virtuosity, building up to g♭" (sounding pitch) towards the end of the solo (ex.1). At the end of 1939 *Down Beat* readers voted Hawkins best tenor saxophonist. He then formed a big band and played in New York at the Golden Gate Ballroom, the Savoy, and the Apollo Theater, and also went on tour. In 1941, however, he resumed working

with small groups, and for the next two years played in Chicago and the Midwest.

Hawkins spent most of 1945 in California, performing and recording with a group that included the young modernists Howard McGhee and Oscar Pettiford (this group also appeared in the film *The Crimson Canary*). He returned to the East Coast, then joined a Jazz at the Philharmonic tour that took him back to California in April 1946. During the next five years Hawkins usually joined these tours for at least a few concerts, while spending most of the year with his own groups in New York. He returned to Europe in May 1948, in late 1949, in 1950, and again in 1954 as part of Illinois Jacquet's tour of American service bases. He continued to lead recording groups with such young talented players as Miles Davis, Fats Navarro, J.J. Johnson, and Milt Jackson. Around 1948 he recorded a fascinating unaccompanied improvisation, "Picasso," a feat that still lay beyond many of the younger generation.

During the late 1950s Hawkins continued to appear at all the major jazz festivals, often as co-leader of a group with Roy Eldridge. He joined the Jazz at the Philharmonic tour of 1957 and the "Seven Ages of Jazz" tours in 1958 and 1959, traveled to Europe for brief engagements, and played on television on *The Tonight Show* (1955) and *The Sound of Jazz* (1957). He also recorded prolifically during this time, beginning with a series of albums for the subsidiaries of Prestige in 1958 and followed by several for Impulse, including his only collaboration with Duke Ellington and his orchestra (1962). During the 1960s he appeared in films and on television. He often recorded and performed at the Village Gate and the Village Vanguard with a quartet including Tommy Flanagan (piano), Major Holley (double bass), and Eddie Locke (drums).

During the last two years of his life Hawkins began to exhibit signs of emotional distress and the ravages of alcoholism. He collapsed while playing in Toronto in February 1967 and again in June while on the last tour of Jazz at the Philharmonic. He traveled to Europe with the Oscar Peterson trio and played for a month at Ronnie Scott's Club in London with an English rhythm section, but a tour of Denmark the following year was canceled due to his ill health. His last concert was on 20 April 1969 at the North Park Hotel, Chicago.

2. MUSICAL STYLE. Hawkins's powerful and original style was largely responsible for the popularity of the tenor saxophone as a jazz instrument. On his early recordings he made much use of the characteristic technique of the day—heavily articulated "slap tonguing"—but he later developed a more legato approach that eventually became the norm. During his years with Henderson he absorbed musical ideas from many non-saxophonists, including his fellow band members. Most important among these was Louis Armstrong, whose smooth melodic lines and advanced sense of swing strongly influenced Hawkins, as may be heard on the recordings made from the end of September 1924 to November 1925. By 1926 Hawkins was also beginning to absorb the harmonic ideas of Art Tatum. On "The Stampede" (1926) he develops

question-and-answer phrasing after the fashion of Armstrong along with his own trills and triplet ornaments. Highly technical patterns and chromatic sequences are introduced on the third take of "St. Louis Shuffle" (1927), which devices achieve even greater virtuosic complexity on "Wherever There's a Will, Baby" (1929). A comparison of the two issued versions of this piece shows that the patterns at crucial points, such as at the beginning and the middle, are memorized and repeated verbatim, but the rest is freely improvised. During the same session, Hawkins recorded a solo on "One Hour" that won widespread acclaim among musicians for its richness of ideas, sensitive tone, rhythmic flexibility, and mixture of speechlike rubato phrases with moments in double time. All of Hawkins's playing is characterized by intense emotional conviction.

Hawkins continued to experiment with a complex rubato approach for the next few years, creating highly elaborate structures even at fast tempos, as on "New King Porter Stomp" (1932). His solo on "Can you take it?" (1933), however, suggests a return to playing on the beat and demonstrates Hawkins's increasing ability to improvise memorable and logically constructed melodies. At the same session, Henderson's band recorded a tune by Hawkins, "Queer Notions," which explores the whole-tone scale.

Hawkins was a brilliant musical thinker who was remarkably open to new developments in jazz as well as classical music; this was reflected in both the personnel and the repertory of his groups. In February 1944 he led a band that featured Dizzy Gillespie, Max Roach, and others in what are generally considered to be the first bop recordings. Another session later the same year was the first to include Thelonious Monk, whom Hawkins also used for live performances.

By the late 1950s Hawkins's tone had hardened somewhat, and he developed a fierce approach to the blues, although he still found new ideas during a sensitive, rhythmically complex treatment of "Body and Soul" (1959). He easily accepted the new bossa nova songs, recording some in 1962, and managed to hold his own during a session the following year that paired him with Sonny Rollins and Paul Bley, both of whom were exploring ideas similar to those of Ornette Coleman.

Young saxophonists continue to find inspiration in Hawkins's recordings. His influence has endured, even though it was somewhat eclipsed during the 1940s by that of Lester Young and after 1960 by that of John Coltrane—a testament to the intelligence and technical authority of his music. Hawkins recorded an interview for Riverside in 1956, *Coleman Hawkins: a Documentary*.

RECORDINGS
(selective list)

As leader or co-leader: Crazy Rhythm/Honeysuckle Rose (1937, Swing 1); Body and Soul (1939, Bluebird 10523); Woody 'n you (1944, Apollo 751); On the Bean (1944, Joe Davis 8251); Picasso (c1948, Jazz Scene [unnumbered]); *Coleman Hawkins and Roy Eldridge at the Opera House* (1958, Verve 8266), incl. The Walker; Body and Soul (1959, Playboy 1959A); *Duke Ellington Meets Coleman Hawkins* (1962, Imp. 26), incl. Self Portrait (of the Bean); *Desafinado* (1962, Imp. 28), incl. Desafinado, Samba para Bean; with S. Rollins: *Sonny Meets Hawk* (1963, RCA LSP2712), incl. Lover Man, Just Friends

As sideman: M. Smith: I'm gonna get you (1922, OK 4781); F. Henderson: Dicty Blues (1923, Voc. 14654), The Stampede (1926, Col. 654D), St. Louis Shuffle (1927, Vic. 20944); McKinney's Cotton Pickers: Wherever There's a Will, Baby (1929, Vic. 22736); Mound City Blue Blowers: Hello, Lola/One Hour (1929, Vic. 38100); F. Henderson: New King Porter Stomp (1932, OK 41565), Queer Notions/Can you take it? (1933, Voc. 2585)

BIBLIOGRAPHY

GroveJ2
AllenH
M. Levin: "Coleman Hawkins: One of the Great Forces in Jazz," *DB*, xvii/21 (1950), 2–3
N. Hentoff: "The Hawk Talks," *DB*, xxiii/22 (1956), 13
L. Feather: "Coleman Hawkins," *The Jazz Makers: Essays on the Greats of Jazz*, ed. N. Shapiro and N. Hentoff (New York, 1957/R), 163–74
M. James: "Coleman Hawkins Today," *JazzM*, viii/1 (1962), 7–12
D. Heckman: "Pres and Hawk: Saxophone Fountainheads," *DB*, xxx/1 (1963), 20–22 [incl. transcrs.]
A. McCarthy: *Coleman Hawkins* (London, 1963); repr. in *Kings of Jazz*, ed. S. Green (South Brunswick, NJ, 1978)
R. Stewart: *Jazz Masters of the Thirties* (New York, 1972), 60
S. Dance: *The World of Swing* (New York, 1974), 140
J. Evensmo: *The Tenor Saxophone of Coleman Hawkins, 1929–1942* (Oslo, Norway, 1975)
A.E. Henderson: *Improvisation in the Recorded Works of Coleman Hawkins, 1932–34* (thesis, York U., 1981)
Y. Delmarche and I. Fresart: *A Discography of Coleman Hawkins, 1922–1969* (n.p., c1983)
B. James: *Coleman Hawkins* (Tunbridge Wells, UK, 1984)
J.-F. Villetard: *Coleman Hawkins*, i: *1922–1944* (Amsterdam, 1984); ii: *1945–1957* (Amsterdam, 1985) [discography]
S. Deveaux: *Jazz in Transition: Coleman Hawkins and Howard McGhee, 1935–1945* (diss., U. of California, Berkeley, 1985)
G. Schuller: "The Great Soloists: Coleman Hawkins," *The Swing Era: the Development of Jazz, 1930–1945* (New York, 1989), 426–50
J. Chilton: *The Song of the Hawk: the Life and Recordings of Coleman Hawkins* (London, 1990)
S. DeVeaux: *The Birth of Bebop: a Social and Musical History* (Berkeley, Los Angeles, and London, 1997)
T. Doering: *Coleman Hawkins: sein Leben, seine Musick, seine Schallplatten* (Waakirchen, Germany, 2001)

LEWIS PORTER

Hawkins, Edwin R. (*b* Oakland, CA, 18 Aug 1943). Gospel singer, songwriter, and producer. He began piano at five and by seven accompanied the Hawkins family group. In 1967 along with Betty Watson, he founded the Northern California State Youth Choir with the aim of singing at the annual COGIC youth conference in Washington DC. As a fundraiser, the choir recorded *Let Us Go Into the House*. Although the group planned to sell the album locally, "Oh Happy Day," played on San Francisco's KSAN and became an instant hit. Renamed the Edwin Hawkins Singers, the choir signed to the Budda label in 1969 and toured worldwide, including many non-religious venues such as jazz clubs, concert halls, and stadiums. Since 1969, "Oh Happy Day" has sold over seven million copies and Hawkins's arrangement remains the signature arrangement in gospel music.

Throughout the 1970s, 80s, and 90s Hawkins continued to tour, compose, and record. He has produced some 20 albums, though none has matched the success of his first. In 1979 he founded the Edwin Hawkins Music & Arts Seminar as a non-profit organization to mentor and develop new gospel talent. On the occasion of the 30th anniversary of the recording of "Oh Happy

Day," Hawkins recorded a revised version of the song on the album *Love is the Only Way* (1998). He founded his own record label, TRI Recordings, in 2004, and released *All the Angels: Music & Arts Love Fellowship Mass Choir*. A multi-Grammy Award winner and 2007 inductee into the Christian Music Hall of Fame, he is now highly regarded as an elder statesman of contemporary gospel music.

EMMETT G. PRICE III

Hawkins, Erick [Frederick] (*b* Trinidad, CO, 23 April 1909; *d* New York, NY, 23 Nov 1994). Dancer and choreographer. After graduating from Harvard University in 1930, Hawkins went to Austria to study modern dance with Harald Kreutzberg. Upon returning to the United States, he enrolled in the School of American Ballet in 1934, founded that year by George Balanchine and Lincoln Kirstein. Hawkins danced from 1935 to 1937 in the American Ballet (later the New York City Ballet). In 1937 he received his first commission for a ballet, *Show Piece*, to a score by Robert McBride. After studies with noted American dancer and choreographer Martha Graham, Hawkins joined her company as its first male dancer and created leading roles in many of her most celebrated works, such as the Husbandman in *Appalachian Spring* (1944). (Hawkins and Graham were married from 1948 to 1954.) After leaving Graham's company in 1950, Hawkins began to develop his own vision of a new dance technique. In 1951 he began his long collaboration with the composer Lucia Dlugoszewski, whom he married in 1962. In 1957 he formed the Erick Hawkins Dance Company. Hawkins was known for his collaborations with some of the leading composers of his generation, including David Diamond, Henry Cowell, Ross Lee Finney, Alan Hovhaness, Wallingford Riegger, and Virgil Thomson. In 1972 Hawkins expanded his collaborations to include performances with symphony orchestras, and his works *Classic Kite Tails* (Diamond) and *Dawn Dazzled Door* (Tōru Takemitsu) were premiered with the Detroit SO. In 1975 the San Francisco SO presented Hawkins's *Hurrah!* (Thomson) and *Meditation on Orpheus* (Hovhaness), with conductor Seiji Ozawa. Overall, the Erick Hawkins Dance Company performed with 25 orchestras, including the National SO, the American SO, the Cleveland Orchestra, the Denver SO, the Buffalo PO, the St. Paul Chamber Orchestra, and the St. Louis SO. His archives are held by the Music Division, Library of Congress.

WRITINGS

The Body is a Clear Place and Other Statements on Dance (Princeton, NJ, 1992)

BIBLIOGRAPHY

R. Lorber, ed.: *Erick Hawkins: Theory and Training* (New York, 1979)
F. Mason: "A Conversation with Erick Hawkins and Lucia Dlugoszewski," *Ballet Review* xxi (Winter 1993)
International Encyclopedia of Dance (New York, 1998)

ELIZABETH ALDRICH

Hawkins, Gordon (*b* Washington, DC, 1959). Baritone. Hawkins is known for his rich and nuanced voice, which some critics have called "luxuriant," and his impressive acting abilities. He made his debut with the Metropolitan Opera in 1989, when he portrayed Jake in Gershwin's *Porgy and Bess*. He also has played the role of Porgy on a number of occasions, making the character nobler than he often appears; he has taken on the role with Washington National Opera, Lyric Opera of Chicago, Dallas Opera, and the San Francisco Symphony. In 1990, he made his first appearance with the New York City Opera in the role of Escamillo in *Carmen*. Throughout the 1990s and 2000s, Hawkins has made a significant impression in works by Verdi, appearing in *Rigoletto* with the Washington National Opera and the Arizona Opera, *Il trovatore* and *Macbeth* with the Seattle Opera, and *Aida* with the Cincinnati Opera and the Houston Grand Opera, among others. Additionally, he has become an important Wagner interpreter, appearing in London, Tokyo, and Seville with major roles in *Götterdämmerung* and *Das Rheingold*. He has also appeared in contemporary works, including the premiere of Jake Heggie's *A Great Hope Fell*.

JONAS WESTOVER

Hawkins, John Isaac (*b* Hillfarrance, Somerset, 14 March 1772; *d* Elizabeth, NJ, 24 June 1854). English inventor, civil engineer, patent agent, and musical instrument maker. Hawkins immigrated to the United States in 1794 and lived in the Philadelphia area until 1803, when he returned to England. He invented numerous devices during his career, including (while in the United States) the upright piano, a polygraph (a writing/copying instrument favored by Thomas Jefferson), a physiognotrace, and (while in England) a self-propelled pencil, an iridium-tipped gold pen, and trifocal lenses.

Interested in music, he conceived of the "portable grand" piano in 1796, and patented it in America and Britain in 1800 with his father, Isaac Hawkins, acting as his agent in England. (Matthias Müller invented the upright piano independently in Vienna about the same time.) Previously, upright pianos were either grands or squares turned on end and placed on a stand, but Hawkins's achievement was to use the space below the keyboard down to the floor. The patent contains a wide range of additional inventions, including the addition of an iron frame to support the wooden soundboard structure. This was the first use of metal to stabilize the frame in any piano; the compensation frame was later developed further by others. However, the instrument did not stay in tune long, and its tone was unsatisfactory, so it was the refinements of later makers that made such a version of the piano acceptable to the market.

Hawkins also invented the "Claviole" in 1798, which was a bowed keyboard instrument housed in an upright cabinet and worked by wheels operated by a foot treadle. It was first displayed in Philadelphia in 1802. He manufactured both instruments for a time, but did not find adequate numbers of customers, and abandoned the endeavors after filing for bankruptcy in 1807. He tried to revive interest in the Claviole by promoting it again in exhibitions in 1813–1814 without success, prior to the expiration of his patent. A museum of inventions that Hawkins established in 1808 displayed other musical inventions, but they were largely impractical.

Hawkins returned to the United States in 1848 to re-establish himself, but was unsuccessful. He died in poverty and obscurity.

WRITINGS

A New System of Musical Notation (London, 1808)
Plan and Catalogue of Hawkins's Museum of Useful and Mechanical Inventions (London, 1808; 2nd ed., 1810)
The History and Resuscitation of the Claviole, or Finger-Keyed Viol (London, 1845)

BIBLIOGRAPHY
ClinkscaleMP and *Clinkscale Database of Early Pianos, 1700–1860* (<http://www.EarlyPianos.org/>)
R.E.M. Harding: *The Piano-Forte: Its History Traced to the Great Exhibition of 1851* (Cambridge, 1933/R, 2/1978/R)
W.E. Mann: *Piano Making in Philadelphia before 1825* (diss., U. of Iowa, 1977)
A.W.J.G. Ord-Hume: "Hawkins' Claviole or Finger-Keyed Viol," *Music & Automata*, 11 (1988), 139–41
M. Cole: *The Pianoforte in the Classical Era* (Oxford, 1988)
M.D. Friesen: *"Mentor-General to Mankind": the Life and Work of John Isaac Hawkins in America* (Master's thesis, Northern Illinois University, 2001)

MICHAEL D. FRIESEN

Hawkins, Margaret B. (*b* Binghamton, NY, 28 Jan 1937; *d* Milwaukee, WI, 13 Nov 1993). Conductor and music educator. After graduating from the University of Wisconsin-Milwaukee (BME 1959), Hawkins became the first vocal teacher at Pewaukee High School (1959–71), where she led the choir in exceptionally polished performances of challenging classical repertoire. Hawkins earned a master's degree from Indiana University during summers, and founded the 80-voice Wisconsin Conservatory Singers (1969). Later, she established the Wisconsin Conservatory Chamber Singers, which appeared at ADCA (1975) and the Kennedy Center for the Performing Arts (1976), and became Director of Performance Activities at the Conservatory (1976). Hawkins began preparing choral groups for the Milwaukee Symphony Orchestra in 1969, and in 1976, Music Director Kenneth Schermerhorn invited her to found the 200-voice Wisconsin Conservatory Symphony Chorus, which was renamed the Milwaukee Symphony Chorus in 1985. They performed at Carnegie Hall (1980) and also with the Chicago Symphony Chorus and Orchestra. In 1979, Hawkins made her debut with the Milwaukee Symphony and became a regular guest conductor with them as well as with other orchestras and choruses. According to Nancy Raabe, typical Milwaukee Symphony Chorus performances had not only "riveting textual and textural clarity including diction like you've never heard it before but the warmth, suppleness and vitality of a vibrant living entity. Through sheer force of personality Hawkins got her 200 voices to think, feel and respond as one" (*Milwaukee Sentinel*, 19 November 1993). Hawkins, who died after defying cancer for seven years, was known for allowing singers to sing out freely, minimal conducting gestures, intense rehearsals, and wicked wit. Twice, the *Milwaukee Sentinel* named her

"Musician of the Year" and in 1991 she received the Michael Korn Founders Award for Development of the Professional Choral Art from Chorus America.

BIBLIOGRAPHY
"1977 ACDA National Convention," *The Choral Journal*, xvii/5 (1977), 24, 26
Obituaries: *Milwaukee Sentinel* (19 Nov 1993), *Milwaukee Journal* (21 Nov 1993)
M. Gresham: "Margaret Hawkins: Preparing a Chorus for the Orchestral Conductor (Dec 1990)," *Choral Conversations. Selected Interviews from* Chorus! *Magazine*, ed. M. Gresham (San Carlos, CA, 1997), 159–70
J. Whittemore: "Margaret Hawkins," *Wisdom, Wit, and Will. Women Choral Conductors on Their Art*, ed. J.C. Conlon (Chicago, 2009), 379–89

J. MICHELE EDWARDS

Hawkins, Micah (*b* Head of the Harbor, nr Stony Brook, NY, 1 Jan 1777; *d* New York, NY, 29 July 1825). Composer. Largely self-educated, Hawkins moved to New York in 1798, where at age 14 he was first a bound apprentice at the coach-making business to Frederick King of Morristown, then a grocer and innkeeper. His first music teacher was a family slave, the fiddler Toney Clapp. Hawkins was an amateur violinist, pianist, and flutist in the Euterpian and Apollo societies, and he compiled several manuscript collections of tunes and arrangements; his *Book of Notes for the German Flute* contains over 200 melodies copied by hand. In 1815, Hopkins Robinson introduced the song "Backside Albany" (1815), with words by Hawkins set to a traditional Irish tune, *The Bayne Water*; this dialect song, performed in blackface, anticipated minstrelsy and remained popular for nearly half a century. Hawkins wrote a second song, "Massa Georgee Washington and General La Fayette," for Lafayette's visit to America in 1824. His opera *The Saw-Mill, or, a Yankee Trick* was given six performances at the Chatham Garden Theatre in 1824–5 and is an early work by an American on a patriotic theme; its characterizations anticipated later "Yankee" shows like Woodworth and Davies's *The Forest Rose* (1825). Collections of Hawkins's manuscripts are in the Watkinson Library of Trinity College, Hartford; the Library of Congress; the New-York Historical Society; and the Museums at Stony Brook, Long Island.

BIBLIOGRAPHY
B.F. Thompson and others: *The History of Long Island, from Its Discovery to the Present Time*, i (New York, 1843), 434
O. Wegelin: *Micah Hawkins and the Saw-Mill* (New York, 1917); repr. in *Magazine of History, with Notes and Queries*, xxxii/3 (1927), 153–210
V.B. Lawrence: "Micah Hawkins, the Pied Piper of Catherine Slip," *New-York Historical Society Quarterly*, lxii (1978), 138–65
M. Barnes-Ostrander: "Domestic Music Making in Early New York State: Music in the Lives of Three Amateurs," *MQ*, lxviii/3 (1982), 353–72
P.G. Buckley: *The Place to Make an Artist Work: Micah Hawkins and William Sidney Mount in New York City, Catching the Tune: Music and William Sidney Mount* (Stony Brook, NY, 1984)
W.J. Mahar: "'Backside Albany and Early Blackface Minstrelsy': a Contextual Study of America's First Blackface Song," *American Music*, vi/1 (1988), 1–27

WILLIAM BROOKS/R

Hawkins, Ronnie [Ronald] (*b* Huntsville, AR, 10 Jan 1935). Rockabilly vocalist. At age nine Hawkins moved to Fayetteville, Arkansas, later forming the first version of his backing band, the Hawks, while studying physical education at the University of Arkansas. Touring on a circuit that included Arkansas, Oklahoma, and Missouri, on the advice of Conway Twitty, in 1958 Hawkins headed 1000 miles north to play gigs across the border in Ontario. Achieving instant acclaim, Hawkins and the Hawks relocated to Toronto in 1959. Signing with Roulette Records, Hawkins had two minor pop hits in 1958 and 1959 with covers of Chuck Berry's "Thirty Days" (retitled as "Forty Days") and Young Jessie's "Mary Lou."

As the various members of the Hawks, with the exception of Levon Helm, succumbed to homesickness and headed back South, Hawkins replaced them with four Canadians: Robbie Robertson, Rick Danko, Richard Manuel, and Garth Hudson. This version of the Hawks, minus Hudson, backed Hawkins on what is generally considered to be his greatest recording, January 1963's incendiary cover of Bo Diddley's "Who Do You Love." Robertson, Danko, Manuel, Hudson, and Helm would leave Hawkins in late 1963 and, after releasing a few singles—as Levon and the Hawks and also as the Canadian Squires—and a groundbreaking tour with Bob Dylan in 1965 and 1966, would emerge as THE BAND in 1968 with *Music from Big Pink*. Hawkins's backing band would similarly be a training ground for future members of Janis Joplin's Full-Tilt Boogie Band, Crowbar, and Pat Travers. In 1975, Bob Dylan cast Hawkins for the film *Renaldo and Clara*. The following year, Hawkins was invited by the Band to play *The Last Waltz*. In 2004 Hawkins was inducted into the Canadian Music Hall of Fame.

BIBLIOGRAPHY
R. Hawkins and P. Goddard: *Ronnie Hawkins: Last of the Good Ol' Boys* (Toronto, 1989)

ROB BOWMAN

Hawkins, Screamin' Jay [Jalacy] (*b* Cleveland, OH, 18 July 1929; *d* Neuilly-sur-Seine, France, 29 Feb 2000). Rhythm and blues songwriter, pianist, and singer. Classically trained as a pianist, Hawkins's primary vocal influence was Paul Robeson and his original goal was to sing opera. In 1951, he joined R&B guitarist Tiny Grimes's band. Over the next few years he served similar stints with Johnny Sparrow, James Moody, Arnett Cobb, Bill Doggett, and Lynn Hope while recording as a solo artist for Atlantic, Timely, Mercury, and its subsidiary, Wing.

Hawkins's career took on significance with his 1955 recording of his self-penned "I Put a Spell on You." Although the song was originally conceived as a romantic ballad, an inebriated Hawkins screamed and grunted his way through the studio recording. The result was an over-the-top performance that was unprecedented in popular music history. Banned by many radio stations, "I Put a Spell on You" holds the distinction of selling over one million copies while never charting.

Encouraged by famed radio DJ and concert promoter Alan Freed, Hawkins's already outlandish live performances began to feature horror movie props such as a smoking skull on a stick and rubber snakes; the singer opened his performances by emerging out of a coffin. All the while Hawkins would dress in a green turban, red tuxedo, purple tie, and white shoes. A case could easily be made that this was the beginning of shock rock with Hawkins directly or indirectly influencing Screamin' Lord Sutch, Alice Cooper, Marilyn Manson, and many others.

Despite his notoriety, none of Hawkins's recordings ever charted in the United States, although his 1993 version of Tom Waits's "Heart Attack and Vine" reached number 42 in the UK singles charts. Over the years "I Put a Spell on You" has been covered dozens of times by artists as far ranging as Nina Simone, Creedence Clearwater Revival, Manfred Man, and Nick Cave.

BIBLIOGRAPHY
B. Millar: liner notes, *Screamin' Jay Hawkins: Spellbound! 1955–1974* (Vollersode, Germany, 1990)

ROB BOWMAN

Hawkins [née Davis], **Tramaine (Aunzola)** [Lady Tramaine Hawkins; The Lady] (*b* San Francisco, CA, 11 Oct 1951). Gospel singer. Raised in the Ephesian Church of God in Christ, pastored by her grandfather, Bishop Elmer Elisha Cleveland, Tramaine Davis emerged as one of the most noted voices in contemporary gospel music during the 1970s. Her first recording was "I Love the Lord" as a member of the Heavenly Tones, a group that would later sing background with Sly & The Family Stone as Little Sister. In 1967 Edwin Hawkins assembled the Northern California State Youth Choir, with Tramaine as soloist. In addition to touring with the Edwin Hawkins Singers she also spent time with Andraé Crouch & the Disciples. In March of 1971 she and gospel songwriter and singer WALTER HAWKINS married. Although the two would later divorce, together they built a gospel music dynasty and dynamic ministry through the *Love Alive* album series and established the Love Center Ministries, Inc. in Oakland, California.

After two solo albums on the Light label, Tramaine's breakout occurred in 1985 with "Fall Down (Spirit of Love)" from the album *The Search is Over*. Quickly rising to the top of dance and club charts as a gospel crossover hit, it ministered to a new generation who had either grown up outside of the church or grown away from the church. Further cementing her rich legacy as a powerful and tasteful soprano was album *Tramaine Hawkins Live!* (1990), which featured appearances by musicians Carlos Santana, Jimmy McGriff, and Stanley Turrentine.

A Grammy, Dove, and Stellar award winner, Hawkins was inducted into the International Gospel Music Hall of Fame in 1999. Known in gospel circles as "The Lady," Hawkins has continued to enjoy success in the 21st century with albums such as *Still* (2001) and *I Never Lost My Praise* (2007).

EMMETT G. PRICE III

Hawkins, Walter (*b* Oakland, CA, 18 May 1949; *d* Ripon, CA, 11 July 2010). Gospel songwriter and singer. Walter Hawkins is celebrated by gospel musicians and audiences for his passionate voice, gripping song interpretations, and enduring compositions. Although his first solo album was released in 1972, he was already contributing cutting-edge developments in gospel music— he sang in the recording choir for Edwin Hawkins's classic song "Oh Happy Day." Hawkins founded the Love Center Church (Oakland, CA) in 1973 and the choir recorded their first album *Love Alive* in 1975. This album was the first of a series of *Love Alive* recordings: *Love Alive II* (1978), *Love Alive III* (1982), *Love Alive IV* (1989), and *Love Alive V* (1998). This series contains a number of his notable and popular gospel songs such as "Changed," "Goin' Up Yonder," "Be Grateful," "Thank You," and "Marvelous." Active as a songwriter, producer, and developer of young talent through the 1980s and 90s, Hawkins released six other albums during his recording career and collaborated with a number of gospel artists including John P. Kee, Mary Mary, Kirk Franklin, Yolanda Adams, and Richard Smallwood. Hawkins's influence and artistry connected with more urban-contemporary audiences in the 21st century through his featured appearance with Donald Lawrence ("Seasons" on *Go Get Your Life Back* (2002)) and his last studio album entitled *Song in My Heart* (2005). These modern projects offered performance styles and production approaches that contrast the more traditional renderings often associated with Hawkins, but these elements did not temper the power, sensitivity, and dexterity that characterize his signature voice.

BIBLIOGRAPHY
R. Darden: *People Get Ready: a New History of Gospel Music* (New York, 2004)
                                            HORACE J. MAXILE JR.

Hawley, C(harles) B(each) (*b* Brookfield, MA, 14 Feb 1858; *d* Eatontown, NJ, 29 Dec 1915). Composer and church musician. The young Hawley attended the Cheshire Military Academy. In 1875 he went to New York, where he studied voice and composition with several teachers, principally DUDLEY BUCK. The following year he was appointed bass soloist at Calvary Episcopal Church and later became assistant organist to George W. Warren at St. Thomas Church. From 1883 until 1900 he was bass soloist and choir director at the Broadway Tabernacle. He also directed the summer music program at St. James Chapel in Elberton, a fashionable New Jersey seaside resort. Hawley later served as organist of the West End Presbyterian Church and for four years as organist and choirmaster of the Madison Avenue Methodist Episcopal Church. He was a cofounder and for a decade director of the Metropolitan College of Music, and maintained a private voice studio in New York for twenty-five years. He was a founding member of both the Mendelssohn Glee Club and the New York Manuscript Society.

Hawley was an enormously prolific and successful composer of solo songs, some of them recorded as

early as 1902. He relied on prominent literary figures of the day for his lyrics, for example, Frank L. Stanton (*A Song of the South*, 1907), Harriet Beecher Stowe (*Still, still with Thee*, 1908), or Clinton Scollard (*The Love-light of your Eyes*, 1910). He also wrote part songs for both female and male voices. A comic glee, *They Kissed! I Saw them Do it*, was especially popular. He also left examples of sacred choral writing, including a Trisagion and Sanctus and *The Christ Child* (1912).

BIBLIOGRAPHY
R. Hughes: *Contemporary American Composers* (Boston, 1900), 323–9
                                            WILLIAM OSBORNE

Hawthorne [Hathorne], **Nathaniel** (*b* Salem, MA, 4 July 1804; *d* Plymouth, NH, 19 May 1864). Novelist and short-story writer. He studied at Bowdoin College (1821–5) in Brunswick, Maine, and worked in the customs houses of Boston (1839–41) and Salem (1845–9). From 1853 to 1857 he served as the US consul in Liverpool, England. His principal writings include five novels and several volumes of short stories. Hawthorne's fiction has inspired more musical adaptations than that of any other American writer. There are more than 11 operas on *The Scarlet Letter* alone, the earliest of which was written around 1855 by Lucien Southard (1827–81). Walter Damrosch's version is set to a libretto by George Parsons Lathrop, Hawthorne's son-in-law. Twentieth-century settings include those of Vittorio Giannini and Walter Kaufmann.

The most frequently set short stories are *Rappaccini's Daughter*, *Dr. Heidegger's Experiment*, and *Young Goodman Brown*. Howard Hanson based a portion of his *Merry Mount* on Hawthorne's *The Maypole of Merry Mount*. Other operas based on Hawthorne's short stories include *Feathertop* by Joyce Barthelson, *The Scarecrow* by Normand Lockwood (from *Feathertop*), *The Great Stone Face* by Martin Kalmanoff, *My Kinsman, Major Molineux* by Bruce Saylor, *Pandora* (from *The Paradise of Children*) by Clarence E. Le Massena, *The Poisoned Kiss* by Ralph Vaughan Williams, and *The Garden of Mystery* by Charles Wakefield Cadman (the last two from *Rappaccini's Daughter*). Later operas include *Rappaccini's Daughter* by Daniel Catán, *The House of Seven Gables* by Scott Eyerly, and *Infinite Fraternity* by Charles Fussell, based on letters between Hawthorne and Herman Melville.

Program music includes Cecil Burleigh's *Land of Olympus* for piano and John Tasker Howard's *Mosses from an Old Manse*, a ballade for string orchestra. The only known published song is "The Ocean" by George Willig, based on the poem of the same title. The singer and composer Nancy Harrow has written songs that draw from Hawthorne. The scherzo of Ives's Second Piano Sonata is an impressionistic picture of Hawthorne. The Tanglewood Festival traces its name to Nathaniel Hawthorne's retelling of Greek myths in his *Tanglewood Tales*. The Berkshire Music Center at Tanglewood also houses the restored Tanglewood cottage where Hawthorne once worked.

BIBLIOGRAPHY
GroveA
A.W. Kelley: *Music and Literature in the American Romantic Movement: a Study of the Knowledge of, Use of, and ideas Relating to the Art of Music in Emerson, Hawthorne, Longfellow, Poe, Thoreau, Lowell, Whitman, and Lanier* (diss., U. of North Carolina, 1929)
C. McGlinchee: "American Literature in American Music," *MQ*, xxxi (1945), 101
H.E. Johnson: *Operas on American Subjects* (New York, 1964)
H.E. Johnson: "Musical Interests of Certain American Literary and Political Figures," *JRME*, xix (1971), 272
C.E.F. Clark Jr.: *Nathaniel Hawthorne: a Descriptive Bibliography* (Pittsburgh, 1978)
B.E. Chmaj: "Sonata for American Studies: Perspectives on Charles Ives," *Prospects: an Annal of American Cultural Studies*, ed. J. Salzman (New York, 1979), 1–58
P. Catalano, "Coro Allegro: Fussell 'Infinite Fraternity'," *American Record Guide*, lxvi/5 (2003), 46
J.K. Law: "The Poisoned Kiss," *OQ*, xxi (2005), 561–3

MICHAEL HOVLAND

Hay, George Dewey (*b* Attica, IN, 9 Nov 1895; *d* Virginia Beach, VA, 8 May 1968). Journalist, radio producer, and founder of the GRAND OLE OPRY. Trained as a print journalist, Hay was reluctantly drawn into radio during the early 1920s. Hay wrote for the Memphis *Commercial Appeal* before honing his air persona on the paper's radio station, WMC. He then took his signature steamboat whistle and nickname "The Solemn Old Judge" to WLS in Chicago, where he helped produce the *National Barn Dance* and was voted the nation's most popular radio announcer. Edwin Craig, founder of WSM-AM, invited Hay to his station's grand opening on 5 Oct 1925 and offered him the post of "radio director" shortly thereafter. Within weeks of starting his new job, Hay invited fiddler Uncle Jimmy Thompson to perform live on a Saturday night. The slot became a weekly "barn dance," which Hay would name the *Grand Ole Opry* in 1927. Hay programmed an expanding lineup of talent and vigorously promoted the show through press releases and newspaper and magazine stories. He established a touring bureau within WSM to keep Opry artists working through the week. Health issues troubled Hay during the 1930s, but he was a key part of the show's identity in the 1940s, including the post-war period when, among other things, he endorsed the new bluegrass style pioneered by Bill Monroe, Lester Flatt, and Earl Scruggs. Hay wrote a short book chronicling the birth of the *Opry* in 1945 and edited an early country music magazine, *Pickin' and Singin' News*. In the late 1950s, Hay moved to Virginia Beach, Virginia, where he died in 1968.

BIBLIOGRAPHY
G.D. Hay: *A Story of the Grand Ole Opry* (1945)
C. Wolfe: *A Good Natured Riot: the Birth of the Grand Ole Opry* (Nashville, 1999)
C. Havighurst: *Air Castle of the South: WSM and the Making of Music City* (Urbana and Chicago, 2007)

CRAIG HAVIGHURST

Hayden, Philip C(ady) (*b* Brantford, ON, 2 Nov 1854; *d* Keokuk, IA, 15 May 1925). Music educator. Hayden was born in Ontario while his mother, of Geneva, New York, was visiting family there. He was educated at Oberlin College (1878–83) though there is no record of his completing a degree. He taught voice and choir at various institutions in the Quincy, Illinois area (1883–8) until becoming supervisor of music in the Quincy schools (1888). In 1900 he became supervisor in nearby Keokuk, Iowa and taught there until his death. Hayden was the founding editor of *School Music Monthly*, later *School Music* (1900–25), the nation's most prominent music education journal at the time. He was also a leader in the Music Department of the National Education Association (NEA). When the annual NEA conference was cancelled in 1907 due to the San Francisco earthquake the previous year, he organized a three-day meeting of some 104 supervisors to discuss matters of mutual interest and to observe his teaching of sight-reading using a method called "rhythm forms." This meeting in Keokuk led to the founding of the Music Supervisors National Conference (later Music Educators National Conference). Hayden served as the organization's first president (1907–9). He was inducted into the Music Educators Hall of Fame in 1986.

BIBLIOGRAPHY
C.N. Cannon: *The Contributions of Philip Cady Hayden to Music Education in the United States* (diss., U. of Michigan, 1958)
C.L. Gerber: *Ear Training and Music Reading Methods Used by Philip C. Hayden, Music Literacy through Rhythm Forms* (diss., U. of Mississippi, 2008)

ALAN L. SPURGEON

Hayes, Catherine (*b* Limerick, Ireland, baptized 25 Oct 1818; *d* London, 11 Aug 1861). Irish opera singer. She studied with Antonio Sapio in Dublin and made her concert debut in 1839. Following further study in Paris and Milan she made her operatic debut in Bellini's *I Puritani* in May 1845, followed by performances in Donizetti's *Lucia di Lammermoor* and Rossini's *Mosé*. Her debut at La Scala in 1845 was an overwhelming success and she subsequently performed in all major Italian cities, becoming the most heralded Lucia of the decade. In 1849, Hayes agreed to sing at Covent Garden in London in *Linda di Chamounix* in April. In June 1849, she received an invitation to sing for Queen Victoria. At this performance the Queen requested an encore to which Hayes obliged with a rendition of "Kathleen Mavourneen," a tune which became her signature.

P.T. Barnum sponsored Hayes's tour of the United States in 1851. Hayes performed with great fanfare in New York, Boston, Philadelphia, Washington D.C., Charleston, Savannah, New Orleans, many other cities along the Mississippi River, and as far west as Sacramento and San Francisco. Her tour continued with engagements in Peru and Chile before she traveled to Hawai'i and gave a concert for King Kamehameha II. She then made her way to Australia, India, Singapore, and Java, where she sang for the British military. She returned to London in 1856. She is said to have been "a true soprano, with more than an average share of the middle voice, which enabled her to sing music beyond the means of ordinary sopranos" (*Musical World*, 17 Aug 1861).

BIBLIOGRAPHY

B. Walsh: *Catherine Hayes 1818–1861: The Hibernian Prima Donna* (Dublin, 2000)

TIMOTHY M. CRAIN

Hayes, Isaac (Lee, Jr.) (*b* Covington, TN, 20 Aug 1942; *d* Memphis, TN, 10 Aug 2008). Soul singer, keyboard player, saxophonist, songwriter, and producer. He first recorded for the Memphis-based Youngstown label in 1962. In the first half of the 1960s Hayes also wrote songs and played sessions for the Goldwax and Phillips labels in Memphis, backing singers such as Jeb Stuart, Dorothy Williams, and Spencer Wiggins. As a member of saxophonist Floyd Newman's band, he eventually found his way into STAX, where he co-wrote one side and played on both sides of Newman's solitary single in 1963. Hayes was then hired for a variety of Stax sessions to replace keyboard player Booker T. Jones while Jones was at college. Soon thereafter Hayes began helping with arrangements and by 1965 had formed a songwriting partnership with lyricist David Porter. Hayes and Porter became the foremost writing and production team at Stax, creating seminal chart hits for artists such as Sam and Dave ("You don't know like I know," "Hold on! I'm a comin'," "Said I wasn't gonna tell nobody," "You got me hummin'," 1966; "When something is wrong with my baby," "Soul Man," 1967; "I thank you," 1968), Ruby Johnson ("I'll run your hurt away," 1966), Mable John ("Your good thing is about to end," 1966), Carla Thomas ("B-A-B-Y," 1966), the Soul Children ("I'll understand," "The sweeter he is," 1969), and the Emotions ("So I can love you," 1969). Their material leaned heavily on gospel roots; some songs, such as Sam and Dave's "Said I wasn't gonna tell nobody," were secular rewrites of traditional gospel material.

Although a successful writer, producer, and session musician, Hayes desired to resume his career as a recording artist. His first album for the Stax subsidiary Enterprise, a trio-based jazz-oriented recording entitled *Presenting Isaac Hayes*, was released in the spring of 1968 to little acclaim. However, his second album, *Hot Buttered Soul* (1969), was a drastic departure from the norm: it included only four songs, two of which were 12 and 18 minutes long. Even more surprising was that three of the four tracks were covers of pop songs written by white songwriters such as Burt Bacharach and Hal David ("Walk on by") and Jimmy Webb ("By the Time I Get to Phoenix"). The length of the songs; the arrangements that equally fused rock, soul, pop, jazz, and classical; the massive and majestic orchestrations; the long spoken rap that preceded Hayes's cover of "By the Time I Get to Phoenix"; and Hayes's crooning baritone vocal style were all radically different from what was going on in mainstream R&B at the time. The album initially broke in the jazz masrket before crossing over first to R&B and then to pop. Ultimately, *Hot Buttered Soul* sold over a million copies and spent months near the top of the R&B, pop, jazz, and easy listening charts, thus redefining the possibilities for black popular music. Contrary to the beliefs of major and independent record companies at the time, it demonstrated that black artists could enjoy success with the more prestigious and potentially creative format of the album as opposed to the single. With *Hot Buttered Soul*, Hayes pioneered the use of extended forms in black popular music. He also initiated the vogue in the first half of the 1970s for spoken monologues, or "raps," as they were then known.

Hayes followed *Hot Buttered Soul* with the equally successful *The Isaac Hayes Movement* and *To Be Continued* (both 1970). In 1971, with the double album *Shaft*, Hayes pioneered the black film soundtrack, winning an Academy Award and two Grammys. Hayes's score for *Shaft* opened the door for such artists as Curtis Mayfield, Marvin Gaye, and Bobby Womack to work in the soundtrack medium. The hi-hat pattern and wah-wah guitar on the single, "Theme from *Shaft*," had an inordinate influence on disco music. Hayes subsequently composed the soundtracks for *Truck Turner* and *Three Tough Guys*.

Hayes continued to record, appearing regularly on the charts through 1980. New albums also appeared in 1986 and 1995, but he spent most of the 1980s and 90s developing an acting career. In 1997, Hayes landed the part of Chef in the animated late-night series *South Park*. He continued to play the voice of Chef through nine seasons and enjoyed a number-one UK hit in 1998 with "Chocolate Salty Balls," taken from the album *Chef Aid: the South Park Album*.

In 1999, Hayes received an R&B Foundation Pioneer Award. Three years later he was inducted into the Rock and Roll Hall of Fame.

BIBLIOGRAPHY

J. Abbey: "Isaac Hayes: the Most Important Soul Man of Today," *Blues and Soul*, no.36 (1970), 6–7

R. Malo: "Recording 'Shaft' at Stax," *Recording Engineer/Producer*, iii/4 (1972), 15–19

J. Abbey: "Black Moses: Back from the Wilderness," *Blues and Soul*, no.166 (1975), 12–13

G. Hirshey: *Nowhere to Run: the Story of Soul Music* (New York, 1984)

P. Guralnick: *Sweet Soul Music* (New York, 1986)

R. Bowman: *Soulsville U.S.A.: the Story of Stax Records* (New York, 1997)

ROB BOWMAN

Hayes, Martin (*b* Feakle, Co. Clare, Ireland, 4 July 1962). Fiddler of Irish birth, naturalized American. Hayes is among the most esteemed and influential of Irish traditional musicians. He was born into a musical family in East Clare; his father P.J. Hayes was a fiddler with the famed Tulla Céili Band for over fifty years, and his uncle was the superb master fiddler Paddy Canny. Hayes's musicianship was recognized early; he won six all-Ireland fiddle championships before the age of eighteen. He immigrated to the United States as a young man, settling first in Chicago, where he formed the trad-rock ensemble Midnight Court with guitarist Dennis Cahill. Hayes and Cahill then returned to Irish traditional dance music, and their collaboration has grown into a unique and intense musical relationship. Hayes is renowned for his experimental approach to traditional tune performance.

His improvisatory exploration of tempos as well as the rhythmic and melodic possibilities of this music results in performances that are emotive and soulful, yet deeply rooted in the tradition. Hayes has developed a highly personalized fiddle style, which is ably supported by Cahill's spare and brilliant guitar accompaniment. Hayes is sought after throughout North America and Ireland as a performer and teacher. His recordings, although infrequent, showcase his singular artistic vision for traditional music performance.

RECORDINGS

Martin Hayes, 1993, Green Linnet, GLCD 1127; *Under The Moon*, 1995, Green Linnet, GLCD 1155; *The Lonesome Touch* (with Dennis Cahill), 1997, Green Linnet, GLCD GLI 1181; *Live in Seattle* (with Dennis Cahill), 1999, Green Linnet, GLCD 1195; *Welcome Here Again* (with Dennis Cahill), 2008, Compass Records, GLI 1233

BIBLIOGRAPHY

M. Larsen: "A Lilt All his Own: Martin Hayes," *Fiddler Magazine*, i/1 (Spring 1994) 4–11
F. Vallely: "Hayes, Martin," *The Companion to Irish Traditional Music*, (Cork, 1999) 183–4

SALLY K SOMMERS SMITH WELLS

Hayes, Roland (*b* Curryville, GA, 3 June 1887; *d* Boston, MA, 1 Jan 1977). Tenor. He received his general education at Fisk University (beginning in 1907) and had several singing teachers, including Arthur J. Hubbard, SIR GEORGE HENSCHEL, and Victor Beigel. Hayes sang with the Fisk Jubilee Singers on a tour to Boston; he remained in the city at the end of the tour and became a popular soloist. He made concert tours throughout the United States (1916–20); in 1921 he went to Europe, becoming a highly successful recitalist and appearing with major orchestras in London, Paris, Amsterdam, Berlin, and Vienna. An outstanding interpreter of African American spirituals (he termed them Aframerican religious folk music), he was equally successful in the classics and the music of Schubert, Schumann, Brahms, Debussy, and Fauré. His sensitive voice and eloquent delivery contributed to an effective performance style. He made a few appearances as late as the 1960s.

Hayes taught at Boston University and served as mentor to aspiring musicians. He was awarded honorary doctorates at Fisk University and Ohio Wesleyan University. He was inducted posthumously into the Georgia Music Hall of Fame (1991), and the city of Calhoun, Georgia, has erected historic markers in his honor. He published arrangements of a number of spirituals as *My Songs* (Boston, 1948).

BIBLIOGRAPHY

A.E. Knight: "Roland Hayes," *Record Collector*, x (1955–6), 29–47; see also xii (1958–60), 116, 215
R. Hayden: *Singing for All People: Roland Hayes, A Biography* (Boston, 1989; R/1995)
"Roland Hayes," *The New Georgia Encyclopedia*, <http://www.georgiaencyclopedia.org>

MAX DE SCHAUENSEE/KAREN M. BRYAN

Hayman, Richard (Warren) (*b* Cambridge, MA, 27 March 1920). Conductor, arranger, harmonica player, and composer. He began his professional career in 1938 as a performer and arranger with the Borrah Minevitch Harmonica Rascals. His arrangements for this ensemble brought him to the attention of commercial musicians, and within a few years he was working as an orchestrator for Metro-Goldwyn-Mayer studios on musical films that included *Girl Crazy, Meet me in St. Louis*, and *As Thousands Cheer*. After returning to Boston, where he was music director of the Vaughn Monroe Orchestra in the late 1940s, Hayman was named principal arranger for the Boston Pops Orchestra in 1950. In the decades that followed he served as music director for numerous leading entertainers, including Bob Hope, Johnny Cash, Red Skelton, Johnny Carson, Andy Williams, Pat Boone, Olivia Newton-John, and Bobby Vinton. His tune "Ruby" (from the soundtrack for the film *Ruby Gentry* [1953], featuring Hayman's own solo harmonica playing) was a best-selling recording, as was his disco arrangement of themes from Beethoven's Fifth Symphony ("A Fifth of Beethoven") in the late 1970s. Hayman expanded his activities in the early 1970s to include appearances as guest conductor for "pops" concerts presented by symphony orchestras, eventually obtaining the title of principal pops conductor with the orchestras in Detroit and St. Louis. Something of a showman, Hayman has a flamboyant style on the podium that is augmented by his extravagant costumes and quick-witted banter.

JAMES WIERZBICKI/R

Haynes, Bruce (*b* Louisville, KY, 14 April 1942). American and Canadian oboist, recorder player, and musicologist. He studied the oboe with Raymond Dusté (1958–61) and JOHN DE LANCIE (1960), and joined the San Francisco Ballet and Opera orchestras in 1960. From 1964 to 1967 he studied early music performance in the Netherlands, where his teachers included Frans Brüggen (recorder) and Gustav Leonhardt (ensemble performance and interpretation). In 1966 he began to play the early oboe. He was one of the first 20th-century performers to master the instrument and a key figure in setting professional performance standards for it. From 1972 to 1983 he taught the recorder and the early oboe at the Royal Conservatory in The Hague. During this period he pursued an active performing career and made a number of recordings. In 1979 he was a founding member of the Philharmonia Baroque Orchestra, and during the 1980s he performed with many period instrument ensembles. In 1984 he was appointed to teach the early oboe at the University of Montreal. Haynes's interest in the instrument and its performing practices led to much scholarly investigation; his research has encompassed the construction, repertory, and playing techniques of the instrument. This aspect of his career had become dominant by the late 1980s, and, while concentrating on the early oboe, he has also produced important studies on the history of pitch and period performance practices. Although retired from performing since the early 2000s, he remains an active researcher, writer, and teacher.

WRITINGS
(selective list)

Music for Oboe, 1650–1800: a Bibliography (Berkeley, 1985, 2/1992)
"Lully and the Rise of the Oboe as seen in Works of Art," *Early Music*, xvi/3 (1988), 324–38

Pitch Standards in the Baroque and Classical Periods (diss., U. of Montreal, 1995)

The Elegant Oboe: a History of the Hautboy, 1640–1760 (Oxford, 2001)

The Oboe (with G. Burgess) (New Haven, CT, 2004)

The End of Early Music: a Period Performer's History of Music for the Twenty-First Century (New York, 2007)

JANET K. PAGE/NATHAN PLATTE

Haynes, John Cummings (*b* Brighton, MA, 9 Sept 1829; *d* Boston, MA, 3 May 1907). Instrument manufacturer and dealer. Haynes first entered the music business in 1845, when he was hired by the successful Boston music merchant OLIVER DITSON (1811–1888), who ten years earlier had begun publishing music and selling instruments. By 1853 Haynes was given a financial interest in Ditson's company, and in 1857 was made a co-partner. After the death of Ditson, Haynes became president of the corporation. By 1864 (though one source says as early as 1858), a separate entity known as J.C. Haynes & Company was formed at 33 Court Street to manufacture and distribute musical instruments, backed by the parent company of Ditson. By 1891 the business had added an address at 453 Washington Street, and by 1900 had discontinued the Court Street location. That same year Haynes's company was amalgamated with Oliver Ditson and Company. An 1879 billhead states that Haynes was an importer, wholesaler, and retailer of instruments, strings, sheet music, and other musical merchandise. A wide variety of instruments were offered, including bowed and plucked strings, woodwinds, brasses, accordions, and music boxes. The firm was perhaps best known for its banjos, mandolins, and guitars, issued under the trade names Bay State and Excelsior. At various times the production of guitars was supervised by a Swedish immigrant named Pehr Anderberg, assisted by his son, Ernest. Boston flute maker George Haynes reportedly made flutes for the company in the late 1890s, but he was apparently not directly related to John. Music Trades Magazine stated in 1900 that J.C. Haynes & Company was the largest manufacturer of small goods in Boston, excelling in the quality of its products. Haynes himself reportedly retired at the beginning of 1904.

BIBLIOGRAPHY

W.A. Fisher: *Notes on Music in Old Boston* (Boston, 1918), 40, 73–4, 77

C.M. Ayars: *Contributions to the Art of Music in America by the Music Industries of Boston, 1640 to 1936* (New York, 1937), 215, 234, 265–6

DARCY KURONEN

Haynes, Roy (Owen) (*b* Roxbury, MA, 13 March 1925). Jazz drummer and bandleader. He has had one of the longest, most prolific careers of any jazz drummer. He taught himself drums and began performing professionally in 1942 in the Boston area, where he worked with Tom Brown, Frankie Newton, Sabby Lewis, and Pete Brown. After moving to New York to join Luis Russell's big band (September 1945), Haynes worked with with Lester Young (1945–7), Charlie Parker (1949–52), and Sarah Vaughan (1953–8). He later played with John Coltrane intermittently (1961–5) and toured with Stan Getz (1965–7), Gary Burton (1967–8), Chick Corea (1981, 1984), and Pat Metheny (1989–90). As a sideman, he has performed and recorded with an array of artists, including Louis Armstrong, Count Basie, Sidney Bechet, Miles Davis, Eric Dolphy, Ella Fitzgerald, Dizzy Gillespie, Stephane Grappelli, Andrew Hill, Billie Holiday, Dave Holland, J.J. Johnson, Hank Jones, Roland Kirk, Thelonious Monk, Gerry Mulligan, Art Pepper, Danilo Pérez, Michel Petrucciani, Bud Powell, Joshua Redman, Sonny Rollins, Horace Tapscott, Lennie Tristano, and McCoy Tyner. Haynes led his first recordings in 1954 and performed with his own groups from the 1960s, including his Hip Ensemble and Fountain of Youth Quartet. Rooted in swing and bebop, his innovative and influential approach accommodates an eclectic range of jazz styles. His recognitions include the Jazzpar Prize in Denmark (1994), the French government's Chevalier dans l'ordre des artes et des lettres (1996), induction into *Down Beat* magazine's hall of fame (2004), the BNY Mellon Jazz Living Legacy Award (2010), and a Grammy Lifetime Achievement Award (2011).

SELECTED RECORDINGS

As leader:*Out of the Afternoon* (1962, Imp.); *We Three* (1966, Col.)

As sideman: C. Parker: *Carnegie Hall X-Mas '49* (1950, Jass); B. Powell: *The Amazing Bud Powell*, i (1951, BN); T. Monk: *At the Five Spot* (1958, Mlst.); E. Dolphy: *Out There* (1960, NewJ); S. Getz: *Focus* (1961, Verve); S. Lacy: *The Straight Horn of Steve Lacy* (1961, Cand.); O. Nelson: *The Blues and the Abstract Truth* (1961, Imp.); J. Coltrane: *Newport '63* (1993, Imp.); A. Hill: *Black Fire* (1963, BN); J. McClean: *Destination…Out!* (1963, BN); C. Corea: *Now he Sings, Now he Sobs* (1968, SolS); P. Metheny: *Question and Answer* (1989, Geffen)

BIBLIOGRAPHY

H. Mandel: "Roy Haynes: Respect," *DB*, lxiii/11 (1996), 18–23

I. Gitler: "Roy Haynes: a Legend at 80," *Modern Drummer*, xxix/8 (2005), 44–8, 50, 52–6.

A. Kahn: "Snap Crackle: Roy Haynes still Brings the Boom-Bap at 80," *JT*, xxxv/9 (2005), 56–61

J. Riley: "Jazz Drummers' Workshop: Roy Haynes, Style & Analysis," *Modern Drummer*, xxix/8 (2005), 58–62

C. McBride: "I'm not a Metronome: the Roy Haynes Interview," *JT*, xxxvii/9 (2007), 50–55, 126–7

B. Ratliff: *The Jazz Ear: Conversations over Music* (New York, 2008), 155–68

THOMAS H. GREENLAND

Haynes, William S(herman) (*b* East Providence, RI, 27 July 1864; *d* Winter Park, FL, 28 Jan 1939). Flute maker. Haynes was trained as a silversmith in the Gorham factory in Providence. By 1888 he had completed his first flute, and for the next six years he was in business with his brother, George W. Haynes. From 1894 to 1900 he was superintendent of John C. Haynes & Co., Boston. In 1900 he started his own company at 180–86 Washington Street, Boston.

Haynes originally made Boehm flutes in wood but in 1913 finished his first silver instrument; he made very few wooden flutes after 1918. At this time he experimented with aluminum tubes and was awarded several US patents (including one in 1914) for a method of drawing integral tone holes from the flute tube.

In 1914 Haynes made his first gold flute and in 1935 the first platinum flute in the United States (for Georges

Barrère). He also made piccolos, alto flutes, and double-walled silver clarinets (built on the Thermos model), for which he received a US patent (1926). The company maintained a New York sales office from 1923 to 1978. Haynes retired in 1936, but the company continued in the ownership of the Haynes family until 1976, when it was sold to long-standing employee Lewis Deveau, who subsequently made modifications in the Haynes scale. Following the deaths of Deveau and his wife, the company was sold to the foreman, John Fuggetta. The firm, Wm. S. Haynes Co., relocated from its original Boston location to a new site in Acton, Massachusetts, in 2010.

Haynes and his foreman VERNE Q. POWELL were the most influential flute makers in the United States in the first half of the 20th century and were responsible for introducing the manufacture of French-style silver flutes to the United States. Haynes also trained many important flute makers, including Arthur Gemeinhardt, and achieved an international reputation.

BIBLIOGRAPHY

L.R. Gallese: "Two Countries are Most Noteworthy," *Wall Street Journal* (1 Feb 1977)

N. Toff: *The Development of the Modern Flute* (New York, 1979/R)

M. Goodman: *The Economics of Flute Production: an In-Depth Survey of the William S. Haynes and Verne Q. Powell Flute Companies* (diss., U. of Southern California, 1983)

M. Silk: "Boston's flutemakers found excellence just wasn't enough," *Boston Globe* (11 Sept 1984)

S. Berdahl: *The First Hundred Years of the Boehm Flute in the United States, 1845–1945: a Biographical Dictionary of American Boehm Flutemakers* (diss., U. of Minnesota, 1986)

S. Berdahl: "Haynes, Haynes, and Haynes," *Woodwind Quarterly*, no.1 (1993), 102–16

FRIEDRICH VON HUENE/NANCY TOFF/R

Hays, Lee (Elhardt) (*b* Little Rock, AR, 14 March 1914; *d* Cortlandt, NY, 26 Aug 1981). Singer, songwriter, and activist. Hays's father, William Benjamin Hays, was a Methodist preacher, who died when Lee was 14 years old. Though he later rejected his father's religious convictions, the hymns he learned as a child and, in particular, the communal aspect of the congregational singing profoundly shaped his musical development. Lee attended Commonwealth College, singing with other students and becoming involved with the union movement. Following college, he began singing with Pete Seeger, Woody Guthrie, and other folk singers and created the ALMANAC SINGERS in the 1940s. After the group disbanded, Hays continued to work with Seeger in the People's Songs, an organization dedicated to creating and disseminating labor songs. The two came together in 1948 with Ronnie Gilbert, and Fred Hellerman to form THE WEAVERS. The group's tight-knit harmony was underpinned by Hays's deep, resonant bass voice. They quickly achieved phenomenal commercial success before their suppression under a McCarthy blacklist in 1953, with both Seeger and Hays accused of communist activity. The group was revived in 1955, finally disbanding in 1964. Because of poor health, Hays semi-retired, living on royalties and mentoring younger singers.

Hays's best known song is "If I Had a Hammer" (1949), written with Pete Seeger, which became a Civil Rights anthem in the 1960s, especially through performances by Peter, Paul, and Mary. Other enduring songs include his collaborations with Seeger on "Kisses Sweeter than Wine" (1950) and "Wasn't That a Time." Hays was also known for his adaptation of spirituals, hymns, and traditional songs into labor and protest songs.

BIBLIOGRAPHY

D. Willens: *The Lonesome Traveler: a Biography of Lee Hays* (New York, 1988)

L. Hays and R.S. Koppelman: *Sing Out, Warning! Sing Out, Love!: the Writings of Lee Hays*, ed. R. Steven (Amherst, MA, 2003)

JOANNA R. SMOLKO

Hays, Sorrel [Doris] **(Ernestine)** (*b* Memphis, 6 Aug 1941). Composer, pianist, and mixed-media artist. She studied at the University of Tennessee, Chattanooga (BM 1963), the Munich Hochschule für Musik (piano and harpsichord diploma 1966), the University of Wisconsin (MM 1968) and the University of Iowa (composition and electronic music, 1969). After winning first prize in the International Competition for Interpreters of New Music (Rotterdam) in 1971, she toured Europe and the USA numerous times as a performer and advocate of new music. In the 1970s and 80s she gave between 60 and 70 premieres of other composers' music, including Cowell's Piano Concerto (1978) and works by Cage, Annea Lockwood, Oliveros, Mimaroglu, and Marga Richter.

She has worked extensively for women composers, producing *Expressions*, a radio series sponsored by the International League of Women Composers, of which she was assistant chairman from 1979 to 1982. Her involvement in the feminist and peace movements became central to her work as a composer during the 1980s. *Exploitation* (1981), written for the first International Congress on Women in Music, commented wryly on the status of women as performers and composers at that conference and elsewhere. She took the name Sorrel in place of Doris in 1985.

Hays's piano writing, in the tradition of Ives and Cowell, juxtaposes fiercely bombastic tone clusters with hymn-like passages of extreme serenity; finger stopping of the strings and microtonal experiments contribute to the great range of sonorities explored. The various chamber works entitled *Tunings* (1978–80), incorporating Appalachian fiddle riffs and a hymn tune, combine fine instrumental writing with rhythmic vitality and lyric beauty. The piano work *Sunday Nights* (1977) was the first of a number of pieces to evoke her Southern background. Her research into the musical aspects of Southern speech resulted in the tape music of *UNI* (1978) and *Southern Voices for Tape* (1980). These speech patterns also became the basis of *Southern Voices for Orchestra* (1981, commissioned for the 50th anniversary of the Chattanooga Symphony), which translates spoken dialects into orchestral and vocal sound, and is the subject of the documentary *Southern Voices: a Composer's Exploration* (dir. G. Stoney, 1985).

Hays has written many mixed-media compositions: the radio drama commissions from Radio Cologne (1984–98) enabled her to create substantial works in this genre, produced in studios in Cologne and New York. Her opera *The Glass Woman* (1989–93), an ambitious work commissioned by the National Endowment for the Arts and Opera America, concerns six renowned women collectors, including Bessie Smith and Peggy Guggenheim, commemorated by their own museums. Another work dedicated to influential women, among them Ethel Smyth and Ruth Crawford, is *90s: a Calendar Bracelet* (1990), a cycle of pieces for MIDI grand piano, a result of her artist residency at the Yamaha Communications and Research Center in New York. *The Clearing Way* (1992), for contralto and orchestra, is based on Amerindian rituals for the passing of the spirit of the dead. Her increasing interest in integrating music with other media is exemplified in *Dream in her Mind* (1995) and *Mapping Venus* (1996), which combine text collage and electronic music with operatic lyrical forms. *Debushing America* (2003), created in collaboration with soprano and avant-garde composer Kristin Norderval, is the latest in a decade long series of pieces called *Traveling*, based on the microtonal fluctuations of tone generators.

Since the late 1990s, the composer has concentrated for the most part on dramatic stage works, finding opera to be an ideal medium in which to combine the lyrical and dramatic elements in her music. After composing avant-garde music for many years, Hays has renewed her earlier interest in writing "acoustic" works for singers and instrumentalists, entwining melody and harmony in collage and contrapuntal textures. Recent stage works include *The Bee Opera* (2003), a comic "postmodern" pocket opera for soloists, chorus, and chamber orchestra; *Our Giraffe* (New York City Opera VOX Festival 2008), a tragicomic romp concerning the arrival of the first giraffe in France from Africa in the 1820s, for soloists, chorus and orchestra; and *Toowhopera* (2009), a comic fantasy about love in outer space, for soloists, chamber orchestra and video. The recipient of numerous awards, Hays has performed, taught, and lectured widely. She is presently based outside of Atlanta and is on the faculty of the University of West Georgia.

WORKS
(selective list)

OPERA
Love in Space (radio op), 1986; Touch of Touch (video op), 1989; The Glass Woman (Hays, S. Ordway, N. Rhodes), 1989–93; The Everybodydom (children's radio op, Hays), 1994; Dream in her Mind (radio op), 1995; Mapping Venus (radio op, G. Stein, Hays and others), 1996; The Bee Opera (D. Duhamel, Hays, G. Stein) 2003; Our Giraffe (C. Flowers), 2008; Toowhopera (Hays), 2009

CHAMBER AND SOLO INSTRUMENTAL
Tunings [nos.1–8]: [1] db, 1978, [2] fl, cl, bn, 1979, [3] solos for S, fl, cl, vn, 1979, [4] S, cl, pf, 1979, [5] str qt, 1980, [6] va, 1980, [7] 2 vn, 1980, [8] S, vn, vc, pf, 1981
Other: SensEvents, 6 insts, tape, 1970–77 [several versions]; Pieces from Last Year, 16 insts, 1976; For A. B., cl, pf, 1977; Breathless, b fl, 1978; Characters, conc., hpd, str qt, 3 ww, 1978; Segment/Junctures, va, cl, pf, 1978; UNI, dance suite (D. Hays), str qt, fl, chorus, tape, 1978; Winded, pic, 1978; Lullabye, fl, vn, pf, 1979; Tommy's Trumpet, 2 tpt, 1979
Fanfare Study, hn, tpt, trbn, 1980; Homing, vn, pf, 1981; Rocking, fl, vn, va, 1983; After Glass, 10 perc, 1984; Harmony, str, 1986; Bits, pf, kbd, 1987; Juncture Dance III, 7 perc, 1988; It All Sounds Like Music to

Me, solo perc, 1994; Structures, orch, 1995, version for elecs; Split Tree Festival March, sym. band, 1996; Travelling, didjeridu, elec sax, sound generator, ob, Tibetan singing bowl, 1997; On the Wind, 5 fl, 1973/2002; Wednesday Nights, pf, cl, trbn, 2010

PIANO
Chartres Red, 1972; If, pf, tapes, 1972; Wildflowers, pf, synth, 1972–9; PAMP, pf, tape, bird whistles, 1973; Sunday Nights, 1977; Etude Base Basses, 1978; Past Present, 1978; Saturday Nights, pf, tape, 1980; Sunday Mornings, 1980; M.O.M. 'N P.O.P, 3 pf, 1986; 90s: A Calendar Bracelet, MIDI grand pf, 1990; Windy Gestures, 1996; Rocker Parts, 2 pf, 1997

ELECTRONIC AND MIXED-MEDIA
Hands and Lights, pf, lights, 1971; Duet for Pianist and Audience, 1971; Translations and Comments, pf, tape, 1971; Round Around, plastic sculptures, lights, tape, 1974; SensEvents for Lincoln Center Out of Doors Festival, 6 insts, dancers, sound sculpture, lights, tape, 1977; Certain: Change, pic, b fl, tape, 1978; Reading Richie's Paintings, synth, fl, slides, 1979; Southern Voices for Tape, tape, slide projections, S/nar, 1980; Exploitation, S/chanter, tape, 1981; The Gorilla and the Girl, tape, 1981; Only, pf, 2 tapes, slide projections, film, 1981; Water Music, S, tape, water pump, slides, opt. vn, opt. baby pool, 1981; Celebration of No, tape, film, opt. vn/S/pf trio, 1983 [several versions]; The Needy Sound, tape, 1983; M.O.M 'N P.O.P, 3 pf, tape, film, slide projections, mime, 1984; Something (to Do) Doing (G. Stein, Hays), 16 chanters, tape, 1984
Weaving (Interviews), opt. S, pf, film, slide projections, 1984; Flowing Quilt (M. Ries), video, soundtrack, 1987; CD: Civil Disobedience, documentary film with music and choreog., 1988; Echo US Continental, 1988; Whatchasay/Wie bitte? (radio play), 1988; Take a Back Country Road, DX7 kbd, elec sax, ob, opt. v, 1989; The Hub: Megopolis Atlanta, 1989; Sound Shadows, ob, didjeridu, synth, dancer + perc, video, tape, 1990–; Scaling, synth, didjeridu, 1991; Echo U.S.A., audio art, 1991; Take Another Back Country Road, elec sax, kbd, sound generator, 1996; Deconstruction, video, electr soundtrack, 2002; Wake Up and Dream, trbn, electr sound, 2002; Debushing America (in collaboration with K. Norderval), S, sampler, laptop, synth, 2003

VOCAL
Star Music (Hays), chorus, tape, bells, 1974; For Women, 5 songs (A. Aldrich, B. Anderson, Hays, E. St V. Millay, A. Waldeman), S, pf, 1976; Set of Cheeky Tongues, S, pf, 1976; Hands Full, 2-pt chorus, drums, tape, 1977; Delta Dad (S. Ordway), 1v, pf, 1979; In-de-pen-dance, chanter, nylon str, 1979; Circling Around (B. Swan), 4 songs, Bar, fl, pf, 1981; Hush, 1v, reco-reco, sand block, 1981; Rest Song, SATB, opt. fl, 1981
Southern Voices for Orch, S, orch, 1981, excerpt Blues Fragments, arr. S, pf; Ex-, Rock-, In-, Re-, chant, tape, 1982; Rest Song, mixed chorus, 1982; Lullago, B, scat singer, 1982; Celebration of No, taped women's vv/(tape, vn, vc, prepared pf, slides, chanters), 1983; Hei-Ber-Ny-Pa-To-Sy-Bei-Mos, S, fl, perc, 1990; Searching Song, S, pf, 1990; The Clearing Way, C, chorus, orch, 1990; Dreaming the World, B, 4 perc, pf, 1993; A Birthday Book (Stein), B, ob, tuba, 1997; Stop Throwing My Country to the Wind (S. Behbahani, trans. K. Safa, F. Milani), S MS A soloists, women's chor, orch, 2010
Film scores, docudramas, videos, 1980–2000
Works for children, incl. vocal, ens, tape, pf pieces

Principal publishers: Peer-Southern, C.F. Peters, Hildegard, Tallapoosa Music

BIBLIOGRAPHY
CC (L. Goldberg); *GroveW* (M.S. Nachman, C.P. Smith) [incl. further bibliography]
M. Campbell: "Doris Hays: Artist with a Vision," *Pittsburgh Post-Gazette* (10 Oct 1977)
K. Gann: "Opera Glasses," *Village Voice* (22 Aug 1989)
M. Sheridan: "New York City Opera: Women's Work," *Playbill Arts* (30 April 2008)
R. Platt: "Our Giraffe," *New York Observer* (26 May 2008)
K. Alenier: "The Politics of Contemporary Opera," *Scene4 Magazine* (June 2008), <http://www.scene4.com/archivesqv6/jun-2008/html/karrenalenierj-r0609.html>

MYRNA S. NACHMAN

Hays, Will(iam) S(hakespeare) (*b* Louisville, KY, 19 July 1837; *d* Louisville, KY, 23 July 1907). Composer. He spent his early adult years working on the riverboats of the Ohio and Mississippi, where he acquired some of the knowledge that served him when he came to write his long-running "River" column for the *Louisville Courier-Journal*. He wrote verse and often set it to his own music, although he had no formal training. He made free use of the important styles and genres of the day: his first ballad, the sentimental and extremely popular "Evangeline" (1857), for example, shows the strong influence of Italian opera; the Irish style is seen in songs like "Nora O'Neal" (1866), "Mollie Darling" (1873), and "Nora, the Pride of Kilkee" (1874). Hays's famous song of the Civil War, "The Drummer Boy of Shiloh" (1862), was influenced by both styles. He also wrote call-and-response spirituals, such as "Keep in de Middle of the Road" (1880), and dialect minstrel songs. Of the latter, "The Little Old Cabin in the Lane" (1871) achieved great popularity and has endured in the folksong repertoire, especially when set with parody verses (eg, "The Little Old Sod Shanty on the Claim"). Hays maintained that he was the first to set Emmett's tune "Dixie" to a minstrel text, and supported his claim with testimonials, but the evidence remains inconclusive (*see* EMMETT, DAN). He wrote at least 546 poems, and published three books of poetry, nine piano pieces, and 322 songs. A measure of his importance is suggested by the fact that over 20 million copies of his songs are estimated to have been sold. The Kentucky Library at Western Kentucky University holds Hays's papers and music.

BIBLIOGRAPHY

F.E. Stoll: *Will S. Hays: Kentucky Composer, Marine Editor, and Poet* (thesis, U. of Kentucky, 1943)

G.C. Grise: *Will S. Hays: his Life and Works* (thesis, Western Kentucky State Teachers College, 1947)

M.C. Chrisman: *Popular Songs of the Genteel Tradition: Their Influence on Music Education in Public Schools of Louisville, Kentucky, from 1850 to 1880 (Will S. Hays)* (diss., U. of Minnesota, 1985)

B.C. Malone: *Singing Cowboys and Musical Mountaineers: Southern Culture and the Roots of Country Music* (August, GA, 1993), 60–66

DALE COCKRELL

Hayter, A(aron) U(pjohn) (*b* Gillingham, UK, 16 Dec 1799; *d* Boston, MA, 28 July 1873). Organist and conductor of English birth. After entering the choir school of Salisbury Cathedral as a youth, Hayter studied music with Arthur Thomas Corfe (1773–1863), the cathedral organist. In 1818, he became the organist of Hereford Cathedral, but after disgracing himself two years later, moved to the collegiate school of Brecon, serving until 1835. At the urging of the Rev. Jonathan M. Wainwright (1792–1854), he immigrated to New York and worked as the organist of Grace Church between 1835 and 1837. He then served Boston's Trinity Church between 1837 and July, 1862, when a stroke paralyzed him. He also served as the organist and conductor of Boston's Handel and Haydn Society between 1839 and 1848. Hayter was highly regarded for his musical skills and premiered a number of prominent European oratorios for American audiences. One of his sons, George F. Hayter, was also an organist.

BIBLIOGRAPHY

"Obituary," *Dwight's Journal of Music* (9 Aug 1873)

W. Shaw: *The Succession of Organists* (Oxford, 1991)

STEPHEN L. PINEL

Hayton, Lennie [Leonard] **(George)** (*b* New York, NY, 13 Feb 1908; *d* Los Angeles, CA, 24 April 1971). Musical director, conductor, and arranger. He began his career as a pianist, playing and arranging for jazz artists, in particular for the Paul Whiteman Orchestra in the late 1920s. His arrangements of classic songs for Whiteman, such as "Nobody's Sweetheart," are considered among the finest of their era, blending jazz instruments with those of the traditional orchestra. His later arrangement of "Star Dust" provided a hit in the early 1940s for clarinetist Artie Shaw. In 1940 he became musical director for Metro Goldwyn Mayer studios before moving to Twentieth Century-Fox in 1953. He was involved in arranging scores for a number of films and musicals, including *The Harvey Girls* (1945) and *The Pirate* (1948); the arrangements reflect the complexity achieved in his work for Whiteman, although film music had only recently incorporated jazz into its idioms. He was nominated for Academy Awards for his work on several notable musicals, including *Singin' in the Rain* (1952) and *Hello Dolly!* (1969). He received the Oscar in 1949 for his musical direction, with Roger Edens, of *On the Town*, based on Leonard Bernstein's ballet *Fancy Free*. His connection with jazz was sustained alongside his film music career through his marriage to jazz vocalist LENA HORNE. She credited Hayton with helping her to develop her voice, and he managed her professional singing career.

BIBLIOGRAPHY

SchullerEJ

SchullerSE

L. Horne and R. Schickel: *Lena* (New York, 1965)

KATE DAUBNEY

Haywood, Lorna (Marie) (*b* Birmingham, England, 29 Jan 1939). English soprano, vocal teacher/coach, and stage director. She studied at the Royal College of Music and the Juilliard School; while a student she made her professional debut in 1964 in the first New York performance of *Kát'a Kabanová*. Her Covent Garden debut in 1966 was as the First Lady in *Die Zauberflöte*, and she first sang with Sadler's Wells Opera (later the English National Opera) as Micaëla in 1970. She appeared widely in the United States, and her repertory included Countess Almaviva, Mařenka, Mimì, Butterfly, Pamina, Tosca, Musetta, Nedda, and Hanna Glawari. Her voice has been described as strong and clear, yet warm, and her considerable talent as a singing actress has made her a leading interpreter of the operas by Leoš Janáček. Her recordings include Menotti's *Amahl and the Night Visitors* with the Royal Opera Covent Garden Orchestra and Chorus, and Britten's *War Requiem* with Robert Shaw and the Atlanta Symphony, which won a Grammy.

In 1982 Haywood joined the voice faculty of the University of Michigan School of Music, teaching there until 2002. She retired from singing professionally in 1988, but by that point she was already well into a successful third career, that of operatic stage direction. Haywood worked most frequently with Madison Opera, receiving the greatest critical acclaim for her stagings of *Le Nozze di Figaro*, *Cavalleria Rusticana*, and *I Pagliacci* for Virginia Opera, *Die Zauberflöte* and *Fidelio* for Atlanta Opera, and *Il Trovatore* and *Don Giovanni* for Opera San Jose. Critics have noted especially her innovative yet sensible approach to blocking and stage movement, as well as her ability to develop character using subtle directorial touches.

ELIZABETH FORBES/KATHLEEN SEWRIGHT

Headphones. Form factors for loudspeakers designed for proximity to the ear. Ear buds and in-ear headphones are inserted into the ear canal, circum-aural headphones fit over the entire outer ear, and supra-aural headphones are placed against the outer ear. The addition of a microphone near the mouth produces a headset useful for two-way communication.

Two important implications of the closeness of the loudspeaker drivers to the ears are binaural listening and electro-acoustic efficiency. Binaural listening, in which each ear receives a dedicated signal without inter-aural crosstalk and devoid of the acoustic signature of the actual listening space, is essential to some forms of audio research and opens the door to the creation of new perceived environments through a range of signal processing techniques focused on the localization and spatialization of sound. Headphones need only a small fraction of the sound power required by traditional loudspeaker enclosures placed at a distance, and this efficiency is crucial for the portability of battery-powered devices.

Headphones offer opportunities for sound isolation and privacy, separating the user from the sound of his or her surroundings and the outside world from the sound within the headphones. Passive isolation relies on the physical obstruction of the headphones to attenuate sound. With active isolation, a signal is generated within the headphones tailored to cancel the outside signal as it reaches the headphones' listening environment. This makes headphone listening practical for planes, trains, stages, and other noisy environments.

Headphones have become an essential feature of contemporary urban society, often used by individuals to defend themselves from the dense, noisy crowds around them by obtaining a personal listening space. The human desire for portable sound was anticipated from the first work of science fiction, Cyrano de Bergerac's *Voyage to the Moon* (1657): it describes a device worn like earrings that might be used when one goes for a walk and from which sound "comes out as if from the mouth of a man, or a musical instrument."

See also LOUDSPEAKER, RECORDED SOUND.

BIBLIOGRAPHY

J. Borwick, ed.: *Loudspeaker and Headphone Handbook* (New York, 3/2001)

J. Eargle: *Loudspeaker Handbook* (Boston, 2/2003)

ALEX U. CASE

Heaney, Joe [Seosamh Ó hÉanaí/hÉiniú] (*b* Carna, Co. Galway, Ireland, 1920; *d* Seattle, WA, 1 May 1984). Irish traditional singer and storyteller. From a western maritime area noted for *sean-nós* ("old-style" unaccompanied Irish-language) singing, Heaney became a leading and magisterial exponent of this style, with a large repertory of several hundred songs, including many in English, which he learned mostly from his father, aunt, and neighbors. His repertory ranged from religious songs and other items of medieval survival to local love and comic songs and political ballads. After an uncompleted period of study at teacher-training college and successes in singing competitions at Irish-language festivals, he emigrated in 1947, going first to Scotland and then to England, where he worked as a laborer. He came to the attention of folk revivalists there and, having returned to Ireland in 1957, was one of the first *sean-nós* singers to record commercially. Heaney emigrated again in the late 1950s, this time moving to New York, where he worked as a doorman and performed at folk festivals and academic workshops. In the 1970s he became a visiting artist at the University of Washington, Seattle, where an archive of his music is now kept. He performed at many festivals, including the Newport Folk Festival (1965), the Smithsonian Institution's Festival of American Folklife, and the National Folk Festival. He collaborated with John Cage on a theater piece based on James Joyce's *Finnegans Wake*, which received its premiere at the Pompidou center in Paris, France, in 1980. He received a National Heritage Fellowship from the NEA in 1982.

RECORDINGS

Sing the Dark Away, RTÉ TV documentary, dir. M. Davitt (Dublin, 1995)

Say a Song, Northwest Archives NWAR CD 001 (1996)

Ó Mo Dhúchas, Gael-Linn CEFCD 051 (1997)

BIBLIOGRAPHY

S. Williams and L.Ó. Laoire: *Bright Star of the West: Joe Heaney, Irish Song-Man* (New York, 2011)

NICHOLAS CAROLAN/R

Hearn, George (*b* St. Louis, MO, 18 June 1934). Actor and singer. He began his career in New York in 1963 with Shakespeare in the Park and subsequently has performed in more than 185 plays and about 20 musicals. He first appeared on Broadway as Ianto Morgan in *A Time for Singing* by John Morris (1966). He also played the role of John Dickinson in Sherman Edwards's *1776* (1971) and replaced Len Cariou in the title role of Stephen Sondheim's *Sweeney Todd* (1979). He originated the role of Papa in *I Remember Mama* (1979), with music by Richard Rodgers. For his portrayal of Albin in *La Cage aux Folles* (Jerry Herman, 1983) he earned a Tony Award for Best Actor in a Musical. Albin's character introduced the anthem "I Am What I Am," which made a powerful statement about homosexual tolerance that coincided with the recognition of AIDS in America. In 1995 he received a Tony Award for Best Featured Actor in a Musical for his portrayal of Max von Mayerling in Andrew Lloyd Webber's *Sunset Boulevard* (1995). Of this performance

New York Times theater critic Vincent Canby observed that Hearn's "fluid baritone…nearly brings the show to a halt." His voice has substantial size and strength, coupled with keen textual interpretation. Hearn played the husband to Carol Burnett's wife in Sondheim's *Putting It Together*, for which he won the 2000 Tony Award for Best Actor in a Musical. He returned to Broadway in 2004–5 and in 2006 to portray the Wonderful Wizard of Oz in Stephen Schwartz's *Wicked*.

SYLVIA STONER-HAWKINS

Hearne, Ted (*b* Chicago, IL, 2 May 1982). Composer and conductor. He attended the Manhattan School of Music (BM 2004) and Yale School of Music (MMA 2009) and has studied composition with MARTIN BRESNICK, AARON JAY KERNIS, EZRA LADERMAN, DAVID LANG, Nils Vigeland, and JULIA WOLFE. Hearne's compositions engage social issues and explore contemporary experience with visceral power and raw emotion. He aims to write works that create something original from varied musical traditions. His *Katrina Ballads,* an oratorio with a primary source libretto, addresses media perspectives on the major hurricane that hit the US gulf coast in 2005. *Katrina Ballads* was awarded the 2009 Gaudeamus Prize by the Music Center of the Netherlands, and the 2010 recording of the work (New Amsterdam Records) was critically acclaimed. Hearne's music has been performed by the Minnesota Orchestra, the Calder Quartet, the Pittsburgh New Music Ensemble, and the New York City Opera, and programmed at the MATA Festival, the Bang on a Can Marathon, and the Carlsbad Music Festival. Hearne has received commissions from Third Coast Percussion (Chicago), the New Music Collective (Charleston), Newspeak, the Huntsville Symphony, the Albany Symphony, and Ensemble ACJW. Hearne is the artistic director of Yes is a World and resident conductor of Red Light New Music, and was for five years composer-in-residence of the Chicago Children's Choir. He served as music director for the premieres of Lang's opera *Anatomy Theatre* (performed by ICE, 2005), Michael Gordon's *Lightning at our Feet* (BAM Next Wave Festival, 2008), and Bryan Senti's *From the margins, this, unmentioned* (Brooklyn Lyceum, 2009). He received a 2008 Charles Ives Scholarship from the American Academy of Arts and Letters, was an artist-in-residence at the MacDowell Colony in the fall of 2009, and has collaborated with composer J.G. Thirlwell and filmmaker Bill Morrison. Also active as a singer, Hearne has performed Matt Marks's *The Little Death Vol. 1* and Jacob Cooper's *Timberbrit*.

ELIOT GATTEGNO

Heart. Rock group. It formed in Vancouver, British Columbia, in 1973. Heart is composed of Seattle-born sisters Ann (*b* San Diego, CA, 19 June 1950) and Nancy (*b* San Francisco, CA, 16 March 1954) Wilson supplemented by a changing lineup of side musicians. The two collaborate as songwriters, with older sister Ann serving as the lead vocalist on the majority of the group's recordings and Nancy as the group's primary rhythm and lead guitarist. They were among the first women in rock to both write and play their own songs. The band achieved major success in the mid-1970s with their first two albums, *Dreamboat Annie* (1976) and *Little Queen* (1977), which spawned a number of top ten singles, including "Dreamboat Annie," "Crazy on You," "Magic Man," and "Barracuda." After a decline in popularity in the early 1980s, Heart again achieved chart success in 1985 with a self-titled album including the top ten hits "What About Love," "Never," "These Dreams," and "Nothin' at All." Their band's sound has ranged from hard rock and metal numbers ("Barracuda") to folk-influenced ballads ("Dreamboat Annie"). In 2010 they released *Red Velvet Car*, a return to their hard rock-influenced roots of the late 1970s. Nancy Wilson also has composed music for many of Cameron Crowe's movies, including *Jerry Maguire* (1996), *Almost Famous* (2000), and *Vanilla Sky* (2001). With *Billboard* Top Ten albums in every decade since the 1970s, and sales of more than 35 million albums worldwide, Heart remains one of the most enduring and successful bands of all time.

KEN McLEOD

Heath [Kuumba], **Albert** [Al; Tootie] (*b* Philadelphia, PA, 31 May 1935). Drummer, brother of bass player Percy Heath and saxophonist Jimmy Heath. He was exposed to jazz through his brother Jimmy's work with John Coltrane and Charlie Parker and the success of the Modern Jazz Quartet, which his brother Percy helped develop. While in his early twenties, he moved to New York City. His propulsive yet sensitive drumming was apparent on key recordings, including Coltrane's first release, *Coltrane*. While in New York, he worked with J.J. Johnson, Nat Adderley, Blue Mitchell, Dexter Gordon, and others. From 1965–8, he lived in Denmark, where he earned respect along with other expatriate American jazz musicians. After returning to the United States, he performed in a jazz-funk sextet led by pianist Herbie Hancock and also participated with Billy Taylor's Jazzmobile, an outreach program that helped popularize jazz in the States. He released his first album, *Kawaida*, in 1969. After a short period of retiring from music, he spent the remainder of the 1970s performing with Yusef Lateef, the Heath Brothers, and Anthony Braxton, among others. He continued to be a supportive sideman for the next two decades for leaders such as Warne Marsh, Joe Pass, Art Farmer, and Frank Morgan, and occasionally led his own ensemble.

BIBLIOGRAPHY

Feather-Gitler BEJ

T.B. Wittet: "Albert 'Tootie' Heath: Drum Brother," *Modern Drummer*, xxii/6 (1998), 72

R. Condit: "The Heath Brothers: Giants of Jazz," *Jazz Education Journal*, xxxv/5 (2003), 42–52

MICHAEL CONKLIN

Heath, Fenno (Follansbee), Jr. (*b* Hampton, VA, 30 Dec 1926; *d* Hamden, CT, 5 Dec 2008). Choral director. He studied with QUINCY PORTER and PAUL HINDEMITH at Yale University (MusB 1951, MusM 1952), where he sang in several choral groups and directed the Apollo Glee

Club. In 1953, Heath succeeded Marshall Bartholomew as director of the Yale Glee Club, a position he held until 1992 as the first Marshall Bartholomew Professor of Choral Conducting. Heath's honors included the Yale Medal, Sanford Medal, Yale Glee Club Medal, University Glee Club of New York City Medal, Mory's Cup, and the Vernon Prize for composition. His works include incidental music for the play *John Brown's Body* (1961), music for the inaugurations of four Yale presidents—including settings of *Thy Word is a Lantern* (1964) and an extract from Spenser's *The Faerie Queen* (1978)—and choral arrangements of traditional spirituals for male chorus and mixed chorus.

BIBLIOGRAPHY

In Memoriam: Fenno Heath, Inspired Song in Many as Yale Glee Club Director, Yale University Office of Public Affairs pamphlet (New Haven, 6 March 2009)

SORAB MODI/PATRICE MADURA WARD-STEINMAN

Heath, Jimmy [James Edward; Little Bird] (*b* Philadelphia, PA, 25 Oct 1926). Saxophonist, flutist, composer, arranger, and educator, father of the percussionist Mtume Heath and brother of the bass player PERCY HEATH and the drummer ALBERT HEATH. He was born into a musical family and was influenced by Charlie Parker on alto saxophone and by John Coltrane on tenor. During the 1940s and early 1950s he played with Howard McGhee, Dizzy Gillespie, and Miles Davis. On tenor, he developed a pleasant hard-bop style, featuring a warm timbre, neat, consequential phrasings, and an efficient rhythmical drive. After working with Kenny Dorham, in the 1960s and 1970s Heath led groups that included Art Farmer and Stanley Cowell. During the same period he worked as a sideman for many players associated with the modern mainstream style, including Ray Brown, Benny Carter, Gil Fuller, Red Garland, Milt Jackson, and Freddie Hubbard. He also recorded for Riverside, Cobblestone, Impulse, and Verve, among other labels. In 1974 he and his brothers formed with Cowell the Heath Brothers, which toured and recorded for various labels including Columbia, Strata-East, and Concord. Heath has written modern standards, notably "CTA," "Gingerbread Boy," and "Gemini"; orchestral arrangements, including "Afro-American Suite of Evolution," "Three Ears," and "In Praise"; and scores for Cannonball and Nat Adderley, Milt Jackson, and Clark Terry, among others. He has taught at Housatonic Community College, CUNY, and the Aaron Copland School of Music and has been nominated three times for a Grammy Award.

BIBLIOGRAPHY

P. Welding: "The Return of Jimmy Heath," *DB*, xxviii/5 (1961), 16

D. Salemann: *Jimmy Heath: Solography, Discography, Band Routes, Engagements, in Chronological Order* (Basel, 1986)

A. Nahigian: "'You can't Buy Experience': the Heath Brothers," *DB*, lxv/1 (1998), 31

W. Friedwald: "A Jazz Colossus Steps Out," *Wall Street Journal* (19 July 2010)

LUCA CERCHIARI

Heath, Percy (*b* Wilmington, NC, 30 April 1923; *d* Southampton, NY, 28 April 2005). Double bass player, oldest brother of the saxophonist JIMMY HEATH and the drummer ALBERT HEATH. He grew up in Philadelphia and started playing violin in junior high school. After his discharge from the army in 1946, he took up bass, studying at the Granoff School of Music in Philadelphia. Heath played with Joe Morris's rhythm-and-blues band in 1947, after which he worked with the trumpeter Howard McGhee, with whom he performed at the Paris Jazz Festival in 1948. In 1949 he moved to New York and was soon playing with Miles Davis, Art Blakey, and Bud Powell at the newly opened club Birdland. Heath joined Dizzy Gillespie's band in 1950 and was a permanent member of the Modern Jazz Quartet (MJQ) from 1952 until it broke up in 1974. He also recorded with Davis (1951–5), Clifford Brown, Kai Winding, and J.J. Johnson (1953), Sonny Rollins, and Thelonious Monk (1954) and participated in projects with both John Lewis and Milt Jackson outside the MJQ. In the late 1950s and early 1960s he recorded with Ornette Coleman (1959), Paul Desmond (1959, 1965), Wes Montgomery (1960), and frequently with his brother Jimmy. After the MJQ broke up in 1974, Heath formed a band with his brothers Jimmy and Albert called the Heath Brothers. When the MJQ came together again for regular tours from 1981, Heath divided his time between these two bands. In 2002 he recorded his only album as a leader, *A Love Song* (Daddy Jazz).

BIBLIOGRAPHY

V. Wilmer: "Percy Heath," *Jazz Journal*, xvii/5 (1964), 6–8

L. Feather: "The Heath Bros: Together again for the First Time," *DB*, xlii/17 (1975), 18–20

W. Knauer: *Zwischen Bebop und Free Jazz: Komposition und Improvisation des Modern Jazz Quartet* (Mainz, 1990)

WOLFRAM KNAUER

Heavy metal. A term used since the early 1970s to designate a style of rock music characterized by loud, sustained "power chords" played on electric guitar and a stomping beat that may be aggressively fast or deliberately ponderous. The lyrics, which concern power, individual freedom, history, sex, rebellion, and violence, are delivered in a screeching or barking vocal style that often explores extremes of vocal register (both high and low). Although heavy metal shades into hard rock at its most melodic and into progressive rock at its most intricate, heavy metal performers usually produce a deliberately stereotyped music. Integral to the style are certain conventions of dress and performance that have marked particular sub-genres. For example, black leather jackets, studded accessories, ripped, tight jeans, and the wearing of long hair became characteristic in the 1970s and in later decades when a "traditional" look was desired; elaborate hair and makeup produced a highly stylized, androgynous look popular with glam metal groups of the 1980s; and black-and-white "corpse paint" and costumes drawn from dark fantasy worlds characterized black metal of the 1990s and the early 21st century. In all its subgenres, performances are marked by an energetic stage presence and often accompanied by flashing lights, the explosion of smoke bombs, and other elaborate stage effects, sometimes

Eddie Van Halen, 2004. (AP Photo/Tom Hood)

involving satanic or horror imagery. Because heavy metal is typically less melodic than most rock, bands tend to build audiences through live performances and through videos, rather than exposure on radio (although many metal groups in the 1980s were successful on radio as well). It has appealed primarily to white males aged 13–35, although the style and its audience have grown more diverse since the late 1980s.

Heavy metal evolved in the late 1960s from American hard rock and psychedelic rock, the British blues revival, and the guitar improvisations of Cream and Jimi Hendrix. The Who perfected the power chord, American hard-rock groups such as Blue Cheer and the Stooges established the use of high volume levels, and Hendrix, Jeff Beck, and Jimmy Page of Led Zeppelin explored the extremes of timbre obtainable on the guitar. The vocal style of Led Zeppelin and the Who dominated one school of heavy metal, and the low-pitched rhythmic chugging and philosophical lyrics of Black Sabbath another. Indeed, following a complex historiographical process over the course of two decades, early 21st-century metal artists usually cite only Black Sabbath as the ultimate root of their music. The effect of this shift has been that Led Zeppelin and other once-popular acts such as Blue Öyster Cult, Grand Funk Railroad, Aerosmith, Van Halen, and KISS have largely been written out of the history of metal. Instead, fans and writers tend to view these groups as exemplars of hard rock.

The most commercially visible groups of the late 1970s and early 1980s were part of the "New Wave of British Heavy Metal," but after 1983 American bands such as Metallica, Mötley Crüe, Bon Jovi, and Queensrÿche dominated sales charts and magazine covers worldwide, although each of these groups had a distinct identity. American metal, in particular, flourished in two competing locations: the thrash metal scene in the San Francisco Bay Area and the glam metal scene based along Sunset Boulevard in West Hollywood, California. Indeed, attempts to lump various substyles together for large, festival-style concerts typically failed owing to fans' very specific allegiances. For example, Metallica's style of thrash metal foregrounded speed and a high degree of ensemble virtuosity to support lyrics about power and personal independence in the face of various social controls. On the other hand, Mötley Crüe's brand of "sleaze" metal (later perfected by Guns N' Roses) emphasized themes of male sexual prowess (sometimes tainted by violent misogyny) and hard drug use over a blues-based sound reminiscent of mid-70s Aerosmith.

With the decline of heavy metal as a commercial juggernaut in the early 1990s, so-called extreme styles of metal such as death metal and black metal proliferated, particularly in Scandinavia. In the United States, Pantera incorporated a heavy groove into its music, and progressive metal groups Dream Theater and Tool combined traditional gestures of metal (powerful vocals, aggressive drumming) with advanced instrumental technique and extended song structures. The audience for metal, like that for rap, became thoroughly global in the 1990s and early 21st century, while the hybrid approaches of Linkin Park and Korn generated enthusiasm for a "New Wave of American Heavy Metal." Although it has often been held in low esteem by rock critics because of its youthful audience and perceived simplicity, it is among the most commercially successful forms of popular music.

BIBLIOGRAPHY

J. Obrecht: *Masters of Heavy Metal* (New York, 1984)
P. Bashe: *Heavy Metal Thunder* (Garden City, NY, 1985)
D. Weinstein: *Heavy Metal: a Cultural Sociology* (New York, 1991, rev. 2/2000 as *Heavy Metal: The Music and its Culture*)
C. Larkin, ed.: *The Guinness Who's Who of Heavy Metal* (Enfield, 1992, 2/1995)
M. Hale: *Headbangers: The Worldwide MegaBook of Heavy Metal Bands* (Ann Arbor, 1993)
R. Walser: *Running with the Devil: Power, Gender, and Madness in Heavy Metal Music* (Hanover, NH, 1993)
I. Christe: *Sound of the Beast: The Complete Headbanging History of Heavy Metal* (New York, 2004)
S. Waksman: *This Ain't the Summer of Love: Conflict and Crossover in Heavy Metal and Punk* (Berkeley, 2009)

JON PARELES/GLENN T. PILLSBURY

Heckscher [née Massey], **Celeste de Longpré** (*b* Philadelphia, PA, 23 Feb 1860; *d* Philadelphia, PA, 18 Feb 1928). Composer. She was born into an artistic family and began composing at the age of ten. Her early training in piano and composition, however, was obtained in spite of her parents' objections. In 1883 she married Austin Stevens Heckscher; they had two daughters and two sons. In the 1890s Heckscher studied composition with Henry Albert Lang and orchestration with Wasili Leps in Philadelphia; she is also reported to have studied in Europe. She composed two operas, *The Flight of Time* and *Rose of Destiny* (Philadelphia, 1918); an orchestral suite, *Dances of the Pyrenees*, which was also staged as a ballet (Philadelphia, 1916); and chamber music, piano works, and songs. In 1913 she gave a concert of her own compositions at the Aeolian Hall in New York. For many years she was president of the Philadelphia Operatic Society.

CAROL NEULS-BATES

Hedmont, Charles [Hedmondt, Emanuel Christian] (*b* Portland, ME, 24 Oct 1857; *d* London, England, 25 April 1940). Tenor. He studied in Montreal, London, and Leipzig, then made his debut in Berlin as Tamino in 1881. He sang with the Leipzig Opera from 1882 to 1889, notably as Max, Don Ottavio, Belmonte, Tamino, and Idomeneo. He appeared in the premiere of Gustav Mahler's completed version of Carl Maria von Weber's *Die drei Pintos* in 1888. He toured the United States with the Emma Juch English Opera Company in 1889 and 1890, serving for a time as their treasurer, and from 1891 lived in England, singing with the Carl Rosa Opera Company and the Quinlan Opera Company. He was Lohengrin in 1891 at Covent Garden and in 1895 presented his own season of opera there, during which he sang the roles of Tannhäuser, Lohengrin, and Siegmund and gave the first performance in English of *Die Walküre*. He was Loge in the 1908 English Ring cycle and performed Wagner in Montreal in 1914 with the Quinlan Opera Company.

HAROLD ROSENTHAL/BETH McGINNIS

Heed, John C. (*b* Hackettstown, NJ, 23 April 1862; *d* Newark, NJ, 12 Feb 1908). Cornetist and composer. Heed showed considerable aptitude for music at an early age, and soon became noted for his skill on the cornet. At seventeen he was in Providence, Rhode Island, where he became director of George Herrick's Band. He was known for his acute sense of rhythm accompanied by an equally sensitive faculty for tune and pitch. After moving to Newark with his wife, Heed was featured as a cornet virtuoso soloist with Voss's First Regiment Band, described as "the crack band of New Jersey." Described as a "bundle of nerves," he apparently suffered from a nervous condition throughout his life. This, plus a general decline in his health, caused him to give up cornet playing and conducting and devote himself to composition. He composed cornet solos, overtures, polkas, waltzes, and other dances, but is mainly known for the spirit and lilting nature of his marches, for which he gained the appellation "The March Wizard." His most famous march, *In Storm and Sunshine*, has long been a staple of circus band repertoire. Many of his marches are recorded in Robert Hoe's *Heritage of the March* series (10, 30, 35, A, E, BBB, OOO, SSS).

BIBLIOGRAPHY

W.H. Rehrig: *The Heritage Encyclopedia of Band Music* (Westerville, OH, 1991, suppl. 1996); CD-ROM (Oskaloosa, IA, 2005) [includes selective list of works]

LOREN D. GEIGER

Hee Haw. Television show. *Hee Haw* featured country-camp humor and the most popular country music acts of the day. Although it was a success upon first airing on CBS in 1969, it was cancelled in 1971 along with the network's other rural-themed shows. *Hee Haw* continued in syndication until 1993, making it one of the longer-running shows in television history and one of the only outlets for televised country music during the 1970s and early 1990s.

Hee Haw's reoccurring comedy skits frequently featured former *Grand Ole Opry* stars Minnie Pearl, Grandpa Jones, and David "Stringbean" Akeman, as well as Archie Campbell, Gordie Tapp, Junior Samples, and Lulu Roman. Musicians Buck Owens and Roy Clark hosted and performed during most of its episodes, and the Hee Haw Gospel Quartet, featuring Owens, Clark, Grandpa Jones, and Kenny Price gained enough popularity to release its own albums. Almost every important country group or performer active during its long run performed on the show. In an attempt to attract new, younger viewers, sets featuring a city street and a shopping mall replaced the barnyard and cornfield sets in the 1991–2 season, and the renamed *The Hee Haw Show* featured more pop-country musicians. In 1992–3, *Hee Haw Silver*, hosted by Roy Clark, featured clips from previous episodes, and, as ratings continued to decline, the show was cancelled at the end of that season.

BIBLIOGRAPHY

J. Aylesworth: *The Corn Was Green: the Inside Story of Hee Haw* (Jefferson, NC, 2010)

CLAY MOTLEY

Hefti, Neal (*b* Hastings, NE, 29 Oct 1922). Jazz composer, arranger, and trumpeter. He began his career as a trumpeter with Charlie Barnet's band and developed into a distinctive arranger during his stay with Woody Herman (1944–5). He gave up full-time playing to concentrate on composition and recorded under his own name with studio bands from the late 1940s. The popularity of a number of these recordings—notably "Repetition" featuring Charlie Parker and "Coral Reef", originally written for Count Basie under the title "Ours Alone"—led Hefti to form a touring band for a couple of years from 1952. Thereafter his writing diversified to include original music for a large number of films, such as *Harlow* (1965, for which he composed "Girl Talk") and *Barefoot in the Park* (1967), as well as for the television series *Batman* and compilations of Harold Lloyd. Although well regarded for his film work, he is likely to be best remembered for his earliest and most jazz-inflected writing. The unpretentiousness, firm sense of textural balance, and melodic architecture of his compositions often inspired dynamic renditions. His many pieces for Count Basie from 1950 display these qualities, although the pace-setting performances on the album *Basie* (1957, including "Lil' Darlin'" and "Whirly-bird") exerted a stultifying influence on most big-band arranging thereafter.

BIBLIOGRAPHY

R. Horricks: *Count Basie and his Orchestra: its Music and its Musicians* (London, 1957/R), 239

M. Ullman: *Jazz Lives: Portraits in Words and Pictures* (Washington, DC, 1979), 45

BRIAN PRIESTLEY/R

Heggie, Jake [John Stephen] (*b* West Palm Beach, FL, 31 March 1961). Composer and pianist. He learned piano as a child and was exposed to jazz standards by his father, an amateur saxophonist. He was also influenced by American musicals and by the voices of Julie Andrews and Barbra Streisand. At 16, he studied composition with ERNST BACON, who ignited Heggie's passion for text and introduced him to the works of Emily Dickinson. Subsequent settings of her poems include *Faith Disquiet* (1987) for a cappella chorus and *From Emily's Garden* (1999), for soprano with chamber accompaniment.

Heggie spent a year at the American University in Paris before enrolling at UCLA to study piano with Johana Harris. They married in 1982 and toured together before and after he graduated (BA 1984). A hand injury curtailed Heggie's piano career, and he turned his focus to composing. A self-described melodist, Heggie is drawn to the music of Leonard Bernstein, Samuel Barber, and Stephen Sondheim. The combination of lyricism with thoughtful text-setting that enables dramatic storytelling has attracted established singers such as Frederica von Stade, who has commissioned and performed his work, and has identified him with theater. In 1998 he became San Francisco Opera's composer-in-residence. He worked on the opera *Dead Man Walking* (2000) with librettist Terrence McNally, the novel's author, Sister Helen Prejean, and conductor Patrick Summers. Heggie's operas have been praised and criticized for their accessibility and invocation of musical theater. *Dead Man Walking* is rich with arioso-style writing and motifs, such as the poignant "He Will Gather Us Around," that unify the drama. The opera has been performed internationally over 150 times and recorded twice.

Whereas earlier song cycles tend toward the playful and jazzy, with musically discrete songs, later cycles often treat themes involving social justice and display some of the theatrical and unifying elements that distinguish his operas. *The Deepest Desire* (2002), which sets poems by Prejean, features a motif that recurs in various incarnations, as well as angular and sometimes declamatory vocal writing. The piano and flute accompaniment suggests the work of Claude Debussy, with its modal touches, sustained pedal work, and extremes of register. The harmonic language is shaped more by gestures and textures than by any clear tonal center. *The Breaking Waves*, also with a text by Prejean, was commissioned by Carnegie Hall in 2011; the premiere was sung by Joyce DiDonato.

Heggie's ability to seamlessly blend genres is exemplified in the one-act opera *To Hell and Back* (Gene Scheer, libretto) for Baroque period instruments, soprano, and Broadway soprano, composed in 2006 during a Guggenheim Fellowship. Ben Heppner accepted the heldentenor role of Ahab in *Moby-Dick* (Scheer), a co-commission by four international opera companies that was given its premiere at the Dallas

Opera in 2010. Heggie spent 2010–11 in residence at the University of North Texas at Denton, composing a symphony with a solo tenor part based on the Ahab monologues from *Moby-Dick*. A commission from the Houston Grand Opera commemorated the 10th anniversary of the 9/11 terrorist attacks.

WORKS
(selective list)

Op: Dead Man Walking (2, T. McNally), 2000, War Memorial Opera House, San Francisco; The End of the Affair (H. McDonald), 2003, rev. 2004–5; To Hell and Back (1, G. Scheer), 2006; For a Look or a Touch (Scheer), drama for actor, lyric Bar, fl, vn, vc, and pf, 2007; Three Decembers (1, Scheer), 2008; Moby-Dick (2, Scheer), 2010, Dallas Opera, Dallas

Choral: Faith Disquiet (E. Dickinson), 1987; I Shall Not Live in Vain (Dickinson), SATB chorus a cappella, 1995, rev. 1998; Patterns (A. Lowell), Mez, SSAA, piano, 1999; My Grandmother's Love Letters (H. Crane), SATB, orch, 2000

Pf song cycles: Encountertenor (J. Hall), 1995; How Well I Knew the Light (Dickinson), 2000; The Deepest Desire (H. Prejean), 2002; Statuesque (Scheer), 2005; Rise and Fall (Scheer), 2007; Friendly Persuasions: Songs in Homage to Poulenc (Scheer), 2008; The Breaking Waves (Prejean), 2011

Orch: Holy the Firm, vc, orch, 2002; Fury of Light, fl, orch, 2010; Ahab Sym., T, orch, 2011

BIBLIOGRAPHY

A. Keenan: *A Performer's Guide to Jake Heggie's* The Deepest Desire: *Four Meditations on Love* (diss., Louisiana State U., 2009)
D. Wylie: "Jake Heggie: a Singer's Composer," Classical Singer (Jan 2011), 24–35

MELANIE FEILOTTER

Heiden, Bernhard (*b* Frankfurt, Germany, 24 Aug 1910; *d* Bloomington, IN, 30 April 2000). Composer of German birth. He studied with PAUL HINDEMITH at the Berlin Hochschule für Musik (1929–33). At the end of this period Heiden was awarded the prestigious Mendelssohn Prize for a piano concerto. He moved to the United States in 1935; six years later he became a naturalized American. He studied musicology with Grout at Cornell University (MA 1946). Later that year he was appointed to the music school of Indiana University, eventually becoming professor of music and chair of the composition department; in 1981 he became professor emeritus. Heiden was the recipient of many awards and commissions, among them a Guggenheim fellowship (1966–7) and an NEA grant (1976). Recently, a manuscript score and parts to his previously unknown Klavierkonzert (1933) were discovered in the collection of the Netherlands Radio Music Library, Hilversum. Whether or not this work is the one for which Heiden won the Mendelssohn Prize in composition from the Berlin Hochschule that year has not been fully documented. This work is being digitized by the library and will be made available to the public.

Heiden's music is neoclassical in its formal structure, the early works portraying the influence of his teacher, Hindemith. Strongly polyphonic in texture, his prolific output, especially in the genre of chamber music, demonstrates a mastery of sonorous balance and effective instrumentation. He made an important contribution to the solo sonata and concerto repertories, writing for many relatively neglected instruments like the horn, tuba, and viola. His Sonata for viola and piano (1969) is intensely lyrical, with clear contrapuntal writing and chromatic melodies. The Sinfonia for wind quintet (1949), a staple of the woodwind repertory, employs modal harmonies, accentuated by the lyrical shapes of his melodic lines and sonorous voicings. In his vocal music the melodies are often free and daring (as in the *Sonnets*), while never obliterating the text. Unlike other composers, he did not take part in the postwar avant-garde movement but remained true to his own musicality.

WORKS

Dramatic: Conspiracy in Kyoto (film score), 1953; Dreamers on a Slack Wire (dance drama), 2 pf, perc, 1953; The Darkened City (op, 3, R.G. Kelly), 1961–2, Indiana U., Feb 1963; incid music to 2 Shakespeare plays

Orch: Conc., pf, orch, 1933 [ms]; Sym. no.1, 1938; Conc., small orch, 1949; Euphorion, 1949; Sym. no.2, 1954; Memorial, 1955; Conc., pf, vn, vc, orch, 1957; Philharmonic Fanfare, 1958; Variations, 1960; Envoy, 1963; Concertino, str, 1967; Vc Conc., 1967; Hn Conc., 1969; Partita, 1970; Tuba Conc., 1976; Conc., tpt, wind orch, 1980; Recitative and Aria, vc, orch, 1985; Fantasie concertante, a sax, wind orch, perc, 1987; Conc., rec, chbr orch, 1987; Salute, 1989; Conc., bn, chbr orch, 1990; Voyage, band, 1991

Vocal: Divine Poems (J. Donne), SATB, 1949; In Memoriam (H. Borland), SATB, 1963; Sonnets of Louise Labé (trans. Barnstone), S, str qt, 1977; Triptych (Beckmann), Bar, orch, 1982; A Bestiary, S, T, chbr orch, 1986; other choral works and solo songs

Chbr and solo inst: Sonata, a sax, pf, 1937; Sonata, hn, pf, 1939; Sonata, pf duet, 1946; Str Qt no.1, 1947; Sinfonia, ww qnt, 1949; Str Qt no.2, 1951; Qnt, hn, str qt, 1952; Sonata, vn, pf, 1954; Serenade, bn, str trio, 1955; Qnt, ob, str, 1962; 7 Pieces, str qt, 1964; 4 Dances, brass qnt, 1965; Ww Qnt, 1965; Sonata, va, pf, 1969; Intrada, wind qnt, a sax, 1970; Variations, tuba, 9 hn, 1974; Qnt, fl, vn, va, bn, db, 1975; Terzetto, 2 fl, vc, 1979; Hn Qt, 1981; Sextet, brass qnt, pf, 1983; Qt, hn, vn, vc, pf, 1985; Trio Serenade, cl, vn, pf, 1987; Préludes, fl, hp, db, 1988; Divertimento, tuba, ens, 1992; Trio, ob, bn, pf, 1992; Serenata, 4 vc, 1993; Prelude, Theme and Variations, a rec, 1994

Principal publishers: Associated, A. Broude, European American, Peer

BIBLIOGRAPHY

M. Laugosch: *The Instrumental Chamber Music of Bernhard Heiden* (diss., Indiana U., 1973)

A.S. Yama: "The Darkened City: a Lyrical Opera," *Opera Journal*, xii/4 (1979), 29–36

J.M. Filkins: *The Horn Music of Bernhard Heiden* (diss., U. of Kentucky, 1994)

M.P. Schaff: *The Wind Ensemble Works of Bernhard Heiden* (diss., Indiana U., 1996)

JAMES P. CASSARO

Heifetz, Daniel (Alan) (*b* Kansas City, MO, 20 Nov 1948). Violinist. He began formal violin study at the age of six with Theodore Norman and continued with Sascha Jacobson. In 1962 he entered the Los Angeles Conservatory (now the California Institute of the Arts), where he studied with Jacobson, ISRAEL BAKER, and Heimann Weinstine until 1965. He then attended the Curtis Institute, where his teachers were EFREM ZIMBALIST, IVAN GALAMIAN, and JASCHA BRODSKY (1966–71). In 1969 he won first prize in the Merriweather-Post Competition in Washington, DC; as a result, he was engaged as a soloist by the National SO for an East Coast tour and made his debut with that orchestra at Avery Fisher Hall in January 1970, playing the Tchaikovsky Violin Concerto. He has since performed extensively in Europe (after a 1976 debut in Brighton, England), Canada, and Central and South America. In the United States, he has appeared with, among others, the Los Angeles PO, the Cleveland Orchestra, and the Philadelphia Orchestra. He was the soloist in the first nationally televised unaccompanied violin recital (1975, for CBS), and won fourth prize in the 1978 Tchaikovsky International Violin Competition. He taught at the Peabody Conservatory (1979–88), the University of Maryland at College Park (1988–2006), and at Mellon University (1994–99).

Heifetz has acknowledged a preference for the Classical and Romantic repertory, but he also performs contemporary works; he is the dedicatee of Marga Richter's *Landscapes of the Mind II* and Lee Hoiby's *Serenade* for violin and orchestra. He has made a priority of performing outside concert halls for audiences not normally exposed to classical music. In 1996 he founded the Heifetz International Music Institute (<http://www.heifetzinstitute.org>), a six-week summer chamber music program held at Brewster Academy in Wolfeboro, New Hampshire. Attracting some of the nation's top pedagogues and students, the institute focuses on cultivating holistic performance practice. With a unique program structure that combines intense musical study with courses in subjects such as public speaking, voice, drama, and movement, the institute has received acclaim for fostering more expressive, communicative, and versatile artists. He performs on a violin made by Samuel Zygmuntowicz.

BIBLIOGRAPHY

S. Applebaum and H. Roth: *The Way they Play*, viii (Neptune, NJ, 1980)

SORAB MODI/JONATHAN KUUSKOSKI

Heifetz, Jascha (*b* Vilnius, Russia [now Lithuania], 2 Feb 1901; *d* Los Angeles, CA, 10 Dec 1987). Violinist of Russian birth, naturalized American. He had his first lessons from his father, Ruvim, a professional violinist. Soon afterwards he went to Elias Malkin, a noted teacher, and at the age of six was able to perform Felix Mendelssohn's Violin Concerto. In 1910 he was admitted to the St. Petersburg Conservatory, studying first with Leopold Auer's assistant Ioannes Nalbandyan, then with Auer himself. On 30 April 1911 he played at a concert in St. Petersburg, and he made a sensational debut in Berlin on 23 May 1912. As a result, Arthur Nikisch invited him to play Pyotr Il'yich Tchaikovsky's Violin Concerto with the Berlin PO on 28 October 1912. The offer of a tour of the United States enabled Heifetz to leave Russia in 1917; his debut at Carnegie Hall on 27 October was a triumphant success. In 1925 he became an American citizen.

Heifetz first appeared in the Queen's Hall, London, on 5 May 1920. He toured Australia (1921) and East Asia (1923). He played to enthusiastic audiences in Palestine in 1926 and in 1967 went back there to play with the Israel PO. No less emotional was his return to Russia in 1934. After World War II Heifetz reduced his appearances. From 1962 he taught at the University of Southern California, Los Angeles, where the Heifetz Chair in Music was established in 1975, with Heifetz as its first occupant. In 1964 he gave three chamber music concerts at Carnegie Hall with Gregor Piatigorsky and other artists. For his 70th birthday a one-hour film made in France was shown on television: he played J.S. Bach's

Chaconne and Max Bruch's Scottish Fantasy and demonstrated his accustomed mastery.

The name of Heifetz has become synonymous with violinistic perfection. Yet he did not stress technical exhibitionism. His stance was almost immobile; he held his violin high and far back, with his face turned towards his fingers. His right elbow was held rather high, owing to an almost exaggerated "Russian-style" grip of the bow. His tone was powerful and produced with great pressure; equalizing this was an intense vibrato giving a glowing tone without a trace of sentimentality. Heifetz's interpretations were sometimes criticized as cold, an impression reinforced by his severe appearance—a chiseled, unsmiling face, even when acknowledging an ovation. But this immobility concealed the utmost concentration, boldness, grandeur, and impetuosity. His preference for fast tempos was encouraged by his technical virtuosity, but the speed was always controlled. He had the ability to blend his tone and interpretation with other artists, as is proved by his chamber music playing with Emanuel Feuermann, William Primrose, Piatigorsky, and Artur Rubinstein.

Heifetz commissioned and performed a number of concertos, including those by William Walton, Mario Castelnuovo-Tedesco, Erich Korngold, and Louis Gruenberg. Among his many transcriptions the most famous is the Hora staccato by Grigoraş Dinicu.

BIBLIOGRAPHY

CampbellGV
SchwarzGM
C. Flesch: *Memoirs* (London, 1957/*R*; Ger. orig., Freiburg, 1960, 2/1961)
L. Raaben: *Zhizn´ zamechatel´nïkh skripachey* [The lives of famous violinists] (Leningrad, 1967)
J.W. Hartnack: *Grosse Geiger unserer Zeit* (Munich, 1967, 4/1993)
J. Creighton: *Discopaedia of the Violin, 1889–1971* (Toronto, 1974)
H.R. Axelrod, ed.: *Heifetz* (Neptune City, NJ, 1976)
The Strad, xcvi (1985–6) [Heifetz issue]
A. Weschler-Vered: *Jascha Heifetz* (New York and London, 1986)
The Strad, xcix (1988) [Heifetz issue]
K. Lee: "Premier Violinist," *The Strad*, cvi (1995), 45–9
J.-M. Molkhou: "Heifetz on Disc and Film," *The Strad*, cvi (1995), 90–97
E. Wen: "Heifetz: a Legend on Record," *The Strad*, cvi (1995), 36–41

BORIS SCHWARZ/MARGARET CAMPBELL/R

Heifetz, Robin Julian (*b* Los Angeles, CA, 1 Aug 1951). Composer. He studied composition at UCLA with PAUL CHIHARA (BA 1973), ROY TRAVIS, and BORIS KREMENLIEV (MA 1975) and at the University of Illinois with SALVATORE MARTIRANO, HERBERT BRÜN, and BEN JOHNSTON (DMA 1978). He became composer-in-residence at Stiftelsen Electronic Studio, Stockholm, Sweden (1978–79) and taught at several universities in the United States and Canada before being appointed director of the Center for Experimental Music at the Hebrew University of Jerusalem in 1980. He has received many honors, including an NEA grant (1981) and awards at the Concours International de Musique Electroacoustique, Bourges, France (1979, 1981) and the International Computer Music Competition in Boston (1983). Heifetz wrote exclusively vocal and instrumental works until 1976, when he first encountered electro-acoustic music at Illinois. Since 1977, nearly all his works have used an electro-acoustic medium. The titles of his tape pieces often serve almost as programs and strongly reflect the music. His compositions show a leaning toward simple forms, such as ternary form (*For Anders Lundberg*) and monothematicism (*In the Last, Frightened Moment*). In 1989 his anthology *On the Wires of Our Nerves* was published by Bucknell University Press. Since 2000, Heifetz has been adjunct professor of music at Antelope Valley College in Lancaster, California. His works have been released by Electroshock Records, including the solo CD *Out of Kilter* (2008).

WORKS

Inst: Two Pieces, pf, 1972; Leviathan, pf, 1975, rev. 1983; Chirp, euph, pf, 1976; Child of the Water, pf, 1978; The Unforgiving Minute for 9 insts, 1981; A Bird in Hand is Safer than One Overhead, 2 or more pfmrs, 1983
Elec-ac: Susurrus, cptr, tape, 1978; For Anders Lundberg: Mardrom 29 30 10, tape, 1978; Harbinger/18:30 PST, 2 tpt, 2 hn, 2 trbn, tape, 1978; Flykt, pf, cptr, 1979; Wasteland, tape, 1979; A Clear and Present Danger, tape, 1980; Spectre, tape, 1980; Wanderer, synth, 1980; In the Last, Frightened Moment, tape, 1980; The Vengeance, synth, 1980; The Arc of Crisis, tape, 1982; At Daggers Drawn, tape, 1983

Principal publisher: Seesaw

STEPHEN MONTAGUE/ANYA LAURENCE

Heindorf, Ray (*b* Haverstraw, NY, 25 Aug 1908; *d* Los Angeles, CA, 3 Feb 1980). Musical director, orchestrator, and conductor. His association with cinema music began as a young man with employment as a pianist and organist for a silent movie theater in Mechanicsville, New York. He became a protégé of LEO FORBSTEIN, the first musical director at Warner Bros.' studios, after helping with the scoring of the first sound film, *The Jazz Singer* (1927). He effectively served his apprenticeship with Warner Bros., rising through the music department as a performer and orchestrator-arranger. During this period he orchestrated for Max Steiner on *Daughters Courageous* (1939). When Forbstein retired in 1947, Heindorf succeeded him, remaining as head of the department until 1959, although he continued to conduct and arrange scores. He was nominated for 18 Academy Awards between 1942 and 1968 and received three: for the musical direction on *Yankee Doodle Dandy* (1942) and *This is the Army* (1943), the latter of which was based on the songs of Irving Berlin; and for the adaptation to film of the Broadway musical *The Music Man* (1962). Despite the traditional pedigree of the Warners' department, Heindorf was supportive of developments in film scoring style, most notably in his conducting of Alex North's original jazz score for *A Streetcar Named Desire* (1951). Among the few scores for which he was principal composer are *Hollywood Canteen* (1944), *Young Man with a Horn* (1950), a biography of Bix Beiderbecke, and *Pete Kelly's Blues* (1955), which achieved minor cult status largely due to its score.

BIBLIOGRAPHY

W. Darby and J. Du Bois: *American Film Music: Major Composers, Techniques, Trends, 1915–1990* (Jefferson, NC, 1991)

KATE DAUBNEY

Heinrich, Anthony Philip [Anton Philipp] (*b* Schön-büchel, Bohemia [now Krásný Buk, Czech Republic], 11 March 1781; *d* New York, NY, 3 May 1861). Composer and violinist of German-Bohemian birth. The adopted son of a wealthy uncle, Heinrich inherited property and a prospering business on his uncle's death in 1800. He visited the United States in 1805, and in 1810 tried to establish his business there. The devastation of the Napoleonic wars and the ensuing European financial depression, however, destroyed his entire inheritance. In the midst of these disasters, he became music director at Philadelphia's Southwark Theatre but returned to Bohemia in 1813. On returning to the United States in 1816, Heinrich traveled on foot from Philadelphia to Pittsburgh, where he briefly directed music at a local theater, only to lose his job amid more financial turmoil. He then traveled along the Ohio River to Kentucky, again on foot.

There, Heinrich began what would become one of the most distinguished musical careers in America before the Civil War. He directed one of the nation's first performances of Beethoven's Symphony no.1 in Lexington (12 November 1817) on a program that also included works by Mozart and Haydn. Shortly thereafter, he moved to a log cabin near Bardstown and began composing in earnest, setting several texts by local authors, as well as works by Robert Burns, Lord Byron, and other noteworthy poets. In 1820 he moved to nearby Farmington, where he composed shorter works for solo piano and for small ensembles of piano and strings. The firm of Bacon and Hart in Philadelphia published *The Dawning of Music in Kentucky* (1820); a supplementary volume, *The Western Minstrel*, followed a month later. Taken together, they formed one of the largest publications of music by any composer living in America up to that time. They tended to be received well by critics. In a review of the first volume, Boston critic John Rowe Parker enthusiastically dubbed Heinrich "the Beethoven of America." In 1823 Heinrich moved to Boston, where the third collection of his works, *The Sylviad,* was published (1823, 1825–6). Bostonians honored him with benefit concerts on his arrival and at his departure for London three years later.

Heinrich returned to Europe in 1826, presumably to reunite with his estranged daughter, whom he had left in the care of a relative, and to disseminate his music more widely. He planned to earn an income as a violinist, but a freak accident on the transatlantic journey crushed his violin and a finger on his left hand. He nevertheless secured a position in the orchestra of the Drury Lane Theatre in London. Although efforts to have his music performed were rebuffed, he managed to arrange for a London publisher to print a handful of his songs. In 1831 he composed his first orchestral work, *Pushmataha*, and a fiendishly difficult work for violin written after hearing Paganini perform. Heinrich left London without reuniting with his daughter, and after a two-year residence in Boston, where several more of his songs were published, he rejoined the Drury Lane orchestra. During the next two years, Heinrich wrote several large-scale works for orchestra: *The Tower of*

Babel, Logan the Mingo Chief, his first symphony ("Schiller"), and *The Treaty of William Penn with the Indians.* He left London for Bohemia in 1835 and oversaw a performance of four of his works, most notably *The Ornithological Combat of Kings,* in Graz, Austria (25 May 1836); his music was received warmly. After learning that his daughter had left Bohemia for America, he prepared to return to the United States.

In 1837 Heinrich moved to New York, where he would reside until his death. After five years of moderate success publishing smaller pieces, he achieved greater recognition in 1842. In April of that year, he presided over the meeting that formed the New-York Philharmonic Society. Two months later he mounted a grand musical festival where several of his works received their premieres, including the overture to an oratorio based on the story of the pilgrims, *The Wild Wood Spirits' Chant.* Critics received the music favorably, calling it a "complete success," though Heinrich did not earn a profit from the concert's receipts. The following year he unsuccessfully attempted to solicit enough subscriptions to have excerpts from the oratorio published; the work was performed again in 1845. In that year he produced a concert overture (*Boadicea*) and three symphonies. He mounted three more grand concerts featuring his compositions: two in New York (1846 and 1853) and one in Boston. After a hearty reception by New York audiences in 1846, the latter concerts were disappointments. Certain pieces had to be omitted owing to lack of rehearsal time, and audiences did not understand the composer's often difficult music. Despite these setbacks, Heinrich continued to eke out a living by publishing songs, teaching pupils, and assisting with local concerts.

In 1857 he traveled to Prague, where he hoped he could achieve greater recognition. Within a year of his arrival, the city's Sophien-Akademie sponsored three concerts that featured his compositions, including excerpts from two of his symphonies. Audiences and critics alike praised his music. His health declined rapidly over the next two years, and he returned to the United States in 1860. He died the following year.

Heinrich's life is prominently linked with the history of concert music, and learned culture more broadly, in the United States during the first half of the 19th century. Notices of his music were given by two distinct generations of musical editors: John Rowe Parker and John Sullivan Dwight, both of Boston. He witnessed the rise of the New-York Philharmonic Society, the decline of the orchestra of Philadelphia's Musical Fund Society, and the successes of the Germania Orchestra and Louis-Antoine Jullien's virtuosic orchestra. The scope of his personal contacts and acquaintances with key figures in fields outside music is astonishing. He was well known to jurists, doctors, and writers; he was also a personal friend of John James Audubon. Unlike most American composers of this period, Heinrich was included in Gustav Schilling's *Encyclopädie* (1836) and in Fétis's *Biographie universelle* (1839).

Like many other 19th-century composers, Heinrich was acutely fond of writing descriptive music. He wrote no fewer than seven large-scale works depicting Native American rituals and historical events relating to their cultures. Although it is unclear whether he ever personally interacted with Native Americans, he learned about their customs from the writings of the anthropologist John McIntosh. Two other orchestral works show the fruits of his friendship with Audubon: *The Columbiad, or Migration of American Wild Passenger Pigeons* (1837), and *The Ornithological Combat of Kings* (1847), which Heinrich considered his best work. His patriotism found expression in several works, including *The War of the Elements and the Thundering of Niagara* and *The Columbiad: A Grand American National Chivalrous Symphony*. Perhaps in an effort to secure financial backing beyond the United States, he also wrote patriotic works for other countries (for example, *The Empress Queen Maria Theresa and the Magyars* and *National Memories; Or, Gran Sinfonia Britanica*). Finally, he wrote symphonic tributes to Mendelssohn, Schiller, and Beethoven, the last of which depicts the ceremonial installation of a statue of Beethoven in Bonn.

Heinrich's compositions are often unusually complex and elaborate. The sources of his musical style are found in Haydn and to a lesser extent Beethoven, but they have the ornateness of Italian opera and often a freer use of chromaticism. He frequently quoted popular, patriotic tunes (for example, "Hail Columbia" and "Yankee Doodle"). The forms Heinrich favored most are those of the dance and the theme with variations. Generally, he did not develop material thematically or formally but instead juxtaposed successive sections. As a result, his works often have the characteristics of an extemporized fantasy. Heinrich composed for a wide variety of forces and consistently rewrote his works, frequently employing the same musical materials in different pieces. Although he wrote many songs and piano pieces, he was an orchestral writer by temperament and choice, and his works for orchestra form the truest expression of his unique musical personality. His scores employ up to 44 individual parts. Although none of his orchestral music was published, the great majority of Heinrich's other work was. His orchestral manuscripts, personal scrapbook, and a large number of printed scores are in the Library of Congress. A smaller collection of his sheet music is in the Národní Múzeum, Prague.

WORKS

EDITIONS

Heinrich: Complete Works, ed. A. Stiller (Philadelphia, 1991–)

The Dawning of Music in Kentucky, or The Pleasures of Harmony in the Solitudes of Nature, op.1 (Philadelphia, 1820, rev. 1820–23) [DMK]

The Western Minstrel, op.2 (Philadelphia, 1820, rev. 1820–23) [WM]

The Sylviad, or Minstrelsy of Nature in the Wilds of N. America, 2 collections, op.3 (Boston, 1823, rev. 1825–6) [Sa, Sb]

SONGS

1v, pf, unless otherwise noted

1819: While the Heart (H.C. Lewis): see INSTRUMENTAL

1820 (in DMK): A Bottle Song (Burns): see VOCAL ENSEMBLES; Coda (W.B. Tappan); Columbia's Plaint (Lewis); From thee Eliza (Burns); Hail to

Kentucky (P.W. Grayson); How Sleep the Brave (W. Collins): see VOCAL ENSEMBLES; Ode to the Memory of Commodore O.H. Perry (Lewis): see INSTRUMENTAL; Prologue Song (Lewis), 2 settings; Say What Is that Heart! (Grayson); Sensibility, and Sensibility's Child (Lewis), 2 songs [no.1 see VOCAL ENSEMBLES]; Sweet Maid; The Birthday of Washington (*The National Intelligencer*); The Bohemian Emigrant (Lewis); The Bride's Farewell (Lewis); The Musical Bachelor (J.R. Black), also for 1v, fl/vn, pf; The Young Columbian Midshipman (Lewis), 2 versions; 'Tis not in Dreams (Tappan); To my Virtuoso Friends (R.S. Coffin); Visit to Philadelphia (Lewis); Where Is that Heart? (Grayson)

1820 (in WM): Hast thou Seen! (Tappan); Image of my Tears (Byron, Lewis); Irradiate Cause! (Tappan); Love in Ohio (Lewis); Maid of the Valley (Tappan); O Smile upon the Deaf and Dumb (Tappan); Remember Me (Lewis), 2 versions; Sailor Boy's Dream (W. Diamond); The Musical Bachelor (Black); There Is an Hour (Tappan); The Yager's Adieu (Grayson); Venez ici! (Lewis); Where are the Pleasures? (G. Dutton)

1822: Ode to the Memory of Commodore Perry (Lewis)

1823: Fair Pupil (M. Neville); Philanthropy (Tappan): see VOCAL ENSEMBLES and KEYBOARD (Sa)

1825 (in Sb): Fill your Goblets (H. McMurtrie): see VOCAL ENSEMBLES; Mary (T. Moore); Overture to the Fair Sylph of America (Neville); The Sylph of Music (C.H. Locke); The Yager's Adieu (Grayson), 2 versions; Where Is the Nymph? (T. Moore, M. Osborne); Where's the home? (Locke)

1826 (in Sb): Sequel, or Farewell to my Log House (J.M. Brown): see VOCAL ENSEMBLES; The Log House (Brown); The Western Minstrel's Recollection (A.G. Whipple)

1828: Fantasia vocale (J.H. Payne); The Twin Brothers (L.E. Landon), 2 settings; The Twin Sisters (W. Steele), 2 settings

c1828: Be Silent Now (Steele); Dean Swift's Receipt to Roast Mutton (J. Swift); I Love the Brilliant Courtly Scene (T. Gaspey), rev. as The Glorious Day Shall Dawn at Last; The Absent Charm (Gaspey)

1832: I Love Thee! (T. Hood); The Voice of Faithful Love (Gaspey), 1v, fl, pf

c1832: Nay, Lady (N.G[reene]); We Wander in a Thorny Maze (Tappan)

?1832: Song of Jacob to Rachel (Tappan), 1v, org

1838: The Bonny Brunette (J.M. Moore), 2 versions

1842: The Loved One's Grave (W. Wordsworth)

1846: Breezes from the Wild Wood: no.1, Imoinda (O.H. Mildeberger), no.2, Ne-La-Me (W. Wallace); Cantilene d'affetto: no.6, La Toilette de la reine (Mrs. G. Killick, G. von Kienbusch), no.7, The Maid of Honor (Steele, von Kienbusch), 2 versions, no.8, Eleanor (A. Mensbier, von Kienbusch), no.9, Love's Confiding (W.L. Jeffers, von Kienbusch); Reminiscences of Kentucky: no.1, The Parting (D.C. Driscoll): see VOCAL ENSEMBLES; The Minstrel's Friend (Tappan); The Tribute: no.1, Sweet Music (Tappan): see VOCAL ENSEMBLES; The Young Columbian Midshipman (Lewis); Une Petite fantaisie d'amour (M.S. Pile)

1847: La Toilette de la cour (Killick)

1848: An Offering of Song: no.1, The Rose of the Sea (M.E. Hewitt), no.2, The Broken Heart (Moore); Sacred Meditations (Tappan): no.1, An Evening Reflection, 1v, org, no.2, Sweet Is the Hour of Solitude; The Harp's Last Echoes: no.1, 'Tis Echo's Voice (Steele, von Kienbusch), also for 1v, fl, pf, no.2, The Soul Released (Tappan), 1v, org, no.3, Heaven and my Harp (Mrs. A.R. Luyster)

1849: La bohémienne (F. Koller, H.B. Gay); La Toilette de la cour (Killick, von Kienbusch); Mým slovanským bratrům v Europě! [To my Sclavonian [*sic*] Brethren in Europe] [see KEYBOARD]: no.1, Home of my Youth (Tappan, von Kienbusch), no.2, The Cypress (W.J. Edson, von Kienbusch); Recollections from a Log House [see KEYBOARD]: no.1, Love in Ohio (Lewis); The Calm Sequester'd Cell [Süss ist die Ruh] (Gaspey, A. Mandel)

1850: Father Heinrich's Klage, 1v; Love's Enchantment (Tappan); Melodie (H. Harring), 1v

?1850: An Elegiac Song (A. Carey); The Garland (Luyster)

1851: How Sleep the Brave (Collins); Must I Resign; The Yager's Adieu (Grayson)

1852: The Unknown Man

?1852: Our Hearts Were Bowed; Remember Me (Lewis)

1852–3: Sunset Chimes, 1v, pf, org: no.1, I Have Something Sweet to Tell You (Mrs F.S. Osgood), no.2, O! Say, my Leila (F.W. Fish), no.3, Loving Hearts (A. Duganne), no.4, The Forsaken (Duganne), no.5,

Hope On (Duganne), no.6, Hope's Diadem (H.T. Drowne), no.7, Remember Me (Lewis), no.8, Forget Me Not (Tappan), no.9, Capriccio vocale, 2 versions, no.10, The Boston Bard (Coffin), no.11, Must I Resign?, no.12, That Awful Day (I. Watts)

1854: A Votive Wreath [Dem Verdienste seine Krone] [see KEYBOARD, ORCHESTRAL]: no.3, Love's Enchantment [see SONGS1850], no.4, La bohémienne [see SONGS1849], no.5, The Spirit Bond [Das Geister Band] (Hewitt, G. Aigner); Legends of the Wild Wood [Urwald Sagen] [see KEYBOARD, ORCHESTRAL]: no.4, Fleeting Hours (W.J. Wetmore, M. Langenschwartz), no.5, The Old Harper (Wetmore, Aigner)

?1858: Balladen: no.1, Die Liebe, no.2, Der Engel Wanderung (E. Vacano)

Uncertain date: Accettate gli ossequi; A Lone Trembling Flower (Steele); Du bist gestorben (H. Heine), 2 settings; Fantasia amorosa (S.S. Fitch); Hark! I Heard; I Love to Watch the Evening Sky; In Lebanon (Tappan), 1v, org; I've Something Sweet to Tell You (Osgood); Oh Happy Land (Wetmore); Shadows of Memory (Wetmore); The Home of Childhood's Hour (Drowne); The Lilac, 3 settings; The Spirit Bond (Hewitt)

VOCAL ENSEMBLES

1820 (in DMK): A Bottle Song (Burns), solo vv, STB, pf: see SONGS; How Sleep the Brave (Collins), 1v, unison vv, pf, also for STB: see SONGS; Sensibility, 2vv, fl, pf: see SONGS; The Sons of the Woods (Lewis), 1v, unison vv, pf

1823 (in Sa): Philanthropy (Tappan), SATBB, pf: see SONGS, KEYBOARD; The Minstrel's Catch, S, 8–40 mixed vv (more ad lib), pf

1825 (in Sb): Epitaph on Joan Buff (W. Stanton, Osborne), 5vv, pf; Fill your Goblets (McMurtrie), 4vv, pf: see SONGS

1826 (in Sb): Bohemia (Watts), SS(A)BB, org; Sequel, or Farewell to my Log House, 4vv, pf: see SONGS; The Minstrel's Adieu (Locke), SSB, pf; The Western Minstrel's Musical Compliments (Grayson), SSB, pf

1832: 4 hymns in N.D. Gould: *National Church Harmony* (Boston, 1832): Antonia, 4vv, Death of a Christian (A.L. Barbauld), SSTBB, org, Harmonia, 4vv, On Judah's Plain (Tappan), 4vv; Funeral Anthem (C. Murray), 2 Tr, T, 2 B, chorus, org/pf; Hail Beauteous Spring (Tappan), ST(S)B, pf

1836: Des Christen Tod (Barbauld, Mandel), SSTBB, pf/org

1845: The Adieu, opening from oratorio The Wild Woods' Spirits Chant (Eng. text Edson, Ger. text C.J. Hempel), S, A, T, 2 B, chorus, org/pf

1846: Elegiac quintetto vocale (Wallace), SATBB, org/pf; Reminiscences of Kentucky: see SONGS: The Valentine, "Lovely Are Maidens" (G.B. King), S, T, pf; The Tribute: see SONGS: no.2, The City of Fraternal Love (Lewis), 1v, SATB, pf

1847: Funeral Anthem (Hewitt), S, A, T, 2 B, chorus, org

1851: Music, the Harmonizer of the World (King), 1v, SATB, pf

1854: Musa sacra, no.4: The Death of a Christian [Des Christen Tod] (Barbauld, Mandel), SATBB, org/pf

?1858: 2 choruses from The Columbiad, pt.2: Erkenne Gott! (Langenschwartz), SATB, pf, Soli Deo gloria, S, A, T, B, chorus, pf

Uncertain date: Our Hearts, 2vv, pf, also for S, A, T, 2 B, chorus, pf

KEYBOARD
(pf 2 hands, unless otherwise noted)

1820 (in DMK): A Chromatic Ramble, pf, 1v; A Divertimento; A Serenade, pf, ?vv; Avance et retraite; Farewell to Farmington, arr. pf; Hail Columbia!; Kentucky March, Trio, and Quick-step Waltz; La buona mattina, pf, 1v; Lord Byron's Cotillion (incl. Fair Haïdée's Waltz); Marche concertante, arr. pf, 1v; Marcia di ballo; Rondo Waltz; The Fair Bohemian; The Henriade; The Minstrel's Petition, pf, 1v, vn; The Prague Waltz; The Sarah; The Unamiable; Three Cotillions, pf, ?fl, 1v; Visit to Farmington; Yankee Doodle Waltz

1820 (in WM): Gipsey Dance; Ländler of Austria; Philadelphia Waltz; The Minstrel's March

1823 (in Sa): A Divertimento di ballo; Canone funerale; Philanthropy: see SONGS, VOCAL ENSEMBLES; The Minstrel's Musical Compliments; Toccatina capricciosa; Valsetto triangolo

1825 (in Sb): A Sylvan Scene; Bernhard, Duke of Saxe Weimar's March; Overture de la cour; The Four-Pawed Kitten Dance, pf 4 hands; The Minstrel's Entertainment with his Blind Pupil, pf 4 hands; The Minstrel's March; The Minstrel's Vote; The Students' March; Toccata grande cromatica

1826 (in Sb): The Debarkation March; The Embarkation March; Vivat Britain's Fair!

c1830: Avance et retraite, arr. pf

c1832: A Divertimento di ballo; A Recollection of England; Il divertimento di Londra; La promenade du diable; Multum in parvo; Paganini's Incantation [with T. Welsh]; The First Labour of Hercules; The Waltz of the N. York Graces

1835: Le Départ d'Angleterre

c1835: Musical Week: The Amaranth, The Brown Beurré, The Hickory, pf, vc, The Phoenix, The Sensitive Plant

1838: The May Day Waltz

1839: L'Esprit et la bonté; Pocahontas

1840: An Elegiac Impromptu Fantasia; The Nymph of the Danube; 3 Elssler Dances: The Laurel Waltz, The New York Capriccio, The Zephyr Dance

1841: The Maiden's Dirge; The President's Funeral March, pf/org; 3 Indian Fanfares; 3 petits caprices; 2 Waltzes Pastorale

1842: The New York Rondo; The Yankee Welcome to Boz, 2 waltzes; 3 Images of Musical Thought: The March and Waltz of the Muses, The Return from School

1844: Texas and Oregon Grand March; Tyler's Grand Veto Quick Step

1847: The Laurel and the Cypress

1848: Der Triller; Valentine Wedding Waltz

1849: A Valentine, pf, vn ad lib; Divertimento leggiadro: Capriccio volante, Finale trionfante, St. Valentine's; Marcia della regina e Passo doppio Coburg; Mým slovanským bratrům v Europě! [To my Sclavonian [*sic*] Brethren in Europe] [see SONGS]: no.3, Žalost Čechů! Bohemia's Funeral Honors to Josef Jungmann (1847), no.4, The Moan of the Forest; Recollections from a Log House [see SONGS]: no.2, The Wood-land Stroll Waltz; The Festival of the Dead and the Cries of the Souls, pf, org ad lib; The Indian Carnival, toccata

1850: Barnum's Invitation to Jenny Lind: Museum Polka; General Taylor's Funeral March; Song without Words

c1850: Jenny Lind and the Septinarian [see ORCHESTRAL]: Jenny Lind's Maelstrom

1851: Voluntary, org

1853: Caprice dansante concertante: Le minuet du grand-père et La valse des grands enfants

1854: Adieu to America; A Votive Wreath [Dem Verdienste seine Krone] [see SONGS]: no. 2, The First Labour of Hercules; Legends of the Wild Wood [Urwald Sagen] [see SONGS]: no.2, Ischl or Union of Spirits, no.3, Ouisahiccon

1855: Katinka: Caprice; Yäger's Adieu

1858: Zerrinnen des geisterhaften Traumbildes

Uncertain date: An Elegy, org; Divertimento di ballo; La Colombiade; Phantasy, org/pf; Pushmataha; 4 capricci: Il dilettante, Il filosofo, Il professore, Il romantic; The Virtuoso's March to Olympus; 2 pieces (unidentified)

VOICES AND ORCHESTRA

O Santa Maria (2 texts: sacred Lat., secular by Steele), S, T, chbr orch, 1834

Musa sacra, no.2: Adoramus te Christe, offertorio, 3vv, orch, 1835, no.3: O Santa Maria, motetto, STBB, chbr orch, ?1835

The Jubilee (Edson), S, A, T, 2 B, chorus, orch, 1841

The Warriors' March to the Battlefield (Grayson), S, A, T, B, chorus, orch, 1845

Coro funerale (Hewitt), S, A, T, 2 B, chorus, semichorus, orch, org, ?1847

Amor patriae—Our Native Land (Eng. Wetmore), S, A, T, 2B, chorus, orch/pf, before 1854

Noble Emperor (Wetmore), S, A, T, 2B, chorus, orch; perf. as orch piece (vv tacent) as Hoch Oesterreich, ?1854

The Columbiad (Langenschwartz, E. Rosenbaum), pt.1, orch; pt.2, S, A, T, 2B, chorus, pf, 1857–8

Der Felsen von Plymouth, pt. 1, orch; pt. 2 borrowed from Adoramus te Christe, Soli Deo gloria, 1858–9

ORCHESTRAL

Schiller, grande sinfonia dramatica, 4 of the 5 movts, 1830s, rev. with addns 1847

Pushmataha, a Venerable Chief of a Western Tribe of Indians, fantasia, 1831

A Concerto for the Kent Bugle or Klappenflügel; Complaint of Logan, the Mingo Chief, fantasia; The Indian War Council; The Mocking

Bird to the Nightingale, capriccio; The Tower of Babel, oratorical divertissement; Washington's Centenial [*sic*] Overture; 1834

The Treaty of William Penn with the Indians, conc. grosso, 1834, rev. 1847

The Wildwood Troubadour, ov., 1834–53

The Yäger's Adieu, 1835

Gran sinfonia eroica, *c*1835

Pocahontas, fantasia romanza; The Columbiad, sym. [see VOICES AND ORCHESTRA]; The Hunters of Kentucky, sym.; 1837

The Wild Wood Spirits' Chant, fantasia, *c*1842

Musa sacra, no.1: The Tower of Babel, sinfonia canonicale, 1843 [based on music of 1834], addns 1852

National Memories, sym., 1844–52

Johannis Berg, grand potpourri dansante; Manitou Mysteries, sym.; The Indian Carnival, sinfonia eratico-fantastica; The War of the Elements, capriccio grande, before 1845

Boadicèa, concert ov.; The Empress Queen and the Magyars, sinfonia patriotica-dramatica; The Mastodon, sym.; To the Spirit of Beethoven, sym.; ?1845

The Ornithological Combat of Kings, sym., 1847, rev. 1856

The Tomb of Genius: to the Memory of Mendelssohn-Bartholdy, sinfonia sacra, ?1847

The Castle in the Moon, orch romanza, 1850

Jenny Lind and the Septinarian [see KEYBOARD]: Jenny Lind's Journey, divertissement, *c*1850

Austria: The Flight of the Double Eagle, ov.; Bohemia, sinfonia romantica; before 1854

A Votive Wreath [see SONGS]: no, 1, The Empress Queen and the Magyars; Legends of the Wild Wood [Urwald Sagen] [see SONGS]: no.1, The Wild Wood Troubadour; 1854

Homage à la Bohème, sym., 1855

Marcia [?Das Schloss im Monde]; The Harper of Kentucky, ov.; uncertain date

INSTRUMENTAL

While the Heart, fl/cl/vn, 1819: see SONGS

Ode to the Memory of Commodore O.H. Perry, pf, vn/fl see SONGS; Tema di Mozart and an Original Air, 2 vn, db/vc, pf ad lib; The Yankee Doodleiad, 3 vn, db/vc, pf; 1820 (DMK)

Storia d'un violino, vn, 1831

2 Scores for 11 Pfmrs: The Columbiad and The Tower of Babel, fl/pic, 2 cl, bn, 2 hn, tpt, 2 vn, va, vc, db [bn, 2nd cl ?added later], 1837

Marcia funèbre for the Heroes, brass band, perc, ?1850–54

Marcia funerale, brass band, perc, after 1850

Souvenir of the Hudson Highlands, pf, vn; Trip to the "Catskill Mountain House," vn, pf, 1851

Otetto, 3 vn, 2 va, 2 vc, db, triangle, ?1857–8

Scylla and Charybdis, pf, vn; The Adieu, fl, 2 vn, 2 va, vc, db, ?inc. [incl. The Greeting]; unknown date

LOST (L.) OR INCOMPLETE (INC.)

Heinrich habitually assigned new titles to old works, so some works listed here may exist under other titles.

V(v) with kbd: I Enter thy Garden of Roses (Byron), with vn, perf. 1821, l.; Maidens in your Mystic Bower (?McMurtrie), perf. 1821, l.; Youths who Merit (McMurtrie), perf. 1821, l.; Lover's Prayer (Coffin), before 1825, l.; Away, away, perf. 1825, l.; The Stranger's Requiem (Edson), duet, perf. 1842, l.; Stay with Me (?Oterman), 1854, inc.; Fantasia amorosa (Fitch), inc.; Funeral Anthem (Hewitt), SATBB, org, inc.; Gloria, inc.; I've Something Sweet to Tell You (Osgood), inc.; Sensitive Plant (Tappan), inc.; Sweet Is the Hour of Solitude (Tappan), inc.; Take Back the Token, inc.

Kbd: The Bachelor's Quick Step and Wedding Waltz, pf, perf. 1832, l.; A Chromatic Ramble, toccata, pf, inc. [see version in DMK]; An Offertorio, l.; Denmark's Funeral Honors to Thorwaldsen, pf, l.; The Dedication Waltz, l.; Toccata grande, org, l.

Vv and orch: The Minstrel, opera, 1835, l.; The Ornithological Combat of Kings, oratorio, 1837, l.; The Maiden Queen, oratorio, l.; The Child of the Mountain (McMurtrie), melodrama, some inst pieces, arr. pf, extant

Orch: A National Olio, perf. 1821, l.; Capriccio, perf. 1821, l.; Finale (Tutti), perf. 1821, l.; Ov., perf. 1821, l.; A New Divertimento, perf. 1832, l.; The Washingtoniad, or the Deeds of a Hero, ov., ?1843, l.; The Mythological Concerti Grossi for a grand orch, before 1845,

only 1 page extant; Tecumseh, ov., perf. 1846, l.; The New England Feast of Shells, divertimento, perf. 1853, tpt extant; A Concertante, ob, orch, l.; Potpourri, l.; The Cosmopolitan Grand March, l.; The "Nec Plus Ultra" Yankeedoodleiad, l.

Miscellaneous: Postillion Waltzes, vn, perf. 1819, l.; Variations on Marlboro, vn, perf. 1819, l.; Divertimento (alla marcia), 11 wind insts, timp, perf. 1821, l.; Solos pastorale, cl/fl, perf. 1821, l.

BIBLIOGRAPHY

A.P. Heinrich: *Scrapbook* (Library of Congress, Washington, DC)

F.A. Mussik: *Skizzen aus dem Leben des sich in Amerika befindenden deutschen Tondichters Anton Philipp Heinrich, nach authentischen Quellen bearbeitet* (Prague, 1843)

Anthony Philip Heinrich ("Vater Heinrich"): zur Lebensgeschichte des Veteran Kompositeurs, unsers aus der neuen Welt heimgekehrten Landsmannes (Prague, 1857)

W.T. Upton: *Anthony Philip Heinrich: a Nineteenth-Century Composer in America* (New York, 1939)

I. Lowens: "The Triumph of Anthony Philip Heinrich," *Music and Musicians in Early America* (New York, 1964), 203

F.N. Bruce: *The Piano Pieces of Anthony Philip Heinrich Contained in "The Dawning of Music in Kentucky" and "The Western Minstrel"* (diss., U. of Illinois, 1971)

D. Barron: *The Early Vocal Works of Anthony Philip Heinrich* (diss., U. of Illinois, 1972)

W.R. Maust: *The Symphonies of Anthony Philip Heinrich Based on American Themes* (diss., Indiana U., 1973)

L.H. Filbeck: *The Choral Works of Anthony Philip Heinrich* (diss., U. of Illinois, 1975)

W.R. Maust: "The American Indian in the Orchestral Music of Anthony Philip Heinrich," *Music East and West: Essays in Honor of Walter Kaufmann*, ed. T. Noblitt (New York, 1981), 309

B. Chmaj: "Father Heinrich as Kindred Spirit: or, How the Log-House Composer of Kentucky Became the Beethoven of America," *American Studies*, xxiv (1983), 35

J.B. Clark: "The Solo Piano Sonata in Early America: Hewitt to Heinrich," *AM*, ii (1984), 27

J.B. Clark: *The Dawning of American Keyboard Music* (Westport, CT, 1988)

V.B. Lawrence: *Strong on Music*, i (New York, 1988), ii (Chicago, 1995)

J.B. Clark: "Anthony Philip Heinrich: a Bohemian Predecessor to Dvořak in the Wilds of America," *Dvořak in America, 1892–1895* (Portland, OR, 1993)

D. von Glahn: *The Sound of Place: Music and the American Cultural Landscape* (Boston, 2004)

M. Broyles: *Mavericks and Other Traditions in American Music* (New Haven, 2004)

W. Gibbons: "The Musical Audubon: Ornithology and Nationalism in the Symphonies of Anthony Philip Heinrich," *JSAM,*, iii (2009), 465–91

DAVID BARRON/DOUGLAS W. SHADLE

Heinsheimer, Hans (Walter) (*b* Karlsruhe, Germany, 25 Sept 1900; *d* New York, NY, 12 Oct 1993). Music publishing executive and writer of German birth. Following law studies in Heidelberg, Munich, and Freiburg (JD 1923), he was employed by Universal Edition in Vienna. At Universal he headed the opera department (1924–38), working with such composers as Alban Berg, Ernst Krenek, Jaromir Weinberger, Kurt Weill, and George Antheil, and supervising the publication of many works, including Berg's *Wozzeck,* Weinberger's *Schwanda the Bagpiper,* and Weill's *Rise and Fall of the City of Mahagonny,* which he directed in the late 1930s. Heinsheimer narrowly managed to escape the Anschluss in 1938; after that he did not return to Austria but joined Boosey & Hawkes in New York. He is known for championing contemporary composers such as Béla Bartók. From 1947 to 1974 he was associated with G. Schirmer, first as head of the symphonic and operatic divisions, then, from 1957, as director of publications, and finally, from 1972, as vice president; among the composers whose works he promoted were Menotti, Bernstein, and Barber. In addition to contributing music articles to various periodicals, Heinsheimer contributed significantly to radio programs, especially promoting new voices in opera.

PAULA MORGAN/JONAS WESTOVER

Held, Alan (*b* Washburn, IL, 20 Nov 1959). Bass-baritone. He studied at Millikin University and Wichita State University under Richard Cross and George Gibson. In 1986, he made his debut with Central City Opera in Denver as Colline in *La Bohème*. He made his Metropolitan Opera debut in 1989 as Mr. Redburn in *Billy Budd*. He has since been heard with many major companies, including those in Washington, Chicago, San Francisco, Vienna, Salzburg, London, Paris, and Milan. He is a winner of the Birgit Nilsson Prize. His rich-hued, powerful voice is especially well suited to the operas of Wagner and Strauss, including such roles as Wotan, Kurwenal, the Dutchman, Jochanaan, and Orestes. He has also been successful in such dramatically demanding roles as Wozzeck in in comic roles such as Leporello and the Four Villains in *Les contes d'Hoffmann*. As a concert soloist, he has performed with the Chicago Symphony, the Cleveland Orchestra, the National Symphony, the Los Angeles Philharmonic, the Berlin Philharmonic, the Paris Orchestra, and the Kirov Opera Orchestra. His recordings include Donner in Wagner's *Ring* cycle under James Levine, Don Pizzaro in *Fidelio* under Simon Rattle, and the title role of Hindemith's *Cardillac* under Kent Nagano.

PETER MONDELLI

Held, (Helena) Anna (*b* Warsaw, Poland, 8 March ?1873; *d* New York, NY, 12 Aug 1918). Singer of Polish birth. She spent her early years in poverty. After her father's death Held and her mother moved to London, where she obtained work as a chorus girl; she also performed on the continent. FLORENZ ZIEGFELD JR. saw her in London and offered her a major part in his production of Hoyt's *A Parlor Match* (1896), in which she won instant celebrity with her coquettish songs. Between 1897 and 1908 Held, a petite, slightly plump woman with reddish-brown hair and large brown eyes, starred in a succession of Ziegfeld's musicals, becoming known particularly for her performance of songs such as "I just can't make my eyes behave," "It's delightful to be married," and "Won't you come and play with me?". After her professional and personal separation from the producer, Held appeared mainly in vaudeville. Her papers are held at the NYPL for the Performing Arts.

BIBLIOGRAPHY
E. Golden: *Anna Held and the birth of Ziegfeld's Broadway* (Lexington, KY, 2000)

GERALD BORDMAN/R

Heller, George N(orman) (*b* Ypsilanti, MI, 19 Dec 1941; *d* Lawrence, KS, 3 July 2004). Music educator and scholar. He earned degrees in music education from the University of Michigan (BM 1963, MM 1969, PhD 1973), taught music privately and in Michigan public schools (1963–6, 1971–3), and was an Army bandsman (1966–8). He spent the bulk of his career at the University of Kansas (1973–2002) and served as a visiting professor at the University of North Carolina at Greensboro (1985–6, summer 1998, summer 2000), University of Washington (summer 1994), and University of Miami (spring 2001, spring 2002). Among his more than one hundred publications are *Ensemble Music for Wind and Percussion Instruments: A Catalog* (Reston, VA, 1970) and *Charles Leonhard: American Music Educator* (Metuchen, NJ, 1995). He was the founding editor of *The Bulletin of Historical Research in Music Education* (1980–99), first chair of the Music Educators National Conference History Special Research Interest Group, and music education area advisor for *The New Grove Dictionary of American Music* (1986). He was inducted into the Kansas Music Educators Association Hall of Fame (2003) and received a (posthumous) Presidential Award from the American Music Therapy Association.

BIBLIOGRAPHY
J.T. Humphreys: "In Memoriam: George N. Heller (1941–2004): *JHRME* Founding Editor," *Journal of Historical Research in Music Education*, xxvi/1 (2004), 5–7

JERE T. HUMPHREYS

Heller, Jack (Joseph) (*b* New Orleans, LA, 30 Nov 1932). Music educator and conductor. He graduated from the Juilliard School (diploma 1952), University of Michigan (MM 1958), and University of Iowa (PhD 1962). He was professor of music education at the University of Connecticut (1960–85), and held post-doctoral fellowships Ohio State University (1966–7) and Yale University (1982–3). He served as director of the School of Music at the University of South Florida (1985–95) and Professor Emeritus (1998–). He was a member of the Music Educators National Conference Music Education Research Council (1968–74), president of the Connecticut Music Educators Association (1977–9), and chair of the International Society for Music Education Research Commission (1983–6). His research interests are in music cognition, and he has served on editorial committees for the CRME *Bulletin*, *Journal of Research in Music Education*, *Research Perspectives in Music Education*, and *Psychomusicology*. Heller's conducting posts include music director of the University of Connecticut Orchestra (1960–66), Manchester (Connecticut) Symphony Orchestra and Chorale (1968–85), Nutmeg Chamber Orchestra (Connecticut) (1984–6), Tampa Spanish Lyric Theatre (1992–2002), and Tampa Bay Symphony (1986–). He has been guest conductor of orchestras from New York (New York City Ballet) to Prague (Czech Radio Orchestra).

JERE T. HUMPHREYS

Hellermann, William (David) (*b* Milwaukee, WI, 15 July 1939). Composer and guitarist. He studied mechanical engineering at the University of Wisconsin (BS 1962) and composition at Columbia University (MA 1965,

DMA 1969); his teachers included STEFAN WOLPE, CHOU WEN-CHUNG, OTTO LUENING, and VLADIMIR USSACHEVSKY. He taught at Columbia University from 1965 to 1972 and was general manager of the Composers' Forum from 1968 to 1980. From 1978 he has served as editor of the *Calendar for New Music* in New York. He has also taught at Farleigh Dickinson University, Western Connecticut University, and the NYU Graduate School.

Hellermann made his New York debut as a classical guitarist and composer at the Kitchen in 1972 and his Paris debut at the Musée d'Art Moderne in 1973. He has since played as a member of the Composers' Group for International Performance (later called the Composers'/Performers' Group), RSVP Ensemble, and Sounds out of Silent Spaces, all of which specialize in new music. He has had a long record of managing and directing series of contemporary music in New York. Hellermann has given the premieres of numerous works for the guitar, many employing new instrumental techniques which he has devised. His solo recital appearances have taken place principally in Europe.

A prolific composer, he has had several gallery exhibitions of his visually oriented works, called Eyescores, and often crosses the boundaries between visual and aural art in creating "music sculptures." Hellermann was traditionally trained, but his work from the mid-1970s can be considered performance art, although it always retains a distinctly musical orientation and sensibility. His honors, among many others, include a Rome Prize (1972–4), Martha Baird Rockefeller Fund grants (1975, 1980), NEA fellowships (1976, 1979, 1991), and a residency at SUNY, Buffalo (1977). His works have been recorded on the Ariel, CRI, Turnabout (Vox), Edipan Records, and Nonesuch labels.

WORKS

Orch: Time and Again, 1969; On Another Level, 21 mallet insts, 1974; But, the Moon, gui, 13 insts, 1975; Anyway, 1977; Can of Sourdines, str, 1979

Variable ens: Stop/Start, 1973; Long Island Sound, 1974; Experimental Music, 1975; Frozen Music Is not Melted Architecture, 1975; One-A-Day Music Pills, 1975; To Get a Peep Out Of, 1976; To Prevent Decay, hp, variable ens, 1976; Clash/Clash/Clash/Clash, 1977; Florida Sym., 1977; Evening the Score, 1979; For John Cage, 1992

4–6 insts/pfmrs: Resonata, brass qnt, 1967; Circle Music I, 4 insts, 1971; Circle Music III, 6 pfmrs, 1971; To the Last Drop, 6 vib, 1974; To Brush Up On, 6 vc, 1976; Sextet, 6 pfmrs, 1977; Hit Tune, 5 perc, 1983; Squeeze me Loose I Get Hot so Easy, 5 accdn, 1983; Tweet Suite, 5 tubas, 1983; Vowel Movement, soloist, qt, 1983; Wind-Up Sym., qnt, surprise guest artists, 1983; Juicy Music, B♭ cl, vn, vc, mar, pf, 1990; On the Vanishing Point, 4 insts, 1990; Post/Pone, B♭ cl, trbn, va, pf, 1990; Hoist by your Own Ritard, B♭ cl, mar, accdn, pf, 1993; several other works

1–3 insts/pfmrs: Round and About, 2 or more insts, 1970; Circle Music II, 2 or more insts, 1971; For the Third Time, 3 ww, 1973; On the Edge of a Node, gui, vn, vc, 1974; Italian Sym. no.1, soloist, 1975; Hidden Drives II, vn, vc, 1976; Meaty Music, soloist, 1977; Squeek, chair, 1977; 3 Weeks in Cincinnati in Dec, fl, 1979; Tremble II, db, 1981; The Violin between Us, vn, 1981; The Bartered Bird, duet, 1983; French Ov., soloist, 1983; Ancient Virtues, 3 insts, 1987; more than 10 other works

Gui: 4 Pieces, 1968; Exchanges, 1969; Distances/Embraces, 1972; Still and All, 1975; Tremble, 1978

Pf: Inter-polations, 1966; On the Vanishing Point, pf, tape delay, 1973; Row Music (Tip of the Iceberg), 1973; For Otto (A Line in Return), 1974; At Sea, 1976; Hidden Drives I, 1976; Chops, toy pf, 1989

Vocal: Poem, S, 4 insts, 1967; Countenormusic, Ct, variable ens, 1972; Entrances, chorus, 1976; Local Exits, S, chbr ens, 1976; Nests (textless), solo v, chorus, 1976; 3 Sisters who Are not Sisters, 5 actors/musicians, 1984; Blood on the Dining Room Floor (G. Stein), 1991

Tape, sculpture: City Games (Hellermann), with 3 vn, 1978; Musical Drawers, 1979; Wind Music, 1979; Morning Music (Staff of Life), 1981; Battery Park, 1982; Chin Music, 1982; Homage to Chubby Checker—Doin' the Twist, 1982; Juicy Music, 1982; Music Plane and Fancy, 1982; Progress in Music Demands Daily Drill, 1982; Smoke Gets in your Ears, 1982; After Dinner Music, with acc., 1983; I Brake for Music, with ens, 1983; many other pieces

Tape: Ariel, 1967; Ek-stasis I, 1968; Mai '68, 1969; Ek-stasis II, with timp, pf, 1970; Passages 13—The Fire (R. Duncan), with tpt, 1971; Parted…, with 3 pfmrs, 1972; One into Another (Ariel), with eng hn, 1972

Other mixed-media works, incid music

Principal publishers: ACA, Presser, Soundings

BIBLIOGRAPHY

N. Slonimsky: *Baker's Biographical Dictionary of Twentieth-Century Classical Musicians* (New York, 1997, ed. L. Kuhn, assoc. ed. D. McIntire)

T. Sauer: *Notations 21* (Brooklyn, 2009)

JOAN LA BARBARA/GREG A STEINKE

Helm, Everett (Burton) (*b* Minneapolis, MN, 17 July 1913; *d* Berlin, 25 June 1999). Composer and writer on music. He was educated at Harvard University (MA 1936, PhD 1939); in Europe (1936–9) he studied composition with Gian Francesco Malipiero and Ralph Vaughan Williams and musicology with Alfred Einstein. He held several teaching positions in the United States including that of head of the music department of Western College, Oxford, Ohio (1944–6). In 1948 he moved to Europe, where he remained except for a period in New York as editor of *Musical America* (1961–3). He contributed reviews and articles to newspapers and journals in the United States, Britain, and West Germany; his books include popular biographies (1971) and sociological studies (1970, 1981). He composed the opera *The Siege of Tottenburg* (1956), commissioned by the Süddeutscher Rundfunk and broadcast in November 1956. Simple folk-like melodies form the basis of this work, accompanied by some imaginative atonal orchestral writing. Other works include two piano concertos (1951, 1956), a Sinfonia da camera (1961), a concerto for strings and five solo instruments, chamber music, and songs. Several of his orchestral works have been performed by the New York PO under Dmitri Mitropoulos, the Berlin PO under Joseph Keilberth, and the BBC SO under Antal Dorati. His music manuscripts are housed at the American Music Center in New York.

WRITINGS

"Charles Ives, Pionier der modernen Musik," *Melos*, xxv (1958), 119–23

Composer, Performer, Public: a Study in Communication (Florence, 1970)

Bartók (London, 1971)

BIBLIOGRAPHY

A.C. Beal: Obituary, *The Sonneck Society for American Music Bulletin*, xxv/3 (1999), 81

PATRICK J. SMITH/R

Helm, George (Jarrett, Jr.) (*b* Molokai, HI, 23 March 1950; disappeared at sea off Kahoolawe, HI, 7 March

1977). Hawaiian falsetto singer, musician, and activist. Helm is widely admired for his *leo ki'eki'e* (Hawaiian falsetto) and commitment to social activism. He grew up on Hawaiian Homes land on the rural island of Moloka'i but moved to Honolulu at age 15 to attend St. Louis High School on an athletic scholarship. Respected performer and arranger Kahauanu Lake became his mentor, and Lake's elegant style is reflected in Helm's performance of classic repertoire such as "Kalamaula" and "Kimo Hula." Helm generally accompanied himself with subdued slack key guitar, favoring complex chording and idiosyncratic picking sometimes called the Moloka'i stroke.

After graduation Helm continued performing and immersed himself in Hawaiian causes. He helped found the Protect Kaho'olawe 'Ohana to stop the US military from using the island for bombing practice. A gifted orator, Helm often spoke and sang at public gatherings, helping establish a link between current political issues and traditional cultural values. Lake always advised his students to delay recording until they were ready, but in October 1976, Richard Wong taped Helm's appearance at his restaurant, the Gold Coin. On 7 March 1977, Helm and Kimo Mitchell were lost at sea while attempting to land on Kaho'olawe. Wong quickly released his home-made tapes on an album called *A True Hawaiian*. Volume 2 soon followed. They became local hits and helped establish Helm's legacy.

Songs such as "Hawaiian Soul" by fellow activist Jon Osorio and "Moloka'i Sweet Home" by Malani Bilyeu have been written in Helm's honor. In 1997 rappers Sudden Rush referenced Helm's death in "Think about It." In 2003 Helm's niece Raiatea launched a successful music career in a style showing some traces of his influence. In 2009 he received a Lifetime Achievement Award from the Hawaiian Academy of Recording Arts. In 1987 a plaque was placed on Kaho'olawe in memory of Helm and Mitchell. The bombing there was officially halted in 1990.

JAY W. JUNKER

Helmecke, August [Gus], **Jr.** (*d* ?New York, NY, 26 Feb 1954). Bass drummer. Little is known of his early life. He was a member of the Musicians' Mutual Protective Union in New York City in 1892 and was one of the honorary pallbearers for Patrick Gilmore. He joined the Sousa Band for the 1916–17 tour and performed with them until 1931. Of him, Sousa stated, "No one who has watched and heard Helmecke with my band playing a march will differ with me when I declare that my bass drummer has the spirit and the soul of a great artist." Helmecke also played with other notable groups, including the New York Po, the Metropolitan Opera, Bachman's Million Dollar Band, the Conway Band, and the Goldman Band. He also performed with orchestras and bands on recordings released by RCA Victor and Columbia. A co-founder of the Sousa Band Fraternal Society in 1944, he served as its first president (1944–7) and was later voted honorary life president. Something of a prankster, he was the central figure in numerous stories told by Sousa band members. In 1951 Theodore

Presser published nine Sousa marches edited by Helmecke to reflect Sousa's performance practices.

BIBLIOGRAPHY
P.E. Bierley: *John Philip Sousa, American Phenomenon* (Westerville, OH, 1973)
W.H. Rehrig: *The Heritage Encyclopedia of Band Music* (Westerville, OH, 1991, 2/1996); CD-ROM (Oskaloosa, IA, 2005)
P.E. Bierley: *The Incredible Band of John Philip Sousa* (Urbana, IL, 2006)

WILLIAM H. REHRIG

Helps, Robert (Eugene) (*b* Passaic, NJ, 23 Sept 1928; *d* Tampa, FL, 24 Nov 2001). Composer, pianist, and teacher. He attended Columbia University (1947–9) and the University of California, Berkeley (1949–51); he also studied piano with ABBY WHITESIDE and composition with ROGER SESSIONS (1943–56). He taught piano at the San Francisco Conservatory (1968–70), Stanford University (1968–9), the University of California, Berkeley (1969–70), the New England Conservatory (1970–2), and the Manhattan School of Music and Princeton University (both 1972–8); he was appointed professor of music at the University of South Florida, Tampa, in 1980, serving until his death. He received a Naumburg Foundation award for his Symphony no.1 (1957), a Guggenheim Fellowship (1966), awards from the Fromm Foundation (1957, 1971) and the American Academy and Institute of Arts and Letters (1976), an honorary Doctor of Humane Letters from the University of St. Thomas in St. Paul Minnesota, and commissions from the Thorne Music Fund and the Ford Foundation (1975, for the Piano Concerto no.2), among others. A noted interpreter of 20th-century piano music, Helps performed widely as a soloist and in partnership with Bethany Beardslee, Isidore Cohen, Rudolf Kolisch, Phyllis Curtin, and Aaron Copland. His many recordings include important works by Schoenberg, Babbitt, Mel Powell, Perle, and Sessions.

In his early works Helps generated pitch centers from a prevailing chromatic context. Often densely polyphonic, his later music makes use of 12-tone resources in a highly individual and expressive manner. The quartet for piano (1971) divides the keyboard into four equal parts of 22 keys each and explores the structural significance of registral pitch identities. *Gossamer Noons* (1977) is a setting for soprano and orchestra of four poems by James Purdy; its instrumental contexts and vocal contours sensitively reflect and enlarge on the verbal sonorities and rhythms of the text.

The University of South Florida's Special Collections holds the Robert Helps Archive. The university also sponsors a Robert Helps Festival and awards an annual Robert Helps Prize for young composers.

WORKS
(selective list)
Inst: Str Qt, 1951; Pf Trio, 1957; Sym. no.1, 1957; Serenade: Fantasy, vn, pf, 1963; Postlude, vn, hn, pf, 1965; Nocturne, str qt, 1966; Conc. no.1, pf, orch, 1969; Conc. no.2, pf, orch, 1976; Qnt, fl, cl, vn, vc, pf, 1976; Second Thoughts, fl, 1978; A Mixture of Time, gui, pf, 1990; Pf Trio no.2, 1996; Pf Qt, 1997; Sym. no.2, 2000

Pf: 3 Etudes, 1956; Images, 1957; Starscape, 1958; Recollections, 1959; Portrait, 1960; Solo, 1960; Saccade, 4 hands, 1967; Qt, pf, 1971;

3 Hommages, 1973; Nocturne, 1973; Music for Left Hand, 1974; Valse mirage, 1977; Eventually the Carousel Begins, 2 pf, 1987; Shall We Dance, 1994; Berceuse, 2 pf, 1995

Vocal: 2 Songs (H. Melville), S, pf, 1950; The Running Sun (J. Purdy), S, pf, 1972; Gossamer Noons (Purdy), S, orch, 1977

Principal publishers: Associated Music Publishers, E.B. Marks, C.F. Peters, and the American Composers Edition

BIBLIOGRAPHY

J. Vinton, ed.: Dictionary of Contemporary Music (New York, 1974)

E.W. Flemm:The Solo Piano Music of Robert Helps (diss., U. of Cincinnati, 1990)

N. Slonimsky: Baker's Biographical Dictionary of Twentieth-Century Classical Musicians (New York, 1997, ed. L. Kuhn, assoc. ed. D. McIntire)

RICHARD SWIFT/GREG A STEINKE

Hemans [née Browne], **Felicia (Dorothea)** (b Liverpool, England, 25 Sept 1793; d Dublin, Ireland, 16 May 1835). English poet. She spent most of her life in Wales and became well known in literary circles, being much admired by Byron, Scott, Shelley, and Wordsworth. Her works were extremely popular at home and abroad, notably in the United States before the Civil War. She rivaled Thomas Moore in the extent to which her works were included in literary anthologies and equaled Tennyson in the degree to which her poems became part of the conventional education of American youth. "Cassabianca" (The boy stood on the burning deck) and "Pilgrim Fathers" (The breaking waves dash high) were standard school recitations until the early 20th century. Four collected editions of Hemans's verse appeared in the United States between 1825 and 1850. Her importance to American musical life lies in the settings made of her poetry by her sister, Harriet Mary Browne (later Mrs. Hughes, d 1858). Many of these became parlor classics, numbered among the most popular songs of the 1830s and 40s. They originated as solo songs or duets and were subsequently arranged by Americans for vocal classbooks, vocal quartets, keyboard, and guitar. The original imprints listed the composer simply as "Mrs. Hemans' Sister" or "Miss Brown," so she was later confused with Augusta Browne. Among the most famous parlor songs by the Hemans sisters were "Tyrolese Evening Hymn" (1827), "The Captive Knight" (1827–32), "The Messenger Bird" (1835), "Pilgrim Fathers" (1835), and "Evening Song to the Virgin" (1835), all of which appeared in collections issued in the middle and at the end of the 19th century (for example, The Parlour Companion, 1836, and the Franklin Square Song Collection, 1884–92).

Other composers to have set Hemans's verses include George Whitefield Chadwick, who used "Pilgrim Fathers" in The Pilgrims for chorus and orchestra (1918). Her poetry was extolled most frequently for its mixture of respectable sentiment and Romanticism or, in the words of the journalist Sarah Josepha Hale, "its sweet feminine delicacy and purity of tone." Her verses are best understood within the context of Victorian-American culture, as is the music based upon them.

JUDITH TICK/LAURIE BLUNSOM

Hemke, Frederick (LeRoy) (b Milwaukee, WI, 11 July 1935). Saxophonist and teacher. He holds degrees from the University of Wisconsin, Milwaukee (BS 1958), the Eastman School of Music of the University of Rochester (MM 1962), and the University of Wisconsin, Madison (DMA 1975). He also studied at the Conservatoire National Supérieur de Musique in Paris, where as a student of Marcel Mule he became the first American saxophonist to win the Premier Prix (1956). Since 1962 Hemke has served as professor of music at Northwestern University, where he is currently Louis and Elise Snydacker Eckstein Professor of Music. He has been a visiting professor at the Conservatoire National de Musique (Paris), the Moscow Tchaikovsky Conservatory, the Basel Conservatory of Music (Switzerland), the Sweelinck Academy of Music (Amsterdam), and numerous institutions throughout the United States. Hemke has recorded on the Saxo, Brewster, New World, SRI, Nonesuch, Swedish Heritage Discophile, Lapider, and other labels. He has recorded as an orchestral saxophonist with the Chicago Symphony Orchestra and with various conductors including Georg Solti, Jean Martinon, Leopold Stokowski, and Seiji Ozawa. He has served as president of the North American Saxophone Alliance and has published a significant collection of saxophone music with Southern Music Company. He has also written extensively about the instrument and its music: he is the author of The Early History of the Saxophone (1975), an expansion of his doctoral dissertation, and The Teacher's Guide to the Saxophone (1977), among other publications, and has contributed many articles to music education journals.

SORAB MODI/JOSEPH WYTKO

Hemmenway, James (b 1792; d Philadelphia, PA, 8 May 1859). Bandmaster, trumpeter, and composer. He was probably active in Boston before coming to Philadelphia and may be related to John Hemmenway, musician of Boston. He is contemporary with Francis Johnson especially as a composer and trumpeter performing with Johnson in the 1820s. Hemmenway was a barber and peruker by profession and first came to public notice around 1818 with his Cupid's Frolic. His fame increased in 1824 with the publication of General Lafayette's Trumpet March and Quick Step, two weeks before Johnson's tribute to "the Nation's Guest." On 12 July 1825 Captain Childs paid $33.37 for two drummers, two fifers and a bass drummer for military exercises at Reading with Hemmenway in charge. By 1826 he had established himself as a worthy rival of Johnson's by organizing his own group of "one to twelve" musicians. On 18 May 1827 he was hired by the Artillery Corps of the Washington Grays. He performed for them again with five musicians on 29 October 1827. Other notable musicians in his band included Peter Lober and Thomas Williams. His activities in the black community included the presidency of the Archer's Literary Club in 1828. During the 1830s he was active in many church-sponsored programs especially when Johnson was not available and in 1838 he was called upon to lead an all-black orchestra at the Second Presbyterian Church performing the works of Haydn. When Johnson prepared to leave for Europe in 1837 Hemmenway was selected to lead his band and issued a notice on 23 October 1837, but then declined, probably due to objections from Johnson's family and other bandsmen. After issuing a correction, he announced the organization of his own cotillion band. He married Harriet R. Lewis on 9 August 1840; a daughter, Harriet James, died in childhood. Hemmenway died in 1859 and is buried at Lebanon Cemetery. His music in many instances is better than Johnson's and was published as far away as New Orleans during his lifetime.

WORKS
(selective list)

Pf unless otherwise stated: Cupid's Frolic, ?1818; Miss Billing's Waltz, ?1819; The Philadelphia Grand Entre, March, 1819–31; Washington Grays' Bugle Quick Step, 1821–5; The Philadelphia Grand March, 1823–4; Washington Grays' Grand March, 1823–4; General LaFayette's Trumpet March and Quick Step (1824); A Set of New Cotillions for the Year 1825, 1825: Eliza, Maria, Emma, James, William, 1825; A favorite cotillion inscribed to Mad Zema Boyer, 1825; Second Set of Quadrilles: Independence, The Arcade, Washington Hall, Bolivar, The Patriot, 1825; That Rest So Sweet Like Bliss Above, 1826; The Philadelphia Hop Waltz, 1826–36; The Philadelphia Serenading Grand March, fl/vn, pf, 1826–51; Third Set of Quadrilles, 1827; Fourth Set: Olevia, Comin' Thro' The Rye, Mermaid, Albert, Love Was Once A Little Boy, ?1827; Fifth Set, ?1827; The New Year's and Curtsy Cotillions, 1827–44; Sixth Set of Quadrilles: Tancredi, La Dame Blanche, Elizabeth, Tancredi, Napoleon, ?1828; Hunter and Hop Waltz, 1840

Principal publisher: Willig

BIBLIOGRAPHY

R.J. Wolfe: *Secular Music in America, 1801–1825: a Bibliography* (New York, 1964)

A.R. LaBrew: *Studies in Nineteenth Century Afro-American Music* (Detroit, 1974)

A.R. LaBrew: *Captain Francis Johnson: Great American Black Bandsman: Life and Works* (Detroit, 1994)

ARTHUR R. LABREW

Hempel, Frieda (*b* Leipzig, Germany, 26 June 1885; *d* Berlin, Germany, 7 Oct 1955). German soprano, later naturalized American. She studied in Leipzig and Berlin, and her early career was centered at the Berlin Königliche Oper from 1905 until 1912. Her fine schooling and purity of tone helped her achieve success. She made her Metropolitan Opera debut on 27 December 1912 as the Queen in a brilliantly cast production of *Les Huguenots*, beginning a period of seven years with that company, during which she settled in New York. She sang Eva (*Die Meistersinger*) and Weber's Euryanthe there under Toscanini, besides many of the lighter Verdi, Rossini, and Donizetti parts, in which she was regarded as the natural successor of Marcella Sembrich. Her big London success came during Thomas Beecham's Drury Lane season of 1914, when she sang the Queen of Night (perhaps her most famous role) and the Marschallin in *Der Rosenkavalier*, a role she had introduced to Berlin in 1911 and to New York in 1913. After a farewell performance as Violetta at the Metropolitan on 6 February 1919, she made a few appearances with the Chicago Grand Opera Company in San Francisco in 1921 but devoted herself mainly to a concert career, in which her great success was sometimes enhanced by the rather dubious device of giving Jenny Lind recitals in period costume. Her refined, exhilarating style is worthily represented on her many recordings.

BIBLIOGRAPHY

GV (R. Celletti, with discography)

F. Hempel: *Mein Leben dem Gesang* (Berlin, 1955)

P.H. Reed, G.T. Keating, and B.F. Stone: "The Recorded Art of Frieda Hempel," *Record Collector*, x (1955–6), 53–71 [with discography]

H. Brower and J.F. Cooke: *Great Singers on the Art of Singing* (Mineola, NY, 1996)

F. Hempel and W.R. Moran: *My Golden Age of Singing* (Portland, OR, 1998)

DESMOND SHAWE-TAYLOR/R

Hemphill, Julius (Arthur) (*b* Fort Worth, TX, 24 Jan 1938; *d* New York, NY, 2 April 1995). Composer, bandleader, and altosaxophonist. He studied at North Texas State College and subsequently served in the US Army (from 1964), during which time he played in the US Army Band. After moving to St. Louis in 1968, he co-founded the Black Artists Group (BAG), modeled on the Association for the Advancement of Creative Musicians in Chicago. Hemphill's multi-media interests, which included dance, chamber music, and drama, helped define the BAG as more than a musicians' collective. While in St. Louis, Hemphill founded his record label, Mbari, and began his recording career with the album *Dogon A.D.* (1971, Mbari, later reissued on the label Arista/Freedom). In 1976 he founded the WORLD SAXOPHONE QUARTET with Hamiet Bluiett, Oliver Lake, and David Murray. In addition to making many recordings with the famed quartet, until he departed the group in 1989, Hemphill recorded more than 20 albums as a leader with musicians as diverse as Anthony Braxton, Björk, James Carter, Olu Dara, Marty Ehrlich, Bill Frisell, and Abdul Wadud.

BIBLIOGRAPHY

B. Looker: *Point from which Creation Begins: the Black Artists' Group of St. Louis* (St. Louis, 2004)

G. Lewis: *A Power Stronger than Itself: the AACM and American Experimental Music* (Chicago, 2008)

ANDREW BARTLETT

Hempsted, Henry N. (*b* Albany, NY, 29 Dec 1830; *d* Kasson, MN, 22 Dec 1898). Music publisher and composer. He moved in 1849 to Milwaukee, where he established himself as a music teacher; he opened a music store two years later that eventually became one of the largest in the upper Midwest. He published editions of the works of 19th-century composers (Schumann, Liszt, Strauss) as well as his own works, the most popular of which were "Iron Brigade Quickstep," "Garibaldi's Sicilian March," and "The Milwaukee Light Guard Quickstep." From 1873 to 1875 he edited and published the *Musical Echo*.

BIBLIOGRAPHY

J.S. Buck: *Milwaukee under the Charter from 1847 to 1853*, iii (Milwaukee, 1884)

FRANKLIN S. MILLER

Henahan, Donal (Joseph) (*b* Cleveland, OH, 28 Feb 1921; *d* New York, NY, 19 Aug 2012). Music critic. He attended Kent State and Ohio Universities before serving in the US Air Force during World War II from 1942 to 1945. He studied at Northwestern University (BA 1948) and later attended the University of Chicago and the Chicago School of Music. He studied piano and classical guitar and was a teacher of the latter instrument for several years. Henahan wrote for the *Chicago Daily News* from 1947 to 1967 and for the *New York Times* from 1967 until his retirement in 1991, becoming chief music critic at both papers. He also contributed to numerous other journals and magazines, including *The Musical Quarterly, American Choral Review, Guitar Review, High Fidelity & Musical America, Down Beat, Gramophone,* and *Esquire.* He was a finalist for the Pulitzer Prize for Criticism in 1982 and won the award in 1986. The vast majority of his reviews addressed orchestral, operatic, and chamber repertoire; he wrote about popular music on occasion. Henahan's writings reveal a complex relationship with 20th-century musical culture. Atonality, minimalism, and electronic music were among the styles about which he expressed negative opinions, but he was an advocate of new music that he considered accessible as a means of perpetuating the classical tradition.

BIBLIOGRAPHY

H.D. Fischer and E.J. Fischer, eds.: *Cultural Criticism, 1969–1990: From Architectural Damages to Press Imperfections* (Munich, 1992)
R. Schick: *Classical Music Criticism* (New York, 1996)
E. Brennan and E. Clarage: *Who's Who of Pulitzer Prize Winners* (Phoenix, AZ, 1999)

LARS HELGERT

Henderson, Eddie [Jackson, Edward Hank] (*b* New York, NY, 26 Oct 1940). Trumpeter. He was born into a musical family. His father Ed Jackson sang with the Charioteers and his mother Vivian Brown was a dancer at the Cotton Club. Henderson's first informal lessons came at the age of nine with LOUIS ARMSTRONG. After taking private lessons in the Bronx, he moved to San Francisco at the age of 14, following his father's death, and took his adoptive father's surname. There he studied at the San Francisco Conservatory and played with its orchestra. Following a stint in the air force, he was a pre-med student at the University of San Francisco and the University of California at Berkeley, graduating in 1964. He earned his MD at Howard University, while playing with local musicians in Washington, DC. After returning to San Francisco, he held a residency in psychiatry (1969–71) while playing in the saxophonist John Handy's group. Having been invited by Herbie Hancock to substitute for Johnny Coles in 1970, he remained with Hancock's band Mwandishi for three years, a high-profile gig which earned him tours with Art Blakey and Norman Connors, a reputation as the first-call trumpeter for artists playing at Keystone Korner in San Francisco—including Dexter Gordon, Joe Henderson, Pharoah Sanders, and Jackie McLean—and five fusion recording dates as a leader. From 1975 to 1985 he practiced medicine during the day and played trumpet at night, after which he returned to New York to tour and record with Kenny Barron, Gary Bartz, Billy Harper, and McCoy Tyner, among others. Since 1994 Henderson has made a series of well received mainstream records with his own groups. In 2007 he joined the faculty of

the Juilliard School and later become a member of the Juilliard Jazz Quintet. Influenced strongly by Miles Davis, Freddie Hubbard, Lee Morgan, and Booker Little, Henderson has forged his own identity as one of the finest players in jazz.

BIBLIOGRAPHY

B. Milkowski: "Dr. Trumpet: Eddie Henderson," *JT*, xxxi/8 (2001), 46–51
T. Erdmann: "Knowledge Enhances all Gifts: an Interview with Eddie Henderson," *ITG Journal*, xxvii/4 (2003), 39–48
R.J. DeLuke: "Eddie Henderson: Healing with Music," *All About Jazz* <http://www.allaboutjazz.com/php/article.php?id=573> (2003)

RUSS MUSTO

Henderson, Fletcher (Hamilton) [Henderson, James Fletcher; Smack] (*b* Cuthbert, GA, 18 Dec 1897; *d* New York, NY, 28 Dec 1952). Jazz bandleader and arranger. The eldest of three children, he grew up in a small segregated town in southwestern Georgia near the Alabama border. As teachers from the black middle class, his parents Fletcher and Ozie Henderson placed high value on education, which included a strict routine of piano practice for their son. Soon after matriculating at Atlanta University, James changed his first name to Fletcher, Jr. In 1920 he graduated, having majored in chemistry. He also played piano at social occasions and led a small band. After graduating he went to New York, ostensibly seeking a graduate degree in chemistry. Harlem's burgeoning music scene drew him in, however, and he quickly began getting musical jobs. He met his future wife, Leora, a trumpeter, while playing with a riverboat orchestra. The couple got married on Christmas Day 1924. Leora later served in several crucial roles supporting her husband's career: booking jobs, copying parts, scouting for and auditioning new band members, and even substituting on trumpet in his otherwise all-male band.

In the fall of 1920, the Pace and Handy Music Company hired Henderson as a song plugger—promoting new songs from the publisher's catalog. Embodying the black middle-class values with which Henderson grew up, Pace and Handy aspired to make black music more respectable. At a time when race records had begun attracting a larger market, Harry Pace then opened a record company to further disseminate black music-making, from opera arias to blues, and hired Henderson as the staff accompanist and orchestra leader. While emphasizing the classics, Pace soon realized that the public favored the blues, especially Ethel Waters' recording of "Down Home Blues" (1921, Black Swan) accompanied by Henderson and a small band.

Henderson's first band grew out of his early recording experiences, and so the ensemble known as Fletcher Henderson and his Orchestra was first and foremost a recording band. In an 18-month period (1923–4) it made nearly 100 recordings, mostly popular songs and blues tunes which combined arranged ensemble passages and limited solo improvisation, and inevitably labeled "fox trot—for dancing." In this period, the band's principal arranger was the clarinetist and saxophonist Don Redman, who typically adapted published, or stock, arrangements by chopping the melody into short phrases distributed among band members and spiced with "hot" solos. One of the regular soloists was the tenor saxophonist Coleman Hawkins. Henderson's piece "Dicty Blues," which his band recorded several times in 1923, represents his early work; it is a witty mix of high class ("dicty") and lowdown during the period's blues craze. For such early efforts, Henderson earned the moniker the Paul Whiteman of the Race, a mixed blessing that linked the young bandleader to the most successful white dance-band leader of the 1920s. In 1924 the band found work in downtown Manhattan, first at the Club Alabam near Times Square, and then at the Roseland Ballroom, where the band performed regularly for radio broadcasts and established a home base for several years.

At the Roseland, the band was joined by the trumpeter Louis Armstrong, whom Henderson had met on a tour with Ethel Waters. With a powerful new weapon in its musical arsenal, the band continued to feature arrangements with a snappy cut-and-paste style that mixed improvised solos and tight ensemble playing, as in "Copenhagen" (1924, Voc.), "T.N.T. (1925, Col.), and a blues piece that Armstrong had brought from Chicago, "Dippermouth Blues." With an arrangement customized for a New York dance band, the number became known as "Sugar Foot Stomp" (1925, Col.) and stood among Henderson's most popular records of the 1920s. Armstrong remained with the band for 13 months, but his virtuosic range, harmonic sense, supple rhythmic style, and sheer loudness offered a challenge to the band's most ambitious players, notably Hawkins and the trumpeter Rex Stewart, who, when hired as Armstrong's replacement, was simply told to "play like Louis." Both Stewart and Hawkins do just that in Henderson's piece "The Stampede" (1926, Col.), a recording that stands as a dramatic document of the band's post-Armstrong style. "Hop Off" (1927, Col.) and "King Porter Stomp" (1928, Col.) represent prototypical big-band jazz that opened up large spaces for improvisation by the band's increasingly virtuosic jazz soloists. In sharp contrast "Whiteman Stomp" (1927, Col.) shows the band reaching for and parodying the symphonic effects popularized by Whiteman, with minimal solos in a musical style designed for listening, not dancing. Unexpected from Henderson, the record caught the attention of listeners and musicians alike. According to the lead trumpeter Russell Smith, it was "the biggest thing Fletcher ever did," and "all the bands wanted that one." Henderson's repertory in this period also featured waltzes, prized by dancers at the Roseland. But racial stereotypes in the recording business meant that a black band could not record waltzes. "There was an unwritten custom among record people that no negro orchestra should be allowed to record anything that wasn't blues or hot stuff," recalled Stewart. Throughout the 1920s Henderson cemented his reputation as "one of the best... 'blues' specialists," as one publication put it, accompanying more than a dozen female singers, including Ma Rainey and Bessie Smith.

After the stock market crash of 1929, the band continued to thrive, at first, on a routine of public appearances, radio play, and records. Its recording of the old orientalist Tin Pan Alley hit "Chinatown, my Chinatown" (1930, Col.) sprints through the familiar tune at a frenzied tempo, conjuring what one critic had called the "dionysiac heat" of its public performances. In 1931 it began a stint at Connie's Inn, an elite nightclub in Harlem where it accompanied floor shows with a varied repertory reflected in its recordings. During the period 1932–5 the band experienced mixed fortunes: vivid reports of exciting performances and a series of what became classic recordings combined with Henderson's intermittent difficulties meeting his payroll. It was in this period, in 1932, that the young Ivy League dropout and aspiring band promoter John Hammond met Henderson and arranged public and recording jobs for the scuffling band.

The recordings give a glimpse of what had become the band's standard operating procedure in a particularly busy period: taking the chords of a well known jazz standard or pop song and collaboratively building an arrangement through rehearsal, discussion, and little if any written music. "Yeah Man" (1933, Voc.) and "Hotter than 'ell" (1934, Decca) became two of the first big-band arrangements of George Gershwin's hit "I got rhythm." "Wild Party" (1934, Voc.) uses the chords of another contemporary Broadway favorite, Jerome Kern's "Ol' Man River." And "Can you take it?" (1933, Col.) in the rare band key of A major, resonates with the harmony of Irving Berlin's "Blue Skies." The period also featured new, faster versions of "Sugar Foot Stomp" (1931, Col.) and "King Porter Stomp" (1932, Voc. and 1933, Col.), which became swing-era anthems. Henderson composed more of the band's material, and in a final group of recordings for Decca, the band recorded his swing-era masterpieces "Down South Camp Meeting," and "Wrappin' it Up" (both 1934, Decca). The pieces show the traits of Henderson's music that influenced the entire swing era: brass and reeds in call-and-response dialogue, elegant ensemble riffs supporting improvised solos, long chains of syncopation, and an overall sense of joyful yet controlled dance music.

By late 1934 Henderson was no longer able to pay his bandmembers. After performing in Detroit, the musicians went their separate ways. Henderson went back to New York, where Benny Goodman, having just won a job playing on the new NBC radio program "Let's Dance" was in search of jazz-oriented arrangements for his band. His path led to Henderson, who subsequently arranged hundreds of charts for Goodman in the latter's rise to become the King of Swing. Henderson's work primarily involved arranging pop tunes such as "Blue Skies," "Between the Devil and the Deep Blue Sea," "Honeysuckle Rose," and "I would do anything for you," in tight block harmonies, call-and-response patterns, and elegant melodic variations inflected with the audible legacy of Armstrong and other soloists from Henderson's band.

Goodman's success emboldened Henderson to form a new band, which included such exciting young musicians as the tenor saxophonist Chu Berry and the trumpeter Roy Eldridge. The band had a hit record with a tune called "Christopher Columbus" (1936, Vic.) and played many of the arrangements that Henderson had written for Goodman, but the latter's success tended to eclipse Henderson's comeback in a segregated America where white achievements received more attention than black achievements in the same field. Such experiences inspired Hammond's description of Henderson's career as "a study in frustration," the title of a commemorative album issued in the early 1960s, a decade after Henderson's death. After leading bands intermittently through the 1940s, sometimes in collaboration with his brother Horace, Henderson had suffered a series of strokes and died in 1952.

RECORDINGS
(selective list)
As leader: Dicty Blues (1923, Voc.); Copenhagen (1924, Voc.); Shanghai Shuffle (1924, Pathé); Sugar Foot Stomp (1925, Col.); T.N.T. (1925, Col.); The Stampede (1926, Col.); The Henderson Stomp (1926, Col.); Hop Off (1927, Col.); Whiteman Stomp (1927, Col.); King Porter Stomp (1928, Col.); Chinatown, my Chinatown (1930, Col.); Sugar Foot Stomp (1931, Col.); King Porter Stomp (1932, Vocalion.); King Porter Stomp (1933, Col.); Queer Notions (1933, Col.); Hotter than 'ell (1934, Decca); Wrappin' it Up (1934, Decca); Down South Camp Meeting (1934, Decca); Shanghai Shuffle (1934, Decca); Christopher Columbus (1936, Voc.)

ARRANGEMENTS
(selective list)
Between the Devil and the Deep Blue Sea (1935); Blue Skies (1935); I would do anything for you (1935); King Porter Stomp (1935); Sometimes I'm Happy (1935); Sugar Foot Stomp (1935); When Buddha Smiles (1935); Wrappin' it Up (1935); Down South Camp Meeting (1936); Honeysuckle Rose (1939)

BIBLIOGRAPHY
G. Schuller: Early Jazz: its Roots and Musical Development (New York, 1968/R)
W.C. Allen: Hendersonia: the Music of Fletcher Henderson and his Musicians, a Bio Discography (Highland Park, NJ, 1974)
M.P. Dews: Remembering: the Remarkable Henderson Family (Chicago, 1978)
G. Schuller: The Swing Era: the Development of Jazz, 1930–1945 (New York, 1989/R)
J. Magee: The Music of Fletcher Henderson and his Orchestra in the 1920s (diss., U. of Michigan, 1992)
J. Magee: "Revisiting Fletcher Henderson's 'Copenhagen'," JAMS, xlviii/1 (1995), 42–66
J. Magee: "'King Porter Stomp' and the Jazz Tradition," CMc, nos.71–3 (2001–2), 22–53
J.L. Clark: "Stock-in-Trade": Investigating the Role of Stock Arrangements in the Development of the Orchestral Repertoire of Fletcher Henderson and his Contemporaries (diss., Brandeis U., 2003)
J. Magee: The Uncrowned King of Swing: Fletcher Henderson and Big Band Jazz (New York, 2005)

JEFFREY MAGEE

Henderson, Joe [Joseph Arthur] (*b* Lima, OH, 24 April 1937; *d* San Francisco, CA, 30 June 2001). Jazz tenor saxophonist. He emerged in the 1960s as one of jazz's most creative improvisers and forged a distinctive style primarily from the influences of Sonny Rollins and John Coltrane. The third youngest of 15 children, he had to earn enough money to buy his first saxophone by delivering newspapers. He learned Lester Young solos with the help of an older brother and later received further mentoring from older musician friends, who included him at jam sessions and hired him to play in Lima's nightclubs. Following high school Henderson moved to Detroit and quickly became a major player. In 1962, after a two-year stint in the army, he worked briefly in Baltimore with the organist Jack McDuff before moving to New York. Shortly after his arrival, Henderson began what became a long-standing association with Kenny Dorham, who introduced him to Blue Note Records; he recorded prolifically with the label as both a leader and sideman from 1963 to 1966. Heralded as some of his best work, these sessions capture Henderson alongside the leading players of the 1960s and reveal his command of both the prevailing hard-bop style and the blues, and his nascent explorations into free jazz. Around this time Henderson gained increased visibility as a member of Horace Silver's quintet (1964–6). After leaving Silver, Henderson formed his own groups and collaborated with other prominent artists, including Miles Davis, Freddie Hubbard, Herbie Hancock, and the Thad Jones–Mel Lewis Orchestra.

Henderson recorded 12 albums for Milestone Records (1967–78), many of which delve into jazz-rock and psychedelic free-jazz styles, and increasingly reflect an Afro-centric awareness. Despite their high artistry, most were met with an underwhelming response. One attempt to counteract this indifference occurred in 1971, when Henderson dissolved his quintet and briefly joined Blood, Sweat, and Tears. Lagging sales forced Milestone to drop him in the late 1970s. Henderson subsequently recorded intermittently for various independent labels, including Blue Note (1985). Although active throughout the 1980s, he continued to receive scant publicity. This changed dramatically in 1991 when he signed with Verve, whose vigorous promotional campaigns catapulted him into the limelight. Of his five recordings for the label, three received Grammy awards, including the tribute album *Lush Life*. However, Henderson's health steadily declined during this period, and in 1998 he suffered a stroke that rendered him slightly paralyzed and ended his career.

RECORDINGS
(selective list)
As leader: Page One (1963, BN); Inner Urge (1964, BN); Live at the Lighthouse (1970, Mlst.); The State of the Tenor, i–ii (1985, BN); Lush Life: the Music of Billy Strayhorn (1991, Verve); So Near, So Far: Musings for Miles (1993, Verve)
As sideman: K. Dorham: Una Mas (1963, BN); H. Silver: Song for my Father (1964, BN); F. Hubbard: Red Clay (1970, CTI); The Griffith Park Collection: In Concert (1982, Elektra Musician); M. Miller: Hand in Hand (1993, Novus)

BIBLIOGRAPHY
P. Carles: "Joe Henderson," Jm, no.159 (1968), 14–19, 43–4
R. Townley: "The Herculean Tenor of Joe Henderson," DB, xlii/1 (1975), 18–20, 40
M. Martin: "Joe Henderson," Saxophone Journal, xv/5 (1991), 12–20
M. Mannucci: "La storia della musica afro-americana, personaggi, stili, epoche, strumenti: Joe Henderson," Musica Jazz, xlviii/ 4 (1992), 35–49

JEFFREY L. LOVELL

Henderson, Luther (*b* Kansas City, MO, 14 March 1919; *d* New York, NY, 28 July 2003). Arranger, composer, and orchestrator. Born into a well-educated family, he grew up in the Sugar Hill neighborhood of New York, where he was steeped in the culture of the Harlem Renaissance. He began playing piano when he was very young, and although he majored in mathematics at the City College of New York he eventually was accepted into the music department of the Juilliard School in the late 1930s. After his graduation from that institution in 1942, Henderson was drafted into the navy, where he found a position as an orchestrator and arranger with its jazz band. While continuing to work in this role, he also served as the staff orchestrator for the Navy School of Music in Washington, DC (1944–6). After the war he worked as an orchestrator for Broadway shows, first with Duke Ellington on *Beggar's Holiday* (1946) and later with Rodgers and Hammerstein on *Flower Drum Song* (1958), Jule Styne on *Do re mi* (1960) and *Funny Girl* (1964), and on Fats Waller's revue *Ain't Misbehavin'* (1978). Henderson received two Tony nominations, for *Jelly's Last Jam* and *Play On!*, and worked with many of the industry's top composers. On many occasions he composed and arranged the dances for these shows, although he was not always given credit. He also lent his talents to music for such television shows as *The Ed Sullivan Show* and orchestrated music for several stars, including Dean Martin and Lena Horne. His longest relationship was with the Canadian Brass, with which he worked for more than two decades.

JONAS WESTOVER

Henderson, Ray [Brost, Raymond] (*b* Buffalo, NY, 1 Dec 1896; *d* Greenwich, CT, 31 Dec 1970). Composer. He studied at the Chicago Conservatory of Music, then taught the piano, served as organist, and played in dance bands in his hometown before moving to New York. He worked initially as a song plugger for Leo Feist and started to compose his own tunes, then in 1922 met lyricist LEW BROWN; one of their earliest songs, "Georgette" (for the *Greenwich Village Follies* of that year), became a hit. BUDDY DESYLVA joined the team in 1925, and they subsequently collaborated on many popular revues and musicals. Their first success, *George White's Scandals of 1926*, included "The Birth of the Blues," "Black Bottom," and "Lucky Day"; this was followed by the quintessential Broadway musical of the 1920s, *Good News* (1927). They also wrote songs for early sound films: "Sonny Boy" was performed by Al Jolson in *The Singing Fool* (1928) and "If I had a talking picture of you" by Janet Gaynor in *Sunny Side Up* (1929). Henderson's music was filled with the lively "lowdown" rhythms and basic harmonies of the period; his love songs were made piquant by the lyrics of DeSylva and Brown. From 1940 DeSylva remained in Hollywood, but Henderson continued to work with Brown, producing the Broadway shows *George White's Scandals of 1931*, *Hot-Cha* (1932), and *Strike me pink* (1933). His ability to create melodies of wide popular appeal seemed to wane, however, and his last theater score (for *Ziegfeld Follies of 1943*) owed its success to the nostalgia it inspired for an earlier era. A film of the

careers of DeSylva, Brown, and Henderson, *The best things in life are free*, appeared in 1956.

WORKS
(selective list)
(unless otherwise stated, lyrics are by B.G. DeSylva and L. Brown)

STAGE
(book musicals unless otherwise stated; dates are those of first New York performance)

George White's Scandals of 1925 (revue), 22 June 1925; George White's Scandals of 1926 (revue), 14 June 1926 [incl. The Birth of the Blues, Black Bottom, Lucky Day]; Good News, 6 Sept 1927 [incl. The best things in life are free, Just imagine, Lucky in Love, Varsity Drag, Good News], films, 1930, 1947; Manhattan Mary, 26 Sept 1927; George White's Scandals of 1928 (revue), 2 July 1928; Hold everything, 10 Oct 1928 [incl. You're the cream in my coffee]; Follow Thru, 9 Jan 1929 [incl. Button up your overcoat], film, 1930; Flying High, 5 March 1930 [incl. Thank your father]; George White's Scandals of 1931 (revue, Brown), 14 Sept 1931 [incl. Life is just a bowl of cherries, The thrill is gone]; Hot-Cha (Brown), 8 March 1932; Strike me pink (Brown), 4 March 1933; Say when (T. Koehler), 8 Nov 1931; George White's Scandals of 1936 (revue, J. Yellen), 25 Dec 1935; Ziegfeld Follies of 1943 (revue, Yellen), 1 April 1943

FILMS
The Singing Fool, 1928 [incl. Sonny Boy]; Say it with songs, 1929; Sunny Side Up, 1929 [incl. If I had a talking picture of you, I'm a dreamer, aren't we all?, Sunny Side Up]; Just imagine, 1930; Indiscreet, 1931; George White's Scandals (Yellen and I. Caesar), 1934; Curly Top (Caesar and Koehler), 1935

OTHER SONGS
Georgette (Brown), in Greenwich Village Follies of 1922, 1922; That Old Gang of Mine (B. Rose and M. Dixon), 1923; Follow the swallow (Rose and Dixon), 1924; Alabamy Bound (B. Green and DeSylva), 1925; Five Foot Two, Eyes of Blue (S. Lewis and J. Young), 1925; I'm sittin' on top of the world (Lewis and Young), 1925; Bye, bye, blackbird (Dixon), 1926

BIBLIOGRAPHY
D. Ewen: *Complete Book of the American Musical Theater* (New York, 1958, rev. 1970 as *New Complete Book of the American Musical Theater*), 639–43
S. Green: *The World of Musical Comedy* (New York, 1960, rev. and enlarged 4/1980), 131–42, 416–20

GERALD BORDMAN

Henderson, Skitch [Lyle Russell Cedric] (*b* Birmingham, UK, 27 Jan 1918; *d* New Milford, CT, 1 Nov 2005). Conductor, pianist, composer, and arranger of English birth, though Henderson may have been born in Halstad, Minnesota, and prevaricated to add prestige to his background.

During the 1930s Henderson worked as a pianist with dance bands and as a studio musician in films and radio. He led his own band in the late 1940s and served both before and after World War II as pianist and music director for Frank Sinatra and Bing Crosby, who gave him his distinctive nickname. During the war years, he first joined the Royal Canadian Air Force, and later became an American citizen and served in the US Air Force. He studied theory and harmony with SCHOENBERG at UCLA after the war. In 1949, Henderson joined the music staff of NBC; his appearances on Steve Allen's *Tonight* (1954–6, during which time he studied conducting with Riener), and on Johnny Carson's *The Tonight Show* (1962–6) brought him the widest recognition. The band assembled for the latter was especially noteworthy, and the first-rate jazz musicians in its ranks set high standards of musicianship. He also conducted the NBC SO on many occasions. He won a Grammy award in 1963 for an album of *Porgy and Bess* scenes with Leontyne Price and William Warfield. After leaving NBC in 1966, Henderson concentrated on arranging and conducting, appearing with orchestras in the United States and Europe in programs of both classical and popular music. In 1983 he formed the New York Pops Orchestra with freelance musicians, and he continued to lead the group into the 21st century. He was awarded the Handel Medallion, New York City's highest cultural honor, in 1997, and the Smithsonian Institution's James Smithson Bicentennial Medal in 2005. In 2004 Henderson and his wife founded a cultural center at their farm in New Milford, which comprised their long-standing art gallery and cooking school, as well as a museum with rare audio and film recordings from across his career.

BIBLIOGRAPHY

"Henderson, Skitch," *CBY 1966*
R. Severo: Obituary, *New York Times* (3 Nov 2005)

MARK TUCKER/JOHN J. SHEINBAUM

Henderson, Wayne (*b* Rugby, Grayson County, VA, 13 March 1943). Guitar maker and player. He is a noted luthier and player of fingerstyle steel-string guitar (in the manner of his relative Estil Ball) and a 1995 NEA National Heritage Fellow. Both his family and his immediate neighborhood were rich in players of traditional Appalachian music. He built his first guitar because he could not afford the instrument he wanted. After a few initial attempts that he has recalled with rueful humor, he has made and sold several hundred finely crafted guitars. The models he makes and the qualities he seeks recall the best of steel-string guitars made by C.F. Martin and Company before World War II. His principal teacher in the art of lutherie was Albert Hash, who is better known as a seminal figure in the White Top (Virginia) style of old-time Appalachian fiddling. Henderson now makes about 20 guitars per year—entirely by hand—plus a handful of mandolins. His craftsmanship has inspired many American luthiers, and his mandolin is played by Doc Watson. He spearheads the annual Wayne C. Henderson Music Festival and Guitar Competition, through which he raises funds to support students of Appalachian traditional music. He has toured Asia under the auspices of the United States Information Agency.

BIBLIOGRAPHY

"Wayne Henderson," National Endowment for the Arts, 1995, <http://www.nea.gov/honors/heritage/fellows/fellow.php?id=1995_05&type=bio>
A. St. John: *Clapton's Guitar: Watching Wayne Henderson Build the Perfect Instrument* (New York, 2005)

CHRIS GOERTZEN

Henderson, William James (*b* Newark, NJ, 4 Dec 1855; *d* New York, NY, 5 June 1937). Music critic. A child of two actors (his father was a theatrical manager as well), Henderson studied at Princeton (BA 1876, MA 1886,

honorary DLitt 1922). He took piano lessons with Carl Langlotz (1868–73) and singing lessons with Angelo Torriano (1876–77), mostly teaching himself music theory. Henderson wrote for newspapers from the time he was a teenager, contributing to the *New York Times* during his freshman year in college and reporting for the *New York Tribune* after college. From the late 1870s to the early 1880s, he briefly abandoned journalism to work with his father but returned to writing as a music critic for the *New York Times* (1887–1902), the *New York Sun* (1902–20 and 1924–37), and the *New York Herald* (1920–24).

From the early stages of his career, he was an ardent supporter of Richard Wagner's music in the United States; however, during the 1890s he was also among the first American critics to recognize a new generation of young Italian composers that included Pietro Mascagni, Ruggero Leoncavallo, and Giacomo Puccini. Among the composers he held in highest regard throughout his life—besides Wagner—were Johannes Brahms and Giuseppe Verdi. Henderson's insightful comments spanned both instrumental and vocal repertory, but his main interest was singing.

Henderson taught music history at the New York College of Music (1889–95) and served as a lecturer on vocal art at the Institute of Musical Art (now the Juilliard School) from 1905. He also wrote novels, poems, and the libretto for Walter Damrosch's opera *Cyrano de Bergerac*, which received its premiere at the Metropolitan Opera on 27 February 1913. In 1914 Henderson was elected to the American Academy of Arts and Letters in the Literature Department. His advocacy for the presence of female musicians in orchestras and his increasing skepticism concerning modernist composers were themes in his writing near the end of his life; still, he acknowledged the importance of Claude Debussy, Arnold Schoenberg, and Igor Stravinsky in the development of music. Henderson offered still-relevant comments on the parallels between musical style and intellectual tendencies in his 1915 article "The Function of Musical Criticism." His 1898 book *What Is Good Music?* was his artistic credo, in which he drew a parallel between his ideas in music and Kant's concept of beauty.

WRITINGS

The Story of Music (New York, 1889, rev. 2/1912)
Preludes and Studies (New York, 1891)
How Music Developed (New York, 1898)
What Is Good Music? (New York, 1898/R1972, 6/1935)
The Orchestra and Orchestral Music (New York, 1899)
Richard Wagner: His Life and His Dramas (New York, 1901, 2/1923/R1971)
Modern Musical Drift (New York, 1904)
The Art of the Singer (New York, 1906, enlarged 2/1938/R1938 as *The Art of Singing*)

BIBLIOGRAPHY

Obituary, *New York Times* (6 June 1937)
O. Downes: "Brilliant Epoch in Criticism," *New York Times* (13 June 1937)
O. Thompson: "An American School of Criticism," *MQ*, xxiii (1937), 428
M. Sherwin: *The Classical Age of New York Musical Criticism, 1880–1920: A Study of Henry T. Finck, James G. Huneker, William J. Henderson, Henry E. Krehbiel, and Richard Aldrich* (diss., City College of New York, 1972)

H.P. Schurtz: *William James Henderson: his Views on the New York Musical World, 1887–1937* (diss., U. of Colorado, Boulder, 1980)

RAMONA H. MATTHEWS/DAVIDE CERIANI

Hendl, Walter (*b* West New York, NJ, 12 Jan 1917; *d* Erie, PA, 10 April 2007). Conductor and teacher. After studying with FRITZ REINER at the Curtis Institute, he taught at Sarah Lawrence College, New York, from 1939 to 1941. In 1941–2 he was a pianist and conductor at the Berkshire Music Center under Sergey Koussevitzky. In 1945 he became associate conductor of the New York PO, in 1949 he was appointed conductor of the Dallas SO, and from 1958 to 1964 he was associate conductor of the Chicago SO. He was also active with the Symphony of the Air and conducted its 1955 tour of East Asia. From 1964 to 1972 Hendl served as director of the Eastman School of Music at Rochester, New York, and was also musical adviser to the Rochester PO and its part-time conductor. In 1976 he was appointed music director of the Erie (Pennsylvania) PO, and in 1990 he became professor of conducting at Mercyhurst College in Erie. An advocate of contemporary music, he conducted the premieres of Peter Mennin's Symphony no.3 (with the New York PO, 1947), Bohuslav Martinů's Piano Concerto no.3 (with Rudolf Firkušný and the Dallas SO, 1949), and Heitor Villa-Lobos's Cello Concerto no.2 (with Aldo Parisot and the New York PO, 1954), as well as the American premiere of Dmitry Kabalevsky's Requiem (with students of the Eastman School, 1965). He composed incidental music for various stage productions and made several orchestral transcriptions.

GEORGE GELLES/JACOB HOSLER

Hendricks, Barbara (*b* Stephens, AR, 20 Nov 1948). American-Swedish soprano. After taking the BSC in mathematics and chemistry at the University of Nebraska, she studied at the Juilliard School with JENNIE TOUREL and first established herself as an accomplished concert singer. In 1973 she recorded the role of Clara in *Porgy and Bess* with Lorin Maazel, and the following year made her American debut in San Francisco and her European deébut at Glyndebourne; she also sang the role of Jeanne in Werner Egk's *Die Verlobung in San Domingo* at the St. Paul Opera summer festival. In 1975 she sang the title role in Leoš Janáček's *The Cunning Little Vixen* at Santa Fe and Nannetta (*Falstaff*) at Boston; in 1976 she sang the demanding solo role in the world premiere of David Del Tredici's *Final Alice* under Georg Solti. That year she also made her Salzburg Festival debut in Gustav Mahler's Symphony no.2. In 1982 Hendricks first sang at the Paris Opera as Gounod's Juliet and the same year sang Nannetta in Los Angeles and at Covent Garden. In 1985 she sang Liù at Bonn, and in 1987 she made her Metropolitan Opera debut as Strauss's Sophie. She also sang Liù with Zubin Mehta in the first performance of *Turandot* in Beijing's Forbidden City in 1998. Her repertory consists of more than twenty soubrette and lyric roles, including Susanna, Ilia, Antonia, Norina, and Mimi, all of which she has recorded. As a recitalist Hendricks specializes in Lieder and is known for her performances of French, American, and Scandinavian art song. She is an organizer of chamber music festivals and added jazz to her repertoire with her appearance at the Montreux Jazz Festival in 1994. She became a Swedish citizen after her marriage in 1978 to the music manager Martin Engstrom.

Hendricks is an activist with the United Nations High Commission for Refugees (UNHCR) and has been honored widely for her activism and her artistic achievements. In 1987 she was named UNHCR Goodwill Ambassador and has since been named Honorary Ambassador for Life. In 1998 she founded the Barbara Hendricks Foundation for Peace and Reconciliation.

BIBLIOGRAPHY

B. Scherer: "Mimi with a Method: on Becoming Barbara Hendricks." *ON,* liii (Aug 1988), 8–12

F.W. Martin: "Barbara Hendricks." *Encyclopedia of Arkansas,* <http://encyclopediaofarkansas.net/encyclopedia/entry-detail.aspx?entryID=2748>

ELIZABETH FORBES/KAREN M. BRYAN

Hendricks, Jon [John Carl] (*b* Newark, OH, 16 Sept 1921). Jazz singer, lyricist, and composer. One of 17 children he is the son of a preacher in the African Methodist Episcopal Church. Billed as the Sepia Bobby Breen, as a teenager Hendricks sang on local radio and performed with the pianist Art Tatum. After serving in the army during World War II (1942–6) he studied pre-law on the GI Bill at the University of Toledo. Encouraged by Charlie Parker he then moved to New York to pursue a singing career.

Hendricks is best known for his work with the pioneering vocal trio Lambert, Hendricks and Ross. The group's album *Sing a Song of Basie* (1957, ABC-Para.) made early use of overdubbing techniques; Dave Lambert transcribed and arranged the horn parts from Count Basie originals for the three singers and Hendricks wrote lyrics for them. The original trio disbanded in 1962, but Hendricks became known as the premiere writer of vocalese: the jazz critic and historian Leonard Feather called him the Poet Laureate of Jazz and *Time* dubbed him the James Joyce of Jive.

Hendricks wrote and directed *Evolution of the Blues*, a stage production depicting the history of African American music, for the Monterey Jazz Festival in 1960. His song "Yeh-Yeh" became a pop hit for Georgie Fame in 1965 and he recorded "Fire in the City" with the Warlocks (which changed its name to the Grateful Dead shortly thereafter) in 1966. After a period in Europe (1968–73), he moved to California, where he served as jazz critic for the *San Francisco Chronicle* and taught at California State University at Sonoma and the University of California at Berkeley. He often appeared with a family group including his wife Judith, son Eric, and daughters Michelle and Aria, as well as guests including Bobby McFerrin.

Hendricks was featured in Wynton Marsalis's jazz oratorio, *Blood on the Fields*. He reunited with his former trio-mate Annie Ross in 1999. The following year he was appointed Distinguished Professor of Jazz Studies at the University of Toledo, where he has arranged classical repertoire such as Rimsky-Korsakov's *Sheherazade* for his group Vocalstra. He was named an NEA Jazz Master in 1993.

BIBLIOGRAPHY

L. Pellegrinelli: *The Song is Who? Locating Singers on the Jazz Scene* (diss., Harvard U., 2005)

S. Josephson: *Jazz Notes: Interviews across the Generations* (Santa Barbara, 2009)

LARA PELLEGRINELLI

Hendrix, Jimi [Johnny Allen; James Marshall] (*b* Seattle, WA, 27 Nov 1942; *d* London, England, 18 Sept 1970). Rock guitarist, singer, and songwriter. Growing up in Seattle, he acquired his first electric guitar at age 16 after years of budding fascination with the instrument. A self-taught, left-handed guitarist he developed an unorthodox technique that involved playing the guitar upside down. Duane Eddy was an important early influence for Hendrix, evident in the repertory of his first band, the Velvetones. In his next venture, the Rocking Kings, he began to incorporate more elements drawn from B.B. King and other blues guitarists of the time. He left high school during his senior year and joined the US Army paratroopers, with which he was stationed at Fort Campbell, Kentucky. With another paratrooper, Billy Cox, he formed a group called the Kasuals; following his discharge from the army in 1962, Hendrix and Cox renewed their partnership as the King Kasuals. After a brief move back to the Northwest, Hendrix returned to the South and became a guitarist for hire.

The critic Nelson George aptly observed that Hendrix's rise to success could be considered "the revenge of the R&B sideman." From 1963 to 1965 the guitarist accompanied a number of African American performers on the so-called Chitlin' Circuit; these included Carla Thomas, Jerry Butler, Chuck Jackson, and Solomon Burke. In 1964 he moved to New York, where he soon began playing with the Isley Brothers, who encouraged his exhibitionist performing routine, which included playing the guitar with his teeth, with one hand, behind his back, and between his legs. His next significant assignment, as a member of Little Richard's Upsetters, was more difficult, as Richard admired Hendrix's skill but resented his budding flamboyance. Late in 1965 Hendrix joined Curtis Knight's band and played on some of its recordings; he subsequently toured with Joey Dee and the Starlighters, then joined the band of the saxophonist King Curtis.

By 1966 the center of Hendrix's musical and social life had moved from Harlem to Greenwich Village. Soaking up the influence of the Village's folk scene, and especially the music of Bob Dylan, he began playing at the Café Wha? on MacDougall Street with his own group, Jimmy James and the Blue Flames. During his tenure at the Wha?, he began experimenting in a more concerted way with the expressive potential of amplified sound; feedback, distortion, and high volume became principle creative tools. He won the admiration of several leading musicians, including Chas Chandler, the former bass player of English R&B group the Animals. Chandler became Hendrix's manager—soon joined by the Animals' manager Michael Jeffery—and took him to England in 1966.

Under Chandler's stewardship, Hendrix formed the Jimi Hendrix Experience with the bass guitarist Noel Redding (*b* Folkestone, England, 25 Dec 1945; *d* Clonakilty, Ireland, 11 May 2003) and the drummer Mitch Mitchell (*b* London, 9 July 1946; *d* Portland, OR, 12 Nov 2008). The group released its first single, "Hey Joe/ Stone Free," in December 1966. Hendrix's blackness lent him an air of exoticism to British audiences, which combined with his outrageous showmanship and the unusual racial constitution of the group—a black American guitarist and singer leading a white rhythm section—contributed to his becoming a highly visible figure in the world of British pop. At the same time, his exceptional guitar technique made an enormous impression on a range of British guitarists, including Eric Clapton, Jeff Beck, and Pete Townshend, who embraced Hendrix's innovations even as they felt challenged by his extravagant virtuosity.

Hendrix's first album, *Are you Experienced?* (Rep., 1967), combined the guitarist's exploratory approach to amplified sound with state of the art recording techniques facilitated by the recording engineer Eddie Kramer. "Purple Haze" was its most widely recognized track, its off-kilter guitar riff and drug-inspired lyric making it one of the hallmarks of psychedelic rock. Hendrix's solo on the album's title track was recorded and then played backwards for the final mix; on the songs "Third Stone from the Sun" and "I don't live

Jimi Hendrix, 1970. (AP Photo)

today" he demonstrated his acute ability to control the sound of guitar feedback through the manipulation of the tremolo arm and the toggle switch controlling the selection and combination of the pickups. As much as any album of the 1960s, *Are you Experienced?* expanded the sonic vocabulary of rock and provoked new recognition of the electric guitar's possibilities.

In the summer of 1967 the Experience made its first American appearance, at the Monterey International Pop Festival. Hendrix's set was one of the highlights of the festival, and his climactic cover of the Troggs' "Wild Thing" subsequently became etched in popular memory through D.A. Pennebaker's film documentary *Monterey Pop* (1968): Hendrix finished the song in a storm of distortion and feedback as he first simulated sex with his guitar thrusting into his amplifier, and then set his guitar on fire, smashed it to bits, and tossed its remains to the audience. Following this sacrificial act, Hendrix became a source of sensation and scandal. He began a tour of the United States with the pop group the Monkees, but his performances proved controversial and the engagement was soon canceled.

While his live performances drew notice for their unpredictable character, in the studio Hendrix showed increasing mastery of song craft and recording methods. His second album, *Axis: Bold as Love* (Rep., 1968), found him merging contemporary soul and R&B with rock to a greater degree than on his debut. "Little Miss Lover" was hard funk that foreshadowed the likes of Funkadelic, while "If Six was Nine" was a psychedelic blues anthem to countercultural independence. In a different register, "Little Wing" and "Castles Made of Sand" were two of the most affecting songs Hendrix recorded, the former a showcase for the guitarist's ability to merge rhythm and lead parts into a single unified voice.

The double album *Electric Ladyland* (Rep., 1968) was the last studio album Hendrix completed. During its recording Hendrix broke with Chandler, who was his producer as well as his co-manager, and subsequently completed it on his own with the assistance of Kramer. A sprawling two-record work, it spotlighted the range of Hendrix's creative concerns, from the improvisatory space-age blues of "Voodoo Chile" and "Voodoo Child (Slight Return)" to the acid funk of "Gypsy Eyes" and "House Burning Down," to the electronic soundscape that occupied most of the album's third side.

By the start of 1969 Hendrix was feeling burdened by his image as rock's wild man and when interviewed often gave voice to exhaustion and a desire to live free of his audience's expectations. In the spring of that year the Experience embarked on an extensive North American tour that culminated in the guitarist's arrest in Toronto, charged with possession of heroin and hashish. After a disastrous concert at Mile High Stadium in Denver, Redding departed the Experience, leaving Hendrix to reconfigure the band. After moving to a country house in rural New York, Hendrix invited a trio of African American and Latin American musicians—the guitarist Larry Lee and the percussionists Juma Sultan and Jerry Velez—to join him and his old musical comrade

Cox, who played bass guitar. Along with Mitchell, this group played the closing set of the Woodstock Music and Arts Fair on the morning of Monday 19 August 1969 to the remnants of the festival's estimated half-million attendees. Hendrix's Woodstock rendition of the "Star Spangled Banner," reproduced in the film and recording of the event, became one of the signature musical statements of the late 1960s, staging a battle between music and noise that articulated the ambivalence of a black artist's perspective on war and patriotism in the middle of the Vietnam War.

Hendrix and Cox subsequently began playing with the African American drummer Buddy Miles, calling themselves the Band of Gypsys. The trio's New Year's Eve concerts at Bill Graham's Fillmore East formed the basis for a live album, *Band of Gypsys* (Cap., 1970), which featured the stirring "Machine Gun," a 12-minute piece that extended Hendrix's use of the electric guitar as a vehicle for both meditating on and sonically evoking the violence of American politics and culture. By the following spring Mitchell had returned to play drums, and the trio of Hendrix, Cox, and Mitchell toured widely in the ensuing months. After the long awaited completion of Hendrix's Electric Lady recording studio in New York later that summer, they began to work on a new set of recordings. At the end of August Hendrix returned to England for his first concert appearance there in 18 months, at the Isle of Wight Festival. Less than three weeks later, on the morning of 18 September 1970, Hendrix was found dead in the London hotel room of a female companion, Monika Dannemann, from asphyxiation caused by drug-induced vomiting.

Hendrix has had one of the most productive posthumous careers of any major rock star. Music from his last sessions at Electric Lady studios formed the basis for two releases, *The Cry of Love* and *Rainbow Bridge* (both Rep., 1971), much of which compares favorably to his best studio work. Over the next decade, further studio tracks—many unfinished at the time of his death—formed the basis for several subsequent releases. The producer Alan Douglas drew considerable criticism for adding studio musicians to the material that was released on the albums *Midnight Lightning* and *Crash Landing*. Received more favorably were issues of Hendrix's live recordings, which have included *Hendrix in the West* (1972), *The Jimi Hendrix Concerts* (1982), and *Live at Winterland* (1987). Something of a milestone in the curation of Hendrix's legacy was reached in 1995, when his father Al Hendrix successfully sued for full control of his son's estate and then established Experience Hendrix, a family run corporation. Since then various efforts have been made to revisit the recordings Hendrix was working on at the time of his death in order to reconstruct the album he planned to call *First Rays of the New Rising Sun*. Further unreleased material has been issued on collections such as *Valleys of Neptune* (Legacy, 2010).

SELECTED RECORDINGS
Are you Experienced? (Rep., 1967); *Axis: Bold as Love* (Rep., 1968); *Electric Ladyland* (Rep., 1968); *Smash Hits* (Rep., 1969); *Band of Gypsys* (Cap., 1970); *The Cry of Love* (Rep., 1971); *Rainbow Bridge*

(Rep., 1971); *War Heroes* (Rep., 1972); *Hendrix in the West* (Pol., 1972); *Crash Landing* (Rep., 1975); *Midnight Lightning* (Rep., 1975); *Nine to the Universe* (Rep., 1980); *The Jimi Hendrix Concerts* (Rep., 1982); *Live at Winterland* (Ryko, 1987); *Radio One* (Ryko Analogue, 1988); *Blues* (MCA, 1994); *Valleys of Neptune* (Legacy, 2010)

BIBLIOGRAPHY

C. Knight: *Jimi: an Intimate Portrait of Jimi Hendrix* (New York, 1974)

D. Henderson: *'Scuse me while I Kiss the Sky: the Life of Jimi Hendrix* (Toronto, 1981)

N. George: *The Death of Rhythm and Blues* (New York, 1988)

C.S. Murray: *Crosstown Traffic: Jimi Hendrix and the Rock 'n' Roll Revolution* (New York, 1989)

C. Glebbeek and H. Shapiro: *Jimi Hendrix: Electric Gypsy* (New York, 1990)

M. Mitchell and J. Platt: *Jimi Hendrix: inside the Experience* (New York, 1990)

J. McDermott and E. Kramer: *Hendrix: Setting the Record Straight* (New York, 1992)

M. Willix: *Jimi Hendrix: Voices from Home* (Seattle, 1995)

N. Redding: *Are You Experienced? The Inside Story of the Jimi Hendrix Experience* (New York, 1996)

S. Waksman: "Black Sound, Black Body: Jimi Hendrix, the Electric Guitar, and the Meanings of Blackness," *Popular Music and Society*, xxiii/2 (1999), 75–114

G. Tate: *Midnight Lightning: Jimi Hendrix and the Black Experience* (Chicago, 2003)

C. Cross: *Room Full of Mirrors: a Biography of Jimi Hendrix* (New York, 2005)

STEVE WAKSMAN

Hengel, Christy [Christian] (*b* Wanda, MN, 25 Dec 1922; *d* New Ulm, MN, 11 Dec 2007). Maker and player of concertinas. Of Bohemian ancestry, he grew up listening to his mother, Anna Schroeder Hengel, sing German folk songs and popular tunes while accompanying herself on the organ. He was greatly influenced and inspired by concertina player "Whoopee" John Wilfahrt, also of Bohemian ancestry, whose recordings he heard as a child. At the age of 14 Hengel acquired his first button accordion, a mail-order Hohner factory-built instrument. He later switched to the Chemnitzer-style concertina (a bisonoric button instrument that sounds different pitches on the pushing in or pulling out of thee bellows). He never learned to read music instead playing entirely by ear. He performed with the Jolly Brewers Band and the Six Fat Dutchmen during the 1950s; he also played with Wilfahrt's band. In 1953 Hengel acquired the entire contents of the Chicago factory of Otto Schlicht (maker of concertinas under the brand names Patek and Pearl), and in 1955 he built his first accordion. He later made several innovations to older concertina designs, including a lighter body and improvements on its reeds. In 1965 he moved to New Ulm, where he continued to build accordions. He was inducted into the Minnesota Music Hall of Fame in that year and was honored as a National Heritage Fellow by the National Endowment for the Arts in 1989. In 1997 Jerry Minar of New Prague, Minnesota, purchased Christy Hengel's accordion manufacturing business, and has continued to build Hengel concertinas.

BIBLIOGRAPHY

M. Hunt and B. Weintraub: "Masters of Traditional Arts," *National Geographic*, clxxix/1 (1991), 74–101

L.J. Rippley: *The Chemnitzer Concertina: a History and an Accolade* (Northfield, MN, 2006)

RON EMOFF

Henley, Don(ald Hugh) (*b* Gilmer, TX, 22 July 1947). Singer/songwriter and drummer. He began his career as a drummer and singer for the country rock band Shiloh. He co-founded the EAGLES in 1971, his songwriting partnership with bandmate Glenn Frey resulting in some of the best-selling songs of the 1970s. Henley launched a solo career in the early 1980s with the hit "Dirty Laundry" from the album *I Can't Stand Still* (1982). His early work departed from the country rock sound of the Eagles in its reliance on a new guitarist/producer (Danny Kortchmar) and the synthesizer, an instrument Henley would feature throughout the 1980s. His second album, *Building the Perfect Beast* (1984), established him as a pop star, delivering the hits "Boys of Summer" and "All She Wants to Do Is Dance." His most commercially successful project was *The End of the Innocence* (1989), a work that most directly expressed the themes of his songwriting career: coming of age, nostalgia, regret, and biting social critique. As with his second album, this one was supported by multiple guitarists, backing vocalists, and keyboard players employed to create a full and varied pop sound. Heavily influenced by soul, Henley's rough-timbred tenor is easily recognizable and characterized by a straight tone, short falling melismas at the ends of phrases, and a subtle accent that also lends a country sound to his singing. He paused from recording during the 1990s for reasons pertaining to his recording contract and to participate in an Eagles reunion. He resumed with *Inside Job* (2000). He has founded environmental nonprofits (for example, the Walden Woods Project) and co-founded the Recording Artists Commission, an organization that advocates for the interests of artists in the music industry.

OLIVIA CARTER MATHER

Henschel, Jane (*b* Appleton, WI, 2 March 1952). Mezzo-soprano. She studied with Ruth Michaelis and Nina Hinson at the University of Southern California. At the time there were limited opportunities in the United States for big voices, so Henschel worked her way up in the European tradition, moving through the German repertory opera houses and starting her career in concerts and oratorios. In 1978 she joined the opera company at Aachen, moving to Wuppertal in 1981 and Dortmund in 1983, ending up with the Deutsche Oper am Rhein. In these years she built up a large repertory, including the major mezzo roles in Verdi and Wagner. Her international career gained momentum when at the Netherlands Opera in 1992 she first sang the high dramatic role of the Nurse in Richard Strauss's *Die Frau ohne Schatten*. A critic for *Opera* asserted that she was "the controlling presence whenever she was on stage." In the following years her reputation was built on dramatic mezzo roles such as Waltraute and Fricka, a role she sang also in the *Ring* at La Scala. Henschel has been closely associated with 20th-century operas such as those of Leoš Janáček, Arnold Schoenberg's *Erwartung*, Harrison Birtwistle's *Punch and Judy*, and Isaac Albeniz's *Henry Clifford*. Her recordings include Mahler's Symphony no.8, the Witch in *Hansel and Gretel* under Charles Mackerras, and a vibrant, richly characterized portrayal of Baba the Turk in *The Rake's Progress* conducted by Seiji Ozawa. One of the most adaptable of singers, with an extensive repertory beyond opera, Henschel currently resides in Düsseldorf, Germany and remains in steady demand internationally.

J.B. STEANE/MEREDITH ELIASSEN

Henschel, Sir (Isidor) George [Georg] (*b* Breslau [now Wrocław, Poland], 18 Feb 1850; *d* Aviemore, Scotland, 10 Sept 1934). English baritone, conductor, and composer of German birth. His early career was spent in Europe after he had studied at the Leipzig and Berlin conservatories. In 1877 he moved to England, where he met his future wife, the American soprano Lillian Bailey. While in Boston before their wedding, they performed several recitals and appeared as Mephistopheles and Gretchen, respectively, in B.J. Lang's performance of Berlioz's *La damnation de Faust* on 12 November 1880.

In March 1881, Henschel led the Harvard Musical Association orchestra in an overture of his own composition, and his conducting attracted considerable attention. Henry Lee Higginson, who wished to establish a permanent symphony orchestra for Boston and was looking for a conductor, engaged him immediately. There was some criticism of the selection at first, in part because Henschel's appointment was deemed a slight to local conductors and in part because his multiple talents aroused suspicion as to his competence in any one area, but he came to be regarded as a fine musician, if not a stern drillmaster; he also established the orchestra's score library. His first season included all the Beethoven symphonies played in chronological order; the Ninth was performed at the last concert of the season with a volunteer chorus of subscribers and others. He conducted the same cycle in his second and third seasons as well. Toward the end of his career, in 1927, Henschel participated in the first cycle of the recorded Beethoven symphonies; in his only recording as a conductor, he led the Royal Philharmonic in a performance of Symphony no.1.

During his three seasons with the Boston SO, he conducted nearly 200 concerts, including public rehearsals for which admission was 25 cents; he also sang often with the SO and composed a number of works that received their premieres there. Henschel worked hard to promote the music of his friend Brahms, who was regarded by the Boston public and critics as a difficult and unrewarding composer. He was an extremely adventuresome programmer, presenting music from England, Scandinavia, and Russia. He also supported American composers and conducted the first performance of George Whitefield Chadwick's *Thalia* and the scherzo of his then-unfinished Second Symphony. As a baritone soloist, he appeared 14 times with the Handel and Haydn Society, in addition to vocal performances with

other organizations, and recitals with his wife. He served as his own accompanist when singing in performance and on his recordings.

After three seasons in Boston, Henschel moved to England, though he returned to Boston as a singer and conductor on several occasions. These included a performance by the Boston Cecilia Society of his *Missa pro defunctis*, composed in memory of his wife, in which he and his daughter Helen took the leading vocal parts, and a concert in 1930 by the Boston SO, which, for the opening of the orchestra's 50th season, re-created Henschel's first program. His compositions include two operas, a number of sacred choral works, about 20 piano pieces, and many songs and duets. Besides his book of memoirs, he published *Personal Recollections of J. Brahms* (1907) and *Articulation in Singing* (1918).

Henschel composed three works for the stage. Nothing seems to have come of his first opera, *Friedrich der Schöne*. At the end of his last season with the Boston SO, he collaborated with the American writer William Dean Howells on a comic opera conceived in the style of Gilbert and Sullivan and planned for production in the United States and England. He composed *A Sea-Change, or Love's Stowaway,* in 1884. The work was to be performed at the Bijou Theatre in Boston in November, but the death of the impresario brought the production to a halt. A small orchestra at the Boston Museum performed a read-through of the music on 27 January 1885, possibly to attract backers for a production; it received a generally favorable reaction, though one reviewer thought the music more suitable for a cantata performed by the Handel and Haydn Society. Sullivan's influence shows in a mock-Handelian number, and a march with "a flavor of Lohengrin about it" is set in counterpoint to "Yankee Doodle." The action takes place aboard the steamer *Mesopotamia,* two days out from Boston. An edited version of the opera finally received two broadcast performances on the BBC in 1929.

Henschel's serious three-act opera, *Nubia*, was composed in 1898–9 to a libretto by Max Kalbeck based on a novel by Richard Voss. The story, set in the Sabine hills of Italy, concerns a fatal love triangle between an Italian peasant girl, a German painter, and a rival suitor. The work was first performed in Dresden on 9 November 1899. Most of the critics described it as "aristocratic music" that remained uninvolved with the drama; there were also complaints of thinness and lack of variety in the scoring. Two days after the first performance, one of the singers became ill and Henschel himself (in his only operatic appearance) sang the role of Fra Girolamo.

BIBLIOGRAPHY

H.T. Parker and A. Foote: "George Henschel's Fifty Years: the Symphony's First Conductor," *Boston Evening Transcript* (30 Oct 1912)

M.A.D. Howe: *The Boston Symphony Orchestra: an Historical Sketch* (Boston, 1914, rev. and enlarged 2/1931/R1978)

G. Henschel: *Musings and Memories of a Musician* (New York, 1919/R1979)

B. Perry: *The Life and Letters of Henry Lee Higginson* (Boston, 1921)

H. Henschel: *When Soft Voices Die* (London, 1944)
H. Bloch: *Directory of Conductors' Archives in American Institutions* (Lanham, MD, 2006)
G.S. Bozarth: *Johannes Brahms & Georg Henschel: An Enduring Friendship* (Sterling Heights, MI, 2008)

STEVEN LEDBETTER/BRIAN BELL

Henson-Conant, Deborah (*b* Stockton, CA, 11 Nov 1953). Harpist, composer, and entertainer. She studied classical harp with Linda Wood at the University of California, Berkeley. An NEA grant supported her study of jazz and, in 1982, she launched a touring career. About this time, she started to amplify the instrument. In 1989, Henson-Conant was signed to GRP Records, with which she made three recordings. She also went on a world tour and recorded for the Laika label (in Germany) as well as her own White Cat company. In 1998, tiring of transporting a concert harp on tour, she asked the Camac Harp Company to design an 11-pound solid-body electric lever harp that could be strapped onto her body. Describing herself as a jazz-pop-comedy-folk-blues-flamenco-Celtic harpist, Henson-Conant mixes music with theatrical and storytelling elements in her performances. She writes solo harp music and symphonic music featuring her harp and voice. The soundtrack of her 2006 DVD release *Invention & Alchemy* received a Grammy nomination. To date, she has released more than a dozen albums.

BIBLIOGRAPHY
K. Rowe: "More Power to Her," *Harp Column* iii/3 (1995), 18–23
A. Reese: "Reinventing Deborah," *Harp Column* xv/1 (2006), 18–23, 26, 28–33
J. Otis: "Feature Interview: Deborah Henson-Conant," *International Musician Magazine* (2007), 20–21.

SUZANNE L. MOULTON-GERTIG

Hentoff, Nat(han Irving) (*b* Boston, MA, 10 June 1925). Writer. As a young man, he attended the Boston Latin School and Northeastern University (BA 1945), where he wrote for the *Northeastern University News*. He briefly pursued postgraduate work in American studies at Harvard University (1946) and received a Fulbright Fellowship to study in Paris (1950) before leaving academia to pursue a career in jazz. Hentoff worked as a staff announcer at radio station WMEX (1944–53) and convinced the station to let him program a jazz show that ran for several years. He left Boston in 1953 and became the New York editor of *Down Beat* (1953–7), a position from which he was fired for hiring a staff person of color. In 1957, Hentoff was hired as a columnist for the *Village Voice*, for which he continued writing until 2009. He was also co-founder and editor of *Jazz Review* (1958–61). His first book, *Hear Me Talkin' to Ya* (1955, with Nat Shapiro), proved widely influential as the first jazz history told exclusively in the words of musicians. The text weaves together quotes from dozens of musician interviews into a linear narrative of music's history, an approach that would be imitated by several subsequent jazz researchers. He has written and edited over 30 books on music and politics, as well as several novels. In 1957 he served as a music consultant for *The Sound of Jazz*, a historic live television show

featuring performances by 32 major jazz figures. From 1960 to 1961 he worked as A&R director for Candid Records, during which time the label produced several significant recordings including Max Roach's *We Insist! Freedom Now Suite.*

Although jazz remained a major interest, much of Hentoff's writing shifted to political issues after 1960. His *Village Voice* column generally focused on politics, though he continued to write about jazz in other publications including the *New Yorker, Jazz Times,* and the *Wall Street Journal.* In cases when these interests overlap, his writing highlights connections between jazz, civil rights, and American political history. He is considered a foremost authority on the First Amendment and in 2009 was named a senior fellow at the Cato Institute in Washington DC. In 2004, Hentoff became the first nonmusician to be named a Jazz Master by the National Endowment for the Arts.

WRITINGS
ed., with N. Shapiro: *Hear Me Talkin' to Ya: the Story of Jazz by the Men who Made it* (New York, 1955/R)
ed., with N. Shapiro: *The Jazz Makers* (New York, 1957/R)
ed., with A.J. McCarthy: *Jazz: New Perspectives on the History of Jazz* (New York, 1959/R)
with D. Stock: *Jazz Street* (Garden City, NY, 1960)
The Jazz Life (New York, 1961/R)
Jazz Is (New York, 1976/R)
Boston Boy (New York, 1986, 2/2001) [autobiography]
Listen to the Stories (New York, 1995)
Speaking Freely: a Memoir (New York, 1997)
American Music Is (Cambridge, 2004)
with L. Porter: *At the Jazz Band Ball: Sixty Years on the Jazz Scene* (Berkeley, 2010)

MICHAEL C. HELLER

Heppner, Ben (*b* Murrayville, BC, 14 Jan 1956). Canadian tenor. He studied at the University of British Columbia and during the mid-1980s sang lyrical roles with the Toronto-based Canadian Opera Company Ensemble. In 1986 he sang Sandy in Peter Maxwell Davies's *The Lighthouse* at the Guelph Spring Festival, then decided to study as a dramatic tenor with William Neill. He won the Birgit Nilsson prize from the American-Scandinavian Foundation (1988), then sang Bacchus (*Ariadne auf Naxos*) in Melbourne. He went on to sing the roles of Lohengrin in Stockholm and San Francisco (1989), Walther von Stolzing at Seattle, La Scala, and Covent Garden (1990), Bacchus at Santa Fe and Frankfurt, and Florestan at Cologne and Vienna. In 1991 Heppner performed as Laca (*Jenůfa*) in Brussels, Erik (*Der fliegende Holländer*) in Geneva, and Idomeneo in Amsterdam; the following year he sang Dvořák's Dimitrij in Munich and Mozart's Titus at Salzburg. He created the title role of William Bolcom's *McTeague* at Chicago and made his Metropolitan Opera debut as Laca. He returned to Covent Garden as Peter Grimes (1995) and to Toronto as Canio (1996). In 2000 Heppner sang the Emperor in *Die Frau ohne Schatten* at the Vienna Staatsoper, and the same year sang Florestan in a new production of *Fidelio* at the Metropolitan. In 2001 he made his Paris Opéra debut as Peter Grimes and sang Berlioz's Aeneas in concert, under Colin Davis, at the Barbican in London. In the 21st century Heppner has turned to Wagner's *heldentenor* roles. In 1998 he made his debut as Tristan in Seattle and has returned to the role at the Metropolitan (2001), Covent Garden (2009), and the Bavarian State Opera (2011). He has sung the title role in *Siegfried* as well as Siegfried in *Götterdämmerung* (Aix-en-Provence and Salzburg) and the title role in *Lohengrin* (Berlin and Los Angeles).

He has made notable recordings of Walther von Stolzing, Lohengrin, Grimes, Erik, Florestan, Huon (*Oberon*), Jean (*Hérodiade*), Chénier, and Calaf, all of which display his powerfully dramatic voice, with its solid middle register and ringing top notes, and his vivid sense of character. Heppner is also a noted interpreter of such non-operatic works as Mahler's Symphony no.8 and *Das Lied von der Erde* and Arnold Schönberg's Gurre-Lieder. Important appearances on video include *Tristan und Isolde* (Metropolitan Opera, 2001) and *Die Meistersinger von Nürnberg* (Metropolitan Opera, 2003).

BIBLIOGRAPHY
P. Dyson: "Ben Heppner," *Opera*, xlvi (1995), 1146–53
I. Siff: "Returning Champion," *ON*, lxix/7 (2005), 16–20

ELIZABETH FORBES/JOSEPH E. MORGAN

Herbert [Hostetter; Houstellier], **Evelyn** (*b* Philadelphia, PA, 18 March 1898; *d* Newport Beach, CA, 22 Feb 1975). Soprano. Trained as an opera singer, Herbert became one of the leading operetta stars of the 1920s and early 1930s. She appeared on Broadway in Jerome Kern and Anne Caldwell's *Stepping Stones* (1923) and an adaptation of Offenbach's *The Love Song* (1925) before creating the female leads in four operettas by Sigmund Romberg: Princess Flavia in *Princess Flavia* (1925), Barbara Frietchie in *My Maryland* (1927), Marianne Beaunoir in *The New Moon* (1928), and Andrée De Nemours/Paula DeLaurier in *Melody* (1933). Herbert was known for her full-bodied lyrical singing and fluid coloratura as well as her physical beauty. She married baritone Robert Halliday, her co-star in *The New Moon*; the couple appeared together in *Princess Charming* (1930) and the London production of *Waltzes from Vienna* (1931). Her final Broadway appearance was in the 1934 revival of *Bitter Sweet*.

WILLIAM A. EVERETT

Herbert, Victor (August) (*b* Dublin, Ireland, 1 Feb 1859; *d* New York, NY, 26 May 1924). Composer, conductor, and cellist of Irish birth. He was the most talented and successful American operetta composer and important also as an advocate of copyright and performance-rights protection for composers.

1. Life. 2. Stage works. (i) Operettas. (ii) Operas. 3. Instrumental music.

1. LIFE. Herbert's father died when the boy was an infant, and he grew up in London with his maternal grandfather, the celebrated Irish novelist, poet, and composer Samuel Lover (1798–1868). In 1866 Fanny Lover Herbert married a German physician; the family settled in Stuttgart, where Victor received musical training as well as a strong liberal education. He retained a lasting pride in his Irish (Protestant) heritage, reflected in many of his operettas.

He turned to music when financial difficulties prevented him from pursuing medicine, studied the cello with Bernhard Cossmann (1874–6), and entered the Stuttgart Conservatory, where he studied with Max Seifritz. He spent a year in the orchestra of the wealthy Russian baron Paul von Derwies and another year in Vienna as a soloist with the orchestra of Eduard Strauss, who had succeeded his brother Johann. In the light of his operetta work, the time in Vienna must be regarded as a significant formative experience. In 1881 he joined the court orchestra in Stuttgart, where he met his future wife, Therese Foerster (1861–1927), a soprano in the court opera. During five years there, he appeared as a soloist in his first two large-scale works, the Suite for Cello and Orchestra op.3 and the Cello Concerto no.1 op.8. Soon after their marriage on 14 August 1886, the Herberts sailed for the United States. Therese had been engaged by the Metropolitan Opera to sing (in German) the title role in the American premiere of *Aida*; Victor was to be principal cellist in the orchestra.

Herbert immediately began to play an active role in New York musical life as a cello soloist, a member of the New York String Quartet, and assistant conductor to Anton Seidl during summer concerts at Brighton Beach. He went on to conduct at summer concerts and festivals, where his programming of lighter works along with more serious repertory created the model for the Victor Herbert Orchestra. He joined the faculty of the National Conservatory of Music, probably in autumn 1889. His compositions at this time were concert works, culminating in the Cello Concerto no.2, op.30 (1894). In 1893 he became director of the 22nd Regiment Band, founded by Patrick S. Gilmore; with this ensemble he toured widely for seven years, performing original band compositions and transcriptions from the orchestral repertory. He composed his first operetta, *Prince Ananias*, in 1894 for a popular troupe called the Bostonians. From then on he occasionally drew upon material from his operettas for a number of fine band marches.

By the turn of the century Herbert had achieved considerable success as an operetta composer (*The Serenade*, 1897, and *The Fortune Teller*, 1898), but he withdrew from the theater to concentrate on his position as conductor of the Pittsburgh SO (1898–1904). He developed the orchestra to the point where it was compared favorably with the Boston SO and the New York PO. A disagreement with the management led to his resignation, whereupon he founded the Victor Herbert Orchestra, which he conducted on tours and at summer resorts for most of the rest of his life in programs of light orchestral music.

Before resigning his Pittsburgh position, Herbert had returned to the theater with *Babes in Toyland* (1903), the first of a series of hits that made him one of the best-known figures in American music. It was followed by *Mlle Modiste* (1905) and *The Red Mill* (1906), both signal successes. In 1908 he was elected to the National Institute of Arts and Letters. After an extended search for a serious opera libretto, he composed *Natoma*,

Victor Herbert. (Lebrecht Music & Arts)

By the end of World War I, musical styles in the popular theater were greatly changed. Herbert changed with them to a degree, writing several "musical comedies" with simpler songs and less elaborate ensembles, but his heart remained with the European-style operetta created for highly trained singers. In the last decade of his career, he was often called upon to provide the ballet music for elaborate production numbers in revues or shows by such composers as Irving Berlin or Jerome Kern.

2. STAGE WORKS.

(i) Operettas. Herbert was a prolific composer for the theater, occasionally working on as many as four shows simultaneously. He wrote well over 50 full scores for the stage, in addition to numbers for the Ziegfeld Follies and elaborate private skits for entertainments of the Lambs, a theatrical club. Although he had as thorough a grounding in his craft as any American composer of his day, he never lost the popular touch or the desire to reach large audiences with his music.

During the early part of Herbert's career, activity in the musical theater was widely dispersed via traveling companies that commissioned shows and produced them in their home base, though usually with a New York run as well. A long run on Broadway was not necessary for success on the road, although acclaim in New York naturally publicized the show and helped receipts elsewhere. Gradually, as Broadway became the focus of American theatrical life, shows were crafted specifically to meet New York tastes. Besides those for the operettas mentioned above, other strong scores are those for *The Serenade* (1897), *The Fortune Teller* (1898), *Cyrano de Bergerac* (1899), *The Singing Girl* (1899), *The Enchantress* (1911), *The Madcap Duchess* (1913), and *The Only Girl* (1914). In musical quality they compare favorably with the works of the principal European operetta composers.

During the 1890s American musical theater productions were likely to be imitations either of Gilbert and Sullivan or of Viennese operetta. Several Millöcker works and Suppé's *Boccaccio* were exceptionally popular in America (the latter always bowdlerized). Herbert's German education and his experience in the Strauss orchestra assured his thorough understanding of the Viennese style (the Viennese lilt is evident in his own recordings of waltz tunes from his operettas). Although Herbert had never heard the work of Gilbert and Sullivan before his arrival in America in 1886, he learned their style because American theatrical companies such as the Bostonians had been founded to perform *HMS Pinafore*, and newer works written to suit the talents of the members inevitably bore at least a family resemblance to the Savoy operas.

Herbert preferred to compose for trained singers rather than for comedians who sang, and the operettas he wrote for such stars as Alice Nielson (*The Fortune Teller*), Fritzi Scheff (*Mlle Modiste*) or Emma Trentini (*Naughty Marietta*) placed great demands on the chorus and orchestra as well as the principals. These operettas

which was produced in Philadelphia by the Philadelphia-Chicago Opera Company on 25 February 1911 and remained in its repertory for three years. *Madeleine*, a lighter work in one act, was produced at the Metropolitan Opera on 24 January 1914 but proved too slight to retain a hold in the repertory.

While composing two operas, Herbert was working on more operettas, including two of the finest, *Naughty Marietta* (1910) and *Sweethearts* (1913). His longstanding wish to compose an Irish operetta was finally gratified with the production of *Eileen* (1917; originally titled *Hearts of Erin*), which boasts a solid libretto concerning the Irish rebellion of 1798 and a rich score, but which marks the end of the production of his greatest theater pieces. He had also composed one of the first original orchestral scores for a full-length film, *The Fall of a Nation* (1916). Long thought to be lost, the score was rediscovered in the film-music collection of the Library of Congress and recorded in 1987.

Herbert was an active fighter for the legal rights of composers. His testimony before Congress had great impact on the American copyright law of 1909, which, among other provisions, secured composers' royalties on the sales of sound recordings. In 1914 he was one of the founders of ASCAP, of which he remained a vice president and director until his death, and in 1917 he won a landmark suit carried to the Supreme Court giving composers the right to collect performance fees (through ASCAP) for public performance of their work.

tended to reflect the Viennese tradition, though Herbert was perfectly capable of writing in the Gilbert and Sullivan tradition when required, as in the quintet "Cleopatra's Wedding Day" from *The Wizard of the Nile*. Harry B. Smith's libretto for *The Serenade*, Herbert's first major success, consists largely of situations taken from *The Pirates of Penzance* and *The Gondoliers*, reassembled into an effective comic plot. Smith's habit of reusing Gilbertian ideas continued to draw forth Sullivanesque music from Herbert. In *The Singing Girl*, an Austrian minister of police named Aufpassen enforces a dreaded law against kissing without a license in obvious imitation of *The Mikado*.

Vienna was a stronger influence in Herbert's operettas, including those with librettos by Smith. The most characteristic Herbert song was the waltz. Many of his waltzes achieved remarkable popularity, although they were beyond the technique of most amateurs. Another specialty was the variation song, with a series of refrains in different styles (for example, "Serenades of All Nations" from *The Fortune Teller*, in which a ballerina demonstrates serenades by admirers from Ireland, Spain, China, Italy, France, and Haiti) or actual variations of the same tune ("The Song of the Poet" from *Babes in Toyland*, which turned the familiar lullaby "Rock-a-Bye Baby" into a brassy march, a Neapolitan song, or a ragtime song).

Herbert also excelled in imitations of traditional music in operettas with exotic settings. These include evocations of Spain (*The Serenade*), Italy (*Naughty Marietta*), Austria (*The Singing Girl*), and the East (*The Wizard of the Nile*, *The Idol's Eye*, *The Tattooed Man*, and other works with settings from Egypt to India). In *The Fortune Teller* he managed to match Strauss for a vigorous *csárdás*. Except for *Eileen*, the frequent Irish songs in his operettas are incidental to the plot.

Herbert's career in the theater lasted from 1894 to 1924, a period of great changes in the style of popular musical shows. In the last decade of his life he wrote in the musically simpler style coming into favor and imitated popular new song types including ragtime, the tango, and the foxtrot. He collaborated with Irving Berlin in *The Century Girl* (1916). These later shows contain memorable numbers, but the real Herbert personality remained evident in the more elaborate operettas of the older style, and by far the biggest hit in this late period was the waltz song "A Kiss in the Dark" from *Orange Blossoms* (1922). Nonetheless, with *The Red Mill* (1906) he was already approaching the fast-moving directness of the later musical comedy with considerable success.

Henry Blossom's libretto for *The Red Mill* features a low-comedy pair of traveling Americans, Con Kidder and Kid Conner, who arrive penniless in Katwyk-ann-Zee. The plot contains all the requisite features of comic opera integrated into a scenario far better than most; its complications allow Con and Kid to adopt various disguises, including those of Sherlock Holmes and Dr. Watson. Herbert's score incorporates popular idioms and contains some of his most enduring music, including "Every Day Is Ladies' Day with Me," the waltz "The

Streets of New York," and the ragtime ensemble "Go While the Goin' Is Good," which characterizes the main characters.

Herbert was equally comfortable with comedic plots and romantic, escapist tales, creating music appropriate to each style. *Naughty Marietta* (1910) demonstrates the latter approach. Commissioned by Oscar Hammerstein, the operetta showcased the temperamental diva Emma Trentini, tenor Orville Harrold, and contralto Marthe Duchne (all of whom had performed at the Metropolitan Opera House). Rida Johnson Young's libretto, set in the 18th century, concerns a European countess who, escaping an unhappy union, finds her way to New Orleans and falls in love with the pirate-hunting Captain Dick Warrington. Comedic elements are present but of limited importance in this swashbuckling story that allowed Trentini to dress as a boy and provided ample scope for some of Herbert's most enduring and expansive numbers: "'Neath the Southern Moon," "Tramp, Tramp, Tramp," "I'm Falling in Love with Someone," "Italian Street Song," and "Ah! Sweet Mystery of Life." The 1935 film version, starring Jeanette MacDonald and Nelson Eddy, had a revised storyline.

Herbert used a slightly larger orchestra than did Sullivan, often employing a harp and more varied percussion instruments to colorful effect. Except when short of time, he wrote his own orchestrations, and his handling of the theater orchestra consistently attracted the highest praise from critics and fellow composers. Almost without exception, later revivals used updated orchestrations, heavy with saxophones and far from his own string-dominated sonorities.

Many of Herbert's stage works were criticized for poor librettos and conventional lyrics though he repeatedly collaborated with some of the era's most prolific writers, including Harry Bache Smith (*The Fortune Teller*, *Miss Dolly Dollars*), Henry Blossom (*Mlle Modiste*, *The Red Mill*), and Glen MacDonough (*Babes in Toyland*). A large-scale rediscovery of Herbert's operettas has been hindered by weaknesses in their books, and several revivals have used heavily rewritten librettos. Herbert's theater works continue to be resurrected, most often by regional operetta companies whose productions may not be fully staged and which may not employ full orchestra. Among the most successful are those by the Ohio Light Opera, the Canton Comic Opera Company (also in Ohio), and the Comic Opera Guild (Ann Arbor, MI). In addition, an annual Victor Herbert Festival takes place in Saratoga Springs, New York. In spite of alterations to libretto or orchestration, such presentations successfully reacquaint audiences with Herbert's musical charms and may be harbingers of a more general reconsideration of his art.

(ii) Operas. With his thorough musical training and extensive theatrical experience, Herbert naturally wished to compose a serious opera. Because of his popularity, the mere announcement that he had signed a contract with Oscar Hammerstein I to produce a grand opera and that the impresario had offered $1000 for a libretto (*Musical America*, 13 April 1907) triggered nationwide

speculation and enthusiasm. The choice of libretto and the progress of the composition and production were followed eagerly by the press, raising expectations that could hardly be filled with the most glorious of successes. Although *Natoma* was produced with great care and with a cast featuring John McCormack and Mary Garden, the 1911 premiere enjoyed only a succès d'estime, mainly because of the weakness of Joseph Redding's book and the use of French, Irish, and Italian singers in what was proclaimed as an American opera (it is set on the Californian coast in the 1820s and concerns the love of an American naval officer for an Amerindian princess). Herbert, an ardent admirer of Wagner, wrote a score that effectively mingled leitmotif construction in a continuing orchestral counterpoint with colorful and melodious set pieces.

Herbert's only other opera was *Madeleine*, a one-act comedy based on a French play about a prima donna. At the premiere in 1914 it was paired with *IPagliacci*, with Caruso in the principal part. *Madeleine* functioned as little more than a curtain-raiser. Its style is conversational throughout, with continuing motivic commentary from the orchestra. The one real set piece, "A Perfect Day," was added at the last moment at the insistence of Frances Alda, who refused to sing the title role otherwise.

Madeleine was dropped from the repertory of the Metropolitan Opera after half a dozen performances, though G. Schirmer published the work in full score, an unprecedented distinction for an American opera.

3. INSTRUMENTAL MUSIC. Herbert's instrumental music fell out of favor after his death, though it has begun to reappear in concerts and recordings. The one substantial exception was the Cello Concerto no.2 in E minor, first performed by the composer with the New York PO under Anton Seidl in 1894. The work is Lisztian in its thorough-going employment of thematic transformation in all three movements. Not only did it enjoy an immediate success with the audience, but it also inspired Antonín Dvořák, who knew Herbert well as a colleague at the National Conservatory, to compose his own Concerto in B minor. Two earlier compositions have begun to return to the repertory. The Suite for Cello and Orchestra (1884), which, despite being identified as op.3 on the published score, is Herbert's earliest known composition, already foreshadows the successful composer of light music (especially in the fourth movement, which was arranged for many instruments and combinations), and the finale, filled with virtuoso runs in octaves, gives some indication of the composer's technical abilities. Herbert gave the first performance of the Cello Concerto no.1 in Stuttgart shortly before leaving for the United States. The work remained in manuscript, evidently unperformed, although a 1986 recording reveals an attractive composition that effectively balances the requirements of lyrical expression and virtuosity.

Herbert composed his most important purely orchestral work, the tone poem *Hero and Leander* (1901), for the Pittsburgh SO during his time there. The work reflects his admiration for Liszt and Wagner in its programmatic outline, its thematic transformations, and the Tristanesque climax of the storm that brings about Leander's death. Also dating from the Pittsburgh years is a four-movement programmatic suite, *Columbus*, op.35; the first and last movements had been composed to accompany a theatrical spectacle at the 1893 Columbian Exposition in Chicago, but the project was never completed. Herbert added two middle movements in 1902 and gave the first performance himself in 1903. It was his last score of a symphonic nature.

Herbert also regularly composed smaller works—miniatures either for his own performance as a cellist or for the Victor Herbert Orchestra. In his last years he concentrated on overtures commissioned for feature films (for which, with the exception of *The Fall of a Nation*, he did not write the rest of the score). His last appearance as the composer of a new work was in the famous Aeolian Hall concert of 12 February 1924, the "Experiment in Modern Music" produced by Paul Whiteman and best known for being the occasion of the premiere of George Gershwin's *Rhapsody in Blue*. Herbert's work for this occasion, *A Suite of Serenades*, was a set of exotic character pieces not notably modern in spirit, but he also made suggestions regarding Gershwin's piece (which he admired greatly) to its composer. Evidently a healthy man at 65, Herbert died suddenly of a heart attack three months later, shortly after his final show, *The Dream Girl*, began its pre-Broadway run in New Haven, Connecticut.

WORKS
(Printed works published in New York unless otherwise stated)

STAGE
(Unless otherwise stated, dates are of first performance)
Prince Ananias (2, F. Neilson), 1894 (1895); The Wizard of the Nile (3, H.B. Smith), 1895; The Gold Bug (musical blend, 2, G. MacDonough), 1896, excerpts (1895); The Serenade (3, Smith), 1897; The Idol's Eye (3, Smith), 1897; The Fortune Teller (3, Smith), 1898; Cyrano de Bergerac (3, Smith; S. Reed, after E. Rostand), 1899; The Singing Girl (3, Smith; S. Strange), 1899; The Ameer (extravaganza, 3, K. La Shelle; F. Ranken), 1899; The Viceroy (3, Smith), 1900; Babes in Toyland (extravaganza, 3, MacDonough), 1903; Babette (romantic comic op, 3, Smith), 1903; It Happened in Nordland (musical extravaganza, 2, MacDonough), 1904 (1905); Miss Dolly Dollars (musical comedy, 2, Smith), 1905; Wonderland [Alice and the Eight Princesses] (musical extravaganza, 3, MacDonough), 1905; Mlle Modiste (2, H. Blossom), 1905; The Red Mill (musical comedy, 2, Blossom), 1906; Dream City (2, E. Smith), 1906 (1907); The Magic Knight [Night] (operatic burlesque, 1, E. Smith), 1906 (1907); The Tattooed Man (2, H.B. Smith and A.N.C. Fowler; H.B. Smith), 1907; Miss Camille (musical skit, G.V. Hobart), 1907, excerpts (1907); The Song Birds (musical skit, Hobart), 1907, excerpts (1907); Algeria (musical play, MacDonough), 1908, rev. as The Rose of Algeria, 1909; Little Nemo (?musical play, 3, H.B. Smith, after comic strip by W. McKay), 1908; The Prima Donna (3, Blossom), 1908; Old Dutch (musical farce, 2, Hobart; E. Smith), 1909; Naughty Marietta (2, R.J. Young), 1910; When Sweet Sixteen (song play, 2, Hobart), 1910; Natoma (op, 3, J.D. Redding), 1911 (1913); Mlle Rosita [The Duchess] (3, H.B. Smith; J. Herbert), 1911; The Enchantress (2, H.B. Smith; F. de Gresac), 1911; The Lady of the Slipper (musical comedy, 3, J. O'Dea; A. Caldwell and L. McCarty), 1912; Sweethearts (2, R.B. Smith; H.B. Smith and De Gresac), 1913; The Madcap Duchess (2, D. Stevens, after J.H. McCarthy), 1913; Madeleine (lyric op, 1, G. Stewart, after A. Decourcelle and L. Thibaut: *Je dîne chez ma mère*), composed 1913, perf. 1914, fs and vs (1913); The Debutante (musical comedy,

2, H.B. and R.B. Smith), 1914; The Only Girl (musical farcical comedy, 3, Blossom, after L. Fulda), 1914; The Princess Pat (3, Blossom), 1915; Hearts of Erin [Eileen] (3, Blossom), 1917; Her Regiment (?musical play, 3, W. Le Baron), 1917; The Velvet Lady (musical comedy, 3, Blossom), 1918; Angel Face (musical play, 3, R.B. Smith; H.B. Smith), 1919 (1920); My Golden Girl (?musical comedy, 2, F.A. Kummer), 1919, excerpts (1920); Oui Madame (musical play, 2, R.B. Smith; G.M. Wright), 1920, excerpts (1920); The Girl in the Spotlight (?musical play, 2, R. Bruce), 1920, excerpts (1920); Orange Blossoms (?comedy with music, 3, B.G. de Sylva; De Gresac), 1922; The Dream Girl (musical play, 3, H. Atteridge; Young), 1924, excerpts (1924)

Other music for revues, incl. The Century Girl, New York, 1916, collab. I. Berlin, excerpts (1916); scores for stage works (Seven Little Widows, The House that Jack Built, The Lavender Lady, Hula-Lula, The Garden of Eden and unidentified material) in Wc

VOCAL

Choral: Aus "Liedern eines fahrenden Gesellen," male vv, op.20/2 (Berlin, 1890); Der Gefangene (dramatic cant., R. von Baumbach), solo vv, chorus, orch, 1891 (Berlin, 1891), Eng. trans. as The Captive, op.25 (1915); Christ Is Risen, anthem, solo vv, chorus, orch/org, 1904 (1908); The Cruiskeen Lawn (trad. Irish), male vv (1913); Widow Machree (S. Lover), male vv (1915); The Call to Freedom (patriotic ode, Herbert), S, chorus, pf (Boston, 1918); Lora Lee (Clarke), male vv (1922)

c80 songs, 1v, pf, incl. Frühlingslied, op.14 no.1 (Berlin, 1889); If Love Were What the Rose Is (A.C. Swinburne) (1907); I Want to Be a Good Lamb (Hobart), 1909 (1940); Farewell (E. Locke) (1919); Molly (Young) (1919); The Equity Star (Stewart) (1921)

INSTRUMENTAL

Orch: Suite, vc, orch, op.3, 1884; Vc Conc. no.1, op.8, 1884; Royal Sec, champagne galop, before 1885; Serenade, str orch, op.12, 1889; Fantasie on "The Desire" of Schubert, vc, orch, 1891; Irish Rhapsody, 1892; Fantasia on Mascagni's Cavalleria rusticana, vn, orch, ?1983; The Vision of Columbus, 1893; Légende, vc, orch, before 1894; Vc Conc. no.2, e, op.30, 1894; America Fantasia, 1898; Suite romantique, op.31, 1901; Pan-Americana, morceau caractéristique, 1901; Hero and Leander, sym. poem, op.43, 1901; Woodland Fancies, suite for orch, op.34, 1901; Columbus, suite, op.35, 1903; L'Encore, fl, cl, orch, c1904; Western Ov., ?1906; A Suite of Serenades, 1924

Marches (for band unless otherwise stated; also pubd in versions for pf): Eldorado, 1894; The Belle of Pittsburgh, 1895; The American Girl, band/orch, 1896; Baltimore Centennial, 1896; The Veiled Prophet, 1896; McKinley Inauguration March, 1897; March of the 22nd Regiment, band/orch, 1898; The President's March, band/orch, 1898; Auditorium Festival March, orch, 1901 [pubd as Festival March]; Aschenbrödel March, orch, 1910; The Lamb's March, orch, 1914; The World's Progress, pf, 1916; Defendam March, 1919; The Marion Davies March, pf, 1923 [for the film When Knighthood Was in Flower]; Cosmopolitan March, orch, ?1923; Salute to America, orch, n.d.

Light orch scores, many pubd or orig. composed for pf, incl. Badinage (1895); Yesterthoughts (1900); Under the Elms: Souvenir de Saratoga (1903); Spanish Rhapsody (?1905); The Jester's Serenade (1908); 3 Compositions, str orch: Air de ballet, Sunset, Forget-Me-Not (1912); Danse baroque (1913); Whispering Willows (1915); Indian Summer (1919); Indian Lullaby (1922) [later titled Dream On]

c22 chbr works, incl. Einsamkeit and Humoresque, 3 fl, 2 ob, 4 cl, s sax, a sax, b cl, cb cl, 2 bn, c1898, lost; Petite valse, vc/vn, pf (Milan, 1905); Duo, 2 vn, pf (1923); many short works for vc, pf

Film scores: The Fall of a Nation, complete film score, 1916, excerpts (1925–6); Under the Red Robe, ov., 1923, as Dramatic Ov. (1938); The Great White Way, ov., 1923, as Golden Days Ov. (1939); Little Old New York, ov., 1923; Star of the North, ov., 1923

Principal publishers: Harms, Schuberth, Witmark
Most MSS in Wc

BIBLIOGRAPHY

J. Kaye: Victor Herbert (New York, 1931/R) [incl. list of compositions]
H.B. Smith: First Nights and First Editions (Boston, 1931)
C.L. Purdy: Victor Herbert, American Music Master (New York, 1944)
E.N. Waters: Victor Herbert: a Life in Music (New York, 1955) [incl. lists of compositions and recordings]

G. Bordman: American Musical Theatre: a Chronicle (New York, 1978, 2/1986)
A.G. Debus: "The Early Victor Herbert," Music of Victor Herbert, Smithsonian Collection (1979) [liner notes]
C. Hamm: Yesterdays: Popular Song in America (New York, 1979)
F.S. Roffman: Naughty Marietta, Smithsonian Collection (1981) [liner notes]
W. Shirley: "A Bugle Call to Arms for National Defense! Victor Herbert and his Score for The Fall of a Nation," Quarterly Journal of the Library of Congress, xl (1983), 26–47
R.F. Schmalz: "Paur and the Pittsburgh: Requiem for an Orchestra," AM, xii/2 (1994), 125–47
W.E. Studwell: "Foreigners and Patriots: the American Musical, 1890–1927: an Essay and Bibliography," Music Reference Services Quarterly, iii/1 (1994–5), 1–10
E.H. Pearson: "Victor Herbert's Madeleine," Opera Quarterly, xiii/4 (1997), 59–75
N. Gould: Victor Herbert: a Theatrical Life (New York, 2008)

STEVEN LEDBETTER/ORLY LEAH KRASNER

Herbig, Günther (b Ústí nad Labem, Czechoslovakia [now Czech Republic], 30 Nov 1931). German conductor of Czech birth. At age nine he began to study the cello, the piano, and the flute and then had conducting lessons with Hermann Abendroth at the Musikhochschule in Weimar (1951–6) and finally with Hermann Scherchen, Arvids Jansons, and Herbert von Karajan. He made his debut in 1957 at the opera house in Erfurt and was soon appointed conductor of the Deutsches Nationaltheater in Weimar (1957–62), where he also taught at the conservatory. In Potsdam he became the director for the Hans-Otto-Theater (1962–6) until he was called to the (East) Berlin SO (1966–72), when he received the title of Generalmusikdirektor. Herbig moved to the Dresden PO (1972–7) as Generalmusikdirektor but returned to the Berlin SO (1977–83) and began to increase his exposure in the West by taking principal guest conductorships with the Dallas SO (1979–81) and the BBC Northern SO in Manchester (1981–4). He moved to the West as music director of the Detroit SO (1984–90) and then of the Toronto SO (1988–94), but he continued to conduct in the eastern part of Germany, where he had won the national arts prize in 1973. Herbig served as principal conductor of the Saarbrücken Radio Symphony Orchestra from 2001 to 2006 and later took advisory positions with the Columbus SO (Ohio) and the National SO in Taiwan. He has recorded with his orchestras in Berlin, Dresden, Manchester, and Toronto, and also with the RPO and the Philharmonia. While conducting mostly traditional Austro-German repertory, Herbig has given the premieres of many works by composers from the former East Germany, including Hanns Eisler, Siegfried Matthus, Siegfried Thiele, Manfred Schubert, and Ruth Zechlin.

CHARLES BARBER

Herbst, Johannes (b Kempten, Swabia, Germany, 23 July 1735; d Salem [now Winston-Salem], NC, 15 Jan 1812). German Moravian composer, organist, and minister. He joined the Moravian Church in 1748 and received his education at the Moravian school in Herrnhut, Germany. He served the Moravian congregations of Neusalz, Gnadenfrey, Gnadenberg, and Kleinwelke (in Germany) and Fulneck (England) as an organist as well as a bookkeeper and teacher, before being ordained in 1774. After that he, was superintendent of the communities at Neudietendorf and Gnadenfrey. With his wife, he came to America in 1785 to serve as pastor in Lancaster, Pennsylvania. In 1791 he was appointed pastor of the Lititz congregation and principal of the girls' boarding school in the town (now called Linden Hall). During his nearly 20 years in Lititz he cataloged that congregation's music library and prepared performance parts for approximately 500 compositions; these parts form a major portion of the Lititz Congregation Collection. He may also have been paid to copy music for use in the girls' boarding school in Bethlehem. He was consecrated a bishop in Lititz on 12 May 1811, two days before leaving to serve as pastor in Salem, North Carolina. During his service there of less than eight months, he contributed manuscripts of performance parts to the congregation's library and made corrections to that library's 1808 catalog.

Herbst was a prolific composer, producing approximately 180 anthems for chorus with orchestra, a large number of vocal solos and duets with orchestra, and about 150 sacred songs with keyboard. He is not known to have written instrumental music, although six short sonatas in a manuscript keyboard book that he compiled may be his own work. Herbst was a gifted melodist whose works are characterized by smooth-flowing yet dramatically appropriate melodies that enhance his texts. His harmonic language, rooted in the Classical style, is somewhat more chromatic than that of his Moravian contemporaries working in America. His rhythms are strong and simple, and strings of dotted 8th- and 16th-note groups are a favorite device. He wrote most effectively for voices, and the instrumental parts of his songs and anthems generally do not carry independent thematic material.

He was also an avid copier of other composers' music, and his personal collection, copied over the course of a 50-year period, is the most important single collection for the study of Moravian music in America and Europe. Unlike the congregations' music collections, Herbst's copies are full scores and often include information about the occasions for which individual pieces were written or used. The collection contains more than 1000 anthems, of which the vast majority are by Moravians, as well as many larger works by composers including C.P.E. Bach, K.H. Graun, G.F. Handel, J.A. Hasse, F.J. Haydn, G.A. Homilius, W.A. Mozart, G.B. Pergolesi, J.H. Rolle, J.A.P. Schulz, and E.W. Wolf. In 1811 he brought it to Salem, where it now resides among the holdings of the Moravian Music Foundation. His personal copy of contemporary Moravian hymnals is also of inestimable value for research into Moravian hymnody and worship, in that his marginal notes identify hymn text writers and translations from the original German to the English language that was becoming more widespread among American Moravians.

BIBLIOGRAPHY

D.M. McCorkle: *Moravian Music in Salem: a German-American Heritage* (diss., Indiana U., 1958)

J.O. Falconer: *Bishop Johannes Herbst* (diss., Columbia University, 1969)

M.P. Gombosi: *Catalog of the Johannes Herbst Collection* (Chapel Hill, 1970)

R. Steelman: *Catalog of the Lititz Congregation Collection* (Chapel Hill, NC, 1981)

F. Cumnock, *Catalog of the Salem Congregation Collection* (Chapel Hill, NC, 1980)

N.R. Knouse, ed.: *The Music of the Moravian Church in America* (Rochester, 2008)

KARL KROEGER/NOLA REED KNOUSE

Herford [Goldstein], **Julius** (*b* Anklam, Germany, 22 Feb 1901; *d* Bloomington, IN, 17 Sept 1981). Pianist, conductor, and teacher of German birth. He studied piano with James Kwast and composition with Wilhelm Klatte and Arthur Willner at the Sternsches Konservatorium in Berlin (1917–23). He then toured in Europe for two years before returning to Berlin to teach. In 1939 he emigrated, took the name Herford, and enjoyed a distinguished teaching career at Columbia University Teachers College (1939–41), the Juilliard School (from 1946), Berkshire Music Center (from 1946), Union Theological Seminary (from 1949), the Manhattan School (from 1949), Westminster Choir College, and Indiana University (1964–80), where he was director of graduate studies in choral conducting. His students include some of the biggest names in American choral conducting: ROBERT SHAW, MARGARET HILLIS, ROGER WAGNER, and ELAINE BROWN (I). His influence on Shaw's approach to score preparation made him famous among American choral conductors (see his chapter in *Choral Conducting: A Symposium*, H. Decker, ed., Englewood Cliffs, NJ, 1973). In 1981 the American Choral Directors Association created a dissertation award in his name to recognize exceptional contributions to choral scholarship. His writings include book chapters, articles, edited scores, and several choral works. His papers are held in the William and Gayle Cook Music Library, Indiana University.

BIBLIOGRAPHY

E. Pierce: *Julius Herford: His Life, Teaching, and Influence on the Choral Art in the United States* (diss., U. of Northern Colorado, 1988)

STEVEN M. DEMOREST

Heringman, Jacob (Walter) (*b* Berea, OH, 1 April 1964). Lutenist. Initially a guitar player in various styles, he studied English and philosophy at Grinnell College (BA 1986). His primary lute studies were with Jakob Lindberg at the Royal College of Music in London from 1987 to 1989 (ARCM diploma), and he later received further instruction from Patrick O'Brien in New York. Specializing in Renaissance lute, Heringman has performed and recorded as a soloist, accompanist, and ensemble member. Notable solo recordings include *Josquin des Prez: Sixteenth Century Lute Settings* (2000), a collection of early lute intabulations of Josquin's sacred and secular vocal music, and *The Siena Lute Book* (2004), which features selections from two Italian manuscripts. As an accompanist he appears on *A Renaissance Songbook: Philippe Verdelot: The Complete Madrigal Book of 1536* (2000) and singer Barbara Bonney's Grammy-nominated album *Fairest Isle* (2001). Ensemble recordings such as

Dowland: Consort Music and Songs (1997, with the Rose Consort of Viols), *Ther Is No Rose: Renaissance Music for the Christmas Season* (1997, with Virelai, a group he helped found), and *Cancionero: Music for the Spanish Court, 1470–1520* (2002, with the Dufay Collective) form a significant part of his discography. Heringman has also played the lute on various film soundtracks and worked with popular musicians such as Sting and Joni Mitchell. As a teacher and practitioner of Alexander Technique, he has often cited its importance to his musicianship.

BIBLIOGRAPHY

M. Dalton: "An Interview with Jacob Heringman," *Lute Society of America Quarterly*, xxxviii–xxxix/4–1 (2003–2004), 7–11

J. Heringman: "The Alexander Technique and the Lute," *Lute News*, 73 (2005), 7–18

LARS HELGERT

Herman, Jerry [Gerald Sheldon] (*b* New York, NY, 10 July 1933). Composer and lyricist. He was self-taught as a musician and gained his first practical experiences of musical theater by writing and staging shows for the summer camp run by his parents. He studied drama at the University of Miami, where he also began writing for revue. He moved to New York, working as a nightclub pianist and writing for television, and reused some of his material from Miami for the revue *I feel wonderful*, presented off-Broadway (1954), and revised the revue *Nightcap* (1958) as *Parade* (1960). His first full-scale musical was *Milk and Honey* (1961), which gave him a hit song in "Shalom"; it starred the opera singers Robert Weede and Mimi Benzell and the long-established Yiddish performer Molly Picon. *Hello, Dolly!* (1964) reinforced Herman's breezy style, and the show won ten Tony Awards, including Best Actress for Carol Channing's famous portrayal of Dolly Levi and Best Composer for Herman. With *Mame* (1966) Herman wrote a fine score that again incorporated a rousing title song; other numbers ranged through vaudeville ("Bosom Buddies"), ballad ("If he Walked into my Life"), and the incorrigibly cheerful ("We need a little Christmas"). Angela Lansbury established a long association with Herman's work in playing the title role and took the lead in his considerably less successful but more adventurous next piece, *Dear World* (1969). An adaptation of Jean Giraudoux's *La folle de Chaillot*, its complex and dark themes allowed Herman to develop intense characterization through such songs as "I don't want to know" and "And I was beautiful." "The Tea Party" is a prime example of Herman's quodlibet ensemble writing, while "The Spring of Next Year" demonstrates his playful and integrated approach to combining words with music by setting witty lyrics about pollution to a sweeping waltz, a musical form with which Herman had previously demonstrated a warm affinity in "Dancing" (*Hello, Dolly!*). With *Mack and Mabel* (1974) he wrote one of the most instantly appealing and tuneful Broadway scores (although dramatic unevenness has made stagings less consistently effective). The show allowed full rein to Herman's revue-based style through its setting in the early days of silent films, with novelty numbers ("Tap your troubles away"), a trademark cumulative chorus ("When Mabel Comes in the Room"), and a love song typically approached at a tangent ("I won't send roses").

The Grand Tour (1979) gained some critical approval but was a commercial failure; *La cage aux folles* (1983) succeeded on both counts. The show is distinguished by its light farce underpinned by songs of unusual intensity, a marriage of direct, accessible popular song forms to strong dramatization that summarizes the best of Herman's considerable and often underrated technical achievement. It was an unexpected success and has become a standard of the repertory. Since 1983 Herman has been represented by revivals and the compilation show *Jerry's Girls* (1985), which drew on the strong female characters at the center of most of his shows. In 1996 he wrote the television musical "Mrs. Santa Claus," whose title role was played by Lansbury; a pleasantly serviceable score, it lacks the variety of previous works. *Miss Spectacular*, commissioned as a Las Vegas show, was recorded in 1998 but remains unstaged. The same year, Herman received the ASCAP Foundation Richard Rodgers Award for lifetime achievement in musical theater.

Milk and Honey established that essential Herman quality of a determined, optimistic and aspirational spirit which runs through his shows in, for example, "Before the Parade Passes by" (*Hello, Dolly!*) and "Open a New Window" (*Mame*), and was expressed in its most assertive form in *La cage aux folles* through "I am what I am," which became a major disco hit for Gloria Gaynor and subsequently a quintessential gay liberation anthem. In "Let's not waste a moment" and "I will follow you" *Milk and Honey* also presaged the haunting lyricism of "Ribbons Down my Back" (*Hello, Dolly!*). Herman's distinctive use of multi-section chorus numbers was first most clearly established in *Hello, Dolly!* through "Put on your Sunday clothes" and the now-classic title song; the former also used the climactic device of a slowed-down melody over a double-time accompaniment, a recurring feature in Herman's shows that reached its extreme in "I am what I am." Characterized by an immediate tunefulness and joie de vivre, Herman's writing is often viewed as formulaic, but within its reliance on established popular song structures are subtle adaptations for each new dramatic setting, for example with the Israeli local color of *Milk and Honey* ("Independence Day Hora"), the silent-film-music figurations of *Mack and Mabel* ("Movies were movies"), and the evocative French lyricism of *Dear World* (the waltzes "I don't want to know" and "The Spring of Next Year"). As a lyricist, Herman imbues his songs with strong emotions through everyday language carefully crafted, as in the ballad "Time heals everything" (*Mack and Mabel*) or "Song on the Sand (La Da Da Da)" (*La cage aux folles*). The easy appeal of the latter belies its technical command in integrating the flow of text and music, a quality characteristic of Herman: its subject is a half-forgotten lyric, musically matched by "incomplete" phrases, six rather than eight bars in length.

From a relatively small output, Herman has achieved a rare degree of lasting popular appeal, with individual songs and complete works established as defining in their respective canons. His shows encapsulate a particular strand of the Broadway musical in the second half of the 20th century that has defied the trend to elevate psychological subtexts expressed through fragmentary musical motifs over direct storylines, memorable tunes, and an uplifting spirit.

WORKS
(selective list)
(unless otherwise stated, all stage musicals in 2 acts, music and lyrics by Herman and dates those of first New York performance; other writers shown as "co-lyricist"; "book author")

I feel wonderful (revue, B.A. Grael), Theatre de Lys, 18 Oct 1954

Nightcap (revue), Showplace, 18 May 1958, rev. as Parade, Players, 20 Jan 1960

Milk and Honey (D. Appell), orchd H. Kay and E. Sauter, Martin Beck, 10 Oct 1961 [incl. Shalom]

Madame Aphrodite (T. Mosel), Orpheum, 29 Dec 1961

Hello, Dolly! (B. Merrill; M. Stewart, after T. Wilder: *The Matchmaker*), orchd P.J. Lang, St. James, 16 Jan 1964 [incl. title song, Before the Parade Passes by, Dancing, It only takes a moment, Put on your Sunday clothes, Ribbons Down my Back; film 1969]

Mame (J. Lawrence and R.E. Lee, after P. Dennis: *Auntie Mame*), orchd Lang, Winter Garden, 24 May 1966 [incl. title song, If he Walked into my Life, My Best Girl, We need a little Christmas; film 1974]

Dear World (Lawrence and Lee, after J. Giraudoux: *La folle de chaillot*), orchd Lang, Mark Hellinger, 6 Feb 1969 [incl. title song, The Spring of Next Year, Kiss her now]

Mack and Mabel (M. Stewart), orchd Lang, Majestic, 6 Oct 1974 [incl. I won't send roses, Time heals everything]

The Grand Tour (Stewart and M. Bramble, after F. Werfel: *Jacobowsky und der Oberst*), orchd Lang, Palace, 11 Jan 1979 [incl. I'll be here tomorrow]

La cage aux folles (H. Fierstein, after J. Poiret), orchd J. Tyler, Palace, 21 Aug 1983 [incl. The Best of Times, I am what I am, Look over there, Song on the Sand (La Da Da Da)]

Mrs. Santa Claus (television musical, M. Saltzman), orchd L. Blank, 1996

Miss Spectacular (Herman and R. Freedman), orchd Blank, 1998 [concept album]

Contribs to: From A to Z, Brooks Atkinson, 20 April 1960 [music mostly by J. Kander]; Ben Franklin in Paris, Lunt Fontanne, 27 Oct 1964 [music mostly by M. Sandrich Jr.]; A Day in Hollywood/A Night in the Ukraine, John Golden, 1 May 1980 [music mostly by D. Vosburgh]

Principal publisher: Hal Leonard

BIBLIOGRAPHY
S. Suskin: *Opening Night on Broadway: a Critical Quotebook of the Golden Era of the Musical Theater: "Oklahoma!" (1943) to "Fiddler on the Roof" (1964)* (New York, 1990), 297–301, 441–3

S. Suskin: *Show Tunes…: the Songs, Shows, and Careers of Broadway's Major Composers* (New York, 1986, enlarged 3/2000), 323–9

J. Herman with M. Stasio: *Showtune: a Memoir* (New York, 1996)

M. Steyn: *Broadway Babies Say Goodnight: Musicals Then and Now* (London, 1997)

S. Suskin: *More Opening Nights on Broadway: a Critical Quotebook of the Musical Theater, 1965 through 1981* (New York, 1997), 225–31, 357–61, 559–66, 575–81

S. Citron: *Jerry Herman: Poet of the Showtune* (New Haven and London, 2004)

JOHN SNELSON

Herman, Reinhold Ludwig (*b* Prenzlau, Brandenburg, 21 Sept 1849; *d* New York, 1919). German singer, pianist, composer, and conductor. Herman received his musical education at the Stern Conservatory from Heinrich Ehrlich (piano), Friedrich Kiel (composition) and Julius Stern (singing). From 1871–8 he taught voice and conducted in New York. In 1878, he was called back to Berlin as temporary head of the Stern Conservatory. After being at the Stern Conservatory, he returned to New York in 1881. Herman conducted the Liedertafel from 1884 and was instructor in music and professor of sacred history at the Union Theological Seminary from 1887, before moving to Boston in 1898 as conductor of the Handel and Haydn Society. He returned in 1900 to Berlin, where he conducted the Meyer Symphony Concerts. Until 1917 he lived in Rapallo, Italy, then moved back to New York. He toured Europe and America with Lilli Lehmann giving recitals and lectures on Wagner.

Herman was the author of *An Open Door for Singers* (New York, 1912). He wrote the operas *Vineta* (1872), *Lancelot, Spielmannsglück* (1894), *Wulfrin* (1896) and *Sundâri* (1911). He composed various cantatas, the orchestral works *Die Seufzerbrücke* and *Der Geiger von Gmünd*, overtures, a piano concerto, piano suites, sonatas, and many songs.

BIBLIOGRAPHY
Baker4 Grove3, Amer. suppl.

W.S. Pratt, ed.: *The New Encyclopedia of Music and Musicians* (New York, 1929)

JOSEPH A. BOMBERGER

Herman, Woody [Herrmann, Woodrow Charles Thomas] (*b* Milwaukee, WI, 16 May 1913; *d* Los Angeles, CA, 29 Oct 1987). Bandleader, clarinetist, saxophonist, and vocalist. For a full half century, Herman led a series of widely popular big bands boasting some of the most skilled players in jazz as sidemen. He was playing saxophone professionally by the age of nine and sang in vaudeville as a teenager. Following his apprenticeship under Tom Gerun, Harry Sosnik, and Gus Arnheim, Herman's big band career began in earnest when he assumed leadership of Isham Jones's group in 1936 and re-formed the ensemble as a cooperative. Marketed as the "Band that Plays the Blues," this first group gained considerable renown following the release of "Woodchopper's Ball" (1939) under Decca. A 30-year collaboration with the arranger Ralph Burns begun in 1944 quickly distinguished Herman's Herd—the first of many eponymous references by which his bands were known—with increasingly sophisticated charts including a hit cover of Louis Jordan's "Caldonia" (1945). His small group the Woodchoppers, made up of members of his big band, also formed during this period.

After disbanding his first group, Herman launched his Second Herd in 1947, promoting it on network radio and signing with both Capitol and Columbia. Also known as the Four Brothers band, after its saxophone section, this Herd featured bop-inspired writing that marked the peak of Herman's adaptability and inventive output. Charts by newcomers Shorty Rogers and Jimmy Guiffre—including Guiffre's "Four Brothers" (1947), which showcased tenor saxophonists Stan Getz, Zoot Sims, and Herbie Steward, along with baritone saxophonist Serge Chaloff—signaled a decidedly modernist direction. After the 1948 American Federation of Musicians recording ban frustrated attempts to establish a new audience, Herman disbanded the group again in December 1949. A Third Herd—started promptly in 1950—suffered amid the emergent rock-and-roll scene. Herman continued to lead groups in various forms into the 1980s and performed until shortly before his death.

Ahead of its time, Herman's work was progressive on a number of fronts. Musically, his big band was among the first to introduce new trends in bebop to the mainstream white audience successfully. This trailblazing provided important models for Claude Thornhill, Boyd Raeburn, and, most notably, the remarkably successful Stan Kenton, who—having collected a number of former Herman personnel along the way—started his own progressive experiments in the mid-1940s. Herman's achievements even attracted Stravinsky, a long admirer and liberal adapter of ragtime and jazz. Herman premiered his "Ebony Concerto" (1946) at Carnegie Hall to mixed reviews from popular and art music camps alike.

Many of the Herds also integrated race and gender. An enthusiastic devotee of Ellington—whose suite *Black, Brown, and Beige* inspired Burns's multi-movement work *Summer Sequence* (1946)—Herman eagerly recorded with Johnny Hodges, Ben Webster, Ray Nance, and Juan Tizol. He also hired Gene Ammons, Oscar Pettiford, and Ernie Royal as regular members of the Second Herd despite repeated cancellations at segregated venues. In the mid-1940s vibraphonist Marjorie Hyams and trumpeter Elizabeth Rogers briefly joined Herman's ranks.

Despite Herman's considerable legacy, historians remain divided over his contribution. Some cite a clear pre-eminence of the First Herd over the Second; others, the opposite. Recent assessments are no more aligned. Where one survey lavishes copious coverage of Herman's career, another downplays his role as marginal, his popularity having been hopelessly devastated in bebop's wake.

SELECTED RECORDINGS

The Isham Jones Centennial Album (1935, Viper's Nest 156); Woodchopper's Ball (1939, Decca 2440); The music stopped (with Ben Webster) (1943, Decca 18577); Perdido (with Ray Nance and Juan Tizol) (1944, Coral 56090); Caldonia (1945, Col 36789); Northwest passage (with Marjorie Hyams) (1945, Stash 113); Esquire Third Annual Jazz Concert (Duke Ellington and Woody Herman orchestras with the King Cole Trio) (1946, Session Disc 125); Ebony Concerto (1946, Col 7479M); Four Brothers (1947, Col 38304)

BIBLIOGRAPHY

E. Edwards, Jr.: *Woody Herman and his Orchestra: a Discography*, i, ii (Brande, 1961); iii: *1959–1965* (Whittier, CA, 1965)
J.A. Treichel: *Woody Herman: the Second Herd* (Spotswood, NJ, 1980)
W.C. Herman and S. Troup: *The Woodchopper's Ball: the Autobiography of Woody Herman* (New York, 1990)
D. Morrill: *Woody Herman: a Guide to the Big Band Recordings, 1936–1987* (Westport, CT, 1990)
W.D. Clancy and A.C. Kenton: *Woody Herman: Chronicles of the Herds* (New York, 1995)
G. Lees: *Leader of the Band: the Life of Woody Herman* (New York, 1995)

RYAN PATRICK JONES

Hernández, Rafael (*b* Aguadilla, PR, 1891; *d* San Juan, PR, 1965). Puerto Rican composer, bandleader, and instrumentalist. Born into a humble musical family, he and his siblings Victoria and Jesús were skilled multi-instrumentalists. During World War I, Hernández played in the Infantry Hellfighters Band of James Reese Europe. Later, he established the trend for guitar-based trios and quartets among New York Puerto Ricans in the 1920s and 30s, founding the Trio Borinquén (1926) and the Cuarteto Victoria (1932). In the period 1932–47 Hernández lived in Mexico, continuing to compose and also conducting radio and dance orchestras, between frequent visits to New York and back to Puerto Rico. He returned permanently to Puerto Rico in 1947, remaining active as a composer and bandleader until his death.

Revered as Puerto Rico's greatest and most prolific popular composer, Hernández is said to have written over 2000 songs. He is best known for *Lamento Borincano* (1930), a bolero that became an anthem for Puerto Ricans. Hernández composed sophisticated songs in a semiclassical vein, reflecting his extensive training and conservatory background. Focusing on romantic and poetic themes, his compositions feature complex melodic lines, contrapuntal vocal parts, and frequent major–minor tonal shifts.

BIBLIOGRAPHY

R. de la Fuente Escalona: "Rafael Hernández y Cuba," *Revista Universidad de América*, v/1 (May 1993), 4–7
R. Glasser: *My music is my flag: Puerto Rican Musicians and their New York Communities, 1917–1940* (Berkeley, 1995)
M. Arce: "The Songs of Rafael Hernández," *Music in Puerto Rico: a Reader's Anthology*, ed. and trans. D. Thompson (Lanham, MD, 2002), 108–11

LISE WAXER/R

Hernried, Robert (Franz Richard) (*b* Vienna, Austria, 22 Sept 1883; *d* Detroit, MI, 3 Sept 1951). Composer, conductor, and musicologist of Austrian birth. He studied at the Vienna Conservatory under Richard Heuberger, JOSEPH FUCHS, and Eusebius Mandyczewski, and at the University of Vienna. Between 1908 and 1914 he conducted opera in various provincial theaters in Austria and Germany, wrote two operas (one later performed), and published the first of his many articles. After World War I he taught in Mannheim (1919–22) and Erfurt (1924–6) before being invited to Berlin as editor and administrator for the Reichsverbandes Deutscher Orchester und Orchestermusiker. He taught at the Stern Conservatory (1926–8) and at the Akademie für Kirchen- und Schulmusik (1927–34); concurrently he carried on research and editing, published several books and numerous articles and reviews, and composed a great deal of music.

Deprived of his position by the Nazis in 1934, Hernried went to Vienna, and in 1939 to the United States, where he taught at St. Ambrose College in Davenport, Iowa (1940–42), the State Teachers College in Dickinson, North Dakota (1942–3), and St. Francis College in Fort Wayne, Indiana (1943–6). In 1946 he became professor of theory and composition at the Detroit Institute of Musical Art, and lecturer on music history and education at the University of Detroit. As a long-standing friend of Wilhelm Furtwängler, Hernried was convinced that the conductor had remained in Germany during the war for the noblest reasons, and he tried to restore Furtwängler's good reputation in the United States.

Hernried's music is well written in a solidly tonal idiom which he himself characterized as "progressive Romantic." About 100 of his pieces have been published. Apart from his two operas, *Francesca da Rimini* and *Die Bäuerin*, he wrote a concert overture for orchestra, many songs, several pieces for woodwind solo with piano, and a Concerto in the Old Style for violin. He also produced a large number of choral works, both sacred and secular, among them a Mass in D which employs both a modal style and modern dissonance. He prepared the first modern edition of Francesco Geminiani's Concerti grossi op.3 (Leipzig, 1935) from the original 1732 parts. His numerous articles in European and American publications cover a wide range of subjects and include several in the *Musical Quarterly*, in which he published some hitherto unknown music of Robert Schumann, and letters of Carl Maria von Weber, Franz Liszt, and Hugo Wolf.

WRITINGS

Emile Jaques-Dalcroze's Lebenswerk (n.p., c1929)
ed.: S. Krehl: *Allgemeine Musiklehre* (Berlin and Leipzig, 3/1933)
Johannes Brahms (Leipzig, 1934)
Systematische Modulation (Berlin, 1935, 2/1949)
"Hugo Wolf's *Corregidor* at Mannheim," *MQ*, xxvi (1940), 19–30
"Four Unpublished Compositions by Robert Schumann," *MQ*, xxviii (1942), 50–62
"Discoveries in Vienna: Unpublished Letters by Weber and Liszt," *MQ*, xxxii (1946), 537–44

RAMONA H. MATTHEWS

Herrmann, Bernard (*b* New York, NY, 29 June 1911; *d* Los Angeles, CA, 24 Dec 1975). Composer and conductor. In 1929, while still a student at DeWitt Clinton High School, he enrolled for classes in composition and conducting at New York University. The subsequent year he followed his conducting teacher ALBERT STOESSEL to the Juilliard School of Music, where he was taught composition by the Dutch émigré BERNARD WAGENAAR. He left the Juilliard School after less than two years, apparently because he found the institution too conservative, and returned informally to New York University during the academic year 1932–3 to attend a course in composition and orchestration given by PERCY GRAINGER. Grainger's eclectic approach revealed to Herrmann the range and diversity of the musical materials available to the contemporary composer. Early in 1933 he formed the New Chamber Orchestra from a group of unemployed musicians as a vehicle for his talents as both conductor and composer. The orchestra's repertory brought together contemporary compositions (including those of Charles Ives, with whom Herrmann formed a lasting friendship) and works by English composers such as Henry Purcell and Edward Elgar, symptomatic of his anglophile tendencies.

In 1934 Herrmann was appointed assistant to Johnny Green, a conductor and composer at CBS, and from 1936 to 1940 composed a considerable quantity of incidental music for the radio series *The Columbia Workshop* (1936–7, at least 75 shows), *The Mercury Theater on the Air* (1938, 22 shows directed by Orson Welles), and *The Campbell Playhouse* (1938–40, 56 shows, also directed by Welles). During his apprenticeship in radio theater he developed a musical style that was immediate and economical, both in terms of the instrumental resources employed and melodic and harmonic language. The partnership he forged with Welles resulted in his first film score, *Citizen Kane*, composed in 1940 and released by RKO in 1941. In 1942 he scored a second film for Welles, *The Magnificent Ambersons*, but refused to let his name appear in the credits after the savage cutting of his music following poor audience response to the preview.

In the subsequent 12 years, Herrmann composed a number of scores for Fox studios, but it was his partnership with Alfred Hitchcock at Paramount and MGM (1955–64) that cemented his reputation. *Vertigo* (1958), *North by Northwest* (1959), and *Psycho* (1960) are generally held to represent the summit of his film scoring achievement; the infamous shower scene of *Psycho*, which Hitchcock initially intended to be unscored, is one of the most frequently referenced and influential cues in cinematic history. Throughout this period he composed cues and stock scores for CBS TV series such as *Rawhide*, *The Twilight Zone*, and *The Alfred Hitchcock Half Hour*. In 1966 Herrmann felt unable and unwilling to acquiesce to Hitchcock's demand for a more overtly popular score for *Torn Curtain*, and composed no further music for him thereafter. During the final ten years of his career, he worked with the directors François Truffaut (*Fahrenheit 451*, 1966, and *La mariée était en noir*, 1967), Brian de Palma (*Sisters*, 1973, and *Obsession*, 1976), and ultimately Martin Scorsese on *Taxi Driver* (1976).

For Herrmann, orchestration was a composer's musical thumbprint. Unlike most other Hollywood composers of his generation, he orchestrated his own music rather than passing a short score to a team of orchestrators. His instrumentation was often unusual: *The Day the Earth Stood Still* (1951) uses two theremins (an electronic instrument previously used by Miklós Rózsa in his 1945 scores for *The Lost Weekend* and *Spellbound*), electronic violin, bass and guitar, four harps, four pianos, percussion, and brass; *Psycho* is scored for string orchestra; *Journey to the Center of the Earth* (1959) requires five organs; *On Dangerous Ground* (1951) has a solo part for viola d'amore. Herrmann generally avoided the "leitmotif" system adopted by many film composers, finding that short phrases were less limiting to the composer than the closed forms of 8- and 16-bar melodies. Ostinato figures built around one- or two-bar units feature prominently in his later scores, often being associated with obsessive behavior. Although his musical language is fundamentally tonal, he makes sustained use of dissonance and chromatic embellishment, and employs complex harmonic units such as the superimposed E♭ minor and D major triads near the beginning of *Vertigo*.

Despite his wide acclaim as a film composer, Herrmann's concert works and operas have not had the same level of public success. His opera *Wuthering Heights* (1943–51) is perhaps his finest and most sustained achievement in this field. A complex and enigmatic figure who could be egotistical and irascible, refined and sentimental by turns, who hustled at the center of the American culture industry, yet yearned for the English pastoral, he remains one of the central figures of film-music composition.

WORKS
FILMS
Citizen Kane, 1941; All that Money can Buy, 1941; The Magnificent Ambersons, 1942; Jane Eyre, 1943; Hangover Square, 1945; Anna and the King of Siam, 1946; The Ghost and Mrs. Muir, 1947; The Day the Earth Stood Still, 1951; On Dangerous Ground, 1951; Five Fingers, 1952; The Snows of Kilimanjaro, 1952; Beneath the Twelve Mile Reef, 1953; King of the Khyber Rifles, 1953; White Witch Doctor, 1953; The Egyptian, 1954 [collab. A. Newman]; Garden of Evil, 1954; The Kentuckian, 1955; The Trouble with Harry, 1955; Prince of Players, 1955; The Man in the Gray Flannel Suit, 1956; The Man who Knew Too Much, 1956; Williamsburg, the Story of a Patriot, 1956; The Wrong Man, 1956; A Hatful of Rain, 1957; The Naked and the Dead, 1958; The Seventh Voyage of Sinbad, 1958; Vertigo, 1958; Blue Denim, 1959; Journey to the Center of the Earth, 1959; North by Northwest, 1959; The Three Worlds of Gulliver, 1960; Psycho, 1960; Cape Fear, 1961; Mysterious Island, 1961; Tender is the Night, 1961; The Birds, 1963 [as sound consultant]; Jason and the Argonauts, 1963; Marnie, 1964; Joy in the Morning, 1965; Fahrenheit 451, 1966; Torn Curtain, 1966 [rejected score]; La mariée était en noir [The bride wore black], 1967; Twisted Nerve, 1968; The Battle of Neretva, 1969; The Road Builder [The Night Digger], 1971; Endless Night, 1971; Sisters, 1973; It's Alive, 1974; Obsession, 1976; Taxi Driver, 1976

TELEVISION AND RADIO
Television (all series or compilations partly scored by Herrmann): The Alfred Hitchcock Half Hour; Alfred Hitchcock Presents; The Americans; Collector's Item; Convoy; Ethan Allan; Forecast; Gunsmoke; Have Gun Will Travel; House on "K" Street; Impact; The Kraft Suspense Theatre; Landmark; Pursuit; Rawhide; Studio One; The Twilight Zone; The Virginian
Radio: The Campbell Playhouse; Columbia Presents Corwin; The Columbia Workshop; Crime Classics; Mercury Summer Theatre; The Mercury Theater on the Air; Orson Welles Show; Suspense; others

VOCAL
Ops: Wuthering Heights (op, L. Fletcher, after E. Brontë), 1943–51; A Christmas Carol (M. Anderson, after C. Dickens), 1954 [television]; A child is born (after S.V. Bénet), 1955 [television]
Musl: The King of Schnorrers (D. Lampert and S. Wencelberg after I. Zangwill), 1968
Cants.: Moby Dick (W.C. Harrington, after H. Melville), solo vv, male chorus, orch, 1937–8; Johnny Appleseed, solo vv, chorus, orch, 1940, inc.
Other: The Fantasticks (N. Breton), song cycle, S, A, T, B, chorus, orch, 1942

INST
Orch: Variations on Deep River and Water Boy, 1933; Currier and Ives, suite, 1935; Nocturne and Scherzo, 1936; Sym., 1939–41; For the Fallen, 1943; Welles Raises Kane, suite, 1943
Chbr: Aria, fl, hp, 1932; Marche Militaire, chbr orch, 1932; Aubade, 14 insts, 1933 [rev. as Silent Noon, 1975]; Prelude to Anathema, 15 insts, 1933; Sinfonietta, strs, 1935; Echoes, str qt, 1965; Souvenirs de voyage, cl, str qt, 1967

Principal publisher: Novello

BIBLIOGRAPHY
E. Johnson: *Bernard Herrmann: Hollywood's Music Dramatist* (Rickmansworth, UK, 1977)

G. Bruce: *Bernard Herrmann: Film Music and Narrative* (Ann Arbor, 1985)
L.T. Zador and G. Rose: "A Conversation with Bernard Herrmann," *Film Music 1*, ed. C. McCarty (Los Angeles, 1989, 2/1998), 209–254
C. Palmer: *The Composer in Hollywood* (London and New York, 1990)
S.C. Smith: *A Heart at Fire's Center: the Life and Music of Bernard Herrmann* (Berkeley and Los Angeles, 1991)
R.S. Brown: *Overtones and Undertones: Reading Film Music* (Berkeley and Los Angeles, 1994)
H.S. Wright: "Bernard Herrmann: a Selected Secondary Bibliography," *Music Reference Services Quarterly*, iv/1 (1995), 49–68
F. Thomas: "Musical Keys to *Kane*," *Perspectives on Citizen Kane*, ed. R. Gothesman (New York, 1996), 172–96
D. Neumeyer: "Tonal Design and Narrative in Film Music: Bernard Herrmann's *A Portrait of Hitch* and *The Trouble with Harry*," *Indiana Theory Review*, xix/1–2 (1998), 87–123
D. Cooper: *Bernard Herrmann's "Vertigo": a Film Score Handbook* (Westport, CT, 2001)
The Journal of Film Music, i/2–3 (2003) [issue devoted to Herrmann]
D. Cooper: *Bernard Herrmann's "The Ghost and Mrs. Muir": a Film Score Guide* (Latham, MD, 2005)
L. Whitesell: "Concerto Macabre," *MQ*, lxxxviii/2 (2005), 167–203
J. Sullivan: *Hitchcock's Music* (New Haven, CT, 2007)

DAVID COOPER

Herrmann, Eduard (*b* Oberrottweil, Germany, 18 Dec 1850; *d* New York, NY, 24 April 1937). Violinist of German birth. He studied at the Stuttgart Conservatory and the Berlin Hochschule für Musik. He served as Concertmaster at Schwerin from 1871 and at the Hamburg Opera from 1875. In 1877 he toured as soloist through Germany, Switzerland, and Holland and became concertmaster at the Saint Petersburg Opera from 1878. In 1881 he immigrated to New York City where he formed a quartet with violinist Miska Hauser, violinist Abraham Wolf Lilienthal, and cellist Emil Schenck, and later, with C. Hermann and Schenck, a trio. These chamber music groups proved to be highly successful for many years. His compositions include a violin concerto, a sextet (with oboe and clarinet), a string quartet, a string quintet, violin works, études for the violin, and three cadenzas for Beethoven's Violin Concerto, op.61. He also made many editions and arrangements of compositions by Bach, Handel, Mozart, Beethoven, and Tchaikovsky. He wrote a violin method and works on theosophy, in which he was extremely interested.

BIBLIOGRAPHY
W.S. Pratt, ed.: *The New Encyclopedia of Music and Musicians* (New York, 1927)
V.B. Lawrence, ed.: *Strong on Music: The New York Music Scene in the Days of George Templeton Strong. 1836–1862* (New York and Chicago, 1988–1999)

ANYA LAURENCE

Hersch, Fred(erick S.) (*b* Cincinnati, OH, 21 Oct 1995). Pianist and composer. He started piano lessons while very young, began playing the mandolin soon thereafter, and had written his first symphony by the age of 12. He attended Grinnell College in Iowa and Cincinnati College-Conservatory, before finishing his undergraduate education at the New England Conservatory of Music (BM 1977), where he studied with Sophia Rosoff. After moving to New York Hersch was quickly accepted into the jazz scene and eventually played with such renowned artists as Ron Carter, Art Farmer, Stan Getz,

Charlie Haden, Woody Herman, Clifford Jordan, Art Pepper, and Joe Henderson. He also became an instructor at the New School and taught at the New England Conservatory (1980–86). During the early 1980s he began to record extensively as a leader and soloist; his first album, *Horizons* (1984), introduced his bop and post-bop versatility. Since that time he has remained a highly sought-after performer, working mostly in the jazz idiom, but also recording classical and Broadway albums with some of the world's top singers, including Audra McDonald and Renée Fleming. As a pianist he is known as a sensitive accompanist, a delicately lyrical soloist, and a consummate interpreter of ballads. In 2006 he became the first solo pianist to play a full week's engagement at the Village Vanguard. One of his most important compositions is *Leaves of Grass* (2005, based on the poetry of Walt Whitman) for two voices and octet. A set of four documentaries about his life, *Let yourself Go: the Lives of Fred Hersch* (2006) by the filmmaker Katja Duregger, covers his experiences as a pianist, composer, teacher, and openly gay jazz performer during a two-year period.

BIBLIOGRAPHY

N. Chinen: "Fred Hersch: Songs of Himself," *JT*, xxxiii/1 (2003), 80–87

F. Hersch: "Respiration and Inspiration," *Ask me Now: Conversations on Jazz and Literature*, ed. S. Feinstein (Bloomington, IN, 2007), 151–69

D. Hajdu: "Walt Whitman and Fred Hersch: the Jazz Leaves of Grass," *Heroes and Villains: Essays on Music, Movies, Comics, and Culture* (Cambridge, MA, 2009), 255–60

JONAS WESTOVER

Hersch, Michael (*b* Washington, DC, 25 June 1971). Composer and pianist. When Hersch was 18, his brother Jamie convinced him to watch a video of Georg Solti conducting Beethoven's Symphony no.5. Inspired, Hersch began composition studies at the Peabody Institute, predominantly with Morris Cotel. He continued his studies at the Moscow Conservatory with Albert Leman and Roman Ledenev (Certificate of Composition, 1995), had lessons with JOHN CORIGLIANO, GEORGE ROCHBERG, and JOHN HARBISON, and completed his education at Peabody (MA 1997). Since 2006 he has taught composition there. In 1996 his *Elegy* for strings was chosen by Marin Alsop as the winner of the American Composers Prize and was given its premiere by Alsop at Lincoln Center the following year. Prior to his commencement, Hersch was awarded a Guggenheim Fellowship, and that same year became a fellow at the Tanglewood Music Center, studying under CHRISTOPHER ROUSE. He has since received the Charles Ives Scholarship (1996) and the Godard Lieberson Fellowship (2006) from the American Academy of Arts and Letters, as well as fellowships from the Norfolk Festival for Contemporary Music and the Pacific Music Festival. In addition to the New York Youth Symphony's First Music Prize, he has won the Prix de Rome (2000), working with LUCIANO BERIO, and the Berlin Prize (2001), working with Hans Werner Henze, and was named the Pittsburgh SO's Composer of the Year by Mariss Jansons for the 2002–2003 season. Hersch writes music in a style

that combines dramatic, neo-romantic expression with a muscular, assertive energy and the use of dissonant clusters in harmonies that are extensions of the early- to mid-20th-century legacy of such American symphonists as David Diamond, William Schuman, and Peter Menin. Along with symphonic music, he writes for chamber groups, solo instruments, chorus, solo voice, and soloists with ensemble. Alsop also continues to champion his works: she has recorded his Symphony no.1 (commissioned by the Dallas SO) and Symphony no.2 (a Pittsburgh SO commission) and the symphonic works *Fracta* and *Arraché* (commissioned by the Baltimore SO) with the Bournemouth SO for the Naxos label. He has also written *Umbra* for the Brooklyn PO and Robert Spano (given its premiere in 2001), the Piano Concerto for Garrick Ohlsson (first performed in 2002 by the St. Louis SO and Alsop), and *The Wreckage of Flowers* for violin and piano, written for Midori, who performed the work in Lisbon, London, and New York in 2004; the work has been recorded by Miranda Cuckson. Other ensembles and artists who have performed his works include James DePriest, Alan Gilbert, Gerard Schwarz, the orchestras of Seattle, Atlanta, and Cincinnati, the String Soloists of the Berlin Philharmonic, Boris Pergamenschikow, Walter Boeykens, and Peter Sheppard Skaerved. His discography includes his own performance of his large-scale solo piano work *The Vanishing Pavillions* and Vanguard Classics collections of his Sonatas 1 and 2 for unaccompanied cello , performed by Daniel Gaisford; Hersch playing works by Morton Feldman, Wolfgang Rihm, and his own arrangements of music by Josquin des Prez; and chamber music with Hersch and the Berlin Philharmonic String Soloists.

GEORGE J. GRELLA JR.

Herseth, Adolph S(ylvester) [Bud] (*b* Lake Park, MN, 25 July 1921; *d* Oak Park, IL, 13 April 2013). Trumpeter. He studied with Marcel LaFosse and Georges Mager at the New England Conservatory (1947–48). In 1948 he became first trumpeter with the Chicago SO, a post he held for 53 years. Among the innovations adopted by the orchestra during his time were the use of four identical trumpets (Vincent Bach large-bore C trumpets with no. 229 bell), resulting in a previously unknown homogeneity of sound, and, from 1965, the use of German rotary valve trumpets (J. Monke, L.A. Schmidt) in certain older works for reasons of timbre. Herseth also had a career as a teacher, soloist, and chamber musician, appearing at the Ravinia and Mostly Mozart (1975) festivals and with the Chicago Symphony Brass Ensemble. He nevertheless preferred to concentrate on his orchestral work, with a certain amount of private teaching at his home. During his tenure with the Chicago SO he was perhaps the most respected and influential American orchestral trumpeter. He received several honorary doctorates from American universities, was elected a charter member of the Trumpet Hall of Fame (1970), and was the first orchestral musician to be named Instrumentalist of the Year by *Musical America* (1996).

BIBLIOGRAPHY
K.L. Neidig: "'Man Alive, what a Kick this Is': An Interview with Adolph 'Bud' Herseth," *Instrumentalist*, xxxi/9 (1977), 38
G. Frigerio: "Adolph Herseth: the Great Storyteller," *International Trumpet Guild Journal*, viii/4 (1984), 19
W.N. Woolworth: *A Biography of Adolph S. Herseth: his Performance and Pedagogical Contributions* (diss., Arizona State U., 1993)
M. Tunnell: "Adolph Herseth: in a Class by Himself," *International Trumpet Guild Journal*, xxii/3 (1998), 4–23
F. Keim: *Das grosse Buch der Trompete* (Mainz, 2005), 356
T. Kent: *Within the Sphere of the Master (Adolph Herseth)* (Woodbridge, NJ, 2005)

EDWARD H. TARR

Hertz, Alfred (*b* Frankfurt, 15 July 1872; *d* San Francisco, CA, 17 April 1942). Conductor. After completing his studies at the Frankfurt conservatory, he held positions at Halle (1891–92), Cöthen (summer 1892), Altenburg (1892–95), and Elberfeld (1895–99), where he first conducted Richard Wagner's operas (for which he later became renowned). At the invitation of Frederick Delius, Hertz conducted in London in 1899; Maurice Grau, manager of the Metropolitan Opera, attended the concert and invited him to New York. Hertz was committed to a contract in Breslau, however, and therefore did not start work at the Metropolitan until 1902. He was not unhappy to leave Germany. In his informal autobiography, he recounts several anti-Semitic incidents and notes that he was offered work in Dresden and Berlin but would have been forced to convert to Christianity.

Hertz's debut at the Metropolitan Opera (*Lohengrin*) took place on 28 November 1902. On Christmas Eve 1903 he conducted the first fully-staged complete performance of *Parsifal* outside Germany to the displeasure of Cosima and Siegfried Wagner, who had initiated an unsuccessful lawsuit to prevent it. Hertz also directed the US premiere of Richard Strauss's *Salome* on 22 January 1907, which closed after a single performance due primarily to religious objections.

On 16 April 1906 Hertz opened what was scheduled to be a 12-day residency of the Met in San Francisco with Karl Goldmark's *Die Königin von Saba*. Two days later the city was struck by a devastating earthquake and fire. The members of the opera company (numbering more than 200) found their way by ferry to Oakland and returned to New York, aborting a cross-country tour. The company lost scenery, costumes, properties, and music for 19 operas.

Although Hertz characterized his seven seasons at the Met under general manager Giulio Gatti-Casazza as "the most satisfactory years of my conducting opera," disagreements with the manager, in particular those concerning cuts in *Der Rosenkavalier*, prompted him to resign in 1915. While he was in Los Angeles that July conducting the premiere of Horatio Parker's *Fairyland*, Hertz received an offer to become the conductor of the San Francisco Symphony, which had been founded four years earlier under the direction of Henry Hadley.

Hertz began his San Francisco duties by directing a Beethoven Festival (6–8 August 1915), which was highly successful in musical terms but problematic politically. He was falsely accused of refusing to conduct "The Star-Spangled Banner" following the performance of the Ninth Symphony (the concertmaster had taken it upon himself to do so while Hertz was off-stage), beginning a tension that continued for many years with some members of the orchestra's board of directors who had supported Hadley's reappointment. During his 15-year tenure (1915–30), Hertz dramatically improved the orchestra's quality, as demonstrated by a series of Victor recordings beginning in 1925. Indeed, the orchestra was one of the first in the country to make recordings as well as to broadcast on radio (Standard Oil broadcasts began in 1926). Hertz successfully reached new audiences through run-out concerts in the Bay Area, spring music festivals (1923–25), a summer season (from 1926), and, most important, an annual series of Municipal Concerts consisting of five performances per year underwritten by the city and featuring renowned soloists at low prices (1922–30). Eleven-year-old Yehudi Menuhin played the Beethoven Violin Concerto at one of them in 1928, attracting nearly 11,000 auditors.

Hertz was the first conductor of the Hollywood Bowl concerts in 1922 and he returned there frequently in later years. He was also the first conductor of a major symphony to admit women other than harpists. Five female string players appeared in the San Francisco Symphony's ranks during the 1924–25 season. After retiring in 1930, Hertz conducted the orchestra occasionally, but his health declined. In June 1937 he was tapped by Harlé Jervis, state director of the Federal Music Project, to serve as administrative head of the Northern California FMP after Jervis clashed with the former San Francisco supervisor (composer Ernst Bacon). Hertz served until December 1938 in an advisory (nonconducting) capacity.

Hertz and his wife, Austrian soprano Lilly Dorn, had no children. At his death he left a $300,000 endowment to the music department of the University of California, Berkeley, launching the present 678-seat Hertz Hall and supporting student scholarships.

WRITINGS
"Facing the Music," informal autobiography published in installments in the *San Francisco Chronicle* (3 May–14 July 1942); typescript at the Jean Hargrove Music Library, UC Berkeley

BIBLIOGRAPHY
L.E. Miller: "'The Multitude Listens with the Heart': Orchestras, Urban Culture, and the Early Years of the San Francisco Symphony," *Music, American Made: Essays in Honor of John Graziano*, ed. J. Koegel (Sterling Heights, MI, 2011), 161–90
L. Rothe: *Music for a City, Music for the World: 100 Years with the San Francisco Symphony* (San Francisco, 2011)

LETA E. MILLER

Hervig, Richard B(ilderback) (*b* Story City, IA, 24 Nov 1917; *d* Iowa City, IA, 6 Sept 2010). Composer and educator. He studied English at Augustana College, Sioux Falls, South Dakota (BA 1939), and after teaching for a time in the public schools, studied composition with PHILIP GREELEY CLAPP at the University of Iowa (MA 1942, PhD 1947). He joined the faculty there in 1955 and became the founding director of the Center for New Music in 1966. Upon his retirement in 1988, he was appointed to a post at the Juilliard School, where he co-chaired the Literature & Materials of Music Department and taught until 2000. His pupils have included CHARLES DODGE and WILLIAM HIBBARD, among others. He has received commissions from the National Music Council, the National Federation of Music Clubs, and numerous performers.

Hervig's compositions, most of which are instrumental and tonal, show a disciplined approach to standard forms and an exploration of timbral possibilities. In two early works, the Clarinet Sonata no.1 and the String Quartet, he casts sections in conflicting rhythms, exploiting the resulting tensions. In the Chamber Music for Six Players, he continued his concern for establishing relationships between the parts while maintaining a separate musical personality for each instrument; in this way, his compositional approach takes on concerns more readily associated with the theater.

WORKS

Orch: Music for a Concert, 1959; Sym., 1960; A Diversion, band, 1963; Iowa Festival, band, 1964; The President's Fanfare, band, 1964; In Those Days, 1987; In Summer Season, str, 1988; Conc., vn, chbr orch, 1992, Iowa 150, A Diversion for Orchestra, 1996

Vocal: Ubi sunt? (*The Wanderer*, anon., medieval), SATB, brass qt, 1964; Quid est musica? (Cassiodorus: *Musica enchiriadis*), chbr chorus, 12 insts, 1972; 5 Romantic Songs (Byron, P.B. Shelley, W. Wordsworth, A. Tennyson), medium v, pf, 1982; 3 Modern Parables (S. Crane), SATB, 1983; Epitaph (B. Franklin), SATB, 1985; Woman with a Torch (T. Jefferson, E. Lazarus), SATB, pf, 1986; 3 Sandburg Songs (C. Sandburg), SATB, org, 1987; see also CHBR AND SOLO INST [The Subtle Thief, arr. 1997]

Chbr and solo inst: Sonata no.1, cl, pf, 1953; Str Qt, 1955; Music, wind, perc, 1960; Diversion, trbn, perc, 1969; Sonata no.2, cl, pf, 1971; Chbr Music for Six Players, fl, cl, vn, db, pf, perc, 1976; An Entertainment, cl, vib/mar, 1978; Sonata, vn, pf, 1979; Lyric Piece, tpt, hp, 1981; Suite, vib/mar, 1981; Airs and Roulades, cl, wind, 1982; The Tree, 9 insts, 1984; Blue Horns, 6-pt hn choir, 1990; The Subtle Thief, fl, cl, vn, va, vc, 1990 [arr. (J. Milton), Mez, pf, 1997]; Off Center, cl, vc, perc, 1991; 4 Impressions, gui, 1993; Fantasy and Toccata, pf, 1998; For Andy Carlson, vn, pf, 1999; A Diversion for Viola and Contrabass, 1999; Suzuki Variation for 4 Violas, 2000; A Diversion, vc, pf, 2004

MSS in *IO*

Principal publishers: ACA, Associated, Columbia, Southern

J. GOTTLIEB/CHRISTIAN CAREY

Herz, Eric (*b* Cologne, Germany, 10 Dec 1919; *d* Barton, VT, 25 May 2002). Keyboard instrument maker of German birth. In 1938 he moved to Israel, where he trained as a cabinetmaker (1939–42) and graduated from the Jerusalem Conservatory of Music (1942). He was a bandsman for the British army (1942–5) and then became a flutist in the Israel PO (1946–52). He immigrated to the United States in 1952 and for a short time was a piano technician for the Baldwin company and concert tuner for Claudio Arrau. From 1952 to 1954 Herz was associated with the harpsichord makers Frank Hubbard and William Dowd, and then set up his own workshop in Harvard, Massachusetts. In 1964, as Eric Herz Harpsichords, Inc., the business moved to Cambridge, Massachusetts. For a brief period during the 1960s Herz was a consultant for the Cannon Guild, an ill-fated attempt at commercial harpsichord production.

Herz's shop produced about 500 instruments before he retired in 1995. His early efforts were aimed at producing extremely stable all-purpose harpsichords; for example, he laminated his soundboards with fiberglass. Later he turned to more historically oriented models, including English harpsichords after Jacob Kirckman, Franco-Flemish-style single and double harpsichords, and clavichords after Johann Christoph Schiedmayer. One of the most respected makers of his generation, his instruments are noted for their excellent workmanship and fine tone, as well as their reliability.

BIBLIOGRAPHY

W.J. Zuckermann: *The Modern Harpsichord* (New York, 1969), 127–29

MARIBEL MEISEL/EDWARD L. KOTTICK

Herz, Henri [Heinrich] (*b* Vienna, Austria, 6 Jan 1803; *d* Paris, France, 5 Jan 1888). Austrian pianist, composer, and teacher. He studied piano with his father and with Daniel Hünten and in 1816 entered the Paris Conservatoire, where he was a piano student of Louis-Barthélemy Pradher. He soon established himself as one of the leading virtuoso pianists of the 1820s and 1830s, noted for his graceful and immaculate technique, and toured frequently. He eventually served as professor of piano at the Paris Conservatoire (1842–74), built an important concert hall in Paris (Salle Herz), and founded a factory that manufactured award-winning pianos. He became one of the most popular composers for the piano during the second quarter of the 19th century, producing primarily brilliant variations on popular tunes and fantasias on opera themes—genres typical of the period. He also designed many of his works for the growing number of amateur pianists. Despite the vilification of his compositions by Robert Schumann, through which he is primarily known today, his works were performed by Clara Wieck Schumann (before her marriage) and Franz Liszt; the latter invited Herz to contribute a variation (along with Frédéric Chopin, Carl Czerny, Johann Peter Pixis, and Sigismond Thalberg) to *Hexaméron*, a set of variations on a theme from Bellini's *I puritani*, whose publication was to benefit Italian refugees.

After Leopold de Meyer, Herz was the first important European pianist to appear in the United States, making his debut in New York on 29 October 1846. He soon engaged as his manager Bernard Ullman, under whose guidance in 1847 he toured the East Coast and Midwest with the violinist Camillo Sivori; they were joined that autumn by the cellist George Knoop. In 1849 Herz appeared with the violinist Frans Coenen and former soloists of the Astor Place Italian Opera Company. The following year, after an extended stay in Mexico, he became the first virtuoso to appear in California; he then toured western South America before returning in 1851 to Europe, having given approximately 200 concerts in more than 50 American cities. Herz played chiefly his own works—concertos, variations, and operatic fantasias—but with Sivori and Knoop also performed trios by Beethoven. He composed a number of works while in the United States, including variations on "The Last Rose of Summer" and two minstrel tunes in one set, "Oh! Susanna" and "Carry Me Back to Old

Virginia." He was the first to organize performances in the United States of works arranged for multiple pianos (Rossini's overtures to *Guillaume Tell* and *Semiramide*), played by sixteen pianists on eight pianos. During his American tour, he also promoted and sold pianos made at his Paris factory. His memoirs of his American travels are often cited but are frequently untrustworthy. His claim that Americans covered piano legs for the sake of decency has been proven false; the legs were covered to protect them (Lott, 2003, 92–95).

BIBLIOGRAPHY
GMO

H. Herz: *Mes voyages en Amérique* (Paris, 1866; Eng. trans. Madison, WI, 1963)

D. Garvelmann: Introduction to *H. Herz: Variations on Non più mesta* (New York, 1970)

L.M. Lerner: *The Rise of the Impresario: Bernard Ullman and the Transformation of Musical Culture in Nineteenth Century America* (diss., U. of Wisconsin, 1970)

R.A. Lott: *The American Concert Tours of Leopold de Meyer, Henri Herz, and Sigismond Thalberg* (diss., CUNY, 1986)

J. Kallberg, ed.: *Piano Music of the Parisian Virtuosos: 1810–1860*, iv: *Henri Herz: Selected Works* (New York, 1993)

S. Lindeman: *Structural Novelty and Tradition in the Early Romantic Piano Concerto* (Stuyvesant, NY, 1998)

C. Kammertöns: *Chronique scandaleuse: Henri Herz, ein Enfant terrible in der französischen Musikkritik des 19. Jahrhunderts* (Essen, Germany, 2000)

R.A. Lott: *From Paris to Peoria: How European Piano Virtuosos Brought Classical Music to the American Heartland* (New York, 2003)

L. Schnapper: "La tournée Henri Herz aux Amériques (1846–1851)," *Le musicien et ses voyages: Pratiques, réseaux et représentations*, ed. C. Meyer (Berlin, 2003), 203–22

L. Schnapper: "Bernard Ullman-Henri Herz: an Example of Financial and Artistic Partnership, 1846–1849," *The Musician as Entrepreneur, 1700–1914: Managers, Charlatans, and Idealists*, ed. W. Weber (Bloomington, IN, 2004), 130–44

R. ALLEN LOTT

Herzog, George (*b* Budapest, Hungary, 11 Dec 1901; *d* Indianapolis, IN, 4 Nov 1983). Ethnomusicologist of Hungarian birth. He studied at the Royal Academy of Music, Budapest (1917–19), at the Berlin Hochschule für Musik (1920–22), and with EGON PETRI (piano) in 1921; while at Berlin University (1922–4) he was an assistant to Erich von Hornbostel at the Phonogramm-Archiv. On immigrating to the United States in 1925 he studied anthropology at Columbia University, where he was influenced by Franz Boas, at the University of Chicago (1929–31), and at Yale University (1932–5), and participated in the University of Chicago Anthropological Expedition to Liberia (1930–31). In 1935 and 1947 he was awarded Guggenheim fellowships. He took the doctorate at Columbia (1937) with a dissertation on the musical styles of the Pueblo and the Pima and taught anthropology there until 1948, when he was appointed professor of anthropology at Indiana University, Bloomington. With him he brought the Columbia University Archives of Folk and Primitive Music (established by him in 1936), which became the Indiana University Archives of Traditional Music. He retired as emeritus professor in 1962.

Herzog was a pioneer of ethnomusicological studies at American academic institutions. Besides teaching courses in linguistics and cultural anthropology he introduced courses in primitive and folk music (1936) and comparative musicology (1941) at Columbia, later amalgamating them as a course in folk, primitive, and oriental music (1944). A leading authority on North American Indian music, he engaged in field research among such western tribes as the Yuma, the Pima, the Maricopa, the Pueblo, the Comanche, the Dakota, and the Navajo. His early interest in methods of transcription and analysis extended his research into the traditional folk music of such European cultures as the Irish, Yugoslavs, Greeks, Spanish, and Jewish (Judeo-Spanish). Besides developing an important archive of commercial and field recordings, he undertook invaluable bibliographical surveys of published materials and compiled descriptive catalogs of archives in museums, institutions, and private collections. In addition to his dissertation, Herzog wrote two books, *Research in Primitive and Folk Music in the United States: a Survey* (1936) and, with C.G. Blooah, *Jabo Proverbs from Liberia: Maxims in the Life of a Native Tribe* (1936).

WRITINGS
(selective list)

"The Yuman Musical Style," *Journal of American Folklore*, xli (1928), 183–231

"Musical Styles in North America," *Proceedings of the Twenty-Third International Congress of Americanists: New York 1928* (New York, 1930/R), 455–8

"The Collections of Phonograph Records in North America and Hawaii," *Zeitschrift für vergleichende Musikwissenschaft*, i (1933), 58–62

"Maricopa Music," in L. Spier, *Yuman Tribes of the Gila River* (Chicago, 1933), 271–9

Appx of song transcrs. in T. Adamson, *Folk Tales of the Coast Salish* (Philadelphia, 1934), 422–30

"Speech-Melody and Primitive Music," *MQ*, xx (1934), 452–66

"Plains Ghost Dance and Great Basin Music," *American Anthropologist*, new ser., xxxvii (1935), 403–19

"Special Song Types in North American Indian Music," *Zeitschrift für vergleichende Musikwissenschaft*, iii (1935), 1–6, 23–33

"Recording Primitive Music in Africa and America," *The Folk-Song Society of the Northeast* (1935), 180-1

A Comparison of Pueblo and Pima Musical Styles (New York, 1937; *Journal of American Folklore*, xlix (1936), 283–417 [diss.])

"Musical Typology in Folksong," *Southern Folklore Quarterly*, i (1937), 49–55

"The Study of Folksong in America," *ibid.*, ii (1938), 59–64

"Etats-Unis d'Amérique," *Folklore musical* (Paris, 1939), 85–128

"The Study of Native Music in America," *Proceedings of the Eighth American Scientific Congress: Washington DC 1940*, ii, ed. P.H. Oehser (Washington DC, 1942), 203–9

"African Influences in North American Indian Music," *PAMS Congress of Musicology: New York 1939*, ed. A. Mendel, G. Reese, and G. Chase (New York, 1944), 130–43

The Cow-Tail Switch (New York. 1947) (with H. Courlander)

"Salish Music," *Indians of the Urban Northwest*, ed. M.W. Smith (New York, 1949), 93–109

BIBLIOGRAPHY
GMO

B. Krader: "George Herzog: Bibliography of his General and Theoretical Works, Area and Special Studies, and Reviews," *Ethno-Musicology Newsletter*, no. 6 (Jan 1956), 11–20

B. Nettl: "George Herzog: an 80th Birthday Appreciation," *EM*, xxv/3 (1981), 499–500

D.P. McAllester: "George Herzog (1901–1984)," *EM*, xxix/1 (1985), 86–87

C.V. Inman: "George Herzog: Struggles of a Sound Archivist," *Resound*, v/1 (1986), 1–5

C.E. Steinzor: *The First Generation of American Musicologists: a Bio-Bibliography* (Buffalo, 1987)

B. Nettl: "The IFMC/ICTM and the Development of Ethnomusicology in the United States," *YTM*, xx (1988), 19–25

D.B. Reed: "The Innovator and the Primitives: George Herzog in Historical Perspective," *Folklore Forum*, xxvi/1-2 (1993), 69–92

D.B. Reed: "George Herzog: a Contemporary Look at his Work and Ideas. I & II," *Resound*, xiii/3–4 (1994), 1–6; xiv/1–2 (1995–6), 1–8

E. Gooding: "'We Come to You as the Dead': Ethnomusicology, Colonialism, and the Standing Rock Reservation, 1868–1964," *Resound*, xvi/1–2 (1997), 1–14

G. List: "The Early Days of the Archives," *Resound*, xviii/1 (1999), 4–5

M. McLean: *Pioneers of Ethnomusicology* (Cold Springs, FL 2006)

ISRAEL J. KATZ

Heth, Charlotte Anne Wilson (*b* Muskogee, OK, 29 Oct, 1937). Ethnomusicologist, educator, and administrator. A member of the Cherokee Nation, Heth was one of the first ethnomusicologists to provide an insider's perspective on the scholarly study of Native American music. She studied first at the University of Tulsa (BA 1959, MM 1960). She taught at various secondary schools and served in the Peace Corps in Ethiopia before returning to UCLA for doctoral studies, where she received the PhD (1975) with a dissertation on the stomp dance music of the Oklahoma Cherokees.

Between 1974 and 1987 Heth served as professor of music and ethnomusicology at UCLA. In addition, she served as department chair, director of American Indian Studies Center, and Assistant Dean for the School of Arts and Architecture at various times during her tenure at UCLA. From 1994 to 1999 Charlotte Heth served as the Assistant Director for Public Programs at the National Museum of the American Indian (Washington, DC). After her retirement, Heth worked with the UCLA Ethnomusicology Archive in repatriating digital copies of her field recordings to members of the Cherokee Nation. She has produced numerous audio and video recordings, including those of Cherokee, Navajo, Pueblo, Seneca, Northern Arapaho, Northern Plains, Creek, Yurok, and Southern Plains performances. Heth is also author of many articles and books on Native American music and served as President for the Society of Ethnomusicology (1993–5). She is currently Professor Emerita in Ethnomusicology at UCLA.

WRITINGS

"Sharing a Heritage," *Contemporary American Indian Issues Series*, no. 5 (1984)

Native American Dance: Ceremonies and Social Traditions (Washington, DC, 1992)

Issues for the Future of American Indian Studies: A Needs Assessment and Program Guide (Los Angeles, 1992)

JOHN B. VALLIER

Hewitt. Family of musicians.

(1) Hewitt, James (*b* Dartmoor, England, 4 June 1770; *d* Boston, MA, 2 Aug 1827). Musician of English birth and father of a large musical family. Hewitt made a significant contribution to musical life in the new nation through his active engagement as a composer, music publisher, merchant, and orchestra conductor in New York, Boston, and other American cities between 1792 and 1825. All of his six children and three of his grandchildren pursued careers in music or music-related professions, which ensured the Hewitt family's continuing influence on American musical life through the early 20th century. His children include Sophia Henrietta Emma Hewitt Ostinelli (1799–1845), a recognized concert pianist; John Hill Hewitt (1801–90), a renowned composer of parlor music; James Lang Hewitt (1803–53), a successful publisher; Eliza Helena Hewitt (1805–76), a music educator; Horatio Nelson Hewitt (1807–56), a manager of a music store; and George Washington Hewitt (1811–93), a music educator and composer. Of his grandchildren, Eliza Ostinelli Biscaccianti (1824–96) was an opera singer, Horatio Dawes Hewitt (1829–94) a composer, and Hobart Doane Hewitt (1851–1932) a composer and music editor at the Theodore Presser Company.

Early documents indicate that James Hewitt resided at 12 Hyde Street, Bloomsbury, London, during 1791–92. Hoping to better his fortunes, in 1792 he sailed on the *Bristol* to America, where he and some of his fellow passengers were recruited by the Old American Company, a theatrical troupe active in New York. Upon his arrival, he advertised himself as a "professor of music from the Opera House, Hanover Square, and Professional Concerts under the direction of Haydn, Pleyel, etc., London," although no evidence of these activities remains. He lived in New York until 1811, his longest period of residence at one address being from 1801 to 1810 at 59 Maiden Lane. From 1792 until the end of March 1808, he was conductor of the orchestra of the Old American Company at the Park Street Theatre, where his duties included arranging and composing music for many ballad operas and other musical productions. He also operated his own musical repository, where he gave lessons and sold musical instruments and music composed by himself and others. In addition, Hewitt was quite active as a violinist and orchestra conductor in various benefit and subscription concerts.

His musical activities in Boston began as early as 1805, though the family did not move there until 1811. He pursued the same musical interests there as in New York, conducting the orchestra at the Federal Street Theatre, giving lessons, and composing and publishing music; he was also the organist at Trinity Episcopal Church. In 1816 he returned to New York, taking his two eldest sons with him. Between 1820 and 1825 he traveled often between Boston, New York, and several southern cities, in particular, Charleston, South Carolina, and Augusta, Georgia. In late 1826 he underwent an unsuccessful operation in New York, and in early 1827 he was brought back to his family in Boston, where he died.

Hewitt published at least 639 compositions, most by British composers such as William Shield, Michael Kelly, and James Hook, though he also issued works by George Frederick Handel, Franz Joseph Haydn, and Wolfgang Amadeus Mozart and approximately 167 of his own compositions. These extant works include 75 instrumental and 92 vocal compositions and stage works (largely ballad operas), many making use of American patriotic and popular tunes. His music is well structured and pleasant and is on a par with that of his English brethren such as Kelly, Shield, and Stephen Storace, and of the American composers Alexander Reinagle, Benjamin Carr, and Gottlieb Graupner. Hewitt also arranged instrumental and vocal works by others, was a prolific craftsman of medleys, and was the author of three pedagogical treatises, of which *A Complete Instructor for the Pianoforte* (*c*1805) is the most widely recognized.

In keeping with many emigrant professionals, Hewitt was an influential figure in the musical cultural of his time, effectively instigating an extension of the London stage. His position as conductor of the Park Street Theatre orchestra and many others gave him a key role in the musical life of New York. His publishing endeavors figured in the rapid growth of music trades in the city, where English popular music and American patriotic songs were the mainstays of sheet music sales. In Boston, his activities included business dealings with Carr, from whom he purchased a music shop in 1797, and Graupner.

BIBLIOGRAPHY

O.G.T. Sonneck: *A Bibliography of Early Secular American Music* (Washington DC, 1905; rev. and enlarged by W.T. Upton, 2/1945/R)

O.G.T. Sonneck: *Early Concert-Life in America* (Leipzig, 1907/R, 2/1949)

J.T. Howard: "The Hewitt Family in American Music," *MQ*, xvii/1 (1931), 25–39

I. Lowens: *Music and Musicians in Early America* (New York, 1964)

R.J. Wolfe: *Secular Music in America, 1801–1825: a Bibliography* (New York, 1964)

J.W. Wagner: *James Hewitt: his Life and Works* (diss., Indiana U., 1969)

J.W. Wagner: "James Hewitt, 1770–1827," *MQ*, lviii/2 (1972), 259–76

J.W. Wagner: "Some Early Musical Moments in Augusta," *Georgia Historical Quarterly*, xvi (1972), 529

J.W. Wagner: "The Music of James Hewitt: a Supplement to the Sonneck-Upton and Wolfe Bibliographies," *Notes*, xxix/2 (1972), 224–27

J.B. Clark: *Anthology of Early American Keyboard Music, 1787–1830*, RRAM, i (Westport, CT, 1977)

R.J. Wolfe: *Early American Music Engraving and Printing* (Urbana, IL, 1980)

J. Hewitt: *Selected Compositions*, ed. J. R. Wagner, RRAM, vii (Madison, WI, 1980)

V.B. Lawrence: "Mr. Hewitt Lays It on the Line," *19th-Century Music*, v/1 (1981), 3–15

J. Ogasapian: *Music of the Colonial and Revolutionary Era, American History through Music* (Westport, CT, 2004), 160–67

JOHN W. WAGNER/KIMBERLY GREENE

(2) Hewitt, John Hill (*b* New York, NY, 11 July 1801; *d* Baltimore, MD, 7 Oct 1890). Composer, music teacher, and writer; son of (1) James Hewitt. After apprenticeships in various trades in New York and Boston, he secured a commission to the military academy at West Point in 1818 but resigned in 1822. He received his only known instruction in music from the academy's bandmaster, Richard Willis. In 1823, Hewitt accompanied his father on a theatrical tour of the Southeast that ended unsuccessfully when a fire destroyed the theater in Augusta, Georgia. He then began a long and largely itinerant career as a music teacher and journalist spent almost entirely in the Southeast.

Hewitt returned to Boston in 1827. After his father's death later that year, he married Estelle Magnin of New York; the couple had seven children. Their eldest son, Horatio Dawes Hewitt (1829–94), operated music stores in New Orleans, Baltimore, and possibly St. Louis. He composed several dances for the piano and a three-act opera, *The Pearl of Granada*. From 1828 to 1840 John Hill Hewitt resided in Baltimore, where he won a poetry competition under a nom de plume with his selection "The Song of the Wind" in which Edgar Allan Poe had submitted "The Coliseum." After more traveling, including a stay in Washington, DC, where he gave music lessons to President John Tyler's daughter Alice and edited the newspaper *Capitol*, Hewitt was offered a position as a music teacher at the Chesapeake Female College near Hampton, Virginia, in 1848. He taught there until his wife's death in 1859.

In 1863 Hewitt married a former pupil, Mary Alethia Smith, who bore him four more children. After spending the remainder of the Civil War in Augusta and Savannah, Georgia, and the immediate postwar years at various colleges in Virginia, he moved his family to Baltimore around 1874 and remained there until his death in 1890.

Best known of the Southern composers, Hewitt wrote prolifically. His music is characterized as conforming to the "genteel tradition" of elegance, artificiality, and sentimentality. He wrote more than 300 songs, most of which were published; the most popular, "The Minstrel's Return from the War" (1825), was also his first attempt at composition. Hamm (1983) considers "All Quiet along the Potomac Tonight" (1863)—"powerful, dramatic, antiwar"—to be Hewitt's best song. He composed six musical stage works during the Civil War, the most popular being the three-act operetta *The Vivandière* (1862). Hewitt's prose, poetry, and plays remain largely unpublished; four volumes of his autobiographical writings are held at Emory University Library, Atlanta, with a fifth at the New York Public Library. N. Hickman of Baltimore published a volume of Hewitt's early poems (1838); his memoir, *Shadows on the Wall* (1877), contains his later poetry.

BIBLIOGRAPHY

J.T. Howard: "The Hewitt Family in American Music," *MQ*, xvii/1 (1931), 25–39

C.E. Huggins: *John Hill Hewitt: Bard of the Confederacy* (diss., Florida State U., 1964)

W.C. Winden: *The Life and Music Theatre Works of John Hill Hewitt* (diss., U. of Illinois, 1972)

C. Hamm: *Yesterdays: Popular Song in America* (New York, 1979)

F.W. Hoogerwerf: *John Hill Hewitt: Sources and Bibliography* (Atlanta, GA, 1981)

C. Hamm: *Music in the New World* (New York, 1983)

N. Tawa: *A Music for the Millions* (New York, 1984)

C.S. Watson: "Confederate Drama: The Plays of John Hill Hewitt and James Dabney McCabe," *Southern Literary Journal* xxi/2 (1989), 100–12

N.L. Orr and L.W. Bertrand: *The Collected Works of John Hill Hewitt* (New York, 1994)

N.L. Orr: "John Hill Hewitt: Bard of the Confederacy," *American Music Research Center Journal*, iv (1994), 31–75

V.B. Lawrence: *Strong on Music: The New York Music Scene in the Days of George Templeton Strong. 1. Resonances, 1836–1849* (Chicago, 1995), 396–99

M.A. Snell and B.C. Kelly: *Bugle Resounding: Music and Musicians of the Civil War Era, Shades of Blue and Gray* (Columbia, MO, 2004)

JOHN W. WAGNER/KIMBERLY GREENE

(3) Sophia Henrietta Emma Hewitt Ostinelli (*b* New York, NY, 13 June 1799; *d* Portland, ME, 3 Sept 1845). Pianist, organist, singer, harpist, and music teacher; daughter of (1) James Hewitt. She studied piano with George K. Jackson and Peter K. Moran and harp with Ferrand. She made her debut as a concert pianist at the age of seven in New York on 21 April 1807. Her numerous concert appearances in New York and Boston over the next several years brought the music of Haydn, Handel, Ludwig van Beethoven, and other premier composers to American audiences and included what may have been the first public performance in America of a piano sonata by Beethoven (op.26, Boston, 27 February 1819). She became the organist for the Handel and Haydn Society (Boston) in 1819 and the organist for the Philharmonic Society of Boston the following year. Her performances were favorably received but conformed to the conventions of appropriateness for women at this time. An accomplished singer as well, she appeared at the New York concerts of the Euterpean Society. In 1822 she married the violinist Louis Ostinelli, who collaborated with Gottlieb Graupner in the founding of the Philharmonic Society in Boston, and soon after their wedding the couple embarked on a concert tour of Maine and other New England states. The Ostinellis had two children; their daughter, Eliza (*b* Boston, MA, 1824; *d* Paris, France, July 1896), was a well-known soprano. She made her debut in Vincenzo Bellini's *La sonnambula* (The Sleepwalker) in New York on 8 December 1847 and subsequently achieved considerable success in the United States (especially Gold Rush–era California), Europe, and South America with her performances of Italian opera. She married the Italian cellist Count Alessandro Biscaccianti.

BIBLIOGRAPHY
J.T. Howard: "The Hewitt Family in American Music," *MQ*, xvii/1 (1931), 38
H.E. Johnson: *Musical Interludes in Boston* (New York, 1943)
C.H. Horton: *Serious Art and Concert Music for the Piano in America in the 100 Years from Alexander Reinagle to Edward MacDowell* (diss., U. of North Carolina, 1965)
J.W. Wagner: *James Hewitt: his Life and Works* (diss., Indiana U., 1969)
B. Owen: "Sophie Hewitt Ostinelli," *American Organist*, 25 (1991), 50–52
V.B. Lawrence: *Strong on Music: The New York Music Scene in the Days of George Templeton Strong. 1. Resonances, 1836–1849* (Chicago, 1995), 461–62

JOHN W. WAGNER/R

(4) James Lang Hewitt (*b* New York, NY, 28 Sept 1803; *d* New York, NY, 24 March 1853). Music publisher, son of (1) James Hewitt. He established a music publishing firm (unconnected with that of his father) in Boston in 1825 in partnership with James A. Dickson. In 1829 he moved to New York and became a prominent dealer and publisher until his death. For many years, his store on Broadway remained a popular gathering place for musicians. He issued works by Haydn, Gioachino Rossini, Carl Maria von Weber, and Lowell Mason, in addition to compositions by his father and his elder brother John Hill Hewitt. Horatio Nelson Hewitt (*b* New York, NY, 7 Oct 1807; *d* New York, NY, 12 Oct 1856), another son of (1) James Hewitt, was listed as a music publisher in the Boston city directory from 1830 to 1832. No publications by his firm are extant, but he may have been the Boston representative for his brother's firm. After James Lang Hewitt's death, his plates were used by many other publishing companies, including Firth, Hall, and Pond.

BIBLIOGRAPHY
J.T. Howard: "The Hewitt Family in American Music," *MQ*, xvii/1 (1931), 25–39
J.W. Wagner: *James Hewitt: his Life and Works* (diss., Indiana U., 1969)
J.W. Wagner: "James Hewitt, 1770–1827," *MQ*, lviii/2 (1972), 259–76
D.W. Krummel and S. Sadie: *Music Printing and Publishing* (New York, 1990)

JOHN W. WAGNER/R

(5) George Washington [Thomas] **Hewitt** (*b* New York, NY, 23 Feb 1811; *d* Burlington, NJ, 4 May 1893). Teacher and composer, son of (1) James Hewitt. Baptismal records give his name as George Thomas; the proximity of his birthday to that of George Washington no doubt influenced the change. By 1832 he was in Portland, Maine, teaching piano and organ and arranging music for military bands. He pursued a disastrous music-publishing career in Philadelphia from 1839 to 1841 and then settled in Burlington, New Jersey, where he taught music in St. Mary's Hall, an Episcopal school for girls. His sister Eliza Helena Hewitt (*b* New York, NY, 15 Sept 1805; *d* Burlington, NJ, 22 Sept 1876) also taught music at the school. George Washington Hewitt composed some short piano pieces and parlor songs, at least one of which was published. His son Hobart Doane Hewitt (*b* Burlington, NJ, 15 March 1851; *d* Burlington, NJ, 30 March 1932) was also a teacher and composer; he played violin in the Germania Orchestra of Philadelphia and served for several years as a music editor for Theodore Presser & Company.

BIBLIOGRAPHY
J.T. Howard: "The Hewitt Family in American Music," *MQ*, xvii/1 (1931), 25–39
J.W. Wagner: *James Hewitt: his Life and Works* (diss., Indiana U., 1969)
J.W. Wagner: "James Hewitt, 1770–1827," *MQ*, lviii/2 (1972), 259–76
C.H. Kaufman: *Music in New Jersey, 1655–1860: a Study of Musical Activity and Musicians in New Jersey from its First Settlement to the Civil War* (London, 1981), 96, 116

JOHN W. WAGNER/R

Hewitt, Angela (Mary) (*b* Ottawa, ON, 26 July 1958). Canadian pianist. Born into a musical family, she first studied the piano with her mother (her parents have been a profound influence throughout her career) before studying from the age of six at the Royal Conservatory of Music in Toronto, where her teachers included Myrtle Rose Guerrero. Her most important teacher was Jean-Paul Sévilla, with whom she studied at the University of Ottawa. She graduated at the age of 18, and after a seven-year spell in Paris settled in London in 1985. That year she won first prize at the Toronto International Bach Piano Competition, and it is as an interpreter of Bach that she has laid the bedrock of her reputation. Her Bach has been described as having a poetic verisimilitude that transcends the issue of instrumental representation. She explained: "I never think about the fact that I'm playing Bach on the piano. I'm thinking more of the human voice, of the violin, of an orchestra." Her playing is widely applauded for its rhythmic vitality and tonal clarity, and for showing an idiomatic empathy that has drawn comparisons with some of the most exalted Bach pianists, including Rosalyn Tureck and Edwin Fischer. In 1994 she signed with the Hyperion record label to record the entire cycle of Bach's keyboard music; that project was completed 11 years and 14 discs later. Her large repertory extends far beyond Bach, and she is especially renowned for her warm and colorful playing of French music, particularly François Couperin, Emmanuel Chabrier, Maurice Ravel, and Olivier Messiaen. She has also received accolades for her recordings of works by Robert Schumann, G.F. Handel, and Joseph Haydn, as well as Ludwig van Beethoven's complete cycle of cello sonatas, recorded with cellist Daniel Müller-Schott. Hewitt founded the annual Trasimeno Music Festival, held in Magione, Italy, in 2004.

BIBLIOGRAPHY

H. Finch: "Redefining Bach," *Gramophone*, lxxix/Sept (2001), 8–11

TIM PARRY/MEGAN E. HILL

Hewitt, Helen (Margaret) (*b* Granville, NY, 2 May 1900; *d* Denton, TX, 19 March 1977). Musicologist. She attended Vassar College (BA 1921) and the Eastman School of Music (BM 1925). She completed graduate degrees at Union Theological Seminary (Master of Sacred Music 1932) and Columbia University (MA 1933) and then studied under Heinrich Besseler at the University of Heidelberg. She was awarded the PhD at Radcliffe College in 1938. She also studied the organ with Charles-Marie Widor and harmony with NADIA BOULANGER at the American Conservatory, Fontainebleau (1926) and organ with W. LYNNWOOD FARNAM at the Curtis Institute, Philadelphia (1928–30). She taught at the State Normal School, Potsdam, New York (1925–8), Florida State College for Women (1938–9), and Hunter College (1942) before arriving in 1942 at North Texas State University, where she taught until her retirement in 1969. She prepared exemplary editions of two of Petrucci's chanson collections, *Harmonice Musices Odhecaton A* (1942, 2/1946/R1978) and *Canti B* (1967), providing a scholarly introduction with extensive lists of sources, concordances, and textual and musical analyses. She also compiled the first four editions of the comprehensive *Doctoral Dissertations in Musicology* (1952, 4/1965). Upon her retirement, Hewitt gave her significant collection of organ music to the Music Library at the University of North Texas. The library received the balance of her personal collection and her papers, including correspondence with Willi Apel and Jean Langlais, after her death.

BIBLIOGRAPHY

J.M. Bowers: "Women and the American Musicological Society: Pioneering Scholars and Officers," *Frauen in der Musikwissenschaft/ Women in Musicology*, ed. M. Grassl and C. Szabo-Knotik (Vienna, 1999)

The Helen Hewitt Collection, <http://www.library.unt.edu/music/special-collections/helen-hewitt/>

PAULA MORGAN/VIRGINIA DANIELSON

Heyer, Anna Harriet (*b* Little Rock, AR, 30 Aug 1909; *d* Fort Worth, TX, 12 Aug 2002). Music librarian. She studied mathematics and piano performance at Texas Christian University (BA, BM 1930) and library science at the University of Illinois (BS 1933). In the summer of 1938 she enrolled in Richard Angell's "Music Library Administration" course at Columbia University and remained there the following academic year, studying library service (MS 1939). Following a year as cataloger at the University of Texas in Austin, she was invited to North Texas State Teachers College in Denton (now University of North Texas), to establish a music library for the university, the first full-time music library position in Texas. In order to increase her knowledge of music history and literature, Heyer took a leave of absence for graduate study in musicology at the University of Michigan, where she received her Masters degree in 1943. Returning to North Texas, Heyer concurrently served as assistant professor in the School of Library Service and taught music librarianship. At the time of her retirement in 1965, Heyer had built the largest music library in the Southwest. She became consultant on music library materials at Texas Christian University (Fort Worth) after her retirement, where she reorganized the music collection, set up listening facilities, and standardized the cataloging of scores. She retired from TCU in 1979.

Heyer is best known for her indispensable research tool, *Historical Sets, Collected Editions, and Monuments of Music: a Guide to their Contents*. She received several awards during her life, including honorary life membership in the American Library Association, the Music Library Association Citation for lifetime achievement, and a special citation in 1983 by the Texas Chapter of MLA for her pioneer contributions to music librarianship in Texas.

WRITINGS

A Check-list of Publications of Music (Ann Arbor, MI, 1944)

"Music Activities at North Texas State College," *Notes*, iv (1947), 234–40

A Bibliography of Contemporary Music in the Music Library (North Texas State College, March 1955) (Denton, TX, 1955)

Historical Sets, Collected Editions, and Monuments of Music: a Guide to their Contents (Chicago, 1957, 3/1980)

Bibliography of Music Bibliographies (Fort Worth, TX, 1967)

BIBLIOGRAPHY

C. Rabson: "Anna Harriet Heyer," *The Musical Woman*, ed. J. Zaimont, iii (Westport, CT, 1991), 238–92

C.J. Bradley: "Anna Harriet Heyer, an Isolated Pioneer," *Notes*, cxiii (2007), 798–805

MARK McKNIGHT

Heyman, Sir Henry C. (*b* Oakland, CA, 13 Jan 1855; *d* Paso Robles, CA, 28 March 1924). Violinist and teacher. He received his early education at the Oakland College School, a preparatory department of the College of California (1860–67), and was one of the first musicians born in California to seek an advanced musical education abroad. He studied at the Leipzig Conservatory (1870–77), where he won the Mendelssohn Prize and played in the Gewandhaus Orchestra; his teachers were Ferdinand David, Friedrich Hermann, and Engelbert Röntgen. During this time, he attended Joachim's master classes in Berlin. Upon his return to San Francisco in 1877, he established himself as a popular and flamboyant member of the musical community and as a patron of the fine arts. He was one of the founders (and concertmaster) of the Philharmonic Society in 1881, and with Gustav Hinrichs gave many successful orchestral concerts. He also formed the Henry Heyman String Quartet, which attracted wide attention. Heyman toured widely in the area, giving concerts as far south as San Diego and as far north as Victoria. On a visit to Hawaii to give concerts in the summer of 1884 he was knighted by King Kalākaua, and he steadfastly employed his title, despite the merriment it caused. He amassed a notable personal library of music, books, and memorabilia, but this was destroyed in the earthquake and fire of April 1906. Heyman returned several times to Europe, in the process accepting several honorary degrees from such institutions as the University of Bologna. Heyman was a competent violinist and teacher, and he probably advanced the status of music in San Francisco's social life more than any other person of his time. His legendary luncheons in the Red Room of the San Francisco Bohemian Club brought world-famous musical celebrities into contact with the political, business, and cultural leaders of the city; among his guests were Paderewski, Rachmaninoff, Saint-Saëns, Henryk Wieniawski, Heifetz, Ysaÿe, and Elman. Saint-Saëns's *Elegie* for violin and piano and Jadassohn's *Romanza*, op.87, are two of several works that are dedicated to Heyman.

BIBLIOGRAPHY

Grove2, Amer. Suppl.
The Bay of San Francisco: a History, ii (Chicago, 1892), 511
"Henry Heyman, K.S.O." *Strad*, v (1895), 180–81
The Musical Courier, lii/19 (1906), 31
M.B. Alverson: *Sixty Years of California Song* (Oakland, CA, 1913), 221–2
E.M. Nesfield: "A California Musician: Sir Henry Heyman," *San Francisco News Letter* (11 Dec 1920)
C. Woodman: "Musical Notables: Sir Henry Heyman," *San Francisco Call and Post* (18 Aug 1923)
Obituary, *Pacific Musical Review*, xlvi/1 (1924), 3
C. Lengyel: *Early Master Teachers, History of Music in San Francisco*, vi (San Francisco, 1940), 13
O. Thompson, ed.: "Heyman, Henry," *International Cyclopedia of Music and Musicians* (New York, 1946), 792

JOHN A. EMERSON/JONAS WESTOVER

Hiatt, John (*b* Indianapolis, IN, 20 Aug 1952). Guitarist, singer, and songwriter. He learned the guitar at age 11 and played with several bands throughout Indiana. Hiatt's career blossomed in 1970, when he moved to Nashville and became a songwriter for Tree Music Publishing and also played with the group White Duck. He secured a deal with Epic Records in 1973. His first hit came with the song "Sure as I'm Sitting Here," which was recorded by Three Dog Night in 1974. He eventually found a home in 1979 at MCA Records, where he experimented with different rock and country sounds. Many established artists, including Johnny Cash and Elvis Costello, recorded with him, but personal fame eluded him until 1987 with the release of his album *Bring the Family* and its popular singles "Have a Little Faith in Me" and "Thing Called Love." His next several albums would all find commercial and critical success and included hits such as "Slow Turning," "Tennessee Plates," and "Angel Eyes." Although Hiatt is a prolific performer and recording artist, he is known best for his songs, which have been covered by artists as varied as Bonnie Raitt, Mandy Moore, Iggy Pop, B.B. King, and Keith Urban. He remains active in the studio and on tour in the 21st century.

JONAS WESTOVER

Hibbard, William (Alden) (*b* Newton, MA, 8 Aug 1939; *d* San Francisco, CA, 5 April 1989). Composer. He studied at the New England Conservatory (BM 1961, MM 1963) and the University of Iowa (PhD 1967); his composition teachers included DONALD MARTINO and RICHARD B. HERVIG. In 1966 he became a member of the composition and theory faculty at the University of Iowa and music director of the university's Center for New Music, which he helped to found; from 1969 to 1976 he also served as director of the Center for New Performing Arts. Hibbard's compositions wed a rigorous exploration of the possibilities of serialism to an increasing fascination with unusual sonorities and complex cross-rhythms. Once having determined a medium, he generated a prodigious quantity of episodes during which the larger aspects of the work took shape. In 1975, while at work on the *P/M Variations* for two double basses, he created a row based on a trichord comprising a perfect 4th and a major 2nd, which occupied his creative imagination throughout the rest of his productive life. In his notes for a 1988 performance of his last composition, *Handwork* for piano, he characterized the row thus: "To my ear the overtone series and sympathetic resonances created by these intervals produce a vibrant… sonority, sharply etched and well-defined, seductive without being voluptuous."

WORKS

Orch: Reliefs, 1962; Va Conc., 1977; Processionals, 1980; Sinfonia on Expanding Matters, str, 1983; Consorts for Ww, Brass, Perc, 1984
Chbr and solo inst: Trio, vn, cl, gui, 1959; Variations, 9 brass, 1960; 4 Pieces, large chbr ens, 1962; Gestures, fl, db, perc, 1963; Portraits, fl, pf, 1963, rev. 1964; Str Trio, 1963; Fantasy, org, tpt, trbn, perc, 1965; Girl on a Landscape (film score), pf, perc, 1966; Intersections I, II, ww qnt, pf, 5 perc, 1966; Stabiles, 13 insts, 1968; Parsons' Piece, 1 perc, 1968, rev. 1974; Variations, vc, 1969; Str Qt, 1971; B Trbn, B Cl, Hp, 1973; P/M Variations, 2 db, 1975–82; One Round…and Another One, vib, 2 pf, 1979; Caprice, va, 1979; Schickstück, vib, 1981; Euphonious Duet on Expanding Matrices, 2 vn, 1982; 3 Pieces, va, 1983; Handwork, pf, 1986
Vocal: The Dream Lady, song cycle, A, ens, 1958; Super flumina Babylonis, motet, S, Mez, A, T, B, B, str sextet, 1967; Reflexa, S, 5 insts,

1970; Ménage, S, tpt, vn, 1974, rev. 1978; 3 Whitman Miniatures, SSATBB, pf, 1983

Principal publishers: Associated, Lone Press, E.C. Schirmer

BIBLIOGRAPHY

Anderson 2
W. Hibbard: "Charles Wuorinen: the Politics of Harmony," *PNM*, vii/2 (1968–9), 155–70

CAROL J. OJA/D. MARTIN JENNI

Hickerson, Joe [Joseph C.] (*b* Lake Forest, IL, 20 Oct 1935). Folklorist and folksinger. He was exposed to folk songs by his parents when he was a child and began to play the guitar as a teenager. His interest in folk music deepened during his undergraduate years at Oberlin College (BA 1957). Among other musical activities while in college he hosted a radio program and served as local agent for the Folkways, Stinson, and Elektra record labels. He pursued graduate studies in folklore (MA 1961) and ethnomusicology at Indiana University and began to hone his skills as a performer in parallel with his academic and archival work there. In 1963 he was hired as librarian at the Archive of Folk Song at the Library of Congress (now the Archive of Folk Culture); this marked the beginning of a 35-year career at that institution. He was promoted to head of the archive in 1974. During his time there Hickerson was active with numerous professional societies and other organizations including the Society for Ethnomusicology, the American Folklore Society, the John Edwards Memorial Foundation, Old Town School of Folk Music Resource Center, the Folklore Society of Greater Washington (of which he was a founder), *Sing Out!* magazine, and Foxfire. Since his retirement from the library in 1998 Hickerson has actively pursued his performing career. His performances have earned him awards from numerous folk festivals.

RECORDINGS
(selective list; all on Folk-Legacy)
Joe Hickerson with a Gathering of Friends, 1970; *Drive Dull Care Away*, vols. 1 & 2, 1976

PAUL F. WELLS

Hickman, David Russell (*b* Duncan, OK, 1950). Trumpeter. An international trumpet soloist and master teacher, he is the founder of the Summit Brass and Summit Records, a co-founder of the Rafael Méndez Brass Institute, and the proprietor of Hickman Music Editions. From 1974 to 1982 Hickman taught at the University of Illinois, then moved in 1982 to Arizona State University, where he serves as the Regents Professor of Trumpet. His many students hold positions in symphony orchestras, military bands, chamber groups, and universities. Through his instigation and with the support of the Méndez family, he established the Rafael Méndez Library in the School of Music at Arizona State in 1993. In addition to performing and teaching, Hickman has written many pedagogical trumpet texts. He also served as president of the International Trumpet Guild from 1977–9 to 1979 and hosted its conference in 1977. In 2005, he received the guild's prestigious ITG Award of Merit. Hickman has performed with hundreds of orchestras around the world and can be heard on 17 solo albums, 11 Summit Brass recordings, and 4 St. Louis Brass Quintet albums.

BIBLIOGRAPHY

J. Bowman: "David Hickman Goes on Record," *International Trumpet Guild Journal* (June 2003), 27–38
H. Morgan: "David Hickman," *The Brass Herald*, no.issue 25 (Oct 2008), 14–16
M. LaPlace: *Trompette, Cuivres & XXe Siècle* (CD-Rom, 2008)

AMANDA PEPPING

Hicks, (Charles) Barney (*b* Baltimore, MD, *c*1840; *d* Surabaya [now in Indonesia], 1902). Minstrel-troupe manager. He became one of the most successful African American managers of minstrel groups. In about 1865 he organized the Original Georgia Minstrels, probably named after a 15-member troupe of former slaves called the Georgia Minstrels, established in April of that year by W.H. Lee in Macon. Hicks's troupe began touring in the Northeast and the West and, within three years, included a 13-piece brass band. In 1870 Hicks and some of his members joined with Sam Hague's Great American Slave Troupe (formerly Lee's group) for a tour of the British Isles. In July of the following year there was a disagreement and Hicks returned to the United States. He sold his company to Charles Callender in 1872 but continued to work as its manager. From 1877 to 1880 he toured Australia with a new troupe, also called the Georgia Minstrels. Returning once more to the United States, he worked with various groups including Hicks and Kersands' Minstrels, McIntosh and A.D. Sawyer's Colored Minstrels, and Callender's Minstrels, with whom he presented the Callender Consolidated Minstrel Festival in the Grand Opera House, New York, in July 1883. Hicks became part owner of the Hicks and Sawyer Refined Colored Minstrels in 1886 and took them on a tour of Australia and the Far East. He managed Harnstron's Circus in Auckland, New Zealand, before moving to Java in 1900.

BIBLIOGRAPHY

SouthernB

DOMINIQUE-RENÉ DE LERMA/R

Hicks, George (*b* England, *c*1818; *d* Brooklyn, NY, 21 Feb 1863). Manufacturer of and dealer in cylinder pianos and barrel organs. He was probably related to the Hicks family of street organ and piano makers in Bristol, Great Britain. He arrived in the United States after 1845 and his name first appeared in Brooklyn street directories in 1849. By 1856 he maintained a retail or manufacturing operation in Manhattan, but in 1860 he was again listed only in Brooklyn, where his family resided after his death. Although he was described in advertisements as a "maker," it is uncertain whether he manufactured all the parts of his instruments, including their laboriously pinned cylinders, or assembled parts imported from England; the latter seems more likely. His products, of standard design and quality, were intended mainly for sale or rental to street musicians who carried the instruments on their backs. Some examples are equipped with percussion devices and with articulated, costumed figures that move in time to the music. Examples at the Metropolitan Museum of Art (New York), the Smithsonian Institution (Washington, DC), and the Henry Ford Museum (Dearborn, Michigan) share a popular repertory that includes American patriotic tunes and ethnic pieces suitable for different neighborhoods. Their range, of approximately two octaves, is chiefly diatonic, with some chromatic notes.

BIBLIOGRAPHY

N. Groce: *Musical Instrument Making in New York City during the Eighteenth and Nineteenth Centuries* (diss., U. of Michigan, 1982)

L. Libin: *American Musical Instruments in the Metropolitan Museum of Art* (New York, 1985)

LAURENCE LIBIN

Hicks, John (Josephus) (*b* Atlanta, GA, 12 Dec 1941; *d* New York, NY, 10 May 2006). Pianist and composer. He was one of the most versatile and respected pianists of his generation. He moved with his family to Los Angeles, then St. Louis. After receiving piano lessons from his mother, he studied at Lincoln University, the Berklee College of Music, and the Juilliard School. He began playing professionally in his father's church, then worked with local blues, rhythm-and-blues, and jazz bands. His first jazz gig of note was with the Al Grey–Billy Mitchell group featuring Bobby Hutcherson. In 1962 he moved to New York and played with Lucky Thompson, Kenny Dorham, Lou Donaldson, and Joe Farrell, before working with Art Blakey's Jazz Messengers (1964–5); he made his recording debut on the group's album *'S Make It* (Verve). Thereafter he played with both mainstream and avant-garde figures, including Sonny Simmons, Pharoah Sanders, Sonny Rollins, Hank Mobley, Anita O'Day, and Dionne Warwick. At the end of the 1960s he was working with Woody Herman. In the 1970s he played with Betty Carter, Oliver Lake, Lester Bowie, Julius Hemphill, Charles Tolliver, and Woody Shaw. He became one of the most in-demand jazz musicians, performing with Arthur Blythe, David Murray, Chico Freeman, Big Nick Nicholas, Bobby Hutcherson, James Moody, Bobby Watson, Roy Hargrove, Mingus Dynasty, and Joe Lovano, among others. He also led his own duos, trios, small groups, and big band, and co-founded Hicks–Wood, Inc. with Elise Wood, whom he later married. A rare virtuoso, equally at home with mainstream and avant-garde groups, instrumentalists, and vocalists, Hicks possessed a unique style that was both sensitive and exciting.

BIBLIOGRAPHY

G. Kalbacher: "John Hicks: First Call Piano," *DB*, liii/6 (1986), 26

C. Henry and P. Richard: "Some other Time: John Hicks," *Jb*, no.539 (1997), 17

Obituary, *New York Times* (13 May 2006)

RUSS MUSTO

Hicks, Stanley (*b* Watauga Co., NC, 13 Oct 1911). Banjoist, folksinger, and instrument maker. He was born into a family of Appalachian folk musicians; his father, Roby Monroe Hicks, taught him to make banjos (the first of which he built when he was 15) and Appalachian dulcimers, and from his father and his mother, Buna Presnell Hicks, he learned Anglo-American ballads and instrumental techniques. His grandfather, a storyteller, taught him "Jack tales," Appalachian stories of German American origin. Hicks also learned to dance in a flat-footed, "jumping jack" style. His instruments, which are notable for their high level of craftsmanship, are made from cherry and walnut wood grown near his farm in Vilas, North Carolina; the heads of his banjos are made of groundhog hides. He also produces a number of folk toys. Hicks has appeared at the North Carolina Folk Festival, the National Folk Festival, and the Smithsonian Institution's Festival of American Folklife. Hicks received the Brown-Hudson Award from the North Carolina Folk Society in 1980 and was awarded a National Heritage Fellowship from the NEA in 1983. Hicks has appeared in Mike Seeger's documentary *Talking Feet: Solo Southern Dance* (1987) and Alan Lomax's film *Appalachian Journey* (1991). Appalachian State University holds several videos of his performances.

BIBLIOGRAPHY

E. Wigginton: *Foxfire 3* (New York, 1973), 139

JOE WILSON/R

Hier, Ethel Glenn (*b* Cincinnati, OH, 25 June 1889; *d* Winter Park, FL, 14 Jan 1971). Composer, teacher, and pianist of Scottish origin. She received a diploma in piano from Cincinnati Conservatory in 1908 and immediately established what became a thriving piano studio. In 1911 she returned to the Conservatory for further piano study and took composition lessons with EDGAR STILLMAN KELLEY; in Germany during the summer of 1912 she studied composition with Hugo Kaun. In 1917 she moved to New York, opening teaching studios there and in New Jersey, and continued composition studies at the Institute of Musical Art, first with PERCY GOETSCHIUS and later with ERNEST BLOCH. During subsequent summers she worked in Europe with Alban Berg, Egon Wellesz, and Gian Francesco Malipiero, and in 1923 she resumed piano study with Carl Friedberg.

Hier began publishing teaching pieces for piano in 1912. By 1918 her more ambitious works had won her the first of 14 fellowships at the MacDowell Colony. In 1925 her works were included in the Festival of American Women Composers in Washington, DC, and later that year, with Amy Beach, Mary Howe, Gena Branscombe, Marion Bauer, and others, she founded the Society of American Women Composers. She organized the Composers Concerts in New York in 1948 and frequently gave lectures on modern music and other topics. *Asolo Bells* was played at the Festival of American Music at the Eastman School of Music in 1939, and in 1945 by the Cincinnati SO; as part of Three Orchestral Pieces it won a Composers Press publication award in 1953. Hier's music combines impressionist elements with popular and jazz styles (as in *Click o' the Latch* and *Badinage*). Her use of coloristic effects can be heard in *Asolo Bells*; in *A Day in the Peterborough Woods* and *The Song Sparrow* Hier drew on birdsong. Within an extended tonal scheme she often used parallel triads and tone clusters in a nonfunctional manner. Hier also wrote a play, *The Boyhood and Youth of Edward Mac-Dowell* (1926). Her manuscripts are held at the American Music Center, the College Conservatory of Music at the University of Cincinnati, and the Delta Omicron Library, Cincinnati.

WORKS

Orch: 5 works, 1926–9, incl. Carolina Christmas; 3 Orch Pieces: Foreboding, Asolo Bells, Badinage (Study in Blues), 1954

Chbr: 9 works, incl. 2 str qts, 3 qnts, suites

Pf: 34 works, incl. Theme and Variations, op.17, 1921; A Day in the Peterborough Woods, op.19, 1924

Vocal: 20 songs, incl. Hail! Glorious Morn!, sacred song, 1912; The Time to Woo (S.M. Peck), 1914; Dreamin' Town (P.L. Dunbar), 1919; La chanson du cordonnier (J. Bois), 1923; Click o' the Latch (N.B. Turner), 1938; The Hour (J. Rittenhouse), 1949; The Song Sparrow (N. Kreymborg), 1955

Choral: 3 works, incl. The Mountain Preacher (J. Still), 1966

Principal publishers: CFE, Composers Press, Willis

BIBLIOGRAPHY

"Contemporary American Musicians, no.168: Ethel Glenn Hier," *MusAm*, xxxiv/2 (1921), 29

K. Pendle: *Ethel Glenn Hier* (MS, American Music Center)

ADRIENNE FRIED BLOCK

Higdon, Jennifer (*b* Brooklyn, NY, 31 Dec 1962). Composer and flutist. Higdon spent her early childhood in Atlanta, Georgia until the age of ten, when her family relocated to Seymour, Tennessee. At age 14, she began her initial applied music training as a percussionist in the marching band; shortly thereafter, Higdon became self-taught on the flute and subsequently attended Bowling Green State University as a flute performance major studying with Judith Bentley. The latter initially encouraged Higdon in composition, which resulted in her first work, *Night Creatures*, for flute and piano. While at Bowling Green, she participated in ROBERT SPANO's conducting course; as the current music director of the Atlanta Symphony Orchestra, Spano has maintained a significant role in commissioning Higdon's music that places her at the forefront of the Atlanta School of Composers.

Higdon received an Artist's Diploma from the Curtis Institute of Music, and a Master of Arts and Doctor of Philosophy in composition from the University of Pennsylvania where she studied with George Crumb. She currently holds the Milton L. Rock Chair in Composition at the Curtis Institute of Music. Higdon's work has been commissioned by the Philadelphia Orchestra, the Atlanta SO, the Chicago SO, the Pittsburgh SO and the Tokyo String Quartet, among numerous other ensembles.

Higdon's music has received many awards, including the 2010 Pulitzer Prize in Music for the Violin Concerto and a Grammy for Best Contemporary Classical Composition for the Percussion Concerto, as well as prizes from the Guggenheim Foundation, the American Academy of Arts & Letters, the Pew Fellowship in the Arts, and the National Endowment for the Arts. Higdon has been featured at numerous festivals and in symphonic residencies. All publication rights are maintained through her company, Lawdon Press.

Higdon's orchestral music features extensive use of percussion, which governs the fourth movement of her Concerto for Orchestra. Additionally, her style is noteworthy for its use of open fifth intervals and attention to tone color accomplished primarily through unorthodox string soli, which are highly prevalent in her most popular work, *blue cathedral*.

WORKS

Orch: Shine, 1995; blue cathedral, 2000; Fanfare Ritmico, 2000; Conc. for Orch, 2002; City Scape, 2002; Machine, 2003; Dooryard Bloom, baritone, 2004; Oboe Conc., 2005; Perc. Conc., 2005; The Singing Rooms, vn, SATB, 2006; Vn Conc., 2008

Chbr inst: Voices, str qt, 1993; wissahickon poeTrees, fl, cl, vn, vc, pf, perc, 1993; Autumn Music, wind qnt, 1995; Sky Quartet, str qt, 1997, rev. 2000; Legacy, fl, pf, 1999; Celestial Hymns, cl, vn, va, vc, pf, 2000; Dark Wood, bn, vn, vc, pf, 2001; Dash, cl, vn, pf, 2001; Bentley Roses, Mez, fl, pf, 2002; Impressions, str qt, 2003; Piano Trio, vn, vc, pf, 2003; Southern Harmony, str qt, 2003; Zaka, fl, cl, vn, vc, pf, perc, 2003; Exaltation of Larks, str qt, 2005; String Poetic, vn, pf, 2006

Choral: Deep in the Night, SATB, 1997; Southern Grace, SATB, 1998; A Quiet Moment, TTBB, 1999; O Magnum Mysterium, SATB, 2 fl, glasses, perc, 2002

BIBLIOGRAPHY

B.R. Phillips: *Jennifer Higdon: a Stylistic Analysis of Selected Flute and Orchestral Works* (diss., Arizona State U., 2005)

C. Reitz: *A Comprehensive Analysis of Selected Orchestral Works by Jennifer Higdon* (diss., U. of Florida, 2007)

CHRISTINA L. REITZ

Higginbotham, J.C. [Jay C.] (*b* Social Circle, GA, 11 May 1906; *d* New York, NY, 26 May 1973). Jazz trombonist. In his youth he played with obscure bands in the South and Midwest. He moved to New York in the late 1920s, where he joined Luis Russell in 1928. In the early 1930s he worked with other leading African American bands including those of Fletcher Henderson, Chick Webb, and Benny Carter. Higginbotham achieved his widest acclaim for the many solos he performed with Russell's band, which he worked with again during the period it was backing Louis Armstrong (1937–40). He also recorded with numerous small groups, especially ones whose music had a New Orleans flavor, including those led by Sidney Bechet and Henry "Red" Allen, and a group of his own. During these years he was considered one of the best of the swing trombonists; he played essentially in the legato style pioneered by Jimmy Harrison, but employed smears and rips to create a rougher and more raucous sound that seemed closer to the older New Orleans approach. With the decline of the swing style in the late 1940s he often performed freelance for the remaining decades of his career.

BIBLIOGRAPHY

C. Jones: *J.C. Higginbotham* (London, 1944)

F. Hoffman: *Henry "Red" Allen/J. C. Higginbotham Discography* (Berlin, 1982)

Oral history material in *NjR (JOHP)*

JAMES LINCOLN COLLIER/R

Higgins, Billy [William] (*b* Los Angeles, CA, 11 Oct 1936; *d* Inglewood, CA, 3 May 2001). Jazz drummer, recording artist, and educator. He played drums from an early age, and his first professional experiences came backing up the rhythm-and-blues performers Amos Milburn and Bo Diddley. After turning his attention to jazz in the late 1950s, Higgins performed and recorded with Dexter Gordon and Thelonious Monk. He was also a member of the Jazz Messiahs with the trumpeter Don Cherry and of Ornette Coleman's quartet with Cherry and the bass player Charlie Haden; he played with the latter group during a residency at the Five Spot in New York. Higgins performed on three of Coleman's recordings: *Something Else!!!! The Music of Ornette Coleman* (1958, Cont.), which included the bass player Don Payne and the pianist Walter Norris; *The Shape of Jazz to Come* (1959, Atl.); and *Change of the Century* (1959, Atl.). All of these albums were significant in the emerging free-jazz movement.

While Higgins continued to perform with Coleman and Cherry on avant-garde projects into the 1960s, the drum chair responsibility in these groups gradually shifted to Ed Blackwell, who was a mentor to Higgins (both drummers performed as members of the double quartets on Coleman's album *Free Jazz*, 1960, Atl.). During this period Higgins became a fixture on the hard-bop scene and was among the most recorded drummers of the decade. Among the many musicians with whom he recorded and performed in the 1960s are Dexter Gordon (*Go!*, 1962, BN), Sonny Rollins (*Our Man in Jazz*, 1962, RCA), Lee Morgan (*The Sidewinder*, 1963, BN), Jackie McLean (*Action*, 1964, BN), and Hank Mobley (*Dippin'*, 1965, BN). During this period he was a member of the house band at Blue Note Records.

Higgins moved from New York to Los Angeles in the 1970s, but continued recording and performing and remained one of the most in-demand drummers in jazz. Between the 1970s and the 1990s he worked with Cedar Walton, Pat Metheny (*Rejoicing*, 1983, ECM), Joshua Redman (*The Wish*, 1993, WB), Joe Henderson, and Slide Hampton and occasionally performed with Ornette Coleman (notably in 1977 and 1987). He also led his own quartet (late 1970s) and appeared in the film *Round Midnight* (1986).

In 1989, with sponsorship from the actress Marla Gibbs, Higgins opened the World Stage with the poet Kamau Daaood at Leimert Park in Los Angeles. This is a cultural arts center that offers a venue for musicians, especially aspiring ones, to perform and interact with others. Among the weekly events hosted at the World Stage have been workshops focusing on drumming (led by Higgins), poetry, and creative writing, as well as jam sessions and a weekend concert series. Higgins also served on the faculty at UCLA in the jazz studies program.

Higgins's work slowed in the mid-1990s due to kidney disease, but resumed after his recovery from a kidney transplant and included an album with the saxophonist Charles Lloyd (*The Water is Wide*, 2000, ECM). His style was always hard-swinging, yet subtle, and he had the ability to adapt to a wide variety of performing situations and styles.

BIBLIOGRAPHY

B. Milkowski: "Billy Higgins: Transcendent Soul," *JT*, xxviii (1998), 38–41

L. Feather and I. Gitler: *The Biographical Encyclopedia of Jazz* (New York and Oxford, 1999/*R*)

D. Chapman: "Enlighten the Spirit: Billy Higgins, the World Stage, and Transforming Society through Jazz," <http://www.echo.ucla.edu/volume2-issue1/chapman-berish/higgins-title.html> (2000)

Obituary, *New York Times* (4 May 2001)

A. Kahn: "The Seekers," *JT*, xxxiv (2004), 76–83

J.H. Costa Vargas: "Jazz and Male Blackness: the Politics of Sociability in South Central Los Angeles," *Popular Music and Society*, xxxi (2008), 37–56

JOHN BASS

Higgins, Dick [Richard Carter] (*b* Cambridge, England, 15 March 1938; *d* Quebec, QC, 25 Oct 1998). Composer, performer, writer, artist, and publisher of English birth. He studied composition and orchestration privately with Harry Levenson (1953), with HENRY COWELL at Columbia University (BS 1960), and with JOHN CAGE at the New School for Social Research (1958–9). In the late 1950s, partly as a result of his studies with Cowell and Cage, Higgins began to explore the areas between music and the other arts—the "intermedia." (*See* INTERMEDIA ART.) He was associated with the first "happenings" (1958) and was one of the original adherents of the Fluxus movement (from 1961), collaborating in performances with such artists as Cage, Philip Corner, Jackson Mac Low, Meredith Monk, and James Tenney. During the 1960s Higgins became one of the chief exponents of avant-garde music through his writings and other activities. He founded and directed the Something Else Press (1964–73), a major publisher of avant-garde intermedia works, and ran its performance gallery (1966–9). He also founded Unpublished Editions (1972, renamed Printed Editions in 1978). He received two grants from the Deutscher Akademischer Austauschdienst (1975, 1982) and held teaching posts at the California Institute of the Arts (1970–71) and as a research associate in the visual arts department of SUNY, Purchase (from 1983). He wrote more than 50 books and numerous articles on theater, visual arts, architecture, and poetry, as well as music.

Many of his performance pieces can best be described as intermedia works. Many of his musical works rely heavily on improvisatory techniques and employ a variety of media with which the performer interacts. Higgins uses graphic notation effectively both in works for solo instruments (as in *Piano Album*, 1980) and in larger works (for example, *Variations on a Natural Theme* for orchestra, 1981). His manuscripts are housed in the Archiv Sohm, Stuttgart (works of 1958–71), the Getty Center for the Arts and Humanities (works of 1968–93), and the Archives of American Art, New York.

WORKS
(selective list)

Dramatic: Hrušalk (op), 1965; 26 Mountains for Viewing the Sunset From, singers, dancers, chbr orch, 1980; Scenes Forgotten and Otherwise Remembered (radio performance piece), 1985; Girlande für John (radio performance piece), 1987; 3 Double Helixes that aren't for Sale (radio performance piece), 1990; Saint Columba (op), 1994

Inst: Danger Music, various insts, incl. Danger Music no.17, 1961–4; Softly for Orchestra (Graphic no.143), 1967; Wipeout for Orchestra (Graphic no.141), 1967; Telephone Music; The 1000 Syms., series, orch, 1968–; Pf Album, 1962–84, 1980; Testing the Boundaries, 1980; 10 Ways of Looking at a Bird, vn, hpd, 1980; Sonata, prepared pf, 1981; Trinity, pf, perc, 1981; Variations on a Natural Theme, orch, 1981; Pf Sonata no.2, 1982; St. Columba, str qt, orch/4vv, chorus,

tubular chimes, 1983; Song (P. Optianus Porphyrius), any vv/insts, 1983; Music for Tpts and Trees, 1995
Many vocal works; many performance pieces with music; film scores

Principal publishers: Printed Editions, Something Else Press

WRITINGS
(selective list)

What are Legends (New York and Calais, ME, 1960)
Jefferson's Birthday/Postface (New York, 1964; Postface repr. in D. Higgins and others: *The Word and Beyond*, New York, 1982)
Foew&ombwhnw (New York, 1969)
Computers for the Arts (Somerville, MA, 1970)
For Eugene in Germany (Barton, VT, 1973)
Everyone has sher Favorite (his or hers) (West Glover, VT, 1977)
The Epikall Quest of the Brothers Dichtung and other Outrages (West Glover, VT, 1977)
A Dialectic of Centuries: Notes towards a Theory of the New Arts (New York, 1978, rev. 2/1979)
Some Recent Snowflakes and other Things (New York, 1979)
Horizons: the Poetics and Theory of the Intermedia (Carbondale, IL, 1983) [incl. essays on the Fluxus movement and on Higgins's works]
Pattern Poetry: Guide to an Unknown Literature (New York, 1987)
Modernism since Postmodernism (San Diego, 1997)

BIBLIOGRAPHY
H. Sohm, ed.: *Happenings and Fluxus* (Cologne, 1970)
R. Kostelanetz: "Dick Higgins," *The Twenties in the Sixties* (New York, 1980)
H. Sayre: *The Object of Performance: the American Avant-Garde since 1970* (Chicago, 1989)
C. Xatrec: "Dick Higgins: la Something Else Press," *Art Press*, no.188 (1994), 16–19
I. Blom, ed.: *Dick Higgins*, Heine Onstad Art Centre, 1995 (Oslo, 1995) [exhibition catalog]
G. Zanchetti, ed.: *Dick Higgins* (Milan, 1995) [exhibition catalog]
R. Kostelanetz: "Dick Higgins (1938–1998)," *PAJ: a Journal of Performance and Art*, xxi/2 (1999), 12–17
N. Zurbrugg: "Dick Higgins," *Art, Performance, Media: 31 Interviews* (Minneapolis, MN, 2004), 197–212

STEPHEN RUPPENTHAL/DAVID PATTERSON/R

Higgins, H(iram) M(urray) (*b* Sherburne, NY, 13 Oct 1820; *d* San Diego, CA, 13 July 1897). Music publisher and dealer. He taught music until 1855, when he established a publishing partnership with his brother Adoniram Judson Higgins at 54 Randolph Street, Chicago. Higgins Brothers catered to the local market; in 1856 they issued J.P. Webster's "Lorena," which was widely popular in the Confederacy during the Civil War. The partnership was dissolved on 1 February 1859, but the brothers continued to run independent businesses. Adoniram ceased operations in November 1861; Hiram continued to publish until he sold his plates to J.L. Peters of St. Louis in May 1867. Hiram Higgins was also a composer; his best-known songs are "The Old Musician and his Harp" and "Hang up the Baby's Stocking."

BIBLIOGRAPHY
Obituary, *San Diego Union* (14 July 1897)
D.J. Epstein: *Music Publishing in Chicago before 1871: the Firm of Root & Cady, 1858–1871* (Detroit, 1969)

DENA J. EPSTEIN

Higginson, Henry Lee (*b* New York, NY, 18 Nov 1834; *d* Boston, MA, 14 Nov 1919). Patron and orchestra founder. He moved to Boston at the age of four. Though his family, on both sides, was of distinguished Boston stock, his father was not wealthy. He attended the elite Boston Latin School and proceeded to Harvard University, but poor eyesight forced him to abandon college. He wound up a diligent music student in Vienna forced to skip meals for lack of means. When he discovered he had no special talent for music, he returned to Boston and was swallowed up by the Civil War; as Major Higginson, he was severely wounded in hand-to-hand combat. Having acquired French and German, soldiered with Americans from every walk of life, married the daughter of Louis Agassiz, and failed in business (an oil venture in Ohio, a cotton plantation with freedman in Georgia), he became a banker. Once he had amassed sufficient capital, he realized his life's dream and founded a "Boston Symphony Orchestra." According to a 30 March 1881 announcement, it would offer 20 concerts per season and an equal number of public rehearsals. Single tickets would sell for as little as 25 cents. Higginson would hire the conductor, make good all deficits, and pay all salaries.

At the time, Boston lacked a stable orchestra of quality. Higginson pointedly engaged an outsider—George Henschel—as his first conductor. When Henschel proved insufficiently disciplined, Higginson hired a disciplinarian in 1884: Vienna's Wilhelm Gericke. Gericke imported key players and demanded polish; he made the young orchestra world-class. In 1889 Higginson hired Arthur Nikisch, a conductor as fiery as Gericke had been methodical. Though Higginson acknowledged the genius in Nikisch, his aesthetics proved anathema to Higginson and to Boston. Conducting a search informed by his exceptional European brain trust and his own considerable musical prowess, Higginson ultimately found in Karl Muck his conductor of choice, beginning in 1906. Meanwhile, he had in 1885 initiated the summer concerts later to be called the Boston Pops and in 1900 built Symphony Hall, still the orchestra's superb home. No previous concert hall had been constructed with input from a professional acoustician (Harvard's Wallace Sabine).

Though Symphony Hall's plain décor documents a notably plainspoken and even puritanical strain in the Higginson personality, he was widely esteemed for the personal warmth of his innumerable friendships; Bliss Perry tellingly testified that "to his true comrades," he "was like a lover." Higginson's singular range of acquaintances—effortlessly including Henry and William James, Charles Eliot, J.P. Morgan, Theodore Roosevelt, and Hans Richter—straddled Brahmin and Viennese culture as well as "barbarian" business. Though he has been portrayed as a cultural plutocrat, he was a cultural democrat driven to share his informed passion for the symphonic experience. He gratefully observed that his audiences were "not from…any particular set of people." Beethoven was his moral lodestar; of the *Eroica* Symphony's slow variations, he wrote: "The gates of Heaven open, and we see the angels singing and reaching their hands to us with perfect welcome. No words are of any avail, and never does that passage of entire relief and joy come to me without tears—and I wait for it, through life, and hear it, and wonder." The most famous portrait of Higginson, by John Singer Sargent, suggests aloofness or arrogance. Though Higginson disliked this picture, it rendered his idealism decisively and bluntly. His relationship to his musicians was paternalistic: he scrutinized them in performance, he promoted or fired them, he supported them in illness or misfortune, he censured those who drank or gambled, he advised them on investments. Through he was criticized for insisting they not play for dancing on days the orchestra rehearsed or performed, his strictness in this and other matters—including forbidding the players to unionize—was productive. He did not interfere with the artistic policies of his conductors but removed conductors he found inadequate or inappropriate.

In combination with World War I and attendant Germanophobia, Higginson's discovery that Muck, whom he considered "indispensable," had privately expressed a withering disdain for Boston delivered a crushing blow to his sanguine commitment to art and uplift. On 4 May 1918, weeks after Muck's arrest by US marshals, Higginson announced that he was retiring from orchestra work. Though he feared the Boston SO would not survive him, a committee of directors was put in charge (and has presided ever since). Few individuals have had a mightier impact on the institutionalization of classical music than Higginson did in the United States. His Boston SO was the first world-class American orchestra to be based in a single city. By 1900 it performed roughly 150 concerts per season. It was already a crucial embodiment of civic purpose and identity. Its self-evident success proved a powerful catalyst and inspiration elsewhere. Alongside Theodore Thomas, Higginson bears major responsibility for making the concert orchestra an American specialty, distinct from the pit orchestras prevalent in Europe.

See also BOSTON.

BIBLIOGRAPHY

B. Perry: *Life and Letters of Henry Lee Higginson* (Boston, 1921)

M.A.D. Howe: *The Boston Symphony Orchestra, 1881–1931* (Boston, 1931/R 1978)

P. Hart: "Henry Lee Higginson—Patron," *Orpheus in the New World* (New York, 1973)

L. Levine: *Highbrow/Lowbrow: The Emergence of Cultural Hierarchy in America* (Cambridge, MA, 1994)

R. Stebbins: *The Making of Symphony Hall, Boston* (Boston, 2000)

J. Horowitz: *Classical Music in America: a History* (New York, 2005)

J. Horowitz: *Moral Fire: Portraits from America's Fin-de-Sieèle* (Berkeley, 2012)

JOSEPH HOROWITZ

Hilburn, [Charles] **Robert** (*b* Natchitoches, LA, 25 Sept 1939). Popular music critic. As the stepson of an electronics engineer in the aerospace industry, he moved frequently as a child. From his native Louisiana, he went first to Dallas and then to various locales in southern California. This helped him develop wide-ranging tastes, as he was exposed at an early age to a variety of popular genres, from country to rhythm and blues and from crooners to rock and roll.

By the sixth grade Hilburn had discovered his love of writing, and he became the editor of his high school and college newspapers. Upon graduation from the

California State University, Northridge (1961), he worked briefly as a journalist for a San Fernando Valley newspaper, the *Valley Times* (1961–63) and then in the public relations department of the Los Angeles Unified School District. In 1966 he began freelancing at the *Los Angeles Times*. His first assignments were in country music, and he was the only journalist to cover Johnny Cash's Folsom Prison show in 1968. In the summer of 1970, he became the paper's first full-time pop critic, a position he maintained until his retirement in 2005. He published his memoirs, *Corn Flakes with John Lennon and Other Tales from a Rock 'n' Roll Life* (Emmaus, PA, 2009).

Hilburn's writings for the *Los Angeles Times* established him as one of the world's preeminent pop critics. He believes that a critic's main tasks are to discover great young talent and to follow the careers of major artists. Some find his writings to be flowery and overly reverential to his favorite musicians, such as John Lennon, Bruce Springsteen, Bob Dylan, and Bono. His ability to conduct insightful interviews with difficult and reticent artists, however, is widely acknowledged.

Throughout his career, Hilburn has subscribed to the romantic notion that great artists have visions that they need to impart to the world, no matter how high the personal costs. This "auteurist" ideology is reflected in his criticism's emphasis on songwriting. His love of Elvis Presley notwithstanding, he generally prefers musicians who write their own materials, bring out socially relevant issues, and have an edgy sound.

ERIC HUNG

Hill, Andrew (*b* Chicago, IL, 30 June 1931; *d* Jersey City, NJ, 20 April 2007). Jazz pianist and composer. He began playing piano at the age of 13 and worked shortly afterwards in Paul Williams's rhythm-and-blues band. Between 1950 and 1952 he studied informally with WILLIAM RUSSO. He subsequently accompanied Charlie Parker in Detroit (1953), Coleman Hawkins, Miles Davis (both *c*1955), and Johnny Griffin, among others, in Chicago, before recording his debut album *So in Love* with Malachi Favors in 1959. Having toured as Dinah Washington's accompanist for several months, in 1961 Hill moved to New York where he worked with Johnny Hartman and Al Hibbler. In late 1962 he followed Roland Kirk to Los Angeles where he recorded with Jimmy Woode. In 1963 he returned to New York to record with Joe Henderson and Hank Mobley. As a personal protégé of Alfred Lion and Francis Wolff, Hill recorded 24 sessions as a leader for Blue Note between November 1963 and March 1970; from these the label released nine albums at the time—including the crowning achievement *Point of Departure* (1964)—and three more, in 1980, 2003, and 2006. Unlike other Blue Note-contracted musicians, he only appeared on one other album as a sideman, Bobby Hutcherson's *Dialogue* (1965). From 1970 Hill rarely worked as a sideman, preferring instead to perform his own compositions. During the period 1972–5 he toured with the Smithsonian Heritage Program and in 1975 he received a Smithsonian Fellowship. Between that year and 1989 he performed and recorded primarily as an unaccompanied soloist (including *Live at Montreux*, 1975, and *From California with Love*, 1978) or in a trio (*Nefertiti*, 1976). Having lived in upstate New York in the early 1970s, he lived in Pittsburg, California, from the late 1970s until 1989, working as a music therapist and giving concerts and classes. He returned to New York in 1990 and performed a season there at the Knitting Factory. The following spring he toured the UK with the pianists Joachim Kühn, Howard Riley, and Jason Rebello. In 1989 and 1990 he recorded two Blue Note albums with Greg Osby, Robin Eubanks, and Hutcherson. After recording in a duo with Chico Hamilton and a quartet with Reggie Workman, Julian Priester, and Sam Rivers (1993), he formed the New Point of Departure Sextet in 1998; the group included Marty Ehrlich, Greg Tardy, and Osby and recorded the album *Dusk* in 1999. Hill also participated with Jim Hall in Osby's Blue Note album *The Invisible Hand* (1999) and recorded a big band album *A Beautiful Day* (2002). Having suffered from lung cancer since 2004, he recorded his final album, *Time Line*, for Blue Note in 2005. Hill received the Danish Jazz Center's Jazzpar Prize in 2003 and a posthumous honorary doctorate from the Berklee College of Music in 2007.

BIBLIOGRAPHY

R. Riggins: "Andrew Hill: Quiet Pioneer," *DB*, lx/2 (1973), 14

A. Dutilh: "Andrew Hill: la periode bleue," *Jh*, no.321 (1975), 16–18

S. Crouch: "Andrew Hill's Alternative Avant-garde," *VV* (1984), 93–4

P. Watrous: "60's Jazz Innovator Returns from End of an Era," *New York Times* (28 Jan 1989)

A. Dupuy-Raufaste: *Strange Serenade: the Andrew Hill Discography* (Mirande, 1998)

B. Shoemaker: "Andrew Hill: Point of Return," *JT*, xxx (2000), July–Aug, 52–5

J. Murph: "Now's the Time," *DB*, lxxiii/3 (2006), 40–44

J. Hale: "Defying the Odds: Andrew Hill's Two-act Career," *DB*, lxxiv/8 (2007) 44–7

Z. Wallmark: "An Alternative Temporal Approach to Jazz Improvisation in the Music of Andrew Hill," *Tijdschrift voor muziektheorie*, xiii/1 (2008), 69–75

B. Ratliff: *The Jazz Ear: Conversations over Music* (New York, 2008)

MICHAEL BAUMGARTNER

Hill, Douglas [Doug] (*b* Lincoln, NE, 6 Feb 1946). Horn player and pedagogue. Hill began studying horn in his early teens in Lincoln, Nebraska, with Jack Snider and later studied with PHILIP FARKAS and Paul Ingraham. He received the bachelor's degree from Indiana University and the Master of Music *cum laude* from Yale University. He taught at the Oberlin Conservatory of Music before joining the faculty of the University of Wisconsin, Madison in 1974. He has been a member of the Spoleto Festival Brass Quintet, the Wisconsin Brass Quintet, the Wingra Wind Quintet, the New York Brass Quintet, and the American Brass Quintet. He also has served as principal horn for the Rochester PO and the Madison SO and has toured with the Henry Mancini and Andy Williams orchestras. Hill's recordings include *The Modern Horn* (1996) and *Music for Horn and Piano* (1999), both with Karen Zaczek Hill. He has also composed dozens of works, including those recorded on *Thoughtful Wanderings: Compositions by Douglas Hill*

(2001). Among his many publications are *Collected Thoughts on Teaching, Learning, Creativity and Horn Performance* (Miami, FL, 2001); *Extended Techniques for the Horn: A Handbook for Students, Composers and Performers* (Van Nuys, CA, 1981, 2/1996); and, with James Froseth, *Introducing the French Horn* (Chicago, 1976). Hill has also developed an instructional video on horn playing titled *Hill on Horn* (1986).

PATRICK RICHARDS

Hill, Edward Burlingame (*b* Cambridge, MA, 9 Sept 1872; *d* Francestown, NH, 9 July 1960). Composer. His father was an accomplished lieder singer and a friend of the distinguished Boston music critic William F. Apthorp, and his grandfather was a president of Harvard University. While attending Harvard, Hill pursued his interest in music and studied with JOHN KNOWLES PAINE and FREDERICK FIELD BULLARD. After graduation (1894) he spent two years in New York, where he studied the piano with ARTHUR BATTELLE WHITING; he also received lessons in composition from Charles-Marie Widor in Paris in 1898 and took a course in orchestration from GEORGE WHITEFIELD CHADWICK at the New England Conservatory in 1902. He taught theory and piano in Boston until 1908, when he accepted a post in the department of music at Harvard. There he was made full professor in 1928 and later chair of the department, a position he held until his retirement to New Hampshire in 1940. Among his students there were LEONARD BERNSTEIN, ELLIOTT CARTER, VIRGIL THOMSON, ROSS LEE FINNEY, and RANDALL THOMPSON. He also was an important contact in the United States for Serge Koussevitzky.

Hill's interest in French Impressionist music was reflected in his own compositions and in his book *Modern French Music* (Boston, 1924); he was a friend of Maurice Ravel and other French composers for whom he had high esteem. Material for the book originated in a series of lectures he gave in 1921 at the University of Strasbourg and at the Congrès d'Histoire et de l'Art at Lyons. His early compositions carry traces of Edward MacDowell's influence, but contemporary critics found the mature style of the tone poem *Lilacs* (1927) evocative of French Impressionism. These French influences notwithstanding, his style had a highly individual stamp that featured lucid details and clearly delineated structures. His later works tended toward more propulsive rhythms and simpler textures; in Jazz Studies for two pianos (1924–35) and the Piano Concertino (1931), he gently parodied the jazz idiom, although he praised jazz itself in lectures at Harvard.

Hill was a member of the National Institute of Arts and Letters (elected 1916) and of the American Academy of Arts and Sciences and a Chevalier of the Légion d'honneur.

WORKS

Orch: Nuns of the Perpetual Adoration (cant., after E. Dowson), female vv, orch, 1908; Jack Frost in Midsummer (ballet-pantomime), 1908; The Parting of Lancelot and Guinevere, tone poem, 1915; Stevensonia I, suite, 1916–7; Prelude to the Trojan Women, 1920; Fall of the House of Usher, 1920; Stevensonia II, suite, 1921–2; Scherzo, 2 pf, orch, 1924; Lilacs, tone poem, 1927; Sym. no.1, 1927; Sym. no.2,

1929; Ode for the 50th Anniversary of the Boston Sym. Orch (R. Hillyer), chorus, orch, 1930; Pf Concertino, 1931; Sinfonietta, str orch, 1932; Vn Conc., 1933–4, 1st movt rev. 1937; Sym. no.3, 1936; Music, eng hn, orch, 1943; Conc., 2 fl, small orch, 1947; 4 Pieces, small orch, 1948; Prelude, 1953; other works

Chbr and solo inst: At the Grave of a Hero, ob, pf, 1903; Jazz Studies no.1, 2 pf, 1924; Sonata, fl, pf, 1925; Sonata, cl, pf, 1925; Sextet, ww, pf, 1934; Jazz Studies nos.2–4, 2 pf, 1935; Str Qt, 1935, arr. str orch 1938; Pf Qt, 1937; Sonata, 2 cl, 1938; Diversion, small ens, 1946; Sonata, bn, pf, 1948; Sonatina, vn, pf, 1951; other chbr and pf works

Songs: Three songs, op.13: In Kensington Gardens, Peace at Noon, Spring Twilight, 1906; The Surges Gushed, others

Principal publisher: Boosey & Hawkes

BIBLIOGRAPHY

EwenD

G.H.L. Smith: "Edward Burlingame Hill," *MM*, xvi (1938–9), 11–16 [incl. list of works]

J.T. Howard: *Our Contemporary Composers* (New York, 1941)

V. Thomson: *American Music since 1910* (New York, 1970)

E. Brody: "Vive la France: Gallic Accents in American Music from 1880 to 1914," *MQ* lxv/2 (1977), 200–11

L.L. Tyler: *Edward Burlingame Hill: a Bio-Bibliography* (Westport, CT, 1989)

C. Oja: "Virgil Thomson's Harvard Years," *A Celebration of American Music,* ed. R. Crawford, R.A. Lott, and C.J. Oja (Ann Arbor, MI, 1990), 323–45

N.E. Tawa: *Mainstream Music of Early Twentieth-Century America* (Westport, CT, 1992)

CHARLES H. KAUFMAN/JONAS WESTOVER

Hill, [Audrey] Faith (née Perry) (*b* Jackson, MS, 21 Sept 1967). Country music singer. Born to an unwed mother, she was raised by adoptive parents in Jackson and, later, Star, Mississippi. At age three, she made her public singing debut at the Star Baptist Church, where she sang through her teens. Following a brief stint at Hinds Community College in nearby Raymond in 1986, Hill dropped out of college and moved to Nashville, Tennessee in 1987 to pursue a career in music. She worked at Fan Fair (later CMA Music Fest) and as a receptionist at Gary Morris Productions; this led to additional experience as a demo singer. In 1992 her collaborations with songwriter Gary Burr brought Hill several performances as a back-up singer at Nashville's legendary Bluebird Café, where she was discovered by Warner Bros. executive Martha Sharp and signed to the label later that year.

Hill's musical career developed rapidly following her 1993 debut album *Take me as I Am* (Warner Bros.), which contained the number-one country singles "Wild One" and "Piece of my Heart." Her follow-up album, *It Matters to Me* (Warner Bros., 1995) was certified quadruple-platinum by the Recording Industry Association of America. In 1996 she toured with vocal partner Tim McGraw, whom she married later that year. In 1997 they released "It's Your Love," the first of many hit duets,

Hill's statuesque beauty, powerful vocals, and musical sensitivity distinguish her from many other country artists of her generation. She received the Academy of Country Music's Top Female Vocalist award in 1998, 1999, and 2000 and was the Country Music Association's Female Vocalist of the Year in 2000. Between 1994 and 2006, Hill scored more than 30 top-10 hits as a solo artist, including seven number-one country singles, four number-one adult contemporary singles, and three number-one country albums. Independent of her recording career, Hill developed an occasional acting career, appearing in a guest role in an episode of the CBS television drama *Touched by an Angel* (1995) and co-starring opposite Nicole Kidman, Glenn Close, and Bette Midler in *The Stepford Wives* (2004).

BIBLIOGRAPHY

J.L. Dickerson: *Faith Hill: Piece of My Heart* (New York, 2001)

J. Neal: "The Voice behind the Song: Faith Hill, Country Music, and Reflexive Identity," *The Women of Country Music,* ed. C.K. Wolfe and J. Akenson (Lexington, KY, 2003), 109–30

DAVID B. PRUETT

Hill, Jackson (*b* Birmingham, AL, 23 May 1941). Composer and musicologist. He received his musical training at the University of North Carolina, Chapel Hill (BA 1963, MA 1966, PhD 1970), where his principal composition teacher was ROGER HANNAY. He also studied composition privately with Iain Hamilton of Duke University. From 1968 he taught at Bucknell University, where he was conductor of the school orchestra (1969–79) and chair of the department of music (1980–90). He was named Presidential Professor of Music in 1996. He was a visiting scholar at Exeter College, Oxford (1974–5) and a visiting fellow at Clare Hall, Cambridge (1982–3). Hill traveled to Japan on a Fulbright Grant in 1977 to study Buddhist liturgical music in Kyoto. He is the author of *The Harold E. Cook Collection of Musical Instruments: An Illustrated Catalog* (Lindburg, PA, 1975) and several scholarly articles on Japanese Buddhist and traditional music.

Hill's compositional style ranges from complex, often experimental procedures in his orchestral and chamber works to the harmonically conservative, utilitarian approach of his many sacred choral compositions. The major influences on his development as a composer have come from Renaissance polyphony and traditional Japanese music. His more recent works, such as the a cappella choral work *Remembered Love, Unforgotten Dreams*, combines both of these influences, with a hint of medieval inspiration. Among the awards he has won for his compositions are the McCollin Prize of the Musical Fund Society of Philadelphia (1979) and a National Flute Association Award (1981).

WORKS
(selective list)

Orch: Variations, 1964; Mosaics, 1965; Ceremonies of Spheres, 1973; Paganini Set, 1973, Sangraal, 1977; Chambers, 1988; Toccata Nipponica, 1989; Secrets (Himitsu), 1990, Sym. no.1 (Sinfonia Nipponica), 1988–90; Sym. no.2 (Sinfonia Canonica), 1986–90; Sym. no.3, 1997

Inst: Music for Str, 1959; Episode for Vn and Pf, 1959; Three Vn Duets, 1959; Poem for Str, 1959; Cortege, vn, pf, 1961; Adagio, vn, pf, 1962; Four Studies, vn, 1964; Improvisation and Dance, vn, 1964; Sonata, vn, 1966; Synchrony, fl, cl, vn, vc, pf, perc, 1967; Serenade, fl, vn, vc, pf/harp, 1970; Entourage, sax qt, 1973; Whispers of the Dead, fl, 1976; Remembered Landscape, vn, va, vc, pf, 1984; Contrafactum III, brass qnt, 1987; Abeunt omnia in mysterium, brass ens, 1987; Enigma Elegy, vc, pf, 1987; Third Elegy, str orch, 1988; Gothic Shadows, fl, ob, vc, 1989; Introspections, ww qnt, perc, 1991; Trio da Camera, fl, ob, vc, 1993

Kbd: 3 Mysteries, org, 1973; Pf Sonata: Super flumina Babylonis, 1976; Toro Nagashi [Lanterns of Hiroshima], 2 pf, 1977; Fanfare and Alleluia, org, brass, 1979; 5 Zen Fragments, org, 1979

Chorus: Magnificat and Nunc dimittis, chorus, org, 1972; O salutaris Hostia, 1973; In Mystery Veiled (Thomas Aquinas, trans. Hill), 1974; Missa brevis, 1974; Tantum ergo, 1974; 3 Motets for Holy Week, 1977; Song of the Sea (S. Williams), 1977; Three Tennyson Lyrics (Tennyson), 1981; Voices of Autumn (Aki no ko-e) (9th-century Japanese), 1982; Remembered Love, Unforgotten Dreams, 2004

Solo vocal: Death Cycle, S, str qt, 1964; 6 Mystical Songs, 1v, pf, 1972; Songs of Wind, Rain, and Liquid Fire, 1v, fl, vc, pf, 1984; Long Hidden Deep in Winter's Keeping, 1v, str qt, 2001; Philomel, 1v, rec, vc, hp, 2002

Other works: 1 theater piece, 1969; incidental music to 2 plays, 1974, 1982; Chameleon Chant, dance music, 1974; 3 band works, several tape works, musical jokes [Spassmusik], and pieces in experimental notations

Principal publishers: Henshaw, Peters, G. Schirmer

DON C. GILLESPIE/REBA WISSNER

Hill, Lauryn (Noelle) (*b* South Orange, NJ, 25 May 1975). Singer, songwriter, and actress. She is acclaimed for her distinctive fusion of soul, rhythm and blues, reggae, and rap in her groundbreaking 1998 debut album *The Miseducation of Lauryn Hill*, which helped usher hip hop into mainstream culture and music.

Hill's early musical aesthetic was heavily shaped by the sounds of Motown and soul music found in her parents' record collection. At age 13, Hill performed Smokey Robinson's classic "Who's Lovin' You" at the Apollo Theater's Amateur Night. She also pursued acting and was featured on the soap opera *As the World Turns* and as a lead in the movie *Sister Act 2*.

After Hill met Prakazrel "Pras" Michel and Wyclef Jean in her teens, the three formed the rap trio that became known as the Fugees (short for "Refugees") and released their first album, *Blunted on Reality,* in 1994. Their second album, *The Score* (1996), as the top-grossing rap album to that date, propelled the Fugees to international acclaim. The lead single from the album was a cover of Roberta Flack's "Killing Me Softly," and Hill's unique vocal sound and abilities were well received.

Hill gained unprecedented recognition as a rapper/singer with *The Miseducation of Lauryn Hill*—one of the most critically acclaimed and highest-grossing albums of the 1990s. The album's songs reflect Hill's musical roots as well as her personal takes on love and life. Her 2000 album, *Lauryn Hill: MTV Unplugged No. 2.0*, met with mixed reviews.

Hill continues to be recognized as a distinct voice within modern American music, and although performances and appearances in the 21st century are less frequent, her effortless musical fusion has set a precedent for subsequent developments in hip hop and popular music.

MATTHEW D. MORRISON

Hill, Richard S(ynyer) (*b* Chicago, IL, 25 Sept 1901; *d* Naples, FL, 7 Feb 1961). Music librarian and musicologist. He received a BA (1924) in general studies and a master's degree in engineering (1931), both from Cornell University. While there he came under the influence of OTTO KINKELDEY, who had been appointed professor of musicology at Cornell and would become the first president of the Music Library Association in 1931. Music, which had previously been Hill's recreation and private study, was transformed into his vocation. In September 1939 he entered the music division of the Library of Congress and before long became head of its reference section, a position he occupied with distinction for more than 20 years. In 1943 he became editor of *Notes*, the journal of the Music Library Association. Initially at his own expense, Hill enlarged—and revolutionized—the scope of *Notes* until it exercised a unique influence in the world of music libraries and beyond. He remained that journal's editor until his death in 1961. In 1951 Hill was elected president of the newly formed International Association of Music Libraries (IAML), and he remained in that role until 1955. As such, he was in a position to strongly influence IAML's agenda, and since he had been a vice president of the American Musicological Society just before his election to IAML, it was to be expected that he brought both a musicologist's and a librarian's perspective to the organization (perhaps he had the model of his teacher, Kinkeldey, in mind when seeking to combine these two disciplines). The musicologist in him was especially concerned with the early planning for the International Inventory of Musical Sources (*RISM*), while the expansion of the network of music libraries in IAML reflected his belief as a professional librarian that action at an international level was the right path to follow.

Because of his work for MLA and IAML, Hill is remembered with great affection as an indefatigable advocate for music libraries and librarians and as a person of great character and generosity of spirit. Since 1978 the Music Library Association has awarded an annual prize named in his honor for the best article on music librarianship or article of a music-bibliographic nature. A *Gedenkschrift* volume published in 1987 pays warm tribute to his dual role as musicologist and library professional.

WRITINGS

"The Plate Numbers of C.F. Peters' Predecessors," *PAMS* (1938), 113–34

ed.: *Music and Libraries: Selected Papers of the Music Library Association* (Washington DC, 1943)

"The Melody of the 'Star Spangled Banner' in the United States before 1820," *Essays Honoring Lawrence C. Wroth*, ed. F.R. Goff (Portland, ME, 1951), 151–93

"International Inventory of Musical Sources: the Joint Committee Meeting in Paris, Jan 1952," *Notes*, ix (1951–52), 213–25 [repr. Washington DC, 1953]

"The Mysterious Chord of Henry Clay Work," *Notes*, x (1952–53), 211–25, 367–90

"The Growing of IAML," *FAM* 1 (1954), 7–11

"A Proposed Official Version of 'The Star Spangled Banner,'" *Notes*, xv (1957–8), 33–42

BIBLIOGRAPHY

V. Duckles: "Richard S. Hill, 1901–1961," *Notes*, xviii (1960–61), 193–6

C.W. Fox: "Richard S. Hill: a Reminiscence," *Notes*, xviii (1960–61), 369–80 [incl. complete list of writings]

V. Duckles: "Richard S. Hill," *AcM*, xxxiii (1961), 69–71

D. Epstein: "Buying Music in War-Torn Germany with Richard S. Hill," *Notes*, xxxvii (1980–81), 503–19

W. Lichtenwanger: "When *Notes* Was Young, 1945–1960," *Notes*, xxxix (1982–83), 7–30

C.J. Bradley and J.B. Coover, eds.: *Richard S. Hill: Tributes from Friends*, (Detroit, 1987), 3–65 [incl. C.J. Bradley, "Richard Synyer Hill, 1901–61"]

C.E. Steinzor: *American Musicologists, c. 1890–1945: a Bio-Bibliographical Guide to the Formative Period* (New York, 1989), 117–25 [incl. list of writings]

ALEC HYATT KING/JOHN WAGSTAFF

Hill, Ureli Corelli (*b* Hartford, CT, 1802; *d* Paterson, NJ, 2 Sept 1875). Violinist, conductor, and founding president of the Philharmonic Society of New York. His father, URI K. HILL, was his first teacher. A member of the second New York Philharmonic (1824–27)—the ensemble known by that name in the 21st century was the third such group to form in New York—Hill played in the orchestra for the Garcia Opera Company performances that included Maria Garcia Malibran. From 1828 to 1835 he was the leader or conductor of the New York Sacred Music Society, which gave the first complete performance in that city of Handel's *Messiah*. In June 1835 he sailed for England, the first American musician to travel abroad for the purpose of studying music. During the next two years he spent nine months in Kassel, Germany, studying the violin with Louis Spohr (46 lessons) and composition with Moritz Hauptmann (52 lessons). In London, Hill played in the Drury Lane orchestra and was invited by Felix Mendelssohn to assist in the 1836 music festival in Düsseldorf, where he participated in the premiere of the oratorio *St. Paul* as well as Beethoven's Ninth Symphony. In April 1842 Hill was elected the first president of the New York Philharmonic and conducted Beethoven's Fifth Symphony at its first concert on 7 December 1842. In 1846 he organized a fundraising concert to build a new music hall in New York at which the Philharmonic gave the American premiere of Beethoven's Ninth Symphony, sung in English; Hill filed the copyright for the translation. He last conducted the orchestra in 1847 but remained a member until 1873, except for the period 1848–51, when he moved to Cincinnati, Ohio. Despondent about no longer being able to play and make a living for his wife and three children, Hill committed suicide in 1875. In addition to his performance activities and composing several sacred and secular works, he published a violin instruction book (Firth, New York, 1855) modeled after Spohr's and was the editor of the *New York Sacred Music Society's Collection of Church Music* (New York, 1843). He was also the inventor of the unsuccessful "tuning-fork piano," which was designed never to go out of tune.

BIBLIOGRAPHY

U.C. Hill Diary, 1831–1837, unpublished (NY Philharmonic Archives)

U.C. Hill's United States passport, issued 1835 (NY Philharmonic Archives)

NY Philharmonic Archives, business records

NY Philharmonic Performance History Database

Newspapers: *Evening Star* (2 Dec 1836), *The Atlas* (8 Feb 1846)

Obituaries, *New York Tribune* (6 Sept 1875), *New York Times* (4 Sept 1875)

H. Shanet: *Philharmonic: a History of New York's Orchestra* (Garden City, NY, 1975)

V.B. Lawrence: *Strong on Music*, vol. 1 (Chicago, 1988)

ROBERT STEVENSON/BETTY BANDEL/BARBARA HAWS

Hill, Uri K(eeler) (*b* ?Richmond, MA, 24 April 1780; *d* Philadelphia, PA, 9 Nov 1844). Music teacher and composer. His father, Frederick Hill, had been a fifer in the revolutionary army. The family moved to Rutland County, Vermont, where Hill spent the first 20 years of his life. His first collection of sacred pieces, *The Vermont Harmony* (1801), and book of secular songs, *A Number of Original Airs, Duetto's and Trio's* (1803), were issued in Northampton, Massachusetts; he published another tunebook, *The Sacred Minstrel* (1806), in Boston. In 1810 he moved to New York, where he founded the Handelian Academy in 1814 (renamed the American Conservatorio, 1820) and compiled *The Handelian Repository* (1814) and *Solfeggio Americano…with a Wide Variety of Psalmody* (1820) for the pupils there. In the latter he called himself a convert to Italian seven-syllable solmization after studying with Philip Trajetta (who contributed some exercises to it). From about 1815 he engraved light music for the publisher Adam Geib, and from 1822 until his death taught in Philadelphia.

Hill was most significant as a composer and arranger of tunebooks. Throughout his career, however, he advertised himself as an expert teacher of several instruments. In Boston (*Gazette*, 13 March 1806) he described himself as a vocal and instrumental teacher of a "stile perfectly novel" and as a piano tuner "in a new method"; he opened a studio there in Joy's Buildings (April 1806), offering to teach the violin, viola, cello, German flute, and other instruments. In New York he advertised himself (18 October 1810) as the "first performer on violin in America." His preface to *The Vermont Harmony* asks the user's indulgence for "deviations from the grammatical rules of composition" in his seven original pieces of the 46 in the book. Hill had two sons: one, URELI CORELLI HILL, became a prominent musician, and the other, George Handel ("Yankee") Hill (1809–49), a writer and actor, was noted for his portrayal of Yankee characters.

BIBLIOGRAPHY

F.L. Ritter: *Music in America* (New York, 1890/*R*1970)

H.E. Johnson: *Musical Interludes in Boston, 1795–1830* (New York, 1942/*R*1967)

R.J. Wolfe: *Secular Music in America, 1801–1825: a Bibliography* (New York, 1964)

C.E. Lindsley: *Early Nineteenth Century Collections of Sacred Choral Music, 1800–1810* (diss., U. of Iowa, 1968)

P.R. Osterhout: *Music in Northampton, Massachusetts, to 1820* (diss., U. of Michigan, 1978)

R.J. Wolfe: *Early American Music Engraving and Printing* (Urbana, IL, 1980)

P.R. Osterhout: "Andrew Wright: Northampton Music Printer," *American Music* i/4 (1983), 5–26

A.P. Britton, I. Lowens, and R. Crawford: *American Sacred Music Imprints, 1698–1810: a Bibliography* (Worcester, MA, 1990)

ROBERT STEVENSON/BETTY BANDEL/R

Hillbilly music. A genre of American popular music, also known less pejoratively as "old-time music," that was commercially broadcast and recorded between approximately 1922 and 1942 and that eventually evolved into modern COUNTRY MUSIC and various regional offshoots including WESTERN SWING, HONKY TONK, and BLUEGRASS

MUSIC. The generic term "hillbilly music," coined in 1925 by the OKeh Records artists and repertoire man Ralph S. Peer, was intended to evoke this music's supposed racial, rural, and regional origins. It typically featured stringed instruments, primarily fiddles, guitars, banjos, and mandolins, but occasionally included pianos, autoharps, basses, harmonicas, and sometimes even woodwind and brass instruments.

The first musicians to record what is now considered hillbilly music were fiddlers A.C. "Eck" Robertson of Texas and Henry C. Gilliland of Oklahoma in 1922, but it was the brisk sales of the 1923 OKeh record "The Little Old Log Cabin in the Lane"/"The Old Hen Cackled and the Rooster's Going to Crow" by Fiddlin' John Carson of Georgia that revealed the potential market for this music. Shortly thereafter Columbia, Victor, Brunswick, and other major companies began recording similar old-time selections, usually at permanent studios in the New York area, Chicago, and, eventually, Los Angeles. But after 1925, with the adoption of the electrical recording process, many hillbilly discs were made at field recording sessions in Atlanta, Memphis, Dallas, New Orleans, San Antonio, and other southern cities.

Prior to the mid-1930s, all of the major labels except Gennett released such records in specially designated numerical series, including Columbia's "Familiar Tunes, Old and New," OKeh's "Old Time Tunes," and Vocalion's "Old Southern Melodies," that targeted primarily rural and small-town white consumers, particularly in the South and the Midwest. National radio broadcasts also played an important role in disseminating hillbilly music; among the leading national radio programs in the field between the mid-1920s and World War II were *The National Barn Dance* (on WLS in Chicago), which had its premiere in 1924, and *The Grand Ole Opry* (on WSM in Nashville), which went on the air in 1925. Among the notable hillbilly artists of the 1920s were Vernon Dalhart, Uncle Dave Macon, Charlie Poole and the North Carolina Ramblers, Gid Tanner and His Skillet Lickers, Jimmie Rodgers, and the Carter Family.

At first, most artists who performed on hillbilly records and radio shows were white southerners, often self-taught musicians from the rural and working classes of the Southeast, but some of the recordings were also made by professional New York studio singers, New England old-time fiddlers, African American string bands, Hawaiian guitarists, Cajun duos, Minnesota polka bands, and hotel dance orchestras. Eventually, the genre came to encompass a remarkably diverse range of performers and musical styles including solo fiddlers, southeastern string bands, white blues guitarists, gospel quartets, singing cowboys, Cajun groups, western swing bands, and mandolin-guitar brother duos.

From the beginning, record companies marketed hillbilly records as the authentic folk music of the rural mountain South, often employing quaint pastoral images of square dances and log cabins in their advertising literature. But this music often developed in urban settings, particularly in southern cities, mill villages, and coal-mining towns, and encompassed a broad range of primarily southern vernacular music and musical styles. Although often considered a folk music, it reflected the deep influences of American popular music, African American blues and jazz, and Hawaiian music; its repertoire actually derived from an eclectic array of songs and tunes including traditional ballads and fiddle tunes, minstrel stage numbers, sentimental parlor songs, gospel hymns, ragtime instrumentals, blues, cowboy songs, and even the latest Tin Pan Alley hits. Increasingly, though, the demand for fresh unrecorded material led to the composition of new songs specifically for the hillbilly music market, and during the 1930s the genre became decidedly more conventional and more oriented toward mainstream popular music.

The Great Depression devastated the hillbilly recording industry, but by 1935 it began to recover, in part as a result of the creation of budget-priced labels such as Decca and RCA Victor's Bluebird. Meanwhile, the hillbilly music business became increasingly dominated by full-time professional musicians and more focused on the western United States, particularly Texas and California. New stars and musical styles came to dominate the field during the 1930s and early 1940s, including Grand Ole Opry string bands such as Roy Acuff and His Smoky Mountain Boys, close-harmony brother duos such as the Monroe Brothers and the Delmore Brothers, western swing bands such as Milton Brown and His Musical Brownies and Bob Wills and His Texas Playboys, Texas honky-tonk singers Ernest Tubb and Al Dexter, and cowboy singers such as Gene Autry and Roy Rogers. By the end of 1942, approximately 23,000 hillbilly records had been released in the United States alone, with hundreds more issued in foreign markets, and dozens of hillbilly radio shows and barn dances were being broadcast on radio stations nationwide. Hillbilly music, in short, had become a multifaceted, multi-million-dollar global industry.

BIBLIOGRAPHY

A. Green: "Hillbilly Music: Source and Symbol," *Journal of American Folklore*, lxxviii (1965), 204–28

B.C. Malone: *Country Music U.S.A.: a Fifty-Year History* (Austin, TX, 1968, 3/2010)

C.K. Wolfe: "The Birth of an Industry," *The Illustrated History of Country Music*, ed. Patrick Carr (Garden City, NY, 1979, repr. New York, 1995), 33–75

R.A. Peterson: *Creating Country Music: Fabricating Authenticity* (Chicago, 1997)

T. Russell: *Country Music Records: a Discography, 1921–1942* (New York, 2004)

T. Russell: *Country Music Originals: the Legends and the Lost* (New York, 2007)

P. Huber: *Linthead Stomp: the Creation of Country Music in the Piedmont South* (Chapel Hill, NC, 2008)

K.H. Miller: *Segregating Sound: Inventing Folk and Pop Music in the Age of Jim Crow* (Durham, NC, 2010)

PATRICK HUBER

Hiller, Lejaren (Arthur) (*b* New York, NY, 23 Feb 1924; *d* Buffalo, NY, 26 Jan 1994). Composer. Renowned as an innovator in the field of computer music, he created much of importance in other genres as well. From his father, a photographer of lurid *tableaux-vivants*, Hiller absorbed a flamboyant theatricality that informs all his best work, especially the large body of mixed-media pieces at the core of his output. He started composing at an early age and studied the piano, oboe, clarinet, and saxophone in his youth. An early passion for big band jazz proved a lifelong influence. While pursuing three chemistry degrees at Princeton (PhD 1947), he studied composition with ROGER SESSIONS, who strongly urged him to take up a musical career, and with MILTON BABBITT. Upon graduation he found employment as a research chemist with the Dupont company in Waynesboro, Virginia, while at the same time composing his earliest major works (notably the imposing *Seven Artifacts*, 1948, rev. 1973, 1984), and receiving his first public performances.

Increasingly disenchanted with corporate culture, he sought refuge in academia, becoming a chemistry research associate at the University of Illinois in 1952. His work with computers there led to experiments (from 1955) in computer composition, ultimately resulting in the *ILLIAC Suite* (1957, later retitled String Quartet no.4)—the first work composed by means of a computer. In the ensuing storm Hiller completed an MA in music (1958) and moved to the music department, where he established an electronic music studio. He documented his computer work in *Experimental Music* (1959).

The interloping "scientist" encountered suspicion, hostility, and contempt from the musical world for many years, finding greater acceptance in the theater, which provided him with a series of commissions while he remained virtually unheard on the concert stage. A breakthrough came with the 1966 phonograph recording *Computer Music from the University of Illinois* (Heliodor HS-25053), which for the first time brought Hiller's music to a wide audience. Shortly thereafter Cage asked him to collaborate on the multimedia extravaganza *HPSCHD* (1968), an immediate and resounding success. Also in 1968, Hiller left the University of Illinois for the State University of New York at Buffalo, where he held an endowed professorship of composition until his retirement. Together with Foss, he directed the university's Center of the Creative and Performing Arts, a nationally prominent new music ensemble. He devoted his sabbaticals to extended residencies in Poland, Malta, and Brazil, from each of which he returned with musical souvenirs that he worked up into compositions. Declining powers of memory following a 1987 encephalitis attack left him unable to teach or compose after 1989.

A determined eclectic, Hiller was unusual in his generation for his willingness to combine the avant-garde and the ultratraditional, a rare carrier of the torch for sonata form and fugue during the turbulent 1960s and 70s. The epic *Electronic Sonata*, for example, sets computer-synthesized sounds against *musique concrète* in place of the traditional key contrasts, while otherwise strictly observing "textbook" sonata form. His algorithmic compositions typically resemble demonstrations, presenting extremes of stasis and chaos before resolving them into a sophisticated mixture. His theater and mixed-media works similarly revel in the contrast of technical and stylistic extremes, while the chamber and piano music tends to focus on specific compositional techniques peculiar to each piece, such as the use of quarter-tones in the String Quartet no.5. Many of his finest works have received only one or two performances, and the full measure of his achievement has yet to be taken.

WORKS

STAGE AND MIXED MEDIA

A Dream Play (incid music, A. Strindberg), 1957; The Birds (incid music/muscm, W. Kerr, after Aristophanes), 1958, concert suite, 1984; Blue is the antecedent of it (elec theater fantasy, J. Leckel), 1959; Cuthbert Bound (theater piece, C. Newton), 4 actors, tape, 1960; Man with the Ob (incid music, W. Smalley), 1962; A Triptych for Hieronymus (Smalley), actors, dancers, orch, tape, slides, film, 1966; An Avalanche (F. Parman), pitchman, prima donna, player pf, perc, tape, 1968; HPSCHD, 1–7 amp hpd, 1–51 tapes, 1968, collab. J. Cage; 3 Rituals, 2/4 perc, film, lights, 1969; Rage over the Lost Beethoven (Parman), 1972 [uses Pf Sonata no.6/portions only of Pf Sonata no.6/any music], 1972; Midnight Carnival, principal tape, secondary tapes, urban environmental events, 1976; Ponteach (mel, after R. Rogers), nar, pf, 1977; Chang Fu, the Witch of Moon Mountain (incid music/op, Smalley), 1982; John Italus (11th-century mel, anon.), nar, 8 insts, 1989

OTHER WORKS

3 syms.: 1953; 1960; 1987–9, inc.

Other orch: 2 Short Pieces, 1941, 1942; Pf Conc., 1949; Suite, small orch, 1951; Time of the Heathen, suite, chbr orch, 1961; A Preview of Coming Attractions, 1975

Tape: Nightmare Music, 1961; 7 Elec Studies, 1963; Elec Sonata, 1976; 3 Compositions (text of no.3 by E. Dickinson), 1983; Expo '85, 1985, collab. C. Ames, J. Myhill

Inst and tape: Amplification, tape, jazz band, 1962; Machine Music, pf, perc, tape, 1964; Suite, 2 pf, tape, 1966; HPSCHD, 1968 [see STAGE AND MIXED MEDIA]; 3 Algorithms, inst ens, tape, 1968, 1972, assisted by R. Kumra, 1984; Computer Music, perc, tape, 1968, rev. (S, pic, perc, tape)/(S, pf), 1981, assisted by G.A. O'Conner; A Portfolio, various performers, tape, 1974; Malta, tuba, tape, 1975; Quadrilateral, pf, tape, 1981

6 pf sonatas, 1946, rev. 1968; 1947; 1950; 1950; 1961; 1972

Other pf: 7 Artifacts, 1948, rev. 1973, 1984; Children's Suite, 1949; Fantasy, 3 pf, 1951; 12-Tone Variations, 1954; 2 Theater Pieces, 1956; Scherzo, 1958; A Cenotaph, 2 pf, 1971; Staircase Tango, 1984

7 str qts: no.1, 1949; no.2, 1951; no.3, 1953; no.4 "ILLIAC Suite," 1957, assisted by L. Isaacson; no.5 "In Quarter-Tones," 1962; no.6, 1972; no.7, 1979

3 vn sonatas: 1949; 1955, arr. as Vc Sonata; 1970

Other inst: Pf Trio, 1947; Divertimento, chbr ens, 1959; 6 Easy Pieces, vn, pf, 1974; Persiflage, fl, ob, perc, 1977; Diabelskie skrzypce, str inst, hpd, 1978; An Apotheosis of Archaeopteryx, pic, berimbau, 1979; Minuet and Trio, 6 pfmrs, 1980; Tetrahedron, hpd, 1982; Fast and Slow, 4 sax, 1984; The Fox Trots Again, 8 insts, 1985; Metaphors, 4 gui, 1986

Vocal: Wordless Chorus, 1940; Jesse James (W.R. Benét), 4 solo vv, pf, 1950; 5 Appalachian Ballads, 1v, gui/kbd, 1958; Spoon River, Illinois (E.L. Masters), 2 nars, 6 insts, 1962; Computer Cant., S, tape, 10 perc, chbr ens, 1963, assisted by R. Baker

Recorded interviews in *NHob*

Principal publishers: Peters, Presser, Kallisti

WRITINGS

with L.M. Isaacson: *Experimental Music: Composition with an Electronic Computer* (New York, 1959/R)

with R.A. Baker: "Computer Music," *Computer Applications in the Behavioral Sciences*, ed. H. Borko (Englewood Cliffs, NJ, 1962), 424

with R.A. Baker: "Computer Cantata: a Study in Composition using the University of Illinois IBM7090 and CSX1-Electronic Digital Computers," *Technical Report of the Experimental Music Studio of the University of Illinois* (Oct 1963)

"Electronic Music at the University of Illinois," *JMT*, vii (1963), 99–126

with R.A. Baker: "Computer Cantata: a Study in Compositional Method," *PNM*, iii/1 (1964–5), 62–90

"Informationstheorie und Computermusik," *Darmstädter Beiträge zur neuen Musik*, viii (1964) [whole issue]

"Electronic Synthesis of Microtonal Music," *Proceedings of the American Society of University Composers*, ii (1967), 99–106

"Music Composed with Computers—a Historical Survey," *The Computer and Music*, ed. H.B. Lincoln (Ithaca, NY, 1970), 42–96

"Composing with Computers: a Progress Report," *Computer Music Journal*, v/4 (1981), 7–21

with C. Ames: "Automated Composition: an Installation at the 1985 International Exhibition in Tsukuba, Japan," *PNM*, xxiii/2 (1984–5), 196–215

BIBLIOGRAPHY

EwenD; *VintonD*

"Lejaren Hiller," *Compositores de América/Composers of the Americas*, xviii (1972), 33–45

C. Gagne and T. Caras: *Soundpieces: Interviews with American Composers* (Metuchen, NJ, 1982)

S. Husarik: "John Cage and LeJaren Hiller: HPSCHD, 1969," *AM*, i/2 (1983), 1–21

L. Austin: "An Interview with John Cage and Lejaren Hiller," *Computer Music Journal*, xvi/4 (1992), 15–29

J.B. Smith: *Parallels in the Development of Electronic and Percussion Music and an Examination of Performance Problems in Lejaren Hiller's "Machine Music" for Piano, Percussion and Two-Channel Tape Recorder* (thesis, U. of North Texas, 1992)

C.A. Wamser and C.C. Wamser: "Lejaren A. Hiller, Jr.: a Memorial Tribute to a Chemist-Composer," *Journal of Chemical Education*, lxxiii/7 (1996), 601–7

J. Bohn: *An Overview of the Music of Lejaren Hiller, and an Examination of His Early Music Involving Technology* (diss., U. of Illinois, 1997)

D. Eisenman and J. Chadabe: "John Cage and Lejaren Hiller's HPSCHD: a Reminiscence and a New Recording," *Musicworks: Explorations in Sound*, xcviii (2007), 36–43

ANDREW STILLER/R

Hilliard, John Stanley (*b* Hot Springs, AR, 29 Oct 1947). Composer, conductor, and educator. His early musical training was in piano and trumpet. He began studying composition and was influenced by the music of Johann Sebastian Bach, Bela Bartók, Ludwig van Beethoven, Paul Hindemith, Charles Ives, Arnold Schoenberg, Jean Sibelius, and Igor Stravinsky. Hilliard attended Ouchita Baptist University in Arkadelphia, Arkansas (BM 1969), where he studied composition with W. FRANCIS MCBETH. He also studied composition with Donald H. White and George B. Wilsonat the Interlochen Arts Academy, where his works came to the attention of KAREL HUSA. Hilliard next studied composition and conducting at Virginia Commonwealth University (MA 1972) and received private composition lessons from WILLIAM GRANT STILL. In 1975 Husa invited Hilliard to study with him at Ithaca College, then at Cornell University (DMA 1980) with Husa and ROBERT PALMER. During this period he also served as assistant conductor of the Cornell Symphony Orchestra. He joined the music faculty at the Interlochen Center for the Arts (1967–90) and Howard Payne University in Brownwood, Texas, where he was appointed composer-in-residence (1981). From 1981 to 1985 Hilliard completed postdoctoral work in composition with DONALD ERB at Southern Methodist University and with Eugene Kurtz at the University of Texas, Austin. He served on the faculty at Washington State University (1986–88) and is professor of music at James Madison University, where he is also composer-in-residence and chair of the Contemporary Music Festival. Hilliard's activities as a conductor include directing Interlochen's 20th-Century Chamber Players, a group he founded in 1976 to perform new music, the Interlochen Orchestra, the Cornell University Symphony, and the Collegium Musicum at Virginia Commonwealth University.

Hilliard's compositions have been widely performed at dozens of new music festivals and by leading orchestras in North America, Europe, South America, and Asia. His many honors and awards include annual ASCAP awards, a commission from the International Horn Society (1991), a residency grant from the Japan Foundation that enabled him to study shakuhachi and gagaku (1995), a grant as a Senior Fulbright Scholar-Artist in composition and composer-in-residence in Hong Kong (1998–99), and commissions from James Madison University, Cornell University, Virginia Commonwealth University, the Mid-America Arts Council, the American Symphony Orchestra League, Meet the Composer, the Virginia Commission for the Arts in conjunction with the National Endowment for the Arts, and the Mozartfest (Augsburg, Germany), which commissioned him to complete the only known fragment of a work for violoncello and cembalo by Mozart.

Hilliard lived for twelve years in Japan, where he studied traditional Japanese music as well as Buddhism, and his works are influenced by both his training in classical Western practices and by the culture, religion, and music of China, India, and Japan and by the Javanese gamelan. While many of his compositions remain within the spheres of the Romantic Western musical tradition and contemporary popular styles, a number of his works show an eclectic blending and synthesis of these multicultural influences.

WORKS

Pf: Sonata for the Sun, 1985; Kado Partita I, 1994; Pf Conc. no.1, Okeanos, pf, winds, 1999; Partita II, Michangelolesca, 2001; Four Partita Movts, 2002; Music for 50 Players, pf ten hands, (2003); Pf Conc. no.2, 2004; Preludes and Fugues, 2007; Pf Conc. no.3, 2009

Chbr: Three Colloquial Pieces, cl, pf, 1967; For the Night Is Dark, brass qnt, 1970; Two Solos for Unacc. Solo Fl, 1971, 1972; Sonata, vn, pf, 1976; Sunrise Fires, 8 trpt, 1987; Three Japanese Sketches, fl choir, 1995; Sonata, vc, pf, 2007) Nihon No Kawa, ww qnt, 2008

Orch: Conc. for Trpt, The Grand Traverse, 1975; Sym. no.1 in Two Movts, orch, s sax, 1983; Sym. no.2, Appearance-Disappearance, chbr. orch, 1986

Vocal: Three Trees (D. Thomas), med. v, pf, 1978; Magnificat, chorus SATB, orch, org, nar, 1972; Love Songs of the New Kingdom, Mez, ob, Fr. hn, pf, (1994); Mass, chorus SATB, soloists, orch, 1999

Winds: Variations on a Theme from "l'Oiseau de feu," 2006; other works

Principal publisher: Gitchi-Mukwa

ROBERT PAUL KOLT

Hilliard Ensemble. British male vocal ensemble. Founded in 1974, the Hilliard Ensemble is best-known for their early music recordings. The ensemble's commissions, recordings, and programs of contemporary vocal music are as numerous as their early music output, however, and the group makes efforts to separate the genres in performance and especially on its recordings. Current American vocal ensembles that reflect the Hilliard

Ensemble's dedication to Medieval and Renaissance music include the Minneapolis-based Rose Ensemble and Seattle's Tudor Choir.

The Hilliard Ensemble has released dozens of commercial recordings with labels such as Saga Classics, Hamonia Mundi, Virgin, EMI, and ECM. Many of the ensemble's early recordings are unaccompanied, but later releases include several collaboration albums, including three produced with Norwegian saxophonist Jan Garbarek—*Officium* (1994), *Mnemosyne* (1999), and *Officium Novum* (2010)—and works that require larger instrumentation, such as their many recordings of major works by Arvo Pärt (*Passio, Miserere, Lamentate, Arbos*, and the world premiere of *Litany)*. The group's landmark two-disc recording titled *A Hilliard Songbook: New Music for Voices* was significant in defining the Hilliard Ensemble's role beyond that of an early music ensemble.

The Hilliard Ensemble is well-known to American audiences. They celebrated their 30th anniversary with the release of an all-Machaut album (*Motets*, 2004) that won a Grammy nomination and also appeared on *The New York Times*'s "Best of the Year" list (2005). Their regular tours of the United States have included several collaborative ventures with American ensembles, including the Philadelphia Orchestra and the New York PO.

ANNE SHELLEY

Hillis, Margaret (*b* Kokomo, IN, 1 Oct 1921; *d* Evanston, IL, 5 Feb 1998). Conductor. After graduating from Indiana University in 1947 she studied choral conducting at the Juilliard School of Music, 1947–9. Further study with ROBERT SHAW followed, and led to her becoming director of the American Concert Choir (1950). She taught choral conducting at the Juilliard School of Music, 1951–3, and the Union Theological Seminary, 1950–60. In 1954 she formed the American Choral Foundation, which did much to promote choral groups and encourage higher standards of performance. She was appointed choral director of the Chicago Symphony Chorus in 1957, the Cleveland Orchestra (1969–71), and the San Francisco SO (1982–3). She conducted performances with the Santa Fe Opera (1958–9) and was music director of the Kenosha Civic Orchestra (1961–8), the Chicago Civic Orchestra (from 1967), and the Elgin SO (from 1971). From 1968 to 1970 she directed the Department of Choral Activities at Northwestern University. Hillis's activities noticeably raised standards of choral singing in the United States. Her thorough preparation resulted in a large, unforced sound, with clear articulation of each part and remarkably idiomatic pronunciation; these qualities can be most clearly heard on Georg Solti's recordings of Ludwig van Beethoven's Ninth Symphony and Joseph Haydn's *The Creation* and *The Seasons*.

RICHARD BERNAS

Hillman, Chris (*b* Los Angeles, CA, 4 Dec 1944). Country-rock singer, songwriter, bassist, mandolinist, and guitarist. He was a mainstay of Los Angeles–area folk-rock and country-rock music of the 1960s and 1970s and a successful commercial country music artist in the 1980s. Since the early 1980s he has been a purveyor of a seamless hybrid of bluegrass, country duo harmony, Bakersfield honky tonk, and West Coast country rock.

Hillman took up the guitar and the mandolin during the urban folk revival. Focusing on the latter, he played traditional bluegrass with the Scottsville Squirrel Barkers (1962–3) and the Golden State Boys, which became The Hillmen (1963–4). In 1964 he joined the BYRDS. At first the group's reticent bassist, he increasingly contributed as songwriter and vocalist to albums starting with the group's fourth, *Younger Than Yesterday* (Columbia, 1967). Recruiting local bluegrass and country players, especially guitarist Clarence White, Hillman helped lay the foundations of country rock. With later Byrds recruit Gram Parsons, he firmly established that genre with the Byrds' *Sweetheart of the Rodeo* (Columbia, 1968) and on *Gilded Palace of Sin* (Columbia, 1969) by the splinter group The Flying Burrito Brothers. On the latter group's eponymous third album (1970), he, with Rick Roberts, augured a lusher soft-rock variant of country rock that became one of the dominant sounds of the 1970s. Hillman had limited commercial success with that sound because he was waylaid by a number of superstar projects including Manassas, the Souther-Hillman-Furay Band, and McGuinn, Clark, and Hillman.

He began emphasizing his bluegrass and country roots in the early 1980s, recording *Morning Sky* (1982) and *Desert Rose* (1984). His greatest commercial success as a leader came when the studio band assembled for the latter morphed into the slicker Desert Rose Band, a unit that was able to endear itself to mainstream country audiences. Since the mid-1990s, Hillman has returned to the progressive bluegrass and Bakersfield country hybrid that marked his early 1980s work, mostly working in tandem with Herb Pedersen and often collaborating with other West Coast bluegrass luminaries, especially Larry and Tony Rice.

BIBLIOGRAPHY

P. Doggett: *Are you Ready for the Country: Elvis, Dylan, Parsons, and the Roots of Country Rock* (London, 2001)
J. Einarson: *Desperados: the Roots of Country Rock* (London, 2001)
J. Einarson: *Hot Burritos: the Story of the Flying Burrito Brothers* (London, 2008)

AJAY KALRA

Hills, Durham (*b* Newcastle-upon-Tyne, England, 4 Oct 1730; *d* Cashaway, SC, *c*Aug 1771). Singing master, compiler, and composer. He was the compiler of *The Cashaway Psalmody* (1770), a South Carolina manuscript that is the earliest surviving collection of sacred music from the colonial South. Born into poverty and orphaned by the age of 10, Hills acquired enough education to become a schoolmaster in Newcastle before 1751. In that year he was arrested for stealing books, tried, and banished to South Carolina for a term of seven years. He settled in the province's remote Pee Dee River country, where he worked as a secretary, accountant, and tutor for local indigo planters. Hills served in the

Cherokee War of 1759 and was appointed clerk of St. David's Anglican parish at Cheraw Hill ten years later.

Hills became a singing master during an extended visit to Newcastle in the mid-1760s. By 1765 he had returned to the Pee Dee region, where he taught singing schools and composed instructional psalm tunes. He was hired by the Reverend Evan Pugh of the Regular Baptist Church in Cashaway to teach English parish-style psalmody to his congregation in 1769–1770. *The Cashaway Psalmody* was Hills's wedding gift to Pugh's bride, Martha "Patty" Magee.

The manuscript tunebook includes 28 pages of musical instruction, 87 untexted "common" psalm tunes (tunes that could be paired with any text in the tunes' own meter), and 63 "particular psalms and hymns" paired by Hills with specific Anglican and Dissenting texts. The collection documents dozens of psalm tunes previously unknown in colonial American use, many of them associated with George Whitefield's Methodist followers, and his musical instructions represent an independent transatlantic transmission of English music theory. Hills's compositional style, best expressed in his tune Cashaway, embodies the expressionistic qualities of the late English Parish style.

BIBLIOGRAPHY

D. Hills: *The Cashaway Psalmody,* in Pugh, Evan, 1729–1802. Papers, 1762–1801 (1292.00) South Carolina Historical Society, Charleston

N. Temperley: *The Music of the English Parish Church,* vol. 1. Cambridge Studies in Music (Cambridge, UK, 1983)

STEPHEN A. MARINI

Hill(strom), Joe [Joseph; Hägglund, Joel] (*b* Gävle, Sweden, 7 Oct 1879; *d* Salt Lake City, UT, 19 Nov 1915). Songwriter and labor leader. He immigrated to the United States in 1902. He played piano in a saloon on the Bowery in New York, worked as a manual laborer on the West Coast, and began writing songs about work and the labor movement; in 1910 he joined the International Workers of the World. His songs gained currency as they were sung at marches and on picket lines and published in the *Little Red Song Book*; the best known, which were written after 1909, include "The Preacher and the Slave," "Casey Jones," "Where the Fraser River Flows," "There Is Power," and "The Rebel Girl." He was convicted of murder and robbery and executed before a firing squad; owing to the political climate in which he was tried, there remains considerable doubt as to his guilt.

Hill's songs are uncomplicated and metrically regular. His wry, parodistic lyrics combine the language of everyday speech with rhetorical appeals to class struggle. He once described his approach to songwriting as follows: "If a person can put a few cold, common-sense facts into a song and dress them up in a cloak of humor to take the dryness out of them, he will succeed in reaching a great number of workers who are too unintelligent or too indifferent to read a pamphlet or an editorial on economic science." He sometimes fitted popular songs and hymns (such as "The Sweet Bye and Bye") with new lyrics. Hill was, with Ralph Chaplin and T-Bone Walker, one of the early leaders of the political

folksong movement; his music influenced the People's Songs movement and such musicians as the Almanac Singers (and, among them, Woody Guthrie and Pete Seeger). Although most of his songs are forgotten today, Hill himself has become a symbol for the social-protest movement, at least in its first generation, thanks to the song "Joe Hill," written by lyricist Alfred Hayes and activist composer Earl Robinson in 1938. The song associates Hill's death with his union activities and asserts that wherever there are labor struggles, Hill remains "alive and well."

BIBLIOGRAPHY

R. Chaplin: "Joe Hill: a Biography," *Industrial Pioneer,* i/7 (1923), 23

W. Alderson: "On the Wobbly 'Casey Jones' and Other Songs," *California Folklore Quarterly,* i (1942), 373

B. Stavis and F. Harmon, eds.: *The Songs of Joe Hill* (New York, 1960)

W. Hille: "Joe Hill," *Reprints from the People's Songs Bulletin* (New York, 1961), 59 [orig. pubd 1948]

J. Kornbluth, ed.: *Rebel Voices: an IWW Anthology* (Ann Arbor, MI, 1964)

P. Foner: *The Case of Joe Hill* (New York, 1966)

G. Smith: *Joe Hill* (Salt Lake City, 1969)

D.A. Carter: "The Industrial Workers of the World and the Rhetoric of Song," *Quarterly Journal of Speech,* lxvi/4 (1980), 365–74

F. Rosemont: *Joe Hill: the IWW and the Making of a Revolutionary Working Class Counterculture* (Chicago, 2003)

DAVID K. DUNAWAY/RICHARD CARLIN

Hillyer [née Tatsumura], **Kazuko** (*b* Osaka, Japan, 6 Sept 1938). Impresario and concert manager of Japanese birth. She studied piano at the Tōhō Gakuen School of Music, Tokyo, before coming to the United States to study at the Berkshire Music Center. She then attended Boston University (BA) and New York University (MA in musicology). She married the violist Raphael Hillyer. In 1968 she founded Pacific World Artists to promote cultural exchange between Asia and the United States. This organization worked with the Japanese government to bring about the first American tours of the Grand Kabuki Theater (1970) and the Noh National Theater (1971) and to take American musicians, including the Cleveland Orchestra, to Expo '70 in Osaka; it also arranged Pacific tours for the Los Angeles PO. Its other activities have included setting up cultural exchanges between East Germany and the United States, and it was responsible for the first foreign tours of the Leipzig Gewandhaus Orchestra (1971) and the Dresden Staatskapelle (1973). In 1972 Hillyer founded Kazuko Hillyer International, which produced and presented thousands of cultural events in more than 100 countries. In 1992 she changed careers, obtained the O.M.D. degree, and established the Okido Holistic Health Center in 1994 and the GAIA Holistic Center in 2001.

ELLEN HIGHSTEIN/R

Hilsberg [Hillersberg], **Alexander** (*b* Warsaw, Poland, 24 April 1900; *d* Camden, ME, 10 Aug 1961). Violinist and conductor of Polish birth. A child prodigy as a violinist, he toured Poland and Russia before studying with Auer at the St Petersburg Conservatory from 1910. In 1917–18 he taught at the Tomsk Conservatory in Siberia, then at Harbin in Manchuria, coming to the United States from Japan in 1923, later becoming a naturalized

American citizen. He joined the Philadelphia Orchestra in 1926, becoming concertmaster in 1931. In 1930 he was appointed to the Curtis Institute as associate conductor and violin teacher, and was head of the orchestra department from 1947 to 1953. He conducted the Philadelphia Orchestra at the Robin Hood Dell concerts of 1936, and from 1945 to 1952 he was Ormandy's associate conductor. Hilsberg's conducting came to further attention following favorable reviews of a concert in Carnegie Hall with the Philadelphia Orchestra (1950); he then became music director of the New Orleans Philharmonic SO (1952–60). Shortly before his death he was appointed head of the orchestra department at the New School of Music in Philadelphia.

BIBLIOGRAPHY

S. Applebaum and S. Applebaum: *With the artists; world famed string players discuss their art* (New York, 1955), 229–36

Obituary, *New York Times* (11 Aug 1961)

H. Kupferberg: *Those Fabulous Philadelphians: the Life and Times of a Great Orchestra* (New York, 1969), 142 only

MARK A. LEACH/R

Hindemith, Paul (*b* Hanau, nr Frankfurt am Main, Germany, 16 Nov 1895; *d* Frankfurt am Main, 28 Dec 1963). Composer, theorist, teacher, violist, and conductor of German birth. From 1940 to 1953 he taught at Yale University; in 1946 he became an American citizen.

1. Life. 2. Works. 3. Influence in the United States.

1. Life. Hindemith's father subjected him from an early age to a strict regimen of musical training. He then began violin lessons at the age of six and was a student at the Hoch Conservatory, Frankfurt, from 1909 to 1917. He had an exceptional gift for learning instruments, and at the age of 19 became second violinist in a well-recognized string quartet and concertmaster of the Frankfurt Opera orchestra. By the early 1920s, he stopped playing the violin in public in favor of the viola. He had begun writing music before becoming a student; by the time of the first public concert of his music (2 June 1919) he had already developed a style of some individuality, and shortly afterward his music began to be published. With the premieres of his one-act operas *Mörder, Hoffnung der Frauen* (1919) and *Das Nusch-Nuschi* (1920) in June 1921, and especially of his String Quartet no.2 op.16 (1921) and the *Kammermusik no.1* (1922) at the Donaueschingen festivals, his reputation as the leading young composer in Germany was established.

In 1927 Hindemith was appointed professor of composition at the Hochschule für Musik in Berlin. His experience with music students and amateur players led to the writing of the theoretical work *Unterweisung im Tonsatz* (1937) and to the composition of music for amateurs. He also continued performing, especially on viola and viola d'amore; his versatility on stage and his compositional fertility became almost legendary. When the Nazis came to power they did not immediately seek to discredit Hindemith, but in 1934 a campaign was launched against him, and in January 1935 he was given a six-month "leave of absence" from the Hochschule.

Several years of unsettled relations with the German authorities followed, but he was allowed to undertake concert tours abroad (notably to the United States, where he made his debut at the eighth Coolidge Foundation Festival of Chamber Music at the Library of Congress on 10 April 1937, playing his solo viola sonata). In 1938 he emigrated, first to Switzerland, and then in February 1940 to the United States. He lectured briefly at Wells College (Aurora, New York), Cornell University, and the New York State College at Buffalo, and he taught during the summer of 1940 at the Berkshire Music Center (now Tanglewood). In the autumn he was appointed visiting lecturer at the Yale University School of Music; a year later, after another summer's teaching at the Berkshire Music Center, he was made a professor, a post he held until 1953.

At Yale Hindemith taught not only composition but traditional harmony and theory; for these classes he used a translation by Arthur Mendel and Otto Ortman of his treatise *Unterweisung im Tonsatz* titled *The Craft of Musical Composition* (1941–2), and from his teaching came other books: *A Concentrated Course in Traditional Harmony* (1943), *Elementary Training for Musicians* (1946), and the second volume of *A Concentrated Course* called *Exercises for Advanced Students* (1948). He also lectured on the history of theory, having mastered the major medieval and later treatises. In order to illustrate these lectures he began in 1945 to direct concerts of early music by the Yale Collegium Musicum, which had been established by Leo Schrade. They were immensely successful and were presented in New York as well as New Haven; the last of them (18 May 1953) was described in the New York *Herald-Tribune* as "the season's brightest treasure." Hindemith's success as a teacher was matched by his success as a composer. His music, virtually unknown in the United States in 1940, within a short period of time became more frequently performed than that of any other composer living in the country. He gave serious thought to writing an opera on an American subject but abandoned the idea in light of the difficulty of getting such a work performed. He also did not want to involve himself in the problems of writing authentically American music or a genuinely American opera. He had originally imagined that he would be unable to compose in a foreign environment and was homesick for Germany, but it was while he was in the United States that he became known throughout the world.

In 1947 Hindemith visited Europe for the first time since World War II, giving lectures and appearing as a conductor. That same year he was elected to the National Institute of Arts and Letters. In 1949–50 he occupied the Charles Eliot Norton chair at Harvard University; his lectures were published as *A Composer's World* (1952). In 1951 he accepted a position at the University of Zurich, planning to alternate yearly between Yale and Zurich; after the 1952–3 year at Yale, however, he settled permanently in Switzerland. He taught his last courses in 1957, devoting himself increasingly to conducting and undertaking several major international tours before his death.

2. WORKS. After his graduation, Hindemith's output may conveniently be divided into three periods: from 1918 to 1923, from 1924 to 1933, and from 1933 to 1963.

In the period 1918–23 the young composer was exploring a variety of styles after producing student works that were based on traditional models and heavily influenced by Brahms. The dominant impression is of provocative and aggressive novelty. Hindemith first made his name with music that proclaimed an allegiance with expressionism, notably the operas *Mörder, Hoffnung der Frauen* and *Sancta Susanna* (1921), the String Quartet no.2, and the ballet *Der Dämon* (1922). In the transitional Quartet no.3 (1922) he acknowledged the stimulus of Bela Bartók, while in the *Kammermusik no.1* he abruptly aligned himself with Igor Stravinsky and Darius Milhaud; in 1922: Suite for Piano his interest in the world of jazz and the nightclub took even more concrete form. The first work to reveal the poised hand of distinction is the *Kleine Kammermusik* for wind quintet (1922). The witty chamber works tended to belie Hindemith's underlying seriousness of purpose, which, however, made unobtrusive appearances in *Die junge Magd* (1922) for voice and six instruments and thoroughly informed the sonata for viola d'amore, the song cycle *Das Marienleben*, and the String Quartet no.4, all of 1922–3.

The period 1924–33 saw Hindemith achieve a mature neo-Baroque style of considerable harmonic asperity; his work with amateurs during the latter part of the period, however, led to a more lyrical and euphonious mode of expression. The first important works of the period, the solo concertos comprising the *Kammermusiken nos.2–7* (1924–7), take their stimulus from Johann Sebastian Bach's Brandenburg Concertos. In the two other important works, the Concerto for Orchestra of 1925 and the opera *Cardillac* of 1926, Hindemith used his orchestra like a large-scale chamber ensemble. All these works evoke Baroque models in their other characteristics, notably rhythmic phraseology, formal structure based on ritornellos, and harmonies deriving from, rather than dictating the course of, linear counterpoint. Two other operas of the period, the 12-minute *Hin und zurück* (1927) and the full-length *Neues vom Tage* (1928–9), recall the irreverent younger composer in their subject matter and occasional use of jazz rhythms. In 1929 came *Lehrstück*, to a text by Bertolt Brecht, a politically motivated "teaching piece" designed to be performed by amateurs—and, as such, Hindemith's most substantial contribution to what became known as *Gebrauchsmusik*. Related to the aesthetic of *Lehrstück* are other works of *Sing- und Spielmusik* (a term preferred by Hindemith to *Gebrauchsmusik*), such as the *Spielmusik* (1927) for strings, flutes, and oboes, the short children's opera *Wir bauen eine Stadt* (1930), and the *Plöner Musiktag* (1932). The three *Konzertmusik* works of 1930—that for viola and orchestra, that for piano, brass, and two harps, and that for strings and brass—combine practicability and adventurousness. The last of these pieces is notable for the abundance of blue notes at its close, Hindemith's characteristic way of offering his respects to the American orchestra that had commissioned the work (the Boston SO). All three compositions revive a style of lyric melody that is overtly diatonic; even when in a chromatic form, it is still grounded on diatonic intervals and constructed in clear phrase groups.

From 1933 to 1963 Hindemith adapted this new and clearly tonal style to Classical sonata forms and conventional genres. In the first three years his compositional energies were concentrated almost entirely on the opera *Mathis der Maler* (first performed in 1938 in Zurich) and its attendant symphony (which was written before work on the opera began, and received its premiere performance on 12 March 1934 by the Berlin PO under Wilhelm Furtwängler). In the post-*Mathis* works of the 1930s and 1940s Hindemith's style became more diatonic and explicitly tonal and at the same time more abstract. The first important work to follow the symphony *Mathis der Maler* was the Violin Sonata in E (1935), the first of an extensive corpus of sonatas, eventually numbering 25, for almost every instrument. In 1939 he wrote his Violin Concerto, the first of eight concertos that build on the tradition of the genre in the 19th century while not forsaking the concertante approach of the 18th. In 1940 he wrote the Symphony in E♭, the first of five symphonies of similar purpose. One can hear the process of increasing abstraction developing from the still humanistic basis of the ballet *Nobilissima visione* of 1938 to the almost geometric design of *Ludus tonalis* (1942, a cycle of fugues and interludes for piano), the extensive revision (1948) of *Das Marienleben* (with an elaborate new preface), and the last full-length opera, *Die Harmonie der Welt* (1956–7), an overtly mystical dramatization of the work of the Renaissance astronomer Johannes Kepler.

In the music of his final years Hindemith explored an increasingly dissonant harmonic vocabulary and even attempted some elements of Arnold Schoenberg's technique: in the Tuba Sonata of 1955, for example, he used a 12-tone theme. Yet his faith in the triad never wavered: the sextet in the one-act opera *The Long Christmas Dinner* (1960), for example, is harmonized exclusively in triads, and in the final bars of his last work, the Mass of 1963, he was still able to draw great beauty from the harmonic language he had espoused for the last 30 years of his life.

3. INFLUENCE IN THE UNITED STATES. In addition to the impact of his practical and theoretical work, which, especially in the 1940s and 1950s, was seen by young American composers as offering an alternative model to those of the three other immigrant giants (Schoenberg, Stravinsky, and Bartók), Hindemith had a powerful influence in the United States as a teacher and author, and as a proponent of Baroque and earlier music. From his first summer of teaching at the Berkshire Music Center (1940) throughout his years at Yale, Hindemith was known to be a demanding and critical mentor (he awarded only 12 master's degrees in composition during his entire professorship), and relationships with students were sometimes tense. But he attracted some of the best talent in the United States; among his

composition and theory students at Yale were EASLEY BLACKWOOD, HOWARD BOATWRIGHT, NORMAN DELLO JOIO, ALVIN ETLER, LUKAS FOSS, ULYSSES KAY, MEL POWELL, HAROLD SHAPERO, and YEHUDI WYNER. In stylistic terms his students did not form a "Hindemith school" of composers, but many of them went on to attempt to inculcate in their own students Hindemith's very high standards of craftsmanship and taste; his books were useful in this mission. Perhaps more important was his role as a director of performances of medieval and Renaissance music on authentic instruments. In the 1940s there was virtually no activity in early music in the United States, and a remarkable number of the best-known performers and leaders of early music ensembles since the 1950s were first inspired as members of Hindemith's Collegium Musicum—as were, in the role of auditors at his concerts, other students, scholars, and listeners. Continuing interest in Hindemith has been sustained through the efforts of the Hindemith Foundation, including support for the publication of the complete edition of his work, as well as by the publication of his correspondence, biographical documents, drawings, and documents. In 1971 the *Hindemith-Jahrbuch* became the forum for Hindemith research, and the celebrations of the centenary of his birth drew widespread attention.

WORKS
(from 1940 on only; all published unless otherwise stated)

EDITION
P. Hindemith: *Sämtliche Werke,* ed. K. von Fischer and L. Finscher (Mainz, 1975–)

STAGE
op
— Hérodiade (Orchester-Rezitation, S. Mallarmé), 1944, Washington DC, 30 Oct 1944
— Die Harmonie der Welt (op, 5, Hindemith), 1956–7, cond. Hindemith, Munich, Prinzregententheater, 11 Aug 1957
— Das lange Weihnachtsmahl [The Long Christmas Dinner] (op, 1, T. Wilder, Ger. trans. Hindemith), 1960–61, cond. Hindemith, Mannheim, Nationaltheater, 17 Dec 1961

ORCHESTRAL
— Vc Conc., 1940
— Sym., E♭
— Theme and Variations, The Four Temperaments, pf, str, 1940, also ballet (choreog. G. Balanchine), 1946
— Poor Lazarus and the Rich Man, Virginian ballad, 1941, frag.
— Amor und Psyche (Farnesina), ballet ov., 1943
— Symphonic Metamorphosis after Themes by Carl Maria von Weber, 1943
— Piano Concerto, 1945
— Symphonia serena, 1946
— Clarinet Concerto, 1947
— Concerto, tpt, bn, str, 1949–52
— Concerto, ww, hp, orch, 1949
— Horn Concerto, 1949
— Sinfonietta, E, 1949–50
— Symphony, B♭, concert band, 1951
— Symphony Die Harmonie der Welt, 1951
— Pittsburgh Symphony, 1958
— Marsch über den alten Schweizerton, 1960
— Organ Concerto, 1962–3

CHORAL
With orch
— Das Unaufhörliche (orat, G. Benn), S, T, Bar, B, mixed chorus, children's chorus, orch, org, 1931

— When lilacs last in the door-yard bloom'd [Als Flieder jüngst mir im Garten blüht] (requiem, W. Whitman, Ger. trans. Hindemith), Mez, Bar, mixed chorus, orch, org, 1946
— Apparebit repentina dies (medieval poems), mixed chorus, brass, 1947
— Ite angeli veloces (cant., P. Claudel, Ger. trans. Hindemith), A, T, mixed chorus, audience, orch, 1953–5: Chant de triomphe du roi David; Custos quid de nocte; Cantique de l'espérance
— Mainzer Umzug (C. Zuckmayer), S, T, Bar, mixed chorus, orch, 1962–
— Credo, 1963, frag.

Unacc.
— Das Galgenritt (The Demon of the Gibbet) (F.J. O'Brien, trans. Hindemith), male vv, 1949
— 12 Madrigals (J. Weinheber), SSATB, 1958: Mitwelt; eines Narren, eines Künstlers Leben; Tauche deine Furcht; Trink aus!; An eine Tote; Frühling; An einen Schmetterling; Judaskuss; Magisches Rezept; Es bleibt wohl; Kraft fand zu Form; Du Zweifel
— Mass, mixed chorus, 1963

SOLO VOCAL
With piano
— 14 Motets (Bible), S/T, pf, 1940–60: Exiit edictum (2 versions); Cum natus esset; In principio erat verbum; Ascendente Jesu in naviculam; Pastores loquebantur; Nuptiae factae sunt; Angelus Domini apparuit; Defuncto Herode; Dicebat Jesus scribis et pharisaeis; Dixit Jesus Petro; Erat Joseph et Mari; Vidit Joannes Jesus venientem; Cum factus esset Jesus annorum duodecim; Cum descendisset Jesus de monte
— Lieder, S, pf, 1942: Frauenklage (Burggraf zu Regensburg); On arrange et on compose (Rilke); To a Snowflake (F. Thompson); Zum Abschiede meiner Tochter (J.F. von Eichendorff); Nach einer alten Skizze (C.F. Meyer); Abendständchen (Brentano); La cigale et la fourmi (J. de La Fontaine); Lampe du soir (Rilke); Ranae ad solem (Phaedrus); Tränenkrüglein (Rilke); Trübes Wetter (Keller); Ich will Trauern lassen stehen (anon.); Abendwolke (Meyer); O Grille sing (M. Dauthendey); Wer wusste je das Leben recht zu fassen (A. von Platen); Eau qui se presse (Rilke); The Moon (P.B. Shelley); On a Fly Drinking Out of his Cup (W. Oldys); The Wild Flower's Song (W. Blake); C'est de la côte d'Adam (Rilke); Envoy (Thompson); La belle dame sans merci (J. Keats); On Hearing 'The Last Rose of Summer' (C. Wolfe); Echo (T. Moore); The Whistlin' Thief (S. Lover)
— Levis exsurgit Zephyrus (anon.), 1943
— Sing On there in the Swamp (Whitman), 1943
— Bal des pendus (A. Rimbaud, Eng. trans. Hindemith, Ger. trans. K.W. Bartlett), 1944
— Le revenant (C. Baudelaire), 1944
— Sainte (S. Mallarmé), 1944
— To Music, to Becalm his Fever (R. Herrick), 1944
— Two Songs (O. Cox), 1955: Image; Beauty touch me

CHBR
For 3 or more inst
— String Quartet [no.7], E♭, 1945
— Septet, fl, ob, cl, tpt, hn, b cl/bn, bn, 1948
— Sonata, 4 hn, 1952
— Octet, cl, bn, hn, vn, 2 va, vc, db, 1958

For 1 or 2 insts
— A frog he went a-courting, variations, vc, pf, 1941
— Sonata, eng hn, pf, 1941
— Sonata, trbn, pf, 1941
— Echo, fl, pf, 1942
— Sonata, a hn, pf, 1943
— Sonata, vc, pf, 1948
— Sonata, db, pf, 1949
— Sonata, b tuba, pf, 1955

CANONS
Richard Donavan has Birthday, 5vv, 1941; Sing, hevin imperial, 4vv, 1942; Dolorum solacium (P. Abelard), 4vv, 1943; Sine musica nulla disciplina (Hrabanus Maurus), 3vv, 1944; Oh, Threats of Hell and Hopes of Paradise (Rubayat), 4vv, 1945; Musica divinas laudes, 3vv,

brass, 1949 [arr. pf 4 hands]; Unusquisque eum cantum (Guido of Arezzo), 3vv, 1949; Du Komponist bist trist?, 5vv, 1952; Wir sind froh (sowieso), 6vv, 1952; Igitur Daniel, 3vv, 1953; Gar viele gibt's, die halten sich für Amigos, 3vv, brass, 1954; Siebzig, ja siebzig ist ein gutes Alter, 11vv, 1954; Canon, 4 insts, 1955; 40, 40, 40, 40, es lebe hoch das Konzerthausleben, 3vv, 1956; Othmar Sch Sch Sch Schoeck, 4vv, 1956; Unsre Amseln lassen sich's nicht verdriessen, 3vv, 1957; Was wäre die Welt ohne unsren Igor, 3vv, 1957; Mit Freuden seinen Wunsche entbiet', 3vv, 1958; Obgleich verspätet, gratulieren, 3vv, 1958; Dem RIAS-Kammerchor viel Glück, 7vv, 1958; Dem RIAS-Kammerchor zu seinem 10 jährigen Bestehen, 9vv, 1958; Wir gratulieren, wünschen Glück, 4vv, 1958; Festmarsch, 3 male vv, tuba, 1959; Joseph, lieber Joseph, 4vv, 1959; Wollte ich allen brieflich danken, 3vv, 1960; Et obstinati quidam cantare volentes (Johannes de Muris), 3vv, 2 insts, 1962; Hoch leb' der Jubilar, er lebe hoch, 3vv, 1962; Hoch soll er dreimal leben, 3vv, 1962; Cum sit eum proprium, 4vv, 1963

SING- UND SPIELMUSIK, ÜBUNGSTÜCKE, ETUDES AND TEACHING PIECES

— A Song of Music (Lied von der Musik) (G. Tyler, Ger. trans. Hindemith), chorus, pf/str, 1940
— 2 Fugues, pf, 1940
— Old Irish Air (trans. Hindemith), mixed chorus, hp, pf/str orch, 1940, collab. Berkshire Music Center students
— Agnus Dei und Dona nobis, male chorus, 1941
— Enthusiasm, fl, pf, 1941
— Introduction and Passacaglia, str trio, 1941
— Lied (I am thee), 1v, pf, 1941
— Sonata, pf, 1941, 1st movt only
— Stücke, bn, vc, 1941
— 6 ganz leichte Stücke, bn, vc, c1942
— Gay, 2 vc, c1942
— Kleine Sonata, vc, pf, 1942
— Trio, rec ens, ?1942
— Ludus minor, cl, vc, 1944

PARODIESTÜCKE

Dramatic: Melodrama (instructions for US tax form 1040), 1v, inst, 1944
Inst: The Expiring Frog (Recitative e aria ranatica) (*Encyclopaedia Britannica*, C. Dickens), 1v, pf, 1944

EDITIONS, ARRANGEMENTS, ETC.

C. Monteverdi, Orfeo, 1943; Suite französischer Tänze, after Gervaise, du Tertre, 1958

Principal publisher: Schott

WRITINGS
(selected)

Unterweisung im Tonsatz, i: *Theoretischer Teil* (Mainz, 1937, 2/1940; Eng. trans., 1942, as *The Craft of Musical Composition*, i: *Theory*, 2/1948)
Unterweisung im Tonsatz, ii: *Übungsbuch für den zweistimmigen Satz* (Mainz, 1939; Eng. trans., 1941)
A Concentrated Course in Traditional Harmony, i (New York, 1943, 2/1948; Ger. orig., London, 1949, as *Aufgaben für Harmonieschüler*)
Elementary Training for Musicians (New York, 1946, 2/1949)
A Concentrated Course in Traditional Harmony, ii: *Exercises for Advanced Students* (New York, 1948, 2/1953; Ger. orig., London, 1949, as *Harmonie-Übungen für Fortgeschrittene*)
Johann Sebastian Bach: Heritage and Obligation (New Haven, 1952; Ger. orig., Frankfurt, 1953, as *Johann Sebastian Bach: ein verpflichtendes Erbe*); repr. in *Paul Hindemith: Aufsätze—Vorträge—Reden*, ed. G. Schubert (Zurich, 1994)
A Composer's World (Cambridge, MA, 1952; Ger. trans., 1959) [Ger. edn incl. addn to chap.5; Eng. trans. in *JMT*, v (1961), 109–12]
Unterweisung im Tonsatz, iii: *Übungsbuch für den dreistimmigen Satz* (Mainz, 1970)
ed. G. Schubert: *Aufsätze—Vorträge—Reden* (Zürich, 1994)

BIBLIOGRAPHY
CATALOGS AND BIBLIOGRAPHIES

K. Stone: *Paul Hindemith: Catalogue of his Works and Recordings* (London, 1954)
Paul Hindemith: Werkverzeichnis (Mainz, 1969)
H. Rösner: *Paul Hindemith: Katalog seiner Werke, Diskographie, Bibliographie, Einführung in das Schaffen* (Frankfurt, 1970)
E. Kraus: "Bibliographie: Paul Hindemith," *Musik und Bildung*, iii (1971), 249–52
H. Rösner: "Zur Hindemith-Bibliographie," *Hindemith-Jahrbuch* 1971, 161–95
O. Zickenheiner: "Hindemith-Bibliographie 1971–73," *Hindemith-Jahrbuch* 1973, 155–94
A. Laubenthal: "Hindemith-Bibliographie 1974–8," *Hindemith-Jahrbuch* 1978, 229–39
G. Metz and D. Neumeyer: "Hindemith-Bibliographie 1979–81," *Hindemith-Jahrbuch* 1986, 159–84
G. Metz: "Hindemith-Bibliographie 1982–4," *Hindemith-Jahrbuch* 1990, 118–38

LIFE AND WORKS
GMO

H. Strobel: *Paul Hindemith* (Mainz, 1928, 3/1948)
N. Cazden: "Hindemith and Nature," *MR*, xv (1954), 288–306
R. Stephan: "Hindemith's Marienleben," *MR*, xv (1954), 275–87
H. Tischler: "Hindemith's Ludus tonalis and Bach's Well-tempered Clavier," *MR*, xx (1959), 217–27
H. Boatwright: "Paul Hindemith as a Teacher," *MQ*, 1 (1964), 279–89
W. Thomson: "Hindemith's Contribution to Music Theory," *JMT*, ix (1965), 52–71
W.W. Austin: "Hindemith," *Music in the 20th Century* (New York, 1966), 396–416
T.W. Adorno: "Ad vocem Hindemith: the Case Against Gebrauchsmusik," *Impromptus* (Frankfurt, 1968), 51–87
I. Kemp: *Hindemith* (London, 1970)
Hindemith-Jahrbuch 1971–
G. Skelton: *Paul Hindemith: the Man behind the Music* (New York, 1975)
H.W. Hitchcock: "Trinitarian Symbolism in the 'Engelkonzert' of Hindemith's *Mathis der Maler*," *A Festschrift for Albert Seay*, ed. M. Grace (Colorado Springs,1982), 217–29
D. Rexroth: *Paul Hindemith Briefe* (Frankfurt, 1982)
D. Neumeyer: *The Music of Paul Hindemith* (New Haven, 1986)
S. Hinton: *The Idea of Gebrauchsmusik* (New York, 1989)
L. Noss: *Paul Hindemith in the United States* (Urbana, IL, 1989)
D. Neumayer and G. Schubert: "Arnold Schoenberg and Paul Hindemith," *Journal of the Arnold Schoenberg Institute*, xiii (1990), 3–46
S. Schaal and A. Storm-Rusche: *Paul Hindemith: der Komponist als Zeichner* (Zurich, 1995)
G. Skelton: *Selected Letters of Paul Hindemith* (New Haven, 1995)
N. Bolín: *Paul Hindemith: Komponist zwischen Tradition un Avantgarde* (Mainz, 1999)
K.H. Kowalke: "For those we Love: Hindemith, Whitman and 'An American Requiem,'" *JAMS*, 1 (1997), 133–74
M.H. Kater: "Paul Hindemith, the Reluctant Emigré," *Composers of the Nazi Era: Eight Portraits* (New York, 2000)
S. Luttmann: *Paul Hindemith: a Research and Information Guide* (New York, 2009)

IAN KEMP/H. WILEY HITCHCOCK/GISELHER SCHUBERT/R

Hinderas [Monagas], **Natalie (Henderson)** (*b* Oberlin, OH, 16 June 1927; *d* Philadelphia, PA, 22 July 1987). Pianist. She was born into a musical family; her father was a jazz pianist and her mother a classically trained pianist who taught at the Cleveland Institute of Music. As a child, Hinderas displayed an affinity for the piano, and she made her recital debut at age eight. By age twelve, she was the soloist in Edvard Grieg's Piano Concerto with the Cleveland Women's SO. After study with OLGA SAMAROFF at the Juilliard School and with EDWARD STEUERMANN at the Philadelphia Conservatory, she made her first European tour, returning in 1954 to play a Town Hall concert in New York featuring works by Wolfgang Amadeus Mozart, Alban Berg, and Paul

Hindemith. Hinderas's recital repertoire promoted 20th-century composers, often championing the new music of African American composers. In 1959 and 1964, the US State Department sent Hinderas on concert tours of Europe, the Middle East, and Southeast Asia. In 1966 she joined the faculty at Temple University. In 1971 Eugene Ormandy invited her to perform Alberto Ginastera's Piano Concerto no.1 with the Philadelphia Orchestra, marking the first time an African American woman performed as soloist with a major symphony. After her acclaimed performance, she received offers to play with the New York Philharmonic, the Chicago SO, the Pittsburgh SO, and the Los Angeles Philharmonic at the Hollywood Bowl. In 1971 she recorded an important two-disk album titled *Natalie Hinderas Plays Music by Black Composers* on the Desto label. This landmark recording featured works by R. Nathaniel Dett, Thomas H. Kerr Jr., William Grant Still, Olly Wilson, and many others. In 1976 she was awarded an honorary doctorate by Swarthmore College.

GEORGE GELLES/ALYSON PAYNE

Hindsley, Mark Hubert (*b* Union City, IN, 18 Oct 1905; *d* Urbana, IL, 1 Oct 1999). Conductor, writer on music, and arranger. He began playing cornet at the age of ten. In 1921 he enrolled at Indiana University, graduating at age 19 with a chemistry degree. While attending IU, he was first cornet and student assistant director of the band. After graduating, he accepted a position directing the IU band as an instructor. During this time, he pursued a music degree (MA 1927). After five years as supervisor of instrumental music in Cleveland Heights, OH (1929–34), Hindsley was appointed assistant director of bands at the University of Illinois. During World War II he served as staff music officer of the Army Air Forces Training Command (1942–6). Hindsley returned to Illinois in 1946, and was appointed director of bands in 1950, a position he held until his retirement in 1970. Under his direction the Illinois Band issued many recordings that have been widely distributed and highly praised.

He was a widely published author on bands and music education, writing seven books and over forty articles. He was particularly recognized as an authority on wind instrument intonation. An accomplished arranger, Hindsley transcribed more than 75 orchestral works for band. He held offices in many national organizations, including president of the College Band Directors National Association (1947) and American Bandmasters Association (1957–8). He was named Honorary Life President of ABA (1996). His papers are at the Sousa Archives at the University of Illinois and the ABA Archives at the University of Maryland.

WRITINGS

Band–at-ten-tion! A Manual for the Marching Band (Chicago, 1932)
School Band and Orchestra Administration (New York, 1940)
Hindsley on Bands (Urbana, IL, 1979)
My Bands and I (Urbana, IL, 1984)

BIBLIOGRAPHY

E.S. Gregory: *Mark H. Hindsley, the Illinois Years* (diss., U. of Illinois, 1982)

W.H. Rehrig: *The Heritage Encyclopedia of Band Music* (Westerville, OH, 1991, suppl. 1996); CD-ROM (Oskaloosa, IA, 2005) [includes selective list of works]

WILLIAM BERZ

Hinduism. Hindu music in the United States comprises the musical traditions of public and domestic worship by immigrant Hindu communities beginning in the 20th century, the influences of transplanted spiritual movements since about 1965, and the impact of classical and devotional music upon classical, jazz, rock, and popular music since around 1960.

Hindu religious traditions exhibit close and persistent associations with chant and the musical arts. The roots of Indian music go back to the Vedas and the Upanishads (4000–1000 BCE), in which the cosmic Absolute (Brahman) is represented by the sound of the syllable Om. In the Tantras and the Purāshas, music is known as Nāda-Brahman and defined as both unmanifest (anāhata) and manifest (āhata). The Hindu divinities themselves are also associated with music and serve as paradigms for musicians and dancers: the goddess Sarasvati holds the vīṇā, Vishnu sounds the conch and plays the flute as Krishna, and Siva plays the damaru drum during his dance of dissolution.

In India and in the diaspora, the daily life of the devout Hindu is laden with mantras, prayers, recitations, songs, and the playing of musical instruments. Based on ancient texts of drama and music, *Nātya-Śāstra* and *Dattilam*, Indian music is viewed by all as both a vehicle for liberation and a source of entertainment. With some differences in lyrical content, the similarity in the fundamental approach to music provides for a pan-Indian artistic and religious expression, whether as devotion to Nirguṇa (Absolute without qualities) or Saguṇa (Absolute with qualities) including Krishna, Vishnu, Śiva, or the various goddesses.

Indian music (Saṅgīta) has three divisions: vocal, instrumental, and dance. The basic scale is made up of seven notes, sa, ri, ga, ma, pa, dha, and ni, (cf. do, re, mi), with flattened and sharpened notes used to create varieties of melodic patterns called rāgas. A rāga is believed to arouse a specific emotional state (bhāva). Indian music does not employ harmony or chords, and is thus essentially monophonic. Rhythmic cycles (tālas) are measured in hand claps and waves, and are rendered in slow, medium, and fast tempos. Traditional genres still performed today include the dhrupad, the dhamar, the khyal, the thumri, the kriti, the kirtana, and the bhajan, which are rendered according to specific rāgas and tālas.

Indian instruments are divided into four classes. The ancient Indian classification system has influenced that of Sachs-Hornbostel (1914): strings or chordophones (tata), wind or aerophones (susira), drums or membranophones (vitata), and idiophones (ghana) like cymbals, clappers, and bells. Drums include the tabla, the pakhavaj, the dholak, the tambourine, and the khole. A drone is provided by a tanpura (four-stringed lute), a harmonium, or a sruti box (a small squeezebox). The harmonium, often used as accompaniment, is a small reed organ brought by 19th-century missionaries.

The metal reed used is similar to that of the harmonica and the accordion.

Before the construction of temples in the 1980s, Hindu families in America held regular pūjā (worship services), including offerings (flowers, water, food, etc.) and songs, at their homes during festivals, weddings, śraddha (funeral services), graduations, and birth ceremonies. As temples appeared, these occasions were facilitated there by formal chanting of Sanskrit verses and the congregational singing of vernacular hymns called bhajan or kīrtan. In time, older styles of devotional music were replaced by the less formal and more egalitarian forms of musical expression.

Despite the appearance of a united Hindu community, separate groups tend to meet according to native region, language, and even cuisine, each cultivating their own musical styles. For example, modern devotional songs combining religious with secular experiences as found in the music of Rabindranath Tagore are popular in Bengal and thus among the American Bengali communities. Yet devotional songs of great Bhakti saints like Sūr Dās and Mirabai are standards in all gatherings, and most Hindus are fond of bhajans sung by Lata Mangeshkar, Anup Jalota, and Mohammad Rafi in films. Worship in the diaspora is often accompanied by the bhajan "Om Jai Jagadisha Hare," from the Hindi film *Purab aur Paschim* (1970). Famous bhajans known to all Hindus such as "Raghupati Rāghava Rāja Rām," a favorite of Mahatma Gandhi, reached wide American audiences in the Oscar-winning film *Gandhi* (1982).

Sectarian leaders of religious movements began entering America after the lifting of immigration restrictions in 1965, some of them serving only Indian members and others reaching out to Americans. The easiest access to Indian music for Americans has been nāmkīrtan, the collective singing of divine names as first brought by the Hare Krishna Movement (ISKCON), and later becoming a mainstay of the Yoga and Vedanta movements. Most recently, Indian-style bhajans are now popular with Christians, Jews, Buddhists, and Muslims (Sufis). Americans such as Krishna Das and Jai Uttal have succeeded with a style employing New Age, Celtic, middle-Eastern, blues, jazz, and African features.

Indian classical music was brought to America by individual performers and sponsors. In 1955, a sarod concert by ALI AKBAR KHAN was arranged in New York by the violinist Yehudi Menuhin. In 1967, the Ali Akbar College of Music was established in San Francisco, and the Kinnara School of Music was founded by RAVI SHANKAR in Los Angeles. Shankar (sitar) and Alla Rakha (tabla drums) gained national attention while featured with the Grateful Dead during large peace concerts. Despite the apparent link between Indian music and alternative mind-states, Ravi Shankar promptly distanced himself from the drug culture in his book *My Music, My Life* (1968).

Nonetheless, Indian music made a major impact on such rock groups as the Grateful Dead, the Byrds, the Doors, the Mahavishnu Orchestra, and the Paul Butterfield Blues Band, wherein the elongated guitar solo is noted as a legacy of Shankar's influence. George Harrison studied the sitar with Ravi Shankar and fostered widespread admiration for Hinduism and its music among the hippie generation. Shankar also made an imprint upon the American composers Philip Glass and Terry Riley, as well as on jazz legend John Coltrane. Shankar's concertos for sitar and orchestra are performed and conducted by sitarist ANOUSHKA SHANKAR, who inherited her father's legacy.

The association of Beatles John Lennon and George Harrison with Maharishi Mahesh Yogi and A.C. Bhaktivedanta Swami made it desirable for musicians to maintain affiliations with Hindu gurus. In the 1970s, Swami Nadabrahmananda taught Nāda-Yoga—Indian music as a spiritual path—to many Americans. Following in the wake of Jon Higgins, the first Westerner to sing South Indian, or Carnatic, music, several Americans including Stephen Slawek (sitar), George Ruckert and Ken Zuckerman (sarod), David Courtney and Ty Burhoe (tabla), and Guy Beck and Warren Senders (Hindustani vocals) perform this style.

Hindu music thus penetrates American life on three fronts: through the practices of immigrant Hindu families, the presence of charismatic religious leaders, and by the effect of classical and devotional music on American musicians. But while Indian instrumental styles have become well-established, the vocal tradition, the foundation of all Indian music, has not achieved the same prominence.

BIBLIOGRAPHY

G.L. Beck: *Sonic Theology: Hinduism and Sacred Sound* (Columbia, SC, 1993)
P. Manuel: *Cassette Culture: Popular Music and Technology in North India* (Chicago and London, 1993)
G. Farrell: *Indian Music and the West* (New York, 1997)
P. Lavezzoli: *The Dawn of Indian Music in the West* (New York, 2006)
R. Shankar: *My Music, My Life* (New York, 1968, 2/2007)

GUY L. BECK

Hines, Earl (Kenneth) [Fatha] (*b* Duquesne, PA, 28 Dec 1903; *d* Oakland, CA, 22 April 1983). Jazz pianist and bandleader. He was one of the most influential pianists of the pre-World War II period, and his Chicago-based Grand Terrace Orchestra one of the most popular black bands that worked outside of New York.

Hines grew up in a lower middle-class home in Duquesne, Pennsylvania (now a suburb of Pittsburgh). Trained primarily in the Western classical tradition by local teachers, in his teens he made his way to Pittsburgh's black Hill District, where he was exposed to popular music and early jazz and crossed paths with such piano luminaries as Luckey Roberts, James P. Johnson, Willie "the Lion" Smith, and Eubie Blake. In 1921 the classical and popular vocalist Lois Deppe hired Hines as his accompanist, and the two worked together steadily for the next three years, both as a duo and in Deppe's Serenaders, a nine-piece ensemble with which Hines made his first recordings in 1923.

In 1925 Hines moved to Chicago to work in the heart of the entertainment district in the South Side. He quickly established himself as a powerful force in Chicago's music life. He also struck up a friendship with the cornetist and trumpeter LOUIS ARMSTRONG, and the

Earl "Fatha" Hines, 1968. (JazzSign/Lebrecht Music & Arts)

result was one of the most famous musical partnerships in early jazz. Beginning in 1927 Armstrong and Hines made a total of 36 recordings together, with various ensembles. In the watershed year of 1928 Hines worked with the clarinetist Jimmie Noone's group at the South Side's Apex Club, recorded his first piano solos and, with Armstrong, made some of the most highly-praised discs in jazz history, including "Skip the Gutter," "Muggles," "Weather Bird" (a duet), and "West End Blues."

At the end of the year Hines organized his first band for the South Side's Grand Terrace Ballroom. For the next 11 years he and his group remained a fixture at the Grand Terrace. The group's first recordings, made in 1929, reveal inconsistent ensemble playing, but Hines refined and expanded his band until, by the late 1930s, it was one of the finest of its type in the country. Through weekly radio broadcasts from the club and extensive touring, the group rose to national prominence. Although 1940 marked the end of the pianist's tenure at the Grand Terrace (he did return for a brief stint there in late 1941), the year also saw the release of Hines's biggest hit, "Boogie Woogie on the St. Louis Blues." "Jelly, Jelly," a blues feature for the vocalist Billy Eckstine, who had joined the group in late 1939, also proved popular.

Eckstine left to form his own band in late 1943, and for a brief period in the same year, Hines led a now-legendary big band that featured the trumpeter Dizzy Gillespie and the saxophonist Charlie Parker, both seminal figures in the creation of bebop; due to the AFM recording ban, however, no recordings were made. Faced with a wartime shortage of male musicians, Hines next tried a short-lived experiment with an expanded complement of women—a harpist, bass player, guitarist, cellist, three violinists, and a vocalist (Sarah Vaughan)—but the complex logistics of the group's tours proved unmanageable.

In 1948, strapped for money and faced with the passing of the big band's heyday, Hines joined Louis Armstrong in a sextet, the All Stars, with which he toured extensively over the next three years. In 1955 he joined the Dixieland house band at San Francisco's Hangover Club. Although not particularly interested in the featured repertory, Hines was drawn by the steady paycheck and the chance to create a stable home for his family. He moved to the West Coast permanently in 1956, bought a house in Oakland a few years later, and spent the rest of his life in the area.

In 1964 he left semi-retirement in California to play three concerts at the Little Theater in New York which received critical acclaim. Invigorated by the enthusiastic response, Hines returned to a regular schedule of performing and recording. He made several tours of Europe, the Soviet Union, and Japan and was a featured performer at the White House in 1969 and 1976. Although he contracted Parkinson's Disease in his later years, he continued performing until a week before his death.

Hines was a true iconoclast at the piano. Especially in the 1920s, no players sounded remotely like him. Although overshadowed by the virtuosity of Art Tatum, beginning in the 1930s Hines was in many ways the more daring pianist, and few players who succeeded him escaped his influence. Early on, he developed what came to be known as trumpet style, in which the right hand played percussive octaves that cut through an ensemble's sound, making him in effect another voice in the front line. Drawing on his early unsuccessful attempts at playing the cornet, as well as Armstrong's influence, he phrased and articulated his right hand much as would a brass player, as in ex.1, which begins with a two-bar pick up much like that of a brass player.

Hines was also one of the most rhythmically audacious jazz pianists, often bringing the flow of a solo to a screeching halt with complex patterns in both left and right hands. These extraordinary moments (ex.2) could give the impression the beat had completely disappeared.

Ex.1 Earl Hines, "Fifty-Seven Varieties" (1928). D2, mm. 1–4. Transcription by Jeffrey Taylor.

Ex.2 Earl Hines, "A Monday Date" (1928). A3, mm. 21–24. Transcription by Jeffrey Taylor.

In later years, Hines gave up the octave texture in favor of a punchy, single-note right hand style, often interrupted by octave glissandos. However, he continued to push the underlying rhythmic structure to its limit, while never mentally losing the beat.

SELECTED RECORDINGS

As leader: *Legendary Little Theater Concert of 1964*, i–ii (1964, Muse); *Earl Hines: 1928–1932* (Classics, 1990); *Earl Hines: 1932–1934* (Classics, 1990); *Earl Hines: 1934–1937* (Classics, 1990); *Earl Hines: 1937–1939* (Classics, 1990); *Earl Hines: 1939–1940* (Classics, 1991); *Hines Collection: 1928–40* (Collector's Classics, 1995); *Earl Hines: 1941* (Classics, 1996)

As sideman with L. Armstrong: *Louis Armstrong with Earl Hines* (Col., 1989)

BIBLIOGRAPHY

R. Hadlock: *Jazz Masters of the Twenties* (New York, 1965/*R*)

G. Schuller: *Early Jazz: its Roots and Musical Development* (New York, 1968/*R*)

S. Dance: *The World of Swing* (New York, 1974/*R*, 2/2001)

S. Dance: *The World of Earl Hines* (New York, 1977/*R*)

S. Dance: disc notes, *Giants of Jazz: Earl Hines*, Time-Life Records TL-J11 (1980)

G. Schuller: *The Swing Era: the Development of Jazz, 1930–1945* (New York, 1989/*R*)

J. Taylor: "Earl Hines's Piano Style in the 1920s: a Historical and Analytical Perspective," *Black Music Research Journal*, xii/1 (1992), 57–77

J. Taylor: "Louis Armstrong, Earl Hines, and 'Weather Bird'," *MQ*, lxxxii/1 (1998), 1–40

J. Taylor: "Earl Hines and 'Rosetta': Jazz Musicians and their Contexts," *CMc*, nos.71–3 (2001–02), 303–23

J. Taylor: *Earl "Fatha" Hines: Selected Piano Solos, 1928–41* (Madison, WI, 2006)

JEFFREY TAYLOR

Hines, Gregory (Oliver) (*b* New York, NY, 14 Feb 1946; *d* Los Angeles, CA, 9 Aug 2003). Tap dancer and actor. He began dance lessons with HENRY LE TANG in 1949, before he was three. When he was five he began performing with his older brother Maurice in a dance act first called The Hines Kids and later The Hines Brothers. Their father, drummer Maurice Hines Sr., joined the act, thereafter known as Hines, Hines and Dad, in 1964. In 1973 Gregory left the act and moved to Venice, California, where he formed a rock band called Severance. He returned to New York in 1978, resuming his stage career as a dancer in *The Last Minstrel Show* and later appearing in *Eubie* (1978–9), which reunited him with Maurice, *Comin' Uptown* (1979-80), and *Sophisticated Ladies* (1981–2), while simultaneously developing an acting career on stage and screen. He appeared again with Maurice in the 1984 film *The Cotton Club*. In 1992 he co-starred with his protégé SAVION GLOVER in *Jelly's Last Jam*, a stage presentation loosely based on the life of Jelly Roll Morton. In the 1990s he appeared on the children's television program *Sesame Street*, often with Glover. In 1997–8, he had his own television sitcom, *The Gregory Hines Show*, and began touring with his own show. In 2001 he played the lead role in the miniseries *Bojangles*, devoted to the dancer Bill Robinson. Hines played a crucial role in transmitting jazz-tap traditions to new generations and promoted forgotten elders as well as promising newcomers.

BIBLIOGRAPHY

R.E. Frank: *Tap!* (New York, 1994)

T. Vallance: Obituary, *The Independent*, 12 Aug 2003

C.V. Hill: *Tap Dancing America: a Cultural History* (New York, 2009)

HOWARD RYE

Hines [Heinz], **Jerome** [Albert Link] (*b* Hollywood, CA, 8 Nov 1921; *d* New York, NY, 4 Feb 2003). Bass and composer. He studied chemistry, mathematics, and physics at the University of California, Los Angeles; he taught chemistry there for a year, then worked briefly in the oil industry. While at UCLA he also studied voice with Gennaro Curci. He made his debut at the San Francisco Opera as Monterone in *Rigoletto* at the age of 20 (1941), afterwards appearing with various American orchestras and the New Orleans Opera. His success influenced his decision to concentrate on singing. In 1946 he won the Caruso Award, which included a debut at the Metropolitan Opera (as the Sergeant in *Boris Godunov*). He spent most of his career with that house, while also establishing a solid international career. In the years immediately following his initial successes, he performed in Rio de Janeiro, Buenos Aires, and Mexico City and in concert with Arturo Toscanini (for a recording of the Ludwig van Beethoven's *Missa solemnis*, 1953). His performances at the Glyndebourne and Edinburgh festivals (1953) as Nick Shadow and in Munich (1954) as Don Giovanni established his European reputation, which was confirmed in 1958 when he made his La Scala debut as Handel's Hercules and sang Gurnemanz at Bayreuth. Subsequent Bayreuth appearances included King Mark and Wotan (*Die Walküre*). In 1962 he sang Boris Godunov at the Bol'shoy. Hines's huge voice and solid technique enabled him to perform a wide repertory, including 45 roles sung at the Metropolitan over the course of 41 seasons. His careful preparation of the historical and psychological aspects of each role led to especially vivid projections of such parts as Boris Godunov and Philip II (*Don Carlo*). His many operatic recordings include Banquo (*Macbeth*) and King Heinrich (*Lohengrin*). He published a number of papers on mathematics, two books about his art, *Great Singers on*

Great Singing (Garden City, NY, 1982) and *The Four Voices of Man* (New York, 1997), and an autobiography, *This is my Story, this Is my Song* (Westwood, NJ, 1968). He held deep religious convictions and was an active volunteer for the Salvation Army in New York. He composed *I Am the Way*, an opera about the life of Christ (1969, Philadelphia), which has been performed in a number of American cities.

BIBLIOGRAPHY

A. Blyth: "Jerome Hines: Operatic Bass with a Voice to Match his Stature," *The Guardian* (14 Feb 2003)

RICHARD BERNAS/KAREN M. BRYAN

Hinners. Firm of organ builders. It was founded in Pekin, Illinois, in 1879 by John L. Hinners (*b* Wheeling, WV, 11 Aug 1846; *d* Pekin, IL, 24 Aug 1906) for the manufacture of reed organs. Late in 1881, Hinners went into partnership with J.J. Fink and became known as Hinners & Fink. In 1885 Uddo J. Albertsen bought out Fink and the company became Hinners & Albertsen, announcing its first pipe organs in 1890 in a special catalog with text in German and English. These organs uniformly had one manual and pedals but were available in a range from three ranks of pipes for $375 to six ranks at the bargain price of $635. After Albertsen left the organ business in 1902 the Hinners Organ Company incorporated under the laws of the State of Illinois. When John L. Hinners died, Jacob Roelfs became president. In 1912 Arthur W. Hinners assumed leadership. In 1928 the company's capitalization increased from $85,000 to $237,500, but, paralleling the national economy, it drifted downward, and by November 1936 the Hinners Organ Company announced that at the completion of its existing contracts pipe organ construction would cease. It finally dissolved in 1942.

The majority of organs were sold in the midwestern states, but Hinners organs were also installed in such remote locations as East India and South Korea. Hinners never became heavily involved in the prevailing trends of organ building. If Hinners was similar to Henry Ford in his product philosophy, he more resembled Montgomery Ward & Co. in his methodology, reaching out to the isolated Midwestern country church with his mail-order pipe organ business. All preliminary business was conducted by catalog and letter, and the first time the buyer had any personal contact with the company was when an employee, whose expenses were included in the contract, turned up to install the new instrument.

BIBLIOGRAPHY

R.E. Coleberd: "Yesterday's Tracker: the Hinners Organ Story," *American Organist*, xliii/9 (1960), 20

J.R. Hinners: "Chronicle of the Hinners Organ Co.," *The Tracker*, vii/2 (1962), 1–4

O. Ochse: *The History of the Organ in the United States* (Bloomington, IN, 1975)

A. Alcorn: *Mail Order Music: the Hinners Organ Company in the Dakotas, 1888–1940* (diss., U. of North Texas, 1997)

A. Alcorn: "A History of the Hinners Organ Company of Pekin, Illinois," *The Tracker*, 44/3 (2000), 13–25

ALLISON A. ALCORN

Hinojosa, (Leticia) "Tish" (*b* San Antonio, TX, 6 Dec 1955). Singer-songwriter. She was born the last of 13 children. The Tejana artist sings in Spanish and in English, in a variety of styles including folk, country, and Tex-Mex. She enjoys an active performance schedule both nationally and internationally. After spending a number of years in New Mexico, she has worked in Nashville, Tennessee, off and on, while residing in Austin, Texas. Her 1995 CD *Frontejas* pays tribute to University of Texas emeritus professor of anthropology Américo Paredes. Her emphasis on country music in the 21st century produced *Our Little Planet* (2008), a CD of country western tunes she composed in "several Nashville chapters" of her life, offering an eclectic mix of bluegrass, folk, and Tex-Mex styles. She has performed live and made recordings with many well-known musicians, among them Flaco Jiménez, her manager Marvin Dykhuis, Rose Reyes, and Kris Kristofferson. *Our Little Planet* also features Rosie Flores, Dale Watson, Carrie Rodríguez, and pedal-steel player Greg Leisz.

BRENDA M. ROMERO

Hinrichs, Gustav (Heinrich Carl) (*b* Grabow, Germany, 10 Dec 1850; *d* Mountain Lakes, NJ, 26 March 1942). Conductor and composer. Trained by his musician father in piano, clarinet, and violin and by Eduard Marxsen in composition, Hinrichs came to San Francisco in 1870. There his expanding reputation as a conductor and teacher led to the founding of the Philharmonic Society. Following his experience as assistant conductor under Theodore Thomas for the American Opera Company, Hinrichs formed his own opera company in Philadelphia and throughout nine seasons presented six American premieres. By the beginning of the 20th century he was well known nationally. In New York he taught at the National Conservatory of Music and Columbia University, and conducted for the Metropolitan Opera. He later composed and arranged film music for Universal Studios including the original Phantom of the Opera.

His compositions reflect his youthful experience playing in orchestras in Hamburg and the styles of German composers of the first half of the 19th century whom he most admired. On his handwritten list of works, Hinrichs includes 47 opus numbers, some published in Germany, some in the United States, and many in manuscript. In addition, there are some 27 works in the San Francisco Performing Arts Library and Museum in manuscript, and in the Free Library of Philadelphia a volume of national patriotic hymns and songs that he arranged and G. Schirmer, New York, published. Other works and arrangements have surfaced in various libraries, some outside the United States. While he composed a number of solo and ensemble instrumental pieces, vocal works, especially songs, constitute the bulk of his creative output.

BIBLIOGRAPHY

G. Hinrichs: "*Memoirs*," Handwritten manuscript, San Francisco Performing Arts Library and Museum

J.C. Ottenberg: "Gustav Hinrichs and Opera in Philadelphia 1888–1896," *Opera Quarterly*, xv/2 (Spring 1999), 197–223

J.C. Ottenberg: *Gustav Hinrichs (1850–1942) American Conductor and Composer* (Michigan, 2003)

JUNE C. OTTENBERG

Hinrichsen, Walter (*b* Leipzig, Germany, 23 Sept 1907; *d* New York, NY, 21 July 1969). Music publisher of German birth. After a brief period of study at the Leipzig Conservatory of Music, Hinrichsen spent the years 1927–30 serving as an apprentice with a number of music publishers: Anton J. Benjamin in Hamburg, Foetisch in Lausanne, Schott Frères in Brussels, and Augener in London. He then returned to Leipzig to work for his father, Henri Hinrichsen, at C.F. Peters. During the early 1930s he also traveled widely, visiting music publishing houses and retailers all over the world. In 1936 Hinrichsen immigrated to the United States and worked in the music publishing industry in Chicago until 1942, when he joined the US Army. He saw combat duty during the war and was stationed in the American Zone in Berlin as a music officer from 1945 until 1947. In 1948 he founded C.F. PETERS in New York. In addition to serving as an agent for a number of European publishers, the New York firm focused on publishing the music of living composers. For his active role in promoting contemporary music, Hinrichsen received several awards, including the citation of the National Association for American Composers and Conductors (1963) and the Laurel Leaf Award of the American Composers Alliance (1964) "for distinguished achievement in fostering and encouraging American music." After Hinrichsen's death his wife Ekvelyn (*b* Chicago, IL, 30 Nov 1910; *d* New York, NY, 14 Jan 2005), who had been vice president of the company, assumed the presidency; she retired in 1978, when she was succeeded by their son, Henry Hans Hinrichsen (*b* New York, NY, 13 April 1949). The Walter Hinrichsen Award, established by the C.F. Peters Corporation in 1984, is given each year by the American Academy of Arts and Letters for the publication of a work by a gifted composer.

BIBLIOGRAPHY

W. Lichtenwanger: "Walter Hinrichsen," *Notes*, xxvi (1969–70), 491

H.W. Hitchcock: "C. F. Peters Corporation and Twentieth-century American Music," *An Introduction to Music Publishing*, ed. C. Sachs (New York, 1981), 15

N. Molkenbur: *C. F. Peters, 1800–2000: ausgewählte Stationen einer Verlagsgeschichte* (Leipzig, 2001)

I. Lawford-Hinrichsen: *Music Publishing and Patronage: C. F. Peters, 1800 to the Holocaust* (Kenton, UK, 2000)

WILLIAM McCLELLAN/LEAH BRANSTETTER

Hinshaw, William Wade (*b* nr Union, IA, 3 Nov 1867; *d* Washington, DC, 27 Nov 1947). Baritone and impresario. He made his debut as Gounod's Méphistophélès with Henry Savage's company in St. Louis in 1899. He then moved to Chicago, where he founded a school of opera and drama that merged with the Chicago Conservatory in 1903. With the tenor James F. Sheehan, Hinshaw formed the Metropolitan Grand Opera Company to produce opera in English at the International Theatre in Chicago; it opened in January 1908 with *Lohengrin,* in which Hinshaw sang Telramund. He became a leading baritone at the Metropolitan Opera (1910–13), where he sang Wotan, and at the Wagner festivals in Graz (1912) and Berlin (1914). He had a strong and sonorous voice; his repertory included more than 50 roles, and he sang in a number of premieres, among them Horatio Parker's *Mona* (1912, as Gloom) and *Fairyland* (1915, as Corvain) and Walter Damrosch's *Cyrano de Bergerac* (1913, as Le Bret).

Hinshaw is chiefly remembered, however, as an enthusiastic promoter of opera in English. He presented hundreds of performances of *opéra comique* and grand opera as president of the Society of American Singers in New York (1918–20) and with his own company in tours of the United States, Canada, and Cuba (1920–26).

BIBLIOGRAPHY

O. Thompson: *The American Singer* (New York, 1937), 245

ANNE MINKO

Hinton, Milt(on John) [The Judge] (*b* Vicksburg, MS, 23 June 1910; *d* New York, NY, 19 Dec 2000). Double bass player, music educator, and photographer. Raised in a musical family, he moved with them to Chicago in 1919. He studied classical music, first at Crane Junior College and later at Northeastern University of Music, and learned various instruments, including violin and tuba, before switching to the bass. He started his professional career in jazz at the end of the 1920s and played with such musicians as Freddie Keppard, Jabbo Smith, Erskine Tate, and Art Tatum. After moving to New York in the mid-1930s, he worked with the Cab Calloway orchestra from 1936 to 1951. He also played with groups led by Fate Marable, Chu Berry, Lionel Hampton, Billie Holiday, and Pete Brown, among others, and recorded as a sideman and as a leader.

Hinton developed an influential slapping technique on the bass and was also proficient in bowing and jazz pizzicato. Playing with Dizzy Gillespie in the bebop years, he developed a distinctively modern harmonic approach. All of these qualities made him one of the most versatile and soughafter jazz musicians of the post-war period, when he recorded nearly 1200 tracks. During the 1950s and 1960s he worked with such luminaries as Count Basie, Louis Armstrong, Benny Goodman, Coleman Hawkins, George Russell, Teddy Wilson, Ben Webster, Paul Gonsalves, and Sonny Stitt. In the 1970s he visited Europe several times, including a tour with Bing Crosby, and taught at institutions including CUNY, Hunter College, and Baruch College. Hinton's passion for photography has also become part of his legacy; some of his photos of the jazz world are featured in his autobiography, *Bass Lines: the Stories and Photographs of Milt Hinton* (Philadephia, 1988), written with David Berger. In addition to his constant work in jazz, he accompanied the pop musicians Bobby Darin, Paul Anka, and Barbra Streisand, and appeared on television and in films, including *Hi-de-ho* (1937), *Minnie the Moocher* (1942), *The Sound of Jazz* (1957), *After Hours* (1961), *L'aventure du jazz* (1970), *A Great Day in Harlem* (1985), and *Old Man Time: Milt Hinton's Jazz Life and Legacy* (1988). In his later years he took part in the Grande parade du jazz in Nice, France, and received numerous honorary doctorates and awards, including recognition as an American Jazz Master from the National Endowment of the Arts. Known as the Judge for his competent and sometimes severe attitude in the studio, he played a Gofriller double bass, a rare instrument he purchased in Italy.

SELECTED RECORDINGS
As leader: *Milt Hinton Quartet* (1955, Beth.); *The Rhythm Section* (1956, Epic); *Here Swings the Judge* (1975, Prog.); *The Trio* (1977, Chi.); *Old Man Time* (1990, Chi.)

As sideman: G. Russell: *The Jazz Workshop* (1956, RCA); I. Quebec: *It might as well be spring* (1961, BN); C. Terry: *The Happy Horns of Clark Terry* (1964, Imp.)

BIBLIOGRAPHY
N. Shapiro and N. Hentoff, eds.: *Hear me Talkin' to Ya: the Story of Jazz by the Men who Made it* (New York, 1955/*R*)

S. Voce: "A Bass for all Seasons," *JJI*, xxxiv (1981), no.11, p.8; no.12, p.10

M. Hinton, D. G. Berger, and H. Manson: *Over Time: the Jazz Photographs of Milt Hinton* (San Francisco, 1991)

Obituary, *New York Times* (21 Dec 2000)

LUCA CERCHIARI

Hip hop. A collective term for urban art forms that emerged in the 1970s beginning in New York City. Initially the term was applied to the artistic outlets of b-boying/b-girling (what cultural outsiders recognized as breakdancing), graffiti writing, MC-ing, and DJ-ing, but as it has grown into a global phenomenon, hip hop has come to embrace fashion, language, and lifestyle.

Hip hop took root in the socio-cultural context of post-Civil Rights era New York City. White flight in the wake of integration depleted local, urban economies of the consumer power necessary to support local businesses. Unemployment in these areas skyrocketed. Urban planning, in particular the Cross-Bronx expressway (spearheaded by Robert Moses), uprooted established South Bronx communities, leaving gangs to rule the neighborhoods. At the same time, a deep fiscal crisis left the state and city of New York unable to support social services in impoverished areas. Landlords burned down their tenement buildings, taking easy insurance money over intermittent rent payments from unemployed tenants, further exacerbating the lack of sufficient housing for Bronx residents. In this context, local youth transformed neglect into numerous creative outlets expressing their frustration, joy, energy, anger, agency, and solidarity. Individual forms of expression associated with this culture—including DJ-ing (manipulating record turntables to provide continuous breakbeats for dancers; *see* DJ (ii); BREAKBEAT), MC-ing (or emceeing, speaking in rhymes over a DJ's beat), b-boying/b-girling (dancing specifically oriented to the beats provided by the DJ; *see* BREAKDANCING), and writing (graffiti or aerosol art)—have come to be known as hip-hop's original "elements."

1. Roots. 2. The elements. 3. Globalization. 4. Hip hop and the academy.

1. ROOTS. By the mid-1970s, versions of all four original elements were in place. Various dance forms that would coalesce into what became known as b-boying were already being practiced in New York. DJ-ing, albeit without the isolation and juggling of breakbeats, already existed in different arenas. Live DJs in disco clubs had already familiarized US club goers with seamless streams of music. More significantly, Jamaican dancehall DJs (known as selectors) used two turntables and a vocalist (known as the DJ) who spoke in rhymes over the selector's beat. This practice was imported to the United States by Caribbean immigrants, among them KOOL HERC, one of hip hop's first significant DJs. Numerous spoken word, poetic, and oral traditions fed into the element that developed into MC-ing. Dancehall selectors provided an immediate influence, as did spoken word political poets such as the Last Poets and Gil Scott-Heron. The swagger and braggadocio typical of MCs have roots in sources as diverse as African oral practices and Blaxploitation films. New York had been attempting to counter graffiti artists since the 1960s. An early graffiti icon, Taki 183, known throughout the boroughs of New York City by the time he was profiled by the *New York Times* in 1971, was only the most notorious of graffiti taggers. By the time hip hop was "born," New York City mayor John V. Lindsay had already declared a war on graffiti. As of the mid-1970s, these four artistic outlets were beginning to express a collective urban experience, catalyzed by a few key visionaries, including AFRIKA BAMBAATAA.

A former gang member, Afrika Bambaataa is commonly credited with the forethought of hip-hop's power for good. (Indeed, he is so revered that he is known by many as the "godfather" of hip hop.) Saddened by the continuous violence of gang life, he envisioned the creation of a safe artistic "space" (as much mental as visceral) as a potential path towards a peaceful existence. Already active in the urban practices of graffiti writing and DJ-ing for neighborhood parties, he founded a performing group that by 1974 he called the Zulu Nation. Grounded in pan-African ideology and Black Nationalist leanings (but boasting a membership of diverse racial backgrounds), the Zulu Nation quickly added b-boys and b-girls, graffiti writers, MCs, and additional DJs to its ranks. Performances were intended to be peaceful gatherings, alternative activities to gang warfare, but these events were not yet known as hip hop. Various apocryphal histories credit several possible "pioneers" (including the MC Keith "Cowboy" Wiggins of the Furious Five, and the DJs Lovebug Starski and Hollywood) with coining the term around 1978. By September of 1979, hip hop was a household word, thanks to the success of The SUGARHILL GANG's single "Rapper's Delight"; "hip-hop" appears in the first line of the song's lyrics and is repeated several times throughout the lengthy song. Further, use of the word "rapper" in the song's title helped to solidify the practice of naming what an MC does as "rapping."

2. THE ELEMENTS. The success of "Rapper's Delight" brought hip hop to public attention, but also began a separation of one element—MC-ing—from the other original elements. The song itself was put together in a manner inauthentic to hip-hop practices. Whereas hip-hop musical events (parties, park jams, club events) were DJ-driven and DJ-centric (and focused on getting the crowd to move, especially the b-boys and b-girls), "Rapper's Delight" was created with a house band and not a DJ. Furthermore, the Sugarhill Gang was comprised of three MCs who had no street credibility. Sylvia Robinson (the owner of Sugarhill Records) put the trio together as a studio project. One member of the Sugarhill Gang, Big Bank Hank, borrowed lyrics from a well-regarded MC (Grandmaster Caz of the Cold Crush Brothers) without

Run-D.M.C., 1986. (Mirrorpix/Lebrecht Authors)

giving due credit. Such unauthorized borrowing of lyrics is anathema in hip-hop culture, referred to pejoratively as "biting." Insiders did not consider "Rapper's Delight" to represent accurately what was practiced on the streets and in clubs. Consumers, however, heard only a compelling, fresh, new approach. Demand for similar products was immediate, spawning more and more RAP, music that featured an MC or group of MCs who spoke in rhymes over a repetitive disco- or funk-based groove. Very little "rap" music involved a DJ. MCs became marketable stars; rap became a fungible commodity.

While the popularity of rap music quickly rose, the other elements developed along quieter pathways. A few DJs tried to enter the public arena with recordings of their own. GRANDMASTER FLASH, for example, released the landmark single "The Adventures of Grandmaster Flash on the Wheels of Steel" (1981), in which he showcased his technical prowess on three turntables. In 1983, the DJ known as Grandmixer D.St. collaborated with Herbie Hancock on the song "Rockit," which quickly became a dance hit. D.St.'s "scratch" solos on this recording became the stuff of legend: a good number of DJs mark hearing his solos as the beginning of their interest in DJ-ing. (*See* SCRATCHING.) Consumer demand for DJ recordings, however, was low, so many DJs placed their efforts into production. Others turned to competing in DJ battles, which has since developed into a worldwide network of spirited contests. (DJs who work primarily to hone virtuosic DJ skills have become known as turntablists; their art is known as TURNTABLISM). DJs compete either as individuals or in crews; famous crews include the INVISIBL SKRATCH PIKLZ and the X-ecutioners. Some DJs have collaborated with rock bands, worked with symphony orchestras, or

fused DJ-ing with other genres in new compositions of their own. DJ SPOOKY collaborated with composer Anthony Paul De Ritis on *Devolution* (2004), a live synthesis of Beethoven's Seventh symphony and Ravel's *Bolero*. And DJ Radar's *Concerto for Turntable* has been performed at Carnegie Hall and various European venues.

B-boying, or early hip-hop dancing, was successfully commodified for a few years by the film industry, taking a central place in films such as *Wild Style, Flashdance*, and *Style Wars* (all from 1983), and *Beat Street* and *Breakin'* (both from 1984). Members of the Rock Steady Crew enjoyed cameo appearances in most of these films, cementing Rock Steady as the nation's best-known b-boy crew. B-boys had a short media life, virtually disappearing from the big screen by the late 1980s until revival films such as *Planet B-Boy* (2007) brought the dance back to public attention. Like their DJ counterparts, b-boys have continued to hone their skills away from the spotlight through local gatherings and regional, national, and international battles (such as those featured in the film *Planet B-Boy*). Battles typically showcase competing crews rather than individuals. Crews from outside of the United States, and especially those from South Korea, France, and Japan, consistently take top prizes at international battles.

Efforts to commercialize graffiti art have not met with the same sustained success. A number of official graffiti shows were curated in the early 1980s as graffiti artists such as Jean-Michel Basquiat and those deeply influenced by graffiti including Keith Haring made a splash in the downtown Manhattan art scene. This crossover was short-lived. In its purest form, graffiti writing happens in outdoor, public, off-limits spaces. Heavily guarded subway train yards held a special appeal for writers, who stood to gain immediate, city-wide notoriety if trains they painted made it out of the yard and into the city. The risk of getting caught was worth the bragging rights. Taking graffiti and its wrong-side-of-the-law essence out of the train yards and putting it in museums seemed to take the life out of the paint. This style of urban art influenced the next generation of visual artists and has heavily influenced commercial design, but the art of making graffiti itself remains an underground art.

Beatboxing (the art of producing drum-like sounds using one's mouth and body; descended from the practice of "patting JUBA"), and knowledge (proposed by Afrika Bambaataa as the fixative that provides cohesion between the other four elements) have been proposed over the years as additional hip-hop elements. Other forms of expression have vied for a place within hip-hop culture after rap was commodified into a mainstream entertainment industry in the mid-1980s. Hip hop and the world of fashion began to merge in 1986 when RUN-D.M.C. released their single "My Adidas"; shell-toe Adidas shoes, Cazal glasses, and fedora hats immediately became fashion musts for hip hop fans, setting in place a trend of product placement and sponsorship in rap songs and videos. Following established designers such as Tommy Hilfiger and Karl Kani benefitted from urban interest in their products, a number of hip-hop entrepreneurs have developed fashion lines that attempt to capture, package, and sell some essence of hip-hop culture.

Beastie Boys on stage at Montreux rock festival, Switzerland, 1987. (Mirror-pix/Lebrecht Authors)

Examples include Sean Jean clothing, founded by SEAN COMBS; Phat Farm, founded by hip-hop mogul RUSSELL SIMMONS; and Rocawear, founded by Damon Dash and megastar JAY-Z.

Hip hop has also infiltrated the world of theater, resulting in initiatives such as the Hip-hop Theater Festival, founded by Danny Hoch, with branches in New York City, Washington, DC, Chicago, and San Francisco. Journalists writing about various aspects of hip-hop culture such as Harry Allen (self described "media assassin"), DaveyD, Kimberly Osorio, Joan Morgan, Oliver Wang, and Akiba Solomon have helped to establish hip-hop journalism. Some commentators argue for the existence of hip-hop politics, a political worldview shaped by growing up in what has been called the hip-hop generation, the generation born after the Civil Rights Movement but before 9/11 (Kitwana, 2002). Hip hop's influence has also extended to the fields of photography, film, literature, philosophy, and language.

Since the late 1990s, journalists have been debating the "death" of hip hop, inferring that the cultural diversity, optimism, and social consciousness of hip hop's earliest days have been replaced by crass commercialism, misogyny, and violence. Nevertheless, grass roots organizations built on hip hop's ideals and aesthetics continue to take root around the globe, even as the industry of hip-hop music continues to thrive in the popular music marketplace.

3. GLOBALIZATION. Many of hip hop's cultural insiders argue that hip hop is merely a modern manifestation of ideals and principles practiced for millennia by Africa's indigenous peoples. Within this framework, the expansion of hip hop outside of the United States could be seen as part of an ongoing dialogue between African peoples around the globe, a construct Paul Gilroy has called the "Black Atlantic." In the 1980s, hip hop as a cultural product quickly expanded beyond US borders, thanks both to hip-hop tours (such as the New York City Rap Tour of 1982, which included MCs, DJs, b-boys, and graffiti writers) and mainstream films that popularized b-boying in other countries. MTV's rising interest in rap helped spread the music as well. As hip-hop culture and rap music took root in other countries, local musical and cultural influences laced hip hop with new flavors. Of particular interest to MCs and MC crews outside of the United States has been the use of rap music as a tool for political, social, and cultural empowerment. Members of minority communities—such as Algerians in France, and Turks in Germany—use rap as a platform to protest racism, poverty, and social strictures. As Tony Mitchell (2000) has documented, the use of local, vernacular languages by MCs is often in itself a political tool.

The story of globalization is not limited to foreign appropriations of a US product. Looking for new sounds, local hip-hop producers have turned to music from around the world for inspiration. For instance, a number of hip-hop producers have incorporated samples from Asian and South-Asian sources, including Missy Elliott's "Get Ur Freak On" (2001), Eric Sermon and Redman's "React" (2002), and Timbaland and Magoo's "Indian Flute" (2003). Producer DJ Quick did not account for the global popularity of Bollywood star Lata Mangeshkar when sampling one of her recordings for the song "Addictive" (2003) by Truth Hurts, which led to a copyright infringement lawsuit. New hybrid forms have also resulted from incorporating East Asian, South-east Asian, Latin American, and Caribbean musical influences. REGGAETON, which combines elements of rap and reggae, represents yet another link in the long-standing musical conversation between Puerto Rico, Jamaica, and the United States.

Public Enemy, 1988. (Mirrorpix/Lebrecht Authors)

4. HIP HOP AND THE ACADEMY. Most early hip-hop scholarship investigated rap music at the expense of the other elements, helping to solidify the public understanding of rap as synonymous with hip hop, a perception instigated by the success of "Rapper's Delight." Once rap became commercially successful in the 1980s, cultural insiders began a movement to differentiate between "hip-hop" as the culture and "rap" as the product, some going so far as to position commercial gain from the culture as a marker of inauthenticity. Legendary MC KRS-ONE is credited with the oft-quoted definition: "hip-hop is something you live; rap is something you do." According to this adage, artists who participate in rap music's commercial juggernaut may or may not be interested in promoting the values and practices of the culture that spawned the music. Within this framework, much rap music could be better described as part of popular culture, not hip-hop culture. The terms "rap" and "hip hop" are fluid enough to inspire lengthy scholarly discussions. Since 2000, scholars have begun to critique rap's dominance in scholarly literature by bringing attention to other elements. Joe Schloss's ethnographic history of hip hop's dance traditions in New York, for example, challenges not only the traditional narrative of DJ-ing as the first element of hip hop, but also the standard history of b-boying (Schloss, 2009). Jeff Chang's 2006 collection *Total Chaos: the Art and Aesthetics of Hip Hop*, deliberately foregrounds scholars and practitioners of dance, filmography, journalism, and graffiti in an attempt to recover the totality of the culture.

A second trend in recent scholarship has been the proliferation of ethnographic research. Most scholarship produced in the 1980s and first half of the 1990s came from an etic standpoint; scholars did not usually engage with members of the culture. Schloss's ground-breaking study (2004) of sample-based DJs, built from many years of work within the DJ community, effectively blended ethnography with rigorous scholarship. Ethnographic work with hip hop "pioneers" has not only provided more balanced accounts of its early diversity but also attempted to offer an undiluted view of the non-commercialized, pre-commodified existence of hip-hop culture (Fricke and Ahern, 2002; Chang, 2006; Schloss, 2009). As part of this resurgence of interest in oral history collection, certain hip hop legends, such as dancer Jorge "Popmaster Fabel" Pabon, are increasingly in demand on the lecture circuit. Some have taught hip-hop-based courses in various university and college settings.

A third scholarly trend involves a general revisionist project, challenging early histories of hip hop that tended to center around African American male subjects without revealing more nuanced understandings of hip hop's early diversity. Such work has sought to critique and re-examine conceptions of race within hip hop history and also to account for the experiences of women in hip hop. Tricia Rose's foundational text *Black Noise* (1994) introduced the topic of female subjectivity in rap scholarship. Despite some work on figures such as graffiti artist Lady Pink, recovering female lost voices from hip hop's earliest years remains a priority. The writings of Joan Morgan helped to establish what has been dubbed hip-hop feminism. A central dilemma at the heart of this concept, which prompted the historic Feminism and Hip-hop conference in 2005 at the University of Chicago, is the difficult challenge of carving out feminist agency within a culture that seems to take women's objectification as its starting point. Documentary films such as Byron Hurt's *Hip-hop: Beyond Beats and Rhymes* (2006) and Rachel Raimist's *Nobody Knows My Name* (1999) brought the discussion to wider audiences. Scholars such as Whitney Peoples, Gwendolyn Pough, and Marcyliena Morgan continue to foreground issues of feminism and women's agency.

Early hip hop scholarship, beginning with David Toop's *The Rap Attack: African Jive to New York Hip Hop* (1984, 3/1993), grounded hip-hop culture within African American and African diasporic aesthetics, a trend continued in subsequent scholarship (Rose, 1994; Keyes, 1996). Whereas this approach acknowledged the significance of African American hip-hop "pioneers," it also effectively erased the many Latina/o contributions to early hip hop. Although this oversight has been gradually addressed since the mid-1990s, such work remains far from complete. Indeed, questions of race in hip hop have only become more complex as hip hop has grown into a global phenomenon. Scholars are presently examining the diverse racial politics at play in hip hop from countries as diverse as Japan, Brazil, France, Croatia, Cuba, Canada, Slovakia, Germany, and the Netherlands.

See also BEAT-MAKING; HIP-HOP DANCE; RAP; SAMPLING AND SEQUENCING, HIP-HOP; TURNTABLISM.

BIBLIOGRAPHY
D. Toop: *The Rap Attack: African Jive to New York Hip Hop* (London, 1984; 2/1992 as *Rap Attack 2: African Rap to Global Hip Hop*; 3/1993 as *Rap Attack 3*)
T. Rose: *Black Noise: Rap Music and Black Culture in Contemporary America* (Middletown, CT, 1994)
R. Potter: *Spectacular Vernaculars: Hip-hop and the Politics of Postmodernism* (Albany, NY, 1995)
W.E. Perkins, ed.: *Droppin' Science: Critical Essays on Rap Music and Hip Hop Culture* (Philadelphia, PA, 1996)
A. Light, ed: *The Vibe History of Hip Hop* (New York, 1999)
J. Morgan: *When Chickenheads Come Home to Roost: My Life as a Hip-hop Feminist* (New York, 1999)
A. Krims: *Rap Music and the Poetics of Identity* (New York, 2000)
T. Mitchell, ed.: *Global Noise: Rap and Hip-hop outside the USA* (Lebanon, NH, 2001)
A. Durand, ed.: *Black, blanc, beur: Rap Music and Hip-hop Culture in the Francophone World* (Lanham, MD, 2002)
M. Forman: *The 'Hood Comes First: Race, Space, and Place in Rap and Hip-hop (Music Culture)* (Middletown, CT, 2002)
J. Fricke and C. Ahern: *Yes yes y'all: the Experience Music Project Oral History of Hip-hop's First Decade* (New York, 2002)
B. Kitwana: *The Hip Hop Generation: Young Blacks and the Crisis in African American Culture* (New York, 2002)
I. Maxwell: *Phat Beats, Dope Rhymes: Hip Down Under Comin' Upper* (Middletown, CT, 2003)
M. Forman and M.A. Neal, eds.: *That's the Joint: the Hip-hop Studies Reader* (New York, 2004)
C.L. Keyes: *Rap Music and Street Consciousness* (Urbana, IL, 2004)
D. Pardue: "Putting Mano to Music: The Mediation of Race in Brazilian Rap," *Ethnomusicology Forum*, xiii (2004), 253–86
J. Schloss: *Making Beats: the Art of Sample-Based Hip-hop* (Middletown, CT, 2004)
J. Chang: *Can't Stop, Won't Stop: a History of the Hip-hop Generation* (New York, 2005)
E. Hisama, ed.: *Critical Minded: New Approaches to Hip Hop Studies* (New York, 2005)
J. Chang, ed: *Total Chaos: the Art and Aesthetics of Hip-hop* (New York, 2006)
I. Condry: *Hip-hop Japan: Rap and the Paths of Cultural Globalization* (Durham, NC, 2006)
A. Leach: "'One Day it'll all Make Sense:' Hip-hop and Rap Resources for Music Librarians," *Notes*, lxv (2008), 9–37
T. Rose: *The Hip Hop Wars: What We Talk About when We Talk About Hip Hop: and Why it Matters* (New York, 2008)
W. Wimsatt: *Bomb the Suburbs: Graffiti, Freight-hopping, Race, and the Fight for Hip-hop's Moral Center* (Washington, DC, 2008)
J. Cohen: "Hip-hop Judaica: the Politics of Representin' Heebster Heritage," *Popular Music*, xxviii/1 (2009), 1–18
J. Schloss: *Foundation: B-boys, B-Girls, and Hip-hop Culture in New York* (New York, 2009)
M. Morgan: *The Real Hiphop: Battling for Knowledge, Power, and Respect in the LA Underground* (Durham, NC, 2009)

FELICIA M. MIYAKAWA

Hip-hop dance. Group of related Afro-diasporic dance forms, characterized by a competitive orientation and a close relationship with hip-hop music and culture. Hip-hop dance generally falls into two categories: dance forms that have been continuously maintained as cultural traditions since hip hop's birth in the 1970s, and relatively short-lived social or "party" dances. As befits a relatively young art form, these categories—and the dances themselves—are both still very much in flux.

(*See also* HIP HOP.)

1. Traditional dances. 2. East Coast traditional forms. 3. West Coast traditional forms. 4. Social dances. 5. Emerging styles. 6. Issues and controversies.

1. TRADITIONAL DANCES. The four traditional dances of hip-hop are rocking, b-boying/b-girling, locking, and popping, all of which trace their origins to the late 1960s or early 1970s. Each of these dances has been passed down continuously since that time through an informal apprenticeship system. These dance forms hold several qualities in common, including an explicitly competitive orientation, adherence to a set of abstract aesthetic principles, an emphasis on improvisation, and a relatively high level of difficulty that requires a substantial commitment on the part of practitioners. East coast and West coast traditional dances originated separately and only later came together under the hip-hop rubric. Significantly, each of the four major traditional dance styles continues to be associated with a specific repertoire of recorded music that was popular at the time the dance first emerged. None of the styles are solely associated with hip-hop music *per se*. In the mid-1980s, several of these forms became pop culture fads (see below), and their subsequent development has in many ways been an ongoing reaction against the perceived exploitation associated with that moment.

2. EAST COAST TRADITIONAL FORMS. East coast hip-hop dance forms developed in a reciprocal relationship with hip-hop's musical practices. Early hip-hop DJs noticed that dancers were particularly enthusiastic about the "breaks" of popular funk and soul recordings, musical passages in which the rhythm section was highlighted and other instruments fell silent. (*See* BREAK (II).) In response to the dancers' enthusiasm, DJs began to use two turntables to repeat these break sections, which in turn led the dancers to develop new moves to accommodate the increased emphasis on this aspect of the music. This then encouraged the DJs to continue

Student Mandi Lewis breakdancing, University of Florida, 2004. (AP Photo/University of Florida, Kristen Bartlett)

their musical and technological experimentation. This ongoing mutual influence led to the development of both hip-hop dance and hip-hop music itself.

The first form of hip-hop dance to emerge on the East Coast was called *rocking* (also known as uprocking, the rock dance, and—in regional variants—Brooklyn rocking or Bronx rocking). Initially, the dance was primarily associated with Latinos, particularly Nuyoricans, though it is currently practiced by dancers of all ethnicities. Rocking is distinctive from other competitive hip-hop dances in that the opponents dance against each other simultaneously, rather than in alternating turns. Partially due to this directly confrontational orientation, the dance became associated with New York City gang culture early in its development, though this association is now more historical than contemporary.

Rocking consists of three types of movement: freestyle, burns, and jerks. The freestyle aspect of the dance consists of solo dancing that draws heavily on Latin dance traditions, including rumba, bomba, salsa and Latin hustle. Burns are pantomimed movements designed to insult the opponent, either by making fun of them or by mimicking physical attacks. The jerk is an aggressive, though stylized, movement in which the dancer charges forward then drops to a crouching position on the beat. Conceptually, rocking resembles a kind of sparring in which dancers are trying to outdo each other in real time through a combination of

superior dance technique, physical intimidation, and specific burns.

Though the exact date of its emergence is unknown—and possibly unknowable, due to variations in the way the dance is defined—rocking's origins are generally traced to the late 1960s and early 70s, predating hip-hop music by several years. In its earliest usage, "rocking" was mainly a generic term used by young Latinos in New York City to refer to the performance of Latin dances to soul, funk and especially rock music. As the dance spread among youth throughout the city, its elements (especially the jerks and burns) became more formalized. Rocking is considered to be a direct ancestor of b-boying, though the exact nature of the influence remains in dispute. Though rocking was largely subsumed into b-boying by the late 70s, it experienced a resurgence as a distinct dance in the 2000s, primarily among b-boys and b-girls who are interested in its historical significance to hip-hop dance culture.

Rocking is usually performed to a specific repertoire of recordings that blend elements from the rock and soul genres with Latin percussion and were recorded at the time that the dance first became popular (between approximately 1969 and 1974). This repertoire includes such songs as "The Mexican," by Babe Ruth (1972), "Give It Up or Turnit a Loose," by James Brown (1969), "Listen to Me," by Baby Huey (1971), and "Yellow Sunshine," by Yellow Sunshine (1973).

B-boying, also known as "breaking," and "breakdancing" (though the latter term is almost universally rejected by dancers themselves [see below]), developed in New York City in the early 1970s. There is widespread disagreement as to what the "b" in the term stands for; possibilities that have been asserted include "Break," "Bronx," "Beat," and "Battle." Though dancers are referred to with the gender-specific terms "b-boys" or "b-girls," the dance itself is usually called "b-boying" regardless of the gender of performers. Although b-boying was created by African American and Latino dancers, dancers of many ethnicities and nationalities currently perform it.

Though competitive in orientation, b-boys or b-girls do not face off directly; rather they take turns in the "cypher," a circle of dancers. Each turn lasts approximately twenty to thirty seconds, and proceeds through four types of moves: "toprock," upright rhythmic dancing derived from rocking; a "go down" or "drop," a transition between toprock and the floor; "floorwork," dancing in a more lateral position where both hands and feet may contact the floor, and the "freeze," a concluding pose. Floorwork is further divided into several subcategories, including—but not limited to—footwork (intricate rhythmic movements on the ground), air moves (acrobatics), and power moves (movements intended to demonstrate physical strength). Different styles of b-boying are often defined by which of these aspects is emphasized.

In 1983 the dance was introduced to the public at large via a brief performance by the Rock Steady Crew (the dance's preeminent crew to the present day) in the film *Flashdance*. B-boying quickly emerged into popular culture through televised performances (including at the closing ceremonies of the 1984 Olympic Games) as well as through a series of low-budget feature films, including *Breakin' (1984), Beat Street* (1984), and *Breakin' 2: Electric Boogaloo* (1984*)*. These popular culture portrayals almost without exception conflated b-boying with other forms of urban dance under the general rubric of "breakdancing." As a result, that term took on connotations of disrespect and exploitation of the culture, which it still holds to the present day.

After going out of fashion with the general public in the late 1980s, b-boying continued primarily as an underground phenomenon that spread internationally through the 1990s. In the 2000s, international competitions such as Battle of the Year (based in Germany), R-16 Korea (based in Korea), and Red Bull BC One (international) led to the dance's re-emergence as a global phenomenon. This perception was reinforced by the independent documentary *Planet B-Boy* (2007), which followed crews from South Korea, France, Japan and the United States as they competed in the 2005 Battle of the Year in Braunschweig, Germany. At this time, dance-oriented reality television programs such as *So You Think You Can Dance?* and *America's Best Dance Crew* also began to showcase b-boying along with other hip-hop dance styles.

The musical repertoire to which b-boying is performed consists primarily of uptempo Latin-influenced soul and rock songs, and overlaps significantly with repertoire of rocking. This repertoire has remained stable from its origins in the early 70s to the present time. These songs include "Apache," by the Incredible Bongo Band (1973), "It's Just Begun," by the Jimmy Castor Bunch (1972), and the previously mentioned "Give It Up or Turnit a Loose," by James Brown (1969).

3. West Coast traditional forms. West Coast styles of hip-hop dance, also known as "Funk Styles" (a term coined by the dancer Popin Pete [Timothy Solomon]), developed separately from hip-hop music but were later integrated into the larger hip-hop culture. The two main styles of traditional West Coast hip-hop dance are locking and popping, which are often mistakenly portrayed as a single dance called "pop-locking."

The first style of West Coast hip-hop dance was locking, which was created in Los Angeles in 1969 by Don "Campbellock" Campbell. Locking is organized around variations on the "lock" movement, which was initially a variation on the social dance "the funky chicken." In its most general form, the lock movement consists of hunching forward, contracting one's body, and briefly freezing on the beat. The form as a whole emphasizes expansion and contraction, with the dancer moving out from a central point in various, often acrobatic, ways, then drawing their limbs in to "lock" to the rhythm. Another important aspect of locking is the expression of "character," which often involves an exaggeratedly sunny disposition and outsized gestures. This goal is often facilitated by the adoption of distinctive clothing, which traditionally includes floppy hats (which emphasize the bounciness of the dance), knickers and striped socks.

As a Los Angeles-based dance form, locking was among the first hip-hop dances to appear on television, popularized via programs like *Soul Train* and the situation comedy *What's Happening?*, on which one of the main actors, Fred "Rerun" Berry, was a real-life member of Don Campbell's dance crew, the Lockers. Locking is traditionally performed to a repertoire of funk music that was produced in the late 1960s and early 70s, by such artists as Sly Stone and James Brown.

The other major form of West Coast traditional hip-hop dance is popping. Like locking, the dance is built around a specific type of movement—popping—but the term itself is used to refer to both the specific movement and the dance form as a whole. The specific popping movement is simply a sharp muscle contraction, usually of the tricep, but often of other muscles as well, which is used to emphasize significant beats of the music. The desired effect is that of a dancer whose body virtually explodes with a mysterious internal energy to the rhythm of the song.

The popping technique can be applied to a variety of different styles of movement. Among the first styles of popping to develop was "boogaloo style," often credited to Fresno, California-based dancer Boogaloo Sam (Sam Solomon), though it has deep roots in older styles of African American dance associated with the San Francisco Bay area. This style is characterized by broad, sweeping gestures and pivots that are set off by pops. Popping was also combined with an earlier party dance—the robot—to create the popular robotic style that is most associated with popping by the general public. Poppers tend to wear loose, flowing clothing, because the natural swirling of the fabric serves to emphasize the popping movement while simultaneously obscuring the way it is produced. The traditional musical repertoire of popping centers primarily around late-1970s and early 80s synthesizer-based funk.

4. SOCIAL DANCES. Social dances associated with hip hop are similar in most respects to social dances associated with other forms of African American popular music, and in fact many of the specific dance forms in this category are not exclusively performed to hip-hop music. (*See* SOCIAL DANCE.) Generally speaking, these dances are fads, and thus tend to be relatively easy to perform, requiring no special training or long-term commitment. The social dance category is primarily solo in its orientation. Even when performed as partner or group dances, there is little direct interaction between the participants. These dances also often appear in choreographed form in hip-hop music videos.

Social dance was a major aspect of hip-hop culture from its birth until the early 1990s. At that time, the tempo of hip-hop music slowed down and its lyrics became more self-consciously artistic and serious-minded. These factors led to an increased perception among fans that hip-hop music was inconsistent with dancing. Even those who still wished to dance moved away from up-tempo, named, dances built around specific movements (e.g. "The Running Man," "The Cabbage Patch," "The Pee Wee Herman") and towards more generic movements. The performance of named dances came back into fashion in the 2000s, largely driven by the Internet. The first significant example of this trend was the "Chicken Noodle Soup" dance, which was designed to accompany the song "Chicken Noodle Soup" by DJ Webstar featuring Young B. The dance was popularized primarily via the website YouTube in 2006, which allowed multiple videos of amateurs performing the dance to spread internationally in a matter of days. Since that time, other such dances—each associated with a specific song—have spread through similar channels. Examples include the "Crank That" dance, designed to accompany the song "Crank That (Soulja Boy)" by Soulja Boy (2007), and the "Dougie," associated with the song "Teach Me How To Dougie," by Cali Swag District (2010).

5. EMERGING STYLES. New competitive dances associated with African American youth clearly overlap in many ways with hip-hop culture, though the exact nature of the relationship has yet to be defined. This is partially because, as hip-hop culture becomes more diffuse, the question of whether any given dance form falls under the hip-hop umbrella becomes increasingly difficult to answer. These dances include jerkin', a Los Angeles-based dance unrelated to the "jerk" movement in rocking; flex dancing, a Brooklyn-based dance that blends

movements from popping with West Indian popular dances; turf dancing, an Oakland-based dance related to popping; krumping, a Los Angeles-based dance popularized by the 2005 film *Rize*; and many others. Each of these new dances is primarily based on one-on-one competition, and all draw on specific movements associated with older forms of hip-hop dance. It remains an open question which, if any, of the established hip-hop categories these dances will come to be associated with, or even if they will ultimately come to be considered hip-hop at all.

6. ISSUES AND CONTROVERSIES. Given the competitiveness of hip-hop dance, and the emotional investment that dancers make in that competition, it should come as no surprise that many aspects of hip-hop dance culture and history are hotly contested. Although this has long been the case, the rise of the Internet has led these debates to increase exponentially. Arguments tend to focus on three general areas: terminology, credit for specific historical innovations, and general historical issues.

Two instructive examples of the first variety of debate are the previously mentioned disavowals of the terms "breakdancing" and "pop-locking." In both cases, the terms represent the dances' association with popular culture, and their rejection thus indicates a kind of artistic purism on the part of dancers. These arguments take a variety of forms, from rejecting the terms themselves as historical inaccuracies to actually using the terms to refer to dance styles that are perceived as inauthentic.

A second subject of debate concerns who should receive credit for specific innovations. Since few if any of hip-hop dance's innovators ever derived a significant economic benefit from their work, many dancers have sought recognition and social status within the hip-hop community as an alternative form of remuneration. This has resulted in historical status as a dance innovator becoming a form of cultural capital that is covetously sought and jealously protected. These debates tend to be particularly difficult to resolve for two reasons. First, the question of what constitutes a "new" dance movement (versus a variation on an existing movement) is extremely subjective even under the best circumstances. In the highly contentious world of hip-hop dance, this issue is magnified substantially. Second, due to the underground nature of hip-hop dances' roots, and the general unavailability of video equipment in the 1970s, virtually no documentary evidence exists from the period in question. Issues thus tend to be determined by the perceived credibility of claimants.

Finally, there are numerous debates over general historical issues, particularly with regard to the way the boundaries of specific dance forms should be defined, and how these boundaries may reflect different understandings of the form's development and significance. As three of the four traditional dance forms originated previous to—and separately from—hip-hop music, their inclusion under the hip-hop umbrella in the first place is primarily a retroactive statement of cultural unity, rather than a self-evident historical reality.

BIBLIOGRAPHY

The Freshest Kids, video, dir. Israel, QD3 Entertainment (USA, 2002)

J. Chang: *Can't Stop, Won't Stop* (New York, 2005)

Rize, video, dir. D. LaChappelle (USA, 2005)

J. Pabon: "Physical Graffiti: the History of Hip-Hop Dance," *Total Chaos*, ed. J. Chang (Cambridge, MA, 2006), 18–26

Planet B-Boy, video, dir. B. Lee (USA, 2007)

J. Schloss: *Foundation: B-boys, B-Girls, and Hip-Hop Culture in New York* (New York, 2009)

JOSEPH G. SCHLOSS

Hipp, Jutta (*b* Leipzig, Germany, 4 Feb 1925; *d* New York, NY, 7 April 2003). Jazz pianist and bandleader. She began learning to play piano at nine years old and apparently first became interested in jazz in her teens. However, she studied painting at the Academy of Arts in Leipzig and it was only around 1940, during World War II, that she began to pursue jazz performance seriously. After the war she formed her own group in Munich. She started recording with Hans Koller in the early 1950s and in 1953 founded a bop group that included Joki Freund and Emil Mangelsdorff. Together they recorded the album *New Faces–New Sounds from Germany* (1954, BN). Her playing impressed the critic Leonard Feather and, with his assistance in obtaining a visa, Hipp decided to move to the United States. After her arrival in New York in November 1955, Feather booked her to play at the jazz club Hickory House in March 1956 with a trio that included the bass player Peter Ind and the drummer Ed Thigpen. During that same year, she performed at the Newport Jazz Festival. Her most highly regarded album is *Jutta Hipp with Zoot Sims* (1956, BN). After a profusion of activity, Hipp retired from jazz in 1958, made her living as a seamstress, and returned to painting. For the next several decades, she lived in obscurity. Unable to pay funeral costs, she arranged to have her body donated to Columbia University.

BIBLIOGRAPHY

F. Manskleid: "I Remember Jutta," *Jazz*, ix/2 (1963), 12

CHADWICK JENKINS

Hipp, (James) William (*b* Guntersville, AL, 2 May 1934). Music educator and administrator. He earned his Bachelor's (1956), Master's (1963), and Doctoral (1979) degrees from the University of Texas at Austin. He taught at Del Mar College, Texas (1960–69), and was director of the School of Music at Illinois Wesleyan University (1973–6) and chair of the Music Division at Southern Methodist University (1976–83). As dean of the Frost School of Music at the University of Miami (1983–2007), he launched new graduate programs, the highly successful Festival Miami, an internationally renowned Salzburg Summer Program, preparatory programs for strings and keyboard, and UM MusicTime, an early childhood program that serves hundreds of preschool children throughout greater Miami. During his tenure as dean, Hipp raised over $100 million in donations, including a $33 million "naming" contribution, at the time the largest single gift to a university-based music school. Hipp also served as a commissioner, treasurer, vice president, and president of the National Association of Schools of Music, and was a visiting evaluator at approximately 70 music schools. He was named a distinguished alumnus by the University of Texas at Austin (2004); after retiring he served as interim dean at the University of the Pacific (2007–9).

STEPHEN F. ZDZINSKI

Hiroshima. Jazz fusion group. Founded in 1974 by the multi-instrumentalist Dan Kuramoto and the koto player June Okida Kuramoto, Hiroshima took its name from one of two Japanese cities to suffer atomic attack during World War II. It consists of third-generation Japanese Americans and first rose to popularity in the late 1970s amid the Asian American movement, which also provided the impetus for the development of Asian American jazz. Hiroshima's early sound mixed Japanese instrumentation, notably koto and bamboo flutes, with a blend of electric jazz, funk, and disco soul. In addition to playing a variety of saxophones, flutes, and keyboards, Dan Kuramoto has served as the group's main arranger and songwriter.

Although Hiroshima's membership and style have shifted over the years, its most consistent feature has been June Kuramoto's virtuosic koto playing. At the age of six, she began lessons with the koto sensei Kazue Kudo. Eventually mastering the instrument's traditional repertoire, she also developed her own approach to improvising.

With its members emerging from Japanese American enclaves in some of Los Angeles's most ethnically diverse neighborhoods, Hiroshima earned the loyal support of many Asian Americans who identified with the band's hybrid background and multicultural stance. The group also earned widespread success after landing a recording contract with Arista in the late 1970s and continuing to record with Epic throughout the 1980s. In addition to the Kuramotos, other long-standing members include the drummer Danny Yamamoto, the guitarist Peter Hata, the taiko player Johnny Mori, the vocalists Teri Kusumoto and Jess Acuna, the keyboard players Richard Mathews and Kimo Cornwell, and the bass players Dane Matsumura and Dean Cortez.

LOREN KAJIKAWA

Hirsch, Louis (*b* New York, NY, 28 Nov 1887; *d* New York, NY, 13 May 1924). Composer. He was a highly regarded composer of Broadway musicals—especially revues—at the turn of the 20 century. He attended the City University of New York and studied piano at the Stern Conservatory in Berlin during his final year. After his return to New York in 1906, Hirsch found employment as a pianist for several music publishers. He composed original music for Lew Dockstader's Minstrels but soon had songs interpolated into several shows produced by the Shuberts, including *The Gay White Way* (1907) and *Up and Down Broadway* (1910). This relationship was essential to Hirsch's career, for the Shuberts eventually hired him as a staff composer. He wrote his first full score for them, *He Came from Milwaukee*, in 1910. The following year, several of his songs were included in *Vera Violetta*, the show that featured a breakout role for

Al Jolson. Hirsch was also the primary contributor to the first of the Shuberts' annual revues, *The Passing Show of 1912*, for which he wrote "The Wedding Glide." He also wrote for several Florenz Ziegfeld productions, beginning with *The Soul Kiss* (1908), and five editions of the Follies (1915, 1916, 1918, 1922, and 1923), with one of his hits being "Hello, 'Frisco!" His collaborations with Otto Harbach, *Going Up!* (1917, including "The Tickle Toe") and *Mary* (1920, featuring "Love Nest"), remain his best-known shows. Hirsch's scores for *The Greenwich Village Follies* (1922 and 1923) also received high acclaim. A founding member of ASCAP, Hirsch served as its director from 1917 until his death in 1924.

BIBLIOGRAPHY
G. Bordman: *American Musical Theatre: a Chronicle* (New York, 3/2001)

JONAS WESTOVER

Hirsch, Shelley (*b* Brooklyn, NY, 9 June 1952). Vocalist, composer, librettist, free-improviser, and performance artist. She studied theater and dance at the High School of Performing Arts, took classical voice and theory lessons at the Manhattan School of Music, and served an apprenticeship with jazz artists in New York and Europe. At the age of 18 she joined the San Francisco Actors Workshop, where, influenced by Antonin Artaud and Jerzy Grotowski, she pursued an interest in sound-as-theater. She has created site-specific works—including *The Passions of Natasha, Nokiko, Nina, Nicole and Norma*, which explored the erotic lives of five women—and personal homages such as her virtual duet, *For Jerry*. Her autobiographical suite, *O Little Town of East New York*, reveals many of her key creative concerns, including a fascination with the nuances of cultural and personal difference. Hirsch's narratives unfold in kaleidoscopic flashes, leaping among sonically embodied characters, glossolalia, and quotations—real and ersatz—from myriad musical sources. She performs with live instrumentalists and over pre-recorded accompaniments, using multiple microphones programmed with contrasting effects, real-time electronic processing, and video projection. *I am a Jew* (1980) presaged the "Radical Jewish Culture" phenomenon of Manhattan's 1990s downtown scene, where her long-standing collaborators include Anthony Coleman, Christian Marclay, David Weinstein, and John Zorn.

WORKS
(selective list)

Radio plays (all collab. D. Weinstein): *#39 (War of Dreams)* (Angela Carter), 1991; *The Vidzer Family*, 1992–93
Interactive multimedia installations: *The Passions of Natasha, Nokiko, Nina, Nicole and Norma,*1993, collab. B. Bloom; *For Jerry*, 1999; *My Father Piece*, 2000; *All the Way with Jim + Shel*, 2002, collab. J. Hodges

SELECTED RECORDINGS

As leader: *Singing* (1985–1987, Het Apollohuis/Apollo); with D. Weinstein: *Haiku Lingo* (1988, Review); with D. Weinstein: *O Little Town of East New York* (1992–95, Tzadik); *States* (1980–1997, Tellus); with K. Uchihashi: *Duets* (2000, Innocent); *The Far In, Far Out Worlds of Shelley Hirsch* (1991–2002, Tzadik); with Simon Ho: *Where Were You Then?* (2012, Tzadik)

As side-musician: R.L. Teitelbaum: *Golem: an Interactive Opera* (1994, Tzadik); D. Maroney: *Music for Words, Perhaps* (2010, Innova)

BIBLIOGRAPHY
A. LeBaron: "Reflections of Surrealism in Postmodern Musics," *Postmodern Music/Postmodern Thought*, ed. J. Lochhead and J. Auner (New York, 2002), 27–73
S. Hirsch: "Wired that Way," *Arcana IV: Musicians on Music*, ed. J. Zorn (New York, 2009), 157–62

TAMAR BARZEL

Hirst, Grayson (*b* Ojai, CA, 27 Dec 1939). Tenor. He studied at the Music Academy of the West, UCLA with MARTIAL SINGHER and from 1963 to 1972 at the Juilliard School with JENNIE TOUREL. He began his professional career as Francesco Cavalli's Ormindo with the Opera Society of Washington (1969) and as Tonio in a concert performance of Gaetano Donizetti's *La fille du régiment* with Beverly Sills at Carnegie Hall (1970, recorded on the Adagio Classics label). Shortly thereafter he made his New York City Opera debut in Benjamin Britten's *The Turn of the Screw* and went on to sing with opera companies in the United States, Mexico, Brazil, France, Switzerland, and England. His repertoire of more than seventy roles includes Wolfgang Amadeus Mozart's Ferrando, Belmonte, and Tamino, Charles Gounod's Faust and Roméo, Georges Bizet's Don José, and Claude Debussy's Pelléas. He has appeared regularly with major American orchestras, choral societies, and music festivals and has performed Franz Schubert's song cycles with fortepiano. Known for his versatility and acute attention to style, he has sung in the premieres of works by Leonard Bernstein, Jack Beeson, Thomas Pasatieri, Alberto Ginastera (*Beatrix Cenci*, at the opening of the Kennedy Center in 1971), Robert Aitken, Ned Rorem, Roger Sessions, Robert Starer, Virgil Thomson (*Lord Byron*, 1972), and Ezra Laderman. A Grammy Award nominee, he has recorded opera and oratorio for Disque VDE Gallo and CRI, Schubert's *Die schöne Müllerin* for Leonarda Records, Leoš Janácek's *Diary of One Who Vanished* for Arabesque Records, songs by Antonin Dvorák for Spectrum Records, George Frederick Handel's opera *Acis and Galatea* and the Heinrich Schütz *Matthäus-Passion* for Newport Classic Recordings, and Britten's *Serenade for Tenor, Horn, and Strings* for Vox Cum Laude. He teaches at the University of Arizona and directs Sons of Orpheus, the Male Choir of Tucson, which he founded in 1991. His lyric tenor voice is of suave beauty, his singing appears effortless, and his performances have shown increasing subtlety in interpretation.

THOR ECKERT JR./BETH McGINNIS

Hirt, Al(ois Maxwell) (*b* New Orleans, LA, 7 Nov 1922; *d* New Orleans, LA, 27 April 1999). Jazz trumpeter and bandleader. The son of a policeman, Al Hirt made his musical debut with the Junior Police Band in 1929. He studied with Mike Cupero at Jesuit High School but showed no interest in jazz until he left New Orleans in 1940 to attend the Cincinnati Conservatory of Music. After 1946 he worked in the big bands of Benny Goodman, Tommy Dorsey, Ray McKinley, and Horace Heidt. While touring with Heidt's "Stars on Parade" revue in

1950 he recorded for the Magnolia label, initiating a recording career that led to 21 Grammy nominations and a Grammy award in 1964 for his hit record of Allen Toussaint's "Java" (Best Non-Jazz Instrumental), as well as to four gold and one platinum long-playing albums for RCA Victor. Although he led jazz bands for five decades and was renowned among musicians for his tone and technical facility, jazz critics ignored Hirt after his success in the popular music market.

BIBLIOGRAPHY
R. Grevatt: "Please, Please, Don't Call Me a Jazzman," *Melody Maker* (29 May 1965)
C. Rose: "Jumbo's Comeback," *New Orleans Times-Picayune* (3 Nov 1991)

BRUCE BOYD RAEBURN

Hirt, Charles C(arleton) (*b* Los Angeles, CA, 4 Nov 1911; *d* Glendale, CA, 3 Feb 2001). Educator and choral conductor. He graduated from Occidental College in 1934 and served for eight years as a music teacher and choral conductor in the Corona and Glendale public schools. He founded the Choral Conductor's Guild of California and received the MS degree from the University of Southern California in 1940. In 1941, he began a 30-year term of service as Minister of Music at First Presbyterian Church of Hollywood. He joined the faculty at USC, in 1942, as Lecturer in Music Education and Director of Choral Organizations. He established two departments, Church Music and Choral Music, in the School of Music and finished work on the PhD in Music History in 1946. From his dissertation studies he became a recognized authority on Greco-Slavonic Chant of the Russian Orthodox Church. An association with Disneyland that began in 1955 led eventually to the annual Christmas Candlelight Processional involving more than 1000 singers. In a period of more than 20 years under his leadership the USC Chamber Singers gained a worldwide reputation for choral excellence. In 1959, he became a founding member of the American Choral Directors Association. His articles on choral conducting were published in several professional journals. During his 35-year tenure on the faculty at USC he served as a guest conductor on numerous occasions, in the United States and abroad. Upon his retirement from USC, he was awarded the title Distinguished Emeritus Professor actively continuing his work as a conductor, lecturer, and editor of works by master composers. The Hirt papers are held in the archives of the American Choral Directors Association.

RECORDINGS
Legacy: 60 Years of the University of Southern California Chamber Singers, USC Choral Recording (2009) [includes monograph by J. Vail: "The Department of Choral and Sacred Music and the Chamber Singers at the USC Thornton School of Music: A Retrospective"]

BIBLIOGRAPHY
C. Hirt and others: "Music Educator's Round Table," *Music Journal*, no.13 (November 1955), 26f
P. Alderman: *We Build a School of Music: The Commissioned History of Music at the University of Southern California* (Los Angeles, 1989)
Obituaries: *Los Angeles Times* (12 Feb 2001); *USC Chronicle* (16 Feb 2001)

WARREN FIELDS

Hisama, Ellie M(ichiko) (*b* Cleveland, OH, 3 Jan 1965). Music theorist. She graduated with the AB in English from the University of Chicago (1987) and the BM in music from Queens College, CUNY (1989). She received the PhD in music theory from the Graduate Center, CUNY (1996), and was appointed Assistant Professor of Music at the Ohio State University (1996) before she became Director of the Institute for Studies in American Music and Associate Professor of music at Brooklyn College and the Graduate Center, CUNY, in 1999. In 2006 she was appointed Professor of Music at Columbia University and became an affiliated faculty member at its Institute for Research on Women and Gender. She has held visiting professorships at various institutions and has received fellowships from the Woodrow Wilson National Fellowship Foundation, the Ethyle R. Wolfe Institute for the Humanities, and Waseda University (Tokyo). She is Founding Editor of the *Journal of the Society for American Music*.

Hisama examines 20th-century art music and 20th- and 21st-century popular music in relation to gender, sexuality, race, and ethnicity, and her work has focused on music by women and on Asian American music and criticism. Using critical theory and interdisciplinary methods, Hisama expands the ways scholars write about music in its social and political contexts. For instance, in *Gendering Musical Modernism*, she uses tools drawn from post-tonal analysis, feminist criticism, and literary theory. She has co-edited essay collections on Ruth Crawford Seeger and on critical approaches to hip hop.

WRITINGS
"Postcolonialism on the Make: The Music of John Mellencamp, David Bowie, and John Zorn," *Popular Music* xii/2, (1993), 91–104; repr. in *Reading Pop: Approaches to Textual Analysis in Popular Music*, ed. R. Middleton (Oxford, 2000), 329–46
"The Question of Climax in Ruth Crawford's String Quartet, Mvt. 3," *Concert Music, Rock, and Jazz Since 1945: Essays and Analytical Studies*, ed. E.W. Marvin and R. Hermann (Rochester, NY, 1995), 285–312
"Voice, Race, and Sexuality in the Music of Joan Armatrading," *Audible Traces: Gender, Identity, and Music*, ed. E. Barkin and L. Hamessley (Zürich, 1999), 115–32
"From L'Étranger to 'Killing an Arab': Representing the Other in a Cure Song," *Expression in Pop-Rock Music: a Collection of Critical and Analytical Essays*, ed. W. Everett (New York, 2000), 59–74
Gendering Musical Modernism: The Music of Ruth Crawford, Marion Bauer, and Miriam Gideon (Cambridge, 2001)
with Evan Rapport, ed.: *Critical Minded: New Approaches to Hip Hop Studies* (Brooklyn, NY, 2005)
with Ray Allen, ed.: *Ruth Crawford Seeger's Worlds: Innovation and Tradition in Twentieth-century American Music* (Rochester, NY, 2007)

BIBLIOGRAPHY
"Feminist Music Theory Into the Millennium: a Personal History," in *Signs: Journal of Women in Culture and Society* 25/4 (Summer 2000), 1287–91, repr. in *Feminisms at a Millennium*, ed. C. Allen and J.A. Howard (Chicago, 2001), 276–280
S. Pahwa: "New Voices at Columbia: Introducing Ellie Hisama," *Feminist News*, xxvi (2008), 8–9

NAOMI ANDRÉ

Hispanic American music. *See* EUROPEAN AMERICAN MUSIC: PORTUGUESE AMERICAN MUSIC; EUROPEAN AMERICAN MUSIC: SPANISH AMERICAN MUSIC; LATINO MUSIC.

Historic Brass Society (HBS). International organization founded in New York in 1988 to offer a forum for the exchange of ideas about the history of brass instruments and their music. Organized by participants in the annual Early Brass Festival (first held in 1985), the HBS is composed of amateur and professional brass musicians and scholars and is concerned with the complete range of brass instruments from ancient times to the present, with a focus on history, the musical literature, and performance practice. The society also aims to bridge the cultural gap between the scholarly music community and musicians who are primarily performers. Since 1989 HBS has published the *Historic Brass Society Journal*. From 1989 through 2005 it published the *Historic Brass Society Newsletter*, which was then supplanted by articles published on the society's website (www.historicbrass.org). It also publishes a book series, BUCINA: The Historic Brass Society Series, in collaboration with Pendragon Press.

The group sponsors the Early Brass Festival, which features lectures, concerts, exhibits of instruments, and playing sessions. It also organizes other historic brass symposia and special study sessions in collaboration with organizations such as the American Musicological Society, the International Musicological Society, and the Galpin Society. The society established the Christopher Monk Award, presented annually to an individual for outstanding contributions to the scholarship of early brass music. In 2011 HBS had about 600 members from 25 countries.

SARAH DETERS RICHARDSON

Histories. Writings on the history of music in the United States have differed widely in scope, regional and chronological coverage, and subject matter. This article is concerned with only the most important of these. For other resource materials of a historical nature, *see* BIBLIOGRAPHIES; BIOGRAPHY; and DICTIONARIES AND ENCYCLOPEDIAS; *see also* articles on individual cities, regions, and musical genres.

1. General histories. (i) Overviews. (ii) African American music. (iii) Native American music. 2. Period and genre studies to 1990. (i) To 1820. (ii) 1820–65. (iii) 1865–1920. (iv) 1920–90. 3. American music studies since 1990.

1. GENERAL HISTORIES.

(i) Overviews. The first history of music in the United States, *Music in America* (1883), was written by German American Frédéric Louis Ritter. Like other music historians of his time, he dealt exclusively with art and religious music, not folk or popular music, claiming with remarkable myopia that "the people's song…is not to be found among the American people." Louis Elson's *The History of American Music* (1904) shared Ritter's orientation, as did W.L. Hubbard's history of 1908. OSCAR G.T. SONNECK, the first great scholar-historian of American music, offered in 1916 "a few suggestions" for a different approach to the history of music in the United States, saying that the existing books and articles "deal more with the history of music and musicians

in America than with the history of America's musical life." But Sonneck did not write such a synthetic history, only specialized studies; nor were his suggestions acted upon by the next major historian of American music.

JOHN TASKER HOWARD's *Our American Music* (1931) was far more extensive than any previous history. Like earlier ones, it was dominated by a preoccupation with art music in the European vein; Howard's view was that the significant story of American music was of a long, arduous struggle to rise to European levels of musical cultivation, as is suggested by the titles of the sections of his book: "Euterpe in the Wilderness [1620–1800]," "Euterpe Clears the Forest [1800–1860]," "Euterpe Builds her American Home [1860 to the present]." Howard brought precision and detail to his work, and in several revisions (1939, 1946, 1965) he sought conscientiously to perfect his book and keep it up to date and reflective of the expanding musical life of the United States.

GILBERT CHASE's *America's Music* (1955) introduced a new scope and stylishness of writing to the history of American music, as well as a new orientation. Chase was influenced by Sonneck, and perhaps even more by Charles Seeger, who had long argued that art music is but one of four idioms in world culture (the others being primitive or tribal, folk, and popular) and that in a dynamic, youthful culture like that of the United States the art idiom may well be the weakest or the least representative. Chase proudly introduced his history with the statement that "some fifteen chapters [of 31] deal…with various phases of American folk, primitive, and popular music." He considered that the importance of a piece of American music was in direct ratio to its difference from European music, and he even suggested that a single popular song by Stephen Foster was worth any number of concertos by Edward MacDowell. In short, he proposed a reversal of attitudes in the criteria for significance in American histories of American music.

The two chief histories that followed—H. WILEY HITCHCOCK's *Music in the United States* (1969) and CHARLES HAMM's *Music in the New World* (1983)—redressed the balance. Both scholars adopted Seeger's pan-cultural approach; both viewed the history of American music as a multilevel, dynamic, kaleidoscopic panorama. But both accepted the inevitability of European influence on the "cultivated" tradition in American music, along with other influences on both the cultivated and "vernacular" traditions. (These terms were introduced by Hitchcock as replacements for "classical" and "popular," which were thought to be imprecise and not sufficiently indicative of the historical reality.) Hamm's book dealt with a wider range of music than any previous history of American music; it reflected very clearly the tendency of American musical scholarship in the early 1980s to concern itself not only with music as an aesthetic object, but with music in its social and cultural context. It was also the first to make consistent and extensive reference to sound recordings as significant sources.

RICHARD CRAWFORD's magisterial *America's Musical Life* (2001) represents at once a synthesis of, and departure from, the approaches of previous general histories.

Foremost among the departures is a strategic shift in historiographic orientation away from the aesthetic and cultural priorities of "composition" towards what Crawford calls "performance." Accordingly, the cultural, social, and institutional contexts and processes of making music are given priority over evaluative consideration of abstract musical works. Crawford also develops an alternative mapping of musical categories according to the specific relationships that are posed between "the composer, the performer, and the written score." This conceptual move results in a tripartite model of musical spheres, one that accounts for, and respects differences in, aesthetic values, genre, style, and practice: classical or "composer's music" is discussed with reference to Euro-American values of "transcendence" and fidelity to the notated score; popular or "performer's music" is explored in relation to the values of "accessibility" and "authority in the audience"; and folk music is discussed within the context of traditional music communities and a "commitment to *continuity*." Yet, because these categories do not neatly map onto wholly separate musical practices and histories, Crawford's narrative also emphasizes the dynamic interaction and interconnectedness between and within spheres, particularly with regard to the foundational musical-racial history of Euro-American and African American music.

Crawford's text counts as one of only a handful of single-authored general histories of American music to have appeared since 1990. The trend of the last few decades has been towards collaborative multi-authored edited collections with essays by leading scholars writing from diverse disciplinary and methodological perspectives. Among the more extended efforts in this category are the *Cambridge History of American Music* (edited by DAVID NICHOLLS, 1998), which contains 20 topical essays organized chronologically and designed to represent the "interrelated diversity of musical experience" that has defined the history of American music with the weight of historical and cultural emphasis falling on the interaction of vernacular traditions ("Native, European, African, Asian and other peoples," xiii); and the *Garland Encyclopedia of World Music—United States and Canada* (edited by ELLEN KOSKOFF, 2001) an extensive collection which eschews chronological narrative entirely for multiple, overlapping sections of essays defined by topic, cultural context, and regional affiliation. This collection is also noteworthy for its comprehensive attention to issues of identity, especially those of gender and sexuality, critical dimensions largely unaddressed in previous general histories. Judith Tick's edited volume *Music in the USA* (2008) provides a resonant record of the nation's diverse musical and cultural voices through extensive source readings spanning nearly five centuries.

(ii) African American music. The first historical text on African American music, *Music and Some Highly Musical People*, was published in 1878 by JAMES MONROE TROTTER (1842–1982) and is considered a landmark survey of the activities of black musicians and musical

organizations in art music during the 19th century. The Harlem (or Negro) Renaissance of the 1920s inspired new directions in historical works on African American music. MAUD CUNEY HARE's *Negro Musicians and Their Music* (1936) drew heavily on Trotter in covering pre-1878 musicians, but Hare departed from Trotter in beginning her study not in Ancient Greece but in Africa, and in advancing the Renaissance ideal of creating an American concert music grounded in black musical idioms. This theme of black cultural nationalism was also developed by the critic and philosopher Alain Locke in *The Negro and His Music* (1936), although Locke's more cosmopolitan orientation gave more critical attention to documenting the history and potential of jazz and black musical theater. Leroi Jones's [later AMIRI BARAKA] *Blues People* (1963) presented a critical social history of African American music from slave songs to the jazz and popular music of the early 1960s; although it sparked a great deal of controversy when it appeared, *Blues People* has since been recognized as a milestone in writing about black music. Both in its sophisticated method and comprehensive scope, EILEEN JACKSON SOUTHERN's detailed survey *The Music of Black Americans* (1971) broke new ground in histories of black music and musical life in the United States. Southern's text played a key role in establishing black music as a scholarly field and, as such, inspired a steady wave of critical-historical studies. SAMUEL A. FLOYD JR.'s *The Power of Black Music* (1995) developed a new type of interpretive-critical approach, derived from the literary theory of Henry Louis Gates Jr. and the historical work of Sterling Stuckey, to understanding the origins and development of black music, applied to a broad range of African American music from ring shouts to contemporary concert music. Floyd's approach has influenced subsequent general studies of black music, notably GUTHRIE RAMSEY JR.'s *Race Music* (2003).

Among collected volumes, *African American Music* (edited by Mellonee V. Burnim and Portia K. Mautlsby, 2006) is the most significant recent contribution, a hefty collection of 30 essays by leading scholars designed to highlight both the rich diversity and the unifying musical characteristics and values of African American musical history and culture. Many of the essays are based on ethnographic research and privilege the perspectives and voices of musicians and listeners. A more modest but valuable text is Burton W. Peretti's *Lift Every Voice* (2009), a compact survey of African American musical history from its origins in West Africa to the present.

(iii) Native American music. The music of Native Americans has engaged the attention of musical scholars since before the turn of the 20th century. The first serious study was done by Theodore Baker, not in English but in German, as a dissertation presented at the University of Leipzig. Among other substantial early contributions were those of a remarkable trio of women (working independently of one another): FRANCES DENSMORE (whose many books for the Bureau of American Ethnology from 1910 on have been reprinted), Natalie Curtis, and ALICE CUNNINGHAM FLETCHER. Later important

studies were made by HELEN ROBERTS (1939), BRUNO NETTL (1954), and DAVID MCALLESTER (1954). More recent ethnographic studies on music in Native American communities include Marcia Herndon (1982) and TARA BROWNER, ed. (2009).

2. PERIOD AND GENRE STUDIES TO 1990. There have been few general surveys of discrete periods in American musical history; rather, writers have tended to study musical genres, institutions, cities, or regions.

(i) To 1820. The psalmody of 17th-century New England is the subject of Waldo Selden Pratt's *The Music of the Pilgrims* (1921), Zoltan Haraszti's *The Enigma of the Bay Psalm Book* (1956), Richard Appel's *The Music of the Bay Psalm Book* (1975), and Lorraine Inserra and H.W. Hitchcock's *The Music of Henry Ainsworth's Psalter* (1981). The later 18th-century singing-schools and their "tunesmith" teacher-composers figure in a number of the articles by IRVING LOWENS gathered into *Music and Musicians in Early America* (1964), and much general information on the same repertory is included in the basically biographical studies by Richard Crawford, *Andrew Law, American Psalmodist* (1968) and *William Billings of Boston* (1975, with David McKay), and in the introductions by Hans Nathan and Karl Kroeger to the volumes of Billings's *Complete Works* (respectively 1977 and 1981). The important early American genres of anthems and military music are discussed by Ralph Daniel (1966) and RAOUL F. CAMUS (1976). Antebellum slave music has proved, understandably, quite resistant to studies in depth, which makes the achievement of DENA J. EPSTEIN's *Sinful Tunes and Spirituals* (1977) all the more remarkable: since its publication, Epstein's collection of primary sources has provided the starting point for much of the research on early African American music. Kenneth Silverman's *A Cultural History of the American Revolution* (1976) is unusual in being a general history that includes informed discussion of music. Two pioneering studies of music in the developing urban culture of the new country were written by Sonneck: *Early Concert-life in America (1731–1800)* (1907) and *Early Opera in America* (1915). Among regional studies, George Hood's *A History of Music in New England* (1846) was the earliest. More recent valuable works are those by George Edwards on Maine (1928), Louis Pichierri on New Hampshire (1960), Joyce Mangler on Rhode Island (1965), and Charles Kaufman on New Jersey (1981).

(ii) 1820–65. Until recently, this period was the *terra incognita* of American music. Some of the most illuminating writing, even if it did not pretend to be scholarly, came from the period itself, for example, Lowell Mason's (*see* MASON) *Musical Letters from Abroad* (1853) and LOUIS MOREAU GOTTSCHALK's journal of 1881, published as *Notes of a Pianist* (re-edited by Jeanne Behrend, 1964). Hamm's *Yesterdays* (1979) and NICHOLAS TAWA's *Sweet Songs for Gentle Americans* (1980) illuminate popular and parlor songs, respectively. The sociocultural aspects of minstrel-show songs are emphasized in

Robert Toll's *Blacking Up* (1974), while Nathan discusses the music itself in his study of a single minstrel-composer, Dan Emmett (1962). The music of Emmett's contemporary Stephen Foster is only one point of focus in the unique contextual study by WILLIAM W. AUSTIN, *"Susanna," "Jeanie," and "The Old Folks at Home"* (1975). Beginning in the 1990s, minstrelsy began to receive an increased amount of scholarly attention, and it has become commonplace to acknowledge its fundamental role in the subsequent history of popular music in the United States. Among the first of these new accounts, and probably the most influential, was Eric Lott's rich archival and psychoanalytically-inflected account, *Love and Theft* (1993). DALE COCKRELL's *Demons of Disorder* (1997) is the most prominent musicological exploration of the topic. Other notable contributions include W.T. Lhamon's *Raising Cain* (1998), and William J. Mahar's *Behind the Burnt Cork Mask* (1998). Most of these authors contributed to *Inside the Blackface Mask*, a volume edited by Bean, Hatch, and McNamara (1996)

(iii) 1865–1920. Broad surveys of American music between the Civil War and World War I are lacking. Two books dealing with art music during the period are Joseph Mussulman's *Music in the Cultured Generation* (1971) and Howard Shanet's history of New York's principal orchestra, *Philharmonic* (1975). One composer-pianist's memoir is enlightening: Richard Hoffman's *Some Musical Recollections of Fifty Years* (1910). The lyric theater of the period, exclusive of opera, is surveyed in DEANE ROOT's *American Popular Stage Music, 1860–1880* (1981). Protestant sacred music is treated with exceptionally rich documentation in ROBERT M. STEVENSON's *Protestant Church Music in America* (1966), which includes discussion of earlier music. The songs of one musically prolific sect are thoroughly discussed and anthologized in Daniel Patterson's *The Shaker Spiritual* (1979). The pioneer work on ragtime was written by Rudi Blesh and Harriet Janis, *They All Played Ragtime* (1950); a riper and more thoroughly documented study is Edward Berlin's *Ragtime* (1980, 2/2002). Several works have appeared since 1990 that examine broad cross-sections of musical activity during this period while focusing on a particular concept or cultural practice; these include William Howard Kenney's early history of sound recording *Recorded Music in American Life* (1999); Karl Hagstrom Miller's study of the formation of separate categories for popular music directed towards different audiences, *Segregating Sound* (2010).

The cultural history of African American music during this period has received a fair amount of attention in the new millennium, with works including Ronald Radano's genealogy of the formation of a distinct category for African American music, *Lying up a Nation* (2003); and Lynn Abbott's and Doug Seroff's painstaking recreation of the establishment of performance networks for African American music in two books: *Out of Sight* (2002), and *Ragged but Right* (2007). Tim Brooks excavates the almost forgotten history of early African American recordings in *Lost Sounds* (2004).

Scholarship on music of a wide range of immigrant groups covering the period from the mid-19th century through the 20th century has blossomed during the past 20 years; among many path-breaking works are Mark Slobin's *Tenement Songs* (1996) on the popular music of Jewish immigrants; Charles Keil and Angeliki Keil's *Polka Happiness* (1996), which explores the centrality of the polka to Polish American social life in the first half of the 20th century; Su Zheng's *Claiming Diaspora* (2010), which traces the roots of the contemporary network of Chinese and Asian American music-making in 150 years of immigrant experiences; and Nancy Newman's *Good Music for a Free People* (2010), which recreates the history of German American performance societies in the mid-19th century.

(iv) 1920–90. Specialized studies of 20th-century American art music abound, with an increasing number of these relating it to more general cultural and social developments. Two early examples are Salzman's *Twentieth-century Music* (1967), which does a particularly good job of discussing American music in the context of Western music in general, and Leonard B. Meyer's *Music, the Arts, and Ideas* (1967), which cunningly relates avant-garde American music after World War II to developments in other arts. In his *Music in a New Found Land* (1964), WILFRID MELLERS, writing from a British perspective, concentrates on American music since 1900. Especially valuable, even though they are not formal histories, are certain composers' writings about their own music and that of their contemporaries, beginning with the symposium of 31 essays edited by Henry Cowell, *American Composers on American Music* (1933). Virgil Thomson's *The State of Music* (1939) speaks of the aesthetic and economic ways and means of the American composer. Other noteworthy books by composer-critics are Aaron Copland's *Music and Imagination* (1952), several collections of essays by John Cage (1961, 1967, 1973, 1979), Roger Reynolds's *Mind Models* (1975), *The Writings of Elliott Carter* (1977), *Roger Sessions on Music* (1979), and *A Virgil Thomson Reader* (1981). Several books have also been devoted to the experimental wing of American art music; David Nicholls' *American Experimental Music 1890–1940* (1990), focuses on the most influential figures before World War II. On the other hand, the postwar avant garde, especially the "downtown" experimental music scene in New York City, is explored in Michael Nyman's *Experimental Music* (1974, 2/1999), which provides a valuable chronicle of the early decades of that scene, while KYLE GANN's *American Music* (1997) provides a more sweeping historical survey through the 1990s.

Popular song up to the mid-1970s is thoroughly charted in Charles Hamm's *Yesterdays* (1979); ALEC WILDER's *American Popular Song* (1972) concentrates on "the great innovators, 1900–1950" among songwriters, and is paralleled by two studies of vocalists in Henry Pleasants's *The Great American Popular Singers* (1974) and in Will Friedwald's *Jazz Singing* (1990). With the increased academic acceptance of popular music have come a number of textbooks, which constitute the major contri-

bution to general histories of popular music published since 1980. Two of the texts with the greatest historical reach are Michael Campbell's *And the Beat Goes On* (1996), and Larry Starr and Christopher Waterman, *American Popular Music* (2003, 2/2007, 3/2010). Two other representative offerings focused more on the 1920s to the present are Reebee Garofalo's *Rockin Out* (1997), and John Covach's *What's That Sound* (2006). DAVID BRACKETT's *Pop, Rock and Soul Reader* (2009) provides source readings for the period from 1910 to the present. Among studies of individual genres, ROBERT ANTON WALSER's *Running with the Devil* (1993) is an influential study of heavy metal that combines musicological analysis of style with cultural analysis, Tricia Rose analyzes hip hop with an approach rooted in cultural studies in *Black Noise* (1994), while Jacqueline Warwick's *Girl Groups, Girl Culture* (2007) combines recent feminist theories of agency with the tools of the music scholar. Another important development is represented by studies that examine the history of popular music in terms of the impact of technology and sound recording. Notable among these are Steve Waksman's *Instruments of Desire* (1999), which presents a series of case studies based around the electric guitar, the most important instrument of the post-rock era; and Albin Zak's *The Poetics of Rock* (2001), which focuses more on the impact of recording on questions of authorship and collaboration.

As with popular music in general, comprehensive histories of jazz published since the 1980s have almost invariably taken the form of textbooks. Thus, historical works of a previous era, such as Marshall Stearns's *The Story of Jazz* (1956) and JAMES LINCOLN COLLIER's *The Making of Jazz* (1978) have been supplanted by books such as (to take the most monumental example) *Jazz* (2009) by GARY GIDDINS and SCOTT DEVEAUX. Publications focused on narrower periods in jazz history have consequently become more common; as a study in depth of jazz's stylistic development up to about 1930, GUNTHER SCHULLER's *Early Jazz* (1968) remains unmatched, and Schuller's *Swing Era*, provides a similar level of musicological detail or music between 1930 and 1945. The swing era has also received detailed attention in terms of its social history, with two excellent examples being David Stowe's *Swing Changes* (1994), and Lewis Erenberg's *Swingin' the Dream* (1999). SHERRIE JEAN TUCKER privileges the perspectives and voices of female musicians in *Swing Shift* (2000) in another excellent study that questions received notions about the agents of history during the swing era. The transition from swing to bebop receives its fullest study in DeVeaux's *The Birth of Bebop* (1997), while Thomas Owens' *Bebop* (1996) provides an in-depth musicological account. Other jazz genre studies include David Rosenthal's *Hard Bop* (1992), and GEORGE LEWIS's magisterial account of the experimental jazz scene in Chicago, *A Power Stronger Than Itself* (2008). INGRID MONSON's *Freedom Sounds* (New York, 2007) explores the impact of the struggle for civil rights and ideas about African roots on jazz from hard bop to avant-garde jazz.

Among other forms of American music existing along a continuum of traditional and popular musics, the folk/country blues and old-time/country music have attracted a significant amount of scholarly attention. Representative of the first wave of scholarship in the blues that appeared in the late 1950s and early 1960s are Samuel Charters's *The Country Blues* (1959) and PAUL OLIVER's *Blues Fell This Morning* (1960). Later additions to this canon include Jeff Todd Titon's *Early Downhome Blues* (1977), Robert Palmer's *Deep Blues* (1981), and David Evans' *Big Road Blues* (1982). The most thorough general history of country music remains BILL MALONE's *Country Music U.S.A.* (1985), although a spate of more specialized and regional studies have appeared in the last two decades; notable among these are Richard Peterson's sociological account of value, *Creating Country Music* (1997); and two studies of country music in California: Gerald W. Haslam's *Workin' Man Blues* (1999) and Peter La Chapelle's *Proud to Be an Okie* (2007).

Sharing much of its source material with old-time/country music but directed towards a very different audience, the music of the various urban folk music revivals has generated a steady stream of scholarly interest over the last two decades. Robert Cantwell's *When We Were Good* (1996) was one of the first, and examined the emergence of the late 1950s to early 1960s folk revival in terms of the seismic changes in US society following World War II. Other influential contributions to this literature include Benjamin Filene's *Romancing the Folk* (2000), Ronald D. Cohen's *Rainbow Quest*, and Dick Weissman's *Which Side Are You On?* (2006). An important and often-cited collection is Neil V. Rosenberg's *Transforming Tradition* (1993).

3. AMERICAN MUSIC STUDIES SINCE 1990. Histories of American music are increasingly placed within transnational and global narratives that have destabilized the US-centric approach that dominated the field prior to 1990. In line with these developments, "American music" is now frequently interpreted as "Music of the Americas" and therefore includes music from Central and South America, the Caribbean, and Canada, an expansion that reflects a new level of diversity in and between musical cultures for which traditional categories no longer suffice. This critical reevaluation of the field is closely related to broader shifts in music scholarship during the 1980s and 90s that were influenced by scholarly approaches adapted from gender/sexuality studies, critical race theory, media studies, postcolonial theory, and the sociology of culture. The emphasis has thus shifted away from overarching historical surveys of American music or, indeed, of the different musical strands implicitly contained within this category. The summaries given above of work on "general histories" as well as the various "period and genre studies" have already indicated the move away in scholarly monographs from such surveys, with the exception of work explicitly designed for adoption as university textbooks. Much of the work published since 1990 cited above in the sections on African American music, Native American music, minstrelsy, contemporary art music, jazz, popular music, country music, blues, and folk music gives

some indication of the range of interdisciplinary work that increasingly focuses on questions specific to these genres within relatively narrow historical periods. Added to this are numerous ethnographic studies that investigate musics in their local geographic contexts across the spectrum of the increasingly capacious category of American music.

LIST

GENERAL

F.L. Ritter: *Music in America* (New York, 1883, 2/1890)

W.S.B. Mathews, ed.: *A Hundred Years of Music in America* (Chicago, 1889/R)

L.C. Elson: *The History of American Music* (New York, 1904; enlarged 2/1915, enlarged by A. Elson 3/1925/R)

W.L. Hubbard, ed.: *The American History and Encyclopedia of Music*, viii: *History of American Music* (Toledo, OH, 1908)

A. Farwell and W.D. Darby: *The Art of Music*, iv: *Music in America* (New York, 1915)

J.T. Howard: *Our American Music* (New York, 1931, 3/1946, suppl. 1954, 4/1965)

G. Chase: *America's Music: from the Pilgrims to the Present* (New York, 1955, 2/1966/R)

W. Mellers: *Music in a New Found Land* (New York, 1964/R)

A.C. Edwards and W.T. Marrocco: *Music in the United States* (Dubuque, IA, 1968)

H.W. Hitchcock: *Music in the United States: a Historical Introduction* (Englewood Cliffs, NJ, 1969, 2/1974)

I. Sablosky: *American Music* (Chicago, 1969)

E. Borroff: *Music in Europe and the United States* (Englewood Cliffs, NJ, 1971)

D. Kingman: *American Music: a Panorama* (New York, 1979/R)

R.L. Davis: *A History of Music in American Life* (Huntington, NY, and Malabar, FL, 1980–82)

C. Hamm: *Music in the New World* (New York, 1983)

M. Campbell: *And the Beat Goes On: an Introduction to Popular Music in America, 1840 to Today* (New York, 1996)

D. Nicholls, ed.: *Cambridge History of American Music* (Cambridge, 1998)

R. Crawford: *America's Musical Life: a History* (New York, 2001)

E. Koskoff: *Garland Encyclopedia of World Music—United States and Canada* (New York, 2001)

J. Tick: *Music in the USA: a Documentary Companion* (New York, 2008)

AFRICAN AMERICAN MUSIC

J.B.T. Marsh: *The Story of the Jubilee Singers, with their Songs* (London, 1875, 3/1892 with suppl.)

J.M. Trotter: *Music and Some Highly Musical People* (Boston, 1878/R)

H.E. Krehbiel: *Afro-American Folksongs: a Study in Racial and National Music* (New York, 1914/R)

J.W. Johnson: *Black Manhattan* (New York, 1930)

M. Cuney-Hare: *Negro Musicians and their Music* (Washington, 1936)

A. Locke: *The Negro and His Music* (1936)

M.J. Herskovits: *The Myth of the Negro Past* (New York, 1941/R)

H. Courlander: *Negro Folk Music U.S.A.* (New York, 1963)

L. Jones: *Blues People* (New York, 1963)

P. Garland: *The Sound of Soul* (Chicago, 1969)

T. Heilbut: *The Gospel Sound: Good News and Bad Times* (New York, 1971)

E. Southern: *The Music of Black Americans: a History* (New York, 1971, 2/1983)

E. Southern, ed.: *Readings in Black American Music* (New York, 1971)

J.S. Roberts: *Black Music of Two Worlds* (New York, 1972)

D. Epstein: *Sinful Tunes and Spirituals: Black Folk Music to the Civil War* (Urbana, IL, 1977)

J. Anderson: *This was Harlem: a Cultural Portrait, 1900–1950* (New York, 1982)

S. Floyd: *The Power of Black Music: Interpreting its History from Africa to the United States* (New York, 1995)

G. Ramsey: *Race Music: Black Cultures from Bebop to Hip-Hop* (Berkeley, 2003)

M. Burnam and P. Maultsby, eds.: *African American Music: an Introduction* (2006)

B. Peretti: *Lift Every Voice: the History of African American Music* (2009)

NATIVE AMERICAN MUSIC

T. Baker: *Über die Musik der nordamerikanischen Wilden* (Leipzig, 1882/*R*)

A.C. Fletcher and F. La Flesche: "The Omaha Tribe," *Annual Report of the Bureau of American Ethnology*, xxvii (1905–6), 17–672

E.S. Curtis: *The North American Indian* (Cambridge, MA, 1907–30)

N. Curtis: *The Indians' Book* (New York, 1907, 2/1923/*R*)

F. Densmore: *The American Indians and Their Music* (New York, 1926/*R*)

H.H. Roberts: *Musical Areas in Aboriginal North America* (New Haven, 1939)

D.P. McAllester: *Enemy Way Music: a Study of Social and Esthetic Values as Seen in Navaho Music* (Cambridge, MA, 1954)

B. Nettl: *North American Indian Musical Style* (Philadelphia, 1954)

C. Hofmann, ed.: *Frances Densmore and American Indian Music: a Memorial Volume* (New York, 1968)

M. Herndon: *Native American Music* (Norwood, PA, 1982)

J. Bierhorst, ed.: *A Cry from the Earth: Music of the North American Indians* (Santa Fe, NM, 1992)

T. Browner, ed.: *Music of the First Nations: Tradition and Innovation in Native North America* (Urbana, IL, 2009)

GENRE AND REGIONAL

To 1820

G. Hood: *A History of Music in New England* (Boston, 1846/*R*)

N.D. Gould: *Church Music in America* (Boston, 1853)

O.G.T. Sonneck: *Early Concert-life in America (1731–1800)* (Leipzig, 1907/*R*)

O.G.T. Sonneck: *Early Opera in America* (New York, 1915/*R*)

W.A. Fisher: *Notes on Music in Old Boston* (Boston, 1918)

W.S. Pratt: *The Music of the Pilgrims* (Boston, 1921/*R*)

A.A. Parker: *Music and Musical Life in Pennsylvania in the Eighteenth Century* (Philadelphia, 1926–7)

G.T. Edwards: *Music and Musicians of Maine* (Portland, ME, 1928)

P.A. Scholes: *The Puritans and Music in England and New England* (London, 1934)

H.E. Johnson: *Musical Interludes in Boston, 1795–1830* (New York, 1943)

Z. Haraszti: *The Enigma of the Bay Psalm Book* (Chicago, 1956)

L. Pichierri: *Music in New Hampshire, 1623–1800* (New York, 1960)

J. Mates: *The American Musical Stage before 1800* (New Brunswick, NJ, 1962)

I. Lowens: *Music and Musicians in Early America* (New York, 1964)

J.E. Mangler: *Rhode Island Music and Musicians, 1733–1850* (Detroit, 1965) [biographical dictionary with chronological and other lists]

R.T. Daniel: *The Anthem in New England before 1800* (Evanston, IL, 1966)

H.A. Kmen: *Music in New Orleans: the Formative Years, 1791–1841* (Baton Rouge, LA, 1966)

R.A. Crawford: *Andrew Law, American Psalmodist* (Evanston, IL, 1968)

E.A. Wienandt and R.H. Young: *The Anthem in England and America* (New York, 1970)

G.D. Yerbury: *Song in America, from Early Times to about 1850* (Metuchen, NJ, 1971)

A. Stoutamire: *Music of the Old South: Colony to Confederacy* (Teaneck, NJ, 1972)

H. Cripe: *Thomas Jefferson and Music* (Charlottesville, VA, 1974)

R.G. Appel: *The Music of the Bay Psalm Book, 9th Edition (1698)*, ISAMm, v (Brooklyn, NY, 1975)

D.P. McKay and R. Crawford: *William Billings of Boston* (Princeton, NJ, 1975)

R.F. Camus: *Military Music of the American Revolution* (Chapel Hill, NC, 1976)

K. Silverman: *A Cultural History of the American Revolution* (New York, 1976)

H. Nathan: Introduction, *The Complete Works of William Billings*, ii (Boston, 1977), xi

B. Lambert, ed.: *Music in Colonial Massachusetts, 1630–1820* (Boston, 1980–85)

F.W. Hoogerwerf, ed.: *Music in Georgia* (New York, 1981)

L. Inserra and H.W. Hitchcock: *The Music of Henry Ainsworth's Psalter*, ISAMm, xv (Brooklyn, NY, 1981)

C. Kaufman: *Music in New Jersey 1655–1860* (East Brunswick, NJ, 1981)

K. Kroeger: Introduction, *The Complete Works of William Billings*, i (Boston, 1981), xiii–lxiii

S. Porter: *With an Air Debonair: Musical Theater in America, 1785–1815* (Washington, DC, 1991)

K. Van Winkler Keller: *Dance and Its Music in America, 1528–1789* (Hillsdale, NY, 2007)

1820 to 1865

L. Mason: *Musical Letters from Abroad* (New York, 1853/*R*)

C. Gottschalk, ed.: *Louis Moreau Gottschalk: Notes of a Pianist*, trans. R. E. Peterson (Philadelphia, 1881); ed. J. Behrend (New York, 1964/*R*)

C.C. Perkins and others: *History of the Handel and Haydn Society of Boston, Massachusetts* (Boston and Cambridge, MA, 1883–1934/*R*)

C. Wittke: *Tambo and Bones: a History of the American Minstrel Stage* (Durham, NC, 1930)

G.P. Jackson: *White Spirituals in the Southern Uplands* (Chapel Hill, 1933/*R*)

R.B. Harwell: *Confederate Music* (Chapel Hill, 1950)

H.E. Johnson: "The Germania Musical Society," *MQ*, xxxix (1953), 75

W.A. Heaps and P.W. Heaps: *The Singing Sixties: the Spirit of Civil War Days Drawn from the Music of the Times* (Norman, OK, 1960)

H. Nathan: *Dan Emmett and the Rise of Early Negro Minstrelsy* (Norman, OK, 1962/*R*)

C. Wunderlich: *A History and Bibliography of Early American Music Periodicals, 1782–1852* (diss., U. of Michigan, 1962)

H.H. Hall: *A Johnny Reb Band from Salem: the Pride of Tarheelia* (Raleigh, NC, 1963)

D.J. Epstein: *Music Publishing in Chicago before 1871: the Firm of Root & Cady, 1858–1871* (Detroit, 1969)

E.C. Krohn: *Music Publishing in the Middle Western States before the Civil War* (Detroit, 1972)

R.C. Toll: *Blacking Up: the Minstrel Show in Nineteenth-century America* (New York, 1974)

W.W. Austin: *"Susanna," "Jeanie," and "The Old Folks at Home": the Songs of Stephen C. Foster from his Time to ours* (New York, 1975)

R.B. Winans: "The Folk, the Stage, and the Five-String Banjo in the Nineteenth Century," *Journal of American Folklore*, lxxxix (1976), 407–37

C. Hamm: *Yesterdays: Popular Song in America* (New York, 1979)

N.E. Tawa: *Sweet Songs for Gentle Americans: the Parlor Song in America, 1790–1860* (Bowling Green, OH, 1980)

K. Olson: Music and Musket: Bands and Bandsmen of the American Civil War (Westport, CT, 1981)

K. Preston: Music for Hire: Professional Musicians in Washington, D.C., 1877–1900 (Hillsdale, NY, 1991)

M. Broyles: *Music of the Highest Class": Elitism and Populism in Antebellum Boston,* (New Haven, 1992)

K. Preston: *Opera on the Road: Traveling Opera Troupes in the United States, 1825–1860* (Urbana, IL, 1993)

1865 to 1920

R. Hoffman: *Some Musical Recollections of Fifty Years* (New York, 1910)

C.E. Russell: *The American Orchestra and Theodore Thomas* (Garden City, NY, 1927/*R*)

P. Rosenfeld: *An Hour with American Music* (Philadelphia, 1929)

W.T. Upton: *Art-song in America: a Study in the Development of American Music* (Boston, 1930, suppl. 1938/*R*)

D. Gilbert: *American Vaudeville: its Life and Times* (New York, 1940)

R. Blesh and H. Janis: *They All Played Ragtime* (New York, 1950, 4/1971)

E.J. Kahn, Jr.: *The Merry Partners: the Age and Stage of Harrigan and Hart* (New York, 1955)

R.F. Goldman: *The Wind Band* (Boston, 1961)

H.N. Roehl: *Player-Piano Treasury* (Vestal, NY, 1963)

Q.D. Bowers: *Put another Nickel in* (Vestal, NY, 1966)

R. Stevenson: *Protestant Church Music in America: a Short Survey of Men and Movements from 1564 to the Present* (New York, 1966)

E.C. Krohn: *Missouri Music* (New York, 1971)

J.A. Mussulman: *Music in the Cultured Generation: a Social History of Music in America, 1870–1900* (Evanston, IL, 1971)

H. Shanet: *Philharmonic: a History of New York's Orchestra* (Garden City, NY, 1975)

D. Patterson: *The Shaker Spiritual* (Princeton, 1979)

E.A. Berlin: *Ragtime: a Musical and Cultural History* (Berkeley, CA, 1980/*R* with addenda)

D.L. Root: *American Popular Stage Music, 1860–1880* (Ann Arbor, MI, 1981)

E. Lott: *Love and Theft: Blackface Minstrelsy and the American Working Class* (New York, 1993)

A. Bean, J.V. Hatch, and B. McNamara, eds.: *Inside the Blackface Mask: Readings in Nineteenth-Century Blackface Minstrelsy* (Hanover, NH, 1996)

C. Keil and A. Keil: *Polka Happiness* (Philadelphia, 1996)

M. Slobin: *Tenement Songs: The Popular Music of the Jewish Immigrants* (Urbana, IL, 1996)

D. Cockrell: *Demons of Disorder: Early Blackface Minstrels and Their World* (Cambridge, 1997)

W.T. Lhamon: *Raising Cain: Blackface Performance from Jim Crow to Hip Hop* (Cambridge, MA, 1998)

W.J. Mahar: *Behind the Burnt Cork Mask: Early Blackface Minstrelsy and Antebellum American Popular Culture* (Urbana, IL, 1998)

W.H. Kenney: *Recorded Music in American Life: the Phonograph and Popular Memory, 1890–1945* (New York, 1999)

L. Abbott and D. Seroff: *Out of Sight: the Rise of African American Popular Music, 1889–1895* (Jackson, MS, 2002)

R. Radano: *Lying up a Nation: Race and Black Music* (Chicago, 2003)

T. Brooks: *Lost Sounds: Blacks and the Birth of the Recording Industry, 1890–1919* (Urbana, IL, 2004)

L. Abbott and D. Seroff: *Ragged but Right: Black Traveling Shows, "Coon Songs," and the Dark Pathway to Blues and Jazz* (Jackson, MS, 2007)

K. H. Miller: *Segregating Sound: Inventing Folk and Pop Music in the Age of Jim Crow* (Raleigh, NC, 2010)

N. Newman: *Good Music for a Free People: the Germania Musical Society in Nineteenth-Century America* (Rochester, NY, 2010)

S. Zheng: *Claiming Diaspora: Music, Transnationalism, and Cultural Politics in Asian/Chinese America* (New York, 2010)

1920–1990

H. Cowell, ed.: *American Composers on American Music: a Symposium* (Stanford, CA, 1933/*R*)

N. Slonimsky: *Music since 1900* (New York, 1937, 4/1971)

V. Thomson: *The State of Music* (New York, 1939/*R*, 2/1962)

A. Copland: *Our New Music* (New York, 1941, rev. and enlarged 2/1968 as *The New Music, 1900–1960*)

S. Spaeth: *A History of Popular Music in America* (New York, 1948)

C. Smith: *Musical Comedy in America* (New York, 1950)

A. Copland: *Music and Imagination* (Cambridge, MA, 1952/*R*)

J. Barzun: *Music in American Life* (Garden City, NY, 1956/*R*)

M. Stearns: *The Story of Jazz* (New York, 1956/*R*)

S.B. Charters: *The Country Blues* (New York, 1959/*R*)

S. Green: *The World of Musical Comedy* (New York, 1960, 4/1980)

P. Oliver: *Blues Fell This Morning: Meaning in the Blues* (Cambridge, 1960)

J. Cage: *Silence* (Middletown, CT, 1961)

W. Mellers: *Music in a New Found Land* (New York, 1964/*R*)

E. Salzman: "*Modern Music* in Retrospect," *PNM*, ii/2 (1964), 4

C. Keil: *Urban Blues* (Chicago, 1966)

J. Cage: *A Year from Monday* (Middletown, CT, 1967)

I. Kolodin: *The Metropolitan Opera, 1883–1966: a Candid History* (New York, 1967)

L.B. Meyer: *Music, the Arts, and Ideas: Patterns and Predictions in Twentieth Century Culture* (Chicago, 1967)

E. Salzman: *Twentieth-century Music: an Introduction* (Englewood Cliffs, NJ, 1967, 2/1974)

E. Schwartz and B. Childs eds.: *Contemporary Composers on Contemporary Music* (New York, 1967)

R. Kostelanetz: *The Theatre of Mixed Means* (New York, 1968)

B.C. Malone: *Country Music U.S.A.: a Fifty-year History* (Austin, 1968, 2/1985)

G. Schuller: *Early Jazz: its Roots and Musical Development* (New York, 1968)

M. Stearns and J. Stearns: *Jazz Dance: the Story of American Vernacular Dance* (New York, 1968)

"The Composer in Academia: Reflections on a Theme of Stravinsky," *College Music Symposium*, x (1970), 55–98

C. Gillett: *The Sound of the City: the Rise of Rock 'n' Roll* (New York, 1970, 2/1972)

M. Williams: *The Jazz Tradition* (New York, 1970)

D. Cope: *New Directions in Music* (Dubuque, IA, 1971, 2/1976)

R. Russell: *Jazz Style in Kansas City and the Southwest* (Berkeley, CA, 1971)

V. Thomson: *American Music since 1910* (New York, 1971)

W. Hays, ed.: *Twentieth-century Views of Music History* (New York, 1972)

A. Wilder: *American Popular Song: the Great Innovators, 1900–1950* (New York, 1972)

J. Cage: *M: Writings '67–'72* (Middletown, CT, 1973)

E. Schwartz: *Electronic Music* (New York, 1973)

M. Nyman: *Experimental Music* (Cambridge, 1974, 1999)

H. Pleasants: *The Great American Popular Singers* (New York, 1974)

J.H. Appleton and R.C. Perera, eds.: *The Development and Practice of Electronic Music* (Englewood Cliffs, NJ, 1975)

C. Hamm, B. Nettl, and R. Byrnside: *Contemporary Music and Music Cultures* (Englewood Cliffs, NJ, 1975)

G. Marcus: *Mystery Train: Images of America in Rock 'n' Roll Music* (New York, 1975, rev. and enlarged 2/1982)

M. Nyman: *Experimental Music: Cage and Beyond* (New York, 1975)

R. Reynolds: *Mind Models: New Forms of Musical Experience* (New York, 1975)

J. Miller, ed.: *The Rolling Stone Illustrated History of Rock & Roll* (New York, 1976, 2/1980)

K. Stone and E. Stone, eds.: *The Writings of Elliott Carter: an American Composer Looks at Modern Music* (Bloomington, IN, 1977)

F. Tirro: *Jazz: a History* (New York, 1977)

J.T. Titon: *Early Downhome Blues* (Urbana, IL, 1977)

G. Bordman: *American Musical Theatre: a Chronicle* (New York, 1978)

J.L. Collier: *The Making of Jazz: a Comprehensive History* (New York, 1978)

D.A. Jasen and T.J. Tichenor: *Rags and Ragtime: a Musical History* (New York, 1978)

A. Shaw: *Honkers and Shouters: the Golden Years of Rhythm and Blues* (New York, 1978)

J. Cage: *Empty Words: Writings '73–'78* (Middletown, CT, 1979)

E.T. Cone, ed.: *Roger Sessions on Music: Collected Essays* (Princeton, NJ, 1979)

C. Hamm: *Yesterdays: Popular Song in America* (New York, 1979)

J.S. Roberts: *The Latin Tinge: the Impact of Latin American Music on the United States* (New York, 1979)

E. Berlin: *Ragtime* (Lincoln, NE, 1980, 2/2002)

R. Palmer: *Deep Blues* (New York, 1981)

V. Thomson: *A Virgil Thomson Reader* (Boston, 1981)

D. Evans: *Big Road Blues: Tradition & Creativity in the Folk Blues* (New York, 1982)

G. Schuller: *The Swing Era* (New York, 1989)

W. Friedwald: *Jazz Singing: America's Great Voices from Bessie Smith to Bebop and Beyond* (New York, 1990)

D. Rosenthal: *Hard Bop: Jazz and Black Music, 1955–1965* (New York, 1992)

N. Rosenberg: *Transforming Tradition: Folk Music Revivals Examined* (Urbana, IL, 1993)

R. Walser: *Running with the Devil: Power, Gender, and Madness in Heavy Metal Music* (Hanover, NH, 1993)

T. Rose: *Black Noise: Rap Music and Black Culture in Contemporary America* (Hanover, NH, 1994)

D. Stowe: *Swing Changes: Big Band Jazz in New-Deal America* (Cambridge, MA, 1994)

M. Campbell: *And the Beat Goes On: an Introduction to Popular Music in America, 1840 to Today* (New York, 1996)

R. Cantwell: *When We Were Good: The Folk Revival* (Cambridge, MA, 1996)

T. Owens: *Bebop: the Music and Its Players* (New York, 1996)

S. Deveaux: *The Birth of Bebop: a Social and Musical History* (Berkeley, 1997)

K. Gann: *American Music* (New York, 1997)

R. Garofalo: *Rockin Out: Popular Music in the U.S.A.* (Upper Saddle River, NJ, 1997, 5/2010)

D. Nicholls: *American Experimental Music 1890–1940* (Cambridge, 1997)

R. Peterson: *Creating Country Music: Fabricating Authenticity* (Chicago, 1997)

L. Erenberg: *Swingin' the Dream: Big Band Jazz and the Rebirth of American Culture* (Chicago, 1999)

G. Haslam: *Workin' Man Blues: Country Music in California* (Berkeley, CA, 1999)

S. Waksman: *Instruments of Desire: The Electric Guitar and the Shaping of Musical Experience* (Cambridge, MA, 1999)

B. Filene: *Romancing the Folk: Public Memory and American Roots Music* (Chapel Hill, NC, 2000)

S. Tucker: *Swing Shift: "All-Girl" Bands of the 1940s* (Durham, NC, 2000)

A. Zak: *The Poetics of Rock: Cutting Tracks, Making Records* (Berkeley, CA, 2001)

R. Cohen: *Rainbow Quest: The Folk Music Revival and American Society, 1940–1970* (Amherst, MA, 2002)

L. Starr and C. Waterman: *American Popular Music: From Minstrelsy to MP3* (New York, 2003, 3/2010)

D. Brackett: *The Pop, Rock, and Soul Reader: Histories and Debates* (New York, 2005, 2/2009)

J. Covach: *What's That Sound: an Introduction to Rock and Its History* (New York, 2006)

D. Weissman: *Which Side Are You On? An Inside History of the Folk Music Revival in America* (New York, 2006)

P. La Chapelle: *Proud to Be an Okie: Cultural Politics, Country Music, and Migration to Southern California* (Berkeley, CA, 2007)

I. Monson: *Freedom Sounds: Jazz, Civil Rights, and Africa, 1950–1967* (New York, 2007)

J. Warwick: *Girl Groups, Girl Culture: Popular Music and Identity in the 1960s* (New York 2007)

G. Lewis: *A Power Stronger Than Itself: the AACM and American Experimental Music* (Chicago, 2008)

G. Giddins and S. Deveaux: *Jazz* (New York, 2009)

BIBLIOGRAPHY

O.G.T. Sonneck: "The History of Music in America: a Few Suggestions," *MTNAP*, xl (1916), 50; repr, in *Miscellaneous Studies in the History of Music* (New York, 1921/R 1968, 1970), 324

O. Kinkeldey: "American Scholarship in Music since 1876," *MTNAP*, lii (1928), 244–56

W.D. Allen: *Philosophies of Music History* (New York, 1939)

H.W. Hitchcock: "Americans on American Music," *College Music Symposium*, viii (1968), 131–42

R. Stevenson: *Philosophies of American Music History* (Washington, DC, 1970)

H.W. Hitchcock: "Sources for the Study of American Music," *American Studies International*, xiv/2 (1975); repr. with "Epilogue" in *Sources for American Studies*, ed. J. B. Kellogg and R. H. Walker (Westport, CT, 1983), 295

R. Stevenson: "American Musical Scholarship: Parker to Thayer," *19CM*, i (1977–8), 191–210

R. Crawford: "Musical Learning in Nineteenth-century America," *American Music*, i/1 (1983), 1–11

R. Crawford: *The American Musical Landscape* (Berkeley, 1993)

H. WILEY HITCHCOCK/LISA BARG AND DAVID BRACKETT

Hitchcock, Benjamin (*b* New York, NY, 1827/1836; *d* Jersey City, NJ, 14 April 1916). Music publisher. He established a music store in New York in 1869 and gradually expanded his business to include publishing. He issued popular instrumental and vocal music such as "The Culprit Fay" (1869), "In the Evening by the Moonlight" (1880), and "With All her Faults I Love her Still" (1888). Although Hitchcock sold his interest in 1893, the firm continued until 1941.

BARBARA TURCHIN

Hitchcock, H(ugh) Wiley (*b* Detroit, MI, 28 Sept 1923; *d* New York, NY, 5 Dec 2007). Musicologist. He attended Dartmouth College (BA 1944) and the University of Michigan (MM 1948), and he studied in Paris with NADIA BOULANGER before resuming graduate work at the University of Michigan (PhD 1954). He taught at Michigan (1950–61) and was professor of music at Hunter College, CUNY (1961–71). In 1971 he became professor of music and founding director of the Institute for Studies in American Music at Brooklyn College, CUNY. In 1980 he was named Distinguished Professor, CUNY, and he retired in 1993. He was among the first group of Getty scholars at the J. Paul Getty Center for Art History and the Humanities (1985–6). In 1994 he was made an honorary member of the AMS, and in 1995 Chevalier of the Ordre des Arts et des Lettres. In 2008, ISAM was renamed the H. Wiley Hitchcock Institute for Studies in American Music.

A versatile scholar, Hitchcock began his career with a dissertation on the music of Marc-Antoine Charpentier (1954), and the next year he published his first article on American music. Throughout his career, his interests remained transatlantic. A meticulous music editor and graceful prose stylist, Hitchcock worked comfortably with both words and music, producing an extraordinary number of musical editions; some fit into the realm of scholarly editions and others were intended for performers. He was fluent in French and Italian, knew Latin well, and was valedictorian of his World War II army class in Japanese. Reaching outside the academy— via journalism, lectures, program notes, and performance editions—remained a lifelong commitment. His research on Charpentier culminated in *Les oeuvres de Marc-Antoine Charpentier* (a catalog raisonné, 1982) and *Marc-Antoine Charpentier* (a synthetic survey of the composer's output, 1990). He also explored the Italian Baroque, notably producing an edition of Giulio Caccini's *Le nuove musiche* (1970) that includes a detailed introduction and an annotated translation of the original preface.

As an Americanist, Hitchcock embraced a broad range of musical repertories, and he founded ISAM as a means of stimulating research and creating an infrastructure for an emerging subdiscipline. His mobilizing leadership not only extended to scholarship focused on the United States but also embraced composers and musicians of the present day. Both of these modes challenged the norms of a Euro-centric academic discipline that privileged study of the distant past. His *Music in the United States* (1969) emerged at a key moment in the historiography of American music. It laid out a crucial distinction between the "vernacular" and "cultivated" traditions, establishing an even-handed analytic paradigm for exploring music that emerged from different social strata, and it has stayed in print through four editions. Over the course of a 22-year directorship of ISAM, he edited and wrote for the informative and engaging *ISAM Newsletter* and produced a series of more than 30 monographs. In the era before the Internet, the newsletter served as a much-needed information hub for scholars, performers, and composers interested in exploring American repertories. Steeped in the activities of the ONCE Group in Ann Arbor during the late 1950s and early 1960s, Hitchcock remained a consistent champion of contemporary American music, from that of Charles Ives to the newest works being performed in New York. In the early 1960s he wrote a series of reviews of new music for "Current Chronicle" in the *Musical Quarterly*, and a solid strain of his subsequent scholarship involved music of the 20th century, whether as writer, editor, or facilitator of research by others, especially his graduate students. Hitchcock worked as an editor or advisor on American music for multiple major scholarly projects, including the sixth edition of *The New Grove* (1980) and *The New Grove Dictionary of American Music* (1986), for which he served as co-editor with Stanley Sadie. He was also editor of the series Recent Researches in American Music (1976–94) and Earlier American Music (1972–91); he served on the inaugural advisory boards of New World Records and Music of the United States of America; and he was founding editor of the Prentice Hall History of Music Series.

Hitchcock was president of the Music Library Association (1966–7) and of the AMS (1991–92). He was also president of the Charles Ives Society (1973–93), serving as scholar, editor, and advocate for that composer's music. He published a compact and insightful study of Ives's music (1977) and a critical edition of Ives's songs (2004), and he supervised a series of Ives editions issued under the auspices of the Ives Society. His final project was a critical edition of Gertrude Stein and Virgil Thomson's *Four Saints in Three Acts* (published posthumously in 2008).

WRITINGS

The Latin Oratorios of Marc-Antoine Charpentier (diss., U. of Michigan, 1954)

"An Early American Melodrama: *The Indian Princess* of J.N. Barker and John Bray," *Notes*, xii (1955), 375–88

"The Latin Oratorios of Marc-Antoine Charpentier," *MQ*, xli (1955), 41–65

and I. Lowens, J. Edmunds, and V. Yellin: "The American Recordings Project: Progress Report of the Committee, 5 Feb 1960), *Notes*, xvii (1960), 213–20

"The Instrumental Music of Marc-Antoine Charpentier," *MQ*, xlvii (1961), 58–72

and R. Crawford: "The Papers of Andrew Law in the William L. Clements Library," *Bulletin of the Clements Library*, 68 (1961)

"Current Chronicle," *MQ* (reviews of contemporary music 1962–65)

"Americans on American Music," *College Music Symposium*, viii (1968), 131–42

"A Monumenta Americana?" *Notes*, xxv (1968), 5–11

Music in the United States: a Historical Introduction (Englewood Cliffs, NJ, 1969, 2/1974, 3/1988, 4/1999 with Kyle Gann)

"Nationalism and Anti-Nationalism in American Music Histories," *Papers of the Yugoslav-American Seminar on Music*, ed. M.H. Brown (Bloomington, IN, 1970), 199–208

"A Footnote on Webern's Variations," *Perspectives of New Music*, viii (1970), 123–26

"Vocal Ornamentation in Caccini's *Nuove musiche*,"*MQ*, lvi (1970), 389–404

ISAM Newsletter (edited by Hitchcock), (1971–93)

"Marc-Antoine Charpentier and the Comédie-Française," *JAMS*, xxiv (1971), 255–81

"Caccini," *MT*, cxiii (1972), 557–58

"Depriving Caccini of a Musical Pastime," *JAMS*, xxv (1972), 58–78

"Deux 'nouveaux' manuscrits de Marc-Antoine Charpentier," *RdM*, lviii/2 (1972), 253–55

"Problèmes d'édition de la musique de Marc-Antoine Charpentier pour *Le malade imaginaire*,"*RdM*, lviii/1 (1972), 3–15

"A New Biographical Source for Caccini," *JAMS*, xxvi (1973), 145–47

"Caccini's 'Other' *Nuove musiche*," *JAMS*, xxvii (1974), 438–60

"Some Aspects of the Notation in an *Alma Redemptoris mater* (c.1670) by Marc-Antoine Charpentier (d.1704)," *Notations and Editions: a Book in Honor of Louise Cuyler*, ed. E. Borroff (Dubuque, IA, 1974), 127–41

"After 100 [!] Years, the Editorial Side of Sonneck: a Lecture, in Memoriam, Oscar George Theodore Sonneck, 1873–1928" (Washington, DC, 1975)

"Charles Ives's Book of 114 Songs," *A Musical Offering: Essays in Honor of Martin Bernstein*, ed. E.H. Clinkscale and C. Brook (New York, 1977), 127–36

Ives: a Survey of the Music (London, 1977, 2/1983 (reprint), 3/1985)

ed., with V. Perlis: *An Ives Celebration: Papers and Panels of the Charles Ives Centennial Festival-Conference* (Urbana, IL, 1977)

ed. *The Phonograph and our Musical Life: Proceedings of a Centennial Conference, 7–10 December 1977*, ISAM Monographs 14 (Brooklyn, NY, 1980)

"Aaron Copland and American Music," *Perspectives of New Music*, xix (1980–81), 31–33

with L. Inserra: *The Music of Henry Ainsworth's Psalter*, ISAM Monographs 15 (Brooklyn, NY, 1981)

Les oeuvres de Marc-Antoine Charpentier: Catalogue raisonné (Paris, 1982)

"Trinitarian Symbolism in the 'Engelkonzert' of Hindemith's *Mathis der Maler*," *A Festschrift for Albert Seay*, ed. M.D. Grace (Colorado Springs, 1982), 216–29

"Sources for the Study of American Music," *Sources for American Studies*, ed. J.B. Kellogg and R. Walker (Westport, CT, 1983), 295–306

"Charpentier's 'Médée,'" *MT*, cxxv (1984), 563–67

"Henry Cowell's Ostinato Pianissimo," *MQ*, lxx (1984), 23–44

"Les oeuvres de Marc-Antoine Charpentier: Post-scriptum à un catalogue," *RdM*, lxx (1984), 37–50

"Marc-Antoine Charpentier: Memoire and Index," *Recherches sur la musique classique française*, xxiii (1985), 5–44

"On the Path to the U.S. Grove," *Notes*, xli (1985), 467–70

and N. Zahler: "Just What Is Ives's Unanswered Question?" *Notes*, xliv (1988), 437–43

Marc-Antoine Charpentier (Oxford, 1990)

English translation, critical edition, and introduction to *André Maugars, Response faite à un curieux sur le sentiment de la musique d'Italie: Escrite à Rome le premier Octobre 1639* (Geneva, 1993)

"Editing Ives's 129 Songs," *Ives Studies*, ed. Philip Lambert (New York, 1997), 57–76

"'A Grand and Glorious Noise!': Charles Ives as Lyricist," *American Music*, xv/1 (1997), 26–44

"Ives's '114[+15] Songs' and What He Thought of Them," *JAMS*, lii/1(1999), 97–144

and J.P. Burkholder, S. McClary, and K.K. Shelemay: "The Symbiosis of Teaching and Research: A Forum," *College Music Symposium*, xliv (2004), 1–14

EDITIONS

Marc-Antoine Charpentier: *In nativitatem Domini Nostri Jesu Christi canticum* (St. Louis, 1959)

Leonardo Leo: *Miserere: concertato a due chori, con una ideale cantilena gregoriana riportata al comodo del tuono del salmo, Marzo 1739* (St. Louis, 1961)

Marc-Antoine Charpentier: *Messe de minuit pour Noël* (St. Louis, 1962)

Marc-Antoine Charpentier: *Judicium Salomonis*, RRMBE i (New Haven, 1964)

Giulio Caccini: *Le nuove musiche e nuova maniera di scriverle*, RRMBE ix (Madison, WI, 1970, 2/2009)

Earlier American Music, facsimile editions with an introduction, 27(?) vols. (New York, 1972–91)

Marc-Antoine Charpentier: *Deux airs de trompette* (Mainz, 1972)

Marc-Antoine Charpentier: *Laudate Dominum omnes gentes: Octo vocibus et totidem instrumentis* (Mainz, 1972)

Marc-Antoine Charpentier: *Noëls pour les instruments* (Mainz, 1972)

Marc-Antoine Charpentier: *Laudate dominum* (Melville, NY, 1973)

Marc-Antoine Charpentier: *Messe de minuit pour Noël* (St. Louis, 1973)

Marc-Antoine Charpentier: *Prologues et intermèdes du Malade imaginaire de Molière* (Geneva, 1973)

Marc-Antoine Charpentier: *Pestis Mediolanensis* (*The Plague of Milan*) (Chapel Hill, NC, 1979)

Marc-Antoine Charpentier: *Le reniement de St. Pierre* (Bryn Mawr, PA, 1982)

Jean-Baptiste Lully: *Chaconne from Roland: for String Orchestra* (New York, 1982)

Marc-Antoine Charpentier: Oeuvres complètes (Paris, 1990–2004)

Henry Cowell: *Three Anti-Modernist Songs* (New York, 1996)

Charles Ives: *129 Songs*, RRAM xlvii; MUSA 12 (Middleton, WI, 2004)

Marc-Antoine Charpentier: *Acteon*; Arts florissants, série I-A, Musique française, œuvres pour le théâtre; 1, M.-A. Charpentier, 3 (Marandeuil, France, 2007)

Virgil Thomson: *Four Saints in Three Acts*, RRAM, lxiv; MUSA, 18 (Middleton, WI, 2008)

BIBLIOGRAPHY

R.A. Crawford, R.A. Lott, and C.J. Oja, eds.: *A Celebration of American Music: Words and Music in Honor of H. Wiley Hitchcock* (Ann Arbor, 1990) [incl. R. Crawford: "H. Wiley Hitchcock and American Music," 3–9; list of writings, 501–6]

F.J. Oteri: "Changing History: at Home with H. Wiley Hitchcock—a Conversation," *NewMusicBox*, 13 Nov 2002, <http://newmusicbox.org/44/interview_hitchcock.pdf>

A. Tommasini: "H. Wiley Hitchcock, Dictionary of Music Editor, Is Dead at 84," *New York Times*, 9 Dec 2007

P. Dickinson: "H. Wiley Hitchcock, Pioneer in American Music Studies," *Independent* (London), 13 Dec 2007

"Professor H. Wiley Hitchcock: Distinguished Musicologist Equally at Home in the European Baroque and the US Contemporary and Vernacular Traditions," *The Times* (London), 14 Dec 2007

S. Feder: "Everbest: Remembering H. Wiley Hitchcock," *NewMusicBox*, 3 Jan 2008, <http://www.newmusicbox.org/article.nmbx?id=5397>

"A Commemorative Issue in Honor of H. Wiley Hitchcock," *Institute for Studies in American Music Newsletter* xxxvii (2008)

R. Crawford, C.J. Oja, and J. Tick: "Remembrances: H. Wiley Hitchcock," *Bulletin of the Society for American Music*, xxxiv (2008), 6–8

P. Dickinson: "Interview with H. Wiley Hitchcock, New York City, 10 May 1981," in *Samuel Barber Remembered: A Centenary Tribute*, ed. Peter Dickinson (Rochester, NY, 2010), 151–56

PAULA MORGAN/CAROL J. OJA

Hiwell, John (*d* Savannah, GA, 15 March 1788). Bandmaster and teacher. He was appointed a sergeant in Knox's Regiment of Artillery in the Continental Army in December 1775, and two months later was made fife major. He was promoted to lieutenant in the Third (Crane's) Regiment of Continental Artillery in January 1777, and in August 1778 was appointed Inspector and Superintendent of Music in the Army, with orders to standardize and improve the army's music; he trained the regimental fife- and drum-majors so that they in turn could train the company musicians and standardize the interpretation of the regulations throughout the army. Through his efforts some units became sufficiently proficient to play hymns in three- and four-part harmony. In 1783 the Third Artillery Band, which Hiwell had been instrumental in developing, performed under the name Crane's Massachusetts Band in concerts at Salem, Massachusetts, and Portsmouth, New Hampshire; the latter performance is recognized as the first public concert given in New Hampshire. The excellence of Hiwell's band and his personal influence probably did much to lay the foundations of the American tradition of military music. After the Continental Army was disbanded, Hiwell moved first to Providence, where he opened a "school of instrumental music," and in February 1785 to Savannah, where he was active in the city's musical life. Hiwell may well be considered an outstanding example of the colonial musician and teacher whose efforts laid the foundation of America's musical culture.

RAOUL F. CAMUS

Ho, Don(ald Tai Loy) (*b* Honolulu, HI, 13 Aug 1930; *d* Honolulu, HI, 14 April 2007). Hawaiian pop singer and bandleader. Often portrayed by the mainstream media as the archetypal lounge lizard, Don Ho was the only Hawaiian musician of his era with an international profile. To his detractors his music was effervescent kitsch that made it hard for outsiders to take any Hawaiian culture seriously. To his supporters, he was a canny entertainer who understood his core audience and catered to their needs for more than four decades. During that time he recorded 15 best-selling records, made guest appearances on every major American talk show, and from 1976 to 1977 hosted his own series on the ABC television network. With his aloha shirt, Beatles haircut, and nonchalant style, his act worked just as well in Las Vegas as in Waikiki. In many ways, he was as much a tourist attraction as a musician, especially for military veterans, whom Ho was always careful to honor in between the joking and the music.

Ho was born in Honolulu but shortly relocated to Kane'ohe, where his mother opened a successful nightclub named Honey's. He attended Kamehameha Schools, then the University of Hawaii, where he earned a degree in sociology. After college, Ho joined the air force and, while stationed at in Hamilton, California, taught himself to play keyboards. He intended to make the military his career but returned home in 1959 when ill health forced his mother to turn over the club. By then Honey's was in decline. Ho assembled a new band, including Sonny Chillingworth, and began experimenting with ways to generate business. Through trial and error he crafted a formula centered on a playful, seemingly casual singer with a tight accompanying band.

Ho's vocal style suggests familiarity with Dean Martin and Elvis Presley as much as the work of Alfred Apaka and other Hawaiian crooners. He tended to slur, even mumble and resolve phrases at the deeper edge of his range. He often sang in a measured pace that seldom varied throughout a song or a set. What he lacked in dynamics he made up for in a relaxed intimacy that made his audience feel comfortable. In accordance with local tradition, he called visiting musicians on stage, which helped create a sense of family.

In 1962 he moved his operation to Waikiki, which led to a showcase engagement at Duke's, a club owned by Duke Kahanamoku. Shortly Ho was performing three shows per day, seven days per week. While he kept the focus on light entertainment, his new backup band, The

Aliis, received high praise for their musicianship and progressive vocal harmonies. Their jazz-inflected arrangements were widely admired and imitated.

In 1965 Ho began recording for Reprise. His first two releases were live albums that sought to capture the high spirits of his club act. He had his first Top 10 single in 1966 with "Tiny Bubbles," an English-language drinking song in the "countrypolitan" style fashionable at the time. Composed by Leon Pober, it is not especially Hawaiian until near the end, when Ho interpolates a translation of the song's only verse as a female chorus intones the English lines. An album quickly followed that featured "Pearly Shells," a hit single in the same style. Pober was again involved, along with Webley Edwards of *Hawaii Calls* fame, but the melody is adapted from the Hawaiian song "Pupu A'O'Ewa" (Shells of Ewa). These easy-listening sing-alongs and catch phrases such as "suck 'em up" resonated with tourist audiences in live shows and on television. From the mid-1960s onward Ho was a regular on the talk show circuit and made cameo appearances playing himself on nearly every major series that shot an episode in Hawaii.

For Hawaiian audiences, Ho is also remembered for popularizing the songs of innovative composer Kui Lee (1932–66), especially "I'll Remember You," "Days of our Youth," and "Ain't No Big Thing." Lee's songs blended Hawaiian sentiments with contemporary trends in rock, pop, and folk. In many regards they showed an entire generation of songwriters how to expand their musical options without compromising their local identity.

In 1969 The Aliis left the act, though a number of them returned over the years, including guitarist and jazz ukulele virtuoso Benny Chong, who stayed with Ho until the end. Bassist Nathan Auweau, now a well-established solo artist, also served a long tenure in the band. Throughout the 1970s and 1980s, as most local venues switched to traditional Hawaiian music or newer pop styles, Ho established his own club, sharing the stage with visiting celebrities such as Herb Alpert and Dionne Warwick as well as young local artists such as Hui Ohana, Palani Vaughan, and Sam Kapu. He also toured regularly, attracting large crowds. In 1995 he began to slow down owing to declining health. He soldiered on through the start of the new millennium performing three times per week, often with his daughter Hoku, until his death in 2007.

JAY W. JUNKER

Ho, Fred [Houn, Fred Wei-han] (*b* Palo Alto, CA, 10 Aug 1957). Jazz saxophonist and composer. Founder of the Afro Asian Music Ensemble and Asian American Arts Ensemble, he was central to the development of Asian American jazz.

Ho grew up near the University of Massachusetts in Amherst where his father was a Chinese political science professor. Feeling alienated by his all-white surroundings, Ho immersed himself in black art and politics. He attended Harvard University and graduated in 1979 with a BA in sociology. Coming of age at the height of the Asian American movement, he joined the I Wor Kuen, which merged with the Marxist League of

Revolutionary Struggle until it disbanded in 1989. Since his first recording, *Tomorrow is Now!* (1985, SN), he has used his music to build political solidarity and highlight connections between the African and Asian experience, both globally as well as in the United States.

Ho's music, which often features the resonant sound of his baritone saxophone, draws from eclectic sources, blending Asian folk music, blues, and free jazz in a big-band setting. He has created and collaborated on a number of stage works and operas, bringing a dramatic, visual sensibility to the Asian American jazz movement. His works often mix instrumental passages and spoken-word storytelling with narratives that reflect his Marxist, anti-patriarchal political commitments. A self-described radical, revolutionary artist, he has discussed his musical endeavors and political aspirations in a variety of publications, including his own edited volume *Sounding Off! Music as Subversion/Resistance/Revolution* (New York, 1996).

LOREN KAJIKAWA

Ho'opi'i Brothers, the. Hawaiian falsetto singers and musicians. Of no direct relation to steel guitarist Sol Ho'opi'i, Solomon (*b* Maui, HI, 28 March 1935; *d* Maui, HI, 2 March 2006) and Richard (*b* Maui, HI, 15 March 1941) Ho'opi'i grew up in Kahakuloa on the remote northwest coast of Maui. From an early age they developed a virtuoso style of duet *leo ki'eki'e* (falsetto) marked by open, robust timbre, and a variety of vocal ornaments. Among these are traditional techniques from Hawaiian chant plus adapted practices such as yodeling, echoing, and percussive effects. Both brothers could sing all four voice parts and complex interplay was common, as on "Kupa Landing" and "I Ali'i No 'Oe." The duo often modulated to higher keys as songs progressed, as in "Haleakala Hula." *Himeni* (Hawaiian hymns) were another specialty. Discreet elements of early rock and roll also filtered into their sound, especially when performing at parties.

The brothers greatly admired Genoa Keawe, who was a major influence along with Bill Ali'iloa Lincoln. They both sang for many local events before forming The Ho'onanea Serenaders in 1968. As The Hoopii Brothers they released *No Ka Oi*, the first of seven albums, in 1975. Generally they worked as a quartet with bass and guitar, accompanying themselves on six-string and eight-string Hawaiian 'ukulele. Beginning around 1982 the brothers developed a close relationship with the University of Hawaii ethnomusicology program, and participated in numerous educational events and media projects throughout the state. In 1989 they performed at the Smithsonian American Folklife Festival along with slack-key master Ledward Kaapana, after which Kaapana began joining them for recordings and important concerts.

In 1996 the brothers received a National Endowment for the Arts Heritage Fellowship. In 1997 they won Group of the Year from the Hawaiian Academy of Recording Arts.

After Sol retired in 2000 Richard began performing solo. He has appeared on three Grammy Award winning anthologies recorded at George Kahumoku's Masters of Hawaiian Music concerts in Maui. In 2008 he returned to singing duets with his son Kalai (*b*1978) singing Sol's parts.

J.W. JUNKER

Hoch, Theodore [Theodor] (*b* Spremberg, Germany, 9 Jan 1842; *d* Brooklyn, NY, 13 Feb 1906). Cornetist of German birth. He began playing the cornet at an early age. At 10 he moved to Berlin, where he became a member of the famed Kaiser Franz Guard Grenadier Second Regiment Band. In 1867 the band won first prize at the Paris Exposition, and Hoch received the gold medal for his solo playing. He visited the United States in 1872 with the band for the World's Peace Jubilee, and on a return trip in 1876, he and the band performed at the Centennial Exposition in Philadelphia.

He immigrated around 1880 to the United States, where he worked as a cornet soloist, teacher, and composer. His *Tutor for the Cornet* (1880) is based on his principle of placing most of the pressure of the mouthpiece against the lower lip, thus allowing the upper lip to vibrate freely. This method gave him an extraordinary range. He also composed orchestral works and solos for the cornet, including "Alpine Flowers," "American Fantasia," "Echoes of the Valley," "Fantasie Brilliante," "Souvenir de Bellini," "Remembrance of Prague," and "Greetings from the Old World." He often performed on an "echo-cornet" built to his design by the Conn Company. He concluded many concerts by unfurling an American flag from the long bell of a Conn herald trumpet while playing "The Star-Spangled Banner."

BIBLIOGRAPHY
G. Bridges: *Pioneers in Brass* (Detroit, 2/1972), 38
R.I. Schwartz: *The Cornet Compendium* (Petersburg, VA 2001)
M. Laplace: *Trompette, Cuivres & XXe Siècle* (CD-Rom, 2008)
MICHAEL ELLZEY

Hoctor, Harriet (*b* Hoosick Falls, NY, 25 Sept 1905; *d* Arlington, VA, 9 June 1977). Dancer, choreographer, and teacher. After ballet studies in New York City, Hoctor made her Broadway debut in the chorus of Jerome Kern's musical *Sally* in 1920. In 1922 she joined the Keith-Orpheum Circuit as a solo ballet dancer. The next year she appeared in Vivian and Rosetta Duncan's (known as the Duncan Sisters) *Topsy and Eva*, a musical comedy adaptation of *Uncle Tom's Cabin*. The show toured the United States and opened on Broadway in 1924. In 1927 Hoctor starred in the Broadway revue *A La Carte*, and critics noted that she was the only member of the cast who "is certain to be pleasantly remembered." Having caught the eye of producer Florenz Ziegfeld, she danced in his sumptuous Broadway production of *The Three Musketeers*, which opened in 1928, and in 1929 she appeared in *Show Girl*, becoming the first dancer to perform Gershwin's *An American in Paris*, with choreography by Albertina Rasch. Between 1930 and 1933, she appeared on Broadway in *Simple Simon, Earl Carroll's Vanities, Hold Your Horses*, and in London in the musical revue *Bow Bells*.

In 1933 Hoctor opened in New York City's RKO Music Hall with her choreography "The Nightingale and the Rose," which critics hailed as an "awe-inspiring performance." She presented six new ballets of her own creation in *Harriet Hoctor Ballet Revue* at New York City's Belasco Theatre in 1934. In 1935 columnist Louella O. Parsons announced the noted dance team of Fred Astaire and Ginger Rogers had split up and Hoctor had been signed to star in Astaire's next film, *Shall We Dance* (1937). However, in the end, Rogers decided to appear in the film and Hoctor's role was diminished to a ballet at the end of the film. She starred in *The Ziegfeld Follies of 1936* and appeared as herself in the film *The Great Ziegfeld* (1936). After several years of touring in revues, Hoctor opened a ballet school in Boston in 1941; she taught there after she ceased performing in 1945. Her archives are held by the Music Division, Library of Congress.

BIBLIOGRAPHY
D. Hering: "Don't Forget the Backbend, Harriet!" *Dance Magazine* (Dec 1965)
ELIZABETH ALDRICH

Hodeir, André (*b* Paris, France, 22 Jan 1921; *d* Versailles, France, 1 Nov 2011). French jazz writer, composer, and musician. At the Paris Conservatoire (1942–8) he was a pupil of Jacques de La Presle, Simone Plé-Caussade, Norbert Dufourcq, and OLIVIER MESSIAEN and won premiers prix in harmony (1944), counterpoint and fugue (1947), and music history (1947). He began his career in jazz music as a violinist (under the name of Claude Laurence) in the Ekyan Sextet (1942–4) and was later musical director of the Jazz Group of Paris (1954–60). Hodeir's compositions include pieces for jazz ensemble (*Evanescence, Oblique, The Alphabet*), two jazz cantatas (*Anna Livia Plurabelle* and *Bitter Ending*), related pairs of compositions called "twin pieces" (*oeuvres jumelles*— for example, *Transplantation I* and *Flautando*) and numerous film scores. Several of his pieces incorporate a technique he developed called "simulated improvisation" (*l'improvisation simulée*), which uses through-composed material to simulate improvised jazz solos.

Hodeir's scholarly publications date to the early 1940s. He began writing for the French journal *Jazz-Hot* in 1945, serving as its editor from 1947 to 1950. Much of his writing explored formal problems and the relation between composing and improvisation. He distinguished himself from his contemporaries by moving away from personal and impressionistic descriptions and toward more precise musical analyses, often including transcriptions of recordings. He achieved wide recognition in the United States in 1956 with the English translation of his first monograph, *Jazz: Its Evolution and Essence*. The book proved influential in its use of an evolutionary framework to describe the music's progression through several discrete periods. Like many of Hodeir's writings, the book has inspired controversy in the years since its publication. Whereas many have praised its rigorous musical analyses (unique for their time) and insistence on demonstrating the value of jazz as an art form, others have critiqued it for overemphasizing the connection between jazz and classical music (especially regarding the role of the composer) and downplaying the significance of African elements.

Although much of Hodeir's early jazz writing is characterized by objective analysis, his approach shifted during the 1960s and 1970s. His second jazz monograph, *Toward Jazz* (1962), is a set of critical essays outlining more personal perspectives on the music, and his third, *The Worlds of Jazz* (1972), is a fictional work—occasionally using real musicians as characters—that dramatizes the author's viewpoints. In addition to his jazz scholarship, Hodeir wrote extensively on European classical music. He retired from composing in 1972, but remained active as a writer, researcher, and teacher until his death.

WRITINGS

Le Jazz, Cet Inconnu (Paris, 1945)

Introduction à la Musique de Jazz (Paris, 1948)

Hommes et Problèmes du Jazz (Paris, 1954, 2/1981; Eng. trans., enlarged, 1956/R, 2/1979, as *Jazz: Its Evolution and Essence*)

"Bibliographie du Jazz," *Précis de Musicologie*, ed. J. Chailley (Paris, 1958), 385–8

"Le Jazz," *Histoire de la Musique*, ed. Roland-Manuel, ii (Paris, 1963), 1075–90

Toward Jazz (New York, 1962/R; Fr. orig. Roquevaire, 1984, as *Jazzistiques*)

Les Mondes du Jazz (Paris, 1970, 3/2004; Eng. trans. 1972 as *The Worlds of Jazz*)

with L. Malson: "Le Jazz: un Enfant Adoptif," *InHarmoniques*, no.2 (1987), 54–62

"Ça Ne Veut Rien Dire/It Don't Mean a Thing," *International Jazz Archives Journal*, i/2 (1994), 75–90

"To Hear All about Anna Livia," *International Jazz Archives Journal*, i/3 (1995), 28–45

"L'improvisation Simulée," *Les Cahiers du Jazz*, 11 (1997), 23–38

The Andre Hodeir Jazz Reader, ed. J. Pautrot (Ann Arbor, MI, 2006)

BIBLIOGRAPHY

GMO

W. Otey: "Hodeir through his own Glass," *Jazz* [Berkeley], i (1958–9), 105–13

L.B. Brown: "The Theory of Jazz Music: 'It Don't Mean a Thing,'" *The Journal of Aesthetics and Art Criticism*, xlix (1991), 115–27

A.H. Levy: "Cultural Resuscitation: The Political Left and Modern Jazz," *Radical Aesthetics and Music Criticism in America, 1930–1950* (Lewiston, NY, 1991), 45–59, esp. 52–7

CHRISTIANE SPIETH-WEISSENBACHER/MICHAEL C. HELLER

Hodges, Donald A(lbert) (*b* Kearney, NE, 9 Oct 1945). Music educator and scholar. He obtained degrees in music education from the University of Kansas (BME 1967) and University of Texas at Austin (MM 1972, PhD 1974). He taught in the public schools of Philadelphia (1963–7), and at the University of South Carolina (1974–7), Southern Methodist University (1977–80), and the University of Texas at San Antonio (1980–2003). Since 2003, he has served as Covington Distinguished Professor and Director of the Music Research Institute (MRI) at the University of North Carolina at Greensboro. At the MRI, he worked with colleagues on projects in Bio-Music, neuroimaging, music-related hearing loss, music education, music performance, and ethnomusicology/ecocriticism. A primary research effort was a series of brain imaging experiments conducted with colleagues in Texas and North Carolina involving pianists, singers,

and conductors. He co-authored (with David Sebald) *Music Psychology for Musicians* (New York), was the (contributing) editor for the *Handbook of Music Psychology* (Lawrence, KS, 1980, 2/1996) and the accompanying *Multimedia Companions* (with Scott Lipscomb, David Sebald, and Jenni Willi-Opalenik) in two volumes (San Antonio, 2000, 2004), published numerous book chapters, articles, and papers in music education and music psychology, and served on editorial boards of several scholarly journals. He has also played a leading role in organizing extensive funding for music education research.

JERE T. HUMPHREYS

Hodges, Edward (*b* Bristol, England, 20 July 1796; *d* Clifton, Bristol, England, 1 Sept 1867). Church musician, composer, organist, and essayist of English birth. As a youth he took piano lessons, later learning to play the organ, and, although from a nonconformist family, he sang bass in the choir of Bristol Cathedral and eventually converted to the Anglican faith. His first appointments were as organist at St. James's (1819–38) and St. Nicholas's (1821–38), Bristol. In both of these churches he was responsible for the rebuilding of older organs, displaying an early interest in novel concepts of organ design in collaboration with local organ builder John Smith, and later working with Smith on the rebuilding of the Bristol Cathedral organ. In 1825 he entered Sydney Sussex College, Cambridge, earning the Doctor of Music degree, and began composing choral music and writing articles about organ construction and church music. After his wife's death in 1835 he applied unsuccessfully for three prestigious academic and cathedral posts; a visiting American clergyman encouraged the idea of emigrating, and in 1838 Hodges was offered a post at St. James's Cathedral in Toronto, to which he and his son George Frederick Handel Hodges traveled the same year. He was at St. James's only six weeks, however, before political unrest and the offer of a post in Trinity Parish precipitated a move to New York.

His first position was at St. John's Chapel, where he superintended the building of a new organ. In 1844 Hodges remarried, enabling him to bring his remaining children to New York, and in 1846 Trinity Church, where he became organist, completed a new building with a Henry Erben organ, the largest in the city, designed by Hodges. At Trinity, he instituted an ambitious music program along English lines, composing much of the liturgical music sung by his choir of men, women, and boys. In 1851 he formed an additional choir, the Church Choral Society, which, though short-lived, helped further the cause of chant and sung liturgy in special services. His involvement with organ design continued, and in 1853 an organ was built to his specifications for Trinity Chapel. He continued to compose choral music, and during the period 1856–8 contributed a number of articles to the *New York Musical World*. Disabled by a stroke in 1858, he continued to compose and publish, and in 1863 he returned to England, ending his days near his birthplace. Hodges fathered eight children, only four of whom reached adulthood; two, FAUSTINA HASSE HODGES and JOHANN SEBASTIAN BACH HODGES, were also active in music.

BIBLIOGRAPHY
GMO
F.H. Hodges: *Edward Hodges, Doctor in Music of Sydney Sussex College* (New York, 1896/R)
A.H. Messiter: *A History of the Choir and Music of Trinity Church, New York* (New York, 1906/R)
C.H. Kaufman: "The Hodges and Newland Collections in the Library of Congress: a Preliminary Report," *CMc*, no.18 (1974), 79–89
J. Ogasapian: *Organ Building in New York City, 1700–1900* (Braintree, MA, 1977)
B.J. Owen: "Dr. Edward Hodges of Bristol and New York: an 'Organ Expert' on Both Sides of the Atlantic," *Bios*, no.14 (1990), 48–61
J. Ogasapian: "New Materials on Edward Hodges," *The Tracker* xxv/1 (1991), 13–18
J. Ogasapian: *English Cathedral Music in New York: Edward Hodges of Trinity Church* (Richmond, VA, 1994)

BARBARA OWEN

Hodges, Faustina Hasse (*b* Malmesbury, England, 7 Aug 1822; *d* Philadelphia, PA, 4 Feb 1895). Organist, composer, and singer of English birth. The daughter of the organist EDWARD HODGES, she followed his example and became a professional musician in New York and Philadelphia. She was a "professor" of organ, piano, and singing at Emma Willard's Troy Seminary for Girls, New York, in 1852 and, in the late 1870s, she became a church organist in Philadelphia. She began composing in the 1850s; her works include several keyboard pieces, a few sacred songs, and about 25 drawing-room songs. Some works were a commercial success, the most famous being the songs "Dreams" (Boston, 1859) and "The Rose Bush" (1859) and a sacred duet "Suffer Little Children." (Ebel claimed that she had sales of more than 100,000 copies for "The Rose Bush".) Hodges skillfully assimilated both Italian and German styles in her more cultivated songs, making them popular light recital pieces for opera singers such as Adelaide Phillipps in the 19th century and Alma Gluck in the early 1900s. She edited some of her father's works and published them in 1891 with her own hymn tunes. She also began writing a memoir of her father that was completed and published by her brother, Reverend J.S.B. Hodges, after her death.

BIBLIOGRAPHY
R. Hughes: "Music in America: the Woman Composers," *Godey's Lady's Book*, cxxxii/Jan (1896), 30–40
O. Ebel: *Women Composers: a Biographical Handbook of Woman's Work in Music* (Brooklyn, NY, 1902, 3/1913)
J. Tick: *American Women Composers before 1870* (Ann Arbor, 1983)

JUDITH TICK/R

Hodges, Fletcher, Jr. (*b* Indianapolis, IN, 6 Aug 1906; *d* Oakmont, PA, 13 March 2006). Archivist and music historian. He received a degree in English from Harvard University. In 1931 he became first curator of the collection of Fosteriana compiled by the pharmaceutical manufacturer Josiah Kirby Lilly, and he continued in the post after Lilly presented the holdings in 1937 for deposit at the University of Pittsburgh. Until his retirement in 1982, Hodges supervised the research, collecting, and cataloging of Foster's manuscripts, of first and early editions of his music, and of iconographical and biographical material. He also oversaw the collected edition of reprints of Foster's music (the first such edition of an American composer's works). For his contributions to Foster scholarship and to 19th-century American studies he was awarded an honorary LLD from Lincoln Memorial University in 1945.

DEANE L. ROOT

Hodges, Johann Sebastian Bach (*b* Bristol, England, 22 Jan 1830; *d* Baltimore, MD, 1 May 1915). Priest and musician, son of EDWARD HODGES. He came to New York in 1845 and studied at Columbia College, receiving the AB in 1850 and the MA in 1853. Afterward he entered General Theological Seminary, graduating in 1853, and was ordained a priest of the Episcopal Church in 1855. After serving churches in Pittsburgh and Chicago, he became rector of Grace Church in Newark, New Jersey, in 1860 and was honored with a doctorate by Racine College in 1867. In 1870 he became rector of St. Paul's Church in Baltimore, where he served for 35 years, during which he founded an outstanding choir of men and boys. The composer of more than 100 hymn tunes and anthems, he compiled the *Book of Common Praise* in 1868, was active in the Episcopal Hymnal commissions of 1874 and 1892, and edited the revised edition of *Hymn Tunes* in 1903.

BIBLIOGRAPHY
C. Fiske: "The Late J.S.B. Hodges, Priest and Musician," *The Churchman* (1915), 667
L. Ellinwood: *The History of American Church Music* (New York, 1953)

JOHN OGASAPIAN/BARBARA OWEN

Hodges, Johnny [Hodge, Cornelius John; Jeep; Rabbit; Rab] (*b* Cambridge, MA, 25 July 1907; *d* New York, NY, 11 May 1970). Jazz alto and sopranosaxophonist, clarinetist, composer, and bandleader. His mother was of Mexican and Native American descent, his father, African American. He is one of the three most significant jazz alto saxophonists, the others being Benny Carter, Hodges's junior by 14 days, and Charlie Parker, who was 13 years younger. Hodges's initial and enduring influence was the soprano saxophonist and clarinetist Sidney Bechet, with whom he studied as an adolescent after a fortuitous introduction by his older sister. He received a thorough grounding on piano and drums but never played either instrument in bands. His teen years were spent in Boston, where he explored the reed instruments with his neighbor Harry Carney; the pair subsequently worked together in Duke Ellington's saxophone section. Hodges worked with Bechet and Lloyd Scott in New York in 1924, abandoning the curved soprano for a straight one given to him by Bechet, and with Chick Webb on both soprano and alto. He joined Ellington in May 1928 on the recommendation of Carney and, according to Barney Bigard, a majority vote of the band members. Hodges continued playing clarinet for two more years until Ellington ceased writing five-clarinet arrangements. He played alto and soprano saxophones in a concert which is now considered historic at Carnegie Hall organized by Benny Goodman on 16 January 1938. The following year Hodges and Bigard brought the double bass player Blanton to Ellington's attention. During the 1930s Hodges recorded with small groups from the big band, with and without Ellington, led by Rex Stewart, Bigard, and Carney and produced by Helen Oakley. A perennial jazz-magazine poll winner, Hodges, as lead saxophonist, favored soloist, and compositional collaborator with Ellington, developed a flawless intonation and the unique, immediately identifiable sound characterized as sensuous, languid, sultry, and, by Ellington, "smeary." Hodges's very personal approach to romping, earthy blues contrasted dramatically with his famous expressionless visage, as did his eloquent, sophisticated, and seemingly emotional rendering of ballads. Ellington, the composer and pianist Billy Strayhorn, and the impressario Norman Granz were all as influential as Bechet in Hodges's career. Many of Strayhorn's most memorable ballads, such as "Day Dream," "Passion Flower," and "Isfahan," were inspired by and specifically written for Hodges, who became their definitive interpreter. Hodges claimed that Ellington's "I let a song go out of my heart" originated with a riff which Hodges played behind the melody of "Once in awhile." Similar stories are attached to Ellington's "Don't get around much anymore," among others. Hodges's own catalog of more than 200 compositions is dominated by blues with many titles employing puns on his nicknames and that of his second wife Edith Porter, Cue. To avoid violating contractual exclusivity on several of his early independent recordings, Hodges is listed as "Cue Porter." Their son, known as Johnny Hodges Jr. (1947–84), was nicknamed Brother and played drums on several recordings made in 1965 with the elder Hodges as leader as well as on Ellington concerts and sessions of that period when Sam Woodyard was temporarily absent. In 1951 Granz persuaded Hodges, the trombonist Lawrence Brown, and the drummer Sonny Greer to leave Ellington, guaranteeing bookings and recording contracts for the Johnny Hodges Septet. The group had one hit record "Castle Rock," composed by the former Ellington tenor saxophonist Al Sears, who preceded John Coltrane as a sideman in the group. On 17 June 1952 Granz staged a coup in the annals of jazz, producing the only recording of Hodges, Carter, and Parker together—an all-star Hollywood jam session. In 1955 Hodges heeded Ellington's repeated invitations to return but continued to record as leader, principally for Granz's labels, making a series of albums with the organist Wild Bill Davis, one with the baritone saxophonist Gerry Mulligan, several with Earl Hines, one in a duo with Lawrence Welk (not a Granz product), and, two months before his death, an album of Ellington tunes arranged by Oliver Nelson and sung by Leon Thomas. After 1940 Hodges was rarely heard on soprano saxophone; however, Ellington was writing him into "A Portrait of Sidney Bechet" in *The New Orleans Suite* when Hodges succumbed to a heart attack.

SELECTED RECORDINGS

As leader: *The Complete Johnny Hodges Sessions 1951–1955* (Mosaic, 1989); *Johnny Hodges and Wild Bill Davis 1965–1966* (Jazz Tribune, 1992); *Jeep's Blues—Johnny Hodges: his Greatest Recordings 1928–1941* (ASV/Living Era, 1995); *Complete Norman Granz Jam Sessions* (Verve, 2004)

As sideman with D. Ellington: *The Centennial Edition* (RCA Victor, 1999); *The Complete 1932–1940 Brunswick, Columbia and Master Recordings of Duke Ellington and his Famous Orchestra* (Mosaic, 2010)

BIBLIOGRAPHY

S. Dance: *The World of Duke Ellington* (New York, 1970/R, 2/2000)

E.K. Ellington: *Music is my Mistress* (New York, 1973/R)

M. Berger, E. Berger, and J. Patrick: *Benny Carter: a Life in American Music* (Metuchen, NJ, 1982, enlarged by E. Berger, 2/2001)

B. Bigard: *With Louis and the Duke: the Autobiography of a Jazz Clarinetist*, ed. B. Martyn (New York, 1986/R)

J. Chilton: *Sidney Bechet: the Wizard of Jazz* (New York, 1987)

E. Lambert: *Duke Ellington: a Listener's Guide*, ed. E. Norsworthy (Lanham, MD, 1999)

L. Massagli and G.M. Volonté: *The New Desor: an Updated Edition of Duke Ellington's Story on Records, 1924–74*, i–ii (Milan, 1999)

W. van de Leur: *Something to Live For: the Music of Billy Strayhorn* (New York, 2002)

S. Lasker: disc notes, *The Complete 1932–1940 Brunswick, Columbia and Master Recordings of Duke Ellington and His Famous Orchestra*, Mosaic MD11-248 (2010)

PATRICIA WILLARD

Hodgkinson, John (*b* nr Manchester, England, *c*7 June 1765; *d* nr Bladensburg, MD, 12 Sept 1805). Actor, singer, and theatrical manager of English birth. He began his career in 1782 with the Tate Wilkinson troupe in York; by 1790 he was playing leading roles in tragedy, comedy, and comic opera at the major English provincial theaters. He made his debut in the United States on 26 September 1792 with the Old American Company in Philadelphia, together with his second wife, Frances Hodgkinson (née Brett) (*b* England, 1771; *d* Philadelphia, PA, 27 Sept 1803). In addition to his varied acting roles and his notable popularity with audiences, Hodgkinson frequently sang in concert. He was credited with "a fine taste for music" and a voice that was "powerful, melodious, variable, and of immense compass" (*Mirror of Taste and Dramatic Censor*, i/3, 1810); he was also said to be proficient on the violin and the flute. He became manager of the Old American Company in 1794 and of the Boston Theatre in 1798. He was considered an arrogant and overbearing theatrical manager, and after a few managerial mishaps, he returned to the ranks of the players. After the death of his wife in 1803 he acted in Charleston, South Carolina, and was traveling to New York when he died of yellow fever. In his time it was agreed that "as a general actor, he was the greatest in America." Frances Hodgkinson was the theater's favorite singing soubrette and owed much of her success to the systematic and insistent support of her husband. She played many roles in comic opera and was a popular concert performer. She was considered a "truly sweet singer" and "the most generally useful female performer" on the New York stage (1794). She remained popular until her death in New York of tuberculosis in 1803.

BIBLIOGRAPHY

J. Hodgkinson: *A Narrative of his Connection with the Old American Company, from 5 Sept 1792—31 March 1797* (New York, 1797)

Mirror of Taste and Dramatic Censor (Philadelphia, March–Nov 1810) [series of biographical articles]

W. Dunlap: *A History of the American Theatre* (New York, 1832/ R2005)

O.G.T. Sonneck: *Early Opera in America* (New York, 1915), 85–86

P.H. Highfill Jr., K.A. Burnim, and E.A. Langhans: "Hodkinson, Mrs. John the Second, Frances, née Brett," *A Biographical Dictionary of Actors, Actresses, Musicians, Dancers, Managers and other Stage Personnel in London, 1660–1800*, xv (Carbondale, IL, 1973–93)

B. Harbin: "The Role of Mrs. Hallam in the Hodgkinson-Hallam Controversy: 1794–1797," *Theatre Journal*, xxxii/2 (1980), 213–22

S.L. Porter: "John Hodgkinson in England: the Early Life of an American Actor–Singer," *Studies in Music: University of Colorado* (Boulder, 985)

S.L. Porter: *With an Air Debonair: Musical Theatre in America, 1785–1815* (Washington, DC, 1991)

SUSAN L. PORTER/R

Hodkinson, Sydney (Phillip) (*b* Winnipeg, MB, 17 Jan 1934). Canadian composer. He studied composition at the Eastman School (BM 1957, MM 1958) with LOUIS MENNINI and BERNARD ROGERS, at Princeton University (1960) with ELLIOTT CARTER, ROGER SESSIONS, and MILTON BABBITT, and at the University of Michigan (DMA 1968) with LESLIE BASSETT, Niccolò Castiglioni, ROSS LEE FINNEY, and George Balch Wilson. He also studied briefly with Benjamin Britten and Luigi Dallapiccola. Following a period as a woodwind instructor in the public schools of Rochester and Brighton, New York, he taught at the University of Virginia (1958–63), Ohio University (1963–6), and the University of Michigan (1968–73), where he conducted the Rockefeller New Music Project. In the period 1970–72 he served as artist-in-residence of Minneapolis with a grant from the Ford Foundation, and in 1973 he joined the faculty of the Eastman School as director of the Eastman Musica Nova and as chairman of the conducting and ensembles department. During the period 1984–86 he served as Meadows Distinguished Professor of Composition at Southern Methodist University. He then spent four years as a visiting professor of composition at the University of Western Ontario (1991–95). In 1995 Hodkinson returned to the Eastman School as a faculty member in the Composition Department; he taught there until his retirement in 1999. Since then, he has conducted the New Music Group at Oberlin College (2001), served as a visiting professor of composition at Indiana University (2002) and Duke University (2003), and in 2004 accepted the Almand Chair of Composition at Stetson University. Hodkinson also conducts the Contemporary Ensemble and teaches composition at the Aspen Music Festival and School.

He has written more than 250 works that span many genres. They include six string quartets, a large amount of choral, operatic, and vocal music, and concerti for horn, voice, violin, cello, clarinet, and piano. He has received commissions from the New York PO (for *Edge of the Olde One*), the St. Paul Chamber Orchestra (*Sinfonie concertante*), the Banff Centre for the Arts (*The Wall*), and the National Arts Centre Orchestra of Ottawa (*Chansons de jadis*), among others; his works have been widely performed by major American orchestras and recorded on numerous labels, including CRI, Grenadilla, Louisville, Advance, Albany, Nonesuch, Centaur, CBC, Novisse, Mark, Innova, and Pantheon. Hodkinson has also enjoyed an active career as a clarinetist and has made frequent appearances in the United States and Canada, conducting concerts of contemporary music with various ensembles including the Rochester PO.

As a composer, Hodkinson is distinguished by his ability to write in idioms as dissimilar as jazz and electronic music with sensitivity and appeal and by his grasp of instrumental capabilities. His experiments in electronic music are among the most engaging in the late 20th-century repertory. In *Edge of the Olde One*, for horn and orchestra, the soloist electronically controls (with foot pedals) echo, octave duplication, reverberation, and modulation, resulting in an endless variety of tone colors and a greatly expanded expressive range. Projects from the early 21st century showcase the ease with which he navigates through various styles and compositional forms. His numerous honors include an award from the American Academy and Institute of Arts and Letters (1971), a Martha Baird Rockefeller Fund grant (1976), NEA grants (1975–6, 1977–8), the Canada Council Senior Arts Award (1977–8), and a Guggenheim Fellowship (1978–9).

WORKS

Orch/band: Caricatures, orch, 1966; Fresco (Sym. no.1), orch, 1968; Drawings: Sets nos.7 and 8, str orch, both 1970; Stabile, orch, 1970; Valence, chbr orch, 1970; Epigrams, orch, 1971; Cortege, band, 1975; Celestial Calendar, 3 pieces, str orch, 1976; Edge of the Olde One, eng hn, elec, chbr orch, 1976; Bach Variations, ww, perc, 1977; Sinfonie concertante (Sym. no.5), 1980; Bumberboom (Scherzo diabolique), hn, orch, elec, 1982; Epitaphion Lament for Sym. Orch, 1990; A Little Travelin' Music: Ov, 1991; Duae Cantatae Breves for Wind Ens and optional Vv, 1995; Tilt, "un gioco burlesco" per Orch, 1997; Monumentum pro umbris for Wind Ens, 2004; Stone for Wind En, 2008; other works include nine symphonies in total, and other smaller works

Solo with orch: Chansons de jadis: Six Songs of Loneliness for High Voice and Chbr Orch, 1978–79; Tango, Boogie, and Grand Tarantella for Solo Db and Orch, 1987; Sym. no.6 for Vn Solo and Sym. Orch, 1988; Threnody: Elegiac Variations for Solo Vn and Orch, 1988; Conc. for Cl and Orch with Str Qt Obbligato, 1989; Pf Conc. no.1: "A Shifting Trek," 1997–2004; Pf Conc. no.2, 2008; and several other works

Chbr: Stanzas, pf trio, 1959; Drawings: Set no.1, perc qt, 1960, Set no.3, cl, drums, 1961, Set no.4, perc trio, 1961, Set no.6, vn, 3 cl, 1965, Set no.9, 3 perc, 1977, Set no.10 (Cerberus), 4 tuba, 1977; Imagined Quarter, 4 perc, 1967; Dance Variations, pf trio, 1977; Night Moves: Four Trio-Nocturines for Pic, Perc, and DB, 1990; Summerwood Concertino for Hp and Chbr Qnt, 1997; Serenata Oscura: "…cinque immagini delle notti tenebrose…" for Chbr Ens, 1999; Stony Brook Jam Variations for Sxt, 1999; Requiescant "In Memoriam Sept Eleven," Elegy for Chbr Sxt, fl(pic), B-flat cl, perc, pf, vn, vl, 2001; Short Cuts for Cl, Vn, and Vc, 2001; Bricks for Solo Vn and Chbr Sxt, 2004; Beguine Again: Encore for Eight Vc, 2005; other works incl. six string qts, three brass qnts, two wind qnts, and pieces for solo org and db

Vocal: Vox populous, oratorio, 1971; November Voices, 1v, speaker, small inst ens, 1975; Maxims and Minims, SATB, 1977; Missa brevis, chorus, bells, 1978; Chansons de jadis, S, orch, 1978–9; The Wall, op, two acts, Alvin Greenberg (librettist), 1980; Adam-Lay-I-Bounden for Mez and Eng Hn, 1989; Cantata Sancta for S and Bar Soli, Mixed Chorus, Org, and Chbr Qnt, 2000; and other choral works

Principal publishers: Associated, Theodore Presser, American Composers Alliance, Associated Music Publishers (G. Schirmer), Ludwig Music Pub. Co., Music for Percussion, Editions Jobert, Ricordi, Columbia University Music Press, Dorn Publications, Transcontinental, and Smith Music Publications

JAMES G. ROY JR./JONATHAN KUUSKOSKI

Hoe, Robert, Jr. [V] (*b* New York, NY, 15 Jan 1922; *d* Poughkeepsie, NY, 16 Feb 1983). Band enthusiast and philanthropist. After attending Pomona College, Claremont, California (BA 1943), he owned and managed an architectural woodworking firm in Poughkeepsie for over 20 years, and later a chain of bowling alleys. An amateur euphonium player, he amassed an encyclopedic collection of band scores, rivaling that of the US Marine band. In conjunction with Commander Donald Stauffer, director of the US Navy Band, he issued a series of 15 recordings made by the band entitled *Heritage of the March*. Each of these records presented unavailable marches by an American composer on one side, and a European composer on the other. Hoe then invited many American and European service, community, college, and high school bands to make recordings. He provided most of the music from his own collection, prepared liner notes and biographies, financed the recordings, and distributed them, free of charge, to schools, libraries, and radio stations. The initial *Heritage of the March* series of 90 LPs was sent to 600 public libraries and music schools in Canada and the United States, and another 400 or so to musicians, directors, students, and band devotees. It was followed by a second set of 94 records labeled A to QQQQ sent to band enthusiasts who were interested in the music. Hoe also subsidized the making of an 18-record set of the complete band works of Sousa performed by the US Marine Band. At the time of his death he had given away over 300,000 long-playing records. The importance of the *Heritage of the March* recordings in preserving the works of undeservedly forgotten composers cannot be understated, and full credit goes to this one man whose dedication, devotion, personal funds, and enthusiasm brought about a renewed interest in this music. He was awarded an honorary doctorate by Central Methodist College in 1978, and a Distinguished Public Service Award by the Department of the Navy.

BIBLIOGRAPHY
W.H. Rehrig: *The Heritage Encyclopedia of Band Music* (Westerville, OH, 1991, suppl. 1996); CD-ROM (Oskaloosa, IA, 2005)

RAOUL F. CAMUS

Hoedown. A term with three principal meanings: (1) a noisy, riotous dance competition held in a social setting, (2) the musical competition associated with it, and (3) a SQUARE DANCE party. The etymology of the term is unknown. It may have been invented to describe a vigorous African American jig or shuffle dance, as in "hoe down the corn field," but this is pure speculation. In any event, the essential element of a hoedown in senses 1 and 2 is not the dance or musical form; it is the element of competition.

Hoedowns involving jigs, reels, and clog dances are mainly associated with rural whites in Appalachia, where fiddling contests often accompany contests in which each of a succession of dancers tries to outdo the previous dancer with a virtuoso display of footwork. In contest fiddling, a hoedown is a tune in fast 2/4 time, typically a jig or a schottische. Hoedowns are also associated with cowboys, ranch hands, and rural social events in the Southwest. In modern western square dance, a hoedown is a piece of music used with a spoken or chanted patter call rather than as accompaniment for sung instructions to the dancers. The best-known hoedown in classical music is the one in Aaron Copland's ballet score for *Rodeo* (1942), choreographed by Agnes de Mille. The best theatrical hoedown captured on film is Michael Kidd's rousing choreography for the barn-raising scene in *Seven Brides for Seven Brothers* (1954).

See BALLET.

BIBLIOGRAPHY
M. Rossoff: *Hoedown Heritage: the Evolution of Modern Square Dancing* (Sandusky, OH, 1977)
J. Duke: *Clog Dance in the Appalachians* (San Francisco, 1984)
G.W. Steele: *Traditional Hoedown Figures for the Appalachian 4-Couple Running Set* (Doraville, GA, 1985)
I.G. Bernstein: *Appalachian Clogging and Flatfooting Steps* (Malvern, NY, 1992)

CLAUDE CONYERS

Hoffer, Charles R(ussell) (*b* East Lansing, MI, 12 Dec 1929). Music educator and author. He received degrees from Michigan State University (MusB 1951, PhD 1955) and the Eastman School of Music (MusM 1952). He taught in the Michigan public schools at Holt (1952–3) and Grand Ledge (1953–6) and at the State University of New York, Buffalo (1956–9); he also was music supervisor in the Clayton, Missouri, public schools (1959–66) and taught at Indiana University (1966–84) and the University of Florida (1984–). Hoffer served as president of the Indiana Music Educators Association (1973–4), the North Central Division of the Music Educators National Conference (MENC) (1976–8), and the national MENC (1988–90). A prolific author of articles and books, his best-known textbooks include *Teaching Music in the Secondary Schools* (1964, 4/1991), *Introduction to Music Education* (1983), *Music Listening Today* (1999, 3/2007), (with Leon Burton and William Hughes) *Adventures in Music Listening* (1996–99), and (with H.F. Abeles and R.H. Klotman) *Foundations of Music Education* (1984, 2/1994). Hoffer received a Distinguished Alumni Award from Michigan State University (1988) and a Hoosier Musician of the Year Award from the Indiana Music Educators Association (1990). He was inducted into the Florida Music Educators Association Hall of Fame (1997) and Music Educators Hall of Fame (2006).

JOHN W. RICHMOND

Hoffman, Al (*b* Minsk, Russia, 25 Sept 1902; *d* New York, NY, 21 July 1960). Composer of Russian birth. His family moved to Seattle when he was six. After graduating from high school, he started his own nightclub band and moved to New York, where he established a reputation as a drummer and collaborator on songs with Tin Pan Alley performers. He joined ASCAP in 1930 and co-wrote a number of well-known songs with Dick Manning, Mack David, and Jerry Livingston, among many others. His songs were performed by well-known singers such as Perry Como, Frank Sinatra, Tony Bennett,

Ella Fitzgerald, Bette Midler, Patsy Cline, and Louis Armstrong. Two of his better-known songs are "Mairzy Doats" (1943) and "Bibbidi-Bobbidi-Boo" (1948) from the Disney movie *Cinderella*, for which he wrote the film score. Hoffman moved to London in 1934 but returned to the United States in 1938. He was inducted into the Songwriter's Hall of Fame in 1984 and has more than 1500 songs registered with ASCAP. Performances of his music continue to appear in contemporary movies, including *Casino* (1995), *Raging Bull* (1980), *Back to the Future: Part II* (1989), and *Ocean's Eleven* (2001).

BRADFORD LEE EDEN

Hoffman, E(lisha) A(lbright) (*b* Orwigsburg, PA, 7 May 1839; *d* Chicago, IL, 25 Nov 1929). Hymnwriter and publisher of Sunday-school and gospel hymns. He served as pastor and mission worker for the Congregational and Presbyterian churches and for the Evangelical Association (later part of the Evangelical United Brethren). Hoffman operated a small music publishing company with his son Ira, issuing many of his own songs, for which he often supplied both words and music. He also edited song collections for other companies: as the first music editor for Hope Publishing Company, he co-edited the successful series *Pentecostal Hymns*. He also edited approximately 50 hymnals and collections and the periodicals *Living Epistle* (1869–71) and Hoffman's *Musical Monthly: a Journal of Song.* Hoffman wrote more than 2000 gospel hymns, including "Are you washed in the blood of the Lamb?" (words and music, 1878), "Down at the cross" (words, 1878), "Leaning on the everlasting arms" (words, 1887), and "You have longed for sweet peace" (alternate title: "Is your all on the altar," words and music, 1900). The first of these (usually printed, without attribution, as a "Salvation Army hymn") was used by Vachel Lindsay for his poem "General William Booth Enters into Heaven," which was set to music for voice and piano by Charles Ives in 1914. Few of Hoffman's hymns appeared in the seminal *Gospel Hymns* series (edited by Philip Bliss and Ira Sankey); nevertheless, they gained widespread popularity, in part because of Hoffman's contributions to the fledgling Hope Publishing Company's successful collections. His hymns were also popular in Methodist Holiness circles.

BIBLIOGRAPHY
J.H. Hall: *Biography of Gospel Song and Hymn Writers* (New York, 1914/*R*1971)
M.R. Wilhoit and R.S. Wilson: "Elisha Albright Hoffman," *The Hymn*, xxxv.1 (1984), 35–39
W.K. McNeil: "Hoffman, Elisha Albright." *Encyclopedia of American Gospel Music*, ed. W.K. McNeil (New York, 2005), 187–188
MEL R. WILHOIT

Hoffman, Mary (Jane Eckert) (*b* Reading, PA, 18 Oct 1926; *d* Urbana, IL, 18 March 1997). Music educator. She earned degrees from Lebanon Valley College (BA 1948) and Columbia University Teachers College (MA 1951). She taught in urban public schools in Delaware (1948–9, 1952–4), Pennsylvania (1949–51), and Connecticut (1951–2), and held music supervisor positions in Philadelphia (1954–9) and Milwaukee (1959–70). She spent the remainder of her career on the faculty at the University of Illinois at Urbana-Champaign (1972–96). Hoffman was on the Wisconsin Music Educators Association Board of Directors (1963–7) and held several leadership positions with the Music Educators National Conference (MENC), among them North Central Division president (1974–6), Executive Director Search Committee chair (1976), and national president (1980–82). MENC established the Society for General Music and Society for Music Teacher Education and celebrated its 75th anniversary during her presidency. Hoffman was well known for authoring and co-authoring several elementary general music textbooks: *Making Music Your Own* (Morristown, NJ 1971), *Teaching Music, What, How, Why* (Morristown, NJ 1973), *Silver Burdett Music* (Morristown, NJ 1974, 4/1985), *World of Music* (Morristown, NJ 1988), and *The Music Connection* (Parsippany, NJ 1996). She was named a Distinguished Alumna by Lebanon Valley College (1992) and inducted into the Music Educators Hall of Fame (1998). Her papers are in the MENC archives at the University of Maryland Michelle Smith Performing Arts Library.

BIBLIOGRAPHY
"Mary E. Hoffman," *Teaching Music*, iv/6 (1997), 19 only
SHELLY C. COOPER

Hoffman, Richard (*b* Manchester, England, 24 May 1831; *d* Mount Kisco, NY, 17 Aug 1909). Pianist, teacher, and composer of English birth. He was trained by his father, who studied with Johann Nepomuk Hummel and Friedrich Kalkbrenner. When plans to study with Felix Mendelssohn did not materialize, Hoffman studied with the Viennese virtuoso LEOPOLD DE MEYER. After his arrival in New York, Hoffman's first appearance was on 16 November 1847, assisting his friend the violinist Joseph Burke. Hoffman gave his formal debut at the Broadway Tabernacle on 25 November 1847. Soon afterward, he performed Mendelssohn's Piano Concerto in g with the New York Philharmonic Society. This performance marked the beginning of a 50-year association with the society. In 1850 P.T. Barnum contracted with Hoffman to be the accompanist and piano soloist for Jenny Lind's American tours. He became a fixture of the New York music scene for the remainder of the 19th century. He appeared on more than 30 occasions with the New York Philharmonic, giving the local premieres of Wolfgang Amadeus Mozart's Piano Concertos K. 466 and K. 488, and Ludwig van Beethoven's Piano Concerto no.3 in c, op. 37. A respected chamber musician, he frequently assisted Louis Moreau Gottschalk in two-piano literature. Gottschalk dedicated the popular "Le Banjo" to Hoffman. Technical precision, clarity of phrasing, and an impressive sight-reading ability were all aspects of Hoffman's playing. His early repertoire focused on opera fantasies and transcriptions, especially those of Sigismund Thalberg. He also programmed the works of J.S. Bach, Beethoven, Johannes Brahms, Mendelssohn and Frederic Chopin.

Hoffman wrote more than 100 character pieces and transcriptions for the piano, sacred music, and songs. His memoirs, *Some Musical Recollections of Fifty Years*, appeared in 1910 with a biographical sketch by his wife and his essay "How to Stimulate Thought and Imagination in a Pupil." Malvina Hoffman, the well-known sculptor, was his daughter.

WORKS
(selective list)

Souvenir de Trovatore (de Verdi), 1856; La Gazelle, andante elegant, 1858; Caprice de Concert, sur les motifs de Favorita, Huguenots et Traviata, 1860; Dixiana, Caprice on the Popular Negro Minstrel's Melody "Dixie's Land," 1861; Ten Minutes with Mozart, trans. from Don Giovanni, 1862; Solitude pensée fugitive, 1863; Rigoletto, fantaisie caprice, 1864; Crispino e La Comare, 3d caprice de concert, 1866; Impromptu, 1867; Sonata bouffa, 1869; In Memoriam, L.M.G., 1870; Chi-ci Pipi Nini, Cuban dance, 1872; Tarantelle, 1872; Barcarolle, 1876; Beyond, reverie, op. 86, (1885)

BIBLIOGRAPHY

Obituary, *New York Times* (19 Aug 1909)

R. Hoffman: *Some Musical Recollections of Fifty Years: with a Biographical Sketch by his Wife* (New York, 1910)

J. Gillespie and A. Gillespie: *A Bibliography of Nineteenth-Century American Piano Music* (Westport, CT, 1984), 86–8, 264–5

H.C. Schonberg: *The Great Pianists: from Mozart to the Present*, rev. ed. (New York, 1987)

V.B. Lawrence, ed.: *Strong on Music: the New York Music Scene in the Days of George Templeton Strong, 1836–1862*, 3 vols. (New York, 1988–99)

SPENCER A. HUSTON

Hoffmann [Hofman], **Max** (*b* Gnesen [now Gniezno, Poland], 8 Dec 1873; *d* Hollywood, CA, 21 May 1963). Ragtime composer and arranger of Polish birth. He went to the United States in 1875 and was a violinist in an orchestra in Minneapolis at the age of 15. Shortly afterwards he published works that synthesized or collected ragtime themes: *A Rag Medley* (1897) and *Ragtime Rags* (1898). He also wrote ragtime-based popular music, such as *Yankee Land* (1904). He worked subsequently as an arranger and conductor in vaudeville and as a composer of musical scores for Broadway, including *A Parisian Model* (1906), *The Young Turk* (1910), and songs for the Rogers Brothers' burlesques. He also directed ballets featuring his wife, Gertrude Hoffmann.

Hoffmann was an early arranger and notator of ragtime. Beginning in 1896 he made syncopated arrangements of popular coon songs, which led to his larger medley arrangements. In effect, his work became a model of scoring for the nascent piano ragtime industry, and his productions helped popularize the work of such ragtime pioneers as Ernest Hogan and Ben R. Harney. Hoffmann and other transcribers and arrangers paved the way for wide popular interest in piano ragtime as a scored music and contributed to the immense popularity of the major ragtime composers Scott Joplin, Tom Turpin, James Scott, and Joseph Lamb.

BIBLIOGRAPHY

D.A. Jasen and T.J. Tichenor: *Rags and Ragtime: a Musical History* (New York, 1978)

E.A. Berlin: *Ragtime: a Musical and Cultural History* (Berkeley, 1980/*R*1984 with addenda)

WILLIAM J. SCHAFER

Hoffman Watts, Elaine (*b* Philadelphia, PA, 25 May 1932). Percussionist and teacher. She began lessons at age seven with her father, drummer and xylophonist Jake Hoffman. In the 1920s, Jake Hoffman played for Harry Kandel, leader of Philadelphia's foremost klezmer orchestra. Despite mastering traditional Yiddish-style drumming in her teens, Hoffman Watts could only find employment with her father because other orchestras were unwilling to hire a woman drummer. Hoffman Watts attended Temple University in 1951, and, after several stints in regional symphony orchestras, graduated from the Curtis Institute in Philadelphia in 1954, the first woman percussionist to do so. From 1956 to 1963 she taught percussion in that city's public school system and played occasional symphony jobs. For the next 25 years she continued to work primarily outside klezmer music, with parallel careers as a music teacher and theater musician in the Philadelphia area.

In the 1990s Hoffman Watts returned to klezmer music and has since toured and taught widely. In 1995 she and her daughter, trumpeter and singer Susan (*b* Havertown, PA, 2 June 1966) were founding members of the all-female klezmer band *KlezMs,* which was featured in Jackie Borock's documentary film *A Joyful Noise: The Lost Klezmer Music of Philadelphia* (1999). She joined the KlezKamp faculty in 2000, gaining a worldwide reputation as a teacher, performer, and enthusiastic mentor and role model. She was awarded a 2007 NEA National Heritage Fellowship. In 2010, Living Traditions released the CD *Elaine Hoffman Watts: A Living Tradition*, and directors Barry Dornfeld and Deborah Kodish released the biographical film *Eatala: A Life in Klezmer* (2010).

HENRY SAPOZNIK

Hofmann, Josef (Casimir) [József Kazimierz; Dvorsky, Michel] (*b* Kraków, Poland, 20 Jan 1876; *d* Los Angeles, CA, 16 Feb 1957). Pianist of Polish birth, son of Kazimierz Hofmann. His mother, Matylda, sang in light operas at the Kraków Theatre, where her husband was conductor. At the age of three Hofmann learned the rudiments of music from his father, for he was one of the most precocious musical prodigies in history, and equally gifted in mathematics, science, and mechanics. He toured Europe as a pianist and composer at the age of seven, and his American debut on 29 November 1887 at the Metropolitan Opera House caused an unprecedented public furor. He soon retired to Germany for further studies. In 1892, after five unsuccessful lessons with Moritz Moszkowski, he became the sole private pupil of Anton Rubinstein. Rubinstein's musical ideals greatly influenced Hofmann, who later stated that their relationship was "the most important event of my life."

Hofmann's reappearance before the public as a mature artist in late 1894 coincided with Rubinstein's death. Although his renown was limited in Britain, he enjoyed complete success in Russia, central Europe, South America, and the United States. He became director of the recently founded Curtis Institute of Music, Philadelphia, in 1926, a position he held until 1938. He and Mary Louise Curtis Bok, the institute's founder, shaped the policies of the school, which became an ideal conservatory and produced many of the finest performing musicians of the time. After 1940 he curtailed his annual tours, and he gave his final New York recital in 1946. He spent his last years experimenting with improved piano actions and recording techniques.

Between about 1910 and 1935 Hofmann was regarded as being without equal among Romantic pianists. His playing combined faultless pedaling, the most even passagework, and the widest range of dynamics with a pellucid and chaste tone, and his sudden, improvisatory eruptions served to heighten the tension and emotional content of each piece he performed. In the first part of the 20th century his playing became an ideal to which most pianists aspired, and his influence on pianists and composers at that time was pervasive (Serge Rachmaninoff dedicated his Third Concerto to him, although he never played the work, complaining of "too many notes"). He played Beethoven, Chopin, Schumann, Liszt, and much salon music, but no Brahms or 20th-century works. He was the first professional musician ever to record (cutting several cylinders as a souvenir during a visit to Thomas Edison's laboratory in New Jersey in 1887), but ultimately made few commercial recordings. Hofmann composed more than 100 works (many under the pseudonym Michel Dvorsky), held over 70 patents for scientific and mechanical inventions, and wrote two books on piano playing. His place in history adds significance to the many recordings of actual performances by him, discovered after his death. These recordings, and published evaluations of his art left by his contemporaries Anton Rubinstein, Camille Saint-Saëns, Rachmaninoff, and Igor Stravinsky, place him with Franz Liszt and Ferruccio Busoni as one of the most important of the Romantic pianists.

WRITINGS

Piano Playing (New York, 1908/*R*1920 and 1976 with *Piano Questions Answered*)

Piano Questions Answered (New York, 1909/*R*1920 and 1976 with *Piano Playing*)

BIBLIOGRAPHY

A. Chasins: *Speaking of Pianists* (New York, 1957, 2/1961/*R*)

H.C. Schonberg: *The Great Pianists* (New York, 1963, 2/1987)

N.S. Graydon: *The Amazing Marriage of Marie Eustis & Josef Hofmann* (Columbia, SC, 1965)

A.F.R. Lawrence and G. Benko: "Josef Hofmann Discography," *International Piano Library Bulletin*, i (1967), no.2, 9; nos.3–4, 11; ii (1968), no.1, 3; no.3, 3

GREGOR BENKO/*R*

Hogan, Ernest [Crowders, Reuben] (*b* Bowling Green, KY, *c*1860; *d* New York, NY, 20 May 1909). Entertainer, singer, and songwriter. He gained national recognition while touring with the all-black Richards and Pringle's Georgia Minstrel Company, where he modernized the role of the end man. He later toured with the Black Patti Troubadours and in 1900, with Billy McClain, created the Original Smart Set Company, with which he starred for two seasons. His career reached its zenith when he starred in the musical comedy he wrote with Joe Jordan, *Rufus Rastus* (1902), singing the hit song "Oh Say, Wouldn't That Be a Dream." He was also an original member of and soloist with the celebrated Memphis Students, which in 1905 presented the first concert of "syncopated music" in the United States. In 1907, with Will Vodery, he wrote the musical comedy *The Oyster Man* (lyrics by H.S. Creamer), which Hogan produced and starred in when it opened in Lima, Ohio. However, after several months on tour he was forced to retire from the company due to tuberculosis, and he died shortly afterwards.

Hogan was among the most versatile and well-known entertainers of his time, winning worldwide acclaim during his long career on the stage. He caused a certain amount of controversy in 1896 with the publication of his hit song "All Coons Look Alike to Me," which was considered by many to be an insult to his race; Hogan conceived it, however, simply as a popular ragtime song. The song spurred the popularity of the coon song and provided many opportunities to songwriters, black and white.

BIBLIOGRAPHY

SouthernB

H.T. Sampson: *Blacks in Blackface: a Source Book on Early Black Musical Shows* (Metuchen, NJ, 1980)

T. Riis: *Just before Jazz: Black Musical Theatre in New York, 1890–1915* (Washington, DC, 1989)

D. Janson and G. Jones: *Spreadin' Rhythm Around: Black Popular Songwriters, 1880–1930* (New York, 1998)

L. Abbot and D. Seroff: *Out of Sight: the Rise of African American Popular Music, 1889–1895* (Jackson, MS, 2007)

L. Abbot and D. Seroff: *Ragged but Right: Black Traveling Shows, "Coon Songs" and the Dark Pathway to Blues and Jazz* (Jackson, MS, 2007)

HENRY T. SAMPSON/BRANDI A. NEAL

Hogan, Moses (George) (*b* New Orleans, LA, 13 March 1957; *d* New Orleans, LA, 11 Feb 2003). Conductor, arranger, and pianist. In addition to his early piano training, Hogan was influenced by his upbringing in the African American Baptist church, particularly the unaccompanied spiritual arrangements he heard there. Hogan was one of the first graduates of the New Orleans Center for Creative Arts; he received a degree in piano performance from Oberlin College in 1979 and briefly continued his piano studies at Juilliard.

Hogan began arranging choral music in 1980, the same year he formed the New World Ensemble. At that time, Hogan perceived a decrease in popularity of traditional spirituals, so he began composing new arrangements to revive the genre. In 1993, he founded the Moses Hogan Chorale, one of only two American choirs invited to perform at the 1996 World Choral Symposium in Sydney, Australia. In 1998, Hogan assembled his most notable group, the Moses Hogan Singers, whose debut album *Give Me Jesus* was released in 2002.

Hogan's first published arrangement, *Elijah Rock*, came in 1994 at the encouragement of André Thomas (Florida State University) after he heard Hogan's Chorale perform at a convention. Hogan published 80 choral arrangements and eight solo voice arrangements in his lifetime; perhaps the most notable among them are *The Battle of Jericho*, *Ev'ry Time I Feel the Spirit*, and *Give Me Jesus*.

In September 2002, Hogan was hospitalized for a brain tumor-induced stroke and died five months later at the age of 45.

ANNE SHELLEY

Hogg, Ima (*b* Mineola, TX, 10 July 1882; *d* London, England, 19 Aug 1975). Art collector, preservationist, musician, and philanthropist. She was the only daughter of lawyer and Texas governor Colonel James Stephen Hogg. She was named after the heroine in the candid Civil War poem "The Fate of Marvin," written by her uncle, Thomas Hogg [pseudo. Tom R. Burnett]. She never married and was known simply as Miss Ima for most of her life.

Inspired by her mother, Hogg began piano lessons at around five years of age. She attended the University of Texas at Austin for two years before moving to New York in 1901 to study piano at the National Conservatory of Music. Between 1907 and 1908, she studied piano with Franz Xaver Scharwenka (1850–1924) in Vienna and Martin Krause (1853–1918) in Berlin. Upon returning to the United States, Hogg shied away from a career as concert pianist and chose instead to immerse herself in musical events and teach piano. In 1913 she helped establish the Houston SO under the direction of Julian Paul Blitz and served the Houston Symphony Association as vice president from 1913 to 1917 and as president from 1917 to 1918 (the orchestra disbanded from 1918 to 1930) and again from 1946 to 1956.

Discovery of oil on the family property in 1918 became a source of great wealth for Ima and her three brothers and funded the construction of their 14-acre estate, Bayou Bend. Hogg became an avid collector of art and furniture and formed the Houston Child Guidance Center (1929) and Hogg Foundation for Mental Hygiene (later Health) at the University of Texas (1940). She donated her art collection along with Bayou Bend to the Museum of Fine Arts, Houston, and is commonly called "the First Lady of Texas" for her cultural contributions.

BIBLIOGRAPHY
L.K. Iscoe: *Ima Hogg, First Lady of Texas: Reminiscences and Recollections of Family and Friends* (Austin, 1976)
G.C. Neeley: *Miss Ima and the Hogg Family* (Dallas, 1992)
V. Bernhard: *Ima Hogg: the Governor's Daughter* (New York, 1996)
GARY GALVÁN

Hogwood, Christopher (Jarvis Haley) (*b* Nottingham, England, 10 Sept 1941). English conductor, scholar, and harpsichordist. While studying music and classics at Pembroke College in Cambridge University, he was a keyboard student of Rafael Puyana, Mary Potts, and Gustav Leonhardt. After completing his BA he traveled on a scholarship to Prague, where he studied at Charles University with Milan Postolka and at the Academy of Music with Zuzana Ruzickova. In 1965 he joined The Academy of St. Martin-in-the-Fields as the continuo

performer and in 1967 was a founding member along with David Munrow of The Early Music Consort of London. In 1973 he was the founder-director of the Academy of Ancient Music. Among his many contributions as a musicologist are his book *Handel* (London, 2007), and articles on George Frederick Handel (*The Cambridge Handel Encyclopedia*), C.P.E. Bach, Franz Josef Haydn, Wolfgang Amadeus Mozart, Ludwig van Beethoven, and Felix Mendelssohn. Hogwood serves as an advisor to many musical groups, including the Haydn Society of North America and the Harvard Early Music Society. His ongoing contributions are celebrated in the collection *Essays in Honor of Christopher Hogwood: The Maestro's Direction* (Metuchen, NJ, 2010). In 2010 he became general editor of the complete edition of the Geminiani Opera Omnia (Bologna) and a member of the board of the Bohuslav Martinů Complete Edition and C.P.E. Bach Complete Works Edition. He has led many celebrated ensembles throughout the world and in the United States, including stints as principal guest conductor of the St. Paul Chamber Orchestra (Minnesota) and as former conductor and now conductor laureate of the Handel and Haydn Society (Boston).

CHARLES JURGENSMEIER

Hohnstock. German-born duo formed by the brother and sister Carl [Karl, Charles] Hohnstock (*b* Braunschweig, Germany, 1828; *d* Braunschweig, Germany, 5 Aug 1889) and Adelaide [Adèle, Adele] Hohnstock (*b* Braunschweig, Germany, c1830; *d* ?Philadelphia, PA, 1856). Carl was a violinist and pianist, Adelaide a pianist; they were both composers and teachers. They arrived in the United States in 1848 or 1849 after garnering praise during their European concerts. Their American appearances included performances with the Germania Musical Society in Baltimore (February 1849) and the Harvard Musical Association's Chamber Concert Series in Boston (December 1849). They established themselves in Philadelphia, where they taught violin and piano lessons and organized chamber concerts. Adelaide died suddenly in 1856, and Carl returned to Germany during the Civil War.

Adelaide performed and published one of the most challenging keyboard pieces written by a woman composer in antebellum America. The "Hohnstock Polka," which consisted of a polka theme with three variations, showcased her prowess at the keyboard and employed the features of a larger, sonorous piano. This "celebrated" and "famous" polka melody was made into a dance set and simpler version, which were published not only in Philadelphia, but also in New York, Boston, and Baltimore. Stephen Foster included the popular melody in his 1854 published collection *Social Orchestra*.

WORKS

BY ADELAIDE HOHNSTOCK
(selective list)

Pf: Hohnstock concert polka: with variations for the piano forte, op.1 (1849); Le Diamant polka brillante, op.7 (1854; repr. in *Three Centuries of American Music*, vol. 4); Sentimental polka (1855); La gracieuse, polka de salon (1855)

BY CARL HOHNSTOCK
(selective list)

Pf: Grande sonate, op.1 (1846); Marche d'amazones, op.2 (New York, 1850); Une soire à Philadelphie, quadrille (1851); Lieder ohne Worte: Heimweh (Thoughts of home) (1854); Lieder ohne Worte: Wiegelied (Cradle song) (1854); Lieder ohne Worte: Romanze (Romanza) (1854); Choral : Eine feste Burg (1859) [arr. from *Les Huguenots*]

Orch: Hail Columbia! Fest-Ouvertüre für grosses Orchester ([1862])

BIBLIOGRAPHY

H.E. Johnson: "The Germania Musical Society," *MQ*, xxxix (1953), 75–93

P. Paige: "Chamber Music in Boston: the Harvard Musical Association," *JRME*, xviii (1970), 134–42

S. Glickman, ed.: *Three Centuries of American Music: American Keyboard music 1866 through 1910*, iv (Boston, 1990)

J. Tick: *American women composers before 1870* (Rochester, NY, 1995)

JENNIFER C.H.J. WILSON

Hoiby, Lee (*b* Madison, WI, 17 Feb 1926; *d* New York, NY, 28 March 2011). Composer and pianist. He began playing the piano at five; early compositional efforts began soon after. At 15, he began a six-year course of intensive piano study with GUNNAR JOHANSEN, preparing for a career as a concert pianist, although he continued to compose concurrently. In 1944, while studying with Johansen, he entered the University of Wisconsin (BM 1947). Subsequently, he went on to Mills College, working, at Johansen's suggestion, with EGON PETRI, who became Hoiby's second significant mentor. In 1948, he was introduced to GIAN CARLO MENOTTI, who invited him to study at the Curtis Institute. It was Menotti, with whom he worked until 1952, who encouraged him to concentrate on composition. Meanwhile, he returned to Mills to complete his graduate study (MA 1952). His own music soon attracted attention, and he began to garner auspicious performances and commissions. He was disinclined to teach, and his circumstances freed him from having to affiliate himself with educational institutions. Later on he revived his career as a pianist and, in addition to his fruitful compositional career, continued to participate actively in performances of his own works until shortly before his death. He lived for many years in New York City and its environs, before moving to a rural area in the Catskill Mountains of upstate New York, where he spent the final decades of his life.

Largely free of the atonality and harmonic dissonance fashionable during the middle years of the 20th century, Hoiby's music is best characterized as neo-romantic, following the lineage of Barber and Menotti. The influence of the former is evident in his warm lyricism and poignant emotional expressiveness, while that of the latter is found in an effective dramatic sense and an appetite for light, genial humor. Though much of his music is characterized by a disarming diatonic simplicity, his more ambitious works tend toward greater harmonic and textural complexity. Interest in his music has centered chiefly on his operatic, choral, and vocal works, which seemed to stimulate his most deeply felt efforts, while endearing him to singers, from students to such leading figures as Leontyne Price and Marilyn Horne. Some of these works—for example *Summer and Smoke, Galileo Galilei,* and *The Tempest*—achieve an eloquence comparable to the finest works of Barber. Although Hoiby's music suffered the disregard that faced conservative composition during the 1960s and 70s, interest has revived and grown since the early 1980s, to the point where he is regarded as one of the foremost neo-romantic traditionalists of his generation.

WORKS

Opera: The Scarf (1, H. Duncan, after Chekhov), op.12, 1955 (Spoleto, Italy, 1958); Beatrice (3, M. Mardi, after Maeterlinck), op.18, 1959, withdrawn; Natalia Petrovna (2, W. Ball, after Turgenev), op.24, 1964 (New York, 1964) [retitled A Month in the Country, 1982]; Summer and Smoke (2, L. Wilson, after T. Williams), op.27, 1970 (St. Paul, MN, 1971); Something New for the Zoo (1, D. Huppler), op.31, 1979 (Cheverly, MD, 17 May 1982); The Italian Lesson (monologue, after R. Draper), op.34, 1980 (Newport, RI, 1982); The English Painter (monologue, after R. Draper, op.40, 1983; The Tempest (3, M. Shulgasser, after Shakespeare), op.43, 1986 (Des Moines, IA, 1986); Bon Appetit! (monologue, after J. Child), op.45, 1986 (Washington DC, 8 March 1989); This is the Rill Speaking (1, M. Shulgasser, after L. Wilson), op.56, 1992; What Is This Light? (melodrama, after V. Woolf), op.62, 1994 (New York City, 1995); Romeo and Juliet (M. Shulgasser, after Shakespeare), op. 66, 2002

Other stage: Hearts, Meadows and Flags (ballet, R. Wagner), op.3, 1950 (Chicago, 1967); After Eden (ballet, J. Butler), op.25, 1966 (New York, 1967); Landscape (ballet), op.26, 1967 (New York, 1967)

Incid music to c. 20 plays

Choral: Songs of the Fool (Shakespeare), op. 14, SATB, 1955; A Hymn of the Nativity (R. Crashaw), op.19, S, Bar, SATB, orch, 1960; Hymn to the New Age (Hoiby), SATB, org/brass qt/orchestra, 1974; Galileo Galilei (oratorio, B. Stavis), op.29, solo vv, SATB, orch, 1975; Magnificat and Nunc dimittis, op.38, SATB, org/st orch, 1983; Psalm 92, op. 42, SATB, org/brass, timp, 1984; Dona nobis pacem, op.55, SA, pf, 1991; St Mary Magdalene (Crashaw), op.63, SATB, brass, org, 1995; Whitman Symphony, op. 64A, Mez, Bar, SATB, orch, 1988–1996; And the Waters Flow (Psalm 148/9), op. 71, SATB, org, br, 2000; Jacob's Ladder, op. 73, SATB, org, br, 2002; Nature (Emerson), op. 77, SATB, orch, 2011

Solo Vocal: Tides of Sleep (T. Wolfe), op.22, Bar, orch, 1961; 3 French Songs (Rimbaud), op.36, Bar, pf, 1980; Bermudas (A. Marvell), op.37, S, Mez, pf, 1982; O Florida [5 songs] (W. Stevens), op.39, S, pf, 1983; I Have a Dream (M.L. King), op.46, Bar, pf/orch, 1987; Emily Dickinson Songs (4), S, pf, 1987; I Was There [5 songs] (Whitman), op.49, Bar, pf, 1988; 3 Ages of Woman [3 songs] (E. Bishop), op.51, 1v, pf, 1990; Southern Voices [4 songs], op.53, Mez, pf, 1990; Rain Forest [4 songs] (E. Bishop), op.65, Bar, Mez, ww qnt, pf, 1996; The Life of the Bee [5 songs] (J. Beam), op. 68, Mez, vc, pf, 1997; Shakespeare Sonnets and Soliloquies, op. 69, S, st qt, 1998

c. 60 additional solo songs

Orch: Pastoral Dances, op. 4, fl, cham. orch., 1950; Summer Suite, op. 5A, band, 1951; arr. 2006; Suite, op. 8, 1953; Design, op. 9, str, 1955; Overture to a Farce, op. 15, 1957; Pf Conc. No. 1, op.17, 1957; Summer and Smoke: Orch. Suite, op. 27A, 1975; Music for a Celebration, op. 30, 1975; Pf Conc. no.2, op.33, 1980; Serenade, op.44, vn, orch/pf, 1983; Rock Valley Narrative, op.50, 1989; Fl Conc., op.58, 1950, rev. 1993; Prayer and Procession, op. 76, band, 2009

Chbr: Sonata, vn, pf, op.5, 1951, rev. 1979; Diversions, ww qnt, op.10, 1953; rev. 1989; Sextet, op.28, wind qnt, pf, 1974; Ten for Ten, op.35A, dectet, 1982; Overture: To a Song, op.48, ob, pf quartet, 1988; Sonata, op.59, vc, pf, 1993; Dark Rosaleen, op. 67, pf quartet, 1997; Trio, op. 72, vn, cl, pf, 2001

Piano: Toccata, op.1, pf, 1949; Nocturne, op.6, pf, 1950, rev. 1981; 5 Preludes, op.7, pf, 1952, rev. 1977; Capriccio on 5 Notes, op.23, pf, 1962; 10 Variations on a Schubert Ländler, op.35, pf, 1980; Narrative, op.41, pf, 1983; Variations and Theme, op.60, carillon, 1993; Theme and Variations, op.61, org, 1994; Stray Dogs (suite in 6 mvts), op. 74, 2 pf, 2005

Principal publishers: G. Schirmer, Rock Valley Music

BIBLIOGRAPHY

EwenD

L. Hoiby: "Making Tennessee Williams Sing," *New York Times* (13 June 1971)

B. Fischer-Williams: "'Summer and Smoke'—On the Wings of Music with Lee Hoiby," *City Center Arts*, ii/2 (1971–2), 3, 6

G. Schmidgall: "A Long Voyage," *ON*, l/17 (1985–6), 10–13 [on *The Tempest*]

"Lee Hoiby," *CBY*, xlviii/3 (1987), 17–21

W. Krusemark: *Two Early Operas by Lee Hoiby, "The Scarf" and "A Month in the Country": a Stylistic Analysis and Commentary* (diss., U. of Missouri, Kansas City, 1989)

R.A. Crosby: *The Piano Music of Lee Hoiby* (diss., U. of Cincinnati, 1990)

D. Fredrickson: "Lee Hoiby: Incurable Romantic," *Clavier* xxxi/1 (Jan 1992), 16–24

A. Robinson: "An Interview with Lee Hoiby," *American Organist* (Dec 1992), 58–60

L.E. Bade: *Lee Hoiby: the composer and his compositional style, his role in the history of American music, and his song output* (diss., U. of Texas, Austin, 1994)

J.W. Barker (ed.): *"Summer and Smoke": the Opera Prompter* (U. of Wisconsin, Madison, Dec 1995)

J. Forman: "The Song in the Flower: Music of Lee Hoiby," *Fanfare*, xx/2 (Nov–Dec 1996), 132–6

C.G. Neubert: *Lee Hoiby: His Life, His Vocal Writing Style and an Annotation of Selected Songs* (diss., U. of W. Virginia, 2003)

Z. Woolfe: "The Lonely Composer: Lee Hoiby Spent His Career Alone and Against the Grain. Will That Make His Music Survive?," *New York Observer*, 14 Dec 2010

Obituary, *New York Times* (29 March 2011)

WALTER SIMMONS

Hokey pokey. A novelty song and dance. It became a popular phenomenon after the 1952 release of a recording by Ray Anthony and His Orchestra. Typically, dancers form a circle and follow instructions given in the lyrics:

> You put your right hand in,
> You put your right hand out,
> You put your right hand in,
> And you shake it all about,
> You do the hokey pokey
> And you turn yourself around.
> That's what it's all about.

Subsequent verses describe similar movements for the left hand, right foot, left foot, head, shoulders, hips, rear end, and "your whole self." By the mid-1950s, the hokey pokey was being performed as a social mixer at weddings, high school dances, and children's parties all over North America.

Provenance of the song has been a matter of legal dispute. Authorship is usually ascribed to Larry LaPrise, a member of the Ram Trio, which recorded "The Hokey Pokey" in the late 1940s. However, a similar song, "The Hokey Pokey Dance," had been copyrighted a few years earlier, in 1944, by club musician Robert Degen, who sued LaPrise for infringement in 1956. The case was settled out of court, with the competing claimants sharing credit and royalties.

Neither of these two versions may be original. A similar song popular with soldiers in England during World War II was ascribed to various British songwriters. Moreover, some scholastic churchmen have noted that the words "hokey pokey" derive from "hocus pocus" and have claimed that the song was written by 18th-century Puritans to mock the language of the Latin Mass. This matter remains unresolved.

CLAUDE CONYERS

Holcomb [Halcomb], **Roscoe** (*b* Daisy, KY, 5 Sept 1912; *d* 1 Feb 1981). Traditional Appalachian singer and banjoist. A traditional musician from the coalfields of Kentucky's Cumberland Mountains, Holcomb was raised with a background in the Old Regular Baptist hymnody that strongly colored his vocal and instrumental performance.

Holcomb possessed a penetrating singing style characterized by musician John Cohen as the "high lonesome sound." His sense of timing and vocal control were marked by long-held tones, dictated by an inner rhythmic freedom described by Bob Dylan as "an untamed sense of control."

His claw hammer banjo style complemented his fluid vocal technique with quirky rhythmic fills. An accomplished guitarist capable of playing pocket knife "slide" style, he also performed on harmonica and fiddle. Holcomb possessed a large, eclectic repertoire that included Old Regular Baptist and Holiness Pentecostal hymns, traditional mountain frolics, square dance tunes, popular recorded songs, ballads, and blues.

Working as a coal miner, construction worker, and farmer until his health declined, Holcomb became a public performer during the urban folk revival following John Cohen's initial field work visit in 1959. He appeared at the Chicago Folk Festival (1960) and toured Europe with musicians such as the Stanley Brothers (1966). Several coal-dust-related respiratory illnesses terminated his performing career in 1978.

RECORDINGS
(selective list)
The High Lonesome Sound (Folkways Records and Service Corp., 1965, reissued on Smithsonian Folkways 1998)
An Untamed Sense of Control (Smithsonian Folkways, 2003)

RON PEN

Holden, Oliver (*b* Shirley, MA, 18 Sept 1765; *d* Charlestown, MA, 4 Sept 1844). Composer and tunebook compiler. He received a formal education of only a few months' duration in Groton, Massachusetts, was apprenticed briefly to a cabinetmaker in Grafton, and then worked as a farmer in Groton and Pepperell (1779). He served in the Revolutionary War, after which he settled in Charlestown, Massachusetts, and worked for a time as a carpenter. By the early 1790s he had become a prominent public figure there because of his extensive land dealings. He gave the lot and a large sum of money for the erection of a Baptist church in the town, and in 1809, after a congregational split, he became the "teaching minister" of another newly established Baptist church. He also wrote and published hymn texts. Holden served as a town official (selectman, assessor, justice of the peace) for more than 50 years, and between 1818 and 1833 he represented Charlestown in the state House of Representatives.

Holden's early musical training consisted of two months' instruction in a singing school in 1783. Shortly thereafter he began to teach singing schools of his own, and his first published tunes appeared in *The Federal Harmony* (Boston, 1788). During the period from 1792 to 1808 he taught singing schools and composed prolifically; his published compositions consist of approximately 250 works, including 25 anthems, and he had a hand in at least 15 anthologies, some of them later editions of previous collections. After 1796 he stopped signing his name to most of his published pieces and tunebooks, with the notable exception of the last three editions of *The Worcester Collection* (Worcester, MA, 1797–1803), one of the most influential tunebooks of its day. Holden was called upon several times to furnish music for special occasions: for the memorial service for George Washington on 22 February 1800 he brought out *Sacred Dirges* (Boston, 1800). His ode "Auspicious Morn" and hymn tune "Beneficence," commissioned for the Stone Chapel Church, Boston, were for years performed there on Christmas Day and when charitable services were held; both were published in his *Plain Psalmody* (Boston, 1800). His "Coronation" is the only hymn tune by an 18th-century New Englander still found in most present-day Protestant hymnals.

Holden's published music tends to follow European theoretical principles more closely than does that of his native-born contemporaries. He joined Hans Gram and Samuel Holyoke as co-author of the influential, pro-European *Massachusetts Compiler of Theoretical Principles* (Boston, 1795), and in the 1790s he sided with the reform movement. As an old man he expressed regret that he had begun to compose before learning to pay proper "attention to musical science" (McCormick, 1963, 161). Nevertheless, he was remembered in his later years as a Yankee psalmodist; a group that formed in Boston during the 1830s to sing the sacred music of earlier generations of New Englanders called itself the Billings and Holden Society. He is buried in the Phipps Street Cemetery, Charlestown.

Miscellaneous correspondence of Holden's is held by the Massachusetts Historical Society and Phillips Academy in Andover; the Boston Public Library also owns an important Holden letter. The Bostonian Society owns additional manuscripts and an organ that once belonged to Holden.

BIBLIOGRAPHY

DAB

S.P. Cheney: *The American Singing Book* (Boston, 1879/R1980), 178

J. Julian: *A Dictionary of Hymnology* (London, rev. 2/1907/R1957)

F.J. Metcalf: *American Writers and Compilers of Sacred Music* (New York, 1925/R1967)

D.W. McCormick: *Oliver Holden, Composer and Anthologist* (diss., Union Theological Seminary, 1963)

K.D. Kroeger: *The Worcester Collection of Sacred Harmony and Sacred Music in America, 1786–1803* (diss., Brown U., 1976)

D.W. Music: "Oliver Holden (1765–1844): an Early Baptist Composer in America," *Singing Baptists: Studies in Baptist Hymnody in America*, ed. H. Eskew, D.W. Music, and P.A. Richardson (Nashville, 1991), 17–25

D. W. Music, ed.: *Oliver Holden (1765–1844): Selected Works* (New York, 1998)

D. W. Music: "*The Young Convert's Companion* (1806), *The Boston Collection of Sacred and Devotional Hymns* (1808), and Oliver Holden," *Jubilate, Amen!: a Festschrift in Honor of Donald Paul Hustad*, ed. P.A. Richardson and T. Sharp (Hillsdale, NY, 2010), 267–87

RICHARD CRAWFORD/DAVID W. MUSIC

Holden, Stephen (*b* Morristown, NJ, 18 July 1941). Writer on music and film. He graduated from Yale University in 1963 with a BA in English, and in late 1971 began writing pop and rock reviews as a freelancer for *Rolling Stone*. He remained a regular contributor there through 1982, writing reviews and occasional features on a wide range of popular music spanning singer-songwriters, soul, R&B, and more. During this period he also freelanced as a popular music critic and journalist for publications such as the *Village Voice* and *The Atlantic*, and starting in 1972, he worked for RCA Records—first as a photo editor and staff writer, and then briefly as an executive for artists and repertoire in 1976. He wrote a satirical novel inspired by his experiences in the music industry titled *Triple Platinum* (New York, 1980). In 1981 he started writing for the *New York Times* as a freelance popular music critic, but after several years, in the face of a changing popular music landscape, started to gradually transition to covering film for the *Times*. In 1988 he became a staff writer, focusing primarily on film, theater, and cabaret. Holden and six other writers received a Grammy Award for Best Album Notes for *The Voice: The Columbia Years, a Frank Sinatra Anthology* (1986). He appears in the Clint Eastwood documentaries *Tony Bennett: The Music Never Ends* (2007) and *Johnny Mercer: The Dream's on Me* (2009).

ALEX HARRIS STEIN

Holdridge, Lee [Elwood] (*b* Port-Au-Prince, Haiti, 3 March 1944). Composer and arranger of Haitian birth. Born to an American father and a Puerto Rican mother and raised in Costa Rica, where he studied violin with Hugo Mariani, he arrived in the United States in 1958. After studying composition and conducting in high school with Henry Lasker in Boston, he attended the Manhattan School of Music under the tutelage of NICOLAS FLAGELLO and LUDMILA ULEHLA. In New York he specialized in writing dance arrangements for musical productions beginning in 1966. By 1970 he was composing for the contemporary instrumental group The Seventh Century. That same year, for "Summerland," from the Joffrey Ballet's *Trinity*, he combined a rock band with an orchestra. Work as Neil Diamond's music director and arranger led him to adapt the singer's music for the 1973 film *Jonathan Livingston Seagull*. Holdridge went on to score *Mr. Mom*, *The Old Gringo*, and others. His themes for television series include *Eight Is Enough*, *Moonlighting*, and *Beauty and the Beast*. With more than 100 television features, such as *Do You Know the Muffin Man?* and *The Mists of Avalon*, he is one of the most prolific composers in the genre. High-profile miniseries include *East of Eden* and *Tuskegee Airmen*. In addition to composing for the major television and cable networks, he has provided music for Steve Krantz Productions, Wolf Film Productions, and numerous others. His compositional output for the concert hall has been eclectic, encompassing ballet, one-act operas, and symphonic works. He has provided arrangements for recordings artists ranging from John Denver to Placido Domingo. Holdridge has scored six documentaries for Moriah Films, based at the Simon Wiesenthal Center, from *The Long Way Home* to *I Have Never Forgotten You*. Blending contemporary pop and traditional music, Holdridge is equally adept at symphonic, rock, and electronic scoring. His music tends to be lyrical, thematic, and story-driven.

WORKS
(selective list)

FILM SCORES

Jonathan Livingston Seagull, 1973 (arranger for N. Diamond); The Other Side of the Mountain Part 2, 1978; The Beastmaster, 1982; Mr. Mom, 1983; Micki & Maude, 1984; Splash, 1984; Big Business, 1988; Old Gringo, 1989; Unlikely Heroes, 2003; Brothers at War, 2009

TELEVISION MUSIC

East of Eden (ABC miniseries), 1981; Moonlighting (ABC series theme), 1985; Beauty and the Beast (CBS series theme), 1989; Do You Know the Muffin Man? (CBS movie), 1990; Call of the Wild (CBS movie), 1993; Buffalo Girls (CBS movie), 1995; Tuskegee Airmen (HBO miniseries), 1996; Mutiny (NBC movie), 1999; The Mists of Avalon (TNT movie), 2002; Saving Milly (CBS movie), 2005

CONCERT MUSIC

"Summerland," from the ballet Trinity (2d mvt), for orch, choir, rock ens, 1970; Scenes of Summer, sym suite, 1973; Serenade for ob and str, 1973; Conc. for vn and str orch, 1975; Conc. for va and chbr orch, 1977; Conc. for vn and orch no.2, 1981; Ode to Orion, Fantasy for solo hn and orch, 2005

OPERA

Lazarus and his Beloved, op, (1, K. Gibran) 1977, sym suite, 1981; Journey to Cordoba (1, R. Sparks) 1995; Concierto para Mendez (1, R. Sparks), 2006

BIBLIOGRAPHY

M. Humphrey: "Lee Holdridge: Matching the Music to the Moment," *Hollywood Reporter* ccc/41 (22 Jan 1988), S9–S10

L. Barth: "Lee Holdridge: a Man of Many Styles," *The Score* xix/3 (2004), 13, 20, 22

WARREN M. SHERK

Hole. Rock band led by COURTNEY LOVE.

Holeman, John Dee (*b* Hillsborough, NC, 4 April 1929). Piedmont blues guitarist, singer, dancer, and storyteller. He grew up on a farm in rural Orange County, North Carolina. When he was 13 or 14 years old, he learned acoustic guitar by watching his uncle and cousin. He drew repertoire from the artists he heard on the radio, such as Blind Boy Fuller, Brownie McGhee, and Lightnin' Hopkins. He played at social gatherings in the community and added buck- and tap-dancing, which he also learned from his uncle and cousin. In 1954 he moved to Durham where he started to play electric guitar and incorporated more modern blues, including songs by Muddy Waters and Jimmy Reed. Teaming up with pianist Quentin "Fris" Holloway (1918–2008), Holeman performed in and around Durham. In 1976 folklorist Glenn Hinson invited Holeman to a local festival that attracted 5000 audience members. Since then he has been playing professionally. During the 1980s, he toured in and outside the United States with Holloway. While his precise finger picking—as heard in "Step It Up and Go" (1999)—shows influence from Piedmont blues masters, Blind Boy Fuller and Rev. Gary Davis, Holeman employs a more eclectic style, as in "Give Me Back My Wig," also on *Bull Durham Blues*, which recalls the style of Lightnin' Hopkins. Holeman is a recipient of a National Heritage Fellowship Award from the National Endowment for the Arts (1988) and a North Carolina Heritage Award (1994).

RECORDINGS

Bull City After Dark (Silver Spring, 1990); *Piedmont Blues from North Carolina* (Inedit, 1992); *Bull Durham Blues* (Music Maker, 1999); *John Dee Holeman with Taj Mahal* (Music Maker, 2004); *John Dee Holeman and the Wifs Band* (Music Maker, 2006); *You Got to Lose, You Can't Win All the Time* (Music Maker, 2008)

BIBLIOGRAPHY

B.L. Pearson: "North Carolina Blues, John Dee Holeman: Bull City Blues," *Living Blues*, cvii (1993), 31–2

MITSUTOSHI INABA

Holiday, Billie [Harris, Elinore; Fagan, Eleanora; Lady Day] (*b* Philadelphia, PA, 7 April 1915; *d* New York, NY, 17 July 1959). Jazz singer. She heard records by Bessie Smith as a child, but Louis Armstrong was her biggest influence. She was one of the first jazz singers and is still widely regarded as the greatest by those who believe that the essence of jazz singing is to make a lyric come alive with personal meaning. She was usually called Eleanora as a child. Her father, Clarence Holiday, played guitar in Fletcher Henderson's band, but never lived with her; her mother, Sadie, adopted the surname of her father, Charlie Fagan, around 1920, but neither Sadie nor Sadie's mother had been married. The surname Harris, which appears on Holiday's birth certificate, came from her mother's side.

Holiday grew up in the streets of Baltimore. She was locked up twice in the House of Good Shepherd for Colored Girls, once because she was truant from school and again because she had been a victim of statutory rape, but both times mainly because there was no one looking after her. By this time she was already singing in the back rooms of brothels and taverns. She went to New York around 1927, where she and her mother were both arrested for prostitution in 1929. As a teenager she worked in clubs in Harlem, where her strength of personality earned her the nickname Lady. The speakeasies had no sound systems, so she sang the same song at each table, improvising each chorus. John Hammond heard her and produced her first recordings in 1933 with a studio band led by Benny Goodman. These were typical novelties of the time and pitched too high for her. She appeared with Duke Ellington in a short film, *Rhapsody in Black*, in early 1935 and made a sensational debut at the Apollo, where the emcee Ralph Cooper advised Frank Schiffman to book her, famously saying: "It ain't the blues...I don't know what it is, but you got to hear her." The name Billie may have come from the film star Billie Dove; she had been calling herself Halliday, but engaged for a return performance, she came back to the Apollo as Billie Holiday.

In July 1935 Holiday made the first of more than 100 recordings on which her fame mainly still rests. These were made quickly and cheaply for jukeboxes, using head arrangements played by small groups under Teddy Wilson's leadership with whichever jazzmen happened to be in town; many of these turned out to be the greatest players of the era. Holiday's recordings sold well enough that she was engaged to record under her own

Billie Holiday, 1957. (D. Hunstein/Lebrecht Music & Arts)

name as well as with Wilson. It is not true that the songs were second-rate. Holiday and Wilson chose the ones they liked best from a stack of 30 or 40 for each session, and many of them were hits at the time; nobody knew which ones would become standards. In any case she transmuted them into gold, bending notes and often recomposing a melody line. She sang behind the beat, endowing lyrics with languor, irony, resignation, and sexuality, depending on the song, and there was often an infectious joy. She was a musician taking her chorus like one of the others. Her vocal texture was coarse yet girlish, an acquired taste but profoundly affecting to many, and her timbre and time were unique. Some of her best recordings were effectively duets with the tenor saxophonist Lester Young, who named her Lady Day; she named him Prez—short for President— and the nicknames stuck as long as they lived.

Holiday toured with Count Basie in 1937 and Artie Shaw in 1938, and suffered racism on the road. By 1939 her recording contract was owned by Columbia, who allowed her to record for Milt Gable's Commodore label that year because Columbia didn't want to record "Strange Fruit," a setting of a powerful poem by Lewis Allen about the lynching of African Americans; this was a jukebox hit and was backed with her own song "Fine and Mellow." After the musicians' union recording ban of the early 1940s, Holiday made more recordings for Gabler. He subsequently took her to Decca, where he was a producer, because he wanted her to record "Lover Man," which he thought would be a pop hit. Holiday asked for and got backing with strings, and "Lover Man" became her only Billboard chart entry, in 1945. Although her lyrical interpretations were always fine, some of the Decca recordings with strings have a slushy effect, but some of the later ones are better; in 1949 she recorded duets with her beloved Armstrong, including "My Sweet Hunk o' Trash." Her first solo concert, at Town Hall in

New York in early 1946, was a success. In the same year she appeared in the film *New Orleans*, a dire Hollywood version of the history of jazz saved only by its musical content; Holiday and Armstrong played a maid and a butler respectively. Holiday had an addictive personality: she had discovered heroin by the early 1940s and was an alcoholic by the end of the decade. Her husband Jimmy Monroe, whom she had married in 1941, was often accused of introducing her to heroin, but there is no evidence of this, and it is likely that she found it by herself. In 1947 she was sentenced to a year in prison for possession. At a concert in Carnegie Hall in 1948 her excellent accompanist was the pianist Bobby Tucker; she broke the house record and then broke her own record at a return engagement a week later.

After Holiday's year in prison, John Levy regarded her as a business investment, kept her short of money and beat her up. On the West Coast in 1949 they were both arrested for possession of opium; she beat the rap, and the next track she recorded for Decca was "'Tain't nobody's business if I do." (During this period there was another John Levy who played bass for her, who later went into artist management and suffered from having the same name as the wannabe gangster.)

In 1950 Holiday was dropped by Decca and made a short film with Basie's sextet. In 1953 she signed with Norman Granz, who produced her until 1957. The following year she toured Europe and performed at the first Newport Jazz Festival, where Lester Young made a surprise appearance after a period of estrangement from her, probably because of her drug addiction. By this time Holiday's range had narrowed and her voice had deteriorated. Her unique timbre was still there, but she had become more and more unreliable, although some thought she was a better interpreter than ever. With Louis McKay she was arrested again in early 1956 for possession; he became her second husband so they couldn't testify against each other, and they got probation. Accompanists in this period included Carl Drinkard and Mal Waldron, with whom she appeared at the Newport festival in 1957. Holiday made a poignant appearance with Young that year on the CBS TV program "Sound of Jazz."

While making the album *Lady in Satin* for Columbia in 1958, Holiday asked for a string orchestra conducted by Ray Ellis. The latter reported that during the session she had trouble learning new material and was drinking on the job. Later that yeat Holiday appeared at the Monterey Jazz Festival and was clearly not well. Another album with Ellis on MGM was finished just weeks before her final illness, and on some tracks she sounded like a sprightly 70-year-old. She was 43. Holiday collapsed in May 1959 and was taken to a hospital in New York. She never left the hospital, where she was arrested for drug possession at a time when the city was struggling with the police department for more humane treatment for drug addicts.

Difficult, childlike, and a fantasist—she told everyone she was married to her boyfriends, but she didn't divorce Monroe for nearly 15 years—Holiday was nevertheless loyal to friends and was loved by almost everyone who knew her. She roared through her life like an express train, making a lot of money and spending it all, and mostly doing as she pleased. She became and remains an international cult figure, her biographies translated into several languages, her recordings heard from the ceiling in French hypermarkets, but she became all things to all people, and perception of her is often simplistic. She had certainly been damaged by neglect in her childhood, and she associated with violent men because they were the kind she had grown up with, but she was often as tough as they were. She was predisposed to failure of her circulatory systems, like her mother and her grandmother, so her lifestyle was fatal. Famous for being a drug addict, she suffered from cirrhosis, and it wasn't drugs that killed her, but alcohol. Her so-called autobiography, *Lady Sings the Blues* (1956), was as gloomy and doom-laden as possible because it was written to sell to the movies, while her ghost-writer, William Dufty, described her as the funniest woman he had ever known. The film version (1972) was a travesty: McKay had carried her dope, helped himself to her money, and beaten her up; as technical adviser on the film, he had himself written into the script as the hero.

BIBLIOGRAPHY
B. Holiday with W. Dufty: *Lady Sings the Blues* (Garden City, NY, 1956/*R* 1984 with discography by A.J. McCarthy)
G. Schuller: *The Swing Era: the development of Jazz 1930–1945* (New York, 1989/*R*), 527–47
S. Nicholson: *Billie Holiday* (London, 1995)
B. Green: "Billie Holiday," *Reading Jazz: a Gathering of Autobiography, Repotage, and Criticism from 1919 to Now*, ed. R. Gottlieb (London, 1996/*R*), 933–59
D. Clarke: *Wishing on the Moon: the Life and Times of Billie Holiday* (New York, 1994, enlarged 2/2002 as *Billie Holiday: Wishing on the Moon*)

DONALD CLARKE

Holland, Bernard (*b* Norfolk, VA, 26 Feb 1933). Music critic, journalist, and teacher. Holland majored in literature and philosophy at the University of Virginia (BA 1955). Thereafter he studied composition and piano at the Vienna Academy of Music, the Paris Conservatory, and in London. Holland taught piano in Pittsburgh between 1966 and 1981, making his entry into freelance music criticism during that period. After writing for the *Pittsburgh Post-Gazette* (1979–80) he was hired in 1981 as a music critic for the *New York Times*. He was named chief critic at the newspaper in 1995, succeeding Edward Rothstein in a position widely viewed as the most prominent platform for classical music criticism in the United States. Holland also contributed articles to publications such as the *Saturday Review*, the *New York Times Magazine*, and *Harper's Magazine*. He retired in 2008.

BRETT BOUTWELL

Holland, Charles (*b* Norfolk, VA, 27 Dec 1909; *d* Amsterdam, Holland, 7 Nov 1987). Tenor. He began singing at the age of 14, studied with May Hamaker Henley, and in the 1930s sang with Benny Carter and Fletcher Henderson's jazz bands. He appeared in Marc Connelly's drama *Green Pastures* and the film *Hullabaloo* (1941), and had a 13-week concert program on NBC radio. He then became a pupil of Georges Le Pyre, an assistant to Bruno Walter, in Hollywood, California. He moved to New York, where he studied with Clyde Burrows and performed in *Jeb* (1948), Hall Johnson's *Run Little Chillun'*, Thomson's *Four Saints in Three Acts*, and the premiere of Blitzstein's *The Airborne*. Holland felt that he was unable to make a life for himself as a respected singer in the United States due to racial prejudice, and thereafter decided to make his home in Europe. After settling in France in 1949 he sang on the French radio and television network, and made his European operatic debut in *Die Zauberflöte* at the Paris Opéra in 1954; the following year he became the first African American singer to appear at the Opéra-Comique. He sang Verdi's *Otello* in English in London, and enjoyed a successful career in French, German, and Dutch theaters in such works as *Carmen, Boris Godunov*, and Gounod's *Faust*; he also sang in Italy, Switzerland, Scandinavia, Australia, New Zealand, and Canada. He returned to the United States in the 1969 and gave a recital at Carnegie Hall at the age of 72. By 1975 his career continued to expand due to his connection with Dennis Russell Davies. In 1983 he recorded an album of spirituals, *My Lord what a Mornin'* (1750 Arch 1796), and the following year sang in Bolcom's *Songs of Innocence and Experience*. His best-known operatic roles include Monostatos in *Die Zauberflöte*, Gounod's Faust, and Nadir in Bizet's *Les pêcheurs de perles*.

CHARLES JAHANT/JONAS WESTOVER

Holland, Dave [David] (*b* Wolverhampton, England, 1 Oct 1946). English jazz double bass player, bass guitarist, cellist, and composer. He played guitar and electric bass before he switched to double bass in 1961, after hearing recordings by Ray Brown and Leroy Vinnegar. In 1963 he moved to London in order to study privately with James E. Merritt, and from 1964 to 1968 he attended the Guildhall School of Music and Drama where he was the principal bass player in the school's orchestra. From 1966 he played on the London jazz scene with Roy Budd, Kenny Wheeler, Evan Parker, John Surman, John McLaughlin, and the Spontaneous Music Ensemble. In September 1968 he was hired by Miles Davis, replacing Ron Carter, and stayed with the trumpeter until autumn 1970. Holland switched from acoustic to electric bass, as heard on the albums *Filles de Kilimanjaro* (1968, Col.), *In a Silent Way* (1969, Col.), and *Bitches Brew* (1969, Col.). During and after his tenure with Davis, he primarily performed and recorded with his London associate Wheeler as well as with Chick Corea, Anthony Braxton, Barry Altschul, Jack DeJohnette, and Sam Rivers in the 1970s. With Braxton, Corea, and Altschul, Holland collaborated in the acoustic avant-garde group Circle (1970–72). In 1975 he founded the trio Gateway with DeJohnette and John Abercrombie; this group was active until 1977 and held a reunion in 1994. Holland also played regularly with Sam Rivers (1974–80), with whom he recorded an album of duets (*Dave Holland, Sam Rivers*, 1976, ImA). In 1977 he began recording and performing as an unaccompanied soloist on both double bass and cello (notably *Emerald Tears*, 1977, and *Life Cycle*, 1982). After a serious illness Holland led his first quintet from 1983 until 1987, with Wheeler, Steve Coleman, Julian Priester (replaced by Robin Eubanks), and Steve Ellington (replaced by Marvin "Smitty" Smith) as his sidemen. In the late 1980s he also recorded in a trio with Coleman and DeJohnette (1988) and a quartet with Coleman, Kevin Eubanks, and Smith (1989). He established a second quintet in 1997 with Steve Wilson (replaced by Chris Potter), Robin Eubanks, Steve Nelson, and Billy Kilson (replaced by Nate Smith). He has subsequently also led a big band (2001–05), a sextet (2008), and an octet (2010, an extension of his quintet) as well as his group the Overtone Quartet with Potter, Jason Moran, and Eric Harland (2009), a successor of the Monterey Quartet (2007, with Gonzalo Rubalcaba on piano). Holland has engaged in several world-music projects, with the sitar and tablā player Collin Walcott (1975), the Tunisian 'ud player Anouar Brahem (1997), and the flamenco guitarist Pepe Habichuela (2010). As a sideman he has collaborated with numerous musicians, including Joe Henderson (1972–3, 1992, 1997), Herbie Hancock (1992–3, 1996, 2008), Joe Lovano (1991, 1997, 2003), Kevin Eubanks (1991, 1993–4), and Karl Berger (1972–6, 1986, 1991, 1994).

BIBLIOGRAPHY

B. Primack: "Dave Holland: Diverse and Dedicated," *DB*, xlv/10 (1978), 18–20

T. Saccone: "Dave Holland: the Scars of Success," *Modern Drummer*, x/12 (1986), 26–9

G. Turi: "Dave Holland: Future in the Past," *JF* [intl edn], no.112 (1988), 36–40

P. Keepnews: "The Lost Quintet," *A Miles Davis Reader* (Washington, DC, 1997), 184–9

B. Blumenthal: "Prime Time: Dave Holland," *JT*, xxx/3 (2000), 34–41

T. Erdmann: "Dave Holland," *Jazz Player*, vii (2000), Aug–Sept, 18–25

L. Peterson, ed.: *Music and the Creative Spirit: Innovators in Jazz, Improvisation, and the Avant garde* (Lanham, MD, 2006)

E. Nemeyer: "Dave Holland," *Jazz Improv*, viii/3 (2009), 126–131

D. Holland: "Business is Good," *JT*, xl/3 (2010), 40–44

MICHAEL BAUMGARTNER

Holland, Jerry (*b* Brockton, MA, 23 Feb 1955; *d* Sydney, NS, Canada, 16 July 2009). Cape Breton fiddler and composer. Jerry Holland was born in Massachusetts, the son of an expatriate New Brunswick fiddler. He fell in love with the fiddle at an early age and became enthralled with the Scottish traditional fiddle music as performed in Cape Breton, Nova Scotia. The Boston area at the time boasted a thriving community of immigrants from Cape Breton, and Holland quickly became adept at both Cape Breton fiddling and step-dancing, which he occasionally performed together. He was recruited at an early age to perform on Canadian television as a member of the Cape Breton Symphony, and became well known throughout Canada. At age 21 he left Massachusetts permanently and settled in Cape Breton. Holland's technically brilliant, danceable style placed him at the forefront of traditional musicians in Cape Breton. In many ways, his driving, passionate fiddling came to define the evolving sound of Cape Breton traditional music. His repertoire of tunes was enormous, and he was a prolific composer as well as a sought-after concert performer, dance musician, and teacher. His compositions have been published in two collections, and almost every traditional fiddler knows how to play at least one or two of Holland's tunes. Many of his recordings were artfully crafted compilations of his own compositions and traditional melodies. They reveal Holland's firm grasp of the elements of the tradition as well as his artistic vision of the future of Cape Breton music. After his untimely death at age 54, he remains one of the most influential of American traditional musicians.

RECORDINGS

Jerry Holland, 1976, Rounder Records, 7008; *Master Cape Breton Fiddler* 1982, Fiddlesticks Music, FM 1982; *Fiddler's Choice* (Odyssey, 1998); *Crystal Clear*, 2000, Cranford Publications, CP-0200-CD; *Parlor Music*, 2005, Rounder Records, 1166 1–7057–2; *Helping Hands*, 2009, Fiddlesticks Music, FM 2009; *Jerry Holland and Friends*, 2010, Fiddlesticks Music, FM20092

BIBLIOGRAPHY

A. MacGillivray: "Jerry Holland," *The Cape Breton Fiddler* (Cape Breton, NS, 1997), 106–7

B. Feintuch: "Jerry Holland," *In The Blood: Cape Breton Conversations on Culture* (Logan, UT, 2010), 98–113

SALLY K SOMMERS SMITH WELLS

Holland, Justin (*b* Norfolk Co., VA, 26 July 1819; *d* New Orleans, 24 March 1887). Guitarist and composer. Born a free black in the slave state of Virginia, he went in 1833 to Boston, where he began to study the piano, guitar, and flute. While in Massachusetts he changed his name to William J.H. White, but later legally changed it back to Justin Holland (on 13 May 1847). Oberlin College Archives record a William J.H. White (not Justin Holland) studying in its Preparatory Department during 1841–2. Holland next studied in Mexico during the early 1840s. He returned to Oberlin *c*1845 where he married. He resettled in Cleveland, Ohio and remained there as a guitar teacher and composer until 1886. Declining health forced him to retire and move to New Orleans. His numerous pieces for solo guitar include

Elfin Waltzes, Maiden's Prayer, Spanish Fandango, and *Three Tyrolien Airs.* A pioneering composer for the guitar, he also wrote duets for guitar, pieces for guitar and piano, arrangements of operatic airs for guitar and violin or flute, and many songs with guitar accompaniment. He also published the book *Choral Reform* (c1845). His instruction books, *Holland's Comprehensive Method for the Guitar* (1874) and *Holland's Modern Method for the Guitar* (1876), were widely acclaimed in Europe and the United States.

BIBLIOGRAPHY

SouthernB

J. Trotter: *Music and Some Highly Musical People* (Boston, 1881/*R*)

W.A. Banks: *Justin Holland, the Guitar's Black Pioneer* (diss., American U., 1987)

Barbara Clemenson: "Justin Holland: Black Guitarist in the Western Reserve," *Western Reserve Studies Symposium, November 10, 11, 12, 1989* (Cleveland, OH, 1989), 17pp (reprint, n.d., <http://www.case.edu/artsci/wrss/documents/Clemenson.pdf>)

D. Back: *American Pioneers of the Classic Guitar* (Pacific, MO, 1994)

EILEEN SOUTHERN/JOSEPHINE WRIGHT

Holland-Dozier-Holland. Rhythm and blues and soul songwriting and production team. Brian Holland (*b* Detroit, MI, 16 June 1941), Lamont Dozier (*b* Detroit, MI, 15 Feb 1941), and Eddie Holland (*b* Detroit, MI, 30 Oct 1939) all were active participants in the Detroit rhythm and blues scene in the late 1950s and early 1960s—Brian Holland as lead singer of the Satintones, Lamont Dozier with the Romeos, and Eddie Holland with the Fideltones. All three were early recording artists at Motown with Eddie Holland achieving a Top Ten R&B and Top 30 pop hit with "Jamie" in 1962. After co-writing and producing the Marvelettes number one hit single "Please Mr. Postman" in the fall of 1961 with Robert Bateman, Brian Holland formed a writing/production team with his brother Eddie and Freddy Gorman. Two years later Lamont Dozier replaced Gorman. Typically, Lamont Dozier and Brian Holland wrote the music and produced the records while Eddie Holland wrote the lyrics.

Holland-Dozier-Holland from 1963 through 1968 wrote and produced an astonishing number of hit singles for Marvin Gaye ("Can I Get a Witness," 1963; "How Sweet It Is To Be Loved By You," 1965), Martha and the Vandellas ("Heatwave," "Quicksand," 1963; "Nowhere to Run," 1965; and "Jimmy Mack," 1967), the Supremes ("Where Did Our Love Go," "Baby Love," 1964; "Come See About Me," "Stop! In the Name of Love," "Back In My Arms Again," 1965; "You Can't Hurry Love," "You Keep Me Hangin' On," 1966), the Four Tops ("Baby I Need Your Loving," 1964; "I Can't Help Myself," "It's the Same Old Song," 1965; "Reach Out I'll Be There," "Standing in the Shadows of Love," 1966; "Bernadette," 1967), the Miracles ("Mickey's Monkey," 1963), Kim Weston ("Take Me In Your Arms (Rock Me a Little While)," 1965), and the Isley Brothers ("This Old Heart of Mine (Is Weak for You)," 1966). By 1968 they had placed 12 records at the number one spot on the US pop charts. Collectively, Holland-Dozier-Holland's songs and productions were instrumental in defining the Motown sound.

In 1968 Holland-Dozier-Holland left Motown amidst acrimonious lawsuits over royalty payments. They sub-sequently formed the Invictus and Hot Wax labels, achieving success with the Honey Cone ("Want Ads," "Stick Up," 1971), the Chairman of the Board ("Give Me Just a Little More Time," 1970), Flaming Ember ("Westbound #9," 1970), Laura Lee ("Women's Love Rights," 1971; "Rip Off," 1972), 100 Proof Aged in Soul ("Somebody's Been Sleeping," 1970), 8th Day ("She's Not Just Another Woman," "You've Got to Crawl Before You Walk," 1971), and solo recordings by Dozier and Brian Holland. At that point Eddie Holland also was credited as being part of the production team.

Dozier left the team in 1973 to once again pursue a career as a performer. By the mid-1970s their recording companies had ceased operation. Dozier went on to have a successful career as a recording artist in the 1970s and 1980s, placing three singles in the R&B Top Five ("Trying to Hold On To My Woman," 1973; "Fish Ain't Bitin'," 1974; "Let Me Start Tonite," 1974). In 2008 Holland-Dozier-Holland reunited to write 22 new songs for a musical production of the *First Wives Club*.

In 1999 Holland-Dozier-Holland were inducted into the Songwriters Hall of Fame. Two years later they were inducted into the Rock and Roll Hall of Fame.

BIBLIOGRAPHY

A. White: Disc notes *Heaven Must Have Sent You: the Holland/Dozier/Holland Story* (Los Angeles, 2005)

ROB BOWMAN

Hollander, Lorin (D.) (*b* New York, NY, 19 July 1944). Pianist and lecturer. His father was a violinist and Associate Concertmaster for Toscanini and the NBC Symphony. An infant prodigy, Lorin memorized the first book of Bach's *Well-Tempered Clavier* by age 5 and made his Carnegie Hall debut at age 11 playing Mozart's Piano Concerto K467. He attended Manhattan's Professional Children's School. Later at Juilliard, he studied principally with EDWARD STEUERMANN, but also with MAX RUDOLF, LEON FLEISHER, and Olga Stroumillo. He subsequently made over 2500 concert appearances with virtually every major orchestra in the United States and Europe, including the New York PO, Chicago SO, Philadelphia Orchestra, National SO, London PO, Concertgebouw Orchestra, L'Orchestre de la Suisse Romande, and the Warsaw PO. His own concert series was televised nationally on PBS. A compelling public speaker, Hollander has delivered numerous lectures at commencements, symposiums, and conferences on topics including the psychological dynamics of creativity, music therapy, stage fright, and the integration of art, science, and spirituality.

Known for his socially oriented focus and leadership in community outreach programs, Hollander has given many piano recitals in hospitals, prisons, and nursing homes, occasionally performing alongside the residents of those institutions. Among other positions, he has served as advisor to the US National Endowment for the Arts, and advisor to the Office of the Gifted and Talented of the US Department of Health, Education, and Welfare. In 1994, the Tennessee Arts Academy created the Lorin Hollander Award in honor of his dedication to arts education. That same year, he publicly disclosed his 30-year battle with epilepsy, effectively becoming an advocate for others afflicted with the disease.

BIBLIOGRAPHY
"Music: Teen-Age Virtuoso," *Time* (16 Nov 1959)

KAREN MONSON/LINCOLN BALLARD

Hollister, Carroll (*b* Danbury, CT, 6 April 1901; *d* New York, NY, 1 Oct 1983). Pianist. He studied piano with Ernest Carter in Providence, Rhode Island, Edward Sims in Norwalk, Connecticut, and S. Constantino Yon in New York. After a year at Amherst College he entered the Institute of Musical Art in New York, where his principal teacher was Arthur Newstead. He also attended the master class of Carl Friedberg and studied composition with GOETSCHIUS. His debut as a professional accompanist came unexpectedly in 1925, when Elena Gerhardt arrived in New York without her usual pianist. Hollister was recommended and found satisfactory for two recitals in Aeolian Hall, after which he went with Gerhardt for a coast-to-coast tour of the United States and Canada. Thus established, he became associated with many famous artists, including the singers Maria Kurenko, Paul Althouse, James Melton, Elsa Alsen, and Todd Duncan; the violinists Elman and Ricci; the viola player Fuchs; and the dancers Angna Enters, Miriam Marmein, and Janet Collins. From 1933 to 1945 he worked exclusively with John Charles Thomas. In later life he devoted most of his time to the career of his wife, the soprano Beatrice Rippy.

PHILIP LIESON MILLER

Holly, Buddy [Holley, Charles Hardin] (*b* Lubbock, TX, 7 Sept 1936; *d* Clear Lake, IA, 3 Feb 1959). Rockabilly guitarist, singer, and lyricist. As a child he took guitar, violin, and piano lessons and was exposed to many musical styles, including country and western, gospel,

Buddy Holly, 1950s. (AP Photo)

bluegrass, and rhythm and blues. Each influenced his later recordings. As a teen he became known throughout western Texas for his unique voice, songwriting skills, and live performances. In 1955 he signed a recording contract with Nashville's Decca, but left within a year because of creative differences. Holly returned to Texas where he opened for acts such as Bill Haley and His Comets and Elvis Presley. After their 15 October 1956 concert, Presley suggested that Holly focus more on rock as his primary style, rather than country and bluegrass. It was a suggestion that changed Buddy Holly's career.

In 1957 Holly and his band, the Crickets, recorded "That'll Be the Day" for Brunswick Records. The single, Holly's first, topped station playlists across the United States and represented his transformation from country crooner to rock and roll pioneer. During the same year Holly and the Crickets recorded "Maybe Baby," "Not Fade Away," "Oh Boy," and "Peggy Sue." The group became the first all-white band to play Harlem's Apollo Theater, and in 1958 they toured America, Australia, England, and Canada. Yet Holly split with the Crickets before year's end due to a disagreement with the group's manager. Because of the resulting financial hardships Holly joined fellow rock and roll musicians Ritchie Valens, the "Big Bopper" (J.P. Richardson), and Dion and the Belmonts for the "Winter Dance Party" tour of Midwest America in January 1959. The tour's final show occurred in Clear Lake, Iowa, on 2 February. After the concert, Holly, Valens, and Richardson chartered a small plane to fly them to their next stop in Minnesota. Soon after takeoff the plane crashed, killing everyone aboard. Holly was 22 years old. Singer Don McLean memorialized the tragedy "the day the music died" in his 1971 song "American Pie."

Although his recording career lasted less than two years, Holly exerted a lasting influence. Known by many for his iconic black horn-rimmed eyeglasses, he inspired countless musicians through his clever use of the recording studio, innovative sound, and popularization of the two-guitar, bass, and drum band arrangement. The Beatles took their name as an homage to Holly's Crickets. Buddy Holly was inducted into the inaugural class of the Rock and Roll Hall of Fame in 1986 and honored with the National Academy of Recording Arts and Sciences' Lifetime Achievement Award in 1997.

RECORDINGS
(selective)
The Buddy Holly Collection, 1993, MCA; *The "Chirping" Crickets*, 2004, MCA; *Not Fade Away: The Complete Studio Recordings and More*, 2009, Hip-O Select

BIBLIOGRAPHY
J. Tobler: *The Buddy Holly Story* (New York, 1979)
J. Goldrosen and J. Beecher: *Remembering Buddy: the Definitive Biography* (New York, 1987)
E. Amburn: *Buddy Holly: a Biography* (New York, 1995)
P. Norman: *Rave On: the Biography of Buddy Holly* (New York, 1996)

J. MICHAEL BUTLER

Hollywood String Quartet. String quartet. It was founded in 1947 by the conductor and violinist FELIX SLATKIN, with Paul Shure (violin), Paul Robyn (viola, replaced by Alvin

Dinkin in 1954), and Slatkin's wife Eleanor Aller (cello). Because they were active in Hollywood studio orchestras (Slatkin, Dinkin, and Shure at Twentieth Century-Fox, Aller and Robyn at Warner Bros.), they confined their touring activities largely to the West Coast, but they attained an international reputation through their many recordings. The quartet performed at the Edinburgh Festival (1957) and toured New Zealand (1960) before disbanding in 1961.

Although albums devoted to Ludwig van Beethoven (the late quartets), Johannes Brahms, and Franz Schubert were widely admired, the Hollywood String Quartet's chief legacy may be its service to 20th-century music. In recordings of works by Ernő Dohnányi, Heitor Villa-Lobos, Sergey Prokofiev, Zoltán Kodály, Dmitry Shostakovich, William Walton, Arnold Schoenberg, Joaquín Turina, and Paul Creston, the quartet was celebrated for its vigor, impeccable intonation, and sympathetic interpretations of contemporary music. Several of their recordings have been reissued on CD.

TIM PAGE

Holm, Celeste (*b* New York, NY, 29 April 1917; *d* New York, NY, 15 July 2012). Actress and singer. Her stage, film, and television acting career exceeded 50 years and embraced a wide variety of characters and genres. Holm began her Broadway musical career in *Gloriana* (1938), then worked steadily in non-musical plays until originating Ado Annie in *Oklahoma!* (1943). She starred in Broadway's *Bloomer Girl* (1944) before signing a movie contract with 20th Century Fox in 1946. She received an Academy Award for portraying Anne Dettrey in *Gentleman's Agreement* (1947) and nominations for *Come to the Stable* (1949) and *All About Eve* (1950). Movie musicals include *The Tender Trap* (1955), *High Society* (1956), and *Tom Sawyer* (1973); television musicals include *The Yeomen of the Guard* (1957) and Rodgers and Hammerstein's *Cinderella* (1965). On Broadway she replaced first Gertrude Lawrence as Anna Leonowens in *The King and I* (opened 1951) and later Angela Lansbury as Mame Dennis in *Mame* (opened 1966). She played Julia Faysle in the failed *The Utter Glory of Morrissey Hall* (1979).

Holm's success as a musical actress reflects the winning contrast of her sophisticated bearing against a disarming, inventive playfulness combined with stellar comedic timing. Her singing voice was effervescent but small.

BIBLIOGRAPHY
T.S. Hischak: "Celeste Holm," *The Oxford Companion to the Musical: Theatre, Film and Television* (Oxford, 2008), 349
A. Gates: "Celeste Holm, Witty Character Actress, Is Dead at 95," *New York Times* (16 July 2012), D8

SHARON O'CONNELL CAMPBELL

Holman, Libby [Elizabeth Holzman] (*b* Cincinnati, OH, 23 May 1904; *d* Stamford, CT, 18 June 1971). Actress, singer, composer, and lyricist. Holman completed her college education before moving to New York where she began her theatrical career in 1924. Encouraged by the critic Channing Pollock, she appeared in revues, including the *Garrick Gaieties* (1925) and *Merry-Go-Round* (1927). Her most successful performance came in 1929 with *The Little Show*, where she introduced the song "Moanin' Low" (by Ralph Rainger). This blues number became her signature tune, although she had another hit in *Three's a Crowd* (1930) with "Body and Soul" (Heyman, Sour/Green). She appeared in other revues during the 1930s, including *Revenge with Music* (1934), and starred in Cole Porter's *You Never Know* (1938). Holman produced her own one-woman show, *Blues, Ballads, and Sin-Songs*, in 1954. She took this opportunity to showcase her own compositions, including "Good Morning Blues" and "House of the Rising Sun." Her music was deeply rooted in African American idioms, a connection she celebrated through her support of the Civil Rights Movement in the 1950s. Holman's performances are preserved on 25 sides recorded for Brunswick from 1927 to 1931, and on six sides recorded for Decca in 1942, the latter accompanied by African American artist Josh White, with whom she was significantly linked for some years. In addition to her career, Holman was famous for her colorful personal life, which included several lesbian relationships and an accusation of murder.

BIBLIOGRAPHY
H.D. Perry: *Libby Holman, Body and Soul* (Boston, 1983)
J. Bradshaw: *Dreams That Money Can Buy: the Tragic Life of Libby Holman* (New York, 1985)

JONAS WESTOVER

Holmes, Oliver Wendell (*b* Cambridge, MA, 29 Aug 1809; *d* Boston, MA, 7 Oct 1894). Writer. He studied at Harvard University and in Paris. His distinguished medical career included a long tenure as professor of anatomy and physiology at Harvard Medical School (1847–82) and six years as its dean. He wrote three novels, several volumes of poetry and essays, and the well-known "Breakfast-Table" articles originally published in the *Atlantic Monthly* from 1857.

The verses of Holmes have been set by more than 120 composers. The earliest known published setting, by R. Stevenson, dates from about 1831; titled *Love and Oysters*, it is adapted from *The Ballad of the Oysterman*, an early poem popular with the public but one that Holmes later wished he had never written. Although many settings of his work were published in his lifetime and especially in the first 35 years after his death, he has been rarely set by later composers. Most often set have been his hymns and patriotic verses, particularly *Hymn of Trust*, *The Chambered Nautilus*, and *Sunday Hymn*. Along with Emerson, Holmes was one of several writers who made important contributions to Unitarian hymn writing.

Holmes was justly famous for his many occasional poems and was often called upon to write lyrics for public events and celebrations. In 1860 a group of 1,200 schoolchildren sang his *International Ode: Our Father's Land* on the visit of the Prince of Wales to Boston. On 29 January 1880, Holmes shared top billing with Ralph Waldo Emerson, Norwegian violinist Ole Bull, and the Fisk University Jubilee Singers in a program to aid the

Old South Church Preservation Fund in Boston. Sometimes he was asked to write lyrics to existing tunes. He wrote *A Hymn of Peace* to Matthias Keller's "American Hymn" for the National Peace Jubilee of 1869. Occasionally he even sang the songs himself, as he did with "The Stars Their Early Vigils Keep," written for a dinner given in Boston for Charles Dickens in 1842. Holmes wrote additional verses for the song "Hail Columbia!" and a fifth verse for "The Star-Spangled Banner." In 1861 he submitted three poems—*Union and Liberty*, *The Flower of Liberty*, and *Freedom our Queen*—in a contest for the writer of the best national anthem. Although no prize was awarded, all three poems have been set by several composers. One of the few recent settings is "Sweet Are the Lips of All That Sing" by Bradley Nelson.

BIBLIOGRAPHY
GroveA
J. Bishop: "In the Wind…That She Blows – Some More," *The Diapason*, xcvii/5 (2006) 14, 16

MICHAEL HOVLAND

Holmes, Richard (*b* United States). Baritone. One of his earliest professional performances took place at the Lake George Opera Festival, where he performed as Damis in Kirke Mechem's *Tartuffe* in 1982. He appeared there again as Papageno in Mozart's *Die Zauberflöte*, one of his signature roles. His voice, while not overpowering, is full of nuance and carries a light brilliance. A sought after performer, he has served as a principal singer with Glimmerglass Opera, Virginia Opera, Chicago Opera Theatre, New York Grand Opera, El Paso Opera, and the Natchez Opera Festival. By the early 2010s, he had performed nearly 150 different roles in a variety of theatrical productions, including bel canto opera, musical theater, and, especially, light opera. During more than a quarter century singing with the New York Gilbert & Sullivan Players, he has performed in each opera and in more than 20 roles. His international reputation as a premiere interpreter of this repertoire has been built on more than 500 Gilbert and Sullivan performances. Other notable works he has performed in New York include Carlisle Floyd's *Susannah* and Strauss' *Die Fledermaus* at the Metropolitan Opera and the premieres of Jack Beeson's *Sorry, Wrong Number* and Seymour Barab's cantata *Rest Eternal Grant Us*, recorded and performed with the Manhattan Chamber Orchestra.

JONAS WESTOVER

Holmes, Timothy John (*b* Detroit, MI, 22 Aug 1956). Musical instrument maker and restorer, repair technician, and performer. Holmes attended Riverside High School in Dearborn Heights, Michigan, and studied flute with Shaul Ben-Meir and saxophone with Herbert Couf, both of the Detroit Symphony. He apprenticed with the Nieman family as repair technician in Detroit area music shops. In the 1970s he worked as a restorer for the Greenfield Village and the Henry Ford Museum in association with curator Robert Eliason. Their collaboration resulted in restorations of ophicleides, serpents, keyed bugles, and civil war over-the-shoulder brass instruments. In 1978 he started his own business in Detroit, A Sharp in C, in partnership with Marko Navachoff. Holmes constructs Allen valves that are used in his over-the-shoulder reproduction instruments, and builds replicas of ophicleides, horns, keyed bugles, and consorts of over-the shoulder instruments as well as newly designed straight saxophones.

Holmes is also a freelance woodwind player. In 1976-7 he toured as a saxophonist with Marvin Gaye. He has played 19th-century piccolo in reenactment ensembles such as the Wildcat Regimental Band (Pennsylvania) and the Dodworth Saxhorn Band (Detroit, Michigan). He appears as a saxophonist with Immigrant Sons, NINE, and the Scavenger Quartet, often featured at the Motor City Casino, Detroit.

BIBLIOGRAPHY
R.C. Lozon: "The Boys in the Back Room," *Downriver Profile* (July 1989)
J. Rolston: "Transforming Trash to Treasure," *Dodworth Saxhorn Band Newsletter*, (Spring 2008), 2

RALPH T. DUDGEON

Holmquist, John (*b* Lander, WY, 7 Feb 1955). Guitarist and educator. He received a BFA degree from the University of Minnesota in 1978 under the direction of guitarist JEFFREY VAN. He studied with Alirio Díaz in France and Canada. His other teachers include British guitarist and composer Gilbert Biberian and Austrian musicologist and violinist Hans Keller. His awards include a First Prize in the 1978 Toronto Guitar International Competition. He was also a recipient of a National Endowment for the Arts Solo Recitalist Fellowship. His publications and recordings are notable for the introduction of new didactic works for the guitar. He was the first person to edit Giulio Regondi's lost "Ten Études" (1857) for solo guitar upon their rediscovery by Matanya Ophee in a private Russian collection in 1987. His CD *Regondi: 10 Etudes/Introduction and Caprice, Op. 23* (Naxos, 2001) is one of few complete recordings of these études. His CD *Études Esquisses; Celtic Airs by Gerald Garcia* (Naxos, 1997) represents the recording premiere of 25 new études for solo guitar by the British guitarist and composer. He was a contributor to the recordings of the complete music of Fernando Sor (Naxos, 1998). His LP recording *The Music of Edvard Grieg* (Cavata) in duet with guitarist Daniel Estrem expands the repertoire for two guitars through the transcription of Grieg's *Holberg Suite* and 11 of Grieg's *Lyric Pieces*. He is the former Head of the Cleveland Institute of Music Guitar Department, where his students included JASON VIEAUX.

M. RUSTY JONES

Holsinger, David Rex (*b* Hardin, MO, 26 Dec 1945). Composer and conductor. He earned degrees from Central Methodist University (BM 1967), the University of Central Missouri (MA 1975), and the University of Kansas (DMA 2006). His primary composition teachers were Donald Bohlen and Charles Hoag. From 1984 to 1999, Holsinger was music minister and composer in residence at Shady Grove Church in Grand Prairie, Texas, and then joined the music faculty at Lee University in

Cleveland, Tennessee, TN, where he directs the wind ensemble and teaches conducting and composition. He has composed about 100 works at various levels for wind band, twice winning the American Bandmasters Association Ostwald Award for *The Armies of the Omnipresent Otserf* (1982) and *In the Spring at the Time When Kings Go Off to War* (1986). His music features memorable use of shifting meters and accents and is often programmatic. In 1995 Holsinger received an honorary doctoral degree from Gustavus Adolphus College in association with the première of *The Easter Symphony*.

BIBLIOGRAPHY

W.H. Rehrig: *The Heritage Encyclopedia of Band Music* (Westerville, OH, 1991, suppl. 1996); CD-ROM (Oskaloosa, IA, 2005) [includes list of works]

N.E. Smith: *Program Notes for Band* (Lake Charles, LA, 2000), 293–4

D.R. Holsinger: "David Holsinger," *Composers on Composing for Band*, i, ed. M. Camphouse (Chicago, 2003)

S. Clickard: "David Holsinger," *A Composer's Insight*, iii, ed. T. Salzman (Galesville, MD, 2006), 113–28

PAUL LAIRD

Holst, Edward [Edvard, Eduard] (*b* Copenhagen, Denmark, 1843; *d* New York, NY, 4 Feb 1899). Composer, dancer, and playwright of Danish birth. He immigrated to the United States in about 1874 and was active in New York in both music and theater. He provided the music for several musical comedies, including *A Circus in Town* (1887) and *Our Flats* (1897). He also wrote many pieces for military band (including *Marine Band March* and *Battle of Manila*), numerous songs, and a vast quantity of descriptive pieces for piano solo and piano ensemble. Holst's total output amounts to more than 2000 works.

Holt, Bob [Robert] **(Morris)** (*b* Ava, MO, 25 Nov 1930; *d* Ava, MO, 19 March 2004). Old-time fiddler. Holt's musical influences included his uncle Node and fiddler Charlie Deckerd. In the late 1950s and early 1960s he lived in Buffalo, Iowa, where he worked various jobs, including playing country music in nightclubs. In 1965 he moved back to his family's property near Ava, Missouri, to run a dairy farm. Interest in his wide-ranging fiddle repertoire grew steadily. Holt, along with Edna Mae Davis and others, was influential in organizing and maintaining popular square dances in Ava, Cabool, and Forsyth. His national reputation grew through his work as a performer and teacher at venues such as the National Folk Festival, the Augusta Heritage Center, and the Festival of American Fiddle Tunes. Best known for his high-speed dance fiddling, Holt was also an articulate speaker, a capable fiddle teacher, a honky-tonk fiddler with Harley and Betty Newberry, and a frequent presence at festivals, jam sessions, fiddle camps, and dances throughout Missouri. Holt was recognized nationally for his contributions to Ozarks fiddle and dance traditions in 1999 when he was awarded a National Heritage Fellowship from the National Endowment for the Arts.

SELECTED RECORDING

Got a Little Home to Go to (1998, Rounder CD0432)

BIBLIOGRAPHY

B. Holt: "My First Love Is These Old Tunes I Learned from my Dad," *Bittersweet*, 9 (1982), 54–58

J.A. Henigan: "'Play Me Something Quick and Devilish': the Old-Time Square Dance Fiddling of Bob Holt," *The Old-Time Herald*, iv/6 (1994/1995), 26–30, 34

DREW BEISSWENGER

Holt, Hosea E(dson) (*b* Ashburnham, MA, 17 Feb 1836; *d* Lexington, MA, 18 Oct 1898). Music educator and author. Holt learned to sing and play the violin in New England singing schools, music teaching institutes, and churches. He was a bandsman and stretcher-bearer in a Civil War militia unit from Boston for a few months, an experience that brought him into contact with trained Boston musicians. On discharge, he studied piano and voice at the Boston Music School with John W. Tufts and BENJAMIN FRANKLIN BAKER from 1863 to his graduation in 1865. In 1868 he joined the music staff of the Boston Public Schools and became a successful and well-known music supervisor under Luther Whiting Mason. He eventually partnered with John Tufts to produce the widely used *Normal Music Course*, with Tufts writing the exercises and instructions for the teaching methods that Holt had developed. For Holt, studying music consisted of learning to read music, and in his speeches and articles he adamantly opposed using rote songs or the Tonic Sol Fa system. Holt was highly respected as a leader of teachers and taught at Wheaton Seminary, Bridgewater Normal School, and at his own successful Lexington Summer Normal Music School (1884–98). He was inducted into the Music Educators Hall of Fame in 1988.

BIBLIOGRAPHY

J.A. Keene: *A History of Music Education in the United States* (Hanover, NH, 1987)

J.A. Rives: *Hosea E. Holt, 1836–1898: Public School Music Supervisor, Teaching Method Innovator, and Normal School Professor* (diss., U. of Kansas, 1994)

WILLIAM R. LEE

Holt, Nora [Douglas, Lena] (*b* Kansas City, KS, 1885; *d* Los Angeles, CA, 24 Jan 1974). Critic, composer, singer, and pianist. After receiving a BSc from Western Ontario University in Quindaro, Kansas, Holt studied at the Chicago Musical College and earned the first MusM in composition awarded to an African American (1918). During the 1920s she performed as a singer throughout Europe, studied composition briefly with NADIA BOULANGER, and developed close friendships with Harlem Renaissance figures such as Carl Van Vechten and Langston Hughes.

While Holt's career included periods in which she composed (only one of approximately 200 compositions survive) and performed (she sang extensively in private venues during her travels), she always returned to music journalism. She served as critic for *The Chicago Defender* from 1917–21, becoming the first woman music critic in the United States. During this same period she published *Music and Poetry* (1919–21), in which she included new compositions (including her own).

Upon her return to the United States in the late 1930s, Holt served as critic for *The Amsterdam News* (New York, 1943–64). She promoted performances of art music by African American composers, championed new performers, and was noted for her insightful analyses of each. In 1945 Virgil Thomson nominated her for membership in the Music Critics Circle of New York. She was its first African American member. As an advocate for African American composers and performers, Holt was a founding member of the National Association of Negro Musicians (1919) and the Chicago Musical Association.

BIBLIOGRAPHY

"Nora Holt," *The Black Perspective in Music*, ii/2 (1974), 226
J. Karpf: "The Early Years of African American Music Periodicals, 1886–1922: History, Ideology and Context," *International Review of the Aesthetics and Sociology of Music*, xxviii/2 (1997), 143–68
H. Walker-Hill: "Western University at Quindaro, Kansas (1865–1943) and Its Legacy of Pioneering Musical Women," *Black Music Research Journal*, xxvi/1 (2006), 7–37

KAREN M. BRYAN

Holtkamp Organ Co. Organ building firm. It was founded in 1855 in Cleveland, Ohio, by Gottlieb Ferdinand Votteler (1817–94), who had emigrated from Germany in 1847 and previously worked for organbuilders in New York and Baltimore. His son Henry B. Votteler later formed a partnership with J.H. Hettche as the Votteler-Hettche Company, and in 1903 Herman Heinrich [Henry] Holtkamp (1858–1931), who had previously operated a music store in St. Mary's, Ohio, joined the company, becoming manager in 1905. The firm's output in this period was small and conservative, one of its larger organs being that built in 1913 for St. Procop's Church in Cleveland. Allen G. Sparling, a Canadian, joined the firm in 1911, and after 1914 it was known as the Votteler-Holtkamp-Sparling Co. On Henry Holtkamp's death, his son Walter (1894–1962) took control, and under his direction the firm, known simply as the Holtkamp Organ Co. after 1951, began to grow. Walter was one of the first American builders to be influenced by the concepts of the "Organ Reform" movement, and in collaboration with like-minded organists Arthur Quimby and Melville Smith, added an unenclosed *Rückpositiv* of classical tonal design to the Skinner organ in the Cleveland Museum of Art in 1933, which attracted considerable attention. This baroque-influenced division soon appeared on some of Holtkamp's larger church organs such as that for Fairmount Presbyterian Church in Cleveland (1942), which also displayed what would soon become both Holtkamp's trademark and an eventual inspiration to other builders: completely unenclosed pipework arranged in an artistic manner. Another innovation of this period was a small movable one-manual organ of three stops with mechanical action, the first one of which was constructed in 1935.

Following the hiatus of World War II and the more general acceptance of his once radical concepts, Walter Holtkamp soon took his place among the major American builders. Among the influential organs of this period were those for Crouse Auditorium at the University of Syracuse (1950), Massachusetts Institute of Technology (1957), and Fisk University (1960). Although Holtkamp organs still employed electro-pneumatic action, they now often contained note-channel (slider) windchests, and featured trim, functional consoles. Walter Holtkamp Jr. joined his father's firm in 1956, and succeeded him as president in 1961. In 1969 the firm began building some mechanical-action organs in addition to those having electro-pneumatic action. Organs built in this period include those for Church of the Ascension (1967), Union Seminary (1980), and Park Street Christian Church (1982), all in New York. In 1987 F. Christian Holtkamp, son of Walter Jr., entered the firm, becoming president in 1995. Organs built under his direction include those for the Peabody Institute, Baltimore (1998) and the Cathedral of St. Louis King of France in New Orleans (2009).

BIBLIOGRAPHY

"The Holtkamp Portative," *The American Organist*, xix/2 (1936), 57
F.R. Webber: "A Holtkamp Story," *The Diapason*, liii/6 (1962), 28
E.M. Nye: "Walter Holtkamp: A Master Organ Builder," *The Organ*, li/2 (1971), 66–77
O. Ochse: *The History of the Organ in the United States* (Bloomington, IN, 1975)
J.A. Ferguson: *Walter Holtkamp: American Organ Builder* (Kent, OH, 1979)
C. Callahan, ed.: *The American Classic Organ: a History in Letters* (Richmond, VA, 1990)

BARBARA OWEN

Holton, Frank (*b* Allegan, MI, 10 March 1858; *d* Elkhorn, WI, 17 April 1942). Trombonist and brass instrument maker. He studied cornet as a child, and was a member of the village band at 15. He joined the Hi Henry Minstrels, for whom he played slide trombone, and soon appeared as a soloist. In 1885 he was engaged by Ellis Brooks as a soloist; he played with that band at Nantasket Beach, Hull, Massachusetts, during the summer, and with his orchestra at the Hotel Ponce de Leon in St. Augustine, Florida, during the winter. In the winter of 1893 he played duets with Herbert L. Clarke, who later remarked that Holton had "taught him much about lip trills, and the right way to play arpeggios." The same year he became a member of Sousa's first band, with which he played at the World's Columbian Exposition in Chicago. He remained in Chicago, where he opened a small music store selling used instruments and Holton's Electric Oil, a lubricant for brass instruments. He soon introduced a trombone model, and his business, increasingly successful, outgrew its quarters several times; in 1907 he built a factory on the west side of Chicago. By this time he carried a full line of instruments and accessories and published a journal, *Holton's Harmony Hints*. In 1916 he developed a cornet model based on the ideas of his friend Clarke. His business was moved to Elkhorn in 1918. Holton's business continued after his death, and the Frank Holton Band Instrument Manufacturing Company became a subsidiary of the G. Leblanc Corporation, a division of Conn-Selmer, in 1964, which in 2004 was purchased by Steinway Musical Instruments.

BIBLIOGRAPHY
A Trip Through the Holton Factory (Elkhorn, WI, 1920)
G.D. Bridges: *Pioneers in Brass* (Detroit, 1965); CD-ROM (Coupeville, WA, 2000)
M. Fonder: "The Instrument Manufacturing Industry and the School Band Movement: A Look at the 'Holton School Band Plan,'" *Journal of Band Research*, xxiv/1 (1988), 44–51

RAOUL F. CAMUS

Holton Corporation. Firm of brass instrument makers and distributors. Frank Holton (*b* Allegan County, MI, 28 Sept 1857; *d* Elkhorn, WI, 17 April 1942), while trombone soloist with notable bands including Sousa's (1892–3), partnered with James Warren York (*b* 1839; *d* 1927) to form York & Holton, Grand Rapids, Michigan (1884–6). While managing Chicago's Second Regiment Band (1896) Holton sold his own trombone-slide lubricant, "Holton's Electric Oil." Producing his first instruments in 1899, he incorporated in 1904 as Frank Holton & Co. During Ernst Albert Couturier's tenure (1908–12), in 1910 Holton produced the large-bore Couturier model cornet. The Holton-Clarke medium-bore cornet followed during Herbert Clarke's association with the company (1917–8). A large, modern factory was built when Holton relocated to Elkhorn, Wisconsin, in 1918.

Notable innovative products include the Philip Farkas French horn (1960s), Don Ellis' quarter-tone trumpet (1965), and Maynard Ferguson's Superbone (1974) and Firebird trumpet (1974) designed by Larry Ramirez, Holton's chief design technician.

Holton was purchased by the G. Leblanc Corporation, Kenosha, Wisconsin, in 1964, then by Steinway Musical Instruments, Inc., in 2004, becoming a division of Conn-Selmer, Inc., Elkhart, Indiana. Holton's Elkhorn factory closed in 2008, and its assets moved to Conn-Selmer's Eastlake, Ohio, facility. The Holton archive and part of Holton's reference model collection are preserved at the National Music Museum, the University of South Dakota, Vermillion.

MARGARET DOWNIE BANKS

Holyoke, Samuel (Adams) (*b* Boxford, MA, 15 Oct 1762; *d* East Concord, NH, 7 Feb 1820). Composer, tunebook compiler, and singing master. He was descended from two noteworthy New England families, the Holyokes and the Peabodys. Nothing is known about his musical training, though he may have helped to organize the "select band of students" that played in the Harvard College commencement procession in 1787. By 1789, the year of his graduation from Harvard, he was seeking subscribers for *Harmonia Americana*, a book of his own sacred compositions (Harvard awarded him the MA in 1792). During August and September of 1789 he also contributed secular songs to the *Massachusetts Magazine*. Holyoke worked as a schoolteacher in Groton, Massachusetts, in 1793 (and perhaps elsewhere), and was a member of the school committee in Boxford, Massachusetts (1796). However, he seems to have made his living chiefly as a musician, teaching singing-schools, furnishing music for special events, and organizing occasional concerts. He lived and worked mostly in Essex County, where he founded the Essex Musical

Association (1797), though towards the end of his life he moved to Boston (1814).

Holyoke was the most prolific American composer of his generation. He published over 650 of his own pieces, mostly in *Harmonia Americana* (Boston, 1791), the *Columbian Repository* (Exeter, NH, 1803), and *The Christian Harmonist* (Salem, MA, 1804), and left more than 200 works in manuscript. As a psalmodist, Holyoke aligned himself with the forces of musical reform. In 1791, he announced his opposition to the kinds of "fuging pieces" then favored in the United States, on the grounds that "the parts, falling in, one after another, each conveying a different idea, confound the sense, and render the performance a mere jargon of words." With Gram and Holden he introduced *The Massachusetts Compiler of Theoretical Principles* (Boston, 1795), a collection of European and Europeanized music prefaced by the lengthiest exposition of European theory printed in America during the century. Holyoke was also involved with instrumental music. His *The Instrumental Assistant* (Exeter, 1800) contains marches and airs for three-part ensembles, as well as instructions on how to play violin, German flute, clarinet, oboe, and bass viol; the second volume (Exeter, 1807), intended not for "learners" but for more accomplished members of "Instrumental Clubs," consists of longer and more difficult pieces. Reputed to be a clarinetist himself, Holyoke was fond of combining voices and instruments, as he did to celebrate the dedication of the New South Meeting House in Salem on 1 January 1805; in some of his publications, such as *The Occasional Companion* (Exeter, 1806/*R*1810), he printed sacred pieces with orchestral accompaniments.

Holyoke occupies an unusual place in early American musical history. He found no place open to him in the cosmopolitan realm, and spent his life working mostly in the field of provincial psalmody, even though he shared the educated tastes and at least some of the technical skills of the immigrant professionals who took control of American urban musical institutions in the 1780s and 90s. The Yale University Music Library owns three books of his musical manuscripts.

BIBLIOGRAPHY
DAB ("Holyoke, Samuel")
N.D. Gould: *Church Music in America* (Boston, 1853)
S.P. Cheney: *The American Singing Book* (Boston, 1879/*R* 1980)
G.F. Dow: *The Holyoke Diaries, 1709–1856* (Salem, MA, 1911) [with an introduction and annotations by G.F. Dow]
F.J. Metcalf: *American Writers and Compilers of Sacred Music* (New York, 1925/*R* 1967)
J.L. Willhide: *Samuel Holyoke, American Music Educator* (diss., U. of Southern California, 1954)
R. Patterson: *Three American Primitives: A Study of the Musical Styles of Hans Gram, Oliver Holden, and Samuel Holyoke* (diss., Washington U., St. Louis, 1963)
R.J. Wolfe: *Secular Music in America, 1801–1825: a Bibliography* (New York, 1964)
R. Crawford: *Music of the Federal Era* (New World LP album 299, 1978) [liner notes]
A.P. Britton, I. Lowens, and R. Crawford: *American Sacred Music Imprints, 1698–1810: a Bibliography* (Worcester, MA, 1990)
H. Eskew and K. Kroeger, eds.: *Selected Works of Samuel Holyoke and Jacob Kimball* (New York, 1998)

RICHARD CRAWFORD/R

Holzmann, Abe [Abraham] (*b* New York, NY, 19 Aug 1874; *d* East Orange, NJ, 16 Jan 1939). Ragtime composer and arranger. He was a professional staff composer and arranger for music publishers and made his mark in the history of ragtime with three notable early cakewalks, *Smoky Mokes* (1899), *Bunch o' Blackberries* (1900), and *Hunky Dory* (1901), though he also wrote marches and other popular characteristic pieces. His three cakewalks were widely played by military bands, including that of John Philip Sousa, and were also popular in piano scores.

Holzmann's writing is spirited and lively in the late 19th-century quick march tradition and shows a good grasp of melodic invention and the idiomatic syncopation typical of early ragtime. His sympathy with the march form gave him an advantage in writing (and scoring) march-like cakewalk and "patrol" numbers. By popularizing the cakewalk through his band arrangements, Holzmann broadened the scope of early ragtime at a time when the major piano ragtime scores were being published and distributed. His music unites the most popular elements of band music with the new African American stylistic traits that were beginning to be understood by a broad audience at the turn of the century.

BIBLIOGRAPHY

R. Blesh and H. Janis: *They all played ragtime* (New York, 1950, 4/1971)

D.A. Jasen and T.J. Tichenor: *Rags and Ragtime: a Musical History* (New York, 1978)

E.A. Berlin: *Ragtime: a Musical and Cultural History* (Berkeley, 1980/*R*1984 with addenda)

WILLIAM J. SCHAFER

Homer [née Beatty], **Louise (Dilworth)** (*b* Pittsburgh, PA, 30 April 1871; *d* Winter Park, FL, 6 May 1947). Contralto. She studied music at Philadelphia and Boston, then married the composer SIDNEY HOMER in 1895 and went to Paris, where she studied singing and acting with Fidèle Koenig and Paul Lhérie, the first Don José. She made her operatic debut at Vichy in 1898, as Léonor in *La favorite*. At Covent Garden in 1899 she sang Lola and Amneris, returning in 1900 for Ortrud and Maddalena after a winter season at La Monnaie in Brussels. Her American debut (1900) was with the Metropolitan Opera on tour in San Francisco as Amneris, in which role she also made her first New York appearance. Homer began a long and successful Metropolitan career, singing chiefly in Italian and French opera, but she soon assumed leading Wagnerian roles; she was also a notable Orpheus in Arturo Toscanini's 1909 revival of Christoph Willibald Gluck's opera, created the Witch in Engelbert Humperdinck's *Königskinder* (1910), and was the first to sing the title role in Horatio Parker's *Mona* (1912). After resigning from the Metropolitan in 1919, she sang with other major American companies including the Chicago Grand Opera (1920–25) and the San Francisco and Los Angeles operas (1926). She returned to the Metropolitan in 1927 and made her last appearance there in 1929, as Azucena. A performer of great artistic integrity, she had a beautiful voice and a

Louise Homer as Azucena in Giuseppe Verdi's Il Trovatore. *(T.P/Lebrecht Music & Arts)*

majestic stage presence. Among her many recordings, the ensembles with Enrico Caruso, Giovanni Martinelli, Beniamino Gigli, and others are particularly successful. Samuel Barber was her nephew.

BIBLIOGRAPHY

S. Homer: *My Wife and I* (New York, 1939/*R*)

D. Reutlinger: "Louise Homer: a Discography," *The Maestro*, iv–v (1972–3), 62–5

A. Homer: *Louise Homer and the Golden Age of Opera* (New York, 1974)

HERMAN KLEIN/DESMOND SHAWE-TAYLOR/
KATHERINE K. PRESTON

Homer, Sidney (*b* Boston, MA, 9 Dec 1864; *d* Winter Park, FL, 10 July 1953). Composer. He studied with GEORGE WHITEFIELD CHADWICK in Boston and with JOSEPH RHEINBERGER and others in Munich and Leipzig. Returning to Boston, he taught theory from 1888 to 1895, in which year he married the contralto Louise Beatty. He traveled extensively with her in Europe and the United States and attended virtually every rehearsal and performance that his health, frequently precarious, would allow. They lived in New York from 1900. He naturally turned to songwriting, and his wife often presented recitals of his music. His 103 songs, which were extremely popular during his lifetime and were included on many American singers' programs, were almost all published by G. Schirmer. Homer's music, grounded in the Germanic style of Chadwick and Arthur Foote, is predominantly diatonic but has an extensive harmonic vocabulary. The songs, for which he chose texts of generally high quality, encompass a wide emotional range, from the lyrical to the highly dramatic. His most popular pieces include "A Banjo Song" (from the *Bandanna Ballads*), "Song of the Shirt," "How's my boy?," and *Songs from Mother Goose*; "Dearest" is perhaps his best-known love song, and the Requiem well represents the religious side of his output. A quartet and quintet for strings and a few other instrumental works were performed locally in Florida after he retired there in 1939, but he did not seek to have them published.

BIBLIOGRAPHY

H.C. Thorpe: "The Songs of Sidney Homer," *MQ*, xvii (1931), 47–73
S. Homer: *My Wife and I* (New York, 1939/*R*)
S. Barber: Preface to *17 Songs by Sidney Homer* (New York, 1943)
R.V. Beatie: "A Forgotten Legacy: the Songs of the 'Boston Group'," *NATS Journal*, xlviii/1 (1991–2), 6–9, 37

DEE BAILY

Homer and Jethro. Country-music comedy duo. The partnership began in 1932 in Knoxville, Tennessee, after Henry Doyle "Homer" Haynes Jr. (*b* 27 July 1920, Knoxville, TN; *d* 7 Aug 1971, Hammond, IN) and Kenneth Charles "Jethro" Burns (*b* 10 March 1920, Conasauga, TN; *d* 4 Feb 1989, Evanston, IL) were disqualified from a Knoxville station WNOX talent contest for sounding "too professional." Subsequently hired as studio musicians, they formed the Stringdusters in 1936. They first appeared as Homer and Jethro, performing comedic versions of pop songs, in January 1939, and joined the Renfro Valley Barn Dance the next year. Following service in World War II the duo reunited at WLW (Cincinnati, Ohio) and recorded for King Records. Signing with RCA Victor in 1948, they had immediate success with a send-up of "Baby, It's Cold Outside." "How Much is That Hound Dog in the Window" (1953) became the first million-selling country comedy recording, and "The Battle of Kookamonga" earned a Grammy in 1959. They starred in a series of Kellogg's Corn Flakes commercials and appeared on numerous television shows including *The Tonight Show Starring Johnny Carson*. Following Haynes' death, Burns toured briefly with brother-in-law Chet Atkins before beginning a decadelong association with folk singer Steve Goodman. Burns also recorded several jazz albums and taught mandolin until his death. Homer and Jethro were inducted into the Country Music Hall of Fame in 2001.

KAREN RAIZOR

Hommann [Homan], **Charles** (*b* Philadelphia, PA, 25 July 1803; *d* Brooklyn, NY, 28 May 1872). Composer, violinist, violist, organist, pianist, and teacher. Born in Philadelphia to immigrant parents, a German father and British mother, Charles Hommann became America's first symphonist in the early 1820s. He also composed string chamber music, unpublished during his lifetime, and popular music of the day—piano music, songs, and choral/organ works. His teachers were his musician father, John C. Hommann, and his brother-in-law, violinist CHARLES FREDERIC HUPFELD. In 1825 he was elected to professional membership in the Musical Fund Society but had performed in society concerts from their inception (1821). Even earlier he participated in the evenings of chamber music that led to the Society's founding in 1820. When the society established its Academy of Music (12 June 1825), Hommann was chosen to teach string instruments; after the Academy's closure in May 1832 he continued to teach.

He also served as organist for services at St. James's Episcopal Church from 1819 to 1829.

Hommann's second Overture in D, with its colorful harmonic palette, won a gold medal from the Philharmonic Society in 1835. From 1837 to 1849 he was organist at Rev. George Washington Bethune's Third Dutch Reformed Church. This affiliation led in 1852 to Bethune consulting Hommann about the organ for his newly organized Reformed Dutch Church on the Heights in Brooklyn, where Hommann lived after 1854. During the New York-American Music Association's three seasons (1856–8), founder Charles Jerome Hopkins programmed Hommann's string chamber music and a violin sonata. The Hommann surname is spelled Homan in Brooklyn directories for 1855–6 ("prof. music") and 1866–7 ("teacher"), giving credence to the 1872 New York and Brooklyn newspaper death notices for Charles Homan, Tuesday, 28 May, "in the 70th year of his age." Hommann's compositions are his legacy.

WORKS
(selective list)

Orch: Overture in D [1822–3]; Sym., E♭ [1821–3]; "Prize" Overture in D, 1835

Chamber: Str Qt, F [1830s]; Str Qt, G [1830s]; Str Qt, d [1840s]; Str Qnt, f# [early 1850s]

Pf: 6 Valses et un Galop, 1834; Marche brillante, 1835–6; Three Fugues, 1835–9; Galopade Brillante, 1837–9; Rondo in B♭, 1840–5; Spanish Gallopade, arr., 1840–55; Palermo Galopade, 1845; Circassian March (duet), 1847; Notturno (manuscript), 8 April 1856

Organ: Voluntary in F, 1836; Voluntary in E♭, 1836

Choral/organ: 11 titles in Cantus Ecclesiae, 1844; Te Deum Laudamus, 1848

Songs: "Oh [O] Come to Me Beloved One," 1831; "The Desert Flower Afar May Bloom," 1842

BIBLIOGRAPHY

R.A. Gerson: *Music in Philadelphia* (Philadelphia, 1940/*R*)
J. Graziano and J. Swenson-Eldridge: *Charles Hommann: Chamber Music for Strings*, RRAM 30 (Madison, WI, 1998)
J. Swenson-Eldridge: *Charles Hommann: Surviving Orchestral Music*, MUSA 17/RRAM 62 (Middleton, WI, 2007)

JOANNE E. SWENSON-ELDRIDGE

Honea, Sion M. [Ted] (*b* Harrah, OK, 21 April 1952). Conservator, teacher, and hornist. While completing his studies in musicology at the Eastman School of Music (MA 1980) and classical studies at the State University of New York at Buffalo (PhD 1991), Honea designed and built a music conservation laboratory at the Sibley Music Library (Eastman) that remains the foremost facility of its kind in the United States. During his tenure as head of rare books and special collections, Honea instituted a program of bibliographic access to rare materials, supervising the creation of over fifty online finding aids to previously inaccessible collections. His work in preservation and reformatting of music scores provided the foundation for Sibley's current programs of digital access to rare scores and hands-on training in music conservation and preservation.

Since his return to his home state Honea has taught musicology and horn performance at the University of Central Oklahoma. He has received two university teaching awards and has published numerous articles on music history and pedagogy.

WRITINGS

"Music...A Binding Challenge," *New Library Scene*, iv (1985), 1, 8–10

"Preservation at the Sibley Music Library of the Eastman School of Music," *Notes: Quarterly Journal of the Music Library Association*, liii/2 (1996), 381–402

"Transforming Administration in Academic Libraries," *Journal of Academic Librarianship*, xxiii (1997), 183–90

"Old Wine in New Bottles: The Humanities Curriculum in Professional Education," *The Classical World*, xcii (1999), 531–52

"The Impact of Professionalism on Library Administration," *Journal of Library Administration*, xxxi/1 (2000), 1–28

ALICE CARLI

Hong, Hei-Kyung (*b* Gangwon, South Korea, 4 July 1959). Soprano of South Korean birth. After attending Yea Won Music School as a child in Seoul, she moved to the United States in 1974 to study at the Juilliard School. She sang a number of roles at the school's American Opera Center, where she participated in master classes held by luminaries such as Schwartzkopf, Legge, Souzay, and TITO GOBBI. Her debut came in 1981 when she performed at the Spoleto Festival at the invitation of Menotti. In the following year Hong won the Metropolitan Opera's National Council Auditions and in 1984 made her Met debut as Servilia in Mozart's *La Clemenza di Tito*. She performed smaller roles until 1987 when she appeared as Mimi in *La Bohème*, which has become her signature role. Since that time, Hong has performed on all the major stages throughout the world, including the Royal Opera House, La Scala, and L'Opéra de la Bastille, where she has sung a variety of roles, from Countess Almaviva to Liù to Zerlina. Comfortable in a wide variety of languages, she has an extensive repertoire, including many concert works. Giuseppe Sinopoli composed his *Lou Salome Suite* specifically for Hong, who premiered the piece in 1985 with the New York PO.

JONAS WESTOVER

Honky-tonk. Honky-tonk music is a genre of country music that developed in tandem with the burgeoning oil industry of Texas and Oklahoma in the 1930s. Especially after the 1933 repeal of Prohibition, roadhouses, known as honky-tonks, formed in the outlying areas of newly developed communities of laborers from not only the Southwest but also from the depressed conditions of the South. Displaced individuals turned to the honky-tonk to re-establish a sense of community and to escape from the pressures of industrialism through drinking, sexual encounters, and dancing to either live music or recordings played by the jukebox.

Though related to the stylistic features of western swing, honky-tonk music emphasizes the vocalist in songs with diatonic melodies and basic chord progressions that incorporate aspects of the blues, Tin Pan Alley, and gospel hymnody. To project above the noise of the typical roadhouse, the music features amplified guitar solos over the insistent beat of the rhythm section. Providing a boom-chuck rhythmic effect, the string bass stresses the strong beats while the rhythm guitarist usually strikes closed chords on the upbeats or backbeats, a technique known as "sock rhythm." The lead electric guitar or steel guitar typically introduces the song's melody and accompanies the vocal line with single-note rhythmic and melodic fragments. In the mid-1950s drums were added. The pedal steel first replaced the steel guitar in the early 1950s music of Webb Pierce.

Beginning with Al Dexter's "Honky-Tonk Blues" (ARC, 1936), the first song to mention honky-tonk in its title, the music articulated the anxieties of migration and modernity through sexualized and domestic metaphors. In his performances on the *Grand Ole Opry*, Ernest Tubb's 1941 "Walking the Floor Over You" not only demonstrated the prominent theme of masculine vulnerability but also introduced the stylistic features of honky-tonk, notably the use of the electric guitar, to the Southeast. Combining honky-tonk music with the blues and southern music making, a nasal vocality and a fiddle style of playing double stops, Hank Williams redefined the genre for 1950s audiences. Women artists, particularly Kitty Wells and Loretta Lynn, acquired national acclaim with honky-tonk songs in which women protagonists negotiated the conflicts of adult love. Honky-tonk music also thrived in California's displaced southwestern culture with the "Bakersfield Sound" of Buck Owens and Merle Haggard. Contemporary country artists often assert their ties to the sensibilities of the southern working class by incorporating the characteristic sounds of honky-tonk in their songs.

See also COUNTRY MUSIC.

BIBLIOGRAPHY

B. Shank: *Dissonant Identities: The Rock 'n' Roll Scene in Austin Texas* (Hanover and London, 1994)

B. Malone: *Country Music, USA* (Austin, TX, 2002)

A. Fox: *Real Country: Music and Language in Working-Class Culture* (Durham, NC, 2004)

P. Fox: *Natural Acts: Gender, Race, and Rusticity in Country Music* (Ann Arbor, MI, 2009)

STEPHANIE VANDER WEL

Honolulu. Capital city of Hawaii (pop. 377, 256; 2010 US Census). Literally meaning "sheltered bay," Honolulu is the state's most populous city, located on the southeastern side of the island of Oʻahu. It is made up of several distinct neighborhoods and districts, bordered in the west by Moanalua and in the east by Hawaiʻi Kai. Music-making is dominated by several of the areas in central Honolulu, including the Arts district, Kakaʻako, and Waikīkī.

The Arts district is a twelve-block area in downtown Honolulu. Especially popular for its First Friday activities each month, the area is home to several art galleries and cultural institutions. The Hawaii Theatre Center, founded in 1922, is a member of the League of Historic American Theatres and has hosted national and international touring productions. Recently, under Artistic Director and General Manager Burton White, it has supported the work of Hawaiian musicians and kumu hula (hula teachers) with hula drama productions such as *Hānau ka Moku* by Hālau o Kekuhi, and concerts featuring the Brothers Cazimero, the family of Vickie ʻIʻi Rodrigues, and the students of famed kumu hula Maiki Aiu Lake.

Kaka'ako is home to several musical venues of note including the Honolulu Academy of Arts (est. 1922) and the Neil S. Blaisdell Center (est. 1964). The Honolulu Academy of Arts offers a varied musical program ranging from jazz to classical to world music. Artists featured at the Academy in recent years include pianist Helen Huang, Bossa Brazil, Steven Rosenthal, jazz ensemble Hot Club of Hulaville, and guitarists Jeff Peterson and Benjamin Verdery. The Academy's Doris Duke Theatre is also the venue of choice for the Honolulu Chamber Music Series, which included the Los Angeles Guitar Quartet and The Zemlinsky String Quartet in its 2010–2011 season. The Neil S. Blaisdell Center, located in the heart of Honolulu proper, has been the home for Hawaii Opera Theatre productions and touring Broadway musicals. The NBC is the former home of the now-defunct Honolulu Symphony, the oldest symphony orchestra west of the Rocky Mountains. After 110 years in existence, the Symphony's assets were liquidated in Dec 2010. However, the Symphony Exploratory Committee, a group of supporters, purchased the Symphony's assets and devised a plan to revive in 2011 what they intend to call the Hawaii Symphony Orchestra.

While Waikīkī has served as Hawaii's tourist mecca for decades, music-making in the area has seen a decline. In years past, several hotels along Kalākaua Avenue catered to tourists with musical productions such as *Hawaii Calls, Don the Beachcomber,* and *Tavana's South Seas Spectacular.* Hawaiian music-making in Waikīkī has been dominated in recent years by the Royal Hawaiian Center, a large retail complex where Hawaiian music performances take place during most evenings of the week. Cultural Director Manu Boyd has made a concentrated effort to assure that Hawaiian music remains a focal point of the Center.

See also HAWAII.

AARON J. SALĀ

Hood, George (*b* Topsfield, MA, 10 Feb 1808; *d* Minneapolis, MN, 24 Sept 1882). Writer on music and composer. He studied in singing schools in Topsfield and with Lowell Mason in Boston, and in 1848 was ordained at Lawrenceville, New Jersey. He worked as a pastor at Bath, New York (1849–50), and Southport, New York (1851–3), and as a "teacher" or "agent" in Chester, Pennsylvania, and at Princeton, New Jersey; at the time of his death he was superintendent of Shakopee Mission, Minnesota. Hood's fame rests on his *History of Music in New England* (1846/R), which has been quoted extensively by every believer in American musical progress from John Weeks Moore (*Complete Encyclopedia of Music,* 1852) to Ralph T. Daniel (*The Anthem in New England before 1800,* 1966). Its continuing value lies chiefly in the long extracts that he gathered from pronouncements on regular singing in early New England. He included only one musical example, "York," in John Tufts's letter notation. "We know that our music was mean," said Hood in his preface; but it was his desire to "gather it carefully up, and set it with the future that the contrast may appear the more bright and beautiful." Hood was also a composer of congregational hymn tunes.

WRITINGS
Can all learn to sing? (Boston, c1840)
A History of Music in New England with Biographical Sketches of Reformers and Psalmists (Boston, 1846/R)
Musical Manual Designed as a Text-Book for Classes or Private Pupils in Vocal or Instrumental Music (Philadelphia, 1864)

BIBLIOGRAPHY
G. Hood: *Memorials for our Father and Mother: also a Family Genealogy* (Philadelphia, 1867)
G. Hood: "Biography of Daniel Read," *The American Singing Book,* ed. S.P. Cheney (Boston, 1879)
R. Stevenson: "American Musical Scholarship: Parker to Thayer," *19CM,* i (1977–8), 191–210

ROBERT STEVENSON

Hood, Helen Francis (*b* Chelsea, MA, 28 June 1863; *d* Brookline, MA, 22 Jan 1949). Pianist, composer, and teacher. She studied in Boston with D.J. Lang (piano), J.C.D. PARKER and JOHN KNOWLES PAINE (harmony), and GEORGE WHITEFIELD CHADWICK (composition); and in Berlin with Moritz Moszkowski and XAVER SCHARWENKA. She appeared as a pianist with many Boston organizations, had an extensive network of piano students for more than 40 years, and composed steadily from an early age into the 1930s. She received a diploma and medal from the World's Columbian Exposition in Chicago, 1893, where her *Summer Song* was given a triple encore at its performance of 6 July. She is noted for her songs, which evolved from early sentimental ballads to an expansive and expressive idiom in the later works. Elson (2/1925), however, considered her piano trio to be her most important work.

WORKS
(selective list)
Stage: Die Bekehrte
Inst: Pf Trio; Suite de pièces, vn, pf, op.6; Str Qt; Romance, org, op.19; Novelette, A, pf
Vocal: Te Deum, E♭; The Robin, partsong; c100 songs, incl. Song Etchings, op.8 (Boston, 1893), A Disappointment, Message of the Rose, Skating, Sleighing, Summer Song, and The River

MSS in Wc

BIBLIOGRAPHY
A. Elson: *Woman's Work in Music* (Boston, 1903, 2/1931), 207
L.C. Elson: *The History of American Music* (New York, 1904, 2/1925), 306
F.B. Lang: *Diaries* (MS, Bp)

PAMELA FOX

Hood, Margaret F. [née Fullerton, Margaret Holmes] (*b* New York, NY, 19 Nov 1937; *d* Platteville, WI, 7 June 2008). Fortepiano, clavichord, and harpsichord builder. She studied philosophy, religion and art at Mt. Holyoke College, then completed her masters degree at the Pacific School of Religion while doing calligraphic and artifact restoration work for the Bade Archeological Museum. During this time she became noted as a painter. She married Ellsworth Hood in 1961 and had two children. Her interest in harpsichords began in the mid-1960s through kits she completed for others and historically appropriate harpsichord case and soundboard painting. In the 1970s she became a professional builder of her original designs for harpsichords, clavichords, and fortepianos, and was also an agent for

Zuckermann Harpsichords. After researching museum instruments in Europe and the United States, she founded Margaret Hood Fortepianos, in Platteville, in 1976. By the mid-1980s she was well known for her reproductions of 1803 and 1816 pianos by Nannette Streicher, as well as her research and publications about Streicher, Beethoven and the instruments of his time. Her premature death left her extensive work on the Beethoven conversation books incomplete. Her last (unfinished) instrument was based on a Streicher fortepiano from the early 1820s, when Nanette Streicher and her son Johann Baptiste were business partners. In addition, Hood wrote and published technical repair and maintenance manuals for both harpsichords and fortepianos.

ANNE BEETEM ACKER

Hood, Marguerite V(ivian) (*b* Drayton, ND, 14 March 1903; *d* Pomona, CA, 22 Feb 1992). Music educator. She attended Jamestown College, North Dakota (BA 1923) and the University of Southern California (MM 1941). She taught in the Montana public schools (1923–30), and was Montana state music supervisor (1930–36) and radio director for the "Montana School of the Air" (1937–9). Collegiate teaching included the University of Montana (1936–7), University of Southern California (1940–42), and University of Michigan (1942–72). She was music supervisor for the Ann Arbor Public Schools (1942–58), and authored/co-authored five children's music books and over 50 articles. She held several positions in the Music Educators National Conference: first vice-president (1929) and board of directors (1935–7), Northwest Division; president, North Central Division (1945–7); Music Education Research Council (1944–50); editorial board (1947–9) and first female chair (1949–50), *Music Educators Journal*; and national president (1950–52). She helped found the International Society for Music Education and *Journal of Research in Music Education*. She received an honorary doctorate from Jamestown College (1947), and was a Fulbright Scholar (1956–7) and a member of the Music Educators Hall of Fame (1986).

BIBLIOGRAPHY
S.C. Cooper: *Marguerite V. Hood (1903–1992): Her Life and Contributions to Music Education* (diss., Arizona State U., 2004)

GEORGE N. HELLER/SHELLY C. COOPER

Hook, Elias (*b* Salem, MA, 11 March 1805; *d* Boston, MA, 15 June 1881). Organ builder and the brother of George G. Hook (1807–1880). The son of a Salem cabinet-maker, William Hook (1777–1867), Elias began his apprenticeship about 1821 with WILLIAM MARCELLUS GOODRICH (1777–1833) in Boston. He returned to his birth place in 1824 and opened a music store, advertising a "Small Church Organ" for sale in the local papers. In 1831 he and his brother George established the firm E. & G.G. Hook (E. & G.G. Hook & Hastings in 1871, and Hook & Hastings after 1882) in Boston. The firm dominated the organ industry in Boston for much of the 19th and early 20th centuries until it closed in 1936. Elias gravitated

toward the business aspects of running the firm, while George served as the shop foreman.

BIBLIOGRAPHY
B. Owen: *The Organ in New England: An Account of its Use and Manufacture to the End of the Nineteenth Century* (Raleigh, NC, 1979)
F. Mack: "The Hook Family: New Light through Two Letters from Elias Hook to his Sister," *The Tracker* xxxvi/3 (1992), 19

STEPHEN L. PINEL

Hook & Hastings. Organ building firm. It was founded in 1827 by Elias Hook (1805–81) and George Greenleaf Hook (1807–80), under the name of E. & G.G. Hook. The sons of William Hook, a cabinetmaker of Salem, Massachusetts, they had apprenticed with William M. Goodrich in Boston. After building a few organs in Salem they moved to a workshop in Boston where in 1833 they built their first three-manual organ for the First Baptist Church of Providence, Rhode Island. In 1845 they built what was considered the first concert organ in Boston for Tremont Temple. When this was later destroyed by fire the Hooks built their first four-manual organ in 1853 for its successor, and in the following year they built a large new steam-powered factory. By the 1850s the firm had become the leading organ-building establishment in Boston and was producing an average of between 15 and 20 organs a year in this period, largely for locations in the northeastern United States.

Following the Civil War, Hook's production gradually increased to between 30 and 40 organs annually, with a clientele now reaching into the Midwest and beyond, and included a large three-manual organ for St. Ignatius's Church in San Francisco (1868). Other notable organs of the 1860s included those for St. John's Church, Bangor, Maine (1860), Immaculate Conception Church, Boston (1863), Mechanics Hall, Worcester, Massachusetts (1864), Plymouth Church, Brooklyn, New York (1865), and Trinity Church, New Haven, Connecticut (1866). Frank H. Hastings (1836–1916) had joined the Hook firm as an apprentice in 1855, and by the late 1860s had become a part of the firm's design and management team. In 1871 he became a full partner with the Hook brothers, and the firm assumed the name of E. & G.G. Hook & Hastings. Hastings is credited with having taken a prominent part in the firm's more innovative tonal and mechanical developments in the 1870s, exemplified in such notable organs as that for First Presbyterian Church, Pittsburgh, Pennsylvania (1870), Boston's Holy Cross Cathedral (1875), the firm's largest to that date, and the even larger one built for the Music Hall in Cincinnati, Ohio (1877).

Another of Hastings's innovations was the introduction of smaller pre-designed "stock" organs, marketed through descriptive catalogs beginning in 1869 and continuing into the early 20th century. These designs, ranging from a two-rank "chapel" organ to moderate-sized organs of two and three manuals, comprised a large proportion of the firm's production, which sometimes reached 60 or more organs annually during the 1870s, 80s, and 90s. The many extant examples testify to the fact that their tonal and mechanical quality matched that of the firm's more prominent instruments, which included those built for St. Francis Xavier Church, New York (1881), the Industrial Exposition Building in Milwaukee, Wisconsin (1881), the Southern Exposition, Louisville, Kentucky (1883), and King's Chapel, Boston (1884).

In 1889 Hastings, sole owner of the company since the deaths of the Hook brothers, replaced the aging Boston factory with a new and larger one in the suburban town of Weston, where his family owned property through which a convenient railroad line ran, and from this time on the firm's nameplates read simply Hook & Hastings. In the new facility production continued to increase through the 1890s and into the early 20th century. Important organs from this period included those for Grace Episcopal Church, Utica, New York (1890), St. Joseph's Cathedral, Hartford, Connecticut (1890), Temple Emanu-El, San Francisco (1898), First Christian Science Church, Boston (1906), and Trinity Church, New York (1907). Electric action began to be introduced at the end of the 19th century, and was employed for all larger organs thereafter, although some small organs continued for some time to be built with mechanical or tubular-pneumatic action. Production had begun to decline by 1910, however, after the death of Hastings in 1916 control of the company fell into the hands of relatives who seemed unable to cope with competition from newer and more progressive firms. Although the number of organs built was falling to an average of only 15 to 20 organs annually, some of their largest organs dated from this period, including those for the Scottish Rite Cathedral, Dallas, Texas (1912), Central Methodist Church, Winona, Minnesota (1918), St. Paul's Cathedral, Boston (1921), and Riverside Church, New York (1927). The effects of the Depression, increasing competition, and lackluster leadership combined to end production in 1935, when only four small organs were built, and this once-distinguished firm closed its doors in 1936.

BIBLIOGRAPHY

S.H. Lovewell: "Great Organ of 1863 in Church of Immaculate Conception, Boston. *The Diapason*, xix/10 (Sept 1928), 1

W.J. Conner: "Pipe Scaling in Hook Organs, 1849–1895," *The Diapason,* lxii/10 (1971), 18, 26–9

T. Murray: "The Hook & Hastings Organ in Holy Cross Cathedral, Boston," *The Diapason*, lxiii/11 (1971–2), 1, 4–6

B. Owen: "A Salem Chamber Organ," *Essex Institute Quarterly,* cx/2 (1974), 111–9

B. Owen: *The Organ in New England* (Raleigh, NC, 1979)

C. Clutton: "E. & G.G. Hook, Organ Builders of Boston, Mass," *The Organ,* lxvi (1987), 167–79

W.T. Van Pelt, ed.: *The Hook Opus List, 1929–1916 in Facsimile* (Richmond, VA, 1991)

P. Fox: "The Hook & Hastings Organ Factory in Weston," *The Tracker,* xliv/3–4, 32–43 (2001),

B. Owen: "Hook & Hastings: The Boston Years," *The Tracker,* xliv/3–4 (2001), 22–31

R.B. Hastings: *E. & G.G. Hook & Hastings and Nineteenth Century American Romanticism* (MM Thesis, SUNY Potsdam, 2002)

BARBARA OWEN

Hooker, Earl (Zebedee) (*b* ?Clarksdale, MS, 15 Jan *c*1929–30; *d* Chicago, IL, 21 April 1970). Blues singer and guitarist. He was raised in Chicago after his family settled there in 1930, and from the late 1940s he stood out as one of the city's most innovative musicians for his virtuoso slide guitar playing and for his mastery of the *wah wah* pedal. A second cousin of John Lee Hooker, he was influenced by a wide range of musical styles, including the work of country guitarists Merle Travis, Les Paul, and Joe Maphis, as well as jazz and popular music. Although he was one of the most revered Chicago blues musicians on a local scale, he never acquired the stardom of Muddy Waters or Howlin' Wolf, because of his weak vocal abilities and his health problems due to the tuberculosis that affected him from his teens. His public recognition began in the late sixties when he released a few LPs and toured in Europe with his own group, shortly before his death in 1970. His instrumental re-recording of Muddy Waters' "She's All Right" (1952), which he released for Chess in 1962 as "You Need Love" with overdubbed voice from the original mix, is claimed to be a major influence on Led Zeppelin's hit "Whole Lotta Love" (1970).

RECORDINGS
(selective list)
You Need Love (1962, Chess); *Two Bugs and a Roach* (1968, Arhoolie, 1044); *Don't Have to Worry* (1969, Bluesway, 6032); *Hooker and Steve* (1969, Arhoolie, 1051)

BIBLIOGRAPHY
A.J.M. Prévos: "Four Decades of French Blues Research in Chicago: From the Fifties into the Nineties," *Black Music Research Journal*, xii/1 (1992), 97–112

S. Danchin: *Earl Hooker: Blues Master* (Jackson, MS, 2001)

ALESSANDRO BRATUS

Hooker, John Lee (*b* Clarksdale, MS, 22 Aug 1917; *d* Los Altos, CA, 21 June 2001). Blues singer and guitarist. He was first exposed to music at church and constructed his first instrument out of a piece of string and an inner tube. In the 1930s, he moved to Memphis and regularly performed at house parties while occasionally singing in gospel quartets including the Fairfield Four. After World War II, he settled in Detroit where he worked at the Ford Motor Company and played in blues venues and clubs at night. It was during this period that he decided to make the switch from acoustic to electric guitar. He had initially developed a country/rural folk-type blues style on his acoustic guitar, but moved to a more urban style with the electric guitar. In 1948, he recorded his first hit single "Boogie Chillen," featuring vocals, electric guitar and the sound of his foot tapping to the beat. This recording also featured Hooker's TALK-ING BLUES style, which became his trademark. In 1955, he signed with VeeJay Records and started recording with a band, producing such hits as "Dimples" (1956) and "Boom Boom" (1962). By this time he had begun to incorporate jazz and jump blues rhythms into his traditional blues sound. During the 1950s, a new audience discovered his blues style and he began appearing at folk festivals, coffeehouses, and college campuses. He appeared and sang in the film *The Blues Brothers* (1980) and won a 1989 Grammy Award with Carlos Santana for the album *The Healer*. In 1997, he

John Lee Hooker, 1991. (Photofest/Lebrecht Music & Arts)

opened a nightclub in San Francisco's Fillmore District called "John Lee Hooker's Boom Boom Room," named after his 1962 hit. He was inducted into the Rock and Roll Hall of Fame in 1991. In 2000 he was awarded the Grammy Lifetime Achievement Award.

BIBLIOGRAPHY
R. Palmer: *Deep Blues* (New York, 1981)
T. Russell: *The Blues from Robert Johnson to Robert Cray* (New York, 1997)
C.S. Murray: *Boogie Man: the Adventures of John Lee Hooker in the American Twentieth Century* (New York, 2000)
D. Waterman: *Between Midnight and Day: the Last Unpublished Blues Archive* (New York, 2003)

DINA M. BENNETT

Hooley, R.M. (*b* Ballina, Ireland, 13 April 1822; *d* Chicago, IL, 8 Sept 1893). Minstrel performer and manager of Irish birth. He came to the United States in 1844 and began performing with Christy's Minstrels in Buffalo, New York in 1845, remaining with the company two years. He continued to perform, but made his reputation chiefly as a manager, owner, and promoter. He first organized a company of his own in 1851 and took it on a tour of Europe, then during much of the 1850s he managed Maguire's Minstrels, the foremost troupe in San Francisco. He organized Hooley and Campbell's Minstrels in 1860, and after it disbanded in 1861 he opened his own minstrel hall in Brooklyn. He remained in Brooklyn for much of the remainder of his career, though he spent periods in Chicago in the early 1870s, and again in the early 1880s; he built minstrel theaters in both Brooklyn and Chicago, where not only his own troupes but all the important touring companies of the

day performed. He followed the trend for larger companies with the formation of his Megatherian Minstrels in the 1880s.

BIBLIOGRAPHY
E.L. Rice: *Monarchs of Minstrelsy* (New York, 1911)
G.C.D. Odell: *Annals of the New York Stage* (New York, 1927–49)
C. Wittke: *Tambo and Bones: a History of the American Minstrel Stage* (Durham, NC, 1930)

ROBERT B. WINANS

Hootchy-kootchy. A kind of erotic dance done to music whose melodic line is now known worldwide, played in performances at the Chicago World's Columbian Exposition of 1893. The exposition included an attraction called "A Street in Cairo," which featured snake charmers, camel rides, and a troupe of Middle Eastern "belly dancers" who scandalized fairgoers with their "shimmy and shake" dance called the hootchy-kootchy. (The stardom of a dancer called Little Egypt is disputed.) Composition of the tune was claimed by Sol Bloom, the entertainment director of the exposition, but since he failed to copyright the music, several other composers of his time used the melody for their songs, variously entitled "Hoolah! Hoolah!," "Coochi-Coochi," "Danse du Ventre," "Kutchi Kutchi," and "Harem Nights" or "In the Harem" (by Irving Berlin). The only one well known today is "The Streets of Cairo, or the Poor Little Country Maid," copyrighted in 1895 by James Thornton and popularized by his wife Bonnie, who sang it on stage. It soon became the definitive song used by hootchy-kootchy dancers everywhere. Although the origin of the tune is uncertain, it is thought to be from an Arabic popular song called "Kradoutja," known in the Middle East and North Africa from at least 1600.

BIBLIOGRAPHY
D. Carlton: *Looking for Little Egypt* (Bloomington, 1995)
J.J. Fuld: *The Book of World-Famous Music: Classical, Popular, and Folk* (Mineola, NY, rev. 5/2000)

CLAUDE CONYERS

Hoover, Cynthia Adams (*b* Lexington, NE, 16 Dec 1934). Music and cultural historian, and museum curator. She studied at Wellesley College (BA 1957), Harvard University (MAT 1958), and Brandeis University (MFA 1961). She taught at Wellesley (1958–60) before becoming a curator in the Division of Musical Instruments of the Smithsonian from 1961 to 2004. She is currently co-editor of *The William Steinway Diary, 1861–96* and curatorial consultant for MIM, a new musical instrument museum in Phoenix, Arizona. Her concentration has been on the cultural, social, and technological history of musical instruments made and used in America. Hoover has been the curator of numerous exhibitions at the Smithsonian. She was president of the Comité International des Musées et Collections d'Instruments de Musique [CIMCIM] (1989–95), for which she edited several reports. She served on the board of the American Musicological Society and as chair of the AMS Bicentennial Committee, on which she oversaw the publication of the William Billings Edition (four volumes, 1977–90) and from 1981–90 helped shape COPAM, the publisher of the Music in the United States of America series. She also was a member of the editorial board of New World Records, as well as the author of many articles for various editions of *Grove Dictionaries*. She was a founding member and officer of the Sonneck Society (now Society for American Music) and the American Musical Instrument Society; in addition, she organized the Smithsonian Forum on Material Culture (chairperson, 1988–95) and the Yale-Smithsonian Seminar on Material Culture (1988–97).

EXHIBITIONS
Music Making—American Style (Smithsonian, 1966)
Music Machines—American Style (Smithsonian, 1971–5), including catalog (Washington, DC 1971)
with P. Rucker, E.M. Good, eds. and co-curators: *PIANO 300: Celebrating Three Centuries of People and Pianos* (Smithsonian, 2000–1), including catalog performances, chapter in companion volume, and PBS video

WRITINGS
"A Trumpet Battle at Niblo's Pleasure Garden," *Musical Quarterly* lx/3 (July 1969), 384–95
"Epilogue to Secular Music in Early Massachusetts," *Music in Colonial Massachusetts 1630–1820* (Boston, 1973) ii, 715–868
"The Steinways and Their Pianos in the Nineteenth Century," *Journal of the American Musical Instrument Society* 7 (1981), 47–89
"Secular Music in Early Massachusetts," *Music in Colonial Massachusetts 1630–1820*, Vol. II (Boston, 1985), 715–867
"The Great Piano War of the 1870s," *A Celebration of American Music: Words and Music in Honor* of *H. Wiley Hitchcock*, ed. R. Crawford, R.A. Lott, and C. Oja (Ann Arbor, MI, 1990), 132–53
"Music and Theater in the Lives of Eighteenth-Century Americans," *Of Consuming Interests: The Style of Life in the Eighteenth Century* (Charlottesville, VA, 1994), 307–53

BIBLIOGRAPHY
GMO

PAULA MORGAN/CATHERINE PARSONS SMITH

Hoover, Katherine (*b* Elkins, WV, 2 Dec 1937). Composer and flutist. She attended the Eastman School (BM 1959), Bryn Mawr, Yale Summer Session, and the Manhattan School of Music (MM 1974). Hoover's main flute study was with Joseph Mariano at Eastman, later working with WILLIAM KINCAID of the Philadelphia Orchestra. She taught at the Manhattan School and at Juilliard Preparatory, and has performed widely as a flautist. From 1978 to 1981 she organized the Women's Interart Center music festivals in New York. Hoover has received many commissions, residencies, and awards, including an Academy of Arts and Letters Award in Composition in 1994. In 1996 Hoover was named composer-in-residence for the biennial Festival of Women Composers held at Indiana University of Pennsylvania. In recent years Hoover has also become active as a conductor, studying at the Conductors Institute in South Carolina and leading performances of her own works and those of others in Wisconsin, West Virginia, New York, and Pennsylvania.

Although her output includes works for solo voice and chorus, her major works are instrumental. Extramusical references include Barbara Tuchman's *A Distant Mirror* (in *Medieval Suite*) and Amerindian myths (in *Kokopeli* and *Stitch-te Naku*). *Da pacem* takes its name from the 16th-century cantus firmus on which it is based. Her musical rhetoric is clear and eloquent; moments of startling beauty emerge from her sometimes acerbic harmonies. The commissioning, rehearsal, and premiere of her *Dances and Variations* is the subject of a 1996 documentary entitled *New Music* (directed by Deborah Novak). Hoover's flute music, in particular *Kokopeli*, is widely performed and recorded.

WORKS
Orch: Summer Night, fl, hn, str, 1985, arr. fl, hn, pf, 1985; Cl Conc., 1987; Eleni: a Greek Tragedy, 1987; Double Conc., 2 vn, str, 1989; 2 Sketches, 1989; Night Skies, 1992; Stitch-te Naku, vc, orch, 1994; Bounce, orch, 1996
Chbr and solo inst: Trio, 3 fl, 1974; Homage to Bartók, wind qnt, 1975; Divertimento, fl, vn, va, vc, 1975; Sinfonia, 4 bn, 1976; Trio, cl, vn, pf, 1978; Set, cl, 1978; Suite, 2 fl, 1977–81; Suite, s sax, a sax, t sax, b sax, 1980; Images, cl, vn, pf, 1981; Medieval Suite, fl, pf, 1981, orchd 1984; 6 Simple Duets, 2 fl, 1982; Serenade, cl, str qt/pf, 1982; Reflections, 6 fl, 1982; Lyric Trio, fl, vc, pf, 1983; Aria, vc/bn, pf, 1982–5 [arr. of movt from Serenade]; Allegro Giocoso, vc, pf, 1985; Qwindtet, wind qnt, 1987; Da pacem, pf qnt, 1988; Ritual, cl, pf, 1989; Kokopeli, fl, 1990; Sound Bytes, 2 fl, 1990; Sonata, ob, pf, 1991; Canyon Echoes, fl, gui, 1991; Dances & Variations, fl, hp, 1996; Three for Eight, 8 fl, 1996; Winter Spirits, fl, 1997; Kyrie, 12 fl, 1998; Masks, fl, pf, 1998; Str Qt, 1998; Canyon Shadows, native fl, fl, perc, 1999; Trio, 3 fl, 1999; Suite, fl, gui, bn, 2000; Mariposas, 6 fl, 2001; Celebration, 6 fl, 2001; Antics, 2 fl, 2002; El Andalus, vc, pf, 2003; Str Qt no.2, "The Knot," 2004; Three Sketches, pic, pf, 2004; To greet the sun, fl, 2005; Concertante "Dragon Court," fl ens, 2006; Two for Two, a fl, pf, 2006; Mountain and Mesa, fl, pf, 2008; Journey, bn, pf, 2009
Pf: [7] Pieces, 1977–82; Andante e allegro, 1983; Sonata mvt, 1999; Preludes, 2004; At the piano, 2004; Dream Dances, 2008
Choral: 3 Carols, SSA, fl, 1972; Songs of Joy, SATB, kbd/(2 tpt, 2 trbn), 1974; 4 English Songs, SATB, ob, eng hn, pf, 1976; Ps xxiii, SATB, org, 1981, arr. SATB, orch, 1981; Songs of Celebration, SATB, kbd/brass qnt, 1983; The Last Invocation (W. Whitman), chorus, 1984; Sweet Thievery (Hoover), (S, A, T, B)/SATB, 1985; Ps c, SATB, kbd, 1997; Ps c, SATB, org, 1997; Echo, SATB, 1998; Requiem: a Service of Remembrance 1865/2001 (W. Whitman), chorus, SATB soloists, 2 spkrs, br(ass), perc, org, 2002; For Peace: Prayer in Time of War, women's chorus (S, A), 2003; Peace is the Way, women's chorus (S, A), 2003
Other vocal: 7 Haiku, S, fl, 1973; To Many a Well, Mez/S, pf, 1977; Selima, or Ode on the Death of a Favourite Cat, Drowned in a Tub of Goldfishes, S, cl, pf, 1979; From the Testament of François Villon, B-Bar, bn, str qt, 1982; Central American Songs, v, fl, perc, pf, 1995; The Heart Speaks, 7 songs, S, pf, 1997; 3 songs, Bar, 1999; Central American songs, S or Mez, fl, pf, perc, 2004

MSS in *NYamc*
Principal publishers: Carl Fischer, Papagena Press, T. Presser

BIBLIOGRAPHY
F. Rothenberg: *Music for Clarinet and String Quartet by Women Composers* (diss., U. of Arizona, 1993)
N. Sanders: *A Woman's Voice: the Clarinet Concerti of Musgrave, Hoover and Gotkovsky* (diss., U. of Illinois, 1994)
E. Yarrison: *The Medieval Suite for Flute and Piano by Katherine Hoover: an Examination, Analysis and Performance Guide* (diss., U. of Nebraska, 1996)

CATHERINE PARSONS SMITH/ELIZABETH PERTEN

Hope, Bob [Townes, Leslie] (*b* Eltham, London, England, 30 May 1903; *d* Toluca Lake, CA, 27 July 2003). Actor, comedian, and singer of English birth. Son of a stonemason and a light opera singer, Hope moved with his family to Cleveland, Ohio, in 1908. As a boy he danced and entertained on the boardwalk. His vaudeville career began in 1925 and included such varied activities as dancing, acts with various partners, and monologues. His Broadway debut took place in *Sidewalks of New*

York (1927). Hope had major roles in *Ballyhoo of 1932*, *Roberta* (1933), *Say When* (1934), *Ziegfeld Follies of 1936*, and *Red, Hot and Blue* (1936), the latter with Ethel Merman and Jimmy Durante. Hope then began a long career in films, radio, and television, becoming one of the world's most recognizable entertainers. His first major film role was in *The Big Broadcast of 1938*, where he sang (with Shirley Ross) "Thanks for the Memories," which became his theme song. Among his many films were the seven *Road to...* movies that he made with Bing Crosby and Dorothy Lamour, starting in 1940. Hope sang in a pleasant, conversational baritone until late in his career. He made 60 USO tours to entertain American troops between the 1940s and 1990s. Among his many awards were a Kennedy Center Lifetime Achievement Award (1985) and an honorary knighthood from Queen Elizabeth II (1998).

BIBLIOGRAPHY
W.R. Faith: *Bob Hope: a Life in Comedy* (New York, 1982)
R. Strait: *Bob Hope: a Tribute* (New York, 2003)

PAUL LAIRD

Hope, Samuel (Howard) (*b* Owensboro, KY, 5 Nov 1946). Accreditation organization executive. He was educated at the Eastman School of Music (BM 1967) and Yale University (MMA 1970) and studied composition with NADIA BOULANGER. After serving as dean and composer-in-residence at the Atlanta Boy Choir School of Music (1970–73) and as executive director of music alumni at Yale (1974–5), in 1975 he became executive director of the National Office for Arts Accreditation and the organizations it serves: National Association of Schools of Music (founded 1924), National Association of Schools of Art and Design (1944), National Association of Schools of Theatre (1965), and National Association of Schools of Dance (1981). Hope has helped establish national standards and policies for education in the arts at professional and elementary-secondary levels. He has built relations between pre-K–12 and higher education, and has assisted in guidelines development for the National Assessment of Educational Progress for the Arts and several other organizations. He is an executive editor of *Arts Education Policy Review* and has been a consultant to national policy analysis projects, including those of the RAND Corporation and the Association of Specialized and Professional Accreditors. Hope also composes for various media and writes about the arts and education.

GARRY E. CLARKE

Hope-Jones, Robert (*b* Hooton Grange, nr Hooton, Cheshire, UK, 9 Feb 1859; *d* Rochester, NY, 13 Sept 1914). Organ builder and inventor of English birth. Apprenticed as an engineer in the Birkenhead shipyard, he later became chief electrician of the Lancashire and Cheshire Telephone Co., and served as organist in local churches. In 1887 he utilized the skills learnt in this work to rebuild and electrify the organ of St. John's Church, Birkenhead, introducing several new features, including the first movable console. In 1889 he established himself as an organ builder in Birkenhead, experimenting with orchestral pipe voicing and electrically-controlled action mechanisms, but subcontracting the actual building to other firms at first. In 1894 he established his own company, the Hope-Jones Organ Co., and in 1898 moved to Norwich. Bankruptcy soon followed, however, and in 1899 he sold his assets to Norman & Beard, and in 1901 briefly partnered with Eustace Ingram as a designer. In 1903 he embarked for the United States. Carleton C. Michell, an Englishman who had preceded him to America, was then working for the Austin firm, and convinced its proprietors to hire him. However, Hope-Jones's desire to immediately make major tonal and mechanical changes soon caused problems, and, after only a few organs had been built to his designs, both he and Michell were dismissed in 1904. A year later he was hired by Ernest Skinner, and the same scenario ensued, although he had again been given full charge of a few organs before being dismissed in 1906. The last of these was for the Park Church in Elmira, New York, and with the encouragement of certain local businessmen he established the Hope-Jones Electric Organ Co. there in 1907, from which issued the first of his "unit orchestras," highly unified instruments containing some of his unusually scaled and voiced pipes At one point the factory was said to have employed 70 people. The largest organ to be built solely under his direction was completed in 1908 for the Auditorium in Ocean Grove, New Jersey.

In 1910, however, again in financial difficulty, Hope-Jones sold his designs and interests to the Rudolph Wurlitzer Co., staying on more or less as a figurehead while, encouraged by early sales of "unit orchestras" to movie theaters in Chicago and Denver, the Wurlitzer firm amplified on his tonal and mechanical innovations to evolve its highly successful style of theatre organs. Hope-Jones, though, found his opportunities for further invention severely restricted, and in 1914, despondent after a failed attempt to break his contract with Wurlitzer and other problems, he committed suicide. There is no question, however, that he left an indelible mark on the American organ of the early 20th century. In addition to the memorable sounds of the theatre organ, many of his mechanical innovations in console design (stop tablets, tilted keyboards, combination actions) and internal mechanism (improved contact and magnet design, more effective expression shutters) were subsequently adapted in various ways not only by the builders that briefly employed him, but by the organ-building industry at large.

BIBLIOGRAPHY
G.L. Miller: *The Recent Revolution in Organ Building* (New York, 1913)
H.C. Cobb: *The influence of Robert Hope-Jones on the American Organ.* (thesis, American Conservatory of Music, 1934)
F. Webb: "Robert Hope-Jones in the United States," *The Organ*, xiii/51 (Jan 1934), 152–160
R. Whitworth: *The Electric Organ* (London, 1948)
A. Turner: "Father of the Theatre Organ: The Remarkable Story of Robert Hope-Jones" *Tibia*, i/1 (1955), i/2 (1956), i/3 (1956)
M. Sayer: "New Light on Hope-Jones," *The Organ*, lx (1981), 20-24

R. Bramlet: "Robert Hope-Jones, Shadow in the Organ Loft" in *Reaching for the Infinite* (Rochester, NY, 1983), 53–79

G.W. Paulsen: "Ocean Grove Auditorium" *The American Organist,* xxiv/7 (Jul 1990)

D.H. Fox: *Robert Hope-Jones* (Richmond, VA, 1992)

BARBARA OWEN

Hopekirk [Wilson], Helen (*b* Edinburgh, UK, 20 May 1856; *d* Cambridge, MA, 19 Nov 1945). Pianist, composer, and teacher of Scottish birth. Following early studies in piano and composition in Edinburgh, she attended the Leipzig Conservatory from 1876 until 1878. There she studied with Carl Reinecke, Salomon Jadassohn (composition), LOUIS MAAS (piano), and E.F. Richter (counterpoint) and formed lifelong friendships with fellow students Carl Muck and George Whitefield Chadwick. Following successful debuts with the Leipzig Gewandhaus (28 November 1878) and at the Crystal Palace (15 March 1879), London, she toured England and Scotland. She married the music critic, painter, and businessman William A. Wilson in 1882, and, with her husband as manager, made her American debut on 7 December 1883 with the Boston SO. Following three highly successful years touring the United States, she felt the need for further development; in Vienna she studied the piano with Theodor Leschetizky and composition with Karel Navrátil. After returning to the United States for another concert tour, in 1892 Hopekirk moved to Paris to enable further composition study with Richard Mandl. After her husband's severe injury in a traffic accident, Hopekirk accepted Chadwick's offer of a teaching post at the New England Conservatory in 1897. She became involved at every level of music making in Boston and promoted Edward MacDowell's piano works as well as introducing works by Faure, Debussy, and d'Indy. During her Boston years Hopekirk also concentrated on composition, producing primarily piano works and songs. In 1901 she left the Conservatory to teach privately. In 1919 she relocated to Scotland, and though she returned to Boston in 1920, she spent part of each year in Europe. Throughout her years in Boston, Hopekirk was a sought-after teacher and performer, winning admirers among the city's most important cultural elite. Among her supporters were Oliver Wendell Holmes, B.J. Lang, Annie Fields, and Margaret Ruthven Lang. She continued to perform, making her last appearance in April 1939 playing only her own compositions.

Hopekirk's compositions reveal her lifelong interest in Gaelic folk music, and many are characterized by the use of folk-like melodic elements. Of particular interest are her settings of poems by Fiona Macleod employing Gaelic dialect and her arrangements of Scottish songs. Her large-scale works demonstrate her knowledge of classical idioms and strong formal organization. Hopekirk's correspondences and papers are held primarily at the Library of Congress, Washington, DC.

WORKS
(selective list)

Orch: Conzertstück, pf, orch, 1894; Pastorale, 1899; Pf Conc., 1900; Légende, 1910

Vocal: 100 songs, incl.5 Songs (F. Macleod) (New York, 1903); 6 Songs (F. Macleod) (New York, 1907); 70 Scottish Songs (arrs.) (Boston, 1905); choral works

Other inst:2 sonatas, vn, pf, e, 1891, D, 1893; Iona Melodies, pf (1910); Suite, pf (Boston, 1917); A Norland Eve, pf (Boston, 1919)

BIBLIOGRAPHY

A.G. Cameron: *Helen Hopekirk: a Critical and Biographical Sketch* (New York, 1885)

C.H. Hall and H.I. Tetlow: *Helen Hopekirk, 1856–1945* (Cambridge, MA, 1954) [incl. works list]

D. Muller: *Helen Hopekirk (1856–1945): Pianist, Composer, Pedagogue. A Biographical Study; a Thematic Catalogue of her Works for Piano; a Critical Edition of her Conzertstück in* D *minor for Piano and Orchestra* (diss., U. of Hartford, 1995)

L. Blunsom: *Gender, Genre and Professionalism: the Songs of Clara Rogers, Helen Hopekirk, Amy Beach, Margaret Lang and Mabel Daniels, 1880–1925* (diss., Brandeis U., 1999)

A.F. Block: "Women in American Music, 1800–1918," in *Women & Music: A History,* ed. K. Pendle (Bloomington, IN, 2001), 212–5

PAMELA FOX/LAURIE BLUNSOM

Hope Publishing Company. A company devoted principally to the publishing of church and educational music, especially hymns and music for choir, keyboard, and handbells. Founded in Chicago in 1892 by Henry S. Date, the company issued a paperback songbook in that year as a sampler for a larger collection, *Pentecostal Hymns* (1893). Date's cousins George H. Shorney and Francis G. Kingsbury joined the business in 1894 and 1896, respectively. After the deaths of Date and Shorney, Kingsbury became president and brought G.H.'s son Gordon D. Shorney into management. Upon Kingsbury's retirement (1925), his interest was purchased by the Shorney family, which still operates the company. In 1972 the firm relocated to Carol Stream, Illinois.

In its early years Hope's principal aim was to provide hymnals and songbooks for use in less formal services of the church where gospel songs were the norm. With the 1935 publication of *The Service Hymnal,* the company began issuing collections designed for broader use. Among recent significant publications of this type have been *Hymns for the Living Church* (1974), *The Singing Church* (1985), *The Worshiping Church* (1990), and *Worship and Rejoice* (2001).

During the course of its history, Hope acquired several other important church music publishing houses, including Biglow & Main (founded 1861, acquired 1922), E.O. Excell (1878, 1931), and Tabernacle Publishing Company (1916, 1926), as well as the copyrights of such popular gospel songwriters as C.H. Gabriel, G.C. Stebbins, F.J. Crosby, I.D. Sankey, P.P. Bliss, J. McGranahan, W.H. Doane, W.J. Kirkpatrick, and D.B. Towner. More recently, Hope has become the US agent and copyright manager for significant hymn writers of the British Commonwealth, the Hymn Society in the United States and Canada, and numerous American authors and composers of hymnody in standard formats.

BIBLIOGRAPHY

G.H. Shorney Jr.: "The History of Hope Publishing Company and Its Divisions and Affiliates," *Dictionary-Handbook to Hymns for the Living Church,* D.P. Hustad (Carol Stream, IL, 1977), 1–21

1892–1992: 100 Years of Hope (Carol Stream, IL, 1992)

DAVID W. MUSIC

Hopi. Native American Pueblo tribe of northern Arizona. Music is an integral part of Hopi culture; as recently as three or four generations ago there were songs to accompany virtually every activity. As the Hopi Reservation entered the modern era, however, many songs ceased to be sung and remembered. Contemporary Hopi music may be divided into three categories: sacred ceremonial music, secular ceremonial music, and children's game or utility music. The number of children songs is diminishing, but ceremonial songs are in regular use and continue to be composed. Religious ceremonies of the Hopi use songs to communicate with spiritual forces, to tell stories, myths, and legends, and to accompany ceremonial dances. Secular ceremonies consist principally of preparation for and performance of ceremonial dances.

Most Hopi men compose ceremonial songs. Some keep their music secret; a Hopi may work on a song for several years before revealing it to others. During preparation for a ceremony an individual sings his song for the performance group, which then learns it, modifies it as needed to fit the situation as hand, dances to it, and sometimes further modifies it to make it more suitable for actual performance. This collective revision process or communal composition ensures that all are familiar with the song and that it will fit the ceremonial function for which it is intended. Once the song is at this stage it is no longer thought of as belonging to an individual, though its source is still recognized; it may in fact be used in other situations or adopted without the composer's permission.

Hopi music is principally vocal. Instruments are used for accompaniment and include rattles, drums, scrapers, cowbells, jingles, bone whistles, flutes, and sheephoof rattles. Except for flutes all instruments are used only to provide rhythmic backing. Ceremonial vocal music is nearly exclusively monophonic; songs are usually sung in unison but occasionally in octaves. In ceremonies males sing in a low, often forced voice, while females generally sing in a high voice or falsetto. Lullabies, game songs, and utility songs are sung in the natural voice of the singer. The melodic contour is usually characterized by establishment of a base pitch, a large leap upward, and a gradual, terraced return to the base pitch at the end of each song section. The scale of most Hopi music is nearly diatonic. In some songs microtonal intervals are used.

Most Hopi music sounds to Western ears as if in simple duple meter, but there are many sections within a song that use triplets, polyrhythm and counter-rhythms. Rhythmic variations are usually based on multiples or divisions of two and three, but occasional exceptions occur. There are also instances where the vocal and accompanimental lines appear in different meters, one duple and the other triple. Hopi ceremonial music, both sacred and secular, normally follows an AABBA form, with a verse and chorus in each of the five sections; traditionally songs generally last from five to ten minutes. Game, utility, and lullaby songs are through-composed.

Songs are thought to have a function and power only when sung in certain situations by appropriate persons; this is particularly true of sacred songs. In some circumstances, especially in the private sections of religious ceremonies, the songs must be performed with perfect accuracy, a tradition that has endured for centuries.

Several influences have affected changes in Hopi music. New ceremonial songs continue to appear; these sometimes reflect the influence of non-Hopi music, but are altered to present a distinct Hopi style. As new material is introduced, some older songs are forgotten. Occasionally an old song is remembered and revived in performance. Certain performances depend on previously used songs, generally from recent years.

A number of Hopi songs have fallen into disuse. Lullabies, although sometimes sung by grandparents, are rare today, as are children's game songs. Hunting, gambling, swimming, and traveling songs are no longer heard, and only a few women remember corn-grinding songs, though there is presently a revival of some of these genres. In some cases sacred songs are now used for secular purposes; they are, for example, sung by some members of the tribe to accompany farming chores or simply to pace their steps. Ceremonial music is often recorded by the Hopi in a shortened form, but is seldom heard by others due to its very different style. Only a few commercial recordings of secular songs exist, and none of the sacred songs have been record within actual ceremonies.

DISCOGRAPHY

Hopi Kachina Songs, collected by J.W. Fewkes (FW, 1924)
Music of the American Indians of the Southwest, collected by W. Rhodes (FW, 1953)
Indian Music of the Southwest, collected by L. Boulton (FW, 1957)
Hopi Buttery Songs (Canada, 1967)
Pueblo Songs of the Southwest (IH, 1972)
Hopi Social Dance Songs (Canada, 1973)
Hopi Sunshield Singers: *Pow-wow Songs Live* (CR, 1982)
Sounds of Indian America (IH, 1995)
Clark Tenakhongya: *Hear my Song, Hear my Prayer* (CR, 2003)
Clark Tenakhongya: *Hoat'Ve'La* (CR, 2005) [original songs]
Clark Tenakhongya: *Po'li* (butterfly) (CR, 2007)

BIBLIOGRAPHY

W. Hough: "Music of the Hopi Flute Ceremony," *American Anthropologist*, x (1897), 162–3
J.W. Fewkes: "Hopi Basket Dances," *Journal of American Folklore*, xii (1899), 81–96
J.W. Fewkes: "Minor Hopi Festivals," *American Anthropologist*, iv (1902), 482–511
N. Curtis: *The Indian's Book* (New York, 1907)
B.I. Gilman: *Hopi Songs* (Boston, 1908)
J. Collier and I. Moskowitz: *Patterns and Ceremonials of the Indians of the Southwest* (New York, 1949)
H. James: *The Hopi Indian Butterfly Dance* (Los Angeles, 1959)
G. List: "Songs in Hopi Culture, Past and Present," *JIFMC*, xiv (1962), 30–5
R.A. Black: *A Content-analysis of Eighty-one Hopi Indian Chants* (diss. Indiana U., 1964)
R.A. Black: "Hopi Grievance Chants: a Mechanism of Social Control," *Studies in Southwestern Ethnolinguistics: Meaning and History in the Languages of the American Southwest*, ed. E.H. Hymes and W.E. Bittle (The Hague, 1967), 54–67
R.A. Black: "Hopi Rabbit-hunt Chants: a Ritualized Language," *American Ethnological Society, Essays on the Verbal and Visual Arts*, ed J. Helm (Seattle, WA, 1967), 7–11
J. Keali'inohomoku: "Hopi and Polynesian Dance: a Study in Cross-Cultural Comparisons," *EM*, xi (1967), 343–58
G. List: "Hopi as Composer and Poet," *Proceedings of the Centennial Workshop on Ethnomusicology: Vancouver 1967*, ed. P. Crossley-Holland (Vancouver, BC, 1968, 3/1975), 43–53
T. Bahti: *Southwest Indian Ceremonials* (Flagstaff, AZ, 1970)

R. Rhodes: *Selected Hopi Secular Music: Analysis and Transcription* (diss., Arizona State U., 1973)

R. Rhodes: *Hopi Music and Dance* (Tsaile, AZ, 1977)

J. Keali'inohomoku: "The Dance of the Hopi Ogres," *Southwestern Indian Ritual Drama*, ed. C.J. Frisbie (Albuquerque, NM, 1980), 37–69

G. List: "Hopi Melodic Concepts," *JAMS*, xxxviii/1 (1985), 143–52

A.W. Geertz: "Ethnohermeneutics and Worldview Analysis in the Study of Hopi Indian Religion," *Numen* 50 (2003), 309–48

E. Sekaquaptewa and D. Washbum: "They go along singing: reconstructing the Hopi past from ritual metaphors in song and dance," *American Antiquity*, lxix/3 (2004), 457–86

L.A. Heeb: "The Hopi Clown Ceremony (Tsukulalwa)," *American Indian Culture and Research Journal*, xxxii/4 (2008), 107–24

ROBERT W. RHODES/J. RICHARD HAEFER

Hopkins, Asa (*b* Litchfield, CT, 2 Feb 1779; *d* New Haven, CT, 27 Oct 1838). Maker of woodwind instruments. He worked in a section of Litchfield, Connecticut, later known as Fluteville. A clockmaker from before 1810 to 1825, Hopkins had briefly located in 1809 to Prince Edward, Virginia, where he advertised in Richmond newspapers that he made not only clocks but also "Piano Forte-Organs, both finger and barrel, of every description, made to order." Returning within a year to Litchfield, he resumed clockmaking until 1825, when he sold that workshop and began acquiring the property on which he would build a workshop to begin to make woodwind instruments in 1828. In 1832 Hopkins encouraged his former apprentice Jabez McCall Camp (1811–90) to become one of five special partners, with Hopkins as general partner. In June 1837, apparently because of Hopkins's deteriorating health, Camp became the general partner, and for two years all instruments bore his stamp. The Camp firm sold the majority of its stock in 1839 to Firth & Hall of New York, which by 1846 (as Firth, Hall & Pond) owned all shares, evidently stamping its woodwind instruments with that firm's name and "N.YORK" even though they were produced in the Litchfield factory. The factory was sold again in 1867 to Frederick S. Porter, the plant superintendent, who sold it in 1875 to John A. Hall. Not long after, the factory converted to the manufacture of cutlery.

Among the earliest woodwind instrument makers in the United States, Hopkins is noted for producing finely crafted instruments that met the needs of the provincial American musical community. The instruments, usually made of boxwood with ivory mounts, have conservative key systems: the clarinets often have five flat brass keys; the flutes have one to nine brass, cupped, or plug-type silver keys.

BIBLIOGRAPHY

YoungHI

P.T. Young: *Asa Hopkins of Fluteville* (diss., Yale U., 1962)

B. Verminb and S. Taylor, "The Hopkins Clockmakers of Litchfield and Harwinton, CT: Part 1A and 1B: Asa Hopkins, Litchfield," *Watch & Clock Bulletin*, 53/3 (2011), 278–301, and 53/4 (2011), 421–33

CYNTHIA ADAMS HOOVER, PHILLIP T. YOUNG/R

Hopkins, (Charles) Jerome (*b* Burlington, VT, 4 April 1836; *d* Athenia, NJ, 4 Nov 1898). Composer, organist, pianist, conductor, and music critic. Hopkins was the eleventh of 14 children born to John Henry Hopkins, first Episcopal Bishop of Vermont (1832–68) and Melusina Müller. He became a prolific composer and fierce advocate for music by Americans, especially his compositions. Self-taught, except for six harmony lessons with T.E. Miguel, he composed from age 14. Upon moving to New York (1853), positions as parish organist assured his income. In 1854 Cook & Brother published *Harebell Waltz* by Timothy Trill, a Hopkins pen name (likewise Joseph Swift). Writing as Justitia in 1855 (*Musical World*, 16 June), he argued for the "cause of American music," its composers, and its performance, citing Charles Hommann's chamber music as exemplary, and proposed founding what became the New York American-Music Association. It survived for three seasons (1856–58); inadequate performance spaces and lack of sufficient professional musicians' support caused its demise. Hopkins developed new schemes that reveal his philanthropic nature and humanitarian ideals, but simultaneously advanced his reputation as a composer and pianist. Utopian convictions led him to launch the Orpheon Free Schools (1861) for teaching children to sing and read music. *Taffy and Old Munch*, Hopkins's children's opera, was composed specifically for the annual Orpheon Springtide festival concerts. Because of his work, Albany, Rochester, Chicago, and Philadelphia had Orpheon Associations by 1881. In 1884 Hopkins proposed a series of "monster" concerts—hundreds of singing children from New York, Brooklyn, and Jersey City—to benefit the Bartholdi pedestal fund.

His compositions number over 600, most of them unpublished. He was also a prolific writer. In *Music and Snobs* (1888), he enumerates the "disabilities of music in America." His polemic, *Why the Best Music Never Pays Here* (1888), pointed out the need for a literate musical audience. Critics pounced; advocates defended him. His opera *Dumb Love* was panned and *Samuel*, an "operatic oratorio," was tolerated. At Cooper Union Hopkins had lectured on "The Music of the Emotions" (1873–4) and became an engaging speaker at his piano concerts, at times inviting the audience to choose the repertoire from his list of 100 memorized works. In 1892 he completed a successful European concert tour. Described variously as energetic, enthusiastic, passionate, outspoken, opinionated, a self-promoter, even crazy, Hopkins was fundamentally creative. Pianist Amy Fay, his niece, credited him for the lecture-concert concept she emulated. His piano piece *The Wind Demon*, still played today, illustrates his personality and life—a whirlwind of activity on behalf of American music. The Houghton Library at Harvard houses his journals and manuscripts. He wanted his ashes laid beside his wife Sarah's in Burlington, Vermont.

WORKS

PUBLISHED

Pf: Rip Van Winkle Polka, 1855; The Wind Demon: Rhapsodie caracteristique, op.11, 1859; Serenade de Don Pasquale, op.22, 1867; Snow Nymph (Polka Caprice), op.24, 1867

Vocal: "The Sailor's Return," op.5, 1856–60; "The Fairest of Flowers," 1858; The Patriot's Call, op.9, 1861; "God Save Our Fatherland," 1861; "If I Couldn't How Could I?" op.14, 1865; "Yes, Love When Stars are Breathing," 1873; "The Gates of Paradise Hymn," 1873

Choral: Orchestral Vesper Service, 1875; Easter Grand Anthem, 1882; Lord with Glowing Heart, 1883
Opera: Samuel: A Sacred Opera, 1877; Taffy and Old Munch, 8 editions, 1882–96
Editions: *A Collection of Sacred Songs*, 1859; *Jerome Hopkins's Second Collection of Church Music*, 1870

UNPUBLISHED
(selective list; performance dates)
Pf: Sepoy March, duet, 1860; Pearl Drops, 1860; *Caprice* for five grand pianos, 1882; Kangaroo Etude, 1886
Vocal: "A Death-Bed Rhapsody," 1856; "Has Summer Pass'd Away?" 1857; "Ode to Florence Nightingale," 1862
Choral/Orchestral: Gloria in excelsis, 1858; Victory Te Deum, 1862
Opera: Dumb Love, 1886
Chamber/Orchestral: Symphony "Life," 1856; Piano Trio in D minor, 1860; Overture "Manhood," 1866
MSS in *MH*

BIBLIOGRAPHY
Obituary, *New York Times* (6 Nov 1898), 7
R. Jackson: "An American Muse Learns to Walk," *American Musical Life in Context and Practice to 1865*, ed. J.R. Heintze (New York, 1994)
V.B. Lawrence: *Strong on Music*, vol. 2, *Reverberations 1850–1856* (Chicago, 1995)
V.B. Lawrence: *Strong on Music*, vol. 3, *Repercussions 1857–1862* (Chicago, 1999)

JOANNE E. SWENSON-ELDRIDGE

Hopkins, Claude (Driskett) (*b* Alexandria, VA, 24 Aug ?1903; *d* New York, NY, 19 Feb 1984). Jazz pianist and bandleader. He studied music and medicine at Howard University. He led his own bands and played briefly in New York with Wilbur Sweatman before touring Europe as music director for Josephine Baker, leading a band that included Sidney Bechet (1925–6). In 1930 Hopkins took over Charlie Skeete's band; under his leadership the band enjoyed successful extended engagements between 1930 and 1936 at the Savoy Ballroom, the Roseland Ballroom, and the Cotton Club. These appearances led to a number of radio broadcasts, which helped to establish Hopkins's group as one of the most popular African American bands of the decade. The personnel included such notable soloists as the trombonist Vic Dickenson, the trumpeter Jabbo Smith, and the clarinetist Edmond Hall. After the group disbanded in 1940 Hopkins continued to perform in combos of various sizes and also worked as a commercial arranger. Although best known as a bandleader, he was also a fine pianist in the stride tradition, especially noted for the strong, rhythmic playing of his left hand.

BIBLIOGRAPHY
SouthernB
S. Dance: *The World of Swing* (New York, 1974/*R*, 2/2001), 31
Obituary, *New York Times* (23 Feb 1984)
W.W. Vaché: *Crazy Fingers: Claude Hopkins' Life in Jazz* (Washington, DC, 1992)

BILL DOBBINS/R

Hopkins, Kenyon (*b* Coffeyville, KS, 15 Jan 1912; *d* Princeton, NJ, 7 April 1983). Composer, arranger, recording artist, and conductor. He studied theory and composition at Oberlin College and Temple University, where he graduated in 1933. In New York he arranged for Andre Kostelanetz and Paul Whiteman, and for radio and theater. Hopkins joined the Coast Guard during World War II, and returned to a variety of musical activities. During the 1950s he was primary composer and arranger for Radio City Music Hall.

In spite of working mostly in New York, Hopkins was part of the new wave of Hollywood composers in the 1950s who eschewed the heavy sound of classic symphonic scoring and introduced a less-is-more, often jazz-influenced sound into the Hollywood of the post-studio era. His total score for *Twelve Angry Men* (1957) is only eight minutes in length.

Hopkins's first feature score, for Elia Kazan's controversial production of Tennessee Williams's *Baby Doll* (1956), fuses naive lyricism and sensual jazz with a touch of rock-and-roll. Previously he had produced an effective jazz score for Rossen's *The Hustler* (1961). For Sydney Lumet's *The Fugitive Kind* (1960), Hopkins created an intimately minimalist score that both plays against and accentuates the darker Tennessee Williams mythos. He introduced twelve-tone techniques into *The Strange One* (1957). Most of his films from this period produced soundtrack LPs.

Hopkins recorded for Cadence, ABC Paramount Capitol, MGM, and Verve records. His albums include *Shock!*, *Panic!*, *Son of Shock*, and other classic examples of what is now called Space Age Pop. Due to contractual issues some of these albums were credited to the Creed Taylor Orchestra. Hopkins was music director for CBS (1963–4) and Paramount Pictures' television (1970–73), and served as music supervisor for television films during this period.

WORKS
Film scores: Baby Doll, 1956; The Strange One, 1957; 12 Angry Men, 1957; The Fugitive Kind, 1960; Wild River, 1960; Wild in the Country, 1961; The Hustler, 1961; The Yellow Canary, 1963; Lilith, 1964; The Cara Williams Show, 1964; This Property Is Condemned, 1966; Mister Buddwing, 1966; Doctor, You've Got to Be Kidding!, 1967; A Lovely Way to Die, 1968; Downhill Racer, 1969; The Tree, 1969
TV scores: Once Upon a Christmas Tree, 1959; East Side/West Side, 1963; To Tell the Truth, 1963; What's My Line?, 1963; 20th Century, 1963; The Reporter, 1964; Hawk, 1966; The Secret of Michelangelo, 1968; Barefoot in the Park, 1970; The Undersea World of Jacques Cousteau, 1970; Love, American Style, 1970; The Young Lawyers, 1970; Mannix, 1970–71; Mission: Impossible, 1970–72; Funny Face, 1971; The Brady Bunch, 1971–3; Women in Chains, 1972; The New Healers, 1972; The World Turned Upside Down, 1973; The Devil's Daughter, 1973; Lincoln: Trial by Fire, 1974
Orch: Sym. in 2 Movts; Town and Country Dances, chbr orch

BIBLIOGRAPHY
G. Bachmann: "Composing for Films; Kenyon Hopkins Interviewed," *Film and TV Music*, xvi/5 (1957), 15–16
K. Hopkins: "Notes on Three Scores: The Strange One, Twelve Angry Men, Baby Doll," *Film and TV Music*, xvi/5 (1957), 12–15

ROSS CARE

Hopkins, Lightnin' [Sam] (*b* Centerville, TX, 15 March 1912; *d* Houston, TX, 30 Jan 1982). Blues singer and guitarist. At age eight, around the time he started to play a guitar crafted from a cigar box, he became acquainted with Blind Lemon Jefferson, a legendary Texas bluesman. Jefferson appointed Hopkins a musical partner as well as a personal guide. After dropping out of school Hopkins traveled with his cousin Alger "Texas" Alexander, another Texas blues legend, throughout Texas and some parts of Mississippi. By accompanying Alexander's free-form vocals, Hopkins developed his unique free-floating guitar style. In 1946, when they were playing at a club in Houston's Third Ward, they were visited by Lola Anne Cullum, a talent scout from Aladdin Records based in Los Angeles. She picked up only Hopkins and teamed him with pianist Wilson "Thunder" Smith. In the autumn of this year, under the name "Thunder" and "Lightnin'," the duo released a single "Katie May" coupled with "I Feel So Bad." As of 1948 Hopkins cut 43 sides for Aladdin, including "Shotgun Blues," "Sugar Mama," and "Play with Your Poodle,"— some were recorded with Smith while others were recorded with Hopkins's brother Joel or by Hopkins alone. During this time, he also made a contract with Gold Star Records in Houston and recorded such songs as "Tim Moore's Farm," "'T' Model Blues," and "Big Mama Jump," the last of which he also recorded for Aladdin. In the mid-1950s Hopkins became a forgotten figure mainly because of the rise of rock 'n' roll, but near the end of the decade the folk music revival helped him regain popularity. In 1959, folklorists Mack McCormick and Samuel Charters located Hopkins; Charters recorded Hopkins in his apartment, releasing *Lightnin' Hopkins* on Folkway Records. Hopkins subsequently performed in coffee houses and on college campuses. He also appeared at the Newport Folk Festival in 1965, Carnegie Hall in 1974, and the New Orleans Jazz and Heritage Festival regularly from 1974. Hopkins was a prolific composer with an ability to make up songs based on life events. Because he preferred upfront cash payment per song to making an exclusive contract with one company at a time, he ended up recording for over twenty labels throughout his career. Hopkins' whimsical business practice has made his one of the most complicated discography in blues history.

RECORDINGS
(selective list)
Blues Masters: The Very Best of Lightnin' Hopkins (Rhino, 2000); *The Complete Aladdin Recordings* (Capitol, 1991); *The Complete Prestige/Bluesville Recordings* (Prestige, 1991); *His Blues* (Ace, 2010); *Lightnin' And the Blues: The Herald Sessions* (Buddha, 2001)

BIBLIOGRAPHY
A. Govenar: *Lightnin' Hopkins: His Life and Blues* (Chicago, 2010)
MITSUTOSHI INABA

Hopkinson, Francis (*b* Philadelphia, PA, 2 Oct 1737; *d* Philadelphia, PA, 9 May 1791). Author, musician, composer, lawyer, and public servant. Hopkinson was the son of Thomas Hopkinson and Mary Johnson, who emigrated from England in 1731, and a graduate of the College of Philadelphia (later University of Pennsylvania; BA, 1757; MA, 1760). He was admitted to the Pennsylvania bar in 1761. At the outset of the Revolutionary War he allied with the Patriot cause as a delegate to the Continental Congress (1776) and signed the Declaration of Independence. From 1779 until his death he practiced law as well as serving on various federal and state commissions. Hopkinson's interests were varied and his talents many. Besides his musical activities, he wrote essays, poetry, and pamphlets; he was skilled at design and drawing; and his inventions included a shaded candlestick, a new method of quilling a harpsichord, and a spring-block to assist in navigation, for which he was awarded a medal by the American Philosophical Society in 1790.

Interested in music from an early age, Hopkinson began to play the harpsichord at 17. Music he copied in the 1750s shows that his preference ran to the Anglo-Italian repertory favored in mid-18th-century London drawing-rooms: arias, songs, and instrumental pieces by composers including Handel, Corelli, Geminiani, Stamitz, Galuppi, and Thomas A. Arne. As a performer, Hopkinson played an important role in the musical life of Philadelphia during the 1760s and early 1770s. A gentleman amateur, he sometimes joined professional musicians to present concerts, particularly his teacher James Bremner. An Anglican his entire life, he was active in sacred music as well, teaching psalmody to children and playing the organ for services when needed. Hopkinson compiled a *Collection of Psalm*

Portrait of Francis Hopkinson by J.B. Longacre, c1780. (University of Pennsylvania Archives)

Tunes (1763) and *The Psalms of David...for the Use of the Reformed Protestant Dutch Church* (1767).

Hopkinson put his literary talents to political use during the Revolutionary War, writing a number of poems and ballads satirizing the British cause and the Loyalists. His most popular poem, "The Battle of the Kegs" (1778), was widely printed in newspapers. Early printings state that the song was set to the Scots tune, "Maggie Lauder," but later printings indicate "Yankee Doodle" as the model for the song. The lyrics follow the latter much more closely.

In 1781, Hopkinson compiled *America Independent, or The Temple of Minerva*, an "oratorial entertainment" predicting a great future for the new nation. Because the earliest notice of the work's performance announced it as "composed and set to music by a gentleman whose taste in the polite arts is, well known," it has been assumed that Hopkinson composed the music and the text. In the 1970s, Gillian Anderson discovered a broadside showing that his texts were written to fit arias, songs, and choruses by Handel, Thomas and Michael Arne, and other composers popular in England, a common practice throughout the eighteenth century (Anderson, 1976).

Hopkinson's "My Days Have Been So Wondrous Free" (1759), a song for voice and harpsichord, is a setting of lyrics by Thomas Parnell. It is modeled after the British songs he had copied, and is the earliest-known secular composition by a native-born European American in British North America. Nearly three decades after composing that song, Hopkinson issued *Seven* [recte Eight] *Songs for the Harpsichord or Forte Piano* (1788), for which he wrote both text and music. The dedication sets forth his assertion, "I cannot, I believe, be refused the Credit of being the first Native of the United States who has produced a Musical Composition." Hopkinson's claim is accurate as a response to the recent ratification of the Federal Constitution, for his publication followed by less than six months the official birth of the United States as a political entity.

Hopkinson's compositions are lyrical songs with easy melodies in keys accessible to most amateurs or young singers. His themes are sentimental love and pastoral settings. The first seven songs in his 1788 collection are arranged in order of difficulty, advertised as "composed in an easy, familiar style, intended for young Practitioners on the Harpsichord or Forte-Piano." Most have a vocal line with an occasional second part and a simple unfigured bass line. The seventh, a rondo, is more complex with an Alberti bass figuration and shorter note values. It presents more of a challenge to the performer. The last song, Hopkinson's favorite, was sent to the printer after the engraving was nearly done. It would have been placed among the easier songs had it been ready earlier. Hand suggests that James Hook's "The Warning" served as Hopkinson's model for this song (Hand, 111–14).

In 1768, Hopkinson married Ann Borden (1747–1827) of Bordentown, New Jersey. One of their five children, Joseph (1770–1842), continued in his father's footsteps as a judge and author, writing the lyrics beginning, "Hail, Columbia, happy land," to a march by Philip Phile.

The Hopkinson Family archive at the Historical Society of Pennsylvania in Philadelphia contains Hopkinson's correspondence (1765–89). The University of Pennsylvania's Rare Book Library and the Library of Congress (Music Division) hold two musical copybooks probably made by Hopkinson and others credited to him that are not in his hand. In 2002, a large body of manuscript music credited to Hopkinson appeared in the auction market and was soon identified as the work of Charles Weisberg (*d* 1945), a noted forger whose work is in unsuspecting libraries across the nation. Because of this forgery, a report on the investigation of these manuscripts in *Notes* (2004) by Gillian Anderson (and others) recommended that librarians review and validate their autograph holdings of Hopkinson, Benjamin Carr, Rayner Taylor, and Stephen Foster. One item with a wide circulation is a photostat of a forgery of Hopkinson's *The Toast* in manuscript (Whiteman, 9–10). Weisberg probably copied the song from sheet music ("Brother Soldiers All Hail," 1799) and inserted his leaf into an anonymous period copybook now at the Library of Congress (ex Carson, and ex Woehlcke collections) to which he added Hopkinson's "signature."

BIBLIOGRAPHY

O.G.T. Sonneck: *Francis Hopkinson, the First American Poet-Composer (1737–1791) and James Lyon, Patriot, Preacher, Psalmodist (1735–1794): Two Studies in Early American Music* (Washington, DC, 1905/R1967)

G.E. Hastings: *The Life and Works of Francis Hopkinson* (Chicago, 1926)

W.T. Upton: *Art-Song in America: a Study in the Development of American Music* (Boston, 1930)

O.E. Albrecht: "Francis Hopkinson, Musician, Poet, and Patriot," *Library Chronicle of the University of Pennsylvania*, vi (1938), 3–15

O.G.T. Sonneck: "Francis Hopkinson: the First American Poet-Composer and our Musical Life in Colonial Times," *Church Music and Musical Life in Pennsylvania*, ed. Pennsylvania Society of the Colonial Dames of America, iii/2 (Philadelphia, 1947), 427–46

C.S. Lenhart: *Musical Influence on American Poetry* (Athens, GA, 1956)

P.Y. Dew: *Francis Hopkinson and His Music* (diss., U. California at Los Angeles, 1967)

H.E. Johnson: "Musical Interests of Certain American Literary and Political Figures," *JRME*, xix (1971), 272–94

G. Anderson: "'Samuel the Priest Gave up the Ghost' and 'The Temple of Minerva': Two Broadsides," *Notes*, xxxi/3 (1975), 493–516

G. Anderson: "'The Temple of Minerva' and Francis Hopkinson: A Reappraisal of America's First Poet–Composer," *Proceedings of the American Philosophical Society*, cxx (1976), 166–77

C. Hamm: *Yesterdays: Popular Song in America* (New York, 1979), 89–93

F. Hopkinson: *Francis Hopkinson's Lessons: A Facsimile Edition of Hopkinson's Personal Keyboard Book*, (Washington, DC, c1979)

M. Whiteman: *Forgers & Fools, The Strange Career of "Baron" Weisberg and the Incredible Story of Documents Destroyed and Disburdened from the Philadelphia Custom House* (New York, 1986)

H.M. Ward: "Hopkinson, Francis," *ANB* (1999)

A.R. Hand: *Francis Hopkinson: American Poet and Composer* (diss, U. Texas at Austin, 2000)

G. Anderson and others: "Forgery in the Music Library: A Cautionary Tale," *Notes*, lx/4 (June 2004), 865–92

RICHARD CRAWFORD/KATE VAN WINKLE KELLER

Hopper, (William) De Wolf (*b* New York, NY, 30 March 1858; *d* Kansas City, MO, 23 Sept 1935). Bass and comedian. He was expected to follow his family tradition and become a lawyer, but after his father's death he abandoned his studies and used his inheritance to form his own acting company. The company failed, partly because, being exceptionally tall, Hopper towered comically above the rest of his troupe. He then studied singing (he had a fine bass voice), and struck huge success in 1884 when John McCaull cast him in John Philip Sousa's *Désirée*. He solidified his reputation in *The Begum* (1887) and *The Lady or the Tiger?* (1888). He then played leading roles in several shows opposite the diminutive Della Fox, where the disparity in their height was deliberately exploited for its comic effect; productions included *Castles in the Air* (1890), *Wang* (1891), and *Panjandrum* (1893). *El Capitan* (1896), which was also produced by Hopper, was one of the greatest successes of his career; its first New York run tallied 112 performances, and Hopper toured with the production for the next two years. He later appeared in such shows as *The Charlatan* (1898), *Fiddle-dee-dee* (1900), and *Happyland* (1905), but after about 1913 his popularity began to wane, despite still being featured prominently. Hopper was famous for reciting the poem "Casey at the Bat" by Ernest Lawrence Thayer, either in the course of a show or during his curtain calls. There was hardly a performance in which he was not called upon to recite the piece. He wrote an autobiography, *Once a Clown, Always a Clown* (1921).

GERALD BORDMAN

Horenstein, Jascha (*b* Kiev, Russia [now Ukraine], 6 May 1899; *d* London, England, 2 April 1973). Russian-Austrian conductor, naturalized American. He left Russia for Königsberg at the age of six and studied there with Max Brode. In 1911 he moved to Vienna (his mother was Austrian), where he studied philosophy at the university, the violin with ADOLF BUSCH, and, from 1917, music theory with JOSEPH MARX and composition with Franz Schreker at the Music Academy. In 1920 he followed Schreker to Berlin, where he conducted choral societies and became assistant to Wilhelm Furtwängler. His orchestral debut was with the Vienna SO in 1923. After guest appearances with the Berlin PO and the Blüthner Orchestra he became conductor of the Berlin SO in 1925. In 1928 he became chief conductor and later director of music at the Düsseldorf Opera, where his repertory included *Wozzeck*, given in 1930 under Alban Berg's supervision. Horenstein remained at Düsseldorf until the Nazis forced him to leave in 1933. For some years he led a wandering existence, conducting in France, Belgium, Poland, the USSR, Australia and New Zealand (1937), Scandinavia (with the Ballets Russes de Monte Carlo, 1937), and Palestine (1938).

He went to the United States in 1940, conducting the New York PO and other orchestras in both the Americas; subsequently he took American citizenship. After the war, his widespread activity included some notable concert performances of modern operas: in this way he introduced *Wozzeck* (1950) and Leoš Janáček's *From the House of the Dead* (1951) to Paris, and Ferruccio

Busoni's *Doktor Faust* to the United States (American Opera Society, 1964). He conducted at the Städtische (later Deutsche) Oper in West Berlin and at Covent Garden (*Fidelio* in 1961 and *Parsifal* shortly before his death in 1973). During the last years of his life he lived in Lausanne.

Although he disliked being labeled a specialist, Horenstein was an admired interpreter of Anton Bruckner and Gustav Mahler. The program of his Viennese debut included Mahler's First Symphony; his performance of the Eighth with the LSO in 1959 (Royal Albert Hall) remains a landmark in the recognition of Mahler in Britain. To this composer's music Horenstein brought sharp intensity and burning clarity. He started making recordings in the late 1920s, and his gramophone repertory (which included early recordings of Bruckner and Mahler) reveals a versatility he did not always have the opportunity to show in the concert hall.

BIBLIOGRAPHY

A. Blyth: "Jascha Horenstein talks to Alan Blyth," *Gramophone*, xlviii (1970–71), 768 only

R. Osborne: "Horenstein and Mahler: a Conversation," *Records and Recording*, xiv/3 (1970–71), 44 only

J. Diether: "The Recorded Legacy of Jascha Horenstein," *HiFi/MusAm*, xxiii/10 (1973), 76–81, 83 only [with discography]

J. Lazar: "Horenstein at Work," *HiFi/MusAm*, xxiii/10 (1973), 82 only

D. Barber: *The Horenstein Legacy: a Discography* (n.p., 1995)

RONALD CRICHTON/R

Horiuchi, Glenn (*b* Chicago, IL, 27 Feb 1955; *d* Los Angeles, CA, 3 June 2000). Jazz pianist, shamisen player, and composer. Influenced by avant-garde jazz, he incorporated Japanese scales, rhythms, and instrumentation into an improvisatory setting and was integral to the development of Asian American jazz. Released through Asian Improv and Soul Note, much of his music was inspired by the Japanese American experience. His albums *Manzanar Voices* (1989, Asian Improv) and *Poston Sonata* (1992, Asian Improv) take their names from internment camps where Japanese Americans were imprisoned during World War II.

Although born in Chicago, where his parents had relocated after leaving the internment camps, Horiuchi spent most of his childhood in Southern California. He attended the University of California at Riverside and San Diego, pursuing a career in mathematics before dropping out to devote himself to music and politics. His first recordings, including *Next Step* (1988, Asian Improv) and *Issei Spirit* (1989, Asian Improv), feature a quartet composed of the bass player M'Chaka Uba, a founding member of the AACM, the bass player Taiji Miyagawa, and the drummer Leon Alexander.

Horiuchi's music is marked by stylistic eclecticism, ranging from tonal balladry to free improvisation, but much of his work consciously evokes an Asian sound. His piano playing often resembles the percussive style of Cecil Taylor, whom he greatly admired. Towards the end of his life, Horiuchi immersed himself in Zen Buddhism and began playing the shamisen, learning the *nagauta* repertoire from his aunt, Lilian Nakano, and developing his own improvisational approach to the instrument. He also served as an artist in residence at the

Japanese American National Museum in Los Angeles where he taught piano, shamisen, and composition.

LOREN KAJIKAWA

Horn. The orchestral horn, commonly known as the French horn, belongs to the family of conical brasswind instruments. Its immediate predecessors are the hand horn and the hunting horn of the 18th and 19th centuries. The Gallic origins of the manufacture and use of the hunting horn (Trompe de Chasse) are the *raison d'etre* of its name.

The horn has sustained a presence in America since the development of colonial society. A 1565 roster of Huguenot soldiers at Fort Caroline (now San Mateo, Florida) lists one Jean Menin as player of the *cor* (horn). The Moravians brought hunting horns with them to their first settlements, and teachers of the horn advertised in newspapers as early as 1736 (Charleston, South Carolina). Hunting horns and hand horns with crooks, also called "concert horns," were available in stores in most major cities in the colonies by 1738. Performers on the horn were popular soloists in the larger cities throughout the 1700s; composer and horn virtuoso VICTOR PELISSIER traveled and played with the orchestra of the Old American Company during the 1790s. Horns with valves were advertised for sale in Philadelphia by 1837, but until the 1840s musicians in America generally played the hand horn or hunting horn. While storekeepers were adding the new valved horns to their inventories, they still offered hand horns (with crooks) through the 1880s.

American firms have contributed widely to the manufacture of horns, especially after World War II embargos significantly reduced the importation of European-made instruments. While Germany featured prominently in the development of the double horn, and England in the descant and triple horns, American firms have historically followed the players' preferences, providing both double horns following German precepts, as built by Carl Geyer, Conn, Holton (including from the 1960s the Philip Farkas horn), S.W. Lewis, and Kortesmaki; and descant instruments, provided by Holton, Conn, Kortesmaki, and George MacCracken. Daniel Rauch, an American living in Norway, has produced some very highly regarded horns. The firm of Lawson Horns carried out groundbreaking research during the 1960s on the effects of both taper and alloy on the playing characteristics of the horn. The company's horns are generally well respected.

In the modern orchestra the French horn most commonly appears as a double horn pitched in F and B♭, wherein the instrument is played in both of its most common lengths, allowing the more traditional tone quality of the F horn to be combined with the greater security of the B♭ horn in the upper register. Beginning in the 1950s, however, B♭/high F double descant horns, or even triple horns in F/B♭/high F, have become more common, being used especially in daunting high-tessitura passages. Generally the first and third (high) players in orchestral ensembles use the shorter horns and the second and fourth (low) players continue playing the traditional double horns. The assignment of high and low roles is less well-defined in wind ensembles, though the choice of horn remains the double horn.

During the boom in early music performance during the last quarter of the 20th century, several American makers began building natural horns based on Baroque and Classical models, most notably LOWELL GREER, James Patterson, George McCracken, and RICHARD SERAPHINOFF. The unbroken 300 + year French tradition of hunting horn playing (Trompes de Chasse) has only recently gained significance in the United States, and there are no American firms currently producing hunting horns.

While the French horn has had less use in jazz and other popular music forms, it has nevertheless been effectively occupied these roles. Many of the specialists who pursue careers outside of the classical forms often prefer the more recently developed descant horn.

Every city with an orchestra of relative prestige has retained at least one soloist, and foreign soloists have often toured the United States. Joseph Eger is an esteemed American player who had an important influence on American music, as did JOHN BARROWS and Helen Kotas Hirsch, and all had pupils who continued their work. The establishment of enduring international competitions within the United States has brought many recent soloists more popular recognition. Currently, Americans seem to have produced as many solo CDs as Europeans have, thus ending a foreign domination of the art.

The horn's solo literature is rich, ranging from concerti by Mozart, Haydn, Schumann, Strauss, and Hindemith, to superb American works by Adler, Chavez, Harbison, Williams, and others who continue advance the literature.

BIBLIOGRAPHY

GMO ("Horn")

R. Morley-Pegge: *The French Horn* (London, 1960; 2/1973)

K. Janetzky and B. Brüchle: *The Horn*, translated by J. Chater (London & Portland, OR, 1988)

J.Q. Ericson: "The Valve Horn and its Performing Techniques in the Nineteenth Century: an Overview," *The Horn Call Annual*, 4 (1992): 2–32

M. Meckna: *Twentieth Century Brass Soloists* (Westport, CT, 1994)

J.L. Snedeker: "The Horn in Early America," *Perspectives in Brass Scholarship: Proceedings of the International Historic Brass Symposium, Amherst, 1995*, ed. S. Carter (Stuyvesant, NY, 1997), 151–69

LOWELL GREER

Horn, Charles Edward (*b* London, England, 21 June 1786; *d* Boston, MA, 21 Oct 1849). English composer and singer, active in the United States. He was taught music by his father, Karl Friedrich Horn, and Venanzio Rauzzini. He began to write music for the theater in 1810, and his first great success was *The Devil's Bridge* (1812), which enjoyed many revivals in England, Ireland, and the United States. He had several successes with songs that were originally introduced in dramatic pieces, notably "On the banks of Allen Water" in *Rich and Poor* (1812), "I know a bank" in *The Merry Wives of Windsor* (1823), "The deep, deep sea" in *Honest Frauds* (1830), and above all "Cherry ripe," apparently first sung by Lucia Vestris in *Paul Pry* (1826), an opera with which Horn was not otherwise connected.

In 1827 Horn sailed to New York where he appeared in *The Siege of Belgrade* on 20 July. He produced *The Devil's Bridge* (known in New York since 1820) on 22 December, and adapted *Le nozze di Figaro* and other works for the American stage. In 1828 he visited Boston and Philadelphia, and was back in London in 1830 for the production of *Honest Frauds* on 29 July. In 1832 he returned to New York where he became musical director at the Park Theatre. As musical director he conducted operas from the piano, adapted *La Cenerentola* and *Die Zauberflöte*, and introduced several English operas with marked success. He lost his voice through an illness in 1835 but continued to compose and to play the piano and organ in public, and to give lessons in singing. In 1837 he went into partnership with W.J. Davis as a music publisher. After a year Davis withdrew, and Horn's Music Store at 411 Broadway prospered for several years. In 1839 Horn conducted a series of "soirées musicales," and in 1842 he participated in the founding of the New York Philharmonic Society. Five of his operas were first performed in New York, and he won American prizes for two glees, *Wisdom and Cupid* (1834) and *Forest Music* (1835). His oratorio *The Remission of Sin*, performed at the New York Sacred Music Society on 7 May 1835, was the first oratorio composed in the United States. The work greatly enhanced his reputation; apart from one short chorus, however, it has not survived. His one attempt at grand opera was *Ahmed al Ramel, or The Pilgrim of Love*, to a libretto by H.J. Finn after Washington Irving's *Alhambra*, performed at the National Theatre, New York, on 12 October 1840; this, too, is lost, but it was significant as the first opera based on a major American literary work. *The Maid of Saxony*, a three-act opera based on the life of Frederick II of Prussia, was premiered at the Park Theatre, New York, on 23 May 1842.

In 1843 Horn returned once more to London where his oratorio, revised under the title *Satan*, was performed in 1845. For a time he was music director at the Princess's Theatre, but he returned to the United States in 1847, where on 23 July he was elected conductor of the Handel and Haydn Society of Boston. It is doubtful that he returned to England again in 1848 (as stated in *Grove 5* and elsewhere); Boston was his home for the last two years of his life. Horn was twice married, first to a Miss Rae, then to Maria Horton (*d* 1887). A son, Charles Edward Horn Jr., was a tenor.

It has been said that Horn was the first composer with a substantial reputation in the Old World who came to live in the United States. He composed or adapted some 30 light theater pieces for London and another ten for New York. They cannot be taken seriously as operas: typically, they consist of a perfunctory overture, a string of a dozen independent songs with perhaps a duet and a glee, and a finale in one rondo movement. Most of the music is weak, but occasionally one or two of the songs are found to possess great charm, such as "Cherry ripe," in his favorite rondo form with coda. He had a gift for incorporating and imitating elements of folksong (or, as it was termed in his day, "national song"), and it was this that gave many of his songs their appeal. In the United States he was quick to adopt local color, most successfully in *National Melodies of America* (1839), which makes use of African American melodies as well as street songs of New York. The tunes are sentimentalized and allied to inappropriate words, but they nevertheless show a willingness to depart from the musical conventions to which he had been trained.

WORKS
(selective list)
(only those composed in the United States;
*partly adapted; **wholly adapted)

THEATRICAL
All first performed at the Park Theatre, New York, unless otherwise stated. Music lost, unless otherwise indicated; all publications are vocal scores published in city and year of first performance.
**The Marriage of Figaro (opera) [after Mozart], 21 Jan 1828; **Dido (opera) [after various operas by Rossini], 9 April 1828; *Isidore de Merida (opera) [after S. Storace: *The Pirates*], 9 June 1828; **Oberon (opera) [after C.M. von Weber], 9 Oct 1828; The Quartette, or Interrupted Harmony (opera, 1), New York, Bowery Theatre, 27 April 1829; *Il trionfo della musica (opera) [after S. Mayr: *Che originali*], Philadelphia, Chesnut Street Theatre, 5 May 1829; **Cinderella (opera) [after Rossini], 20 Dec 1832; Nadir and Zuleika, 27 Dec 1832; **The Magic Flute (opera) [after Mozart], 17 April 1833; Ahmed al Ramel, or The Pilgrim of Love (grand opera, H.J. Finn, after W. Irving: *Alhambra*), New York, National Theatre, 12 Oct 1840; The Maid of Saxony (opera, 3, G.P. Morris, after M. Edgeworth), 23 May 1842

OTHER
The Remission of Sin (oratorio, after J. Milton), New York, Sacred Music Society, 7 May 1835; rev. as Satan; Ode to Washington, 4vv (New York, 1828); Ode to Music, 4vv (New York, 1839); Many songs, incl. collections: Shakespeare's Seven Ages (New York, c1835); National Melodies of America (New York, 1839); Six Popular Songs (New York, 1839)

BIBLIOGRAPHY
New York Mirror (6 Oct 1827, 14 Aug 1830, 22 Dec 1832, 14 March 1835, 16 Oct 1841)
American Musical Journal, i (1834–5), 45, 238
H.C. Lahee: *Annals of Music in America* (Boston, 1922)
E.E. Hipsher: *American Opera and its Composers* (Philadelphia, 1927)
E.W. White: *The Rise of English Opera* (New York, 1951)
G. Chase: *America's Music* (New York, 1955, 2/1966)
R.A. Montague: *Charles Edward Horn: his Life and Works* (diss., Florida State U., 1959)
J. Mattfeld: *A Handbook of American Operatic Premieres, 1731–1962* (Detroit, MI 1963)
N. Temperley, ed.: *The Romantic Age 1800–1914, Athlone History of Music in Britain*, v (London, 1981), 271, 305
M. Kassler, ed.: *Charles Edward Horn's Memoirs of his Father and Himself* (Aldershot, UK, 2003)

NICHOLAS TEMPERLEY/E. DOUGLAS BOMBERGER

Horn, Shirley (Valerie) (*b* Washington, DC, 1 May 1934; *d* Cheverly, MD, 20 Oct 2005). Jazz singer and pianist. A sensitive interpreter of jazz standards and ballads, she studied classical piano at Howard University in her youth. She began playing at jazz clubs after high school and formed a trio in 1954. After hearing her album *Embers and Ashes* (1960, Hi-Life) Miles Davis hired her to open for him at the Village Vanguard in New York in 1961. This led to a singing contract with Mercury Records; Quincy Jones produced two of her albums. Horn ceased touring in the mid-1960s to raise a daughter, but continued performing locally, leading a trio that included the bass player Charles Ables and the drummer Steve Williams. Over the next two decades she recorded for independent labels and performed at European jazz festivals. After signing with Verve in 1986, she found critical and popular success. Her album *You won't forget me* (1990, Verve) featured guest appearances by Davis and Branford and Wynton Marsalis. Horn played piano on Carmen McRae's album *Sarah: Dedicated to You* (1991, Novus). Her tribute album *I Remember Miles* (1998; Verve) earned a Grammy. Although serious health crises slowed her career from 2001, Horn continued to sing accompanied by the pianist George Mesterhazy. She was honored with a Kennedy Center tribute in 2004 and received an NEA Jazz Masters Fellowship in 2005.

BIBLIOGRAPHY

L. Gourse: *Madame Jazz: Contemporary Women Instrumentalists* (New York, 1996)

Obituaries: *New York Times* (22 Oct 2005); *Washington Post* (22 Oct 2005)

GAYLE MURCHISON

Horne, Lena (Mary Calhoun) (*b* New York, NY, 30 June 1917; *d* New York, NY, 9 May 2010). Popular singer and actress. She began performing at the Cotton Club in 1933 and made her Broadway debut in 1934 in *Dance with Your Gods*. She toured with Noble Sissle's Society Orchestra in 1934 and 1935, and in 1936 recorded with Sissle's band. Her initial, albeit brief film appearance was in *Cab Calloway's Jitterbug Party* in 1935; but in 1938 she gained a more substantial role in *The Duke is Tops,* the first of many films in which she was a featured

Lena Horne in Stormy Weather, *Twentieth Century Fox, 1943. (Twentieth Century Fox Film Corporation/ Photofest)*

soloist. The following year she joined the cast of the short-lived *Lew Leslie's Blackbirds of 1939*. In 1940 she began touring with Charlie Barnet and his Orchestra. Horne and Barnet also made several recordings together, including "Good for Nothing Joe" in 1941, the same year that she began singing at the Café Society in downtown New York.

In 1942 she appeared at the Little Troc in Hollywood, and her move to the West Coast helped her secure a seven-year contract with MGM—a radical arrangement given that studios rarely offered term contracts to African Americans. She appeared in 15 films for MGM and other studios between 1942 and 1956, including *Panama Hattie, Swing Fever, Broadway Rhythm, Ziegfeld Follies*, and *Till the Clouds Roll By*, in which she performed the song "Can't Help Lovin' Dat Man." Her film appearances were generally limited to one or two interpolated songs. She played more significant roles in *Cabin in the Sky, Stormy Weather* (the title song of which became her signature number), and *Boogie Woogie Dream*.

She continued performing at nightclubs throughout her career, working with Luther Henderson, her second husband Lennie Hayton, Jimmie Lunceford, Henry Levine, Duke Ellington, Billy Strayhorn, and Billy Eckstine. Engagements included contracts with the Savoy-Plaza Hotel, and later with the Sands Hotel in Las Vegas, the Cocoanut Grove in Los Angeles, and at New York's Waldorf-Astoria Hotel and Copacabana Club. Horne's first of many television appearances was in 1951, and the recording *Lena Horne at the Waldorf-Astoria* became a best seller for RCA Victor in 1957. That same year she returned to Broadway and earned a Tony Award nomination for her performance in *Jamaica*. However it was not until 1981 that she won a Tony Award for her one-woman revue, *Lena Horne: The Lady and Her Music*. Its recorded soundtrack won her a Grammy award for best female pop vocal performance.

Horne released nearly 30 albums between 1955 and 2006, working with performers including Gábor Szabó, Joe Williams, Harry Belafonte, Sammy Davis Jr., and Michel Legrand. She received a Grammy Lifetime Achievement Award in 1989, another Grammy in 1995, and was nominated on various other occasions. She has been recognized for both musical achievement and civil rights activism by the NAACP, the Songwriters Hall of Fame, the Hollywood Walk of Fame, ASCAP, Howard University, Yale University, the Kennedy Center, and the International Civil Rights Walk of Fame.

BIBLIOGRAPHY

H. Arstein, C. Moses, and L. Horne: *In Person: Lena Horne* (New York, 1950)

L. Horne and R. Schickel: *Lena* (New York, 1965)

J. Haskins and K. Benson: *Lena: a Personal and Professional Biography of Lena Horne* (New York, 1984)

J. Gavin: *Stormy Weather: the Life of Lena Horne* (New York, 2009)

ELIZABETH SURLES

Horne, Marilyn (Berneice) (*b* Bradford, PA, 16 Jan 1934). Mezzo-soprano. The often-encountered birth year of 1929 is erroneous. She studied at the University of

Marilyn Horne, 1990s. (Marion Kalter/Lebrecht Music & Arts)

Southern California where she took part in LOTTE LEH-MANN's master classes. She sang the dubbed voice of Dorothy Dandridge in the film *Carmen Jones* in 1954, the year of her debut in Los Angeles (as Háta in *The Bartered Bride*), then spent three seasons at Gelsenkirchen (1956–9) where she sang soprano and mezzo roles. In 1960 she first appeared in San Francisco as Marie in *Wozzeck*, also the role of her Covent Garden debut in 1964. From 1960 to 1979 she was married to the conductor Henry Lewis. She began an association with Joan Sutherland in New York in 1961 with a concert performance of *Beatrice di Tenda* in which she sang Agnese. Being cast with Sutherland brought her many notable performances—as Arsace to Sutherland's Semiramide (1965, Boston), and as Adalgisa to Sutherland's Norma (1967, Covent Garden; her New York Metropolitan Opera debut, 1970). She sang Néocles in *Le siège de Corinthe* at La Scala (1969), Carmen at the Metropolitan in 1972, and Handel's Rinaldo in Houston (1975). Among her other Rossini roles were Malcolm in *La donna del lago* (1981, Houston; 1985, Covent Garden), Falliero in *Bianca e Falliero* (1986, Pesaro), Andromache in *Ermione* (1987, Pesaro), Calbo in *Maometto II* (1988, San Francisco), and Isabella in *L'italiana in Algeri* (1989, Covent Garden). In the latter part of her career she sang Mistress Quickly (1988, San Francisco) and Delilah (1988, Théâtre des Champs-Elysées).

Horne had a voice of extraordinary range, rich and tangy in timbre, with a stentorian chest register and an exciting top. Her recordings include several Rossini roles such as Laura in *La Gioconda* and Juno in *Semele*. She also recorded in productions of Gluck's *Orpheus*, a historically important version of *Carmen* conducted by Leonard Bernstein, as Anita in Massenet's *La Navarraise*, and as Zerlina. In concert she once managed the feat of singing in a single program Rossini arias and Brünnhilde's Immolation Scene, proof of her exceptional versatil-

ity. She was an equally admired recitalist, singing Lieder, *mélodies*, and Spanish and American songs, all to acclaim. Since retiring from the concert stage in 1999 she has taught vocal master classes at various colleges and universities throughout the United States. In 1993 she created The Marilyn Horne Foundation, Inc., to preserve and promote the art form of the vocal recital. The Foundation offers a forum for young, gifted singers to experience some of the artistic opportunities that Horne was fortunate to have had during her own early career as a singer, and which helped her develop her own musicianship and artistry. The Foundation sponsors an annual festival, *The Song Continues*, as well as a series of vocal recitals, *On the Wings of Song*. It is no exaggeration to describe Horne as one of the greatest artists of the 20th century, and later in her life, an important promoter of young vocal talent.

BIBLIOGRAPHY
M.R. Scott: "Marilyn Horne," *Opera*, xviii (1967), 963–7
J.B. Steane: *The Grand Tradition: Seventy Years of Singing on Record* (New York/London, 1974; repr. Portland, OR, 1993), 387ff
M. Horne and J. Scovell: *Marilyn Horne, My Life* (New York, 1983)
M. Horne and J. Scovell: *Marilyn Horne: the Song Continues* (Fort Worth, TX, 2004)

ALAN BLYTH/KATHLEEN SEWRIGHT

Horner, James (Roy) (*b* Los Angeles, CA, 14 Aug 1953). Film composer and conductor. Son of Bohemian American production designer Harry Horner, James Horner studied at the RCM, where his teachers included György Ligeti. He moved to California in the early 1970s and attended the University of the Pacific and then USC. He then earned a master's degree in composition and music theory at UCLA, where he also taught music theory and worked on a doctorate; his professors included Paul Chihara. In 1978 Horner scored a series of films for the American Film Institute (including *The Watcher*), and in

1979 he began scoring feature-length films, including work for B-movie producer Roger Corman.

Horner often incorporates electronic elements, choral or solo vocal music (including wordless female voices), and Celtic and other "world music" elements. He has scored a large number of science fiction and action films, and also many dramas and children's films, totaling nearly one hundred feature film scores as of 2009. Horner has also written TV scores (*Amazing Stories*, etc.) and themes (*The CBS Evening News*, 2006–), music for short films (including Epcot Center's Captain EO), studio and THX logo themes, and several concert works. Some of his movie themes (such as for *Aliens* and *Glory*) have become familiar through recycling in trailers for other movies.

Horner won Grammys for "Somewhere Out There" (from *An American Tail*), Glory, and the Celine Dion song "My Heart Will Go On" (from *Titanic*); he also won two Oscars and two Golden Globes for *Titanic* (for score and song). The soundtrack album for that film sold 24 million copies worldwide, making Horner a multimillionaire.

WORKS

Film scores: Battle beyond the Stars (1980); Humanoids from the Deep (1980); Star Trek II: The Wrath of Khan (1982); 48 Hrs. (1982); Krull (1983); Gorky Park (1983); The Dresser (1983); Star Trek III: The Search for Spock (1984); Cocoon (1985); Commando (1985); Faerie Tale Theatre (TV ep. "The Pied Piper of Hamelin," 1985); Aliens (1986); Amazing Stories (TV ep. "Alamo Jobe," 1985); An American Tail (1986); The Name of the Rose (1986); Tales from the Crypt (TV ep. "Cutting Cards," 1990); Willow (1988); Honey, I Shrunk the Kids (1989); Field of Dreams (1989); Glory (1989); An American Tail: Fievel Goes West (1991); Crossroads (theme, 1992); Fish Police (TV, theme, 1992); Patriot Games (1992); Swing Kids (1993); Legends of the Fall (1994); Braveheart (1995); Apollo 13 (1995); Titanic (1997); Deep Impact (1998); The Mask of Zorro (1998); Mighty Joe Young (1998); Bicentennial Man (1999); The Perfect Storm (2000); How the Grinch Stole Christmas (2000); Enemy at the Gates (2001); A Beautiful Mind (2001); House of Sand and Fog (2003); Troy (2004); The Legend of Zorro (2005); The CBS Evening News (TV, theme, 2006); The Spiderwick Chronicles (2008); The Boy in the Striped Pajamas (2008); Avatar (2009)

Concert music: Conversations (1976); Spectral Shimmers (1977); A Forest Passage (2000)

BIBLIOGRAPHY

L. Kendall and J. Bond: "Letters about James Horner's Titanic," Film Score Monthly, iii/3 (1997)

A. Ross: "Oscar Scores," The New Yorker (9 March 1998)

DURRELL BOWMAN

Horowitz, Joseph (*b* New York, NY, 12 Feb 1948). Writer on music, music administrator, and concert producer. He studied at Swarthmore College, Pennsylvania (BA 1970). He was a music critic for the *New York Times* (1976–80) and artistic advisor to the Schubertiade at the 92nd Street Y, New York (1987–93). In 1992 he became artistic adviser to the Brooklyn Philharmonic; he was named executive director in 1994. Under his administration the orchestra's subscription concerts became a series of interdisciplinary thematic festivals with complementary educational programming. Since 1999 Horowitz has served as artistic consultant for more than a dozen orchestras, influentially applying the model of thematic festivals to a variety of topics—most frequently Dvořák in America. For the New York Philharmonic and other orchestras, he has scripted and produced contextualized explorations of symphonic works by Dvořák, Brahms, Tchaikovsky, Bruckner, and others. In 2003 he co-founded the Post-Classical Ensemble in Washington DC, through which he fosters eclectic formats, an interdisciplinary scope, and educational linkages (most notably a partnership with Georgetown University); it tours its programs as "Post-Classical Productions."

Horowitz has taught at Colorado College, the Eastman School of Music, the Institute for Studies in American Music (Brooklyn College), the Manhattan School of Music, Mannes College, and the New England Conservatory. He has lectured at Bayreuth and Salzburg, and throughout the United States. He has received a Guggenheim Fellowship, two NEH Fellowships, a National Arts Journalism Program Fellowship, and a commendation from the Czech Parliament. For the NEH he directed the National Education Project and the Teacher-Training Institute, both devoted to "Dvořák and America," and "Music Unwound," a three-year sequence of thematic festivals undertaken by a consortium of four orchestras. For the NEA he served as Artistic Director of an annual Music Critics Institute hosted by Columbia University. The larger goal of much of his activity has been to infuse the humanities into middle and high school classrooms, and to broadly re-envision symphonic institutions as purveyors of education.

Horowitz's writings focus on the institutional history of concert music and opera in the United States. *Understanding Toscanini* treats the "Toscanini cult" as a metaphor for the decline of classical music after World War I. *Wagner Nights,* a history of Wagnerism in America, interprets "meliorist" cultural currents in the late Gilded Age; it challenges pejorative notions of "sacralization" and "social control." *Classical Music in America* treats the history of America's musical high culture as an historical phenomenon that peaked around 1900 and then began receding into a "culture of performance" that sidelines the creative act; it controversially asserts that classical music in the United States is best understood by focusing on performers and institutions of performance, rather than on composers. Horowitz's books provide an alternative to the composer-centric historiography that has long dominated musicology. He is credited (according to Alex Ross in *The New Yorker*) with influentially coining the phrase "post-classical music" to describe an emerging 21st-century musical landscape that merges classical music with popular and non-western genres. He frequently reviews concerts and books for *The Times Literary Supplement*. His blog is "The Unanswered Question" (www.artsjournal.com/uq).

WRITINGS
(selective list)

Conversations with Arrau (New York, 1982, 2/1992)

Understanding Toscanini—How He Became an American Culture-God and Helped Create a New Audience for Old Music (New York, 1987)

The Ivory Trade: Music and the Business of Music at the Van Cliburn International Piano Competition (New York, 1990)

"Anton Seidl and America's Wagner Cult," *Wagner in Performance*, ed. B. Millington and S. Spencer (New Haven, CT, 1992), 168–81
"Mozart as Midcult: Mass Snob Appeal," *MQ*, lxxvi (1992), 1–16
"Dvořák and the New World: A Concentrated Moment," *Dvořák and his World*, ed. M. Beckerman (Princeton, NJ, 1993), 92–103
"Finding a 'Real Self': American Women and the Wagner Cult of the Late Nineteenth Century," *MQ*, lxxviii (1994), 189–205
Wagner Nights: an American History (Berkeley, 1994)
The Post-Classical Predicament: Essays on Music and Society (Boston, 1995)
"Laura Langford and the Seidl Society—Wagner Comes to Brooklyn," *Cultivating Music in America: Women Patrons and Activists since 1860*, ed. R. Locke and C. Barr (Berkeley, 1998), 164–84
"Wagner und der amerikanische Jude—eine persönliche Betrachtung," *Richard Wagner und die Juden*, ed. D. Borchmeyer (Stuttgart, 2000), 238–50
"Musical Boston Reconsidered," special issue of *American Music*, xix/1 (Spring 2001)
Dvořák in America: In Search of the New World (Chicago, 2003)
"Music and the Gilded Age: Social Control and Sacralization Revisited," *Journal of the Gilded Age and Progressive Era*, iii/3 (July 2004), 227–45
Classical Music in America: a History of its Rise and Fall (New York, 2005/R 2007)
Artists in Exile: How Refugees from Twentieth-Century War and Revolution Transformed the American Performing Arts (New York, 2008)
"Henry Krehbiel: German American, Music Critic," *The Journal of the Gilded Age and Progressive Era*, viii/2 (April 2009), 165–87
Moral Fire: Musical Portraits from America's Fin-de-Siecle (Berkeley, 2012)

PAULA MORGAN/E. DOUGLAS BOMBERGER

Horowitz, Richard (Michael) [Ztiworoh, Drahcir] (*b* Buffalo, NY, 6 Jan 1949). Composer and instrumentalist. He studied piano with Daniel Kay, Fine, and Florence Pelton (1955–66). From 1968 to 1974 he lived in Paris, studying piano and composition with Ariel Kalma as part of the Groupe de Recherches Musicales (GRM), and studying synthesized music with George Aragada. He also performed avant-garde jazz with Alan Silva's Celestial Communications Orchestra (other members were Steve Lacy and Anthony Braxton) and formed the ensemble Free Music Formation with Hugh Levick, both in 1971. In 1972 he travelled in Turkey and Morocco; in 1975 he settled in Morocco and studied microtonal modal modulation systems (with Abdelatif Kartuma and Hamid Ben Brahim) and the nāy, a bamboo flute of North African origin (with Kasim Nacquisabundi and Louis Soret). He also studied and made recordings of Berber music with the ethnomusicologist Philip Schuyler. In 1980 he returned to the United States (San Francisco) and was invited to work at Stanford's computer music research lab, CCRMA. He met his longtime collaborator, vocalist, dancer, and composer Sussan Deyhim (*b* Tehran, Iran, 14 Dec 1956) in New York, where they collaborated on their first album, *Azax Attra: Desert Equations,* in 1981, a pioneering effort in world music and early trip-hop. He also performed and recorded with Jon Hassell and Brian Eno (1982–7). After working on several film projects in Los Angeles in the early 1990s, he moved with Deyhim to London in 1993 and then to New York in the late 1990s. In 1997 Horowitz founded and served as artistic director of The Gnaoua Festival in Mogador (Essaouira), Morocco with Neila Tazi and André Azoulay. In the 1990s he also coproduced, with Bill Laswell, the album *Night Spirit Masters: Gnawa Music of Marrakech,* and collaborated with Gnawa musician Hassan Hakmoun and Don Cherry. Currently based in New York, he continues his collaborations (primarily multimedia projects) with Deyhim.

Horowitz's music is a crossover between Western contemporary art music, avant-garde jazz, and non-Western music (principally North African- and Middle Eastern-influenced music). Combining Western and non-Western instruments and "wordless" voices with computer and electronic music, he creates vast, evocative, trance-induced soundscapes. A source of inspiration for his compositions since the late 1960s has been the "ritual drama of ancient music…with motifs and overtones of instruments and voices from the oldest cultures." His studies in North Africa led to music for the nāy, composed in both traditional and contemporary styles. After his first return to the United States, he recorded *Eros in Arabia* (1981), a collection of his music that creates timbral variety through the use of North African instruments (nāy and bendīr), voice, synthesizer, and prepared piano. During the 1990s he focused his attention on film scores. He received both the Golden Globe and the Los Angeles Film Critics Association awards for his scoring of Bertolucci's *The Sheltering Sky,* in collaboration with Ryiuchi Sakamoto. In the early 2000s he continued to write music for several film projects.

WORKS
(selective list)

Multimedia operas: Azax/Attra, New York, 1985; The Ghost of Ibn Sabba, 1988; X-Isle Isle-X, Hong Kong, 1989; Majoun, New York, 1997; Logic of the Birds, New York, 2002 [collab. Deyhim, Shirin Neshat, Ghasem Ebrahimian]
Vocal (all wordless): Queen of Saba, 1v, nāy, 1981; Never Tech No Foreign Answer, 1v, synth, chorus, 1982; Desert Equations, 1v, nāy, bendīr, 1984 [both collab. Deyhim]
Nāy: Oblique Sequences (Solo Nāy Improvisations no.1), nāy and electronics, 1972–9; Mémoire, vn, nāy, synth, 1974–81; Solo Nāy Improvisations no.2, 1979–82; Saharazona, nāy, elec, 1980; Baby Elephant Logic, nāy, synth, 1981; Bandit Narah Master of Rajasthan, nāy, synth, 1981; Eros Never Stops Dreaming, nāy, bendīr, synth, 1981; Elephant Dance, nāy, synth, 1981; Solo Nāy Improvisations no.3, 1984; Au pays des arabes, nāy, synth [collab. A. Kalma]
Synth and inst: Out of Thin Air, vn, synth, 1974–81; 23/8 for Conlon Nancarrow, prepared pf, 1981; Tamara Alexa Interdimensional Travel Agent, synth, 1981
Film scores: Valparaiso, *c*1970; Walls, *c*1970; Saharazona, 1983; The Sheltering Sky, 1990; Lakota Woman, 1994; Any Given Sunday, 1999; Three Seasons, 1999; Tobruk, 2008; Little Johnny, 2011; Love in the Medina, 2011
Other works incl. Joey Shmerda (incid. music for radio drama, J. Strahs), 1980–3, [collab. B. Spencer; DP, mixed-media works, collab. S. Edery]

BIBLIOGRAPHY
M. Dery: "Richard Horowitz: Stalking the Wild Guedra for 'The Sheltering Sky'," *Keyboard*, xvii/5 (1991), 23–4
M. Dery: "World View: Richard Horowitz—a Musical Journey from Morocco to the Fourth World," *Keyboard*, xix/3 (1993), 38–40
S. Hopkins: "Passion Players," *The Wire* (London), no.164 (1997), 14–6
B. Heuzé: "Éros en Arabie," *Crystal*, no.18 (1999), 93–9

STEPHEN RUPPENTHAL/DAVID PATTERSON/
MICHAEL BAUMGARTNER

Horowitz, Vladimir (*b* ?Kiev, Russia [now Ukraine], 18 Sept/1 Oct 1903; *d* New York, NY, 5 Nov 1989). Pianist of Ukrainian birth. All previous reference sources give his year of birth as 1904: when Horowitz left Russia in 1925 his father had Vladimir's passport doctored to make him appear a year younger, thus enabling him to avoid military service. His birthplace is sometimes given as Berdichev, but Horowitz always claimed that he was born in Kiev. His cousin Natasha Saitzoff, in an interview in 1991, said that all four Horowitz children were born in the home of their maternal grandmother in Kiev; so even if the family lived in Berdichev, Vladimir would have been born in Kiev. In any case, he was living there as an infant.

His mother was his first teacher; she also taught his elder sister Regina (1900–84), who became a skilled pianist and teacher. At the age of nine Horowitz entered the Kiev Conservatory along with his sister. His teachers were Vladimir Puchalsky, Sergei Tarnowsky (both pupils of Theodor Leschetizky), and Felix Blumenfeld (who had studied with Anton Rubinstein). After the Revolution, the previously well-off Horowitz family was impoverished. Horowitz started to give concerts, making his debut on 30 May 1920 in Kiev. He then linked up with the violinist Nathan Milstein for concerts throughout Russia. In Leningrad during the 1924–5 season, Horowitz gave some 20 solo recitals of about ten programs, establishing himself as the most prominent of the younger generation of Soviet pianists.

Leaving the USSR in 1925, Horowitz went to Berlin, where he made his debut on 2 January 1926. Two more Berlin appearances and a performance in Hamburg of the Tchaikovsky First Concerto made his name known all over Germany. Extremely successful appearances in Europe followed. On 12 January 1928 Horowitz made his American debut, playing the Tchaikovsky concerto with the New York PO under Thomas Beecham. Horowitz, who thought Beecham's tempos too slow, took his own tempo in the finale, throwing in a shower of octaves that astounded the audience. He was now internationally acclaimed as the most exciting pianist of the new school. He married Wanda Toscanini, daughter of the conductor, in Milan on 21 December 1933. From 1936 to 1938 he was inactive; this was the first of four retirements (the others were 1953–65, 1969–74, and 1983–5). Highly neurotic, Horowitz was plagued by feelings of inadequacy. He never succeeded in resolving his basic problem: Was he living up to his potential? Was he a great musician or a mere entertainer?

He returned to Europe after 1982, playing first in London, then Japan (1983), Paris (1985), and the USSR (1986). From 1975 to 1985 he was under heavy sedation from drugs prescribed by his psychiatrist. His playing suffered; it was often incoherent, with memory lapses and wrong notes. But he finally managed to regain his health and mental stability, and he played with serenity and joy during the last five years of his life. It was as though he felt he no longer had to prove anything. He died suddenly at home from a heart attack.

As a pianist he was unique. It was not only a matter of an awesome technique. At its best his playing had infinite degrees of color, and a sonority that could well have been unparalleled. He could override the greatest orchestral *fortissimo* without ever banging. Above all he had a kind of high-voltage charisma that, in his time, could be matched only by Arturo Toscanini, Maria Callas, and Luciano Pavarotti. An element of neuroticism was almost always present in his playing; and, especially during the period when he was taking drugs in heavy doses, his playing could be mannered. But at all times he was widely considered the greatest living interpreter of Franz Liszt, Robert Schumann, Aleksandr Skryabin, and Serge Rachmaninoff. His repertory was predominantly Romantic, but he also swept audiences away with his performances of Domenico Scarlatti and Muzio Clementi. He introduced to America the Sergey Prokofiev Sonatas nos.6, 7, and 8, as well as the music of other contemporary Russians. He was never regarded as an expert in Ludwig van Beethoven and the Classical composers. Yet his 1932 recording of the Joseph Haydn E♭ Sonata (no.52) has style, grace, bracing rhythm, incredible articulation, and complete responsiveness to the lyricism as well as the music's architecture.

A future revisionist period may pay more attention to Horowitz's performances of Wolfgang Amadeus Mozart, which many have derided as unstylistic. Towards the end of his life Horowitz returned to Mozart, a composer he carefully studied. He had memorized everything that Mozart ever wrote about performing practice, and tried to put those precepts into effect. His recordings of several sonatas, a few shorter pieces, and the A major Concerto K488 were not generally well received. In recent years, however, it has come to be realized that Mozart style is not academic literalism. Rather (as Mozart himself explained in his letters) it demands freedom, a sensuous sound, a degree of rubato, and faster tempos than musicians of the 20th century are generally willing to adopt. It could well be that Horowitz's flexible and expressive approach to Mozart will eventually be recognized as in some sense more authentic than the work of so many late 20th-century "authenticists." In any case, the position of Vladimir Horowitz as one of the supreme pianists in history cannot be challenged.

BIBLIOGRAPHY

J. Kaiser: *Grosse Pianisten in unserer Zeit* (Munich, 1965, 5/1982; Eng. trans., 1971, with enlarged discography)

R.R. Gerig: *Famous Pianists and their Technique* (Newton Abbot, England, 1976), 306–7

G. Plaskin: *Horowitz* (New York, 1983) [with discography by R. McAlear]

J. Horowitz: "Letter from New York: the Transformations of Vladimir Horowitz," *MQ*, lxxiv/4 (1990), 636–48

H. Schonberg: *Horowitz: his Life and Music* (New York, 1992) [with discography by J.M. Samuels]

D. Dubal, ed.: *Remembering Horowitz: 125 pianists recall a legend* (New York, 2000)

D. Dubal: *Evenings with Horowitz: a Personal Portrait* (New York, 2004)

HAROLD C. SCHONBERG/R

Horst, Louis (*b* Kansas City, MO, 12 Jan 1884; *d* New York, NY, 12 Jan 1964). Pianist, composer, music director, writer, and editor. Horst grew up in a German family that prized music and he first studied violin. After elementary school, the end of his formal education, he took up piano, honed his skills, and soon supported himself as a musician, playing ragtime and improvisations in dance and gambling halls, performing with theater pit orchestras, and accompanying solo classical recitalists.

On the West Coast in 1915, Horst encountered Ruth St. Denis and Ted Shawn, who hired him as accompanist for their Denishawn company and subsequently as music director of their new school. He remained for ten years. Immersed in the developing new abstract form of dancing, he examined the relationship of music to dance, especially through St. Denis's "music visualizations." He began to study musical structure and composition, and left Denishawn to continue learning in Vienna and becoming better informed in contemporary theater, art, literature, and film—knowledge he passed on to future choreographers in his book (with Caroll Russell) *Modern Dance Forms in Relation to the Other Modern Arts* (1961).

At Denishawn, Horst also came to know the soon to be revolutionary pioneers of "modern dance": Doris Humphrey, Charles Weidman, and Martha Graham, all of whom he mentored, along with other experimenters. His longtime collaboration with Graham was especially fecund, his spare music supporting her search for spare, impulse-driven movement. Besides providing the score for her notable seminal works *Primitive Mysteries* (1931), *Frontier* (1935), and *El Penitente* (1940), he assisted her interpretation of dissonance, atonality, and polyrhythms in the music she used, and pointed her toward avant-garde composers she commissioned. His rigorous eye ensured the stripping away of choreographic excess.

Horst's classes in choreographic composition at the American Dance Festival, several colleges, and the Juilliard School were a mecca for successive generations of creative artists. Among other disciplines, he applied the rigor of historical dance forms as a requisite to experimental choreography, principles promulgated in his book *Pre-Classic Dance Forms* (1937).

To herald modern dance, Horst founded the periodical *Dance Observer*, which he edited and filled with sapient writing from 1934 until his death. Besides his prolific compositions for dance, he also wrote incidental music for plays and film. His dance scores, which favored sparse instrumentation, functionally related to the dance harmonically and rhythmically.

BARBARA PALFY

Horszowski, Mieczysław (*b* Lemberg, Austria [now L'viv, Ukraine], 23 June 1892; *d* Philadelphia, PA, 22 May 1993). Pianist of Polish ethnicity. He was a remarkable child prodigy, whose playing from an early age was noted for its rare musicality and maturity. His mother, a pupil of Karl Mikuli (who studied with Frédéric Chopin), was his first teacher. Before going to Vienna to study with Theodor Leschetizky, he had piano lessons with Henryk Melcer-Szczawiński and composition with Mieczysław

Soltys. Horszowski made his official recital debut in Vienna in March 1902 and the same year performed Ludwig van Beethoven's First Piano Concerto with the Warsaw PO under Emil Młynarski. After several years spent touring Europe, he made his American debut on 30 December 1906 in Carnegie Hall. From 1914 he lived in Milan, which remained his home until the outbreak of World War II, when he moved permanently to the United States. Invited to become a member of the piano faculty of the Curtis Institute of Music in the early 1940s, he remained there for the remainder of his life. He taught his final lesson at the age of 100, one week before his death.

A short man, with small hands, he did not play certain virtuoso works, but concentrated on works by Chopin, Beethoven, W.A. Mozart, and Claude Debussy. The most significant periods in his concert life were the late 1920s and the decade from 1954, when he gave a cycle of Beethoven's complete piano works in New York. He was also active in chamber music; for 50 years he was the favored duo partner of the cellist Pablo Casals. He married, at the age of 89, Bice Costa, an Italian pianist, who edited his memoirs and retrieved several songs he had composed in 1913–14. After his marriage, he toured widely, giving concerts in Canada, the United States, Japan, and Europe. He had one of the longest known careers of any performer or teacher in history, and was as vigorous in his late years as he was when he was young. Heitor Villa-Lobos and Camargo Guarnieri dedicated compositions to him, and he gave the first performance of Karol Szymanowski's Third Piano Sonata in 1932. Horszowski was invited to play at the White House on two occasions, the first with Pablo Casals and Alexander Schneider for President Franklin D. Roosevelt, and the second a solo recital for President Jimmy Carter. In October 1991, he gave his final public performance in Philadelphia at the age of 99.

BIBLIOGRAPHY

J. and A. Gillespie: *Notable Twentieth-Century Pianists* (Westport, CT, 1995)

JAMES METHUEN-CAMPBELL/ANYA LAURENCE

Horton, Jim (*b* Austin, MN, 6 Sept 1944; *d* Berkeley, CA, 8 June 1998). Composer. He studied philosophy at the University of Minnesota. After moving to the San Francisco area in 1968, he played the analog synthesizer in various ensembles. During the 1970s he studied at the Center for Contemporary Music, Mills College, with ROBERT ASHLEY, among others. He began to compose and perform live computer music in 1976. He co-founded the first computer network band, the League of Automatic Music Composers, with John Bischoff and Rich Gold in 1978, and the Rotaleague live electronic music ensemble with Bischoff, Tim Perkis, K. Atchley, Sam Ashley, Ben Azarm, Barbara Golden, and Jay Cloit in the 1980s. He performed in the computer band AA Bee Removal with Azarm, Ashley, and Bob Gonsalves, and in the multimedia noise collective Cactus Needle Project. His music, which employs algorithmic processes and just intonation, uses the computer as an interactive partner, not a directed tool. From 1994 to 1998 he assembled an extensive archive of texts on the history of experimental music in Northern California.

WORKS
(selective list)

Rebirth, cptr, 1990; Some Pointillism, 1990; Faraway Stations, cptr, 1992; Rave Patterns, cptr, 1992; Simulated Winds and Cries, cptr, 1992

WRITINGS

with J. Bischoff and R. Gold: "Music for an Interactive Network of Microcomputers," *Computer Music Journal*, ii/3 (1978), 24–9

"Horton hears a whole number ratio," *1/1 Just Intonation*, ii/0 (1986), 1 only, 11–14

CARTER SCHOLZ/R

Horton, Lester (*b* Indianapolis, IN, 23 Jan 1906; *d* Los Angeles, CA, 2 Nov 1953). Choreographer, teacher, and dance company director. Having studied various forms of dance, including ballet, Denishawn techniques, and Native American dance forms, he moved to Los Angeles in 1929 and pursued his training with Michio Ito, an influential Japanese teacher of modern dance. Soon Horton had developed his own style of teaching and in 1932 founded a performing group with a repertory of dances with such exotic titles as *Voodoo Ceremonial* and *Allegro Barbaro*. From the mid-1930s until the outbreak of World War II, the Lester Horton Dancers presented appreciative audiences with performances of daringly erotic dance (e.g., *Salome*), Native American pageants (e.g., *Mound Builders*), social and political statements (e.g., *Ku Klux Klan*), and an occasional satirical piece (e.g., *Flight from Reality*). With such a variety of dance styles and forms, he was recognized as the leading practitioner of modern dance on the West Coast. To create jobs for his students, Horton produced Afro-Cuban and Latin nightclub shows and worked on Hollywood films, creating dances for twenty-one movies between 1942 and 1953. He also taught tirelessly throughout all these years, giving sound training to hundreds of students. His importance lies not so much in his choreography as in his eclecticism, his musicianship, and his teaching methods. Major figures to emerge from his school and his company include Bella Lewitzky, Merce Cunningham, Alvin Ailey, Carmen de Lavallade, Joyce Trisler, Janet Collins, James Mitchell, and James Truitte.

BIBLIOGRAPHY
L. Warren: *Lester Horton: Modern Dance Pioneer* (New York, 1977)

N. Prevots: *Dancing in the Sun: Hollywood Choreographers, 1915–1937* (Ann Arbor, 1987)

M.F. Perces and others: *The Dance Technique of Lester Horton* (Pennington, NJ, 1992)

CLAUDE CONYERS

Hoschna, Karl L. (*b* Kuschwarda, Bohemia, 16 Aug 1877; *d* New York, NY, 23 Dec 1911). Composer, arranger, and oboist of Bohemian birth. Best known for the musical comedies he wrote for the Broadway stage, Hoschna studied oboe, piano, and composition at the Vienna Conservatory. Following graduation he became a bandmaster and oboist in the Austrian Army Band. In 1896 Hoschna moved to New York where he played oboe under Victor Herbert. Hoschna's decision to stop playing his instrument came in 1898. He wrote a long letter to Witmark music publishers asking for a job. Hoschna believed that the high pressures involved with the double reed of the oboe were affecting his brain and that a new direction in his musical career was needed in order to literally remain sane. Witmark gave him a job as an arranger and orchestrator and Hoschna stayed with the company until 1908.

While working for Witmark Hoschna arranged music for various stage productions, including *Broadway to Tokio* (1900). He also began to write original scores, including at least three comic operas that did not make it to Broadway. In 1905 he managed to get his music heard in *The Belle of the West*, with lyrics by Harry B. Smith. In 1907 *The Girl from Broadway* was produced, with lyrics by Charles Noel Douglass. None of his songs for these shows, however, managed to ignite the audience's flame.

The composer's successful run of popular shows began in 1908 when he was introduced to the lyricist Otto Hauerbach (later OTTO HARBACH). Given $100 by Witmark to write the score for a new musical, Hoschna was told he would be collaborating with Hauerbach who at the time was working in advertising. Their production, *The Three Twins* (1908), was an immediate success and ran for an impressive 289 performances. The songs "Cuddle Up a Little Closer, Lovey Mine" and "The Yama Yama Man" (lyrics by Collin Davis) became instant hits, and Bessie McCoy, who played Molly Summers (the Yama Yama Girl), gained immediate renown. The Hauerbach-Hoschna partnership blossomed. Between 1908 and 1911 they wrote eight musicals, all of which enjoyed commercial success; these include *Bright Eyes* (1910), *Dr. De Luxe* (1911), and *The Girl of My Dreams* (1911).

Hoschna and Hauerbach's second hit and the work for which they are best remembered is *Madame Sherry* (1910). The most memorable number, "Every Little Movement," is a polka introduced early in the show, which is reprised at structural moments. Both Frances Demarest and Lina Abarbanell, who played the title role, received positive notices. Curiously, the show was subtitled a "vaudeville," demonstrating that American musicals of the time were still struggling with clear genre definitions. Among Hoschna's other famous songs are "Electricity," "The Girl of My Dreams," "The Birth of Passion," "Doctor Tinkle Tinker," and "Fascination."

Hoschna was killed unexpectedly in 1911. Opening posthumously, *The Wall Street Girl* (1912) starred Broadway regular Blanche Ring and introduced a new face—the cowboy Will Rogers—to Broadway stardom.

BIBLIOGRAPHY
Anonymous: "Polka Dominates Madame Sherry," *New York Times*, 31 Aug 1910

I. Witmark: *The Story of the House of Witmark: From Ragtime to Swingtime* (New York, 1939)

J. Burton: "The Honor Roll of Popular Songwriters, No. 28, Karl Hoschna," *Billboard*, 16 July 1949, 40

JONAS WESTOVER

Hot jazz. A term used to describe jazz, particularly early jazz and swing, of an exciting and energetic nature.

House. A genre of ELECTRONIC DANCE MUSIC that originated in Chicago in the mid-1980s following the birth of techno in nearby Detroit. Chicago nightclubs such as the Warehouse (where the name "house" is said to have originated), the Music Box, and the Power Plant hosted predominantly gay, black, and Latino clientele. Pioneering house DJs, such as Frankie Knuckles and Ron Hardy, and key labels, notably Trax and DJ International, introduced house music to a mass audience.

House and techno both feature a 4/4 meter ("four on the floor"), with a kick drum sounding on every beat. Ample use of hi-hats, as well as snare hits or handclaps on the second and fourth beat lend a syncopated "disco" feel to a steady kick drum pulse. House music borrows heavily from disco and soul—producers emphasized melody and vocals, and added embellishments such as drum fills and strings. The tempo of house music tracks hovers around 120 beats per minute (as opposed to techno tracks, which range from 120 to upwards of 140 beats per minute). The Roland TR-808 and TR-909 drum machines were often used to provide the drum tracks for house music. The Roland TB-303, a "bass synthesizer," was often utilized by house producers for its unique timbres—the twitchy, rubbery synth lines produced by the TB-303 spawned the sub-genre of acid house.

By the end of the 1980s house music had become popular in New York City, with acts like the Peech Boys and Junior Vasquez, and was centered in clubs like Larry Levan's Paradise Garage. By 1988 house had taken root in Europe and especially in the UK, where it rapidly grew and mutated, helping to catalyze the rave movement. House music is still a thriving genre today, and has spawned several variants, such as deep house, electro-house, funky house, hip-house, and ambient house.

BIBLIOGRAPHY
H. Rietveld: *This is our House: House Music, Cultural Spaces and Technologies* (Aldershot, England, 1998)
S. Reynolds: *Generation Ecstasy: Into the World of Techno and Rave Culture* (New York, 1999)
B. Brewster & Frank Broughton. *Last Night a DJ Saved My Life: the History of the Disc Jockey* (New York, 2000)
K. Fikentscher: *"You Better Work!" Underground Dance Music in New York City* (Middletown, CT, 2000)
S. Bidder: *Pump Up the Volume: a History of House Music* (London, 2001)

GEETA DAYAL

House, Son [Eddie James, Jr.] (*b* Lyon, nr Clarksdale, MS, 21 March 1902; *d* Detroit, MI 19 Oct 1988). Blues singer and guitarist. Delta blues musician Son House developed a distinctive guitar playing style that incorporated driving, repetitive rhythms and bottleneck sliding techniques. His singing style stemmed from southern gospel music, field hollers, and chain gang work songs that he absorbed as a child in Mississippi and southern Louisiana. At age 15 House began to preach in local churches; his powerful voice and use

of hummed phrases probably derived from his church experiences. At age 20 he moved to St. Louis to work in a steel plant. Upon returning to Mississippi he heard blues singers Willie Wilson and Reuben Lacy; under their influence, and reinforced by an association in 1928 with Charley Patton and guitarist Willie Brown, he began to play guitar and sing blues. House spent time in the Mississippi State Penitentiary in 1928 and 1929 for allegedly killing a man in self-defense in a juke joint shooting. Once released he recorded several remarkable two-part blues for Paramount Records in 1930, including the influential "Preachin' the Blues" and "Dry Spell Blues," an account of the farming crisis in Mississippi. In 1941 ethnomusicologist Alan Lomax recorded House for the Library of Congress. Among the most significant songs from these Cormorant, Mississippi, recording sessions is "Depot Blues," a half-moaned, half-shouted song marked by the use of falsetto and trembling figures on the guitar that showcase House's musical maturity; another is "Walking Blues," on which House is accompanied by a string band that includes Willie Brown. "The Pony Blues" demonstrated his indebtedness to Patton, while "Am I right or wrong" (both 1942, Roots 1) placed him in the unfamiliar role of entertainer. After moving to Rochester, New York, in 1942, House began working for the New York Central Railroad. He continued to perform in a limited capacity in local music halls. In the early 1960s a new generation of blues enthusiasts "rediscovered" him during the US blues revival, although he was unaware of the international enthusiasm for his early recordings. He subsequently played at the Newport Folk Festival in 1964, toured the US and Europe, and recorded two records, "Death Letter" and a new version of "Preachin' Blues" (both 1965, Col. 2417). House can be seen in the documentary *The Howling Wolf Story*, which includes an exchange between the two bluesmen during the 1966 Newport Festival in which Wolf berates the elder House for wasting his talents through alcohol abuse. In 1970 House toured Europe and appeared at the Montreux Jazz Festival; his London concerts were recorded and released by Liberty Records. Poor health curtailed further concert performances, and House retired to Detroit, Michigan, in 1974, where he would remain until his death from laryngeal cancer in 1988. For many blues authorities House remains the epitome of the Delta blues style. He was a primary influence on bluesmen Robert Johnson and Muddy Waters and generations of young rock musicians.

RECORDINGS
(selective)
The Legendary Son House: Father of Folk Blues, 1965, Columbia; *Son House-Delta Blues*, 1991, Biograph Records; *The Very Best of Son House: Heroes of the Blues*, 2003, Shout! Factory

BIBLIOGRAPHY
A. Lomax: *Land Where the Blues Began* (New York, 1993)
J.T. Titon: *Early Downhome Blues: a Musical and Cultural Analysis* (Chapel Hill, NC, 1994)
E. Komara: "Blues in the Round," *Black Music Research Journal*, xvii/1 (1997), 3–36

D. Evans: *Ramblin' On My Mind: New Perspectives on the Blues* (Urbana, IL, 2008)

D. Beaumont: *Preachin' the Blues: the Life and Times of Son House* (New York, 2011)

PAUL OLIVER/MARGARET R. JACKSON

Houseley, Henry (*b* Sutton-in-Ashfield, Notts, England, 20 Sept 1852; *d* Denver, CO, 13 March 1925). Organist, conductor, and composer, of English birth. After studying with Michael Costa and E. H. Turpin, he held posts as an organist in Derby and Nottingham, and was professor of harmony and composition at the University of Nottingham.

Houseley came to Denver in March 1888 as associate organist at the Episcopal Cathedral of St John in the Wilderness, where he remained for 36 years, becoming principal organist in 1892. He was also organist at Temple Emanu-El and music director for the Ancient and Accepted Scottish Rite body of Masons. He was a founding member of the American Guild of Organists. In 1894 he became director of the Denver Choral Society, which won the Salt Lake City Welsh Eisteddfod in 1895; a "select chorus" from the group won first place at the Louisiana Purchase Exposition, St Louis (1904). He was also director of the Apollo Club men's chorus in Denver. His most permanent contribution to Denver's musical culture was the establishment of the first resident symphony orchestra in 1900; he led and developed many areas of musical life in Denver during the next 30 years. As a composer Houseley was best known for his cantata *Omar Khayyám*, which received its première in Denver on 1 June 1916; his anthems and ballads were also well known in his day. His other works include seven operas, a few orchestral compositions, and keyboard pieces.

BIBLIOGRAPHY

M.G. Wyer, ed.: *Music in Denver and Colorado* (Denver, 1927)

S.A. Linscome: *A History of Musical Development in Denver, Colorado, 1858–1908* (diss., U. of Texas, Austin, 1970)

S.A. Linscome: "Henry Houseley, Versatile Musician of Early Denver," *Colorado Magazine*, xlix (1972), 1

SANFORD A. LINSCOME/R

Housewright, L(ee) Wiley (*b* Wylie, TX, 17 Oct 1913; *d* Tallahassee, FL, 13 Dec 2004). Music educator, conductor, scholar, and administrator. He earned degrees from North Texas State College (BS 1934), Teachers College, Columbia University (MA 1938), and New York University (EdD 1943). He was director of music for public schools in Texas (1934–7) and New York (1938–41), and taught at New York University (1941–3) and the University of Texas (1946–7). He served as an Executive Officer in the US Army Medical Administrative Corps in the United States and Philippines (1943–6). He then taught at Florida State University (1947–66), where he was named Distinguished Professor (1961). During those years he held a Fulbright Fellowship to Japan (1956–7) and summer appointments at North Texas State University, University of Michigan, and Indiana University. He served on committees and advisory boards for the US Department of State International Cultural Presentations Program (1958–79), American Council of Learned Societies (1958–60), Ford Foundation Young Composers Project (1959–73), US National Commission of UNESCO (1961–4), and National Endowment for the Arts (1970), among others. He was Southern Division president (1953–5) and national president (1968–70) of the Music Educators National Conference, and chair of the Editorial Board for the *Music Educators Journal* (1958–66). He served as dean of the Florida State University School of Music for 12 years (1966–79). In 1991 he published *A History of Music & Dance in Florida, 1565–1865* (Tuscaloosa, AL). Housewright received a Distinguished Alumni Award from North Texas State University (1968), and was inducted into the Florida Music Educators Association Hall of Fame (1981) and Music Educators Hall of Fame (1994). The Society for American Music presents its annual award for best dissertation in his name. He contributed funds for the Wiley L. Housewright Building for music at Florida State University.

BIBLIOGRAPHY

G.N. Heller: "In Memoriam: Wiley L. Housewright (1913–2003)," *Journal of Historical Research in Music Education*, xxv/2 (2004), 77–8

JERE T. HUMPHREYS

Houston, Whitney (Elizabeth) (*b* Newark, NJ, 9 Aug 1963; *d* Beverly Hills, CA, 11 Feb 2012). Singer. She was one of the top-selling artists of all time. She began singing and playing piano in a church gospel choir as a child. In her teens, she modeled, performed with her mother, singer Cissy Houston, in nightclubs, and sang backup for Chaka Khan and Jermaine Jackson. Houston possessed a rich, strong mezzo-soprano voice and was known for her melismatic embellishments, especially at phrase endings. Arista's Clive Davis signed her to a recording contract in 1983. Houston's 1985 self-titled debut album produced a string of hits including "Thinking About You," "You Give Good Love," and Grammy-winning "Saving All My Love for You," Houston's first number one hit. The video for her fourth single, "How Will I Know," received heavy rotation at a time when MTV was criticized for ignoring black artists. Grammy-nominated "Greatest Love of All," the final single, became Houston's biggest hit to that point. Her second album, *Whitney* (1987), entered at number one on the *Billboard 200* albums chart. Critics suggested that it was too similar to her debut, but it became an even bigger commercial success. "I Wanna Dance With Somebody (Who Loves Me)," "Didn't We Almost Have It All," "So Emotional," and "Where Do Broken Hearts Go" were all number one hits. Houston demonstrated versatility with *I'm Your Baby Tonight* (1990), an album that mixed ballads and dance tracks.

In the 1990s, she appeared in a handful of films, beginning with *The Bodyguard* (1992). The soundtrack won three Grammys and eight American Music Awards, while the single, "I Will Always Love You," became the best-selling single by a female artist, charting on pop, R&B, and adult contemporary charts simultaneously. The films *Waiting to Exhale* (1995) and *The Preacher's Wife* (1996) also generated hit soundtracks. Houston's 1998 album, *My Love Is Your Love*, featuring Grammy-winning

"It's Not Right But It's Okay," did not sell well but garnered strong reviews. By the late 1990s, Houston was struggling with personal and professional difficulties, stemming from her marriage to the R&B singer Bobby Brown. Her career was at a virtual standstill. In 2002, Houston finally released her fifth studio album, *Just Whitney*, which received mixed reviews. It did not provide enough momentum to get Houston's career back on track but some of its singles became popular club hits. After divorcing Brown in 2006, Houston attempted a comeback with *I Look To You* (2009), which placed number one on the *Billboard 200*. In the midst of another attempted comeback in 2012, she was found dead at the age of 48 at the Beverly Hilton Hotel. Throughout her career, Houston influenced many singers, including Mariah Carey, Brandy, Jennifer Hudson, Leona Lewis, Beyoncé Knowles, and Alicia Keys.

COLETTE SIMONOT

Houston. City in Texas (pop. 2,099,451; metropolitan area 5,946,800; 2010 US Census). It was founded in 1836, the same year Texas gained independence from Mexico. Although its history is relatively short, Houston has become the fourth largest city in the United States. Its prosperity derives from successive industries in cotton and lumber, the discovery of oil in 1901, and the dredging of lower Buffalo Bayou from Galveston Bay in 1915, eventually making the Port of Houston the third busiest seaport in the United States. By the 1970s, Houston had become one of a handful of American cities able to maintain a major symphony orchestra, opera, ballet and spoken theater companies, a major art museum, two large university music schools, a steady stream of major touring attractions and numerous smaller resident performing and visual arts organizations.

1. Classical music. 2. Popular music. 3. Ethnic music

1. CLASSICAL MUSIC. In the city's earliest days, professional musical activity was largely imported in the form of traveling performers. The Roncari Opera made the first documented visit in 1867. The Metropolitan Opera staged a production of Wagner's *Lohengrin* in 1901 and returned in a performance of *Parsifal* four years later, Native Houstonian Edna W. Saunders (1880–1963) staged free public concerts on a volunteer basis at City Auditorium during World War I, then opened her own professional management agency, presenting leading national and international soloists, orchestras, opera and ballet companies during the last 45 years of her life. The series included six annual visits by the Chicago Opera Association, 1919–25, and visits by Caruso, Paderewski, the French Army Band, Ballet Russe, a historic 1947 return of the Metropolitan Opera, Rosa Ponselle, Yehudi Menuhin as a child prodigy, and countless others. After a brief hiatus following her death, the nonprofit Society for the Performing Arts was formed in 1966, continuing a tradition of importing many of the world's prime ballet companies, orchestras and solo performers to Houston under vigorous management by Jim Bernhard, Toby Mattox and June Christensen.

Resident musical institutions emerged alongside touring attractions throughout the later 19th and early 20th centuries. In 1866, Thomas W. Goggan opened a music store that lasted until the 1970s, while Theodore Grunewald established a music instrument dealership. By 1860, German immigrants numbered 30 percent of Houston's population and they formed several singing societies: the Houston Männerchor in the 1870s, the Houston Saengerbund in 1883—still in existence in 2011 as Houston's longest surviving musical organization—and the Liederkranz Singing Society prior to 1890. In 1884, the Sweeney & Coombs Opera House became the largest of several theaters built in the 19th century. At midnight mass on New Year's Eve, 1899, the choristers of Annunciation Church, the city's second oldest Catholic church, welcomed the new century with a performance of a Haydn mass. The Tuesday Musical Club, founded in 1911 to present leading recitalists, celebrated its centennial in 2011.

In 1913, a group of 138 citizens sponsored the first symphony orchestra in Houston, at the urging of Miss Ima Hogg (daughter of former Texas Governor James Stephen. Hogg). She remained its most stalwart supporter until her death in 1975. The original ensemble consisted of 35 musicians with a budget of $2500. The orchestra was largely formed out of a café orchestra headed by Julien Paul Blitz, 28, who became the orchestra's first and youngest conductor (1913–16). He was succeeded by Paul Bergé (1916–18). Toward the end of World War I, the orchestra was disbanded but the society continued to function. In 1931 the Houston SO was revived, first under Uriel Nespoli (1931-32), then Frank St. Leger (1932–35) and Ernst Hoffmann (1936–47), its first great builder who established the orchestra as a fully professional ensemble.

Following Hoffmann, Efrem Kurtz (1948–54) introduced then-unfamiliar works by Honegger, Bartók, Ives and others. Ferenc Fricsay oversaw a partial season in 1954, followed by Thomas Beecham (1954–55) and Leopold Stokowski (1955–60). Stokowski's tenure included a number of recordings the by orchestra, guest conducting appearances by Villa-Lobos, Stravinsky and Walter Susskind. During the next six years under Sir John Barbirolli (1961–67), the orchestra was enlarged and undertook a series of tours in the United States. Barbirolli presided over the orchestra's 50th anniversary (1963–64) and its first performances in Jesse H. Jones Hall, completed in 1966, which remains the orchestra's permanent home. André Previn followed Barbirolli for two seasons. From 1969–71, various guest conductors were invited, with Antonio de Almeida as principal guest conductor. At age 29, Lawrence Foster became the orchestra's conductor in chief in 1971 and music director in 1972. After Hoffmann, he became the orchestra's second great builder, greatly improving intonation and general technical discipline, especially in the brass section, while thoroughly modernizing the orchestra's repertoire. Upon his departure in 1978, a full season of guest conductors resulted in the appointment of Sergiu Comissiona, first as artistic adviser (1979), then music director. Comissiona pursued a vigorous program of audio and television recordings and touring, but problems of communication caused considerable frustration and left the orchestra greatly disheartened.

Christoph Eschenbach won instant acclaim when he became music director in 1988. An enthusiastic proponent of new music, he continued commissioning projects begun by Foster and Comissiona, bringing new works by Picker, Reimann, Singleton, Rouse and others into the orchestra's repertoire. Under his leadership, the orchestra grew artistically, undertaking ambitious recording projects and embarking on several international tours. A cycle of Mahler's nine complete symphonies was a significant accomplishment of his 11-season tenure. While well received critically, these activities precipitated a financial crisis that threatened the orchestra's long-term stability. In 1998, two local philanthropic foundations donated a total of $7.3 million to the orchestra, temporarily eliminating its accumulated budget deficit.

Since his appointment in 2001, Viennese-born conductor Hans Graf has proven to be a highly resourceful music director, working patiently and steadfastly to rebuild the orchestra and audience amid three catastrophes that coincided with his appointment: a citywide flood that destroyed the HSO administrative offices, music library and several orchestral instruments; the collapse of the Enron corporation, an important corporate donor to leading Houston arts organizations, and the September 11 bombing of New York's World Trade Center. Working with three different executive directors through two national recessions that saw the reduction of the orchestra by 10 members, and diminished concert attendance, he used great skill to restore the organization with novel, well-designed audience-accessible programs that held genuine artistic value, while overseeing the appointment of 18 new musicians, leading the orchestra on two short-but-acclaimed national tours and a week of sold-out concerts in England in 2010. At the conclusion of his 12-year tenure on the eve of the orchestra's centennial, he became its longest-serving music director, credited for imparting the warm, full-bodied orchestral sound that was characteristic of the Barbirolli years. In January 2013, Colombian-born conductor Andrés Orozco-Estrada was named music director-designate to succeed Graf in a five-year contract beginning with the orchestra's 2013–14 centennial season.

Various chamber orchestras have existed since the mid-1960s, independently as well as under the auspices of the Houston Symphony. Independent organizations have included the Houston Chamber Orchestra, led by Charles Rosekrans in the 1960s and 1970s; the conductorless Texas Chamber Orchestra, active during the 1980s, the River Oaks Chamber Orchestra, (est. 2005), and three baroque ensembles: Mercury Baroque, a period-instrument orchestra (est. 2001), Ars Lyrica and the J.S. Bach Society

Houston Grand Opera was founded in 1955 with Walter Herbert as general director, a post in which he served as artistic and business manager and principal conductor until 1972. Two operas were produced during his first season, gradually increasing in number to five productions in 1965. A sixth was added when the company, along with the Houston Symphony and touring concert attractions, moved from the Houston Music Hall to the new Jesse H. Jones Hall for the Performing Arts in 1966. The company's early repertoire consisted largely of popular operas, with occasional exceptions such as Rimsky-Korsakov's *The Golden Cockerel*, Henze's *Der junge Lord* and Orff's *Der Mond*.

After David Gockley's appointment as general director in 1972, HGO established itself as a champion of new opera and innovatory productions. Beginning in 1974 with Pasatieri's *The Seagull*, Gockley oversaw the world or American premieres of new operas on a nearly annual basis, including Bernstein's *A Quiet Place*, Adams' *Nixon in China,* Tippett's *New Year*, Wallace's *Harvey Milk*, Vaughan Williams' *Hugh the Drover*, Glass's *Akhnaten* and *The Making of the Representative for Planet Eight*. He established a parallel English-language series to the main subscription season and instituted free outdoor springtime performances.

Private funding underwrote the planning and development of the Gus Wortham Center, which opened in 1987 as a permanent home for Houston Grand Opera and Houston Ballet, boasting large (Brown Theater, cap. 2167) and small (Cullen Theater, cap. 1066) auditoriums. In addition to its regular seasons, HGO has been very active in producing educational programs and performances for students, in training young singers. Two small affiliated companies, Texas Opera Theater and Opera to Go, successively provided educational touring productions throughout Houston and Texas, in adjoining states and locations farther afield beginning in 1973. Houston Opera Studio, founded by Gockley and composer Carlisle Floyd in 1977 as a training program for talented young artists, has helped launch the careers of Joyce Di Donato, Richard Paul Fink, Denyce Graves, Erik Halfvarson, John Keyes, Ana Maria Martinez, Suzanne Mentzer and Erie Mills. In 1989, HGO established the Genevieve P. Demme Archives and Resource Center, becoming only the second major American opera company to provide its own research facility. Anthony Freud, director of the Welsh National Opera, succeeded Gockley in 2005, continuing the high level of quality Gockley achieved. Highlights of his tenure have included cycle of Britten operas and a re-focusing of HGO's commissioning policy to reach a broader audience by producing operas based on stories of Houston's many immigrant communities.

Five smaller operatic institutions have added novelty to Houston's operatic scene since the mid-1980s: the University of Houston Opera Theatre, directed by Buck Ross at the UH Moores School of Music; The Shepherd School of Music Opera Theatre at Rice University, directed by Richard Bado; Opera in the Heights, founded in 1995 by William Weibel, who was succeeded by artistic director Enrique Carreón-Robledo in 2011; Ebony Opera, founded by the late Robert C. Henry, currently conducted by Willie Anthony Waters with a mission of presenting African American casts in free performances;

and Opera Vista, specializing in new operas by living composers presented in a festival setting.

Prominent resident chamber music ensembles began with a string quartet headed by violinist Josephine Boudreaux in 1929. Other ensembles have included the Lyric Art String Quartet, founded by Houston concert violinist Fredell Lack in the 1950s, the Virtuoso Piano Trio, Woodwinds of Houston and Symphonic Brass, all associated with the University of Houston School of Music from the 1950s through the 1970s, the Music Guild Quartet, headed by Houston Symphony concertmaster Raphael Fliegel in the 1950s and 1960s, the Shepherd String Quartet, headed by Fliegel's successor, Ronald Patterson, at Rice University's Shepherd School of Music in the mid-1970s, the Cimarron Winds in the 1980s, and two separate ensembles called the Houston Symphony Chamber Players, staffed by the orchestra's principal musicians in the 1970s and 1990s.

Touring string quartets and other chamber music ensembles have regularly been presented by the Houston Friends of Music (now Houston Friends of Chamber Music) since 1960. In 1987, violinist Sergiu Luca founded the Da Camera Society (now Da Camera of Houston), presenting broader historical thematic programs of chamber music at various Houston venues, and combining resident and touring musicians. Pianist Sarah Rothenberg became director of the series in 1994, building its thematic programming to embrace parallel trends in art and literature, instituting a separate series of jazz concerts and bringing Da Camera to its highest level of achievement. Luca and pianist Brian Connelly established a new chamber music series, called Music in Context, in 1995, focusing on historically informed performances of 18th and 19th century works played on period instruments. Several contemporary music groups have existed for various time periods since Stokowski founded a Contemporary Music Society in 1960. Current ensembles include Syzygy at Rice University, Aura at UH's Moores School of Music, and Musiqa (cq), founded by a group of Houston composers in 2002 as an independent ensemble embracing musical, visual, theatrical and movement disciplines

Choral music, both sacred and secular, has figured significantly in Houston's musical life since the early 20th century. Major church choirs providing public concerts as well as service music have included those at First Presbyterian Church under Charles Pabor (1940s–1960s), Christ Church Episcopal Cathedral Choral Society under William Barnard (1950s-1970s), and St. Luke's United Methodist Church under Robert C. Bennett (1960s–1980s), St. Paul's United Methodist Church under Robert Brewer (1980–2005).

The Houston Symphony and Houston Grand Opera developed massive choruses in the mid-20th century, founded respectively by Alfred Urbach in 1949, and Charles Rosekrans in 1958. Their respective current directors, Charles Hausmann and Richard Bado, maintain the choruses at a high level of precision and tonal splendor. Ara Carapetyan founded Houston Oratorio Society (later named Houston Masterworks Chorus in 1986. The Houston Chamber Choir, founded in 1995 by Robert Simpson, is currently the city's leading choral organization. The Singing Boys of Houston (now Houston Boy Choir), celebrates its 50th anniversary in 2012.

Five Houston universities provide degree programs in music, the largest being the University of Houston Moores School of Music, established in 1940, and Rice University's Shepherd School of Music, established in 1975. Both schools are housed in spacious modern facilities, their faculties are staffed with significant performing artists and musical scholars, and they offer a broad range of training through the doctoral degree level. A public High School for the Performing and Visual Arts was established by educator Ruth Denney in the 1970s and the city has two youth orchestras, the Houston Youth Symphony, founded in 1948 by Howard Webb, and the Greater Houston Youth Orchestra, established by violist-conductor Lawrence Wheeler in 1993.

The Houston area has two major summer music festivals each June and July: the month-long Texas Music Festival, founded in 1990 by David Tomatz at UH's Moores School of Music, and the Festival-Institute at Round Top, a six-week festival founded by pianist James Dick in 1971. A 1200-seat Victorian-style concert hall is the centerpiece of this festival, built on a 200-acre campus of new and restored buildings in the rural Texas village of Round Top. Both festivals emphasize orchestral and chamber music training and performance, with students and faculty drawn from an international community of musicians.

Serge Diaghilev's Ballets Russes first performed in Houston 4–5 December 1916, during the company's inaugural American tour, with Pierre Monteux conducting. During the 1930s and early 1940s, the company's successor, Col. de Basil's Ballet Russe de Monte Carlo, made annual week-long Christmas-holiday visits to Houston, followed by Ballet Theatre after the demise of Ballet Russe. These tours inspired a group of citizens, headed by Natasha Rawson, to form a Houston Ballet Foundation in 1955, sponsoring a ballet academy directed by former Ballet Russe dancer Tatiana Semenova. In 1967, Semenova was succeeded by Nina Popova, who formed a 15-member company that engaged in local performances and regional tours during a 21-week season.

Ben Stevenson became artistic director when the company had reached 28 members in 1976, doubling its size to 56 dancers by the time he retired in 2003. During his 27 years, Houston Ballet acquired a vast repertoire representing the world's leading choreographers, toured nationally and internationally, including major engagements in Beijing, Moscow and London, and became the fourth largest ballet company in the United States. In 2003, Australian choreographer Stanton Welch was named artistic director, building further upon Stevenson's accomplishments. In 2011, the company, administration, and academy moved into its new six-story, 115,000 sq. ft. Center for Dance, the largest facility of its kind in the United States.

Numerous smaller dance troupes, representing all aspects of classical, modern and jazz dance, have existed at various times during the last half-century. Dennis

Marshall, son of Greater Houston Civic Ballet founder Margo Marshall Geis, gained prominence as a principal with American Ballet Theatre, and Patrick Swayze, son of Houston Jazz Ballet founder Patsy Swayze, became a well-known film dancer and actor.

2. POPULAR MUSIC. Houston has played an important yet often overlooked role in the development of most modern forms of American popular music, especially boogie-woogie, early rock and roll, country, soul, Southern hip hop, and zydeco. At bottom, Houston is a blues town; scratch the surface of almost any genre and the deep blues lies just below.

The Bayou City is at a trilingual cultural crossroads. To the north is the Deep South, in the form of East Texas, a traditionally cotton-bound Scotch-Irish/African American cultural zone more akin to the Mississippi Delta than the Lone Star State of popular imaginings. To the immediate west is a farming region heavily populated by polka-loving Czechs, Germans, and Poles. To the east sprawl alligator-patrolled swamplands where historically Francophone Creole/Cajun Louisiana folkways and musics at least in part hold sway, and to the southwest is the road to Mexico. All of these cultures have brought their sounds to Houston.

Very little music was recorded in Houston prior to World War II. However, as the city's growth exploded after the excavation of the Houston Ship Channel in 1914, the city did prove fertile ground for musicians. The Thomas family, sons and daughters of a Baptist deacon in Houston's Fifth Ward, were the Bayou City's first native-bred entries into the national "race music" consciousness. George Thomas Jr. was the eldest of a trio of musical siblings that also included classic blues singer Beulah "Sippie" Wallace and doomed teenaged piano prodigy Hersal Thomas. Later boogie-woogie pianists such as Meade Lux Lewis and Albert Ammons credited George and Hersal Thomas with helping lay the groundwork for the influential style.

While the Thomas family made its name in northern cities such as Chicago and Detroit, another Houstonian pianist crafted his legend mainly within Texas. John Dickson "Peck" Kelley (1898–1980) hailed from Houston's Sixth Ward, just across Buffalo Bayou from what was then known as "The Reservation," Houston's early 20th-century red light district. Kelley's prowess was legendary, yet despite offers of tryouts from the likes of Benny Goodman and Artie Shaw, he chose to stay in Houston and perform more for fun than money or fame. The same could be said for trumpeter Milt Larkin, leader of Houston's top Depression-era territory band, which featured Dallas's T-Bone Walker on guitar, and graduated various "Texas tenors," the Houston-bred sax-men (and future bandleaders) Eddie "Cleanhead" Vinson, Arnett Cobb, and Illinois Jacquet.

Houston's country and western scene began making a national impression in the 1930s with the rise of steel guitarist and songwriter Ted Daffan, once a bandmate of both Floyd Tillman and Moon Mullican. Daffan's honky-tonk standards include "Truck Driver's Blues," "Born to Lose," and "No Letter Today." Floyd Tillman's risque "Slippin' Around" (1949) is credited as the first cheatin' song to grace the country charts, and his sly songwriting sensibility, laconic, jazzy vocal phrasing, and electric guitar innovations explain why Willie Nelson called him "the Original Outlaw."

In 1949, Fifth Ward guitarist Goree Carter (1930–90) recorded a song called "Rock Awhile" for Sol Kahal's short-lived Freedom label. Pop critic Robert Palmer would later claim that the amped-up update of the T-Bone Walker sound was the best choice as the very first rock and roll single on wax. While Carter gave up on recording music five years after recording his seminal track, his Grammy-winning, world-touring contemporaries Albert Collins and Johnny Clyde Copeland would enjoy longer careers and gain much wider renown.

With the 1949 signing of volcanic, genre-bending Louisiana-born guitarist-fiddler Clarence "Gatemouth" Brown, Fifth Ward entrepreneur Don Robey would launch Peacock Records, a pioneering black-owned label that became one of Houston's most successful. After absorbing Memphis's Duke, the renamed Duke-Peacock empire would be the driving wheel behind the careers of Johnny Ace, Bobby "Blue" Bland, Junior Parker, Johnny Otis, Big Mama Thornton, and blue-eyed soul artist Roy Head, as well as a host of gospel artists, including the Swan Silvertones, the Mighty Clouds of Joy, and the Dixie Hummingbirds. Robey sold the label to ABC-Dunhill in 1973.

Across the tracks, jukebox vendor Harold "Pappy" Daily founded Starday Records in 1953. Through a partnership with Mercury Records, Starday would launch George Jones, who recorded "The Window Up Above" and "White Lightning" for Daily. Another Daily label, this one simply called D Records, gave the world the Big Bopper's "Chantilly Lace" in 1958.

Louisiana-bred Huey P. Meaux ("the Crazy Cajun") bought the old Gold Star Studios and renamed them Sugar Hill in the late 1960s. In addition to recording important swamp pop regional hits by south Louisiana artists such as Joe Barry, Meaux would produce national hits such as Creole swamp-rocker Barbara Lynn's "You'll Lose a Good Thing," Tejano crooner Freddy Fender's "Before the Next Teardrop Falls," and "Wasted Days and Wasted Nights," and San Antonio Tex-Mex rockers Sir Douglas Quintet's "Mendocino" and "She's About a Mover."

Where Meaux's recordings were steeped deep in Gulf Coast roots music, International Artists looked outward for inspiration. IA is known today chiefly as the home of the psychedelic rock pioneers the 13th Floor Elevators and Bubble Puppy. Out of the fringes of this LSD-drenched blues scene would also emerge ZZ Top, which merged two members of Dallas's American Blues with Billy Gibbons, formerly of Houston's Moving Sidewalks, and went on to join the unofficial classic rock canon.

Though not known as a soul hub, Houston did produce a national smash hit with Archie Bell and the Drell's breezy "Tighten Up"; equally balmy were the reggae-tinged numbers "I Can See Clearly Now" and "Hold Me Tight" by former Houston teen idol Johnny

Nash. Although they were based in Los Angeles by the late 1960s, the Crusaders bore aloft the banner for Houston jazz for much of the 1970s, and Crusaders pianist Joe Sample has since returned home to the city. Houston's R&B scene would enjoy its biggest success to date in the late 1990s with the rise to international superstardom of Destiny's Child and singer Beyoncé, very likely Houston's top-selling act of all time.

Spearheaded by Townes Van Zandt, a local folk music scene started to coalesce around 1965, producing Guy Clark, Rodney Crowell, Steve Earle, Lucinda Williams, Eric Taylor, Lyle Lovett (who remained in Houston), Robert Earl Keen, and K.T. Oslin. Standing as a spiritual forefather to Houston's folk scene is Mickey Newbury, who helped guide its development in the early days.

With the 1980 release of *Urban Cowboy*, blue-collar Houston's city-meets-country aesthetic swept the nation's consciousness. The cowboy hats, snap-button shirts, huge belt buckles, longneck beers, and country sounds of singers like Johnny Lee and Mickey Gilley (whose nightclub in nearby Pasadena served as the centerpiece of the film) were adopted as style accoutrements from coast to coast. Meanwhile, Houston's Kenny Rogers enjoyed crossover pop success with songs like "Coward of the County" and "The Gambler." Not until the rise and relatively brief peak of Clint Black at the end of the 1980s would Houston have a country singer who could rival Rogers's success. In the 21st century Hayes Carll has become Houston's brightest light on the national country stage, though to date he has enjoyed more critical success than commercial.

Under the watchful eye of James Prince, president of Rap-A-Lot records, Houston hip hop took its first big step with the Geto Boys highly-controversial 1990 self-titled major-label debut. Chart success came with the following year's "Mind Playing Tricks on Me." Geto Boy Scarface (Brad Jordan) would go on to a successful solo career. In the early and mid-1990s, DJ Screw (Robert Davis) popularized a post-production technique called "chopping and screwing," in which original recordings are slowed and effects added in order to enhance their enjoyment for listeners intoxicated on codeine. The technique proved widely influential and endures throughout Texas and the South. Davis passed away from the effects of codeine abuse in 2000. Houston rap artists have achieved even greater success in the 21st century. Mike Jones, Paul Wall, Chamillionaire, and Slim Thug all have enjoyed national hits and plaudits, as did Port Arthur's Underground Kingz, whose long rise to national prominence was tragically punctuated by the untimely death of co-leader Chad "Pimp C." Butler in 2007.

3. ETHNIC MUSIC. Creole migration from rural south and southwest Louisiana to Houston began in 1927 after the infamous floods of that year. Many settled in a subsection of the city's Fifth Ward that later came to be known as Frenchtown. This population got another boost during the wartime boom years as jobs were plentiful on the wharves and shipyards of the Port of Houston. In Houston, these rural Creoles were first exposed to prevailing trends in English-language music, which typically included blues and R&B. Rural French-language "la-la" music evolved soon enough into bilingual zydeco in cities like Houston and Beaumont-Port Arthur. Beginning with Clifton Chenier and continuing through Buckwheat Zydeco and beyond, most of the genre's leading lights have lived in Houston for a time, and have made the city's half-dozen or so black Catholic parish halls regular tour stops through their careers. A horseback zydeco culture derived from Creole cowboy traditions still thrives, with trail rides often culminating in concerts redolent of smoky boudin and rouiling gumbo and echoing with wheezing accordions and raspy rub-boards. Although there are tens of thousands of white Cajuns in Houston, Cajun music is rare today. The city was the site, however, of the 1946 recording of fiddler Harry Choate's "Jolie Blond," perhaps the definitive rendition of that unofficial anthem of South Louisiana.

The music of Hispanic Houston has always displayed a tension between recent and earlier arrivals. The city was the birthplace of legendary songstress Lydia Mendoza, and later Orquestas Tejanas performed in the ballrooms and performances halls of the city's Segundo Barrio (or Second Ward) east of downtown. Notable bandleaders of the 20th century included one-armed trumpeter Roberto Zenteno (whose daughter Norma has enjoyed a long locally popular career of her own) and Fito Olivares, who had a big hit with "Juana La Cubana." Mexican-born *cumbia* master Rigo Tovar launched his career in Houston in the early 1970s and was wildly successful on both side of the Rio Grande, even reportedly outdrawing the Pope when both made appearances in Monterrey.

Although the city has never been quite the Tejano hub that Corpus Christi is, nor the conjunto haven that is San Antonio, Houston's La Mafia became the city's biggest latter-day Tejano group. In the late 1990s, taste among more assimilated Hispanics in Houston started running from Tejano and towards hip hop, exemplified by South Park Mexican, Luciano, singer-rapper Baby Bash, and Chingo Bling, a satirist who blends north Mexican styles with black culture into a seamless Aztlan-meets-Dirty South whole.

BIBLIOGRAPHY

Ann Holmes Fine Arts Archive, 1920–2008 (MS, Woodson Research Center, Fondren Library, Rice U., 546)

D.W. Pugh: *Music in Frontier Houston, 1836–1876* (diss., U. of Texas, 1970)

H. Roussel: *The Houston Symphony Orchestra, 1913–1971* (Austin, TX, 1972)

D.W. Looser: *Significant Factors in the Musical Development of the Cultural Life in Houston, Texas 1930–1971* (diss., Florida State U., 1972)

R. Craven, ed.: *Orchestras of the United States: Selected Profiles* (New York, 1986)

G. Schmidgall: "Can Do: How Houston came by its Grand New Arts Complex," "Architect Eugene Aubry," "General Director David Gockley," *ON* lii/4 (1987–88), 12–16, 16–18 and 66–67, 20, 70 only

G. Gart and R. Ames: *Duke/Peacock Records: an Illustrated History with Discography* (Milford, NH, 1989)

W. Albright: "Play it Again: William Albright on Houston's 25 Premieres," *Opera*, li/4 (2000), 426–31

G. Kay: "Championship Seasons," *Opera News*, lxv/3 (2000), 55–61

R. Wood: *Down in Houston: Bayou City Blues* (Austin, TX, 2003)

J. Caramanica: "The Tippin' point: Houston hip-hoppers," *Spin*, xxi/9 (Sept 2005), 64–8

C. Cunningham and R. Giesberg: *Houston Grand Opera at Fifty* (Houston, 2005)

R. Wood and J. Fraher: *Texas Zydeco* (Austin, TX, 2006)

J. Minton: "Houston Creoles and Zydeco: the Emergence of an African American Urban Popular Style," *Ramblin' on My Mind: New Perspectives on the Blues*, ed. D. Evans (Urbana, IL, 2008), 350–98

A. Bradley and R. Wood: *House of Hits: the Story of Houston's Gold Star/Sugar Hill Recording Studio* (Austin, TX, 2010)

LAURIE SHULMAN/CARL CUNNINGHAM (1),
JOHN NOVA LOMAX (2, 3)

Hovda, Eleanor (*b* Duluth, MN, 27 March 1940; *d* Springdale, AR, 12 Nov 2009). Composer and teacher. *Her career also spanned* choreography, arts administration, and advocacy. She studied composition with Gordon Smith, MEL POWELL, KENNETH GABURO, ESTHER BALLOU, and Karlheinz Stockhausen. She also studied dance with LUCIA DLUGOSZEWSKI, ERICK HAWKINS, Bessie Schonberg, and MERCE CUNNINGHAM and worked with choreographers such as Nancy Meehan, Laura Pawel, and Sharon Friedler. After receiving her BA in music at American University in Washington DC, she completed a MFA in dance composition at Sarah Lawrence College.

Her music has been performed extensively in the United States and Europe and at festivals worldwide. In addition to faculty appointments at Princeton and Yale universities, and Bard College in Annandale-on-Hudson, New York, she held residencies at Sarah Lawrence College, Wesleyan University, the College of St. Scholastica, and the American Dance Festival. She was composer-in-residence of the North Arkansas Symphony, for which she wrote *Ground Rounds* and *Beautiful Arkansas: A Fanfare of Songs*, based on old Arkansas state songs and fiddle music. She always explained that the concerns of dance—weight, energy, space—added important dimensions to her thinking about music and about the interaction between time and physical movement.

WORKS
(selective)

Spring music with wind (1973), pf; Ariadne music (1984), fl, cl, vn, vc, db, pf, and perc [Commissioned for Boston Musica Viva]; Song in high grasses (1986), v, fl, vc, and pf; *Guest to Star—Part II* (1986); Fields (1987), orch; Lemniscates (1988), str qt; Nine Leaf Window (1990), ob, elec b; Beginnings (1991), shenai, ob, and elec b; Glosses/Glacier (1991), elec b with superball mallet; Onyx (1991), fl, ob, cl, hn, tpt, vn, va, vc, and db [Commissioned by the Lake Superior Chamber Orchestra]; Shenai sky (1991), shenai; Armonia (1992), gui qt; Cheetah (1992), fl, ob, cl in B♭, bn, perc, elec b, and va; If tigers were clouds…then reverberating, they would create all songs (1993), 2 perc, cls (1 player), and pf [Commissioned by Zeitgeist for the Music in Motion project]; Snapdragon (1993), fl, obs, cls, bns, and hns [Commissioned by The Netherlands Wind Ensemble]; Leaning into and away (1994), fl, ob, cl, vns, va, vc, and 2 perc [Written for the Cuicani Project and commissioned by the US/Mexican Fund for Culture]; Glacier track (1996), ob d'amore and elec b; Coastal traces tidepools 1 (1997), pf innards and waterphone [Composed for the Nancy Meehan Dance Company]; Coastal traces tidepools 2 (1997), bowed pf innards; Dancing in place (1997) harp; Beautiful Arkansas: A fanfare of songs (2003), orch

BIBLIOGRAPHY

K. Pendle: *American Women Composers*, Contemporary Music Review 16 (Amsterdam, 1997)

K. Gann: *Music downtown: writings from The Village voice* (New York, 2006)

E. Arciuli: *Musica per pianoforte negli Stati Uniti. Autori, opere, storia* (Torino, 2010)

DANIELE BUCCIO

Hove, Carolyn (*b* United States). Oboist, English horn player, and pedagogue. Carolyn Hove attended the Oberlin College Conservatory of Music and upon graduation moved to Chicago where she maintained an active performance schedule. While in Illinois she taught at Northern Illinois University and Elmhurst College. In 1986 she became English horn player with the San Antonio Symphony, and two years later secured the same post with the Los Angeles Philharmonic, a position she held until 2011. During the past quarter century Hove has been featured as a soloist with the Los Angeles Philharmonic numerous times and also has been involved in the creation and premiere of many new works for her instrument. Composers that have written pieces for her include Esa-Pekka Salonen and William Kraft. She also recorded two solo CDs for the Crystal Records label, *20th Century Music for English Horn and Oboe* in 1996 and *Ascending to Superlatives* in 2000. A champion of all things related to the English horn, Hove maintains an active recital and teaching schedule in addition to her annual summer event "English Horn Master Classes with Carolyn Hove," where both serious and amateur oboists develop their skills on the English horn under her expert guidance.

ANNA PENNINGTON

Hovey, Nilo Wellington (*b* Cedar Falls, IA, 22 Sept 1906; *d* Elkhart, IN, 14 March 1986). Conductor, educator, and composer. He received his first musical instruction in the Cedar Falls Concert Band, and first conducted in the public schools of Dike, Iowa, while attending Iowa State Teachers College. Following studies at Northwestern and Butler Universities (BME, MM) he served as director of instrumental music in Hammond, Indiana for 18 years. In 1944 he became director of the concert band and chairman of the music education department at Butler University. In 1957 he joined the Selmer Company in Elkhart, Indiana, as educational director, and spent the next 16 years writing methods, instructional guides for band directors, solos for individual instruments, and arrangements of classical symphonic and operatic music for woodwind ensembles.

Hovey was guest conductor, lecturer and clinician in 46 states and five Canadian provinces. He was president of the American Bandmasters Association (1970) and MENC's Music Industry Council, and the recipient of many national, state, and regional awards, including Phi Beta Mu's Hall of Fame Award (1979), Kappa Kappa Psi's Distinguished Service Award, and the National Band Association's Academy of Wind and Percussion Arts and Hall of Fame Awards (1980, 1986).

WORKS

Efficient Rehearsal Procedures for School Bands (Elkhart, IN, 1976)
Seven volumes of band materials; 18 methods and studies for wind instruments; ten arrangements for large woodwind ensembles; and 19 solos for clarinet, some written jointly with Beldon Leonard.

RAOUL F. CAMUS

Hovhaness [Hovaness], **Alan** [Chakmakjian, Alan Hovhaness] (*b* Somerville, MA, 8 March 1911; *d* Seattle, 21 June 2000). Composer. Of Armenian and Scottish descent, he began composing in early childhood and took a youthful interest in meditation and mysticism. In the early 1930s he studied with FREDERICK SHEPHERD CONVERSE at the New England Conservatory and was exposed to the music of India, then little known in the West, through musicians in the Boston area. His early, "first-period" works show little of this influence but reflect that of Renaissance music, and, especially in works composed before 1936, employ a harmonic language reminiscent of late Romanticism. In 1943 Hovhaness rethought his style, influenced by his meditative activities and the disappointments he had experienced that summer at the Berkshire Music Center, where his music was criticized by Leonard Bernstein and Aaron Copland. He destroyed or suppressed many works and studied Armenian music—especially the works of the priest-composer Komitas Vardapet—which he had until then neglected. The music of this second period is more active rhythmically and contrapuntally, but it is significant that the stylistic attitude and the harmonic and melodic vocabulary remain more or less the same. Hovhaness attained a considerable reputation in the 1950s, a decade during which he travelled widely and embarked on a third stylistic period which combined elements of the first two periods as well as various experimental and non-Western procedures. These international tendencies continued into a fourth period, beginning about 1960, in which East Asian elements, particularly features of Japanese and Korean music, predominate. The fifth period, beginning about 1971, was marked by a return to Western influences; the works are particularly rich in scoring and chordal sonority, longer in duration than their predecessors, and generally more spacious and less active.

Although most of Hovhaness's major compositions are instrumental, almost every work is religious in nature. This does not, however, inhibit stylistic and psychological variety; tranquility, fear, ecstasy, mystery, and epic chaos find expression by means of divergent and ever-changing techniques. Hovhaness's melodies are clear, often largely conjunct, and generally confined to the notes of a particular mode. The modes range from diatonic scales to exotic rāgas; the use of the rāga increased in the later periods. *Wind Drum* (1962), for voices and small orchestra, uses one six-note mode for the entire 35-minute work. His harmonies are often quite consonant, but progress modally or chromatically rather than tonally. In the works of his second and fourth periods, long sections may be completely static chordally. Hovhaness also uses harsh dissonances formed by adding semitone-removed pitches to a consonant chord. This collapses the functions of nonharmonic tones and of resolutions into one chord. A surprising harmonic fingerprint, found in the very early and very late works, but entirely absent from 1940 to 1970, is the traditional half-diminished chord (a diminished triad with an added minor 7th) elevated in some fifth-period works to a predominant role. In this

Hovhaness acknowledges the influences of Wagner's operas and the idiom of music for the shō, a Japanese mouth organ.

Hovhaness rarely used standard formal and motivic procedures, but he made frequent and rigorous use of counterpoint throughout his life. For example, the first period has many richly beautiful modal fugues (as in the Missa brevis), the second abounds in vigorous polymodal canons ("St. Vartan" Symphony), and the fourth features slow dissonant canons at the unison (The Holy City). Rhythmic organization is equally strict, often including complex repeated metric patterns related to both Indian tāla and Western isorhythm. A variant of this procedure, which Hovhaness devised in 1944, assigns different short patterns, with pitches and rhythm specified, to several parts, with instructions that players perform the passages repeatedly at their own speed without synchronization with the rest of the ensemble. However, the resultant blur is hardly aleatory, since exact pitches are carefully controlled and any two performances will be substantially the same. Hovhaness uses these sections, which he calls "rhythmless," in many ways, ranging from gentle murmuring accompaniments (in such works of the second period as *Lousadzak*, 1944) to cataclysmic orchestral crescendos (as in *Fra Angelico*, 1967, of the fourth period).

Despite his high mystical intentions, Hovhaness wrote quickly and produced many works of Gebrauchsmusik (Symphony for Metal Orchestra, for flutes, trombones, and percussion, 1963, was written for a metallurgical society's convention). He sometimes reworked material for new pieces, a practice consistent with that of his favorite Western composers, those of the Baroque, especially Handel and Bach, and Renaissance. He was also concerned to make his works easily playable. Just as Hovhaness tended to avoid Classical and Romantic forms, he normally rejected traditional Western orchestration. Many works, particularly of the second period, use small orchestras, and keep instruments and instrumental groups clearly distinct. In later works requiring larger forces he tended to cultivate polyrhythmic or polymodal techniques so that *tuttis*, when they do occur, are accumulations of differentiated colors rather than homogeneous aggregates. There are exceptions in the third period, particularly in the symphonies of the 1950s, where Romantic *tuttis* can be found.

Among the most prolific composers of the 20th century, his surviving corpus of works numbers well over 400, despite his destruction of dozens of works. Age did not impede his productivity; in fact the years after his 60th birthday were the most productive of all, yielding over 30 symphonies. In 1977 he became a member of the Institute of the American Academy and Institute of Arts and Letters.

Hovhaness composed extensively for full orchestra, chamber orchestra, and band. A capable pianist, he wrote many piano works and songs with piano accompaniment. His chamber works often use instruments of diverse types, occasionally including Asian instruments. The short chamber operas are suggestive of mystery plays and *Noh* drama. Of his many choral works, the psalm settings have acquired a permanent place in the repertory of many church choirs.

WORKS

STAGE

Ops (libs by Hovhaness unless otherwise stated): Etchmiadzin, op.62, 1946; Afton Water (operetta, after W. Saroyan), 1951; Blue Flame (chbr op), op.172, 1959; The Burning House (chbr op, 1), op.185, 1960; Spirit of the Avalanche (chbr op, 1), op.197, 1962; Pilate (chbr op, 1), op.196, 1963; Travellers (chbr op), op.215, 1965; The Leper King (music-drama), op.219, 1965; Lady of Light (op-orat), op.227, 1969; Pericles (after W. Shakespeare), op.283, 1975; Tale of the Sun Goddess Going into the Stone House, op.323, 1978; The Frog Man (chbr op, M. Hamma), op.407, 1987

Ballets: Ardent Song (choreog. M. Graham), 1954; A Rose for Miss Emily, op.229/2, 1969; Dream of a Myth, op.257, 1973; Plains Daybreak (E. Hawkins), 1977; Killer of Enemies (Hawkins), op.383, 1983; God, the Reveller (Hawkins), op.408, 1987

SYMPHONIES

no.1 "Exile," op.17, 1937; no.2 "Mysterious Mountain," op.132, 1955; no.3, op.148, 1956; no.4, op.165, wind, 1958; no.5, op.170, 1953, rev. 1963; no.6 "Celestial Gate," op.173, chbr orch, 1959, rev. 1960; no.7 "Nanga Parvat," op.175, wind, 1959; no.8 "Arjuna," pf, chbr orch, 1947; no.9 "St. Vartan," op.80 (op.180), chbr orch, 1950; no.10, chbr orch, op.184, 1944, rev. 1965; no.11 "All Men are Brothers," op.186, 1960, rev. 1969; no.12, op.188, SATB, orch, 1960; no.13, op.190, 1954, rev. 1960; no.14 "Ararat," op.194, wind, 1961; no.15 "Silver Pilgrimage," op.199, 1962; no.16, kayagŭm, op.202, Korean perc, str, 1962; no.17 (Sym. for Metal Orch), op.203, 6 fl, 3 trbn, perc, 1963; no.18 "Circe," op.204a, 1963; no.19 "Vishnu," op.217, 1966; no.20 "Three Journeys to a Holy Mountain," op.223, band, 1968; no.21 "Etchmiadzin," op.234, 2 tpt, str, 1970; no.22 "City of Light," op.236, 1971; no.23 "Ani," op.249, band, 1972; no.24 "Majnun," T, SATB, op.273, tpt, str, 1973; no.25 "Odysseus," op.275, small orch, 1973

no.26 "Consolation," op.280, str, 1975; no.27, op.285, 1976; no.28, op.286, 1976; no.29, op.289, 1976; no.30, op.293, small orch, 1976; no.31, op.294, 1976; no.32 "The Broken Wings," op.296, 1977; no.33, op.307, 1977; no.34, op.310, 1977; no.35, op.311, with Korean orch, 1978; no.36, op.312, fl, orch, 1978; no.37, op.313, 1978; no.38, op.314, S, small orch, 1978; no.39, op.321, gui, orch, 1978; no.40, op.324, 1979; no.41, op.330, 1979; no.42, op.332, 1979; no.43, op.334, ob, tpt, timp, 1979; no.44, op.339, 1980; no.45, op.342, 2 pf, large orch, 1979; no.46 "To the Green Mountains," 1980–1; no.47 "Walla-Walla, Land of Many Waters," 1981; no.48 "Vision of Andromeda," op.355, 1982; no.49 "Christmas Sym.," op.356, str, 1981; no.50, "Mount St. Helens," op.360, 1982; no.51, op.364, tpt, str, 1982; no.52 "Journey to Vega," op.372, 1982; no.53, op.378, 1982; no.54, op.379, 1982; no.55, op.380, 1982; no.57 "Cold Mountain," op.381, T/S, cl, str, 1983; no.58 "Sym. Sacra," op.389, S, Bar, SATB, fl, hn, tpt, timp, chimes, hp, str, 1985; no.59, op.395, str, hp, timp, 4 perc, 1985; no.60 "To the Appalachian Mountains," op.396, str, hp, timp, 4 perc, 1985; no.61, op.397, str, hp, timp, 4 perc, 1986; no.62 "Oh Let Man not Forget these Words Divine," op.402, Bar, tpt, str, 1988; no.64 "Agiochook," op.422, tpt, str; no.65, op.427, str, hp, timp, 4 perc, 1991; no.66, op.428, str, hp, timp, 3 perc, 1992; no.67, op.429, str, hp, timp, 3 perc, 1992

OTHER ORCHESTRAL WORKS

Full orch: Monadnock, op.2, 1935, rev. 1936; Boreas and Mount Wildcat, op.2a, 1931, rev. 1936; Variations and Fugue, op.18, 1964; Suite no.1, op.26, 1937; Hymn to Shasta, op.31, 1938; Conc. no.1 "Arevakal," op.88, 1951; Island Sunrise, op.107, 1965; Conc. no.7, op.116, 1953; Conc. no.8, op.117, 1957; Vision from High Rock, op.123, 1954; Prelude and Quadruple Fugue, op.128, 1936, rev. 1954; 3 Greek Folk Dances, op.150/2; Meditation on Orpheus, op.155, 1957; Mountain of Prophecy, op.195, 1961; Meditation on Zeami, op.207, 1964; Floating World "Ukiyo," op.209, 1964; Ode to the Temple of Sound, op.216, 1966; The Holy City, op.218, 1965; Fra Angelico, op.220, 1967; Shambala, conc., op.228, vn, sitar, orch; And God Created Great Whales, op.229/1, taped whale sounds, orch, 1970; Ov. to Pericles, op.261, 1973; Ode to the Cascade Mountains, op.279, 1974;

Ode to Freedom, op.284, vn, orch; Rubaiyat, op.308, spkr, accdn, orch; 2 gui concs., op.325, op.330, 1979; Copernicus, op.338, 1980; Greek Rhapsody no.2, op.341, 1980; Gui Conc. no.2, op.394, 1985

Chbr orch: Tzaikerk, op.53, 1945; Anahid, op.57, 1945; Vosdan, 1945, rev. 1948; Is There Survival? (King Vahaken), op.59, 1949; Kohar, op.66, 1946; Agori, 1946, version for 2 chbr orch, 1950; Sosi (The Forest of Prophetic Sound), op.75, 1948; Zartik Parkim, op.77, pf, chbr orch, 1949; Janabar, op.81, 1950; Harmonica Conc., op.114, 1952; Accdn Conc., op.174, 1959; Fantasy on Jap. Woodprints, op.211, with xyl, 1965; Ob Conc., op.430, 1992; Vn Conc., op.431, 1993

Str orch: Conc., op.27 (op.17/2), vc, str, 1937; Psalm and Fugue, op.40a, 1941; Alleluia and Fugue, op.40b, 1941; Celestial Fantasy, op.44, 1944; 3 Armenian rhapsodies, opp.45, 51, 189, 1944; Lousadzak, op.48, pf, str, 1944; Khrimian Hairig, op.49, tpt, str, 1944; Elibris, op.50, fl, str, 1944; Prayer of St. Gregory, op.62b, tpt, str, 1946; Haroutiun, op.71, tpt, str, 1948; Artik, op.78, hn, str, 1949; Conc. no.2, op.89a, vn, str, 1951; Talin, op.93, va, str, 1952; Diran, op.94, bar hn/trbn, str, 1949; Partita, op.98, pf, str, 1953; Conc. no.4, op.98b, 1953; Conc. no.5, 1953; Conc. no.6, 1953; In Memory of an Artist, op.163, 1958; Vibration Painting, op.226, 13 str; Hp Conc., op.267, 1973; Dawn at Mount Tahoma, op.272, 1973; Conc., op.344, sax, str; Conc. no.9, op.412, pf, str, 1954; Conc. no.10, op.413, pf, str, 1988

Wind ens: Tapor no.1, op.14, band, 1949; Suite, op.15, band, 1949; 3 Improvisations of Folk Tunes, band, 1951; Hymn to Yerevan, op.83, wind orch, 1969; Khaldis, op.91, pf, 4 tpt, perc, 1951; Tower Music, op.129, large wind ens, 1954; Return and Rebuild the Desolate Places, op.213, tpt, wind orch, 1944, rev. 1965; Requiem and Resurrection, op.244, brass, perc, 1968; Ode to Mount Hood, op.370, band; Star Dawn, op.377, band

ACCOMPANIED CHORAL

Missa brevis, op.4, SATB, org, str, 1935; Easter Anthem, op.18, S, SATB, org, 1937; O Lord our Lord, op.23, B, SATB, org, 1937; Why hast thou forsaken me?, op.24, S, SATB, org, 1937; The Voice of the Lord, op.25, T, SATB, org, 1937; O Lord Rebuke Me Not, op.28, SATB, org; Christmas Song (Watchman, tell us of the night), op.34, B, SATB, org/small orch, 1927, rev. 1962; The Lord's Prayer, op.35, SATB, org, 1958; Protest and Prayer, op.41, T, TTBB, pf, 1941, rev. 1968; I will Rejoice in the Lord, op.42, SATB, org; Jesus, lover of my soul, op.53, 1v, SATB, org; 30th Ode of Solomon, op.76, Bar, SATB, small orch, 1948; I have seen the Lord, op.80, SATB, tpt, org, 1963

I Will Lift up mine Eyes, op.93, SATB, org, 1969; Ave Maria, op.100/1a, SSAA, 2 ob, 2 hn, hp, 1952; The Beatitudes, op.100/2, SATB, small orch, 1955; Easter Cant., op.100/3, S, SATB, small orch, 1953; Make a Joyful Noise, op.105, SATB, brass, org, 1967; Glory to God, op.124, S, A, SATB, brass, perc, 1954; The Stars, op.126, S, SATB, small orch, 1954; Immortality, op.134, S, SATB, org, 1960

O God our Help in Ages Past, op.137, SATB, org, 1963; The God of Glory Thundereth, op.140, T, SATB, org, 1935, rev. 1960; Anabasis, op.141, nar, S, B, SATB, org, 1953; Out of the Depths, op.142/3a, 1v, SATB, org, 1938, rev. 1960; Ad lyram, op.143, solo vv, SSAATTBB, orch, 1955; To the God who is in the fire, op.146, T, TTBB, perc, 1956, rev. 1965; Mag, op.157, solo vv, SATB, orch, 1958; Look toward the Sea, op.158, Bar, SATB, trbn, org, 1957; Alleluia, op.158/11, SATB, org/pf, 1935, rev. 1957

Ps cxlviii, op.160, B, SATB, org, 1958; O for a shout of sacred joy, op.161, SATB, org, 1958; Ps xxviii, op.162, SATB, org, 1958; Glory to Man, op.167, SAB, org, 1958; From the End of the Earth, op.177, SATB, org, 1952; Fuji, op.182, female vv, small orch, 1960; Wind Drum, op.183, unison vv, small orch, 1962; In the beginning was the word, op.206, solo vv, SATB, orch, 1963; Adoration, op.221, (S, A, female vv)/(T, B, male vv), orch; Praise the Lord with Psaltry, op.222, SATB, orch, 1968; The Hermit Bell-Ringer of the Tower, op.256, male vv, fl, chimes, 1972; The Way of Jesus, folk mass, op.278, SATB, unison vv, 3 gui, orch, 1974; A Simple Mass, op.282, solo vv, chorus, org, 1975; Songs, op.315, 1978; On Christmas Eve a Child Cried Out, op.337, chorus, fl, hp, 1979; Revelations of St. Paul, orat, op.343, S, T, Bar, SATB, 1981; God is our Refuge and Strength, op.359, SATB, orch, 1981; The waves unbuild the wasting shores, op.376, T, SATB, org; CanD, op.385, SATB, org; Bless the Lord (cant.), op.401, T, SATB, org, 1986; The Aim was Song, op.410, double chorus (SAB/SATB), 2 fl, pf, 1987; Out of Silence (cant.), op.418, SATB, tpt, str, 1989; Pastime with Good Company, op.432/1, SATB, fl, drum, timp;

The Baby's Dance, op.432/2, SATB, fl, hp; How Lovely are Thy Dwellings, op.433, SATB, gui: see SYMPHONIES [no.58 "Sym. Sacra," op.389]

UNACCOMPANIED CHORAL
For SATB unless otherwise stated

Hear my prayer, O Lord, op.16, 1935; Behold, God is my Help, op.26, 1940, rev. SATB, org/pf, 1967; O Lord God of Hosts, op.27, 1940, rev. SATB, org/pf, opt. brass, 1967; To the blessed there is joy, op.32, S, female vv, 1937; Let us love one another, op.46, T/Bar, SATB, 1941, rev. 1968; Sing Aloud, op.68, 1951; Transfiguration, op.82, T, SATB, 1950; And as they came down from the mountain, op.82/13–6, T, SATB; Make haste, op.86, 1951; 4 Motets, op.87, 1951; The Brightness of our Noon, op.131, 1954; Hear my Prayer, O Lord, op.149, SSATBB, 1935, rev. 1960; 4 Motets, op.246, 1971, rev. 1972; For the waters are come, male vv, op.257, 1973; 3 Madrigals, op.258, 1972; 3 Motets, op.259, 1972; 4 Motets, op.268, 1973; 3 Motets, op.269, 1973; Teach me thy Way, op.320, female vv, 1978

SOLO VOCAL

With orch: Angelic Song (anon.), op.19, S, hn, str, 1948; Avak the Healer, op.64, S, tpt, str, 1945, rev. 1946; As on the Night (Christmas Ode), op.100/1b, S, cel, str, 1952; Canticle (Hovhaness), op.115, S, small orch, 1953; Shepherd of Israel, op.192, 1v, orch, 1951; Adoration, op.221, 1v, orch, 1978 [version of acc. choral work, op.221]; Lalezar, op.353, B, orch, 1981: see SYMPHONIES [no.62 "Oh let Man not forget these words Divine," op.402]

With insts: 2 Motets, op.12, S, fl, 1936; Christmas Song, op.34, 1v, org, 1927; Hercules, op.56/4, S, vn, 1956; O Lady Moon, op.139, 1v, cl, pf, 1955; Out of the Depths, op.142/3, 1v, org, 1938, rev. 1958; Live in the Sun, op.169, 1v, cel, 1954, rev. 1960; Saturn, op.243, 1v, cl, pf, 1971; Glory Sings the Setting Sun, op.292, S, cl, pf, 1977; How I Love thy Law, op.298, S, cl, pf, 1977; Stars Sing Bell Songs, op.350/1, S, gamelan, 1981

With pf unless otherwise stated

3 Odes of Solomon, op.5 (op.30), 1935, rev. 1937; How I Adore Thee, op.7, 1936; 3 Songs, op.19, 1936; Lament, op.20a, 1936; Yar Nazani (Armenian), op.24, 1939; I will Extol Thee, op.28, 1937; Layla (Persian), medium v, pf, op.29, 1935, rev. 1937; 2 Shakespeare Sonnets, op.31, 1942; 2 Songs, op.32; Love Songs of Hafiz, op.33, first version, 1935, rev. 1938, second version, 1957; 4 Songs, op.35, 1938; 2 Songs, op.42, 1938; Pagan Saint (C. Cloos), op.74/1, 1948; Lullaby of the Lake (Cloos), op.74/4, 1948; I Heard Thee Singing (Cloos), op.74/5, 1948; Raven River (Cloos), op.74/8, 1948

Black Pool of Cat (J. Harper), op.84/1, 1949; Innisfallen (Harper), op.84/2, 1949; 3 Songs (Harper), op.95, 1949; O Goddess of the Sea (Hovhaness), op.151, 1957; Dawn at Laona (Hovhaness), op.153, 1957; Persephone (Hovhaness), op.154, 1957; The Moon has a Face (R.L. Stevenson), op.156, 1930; Live in the Sun (Hovhaness), op.169, 1v, cel/pf; Songs with Armenian Words, op.238, 1948; The Flute Player of the Armenian Mountains, op.239, 1946, rev. 1971; 4 Songs, op.242, 1971; Spirit Cat, op.253; 2 Songs, op.254, 1972; 3 Sasa Songs, op.274, 1973; Shiguré, op.365; A Presentiment, op.304, 1977; Celestial Canticle, op.305, 1977; Songs for High S, unacc., op.315, 1978; Shigue (H. Sato), op.365, S, 1982; Love's Philosophy (P.B. Shelley), op.370, 1984; The Spirit's Map (J. Harper), 3 songs, op.391, 1977: Distant Age, the Day, their Ways; A Friendly Mountain (Hovhaness), op.400, B, 1986; 3 Songs, op.425, low v, pf, 1934: Foothills, the Lake, Fog; Why is my verse so barren of new pride? (W. Shakespeare), op.417, Bar, pf, 1988; Dream Flame, op.426, low v, pf

CHAMBER AND SOLO INSTRUMENTAL
For 5 or more instruments

Suite, op.1, str qnt, pf, 1928, rev. 1934; Pf Qnt no.1, op.9, 1927, rev. 1962; Sharagan and Fugue, op.58, brass choir, 1949; 5 Fantasies, op.70, brass choir, 1943, rev. 1967; 6 Dances, op.79, brass qnt, 1967; Pf Qnt no.2, op.103, 1953, rev. 1963; Sextet, vn, perc, op.108, 1967; The World Beneath the Sea no.1, op.133, sax, hp, 3 perc; October Mountain, op.135, 6 perc, 1942; Sextet, op.164, rec, perc, str qt, 1958; Bacchanale, op.203a, 5, perc; Mountains and Rivers without End, op.225, 10 insts, 1968; Khorhoot Nahadagatz, op.251, ud, str qt, 1972; Shah-Nameh, op.252/1, fl, ob, 2 shawms, Oriental insts, 1972;

Suite, op.290, 4 tpt, trbn, 1976; Septet, op.295, 5 wind, db, perc, 1976; Sunset on Mount Tahoma, op.319, hn, 2 tpt, trbn, org, 1978; 2 Sonatas, op.326, 3 tpt, 2 trbn, 1979, op.328, 1979; Pleiades, op.350/2, gamelan, 1981; Lake Winnipesaukee, op.363, fl, ob, vc, 2 perc, pf; Mountain Under the Sea, op.392, a sax, timp, vib, tam-tam, hp, 1984; Sno Qualmie, op.416, cl, timp, chimes, hp, db

For 4 instruments

Str Qt no.1, op.8, 1936; 4 Bagatelles, op.30, str qt, 1964; Divertimento, op.61/5, wind qt/4 cl, 1949; Canzona and Fugue, op.72, hn, 2 tpt, trbn/tuba, 1943, rev. 1967; Upon Enchanted Ground, op.90/1, fl, hp, tam-tam, vc, 1951; Orbit no.1, op.90/2, fl, hp, cel, tam-tam, 1952; Qt no.1, op.97, fl, ob, hpd, vc, 1952; Hanna, op.101, 2 cl, 2 pf, 1952; Qt no.2, op.112, fl, ob, hpd, vc, 1952; The Flowering Peach, op.125, cl, sax, hp, perc, 1954; The World Beneath the Sea no.2, op.133/2, cl, hp, perc, db, 1965; Str Qt no.2, op.147, 1951; Wind Qt, op.159, 1960, rev. 1965; Str Qts nos.3–4, op.208/1–2, 1964; Island of Mysterious Bells, op.244, 4 hp, 1971; Ruins of Ani, op.250, 4 cl, 1972; Cl Qt, op.262, 1973; Adagio and Fugue, str qt, op.265, 1973; Ps to St. Alban, op.281/2, 4 brass, 1974; Str Qt no.5, op.287, 1976; Ps, op.358, brass qt, 1981; Prelude and Fugue, op.373, brass qt; Chomulungma (Sonata for Brass Qt), op.404, 1986

For 3 instruments

Pf Trio, op.3, 1935; Suite, op.99, vn, pf, perc, 1952; Sonata, op.130, 2 ob, org, 1963, rev. 1964; Koke no niwa (Moss Garden), op.181, eng hn, hp, perc, 1954, rev. 1960; Str Trio, op.201, 1962; Spirit of Ink, op.230, 3 fl; St. Nerses the Graceful, op.235, 3 cl, 1970; Firdausi, op.252, cl, hp, perc, 1972; Tumburu, op.264/1, pf trio, 1973; Varuna, op.264/2, pf trio, 1973; Starry Night, op.288, fl, hp, xyl, 1978; Trio, op.331, a sax, t sax, bar sax, 1979; Music, op.384, fl, hp, xyl; Trio, op.403, vn, va, vc, 1986; Trio "Lake Samish," op.415, vn, cl, pf, 1988

For 2 instruments

Oror (Lullaby), op.1, vn, pf, 1927; Prelude and Fugue, op.10, fl, cl, 1936; Prelude and Fugue, op.11, fl, ob, 1936; Sonata, op.11, vn, pf, 1938; Prelude and Fugue, op.13, ob, bn, 1935, rev. 1937, rev. 1967; Nocturne, op.20/2, fl, hp, 1956; Suite, d, op.21, eng hn, bn, 1935, rev. 1937, rev. 1967; Suite, op.23, ob, bn, 1949, rev. 1967; O World, op.32b, trbn, pf, 1948; Varak, op.47, vn, pf, 1944; Arshalouis, op.47b, vn, pf, 1943; Invocations to Vahaken, op.54, pf, perc, 1945; Sonata "Hakhpar," op.54/2, pf, perc; Shatakh, vn, pf, op.63, 1948

Saris, op.67, vn, pf, 1946; Kirghiz Suite, op.73, vn, pf, 1951; Sonata, op.121, (ryūteki, shō)/(fl, org); Duet, op.122, vn, hpd, 1954; 7 Greek Folk Dances, op.150, harmonica, pf, 1956; Sonata, op.171, (hichiriki, shō)/(ob, org); Suite, op.193, vc, pf, 1927, rev. 1961; Yakamochi, op.193/2, vc, pf, 1965; 3 Visions of St. Mesrob, op.198, vn, pf, 1962; Sonata, op.200, tpt, org, 1962; Mysterious Horse Before the Gate, op.205, trbn, perc, 1963; Fantasy on Jap. Wood Prints, op.211, xyl, pf; Nagooran, op.237, db, perc, 1971

The Garden of Adonis, op.245, fl, hp/pf, 1971; Hermes Stella, op.247, pf, tam-tam, 1971; 7 Love Songs of Saris, op.252/3, vn/fl, pf, 1972; Sonata, op.255, vc, pf, 1972; Night of a White Cat, op.263, cl, pf, 1973; Sonata, op.266, 2 bn, 1973; Pastoral and Fugue, op.271, 2 fl, 1973; Fantasy, op.277, db, pf, 1974; Suite, op.291, sax, gui, 1976; Sonata, op.297, 2 cl, 1977; Suite, op.300, fl, gui, 1977; Sonata, op.302, ob, bn, 1977; Sonata, op.322, cl, hpd, 1976; 4 Nocturnes, op.334, s sax, pf, 1979; Campuan Sonata, op.371, va, pf; Sonata "Spirit of Trees," op.374, gui, hp; Sonata, op.375, cl, pf; Sonata, op.387, a rec, hpd, 1984; Dawn on a Mountain Lake, op.393, db, pf, 1977; Srpouhi, op.398, 2 vn, pf, 1977; Sonata, op.406, fl, hp, 1987, Duet, op.409, vn, vc, 1987a

For 1 instrument

Nocturne, op.20, hp, 1938; Lament, op.25, cl, 1935; Chahagir, op.56/1, va, 1945; Yeraz, op.56/2, vn, 1945; Sanahin, op.69, org, 1951, rev. 1968; Gamelan and Jhala, carillon, op.106, 1951; 2 Sonatas, op.110, koto/hp, 1962; Sonata, op.118, fl, 1964; Sonata, op.119, ch'in, 1962; Hp Sonata, op.127, 1954; Dawn Hymn, op.138, org, 1954; Suite, op.166, accdn, 1958; Suite, op.270, hp, 1973; 5 Sonatas for op.306, 1977, op.318, 1978, op.337, 1979, op.357, 1981, op.361; 2 Sonatas, gui: op.316, 1978, op.329, 1979; Sonata, op.317, a fl/b fl, 1978; Sonata, op.352, org, 1981; Sonatina, op.382, org; Org Sonata no.2

"Invisible Sun," op.386; Sonata no.6, op.414, hpd, 1988; Sonata no.7 "Journey to Sanahin," op.420, hpd, 1950; Gui Sonatas no.3, no.4, no.5, op.421; Sonata, op.423, vn; Sonata "Hermit Thrush," op.424, org; Habakkuk, op.434, org

PIANO

3 Preludes and Fugues, op.5 (op.10), 1935; Toccata and Fugue, op.6, 1935, Toccata, rev. 1970; Toccata and Fugue on a Kabardin Tune, op.6/2, 1951; 2 Suites, opp.9, 14, 1936; Sonata ricercare, op.12, 1935; Fantasy, op.15, 1936; Fantasy, op.16, 1953; Lament, op.20b, 1937; Mystic Flute, op.22, 1937; Sonata, op.22, 1937; Ghazal, op.36, 1938; Mazert nman rehani [Thy hair is like basil leaf], op.38, 1944; Artinis, op.39, 1945; 12 Armenian Folk Songs, op.43, 1943; Lousnag Kisher, op.52/1, 1943; Slumber Song, op.52/2, 1938; Siris Dance, op.52/3, 1943; Mountain Idylls, opp.52/4–6, 1953, 1949, 1932; Lullaby, op.52/7, 1951; 2 Pieces, op.55, 1945; Sandra's Dance, op.58, 1941; Dance Ghazal, 1941; Greek Rhapsody no.1, op.63, 1946; Achtamar, op.64/1, 1948; Fantasy on an Ossetin Tune, op.85, 1951; Suite, op.96, 1954, rev. 1967; Orbit no.2, op.102, 1952; Jhala, op.103, 1952; Allegro on a Pakistan Lute Tune, op.104/6, 1951; Pastoral no.1, op.111/1, 1952; Hymn to a Celestial Musician, op.111/2, 1952; 3 Haiku, op.113, 1964; Sonatina, op.120, 1962; 2 Macedonian Mountain Dances, op.144, no.2 rev. 1962; Sonata, op.145, 1956; Do you Remember the Last Silence?, op.152, 1957; Child in the Garden, op.168, 1958; Lake of Van Sonata, op.175, 1946, rev. 1959; Madras Sonata, op.176, 1946, rev. 1960; Yenovk [The Troubadour], op.176/2, 1948, rev. 1951, rev. 1958; Shalimar, op.177, 1949, rev. 1960; Poseidon Sonata, op.191, 1957; Bardo Sonata, op.192, 1959, rev. 1960; 2 Ghazals, op.36a–b, 1963; Bare November Day, pf/hpd/org/clvd, op.210; Dark River and Distant Bell, pf/hpd, op.212; 5 Visionary Landscapes, op.214, 1965; All the World's a Dance of Snobbery, op.233, 1970; Komachi, op.240, 1971; Tsamicos nos.1–2, Tsamico and Fugue, op.241, 1971; Dawn on the Mountain of Initiation, op.248, 1972; 3 Sonatas, op.299, 1977; Sonata "Fred the Cat," op.301, 1977; Sonata "Ananda," op.303, 1977; Sketch Book of Mr Purple Poverty, op.309, 1977; Love Song Vanishing into Sounds of Crickets, op.328, 1979; Sonata "Mount Chocorua," op.335; Sonata "Blue Job Mountain," op.340, 1979; Sonata "Caramount," op.345; Corruption in Office, op.351, 1981; Sonata "Journey to Arcturus," op.354, 1981; Cascade Mountain Dances, op.362; Sonata "Hiroshige's Cat Bathing," op.366; Sonata "On the Long Total Eclipse of the Moon 6 July 1982," op.367; Sonata "Tsugouharu Fujita's Cat," op.368; Sonata "Lake Sammamish," op.369; Lilydale, op.388, 1986; Sonata "Cougar Mountain," op.390, 1985; Sonata, op.399, 1986; Sonata "Mt. Katahdin," op.405, 1987; Consolation, op.419, 1989

For 2 pf: Vijag, op.37, 1946; Mihr, op.60/1, 1945; Ko-Ola-U, op.136, 1962; O Lord, Bless thy Mountains, op.276, 2 pf tuned ¼tone apart, 1974

Principal publishers: Associated, Peer, Peters

BIBLIOGRAPHY

CBY 1965 EwenD VintonD
O. Daniel: "Alan Hovhaness," Bulletin of American Composers Alliance, ii/3 (1952), 3
A. Rosner: Analytical Survey of the Music of Alan Hovhaness (diss., New York U., 1972)
B. Silver: "Henry Cowell and Alan Hovhaness: Responses to the Music of India," Contributions to Asian Studies, xii (1978), 54–79
R. Howard: The Works of Alan Hovhaness, a Catalogue: Opus 1—Opus 360 (New York, 1983)
V. Wolverton: "The Choral Psalm Settings of Alan Hovhaness," The American Organist, xxv/2 (1991), 102–6
V.D. Wolverton: "The Solo Vocal Music of Alan Hovhaness," NATS Journal, xlvii/5 (1991), 4–9, 32–3
V. Wolverton: "From Mountain Climbing to Composing: an Interview with Alan Hovhaness," Choral Journal, xxxiv/3 (1993), 29–36
E. Kunze: Alan Hovhaness: a Discography (Seattle, 1996)
Obituary, New York Times, 23 July 2000
R. Kostelanetz: "Remembering Alan Hovhaness: Making the Right Connections," 21st-century music, vii/9 (Sept 2000), 15–18
D. Bierman: "Interpreting Alan Hovhaness's Fantasy on Japanese Wood Prints," Percussive Notes, xl/6 (Dec 2002), 40–53

ARNOLD ROSNER/R (text), ARNOLD ROSNER/
VANCE WOLVERTON (worklist)

Howard, Emmons (b Brimfield, MA, 1 Oct 1845; d Westfield, MA, 18 March 1931). Organ builder. He received his early training with WILLIAM ALLEN JOHNSON, later worked for JOHN WESLEY STEERE, and in 1883 established his workshop in Westfield, Massachusetts. For some time his operation remained small, building modest-sized mechanical action organs for churches in New England and New York state, one of his larger instruments being a 3-manual organ built in the 1890s for the First Congregational Church of Spencer, Massachusetts. Nonetheless he received a contract for a 4-manual organ to be built in 1901 for the Temple of Music at the Pan-American Exposition in Buffalo, New York, and moved his workshop there to build it. His hopes of obtaining other large commissions were not realized, however, and he returned to Springfield, Massachusetts, where, with the exception of an organ built for the Municipal Auditorium of Lowell, Massachusetts in 1922, he continued to build mostly smaller organs until his retirement in 1929. His son Walter, who had worked for his father as a voicer, was later employed by the Estey firm.

BIBLIOGRAPHY

"Emmons Howard," Westfield Times and News-Letter (6 Oct 1897)
K.F. Simmons: "The Temple of Music Organ," The Tracker, xiv/2 (1970)
B. Owen: The Organ in New England (Raleigh, 1979)

BARBARA OWEN

Howard, George Cunnibell (b Halifax, NS, Canada, 1815; d Cambridge, MA, 19 Jan 1887). Actor and impresario of Canadian birth. An 1842 theatrical engagement in Boston united him with 13-year-old Caroline Emily Fox (1829–1908); they married in 1844. Fox had a family act with her brothers George L., James A., Henry N., and Charles K., which Howard later managed. Howard asked Fox's cousin George L. Aiken (1830–76) to write the first dramatization of Harriet Beecher Stowe's Uncle Tom's Cabin, which debuted at the Troy (NY) Museum on 27 September 1852 and toured until 1857. The cast was a three-generation family affair: Howard as St. Clare; Mrs. Howard as Topsy (in blackface); their 4-year-old daughter Cordelia (1848–1941) as Little Eva; Mrs. E. Fox (Caroline's mother) as Aunt Ophelia; George Fox as Phineas Fletcher; Charles K. Fox as Gumption Cute; and Aiken doubling as George Harris and George Shelby. Howard wrote several songs for the play, including Mrs. Howard's hit "Oh! I'se So Wicked." Although Cordelia Howard retired at age 12 and the extended Fox family eventually dispersed, the Howards devoted their careers to the play. In 1876 they trumped competing productions by incorporating jubilee singers and spirituals and, later, minstrel acts, thus changing the nature of Tom shows for the rest of the century. The Howards had two sons, one of which, Walter S. (1868–1945), was an actor and stage manager.

BIBLIOGRAPHY

Thomas L. Riis: "The Music and Musicians in Nineteenth-Century Productions of Uncle Tom's Cabin," American Music iv/3 (1986), 268–86
S. Railton (director): Uncle Tom's Cabin and American Culture, U. of Virginia, <http://utc.iath.virginia.edu/>

SANDRA JEAN GRAHAM

Howard, George Salladé (*b* Reamstown, PA, 24 Feb 1903; *d* San Antonio, TX, 18 Sept 1995). Conductor. He attended the Conway Military Band School at Ithaca College studying with PATRICK CONWAY and playing clarinet in his professional band. In 1925 he became band director at Ohio Wesleyan University and earned the Bachelor of Arts in Music Education (1929). In 1932 Pennsylvania State Teachers College hired him to direct the summer band, orchestra, and chorus. Other degrees earned by Howard include: New York University (MA, 1936); Chicago Conservatory (BA, 1934; MM, 1935; DM, 1939); and Ithaca College (HD, 1984). In 1942 he accepted a captain's commission in the Army Specialist Corps administering and teaching music, which led to a 1944 appointment as commander and conductor of the US Army Air Forces Band—renamed the US Air Force (USAF) Band in 1947 and eventually becoming the USAF Band and Orchestra—a position he held until 1963, when he retired as a colonel. Other USAF groups he started were Airmen of Note, Singing Sergeants, Strolling Strings, Women in the Air Force Band, and the USAF Bandsman School. He had a 60-year affiliation with the American Bandmasters Association as member (1935), President (1956), Honorary Life Member (1984), and Honorary Life President (1986).

BIBLIOGRAPHY

G.S. Howard: *The Big Serenade: the Exciting Adventures and Travels of the United States Air Force Band.* (Evanston, IL, 1961)

W.H. Rehrig: *The Heritage Encyclopedia of Band Music* (Westerville, OH, 1991, 1996); CD-ROM (Oskaloosa, IA, 2005) (includes selective works list)

G.S. Howard: *A Symphony in the Sky: an Autobiography* (San Antonio, TX, 1992)

N.E. Smith: *Program Notes for Band,* (Chicago, 2002), 301–2

JILL SULLIVAN

Howard, Harlan (*b* Lexington, KY, 8 Sept 1929; *d* Nashville, TN, 3 March 2002). Country-music songwriter. As a child in Detroit Howard listened to the *Grand Ole Opry*; he tried to copy down Ernest Tubb's songs and wrote his own lyrics when he could not remember the original ones. He learned guitar while serving in the US Army and, influenced by Tubb, Fred Rose, Floyd Tillman, and Rex Griffin, soon began composing his own songs. While stationed in Georgia he made a number of trips to Nashville but was unsuccessful in getting his songs recorded. In the late 1950s he moved to Los Angeles where Johnny Bond and Tex Ritter took an interest in his writing and subsequently published his first songs. At this time he met his future wife, Jan Howard (*b* 1932), who recorded a number of his songs, including "Evil on Your Mind" (Decca, 1966). Howard's first significant success was "Pick Me Up on Your Way Down" (1958), which he wrote for Ray Price but which was recorded by Charlie Walker. Price recorded "Heartaches by the Number" for Columbia in 1959, and a cover by Guy Mitchell reached number one on the *Billboard* pop chart later that year. During the 1960s and early 1970s he wrote hit singles for artists such as Buck Owens ("Above and Beyond" and "Excuse Me [I Think I've Got a Heartache]," both 1960), Patsy Cline ("I Fall to Pieces," 1960), Jim Reeves ("The Blizzard," 1961), Johnny Cash

("Busted," 1963), and Buck Owens ("I've Got a Tiger by the Tail," 1965). He wrote "No Charge" for Melba Montgomery (1974), "She Called Me Baby" (Charlie Rich, 1974), and co-wrote "Why Not Me" (The Judds, 1984). Howard recorded several albums of his own songs, but never actively pursued a performing career because he disliked touring. He was elected to the Country Music Hall of Fame in 1997.

DON CUSIC

Howard, James Newton (*b* Los Angeles, CA, 9 June 1951). Composer. Starting piano at age 4, he undertook classical studies at the Music Academy of the West (Santa Barbara, CA) and the University of Southern California (Los Angeles), but left formal education in favor of work as a studio musician (although he later studied orchestration with West Coast jazz arranger Marty Paich). He toured with Elton John in 1975 and 1976, and at that time began arranging and conducting for the rock star. During the late 1970s and early 1980s he continued to perform, arrange, and produce through collaborations with Bob Seger, Rod Stewart, Olivia Newton-John, Randy Newman, Cher, Chaka Khan, and others.

Howard found his niche when he was commissioned to compose for a film (*Head Office*) in 1985. By the 1990s he was scoring dramas (*Grand Canyon*, *The Prince of Tides*), action films (*The Fugitive*), romantic comedies (*My Best Friend's Wedding*), and Westerns (*Wyatt Earp*). By the early 2000s he was considered one of Hollywood's most talented and versatile composers, adding thrillers (especially those of director M. Night Shyamalan, including *The Sixth Sense, Signs,* and *The Village*), animated films (*Dinosaur*), and big-budget fantasy epics (*King Kong*) to his resumé. His understanding of both the traditional orchestra and more contemporary pop idioms kept him in demand. In addition, he has employed non-Western music in his compositions as appropriate (African sounds in *Blood Diamond*, choir and Japanese shakuhachi in *Snow Falling on Cedars*).

He enjoyed a long-running television hit with the theme for *ER*, and partnered with another popular composer, Hans Zimmer, on *Batman Begins* (2005) and the even more successful *The Dark Knight* (2008). In 2009 his first concert commission, a 20-minute orchestral work titled *I Will Plant a Tree*, was debuted by the Pacific Symphony in Costa Mesa, California.

WORKS
(selected list)

Film scores: Pretty Woman, 1990; Flatliners, 1990; The Man in the Moon, 1991; Grand Canyon, 1991; The Prince of Tides, 1991; Glengarry Glen Ross, 1992; Alive, 1993; Dave, 1993; The Fugitive, 1993; Wyatt Earp, 1994; Outbreak, 1995; Waterworld, 1995; Restoration, 1995; Space Jam, 1996; My Best Friend's Wedding, 1997; The Devil's Advocate, 1997; Runaway Bride, 1999; The Sixth Sense, 1999; Snow Falling on Cedars, 1999; Dinosaur, 2000; Unbreakable, 2000; Atlantis: The Lost Empire, 2001; Signs, 2002; Peter Pan, 2003; Hidalgo, 2004; The Village, 2004; Collateral, 2004; The Interpreter, 2005; Batman Begins (with Hans Zimmer), 2005; King Kong, 2005; Lady in the Water, 2006; Blood Diamond, 2006; Michael Clayton, 2007; I Am Legend, 2007; The Dark Knight (with Zimmer), 2008; Defiance, 2008; Duplicity, 2009; The Last Airbender, 2010; Salt, 2010; The Tourist, 2010

Television: Go Toward the Light (TV-movie), 1988; Somebody Has to Shoot the Picture (TV-movie), 1990; Descending Angel (TV-movie), 1990; The Image (TV-movie), 1990; Revealing Evidence: Stalking the Honolulu Strangler, 1990; A Private Matter (TV-movie), 1992; 2000 Malibu Road (theme), 1992; ER (theme), 1994; The Sentinel (theme), 1996; From the Earth to the Moon (one episode), 1998; Gideon's Crossing (theme), 2000

BIBLIOGRAPHY

M. Schelle: *The Score: Interviews with Film Composers* (Los Angeles, 1999) 175–96

J. Burlingame: "He Scores, They Shoot: the Unusual Twist of 'Unbreakable,'" *Los Angeles Times*, 25 Nov 2000, F1, F20

J. Burlingame and S. Knolle: "Billion Dollar Composer: James Newton Howard," *Daily Variety*, 17 July 2006, A1–A6

JON BURLINGAME

Howard, Joe [Joseph] **E.** (*b* New York, NY, 12 Feb 1867; *d* Chicago, IL, 19 May 1961). Composer and singer. He claimed to have run away from home to perform as a boy soprano in vaudeville, especially in concert saloons and "free and easys" along the Bowery in New York. However he also claimed that he had been placed in an orphanage after the deaths of his parents and later ran away to St. Louis. It is likely that he worked as a newsboy, then joined McNish, Johnson, and Slavin's Refined Minstrels, and also performed in a vaudeville act in which he boxed with the former champion Bob Fitzsimmons. What is certain is that by the turn of the century he had settled in Chicago where he began to write songs to supplement his income as a performer. His earliest successes came with the ragtime-influenced songs "Hello, my Baby" (1899) and "Goodbye, my Lady Love" (1904) as he began to interpolate songs in musical comedies in Chicago. In 1904 he joined forces with two young librettists and lyricists, Frank R. Adams and Will M. Hough, to write a succession of popular musical shows; *The Umpire* (1905) and *The Time, the Place and the Girl* (1906) both established records in Chicago for the lengths of their runs. Most of these musicals toured the Midwest with great success, but the few that reached New York were failures there. Although he continued to compose, Howard became more prominent in later years as a performer in vaudeville and nightclubs; he was appearing in an "old-timers" act at the time of his death. For many years his claim to fame was the song "I wonder who's kissing her now," which first appeared in *The Prince of Tonight* (1909). However, after a film based on Howard's life was made with the same title in 1947, a lawsuit was established contending that the true author was Harold Orlob, one of Howard's arrangers. Howard continued to perform later in life, appearing as the host on a radio program called *The Gay Nineties Revue*, which ran from the late 1930s until 1944; the show was moved to television for a season in 1948. Howard's own best songs were either lively commercial rags or warm and simple waltzes.

WORKS
(selective list of songs)
(unless otherwise stated, all lyrics are written by W.M. Hough and F.R. Adams, and all are printed works published in New York)

On the Boulevard (Howard) (1897); Hello, my Baby (Howard). (1899); Honey, will you miss me when I'm gone (Howard) (1902); On a Saturday Night (A.J. Sterling) (1902); Goodbye, my Lady Love (Howard) (1904); I Want a Girl like You, in The Umpire, 1905; I Don't Like your Family, Waning Honeymoon, in The Time, the Place and the Girl, 1906; Oh Gee! Be Sweet to Me, Kid, in The Girl Question, 1907; When you First Kiss the Last Girl you Love, in A Stubborn Cinderella, 1908; Montana (C.C. Cohan) (Helena, MT, 1910); Those Wonderful Eyes (Howard) (1912); You'll Be Sorry when We Say Goodbye (Howard) (1914); Somewhere in France is the Lily (P.C. Johnson) (1918)

Principal publisher: Harris

BIBLIOGRAPHY

J. Burton: *The Blue Book of Tin Pan Alley* (Watkins Glen, NY, 1950, enlarged 2/1962)

GERALD BORDMAN/JONAS WESTOVER

Howard, John Brooks (*b* Plymouth, MA, 3 June 1952). Musicologist and librarian. From 1979 through 1998 he held various positions at Harvard University, including Keeper of the Isham Memorial Library, Richard F. French Music Librarian, and Senior Lecturer in Music. He holds the MA (1976) and PhD (1983) from Bryn Mawr College. During his Harvard years Howard concurrently served as head of the US Working Group of the Répertoire International des Sources Musicales (RISM), overseeing the successful completion the inventory of music manuscripts (*c*1580–1825). In cooperation with the RISM Zentralredaktion in Frankfurt, Germany, he was instrumental in transitioning access to RISM's bibliographic information from printed formats to online databases. He also played a key role in initiating the online publication of the electronic journal *Seventeenth-Century Music* (1995–).

Since 1998 Howard's work has focused on broad issues of computation and data, information and knowledge management. After holding technology administration positions at Harvard College (1998–2001) and Harvard Medical School (2001–04), he was appointed Associate Dean of Libraries and a faculty member in computing and informatics at Arizona State University (2004–09). In 2009 he was appointed librarian at University College, Dublin (Ireland). Howard's research interests extend to digital representation of musical information, musical identity, and musical similarity.

WRITINGS

with J. Schlichte: "Répertoire International des Sources Musicales (RISM)," *Directory of Computer Assisted Research in Musicology*, iv (1988), 11–24

"Bibliographic Databases for Music Research," *Computing in Musicology*, v (1989), 7–32

"*Plaine and Easie Code*: a Code for Music Bibliography," *Beyond MIDI: A Handbook of Computer Codes,* ed. E. Selfridge-Field (Cambridge, MA, 1997), 362–72

"Strategies for Sorting Encoded Music Incipits," *Melodic Similarity: Concepts, Procedures, and Applications, Computing in Musicology,* 11 (Cambridge, MA, 1998), 119–28

"The U.S. RISM Libretto Project: Project Overview and Update," *Info RISM*, ix (1998), 15–29

EDITIONS

Wolfgang Amadé Mozart, Concerto for Horn and Orchestra in E-flat Major, K. 370 b + 371: A Facsimile Reproduction of the Autograph Sources (Cambridge, MA, 1997). Various biographical and bibliographical articles for the forthcoming 7th edition of *Grove's Dictionary of Music and Musicians*

"Thomas Gray's Italian Sojourn of 1740–1741," in *Festschrift for Robert Weaver* (forthcoming, Harmonie Park Press, Sterling Heights, MI)

ELEANOR SELFRIDGE-FIELD

Howard, John Tasker (*b* Brooklyn, NY, 30 Nov 1890; *d* West Orange, NJ, 20 Nov 1964). Writer on music and composer. He studied the piano as a child, and later attended Williams College (1910–13; honorary MA 1937). After further study of the piano and composition he served as managing editor of *The Musician* (1919–22), and then joined the Ampico Corporation as educational director and demonstrator of their mechanized piano. In 1928 he left Ampico and began an intensive involvement with American music that resulted in many articles in periodicals and reference works.

He served as music editor of *McCall's* magazine (1928–9) and *Cue* magazine (1936–8), and for the US George Washington Bicentennial Commission (1931) and the US Constitution Sesquicentennial Commission (1937). He was curator of the Musical Americana collection of the New York Public Library (1940–56), and lecturer in music at Columbia University (1950–54). He also served on the board of directors of the ASCAP, and continued to compose music.

His music has been characterized as romantic and sentimental. Many pieces are based on folksongs, and some on the music of Stephen Foster. He published many works for piano solo, including the *Calendar Suite* (on months of the year), numerous songs for chorus and for solo voice, *Mosses from an Old Manse*, Ballade (after Hawthorne) for String Orchestra, the music for *Wakefield, a Folk-Masque*, written for the George Washington Bicentennial, and several collections of early 19th-century American songs and piano music. He was better known as a writer than as a composer: his important book *Our American Music* (1931) was greeted with enthusiasm as the first comprehensive account of American music, for it included, in addition to a readable history, a discussion of folk music and biographical sketches of many American composers. It was criticized for its overreliance on secondary sources, and much of the older material has become dated, but, with its biographies and bibliography, it retains a place as a useful reference work.

WRITINGS
"The American Composer, the Victim of his Friends," *MQ*, viii (1922), 313–18
"Inevitability as a Criterion of Art," *MQ*, ix (1923), 303–13
A. Walter Kramer (New York, 1926) [comprehensive bio-bibliography]; part of biography repr. as "A. Walter Kramer: the Early Years," *Music Journal*, xxx/3 (1972), 30–31
ed.: *The Music of George Washington's Time* (Washington, DC, 1931/*R*)
Our American Music (New York, 1931, enlarged 4/1965)
Stephen Foster, America's Troubadour (New York, 1934/*R*, 2/1953/*R*)
Ethelbert Nevin (New York, 1935)
with A. Mendel: *Our Contemporary Composers* (New York, 1941/*R*)
This Modern Music (New York, 1942/*R*, enlarged 2/1958 with J. Lyons as *Modern Music*)
The World's Great Operas (New York, 1948/*R*, enlarged 2/1959)
with G.K. Bellows: *A Short History of Music in America* (New York, 1957, 2/1967)

BIBLIOGRAPHY
G.K. Bellows: "John Tasker Howard," *Notes*, xiv (1956–7), 501–14 [biography, bibliography, and list of compositions]

RAMONA H. MATTHEWS

Howard, Willie (*b*, Neustadt, Germany, 13 April 1883; *d* Paramus, NJ, 14 Jan 1949). Actor and comedian of German birth. Howard was an important star in vaudeville and musicals, especially revues, throughout the first half of the 20th century. Howard began his career as a singer while only a boy, performing alongside Anna Held in vaudeville for a brief time, and gaining the attention of Florenz Ziegfeld Jr. Beginning in 1902 he teamed with his brother Eugene (1881–1965), who played the duo's "straight man." The brothers were famous for their openness regarding their Jewish heritage, which they often displayed in their act. Their first appearance on the Broadway stage was in *The Passing Show of 1912*, and the two men became staples of the Shubert-produced revue series. They were engaged as headliners for *George White's Scandals of 1926*, and continued to work with White for many years. In the 1930s Howard began to appear on radio and in short films, and reprise some of the routines he made famous on stage. These include various operatic and dramatic parodies, such as the "Pay the Two Dollars" skit, and his extraordinary impersonations of other entertainers, most famously Al Jolson and Maurice Chevalier.

BIBLIOGRAPHY
A. Slide: *The Vaudevillians: a Dictionary of Vaudeville Performers* (Ann Arbor, MI, 1981)
T.S.D: *No Applause, Just Throw Money: the Book that Made Vaudeville Famous* (New York, 2005)

JONAS WESTOVER

Howard University. University founded in Washington, DC, in 1867, with a music department from 1913; *see* WASHINGTON, DC.

Howe, Elias (*b* Framingham, MA, 1820; *d* Watertown, MA, 6 July 1895). Music publisher and music and instrument dealer. According to several accounts he was a farmhand and fiddler. He compiled a large collection of fiddle tunes popular at local dances and persuaded the Boston publishers Wright & Kidder to publish it as *The Musician's Companion*. As a result of his success in selling this collection from door to door, he opened a music shop in Providence, Rhode Island, in 1842, and set up a similar business in Boston in 1843. His books of arrangements and instrument instruction were popular: *The Complete Preceptor for the Accordeon* (1843) sold over 100,000 copies, and his violin self-mastery volumes sold over 500,000 copies. In 1850 he sold his catalog to the Boston publisher Oliver Ditson and agreed not to publish music for ten years. During that period he lived on his newly acquired estate in South Framingham, managed the South Reading Ice Company, and compiled editions of dance music and dance instruction books.

In 1860 Howe reentered the publishing business in Boston at 33 Court Street, where he also sold drums, fifes, and other instruments needed for Civil War bands. His expanded catalog included numerous arrangements for band, orchestra, solo instruments, and voice. By 1871 he was collecting rare string instruments, and by the late 1880s he was one of the largest dealers in rare violins, violas, cellos, viols, violas d'amore, guitars, and banjos in the United States. After his death his sons William Hills Howe and Edward Frank Howe carried on the business, specializing in the sale and repair of violins, plucked string instruments, and their fittings. When the company was sold in 1931, the music catalog plates were destroyed and the rare instrument collection was dispersed.

BIBLIOGRAPHY

R. Herndon: *Boston of To-Day* (Boston, 1892), 265–6

C.M. Ayars: *Contributions to the Art of Music in America by the Music Industries of Boston, 1640–1936* (New York, 1937/*R*)

CYNTHIA ADAMS HOOVER

Howe, Julia Ward (*b* New York, NY, 27 May 1819; *d* South Portsmouth, RI, 17 Oct 1910). Poet, author, and social activist. In 1843 she married Samuel Gridley Howe and moved with him to Boston, where both became prominent abolitionists and jointly edited an antislavery paper, *The Commonwealth*. She began publishing lyric verse in 1854, but in later life concentrated on writing essays and books, notably *Sex and Education* (1874), *Modern Society* (1881), and a life of *Margaret Fuller* (1883). Her primary focus, however, remained social issues, and throughout her life she supported various liberal causes, including suffrage, the peace movement, public health, and various women's issues. She became and remains most famous, however, for her poem "Battle Hymn of the Republic" ("Mine eyes have seen the glory"), written on 19 November 1861 after a visit to a Union army camp near Washington, DC. The poem was widely circulated after its appearance in the *Atlantic Monthly* (Feb 1862), and was apparently first published by Ditson with the melody of an anonymous revival song, "Glory hallelujah" (or "Say, brothers, will you meet me"), in April of that year. Words and tune soon became inseparably linked, and the song has since become one of the most popular American patriotic hymns.

See also PATRIOTIC MUSIC.

BIBLIOGRAPHY

J.W. Howe: *Reminiscences, 1819–1899* (Boston and New York, 1899)

L.E. Richards and M.H. Elliott: *Julia Ward Howe* (New York, 1915)

M.S. Gerry: "Howe, Julia Ward," *DAB*

B.B. Stutler: *Glory, Glory, Hallelujah!* (Cincinnati, OH, 1960)

J.J. Fuld: "Battle Hymn of the Republic," *The Book of World-famous Music* (New York, 1966, rev. 4/1995)

PAUL C. ECHOLS/LAURIE BLUNSOM

Howe, Mary (*b* Richmond, VA, 4 April 1882; *d* Washington, DC, 14 Sept 1964). Composer and pianist. Her early musical and piano training was under the private tutelage of Herminie Seron. In 1904 she briefly studied the piano with Richard Burmeister in Dresden; subsequently she became a pupil of ERNEST HUTCHESON and Harold Randolph at the Peabody Conservatory and studied composition there with Gustav Strube. At the age of 40, married and the mother of three children, she took the diploma in composition at the Peabody Conservatory (1922). In 1933, having already amassed a considerable output, she studied for a short period with NADIA BOULANGER in Paris.

During her early mature years, Howe gave solo recitals and appeared as accompanist in the Washington area. Her first professional performances were as a duo pianist with Anne Hull (1920–35). With her husband and others she helped found the National SO and served on the board of directors. She was also a founder, with Elizabeth Sprague Coolidge and others, of the Chamber Music Society of Washington (from 1928, the Friends of Music in the Library of Congress); with Amy Beach she helped organize the Society of American Women Composers in 1925.

Howe's music is conservative in style; its harmonic and melodic material stem from what she called "spanning and bridging," a style of composition reaching from the past through to the contemporary. Three of her best-known pieces are cast as tone poems and demonstrate her expansive orchestral and instrumental writing: *Castellana* is based on four Spanish folk tunes remembered from Howe's childhood; *Three Pieces after Emily Dickinson* (1941) is a string quartet inspired by the last lines of three of Dickinson's poems; and *Sand* is described by Howe as evoking the "granular consistency and grittiness and…potential scattering quality" of sand on the shore. Her settings of Johann Wolfgang von Goethe, Rainer Maria Rilke, Elinor Wylie, Amy Lowell, and others demonstrate a combination of artistic and organizational ability in the interpretation of the text and its underlying feeling.

WORKS
(selective list)

Catalog: *Mary Howe: Works*, ed. C. Howe (MS, 1992)

CHORAL
(published unless otherwise stated)

Catalina, 1924; Chain Gang Song, 1925; Cavaliers, 1927, unpubd; Laud for Christmas, 1936; Robin Hood's Heart, 1936, unpubd; Spring Pastoral, 1936; Christmas Song, 1939; Song of Palms, 1939; Song of Ruth, 1939; Williamsburg Sunday, 1940; Prophecy, 1943; A Devotion, 1944; Great Land of Mine, 1953; Poem in Praise, 1955, unpubd; The Pavilion of the Lord, 1957, unpubd; Benedictus es Domine, 1960, unpubd; We praise thee O God, 1962, unpubd

SONGS
(published unless otherwise stated)

Old English Lullaby, 1913; Somewhere in France, 1918; Cossack Cradle Song, 1922; Berceuse, 1925; Chanson Souvenir, 1925; O Mistress Mine, 1925; The Prinkin' Leddie, 1925; Reach, 1925; Red Fields of France, 1925; Ma douleur, 1929; Ripe Apples, 1929; There has fallen a splendid tear, 1930; Der Einsame, 1931; Liebeslied, 1931; Mailied, 1931; Schlaflied, 1931; Abendlied, 1932, unpubd; Avalon, 1932; The Little Rose, 1932; The Rag Picker, 1932; The Lake Isle of Innisfree, 1933; Fair Annet's Song, 1934; Herbsttag, 1934; Little Elegy, 1934; Fragment, 1935; Now goes the light, 1935; Velvet Shoes, 1935; Go down Death, 1936; A Strange Story, 1936; Départ, 1938, unpubd; Soit, 1938; Viennese Waltz, 1938; Irish Lullaby, 1939, unpubd; You, 1939; Am Flusse, 1940; Die Götter, 1940; Heute geh' ich, 1940; Die Jahre, 1940; Ich denke dein, 1940; Trocknet nicht, 1940, unpubd; Zweifel, 1940; The Bird's Nest, 1941; General Store, 1941; Horses of Magic, 1941; Song at Dusk, 1941; Traveling, 1941, unpubd; Were I to Die, 1941, unpubd; L'amant des roses, 1942; Mein Herz, 1942; Men, 1942; Nicht mit Engeln, 1942; Hymne, 1943; In Tauris, 1944; Look on this horizon, 1944, unpubd; To the Unknown Soldier, 1944; Lullaby for a Forester's Child, 1945; Rêve, 1945; O Proserpina, 1946; Spring come not too soon, 1947; The Christmas Story, 1948; The Bailey and the Bell, 1950; Horses, 1951; Einfaches Lied, 1955, unpubd; My Lady Comes, 1957; Three Hokku, 1958

OTHER WORKS

Orch: Poema, 1922; Stars, 1927 (New York, 1963); Sand, 1928 (New York, 1963); Castellana, 2 pf, orch, 1930; Dirge, 1931; Axiom, 1932; American Piece, 1933; Coulennes, 1936; Potomac River, 1940; Paean, 1941; Agreeable Ov., 1948; Rock, 1954 (New York, 1963); The Holy Baby of the Madonna, 1958

Chbr: Fugue, str qt, 1922; Sonata, D, vn, pf, 1922 (New York, 1962); Ballade fantasque, vc, pf, 1927; 3 Restaurant Pieces, vn, pf, 1927; Little Suite, str qt, 1928; Pf Qnt, 1928; Suite mélancolique, vn, vc, pf, 1931; Patria, vc, pf, 1932; Quatuor, str qt, 1939; 3 Pieces after Emily Dickinson, str qt, 1941; Interlude between 2 Pieces, fl, pf, 1942; Wind Qnt, 1957

Pf (pubd unless otherwise stated): Andante douloureux, 1910; Nocturne, 1913 (New York, 1925); Prelude, 1920; Valse dansante, 2 pf, 1922, unpubd; Berceuse, 1924 (New York, 1925); Estudia brillante, 1925, unpubd; 3 Spanish Folk Tunes, 2 pf, 1925 (New York, 1926); Whimsy, 1931; Stars, 1934; Trifle, 1935, unpubd; Cards, ballet, 2 pf, 1936, unpubd; Le jongleur de Notre Dame, ballet, 2 pf, 1959, unpubd

Org: Elegy, 1939, pubd; For a Wedding, 1940, unpubd

Also transcrs. of works by J.S. Bach for 1 and 2 pf

Principal publishers: Oliver Ditson, Edition Musicus, Carl Fischer, Galaxy, H.W. Gray, Mercury Music, OUP, C.F. Peters, E.C. Schirmer, G. Schirmer

BIBLIOGRAPHY

GroveW (D. Indenbaum, C.J. Oja) [incl. further bibliography]

C. Reis: Composers in America: Biographical Sketches (New York, 3/1938 of American Composers, rev. and enlarged 4/1947)

D.N. Allen: The Works of Mary Howe: a Survey of Performance History and Critical Response (diss., George Washington U., 1992)

S.C. McClain: The Solo Vocal Repertoire of Mary Howe with Stylistic and Interpretive Analyses of Selected Works (diss., Teachers College, Columbia U., 1992)

D. Indenbaum: Mary Howe: Composer, Pianist and Music Activist (diss., New York U., 1993)

DOROTHY INDENBAUM, CAROL J. OJA

Howlin' Wolf [Burnett, Chester Arthur] (*b* White Station, MS, 10 June 1910; *d* Hines, IL, 10 Jan 1976). Blues singer, guitarist, and harmonica player. As a mischievous child he was nicknamed "Wolf" by his grandfather after the character in "Little Red Riding Hood." He grew up in the midst of Delta blues culture. While working on a plantation he met CHARLEY PATTON, a legendary blues singer who lived on the nearby Dockery's Farm, an important base for blues performers. Patton inspired Wolf's low, cracking voice as well as his clown-like performing style. He also drew repertoire from songs taught by Patton. In 1933 Wolf's family moved to Arkansas where he learned harmonica from SONNY BOY WILLIAMSON (II) (Rice Miller), who was then married to Wolf's sister. During this time he also played with prominent blues figures such as Robert Johnson, Johnny Shines, Son House, and Willie Brown. In 1948 he formed his first band, the House Rockers, and started his radio show on KWEM in West Memphis, Arkansas, which caught the attention of record producer Sam Phillips of Memphis Recording Service. Phillips leased Wolf's masters to Chess Records and RPM Records. "Moanin' at Midnight," with its spine-chilling moans and the hypnotic repetition of a one-chord guitar and harmonica riff, is representative of this period.

In 1953, after signing an exclusive contract with Chess Records, he moved to Chicago where he made impressive recordings such as "Smokestack Lightning" (1956) and "Killing Floor" (1961). His recordings of compositions by the acclaimed house-songwriter of Chess Willie Dixon, such as "Backdoor Man" (1960), "Spoonful" (1960), "The Red Rooster" (1961), "I Ain't Superstitious" (1961), and "Tail Dragger" (1962), not only constituted the heart of Wolf's repertoire but also became Chicago blues classics. They capture Wolf's soulful vocal performance as well as his partner Hubert Sumlin's excellent guitar work. Wolf had a reputation for giving wild performances. With his huge body—reportedly he was six feet three inches tall and weighed 270 pounds—he howled, shouted, crawled around, and rolled on the stage. Until the mid-1960s, Wolf was known mostly within African American communities, but he became a highly influential artist especially in the British music scene through his performances for the American Folk Blues Festival. In 1965 Wolf performed for more than a million viewers of ABC's music show *Shindig* as a special guest requested by the Rolling Stones, who also performed on the show.

RECORDINGS
(selective list)

The Chess Box: Howlin' Wolf (MCA, Universal, 1991); Definitive Collection (Geffen, 2007); The London Howlin' Wolf Sessions–Deluxe Edition (original Chess, 1971; reissue MCA, Universal 2002); Memphis Days: the Definitive Edition, Vol. 1 and 2 (Bear Family, 1989, 1990)

BIBLIOGRAPHY

J. Segrest and M. Hoffman, Moanin' at Midnight: the Life of Howlin' Wolf (New York, 2004)

MITSUTOSHI INABA

Hoyt, Charles H(ale) (*b* Concord, NH, 26 July 1860; *d* New York, NY, 20 Nov 1900). Librettist, lyricist, and producer. He studied law and worked on a western cattle ranch before becoming a writer for the Boston Post. He then began to write plays, achieving success with *A Bunch of Keys* (1883) and *A Rag Baby* (1884), the latter of which was produced by Tony Pastor. Both works were farce-comedies. Though in Hoyt's hands these rather simplistically conceived shows, with their thin plots and their reliance on existing musical material, were transformed into recognizable musical comedies; he wrote full-length librettos and assigned a single composer to write a basic score (though still allowed for the traditional practice of interpolating of songs). He also preferred to write on American subjects. In collaboration with such composers as Edward Solomon, Percy Gaunt, and Richard Stahl, Hoyt produced a series of popular shows which included *A Parlor Match* (1884), *A Tin Soldier* (1886), *A Brass Monkey* (1888), and *A Trip to Chinatown* (1891). The last was his greatest success, and its run of 657 performances remained unsurpassed for 30 years; the show included Gaunt's popular songs "The Bowery and Reuben and Cynthia," and the well-known interpolation by Charles K. Harris, "After the Ball." Subsequent productions included the satirical *A Temperance Town* (1893), *A Milk White Flag* (1894), *A Black Sheep* (1896), *A Contented Woman* (1897), and *A Day and a Night in New York* (1898). By the late 1890s, however, Hoyt was displaying signs of mental instability, and he died shortly after being committed to an asylum.

BIBLIOGRAPHY

D.C. Dickinson: *The Life and Work of Charles H. Hoyt* (Nashville, TN, 1945)

GERALD BORDMAN

Hsu, Eric (*b* Taipei, Taiwan, 15 Dec 1973). Rock musician and songwriter of Taiwanese birth. Hsu moved to Houston, Texas, with his family in 1989. His brother, Kevin Hsu, was a pop star in Taiwan who signed to Golden Point/BMG. Self-taught in guitar, keyboards, voice, and drums, Hsu formed in 2001 the alternative rock band Johnny Hi-Fi, which has toured extensively in the United States and Asia. As a songwriter Hsu writes songs in both English and Mandarin Chinese. He has collaborated with Taiwanese recording artists and producers and has had success overseas. His song titled "Don't Go," performed by Richie Ren, reached the top 10 pop music chart in Taiwan. Hsu also has toured with Taiwanese rock musician Chang Chen-Yue on his US tour in 2004.

In 2004 Hsu began organizing the Asian Rock Fest in recognition of Asian American Heritage Month in May. An annual festival series, Asian Rock Fest has brought together Asian American artists and showcased rock music talent including Eyes Like Knives, Kite Operations, Carol Bui, Burning Tree Project, Festizio, Vudoo Soul, Jack Tung, and Johnny Hi-Fi. The first Asian Rock Fest took place at The Pianos in New York. The festival continued to feature Asian American musicians after Hsu's relocation to the west coast in 2009. Hsu also worked with former Johnny Hi-Fi bandmate Asif Khan to co-found the non-profit organization Passion and Profession. The organization provides multicultural life and career counseling and motivational workshops for college students contemplating career interests and personal goals. As successful professionals in Internet business and medicine, as well as members of Johnny Hi-Fi, Hsu and Khan highlight aspects of their experiences growing up Asian in America—coping with parental pressure and stereotypes while pursing their passion in rock music performance. Now based in the San Francisco Bay Area, Hsu regularly performs in Johnny Hi-Fi and continues to organize musical events that feature Asian American talent.

WENDY F. HSU

Hsu, John (Tseng-Hsin) (*b* Shantou, China, 21 April 1931). Cellist, viol player, and conductor of Chinese birth. After immigrating to the United States in 1949 he studied the cello and chamber music performance at Carroll College, the Berkshire Music Center, and the New England Conservatory (BMus 1953, MMus 1955, hon. DMus 1971). He began teaching at Cornell University in 1955 and was appointed professor there in 1967. From 1968 to 1983 he gave numerous viola da gamba recitals in Europe and made several radio recordings. With Sonya Monosoff (violin) and Malcolm Bilson (fortepiano) he formed the Amadé Trio (1972–82), a pioneer ensemble in performing and recording the Classical piano trio repertory on period instruments. In 1982 Hsu formed the Haydn Baryton Trio with David Miller (viola) and Fortunato Arico (cello, replaced by Loretta O'Sullivan in 1985), and in 1991 he founded the Apollo Ensemble, a period instrument chamber orchestra with the primary aim of performing and recording the Haydn symphonies composed during the years of his baryton trios. He was appointed a faculty member of Aston Magna in 1972 and served as its artistic director from 1984 to 1990. A player of great refinement and masterly technique, Hsu is considered a leading exponent of the French solo viol literature of Marin Marais, Antoine Forqueray, and their contemporaries, and has made many recordings as a soloist and with his ensembles. He is the editor of the complete instrumental works of Marais (1980–) and the author of *A Handbook of French Baroque Viol Technique* (New York, 1981). Hsu owns a viola da gamba by Francesco Ruggeri, *c*1690, the only known Cremonese seven-string viol. He retired from Cornell in 2005 after 50 years of teaching, performing, and conducting.

HOWARD SCHOTT/R

Hsu-nami, the. Rock band. Formed at Ramapo College in Mahwah, New Jersey, the Hsu-nami is an erhu progressive rock band fronted by Taiwanese American erhu player and composer Jack Hsu. Hsu was classically trained in violin. His erhu training included intensive summer lessons in Nanjing, China. The rest of the group is composed of Tony Aichele (guitar), Brent Bergholm (guitar), Dana Goldberg (keyboard), John Manna (drums), and Derril Sellers (bass). The Hsu-nami integrates an amplified "erhu," a two-string spike fiddle used in Chinese classical and folk music, into an instrumental progressive rock sound. Their music is marked by virtuosic erhu melodies and shredding solos, in place of vocals, intertwined with heavy guitar riffs, funky rhythms, and metal-driven rock drumming. Part of the new-fusion rock movement, the group recasts the sound of its 1960s and 1970s roots.

The band has played alongside international and major recording artists such as Chthonic, Yellowcard, Bowling for Soup, Nightmare of You, and The Parlor Mob. Their music was also featured during the 2008 Summer Olympics in Beijing as entrance music for the Chinese basketball team. In 2011 they toured Taiwan and performed at Spring Scream Festival in southern Taiwan. The band has been showcased at various large-scale North American cultural festivals held in, among other sites, Vancouver, Toronto, and New York; and at *anime* conventions and university campuses in Ohio, Virginia, and along the northeastern coast of the United States.

BIBLIOGRAPHY

W.F. Hsu: "Troubling genre, ethnicity and geopolitics in Taiwanese American independent rock music," *Popular Music* 32/1 (2013), 91–109

WENDY F. HSU

Hua, Wen-yi (*b* Shanghai, China, 21 Feb 1941). *Kunqu* opera singer of Chinese birth. She was a member of the first class of *Kunqu* opera students at the Shanghai Opera School, which she entered in 1954. She graduated as the school's top student in 1961, by which time she was already well known in China, Hong Kong, and Macao. She became a specialist in *guimen dan*, the refined female role-type. As a young actress she had earned the nickname "Little Mei Lan Fang" after the legendary male performer who had been the exemplar of the *dan* role. Today Hua has come to be regarded internationally as the premier model for *Kunqu guimen dan*.

She performed with the Shanghai Youth Beijing and *Kunqu* Troupe from 1961 until 1971. Due to the Chinese government's censuring of traditional Chinese opera because of its links to China's "feudalistic" history, during the Cultural Revolution (1966–76) Hua could only perform revolutionary Beijing-style works. After the Gang of Four were deposed in 1978 she joined the Shanghai Kun Opera Company and eventually became the organization's director in 1985. The next year she received China's highest artistic distinction, the Plum Blossom Award. Four years later, while touring, Hua and members of her company opted to remain in the United States in order to further promote *Kunqu* outside of China. She established the Hua Kun Opera in Arcadia, California, where she still serves as director. She was named a National Heritage Fellow of the United States by the National Endowment for the Arts in 1998. She lives in Los Angeles and continues to perform internationally.

MEGAN E. HILL

Huang, Cham-Ber [Tsing-Barh] (*b* Shanghai, China, 17 Oct 1925). Classical harmonica virtuoso, instrument designer, and manufacturer of Chinese birth. After immigrating to the United States in 1953 he worked for Hohner for many years, designing the first Hohner products made in the United States. These included the Professional 2012 and 2016 CBH (replacing internal metal slides with Delrin plastic resin; trademarked with his initials) and the Chordomonica series (multi-chord instruments with two slides which allow the player to produce melody and accompanying harmony). He founded his own brand in 1983 (Huang Harmonicas, Farmingdale, NY).

Huang plays the instrument "upside-down," with the bass on the right, as his first Hohner instrument had the top and bottom plates installed in reverse; however, he is right-handed, so his personal instruments retain the slide button on the right end. He holds dual degrees in music and engineering from the Shanghai Conservatory and St. John's University, Shanghai (1949). After organizing harmonica bands of up to 125 players in China, Huang gave radio and recital performances in Hong Kong, England, and Germany. He performed on multiple diatonic harmonicas simultaneously before shifting to the modern chromatic harmonica. He debuted at Town Hall in 1953, playing his own arrangements of Bach, Milhaud, and Copland. From 1958–76 he taught harmonica at the Turtle Bay Music School and Kingsborough Community College (NY) and gave master

classes in classical harmonica and chamber music at the Grand Teton Music Festival (1974–9). In 1979 he began touring in China; as a result the harmonica was incorporated into the country's school music programs in the 1980s. Huang premiered Robert Russell Bennett's last major work, the *Concerto for Harmonica and Orchestra* (Hong Kong, cond. Karel Husa, 1981). He recorded his own interpretations of music by Couperin, Telemann, Bach, and Mozart; his instructional books include *Blues and All That Jazz: a Complete Blues Harmonica Method*.

BIBLIOGRAPHY

G. Neilson: "A Little Cham-ber Music: M. Hohner, Inc., the Big Name in Harmonicas, Hits a New Note with 'Delrin' Acetal Resin," *DuPont Magazine* (May–June 1975)

K. Field: *Harmonicas, Harps and Heavy Breathers: the Evolution of the People's Instrument* (New York, 1993; rev. ed. 2000)

IVOR BENYON/LAURA PRICHARD

Hubbard, Frank (Twombly) (*b* New York, NY, 15 May 1920; *d* Newton, MA, 25 Feb 1976). Harpsichord maker. He studied English literature at Harvard (AB 1942, MA 1947), where his growing interest in early music led him and his friend William Dowd to construct a clavichord. Its success encouraged them to abandon academic pursuits and to prepare for careers as builders of early keyboard instruments constructed on historical principles. In 1947 Hubbard went to England to learn the craft and worked briefly at the Dolmetsch workshop before joining HUGH GOUGH at his London premises. He also studied early keyboard instruments in British and continental collections. On his return to the United States in 1949 he and Dowd founded a workshop to build harpsichords on historical principles rather than in the modern fashion then practiced by virtually all professional makers. Their firm produced models based on the surviving instruments made by the leading historical makers of Italy, Flanders, France, and England. Numerous restorations of many such harpsichords from important public and private collections helped them evolve their own designs and refine their methods of construction. The partnership with Dowd continued until 1958, after which each continued to make instruments independently.

Meanwhile Hubbard had been doing the research that led to the publication in 1965 of his authoritative historical study of harpsichord making from the 16th century to the 18th. During 1955–7, partly supported by grants, he had been able to examine many more instruments in Europe and to establish close contacts with museums there. As a result he was asked in 1967 to set up the restoration workshop for the Musée Instrumental at the Paris Conservatoire, where he worked in 1967–8 and taught the restoration of historical instruments and the construction of harpsichords on historical principles.

Hubbard's own production of finished instruments was necessarily limited, but he also developed a harpsichord, based on a Taskin instrument of 1769, which could be produced in kit or semifinished form. By the end of 1975 about 1000 of these kit instruments had been produced. As a dedicated amateur violinist and chamber musician Hubbard also restored a number of early violins to their pre-19th-century state and made bows of a pre-Tourte type for instruments of the viol and violin families.

WRITINGS

"Two Early English Harpsichords," *GSJ*, iii (1950), 12–18

"The *Encyclopédie* and the French Harpsichord," *GSJ*, ix (1956), 37–50

Harpsichord Regulating and Repairing (Boston, 1963/*R*)

Three Centuries of Harpsichord Making (Cambridge, MA, 1965, 2/1967)

"Reconstructing the Harpsichord," *The Historical Harpsichord: a Monograph Series in Honor of Frank Hubbard*, i, ed. H. Schott (Stuyvesant, NY, 1984), 1–16

BIBLIOGRAPHY

H. Haney: "Portrait of a Builder: Frank Hubbard," *The Harpsichord*, v/1 (1972–3), 5–9, 14–17

T. McGeary: "Frank Hubbard," *English Harpsichord Magazine*, i/4 (1975), 98–105

H. Schott: "Tribute to Frank Hubbard," *Early Music*, iv (1976), 252 only

M. Steinberg: "Frank Hubbard 1920–1976," *Boston Sunday Globe* (7 March 1976)

HOWARD SCHOTT

Hubbard, Freddie [Frederick Dewayne] (*b* Indianapolis, IN, 7 April 1938; *d* Sherman Oaks, CA, 29 Dec 2008). Jazz trumpeter. He began playing trumpet in junior high school. At the age of 18 he worked in clubs in Indianapolis with his own group and frequented local jam sessions held by the guitarist Wes Montgomery, who also provided Hubbard with his first professional recording experience. Hubbard moved to New York in 1958 and within two years had already worked with several well-known jazz musicians, including Sonny Rollins, Slide Hampton, J.J. Johnson, Quincy Jones, and John Coltrane. He then completed a three-year apprenticeship with the drummer Art Blakey (1961–4) who recruited Hubbard to play with the Jazz Messengers following Lee Morgan's departure. After Blakey he worked with Max Roach (1965–6) and led his own quintet. From 1960 to 1966 Hubbard recorded several albums for Blue Note Records both as a leader and sideman performing music that has since become recognized as quintessential hard bop. He also displayed an affinity for the avant-garde, playing on landmark recordings such as Ornette Coleman's *Free Jazz* (1960, Atlantic) and Coltrane's *Ascension* (1965, Impulse). His recordings for Atlantic Records (1966–9) initially merged hard-bop with the avant-garde, but later gravitated toward the more commercial soul-jazz style.

By the late 1960s Hubbard was widely regarded as the next trumpet innovator after Dizzy Gillespie, Miles Davis, and Clifford Brown, all of whom were major influences on his own style, particularly Brown. Emulating Hubbard's rich tone, impeccable technique, and fiery soloing style, an entire school of trumpeters emerged. Hubbard also enjoyed success with a string of jazz-rock albums in the early 1970s for the label CTI, including *Red Clay* (1970, CTI), *Straight Life* (1970, CTI), and *First Light* (1971, CTI,), the last of which won a Grammy award. In 1974 Columbia Records won a

bidding war for Hubbard and capitalized on his commercial appeal, recording many over-produced soul-pop and funk albums, replete with lush strings, electronic overdubbing, and rhythm-and-blues background vocals. On these albums Hubbard sometimes sacrificed substance for special effects, as his style relied increasingly on clichés and gimmicks—acrobatic shakes, wide vibrato, and blistering high notes—and less on virtuosic bebop lines. In 1976 he began a gradual return to his hard-bop roots, which led to notable projects including Herbie Hancock's group V.S.O.P. and his own album *Superblue* (1978, Columbia). This trend continued into the 1980s, as Hubbard became a bastion of the 1960s style of hard bop; he took part in several reunion collaborations and in 1985 returned to the revived Blue Note. Hubbard remained active until 1992, when he suffered a lip injury brought on by years of excessive bravura and unrestrained playing. Despite his best efforts Hubbard's attempted comebacks faltered. His collaborations with the New Jazz Composer's Octet were exceptions; these enabled him to showcase his writing while minimizing his shortcomings as a player, allowing him to conclude his career positively.

SELECTED RECORDINGS

As leader: *Open Sesame* (1960, BN); *Hub Tones* (1962, BN); *Breaking Point* (1964, BN); *High Blues Pressure* (1967, Atl.); *Red Clay* (1970, CTI); *Sky Dive* (1972, CTI); *High Energy* (1974, Col.); *Superblue* (1978, Col.); *Skagly* (1979, Col.); *Double Take with Woody Shaw* (1985, BN); *New Colors* (2001, Hip Bop Essence)

As sideman: P. Chambers: *GO* (1959, VJ); O. Coleman: *Free Jazz* (1960, Atl.); O. Nelson: *The Blues and the Abstract Truth* (1961, Imp.); A. Blakey: *Mosaic* (1961, BN); W. Shorter: *Speak No Evil* (1964, BN); H. Hancock: *Maiden Voyage* (1965, BN); V.S.O.P.: *the Quintet* (1977, Col.); *The Griffith Park Collection* (1982, Elek. Mus.)

BIBLIOGRAPHY

I. Gitler: "Focus on Freddie Hubbard," *DB*, xxix/2 (1962), 22

D. Morgenstern: "Toward Completeness: an Interview with Trumpeter Freddie Hubbard," *DB*, xxxiii/24 (1966), 19–21

H. Mandel: "Freddie Hubbard: New Direction, Fresh Perspective," *DB*, xlv/12 (1978), 17–19, 50–51

T. Erdmann: "An Interview with Freddie Hubbard," *ITG Journal*, xxvi/2 (2002), 15–22

H. Mandel: "The Redefinition of Freddie Hubbard," *DB*, lxxv/6 (2008), 34–41

JEFF R. LOVELL

Hubbert, Michael L(ee) (*b* Los Angeles, CA, 10 April 1948). Maker and restorer of woodwind instruments, based in Boonville, California. He grew up playing the clarinet. Primarily self-taught as an instrument maker, he learned by tinkering in his father's home workshop where he made his first musical instrument, a whistle. Upon his return from service in the Vietnam War he worked as an assistant sound editor and music editor in Los Angeles before moving to northern California and working with friends as an instrument maker. He played Irish music with Mickie Zekley for several years in a touring group and opened his own instrument shop in 1980. He served an informal apprenticeship in instrument making with RODERICK CAMERON from 1985 to 1989. He is best known for his Irish and Uilleann pipes based on 19th- and 20th-century models. He also makes reproductions of 17th- through 19th-century French *vielles* or *hurdy gurdies*; Italian *zampogne*; late 18th-century German bassoons; and late 18th-century Viennese clarinets. In addition Hubbert has restored many types of stringed and woodwind instruments, particularly 19th-century orchestral flutes. He has written unpublished papers on his restorations, notably on restoring a basset horn by Franz Doleisch (Prague, 1800), and has lectured on woodwind restoration for the American Musical Instrument Society.

BIBLIOGRAPHY
S. Sparks: "Lives and Times of Valley Folks: Michael Hubbert," *Anderson Valley Advertiser* (20 Jan 2011)

ALBERT R. RICE

Huene, Friedrich (Alexander) von (Hoyningen-) (*b* Breslau, Germany [now Wrocław, Poland], 20 Feb 1929). Maker of recorders and flutes. He was the first American commercial maker of these instruments. He grew up on a farm in Mecklenburg and immigrated to the United States in 1948 at the age of 19. After three years in a US Air Force band he attended Bowdoin College in Brunswick, Maine, and received his BA in music there in 1956. From 1956 to 1960 he worked in the shop of Verne Q. Powell, flute maker, in Boston, and spent his spare time experimenting with the construction of recorders. In 1960 he began to build recorders and Baroque and Renaissance flutes in his own shop, first in Waltham, Massachusetts, and later in Brookline, Massachusetts, where he employed five people during the 1970s. In 1966–7 he held a Guggenheim Fellowship to study instruments built in the 16th, 17th, and 18th centuries, preserved in various museums. Von Huene was one of the first modern makers of recorders to base his instruments on historic designs. He also designed recorders for mass production, including a model based on the work of Jean-Hyacinth-Joseph Rottenburgh (1672–1756), manufactured and distributed by Moeck in Celle, Germany, and a model based on the work of Bressan, manufactured and distributed by Zen-On in Japan. He has also designed and built recorders with modern keywork.

BIBLIOGRAPHY
M. Lewis: "How Recorders are Made: At the Workshop of Friedrich von Huene," *American Recorder*, i/4 (1960), 4–6
C.E. Merger: "Friedrich von Huene: the Man, his Work and his Family," *American Recorder*, xi/1 (1970), 3–7

HOWARD MAYER BROWN/ARDAL POWELL

Huff, Leon (*b* Camden, NJ, 8 April 1942). Songwriter and producer who teamed with Kenneth Gamble starting in the 1960s; *see* GAMBLE AND HUFF.

Huffman, J.C. (*b* Bowling Green, OH, *c*1886; *d* New York, NY, 1935). Director, designer, and producer. Huffman began his directing career at the Alvin Theater in Pittsburgh, Pennsylvania. After he moved to New York, Richard Mansfield engaged him to work at the Volkstheater in Berlin where he met the Shubert brothers. Huffman worked primarily for the Shuberts thereafter, beginning in 1906 with a production of *The Shalumite*. He was involved with many of their musicals, especially

their revues. Huffman served in several capacities, from directing to designing sets and lighting. Two series of revues for which he was especially well known were *The Passing Show* and *The Greenwich Village Follies*. Huffman considered the revue to be the most difficult type of production to stage, stating that the genre required "a shrewdness born of long experience, a psychological setting of pace, and the ability to gauge to precision what the public wants at the time." In the 1920s Huffman directed a string of Shubert-produced operettas, including *The Rose of Stamboul* (1922), *Maytime* (1927), *My Maryland* (1927), *Countess Maritza* (1928), and *The Circus Princess* (1927). As his career expanded so too did his interest in stagecraft; he eventually published a widely used manual on the topic.

BIBLIOGRAPHY
J.C. Huffman: "Revue Proves Hardest Test of Craftsmanship on Stage," *New York American*, 10 June 1928, M-5
M. Seff: "Marching By" Press Release, Shubert Archive, J.C. Huffman Folder, *c*1932
J. Westover: *A Study and Reconstruction of* The Passing Show of 1914: *the American Musical Revue and its Development in the Early Twentieth Century* (diss., City University of New York, 2010)

JONAS WESTOVER

Hughes, Edwin (*b* Washington, DC, 15 Aug 1884; *d* New York, NY, 17 July 1965). Pianist and teacher. He studied with S.M. Fabian in Washington, DC, RAFAEL JOSEFFY in New York, and Theodor Leschetizky in Vienna (1907–10), eventually serving as Leschetizky's assistant (1909–10). After teaching at the Ganapol School of Musical Art in Detroit (1910–12), he made his European debut in Vienna in 1912 and spent the next four years teaching in Munich and performing throughout Germany. He then settled in New York, where he taught at the Volpe Institute of Music (1916–17) and the Institute of Musical Art (1918–23) and was editor-in-chief of piano music for G. Schirmer (1920–25). He made his New York recital debut on 14 March 1917 and thereafter performed extensively in Europe and the United States; he also gave two-piano recitals with his wife, Jewel Bethany Hughes. His memorabilia are held at the University of South Carolina.

R. ALLEN LOTT

Hughes, (James Mercer) Langston (*b* Joplin, MO, 1 Feb 1902; *d* New York, NY, 22 May 1967). Writer, poet, and playwright. Although he is best known as an acclaimed African American poet, novelist, and playwright, music played an important role in his career, as reflected in his writings about African American music and the numerous lyrics and librettos that he wrote for various performing arts venues. He attended Columbia University (1921–2) and Lincoln University, Pennsylvania (BA 1929). In 1937 he created the opera libretto for William Grant Still's *Troubled Island* and between 1940 and 1960 wrote five more opera librettos. After garnering wide acclaim on Broadway in 1947 as the lyricist for Kurt Weill's musical adaptation of Elmer Rice's *Street Scene*, Hughes wrote librettos for other musicals, cantatas, gospel plays, radio plays, and ballets. The idioms of blues, jazz, and gospel figured prominently in his writings. In 1958 he ventured into jazz at the Village Vanguard in New York, giving poetry readings accompanied by Charles Mingus and Phineas Newborn. This resulted in the production of the historic album *Weary Blues*, which features Hughes reciting his blues poetry to music composed and arranged by Mingus and Leonard Feather. The James Weldon Johnson Collection at the Beinecke Rare Book & Manuscript Library, Yale University, houses the Hughes papers, including more than 800 song lyrics, which were set variously by contemporary African American composers, notably Margaret Bonds, Dorothy Rudd Moore, Robert Lee Owens, Florence Bea Price, Hale Smith, and Still, as well as the European American composers Samuel Adler, John Alden Carpenter, William Schuman, and Elie Siegmeister. Hughes's awards included fellowships from the Guggenheim (1935) and Rosenwald foundations (1941), election to the National Institute of Letters (1946), the Spingarn Medal (1960), and honorary DLitt degrees from Lincoln University, Pennsylvania (1943), and Case Western Reserve University (1964).

SELECTED RECORDINGS

As leader: with L. Feather and C. Mingus: *The Weary Blues* (1958)
Recorded by D. Taylor: *Dreams: a Portrait of Langston Hughes* (Naxos, 2002)

BIBLIOGRAPHY

SouthernB
"The Negro Artist and the Racial Mountain," *The Nation* (June 1926); repr. in *Jazz in Print(1866–1922)*, ed. K. Koenig (Hillsdale, NY, 2002), 478–80
L. Hughes: *Famous Negro Music Makers* (New York, 1955)
L. Hughes and M. Meltzer: *Black Magic: a Pictorial History of the Negro in American Entertainment* (Englewood Cliffs, NJ, 1967/*R* as *Black Magic: a Pictorial History of the African-American in the Performing Arts*)
K.P. Neilson: *The World of Langston Hughes Music: a Bibliography of Musical Settings of Langston Hughes' Work with Recordings and Other Listings* (Hollis, NY, 1982)
A. Rampersad: *The Life of Langston Hughes*, ii: *1941–1967, I Dream a World* (New York, 1988)
P.E. Bonner: *Sassy Jazz and Slo' Dragging Blues: Music in the Poetry of Langston Hughes* (New York, 1996)
L.C. Sanders: *The Collected Works of Langston Hughes*, vi: *Gospel Plays, Operas, and Later Dramatic Works* (Columbia, MO, 2004)

JOSEPHINE WRIGHT

Hughes, Rupert (*b* Lancaster, MO, 31 Jan 1872; *d* Los Angeles, CA, 9 Sept 1956). Writer on music and composer. He graduated in 1892 from Adelbert College (now Case Western Reserve University) and received an advanced degree from Yale University in 1899. Best known for his biography of George Washington, Hughes also wrote novels, short stories, and plays, wrote and directed films, and was a radio commentator. His musical activities were equally varied. He composed songs, piano pieces, and a dramatic monologue *Cain*, which was noted at the time for its use of dissonance. He also worked for a short time as a music critic. His musical writings include *Contemporary American Composers* (1900, repr. 1906 as *Famous American Composers*, rev. and enlarged 2/1914 as *American Composers*), *The Musical Guide* (1903, 2/1913 as *Music Lovers' Encyclopedia*;

rev. and ed. D. Taylor and R. Kerr, 1939), and *Love Affairs of the Great Musicians* (1903).

PAULA MORGAN

Hui, Melissa (Ming-Sum) (*b* Hong Kong 21 April 1966). Composer. Raised in Vancouver, BC, Canada, she studied piano at the University of British Columbia (BMus 1987) and composition at the California Institute of the Arts (MFA 1990) and Yale University (MMA 1992, DMA 1996). She also earned an MBA at McGill University (2010). Her composition teachers included JACOB DRUCKMAN, MARTIN BRESNICK, MEL POWELL, MORTON SUBOTNICK, and EARL KIM. Now an associate professor of theory and composition at McGill, she previously taught at Stanford University (1994–2004).

Hui won grand prizes in the CBC Young Composers' Competition and the Winnipeg Symphony Orchestra Canadian Composers Competition in 1996, and was a finalist in that year's International Gaudeamus Music Competition. A founding member of the Common Sense Composers Collective, she has written solo, vocal, choral, orchestral, and chamber music, has served composer residencies at the Marlboro and Yellow Barn Music Festivals, been awarded grants by the Guggenheim and Fromm Foundations, and received commissions from a number of Canadian orchestras as well as new-music organizations across North America and abroad. She composes mainly for Western-style ensembles, sometimes incorporating non-Western instruments (pipa, Chinese gong, African "gankoqui" bells in *Come as you are* [2000]), while creating soundscapes that reference a diversity of world musics—her trumpet concerto, *two sides to the wind* (1990), incorporates musical elements ranging from Charles Mingus to Zairean pygmies and Indian ragas, while *Solstice* (1994), for instrumental ensemble, draws inspiration from Japanese Gagaku music.

Hui's interest in Asian music and other musics from around the world plays a central role in her musical thinking. Although the compositional techniques she uses derive from her Western classical training, she conceives her works according to parameters of non-Western modes of expression and perceptions of time. Referring to "the Chinese delight in succinctness that alludes to an ephemeral wisdom," she opts for "the implicit over the explicit, for non-linear juxtapositions over narratives, and for simple eloquence." Hallmarks of her style include extreme concision, delicacy of sound, transparent scoring, limited pitch materials, use of discreet sound objects (Hui calls them "sonic images"), fragmentation, durational variation, subtle contrapuntal interaction, "color-fields" of flat aural planes, static, non-teleological *tableaux,* and silence elevated to a structural level. In *Common Ground* (1993) and other works she "aimed to create a musical quilt, a patchwork of inviolable musical entities whose diverse natures would be united, and by juxtaposition, strengthened, in a single, integrated whole."

Her compositions have been performed by ensembles as diverse as the Cecilia and St. Lawrence string quartets, American Baroque, American Composers

Orchestra, California EAR Unit, New Millennium Ensemble, Oregon Symphony, La Société de musique contemporaine du Québec, and by orchestras and ensembles in Europe, Asia, and Australia. Among her credits are the soundtrack for the Oscar-nominated documentary film *Sunrise Over Tiananmen Square* (1998) and the opera, *Pimooteewin/The Journey* (2008), based on a Cree myth and with a Cree libretto by Tomson Highway. Her compositions have been recorded on the Centrediscs, CRI, Naxos, Nisapa, Santa Fe New Music, and UMMUS labels.

S. TIMOTHY MALONEY

Hui Ohana. Hawaiian vocal and instrumental trio. Formed in 1969, Hui Ohana (family group) comprised Ledward Kaapana (*b* Kalapana, HI, 25 Aug 1948), Nedward "Nicky Boy" Kaapana (*b* Kalapana, HI, 25 Aug 1948), and Dennis Pavao (*b* Kalapana, HI, 11 July 1951; *d* Maui, HI, 18 Jan 2002). They were one of Hawaii's leading bands in the 1970s, attracting fans of both traditional and popular music. Their popularity extended to other parts of Polynesia, especially Samoa and Tahiti. The trio's soaring falsetto leads by Dennis Pavao, bright harmonies and prominent slack key guitar by Ledward Kaapana, embodied the spirit of the era, a time when artists were seeking to revive Hawaiian music and perpetuate it in a manner conducive to modern musical contexts.

All three grew up in Kalapana village on Hawai'i's remote southeast coast. There was no electricity. While there was some radio, Kalapana was a hotbed of home-made music. Parties lasted for days and families were full of excellent musicians, especially the Kaapana clan with slack key master Fred Punahoa and vocalist Tina Kaapana, mother of Ledward and Nedward. Hui Ohana added discreet elements of country and rock to their music. However, most of their style and repertoire came from performing with older family members as typified by "Sweet Lei Mokihana," "Ku'u Ipo Onaona," and "God Bless My Daddy." They also performed a few newer compositions, such as "Hanalei Moon" and the enormously successful hit "Kona Moon."

Hui Ohana released 14 albums, including compilations, and several with Mama Tina. They disbanded in 1979 with Dennis and Ledward both forging very successful solo careers. They were inducted into the Hawaiian Music Hall of Fame in 2009. Their influence has been widely felt, from early Jawaiian music pioneers Kapena and falsetto singer Darren Benitez to contemporary revivalists such as Pili Oha.

JAY W. JUNKER

Hula. Dance tradition of indigenous Native Hawaiian people that integrates aural and visual presentation of poetic texts called *mele*. Choreographies are creative interpretations of selected aspects of *mele*, with either

Dancers perform an ancient hula at Merrie Monarch Hula Festival, Hilo, Hawaii, 2007. (AP Photo/Tim Wright)

conventional or arranged introductions and conclusions. The movement vocabulary combines hand and arm gestures that illustrate aspects of the poetry and named rhythmic lower-body movement patterns. Accompaniment always includes vocal recitation of the *mele* as well as the use of a variety of instruments (*see* HAWAII).

By the end of the 19th century the hula tradition had developed into two general performance streams, reflecting Hawai'i's layered history of settlement. Indigenous Hawaiians settled the archipelago centuries prior to the arrival of Europeans in 1778, American Protestant missionaries after 1820, and agricultural laborers from Asia, Europe, and Puerto Rico after the 1850s. Innovations in the late 19th century were initially grouped into a category then called hula *ku'i*—hula which combines (*ku'i*) preexisting indigenous features of poetry, vocal recitation, movement, and choreography with elements incorporated from settler introductions, including western practices of melody and harmonization via Christian hymnody, and chordal stringed instruments such as guitar and the Hawai'i-based invention, by Portuguese settlers, of the four-stringed 'ukulele. By the early 20th century this performance stream came to be called "modern hula," distinct from the continuity of the indigenous performance practice then called "ancient hula."

A vigorous cultural revitalization movement in the 1970s brought into use the terms "hula *kahiko*" and "hula '*auana*" as Hawaiian-language counterparts to the respective descriptors "ancient hula" and "modern hula." Hula competitions are popular venues for troupes representing privately-organized hula schools called *halau*, directed by master instructors called *kumu* hula. These events are convened throughout Hawai'i, in communities of resettled Hawaiians across the continental United States, and in locales where hula enjoys great popularity, especially Japan and Mexico.

BIBLIOGRAPHY
A. Stillman: "Hula Competitions: Event, Repertoire, Performance, Tradition," *Journal of American Folklore*, 109 (1996), 357–80
I. Stagner: *Kumu Hula: Roots and Branches* (Honolulu, HI, 2011)

FILMOGRAPHY
R. Mugge, prod.: *Kumu Hula: Keepers of a Culture*, 1989
L. Flanary and E. Siebens, prods.: *American Aloha: Hula Beyond Hawai'i*, 2003 [See also the companion website at <www.pbs.org/pov/americanaloha>
Merrie Monarch Festival [Annual competition event broadcast and webcast live, and released on commercial DVDs]

AMY STILLMAN

Hume, Paul (Chandler) (*b* Chicago, IL, 13 Dec 1915; *d* Baltimore, MD, 26 Nov 2001). Music critic. He studied music and English at the University of Chicago (BA 1937). During his time as music editor of the *Washington Post* (1946–82) he wrote more than 20,000 articles and reviews; his negative assessment of a song recital given by Margaret Truman, daughter of Harry S. Truman, elicited a vitriolic response from the president and made Hume nationally known. He published prolifically outside the *Post*, contributing to such periodicals as *The Critic, The Sign, Americas*, and *Dialogue*, and writing books on music of the Catholic Church, Giuseppe Verdi, and Giacomo Puccini. Hume co-authored biographies of Ignacy Jan Paderewski (*The Lion of Poland*, 1963) and John McCormack (*The King of Song*, 1964) with his wife Ruth Hume. In the Washington area he was also an established radio personality at WGMS. National recognition was afforded to Hume for his promotion and criticism of classical music in the form of a Peabody Award (1977) and numerous honorary doctorates, including one from Georgetown University (1979). Hume also taught at Georgetown University, where he directed the glee club (1950–77), and Yale University (1975–83).

PATRICK J. SMITH/ANDREA F. BOHLMAN

Humes, Helen (*b* Louisville, KY, 23 June 1909; *d* Santa Monica, CA, 13 Sept 1981). Singer. She started to sing as a child at the Baptist church near her house. She also played trumpet in the Sunday school band and piano with a jazz group in Louisville called the Dandies. After hearing the 14-year-old Humes sing at the Palace Theater, the guitarist Sylvester Weaver recommended her to the producer Tommy Rockwell at Okeh Records. Humes recorded for Okeh in 1927 and 1929. After graduating from high school, she worked at a bank and then became a waitress. She began performing professionally soon thereafter, in Buffalo, Albany, and Cincinnati. Humes worked at the Cotton Club in Cincinnati and at the Renaissance Ballroom in New York. In the mid-1930s John Hammond recorded her with Harry James and several of the main personnel from Count Basie's orchestra. Humes subsequently joined Basie's band in 1938 to replace Billie Holiday and stayed until 1941. After working in New York she went to California and participated in Jazz at the Philharmonic for five seasons in the late 1940s. In addition she recorded such hit tunes as "Be-ba-ba-le-ba" (1945, Philo) and "Million Dollar Street" (1950, Modern). Humes toured Australia with Red Norvo in 1956 and went back there as a soloist twice in the early 1960s. In 1962 she toured Europe with a blues festival. After taking care of her parents at home in the late 1960s, she began performing again in 1973 and was active in New York and Europe through the late 1970s.

BIBLIOGRAPHY
W. Balliet: *American Singers* (New York, 1979), 42–9
S. Dance: *The World of Count Basie* (New York, 1980/R), 129–36
L. Dahl: *Stormy Weather: the Music and Lives of a Century of Jazzwomen* (New York, 1984/R), 225–33
B. Josephson and T. Trilling-Josephson: *Café Society: the Wrong Place for the Right People* (Urbana, 2009), 287–92

YOKO SUZUKI

Humphrey, Bobbi [Barbara Ann] (*b* Marlin, TX, 25 April 1950). Jazz and rhythm-and-blues flutist, singer, bandleader, composer, and producer. She started to play flute in the Lincoln High School band in Dallas. Studying both classical and jazz flute, she continued her musical training at Texas Southern University and Southern Methodist University. In 1971 she moved to New York, where a relative, Eddie Preston, played trumpet with Duke Ellington. Because of this connection, she had the opportunity to play with Ellington's band. She also competed in the Apollo Theater's amateur night, winning first place for seven consecutive weeks. Blue Note Records signed Humphrey in 1971 and had recorded six of her albums by 1976, including *Blacks and Blues* (1973, BN). She performed at the Montreux Jazz Festival in 1973 and 1977. She also appeared on "Another Star" from Stevie Wonder's album *Songs in the Key of Life* (1975-1976, Tamia). After switching to Epic she recorded three more albums for that label: *Tailor Made* (1977, Epic), *Free Style* (1978, Epic), and *The Good Life* (1979, Epic). In 1994 she founded her own label, Paradise Records, for which she recorded an album which was reissued in 2008.

BIBLIOGRAPHY

R. Townley: "Bobbi Humphrey," *DB*, xli/11 (1974), 32–3

D.A. Handy: *Black Women in American Bands and Orchestras* (Metuchen, 1981, 2/1998)

YOKO SUZUKI

Humphrey, Doris (*b* Oak Park, IL, 17 Oct 1895; *d* New York, NY, 29 Dec 1958). Dancer, choreographer, teacher, and pioneer in modern dance. Descendants of Pilgrim stock in New England, her well-educated parents moved to the Midwest for better income, first to Chicago and then the suburb of Oak Park. Trained first by the highly regarded dance educator of the time, Mary Wood Hinman, and various itinerant ballet instructors, Humphrey showed early talent and, finishing high school, launched into a cross-country performing tour; there being little other work in dance for a proper young woman, she taught dance classes at home for children and adults, and for actors at a summer theater camp in New England, where she first encountered the music of Edward MacDowell. World War I preserved this status quo until she was finally able to break away in 1920 to join the Denishawn school and company in California, where she was not only a principal dancer but also choreographed many solos and small group works.

By 1928, disaffected with the Denishawn aesthetic, she and several other dancers broke away to explore new ways of moving. After she gave a solo concert in the spring, the company she formed with fellow Denishawn rebel Charles Weidman premiered in October 1928. The Humphrey-Weidman Company remained a primal force in the modern dance movement for close to 20 years, appearing in its New York studio-theater and at colleges, summer dance festivals, and urban theaters across the country.

Humphrey was the movement's innovator, creating a technique based on observations of how the body moves. Three natural rhythms—motor, pulse, and breath—underlay all movement, which had to contend with gravity. Inhaling, rising above gravity's pull to reach perfection and stability she called Apollonian; exhaling, giving in to the ecstasy of abandon, was Dionysian. Between "fall" and "recovery" was what she termed "the arc between two deaths." From the natural rhythms, she built devices to counterpoint dance versus musical

phrasing and she regularly incorporated polyrhythms. Her intellectual approach to craft was tempered by an emotional commitment to humane values: dance had to be an expressive language, classically structured with conflict, development, and resolution, for comment on the human condition. At the same time her spatial patterns had a formal, architectural rigor.

Visualizing a piece of music was not the trigger for her choreography; some early works like *Water Study* (1928) were done in silence. Over her career Bach drew her in *Air for the G String* (1928), the great *Passacaglia in C* (1938), and *Brandenburg Concerto No. 4* (1959), and she looked to the music of Rameau and Purcell, Grieg and Brahms, Ravel and Scriabin. But it was contemporary composers for whom she had the greatest affinity: MacDowell, Wallingford Riegger, Dane Rudhyar, Charles Griffes, Aaron Copland, all the way to the electronics of Otto Luening for her *Theatre Piece No. 2* (1956). Besides those mentioned, her most noted works for the company were *The Shakers* (1931) to traditional hymns arranged by Pauline Lawrence, *New Dance* (1935) and *With My Red Fires* (1936), both with scores by Riegger, and *El Salón México* (1943, Copland), which introduced the dancer José Limón to the company.

Upon the dissolution of the Humphrey-Weidman Company in 1946, Humphrey became choreographer and mentor to the troupe formed by Limón, making use of his striking stage presence and Mexican background to create the starkly dramatic *Lament for Ignacio Sánchez Mejías* (1946), set to the poem by García Lorca and music by Norman Lloyd, and *Ritmo Jondo* (1953) to Carlos Surinach. Also to Copland was the touching *Day on Earth* (1947), a comment on all humanity encapsulated in the life span of a single family.

In the 1940s Humphrey also choreographed with Weidman several successful shows on Broadway, and was instrumental in the formation of the Dance Centre at New York's 92nd Street YMHA. When the Dance Department opened in the early 1950s at the Juilliard School, she was immediately on the faculty and also formed its performance wing, the Juilliard Dance Theater, which relied on music by the conservatory faculty. There she remained until her death.

BIBLIOGRAPHY

D. Humphrey: *The Art of Making Dances* (New York, 1959)

S.J. Cohen, ed.: *Doris Humphrey: an Artist First* (Middletown, CT, 1972)

E. Stodelle: *The Dance Technique of Doris Humphrey and its Creative Potential* (Princeton, NJ, 1978)

M.B. Siegel: *Days on Earth: The Dance of Doris Humphrey* (New Haven, CT, 1987)

D. Humphrey: *New Dance: Writings on Modern Dance*, selected and ed. Charles Humphrey Woodford (Hightstown, NJ, 2008)

BARBARA PALFY

Humphreys, Jere T(homas) (*b* Humboldt, TN, 26 March 1949). Music educator and scholar. Humphreys earned degrees in music education from the University of Mississippi (BM 1971) and University of Michigan (PhD 1984), and in clarinet performance from Florida State University (MM 1976). He taught music in Mississippi public schools (1971–5), and at Huntingdon College

(1977–9), West Virginia University (1981–7), and Arizona State University (1987–). He is a Senior Fulbright Scholar (2002) and the recipient of several awards, including the Citation of Excellence in Research (1985) and the Senior Researcher Award (2006) from the Music Educators National Conference (MENC). He has been an Academic Specialist for the US Department of State (1996) and an investigator in projects funded by the European Union and the National Endowment for the Arts. He has been a featured speaker, visiting professor, endowed chair resident, or consultant in twenty-nine countries, and has advised graduate students at home and abroad on numerous dissertations and theses, several of which won university or national awards. Humphreys has been an editorial committee member for 13 scholarly journals, editor of the *Journal of Historical Research in Music Education* (1999–2003), a section editor for the *Oxford Handbook of Music Education,* and the contributing editor for music education for the *Grove Dictionary of American Music,* second edition. He has served on the boards of many professional and community organizations, including several within the MENC. A prolific and versatile researcher, historical and quantitative, Humphreys has authored over 150 publications, with reprints in six languages.

WILLIAM R. LEE

Hundley, Richard (Albert) (*b* Cincinnati, OH, 1 Sept 1931). Composer and pianist. He studied piano at the Cincinnati Conservatory and the Manhattan School, and composition privately with ISRAEL CITKOWITZ, Harold Knapik, and WILLIAM FLANAGAN. Other particularly formative experiences include singing in the Metropolitan Opera chorus (1960–4), serving as studio accompanist for soprano Zinka Milanov (1967–81), and years of friendship with Virgil Thompson. Hundley has held residencies at the MacDowell Colony and a number of American universities, and has received commissions from the Clarion Music Society, the Robert Page Singers, and the Marilyn Horne Foundation, among others.

Hundley's compositional output consists almost entirely of art song. He has penned more than 75 songs for solo voice with piano, of which almost half are published. Hundley's lyrical and expressive vocal writing set him apart from many of his peers. It was met with criticism early in his career, but his work has typically been well received by performers and audiences. Hundley has drawn texts mainly from 20th-century American poets, and he has since 1971 enjoyed a fruitful collaboration with writer James Purdy.

WORKS
(selective)

SOLO VOICE WITH PIANO
Epitaph on a Wife (anon.), 1957; Softly the Summer (R. Hundley), 1957; The Astronomers (anon.), 1959; Isaac Greentree (anon.), 1960; Epitaph of a Young Girl (anon.), 1961; Wild Plum (O. Jones), 1961; Ballad on Queen Anne's Death (anon.), 1962; Spring (W. Shakespeare), 1962; For Your Delight (R.L. Stevenson), 1962; Maiden Snow (K. Patchen), 1963; My Master Hath a Garden (anon.), 1963; A Package of Cookies (V. Thomson), 1963; Some Sheep Are Loving (G. Stein), 1964; Postcard From Spain (Hundley), 1964; When Children Are Playing Along on the Green (R.L. Stevenson),

1965; Six John Fletcher Songs, 1966; Screw Spring (W.M. Hoffman), 1968; Lions (J. Purdy), 1971; Come Ready and See Me (Purdy), 1971; I'm Going Broke at the Ritz (A. Berger), 1974; I Do (Purdy), 1974; Evening Hours (Purdy), 1975; Bartholomew Green (Purdy), 1978; When Orpheus Played (Shakespeare), 1979; Sweet Suffolk Owl (anon.), 1979; Arise, My Love (King Solomon), 1981; Will There Really Be a Morning? (E. Dickinson), 1987; Waterbird (Purdy), 1988; Maud Muller (J.G. Whittier), cant., 1988; Octaves and Sweets Sounds (multiple), five songs, 1989; Awake the Sleeping Sun (R. Crashaw), 1991; O My Darling Troubles Heaven With Her Loveliness (Patchen), 1998

OTHER VOCAL
Just Why Johnny Was Jimmie (G. Stein) T, B, pf, 1964; Jenny Wren (J. Purdy) S, S, pf, 1971; Vocal Quartets to Poems by James Purdy (Purdy) S, A, T, B, pf, 1971; Ballad On Queen Anne's Death (anon.) v, fl, cl, vcl, pf, 1978; The Sea Is Swimming Tonight (Purdy), cant., S, A, T, B, choir, pf 4h, 1982; Ball (Purdy), S, A, T, B, choir, pf 4h, 1985; Come Ready and See Me (Purdy), choir, pf, 2002; Moonlight's Watermelon (J.G. Villa), choir, pf, 2003

BIBLIOGRAPHY
E.J. Hardenbergh: *The Solo Vocal Repertoire of Richard Hundley: a Pedagogical and Performance Guide to the Published Works* (diss., Columbia U., 1997)
L. Cellucci: *An Examination of Selected Songs of Richard Hundley* (diss., U. of Cincinnati, 2000)
R. Hanshe: "Ready All the Time Like Gunpowder: an Interview with Richard Hundley," *Hyperion,* vi, 1 (2011), 159–85

DAVID ATKINSON WELLS

Huneker, James Gibbons (*b* Philadelphia, PA, 31 Jan 1857; *d* Brooklyn, NY, 9 Feb 1921). Critic and essayist. He studied piano in Paris with Georges Mathias, and in New York with Edmund Neupert and RAFAEL JOSEFFY. From 1888 to 1898 Huneker taught piano at the National Conservatory in New York, while also writing for the *Recorder* (1891–95), the *Morning Advertiser* (1895–97), the *Morning Telegraph* (1898), the *Musical Courier* (1887–1902), and *Etude* (1895). He became a music critic for the weekly magazine *Town Topics* (1897–1902) as well as the *New York Sun* (1900–02) where he also served as drama critic (1902–04) and art critic (1906–12). He later worked as foreign correspondent for the *New York Times* (1912–14) and contributed the "Seven Arts" column of *Puck* magazine (1914–16). In 1916 he returned to the *New York Sun* for a single year as a general critic. He subsequently worked as music critic for the *Philadelphia Press* (1917–19), the *New York Times* (1918–19), and the *New York World* (from 1919). Although he struggled in the early stages of his career he eventually became the highest-paid music critic in the United States.

His breadth of knowledge, spanning nearly all of the arts (apart from cinema), and his authority on piano literature set him apart from other music critics of his era. He championed Chopin and Liszt with articles and one monograph on each of them; however, this admiration was not at the exclusion of other composers. Huneker expressed great interest in many other composers, particularly French, German, and American ones, including those of the 20th-century. He also supported composers such as Edward MacDowell, Charles Martin Loeffler, George Whitefield Chadwick, and Horatio Parker. While his music critic colleagues primarily focused their attention on German music, Huneker was a true cosmopolitan who engaged equally with repertoires of many countries, both vocal and instrumental; the only exception may be Italian opera, since he never showed a marked interest in the music of Italy.

His writing on topics outside of music also showed him to be very perceptive of new trends; he was among the first to recognize the importance of figures such as Ibsen, Nietzsche, Cézanne, Matisse, and Manet. Huneker's approximately 20 trips to Europe (primarily Paris) helped him stay abreast of cultural developments. He wrote books on music, art, and drama, as well as an autobiography. His autobiography and letters are very valuable sources on music in America between 1870 and 1920.

WRITINGS

Chopin, The Man and His Music (New York, 1900/R1966)
Melomaniacs (New York, 1902)
Overtones (New York, 1904/R1970)
Franz Liszt (New York, 1911/R1971)
Old Fogy (Philadelphia, 1913/R1979)
The Development of Piano Music (New York, 1915–6)
The Philharmonic Society of New York (New York, ?1917/R1979)
Unicorns (New York, 1917/R1976)
Bedouins (New York, 1920/R1975)
Variations (New York, 1921)
ed., *Letter of James Gibbons Huneker* (New York, 1922)
ed., *Intimate Letters of James Gibbons Huneker* (New York, 1924)
MSS in *NbD*

BIBLIOGRAPHY

B. De Casseres: *James Gibbons Huneker* (New York, 1925)
W.J. Henderson: "Huneker, James Gibbons," *DAB*
A.T. Schwab: *James Gibbons Huneker: Critic of the Seven Arts* (Palo Alto, CA, 1963) [incl. complete list of Huneker's books, full biography, and a note on sources]
ed.: *Americans in the Arts, 1890–1920: Critiques by James Gibbons Huneker* (New York, 1985)

ARNOLD T. SCHWAB/DAVIDE CERIANI

Hungarian American music. *See* EUROPEAN AMERICAN MUSIC.

Hungarian String Quartet. String quartet, founded in Budapest in 1935. It disbanded in 1970 after a long career in the United States; at the time of its dissolution its members were Zoltán Székely (*b* Kocsola, Hungary, 8 Dec 1903), Michael Kuttner (*b* Budapest, Hungary, 9 Dec 1918), Dénes Koromzay (*b* Budapest, 18 May 1913), and Gabriel Magyar (*b* Budapest, 5 May 1914). There had been several previous changes of personnel, the original members being Sándor Végh, Péter Szervánszky, Koromzay, and Vilmos Palotai. Kuttner trained at the Liszt Academy in Budapest. From 1938 to 1948 he was a member of several string quartets in the United States and also conducted the New York City Opera and other organizations. He became an American citizen and, later, violin professor at the Indiana University. Koromzay was a pupil of Jenő Hubay in Budapest and of Carl Flesch in Berlin. From 1942 to 1944 he was leader of the violas in the Amsterdam Concertgebouw. He later took American citizenship, as did Magyar, who was a pupil of Zoltán Kodály and Léo Weiner in Budapest, and who moved to Venezuela in 1941 and to the United States in 1949. The quartet was resident in the Netherlands before moving to the United States in 1950. It had made a notable reputation in Europe and became one

of the leading quartets soon after its Budapest debut in 1935. In the United States it was equally successful and won a place among the few quartets of international status then resident here. Its repertory was based on the standard quartet literature, its Beethoven interpretations being particularly highly regarded. It also played many works by contemporary Hungarian composers; the most important were Bartók's six quartets, in which its performances had the seal of authenticity because of Székely's close artistic association with the composer, and set a standard by which later interpretations could be judged. The quartet's first performances included works dedicated to it by Bernard Van Dieren, Willem Pijper, and Mario Castelnuovo-Tedesco.

RONALD KINLOCK ANDERSON

Hunkpapa. Native American group belonging to the Teton division of the SIOUX.

Hunsberger, Donald (*b* Souderton, PA, 2 Aug 1932). Conductor, educator, orchestrator, and author. He attended the Eastman School of Music (BM 1954, MM 1959, DMA 1963) and was trombone soloist and chief arranger with the United States Marine Band, Washington, DC (1954–8). He taught at SUNY, Potsdam (1959–62), and returned to Eastman in 1962 where he was appointed conductor of the Eastman Wind Ensemble (EWE) in 1965. He made a US State Department six-week tour of Japan and capital cities of Southeast Asia (1978) and biennial concert tours of Japan (Sony Corporation, 1990–2000) with the Ensemble. A leading advocate of expanded orchestration and coloristic scoring developments for the wind band, he founded the *MCA Symphonic Wind Ensemble Editions* (1968–71), the National Center for the Symphonic Wind Ensemble (1973–) and the *Donald Hunsberger Wind Library* (1997–). A champion of contemporary composers with more than 100 première performances with the EWE, he made first recordings of works by Schwantner, Copland, Mayazumi, Penderecki, Hanson, Persichetti, Dahl, and Vaughan Williams and others with the EWE, the Tokyo Kosei Wind Orchestra, and the Eastman Dryden Orchestra. As researcher and conductor, he has conducted several hundred performances with more than 40 symphony orchestras of his orchestrations of accompaniments for 18 films and numerous Chaplin shorts of the silent era (1914–29). He is active in WASBE (board member and international conducting and repertoire development mentor), CBDNA (president, 1983–5), and as a teacher and mentor in Scandinavia, England, Israel, Japan, the United States, and Canada. He recorded for DGG, Sony Classics, CBS Masterworks, Phillips, Mercury, Arabesque, Toshiba-EMI, Vox, Kosei, Centaur, and Tioch.

Principal publishers: Warner Bros. Music Publishing, MCA Music, Carl Fischer, G. Schirmer, Boosey & Hawkes, Boston Music, Accura Music

WRITINGS

Clef Studies for Trombone (Blazhevich) (New York, 1965)
Emory Remington Warm-up Studies (Athens, OH, 1980)
with R.E. Ernst: *The Art of Conducting* (New York, 1983, 2/1992)
with F.J. Cipolla: *The Wind Ensemble and Its Repertoire* (Rochester, NY, 1994)

BIBLIOGRAPHY
W.H. Rehrig: *The Heritage Encyclopedia of Band Music* (Westerville, OH, 1991, suppl. 1996); CD-ROM (Oskaloosa, IA, 2005) [includes selective works list]

DAVID WHITWELL

Hunt, Jerry (Edward) (*b* Waco, TX, 30 Nov 1943; *d* Canton, TX, 27 Nov 1993). Composer and performer. He studied the piano and composition at the University of North Texas (1960–61) and worked as a pianist up to 1969, performing in concerts of contemporary American and European music. Many of these concerts featured premieres of works that are now considered standard repertory. His own composition was sponsored by such groups as the National Center for Experiments in Television, the Rockefeller Foundation, the National Endowment for the Arts, and the Foundation for Contemporary Performance Art. A commission from the Scottish Arts Council and the British Computing Society resulted in *Haramand Plane: Parallel/Regenerative* (1973), in which aural and visual images relate and interact.

After 1978 Hunt's main work was a series of interrelated electronic, mechanical, and social theatrical events. Telephone transmission of electronic signals provided the impetus behind his series *Quaquaversal Transmission* (1973–83), a collaborative work with the Merce Cunningham Dance Company and a separate bilateral interactive satellite electronic performance (Washington, DC–Austin, TX). *(Field): CYRA* (1983–4) also emphasized the interactive nature of an electronic system, but its performance in 1985 involved larger forces: the Brooklyn Philharmonic SO, conducted by Lukas Foss.

His last works included collaborations with the performance artist Karen Finley (New York), the visual and conceptual artist Maria Blondeel (Belgium), the performer and composer James Fulkerson (Netherlands), the visual and sound artist Paul Panhuysen (Netherlands), and the composer and software designer Joel Ryan (Netherlands). Always searching for new technologies to use or manipulate, Hunt was working on an interactive optical disc performance series at the time of his death.

WORKS
(selective list)

Helix 1–8, variable inst(s), 1961–71; Sur John Dee, 0–11 pfmrs, 1963; Haramand Plane, elec series [audio/video generation], 1972–86; Quaquaversal Transmission, interactive performance descriptor, 1973–83; Cantegral Segment(s), variable insts [groups, solos, elec, mechanical], nos.1–3, 1973, nos.4–17, 1976, nos.18–26, 1977–8, no.27, 1993; Procession, audio/video, 1974; Kelley: (Drape), gesture, 1975; Pounding, perc/gesture, 1977/80; Volta (kernel), 1v/gesture/ live elec, 1977; Transform (stream), 1v/perc, 1977; Lattice, kbd/perc, 1978; Phalba (stream), variable configuration, 1979; Volta (converge 1 & 2), 1v, 1980; Phalba: Ground (extractive: converge 1 & 2), perc, 1980; CANA (overlay): Converge, 1v, 1981; Ground: Field (still-core set), performance descriptor, 1981; Ground: Field (transform de chelly), pfmrs [multiples of 5], 1981–2 [with ROTA, 1984]; CANA (overlay): burst-core, gesture/artefacts/perc, 1983; Birome (ZONE): Cube, installation [mannequin, audio/video], 1983; Tango, pf, 1983; (Field): CYRA, orch, 1983–4; Volta (Birome), 1v, gesture, perc, audio/ video, 1984; Bitom (stream), transactional exercise, 1984; DIOM, transactional exercise with perc, 1985; Phalba (converge), variable insts, 1985; GROUND, performance system, 1985; Tango, ens/accdn,

1985; Transform (stream): pounding (reflex), elec, 1985; Pastos (fixture), system alteration, 1985; deAbano (translation), system alteration, 1985; Fluud, system of translation derivatives, 1985; Birome (zone): Plane, performance translation/variable insts, 1985–6; Mask (Window) [ ]: SOYGA (DIOM), transactional exercise, 1986; Trapani (stream) a & b, (a): pf, (b): perc/1v, 1990; Ground (Birome): Plane, retrieval system, 1990; Chimanzzi (Olun): core, pfmrs (in pairs), 1991; Lattice (stream): ordinal, variable insts, 1991; Bitom (rota): fixture, gesture/objects, 1991; Bitom (stream): link, variable inst(s) (in pairs), 1991; Bitom (fixture); topogram, stationary performer as inst [elec alteration], 1992; Transform (stream): monopole, variable insts, 1992; CANA (bed): overlay, interactive installation, 1992; Bitom (stream): couple, pf/trbn/perc, 1992; Birome (stream): link 1 & 2, elec, 1993; Chimanzzi: link, variable inst(s) (in pairs), 1993

BIBLIOGRAPHY
J. Hunt: *Talk(slice):duplex*, OODiscs bp 5091 (1990) [liner notes]
"...[L]ooking to the long shores": Writings, Reminiscences and Ideas of and about Jerry Hunt (n.p., 1994)
M. Schell: "Unlikely Persona: Jerry Hunt (1943–1993)," *Musicworks*, lxv (1996), 18–23

STEPHEN HOUSEWRIGHT, ROD STASICK

Hunter, Alberta [Alix, May; Beatty, Josephine] (*b* Memphis, TN, 1 April 1895; *d* New York, NY, 17 Oct 1984). Jazz and blues singer. From 1914 she sang in night clubs and cabarets in Chicago, and in 1921 she began recording and performing in theaters in New York, where she finally moved in 1923; because she was under contract to Gennett she sometimes recorded for other labels under the pseudonym May Alix and the name of her half-sister Josephine Beatty. She was accompanied most often by Fletcher Henderson, but also by Louis Armstrong, Fats Waller, and Sidney Bechet. In 1922 she composed and recorded "Downhearted Blues" (Para.), which was recorded in the following year by Bessie Smith and became a popular classic. Another fine recording by Hunter is "Texas Moaner Blues" (1924, Gen.). Between 1927 and 1937 she worked chiefly in Europe, and in 1934 appeared in the film Radio Parade; at the same time she continued to sing occasionally in the United States. She took part from 1944 to 1953 in several tours sponsored by the United Service Organizations, including one of Europe and Korea with Snub Mosley (1952–3). After beginning a career as a nurse in 1954 she worked infrequently in music, apart from recording with Lovie Austin (1961) and Jimmy Archey (1962). From 1977 she again worked full-time as a musician and made recordings, and until the summer of 1984 she sang regularly at the Cookery in New York. The documentary *Alberta Hunter: My Castle's Rockin'* (1998, dir. C. Albertson) mixes interviews with performance footage shot late in her career.

BIBLIOGRAPHY
CBY 1979
W. Balliett: "Let it Be Classy," *American Singers* (New York, 1979), 21–31
F.C. Taylor and G. Cook: *Alberta Hunter: a Celebration in Blues* (New York, 1987)
Oral history material in *NEij (JOHP)*

RONALD M. RADANO/R

Hunter, Charles (*b* Columbia, TN, 16 May 1876; *d* St. Louis, MO, 23 Jan 1906). Ragtime composer. He was born almost totally blind and learned piano tuning at a school for the blind. He later worked as a tuner for the Jesse French Piano Co. and taught himself to play and compose ragtime. In 1902 the company transferred him to St. Louis, where he played in various bordellos in Chestnut Valley and contracted the dissipated habits which, despite belated attempts to reform, hastened his early death from tuberculosis.

Hunter was a pioneer among white ragtime composers. His rags are syncopated country marches with a distinctive folk flair that seem to celebrate rural life, though tempered with the same touch of melancholy that characterizes country band breakdowns and fiddle tunes. Within the traditional march form he delightfully combined the more complex syncopations of sophisticated piano rags with the simpler rhythms of the cakewalk. Like most folk ragtime composers and performers who begin playing by ear, he had a predilection for the flat keys, especially A♭. His most popular rag, *Tickled to Death* (1899), was still available on piano rolls as late as the 1920s. Unpredictable form and key changes abound in *Cotton Bolls* (1901), *Just Ask Me* (1902), and his last piece, *Back to Life* (1905), the title of which is said to be indicative of Hunter's decision to return to a normal life. All but his last rag were published in Nashville, and evidence points to the existence of a distinctive school of ragtime composition in that city. Hunter also wrote a song, "Davy" (1904), from the opera *Josephine*, but the complete work was probably never published.

WORKS

Pf rags: Tickled to Death, 1899; 'Possum and 'Taters, 1900; A Tennessee Tantalizer, 1900; Cotton Bolls, 1901; Queen of Love, 1901; Just ask me, 1902; Why we Smile, 1903; Back to Life, New York, 1905

Other pf: Seraphine Waltzes, St. Louis, 1905

Song: Davy (W.V. Reynolds), 1904

Principal publishers: Frank G. Fite, H.A. French

BIBLIOGRAPHY

GroveA

R. Blesh and H. Janis: *They all played ragtime* (New York, 1950, 4/1971)

T.J. Tichenor, ed.: *Ragtime Rarities* (New York, 1975)

D.A. Jasen and T.J. Tichenor: *Rags and Ragtime: a Musical History* (New York, 1978)

D.T. Roberts: liner notes, *An Album of Early Folk Rags*, Stomp Off 1021 (1982)

TREBOR JAY TICHENOR

Hunter, Charlie (*b* Providence, RI, 23 May 1967). Jazz guitarist. His mother repaired guitars and moved the family to Berkeley, California, in 1974. As a teenager Hunter studied with Joe Satriani, and at the age of 18 he became interested in jazz, citing Charlie Parker, Charlie Christian, and John Coltrane as influences. In the late 1980s he began experimenting with adapting the jazz organ style of Jimmy Smith and Larry Young to the guitar, using a custom-made seven-string guitar to gain additional low range (tuned A–d–a–d′–g′–b′–e″).

After a time as a street musician in Paris, Hunter returned to the Bay Area and began playing with Michael Franti's group the Disposable Heroes of Hiphoprisy (1991–3). He then formed a trio with the saxophonist Dave Ellis and the drummer Jay Lane, and began playing at the Elbo Room in San Francisco. Although the personnel changed, this group became the model for Hunter's future performances and recordings. In 1994 he also began playing an eight-string guitar, which added even more bass range (down to E), although he subsequently returned to the seven-string instrument. His playing shows remarkable virtuosity: he maintains bass lines while providing accompaniment and improvising solos.

Hunter has founded several groups, including T.J. Kirk (1994) and Pound for Pound (1997), and has recorded albums for the labels Blue Note, Thirsty Ear, and Ropeadope. His style is rooted in jazz tradition, but constantly adapts to new trends and mixes elements of rock and popular music, which Hunter cites as a reason for his continued success.

BIBLIOGRAPHY

B. Milkowski: "Charlie Hunter: String Theory," *JT*, xxxiv (2004), 54–8

E. Haga: "In the Pocket, Out of Pocket: after Major Labels and Jamband Hype, Groove-crazy Guitarist Charlie Hunter has the Steady Gaze of a Survivor," *JT*, xl (2010), 38–44

D. Wright: "Charlie Hunter: Seven-String Samurai," <http://www.allaboutjazz.com/php/article.php?id=34575> (2009)

JOHN BASS

Huntington, Jonathan (*b* Windham, CT, 17 Nov 1771; *d* St. Louis, MO, 29 July 1838). Composer, singer, and singing master. Although it is unknown at what schools he taught before 1808, Huntington is said to have been a singing master for all his working life, which was spent until about 1804 in and around his hometown, and thereafter in Troy, New York (1806), Northampton, Massachusetts (1807–11), Boston (1812–29), and St. Louis. On 10 May 1808 he advertised in Northampton, Massachusetts: "Musical Instruments. For sale, and instructions given by J. Huntington"; in 1818 and 1820 he advertised both singing-schools and flute lessons in Boston. His tunebook *The Apollo Harmony* (Northampton, MA, 1807) contained instructions for "Violincello, and German Flute."

Huntington's career as a compiler illustrates the shift in taste that took place in New England between 1790 and 1820. *The Albany Collection* (1800) and *The Apollo Harmony* are both eclectic, mixing American pieces (including a few of Huntington's own) with English compositions. But his last two tunebooks, *The English Extracts* (Northampton, MA, 1809) and *Classical Church Musick* (Boston, 1812), adhere to reformist principles and emphasize European repertoire.

Huntington was a tenor and sang in three successive Independence Day celebrations in Northampton (1809–11). As a founding member of Boston's Handel and Haydn Society (he represented the choir of Old South Church at the organizational meeting on April 20, 1815), he sang "I Know that my Redeemer liveth" from Handel's *Messiah* at the society's first public concert (December 25, 1815); he performed the same piece in public as late as 1822. Two letters from Huntington to the composer Timothy Swan are among Swan's papers at the American Antiquarian Society, Worcester, Massachusetts.

BIBLIOGRAPHY

C.C. Perkins and J. S. Dwight: *History of the Handel and Haydn Society of Boston, Massachusetts*, i (Boston, 1883–93/*R* 1977)

C.G. Burnham: "Olden Time Music in the Connecticut Valley," *New England Magazine*, xxiv/1 (1901), 12–27

The Huntington Family in America (Hartford, CT, 1915), 608–9

F.J. Metcalf: *American Writers and Compilers of Sacred Music* (New York, 1925/*R* 1967)

S.E. Murray: "Timothy Swan and Yankee Psalmody," *MQ*, lxi/3 (1975), 433–63

P.R. Osterhout: *Music in Northampton, Massachusetts to 1820* (diss., U. of Michigan, 1978), 252, 343, 352

P.R. Osterhout: "Andrew Wright: Northampton Music Printer," *American Music* i/4 (1983), 5–26

A.P. Britton, I. Lowens, and R. Crawford: *American Sacred Music Imprints, 1698–1810: a Bibliography* (Worcester, MA, 1990)

T. Swan: *Psalmody and Secular Songs*, ed. Nym Cooke, RRAM, xxvi (Madison, WI, 1997)

RICHARD CRAWFORD/R

Hunt-Lieberson [Hunt], **Lorraine** (*b* San Francisco, CA, 1 March 1954; *d* Santa Fe, NM, 3 July 2006). Mezzo-soprano. She first studied the viola with Lauren Jakey and voice with Edwin Dunning at San Jose State University. She was assistant principal violist with the San Jose Symphony (1972–80) and a member of the Artemis String Quartet at Wheaton College in Massachusetts. She received mixed signals regarding career direction from Tanglewood as she was turned down as a singer and accepted as violist. In 1980 she was a finalist at the Metropolitan Opera's San Francisco regional auditions and committed to a singing career. She told an interviewer, "Now my body's my instrument.... For me health is much more a concern since I've become a singer, and I feel much more vulnerable. It takes on a whole different lifestyle." She initially concentrated on Baroque repertory. One of her earliest successes was playing the role of Sesto in PETER SELLARS's controversial staging of *Giulio Cesare*. She also appeared in Sellars's productions of *Oedipus rex* as Jocasta, *Don Giovanni* as Donna Elvira, *L'incoronazione di Poppea* as Octavia, and the title role in *Serse*. She enjoyed major successes as Irene in Sellars's 1996 staging of Handel's *Theodora* at Glyndebourne, and as the title roles for Charpentier's *Médée* with William Christie's Les Arts Florissants and *Ariodante* at Göttingen. She also achieved great success as Myrtle Wilson in the world premiere of Harbison's *The Great Gatsby* at the Metropolitan Opera. In 1996–7 she sang Charlotte (*Werther*) at the Lyons Opéra, Sesto at the Paris Opéra, and Phèdre (*Hippolyte et Aricie*) with Christie at the Palais Garnier, Paris. She also undertook the title roles in *Carmen* at the Opéra Bastille in 1998 and in a concert performance of *The Rape of Lucretia* at the 1999 Edinburgh Festival. In 2001 she returned to the Edinburgh Festival, singing a magnetic, sensual Dido in *Les Troyens*. On the concert platform her repertory included Berlioz's *Les nuits d'été*, Berg's *Sieben frühe Lieder*, Britten's *Phaedra* (which she subsequently recorded), and Mahler's *Lieder eines fahrenden Gesellen*, with which she made her Proms debut in 1998. She married the composer PETER LIEBERSON in 1999. In December 2000 she sang in the premiere of John Adams's nativity oratorio *El Niño* at the Théâtre du Châtelet in Paris. In 2001 she was widely acclaimed for her singing of two Bach cantatas (nos.82 and 199) in stagings by Peter Sellars. Other recordings include the title roles in *Médée* and *Theodora*, and a disc of Schumann *Lieder*. Her deeply eloquent Irene at Glyndebourne is preserved on video, and discloses her warm, vibrantly expressive tone at its best. A highly spiritual singer, Hunt-Lieberson was asked to headline benefit concerts for HIV/AIDS organizations throughout the San Francisco Bay Area.

BIBLIOGRAPHY

C. Michener: "The Soul Singer: a Mezzo with the Most Potent Voice since Callas," *New Yorker*, lxxix/41 (5 Jan 2004), 42–7

Obituaries: *New York Times* (5 July 2006); *Opera News*, lxxi/3 (2006), 96

ALAN BLYTH/MEREDITH ELIASSEN

Hupa. Native American group of California. Their music bore a resemblance to that of the YUROK.

Hupfeld, Charles Frederic (*b* Germany, 1788; *d* Philadelphia, PA, 15 July 1864). Violinist, conductor, composer, teacher, and music publisher of German birth. In 1801 Hupfeld arrived in Baltimore, likely joining other family. Henry Hupfeld, musician, is listed in the 1799 Baltimore directory and in 1802 as music master. Between 1810 and 1818 Hupfeld gave annual concerts in Philadelphia and also performed with an established string quartet that included J.C. Hommann, whose daughter, Constantia, he married in 1815. In 1816, with Benjamin Carr and others, Hupfeld tried to establish a society for regular music practice. Gradually a grander idea emerged: the MUSICAL FUND SOCIETY of Philadelphia, founded in 1820. Hupfeld became "leader" of the Society orchestra, a post he held for over 20 years. He frequently appeared as violin soloist on Society programs and elsewhere. Hupfeld played the violin at a Philharmonic concert in New York on April 21, 1825, and Grider (*Music in Bethlehem*, 1873) cites Hupfeld as "the best violinist in Philadelphia until 1835." Hupfeld established a music store in Philadelphia; numerous publications by C.F. Hupfeld & Son (importers of music and musical instruments) date from 1843 to 1854. His own works include a waltz for piano, *Leaf of an Album* (1837), three songs (1846–7), and *Cadwalader's Quick Step* (1846). In 1857 Hupfeld was named to honorary membership in the Musical Fund Society, a tribute rarely bestowed.

BIBLIOGRAPHY

L.C. Madeira: *Annals of Music in Philadelphia* (Philadelphia, 1896)

R.A. Gerson: *Music in Philadelphia* (Philadelphia, 1940/*R*)

R.J. Wolfe: *Secular Music in America, 1801–1825*, vol. 1 (New York, 1964)

J. Swenson-Eldridge: *Charles Hommann: Surviving Orchestral Music*, MUSA 17/RRAM 62 (Middleton, WI, 2007)

JOANNE E. SWENSON-ELDRIDGE

Hurok [Gurkov], **Sol(omon Israelovich)** (*b* Pogar, Russia, ?9 April 1888; *d* New York, NY, 5 March 1974). Impresario and manager. Hurok left Russia in 1906 and settled in New York, where he progressed from organizing left-wing political events in Brooklyn to presenting prominent musicians (such as violinists Efrem Zimbalist and Mischa Elman) and dancers (such as Anna Pavlova, Isadora Duncan, and Michel Fokine) at Carnegie Hall and the Hippodrome. In 1921–2 Hurok presented Russian bass Fyodor Chaliapin in a series of highly publicized appearances in the United States; their collaboration lasted until 1927. During the 1930s Hurok concentrated primarily on dance presentations, and introduced audiences across the United States to classical ballet through extensive tours by such companies as the Ballet Russe de Monte Carlo. These tours also introduced a wide audience to ballet music, including new scores by Nicolas Nabokov and Vladimir Dukelsky.

Hurok tirelessly sought out new and up-and-coming musical talent throughout the United States, Europe, and the USSR. One of his most celebrated "discoveries" was the African American contralto Marian Anderson. The recital she gave under Hurok's management at Town Hall in New York in 1935 helped to establish her ground-breaking career in the United States. On 9 April 1939, Anderson gave an historic performance at the Lincoln Memorial in Washington, DC. The performance was organized by Hurok with assistance from Eleanor Roosevelt after the singer was denied permission by the Daughters of the American Revolution to appear in Constitution Hall. Transmitted to millions by radio and film, the recital became a landmark event in the American civil rights movement and led to greater opportunities for African American classical singers and musicians.

In the late 1930s Hurok also began long and successful associations with Polish-born pianist Arthur Rubinstein, whom he promoted as the "Prince of Pianists," and operatic tenor Jan Peerce. Violinist Isaac Stern became a Hurok artist in 1940, eventually becoming not only one of his most steady and profitable "attractions" but also a valued advisor and talent scout. Along with young American soprano Roberta Peters, another Hurok star, Stern appeared in a highly fictionalized 1953 film/musical biography of the impresario, *Tonight We Sing*. Later additions to Hurok's roster included pianist Van Cliburn, cellists Jacqueline Du Pré and Gregor Piatigorsky, and violinists Nathan Milstein, Itzhak Perlman, and Pinchas Zukerman.

The liberalization of Soviet cultural policies following the death of Soviet leader Joseph Stalin in 1953 made it possible for Hurok to realize his life-long dream of bringing major Soviet performing artists to the United States. In 1958 he presented the Moiseyev Folk Dance Ensemble, and in 1959 the Bolshoi Ballet, both on wildly successful cross-country tours. Soviet musicians including pianists Vladimir Ashkenazy, Emil Gilels, and Sviatoslav Richter; violinists David Oistrakh and Leonid Kogan; cellist Mstislav Rostropovich; singers Galina Vishnevskaya and Irina Arkhipova; and conductors Kiril Kondrashin and Yevgeny Svetlanov all eventually appeared in the United States under the "S. Hurok Presents" label, which became synonymous with high-quality musical performance presented stylishly for a popular audience. In his later years Hurok advocated for the establishment of the National Endowment for the Arts.

BIBLIOGRAPHY

S. Hurok (with R. Goode): *Impresario: a Memoir* (New York, 1946)

S. Hurok: *S. Hurok Presents: a Memoir of the Dance World* (New York, 1953)

M. Anderson: *My Lord, What a Morning* (New York, 1956)

A. Levy: *The Bluebird of Happiness: the Memoirs of Jan Peerce* (New York, 1976)

H. Robinson: *The Last Impresario: the Life, Times and Legacy of Sol Hurok* (New York, 1994)

HARLOW ROBINSON

Hurston, Zora Neale (*b* Notasulga, AL, 7 Jan 1891; *d* Fort Pierce, FL, 28 Jan 1960). Writer, playwright, anthropologist, and folklorist. Although Hurston is best known as a novelist and essayist, she was one of the first African Americans to apply the anthropological method to the study and collection of black folklore in the United States and Caribbean. In 1894 her family moved to Eastonville, Florida, where she spent most of her childhood and adolescence. She attended Morgan Academy (now Morgan State University, 1917–18) and Howard University (intermittently from 1919–24). At Howard she came under the influence of Alain Locke, chief architect of the Harlem Renaissance, who brought her to the attention of editor Charles S. Johnson, who published her short story "Drenched in Light" (*Opportunity Magazine*, 1924). Hurston moved to New York City in 1925 and became acquainted with Langston Hughes and Countee Cullen. She attended Barnard College that fall, studying anthropology with Franz Boas and obtaining the BA degree (1928).

Hurston conducted extensive field research during the late 1920s and 30s, collecting hundreds of folksongs, tales, and sayings, recording and describing rituals and dances of the rural black South and Caribbean. Her writings reflect with authenticity this folklore, especially the novels *Jonah's Vine Gourd* (1934), *Their Eyes Were Watching God* (1937), *Moses, Man of the Mountain* (1939), and *Seraph on the Swanee* (1948), the autobiographical *Dust Tracks on a Road* (1942), and her two folklore studies, *Mules and Men* (1935) and *Tell My Horse* (1938), which examines Caribbean Voodoo practices.

WRITINGS

"Songs and Tales from the Bahamas," *Journal of American Folk-Lore*, xliii (1930), 294–312

Zora Neale Hurston Collected Plays, ed. J.L. Cole and C. Mitchell (New Brunswick, NJ, 2008)

BIBLIOGRAPHY

L.L. Crawley and J.C. Hickerson: *Zora Neale Hurston: Recordings, Manuscripts, Photographs, and Ephemera in the Archive of Folk Culture and Other Divisions of the Library of Congress* (Washington, DC, 1992/R)

R.P. Davis: *Zora Neale Hurston: an Annotated Bibliography and Reference Guide* (Westport, CT, 1997)

R.W. Croft: *A Zora Neale Hurston Companion* (Westport, CT, 2002)

V. Boyd: *Wrapped in Rainbows: the Life of Zora Neale Hurston* (New York, 2003)

L. King: *The Cambridge Introduction to Zora Neale Hurston* (New York, 2008)

JOSEPHINE WRIGHT

Hurt, Mississippi John [Hurt, John Smith] (*b* Teoc, MS, c1894; *d* Grenada, MS, 2 Nov 1966). Songster and guitarist. He sang in church as a child and taught himself the guitar from the age of ten, developing an original finger-picking style. He made a few excellent recordings in New York in 1928, then for the next 35 years lived obscurely as a farmer and railroad worker. His rediscovery in 1963 proceeded from the slender clue of the title to his "Avalon Blues" (1928, OK 8759). From then he recorded extensively, including more than 90 titles for the Library of Congress, and re-created with uncanny similarity many of his 1928 performances. Although much admired by eastern audiences for his accomplished playing and wistful blues as well as his agreeable disposition, he soon tired of publicity and lived out the rest of his life quietly in Mississippi. Before his rediscovery Hurt had never played professionally, which attaches special importance to his work; apart from its intrinsic merit, it preserved an old African American tradition. His earliest recordings, including "Frankie" (1928, OK 8560), "Stack o' Lee Blues" (1928, OK 8654), and "Spike Driver Blues" on the "John Henry" theme (1928, OK 8692), were long-established ballads. Hurt's guitar playing was characterized by a light thumb-picked beat and rapid fingerwork, and ideally complemented his gentle, almost whispering singing style. Notable among his later recordings were the little-recorded Mississippi theme "Sliding Delta" (1964, Piedmont 13161), demonstrating his nimble fingering; "Petra-Lee" (1963, Flyright 553), on which he played slide guitar; the mildly erotic "Candy Man Blues" (1964, Van. 9220); and the ballad "Louis Collins" (1963, Piedmont 13157).

BIBLIOGRAPHY
SouthernB
L. Cohn: "Mississippi John Hurt," *Sing Out!*, xiv/5 (1964), 16
D. Waterman: "John Hurt: Patriarch Hippie," *Sing Out!*, xvii/1 (1967), 4
B. Bastin: liner notes, *Mississippi John Hurt: Library of Congress Recordings*, Flyright 553 (1980)
P. Oliver: *Songsters and Saints: Vocal Traditions on Race Records* (Cambridge, England, 1984)
L. Cohn: liner notes, *Mississippi John Hurt: Avalon Blues: the Complete 1928 Okeh Recordings*, Col. CK64986 (1996)
PAUL OLIVER/R

Husa, Karel (*b* Prague, 7 Aug 1921). Composer and conductor of Czech birth. Trained initially as a pianist and violinist, Husa attended the Prague Conservatory (1941–5), studying composition with Řídký and conducting with Dědeček and Talich. His first published work, Sonatina for piano (1943), was composed while he was still a conservatory student. From 1946 to 1951, a fellowship by the French government enabled him to matriculate in Paris at the École Normale de Musique, where he studied composition with Honegger and conducting with Fournet. He took conducting classes at the Paris Conservatoire with Bigot, as well as private lessons with BOULANGER and Cluytens. His String Quartet no.1 (1948) enjoyed a decisive success: after its Parisian premiere, the quartet was performed at the ISCM Festival in Brussels (1950) and at Darmstadt (1951); it was awarded the first prize at the 1951 Gaudeamus Festival. In 1954 he joined the music department at Cornell

University, becoming an American citizen in 1959. As Kappa Alpha Professor of Music, he taught composition, conducting, and orchestration until his retirement in 1992. Major orchestras in Europe, America, and Asia engaged him frequently as a guest conductor. His honors include the Prix Lili Boulanger (1950), two Guggenheim Fellowships (1964, 1965), the Pulitzer Prize (1969), the Friedheim Award of the Kennedy Center (1983), and the Grawemeyer Award (1993). In 1974, Husa was elected to the Royal Belgian Academy of Arts and Sciences; in 1994, he was elected to American Academy of Arts and Letters; and his native land honored him with the Gold Medal of Merit of the Czech Republic (1995).

While his early scores evince a broadly neoclassical style, in the 1950s Husa became fascinated with dodecaphonic techniques. In works such as *Mosaïques* for orchestra (1961), Husa allied a personal adaptation of serial techniques with dynamic rhythms and brilliant timbres. He further explored extended instrumental sonorities in compositions such as the Concerto for alto saxophone and concert band (1967) and the String Quartet no.3 (1968).

Husa is celebrated especially for three major scores that possess a searing expressivity engendered by his compassionate humanitarianism: *Music for Prague 1968* (1968), *Apotheosis of this Earth* (1971, rev. 1972), and the ballet *The Trojan Women* (1981). After the masterful Concerto for Orchestra (1986), commissioned by the New York PO, Husa composed concertos for organ (1987), trumpet (1987), violoncello (1988), and violin (1993). The lyrical intensity of these works is echoed in the chamber music from this period, including the Variations for piano quartet (1984) and the String Quartet no.4 "Poems" (1990). Except for opera, Husa has written in every important musical genre; many of his scores, notably those for wind ensembles, have secured an honored and permanent place in the concert repertory.

WORKS
(selective list)
Ballets: The Steadfast Tin Soldier (H.C. Andersen), nar, orch, 1974, Boulder, CO, 10 May 1975; Monodrama, orch, 1976, Indianapolis, IN, 26 March 1976; The Trojan Women, orch, 1981, Louisville, KY, 28 March 1981
Orch: Ov., orch, 1944; Sinfonietta, chbr orch, 1946; Fresque, 1946, rev. 1963; Divertimento, str, 1948; Concertino, pf, orch, 1949, arr concert band, 1984; Musique d'amateurs, chbr orch, 1953; Portrait, str, 1953; Sym. no.1, 1953; 4 Little Pieces, str, 1955; Fantasies, 1956; Poème, va, chbr orch/pf, 1959; Elégie et rondeau, a sax, orch,1961, arr. a sax, pf; Mosaïques, 1961; Serenade, ww qnt, str, 1963; Conc., brass qnt, str/pf, 1965; 2 Sonnets from Michelangelo, 1971; Pastoral, str, 1980; Sym. no.2 "Reflections,"1983; Sym. Suite, 1984; Conc. for Orch, 1986; Org Conc., 1987; Tpt Conc., 1987; Vc Conc., 1988; Ov. "Youth," 1991; Cayuga Lake (Memories), chbr orch, 1992; Vn Conc., 1993; Celebration Fanfare, 1996; Midwest Celebration, fanfare, 1996; Celebración, 1997
Wind: Divertimento, brass, perc, 1959; Conc., a sax, concert band, 1967; Music for Prague 1968, arr. orch, 1968; Perc Conc., 1970–71; Apotheosis of this Earth, 1971, arr. SATB, orch, 1972; Al fresco, 1973; Tpt Conc., 1973; Fanfare, brass, perc, 1980; Intradas and Interludes, 7 tpt, perc, 1980; Conc., 1982; Smetana Fanfare, 1984; Les couleurs fauves, 1994; Cheetah, 2006
Chamber: Suite, va, pf, 1945; Sonatina, vn, pf, 1945; Str Qt no.1, 1948; Evocations of Slovakia, cl, va, vc, 1951; Str Qt no.2, 1953; 2 Preludes,

fl, cl, bn, 1966; Divertimento, brass qnt, 1968; Str Qt no.3, 1968; Studies, perc, 1968; Sonata, vn, pf, 1973; Drum Ceremony, 5 perc, 1976; Landscapes, brass qnt, 1977; 3 Dance Sketches, 4 perc, 1979; Intradas and Interludes, 7 tpt, timp, 1980; Sonata à tre, vn, cl, pf, 1982; Recollections, ww qnt, pf, 1982; Variations, pf qnt, 1984; Str Qt no.4 "Poems," 1990; Tubafest Celebration Fanfare, 4 tuba, 1992; 5 Poems, ww qnt, 1994; Postcard from Home, a sax, pf, 1997; Three Studies, cl, 2008

Keyboard: Sonatina, pf, 1943; Sonata no.1, pf, 1949; 8 Czech Duets, pf 4 hands, 1955; Elégie, pf, 1957; Sonata no.2, pf, 1975; Frammenti, org, 1987

Vocal: 12 Moravian Songs (folk, trans. R. Martin), 1v, pf, 1956; Festive Ode (E. Blackall), mixed/male chorus, orch/band, 1964, arr. chorus, wind; There are from Time to Time Mornings (H.D. Thoreau), Bar, chorus, 1976; An American Te Deum (H.D. Thoreau, O. Rølvaag, O. Březina), Bar, chorus, band, 1976, arr. chorus, orch, 1978; Every Day (H.D. Thoreau), SATB, 1981; 3 Moravian Songs (folk, trans. Martin), SATB, 1981; Cant., TTBB, brass qnt, 1983; Song (Good Night), SATB, 2000

Principal publishers: Associated, G. Schirmer, Schott, Leduc

BIBLIOGRAPHY

A. Hegvik: "Karel Husa Talks About His Life and Work," *The Instrumentalist*, xxix (1975), 31

L.W. Hartzell: "Karel Husa: the Man and his Music," *MQ*, lxii (1976), 87

K.K. Hestekin: *Structural Elements in Karel Husa's Apotheosis of This Earth* (diss., University of Wisconsin, Madison, 1976)

M.B. Thompson: *Karel Husa: Concerto for Wind Ensemble* (diss., Eastman School of Music, 1985)

D. McLaurin: *The Life and Works of Karel Husa with Emphasis on the Significance of His Contribution to the Wind Band* (diss., Florida State University, 1985)

C.O. Summers: *The Development of Original Band Scoring from Sousa to Husa.* (diss., Ball State University, 1986)

B. Adams: "Karel Husa's Music for Prague 1968: an Interpretive Analysis," *The Instrumentalist*, xlii (1987), 19

M. Scattergay: *Karel Husa's Music for Prague 1968* (diss. Eastman School of Music, 1989)

S.H. Hitchens: *Karel Husa: a bio-bibliography* (New York, 1991)

B. Adams: "Two Scores by Karel Husa," *MLA Notes* (March 1995), 1149

J.A. Treybig: *An Analytical and Historical Study and Performance Guide for Karel Husa's Concerto for Trumpet and Wind Orchestra (1973).* (diss., University of Texas at Austin, 1999)

C.M. Neal: *An Analysis of Karel Husa's Music for Prague 1968: an Exploration of Compositional Process and Historical Background.* (diss., University of Oklahoma, 2002)

M.A. Radice, ed.: *Karel Husa: a Composer's Life in Essays and Documents* (Lewiston, NY, 2002)

D.C. Fullmer: *A Comparison of the Wind Band Writing of Three Contemporary Composers: Karel Husa, Timothy Broege, Cindy McTee.* (diss., University of Washington, 2003)

B. Adams: "Karel Husa's Sinfonietta for Chamber Orchestra," *MLA Notes*, (March 2009), 575

BYRON ADAMS

Hüsker Dü. Hardcore punk band. It formed in 1979 in St. Paul, Minnesota, with guitarist and vocalist Bob Mould (*b* Malone, NY, 16 Oct 1960), bassist Greg Norton (*b* Rock Island, IL, 13 March 1959), and drummer Grant Hart (*b* St. Paul, MN, 18 March 1961). In their early years Hüsker Dü played at a furiously fast and chaotic pace, but their music evolved beyond hardcore into more melodic and varied sounds with the release of their double album *Zen Arcade* on SST in 1984. The band's most praised work, it is a concept album about a young man who runs away from his family and friends into a cruel world of alienation and despair. After two more albums with SST Hüsker Dü signed a major label deal with Warner Bros., but 1986's *Candy Apple Grey*, and its 1987 double-album follow-up, *Warehouse: Songs and Stories*, were both commercial failures by major label standards. This pressure and disappointment intensified ongoing personal conflicts within Hüsker Dü, causing the band to break up in 1987.

BIBLIOGRAPHY

A. Earles: *Hüsker Dü: the Story of the Noise-Pop Pioneers Who Launched Modern Rock* (Minneapolis, MN, 2010)

RYAN MOORE

Husky, Ferlin (Eugene) [Terry Preston] (*b* Flat River, MO, 3 Dec 1927; *d* Hendersonville, TN, 17 March 2011). Country music singer. A pioneer in West Coast country music and a charismatic performer, Husky played a central role in shaping the Nashville Sound of country music in the 1950s and 60s. Following service in the Merchant Marines during World War II, Husky worked as a DJ in Bakersfield, California. In 1949 he signed with Four Star Records, recording under the name Terry Preston. In 1951 Husky replaced Tennessee Ernie Ford on the Los Angeles-based TV show *Hometown Jamboree*. Signing with Capitol Records in 1952, he recorded his first two hits with singer Jean Shepard in 1953: "A Dear John Letter" and the follow-up, "Forgive me, John." Husky's first hit as a solo artist came in 1955 with the two-sided hit "I feel better all over (more than anywhere's else)"/"Little Tom." In 1957 he scored a major hit with "Gone," a song he had first recorded under the name Terry Preston in 1952. Considered the first record to capture the emerging pop-oriented NASHVILLE SOUND, it was produced by Ken Nelson at Owen Bradley's studio in Nashville, and featured the Jordanaires with soprano Millie Kirkham. In its new version, "Gone" reached number one on *Billboard*'s country sales chart for ten consecutive weeks and also crossed over to the pop chart where it reached number four. In 1960 Husky recorded the number-one hit "Wings of a Dove," which remained on the charts for almost nine months. His comic alter ego, Simon Crum, charted singles with "Cuzz Yore So Sweet" (no.5 in 1955), and "Country music is here to stay" (no.2 for three weeks in 1958–9). Husky recorded 41 chart singles for Capitol before signing with ABC Records in 1972. During this time he also appeared in a number of movies, including *Country Music Holiday* (1958), *Las Vegas Hillbillies* (1966), and *Hillbillies in a Haunted House* (1967). He was inducted into the Country Music Hall of Fame in 2010.

DON CUSIC

Huss, Henry Holden (*b* Newark, NJ, 21 June 1862; *d* New York, NY, 17 Sept 1953). Pianist, composer, and teacher. He studied piano with his father, George John Huss (1828–1904), and theory with OTIS BARDWELL BOISE, and then with JOSEPH RHEINBERGER and Josef Giehrl at the Munich Musikschule (1882–5). Upon returning to the United States Huss toured as a solo pianist, with engagements including a White House performance in 1904 and solo performances of his Rhapsody and Concerto with major orchestras. He married soprano Hildegard Hoffmann in 1904. He taught at Hunter College, New York, and at the Masters School, Dobbs Ferry New York. He co-authored with his father *Condensed Piano-Technics*, G. 222 (1904).

A founder of the American Guild of Organists, Huss also published numerous articles on piano pedagogy.

WORKS
(selected list)
Vocal: Ave Maria, op.4, G.135, S, A, female chorus, str org, str orch (1888/rev. 1890); Festival Sanctus, op.7, G.138, S, chorus, orch (1889); Songs from the German, G.11 (1891); Pater Noster, op.15, G.147, chorus (1900); Crossing the Bar, G.148, chorus (1901); Four Songs, op.22, G.28 (1907); Nocturne, chorus, orch, 1913; Two Songs, op.28, G.42 (1917); All the World's a Stage, op.16, G.16 (1928); Shed No Tear, G.96 (1949)

Inst: Rhapsody, op.3, G.371, pf, orch (1885); Concerto, op. 12, G. 384, vn, orch (1889); Concerto, B, op.10, G.372, pf, orch (1898/rev. 1910); Trio, G.337, pf trio (1887); Drei Bagatellen, op.5, G.199, pf (1889); Quatre Préludes en forme d'Étude, op.17, G.214, pf (1901); Sonata, op.19, G.342, vn, pf (1903); La Nuit, op.21, G.220, pf (1904); Romance, G.344, vn/vc, pf (1907); Six Pieces, op.23, G.230, pf (1912); Quartet, b, op.31, G.353, str qt (1921)

BIBLIOGRAPHY
G.A. Greene: *Henry Holden Huss: An American Composer's Life* (Metuchen, NJ, 1995)

GARY A. GREENE

Hussain, Zakir (*b* Bombay [now Mumbai], India, 9 March 1951). Percussionist and tabla player of Indian birth. Hussain began studying music at the age of three with his father, the late Ustad Alla Rakha. He presented his debut performance in Bombay at age 15, providing tabla accompaniment for the master of the Indian santur, Pandit Shiv Kumar Sharma. Hussain's rise to fame was rapid and sustained, leading to international renown after he traveled to the United States in 1970. His first US public performance came as accompanist to Pandit Ravi Shankar. By age 20 he had become one of the most sought-after tabla accompanists; his virtuosic playing also led to collaborations with popular musicians such as drummer Mickey Hart of The Grateful Dead and guitarist John MacLaughlin, whose Mahavishnu Orchestra had fused elements of Indian classical music with rock and jazz. Hussain stands out for his work in creating fusions of Indian music with Western popular idioms, a practice that has grown into a major stream of activity for a large number of Indian musicians. The first of these efforts to receive widespread recognition was Shakti, a group consisting of MacLaughlin, violinist L. Shankar, and South Indian percussionists Ramnad Raghavan and T.H. "Tikku" Vinayakram. While Shakti retained acoustic instrumentation, Hussain's later fusion projects such as *Planet Drum*, with Mickey Hart (later reincarnated as the *Global Drum Project*), *Tabla Beat Science*, and *The Diga Rhythm Band* often included electric instruments and synthesizers. Hussain also has provided music for film, including Ismail Merchant's *In Custody* and *The Mystic Masseur* and Bernardo Bertolucci's *The Little Buddha*, and for dance companies, most notably Alonzo King's Lines Ballet. He has received numerous prestigious honors and awards, including the Indo-American Award (1990), the Sangeet Natak Akademi Award (1991), the Government of India bestowed titles of *Padma Shree* (1988) and *Padma Bhushan* (2002), and the NEA National Heritage Fellowship (1999).

STEPHEN SLAWEK

Hustis, Gregory (*b* White Plains, NY, 10 May 1950). Horn performer. Hustis attended the Curtis Institute of Music (BM 1972) where he studied with MASON JONES. Since 1976 he has performed as principal horn in the Dallas Symphony. He also served for four years as principal horn in the Hamilton Philharmonic, Ontario, Canada. In addition to frequent work as a commercial recording artist for radio, film, and television, he has performed and recorded with many notable ensembles, including the Dallas Symphony, the Philadelphia Orchestra, and Summit Brass. His other recording projects include Joseph Schwantner's *Beyond Autumn*, commissioned by the International Horn Society, and works by composers such as Eric Ewazen, Simon Sargon, Augusta Read Thomas, and Lee Holdridge. In the mid-1990s he co-founded the company TrumCor to manufacture mutes for brass instruments. In 1997 Hustis introduced a Chamber Music series for Music in the Mountains, a festival in Durango, Colorado, and in 2008 he was appointed the Festival Artistic Director. He has taught at Southern Methodist University for over 25 years and was presented the institution's Meadows Foundation Distinguished Teaching Award in 1995.

BIBLIOGRAPHY
J. West: "Mute Design: An Interview with TrumCor Mutes," *International Trumpet Guild Journal* (June 2004), 64–5

HEIDI LUCAS

Hustle. A generic term for a number of forms of disco dance (*see* DISCO (II)). Based on Latin dances such as the mambo and the merengue, the hustle originated as a

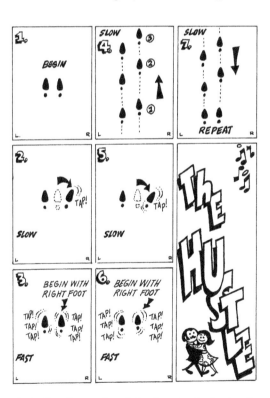

Artist Jim Hummel explains how to do the hustle, 1975. (Sketch by Jim Hummel. AP Photo/Dolores Barclay)

line dance in the Latino communities of New York and Miami in the early 1970s. After some fusion with swing dance and changes in basic foot rhythm, the dance became known variously as Latin hustle, New York hustle, and Brooklyn hustle. Upon publication of the song "The Hustle" by Van McCoy and the Soul City Symphony in 1975, line dances set to it became an international disco craze. Similar line dances set to music by Archie Bell and the Drells, as well as other musicians, dominated the floors of discothèques in 1976–7. Subsequently, a freestyle version for partners supplanted line dances in popularity and was danced by couples in ballrooms and night clubs all over the globe. Both a line dance version and the partnered form for couples can be seen in the movie *Saturday Night Fever* (1977), starring John Travolta and Karen Lynn Gorney in disco numbers created by Leslie Wilson and Lorraine Field. After the publicity created by this movie died down, the popularity of exhibitionistic disco dancing quickly faded and by 1978 the hustle had settled into a more sedate dance for lead-and-follow partners. The ballroom hustle for couples can be seen in the Merchant-Ivory film *Roseland* (1977), in a sequence starring Christopher Walken as a gigolo hired to dance with Geraldine Chaplin, Helen Gallagher, and Joan Copeland.

BIBLIOGRAPHY

J. Forest: *The Hustle, the New Dance Sensation* (Fort Lauderdale, FL, 1975)

K. Lustgarten: *The Complete Guide to Disco Dancing: the Easy Step-by-Step Way to Learn Today's Top Dances* (New York, 1978)

O.M. Ray: *Encyclopedia of Line Dances: the Steps That Came and Stayed* (Reston, VA, 1992)

N. Shell and J. P. Nyemchek: *Hustle* (Austin, TX, 1999)

CLAUDE CONYERS

Huston, (Thomas) Scott (*b* Tacoma, WA, 10 Oct 1916; *d* Cincinnati, OH, 2 March 1991). Composer and teacher. After a brief period of study at the University of Puget Sound (1934–5) he attended the Eastman School of Music (BM 1941, MM 1942, PhD 1952) where his principal teachers were BURRILL PHILLIPS, BERNARD ROGERS, HOWARD HANSON (analysis), and Gustave Soderlund (counterpoint). After periods of teaching at the Universities of Puget Sound and Redlands and at the Kearney State Teachers' College, he joined the staff of the Cincinnati Conservatory in 1952. When the conservatory was merged with the Cincinnati College of Music, he served for a year as dean (1955–6) and then continued to teach at the College-Conservatory, which later became part of the University of Cincinnati, until his retirement in 1987. In his early career his music was influenced by the harmony of Chopin (in particular, the ballades), the polyphony of Bach, and the formal integration of Brahms. He conducted an in-depth study of 16th- and 18th-century counterpoint under Soderlund and worked with Hanson on theories of intervallic projections and the essentials of golden mean proportional concepts; further, his own immersion in the capabilities of all orchestral instruments provided him with an array of compositional possibilities that can be observed in his solo and chamber works. Huston's later music is more eclectic: some works are tonal while others are atonal, and his approach to color is suggestive of both Schoenberg and Debussy. His style is characterized by an increasing formal freedom, a terseness of expression, and a controlled warmth and lyricism that is enhanced by attention to subtleties of timbre. His artistic credo eschewed the concept of composing to amuse or to entertain. *Columbia,* which won the Orchestral Composition Prize for Northeast Composers when Huston was a student at Eastman in 1941, was premiered a year later by Sir Thomas Beecham with the Seattle Symphony; Max Rudolf and the Cincinnati Symphony performed Symphony No.3 "Four Phantasms for Orchestra" in 1968; and *Time Reflections Cantata* (aka *Cantata Enigmatica*), commissioned by Moorehead State University, was introduced by the St. Paul Chamber Orchestra and Moorehead State University Chorus with Bill McGlothlin as conductor in 1979. The one-act television opera *The Blind Girl* was produced by the opera division of the College-Conservatory of Music in 1988. An enthusiastic teacher, Huston made a series of educational tapes that feature conversation with Carolyn Watt. They are devoted to 20th-century music, and have such titles as "The Evolution of Modern Music," "The Arrival of Atonal Music," and "The Avant-Garde Today" (Center for Cassette Studies). When teaching composition he held few restrictions in terms of style, dwelling instead on "the verities of pitch, time, curve, space, silence, and timbre."

WORKS
(selective list)

Stage: Blind Girl (op.1, D. Bredemann), 1982

Orch: Toccata, pf, orch, 1952; Tpt Conc., 1963; 2 Images, str, 1964; Sym. no.3 "4 Phantasms," 1964; Sym. no.4, str, 1972; Fanfare for the 200th, 1975; Sym. no.5, 1975; Sym. no.6 "The Human Condition," 1981; several other works, some withdrawn

Vocal: Ante mortem (R. Jeffers), TTB, brass, org, perc, 1965; The Song of Deborah (Bible: *Judges v*), orat, nar, SATB, 1969; American Trilogy (C. Sandburg, Wolf, W. Whitman), 1v, ob, hpd, 1970; Divinely Superfluous Beauty and Natural Music (R. Jeffers), S, chbr ens, 1971; Tamar (monodrama, Jeffers), S, prepared pf, 1974; Vocal Supremacy (Huston), S, A, 1975; Ecstasies of Janus (J. Lloyd), Ct, chbr ens, 1978; Time/Reflections (B. Thomas), chorus, chbr orch, 1978; Songs of Innocence (W. Blake), T, pf, 1979; Songs of Experience (Blake), Mez, pf, 1981; No More War (Bible: *Isaiah*), SATB, 1983; Pss xxv/xxxiv, SATB, org, 1990; liturgical and other choral works

Chbr and inst: 3 sonatas: fl, pf, 1959; va, pf, 1960; org, 1960; Intensity I, wind ens, 1962; Suite, timp, 1963; Suite of 3, hp, 1963; Pro vita, pf, brass qnt, 1965; Penta-tholoi, pf, 1966; Phenomena, fl, ob, hp, db, 1967; Mercury and Venus, sonata, vn, pf, 1968; Diorama, org, 1968; Life-Styles I–IV, pf trio/cl, vc, pf, 1972; 3 Temperaments, org, 1972; Cool to Hot, jazz qt, 1973; For Our Times, suite, 6 brass, 1974; Eealtron, va, pf, 1975; Intensity II, wind ens, 1975; Quiet Movt, Kanon, Fantasy, 2 March 1975; Impressions from Life, chbr ens, 1976; Fragments, Disputes, Mirrors, 2 ob, 1977; Shadowy Waters, cl, vc, pf, 1977; Trichroma, t sax, 1977; Vc suite, 1977; Variables, 4 sax, 1979; Phonenix, tpt, pf, 1980; Brevity is the Soul, pf, suite, 1982; In memoriam, pf, ens, 1983; Time in Mind, gui, 1983; Tribune, hn, org, 1983; 5 Notes for Ada, 2 pf, 1984; Optimism: a Way of Life, brass qt, 1986; 5 Pieces, org, 1988; many others

Principal publishers: Canyon, Marks, Willis, Screen Gems, EMI, G. Schirmer

Principal record companies: Music Now, Opus One

BIBLIOGRAPHY

EwenD

D.Z. Kushner: "A Profile of Scott Huston," *Music Journal*, xxx/7 (1972), 26–7, 52

A.M. Koukios: "In Memoriam, Thomas Scott Huston: 1916–91," *Music Research Forum*, vi (1991), 1–14

A.M. Koukios: *The Choral Music of Thomas Scott Huston* (DMA document, College-Conservatory of Music, U. of Cincinnati, 1993)

DAVID Z. KUSHNER

Hutcherson, Bobby [Robert] (*b* Los Angeles, CA, 27 Jan 1941). Jazz vibraphonist and composer. As a teenager he was inspired by Milt Jackson to take up vibraphone, which he studied briefly with Dave Pike. After working on the West Coast with Curtis Amy, Charles Lloyd, and the Al Grey–Billy Mitchell group, he moved in 1961 to New York, where he was acclaimed for his fresh, full sound on an instrument that was still a rarity in jazz bands. During this time, he moved from using four mallets to two. Into the 1960s he worked with Archie Shepp, Eric Dolphy, Hank Mobley, Herbie Hancock, Andrew Hill, and other musicians who were beginning to break the traditional limitations of song form in jazz and recorded many albums as a leader and a sideman for Blue Note. Among his own recordings are *Components* (1966, BN, which included his well-known tune "Little B's Poem"), *Stick Up!* (1966, BN), and *Solo/Quartet* (1982). In 1988 Hutcherson was an artist-in-residence at the Monterey Jazz Festival, where he led a band with McCoy Tyner. Based in Los Angeles, he has retained widespread popularity playing both vibraphone and marimba. He has worked with various small groups and with the San Francisco Jazz Collective. His recording and performance schedule remained full into the 21st century, usually centering on hard bop. In 2010 Hutcherson was honored by the National Endowment of the Arts with a Jazz Masters Fellowship.

BIBLIOGRAPHY

SouthernB

"Bobby Hutcherson Discography," *Swing Journal*, xxviii/13 (1974), 244

M. Bourne: "A Natural Player," *DB*, xli/5 (1974), 18

L. Darroch: "Bobby Hutcherson: Tradition's Adventurous Edge," *JT*, (1985), Aug, 12

B. Milkowski: "A Personal Slant: Bobby Hutcherson," *JT*, xxix/2 (1999), 42

LEE JESKE/JONAS WESTOVER

Hutcheson, Ernest (*b* Melbourne, Australia, 20 July 1871; *d* New York, NY, 9 Feb 1951). Pianist of Australian birth. He studied with Max Vogrich in Australia, then entered the Leipzig Conservatory as a student of Carl Reinecke and Salomon Jadassohn, graduating with the Mozart prize. After further study with Bernhard Stavenhagen, he toured the Continent and England, and went to the United States (1900) as head of the piano department of the Peabody Conservatory (Baltimore). He resigned (1912) to resume his concert career, appearing in recitals, with major orchestras, and in a notable series of radio broadcasts. His playing was unpretentious but characterized by technical proficiency and intellectuality. Some critics also noted a lack of warmth and emotion, but he was considered among the finest pianists of his generation. A respected teacher and administrator, he joined the Juilliard School piano faculty at its inception (1924), becoming dean (1927) and later

president (1937–45). His compositions did not receive wide recognition.

WRITINGS

The Elements of Piano Technique (Baltimore, 1907)

The Literature of the Piano (New York, 1948, rev. 2/1964/*R*)

JOHN G. DOYLE

Hutcheson, Jere (Trent) (*b* Marietta, GA, 16 Sept 1938). Composer and educator. He studied composition with Frances Buxton at Stetson University (FL), Helen Gunderson at Louisiana State University, and H. OWEN REED at Michigan State University. He also worked with ERNST KRENEK and GUNTHER SCHULLER at Berkshire Music Center, Tanglewood, Massachusetts. He began teaching at Michigan State University in 1965, chairing the composition area from 1975 until 1992. In addition to offering private composition lessons and teaching theory, he developed specialized courses in scoring for orchestra and wind ensemble and in 20th-century music.

He has composed in numerous genres, producing chamber music, songs, choral music, piano works, concertos, orchestral music, and works for wind ensemble. A hallmark of his style is his distinctively symphonic wind ensemble scoring. Among his better-known works is the series of "Caricatures" for wind symphony, in which he highlighted various creative traits of well-known writers, artists, actors, and composers. His compositions have been performed throughout the world, and recordings of his music have appeared on Crystal, Mark, Klavier, and Arizona University Records.

He has won many commissions and honors, including fellowships from the Guggenheim Foundation, the Berkshire Music Center (Tanglewood), and the Vermont Composers Conference; grants from the National Endowment for the Arts, the Martha Baird Rockefeller Fund for Music, and the Michigan Council for the Arts; and five nominations for the Pulitzer Prize. He was named Distinguished Composer of the Year in 1976 by the National Music Teachers Association. Michigan State University maintains a growing archive of his musical manuscripts, including scores and recordings, drafts, notes on composition, correspondence, programs, and other material (<http://www2.lib.msu.edu/branches/fal/musicmancoll.jsp>).

WORKS

(selective list)

Wind ens: Five sets of Caricatures, each highlighting nine musical portraits, 1997–2005; Desert Flower, 2004; six concs. (pf, fl, sax, cl, ob, and solo perc), 1981–2006; Symphonic Etudes, 2009

Orch: Conc. for Vn and Small Orch, 1987; Dance of Time Symphony, 1994; Three Visions 2000; Taj Mahal, 2004; Reveries, 2010; New England in the Summer, 2011

Choral: Lament for a Lost Child (SATB; SSA), 1972, 2000; Mist of Tears (SATB), 2005

Vocal: The Songbook, T, fl, 1970; Mrs. Dalloway's Party, Mez, pf, 1999; Petals Over Time, Mez, pf, 2003

Dramatic: The Silver Sword, chorus, orch, 2009

Chbr: Designs for Fourteen, brass, perc, 1968; Passing, Mez, cl, vc, trbn, pf, 1975; Interplay a sax, mallet perc, 1984; Three Notions, sax qt, 2000; Three Pieces for Tuba and Piano, 2002–2003; Wild Nights, bn, mixed ens, 2007

Piano: Electrons, 1966; Fantaisie-Impromptu, 1974; Quirky Etudes, 2001

Principal publishers: Walton, Dorn Music, G. Schirmer, Subito, C. Alan, and the American Composers Edition.

WRITINGS

with J. Niblock: *Music for the High School Chorus* (Boston, 1967)

Musical Form and Analysis: A Programmed Course. 2 vol. (Boston, 1967)

with G. Spring: *Musical Form and Analysis* (New York, 1995)

MARY BLACK JUNTTONEN

Hutchings, George Sherburn (*b* Salem, MA, 9 Dec 1835; *d* Cambridge, MA, 1 June 1913). Organ builder. Trained as a carpenter, he entered the E.&G.G. Hook firm of Boston in 1857 as a case maker and was soon appointed foreman of that department. In 1861 he left for two years to serve in the Union Army and shortly after his return was appointed factory superintendent. In 1869 the organist John H. Willcox (1827–75) recruited Hutchings, along with fellow Hook employees Mark Plaisted, G.V. Nordstrom, and C.H. Preston, to form a new company under the name of J.H. Willcox & Co. This firm began attracting business in 1870, and built an impressive 54-stop organ in 1871 for St. Peter's Church in Philadelphia that displayed many then innovative features. In 1872 Willcox left the firm, probably for reasons of ill health, and it reorganized under the name of Hutchings, Plaisted & Co., under which it built an even larger organ for the new building of Old South Church in Boston in 1875. Plaisted withdrew from the partnership in 1883, in which year another influential organ was built for Boston's Church of the Advent, and Hutchings continued under the name of G.S. Hutchings & Co.

Now one of the leaders in the trend toward organs of advanced mechanical and Romantic tonal characteristics, G.S. Hutchings & Co. had become a formidable rival to older firms such as Hook & Hastings, and was soon producing a comparable number of organs annually. During the late 1890s Hutchings became one of the pioneers in the use of electro-pneumatic action, aided by a talented young inventor, Ernest M. Skinner, who would shortly leave to open his own competing business. Important organs in this period included those for the Mission Church in Boston (1898), Holy Trinity Church in Brooklyn (1899), and Symphony Hall in Boston (1900). Between 1901 and 1904 EDWIN SCOTT VOTEY (1856–1931) became a partner under the name of Hutchings-Votey Organ Co., for which a larger factory was built. Under this name a distinguished organ for Woolsey Hall at Yale University was built in 1902, and after Votey's departure the firm reverted to Hutchings's name. A notable organ of this later period was the one built in 1906 for Madison Square Presbyterian Church in New York City. After Hutchings's death the company declined, and business difficulties caused its closure in 1919.

BIBLIOGRAPHY

"Where Church Organs Are Made." *New-England Magazine* (April 1892)

"George Hutchings." *The Organ,* ii (1893), 221–2

E.W. Flint: *The Newberry Memorial Organ at Yale University* (New Haven, CT, 1930)

B. Owen: *The Organ in New England.* (Raleigh, NC, 1979)

E.T. Schmitt: "Letters: Geo. S. Hutchings & Pilgrim Congregational, St. Louis." *TheTracker,* xxxiii/1 (1989), 21–6

B. Owen: "John Henry Willcox, Organist and Organbuilder." *The Tracker,* 36/4 (1992), 13–24

BARBARA OWEN

Hutchins [née Maley], **Carleen** (*b* Springfield, MA, 24 May 1911; *d* Wolfeboro, NH, 7 Aug 2009). Violinmaker, acoustician, and writer. A trumpeter and biology graduate of Cornell University (AB 1933) and New York University (MA 1942), she left both disciplines to embrace string instruments and acoustical physics. While teaching science and woodworking at the Brearley School, chamber music colleagues convinced her to take up viola. A woodcarver since childhood, Hutchins, at age 35, decided to make a viola. Hutchins then studied luthiery with Karl A. Berger (1949–59) and Stradivari expert FERNANDO SACCONI (1960–3). While she and Harvard physicist Frederick A. Saunders performed more than 100 acoustical experiments (1949–63), Hutchins taught herself acoustical physics by making string instruments. In 1963 Hutchins and colleagues Robert Fryxell and John Schelleng founded the Catgut Acoustical Society. She published the CAS journal for more than 30 years, helping bridge the gap between violin makers and acoustical physicists. Hutchins made more than 500 instruments, authored more than 100 technical papers on violin acoustics, and edited *Musical Acoustics, Part I & II, of the Benchmark Papers in Acoustics, 1975, 1976,* and the definitive collection *Research Papers in Violin Acoustics, 1975–1993.* Hutchins developed two electronic testing techniques used by most luthiers today—"free plate tuning" for violin plates using Chladni patterns, and "mode tuning" for finished instruments. Both techniques provide invaluable measurable parameters to augment and qualify traditional violin making techniques. Hutchins is also acclaimed for creating the new violin family, the violin octet—an acoustically matched consort of eight violins that span the tonal range of a piano, ranging in size from an 11-inch treble violin to a 7-foot contrabass violin.

The pioneering Hutchins, a lone female in the male-dominated fields of acoustical physics and violin making, persisted through much criticism from her peers for "demystifying" the art and "magic" of violin making by bringing science into the workshop. She also challenged conventional wisdom of the violin world that claimed an "old" violin was always better than a contemporary one, which furthermore suggested that violin value could be based upon acoustics rather than labels or provenance. A two-time Guggenheim Fellow (1959, 1961) and Martha Baird Rockefeller Fund for Music Grantee (1966, 1968), Hutchins was awarded numerous honorary degrees, including the 1981 Acoustical Society of America Silver Medal, the first award given by the society in Musical Acoustics. In 1998 Hutchins received the ASA Honorary Fellowship Award, the first and only female of 14 recipients in 69 years. It is commonly acknowledged by many in the field of violin making and violin acoustics that the application of new scientific data, knowledge, and techniques to the task of violin making—pioneered and spearheaded by Carleen Hutchins–has provided luthiers unprecedented opportunities to usher in a new "Golden Age" of violin making.

BIBLIOGRAPHY

P. Hormick: "Eight Is Enough," *Strings*, xix/6 (2006), 47–51

Obituary, *New York Times* (8 Aug 2009)

D. QUINCY WHITNEY

Hutchinson. Family of singers, active from 1840 to the 1880s, who were among the most widely known American musicians of the era. The 13 children of Jesse and Mary Leavitt Hutchinson of Milford, New Hampshire, were acclaimed locally as fine musicians. Such was their reputation that when they presented a family concert of sacred and secular pieces at the Milford Baptist Meeting House on November 7, 1840, it was well and enthusiastically attended. Shortly after, several of the younger brothers moved to Lynn, Massachusetts, and continued singing together. By the autumn of 1841, Judson (*b* Milford, NH, 14 March 1817; *d* Lynn, 10 Jan 1859), John (*b* Milford, NH, 4 Jan 1821; *d* Lynn, 29 Oct 1908), and Asa (*b* Milford, NH, 14 March 1823; *d* Hutchinson, MN, 25 Nov 1884) had formed the Aeolian Vocalists, in emulation of the successful Rainer Family, and set out on a short tour of towns and villages near Milford. After their measured success, the boys added to the group their youngest sister Abby (*b* Milford, NH, 29 Aug 1829; *d* New York, NY, 24 Nov 1892), and on January 19, 1842, they began a month-long tour of coastal cities in Massachusetts, New Hampshire, and Maine. By July of that year the quartet was committed to a professional touring career, and traveled from New Hampshire through Vermont to New York, where they began to build a reputation and receive favorable notice. After returning briefly to Lynn, the newly named Hutchinson Family Singers gave its first performance, in Boston on September 13, 1842, to unqualified approbation. Appearances throughout New England that autumn and winter were to full houses; the success they enjoyed at their debut in New York in May 1843 sealed their reputation. The Hutchinsons during this time were wildly popular and among the most influential popular music performers in the United States; soon singing quartets and similar ensembles emerged throughout the nation in emulation of the Hutchinsons. In August 1845 the troupe left for a year-long tour of the British Isles, and attracted large, enthusiastic audiences much in the way they had in the United States; while there they were commended by Charles Dickens, William Macready, Edwin Forrest, Charlotte Cushman, Harriet Martineau, Mary Howitt, and other important cultural and political figures. The popularity of the Hutchinsons remained high throughout the 1840s, and they often appeared before thousands in concert.

Early in 1843 the Hutchinsons began appearing at anti-slavery meetings and temperance conventions. They were at first careful not to identify themselves too closely with the positions adopted at these meetings, doubtless so as not to alienate the large portions of their audience who were pro-slavery. But after spirited debate among themselves, they publicly endorsed the movements and their tenets. The Hutchinsons were long drawn to current radical social and political positions—utopian experiments in communal living, women's rights, dress reform, health reform, universal suffrage—and regularly sang about them. They thus gave early and powerful expression to streams of political activism that continue to this day to permeate American vernacular musics.

With Abby's marriage in 1849 and her decision to retire from touring, the constitution of the group changed. The brothers first formed a trio, but without the foil that Abby provided, the group never regained its former renown. Moreover, contentions between the brothers frequently boiled over. Jesse Hutchinson Jr. (*b* Milford, 29 Sept 1813; *d* Cincinnati, OH, 15 May 1853), who had managed the quartet from the start, left the family troupe in 1851 to manage a rival group, the ALLEGHANIANS. Soon various other combinations of family, relatives, and friends, now often identified as "tribes" of members of the original Hutchinson Family Singers, continued to tour the country for several more decades. Asa, who with the other brothers had founded Hutchinson, Minnesota, in 1855, went to live there, and he and his own family toured extensively throughout the American West. John settled in Lynn, from where his "tribe" made annual tours well into the 1880s; he claimed to have given more than 12,000 concerts during his career. Judson also performed with his family. Abby, constrained by social inhibitions about the public roles of married women, sang only occasionally. Although the name of the Hutchinson Family ensured an audience for several decades to come, the days of such widespread and enthusiastic national interest were over by the 1850s.

Many of the pieces in the Hutchinsons' early repertory were glees. They were often taken from popular music books of the day, such as *The Orphean Lyre* or *The Social Choir*, and from the published songs of the Rainer Family; the solo songs and ballads that they sang were written by popular contemporary composers such as Henry Russell. As time went on the singers increasingly favored music with American themes. Their early concerts were given with the instrumental support of Judson's and John's violins and Asa's cello; later John played harmonium and Abby occasionally guitar. They concentrated on producing a close, "sweet" blend of voices, and placed great emphasis on a "natural" (uncultivated) tone and perfect intonation, all of which was reinforced by an informal stage manner. The Hutchinson Family introduced these characteristics into the mainstream of popular music, where they remained central to the genre until the mid-20th century.

The reputation of the Hutchinson Family Singers was built largely on the performance of the works of others. By the mid-1840s, however, a number of songs written by members of the group had been published. Almost all this music was reworked from existing melodies, with new texts and arrangements. A famous example is the group's signature song, "The Old Granite State" (1843), which sets a text by Jesse to the Millerite hymn "Old Church Yard"; another is the anti-slavery anthem "Get off the track" (1844), which ironically used as its tune "Old Dan Tucker," the blackface minstrel song by DAN EMMETT, set to another text by Jesse. Abby, who composed nothing while a member of the quartet, ultimately became the most successful writer, and was known particularly for her arrangements of black spirituals, such as her "Kind words can never die" (1855), and her setting of Tennyson's "Ring out, Wild Bells" (1891).

There are collections of the Hutchinsons' papers and music in the Wadleigh Public Library, Milford, New Hampshire; the McLeod County Historical Society, Hutchinson, Minnesota; the Minnesota Historical Society, St. Paul, Minnesota; and at Dartmouth College.

See also ABOLITION.

BIBLIOGRAPHY

A.B. Hutchinson: *The Book of Brothers, or History of the Hutchinson Family* (New York, 1852)

J. Hutchinson: *A Brief Narrative of the Hutchinson Family* (Boston, 1874)

J.W. Hutchinson: *Story of the Hutchinsons (Tribe of Jesse)* (Boston, 1896/R1977)

H. Nathan: "The Career of a Revival Hymn," *Southern Folklore Quarterly*, vii (1943), 89

P.D. Jordan: *Singin' Yankees* (Minneapolis, MN, 1946)

C. Brink: *Harps in the Wind: the Story of the Singing Hutchinsons* (New York, 1947/R1980)

C. Moseley: "The Hutchinson Family: the Function of Their Song in Ante-bellum America," *Journal of American Culture*, i (1978), 713

C. Hamm and J. Morris: *There's a Good Time Coming: Songs by the Hutchinson Family* (Smithsonian Collection N020, 1979) [liner notes]

D. Cockrell: *Excelsior!: Journals of the Hutchinson Family Singers, 1842–1846* (Stuyvesant, N.Y., 1987)

S. Gac: *Singing for Freedom: the Hutchinson Family Singers and the Nineteenth-Century Culture of Reform* (New Haven, 2007)

DALE COCKRELL

Hutchinson, Brenda (*b* Trenton, NY, 15 June 1954). Composer. She studied under PAULINE OLIVEROS, ROGER REYNOLDS, BERNARD RANDS, and ROBERT ERICKSON at the University of California, San Diego (MM 1979), and received additional instruction in electronic and computer music from JOHN M. CHOWNING and ALLEN STRANGE. She has served as artist-in-residence at the Exploratorium in San Francisco; at Mills College in Oakland, California; and at Harvestworks, New York, and has worked as an engineer and adviser on a series of recordings for Harvestworks-Tellus. Hutchinson became interested in sound and electronics from an early age. Her principal artistic interest is based on the cultivation and encouragement of openness in her own life and in those she works with. Hutchinson encourages participants to experiment with sound, share stories, and make music. She also improvises on a Long Tube, a 9½-foot tube with a gestural interface she designed, and has been working with an assistive device she designed—a sound initiated drawing interface—to work with memory and cognitive impairment.

WORKS
(selective list)

Long Tube: Star Strangled Banner, 2001; Solos with gestural interface and MAX/MSP, 1999– ongoing; Vorticella, 1997– ongoing

Concert: Every Dream Has Its Number, 1996; How Do You Get To Carnegie Hall?, any number of pf, 1998; Radio: Violet Flame, 1993;

Every Dream Has Its Number, 1996; All Roads: How Do You Get To Carnegie Hall? 2000; New Violet Flame, 2002

Interactive/Invitational Performances: How Do You Get To Carnegie Hall? 1996; Vagabond Vaudeville, 2000; Fun Show, 2006; Thebellproject, 2006; Tiny Offerings, 2010

SoundTracks: collab. A. Chamberlain. Developed sound initiated drawing program to create both drawings on paper and animated line drawings with sound. Created to work with people with severe memory impairment.

Installations: Everyone was a Captain, mixed media, Staten Island, NY, 1992; Listen for a Change, installation and radio series, San Francisco, 1992; Norris, elevator shaftway installation, New York, 1992; Giant Music Box, interactive exhibit, San Francisco, 1992; Whistling Walls and Windows, mixed media, San Francisco, 1994; collab. M. Olexo

Concert pieces: (el-ac): Fly Away All (op, T. Shank), solo vv, mime, sampler, 1987–8, MN, 1988; A Grandmother's Song, 1v, pre-rec. stories, ambiences, 1979; Apple Etudes, 1v, pre-rec. stories, ambiences, 1982; Liquid Sky (film score, dir. S. Tsukerman), elecs, 1982; collab. C. Smith; Joy Chorus, female chorus, sampler, 1988 [from Fly Away All]; EEEYAH!, 1v, bass drum, bell, tape, 1989; Voices of Reason, Giant Music Box, elecs, pre-rec. stories, 1991; Long Tube Trio, vv, long tubes, 1993; Every Dream Has Its Number, live elecs, pre-rec. stories, 1996; How Do You Get To Carnegie Hall?, pf, pre-rec. stories, 1998

Principal recording company: Tellus, Deep Listening, Frog Peak

BIBLIOGRAPHY

B. Hutchinson: "Don't Stop the Music," *Exporatorium Quarterly*, x/4 (1986), 2–7

L. Wendt: "Vocal Neighborhoods: a Walk through the Post-Sound Poetry Landscape," *Leonardo Music Journal*, iii (1993), 65–71

C. Boone: "Vanguard Composers in San Francisco," *P-form Magazine*, xxxiii (1994), 20–2

K. Gann: "Totalism and the 1990s," *American Music in the Twentieth Century* (New York, 1997), 352–86

E. Hinkle-Turner: *Crossing the Line: Women Composers and Music Technology in the United States* (Burlington, VT, 2006)

L. Chernosky: *Ethnographic Experimentalism: the Politics of Representation in Brenda Hutchinson's Music* (diss., Columbia University, 2008)

ELIZABETH HINKLE-TURNER

Hutton, Ina Ray [Cowan, Odessa] (*b* Chicago, IL, 13 March 1916; *d* Ventura, CA, 19 Feb 1984). Singer and bandleader. Born Odessa Cowan, she began singing and dancing professionally as a child. In the early 1930s she appeared in shows, including Ziegfeld's *Follies of 1934*. In late 1934 she signed with Irving Mills to lead an all-female orchestra that became known as Ina Ray Hutton and her Melodears. Dressed in glamorous gowns, she danced as she conducted the 15-piece group of excellent musicians. The band found commercial success, making recordings for Okeh, Victor, Brunswick, and Vocalion and appearing in several short films and the feature *The Big Broadcast of 1937*. Hutton led two more all-female bands and one all-male group in the late 1930s and 40s. A television pioneer, she hosted "The Ina Ray Hutton Show," which ran for four years on WKLA (Los Angeles), beginning in 1952. She then formed another all-female band (1954) and appeared in the film *Girl Time* (1955). After leading a five-piece male group in the 1960s, she ceased performing. Billed alternately as the "Queen of the Name Bands" and the "Blonde Bombshell of Rhythm," Hutton is credited with popularizing the all-female band format, which was adopted by the International Sweethearts of Rhythm, among other groups.

BIBLIOGRAPHY

S. Placksin: *American Women in Jazz, 1900 to the Present: their Words, Lives, and Music* (New York, 1982)

L. Dahl: *Stormy Weather* (New York, 1984)

Obituary, *Los Angeles Times* (21 Feb 1984)

Leo Walker: *The Big Band Almanac* (New York, 1989)

GAYLE MURCHISON

Hutton, J. Warren (*b* Little Rock, AR, 10 Dec 1928; *d* Philadelphia, PA, 1 July 2002). Organist and teacher. He began organ and piano studies with John H. Summer in Little Rock. He received his BMus at Oberlin Conservatory of Music (1950), studying with Arthur Poister and Fenner Douglass, continued his work with Poister at Syracuse University, New York, receiving an MMus (1951), and later studied with various American and European organists. He taught organ at Peabody College, Nashville, Tennessee (1951–4), at Scarritt College, Nashville (1951–2), and at the University of Alabama, Tuscaloosa (1954–96), continuing there as adjunct professor until his death. He was organist and choir director at University Presbyterian Church, Tuscaloosa (1966–2002) and Regional Councillor for Region IV of the American Guild of Organists. He died while attending a National Convention of the AGO. He was one of the most influential post-World War II organ teachers and performers, as attested to by the notable accomplishments of many of his students. The quality of many new organs is a result of his work as a consultant in organ design. The University of Alabama conferred the Fine Arts Award posthumously for his significant impact on the creative and performing arts.

BIBLIOGRAPHY

"Getting to Know Your Council Members," *American Organist*, xxxi/12 (1997), 10 only

"J. Warren Hutton," *American Organist*, xxxvi/10 (2002), 48–9 [obituary]

JUDI CALDWELL

Huybrechts, François (*b* Antwerp, Belgium, 15 June 1946). Belgian conductor. At age nine he entered the Antwerp Conservatory where he studied cello and clarinet. He made his professional debut as a cellist at age 14 and gained an early reputation as a chamber music player on radio and television broadcasts. He studied conducting first with Daniel Sternefelt and subsequently with Jacques Pernoo, Hans Swarowsky, and Bruno Maderna. At age 17 he made his conducting debut with the Royal Flemish Opera. During the 1967 season he conducted at the Salzburg Mozarteum. Huybrechts won the 1968 Dimitri Mitropoulos Competition in New York, which resulted in his appointment as Leonard Bernstein's assistant with the New York Philharmonic and guest appearances with the Los Angeles and Berlin POs. In 1969 he was a prizewinner in the Herbert von Karajan Foundation competition, and in 1970 he became George Szell's assistant with the Cleveland Orchestra. He was music director and principal conductor of the Wichita Symphony Orchestra (1972–7) and from 1978 to 1980 of the San Antonio SO. He has recorded Leoš Janáček's *6 Lachian Dances* with the London PO.

Principal recording companies: Decca, London

ROBERT PAUL KOLT

Hwang, David Henry (*b* Los Angeles, CA, 11 Aug 1957). Playwright. Hwang is known as the pre-eminent Asian American playwright in the United States. His plays often combine humor, pathos, and a sense of awe at ancient rituals. His early works focus on Chinese American experiences. His first success, the Obie Award-winning *FOB* (1980), depicts the conflicts between an American-born young man of Chinese descent and newly arrived Chinese immigrants. One of his best known works is *M. Butterfly* (1988), a play for which he won a Tony Award and a Pulitzer Prize for Drama. It is loosely based on a news report of a relationship between a French diplomat and a male Chinese opera singer. Hwang co-wrote the books for the musicals *Aida* (2000) and *Tarzan* (2006), rewrote the book for a revival of *Flower Drum Song* (2002), and provided the librettos for Philip Glass's works *1000 Airplanes on the Roof* (1988), *The Voyage* (1992), and *The Sound of a Voice* (2004). His collaboration with the Korean composer Unsuk Chin, *Alice in Wonderland* (2007), was hailed as World Premiere of the Year by *Opernwelt* in 2007.

BIBLIOGRAPHY

L.J. Trudeau: *Asian American Literature: Reviews and Criticism of Works by American Writers of Asian Descent* (Detroit, 1999)

HSUN LIN

Hwang, Jason Kao (*b* Lake Forest, IL, 1957). Jazz violinist and composer. Known for his unconventional violin technique, Hwang participated in downtown New York's free jazz scene in the late 1970s and early 80s and became increasingly associated with Asian American jazz in the 1980s and 90s. His more recent work emphasizes cross-cultural themes, especially as they relate to the Chinese experience in the United States.

Hwang spent his childhood in Waukegan and Highland Park, Illinois, before attending New York University. In New York he frequented "loft jazz" performances, which featured experimental players such as David Murray, Lester Bowie, Charles "Bobo" Shaw, and Frank Lowe. Hwang was mentored by alto saxophonist Will Connell Jr. who had come to New York after his tenure with Horace Tapscott's Pan Afrikan Peoples Arkestra in Los Angeles. Hwang and Connell Jr. teamed with bassist William Parker and percussionist Takeshi Zen Matsuura to form the quartet Commitment. Commitment achieved modest local success, toured Germany, and recorded a self-titled album in 1981 which was released on Hwang's own Flying Panda label.

Hwang's ensemble The Far East Side Band, featuring violin, taiko, kayagum, and tuba, released two CDs of his compositions, *Urban Archaeology* (1996) and *Caverns* (1994). He has also collaborated on a chamber opera, *The Floating Box: A Story in Chinatown* (2005). In addition to leading his own groups and writing music for staged works, Hwang has performed and recorded with a number of players, including Anthony Braxton, Henry Threadgill, Butch Morris, and Reggie Workman.

LOREN KAJIKAWA

H. Wiley Hitchcock Institute for Studies in American Music. American music research institute. Founded in 1971 as The Institute for Studies in American Music, the Institute was renamed in 2008 to honor its founding director. It is a research center at Brooklyn College, CUNY, New York, and is also affiliated with CUNY's Graduate Center. As Hitchcock stated, the Institute was established "to provide a suitable academic framework in which to encourage, support, propagate, and evaluate research projects in American music." Hitchcock led the Institute until his retirement in 1993; during this time the center also functioned as the world headquarters of the Charles Ives Society. The Institute has been directed by Carol J. Oja (1993–7), Ellie M. Hisama (1997–2005), and Jeffrey Taylor (2007–present). Hitchcock's extensive files at the Institute and materials related to Henry Cowell were bequeathed to the Performing Arts Division of the New York Public Library upon his death in December 2007.

Although the Institute houses a diverse library and maintains files on composers, musicians, and events, it is not an archive. Rather, it disseminates information about American music through publications, lectures, symposia, and concerts. The Institute's primary publication is the biannual *American Music Review* (formerly *The Institute for Studies in American Music Newsletter*), which contains articles by leading scholars, as well as book, recording, and multimedia reviews, and information about American music events. The Institute also publishes a series of monographs by such prominent figures as Gilbert Chase, Richard Crawford, Charles Hamm, Vivian Perlis, and many others. More recently the Institute has produced *Island Sounds in the Global City: Caribbean Popular Music and Identity in New York* (edited by Ray Allen and Lois Wilcken, 1998), *Behind the Beat: Jazz Criticism* by Mark Tucker (edited by Jeffrey Taylor and Ray Allen, 2003), and *Critical Minded: New Approaches to Hip Hop Studies* (edited by Ellie Hisama and Evan Rapport, 2005).

The Institute's first public event, in 1972, was devoted to ragtime, and in 1974, with the Yale School of Music, it held the first international conference on an American composer, the Charles Ives Centennial Festival-Conference. The centennial celebration of Edison's invention of his phonograph in 1977 featured a performance of John Cage's *33–1/3* for turntable, written specifically for the event. The Institute provided research and editorial assistance for the first edition of *The New Grove Dictionary of American Music and Musicians*, of which Hitchcock was co-editor. The 1990s saw conferences on Amy Beach, contemporary American opera composers, Caribbean traditions, Henry Cowell, and George Gershwin. In the following decade the Institute produced conferences devoted to composer and folklorist Ruth Crawford Seeger, calypso music in Brooklyn, and the folk music revival. It also inaugurated a yearly lecture series, "Music in Polycultural America," on a wide variety of American musics. In the early 21st century the Institute developed a strong interest in Brooklyn's jazz and ethnic music traditions, partnering with the Central Brooklyn Jazz Consortium and the Brooklyn Arts Council to produce events highlighting the borough's diverse music cultures.

BIBLIOGRAPHY
H.W. Hitchcock: "Report from Brooklyn College: the Institute for Studies in American Music," *CMc*, xviii (1974), 37–40
C. Oja, R. Crawford, et al.: "The Institute for Studies in American Music Newsletter: a commemorative Issue in Honor of H. Wiley Hitchcock," *American Music Review* xxxvii/2 (Spring 2008)

JEFFREY TAYLOR

Hybridity. A concept for describing musical mixtures that are explicitly enmeshed in identity politics, most often involving racial and ethnic identity, and its effects on culture. As a concept, scholars and critics began using hybridity in music during the late 1980s and early 1990s as postcolonial and critical race theory expanded in influence in North American music scholarship. Previously, "hybrid" referred to mixture involving genre or form.

Early accounts pitted discourses of hybridity in music against authenticity, or musical purity, and multiculturalism (Gilroy, 1993; Lipsitz, 1997). This was especially the case for musicians who preferred to mix disparate genres from far-flung geographic locations, or for world music musicians who collaborated with pop musicians from the United States or Europe (Taylor, 1997). For example, the collaborations that formed the heart of Ry Cooder's Cuban project were just as entangled with discourses of hybridity and authenticity as were Sérgio Mendes's expressions of Brazilianness in the 1990s and 2000s. For the case of diasporic groups, theorizing hybridity in music provided scholars with a key to understanding political strategies and articulations of the ambiguity of simultaneously feeling connected to more than one place. Some scholars criticized world music and ethnic music hybrids in electronic dance music due to concerns that the producers were replicating colonial power imbalances through appropriation (Hutnyk, 2000). By the late 1990s hybridity had so much traction among music critics that many of them privileged recordings featuring an aggressive mixture of genres as authentic musical expressions, further demonstrating how confused and entangled the two seemingly-opposed concepts had become (Frith, 2000; Taylor, 2007).

Theorizations of hybridity in music emphasize the liminality, or doubleness, of mixing musical genres in identity formation. These hybrids express the negotiations diasporic groups often face as they balance pressures to assimilate with embodied desires to express ethnic or racial pride among audiences (Maira, 2002; Madrid, 2008). Theorizing hybrid music among immigrant communities has gained extended traction in recent years, especially for analyzing music among Latinos in the United States. This is due, in part, to a separate theorization of hybridity from Latin American cultural studies that draws from differing notions of modernity (García Canclini, 1995), the prominence of the border in Latin American cultural expressions, and the legacy of racial mixing (*metissage, mestizaje, mestiçagem*) throughout the Americas. Pacini Hernandez (2010) theorized hybridity to be central to Latino popular musical expressions, due to the ways in which they take place at the center of multiple intersections of race, ethnicity, and culture. By using hybridity to describe the crossroads of culture at the heart of Latino popular music, these scholars can extend our understanding of musical expressions and identifications as they relate to transnational modes of musical expression. For example, Pacini Hernández cites the circulation of *cumbia* between Colombia, Mexico, and the United States, and back again to South America through networks of DJs and dancers. This example of hybridity exemplifies the refusal of "either/or" dichotomies that often characterize the debates surrounding American music.

BIBLIOGRAPHY

P. Gilroy: *The Black Atlantic: Modernity and Double Consciousness* (Cambridge, MA, 1993)

G. Lipsitz: *Dangerous Crossroads: Popular Music, Postmodernism, and the Poetics of Place* (London, 1994)

N. García Canclini: *Hybrid Cultures: Strategies for Entering and Leaving Modernity* (Minneapolis, MN, 1995)

T.D. Taylor: *Global Pop: World Music, World Markets* (New York, 1997)

S. Frith: "The Discourse of World Music," *Western Music and Its Others: Difference, Representation, and Appropriation,* eds. G. Born and D. Hesmondhalgh (Berkeley, CA, 2000)

J. Hutnyk: *Critique of Exotica: Music, Politics, and the Culture Industry* (London, 2000)

S. Maira: *Desis in the House: Indian American Youth in New York City* (Philadelphia, 2002)

T.D. Taylor: *Beyond Exoticism: Western Music and the World* (Durham, NC, 2007)

A.L. Madrid: *Nor-Tec Rifa! Electronic Dance Music from Tijuana to the World* (New York, 2008)

D. Pacini Hernández: *Oye Como Va! Hybridity and Identity in Latino Popular Music* (Philadelphia, 2010)

KARIANN GOLDSCHMITT

Hyers Sisters. Vocal duo. The group comprised soprano Anna Madah (*b* New York?, NY, 1855; *d* ?1920s) and alto/tenor Emma Louise (*b* Sacramento, CA, 1857; *d* by 1901). Born to Samuel B. and Annie E. Hyers, the musically precocious sisters soon abandoned their parents' musical tutelage for private study with German music teacher Hugo Sank (vocalization, piano) and opera singer Josephine D'Ormy (Italian and German, enunciation, intonation, stage presence). Shortly after their debut at the ages of 12 and 10 at the Metropolitan Theatre in Sacramento, the parents separated, and their father Samuel managed their careers.

From 1867 to 1876 the sisters devoted themselves to concerts of operatic excerpts, art songs, popular ballads, and, from 1872, spirituals. Arriving in New York in 1871 after a cross-country tour, Samuel formed a concert company around his daughters, engaging tenor Wallace King, baritone John Luca, violinist John Thomas Douglass, and pianist Alexander C. Taylor. Myriad favorable reviews praised Anna's range and suppleness, Emma's power, and the sisters' well-cultured refinement.

In 1876 the Hyers Sisters turned to musical theater, creating three productions that toured nationwide until the 1890s: Joseph Bradford's *Out of Bondage* (originally titled *Out of the Wilderness*, 1876), E.S. Getchell's

Urlina, the African Princess (1879), and *Uncle Tom's Cabin* (1880). The troupe rendered the earnest narratives of these plays in the manner of comic opera, offering a mélange of minstrel-style comedy, improvisations, jubilee and parlor songs, and dance. In *Out of Bondage* Emma's comedic talents had free rein in the character of Kaloolah, a mischievous field hand, whereas Anna portrayed the demure Narcisse, a house servant. *Urlina,* with Anna as the princess and Emma as the prince, is thought to be the earliest black musical play with an African setting. The Hyerses' production of *Uncle Tom's Cabin* featured the first fully interracial cast (African Americans playing black characters, whites playing white characters), with Emma as Topsy and Anna as Eliza. The sisters also performed in *Peculiar Sam; or The Underground Railroad*, written by Pauline Hopkins and staged by Hopkins' Colored Troubadours (Boston, 1880).

In 1883 Samuel married a much younger woman, and his daughters left their father's management, resulting in two Hyers troupes: the S.B. Hyers Colored Musical Comedy Company (featuring May Hyers, Samuel's new wife) and the Hyers Sisters Combination. The sisters began supplementing their concerts and musical plays with specialty performances for other organizations. These included Callender's Colored Minstrels (1883), Donavin's Famous Tennessee Singers (1886), McCabe and Young's Genuine Darky Minstrels (1892), and Isham's Octoroons (1896). By 1901 Emma had died; in 1902 Anna withdrew from Williams and Walker's *In Dahomey* and retired to Sacramento.

The Hyers Sisters were unique among postbellum African American artists in that they sustained long careers that did not depend for success upon race-based music. Their musical plays laid a foundation for the flowering of African American musical theater at the turn of the century, and provided some of the most preeminent entertainers of the time, including Sam Lucas, Billy Kersands, James Bland, and Wallace King, a respite from the demeaning limitations of minstrelsy.

BIBLIOGRAPHY

J.M. Trotter: *Music and Some Highly Musical People* (Boston, 1878)

E. Southern: "An Early Black Concert Company: the Hyers Sisters Combination," *A Celebration of American Music,* R. Crawford and others eds. (Ann Arbor, MI, 1990), 17–35

E. Hill: "The Hyers Sisters: Pioneers in Black Musical Comedy," *The American Stage: Social and Economic Issues from the Colonial Period to the Present,* ed. R. Engle and T.L. Miller (New York, 1993), 115–30

E. Southern, ed.: *African American Theater: Out of Bondage (1876) and Peculiar Sam; or, The Underground Railroad (1879)* (New York, 1994)

E. Southern: *Music of Black Americans,* 3rd ed. (New York, 1997)

E. Hill and J.V. Hatch: *A History of African American Theatre* (Cambridge, UK, 2003)

SANDRA JEAN GRAHAM

Hykes, David (Bond) (*b* Taos, NM, 2 March 1953). Composer, singer, and teacher. He studied filmmaking, music, and Buddhism at Antioch College, Yellow Springs, Ohio (1970–4), and arts administration at Columbia University (MFA 1984). He lived in New York from 1974 until 1987 when he moved to France. From

1975 to 1977 he studied classical Azerbaijani and Armenian music on the *tār* with Zevulon Avshalomov, and in 1982 became a pupil of Smt. Sheila Dhar, studying North Indian *raga* singing. In 1975 Hykes founded his first group, David Hykes and The Harmonic Choir, an international ensemble of five to ten singers and musicians with whom he developed his own musical language, Harmonic Chant, which combines just intonation modal principles, specific overtone and undertone practices, polyphony, sacred texts and mantra, polyrhythm, and other highly evolved techniques that explore the co-presence of fundamentals and harmonics. For the strongly resonated upper partials and subharmonic low tones his singers produce, he was at first inspired by techniques he borrowed and evolved from Tibetan Chant, the Höömii (throat) singing of Mongolia, and Tuvan folk music. Equally present in his music is an orientation toward just intonation and microtonal, inspired by the music of La Monte Young, Terry Riley, and Tony Conrad. Unprecedented and of a haunting beauty, Hykes's often wordless, partly improvised, contemplative music was received enthusiastically, mixed with amazement that the human voice can produce so wide and varied a spectrum of sound.

From 1979 to 1989 Hykes and the Harmonic Choir were in residence at the Cathedral of St. John the Divine, New York, and he and his groups continue to tour worldwide. Hykes established the Harmonic Presence Foundation, a center for contemplative retreats, seminars, and research in Autainville (Loir-et-Cher), France. In 1981 he studied in Mongolia, and in 1985–90 he participated in a number of collaborative events with His Holiness the Dalai Lama (on the day the latter received the Nobel Peace Prize) and the Gyuto Monks. He continues to offer his music at numerous Tibetan Buddhist events.

Hykes has released 12 albums of his music, and has composed a significant body of film music, particularly for "sacred cinema" films including *Meetings with Remarkable Men, Travelers and Magicians, Journey into Buddhism*, and *Baraka*. His first album, *Hearing Solar Winds*, remains the most popular chant/"throat-singing" album of all time. That album, as well as *Harmonic Meetings*, which explores the congruent harmonies of the sacred words of Christianity, Islam, and Judaism, was recorded in the extraordinary acoustics of Le Thoronet Abbey in southern France. *Windhorse Riders, Let the Lover Be*, and *True to the Times* (1989–93), featuring collaborations with the percussion virtuosos Djamchid Chemirani (Iran) and Zameer Ahmed (India), inaugurated the exploration of solo vocal performance (often using poetic and mystic texts by Rumi and other Sufi poets) that integrates an often impassioned, highly ornamented performance style influenced by his immersion in the musics of India and the Near East. *Earth to the Unknown Power* (1996) marked a return to Hykes's earlier balance of solo voice and chorus, as do his recent recordings *Breath of the Heart, Harmonic Worlds* (2007) and *Harmonic Mantra* (2011). His combined interests in music, neuroscience, healing, and meditation led to his work with the Mind and Life Institute, co-founded by

His Holiness the Dalai Lama and the late neuroscientist Francisco Varela. The organization brings together neuroscientists and other practitioners to study the effects of contemplative practice, including music, on cognitive function, health, and well-being. Hykes served on the faculty of the institute where he presented his Harmonic Presence system, combining music and meditation.

His recordings, accompanying writings, and a large unpublished archive of music and seminar recordings constitute the primary documentation of his music. He has been awarded grants by the NEA, the Rockefeller Foundation, UNESCO, New York State Council on the Arts, the Asian Cultural Council, the Edwards Art Fund, and the Threshold Foundation, among others.

WORKS
(selective list†works as recordings)

Harmonic Tissues, sine waves, 1971; Looking for Gold/Life in the Sun, children's vv, harmonizer, metal detector, 1975; Test Studies for Harmonic Orch, dulcimer, santur, cimbalom, sāz, tār, bagpipes, ẓarb, daff, 1975–; Hearing Solar Winds, vv, 1977–83†; Outside of Being There, vv, 1981; One Up, One Down, 2 solo vv, svarpeṭī, 1982; Subject to Change, 1v, drones, 1983; Current Circulation, vv, 1983–4†; Harmonic Meetings, 8 pieces, vv, tānpura, 1986†; Windhorse Riders, 9 pieces, 1v, ẓarb, tablā, tānpura, elecs, 1989†; Let the Lover Be, 5 pieces, v, zither, ẓarb, sūrpeṭī, elecs, 1991†; True to the Times (How to Be?), 7 pieces, 1v, dobro, oud, windhp, tablā, ẓarb, org, elecs, 1993†; Earth to the Unknown Power, 4 pieces, vv, accdn, ẓarb, tānpura, 1996†; Breath of the Heart, 4 pieces, vv, ney, Turkish tanbur, ẓarb, daff, 1997†; Rainbow Dances, 7 pieces, vv, perc, elecs, 2000†; Harmonic Meditations, 10 pieces, vv, zither, table, elecs, 2005†; Harmonic Worlds, 7 pieces, vv, table, perc, zither, 2007†; Harmonic Mantra, 6 pieces, vv, perc, didjeridu, elecs, 2011†; Meditations: Music from the Heart of the Cosmos, 2011†; Spheres of Harmonic Meeting, 2011†; film scores, music for television

Principal publisher: Harmonic Arts Society

Principal recording companies: Harmonic Presence, Ocora, Celestial Harmonies, New Albion, Auvidis, Catalyst, Fønix Musik

BIBLIOGRAPHY

N. Kenyon: "Tuning the Skies," *New Yorker* (2 Aug 1982)

J. Reinhard: "An Interview with David Hykes," *Ear Magazine East*, vii/5 (1982–3), 22 only

R. Palmer: "Get Ready for the Music of Harmonics," *New York Times* (17 July 1983)

J. Schaefer: *New Sounds: a Listener's Guide to New Music* (New York, 1987), 224–9

D. Hykes: "Harmonic Chant—Global Sacred Music," *Music: Physician for Times to Come*, ed. D. Campbell (Wheaton, IL, 1991), 55–69

DOUGLAS LEEDY/SARAH EYERLY

Hyla, Lee (Leon Joseph) (*b* Niagara Falls, NY, 31 Aug 1952). Composer. After graduating from the New England Conservatory (BMus 1975), he studied at SUNY, Stony Brook (MA 1978). In 1992 he returned to the New England Conservatory to teach. He is currently the Wyatt Chair of Music Composition at Northwestern University's Bienen School of Music. His numerous fellowships and honors include the Stoeger Prize from the Chamber Music Society of Lincoln Center, the Prix de Rome, grants from the Fromm and Koussevitzky Foundations, and a Guggenheim Fellowship. His music finds common ground between the postwar American expressionism of Stefan Wolpe and Elliott Carter and the avant-garde jazz style of musicians such as Cecil Taylor, also integrating aspects of rock music, especially punk. Despite their high energy and raw surface, his works are fully notated. A meticulous attention to pitch organization and dramatic structure allows raucousness to achieve elegance.

Among Hyla's works for chamber orchestra, *Pre-Pulse Suspended* (1984) marks the first thorough integration of the various elements of his musical style. In this pivotal work, the motivic treatment of short-breathed riffs develops a Beethovenian intensity. This rhythmic force enables Hyla to juxtapose music of contrasting tempo and affect. At the same time, a powerful sense of drama unfolds through an adroit manipulation of pedal points, presented either as fixed chords or as extended repeated notes. Hyla develops these techniques in the Concerto for Piano no.2 (1991) and *Trans* (1996). Hyla's chamber music is notable for three highly original string quartets and a sensitive setting of Allen Ginsberg's poem *Howl*.

Hyla's only use of electronics is his detailed and ingenious use of pre-recorded sound in *Wilson's Ivory-bill* (2000), in which a recording of this extinct woodpecker is integrated with piano and baritone voice in ways both humorous and affecting. Hyla's use of abrupt shifts in the manner of cinematic jump cuts is intensified in the 2007 *Polish Folk Songs,* which also extends his expressive palette in its use of folk materials, and the inclusion of organ and melodica in the chamber ensemble.

In Hyla's works for full orchestra, especially *Trans* and the Violin Concerto, his characteristic jump cuts and his short, frequently violent melodic figures are balanced by a shift of focus to the slower, strangely serene background layer. This shift of focus, perhaps motivated by the practicalities of writing for orchestra, has the additional effect of giving the music a greater sense of scope and power. In Hyla's recent focus on vocal works, especially *At Suma Beach* and *Lives of the Saints,* the texts reflect both the ecstasy and the violence of his instrumental music. This approach to vocal music places an emphasis on the dramatic rather than the lyric, and may suggest a move in the direction of opera for this evolving and compelling composer.

WORKS

Orch: Pf Conc. no.1, pf, chbr orch, 1974; Vn Conc., 1987; Cl Conc., b cl, chbr orch, 1988; Pf Conc. no.2, pf, chbr orch, 1991; Trans, 1996; Vn Conc., 2001; The Triadic Coast, 2005; Riff and Consequences, 2008

Chbr: White Man on Snowshoes, fl, a sax, vn, vc, 1973; Str Qt no.1, 1975; Amnesia, sextet, 1979; Str Trio, 1981; In Double Light, va, b cl, pf, perc, 1983; Pre-Pulse Suspended, 12 insts, 1984; Str Qt no.2, 1985; Anhinga, chbr ens, 1987; The Dream of Innocent III, vc, pf, perc, 1987; Amnesia Variance, cl, vn, va, vc, pf, hammered dulcimer, 1989; Str Qt no.3, 1989; Amnesia Breaks, ww qnt, 1990; Ciao, Manhattan, fl, va, vc, pf, 1990; We Speak Etruscan, b cl, bar sax, 1992; Howl, nar, str qt, 1993; Qt, bn, str trio, 1993; How Was Your Weekend, va, vc, 1994; Now Exclusively Cello, 16 vc, 1996; Str Qt no. 4, 1999; Amnesia Redux, vn, vc, pno, 2002; Amore Scaduto, vn, vc, 2004; Zurek, amplified chamb ens, 2004; Paradigm Lost, 4 sax, 2005; Field Guide, fl, cl, vn, va, vcl, pf, perc, 2006; Polish Folk Songs, cl, b cl, vn, va, vc, pf, perc, 2007; Warble (for Fenwick Smith), fl, pf, 2008; Mother Popcorn Revisited, vn, va, vc, 2009; Triptych, vc, perc, 2009; My Life on the Plains, chamb ens, 2010

Solo inst: For Tenor Sax, 1973; Bassius Ophelius, db, 1975; Revisible Light, pf, 1978; Pre-Amnesia, a sax, 1979; Mythic Birds of Saugerties, b cl, 1985; Basic Training, pf, 1994; Riff and Transfiguration, pf,

1997; Third Party, pf, 1998; Detour Ahead, db, 2003; Passagietta, vn, 2007; Message from Auvilliar, mar, 2011

Vocal: Wilson's Ivory-bill, bar, pf, field recording, 2000; Lives of the Saints (Pts I and II), mezzo, 8 instruments, 2000; At Suma Beach, mezzo, 6 instruments, 2003; Quarry, bar, va, 2004; House of Flowers, mezzo, b cl, pf, db, 2007

BIBLIOGRAPHY

S. Wheeler: "Beyond the Flat Surface: Form and Rhetoric in Machover, Hyla and Lindroth," *CMR*, x/1 (1994), 75–100

J. McCalla: *Twentieth-Century Chamber Music* (New York, 1996)

J. Eichler: "Controlled Chaos," Boston Globe (14 Jan 2007)

SCOTT WHEELER

Hyman, Dick [Richard Roven] (*b* New York, NY, 8 March 1927). Pianist and composer. After studying classical music at Columbia University (BA 1948), he became a versatile performer and composer active in jazz, classical music, ballet, musical comedy, popular music, and film music. He started playing bebop and traditional jazz styles in New York with Dizzy Gillespie, Charlie Parker, and Lester Young, among others. He also performed in Europe, recording with such musicians as Benny Goodman, Zoot Sims, and Roy Eldridge. During the 1950s he worked as a studio musician for NBC, led his own groups, and served as a sideman. He also developed a passion for early jazz and pre-jazz styles that led hm to play and record the music of Scott Joplin, Jelly Roll Morton, Fats Waller, and James P. Johnson. Of his more than 100 albums, several are unaccompanied piano works dedicated to key figures in American popular song, including Irving Berlin, Cole Porter, and George Gershwin. He has also played and recorded traditional jazz styles with Warren Vaché, Bob Wilber, Milt Hinton, Ruby Braff, Joe Venuti, Slam Stewart, and Ralph Sutton. As a composer Hyman has written music and arrangements for Count Basie, the Mills Brothers, Cozy Cole, and J.J. Johnson. He has also specialized in staging concerts and recordings dedicated to the many styles of African American piano music. In addition to his work as an author on music, he has served as the music director for a number of films by Woody Allen. He has received honorary doctorates from Hamilton College, Five Towns College, Wilkes University, and the University of South Florida.

BIBLIOGRAPHY

E. Cook: "Dick Hyman," *Ragtimer* (1985), July–Aug, 10

C. Defaa: *Inthe Mainstream: 18 Portraits in Jazz* (Metuchen, NJ, 1992), 311

W. Zinsser: "Doin' the Chameleon," *Atlantic Monthly*, cclxxvi/4 (1995), 98–108

S. Josephson: *Jazz Notes: Interviews across the Generations* (Santa Barbara, 2009)

LUCA CERCHIARI

Hyman, William (*b* New York, 18 Jan 1931; *d* New York, 11 June 1974). Harpsichord maker. He received organ instruction as a youth and was attracted to the harpsichord through a recital by Wanda Landowska. Basically self-taught, he became a master woodworker, decorator, and gilder; he was active as a harpsichord maker in Hoboken, New Jersey, from 1963 until his death. While serving with the US Signal Corps in Germany he studied antique harpsichords in museum collections, purchasing and bringing back a Neupert instrument. He also studied old craft books, his aim being not to copy early instruments but to assimilate their makers' techniques. With his wife Doris and, from 1972, a few apprentices he made about 25 harpsichords; they have been acknowledged for their extraordinarily full tone and light touch. In 1971 Hyman became adviser to David Way, who had recently taken over Zuckermann Harpsichords. After Hyman's death his workshop and apprentices moved to Stonington, Connecticut, where about 20 unfinished orders were completed by Way under the Hyman name.

BIBLIOGRAPHY

W.J. Zuckermann: *The Modern Harpsichord* (New York, 1969), 136ff
Obituary, *New York Times* (14 June 1974)
D. Way: "William Hyman," *Harpsichord*, viii/4 (1975–6), 15

MARIBEL MEISEL

Hymnody. A general term referring to hymns collectively and also to the singing of hymns. The term is used to denote words, music, or their combination. This article surveys hymns written for and sung by Christians in what is now the United States.

1. European inheritance. 2. Awakening and diversity. 3. New tunes and texts. 4. Shape notes. 5. Hymns of insiders. 6. Hymns of outsiders. 7. Hymns for Sunday schools and revivals. 8. Hymns for the unchurched. 9. Different directions. 10. Recent developments.

1. EUROPEAN INHERITANCE. For most of the early settlers and for succeeding generations, hymnody was metrical psalmody. (*See* PSALMS, METRICAL and PSALMODY.) Reformed groups who observed Calvin's strictures on congregational praise sang only versified psalms. Under his guidance these biblical songs had been translated into the vernacular, put in regular poetic meters, and set to tunes crafted for this use. A complete psalter (a book of Psalms in this form), *Pseaumes de David mis en rime-francoises*, was published in Geneva in 1562.

Two early accounts of Europeans in what is now the United States mention the singing of metrical Psalms. Huguenots in Florida in 1564 sang from the new Genevan psalter, and the songs were subsequently recalled by the Native Americans who had heard them. In 1579, Francis Drake and his company in California used Thomas Sternhold and John Hopkins's *The Whole Booke of Psalmes* (London, 1562), the authorized psalter of the Church of England, to similar effect.

In 1607 the Jamestown settlers brought with them the 1592 edition of this psalter, which included tunes collected by Thomas Este. The Pilgrims who arrived at Plymouth in 1620 brought *The Book of Psalmes: Englished both in Prose and Metre* (Amsterdam, 1612). This emblem of separatism had been prepared by Henry Ainsworth for radical Puritans during their exile in Holland. It contains a wide range of poetic meters served by 39 unison tunes. The Puritans who came to Massachusetts Bay in 1629 with the psalter of Sternhold and Hopkins soon decided to prepare a version closer to the biblical language and published *The Whole Booke of Psalmes Faithfully Translated into English Metre* (Cambridge, 1640).

Often called the "Bay Psalm Book," this was the first substantial English-language book published in North America. It had a narrow range of meters (only six patterns, with Common Meter used for 112 psalms). Its fidelity to the biblical language, however, produced poetic deficiencies, and the third edition (1651) was revised by Henry Dunster and Richard Lyon as *The Psalms, Hymns and Spiritual Songs of the Old and New Testament Faithfully Translated into English Metre for the Use, Edification, and Comfort of the Saints*. Though its textual scope was broadened by metrical versions of 36 passages of scripture outside the Psalms, its range of meters became narrower, with Common Meter used for 125 Psalms, permitting a smaller repertory of tunes. The first extant edition with music (9th; Boston, 1698) includes 13 tunes from the 1679 edition of John Playford's *A Breefe Introduction to the Skill of Musick* (London). These reflect British custom in the presentation of letter notation for solfege syllables and a bass line.

Singing of even this limited repertory became lethargic. Many congregations instituted LINING OUT, in which a leader read or sang a line or couplet to remind worshipers of text and tune, the congregation responded by singing, and this pattern was repeated until the entire text had been sung. This method was begun in the Massachusetts Bay Colony by 1647 and by the Plymouth Colony in 1681.

The state of congregational singing had become such a concern by the early 18th century that several clergymen advocated strategies for its renewal. Chief among these was "regular" singing (that is, regulated by musical notation), together with the training that would enable this. Among the promoters of this cause and their works were Thomas Symmes, *The Reasonableness of Regular Singing; or, Singing by Note* (Boston, 1720), and Cotton Mather, *The Accomplished Singer* (Boston, 1721), the subtitle of which discloses the purpose behind this movement: *Instructions How the Piety of Singing with a True Devotion may be obtained and expressed; the Glorious God after an uncommon manner Glorified in it, and His People Edified*. Mather's nephew, Thomas Walter, leader of the Society for Promoting Regular Singing in the Worship of God in Boston (1720–23), issued *The Grounds and Rules of Musick Explained* (Boston, 1721), the source of the tune "Southwel new." John Tufts produced *An Introduction to the Singing of Psalm-Tunes in a Plain and Easy Method* (Boston, 1721). The volumes of Walter and Tufts provided musical instruction and a small body of tunes. Tufts's book placed solfege letters on a staff. Its third edition (1723) is the source of "100 Psalm tune new."

These were the first resources for singing schools, which taught music reading and modestly expanded musical repertory. Though the textual limitation to metrical scriptures remained, new versions of these became available. Cotton Mather's blank-verse *Psalterium Americanum* (Boston, 1718) never took hold, but *A New Version of the Psalms of David* (London, 1696; revised, 1698; first American publication, New York, 1710), by Nahum Tate and Nicholas Brady, gradually replaced the "Old Version" of Sternhold and Hopkins.

Ephrata community hymnal, 1746. (Library of Congress, Music Division)

Regular singing (also called the "new way") revived singing in many places, but it was resisted by proponents of tradition, who held to the "old way," with its lining out, slow tempos, and heterophonic vagaries. (*See* OLD WAY OF SINGING.) Though designed to equip persons for worship, singing schools were social events as well. A singing master, often itinerant, provided instruction for a fee each evening for a week or two. He also sold the tunebook, which he might have compiled. Those who attended could sing from a score and guide the congregation. Those who developed these skills, however, often wished to perform more ambitious music than a congregation could negotiate, and the consequent formation of a choir frequently created contention.

During the same period, the textual boundary was being challenged by the work in England of Isaac Watts. Though a Calvinist, Watts envisioned congregational song that would include both a new approach to the psalms and a type of hymn that was not limited to scriptural paraphrase. His "renovated" psalms were paraphrased for ready application by Christians in the worship of their own time and place. His hymns "of human composure," though grounded in scripture and theology, were expressions of experience and liturgical function. Watts shared his work with American colleagues, among them Cotton Mather, and the first colonial edition of his *The Psalms of David Imitated in the Language of the New Testament* was published by Benjamin Franklin (Philadelphia, 1729), but his innovations were not widely accepted at first, as evidenced by Franklin's complaint about slow sales.

2. AWAKENING AND DIVERSITY. The situation changed dramatically with the period of revival subsequently called the Great Awakening. This shift in religious thought toward personal experience, beginning in the 1730s, created a need for new musical expression, and the

texts of Watts met the need, both because of their subject matter and their craft. Watts's psalms and hymns became the songs of the pro-revival "New Lights." The leading figures of the revival, George Whitefield and Jonathan Edwards, promoted the use of this literature. Recognizing the value of hymns to his ministry, Whitefield issued *A Collection of Hymns for Social Worship, more particularly Design'd for the Use of the Tabernacle Congregation* (London, 1753), which passed through multiple editions and was subsequently published in Philadelphia in1768.

While an Anglican missionary in Georgia and South Carolina, John Wesley compiled the first American book of hymns (not psalms only). *A Collection of Psalms and Hymns* (Charlestown [Charleston], 1737) contains texts from Watts and earlier British poets and translations of German hymns. It did not find broad use, however, and had no significant impact on subsequent American hymnody. It was issued before Charles Wesley began his prolific hymn writing. Whitefield used the hymns of the Wesleys in his 1739–41 preaching tour, but they were slow to find a place in American collections.

The exclusive use of metrical psalmody until the Great Awakening reflected the dominance (and, in many colonies, the establishment) of Anglicans and Congregationalists. Other groups also founded settlements and congregations, and their hymnody differed from that of the dominant groups in textual and musical expression. Pennsylvania, with its guarantee of religious freedom, was the colony most receptive to other practices.

The Dutch Reformed were wedded to metrical psalmody. Their first English psalter was *The Psalms of David...Translated from the Dutch* (New York, 1767). Evert Byvank began this project, but it was completed by Francis Hopkinson, who adapted texts from Tate

Hymn singing, Greenbelt, Maryland. (Library of Congress, Prints & Photographs Division, FSA/OWI Collection, LC-USW3-003564-D)

and Brady's *New Version* to match Genevan tunes. The tunes were printed in *A Collection of the Psalm and Hymn-Tunes* (New York, 1774).

The earliest community to arrive in America with a tradition other than metrical psalmody were Lutherans, who came from Sweden and various parts of Germany to the Philadelphia area and to the Hudson River valley. Most of these Lutherans were Pietists, whose hymnody was more personal and devotional than confessional and liturgical. They brought many hymnals, of which the most prominent was Johann Freylinghausen's *Geistreiches Gesangbuch* (combined with *Neues Geistriches Gesangbuch*, Halle, 1741). It contained nearly 1600 texts and 597 tunes, presented as melody with figured bass. *Vollständiges Marburger-Gesangbuch* (Marburg, many editions from 1549 to the relevant one, 1747) another collection brought from Germany, was subsequently published in America (Germantown, 1757).

Heinrich Melchior Mulhenberg came to America from Germany in 1742 as pastor of congregations in the Philadelphia area and in 1748 organized the first American Lutheran synod. His goal of a single hymnal to serve Lutherans in America led to the appointment of a committee, on which he served, in 1782. It produced *Erbauliche Liedersammlung sum Gottesdienst Gebrauch in den Vereinigten Evangelisch Lutherishen Gemeinen in Nord-America* (Germantaun [Germantown], 1786), a text-only collection, often referred to as "the Muhlenberg Hymnal."

Lutherans faced a dilemma in the choice between their ancestral languages or English for worship. An early resource for English hymnody was *Psalmodia Germanica* (London, first part, 1722; second part, 1725; combined, 1732; reprinted, New York, 1756) that provided rather rough translations of chorales. Muhlenberg used this with English-speaking congregations.

The German Reformed employed both hymns and metrical psalms. Their first American hymnal, *Neuvermehrt-und vollständiges Gesang-Buch* (Germanton [Germantown], 1753) and tune book, *Kern alter und neuer*, (Germanton [Germantown], 1752), were reprints of German publications. The *Gesang-Buch* contains German translations by Ambrosius Lobwasser from the Genevan Psalter and 700 hymns.

Other Protestants from Europe—Mennonites, German Baptist Brethren, Moravians, Schwenkenfelders, and Wissahickon Brethren among them—owned views of hymnody more akin to Luther's than to Calvin's and cultivated bodies of song appropriate to their distinctive theological perspectives. A unique development occurred in the Ephrata Cloister, where hymns by founder Conrad Beissel were preserved in illuminated manuscripts.

Baptists were principally psalm-singers in this period. However, Elias Keach, whose father Benjamin had issued the first English Baptist hymnal in 1691, brought hymn singing to Pennsylvania while ministering there from 1686 until 1692. Accounts strongly suggest that he led the singing of communion hymns during that time. Welsh Baptists who settled in Delaware in 1701 brought with them a vigorous tradition of hymn singing.

Native Americans were offered hymnody in their own languages. John Eliot, an editor of the Bay Psalm Book, versified the psalms in Algonquin under the title *Wame Ketoohomae Uketoohomaongash David* (Cambridge, 1663). Samson Occom, a Mohegan, compiled *A Choice Collection of Hymns and Spiritual Songs* (New-London, CT, 1774). Though the language of Catholic worship was Latin, and though hymns were not part of the Mass, approval was granted for the use of hymns in native vernaculars.

3. NEW TUNES AND TEXTS. In the 50 years following the initiation of SINGING-SCHOOLS, Americans composed few hymn settings. In the succeeding half century, however, more than 300 composers created more than 5000 tunes. The first sizeable tunebook was James Lyon's *Urania; or a Choice Collection of Psalm-Tunes, Anthems, and Hymns* (Philadelphia, 1761), published by subscription. This 198-page volume includes a variety of genres, from congregational tunes to choral pieces, selected from British and American sources. Whereas most tunes before this time had been written for two or three voices, a large portion of *Urania* is scored in four parts. Similar books appeared in the ensuing decades, including Joseph Flagg's *A Collection of the Best Psalm Tunes* (Boston, 1764) and Oliver Brownson's *Select Harmony* (Hartford, 1783).

Prominent among the "Yankee tunesmiths" was William Billings, whose *The New-England Psalm-Singer* (Boston, 1770) contains 127 tunes—all his own. Billings was inventive and iconoclastic, writing in forms from simple canons to anthems and set pieces, and flouting the rules of European harmonic theory as he layered one voice upon another. Most of his compositions are settings of strophic hymns. An emblematic composition that caught the rebellious flavor of the times is his text "Let Tyrants Shake Their Iron Rod," set to "Chester."

Oliver Holden, like Billings, pursued his role as author/composer/compiler/teacher alongside other employment. His "Coronation" has remained in wide use since its publication in his singing-school book, *The Union Harmony* (Boston, 1793). Others who composed and compiled such collections in the latter part of the 18th century include Daniel Read, *The American Singing Book, or a New and Easy Guide to the Art of Psalmody* (New Haven, 1785); Jacob French, *The New American Melody in Three Parts* (Boston, 1789); and Timothy Swan, *The Federal Harmony in Three Parts* (Boston, 1790). Read's "Windham" and Swan's "China" were widely reprinted. The tunes of this era were published with two to four voices, three being typical. The melody, often pentatonic or hexatonic, was found in the tenor, with the bass below and the counter above. Parallel fifths and octaves, as well as dissonant intervals disdained in European practice, were common.

Billings and many of his contemporaries wrote fuging tunes, a form pioneered in England. After a chordal beginning, the parts enter in imitation, typically as the second half of the stanza begins, before concluding with a chordal cadence. This structure provides a display of the skills learned in the singing school, but it served neither the less-prepared singers in the congregation nor the intelligibility of the text. Lewis Edson's "Lenox" is an enduring example of this form.

There was a reaction to American styles as early as Samuel Holyoke's *Harmonia Americana* (Boston, 1791). Andrew Law, having previously published tunes in the New England style, became an advocate of European common-practice harmony by the time of *The Musical Primer* (Cheshire, CT, 1794).

The text repertory also expanded rapidly in the latter decades of the century. Watts's reach beyond biblical paraphrase had been followed by Charles Wesley, by John Newton and William Cowper in *Olney Hymns* (London, 1779; New York, 1787), and by numerous English nonconformists, who were represented in John Rippon's *A Selection of Hymns from the Best Authors, Intended to Be an Appendix to Dr. Watts's Psalms and Hymns* (London, 1787; New York and Elizabethtown, NJ, 1792). American authors such as John Leland and Thomas Baldwin imitated these models.

These textual and musical innovations accompanied the political and ecclesiastical changes of the revolutionary era. Communions that had had ties to European hierarchies now faced decisions about polity, liturgy, and hymnic repertory, as well as the pastoral issue of relation to cultural surroundings. The Protestant Episcopal Church, formed in 1784, undertook its own revision of the *Book of Common Prayer* two years later. It appended "Hymns Suited to the Feasts and Fasts of the Church," with selections from Tate and Brady's *New Version*, 51 hymns, and chants and tunes edited by Francis Hopkinson. When adopted in 1789, this supplement took a more traditional shape of a complete psalter without tunes, but 27 hymns were retained, advancing American practice the beyond Anglican norm.

Also founded in 1784 was the Methodist Episcopal Church, for which John Wesley prepared *A Collection of Psalms and Hymns for the Lord's Day* (London, 1784). However, *A Pocket Hymn Book* (New York, 1786), compiled by American bishops was more widely used. The Dutch Reformed issued *The Psalms and Hymns of the Reformed Protestant Dutch Church in North America* (New York, 1789), proclaiming its new identity only two years after breaking transatlantic ties. Edited by John Henry Livingston, it included 135 hymns, as well as Psalms from Tate and Brady and from Watts. The first General Assembly of American Presbyterians (1788) amended *The Westminster Directory for the Worship of God* to include the "singing of psalms or hymns." It also recommended an end to lining out. The Synod of the German Reformed Church in the United States of America, now distinct from the Dutch Reformed, was organized in 1793. It published *Das neue und verbessert Gesangbuch* (Philadelphia, 1797).

In this same period, African American Methodists established their own churches. The earliest was the African Methodist Episcopal Church, begun in 1784 in Philadelphia. Its pastor, Richard Allen, assembled 54 texts in *A Collection of Spiritual Songs and Hymns* (Philadelphia, 1801), followed in the same year by an expanded edition of 64 items under the title *A Collection of Hymns and Spiritual Songs*. This first anthology by a black compiler for a black congregation provides a glimpse of the broad repertory sung by this church–though to what extent that may be representative of others cannot be known. Found here are hymns by Watts and his imitators, anonymous ballads, three "wandering choruses," and one text that is widely held to be by Allen, "See! How the Nations Rage Together."

Entwined with the awakenings of this era were two new types of hymns. The first is the religious ballad, which often recounts the experience of an individual.

The second is a responsorial structure created by an internal refrain or an appended chorus, or both. Early publications including these types are Richard Broaddus and Andrew Broaddus's *Collection of Sacred Ballads* (Richmond, 1790) and Benjamin Cleaveland's (*sic*; Cleavland) *Hymns on Different Spiritual Subjects* (Norwich, CT, 1786). The *Collection* has the first appearance of the anonymous chorus "When We've Been There Ten Thousand Years"—now found with "Amazing Grace! (How Sweet the Sound)." The second edition of *Hymns* (1792) contains a hymn with the heading "On the worth of true Religion, an Acrostick on the Author's Name, Age, and place of Abode" by Anna Beeman. These new genres are found alongside hymns of British evangelicals in such collections as Joshua Smith's *Divine Hymns or Spiritual Songs* (Exeter, NH, 1791) and Josiah Goddard's *A New and Beautiful Collection of Select Hymns* (Conway, NH, 1798), both of which spread this literature through multiple editions.

Ballads and choruses multiplied in camp meetings at the turn of the 19th century. The outdoor setting, the presence of blacks and whites, and the urgent seeking of the Spirit served to loosen constraints on religious song and to promote an interchange of traditions. Fragmentary evidence makes it difficult to trace specific developments, but camp-meeting songs mixed texts from Watts and the English Evangelicals, biblical stories and language, personal testimonies, invitations to conversion and community, and ecstatic responses. Added to these elements were celebrations of the rituals of gathering, fellowship, prayer, departing, and continuing pilgrimage. Among the musical elements were simple, memorable, and repeated rhythmic and melodic figures; forms suited to large-group participation, such as formulaic interjections, internal refrains, and loosely attached choruses; and African American performance practices, including call-and-response patterns, wholebody engagement, and vocal styles that extended the tonal spectrum from groans to shouts. The earliest collections of camp-meeting songs—among them *Spiritual Song Book* (Halifax, NC, 1805) by David Mintz, *A Collection of the Most Admired Hymns and Spiritual Songs* (New York, 1809) by John Totten, and *The Pilgrim Songster* (Chillicothe, OH, 1815) by Thomas Hinde—contain only texts. The tunes, many of them of folk origin, appear in later books.

Adoption of new guidelines and resources for congregational singing, employment of folk tunes with hymns, composition in novel idioms by the Yankee tunesmiths, and creation of revival texts can all be seen as acts of cultural independence. These changes were not wholly unlike the broad cultural inheritance, but they embodied an essential disregard for it.

4. SHAPE NOTES. Along with new types of text and tunes, and the new practice of singing received texts to folk tunes, came new means of NOTATION. Several systems were developed to make the use of solfege syllables an asset in music reading. The most successful was that of John Connelley of Philadelphia, who devised note heads in distinguishing shapes to signify "fa," "so," "la,"

and "mi." He sold his invention to William Little and William Smith, who displayed the shapes on the customary staff in *The Easy Instructor* (Philadelphia, [1801]). This method was widely adopted, while Andrew Law's similar approach of using shapes without a staff—introduced in the fourth edition of *The Musical Primer* (Philadelphia, 1803)–did not attract imitators.

The first publication to include folk tunes as settings of hymn texts was *The United States' Sacred Harmony* (Boston, 1799), compiled in Charleston, South Carolina, by Amos Pilsbury. Among its unattributed works are "Charleston" and "Kedron." More of this literature appears in Samuel Holyoke's *The Christian Harmonist* (Salem, MA, 1804) and Jeremiah Ingalls's *The Christian Harmony* (Exeter, NH, 1805). Holyoke advertised on his title page that these tunes served all the meters "in the collection of hymns by Mr. Joshua Smith," as well as those from Watts and Rippon. All of these compilers used round notes, but the folk song repertory soon became identified with shape notes. The tunes and shaped notation first appeared together in John Wyeth's *Repository of Sacred Music, Part Second* (Harrisburg, PA, 1813), for which Elkanah Kelsay Dare edited the music. This collection marked the first publication of "Hallelujah" (now known in a modified version as "Nettleton") and promoted the spread of "Morning Song," which had been introduced in *Sixteen Tune Settings* (Philadelphia, 1812), printed by Andrew Law in his staffless notation for John Logan, a Virginia singing master. (*See* SHAPE-NOTE HYMNODY.)

The use of shape notes was not limited to folk tunes. Wyeth's *Repository, Part Second*, contained both folk tunes and works by the Yankee tunesmiths. Oblong shape-note collections in the first half of the 19th century typically included both genres as well as songs from the camp meetings and plain and ornate English tunes. Among the notable publications in this line were *Patterson's Church Music* (Cincinnati, 1813), Freeman Lewis's *Beauties of Harmony* (Pittsburgh, 1813), Ananias Davisson's *Kentucky Harmony* (Harrisonburg, VA, 1816), James Boyd's *The Virginia Sacred Music Repository* (Winchester, VA, 1818), Alexander Johnson's *Tennessee Harmony* (Cincinnati, 1818), Allen Carden's *The Missouri Harmony* (St. Louis [printed in Cincinnati], 1820), William Moore's *The Columbian Harmony* (Cincinnati, 1825), Benjamin Shaw and Charles H. Spilman's *Columbian Harmony* (Cincinnati, 1829), William Caldwell's *Union Harmony* (Maryville, TN, 1837), and John Jackson's *The Knoxville Harmony* (Madisonville, TN, 1838). As the titles and places of publication indicate, the popularity of this notation and the new musical literature was shifting toward the South and the West, and Cincinnati had become a center of publication.

First publications of enduring anonymous tunes include "Bourbon" (Lewis), "Consolation" (Lewis, in an enlarged edition of 1828), "Holy Manna" (Moore), and "St. Mary's/Gallaher" (now called "New Britain" or "Amazing Grace," Shaw and Spilman). "Detroit" appeared in Davisson's *Supplement to Kentucky Harmony* (Harrisonburg, VA, 1820), which more strongly reflected a Southern repertory. A distinctive legacy of collections was published in Virginia's Shenandoah Valley by Mennonite singing school teacher Joseph Funk. He published a German shape-note book, *Die allgemein nützliche Choral-Music* (Harrisonburg, VA, 1816), followed by *A Compilation of Genuine Church Music* (Winchester, VA, 1832). *A Compilation* (renamed *Harmonia Sacra* in 1851) is the source of "Protection" (now known as "Foundation").

The proliferation of oblong shape-note books prompted the propagation of singing schools to teach the method. As with the earlier schools for promotion of regular singing and those of the Yankee tunesmiths, the experience emphasized music education and socialization, not worship; most of the tunebooks contain abbreviated versions of the multi-stanza texts.

Two shape-note collections compiled in the South but published in the North, where printing resources were more adequate, have enduring legacies. *The Southern Harmony* (New Haven, 1835) by William Walker and *The Sacred Harp* (Philadelphia, 1844) by B.F. White and E.J. King are four-shape books that collected a variety of tune types and added to the repertory. "Restoration" was introduced in *The Southern Harmony*, which also had the first pairing of "Amazing Grace" and "New Britain," while "Wondrous Love" was initially printed in its 1840 edition. "Beach Spring" first appeared in *The Sacred Harp*. Gatherings called "singings" using these and similar books continue to the present in the rural South. Rediscovered by folklorists and musicians, this literature is now sung by groups around the country. *The Sacred Harp* has been through many editions (the most recent, Bremen, GA, 1991), and other collections have been revived in reprints. The tunes have also found renewed life in recent hymnals.

By the Civil War, most publishers of shape-note collections had shifted to one of several seven-note systems. The shapes introduced by Jesse Aiken in *The Christian Minstrel* (Philadelphia, 1846) became standard by the 1870s.

5. HYMNS OF INSIDERS. In hymnody, as in other types of church music, the favoring of European models and antipathy toward native works that did not imitate them gained ground in the 19th century. Advocated by American tastemakers, this view garnered support from upwardly mobile urban churchgoers whose aim was cultural sophistication. It was nurtured by similar attitudes in England, where there was a move toward use of tunes excepted from the works of great composers and a reappraisal of aesthetic and educational philosophies.

Thomas Hastings and Lowell Mason—partners and rivals at different times—promoted a style of hymn tune described as "devotional," "meditative," and "chaste" in which musical interest shifted toward attractive melody, harmonies followed common-practice dictates, and rhythms were simple. Hastings was particularly opposed to the use of secular tunes for hymn singing. He addressed hymn singing as part of a wide-ranging philosophy in *Dissertation on Musical Taste* (Albany, 1822;

revised and enlarged edition, New York, 1853). Mason issued the first of his more than eighty collections in the same year: *The Boston Handel and Haydn Society Collection of Church Music* (Boston, 1822). He was an advocate of "scientific" practices of theory and pedagogy. Like those before who had sought to change the style of worship music, Hastings and Mason designed and implemented educational strategies to equip the masses to participate. These included working directly with children and training those who would teach. Among their collaborators and pupils were George Webb, William Bradbury, George Root, Isaac Woodbury, and numerous others who would influence singing in churches and schools. Mason composed or arranged more than 1500 hymn tunes. His varied applications of scientific propriety are represented by "Hamburg" (based on plainsong), "Antioch" (said to have been arranged from fragments from Handel), "Azmon" (arranged from Carl Gläser), and "Olivet" (an original composition in which he modified his own work).

The musical aspirations of Hastings and Mason were paralleled in texts for worship. Their colleagues, Samuel Smith ("My Country, 'tis of Thee") and Ray Palmer ("My Faith Looks up to Thee"; "Jesus, Thou Joy of Loving Hearts," translated from Latin) were early contributors. Two later Christmas hymns, "It Came upon the Midnight Clear" by Edmund Sears and "O Little Town of Bethlehem" by Phillips Brooks, demonstrate literary finesse, with the former also expressing social concern. The tunes for these—"Carol" by Storrs Willis, and "St. Louis" by Lewis Redner, respectively—show the acceptance of a more chromatic romanticism. The work of noted poets, such as Henry Wadsworth Longfellow ("I heard the bells on Christmas Day") and John Greenleaf Whittier ("Dear Lord and Father of Mankind"), was adapted for congregational singing. Whittier's poems were first excerpted as hymns by Samuel Longfellow and Samuel Johnson, who in *A Book of Hymns* (Cambridge, 1846) and *Hymns of the Spirit* (Boston, 1864) voiced the literary, as well as the theological, aims of a more progressive perspective.

An important change in hymnal design was made by Plymouth Congregational Church, Brooklyn, whose pastor was Henry Ward Beecher. Darius Jones, director of music, compiled *Temple Melodies* (New York, 1851), placing a tune and multiple texts in matching meter on the same page. This innovation was repeated in the *Plymouth Collection of Hymns and Tunes* (New York, 1855), a book of 1374 texts selected by Beecher, with music chosen by Charles Beecher and the church's organist, John Zundel, composer of "Beecher." With its size, format, and eclectic content, the *Plymouth Collection* became a model for worship anthologies.

The Oxford Movement had limited influence on American hymnody until the publication of *Hymns Ancient and Modern* (London, 1861). (This Anglican collection included only two American hymns: Charles Everest's "'Take up Thy Cross,' the Savior Said" and George Washington Doane's "Thou Art the Way; to Thee Alone.") Episcopal and Presbyterian hymnals, followed by those of other denominations, borrowed its texts for the liturgical year, translations from Latin and Greek by John Mason Neale and others, and pairings of texts and tunes. The tunes, especially in subsequent editions, reflected a growing choral emphasis. Arthur Messiter ("Marion") and Horatio Parker ("Mount Sion") were among the composers in America influenced by this trend.

6. HYMNS OF OUTSIDERS. African Americans created a distinctive genre, the SPIRITUAL. The term "spiritual song" has a long and varied history (as in the titles of 18th-century collections above), in this instance reaching to the New Testament. Because these spirituals were originally and essentially an oral tradition, evidence to construct a thorough history does not exist. Certain characteristics—call-and-response forms, biblical phrases, text and/or tune fragments shared with other types—link with what we know of singing in the camp meetings. Reports of their use indicate that spirituals were sung in unison or heterophony. The earliest published anthology, *Slave Songs of the United States* (New York, 1867) by William Allen, Charles Ware, and Lucy Garrison, presents them as melody only. Arrangements for choirs and for soloist with accompaniment, though they brought the literature before a wider audience, hid the sound of their use in worship by slaves. Evident in the various versions, however, are an aesthetic framework and musical forms that invite improvisation, and a unity of song with whole-body movement. Texts emphasize the existential perseverance of faith, particularly through the language of biblical stories and allusions, whether facing hardship in the sorrow songs (slow and melancholy) or celebrating deliverance in the jubilees (fast and rhythmic). The variety of versions transcribed in different times and places suggests that transformation was an element of the style, not merely an accident of communication. Anonymous spirituals that are now part of the broader church's hymnody reached print at different times and through different hands. "Go Down, Moses" was the first to be published with music, in 1861. "Give Me Jesus" initially appeared in Theodore Seward's *Jubilee Songs* (New York, 1872). The first printings of "Let us break bread together" and "Were You There" occurred in *Old Plantation Hymns* (Boston, 1899) by William Barton. *Folk Songs of the American Negro* (Nashville, 1907) by Frederick Jerome Work and John Wesley Work, II, provided the first publication of "There is a Balm in Gilead." "Go tell it on the Mountain" did not appear in print until Nathaniel Dett's *Religious Folk-Songs of the Negro* (Hampton, VA, 1927). Many genres beyond the church—jazz, blues, ragtime, various popular and commercial styles—have their roots in spirituals.

Another type of African American song, the RING SHOUT, shows distinct African roots. Its deliberate and holistic engagement of the body in rhythmic chant and movement is a yielding to the Spirit and to the community formed by faith.

A third form of hymnody from the historic black church is called "Dr. Watts" or "meter(ed)" music. The naming of Watts or the reference to poetry recalls the origin of the texts as evangelical hymns of the 18th century. Often led by a solo intonation that approaches lining out, the slow, heterophonic execution is reminiscent of the "old way" of singing. In the style known as surge singing, communities develop their own patterns of ornamentation, at one point changing dynamic level, at another shifting vocal register, at yet another altering tempo as the music surges from one center of gravity to another.

Groups that originated in America such as Shakers, Mormons, and Adventists generated hymnody to express their particular beliefs, but its use did not reach beyond those for whom it was created.

7. HYMNS FOR SUNDAY SCHOOLS AND REVIVALS. The Sunday school came on the American scene in the early years of the 19th century. The earliest book of texts for these schools was *Hymns for Sunday School Teachers* (New York, 1816), a reprint of materials from the London Sunday School Union. The first identifiable American compiler in this field, Hervey Wilbur, edited *A Sunday School Hymn Book for Youth* (Hartford, 1818). *The Sunday School Hymn Book* (Philadelphia, 1818; first extant edition, 1819) was issued by a forerunner of the American Sunday School Union, which published numerous resources after its formation in 1824. Elbert Osborn's *The Sunday School Music Book* (Philadelphia, 1826), a collection of music to serve *The Sunday School Hymn Book*, was the first tunebook created for this purpose. Though most Sunday school music was printed in round notes, Osborn's book uses shape notes. Early collections for Sunday schools did not have a distinctive musical idiom, but a typical style emerged, characterized by simplicity and the sort of theoretical correctness advocated by Mason. There was a natural intersection between this literature and the interests of Hastings and Mason, and each edited a collection: *Juvenile Psalmody* (Utica, 1827) by Hastings, and *Juvenile Psalmist* (Boston, 1829) by Mason. The leading exponent of Sunday school song was Mason's pupil, Bradbury. He wrote devotional tunes in the Mason manner, such as "Woodworth" (for Charlotte Elliott's "Just as I Am, without One Plea"), and for Sunday schools retained the elements that Mason valued but infused them with greater melodic and rhythmic interest. His setting of Anna Warner's "Jesus Loves Me" is the archetype of Sunday school tunes. The first of Bradbury's many collections of Sunday school music was *The Young Choir* (with Charles Saunders; New York, 1841).

A new style of revivalism suited to settled areas developed in the early decades of the century. Its most prominent proponent, Charles G. Finney, was cautious about the use of music, but others employed it as a principal means of popular appeal. Various compilers aimed for different points on the continuum from camp meeting songs to European-style hymns. In the middle was Asahel Nettleton's *Village Hymns* (Hartford, 1824), designed as a supplement to Watts. Its companion tune book, *Zion's Harp* (New Haven, 1824), eschewed folk tunes. Nearer the camp-meeting pole was Joshua Leavitt, who included folk tunes as well as secular melodies such as "Auld Lang Syne" in *The Christian Lyre* (New York, 1831). Its diverse contents range from the folk melody "Pleading Savior" to James Alexander's translation, "O Sacred Head, Now Wounded." *The Christian Lyre* advanced the unity of text and tune by placing them on facing pages. Adopting the same format, but with repertory toward the "good music" end of the spectrum, Hastings and Mason issued *Spiritual Songs for Social Worship* (Boston, 1831). Its folk tunes were "properly" harmonized, and alongside them stood Mason's "Olivet," with the first publication of Palmer's decorous but personal text "My Faith Looks up to Thee" and Hastings's "Toplady" as the setting for "Rock of Ages, Cleft for Me."

8. HYMNS FOR THE UNCHURCHED. The next genre of populist hymnody was the gospel song. (*See* GOSPEL MUSIC.) It built on the style of music developed for the Sunday schools, but also borrowed from camp-meeting songs and revival hymns and incorporated elements from a variety of popular styles. Gospel song texts, though more fully developed than those of the camp meetings, seldom range more widely in content. They are typically concerned with a simple theology of redemption, personal expressions of testimony and invitation, and the rituals of gathering, celebrating, and sending to faithful Christian living. Many of its proponents and producers were careful to note that it was intended for appeal to the unchurched and for informal gatherings, not for regular worship of established congregations.

Bradbury used the style developed in Sunday school songs for gospel song tunes, such as "Solid Rock" (for Edward Mote's "My hope is built on nothing less") and "He Leadeth Me" (for Joseph Gilmore's "He Leadeth Me! O Blessed Thought"). The publishing company he established was succeeded by Biglow and Main, and his role as editor was filled by Robert Lowry. Lowry wrote both text and tunes, demonstrating a range of style: "What Can Wash away My Sin"/"Plainfield" has the inner refrain and chorus of a camp-meeting song; "Marching to Zion" (for Watts's "Come, We That Love the Lord") adds textual repeats and a chorus with echo to a historic text; "Low in the Grave He Lay"/"Christ Arose" juxtaposes a solemn stanza with a celebrative response; "Shall We Gather at the River"/ "Hanson Place" is a military march. Lowry's partner in numerous collections was W. Howard Doane, known for many settings of texts by Fanny Crosby. Among their collaborations were "Jesus, Keep Me Near the Cross," "Pass Me Not, O Gentle Savior," and "To God Be the Glory." Crosby was the most prolific author in this genre, with upward of 8000 texts.

While in England with preacher Dwight Moody, song leader and soloist Ira Sankey published *Sacred Songs and Solos* (London, 1873). He had earlier used *Hallowed Songs* (Cincinnati, 1865) by Phillip Philips, known as the "Singing Pilgrim." Shortly thereafter, another soloist, Philip Bliss, paired by Moody with preacher D.W. Whittle, issued *Gospel Songs* (Cincinnati, 1874). Though this title was not a new term, it provided the generic label for the genre. When Sankey

returned to the states, he proposed to Bliss that they combine their efforts. The product was *Gospel Hymns and Sacred Songs* (Cincinnati and New York, 1875). Following the tragic death of Bliss in 1876, Sankey engaged James McGranahan and George Stebbins—other singing evangelists—as partners in five additional volumes, culminating in *Gospel Hymns, Nos. 1–6 Complete* (Cincinnati and New York, 1894). Its content and proportions—more than 600 gospel songs and, as the book describes them, "over 125 of the most useful and popular standard hymns and tunes of the church"— shaped the congregational song of evangelical groups for decades thereafter.

Though Sankey played a central role in the dissemination of gospel songs, he was not a prolific composer. Exemplary of his writing and his understated performance style is "The Ninety and Nine," said to have been improvised in an evangelistic meeting. Sankey's partners were quite productive. Bliss wrote texts and tunes, including "Sing Them over Again to Me"/"Words of Life" and "Ville du Havre" (for Horatio Spafford's "It Is Well with My Soul"). McGranahan ("Showers of Blessing" for Whittle's "There Shall Be Showers of Blessing") and Stebbins ("Calling Today" for Crosby's "Jesus Is Tenderly Calling Thee Home") composed hundreds of songs. Others who were productive in this genre include John Sweney, William Fisher, William Kirkpatrick, E.O. Excell, and Will Thompson.

The camp meeting form with inner refrain and chorus was retained in treatments by Ralph Hudson of Watts's "Alas, and Did My Savior Bleed" as "At the Cross" and Charles Wesley's "O for a Thousand Tongues to Sing" as "Blessed Be the Name." Gospel songs were written in the 20th century by Charles Gabriel, Charles Alexander, Daniel Towner, Alfred Ackley, B.B. McKinney, and Homer Rodeheaver, each of whom adapted to changing trends in popular music. More recent examples that continue the revival tradition are "Coming Again" by John W. Peterson, "Holy, Holy" by Jimmy Owens, and "Because He Lives" by Bill and Gloria Gaither.

The gospel song became an important hymnic genre, dominating the congregational song of some groups, prompting strong repudiation from others, and finding its way into the extra-liturgical activities of many. One reason for its success was its accessibility to pianists of limited skill, who were eager to play their own instruments as part of the growing middle class.

In a style known as "southern gospel," lyrics and musical forms of the gospel song are blended with close harmonies of male quartet (or female trio) writing. Fast and rhythmic music is undergirded by vigorous improvisational piano accompaniment. The vocal parts are printed in seven-shape notation. Singers gather in "conventions" akin to shape-note "singings."

A distinctive line of "black gospel" evolved in the early 20th century. Combining textual and music forms from the Sunday-school gospel tradition with elements from African American genres, including the spiritual, it is both a performance style and a body of literature. Whereas spirituals were anonymous, black gospel songs have identifiable creators. The earliest prominent figure was Charles Tindley, who wrote "Stand by Me." The introduction of a distinctive blues style is credited to Thomas A. Dorsey, writer of "Precious Lord, Take My Hand." (See GOSPEL BLUES.) The consolidation of standard hymns, gospel songs, and spirituals in *Gospel Pearls* (Nashville, 1921) provides insight into the hymnody of black churches of that era. This was also the period in which the inimitable "Lift Every Voice and Sing" was written by James Weldon Johnson (text) and his brother J. Rosamond Johnson (music). Subsequent composers of black gospel include Lucie Campbell ("He'll Understand and Say 'Well Done'"), Doris Akers ("Sweet, Sweet Spirit"), Andraé Crouch ("Soon and Very Soon"), and Margaret Douroux ("Give Me a Clean Heart").

9. DIFFERENT DIRECTIONS. Three disparate developments early in the 20th century have had lasting import. The first was the creation of texts addressing the social implications of the gospel. Frank Mason North's "Where Cross the Crowded Ways of Life" (titled "A Prayer for the Multitudes," 1903), was earliest in a continuing line that includes Russell Bowie's "O Holy City, Seen of John" (a vision of divine judgment on human injustice), Ferdinand Blanchard's "Before the Cross of Jesus" (an extroverted counterpart to the introverted "Beneath the Cross of Jesus," 1929) and Harry Emerson Fosdick's "God of Grace and God of Glory" (written to focus the monied financiers of New York's Riverside Church on the surrounding city and world, 1930). The second—from England—was the publication of *The English Hymnal* (London, 1906). Music editor Ralph Vaughan Williams selected and arranged a large number of folk melodies from various European cultures; he also composed tunes—notably "Sine nomine"—to promote vigorous unison singing. His American heirs as composers include Winfred Douglas ("St. Dunstan's," ironically, written to replace a Vaughan Williams arrangement) and Tertius Noble ("Ora labora"). His inclusion of folk tunes lent legitimacy that has been increasingly influential. The third was the emergence of Pentecostalism, often traced to the Azusa Street revival that began in 1906. The stylistic traits and function of the hymnody of this branch of the church have shaped hymn singing to the present.

The Hymnal 1940 (New York, 1943) of the Episcopal church not only served its communion well but also set a high standard of selection and editing that influenced American hymnal making for a generation. It introduced the texts of Americans Walter Russell Bowie ("Lord Christ, When First Thou Cam'st to Man"), Howard Chandler Robbins ("And Have the Bright Immensities"), and Bland Tucker ("Father, We Thank Thee Who Hast Planted"). Among its new tunes are "Sursum corda" by Alfred Smith and "Christus Rex" by David McK. Williams.

The middle decades of the century, though neither productive nor innovative in hymnody, featured rising standards for professional training of church musicians and increasing advocacy by non-denominational organizations such as the American Guild of Organists (founded 1896), Hymn Society of America (1922; since 1991 The Hymn Society in the United States and Canada), and

Choristers Guild (1949). All of these promoted hymnody, and searches by the Hymn Society stimulated the writing of new material. Texts disseminated through these searches include "Eternal God, Whose Power Upholds" by Henry Hallam Tweedy, "Hope of the World" by Georgia Harkness, and "Word of God, across the Ages" by Ferdinand Blanchard. Sturdy and serviceable tunes were written during this period by Leo Sowerby ("Rosedale") and Earle Copes ("Vicar").

10. RECENT DEVELOPMENTS. Following World War II a resurgence in church attendance enabled congregations and denominations to grow, and hymnal publication reflected this prosperity. It was soon evident, however, that nostalgia could not sustain vigorous congregational life. Changes in society, in programs of ministry, and in Bible translations prompted liturgical renewal and experimentation. Troubled by a sense of growing irrelevance, some within the church sought to renovate hymnody, building largely on traditional forms. Others outside the church or on its edges, reacting differently to concerns about relevance, began populist movements, influenced by folk and commercial styles.

Proponents of both approaches were energized by the second Vatican Council, called to address the relationship between the church and the world. The council approved congregational singing at Mass, as well as hymnody that was vernacular in text and music. The immediate effect of Vatican II was seen in Roman Catholic hymnody that embraced informal styles. Examples of this genre are "We Are One in the Spirit" (Peter Scholtes), "On Eagle's Wings" (Michael Joncas), "Here I Am, Lord" (Dan Schutte), "I Am the Bread of Life" (Suzanne Toolan), and "Blest Are They, the Poor in Spirit" (David Haas), all of which are used beyond Catholic parishes. The same elements are found in compositions by non-Catholics Karen Lafferty ("Seek Ye First the Kingdom of God"), Marty Haugen ("Gather Us In"), and James Strathdee ("What Does the Lord Require of You").

Shaped by commercial music and concerts are styles labeled "praise and worship" and CONTEMPORARY CHRISTIAN MUSIC. Because the songs often originate as music for solo or small-group performance, they contain rhythmic and melodic complexity that appear daunting in print. Congregational singing is enabled by repeated hearing, either in a given setting or through recordings. "Thy Word Is a Lamp unto My Feet" by Amy Grant and Michael W. Smith, "Lord, I Lift Your Name on High" by Rick Founds, and "How Great Is Our God" by Chris Tomlin, Jesse Reeves, and Ed Cash typify this genre. Such songs, usually sung with repetition, are often assembled in a sequence designed to guide the singer through a series of emotions into a readiness for worship (or, as is sometimes said, "into the presence of God"). This reflects a Pentecostal understanding of worship and the role of hymnody in it.

Those who sought to renew existing traditions were inspired by the "hymn explosion" in Britain. The American publisher George Shorney made the literature accessible, and Erik Routley, an English hymnologist and philosopher of church music, brought insight to the United States as a teacher and writer. American hymn poets avoided archaisms, addressed contemporary issues, and crafted language that was artistic but accessible. Many individuals contributed to fresh multi-stanza hymnody. Representative writers are Omer Westendorf ("Sent Forth by God's Blessing"), Jaroslav Vajda ("God of the Sparrow"), Herman Stuempfle ("Would I Have Answered when You Called"), Rae Whitney ("It Was God Who Ran to Greet Him"), Delores Dufner ("Faithful Cross, O Tree of Beauty"), Jeffrey Rowthorn ("Lord, You Give the Great Commission"), Carl Daw ("Like the Murmur of the Dove's Song"), Thomas Troeger ("Wind Who Makes All Winds That Blow"), Ruth Duck ("Womb of Life, and Source of Being"), Richard Leach ("Told of God's Favor, Told of God's Purpose"), Mary Louise Bringle ("When Memory Fades, and Recognition Falters"), and John Thornburg ("God, the Sculptor of the Mountains"). Hymn tune composers had similar aims but found they could not extend the congregational idiom far toward the era's art music. Among those who achieved creativity within reach of the congregation are Austin Lovelace ("Mustard Seed"), Richard Dirksen ("Vineyard Haven"), David N. Johnson ("Earth and all Stars"), Lee Hastings Bristol ("Dickinson College"), Jane Marshall ("Jacob"), Carlton Young ("Starchild"), Carl Schalk ("Roeder"), Hal Hopson ("Merle's Tune"), Carol Doran ("Authority"), Richard Proulx ("Castlewood"), Calvin Hampton ("St. Helena"), David Hurd ("Julion"), Al Fedak ("Myrrh-bearing Mary"), and Dan Damon ("Mitulski").

An increasing number of Americans do not use English as their language of worship. Hymnals have been produced to serve these groups. Among the several Spanish-language hymnals are *Flor y Canto* (Roman Catholic; Portland, OR: 1989, 3/2011), *Mil Voces para Celebrar* (United Methodist; Nashville: 1996) and *Libro de Liturgia y Cantico* (Lutheran; Minneapolis: 1998).

The black church's vibrant traditions, which cross denominational lines, have prompted the publication of several hymnals by denominations that do not have African American majorities. Among these are *Songs of Zion* (United Methodist; Nashville: 1981), *Lift Every Voice and Sing* (Episcopal; New York: 1981, vol. ii, New York: 1993), *This Far by Faith* (Lutheran; Minneapolis: 1999), and *Lead Me, Guide Me* (Roman Catholic; Chicago: 1987). A collection without denominational identification is the *African American Heritage Hymnal* (Chicago: 2001).

In the early years of the 21st century, congregational song in America is richly varied. Hymnody of nearly every type identified above continues to be written, published, and sung.

BIBLIOGRAPHY

N.D. Gould: *Church Music in America: Comprising Its History and Its Peculiarities at Different Periods, with Cursory Remarks on Its Legitimate Use and Its Abuse* (Boston, 1853/*R*)
L. Benson: *The English Hymn: Its Development and Use in Worship* (New York: 1915/*R*)
F.J. Metcalf: *American Writers and Compilers of Sacred Music* (New York, 1925/*R*)
H.W. Foote: *Three Centuries of American Hymnody* (Cambridge, MA, 1940/*R*)
I. Lowens: *Music and Musicians in Early America* (New York, 1964)
R. Stevenson: *Protestant Church Music in America: a Short Survey of Men and Movements from 1564 to the Present* (New York, 1966)
J. Downey: *The Music of American Revivalism* (diss., Tulane U., 1969)
P. Hammond: *Music in Urban Revivalism in the Northern United States, 1800–1835* (diss., Southern Baptist Theological Seminary, 1974)
W.J. Reynolds: *A Joyful Sound: Christian Hymnody* (New York, 2/1978, rev. 3/1987 with M. Price as *A Survey of Christian Hymnody*, enlarged by D. Music and M. Price, 5/2010)
E. Routley: *A Panorama of Christian Hymnody* (Collegeville, MN, 1979, ed. and expanded P.A. Richardson, Chicago, 2005)
A. Christ-Janer, C.W. Hughes, and C.S. Smith: *American Hymns Old and New* (New York, 1980)
C.W. Hughes: *American Hymns Old and New: Notes on the Hymns and Biographies of the Authors and Composers* (New York, 1980)
M. Wilhoit: *A Guide to the Principal Authors and Composers of Gospel Song of the Nineteenth Century* (diss., Southern Baptist Theological Seminary, 1982)
R. Crawford: *The Core Repertory of Early American Psalmody* (Madison, WI, 1984)
V. Cross: *The Development of Sunday School Hymnody in the United States of America, 1816–1869* (diss., New Orleans Baptist Theological Seminary, 1985)
A. Britton, I. Lowens, and R.S. Crawford: *American Sacred Music Imprints 1698–1810: a Bibliography* (Worcester, MA, 1990)
R.F. Glover, ed.: *The Hymnal 1982 Companion* (New York, 1990–94)
J.M. Spencer: *Black Hymnody: a Hymnological History of the African-American Church* (Knoxville, 1992)
D.P. Hustad: *Jubilate II: Church Music in Worship and Renewal* (Carol Stream, IL, 1993)
C.R. Young: *Companion to the United Methodist Hymnal* (Nashville, 1993)
H. Eskew and H.T. McElrath: *Sing with Understanding: an Introduction to Christian Hymnology* (Nashville, 2/1995)
N. Temperley: *The Hymn Tune Index: a Census of English-Language Hymn Tunes in Printed Sources form 1535 to 1820* (New York, 1998)
M.W. Costen: *In Spirit and in Truth: the Music of African American Worship* (Louisville, 2004)
P. Westermeyer: *Let the People Sing: Hymn Tunes in Perspective* (Chicago, 2005)

PAUL A. RICHARDSON

Hymn Society in the United States and Canada. Organization founded in 1922 as the Hymn Society of America, and renamed in 1991 to its present title, to encourage the singing of hymns in congregations of all faiths, foster research in the field of hymnology, and promote the writing of new hymn words and music. By 2010 the society had approved, copyrighted, and made available to publishers and individuals more than 400 hymns. It publishes a scholarly and practical quarterly, *The Hymn* (1949–), a newsletter called *The Stanza* (1976–), an e-mail newsletter called *The Verse* (2011–), and occasional monographs on hymnology. Each summer it stages annual conferences, including workshops, lectures, and discussion groups; it also schedules occasional tours. In 1984 it published on microfilm the *Dictionary of American Hymnology* (edited by Leonard Ellinwood and Elizabeth Lockwood), a comprehensive index to the texts of more than 8000 hymnals. The headquarters of the society are at Baptist Theological Seminary at Richmond, Virginia.

RITA H. MEAD/R

Hynde, Chrissie (*b* Akron, OH, 7 Sept 1951). Singer, songwriter, and guitarist. Hynde studied art at Kent State University, but in 1973 relocated to London and immersed herself in its burgeoning punk scene. She wrote for *New Musical Express* and worked in Malcolm McLaren's SEX boutique. Hynde was associated with various musicians and groups in the mid-1970s, including Jack Rabbit, Chris Spedding, Berk Brothers, The Unusuals, Moors Murderers, London SS, McLaren's Masters of the Backside, and Mick Farren. In 1978 she co-founded the Pretenders in London. With Hynde as principal songwriter, their debut album *Pretenders* (1980) defined post-punk new wave: tight and lively guitar-driven arrangements buoyed by Hynde's rhythm guitar, radio- and MTV-friendly riffs and hooks, and tough lyrics not devoid of vulnerability ("Tattooed Love Boys," "Kid").

Hynde led the Pretenders through various line-ups and nine studio albums. Their American Top Forty singles—all written or co-written by Hynde—include "Back on the Chain Gang" (1983, their first US Top Ten) and "I'll stand by you" (1994). Particularly in ballads, Hynde's rich alto is shaded by melismas and subtle dynamics revealing the influence of R&B. She also collaborated with Moodswings and INXS, and took part in a charity cover of The Judds's "Love can build a bridge" with Eric Clapton, Cher, and Neneh Cherry (1995). Hynde's 1985 reworking with UB40 of Sonny and Cher's "I got you Babe" reached the US Top Forty.

Hynde has described her rock experience as "escapism" from her Midwestern upbringing—her expansion of the category "women in rock" can be understood in this light. Like her punk-influenced music, Hynde's mascara-encircled eyes, shaggy bangs, t-shirts, jeans and/or leather are often viewed as tough, androgynous, and sexy. Although Hynde has expressed ambivalence toward feminism, her presence on early MTV made her one of the most visible female rockers for a generation; artists such as Courtney Love and Shirley Manson have cited her influence. On and off-stage, Hynde has devoted herself to issues that impact women in unique ways, and she has written a number of songs on parenthood (she raised two daughters, the first fathered by musician Ray Davies).

WAYNE HEISLER JR.

I

Ian [Fink], **Janis (Eddy)** (*b* New York, NY, 7 April 1951). Singer and songwriter. She began playing piano when she was three years old, and learned to play guitar a few years later. Many of her songs deal with themes involving social consciousness. She wrote "Society's Child," her first hit single (no. 14, 1967), when she was only 14. It is an uncommonly perceptive song about a relationship between a white girl and an African American boy that many radio stations refused to play. In April of 1967 she appeared on Leonard Bernstein's television special *Inside Pop: The Rock Revolution,* which helped her gain more recognition by the public and the press. Exposure at such a young age proved detrimental: after the success of her first album, *Janis Ian* (1967), and several concert tours, her career began to falter and she announced her retirement at the age of 20. This withdrawal was short lived, as she signed a contract with CBS Records and released the album *Stars* in 1974. Throughout her career her songs have been recorded by Roberta Flack, Joan Baez, Cher, and Bette Midler, which helped considerably to establish Ian's reputation as a songwriter. Ian's most successful album, *Between the Lines* (1975), contained the hit single "At Seventeen" (no. 3, 1975), which earned her a Grammy Award; the album was awarded a platinum record. To promote the song she appeared as the musical guest on the first episode of NBC's *Saturday Night Live* in October of 1975. Although her success since the mid-1970s has been less spectacular, she continues to record and perform. In 1979 she released the album *Night Rains* which was notable for its range of styles. It included the internationally successful single "Fly Too High," one of two songs on the album co-written and produced by the disco composer Giorgio Moroder, and a piano duet with Chick Corea. Throughout her career she has maintained a folk-rock style, draws upon jazz, and usually accompanies herself on guitar during live performances. In 2008 she published an autobiography, *Society's Child*, and an accompanying CD set, *The Best of Janis Ian: the Autobiography Collection.*

ANTHONY MARKS/CAROLYN BRUNELLE

Iannaccone, **Anthony (Joseph)** (*b* Brooklyn, NY, 14 Oct 1943). Composer. He studied composition with LUDMILA ULEHLA, VITTORIO GIANNINI, and DAVID DIAMOND at the Manhattan School of Music (1961–8, MM) and with SAMUEL ADLER at the Eastman School of Music (1968–71, PhD); he also studied privately with AARON COPLAND between 1959 and 1964. He worked as an orchestral violinist (1962–8) and taught briefly at the Manhattan School (1966–8). In 1971 he was appointed professor of composition at Eastern Michigan University, where he founded the school's electronic music studio. In 1973 he became director of the school's Collegium Musicum. He is an active conductor of contemporary and traditional orchestral music, and has received awards from the NEA, the Phi Mu Alpha Sinfonia Foundation, and other organizations.

After an early phase of nearly orthodox serialism from 1967 to 1975, his music diverged into what the composer described as "small-audience" music—abstract and intense works, such as *Mobiles* for brass and percussion—and "large audience" music, wherein melody and cohesiveness are paramount—such qualities characterize works like the *Divertimento* (1983) and much of his vocal and wind-ensemble writing. His craft reaches its zenith in his synthesis of the two styles in the *Two-Piano Inventions*, which won the SAI/C.F. Peters competition in 1990, and the Third Symphony; in both these works, organic growth inspires music of great strength and formal clarity, as opening bars generate the textural and thematic contours that forge contrasting sections of reflection and cross-rhythmic dynamism. His *Waiting for Sunrise on the Sound* received second prize in the 2001 Masterprize/London Symphony Orchestral Works competition. In addition to the influence of Stravinsky, Bartók, and Debussy, the poetry of Walt Whitman has proved a frequent source of inspiration, culminating in his Third Symphony, with its effective imagery based on Whitman's metaphors of night and rivers.

WORKS

Orch: Suite, chbr orch, 1962; Sym. no.1, orch, 1965; Sym. no.2, orch, 1966; Concertino, vn, orch, 1967; Lysistrata, concert ov., 1968;

Variations, vn, orch, 1969; Interlude, wind band, 1970; Antiphonies, wind band, 1972; Scherzo, sym. band, 1976; Of Fire and Ice, sym. band, 1977; Images of Song and Dance: 1 Orpheus, wind band, 1979–82, 2 Terpsichore, wind band, 1981; After a Gentle Rain, sym. band, 1980; Plymouth Trilogy, wind band, 1981; Divertimento, orch, 1983; Apparitions, wind band, 1986; Sym. no.3 "Night Rivers," orch, 1990–2; Sea Drift, sym. band/wind band, 1993; Concertante, cl, orch, 1994; Crossings, 1996; West End Express, 1997; Waiting for Sunrise on the Sound, orch, 1998; From Time to Time, orch, 2000; Dancing on Vesuvius, orch, 2008

Chbr and solo inst: Parodies, wind qnt, 1958; Pf Trio, 1959; Retail Rags, pf, 1959; Sonata, va, pf, 1961; Sonata no.1, vn, pf, 1964; Str Qt no.1, 1965; Partita, pf, 1967; Hades, brass qt, 1968; Remembrance, va, pf, 1968, arr. a sax, pf, 1971; 3 Mythical Sketches, brass qt, 1971; Sonata no.2, vn, pf, 1971; Anamorphoses, 2 tpt, trb, perc, 1972; Keyboard Essays, pf, 1972; Rituals, vn, pf, 1973; Bicinia, fl, a sax, 1974; Night Song, bn, pf, 1975; Sonatina, tpt, tuba, 1975; Aria Concertante, vc, pf, 1976; Invention, 2 a sax, 1978; Trio, fl, cl, pf, 1979; Toccata Variations, org, 1983; 2 Pf Inventions, 1985; Octet, fl, ob, cl, str qnt, 1985; Sonata no.3, vn, pf, 1985; Mobiles, brass, perc, 1986; Toccata Fanfares, 6 brass, 1986; Pf Qnt, 1996; Str Qt no.2, 1997; Str Qt no.3, 1999; Qnt, cl, str qt, 2002; Sarabande, pf, 2003; Woodwind Qnt no.2: Scenes after Hart Crane, 2004

Vocal: 3 Songs on Immortality (P.B. Shelley, A.E. Housman, E. Dickinson), S, pf, 1959; Magnificat, chorus, orch, 1963; Solomon's Canticle, SATB, 1968; The Prince of Peace (Bible), S, Mez, Bar, B, chorus, orch, 1970; With Music Strong I Come (W. Whitman), SATB, chbr ens/2 pf, 1974; The Sky Is Low, the Clouds Are Mean (Dickinson), SATB, 1976; Song of Thanksgiving (Song of Thanks) (L.N. Woodruff), SATB, 1980; Walt Whitman Song, solo vv, chorus, wind, 1980; Autumn Rivulets, chorus, orch, 1984; A Whitman Madrigal, SATB, pf, 1984; Chautauqua Psalms, chorus, pf, 1987; The Soul's Expression, SATB, 2003; Exsultate, SATB, 2004

Principal publishers: C. Fischer, Ludwig/Kalmus, C. F. Peters, Presser, E.C. Schirmer, Seesaw/Subito

BIBLIOGRAPHY

S. Kalib: "Analysis of Iannaccone's *Apparitions*," *Journal of Band Research*, xxv/1 (1989), 2–64

J. Renshaw: "Conducting Iannaccone's *After a Gentle Rain*," *Instrumentalist* xlviii/9 (1994), 27–32, 79

W. Probst: "Anthony Iannaccone: Musik sowohl für den normalen Konzert Besucher als auch für Kenner," *Clarino*, viii/1 (1997), 37

J. Renshaw: "Analysis: Anthony Iannaccone's *Sea Drift*," *Journal of Band Research* xxxv/1 (1999), 36–61

STEPHEN W. ELLIS/SARAH EYERLY

Ibáñez [Ybañez], **Florencio** (*b* Tarazona, Aragón, Spain, 26 Oct 1740; *d* Mission Soledad, CA, 26 Nov 1818). Spanish musician and Franciscan missionary to Alta California. He entered the Franciscan order at the Convento de Nuestra Señora de Jésus in Zaragoza in 1757, where he served as choirmaster. He traveled to New Spain in 1770, and was assigned to the Colegio de San Fernando, the Franciscan missionary college in Mexico City that established the Alta California missions. He remained there until 1774, serving in the choir. A talented artist and musician, he copied large choirbooks for use at the colegio, at least one of which was brought to Mission Santa Barbara (Santa Barbara, CA) in 1882. After service in San Miguel el Grande (now San Miguel de Allende) in central New Spain, and missionary assignments with the Colegio de Santa Cruz de Querétaro in Northern New Spain, Ibáñez served in the Alta California missions. From 1801 to 1803, he was stationed at Mission San Antonio, and from 1803 until his death in 1818 he was assigned to Mission Soledad. Ibáñez was frank in defending those whom he considered to be oppressed, including the California Indians,

although his lack of knowledge of indigenous languages limited his ability to preach and convert. A well-known teacher of music, he is also credited with a popular pastorela, the Spanish-language nativity play with music, although no such manuscript by him has been found. Chant books copied by Ibáñez are at the Bancroft Library and Santa Clara University.

BIBLIOGRAPHY

O.F. da Silva, ed.: *Mission Music of California: A Collection of Old California Mission Hymns and Masses* (Los Angeles, CA, 1941)

M. Geiger: *Franciscan Missionaries in Hispanic California 1769–1848* (San Marino, CA, 1969), 124–25

C.H. Russell: *From Serra to Sancho: Music and Pageantry in the California Missions* (New York, 2009)

MARGARET CAYWARD

Ibarra, Susie (*b* Anaheim, CA, 15 Nov 1970). Jazz percussionist and composer. Of Filipino heritage, Ibarra grew up in Houston, Texas. She received a music diploma from Mannes College and a BA from Goddard College. She studied drums with Buster Smith and Vernel Fournier and percussion with Milford Graves. She also played with William Parker and his big band, The Little Huey Creative Music Orchestra. In the 1990s, Ibarra became interested in Philippine musical traditions and took lessons on kulintang from master artist Danongan Kalanduyan. She joined the avant-garde free jazz quartet led by David S. Ware and became well known in the New York jazz scene. She collaborated on several albums with a number of respected musicians such as Assif Tsahar, Cooper-Moore, Charles Burnham, Chris Speed, Wadada Leo Smith, and Pauline Oliveros, notably on the album *Flower after Flower* (2000) released on John Zorn's Tzadik label. Combining and improvising in many eclectic styles, Ibarra recorded several albums with classical violinist Jennifer Choi and pianist Craig Taborn as The Susie Ibarra Trio. In *Folkloriko* (2004), Ibarra makes reference to her Filipino heritage and incorporates kulintang melodies. She and her husband Cuban American percussionist and composer Roberto J. Rodriguez formed the duo *Electric Kulintang* and founded *Mundo Niños,* an organization that provides workshops on percussion to teach improvisation to young children.

BIBLIOGRAPHY

D. Mandl: "Rhythm and Radiance," *Wire Magazine* (June 2002)

P. Catapano: "Bang a Gong (or Eight) in a Pan-Cultural Fusion," *New York Times* (18 Feb 2006)

T. Lee: "Filipina-American Percussionist Susie Ibarra," *Azine: The Asian American Movement Ezine* (9 Nov 2009) <http://apimovement.com/susie-ibarra/filipina-american-percussionist-susie-ibarra>

MARY TALUSAN

Ibrahim, Abdullah [Brand, Adolph Johannes; Brand, Dollar] (*b* Cape Town, South Africa, 9 Oct 1934). South African pianist. Born and raised in the cosmopolitan port city of Cape Town, he was surrounded by many musical cultures from which he has crafted a singularly influential and unified voice. He was brought up in the local African Methodist Episcopal Church which his grandmother founded. Moving through the city he was also exposed to *marabi*, Khosa hymns, and jazz recordings. Setting aside his aspirations for a career in medicine, he joined the groundbreaking ensemble the Jazz Epistles in 1960. He was soon subject to oppressive scrutiny under the apartheid regime, which prompted him to move to Zurich, Switzerland, with his future wife, the singer Sathima Bea Benjamin. Duke Ellington heard him perform and arranged a recording session, which earned him more recording dates and festival appearances throughout Europe. In 1965 he and Benjamin moved to New York. Once in the United States, he toured extensively, including work with Elvin Jones and as substitute in the piano chair of Ellington's orchestra. He also recorded a series of duets with Buddy Tate, Max Roach, Archie Shepp, and Randy Weston, among others. In 1968 he converted to Islam and after making a pilgrimage to Mecca he adopted the name Ibrahim. In the mid-1970s he visited Cape Town briefly, sponsoring a jazz festival and recording with South African musicians. It is during this period when he composed and recorded "Mannenburg" which became an anthem for South African freedom. After once again moving from South Africa, Ibrahim led several groups on various tours, including the septet Ekaya. Since 1990 he has lived both in New York and Cape Town, where he played at Nelson Mandela's inauguration in 1994. He has continued to perform outreach work there, including Project M7, an educational initiative for young South Africans. Despite drawing on many musical cultures expressed through multiple genres, Ibrahim has maintained a mission of peaceful unity realized through compelling performance.

SELECTED RECORDINGS

As leader: *Duke Ellington Presents the Dollar Brand Trio* (1963, Rep.); *African Space Program* (1973, Enja); *Blues for a Hip King* (1975, The Sun); *African Marketplace* (1979, Elek.); *African River* (1989, Enja); *Senzo* (2008, Sunnyside)

As sideman with Jazz Epistles: *Jazz Epistle Verse I* (1960, Gallo/Continental)

BIBLIOGRAPHY

GroveJ

H. Willemse: "Abdullah Ibrahim Speaks!" *Staffrider*, vi/4 (1987)

K. Franckling: "Going Home: Abdullah Ibrahim," *DB*, lix/10 (1992), 22

L. Rasmussen: *Abdullah Ibrahim: a Discography* (Copenhagen, 1998)

M. Titlestad: *Making the Changes: Jazz in South African Literature and Reportage* (Pretoria, 2004)

MARK LOMANNO

Ice Cube [Jackson, O'Shea] (*b* Los Angeles, CA, 15 June 1969). Rapper and actor. Born and raised in Compton, California, a city southeast of downtown Los Angeles, Ice Cube began rapping in his teens with a group called C.I.A., which released one single produced by Dr. Dre, "My Posse" (independent, 1987). He joined N.W.A. in 1987, serving not only as a rapper on the group's first album *N.W.A. and the Posse* (Ruthless, 1987), but also as a lyricist. For example, he penned the lyrics for rapper Eazy-E's seminal track "Boyz-N-The-Hood," which helped to put West Coast gangsta rap on the map. Ice Cube also played a major role on N.W.A.'s second, highly influential album *Straight Outta Compton* (Ruthless, 1988). He served as one of the principal rappers, as well as lyricist for Eazy-E and Dr. Dre. He wrote a majority of "Fuck The Police," an outspoken song protesting police brutality and racial profiling by Los Angeles police officers. Cube's storytelling style, which described gang culture and African American lifestyle in South Central Los Angeles, would define his subsequent career as a rapper and actor.

Unhappy with his share of N.W.A.'s profits, Ice Cube left the group in 1989, releasing the critically and commercially successful *Amerikka's Most Wanted* (Priority, 1989), produced by the Bomb Squad. Ice Cube's solo work displayed the continued use of a "shouted" rap style and explicit lyrics. The E.P. *Kill At Will* (Priority, 1990) featured "Dead Homies," a detailed narrative describing the tragic aftermath of gang violence.

His second solo album *Death Certificate* (Priority, 1991) included a telling back cover image: Ice Cube stands at the center, with men in gang clothing under the heading "The Death Side" on his left, and Nation of Islam troops (Fruit of Islam or F.O.I.) under a heading "The Life Side" on his right. The imagery seems to suggest that gangsters, or gangsta rappers like Ice Cube, could turn to Islam to survive. Much of Ice Cube's solo work exhibits similar dualities, including his two disc album *War and Peace*: *War Disc* and *Peace Disc* (Priority, 2002). His lyrics also displayed two sides: sometimes promoting a political agenda and black self-awareness, but more often telling violent, at times sexist, stories related to gangster life. As artistic choices of hip hop musicians are often inextricable from commercial obligations, Ice Cube's work shows the conflicts of navigating artistic expression while fulfilling the buying public's expectations. Ice Cube was also a member of the group Westside Connection with fellow Los Angeles rappers Mack 10 [Dedrick Rolison] (*b* 1971), and WC [William Calhoun] (*b* 1970).

His acting debut in *Boyz n The Hood* (Columbia Pictures, 1991), the John Singleton film inspired by N.W.A., would transform Cube into a successful actor and filmmaker. His movies include the comedy *Friday* (New Line, 1995), a film about life in Compton, the plot of which could be seen as an extension of his rap storytelling style.

WILL FULTON

Ice dancing. A competitive discipline within the sport of figure skating, recognized at world championship level in 1952 and accepted into the Olympic Games in 1976. As in pair skating, ice dancing is performed by a couple skating to musical accompaniment. The two disciplines differ in the technical requirements and restrictions concerning spins, throws, jumps, and lifts, as well as in aesthetic requirements concerning the choreographic use of music. Ice dancers are required to skate to music that has a definite beat or rhythm and are judged partly on their ability to tailor their performance to it. Pair skaters more often skate to the melody or phrasing of their music, a practice that is severely penalized in ice dance.

The modern form of ice dancing, based on ballroom dancing, was introduced in Vienna in 1868 by the American figure skater Jackson Haines and soon became popular throughout Europe. In the United States, a theatrical form of ice dancing was popularized by the movies and ice shows of Sonja Henie in the 1930s and 1940s. After World War II, these were followed by touring troupes such as Ice Capades, Holiday on Ice, Stars on Ice, and the companies of professional skaters such as John Curry in the 1970s and the team of Jayne Torvill and Christopher Dean in the 1980s. Although ice dancing has since evolved into a more acrobatic sport, featuring difficult, awkward tricks and melodramatic expression, Torvill and Dean are still recognized as the supreme exponents of ice dancing in elegant ballroom style. They often danced to Broadway show tunes ("Mack and Mabel") and to American popular songs and dance music ("Tribute to Fred and Ginger," "Let's face the music and dance"). Today, skaters in all disciplines of figure skating sometimes perform to popular music by American songwriters but are equally likely to set their routines to rock, classical, or sacred music.

BIBLIOGRAPHY

L. Copley-Graves: *Figure Skating History: the Evolution of Dance on Ice* (Columbus, OH, 1992)
C. Hilton: *Torvill and Dean: the Full Story* (London, 1994)
J. Torvill, C. Dean, and J. Man: *Torvill and Dean: the Autobiography of Ice Dancing's Greatest Stars* (London and New York, 1996)

CLAUDE CONYERS

Ice-T [Morrow, Tracy] (*b* Newark, NJ, 14 Feb 1958). Rapper and actor. One of the first "gangsta" rappers to succeed in the music industry. Along with artists such as N.W.A., Ice-T helped bring national attention to West Coast rap. As a young teenager, he moved to Southern California from New Jersey. He attended Crenshaw High School in Los Angeles and danced with the West Coast Locksmiths and with the Radio Crew. With these groups, he appeared in the films *Breakin'* (1984) and *Breakin' II: Electric Boogaloo* (1984), two Hollywood films quick to cash in on the breakdancing fad. As an aspiring rapper, Morrow gave himself the name Ice-T, which he derived from one of his inspirations: pimp/poet/novelist Iceberg Slim. He released his major label debut, *Rhyme Pays* (1987, Sire), with assistance from DJ Aladdin and producer Afrika Islam. That same year, he recorded the title track for Dennis Hopper's film *Colors,* which dramatized inner city gang life in Los Angeles. Soon after he formed his own label, Rhyme Syndicate (distributed by Warner/Sire), and released *Power* (1988), which, like much of his early rap work, featured explicit lyrics and sparse beats.

Ice-T also founded Body Count, a heavy metal band that released their eponymous debut album in 1992. Its track "Cop Killer," delivered by Ice-T from the point of view of the murderer, provoked public outcry from watchdog groups and law enforcement agencies. Although the song was thrash metal in style, the discourse surrounding the controversy consistently focused more on Ice-T's rap history than on metal. The band's record label, Time-Warner, withdrew the album from stores and eventually Ice-T chose to remove it from the album. With a higher, if controversial, profile, Ice-T continued to release rap albums throughout the 1990s, and to a lesser extent into the 21st century.

Ice-T has also developed a successful career as an actor on film and television. He has appeared in many feature films, including *New Jack City* (1991), for which he recorded "New Jack Hustler" for the soundtrack album. In 1999, he took the role of Odafin "Fin" Tutuola on the highly successful crime drama *Law and Order: Special Victims Unit,* and, in an ironic twist, has played the role of a police detective for over a decade.

BIBLIOGRAPHY

A. Light: "Body Count Shows Cancelled: 'Cop Killer' Protest Continues after Police Refuse to Provide Security" *Rolling Stone* (4 Feb 1993), 16
B. Higa: "Early Los Angeles Hip Hop," *Vibe History of Hip Hop* (New York, 1999), 111–19

JUSTIN A. WILLIAMS

Ideal Records. Record label. Ideal Records was one of the first Mexican American–owned record labels in the country and was influential in recording, disseminating, and popularizing Texas Mexican *conjuntos, orquestas,* and vocal duos and trios throughout Texas and the Southwest. It was founded in 1946 by Armando Marroquín, a jukebox businessman frustrated by the lack of Spanish-language music available. His first recording was of a female duo, Carmen y Laura (Carmen was his wife), singing about post–World War II sentiments; it was an instant hit among his clients. Marroquín joined with Paco Betancourt, owner of the Rio Grande Music Company in nearby San Benito, to help with distribution. They set up a studio in downtown Alice, Texas. The records immediately sold and the studio attracted the region's top musicians: accordionists Narciso Martínez, Tony de la Rosa, and Valerio Longoria; bandleaders Beto Villa and Paulino Bernal; popular female singer Lydia Mendoza, and others. The Tejano music industry owes a great debt to Ideal. It inspired scores of independent record labels specializing in Spanish-language music like Falcón, Río, Bego, Zarape, Corona, Freddie Records, and Discos Joey. In 1990, Arhoolie Records owner Chris Strachwitz purchased the Ideal masters and reissued many recordings to the delight of new audiences.

CATHY RAGLAND

Iggy Pop. *See* POP, IGGY.

Iglesias, Enrique (*b* Madrid, Spain, 8 May 1975). Spanish pop music singer-songwriter, active in the United States. The third child of singer Julio Iglesias (*b* 1943), he moved to Miami in 1982. He first found commercial success among US Latinos and Latin Americans singing in Spanish. His first three albums, *Enrique Iglesias* (1995), *Vivir* (1997), and *Cosas del amor* (1998), were released by Mexican label Fonovisa. In the wake of the Latin Pop music boom of the late 1990s, Iglesias signed with Interscope Records and released an album in English, *Enrique* (1999). The album was a major crossover success in the United States and internationally. In the aftermath of the 11 September 2001 terrorist attacks on New York and Washington, DC, Iglesias's song "Hero," the first single off his second English-language album *Escape* (2001), was used as a tribute song and became a popular national anthem. His songs feature straightforward and direct lyrics, and his music is strongly rooted in North American pop with only minor references to Latin American or Spanish popular music traditions. His most recognizable trait is the emotional vulnerability of his mildly raspy voice. He continues to record successfully in both Spanish and English.

DANIEL PARTY

Illinois, University of. State university founded in 1867. The School of Music in Urbana-Champaign was established in 1895 and made a unit of the College of Fine and Applied Arts in 1931. The school enrolls approximately 825 students and has over 90 instructors. BM, BME, BA, MM, MME, EdD, DMA, and PhD degrees are offered in performance, conducting, music education, theory, composition, jazz, and musicology. The Music Library contains more than 765,000 holdings, including over 55,000 books, 520,000 scores, 19,000 microforms, 150,000 sound recordings, and 20,000 items in other formats and media. Special collections include those of Rafael Joseffy and Joseph Szigeti, among others. The school maintains a Musicological Archive for Renaissance Manuscript Studies (with more than 90% of known polyphonic sources from 1400 to 1550 on film) and a Hymn Tune Index. The Experimental Music Studios (EMS) were founded by Lejaren Hiller in 1958. Many important compositions were created at the studio; Hiller, Brün, Martirano, Cage, Gaburo, Ben Johnston, and Scott Wyatt are among the composers who have been associated with it. More recently, the EMS was expanded to include the Computer Music Project. In 2008 the school opened the Robert E. Brown Center for World Music. The Sousa Archives and the Center for American Music are part of the University Library and University Archives.

BIBLIOGRAPHY

A.L. Silverberg: *A Sympathy with Sounds: A Brief History of the University of Illinois* (Urbana, IL, 1995)

MARK FONDER

Imbrie, Andrew (Welsh) (*b* New York, NY, 6 April 1921; *d* Berkeley, CA, 5 Dec 2007). Composer. Andrew Imbrie ranks high among composers of his generation for the distinguishing individuality, independence, personal and often passionate expressiveness, and high craft evident throughout a large corpus of works in all of the traditional genres. He began piano studies at the age of four with Ann Abajian, and continued with Pauline and LEO ORNSTEIN until 1942. He also studied briefly with NADIA BOULANGER (1937) and Robert Casadesus (1941). As an undergraduate at Princeton (BA 1942) he studied composition with ROGER SESSIONS. After serving in the US Army (1944–6), he followed Sessions to the University of California, Berkeley, where he received the MA in 1947 and was in the same year appointed an instructor. He postponed the start of his teaching career, however, to accept a fellowship at the American Academy in Rome (1947–9), to which he later returned as composer-in-residence (1967–8). Returning to Berkeley in 1949,

he remained a member of the music department until his retirement in 1991.

Highly respected as a teacher and scholar as well as a composer, Imbrie also taught at the San Francisco Conservatory and held distinguished visiting professorships at the University of Alabama, the University of Chicago, and Brandeis, Harvard, Northwestern, and New York universities. He also served as composer-in-residence at the Tanglewood Music Center (1991) and the Festival at Sandpoint, Idaho (1989, 1990, 1992, 1993). His many honors include the New York Music Critics' Award (1944), the Alice M. Ditson Award (1947), National Institute of Arts and Letters grant (1950), two Guggenheim fellowships (1953–4, 1959–60), the Hinrichsen Award of the American Academy of Arts and Letters (1971), a Citation from the University of California, Berkeley (1991), and commissions from the Koussevitzky (1954), Fromm (1957), Ford (1959, 1974), and Naumburg (1960, 1981) foundations, the New York PO (1977), the San Francisco Opera (1976), and the San Francisco SO (1984). He was elected to the National Institute of Arts and Letters in 1969 and, in 1980, to the American Academy of Arts and Sciences. He also served as a board member of the Koussevitzky Foundation and as governor of the San Francisco SO (1982–91). He was awarded the Doctor of Music degree by the San Francisco Conservatory of Music, 2004.

Imbrie's aesthetic was strongly shaped by his pedagogical encounter with Sessions. Like Sessions, he remained committed to the principles of classical motivic development, harmonic structure, and phrasing throughout his career. While his cosmopolitan outlook and life as well as his assimilation of America's vernacular and jazz music are evident in various compositions, most of his ideas came from internal sources. Indeed, much of his melodic impulse is a vocal one, becoming more impassioned, wide-ranging, ecstatic in instrumental works from the 1960s on. From the earliest to the last works, however, there is a remarkable consistency of craft, character, and his voice as a composer. In published articles on Sessions and Beethoven, he articulated concerns that also inform his compositional work: the construction of long, nuanced musical lines and the embedding of metrical relationships on different structural levels. The harmonic materials of his work are varied, though usually non-triadic. He remained flexible and open to a broad range of possibilities, however. In the opera *Angle of Repose*, for example, he incorporated bits of banjo and fiddle music and other North American folk idioms into a predominantly richly dissonant and elusively tonal harmonic language. A similar sense of personal expression can be heard in many of his "abstract" instrumental works.

WORKS

OPERAS

Three against Christmas (Christmas in Peebles Town) (comic op, 4 scenes, R. Wincor), 1960, Berkeley, CA, 1 Dec 1964

Angle of Repose (3, O. Hall, after W. Stegner), 1976, San Francisco, 6 Nov 1976

INSTRUMENTAL

Orch: Ballad, D, 1947; Vn Conc., 1954; Little Conc., pf 4 hands, orch, 1956; Legend, 1959; Sym. no.1, 1965; Chbr Sym., 1968; Sym. no.2, 1970; Sym. no.3, 1970; Vc Conc., 1972; Pf Conc. no.1, 1973; Pf Conc. no.2, 1974; Fl Conc., 1977; Pf Conc. no.3, 1992

Chbr and solo inst: Str Qt no.1, 1942; Pf Trio, 1946; Pf Sonata, 1947; Divertimento, fl, bn, tpt, pf trio, 1949; Serenade, fl, va, pf, 1952; Str Qt no.2, 1953; Str Qt no.3, 1957; Impromptu, vn, pf, 1960; Sonata, vc, pf, 1966; Dandelion Wine, ob, cl, str qt, pf, 1967; 3 Sketches, trbn, pf, 1967; Here We Stand, fanfare, double brass ens, 1969; Str Qt no.4, 1969; A Hawk for Peace, fanfare, brass, 1970; To a Traveler, cl, vn, pf, 1971; Fancy for Five, 5 trbn, 1972; Short Story, pf, 1982; Pilgrimage, fl, cl, vn, vc, pf, perc, 1983; Daedalus, pf, 1986; Dream Sequence, fl, ob, cl, vn, va, vc, pf, perc, 1986; Prelude, org, 1987; Str Qt no.5, 1987; Three-piece Suite, hp, pf, 1987; Pf Trio no.2, 1989; Reminiscence, gui, 1992; Earplay Fantasy, fl, cl, vn, vc, pf, perc, 1995; Chicago Bells, vn, pf, 1997; Mukashi Mukashi (Once Upon a Time), 2 pf, 1997; Spring Fever, fl, ob, cl, pf, perc, 2 vn, va, vc, db, 1997; Soliloquy, vn, 1998; Piano Quartet, 1999, From Time to Time, fl, ob, cl, bn, perc, 2 vn, va, 2 vc, 2000; Four Hand Fantasy, 2001; In Memoriam Nathan Schwartz, vc, 2002; Duet for Two Friends, cl, vc, 2002; Sonatina for Solo Viola, 2003; Concertino for Vn and Chbr Sym, 2005; To My Son, pf solo, 2006; Kayagum Solo, 2006; Sextet for Six Friends, fl, ob, cl, vn, va, vc, 2007.

VOCAL

On the Beach at Night (W. Whitman), SATB, str orch, 1949; 3 Songs (R. Frost, E.L. Masters, J.C. Ransom), S, orch, 1949; 2 Christmas Carols, male vv, pf, 1955; Introit, Gradual and Alleluia for All Saints' Day, chorus, org, 1956; Drum-Taps (cant., Whitman), SATB, orch, 1960; Ps xlii, TBB, org, 1962; Tell Me Where s Fancy Bred (W. Shakespeare), S, cl, gui, 1964; 3 Songs (e.e. cummings, Euripides, T. Roethke), chorus, pf, 1965; [3 songs], 1966: The Wind has blown the rain away, SAB, pf; Love distills desire upon the eyes, SATB, pf; The Serpent, SAB, pf

Let all the World (G. Herbert), anthem, SATB, brass, perc, org, 1971; Let Us Now Sing the Praises of Famous Men, SATB, org, 1977; Prometheus Bound (D. Grene, after Aeschylus), 3 solo vv, chorus, orch, 1979; 5 Roethke Songs, S, pf, 1980; 3 Campion Songs, S, A, T, B, pf, 1981; A Song for St Cecilia's Day (J. Dryden), SATB, 2 vn, brass, perc, 2 pf, 1981; Requiem: in memoriam John H. Imbrie 1962–1981 (Lat., W. Blake, J. Donne, Herbert), S, SATB, orch, 1984; Adam (cant., late medieval and Amer. Civil War period texts), S, SATB, orch, 1994; Songs of Then and Now (R.L. Stevenson, Cummings, Shakespeare), SA, fl, cl, vn, va, pf, perc, 1998 Four Songs (The Tyger), sop, barit., pf, 2005

Recorded interviews in *NHoh*
Principal publishers: Malcolm, Shawnee

BIBLIOGRAPHY

EwenD; VintonD (J.D. Kramer)
M. Boykan: "Andrew Imbrie: Third Quartet," *PNM*, iii/1 (1964–5), 139–46
E. Soskin: *Cadences and Formal Structure in Four American String Quartets* (diss., U. of California, Berkeley, 1986)
A.P. Basart: "A Three-Dimensional Musical World," *Cum notis variorum*, cxxxi (1989), 1–4 [interview]

ANN P. BASART/MARTIN BRODY/ROBERT COMMANDAY

Imperial. Record label. The company was established by Lew Chudd in 1946 in Los Angeles, where it originally issued records aimed at the local Mexican American market. With the New Orleans bandleader and arranger Dave Bartholomew as the company's A&R man, Chudd extended Imperial's reach into the emergent rhythm and blues market. Their first major signing was the New Orleans pianist and singer Fats Domino. Between 1949 and 1962, Domino had a string of hit records with Imperial beginning with "The Fat Man" (1949) which was a hit on *Billboard*'s R&B chart. Domino also began to achieve increasing crossover success for the small, independent label. His biggest hit, "Blueberry Hill" (1956), reached no.1 on the R&B chart and no.2 on the Hot 100.

Imperial was the first label to promote the New Orleans R&B scene and, with the success of Domino, several others signings followed: Roy Brown, Smiley Lewis, Tommy Ridgely, and The Spiders. In 1952 country singer Slim Whitman signed to the label and had a no.2 hit on the Country chart with "Indian Love Call." In 1957 Ricky Nelson was signed and immediately became a profitable asset for the label with the no.1 hit album *Ricky* followed by a no.1 hit single "Poor Little Fool" the following year. Imperial also issued recordings by blues artists T-Bone Walker, Smokey Hogg, and Lightnin' Hopkins. The label also issued a few significant jazz records, notably by Sonny Criss, Charlie Mariano, and Harold Land. After the departure of Domino and Nelson to other labels, in 1964 Chudd sold Imperial to Liberty Records.

BIBLIOGRAPHY

R. Kennedy and R. McNutt: *Little Labels—Big Sound: Small Record Companies and the Rise of American Music* (Bloomington, IN, 1999)

IAN BROOKES

Imperials, the. *See* LITTLE ANTHONY AND THE IMPERIALS.

Impressions, the. Soul vocal group. Formed in Chicago in 1957 as the Roosters, its original members were JERRY BUTLER (*b* 1939), CURTIS MAYFIELD (*b* 1942–*d* 1999), Sam Gooden (*b* 1942), and the brothers Arthur and Richard Brooks. As the Impressions they made their first recording, "For Your Precious Love," which was released on three different labels, selling most copies on Vee-Jay Records in 1958. Fred Cash (*b* 1938) replaced Butler, who left to pursue a solo career, and having signed for ABC-Paramount the group had a hit with Mayfield's "Gypsy Woman" (1961). Shortly thereafter the Brooks brothers left and the group continued as a trio. In 1970 Mayfield decided to go solo, triggering a number of changes in personnel. Gooden and Cash continued to perform into the second decade of the 21st century.

Led by Mayfield's talent for songwriting, guitar playing, and production, the Impressions defined the sound of Chicago soul and achieved much success throughout the 1960s. Their records commonly featured extensive use of falsetto, a combination of clipped rhythm guitar and bright lead guitar, percussive (often pizzicato) strings, metallic timbres from vibraphone or glockenspiel, brass (as opposed to saxophones), and instrumental vamps instead of solos. A great deal of their success can be attributed to Johnny Pate's innovative arrangements. Through the interplay of their multiple lead vocals, they evoked a palpable sense of community. As earlier songs such as "Keep on pushing" (1964) and "People get ready" (1965) reflected the spirit of the Civil Rights movement, by the end of the decade Mayfield's work showed a more militant stance, notably on "This is my country" (1968), and "Choice of Colors" (1969). The group was inducted into the Rock and Roll Hall of Fame in 1991.

BIBLIOGRAPHY

R. Pruter: *Chicago Soul* (Urbana, IL, 1991)
R. Pruter: *Curtis Mayfield and the Impressions: the Anthology (1961–1977)*, MCA MCAD2-10664 (1992) [liner notes]

R. Bowman: *Movin' On Up: the Music and Message of Curtis Mayfield and the Impressions* (2008) [DVD liner notes]

ROB BOWMAN

Improvisation. The practice of improvisation is widely regarded as a prominent feature of American musical culture as well as a fundamental component of the international image of America's music. While not present in all forms of American music, improvisation serves as a pronounced or even defining element of some of America's best-known musical forms, including jazz, blues, rock, and bluegrass; some forms of American classical music, particularly since the 1950s, also incorporate performance and compositional practices that deploy improvisation.

1. Definitions. 2. Improvisative practice in American music.

1. DEFINITIONS. Constructing a definition of improvisation was once considered a relatively straightforward matter. The *Oxford Dictionary of Music*'s pithy definition was typical, framing improvisation as a performance conducted "according to the inventive whim of the moment, i.e. without a written or printed score, and not from memory." Ethnomusicologist Paul Berliner's 1994 book on improvisation in jazz began to complicate this understanding, describing the practice as involving "reworking precomposed material and designs in relation to unanticipated ideas conceived, shaped, and transformed under the special conditions of performance" (Berliner, p. 241).

These definitions, like many emerging from music scholarship, tend to privilege individual expression in performance over other crucial aspects of the improvisative experience, such as attention, listening, and dialogue. Moreover, these perspectives appear to draw implicitly upon an ideologically driven dialectic between improvisation and composition, reflecting widespread contention regarding not just the nature of improvisation, but its propriety as well. This debate dovetails with improvisation's fraught status in Western classical music history and culture, in which improvisation, particularly since the 18th century, has been compared with the practice of composition, with clear prejudices in favor of the latter practice's presumed advantages in terms of creating unity and coherence in musical utterance. In that light, as ethnomusicologist Bruno Nettl, one of the pioneers of 20th-century scholarship on improvisation, observed in a *Grove Music Online* essay, "the term 'improvisation,' in suggesting a failure to plan ahead or making do with whatever means are available, may have negative implications." Thus, in Western culture, as Nettl continued, "the musics that are most dependent on improvisation, such as jazz, have traditionally been regarded as inferior to art music, in which pre-composition is considered paramount." As Nettl noted in the same essay, while ethnomusicologists in the 1960s produced detailed case studies of improvisation, concentrating on jazz, Indian classical music, and Iranian (Persian) music, "before the 1970s the field of musicology tended to treat improvisation as a 'craft,' in contrast to the 'art' of composition." Since the mid-1970s and moving into the late 1980s, however, musicology's increasing interest in improvisation went hand in hand with the field's turn to cultural history, popular music studies, and the investigation of experimental music scenes.

Art Ensemble of Chicago, 1993. (JazzSign/Lebrecht Music & Arts)

Terry Riley, 2007. (Pascal Saez/Lebrecht Music & Arts)

Writing on improvisation in Western art music, *Grove Music Online* author Rob C. Wegman maintained that "the concept of improvisation has been current in the West since the late 15th century to designate any type, or aspect, of musical performance that is not expressive of the concept of the fixed musical work. Its precise definition depends on the stability and perceived identity of the 'fixed musical work,' which varies widely according to musical culture and historical period." This conceptual dialogue with the historical notion of *Werktreue* leads inevitably to Wegman's observation that "musical traditions that do not rely on a strong conception of the fixed musical work tend not to have a concept of 'improvisation,' but rather qualify performances in terms of a musical idiom or a set of performative conventions." This remark is nuanced, if not entirely contradicted by Nettl's section of the same article on improvisation: "Determining the presence or absence of improvisation in a particular culture depends to a great extent on the culture's own taxonomy of music-making and on its assessing of the relationship between what is memorized or given and the performance."

There is good reason to be circumspect about projecting a Western-centered definition of improvisation on non-Western, popular, or non-art music traditions, or even remote historical periods in Western art music. However, scholars working on non-musical aspects of human experience, and not necessarily working in dialogue with these particular musical histories and aesthetic ideologies have created potentially more generalizable, bidirectional models and definitions of improvisation that may have the potential to cross cultural borders. For instance, researching negotiators in business transactions, a team of investigators in the field of organizational science sought to "define an improvisation in the context of a negotiation as a coherent sequence of relational, informational, and procedural actions and responses created, chosen, and carried out by the parties during the social interaction" (McGinn and Keros, 445).

One notes the irrelevance to this expanded context of ideological debates common in musical research concerning whether or not improvisations must inevitably rely upon preset, memorized formulae, rules, and cultural models. Moreover, the prosaic nature of this definition itself seems to undercut attempts to impose upon the concept of improvisation the special sense of creative autonomy or uniqueness that many commentators in the field of music seem to demand of the practice. Here, improvisation becomes a matter of negotiation, choice, action, and response, incorporating production and perception, process and product—all aspects of human experience that improvisations in music share with improvisations in everyday life. In this context, assumed dialectical relations between composition and improvisation merely serve to warp and obscure attempts at creating workable definitions of the latter.

The British experimental guitarist Derek Bailey's *Improvisation: Its Nature and Practice in Music,* perhaps the most widely cited book on the subject in recent academic literature, manages to simply avoid creating a definition at all, preferring to describe cases in which improvisation as he understands it is practiced, in order to fulfill the remit of the book to divine its nature. Following this approach, we can now turn to some of the many appearances of improvisation in American music.

2. IMPROVISATIVE PRACTICE IN AMERICAN MUSIC. Many discussions of improvisation in American music begin and end with its presence in African American musical culture—from the field hollers and work songs of antebellum days to blues, jazz, rhythm and blues, and hip-hop "freestyling." However, there is considerable evidence indicating that well before the arrival of Europeans and Africans on the shores of North America, improvisation was already present in both contributory and defining roles in the music of many Native American peoples. Particularly noted for their improvised music-making were the YUROK of Northern California, and the CHOCTAW, forcibly removed from their originary Southern United States homelands to Indian territory in what is now Oklahoma. As Bruno Nettl observed,

> Even in societies in which improvisation is not recognized it may play a role in the conception of music. Some Amerindian music is said to be created in a moment of ecstasy, with a suddenness analogous to peoples of the North American Plains who say that in the dream the song was sung to them by an animal guardian spirit only once. The visionary, however, rehearses the song before singing it for other humans. In Plains culture this way of composing is contrasted with another, in which someone may sing through the songs they know and will consciously combine sections to create a new work.

In late 18th-century Yankee folk PSALMODY, improvisation was common and considered an essential aspect of the experience. The sacred harp choral practices of the mid-1800s, performed by amateur church congregations and facilitated by the notationally simplified innovation of shape-note singing, encouraged improvised ornamentation, and those Yankee singing masters who ventured into the Southern United States encountered improvised harmony on the part of congregants. Those social aesthetics, however, played havoc with those whose moral or religious scruples demanded obedience to the text (to set a moral example), and by the mid-19th century, the aesthetics of congregational singing in Northern Euro-American communities were in flux. Leading sacred music reformer Lowell Mason, part of a highly distinguished musical family, moved to stamp out the joyous and energetic improvisational style of yore, in order to restore appropriate decorum and moral order, and to remove secular associations, particularly those associated with "lower" popular music forms (Preston, p. 198).

American theater songs and other forms of popular entertainment throughout the 18th and 19th centuries often featured improvised ornamentation and virtuosic vocal display. One popular solo vehicle was Benjamin Carr and Susanna Rowson's "The Little Sailor Boy," which was described as "a miniature melodrama" (Tick and Beaudoin, 78–9). Blackface MINSTRELSY, perhaps the most important popular performance form to emerge in the United States during the 19th century, featured extensive improvisatory aspects in text, music,

and gesture. SLACK KEY GUITAR, or *Ki ho'alu*, dates back to the mid-19th century, in the wake of the arrival of the guitar on the Hawaiian Islands, brought by Southern Californian, Portuguese, and Mexican workers. By the 1880s, hula troupes featured guitars, and the instrument, along with nose flutes, was heard at the royal court. The style of slack-key performance featured extensive improvisation, and contained elements of the *mele hula* and other chant and dance traditions.

Between 1800 and the Civil War, as music historian Richard Crawford notes, "most African-American music was made by slaves," by which we mean specifically African persons who were brought into bondage against their will, as well as generations of their descendants. "Patting Juba," a body-based rhythmic dance accompaniment, served as an improvised slave substitute for the drum, whose use by slaves was outlawed in many states, as well as for other "loud instruments" that plantation owners feared could be used to literally drum up conspiracies and rebellions (Crawford, pp. 409–10). Traveling chroniclers marveled at the apparently endless variety of improvised choruses that slaves produced in their songs, and despite some owners' insistence that black slaves should not sing hymns of their own composition—a posture analogous to the desires of Lowell Mason, but pursued for rather different ends—black slaves persisted in creating improvised versions of sacred songs that were revered as much for their improvised provenance as for their nominally religious content.

The ubiquitous WORK SONGS of slaves featured improvised verses and responsive choruses, as well as competitive songs—precursors to hip-hop "beef" songs—that featured a form of what literary scholar Henry Louis Gates would later theorize as "signifyin(g)," even if part of what was being signified was the presence of the slaves themselves, as the sounds were often enough mandated as part of the overseers' surveillance strategies. Many of these melodic, rhythmic, and linguistic tropes were retained across the centuries, turning up in the musical games and improvised jump rope songs of young African American girls, and in the freestyling that rappers use, particularly in live settings, as an occasional respite from the otherwise meticulously composed and highly produced sense of flow that characterized 20th- and early 21st-century HIP HOP.

The traditions of today's New Orleans jazz funerals predate jazz; according to Joseph Roach, the "Second Line," in which marchers, dancers, and other musicians follow the main funeral band with improvised accompaniment, exemplifies what Roach calls "memory as improvisation" (Roach, pp. 279–81). The second line becomes a performance of memory in which "improvisation introduces a space for play within memory itself," a dynamic that, by definition, counters the Grove Dictionary's characterization of improvisation as "essentially evanescent." In these and countless other ways and in many venues in Creole New Orleans, from dance halls to brothels, "a new social order was improvised" as Roach put it—an excellent description of what was occurring in America writ large.

Other "pre-jazz" forms of improvised music included the minstrel songs, a form dating from the mid-19th century, one of the forms of music preserved for the early 20th century by southern Appalachian folk musicians, among others. 19th-century fiddlers and banjoists, black and white, embellished and ornamented popular melodies, and white and black Appalachian amateur and folk musicians were listening assiduously to early blues guitarists such as Blind Lemon Jefferson. By the late 1940s, these tendencies had coalesced in BLUEGRASS MUSIC, an extension of the earlier forms that spread to urban areas as it was taken up by the emerging country music industry of the period, led by virtuoso fiddlers such as Vassar Clements, guitarists such as Bill Monroe and Lester Flatt, and banjoists such as Earl Scruggs. Indeed, the BLUES—country and urban—retained and extended its improvised and virtuosic elements in many and varied ways. At the turn of the 20th century, RAGTIME was both a form of composition and a style of improvised performance; as with its direct progeny, 1920s Harlem STRIDE piano, a given rag could go on as long as audience and performer consented.

Moviegoers of the first decades of the 20th century were regularly treated to instrumental improvisations on organ and piano as accompaniment to silent films produced before the appearance of the first "talkies" in the 1920s. (*See* FILM MUSIC.) Among the many performers who practiced this art, known and unknown, was composer Carl Stalling, later famed for his soundtracks to Walt Disney and Warner Brothers cartoons. "I had played in theaters for about twenty years before sound came in," he told an interviewer in 1971. "We improvised all the time, on the organ. I'd have to put music out for the orchestra, for features, but for comedies and newsreels we just improvised at the organ. So I really was used to composing for films before I started writing for cartoons....I just imagined myself playing for a cartoon in the theater, improvising, and it came easier" (Tick and Boudoin, p. 425).

With the sacred traditional music that became known as the spirituals—or what W.E.B. DuBois called the "sorrow songs" in his 1903 classic, *The Souls of Black Folk*, in recognition of their slave provenance—melodic affect eluded precise notation and capacity for improvisation was essentially infinite; in response to a query as to how many stanzas there were in his song, its creator responded, "until you get tired" (Levine, p. 159; *see* SPIRITUAL). The spirituals' immediate descendant, gospel music, retained the capacity for improvisative utterance, as notated forms composed by professional musicians were elaborated and even subverted in virtuoso performance. Acknowledging this, black GOSPEL MUSIC composers of the 1920s, including the "father of gospel," Thomas A. Dorsey, produced separate versions of the music—a carefully notated score for white consumption, and a lead sheet for the black market to facilitate improvised performance (Levine, p. 186).

The tremendous growth in the professionalization (and commercialization) of improvised music-making during the 20th century was arguably an outgrowth of the enormously varied and hugely influential styles of JAZZ music. By the time jazz began to appear as a named entity, the variegated approaches to improvisations promulgated by earlier generations of African American musicians had become widespread; from New Orleans to Chicago to New York to Paris and points around the world, stride, swing, bebop, free jazz, fusion, and styles and substyles too numerous to count have marked the development of the most influential American music to emerge before rock and roll and hip hop. Of these styles of music-making, jazz is the music most centrally identified with improvisation, and to be sure, the music that portrays American culture as inseparable from its improvisative aspect.

By the 1920s, jazz was already straining its boundaries, attracting powerful defenders and detractors alike. European classical composers of the 1920s incorporated its sounds into their work and admonished their American counterparts to make it the foundation of a new American music. But the philosopher Theodor Adorno railed against jazz from 1930 until his death, seeing it as commercial seduction and feigned authenticity of human experience. Nonetheless, jazz and jazz-influenced forms gained homegrown variants, spin-offs, and post-jazz evolutionary developments in Europe, Asia, Latin America, the Caribbean, and Oceania. Mediated by improvisative practice, intercultural hybrids emerged, such as the 1940s collaborations between composer George Russell, trumpeter Dizzy Gillespie, and Cuban conguero Chano Pozo, a "pan-African" musical collaboration which one commentator has termed "one of the germinal moments in the history of intercultural music making of the second half of the twentieth century" (Stanyek, p. 88).

Moving well beyond the image of marvelous and mystifying virtuosity that linked it with earlier black music traditions, jazz became identified, both at home and around the world, with authentic human freedom, creativity, resistance to illegitimate authority, civil and human rights, interculturalism, internationalism, pan-Africanism, social change, and even revolution. The working-class origins of jazz—in fact, its emergence from the history of a formerly enslaved people who still experience racism in the land of their birth—made jazz a symbol of how sound can embed aspirations, hopes, and the possibility of change.

As part of what Daniel Belgrad called a uniquely American "culture of spontaneity," and as the rise of FREE JAZZ in the United States was widely connected, both in Europe and the United States, with challenges to racism and the social and economic order generally, jazz became the musical accompaniment to the BLACK ARTS MOVEMENT, unifying artists from many disciplines (Belgrad, 1998). Blends of poetry, theater, and improvisation, explored by the Beat generation in the 1950s, became a standard feature of 1960s improvisation. Improvised music became part of a multimedia environment that treated sound, visuals, text, and stage dress as integrated features, along with overtly political sub-texts. This improvisative ethos inspired explorations in film, literature, visual art, theatre, photography, and dance, as well as academic investigations in fields as diverse as sociology, philosophy and theology, computer science, psychology, literary theory, and even business management.

The worldwide influence of jazz crossed boundaries of geography, class, race, language, and ethnicity in ways that led, by the 1950s, to a perception of it as rivaling the other great world-music tradition, Western classical music, along a number of axes. Particularly after 1950, alongside bebop's success in cementing jazz's claim to art music status, improvisation became a contentious issue in American classical music. American composers such as John Cage, Christian Wolff, Earle Brown, and Morton Feldman became influential for their experiments with open forms and with more personally expressive systems of notation, designating salient aspects of a composition as performer- or environment-supplied rather than composer-specified.

This advent of what Cage and others termed "indeterminacy" in performance and in the compositional process led some listeners, critics, composers, and performers to conflate that practice with the practice of improvisation. (*See* ALEATORY and EXPERIMENTAL MUSIC.) The issue was a matter of fierce debate and the writings of Cage, one of the most important composers and aesthetic theorists in postwar American music, exhibited considerable ambivalence regarding the practice. Early Cage deployed "considered improvisation," in his compositions, while later Cage avoided it as too related to individual psychology, taste, and the sonic signification of history and memory. Cage and Feldman became very critical of jazz, avoiding overt association with it, while Wolff and Brown (a former jazz trumpeter) were less distanced from this branch of American music. Brown later declared explicitly that he was working with improvisational forms, and both he and Wolff were at times mildly critical of those among their circle of colleagues who crafted more or less rigorously composed secondary scores as realizations of their indeterminate works, rather than simply performing them spontaneously, thereby pursuing an exploration of spontaneity itself as a component of the musical experience. Proceeding from Brown's pioneering work, graphic notation became one pathway linking the practices of improvisation and indeterminacy. (*See* NOTATION.)

In the 1960s and 1970s, the advent of minimalism was attended by the soprano saxophone improvisations of Terry Riley and La Monte Young, both of whom studied with the Hindustani classical singer Pandit Pran Nath. Eventually, improvisation, in concept and practice, became identified with an expansion of the meaning of experimental music itself, and around the same moment as the first stirrings of the free jazz of Ornette Coleman, Albert Ayler, and others in the early 1960s, composers with academic connections also began exploring free improvisation. These musicians, including Pauline Oliveros, Larry Austin, and Lukas

Foss, declared themselves particularly concerned with separating their music from overt association with what they saw as jazz's conventions. These composers, like others such as Alvin Lucier and La Monte Young, sought to avoid not just the structural conventions, but what they saw as the conventions of custom, such as overt displays of individual virtuosity. Some, such as Austin and Foss, later abandoned the practice, while others, such as Oliveros, building on her early work at the San Francisco Tape Music Center, continued to develop their improvisative practices in pan-stylistic and intercultural directions.

Later ensembles in the academic realm extended these experiments, notably at the University of California's Center for Music Experiment in San Diego, where Oliveros worked for a number of years, as well as the ensemble KIVA (violinist Mary Oliver, trombonist John Silber, and percussionist Jean-Charles François). Classically trained violinist Malcolm Goldstein, an early proponent of free improvisation in New York's downtown experimentalist movements of the 1960s, followed the publication of British guitarist Bailey's book with his own exploration of the relationship of improvisation to cultural, political, and social issues in his self-published 1988 book *Sounding the Full Circle*. A few classical interpreters, such as the keyboard player Robert Levin, began in the 1980s to emulate their colleagues of two centuries' distance in improvising cadenzas and fantasias on the spot.

Many forays into improvisation in experimental music incorporated technology. Around 1965, saxophonist Eddie Harris had become one of the first musicians in any field to seriously experiment, in concert and on records, with the new real-time music technologies, forging a trenchant connection between advanced electronic music techniques, extended acoustic instrumental technique, and down-home funk that presaged trumpeter Miles Davis's better-known forays of the late 1960s and after. The 1970s advent of relatively small, portable minicomputers and microcomputers made live, interactive computer music a practical possibility, and during the 1970s and 1980s, composer-performers such as Joel Chadabe, Salvatore Martirano, David Behrman, David Rosenboom, George Lewis, and the California Bay Area scene surrounding the League of Automatic Music Composers (Jim Horton, John Bischoff, Rich Gold, Tim Perkis, Mark Trayle, and others) began creating computer music machines that interacted with each other and human musicians to create music collectively, blurring the boundaries between improvisation in the traditional sense of purposive human activity and machine interactivity. (*See* COMPUTERS AND MUSIC and ELECTROACOUSTIC MUSIC.)

From the late 1950s onward, the palette of instrumental timbre used in jazz was greatly expanded; oboes, bass clarinets, fluegelhorns, and soprano saxophones were rediscovered, as well as percussion, reeds, and flutes from around the world. Reflecting the increasing globalization of sound, musicians such as Yusef Lateef began to listen to music from Africa, Asia, South and Central America, Oceania, and Native

America. Multiphonics and many other extended instrumental and vocal techniques were to be found in the work of people like Abbey Lincoln, Jeanne Lee, Leon Thomas, John Coltrane, and Pharoah Sanders. Traditional distinctions between soloists and "rhythm sections" broke down, as instruments that normally assumed background roles in earlier forms of jazz, such as the bass, came to the front with the work of virtuosi such as Charles Mingus and Scott LaFaro. During this period, meters became irregular, or disappeared entirely, as did regular, steady pulses, and bebop's smooth stepwise melodic textures were expanded into the wide intervallic leaps of Eric Dolphy; harmonic practices ranged through quartal, serial, polytonal, pantonal, microtonal, and so-called atonal techniques. The recycling and subversion of melodies, harmonic sequences, and forms from Tin Pan Alley were no longer inevitably centered, and harmonic and modal schemes became more fluid, as with Bill Evans's "Flamenco Sketches," where a sequence of five modes recurs, with the duration of each mode being chosen by the ensemble and soloist in real time. Collective free improvisations strongly marked the work of Mingus, Ornette Coleman, Sun Ra, Albert Ayler, and late Coltrane.

By the end of the 1970s, the African American experimental musicians' collective known as the Association for the Advancement of Creative Musicians (AACM), founded in Chicago in 1965, had come to prominence. AACM composers such as Anthony Braxton, Amina Claudine Myers, Muhal Richard Abrams, and the members of the Art Ensemble of Chicago created extended-form works that combined improvisation and composition, extended technique and instrumentation, intermedia, and invented acoustic instruments. Another important collective was pianist Horace Tapscott's Los Angeles-based Union of God's Musicians and Artists Ascension, or Underground Musicians Association (UGMAA/UGMA), whose "Arkestra" (recalling Sun Ra's use of the term), familiarly called "The Ark," produced such musicians as saxophonists Arthur Blythe and David Murray, flutist James Newton, and trumpeter Lawrence "Butch" Morris.

In the 1990s, pianists Jon Jang and Glenn Horiuchi, saxophonists Russel Baba, Gerald Oshita, Fred Ho, and Francis Wong, bassist Mark Izu, storyteller Brenda Wong Aoki, and kotoist and electronic musician Miya Masaoka were prominent in the formation of an Asian American improvisation movement in the San Francisco Bay Area that drew upon pan-Asian constructions of American and world history and culture. (*See* ASIAN AMERICAN JAZZ.) A later California collective, Trummerflora, drew upon the energies of San Diego-based experimental musicians and filmmakers such as Hans Fjellestad, Ellen Weller, Marcelo Radulovich, Marcos Fernandes, and Damon Holzborn, to forge creative connections with electronic music improvisers such as Tijuana's Nor-Tec Collective. Another Los Angeles avant-garde improvisation scene included Vinny Golia, Nels Cline (who later joined the important band Wilco), Alex Cline, and G.E. Stinson.

Since the late 1950s, the gradual acceptance of jazz as a form of serious music was leading to the emergence of the United States as a leading site for the study of improvisation in academia, beginning with academic programs that featured the study of jazz, such as the Lenox School of Jazz. The concept of improvisation had already interested music educators who used it to enhance music learning, and by the 1970s, the Berklee School of Music had transformed itself from its early days as an outpost for adherents of Joseph Schillinger's System of Musical Composition to become one of the earliest important degree-granting programs in jazz. Programs at universities such as Wesleyan brought musicians such as saxophonist and free-jazz pioneer Marion Brown, who served as a graduate student assistant, to interact with graduate students in ethnomusicology, and with professors such as Nigerian drummer Abraham Adzenyah and *mṛdaṅgam* performers Ramnad Raghavan and T. Ranganathan. The 1960s push for African American studies in the academy led to the development of curricula in jazz performance, which meant that the pedagogy of improvisation was slowly becoming mainstream.

The Creative Music Studio (CMS), founded by the German vibraphonist Karlhanns Berger and his spouse Ingrid Sertso in the early 1970s in the forests near Woodstock, New York, brought together representatives of the Beats such as Allen Ginsberg; members of the AACM such as Braxton and Roscoe Mitchell; pioneers of experimental 1960s jazz such as Ornette Coleman and trumpeter Don Cherry; and experimental American classical composers and performers such as John Cage, Maryanne Amacher, and Frederic Rzewski. A crucial part of CMS pedagogy and performance drew upon the importance of improvisation to many traditions of music around the world, and performers from Asian and African musical traditions, such as the Zen practitioner and *shakuhachi* performer Watazumi-doso, came together with American improvisers to create a new kind of intercultural music performance think tank and pedagogical site.

Rock guitar, in the United States, particularly since Jimi Hendrix's apocalyptic solos, has become known as a dynamic area for improvisation, even if some scholars have claimed that many of the apparently spontaneous guitar breaks in heavy metal music (themselves an outgrowth of the analogous practice in jazz) were actually scripted in advance (Walser, 1993). California-based bands such as Jefferson Airplane and, most notably, the Grateful Dead, developed devoted followings for their extended improvisations, which the Dead's lead guitarist, Jerry Garcia, described as "anti-authoritarian" (Marre, 1992). In the late 1980s, members of New York's Black Rock Coalition, one of whose members, the band Living Colour, achieved substantial fame, reasserted the place of improvisation in rock, with strong leanings toward avant-garde jazz. Later, indie rock bands such as Chicago's Isotope 217 and the ensembles of Jim O'Rourke utilized rock-based elements in the creation of improvised music works, part of a larger Chicago avant-garde activity in the 1990s with Ken Vandermark and others.

In contrast to the generally tightly produced and scripted nature of recorded rap music, in live performance rap artists pursued two forms of improvisation. First, "freestyling" rappers created lyrics and rhythms in real time to create what was generally termed "flow" (in psychologist Mihaly Csikszentmihalyi's sense of the word). Second, 1990s rap artists and the now-ubiquitous DJs recycled turntables from the dustbin of history, saving them from analog obsolescence in the face of digital compact discs and portable digital music players by transforming them into musical instruments in their own right. (*See* DJ (ii).) A descendent of the traveling disk jockey that was a staple of 1950s African American social life, DJs of the 1980s and after brought arrays of mixers, turntables, effects processors, and vinyl records (and, often enough, laptop computers) to a typical improvised set of dance music. By the 1990s, turntable performance had become TURNTABLISM, as pioneered by artists such as Grandmaster Flash, Afrika Bambaataa, DJ Kool Herc, and GrandWizzard Theodore. SCRATCHING, a particular mode of performance of sound collages using vinyl records, became a primary medium for improvisation in hip hop, as well as in experimental music with the work of Christian Marclay, DJ Spooky, and Marina Rosenfeld.

In the 1980s, improvisation had become as much a collective art as a site for soloistic virtuosity. Saxophonist John Zorn; guitarists Fred Frith, Eugene Chadbourne, and Elliott Sharp; vocalist Shelley Hirsch; pianist Wayne Horvitz; and electronic improviser Bob Ostertag, among others, created hybrids of jazz, rock, country, klezmer, and many other forms of American and European music, oriented toward timbre, extended instrumental and electronic technique, and noise elements, in lieu of melodic and harmonic structure; coming out of the legacy of 1960s free jazz, steady beats had long been basically abandoned. In the late 1980s, a number of these musicians, including Zorn, Hirsch, Sharp, Anthony Coleman, David Krakauer, Gary Lucas, and Annie Gosfield, became prominent in what became known as a "Radical Jewish Culture" musical movement, piqued in partial reaction to an ongoing klezmer revival in which Krakauer, the African American clarinetist Don Byron, and the band The Klezmatics were prominent figures. The movement self-consciously foregrounded Jewish history and culture as structures of feeling for a new musical experimentalism.

Many of these musicians had also forged strong links with the European free improvisation scenes that had been developing since the mid-1960s. Important outposts for American expatriate jazz artists had been established by the 1950s, including such important figures as Randy Weston (Morocco), Dexter Gordon (Denmark), and Johnny Griffin (France). By the mid-1960s, key European countries were producing musicians like pianist Irene Schweizer (Switzerland); guitarist Derek Bailey, saxophonist Evan Parker and vocalist Maggie Nicols (UK); pianist Misha Mengelberg and drummer Han Bennink (Netherlands); and saxophonist Peter Brotzmann and pianist Alexander von Schlippenbach (Germany) with his Globe Unity Orchestra projects.

These and other first-generation European improvisers, who came to prominence in the mid-1960s, were strongly influenced in particular by African American first-generation progenitors of the free jazz movement, including John Coltrane, Ornette Coleman, Cecil Taylor, Eric Dolphy, Sun Ra, and Albert Ayler. At the same time, these Europeans were credited with having been the first to promulgate new, specifically European styles of "free jazz" and free improvisation that moved away from American models toward greater emphasis on European sonic and cultural sources.

At the same time, American experimental improvisers were also establishing footholds outside the United States. One of the most prominent and long-lasting ensembles was Musical Elettronica Viva, formed in Rome in 1968 in the midst of Europe-wide political and social upheaval, with Richard Teitelbaum, Alvin Curran, Frederic Rzewski, Steve Lacy, and Garrett List as central figures. Early AACM figures, such as the Art Ensemble of Chicago, Anthony Braxton, Leo Smith, Steve McCall, and Leroy Jenkins also became closely associated with European scenes during this period. These linkages between American improvisers and their counterparts around the world became more prominent in the late 1990s with the emergence of the yearly Vision Festival, a New York-based project of the bassist William Parker and his partner, choreographer Patricia Nicholson, that provided a forum for performances, workshops, and conferences by improvising musicians from around the world.

Jazz-identified composers had already pioneered the integration of composition with improvisation in large ensemble format as far back as the work of pianist-composer Ferdinand "Jelly Roll" Morton. Bandleader, composer, and pianist Edward Kennedy "Duke" Ellington, widely recognized as one of America's greatest composers, integrated composed and improvised elements in his "extended form" works from the 1930s forward, including *Black, Brown, and Beige* (1944). Pianist Mary Lou Williams's *Zodiac Suite* (1945) moved in a related direction, and saxophonist Ornette Coleman extended the practice to the orchestral realm with his 1971 orchestral work *Skies of America*, which featured his quartet in performance in a kind of quadruple concerto with the orchestra. In 1997, one such work, trumpeter-composer Wynton Marsalis's *Blood On Fields*, garnered the Pulitzer Prize in Music.

In full-length operas such as *X: The Life and Times of Malcolm X* (1983), *Amistad* (1997), and *Wakonda's Dream* (2010), composer Anthony Davis broke new ground within the seemingly unlikely medium of grand opera by forging a tightly coupled experimentalist synthesis of improvisation with acoustic and electronic instruments within the overall composed form. For the most part, however, classical orchestras in the United States (with the notable exception of the American Composers Orchestra) avoided encounters with improvisation, despite the new vistas opened up by the orchestrally conceived "Conduction" practices of former trumpeter Lawrence "Butch" Morris, who refashioned himself in the 1990s as an improvising conductor of ensembles, creating large-ensemble, completely improvised extended works in which a conductor, drawing on Morris's extensive repertoire of codified and documented gestures and symbols, functioned as a centralized conduit of musical current linking other improvisers in real time.

In the 1990s and 2000s, jazz- and rock-identified work continued to produce experimental hybrids. Jam bands such as Phish extended the legacy of the Grateful Dead by collaborations with members of the Sun Ra Arkestra (*see* JAM BAND); saxophonist Steve Coleman, one of the organizers of the M-BASE collective of exploratory musicians in the 1980s, pursued intercultural collaborations with Afrocuba de Matanzas and other Cuban and Brazilian musicians, extending and experimentalizing the Afrodiasporic notion of *clavé* well beyond its standard usages in Latin music. Younger musicians, such as saxophonist Rudresh Mahanthappa and the pianist Vijay Iyer, expanded on Coleman's rhythmic and metric experiments to incorporate Karnatic rhythmic practices. Extending the notion of the intercultural, philosopher and clarinetist David Rothenberg combined essays on improvisation and human nature with forays into what might be termed "interspecies improvisation," in which groups of musicians "jammed" with birds, wolves, elephants, and whales.

It may fairly be said that the human-created portion of the soundtrack that accompanied the development of the Americas was in large measure improvised by its inhabitants; its diversity confounds any single definition.

BIBLIOGRAPHY

GMO (Bruno Nettl, Rob Wegman, et al.

W.E.B. Du Bois: *The Souls of Black Folk* (Nashville, TN, 1903)

T. Adorno: "Perennial Fashion—Jazz," *Prisms*, trans. by S. and S. Weber (Cambridge, MA, 1953 R/1981), 119–32

J. Cage: *Silence: Lectures and Writings by John Cage* (Middletown, CT, 1961)

P. Alperson: "On Musical Improvisation," *The Journal of Aesthetics and Art Criticism*, xliii/1 (1984), 17–29

H.L. Gates Jr.: *The Signifying Monkey: A Theory of African-American Literary Criticism* (New York, 1988)

M. Goldstein: *Sounding the Full Circle: Concerning Music Improvisation and Other Related Matters* (self-published, 1988), <http://www.frogpeak.org/unbound/goldstein/goldstein_fullcircle.pdf>

B. Klitz: "Blacks and Pre-Jazz Instrumental Music in America," *International Review of the Aesthetics and Sociology of Music*, xx/1 (1989), 43–60

M. Csikszentmihalyi: *Flow: The Psychology of Optimal Experience* (New York, 1991)

C.O. Hartman: *Jazz Text: Voice and Improvisation in Poetry, Jazz, Song* (Princeton, NJ, 1991)

D. Bailey: *Improvisation: Its Nature and Practice in Music* (New York, 1992)

R. Keeling: "Music and Culture History among the Yurok and Neighboring Tribes of Northwestern California," *Journal of Anthropological Research*, xlviii/1 (1992), 25–48

J. Marre, dir.: *On the Edge: Improvisation in Music, Part 4: Nothin' Premeditated* (London, 1992)

R. Crawford: *The American Musical Landscape: The Business of Musicianship from Billings to Gershwin* (Berkeley, 1993)

R. Walser: *Running with the Devil: Power, Gender, and Madness in Heavy Metal Music* (Hanover, NH, 1993)

P.F. Berliner: *Thinking in Jazz: The Infinite Art of Improvisation* (Chicago, 1994)

M. Kennedy, ed.: "Improvisation," *The Oxford Dictionary of Music* (Oxford, 1994)

K. Gabbard, ed.: *Jazz Among the Discourses* (Durham, NC, 1995)

S. Feinstein and Y. Komunyakaa, *The Second Set: The Jazz Poetry Anthology* (Bloomington, IN, 1996)

K. Gabbard: *Jammin' at the Margins: Jazz and the American Cinema* (Chicago, 1996)

J. Roach: *Cities of the Dead: Circum-Atlantic Performance* (New York, 1996)

D. Belgrad: *The Culture of Spontaneity: Improvisation and the Arts in Postwar America* (Chicago, 1998)

S. Blum: "Recognizing Improvisation," *In The Course of Performance: Studies in the World of Musical Improvisation*, eds. B. Nettl with M. Russell (Chicago, 1998), 27–45

V.L. Levine: "American Indian Musics, Past and Present," *The Cambridge History of American Music*, ed. D. Nicholls (Cambridge, 1998), 3–29

K.K. Preston: "Art Music from 1800 to 1860," *The Cambridge History of American Music*, ed. D. Nicholls (Cambridge, 1998), 186–213

J. Cruz: "Sound Barriers and Sound Management," *Culture on the Margins: The Black Spiritual and the Rise of American Critical Interpretation* (Princeton, NJ, 1999), 43–66

K.v. Maur: *The Sound of Painting: Music in Modern Art* (Munich, 1999)

C.J. Oja: *Making Music Modern: New York in the 1920s* (New York, 2000)

J. Zorn, ed.: *Arcana: Musicians on Music* (New York, 2000)

D. Rothenberg and M. Ulvaeus, eds.: *The Book of Music and Nature* (Middletown, CT, 2001)

R.K. Sawyer: *Creating Conversations: Improvisation in Everyday Discourse* (Cresskill, NJ, 2001)

M.P.E. Cunha, J. Vieira da Cunha, and K.N. Kamoche: *Organizational Improvisation* (New York, 2002)

K.L. McGinn and A.T. Keros: "Improvisation and the Logic of Exchange in Socially Embedded Transactions," *Administrative Science Quarterly*, xlvii/3 (2002), 442–73

F.J. Hay: "Black Musicians in Appalachia: An Introduction to Affrilachian Music," *Black Music Research Journal*, xxiii/1–2 (2003), 1–19

D. Fischlin and A. Heble, eds.: *The Other Side of Nowhere: Jazz, Improvisation and Communities in Dialogue* (Middletown, CT, 2004)

D. Harris-Kelley: "Revisiting Romare Bearden's Art of Improvisation," *Uptown Conversation: The New Jazz Studies*, ed. R.G. O'Meally, B.H. Edwards, and F.J. Griffin (New York, 2004)

T.S. Jenkins: *Free Jazz and Free Improvisation: An Encyclopedia, Volumes One and Two* (Westport, CT, 2004)

D. Wong: *Speak it Louder: Asian Americans Making Music* (New York, 2004)

J. Robinson: *Improvising California: Community and Creative Music in Los Angeles and San Francisco* (PhD diss., University of California, 2005)

J. Robinson: "The Challenge of the Changing Same: The Jazz Avant-Garde of the 1960s, the Black Aesthetic, and the Black Arts Movement," *Critical Studies in Improvisation/Etudes Critiques en Improvisation*, i/2 (2005), <http://www.criticalimprov.com/article/viewArticle/17/47>

M. Sell: *Avant-Garde Performance and the Limits of Criticism: Approaching the Living Theatre, Happenings/Fluxus, and the Black Arts Movement* (Ann Arbor, MI, 2005)

H.S. Becker, R.R. Faulkner, and B. Kirshenblatt-Gimblett, eds.: *Art from Start to Finish: Jazz, Painting, Writing, and Other Improvisations* (Chicago, 2006)

M. Dessen: "Asian Americans and Creative Music Legacies," *Critical Studies in Improvisation/Études critiques en improvisation*, i/3 (2006), <http://www.criticalimprov.com/article/view/56/89>

K.D. Gaunt: *The Games Black Girls Play: Learning the Ropes from Double-Dutch to Hip-Hop* (New York, 2006)

G.E. Lewis: "Improvisation and the Orchestra: A Composer Reflects," *Contemporary Music Review*, xxv/5–6 (2006), 429–434

L.W. Levine: *Black Culture and Black Consciousness: Afro-American Folk Thought from Slavery to Freedom* (New York, 2007)

G.E. Lewis: "Living with Creative Machines: An Improvisor Reflects," *AfroGEEKS: Beyond the Digital Divide*, eds. A. Everett and A. J. Wallace (Santa Barbara, CA, 2007), 83–99

D.W. Bernstein: *The San Francisco Tape Music Center: 1960s Counterculture and the Avant-garde* (Berkeley, 2008)

A.L. Madrid: *Nor-tec Rifa!: Electronic Dance Music from Tijuana to the World* (New York, 2008)

J. Tick with P.E. Beaudoin, eds.: *Music in the USA: A Documentary Companion* (New York, 2008)

G.E. Lewis: *A Power Stronger Than Itself: The AACM and American Experimental Music* (Chicago, 2008)

G.E. Lewis: "Foreword: After Afrofuturism," *Journal of the Society for American Music*, ii/2 (2008), 139–53

A.C. Beal: "'Music Is a Human Right': Musica Elettronica Viva," *Sound Commitments: Avant-garde Music and the Sixties*, ed. R. Adlington (New York, 2009)

S.M. Feisst: "John Cage and Improvisation: An Unresolved Relationship," *Musical Improvisation: Art, Education, and Society*, ed. G. Solis and B. Nettl (Urbana, 2009)

W.M. Muyumba: *The Shadow and the Act: Black Intellectual Practice, Jazz Improvisation, and Philosophical Pragmatism* (Chicago, 2009)

G. Peters: *The Philosophy of Improvisation* (Chicago, 2009)

D. Ake: *Jazz Matters: Sound, Place, and Time Since Bebop* (Berkeley, 2010)

T. Barzel: "An Interrogation of Language: 'Radical Jewish Culture' on New York City's Downtown Music Scene," *Journal of the Society for American Music* iv (2010), 215–250

A.L. Berkowitz: *The Improvising Mind: Cognition and Creativity in the Musical Moment* (New York, 2010)

D. Goldman: *I Want to Be Ready: Improvised Dance as a Practice of Freedom* (Ann Arbor, MI, 2010)

C. Salter: *Entangled: Technology and the Transformation of Performance* (Cambridge, MA, 2010)

R. Wallace: *Improvisation and the Making of American Literary Modernism* (New York, 2010)

L. Austin and D. Kahn, eds.: *Source: Music of the Avant-Garde, 1966–1973* (Berkeley, 2011)

R.Y. Kim: "The Formalization of Indeterminacy in 1958: John Cage and Experimental Composition at the New School," *John Cage*, ed. J. Robinson (Cambridge, MA, 2011)

GEORGE E. LEWIS

Impulse! Record label. Founded as a subsidiary of ABC-Paramount in 1960, it became known for its strong roster of jazz artists. Through the efforts of the producer Bob Thiele in the 1960s, the label become very successful, recording avant-garde and free-jazz by such musicians as Archie Shepp, Pharoah Sanders, Charles Mingus, and John Coltrane, who became its most prolific artist. It also featured hard-bop by Art Blakey, Freddie Hubbard, Max Roach, and Sonny Rollins; mainstream by Coleman Hawkins, Duke Ellington, and Dizzy Gillespie; and other styles by Oliver Nelson, Gil Evans, and McCoy Tyner. In addition to presenting stylish artwork and a consistent design, the label possessed a memorable logo, which was conceived by Margo Guryan. Most recordings were made in Rudy van Gelder's studio in Englewood Cliffs, New Jersey. After Thiele left in 1969, his successor Ed Michel released other important jazz records by the Liberation Music Orchestra, Ahmad Jamal, Gato Barbieri, Keith Jarrett, and Sam Rivers, among others. MCA purchased the label in 1979 and continued to issue reprints as well as new titles by such musicians as Michael Brecker, Jack DeJohnette, Diana Krall, and Danilo Pérez. Owned by the Universal Music Group since 2000, the label focuses on reissues.

BIBLIOGRAPHY

M. Shera: "A Discography of the Impulse Label," *JJ*, xv/10 (1962), 19

A. Kahn: *The House that Trane Built: the Story of Impulse Records* (New York, 2006)

LUCA CERCHIARI

Ince, Kamran (*b* Glendive, MT, 6 May 1960). Composer of Turkish descent. In 1966 he moved with his parents from Montana to Ankara, where he studied composition with Ilhan Baran (1970–5) and cello and piano at the Ankara Conservatory (1971–7). He entered the Izmir Conservatory in 1977 to pursue composition studies with Muammer Sun. In 1980 he returned to the United States, maintaining dual Turkish and US citizenship. He attended the Oberlin College Conservatory (BM 1982) and the Eastman School (MM 1984, DMA 1987), where his teachers included DAVID BURGE (piano), JOSEPH SCHWANTNER, CHRISTOPHER ROUSE, SAMUEL ADLER, and BARBARA KOLB (composition). In 1987 he won the Rome Prize and a Guggenheim fellowship, followed in 1988 by the Lili Boulanger Memorial Prize. He has taught at the University of Michigan (1990–2) and the University of Memphis (from 1992) and served as composer-in-residence of the California SO, Walnut Creek (1991–3). His commissions include works for the Minnesota Orchestra, Albany SO, Milwaukee SO, Present Music, Meet the Composer, and the Fromm and Koussevitzky foundations.

His musical influences range from Turkish folk tunes to neo-romanticism. His instrumental palette is equally broad, incorporating timbres from serpents to synthesizers. Most of his music is programmatic. *Night Passage* (1992) evokes an evening spent wandering through bars in a Mediterranean town, while the Symphony no.2, "Fall of Constantinople" (1994), was inspired by the victory of the Ottoman Turks in 1453. In 1996 Ince wrote his first film score, *Love Under Siege,* and in 1997 he received a commission for the film *Aphrodisiac.* His first opera, *Judgment of Midas* (2012), with the American Opera Project and the Milwaukee Florentine Opera/Present Music as co-presenters, juxtaposes the folk and vernacular elements of his style with his more classical tendencies, while his contribution to the Gallipoli Symphony, commissioned by the Australian government to mark the centennial in 2015 of the World War I Battle of Gallipoli, employs Turkish ethnic musicians, a military band, and a string ensemble.

WORKS
(selective list)

Film scores: Love Under Siege, 1996; Aphrodisiac, 1997

Orch: Pf Conc., 1984; Infrared Only, 1985; Before Infrared, 1986; Ebullient Shadows, 1987; Deep Flight, 1988; Sym. no.1, "Castles in the Air," 1989; Lipstick, 4 sax, synth, orch, 1991; Hot, Red, Cold, Vibrant, 1992; Domes, 1993; Plexus, 4 sax, 2 elec gui, drum machine, synth, orch, 1993; Sym. no.2, "Fall of Constantinople," 1994; Sym. no.3, "Siege of Vienna," 1995; Remembering Lycia, pf, orch, 1996; F E S T for new music ens and orch, 3 sax, 2 elec gui, vn, vc, pf, synth, orch, 1998; Academica, orch, 1998; Sym. no.4, "Sardis," 2000; Sym. no.5, "Galatasaray" (I. Callslar), S, T, boy S, SATB, orch, 2005; Temple II, tuba, orch, 2006; Hammers and Whistlers, SA, child, orch, 2006; Conc. for Orch., Turkish insts and Vv, 2009; Domes, orch, 2010 (for the film Ondine); The Invasion, Turkish insts, band, str ens, 2011

Chbr: Matinees (J. Merrill), nar, ww qnt, 1989; Waves of Talya, fl, cl, vn, vc, pf, perc, 1988; Hammer Music, fl, cl, vn, va, vc, synth, perc, 1990; Fantasy of a Sudden Turtle, vn, va, vc, pf, 1991; Night Passage, fl, cl, tpt, elec gui, amp vn, vc, synth, drum machine, 1992; Arches, fl, cl, tpt, vn, vc, synth, 1994; Tracing, vc, pf, 1994; Evil Eye, pic, ob, cl, 2 sax, bn, tpt, hn, trbn, pf, synth, drum set, elec gui, str qt, db, 1996; Turqoise, fl, cl, tpt, vn, vc, pf, synth, perc, 1996; Curve, str qt, 1997; Lines, pf, cl/vn, 1997; Split, chbr ens, 1997; MKG Variations, vc, 1998 [arr. gui, 1998]; In White, vn, chbr ens, 1999; One for Eight, 8 vc, 2000; Flight Box, chbr ens, 2001; Strange Stone, chbr ens, 2004; Last

Night, in Istanbul, chbr ens, 2006; Nihavent Longa, wind ens, 2007; Partita in A, vn, perc, 2007; Music for a Lost Earth, vn, chbr ens, 2007; Road to Memphis, va, hpd, 2008; Dreamlines, chbr ens, 2008; Far Variations, pf qt, 2009

Vocal: Love Under Siege, suite, SATB, sax, serpent, pf, synth, perc, elec gui, vn, 1996 [from film score]; Aphrodisiac, suite, SATB, fl, sax, serpent, pf, synth, perc, elec gui, vn, 1997 [from film score]; Istathenople, 1v, chbr ens, 2003; Requiem without Words, vv, chbr ens, synth, 2004; Gloria "Everywhere," SATB, 2006; Judgment of Midas (op, 2, M. Seidel), 2012

Pf: The Blue Journey, 1982; Cross Scintillations, 4 hands, 1986; My Friend Mozart, 1987; An Unavoidable Obsession, 1988; Kevin's Dream, 1994; In Memorian: 8/17/99, 1999; Gates, 2002; Sheherazade Alive, 2 pf, 2004; Requiem for Mehmet, 3 pf, 2009

Principal publishers: Schott, European American

JAMES CHUTE

Inch, Herbert Reynolds (*b* Missoula, MT, 25 Nov 1904; *d* San Diego, CA, 14 April 1988). Composer. He studied with Josephine Swenson and A.H. Weisberg at Montana State University, Missoula, and with HOWARD HANSON and Edward Royce at the Eastman School (BM 1925, MM 1928); he then held a fellowship at the American Academy in Rome (1931–4) and later obtained the PhD from the University of Rochester (1941). Most of his career as a teacher was spent at Hunter College (1937–65); earlier he taught at Eastman (1925–8, 1930–31) and served as a reference assistant at the New York Public Library (1935–8). Many of Inch's orchestral works were given premieres at the Eastman School Festivals of American Music. In 1945 he received the Ernest Bloch Award for *Return to Zion*. His music is characterized by a skillful contrapuntal technique, clear textures, a lyrical line, and moods ranging from the elegiac to energetic protest.

WORKS

Orch: Sym., 1932; 2 concs., pf, 1940, vn, 1946–7; Answers to a Questionnaire, 1942; Northwest Ov., 1943; other works

Inst: Pf Qnt, 1930; 2 str qts, 1933, 1936; Divertimento, brass, 1934; 3 pf sonatas, 1935, 1946, 1966; Pf Trio, 1963; other chamber ens, pf works

Vocal: Return to Zion, SSAA, pf, 1945; 2 other choruses

MSS in *R, GRB*

Principal publisher: C. Fischer

BIBLIOGRAPHY

C. Reis: *American Composers* (New York, 2/1932, rev. and enlarged 4/1947/R1977 as *Composers in America: Biographical Sketches*)

N. Laughbaum: *A Study of the Piano Quintet of Herbert Inch* (MM Thesis, U. of Rochester, 1944)

D. Ewen: *American Composers Today* (New York, 1949)

American Organist, xxii (July 1988), 40–41 [Obituary]

MICHAEL MECKNA

Independent Christian Churches. *See* THE STONE-CAMPBELL TRADITION.

Independent label [indie label]. A type of record label that operates outside the control of major record companies in terms of its distribution, organizational structure, or its function in serving a specialized market. At present, independent labels claim about 25% of the global market share, with major companies Sony-BMG, Warner, and Universal controlling the other 75%.

1. History. 2. Development.

1. HISTORY. Independent or "indie" labels have been a part of the recording industry since about 1915, when several key patents owned by three major phonograph manufacturers—Edison, Columbia, and Victor—began to expire. Since then, waves of independent label activity have generally corresponded with both technological and musical innovations, especially those neglected or ignored by major labels. Indie labels have subsequently earned an important cultural status for their role in pioneering great stylistic changes and helping to launch the careers of many legendary artists. However, their comparative lack of business and economic resources in the major-dominated industry has made them vulnerable to shutdowns and takeovers. Throughout the 20th century, few indie labels lasted more than 20 years without some major label involvement.

Although independent labels are often cast as the ideological opposite of profit-oriented majors, their relative positions within the music industry are better characterized as a web of relationships that continually evolve with developments in technology, industry, and culture. Founders of indie labels often gain experience within the major label system, and many indie labels have distribution, licensing, and production deals with the major companies. Majors also pursue niche markets by creating their own "independent" sublabels, and actively recruiting indie label artists and personnel who demonstrate the capacity for large-scale success.

2. DEVELOPMENT. The first independent labels to impact the music industry emerged in the early 1920s, and targeted underserved, regional markets. Labels such as Paramount, Gennett, and OKeh paved the way for "race" records by recording black-American jazz, blues, and gospel, as well as folk and white country music. Black Swan, the first black-owned label, was the first widely distributed label to market recordings exclusively to black Americans. Although they made some of the most influential records of the decade, which were later recognized as invaluable artifacts of American music, none of these labels survived past the Depression.

In the 1940s, a number of factors increased opportunities for label entrepreneurs, namely wartime shellac rations, the American Federation of Musicians strike, and the founding of Broadcast Music, Incorporated (BMI), which supported black American and rural white musicians. While major labels refused to record the rhythm and blues (R&B) music developing in black American communities on the grounds that it was "morally corrupt," new indie labels capitalized on its growing popularity. By the mid-1950s, hundreds of independent labels were producing and promoting R&B-related styles, including Sun, Chess, Atlantic, King, Mercury, Modern Music, Duke-Peacock, and Savoy. By the mid-1960s, most had either gone out of business or had been purchased by a major label.

Indie labels began to re-emerge in the late 1970s with the punk movement's do-it-yourself ethos and the advent of home recording technology. In this era, musicians often founded their own labels and helped support the underground punk network that spread throughout the 1980s. Among the best known are SST, Twin/Tone, Sub Pop, Touch and Go, dB, Dischord, Matador, Merge, and K Records. Internet technology and increased means of distribution enabled a number of these labels to survive into the 21st century.

Indie label activity surged again in the 2000s as major companies struggled to adapt their business models to digital distribution. With lower overhead costs and willingness to embrace internet technologies, many indie labels navigated dramatic changes in music consumption more successfully than the majors. And, since 2005, the American Association of Independent Music (AAIM) has been providing business and legal resources for independent labels in order to foster greater stability within the record industry.

BIBLIOGRAPHY

R. Peterson and D. Berger: "Cycles in Symbol Production: The Case of Popular Music," *American Sociological Review*, xl/2 (1975), 158–73

S. Lee: "Re-examining the Concept of the 'Independent' Record Company: The Case of Wax Trax! Records," *Popular Music* xiv/1 (1995), 13–32

R. Kennedy and R. McNutt: *Little Labels-Big Sound: Small Record Companies and the Rise of American Music* (Bloomington, IN, 1999)

J. Broven: *Record Makers and Breakers: Voices of the Independent Rock n' Roll Pioneers* (Urbana, IL, 2009)

J. Cook: *Our Noise: The Story of Merge Records, the Indie Label that Got Big and Stayed Small* (Chapel Hill, NC, 2009)

S. Knopper: *Appetite for Self-Destruction: The Spectacular Crash of the Record Industry in the Digital Age* (New York, 2009)

LAURA B. SCHNITKER

Indeterminacy. *See* ALEATORY.

Indian American music. *See* ASIAN AMERICAN MUSIC.

Indianapolis. Capital city of Indiana (pop. 829,718; metropolitan area 1,756,241; 2010 US Census). It was founded in 1821.

1. Early concert life. 2. Orchestras. 3. Opera. 4. Education. 5. Ragtime and jazz.

1. EARLY CONCERT LIFE. The city's early musical life was characterized by church choir performances, notably by the 50-voice ensemble at the Second Presbyterian Church, where Henry Ward Beecher was pastor from 1839 to 1847. Stimulated by German immigration during the 1830s and 40s, singing societies flourished in the mid-19th century. In 1854 the Indianapolis Männerchor was founded and has remained active, and is older than its parallel society in Vienna. It sponsored visits from such international artists as Ernestine Schumann-Heink, Maggie Teyte, George Enescu, Myra Hess, and Nathan Milstein. It was followed in 1885 by the Indianapolis Socialisticher Saengerbund, now named the Saenger Chor, which celebrated the labor movement and US patriotism generally. In 1900 there were some 100 German singing societies in the city.

The May Music Festival, held from 1874 to 1875 and from 1886 to 1898 (when it was also known as the Grand Festival), was modeled on that of Cincinnati. The festival of 1886 had a chorus of about 600 and an orchestra of 60. Visiting orchestras included the Theodore Thomas Orchestra and the Boston SO; among guest conductors were Walter Damrosch and Frederick Stock, who brought the Chicago SO repeatedly to Indianapolis.

The Indianapolis Matinee Musicale (founded in 1877 as the Ladies Matinee Musicale), a society for instrumentalists and singers, continues to play an active part in the city's musical life. Membership by 1927 was no longer restricted to women. After its participation in the World's Columbian Exposition (Chicago, 1893), it became affiliated with the National Federation of Music Clubs. Guest artists in the programs sponsored by the society (usually about 30 a year) have included Alfredo Casella (1920), Wilhelm Backhaus (1925), and Eugene Istomin (1947). Other city choral groups included the Mendelssohn Choir (founded 1916) and the Haydn Festival Choir (1932). Solo recitals flourished from 1900 to 1960; the series at the English Theater was particularly notable and included such performers as Rachmaninoff.

2. ORCHESTRAS. In 1896 Karl Schneider formed a 60-member orchestra, which survived until 1906 and was occasionally referred to as the Indianapolis SO. Other early attempts to form orchestras were the Indianapolis Orchestra and another short-lived Indianapolis SO under Alexander Ernestinoff (1910–14). The latter rehearsed at the German House (Athenaeum), which has remained an important center of musical activity.

The current Indianapolis SO was formed in 1929 and first performed on 2 November 1930 under Ferdinand Schaeffer, a German violinist and conductor. It rehearsed for a brief period at the Jewish Community Center of Indianapolis, then as now a presenter of the arts, before moving to other venues. The orchestra is supported by the Indiana State Symphony Society (founded 1931) and by its women's committee (once numbering 5000). Until 1937 it was a cooperative, semiprofessional orchestra. That year the society was reorganized under the leadership of the industrialist William H. Ball of Muncie. The nephew of the conductor Sergei Koussevitzky, Fabien Sevitzky, was appointed conductor and the orchestra became fully professional. During the 1937–8 season, Lotte Lehmann, Albert Spaulding, and Emanuel Feuermann appeared as guest soloists; the Indianapolis Symphonic Choir was formed as an affiliate of the orchestra; and ten concerts were broadcast by the Mutual Broadcasting Network (broadcasts continued to 1945). In 1943 the state passed legislation permitting the use of tax revenue for the orchestra, although it subsequently has become self-supporting; in 1951–2 it was the first significant orchestra to appear on commercial television and was considered one of the ten best orchestras in the United States. Sevitzky's tenure was marked by his performances of contemporary American music, the hiring of young musicians, several recordings (from 1941) and the initiation of children's and other community concert series. Dissatisfaction over his programming and other issues led to his dismissal in 1955, and Izler Solomon became director in 1956. In 1963 the orchestra moved to Clowes Memorial Hall (cap. 2182) on the Butler University campus. In 1984 a renovated "movie palace," the Circle Theater (cap. 1847) in the city center, became the orchestra's home. The ISO in 2011 is one of 18 US orchestras performing all year, including the summer series Symphony on Conner Prairie.

The orchestra achieved increased international recognition under Solomon, who resigned his post in 1976. Following two seasons of guest conductors, John Nelson became music director in 1976. Raymond Leppard succeeded him in 1987, Mario Venzago became music director from 2002–9 and Krzysztof Urbanski was named director in 2011. In 1982 the quadrennial International Violin Competition was initiated in Indianapolis. Other significant organizations have included the Indianapolis Chamber Orchestra, Festival Music Society for summer early music concerts, and various Broadway musical venues such as those at the Murat and Scottish Rite theatres. The Madame Walker Theater, named for an African American philanthropist, features jazz and gospel as well as concert music.

3. OPERA. Despite frequent appearances by world renowned groups, it was not until World War II had ended that local opera began to develop. An interest in light opera in the 1880s resulted in the founding, by Ora Pearson, of the Indianapolis Opera Company, which lasted about a decade. A professional company, the Indianapolis Opera, was founded in 1975 and gives about four productions a year at the Clowes Memorial Hall of Butler University and the Basile Opera Center. The Indiana Opera Theater, a community-based opera company specializing in school concerts, was founded in 1983 and ceased activity in about 2000.

4. EDUCATION. In 1894 the Metropolitan School of Music was founded, being reconfigured in 1907 as the College of Musical Art. It merged with the Indiana College of Music and Fine Arts in 1918 and by 1922 it had 1000 students and 30 instructors. The Arthur Jordan Conservatory of Music was formed in 1928 when the Indiana College of Music and Fine Arts merged with smaller schools, and it remained independent until it affiliated with Butler University (1855) in 1951. In 1968 the college, named the Jordan College of Fine Arts and incorporating departments of dance and theatre, began sponsoring the Romantic Music Festival, held each April until 1988. Succeeding annual festivals have presented the Soviet arts, contemporary American music, and the works of Brahms and Schubert. There followed in 1994 a centennial celebration of the College, in 1996 a music component of the city-wide festival CalderFest commemorating the artist Alexander Calder, and in 2000 a Copland Centenary. In 2011 200 undergraduate and 70 graduate students were enrolled at Butler, which has a music faculty of 50 and offers BA, BM, BS, and MM degrees in performance, theory, composition, conducting, education, musicology, and arts administration. Bachelor's degree programs are also offered at the University of Indianapolis (founded as Indiana Central University in 1902), Marian University, and the school of music at Indiana University in Bloomington, about 80 kilometers south of Indianapolis.

5. RAGTIME AND JAZZ. Although Indianapolis was not one of the points of origination for ragtime, it became an important center for its publication. After a late start, the publication of ragtime in Indianapolis reached a peak in 1908 and remained high until 1916. Leading local ragtime composers included May Aufderheide, Julia Niebergall, Paul Pratt, J. Russel Robinson, and Russell Smith.

The early history of jazz in the city featured extended visits from the Wolverines with Bix Beiderbecke, Fletcher Henderson, Red Nichols (and his Syncopating Five), and Hoagy Carmichael. From the 1930s a more indigenous jazz evolved around the local jazz clubs, such as the Missile Room, Henri's, and Al's British Lounge, and in the African American neighborhood along Indiana Avenue. Among those whose careers began or were pursued in Indianapolis are the pianist Reginald DuValle Sr., who instructed Hoagy Carmichael and gained a national place with his band the Blackbirds; the trumpeter Freddie Hubbard; the trombonists J.J. Johnson, Slide Hampton and David Baker; the alto saxophonist Jimmy Spaulding; the pianists Leroy Carr and Carl Perkins; the guitarist Wes Montgomery; the double bass players Monk Montgomery and Larry Ridley; and the drummers Earl "Fox" Walker and Sonny Johnson. The most important groups included the Montgomery-Johnson Quintet, the Dave Baker Quartet, and the Wes Montgomery Trio. David Baker of Indiana University at Bloomington has also achieved recognition as a jazz educator, author, and arranger. The city is currently home to the jazz pianists Marvin Chandler and Steve Allee, clarinetist and saxophonist Frank Glover, vocalist Everett Greene, organist Melvin Rhyne, and the Buselli-Wallarab Jazz Orchestra.

BIBLIOGRAPHY

M.F. Bellinger: "Music in Indianapolis," *Indiana Magazine of History*, xli (1945), 345–62; xlii (1946), 47–65

E. Draegert: *Indianapolis: the Culture of an Inland City* (diss., Indiana U., 1952)

S.W. Siurua: *History of the Indianapolis Symphony Orchestra* (diss., Indiana U., 1961)

N.H. Long: "The Development of Musical Educational Organizations in Indiana," *Indiana Musicator*, xxxii/3 (1976–7), 36

J. Hasse: *The Creation and Dissemination of Indianapolis Ragtime, 1897–1930* (diss., Indiana U., 1981)

N. Comiskey: "Historic Indianapolis: the Two-step, Toe-tapping Tempo of Ragtime," *Indianapolis Monthly* (March, 1982), 54

D. Bodenhamer, R. Barrows, and D. Vanderstel: *The Encyclopedia of Indianapolis* (Bloomington and Indianapolis, 1994)

J. Tenuth: *Indianapolis: Circle City History* (Mount Pleasant, SC, 2004)

R. Pierce: *Polite Protest: The Political Economy of Race in Indianapolis, 1920–1970* (Bloomington, IN, 2005)

DAVID E. FENSKE (with WILLIAM McCLELLAN (4))/
JAMES R. BRISCOE

Indiana University. State university in Bloomington founded in 1820. It began to offer music instruction in 1893; a music department was organized in 1910, which became a school of music in 1921. From 1947, under the deanship of Wilfred C. Bain, the school became one of the largest, best-equipped schools of music in the country. Charles H. Webb succeeded Bain in 1973 and remained dean until 1997. During his tenure, the school expanded its range of activities by establishing the Early Music Institute (with Thomas Binkley as its founding director) and the New Music Ensemble (first headed by Frederick Fox). The school also gained an international reputation by increasing the number of tours and performances outside of Bloomington and attracting a larger number of students from other countries. After David Woods served as dean for two years, Gwyn Richards was appointed interim dean in 1999, and assumed the position permanently in 2001. In 2012, the school enrolled over 1,600 students, about equally divided between graduate and undergraduate, and had over 170 faculty members, many of them internationally recognized as leaders in their fields. It offers BM, BMEd, BS, MA, MM, MMEd, MS, DM, DMEd, and PhD degrees in performance, theory, composition, musicology, music education, artist's and performer's diplomas, and a number of programs for children and young adults. The school has unusually strong programs in both opera and ballet, and typically mounts six opera and three ballet productions each year.

The William and Gayle Cook Music Library contains over 700,000 items, including 112,000 books and journals, 155,000 scores, and 165,000 sound recordings. The music library is a leader in providing online access to its collection through the Variations program, which contains over 21,000 digitized recordings and a growing number of scores. The Lilly Library, which houses the university's rare books, manuscripts, and special collections, has 150,000 pieces of sheet music as well as the personal papers of Hoagy Carmichael. Other important resources of the university are the Latin American Music Center, the Archives of African American Music and Culture, and the Archives of Traditional Music.

BIBLIOGRAPHY

G.M. Logan: *The Indiana University School of Music: A History* (Bloomington, IN, 2000)

J.F. Anderies: "Ethel Louise Lyman and the Beginnings of the Indiana University Music Library," *Notes*, lix/2 (2002), 264–87

M.W. Davidson: "Indiana University's William & Gayle Cook Music Library: An Introduction," *Notes*, lix/2 (2002), 251–63

BRUCE CARR/KEITH COCHRAN

Indiana University of Pennsylvania. State-supported university founded in 1875 in Indiana, Pennsylvania. The department of music granted its first music degree in 1906. In 2010 over 300 music majors were served by a faculty of 34. The department offers BA, BFA, BS, and MA degrees in general studies, performance, history and literature, theory and composition, music education, and interdisciplinary fine arts. The University's Orendorff Music Library is home to the Charles Davis Collection of Jazz and Musical Theatre, the Edward R. Sims Collection of Musical Instruments, and the Albert R. Casavant Research Collection of marching band and drill team materials.

WILLIAM McCLELLAN/CHRISTOPHER E. MEHRENS

Indians, American. *See* NATIVE AMERICAN MUSIC.

Indie rock. Indie rock originally referred to music released on independent record labels but has also come to refer to a sonic aesthetic influenced by various forms of post-punk and lo-fi music. Independent labels have played a central role in rock music from the beginning, as most rock 'n' roll of the 1950s was released on small, independently owned labels such as Sun, Chess, and Atlantic. (*See* INDEPENDENT LABEL.) However, the notion of "indie rock" developed in the 1980s and 1990s to describe bands on labels that grew out of the punk and hardcore scenes, especially SST, Touch & Go, and Dischord. Independent labels granted artistic license to musicians, and bands like Hüsker Dü, Sonic Youth, and Dinosaur Jr. expanded their music to the point where generic terms like "punk" or "hardcore" were no longer adequate to describe them.

Independent labels expressed punk's do-it-yourself (DIY) ethic, created because the major labels were not interested in punk and hardcore and it was the only method for getting music recorded and distributed. They also operated under the ideal that music is a creative art and that the commercial bottom line of the major labels restricts musical freedom. Indie rock subsisted as a cultural niche throughout the 1980s, but the success of Nirvana, grunge, and the Seattle scene, followed by the commercial breakthrough of Green Day, the Offspring, and other California punk bands, transformed the relationship between independents and the major labels in the following decade. Major labels returned to signing bands away from independents, as they had in earlier periods of rock history, using them as a kind of farm system for talent scouting, while the music that was once "alternative" in its sound began being assimilated into the mainstream as the new standard of rock.

The sound typically described as indie rock was developed in the 1990s by performers such as Pavement, Guided by Voices, and Elliott Smith. Female musicians also played a significant role in indie rock, from the singer-songwriter Liz Phair to the post-riot grrrl rock of Sleater-Kinney. Indie rock constructed a sense of authenticity by flaunting its low-budget and haphazard conditions of production, typically utilizing lo-fi equipment or home recording and allowing the resulting noise and flaws to be heard by listeners. Over the course of the 1990s, indie rock came to be associated with a particular sound and aesthetic that had less to do with actually recording for an independent label. As a style of music, indie rock has typically been used to describe artists who are more intellectual and ironic in their approach and seemingly not as driven by commercial success as musicians in other subgenres of rock. In the 2000s, the increasing centrality of the Internet and online methods of music exchange allowed independent labels to compete with the majors again: for example, Merge Records, an independent founded in 1989 in North Carolina by two members of Superchunk, has since released albums from the Arcade Fire and Spoon that made it into *Billboard*'s Top Ten.

BIBLIOGRAPHY
G. Arnold: *Route 666: On the Road to Nirvana* (New York, 1993)
M. Azerrad: *Our Band Could Be Your Life: Scenes from the American Indie Underground* (New York, 2001)
J. Sellers: *Perfect From Now On: How Indie Rock Saved My Life* (New York, 2008)
J. Cook: *Our Noise: the Story of Merge Records, the Indie Label That Got Big and Stayed Small* (Chapel Hill, NC, 2009)
R. Moore: *Sells Like Teen Spirit: Music, Youth Culture, and Social Crisis* (New York, 2009)
K. Oakes: *Slanted and Enchanted: the Evolution of Indie Culture* (New York, 2009)

RYAN MOORE

Indigo Girls. Folk rock duo. Its members Emily Saliers (*b* New Haven, CT, 22 June 1963) and Amy Ray (*b* Decatur, GA, 12 April 1964) met as children in Decatur, Georgia, and began performing together as high school students. They first performed under the name Indigo Girls in Atlanta while both women were students at Emory University in the mid-1980s. They released their first full-length album—self-produced—in 1987, and signed with Epic Records the following year. Their self-titled debut with Epic (1989) garnered favorable reviews and eventually went platinum. It won them a Grammy Award for Best Contemporary Folk Album and a nomination for Best New Artist. They continued to release albums with Epic throughout the 1990s and into the early 2000s. In 2006, they signed with Hollywood Records and released their tenth studio album, *Despite Our Differences*, to considerable critical acclaim. The duo has produced albums independently since 2009. Saliers and Ray both self-identify as lesbian, and they have been politically active in the LGBT rights movement. In addition to staging performances in support of gay rights, they have held benefit concerts for the environment, the rights of Native Americans, and the National Coalition to Abolish the Death Penalty.

MEGAN E. HILL

Industrial rock. A musical genre that has its roots in the industrial music genre and the rock and punk music of the 1970s. In the beginning the genre was an international phenomenon with a number of major artists cropping up almost simultaneously in the United States, Great Britain, and Australia, but during the mid-1980s the genre became associated mostly with the American no-wave and hardcore scenes.

Early artists such as the San Francisco group Chrome forged the sound by blending traditional rock instrumentation, a musical vocabulary steeped in distortion and feedback, and elements of synthesized noise and drones. Many later groups embraced this format, including Swans, Big Black, and Killing Joke; some substituted electronic drum machines for live drummers. As industrial rock developed artists like Einstürzende Neubauten turned increasingly to electronic sounds and metal percussion instruments, influenced by earlier groups such as Throbbing Gristle and Cabaret Voltaire. Many industrial rock artists made extensive use of tape techniques such as looping and playback manipulation.

Although bands like Swans and Suicide remained influential on the underground, industrial rock had its first mainstream breakthroughs with the rise of artists such as NINE INCH NAILS and Ministry, whose music was placed on heavy rotation on MTV and alternative radio in the early 1990s. The genre also gave rise to industrial metal, including artists such as KMFDM, Rob Zombie, MARILYN MANSON, Rammstein, and Fear Factory, which in many cases included a return to more traditional instrumentation and the prominent use of electric guitars. Many of these later bands found much commercial success during the 1990s.

BIBLIOGRAPHY
D. Thompson: *Industrial Revolution* (Los Angeles, 1994)
S. Blush: *American Hardcore: A Tribal History* (Los Angeles, 2001)
S. Reynolds: *Rip It Up and Start Again: Postpunk 1978–1984* (London, 2005)

RYAN KIRK

Infante (Cruz), (José) Pedro (*b* Mazatlán, Mexico, 18 Nov 1917; *d* Mérida, Mexico, 15 April 1957). Mexican film actor and singer. Pedro Infante was the third of nine children born into a working-class family. His formative years were spent in Guamúchil, Sinaloa, where his father was a musician and music teacher. In his teen years, Infante apprenticed in carpentry and even made his own guitar. He played violin, guitar, and percussion in his father's orchestra and, by 1937, was leading his own group.

In the hopes of furthering his musical career, Pedro Infante moved to Mexico City in 1939. His singing debut on Radio XEB in 1940 was soon followed by appearances on Radio XEW. Infante's film career coincided with the era identified as the "golden age" of Mexican film. His first significant roles were in *La feria de las flores* and *Jesusita en Chihuahua*, both released in 1942. His lead *charro* (singing cowboy) roles such as in *Los tres García* (1946) and *Vuelvan los García* (1947) established him as successor to Jorge Negrete in the ranch-themed (*ranchera*) film genre. Infante's on- and off-screen persona as a macho, yet good-natured bad-boy, endeared him to audiences throughout the Americas. His numerous recordings, especially of *rancheras* and *boleros*, are classics of the mariachi repertory.

BIBLIOGRAPHY
A. Rubenstein: "Bodies, Cities, Cinema: Pedro Infante's Death as Political Spectacle," *Fragments of a Golden Age*, eds. G. Joseph, A. Rubenstein, E. Zolov (Durham, NC, 2001)
J.I. Quintanilla: *Pedro Infante: el ídolo inmortal* (México, D.F., 2006)

DONALD A. HENRIQUES

Information theory. A theory that seeks to describe, by means of mathematical equations, the properties and behavior of systems for storing, processing, and transmitting information. Here the term "information" is interpreted broadly as covering not only messages transmitted via the familiar communications media (radio, television, telephone, and computer networks), but also the signals (aural, visual, and other sensory stimuli) by means of which an individual perceives his or her immediate environment or communicates with others.

One of the fundamental tenets of information theory is that information can be quantified and measured in terms of the number of bits (binary digits: 0, 1) required to store or transmit a message. Information is understood as the selection by a message source of one particular message from a set of all possible messages. If the alternatives are not all equally likely, then each message in the set will have its own probability of occurrence. The average information content of the message set, or the average number of bits required to represent a message from the set, is called the entropy of the set (H). A music source is not a simple stochastic process; it is a Markov chain, where the probability of a future musical event occurring in the sequence depends explicitly on the occurrence of previous events.

From 1956 a spate of publications appeared applying information theory to many aspects of music analysis and the aesthetics of music. In particular, information theory has been used to determine the relative information rates or entropy profiles of different samples of music in attempting to analyze content, style, or perception objectively. More recently important work has been done on the entropies of music as measured by both human and computational models of music prediction. The computational approach involved learning inductively the rules for generating the musical sequences. The combinatorial complexity of two classes of algorithm for musical similarity and melodic recognition has been analyzed in detail and compared quantitatively. The computational problems associated with approximate string-matching techniques for music analysis and musical information retrieval have also been explored.

BIBLIOGRAPHY

R.C. Pinkerton: "Information Theory and Melody," *Scientific American*, cxciv.ii (Feb 1956), 77–86

L.B. Meyer: "Meaning in Music and Information Theory," *Journal of Aesthetics and Art Criticism*, xv (1957), 412–24

E. Coons and D. Krahenbuehl: "Information as a Measure of Structure in Music," *JMT*, ii (1958), 127–61

J.E. Cohen: "Information Theory and Music," *Behavioral Science*, vii (1962), 137–163

L. Knopoff and W. Hutchinson: "Entropy as a Measure of Style: the Influence of Sample Length," *JMT*, xxvii (1970), 75–97

I.H. Witten, L.C. Manzara, and D. Conklin: "Comparing Human and Computational Models of Music Prediction," *Computer Music Journal*, xviii (1994), 70–80

D. Conklin and I.H. Witten: "Multiple Viewpoint Systems for Music Prediction," *Journal of New Music Research*, xxiv (1995), 51–73

T. Crawford, C.S. Iliopoulos, and R. Raman: "String Matching Techniques for Musical Similarity and Melodic Recognition," *Computing in Musicology*, xi (1998), 73–100

RICHARD E. OVERILL/R

Ingalls, Jeremiah (*b* Andover, MA, 1 March 1764; *d* Hancock, VT, 6 April 1838). Tunebook compiler and composer. He moved to Newbury, Vermont, around 1791 and in 1810 to a farm between Rochester and Hancock, Vermont, where he lived for the rest of his life. He was active in both areas as a choir leader, singing-school master, and bass viol player. Over half of the 137 tunes in his only tunebook, *The Christian Harmony, or Songster's Companion* (Exeter, NH, 1805/*R*1981), were composed in the indigenous New England style prevalent in northern tunebooks before 1820. More significantly, the remaining settings constitute the first appearance in print of the spiritual folksong—a sacred text set to a formerly secular or folk melody—a genre that appeared frequently in southern tunebooks from the second decade of the 19th century. Other characteristics of *The Christian Harmony* that appear rarely in northern tunebooks but commonly in later southern ones are rhythmic and scalar influences from folk and secular music, repeated phrases, three-voice settings, tunes with added choruses, revivalist poetry, the inclusion of complete texts, and tunes named after the texts to which they are set. Ingalls's book thus belongs to both traditions and occupies a unique position in the tunebook literature.

BIBLIOGRAPHY

B.F. White, E.J. King, and J.S. James: *Original Sacred Harp: Containing a Superior Collection of Standard Melodies, of Odes, Anthems, and Church Music* (Atlanta, GA, 1911), 31, 62, 155

D.G. Klocko: *Jeremiah Ingalls's "The Christian Harmony: or, Songster's Companion (1805)"* (diss., U. of Michigan, 1978)

D.W. Patterson: *The Shaker Spiritual* (Princeton, NJ, 1979)

R. Crawford: *The Core Repertory of Early American Psalmody*, RRAM, xi (Madison, WI, 1984)

A.P. Britton, I. Lowens, and R. Crawford: *American Sacred Music Imprints, 1698–1810: A Bibliography* (Worcester, MA, 1990)

J. Bealle: *Public Worship, Private Faith: Sacred Harp and American Folksong* (Athens, GA, 1997)

S. Marini, S. Mampre, and D. O'Brien: *The Norumbega Harmony* (Toronto, 2003)

A.D. McLucas: *The Musical Ear: Oral Tradition in the USA* (Burlington, VT, 2010)

DAVID G. KLOCKO/R

Ink Spots, the. Vocal group. One of the most influential black vocal harmony groups, the Ink Spots recorded over 70 hit recordings over a career that lasted, through various permutations of personnel, for seven decades. The Ink Spots first assembled in 1932 in Indianapolis, Indiana, and initially performed under the names the Four Riff Brothers, the Percolating Puppies, and King, Jack, and Jester. They appeared at New York's celebrated Apollo Theatre in 1934 and were reputedly influenced by Paul Whiteman to change their name so as not to collide with that of his vocal ensemble, the King's Jesters. The group signed with RCA Victor in 1935, but did not achieve commercial success, and switched to Decca the following year. The inimitable Ink Spots sound used a format whereby a track opened with a guitar riff, followed by the tenor lead singer's rendition of the song's lyric, after which the bass would pronounce that same material in the form of an oral recitation and then conclude with a repetition of the lead vocalist's performance. That format first took hold of the public consciousness in 1939, with the release of "If I Didn't Care" on Decca Records. A number of hits followed, including, "We Three (My Shadow and Me)" (1940), "I'm Making Believe," "Into a Life a Little Rain Must Fall," "The Gypsy," and "To Each His Own" (all from 1944). "The Gypsy" remained at no.1 on the charts for 13 weeks. The Ink Spots were inducted into the Rock & Roll Hall of Fame in 1989 and the Vocal Group Hall of Fame in 1999.

DAVID SANJEK

Innes, Frederick Neil (*b* London, England, 29 Oct 1854; *d* Chicago, IL, 31 Dec 1926). Trombonist and bandmaster of English birth. At 13 he joined the band of the First Life Guards, of which his father was a member, while studying the violin, piano, trombone, and harmony. In 1874 he went to Boston, where he played at the Howard Street Theater and in the Boston Cadet Band. In 1876 he performed with Patrick Gilmore at the Philadelphia Centennial Exposition, then moved to New York. By the end of 1879 he was a soloist with the Gilmore Band. In 1880 Innes began playing difficult cornet solos on his trombone, and a "War of Blasters" ensued between Innes and the infuriated Jules Levy, "The Cornet King," much to the delight of Gilmore's audiences at Manhattan Beach. Except for a brief trip to Europe, where he acquired a reputation as a soloist in Hamburg, St. Petersburg, Berlin, and Paris, Innes remained with the Gilmore Band until 1883. A Paris newspaper called him the "Paganini of the trombone." He formed his first band in 1887; from 1888 to 1896 he directed the 13th Regiment Band of Brooklyn, New York, and then Innes's Orchestral Band. With these bands he toured the United States and Canada, performing in various cities, at industrial fairs and at expositions in Chicago (1893), Buffalo (1901), St. Louis (1904), Seattle (1909), and San Francisco (1915). In 1914 he moved to Denver, where he formed a municipal band. In 1916 he founded the Innes School of Music, which offered home-study courses for bandmasters, orchestra directors, and instrumentalists. After his wife's death he moved to Chicago in 1923 to become president of the Conn National School of Music.

Sousa and Clarke considered Innes the greatest trombone player of his time. As a band director, he is recognized as the first to have included the string bass, harp, and chimes as band instruments; to have devoted entire programs to the compositions of Wagner and Beethoven; and to have played complete symphonies. He conducted from memory, even when performing two different programs daily for several weeks. The Innes School had a great impact on the development of instrumental music education in America. Innes's compositions include two comic operas, cornet and trombone solos (including *Sea Shells Waltz* and *Phenomenal Polka*), orchestral suites (including *A Trip to the World's Fair*, *Pictures of the Rockies*, and *Out in the West*), marches (including *The Chronicle Telegraph*, *The Atlanta Constitution*, *Gloria Washington*, *Love Is King*, and *The Washington Times*), waltzes, overtures, humoresques, and cantatas.

BIBLIOGRAPHY

F.R. Seltzer: "Famous Bandmasters in Brief," *Jacobs' Band Monthly*, iv/11 (1919), 18ff

A.H. Rackett: "Frederick Neil Innes: the Supreme Master," *Musical Messenger*, xix/4 (1923), 3ff [a very similar article, by "A.H. Hackett," appeared in *Jacobs' Band Monthly*, viii/5 (1923), 12ff]

F.N. Innes: "The Musical Possibilities of the Wind Band," *Music Supervisor's Journal*, x/5 (1924), 40ff

L.W. Chidester: "Frederick Neil Innes and His Band," *The Instrumentalist*, ix/May (1955), 18–19; x/March (1956), 18, 26; x/April (1956), 29, 77

H.W. Schwartz: *Bands of America* (Garden City, NY, 1957)

G.M. Campbell: "Bandsman Frederick Neil Innes as Trombonist," *Journal of Band Research*, vi/2 (1970), 30–32

G.D. Bridges: *Pioneers in Brass* (Detroit, 1972); CD-ROM (Coupeville, WA, 2001)

D.M. Guion: "Four American Trombone Soloists before Arthur Pryor: Some Preliminary Findings," *ITA Journal*, xx/4 (1992), 32–3, 36–7

W.H. Rehrig: *The Heritage Encyclopedia of Band Music* (Westerville, OH, 1991/R1996); CD-ROM (Oskaloosa, IA, 2005)

RAOUL F. CAMUS

Insixiengmai, Khamvong (*b* Savannakhet, Laos, 1947). Laotian composer and singer. He began his musical training by studying Lao folk songs with Buddhist monks. Before age 20, he already had garnered a reputation as a creative *maulam*, or narrative singer of *lam* (or *lum*)—a genre of traditional vocal music from southern Laos of solo or male–female repartee singing accompanied by *khene* and oftentimes a small ensemble. He later studied composition and performance and was employed in 1965 by the Department of Lao National Fine Arts. In 1968, he entered the army and worked as a singer for the National Radio Broadcast. After the Pathet Lao came to power in 1975, he worked at the military radio station singing propaganda songs. In 1979, he escaped to Thailand, and in 1980, immigrated to the United States, first living with his cousin, Bountong Insixiengmay, in Bowling Green, Kentucky. He soon relocated to Minneapolis—a city with a large population of Lao émigrés—and in 1984 to Fresno, California. In 1982, with folklorist Cliff Sloane, he released *Thinking of the Old Village*, a cassette of *lam* songs, which he composed and sung, that depict life under the Pathet Lao—one of which has been translated by Deborah Wong in *Speak It Louder* (New York, 2004). In 1991, the NEA awarded him a National Heritage Fellowship, highlighting not only his talent for improvising poetry and song melodies, but also his command of many regional styles of *lam* performance. He also directs the Khamvong Insixiengmai Ensemble with female vocalist Thongxhio Manisone and *khene* player Khamseung Syhanone.

ALEXANDER M. CANNON

Inskeep, Alice Carey (*b* Ottumwa, IA, 1 April 1875; *d* Ottumwa, IA, 23 Feb 1942). Music educator. She attended Iowa State Normal School (now University of Northern Iowa) and Northwestern University. She taught and supervised music instruction in the public schools of Ottumwa (1894–8) and Cedar Rapids (1900–01, 1902–41), Iowa, and Sioux Falls, South Dakota (1901–2). From 1911 she had a joint appointment at Coe College in Cedar Rapids, Iowa, where she was involved in music teacher education. She also taught in the influential American Book Company School and American Institute of Normal Methods (school) summer sessions in Chicago (1914–41). A protégé of leading music educator Frances Elliott Clark, Inskeep served on the planning committee for the first meeting of what became the Music Supervisors National Conference in Keokuk, Iowa, and became a charter member of that organization (1907). She held several important positions for MSNC: Nominating Committee (1912), Board of

Directors (1915–33, chairman 1919–20), Educational Council (1918–22), and director of the North Central Division (1931–3), among others. She also helped organize the first school music contests in Iowa (1923), and later became a founding board member of the Iowa Music Educators Association (1938).

BIBLIOGRAPHY

E.B. Birge: Obituary, *Music Educators Journal*, xxviii/2 (1942), 14 only

D.G. Hedden and others: "Alice Carey Inskeep (1875–1942): a Pioneering Iowa Music Educator and MENC Founding Member," *JRME*, lv/4 (2007), 129–47

DEBRA GORDON HEDDEN

Institute of Jazz Studies. An archive of jazz recordings and other jazz-related materials housed by Rutgers University Libraries in Newark, New Jersey. Marshall W. Stearns, a pioneering jazz scholar, donated his personal collection and founded the Institute in 1952 to promote the growing field of jazz scholarship and research.

MICHAEL D. WORTHY

Instruments. The development of musical instruments in the United States through the early 20th century to a large degree reflected the history of European musical instruments. From that time and increasingly since the end of World War II, American practices in the design and manufacture of musical instruments can be said to have led, as much as followed, European practices. By the late 20th century, many American and European manufacturers had become subsidiaries of large international corporations and had moved their manufacturing operations to Japan, China, and Korea. The present article outlines the beginnings of musical instrument industries in the United States, their evolution, and their more important contributions. Within the chronological ordering—generally by 30-year periods—instruments are discussed broadly in the following groups: woodwinds; brass; percussion; bowed strings; plucked or hammered strings; keyboard strings; organs (pipe and reed); and automatic, electronic, and miscellaneous instruments.

1. Before 1780. 2. 1780–1810. 3. 1810–40. 4. 1840–70. 5. 1870–1900. 6. 1900–30. 7. 1930–60. 8. 1960–90. 9. Since 1990.

1. BEFORE 1780. The musical instruments of the early settlers in America were either brought with them or subsequently imported from the colonizing countries. Although some of the early explorers and traders came from Spain and France, the strongest cultural influences on what is now the United States were English and German. During the colonial period a wide variety of instruments were used in churches, theaters, and homes, as well as outdoors, for worship, amusement, dancing, or military purposes. The violin, flute, hautboy (oboe), recorders, viols, lute, guitar, cittern, dulcimer, virginal, and spinet were familiar instruments in wealthy and middle-class urban homes. Fifes, trumpets, bugles, horns, trombones, and drums were common outdoors and in concerts and theatrical events. Most concerts consisted of instrumental and vocal solos, duets, and

chamber music, with one or two selections combining the evening's instrumental resources. A ball often followed. The most popular form of classical music during the 50 years before the Revolution was that from theater productions of English ballad operas. Williamsburg, Virginia, had a theater by 1716 and other important cities soon after.

Inventories show that some early settlers possessed several kinds of wind instrument—recorders, fifes, oboes, even early clarinets and bassoons, and by 1780 several makers of woodwinds had appeared in the colonies. Four of the earliest are Arthur Clarke (*d* 1665) and John Dyer (*d* 1696), fife makers; Gottlieb Wolhaupter, who from 1761 advertised German flutes, oboes, "clareonets," flageolets, bassoons, and fifes in New York; and Jacob Anthony, who made flutes in Philadelphia from about 1764.

Trumpets are known to have been used from the beginnings of colonization and are commonly found in inventories of the late 17th and early 18th centuries. The earliest documented accounts of other brass instruments being played are found among the Moravian settlers in Pennsylvania, who had come from Germany and adapted the German tradition of *Stadtpfeifer* (town musicians) to their own religious and community use. Brass choirs—at first only trumpets and horns but by 1754 trombones as well—were used outdoors to announce and accompany religious and community events. The earliest known American brass-instrument maker, John Balthius Dash, advertised horns in New York as early as 1765 and continued a metals business until the early 1800s.

Percussion instruments were made in America at least by the time of the Revolutionary War, but known examples seldom have a maker's mark.

Bowed string instruments also appear in early accounts and inventories. One of the first American makers was Robert Horne, who advertised in New York as early as 1767: "Makes and repairs violins, bass viols, tenor viols, Aeolius harps, gauiters, German flutes, Kitts, violin bows, & c."

Harpsichords were found in wealthy American homes from colonial times until the early 19th century. Gustavus Hesselius, a Swedish organ builder, made spinets in Philadelphia in 1742 or earlier, and JOHN HARRIS, an English maker, set up shop in Boston in 1768. Their instruments were soon considered obsolete, however, as pianos began to be imported and made in America. A piano of 1775 by John Behrent of Philadelphia is the earliest known American example.

Although a few organs are heard of in America as early as 1703, the first significant organ builders were the Moravians Johann Gottlob Klemm, active from 1739 until his death in 1762, and David Tannenberg, who began with Klemm in 1758 and continued until his death in 1804. In New England, the first builder was Thomas Johnston, in the 1750s.

Miscellaneous instruments during the colonial period included the jew's harp, which was traded to the Indians in great quantities; Aeolian harps (string instruments sounded by natural wind), advertised by Robert

Horne in New York; and BENJAMIN FRANKLIN's armonica of 1762, an important improvement on the musical glasses then popular in Europe.

2. 1780–1810. Although opera and concert performances were suppressed during and for a time after the Revolutionary War, military bands flourished, since they played for a variety of activities, including concerts and dancing. As theaters reopened and concerts resumed after the war, ballad opera regained its importance, and subscription and benefit concerts were again offered. Musicians from the opera troupes were often prominent in other concerts, both instrumental and vocal. Musical societies were established for the performance of, especially, larger choral and instrumental works; the ST. CECILIA SOCIETY, founded in Charleston (1766), is thought to be the first, and others soon followed in most of the larger cities.

The first important maker of woodwind instruments after the Revolution was GEORGE CATLIN of Hartford, Connecticut. He began business about 1799, and advertised in 1800 that he made "almost every kind of musical instrument now in use, such as pianofortes, harpsichords, violoncellos, guitars, bassoons, clarinets & Hautboys of different keys, tenor clarinets, flutes of various kinds, fifes, reeds, etc. etc." Oboes, clarinets, horns, and bassoons, with an occasional flute, trumpet, bugle, trombone, or serpent, made up most of the military or community bands during these years. Samuel Holyoke's *The Instrumental Assistant* (1800) and several similar works offered instruction on most instruments and included short pieces too. There is little evidence of brass-instrument making in the period following the Revolution.

Percussion instruments were usually made by makers of other instruments or by craftsmen in related trades. BENJAMIN CREHORE, better known for his pianos, made violins, cellos, bass viols, guitars, drums, flutes, and at least one harpsichord before 1800. The most famous early American maker of bells was Paul Revere of Boston, whose first bell was cast in 1792.

Several American string-instrument makers began business after the Revolution. The earliest of them, Crehore, Joseph Minot, William Green, and ABRAHAM PRESCOTT, made bass viols peculiarly American in construction used in churches and for dancing.

Among the plucked and hammered strings, the guitar and hammered dulcimer were in use, the former made by makers such as Catlin and Crehore, the latter more often made at home or by local craftsmen. By this time also a banjo made of simple materials in the tradition of similar African instruments was being played by African Americans in the south.

A few harpsichords continued to be made during this period (and Francis Hopkinson invented a new method of quilling them), but most new keyboard instruments were pianos. The short-lived firm of DODDS & CLAUS was among the earliest to establish the piano industry in New York, though the partners are known to have produced other types of instrument as well. CHARLES ALBRECHT began making pianos in Philadelphia some time before 1789, and CHARLES TAWS had begun to do so

there by 1792. By 1791 Crehore had established a shop in Milton, Massachusetts, where several important piano makers were trained. He made his first piano about 1797, and was well known in Boston, New York, and Philadelphia. In 1800 JOHN ISAAC HAWKINS of Philadelphia made a significant contribution to piano design. Grand and square pianos had formerly been erected on stands to form upright pianos, but Hawkins (and, at about the same time, Matthias Müller of Vienna) designed an upright to sit on the floor without a stand. Other innovations on his "portable grand pianoforte" included a metal frame, improved wrest pins, and a keyboard that could be closed.

New makers of organs in New England during the 1780s and 1790s included Josiah Leavitt and Henry Pratt. The first important maker was William Marcellus Goodrich, who opened a shop in Boston in 1804. Taws seems to have been one of the first to make automatic instruments in America, offering to build or repair "finger and barrel organs" as early as 1786.

3. 1810–40. Early in this period the manufacture of musical instruments in the United States was stimulated by the import restrictions of the embargo of 1807 against foreign trade, and by the War of 1812, after which protective tariffs of 20–30% continued to encourage American manufacture. A far greater stimulus, however, was provided by the expanding population, an improving standard of living, and confidence in scientific and mechanical improvements.

This period and the early part of the next saw enormous changes in wind instruments. Woodwind and brass developed the key and valve mechanisms that made them fully chromatic. Far from being merely observers and copiers of these developments, which occurred mainly in Europe, Americans contributed many experimental designs and some lasting inventions and improvements.

About 1810 George Catlin invented his "clarion," a bassoon-shaped bass clarinet that was more successful than any of the European designs during the next two decades. Other important makers of woodwind instruments beginning business in New York included John Meacham at Albany and WILLIAM WHITELEY at Utica, both about 1810, and John Firth and William Hall, who, after working in the shop of Edward Riley in New York, started on their own there about 1821. In the 1820s many more woodwind makers started up, among them H.C. EISENBRANDT, CHARLES G. CHRISTMAN, and Chabrier Peloubet. The most influential firms were those of SAMUEL GRAVES and ASA HOPKINS. Graves started about 1824 in West Fairlee, Vermont, established a large shop at Winchester, New Hampshire (1830), and turned out top-quality woodwind instruments until he moved to Boston in 1850. Hopkins's shop, established in 1831, became important as the woodwind manufactory of FIRTH, HALL & POND. Most sizes of fife, flute, and clarinet were made by makers of this period as well as single and double flageolets, but only a few oboes and bassoons.

Two European innovations—the application of keys to the bugle (1800) and the addition of valves to brass instruments (1815)—were soon imported and had been adopted by American inventors and manufacturers by the 1830s. NATHAN ADAMS of Lowell, Massachusetts, invented two experimental valve designs about 1830, and Graves was producing both keyed and valved brass instruments by 1837. The keyed bugle was quickly made obsolete by valved instruments in Europe, but in the United States the small E♭ keyed bugle became a popular solo instrument and was played by nearly every military and dance bandleader.

A few names of drum makers are known from this period, among them ELI BROWN of Bloomfield. Connecticut, who was active between 1818 and 1840. Drums were available from most music stores; in 1822 Meacham's, in Albany, advertised "double bass drums with the bust of Washington in the center and all other kinds of drums; plain, eagle & ornamental painting." Kettledrums were probably in use earlier but are specifically mentioned as early as 1816. References to triangle and cymbals in the instrumentation of bands also appear at this time. In 1808 William Barton (1762–1849) opened a bell-making business in East Hampton, Connecticut, that became the center of small bell manufacturing in the United States.

The manufacture of bowed string instruments continued to feature the New England bass viol as well as violins and cellos. About 1820 Abraham Prescott began making double-bass viols, some of which were of outstanding quality and are still in use in American symphony orchestras. William Darracott Jr., also made bass viols during this period.

Guitars and hammered dulcimers continued in use and were joined in the 1830s by improved models of the banjo. Joel Walker Sweeney was the first known white banjo player to perform in public, and he helped standardize its construction. The C.F. Martin guitar company was formed in 1833 and began making fine plucked-string instruments.

The piano industry grew rapidly during this period, with many new makers starting up. From Benjamin Crehore's shop came ALPHEUS BABCOCK, who opened his own shop in 1809, and John Osborne, who started on his own in 1815 or earlier. In 1825 Babcock patented a complete cast-iron frame for pianos, an invention that was to have a significant influence on first American and then European piano making. Other important makers starting in this period included Thomas Loud, Jr. (1817), Jonas Chickering (1823), R. & W. Nunns (1823), Boardman & Grey (1835), and William Knabe (1837).

Organ building in Boston continued with William Goodrich and several builders who had worked in his shop; the most important were Thomas Appleton and Elias Hook, who both began in the 1820s. Hook's firm, as well as the New York builders Henry Erben (1824) and George Jardine (1837), established shops that were large for this time and introduced factory methods to the trade. Henry Pilcher began in 1833 at Newark, New Jersey, before moving to New Haven in 1839 and eventually to St. Louis and Chicago.

The earliest known American reed organ was made by Ebenezer Goodrich, brother of William, possibly as early as 1809. Suction bellows (as opposed to those activated by air under pressure) were patented by Aaron M. Peasley of Boston in 1818 and eventually became a distinctive feature of American reed-organ design. Some time in the 1830s JAMES A. BAZIN of Boston devised the "elbow melodeon," an accordion-like reed organ pumped with the left forearm or elbow that became very popular in the 1840s. Abraham Prescott also began making reed organs, about 1836. Barrel organs continued to be made by rural craftsmen such as Erastus Wattles of Lebanon, Connecticut, and William Whiteley of Utica, New York, for use in both churches and homes.

Among the miscellaneous instruments of the period probably the most fascinating were the "Grand Harmonicons" patented by Francis Hopkinson Smith in 1825 and made until about 1833. These were sets of musical glasses arranged to produce a chromatic scale and housed in handsome wooden cases. An Aeolian harp was among the instruments offered at the opening of the C.F. Martin music store in New York in 1833.

4. 1840–70. The populations of American towns and cities of 8000 or more inhabitants increased by a phenomenal 90% during the 1840s alone, reflecting the effects of immigration, industrialization, and improved transportation. Urban musical entertainment developed at an equally rapid rate in many forms: pleasure-garden, musical-society, and theater concerts, Italian opera, traveling virtuosos, minstrel shows, popular songs, dancing, traveling concert troupes, circuses, brass bands, and many others. All types of musical instrument maker flourished, especially those making brass instruments, reed organs, and pianos.

During the early part of this period American players and manufacturers of flutes sorted out the advantages and disadvantages of three types of flute: the simple eight-key instrument, Abel Siccama's diatonic model, and the Boehm flute. All three were made by American makers and competed at mechanic fairs between 1846 and 1855. The Boehm was the undisputed winner; its rapid acceptance by professional and amateur players alike was due in part to its avid promotion by America's foremost flute maker of that time, ALFRED G. BADGER. From 1851 he also pioneered the use of ebonite in flute making and in 1866 apparently produced the first American metal flutes.

It was during the 1840s that the full effects of the revolution in brass-instrument construction were first felt in the United States. By 1840 practically every community and military band in the country had switched entirely to brass. The making of brass instruments increased by leaps and bounds, spurred on by the popularity of brass bands in the 1840s and 1850s and by the needs of military bands during the 1860s. E.G. WRIGHT of Boston perfected the small keyed bugle in E♭ with 10–12 keys used by most bandleaders and soloists. In the 1840s Samuel Graves made the first American alto, tenor, and bass valved instruments called "trombacellos." THOMAS D. PAINE of Woonsocket, Rhode Island, also made larger brasses called "bassonetts," invented a rotary valve, and was the first to use string linkage for rotary valves. J. LATHROP ALLEN contributed a valve design that was very successful in the United States, and ISAAC FISKE patented several experimental brass instrument designs. American brass bands developed with the small E♭ keyed bugle as their leading solo voice, and until after the Civil War, they played at a pitch level a perfect 4th higher than most bands in other countries. This has exacerbated the confusion in terminology whereby instruments playing soprano and alto parts in European bands would have to play alto and tenor parts (respectively) in the United States. Not until the 1870s did American bands begin to conform to standard practice elsewhere. Allen Dodworth of New York is credited with suggesting the over-shoulder design of brass instruments used from the 1830s through this period. Louis Schreiber's teardrop-shaped design (1867) is found only in American brass instruments. With these, as well as the upright saxhorns imported from France from the 1840s, and circular cavalry or helicon instruments based on eastern European design, American brass bandsmen of the Civil War shouldered instruments of amazing variety in their shape and size.

Two percussion instruments, tambourine and bones, came into popular use with the minstrel shows of this period. They were used both as solo instruments and as rhythm background for the banjo and fiddle. A drum-making industry developed in Philadelphia during the 1850s. Prominent makers included William H. Horstmann (who began about 1845), Charles and Francis Soistman (1854), A. Eggling & Co. (c1855), and William Ent (c1856). The Civil War encouraged these and many other makers with large orders for military drums. Other well-known makers of drums at this time included Ernest Vogt and C.M. Zimmerman of Philadelphia, and WILLIAM BOUCHER of Baltimore. Heads for drums and banjos were produced by Joseph Rodgers in Farmingdale, New Jersey, from 1849. The bell-manufacturing shops in East Hampton, Connecticut, continued to produce most of the handbells, sleigh bells, and other such instruments used in the United States and Canada.

Several good violin-making shops were established during this period, including those of Ira J. White (Boston, 1835–90); Asa W. White (Boston, 1849–70); John Albert (New York, c1848, Philadelphia from c1859); Charles Mercier (New York, 1842–68); William B. Tilton (New York, 1853–67); and Joseph Urban (New York, 1847, San Francisco, 1863–93). The first outstanding violin maker in the United States was George Gemunder, who had worked with J.-B. Vuillaume in Paris and immigrated in 1847, working first in Boston and from 1851 to 1899 in New York.

Plucked string instruments were widely used during this period. Virtually all the above-named violin makers also made guitars. The guitar maker C.F. Martin moved his business to Nazareth, Pennsylvania, in 1839, expanding production and offering several innovations. From about 1842 until at least 1863 Charles Stumcka made fine guitars in Boston. About 1840 the harp maker J.F. Browne established a shop in New York and made excellent harps until the early 1870s. The firm was continued by Edgar J. Browne, probably his son, and

George H. Buckwell until 1942. The harp-making business of Reese and Laban Lewis in New York lasted from 1848 at the latest until 1868.

Boucher, who worked in Baltimore from about 1845 to 1870, was probably the first commercial manufacturer of the increasingly popular banjo. Other performers and makers who helped improve the instrument during the 1850s and 1860s were Henry C. Dobson (1831–1908), his younger brothers Charles and George, and James W. Clarke (d 1880). Clarke is credited with evolving the perch pole or extension of the neck through the hoop, thus strengthening the construction of the banjo. Frets were first used on it in the 1840s, though they were not in general use until the 1870s. Although the hammered dulcimer was often made by local craftsmen or by players themselves, a few small factories can be identified in the 1850s and 1860s. Harrison and Lewis S. Wade operated a shop in Stedman, New York, which according to census data employed six men and produced 500 dulcimers in 1855. John Low patented an improved bridge in 1860 and evidently operated a shop in Clinton, Massachusetts. Ezra Durand of Norwich, Connecticut, was the most prominent maker, even though his shop operated only during 1867–9.

The years 1840–70 saw a phenomenal growth in the American piano-making industry in spite of the difficulties caused by the Civil War. Several well-known piano firms originated during this period, including Haines Brothers (in 1851), WEBER (1852), STEINWAY & Sons (1853), Decker & Son (1856), and BALDWIN (1862). The new ideas of metal framing, increased tension, overstringing, better hammer action, and improved scaling were gradually proved and applied, and for the first time American makers competed successfully in international exhibitions. Jonas Chickering won a gold medal in the Great Exhibition of 1851 at the Crystal Palace, London, and both Chickering and Steinway pianos won worldwide acclaim at the Universal Exhibition of 1867 in Paris.

Among the most important organ-building firms established during this period were those of William Allen Johnson of Westfield, Massachusetts, in 1854, and John H. and Caleb S. Odell in 1859. The Odells contributed several important inventions to organ building in the 1860s and 1870s, including an early combination action that proved very successful.

The fastest-growing sector of the organ-building trade at this time was that of the reed organ. This was a less expensive substitute for the pipe organ or piano and was frequently bought for small churches, modest homes, and rural communities. Concord, New Hampshire, became a center of this industry in the 1840s as a result of the activities of the firm of Abraham Prescott and such makers as Charles Austin, D.B. Bartlett, David Dearborn, and John A. Farley. Their first products were the little elbow melodeons of James A. Bazin's design. George A. Prince ran an extensive reed-organ business in Buffalo, New York, from 1846 until about 1879. While working for Prince in 1846, Jeremiah Carhart developed an exhaust bellows similar to that invented by Peasley that was soon characteristic of most American reed organs. Carhart went into partnership with Elias Needham about 1846 and contributed improvements to the trade until the mid-1860s, the firm lasting until the 1870s. Emmons Hamlin, who also worked for Prince, discovered about 1848 how to voice metal reeds for differing tone qualities. In 1854, with Henry Mason, he founded the firm of MASON & HAMLIN, whose important inventions included the double bellows and the knee swell lever. The harmonica and accordion, instruments of the reed-organ family, also found a ready market. Charles G. Christman of New York had advertised their manufacture as early as 1831 and continued in business until 1858. Other New York producers included John Jacobs (active from 1846 to 1856), Frederick Goetze (1855 to at least 1890), and Francis Ludwig (1857–72).

About 1845 Joshua C. Stoddard of Worcester, Massachusetts, built his first steam calliope, a cylinder-operated model with 15 whistles. It was first heard in public in 1855, when the patent was also obtained, and in 1856 the American Steam Piano Company was formed to manufacture it. Models of the calliope with up to 150 lbs of steam pressure could be heard as far as 12 miles away, and they immediately became popular on riverboats. Other automatic musical instruments popular between 1840 and 1870 included barrel organs and pianos made for street use, and Swiss music boxes. Barrel organ and piano makers included GEORGE HICKS (in Brooklyn, 1849–62), Henry S. Taylor (New York, 1854–1900), and Antonio Ginocchio (New York, 1855–c1900).

5. 1870–1900. During this period the larger American cities enjoyed a flourishing concert life, which included opera, symphony orchestras, choral societies, concert bands, theater music, recitals and chamber music of many kinds, and pleasure-garden and park concerts, as well as casual performances by a variety of street musicians. Throughout the country in cities and towns of all sizes the phenomenon of the community band led to the training of thousands of musicians, the sale of at least as many band instruments, and the development of audiences who appreciated music by some of the better 19th-century composers. In their homes people continued to enjoy singing and playing the ever-mounting tide of popular sheet music, using the piano, reed organ, guitar, and other instruments. Many of those less skilled in singing or playing were increasingly drawn to one of the many models of automatic musical instrument, and thousands of hand-cranked machines in all price ranges were sold.

Following the Civil War a movement began to reinstate woodwind instruments in military and community bands. Contact with European bands at Patrick S. Gilmore's huge music festivals and by Americans traveling abroad convinced bandleaders in the United States of the improved effects of mixed bands of wind and brass. During the 1870s bands acquired flutes, clarinets, oboes, bassoons, and saxophones, including the larger members of the clarinet, bassoon, and saxophone families. Although American manufacturers continued to produce flutes of competitive quality, most of the other instruments were imported: the American fascination with brass instruments from 1840 through the Civil War had stunted the woodwind industry and left it far behind its European competitors. Important flute makers continuing from the previous period were Alfred G. Badger, THEODORE BERTELING, John Pfaff (active 1839–86), and William Ronnberg (active 1835–89). Those starting in business included George Cloos (active 1869–1913), William Meinell (from 1874 to at least 1900), and George W. and WILLIAM S. HAYNES. C.G. Conn began producing clarinets of metal and of an ebonized composite material in the late 1880s and offered the first American-made saxophone in 1889.

The most significant development in American brass-instrument making after the Civil War was the gradual shift from mostly rotary valves to piston valves of the Périnet type. This change seems to have been brought about first by the influence of HENRY DISTIN, an English brass player and manufacturer who had toured the United States before immigrating in 1877. Distin's "light piston valves," patented in 1864, rapidly found favor with American brass players and influenced other American manufacturers to offer similar valves. Distin first joined with MOSES SLATER but by the mid-1880s had established his own firm near Philadelphia. Other important brass firms continuing during this period include Benjamin F. Quinby, who patented another valve design in 1872; JOHN HOWARD FOOTE, a New York importer and manufacturer who was the founding patron of the instrument collection at the Smithsonian Institution; John F. Stratton, whose large European factories supplied instruments for his New York store and for that of his brother George W. Stratton in Boston; Louis Schreiber (active in New York, 1865–84) and Henry Lehnert (Philadelphia, 1865–1914), whose teardrop-shaped and "Centennial" model brasses respectively were more distinctive than successful; and the BOSTON MUSICAL INSTRUMENT MANUFACTORY, formed from the shops of SAMUEL GRAVES and E.G. Wright and known for high-quality instruments. A new firm, C.G. Conn of Elkhart, Indiana (1875), invented the double-bell euphonium about 1890 and produced the first successful sousaphone in 1898 (a prototype may have been built by J.W. PEPPER in 1892). Other new firms that were to become famous in the 20th century included York Brothers of Grand Rapids, Michigan (1882), the BUESCHER Band Instrument Co. of Elkhart (1888), and the H.N. White Co. (KING instruments) in Cleveland (1893).

Percussion instruments increased in variety as minstrel shows and vaudeville introduced new effects, and symphony orchestras, bands, and theater orchestras performed works demanding new kinds of sound. The firm of J.C. DEAGAN was established in St. Louis as the J.C. Deagan Musical Bells Company in 1880 and soon produced a large range of novelty instruments, including many models of glockenspiel, improved chimes, and xylophones. After a short period in San Francisco (1891–7) the firm moved to Chicago and offered a continuing stream of new tuned idiophonic instruments.

Gemunder remained the most important American violin maker throughout this period. Other makers of some importance were Walter S. Goss (active in Boston, 1870–1925) and Jerome Bonaparte Squier (Boston, 1886–1906). Hugo Schindler made violin strings in Boston (1889–1934) and was evidently the first to make aluminum-wound D strings. William Lewis & Son of Chicago and John Friedrich & Bros. of New York were important new firms, starting in 1874 and 1884 respectively; the writer Ernest N. Doring, an expert on violins and bows, joined the latter in 1893. Between 1866 and 1869 John F. Stratton, previously a brass-instrument manufacturer and dealer in musical merchandise, established musical instrument factories in Germany, including a large one at Gohlis (now a suburb of Leipzig), to manufacture violins by machine. More than 100 violins per day were produced for sale in New York and Boston stores, some priced as low as $3.

Plucked and hammered string instruments were increasingly popular during this period. Several new designs appeared, a few older instruments were reintroduced, and others continued to be developed and improved. String bands, which eventually used several sizes of banjo, mandolin, and guitar, were first formed late in the century. The Appalachian dulcimer, a distinctive American instrument of the zither family, seems to have evolved in some areas of the southern Appalachian Mountains shortly after the Civil War, but its use was not widespread, and it was made largely by those who played it. Traditional zithers were also made in the United States during this period by Franz Schwarzer of Washington, Missouri, who arrived from Austria in 1864 and began making zithers about 1869. By the early 1870s these were winning top prizes in Vienna and had found a ready market throughout the world. Schwarzer was noted for his improvement of the bracing of the instrument, for his patented means of steadying it on a specially designed table, for a model with additional bass strings, and for his outstanding engraving and inlay work. His firm had made over 10,000 instruments, including some mandolins and guitars, by Schwarzer's death in 1904; production declined after

Lucie Bigelow Rosen, playing a theremin, 1930s. (From the Archives of Caramoor Center for Music and the Arts, Inc.)

World War I and the factory was demolished in the 1950s. Another zither-like instrument made during this period was the autoharp, probably a German invention, patented in the United States in 1882 by Charles F. Zimmermann, who opened a factory to produce it in 1885. His business and patents were acquired in 1892 by Alfred Dolge and moved to Dolgeville, New York. In the mid-1890s Dolge made and sold over 3000 autoharps a week.

The banjo, professionally played and increasingly popular, was being improved by many manufacturers. Epiphone, established in 1873 by A. Stathopoulo, first made banjos in 1876; S.S. Stewart had opened his factory in Philadelphia by 1880; and A.C. Fairbanks and William E. Cole formed Fairbanks & Cole in Boston in 1880. Another important firm, the Vega Co. of Boston, began in 1889. By the 1880s the banjo had acquired frets on its fingerboard as well as other details of construction that improved its playing qualities and sound, and in general had arrived at the design that has become standard.

Hammered dulcimers were widely used during this period in New England and westward through New York, parts of Canada, and Michigan. They were also common in other parts of the country among German settlers. A number of small factories produced them, and they were offered in both the Sears and Montgomery Ward catalogs. Fine guitars continued to be made by C.F. Martin & Co., which by 1890 was also producing mandolins. Angelo Mannello made outstanding mandolins after his arrival in New York from Italy in 1885. Because inexpensive guitars and mandolins were available from mail-order companies, and the instruments were promoted by players and teachers, they became increasingly popular. Lyon & Healy, a large musical merchandise firm in Chicago, began to make fine harps in 1889 and was also prominent in the manufacture of other plucked string instruments. In Hawaii a small Portuguese instrument, introduced in the 1890s, began to be developed as the ukulele.

The American piano industry, having won international honors at the Universal Exhibition of 1867 in Paris, now looked for ways to profit by its success. While Chickering and Steinway continued to make fine pianos and bickered about who had received top honors in Paris, a number of new or lesser-known piano firms cashed in on the new interest in pianos. A trend towards specialization is best illustrated by the career of ALFRED DOLGE. He mechanized the making of felts for piano hammers, establishing a factory for the purpose in 1871, and in 1876 he began making soundboards; by 1880 he was supplying most other makers with both. Many other specialized shops produced other parts such as legs, cases, actions, keyboards, and frames, making it possible for manufacturers to buy any or all of the parts of a piano. Such specialization was encouraged by the change during the late 19th century to a somewhat standardized upright piano from the previously popular square model. Another practice that became widespread during this period was that of stenciling any name on a piano that the sales firm preferred.

JOSEPH P. HALE was the most notorious manufacturer in this regard. Between 1860 and 1891 he built up a huge business by assembling inexpensive pianos from discounted parts produced by the specialty shops and selling them with any name desired on the fallboard. Briefly after 1876 Hale built more than 5000 pianos a year, more than any other manufacturer.

Piano making followed the population westward, and in the years after the fire of 1871 in Chicago a small piano and organ dealer there, W.W. Kimball, who had founded his company in 1857, grew to be the largest piano manufacturer in the world as well as one of the largest makers of reed organs. One other notable firm that began piano making in this period was Mason & Hamlin (founded in Boston in 1854), makers of reed organs, which had offered its first upright piano by 1883 and went on to build grands of a quality to compete in some ways with those of Chickering and Steinway.

Important pipe-organ companies now included HOOK & HASTINGS, Johnson & Son, the George S. Hutchings Co., J.H. & C.S. Odell, GEORGE JARDINE, and HILBORNE LEWIS ROOSEVELT. Water and then electric motors gradually superseded the pipe-organ pumper; electric action allowed disbursement of organ sections anywhere in the church and resulted in new keyboard controls; louder and more colorful voicing, together with more open installation, gave a more dramatic sound and appearance; and huge installations for exhibitions and fairs excited public interest as never before.

The reed organ reached the pinnacle of its development and production during this period. Jacob Estey, who had gradually been involved in the industry over the previous 20 years, reorganized his firm as the ESTEY ORGAN CO. at Brattleboro, Vermont, in 1866, and by 1898 had produced 300,000 instruments. Kimball began building reed organs in Chicago in 1880 and used new mass sales techniques to market a similar number in the Midwest. Daniel F. Beatty operated a large reed-organ business from about 1868 to 1889 and pioneered in accepting payments by installments. But he also indulged in more dubious selling practices and was eventually convicted of fraud for receiving prepaid orders but neglecting to ship the merchandise.

Swiss music boxes had long been imported into the United States, and the barrel organ was also well known, but in the 1870s a new and less expensive type of automatic musical instrument was introduced. The organina—or organette, as it has come to be called—was a small hand-cranked reed organ operated by a paper roll or pinned cylinder. The most important companies to produce them were the Monroe Organ Reed Co. of Worcester, Massachusetts, and the Massachusetts Organ Co. of Boston. The Monroe Co. was founded in 1869, began producing organettes in 1879, and in 1892 sold out to the Aeolian Organ & Music Co. (from 1895 the AEOLIAN Co.). By 1887 this firm was producing over 50,000 instruments a year, mostly for the Mechanical Orguinette Co. of New York (founded 1878). The Massachusetts Organ Co. (1880) produced even more and sold most of them by mail order under various brand names, such as "Gem Organetta." The technology of the organette, widely developed in Europe as well as in the United States, led directly to the automatic-playing reed organ introduced by the Monroe Organ Reed Co. in 1883 and to the pneumatic paper-roll player pianos and orchestrions that followed.

Another invention important in the American automatic instrument market was the music box operated by a disc mechanism (rather than a cylinder). Between 1882 and 1889 patents were issued in the United States and Germany covering its basic mechanisms, and in 1892 the Regina Music Box Company was formed in Jersey City, New Jersey, by Gustave Brachhausen from the German firm of Polyphon. It was less expensive to produce than cylinder machines, and any number of the inexpensive discs with the latest songs could be played. The firm moved to Rahway, New Jersey, in 1895, and in 1897 Brachhausen patented a mechanism for automatically changing the discs. By 1921 the firm had sold 100,000 disc players.

Accordions and harmonicas continued to be popular, but most were imported: in 1879 over 60% of the production of harmonicas by the Hohner Co. of Trossingen, Germany, was exported to the United States. The English concertina was also imported and sold by American firms.

6. 1900–30. During the first decade of the 20th century most woodwind instruments were imported, but an increased market and the trade difficulties caused by World War I soon persuaded band-instrument companies to begin making them; craftsmen with the necessary skills often had to be imported. It was now that the Buffet clarinet with a Boehm-inspired key system began to compete with the Albert- or Muller-system clarinet in the United States. W.H. Cundy and Harry Bettoney, who had been importing this clarinet for some time, formed the Cundy–Bettoney Co. Inc. in 1907 and began manufacturing as well as importing. William S. Haynes continued to make fine flutes and in 1914 patented the drawn (i.e., integral) tone-hole now used on all metal woodwinds. VERNE Q. POWELL, who had worked for Haynes, formed his own company in 1927 and also made flutes of the finest quality. The craze for saxophones after the war and well into the 1920s was met by band-instrument companies such as Conn, Buescher, King Musical Instruments, and Martin. Three minor innovations in the shape of the saxophone bell were offered in the late 1920s: the Connosax, with an english-horn-like ball instead of a bell; Buescher's tipped (forward) bell; and the King Saxello, with the bell turned 90° forward. Various sizes of the sarrusophone were introduced by Conn in 1921.

The brass-instrument industry expanded very rapidly, first on the strength of popular touring bands like those of Conway, Creatore, Innes, Liberati, Pryor, Kryl, and Sousa, and then, in the mid-1920s, as a result of successful efforts to establish bands in the public schools. New companies included E.K. Blessing (1906), Martin (1907), F.E. Olds (1912), VINCENT BACH (1924), and Lorenzo Sansone (1925). The bell-front sousaphone was first offered by Conn in 1908.

Beginning late in the 19th century and continuing into the 20th, drummers for vaudeville, theatrical shows, and jazz bands developed the trap-drum set, which included an ever wider variety of percussion instruments and special effects. Ludwig Industries began in 1909 (as Ludwig & Ludwig) with the production of a trap-drum pedal and continued with many other items for drummers, including notably improved pedal timpani. The Leedy Manufacturing Co., established in 1900, also specialized in percussion products and contributed significantly to the design of pedal timpani in 1923. The Slingerland Drum Company was established in 1921 and also offered improvements in pedal timpani as well as in other types of drum. Mallet instruments were increasingly popular during this period, and in 1916 Hermann Winterhoff of the Leedy Co. invented an early version of the vibraphone; its definitive features were established in 1923. The J.C. Deagan Co. continued to offer vital innovations in glockenspiels, xylophones, marimbas, carillons, chimes, and mallet-instrument mechanisms for automatic musical instruments.

The late 19th and early 20th centuries saw violin making in the United States grow both in the manufacturing of inexpensive copies and in the number of makers of good-quality instruments. Players could choose from instruments offered by mail-order catalogs for only a few dollars or traditional handcrafted instruments costing hundreds. Jalovec (1968) lists over 500 American violin makers during this period, the most notable including Rudolph Henry Wurlitzer and James R. Carlisle in Cincinnati; William Heinrich Moennig in Philadelphia; Emil Herrmann in New York; and John Hornsteiner, Carl H. George, Frank Sindelar, and Carl Becker in Chicago. Ernest N. Doring's reputation as an expert on violins and bows increased through his work in New York and Chicago.

During the years 1900–1930 plucked string instruments were very popular in the United States. Mandolins, guitars, and especially banjos were used in many kinds of entertainment and provided recreation for many amateurs in string bands as well. Important manufacturers included Lyon & Healy under the "George Washburn" brand name; the Fred Gretsch Manufacturing Company; H.A. Weymann & Son, whose "Keystone" instruments were offered in 1903; William L. Lange, whose "Orpheum" and "Paramount" brands were introduced in 1908 and 1921 respectively; the Gibson Mandolin-Guitar Manufacturing Co., established in 1902; the Vega Co., which acquired A.C. Fairbanks & Co. in 1904; Epiphone; and the Bacon banjo company, which with David L. Day initiated the Bacon & Day "Silver Bell" model in 1923. Orville H. Gibson's arch-top guitars and flat-back mandolins were introduced at the beginning of the century, and by 1910 tenor and plectrum banjos had also appeared. The Hawaiian and Dobro guitars were also products of this period. From 1909 the Rudolph Wurlitzer Co. competed with Lyon & Healy in building fine concert harps suitable for the American climate.

In the United States from about 1895 to 1914, according to Loesser (1954), the piano "gave the most substantial pleasure of which it was capable to the greatest number of people." Pianos were produced during the first decade of the 20th century at a rate far exceeding the increase in the country's population. The piano was the focal point of home entertainment, a favorite solo instrument, and used in almost every kind of musical ensemble. It was during this period that W.W. Kimball became the largest piano manufacturer in the world and many small and medium-sized companies joined together to form large conglomerates. The Aeolian Co. joined with Weber in 1903, and they gradually absorbed other, smaller firms. In 1908 the American Piano Co. acquired several important firms, including Chickering, Knabe, Marshall & Wendell, and, in 1922, Mason & Hamlin. Steinway and Baldwin were among the firms that continued separately. The rapid growth of the piano industry before World War I began to wane in the 1920s. The phonograph and radio captured the public interest along with motion pictures and such costly consumer goods as automobiles. The sales of player pianos held up for a time, but by the late 1920s production was falling.

The pipe organ reached a degree of popularity unknown before or since in the United States during the early 20th century. In addition to more traditional installations in churches, a new kind of organ with resources simulating the sounds of orchestras, bands, or popular dance ensembles evolved; such organs were widely installed in municipal auditoriums, schools, convention and exhibition halls, theaters, and even homes. Robert Hope-Jones and George Ashdown Audsley were particularly involved in these new trends. Important firms during this period included Moller, Austin, Skinner, Kimball, and Kilgen. Wurlitzer began making pipe organs in 1910 and specialized in theater models. The Aeolian Co. was foremost in providing organs for home use, many of them with automatic playing devices. Other well-known firms joining the market included Estey, whose first pipe organs were produced in 1901, and Wicks, founded in 1906. Reed organs had been taken westward as the plains were settled, but production gradually declined, and in 1922 Kimball, in previous decades the world's largest producer of reed organs, stopped making them altogether.

Automatic musical instruments were much favored in this era. During the 1890s various types of piano player (an exterior apparatus pushed up to and operating an ordinary piano) first gained public attention, notably the Cecilian by the Farrand Organ Co. of Detroit and the Pianola invented by Edwin Scott Votey and marketed by the Aeolian Co. of New York. In the early 1900s player pianos with built-in mechanism became very popular for home entertainment, and coin-in-slot models were made for use in public places. Gradually the paper-roll mechanism was used to play a wide variety of automatic instruments including reed organs, pipe organs, violins, banjos, mandolins, and band organs (which simulated an entire band or orchestra). Aeolian was the leading manufacturer of player pianos, as of automatic organs, but almost all other makers offered them as well. Most of the mechanisms were built by either the Standard Pneumatic Action Co. or the Auto

Pneumatic Action Co., both of New York. The most important producer of rolls was Q-R-S Music Rolls Inc., formed by the Melville Clark Piano Co. of Chicago about 1900. Band organs, or orchestrions, with pipes simulating a variety of instruments, often including even percussion instruments and xylophone, were first made in the United States by several firms located in North Tonawanda, New York. Eugene DeKleist began in 1893 and was associated with Wurlitzer from 1897. The Niagara Musical Instrument Manufacturing Co. started in 1905, and the North Tonawanda Musical Instrument Works followed in 1906. Wurlitzer was soon the leading manufacturer and provided thousands of these machines for skating rinks, carnivals, merry-go-rounds, circuses, amusement parks, and theaters.

From about 1915 calliopes were made using compressed air instead of steam. These were played either from an automatic paper-roll system or a keyboard, and they also competed for the outdoor music business. The Tangley Co. of Muscatine, Iowa, was the leading producer, followed by the National Calliope Co. of Kansas City. One of the most ingenious of the music machines was the Violano Virtuoso developed for the Mills Novelty Co. of Chicago by Harry K. Sandell from about 1904. Using a paper roll combined with electromagnets, the Violano automatically played a violin with piano accompaniment.

The most significant of the automatic instruments was the reproducing piano, a player piano with a built-in mechanism that reproduced such subtleties as the dynamics, tempo, pedaling, and accentuation of a particular artist's performance. The first of these was introduced in Germany in 1904 by M. Welte & Söhne of Freiburg. About 1913 two American firms entered the market. The American Piano Co. called its reproducing mechanism the Ampico; and the Aeolian Co. offered the Duo-Art. Most of the great pianists of the early 20th century—among them Paderewski, Rachmaninoff, and Rubinstein—made rolls for these companies and verified that they were accurate reproductions of their performances. Because recording was still in its infancy these rolls played on a good piano with mechanism in good repair are the best surviving evidence of the playing of many fine artists.

Although electronic devices had been made earlier to produce musical sounds it was in the early 20th century that the first workable instruments were demonstrated. Between 1895 and 1900 THADDEUS CAHILL built the first of his three Telharmoniums in Washington, DC. The second improved model, built at Holyoke, Massachusetts, was completed in New York in 1906 and the third in 1911. The Telharmonium consisted of tons of equipment and produced a wide range of sounds controlled by a keyboard. Its music was to be distributed over telephone lines to subscribing hotels, restaurants, and homes, but it had little success. Engineers at the Gibson Guitar Co. experimented with electrically amplified instruments in the early 1920s. The ViviTone Co., formed by Lloyd Loar and others from the Gibson Co., was unsuccessful in an attempt to produce and market electric guitars and basses in 1924. In the late 1920s Lev Termen

(Leon Theremin) left Russia for the United States and demonstrated his theremin, an electronic musical instrument controlled in pitch and volume by movements of the player's hands. A number of them were manufactured by the RCA Corporation in the late 1920s and early 1930s, and several American composers wrote for the instrument.

Miscellaneous instruments of this period include a widespread group on which a melody and four chords could be played, such as the ukelin. They were marketed by door-to-door salesmen from several firms beginning in the 1920s, including the Pianoharp Co. of Boston, which merged with Oscar Schmidt International of Jersey City in 1926, and the Marxochime Colony, New Troy, Michigan.

7. 1930–60. In instrument making as well as in other business activities the Depression and World War II accelerated change by ending many established companies and technologies, providing added incentive for new technological developments during the war, and then encouraging new industries using these new ideas in the recovery that followed. The automatic musical instrument industry ended with the Depression; but already newer technologies—sound film, radio, and the phonograph—had begun to take its place. The war stimulated rapid advances in electronics that were then applied to these devices when production of consumer goods resumed. The Depression also terminated the era of the professional concert band, and band-instrument makers turned to the production of special lines of instruments for the expanding school market. New interests and tastes in music also affected the music business. A concern for historically accurate performance of early music, apparent in the United States from the 1930s, led to new concepts in organ building and to the founding of new firms making harpsichords, recorders, and other early instruments. Styles such as country-and-western, bluegrass, swing, and rock-and-roll were also influential.

High-quality flutes, piccolos, and saxophones continued to be made in the United States, while most of the best oboes, clarinets, and bassoons were imported. New firms making and dealing in woodwind instruments included W.T. Armstrong (flutes, established in 1932), the Artley Flute Co. (1939), the Linton Manufacturing Co. (all woodwinds, 1944), the K.G. Gemeinhardt Co. (flutes, 1945), the Lesher Woodwind Co. (bassoons and oboes, c1945), Larilee Woodwinds (oboes, 1946), the G. LEBLANC Corp. (flutes, clarinets, saxophones, 1947), and the Fox Products Corporation (bassoons, 1949). Although SELMER was established in the United States early in the 1900s, its actual production of instruments began only in the 1940s. Almost all of these firms concentrated on making school-model instruments, mostly of metal or composite construction. From the 1940s until 1959 Alfred B. LAUBIN of Scarsdale, New York, made fine oboes (promoted by Fernand Gillet); so did A. Lym and his son, William R. Lym, of Los Angeles during the 1950s, but from the mid-1960s they catered mainly to the student market.

Brass-instrument companies also concentrated on school instruments, often expanding their businesses to

EMS VC53 synthesizer, c1969. *(Susurreal/Lebrecht Music & Arts)*

include woodwinds as well. Although only a few of their products were directed at the professional performer, most of the following established firms could boast a few outstanding models: Conn, York, Buescher, Holton, White, Blessing, Martin, Olds, Bach, and Sansone. New companies included F.A. Reynolds in Cleveland from 1935 and the GETZEN Co., a repair shop from 1939 and a manufacturer from 1945. Outstanding small shops include Vincent Bach, who began making trumpets in 1924, and RENOLD O. SCHILKE of Chicago, a full-time trumpet maker from 1956. During the early 1950s a neglected brass instrument, the valved bugle or flugelhorn, was revived by some popular players of the trumpet for its smooth and mellow tone quality.

The refinement of percussion instruments continued during this period with significant improvements in pedal timpani, drums, and mallet instruments. The C.G. Conn Co. acquired the Leedy Manufacturing Co. in 1927 and the firm of Ludwig & Ludwig in 1930, giving it a strong line of percussion instruments. In 1936 William F. Ludwig left Conn to set up his own percussion business under the name W.F.L. Drum Co.; in 1955 he purchased the Ludwig division from Conn and set up the Ludwig Drum Co. The Slingerland Drum Co. was also a strong competitor during this period

and in 1955 purchased the Leedy patents from Conn. Deagan continued its dominance in bells, chimes, and mallet instruments, and it drew attention to new marimba designs by staging concerts by 100-player marimba orchestras in the 1930s. In 1929 Avedis ZILDJIAN, a nephew of the famous Armenian cymbal-making family who was living in the United States, inherited the family business and established a foundry at North Quincy, Massachusetts, and later at Norwell. Since then, most of the best orchestral cymbals have been produced by Zildjian.

Because of the widespread use of instruments made in earlier centuries, the fine string-instrument businesses in the United States revolved more around dealers, experts, and repairers than actual makers. Foremost among the dealers and experts were Emil Herrmann of New York; Rembert Wurlitzer, who continued his father's business with branches in several cities; William Moennig, Jr., who also continued a family business, in Philadelphia; Kenneth Warren in Chicago; and Jacques Français, who began in New York. Outstanding repairers included three immigrants, Fernando Sacconi, Dario D'Attili, and Zenon Petesh, who arrived in 1931, 1935, and 1949 respectively. Makers included Carl Becker, Jr., in Chicago, and Hana Wiesshaar in Hollywood.

The 1930s saw a decline in the use of banjos and mandolins as dance bands turned more to the smooth sound of the guitar. Country-and-western music also favored the guitar, and new models by Gibson in 1932 and 1934 set standards of tone and volume. C.F. MARTIN & Co. introduced the Dreadnought model guitar in 1931; its variant models are identified with the prefix "D," among them the well-known D-45 model made for Gene Autry in 1933. The RICKENBACKER brand name was introduced by the Electro String Instrument Company for various types of electric steel guitar in 1931. For a time most interest centered on the amplified acoustic guitar, but by the 1940s several performers, notably LES PAUL, were interested in the increased sustaining power and easier amplification of solid-body electric guitars. In 1946 Leo Fender formed the FENDER Electric Instruments Company and by 1948 was marketing a solid-body electric guitar called the Broadcaster (renamed the Telecaster in 1950), followed by the Stratocaster in 1954; from 1951 electric bass guitars were also offered. With the help of Les Paul, the firm of Gibson introduced solid-body instruments in 1952, and in 1957 set a standard for the industry with their "humbucking" (hum-cancelling) pickup. In 1944 Gibson became part of the Chicago Musical Instrument Co.

Bluegrass music, featuring a fast finger-picking style of five-string banjo playing, prompted renewed interest in the banjo, particularly from the late 1950s. Gibson began making banjos again in 1948; the Fred Gretsch Manufacturing Co., which had acquired the Bacon Banjo Co. in 1940, also began soon after the war; and Epiphone offered banjos again in the 1950s and continued to do so after being purchased by the Chicago Musical Instrument Co. in 1957.

The Depression forced many piano makers out of business and led others to join together for survival. The merger in 1932 of the Aeolian Co. and the American Piano Corporation brought nearly 20 once independent piano companies together under the new Aeolian American Corporation. The most significant new products during this period were the small spinet and console model upright pianos first produced in 1934. The interest in historically accurate performance of early music led to the manufacture of harpsichords: JOHN CHALLIS of Detroit set up as a maker in the early 1930s, and two of the most influential American harpsichord makers, FRANK HUBBARD and WILLIAM DOWD, followed in Boston during the 1950s.

The 1930s saw the decline of the large orchestral organ and spreading interest in smaller-scale instruments based on the principles of Baroque and earlier organs. G. DONALD HARRISON, who joined the Skinner Organ Co. in 1927, was the leading proponent of the new style. Also important was Walter Henry Holtkamp (see HOLTKAMP ORGAN CO.), who made the first American tracker-action instruments inspired by this trend. Other important pipe-organ firms during this period included Austin, Moller, Aeolian-Skinner (merged in 1931), and Schlicker (formed in 1932). Imported tracker-action organs by Dirk Flentrop of the Netherlands and other European makers were also influential. Strong interest

in organs was provoked by the controversy over whether the Hammond electronic organ (introduced in 1935) could be considered an organ. Claims by Hammond that its instrument could do everything a pipe organ could do, for much less money, were disputed in court by the American Guild of Organists. The instrument rapidly achieved commercial success, and the more advanced but less successful Hammond novachord followed about 1939. The Allen organ was also first produced in 1939. There followed electronic organs of many kinds produced by such companies as Baldwin, Conn, Gulbransen, Kimball, Lowrey, Rodgers, and Wurlitzer. The first successful electronic pianos began to appear after the war. The making of automatic musical instruments ceased almost entirely during the Depression, and except for toys and novelties the market was entirely taken over by the phonograph, jukebox, radio, sound movies, and other forms of electronically recorded and reproduced music.

8. 1960–90. A growing dissatisfaction with work in large corporations and with mass-produced products, together with the suitability of many popular instruments for handcrafting, led to the setting up of many small instrument-making shops. Over 1000 makers of all kinds of instrument are listed in Susan Caust Farrell's *Directory of Contemporary American Musical Instrument Makers* (1981). This trend was further stimulated by the ever-increasing enthusiasm for the revival of medieval, Renaissance, and Baroque music and the concomitant demand for faithful copies of appropriate instruments. Interest in the collecting and study of instruments resulted in the formation in 1971 of the AMERICAN MUSICAL INSTRUMENT SOCIETY "to promote study of the history, design, and use of musical instruments in all cultures and from all periods." The instruments of popular music, electric guitars, drum kits, and the new electronic instruments and accessories began a spectacular rise.

Haynes and Powell continued to produce top-quality flutes and piccolos during this period, and the Fox Products Corporation of South Whitley, Indiana, improved their bassoons to very nearly the same level. Oboes and clarinets for professionals were still made largely in France, though many school models made in the United States were now much improved. Excellent saxophones continued to be produced by King Musical Instruments and C.G. Conn. During the 1960s a reshaped metal mouthpiece for saxophones provided the cutting sound desired in new styles of popular music. The instruments demanded by the early-music revival—recorders, Baroque flutes and oboes, early bassoons, natural trumpets and horns, cornetts, early trombones, serpents, and so on—were largely imported, but some were made by knowledgeable American craftsmen; FRIEDRICH VON HUENE of Brookline, Massachusetts, who started his business in 1960, has been among the most successful of them. Outstanding American brass instruments included Selmer's Bach trumpets, Renold Schilke trumpets, Conn trombones and horns, King trombones, and horns by Reynolds and Holton. During the 1960s European tubas began to capture the American professional market, and the contrabass tuba in *16'C* became the favorite of American symphony orchestra players.

The most important American makers of percussion instruments during this period were Conn, with its Slingerland and Deagan subsidiaries, and the Ludwig division of Selmer. Advances in design included plastic heads for all kinds of drums and timpani developed by REMO INC. of North Hollywood from 1957 on and, from the same firm, pre-tuned drumheads, introduced in 1983. Another development of the 1980s was the drum computer, which allowed electronically stored drum sounds of all kinds to be programmed for the entire length of a composition and then reproduced; they were made by such firms as LINN Electronics Inc. of Tarzana, California, and Oberheim Electronics Inc. of Los Angeles.

A surge of interest in the traditions of violin and bow making brought to the United States by earlier 20th-century craftsmen and dealers resulted in many new makers of fine string instruments. Formal schools for the technical training of aspiring makers were established by Peter Prier of Salt Lake City in 1972 and Kenneth Warren of Chicago in 1975. The founding of the VIOLIN SOCIETY OF AMERICA in 1973 and the American Federation of Violin and Bow Makers in 1980 further encouraged the trade. Modern American string instruments began to compete in American symphony orchestras with the more expensive and therefore less accessible violins of previous centuries.

Plucked string instruments now enjoyed a popularity unequaled even by the banjo and mandolin 60 or so years earlier. Electric guitars and bass guitars for rock music were increasingly in demand, especially from major companies such as Fender and Gibson. The Adamas model solid-body guitar by the Kaman Corporation, makers of Ovation guitars, offered innovations in materials and better sound control. The Avatar, a guitar synthesizer (i.e., one played from a guitar rather than from a keyboard) was introduced—not very successfully—in 1978 by ARP of Lexington, Massachusetts. A firm that increased in importance during the 1980s was PEAVEY of Meridian, Mississippi, formed to produce amplifiers and public address systems in 1966 and offering electric guitars and basses from 1977. Heightened interest in folk music as well as in the classical and flamenco guitar, together with the continued popularity of country-and-western music, led to intensive production by the leading makers of acoustic guitars, Martin and Gibson, as well as by many other companies and small craftsmen. In addition the banjo enjoyed renewed interest both in its tenor and plectrum forms— prompted in part by the revived enthusiasm for ragtime and 1920s songs—and in the five-string version used for bluegrass music. Revivals of traditional folk music also encouraged the making of hammered and Appalachian dulcimers by local craftsmen.

The leading concert pianos used in the United States continued to be Steinway, followed by Baldwin, but imports from Japan and Germany took an increasing share of the market from the 1970s on. Interest in historical performance continued to encourage builders of harpsichords. The leading firm was that of William Dowd of Boston. A new phenomenon, going back to the mid-1950s, was the build-it-yourself harpsichord kit. WOLFGANG JOACHIM ZUCKERMANN was the first to produce such kits, followed in the 1960s by Frank Hubbard and others. Early pianos—fortepianos—also began to be built again in the 1960s, by PHILIP R. BELT and other craftsmen.

The most significant development in pipe organs of this period was the growing interest in instruments with mechanical or tracker action and tonal resources patterned after organs of the Baroque period. Builders offering such organs in the 1960s included the ANDOVER Organ Co. of Methuen, Massachusetts; John Brombaugh of Middletown, Ohio (from 1977 of Eugene, Oregon); C.B. Fisk of Gloucester, Massachusetts; Otto Hofmann of Austin, Texas; Charles McManis; the Noack Organ Co.; and the Schlicker Organ Co. Although many smaller instruments had been built earlier, the first modern three-manual tracker organ produced in the United States, by CHARLES BRENTON FISK, was installed in King's Chapel, Boston, in 1964. Electronic home organs enjoyed enormous appeal during the 1960s and 1970s. Baldwin, Kimball, Lowrey, Gulbransen, and Thomas were the leading manufacturers.

A revival of interest in automatic musical instruments fueled the antiques market in them, but few new instruments were offered. Player pianos operated by electronic tape were developed by Super Scope, a division of Sony, in the late 1970s and marketed in the United States by Marantz, but they were not very successful.

Electronic instruments enjoyed faster development than any other segment of the musical instrument industry in this period, and an enormous range of inventions drawing on the latest electronic technology resulted. Wurlitzer's "Sideman" introduced in 1959 was the first commercially available drum machine. The first portable performing music synthesizers were produced in 1965 by ROBERT A. MOOG at Trumansburg, New York, and brought to public attention by Wendy Carlos's recording *Switched-on Bach* in 1968. The firm of BUCHLA in Berkeley, California, has produced voltage-controlled synthesizers, since 1970 including computerized elements. By the early 1970s the ARP company of Lexington, Massachusetts, was rapidly developing synthesizers for the performing market alongside Moog Music Inc., which by then had moved to Williamsville, New York. Other, new companies soon to be prominent included Roland (a Japanese firm), E-MU SYSTEMS Inc. of Santa Cruz, California, and Oberheim Electronics Inc. of Los Angeles s (*see* OBERHEIM, THOMAS ELROY).

From 1976 the Synclavier, the first commercially manufactured digital synthesizer, was developed by the New England Digital Corporation of White River Junction, Vermont, offering a new range of possibilities in sound manipulation. In the 1980s guitar synthesizers were developed by Roland and others more successfully than by ARP a few years earlier. Another exciting development of the 1980s was the Musical Instrument Digital Interface (MIDI), a standard system that enabled instruments made by different manufacturers to be compatible with each other when they are connected. Several companies, including Sequential Circuits Inc.

TABLE 1: American Instrument Making Brand Names by Company

Gibson Guitar Corp., Nashville, TN

Gibson USA	Electric and acoustic guitars and basses, electronics
Gibson Custom, Hist. & ES	Electric guitars/basses
Epiphone	Electric and acoustic guitars, mandolins, banjos, Dobros, and basses, electronics
Kramer	Electric and acoustic guitars and basses
Steinberger	Electric guitars/basses
Tobias	Electric guitars/basses
Valley Arts	Electric guitars/basses
Avante Baritone	Acoustic guitars/basses
Gibson Original Instrs.	Mandolins, banjos, Dobros
Maestro	Mandolins, banjos, Dobros, band instrs.
Slingerland	Drums
Baldwin	Pianos
Chickering Grands	Pianos
Hamilton	Pianos
Howard Grands	Pianos
Wurlitzer Grands	Pianos
ConcertMaster	Player piano systems

Steinway Musical Instrs., Waltham, MA

Steinway & Sons	Pianos
Boston	Pianos
Essex	Pianos
Conn-Selmer	
Vincent Bach	
Selmer USA	Woodwinds
C. G. Conn	Brass
King	Brass
Armstrong	Woodwinds
Ludwig	Percussion
Musser	Percussion
Glaesel	Strings
Scherl & Roth	Strings
William Lewis & Son	Strings
Emerson	Flutes
Benge	Brass
Artley	Woodwinds
Leblanc, Inc.	
Leblanc	Band instrs.
Holton	Band instrs.

Steinway Musical Instrs., Waltham, MA

Noblet	Band instrs.
Vito	Band instrs.

Fender Musical Instruments, Scottsdale, AZ

Squier	Electric and acoustic guitars and basses
Tacoma	Acoustic guitars and mandolins
Charvet	Electric guitars
Jackson	Electric guitars
Guild	Acoustic and acoustic-electric guitars
Benedetto	Archtop and electric jazz guitars
Manuel Rodriguez	Classical guitars
Kaman Music, Bloomfield, CT; Mississauga, ON, Canada	
Ovation	Guitars
Applause	Guitars
Adamas	Guitars
Takamine	Guitars
Jasmine	Guitars
Hamer	Guitars
Slammer	Guitars
Toca	Percussion (primarily Latin style)
Gibraltar	Percussion
Gretsch Drums	Percussion
LP Music	Percussion (primarily Latin style)
LP Rhythmix	Student percussion
Sabian	Percussion (cymbals)
Lee Oscar	Harmonicas
Becker Instrs	Student violins
CB Percussion	Student percussion
Vic Firth	Student percussion

Gemstone Musical Instruments, Elkhart, IN

Stephanhouser	Saxophones
Sankyo (Japan)	Flutes
Trevor James (England)	Alto flutes
Artisan	Flutes
W. Nirschl (Germany)	Brass
Andino (Chile)	Clarinets
Weril (Brazil)	Brass and woodwinds
Brio	Flutes
W. Schreiber (Germany)	Bassoons, clarinets, oboes

and Passport Designs, developed industry-standard software and interface cards for micro-computers to enable them to be used to control instrument and synthesizer sounds, audio mixing, and lighting. The most advanced synthesizers allowed composition, manipulation, editing, performance, and even printing of score and parts (*see* COMPUTERS AND MUSIC, ELECTRONIC INSTRUMENTS, and ELECTROACOUSTIC MUSIC).

9. SINCE 1990. Classical, early, and school musical instrument making continues to grow; pianos are made in similar numbers but organ sales have declined. Production of fretted, electronic, and percussion instruments of popular music, however, has grown to nearly three times that of woodwinds, brass, strings, pianos, and organs combined. Many small, specialized instrument making shops thrive independently, while most larger musical instrument makers have been consolidated into a few large corporations. Table 1 shows a list of the brand names controlled by just four American companies as of 2011.

Many other familiar American brands are now subsidiaries of large international companies. For example,

Knabe, Epiphone, Squier, Washburn, and Hohner are owned by Korean based Samick; and the Gemeinhardt flute company is now a part of Angel Industries Co. of Taiwan. Over all about 60% of the instruments sold in the United States are imported, mostly from Yamaha and Kawai of Japan and Samick. On the other hand, about 40% of the instruments made in the United States are exported.

Fretted instruments, mainly guitars, but also banjos, mandolins, and ukuleles, are the most popular instruments today. Enormous sales support several large manufacturers as well as hundreds of small shops. In 2006, *Guitar World* published a list of the "10 most earth shaking guitar innovations in the last 25 years." This included such innovations as the inexpensive wireless systems developed in the 1990s by companies such as Nady of Emeryville, California, and Samson Technologies of Hauppauge, New York, that allow musicians to roam the stage without ending up in a tangled mess of cords. Hybrid electric-acoustic guitars made by Parker Guitars, Mundelein, Illinois, and Hamer enable players to switch from electric sounds to convincing acoustic tones in the middle of a song, without changing instruments. Modeling amps by the Line 6 company of Calabasas, California, can summon a variety of amp tones with the flick of a switch. Direct recording boxes by companies like Rockman, Zoom, and Line 6, along with Digidesign Pro Tools and plug-ins including Sound Replacer, Beat Detective, and Auto-Tune, make it possible for anyone with a decent computer to make studio-quality recordings. The Whammy pedal by Digitech and Molten Voltage with its harmony effects and ability to sweep pitch up or down two octaves may be the wildest effect ever invented. Switching systems like Bradshaw's RS-10 eliminate the challenges of using multiple amps, rack effects and pedals onstage by enabling users to program complex signal-routing setups that can be accessed instantly by stomping on a single switch.

Electric and electronic devices that create, manipulate, mix, edit, and record sounds have become a major part of the musical instrument industry. New, less expensive equipment with even more capability has replaced the Synclavier and similar synthesizing and sound manipulation products. Top producers of synthesizers, digital pianos, and recording products include Roland of Los Angeles as well as the Japanese firms Yamaha, Casio, Kawai, and KORG. Equipment for sound manipulation and editing has become an integral part of musical instrument use: "In an era where there are fewer opportunities for live performance, recording is an increasingly important way to make and share music. For many players under the age of 35, recording is making music." ("2011 Music Industry Census Report," *Music Trades*, April 2011). Avid Technology of Burlington, Massachusetts, has become the leading American producer of sound and film editing software. Recording studios are being used less as artists find it possible with new equipment to record and edit at home. Other American sound editing companies include WaveFrame, Emeryville, California, and SonicSolutions (part of Rovi Corp., Santa Clara, CA).

Percussion instruments have seen synthetic materials for drumheads from companies such as Remo, Valencia, California; Acquarian, Anaheim, California; and Evans, Farmingdale, New York, almost totally replace traditional materials. Kevlar heads, introduced in 1978, have become standard in marching bands and pipe bands where high tension is desired. Other new developments in percussion involve electronic alteration and creation of sounds and effects. Anderson FX Percussion, Winchester, California, designs devices that are "sonically reactive, utilizing the vibrations of your current instruments to create altered sound possibilities." Top quality cymbals continue to be made by Zildjian (Norwell, MA) and Sabian (Meductic, New Brunswick, Canada), led respectively by the brothers Robert and Armond Zildjian.

Some of the finest professional flutes continue to be made by American companies Wm. S. Haynes and Verne Q. Powell, and new companies such as Emanual Flutes, North Andover, Massachusetts; but most professional oboes, clarinets, and bassoons are still imported from European companies. In 2005 the William S. Haynes company became part of Eastman Strings, continuing to

employ most of the same craftsmen. Fox Products, South Whitley, Indiana, continues to improve its line of bassoons, contrabassoons, and oboes. The top four saxophone makers are now Keilwerth (Germany), Selmer (United States and France), Yanagisawa (Japan), and Yamaha (Japan). Wooden flutes and wooden heads for flutes have become more common as players search for unique tone quality. An increasing number of small American firms have been established to make custom accessories, flute head joints, clarinet mouthpieces, barrels, bells, ligatures, and so on. Non-Western wooden flutes are also made by many small American craftsmen. Baroque and Renaissance flutes and recorders continue to be made by the Von Huene Workshop, Brookline, MA; Charles Collier, Berkeley, CA; the Prescott Workshop, Hanover, NH; and Peter Noy, Seattle, WA. Sweetheart Flute, of Enfield, CT, makes Baroque and Renaissance flutes, fifes, pennywhistles, tabor pipes, and other wind instruments. FOLKERS & POWELL, Hillsdale, New York, builders of historical flutes, ceased business in 2009.

The brass instrument divisions of large corporations produce mostly for schools, but the C.G. Conn, Vincent Bach, King, and Benge divisions of Steinway Musical Instruments also make fine professional brasses. The Getzen Co. and many small specialty shops also compete in making top quality brasses, especially Kanstul (full line), Calicchio and Marcinkiewicz, Monette, Blackburn, and Schilke (trumpets); Atkinson, S.W. Lewis, and Kendall Betts, which now owns Lawson (horns); and S.E. Shires (trombones and trumpets). Almost all professional quality tubas are now imported from Europe or Japan. Interesting recent developments and trends include the unique trumpets of Monette, growing use of triple horns in F/B♭/F alto, half size horns for young students, new valve designs for trombones by S.E. Shires (Thayer axial-flow, Trubore) and Conn (Christan Lindberg valve); and the growing use of tubas in E♭ and F along with the more common B♭ and C models. Balu Mutes beginning in 2002 has been successful in designing a number of outstanding mutes for brasses.

Traditional bowed string instruments continue in school and professional use, and are produced by many small shops and some large manufacturers in this country and abroad. Recently, however, stringed instrument use in popular music has driven the development of new violins, violas, cellos, and basses specifically designed for electronic amplification. Instruments like those made by Ithica Stringed Instruments (Trumansburg, New York), Wood Violins (Port Washington, New York), and NS Design (Nobleboro, Maine) have taken these instruments from simply amplified acoustical instruments to new designs specifically built for electronic amplification and manipulation.

Piano manufacturing has migrated almost completely to Japan, China, and Korea. The few companies still making any quantity of pianos in the United States include Steinway, Long Island, New York; Mason & Hamlin, Haverhill, Massachussetts; and the WALTER PIANO CO., Elkhart, Indiana. Improved actions made of composite materials have been developed by Wessell, Nickel & Gross, Haverhill, Massachussetts, and are available for most top-quality pianos. A growing industry has developed to rebuild and restore pianos. Some of the leaders in the field are: the Cunningham Piano Company, Philadelphia, Pennsylvania; Lindeblad Piano Restoration, Pine Brook, New Jersey; and Precision Piano Services, North Hollywood, California. A new generation of harpsichord builders is represented by RICHARD KINGSTON, Ft. Mill, South Carolina. Probably the most important recent change in harpsichord making is the reinstatement of side damping systems as commonly used in historical harpsichords rather than flag dampers. When a register is "off," side dampers do not contact the strings, allowing them to vibrate sympathetically.

Organ production has fallen by half from the previous period, and new installations are more likely to be in auditoriums and civic buildings than in churches. There is growing diversity in the style of these new organs, but a general trend is evident toward the late 19th-century romantic in terms of stop choice, size, and general sound. As in so many other areas of instrument design, the incorporation of electronic sounds and devices has grown. Many pipe organs now have digital electronic stops, multiple electronic memory levels for piston pre-sets, and MIDI or newer faster interface capability. Deluxe electronic instruments by makers such as Marshall & Ogletree, Needham, Massachussetts, have no pipes at all and challenge the pipe organ industry in sound, versatility, upkeep, and cost. The quality of organ restorations has improved measurably over recent decades, and there is more clarity on what constitutes a restoration versus a rebuild of an older instrument. Since the economic downturn of 2008, there is growing demand for restorations or rebuilds of existing instruments rather than for new instruments.

There are separate entries on the following instruments: ACCORDION; APPALACHIAN DULCIMER; AUTOHARP; BAJO SEXTO; BAND ORGAN; BANJO; BASSOON; BONES; BONGOS; CALLIOPE; CHORALCELO; CLARINET; CLAVES; CONCERT ORGAN; CONGA DRUM; CORNET; CUATRO; DIDDLEY BOW; DOLCEOLA; DOUBLE BASS; DRUM; DRUM SET; ELECTRIC BASS GUITAR; ELECTRIC GUITAR; ELECTRIC PIANO; ELECTRONIC INSTRUMENTS; ELECTRONIC PERCUSSION; EUPHONIUM; FLUTE; GUITAR; HAMMERED DULCIMER; HAMMOND ORGAN; HARMONICA; HARP GUITAR; HAWAIIAN GUITAR; HORN; KAZOO; KEYED BUGLE; LAPTOP; MANDOLIN; MARIMBA; MA'WO; MÁ'XE ONÉHAVO'E; MECHANICAL INSTRUMENT; NATIVE AMERICAN FLUTE; OBOE; ORGAN; PEDAL STEEL GUITAR; PIANO; PEYOTE DRUM; PEYOTE RATTLE; PLAYER PIANO; PLAYER ORGAN; PREPARED PIANO; REED ORGAN; RESONATOR GUITAR; ROLAND TB-303; ROLAND TR-808; SAXHORN; SAXOPHONE; SOUSAPHONE; SYNCLAVIER; SYNTHESIZER; TELHARMONIUM; THEATER ORGAN; THEREMIN; TIMPANI; TOY INSTRUMENT; TROMBONE; TRUMPET; TSLI'EDO'A'TL; TUBA; TURNTABLE; UKULELE; VIBRAPHONE; VIHUELA; VIOLA; VIOLIN; VIOLONCELLO; WASHTUB BASS; WATERDRUM; XYLOPHONE; ZITHER, FRETLESS; ZITHER, FRETTED.

Further discussion of instruments is contained in broad entries such as ASIAN AMERICAN MUSIC, EUROPEAN AMERICAN MUSIC, LATINO MUSIC and NATIVE AMERICAN MUSIC. For modern makers of early instruments *see* INSTRUMENTS, HISTORICAL and EARLY-MUSIC REVIVAL. *See also* BAND; ELECTROACOUSTIC MUSIC, GAMELAN; INSTRUMENTS, COLLECTIONS OF, and TUNING SYSTEMS.

BIBLIOGRAPHY

D. Spillane: *History of the American Pianoforte* (New York, 1890/*R*)
C.M. Ayars: *Contributions to the Art of Music in America by the Music Industries of Boston, 1640–1936* (New York, 1937/*R*)
A. Loesser: *Men, Women and Pianos: a Social History* (New York, 1954)
A. Baines: *European and American Musical Instruments* (London, 1966)
K. Jalovec: *Encyclopedia of Violin-makers* (London, 1968)
Ḍ.Q. Bowers: *Encyclopedia of Automatic Musical Instruments* (Vestal, NY, 1972)
R.F. Gellerman: *The American Reed Organ* (Vestal, NY, 1973)
O. Ochse: *The History of the Organ in the United States* (Bloomington, IN, and London, 1975)
C.H. Kaufman: "Musical-instrument Makers in New Jersey, 1796–1860," *JAMIS*, ii (1976), 5–33
R.E. Eliason: "Oboes, Bassoons, and Bass Clarinets, Made by Hartford, Connecticut, Makers before 1815," *GSJ*, xxx (1977), 43
U. Pape: *The Tracker Organ Revival in America* (Berlin, 1978)
R.E. Eliason: *Early American Brass Makers* (Nashville, 1979/Vuarmarens, 2/1999)
B. Owen: *The Organ in New England: an Account of its Use and Manufacture to the End of the Nineteenth Century* (Raleigh, NC, 1979)
A.W.J.G. Ord-Hume: *Pianola: the History of the Self-playing Piano* (London, 1984)
B. Lambert, ed.: *Music in Colonial Massachusetts, 1630–1820*, ii: *Music in Homes and in Churches* (Boston, 1985)
L. Libin: *American Musical Instruments in the Metropolitan Museum of Art* (New York, 1985)
B. Majeski, ed.: *The Music Trades 100th Anniversary Issue: A History of the US Music Industry* (Englewood, 1990)
N. Groce: *Musical Instrument Makers of New York: A Directory of Eighteenth- and Nineteenth-Century Urban Craftsmen* (Stuyvesant, New York, 1991)
M. Vail: *Vintage Synthesizers: Groundbreaking Instruments and Pioneering Designers of Electronic Music Synthesizers* (San Francisco, 1993)
P. Théberge: *Any Sound You Can Imagine: Making Music/Consuming Technology* (Middletown, 1997)
D. Kuronen: "Early Violin Making in New England, *JAMIS*, xxviii (2002), 5–62
J. Montagu: *Timpani and Percussion* (New Haven, 2002)
T. Pinch and F. Trocco: *Analog Days: The Invention and Impact of the Moog Synthesizer* (Cambridge, MA, 2002)

For further bibliography, see also articles on individual instruments and makers.

ROBERT E. ELIASON

Instruments, collections of. Musical instruments are collected for many reasons—for use in performance, as objects of veneration or visual art, to furnish ethnological and historical evidence, to illustrate technical developments and to serve as models for new construction, for financial investment and sale, and merely to satisfy curiosity. This article is an account of public and private collections in the United States; instruments awaiting dispersal (e.g., in a dealer's or maker's shop) or accumulated by chance are not considered.

Instruments for use in performance have long been collected in the United States by individuals and by religious, civic, and military institutions, notably since the mid-18th century among the music-loving Moravian communities of Bethlehem, Lititz, and Nazareth, Pennsylvania, where instruments are still cherished and displayed. The large-scale, systematic accumulation of instruments for non-musical purposes, however, began in the United States only in the last quarter of the 19th century, chiefly in connection with ethnographic fieldwork sponsored by schools and government agencies, but also under the auspices of wealthy private collectors. Extensive permanent repositories of exotic instruments originated at research centers, mainly on the East Coast, where musical artifacts were preserved for anthropological comparison and analysis. Smaller, more casual assemblages of attractive instruments often decorated the music rooms of urban mansions; occasionally such domestic collections were donated to local museums, where they might be supplemented by acquisitions of high artistic quality. More recently, instruments have been collected widely not only by investors for eventual profit through resale but by musicians seeking information about the performance practices and tone colors of earlier times and by instrument makers studying antiques as models.

Although prestige and tax advantages encourage public-spirited donations of instruments to cultural institutions, most American collections are privately owned. A survey carried out in 1998 for the online International Directory of Musical Instrument Collections (sponsored by the International Committee of Musical Instrument Museums and Collections and the American Musical Instrument Society) lists 372 significant instrument repositories throughout the United States, many in small museums and historical societies where the instruments are integrated with the general collections; only about 50 institutions separate their instruments administratively from other holdings.

In 1879, G. Brown Goode, an assistant secretary of the Smithsonian Institution and an amateur musician, established sound-producing implements as a distinct category within the US National Museum's system of objects classification. Musical instruments were separately categorized after 1884 by Edwin H. Hawley, also of the Smithsonian, who based the institute's classification system on those used in Europe and that of the Metropolitan Museum of Art in New York. Hawley, a pioneer American organologist, was one of several experts consulted by Mary Elizabeth Brown (Mrs. John Crosby Brown), the foremost instrument collector of her generation. She began acquiring instruments in 1884 to decorate her family's music room; when her display became too large she offered more than 270 items to the Metropolitan in 1889 with the stipulation that she could continue to enlarge and improve the collection as she saw fit. Her efforts, combined with gifts from Joseph W. Drexel and later donors, resulted in a repository of national preeminence; at the time of her death in 1918 it comprised 3400 items. The catalog of that collection, completed in 1914, was the first significant one to be published in the United States.

The extraordinarily rapid growth of Brown's collection typifies the enthusiastic, if sometimes undiscriminating, approach of private collectors in the 19th century. Sarah Frishmuth, who donated her collection (now dispersed) to the University of Pennsylvania Museum, and Frederick Stearns, whose collection was accepted by the University of Michigan, Ann Arbor, in

1899, are other examples of non-musicians who were either inspired by the visual elegance of the instruments they collected or who wished to illustrate the Darwinian notion of musical "progress." In contrast, the professional musician and piano merchant Morris Steinert assembled a representative group of European keyed and bowed instruments that he restored to playing order for didactic purposes. Exhibited in part in Vienna (1892) and at the World's Columbian Exposition in Chicago (1893), his collection (now at Yale University) revealed the value of antique instruments in reconstructing the sounds of early music. Subsequent donations, including Belle Skinner's collection of keyboards, strings, and a number of other Western and Eastern examples, have made Yale's holdings one of the most significant at an American university.

In 1941 Nicholas Bessaraboff published a scholarly catalog of the Leslie Lindsey Mason collection at the Museum of Fine Arts in Boston, which had been bought from the English authority on instruments Francis W. Galpin in 1916; Galpin intended these instruments to be used to exemplify audibly as well as visually the history of European music. The Mason collection and Bessaraboff's seminal catalog did much to establish Boston as the leading center for early-music study and instrument construction in the United States. Also in 1941 Dayton C. Miller left to the Library of Congress a unique collection of about 1500 flutes and closely related types, as well as a library of relevant music, photographs, books, and other documents.

The collector and band director, Arne B. Larson began collecting instruments during the 1920s and donated his collection of over 2500 instruments in 1973 to the University of South Dakota in Vermillion. The Shrine to Music Museum (now the National Music Museum) grew to some 14,500 instruments under the leadership of André Larson. Its collections of keyboards, bowed strings, brasses, woodwinds, guitars, and harmonicas are among the most comprehensive in the world.

The second half of the 20th century saw a significant increase in cooperation between museums. The Comité International des Musées et Collections d'Instruments de Musique (CIMCIM) was formed in 1960 with members from fourteen countries, becoming part of the International Council of Museums. In 1971 CIMCIM gave birth to the International Association of Instrument Collections, reabsorbed into an enlarged CIMCIM in 1975. The organization provides a forum for the exchange of professional experience and has produced publications of value to public and private collectors of instruments alike.

LIST

The list includes the most important and largest permanent collections accessible to the public and a selection of private ones. Detailed information about particular collections is available from such organizations as the American Musical Instrument Society and the Violin Society of America, as well as from publications listed in the bibliography below. The number of instruments given for each collection is approximate.

ALBUQUERQUE, NM. Maxwell Museum of Anthropology, University of New Mexico: 600, mostly indigenous American and East African, incl. the Kidd collection.

ANN ARBOR, MI. Stearns Collection, University Michigan: 2500 general, esp. European and East African. A.A. Stanley: *Catalogue of the Stearns Collection of Musical Instruments* (Ann Arbor, 1918, 2/1921); R.A. Warner: "The Stearns Collection of Musical Instruments," *JVdGSA*, ii (1965), 38–48; B.M. Smith: "Two-Hundred Forty-One European Chordophones in the Stearns Collection," U. of Michigan, Ph.D. diss., (1977); W. Malm: "Stearns Musical Instruments: an Exotic Collection," *Ann Arbor Magazine* (1986), 14–19; J.M. Borders: *European and American Wind and Percussion Instruments: Catalogue of the Stearns Collection of Musical Instruments, University of Michigan* (1988).

ASHBURNHAM, MA. Frederick Historic Piano Collection (Patricia and Edmund Michael Frederick): more than 30 grand pianos. G. Hayes: "How Many Pianos Does It Take to Fill A House?," *Early Keyboard Studies Newsletter*, i/2 (1985); M. Boriskin: "They Prefer Pianos to Furniture," *Piano Quarterly* 130 (1985), 41–3.

BAKERSFIELD, CA. Kern County Museum: c30, half mechanical, also country-and-western.

BALTIMORE, MD. Maryland Historical Society: c40 locally made or owned incl. 15 Baltimore pianos. G.R. Weidman: *Furniture in Maryland, 1740–1940* (1984).

BARTLESVILLE, OK. Woolaroc Museum, Frank Phillips Foundation: incl. c25 Native American.

BELOIT, WI. Logan Museum of Anthropology, Beloit College: c150, half Native North and Central American, African and from the Pacific Rim.

BENNINGTON, VT. Bennington Museum: c30 with local associations.

BEREA, KY. Berea College Appalachian Museum: c25 traditional Appalachian.

BERKELEY, CA. Department of Music, University of California: c110 Western art, also African and Asian incl. the Ansley K. Salz collection (strings). D.D. Boyden: *Catalogue of the Collection of Musical Instruments in the Department of Music* (1972); J.A. Emerson: *Musical Instruments, East and West*, i (1972); *Catalog of an Exhibit on the Occasion of the 12th Congress of IMS* (1977).

BERKELEY, CA. Phoebe Hearst Museum of Anthropology (formerly Robert H. Lowie Museum of Anthropology), University of California: 1050 mainly Native North and Latin American ethnological and archaeological, esp. Californian and Peruvian, also African, Asian, Australian, Oceanian, and European.

BETHLEHEM, PA. Moravian Museum of Bethlehem: c35, many trombones, used by Moravian congregations. C.S. Mayes: *A Descriptive Catalogue of Historic Percussion, Wind and Stringed Instruments in Three Pennsylvania Museums* (thesis, Florida State U., 1974).

BISMARCK, ND. Museum of State Historical Society of North Dakota: c160 Western and Native American.

BLOOMFIELD HILLS, MI. Cranbrook Institute of Science: c80 worldwide ethnological.

BLOOMINGTON, IN. Musical Instrument Collection, William Hammond Mathers Museum of World Cultures, Indiana University: c1800 worldwide, esp. American, African, Southeast Asian, and Balkan traditional and ethnological, incl. Robert Ellison (Native North American Plains), Frances Cossard (mainly Japanese), Georg Herzog-Erich von Hornbostel, Carl Anton Worth (Sudanese and Javanese puppet and gamelan), and Laura Boulton collections. P. Gold: *Traditional Music of the World* (1968); L. Boulton: *Musical Instruments of World Cultures* (1972); "Boulton Collection Donated to Arizona State," *AMIS Newsletter*, xii/2 (1983).

BOISE, ID. Idaho State Historical Society: c50 Western art, traditional, and popular.

BOSTON, MA. Boston SO, Symphony Hall: c100 Western and non-Western art, traditional, ethnological, incl. the Henri Casadesus and John S. Barnet collections.

BOSTON, MA. Musical Instruments Collection, Museum of Fine Arts: c1200 Western art, traditional, and ethnological, incl. North and South American; African, Asian, esp. 1840 Blora Javanese gamelan; the Leslie Lindsey Mason (formerly Francis W. Galpin [Western art, traditional, and non-Western], and Moule [Chinese]), Edwin M. Ripin (keyboards), Douglas Diehl, Peggy Stewart Coolidge, Harold Priest and Searles/Rowland collections. N. Bessaraboff: *Ancient Musical Instruments: An Organological Study of the Musical Instruments in the Leslie Lindsey Mason Collection* (1941); B. Lambert: *Musical Instruments Collection: Checklist of Instruments on Exhibition* (1983); J. Koster: *Keyboard Musical Instruments in the Museum of Fine Arts, Boston* (1994); D. Kuronen: *Musical Instruments: Museum of Fine Arts, Boston* (2004).

BOSTON, MA. New England Conservatory of Music: c125, mostly Asian, also Western, incl. Eben Tourjee collection. E. Burnett: "A Catalogue of the Collection of Ancient Instruments Owned by the New England Conservatory" (MA thesis, New England Conservatory of Music, 1967).

BOSTON, MA. Sheridan Germann collection: c20, half string keyboards. S. Germann: "The Accidental Collector," *Early Keyboard Studies Newsletter*, v/3 (1991), 1–3.

BOSTON, MA. Society for the Preservation of New England Antiquities: over 50 Western art and popular.

BOWLING GREEN, KY. Kentucky Museum, Western Kentucky University: c35 mainly Western popular, art and traditional, a few non-Western.

BROWNING, MT. Museum of the Plains Indian and Crafts Center: c30 Plains Native American, esp. Sioux.

BURLINGTON, VT. Robert Hull Fleming Museum, University of Vermont: c170 worldwide ethnological, some American popular.

CAMBRIDGE, MA. Department of Music, Harvard University: c100 Western and Asian art, traditional, ethnological, incl. Ralph Isham and Edward R. Hewitt collections. S.E. Thompson: *Checklist of Items in the Collection of Musical Instruments, Harvard University* (1990) [typescript].

CAMBRIDGE, MA. Peabody Museum of Archeology and Ethnology at Harvard University: c2000 worldwide, half Native North American.

CARBONDALE, IL. Southern Illinois University Museum: c250 Middle Eastern, American, Asian ethnological, and some archaeological.

CARLSBAD, CA. Museum of Making Music, founded 1998 by National Association of Music Merchants (NAMM): More than 500 instruments primarily made after 1900.

CHARLESTON, SC. Charleston Museum: c75 used locally, incl. Siegling Music House collection.

CHARLOTTESVILLE, VA. Thomas Jefferson Memorial Association: 7 Jefferson-related musical instruments. W.H. Adams: *The Eye of Thomas Jefferson* (1976); H. Cripe: *Thomas Jefferson and Music* (1974); S. Stein: *The Worlds of Thomas Jefferson at Monticello* (New York, 1993).

CHICAGO, IL. Department of Anthropology, Field Museum of Natural History: c3800, over half American ethnological and archaeological, also African, Middle Eastern, Asian, Oceanian, and European.

CHICAGO, IL. Oriental Institute Museum, University of Chicago: c40 archaeological Egyptian and Near Eastern.

CINCINNATI, OH. Cincinnati Art Museum: c775 general, incl. the William Howard Doane collection. E. Winternitz: *Musical Instruments: Collection of the Cincinnati Art Museum* (1949) [catalog]; *Cincinnati Art Museum Handbook* (1977).

CLARKSDALE, MS. Delta Blues Museum: over 30, American acoustic and electric guitars, also traditional and popular.

CLEVELAND, OH. Western Reserve Historical Society Museum: c100. T. Albrecht: "An Annotated Catalogue of Musical Instruments in the Collection of the Western Reserve Historical Society" (1978) [typescript].

COLORADO SPRINGS, CO. Colorado Springs Museum: over 100 mainly music boxes, also Western, and Native American archaeological and ethnological.

CONCORD, NH. New Hampshire Historical Society Museum: c65 Western art, traditional and popular used locally.

CORNING, NY. Corning Museum of Glass: c15, 7 glass instruments and whistles.

COSTA MESA, CA. Christian and Kathleen Eric collection: c300 music boxes.

DAVENPORT, IA. Putnam Museum of History and Natural Science: c35 European art, traditional, popular, and Native North American.

DEARBORN, MI. Henry Ford Museum and Greenfield Village: over 600 mainly American art, popular, and band, incl. D. S. Pillsbury Collection of American Brass and Chickering (piano) collection. *Chickering & Sons: Pianofortes at the Exhibition of 1856* (1857); *Under the Auspices of Chickering & Sons: Catalogue of the Exhibition, Horticultural Hall, Boston* (1902); R.E. Eliason: *Brass Instrument Key and Valve Mechanisms Made in America Before 1875, with Special Reference to the D.S. Pillsbury Collection* (diss., U. of Missouri, 1969); V. Angelescu: "The Henry Ford Collection of Instruments," *Violins*, xxi (1960), 3–9, 46, 48–53, 97–102, 138–44, 173; R.E. Eliason: *D.S. Pillsbury Collection of Brass Instruments* (Dearborn, MI, 1972).

DECORAH, IA. Vesterheim Norwegian-American Museum: c100 European art and traditional having belonged to Norwegian Americans.

DENVER, CO. Denver Museum of Natural History: c725 mainly Native North and Latin American archaeological, ethnographic, also African, Oceanian, and Asian.

DETROIT, MI. Children's Museum: c300 African, Asian, and American.

DETROIT, MI. Detroit Institute of Arts: c70 Western art, traditional, and some ethnological (formerly exhibited as the Edith J. Freeman collection). *Musical Instruments Through the Ages* (1952) [exhibition catalog, Toledo, Ohio, Museum of Art]; *Music and Art* (1958) [exhibition guide, University of Minnesota].

DURHAM, NC. Duke University Musical Instrument Collections: G. Norman Eddy and Ruth G. Eddy collection and the Frans and Willemina de Hen-Biji Collection of Musical Instruments. 600 pianos, woodwinds, and brass; 50 illustrative oil paintings, 100 reel-to-reel field recordings, 1000 slides of musical instruments. T. Good and G.N. Eddy: *The Eddy Collection of Musical Instruments: A Checklist* (San Francisco, 1985).

EDWARDSVILLE, IL. University Art Museum, Southern Illinois University: c125 mainly European art, also Asian incl. Carl H. Tollefsen, Kiburz Flute, and African collections.

ELMIRA, NY. Chemung County Historical Centre: c50 Western art and popular.

FAYETTEVILLE, AR. Nophachai Cholitchantka collection: c250 clarinets and other woodwinds.

FLAGSTAFF, AZ. Museum of Northern Arizona: c350 southwest Native American.

FRANKLIN, PA. DeBence Antique Music World: 125 mechanical. "DeBence Antique Music World," *AMIS Newsletter*, xxiv/1 (1995, 10).

HARTFORD, CT. Connecticut Historical Society Museum: c35 Connecticut-origin.

HARVARD, MA. Fruitlands Museums: c35 incl. Native American, Shaker, Western art and traditional.

HOMER, NY. The Ralph and Virginia Dudgeon collection: c200 Western, half brass.

HONOLULU, HI. Bernice Pauahi Bishop Museum: c640, mainly Hawaiian and Oceanian. Te Rangi Hiroa [Peter H. Buck]: "Section 9: Musical Instruments," *Arts and Crafts of Hawaii* (1957); *Pahu and Pūnio* (1980) [drum exhibition catalog]; J. Koster: "Report from Hawaii," *AMIS Newsletter*, xxi/3 (1992, 9–11).

HONOLULU, HI. Music Department, University of Hawaii: c4500 ethnological.

HOUSTON, TX. Anthropology Department, Houston Museum of Natural Science: c35 ethnological.

INDIANAPOLIS, IN. Indiana State Museum: c70 European art, popular, and mechanical.

INDIANAPOLIS, IN. Percussive Arts Society's Rhythm! Discovery Center: c700, mainly acoustic percussion, including prototype and electronic instruments.

IOWA CITY, IA. University of Iowa: c40. D. Ross: *Musical Instruments at the University of Iowa: A Catalogue* (1979).

IVORYTON, CT. The Company of Fifers and Drummers: c195 mainly American and European fifes and drums, also bugles. S. Cifaldi: "The Company of Fifers and Drummers," *Sonneck Society for American Music Bulletin*, xvi/2 (1990), 50–53.

JACKSONVILLE, AL. E. Lee Chaney collection: c30 reed organs. E.L. Chaney: "Three Rare Organs," *ROS Bulletin*, viii/1 (1989), 20–23.

KALAMAZOO, MI. Kalamazoo Valley Museum: c95 esp. Kalamazoo-made, also African and Asian ethnological.

KENT, OH. Hugh A. Glauser School of Music, Center for the Study of World Musics, Kent State University: c100 African, Asian, Pacific, Middle Eastern.

LE MARS, IA. Parkinson Collection of Historical Musical Instruments, Plymouth County Historical Museum: 176 European, American, and worldwide.

LEWISBURG, PA. Harold E. Cook Collection of Musical Instruments, Department of Music, Bucknell University: c150, many Asian, also African, some European, Ecuadorean, and United States. J. Hill: *The Harold E. Cook Collection of Musical Instruments* (Cranberry, NJ, 1975).

LINCOLN, NE. Anthropology Division, State Museum, University of Nebraska: c115 African, East Indies, Philippines, South American, and Plains Native American ethnological.

LITITZ, PA. Lititz Moravian Congregation Archives and Museum: over 50.

LOS ANGELES, CA. Albert Gale and Leonardo De Lorenzo collections, University of Southern California: c180 mainly Native American, Asian, European and American. P.J. Norvel: "A History and Catalogue of the Albert Gale Collection of Musical Instruments" (thesis, University of Southern California, 1952).

LOS ANGELES, CA. Department of Ethnomusicology, University of California (UCLA): 1000 non-Eastern art instruments, esp. Southeast Asian, most in playing condition.

LOS ANGELES, CA. Fowler Museum of Cultural History, University of California (UCLA): 4300 worldwide, esp. African.

MANHATTAN, KS. Riley County Historical Society and Museum: c60 European popular, traditional and art.

MANOA, HI. Music Department, University of Hawaii: over 1500 from the Pacific Rim.

MEMPHIS, TN. Memphis Pink Palace Museum: c35 Western art, popular, and ethnological.

MIDDLETOWN, CT. Collection of Music Instruments, Wesleyan University: 500, mainly non-Western esp. Ghanaian, Javanese, Indian, East Asian, also electronic and experimental.

MILWAUKEE, WI. Milwaukee Public Museum (affiliated with University of Wisconsin): c400 worldwide art and ethnological.

MINDEN, NE. Harold Warp Pioneer Village: c60 Western, regional, some ethnological.

MONROE, MI. Monroe County Historical Museum: c40 mainly band.

MONTCLAIR, NJ. Montclair State University: Harry Partch collection. T. Kakinuma: *The Musical Instruments of Harry Partch as an Apparatus of Production in Musical Theatre* (diss., U. of California, 1989); D.A. Savage: *Voice and Soul: Intrinsic Description of Harry Partch's Keyboard and String Instruments* (diss., U. of California, 1994).

MORRISTOWN, NJ. Morris Museum, Murtogh D. Guinness Collection: 700 mechanical musical instruments and automata.

NASHVILLE, TN. Country Music Hall of Fame and Museum: c600 American made instruments mainly guitars and mandolins.

NASHVILLE, TN. Cumberland Science Museum: c85 mainly African, Asian, and Middle Eastern ethnological.

NAZARETH, PA. C.F. Martin Guitar Museum: over 170, mainly guitars, other fretted.

NAZARETH, PA. Museum of Moravian Historical Society: c60. L. Libin: "Nazareth Piano may be among America's First," *Moravian Music Journal*, xxxiii/1 (1988), 2–6.

NEWARK, NJ. Newark Museum: 300, mainly ethnological, esp. African and Tibetan, but incl. the Russell Barkley Kingman collection (European art instruments). R.R. Kerr: "Musical Instruments in the Museum's Collection," *The Museum*, xiv/1 (1962) [whole issue]; *Catalogue of the Tibetan Collection* (1950, 2/1973).

NEW HAVEN, CT. Peabody Museum of Natural History, Department of Anthropology, Yale University: 1000 African, Oceanian, and North American.

NEW HAVEN, CT. Yale University Collection of Musical Instruments: c1000, mainly European art instruments, incl. the Belle Skinner, Emil Herrmann (strings), Albert Steinert (formerly at Rhode Island School of Design), Morris Steinert, and Robyna Neilson Ketchum (bells) collections. M. Steinert: *Catalogue of the Morris Steinert Collection* (1893); W. Skinner: *The Belle Skinner Collection of Musical Instruments* (1933); S. Marcuse: *Musical Instruments at Yale* (1960); R. Rephann: *Checklist: Yale Collection of Musical Instruments* (1968); R. Rephann and N. Renouf: *The Robyna Neilson Ketchum Collection of Bells* (1975); "Dolmetsch-Chickering Instruments at Yale," *AMIS Newsletter*, xxi/2 (1992, 1–2); *Tintinnabulation!* (2006) [exhibition catalog, Yale University Collection of Musical Instruments, 20 June–21 December 2006].

NEW ORLEANS, LA. The Louisiana State Museum, Music Collection: c240 instruments, many from the New Orleans Jazz Club.

NEWTON CENTER, MA. Marlowe A. Sigal sollection: c500 European and American keyboards and woodwinds.

NEW YORK, NY. Department of Anthropology, American Museum of Natural History: 4000 ethnographic esp. African, Asian, Siberian, Melanesian, North and South American, esp. pre-Columbian.

NEW YORK, NY. Metropolitan Museum of Art: c5000 worldwide, esp. European, American, Asian, African art, traditional, popular, ethnological and archaeological, incl. Mrs. John Crosby Brown, Joseph W. Draxel, Getty, some of Tagore, part of Mrs. W.D. Frishmuth, Herbert J. Harris (worldwide percussion), Robert A. Lehman and other collections. See also private collection of Nathaniel Spear, Jr., below. M.E. Brown and W. Adams Brown: *Musical Instruments and Their Homes* (1888); F. Morris and others: *Catalogue of the Crosby Brown Collection of Musical Instruments of All Nations* (1901–14); E. Winternitz: *Keyboard Instruments in the Metropolitan Museum of Art* (1961); E. Winternitz: "The Crosby Brown Collection…Its Origin and Development," *Metropolitan Museum Journal*, iii (1970), 337–356; L. Libin: *American Musical Instruments in the Metropolitan Museum* (1985); *Recent Acquisitions: A Selection, 1985–1986* (1986); J.K. Moore: *Sounding Forms: African Musical Instruments*, Washington, DC: National Museum of African Art, 25 April–18 June 1989 (1989) [exhibition catalog]; L. Libin: "Keyboard Instruments," *Metropolitan Museum of Art Bulletin*, lxvii/1 (1989, 5–56); "Musical Instruments Retell African-American History at the Metropolitan Museum," *AMIS Newsletter*, xxv/3 (1996, 3–4); S. Pollens: "Flemish Harpsichords and Virginals in the Metropolitan Museum of Art: An Analysis of their Alterations and Restorations," *Metropolitan Museum Journal*, xxxii (1997), 85–110; H. Heyde: "The brass instrument collection of the Metropolitan Museum of Art in New York," *HBSJ*, xi (1999), 113–47; H. Heyde: "Ars vitraria: Glass in the Metropolitan Museum of Art: Musical instruments," *The Metropolitan Museum of Art Bulletin*, lix/1 (2001), 52.

NEW YORK, NY. Museum of the City of New York: c30 Western art and popular.

NEW YORK, NY. Research Branch, National Museum of the American Indian, Smithsonian Institution: 6150 (3210 ethnological, 2940 archaeological) Native North, Central and South American. Exhibitions held at NMAI's George Gustave Heye Center, New York City.

NEW YORK, NY. Nathaniel Spear, Jr. collection: 1000 bells some transferred to Metropolitan Museum of Art. N. Spear, Jr.: *A Treasury of Archaeological Bells* (New York, 1978).

NORRIS, TN. Museum of Appalachia: c200 traditional. J.R. Irwin: *Musical Instruments of the Southern Appalachian Mountains* (West Chester, PA, 2/1983)

NORTH NEWTON, KS. Kauffman Museum: c100, more than half European-American origin, also Native North American, Asian, and Central African ethnological.

OAKLAND, CA. Pardee Home Museum: c60 Western, many popular.

OBERLIN, OH. Oberlin Conservatory, the Frederick R. Selch Collection of American Music History: 700 American-made stringed, keyboard, woodwind, and brass instruments and 7000 rare books. F.R. Selch: *An Exhibition of Early Musical Instruments* (Fredericksburg, MD: Washington College, Dupont Galleries, 12 March–5 April 1959) [exhibition catalog]; Frederick R. Selch and H. Reynolds Butler, *The Legacy of Sebastian Virdung: An Illustrated Catalogue of Rare Books from the Frederic R. Selch Collection Pertaining to the History of Musical Instruments* (New York, 2005).

OKLAHOMA CITY, OK. National Cowboy Hall of Fame: c35 mainly US military.

OKLAHOMA CITY, OK. Oklahoma Historical Society Museum: c50 Western, Native American, some non-Western.

OKLAHOMA CITY, OK. Richard W. Payne collection: over 500 archaeological and ethnological American winds, esp. flutes.

ONCHIOTA, NY. Six Nations Indian Museum: c30.

ORONO, ME. Hudson Museum, University of Maine: c60 Meso- and North American, African, and Southeast Asian ethnological and archaeological.

PHILADELPHIA, PA. Independence Seaport Museum: c60 non-Western. Joseph Barone, *A Handbook of the Musical Instrument Collection of the Commercial Museum Philadelphia* (1961).

PHILADELPHIA, PA. Museum of Archaeology and Anthropology, University of Pennsylvania: c3500 North-, Central-, South American, African, Near Eastern, and Oceanian mainly ethnological, also some Western incl. Mrs. William D. Frishmuth collection.

PHOENIX, AZ. Heard Museum of Native Cultures and Art: c600 ethnological primarily Native North American, African.

PHOENIX, AZ. The Musical Instrument Museum. 14,500 general collection including the Kenneth G. Fiske Museum, Claremont University Consortium (multiple countries); Walter J. Erdmann Collection (multiple countries), Horacio Quintana Collection (Brazil); David Kilpatrick Collection (multiple countries); Gérard Coppéré Collection (Africa, Europe, Asia); René Grémaux Collection (mostly Balkans); Guillermo Contreras Collection (Mexico); Garry Harrison Collection (American zithers); Robert Garfias Collection (multiple countries). A.R. Rice: "The Curtis W. Janssen Collection," *Journal of the International Trumpet Guild*, xiv/3 (1990, 30); A.R. Rice: "Curtis Janssen and a selection of outstanding brasses at the Fiske Museum, The Claremont Colleges, California," *HBSJ*, xvii (2005), 85–113; MIM: Highlights from the Musical Instrument Museum, ed. K. Werner (Phoenix, 2012).

PITTSBURGH, PA. Carnegie Museum of Natural History, Division of Anthropology: c460 instruments, mostly ethnographic, worldwide distribution, including 150 ocarinas from Costa Rica and Colombia; drums from North America and Africa; flutes, mostly from Amazon Basin; rattles from North and South America; stringed instruments from China, India, and Japan.

PORTLAND, ME. Maine Historical Society Museum: c30 Western art and traditional.

PORTLAND, OR. Oregon Historical Society Museum: c60 Western used locally, some Native American.

PORTLAND, OR. Rasmussen Collection of Northwest Coast Indian Art, Portland Art Museum: c15. E. Gunther: *Art in the Life of the Northwest Coast Indians* (Portland, 1966).

POTSDAM, NY. Crane School of Music, State University College: Charles N. Lanphere collection, over 100 Middle Eastern from Biblical period, incl. reconstructions, Asian, Australian, from Madagascar, the Philippines and Siberia; Washburn Collection, c150 African and Asian. C.N. Lanphere: *The First Ten Thousand Years of Music: Music of the Bible* (2/1972); *African and Asian Musical Instruments* (Postdam, NY: State University College of Arts and Science, Brainerd Art Gallery, 4 December 1981–15 January 1982, 1981) [exhibition catalog].

POUGHKEEPSIE, NY. Treasure Room, Historical Musical Instruments Collection, Department of Music, Vassar College: over 50 Western, art esp. keyboards. "Instruments in Vassar's Collection (partial listing)," *AMIS Newsletter*, xxvii/3 (1998, 11).

PROVIDENCE, RI. Rhode Island Historical Society Museum: *c*40, mainly brass.

PROVO, UT. Brigham Young University, Museum of Art: *c*150 non-Western and Western, incl. Lloyd Miller and Lotta Van Buren collections.

RED WING, MN. Goodhue County Historical Society Museum: *c*40 mainly Western art and traditional.

ROCHESTER, NY. Helen R. and Charles R. Valenza flute collection: over 60 European and American art. *Historic Flutes from Private Collections* (1986) [exhibition catalog, Metropolitan Museum of Art, New York].

ST. JOHNSBURY, VT. Fairbanks Museum of Natural Science and Planetarium: *c*75 mainly ethnological, and some American winds and string instruments.

ST. JOSEPH, MO. St. Joseph Museum: *c*75, mainly Native American, also non-Western ethnological and some Western.

ST. LOUIS, MO. Aurelia W. Hartenberger collection: 2500 European and instruments of world cultures.

ST. PAUL, MN. Minnesota Historical Society Museum: *c*175 Western.

ST. PAUL, MN. The Schubert Club Museum of Musical Instruments: *c*2100 worldwide, incl. 100 keyboards, Western art, traditional, band, mechanical, and ethnological, esp. African and Indian, and 60 phonographs, most from William and Ida Kugler collection. B. Carlson: *The Schubert Club Museum* (St. Paul, 1991).

SALEM, MA. Peabody Essex Museum: *c*300 mainly Asian (particularly Chinese), Native American, from Hawaiian Islands, African ethnological, and some Western art.

SALT LAKE CITY, UT. Museum of Church History and Art, Church of Jesus Christ of Latter-Day Saints: *c*75 Western art and popular.

SAN DIEGO, CA. San Diego Museum of Man: *c*300 ethnological mainly North American and Mexican, also African, Asian, and Oceanian.

SAN FRANCISCO, CA. Fine Arts Museums of San Francisco: *c*270 Western and ethnological incl. Jascha Heifetz's 1742 Guarneri del Gesu violin.

SANTA ANA, CA. Bowers Memorial Museum: *c*70 pre-Columbian, archaeological and a few Western.

SANTA BARBARA, CA. Santa Barbara Historical Society Museum: *c*300 bells worldwide, *c*15 Western.

SANTA BARBARA, CA. Department of Music, University of California: *c*900 East Asian, southeast Asian, African, Middle Eastern, pre-Columbian and Western, incl. Henry Eichheim collection. D.M. Hsu: *Henry Eichheim Collection of Oriental Instruments* Santa Barbara: U. of California, U. Art Museum, 26 September–28 October 1984 (1984) [exhibition catalog].

SANTA FE, NM. Wheelwright Museum of the American Indian (formerly Museum of Navajo Ceremonial Art): *c*50 Navajo, Pueblo, and Apache Native American.

SEATTLE, WA. Anthropology Division, Thomas Burke Memorial Washington State Museum, University of Washington: *c*500 from the Pacific Rim and Native North American Amerindian.

SEATTLE, WA. EMP Museum (formerly Experience Music Project): *c*100, mainly acoustic and electric guitars.

SEATTLE, WA. Museum of History and Industry, Historical Society of Seattle and King County: *c*70 Western art and popular, some ethnological.

SEATTLE, WA. School of Fine and Performing Arts, Seattle Pacific University: *c*25 art and ethnological flutes from Jim Buck collection.

SEATTLE, WA. Seattle Art Museum: *c*175 from the Pacific Rim, African, North and South American art and ethnological.

SHELBURNE, VT. Shelburne Museum: *c*40 mainly music boxes incl. Wilmerding collection.

SITKA, AK. Sheldon Jackson Museum: *c*25 Inuit, and a Russian organ, 1846, first used in Alaska.

STANFORD, CA. Department of Music, Stanford University: *c*65 string instruments esp. bowed, Harry R. Lange collection. H.W. Myers: "Stanford's Lange Collection Profiled," *AMIS Newsletter*, xiv/3 (1985), 8–9.

STERLING, CO. Overland Trail Museum: *c*50 mainly Western used locally.

STURBRIDGE, MA. Old Sturbridge Village: *c*110 made or used in New England before 1840.

SUPERIOR, WI. Douglas County Historical Society: *c*50 Western used locally.

TALLAHASSEE, FL. Department of Anthropology, Florida State University: *c*65 worldwide, especially Peru, Panama, and Montana.

TALLAHASSEE, FL. James Roberts Instrument Collection, Florida State University: K.R. Gengo: "The James Roberts Instrument Collection: A Documentation and Description" (thesis, Florida State U., 1994).

TOLUCA LAKE, CA. Emil Richards collection: *c*600 percussion worldwide.

TOPEKA, KS. Kansas State Historical Society and Kansas Museum of History: *c*150 Western art, popular, and traditional made or used in Kansas.

TUCSON, AZ. Arizona State Museum, The University of Arizona: *c*500 ethnological and archaeological southwestern and Mexican Native American instruments and some Asian. R.W. Payne: "Indian Flutes of the Southwest," *JAMIS*, xv (1989), 5–31.

TULSA, OK. Anthropology Department, Gilcrease Museum: *c*40 mainly Native American.

TULSA, OK. Native American Collection, Philbrook Museum of Art: *c*30 mainly Plains tribes.

URBANA-CHAMPAIGN, IL. School of Music, Division of Musicology, University of Illinois: *c*90 Middle Eastern, Asian, Native North and Latin American incl. permanent loan of Peruvian archaeological from Krannert Art Museum. J.R. Haefer: "A Checklist of Folk and Non-European Musical Instruments in University of Illinois Collections" (1974) [typescript].

URBANA-CHAMPAIGN, IL. Sousa Archives and Center for American Music, University of Illinois: worldwide incl. Carl Busch, some from Lloyd Farrar collections. C.T. Carrell: *A Catalogue of the Brass Musical Instruments of the Carl Busch Collection at the University of Illinois* (diss., U. of Illinois, 1996); K.L. Cox: *A Catalog of the Clarinets in the University of Illinois Bands Museum* (diss., U. of Illinois, 1997).

URBANA-CHAMPAIGN, IL. University of Illinois: small collections in the Afro-American Culture Centre, Department of Anthropology Laboratory, and Natural History Museum.

VERMILLION, SD. National Music Museum, University of South Dakota: 14,500 general, incl. the Arne B. Larson, Wayne Sorensen (band), Lawrence Witten (string instruments), Cecil Leeson (saxophone), John Powers (saxophone), Rosario Mazzeo (clarinets), Bill Maynard (clarinets), Joe and Joella Utley (brass), Alan Bates (harmonicas), and D'Angelico (guitar workshop) collections. Extensive archives of advertising material, pamphlets, and sales records of the C.G. Conn, Leblanc, and Holton firms. A.P. Larson: *A Catalogue of the Double Reed Instruments in the Arne B. Larson Collection of Musical Instruments* (diss., U. of South Dakota, 1968); A.P. Larson: *Catalog of the Nineteenth-Century British Brass Instruments in the Arne B. Larson Collection* (diss., West Virginia University, 1974); G.M. Stewart: "Restoration and Cataloging of Four Serpents in the Arne B. Larson Collection of Musical Instruments" (thesis, U. of South Dakota, 1978); G.M. Stewart: *Catalog of the Collections, the Shrine to Music Museum*, i: *Arne B. Larson Collection: Keyed Brass Instruments* (1980); "The Wayne Sorensen Collection," *AMIS Newsletter*, xii/3 (1983, 4); M.D. Banks: "North Italian Viols at the Shrine to Music Museum," *JVdGSA*, xxi (1984), 7–27; L. Kitzel: *The Trombones of the Shrine to Music Museum* (diss., U. of South Dakota, 1985); G.R. Moege, ed.: *A Catalogue of the Alto Brass Instruments in the Arne B. Larson Collection of Musical Instruments* (1985); J.J. Swain, ed.: *A Catalog of the E-Flat Tubas in the Arne B. Larson Collection* (diss., U. of Michigan, 1985); M.D. Banks: "The Witten-Rawlins Collection and other Early Italian Stringed Instruments at the Shrine to Music Museum," *Journal of the Violin Society of America*, viii/3 (1987), 19–48; M.D. Banks: "The 'Harrison' Violin, the 'Rawlins' Guitar, and Other Stradivari Materials at the Shrine to Music Museum," *Journal of the Violin Society of America*, ix/3 (1988), 13–35; M. Schlenz: *The Shrine to Music Museum: A Pictorial Souvenir* (1988); M.L. Scott: *The American Piston Valved Cornets and Trumpets of the Shrine to Music Museum* (diss., U. of South Dakota, 1988); D.W. Knutson: *A Catalogue of the European Cornets and Trumpets at the Shrine to Music Museum* (diss., U. of Illinois, 1992); S. Carter: "Early Trombones in America's Shrine to Music Museum," *HBSJ*, x (1998), 92–94, 102–104; *Beethoven & Berlioz, Paris & Vienna: Musical Treasures from the Age of Revolution & Romance 1789–1848* (Vermillion, SD, 2003); S. Klaus: "The Joe R. and Joella F. Utley Collection of High Brass Instruments: A Trumpeter's Dream Comes True," *International Trumpet Guild Journal*, xxxiv/4 (2010), 38–45.

WARRENSBURG, MO. Music Division, University of Central Missouri: *c*300 mainly winds, worldwide: the Don Essig collection. "Essig Collection is Cataloged and Exhibited," *AMIS Newsletter*, x/2 (1981, 1).

WASHINGTON, DC. Daughters of the American Revolution (DAR) Museum: *c*45 European and American. E.D. Garrett: *The Arts of Independence, the DAR Museum Collection* (1985); *Strike Up the Band* (1988) [exhibition checklist].

WASHINGTON, DC. Library of Congress, Music Division: Collections of Dayton C. Miller (*c*2000 flutes), the Thai-Laotian Ceremonial, Robert E. Sheldon (winds loan) collections, Gertrude Clarke Whittall Foundation (5 Stradivari), and H. Blakiston Wilkins (5 strings). W.D. Orcutt: *The Stradivari Memorial at Washington, the National Capitol* (Washington, 1938); L.E. Gilliam and W. Lichtenwanger: *The Dayton C. Miller Flute Collection: A Checklist of the Instruments* (Washington, 1961); R.E. Sheldon: *Wind Instruments* (1968) [exhibition brochure, Museum of History and Technology, Smithsonian]; F. Traficante: "Henry Blakiston Who? Or Some Early Instruments at the Library of Congress," *JVdGSA*, x (1973, 29–80); C.A. Goodrum: *Treasures of the Library of Congress* (1980); M. Seyfrit: *Musical Instruments in the Dayton C. Miller Flute Collection: A Catalog*, i: *Recorders, Fifes and Simple System Transverse Flutes of One Key* (1982); *The Stringed Instrument Collection in the Library of Congress* (Tokyo, 1986); M.J. Simpson: "Dayton C. Miller and the Dayton C. Miller Flute Collection," *Flutist Quarterly*, xv (1990), 5–11; R. Sheldon: "The Musical Instrument Collections of the Library of Congress," *Flutist Quarterly*, xvi/3 (1991, 19–23); *Music, Theater, Dance: An Illustrated Guide* (1993); R. Hargrave: *Amati, Stradivari & Guarneri: The Library of Congress Violins* (1997).

WASHINGTON, DC. National Park Service, US Department of the Interior: western art and traditional, ethnological, archaeological, esp. Native American.

WASHINGTON, DC. Smithsonian Institution, National Museum of African Art: 119, mainly percussion.

WASHINGTON, DC. Smithsonian Institution, National Museum of American History: *c*5000 American and European art, traditional, jazz, and popular, incl. 268 keyboards and Hugo Worch (keyboards), part of Mrs. W.D. Frishmuth, Janos Scholz (cello bow) collections, and Herbert and Evelyn Axelrod collection of quartets (two violins, viola, cello) by Stradivari, Nicolo Amati, Vuillaume, and Peresson. F. Densmore: *Handbook of the Collection of Musical Instruments in the United States National Museum* (1927); C. Hoover and S. Odell: *A Catalogue of Keyboard Instruments at the Smithsonian Institution* (1967, 2/1975); J. Fesperman: "Music and Instruments at the Smithsonian Institution," *CMc*, no.6 (1968), 63–5; C. Hoover: *Harpsichords and Clavichords* (1969); C. Hoover: *Music Machines—American Style: A catalog of the exhibition*, Washington, DC: National Museum of History and Technology (1971) [exhibition catalog]; J.S. Odell: *Plucked Dulcimers: A Checklist of Appalachian Dulcimers and Similar Instruments in the Collection of the Division of Musical Instruments* (1971); H. Hollis: *Pianos in the Smithsonian Institution* (1973); J.S. Odell: *A Checklist of Banjos in the Collections of the Division of Musical Instruments* (1973); G. Sturm: "Exhibition of Violins and Bows in the Smithsonian Collection," *Journal of the Violin Society of America*, v/2 (1979), 75–102; L.E. Herman: *The Harmonious Craft: American Musical Instruments* Washington, DC: Renwick Gallery, 29 September 1978–5 August 1979 (1979) [exhibition brochure]; *Classical Bowed Stringed Instruments from the Smithsonian Institution* (1986); G. Sturm and W. Monical: *An Exhibi-*

tion of American Violin Makers before 1930 Washington, DC: National Museum of American History, 12 June–23 August 1987 (1987) [exhibition catalog]; M.K. O'Brien: "The Smithsonian Clavichords," *Early Keyboard Journal*, x (1992), 121–78; C. Hoover and others, *Piano 300: Celebrating three centuries of people and pianos* Washington, DC: National Museum of American History, Behring Center, 9 March 2000–21 October 2001 (2001) [exhibition catalog].

WASHINGTON, DC. Smithsonian Institution, National Museum of Natural History, Department of Anthropology: 3300 ethnological, mainly African, Asian, indigenous American, and Oceanian. F. Densmore: *Handbook of the Collection of Musical Instruments in the United States National Museum* (1927); D.L. Thieme: *A Descriptive Catalogue of Yoruba Musical Instruments* (diss., Catholic U. of America, 1969).

WASHINGTON, DC. Smithsonian Institution, National Museum of the American Indian: *c*6100 ethnological or archeological items from North, Central, and South America, including panpipes, ocarinas, whistles, flutes, trumpets, clarinets, violins, fiddles, guitars, harps, drums, marimbas, bells, rattles, time keeping and song sticks, buzzers, and bullroarers.

WICHITA, KS. Flutes of the World, Betty Austin Hensley Collection: over 350 Western art, traditional, popular, and non-Western ethnological flutes. B.A. Hensley: *Flutes of the World: A Checklist* (1983).

WICHITA, KS. Thurlow Lieurance Indian Flutes, Wichita State University: *c*25 flutes, half Native North American. B.A. Hensley: *Thurlow Lieurance Indian Flutes* (1990).

WILBRAHAM, MA. Robert S. Howe collection: *c*250 woodwinds and some brasses.

WILLIAMSBURG, VA. DeWitt Wallace Gallery, Colonial Williamsburg: *c*80 mainly English and American 18th-century art.

WILLIAMSTOWN, MA. Department of Music, Williams College: *c*50 Western art, incl. Telford Taylor collection.

WINSTON SALEM, NC. Old Salem Museums & Gardens: Wachovia Historical Society collection and instruments from Moravian congregations. J. Watson: "Claviers for Salem: Historic Instruments in the Salem Moravian Community," *Moravian Music Journal*, xxxi/1 (1986, 9–12); "Historic Tannenberg Organ from Old Salem," *AMIS Newsletter*, xxviii/3 (1999, 14–15).

WISCASSET, ME. The Musical Wonder House: Music boxes, disc and cylinder types 1815–1915; also crank organs, player pianos, reproducing pianos, and other mechanical.

YORK, PA. York County Heritage Trust (formerly Historical Society of York County): *c*50 Western art, traditional used locally.

BIBLIOGRAPHY
Waterhouse-LangwillI
A. Baines: *European and American Musical Instruments* (New York, 1966)
W. Lichtenwanger and others: *A Survey of Musical Instrument Collections in the United States and Canada* (Ann Arbor, 1974)
J. Jenkins, ed.: *International Directory of Musical Instrument Collections* (Buren, Netherlands, 1977)
J. Coover: *Musical Instrument Collections, Catalogues and Cognate Literature* (Detroit, 1981)
CIMCIM/AMIS International Directory of Musical Instrument Collections: <http://www.music.ed.ac.uk/euchmi/cimcim/id/index.html>

LAURENCE LIBIN/ALBERT R. RICE

Instruments, electronic. *See* ELECTRONIC INSTRUMENTS.

Instruments, historical. A general term for instruments of previous eras, particularly those considered appropriate for the historically informed performance of early music. The term should not be confused with "historic instruments," which denotes those individual instruments distinguished by their rarity, symbolic

Grand piano built by Bartolomeo Cristofori, 1720. (Image copyright © The Metropolitan Museum of Art. Image source: Art Resource, NY)

value, association with prominent persons or events, innovatory significance, and so on.

Within the Western classical tradition, interest in historical instruments has tended to be a subcultural activity, with the majority of musicians and audiences preferring instruments of their own day to earlier types. Particularly in the 19th and early 20th centuries, historical instruments were often derided as "primitive" in sound and mechanism, and as unsuited for the performance of either modern or historical music. Thus, for example, the increased dynamic range, pitch range, and durability of 19th-century pianos were seen as "improvements" over fortepianos, harpsichords, and clavichords of previous eras. Though evidence of this view appears in the popular press as late as the 1980s (when *New York Times* music critic Bernard Holland referred to period instruments as "the dead ends of instrumental evolution"), in general the zeitgeist of European and American early-music scenes has shifted to revere antique instruments over modern ones for the performance of pre-19th-century repertoire.

The accelerating pace of innovation and mass production during the industrial revolution led, by the late 19th century, to a reaction in some quarters aimed at fostering higher quality and greater individuality and simplicity in instrument manufacture, as exemplified by fine hand-made examples from the past. This nostalgia, writ large by the British Arts and Crafts movement, was

bolstered by exhibitions of historic instruments (for instance at the 1893 World's Columbian Exposition in Chicago, where antique keyboard instruments owned by Morris Steinert were displayed) and by the formation of important permanent collections in museums such as the Kensington, later the Victoria and Albert, in London, and the Metropolitan Museum of Art in New York. Here, in the context of fine art, displays of especially beautiful or curious old instruments aroused interest in their sounds.

The prominent British instrument collectors and scholars Carl Engel, A.J. Hipkins and F.W. Galpin influenced this development through their publications and by advising American antiquarians such as Mrs. John Crosby Brown, James Henry Darlington, Sarah Frishmuth, Belle Skinner, and Frederick Stearns, whose instrument holdings became the nuclei of public collections that offered examples for careful study by contemporary makers, as well as for occasional performance in educational concerts. For example, in the 1890s, music critic Henry Edward Krehbiel and collector MORRIS STEINERT gave lectures in New York City on historical keyboards, illustrated with short performances on instruments from Steinert's collection. American concert-goers also enjoyed increasing exposure to 18th-century music, for example through Ferruccio Busoni's keyboard recitals (1910, 1911), Gustav Mahler's performances of Bach with the New York Philharmonic (using a Steinway piano with tacks in its hammers to replicate the sound of a harpsichord), and concerts by the Handel & Haydn Society of Boston (founded 1815) and the Bethlehem Bach Choir (founded 1898).

By the turn of the 20th century ensembles had formed in America to specialize in performance on historical instruments. For example, from 1891 through 1905 the Mozart Symphony Club of New York offered "Three Centuries of Romantic, Classic and Popular Music Interpreted on the Instruments of the Times." George Proctor in Boston played the harpsichord for a private performance organized by Isabella Stewart Gardner in 1900 at which the viola d'amore was also heard. Also in Boston, from 1905 to 1911 ARNOLD DOLMETSCH supervised a department of CHICKERING & Sons devoted to making harpsichords, clavichords, virginals, lutes and viols. The availability of Dolmetch-Chickering instruments, which were unsurpassed in their day for fidelity to historical models, facilitated the more "authentic" performance of early music. Busoni's advocacy of Dolmetsch's work, and Dolmetsch's own somewhat eccentric performances, gained American adherents for his instruments, some of which were acquired by prestigious schools such as Vassar College. The American harpsichord maker JOHN CHALLIS began his career in 1925 by attempting to copy a Dolmetsch–Chickering clavichord. By such means the groundwork was laid for the EARLY-MUSIC REVIVAL of the mid-20th century.

Charismatic performers, notably the harpsichordist WANDA LANDOWSKA, promoted this endeavor in America after World War I (Landowska first performed in the United States in 1923). While Landowska's Pleyel harpsichords were remote from Baroque models in design and sound, her fame inspired American performers to explore more deeply the resources of historical instruments. Organists in particular received encouragement from Albert Schweitzer, who championed a return to "classical" principles in organ building. A major step toward this goal was the installation in 1937 of a German Baroque-style organ by Aeolian–Skinner (designed by G. Donald Harrison) in the Busch-Reisinger Museum of Germanic Culture at Harvard University, from which E. POWER BIGGS broadcast recitals nationwide beginning in 1942 (that famous organ was replaced in 1958 by an equally influential, mechanical-action instrument by Flentrop). Harrison's retrospective approach was prefigured in the early 1930s by neo-Baroque organs of Walter Holtkamp.

During and after World War II some aspiring American craftsmen first beheld antique instruments in Europe; in 1947, for example, FRANK HUBBARD went abroad to study museum collections and worked in England for Dolmetsch and the clavichord builder HUGH GOUGH before returning to open a harpsichord workshop with WILLIAM DOWD, a former apprentice of Challis's (Gough himself settled in New York in 1959 to produce clavichords, harpsichords, and several lutes). Meanwhile the 1930s and 40s saw an influx of European early music performers to the United States, notably Anne (Tschopp) Gombosi, who brought to Boston the instrumental traditions of the Schola Cantorum Basil-

iensis. The BOSTON CAMERATA, which Gombosi co-founded, in turn promoted the success of Hubbard & Dowd, the recorder and flute maker FRIEDRICH VON HUENE, and other Boston-area pioneers who trained the next generation of makers of "revival" instruments, among them Walter Burr, Eric Herz, Robert Marvin, Thomas Prescott, and others who helped establish Boston's primacy in the American early music scene.

Indeed, across the United States, the youth-oriented counterculture of the 1960s and 70s brought increasing attention to historical instruments associated with the Western Classical tradition, such as the harpsichord and recorder, as well as to historical instruments associated with folk traditions, such as the Appalachian dulcimer. These young people provided a market for newly built instruments, as well as cheap labor for instrument shops like Hubbard's and Dowd's. During this period, the amateur market for historical instruments became such that a number of makers began offering dulcimers, psalteries, clavichords, harpsichords inexpensively in kit form. Among the most successful were the harpsichord kits produced by Zuckermann Harpsichords. Though the instruments resulting from these instrument kits tended not to be of high quality, they were the start of many harpsichord makers' careers.

Also during this period, some folk and rock musicians began incorporating harpsichords, recorders, clavichords, or lutes into their recordings, including Pete Seeger, the Weavers, the Beach Boys, the Monkees, Jimi Hendrix, and Jefferson Airplane. Jazz pianists Erroll Garner, John Lewis, Junior Mance, Sun Ra, and McCoy Tyner recorded songs on harpsichord; Oscar Peterson played clavichord on his 1976 recording of "Porgy and Bess." Combined with the already copious number of period ensemble recordings of Classical repertoire released between the 1940s and 70s, these musicians helped historical instruments to reach mainstream status.

Another avenue by which historical instruments became more widely available during the 20th century was through repair or restoration of original examples. Civil War reenactment bands, for example, could often acquire 19th-century brasses and drums for less than the cost of new equivalents, and for some old forms, such as over-the-shoulder saxhorns, no modern equivalents existed (until the 1980s, when brass maker ROBB STEWART began making them). Similarly, 19th-century square pianos could sometimes be obtained cheaply and restored to reasonable working order for use at historic sites where "authentic" music performance was desired. Also, Baroque-era bowed instruments that had previously been modernized began to be returned to approximations of their original condition, and manufacture of appropriate gut strings and Baroque-style bows resumed on a small scale.

This development was paralleled by an outpouring of reprint and Urtext editions of 19th-century and earlier music, giving performers unprecedented access to repertoire suited to historically informed performances—which were increasingly recorded commercially. The quality of these editions, performances, and replica or restored instruments varied greatly, but the net effect was to spur excitement about early music, particularly among young aficionados who participated in collegiate ensembles that served as laboratories for "authentic" performance practices. Remarkably, the American COLLEGIUM MUSICUM movement took root not in conservatories, which train professional performers, but in university departments of musicology that married analysis of original source materials (manuscripts, treatises) with practical application through student performance.

From the mid-20th century, proliferating collegiate ensembles and a growing number of successful professional groups such as the NEW YORK PRO MUSICA ANTIQUA (founded 1952) constituted a substantial market for replicas of historical instruments. American builders received further orders from the members of specialized performance-oriented organizations such as the American Recorder Society (1939), the Organ Historical Society (1956; devoted mainly to preservation), the Viola da Gamba Society of America (1963), the Lute Society of America (1966), the Westfield Center for Early Keyboard Studies (1979), and Early Music America (1985). Interest went so far as to encourage speculative reconstruction of instruments for which no historical prototypes exist (e.g., Willard Martin's *Lautenwerk*), "copies" without validity ("natural" trumpets with fingerholes), and even production of novel types (e.g., George Kelischek's Kelhorns, plastic gemshorns).

This growing enthusiasm among academics, amateurs, and, increasingly, music critics, for historical instruments and their music was presaged, years earlier, by the warm reception accorded RALPH KIRKPATRICK's sensational performance, at a meeting in 1939 of the American Musicological Society in New York, on the world's oldest piano (by Bartolomeo Cristofori, 1720), which had been rebuilt at the Metropolitan Museum of Art under supervision of Curt Sachs. Sachs, a former museum curator, believed that museums have a responsibility to return instruments in their collections to playing condition so that they can be heard and fully appreciated. He observed that, otherwise, fragile old instruments might be allowed to deteriorate structurally while serving only to delight the eye. His view, however, raised troubling questions about how best to balance the desire to hear these intriguing relics against the need to preserve the irreplaceable evidence they embody.

With the emergence of conservation (as opposed to restoration) as a distinct discipline within museums, attention turned to the unique problems posed by historical instruments, which, unlike most museum pieces, were wanted to fulfill their original working function. Conservators experienced in instrument making, most prominently J. Scott Odell of the Smithsonian Institution, John R. Watson of the Colonial Williamsburg Foundation, and Robert Barclay of the Canadian Conservation Institute, focused attention on fundamental issues having to do with authentication, deterioration both from natural causes and through use, and ambiguity of context.

Connoisseurship regarding instruments lagged expertise about fine arts, and new research involving techniques such as dendrochronology proved that many prized instruments in museums were fakes, forgeries, or too optimistically attributed, hence not suitable subjects for costly restoration or replication. Most instruments, especially those incorporating biological materials such as wood or leather, deteriorate over long timespans whether they are played or not, and these effects often cannot be corrected unless original material is replaced. In addition, playing itself is destructive due to unavoidable wear and tear, accidents, replacement of ephemeral parts such as drum heads or violin strings, and routine maintenance procedures such as cleaning and lubrication that subtly erode original surfaces, gradually change critical dimensions, and further obscure the original state. Hence, instruments that are regularly played are endangered, and repair and restoration, especially if inadequately documented, compound uncertainty as to the maker's intentions. Considering that extant historical instruments are all more or less altered (admittedly, sometimes improved) from their intact condition, and knowledge of their contemporary playing techniques, voicing, tuning, mechanical regulation, and so on is incomplete at best, we cannot know with certainty and precision how they were intended to sound and work. Consequently, every restoration involves subjective judgments that might be overturned by future discoveries, and risks obliterating precious evidence that had not been recognized.

With these caveats in mind, and because old instruments provide practically the only tangible evidence for how music sounded before the advent of recording, the need to preserve at least the best, rarest, and most representative of them unaltered to the extent possible, and documenting them thoroughly, is imperative. Fortunately, copying them offers a solution, albeit imperfect, to the problems enumerated above. An accurate copy might play and sound more like the subject instrument did when it was new than it could today. Making a copy greatly reduces risk of wear and tear on the original, and copies can be multiplied so that many musicians can benefit from playing them. Also, copies can be altered and experimented upon without endangering the original. And the process of comprehensive documentation and precise replication (facilitated by provision of technical drawings, x-rays, material analyses, etc.) generally require more careful observation of all aspects of the original than simply repairing it would do. Finally, the insights gained from copying can contribute to advances in instrument making and organology, among other ways by disclosing long-forgotten systems of design (e.g., proportional schemes) and methods of construction (e.g., sand-casting organ pipe metal) that can be applicable today.

BIBLIOGRAPHY

W.L. Johnson: "The Harpsichord in America 1884–1946," *Harvard Musical Association Bulletin* (April 1946)

H. Schott: "The Harpsichord revival," *EMc*, ii (1974), 85–95

F. Hubbard: "Reconstructing the Harpsichord," *The Historical Harpsichord: a Monograph Series in Honor of Frank Hubbard*, ed. H. Schott (New York, 1984), 3–16

L. Palmer: *Harpsichord in America: a Twentieth Century Revival* (Bloomington, IN, 1989)

M. Elste: "Nostalgische Musikmaschinen: Cembali im 20. Jahrhundert," *Kielklaviere: Cembali, Spinette, Virginale,* ed. J. H. van der Meer and others (Berlin, 1991), 239–77

J.B. Rutledge: "Late 19th-century viol revivals," *EMc,* xix (1991), 409–18

R. Taruskin: *Text and Act: Essays on Music and Performance* (Oxford, 1995)

K.K. Shelemay: "Toward an Ethnomusicology of the Early Music Movement: Thoughts on Bridging Disciplines and Musical Worlds," *EthM,* xliv (2001), 1–29

H. Schott: "The Clavichord Revival, 1800–1960," *EMc,* xxxii (2004), 595–603

J.-C. Battault: "Les clavecins Pleyel, Érard, et Gaveau, 1889–1970," *Musique ancienne: instruments et imagination,* ed. M. Latcham (Berne, 2006), 193–212

K. Yri: "Noah Greenberg and the New York Pro Musica: Medievalism and the Cultural Front," *American Music,* xx/4 (2006), 421–44

M. Bixler: "A History of the American Recorder Society: A Memoir. Part I" *American Recorder,* xlviii (2007), 9–18

B. Haynes: *The End of Early Music: a Period Performer's History of Music for the Twenty-First Century* (Oxford, 2007)

LAURENCE LIBIN, JESSICA WOOD

Instrument societies. Organizations devoted to a particular musical instrument or group of instruments. Groups state their purpose and goals in many different ways, but common ideas include fostering communication between members, providing a forum for the exchange of information and ideas, and promoting interest in and study of the instrument(s) to which the society is dedicated. Some societies emphasize the history of instruments, disseminating information about them, and preserving historic instruments. Others emphasize collecting or making instruments. A common theme is bringing together amateur and professional players or instrument makers of all experience levels.

A number of groups, including what is probably the first instrument society—the American Recorder Society (ARS), founded in 1929 by lutenist Suzanne Block—were an outgrowth of the early music revival, through which instrumental ensembles brought recorders, viols, lutes, and other little-known instruments to the notice of a wider audience. The ARS continues to facilitate meetings between recorder players and to offer help and support as members choose, learn, play, and care for their instruments. Interest in early instruments has prompted the formation of similar groups such as the Viola da Gamba Society of America (founded 1963), the Lute Society of America (1966), the Viola d'Amore Society (1977), the Historical Harp Society (1990), and the Clavichord Society of Boston (1995).

The 1960s and 1970s saw the formation of many societies devoted to standard band and orchestral instruments. These were generally organized by educators who sought to improve teaching and performance standards, and to provide a forum for communication among members. These typically large societies often schedule national conventions that include competitions and contests for high school, college, and young professional musicians. In 1960 a group of percussionists and educators attending the Midwest Band and Orchestra Clinic in Chicago sought to stimulate greater interest and higher standards in percussion performance and teaching; the PERCUSSIVE ARTS SOCIETY was established the following year. Other new organizations included the AMERICAN HARP SOCIETY (1962), the International Society of Bassists (1967), the INTERNATIONAL HORN SOCIETY (1970), the INTERNATIONAL DOUBLE REED SOCIETY (1971), the NATIONAL FLUTE ASSOCIATION, the International Trombone Association (1972), the INTERNATIONAL CLARINET ASSOCIATION (1973), and the INTERNATIONAL TRUMPET GUILD (1974). In 1973, the Tubists Universal Brotherhood Association (TUBA) (1973), sought to reach composers as well; the group's first symposium resulted in some 150 new compositions for the tuba, leading to a rise in the performance level of the tuba. The group was renamed the International Tuba and Euphonium Association in 2000. The American Viola Society was organized in 1978, encouraging wider participation than in its original format as the Viola Research Society (1971–77); in addition to promoting performance and recording at the highest level, the group encourages "development of the fraternal bond among violists."

Societies that particularly emphasize the historical aspect of instruments include the ORGAN HISTORICAL SOCIETY (1956), which promotes historical interest in American organ building, and the AMERICAN MUSICAL INSTRUMENT SOCIETY (1971), which is dedicated to the study of musical instruments in all cultures and from all periods. The Southeastern Historical Keyboard Society, formed in 1980, along with two later regional groups—the Midwestern Historical Keyboard Society and the Western Early Keyboard Association—provide forums for all aspects of early keyboard instruments and their music. The HISTORIC BRASS SOCIETY (1988) focuses on history, music literature, and performance practice.

Two groups oriented toward collectors are the Musical Box Society International (1949) dedicated to the "enjoyment, study and preservation of all automatic musical instruments" and AMICA—the Automatic Musical Instrument Collectors' Association (1963)—which focuses on player-pianos, roll-playing, and automatic instruments, facilitating collecting but also attempting to place instruments in locations where the general public can see and hear them.

Nearly all instrument societies include makers among their members; two that focus especially on instrument making are the GUILD OF AMERICAN LUTHIERS (1972), which encourages the sharing of information about building string instruments, and the VIOLIN SOCIETY OF AMERICA (1973), which promotes the art and science of making, repairing, and preserving stringed musical instruments and their bows.

By the late 20th century, the growth of the Internet had revolutionized communications between societies, their members, and the general public. Society websites, online forums (officially sponsored or informally organized), and online storehouses of information devoted to instruments or instrument makers now proliferate. The importance of making personal connections and exchanging ideas through local gatherings and annual conventions remains significant to today's members of instrument societies. The American Musical Instrument Society maintains a list of additional instrument societies (<http://www.amis.org/resources/index.html#org>).

See also AMERICAN THEATRE ORGAN SOCIETY, EARLY MUSIC AMERICA, EARLY-MUSIC REVIVAL, INSTRUMENTS, INSTRUMENTS, HISTORICAL, and PIANO TECHNICIANS GUILD.

CAROLYN BRYANT

Intellectual property. Intellectual property (IP) has no physical or tangible characteristics, and must be instantiated or demonstrated in an observable way before the legal system can acknowledge a claim to protection. Its creation is said to belong to an original author, and its value is presumed to accrue in the market and through enforcement of legal property claims. The IP system is credited with creating public and private benefits: incentives for private creators to continue creating, and public benefits of knowledge from imposing limits and restrictions on monopolies to IP owners.

The notion of private IP is a product of juridical thinking about property rights that has developed since about 1450 in the Republic of Venice. The English Statute of Monopolies codified IP rights in the Anglo world in 1624. Article 1, Section 8 of the US Constitution is the intellectual property clause that empowers the US Congress to "promote the Progress of Science and useful Arts, by securing for limited Times to Authors and Inventors the exclusive Right to their respective Writings and Discoveries." In the United States, the US Copyright Office and Patent and Trademark Office register intellectual property, while Congress has authority to change the terms or durations of rights. Most of the world's countries have established formal IP law systems similar to the US. The Berne Convention created a world-wide protection scheme for IP in 1886, and was mostly superannuated by the World Intellectual Property Rights Organization (WIPO) in 1970 and TRIPS (Trade Related Aspects of Intellectual Property Rights) in 1995. TRIPS is administered by the WTO (World Trade Organization).

Within the natural law framework for thinking about creative production, intellectual property rights guarantee a monopoly of ownership and disposition of a creative work, device, trademark, or trade secret, thereby restricting its use by others. The IP system is predicated on the notion of an original author of an innovation, who can subsequently transfer or license ownership of IP. Legal treatment of IP has increasingly wrestled with the notion of original authorship, as the growth of media conglomerates has depended upon assembly-line like production of audiovisual works, and as youth culture produces and consumes digitally remixed and mashed-up productions.

IP law provides the economic basis for the culture industries by turning intangible, symbolic products into saleable goods and services. Record labels, music publishers, and movie studios, among others, generate and license music commodities through their production lines of creative talent, their writers, composers, and performers. Rights agencies collect and redistribute royalties paid by licensees. Retailers buy and sometimes resell physical music media, while distributors supply sales channels with retail catalog content.

1. Copyright. 2. Patents. 3. Trade secrets. 4. Trademarks and service marks. 5. International political economy of intellectual property. 6. Critiques of intellectual property law.

1. COPYRIGHT. Songs, advertising jingles, motion pictures, audiovisual works, sound recordings, and instrumentals are examples of musical works covered by copyright law. Copyrights provide "an exclusive right to reproduce an original work of authorship fixed in any tangible medium of expression, to prepare derivative works based upon the original work, and to perform or display the work in the case of musical, dramatic, choreographic, and sculptural works" (Hefter and Litowitz, 2008, p. xxviii). Originality of work of authorship is the key to copyright. Protection subsists from the moment the work is fixed in a tangible expression, but registration options are available. Duration has changed frequently through legislative copyright term extensions. The United States does not recognize the moral rights of creators, whereas moral rights are obtained for works by European creators. Moral rights convey more authorial control over the disposition and use of works that may or may not be owned by the creator.

When the terms of copyrights and patents expire, rights to their creations are released to the public domain. The public domain contains the universe of creative works for which copyright and patent protections no longer apply. Fair use is the exemption to copyright that ensures that the public has the right to an ongoing and open access to use copyrighted works in ways that do not harm the copyright owner economically. For example, no permissions are required for noncommercial home taping, criticism, comment, journalism, teaching, and researching on audiovisual materials, including music. A body of critical scholarly work on music and fair use developed after the 1998 Digital Millennium Copyright Act (US-DMCA) was codified in Section 1201 of the US Copyright Act. Researchers have discovered many unintended consequences of the DMCA for fair use and access to digitally encoded culture. Artists and other creators have created CreativeCommons.org as an alternative licensing scheme for publishing. It uses the existing IP law system for enabling creators to secure broader, public rights for fair use of creative works.

See also COPYRIGHT.

2. PATENTS. Patent law developed as a variety of contract between society as a whole and an individual inventor. As with copyright, the inventor of a patent is granted, for a limited time, the exclusive right to block access to the creation, use, and sale of a patented invention. The inventor is required to publish the details of the invention in a public archive, in exchange for the monopoly. The patent is the legal means by which the market and society typically distinguish between an idea and its expression in an invention, although the line between idea and expression is often difficult or impossible to identify in patentable "inventions" such as software and

business processes. In the United States, useful inventions that are also new are generally patentable; in the UK, a new invention must be capable of "industrial application." Besides being useful and novel, a patent must also be nonobvious.

Patent protections have been extended to agriculture, pharmaceuticals, and software. Software patents, in particular, intersect with music in a growing number of contexts, including the production and development of commercial software for producing, storing, encrypting, and distributing digital music and audiovisual files. A patent by Clear Channel/Live Nation called "System and method of creating digital recordings of live performances" captured the attention of a "patent-busting" campaign by the Electronic Frontiers Foundation because it appeared to cover the general concept of recording live events such as concerts.

As with copyright, enforcement responsibilities fall to the IP owner making a legal claim. Infringing acts, such as unauthorized use of a patent, create liability, even if the infringer did not have ill intent or know of the patent. Remedies are available to patent owners who prove infringement cases. "Patent thickets" are anticompetitive patents set up by corporations to forestall competition in an innovative market. Issued patents can be challenged in court for invalidity. Finding the existence of "prior art" challenges the novelty required of a granted patent.

3. TRADE SECRETS. A trade secret is information that is known only by its "owner," used for competitive advantage in business, and successfully protected from disclosure. If a trade secret is lawfully and independently shared, it loses its value as intellectual property. The only markets for trade secrets that exist are black markets, and trade secrets are often the domain of corporate espionage. Disputes over trade secrets have not generated as much legal activity in the audio-visual industries, or scholarship, as have copyright contests.

4. TRADEMARKS AND SERVICE MARKS. These are developed to indicate the commercial origin of goods and services and to distinguish between trademarked goods and services. A trademark owner who uses a distinctive name, logo, image, symbol, or some combination of these, can register the trade mark, use it on its products, and restrict its use by others. A service mark functions similarly to the trademark, but is intended for services, including transportation, telecommunications, and audio-visuals including film. A sound trademark, such as the 20th Century-Fox Studios' introductory fanfare composition by Alfred Newman, uniquely identifies the origin of the product or service.

5. INTERNATIONAL POLITICAL ECONOMY OF INTELLECTUAL PROPERTY. Hollywood, Madison Avenue, Silicon Valley, and the other engines of the North American culture industries produce tradable IP goods and services valued, on average, at 18% of the US Gross Domestic Product between 1998 and 2003. After aerospace and defense, IP trade—in software, audiovisual, and other personal, cultural, and recreational service products—is the most valuable sector for the US balance of payments. All IP dependent sectors together, including aerospace, automotive, computer, pharmaceutical, semiconductor, motion picture, and recording industries, employ 13% of the US labor force in higher-wage jobs (US GAO, 2008).

Countries with free trade agreements with the United States face high competition from US products in local markets for music, film, television, other audiovisual goods and services, and software. The United States aggressively pursues media and software exports through the US Trade Representative's office Enforcement, while several federal agencies including ICE, FBI, DOJ, and the FDA pursue international IP policing programs.

6. CRITIQUES OF INTELLECTUAL PROPERTY LAW. Realist legal critiques of intellectual property law include objections to the theory of natural rights imposing yet another variety of "transcendental nonsense" (Cohen, 1935) to justify unjust labor practices and wealth distribution in the creative industries. Other legal scholars have embraced various environmentalist, anarchist, and cyberlibertarian critiques of IP law that reconceptualize intellectual property as a cultural commons or lost public domain. The non-rival nature and public goods characteristics of intellectual property, and information generally, mean that impositions of scarcity on IP, such as DRM (Digital Rights Management), or copy protections, are broadly perceived to be abusive, or too easy to abuse. Critical media studies of IP law investigate the sources of widespread anxieties about intellectual property PIRACY, document abusive IP practices in the media and software industries, and develop comparative cases of resistance to the global IP regime. The record and movie industries' massive confrontations with FILE SHARING fans and their sharing sites Napster and Grokster sparked popular rebellions against the Recording Industry Association of America, representing the major labels, and the Motion Picture Association of America, representing the Hollywood studios.

A frequent economic critique of IP law is that it perpetuates market failures such as media monopolies. Media economics and political economy of media have explored the consequences of media consolidation for consumers, culture, and society at large. Critics of copyright term extension have pressed for an "information politics" for "balanced copyright," to restore the social value of limiting the terms of copyright, and expanding the basis for the public domain. However, the "copyfight" continues, partly because copyright term extensions are politically popular, and because most publishing, licensing, manufacturing, design, and artistic creation use business models based on exclusive, enforceable, and long-lasting intellectual property rights protections.

REFERENCES

F.S. Cohen: "Transcendental Nonsense and the Functional Approach," *Columbia Law Review* xxxv/6 (1935), 809–49

F.D. Prager: "History of Intellectual Property from 1545 to 1787," *Journal of Patent Office Society*, xxvi (1944), 711 ff.

R. Peterson and D. Berger: "Cycles in Symbol Reproduction: The Case of Popular Music," *American Sociological Review*, xl (1975), 158–73

E.W. Rothenbuhler and J.W. Dimmick: "Popular Music: Concentration and Diversity in the Industry, 1974–1980," *Journal of Communication*, xxxii/1 (March 1982), 143–9

S. Frith: "Copyright and the Music Business," *Popular Music* vii (1988), 57–75

P. Jaszi: *The Construction of Authorship: Textual Appropriate in Law and Literature* (Durham, NC, 1994)

J.D. Brinson and M.F. Radcliffe: *An Intellectual Property Law Primer for Multimedia and Web Developers* (1996), <http://w2.eff.org/Censorship/Academic_edu/CAF/law/multimedia-handbook>

P. Jaszi: "Caught in the Net of Copyright," *Oregon Law Review* lxxv (Spring 1996), 299–307

J. Boyle: "A Politics of Intellectual Property: Environmentalism for the Net?" *Duke Law Journal*, xlvii/1 (Oct 1997), 87–116

M. Kretschmer, G.M. Klimis, and R. Wallis: "The Changing Location of Intellectual Property Rights in Music: A Study of Music Publishers, Collecting Societies and Media Conglomerates," *Prometheus*, xvii/2 (1999), 163–86

B.H. Bagdikian: *Media Monopoly* (Boston, 2000)

S. Frith and L. Marsall, eds.: *Music and Copyright*, 2nd ed. (New York, 2004)

C. May: "The Denial of History: Reification, Intellectual Property Rights and the Lessons of the Past," *Capital and Class*, xxx/1 (Spring 2006), 33–56

IMF [International Monetary Fund]: *Committee of Balance of Payments Statistics, Annual Report* (2007)

C. Doctorow: "Why I Copyfight" (2008), <http://www.locusmag.com/Features/2008/11/cory-doctorow-why-i-copyfight.html>

L.R. Hefter and R.D. Litowitz: "Overview: What is Intellectual Property?" *Intellectual Property Law Dictionary*, ed. R. Gader-Shafran (New York, 2008), xvii–xxxvi

US General Accounting Office: *Enforcement Efforts* (March 2008)

US General Accounting Office: *Intellectual Property: Federal Enforcement Has Generally Increased, But Assessing Performance Could Strengthen Law* (11 March 2008), <http://www.gao.gov/products/GAO-08-157>

Electronic Frontiers Foundation: "Unintended Consequences: Twelve years under the DMCA" (March 2010), <http://www.eff.org/wp/unintended-consequences-seven-years-under-dmca>

P. Burkart: *Music and Cyberliberties* (Middletown, CT, 2010)

Electronic Frontiers Foundation: "Patent Busting's most Wanted" [n.d.], <http://w2.eff.org/patent/wanted/prior.php?p=clearchannel>

PATRICK BURKART

Interior Salish. Native American group of the North American plateau; *see* FLATHEAD.

Interlochen [National School Music Camp, Interlochen Arts Academy, Interlochen College of Creative Arts]. Summer music camp, year-round arts academy, and arts college for adults located at Interlochen, Michigan, all known as "Interlochen." Under the leadership of Joseph E. Maddy and Thaddeus P. Giddings, with support from the Music Supervisors National Conference, Interlochen was established as the National High School Orchestra Camp in Interlochen, Michigan in 1927. It was expanded to include instrumental and vocal music education and renamed the National Music Camp in 1928. It soon began to receive support from the University of Michigan School of Music (1930), and from individuals and corporations. This support, together with a renowned faculty and radio broadcasts by NBC and ABC from the 1930s through the 1950s, helped Interlochen become a preeminent center for summer music instruction. In 1962 the Interlochen Arts Academy was established as the nation's first independent boarding school for the arts. It offers comprehensive college-preparatory academics along with rigorous arts instruction. In 1963 Interlochen also launched an FM public radio station, WIAA, which later affiliated with National Public Radio. The Interlochen College of Creative Arts was established in 2004 to provide education in the arts for adults.

BIBLIOGRAPHY
T.A. Brandt: "Summer Music Camps: a Historical Perspective," *Bulletin of Historical Research in Music Education*, ix/2 (1988), 119–30

D. Boal: *Interlochen: a Home for the Arts* (Ann Arbor, 2001)

P.M. Hash: "National High School Orchestra 1926–1936," *JRME*, lvii/1 (2009), 50–72

ROBERT A. AMCHIN

Intermedia art. The term intermedia art describes creative work that makes artistic connections between disciplines. When used in contrast to "multimedia" it is meant to imply a sense of integration of diverse media rather than just the presence of multiple media. The term came into prominence through a 1965 article by the Fluxus artist Dick Higgins and was used to characterize a large body of work that did not fit into discrete studio art practices. Increasingly, intermedia art has grown to incorporate digital and emerging technologies and to rely on the ability for digital data to be easily mapped from one medium (e.g. visual image or sound) to another.

See also EXPERIMENTAL MUSIC THEATER; FLUXUS; NEW MEDIA; PERFORMANCE ART; SOUND INSTALLATION; SOUND SCULPTURE.

BIBLIOGRAPHY
R. Goldberg: *Performance Art—From Futurism to the Future* (London, 2001)

D. Higgins and H. Higgins: "Intermedia," *Leonardo*, xxxiv/1 (2001), 49–54

S. Dixon: *Digital Performance—a History of New Media in Theater, Dance, Performance Art, and Installation* (Cambridge, MA, 2007)

DAVID BITHELL

International Alliance for Women in Music [IAWM]. International organization created in 1994 through the merging of the International Congress on Women in Music (ICWM), American Women Composers (AWC), and the International League of Women Composers (ILWC). The International Alliance for Women in Music aims to build on the work of the three original organizations in celebrating and encouraging the activities of women in music.

The League of Women Composers was founded by composer NANCY VAN DE VATE in 1975 and renamed the International League of Women Composers in 1979. In the words of its founder, the ILWC aimed "to create change and to provide a larger number of women musicians their first real opportunity to enter the professional mainstream." At the time of the merger it was a networking organization operating in over 36 countries, with a well-established journal. The ILWC supervised various projects, including the publication of a directory of music by women, several radio series, an association with Arsis Press (which specializes in the publication of music by women), and a competition for student composers.

American Women Composers was founded by composer Tommie E. Carl in 1976. The organization aimed to promote the work of American women composers by establishing a library of scores (housed at George Washington University), publishing the biannual *AWC NewsForum*, mounting concerts, and producing recordings of music by American women.

The International Congress on Women in Music, initially organized by Jeannie Pool, held its first event in 1980, and thereafter held regular congresses in the United States and Europe consisting of concerts, workshops, and academic papers all aimed at an international exchange of information about music by women. In 1990 the organization merged with the ILWC.

The IAWM publishes the *IAWM Journal* twice a year and, from 1997 to 2008, published a scholarly journal *Women and Music: a Journal of Gender and Culture*. It also sponsors the Search for New Music Competition and administers the Pauline Alderman Award for new research on women in music. It holds regular IAWM congresses (in the tradition of the ICWM) and maintains an extensive website (<http://www.iawm.org>) which includes links to bibliographies, discographies, and course syllabi on women, gender, and music; women in music organizations worldwide; music publishers, archives, and libraries; and many other resources.

BIBLIOGRAPHY

B. Beath: "The International League of Women Composers," *ILWC Journal* (July 1991), 1–2

S. Fry: "The ICWM Legacy: a Chronicle and Review of the International Congress on Women in Music," *IAWM Journal*, i/1 (1995), 4–8

J. Shatin: "American Women Composers, Inc.," *IAWM Journal*, i/1 (1995), 3–4

G. Straughn: "The International League of Women Composers," *IAWM Journal*, i/1 (1995), 8–10

SOPHIE FULLER/R

International Association for the Study of Popular Music—US [IASPM-US]. The US branch of the International Association for the Study of Popular Music (founded in 1981) promotes research and analysis of popular music. With the guidance of organization leaders such as Harris Berger, Paul Fischer, Reebee Garofalo, Charles Hamm, Anahid Kassabian, Portia Maultsby, and Robert Walser, IASPM-US has embraced the philosophy that the study of popular music is both serious and vital, whether in the areas of personal, collective and geographic identity, or in the realms of technology, economics, politics, and sociology. The organization is built on the principle that popular music has been and remains one of the most important and influential forms of art and communication.

IASPM-US, a 501 (c)(3) organization, is an interdisciplinary association that provides a virtual and physical gathering place for kindred spirits from various backgrounds—music, communications, English, history, cultural studies, sociology, and more—to share and explore their common passion for and abiding interest in popular music. In addition, it remains committed to its founders' goal of not limiting membership to those strictly from academic circles; journalists, musicians, independent scholars, and many others are members of the organization, which in 2011 numbered about 300. The diversity of its members' interests, backgrounds, and expertise is one of the association's greatest strengths and enables wide-ranging contributions to popular music studies. In recent years, IASPM-US has made a concerted effort to improve its diversity through roundtable discussions and organizational committees to ensure that it remains inclusive and welcoming to voices from all walks of popular music life.

Through its partnership with Blackwell Publishing, IASPM-US publishes the *Journal of Popular Music Studies* (1988–), a peer-reviewed journal published three times a year that is dedicated to research on popular music throughout the world. It also sponsors an annual book award, renamed The Woody Guthrie Book Award in 2006, which honors an outstanding book in the field of popular music studies written in the English language.

The foundation of IASPM remains its annual conference, which addresses a theme relevant to significant issues in popular music studies or central to musical life in the host city. For instance, the organization's 2010 conference in New Orleans focused on "Births, Stages, Declines, Revivals"; the San Diego conference a year earlier was titled "Don't Fence Me In: Borders, Frontiers and Diasporas." Conferences offer members a chance to present research, hold discussions, and explore issues in the field. Papers address a wide range of topics, from music in advertising or Bollywood film, to an individual recording artist's body of work or trends in a musical genre, to analyses of the specific musical notes used in a pop song. A productive partnership with the Rock and Roll Hall of Fame has provided opportunities for conference goers to hear firsthand from some of the producers and musicians who created music studied by IASPM-US members.

BEVERLY KEEL

International Association of Music Libraries–US Branch [IAML-US]. American branch of an organization that fosters international cooperation and standardization in cataloging, standards of service, personnel training, and the exchange of materials between libraries. Founded in 1951, the International Association of Music Libraries, Archives, and Documentation Centres (IAML) quickly developed national branches serving as professional associations for music librarians within individual countries. The United States had the largest of the national groups by October 1952, according to IAML's first *Bulletin d'Information*, though the exact date of the organization of the IAML-US branch is not documented. At the founding of IAML, however, music librarians in the United States already supported a much larger and vigorous national professional organization—the Music Library Association (MLA, organized in 1931). Historically, MLA has continued to overshadow IAML-US in its membership numbers and professional activity, thus playing a mixed role in the development of IAML-US as a commensal association within American music librarianship.

The two associations share professional goals and interests and "a powerful symbiotic relationship," but there was no formal affiliation for 60 years. In 2011, with the support of the membership of both IAML-US and MLA, MLA became the US Branch of IAML, retaining the name MLA, and IAML-US was dissolved as an independent entity. The legal process of the merger was finalized in 2012. IAML-US had been incorporated as a 501(c)(3) charitable organization in 2002 with a governing board of six officers. It held its business and board meetings during the MLA national conference (winter) and a board meeting during the IAML annual conferences (summer); news was disseminated using the MLA listserv, as well as on its own website. In addition to providing support for the parent IAML organization and its projects at the national level, such as RILM-US, IAML-US activities include the Donated Music Materials Program, facilitating the donation of music materials to libraries in Third World countries. The association also hosted its own international conferences in 1968 (New York), 1983 (Washington), and 2002 (Berkeley).

MANUEL ERVITI

International Church of the Foursquare Gospel. *See* MCPHERSON, AIMEE SEMPLE.

International Clarinet Association. An international organization based in the United States dedicated to "fostering communication and fellowship of clarinetists on a worldwide basis through publishing a quarterly scholarly journal, producing an annual clarinet festival, supporting a research library with materials available to all members, and promoting other endeavors related to the clarinet and clarinet playing." The organization was founded in Denver in 1973 as the International Clarinet Society. In 1981–82 another clarinet group, ClariNetwork International, Inc., was formed, and in 1988 the two organizations merged. The name was officially changed to the International Clarinet Association (ICA) in 1991. In 2011 its membership was about 4000, with 18% of the members coming from outside the United States.

In the fall of 1973, the organization began issuing the quarterly journal *The Clarinet*. Its conferences are held most often in the United States, but increasingly in Canada (since 1978) and Europe (since 1981), with one in Japan in 2005. The conferences offer scholarly papers, performances, and presentations, as well as competitions with prizes, including awards for composition and research, and for performance at the high school, young artist, and orchestral audition levels.

A research and music-lending library is located at the University of Maryland, Special Collections in Performing Arts (originally at the University of Idaho, in Moscow, Idaho). ICA maintains a website with information on its activities (<www.clarinet.org>).

CAROLYN BRYANT

International Composers' Guild. Organization formed in 1921 in New York by Edgard Varèse and Carlos Salzedo to assure performances of contemporary music. Membership was open to composers, who often performed their own music. Concerts were restricted to previously unheard works, a policy that so disturbed some members that they formed the LEAGUE OF COMPOSERS. Before it disbanded in 1927 the guild gave first performances of Varèse's *Hyperprism*, *Octandre* and *Intégrales*, and American premieres of Berg's *Kammerkonzert*, Schoenberg's *Pierrot lunaire*, Stravinsky's *The Wedding*, and Webern's op.5. Guest conductors included Klemperer, Reiner, and Stokowski.

BIBLIOGRAPHY
D.L. Root: *The Performance Guilds of Edgard Varèse* (thesis, U. of Illinois, 1971)
R.A. Lott: "'New Music for New Ears': the International Composers' Guild," *JAMS*, xxxvi/2 (1983), 266–86

RITA H. MEAD/R

International Conference of Symphony and Opera Musicians. Musicians' union for orchestral players, founded in 1962; *see* UNIONS, MUSICIANS.

International Congress on Women in Music. *See* INTERNATIONAL ALLIANCE FOR WOMEN IN MUSIC [IAWM].

International Contemporary Ensemble [ICE]. Chamber ensemble founded in 2001 by the flutist Claire Chase and the composer Huang Ruo. With more than 30 premieres, it has demonstrated the instrumental and organizational flexibility, as well as the musical virtuosity, to perform a broad range of music from the 20th and 21st centuries. It has operated as a collective with Chase as its executive director and the musicians taking responsibility for its management and selecting repertoire and projects. Among the premieres the ICE has presented are works by Georges Aperghis, Julio Estrada, Philippe Manoury, David Lang, and Dia Fujikura. They have also recorded John Adams's *Son of Chamber Symphony* and given multiple US premieres of music by Kaija Saariaho, including her ballet *Maa*. They have engaged conductors and soloists on a performance-by-performance basis and collaborated with Steven Schick, Matthias Pintscher, Ludovic Morlot, Pierre-Laurent Aimard, and Peter Serkin. Their performance history includes a number of Composer Portraits (Miller Theater, Columbia University), the chamber music of Edgard Varèse (Alice Tully Hall, New York, 2010), Mostly Mozart (Lincoln Center, 2010), and the music of Morton Feldman, John Cage, Iannis Xenakis, and Anton Webern (Alice Tully Hall, 2011). In that year ICE created ICElab, an initiative in which small groups from within the ensemble collaborated with six emerging composers to produce 24 evening-length works. The initial concerts were presented free of charge at (le) Poisson Rouge in New York. In 2010 the ensemble was given the American Music Center's Trailblazer Award, and in 2012 Chase was awarded a MacArthur Fellowship.

GEORGE J. GRELLA JR.

International Double Reed Society [IDRS]. International organization established in 1971, dedicated to double reed players, instrument manufacturers, and enthusiasts. The society aims to enhance the art of double reed playing; encourage the performance of double reed literature; improve instruments, tools, and reed-making material; encourage the composition and arranging of music for double reeds; act as a resource for performers; assist teachers and students of double reed instruments; encourage cooperation and an exchange of ideas between the music industry and the society; and foster a world-wide communication between double reed musicians (IDRS Constitution, 1997). IDRS has over 4,400 members from 56 countries. The society's website (www.idrs.org) hosts archives of its publications, conferences, and competitions, along with information on double reed performance, pedagogy, and research.

The society grew out of a thrice-yearly newsletter, *To the World's Bassoonists* (1969–77). In the second year of its existence, a parallel newsletter, *To the World's Oboists* (1972–77), was introduced. In the third year, a scholarly publication was added: *The Journal of the International Double Reed Society* (published annually 1973–99). Beginning in 1978, the two newsletters were combined into *The Double Reed*, published thrice yearly. The *Journal* was discontinued after 1998, in favor of a fourth issue per year of *The Double Reed*.

The society sponsors an annual conference held either in the United States or an international location; in addition to concerts, workshops, and lectures, each conference includes two competitions—the Gillet-Fox International Competition (for bassoonists and oboists under age 31) and the Young Artist Competition (for those younger than age 22). IDRS also maintains diplomatic relations with other national double reed organizations from around the world.

SARAH DETERS RICHARDSON

International Exhibition of Arts, Manufacturers, and Products of the Soil and Mine. Exhibition held in Philadelphia, 1876, known as the Centennial Exhibition. *See* CENTENNIAL EXHIBITION.

International Federation for Choral Music [IFCM]. A non-profit membership organization that was founded in 1982 by seven national and international choral organizations from five continents: American Choral Directors Association (United States), A Coeur Joie International (France), Arbeitsgemeinschaft Europäischer Chorverbände (Germany), Asociación Interamericana de Directores de Coros (Latin America), European Choral Association—Europa Cantal, formerly Europa Cantat—Federation Européenne des Jeunes Chorales (Europe), Japan Choral Association (Japan), and Nordisk Korforum NKK (Scandinavia).

The purpose of this newly formed organization was to facilitate communication and exchange between choral musicians throughout the world. Over the past 29 years IFCM has created a variety of projects to fulfill its mission: the tri-annual World Symposia on Choral Music, World Youth Choir, Conductors Without Borders, World Day of Choral Singing, conducting masterclasses,

and publications such as the *International Choral Bulletin, World Choral Census, Cantemus*, and *CarminaMundi*.

In November 2010, IFCM established its first project with China, the *11th International Choral Festival and IFCM World Choral Summit*. Among other things, the project focused on bringing executives from 30 national and international choral organizations to share ideas from their respective choral traditions and to open the windows of opportunity for the world to know and experience the choral music of China.

IFCM is the official representative of choral music on the International Music Council of the UNESCO. In 2011, IFCM numbers more than 2000 direct members on all continents, divided into four categories: individuals, choirs, organizations, and businesses.

MICHAEL J. ANDERSON

International Horn Society [IHS]. International organization dedicated to horn performance, teaching, composition, and research, and the preservation and promotion of the horn as a musical instrument. The society was formed in June 1970 at the Second International Horn Workshop, in Tallahassee, Florida. It began publishing a refereed journal, *The Horn Call*, in Feb 1971; since its inception the journal has grown from a biannual to a quarterly publication. The society holds workshops, lectures, and seminars; awards grants and scholarships; encourages new compositions and arrangements for the horn; and presents honors and recognition for distinctive service related to the horn. It also maintains the IHS Archive, housed in the Sibley Music Library at the Eastman School of Music, as a repository for documents and memorabilia related to the history and development of the society, as well as for specially donated material relating to the horn. Its website <http://www.hornsociety.org> contains information on society activities and events of interest to horn players. IHS has over 3500 members from 55 countries, including university teachers, students, horn designers/builders, composers, music libraries, music publishers, internationally renowned touring artists, symphony musicians, and amateur players.

BIBLIOGRAPHY
W. C. Robinson: "Formation of the International Horn Society," *The Horn Call*, i/2, (May, 1971), 40

SARAH DETERS RICHARDSON

International League of Women Composers [ILWC]. *See* INTERNATIONAL ALLIANCE FOR WOMEN IN MUSIC.

International Music Company. Firm of music publishers. It was founded in New York in 1941 by A.W. Haendler (1894–1978). International Music Company (IMC) publishes solo instrumental music, chamber music, vocal music, and miniature scores of works in the standard repertory. After Haendler's death Frank Marx became head of the company. Marx served as president until IMC was sold to the Bourne Company in 1979.

FRANCES BARULICH/R

International Society for Contemporary Music [ISCM]. Founded on 11 August 1922 and inspired by that year's Salzburg Festival of Contemporary Music, the ISCM aimed to override national barriers and personal prejudices in order to support and promote living composers' works through annual World Music Days festivals. The society served as an important channel for composers to engage in the international exchange of new music, especially during the Cold War. ISCM was first headquartered in London with music critic Edward J. Dent as president (1922–38, 1945–7). Although an early draft of the organization's constitution specified that only works by European composers would be considered for festival performances, American composers gained equal acceptance in 1923 after Oscar Sonneck endorsed a petition for an amendment. In 1954, the US branch of the ISCM officially merged with the League of Composers.

American composers working in the 1920s and 1930s gained invaluable exposure through ISCM concerts, and the festival's first few decades witnessed important performances of works by Emerson Whithorne, Louis Gruenberg, and Frederick Jacobi. Other significant premieres at festivals throughout the century include Schoenberg's *Erwartung* (Prague, 1924), Webern's Concerto for Nine Instruments Op. 24 (Prague, 1935), Berg's Violin Concerto (Barcelona, 1936), and Boulez's *Le marteau sans maître* (Baden-Baden, 1955). The United States has hosted the World Music Days festival three times, in New York (1941), Berkeley (1942), and Boston (1976). In 1949, ISCM published the first and only issue of the journal, *Music Today*, and in 1991 founded a new journal, *World New Music Magazine*.

BIBLIOGRAPHY

N. Slonimsky: *Music Since 1900* (New York, 1937, 5/1994)

E. Wellesz: "E. J. Dent and the International Society for Contemporary Music," *Music Review*, vii (1946), 205–8

C. Oja: *Making Music Modern: New York in the 1920s* (New York, 2000)

LINCOLN BALLARD

International Society for Music Education [ISME]. International professional organization for music education. ISME was founded in Brussels in 1953 during the International Conference on the Role and Place of Music in the Education of Youth and Adults. The conference was organized under the auspices of the United Nations Educational, Scientific, and Cultural Organization (UNESCO), in collaboration with the International Music Council. The society's mission is to build a worldwide community of music educators, foster intercultural understanding and cooperation, and nurture and promote music education worldwide. Its seven commissions are: Research; Community Music Activity; Early Childhood Music Education; Education of the Professional Musician; Music Policy: Cultural, Educational and Mass Media; Music in Schools and Teacher Education; and Music in Special Education, Music Therapy, and Music Medicine.

North Americans have played important roles in the society. Vanett Lawler, Charles Seeger, and Arnold Walter contributed significantly to its founding. The office of President was held by Arnold Walter (1953–56), Karl Ernst (1964–68), Robert Werner (1984–86), and Giacomo Oliva (2002–04); Secretary General by Vanett Lawler (1953–55) and Joan Therens (1992–2000); and Treasurer by Vanett Lawler (1953–1972) and Robert Werner (1988–97). Honorary life members from North America are James Carlsen, Paul Lehman, Donald Robinson, Joan Therens, and Robert Werner. ISME biennial conferences in North America were held in Interlochen, Michigan (1966), London, Ontario (1978), Eugene, Oregon (1984), Tampa, Florida (1994), and Edmonton, Alberta (2000). Of the 1553 ISME members in 2009, 404 were from North America. Two North American organizations are ISME affiliates: The National Association for Music Education (NAfME) and the Canadian Music Educators Association.

MARIE McCARTHY

International Sweethearts of Rhythm. Big band. One of the most celebrated all-female bands of the 1940s, this group was founded in 1937 by Laurence Clifton Jones as a fundraising initiative for the Piney Woods Country Life School in Piney Woods, MI. The Sweethearts' international theme referred to the racial and ethnic variety of its members, which included African American, biracial, Latino, Asian, and Native American women. Although the group initially played for regional dances and games, by 1940 they had made successful debuts at the Apollo Theater in New York and the Howard Theater in Washington.

In 1941 the band left the school and moved to northern Virginia where it worked with a number of arrangers and music directors to make the transition to a professional band. Anne Mae Winburn, who had garnered a reputation singing with and leading male bands throughout the Midwest, served as the band's leader from this year until its demise in the late 1940s. The band included a number of professional musicians during this period, notably the tenor saxophonist Vi (Viola) Burnside, the trumpeter Tiny (Ernestine) Davis, and the alto saxophonist Roz (Rosalind) Cron. Beginning in 1943 its membership routinely included one or two white women, who passed as African American in an attempt to skirt Jim Crow laws in the southern United States. Rumors of their integration won these white musicians admirers in some circles, but also added to the dangers they already faced as members of a black band traveling in the South; along with some of the lighter-skinned African Americans, who were mistaken for being white, they were harassed and even arrested. The popularity of the group's live and recorded performances, however, led to the band being one of the few predominantly black all-female bands to be featured in soundies. Their biggest hits from this period included their renditions of such standards as "Tuxedo Junction" and "Sweet Georgia Brown" as well as an original, "Jump Children."

In 1945 the group participated in a six-month European USO tour, which marked the first time African American women musicians toured with the USO and was highly successful. Unfortunately it also marked the

Tiny Davis, trumpet, with the International Sweethearts of Rhythm in a still from That Man of Mine, *1946. (Film still, William Alexander, Alexander Productions)*

swan song for the group. The next few years were defined by numerous personnel changes, notably the departure of the group's star soloist Davis, and poor management. It disbanded in 1949.

SELECTED RECORDINGS
Hot Licks: 1944–1946 (Sounds of Yesteryear, 2006)

BIBLIOGRAPHY
D.A. Handy: *The International Sweethearts of Rhythm: the Ladies Jazz Band from Piney Woods Country Life School* (Lanham, MD, 1998)
S. Tucker: *Swing Shift: All-Girl Bands of the 1940s* (Durham, 2000)
K. McGee: *Some Liked it Hot: Jazz Women in Film and Television 1928–1959* (Middletown, 2009)

TAMMY L. KERNODLE

International Trumpet Guild [ITG]. International organization established in 1974 by Charles Gorham and Robert Nagel with the mission "to promote communications among trumpet players around the world and to improve the artistic level of performance, teaching, and literature associated with the trumpet." ITG welcomes professional and amateur performers, teachers, students, manufacturers, publishers, and others interested in belonging to an organization dedicated to the trumpet profession. Its members number more than 5000 individuals from 56 countries.

From 1975 through 1982, ITG published the quarterly *ITG Newsletter* and the annual *International Trumpet Guild Journal*. In 1982, the newsletter was discontinued and replaced by the quarterly *ITG Journal*. In additional to its scholarly publications, the ITG hosts an annual conference, the first of which was held in Bloomington, Indiana, in 1975, as well as many competitions and conferences for trumpet players of all levels and interests, including the Carmine Caruso International Jazz Trumpet Solo Competition and the Ellsworth Smith International Trumpet Solo Competition. ITG underwrites scholarly works on the trumpet and sponsors new compositions for trumpet. It has affiliate chapters throughout the United States and in many other countries.

BIBLIOGRAPHY
D.K. Dunnick: "Twenty Years of the International Trumpet Guild" *ITG Journal* xx/3 (1996), 42–47

SARAH DETERS RICHARDSON

Internet, the. The inter-connection of personal and institutional computers and computer networks known as "the Internet" forms the backbone of much contemporary digital communications. The World Wide Web (WWW)—the linked collection of various digital texts, images, audio, and video, accessible via a web browser—has become a primary means for the promotion, production, distribution, consumption of music. The WWW is also an important forum for discourse about music. Since the rise of Internet Communication Technologies (ICTs) novel practices have emerged, such as widespread sharing of amateur and user-created music-related content (and corollary attempts by incumbent and existing media companies to generate profit from such activity). Additionally, musical practices that predate the Internet have been magnified and intensified, such as sharing music without regard for profit, word-of-mouth promotion, and the commodification of ancillary merchandise.

1. Promotion. (i) Websites. (ii) Social networks. (iii) Video. 2. Journalism. 3. Fandom. (i) Fan production. 4. Information efficiency. (i) Databases. (ii) Communication. 5. Distribution/consumption. 6. Research. (i) Scholarly publishing. (ii) Pedagogy.

1. PROMOTION.
(i) Websites. Websites, essentially linked digital documents that often contain text, images, audio, and increasingly video, have become fundamental to the promotional strategies of most musicians. Websites are typically used in combination with traditional forms of broadcast and print media. In the early years of the WWW artist websites were largely text-based with few images. They contained biographical and discographical information, appearance schedules, and discussion forums through which fans and artists could communicate with and among each other. As of 2011, following a decade of improvements in Internet speed and network capacity, most websites included images, video, and sound that augmented greater interactivity in the form of live chat, webcasts, and expanded discussion forums. Websites that are said to represent a musician's or record label's promotional strategies are often explicitly denoted as "official." In contrast, many "unofficial" websites are maintained by fan clubs or individuals; such sites may or may not carry the approval of the artist. Whereas mainstream popular music artists' websites have come to mimic broadcast media (more information-driven with less fan/artist interactivity), musicians who have little or no affiliation with mainstream record labels and management often rely on the interactive possibilities of the WWW to facilitate word-of-mouth promotion and information distribution.

(ii) Social networks. "Social media," a catch-all term that emerged in the first decade of the 2000s, describes both commercial and non-commercial online services that focus primarily on facilitating connections between users through the sharing of personal information, images, and links to other web content. Growing out of the widespread usage of MYSPACE (<http://www.myspace.com/music/>) in the early 2000s, musicians and promoters embraced social media of all forms to their online promotional strategies. By 2010 *Facebook* (<http://www.facebook.com>) had become popular among musicians, venues, record companies, websites, and media companies as a promotion vehicle, offering pages where fans could interact among one another in ways similar to the earliest website-based forums. Some *Facebook* artist pages are "official," as in the official websites above; others are maintained by fans. *Twitter* (<http://www.twitter.com>), a service for short and timely public and/or private communication is used by artists to update fans

about their musical progress, tour reflections, and personal thoughts.

(iii) Video. Since the 1980s, music VIDEO has played a central role in the promotion of music, especially mainstream popular music. By the mid-2000s the video sharing site *YouTube* (<http://www.youtube.com>), which was initially driven by users who submitted their own amateur video creations, had begun to play an increasingly important role in music promotional strategies. *YouTube* has since grown into a major media venue with record label pages that feature official music videos, independent artists' video work, live streaming music events, and concert footage posted by music fans. Though *YouTube* dominates the online video realm and has developed agreements with many major video content providers, other video sites also compete for music fans' attention, such as *Vimeo* (<http://www.vimeo.com>), *Hulu* (<http://www.hulu.com>), and *Dailymotion* (<http://www.dailymotion.com>).

2. JOURNALISM. The World Wide Web has also become a central venue for music journalism. (*See* CRITICISM.) Most of the major print publications covering all genres of music maintain websites that offer "web-only" content in addition to the content of their print publications; examples include *Rolling Stone* (<http://www.rollingstone.com>), *DownBeat* (<http://www.downbeat.com>), and *American Record Guide* (<http://www.americanrecordguide.com/>). Additionally, several publications that originated online have emerged as leaders in both mainstream and alternative arts news and criticism, such as *Pitchfork* (<http://www.pitchfork.com>) and *PopMatters* (<http://www.popmatters.com>). Content featured on such sites may include video clips of interviews, concerts, or promotional materials; extended text of interviews that may have appeared in a print publication; image galleries of musicians and events; and advance releases of upcoming singles. One of the challenges faced by traditional print media, not only music-related, has been the rapidity with which new content can be added to a website given that online publications need not adhere to traditional publication deadlines. Such a change has resulted in many publications attempting to make up for lost print sales by offering access to premium web content for a fee or accompanying a print subscription. The individualized nature of much online media consumption has hastened a somewhat fragmented musical discourse; many sites offer only coverage of one particular genre or style of music or particular "scene." However, traditional print magazines (and their online variants), which traditionally cover a wider range of musical styles, still retain a certain amount of authority in relation to online-only publications, though this relationship is changing rapidly.

3. FANDOM. For fans, the World Wide Web is an endless resource of information, media, and opportunities to communicate about music. There are countless fan-run blogs that range from personal reflections on music

tastes to "citizen journalism," including concert and recording reviews produced by individuals and small fan groups; many now authoritative sites have their beginnings as such endeavors, such as *Stereogum* (<http://stereogum.com>) and *PopMatters* (<http://www.popmatters.com>). There are also numerous music-related discussion forums, and, mimicking offline socializing, discussions about music will often take place in non-music-related online forums. Social networks, as noted above, also play a significant role in word-of-mouth promotion of artists and events, and they represent one of the dominant areas in which fans discuss and critique music.

(i) Fan production. The increased availability of music online, combined with the increasing capacity for music consumers to produce their own creations and distribute these online, has led to a much broader and highly visible practice of reconfiguring existing musical texts. Often called MASH-UPS (combining existing digital musical texts to create a new text), these new pieces are circulated through blogs, fan forums, social networks, and video hosting sites. Sites such as *MixMatchMusic* (<http://www.mixmatchmusic.com>) and *Turntable.fm* (<http://www.turntable.fm>) encourage online musical collaborations ranging from sharing original musical creations to "live" mixing and performing of musical pieces. Creators usually seek nothing more than moderate notoriety for their contributions and rarely if ever seek to be remunerated. Such "user-generated content" often makes use of existing musical texts and circulates without permission from rights holders. At times creators are threatened with legal action. *YouTube*'s initial success was largely a result of its capitalization on the labor of unpaid amateur video makers whose creations would sometimes include copyrighted works. By 2010, as a result of increased industry pressures to prohibit use of copyrighted materials, *YouTube* and other such sites were actively policing content for copyrighted images and music.

4. INFORMATION EFFICIENCY.
(i) Databases. A variety of Internet-based music information technologies have emerged. Meta-data databases store information about CDs and digital music. Examples include *Gracenote*, a commercial database service formerly known as CDDB (<http://www.gracenote.com>), and *FreeDB* (<http://www.freedb.org/>) and *MusicBrainz* (<http://musicbrainz.org/>), which are free and open-source database services. These databases assist users in categorizing their digital media and managing information about music in their collections. Many contemporary computer media players integrate such databases into their software.

(ii) Communication. As with all modern industries, email and instantaneous communications such as Internet Relay Chat have had a profound impact on the organization of music production, from scheduling recording sessions to the transmission of recorded music files across great distances in short time periods. ICTs

have thus increased efficiency in collaborative projects (e.g., musicians need not be in the same location at the same time for recording or mixing sessions).

5. DISTRIBUTION/CONSUMPTION. Since the emergence of the MP3, a form of digital compression that decreases the size of a digital music file, one of the primary uses of the Internet has been to distribute music. There are two predominant forms of "legitimate" distribution featuring agreements with content providers and copyright holders to sell digital music files: (1) music download, where a user purchases a digital copy he or she can store locally on his or her hard disk; (2) music streaming, where a user plays music directly from the Internet without storing a local copy. The former usually involves a one-time fee per music track or album and as of 2011 is dominated by Apple's *iTunes Music Store* (<http://www.itunes.com>) and Amazon's *Amazon MP3* (<http://www.amazon.com>). The latter may be a free service supported by advertising or a paid subscription service. Such services include *Grooveshark* (<http://www.grooveshark.com>), *Pandora* (<http://www.pandora.com>), or *Spotify* (<http://www.spotify.com>). There are also online radio stations, which may deliver simultaneous webcasts of an existing commercial or non-commercial FM or AM radio broadcast, or a "web only" broadcast. Many online radio stations archive their programs and offer these as downloadable MP3s and in most cases online radio is freely accessible. For forms of "illegitimate" online music distribution, *see* PIRACY.

Music is also transferred via online chat and email, a one-to-one transfer by which users send each other digital music files. Internet forums, file hosting services, and "MP3 blogs" are all forms of distribution that make music available as a direct download (i.e., not through P2P file sharing but through the download of files hosted on a server).

The distribution of music without the permission of copyright holders constitutes one of the most pressing debates surrounding the relationship between music and the Internet, with industry lobby groups suggesting that the size and scope of sharing are justification for their efforts to curtail the activity through legal, discursive, and technological means, regardless of whether individuals or groups are seeking to profit via sharing. Artists are divided as to whether FILE SHARING helps or hinders their ability to profit from their music careers. Some are of the opinion that widespread exposure facilitated by file sharing creates greater opportunities for live performances while others suggest that the practice detracts from record sales and licensing revenues. Music fans appear to favor the practice, as evidenced by the high levels of adoption of various P2P technologies.

6. RESEARCH.
(i) Scholarly publishing. As with all scholarly disciplines, the Internet has impacted the administration, organization, and dissemination of music scholarship. ICTs have facilitated greater, though not universal, access to scholarly publications about music. Most are online versions of print journals published by for-profit entities

and available only to those who pay for access individually or through institutional fees. However, there are also several open access music journals that operate from the perspective that scholarly work ought to be freely and universally accessible to anyone with an Internet connection. A similar egalitarian perspective underpins many online encyclopedias and dictionaries and in the adoption of blogs by some individual music scholars. The *All Music Guide* (<http://www.allmusic.com>) and *Wikipedia* (<http://wikipedia.org>), which contains a vast corpus of music entries of varying quality, are two examples of freely accessible reference sites. *All Music Guide* also functions as a music news site that features recording reviews and articles. *Wikipedia* articles are created and maintained entirely by users of the service.

(ii) Pedagogy. At the time of writing, music teaching faces challenges with regard to the use of copyrighted music on class websites. Licensing fees often prohibit posting copyrighted music on educational websites, but library CD collections often do not offer the diverse selection of music used by music instructors, nor are they always able to respond in a timely manner to the diversity of music taught in schools today. At the same time, the flexibility of fair use or fair dealing provisions for education is under threat from intensified efforts to expand the scope of intellectual property rights to require greater licensing fees for a wider variety of uses of recorded and printed music.

BIBLIOGRAPHY

L. Lessig: *Free Culture: How Big Media Uses Technology and the Law to Lock Down Culture and Control Creativity* (New York, 2004)

S. Vaidhyanathan: *The Anarchist in the Library: How the Clash Between Freedom and Control is Hacking the Real World and Crashing the System* (New York, 2004)

W. Wang: *Steal This File Sharing Book: What They Won't Tell You About File Sharing* (San Francisco, 2004)

K. Mcleod: *Freedom of Expression®: Overzealous Copyright Bozos and other Enemies of Creativity* (New York, 2005)

M. Strangelove: *Empire of the Mind: Digital Piracy and the Anti-Capitalist Movement* (Toronto, 2005)

P. Burkart: *Digital Music Wars: Ownership and Control of the Celestial Jukebox* (Lanham, MD, 2006)

F. Vincent: *Myspace for Musicians* (Boston, 2007)

P. Burkart: *Music and Cyberliberties* (Middletown, CT, 2010)

PAUL A. AITKEN

Interscope. Record label. Interscope was founded in 1990 in Los Angeles by producer Jimmy Iovine and Ted Field. Warner Music Group initially purchased 50% of the label and distributed material through Atlantic Records; albums by Gerardo, Primus, and Marky Mark and the Funky Bunch were among the first releases. Its first large scale success came from promoting "gangsta rap" in the early 1990s, largely through a partnership with Death Row Records, founded by former football player Marion "Suge" Knight and rapper/producer Dr. Dre (Andre Young). Dr. Dre's debut album, *The Chronic* (1992), would be a huge success for the label, as would the Dr. Dre-produced Snoop Doggy Dogg debut *Doggystyle* (1993). In 1996, Universal Music Group purchased Interscope and in 1999, the label merged with Geffen and A&M records.

Interscope has worked with a number of rap subsidiary labels, including Dr. Dre's Aftermath Entertainment (founded in 1996 after he left Death Row), Eminem's Shady Entertainment, and 50 Cent's G-Unit Records. The label has released and distributed a variety of artists and groups including Nine Inch Nails, Marilyn Manson, No Doubt, Common, Black Eyed Peas, The Game, La Roux, James Morrison, One Republic, U2, Timbaland, Sting, Soulja Boy, Limp Bizkit, 2Pac, Jurassic 5, and Lady Gaga.

BIBLIOGRAPHY

R. Marriott: "Gangsta, Gangsta: The Sad, Violent Parable of Death Row Records," *The Vibe History of Hip Hop* (New York, 1999), 319–25

S.C. Watkins: *Hip-hop Matters* (Boston, 2005), 33–53

JUSTIN A. WILLIAMS

Intertextuality. A term coined by literary critic Julia Kristeva that encompasses the entire range of interrelationships between texts, from direct incorporation or reworking through shared conventions or language. It posits a view of texts as responses to other texts, embedded in a perpetual stream of interrelated texts. Applied to music since the 1980s, it is a broader term than BORROWING, which typically focuses on the use in one piece of one or more elements taken from another. By embracing everything from QUOTATION to stylistic ALLUSION and use of conventions, an intertextual approach can address the entire range of ways a musical work refers to or draws on other musical works. Some writers propose a more limited definition, using "intertextuality" for direct incorporation and "hypertextuality" for other forms of modeling a new text on an existing one (Lacasse, 2000).

The related terms "intertexturality" (Hertz, 1993) and "intermusicality" (Monson, 1996) have been proposed to focus on the characteristics of music as a sounding art and to avoid the implications of the word "textual" that music can be reduced to a text that must be read. The former allows discussion of relationships between music, the other arts, and the realm of ideas, and the latter focuses on music as improvised, performed, and heard.

See also POSTMODERNISM.

BIBLIOGRAPHY

GMO (J.P. Burkholder)

D.M. Hertz: *Angels of Reality: Emersonian Unfoldings in Wright, Stevens, and Ives* (Carbondale and Edwardsville, IL, 1993)

I. Monson: *Saying Something: Jazz Improvisation and Interaction* (Chicago, 1996)

S. Lacasse: "Intertextuality and Hypertextuality in Recorded Popular Music," *The Musical Work: Reality or Invention?*, ed. Michael Talbot (Liverpool, 2000), 35–58

R. Middleton: "Work-in(g)-Practice: Configurations of the Popular Music Intertext," *The Musical Work: Reality or Invention?*, ed. Michael Talbot (Liverpool, 2000), 59–87

For further bibliography *see* BORROWING.

J. PETER BURKHOLDER

Intertribal powwow. *See* POWWOW.

Inuit [Eskimo]. The inhabitants of the circumpolar region; around 50,000 live in Alaska, and this article refers specifically to the music of the Alaskan people. The traditional reliance of the coastal Inuit on sea mammals as a source of food, clothing, and other materials, and of the inland Inuit on caribou hunting, have been the principal determinants of their ceremonialism. Although there are considerable differences in culture and race between the Inuit and Native Americans, the music of the two groups is stylistically related.

1. Genres and functions. 2. Instruments. 3. Style.

1. GENRES AND FUNCTIONS. Most indigenous explanations of songs, dances, and drumming distinguish between social, secular, and religious functions. St. Lawrence Islanders refer to *ilaegaek* as "nighttime singing" or shamanistic song, and to *aetok* as "daytime singing" or secular song used for entertainment (Hughes, 1960, p.304). A similar distinction is reported for the Northwest; of the four generic categories of song recognized there, three are secular and the fourth is literally translated as "songs of group of things done in a trance": (1) *qitkutim atuutaa*, game songs; (2) *unipkaaq atuutilik*, songs in stories; (3) *uamipiaq*, dance songs; (4) *angaiyutikun atuutit*, ceremonial dance songs (Johnston, "The Eskimo Songs of Northwestern Alaska," p.8). By the 1970s the last category had been subdivided into six subgenres: (i) *kiapsaq*, whalers' spinning-top dance songs; (ii) *tohoyaqhuuqaun*, puppet ceremony dance songs; (iii) *nalukataun*, whalers' skin-toss dances; (iv) *uingarung*, whalers' masquerade dance songs; (v) *kigugiyataun*, northern lights dance songs; (vi) *kalukhaq*, box-drum dance songs. Most of these are mod-

ified fragments of such larger ceremonials as the Messenger Feast (*kalukhaq*) or whaling rituals (first four categories), which flourished in the 19th century.

In coastal communities of the Northwest, communal religious festivals were related to whaling and centered around the hunting-group leader (*ümealiq*) and his crew or lodge. In the interior similar lodges were traditionally associated with the annual caribou drive. A large cycle of songs was sung by the *ümealiq*, the *kaakliq* (an older, more experienced whaler who was also often a shaman), and the crew to accompany each stage of the whaling operation (Spencer, 1959). Songs thought to ensure the efficacy of the harpoon, lances, lines, and floats; to control the weather; and to attract the whale were also sung. The season ended with a spring whaling feast. Special dances performed in recent decades in Point Hope on New Year's Eve and at the June Whaling Feast derive from these practices. Traditional festivals involved social dancing, distribution of whale meat, ceremonial masked dances, and, at their culmination, the *nalukataq* or blanket toss, in which an individual was thrown into the air from a walrus skin to the accompaniment of a song.

The second important ceremonial of the Northwest was the social Messenger Feast, last held at Wainwright in 1914–15. This event, which has some features in common with the Northwest Coast Indian potlatch, demanded a long period of preparation to amass food and gifts, prepare songs, dances, and costumes, build a *karigi* (dance house), and train participants. Songs of invitation bearing a symbolically marked staff were sent by messenger from one village to another. The festival

Inuit dancers performing at the Alaska Native Heritage Center, Anchorage. (Nativestock.com/Marilyn Angel Wynn)

Inuit men with wolf dancers. (Nativestock.com/Marilyn Angel Wynn)

included the formal announcing and greeting of guests, pretended insults between the messengers and the chief host, footraces between the guest and host camps, stomping dances accompanied by a box drum, distribution of gifts, dances by hosts and guests either separately or together, a soccer game, and social dances. A contemporary box-drum dance cycle at Wainwright has evolved from this feast.

In the Southwest whaling rituals culminated in the annual Bladder Festival. For approximately one month the spirits of animals taken during the year's hunt were honored, and through the action of returning the bladders to the sea the rebirth of the spirits in new creatures was requested. Rival groups practiced new songs in darkness until correct performance was assured; wild parsnip was burned to the accompaniment of a special song as a purification rite. Modified parts of this festival continued into the 1970s in some communities (e.g., the April Walrus Carnival and June Whaling Feast in Savoonga).

An ancient Feast for the Dead shared some characteristics with the Bladder Festival: the careful preparation of ceremonial songs in the darkness of the dance house, and the singing of songs to honor the spirits of the dead and encourage their return. Ghost songs unassociated with dance continue to constitute a special repertory in this area, but their relationship to earlier ritual is unclear.

A third ceremonial in the Southwest and on St. Lawrence Island is the Inviting-in Feast, which relates to some extent to the northern Messenger Feast. Originally involving elaborate wooden masks that represent animal protectors (Nelson, 1899, p.358), these dances are now intercommunity events at which dance teams display story dancing.

Central to ceremonial and recreational life in the 19th century was the *karigi* (also called *kashgee*, *kashim*, *kudyigi*, or *kazigi*), a large house built either temporarily for the winter season or remaining permanently in the community (as at Point Hope). In southern areas the semi-subterranean building was a men's house for hunt-related chores, meetings, socializing, bathing, and sleeping, while in the north women were more freely admitted. Shamanistic performances and ritual and recreational dancing occurred there.

In addition to the role that music played in these festivals, songs could be used for many non-secular purposes to extend personal power. Power songs were sung to attempt control of the weather, to encourage game, to seek protection in conjunction with amulets, or to facilitate shamanistic actions. There were songs designed to prevent conception, to ease the birth of a child, to raise a boat or house, to cure illness, to find objects, and to effect love magic. Such songs were personal property, not always the shaman's, and could be sold. The power of such songs was feared; children were told not to learn the songs sung by the shaman lest they themselves become imbued with shamanistic power.

Secular, recreational, non-ceremonial songs and dances are either composed or, in some instances, improvised. In northwestern communities dances for which the choreography is fixed, taught, and rehearsed by dance teams are called *sayuun*. This category includes specific items such as the women's bench dance, often with paddling motions (*taliq* in Point Hope, *paagurraqtuq* in Wainwright). The permanently assigned motions that accompany the drum rhythms and musical motives of a song are often devised by the composer's male hunting partner or trading associate. The *atuutipiaq* dances, on the other hand, have freely improvised motions, often including jumping or stomping for men and knee-bending or arm-curving for women. Both dance categories frequently imitate hunting or other subsistence activities. The Southwest region does not recognize a division between fixed-motion and freely improvised dances, but rather classes dance styles according to the body position of the dancers. The men's *arula* is done in a kneeling position; during an *arula* performance women do a gentler style known as *putuluteng*, standing behind and to the side of the men with eyes downcast. The *pualla* is a men's stomping dance; the *talirluteng* (like the Inupiaq *taliq*) is a seated bench dance with arm motions executed both by men and women.

In the game-song category juggling songs are the most widespread. These are characterized by texts containing sexual allusions and indelicate references, features shared by juggling songs in northern Canada. In a hopping game called *mitquliksraq*, in which opposing lines of boys and girls hop toward each other and try to break through the linked arms of the other team, the hopping is timed to the asymmetrical rhythm of the song's words (Johnston, *Eskimo Music*, 1976, p.57). A song also accompanies *annami-analuuraq*, a chasing game. Short chants accompany string games, in which cat's-cradle figures represent segments from stories. Songs associated with stories range from short, half-spoken dialogues between animals to longer, dramatic performances with masked dance (e.g., the Beautiful Woman and the Three Suitors dance, performed in Point Hope on New Year's Eve).

Thus fragments of traditional festivals continue, usually in conjunction with recreational dances by community dance teams. Ritual items are now often associated with US holidays (Christmas, New Year's Day, Independence Day), or with special community events (the Point Hope Northern Lights Dance, the Barrow Eskimo games, the Dillingham Beaver Round-up).

2. INSTRUMENTS. The Alaskan Inuit use a wider variety of traditional instruments than do the Inuit of Canada and Greenland, where the single-headed frame drum is often the only indigenous instrument. In Alaska this type of drum—called *tchauyuk* (by Koranda) or *cauyuk* (by Johnston) in Yupik, and *keylowtik* (Koranda) or *gilaun* (Johnston) in Inupiaq—has a thin, wooden, circular frame covered with a natural membrane that is wetted and stretched tight in preparation for playing.

On the northwest coast the Inuit frame drum is cylindrical, around 60 cm in diameter and 4 cm deep, with a membrane usually made from the stomach or liver of a whale, walrus, or (inland) caribou. The beater, a thin, slightly curved stick, is used to strike the instrument from below. The player strikes the rim either in

one or two places, or strikes both the rim and membrane. The southwestern frame drum differs in that the diameter of the head may vary from 55 to 65 cm; plastic membranes have sometimes been used since the 1970s. The beater strikes the instrument from above or on the edge, the membrane, or both. On St. Lawrence Island a pyriform frame drum, with a membrane made from walrus tissue, is used. The beater, a sharply curved stick with a paddle carved at each end, strikes the membrane from above.

Another important type of "drum" is the *kalukhaq* (also spelled *kalluraq, kaylukuk,* or *kotlookuk*), an idiophonic box drum associated originally with the Messenger Feast. In the myth that explains the feast's origin the drum is said to represent an eagle's heartbeat. The instrument consists of a wooden, rectangular case of variable size with a decorative, zigzag top edge and eagle feathers. A fur-padded rail along one side is struck with a short stick. The drum is suspended from the roof and played by a seated drummer.

Other instruments include rattles made of bone, bird beaks, animal teeth, or cartridge shells, which are attached to the northwest-coast dance mittens worn in deference to whaling spirits. Arm gauntlets with puffin-beak rattles are worn on King Island. Rattles are sometimes attached to other items of apparel; an interesting historical example is the tall, conical cap covered with rows of mountain-sheep teeth (Murdoch, 1892, p.365). Bullroarers are found chiefly as children's toys. Rare instances of chordophones have been observed, one a one-string fiddle (*kelutviaq*) tapped with a small wand or quill (Johnston, *Eskimo Music*, 1976, p.107).

3. STYLE. Dance songs vary from one region to another, but most are pentatonic. Certain scale notes (especially the note below the tonal center) may be microtonally inflected according to context. A tonal center, defined by its reiteration and position at the end of a phrase, is often the second lowest scale tone. The range of dance songs is usually around an octave but may be as great as a 12th; intervals differ according to region but large, ascending leaps are rather common. An exception to this is the style of the riverine communities of the southwest (such as Pilot Station and St. Mary's), where narrow-ranged, tetratonic melodies with many ascending 4ths and descending minor 3rds were analyzed by Johnston (*Eskimo Music*, 1976, p.109).

Text settings are generally syllabic; there is some melismatic prolongation of certain vowels in large, downward melodic leaps, but only in specific positions within words. Dance songs are generally single strophes (except in some inland communities of the southwest, such as Pilot Station), but many are performed twice, first with vocables and light drumming on the rim, then slightly faster with lexical text and heavier drumming involving membrane strokes. More vigorous dancing parallels the appearance of song words in the second part.

The most common meter is 5/8, but heterometric sections, often parallel to the rhythms of the text, are frequent. Some areas have distinctive meters; for example,

7/8, related to Siberian styles, is characteristic of St. Lawrence Island Song and drum pulses (as well as dance motions) generally coincide, but the metric grouping of vocal and drum rhythms often diverges, producing polyrhythms and syncopation.

Game songs, such as those for juggling, usually have a range exceeding an octave and a modular, motivic structure that might be represented *AA'*...*BB'*...*CC'*...(ellipses denote a variable number of repetitions of the same motive). Some motives are iterated at a later point in the song. Although pebble-juggling implies a regular, duple rhythm (many transcriptions are written in 2/4 meter), not all musical motives are consistently duple, and the resulting cross-rhythms add a dimension of complexity to the juggling performance.

Songs-in-stories and string figure songs are generally narrow-ranged and sometimes use speech-song in which relative, rather than exact, pitch levels are important; animal calls are sometimes interspersed. The most wide-ranging melodic motion occurs at the beginning of the song, and tone reiterations increase toward the end.

Acculturation in musical style ranges from the parodying of Euro-American song features to the complete imitation of new styles (e.g., four-part hymns, pop songs accompanied by guitar). The continuity of traditional music varies widely, depending on such factors as the relative tolerance of religious authorities and the influence of the mass media. Inuit music features in two documentary films by Sarah Elder and Leonard Kamerling, *Tununeremiut: the People of Tununak* (1972) and *The Drums of Winter: Uksuum Cauyai* (1988).

SELECTED RECORDINGS

The Eskimos of Hudson Bay and Alaska (Folkways, 1956); *Eskimo Songs from Alaska* (Folkways, 1966); *Alaskan Eskimo Songs and Stories* (U. of Washington Press, 1972); *Music of the Alaskan Kutchin Indians* (FE, 1974)

BIBLIOGRAPHY

J. Murdoch: "The Ethnological Results of the Point Barrow Expedition," *Ninth Annual Report of the Bureau of American Ethnology* (Washington, DC, 1892), 3–441

E.W. Nelson: "The Eskimo about Bering Strait," *18th Annual Report of the Bureau of American Ethnology* (Washington, DC, 1899/*R*)

E.W. Hawkes: *The Dance Festivals of the Alaskan Eskimo* (Philadelphia, 1914)

M. Lantis: "Social Culture of the Nunivak Eskimo," *Transactions of the American Philosophical Society*, xxxv/3 (1946)

E. Groven: *Eskimo melodier fra Alaska: Helge Ingstads samling av opptak fra Nunamiut studier over tonesystemer og rythmer* [Eskimo melodies from Alaska: Helge Ingstad's Nunamiut collection studied with regard to tonal and rhythmic system] (Oslo, 1956)

R. Spencer: *The North Alaskan Eskimo: a Study in Ecology and Society* (Washington, DC, 1959/*R*)

C.C. Hughes: *An Eskimo Village in the Modern World* (Ithaca, NY, 1960)

J.L. Giddings: *Kobuk River People* (Fairbanks, AK, 1961)

J.W. Van Stone: *Point Hope: an Eskimo Village in Transition* (Seattle, 1962)

W. Oswalt: *Napaskiak: an Alaskan Eskimo Community* (Tucson, 1963)

N. Gubser: *The Nunamiut Eskimos: Hunters of Caribou* (New Haven, 1965)

L. Koranda: *Alaskan Eskimo Songs and Stories* (Seattle, 1972)

L.P. Ager: "Eskimo Dance and Cultural Values in an Alaskan Village," *Dance Research Journal*, viii/1 (1975–6), 7–12

T. Johnston: *Eskimo Music by Region: a Comparative Circumpolar Study* (Ottawa, 1976)

T. Johnston: "The Eskimo Songs of Northwestern Alaska," *Arctic*, xxix/1 (1976), 7–19

T. Johnston: *Inupiat Dance Songs* (Anchorage, 1979)

L.D. Koranda: "Music of the Alaskan Eskimos," *Musics of Many Cultures*, ed. E. May (Berkeley, CA, 1980), 332–62

M. Maguire: *American Indian and Eskimo Music: a Selected Bibliography through 1981* (Washington, DC, 1983)

D. Damas, ed.: *Handbook of North American Indians*, v: *Arctic* (Washington, DC, 1984)

P. Morrow: "It Is Time for Drumming: A Summary of Recent Research on Yupik Ceremonialism," *Études/Inuit/Studies*, ii (1984), 113–40

T. Johnston: "Community History and Environment as Wellspring of Inupiaq Eskimo Songtexts," *Anthropos*, lxxxiii (1988), 161–71

T. Johnston: "Drum Rhythms of the Alaskan Eskimo," *Anthropologie*, xxvi/1 (1988), 75–82

T. Johnston: "Song Categories and Musical Style of the Yupik Eskimo," *Anthropos*, lxxxiv (1989), 423–31

M. Williams: "Contemporary Alaska Native Dance: the Spirit of Tradition," *Native American Dance: Ceremonies and Social Traditions*, ed. C. Heth (Washington, DC, 1992), 149–67

C. Mishler: *The Crooked Stovepipe: Athapaskan Fiddle Music and Square Dancing in Northeast Alaska and Northwest Canada* (Urbana, IL, 1993)

A. Fienup-Riordan and J.H. Barker: *Yupiit Yuraryarait: Yup'ik Ways of Dancing* (Anchorage, 2010)

BEVERLEY DIAMOND/R

Invictus. Record company. Based in Detroit, Invictus was an independent record company that specialized in dance-based rhythm-and-blues and psychedelic soul. Invictus was founded by the songwriter-producer team of Edward Holland, Jr., Lamont Dozier, and Brian Holland, after the trio left Motown, where they had produced dozens of chart-topping hits during the 1960s. Holland, Dozier, and Holland, also founded the Hot Wax label and wrote, produced, and owned much of the music on both labels. New York-based Buddah Records distributed Hot Wax. Invictus releases were distributed by Capitol from 1969 to 1972 and Columbia from 1972 to 1978, at which point Invictus and Hot Wax reformed into H-D-H records. The most popular singles released on Invictus and Hot Wax were by Freda Payne ("Band of Gold," 1970), Chairmen of the Board ("Give Me Just a Little More Time," 1970), and Honey Cone ("Want Ads," 1971). Invictus also released the first single and album recorded by the Detroit-based psychedelic soul group Parliament.

ANDREW FLORY

Invisibl Skratch Piklz. Hip-hop DJ collective. The group included some of the most lauded and respected artists in the world of turntablism. Filipino-Americans DJ Q-Bert [Richard Quitevis] and Mix Master Mike [Michael Schwarz] formed the core of the group. With DJ Apollo, they formed a trio in 1992 called the Rock Steady DJs. Adopting the "Piklz" moniker in 1995, Mike and Q-Bert were joined by a rotating cast over the next five years that included DJ Disk [Luis Quintanilla], Yogafrog [Ritchie Desuasido], D-Styles [David Cuasito], DJ Shortkut [Jonathan Cruz], and others.

The Piklz presented themselves as an all-turntable band, rather than a group of individual artists. With an approach to performance not dissimilar from a jazz combo, members would improvise solos in alternation while the others held down a supporting musical framework. "Invasion of the Octopus People," included on 1995's turntablist compilation album *Return of the DJ vol. 1*, is an early example of this "turntable band" sound. Recordings of *The Shiggar Fraggar Show*, a 1990s Bay-Area pirate radio program, also showcase the group's characteristic mixture of boyish humor and extreme technical virtuosity.

While they remained together for less than a decade, the Piklz are widely acknowledged as one of the most influential and innovative forces in the development of turntablism. After a final performance in San Francisco on 1 July 2000, the group cordially disbanded. Members of the group—DJ Q-Bert in particular—went on to pioneer efforts in turntablist education.

BIBLIOGRAPHY

O. Wang: *Spinning Identities: A Social History of Filipino American DJs in the San Francisco Bay Area* (diss., Univ. of California, Berkeley, 2004)

M. Katz: *Groove Music: The Art and Culture of the Hip-Hop DJ* (New York, 2012)

WILL BOONE

Iowa, University of. State university in Iowa City, Iowa. The institution was founded in 1855 and began offering vocal lessons in 1860. The School of Music first appeared in 1906 and was fully incorporated into the College of Liberal Arts in 1915. Philip Greeley Clapp was director from 1919–54. Early work in musical aptitude testing was done by Carl E. Seashore, professor of philosophy and psychology, who as dean of the Graduate College (1908–37, 1942–6) led the university's pioneering efforts in awarding graduate degrees for creative scholarship. Numbering approximately 550 students and 50 faculty and known for its Center for New Music, rare books collection, and Goldman Band Library, the school awards degrees in performance, music education, theory, composition, and musicology. In 1971 the school moved into a building named in 1995 to honor Himie Voxman, director from 1954–80. Voxman was succeeded by Marilyn Somville (1980–90), David Nelson (1991–2000, 2008–10), Kristin Thelander (2000–08), and David Gier (2010–). Distinguished alumni include Thomas J. Anderson, Eugene Rousseau, Robert Glidden, Himie Voxman, and Edwin E. Gordon. The music building was closed in 2008 because of a flood of the Iowa River. The estimated completion date for a new building (and location) is 2015.

DON D. COFFMAN

iPod. *See* PORTABLE MEDIA DEVICE.

Irakere. Cuban jazz and popular dance band. The ensemble is widely recognized as one of the most significant to have emerged in Cuba since the 1959 Revolution. Through the 1970s and 1980s, Irakere gained international acclaim for its innovative compositions, dynamic musical fusions, and the dazzling virtuosity of its soloists. Their sound draws on jazz, rock, funk, Cuban popular dance music, and Afro-Cuban folkloric and sacred music. Irakere mixes Afro-Cuban percussion instruments, rarely heard in earlier popular Cuban music, with electronic guitar, bass, and synthesizers. They also have engaged with the Western European art music tradition in compositions such as "Adagio on a Mozart Theme" and in collaboration with the Cuban guitarist and composer Leo Brouwer.

Pianist, composer, and bandleader Jesús Chucho Valdés officially founded Irakere in 1973 in La Habana. The Cuban Ministry of Culture was slow to officially approve the group Irakere in part because many in the Cuban establishment viewed jazz and rock as signs of North American imperialism. The group's roots can be found a decade earlier in Chucho Valdés y su Combo, his initial attempt to break away from Cuban music conventions. To form Irakere, Valdés drew from his fellow musicians in the Orquesta Cubana de Música Moderna, an all-star ensemble that specialized in complex arrangements of avant-garde jazz, rock, and popular Cuban dance tunes. In 1972 Valdés recorded a trio album, *Jazz Batá*, along with future Irakere members: vocalist and percussionist Oscar Valdés (no relation) and bassist Carlos del Puerto. This album foreshadowed the Irakere sound by replacing the drum set of the standard jazz trio format with Afro-Cuban folkloric drums, including the batá, and featured the track "Irakere," which means thick, dense jungle in Lucumí, the Cuban Yoruba language. The classic Irakere line up includes the trio from *Jazz Batá* joined by conguero Jorge "El Niño" Alfonso, saxophonists Paquito D'Rivera and Carlos Averhoff, trumpet players Arturo Sandoval and Jorge Varona, electric guitarist Carlos Emilio Morales, and drummer Enrique Plá. Other notable alumni include José Luis Cortéz, Orlando Valle, Miguel Díaz, and Germán Velasco.

Despite several changes in personnel and the departure of many original members, Irakere continued to perform and record into the late 1990s under the direction of Valdés. Significant works include *Misa negra* (the Black Mass, based on Afro-Cuban sacred music), "Bacalao con pan," and "Juana 1600." A recording of their 1978 performances at the Newport and Montreux jazz festivals won a US Grammy Award. The orchestration and timbre of Irakere's brass section and the arrangement of percussion and bass breaks also influenced *timba*, a popular Cuban dance genre that responded to North American salsa. In recent years, Valdés has stopped touring with the band to focus on his career as a soloist and other small ensembles.

RECORDINGS
(selective list)

The Best of Irakere (1994, Sony Music CK57719); *Irakere Vol. II* (1995, EGREM 146); *Great Moments* (1996, Milan 35778); *The Legendary .../ exuberancia* (1999, Jazz House Music 6603); *Jazz Batá* (2007, Malanga Music 802); *Irakere* (2008, Sony BMG Legacy 88697122762)

VIDEOGRAPHY

Chucho Valdés: Latin Jazz Founders Featuring Irakere, Music Video Distributors, 2869048 (2005)

BIBLIOGRAPHY

L. Acosta: *Cubano Be Cubano Bop: One Hundred Years of Jazz in Cuba* (Washington, DC, 2003)

LISE WAXER/CARLOS PALOMARES

Irish American music. *See* EUROPEAN AMERICAN MUSIC.

Iroquois. A confederacy founded in the late 16th century that originally comprised five Iroquoian-speaking Native American tribes of the lower Great Lakes region: the Seneca, Cayuga, Onondaga, Oneida, and Mohawk. It was also known as the Five Nations and the League of the Iroquois. Five Nations became Six Nations with the inclusion of the Tuscarora in 1722. Today, most Iroquis live in New York state, southern Ontario, and Quebec; others live in Wisconsin and Oklahoma.

The Iroquois homeland was northern New York state between the Adirondack Mountains and Niagara Falls. The Iroquois called themselves the Haudenosaunee ("people of the longhouse"), referencing both their traditional communal dwellings, as well as their metaphorical longhouse of territories from west to east: the Mohawk (keepers of the Western Door), the Oneida, the Onondaga (keepers of the Central Fire), the Cayuga, and the Seneca (keepers of the Eastern Door). The Oneida and Cayuga were referred to as the Little Brothers.

During the 17th century the Iroquois confederacy conquered neighboring tribes. At the height of its power and influence, the confederacy controlled the Northeast from the Ottawa River to the Tennessee, and from the Kennebec River to today's Illinois and Lake Michigan.

Tuscarora Indian Randy Green dances at New York State Fair, 1997. (AP Photo/Mike Okoniewski-New York State Fair/HO)

Wars of expansion brought the Iroquois into contact with various tribes, such as the Huron and Cherokee, from which elements of musical style and culture were adopted. In 1722 the Iroquoian-speaking Tuscarora from North Carolina were formally admitted into the confederacy as its sixth nation, and in 1753 the Cayuga adopted the Tutelo, a Siouan tribe from Virginia. During the American Revolution most Iroquois fought on the side of the British, their traditional ally. As no provisions were made for the Iroquois in the Treaty of Paris (1783), they were compelled to move to Canada or to negotiate separate treaties with the Americans. Many were removed from their lands and relocated to reservations. Today the Iroquois live within 14 communities, a huge contrast to their once vast territory.

The Iroquois have successfully maintained much of their native culture despite more than 300 years of contact with whites. Three classic oral narratives provided a basis for Haudenosaunee beliefs, customs, values, and relationships: the Great Law of Peace, the Code of Handsome Lake, and the Thanksgiving Address.

The Great Law of Peace emphasized the need for peace and justice among the tribes. It outlined the structure of the confederacy as the aforementioned metaphorical longhouse. A council of 50 members became the decision-making body. Only men were allowed to serve as council members; however, as a matriarchal society, only clan mothers could chose the council members.

The Code of Handsome Lake was brought to the Haudenosaunee during a time of stress and despair, due primarily to colonialism. Under the leadership of the prophet Handsome Lake, a religious revitalization movement took place, synthesizing elements of native culture with select Christian teachings of the Quakers. The internal coherence provided by this Longhouse Religion and the adherence to the prescribed yearly system of rituals made it possible for the Iroquois to adopt aspects of white culture without compromising their own ideology.

Today, the longhouse serves as the central community gathering place. There, the followers of Handsome Lake meet to perform the religious rituals prescribed in his code, and to discuss tribal policy; the longhouse serves as the center for moral education and traditional socialization, as well as a social club that provides feasts, dances, and receptions for visitors.

The third narrative is the Thanksgiving Address, a speech given at the beginning of every community event. In this address, the entire Haudenosaunee universe of spirit forces is invoked and thanked in a hierarchy of categories, beginning with the terrestrial and proceeding skyward, ending with the Creator. This obligation to give thanks permeates Haudenosaunee dance and song tradition.

In the calendric rites, based on the old agricultural economy and repeated annually in the various longhouses, participants perform ceremonies in honor of creation. Sets of songs and dances are central features of all the ceremonies; however, individual differences exist. All longhouses hold the Midwinter ceremony, the longest and most important event of the year. This ceremony incorporates every aspect of longhouse activity within a nine-day festival with two distinct parts. The initial days focus on personal well-being and healing through rites sponsored by individuals; this portion is very old and is related to the Huron dream-divining and healing feasts described by the Jesuits in the 17th century. The latter days are devoted to the Four Sacred Rituals given by the Creator and reaffirmed by Handsome Lake—the Great Feather Dance (*hostowehgo'wa*), the Thanksgiving Dance (*koneo'uh*), the Personal Chant (*ado'wa*), and the Bowl Game (*kaje'kekha*)—and to dances honoring the various food spirits.

Because the teachings of Handsome Lake have been incorporated into the second part of the Midwinter ceremony, repetition for didactic purposes is found in the song texts of the Great Feather Dance and the Thanksgiving Dance prayers. Both are patterned after the Thanksgiving Address. The Great Feather Dance, also performed as part of other ceremonies during the year, is sung by two male singers, each with a turtle-shell rattle; it is a costumed dance for the longhouse faithful. A fast, iambic rhythm is provided by the rattles, as accompaniment to a series of short songs (from a repertory of more than 100) that invoke the various spirit forces. The Thanksgiving Dance, performed only at the Midwinter and the Green Corn ceremonies, is another costumed dance consisting of a long, elaborate song cycle interspersed with prayers of thanksgiving. Personal Chants and individual songs of thanksgiving are addressed to the Creator; each man has his own set of songs that are, to some degree, the property of his family or clan. The Bowl Game, also part of Midwinter, is symbolic of the struggle between good and evil; it has no associated music or dance.

After Midwinter comes a series of ceremonies giving thanks to the food spirits; these include the Bush, Maple, Seed Planting, Corn Sprouting, Strawberry, Raspberry, Green Bean, Corn Testing, Green Corn, and Harvest ceremonies. Each of these is timed to coincide with the appearance, or change in appearance, of the item to be honored. Thus, the Maple ceremony is held when the sap begins to flow, while others take place when the various fruits and vegetables ripen. Associated with the agricultural cycle, but performed infrequently, are the Sun, Moon, and Thunder ceremonies, which include music and dance from the obsolete war dance.

Because agriculture is traditionally the women's domain, most of the food-spirit ceremonies are organized by matrons. Female symbolism is inherent in the set of dances performed to thank the corn, beans, and squash (called the Three Sisters). In addition, at the Midwinter, Seed Planting, and Green Corn ceremonies, members of the Society of Women Planters (*towisas*) sing individual chants, and dance while holding ears of corn.

Medicinal societies exist within the Haudenosaunee community to uphold and preserve rituals that guard and protect their people. These societies are renewed yearly at Midwinter and usually meet in private homes when an individual is sick. Once banned by Handsome Lake, these societies, each specializing in specific ailments, are numerous and continue to function in the longhouse community. One of the most important is the Society of Medicine Men, derived from an older society of shamans; its extensive ritual involves a company of 12 to 15 men, each singing individual songs, followed by 50 or more songs sung in unison for the Medicine Dance. The Bear, Buffalo, Eagle, and Otter societies are collectively known as the Company of Mystic Animals. Each society, except that of the Otter, has a distinctive set of songs and dances in which its animal tutelary is imitated. The False Face (*kakoh'sa*) and Husk Face (*gadjisa*) societies, whose tutelaries are respectively forest and agricultural spirits, attempt to heal by blowing hot ashes on the patient. The Little Water Medicine Society sings not to heal an individual, but to renew the strength of a particular medicine. Women maintain four medicine societies, including that of the Feast of the Dead (*ohgi'we*), an important communal memorial that lasts a full night. In all cases the society's performance is considered therapeutic, and the songs are sung only at the specific ritual for which they are intended. Both musical (Kurath, 1951) and linguistic (Chafe, 1964) evidence suggest that the medicine rites are older than the agricultural ones.

Iroquois musical style is essentially conservative and lacking in extremes. Traditionally, most singers are men; their singing style is characterized by a moderate amount of tension in the throat, pulsation on sustained notes, downward glides, and grace notes. Apart from an individual's singing style, some songs are marked by a specific vocal quality; for example, the Bear Dance is sung in a low-pitched, husky voice, whereas the Bean Dance is sung smoothly and with resonance.

Tonally, songs range from the simple, monotone chants of the Husk Face society and the prayers of the Thanksgiving Dance, through agricultural, animal, and bird songs based on four- and five-tone scales, to newer social dance compositions based on larger scales. Most songs, such as agricultural song cycles and the Stomp Dance, lie within a one-octave range; the smallest ranges are found in shamanistic rites, the largest in Thanksgiving Dance songs and new compositions. The melodic contour of Iroquois music is undulating, with slightly more descent than ascent overall. Many songs focus strongly on their main, or ground, tone by repeated returns from upper and lower notes; a stylistic analogue is suggested in the earth-bound shuffle of the ubiquitous stomp step. The most frequently used intervals are the major second and minor third; by contrast, some new compositions for Women's Shuffle Dances open with a bold octave leap and descend rather freely and rapidly.

Rhythmically, the voice and accompaniment generally coincide; the instrumental rhythm is most often a moderate to fast duple beat. Song cycles tend to begin slowly, with gradual acceleration to the prescribed tempo. Changes in percussive accompaniment patterns cue changes in dance steps. Melodic rhythms usually consist of eighth, quarter, and half notes with some use of syncopation and triplets. Songs are built of one, two, or occasionally three short themes that are simply alternated or varied in repetition (*AA′, AABA, ABAB, ABA′B′*). In songs with leader and chorus a typical pattern is as follows: first theme sung by leader; first theme repeated by chorus; second theme sung by all; entire song repeated (*AABAB*). Introductory and coda phrases are common in many song types. Call and response occurs in about 20% of all songs and is the sole structural device of the Stomp Dance. Meaningful texts are most often used in ceremonial songs, while vocables are used in most social dance songs.

Social dance songs are short (about one minute) and strung together, usually in groups of seven, to form a set or cycle. The typical religious or secular dance is performed by a group arranged in a circle, either in single- or double-file, moving counterclockwise around a central singers' bench.

The Iroquois have many instruments. The water-drum (*ka'nohko'wah*) and cow-horn rattle (*ono'kah kastawe'sha*) provide percussive accompaniment for most social dance songs and many ceremonies. The water drum is a small, watertight keg, 12 to 15 centimeters in diameter, covered with a soft, tanned skin held in place by a hoop. A small amount of water is always kept in the drum; before playing, the head is thoroughly soaked and pulled taut until the characteristic high, pinging sound is obtained when the instrument is struck with a small, wooden beater. The cow-horn rattle is made from a conical piece of cow horn mounted on a wooden handle; the horn contains steel pellets and is closed at the top by a wooden disc. Use of the turtle-shell rattle (*kan-yahte'ka'nowa*), with its symbolic associations to Iroquois cosmogony, is restricted to the Great Feather and False Face dances. Gourd rattles are used only in agricultural and medicine rites.

Iroquois music varies from one longhouse to another. In social dance music, a singer may express his personality and creativity via his singing style and his compositions, but always within prescribed limits. Ritual singers can develop their own versions of ceremonies by choosing and determining the sequence of songs, selected from a large, traditional repertory. The ceremonial calendars of individual longhouses vary, in part, for historical reasons. For example, three longhouses at Six Nations Reserve in Ontario perform the unique Tutelo harvest songs and the Spirit Adoption Ceremony, in addition to the usual Iroquoian rites. The Mohawk of St. Regis, who were Christianized by Jesuits in the 17th century, but did not adopt the Longhouse Religion until the 1930s, omit some shorter ceremonies and perform abbreviated versions of others.

A body of traditional and newly composed song exists for social dancing, which takes place on many occasions. Traditional social dance songs can be classified into two groups—stomp-type and fish-type—according to the basic dance step used. Stomp-type dances include the food-spirit dances, the Pigeon, Duck, Robin, and Alligator dances, and the Standing Quiver

(or Stomp) dance. Call-and-response singing, a characteristic shared with tribes in the Southeast, is a distinct structural feature of this group. The fish-type dances include the Old Moccasin, Sharpening-a-stick, and Raccoon dances; they have a more complicated step and are somewhat less common.

Beginning in the mid-20th century, social gatherings called sings featured community Singing Societies to raise money for members in need. The sing begins with the Thanksgiving Address delivered by one of the elders. Then the singing begins with a series of Women's Shuffle Dances (*eskanye*), a favorite genre for new song creation. The singing is accompanied by the water drum and cow-horn rattles. After a dinner break, the evening dance social continues with a variety of traditional dances.

In contrast, the powwow, developed in the southern plains, is a more recent addition to Native American gatherings in the Northeast. Many are competitive events with costumes and fancy footwork.

Historic recordings of Iroquois music are held at the Archive of Folk Culture at the Library of Congress, Washington, DC; the Archives of Traditional Music at Indiana University, Bloomington; the American Philosophical Society Library, Philadelphia; and the National Museum of Canada, Ontario. Contemporary Iroquois music, a blending of traditional and cross-cultural music, is performed by musicians such as the Six Nation Women's Singers, the Allegheny River Singers, Joanne Shenandoah, and Robbie Robertson.

SELECTED RECORDINGS

Songs from the Iroquois Longhouse (Library of Congress, 1942); *Seneca Songs from Coldspring Longhouse* (Library of Congress, 1947); *Seneca Social Dance Music* (Smithsonian Folkways, 1980); R. Robertson: *Music for Native Americans* (Cap., 1994); J. Shenandoah: *Matriarch: Iroquois Women's Songs* (Silver Wave, 1996); Six Nation Women Singers: *We will all sing* (Soar Records, 1996); R. Robertson: *Contact from the Underworld of Redboy* (Capitol, 1998); J. Shenandoah: *Orenda: Native American Songs of Life* (Silver Wave, 1998); Allegheny River Singers: *Social Dance Songs of the Iroquois* (JVC/XRCD, 1998); M. Shenandoah and E. Roberts: *Sisters: Oneida Iroquois Hymns* (Silver Wave, 2003)

BIBLIOGRAPHY

W.N. Fenton and G.P. Kurath: "The Feast of the Dead, or Ghost Dance, at Six Nations Reserve, Canada," *Symposium on Local Diversity in Iroquois Culture: Washington DC 1949* [*Bureau of American Ethnology Bulletin*, no.149 (1951)], 139

G.P. Kurath: "Iroquois Midwinter Medicine Rites," *JIFMC*, iii (1951), 96

G.P. Kurath: "Local Diversity in Iroquois Music and Dance," *Symposium on Local Diversity in Iroquois Culture: Washington DC 1949* [*Bureau of American Ethnology Bulletin*, no.149 (1951)], 109

G.P. Kurath "Indian Tribes of Aboriginal America, iii: Matriarchal Dances of the Iroquois," *International Congress of Americanists: New York 1949*, ed. S. Tax (Chicago, 1952), 123

H.C. Conklin and W.C. Sturtevant: "Seneca Indian Singing Tools at Coldspring Longhouse: Musical Instruments of the Modern Iroquois," *Proceedings of the American Philosophical Society*, xcvii (1953), 262

W.N. Fenton and G.P. Kurath: "The Iroquois Eagle Dance: an Offshoot of the Calumet Dance," *Bureau of American Ethnology Bulletin*, no.156 (1953/R)

G.P. Kurath: "Antiphonal Songs of Eastern Woodland Indians," *MQ*, xlii (1956), 520

G.P. Kurath: "The Effects of Environment on Cherokee-Iroquois Ceremonialism, Music and Dance," *Symposium on Cherokee and Iroquois*

Culture: Washington DC 1958 [*Bureau of American Ethnology Bulletin*, no.180 (1961)], 173

A. Shimony: "Conservatism among the Iroquois at the Six Nations Reserve," *Yale University Publications in Anthropology*, no.65 (New Haven, 1961)

G.P. Kurath: "Iroquois Music and Dance: Ceremonial Arts of Two Seneca Longhouses," *Bureau of American Ethnology Bulletin*, no.187 (1964/R)

G.P. Kurath: *Dance and Song Rituals of Six Nations Reserve, Ontario* (Ottawa, 1968)

A.F.C. Wallace: *The Death and Rebirth of the Seneca* (New York, 1970/R)

D.S. Gaus: *Change in Social Dance Song Style at Allegany Reservation, 1962–1973: the Rabbit Dance* (diss., Catholic U. of America, 1976)

C. Heth: "Stylistic Similarities in Cherokee and Iroquois Music," *Journal of Cherokee Studies*, iv (1979), 128–62

G.P. Kurath: *Tutelo Rituals on Six Nations Reserve, Ontario* (Ann Arbor, MI, 1981)

R. Cornelius and T.J. O'Grady: "Reclaiming a Tradition: the Soaring Eagles of Oneida," *EthM*, xxxi/2 (1987) 261–72

T. Alfred: *Peace, Power, Righteousness: an Indigenous Manifesto* (New York, 1999)

M. Paul: "Every Song You Sing Just Keeps Getting Better and Better," *In the Words of Elders: Aboriginal Cultures in Transition*, ed. P. Kulchyski (Toronto, 1999)

S.A. Krouse: "Traditional Iroquois Socials: Maintaining Identity in the City," *American Indian Quarterly*, xxv/3 (2001), 400–408

W.F. Fenton: *The Little Water Medicine Society of the Senecas* (Oklahoma, 2003)

B. Diamond: *Native American Music in Eastern North America* (New York, 2008)

W. Wonderley: *At the Font of the Marvelous: Exploring Oral Narrative and Mythical Imagery of the Iroquois and their Neighbors* (Syracuse, 2009)

MARIE RIEMER-WELLER/ANN McFARLAND

I.R.S. Record company. It was originally established in the United States in 1979 by music entrepreneur Miles Copland as an outgrowth of his Faulty Products/Illegal Records company in the United Kingdom. After having negotiated a contract for the rock band the Police with A&M Records, Copland and A&M reached a distribution and production deal for the International Record Syndicate (a/k/a I.R.S.), for which he named 21-year-old Jay Boberg to oversee American operations. I.R.S. not only reissued Illegal releases originally distributed in the United Kingdom, but also became the umbrella group for a host of labels, including Industrial Records, Spy Records, Deptford Fun City Records, No Speak, the independent label Rough Trade, and others, as well as issuing records under the I.R.S. banner. Notable artists included the Buzzcocks, the Cramps, Oingo Boingo, Renaissance, Wall of Voodoo, the Go-Go's, and R.E.M.

In 1985 I.R.S. switched its distribution to MCA Records for new releases, remaining there until 1990, at which point new releases were distributed through CEMA (EMI's then-distributor, now EMI Music Distribution, or EMD). The label was purchased outright by EMI in 1992, and ceased operations in July of 1996 after EMI rebuffed an offer from Copland to repurchase the label.

BIBLIOGRAPHY
C. Campion: *Walking on the Moon: the Untold Story of the Police and the Rise of New Wave Rock* (Hoboken, NJ, and Mississauga, ON, 2010), 107

THANE TIERNEY

Irving, Washington (*b* New York, NY, 3 April 1783; *d* New York, NY, 28 Nov 1859). Writer. He studied law in various legal offices, but did not practice as a lawyer, and contributed essays to society and comic journals in New York. His experiences in Europe, first as a traveler (1804–6) and subsequently as a resident (1812–29) and diplomat (England, 1829–32; Spain, 1842–6), gave him a wealth of colorful material for his published collections of stories, verse, sentimental tales, history, and folklore. Although much of his work was borrowed, he was widely acclaimed both in Europe and the United States. He is perhaps most closely associated with the characters Ichabod Crane from "The Legend of Sleepy Hollow" and Rip Van Winkle, a deft appropriation of an ancient German folktale, both of which first appeared in Irving's *The Sketch Book of Geoffrey Crayon*.

Irving was a flute player of some ability and an enthusiastic opera, concert, and theater goer. He heard more than 130 operas in Europe and was presented at a performance of *Fidelio* in the Kärntnertortheater in Vienna on 23 May 1814. In London and Paris he heard the music of Bach, Gluck, Handel, Beethoven, Mozart, Rossini, and Weber.

George Frederick Bristow's *Rip Van Winkle*, produced in New York in 1855, is regarded as the first American grand opera on an American subject; other operatic adaptations based on this character include those of the French composer Robert Planquette (1882), Reginald De Koven (1920), and Edward Manning (1932), and there is an early overture on the subject by George Whitefield Chadwick. Maxwell Anderson borrowed the despotic character of Peter Stuyvesant from Irving's *A History of New York* for his musical satire *Knickerbocker Holiday*. "The Legend of Sleepy Hollow" has also received several operatic treatments (e.g., by Max Maretzek); one of the more interesting is Douglas S. Moore's *The Headless Horseman*, for which Stephen Vincent Benét provided a one-act libretto that satirizes progressive education. Several composers have set stories from Irving's *The Alhambra*, notably Rimsky-Korsakov in *The Golden Cockerel*, and Dudley Buck composed a cantata on six scenes from *A History of the Life and Voyages of Christopher Columbus*. Other program music includes *Zorahayda*, drawn from *The Alhambra* by the Norwegian violinist, composer, and conductor Johan Svendsen, and Aaron David Miller's *Sleepy Hollow: A Tone Poem for Organ and Orchestra*.

BIBLIOGRAPHY
C. McGlinchee: "American Literature in American Music," *MQ*, xxxi (1945), 101

G.R. Price: "Washington Irving's Librettos," *ML*, xxix (1948), 348

P.R. Kirby: "Washington Irving, Barhum Livius and Weber," *ML*, xxxi (1950), 133

H.E. Johnson: "Young American Abroad," *MQ*, xxxiv (1958), 65

H.E. Johnson: *Operas on American Subjects* (New York, 1964)

H.E. Johnson: "Musical Interests of Certain American Literary and Political Figures," *JRME*, xix (1971), 272

JOHN McLAUGHLIN/MICHAEL HOVLAND

Irwin, May [Campbell, Georgina May] (*b* Whitby, ON, 27 June 1862; *d* New York, NY, 22 Oct 1938). Canadian actress, singer, and producer. It is believed that Irwin made her debut in Buffalo, New York, in 1875 alongside her sister. Between 1875 and 1883, the Irwin Sisters performed in a vaudeville song-and-dance act in Rochester and Buffalo, eventually becoming regulars at Tony Pastor's Theatre in New York. When the sister act split, May joined Augustin Daly's stock company, where she spent the next three years refining her comic timing in ensemble work before joining the Howard Athenaeum Company. Beginning in 1893, Irwin appeared in a series of farce comedies, where her rendition of songs in African American dialect led to her reputation as a "coon shouter." Despite her early successes, it was *The Widow Jones* (1895) that first established May Irwin as a star of the Broadway stage. Here she introduced her signature song, "The Bully Song," and performed the scene with John C. Rice that would later be immortalized as the first cinematic kiss. This was followed by leading roles in other successful Broadway shows, including *Sister Mary* (1899), *Madge Smith, Attorney* (1900), *Mrs. Black is Back* (1904), *Mrs. Wilson, That's All* (1906), *Mrs. Peckham's Carouse* (1908), and *Widow by Proxy* (1913). Her final Broadway appearance was in the musical revue *The 49ers* (1922). During her nearly 50 year career, Irwin was dubbed "The Funniest Stage Woman in America" and was a particular favorite of President Woodrow Wilson, who joked about appointing her "Secretary of Laughter."

GERALD BORDMAN/MARIA PURCIELLO

Isaac, Merle J(ohn) (*b* Pioneer, IA, 12 Oct 1898; *d* Chicago, IL, 11 March 1996). Music educator, arranger, and administrator. Isaac graduated from the VanderCook College of Music (BM 1932), the Lewis Institute (BSc 1936), and Northwestern University (MA 1937). He learned to sing in the Chicago public schools and studied piano and organ privately. From 1919 to 1929 he performed as a silent movie organist. When the silent film era ended, Isaac taught at John Marshall High School in Chicago, where he developed an award-winning orchestra (1929–43) before becoming principal of Talcott Elementary School, also in Chicago (1943–64). Noticing an absence of easier pieces for children to play, he began arranging and composing for band and orchestra, producing hundreds of works. Isaac also authored many articles and books on education and on arranging. His arrangements and the famous *Merle Isaac String Class Method* (1938, 2/1966) sold millions of copies and made him a well-known clinician and lecturer. He received awards from the American Society of Composers, Authors and Publishers; the National School Orchestra Association; and the American String Teachers Association. In 1996 he was inducted into the Music Educators Hall of Fame (1996) of the Music Educators National Conference.

BIBLIOGRAPHY

W.H. Rehrig: "Isaac, Merle," *The Heritage Encyclopedia of Band Music*, i (Westerville, OH, 1991), 366 only

"In Memoriam: Merle J. Isaac," *American String Teacher*, xl/3 (1996), 101 only

"Merle Isaac Passes," *Teaching Music*, iii/6 (1996), 22 only

"Merle J. Isaac (1898–1996)," *The Instrumentalist*, l/10 (1996), 75 only

F.M. Harley: "Merle, Magical Musician," *American String Teacher*, xl/2 (1997), 25–32

WILLIAM R. LEE

Isaacs. Family of Hawaiian musicians. Alvin Kaleolani ("Papa") Isaacs (1904–1984) was an important bandleader, singer, musician, and composer. He wrote over 300 songs ranging from sentimental ("Kau`ionalani") to swinging ("Auhea Oe") and humorous ("No Huhu"). Isaacs started on steel guitar, inspired by Joseph Kekuku and Pali K. Lua, but also learned ukulele, guitar, mandolin, piano, bass, and various wind instruments. He formed his first band at 13 but kept music a hobby until a motorcycle accident in 1929 forced him to retire from the police force. He worked the club circuit before joining Harry Owens in 1935 at the prestigious Royal Hawaiian Hotel as singer and comic hula dancer.

During World War II, Isaacs ran two groups simultaneously, including the house band for NBC radio's "Voice of Hawaii" program. In 1947 he created The Royal Hawaiian Serenaders, a local super group with Tommy Castro (steel guitar/bass vocals), Benny Kalama (standup bass/falsetto vocals), and George Kainapau ('ukulele/falsetto vocals). Based at the hotel of the same name, they recorded for the Bell label as featured artists and accompanists. Isaacs also worked on the West Coast with Harry Owens and Bing Crosby, whose close connections to Hawaiian music are often forgotten today. Isaacs hosted legendary jam sessions at his home and trained three of his sons, making sure each played a different instrument so they could play together.

One of his sons, Alvin "Barney" Isaacs, Jr. (1924–96), played steel guitar. He joined his father's quartet in 1948, and then worked with many top artists such as Alfred Apaka and Danny Kaleikini. He was music director at Waikiki Records and served 25 years at the Hawaii Calls radio program. His recording credits number in the hundreds, often with one or both of his brothers. Like all leading Hawaiian steel players of his era, Barney played electric without pedals. He made his last recordings in 1995 on acoustic steel with guitarist George Kuo for the Dancing Cat label.

Another of Papa Isaacs' sons, Leland "Atta" Isaacs (1929–83), was a musician's musician, highly regarded for his lead work and jazzy chord variations. Atta performed in a variety of club bands but is best remembered for his work with longtime friend Gabby Pahinui, especially the album *Two Slack Key Guitars* (1969), and the extremely popular Gabby Pahinui Hawaiian Band records in the 1970s. Atta frequently recorded as an accompanist with singers such as Linda Dela Cruz and Bill Kaiwa, and occasionally in groups such as The Maile Serenaders, The New Hawaiian Band, and The Sons of Hawaii. He released his only solo album in 1971 for Tradewinds.

Known for his humor and his solid musicianship, Norman Isaacs (1925–80), a third musical son of Papa Isaacs, was a leading bassist and singer. He worked with Hawaii Calls, Jerry Byrd, Charles K.L. Davis, Benny Kalama, and sometimes substituted for Joe Marshall in

The Sons of Hawaii. He often performed and recorded with his brothers as well.

The Isaacs family received a Lifetime Achievement Award from the Hawaii Academy of Recording Arts in 2010.

JAY W. JUNKER

Isbin, Sharon (*b* Minneapolis, MN, 7 Aug 1956). Classical guitarist. She studied guitar with Aldo Minella, JEFFREY VAN, and Alirio Diaz; she also received instruction from ANDRÉS SEGOVIA and Oscar Ghiglia. Isbin's studies with ROSALYN TURECK began during her years at Yale (BA 1978, MM 1979). She won first prize at the Toronto International Guitar Competition (1975), top prize at the Munich International Competition (1976), and was a winner of the Queen Sofia Competition in Madrid (1979). Her New York debut was at Alice Tully Hall in 1979. Isbin teaches at the Juilliard School, where she founded the guitar department in 1989; she has also taught at the Manhattan School of Music and the Aspen Music Festival. Having established an international reputation as a recitalist and concerto soloist, she also contributed to the expansion of the classical guitar repertoire by commissioning new works for the instrument. Her 1995 recording *American Landscapes* includes pieces for guitar and orchestra written for her by John Corigliano, Lukas Foss, and Joseph Schwantner. Isbin has won two Grammy Awards for her recordings: in 2001 for *Dreams of a World*, and in 2010 for *Journey to the New World*. Her 2001 recording of the Grammy-winning composition *Concert de Gaudi for Guitar and Orchestra* by Christopher Rouse was itself nominated for a Grammy, and she performed on Howard Shore's Grammy-nominated soundtrack to the film *The Departed* (2006). Though Isbin's repertoire comprises of many standard classical works by composers such as Rodrigo, Vivaldi, and Bach, she has also shown eclectic musical tastes by working with musicians such as rock guitarist Steve Vai and jazz guitarist Larry Coryell.

BIBLIOGRAPHY
J. Lehmann-Haupt: "American Tunes: Sharon Isbin and Three Leading Composers Breathe New Life into the Guitar Concerto," *Acoustic Guitar*, vi/9 (1996), 64–69
J. Tosone: *Classical Guitarists: Conversations* (Jefferson, NC, 2000)
M. Summerfield: *The Classical Guitar: Its Evolution, Players and Personalities Since 1800* (Blaydon on Tyne, England, 1982, 5/2002)
G. Orens: "Isbin, Sharon," *Current Biography*, lxiv/8 (2003), 50–57
R. Tuttle: "'Ms. Guitar, Inc.': A Chat with Sharon Isbin," *Fanfare—The Magazine for Serious Record Collectors*, xxvii/5 (2004), 14–24
L. Del Casale: "Sharon Isbin," *Classical Guitar*, xxvii/9 (2009), 11–16

THOMAS F. HECK/LARS HELGERT

Iseler, Elmer (Walter) (*b* Port Colborne, ON, 14 Oct 1927; *d* Caledon East, ON, 3 April 1998). Canadian choral conductor, arranger, editor, and teacher. After graduating from the University of Toronto (BM 1950), he conducted the University of Toronto Symphony Orchestra and All-Varsity Mixed Chorus, was a choir member at St. Mary Magdelene Church under Healey Willan, and apprenticed with Sir Ernest MacMillan as assistant conductor of the Toronto Mendelssohn Choir. In 1964 he was appointed conductor of the Toronto Mendelssohn Choir, a position he held until 1997. He taught choral music at the University of Toronto from 1965 to 1968, and was Adjunct Professor from 1997 until his death in 1998. After his death, the University of Toronto's Elmer Iseler Chair in Conducting was established in his honor.

Iseler's work with his professional choirs established his reputation in Canada and internationally. In 1954 he helped found Canada's first professional choir, the Toronto Festival Singers. He founded the Elmer Iseler Singers in 1979, and with this choir he toured nationally and internationally. In 1984 and 1985 they joined the Netherlands Chamber Choir for a series of concerts and a critically acclaimed recording. They made appearances at the Seoul Olympics, the 1985 American Choral Directors Association National Convention and the 1987 World Symposium of Choral Music in Vienna. Through his efforts as a conductor and editor of the Elmer Iseler Choral Series, published through Gordon V. Thompson, Iseler introduced significant Canadian composers to American conductors. The technical and artistic excellence of his performances and recordings helped to raise the standards of Canadian choral music in the last half of the 20th century.

RECORDINGS
Sacred and Profane Somers, Centrediscs, CMC-2385 (1985)
Canadian Choral Classics, CBC Records, SMCD 5115 (1992)
Spirituals, Marquis, 7741 8111524 (1993)
Elmer Iseler Conducts Canadian Music, Centrediscs, CMC-6599 (1999)

BIBLIOGRAPHY
W. Pitman: *Elmer Iseler: Choral Visionary* (Toronto, 2008)

L. BRETT SCOTT

Isham, Mark (*b* New York, NY, 7 Sept 1951). Composer and trumpeter. Born into a musical family, he learned piano and violin at an early age before taking up the trumpet. He left high school and moved to San Francisco, where he played classical trumpet. Once there, he quickly took an interest in jazz and rock, especially the music of Miles Davis, Wayne Shorter, Chick Corea, Carlos Santana, and Cold Blood. He also became involved with the electronic music scene in San Francisco. Isham has released several solo jazz albums and has collaborated with such artists as the Rolling Stones, Willie Nelson, Joni Mitchell, and Bruce Springsteen. Isham has also been a prolific film composer, although he did not initially intend to pursue film music as a career. In 1982, an electronic piece for Chinese instruments and synthesizers made its way into director Carroll Ballard's hands, and he was asked to compose the score for the film *Never Cry Wolf*. Since 1990, Isham has been a notably prolific and versatile composer, working closely with directors Alan Rudolph and Paul Haggis. Many of his film scores, particularly early ones including *Reversal of Fortune* and *Point Break*, combine Isham's interest in electronic music with orchestral instruments. Other scores reflect his background in jazz, such as *Short Cuts*, *The Cooler*, *Bad Lieutenant: Port of Call New Orleans*, and the period films *Mrs. Parker and the Vicious Circle* and *Quiz Show*. Director Brian DePalma admired Isham's mournful trumpet work and specifically sought him out to score his *The Black Dahlia*. His warm, lush score for *A River Runs Through It*, a departure from his sparer style, earned him an Academy Award nomination.

WORKS
(selected)

FILM AND TELEVISION SCORES

Never Cry Wolf, 1983; The Times of Harvey Milk, 1984; Mrs. Soffel, 1984; Trouble in Mind, 1985; The Hitcher, 1986; Made in Heaven, 1987; The Moderns, 1988; Love at Large, 1990; Reversal of Fortune, 1990; Mortal Thoughts, 1991; Crooked Hearts, 1991; Point Break, 1991; Little Man Tate, 1991; Billy Bathgate, 1991; Cool World, 1992; A River Runs Through It, 1992; Of Mice and Men, 1992; Nowhere to Run, 1993; Made in America, 1993; Short Cuts, 1993; The Getaway, 1994; Mrs. Parker and the Vicious Circle, 1994; Quiz Show, 1994; Timecop, 1994; Nell, 1994; Miami Rhapsody, 1995; Losing Isaiah, 1995; The Net, 1995; Home for the Holidays, 1995; Last Dance, 1996; Fly Away Home, 1996; Night Falls on Manhattan, 1996; Kiss the Girls, 1997; The Gingerbread Man, 1998; Blade, 1998; At First Sight, 1999; Varsity Blues, 1999; October Sky, 1999; Rules of Engagement, 2000; Life as a House, 2001; The Majestic, 2001; Moonlight Mile, 2002; The Cooler, 2003; Spartan, 2004; Miracle, 2004; Crash, 2004; Racing Stripes, 2005; Kicking and Screaming, 2005; Running Scared, 2006; Eight Below, 2006; The Black Dahlia, 2006; Invincible, 2006; Freedom Writers, 2007; Next, 2007; Reservation Road, 2007; The Secret Life of Bees, 2008; Pride and Glory, 2008; The Express, 2008; My One and Only, 2009; Crossing Over, 2009; Bad Lieutenant: Port of Call New Orleans, 2009; Fame, 2009; The Crazies, 2010; The Mechanic, 2011

DAN BLIM

Islam.

1. Islamic sonic arts in the United States. 2. Music of Muslim-Americans.

1. ISLAMIC SONIC ARTS IN THE UNITED STATES. Islamic doctrine regarding the role and permissibility of music is hotly debated. For some, music is forbidden; for others, music is permissible so long as it does not encourage immoral thoughts or activities; and for others still, music is an integral component of their devotional practices. Although the Qur'ān makes no specific mention of music, several passages as well as sayings and narratives of the life of the Prophet Muhammad (*hadīth*) have been interpreted to support various perspectives on the debate.

For even the most austere interpretations of Islam (those that forbid music), a collection of sonic arts is central to their devotional practice and, even for more liberal schools of thought, these practices are not considered "music." A source of confusion is that while the Arabic term *musīqa* has the same Greek origin as "music" in the English language, these terms do not have the exact same meaning. In Arabic, *musīqa* is thought to pertain to entertainment music and traditions that include instruments, especially winds and strings. Forms of chanting or chanting with drums are not viewed as *musīqa* and thus are permissible. The call to prayer (*adhān*) and the system for the recitation of the Qur'ān (*tajwīd*) are the two most important practices. Both can be performed at a fairly rudimentary level, with an emphasis on proper enunciation, or in a very sophisticated manner that takes years of training and employs advanced use of the Arab melodic modes

(*maqām*) with improvisation and even modulations. Both of these are non-metrical, solo traditions with fixed texts, whose melodic rules are transmitted orally. There are some characteristic upward leaps, but the contour of the melody tends to be based on small intervals in a relatively small range. Devotional a cappella chanting (*nashīd*), sometimes performed with percussion, is also a widely permitted tradition that is not seen as *musīqa*. These are usually performed by a chorus and can feature old and new texts in Arabic and other languages.

Hollywood has used the *adhān* (and melodic figures reminiscent of the *adhān*) in numerous films, but broadcasting the call from local mosques, as it is done in the Muslim world, has been a contentious issue in many American communities. As a compromise, some mosques are permitted to broadcast an amplified *adhān* only for the main Friday service, as opposed to the traditional five times per day, and others simply perform the *adhān* inside the worship hall without amplification to the outside. Although the *adhān* and *tajwīd* are central to Islamic practice, there is a lack of formal training opportunities in the United States, and many American Muslims seek advanced training overseas in places such as Al Azhar University in Egypt. A typical worship service at a mosque will begin with the worshipers' performing a ritual ablution with water when they arrive. The appropriate time for prayer (determined by the position of the sun) is announced by the *adhān* and congregants segregate by gender and form shoulder-to-shoulder lines facing the direction of Mecca, Saudi Arabia, and perform a series of positions (e.g., standing, bowing, prostrating). The prayer leader then recites passages from the Qur'ān at specific points in these series in the *tajwīd* style if they have the appropriate level of training.

Typically prayers are fairly short (5–15 minutes) except on Friday afternoons, when the prayer leader (usually a cleric or someone with religious training) will deliver a sermon.

For some Muslim groups, particularly those who subscribe to various forms of Islamic mysticism (Sufism), music itself is a key devotional act. It is commonly felt that music can be a conduit to subvert the sense of individuality and achieve a temporary sense of unity with the divine. Whereas the previously mentioned orthodox practices are for the most part standardized, Sufi music varies greatly and tends to be highly syncretic with other traditions. Sufism has been quite popular in the United States, through the work of figures such as the poet Rumi, whose 13th-century verse remains widely circulated today, and the Pakistani singer Nusrat Fateh Ali Khan (1948–97), who collaborated with prominent American musicians including Eddie Vedder and contributed to the soundtracks of several Hollywood films.

2. MUSIC OF MUSLIM AMERICANS. The first Muslim populations in North America were brought from Africa as slaves. There is a range of estimates, and the percentage undoubtedly varies greatly over time and location, but may have been as high as 30% of men in some areas.

Among those brought as slaves were *marabout*s (religious scholars) and *griot*s (praise singers), but religious practice was forbidden, and the Muslim population was absorbed into the larger African American community. The earliest known African American writings were by Muslim slaves (often in Arabic) and include the autobiography of Omar Ibn Said, a Fula Islamic scholar who noted the difficulties of following his faith as a slave in the United States. Communities like the Gullah in the Low-country region of Georgia and South Carolina retained a host of Muslim names and Arabic loanwords in the Geechee language. Although these early African Muslims were an integral component of the formulation of African American culture and musical practices, it is difficult to ascertain any direct links to contemporary practice.

Starting in the mid-19th century, immigration from primarily Ottoman territories to the Americas began to build. Although many of these immigrants were Christians from the Eastern Mediterranean, this migration included Muslims from the Balkans, Turkey, and Arabic-speaking regions who settled primarily on the Eastern seaboard and in the Midwest. In the early 20th century, Islamic or Islamic-inspired movements including the Moorish Science Temple, the Ahmadiyya Mission to America, and the Nation of Islam, began to attract American converts. By the 1940s and 1950s, many prominent jazz musicians had joined Islamic movements, especially the Ahmadiyya, including Art Blakey, Yusef Lateef, Ahmad Jamal, Larry Young, and Idris Muhammad. Many others were influenced by Islam, including John Coltrane (whose first wife, Naima, was a Muslim convert). The attraction to Islam had various sources ranging from the esoteric Sufi concept of achieving oneness with God through music, to a theology that was seen as more muscularly demanding equal rights, to a way to subvert social hierarchies (in some instances being Muslim was a way to make an end-run around Jim Crow laws).

While African Americans continue to be the largest percentage of American Muslims, immigrant Muslim communities started to increase dramatically after the passage of national immigration reform acts in 1952 and 1965. This legislation removed most of the previous quotas and restrictions based on national origin and ethnicity and shifted to immigration based on skills, education, or refugee status. In the period after the passage of these acts, much of the immigration came from South and Southwest Asia, but it has since broadened to include communities from every corner of the Muslim world. The Pew Forum on Religion and Public Life estimated that in 2010 there were almost 2.6 million Muslims in the United States.

Members of various Islamic communities have continued to be involved in American popular music. The symbols and rhetoric of the Nation of Gods and Earths (or Five-Percent Nation), an offshoot of the Nation of Islam, have been an important component of hip-hop culture, especially in the 1980s and 1990s. (*See* FIVE PERCENTER RAP.) Other notable artists who have either referenced Islam in their work or have self-identified as Muslim are Rakim, Nas, Busta Rhymes, Public Enemy, Wu-Tang Clan, Black Thought, Mos Def, Common,

Q-Tip, Ali Shaheed Muhammad, Ice Cube, Eve, and Lupe Fiasco. Muslims such as DJ Khaled (Palestinian American) and Akon (Senegalese American) have also found success in hip-hop and R&B. Members of Muslim communities are involved in a wide range of popular music styles, such as Munaf Rayani of the influential post-rock band Explosions in the Sky.

In recent years, groups that perform a mixture of *nashīd*, hip-hop, and other pop styles have become popular and perform regularly at conferences of organizations like the Islamic Society of North America. One of the most well known is Native Deen. Devotional singers from the Middle East and elsewhere have also started to tour in the United States.

The TAQWACORE movement of punk rock—the name is a combination of "hardcore" and *taqwā* ("piety" in Arabic)—has received a fair amount of media attention. While outside of mainstream Islamic practice, this loose collection of bands, including the Kominas and Al Thawra, incorporate Islamic philosophy and references into their music and often take sharp political stands concerning the religion and the treatment of Muslims in North America.

See also ARAB AMERICAN MUSIC.

BIBLIOGRAPHY

S. Diouf: *Servants of Allah: African Muslims Enslaved in the Americas* (New York, 1998)
M. Frishkopf: "Inshad Dini and Aghani Diniyya in Twentieth Century Egypt: A Review of Styles, Genres, and Available Recordings," *Middle Eastern Studies Association Bulletin*, xxxiv/2 (2000) <http://fp.arizona.edu/mesassoc/Bulletin/34-2/34-2%20Frishkopf.htm>
J. Curiel: "Muslim Roots, U.S. Blues," *Saudi Aramco World*, lvii/4 (2006), 8–13 <http://www.saudiaramcoworld.com/issue/200604/muslim.roots.u.s.blues.htm>
E. Curis: *Muslims in America: A Short History* (New York, 2009)

LAITH ULABY

Island. British record company. It was formally established in 1959 by Chris Blackwell in Kingston, Jamaica. Three years later, Blackwell relocated the label's headquarters to London, in part due to the large Jamaican expatriate community living there. By 1964, the Island family of labels included Sue, Black Swan, and Jump-Up. Although the label was located in England during the "British Invasion" era, it wasn't until 1967 that Island turned its focus to rock, signing Traffic, King Crimson, Jethro Tull, and others, with the likes of John Cale and Marianne Faithfull to follow. The British folk scene also yielded some of Island's most notable artists of the era, including Nick Drake, Fairport Convention, Sandy Denny, Richard Thompson, Cat Stevens, and more. Many of these artists were licensed out to other American labels, as Island didn't develop a substantial presence in the United States until its distribution deal with Capitol in 1971. Throughout this time, Blackwell never abandoned his musical roots; he and producer Denny Cordell launched the reggae imprint Mango in 1972, and after singer/actor Jimmy Cliff departed the label in 1973, Island signed Bob Marley.

Over the course of the 1970s, Island's distribution shifted to PolyGram and then Warner Bros. In 1975, the label launched a subsidiary, Antilles, as a mid-price line, featuring albums from Eno & Fripp, Ashley Hutchings, and others. In 1982, Island's agreement with Warner Bros. had run its course, and Blackwell threatened to take the imprint independent, only to return to the WEA fold with a distribution deal through Atlantic. The following year, Island's biggest rock signing, U2, cracked the top 20 album chart, hinting at future achievements. Through the 1980s, rock artists such as Steve Winwood, Tom Waits, and Grace Jones also provided the label with hits. The 4th and B'Way subsidiary label, featuring rap and hip-hop artists including Stereo MCs and Eric B. & Rakim, was launched in 1984.

In July 1989, Blackwell sold the Island Records Group to PolyGram UK. In 1998, PolyGram was acquired by Seagram, which subsequently folded the company into the newly created Universal Music Group, and Island became part of Universal's Island Def Jam Music Group. Current artists of note include Justin Bieber, Jennifer Lopez, Mariah Carey, Bon Jovi, Melissa Etheridge, and others.

BIBLIOGRAPHY
C. Larkin: *The Virgin Encyclopedia of Sixties Music* (London, 1997), 127.
F. Sturges: "Island: The Record Label that Changed the World," *The Independent* (1 May 2009)
S. Newman, C. Salewicz, eds.: *The Story of Island Records: Keep On Running* (New York, 2010)

THANE TIERNEY

Isleta. Native Americans belonging to the Tiwa subgroup of the EASTERN PUEBLO.

Isley Brothers, the. Soul and funk group. The original members, lead singer Ronald Isley (*b* 21 May 1941), O'Kelly Isley (*b* 25 Dec 1937; *d* 31 March 1986), and Rudolph Isley (*b* 1 April 1939), began singing gospel in their native Cincinnati. In 1958 they moved to New York and recorded a series of singles for the Teenager, Mark X, Cindy, and Gone labels before signing to RCA. They achieved success in 1959 and again in 1962 with their composition "Shout." Their next hit was a cover of the Top Notes' "Twist and Shout" (Wand, 1962) using an arrangement which was subsequently copied by the Beatles for their version of the song. After a short-lived attempt at starting their own label, T-Neck Records, in the mid-1960s the Isley Brothers recorded for Motown. Here the production team of Holland, Dozier, and Holland wrote four hits for the group, including "This Old Heart of Mine (Is Weak for You)" (1966).

In 1969 the Isley Brothers reactivated their T-Neck label and added two younger brothers, Ernie on guitar and Marvin on bass, plus cousin Chris Jasper on keyboards. At this point, the group followed the recent development of funk by James Brown and Sly and the Family Stone and, with Ernie Isley's Hendrix-influenced guitar, recorded a series of hit singles that dominated the rhythm and blues charts until 1983, while hardly reaching a white audience. These included original songs such as "It's Your Thing," "That Lady," "Fight the Power" and "The Pride" juxtaposed with covers of pop

material such as Steve Stills's "Love the One You're With" and Seals and Crofts's "Summer Breeze."

In 1984 Ernie and Marvin Isley and Jasper left the original trio and went on to form Isley-Jasper-Isley and had a no.1 R&B hit in 1985 with "Caravan of Love." Ronald and Rudolph continued as the Isley Brothers after O'Kelly's death in 1986, finally disbanding in 1990. A year later Ernie, Marvin, and Ronald Isley reformed the group, now billed as the Isley Brothers featuring Ronald Isley. Between 1987 and 1994, Ronald Isley's wife, Angela Winbush, wrote and produced a number of hits for the group. In 1997 Marvin became diabetic and retired from the group. In 2001 Ernie and Ronald Isley had one final top-five R&B and top-20 Pop hit with the R. Kelly produced "Contagious," making the Isley Brothers the only group to have a hit in six different decades. Marvin Isley died in Chicago in June 2010. On a handful of occasions each year Ronald and Ernie continue to perform together. The Isley Brothers' contributions to popular music were recognized in 1992 when they were inducted into the Rock and Roll Hall of Fame.

BIBLIOGRAPHY
R. Palmer: "Black, Proud and Not Ashamed to be Loud: the Isley Brothers Keep on Fighting the Power," *Rolling Stone* (28 Aug 1975)
A. Peck: "The Isley Brothers Are Ready for Their Next Phase," *Rolling Stone* (10 Aug 1978)
D. Nathan: *The Isley Brothers Story Volume 2: the T-Neck Years (1969–85)*, Rhino R2 70909 (1991) [liner notes]
A. White: *The Isley Brothers Story Volume 1: Rockin' Soul (1959–68)*, Rhino R270908 (1991) [liner notes]

ROB BOWMAN

Istomin, Eugene (George) (*b* New York, NY, 26 Nov 1925; *d* Washington, DC, 10 Oct 2003). Pianist. He first studied with Kiriena Siloti, and then at the Mannes College. When he was 12 he entered the Curtis Institute, where he studied with RUDOLF SERKIN and MIECZYSLAW HORSZOWSKI. In 1943 he won the youth competition sponsored by the Philadelphia Orchestra, with which he made his orchestral debut playing Chopin's F minor Concerto the same year. That year he also won the Leventritt Award, which led to an appearance with the New York PO, playing Brahms's Second Concerto (1943). Around this time he also played with the Busch Chamber Players; his first recording, which brought him considerable attention, was of Bach's D minor Concerto with that ensemble. He then appeared regularly as a soloist with leading American orchestras, embarking on major tours abroad from 1956; he was associated primarily with 19th-century works. In 1961 he formed a trio with Isaac Stern and Leonard Rose; his performances of chamber music represent the delicate end of the expressive spectrum. In 1975 he married Marta Casals, the widow of Pablo Casals; she became artistic director of the Kennedy Center in 1980.

MICHAEL STEINBERG/DENNIS K. McINTIRE

Italian American music. *See* EUROPEAN AMERICAN MUSIC.

Ithaca College. Private college in Ithaca, New York. It was founded by Grant Egbert in 1892 as the Conservatory of Music. In 1931 several affiliated institutions merged to form the comprehensive Ithaca College: Patrick Conway Military Band School, Williams' School of Expression and Dramatic Art, Ithaca School of Physical Education, and Westminster Choir School. As of 2009 the School of Music enrolls about 575 students and employs 62 full-time instructors. It offers the BM, BA, MM, and MS degrees in performance, music education, composition, jazz studies, sound recording technology, theory, conducting, Suzuki pedagogy, and music in combination with another field. The school has established archives of Walter Beeler, Karel Husa, and Frank Battisti, and sponsors the publication of the *Journal of Historical Research in Music Education*.

MARK FONDER

Iturbi, José (*b* Valencia, Spain, 28 Nov 1895; *d* Los Angeles, CA, 28 June 1980). Pianist and conductor of Spanish birth. He studied at the Valencia Conservatory and then with Victor Staub at the Paris Conservatoire, where he gained a *premier prix* in piano in 1913. During World War I he played in Swiss cafés, then taught at the Geneva Conservatoire, 1919–23. Extensive tours followed. He first played in the United States (where he settled) in 1928; in 1930 he gave 77 concerts on one American tour. In 1936 he was appointed conductor of the Rochester PO, a post he held for several seasons. His connection with films began when his fingers impersonated Chopin's in *A Song to Remember*; he then appeared in several more films. He was the most famous Spanish pianist of his day, with a large popular following; in 1950 he became the first classical musician whose sales of a single record exceeded a million copies. Some critics held reservations about his Beethoven and Chopin, but his playing of the music of his native land was idiomatic, ebullient, and vital. Iturbi composed a number of pieces in a Spanish idiom, including the *Pequeña danza española* for piano and *Seguidillas* for orchestra. His sister Amparo (1898–1969), with whom he often performed, was also a pianist.

BIBLIOGRAPHY
R. Pons Server: *José Iturbi* (Valencia, Spain, 1995)

FRANK DAWES/R

Ivers, Eileen (*b* New York, NY, 13 July 1965). Traditional Irish fiddler, banjo player, and bandleader. Eileen Ivers was raised in the Bronx by Irish parents. She took up the fiddle at age nine, taking lessons with Irish fiddler MARTIN MULVIHILL. She began competing in the All-Ireland championships as a teen, and ultimately won 35 championships, including nine solo fiddle titles and a tenth on tenor banjo, making her the most successful American-born competitor in the All-Ireland's history.

During the 1980s, Ivers was a founding member of Cherish the Ladies, played with Mick Moloney's ensemble The Green Fields of America, and toured and recorded in an influential duo with accordionist John Whelan. In 1990, she was invited to record and tour with the pop duo Hall & Oates, which she did for over a year. She then returned to New York, where she immersed herself in the multicultural music scene. In

1994, she released her first solo album, and in 1995, she joined the touring cast of *Riverdance*, an acclaimed theatrical production based on Irish traditional music and dance. Drawing inspiration from all these experiences, Ivers experimented with a style of music based in Irish traditional forms, incorporating classical, pop, and world-music elements, as well as elements of musical theater. The result is her ensemble Immigrant Soul, which she launched in 2003. As one of the most sought-after Irish fiddlers for pop music projects, in recent years Ivers has also become a popular guest artist for symphony and pops orchestras.

STEPHEN D. WINICK

Ives, Burl (Icle Ivanhoe) (*b* Hunt Township, Jasper Co., IL, 14 June 1909; *d* Anacortes, WA, 14 April 1995). Singer and actor. Ives began singing in public as a child. In 1929 he dropped out of Eastern Illinois State Teachers College to pursue a career as a performer. He auditioned, albeit unsuccessfully, for Gennett Records in 1929. In 1931 he moved to New York City where he landed some minor stage roles. His first major success came as the host of a CBS radio program, "The Wayfaring Stranger," which ran from 1940 until 1942. He began recording folk songs in the 1940s, with releases on the Columbia, Asch, and Decca labels. In 1945 he gave his first important concert at Town Hall in New York City. That same year he portrayed a singing cowboy in the film *Smoky*, and received a Donaldson Award for his appearance in the Broadway production *Sing Out, Sweet Land*. He later produced an ambitious educational series of recordings for Encyclopedia Britannica Films, *Historical America in Song* (1950), and compiled several printed collections of folk songs. During the 1960s and 1970s he continued to record and to perform in films and theatrical productions. His notable screen appearances include *East of Eden* (1955), *Cat on a Hot Tin Roof* (1958), *The Big Country* (1958, for which he won an Academy Award as Best Supporting Actor), and the television mini-series *Roots* (1977). In spite of the fact that Ives had built his identity as a performer of folk songs, his greatest successes as a singer came with the pop/country hits "A Little Bitty Tear" (1961) and "Funny Way of Laughin'" (1962). It is ironic that by the time the folk revival was in full gear, Ives, who had played an important role in instigating it, had largely moved on to other creative pursuits.

RECORDINGS
(selective list; all recorded for Decca)
Ballads and Folk Songs (1949); *Ballads, Folk and Country Songs* (1949); *Down to the Sea in Ships* (1956); Marianne (1957); A Little Bitty Tear (1961); Call Me Mr. In-between (1962); *It's Just my Funny Way of Laughing* (1962); Mary Ann Regrets (1962); The Same Old Hurt (1963); This is All I Ask (1963); True Love Goes on and on (1963); Pearly Shells (1964)

BIBLIOGRAPHY
B. Ives: *The Wayfaring Stranger* (New York, 1948)
"Ives, Burl (Icle Ivanhoe)," *CBY 1960*
R.M. Lawless: *Folksingers and Folksongs in America: a Handbook of Biography, Bibliography, and Discography* (New York, 1960, rev. 2/1965)
Obituary: *New York Times* (15 April 1995)

R.D. Cohen: *Rainbow Quest: the Folk Music Revival and American Society, 1940–1970* (Amherst, MA, 2002)

CHERYL A. BRAUNER/PAUL F. WELLS

Ives, Charles (Edward) (*b* Danbury, CT, 20 Oct 1874; *d* New York, NY, 19 May 1954). Composer. His music is marked by an integration of American and European musical traditions, innovations in rhythm, harmony, and form, and an unparalleled ability to evoke the sounds and feelings of American life. He is regarded as the leading American composer of art music of the early 20th century.

1. Unusual aspects of Ives's career. 2. Youth, 1874–94. 3. Apprenticeship, 1894–1902. 4. Innovation and synthesis, 1902–8. 5. Maturity: modernist nationalism, 1908–18. 6. Completions and last works, 1919–29. 7. Revisions and premieres, 1929–54.

1. UNUSUAL ASPECTS OF IVES'S CAREER. Ives had an extraordinary working life. After professional training as an organist and composer, he worked in insurance for 30 years, composing in his free time. He used a wide variety of styles, from tonal Romanticism to radical experimentation, even in pieces written during the same period, and in his mature music frequently used multiple styles within a single work as a formal and expressive device. His major works often took years from first sketch to final revisions, and most pieces lay unperformed for decades. His self-publications in the early 1920s brought a small group of admirers who worked to promote his music. Around 1927 he ceased to compose new works, focusing instead on revising and preparing for performance the works he had already drafted. By his death he had received many performances and honors, and much of his music had been published. His reputation continued to grow posthumously, and by his centenary in 1974 he was recognized worldwide as the first composer to create a distinctively American art music. Since then his music has been frequently performed and recorded and his reputation has broadened further, resting less on his innovations or nationality and more on the intrinsic merits of his music.

The unique circumstances of Ives's career have bred misunderstandings. His work in insurance, combined with the diversity of his output and the small number of performances during his composing years, led to an image of Ives as an amateur. Yet he had a 14-year career as a professional organist and thorough formal training in composition. Since he developed as a composer out of the public eye, his mature works seemed radical and unconnected to the past when they were first published and performed. However, as his earlier music has become known, his deep roots in 19th-century European Romanticism and his gradual development of a highly personal modern idiom have become clear. The first of Ives's major works to appear in performance and publication, such as *Orchestral Set no.1: Three Places in New England*, the *Concord Sonata*, and movements of the Symphony no.4 and *A Symphony: New England Holidays*, were highly complex, incorporated diverse musical styles, and made frequent use of musi-

cal borrowing. These characteristics led some to conclude that Ives's music could be understood only through the programmatic explanations he offered and was not organized on specifically musical principles. Yet by analyzing his techniques in depth and tracing their evolution through his earlier works, scholars have demonstrated the craft that underlies even seemingly chaotic scores and have shown the close relationship of his procedures to those of his European predecessors and contemporaries.

One result of Ives's unusual path is that the chronology of his music is difficult to establish beyond general outlines. His practice of composing and reworking pieces over many years often makes it impossible to assign a piece a single date. That he worked on many compositions and in many idioms simultaneously makes the chronological relationships between works still more complex. There is often no independent verification of the dates Ives assigned to his works, which can be years or decades before the first performance or publication. It has been suggested that he dated many pieces too early and concealed significant revisions in order to claim priority over European composers who used similar techniques (Solomon, C1987) or to hide from his business associates how much time he was spending on music in the 1920s (Swafford, C1996). Recent scholarship, however, has established firmer dates for the types of music paper Ives used and refined estimated dates for various forms of his handwriting, allowing most manuscripts to be placed within a brief span of years (Sherwood, C1994 and E1995, building on Kirkpatrick, A1960, and Baron, C1990). These methods have often come to support Ives's dates, confirming that he did indeed develop numerous innovative techniques before his European counterparts, including polytonality, tone-clusters, chords based on 4ths or 5ths, atonality, and polyrhythm. Where a discrepancy exists—in the case of several longer works for example—this may well result from his practice of dating pieces by their initial conception, the first ideas worked out at the keyboard or in sketches now lost. The dates provided here are, then, estimates based on the manuscripts when extant, supplemented by contemporary documents and Ives's testimony.

2. YOUTH, 1874–94. The Iveses were one of Danbury's leading families, and they were prominent in business and civic improvement and active in social causes, such as the abolition of slavery. Ives's father George E. Ives (1845–94) was an exception in making music a career. He took lessons on the flute, violin, piano, and cornet, following which, during 1860–62, he studied harmony, counterpoint, and orchestration with the German-born musician Carl Foeppl in New York. After Civil War service as the youngest bandmaster in the Union Army and two more years in New York, he returned to Danbury and pursued a variety of musical activities, performing, teaching, and leading bands, orchestras, and choirs in and near Danbury, and sometimes touring with traveling minstrel shows. He also worked in businesses connected to the Ives family. He married Mary

("Mollie") Elizabeth Parmalee (1850–1929) on 1 January 1874, and Charles was born on 20 October the same year, followed by J. Moss (1876–1939), who became a lawyer and judge in Danbury.

As a youth Ives was exposed to the entire range of music-making in Danbury, from the band music and gospel hymns he associated with his father to the cultivated repertoire fostered by the local school of music. He studied the piano and organ from a young age with a series of teachers and was playing in recitals by his early teens. He became an accomplished performer in three musical traditions: American vernacular music, Protestant church music, and European classical music. Additionally, he was an avid athlete and was captain of several baseball and football teams.

Ives played the drums with his father's band, and the spirit of band performance echoes in many works of his maturity. He wrote marches for piano, band, and theatre orchestra, several of which adopt the by then longstanding practice of setting a popular song in one section of the march. His first publicly performed piece may have been the march *Holiday Quickstep*, written when he was 13; despite the work's somewhat old-fashioned style, the review in the *Danbury Evening News* of the January 1888 premiere called him "certainly a musical genius" and declared "we shall expect more from this talented youngster in the future."

At the age of 14 he became the youngest salaried church organist in the state, and he worked regularly as one until 1902. He wrote anthems and sacred songs for church services, at first using hymn texts and a hymn-like style, as in *Psalm 42*. The hymns he knew from church, and the gospel hymns he knew from camp-meeting revivals where his father sometimes led the singing with his cornet, he later regularly borrowed or reworked as themes in sonatas, quartets, and symphonies. He heard some classical music in concert performances in Danbury, New York, and Chicago (at the 1893 World's Fair) and learned rather more through his own study and performance of works by Bach, Handel, Beethoven, Rossini, Schubert, Mendelssohn, Wagner, John Knowles Paine, and others on the piano or organ, including many transcriptions. His virtuoso *Variations on "America"* (1891–2) shows just how skilled an organist Ives was while still in his late teens. Many of the distinctive features of Ives's mature music stem from his experience as an organist, including his penchant for improvisation, virtuosic demands on performers, orchestration with layering or juxtaposition of contrasting timbres (akin to contrasting ranks of pipes on the organ's different keyboards), spatial effects (based on alternating Great and Swell keyboards), and frequent use of pedal points, fugal textures, and hymn tune elaborations, all characteristics of the organ repertoire (Burkholder, D2002).

Although he had many teachers for performance, his father taught him harmony and counterpoint and guided his first compositions. Several of these take existing works as models, following the traditional practice of learning through imitation, such as the *Polonaise* for two cornets and piano (*c*1887–9), modeled on the

sextet from Donizetti's *Lucia di Lammermoor*. At the same time, Ives's father had an open mind about musical theory and practice and encouraged his son's experimentation. Bitonal harmonizations of *London Bridge*, polytonal canons and fugues, and experiments with whole-tone pieces, triads in parallel motion, and chromatic lines moving in contrary motion to create expanding or contracting wedges, all dating from the early 1890s, show Ives's interest in testing the rules of traditional music by trying out alternative systems, as if the rules of music theory were as arbitrary as those of baseball (whose rules changed several times during his youth). Many of Ives's experiments derive from extending European classical precedents: for example, the fugue in four keys (C, F, B♭, E♭) that opens his *Song for Harvest Season* was modeled on a fugal modulating sequence in the same keys in Mendelssohn's organ Prelude and Fugue in C Minor, op.37, no.1, which Ives played in church and in recital. At the time, Ives apparently conceived of such experimentation merely as playing with music theory, a private activity shared primarily with his father, rather than regarding these new systems as a serious basis for composing concert music. On still another musical plane, it was his father whom he credited with teaching him the songs of Stephen Foster, whose tunes he would later borrow and whose simple diatonic lyricism informs many of Ives's own melodies.

Ives moved to New Haven in early 1893 to attend Hopkins Grammar School and prepare for entrance examinations at Yale. He pitched for the Hopkins baseball team and led them to victory over the Yale freshmen in April 1894 for only the second time in the school's history. He was the organist at St. Thomas's Episcopal Church for a year, and then moved to Center Church on the Green in September 1894, the same month he matriculated at Yale. Just six weeks later, on 4 November,

Charles Ives. (Lebrecht Music & Arts)

his father died suddenly of a stroke. Leaving home, starting university, and especially the death of his principal teacher and supporter marked a sharp break from the past and the end of his youth.

3. APPRENTICESHIP, 1894–1902. Ives began his time at Yale as a virtuoso organist and an experienced composer of popular and church music but with limited exposure to classical music. He continued to compose vernacular works including songs, marches, and glee club and fraternity-show numbers. Several works were published, including three glees, a march, and an 1896 presidential campaign song for William McKinley. His church music also grew in maturity. The choirmaster at Center Church, John Cornelius Griggs, was a supportive colleague and mentor and became a lifelong friend. For the Center Church choir, which was led by a quartet of paid soloists, Ives wrote anthems such as *Crossing the Bar* in a chromatic late-Romantic style modeled on the anthems of Dudley Buck, the leading composer of music for quartet choir, with whom he briefly studied the organ around 1895. Later, he gradually adopted the elevated choral style of his teacher at Yale, Horatio Parker, in works such as *All-Forgiving, look on me.*

But it was in classical music that Ives learned the most. For the first time, he had regular access to chamber and orchestral concerts. He audited Parker's courses in harmony and music history during his first two years, and then studied counterpoint, instrumentation, and strict composition with Parker. In his senior year he took the capstone course in free composition (as an unregistered student because he lacked one prerequisite); Parker's willingness to admit him to the class shows his high esteem for Ives's potential as a composer. Ives assimilated the German lied by resetting texts from well-known examples, typically incorporating some aspects of the model's structure or contour while seeking a different figuration and mood. He later recalled that his *Feldeinsamkeit* earned the praise of Parker's teacher George Chadwick for taking "a more difficult and almost opposite approach" that was "in its way almost as good as Brahms" and "as good a song as [Parker] could write." Comparison of Ives's earlier exercises with the works of his last term at Yale shows how much he learned from Parker, whose thorough instruction provided the firm foundation he needed in theory and composition.

Ives began his Symphony no.1 under Parker, and later recalled that the second and fourth movements were accepted as his final thesis, although he continued to work on it after graduation. In this work there are strong echoes of the symphonic masterpieces he used as models, especially Schubert's "Unfinished" in the first movement, Dvořák's "New World" in the slow movement and the work as a whole, Beethoven's Ninth Symphony in the scherzo, and the third movement of Tchaikovsky's "Pathétique" in the finale. Yet even the most direct references are reworked in fresh and interesting ways. Ives owed to Parker his new found skills in counterpoint, thematic development, orchestration, and composing large forms, along with the concept, foreign to

the utilitarian music of Danbury, of music as an experience to be savored for its own sake. The simultaneous citation of the familiar and assertion of an individual personality is a distinguishing Ives trait, evident even in the music he wrote in a late-Romantic style. This work also set the pattern for Ives's later symphonies and for many of his sonatas in linking movements through the cyclic repetition of themes.

Although he studied music diligently, Ives may not have intended to make music his career. He took the usual round of Greek, Latin, German, French, mathematics, history, and political science, and he remembered especially fondly his English and American literature courses with William Lyon Phelps, who helped to form Ives's taste in poetry. A Yale education was regarded as a preparation for success in business, and much of the social life on the all-male campus was organized around groups through which one could develop friendships and potentially useful connections. Ives was no great scholar outside his music courses, but he was well-regarded and socially successful, chosen as a member of the Delta Kappa Epsilon fraternity and of Wolf's Head, one of Yale's elite secret senior societies. Songs of both groups figure in later works recalling his college days, such as *Calcium Light Night* and the middle movement of the Trio for Violin, Violoncello, and Piano. One of his best friends was David Twichell, who invited him to Keene Valley in the Adirondacks for a family vacation in August 1896; there Ives met his future wife, David's sister Harmony (1876–1969).

After graduation in 1898, he moved to New York, living for the next decade in a series of apartments, all wryly dubbed Poverty Flat, with other bachelors with Yale connections. Through his father's cousin, Ives gained a position in the actuarial department of the Mutual Insurance Company. In early 1899 he moved to Charles H. Raymond and Co., agents for Mutual, where he worked with sales agents and developed ways to present the idea of insurance. There he met Julian Myrick (1880–1969), who would later become his partner.

While working in insurance, Ives did not give up all hope of a musical career. He continued to serve as an organist, first in Bloomfield, New Jersey (where for the first time he was also choirmaster), and then from 1900 at the Central Presbyterian Church in New York, a prestigious post. After university, he ceased writing vernacular music and sought to consolidate his training as a composer of church music and art music in the Parker mold. He continued to write lieder to established texts and composed a seven-movement cantata, *The Celestial Country*, modeled in its format on the quartet choir cantatas of Buck and in specific details on Parker's oratorio *Hora novissima*, whose 1893 premiere had established Parker's reputation.

He also pursued some new avenues. Parker had focused on German music; now Ives wrote French chansons, modeled on those of composers such as Massenet. He reworked some of the German songs with new English texts; it would become characteristic of him to reshape older pieces into newer ones, often in different media. In similar fashion, he developed what may have been church service music from his Yale years into a string quartet that used paraphrased hymn tunes as themes. The opening theme of the First Symphony had used elements of two hymns, but the String Quartet no.1 established the pattern for many later works in that it derived virtually every one of its themes from a hymn tune source. Unaltered hymn tunes were too predictable and repetitive in rhythm, melody, and harmony to serve well as themes for movements in classical forms, so Ives ingeniously reshaped them into irregular, Brahmsian themes ripe for development, while preserving a hymn-like, American character. Ex.1 shows the derivation of the opening theme of the third movement from its source, the hymn-tune *Nettleton* ("Come, Thou Fount of Ev'ry Blessing"). With this work Ives began to integrate the different traditions he had learned, bringing the spirit and sound of Protestant hymnody into the realm of art music.

Most remarkably, Ives's experimentation took on a new seriousness. Armed with techniques learned from Parker and perhaps inspired by compositional systems of the Middle Ages and Renaissance that

Ex.1 Opening theme of String Quartet no.1, 3rd movt, and its source

Parker described in his music history lectures, such as organum, counterpoint, and rhythmic stratification, Ives began to produce, not mere sketches or improvised "stunts," but finished pieces that explore new procedures. Most significant is a series of sacred choral works, mainly psalm-settings, that Ives may have tried out with singers where he was organist, although no performances are registered. *Psalm 67* uses transformations of a five-note chord (arranged to create the impression of bitonality) to harmonize a simple melody in a style resembling Anglican chant. *Psalm 150* features parallel triads that are dissonant against sustained triads. *Psalm 25* deploys angular, dissonant two-voice canons over pedal points and includes a whole-tone passage that expands from a unison to a whole-tone cluster spanning almost three octaves. In *Psalm 24* the outer voices move in contrary motion, expanding from a unison in each successive phrase and moving first by semitones (often displaced by octaves), then by whole tones, 3rds, 4ths, 4ths and tritones, and finally 5ths; after the golden section of the work, there is a contraction, phrase by phrase, using the same intervals in reverse order, to make an approximate palindrome.

Each piece finds new ways to establish a tonal center, create harmonic motion and resolution, and regulate counterpoint. The technique chosen often responds to the text; for example, the central image of *Processional: Let There Be Light* is perfectly conveyed by the procession of chords formed of 2nds, 3rds, 4ths, and 5ths, through increasingly dissonant chords of 6ths and 7ths, to pure octaves. In these systematic experiments in compositional method, Ives established what was to become a 20th-century tradition of experimental composition, one that included the work of Henry Cowell, Charles Seeger, Ruth Crawford Seeger, John Cage, and many later composers. These experimental works remained distinct from his concert music, which continued to use the language of European Romanticism.

The climax of Ives's apprenticeship was the premiere of *The Celestial Country* at the Central Presbyterian Church in April 1902, his most ambitious piece to be performed up to that point. It received pleasant, if mild, reviews from the *New York Times* and *Musical Courier*. Yet soon after, Ives resigned as organist, the last professional position in music he was to hold. He recalled that he left behind much of his church music, which was later discarded by the church, so that what survives of his anthems, songs, and organ music for services is only part of what may have been a much larger body of work. Ives apparently concluded that he did not want or would not achieve a career like that of Parker, who survived as a composer by serving as a church organist and teaching at Yale. Ives would later ironically describe this as the time he "resigned as a nice organist and gave up music."

4. INNOVATION AND SYNTHESIS, 1902–8. Having abandoned music as a career, Ives cast his lot with insurance. However, in 1905 the New York state legislature launched an investigation of scandals in the insurance business, with Mutual and the Raymond agency as

particular targets. Although Ives was not implicated, higher executives were, including two of Ives's relatives, and the agency was ultimately dissolved. The investigation coincided with two bouts of illness for Ives in the summer of 1905 and late 1906, diagnosed as neurasthenia (nervous exhaustion) with irregular heartbeat, a condition associated at the time with overwork, especially among upper-class businessmen (Magee, C2001). The usual prescribed remedy was a rest cure. Ives spent the late summer of 1905 at Saranac Lake in the Adirondacks with David Twichell and family, including Harmony, by then a registered nurse. While recuperating from the second, more serious illness over Christmas 1906 at Old Point Comfort, Virginia, Ives finalized plans with Myrick to launch an agency affiliated with Washington Life, which had begun as a Mutual subsidiary; it appears that Mutual's management helped with the arrangements. Ives & Co. opened on 1 January 1907, with Myrick as Ives's assistant. The two became central figures of the generation that professionalized the insurance business and cleaned up its image after the 1905 scandals. The ideals Ives stated and pursued as a businessman were, ironically, those articulated at the New York legislature's hearings by the president of Mutual: that life insurance was not a scheme for profit, but a way for each policyholder to provide for his family while "participating in a great movement for the benefit of humanity at large" through mutual assistance.

The year 1905 also began the other key partnership of Ives's adulthood, as he renewed his acquaintance with Harmony Twichell. Their courtship was slow, hindered by long absences, infrequent times together, and Ives's shyness. She wrote poems, some of which he set to music in a tonal, Romantic style meant to please her and her family, and they planned an opera that never materialized. Their friendship grew in intensity until they professed their love for each other on 22 October 1907. They were married on 9 June 1908 by Harmony's father, the Rev. Joseph Twichell, at his Congregational church in Hartford, and settled in New York.

Harmony rekindled Ives's interest in composition after three years in which he had composed little. Without a church position, he had evenings and weekends free for composition, and forgoing regular performance allowed Ives freedom to explore without having to please anyone but himself. No longer a Parker apprentice, nor a composer of popular or sacred music, Ives entered a period of innovation and synthesis.

Ives now sought increasingly to integrate vernacular and church style into his concert music. In his Second Symphony (begun by 1902, completed c1907–9), the major work of this period, he introduced for the first time both hymn tunes and American popular songs into a piece in the classical tradition. The framework is still European, a cyclic five-movement symphony in late Romantic style with direct borrowings from Bach, Brahms, Wagner, Dvořák, and Tchaikovsky; the final two movements are modeled on the finale of Brahms's First Symphony. But the themes are all paraphrased from American melodies, reshaped to suit sonata and ternary forms. Like many symphonies that employ national material, the work celebrates the nation's music while conforming to an international style. What is especially striking is that the national material is not primarily folk music (only three fiddle tunes fit that category) but rather types of popular music, including Stephen Foster songs, patriotic songs, popular songs, gospel songs, and hymn tunes. From this time on, most of Ives's major works would integrate sounds and melodies of popular music into classical genres. This was a radical departure from the traditional focus on privileging folk material, but it was a choice that represented his own experience and that of many urban Americans, who were more familiar with popular music from several generations than with any folk music.

In other pieces, such as the improvisations and sketches that became the *Ragtime Dances*, Ives began to create a more modern and individual idiom that drew on American melodic and rhythmic characteristics, including ragtime, the currently popular style. Ives had grown familiar with ragtime at Yale and in New York, primarily East Coast performing styles and Tin Pan Alley ragtime songs, and he was one of the first composers to integrate its gestures into classical genres. In such works, Ives was writing music about music, evoking the sounds and spirit of American music-making, placing both himself and his listeners in the role of spectators. The many guises the *Ragtime Dances* would eventually assume—from a set of dances for theatre orchestra to movements in his Piano Sonata no.1, *Set for Theatre Orchestra,* and *Orchestral Set no.2*, and passages in his second Quarter-Tone Piece for two pianos—illustrate again his penchant for reworking his own music into new forms.

He continued experimenting, especially now in chamber music, whose greater range of sonorities allowed him to extend traditional counterpoint and increase the independence between the parts to create an effect of separate layers. Works such as the *Fugue in Four Keys on "The Shining Shore," From the Steeples and the Mountains,* and *The Unanswered Question* display polytonal and atonal canons, multiple layers distinguished by rhythm, pitch content, and sonority, and the combination of atonal and tonal planes, often with a program to explain the unusual musical procedures. For example, *Scherzo: All the Way Around and Back* gradually builds up six distinct layers, subdividing each bar into 1, 2, 3, 5, 7, and 11 equal divisions respectively, over which a bugle plays fanfares in common time (Ex.2); the piece is palindromic, swelling to a climax and returning in an exact retrograde, a musical analogue to "a foul ball [in baseball]—and the base runner on 3rd has to go all the way back to 1st." Several of his experimental works use such images from baseball, which became a proving ground for musical ideas as it had been for his athletic abilities in his teens (Johnson, D2004). In works like this Ives developed approaches using interval cycles, pitch class sets, and other organizing principles that he later used to great effect in his mature music.

Ex.2 *Scherzo: All the Way Around and Back*, bars 17–18

5. MATURITY: MODERNIST NATIONALISM, 1908–18. Ives's wife Harmony played a crucial role in his development. As he noted in his *Memos*, her unwavering faith in him gave him confidence to be himself, although she did not claim to understand all of his music. Moreover, she helped him to find the purpose and the subject matter for his mature work. She wrote to him in early 1908 stating that

> inspiration ought to come fullest at one's happiest moments—I think it would be so satisfying to crystallize one of those moments at the time in some beautiful expression—but I don't believe it's often done—I think inspiration—in art—seems to be almost a consolation in hours of sadness or loneliness & that most happy moments are put into expression after they have been memories & made doubly precious because they are gone.

This upholds the Romantic idea of music as an embodiment of individual emotional experience, but adds two elements that were to become characteristic of Ives's mature music: capturing specific moments that are individual and irreplaceable, and doing so through memory. Her interest in Ives's father and family revived his own, and several pieces over the next decade recall the town band (*Decoration Day, The Fourth of July, Putnam's Camp*), the American Civil War (*The "St Gaudens" in Boston Common*), camp meetings (Symphony no.3, Violin Sonata no.4, *The Rockstrewn Hills Join in the People's Outdoor Meeting*), and other memories Ives connected to his father. Harmony's interest in literature rekindled his, which had apparently lain dormant since college, and he produced a series of works on Emerson, Browning, Hawthorne, Thoreau, and others. Her sense of idealism about America echoed in him, stimulating a rush of pieces on American subjects. The socially committed Christianity of the Twichells reinforced that of the Ives family, as Ives took up subjects from Matthew

Arnold's *West London* to the movement to abolish slavery (*Study no.9: The Anti-Abolitionist Riots in the 1830s and 40s*). Although her influence and support were crucial, Harmony was of course not his only inspiration; some pieces respond to current events or set poetry he read in newspapers, and several works begun in the mid-1910s focus on war or memorials to war, inspired by the 1911–15 50th anniversary of the Civil War and by the events of World War I.

Ives's successes in insurance must also have bolstered his self-confidence. After Washington Life was sold in 1908, he took Myrick into full partnership in an agency with Mutual, launched on 1 January 1909. Within a few years, they were selling more insurance than any agency in the country, during a time of dramatic expansion in the industry. Their secret lay in recruiting a wide network of agents to sell policies for them and in preparing detailed guidelines for selling insurance, summarizing the best arguments to be made. Ives established the first classes for insurance agents at Mutual and helped to devise and promote "estate planning," a method still used to calculate the amount of life insurance one should carry based on a family's expected expenses and income should they lose their main breadwinner. His pamphlet *The Amount to Carry* became a classic of its kind. He composed during the evenings, at weekends and on vacations, finding particular inspiration at a weekend cabin on Pine Mountain in Connecticut and during family vacations in the Adirondacks. Family letters suggest that Harmony chose these getaways, at rural locations suitable for rest cures, as part of Ives's ongoing treatment for neurasthenia, but increasingly composition seems to have played a role as a relief from the pressures of business.

The works of 1908–18 have been aptly described as examples of modernist nationalism (Magee, C2008), using modernist techniques to ruminate on American music and culture. Ives continued to use American melodies as themes, but turned from the traditional ternary and sonata forms of the First Quartet and Second Symphony to a new pattern that has been called cumulative form. In the outer movements of the Symphony no.3, most movements of the four violin sonatas and the Piano Sonata no.1, and several other works from c1908–17, the borrowed hymn tune used as a theme appears complete only near the end, usually accompanied by a countermelody (often paraphrased from another hymn). This is preceded by development of both melodies, including a statement of the countermelody alone. The harmony may be dissonant, and the key is often ambiguous until the theme appears, but the music remains essentially tonal. Cumulative form drew on traditional sources, including thematic development and recapitulation; the 19th-century conventions of a large work culminating with a hymn-like theme and of combining themes in counterpoint; and the church organist practice of preceding a hymn with an improvised prelude on motives from the hymn. Indeed, Ives commented that many of these movements developed from organ preludes he had played or improvised in church, all now lost. However, Ives's synthesis was new. The avoidance of large-scale repetitions, inherent in older forms, allowed him to use hymns essentially unaltered as themes, for the rhythmic and melodic plainness and lack of harmonic contrast that made them unsuitable for the opening theme of a sonata form were perfect for the culmination of a movement. The process of developing motives and gradually bringing them together in a hymn paralleled, on a purely musical level, the experience Ives remembered of hymn-singing at the camp-meetings of his youth, as individuals joined in a common expression of feeling. The combination in many of these works, such as the Third Symphony, of source tunes from the camp-meeting repertoire with hymns from middle-class mainline churches, all in a compositional framework derived from European symphonies and sonatas, embodies a reconciliation of rural and urban, lower- and middle-class, and American and European traditions.

In other works, Ives sought to capture American life, especially American experiences with music, in a more directly programmatic way. *The Housatonic at Stockbridge* (Ex.3) evokes a walk by the river Ives and his wife shared soon after their marriage. The main melody (given to second violas, horn, and English horn), harmonized with simple tonal triads (in the lower strings and brass, notated enharmonically), suggests a hymn wafting from the church across the river, while repeating figures in distant tonal and rhythmic regions (upper strings), subtly changing over time, convey a sense of the mists and rippling water. Like this work, most of Ives's music about life experiences is composed in layers, distinguished by timbre, register, rhythm, pitch content, and dynamic level, to create a sense of three-dimensional space and multiple planes of activity; here

the earlier experiments in layering bear rich fruit. *Central Park in the Dark* pictures the noises and music of the city against the background sounds of nature, rendered as a soft series of atonal chords in parallel motion. In *From Hanover Square North*, background ostinatos represent city noises in New York, over which commuters on a train platform gradually come together to sing a hymn for those lost in the sinking of the *Lusitania* that morning. When suggesting a memory of his youth, as in *Putnam's Camp, The Fourth of July,* and *Washington's Birthday*, Ives often infused the background with a collage of tunes related by motif or genre to his main theme, evoking the way one memory will summon up others in a stream of consciousness. Songs such as The Last Reader and The Things Our Fathers Loved suggest a similar fount of memory through a patchwork of fragments from songs of the past. These collages and patchworks present a multiplicity of references, but they build on Ives's experience with more traditional forms of borrowing.

These programmatic pieces and songs mix tonality with atonality, traditional with experimental procedures, direct quotation with paraphrases and original melodies. Having developed an impressive range of tools, Ives used them all in his mature works, choosing whatever was appropriate to fit the image, event, or feeling he was attempting to convey. Ives wrote in 1925, "why tonality as such should be thrown out for good, I can't see. Why it should be always present, I can't see. It depends, it seems to me, a good deal—as clothes depend on the thermometer—on what one is trying to do." Ives's willingness to break rules, even his own, for expressive ends places him with the likes of Monteverdi, Beethoven, Mahler, Strauss, and Berg as an essentially dramatic and rhetorical composer. Like them he often coordinated diverse styles within a single movement, using the contrasts to delineate sections and create form as well as for emotional effect. Though this eclecticism has been criticized by those who value systems, refinement, and homogeneity more than rhetorical power, many others have found the mix of elements in Ives's music an apt expression of the heterogeneity of modern, especially American, life.

In 1912 Ives and his wife bought farmland in West Redding, near Danbury, and built a house, soon settling into a pattern of spending May to November in West Redding and the rest of the year in New York. Unable to have children after Harmony miscarried in April 1909 and underwent an emergency hysterectomy, they found a partial outlet for their parental energies in Moss's six children, often hosting one or two of them for extended periods. They opened a cottage on their property to poor families from the city through the Fresh Air Fund; the second family to visit had a sickly infant daughter, whom they cared for and eventually adopted as Edith Osborne Ives (1914–56).

From time to time Ives sought out performances or at least readings of his music, and this encouraged him to have clean scores and parts copied by a series of professional copyists. Walter Damrosch conducted an

Ex.3 *The Housatonic at Stockbridge*

Charles Ives manuscript, "Fourth of July." (Lebrecht Music & Arts)

informal reading of movements from the First Symphony in March 1910; attempts to interest him in the Second and Third had no result. Periodically, Ives invited or hired professional musicians to try out some of his music; the reactions he recorded in his *Memos* ranged from incomprehension to apoplectic criticism of its dissonance and complexity. The United States' entrance into World War I in April 1917 inspired him to write the song In Flanders Fields to a text by a Mutual medical examiner, and Myrick arranged for a performance at a meeting of insurance executives. Later the same month David Talmadge (violin teacher to Ives's nephew Moss White Ives) and Stuart Ross performed the Third Violin Sonata for an invited audience at Carnegie Chamber Music Hall.

6. COMPLETIONS AND LAST WORKS, 1919–29. The war pulled Ives away from composition into work for the Red Cross and Liberty Loan appeals. He even tried to enlist in 1918 to serve six months in France with the YMCA but did not pass the physical examination. On 1 October 1918, he suffered a debilitating illness, apparently a serious recurrence of his cardio neurasthenia, which kept him from work for a year.

Mindful of his mortality, Ives set about finishing and making available the music he had been composing. Two months in early 1919 were spent on a rest cure at Asheville, North Carolina, where he completed his Second Piano Sonata, subtitled *Concord, Mass., 1840–60*, with musical impressions of Emerson, Hawthorne, the Alcotts, and Thoreau, and wrote most of

an accompanying book of *Essays before a Sonata*, his most detailed statement of his aesthetics. The importance of transcendentalism in the sonata and essays has obscured other influences, including those of Beethoven, Debussy, Liszt, and Skryabin on the sonata (and on much of Ives's other music) and those of Romantic aesthetics and liberal Christianity on his philosophy. The famous distinction Ives makes in the essays between "substance" (more or less, the spiritual content of a work) and "manner" (the means of its expression) derives largely from a 1912 essay on Debussy by Ives's friend John C. Griggs. The sonata and the essays were privately printed in 1920–21 and sent free to musicians and critics whom he hoped to interest in his music. Most reviews were mocking, and the sonata's programmaticism and nationalism were out of step with the postwar mood, but a perceptive notice by Henry Bellamann praised the sonata's "loftiness of purpose" and its "elevating and greatly beautiful" moments. Bellamann became Ives's first advocate, lecturing and writing on his music, and Ives later set two of Bellamann's poems.

Between 1919 and 1921 Ives gathered most of his songs, including 20 new ones, 20 adapted to new texts, and 36 newly arranged from works for chorus or instruments, into a book of *114 Songs*, privately printed in 1922. Many of the songs use words by Ives or by Harmony, while others set a wide range of texts, from the great English and American poets Ives studied with Phelps at Yale to hymns and poems he found in newspapers, or other such sources. The volume encompasses the diversity of Ives's output, from the vast clusters that open *Majority* and the quartal chords and whole-tone melody of *The Cage* to his German lieder and parlor songs from the 1890s. The late songs include a new style for Ives: more restrained, simpler, and with less overt quotation, although still often dissonant and full of contrasts used to delineate phrases and highlight the text. This is illustrated in the song *Resolution* (Ex.4), which features four distinctive figurations in its brief eight measures, each using a different collection of pitches and each subtly linked to images in the text: in *a*, a pentatonic melody with dotted rhythms recalls American folksong style, associated with rugged strength and the outdoors, while the wide spacing in voice and piano evokes the spaciousness of "distant skies"; in *b*, tonal harmonies and secondary dominants suggest hymnody, representing faith; *c* mimics the style Ives associated with sentimental parlor songs, with an undulating melody in dotted rhythm over harmonies tinged with chromaticism, while the reiterated chords and emphasis on G create a sense of marking place; *d* is again diatonic, suggesting Romantic song through a leap and descent; and *a* returns at the close, as "journey" harks back to "walking."

Once again Ives distributed his publication to musicians and critics, hoping to attract some interest, with little initial success; John Philip Sousa found some songs "most startling to a man educated by the harmonic methods of our forefathers," and the *Musical Courier* called Ives "the American Satie, joker par excellence." Nevertheless, several of the songs were

Ex.4 *Resolution*

Walk-ing strong-er un-der dis-tant skies, Faith e'en needs to mark the sen - ti-men-tal pla - ces; Who___ can tell where___ Truth may ap - pear, to guide the journ - ey!___

given their premieres in recitals in Danbury, New York, and New Orleans, between 1922 and 1924, and were apparently well received. Ives also completed or revised many other works between 1919 and the early 1920s, including the First Piano Sonata, the Second Violin Sonata, and most movements of *A Symphony: New England Holidays, Orchestral Set no.1: Three Places in New England, Orchestral Set no.2,* and the Symphony no.4. Many of these multi-movement cycles brought together movements first conceived separately, sometimes at different times. The Second Violin Sonata was first performed in 1924 to respectful reviews, but the others had to wait.

In 1923 Ives met E. Robert Schmitz, pianist and head of the Franco-American Musical Society, later renamed Pro-Musica Society. The relationship was mutually beneficial; Ives supported the Society financially (though anonymously), and Schmitz arranged performances of the newly composed *Three Quarter-Tone Pieces* for two pianos in 1925, the first two movements of the recently completed Fourth Symphony in 1927, and the piano piece *The Celestial Railroad* in 1928. The symphony was a summation of all Ives had done, drawing on more than a dozen earlier works and encompassing the range

of his techniques from pure tonality to the most rhythmically complex textures any conductor had ever seen. It traces a mystical inner journey: the brief opening movement poses "the searching questions of What? and Why? which the spirit of man asks of life" (in the words of Bellamann's program note) by means of a choral setting of the hymn tune "Watchman, Tell Us of the Night"; the second movement, adapted from *The Celestial Railroad*, is a dream-like collage based on Hawthorne's tale of the same name, a satire of the search for an easy way to heaven; the third movement, based on the first movement of the First Quartet, depicts religious "formalism and ritualism" through a tonal fugue on hymn tunes; and after these two false answers to the questioning prelude the finale suggests the truer path through a meditation on *Bethany* ("Nearer, My God, to Thee") in cumulative form. Despite the work's novelty and complexity, it won encouraging reviews from Olin Downes of the *New York Times* and Lawrence Gilman of the *Herald Tribune,* two of the leading critics of the day.

Ives stopped composing new works by early 1927; as Harmony later told John Kirkpatrick, "he came downstairs one day with tears in his eyes and said he couldn't seem to compose any more—nothing went well—nothing sounded right." Theories abound for his cessation, from the psychological effects of his double life in business and music to the physical illnesses he continued to endure. He may have exhausted himself from the push to complete the Fourth Symphony and other major works. He had started no new orchestral compositions since an attempt at a third orchestral set in *c*1921, which remained unfinished. The early 1920s had produced a few songs and his choral masterpiece *Psalm 90*, essentially rewritten from scratch around 1923. Around the same time he returned to his ambitious *Universe Symphony* (begun *c*1915), the capstone of his exploration of systematic methods of composition, which features over 20 wholly independent musical strands, each moving in its own subdivision of a metric unit eight seconds in length. This too would remain unfinished, finally appearing in three separate realizations in the 1990s. His last new work was the song Sunrise in August 1926, left incomplete. He had still received very few performances, and no professional publications since the 1890s. Ives may have followed the same steps as most composers—first conceiving a piece, then drafting, revising, completing and copying it, and seeing it through to performance and publication—but instead of doing this for each piece in a short span of time, he did it for dozens of pieces at once, stretched over decades.

7. REVISIONS AND PREMIERES, 1929–54. After years of health problems, eventually diagnosed as diabetes (for which he was among the first to receive insulin treatments), Ives retired from business on 1 January 1930. His music was written, but its public career was just beginning. After Bellamann and Schmitz, Ives found an ever-increasing series of advocates who promoted and performed his music. Most important was Henry Cowell, whose activities in support of new American music

(including Ives's own) Ives supported financially. Cowell's quarterly *New Music,* whose first issue in 1927 brought Cowell to Ives's attention, printed several Ives works, starting with the second movement of the Fourth Symphony in 1929, and Cowell's New Music Society sponsored the premiere of the First Violin Sonata in San Francisco in 1928. In the late 1920s and 30s, Cowell wrote a series of appreciations of Ives's music emphasizing its pioneering use of innovative techniques and reframing Ives as a uniquely American experimentalist composer, one who created the first truly American art music by using American tunes and representing in art music distinctively American folk performance traditions. Also at Cowell's urging, Nicolas Slonimsky approached Ives for a piece for his Boston Chamber Orchestra, and Ives responded by rescoring *Three Places in New England,* which Slonimsky performed in New York, Boston, Havana, and Paris in 1931 to generally favorable reviews. The combination in this and other works of modernist sounds, nationalist subjects, and recognizable borrowings from familiar American tunes was well suited to the Depression-era interest in cultivating a wide audience for modern classical music. That September, Slonimsky conducted the premiere of *Washington's Birthday* at a New Music Society concert in San Francisco, and the following year he conducted *The Fourth of July* in Paris, Berlin, and Budapest. In May 1932 Hubert Linscott and Aaron Copland presented seven of Ives's songs at the first Yaddo Festival of Contemporary American Music, and Ives began to be seen as a forerunner of the current generation of American modernists. These seven songs, *The Fourth of July,* and the *Set for Theatre Orchestra* were published in 1932, followed by more songs in 1933 and 1935, *Three Places in New England* in 1935, *Washington's Birthday* in 1936, and *Psalm 67* in 1939. Numerous songs were given premieres in recitals during the 1930s in New York, San Francisco, Boston, Dresden, Vienna, Paris (with Messiaen at the piano), and elsewhere. The January 1939 New York premiere of the *Concord Sonata* by John Kirkpatrick (who had played the world premiere the previous November in Cos Cob, Connecticut) drew high praise from Gilman in the *Herald Tribune,* who called it "exceptionally great music…the greatest music composed by an American, and the most deeply and essentially American in impulse and implication." More premieres followed, including the Fourth Violin Sonata in 1940, the Symphony no.3 and the String Quartet no.2 in 1946, and the Piano Sonata no.1 in 1949, each more than two decades after its completion. Ives was elected to the National Institute of Arts and Letters in 1945, and the Symphony no.3 won the Pulitzer Prize in 1947. Bernstein conducted the New York PO in the premiere of the Symphony no.2 in 1951, over 40 years after its completion, and the Symphony no.1 was finally performed for the first time in 1953, almost half a century after it was finished.

Throughout this time, Ives continued to work on his music, copying the full score for *Thanksgiving* during a year in Europe with Harmony in 1932–3, recording his own piano performances and improvisations in London and New York, adding a new ending to the Second Symphony, and pulling old pieces out of his piles of manuscripts. He had photocopies made of his manuscripts and sent them to those who expressed interest in a work. In the early 1930s he dictated reminiscences about his life and his music, intended only to provide information for those writing about him, but published four decades later as *Memos.* Although in *Essays before a Sonata* he had seemed a follower of Beethoven, in *Memos* he emphasized his experimental works and his invention of novel techniques, presenting himself as the pioneer Cowell and others seemed to want him to be, and credited so much influence to his father that he obscured for decades his deep debts to Parker, to the 19th-century Romantic tradition, and to older contemporaries such as Debussy, Strauss, and Skryabin. He worked for years on a revised edition of the *Concord Sonata,* finally published in 1947. His health gradually weakened, and in May 1954 he died of a stroke while recovering from an operation.

Music continued to appear after his death, and his reputation continued to grow. Harmony Ives gave his manuscripts to the Library of the Yale School of Music in 1955, and John Kirkpatrick published a meticulous catalog in 1960. The first biography, by Henry and Sidney Cowell in 1955, was followed by a steady stream of theses and articles. The Fourth Symphony was finally played in its entirety in 1965. *Memos* and other writings appeared in 1972. The Charles Ives Society, which became active in 1973, has sponsored a series of critical editions of individual works with Kirkpatrick and James B. Sinclair the most prominent editors. The 1974 centennial brought the first festivals devoted to Ives's music, and there have been several since. He is now regarded as one of the leading composers of his time from any nation, with a secure place in the concert repertoire and a growing body of scholarly studies of his music and life.

Although the legend of Ives as an isolated, idiosyncratic, and uniquely American figure was useful to those seeking to promote his music in the 1920s through 1950s, it led to a distorted picture of him. As a result, much of the scholarship on Ives has been revisionist, correcting earlier misimpressions and reframing him to suit new perspectives. Influenced by Cold War politics, the Cowells' 1955 biography already portrayed Ives differently than Cowell had done in the 1930s, now highlighting his individualism and links to Transcendentalism. Later biographies by Frank Rossiter (C1975), J. Peter Burkholder (C1985), Stuart Feder (C1992), Jan Swafford (C1996), and Gayle Sherwood Magee (C2008) have repeatedly challenged earlier views, revealing an Ives who was very much of his time, influenced by a variety of intellectual currents beyond Transcendentalism, and much less isolated or idiosyncratic than he once appeared. Other studies have revealed Ives's strong links to European composers from Bach and Beethoven to Debussy and Skryabin, have shown how his techniques from musical borrowing to pitch organization draw on traditional practices while also developing new innovations, and have shown how his political views, use of gendered language, and activities both in and outside of music relate to contemporary currents in American life. Successive waves of reconsideration are deepening our understanding of his unusual career and of the genesis, structure, and meaning of his music. The picture that is emerging is increasingly well-rounded, embracing the contrasts and contradictions that both Ives and his music so richly embodied.

See also BORROWING, EXPERIMENTAL MUSIC.

WORKS

A chronological listing of Ives's works is neither possible nor appropriate as dates for many works are uncertain, and Ives tended to work on a number of pieces simultaneously, often taking years from first sketch to final revision.

This work-list follows the ordering, numbering and title style in James B. Sinclair, *A Descriptive Catalogue of the Music of Charles Ives* (New Haven, 1999), grouping works by genre and numerically or alphabetically within each genre. Most incomplete works, exercises, arrangements of works by others, unidentified fragments, and lost or projected works are omitted. Dates are of manuscripts when extant; these are based on Gayle Sherwood's datings of the manuscripts by paper type and handwriting, and they may not reflect the entire period of composition if the earliest sketches or final revisions do not survive. Dates in square brackets are from Ives's own hand but represent pieces or stages of composition for which no manuscripts are extant. Printed works are published in New York unless otherwise stated (reprints are not listed). For full details of publication and first performances, see Sinclair.

MSS in *NH*, photocopies in *NYp*, *Wcg*

corr. edn	corrected edition
crit. edn	critical edition sponsored by The Charles Ives Society
real.	realized by
rej.	rejected
>	derived from
<	developed into

Principal publishers: Arrow, Associated, Mercury, Merion, New Music, Peer, Peters, Presser, G. Schirmer

ORCHESTRAL

Symphonies

No.	Title and instrumentation	Dates	First known performance	Remarks and publication
1	Symphony no.1	c1898–c1902, c1907–8	Washington, DC, 26 April 1953	ed. R. Cordero (1971); crit. edn J. Sinclair (1999)
	i. Allegro	c1898–c1902, c1908		first theme <318 (itself <339)
	rej. ii. Largo	c1898–9		inc.; <2/iii
	ii. Adagio molto	c1898–9, c1907–8		
	iii. Scherzo: Vivace	c1898–9, c1907–8		
	iv. Allegro molto	[1898], c1907–8		part of coda <part of 122/ii
2	Symphony no.2	[1899–1902], c1907–9	New York, 22 Feb 1951	ed. H. Cowell and L. Harrison (1951); corr. edns (1988, 1991); crit. edn J. Elkus (2007)
	i. Andante moderato	c1907–8		?>lost org sonata, lost ov.
	ii. Allegro	c1908–9		?>lost ovs.
	iii. Adagio cantabile	c1908–9		>1/rej. ii; portion <part of 105
	iv. Lento (maestoso)	c1908		?>lost ov. or lost org sonata
	v. Allegro molto vivace	c1907–9, new ending c1950		?>lost ov./ovs.; portions <part of 105
3	Symphony no.3: The Camp Meeting, small orch	[1904], c1908–11	New York, 5 April 1946	ed. L. Harrison (1947); rev. and corr. edn H. Cowell (1964); crit. edn K. Singleton (1990)
	i. Old Folks Gatherin'	c1909–10		>lost org prelude
	ii. Children's Day	c1908–10		>lost org postlude
	iii. Communion	c1909–11		>lost org communion piece; <222
	rej. iv. Allegro	c1910		inc.; <9/i
4	Symphony no.4, pf, orch, opt. SATBB	c1912–18, c1921–5	New York, 26 April 1965 [complete work]	(1965)
	i. Prelude	c1916–17, c1923–4	New York, 29 Jan 1927	portion >386 or part of 60/iii
	ii. Allegretto	c1916–18, c1923–5	New York, 29 Jan 1927	>116 (itself >88/ii, which borrows from 36); ?>lost Hawthorne Concerto; (San Francisco, 1929)
	iii. Fugue	c1912–13, c1923–4	New York, 10 May 1933	>57/i
	iv. Largo	c1915–16, c1921–4		?>lost slow march; ending>ending of 58/iii
5	A Symphony: New England Holidays	assembled ?c1917–19	Minneapolis, 9 April 1954 [complete work]	
	i. Washington's Birthday, small orch	[1909–13], c1915–17	San Francisco, 3 Sept 1931	(San Francisco, 1936); crit. edn J. Sinclair (1991)
	ii. Decoration Day	[1912–13], c1915–20, rev. c1923–4	Havana, 27 Dec 1931	early version <64; crit. edn J. Sinclair (1989)
	iii. The Fourth of July	[1912], c1914–18, rev. c1930–31	Paris, 21 Feb 1932	portions > or < parts of 315; portion > trio of 24; (San Francisco and Berlin, 1932); crit. edn W. Shirley (1992)
	iv. Thanksgiving and Forefathers' Day, orch, opt. SSATTB	c1911–16, rev. 1933		?>lost 1904 version; >lost 1897 org prelude and postlude; crit. edn J. Elkus (1991)

No.	Title and instrumentation	Dates	First known performance	Remarks and publication
6	Universe Symphony	1915–28	Greeley, CO, 29 Oct 1993 [i and iv, ed. D. Porter]; Cincinnati, 28 Jan 1994 [real. L. Austin]; New York, 6 June 1996 [real. J. Reinhard]	portions >part of 49/1; chord structures used in 319
	i. Prelude no.1	c1923		
	ii. Prelude no.2	c1923		inc.
	iii. Prelude no.3, lost			
	iv. Section A	1915–28		
	v. Section B	1923–8		inc.
	vi. Section C	1923–8		inc.

	Orchestral sets			
7	Orchestral Set no.1: Three Places in New England	c1912–17, c1919–21	New York, 10 Jan 1931 [small orch version]	version for small orch 1929, rev. 1933–5, ed. N. Slonimsky (Boston, 1935); crit. edn J. Sinclair, with full orch (Bryn Mawr, PA, 1976, 2/2008)
	i. The "St Gaudens" in Boston Common (Col. Shaw and his Colored Regiment)	c1915–17		>version for piano (Black March)
	ii. Putnam's Camp, Redding, Connecticut	c1914–15, c1919–20		>36 and 24
	iii. The Housatonic at Stockbridge	[1908], c1912–17, rev. c1921		>early song version; <266
8	Orchestral Set no.2	assembled c1919	Chicago, 11 Feb 1967	crit. edn J. Sinclair (2001)
	i. An Elegy to Our Forefathers	c1915–19, c1924–5		
	ii. The Rockstrewn Hills Join in the People's Outdoor Meeting	c1915–16, c1920–22		>43/iii, borrows from 43/i and ii
	iii. From Hanover Square North, at the End of a Tragic Day, the Voice of the People Again Arose, orch, opt. unison vv	1915–c1916, c1918–19, c1926, c1929		
9	Orchestral Set no.3	assembled c1921		transcr. of MSS in Porter, 1980
	i.	c1921–2, c1925–6	Fullerton, CA, 16 March 1978 [real. D. Porter]	>3/rej. iv
	ii. An Afternoon/During Camp Meetin' Week—One Secular Afternoon (In Bethel)	c1912–14, c1921–2		inc.; partly >24; portion >part of 51; borrows from 104
	iii.	c1921		inc.; borrows from 27

	Sets for chamber orchestra			
10	Set no.1	assembled c1915–16		
	i. Scherzo: The See'r	[1913], c1915–16		=18/ii; <344; portions reworked in 128/ii
	ii. A Lecture	[1909], c1915–16		<377
	iii. The Ruined River	[1912], c1915–16		>or <186 and 308 (itself <14/i and 17/i); portions reworked in 128/ii
	iv. Like a Sick Eagle	[1909], c1915–16		=19/i; <288
	v. Calcium Light Night	[1907], c1915–16	New Haven, 22 Feb 1956 [ed. and arr. H. Cowell]	portion borrowed from 70, reused in 117/i
	vi. Allegretto sombreoso	c1915–16	New York, 10 May 1951	<280; (1958)
11	Set no.2	assembled c1916–17	New Haven, 3 March 1974 [ed. K. Singleton]	
	i. Largo: The Indians	[1912], c1916–17		<283 (itself <14/ii and 17/ii), <19/iii; first half <part of 128/ii
	ii. "Gyp the Blood" or Hearst!? Which is Worst?!	?1912, c1916–17		?inc.; crit. edn real. K. Singleton (1978)
	iii. Andante: The Last Reader	[1911], c1916–17		<18/i, 286
12	Set no.3	assembled c1919	New York, 6 Dec 1962 [arr. G. Schuller]	
	i. Adagio sostenuto: At Sea	c1918–19		<213; ?<16/i; (1969)
	ii. Luck and Work	c1919	New York, 10 May 1951	<or>293; <19/ii
	iii. Premonitions	c1918–19		<328

No.	Title and instrumentation	Dates	First known performance	Remarks and publication
13	Set no.4: Three Poets and Human Nature	?c1925–30		not fully orchestrated
	i. Robert Browning			>324; arr. D. Porter
	ii. Walt Whitman			>384; arr. G. Smith
	iii. Matthew Arnold		New Haven, 20 Oct 1974 [real. J. Kirkpatrick]	>388
14	Set no.5: The Other Side of Pioneering, or Side Lights on American Enterprise	?after c1925		<17
	i. The New River			=17/i; >308 (itself > or <10/iii and 186)
	ii. The Indians			=17/ii; >283 (itself >11/i)
	iii. Charlie Rutlage		New Haven, 3 March 1974	>226; crit. edn K. Singleton (1983)
	iv. Ann Street			=17/iii; >211; not fully orchd
15	Set no.6: From the Side Hill	?c1925–30		
	i. Mists		New Haven, 3 March 1974	>301 version 2; crit. edn real. K. Singleton (Bryn Mawr, PA, 1976)
	ii. The Rainbow			>330 (itself >45)
	iii. Afterglow			>207
	iv. Evening		New Haven, 3 March 1974	>244; crit. edn real. K. Singleton (1983)
16	Set no.7: Water Colors	?c1925–30		
	i. At Sea			>213, ? >12/i; not fully orchd
	ii. Swimmers		New Haven, 3 March 1974 [real. J. Sinclair]	>366
	iii. The Pond		New Haven, 3 March 1974	>332; crit. edn real. K. Singleton (1977)
	iv. Full Fathom Five			>324; orchestration lost
17	Set no.8: Songs without Voices	?c1930	New York, 21 April 1930 [in a version for tpt, pf]	>14
	i. The New River			=14/i
	ii. The Indians			=14/ii
	iii. Ann Street			=14/iv
18	Set no.9 of Three Pieces	assembled ?1934		
	i. Andante con moto: The Last Reader			>11/iii (itself <286)
	ii. Scherzo: The See'r			=10/i
	iii. Largo to Presto: The Unanswered Question			=50 rev. version
19	Set no.10 of Three Pieces	assembled ?1934		
	i. Largo molto: Like a Sick Eagle			=10/iv (itself <288)
	ii. Allegro-Andante: Luck and Work			>12/ii (itself >293)
	iii. Adagio: The Indians			>11/i (itself <283, which <14/ii and 17/ii)
20	Set for Theatre Orchestra	assembled c1915	New York, 16 Feb 1932 [complete work]	(San Francisco, 1932)
	i. In the Cage	[1906], c1907–8, rev. c1911–12		<or >221
	ii. In the Inn	[1904–11], c1915–16, rev. c1929–30		>43/i and 87/iib; portions reworked in 128/ii
	iii. In the Night	[1906], c1915–16, rev. c1929–30	St. Paul, MN, 7 Dec 1931	>80 and lost choral hymn-anthem

Overtures

No.	Title and instrumentation	Dates	First known performance	Remarks and publication
22	Emerson Overture for Piano and Orchestra	c1910–14, rev. c1920–21	Cleveland, 1 Oct 1998 [real. D. Porter]	inc.; portions >90, 91, 97; portion < or >99; portion <part of 107; portions <88/i, 123
24	Overture and March "1776," small orch	[1903–4]; c1909–10	New Haven, 3 March 1974	outer sections <portions of 7/ii; part of trio <part of 5/iii; partly <9/ii; portion used in 74; crit. edn real. J. Sinclair (Bryn Mawr, PA, 1975)
25	Overture in G Minor	c1899		inc.
27	Robert Browning Overture	c1912–14, rev. c1936–42	New York, 14 Oct 1956	portions <portions of 324; borrowed from in 9/iii; ed. H. Cowell and L. Harrison (1959)

Marches

No.	Title and instrumentation	Dates	First known performance	Remarks and publication
28	Holiday Quickstep, pic, 2 cornets, pf, 2 vn	1887	Danbury, 16 Jan 1888	> or <lost band Holiday March; <lost org arr.; crit. edn J. Sinclair (Bryn Mawr, PA, 1975)
29	March no.2, with "Son of a Gambolier," small orch	1892, c1895	New Haven, 3 March 1974	<or >110; crit. edn K. Singleton (1977)
31	March no.3, with "My Old Kentucky Home," small orch	c1895	New Haven, 19 Oct 1973	portion <part of 396; crit. edn K. Singleton (Bryn Mawr, PA, 1975)
33	March: The Circus Band, chbr orch, opt. SSATTBB	c1898–9, arr. c1932–3		early version >115; final version >229 (itself >115); arr. G. Roberts (1969)

No.	Title and instrumentation	Dates	First known performance	Remarks and publication
		Other orchestral		
	Adagio sostenuto: see 12/i			
	Allegretto sombreoso: see 10/vi			
	Ann Street: see 14/iv			
	Calcium Light Night: see 10/v			
34	Central Park in the Dark, small orch	[1906], c1909, rev. c1936	New York, 11 May 1946	crit. edn J.-L. Monod and J. Kirkpatrick (Hillsdale, NY, 1973)
	Charlie Rutlage: see 14/iii			
35	Chromâtimelôdtune, small orch	c1923	New York, 6 Dec 1962 [real. G. Schuller]; New Haven, 3 March 1974 [real. K. Singleton]	real. and arr. G. Schuller (1963)
36	"Country Band" March, small orch	[1905], c1910–11, c1914	New Haven, 3 March 1974	inc.; borrows from 43/i; <part of 7/ii; portions borrowed in 88/ii (itself <116, which <4/ii) and in 262 (itself <182, 188, 371); crit. edn real. J. Sinclair (Bryn Mawr, PA, 1974)
	Decoration Day: see 5/ii			
	Evening: see 15/iv			
	The Fourth of July: see 5/iii			
37	The General Slocum	[1904], c1909–10	New York, 29 Nov 1970 [real. G. Schuller]	inc.
38	The Gong on the Hook and Ladder/Firemen's Parade on Main Street, small orch	arr. c1934	New York, 22 April 1934	>70; (San Francisco, 1953); (1960); corr. edn J. Sinclair (1979)
	"Gyp the Blood" or Hearst?! Which is Worst?!: see 11/ii			
	Holidays Symphony: see 5			
	Mists: see 15/i			
40	The Pond, small orch	[1906], c1912–13	New York, 22 April 1934	<332, 16/iii; crit. edn J.-L. Monod and J. Kirkpatrick (Hillsdale, NY, 1973)
41	Postlude in F	c1898–9	New Haven, 6 June 1971	>lost org postlude; crit. edn K. Singleton (1991)
43	Four Ragtime Dances, small orch	[1902–11], c1915–16, c1920–21		crit. edn J. Sinclair (1990)
	i. no.1		New Haven, 22 April 1976	partly >46; < 87/iib, 20/ii; portions reworked in 8/ii, 36, 128/ii
	ii. no.2		New Haven, 21 Oct 1974	partly >46; <87/iia; portions reworked in 8/ii
	iii. no.3		New Haven, 25 Feb 1976	<8/ii
	iv. no.4		New Haven, 21 Oct 1974	<87/ivb; portion reworked in 128/ii
45	The Rainbow, small orch	1914	Danbury, 11 April 1969	<330, 15/ii; (1959)
46	Skit for Danbury Fair	[1902], c1909	West Redding, CT, 17 Aug 1974 [real. K. Singleton]	inc.; portions <portions of 43/i (itself <87/iib, 20/ii), 43/ii (itself <87iia)
47	Take-Off no.7: Mike Donlin—Johnny Evers	1907	West Redding, CT, 17 Aug 1974 [real. K. Singleton]	inc.
48	Take-Off no.8: Willy Keeler at Bat	c1907	West Redding, CT, 17 Aug 1974 [real. K. Singleton]	inc.
	Thanksgiving and Forefathers' Day: see 5/iv			
	Three Places in New England: see 7			
49	Tone Roads et al.			
	i. Tone Roads no.1	c1913–14	San Francisco, 10 Aug 1950	portion <part of 6; (1949)
	ii. Tone Roads no.2			lost
	iii. Tone Roads no.3	c1911, c1913–14	New York, 20 Dec 1963	(1952)
50	The Unanswered Question, 4 fl/(2 fl, ob, cl), tpt/(ob/ eng hn/cl), str orch/str qt	1908, rev. c1930–35	New York, 11 May 1946 [rev. version]; New York, 17 March 1984 [first version]	rev. version = 18/iii; (Montevideo, 1941); (1953); both versions, crit. edn P. Echols and N. Zahler (1985)
	Washington's Birthday: see 5/i			
51	Yale-Princeton Football Game	[1899], c1910–11	New York, 29 Nov 1970 [real. G. Schuller]; New Haven, 2 Oct 1976 [real. J. Sinclair]	?inc.; portion <part of 9/ii
			BAND	
52	Fantasia on "Jerusalem the Golden"	[1888]	West Caldwell, NJ, 5 Feb 1972 [arr. K. Brion]	only short score extant; arr. K. Brion (1974)
53	March in F and C, with "Omega Lambda Chi"	1895–6		>111; ed. and arr. K. Brion (1974)

No.	Title and instrumentation	Dates	First known performance	Remarks and publication
54	March "Intercollegiate," with "Annie Lisle"	c1895	Washington, DC, 4 March 1897	>112; (Philadelphia, 1896); ed. and arr. K. Brion (Hackensack, NJ, 1973)
55	Runaway Horse on Main Street	c1907–8	New Haven, 18 Nov 1977 [real. J. Sinclair]	inc.; partly <portion of 226

CHAMBER ENSEMBLE

String quartets

57	String Quartet no.1: From the Salvation Army	c1897–c1900, c1909	New York, 17 March 1943 [movts ii–iv only]; New York, 24 April 1957 [complete work]	(1961 and 1963)
	i. Chorale	c1897–8		<lost org fugue; <4/iii
	ii. Prelude	c1900, c1909		? <lost org prelude
	iii. Offertory	c1897–8, c1909		>lost org prelude
	iv. Postlude	c1900, c1909		>lost org postlude
58	String Quartet no.2	c1913–15	New York, 11 May 1946	(1954); corr. edn J. Kirkpatrick (1970)
	i. Discussions	[1911], c1913–14		
	ii. Arguments	[1907], c1913–14		
	iii. The Call of the Mountains	[1911–13], c1914–15		ending <ending of 4/iv

Sonatas for violin and piano

59	Pre-First Sonata for Violin and Piano	[1901–3], c1908–13		inc.; mostly <61
	i. Allegretto moderato	[1902–3], c1909–10, rev. c1911–12		>lost org postlude; portion <part of 61/ii
	rej. ii. Largo	[1901], c1909–10		<73; pubd as Largo for Violin and Piano, ed. P. Zukofsky (1967)
	ii. Largo	[1902, 1908], c1911–12		<60/ii
	rej. iii. Scherzo	c1908–9		inc.; <part 61/ii
	iii. Largo–Allegro	[1908–10], c1911–13		inc.; <61/i
60	Sonata no.1 for Violin and Piano	assembled c1914 or c1917	San Francisco, 27 Nov 1928	(1953)
	i. Andante–Allegro vivace	[1906], c1910–12, c1914, rev. c1917		
	ii. Largo cantabile	c1914, rev. c1917		>59/ii
	iii. Allegro	[1909], c1911–12, rev. c1917–18, c1924–5		portion >lost song "Watchman"; <386; used in 4/i
61	Sonata no.2 for Violin and Piano	assembled c1914–17	New York, 18 March 1924	mostly >59; ed. J. Kirkpatrick (1951)
	i. Autumn	c1914, rev. c1920–21		>59/iii; ending <265
	ii. In the Barn	c1914, rev. c1920–21		>59/rej. iii, part of 59/i
	iii. The Revival	c1915–17, rev. c1920–21		>63/rej. iv
62	Sonata no.3 for Violin and Piano	1914	New York, 22 April 1917	ed. S. Babitz and I. Dahl (1951)
	i. Adagio			>lost org prelude
	ii. Allegro			>lost org toccata, lost ragtime piece
	iii. Adagio cantabile			>lost org prelude
63	Sonata no.4 for Violin and Piano: Children's Day at the Camp Meeting	assembled c1914–16	New York, 14 Jan 1940	(1942)
	i. Allegro	c1911–12		>lost sonata for tpt and org
	ii. Largo–Allegro (conslugarocko)–Andante con spirito–Adagio cantabile–Largo cantabile	c1914–15		
	iii. Allegro	c1916		>lost piece for cornet and str; portion <214
	rej. iv. Adagio–Faster	[1906, 1909–10], c1915–17		<61/iii

Other chamber

	Adagio cantabile: The Innate: see 84/iii			
64	Decoration Day for Violin and Piano	arr. c1919	New Haven, 19 Oct 1973	>early version of 5/ii
65	From the Steeples and the Mountains, tpt, trbn, 4 sets of bells	[1901], c1905–6	Waltham, MA, 26 April 1963	(1965)
69	Fugue in Four Keys on "The Shining Shore," fl, cornet, str	c1903	New Haven, 3 March 1974	crit. edn real. J. Kirkpatrick (Bryn Mawr, PA, 1975)

No.	Title and instrumentation	Dates	First known performance	Remarks and publication
70	The Gong on the Hook and Ladder/Firemen's Parade on Main Street, str qt/str qnt, pf	c1912		<38; portion borrowed in 10/v, 117/i
71	Hallowe'en, str qt, pf, opt. b drum/timp/any drum	[1911], c1914	New York, 22 April 1934	(1949)
72	In Re Con Moto et al., str qt, pf	[1913], c1915–16, rev. c1923–4	New York, 11 Feb 1970	(1968)
	Largo for Violin and Piano: see 59/rej. ii			
73	Largo for Violin, Clarinet and Piano	arr. ?1934	New York, 10 May 1951	>59/rej. ii; (1953)
	Largo cantabile: Hymn: see 84/i			
74	Largo risoluto no.1, str qt, pf	c1908–9	Washington, DC, 4 May 1958	portions < or >parts of 24, 82; (1961)
75	Largo risoluto no.2, str qt, pf	c1909–10	Washington, DC, 4 May 1958	(1961)
76	An Old Song Deranged, cl/ eng hn/1v, hp/gui, vn/va, va, 2 vc	arr. c1903	New Haven, 3 March 1974	>361
78	Polonaise, 2 ?cornets, pf	c1887–9		?inc.
79	Practice for String Quartet in Holding Your Own!, str qt	1903		<middle section of 84/ii
80	Prelude on "Eventide," Bar/ trbn, 2 vn/echo org, org	[by 1902], c1907–8	New Haven, 21 Oct 1974	<20/iii
81	Scherzo: All the Way Around and Back, cl/fl, bugle/tpt, bells/hn, vn, 2 pf/pf 4 hands	c1907–8		(1971)
82	Scherzo: Over the Pavements, pic, cl, bn/bar sax, tpt, 3 trbn, cymbal, b drum, pf	c1910, rev. c1926–7	New York, 20 Dec 1963	portions >parts of 85 (also used in 87/iva, 107, 321); portions > or <part of 74, part of 90; (1954)
83	Scherzo for String Quartet	1904		<outer sections of 84/ii
84	A Set of Three Short Pieces	assembled ?c1935	Syracuse, NY, 8 Feb 1965	
	i. Largo cantabile: Hymn, (str qt, db)/str orch	[1904], c1907–8		<267; (1966)
	ii. Scherzo: Holding Your Own!, str qt	assembled c1935		combines 83 and 79; (1958)
	iii. Adagio cantabile: The Innate, str qt, pf, opt. db	c1908–9		<284; (1967)
85	Take-Off no.3: Rube Trying to Walk 2 to 3!!, cl, bn, tpt, pf	c1909		portions <parts of 82, 87/iva, 88/ii, 107, 321
86	Trio for Violin, Violoncello and Piano	c1909–10, rev. c1914–15	Berea, OH, 24 May 1948	(1955); crit. edn J. Kirkpatrick (1987)
	i. Moderato	c1909–10		
	ii. Presto ("TSIAJ" or Medley on the Fence or on the Campus!)	c1909–10		"TSIAJ" stands for "This Scherzo Is A Joke"
	iii. Moderato con moto	c1909–10, rev. c1914–15		portions >209

PIANO

Sonatas

No.	Title and instrumentation	Dates	First known performance	Remarks and publication
87	Sonata no.1 for Piano	assembled c1915–16, c1921	New York, 17 Feb 1949	ed. L. Harrison and W. Masselos (1954); corr. edn (1979); 2nd corr. edn (1990)
	i. Adagio con moto–Allegro con moto–Allegro risoluto–Adagio cantabile	c1909–10, c1915–16, rev. c1921, c1926–7		>lost organ piece
	iia. Allegro moderato–Andante	c1915–16, c1920–21		>43/ii
	iib. Allegro–Meno mosso con moto (In the Inn)	c1915–16, c1920–22		>43/i; <20/ii; portions reworked in 128/ii; (San Francisco, 1932)
	iii. Largo–Allegro–Largo	c1915–16, rev. c1921–2		
	iva.	c1921		portion >part of 85 or 82 (also used in 107)
	ivb. Allegro– Presto–Slow	c1921	>43/iv; portion reworked in 128/ii	
	v. Andante maestoso–Adagio cantabile–Allegro–Andante	c1920–22, rev. c1926–7		portion >part of 122/iv; borrows from 106
88	Sonata no.2 for Piano: Concord, Mass., 1840–60	c1916–19; rev. 1920s–40s	Cos Cob, CT, 28 Nov 1938 [complete work]	(Redding, CT, 1920); edn (1947)
	i. Emerson	c1916–19	Paris, 5 March 1928	>22; uses portions of 90, 91, 97, 99; portion used in 107; <123
	ii. Hawthorne	c1916–17		>lost Hawthorne Concerto; borrows from 36, 85, 262; <116 (itself <4/ii)
	iii. The Alcotts	c1916–17	3 Aug 1921	>lost Alcott Overture
	iv. Thoreau	c1918–19	Hartford, CT, 12 Dec 1928	portions <parts of 373

No.	Title and instrumentation	Dates	First known performance	Remarks and publication
89	Three-Page Sonata	[1905], c1910–11, rev. c1925–6	New York, 25 April 1949	ed. H. Cowell (1949); crit. edn J. Kirkpatrick (Bryn Mawr, PA, 1975); other edns in Joyce (E1970), Baron (D1987)

Studies

No.	Title and instrumentation	Dates	First known performance	Remarks and publication
90	Study no.1: Allegro	c1910–11	New York, 23 March 1968	inc.; portion < or >part of 82; portions used in 22, 88/i, 91, 123/i
91	Study no.2: Andante moderato–Allegro molto	c1910–11, rev. c1925	New York, 23 March 1968	borrows part of 90; <part of 22, 123/i; portion used in 88/i; portion = 117/ii
93	Study no.5: Moderato con anima	c1912–13	New York, 23 March 1968	crit. edn A. Mandel (Bryn Mawr, PA, 1988)
94	Study no.6: Andante	c1912–13	New York, 23 March 1968	
95	Study no.7: Andante cantabile	c1912–13	New York, 23 March 1968	
96	Study no.8: Trio (Allegro moderato–Presto)	c1912–13	New Haven, 21 Nov 1966	borrows from 125
97	Study no.9: The Anti-Abolitionist Riots in the 1830's and 1840's	c1912–13	New York, 3 April 1950	<parts of 22, 123/i; portions used in 88/i; ed. H. Cowell (1949)
99	Study no.11: Andante	c1915–16		inc.; > or <part of 22; portion <part of 88/i, part of 123/iv
100	Study no.15: Allegro moderato	c1917–18	New York, 23 March 1968	inc.
101	Study no.16: Andante cantabile	c1917–18	Middletown, CT, 19 April 1991	inc.; real. J. Kirkpatrick and D. Berman (with 103)
103	Study no.19: Andante cantabile	c1914	Middletown, CT, 19 April 1991	inc.; real. J. Kirkpatrick and D. Berman (with 101)
104	Study no.20: March (Slow Allegro or Fast Andante)	c1917–19	New York, 23 March 1968	portion borrowed in 9/ii; crit. edn J. Kirkpatrick (Bryn Mawr, PA, 1981)
105	Study no.21: Some Southpaw Pitching	c1918–19	New York, 3 April 1950	>parts of 2/iii and 2/v; ed. H. Cowell (1949); crit. edn J. Kirkpatrick (Bryn Mawr, PA, 1975)
106	Study no.22: Andante maestoso–Allegro vivace	c1918–19, c1922–3		portion borrowed in 87/v; ed. H. Cowell (San Francisco, 1947); crit. edn J. Kirkpatrick (Bryn Mawr, PA, 1973)
107	Study no.23: Allegro	c1920–22	New York, 23 March 1968	portion >part of 85 or 82 (also used in 87/iva); portions >part of 22, part of 88/i; portion used in 123/ii; crit. edn J. Kirkpatrick (Bryn Mawr, PA, 1990)

Marches

No.	Title and instrumentation	Dates	First known performance	Remarks and publication
109	March no.1 for Piano, with "Year of Jubilee"	[1890], c1894–5		<lost chbr orch arr.
110	March no.2 for Piano, with "Son of a Gambolier"	1895		inc.; > or <29; <353
111	March no.3 for Piano, with "Omega Lambda Chi"	c1895–6		<53
112	March no.5 for Piano, with "Annie Lisle"	c1895		<54
113	March no.6 for Piano, with "Here's to Good Old Yale"	c1895–6	New York, 16 Feb 1975	three versions, first and third inc., third without borrowed tune; second <lost chbr orch arr.
114	March in G and C for Piano, with "See the Conquering Hero Comes"	c1896–7		
115	March for Piano: The Circus Band	c1898–9		<229, 33 (early version)

Other works

No.	Title and instrumentation	Dates	First known performance	Remarks and publication
116	The Celestial Railroad	c1922–5	Albany, NY, 30 Oct 1928	>88/ii (which borrows from 36), ?>lost Hawthorne Concerto; <4/ii
117	Three Improvisations	1938	recorded New York, 11 May 1938	transcr. from recording and ed. G. and J. Dapogny (1983)
	i. Improvisation I			borrows from 10/v or 70
	ii. Improvisation II			=part of 91
	iii. Improvisation III			borrows from 96 or 125
118	Invention in D	c1898	New York, 16 Feb 1975	
119	Minuetto, op.4	1886		
120	New Year's Dance	1887		?inc.
	Three Protests: see 124			

No.	Title and instrumentation	Dates	First known performance	Remarks and publication
122	Set of Five Take-Offs	c1909	New York, 23 March 1968	crit. edn J. Kirkpatrick (1991)
	i. The Seen and Unseen?			
	ii. Rough and Ready et al.			borrows part of 1/iv coda
	iii. Song without (good) Words/The Good & the Bad (new & old)			
	iv. Scene Episode			portion <part of 87/v
	v. Bad Resolutions and Good WAN!			
123	Four Transcriptions from "Emerson"	c1923–4, c1926–7	New York, 12 March 1948 [complete work]	
	i. Slowly	c1923–4, c1926–7	New York, 6 Jan 1931	>part of 88/i, part of 22; borrows from 90, 91, 97
	ii. Moderato	c1926–7		>part of 88/i, part of 22; borrows from 107
	iii. Largo	c1926–7		>part of 88/i, part of 22
	iv. Allegro agitato– Broadly	c1926–7		>part of 88/i, part of 22; borrows from 99
124	Varied Air and Variations	c1920–22	New Haven, 18 May 1967	portions ed. as Three Protests (San Francisco, 1947); ed. J. Kirkpatrick and G. Clarke (Bryn Mawr, PA, 1971)
125	Waltz-Rondo	1911	Syracuse, NY, 8 Feb 1965	crit. edn J. Kirkpatrick and J. Cox (1978); portions borrowed in 96, 117/iii

	Two pianos			
128	Three Quarter-Tone Pieces	1923–4		ed. G. Pappastavrou (1968)
	i. Largo		New York, 14 Feb 1925 or 9 April 1929	
	ii. Allegro		New York, 14 Feb 1925	reworks parts of 308 [or 10/iii or 186], 283 [or 11/i], 344 [or 10/i], 43/i [or 87/iib or 20/ii], 43/iv [or 87/ivb]
	iii. Chorale		New York, 8 Feb 1925	>lost quarter-tone chorale for str, reconstructed by A. Stout (1974)

	ORGAN			
131	"Adeste Fideles" in an Organ Prelude	[1898], c1903		ed. E.P. Biggs (1949)
134	Canzonetta in F	c1893–4	New Haven, 21 Oct 1974	
135	Fugue in C Minor	c1898	New Haven, 21 Oct 1974	?inc.
136	Fugue in E♭	c1898	New Haven, 21 Oct 1974	
137	Interludes for Hymns	c1898–1901	New Haven, 21 Oct 1974	
140	Variations on "America"	1891–2, additions c1909–10, rev. c1949	Brewster, NY, 17 Feb 1892	polytonal interludes added c1909–10; ed. E.P. Biggs (1949)

	CHORAL			
	Sacred (more than one movement)			
143	The Celestial Country (H. Alford), T, Bar, 2 vocal qts (both S, A, T, B), SATB, tpt, euphonium, timp, org, str qt/str orch	1898–1902, additions c1912–13	New York, 18 April 1902	org part lost; ed. J. Kirkpatrick (1973) [org part reconstructed]
	Introduction before no.1	added c1912–13		
	i. Prelude, Trio, and Chorus			>inc. or lost anthem
	Prelude before no.2	added c1912–13		
	ii. Aria for Baritone			<307
	iii. Quartet			
	Interlude before no.4	added c1912–13		
	iv. Intermezzo for String Quartet			
	Interlude after no.4	added c1912–13		
	v. Double Quartet, a cappella			
	vi. Aria for Tenor			<252
	Introduction to no.7	added c1912–13		
	vii. Chorale and Finale			
144	Communion Service, SATB, org	c1894		
	i. Kyrie			three settings, the first inc.
	ii. Gratias agimus			
	iii. Gloria tibi			

No.	Title and instrumentation	Dates	First known performance	Remarks and publication
	iv. Sursum corda			
	v. Credo			inc.
	vi. Sanctus			two settings
	vii. Benedictus			
	viii. Agnus Dei			
145	Three Harvest Home Chorales, SATB divisi, 4 tpt, 3 trbn, tuba, org	c1902, c1912–15	New York, 3 March 1948	ed. H. Cowell (1949)
	i. Harvest Home (G. Burgess)	c1902, c1915		
	ii. Lord of the Harvest (J.H. Gurney)	c1915		
	iii. Harvest Home (Alford)	c1912–15		

Psalms

No.	Title and instrumentation	Dates	First known performance	Remarks and publication
146	Psalm 14, SATB, SATB	c1902, rev. c1912–13		crit. edn J. Kirkpatrick (Bryn Mawr, PA, 1995)
147	Psalm 24, SSAATTBB	c1901, rev. c1912–13		(1955)
148	Psalm 25, SSAATTBB, org	c1901, rev. c1912–13	Washington, DC, 24 Oct 1967	org part inc.; crit. edn J. Kirkpatrick and G. Smith (Bryn Mawr, PA, 1979) [org part reconstructed]
149	Psalm 42, T, SATB, org	c1891–2		org part inc.
150	Psalm 54, SSATBB	c1902	Los Angeles, 18 April 1966	ed. J. Kirkpatrick and G. Smith (Bryn Mawr, PA, 1973)
151	Psalm 67, SSAATTBB	c1898–9	New York, 6 May 1937	(1939)
152	Psalm 90, SSAATTBB, bells (4 players), org	1923–4	Los Angeles, 18 April 1966	ed. J. Kirkpatrick and G. Smith (Bryn Mawr, PA, 1970)
153	Psalm 100, SSAATTBB, boys' choir (TrTrAA), opt. bells, opt. vns/org	c1902	Los Angeles, 18 April 1966	ed. J. Kirkpatrick and G. Smith (Bryn Mawr, PA, 1975)
154	Psalm 135, SSAATTBB, tpt, trbn, timp, drums, org	c1902, rev. c1912–13		crit. edn J. Kirkpatrick and G. Smith (Bryn Mawr, PA, 1981)
155	Psalm 150, SSAATTBB, boys' choir (TrTrAA), opt. org	c1898–9	Los Angeles, 18 April 1966	ed. J. Kirkpatrick and G. Smith (Bryn Mawr, PA, 1972) [org part added by ed.]

Other sacred

No.	Title and instrumentation	Dates	First known performance	Remarks and publication
156	All-Forgiving, look on me (R. Palmer), SATB,	c1898–9		?org part lost
159	Benedictus in E, T/S, SATB, org	c1894		
161	Bread of the World (R. Heber), unison vv, org	c1896–7		inc.
164	Crossing the Bar (A. Tennyson), SATB, org	c1894		org part inc.; ed. J. Kirkpatrick (1974) [org part reconstructed]
165	Easter Anthem, SATB, org	c1890–91		inc.
166	Easter Carol, S, A, T, B, SATB, org	c1896, rev. c1901	New York, 7 April 1901	crit. edn of rev. version J. Kirkpatrick (1973)
167	Gloria in Excelsis, A, unison vv, org	c1893–4		inc.
169	I Come to Thee (C. Elliott), SATB, ?org	c1896–7		no org in sources; opening figure reused in 219; crit. edn J. Kirkpatrick (1983) [org part added by ed.]
170	I Think of Thee, My God (J.S.B. Monsell), SATB	c1895–6		inc.; <375
173	The Light That Is Felt (J. Whittier), B, SATB, org	c1898		inc.; <287
174	Lord God, Thy Sea Is Mighty, SATB, org	c1900–01		org part mostly missing; crit. edn J. Kirkpatrick (1983) [org part reconstructed]
176	Processional: Let There Be Light (J. Ellerton), (TTBB and/or 4 trbn)/SSAATTBB, org/str orch, org/4 vn	c1902–3, rev. c1912–13, late 1930s	Danbury, 25 March 1966	choral/kbd reduction (1955); full score (1967); first version for SATB, org
178	Turn Ye, Turn Ye (J. Hopkins), SATB, org	c1896		org part inc.; (1952); crit. edn J. Kirkpatrick (Bryn Mawr, PA, 1973) [org part reconstructed]

Secular works for chorus and ensemble

No.	Title and instrumentation	Dates	First known performance	Remarks and publication
179	Dec (D.G. Rossetti, after Folgore), unison male vv, pic, 2 cl, 2 hn, 3 tpt, 3 trbn, tuba	c1914, rev. 1934	New York, 15 April 1934	> or <234; ed. N. Slonimsky (1963)

No.	Title and instrumentation	Dates	First known performance	Remarks and publication
180	An Election (Ives), unison male vv divisi, orch	[1920], c1923	New York, 16 Oct 1967	< or >313; borrows part of 184 or 289
181	General William Booth Enters Into Heaven (V. Lindsay), unison vv divisi, chbr orch	arr. 1934	Los Angeles, 18 April 1966	arr. of 255 by J.J. Becker under Ives's supervision
182	He Is There! (Ives), unison vv, orch	c1918–21	Norwalk, CT, 19 Oct 1959	>262 (itself partly >187 and borrowing from 36); <188, 371
183	Johnny Poe (B. Low), TTBB, orch	c1927–9	Miami, 20 Oct 1974	inc.; crit. edn real. J. Kirkpatrick (1978)
184	Lincoln, the Great Commoner (E. Markham), unison vv divisi, orch	c1922–3	New York, 16 Oct 1967	>289; (San Francisco, 1932)
185	The Masses (Majority) (Ives), unison vv divisi, orch	c1916, rev. c1920–21	New York, 16 Oct 1967	<294
186	The New River (Ives), unison vv divisi, orch	c1915	New York, 15 April 1934	> or <10/iii, 308 (itself <14/i and 17/i); portions reworked in 128/ii; (1971)
187	Sneak Thief (Ives), unison vv divisi, tpt, pf	1914	New Haven, 21 Oct 1974	inc.; portion reworked in 262
188	They Are There! (A War Song March) (Ives), unison vv, orch	adapted 1942	Danbury, 25 March 1966 [with pf]; New York, 16 Oct 1967 [with orch]	>182 and 371 (themselves >262); ed. L. Harrison (1961)
189	Two Slants (Christian and Pagan)	c1912–14, c1916–17	Los Angeles, 18 April 1966	<380
	i. Duty (R.W. Emerson), unison male vv, orch			
	ii. Vita (Manilius), unison vv, org			
190	Walt Whitman (W. Whitman), SATB, chbr orch	c1914–15, rev. c1920–21	Los Angeles, 18 April 1966	inc.; >384 and lost earlier version
		Secular partsongs		
192	The Bells of Yale (H. Mason), Bar, unison male vv, pf, vn	c1897, rev. c1900–01	South Norwalk, CT, 1 Dec 1897	three versions, first two for Bar, TTBB, vc [one adds bells, pf]; third version (1903)
193	The Boys in Blue, TTBB	c1895–6	New Haven, 21 Oct 1974	
194	For You and Me!, TTBB/ SATB	?1895–6		(1896); ed. and arr. C.G. Richter (Hackensack, NJ, 1973)
195	My Sweet Jeanette, TTBB	c1900		?inc.
196	O Maiden Fair, Bar, TTBB, pf	c1900		inc.
200	Serenade (H. Longfellow), SATB	c1895–6	New Haven, 14 Oct 1973	
201	A Song of Mory's (C.E. Merrill jr), TTBB	c1896	New Haven, 21 Oct 1974	(New Haven, 1897)
202	The Year's at the Spring (R. Browning), SATB	c1892		

SONGS

Editions
A 114 Songs (Redding, CT, 1922, 2/1975)
A* in A and also in 50 Songs (Redding, CT, 1923, from plates of A)
B Seven Songs (1932)
C Thirty-Four Songs (San Francisco, 1933)
D Nineteen Songs (San Francisco, also as Eighteen [sic] Songs)
E Four Songs (1950)
F Ten Songs (1953)
G Twelve Songs (1954)
H Fourteen Songs (1955)
J Nine Songs (1956)
K Thirteen Songs (1958)
L Sacred Songs (1961)
M Eleven Songs and Two Harmonizations, ed. J. Kirkpatrick (1968)
N Three Songs (1968)
P Forty Earlier Songs, crit. edn J. Kirkpatrick (1993)
Q 129 Songs, crit. edn H.W. Hitchcock (Middleton, WI, 2004)

No.	Title and instrumentation	Dates	First known performance	Remarks and editions
205	Abide with me (H.F. Lyte)	c1890–91, rev. c1921	New York, 11 April 1962	new acc. added c1921; K, L, Q
206	Aeschylus and Sophocles (W.S. Landor), 1v, pf, str qt/str orch	1922–c1924	Los Angeles, 2 April 1951	>inc. Fugue in Four Greek Modes; D, Q
207	Afterglow (J.F. Cooper jr)	1919	New York, 6 Feb 1933	<15/iii; A, C
208	Allegro (Ives)	adapted after c1902–3	Danbury, 25 March 1966	>345; A, K, Q
209	The All-Enduring	c1898–c1900		? >lost TTBB version; <parts of 86/iii; P
210	Amphion (Tennyson)	adapted after c1896–7		>275; A*, F, Q
211	Ann Street (M. Morris)	1921	New York, 6 Feb 1933	<14/iv, 17/iii; A, C, Q
212	At Parting (F. Peterson)	c1897–c1900	Milwaukee, 28 March 1950	?>lost earlier version; C, Q
213	At Sea (R.U. Johnson)	arr. 1921	New York, 17 Nov 1936	>12/i; <16/i; A*, C, Q
214	At the River (R. Lowry)	arr. [1916]	Vienna, 15 Feb 1935	>part of 63/iii; A, C, Q
216	Aug (D.G. Rossetti, after Folgore)	1920		A, G, Q
217	Autumn (H. Twichell)	c1907–8	New York, 24 Feb 1939	A, J, Q
	Ballad from Rosamunde: see 337 (1st version)			
218	Because of You	1898		P
219	Because Thou Art	c1901–2		opening figure >169; P
220	Berceuse (Ives)	adapted c1920	New York, 24 Feb 1939	>395; A*, K, Q
221	The Cage (Ives)	[1906]	Philadelphia, 1 Nov 1962	> or <20/i; A, (San Francisco, 1932), H, Q
222	The Camp Meeting (Ives, C. Elliott)	arr. [1912]		>3/iii; A, K, L, Q
223	Canon [I]	[1893], c1895–6		<224; P
224	Canon [II] (T. Moore)	adapted after c1895–6	New York, 19 April 1942	>223; A, D, Q
225	Chanson de Florian (J.P.C. de Florian)	c1898	New York, 27 Dec 1949	A, (1950), Q
226	Charlie Rutlage (D.J. O'Malley, as collected by J.A. Lomax)	1920/1921	New Orleans, 17 Jan 1924	partly >portion of 55; <14/iii; A*, B, Q
227	The Children's Hour (Longfellow)	c1912–13	Vienna, 15 Feb 1935	A*, C, Q
228	A Christmas Carol (Ives)	before 1898	Los Angeles, 1 Feb 1942	A*, D, Q
229	The Circus Band (Ives)	adapted ?c1899 or ?c1920–21	New Haven, 5 Nov 1966	>115; <33; A*, F, Q
230	The Collection (J. Edmeston)	1920		A, K, L, Q
232	Country Celestial (J.M. Neale, after Bernard of Cluny)	c1895–8		>or <240; <389; P
233	Cradle Song (A.L. Ives)	1919	New York, 5 Feb 1965	A*, D, Q
234	Dec (D.G. Rossetti, after Folgore)	c1913–14		<or >179; A, C, Q
235	Disclosure (Ives)	1921		A*, G, L, Q
236	Down East (Ives)	1919	New York, 24 Feb 1939	A, K, L, Q
238	Dreams (Baroness Porteous, trans. A. Streleski)	[1897]		A, J, Q
239	Du alte Mutter (A.O. Vinje, Ger. trans. E. Lobedanz) [Eng. version My dear old mother (trans. F. Corder)]	[1900], c1902	New York, 28 Nov 1922	second setting of Eng. version [see 316]; A, K, Q
240	Du bist wie eine Blume (H. Heine)	c1896–7		>or <232; <389; P
	Duty: see 380/a			
241	Ein Ton (P. Cornelius) [Eng. version I hear a tone (trans. C.H. Laubach)]	c1900		<309; P
	An Election: see 313			
242	Elégie (L. Gallet)	c1901–2	Danbury, 17 March 1967	A*, J, Q
243	The Ending Year	1902		?>lost song, arr. J. Kirkpatrick as 357; <382; P
244	Evening (J. Milton)	1921	Saratoga Springs, NY, 1 May 1932	<15/iv; A*, B, Q
245	Evidence (Ives)	adapted [1910]		>394; A, J, Q
	Eyes so dark: see 387			
246	Far from my heav'nly home (Lyte)	c1893–4		M
247	Far in the wood	c1900		<310; P
248	A Farewell to Land (Byron)	c1909–10	Minneapolis, 18 Jan 1944	D, Q

No.	Title and instrumentation	Dates	First known performance	Remarks and editions
249	La Fede (Ariosto)	1920		A*, D, Q
250	Feldeinsamkeit (H. Allmers) [Eng. version In Summer Fields (trans. H.C. Chapman)]	c1897–8	Los Angeles, 12 Nov 1946	A*, D, Q
251	Flag Song (H.S. Durand)	[1898], c1900		(1968), Q
252	Forward into Light (H. Alford)	1902		>143/vi; A, F, L, Q
253	Friendship	c1898–9		P
254	Frühlingslied (Heine)	c1898		<270; P
255	General William Booth Enters into Heaven (V. Lindsay)	1914, rev. c1933	San Francisco, 26 Sept 1933	?>lost version for unison male vv, band; <181; D, Q
256	God Bless and Keep Thee	c1898, c1901–2		M
257	Grace	c1900–03		<390; P
258	Grantchester (R. Brooke)	1920	New York, 13 Nov 1933	A*, J, Q
259	The Greatest Man (A.T. Collins)	1921	New York, 28 Feb 1924	A*, C, N, Q
260	Gruss (Heine)	c1898–9, c1902–3		<398; P
261	Harpalus (anon., coll. T. Percy)	adapted [1902] or c1920	Houston, 3 May 1943	>323; A, C, Q
262	He Is There! (Ives), 1v/vv, pf, opt. vn/fl/fife	1917	Danbury, 18 Jan 1940	portion >part of 187; borrows from 36; <182, 371, 188; portion borrowed in 88/ii; A, Q
	Hear My Prayer, O Lord: see 355c			
263	Her Eyes	c1898		<299; P
264	Her gown was of vermilion silk	1897		P
265	His Exaltation (R. Robinson)	arr. [1913]		>ending of 61/i; A, J, L, Q
266	The Housatonic at Stockbridge (R.U. Johnson)	arr. 1921	New York, 11 May 1946	>7/iii, early song version; A, G, Q
267	Hymn (J. Wesley, after G. Tersteegen)	arr. 1921	San Francisco, 26 Sept 1933	>84/i; A*, C, Q
268	Hymn of Trust (O.W. Holmes sr), 1v, org/pf	adapted c1899–c1900		inc.; >312; P [org part added by ed. J. Kirkpatrick]
	I hear a tone: see 241			
269	I knew and loved a maid	c1898–9, c1901–2		P
270	I travelled among unknown men (W. Wordsworth)	adapted [1901]		>254; A*, F, Q
271	Ich grolle nicht (Heine) [Eng. version I'll not complain (trans. J.S. Dwight)]	c1898–9, rev. c1900–01	Milwaukee, 28 March 1950	A, C, Q [latter two incl. Eng. version]
272	Ilmenau (J.W. von Goethe) [Eng. version Over all the treetops (trans. H. Twichell)]	c1903	Danbury, 8 June 1922	A*, (1952), Q
273	Immortality (Ives)	1921	Vienna, 15 Feb 1935	A*, C, Q
275	In April-tide (C. Scollard)	c1896–7		<210; P
276	In Autumn	c1896		P
277	In Flanders Fields (J. McCrae)	1917, rev. 1919	New York, 15 April 1917	A, H, Q
278	In My Beloved's Eyes (W.M. Chauvenet)	c1899		<311; P
	In Summer Fields: see 250			
279	In the Alley (Ives)	[1896]	Danbury, 18 Jan 1940	A, K, Q
280	The "Incantation" (Byron)	arr. 1921		>10/vi; A, C, Q
283	The Indians (C. Sprague)	arr. 1921	Saratoga Springs, NY, 1 May 1932	>11/i (itself <19/iii); <14/ii and 17/ii; first half <part of 128/ii; A*, B, Q
284	The Innate (Ives)	arr. [1916]	Paris, 5 March 1936	>84/iii; A, D, Q
285	Kären (P.K. Ploug, trans. C. Kappey)	c1900, c1905–6	New Haven, 1 March 1968	A*, G, Q
286	The Last Reader (O.W. Holmes)	arr. 1921	New York, 2 Nov 1942	>11/iii, 18/i; A*, C, Q
287	The Light That Is Felt (Whittier)	adapted c1899–1900, [1903–4], c1919–20	New Haven, 7 Sept 1961	>173; A*, (1950), Q
288	Like a Sick Eagle (J. Keats)	arr. 1920	New York, 6 Feb 1933	>10/iv (itself <19/i); A*, C, Q
289	Lincoln, the Great Commoner (E. Markham)	c1919–20	New York, 27 Dec 1949	<184; portions borrowed in 313 (itself <180); A, (1952), Q
291	Die Lotosblume (Heine) [Eng. version The Lotus Flower]	c1897–8, rev. c1900–01 and c1908–9		<362; pubd as alternative text for 362 in A*, C, Q

No.	Title and instrumentation	Dates	First known performance	Remarks and editions
292	The Love Song of Har Dyal (R. Kipling)	c1899–c1900, c1902–3		P
293	Luck and Work (R.U. Johnson)	c1919–20	Dallas, 7 Feb 1965	> or <12/ii (itself <19/ii); A, C, E, Q
294	Majority (Ives)	arr. 1921	Paris, 5 March 1936	>185; A, D, Q
295	Maple Leaves (T.B. Aldrich)	1920	Saratoga Springs, NY, 1 May 1932	A, B, Q
296	Marie (R. Gottschall) [Eng. version trans. E. Rücker]	[1896], c1901–2, second version c1903–4		first version in P; second version A*, H
297	Memories: a. Very Pleasant, b. Rather Sad (Ives)	[1897]	Pittsburgh, 29 April 1949	A, F, Q
298	Minnelied (L.H.C. Hölty)	c1901		<306; P
299	Mirage (C. Rossetti)	adapted [1902]	Minneapolis, 29 May 1955	>263; A*, F, Q
300	Mists [I] (H.T. Ives)	1910, c1912–13		<301
301	Mists [II] (H.T. Ives)	c1912–13, rev. c1920	Vienna, 15 Feb 1935	>300; <15/i; first version inc., second version in A*, C, Q
	My dear old mother: see 239, 316			
302	My Lou Jennine	c1894		P
303	My Native Land [I] (after Heine)	c1897–c1900		?first setting; A, G, Q
304	My Native Land [II] (after Heine)	c1900–01		?second setting; P
306	Nature's Way (Ives)	adapted [1908], c1909–10		>298; A*, H, Q
307	Naught that country needeth (H. Alford)	c1898–9, rev. 1902		>143/ii; A*, H, L, Q
308	The New River (Ives)	1914–15, ?rev. 1921	Dresden, 11 March 1932	> or <10/iii, 186; <14/i, 17/i; portions reworked in 128/ii; A*, C, Q
309	Night of Frost in May (G. Meredith)	adapted [1899] or c1920	New York, 30 March 1940	>241; A*, D, Q
310	A Night Song (T. Moore)	adapted ?c1920	New York, 10 Feb 1950	>247; A, (1952), later printings of K, Q
311	A Night Thought (Moore)	adapted c1916	New York, 28 Nov 1922	>278; A*, C, Q
312	No More (W. Winter)	1897	New Haven, 22 Feb 1956	<268; M
313	2 Nov 1920 (An Election) (Ives)	c1921	Bennington, VT, 17 June 1959	> or <180; borrows part of 184 or 289; A, D, (1949), Q
314	An Old Flame (Ives)	c1898, c1901	New York, 15 May 1901	A, K, Q
315	Old Home Day (Ives), 1v, pf, opt. vn/fl/fife	c1920	London, 17 June 1965	portions> or <parts of 5/iii; A*, K, Q
316	The Old Mother (Vinje, trans. Corder)	?1898, c1902		first setting: see also 239; P
317	Omens and Oracles (O. Meredith)	[1899], c1902	Danbury, 17 March 1967	A, F, Q
318	On Judges' Walk (A. Symons)	c1901–2	New Haven, 7 Sept 1961	>first theme of 1/i; <339; P
319	On the Antipodes (Ives), 1v, pf 4 hands	c1922–3	New York, 11 May 1963	chords derived in part from 6; D, Q
320	On the Counter (Ives)	1920		modeled on 355; A, H, Q
321	"1, 2, 3" (Ives)	1921	Philadelphia, 23 April 1940	portion >part of 85 or 82; A, E, Q
322	The One Way (Ives)	c1922–3		M
323	The Only Son (Kipling)	c1898–9		<261; P
	Over all the treetops: see 272			
324	Paracelsus (Browning)	1921	Paris, 5 March 1936	portions >parts of 27; <13/i; A*, D, Q
325	Peaks (H. Bellamann)	c1923–4		M
326	A Perfect Day	1902		P
327	Pictures (M.P. Turnbull)	1906	Germantown, PA, 11 Oct 1963	M
328	Premonitions (R.U. Johnson)	arr. 1921	San Francisco, 15 Feb 1934	>12/iii; A, C, Q
329	Qu'il m'irait bien (trans. M. Delano)	c1897–9		A, G, Q
330	The Rainbow (So May It Be!) (Wordsworth)	arr. 1921	New York, 27 Dec 1949	>45; <15/ii; A, C, Q
331	Religion (L.Y. Case)	arr. c1910–11		>lost anthem; A*, G, L, Q
332	Remembrance (Ives)	arr. 1921		>40; <16/iii; A*, G, Q
333	Requiem (R.L. Stevenson)	1911	Paris, 5 March 1936	D, Q
334	Resolution (Ives)	1921	Paris, 5 March 1936	A*, D, Q
335	Rock of Ages (A.M. Toplady), 1v, pf/org	c1892	? Danbury, 30 Apr 1893	M
336	Romanzo (di Central Park) (L. Hunt)	[1900], c1911	Bennington, VT, 17 June 1959	A, H, Q
337	Rosamunde (H. von Chézy, Fr. paraphrase by Bélanger)	c1898–9, c1901–2		first version (Ger. only) in P; Fr. text substituted in second version in A, H, Q
338	Rosenzweige (K. Stieler)	c1902–3		>345; <208; P

No.	Title and instrumentation	Dates	First known performance	Remarks and editions
339	Rough Wind (P.B. Shelley)	adapted [1902]	New York, 1 March 1932	>318 (itself >first theme of 1/i); A, C, Q
341	A Scotch Lullaby (Merrill)	1896		(New Haven, 1896), M
342	A Sea Dirge (W. Shakespeare)	1925	New Haven, 22 Feb 1956	<16/iv; M
343	The Sea of Sleep	1903		<374; P
344	The See'r (Ives)	c1914–15, arr. 1920	Saratoga Springs, NY, 1 May 1932	>10/i; portions reworked in 128/ii; A, B, Q
345	Sehnsucht (C. Winther, Ger. trans. E. Lobedanz)	c1902–3		<338, 208; P
346	Sept (D.G. Rossetti, after Folgore)	c1919–20	New York, 11 May 1963	A, C, Q
347	Serenity (Whittier)	arr. [1919]	New York, 15 March 1929	>inc. or lost choral version; A, B, Q
348	The Side Show (Ives)	adapted 1921	New York, 24 Feb 1939	>lost piece for 1896 college show; A, G, Q
349	Slow March (L. Brewster, Ives family)	c1887, rev. 1921		A, F, Q
350	Slugging a Vampire (Ives)	adapted [1902] or c1920	New York, 21 Feb 1947	>367; D, Q
	So May It Be!: see 330			
352	Soliloquy (Ives)	c1916–17	Philadelphia, 1 Nov 1962	C, Q
353	A Son of a Gambolier, 1v, pf, opt. fls/vns/other insts	arr. c1919–21		>110; A, J, Q
354	Song (H. Coleridge)	c1897		P
No.	Title and instrumentation	Dates	First known performance	Remarks and editions
355	A Song—For Anything	c1921		A, H, Q; 355c reused for 355a and 355b; in assembling *114 Songs* Ives combined all three texts to make 355; used as model for 320
	a. When the waves softly sigh (?Ives)	[1892]		
	b. Yale, Farewell! (?Ives)	c1898–9		
	c. Hear My Prayer, O Lord (N. Tate, N. Brady)	c1889–90		
356	Song for Harvest Season (G. Phillimore), 1v (cornet/tpt, trbn, b trbn/tuba)/org	1894, rev. c1932–3	Minneapolis, 18 Jan 1944	C, Q
357	The Song of the Dead (Kipling)	?1898		conjectured first text for music of 243 (itself <382); arr. J. Kirkpatrick, P
361	Songs my mother taught me (A. Heyduk, Eng. trans. N. Macfarran)	[1895], c1899–c1901	Danbury, 17 March 1967	<76; A*, H, Q
362	The South Wind (H. Twichell)	adapted 1908		>291; A*, C, Q
363	Spring Song (H. Twichell)	1907	Danbury, 8 June 1922	?>lost song; A*, G, Q
365	Sunrise (Ives), 1v, pf, vn	1926	New Haven, 7 Sept 1961	crit. edn J. Kirkpatrick (1977)
366	Swimmers (L. Untermeyer)	[1915], ?rev. 1921	San Francisco, 26 Sept 1933	<16/ii; A, C, Q
367	Tarrant Moss (Kipling)	c1902–3	New Haven, 2 June 1960	<350; A, K, Q
369	There is a certain garden	[1893], c1896–8	New Haven, 22 Feb 1956	M
370	There is a lane (Ives)	adapted [1902] or c1920		>393; A*, J, Q
371	They Are There! (Ives), 1v/vv, pf, opt. vn/fl/fife, opt. 2nd pf	adapted 1942	New Haven, 19 Oct 1973	>182, 262 (which borrows from 187 and 36); <188; J, Q
372	The Things Our Fathers Loved (Ives)	1917	New York, 15 March 1929	>inc. or lost orch work; A, H, Q
373	Thoreau (Ives, after H. Thoreau)	arr. c1920	Poughkeepsie, NY, 19 April 1934	portions >parts of 88/iv; A, C, Q
374	Those Evening Bells (T. Moore)	adapted [1907]		>343; A, H, Q
375	Through Night and Day (after J.S.B. Monsell)	adapted c1897–8		>170; P
376	To Edith (H.T. Ives)	1919		?>lost song; A*, F, Q
377	Tolerance (R. Kipling)	arr. 1921	Minneapolis, 18 Jan 1944	>10/ii; A, C, Q
378	Tom Sails Away (Ives)	1917	New York, 11 May 1963	A, D, Q
	Ein Ton: see 241			
379	Two Little Flowers (C. Ives, H.T. Ives)	1921	New York, 24 Feb 1939	A*, D, N, Q
380	Two Slants (Christian and Pagan)		Dallas, 7 Feb 1965 [complete work]	>189; A*, C, E, Q
	a. Duty (Emerson)	arr. 1921	Dallas, 7 Feb 1965	
	b. Vita (Manilius)	arr. 1921	Boston, 22 April 1934	

No.	Title and instrumentation	Dates	First known performance	Remarks and editions
381	Vote for Names! Names! Names! (Ives), 1v, 3 pf	1912		inc.; (1968); ed. N. Schoffman, *CMc*, no.23 (1977); Q
382	The Waiting Soul (J. Newton)	adapted [1908]		>243; A*, G, L, Q
383	Walking (Ives)	c1912	Saratoga Springs, NY, 1 May 1932	>inc. or lost anthem; A*, B, Q
384	Walt Whitman (Whitman)	c1920–21	Poughkeepsie, NY, 19 April 1934	>lost early version of 190; <190, 13/ii; A*, C, Q
385	Waltz (Ives)	c1894–5, rev. 1921		A, G, Q
386	Watchman! (J. Bowring)	adapted [1913]		>lost early song version or part of 60/iii; <part of 4/i; A*, H, L, Q
387	Weil' auf mir (N. Lenau) [Eng. version Eyes so dark (trans. after E. Rücker and W.J. Westbrook)]	[1902]		A, H, Q
388	West London (M. Arnold)	1921	Colorado Springs, CO, 28 April 1939	>inc. Matthew Arnold Overture; <13/iii; A*, C, Q
No.	Title and instrumentation	Dates	First known performance	Remarks and editions
389	When stars are in the quiet skies (E.G. Bulwer-Lytton) When the waves softly sigh: see 355a	adapted c1899–c1900	Oxford, OH, 14 May 1950	>240 or 232; A*, C, Q
390	Where the eagle cannot see (M.P. Turnbull)	adapted c1906	Saratoga Springs, NY, 1 Oct 1933	>257; A, (1935), early printings of K, L, N, Q
391	The White Gulls (M. Morris, after Russian poem)	c1920–21	Danbury, 8 June 1922	A*, C, Q
393	Widmung (W.M. von Königswinter)	?1898		<370; P
394	Wie Melodien zieht es mir (K. Groth)	c1898–1900		<245; P
395	Wiegenlied (*Des Knaben Wunderhorn*)	c1906	Germantown, PA, 11 Oct 1963	<220; P
396	William Will (S.B. Hill)	1896		portion >part of 31; (1896), P
397	The World's Highway (H. Twichell)	1906/1907		A, K, Q
398	The World's Wanderers (Shelley) Yale, Farewell!: see 355b	adapted after c1898–9	Danbury, 17 March 1967	>260; A*, F, Q
399	Yellow Leaves (Bellamann)	1923	New Haven, 22 Feb 1956	M

ARRANGEMENTS

No.	Title and instrumentation	Dates	First known performance	Remarks and editions
439	Beethoven: Adagio in F from Piano Sonata op.2 no.1, str qt	c1898	New Haven, 21 Oct 1974	
440	E. Ives: Christmas Carol, 1v, pf, opt. bells	1924/1925	New York, Dec 1925	M
441	In the Mornin', 1v, pf	1929		M

WRITINGS

Essays Before a Sonata (New York, 1920/*R*)

"Some 'Quarter-tone' Impressions," *Franco-American Music Society Bulletin* (25 March 1925)

"Music and its Future," *American Composers on American Music*, ed. H. Cowell (Stanford, CA, 1933/*R*)

Essays Before a Sonata and Other Writings, ed. H. Boatwright (New York, 1962, rev. 2/1970 as *Essays Before a Sonata, The Majority, and Other Writings*)

Memos, ed. J. Kirkpatrick (New York, 1972)

Selected Correspondence of Charles Ives, ed. T.C. Owens (Berkeley, 2007)

BIBLIOGRAPHY

A: CATALOGS, BIBLIOGRAPHIES, AND REFERENCE WORKS

J. Kirkpatrick: *A Temporary Mimeographed Catalogue of the Music Manuscripts and Related Materials of Charles Edward Ives 1874–1954* (New Haven, CT, 1960)

R. Warren: *Charles E. Ives: Discography* (New Haven, CT, 1972)

V. Perlis, ed.: *Charles Ives Papers* (New Haven, CT, 1983)

G. Block: *Charles Ives: a Bio-Bibliography* (New York, 1988)

W. Rathert: *Charles Ives* (Darmstadt, 1989, 2/1996)

C.W. Henderson: *The Charles Ives Tunebook* (Warren, MI, 1990, 2/2008)

J.B. Sinclair: *A Descriptive Catalogue of the Music of Charles Ives* (New Haven, CT, 1999; rev. 2/2010, available at <http://hdl.handle.net/10079/fa/music.mss.0014.1>)

G. Sherwood: *Charles Ives: a Guide to Research* (New York, 2002; rev. 2/2010 by G.S. Magee as *Charles Ives: a Research and Information Guide*)

J.M. Burk and M.J. Budds: *A Charles Ives Omnibus* (Missoula, MT, 2008)

B: COLLECTIONS OF ARTICLES

H.W. Hitchcock and V. Perlis, eds: *An Ives Celebration: Brooklyn, NY, and New Haven, CT: 1974* [incl. articles by R.M. Crunden, F.R. Rossiter, N. Bruce, R.P. Morgan, A. Forte, W. Brooks]

Charles Ives und die amerikanische Musiktradition bis zur Gegenwart: Cologne 1988 [incl. articles by J.P. Burkholder, D. Kämper, R.P. Morgan, W. Rathert]

G. Block and J.P. Burkholder, eds: *Charles Ives and the Classical Tradition* (New Haven, CT, 1996) [incl. articles by G. Block, A. Buchman, J.P. Burkholder, P. Lambert, R.P. Morgan, N.E. Tawa, K.C. Ward]

J.P. Burkholder, ed.: *Charles Ives and his World* (Princeton, NJ, 1996) [incl. articles by L. Botstein, M. Broyles, J.P. Burkholder, D.M. Hertz, and M. Tucker, with selected correspondence 1881–1954, reviews 1888–1951, profiles 1932–55]

P. Lambert, ed.: *Ives Studies* (Cambridge, 1998) [incl. articles by L. Austin, G. Block, J.P. Burkholder, S. Feder, H.W. Hitchcock, P. Lambert, R.P. Morgan, W. Rathert, G. Sherwood, J. Tick]

H.-W. Heister and W. Kremp, eds: *Charles Ives, 1874–1954: Amerikanischer Pionier der neuen Musik* (Trier, 2004) [incl. articles by J. Barnieck, R. Flender, T. Giebisch, P Gläfcke, H.-W. Heister, H. Henck, H. Lück, F. Mehring, H.-C. Müller, T. Phelps, W. Rathert, L. Schmidthals, M. Tischer]

U. Tadday, ed.: *Charles Ives* [*Musik-Konzepte* 123] (Munich, 2004) [incl. articles by L. Fenner, D. Gail, W. Rathert, G. Schubert, D. Schulz, D. Von Glahn]

C: LIFE AND WORKS

H. Cowell: "Charles Ives," *MM*, x (1932–3), 24–33

H. Bellamann: "Charles Ives: the Man and his Music," *MQ*, xix (1933), 45–58

H. Cowell: *American Composers on American Music* (Stanford, CA, 1933/R), 128–45

H. and S. Cowell: *Charles Ives and his Music* (New York, 1955, 2/1969)

J. Bernlef and R. de Leeuw: *Charles Ives* (Amsterdam, 1969); partial Eng. trans. in *Student Musicologists at Minnesota*, vi (1975–6), 128–91

L. Wallach: *The New England Education of Charles Ives* (diss., Columbia U., 1973)

V. Perlis: *Charles Ives Remembered: an Oral History* (New Haven, CT, 1974/R)

R.S. Perry: *Charles Ives and the American Mind* (Kent, OH, 1974)

G. Vinay: *L'America musicale di Charles Ives* (Turin, 1974)

D. Wooldridge: *From the Steeples and Mountains: a Study of Charles Ives* (New York, 1974); repr. as *Charles Ives: a Portrait* (London, 1975)

F.R. Rossiter: *Charles Ives and his America* (New York, 1975)

S. Feder: "Charles and George Ives: the Veneration of Boyhood," *Annual of Psychoanalysis*, ix (1981), 265–316; repr. in *Psychoanalytic Explorations in Music*, ed. S. Feder, R.L. Karmel and G.H. Pollock (Madison, CT, 1990), 115–76

P.J. Conn: "Innovation and Nostalgia: Charles Ives," *The Divided Mind: Ideology and Imagination in America, 1898–1917* (Cambridge, 1983), 230–50

M.S. Harvey: *Charles Ives: Prophet of American Civil Religion* (diss., Boston U., 1983)

J.P. Burkholder: *Charles Ives: the Ideas Behind the Music* (New Haven, 1985)

J.J. Gibbens: *Debussy's Impact on Ives: an Assessment* (diss., U. of Illinois, 1985)

M.S. Moore: *Yankee Blues: Musical Culture and American Identity* (Bloomington, IN, 1985)

K.C. Ward: *Musical Idealism: a Study of the Aesthetics of Arnold Schoenberg and Charles Ives* (diss., Northwestern U., 1985)

J. Maderuelo: *Charles Ives* (Madrid, 1986)

D. Rostkowski: *Ives* (Gdańsk, 1987)

M. Solomon: "Charles Ives: some Questions of Veracity," *JAMS*, xl (1987), 443–70 [response: J.P. Lambert, *JAMS*, xlii (1989), 204–9; counter-response: M. Solomon, *JAMS*, xlii (1989), 209–18]

R.N. Bukoff: *Charles Ives: a History and Bibliography of Criticism (1920–1939), and Ives' Influence (to 1947) on Bernard Herrmann, Elie Siegmeister, and Robert Palmer* (diss., Cornell U., 1988)

J.P. Burkholder: "Charles Ives and his Fathers: a Response to Maynard Solomon," *Institute for Studies in American Music Newsletter*, xviii/1 (1988), 8–11

C.K. Baron: "Dating Charles Ives's Music: Facts and Fictions," *PNM*, xxviii/1 (1990), 20–56

A. Ivashkin: *Charlz Aivz i muzïka XX veka* [Charles Ives and Twentieth-Century Music] (Moscow, 1991)

C.K. Baron: "Georges Ives's Essay in Music Theory: an Introduction and Annotated Edition," *American Music*, x (1992), 239–88

S. Feder: *Charles Ives, "My Father's Song": a Psychoanalytic Biography* (New Haven, CT, 1992)

R.V. Wiecki: "Two Musical Idealists, Charles Ives and E. Robert Schmitz: a Friendship Reconsidered," *American Music*, x (1992), 1–19

J. Tick: "Charles Ives and Gender Ideology," *Musicology and Difference: Gender and Sexuality in Music Scholarship*, ed. R.A. Solie (Berkeley, 1993), 83–106

G. Sherwood: "Questions and Veracities: Reassessing the Chronology of Ives's Choral Works," *MQ*, lxxviii (1994), 429–47

D.V.G. Cooney: *Reconciliation: Time, Space and the American Place in the Music of Charles Ives* (diss., U. of Washington, 1995)

L. Kramer: "Cultural Politics and Musical Form: the Case of Charles Ives," *Classical Music and Postmodern Knowledge* (Berkeley, 1995), 174–200

J. Swafford: *Charles Ives: a Life with Music* (New York, 1996)

J.P. Burkholder: "Ives and Yale: the Enduring Influence of a College Experience," *College Music Symposium*, xxxix (1999), 27–42

S. Feder: *The Life of Charles Ives* (Cambridge, 1999)

T.C. Owens: *Charles Ives and His American Context: Images of "Americanness" in the Arts* (diss., Yale U., 1999)

P.K. Fairfield: *Representations of Gender and Sexuality in the Music and Writings of Charles Ives* (diss., Brandeis U., 2000)

G. Sherwood: "Charles Ives and 'Our National Malady'," *JAMS*, liv (2001), 555–84

B. Marshall: *Charles Ives and the Absent Presences of Life and Work* (diss., U. of Wales, 2003)

C.K. Baron: "Efforts on Behalf of Democracy by Charles Ives and His Family: Their Religious Contexts," *MQ*, lxxvii (2004), 6–43

M. Broyles: *Mavericks and Other Traditions in American Music* (New Haven, 2004)

T.A. Johnson: *Baseball and the Music of Charles Ives: a Proving Ground* (Lanham, MD, 2004)

D.C. Paul: "From American Ethnographer to Cold War Icon: Charles Ives through the Eyes of Henry and Sidney Cowell," *JAMS*, lix (2006), 399–457

D. Massey: "The Problem of Ives's Revisions (1973–1987)," *JAMS*, lx (2007), 599–645

G.S. Sherwood: *Charles Ives Reconsidered* (Urbana, IL, 2008)

D. Nicholls: "'The Unanswered Question of Her Son's Biography': New Thoughts on Mollie Ives," *Journal of the Society for American Music*, v (2011), 95–111

D.C. Paul: *Charles Ives in the Mirror: American Histories of an Iconic Composer* (Urbana, IL, 2013)

D: STUDIES OF THE MUSIC

H. Bellamann: "The Music of Charles Ives," *Pro-Musica Quarterly*, v/1 (1927), 16–22

P. Rosenfeld: *Discoveries of a Music Critic* (New York, 1936/R), 315–24

W. Mellers: "Realism and Transcendentalism: Charles Ives as American Hero," *Music in a New Found Land: Themes and Developments in the History of American Music* (London, 1964/R), 38–64

D. Marshall: "Charles Ives's Quotations: Manner or Substance?," *PNM*, vi/2 (1967–8), 45–56; repr. in *Perspectives on American Composers*, ed. B. Boretz and E.T. Cone (New York, 1971), 13–24

C.W. Henderson: *Quotation as a Style Element in the Music of Charles Ives* (diss., Washington U., 1969)

J.M. Rinehart: *Ives' Compositional Idioms: an Investigation of Selected Short Compositions as Microcosms of his Musical Language* (diss., Ohio State U., 1970)

R.P. Morgan: "Rewriting Music History: Second Thoughts on Ives and Varèse," *Musical Newsletter*, iii (1973), no.1, pp.3–12; no.2, pp.15–23, 28

C. Ward: *Charles Ives: the Relationship Between Aesthetic Theories and Compositional Processes* (diss., U. of Texas, 1974)

H.W. Hitchcock: *Ives* (London, 1977, 3/1988)

L. Starr: "Charles Ives: the Next Hundred Years: Towards a Method of Analyzing the Music," *MR*, xxxviii (1977), 101–11

N.S. Josephson: "Charles Ives: intervallische Permutationen im Spätwerk," *Zeitschrift für Musiktheorie*, ix/2 (1978), 27–33

R.P. Morgan: "Ives and Mahler: Mutual Responses at the End of an Era," *19CM*, ii (1978–9), 72–81; repr. in *Charles Ives and the Classical Tradition*, ed. G. Block and J.P. Burkholder (New Haven, CT, 1996), 75–86

C. Ballantine: "Charles Ives and the Meaning of Quotation in Music," *MQ*, lxv (1979), 167–84

S.S. Pavlyshyn: *Charlz Aivz* (Moscow, 1979)

N. Schoffman: "Serialism in the Works of Charles Ives," *Tempo*, no.138 (1981), 21–32

J.P. Burkholder: *The Evolution of Charles Ives's Music: Aesthetics, Quotation, Technique* (diss., U. of Chicago, 1983)

L.L. Gingerich: *Processes of Motivic Transformation in the Keyboard and Chamber Music of Charles E. Ives* (diss., Yale U., 1983)

L. Starr: "The Early Styles of Charles Ives," *19CM*, vii (1983–4), 71–80

L.L. Gingerich: "A Technique for Melodic Motivic Analysis in the Music of Charles Ives," *Music Theory Spectrum*, viii (1986), 75–93

T.D. Winters: *Additive and Repetitive Techniques in the Experimental Works of Charles Ives* (diss., U. of Pennsylvania, 1986)

C.K. Baron: *Ives on his Own Terms: an Explication, a Theory of Pitch Organization, and a New Critical Edition for the "3-Page Sonata"* (diss., CUNY, 1987)

H.W. Davies: *The Correlation Between Source and Style in the Music of Ives* (diss., U. of Wales, Cardiff, 1987)

Y. Sakae: "Charles Ives no ongakukozo ni okeru de-composition" [De-composition in the structure of Ives's music], *Ongaku-gaku*, xxxiv/2 (1988), 97–111

J.P. Lambert: "Ives's 'Piano-Drum' Chords," *Intégral*, iii (1989), 1–36

J.P. Burkholder: "The Critique of Tonality in the Early Experimental Music of Charles Ives," *Music Theory Spectrum*, xii (1990), 203–23

J.P. Lambert: "Aggregate Structures in Music of Charles Ives," *JMT*, xxxiv (1990), 29–55

J.P. Lambert: "Interval Cycles as Compositional Resources in the Music of Charles Ives," *Music Theory Spectrum*, xii (1990), 43–82

D. Nicholls: *American Experimental Music, 1890–1940* (Cambridge, 1990)

C.K. Baron: "Meaning in the Music of Charles Ives," *Metaphor: a Musical Dimension*, ed. J.C. Kassler (Sydney, 1991), 37–50

J.P. Lambert: "Ives and Counterpoint," *American Music*, ix (1991), 119–48

W. Rathert: *The Seen and Unseen: Studien zum Werk von Charles Ives* (Munich, 1991)

L. Starr: *A Union of Diversities: Style in the Music of Charles Ives* (New York, 1992)

T. Giebisch: *Take-Off als Kompositionsprinzip bei Charles Ives* (Kassel, 1993)

D.M. Hertz: *Angels of Reality: Emersonian Unfoldings in Wright, Stevens, and Ives* (Carbondale, IL, 1993)

J.P. Lambert: "Toward a Theory of Chord Structure for the Music of Ives," *JMT*, xxxvii (1993), 55–83

T.M. Brodhead: "Ives's *Celestial Railroad* and his Fourth Symphony," *American Music*, xii (1994), 389–424

A.B. Scott: "Medieval and Renaissance Techniques in the Music of Charles Ives: Horatio at the Bridge?," *MQ*, lxxviii (1994), 448–78

J.P. Burkholder: *All Made of Tunes: Charles Ives and the Uses of Musical Borrowing* (New Haven, CT, 1995)

P. Lambert: *The Music of Charles Ives* (New Haven, CT, 1997)

D. Metzer: "'We Boys': Childhood in the Music of Charles Ives," *19CM*, xxi (1997–8), 77–95

J.P. Burkholder: "The Organist in Ives," *JAMS*, lv (2002), 255–310

M.E. Johnson: "Charles Ives's (Utopian, Pragmatist, Nostalgic, Progressive, Romantic, Modernist) Yankee Realism," *American Music*, xx (2002), 188–231

M. Betz: "The Voice of the City: New York in der Musik von Charles Ives," *AMw*, lxi (2004), 207–25

M.J. McDonald: *Translating Experience, Transcending Time: Temporal Procedures and Their Expressive Meanings in the Music of Charles Ives* (diss., Yale U., 2004)

L. Fenner: *Erinnerung und Entlehnung im Werk von Charles Ives* (Tutzing, 2005)

H.-C. Liao: *The Evolving Perception of Charles Ives and His Music* (diss., U. of West Virginia, 2006)

J.P. Burkholder: "Stylistic Heterogeneity and Topics in the Music of Charles Ives," *Journal of Musicological Research*, xxxi (2012), 166–99

E: STUDIES OF INDIVIDUAL WORKS OR GENRES

Orchestral

D. Eiseman: *Charles Ives and the European Symphonic Tradition: a Historical Reappraisal* (diss., U. of Illinois, 1972)

W. Brooks: "Unity and Diversity in Charles Ives's Fourth Symphony," *YIAMR*, x (1974), 5–49

N.S. Josephson: "Zur formalen Struktur einiger später Orchesterwerke von Charles Ives (1874–1954)," *Mf*, xxvii (1974), 57–64

S. Feder: "Decoration Day: a Boyhood Memory of Charles Ives," *MQ*, lxvi (1980), 234–61

D. Porter: *The Third Orchestral Set of Charles Edward Ives* (thesis, California State U., 1980)

A. Maisel: "*The Fourth of July* by Charles Ives: Mixed Harmonic Criteria in a Twentieth-Century Classic," *Theory and Practice*, vi/1 (1981), 3–32

W. Rathert: "Charles Ives: Symphonie Nr.4, 1911–1916," *Neuland*, iii (1982–3), 226–41

M.D. Nelson: "Beyond Mimesis: Transcendentalism and Processes of Analogy in Charles Ives' 'The Fourth of July'," *PNM*, xxii/1–2 (1983–4), 353–84

W. Brooks: "A Drummer-Boy Looks Back: Percussion in Ives's *Fourth Symphony*," *Percussive Notes*, xxii/6 (1984), 4–45

N.S. Josephson: "The Initial Sketches for Ives's *St. Gaudens in Boston Common*," *Soundings* [Cardiff], xii (1984–5), 46–63

L. Austin: "Charles Ives's Life Pulse Prelude for Percussion Orchestra: a Realization for Modern Performance from Sketches for his Universe Symphony," *Percussionist*, xxiii/6 (1985), 58–84

R. Pozzi: "Polemica antiurbana ed isolamento ideologico in Central Park in the Dark di Charles Ives," *NRMI*, xix (1985), 471–81

W. Rathert: "Paysage imaginaire et perception totale: l'idée et la forme de la symphonie *Universe*," *Contrechamps*, no.7 (1986), 129–54

W. Shirley: "Once More Through *The Unanswered Question*," *Institute for Studies in American Music Newsletter*, xviii/2 (1989), 8–9, 13

W. Shirley: "'The Second of July': a Charles Ives Draft Considered as an Independent Work," *A Celebration of American Music: Words and Music in Honor of H. Wiley Hitchcock*, ed. R.A. Crawford, R.A. Lott and C.J. Oja (Ann Arbor, 1990), 391–404

J.B. Roller: *An Analysis of Selected Movements from the Symphonies of Charles Ives Using Linear and Set Theoretical Analytical Models* (diss., U. of Kentucky, 1995)

D.V.G. Cooney: "A Sense of Place: Charles Ives and 'Putnam's Camp, Redding, Connecticut'," *American Music*, xiv (1996), 276–312

D.V.G. Cooney: "New Sources for The '*St. Gaudens*' in Boston Common (*Colonel Robert Gould Shaw and his Colored Regiment*)," *MQ*, lxxxi (1997), 13–50

D. Von Glahn: "From Country to City in the Music of Charles Ives," in *The Sounds of Place: Music and the American Cultural Landscape* (Boston, 2003), 64–109

C.H. Garrett: "Charles Ives's *Four Ragtime Dances* and 'True American Music'," *Struggling to Define a Nation: American Music and the Twentieth Century* (Berkeley, CA, 2008), 17–47

D. Von Glahn: "Charles Ives at 'Christo's Gates'," *Twentieth-Century Music*, v (2008), 157–78

D. Gail: *Charles E. Ives' Fourth Symphony: Quellen—Analyse—Deutung* (Hofheim, 2009)

M.A. Zobel: *The Third Symphony of Charles Ives* (Hillsdale, NY, 2009)

Band

J. Elkus: *Charles Ives and the American Band Tradition: a Centennial Tribute* (Exeter, 1974)

Chamber

E. Gratovich: *The Sonatas for Violin and Piano by Charles Ives: a Critical Commentary and Concordance of the Printed Editions and the Autographs and Manuscripts of the Yale Ives Collection* (diss., Boston U., 1968)

U. Maske: *Charles Ives in seiner Kammermusik für drei bis sechs Instrumente* (Regensburg, 1971)

A. Forte: "The Diatonic Looking Glass, or An Ivesian Metamorphosis," *MQ*, lxxvi (1992), 355–82 [on Sonata no.2 for violin and piano, 3rd movement]

Piano

S.R. Clark: *The Evolving "Concord Sonata": a Study of Choices and Variants in the Music of Charles Ives* (diss., Stanford U., 1972)

S.R. Clark: "The Element of Choice in Ives's *Concord Sonata*," *MQ*, lx (1974), 167–86

B.E. Chmaj: "Sonata for American Studies: Perspectives on Charles Ives," *Prospects: an Annual of American Cultural Studies*, iv (1978), 1–58

M.J. Alexander: *The Evolving Keyboard Style of Charles Ives* (New York, 1989)

F. Meyer: *"The Art of Speaking Extravagantly": eine vergleichende Studie der "Concord Sonata" und der "Essays before a Sonata" von Charles Ives* (Berne, 1991)

G. Block: *Ives: Concord Sonata* (Cambridge, 1996)

W. Rathert: "'Sonate, que me veux-tu?': Die Concord Sonata von Charles Ives als musikalische Utopie," *Bayerische Akademie der Schönen Künste Jahrbuch*, xxii (2008), 160–74

C. Bruhn: "The Transitive Multiverse of Charles Ives's 'Concord' Sonata," *JM*, xxviii (2011), 166–94

Choral

W.C. Kumlien: *The Sacred Choral Music of Charles Ives: a Study in Style Development* (diss., U. of Illinois, 1969)

G. Sherwood: *The Choral Works of Charles Ives: Chronology, Style, Reception* (diss., Yale U., 1995)

G. Sherwood: "'Buds the Infant Mind': Charles Ives's *The Celestial Country* and American Protestant Choral Traditions," *19CM*, xxiii (1999), 163–89

Songs

P.E. Newman: *The Songs of Charles Ives* (diss., U. of Iowa, 1967)

L. Starr: "Style and Substance: 'Ann Street' by Charles Ives," *PNM*, xv/2 (1976–7), 23–33

N. Schoffman: *The Songs of Charles Ives* (diss., Hebrew U. of Jerusalem, 1977)

L. Kramer: "'A Completely New Set of Objects'," *Music and Poetry: the Nineteenth Century and After* (Berkeley, 1984), 171–202

K.O. Kelly: *The Songs of Charles Ives and the Cultural Contexts of Death* (diss., U. of North Carolina, 1988)

L. Whitesell: "Reckless Form, Uncertain Audiences: Responding to Ives," *American Music*, xii (1994), 304–19

T.A. Johnson: "Chromatic Quotations of Diatonic Tunes in Songs of Charles Ives," *Music Theory Spectrum*, xviii (1996), 236–61

H.W. Hitchcock: "'A grand and glorious noise!': Charles Ives as Lyricist," *American Music*, xv/1 (1997), 26–44

A. Houtchens and J.P. Stout: "'Scarce Heard amidst the Guns Below': Intertextuality and Meaning in Charles Ives's War Songs," *JM*, xv (1997), 66–97

H.W. Hitchcock: "Ives's *114 [+ 15] Songs* and what he thought of them," *JAMS*, lii (1999), 97–144

J. PETER BURKHOLDER (WORK-LIST WITH JAMES B. SINCLAIR AND GAYLE SHERWOOD MAGEE)

Ives, Edward D. [Sandy] (*b* White Plains, NY, 4 Sept 1925; *d* Bangor, ME, 1 Aug 2009).Folklorist, folksinger, and song collector. Ives was educated in English (MA, Columbia) and folklore (PhD, Indiana University), and taught for more than 40 years at the University of Maine. His travels in Maine and the Maritime Provinces of Canada brought him into contact with the traditions of local song-making and storytelling, particularly among men working in the woods in lumber camps and as guides. Ives' reflexive studies of New England songmakers from the late 19th and early 20th centuries show a keen intelligence and generosity of spirit. His eight books concentrated on deceased working-class songsters and storytellers (Larry Gorman, Lawrence Doyle, Wilbur Day, George Magoon, and Joe Scott), and on creativity within traditional forms. He claimed that vernacular literature and song had social and aesthetic values that transcended its sentimentality. His teaching and writing inspired two generations of New England folklorists, and he was active as an educator and public speaker throughout the state of Maine, where he is remembered with affection. He founded the Northeast Archives of Folklore, which later became incorporated into the Maine Folklife Center at the University of Maine, and which houses thousands of recorded interviews, photographs, and artifacts related to traditional music and lifeways in Maine and the Maritimes.

WRITINGS

Larry Gorman: The Man Who Made the Songs (Bloomington, 1964; repr. New York, 1977; repr. Fredericton, New Brunswick, 1993)

Joe Scott: The Woodsman Songmaker (Champaign, 1978)

George Magoon and the Downeast Game War (Champaign, 1988)

JEFF TODD TITON

Ives, Elam, Jr. (*b* Hamden, CT, 7 Jan 1802; *d* Hamden, CT, 10 Feb 1864). Music educator. He taught piano, violin, and singing, and also worked as a church choir director and singing-school master. From 1830 to 1836 he lived in Philadelphia, where he was the principal of the Philadelphia Musical Seminary. He then established a music school in New York, where he continued to teach and write. He published many school songbooks, collections of sacred music, and art songs, some in collaboration with Deodatus Dutton, Jr, and Lowell Mason; he also contributed to nonmusical periodicals, such as *The Harbinger*. He was one of the first Americans to apply the theories of the Swiss educational philosopher Johann Heinrich Pestalozzi to the field of music education, and became an important figure in American public school music; his ideas exercised an influence on both Thomas Hastings and Lowell Mason.

BIBLIOGRAPHY

R.W. John: "Elam Ives and the Pestalozzian Philosophy of Music Education," *JRME*, viii/1 (Spring 1960), 45–50

WILLIAM McCLELLAN

Ivey, Jean Eichelberger (*b* Washington, DC, 3 July 1923; *d* Baltimore, MD, 2 May 2010). Composer and pianist. She studied at Trinity College (BA 1944), the Peabody Conservatory (MM in piano, 1946), the Eastman School (MM in composition, 1956), and the University of Toronto (DMus in composition, 1972). In 1967 she founded the electronic music studio at Peabody, and from 1982 until her retirement in 1997 she coordinated its composition department. Ivey summarized her compositional ideals at the 30th anniversary of computer music at Peabody: "I consider all the musical resources of the past and present as being at the composer's disposal, but always in the service of the effective communication of humanistic ideas and intuitive emotion." Her early music was tonal and neo-classical, drawing particularly on the styles of Bartók and Ravel; in the 1960s she began to incorporate serial and electronic elements which gave her music greater fluidity. She was especially fond of writing for the voice in combination with orchestra, ensemble, piano, or tape. Some of her works, including the monodrama *Testament of Eve* (1976), are to her own texts; in general she preferred poems with philosophical content, as in *Night Voyage* (1975), after Matthew Arnold's *Self-Dependence*. As a pianist she toured Europe, Mexico, and the United States. She was a director of the League of Composers of the ISCM

(1972–5, 1979). Her awards include an Artists' Fellowship from the New York Foundation for the Arts (1992) and grants from the NEA to compose *Sea-Change* (1979) and the Cello Concerto (1983–5). She wrote many articles on music and is herself the subject of the WRC-TV documentary *A Woman is…a Composer.*

WORKS
(selective list)

Stage: Birthmark (op, 1, Ivey, after N. Hawthorne), 1980–82

Vocal: Woman's Love (S. Teasdale), cycle of 5 songs, Mez, pf, 1962; Tribute: Martin Luther King (spirituals), Bar, orch, 1969; Terminus (R.W. Emerson), Mez, tape, 1970; 3 Songs of Night (W. Whitman, Hovey, Callimachus-Cory), S, a fl, cl, va, vc, pf, tape, 1971; Hera, Hung from the Sky (C. Kizer), Mez, 7 wind, 3 perc, pf, tape, 1973; Night Voyage (M. Arnold), 1975; Testament of Eve (monodrama, Ivey), Mez, orch, tape, 1976; Solstice (Ivey), S, fl + pic, perc, pf, 1977; Prospero (scena, W. Shakespeare), B, hn, perc, 4-track tape, 1978; Crossing Brooklyn Ferry (Whitman), Bar, pf, 1979; Notes toward Time (J. Jacobsen), 3 songs, Mez, fl + a fl, hp, 1984; My Heart is Like a Singing Bird (C. Rossetti), SSA, fls, 1994

Orch: Little Sym., 1948; Passacaglia, chbr orch, 1954; Festive Sym., 1955; Ov., small orch, 1955; Forms in Motion, sym., 1972; Sea-Change, large orch, tape, 1979; Vc Conc., 1983–5; Voyager, vc, orch, 1987; Short Sym., 1988

Chbr and solo inst: Theme and Variations, pf, 1952; Scherzo, wind septet, 1953; Pf Sonata, 1957; 6 Inventions, 2 vn, 1959; Str Qt, 1960; Sonatina, cl, 1963; Ode, vn, pf, 1965, arr. orch, 1965; Aldebaran, va, tape, 1972; Skaniadaryo, pf, tape, 1973; Music, va, pf, 1974; Triton's Horn, t sax, pf, 1982; Ariel in Flight, vn, tape, 1983; Sonata da chiesa, hp, 1986; Suite, vc, pf, 1993; Flying Colors, brass fanfare, 1994

Elec: Enter 3 Witches, 4-track tape, 1964; Pinball, 1965 [from film score]; Continuous Form, 1967; Theater Piece, 1970; Cortège—for Charles Kent, 1979

2 incid music scores, 1963; 2 film scores, 1963, 1965

Principal publishers: Boosey & Hawkes; C. Fischer; E.C. Schirmer

BIBLIOGRAPHY

B.E. Maris: *American Compositions for Piano and Tape-Recorded Sound* (diss., Peabody Conservatory, 1976) [incl. analysis of Skaniadaryo]

J.W. LePage: *Women Composers, Conductors, and Musicians of the 20th Century*, i (Metuchen, NJ, 1981)

R.M. Muennich: *The Vocal Works of Jean Eichelberger Ivey* (diss., Michigan State U., 1983)

H. Woodworth: *Jean Eichelberger Ivey: Current Research and Interviews with Former Colleagues and Students* (M.M. thesis, Peabody Conservatory of Music, 2010)

H.W. Brannon: "A Tribute to Jean Eichelberger Ivey," *Journal of the International Alliance for Women in Music*, xvii/1 (2011), 1–4

SAM DI BONAVENTURA/GEOFFREY WRIGHT/R

Ivy Queen [Pesante, Martha Ivelisse] (*b* Añasco, PR, 4 March 1972). Puerto Rican singer. Ivy Queen has reigned as reggaeton's practically sole female voice for well over a decade, remaining a central and respected figure while transforming herself from fierce battle rapper to sentimental sophisticate. She started singing to her father's guitar accompaniment and identifies Celia Cruz and Selena as role models. She lived in New York City from childhood into her teenage years, moving to San Juan after high school. While writing for other acts and performing in talent shows, she grabbed the attention of DJ Negro, who added her to the roster of The Noise, an influential crew of DJs and performers. After making a splash on several mixtapes by The Noise, she embarked on a solo career, in part to distance herself from sexually explicit and violent lyrics, addressing a range of topics from domestic violence to single mothers, fidelity to feminism. Her first album, *En mi imperio* (1996), sold briskly in Puerto Rico and was picked up by Sony. She has since released a steady stream of albums, broadening her audience, garnering industry awards, and settling into a style that finds her crooning bachata-infused ballads as often as rapping in her distinctively deep rasp.

WAYNE MARSHALL

Iyer, Vijay (*b* Albany, NY, 26 Oct 1971). Pianist. His family moved to Rochester, NY, soon after his birth. He studied classical violin from the ages of three to 18, while exploring piano on his own. He was introduced to jazz in high school where he began playing in rock bands and in the school jazz ensemble. Recordings from the local library introduced him to the music of Miles Davis, Herbie Hancock, and, most importantly, Thelonious Monk, whose physicality at the keyboard, along with an insistent logical rigor, touched a deep emotional chord. After Iyer saw the Monk documentary, *Straight, No Chaser* (1988), his aesthetic was sealed: seeing Monk in action, he explained, made the musical experience even more vivid and intense.

Iyer studied physics at Yale University and moved to California to pursue a PhD in the subject at the University of California at Berkeley. However, after winning a local music contest, he decided to change directions. Several musicians became mentors, including the saxophonist Steve Coleman, with whom he toured and recorded, and the trombonist George Lewis. With his school advisor, the research scientist David Wessel, he redirected his scholarly focus to integrate his musical side and wrote a dissertation (*Macrostructures of Sound: Embodied Cognition in West African and African-American Musics*, 1988) in which he explored the role of the body in music perception and cognition.

Iyer's percussive approach, although influenced by Monk, draws on African and Indian traditions, which manifest themselves in complex rhythmic cycles, arpeggiation, and melodic permutation. Iyer has received many awards and honors, winning *Downbeat* Album of the Year for *Historicity* (2010, ACT) and being named Musician of the Year by the Jazz Journalists Association (2010). He collaborates frequently with the saxophonist Rudresh Mahanthappa.

STUART ISACOFF

Iznaola, Ricardo (*b* Havana, Cuba, 21 Feb 1949). Guitarist of Cuban birth. After the Cuban Revolution his family moved to Columbia and then to Venezuela. He studied at the Escuela Superior de Música in Caracas with Manuel Pérez Díaz and subsequently with Regino Sáinz de la Maza in Madrid and Alirio Díaz at the summer school in Caracas. He won many international prizes including first prize at the Francisco Tárrega Competition in 1968 and 1971. In 1969 he began his international career, touring Asia, Europe, and North and South America, and the next year made the first of many recordings, concentrating particularly on Spanish and South American music. He gave his London debut in 1976.

In 1983 he became professor of guitar at the Lamont School of Music, University of Denver, being appointed in 2004 to the John Evans Distinguished Professorship, the faculty's highest distinction. He has published many articles, compositions, and arrangements, and several books on the guitar including *Kitharologus: The Path to Virtuosity* (Heidelberg, 1993) and *On Practicing* (Aurora, CO, 1992). Iznaola is a virtuoso recitalist of immense technical resources and powerful intellect with a deep awareness of Hispanic culture. He has been on the juries of many international competitions, and in addition to his hundreds of concerts is much in demand for lectures and master classes.

BIBLIOGRAPHY

S. McReadie: "Ricardo Fernandez Iznaola," *Guitar,*viii/9 (1979–80), 16–18
C. Postlethwaite: "Iznaola," *Guitar International,* xiv/7 (1985–6), 15–19 [interview]
C. Cooper: "Ricardo Iznaola and the Long-Term Approach," *Classical Guitar,* ix/12 (1990–91), 11–16
G. Wade: *A Concise History of the Classic Guitar* (Pacific, MI, 2001), 185

GRAHAM WADE

Izu, Mark (George) (*b* Vallejo, CA, 30 Sept 1954). Composer and bass player. He studied bass as a youth with Charles Manning and then under Charles Siani at San Francisco State University, where he received a BA in music. He also studied Japanese *gagaku* music with Togi Suenobu and has become proficient on the *shō*, *sheng*, and other Asian instruments. Izu has performed with Cecil Tayor, Steve Lacy, and James Newton, and has been an important figure in Asian American jazz. He was a founding member of the groups United Front and Anthony Brown's Asian American Orchestra, performing on the latter's Grammy-nominated recording of Duke Ellington and Billy Strayhorn's *Far East Suite* (1999, Asian Improv). He has also worked with Jon Jang's Pan Asian Arkestra. Izu has served as artistic director of the Asian American Jazz Festival and on the faculty of Stanford University's Institute for Diversity in the Arts.

A combination of jazz (especially free jazz) and Asian influences, Izu's compositions blend the improvisation and texture of jazz with the Japanese concept of *ma*. *Hibakusha! (Survivors)* (1995) combines Western orchestral and Asian instruments, while *Navarasa* (2009) is a collection of improvised duets for bass and *shakuhachi*. Izu's works sometimes depict difficult events in Asian American history: *Last Dance* (1998), for example, was inspired by the internment of Japanese Americans during World War II. His scores for film and television include the Academy Award-winning film *Days of Waiting* (1990) and the Emmy-winning documentary *Bolinao 52* (2008). He has also written scores for dramatic works, particularly those of his wife, Brenda Wong Aoki. Izu's compositions have been performed by Kent Nagano and George Lewis.

WORKS
(selective list)
DRAMATIC

Dreams and Illusions: Tales of the Pacific Rim (B. W. Aoki), 1990; Dragonwings (L. Yep), 1992; The Queen's Garden (Aoki), 1992; Mermaid (Aoki), 1997; Uncle Gunjiro's Girlfriend (Aoki), 1998, rev. 2007; Last Dance (G. Yoshida, Aoki, and others), 1998; Ballad of the Bones (J. O'Neal and Aoki), 2000; Kuan-Yin: Our Lady of Compassion (Aoki), 2002; Mermaid Meat (Aoki), 2007; The Legend of Morning Glory (Aoki), 2008; Return of the Sun (Aoki), 2009

FILM AND TELEVISION SCORES

Dim Sum Take Out (W. Wang), 1987; Westward to China (TV, J. Culp), 1989; Days of Waiting (S. Okazaki), 1990; The Tong Man (W. Worthington, new score to a 1919 silent film), c1990; The Dragon Painter (Worthington, new score to a 1919 silent film), 1993; Notes On a Scale (K. Kashima), 1994; The Lady and the Beard (Y. Ozu, new score to a 1931 silent film), 1994; American Sons (Okazaki, music by M. Izu, F. Wong, and M. Masoaka), 1994; Return to the Valley (TV, S. Gracheff), 2003; What's Wrong With Frank Chin? (C. Choy, music by Izu and L. Choy), 2005; The Dancing Girl of Izu (G. Heinosuke, new score to a 1933 silent film), 2005; Bolinao 52 (TV, D. Nguyen, music by Izu and V.-A. Vo), 2008

SELECTED RECORDINGS

Circle of Fire (Asian Improv, 1992); *Threading Time* (Belly to Belly, 2007); *Navarasa* (with C. Yohmei Blasdel, Belly to Belly, 2009)

BIBLIOGRAPHY

S. Asai: "Sansei Voices in the Community: Japanese American Musicians in California," *Musics of Multicultural America: A Study of Twelve Musical Communities*, eds. K. Lornell and A.K. Rasmussen (New York, 1997), 257–285
D. Wong: *Speak it Louder: Asian Americans Making Music* (New York, 2004)
S. Asai: "Cultural Politics: the African American Connection in Asian American Jazz-based Music," *Asian Music,* xxxvi/1 (2005), 87–108

LARS HELGERT

Jabbour, Alan (*b* Jacksonville, FL, 21 June 1942). Folklorist and fiddler. An orchestral violinist early in life, he studied folklore and medieval literature at Duke University, earning the PhD in English in 1968. He documented the playing of Appalachian traditional fiddlers and drew upon their repertoire as a member of the Hollow Rock String Band, which contributed significantly to the 1960s folk revival. After teaching at UCLA (1968–9), Jabbour held influential positions with national cultural institutions. He was head of the Archive of Folk Song at the Library of Congress (1969–74); founding director of the NEA's Folk Arts Program (1974–6); and founding director of the American Folklife Center at the Library of Congress (1976–99).

As a scholar Jabbour has edited and annotated several significant collections of sound recordings. *American Fiddle Tunes* (Library of Congress, 1971; Rounder, 2000) consists of early field recordings drawn from the Archive of Folk Culture at the Library of Congress. *The Hammons Family: the Traditions of a West Virginia Family and their Friends* (Rounder, 1998) is based on ethnographic research that Jabbour and Carl Fleischhauer conducted in the early 1970s. *The Edden Hammons Collection: Historic Recordings of Traditional Fiddle Music from the Louis Watson Chappell Archive* (1999), co-edited with John A. Cuthbert, is a two-volume collection of home recordings of a West Virginia fiddler. More of the fruits of Jabbour's fieldwork have been published on a website hosted by the Library of Congress, "Fiddle Tunes of the Old Frontier: the Henry Reed Collection" (<http://memory.loc.gov/ammem/collections/reed/>); it features Jabbour's recordings of the fiddler Henry Reed of West Virginia and Virginia, and includes written and video commentary.

BIBLIOGRAPHY

J. Bernhardt: "The Hollow Rock String Band," *Bluegrass Unlimited*, xxi/6 (1986), 74–81

T. Carter: "Looking for Henry Reed: Confessions of a Revivalist," *Sounds of the South*, ed. D.W. Patterson (Durham, NC, 1991), 73–89

S. Goldfield: "Alan Jabbour: Fiddler, Scholar, and Preserver of Tradition," *Fiddler Magazine*, xiii/2 (2006), 14–20

MATT MEACHAM

Jackson. City in Mississippi (pop. 173,514; metropolitan area 568,163; 2010 US Census). It was designated the state capital in 1822. The city's musical life in the 19th century is largely undocumented. In the latter part of the 19th century a local blues tradition emerged, having spread from the Mississippi Delta. In the mid-1920s and early 1930s the Jackson businessman and talent scout Henry C. Speir recorded the blues musicians Ishman Bracey, TOMMY JOHNSON (I), Charley Patton, and Skip James, all of whom lived in Jackson at one time. The recording scene in Jackson continued to flourish for decades. Lillian McMurry founded Trumpet Records in 1950 and was the first to record SONNY BOY WILLIAMSON (I) and Elmore James. Ace Records, started in 1955 by Johnny Vincent, recorded such artists as Lightnin' Hopkins, Dr. John, and Sam Myers and the Five Blind Boys of Mississippi. Two important performance venues on N. Farish Street helped to sustain local blues, jazz, and pop artists: the Alamo Theater (opened in 1942) and the Subway Lounge (opened in 1966, and featured in Robert Mugge's documentary *Last of the Mississippi Jukes*, 2003). In 1968 Tommy Couch and Mitchell Malouf founded Malaco Records, which recorded Mississippi Fred McDowell, Bobby Rush, Denise LaSalle, Bobby Bland, Dorothy Moore, the Jackson Southernaires, and the award-winning Mississippi Mass Choir. The popular music scene has remained vibrant into the 21st century. Between 1987 and 2009 the Jubilee! Jam arts and music festival attracted national and international acts to Jackson.

Concert music in the mid-20th century was staged in various high schools, the Heidelberg Hotel, and the old City Auditorium. The 2362-seat Municipal Auditorium opened in 1968 and was renamed Thalia Mara Hall in 1994 after the renowned dancer and teacher. It has become the major arts venue of downtown Jackson, providing space for touring musical theater productions and serving as the home of the Mississippi SO and the USA International Ballet Competition which is held quadrennially in Jackson, alternating with sister competitions in Bulgaria and Russia.

The Mississippi SO began in 1944 as the all-volunteer Jackson SO, with an operating budget of $2,000. Theodore

Caskey Russell was its first conductor (1945–65), followed by Lewis Dalvit (1965–89), and Colman Pearce (1989–99). Crafton Beck took over the role in 2001, and Michael Beattie became its president and executive director in 2004; in the early 2010s the MSO was a professional orchestra with an annual budget of $1.6 million. A nationally recognized strings education program has reached 800 students in under-served areas, and the orchestra has performed before 25,000 elementary school children each year.

Mississippi Opera has a history of continuous productions beginning in 1945. As Jackson Opera, it was supported by the Jackson Opera Guild (incorporated in 1947), which changed its name to the Mississippi Opera Guild (1970). Opera/South began in 1971 as a joint venture between Tougaloo College, Utica Junior College, and Jackson State University, chartered as the Mississippi Intercollegiate Opera Guild. Its purpose was to promote young African American vocal talent and the music of African American composers such as William Grant Still.

Five institutions of higher learning in the greater Jackson area have offered degrees in music: Belhaven University (from 1883, BM and BA), Jackson State University (1877, BM, BMEd, and MME), Millsaps College (1890, BA and BS), Mississippi College (1826, BM, BA, and MM), and Tougaloo College (1869, BA). Hinds Community College (1917) in nearby Raymond has offered music courses as well.

The list of notable musicians who have emerged from Jackson is both eclectic and remarkable, given the city's size: Jackson natives include the Broadway composer and producer Lehman Engel (1910–82) and the composer and theorist Milton Babbitt (1916–2011); the latter's early musical experiences came as a talented young clarinetist, and he famously sat in at age 12 with touring New Orleans jazz bands. Other musicians of note include the jazz vocalist Cassandra Wilson (*b* 1955), the composer Samuel Jones (*b* 1935), and the music educator Willard Palmer (1917–96).

BIBLIOGRAPHY
N. Colee: *Mississippi Music and Musicians* (Magnolia, MS, 1948)
B. Bailey: "Opera/South: a Brief History," *BPM*, xiii/1 (1985), 48–78
G. Wardlow: *Chasin' that Devil Music: Searching for the Blues* (San Francisco, 1998)
J. Brewer, ed.: *Mississippi Musicians Hall of Fame: Legendary Musicians whose Art has Changed the World* (Brandon, MS, 2001)
LYNN RALEY

Jackson, Alan (Eugene) (*b* Newnan, GA, 17 Oct 1958). Country recording artist. Entering the national country music scene in the early 1990s amid the rise of Garth Brooks, Tim McGraw, and the other "hat acts" of the era, he distinguished himself among his contemporaries as both a talented singer and songwriter. The lyrical content of Jackson's music underscored his working class upbringing in rural west Georgia, where he worked as an auto mechanic and a used-car salesmen, married his high-school sweetheart, and performed country music as a side job to help pay bills. In 1985 he relocated to Nashville, where he eventually secured a staff songwriting position at Glenn Campbell's music publishing company. In 1989 he signed with Arista Records; his debut album, *Here in the Real World* (Arista, 1990), produced five singles, including his first number-one hit "I'd love you all over again." An industry favorite, Jackson won the Academy of Country Music's Top New Male Vocalist award in 1990. His sophomore album, *Don't rock the jukebox* (1991), was already quadruple platinum by 1995, and its title track became Jackson's second number-one hit; this feat was surpassed by his third recording with Arista, *A Lot about Livin' (and a Little 'bout Love)* (1993), which had sold more than six million copies by 1995 and produced a number-one hit, "Chattahoochee." Jackson received the Academy of Country Music's Top Male Vocalist award in 1994 and the Country Music Association's Entertainer of the Year award in 1995, 2001, 2002, and 2003. Jackson's compilation albums, *Greatest Hits Collection* (Arista, 1995) and *Greatest Hits Volume II* (Arista, 2003), had each sold more than six million copies by the early 2010s. Notable in Jackson's career has been his performance at the Country Music Awards in 2001 when he debuted "Where were you (when the world stopped turning)," his number-one ballad written about the events of 11 September 2001; it brought him his first Grammy Award, for Best Country Song. By 2011 Jackson had scored more than 25 number-one country singles, including "Drive (for Daddy Gene)" (2002), "It's Five O'Clock Somewhere" (2003), "Remember When" (2004), and "Country Boy" (2009), and sold more than 43.5 million albums worldwide.

DAVID B. PRUETT

Jackson, Aunt Molly [née Garland, Mary Magdalene] (*b* Clay County, KY, 1880; *d* Sacramento, CA, 1 Sept 1960). Folksinger. She grew up in a coal-mining region, where her father was a minister and a supporter of labor unions. During the first two decades of the 20th century she worked as a labor organizer and wrote protest songs. In 1931 she left Kentucky for New York, then joined a national music tour in support of striking miners. She made the acquaintance of Alan Lomax, who introduced her to Woody Guthrie and persuaded the Archive of American Folksong at the Library of Congress to record her repertory of 204 songs in 1939. She lived in New York and then in Sacramento, California. Jackson's songs are in regular meter and characterized by a dark, unforgiving mood. Some consist of traditional melodies fitted with new lyrics; "Dreadful Memories," for example, is a parody of the white gospel song "Precious Memories." Her other well-known songs include "Poor Miner's Farewell," "Death of Harry Sims," and "I am a Union Woman." Some of her early recordings have been reissued by Rounder Records.

BIBLIOGRAPHY
G. Friesen: "Aunt Molly Jackson," *Daily Worker* (10 Jan 1942)
J. Greenway: "Aunt Molly Jackson and Robin Hood: a Study in Folk Re-creation," *Journal of American Folklore*, lxix/1 (1956), 23
A. Lomax: "Aunt Molly Jackson," *Kentucky Folklore Record*, vii/4 (1961), 131

A. Lomax and W. Guthrie, eds.: *Hard Hitting Songs for Hard Hit People* (New York, 1967) [orig. on mimeograph, 1940]

S. Romalis: *Pistol Packin' Mama: Aunt Molly Jackson and the Politics of Folksong* (Urbana, IL, 1999)

DAVID K. DUNAWAY/R

Jackson, D.D. [Robert Cleanth Kai-Nen] (*b* Ottawa, ON, 25 Jan 1967). Jazz pianist and composer with dual Canadian-American citizenship. Of mixed African American and Chinese heritage, he was called Di-di (Mandarin Chinese for "little brother") at home. He studied classical piano at Indiana University (BMus 1989), jazz at the Manhattan School of Music (MM 1991), and later had private tuition with JAKI BYARD and DON PULLEN in New York, where he has lived since 1989. He began playing with David Murray and Billy Bang in the early 1990s and has played frequently with Murray in both small-group and big-band settings since then. He has toured internationally and has performed with such notable musicians as Nat Adderley, Jack DeJohnette, Dewey Redman, and James Spaulding. A virtuoso who recorded Gershwin's *Rhapsody in Blue* for Summit Records in 2002, Jackson has also made nine albums of mostly his own material for RCA and Justin Time 1994-2006, and another three in trio formations with Hamiet Bluiett and Mor Thiam or Kahil El'Zabar 1998-2000. For five years he wrote a column, "Living Jazz," for *Down Beat*, and he has taught at Hunter College since 2009 and at the Harlem School of the Arts since 2011.

In 1999 Jackson was the music director for a Broadway production of *Mytholojazz*, in which his trio performed onstage and he played the role of Lord Hades. In the same year he performed on a John Coltrane tribute album with the David Murray Octet and collaborated on Murray and Bob Weir's opera *Satchel Paige*. He has also written two operas, *Quebecité* and *Trudeau: Long March/Shining Path*, which premiered in Canada in 2003 and 2006, respectively, and the musical comedy *Depressed, Depressed*, which was first performed in Chicago in 2006. He wrote the music for all 26 episodes of *The Ocean Room*, a Canadian children's television show, and has also composed for *The Wonder Pets*, another children's show which has won three Emmy Awards for Outstanding Musical Direction and Composition. Known for an energetic, even daring, approach to keyboard playing, Jackson routinely pushes his technical limits, using cross-rhythms or different meters in each hand, playing clusters with his palms or arms, and standing to sound thunderous chords at both ends of the piano simultaneously. His compositions, like his improvisations, feature an eclectic blend of blues, Latin, funk, gospel, and pop styles. Jackson was awarded a Juno prize in 2000.

S. TIMOTHY MALONEY

Jackson, George K(nowil) (*b* Oxford, England, baptized 15 April 1757; *d* Boston, MA, 18 Nov 1822). Composer, teacher, and editor of English birth. Around 1766 his widowed mother moved to London, and Jackson is reported to have studied under James Nares at the Chapel Royal. In 1774 he was appointed organist of St. Alban, Wood Street, a post he held until 1790. While in London he also taught privately, wrote a number of sacred and secular compositions, and published a *Treatise on Practical Thoroughbass* (1785). St. Andrews University granted him a doctorate in music in 1791, probably an honorary award.

In 1796 or 1797 Jackson immigrated to the United States. He settled in New Brunswick, New Jersey, where he taught until 1801, possibly spending a short time in Newark in 1801. His public concerts received considerable attention in New Jersey, and their sophistication and popularity was reported in New York newspapers. From 1802 to 1807 he served as organist of St. George's Church, New York, and also gave concert performances in the city, often of his own works. Between September 1805 and October 1806 he spent some time in Hartford, Connecticut, where he advertised his services as teacher and presented several concerts.

Jackson moved in 1812 to Boston, where he continued to teach and serve as church organist. During the War of 1812 he was exiled from Boston to Northampton, Massachusetts, for failing to register as an enemy (British) alien. His sentence quickly became the focus of an argument between opponents and proponents of the War; newspaper accounts make it clear that Jackson had already assumed a leading role in Boston's musical life, and improvements in standards of musicianship and performance were attributed directly to his influence. Nonetheless, he was forced to spend three years in Northampton, where he taught, and, despite limited resources, managed to mount an occasional concert.

On his return to Boston, Jackson became organist at Trinity Church and opened a music store. He was frequently in dispute with other musicians, often because of his discontent with what he believed to be unsatisfactory standards of musicianship and his insistence on complete control of all performances; he was sometimes accused of arrogance and of over valuing his services. His opinion was often sought, but his active participation in Boston's musical life declined steadily after 1817. In autumn 1821 he advised Lowell Mason in the preparation of *The Boston Handel and Haydn Society Collection of Church Music* (1822/R1973), which the society subsequently dedicated to Jackson; the first edition bore a testimonial to his great skill in music.

Although Jackson's reputation rested largely on his skills as organist and teacher, he also wrote nearly 100 compositions. He was essentially a conservative composer, making much use of figured bass and fugal techniques. His keyboard pieces do not reflect his proficiency as a performer, but often fulfilled a pedagogical role. His few surviving hymns and chant settings are stolidly harmonized; but the settings of *Dr. Watts's Divine Songs* (c1791) are tuneful and show a degree of sophistication in their use of chromatic inflection and broad melodic curves not usual in contemporary settings of Watts.

WORKS
(printed works published in New York unless otherwise stated; for fuller list see Kaufman)

SACRED VOCAL
Ponder My Words (Ps.v), anthem, 3vv, op.2 (London, c1790); Dr. Watts's Divine Songs Set to Music, op. 1, 28 hymn tunes, 9 morality songs (London, c1791); David's Psalms, 1v, org (1804); Sacred Music for the Use of Churches, Sanctus, doxology, 3 psalm tunes, 2 chants, *GEU*; Pope's Universal Prayer and his Celebrated Ode, The Dying Christian (A. Pope), SST, vn (n.d.); 7 hymn tunes, 2 canons pubd in The Boston Handel and Haydn Society Collection of Church Music (Boston, 1822/*R*1973); Benedictus No. 1, Gloria Patri no.5, pubd in Music of the Church (Philadelphia, 1828); Te Deum, 4vv, org, *INS*; Two Books of Sacred Amusements, *INS*

Edns: A Choice Collection of Chants, 4vv (Boston, 1816), incl. chants by Jackson; The Choral Companion (Boston, 1817)

SECULAR VOCAL
A Favorite Canzone (J. Jackson), 1/2/3vv/pf (c1787–91); A Favorite Collection of [10] Songs and Duetts, 1v, hpd/pf, op.3 (London, 1791); A Prey to Tender Anguish, song (n.d. [c1801]); Freedom and our President (Jefferson's March), 1v, pf, c1801, *MBHM*; New Ode to Liberty, c1801, lost; [6] New Bagatelles, 1v, pf (c1801); A Winter's Evening, c1801, *MBHM*; President Jefferson's New March and Quick Step (J. Jackson) (c1803); The Sylph (T. Moore), pubd in Dr. Jackson's Selection, iii (c1803); Verses for the Fourth of July (J. Jackson) (c1803), lost; Ode for Gen'l Hamilton's Funeral, 4vv (c1804)

Elegy (No more the mounting lark), c1805, lost; The Humours of Vauxhall (J. Jackson), c1805, lost; Huzza for Masonry, c1805, lost; Ode to Harmony, c1805, lost; Ode to Peace (J. Jackson), c1805, lost; Say Lovely Maid, song, c1805, lost; Content, 3vv (1806); Drink to Me Only, glee, pubd in A Favourite Selection of Music (Dedham, MA, 1806); A New Musical Score of [13] Easy Canons: Sacred to Masonry, 1–12vv (c1807); The Fairies to the Sea Nymphs (Miss Seward), song (1808); Song and Martial Chorus, c1808, lost; Ode for the Fourth of July (Mr. Townsend) (c1808); Friendship Is the Joy of Reason, 1/2/3vv (c1809)

American Serenade (J. Jackson), *MBHM*; Canon in Praise of Liberty, *INS*; Close Canon for the Use of Masonic Lodges, 6vv, lost; The Delights of Married Life, *INS*; The Fatal Hours are Wondrous Near, 3vv, *INS*; 5 songs: The Lover's Invocation, The Lover's Watch, The Wish, The Dream, The Jealous Lover, *INS*; Here Ye Powr's O Let Me Rove, *INS*; New Miscellaneous Musical Work, 12 songs, 1–3vv, pf, *MBHM*; An Ode on Painting, *INS*

INSTRUMENTAL
Kbd: A Favorite Sonata, hpd/pf, op.4 (London, c1795); Overture with Double Fugue and Grand March, c1801, lost; 2 petits duos, pf, 4 hands (c1807); Duo, pf, 4 hands (Philadelphia, c1808); Dr. Jackson's Selection, pf, ?8 vols. (1801–12) [transcrs., arrs.]: vol.iii incl. March and Quick Step, The Sylph by Jackson]; Toccamento, org/hpd/pf, *INS*

Other: A Musical Coalition…to Which is Added A Musical Parody, fl, pf, drum (n.d.); Va Conc., c1805, lost

Pedagogical: A Treatise on Practical Thoroughbass with General Rules for its Composition and Modulation, op.5 (London, 1785); Instruction Book to the Piano Forte (1825), lost; I rudimenti da musica, or Complete Instructor for the Piano Forte, lost; Book…for the Theoretic Part of Instruction, *INS*

BIBLIOGRAPHY
J.R. Parker: *Musical Biography, or Sketches of the Lives and Writings of Eminent Musical Characters* (Boston, MA, 1824)

F.J. Metcalf: *American Writers and Compilers of Sacred Music* (New York, 1925/*R*1967)

H.E. Johnson: "George K. Jackson, Doctor of Music (1745–1822)," *MQ*, xix/1 (1943), 113–21

C.H. Kaufman: *George K. Jackson: American Musician of the Federal Period* (diss., New York U., 1968)

R.M. Wilson: *Anglican Chant and Chanting in England and America: 1660–1811* (diss., U. of Illinois, 1988)

H.E. Smither: *A History of the Oratorio. Volume 4: the Oratorio in the Nineteenth and Twentieth Centuries* (Chapel Hill, NC, 2000)

N. Temperley: *Bound for America: Three British Composers, Music in American Life* (Urbana, IL, 2003)

CHARLES KAUFMAN/R

Jackson, George Pullen (*b* Monson, ME, 20 Aug 1874; *d* Nashville, TN, 19 Jan 1953). Folksong scholar. He was educated at Dresden Conservatory (1897–8), Vanderbilt University, the universities of Munich and Bonn, and the University of Chicago, where he took the doctorate in 1911 with a dissertation on Romantic literature. Shortly after joining the German department of Vanderbilt University in 1918 he became interested in the music of the large southern singing groups such as the Sacred Harp Singers (together with Alan Lomax he made recordings of their performances, 1942). His study of the music, as found in collections published in the early 19th century, resulted in the book *White Spirituals in the Southern Uplands* (Chapel Hill, NC, 1933/*R*), which introduced an important body of American folk music to scholarly and general readers. It was followed by two collections of the music, *Spiritual Folk-Songs of Early America* (Locust Valley, NY, 1937/*R*) and *Down-East Spirituals* (New York, 1943/*R*), two further studies, *White and Negro Spirituals…with 116 Songs as Sung by both Races* (New York, 1943/*R*) and *The Story of 'The Sacred Harp', 1844–1944* (Nashville, TN, 1944), and a final anthology, *Another Sheaf of White Spirituals* (Gainesville, FL, 1952/*R*). He also founded and directed numerous organizations, including the Nashville SO (1920) and the Tennessee State Sacred Harp Singing Association (1939).

BIBLIOGRAPHY
K. Norton: "Who Lost the South?" *American Music*, xxi/4 (2003), 391–411

K. Norton: "Anne Geddes Gilchrist, George Pullen Jackson, and American Sacred Folksong," *On Bunker's Hill: Essays on Music in Memory of J. Bunker Clark*, eds. W.A. Everett and P. Laird (Sterling Heights, MI, 2007), 89–98

RICHARD JACKSON/R

Jackson, Howard (Manucy) (*b* St. Augustine, FL, 8 Feb 1898; *d* St. Augustine, FL, 4 Aug 1966). Composer, conductor, arranger, music director, and pianist. He learned to play the piano from his mother who was a pianist. As a teenager, Jackson played piano for vaudeville shows and at movie theaters. He studied harmony and counterpoint with RUBIN GOLDMARK, a student of Dvořák. He served as conductor and music arranger for Fanchon and Marco, the vaudeville dance troupe that performed elaborate live stage shows before feature films in the mid-1920s. For the Broadway stage he composed music for Earl Carroll's Vanities, George White's Scandals, and Ziegfeld Follies. By 1928 he was in California, where he arranged music for two stage productions at the Hollywood Playhouse. He found success with his arrangements of Negro spirituals for *Hearts in Dixie* (1929) and for other early sound musicals. After a stint at Columbia in the mid-1930s, where his music became associated with a handful of Three Stooges short films, he settled in at Warner Bros. where he worked almost exclusively from 1936 to 1964. In addition to his work on close to 200 feature films, he was a prolific composer of music for documentaries, short films, travelogues, trailers, and industrial films, as well as US Army orientation films during World War II. Drawing on his experience with live-action shorts at Columbia and Universal, he found a niche in the genre at Warner Bros., where for nearly three decades he composed music for hundreds of the studio's shorts. These topical films covered a potpourri of subjects, such as animal antics, comedies, musicals, and educational and sports films. For ten years, beginning in 1948, he supplied music to shorts produced by Dudley, including lavishly filmed VistaVision travelogues released by Paramount. In addition to composing music for industrial films for Trans World Airlines, Union Pacific, and others, he arranged music for radio programs sponsored by Chrysler and Goodyear.

WORKS
(selective list)

FILM SCORES
as music director and/or arranger
Broadway, 1929; Hearts in Dixie, 1929; Sunny Side Up, 1929; The Great Gabbo, 1930; And So They Were Married, 1936

FILM SCORES
as composer
Sing Sinner Sing, 1933; This Day and Age, 1933; Beloved, 1934; Glamour, 1934; It Happened One Night, 1934, uncredited; Dizzy Dames, 1935; Counterfeit, 1936; The King Steps Out, 1936; Mr. Deeds Goes to Town, 1936; Torchy Runs for Mayor, 1939; River's End, 1940; Law of the Tropics, 1941; Singapore Woman, 1941; You're in the Army Now, 1941; Wild Bill Hickok Rides, 1942; Club Havana, (1945); Lullaby of Broadway, 1951; Appointment in Honduras, 1953; Run for Cover, 1955; Cry Terror!, 1958; Yellowstone Kelly, 1959; The Lost World, 1960, with others; Sergeant Rutledge, 1960; Merrill's Marauders, 1962

FILM
title songs
Hearts in Dixie, 1929; Run for Cover, 1955

STAGE
Tattle Tales, music revue, New York, 1933 [collab. with others]

ORCHESTRAL
Lazy Rhapsody, 1929 [sym. jazz]

WARREN M. SHERK

Jackson, Isaiah (Allen) (*b* Richmond, VA, 22 Jan 1945). Conductor. After conducting several undergraduate opera productions and the Bach Society Orchestra at Harvard (where he received a BA in 1966), he decided to study conducting at Stanford (MA 1967). A summer studying with NADIA BOULANGER at the American Conservatory at Fontainebleau confirmed his direction and he entered the Juilliard School in 1968 (MS 1969, DMA 1973). During his time there Jackson held a variety of positions, including music director of the Youth SO, New York, assistant conductor of the American SO and the Baltimore SO, and associate conductor of the American Ballet Theatre. His debut with the National SO at the Kennedy Center in June 1972 marked his first appearance with a major orchestra in a major hall. He made his European debut with the Vienna SO in July 1973 and that summer, at the suggestion of Leonard Bernstein, he served as artistic director of Vienna's Youth Music Festival. In 1973 he became associate conductor of the Rochester PO and in 1982 he was appointed music director of the Flint SO.

He has also conducted the Detroit SO, Toronto SO, Oakland SO, and the Royal Ballet at Covent Garden. In the 1980s he became an important conductor in Australia, where he worked with most of that country's major symphony orchestras. One of the most renowned African American conductors of his generation, Jackson received the Signet Society Medal for Achievements in the Arts from Harvard University in 1991. He finished a seven-year tenure with the Pro Arte Chamber Orchestra in Boston in 2006. His experience has chiefly involved symphonic and ballet music. The elegance of his style is noteworthy: he has exhibited a particular flair for generating an infectious rhythmic vitality and creating finely shaped lines within clearly defined orchestral textures. He has taught at a variety of institutions, including the Berklee College of Music, the Longy School, and the Harvard Extension School.

BIBLIOGRAPHY
SouthernB

JOANNE SHEEHY HOOVER/JONAS WESTOVER

Jackson, Janet (Damita Jo) (*b* Gary, IN, 16 May 1966). R&B and pop singer and actress, sister of MICHAEL JACKSON. She is the youngest of the ten children of Katherine and Joseph Jackson and part of one the most influential musical families in the history of American popular music. Her brothers had already formed a successful group, the Jackson 5 (*see* JACKSON 5), by the time she was a young child, and she grew up with family expectations that she would also enter show business. She made her first television appearance on the family's variety show, *The Jacksons*, in 1976 and quickly became a child star actress in other programs, including *Good Times*. She recorded her first song with her brother Randy, a duet titled "Love Song for Kids" (1978). Although she was hesitant to continue singing, her father insisted that she record her first album, *Janet Jackson* (A&M, 1982). Its success encouraged her to continue a music career, and after a second album she decided to keep recording, but she broke away from her father's management and her family's producers. Instead, A&M hired Jimmy Jam and Terry Lewis to produce her next record, *Control* (1986), which rocketed Jackson to new heights as a performer and garnered glowing reviews. The album hit number one on the Billboard Hot 200 and produced numerous popular singles, including "Nasty," "What have you done for me lately," "Control," "When I think of you," and "Let's wait awhile," each of which broke into the top five on the charts. In addition to praising the album, critics lauded her dancing skills, demonstrated on tour and in her infectious music videos (choreographed by Paula Abdul). Although her voice was described by some as wispy and light, her producers placed it carefully in the mix to highlight her best vocal qualities. Her work became important for its demonstration of female independence, and she became a pop icon. *Control* was nominated for Album of the Year at the Grammys and won four American Music Awards. Her next record, *Janet Jackson's Rhythm Nation 1814* (A&M, 1989), received similar attention and accolades, spawning more successful singles and resulting in a tour that made her an international superstar. As Jackson has continued to release albums, including *The Velvet Rope* (Virgin, 1997) and *20 Y.O.* (Virgin, 2006), she has won a slew of awards and influenced many newcomers, from Beyoncé Knowles to Britney Spears. She has continued to produce hits, including "Feedback" (2008) and "Nothing" (2010), and to land roles in popular films such as Tyler Perry's *Why did I get Married?* (2007). Over the course of her career, she has combined R&B, hip-hop, and dance styles to create successful new fusions. Maintaining a high profile, she has continued to act, sing, dance, and tour widely into the 21st century.

BIBLIOGRAPHY

J. Cornwell: *Janet Jackson* (London, 2002)
R. Ripani: *The New Blue Music: Changes in Rhythm & Blues, 1950–1999* (Jackson, MS, 2006)

JONAS WESTOVER

Jackson, John (*b* Rappahanahock County, VA, 24 Feb 1924; *d* Fairfax, VA, 20 Jan 2002). Blues singer, banjoist, and guitarist. One of the most important bluesmen on the East Coast, and a master of the Piedmont tradition, he grew up in a family of amateur musicians, started playing guitar at the age of four, and learned slide guitar from a chain gang convict nicknamed Happy. Influenced by early blues musicians heard on records, such as Blind Lemon Jefferson, Blind Blake, and Blind Boy Fuller, as well as by country singer Jimmie Rodgers, he developed a distinctive style of finger picking especially on the banjo. A gifted guitarist, he embraced both blues and country music, blending black and white tradition of the Appalachian area. By 1950, when he married his wife Cora and started working for a farmer in Fairfax, he had come to believe that music encouraged violent behavior, so he quit playing. In the mid-1960s Jackson was rediscovered by Chuck Perdue, president of the Great Washington Folklore Society, and started performing again, in coffeehouses. Although his fame extended beyond his local community, leading him to perform occasionally outside the United States, he always maintained a strong commitment to his family and hometown, where he kept his job as a gravedigger until his death in 2002.

RECORDINGS
(selective list)

Blues and Country Dance Tunes from Virginia (1966, Arhoolie 1025); *John Jackson in Europe* (1970, Arhoolie 1047); *Deep in the Bottom* (1983, Rounder 2032); *Step It Up and Go* (1990, Rounder 2019); *Don't Let Your Deal Goin' Down* (1992, Arhoolie CD 378)

BIBLIOGRAPHY

J. Pareles: "John Jackson, 77, Guitarist and Singer in Piedmont Style," *New York Times* (29 Jan 2002) [obituary]
B.L. Pearson: "Appalachian Blues," *Black Music Research Journal*, xxiii (2003), 23–51

ALESSANDRO BRATUS

Jackson, Judge [J.] (*b* Montgomery County, AL, 12 March 1883; *d* Ozark, AL, 7 April 1958). Composer, music teacher, and songster. He was the youngest child of an African American sharecropper family and received no more than two years of education in public school before leaving home at age 16 with his clothes in a flour sack and a half-dollar in his pocket. He eventually found farm work in Dale County, Alabama, where he spent the rest of his life, earning a livelihood as a farmer, a real-estate developer, and a door-to-door salesman of religious books. He was baptized in May 1902 and married Lela Campbell in October of that same year.

At an early age, around 1899, Jackson was attracted to Sacred Harp singing (*see* SHAPE-NOTE HYMNODY). Unable to attend Sacred Harp singing schools as a youth because his employer on the farm refused to permit it, he learned by interviewing other youths who were allowed to attend and quickly mastered the art. He evolved from curious student to teacher and in 1922 helped organize the Alabama and Florida Union State Sacred Harp Singing Convention. He began composing lyrics in 1904 and music in the 1920s. In 1928 he published his first song, "My Mother's Gone," which later appeared in his compilation *The Colored Sacred Harp* (1934) authorized by the Dale County Colored Musical Institute. This 77-song, 98-page songbook was intended both for use by the African American songster community and as Jackson's personal testament to racial achievement. Forty-two years after Jackson's death the song "My Mother's Gone" appeared as number 519 in the Cooper revision (the version of *The Sacred Harp* preferred by white and African American songsters of south Alabama), from which Jackson had earlier adopted the architecture and mission statement for his own collection. Of the 18 songs attributed to Jackson in *The Colored Sacred Harp*, he deserves full credit for 17 and credit for the music of one other. Of the songs in *The Colored Sacred Harp* for which primary credit is assigned to another composer, 24 acknowledge Jackson's contributions by also bearing his name.

The Colored Sacred Harp was a labor of love for Jackson, who brought it to fruition during the Great Depression; he eventually subsidized, along with his associate author Bishop J.D. Walker, the cost of publishing 1000 copies of the softcover songbook by a Chicago printer and relied on his personal reputation to sell them for $1 each at singing schools and conventions. Although the collection never achieved the level of success for which Jackson must have hoped, its legacy has been profound. According to the scholar Doris Dyen, *The Colored Sacred Harp* stands as the community's premier musical document and serves as a record of African American Sacred Harp singing at the height of the tradition.

BIBLIOGRAPHY

J. Jackson: *The Colored Sacred Harp* (Chicago, 1934/R)
J. Work: "Plantation Meistersinger," *MQ*, xxvii (1941), 97–106
D.J. Dyen: *The Role of Shape-Note Singing in the Musical Culture of Black Communities in Southeast Alabama* (diss., U. of Illinois, 1977)
J.D. Boyd: *Judge Jackson and the Colored Sacred Harp* (Montgomery, AL, 2002)

JOE DAN BOYD

Jackson [Jackson McKim], **Leonora** (*b* Boston, MA, 20 Feb 1879; *d* 7 Jan 1969). Violinist. She was one of the first American female concert violinists to achieve international acclaim. Frances Cleveland, the wife of US President Grover Cleveland, was one of her early patrons, and it was her support that enabled Jackson to study in Chicago, Paris, and Berlin. Jackson performed for royalty in Britain, Germany, and Sweden, and was honored by Queen Victoria. She performed as a soloist with leading European and American orchestras including the London PO and the Boston SO. She was remarkably active, giving 160 concerts in the United States during the 1900–01 season alone.

Jackson retired from performing in 1915 after marrying Dr. William Duncan McKim, but her involvement in music and the arts continued. The McKims held musical programs in their home and collected art. After William's death in 1935, many of their artworks were donated to the Smithsonian Institute and the Maryland Historical Society. In 1970, shortly after Jackson's death, the McKim Fund was established for the creation and appreciation of music for violin and piano. This fund has supported the commissioning of new works by a number of acclaimed contemporary composers, including Ellen Taaffe Zwilich, Anne LeBaron, and Daria Semegen.

During her performance career Jackson played a 1714 Stradivarius. That instrument has continued to be associated with her and has come to be known as the "Leonora Jackson" Stradivarius. Her papers and other materials are housed in the Leonora Jackson and William Duncan McKim Collection by the Library of Congress Music Division.

BIBLIOGRAPHY

H. Roth: *Violin Virtuosos: from Paganini to the 21st Century* (Los Angeles, 1997)

MEGAN E. HILL

Jackson, Mahalia (*b* New Orleans, LA, 26 Oct 1911; *d* Chicago, IL, 27 Jan 1972). Gospel singer. Growing up in the Baptist faith, she also drew influences from the worship practices of the Holiness church and the blues. She moved to Chicago in 1927 and joined the choir of the Greater Salem Baptist Church. She formally started her career with the Johnson Gospel Singers, an early professional gospel quintet. With greater frequency, she made appearances as a soloist, eventually coming under the tutelage of THOMAS A. DORSEY, who maximized the blues-inspired quality of her voice while tempering the excitable, shouting manner of gospel singing, which was her initial approach. Jackson's earliest recording, "God's gonna separate the wheat from the tares" (1937, Decca) received only moderate success, but exemplifies her developing sound. Rhythmically unfettered, her slow, intentional execution of phrases and the careful manipulation of text became synonymous with her maturing style. However, she retained the folk qualities of moans, hums, and hollers that readily identified her upbringing and the black cultural experience. "Move on up a Little Higher" (1948, Apollo) affirmed her position as the Queen of Gospel, demonstrating her broad vocal range and her ability to create dramatic tension in her delivery. This song, along with Dorsey's similarly executed "Take my Hand, Precious, Lord" (1932), became staples in her repertoire. Jackson was among a growing number of artists who performed gospel in venues outside of the black church during the post-World War II years. She appeared in an unprecedented gospel celebration program at Carnegie Hall (1950) and later at the Newport Jazz Festival (1958). She was invited to appear in nightclubs and to perform secular music, but always rejected such offers. However, numerous radio and television appearances, including hosting her own radio and television programs, broadened her appeal. Appearing in films, notably *Imitation of Life* (1959), collaborating with large choruses and string orchestras, and recording with Duke Ellington (*Black, Brown, and Beige*, 1958, Col.) set a new bar for gospel performance. Flourishing in the 1950s and 1960s, Jackson's powerful voice provided natural counterpoint to the era's political and social movements. She joined Martin Luther King in the Civil Rights crusade, singing for rallies and marches, including the historic March on Washington (1963). She also sang for the inauguration of President John F. Kennedy (1961). Jackson developed an international following and made numerous trips abroad during the last decade of her life. She secured two prizes from the French Academy, the first for "Let the Power of the Holy Ghost Fall on Me" (1949) and second for "I can put my trust in Jesus" (1952).

SELECTED RECORDINGS

In the Upper Room, i–ii (1952, Apollo); *Bless this House* (1956, Col.); *Live at Newport!* (1958, Col.); *Come on Children, Let's Sing!* (1960, Col.); *Complete Mahalia Jackson*, i: *1937–46* (Frémeaux & Associés, 1998)

BIBLIOGRAPHY

M. Jackson and E.M. Wylie: *Movin' On Up* (New York, 1966)

P. Oliver: *Mahalia Jackson* (Milan, 1968)

H.C. Boyer: "Contemporary Gospel Music: Characteristics and Style," *BPM*, vii (1979), 22–58

M.W. Harris: *The Rise of the Gospel Blues: the Music of Thomas Andrew Dorsey in the Urban Church* (New York, 1992)

J.V. Schwerin: *Got to Tell it: Mahalia Jackson, Queen of Gospel* (New York, 1992) [incl. bibliography and discography]

HENRY PLEASANTS/HORACE CLARENCE BOYER/
ROXANNE R. REED

Jackson, Michael (Joseph) (*b* Gary, IN, 29 Aug 1958; *d* Los Angeles, CA, 25 June 2009). Pop singer, songwriter, dancer, and producer. From soul-singing child prodigy to the self-styled "King of Pop," Michael Jackson's career spanned five decades, explored a myriad of pop styles, and, in *Thriller*, produced the best-selling album of all time.

Jackson first catapulted to fame as the 11-year-old lead singer of the JACKSON 5, a group consisting of Michael and his four older brothers. Michael was clearly the focal point of the group, with a vocal style and dance moves heavily indebted to James Brown. His precocious mastery of soul-singing was fully evident on the group's first release for Motown, "I want you back," in which he displayed an infectious sense of up-tempo timing and an impressive range of vocal resources, effectively showcased on a finely crafted tune. In 1971 Michael released his first record as a solo artist which revealed a predilection towards ballads. Like those of the Jackson 5, Michael's early solo recordings were remarkably successful.

However, Jackson's solo career did not really take off until the late 1970s. In 1978, while starring in the film musical, *The Wiz*, as the Scarecrow, Jackson met producer Quincy Jones. The two collaborated on Jackson's next album, *Off the Wall*, which outsold his previous solo efforts and garnered favorable critical notices. Jones and Jackson successfully updated Jackson's sound, presenting him as a mature artist capable of appealing to dancers and top 40 radio programmers alike. Jackson's voice had deepened somewhat, but retained its trademark flexibility, timbral variety, rhythmic subtlety, and melodic sensitivity that perfectly fit the album's combination of funk, pop, and disco. *Off the Wall* only hinted at what was to come. Jackson's next album (again produced by Jones), *Thriller*, released late in 1982, became an international phenomenon, breaking all sales records, and selling an estimated 110 million copies to date. *Thriller* did not so much create a new style as it successfully synthesized aspects of preexisting ones: on it, one hears soulful, middle-of-the-road ballads ("The Girl Is Mine," sung with Paul McCartney), funk-disco ("Billie Jean"), and funky heavy-metal ("Beat It"). This stylistic blending enabled Jackson to transcend boundaries between audiences that music industry experts believed were unassailable. Additionally, Jackson began conceiving of his songs as soundtracks for videos. Aware that MTV had become the most effective tool for promoting recordings, the videos for "Billie Jean," "Beat It," and "Thriller" were more than mere promotional vehicles for the recordings: they were "mini-films," small narratives with relatively huge budgets that dwarfed preceding videos. "Billie Jean," released first, did not receive much airplay on MTV due to the channel's de facto color line; "Beat It," however, with its funk-metal fusion, entered heavy rotation on the video channel amid rumors of strong-arm tactics on the part of Walter Yetnikoff, the head of CBS/Epic (Jackson's recording company). Jackson's understanding of how to employ his singing and dancing skills within the rhetoric of video enabled him to exploit his abilities as a *performer* rather than as a *musician* per se. Viewed in this way, the magnitude of his success is inextricable from the age of music VIDEO.

The years following *Thriller* were tumultuous ones for Jackson: he released "We are the world" (1985, co-written with Lionel Ritchie and co-performed with many other stars to benefit famine relief), another Jones-produced album, *Bad* (1987), and an autobiography, *Moonwalker* (1988); and he began to receive an increasing amount of media attention, much of it sensationalistic. *Bad* was a very successful recording by any standard other than that set by *Thriller*, and, like its predecessor, was extremely eclectic, featuring funk, heavy metal-influenced songs, love ballads, and humanitarian anthems in the vein of "We are the world." But the reception of the album betrayed a split between the rapturous adoration of Jackson's fans and the lukewarm reaction of critics, especially in the United States, a reaction probably fanned by negative media attention over changes in Jackson's appearance and rumors about other personal eccentricities.

After the record-setting "Bad" tour, Jackson released *Dangerous* late in 1991. With the assistance of producer Terry Riley, Jackson updated his sound to incorporate elements of hip hop and new jack swing. Like *Bad*, the album was hugely successful in commercial terms (with worldwide sales eventually surpassing 40 million), but drew mixed critical notices. The release of the album was preceded by a single, "Black or White," the video of which premiered simultaneously on television channels around the world. The 14-minute video attracted attention for a famous "morphing" sequence towards the end of the song, in which people of various races, ages, and genders blurred into one another, and for a long music-less coda in which Jackson dances, destroys property in a rage, and grabs his crotch. The song itself broke new ground for Jackson, revisiting the rock-funk fusions he had previously explored, but in a new form: the song was based on a guitar riff reminiscent of the Rolling Stones, a blues harmonic pattern, and a rhythm section groove derived from funk and reggae.

In 1993 negative media attention came to a head when Jackson became involved in a court case on charges of child molestation that was eventually settled out of court. The firestorm of publicity led to cancellation of Jackson's ongoing *Dangerous* tour and the withdrawal of tour sponsorship by Pepsi. Although he had devoted much effort to humanitarian causes throughout the 1980s and early 1990s—donating huge sums to charities for children, AIDS research, and scholarships funds for African Americans—by the mid-1990s his career was in danger of being overshadowed by scandals. His brief marriage to Lisa Marie Presley (daughter of Elvis) from 1994 to 1996 only seemed to add to the aura of strangeness that increasingly engulfed him.

Despite these personal setbacks, throughout the rest of the 1990s and into the early years of the new millennium Jackson remained quite active artistically, producing *HIStory: Past, Present and Future, Book I* (1995), a double-CD, which combined a greatest hits collection with 15 new tracks; *Ghosts* (1996), a mini-film with Stephen King described as the longest music video ever (it ran 38 minutes); *Blood on the Dance Floor: HIStory in the Mix* (1997), a CD combining remixes of tracks from *HIStory* with five new songs; and, finally, *Invincible* (2001), the last album of new material released during his life. While the music and the videos all featured new touches (e.g., the increase of "industrial"-derived timbres and other sounds associated with techno, sampling, the collaborations with rappers, the setting of a Rio de Janeiro *favela* for the video of "They don't care about us" in 1996), the dominant themes in his lyrics of paranoia, predatory women, and the need to address various humanitarian crises could all be traced back to his work in the 1980s, as could the seamless musical blend of different genres that he pioneered in *Thriller*.

At the time of his death in 2009 Jackson had established himself as the most successful individual popular musician of all time, surpassing the sales records and global reach of Elvis Presley. To understand the international reach of his popularity, one needs to consider the fact that only 10% of the sales of his last three albums came from the United States, and that his record-setting tours after 1989 avoided the United States except for Hawaii. He virtually redefined the music-stylistic basis of the popular music mainstream in the early 1980s, and established the music video as both a central feature of popular music promotion and as an art form. Even as he experienced unprecedented celebrity, his physical transformations, androgynous appearance, and reclusive lifestyle provoked public debates on the nature of his identity. When he died on 25 June 2009, Jackson was in the midst of preparations for a series of 50 concerts planned for the O2 arena in London. These preparations were edited into a film, *This Is It* (2009), which showed Jackson in top form working with musicians and dancers. *Michael*, a CD released in 2010, began what promises to be a long string of posthumous releases.

BIBLIOGRAPHY

N. George: *The Michael Jackson Story* (London, 1984)

K. Mercer: "Monster Metaphors: Notes on Michael Jackson's 'Thriller,'" *Sound and Vision: the Music Video Reader*, ed. S. Frith, A. Goodwin, and L. Grossberg (London/New York, 1986/1993), 93–108

M. Jackson: *Moonwalk* (New York, 1988)

M. Wallace: "Michael Jackson, Black Modernisms, and 'The Ecstasy of Communication'," *Invisibility Blues: From Pop to Theory* (London, 1990), 77–90

G. Brown: *The Complete Guide to the Music of Michael Jackson and the Jackson Family* (New York, 1996)

J. Taraborrelli: *Michael Jackson: the Magic, the Madness, the Whole Story* (New York, 2009)

S. Hidalgo and R. Weiner: "'Wanna Be Startin' Somethin': MJ in the Scholarly Literature: a Selected Bibliographic Guide," *The Journal of Pan African Studies*, iii/7 (March 2010), 14–28

Special Issue on Michael Jackson, *Journal of Popular Music Studies*, xxiii/1 (2011)

Special Issue on Michael Jackson, *Popular Music and Society*, xxxv/3 (2011)

DAVID BRACKETT

Jackson, Millie [Mildred] (*b* Thomson, GA, 15 July 1944). Soul and R&B singer, songwriter, and radio broadcaster. She was brought up by her grandparents in Georgia and moved to New Jersey in 1959. She began singing professionally in New York in the mid-1960s, and in 1972 her single "A Child of God" performed well on the rhythm-and-blues chart. Her next two releases, "Ask me what you want" (1972) and "Hurts so good" (1973), were successful with pop audiences as well. Her album *Caught Up* (1974) was the first of several that included soul, country music, and rock standards, as well as her own material which seemed to comment upon them. This recording and *Still Caught Up* (1975) tell the stories of love affairs from the viewpoints of both wife and mistress in blunt, uncompromising language. In 1979 Jackson recorded an album of duets, *Royal Rappin's*, with Isaac Hayes. Her early releases reflect the rough, shouting soul style of the 1960s; later her voice displayed

greater warmth and subtlety. Despite the fact that the explicit language of her live performances and the poor taste of some album covers gradually increased to the point of unintentional self-parody, Jackson has written and recorded songs that are remarkable for their sensitivity. She has released country songs and disco tracks, and she also worked for many years as an afternoon radio show host. From the late 1980s her daughter, Keisha Jackson, has pursued her own career as an R&B singer.

Jackson, Milt(on) [Bags] (*b* Detroit, MI, 1 Jan 1923; *d* New York, NY, 9 Oct 1999). Jazz vibraphonist. He taught himself to play guitar at the age of seven. He received piano lessons at 11 and took up other instruments in high school, including timpani, violin, and xylophone. His first public appearance was as a singer in a local gospel quintet; around the same time he also performed in the band of George E. Lee. In the late 1930s Jackson began to study music at Michigan State University, but was soon drafted into the army, in which he served until 1944. After his release he formed his own quartet with vibraphone, guitar, piano, and double bass. In 1945 Dizzy Gillespie convinced Jackson to move to New York and become part of the trumpeter's sextet. In December of that year Jackson made his first recordings, with the vocalist Dinah Washington and the Lucky Thompson All Stars. Soon he was playing with such major bebop figures as Gillespie, Charlie Parker, Howard McGhee, Tadd Dameron, and Thelonious Monk. The rhythm section of Gillespie's orchestra, in which he worked from 1946 to 1947, subsequently became the nucleus of the Modern Jazz Quartet.

Jackson was then a member of the Woody Herman Orchestra (1949) before working again in Gillespie's sextet (1950–52). In 1952 he formed his own quartet with the pianist John Lewis. Later that year this group was incorporated as the MODERN JAZZ QUARTET (MJQ), which became one of the most successful ensembles in modern jazz; it broke up in 1974 but came together again for regular tours between 1981 and 1997. During the MJQ's annual summer breaks from performing Jackson recorded with such musicians as Miles Davis (1954–5), Ray Charles (1957–8), Coleman Hawkins, Cannonball Adderley (1958), John Coltrane (1959), Oscar Peterson, and Wes Montgomery (1961). In the 1970s he tried with moderate success to reach the popular market, but in the late 1970s, strengthened by the bebop revival of that time, he returned to a more conventional acoustic quartet instrumentation, often playing with either Cedar Walton or Monty Alexander.

Jackson is one of the most influential vibraphonists in jazz. Following in the steps of Lionel Hampton and Red Norvo, he succeeded in transferring the bebop idiom to his instrument. Especially in his early recordings with the Gillespie orchestra and his first quartet, the influence of Charlie Parker is clearly discernible. Jackson developed a more mature style in the 1950s, when in the formally stricter music of the MJQ he found a voice beyond the bebop idiom. He used a relatively slow vibrato on his instrument, which gave a warm sound especially to sustained notes. His playing is marked by his virtuoso skills, but also laced with blues and soul phrases that refer to his musical upbringing in the black church.

SELECTED RECORDINGS

As leader: *Bluesology* (1951, Dee Gee); *Milt Jackson Quartet* (1955, Prst.); with J. Coltrane: *Bags and Trane* (1959, Atl.); with W. Montgomery: *Bags Meets Wes!* (1961, Riv.); *Sunflower* (1973, CTI); with C. Basie: *Milt Jackson + Count Basie + the Big Band* (1978, Pablo); with O. Peterson: *Two of the Few* (1983, Pablo); *The Prophet Speaks* (1994, Qwest)

As sideman: D. Gillespie: *Anthropology/A Night in Tunesia* (1946, Vic.); T. Monk: *Misterioso* (1948, BN); M. Davis: *Miles Davis All Stars* (1954, Prst.)

BIBLIOGRAPHY

H. Renaud: "Milt Jackson: a renouvelle le style du vibraphone," *Jazz Hot*, no.56 (1951), 12–13

M. Williams: "Recording with Bags," *DB*, xxx/24 (1963), 14–16

L. Tomkins: "Personal Account: the MJQ is no Straightjacket, says Milt Jackson," *Crescendo*, vi/6 (1968), 26–7

B. Rusch: "Milt Jackson Interview," *Cadence*, ii/9 (1977), 3–4, 6

W. Knauer: *Zwischen Bebop und Free Jazz: Komposition und Improvisation des Modern Jazz Quartet* (Mainz, 1990)

C. Sheridan: *Bags' Groove: a Discography of Milt Jackson* (Almere, 2006)

WOLFRAM KNAUER

Jackson, Richard (Hammel) (*b* New Orleans, LA, 15 Feb 1936). Music librarian, musicologist, and organist. He studied organ at Loyola University (BM 1958), musicology at Tulane University (MA 1962), and library science at Pratt Institute (MSLS 1968). After holding positions at the New Orleans Public Library (1958–9), the Maxwell Music Library at Newcomb College, Tulane University (1959–62) and the library of the New School (1962–5), he became head of the Americana Collection in the music division of the New York Public Library (1965–91), where he prepared major exhibitions on Aaron Copland, Carter, Louis Moreau Gottschalk, and the New York PO, among other subjects. After his retirement he volunteered for ten years at the Historic New Orleans Collection.

As a musicologist Jackson has specialized in 19th- and early 20th-century American classical and popular music. He edited collections of Gottschalk's piano music (1973, 1976) and songs (1992), Stephen Foster's songs (1974) as well as individual works by Caryl Florio and Edward Everett Rice. He has compiled two anthologies, *Popular Songs of Nineteenth-century America* (1976) and *Democratic Souvenirs* (1988), and was editorial consultant for the collected works of Scott Joplin (1971–81) and for the five-volume anthology *The Wa-Wan Press: 1901–1911* (1970). His other publications include articles and reviews, program notes for recordings, and bibliographies of American music (1973, 1977). He was also associate editor of *American Choral Review* (1967–91).

WRITINGS

The Operas of Gertrude Stein and Virgil Thomson: a Binomial Study (thesis, Tulane University, 1962)

United States Music: Sources of Bibliography and Collective Biography (Brooklyn, NY, 1973)

U.S. Bicentennial Music (Brooklyn, NY, 1977)

"Salvaging a Treasure: Pop Songs in the New York Public Library," *Popular Music Perspectives II: Papers from the Second International Conference on Popular Music Studies: Reggio Emilia 1983*, ed. D. Horn and P. Tagg (Göteborg, Exeter, 1985), 190–95

with D. Horn: *The Literature of American Music in Books and Folk Music Collections* (Metuchen, NJ, 1988)

"More Notes of a Pianist: a Gottschalk Collection Surveyed and a Scandal Revisited," *Notes*, xlvi (1989–90), 325–75

"An American Muse Learns to Walk: the First American-Music Group," *American Musical Life in Context and Practice to 1865*, ed. J.R. Heintze (New York, 1994), 265–336

"*Maple Leaf Rag*: Bill Russell and his Jazz Collection at the Historic New Orleans Collection," *Southern Quarterly*, xxxvi/2 (1998), 63–72

EDITIONS

L.M. Gottschalk: *Piano Music* (New York, 1973)

Stephen Foster Song Book (New York, 1974)

Popular Songs of Nineteenth-century America (New York, 1976)

with N. Ratliff: *The Little Book of Louis Moreau Gottschalk* (New York, 1976) [seven piano pieces]

Democratic Souvenirs: an Historical Anthology of 19th-Century American Music (New York, 1988)

C. Florio: *Quartette, Soprano, Alto, Tenor, and Baritone Saxophones: allegro de concert* (New York, 1988)

Louis Moreau Gottschalk: the Complete Published Songs, with a Selection of Other Songs of mid-nineteenth Century America (Newton Centre, MA, 1992)

E.E. Rice: *Early Burlesque in America: "Evangeline" (1877)* (New York, 1994)

PAULA MORGAN/MARY WALLACE DAVIDSON

Jackson, Ronald Shannon (*b* Fort Worth, TX, 12 Jan 1940). Drummer and composer. He is best known for his contributions to avant-garde jazz and related improvisational musics. He absorbed a variety of musical traditions, including country, marching band music, jazz, and blues, during his youth in the southwest, and had started performing professionally by the age of 15. In 1966 he arrived in New York, where he found frequent work with jazz groups, including a spot in Albert Ayler's ensemble and dates with Betty Carter. Soon thereafter he fell into relative obscurity for almost a decade.

Jackson's music career was transformed in 1975 when he joined Ornette Coleman's electric band Prime Time. He studied Coleman's harmolodic system and with Coleman's encouragement began to write his own compositions. During this period he also performed in one of Cecil Taylor's ensembles, giving him the distinction of being the only musician known to have ever worked with Ayler, Coleman, and Taylor.

Jackson's critical visibility and creative output ascended in 1980, as he began to direct a series of medium-sized, New York-based ensembles known as the Decoding Society. The Decoding Society primarily performed Jackson's compositions and was propelled by his powerful and jubilant drumming. The group's sound could be both flashy and serene. Exotic horn melodies floated above a polyphonic weave of bass and electric guitars, and sometimes also vibraphone or violin. Stylistically, it reflected the broad range of musics—Western, Eastern, and African—that Jackson had assimilated throughout his career.

During the 1980s Jackson also participated in session work with other avant-garde musicians and performed in the hard-edged, improvising ensemble Last Exit with Sonny Sharrock, Bill Laswell, and Peter Brötzmann.

By the mid-1990s he had returned to Texas and effectively dissolved the Decoding Society. He has subsequently kept a relatively low profile, leading educational clinics and occasionally performing with notables such as Wadada Leo Smith.

JEFFREY T. ELDREDGE

Jackson, Samuel P. (*b* Manchester, England, 2 Feb 1818; *d* Brooklyn, NY, 27 July 1885). Organist and composer of English birth. The son of an organ builder, Jackson immigrated to New York in 1825 and played the organ at St Clement's at the age of 12, the first of various posts at New York churches in a career that spanned 45 years: St Clement's (1830–42), St Bartholomew's (1842–61), the Church of the Ascension (until 1874), Christ Church, the Anthon Memorial Church, and others. He also taught piano and harmony privately and was for nearly 30 years G. Schirmer's chief proofreader. Of the several hundred compositions he is reputed to have written, few survive, among them four volumes of organ voluntaries (1865–74) and other works for the instrument. He also published a study of *Major and Minor Scales*.

WILLIAM OSBORNE

Jackson, Tony [Anthony; Antonio] (*b* New Orleans, LA, 25 Oct 1884; *d* Chicago, IL, 20 April 1921). Pianist, singer, and composer. Born to a poor family and self-taught, he began playing a harpsichord of sorts at ten, until neighbors let him practice on their pianos and organs. He was a professional at 13 and was considered the best pianist in town at 15. He was much in demand in the red-light district because of his musical memory and vast repertoire, embracing classical, light classical, opera, cake-walk (which he danced while playing), popular songs from the United States, Europe, and Latin America, blues, and, above all, ragtime. He could read and improvise, sing in a powerful operatic style in any range from baritone to soprano, and even adopt blues inflections. His attire was widely imitated. Jelly Roll Morton considered him a great pianist-entertainer and his principal role model.

In 1907 Jackson went to Chicago and by 1912 had settled there, possibly looking for better offers from publishers, as well as seeking privacy in a city where his homosexuality could pass unnoticed. He had residencies at the De Luxe, Elite, and Pekin cafes and published nine compositions, notably "Pretty Baby" (issued 1916 but known in town for years). Rumors suggest that more songs were stolen from him; Morton's "The Naked Dance" is likely by Jackson. By 1920 he was impaired by syphilis and cyrrhosis; he never recorded. Louis Malle's movie *Pretty Baby* (1978) is named after Jackson's song, and Clare Brown's play *Don't you leave me here* (2008) explores the Morton–Jackson relationship.

BIBLIOGRAPHY
R. Blesh and H. Janis: *They all Played Ragtime* (New York, 1950, 4/1971)
R.J. Carew: "He Knew a Thousand Songs: a Recollection of Tony Jackson," *JJ*, no.3 (1952), 1; repr. <http://www.doctorjazz.co.uk/page29.html>

A. Rose and E. Souchon: *New Orleans Jazz: a Family Album* (Baton Rouge, 1967)
A. Rose: *New Orleans* (Birmingham, 1978)

MARCELLO PIRAS

Jackson, Wanda (Lavonne) (*b* Maud, OK, 20 Oct 1937). Country and rockabilly guitarist, songwriter, and singer. While still in high school, Jackson signed with Decca Records and performed traditional country music on her own radio show on Oklahoma City's KLPR. She was influenced by Jimmie Rodgers, Hank Williams, and Hank Thompson, who invited her to perform with his band and became a mentor and friend. On one of her earliest tours, in mid-1955, the headline act was Elvis Presley; according to Jackson, he strongly encouraged her to sing and play rock and roll in the style that he, Carl Perkins, and Jerry Lee Lewis were fast popularizing, later known as rockabilly. Addressing the lack of repertoire for women in this new form, Jackson began writing her own material.

Chart success eluded Jackson until she recorded Earl Burrows's composition "Fujiyama Mama," which reached number one in Japan in 1958, prompting a lengthy and successful Japanese tour. "Let's have a party," released as a single in 1960, was a hit in the United States, as was "Right or Wrong," a self-penned mainstream country song that reached number 29 on the pop charts. After spending several years on the Vegas circuit, Jackson embraced Christianity in 1971 and made religiously themed recordings for the Word and Myrrh labels. She returned to rockabilly in 1985, and recordings and a tour with Rosie Flores followed, as well as shows in Europe, where Jackson has remained in demand. She was inducted into the Rock and Roll Hall of Fame in 2009 and is acknowledged as the Queen of Rockabilly. Jackson recorded a critically acclaimed album, *The Party Ain't Over* (Nonesuch), with Jack White in 2011.

BIBLIOGRAPHY
D. Sanjek: "Can a Fujiyama Mama be the Female Elvis? The Wild, Wild Women of Rockabilly," *Sexing the Groove: Popular Music and Gender*, ed. S. Whiteley (London, 1997), 137–67
C. Escott: "Wanda Jackson: Did She or Didn't She?," *Roadkill on the Three-Chord Highway: Art and Trash in American Popular Music* (New York, 2002), 145–62
S. Homer: "Louisiana Hayride Stars: Wanda Jackson," *Catch that Rockabilly Fever: Personal Stories of Life on the Road and in the Studio* (Jefferson, NC, 2010), 52–7

LISA MACKINNEY

Jackson 5 [Jackson Five; Jacksons]. Soul group. Its original members were the Jackson brothers, Jackie (Sigmund Esco; *b* Gary, IN, 4 May 1951), Tito (Toriano Adaryll; *b* Gary, IN, 15 Oct 1953), Jermaine [La Jaune] (*b* Gary, IN, 11 Dec 1954), Marlon [David] (*b* Gary, IN, 12 March 1957), and Michael [Joseph] (*b* Gary, IN, 29 Aug 1958; *d* Los Angeles, CA, 25 June 2009). Although the Jackson 5 was first marketed in 1969 by Motown Records toward pre-teen audiences, their music had a broader appeal, and the group—and especially its youngest member, MICHAEL JACKSON—displayed precocious talent. Their sound was initially modeled on the music of another African

American group, the Temptations, which by the late 1960s had developed an ensemble approach featuring rapid trade-offs among the vocalists, all of whom occupied a different tessitura. Between 1969 and 1974 the group recorded a remarkable string of top 20 hit singles, including "I want you back," "ABC," and "I'll be there," all of them written and produced by the Motown staff. In 1976, Randy [Steven Randall] Jackson (*b* Gary, IN, 29 Oct 1961) replaced Jermaine, and the group changed direction, moving to Epic Records and changing their name to the Jacksons. They wrote and produced the material for two albums, *Destiny* (Epic, 1978) and *Triumph* (Epic, 1980), both of which surpassed their earlier efforts for Epic and which initiated the second successful phase of their career. These records nestle securely within the disco mainstream of the time and feature their trademark superlative vocal abilities. Their album *Victory* (Epic, 1984) was accompanied by the largest-grossing and most widely covered tour of its time, but Michael's unprecedented success produced unmanageable tensions within the group. In 1989 the Jacksons, without Michael, released *2300 Jackson Street*, an album which found them treading water artistically amid increasing scandals and controversies surrounding the family.

BIBLIOGRAPHY

G. Brown: *The Complete Guide to the Music of Michael Jackson and the Jackson Family* (New York, 1996)

DAVID BRACKETT/R

Jackson-Guldan. Manufacturer of bowed and fretted string instruments based in Columbus, OH. It is significant as one of the first factory-based producers of bowed string instruments to use machine carving for the fabrication of such components as the front, back, and scroll. An announcement was made in *Music Trade Review* (30 December 1916) that the Guldan Violin Company was established at 171 West Main St., the first known information about the company. Beginning in 1920 advertisements for Jackson-Guldan Violin Company appeared in *The Violinist*, some of which offered the production of violins for stencil, or secondary company, branding. Some such Jackson-Guldan instruments survive, notably with the decaled logos of music schools on the back, such as the First National Institute of Allied Arts, South Bend, IN, or with the paper label of Slingerland's Correspondence School of Music, Chicago, the predecessor to the Slingerland Drum Company, inside the body. The establishment of this line of work was related to the end of the dominant supplies of mass-produced violins from Germany, Austria-Hungary, France, and Japan due to World War I. By the time that these foreign suppliers resumed exports to the United States, Jackson-Guldan was sufficiently established to compete with these larger-volume producers. Nevertheless, in the 1930s the company also produced toys in addition to musical instruments. Jackson-Guldan instruments were offered in various grades ranging from machine-carved and spray-finished student instruments to hand-finished examples which, unlike most foreign violins, were still handmade, although often of poor quality.

In addition to violins, Jackson-Guldan produced acoustic and electric guitars after World War II. In 1954 the company's name changed to Jackson-Guldan, Inc., probably to reflect the increased importance of non-violin-family instruments to their product line. The company remained in directories as late as 1976, listed as a guitar maker. It is notable for its period of success which coincided with the rise of for-profit music schools, with which they established business relationships, and of public school music programs, which provided a strong customer base for machine-made, inexpensive domestic string instruments.

ARIAN SHEETS

Jackson Southernaires. Gospel vocal group. It was organized in the mid-1960s and took its name from the city in Mississippi from which it originated. The original singers were Luther Jennings, Franklin Williams, Huey Williams, Paul Peters, Haran Griffin, Brian Williams, and Roger Bryant Jr. The group soon established a reputation for the performance of traditional gospel music, and much of their hard gospel quartet style was inherited from Archie Brownlee and the Five Blind Boys of Mississippi, particularly Peters's high falsetto and the use of alternating leads. After the success of their recording of an old church refrain, "Too Late" (1970), which sold more than 100,000 copies, the group turned towards a softer style in the tradition of the Pilgrim Travelers and the Dixie Hummingbirds. They also revived traditional pieces, such as Dorothy Love Coates's "You can't hurry God." By the 21st century the group had transformed into a trio comprising Huey Williams, Maurice Surrell, and James Burkes.

HORACE CLARENCE BOYER/JONAS WESTOVER

Jacksonville. City in Florida (pop. 821,784; metropolitan area 1,313,228; 2010 US Census). Named after President Andrew Jackson, the first military governor of the Florida Territory, Jacksonville is the largest city in terms of population in Florida and the 11th most populous city in the United States. It is also the largest city in the United States in terms of area due to the consolidation of Duval County and the city government in 1968. Located in the extreme northeastern corner of Florida, it is culturally a city of the Deep South, distinct from the urban centers in the southern part of the state. Although it is barely 40 kilometers north of the former Spanish settlement of St. Augustine, the city's main influences have been British and African American.

1. Art music. 2. Folk and popular music.

1. ART MUSIC. Until the Civil War there was little organized art music in Jacksonville, which was not incorporated as a town until 1822. After the war the city began to develop as a cultural center, and by 1890 the Friday Musicale, the oldest ongoing music organization in Florida and second oldest in the country, began sponsoring concerts which included such well-known artists

as Dame Nellie Melba, Fritz Kreisler, Serge Rachmaninoff, and Ignacy Jan Paderewski. The Jacksonville PO was founded in the 1930s. Renamed the Jacksonville SO in 1949, this ensemble is a regional professional symphony orchestra serving north Florida and has given regular concert series in the Jacoby Symphony Hall, one of three venues at the Times–Union Center for the Performing Arts. The other two are the Jim and Jan Moran Theater for touring Broadway shows and the Terry Theater for small shows and recitals. The building was originally erected as the Civic Auditorium in 1962 and underwent a major renovation in 1996. Jacksonville SO conductors have been Van Lier Lanning (1949–52), James Christian Pfohl (1952–61), John Canarina (1962–9), Willis Page (1971–83), Roger Nierenberg (1984–98), and Fabio Mechetti (from 1999). The Jacksonville Symphony Chorus was founded in 1985. Other music groups include the Jacksonville Symphony Youth Orchestra, choral and instrumental ensembles, and ballet groups, most of them semi-professional or amateur. From 1930 to 1984 the Jacksonville Civic Music Association sponsored performances by nationally known groups. In the early 2010s there were at least six concert series, sponsored by the public library, art gallery, and local churches, which presented artists and musicians with local to national and international reputations.

One of the most notable organizations in the city was the Delius Association of Florida (1961–2004), which sponsored a Delius Festival each spring and attracted scholars and musicians, especially from England and the United States. During 1884 and 1885 the English composer FREDERICK DELIUS (1862–1934) lived at Solano Grove on the St. Johns River, near Jacksonville, and spent time studying there with Thomas Ward, a gifted musician whom he befriended. Delius became so enamored of the African American melodies and rhythms he heard that he incorporated them into some of his own compositions, notably the suite *Florida* (1887, for orchestra), the lyric drama *Koanga* (1895–7), and *Appalachia* (1902–03, for baritone, chorus, and orchestra). Several Delius manuscripts are housed in the library of Jacksonville University, and the Solano Grove house has been transported to the university's campus.

Jacksonville's most famous native son is the author, educator, and early civil rights activist James Weldon Johnson (1871–1938). He and his brother J. ROSAMOND JOHNSON (1873–1954), a composer and singer, wrote the words and music to *Lift Every Voice and Sing* (1900), sometimes known as the Negro National Anthem. Another composer and folk music specialist with Jacksonville roots was Ruth Crawford Seeger (1901–53). Although born in Ohio, she received her early musical training in Jacksonville between 1912 and 1921. She was the first woman to be awarded a Guggenheim Fellowship in music.

In the early 2010s there was a vibrant musical community for young musicians in Jacksonville which had a number of music schools spanning the gamut from primary through college education. The First Coast Community Music School has offered various levels of instruction with ties to the youth orchestra. Music magnet schools on the primary, middle, and high school levels, such as the Douglas Anderson School of the Arts, have fed into the main academic institutions offering degrees in music. Florida State College (formerly known as Florida Community College) has offered a two-year program. Undergraduate degree programs have been offered by two academic institutions: Jacksonville University (founded 1934), which joined the Jacksonville College of Music (1926) to form its music division (1958); and the University of North Florida (UNF, 1972). The jazz studies program (1987) at UNF has been a leading program and has become internationally renowned.

2. FOLK AND POPULAR MUSIC. Band music has long been popular in Jacksonville. The Morocco Shrine Temple has supported a variety of performing ensembles with a tradition going back to 1910. Also important in local parades and other events has been the Navy Band Southeast, connected to the Naval Air Station. The St. Johns River City Band (founded in 1984) and First Coast Wind Ensemble (1990) have provided performance outlets for professional and amateur musicians.

Quartet singing has constituted another important popular activity. In addition to the active local chapters of the Barber shop Harmony Society and the Sweet Adelines International for barbershop music, there has been a longstanding tradition of gospel quartet singing. In the black community, quartet singing goes back to the 1920s, when jubilee singing developed out of local church practices. From the 1930s to the 1960s, black jubilee quartets from Jacksonville, such as the Royal Harmony (later known as the CBS Jubilaires), toured the Deep South and beyond. A local promoter and composer of quartet songs was Otis Jackson (active around the period 1920–60 in Jacksonville and later Orlando), some of whose pieces have remained in the repertory. Historically, the Ritz Theatre—which opened in 1929 and was renovated in 1999—has hosted leading African American performers. It is located in LaVilla, a neighborhood in the northern part of the downtown area, which was known as the Harlem of the South in the 1930s.

The Florida Theatre (1927), built in the style of the Mediterranean Revival and designed for both stage shows and motion pictures, has possessed a seating capacity of 1900. Elvis Presley gave one of his first headline concerts on an indoor stage here in 1956. Native son Jack Sheldon (*b* Jacksonville, FL, 1931) led a career as a trumpeter, singer, and actor, and performed for many years on *The Merv Griffin Show*. The jazz pianist MARCUS ROBERTS, born and raised in Jacksonville, was appointed assistant professor of the music faculty of Florida State University in 2004. Another well-known educator is the alto saxophonist Bunky Green, who began directing the jazz studies program at the University of North Florida in 1993. The city has also hosted the Jacksonville Jazz Festival since 1979, which has presented star performers and attracted thousands of spectators.

Jacksonville has also been home to many well-known rock bands, including Classics IV, which popularized the soft Southern rock sound with such hits as "Spooky" (1967), "Stormy" (1968), and "Traces" (1969). Jacksonville bands LYNYRD SKYNYRD and the ALLMAN BROTHERS BAND both became pioneers of Southern rock. Successful hard rock and heavy metal groups from the 1970s and early 1980s included Blackfoot, Molly Hatchet, and 38 Special. Among the many notable Jacksonville groups of subsequent years is the nu-metal band Limp Bizkit, which formed in 1995 and had sold millions of albums and been nominated for three Grammy Awards by the early 2010s.

Jacksonville also has several large ethnic groups which have carried on music traditions of their homelands, especially those from the Mediterranean region. One of the oldest such groups is the Arab community. In the late 19th century Syrian Arabs began to settle in Jacksonville as merchants. In the early 2010s the Lebanese and Palestinian immigrant communities, most of them Christian, were dancing the traditional Middle Eastern circle dance *debke* at local weddings and other celebrations. For such events they have called upon local musicians or those from Miami to play the *derbekke* (pot drum) and oud, since a sizable Arab population has developed in southern Florida.

BIBLIOGRAPHY

Florida: a Guide to the Southernmost State (New York, 1939)
R. Smith: *Culture in Florida* (Tallahassee, 1963)
D.L. Root: *Music in Florida Historic Sites* (Tallahassee, 1982)
W.L. Housewright: *A History of Music and Dance in Florida, 1565–1865* (Tuscaloosa, 1991)
P.D. Smith: *Ashley Street Blues: Racial Uplift and the Commodification Vernacular Performance in Lavilla, Florida, 1896–1916* (diss., Florida State U., 2007)

PETER MATHEWS

Jacobi, Frederick (*b* San Francisco, CA, 4 May 1891; *d* New York, NY, 24 Oct 1952). Conductor and composer. In New York he studied with Gallico, RAFAEL JOSEFFY, RUBIN GOLDMARK, and ERNEST BLOCH, and, at the Hochschule für Musik in Berlin, with Juon. From 1916 to 1917 he was assistant conductor of the Metropolitan Opera in New York; he taught harmony at the Master School of United Arts (1924) and composition at the Juilliard School (1934–50), where his pupils included ALEXEI HAIEFF, NORMAN DELLO JOIO, Ratner, ROBERT STARER, and ROBERT WARD. As a director of the American section of the ISCM and a member of the executive board of the League of Composers, he worked to further the cause of living composers in the United States. His frequent contributions to *Modern Music* focus on American composers, on Igor Stravinsky, and on more general topics, as in the article "In Defense of Modernism" (May–June 1940). Jacobi also lectured at the University of California, Berkeley, at Mills College, and for the Julius Hartt Musical Foundation at Hartford, Connecticut. He won an honorable mention in the Coolidge Competition of 1924, and in 1945 he was given the David Bispham Award for his opera *The Prodigal Son*, based on early 19th-century prints illustrating the biblical story. Well known in his day, his music was performed by leading orchestras in the United States and Europe.

Jacobi's compositions reflect a modernism informed by American, Jewish, Classical, and Romantic traditions.

In the 1920s his study of Native American music, supplemented by visits to Pueblo and Navajo tribes in the Southwest, led him, like many of his contemporaries, to work with indigenous material: his String Quartet no.1 (1924) and the *Indian Dances*, given their premiere by Serge Koussevitzky with the Boston SO in 1928, were products of this synthesis. It was in the 1930s, however, after being commissioned to write a Friday evening service for Temple Emmanuel in New York, that he turned toward the path of stylistic development for which he remains best known. After composing *Sabbath Evening Service*, sung in Hebrew, his music began to include more of such elements as mysticism (framed within a neo-classical structure), Hebraic melody, and many other aspects of his Jewish spiritual and cultural heritage. Examples are the Cello Concerto (1932), *Hagiographa* (1938), three biblical narratives based on the books of Job, Ruth, and Joshua, *Ode to Zion* (1948), and his final work, the *Friday Evening Service* no.2 (1952). He further explored these interests through his involvement with the Jewish Music Forum and the National Council for Jewish Music of the Jewish Welfare Board.

WORKS
(selective list)

Op: The Prodigal Son (3, H. Voaden), 1943–4, concert perf., Chicago, 1947; staged Toronto, Arts and Letters Club, 22 April 1952
Choral: The Poet in the Desert (C.E.S. Wood), Bar, 4vv, orch, 1925; Sabbath Evening Service, Bar, 4vv, 1930–31; Saadia, hymn, male vv/SATB, 1942; Ahavas Olom, T, 4vv, org, 1945; Contemplation (W. Blake), 4vv, pf, 1947; Ode to Zion (J. Halevi), 4vv, 2 hp, 1948; Ashrey Haish (Zionist song by M. Zaira), arr. 4vv, str, 1949; Arvit l'shabbat, Friday Evening Service no.2, cantor, 4vv, org, 1952
Orch: The Pied Piper, sym. poem, 1915; A California Suite, 1917; The Eve of St Agnes, sym. poem, 1919; Sym. no.1, "Assyrian," 1922; Indian Dances, 1927–8; Conc., vc, orch, 1932; 3 Psalms, vc, orch, 1932; Pf Conc., 1934–5; Vn Conc., 1936–7; Ave rota: 3 Pieces in Multiple Style, small orch, pf, 1939; Rhapsody, hp, str, 1940; Night Piece, fl, small orch, 1941 [after Sym. no.1, movt 2], arr. fl, ob, cl, str qt, pf, 1944; Ode, 1941; Concertino, pf, str, 1946; 2 Pieces in Sabbath Mood, 1946; 4 Dances from The Prodigal Son, 1946; Sym. no.2, 1947; Yeibichai: Variations for Orch on an Amer. Indian Theme, 1947; Music Hall, ov., 1948
Chbr and solo inst.: Nocturne, str qt; 3 Preludes, vn, pf, 1921; Str Qt on Indian Themes, 1924; Str Qt no.2, 1933; 6 Pieces for Use in the Synagogue, org, 1933; Scherzo, ww qnt, 1936; Swing Boy, vn, pf, 1937; Hagiographia: 3 Biblical Narratives, str qt, pf, 1938; Shemesh, Palestinian folksong arr., vc, pf, 1940; Fantasy, va, pf, 1941; Ballade, vn, pf, 1942; Impressions from the Odyssey, vn, pf, 1945; Music for Monticello, fl, vc, pf, 1945; Str Qt no.3, 1945; Meditation, trbn, pf, 1947; Sonata, vc, pf, 1950; 3 Quiet Preludes, org, 1950; Night Piece and Dance, fl, pf, 1951
Pf: 6 Pieces, 1921; Pieces for Children, 1935; Dances from The Prodigal Son, 2 pf, 1944; Fantasy Sonata, 1945; Moods, 1946; Prelude, 1946; Toccata, 1946; Introduction and Toccata, 1946; Suite fantastique, 1948
Songs: 3 songs (F.L. Koch, S. Teasdale, A. Brome), 1v, pf, 1914; 3 Songs (S. Naidu), 1v, pf, 1916; Vocalise, 1921; 3 Poems (G. Chaucer), 1v, pf, 1922; 2 Assyrian Prayers, 1v, orch, 1923; Vocalise, 1930; Dunam Po, Palestinian folksong arr., 1939; From the Prophet Nehemiah, 3 excerpts, 1v, 2 pf, 1942; 3 Songs (P. Freneau), 1v, pf, 1948

MSS and other materials in *PHff*
Principal publishers: Boosey & Hawkes (New York), Leeds, Marks, G. Schirmer, Southern

BIBLIOGRAPHY

D. Diamond: "Frederick Jacobi," *MM*, xiv (1936–7), 124–31
O. Downs: "American Composer: Contributions of F. Jacobi to his Time and Art," *New York Times* (2 Nov 1952)

F. Croche: "Jacobi's Tinge of Mysticism," *The Sun* [Baltimore] (3 May 1964)

N.W. Levin: "Frederick Jacobi," *Milken Archive of Jewish Music*, <http://milkenarchive.org/people/view/volume-10/544/Jacobi+Frederick>

GUSTAVE REESE/MARJORIE MACKAY-SHAPIRO/R

Jacobs, Arnold (Maurice) (*b* Philadelphia, PA, 11 June 1915; *d* Chicago, IL, 7 Oct 1998). Tuba player and educator. He entered the Curtis Institute in 1930 and studied with Philip Donatelli of the Philadelphia Orchestra. After graduating in 1936, he was a member of the Indianapolis SO (1937–9), the Pittsburgh SO (1939–44), and the Chicago SO (1944–88). He also performed with the All-American Youth Orchestra under Leopold Stokowski in 1941 and recorded with the Philadelphia Orchestra in 1949. With colleagues from the Chicago SO he performed in the Chicago Symphony Brass Quintet. He recorded numerous times with the Chicago SO, but only once as a soloist: Ralph Vaughan Williams's Tuba Concerto (1977).

Jacobs is widely regarded as one of the most influential brass pedagogues of the 20th century. Although largely self-taught, he was considered by many to be the foremost expert on the study of breathing as it applies to wind instruments. Widely sought after as a teacher by tuba players and other brass performers, Jacobs also developed a reputation as a pedagogue among woodwind players. In addition to teaching in his private studio, he was on the faculty of Northwestern University. His former students have occupied orchestral and teaching positions throughout the United States.

BIBLIOGRAPHY

B. Frederickson: *Arnold Jacobs: Song and Wind* (Chicago, 1996)

R.W. Morris and E.R. Goldstein, eds.: *The Tuba Source Book* (Bloomington, IN, 1996)

RICHARD H. PERRY

Jacobs, Paul (*b* New York, NY, 22 June 1930; *d* New York, NY, 25 Sept 1983). Pianist and harpsichordist. He studied with ERNEST HUTCHESON and at the Juilliard School, and appeared both as soloist and ensemble pianist with the Composers Forum and Robert Craft's Chamber Arts Society before the age of 20. In 1951 he made his official New York debut, and then moved to Europe, where he worked for the next nine years, performing with the Domaine Musical, at the Darmstadt and Dartington summer schools, and for the ISCM in Italy and Austria. He also lectured on American music and in 1956 gave the first complete performance of Schoenberg's piano music in a series of concerts in Paris. On his return to the United States he taught at the Mannes College and Manhattan School and at the Berkshire Music Center, and performed with ensembles directed by Schuller and Weisberg. In 1962 he was appointed pianist of the New York PO and, in 1974, harpsichordist. He was on the faculty at Brooklyn College and gave many solo recitals each year.

Although he frequently performed Baroque music, Jacobs was best known for his interpretations of 20th-century music; he played pieces by Boulez, Busoni, Cage, Carter, Copland, Messiaen, Stockhausen, Stravinsky, and Thomson, among many others. With the pianists Ursula Oppens (his frequent collaborator in the two-piano repertory), Gilbert Kalish, and Charles Rosen, he commissioned Carter's *Night Fantasies* (1980), which he recorded. Jacobs was a thoughtful performer, whose recording of Schoenberg's piano music is notable more for its careful placing and weighting of each detail than for a range of color. This insistence on the music rather than the musician made his ensemble and orchestral work especially valuable, and his contributions to such works as Bartók's *Music for Strings, Percussion and Celesta* and Carter's Double Concerto were noted for their crisp accuracy and confident articulation.

BIBLIOGRAPHY

W. Crutchfield: "Paul Jacobs Talks about Carter and Messiaen," *Keynote*, vii/10 (1983), 19–24

Obituary, *New York Times* (26 Sept 1983)

RICHARD BERNAS/R

Jacobsohn, Simon E(berhard) (*b* Mitau, Kurland, Russia [now Jelgava, Latvia], 24 Dec 1839; *d* Chicago, IL, 3 Oct 1902). Violinist of Russian birth. He studied music at home and supported his family by playing for balls and parties. The Mitau organist R. Postel raised funds to support his studies, at age 15, with the concertmaster Weller at Riga, where he played in Weller's quartet, and, when almost 20 years old, at the Leipzig Conservatory, with the concertmaster Ferdinand David. After a successful appearance as soloist on a Gewandhaus concert, he took a concert tour through western Russia, and in 1860 became concertmaster in Bremen. In 1872 Jacobsohn came to the United States to be concertmaster with Theodore Thomas's orchestra (1872–8). He also joined the Mendelssohn Quintette Club in 1876, with which he played for two seasons. In 1878 he became violin professor at the Cincinnati College of Music and established a violin school there. He moved to the Chicago Musical College in 1886 to head the violin department and became associate director in 1900. His students included Michael Banner, Max Bendix, Theodore Binder, Henry Burke, Charles Henzen, and Nicholas Longworth.

BIBLIOGRAPHY

"S.E. Jacobsohn," *Brainard's Musical World* (July 1879); repr. in *Brainard's Biographies of American Musicians*, ed. E.D. Bomberger (Westport, CT, 1999), 153–4

Chicago Daily Tribune (18 Sept 1886)

W.S.B. Mathews: *A Hundred Years of Music in America* (Chicago, 1889/R), 288, 290

"Jacobsohn, Simon Eberhard," *Who's Who in America* (Chicago, 1899), 374 only

Chicago Daily Tribune (5 October 1902)

"Jacobsohn, Simon E.," *The American History and Encyclopedia of Music: Musical Biographies*, i, ed. W.L. Hubbard (Toledo, 1908), 406 only

JOHN C. SCHMIDT

Jacob's Pillow Dance Festival. It is widely regarded as the oldest and most extensive dance festival in the world, located on a National Historic Landmark site in the Berkshire Hills of western Massachusetts. Founded by the modern dance pioneer TED SHAWN in 1933, the

Pillow dates its origins to the first performance by Shawn and his Men Dancers, a company that was synonymous with the festival until it disbanded in 1940. For the first decade, all performances were afternoon events in a simple barn studio with no electricity. In 1942 a formal board organized and raised funds to build America's first theater especially for dance, designed by Joseph Franz, who also built the Music Shed at nearby Tanglewood. In this 620-seat theater, which has continued to bear his name, Shawn instituted an ambitious program encompassing a full range of dance styles, nurturing indigenous American dance and importing international artists, while serving as a showcase for leading performers and newcomers alike.

In the 1950s and 1960s Shawn began introducing US audiences to a number of prominent international companies, including the National Ballet of Canada, the Royal Danish Ballet, Nederlands Dans Theater, and Ballet Rambert. The international focus has continued into the 21st century, with companies from around the world making their US debuts at the Pillow or presenting US premieres each season. Among the choreographers who have premiered works at the festival are Merce Cunningham, Paul Taylor, Alvin Ailey, Mark Morris, Twyla Tharp, and Meredith Monk. Live music has often been featured, with prominent artists including Yo-Yo Ma, Dave Douglas, Fred Hersch, and Cecil Taylor, among others.

The Pillow has operated a summer school since 1934, training generations of dancers in ballet, modern, and other techniques. Some of the world's finest dance artists and educators have taught at Jacob's Pillow, including Bronislava Nijinska, Antony Tudor, José Limón, La Meri, Bessie Schönberg, Margaret Craske, Judith Jamison, Trisha Brown, and Ann Hutchinson Guest.

At the time of Shawn's death in 1972, there were doubts that Jacob's Pillow could remain viable as an institution. Following a succession of directors throughout the 1970s, Liz Thompson brought new life to the festival in a transformational decade, adding new performance spaces and opening up the grounds to the public. Subsequent developments have increased visitor experiences, with free access to talks, exhibits, informal showings, and archives. Under the direction of Ella Baff from 1998, Jacob's Pillow has continued to be a major cultural force.

NORTON OWEN

Jacquet, (Jean-Baptiste) Illinois (*b* Broussard, nr Lafayette, LA, 31 Oct 1922; *d* New York, NY, 22 July 2004). Saxophonist, bassoonist, composer, and bandleader. Born to a black Creole father and a Sioux mother—in a musical family, which had moved to Texas by 1923—he grew up onstage, sang on the air at three, and tap-danced before his father's band in Houston. He learned the drums, then soprano and alto saxophone, which he played in Milt Larkin's band (1939–40). After moving to California, he worked with Floyd Ray (1941) and Lionel Hampton (1941–2), who had him concentrate on tenor. At 19, on his second recording session, he played a powerful solo on "Flying Home," in a simplified Coleman

Hawkins style, which won him overnight stardom; the solo was to be regularly repeated by him and later Hampton tenors. Jacquet next worked with Cab Calloway (1943–4), in whose band he appeared in the movie *Stormy Weather* (1943). In 1944 he was filmed again in *Jammin' the Blues* and joined Jazz at the Philharmonic (JATP). In the latter setting he began to exploit the tenor saxophone's altissimo register—using harmonics and false fingerings—a device well suited to such a competitive environment. His solos, which had a stirring effect on audiences, often opened in a subdued melodic vein and built up towards forte and the treble register before giving way to shorter and shorter riffs and finally climaxing on a repeated high note. His combination of piercing whistles and low-register honks characterized the rhythm-and-blues tenor saxophone formula.

Jacquet worked with Count Basie (1945–6) and toured with JATP (1946–7, 1955, 1957), while leading his own group, whose records, produced by Norman Granz, sold well. One of them contained his best-known composition, "Robbins' Nest" (1947). In 1954 Jacquet visited Europe for the first time. Subsequent albums displayed his soulful ballad style. After leaving Granz (1958), Jacquet reduced his recorded activity in favor of European tours, and France became his second homeland. From 1963 he also played bassoon, and from 1966 he worked with the pianist Milt Buckner until the latter's death in 1977. A lecture at Harvard University (1982) led to his working there as the Kayden Artist-in-Residence (1983–4), making him the first jazz musician to be so honored. This experience prompted him to lead a big band (1985–2004), which toured the United States and Europe and was the subject of Arthur Elgort's award-winning documentary, *Texas Tenor: the Illinois Jacquet Story* (1991). Jacquet received the Award for Artistic Excellence from Lincoln Center (2000) and a doctorate from the Juilliard School (2004). The Illinois Jacquet Scholarship in Jazz Studies at Juilliard honors his memory.

BIBLIOGRAPHY

D. Gillespie and A. Fraser: *To Be, or not…to Bop: Memoirs* (Garden City, NY, 1979/R1980 as *Dizzy: the Autobiography*)
J. Evensmo: *The Flute of Wayman Carver, the Trombone of Dickie Wells, 1927–1942, the Tenor Saxophone of Illinois Jacquet* (Oslo, c1983) [discography]
G. Giddins: *Rhythm-a-Ning: Jazz Tradition and Innovation in the 80's* (New York, 1985), 178
F.P. Miller, A.F. Vandome, and J. McBrewster, eds.: *Illinois Jacquet* (Beau Bassin, Mauritius, 2010)

MARCELLO PIRAS

Jaffe, Stephen (*b* Washington, DC, 30 Dec 1954). Composer and educator. He studied composition at the Geneva Conservatoire and the University of Massachusetts, Amherst, and received degrees from the University of Pennsylvania (BA 1977, MA 1978), where he studied with GEORGE CRUMB, GEORGE ROCHBERG, and RICHARD WERNICK. In 1981 he joined the music faculty at Duke University and established the prominent concert series Encounters: with Music from our Time. He also was awarded the Rome Prize (1981) and later received the

Brandeis University Creative Arts Citation (1989). Other honors include the Kennedy Center Friedheim Award (1991) and the American Academy of Arts and Letters' lifetime achievement prize (1993), as well as fellowships from the Guggenheim Foundation, Tanglewood, and the NEA. In 1999 Jaffe was named Mary D.B.T. and James H. Semans Professor of Music at Duke University. Jaffe is well represented on recordings (Bridge, Neuma, Albany, and CRI) and has received commissions from the Fromm Music Foundation, the Walter W. Naumburg Foundation, the National SO, and the North Carolina Symphony, among others. His lyrical style balances familiar tonal harmonies with denser materials in colorful instrumental combinations. He sometimes augments more traditional instrumental writing with surprising additions (mandolin and steel drums in the cello concerto and an oboist doubling on harmonica in *Homage to the Breath*).

WORKS

Orch: Sym. "Three Lives," 1973–5, unpubd; Rega-Raga, jazz ens, 1974, unpubd; 4 Images, 1983, rev. 1987; The Rhythm of the Running Plough, chbr orch, 1985–8; Autumnal, 1986; Vn Conc., 1999; Vc Conc., 2003; Cut-Time, orch, 2004; Poetry of the Piedmont, orch, 2006;

Vocal: 3 Yiddish Songs (L. Rudnitsky, A. Suztkever, S. Kacerzinsky), Mez, orch/chbr orch, 1975–7, arr. S, hn, vn, vc, pf, 1987; 3 Images (H. Martinson, F. García Lorca, W. Whitman), nar, vv soloists, chorus, chbr orch, 1979; Four Songs with Ensemble (Martinson, R. Francis, D. Levertov), Mez, a fl + fl, va, vc, pf, 1988; Fort Juniper Songs (Francis), S, Mez, pf, 1989; Pedal Point (Francis, M. Oliver), Bar, 3 va, 4 vc, hp, timp, 1989, rev. 1993; The Reassurance (T. Gunn), high v, pf, 1995 [contribution to AIDS Quilt Songbook]; Songs of Turning (Jaffe, after A. Landers, H. Kushner, M. Oliver, Levertov, D. Rosenberg, Pss, Bible: Jeremiah) S, B, SATB, chbr orch, 1996; Homage to the Breath (Thich Nhat Hanh), Mez, 10 insts, 2001

Chbr: Fantasies, Etudes and Interludes, solo pf, pf 4 hands, 1975–7, unpubd; 4 Nocturnes, cl, vn, va, vc, hp, perc, 1975; Un dialogo possibile, fl + pic + opt. b fl, va, pf, perc, 1976, unpubd; Centering, 2 vn, 1978; Concert, vn, pf + cel + org, 1978, unpubd; Partita, vc, pf, perc, 1980, rev. 1987; Arch, fl + pic, cl, b cl, vn, vc, db, cel, pf, 1981; Ballade (Qt from Arch), cl, vn, vc, pf, 1981; A Nonesuch Serenade, fl, cl, vn, vc, pf, 1984; The Rhythm of the Running Plough, a fl + pic + fl, vn, vc, perc, 1985; Impromptu, pf, 1987; 3 Figures and a Ground, fl, pf, 1988; Double Sonata, 2 pf, 1989; Str Qt no.1, 1991; Triptych, wind qnt, pf, 1992; Chbr Conc. "Singing Figures," ob, vn, va, vc, hpd, cel, 1994, arr. ob, 5 insts, 1996; Offering, fl, va, hp, 1996; Spinoff, gui, 1997; Designs, fl, gui, perc, 2001; String Quartet no.2 "Sylvan and Aeolian Figures," 2005; Chbr Conc. no.2 "Light Dances," fl, cl, vn, vc, perc, pf, 2010

Principal publishers: Merion (Presser), MMB, Mobart

BRYAN GILLIAM/ALAN SHOCKLEY

Jaffee, Michael (*b* Brooklyn, NY, 21 April 1938). Lutenist, guitarist, and musicologist. He studied at New York University (BA in music 1959, MA in musicology 1963). In 1964 with his wife Kay (*b* Lansing, MI, 31 Dec 1937) he founded the early music ensemble the WAVERLY CONSORT. After its New York debut in 1965, with Jaffee as artistic director it performed music from the 12th to the 18th centuries in concerts throughout North and South America, Asia, and Europe, as well as on records and television. A versatile player of many antique plucked and bowed string instruments and woodwind instruments, Jaffee has also appeared as a lutenist and guitarist with the Bach Aria Group, the Fine Arts Quartet, Clarion Concerts, and the New York City Orchestra. He

was founding president of Chamber Music America (1978–83).

HOWARD SCHOTT/R

Jagel, Frederick [Jeghelli, Federico] (*b* Brooklyn, NY, 10 Jan 1897; *d* San Francisco, CA, 5 July 1982). Tenor. After war service in France, he studied singing in New York and Milan; he made his debut in 1924 at Livorno in *La bohème*. As Federico Jeghelli he sang for three years in Italy and with an Italian company in the Netherlands. Under his own name, he made his American debut at the Metropolitan Opera in 1927 as Radames, the part he sang most frequently there; in the same season, he made a strong impression in the local premiere of Franco Alfano's *Risurrezione*. He remained with the Metropolitan until 1950, also singing in Chicago, San Francisco, and South America, and with the New York City Opera (1947–9). His most important new role at the Metropolitan (and his last) was probably Peter Grimes, which he sang in the first production there of Benjamin Britten's opera (1948); other American premieres in which he took part include Musorgsky's *The Fair at Sorochintsï* (1930). His repertory also included the Drum Major in *Wozzeck* and Luka in *From the House of the Dead* (which he sang in a televised performance in 1969). His singing of Alfredo with Rosa Ponselle as Violetta can be heard in a primitive recording of a Metropolitan performance in 1935, the voice clearly projected, the bright tone sensitively shaded.

J.B. STEANE

Jager, Robert (*b* Binghamton, NY, 25 Aug 1939). Composer and educator. Beginning with trumpet lessons from his father, a Salvation Army musician and later a minister, Jager began composing by writing duets for his father and himself. Jager studied trumpet at the University of Michigan with Clifford Lillya. He joined the Navy's music program in 1962 and was assigned to the Navy School of Music, where he taught basic music theory. He was reassigned as Staff Arranger/Composer after winning his first Ostwald Award. Returning to the University of Michigan he earned the BME (1967) and MME (1968) degrees. In 1971, he joined the faculty at Tennessee Tech University in Cookeville, TN, retiring in 2001 as emeritus professor of music.

His music has been performed throughout the United States, Canada, Europe, and Asia. His numerous commissions include works for all the Washington-based military bands and military academies, many United States and Japanese universities, the Tokyo Kosei Wind Orchestra, and the Republic of China Band Association.

BIBLIOGRAPHY
W.H. Rehrig: *The Heritage Encyclopedia of Band Music* (Westerville, OH, 1991, suppl. 1996); CD-ROM (Oskaloosa, IA, 2005) [includes selective list of works]

R. Jager: "Robert Jager," *Composers on Composing for Band*, ed. Mark Camphouse, ii (Chicago, 2004), 125–67

DAVID WHITWELL

Jagiello, Walter [Maly Wladziu; Li'l Wally] (*b* Chicago, IL, 1 Aug 1930; *d* Miami Beach, FL, 17 Aug 2006). Polka bandleader and musician. He was the musician most responsible for developing and popularizing the Chicago style of Polish American POLKA (III), which in updated form has remained the dominant style of Polish polka in the United States. The son of immigrants, he was born in a predominantly Polish ethnic community. Growing up immersed in the community's culture and music, he was a musical prodigy who began singing at Polish picnics at age eight, acquiring his lifelong nickname Maly Wladziu (Li'l Wally). He learned drums and concertina and at age 14 became a bandleader.

Jagiello pioneered a small combo sound nicknamed honky style, a core of trumpet, concertina, and drums, plus a clarinet and/or string bass for bigger gigs. Vocals were strongly emphasized. Moreover, he favored a slower tempo that corresponded to and enabled the rising popularity of a new polka dance step, the Polish hop, danced in double time to the music.

Jagiello was dissatisfied with his experience recording eight sides for Columbia in 1949, so in 1951 he established Jay Jay, his own label. He also acquired a studio and record pressing equipment. He recorded prodigiously, often issuing ten albums per year in the 1950s and 1960s. "Puka Jasiu" and "I wish I was single again" were among his many hits. From the mid-1960s he lived Miami Beach, where he continued his recording efforts, and toured extensively, especially in the Midwest. He remained active until his death in 2006, ultimately recording more than 150 albums.

RICHARD MARCH

Jagoda [née Kabilio], **Flory** (*b* Sarajevo, Yugoslavia [now Bosnia and Herzegovina], 1925). Singer and guitarist. Growing up in a Sephardic Jewish community, she learned Balkan folklore as well as traditional songs in the Ladino language with guidance from her grandmother. In 1946 she married a serviceman and immigrated to the United States, where she has become known as the Flame of Sephardic Music because of the strength of her commitment to this unique musical heritage. In addition to transcribing, performing, and teaching traditional Ladino material, Jagoda has composed and arranged new Sephardic songs. She also has performed material drawn from biblical verses, poems, and prayers. She has recorded several albums, which often recall her early experiences, including *Memories of Sarajevo* (1996) and *Kantikas di mi Nona* (Songs of my Grandmother) (1996). She also published *The Flory Jagoda Songbook: Memories of Sarajevo* (1996), which includes songs and stories about her family history. She is featured in the documentary *The Key from Spain: the Songs and Stories of Flora Jagoda* (2000). To honor her distinctive musical contributions, Jagoda received an NEA National Heritage Fellowship (2002).

CATHERINE WOJTANOWSKI

Jamal, Ahmad [Jones, Frederick Russell] (*b* Pittsburgh, PA, 2 July 1930). Jazz pianist and composer. He studied with the singer MARY CARDWELL DAWSON and the pianist JAMES MILLER in Pittsburgh where he began playing professionally at the age of 11. After attending Westinghouse High School, he left in the late 1940s to join the George Hudson Orchestra. In 1951 he formed his first trio, the Three Strings, and after an extended engagement at the Blue Note club in Chicago, he appeared at the Embers in New York, where he attracted the critical support of John Hammond. He changed his name on his conversion to Islam in the early 1950s. In 1958, with the bass player Israel Crosby and the drummer Vernel Fournier, Jamal recorded his most popular and influential album, *Ahmad Jamal at the Pershing*, which included influential versions of "But not for me" and "Poinciana." Miles Davis admired the album's lean style, use of space, and simple embellishments, all of which characterized Davis's own bands and recordings in the 1950s. Jamal's trio disbanded in 1962, but with new personnel, notably the bass player Jamil Nasser, he continued to tour and record for Argo/Cadet, Impulse, and 20th Century-Fox. Jamal's trio style has featured orchestrated performances with harmonic and rhythmic elaborations, extended forms, and finely calibrated dynamics. Since the 1980s Jamal has worked with the bass player James Cammack and the drummer Idris Muhammad, among others. His recording *The Essence Part One* featured the tenor saxophonist George Coleman, the first appearance of a horn player with Jamal's trio. Jamal received an NEA Jazz Masters Fellowship in 1994.

SELECTED RECORDINGS
Chamber Music of the New Jazz (1955, Argo); *Ahmad Jamal at the Pershing* (1958, Argo); *At the Top: Poinciana Revisited* (1968, Imp.); *The Awakening* (1970, Imp.); *Jamal Plays Jamal* (1974, 20C); *The Essence Part One* (1995, Birdology)

BIBLIOGRAPHY
N. Tesser: "'Cut out the Jass': Ahmad Jamal," *DB*, xli/1 (1974), 14
L. Lyons: "Ahmad Jamal: Mainstream Jazz Pianist," *CK*, iii/6 (1977), 8
L. Goddet: "Ahmad Jamal: une musique du désir," *Jb* (1979), no.359, p.4; no.360, p.6
W. Jenkins: "Ahmad Jamal's Orchestral Designs," *JT*, xxiii/4 (1993), 33
A. Kahn: "Walking History," *JT*, xxxiii/6 (2003), 72–80

RICHARD WANG/BRAD LINDE

Jam band. A term that gained popularity in the mid-1990s to refer to a subgenre of improvisational rock music. Both the bands and their individual repertoires are stylistically heterogeneous, encompassing myriad rock genres, folk, jazz, bluegrass, and electronica. Although most remain outside the popular mainstream, some jam bands, including the DAVE MATTHEWS BAND and Blues Traveler, have had crossover hits. Others, such as PHISH and Widespread Panic, have achieved tremendous success as touring acts, despite no commercial radio airplay.

Jam bands share a number of musical traits, the foremost being a propensity for lengthy improvisation and stylistic variation. They often tend towards more progressive songwriting and avoiding pop conventions. Jam bands take a democratic approach to jamming, establishing a groove with full-band improvisation, rather than featuring successive soloists improvising over chord changes. Jams often leave the harmonic and/or rhythmic foundation from which they sprang and segue into other songs. Tempos tend to be fast, which encourages dancing and keeps the music fresh during long improvisatory passages.

Some have applied the term retroactively to the Grateful Dead and the Allman Brothers Band. Whether or not the former are considered a jam band, they provided a model, as well as cover song opportunities, for later jam bands. Like the Grateful Dead, jam bands rely on incessant touring and word of mouth for promotion, and many fans hold the live show in higher regard than studio efforts. Jam bands have tended not to repeat concert set lists, and some garner a following of fans who attend multiple shows on a tour. Most allow amateur audience recording and trading of concerts.

The H.O.R.D.E. touring festival, which began in 1992, helped to define the genre, with internet newsgroup users and amateur tapers already calling these groups jam bands. Organized by Blues Traveler, the original lineup also included Phish, Widespread Panic, Spin Doctors, and the Aquarium Rescue Unit. As the decade wore on, fans of these bands helped others gain popularity, such as moe., the String Cheese Incident, the Disco Biscuits, and Umphrey's McGee. In this sense jam bands also constitute an audience-defined genre, since bands who have been absorbed by this community of fans have tended to acquire the moniker. Although some originally perceived the term as derogatory, akin to meandering improvisation, it became much more commonplace in mainstream media by the late 1990s and early 2000s, thanks to *Relix* magazine and websites such as *jambands.com* (<http://www. jambands.com/>).

BIBLIOGRAPHY

D. Budnick: *Jambands: the Complete Guide to the Players, Music, & Scene* (San Francisco, 2003)

JACOB A. COHEN

James, Bob [Robert] (*b* Marshall, MO, 25 Dec 1939). Pianist, keyboard player, arranger, composer, and record producer. After studying composition at the University of Michigan (MA 1962) he was discovered by Quincy Jones at the Notre Dame Collegiate Jazz Festival in 1963. That year he recorded his first solo album, *Bold Conceptions*, for Mercury Records. He began performing as a freelance musician with such artists as Jones, Morgana King, Roberta Flack, and Dionne Warwick, but credits the producer Creed Taylor for the launch of his career in 1973, when he became an arranger for Taylor's label Creed Taylor Incorporated (CRI). The following year he joined CBS and worked with the singers Neil Diamond and Paul Simon. In 1977 he formed his own record company, Tappan Zee, and used it to promote the music of several musicians, including Richard Tee and Mongo Santamaria.

James became associated with the smooth-jazz sound, and his first big instrumental hit in that vein, "Angela," was used as the theme song for the television series *Taxi*, for which James became resident composer. The first of his three albums with the guitarist Earl Klugh, *One on One*, was awarded a Grammy in 1980 and sold more than a million copies. In an unusual turn, James also recorded three classical albums using electronic

instrumentation for CBS Masterworks, the first of which, in 1984, was devoted to Jean-Phillipe Rameau. He was surprised at the time that no-one detected the fact that one of the pieces was his own composition.

In 2006 James received the George Benson Lifetime Achievement Award at the Canadian Smooth Jazz Awards. He is the subject of two video documentaries, *Bob James Live* (*c*1989) and *Bob James: for the Record* (*c*1990s), and can be seen performing in the video documentary *Sinatra: Portrait of an Album* (1986).

STUART ISACOFF

James, Dorothy (*b* Chicago, IL, 1 Dec 1901; *d* St Petersburg, FL, 1 Dec 1982). Composer and teacher. She studied with Adolf Weidig, HOWARD HANSON, LOUIS GRUENBERG, HEALEY WILLAN, and ERNST KRENEK. From 1927 to 1968 she taught at Eastern Michigan University, Ypsilanti, where she became professor in 1962; she was also music critic for the *Ypsilanti Press*. Her music is for the most part chromatic, well wrought, and finely balanced; although based in 19th-century technique, it is not limited to traditional content. The clarity and fluidity of her choral writing create a quite individual luminous sound. James was an allied member of the MacDowell Colony Fellows. She published *Notes on Living Michigan Women Composers* (1975).

WORKS
(selective list)

Op: Paola and Francesca, 1933

Orch: 3 Sym. Fragments, 1931; Elegy for the Lately Dead, 1938; Suite, small orch, 1940

Choral: Tears (W. Whitman), SATB, orch, 1930; Christmas Night (E. Tatum), SATB, 1933; The Jumblies (E. Lear), SSAA, orch, 1935; The Little Jesus Came to Town (L. Reese), SATB, 1935; Mary's Lullaby (E. Coatsworth), SSAA, 1937; Paul Bunyan (Tatum), Bar, SSAA, orch, 1937; Niobe (J.H. Noyes), SSAA, chamber orch, 1941; The Night (H. Belloc), TTBB, pf, 1950; The Golden Years (A. Tennyson), SATB, orch, 1953; The Nativity Hymn (J. Milton), SSAA, 1957; Envoy (F. Thomson), SSAA, pf, 1958; Mutability (P.B. Shelley), SSAA, ens, 1967

Inst: 3 Pastorales, cl, str, cel, 1933; Autumnal, org, 1934; 2 Satirical Dances, pf, 1934; Recitative and Aria, 2 vn, va, 2 vc, 1944; Dedication, org, 1958; Dirge, pf, 1962; Impressionistic Study, pf, 1962; Tone Row Suite, pf, 1962; Two in One, pf, 1962; Morning Music, fl, pf, 1967; Motif, ob, org, 1970; Patterns, harp, 1977

Solo vocal: The White Moon (P. Verlaine), 1v, pf, 1924; Lacquer Prints (A. Lowell), 1v, pf, 1925; 4 Preludes from the Chinese, A/B, pf qnt, 1930: So Sleeps the Night (G. Goff), 1v, pf, 1930; Songs for Emily (E. Dickinson), 1v, pf, 1965; Sonnet after Michelangelo, Mez/Bar, hn, pf, 1967

Principal publishers: J. Fischer, Fitz Simmons

EDITH BORROFF

James, Elmore [Brooks, Elmore] (*b* Richland, Holmes County, MS, 27 Jan 1918; *d* Chicago, IL, 24 May 1963). Blues guitarist, singer, and bandleader. An influential slide guitarist whose impact transcends blues, James first made music on a "diddley bow" and later a homemade guitar constructed from a can, board, and wire. During his teen years James performed at juke joints in the Delta region and furthered his musical education via encounters with Robert Johnson and Sonny Boy Williamson II. His music, although rooted in traditional blues, took a more progressive turn than that of these early role models. His most famous recording, "Dust My Broom," a top-ten rhythm and blues hit in 1952, not only showed his stylistic links to Robert Johnson but also anticipated the electrified sounds of later rock, funk, and soul music. Following the success of this record, James moved to Chicago and recorded for several independent labels. Although he never achieved the commercial success of Muddy Waters or Howlin' Wolf, James's mastery of slide-guitar techniques, as well as his innovative use of distortion and sustain, helped shape the vocabulary of postwar electric guitar. His wailing vocal work was also immediately recognizable to blues fans and equally adaptable to slow tearjerkers such as "The Sky Is Crying" and faster groove numbers such as "Rollin' and Tumblin'." James suffered a fatal heart attack at age 45, his passing largely unnoticed by the media. Yet his fame has grown posthumously, and a cult following continues to revere him as one of the leading guitarists of the mid-20th century.

RECORDINGS

The Sky Is Crying: the History of Elmore James (1993, Rhino); *King of the Slide Guitar: the Complete Trumpet, Chief, and Fire Sessions* (2005, Snapper)

BIBLIOGRAPHY

S. Franz: *The Amazing Secret History of Elmore James* (St. Louis, 2002)

M. Ryan: *Trumpet Records: Diamonds on Farish Street* (Jackson, MS, 2004)

TED GIOIA

James, Etta [Hawkins, Jamesetta] (*b* Los Angeles, CA, 25 Jan 1938; *d* Riverside, CA, 20 Jan 2012). Pop and R&B singer and songwriter. Born to an unmarried 14-year-old mother, she began her career by auditioning for R&B bandleader Johnny Otis. She quickly rose to fame, at the age of 15, as the co-writer and singer of the 1955 R&B hit "Wallflower (Roll with Me Henry)," an answer record to Hank Ballard and the Midnighters' "Work with Me Annie." In 1960, she signed a recording contract with Chess Records, releasing many records on its subsidiary labels. That year she also recorded her signature song, "At Last" (1960), which hit number two on the R&B chart. Leonard Chess recognized James's crossover appeal and backed many of her tracks with lush string accompaniments. Subsequent hits in the 1960s included "I'd Rather Go Blind" and "Tell Mama," the latter of which charted on both the R&B and Hot 100 lists. The decade saw James establish her reputation as a recording artist and songwriter; it was also marked by her battle with a serious heroin addiction.

During the 1970s she released a mixture of fast R&B and slow soul ballads. She was deeply influenced by Otis Redding, an artist whose music she often remade; her version of "Security" made it to number 11 on the R&B chart. Other successful songs from the 1970s included "Losers Weepers" and "I Found a Love." By the early 1980s, James's career had stalled, but she picked up momentum by the end of the decade (including the release *Seven Year Itch*), and the 1990s saw a return to popularity, especially as a stage draw. In 1993 she was

inducted into the Rock and Roll Hall of Fame and in 1999 "At Last" was inducted into the Grammy Hall of Fame. She has since been honored repeatedly for her accomplishments in music, and was also remembered in the film *Cadillac Records* (2008), a biopic about Leonard Chess, in which James was portrayed by Beyoncé Knowles. In 2010, James was diagnosed with leukemia and in the final years of her life she also suffered from dementia and hepatitis C.

RECORDINGS
(selective list)

Etta James (Argo, 1963); *Tell Mama* (Cadet, 1967); *Etta is Betta Than Evah!* (Chess, 1977); *Seven Year Itch* (Island, 1989); *Matriarch of the Blues* (Private, 2000)

BIBLIOGRAPHY

N. Cohodas: *Spinning Blues into Gold: the Chess Brothers and the Legendary Chess Records* (New York, 2000)

E. James and D. Ritz: *Rage to Survive: the Etta James Story* (Cambridge, MA, 2003)

DAVID MOSKOWITZ

James, Harry (Haag) (*b* Albany, GA, 15 March 1916; *d* Las Vegas, NV, 5 July 1983). Jazz and popular trumpeter and bandleader. He began playing professionally at an early age with his father's circus band, and worked for a year with Ben Pollack (1935–6) before becoming a leading member of Benny Goodman's band (1937). James's exciting playing was given great prominence by Goodman, and is shown at its most typical on his recording of "Ridin' High" (1937, on the album *Jazz Concert, no.2*, Col.). After leaving Goodman in late 1938 James formed his own big band, which by the early 1940s had an enormous following. This was one of the first big bands to add a string section. One of its greatest hits was "You made me love you" (1941, Col.), on which James delivered the melody in a highly sentimental manner with a distinctive, wide vibrato. Further wartime successes featuring the singers Helen Forrest ("I don't want to walk without you," 1941, "I cried for you," 1942, Col.) and Dick Haymes (who replaced Frank Sinatra) made the band even more popular than Glenn Miller's. James reoriented towards jazz from the mid-1940s. He appeared in several films, including *Springtime in the Rockies* (1942, with his second wife, the film star Betty Grable), *Best Foot Forward* (1943), and *The Benny Goodman Story* (1955), and in the 1950s made regular tours with the band, traveling to Europe in 1957. From the 1960s to his death, although he spent long periods in Nevada, he performed frequently in New York and occasionally toured abroad.

James's admiration for the playing of Louis Armstrong never overwhelmed his individuality; he was noted for the boldness of his style, the richness of his tone, his range, and his stamina. The popularity that he gained with his bravura performances of such showpieces as "Carnival of Venice" and "Flight of the Bumble Bee" (both 1940, Var.) has tended to obscure the fact that he was a very fine jazz improviser, possessing a verve that enhanced many small-group and big-band recordings. A collection of his scores and other materials is held in the American Heritage Center of the University of Wyoming in Laramie.

BIBLIOGRAPHY

SchullerSE

C. Emge: "James Still Fronts Crack Band," *DB*, xviii/4 (1951), 3, 18

J. Tynan: "The Horn Still Blows," *DB*, xxv/2 (1958), 17, 34–5

G.T. Simon: *The Big Bands* (New York, 1967, enlarged 2/1971, 4/1981), 262–76, 534–7

L. Tomkins: "The Harry James Story," *Crescendo International*, ix/4 (1970–71), 20–3

G. Hall: *Harry James and his Orchestra* (Laurel, MD, 1971) [discography]

A. McCarthy: *Big Band Jazz* (New York, 1974), 240–2, 348–51

C. Garrod and P. Johnston: *Harry James and his Orchestra, i: 1937–1946, ii: 1947–1954* (Zephyrhills, FL, 1975); *iii: 1955–1982* (Zephyrhills, FL, 1985) [discography]

F. Hall: *More Dialogues in Swing: Intimate Conversations with the Stars of the Big Band Era* (Ventura, CA, 1991), 179–202

P. Levinson: *Trumpet Blues: the Life of Harry James* (Oxford, 2000)

JOHN CHILTON/R

James, Henry (*b* New York, NY, 15 April 1843; *d* London, England, 28 Feb 1916). Novelist. He received an eclectic and cosmopolitan private education, thus gaining the intimate knowledge of Europeans and Americans that figures prominently in his writings. James ranks as one of the most acclaimed writers and critics of the United States. His novels include *Daisy Miller* (1879), *The Portrait of a Lady* (1881), *The Wings of the Dove* (1902), and *The Ambassadors* (1903). After 1876 he made his home in England and in 1915 became a British citizen.

The best known operatic adaptations of James's fiction are Benjamin Britten's *The Turn of the Screw* and *Owen Wingrave*, both based on novels of the same titles. Other operas include Thea Musgrave's *The Voice of Ariadne* (based on James's short story "The Last of the Valerii"), Oakley Hall's *The Portrait of a Lady,* and Douglas S. Moore's *The Wings of the Dove.* Aaron Copland composed music for the film *The Heiress* (1949), derived from James's *Washington Square*. In 1988 Dominick Argento wrote the opera *The Aspern Papers* based on James's novella of the same name.

BIBLIOGRAPHY

GroveA

B. Ivry: "Portrait of an Author," *ON*, liii/5 (1988–9), 20–22

H. Blumenfeld: "The Henry James–Dominick Argento 'Aspern Papers'," *Opera Journal*, xxii/1 (1989), 34–7

R. Jordan and E. Kafalenos: "The Double Trajectory: Ambiguity in Brahms and Henry James," *19CM*, xiii (1989–90), 129–44

C. Hindley: "Why does Miles Die? A Study of Britten's 'The Turn of the Screw'," *MQ*, lxxiv (1990), 1–17

J. Rosen: "Dramatic Music," *Notes: Quarterly Journal of the Music Library Association*, li (1995), 1152

S. McClatchie: "Benjamin Britten, 'Owen Wingrave,' and the Politics of the Closet; or, 'He shall be Straightened out at Paramore'," *COJ*, viii (1996), 59–75

S. McKellar: "Re-visioning the 'Missing' Scene: Critical and Tonal Trajectories in Britten's *Billy Budd*," *JRMA*, cxxii (1997), 258–80

S. McKellar: "Music, Image and Ideology in Britten's 'Owen Wingrave': Conflict in a Fissured Text," *ML*, lxxx (1999), 390–410

L. Whitesell: "Britten's Dubious Trysts" *JAMS*, lvi (2003), 637–94

M. Stimpson: "Owen Wingrave's *Pacifism*," *MO*, no.1457 (2007), 34–5

MICHAEL HOVLAND

James, Philip (*b* Jersey City, NJ, 17 May 1890; *d* Southampton, NY, 1 Nov 1975). Composer and conductor. He studied the organ with J.W. Andrews, J.F. Bridges, and Alexandre Guilmant, and composition with Homer Norris, RUBIN GOLDMARK, ROSARIO SCALERO, and Elliott Schenck, with whom he also studied conducting. James received a baccalaureate degree from City College, CUNY (1910), and an honorary doctorate from New York College of Music (1946). During World War I he served in the 308th Regimental US Army Band and after the armistice became associate conductor of General John Pershing's American Expeditionary Forces General Headquarters Band. James went on to conduct the Broadway production of Victor Herbert's *My Golden Girl*. He co-founded and conducted the New Jersey Orchestra (1922–9) and conducted the Little Bamburger Orchestra in its weekly broadcasts on WOR radio (1929–36). In 1923 James assisted Albert Stoessel in founding the music department at New York University, acting as department chair from 1934 to 1955. He also served as secretary of the MacDowell Association, vice-president of the Institute of Arts and Letters, president of the Society for the Preservation of American Music, and as a juror for the Naumburg award, the Prix de Rome, and other competitions.

James's choral works are strongly influenced by English cathedral music and his Welsh heritage, while his orchestral works respond to French and German late-Romanticism. Progressive in their use of polyrhythms and polytonality, these works reveal a mastery of orchestration. The compositions for organ are virtuosic in nature and the songs, in a Victorian style, were popular with major artists of the time.

WORKS

(selective list)

INSTRUMENTAL

Orch: Col. Averill March, band, 1917; Ov. in Olden Style on French Noëls, 1926; Song of the Night, sym. poem, 1931; Station WGZBX, suite, 1931; Suite, vn, vc, db, str orch, 1933; Bret Harte Ov. no.3, 1934; Gwalia (A Welsh Rhapsody), 1937; Festal March "Perstare et praestare," band, 1942; Sym. no.1, 1943; E.F.G. Ov., band, 1944; Sym. no.2, 1946; Miniver Cheevy and Richard Cory (melodramas), spkr, orch, 1947; Fanfare and Ceremonial, march, band, 1955

Chbr and solo inst: Pensée d'automne, org, 1907; Meditation à Ste Clotilde, org, 1915; Fête, org, 1921; Org Sonata no.1, 1929; Suite, ww qnt, 1936; Alleluia-Toccata, 1949; Passacaglia on an Old Cambrian Bass, org, 1951; Requiescat in pace, org, 1955

VOCAL

Sacred choral (all with org): Mag and Nunc, D, S, T, B, SATB, 1910; By the Waters of Babylon (Ps cxxxvii), anthem, 1920; The Nightingale of Bethlehem (cant., F.H. Martens) S, A, B, SATB, 1920; The Lord is My Shepherd (Ps xxiii), anthem, S, SATB, 1926; Hark! A Thrilling Voice is Sounding (16th-century, trans. E. Caswall), anthem, 1958; Mass in Honor of St Mark, 1966

Secular choral: I Know a Maiden Fair to See (H.W. Longfellow), madrigal, SATB, 1913; General William Booth Enters into Heaven (V. Lindsay), TTBB, tpt, trbn, perc, 2 pf/(pf, org), 1932; The World of Tomorrow (V. Hitchcock, rev. H. Thompson) (cant.), SATB, orch, 1938; Skyscraper Romance (A. Bonner) (cant.), S, B, SSA, pf, 1949; Chorus of Shepherds and Angels (W.H. Auden) (cant.), SSA, str orch, 1956

Solo (all 1v, pf): Transit (A.McC. Sholl), 1914; Evening (W. Griffith), 1919; The Victory Riders (T. Garrison), ballad, Bar, 1919; My Heart is Like a Sweet-Toned Lute (Martens), 1927; Uncertainty (M. Moore), 1945

MSS, diaries and memorabilia in *STO*

BIBLIOGRAPHY

H. James: *A Catalog of the Musical Works of Philip James (1890–1975)* (New York, 1980, suppl. Southampton, NY, 1984)

D. ROYCE BOYER

James, Rick [Johnson, James Ambrose] (*b* Buffalo, NY, 1 Feb 1948; *d* Burbank, CA, 6 Aug 2004). Singer, songwriter, multi-instrumentalist, and record producer. After growing up singing on street corners in Buffalo, New York, he fled to Toronto, Canada, to avoid the draft in 1964. Using the pseudonym Big Jimmie, he formed the group the Sailorboys with future members of Steppenwolf. The band changed its name to the Mynah Birds and released "Mynah Bird Hop/Mynah Bird Song" for Columbia Records Canada. After auditioning unsuccessfully in 1966 for Motown Records, the band re-formed, including Neil Young, and recorded an album. However, its release was canceled following disputes with their manager, who reported James absent without leave and he was briefly imprisoned.

James returned to Detroit, where he was hired by Motown Records as a songwriter and producer; he worked with Smokey Robinson and the Miracles, the Spinners, and Bobby Taylor and the Vancouvers, before leaving in 1968. After spending a decade as a journeyman bass player in Los Angeles and Toronto, he released his first album, *Come and Get it* (Motown, 1978). With James playing most instruments himself, it spanned the R&B hits "You and I" and "Mary Jane." Combining funk grooves and R&B harmonies with rock arrangements, it anticipated later styles of funk rock. His music ranged from hard, aggressive funk with gritty lyrics about everyday life to sweeter, romantic songs. The tour promoting the album also helped launch the career of its opening act, Prince.

James's next three albums were more modestly successful and included the hit "Bustin out of L Seven" (1979). In 1981 he became a pop star with *Street Songs*, which hit number three on the pop chart and number one on the R&B chart. Employing strident synthesizer sounds that evoked new wave and containing his most enduring songs, including "Super Freak," the album earned a Grammy nomination. MC Hammer subsequently appropriated "Super Freak" for the international hit "U can't touch this" (1989), precipitating a lawsuit that was settled by giving James a co-composer credit and his only Grammy Award.

James continued working as a writer and producer, with Teena Marie, the Temptations, Robinson, and the actor Eddie Murphy, and created a band featuring his backup singers, the Mary Jane Girls. Cocaine abuse and accompanying sexual violence compromised his health and led to his imprisonment several times between 1991 and 1996.

Releasing 13 albums and 28 hit singles, James contributed heavily to the development of funk; his music has been widely sampled by hip-hop artists and his flamboyant style made lasting impressions upon urban fashion.

BIBLIOGRAPHY

M. Barackman: "Rick James' Funky Realism," *Rolling Stone* (24 Jan 1980)

R. Vincent: *Funk: the Music, the People, and the Rhythm of the One* (New York, 1996)

Obituary: *New York Times* (26 Dec 2004)

LUKAS PEARSE

James, Skip [James, Nehemiah Curtis] (*b* Bentonia, MS, 9 June 1902; *d* Philadelphia, PA, 3 Oct 1969). Blues guitarist, pianist, singer, and composer. Often cited as the leading exponent of the "Bentonia school" of blues playing, James spent only a brief time in that community. He moved to Sidon in the Delta region of Mississippi at age twelve and ran away from home in his early teens, visiting Florida and Georgia. While still a teenager, he worked in manual labor jobs, but eventually learned he could earn more money from bootlegging and his guitar playing. In 1931 James auditioned for Jackson, Mississippi, talent scout H.C. Speir, who was impressed with the guitarist's songwriting and the haunting quality of his vocals. James was enlisted to travel to Grafton, Wisconsin, to record for the Paramount label. These 1931 recordings represent the core of James's legacy, marked by his distinctive guitar playing, which relied on open D-minor tuning, and the poetry of his artfully constructed songs, such as "Hard Time Killing Floor Blues" and "Devil Got My Woman." Paramount also allowed James to play piano on several tracks, and his percussive, self-taught approach to the instrument stands out as one of the most distinctive blues keyboard styles of the day.

The Paramount recordings did not sell well, although James's music clearly influenced other players, most notably Robert Johnson. James left music behind, was ordained a minister, and undertook a range of employments, including farming, cutting timber, tuning pianos, and driving a delivery truck. Three fans—John Fahey, Bill Barth, and Henry Vestine—traversed the state of Mississippi in 1964 in search of James, eventually tracking him down in a Tunica hospital. With their encouragement, he resumed his performing career and returned to the recording studio after a hiatus of more than three decades. His performance at the 1964 Newport Folk Festival caused a sensation and was followed by regular touring until shortly before James's death five years later. James's largest payday from this period, however, derived from royalties from his song "I'm So Glad," which was recorded by Eric Clapton and the rock trio Cream as part of their 1966 album *Fresh Cream*.

RECORDINGS

Skip James Today! (1988, Vanguard 79219); *She Lyin'* (1993, Genes 9901); *Complete Early Recordings* (1994, Yazoo 2009); *Rare and Unreleased* (1998, Vanguard 79715)

BIBLIOGRAPHY

S. Calt: *I'd Rather Be the Devil: Skip James and the Blues* (New York, 1994)

P. Guralnick: *Feel Like Going Home: Portraits in Blues and Rock and Roll* (New York, 1999)

TED GIOIA

Jamison, Judith (*b* Philadelphia, PA, 10 May 1943). Modern dancer, choreographer, and company director. She studied with Marion Cuyjet and at the Philadelphia

Dance Academy. There, Agnes de Mille saw her in a class and invited her to dance in her ballet *The Four Marys* (1965) for American Ballet Theater. Jamison moved to New York City, continued her training with several prominent ballet and modern dance teachers, and soon joined the Alvin Ailey company, where she remained as a principal dancer until 1980. Of her many roles, the most remarkable was *Cry* (1972; music by Alice Coltrane, Laura Nyro, and The Voices of East Harlem), a 15-minute solo that was Ailey's tribute to "black women everywhere, especially our mothers." After leaving the Ailey company, Jamison starred in Donald McKayle's *Sophisticated Ladies* (1981) on Broadway, formed her own company, and began to choreograph. Upon Ailey's death in 1989, she was appointed artistic director of the Alvin Ailey American Dance Theater. Among her works for the company are *Divining* (1984; music by Kimati Dinizulu and Monti Ellison), *Hymn* (1993; music by Robert Ruggeri, libretto by Anna Deavere Smith), *Reminiscin'* (2005; music by various jazz artists), and *Among Us (Private Spaces: Public Places)* (2009; music by Eric Robert Lewis).

BIBLIOGRAPHY

O. Maynard: *Judith Jamison: Aspects of a Dancer* (New York, 1982)
J. Jamison: *Dancing Spirit* (New York, 1993)

CLAUDE CONYERS

Jam session [Jam]. An informal gathering of jazz or rock or other improvisational musicians playing for their own pleasure. Jam sessions originated in the 1930s as spontaneous diversions among jazz musicians, free from the constraints of professional engagements; they also served the function of training young musicians in a musical tradition that was not formally taught and accepted in music schools and academic institutions until the 1960s. In the late 1930s jam sessions came to be organized by entrepreneurs for audiences; this undermined their original purpose, and by the 1950s true jam sessions were becoming increasingly rare. However, in the 1970s and 1980s jam sessions made a comeback among younger jazz musicians, especially those trained in conservatories. The loft scene of the late 1970s, so-called because of its establishment of abandoned lofts as concert venues in the Village in New York, can also be seen as a quasi-commercial offshoot of the jam session. The idea of a jam session, or simply jamming, has come to mean any meeting of musicians, in private or public, where the emphasis is on unrehearsed material and improvisation.

BIBLIOGRAPHY

W.B. Cameron: "Sociological Notes on the Jam Session," *Social Forces*, xxxiii/2 (Dec 1954), 177–82
J.F. Behling: *Music Practices as Social Relations: Chicago Music Communities and the Everyday Significance of Playing Jazz* (diss., U. of Michigan, 2010)

GUNTHER SCHULLER/R

Jan and Dean. Rock-and-roll male vocal duo. The singer, songwriter, and producer Jan Berry (*b* Los Angeles, CA, 3 April 1941; *d* Brentwood, CA, 26 March 2004) had his first success with the singer Arnie Ginsberg in the hit song, "Jennie Lee" (1958) which was recorded in Berry's garage. He then formed a permanent partnership with the singer Dean Torrence (*b* Los Angeles, CA, 10 March 1941), and until 1966, when Berry was disabled in an automobile accident, Jan and Dean represented rock and roll as mindless fun, following and exploiting every new pop trend; their songs were based on doo-wop harmony and celebrated aspects of southern Californian hedonism such as surfing ("Surf City," 1963, no.1) and fast cars ("Drag City," 1963, no.10). Although Berry's vocal abilities were not up to par and Torrence was little better, each managed to make at least one classic rock recording—Berry on Jan and Dean's brilliantly orchestrated melodrama "Dead Man's Curve" (1964, no.8) and Torrence as the (uncredited) lead singer on the Beach Boys' "Barbara Ann" (1966, no.2). The duo gave occasional reunion concerts in the late 1970s; they were the subject of *Dead Man's Curve*, a film made for television. From the 1980s until Berry's death, Jan and Dean performed their 1960s repertoire for a faithful nostalgic national audience.

SELECTED RECORDINGS

Jennie Lee (Arwin, 1958); *Baby Talk* (Dore, 1959); *Heart and Soul* (Challenge, 1961); *Surf City* (Liberty, 1963); *Drag City* (Liberty, 1963); *Dead Man's Curve/The New Girl in School* (Liberty, 1964;); *The Little Old Lady from Pasadena* (Liberty, 1964); *Jan and Dean Meet Batman* (Liberty, 1966)

BIBLIOGRAPHY

D. Marsh: liner notes, *Jan and Dean Anthology Album* UA (1971)
P. Morantz: "The Road Back from Dead Man's Curve," *Rolling Stone* (12 Sept 1974)
B. Greene: *When we Get to Surf City: a Journey through America in Pursuit of Rock and Roll, Friendship, and Dreams* (New York, 2009)

GREIL MARCUS/MICKEY VALLEY

Jane's Addiction. Rock band. It was formed in Los Angeles in 1985 by the singer Perry Farrell (Peretz Bernstein; *b* New York, NY, 29 March 1959), who named the group for the heroin addiction of his housemate. While Farrell embodied theatrical hedonism, the guitarist Dave (Michael) Navarro (*b* Santa Monica, CA, 7 June 1967) gave the band a harder psychedelic rock sound, and the bass player Eric (Adam) Avery (*b* Los Angeles, CA, 25 April 1965) and the drummer Stephen (Andrew) Perkins (*b* Los Angeles, CA, 13 Sept 1967) added dashes of funk to the mix. Following a live album with the independent label XXX Records, Jane's Addiction signed with Warner Bros. to release their first studio album, *Nothing's Shocking* (WB, 1988), and its follow-up, *Ritual de lo habitual* (WB, 1990). In the summer of 1991 Farrell organized the LOLLAPALOOZA festival that featured a musical lineup of alternative rock, industrial, and hip-hop artists but also created a vaudevillian environment that incorporated everything from freak shows to political activism. Jane's Addiction broke up at the end of the first Lollapalooza tour, but have since reunited to tour and record new material (1997, 2002–04, and after a tour with Nine Inch Nails, 2009).

Singer Perry Farrell and bassist Chris Chaney, members of Jane's Addiction, 2003. (Reuters/Ethan Miller/Landov)

BIBLIOGRAPHY

B. Mullen: *Whores: an Oral History of Perry Farrell and Jane's Addiction* (New York, 2005)

D. Navarro (with N. Strauss): *Don't Try this at Home: a Year in the Life of Dave Navarro* (New York, 2005)

RYAN MOORE

Jang, Jon (*b* CA, 11 March 1954). Jazz pianist and composer. A central figure in the Asian American jazz movement, he has made numerous recordings on such political themes as anti-Asian violence, Japanese American reparations, and workers' rights. In addition to leading his own groups, he has recorded and performed extensively with Anthony Brown, Mark Izu, David Murray, James Newton, Max Roach, and Francis Wong. As a co-founder of ASIAN IMPROV RECORDS, he has helped to establish and document the music of other Asian American musicians.

After earning a piano performance degree from Oberlin Conservatory in 1978, Jang concentrated his efforts on political work and union organizing. After attending the first Asian American Jazz Festival in San Francisco in 1981, however, he found himself called back to music. His early recordings, such as *Are you Chinese or Charlie Chan?* (1983, RPM) and *The Ballad or the Bullet?* (1988, Asian Improv), reflect themes of self-empowerment and political struggle central to the Asian American movement of the 1980s. Around 1995 Jang's focus shifted towards a musical engagement with Chinese American history. His work *Island: the Immigrant Suite No.2* (1996) drew inspiration from the Chinese experience at San Francisco Bay's Angel Island Immigration Station, and his programmatic composition *Chinese American Symphony* (2007) portrayed the difficult experience of Chinese immigrant railroad workers in the 1860s.

Over the course of his career, Jang has sought to deepen his interest in traditional Chinese musics, coining the phrase "paper songs" to describe his Americanized Chinese musical material. Jang's arrangement of the "Butterfly Lovers Song" (1994) and his composition "Two Flowers on a Stem" (1995) feature improvisation, pentatonic scales, and percussive octave trills on the piano meant to evoke the *yanqin*, a Chinese hammered dulcimer. Jang has also worked to forge connections between Asian American and African American communities through music. In 2000 he and Newton teamed up to compose and perform *When Sorrow Turns to Joy*, a musical tribute to Paul Robeson and Mei Lanfang. In 2011 he and Marcus Shelby co-led Meditations on Integration, a celebration of peace and progress between the Chinese American and African American communities.

LOREN KAJIKAWA

Janis [née Bierbower], **Elsie (Jane)** (*b* Columbus, OH, 16 March 1889; *d* Beverly Hills, CA, 26 Feb 1956). Actress, singer, songwriter, and entertainer. Her stage career began when she was just a child and was promoted tirelessly by her mother, Jennie Cockrell Bierbower, a woman whose own theatrical aspirations had been thwarted. Janis's first roles on the stage were with the Ohio Valentine Stock Company in 1897. Her career in vaudeville lasted into the 1920s, and the format of her act varied little. She opened with a song and then moved through imitations of popular stars of the period; her imitations varied from year to year and included a wide range of celebrities including Weber and Fields, Lillian Russell, Pat Rooney, Anna Held, Ethel Barrymore, Alla Nazimova, Fanny Brice, and George M. Cohan. By the 1920s she had begun to move into musical comedy and revue.

Janis was a tireless supporter of the troops during World War I and traveled to France and England to entertain them. She found equal popularity with English and French audiences. After her mother's death in 1930, Janis's career lost focus and the fading star did not work regularly on the stage. She found work as a scriptwriter for the film industry and wrote lyrics for several songs that appeared in Paramount films. She was also periodically hired to work on radio shows for NBC and ABC. She married Gilbert Wilson, 16 years her junior, in 1931. The marriage was not successful, and they quickly separated although they never divorced. Janis died of cancer at the age of 67.

WORKS
(selective list)
SONGS

I'd rather love what I cannot have (than have what I cannot love), 1911; Anti Rag-time Girl, 1913; I never knew (music by I. Berlin), 1919; Love (your spell is everywhere) (music by E. Goulding), 1929; Anytime's the time to fall in love, I'm true to the navy now, Paramount on Parade, What did Cleopatra Say (all music by J. King), 1930 [from the film revue Paramount on Parade]

BIBLIOGRAPHY

Who's Who on the Stage, 1908: the Dramatic Reference Book and Biographical Dictionary of the Theatre (New York, 1908)

The American Stage of To-day: Biographies and Photographs of One Hundred Leading Actors and Actresses (New York, 1910)

R.A. Schanke: "Elsie Janis: a Comfortable Goofiness," *Passing Performances: Queer Readings of Leading Players in American Theater History* (Ann Arbor, MI, 1998), 151–72

GILLIAN M. RODGER

Janis [Yanks, Yankelevitch], **Byron** (*b* McKeesport, PA, 24 March 1924). Pianist. He studied with the pianist ADELE MARCUS, then attended the Juilliard School, where he worked with JOSEF LHÉVINNE and ROSINA LHÉVINNE. In 1943 he made his orchestral debut with Frank Black and the NBC SO in Rachmaninoff's Piano Concerto no.2. The following year he played the same work with the Pittsburgh SO conducted by Lorin Maazel; VLADIMIR HOROWITZ was in the audience and offered to teach Janis, who worked with him for three years. After his Carnegie Hall debut in 1948, Janis appeared with the world's leading orchestras and as a recitalist, making many tours, including an outstandingly successful one of the USSR in 1960. On his return to the United States he celebrated the 150th anniversary of Liszt's birth by performing both of Liszt's piano concertos with Charles Münch and the Boston SO in Boston and New York. His career was interrupted by illness in the 1960s but he began to make regular appearances again in 1972. He continued to pursue his concert career with notable success despite the onset the following year of arthritis, which affected his hands and wrists. He played at the White House in 1985 and the same year was made Ambassador for the Arts of the National Arthritis Foundation. Janis was a keen advocate of Louis Moreau Gottschalk before that composer's music became fashionable, but he remains best known in the repertory from Rachmaninoff to Prokofiev. He has also composed popular songs, ballads, and music for film and television. In 1967 at the Château de Thoiry, Yvelines, Janis discovered autograph manuscripts of two Chopin waltzes (G♭, op.70 no.1, of which no autograph had

previously been known, and E♭, op.18), then two variant autographs of the same waltzes in the Yale University library in 1973; a film entitled *Frederic Chopin: a Voyage with Byron Janis* relates his French discoveries. Having made no recordings since the age of 30, Janis returned to the studio in 1996 to make a Chopin recording for EMI. He was the first American to win a Grand Prix du Disque, and he also received a Harriet Cohen International Music Award. In 1965 the French government bestowed upon him the rank of Chevalier in the Ordre des arts et des lettres, the first American pianist to be so honored. In 2010 he published *Chopin and Beyond: my Extraordinary Life in Music and the Paranormal* (Hoboken, NJ).

MICHAEL STEINBERG/ANYA LAURENCE

Janssen, Werner (*b* New York, NY, 1 June 1899; *d* Stony Brook, NY, 19 Sept 1990). Conductor and composer. He studied with PHILIP GREELEY CLAPP at Dartmouth College (BMus 1921, honorary DMus 1935) and with FREDERICK SHEPHERD CONVERSE, Arthur Friedheim, and GEORGE WHITEFIELD CHADWICK at the New England Conservatory. Subsequently he was a conducting pupil of Weingartner in Basel (1920–21) and of Hermann Scherchen in Strasbourg (1921–5). He received a fellowship from the Juilliard Music Foundation and the Rome Prize, which took him to the St. Cecilia Conservatory for orchestration studies with Ottorino Respighi (1930–33). His formal creative work received some impetus from the success of his work *Kaleidoscope* for string quartet in Rome (1930). His international reputation was established when he conducted an all-Sibelius concert in Helsinki (1934); the composer himself declared the performances definitive, and Janssen was awarded the Order of the White Rose for his services to Finnish music. During the 1934–5 season he became the first native New Yorker to conduct the New York PO. He later held appointments as music director of the Baltimore SO (1937–9), the Janssen SO of Los Angeles (1940–52, which he founded for the performance of new works), the Utah SO (1946–7), the Portland SO (OR, 1947–9), and the San Diego SO (1952–4); he also conducted major orchestras throughout the world.

In addition to his classical career, Janssen worked in both American musical theater and film. In the 1920s he played piano in New York cabaret theaters and composed for several musical shows on Broadway including *Love Dreams* (1921), *Letty Pepper* (1922), *Ziegfeld Follies of 1925* (1925), *Lady Butterfly* (1923), *Nic Nax of 1926* (1926), and *Boom Boom* (1929). He later scored Hollywood films across a wide range of genres including *The General Died at Dawn* (1936), *Blockade* (1938), *Winter Carnival* (1939), *Eternally Yours* (1939), *Slightly Honorable* (1939), *The House across the Bay* (1940), *Guest in the House* (1944), *The Southerner* (1945), *Captain Kidd* (1945), *A Night in Casablanca* (1946), *Ruthless* (1948), and *Uncle Vanya* (1957). In total his film scores received five Academy Award nominations. Janssen wrote the music for the wartime documentary *Lights Out in Europe* (1940). He also wrote the score and appeared in the Musicolor documentary short film

Enchanted Lake (1947), conducting the Janssen SO. In general his music incorporates descriptive effects and the idioms of jazz, which he considered modern folk music, within traditional structures.

BIBLIOGRAPHY
A. Johnston: "Profiles: American Maestro," *New Yorker* (20 Oct, 27 Oct 1934)
Obituary, *New York Times* (21 Sept 1990)

GUSTAVE REESE/BARBARA A. RENTON/
IAN BROOKES

Japanese American music. *See* ASIAN AMERICAN MUSIC.

Jaques-Dalcroze, Emile (*b* Vienna, Austria, 6 July 1865, *d* Geneva, Switzerland, 1 July 1950). Swiss educator and composer. He created the Dalcroze Eurhythmics method of music education. The three-part approach—rhythmic movement, solfège, and piano improvisation—focuses on the use of the body to comprehend and express musical energy in all its forms. Based on the idea that the body's automatic processes are inherently rhythmic, Eurhythmics uses the kinesthetic experience of musical energy to explore concepts both basic (e.g., tempo and dynamics) and complex (e.g., unequal beats, phrasing, and nuance). The approach stresses aural and physical experiences of music as precursors to written notation or instrumental study. Classes feature rhythmic and expressive movement, singing, and improvisation, the last of these practiced not only by the students but also by the teacher, who accompanies class activities with music improvised at the piano. Working with the psychologist Édouard Claparède, Jaques-Dalcroze broadened his educational theories to apply to students' development outside the musical sphere. His major pedagogical writings include *La rhythme, la musique et l'éducation* (Paris, 1920; Eng. trans. 1921) and *Eurhythmics, Art, and Education* (ed. C. Cox, London, 1930; essays written 1922–5, trans. by F. Rothwell). His ideas spread worldwide during the mid-1910s. In the United States, Dalcroze Eurhythmics has been most widely known as an educational method for children, either in dedicated Eurhythmics classes or as one component in an eclectic music curriculum (generally alongside the methods of Orff and Kodály). Into the 21st century it is still taught at various universities and conservatories and in teacher certification programs throughout the country.

BIBLIOGRAPHY
GMO
M.-L. Bachmann: *La rhythmique Jaques-Dalcroze: une education par la musique et pour la musique* (Neuchâtel, 1984; Eng. trans., 1991)
I. Spector: *Rhythm and Life: the Work of Emile Jaques-Dalcroze* (Stuyvesant, NY, 1990)
S.F. Moore: *The Writings of Emile Jaques-Dalcroze: toward a Theory for the Performance of Musical Rhythm* (diss., Indiana U., 1992)
J.T. Caldwell: *Expressive Singing: Dalcroze Eurhythmics for Voice* (Englewood Cliffs, NJ, 1995)

NICOLE M. BROCKMANN

Jara (Martínez), Víctor (Lidio) (*b* Chillán Viejo, Chile, 28 Sept 1932; *d* Santiago, Chile, 16 Sept 1973). Chilean protest singer and guitarist. The son of agricultural laborers, he was raised in rural Chile and in the peripheral communities of peasant migrants to Santiago. His mother, a gifted traditional singer and guitarist, was his principal musical influence. Although he initiated studies in accounting and in the seminary, Jara completed programs in theater at the University of Chile and enjoyed a successful career during the 1950s and 1960s; he received numerous national and international honors for his achievements as a director.

Parallel to his theatrical pursuits, Jara participated in the burgeoning youth folk-music scene of the mid-20th century as a core member of the ensemble Cuncumén. Along with Patricio Manns and Ángel and Isabel Parra, he also performed his own songs at the Peña de los Parra and campaigned in support of candidates of the Unidad Popular. After a series of successful solo albums in the late 1960s, Jara devoted most of his time to his music career and political activism. Shortly after the coup d'état in Chile in 1973, Jara was detained, tortured, and killed by military forces. His songs, including "Plegaria a un labrador," "El aparecido," and "Te recuerdo Amanda," are considered anthems of the *nueva canción* movement, and his legacy of compassionate and committed art has continued to be memorialized in performance by artists in Latin America and beyond.

BIBLIOGRAPHY
GMO
J. Jara: *Víctor: an Unfinished Song* (London, 1998)
R. Acevedo and others: *Víctor Jara: Obra musical completa* (Santiago, Chile, 2/1999)

EMILY PINKERTON

Jarana. A regional dance from the Yucatán peninsula in Mexico. It originated in the 18th century and contains Spanish as well as pre-Hispanic elements associated with the Maya. Performed during hacienda celebrations, it has historically been linked to *la vaquería* (cattle fiesta), an event popular among the regional criollo population. *Jarana* performance also became part of Catholic festivities associated with patron saints and, in some communities, with Christmas ceremonies.

In terms of tempo, there is a slow, waltz-like *jarana* in 3/4 time and a quicker version in 6/8. Similarities exist with the Spanish *jota* and *fandango*. However, Mayan influence is evident in the song titles and lyrics which refer to the natural world. The modern *jarana* music ensemble has typically included wind, brass, and percussion instruments. In terms of dance attire, women have worn elegant regional costumes. For men, traditional dress has included a white, long-sleeved cotton shirt, white pants, and a white Panama hat.

The term "*jarana*" also refers to a medium-sized instrument of the guitar family, most frequently with five double courses of strings. Presumably the instrument's name arose from its association with the Yucatán dance. The instrument is characteristically used by *son jarocho* ensembles by Mexican American musicians.

BIBLIOGRAPHY
M. Jardow-Pedersen: "La música maya: producción del significado musical en el oriente del estado de Yucatán," *Sabiduría Popular*, ed. A. Chamorro (Mexico City, 1997)

R. Loewe: "Euphemism, Parody, Insult, and Innuendo: Rhetoric and Ethnic Identity at the Mexican Periphery," *Journal of American Folklore*, cxx (2007), 284–307

E.THOMAS STANFORD/DONALD A. HENRIQUES

Jarboro, Caterina [Yarborough, Katherine] (*b* Wilmington, NC, 24 July 1903; *d* New York, NY, 13 Aug 1986). Soprano. After leaving school she went to New York in 1916. She began her stage career singing and playing the trombone in all-black musical comedies, Sissle and Blake's *Shuffle Along* (1921) and James P. Johnson's *Runnin' Wild* (1923). She subsequently went to study in Europe (late 1920s) and made her debut in Milan at the Teatro Puccini as Aida (1930–31). She sang in France, Poland, and Switzerland, adding the title roles of Gounod's *La reine de Saba* and Meyerbeer's *L'Africaine* to her repertory before returning to the United States, where she sang Aida in Chicago and New York (at the Hippodrome, with Jules Bledsoe as Amonasro). After several further years in Europe, based in Belgium, she eventually settled in New York, where she gave her first recital at Town Hall (16 January 1942); it included arias by Piccinni, Gluck, Weber, and Wagner. She continued to sing in recital until the early 1950s. Jarboro appears to have been the first African American singer to have achieved a significant career on the opera stage. "A beautiful woman," wrote Virgil Thomson (*New York Herald-Tribune*, 17 January 1942), "superb of presence, gifted with a lyrico-dramatic voice handsome in range and quality, she is also the possessor of a truly great dramatic temperament."

BIBLIOGRAPHY

SouthernB

W. Bolcom and R. Kimball: *Reminiscing with Sissle and Blake* (New York, 1973)

A.F. Block and C.N. Bates: *Women in American Music* (Westport, CT, 1979)

J. Gray: *Blacks in Classical Music* (Westport, CT, 1988)

PATRICK O'CONNOR

Jardine, George (*b* Dartford, England, 1 Nov 1800; *d* New York, NY, 12 Feb 1882). English organ builder, naturalized American. He apprenticed in London with Flight & Robson and Joseph W. Walker and immigrated to New York in 1837 with his wife, four children, and a nephew, Frederick Wincott Jardine, who was also his apprentice. He worked briefly for FIRTH, HALL & POND before establishing his own workshop, where he began building small chamber and church organs, some of which were playable from either a keyboard or a barrel, patterned after those made by Flight & Robson. One of these, built in 1842, is still extant in the small Episcopal Church in Pierrepont Manor, NY. His first church organ is said to have been built for St. James's Church in New York, and in 1841 he built a good-sized two-manual organ for Chelsea Presbyterian Church there. In 1843 his nephew Frederick, having completed his apprenticeship, returned to England, where he eventually founded the firm of Kirtland & Jardine, but by this time some of George's sons were beginning to enter the workshop as apprentices, and Jardine's business was expanding. In 1845 a large

organ was built for the Franklin Street Reformed Church, but two years later his factory was destroyed by fire. Jardine seems to have quickly recovered and by the 1850s was building substantial organs such as the instrument in the First Presbyterian Church in Rome, NY (1853), and that for Christ Methodist Church, Pittsburgh (1854).

Around 1860 George's eldest son Edward (1830–96) became a partner under the company name of Jardine & Son, and by 1869 the firm had built more than 300 organs. Some of these, such as the large instrument for St. John's Church in Ogdensburg, NY (1864), and that built for St. George's Church, New York (1870), were showing European tonal influences, presumably due to trips made to the continent by Edward. Composition pedals, reverse-fold reservoirs, and radiating pedal sharps also appeared in this period. The organ for Fifth Avenue Presbyterian Church (1875) boasted a water motor, pneumatic action assistance, and three different wind pressures. In 1871 control of the company had largely passed to Edward, and George formally retired in 1880. After his death interest in the company was passed on to his three surviving sons and two grandsons, and they continued to build a good number of organs through the 1880s and into the 1890s, among them a large four-manual organ for Brooklyn Tabernacle (1890). In 1896, however, Edward and Joseph Jardine both died within days of each other, and although two grandsons tried to carry it on, the Jardine firm closed in 1899.

BIBLIOGRAPHY

B. Owen: "Hymn Tunes from an American Barrell-Organ of 1842," *The Hymn*, xi (1960), 69–73

E.A. Kraege: "The Early Organs of the Fifth Avenue Presbyterian Church," *The Tracker*, xviii/2 (1974), 3-10

J. Ogasapian: *Organ Building in New York City, 1700–1900* (Braintree, MA, 1977)

W.T. Van Pelt: "A Survey of Jardine Cases," *The Tracker*, xxvii/3 (1983), 6–10

P. Cameron: "Three Generations of Jardines," *The Tracker*, xxxi/2 (1987), 24–5

J.L. Speller: "Transatlantic Relations: the Jardine Connection," *The Organ*, lxxii (1992–3), 122–7

BARBARA OWEN

Jarecki, Tadeusz (*b* Lwów, Austria-Hungary [now Lviv, Ukraine], 1 Jan 1889; *d* New York, NY, 2 May 1955). Polish composer and conductor naturalized American. He studied with Stanisław Niewiadomski in Lwów, Sergey Ivanovich Taneyev in Moscow, and Emile Jaques-Dalcroze in Hellerau (1912–13), where he remained for some time as a teacher. In 1917 he moved to the United States and won first prize at the Berkshire Festival for his String Quartet op.16. After living in Poland for two years (1918–20) he settled in New York, where he worked first for NBC and then directed the Chamber Ensemble of New York with his wife, the soprano Louise Llewellyn (1889–1954), and Polgar. He was also active as a conductor. From 1932 to 1935, his last years in Poland, he directed the Stanisławów Musical Society and conducted the Lwów

SO. During World War II he was in Paris and London, where he formed the association the Musicians of Poland. He returned to New York in 1946 to continue his conducting and composing and to lecture at Columbia University. As a composer he drew directly on the harmonic and orchestral resources of Wagner and Strauss; his works include five symphonies, symphonic poems, and chamber music including three string trios and three string quartets. Most of his works were not published. He wrote a book on Chopin, which was published in 1949.

TERESA CHYLIŃSKA/R

Jarman, Joseph. Jazz musician and founding member of the ART ENSEMBLE OF CHICAGO.

Jarre, Maurice (Alexis) (*b* Lyons, France, 13 Sept 1924; *d* Malibu, CA, 28 March 2009). French composer. He studied engineering at the University of Lyons and at the Sorbonne, then attended the Paris Conservatoire, studying percussion with Passerone and composition with Honegger and Joseph Martenot, inventor of the ondes martenot. He served in the army during World War II, and in the late 1940s played percussion in the navy band, with the Orchestre Radio-Symphonique, and with the Compagnie Renaud-Barrault, where he became friends with Boulez and Delerue. When Jean Vilar became director of the Théâtre National Populaire, he made Jarre his musical director, resident composer, and conductor. In 1952 Georges Franju asked him to write the score for *Hôtel des invalides*. The film went on to become a minor classic, and Jarre turned henceforth almost exclusively to film music, writing scores for many French directors, including Jacques Demy, Alain Resnais, and Jean-Paul Rappeneau. His score for *Cybéle* (1961) brought him to the attention of American producer Sam Spiegel, which led to Jarre's first Hollywood scores: *The Crack in the Mirror* (1960), *The Big Gamble* (1961), and *The Longest Day* (1962). In 1962, David Lean commissioned the score for *Lawrence of Arabia*, originally to be co-written by Jarre, Khachaturian, and Britten. After the latter two dropped out, Richard Rogers was briefly considered, before the entire score was given to Jarre. Thus began a collaboration that would produce four films and three Academy Awards for the composer, for *Lawrence of Arabia*, *Doctor Zhivago* (1965), and *A Passage to India* (1984). After the immense success of *Lawrence of Arabia*, Jarre moved permanently to the United States, where he worked with some of the biggest directors in Hollywood, notably John Frankenheimer, Joseph Hardy, John Huston, Paul Mazursky, Alfred Hitchcock, and Peter Weir. But he never abandoned his European roots, scoring films for such luminaries as Luchino Visconti, Franco Zeffirelli, and Volker Schlöndorff. Jarre became, along with Delerue, France's most prominent and sought-after film composer of the second half of the 20th century. In addition to his three Academy Awards, he received Oscar nominations for his contributions to *Cybéle* (1961),

The Life and Times of Judge Roy Bean (1972), *Witness* (1985), *Gorillas in the Mist* (1988), and *Ghost* (1989). He received British Academy Awards for *Witness* and *Dead Poets Society* (1989), and a special César Award in 1985. He was the father of the composer Jean-Michel Jarre.

Jarre wrote more than 180 scores for film and television, as well as ballets, orchestral works, incidental music, and operas. His early concert music reflected his interest in 12-note composition, in contrast to the more popular style of his theater works, of which the ballet *Notre Dame de Paris*, written in 1964 for the Paris Opéra, was the most successful. Jarre's earlier film scores use sparse, chamber music scoring, for example in *Cybèle*, written for double bass, zither, and flute. His eight scores for the poignant films of Franju were subtle but evocative. Once in Hollywood, however, he preferred a richer, more symphonic style, using full orchestral forces. A ceaseless experimenter, he took advantage of the exotic locations and subjects of Lean's films: the sweeping score for *Lawrence of Arabia* made extensive use of chromatic modes and wide interval leaps to evoke immense panoramas, and included in its scoring the ondes martenot, an instrument not used before in an American film. *Doctor Zhivago*'s melancholy score suggests the influence of composers such as Borodin, and makes use of the balalaika, as well as Russian folksongs and modes. For the score of *Ryan's Daughter* (1970), however, Jarre and director Lean decided against the evocation of traditional Irish music. His scores for Luchino Visconti's *La caduta degli dei* (1969) and Volker Schlöndorff's *Die Blechtrommel* (1979) both use an orchestra made up entirely of cellos and double basses, augmented only by human whistling and the fujara, a Slovakian folk instrument. In the 1980s Jarre became interested in blending electronic sounds with those of traditional orchestral and occasionally non-Western instruments, often by means of digital sampling techniques. His most successful film scores involving electronics are *Witness* (1985), which required only five performers to evoke the early American feel of the Amish community; and *The Year of Living Dangerously* (1982), a subdued, evocative score that makes use of traditional Javanese gamelan. In *Jacob's Ladder* (1990), he again attempted a score that was "atmospheric rather than thematic," making use, alongside electronics, of Indian instruments and a Bulgarian women's chorus.

WORKS

FILM SCORES
(English-language films only)
The Big Gamble, 1961; The Longest Day, 1962; Lawrence of Arabia, 1962; The Train, 1964; Behold a Pale Horse, 1964; Doctor Zhivago, 1965; The Collector, 1965; The Professionals, 1966; Grand Prix, 1966; The Night of the Generals, 1966; Gambit, 1966; Barbarella, 1967; The Extraordinary Seaman, 1968; The Fixer, 1968; Five Card Stud, 1968; Villa Rides, 1968; Isadora, 1968; Topaz, 1969; The Only Game in Town, 1969; Plaza Suite, 1970; Ryan's Daughter, 1970; Pope Joan, 1972; The Life and Times of Judge Roy Bean, 1972; The Effect of Gamma Rays on Man-in-the-Moon Marigolds, 1972; The

Mackintosh Man, 1973; Ash Wednesday, 1973; Mrs. Uschyck, 1973; The Island at the Top of the World, 1973; Mr. Sycamore, 1974; Posse, 1975; Mandingo, 1975; Great Expectations, 1975; The Silence, 1975; The Man Who Would Be King, 1975; Shout at the Devil, 1976; The Last Tycoon, 1976; The Prince and the Pauper, 1977; March or Die, 1977; Two Solitudes, 1978; The Users, 1978; Mourning Becomes Electra, 1978; One of a Kind, 1978; Ishi, the Last of His Tribe, 1978; The Black Marble, 1979; Magician of Lublin, 1979; The American Success Company, 1979; Winter Kills, 1979; Lion of the Desert, 1980; The Last Flight of Noah's Ark, 1980; Resurrection, 1980; Enola Gay: The Men, the Mission, the Atomic Bomb, 1980; Taps, 1981; Shogun, 1981; Chu Chu and the Philly Flash, 1981; Firefox, 1982; Coming Out of the Ice, 1982; Young Doctors in Love, 1982; The Year of Living Dangerously, 1982; Don't Cry, It's Only Thunder, 1982; Samson and Delilah, 1983; Top Secret!, 1983; A Passage to India, 1984; The Sky's No Limit, 1984; Dreamscape, 1984; Mad Max: Beyond Thunderdome, 1985; Enemy Mine, 1985; The Bride, 1985; The Mosquito Coast, 1985; Witness, 1985; Apology, 1986; Tai-Pan, 1986; Solarbabies, 1986; Julia and Julia, 1987; No Way Out, 1987; Fatal Attraction, 1987; Gaby—A True Story, 1987; Gorillas in the Mist, 1988; Buster, 1988; The Murder of Mary Phagan, 1988; Wildfire, 1988; Moon Over Parador, 1988; Distant Thunder, 1988; Chances Are, 1989; Prancer, 1989; Enemies, A Love Story, 1989; Dead Poets Society, 1989; After Dark, My Sweet, 1990; Jacob's Ladder, 1990; Solar Crisis, 1990; Ghost, 1990; Almost An Angel, 1990; Fires Within, 1991; Only The Lonely, 1991; School Ties, 1992; Shadow of the Wolf, 1992; Mr. Jones, 1993; Fearless, 1993; A Walk In The Clouds, 1995; The Sunchaser, 1996; The Mirror Has Two Faces, 1996; Sunshine, 1999; I Dreamed of Africa, 2000; Uprising, 2001

BIBLIOGRAPHY

J. Burlingame, "Maurice Jarre," *The Cue Sheet*, xiii/3 (July 1997), 21–26

J. Westby: "Film scores of Maurice Jarre," *The Cue Sheet*, xiii/3 (July 1997), 27–34

MARK BRILL

Jarreau, Al(win Lopez) (*b* Milwaukee, WI, 12 March 1940). Singer. He was born into a large, musical family and began singing at the age of four. By the time he attended Ripon College, he was regularly appearing with a vocal quartet called the Indigos. After graduating in 1962, he moved to San Francisco, where he continued to sing as a side interest while pursuing a career as a rehabilitation counselor. After a brief time with George Duke's jazz trio, he connected with the guitarist Julio Martinez and received so much attention that he decided to pursue music as a career. While playing in small clubs like Dino's and the Bitter End, Jarreau and Martinez landed television spots on *The Tonight Show* and *The Merv Griffin Show*. Jarreau began performing in New York, which led to Warner Bros. signing him in 1975. His debut album, *We Got By* (1975, WB), was hailed as a major achievement by fans and critics alike. Although *This Time* (1980) hit the top spot on the jazz charts, Jarreau's biggest early success came with *Breakin' Away* (1981, WB), which reached number nine on the pop charts and topped the jazz and R&B charts; the album included the popular single "We're in this Love Together." His smooth and entrancing voice is well matched to the lyrically rich material provided by the songwriter Bill Withers, who wrote many of Jarreau's songs. Jarreau continued to record regularly throughout the 1980s and toured extensively in the 1990s and 2000s. The winner of seven Grammy awards, he became the first to win in three separate categories: pop, jazz, and R&B.

BIBLIOGRAPHY

J. Scheytt: *Al Jarreau: Studien seiner Entwicklung vom Jazz zum Pop-interpreten* (Stuttgart, 2008)

JONAS WESTOVER

Jarrell, Tommy [Thomas Jefferson] (*b* Round Peak, nr Mount Airy, NC, 1 March 1901; *d* Mount Airy, 28 Jan 1985). Appalachian music fiddler, banjoist, and singer. He began performing as a fiddler and banjoist at an early age. He learned much of his vast repertory of traditional instrumental tunes, Baptist hymns, and ballads from his father, Ben Jarrell, who was known throughout the Blue Ridge Mountains as a fine fiddler. His musical style changed little over seven decades as a performer. Although Jarrell was well known and respected as a musician in his native Surry County, he did not receive widespread recognition until the 1970s, when he was sought by many young musicians as a mentor. He performed at the Festival of American Folklife organized by the Smithsonian Institution (1968, 1981, 1982, 1984) and played on many recordings, including his own album *Tommy Jarrell: Sail away Ladies* (County, 1976). He received the Brown-Hudson Folklore Award from the North Carolina Folklore Society in 1981 and a National Heritage Fellowship from the NEA in 1982.

BIBLIOGRAPHY

C. Conway: "Thomas Jefferson Jarrell," *North Carolina Folklore Journal*, xxx/1 (1982), 3

R. Alden: "Tommy Jarrell & Fred Cockerham," *Musical Traditions*, no.11 (1993); repr. <http://www.mustrad.org.uk/articles/jarrell.htm> (2012)

P. Anick: "An Afternoon with Tommy Jarrell, 1982," *Fiddler Magazine*, ii/1 (1995), 22–8

DANIEL SHEEHY/R

Jarrett, Keith (*b* Allentown, PA, 8 May 1945). Jazz pianist and composer. He began learning piano at the age of three, and by the time he was seven had presented a full recital and was composing and improvising. He played professionally throughout his elementary school years, performing at the Academy of Music in Philadelphia, and during his teens toured for one season as a piano soloist with Fred Waring's Pennsylvanians. He turned down an offer to study classical composition in Paris with Nadia Boulanger and instead chose to pursue jazz by working with Dave Brubeck, who was an early influence. In 1962 Jarrett moved to Boston where he spent a year on scholarship studying at the Berklee College of Music. He then began working in the Boston area with his own trio and with such visiting artists as Tony Scott and Roland Kirk. He moved to New York in 1965 but, having decided to avoid commercial work, was scarcely noticed until Art Blakey heard him during a jam session at the Village Vanguard. He joined Blakey's Jazz Messengers in December of that year and stayed with them for three months, gaining critical notice and making his first recording with an established group, *Buttercorn Lady* (Lml, 1966).

While a Jazz Messenger he attracted the attention of Jack DeJohnette who recommended him to the saxophonist Charles Lloyd, with whom Jarrett subsequently rose to international acclaim (1966–9). One of the first groups to explore a broad range of improvisational styles, Lloyd's quartet attracted a large youthful following extending as far as the USSR, where it toured in 1967; Jarrett's flawless technique, intense lyricism, and total physical involvement with the piano were among its strongest assets, as may be heard on the album *Forest Flower* (Atl., 1966). Jarrett also played soprano saxophone and percussion for Lloyd, a practice he has continued throughout his career. He recorded his first album as a leader, *Life between the Exit Signs* (Vortex, 1967), with Charlie Haden and Paul Motian. From 1970 to 1971 he worked with Miles Davis, first on electric organ while Chick Corea was playing electric piano (as on *Miles at Fillmore*, Col., 1970), then playing both instruments (*Live Evil*, Col., 1970) after Corea left the group. Jarrett made good use of Davis's frequent periods of inactivity to work and record further with his own band, which included Haden, Motian, and later Dewey Redman. This so-called American quartet had a fruitful performing and recording career until 1976. Although encompassing a much broader stylistic range, its music revealed a strong kinship with the earlier work of Bill Evans, Paul Bley, and Ornette Coleman.

Jarrett began a long and successful relationship with Manfred Eicher's ECM Records in 1971, when he made his first solo piano recording, *Facing You*. In 1972 he began performing solo concerts that consisted simply of two extended improvisations, each usually 30 to 45 minutes in length (for example, *Solo Concerts*, ECM, 1973). The music spanned a rich variety of traditions but was developed in a manner that seemed holistic rather than merely eclectic, illuminating Jarrett's reference to his work as universal folk music. Through the international success of these concerts he became the only jazz artist of the 1970s to capture a mass audience without conforming to commercial trends. His recording *The Köln Concert* (ECM, 1975) became one of jazz's best-selling albums, and Jarrett named his album *The Vienna Concert* (ECM, 1991) in the liner notes as his greatest achievement. Furthermore he spearheaded a revival of interest in acoustic music, having refused to play electronic instruments after he left Davis's band. His highly acclaimed European quartet with Jan Garbarek, Palle Danielsson, and Jon Christensen released four albums including *My Song* (ECM, 1977) and *Personal Mountains* (ECM, 1979). Beginning in the early 1980s Jarrett led a trio with Gary Peacock and Jack DeJohnette that has remained his primary working group. Inspired by Ahmad Jamal, their interpretive performances and recordings of standards have been among the most influential jazz of the late 20th and early 21st centuries. Jarrett suspended his touring when he was diagnosed with chronic fatigue disorder in the late 1990s but had returned to the stage by 2000 in both solo and trio formats. He has also been a frequent essayist and an outspoken critic of the neo-traditional jazz movement, in particular, the vision advocated by Wynton Marsalis and Jazz at Lincoln Center.

Avoiding easy categorization, Jarrett's projects have remained extremely varied. Chamber recordings *In the Light* (ECM, 1973), *Luminessence* (ECM, 1974), and *Arbour Zena* (ECM, 1975) explore classical styles and the fusion of composed works with improvisation. He has recorded solo improvisations on the pipe organ and works from the classical piano repertory, including Bach's *Wohltemperierte Clavier* and Goldberg Variations, selected Mozart piano concertos, Shostakovich's 24 Preludes and Fugues, and Barber's Piano Concerto. His own compositions include pieces for classical chamber groups, symphony orchestra, and orchestra with improvising soloists.

BIBLIOGRAPHY

J. Klee: "Keith Jarrett: Spontaneous Composer," *DB*, xxxix/1 (1972), 12

B. Palmer: "The Inner Octaves of Keith Jarrett," *DB*, xli/17 (1974), 16

J. Aikin: "Keith Jarrett," *Contemporary Keyboard*, v/9 (1979), 38

L. Lyons: "Keith Jarrett," *The Great Jazz Pianists: Speaking of their Lives and Music* (New York, 1983), 294–300

J. Rockwell: "Mystical Romanticism, Popularity and the Varied Forms of Fusion: Keith Jarrett," *All American Music: Composition in the Late Twentieth Century* (New York, 1983), 176–84

A. Lange: "Keith Jarrett," *DB*, li/6 (1984), 16 [interview]

U. Andresen: *Keith Jarrett: sein Leben, seine Musik, seine Schallplatten* (Gauting, 1985)

B. Doerschuk: "Keith Jarrett," *Keyboard*, xii/9 (1986), 80–103 [incl. discography]

I. Carr: *Keith Jarrett: the Man and his Music* (London, 1991)

B. Sidran: "Keith Jarrett," *Talking Jazz* (New York, 1995), 283–94

T. Moon: "Keith Jarrett: Order and Ordeal," *JT* (5/1999)

M. Nordal: "Keith Jarrett: Whisper Not," *JT* (2004)

D. Adler: "Keith Jarrett, Jack DeJohnette, and Gary Peacock: Standard Bearers," *JT* (2008)

D. Terefenko: *Keith Jarrett's Transformation of Standard Tunes: Theory, Analysis, and Pedagogy* (Saarbrücken, 2009)

Oral history material in *NEij*

BILL DOBBINS/BARRY LONG

Järvi, Neeme (*b* Tallinn, Estonia, 7 June 1937). Estonian conductor, naturalized American. He studied percussion and choral direction at the Tallinn Music School before taking his degree in conducting with Nicolai Rabinovich and Evgeny Mravinsky at the Leningrad Conservatory (1955–60). He made his debut in Tallinn in 1954 and began working there as percussionist in the Estonian State SO. He was subsequently the music director of this orchestra (1960–80) and of the Tallinn Opera (1966–79). He also formed the Chamber Orchestra of Tallinn, conducted opera and ballet in Moscow and Leningrad, and after winning first prize in the Accademia Nazionale di Santa Cecilia conducting competition in 1971 he began to appear elsewhere in Europe and in Canada, Mexico, and Japan. In 1979 he toured the United States, making his Metropolitan debut with Yevgeny Onegin and appearing with major American orchestras; he immigrated to the United States the following year. He continued to appear as a guest conductor with the New York PO, the Philadelphia Orchestra, and the Boston SO, among others, before serving as the principal guest conductor of the CBSO (1981–4). After conducting *Salome* at the Swedish Royal Opera he was the principal conductor of the Göteborg SO (1982–2004), principal conductor of the Royal Scottish National Orchestra in Glasgow (1984–8), and music director of the Detroit SO (1990–2005). In 2005 he was appointed music director of the New Jersey SO and in 2010 the music director of the Estonian National SO. Järvi has conducted all the major orchestras in Europe and America and has kept up an active career in the studio, making more than 400 albums. His repertory is centered on Slavonic and Scandinavian composers, including Sibelius, Prokofiev, Dvořák, and Martinů, and he has been a champion for Berwald, Gade, Svendsen, Stenhammar, Tubin, and Maximilian Steinberg; he has also conducted the premieres of many works by Tubin and Arvo Pärt. He gave the Soviet premieres of *Porgy and Bess, Der Rosenkavalier*, and *Il turco in Italia*. His interests, however, have ranged wide and he has been able to give a solid account of anything that has come his way. Järvi's enterprising recordings of rare American music have had a beneficial effect on concert programming throughout the United States. His conducting is particularly admired for its warmth and lyrical line. He became an American citizen in 1987 and is a Knight of the Order of the Polar Star in Sweden.

JOSÉ A. BOWEN/R

Järvi, Paavo (*b* Talinn, Estonia, 30 Dec 1962). Conductor of Estonian birth, naturalized American. The son of NEEME JÄRVI, he studied percussion and conducting at the Talinn Music School before moving to the United States in 1980 to continue his studies at the Curtis Institute (graduating in 1988) and with LEONARD BERNSTEIN at the Los Angeles Philharmonic Institute. He became a US citizen in 1985. Järvi was music director of the Malmö SO (1993–7) and principal guest conductor of the Royal Stockholm PO (1995–8) and the CBSO (1996–9). He has also appeared as guest conductor with other leading orchestras in Europe and the United States, including the Orchestre de Paris, the LSO, the Berlin PO, the Czech PO, the Philharmonia, the Concertgebouw (with whom he conducted the premiere of Aulis Sallinen's Eighth Symphony in 2004), the Israel PO, the Boston SO, the Los Angeles PO, the New York Philharmonic, and the Chicago SO.

In 2001 Järvi became music director of the Cincinnati SO, which he brought to a new level of excellence through a series of enterprising programs and recordings. A renowned champion of Estonian composers (notably Arvo Pärt, Eduard Tubin, Lepo Sumera, and Erkki-Sven Tüür), he was appointed artistic adviser to the Estonian National SO in 2002. In 2004 he became artistic director of the Deutsche Kammerphilharmonie, leading the ensemble in acclaimed performances and recordings of Ludwig van Beethoven's symphonies between 2007 and 2010. Since the 2006–7 season, he has been music director of the Frankfurt Radio SO. In 2010–11 he became music director of the Orchestre de Paris. He announced his retirement from his post at the Cincinnati SO, effective May 2011. He has also worked with youth orchestras, including the European Union

Youth Orchestra (with whom he toured the Baltic states in 2004), the Gustav Mahler CO, and the Russian-American Youth Orchestra. In 2003 he made his Italian opera debut conducting *Fidelio* at the Florence Maggio Musicale. Järvi's wide-ranging list of recordings includes works by Hector Berlioz, Claude Debussy, Maurice Ravel, Sergey Prokofiev, Igor Stravinsky, Strauss, Pärt, Tüür, and Tubin, and an award-winning disc of Jean Sibelius's cantatas with the Estonian National SO.

RICHARD WIGMORE/CHRISTINA TAYLOR GIBSON

Jarvinen, Arthur (*b* Ilwaco, WA, 27 Jan 1956; *d* Los Angeles, CA, 2 Oct 2010). Composer and performer. Originally trained as a percussionist, he studied at Ohio University in Athens, Ohio (BM 1978), and at the California Institute for the Arts (MFA 1981), where his teachers included John Bergamo, Ruth Underwood, and Karen Ervin (percussion) and STEPHEN MOSKO, MORTON SUBOTNICK, and EARLE BROWN (composition). In 1981, he began teaching at CalArts and co-founded the CALIFORNIA E.A.R. UNIT; he also performed with the Antenna Repairmen percussion trio and his ensemble Some Over History.

Jarvinen was the West Coast's most prominent practitioner of the Totalist phenomenon, a minimalist-derived movement of composers creating music accessible to wide audiences but full of complex structures for the initiated. His music, mostly for small instrumental ensembles featuring percussion, elegantly combined experimental techniques and intricate rhythmic structures with timbres that grew out of his involvement with rock and blues. In *Murphy-Nights* (1989), scored for synthesizer, bass, baritone sax, electric violin, and percussion, he set up two recurring patterns (one in 33/16 and one in 8/4) that slowly move out of phase with each other at the rate of a 16th note. He also had a fondness for idiosyncratic instrumental combinations and unusual sonorities: *Egyptian Two-Step* (1986) uses two spray cans of compressed air and *The Paces of Yu* (1990) employs window shutters, pencil sharpeners, eight mousetraps, and Brazilian *berimbau*. Much of his music has an air of puckish theatricality that extended from his ensemble works to his own genre of non-narrative audiovisual stage compositions called "physical poetry." His searching musical mind even led him to compose for the Internet, such as *The Invisible Guy* (2005), which Jarvinen described as "a real soundtrack for an imaginary spy film."

WORKS
(selective list)

Ens: Through Birds, Through Fire, but Not Through Glass, perc qt, 1979; Vote of Confidence, amp triangles, 1979; Viscous Linings, va, b cl, cel, perc, 1981; Elec Jesus, pf, 19 insts, 1985; A Book of Five Rings, pf, prep pf, perc, 1986; Egyptian Two-Step, pic + b fl, chromatic harmonica, bar sax, pf, mar, elec b gui, 2 spray cans, 1986; Mass Death of a School of Small Herring, chbr orch, 1986; Goldbeater's Skin, bn + b cl, vn, vc, ratchet, glock, synth, 1987 [arr. cl + b cl, 1987; vn, 1988]; The Seven Golden Vampires, 2 pf, 1987; The Queen of Spain, 2 elec hpd, 2 perc (1988–90); Murphy-Nights, bar sax, elec vn, elec b gui, perc, synth, opt. solo inst, 1989; The Paces of Yu, berimbau, perc, 1990; The Trio with Time Machines, 3 glock, 3 ratchets, 3 kitchen timers, 1990; Vulture's Garden, fl + pic, cl + b cl, vn, vc, pf, 2 perc, 1990; Jaltarong, 26 porcelain bowls, 1992; The Modulus of Elasticity, crumhorn + ob, b cl, bn, vn, va, vc, perc, 1992;

Toys do not Walk and Talk, vn, b cl, trbn, elec b gui, 1992; Bong's Garbo, gongs, 1993; Bong's Other Garbo, perc trio, 1993; Breaking the Chink, s sax, bar sax, b cl, trbn, kbd, 2 perc, 2 elec gui, elec b gui, vn, va, 1993; God B's Lullaby, 1v, pf, 1994; The Aten, vn + cl, db, pf, perc, 1995; Chasing the Devil, 4 melody insts, low inst, b inst, perc, 1995; Microscoperas, spkr, elec org, 1995; Solving for X(tet), 10 insts, 1995; Broken Ostinato, 2 pf/gui, 1996; The Hole-Flow Symphony, elec, vn, v cl, trbn, har, 1997; A Conspiracy of Crows, 3 ob, 2000; Tango Suburbio, str qt, 2002; Blue Tango/Open Water, dobro, str qt, 2005; The Invisible Guy, internet, 2005; Defrag 1, mix en, 2006; 100 Cadences, with Four Melodies, a Chorale and Coda ("With Bells On!"), str qt, 2007; Percy Grainger Fans the Muse, 3 s rec, 2007

Solo inst: Mercury at Right Angles, cel, 1980; Soluble Furniture, pf, 1980; Carbon, b cl, 1982; Deductible Rooms, mar, 1982; The Fifteen Fingers of Doctor Wu, ob, 1987; Bench Ads Works, gui, 1990; The Meaning of the Treat, pf, 1995; Pizzicato, vc, 1996; Serious Immobilities (840 Variations on Satie's Vexations), pf, 1997; No Blues, har, 1997; The Flute of Shame, fl, 1999; Sgt. Pekker, v, 2001, Boardplay, perc, 2007

Recorded interviews in *NHob*.
Principal publisher: Leisure Planet

BIBLIOGRAPHY
K. Gann: *American Music in the Twentieth Century* (New York, 1997), 279ff

JOSHUA KOSMAN/S. ANDREW GRANADE

Jarvis, Charles H. (*b* Philadelphia, PA, 20 Dec 1837; *d* Philadelphia, PA, 25 Feb 1895). Pianist and teacher. Jarvis made his début as a pianist at the age of seven while studying with his father, Charles W. Jarvis. His father immigrated to Philadelphia from England *c*1835 and died in 1854. A pianist, teacher, and composer of songs and piano music, the elder Jarvis gave the premiere of his opera *Luli, or the Switzer's Bride* in 1846. Charles H. Jarvis attended Philadelphia public schools, where he excelled in mathematics. He studied music theory with Leopold Meignen, played solo piano recitals and performed concertos with the New York Philharmonic and Theodore Thomas Orchestra. A teacher of almost 1000 students, Jarvis began the Classical Soirées in 1862, a series of chamber music concerts and recitals with lectures in Philadelphia that continued until shortly before his death. With Jarvis as soloist, programs frequently featured chamber works with piano. He presented over 800 compositions by various composers at the Soirées held at several locations in the city. His few compositions remain unpublished.

BIBLIOGRAPHY
Grove2, Amer. suppl.DAB (F.L. Gwinner Cole)
T.C. Whitmer: "Charles H. Jarvis: Man and Music," *Music* (May 1900)
R.A. Gerson: *Music in Philadelphia* (Philadelphia, PA, 1940)

MARTHA FURMAN SCHLEIFER

Jausoro, Jimmy [Jim] **(Mallea)** (*b* Nampa, ID, 30 Dec 1920; *d* Boise, ID, 2 Dec 2004). Accordionist. His parents migrated to the United States from the Basque region of Spain. He grew up listening to the music of guitars and button accordions played by travelers at his parent's boarding house. When he was 12 years old, Jausoro purchased his first accordion and began taking lessons. By age 15 he had become skilled enough to win an amateur contest and the opportunity to play on a national radio program in Portland, Oregon. In 1957 he started the Jim Jausoro Band, which played Basque and modern dance music until 2000. Three years later he began to perform music with the Oinkari Basque Dancers, a group which has continued to showcase Basque dance today. In addition to four decades working for the Union Pacific Railroad, he performed at countless dance rehearsals, community dances, weddings, cultural events, state festivals, and world's fairs. He taught budding accordionists through apprentice programs and at music camps. He became known in Boise as an accomplished Basque accordionist as well as a culture bearer for Basque tradition. The many honors he received include the Idaho Governor's Award in the Arts for Lifetime Achievement (2000) and the National Heritage Award from the NEA (1985).

CATHERINE WOJTANOWSKI

Jawaiian music. The term "Jawaiian" was used in Hawaii through the 1990s for a pop music trend that has continued to evolve. The musician Brickwood Galuteria coined it in 1986 as a conflation of "jamming" and "Hawaiian," although as its use spread, most people assumed it came from "Jamaican" and "Hawaiian." While this is incorrect, it is not inappropriate as Jawaiian music reflected the innovative transformation of reggae by musicians in Hawaii.

In the mid-1980s reggae's popularity in Hawaii increased, and local musicians began to experiment with it, first as a grassroots movement and then as a commercial fad. It was mainly used for leisure dance and casual listening although there was a strong social undercurrent. As throughout the world, Rastafarian symbols were localized. Critics point to an overabundance of cover tunes, branding Jawaiian music an invasive species. Academics tend to stress the abundance of island themes in original songs. These include surfing ("Wave Rider" by Butch Helemano); ethnic and regional pride ("Hawaiian Born" by Norm and "Masese" by Kapena); cuisine ("Fish and Poi" by Sean Na`auao); and Hawaiian sovereignty ("Keep Hawaiian Lands in Hawaiian Hands" by Bruddah Waltah Aipolani).

Many early adopters, such as the Peter Moon Band, Kapena, Brother Noland, and the Mana`o Company, tended to include reggae as one of several styles they played, but some artists focused on it exclusively, notably Ho`aikane and Simplisity. Most subsequent groups, such as Ooklah the Moc, Rebel Souljahz, Maoli, and Kolohe Kai, have taken the latter approach, especially as local media and clubs have become more niche oriented. Some groups, such as Three Plus, maintain a Hawaiian reliance on ukulele, guitar, and bass with harmony vocals. Others including B.E.T. (Big Every Time) perform hybrids of hip-hop and reggae. By the early 2010s Hawaiian reggae had had no significant impact on Hawaiian traditional music. The two tended to be regarded as separate entities, although fans and some musicians freely moved between them.

J.W. JUNKER

Jay-Z [Jay Z] [Carter, Shawn Corey] (*b* New York, NY, 4 Dec 1969). Hip-hop artist, producer, and entrepreneur; husband of singer and actress BEYONCÉ KNOWLES. He emerged in the early 1990s to become one of hip-hop's most influential artists. Born Shawn Carter, he was raised in the Marcy housing projects in Brooklyn, New York, and used his adolescent experiences selling crack cocaine as fodder for his autobiographical rap songs.

Jay-Z's recording career began when he was featured on the tracks "The Originators," and "Hawaiian Sophie" by East Coast rapper Jonathan Burks (Jaz-O), and on "Show and Prove" from Big Daddy Kane's 1994 release *Daddy's Home*. Soon after, he founded ROC-A-FELLA Records with friends Damon Dash and Kareem Burke and released his debut album *Reasonable Doubt* (1996). The album showcased the young rapper's inventiveness and lyrical dexterity as he spun a coming-of-age tale shaped by crime, bravado, and quick wit. With a distribution agreement with Def Jam Records and production assistance from Sean "P-Diddy" Combs, Jay-Z released *In My Lifetime, Vol. 1*, in 1997; he was featured on the Notorious B.I.G's *Life After Death* that same year. Widespread commercial success came in 1998 with *Vol. 2…Hard Knock Life*, the title track of which liberally sampled the chorus of "Hard Knock Life" from the Broadway musical *Annie*. Selling over five million copies in the United States, the album established Jay-Z's commercial viability. He followed with 1999's *Vol. 3…Life and Times of S. Carter*, which included "Big Pimpin'," a collaboration with southern rap duo UGK. After releasing *The Black Album* in 2003, Jay-Z announced his retirement. In 2005, he became president of Def Jam Recordings. He emerged from retirement to release *Kingdom Come* in 2006, a politically conscious work that tackled themes such as Hurricane Katrina and drought in Africa. In partnership with the United Nations, Jay-Z used the *Kingdom Come* tour to raise awareness of global water shortages. He followed this with the soul-influenced *American Gangster* (2007) and eclectic *The Blueprint 3* (2009). Jay-Z has received ten Grammy Awards for his musical work.

As one of the most prominent and successful rappers in the music industry, Jay-Z has been involved in a number of controversies. In December of 1999, Jay-Z was accused of stabbing a record producer, a crime to which he later confessed. He was sentenced to three years probation. In 2001 the rapper publicly provoked artists including Nas and Mobb Deep, igniting a public feud with the former that would last for five years. Nas and Jay-Z reconciled in 2005 when they appeared onstage together on Jay-Z's "I Declare War" concert. In 2008, when chosen as the first hip-hop artist to headline Britain's Glastonbury Music Festival, the rapper drew criticism from British rocker Noel Gallagher of the band Oasis. Jay-Z publicly defused the controversy by opening his set with Oasis's signature tune, "Wonderwall."

Jay-Z has also proven successful in a number of extra-musical ventures. Launched in 1999, his Rocawear clothing line reports annual sales of more than $700 million. He was part-owner of the Brooklyn Nets basketball franchise until 2013, and he is part-owner of the 40/40 Clubs in New York, Atlantic City, and Chicago. Inspired by the life of Nigerian musician and political figure Fela Kuti, Jay-Z became a co-producer of the Broadway musical *Fela!* in 2009. In 2010, he released a critically acclaimed memoir *Decoded* that discusses his life and music. In 2013 it was officially announced that he had dropped the hyphen from his name, electing to be now known as Jay Z.

BIBLIOGRAPHY

J. Brown: *Jay-Z and the Roc-A-Fella Dynasty* (Phoenix, AZ, 2005)
C. Kubrin: "I See Death Around the Corner: Nihilism in Rap Music," *Sociological Perspectives*, xxxxviii (2005), 433–59
M. Reeves: *Somebody Scream!: Rap Music's Rise to Prominence in the Aftershock of Black Power* (New York, 2008)
D. Ross: *The Nightmare and The Dream: Nas, Jay-Z and the History of Conflict in African-American Culture* (Jersey City, NJ, 2008)
Jay-Z: *Decoded* (New York, 2010)

MARGARET JACKSON

Jazz. The term conveys different although related meanings: 1) a musical tradition rooted in performing conventions that were introduced and developed early in the 20th century by African Americans; 2) a set of attitudes and assumptions brought to music-making, chief among them the notion of performance as a fluid creative process involving (group) improvisation; and 3) a style characterized by melodic, harmonic, and timbral practices derived from the blues and African American religious musics, cyclical formal structures, and a supple approach to rhythm and phrasing known as swing.

1. Introduction. 2. Jazz and the New Orleans background (1895–1916). 3. Early recorded jazz (1917–23). 4. The jazz age (1920–30). 5. Swing and big bands (1930–45). 6. Small groups and soloists of the swing era. 7. Traditional and modern jazz in the 1940s. 8. Post-bop developments in the 1950s. 9. Mainstream, third stream, and the emerging avant garde. 10. Free jazz, fusion, and beyond (1960–79). 11. In the tradition? Eclecticism, canonicity, and conservatism (1979–2001). 12. Jazz in the new century

1. INTRODUCTION. Historians and critics using studies of concert music and literature as models have often portrayed the development of jazz as a narrative of progress. Their accounts suggest that jazz started as unsophisticated dance music but grew into increasingly complex forms, gradually gaining prestige and becoming recognized around the world as an art. Over that same period, the attitudes of cultural and institutional gatekeepers toward the music changed dramatically. In 1924 an editorial writer for the *New York Times* called jazz "a return to the humming, hand-clapping, or tomtom beating of savages;" in 1987 the US Congress passed a resolution designating jazz "an outstanding model of individual expression" and "a rare and valuable national American treasure." Those promoting this narrative of progress have emphasized innovation as a primary driving force, identifying new techniques, concepts, and structures that presumably inspired musicians to reach ever higher stages of development.

Narratives of evolution and innovation, however, oversimplify a story much broader in scope and more complex in structure. If some musicians have striven to be innovators, many others have viewed themselves as proud bearers of tradition. If some have struggled as uncompromising creative artists whose work reaches only a small, select audience, still others have flourished providing entertainment with deliberate mass

The Original Dixieland Jazz Band: Henry Ragas, Larry Shields, Eddie Edwards, Nick La Rocca, and Tony Spargo, 1917. (JazzSign/Lebrecht Music & Arts)

appeal. While its contours are not wholly determined by audiences and markets or technologies of production and reproduction, jazz is inextricably bound by them. And if the music has gradually been accorded greater status and respect over the years, it has also consistently provoked controversy. The term "jazz" itself has often carried negative associations, which is partly why Duke Ellington and other musicians spurned it, and why Max Roach once told an interviewer, "I resent the word unequivocally" (Taylor, H1977, p. 110).

The denotative instability of the word complicates efforts to write the music's history in at least three ways. First, the music's sonic identity is difficult to isolate or delimit: although "jazz" seems to refer to a single musical idiom, like "classical" or "rock" it describes an extended family of styles, with all members sharing at least some traits in common yet none capable of representing the whole. Second, the varying functions of what has been labeled jazz conspire against the perception of those items as a unified entity. Jazz can present a musical background for social recreation, lively accompaniment for dancing, or an invitation to close listening and deep concentration—and the same performance or recording might operate in these different ways simultaneously. Third, the question of the music's racial provenance has generated heated debate over the years and shaped its reception. While jazz is a product of African American expressive cultures, its practitioners have always incorporated influences from other musical traditions, and since the 1920s jazz has been performed by musicians of varying backgrounds throughout the world. In different eras, for example, commercially successful white musicians such as the bandleader Paul Whiteman and the saxophonist Kenny G have been identified by large segments of the public as major exponents of jazz. Many others, however, have seen these

two as standing outside the tradition and have considered jazz to be a form of black music in which African Americans have been the leading innovators and most authoritative practitioners. Complications in attempts to describe the identity, function, and racial character of jazz—and the shifting ideological terrain on which one encounters them—are, however, unavoidable: they have been intrinsic to the discussion from the beginning.

2. JAZZ AND THE NEW ORLEANS BACKGROUND (1895–1916). The word "jazz" took on musical connotations in the United States during World War I; before then it was a colloquialism possibly southern and African American in origin, perhaps derived from (Central) African roots. Writers have offered several definitions of the term from this pre-war period, claiming it to be a verb that meant to make something livelier or faster, to demonstrate pep and energy, or to engage in sexual activity. In its earliest printed appearances, "jazz" turns up as a noun. A San Francisco sportswriter in 1913 used the word to describe a kind of spirited liveliness shown by baseball players, for example: "Everybody [on the team] has come back full of the old 'jazz'" and "Henley the pitcher put a little more of the old 'jazz' on the pill [ball]" (Porter, E1997, p. 5).

A few years later small ensembles from New Orleans playing spirited, sometimes crude dance music began featuring the term—also spelled as "jass"—in their names. One was Stein's Dixie Jass Band, a white group from New Orleans which in 1917 performed and recorded with slightly different personnel in New York as the Original Dixieland Jazz Band. Another was the Creole Band, a group of black American musicians that toured on vaudeville circuits in various parts of the United States (1914–18) and was occasionally advertised as a "New Orleans Jazz Band" or as the "Creole

Duke Ellington Orchestra: Kay Davis, singer; Al Sears, saxophone; Junior Raglin, bass; Ray Nance trumpet; and trombonist Tricky Sam Nanton, 1945. (JazzSign/Lebrecht Music & Arts)

Band/Sometimes called the Jazz Band." These ensembles gave northern urban audiences their first exposure to an energetic, blues-tinged musical idiom derived from southern black performing traditions. A New York newspaper article commented on the phenomenon in 1917 (Osgood, G1926, p. 11):

> A strange word has gained wide-spread use in the ranks of our producers of popular music. It is "jazz," used mainly as an adjective descriptive of a band. The group[s] that play for dancing, when colored, seem infected with the virus that they try to instil as a stimulus in others. They shake and jump and writhe in ways to suggest a return to the medieval jumping mania.

Novel and entertaining, this music usually accompanied dancing and was performed in places serving alcoholic beverages: restaurants, nightclubs, cabarets, and dance halls. Such places were themselves elements of an emergent culture of nightlife which brought patrons into more intimate contact with performers than concert or theater performances did and which often hinted at illicit pleasures of various kinds (Erenberg H1984, pp. 119–30). The combination of the music and such spaces led some reformers to see both jazz and nightlife as threats, as forms of social contagion.

Yet while jazz first drew widespread notice in the years leading up to 1920, some musicians and historians have claimed that it originated much earlier. Bunk Johnson stated that he and Buddy Bolden were playing jazz in New Orleans around the period 1895–6; Jelly Roll Morton said he invented jazz in 1902 (he was 12 at the time). Various brass bands from New Orleans, in-

cluding the Olympia, Golden Rule, and Eagle, have also been cited as playing in a jazz style before 1910. Since these assertions have been made retrospectively, often by individuals with a strong personal investment in the histories they have related, and since there is little contemporary evidence to put such claims in perspective, questions of specifically when and how jazz performance practices emerged remain unanswerable. What is more certain, at least for most historians, is that the area in and around New Orleans was the principal site of emergence for jazz.

New Orleans residents in the early 1900s displayed a syncretic blend of African, Caribbean, and European cultures unique among American cities. Morton's Catholicism and belief in vodoun exemplified the cultural fusions that also characterized the city's music traditions. A major port and commercial center, New Orleans attracted black Americans from rural communities in Louisiana and neighboring states, offering economic incentives, educational opportunities, and more relaxed racial codes. At the same time many residents had to endure poverty and sharp tensions that divided neighborhoods and districts according to the skin color, language, religion, ethnicity, and class of their inhabitants: Protestant, English-speaking blacks; Catholic, French-speaking blacks known as "Creoles of color" (*gens de couleur*, henceforth designated by "Creoles") of mixed African and European ancestry; and native-born and immigrant whites with a variety of religious, ethnic, and class affiliations.

Charlie Parker, 1949. (JazzSign/Lebrecht Music & Arts)

The foundations of jazz were established by African Americans in this urban environment before the music had a name, or when it was still referred to as ragtime or ratty music. The process unfolded as musicians gradually developed distinctive ways of interpreting a varied repertory that circulated widely in the United States, the Caribbean, and Western Europe through the movement of people, published music, and eventually recordings (Bilby, H1985, pp. 140–41). That repertory included marches, dance music (two-steps, quadrilles, waltzes, polkas, schottisches, and mazurkas), popular songs, traditional hymns, and spirituals. What might be called a nascent jazz sensibility arose when musicians started loosening the strictures of that repertory and adopting an individualistic, liberating approach that has remained at this musical tradition's core.

Although we lack documentation that shows this process unfolding, it is possible to hypothesize some of the stages involved. Rhythms, for example, gradually may have come to be interpreted more freely than in earlier 19th-century marches, ragtime, and cakewalks. Phrases were stretched out and either played in a more relaxed manner or with more vigorous offbeat accents, not just in one instrumental part but in two or more simultaneously. Drummers enlivened simple duple and triple meters by introducing multi-metric or hemiola-like patterns and phrasing over bar lines. Players began embellishing and ornamenting melodies, inventing countermelodies, weaving arpeggiated lines into the texture, and coloring diatonic harmonies with the pitch-play of blue notes (*see* Blue note (i)).

Although such techniques may have been applied to music by solo pianists active in New Orleans, among them Jelly Roll Morton and Tony Jackson, they generally came to characterize a style of ensemble playing. Precursors to the jazz bands during the period 1915–20 included small dance groups led by such players as Buddy Bolden, Lorenzo Tio Sr., and Papa Celestin, together with brass bands (often featuring some of the same players) that provided music for such community functions as parades, picnics, parties, and funerals. In a Library of Congress interview with Alan Lomax in 1938, Morton recalled the typical brass band instrumentation as including "a bass horn [e.g. tuba or euphonium], one trombone, one trumpet, an alto [horn] and maybe a baritone [horn] or clarinet, and a bass drum and snare drum." These bands gave employment and ensemble experience to early New Orleans jazz musicians such as Bunk Johnson, King Oliver, and Louis Armstrong, while in the process fostering a sense of group identity, pride, and competitiveness. They contributed as well to the solidifying of a professional sphere comprised almost exclusively of men, a trait that characterized jazz in the following years, except in the area of singing, where women gained more opportunities; these bands also helped to create a performance environment in which individual expression was encouraged yet closely coordinated with the activities of other ensemble members. As the writer Ralph Ellison later observed, "True jazz is an art of individual assertion within and against the group... Each solo flight, or improvisation, represents... a definition of [the jazz artist's] identity: as individual, as member of the collectivity, and as a link in the chain of tradition" (Ellison, H1986, p. 234).

Given the scanty documentation for New Orleans jazz during these formative stages (*c*1895–1915), it is unclear to what extent musicians in the early dance and brass bands improvised. Judging from later exponents of the style, a description like "collective improvisation"—used by writers to suggest a basic approach to performing—might lead some to assume that the music was entirely spontaneous, invented in the moment. Like improvisers in other traditions, however, these musicians developed conventions that guided their individual and ensemble work: familiar formal plans, ordered sequences of themes and keys, specific functions for individual instruments within ensembles, and common techniques of embellishment. When they invented compelling new rhythmic devices and melodic patterns, these were imitated by others and repeated in different pieces, then passed on through oral tradition. The way Armstrong once described his approach to soloing—"First I plays the melody, then I plays the melody 'round the melody, then I routines"—hints at the conventional practice that shaped his approach to improvising, belying the primitivist myth that "instinct" or "natural feeling" produced the music and challenging the undisciplined connotations some attach to "collective improvisation." Moreover, musicians working in certain New Orleans contexts—at high society balls and parties and on the excursion boats that went up the Mississippi River—were required to play from written parts, and their opportunities to improvise were limited accordingly. Many Creole musicians in particular, who lived in and around the city's French Quarter, were proficient readers who combined an ability to play from notation with techniques of embellishment and variation.

Who created jazz? This has been a controversial issue in the jazz literature, especially since much of the evidence concerning its origins comes from vague and often conflicting oral testimony. Nevertheless, extant documents and the most reliable accounts support the contention that New Orleans musicians of African descent—both the blacks living uptown and the Creoles downtown—played a leading role both as inventors and expert practitioners of the techniques that came to characterize jazz. In doing so they drew both on a fund of African-derived musical practices and on performing techniques and dance forms widely dispersed in Western Europe, the Caribbean, and Latin America. Concurrently members of other racial and ethnic groups became involved in the development and dissemination of these same techniques. The white musician Papa Jack Laine, for example, led brass and dance bands that trained other white musicians later active in jazz, among them Tom Brown, George Brunis, and Nick LaRocca. These bands furnished music for similar social functions as their African American counterparts, such as parades and riverboat entertainment. As with the early black bands, the lack of recorded documentation makes it difficult to know the styles in which these white groups played. It is conceivable, though, that white New Orleans musicians in the early 1900s were also beginning to adopt a looser and more rhythmically lively approach to the repertory of brass and dance bands.

Musicians of Caribbean ancestry and of mixed racial and ethnic heritage also contributed to the formation of a jazz performance practice. One was the Cuban American cornetist and cellist Manuel Perez, who played with the Onward Brass Band and led a well-known dance band called the Imperial Orchestra. The Creole population of New Orleans included many descendants of Haitians and Cubans who had immigrated to the city in the 19th century, and the New Orleans–Caribbean connection proved especially important for jazz rhythm. When Morton spoke of the "Spanish tinge" present in jazz, he partly had in mind patterns like the *tresillo* (ex.1*a*), habanera (ex.1*b*), and *cinquillo* (ex.1*c*) that defined the rhythmic composites of Cuban and other Caribbean and Latin American dance genres. Such rhythms turn up in some of his own compositions, such as "New Orleans Blues" (*c*1902–5; 1923, Gen.) and "The Crave" (*c*1910–11; 1939, General). They also appear in late 19th-century pieces published in New Orleans such as W.T. Francis's "The Cactus Dance," "Danza Mexicana" (1885), and his arrangements of pieces played by the Mexican Military Band at the 1885 World's Exposition in New Orleans.

The racial and ethnic profile of early New Orleans jazz, then, was multifaceted, reflecting and refracting the mixed heritage of the city's residents. At the same time most of the leading musicians identified with jazz

Ex.1a

Ex.1b

Ex.1c

were African Americans. These two generalizations would remain constant as the music spread beyond New Orleans in the years that followed.

It is likely that characteristic rhythmic and metric practices and embellishing techniques employed by black, Creole, and white musicians in New Orleans might have been heard in small ensembles elsewhere in the country. Groups that played instrumental ragtime, dance genres such as the habanera, rumba, and tango, and blues pieces like W.C. Handy's "Memphis Blues" (1912) and "St. Louis Blues" (1914) probably displayed features that resembled what might be called protojazz. The Ohio-born reed player Garvin Bushell recalled playing with a circus band in 1916 that performed marches, ragtime, and blues throughout the South and Midwest; he also identified several accomplished black clarinetists—Percy Glascoe, J. Paul Wyer (known as the Pensacola Kid), and Fred Kewley—who traveled with circus and minstrel bands and later could be heard in jazz and blues settings. Nevertheless, there was something distinctive about the musical fusion that occurred in New Orleans, a flavor and piquancy that resulted from a subtle blending of many different ingredients. Together with this intermingling of musical traits, other extra-musical qualities helped to shape an emerging jazz aesthetic.

In the decade before 1920 players from New Orleans took this emerging style to California, Chicago, and other parts of the United States offering them employment opportunities. They also began recording jazz, which quickly catapulted a regional American vernacular idiom into the international arena.

3. EARLY RECORDED JAZZ (1917–23). Audio recordings have played a crucial role in disseminating jazz. From 1917 to 1920, the years when "jazz" began appearing with increasing frequency as a stylistic label, record companies were mainly issuing 8-, 10-, and 12-inch discs which were played at 78 r.p.m. and which targeted markets segmented along lines of race, region, class, and ethnicity. The recordings, most lasting between three and four minutes, were made using acoustical methods (microphones did not come into widespread use until after 1925), and their relatively low fidelity

Sarah Vaughan, 1946. (Library of Congress, Prints & Photographs Division, William P. Gottlieb Collection, LC-USZ62-89643)

limits what they can reveal about early jazz performance practice. For one thing, their balances of sound and timbral qualities may have been quite different in live settings. In those same settings, likewise, the durations of individual selections might have been extended beyond those of their recorded counterparts. The acoustical recording process also affected instrumentation: drummers often had to limit their activity to wood blocks and cymbals since drums might have created distortion or overwhelmed other instruments. In addition, the pieces recorded by bands may not have reflected what they performed regularly outside the studio: record producers and publishers often selected the repertory as part of a larger effort to market sheet music copies of newly published compositions. Finally, race influenced producers' decisions regarding whom to record and what styles were appropriate for them. Black jazz musicians only started recording in significant numbers during the period 1923–5 and often found themselves expected to play a repertory emphasizing blues and "hot" jazz (fast, rhythmically energetic dance music) that ostensibly would appeal to the African American consumers targeted by record companies in their segregated race series (*see* Race record). As Duke Ellington's saxophonist Otto Hardwick observed, "The field for recording was quite limited…If you didn't play the blues, there was no room for you." (White musicians from rural areas of the southern United States were similarly discouraged from recording anything other than what Ralph Peer later called hillbilly music.) For all these reasons, recordings may offer unreliable sonic representations of early jazz performing practice while preserving echoes of the varied jazz styles that

had begun to circulate in the United States and overseas by the early 1920s.

The historical distinction for being the first group to record jazz goes to the Original Dixieland Jazz Band. A quintet of white musicians from New Orleans, it made its first recordings early in 1917 in New York, where the band had been attracting attention through appearances at Reisenweber's Restaurant on 58th Street. Although the Original Dixieland Jazz Band lacked both banjo and a bass instrument (string bass or tuba), its other instruments became standard for small New Orleans jazz units, which included three lead or melody-carrying instruments (cornet, clarinet, and trombone) with piano and drums providing accompaniment in the rhythm section. The pieces they recorded show a mixture typical for early jazz bands: blues, ragtime, popular songs, and novelty numbers. Improvisation, however, is minimal. Often the band seems to be following set routines: "Livery Stable Blues" (Vic., 1917), for example, uses a common multi-part strain form derived from 19th-century marches and ragtime (e.g., *AABBCCABC*), and successive iterations of individual strains vary little from their predecessors. The band must have impressed listeners with both its ebullience and its extroverted humor: the group was a seasoned vaudeville act, and its crowd-pleasing tactics—including the imitation of animal noises in the recorded version of "Livery Stable Blues"—may have reflected its stage experience more than its New Orleans jazz background. The New Orleans Rhythm Kings, another white band, showed more restraint: their rendition of "Livery Stable Blues" (Para., 1922) is smoother and more rhythmically supple than recordings of the same piece made by the Original Dixieland Jazz Band in 1917 and again in 1923, the latter for OKeh under the title "Barnyard Blues" (*see* Dixieland jazz).

Kid Ory and a five-piece band (cornet, clarinet, trombone, piano, and drums) provide another example of early jazz by New Orleans musicians, this time an African American group recorded in Los Angeles in 1922. Although its instrumentation is identical to that of the Original Dixieland Jazz Band, Ory's group displays both a gentler, more lilting rhythmic style and a greater sense of relaxation on "Ory's Creole Trombone/Society Blues" (Nordskog) than is evident in work by the Original Dixieland Jazz Band. In other respects, however, the multi-strain formal patterns, the "set" quality of many of the instrumental lines (although the cornetist Mutt Carey does take liberties in embellishing parts), the functions of instruments within the ensemble, and the use of breaks (short passages played by soloists while the rest of the band stops) all resemble aspects heard in the earlier recordings. As with the Original Dixieland Jazz Band, virtually nothing played by Ory's band would qualify as unscripted "collective improvisation." Instead it was highly ordered and predictable music with built-in repetitions, probably intended for dancers; however, as Gushee has suggested (G1977, p. 5), it is likely that the band's lack of a full rhythm section (notably bass, banjo, and a complete drum kit) made it sound different on record from what listeners heard live.

In addition to these early recorded examples by small groups from New Orleans, larger ensembles playing "syncopated" dance music showed another side of the emerging jazz phenomenon. Black bandleaders in New York such as James Reese Europe, Ford Dabney, Tim Brymn, and Leroy Smith performed with groups of up to 15 or more players, including strings together with brass, reeds, and percussion. The relatively few recordings made by these ensembles during the period 1914–23 have often been cited as examples of late instrumental ragtime or pre-jazz music. Indeed, in some ways they seem closer in sound and spirit to the bands of John Philip Sousa and Arthur Pryor or to theater pit orchestras and polite society dance orchestras than to the convention-flouting strain of jazz that characterized the Roaring Twenties. Nevertheless, the energy and rhythmic verve of Europe's orchestra—especially when the drummer Buddy Gilmore was driving the ensemble as on "Castle Walk" (Vic., 1914)—along with its loosely embellished performance practice and repertory of rags, pop songs, and blues, relate his group to the Original Dixieland Jazz Band, the New Orleans Rhythm Kings, and Ory's band, even if its overall sonic identity seems quite different. (The frequent unison melody lines, not just the larger size or stiffer rhythmic practice, account in large part for the difference of Europe's orchestra.) Europe, who directed the celebrated 369th US Infantry Regiment Band in France during World War I, linked his approach to that of jazz players in 1919, explaining that "jazz" was associated with certain instrumental effects (mutes, flutter-tonguing), strong rhythmic accents, and "embroidery" and "discordance" in the instrumental parts. He also made clear his belief that jazz originated in African American culture: "The negro loves anything that is peculiar in music, and the 'jazzing' appeals to him strongly…We have our own racial feeling and if we try to copy whites we will make bad copies" (Porter, E1997, pp. 126–7). A contemporary of Europe who led a large ensemble that included early jazz or pre-jazz in its repertory was Will Marion Cook. Although his Southern Syncopated Orchestra made no recordings, it traveled to Europe in 1919 and made a deep impression on listeners, among them the Swiss conductor Ernest Ansermet who, while describing Sidney Bechet in primitivist terms, found the latter's blues solos "admirable equally for their richness of invention, their force of accent, and their daring novelty and unexpected turns" (Walser, H1999, p. 11).

Other bandleaders provided models for organizing and standardizing the instrumental components of dance orchestras playing jazz. On the West Coast during the mid- to late-1910s, Art Hickman led a ten-piece ensemble consisting of two brass instruments (cornet and trombone), two saxophones, violin, piano, two banjos, string bass, and drums. He took the orchestra east in 1919. Evidence of the impact of New Orleans jazz style upon Hickman can be heard in the final chorus of "Whispering" (Col., 1920), both in the arpeggiated embellishing techniques of the soprano saxophonist (emulating a New Orleans clarinetist) and the loose connecting phrases of the trombonist, playing in tail-gate fashion. Hickman's configuration of brass, reeds, violin, and rhythm section was emulated by Paul Whiteman, another California-based bandleader who came to New York in 1920. The instrumental line-up of Hickman's and Whiteman's bands required arrangers skilled in composing embellished melodic variations and exploring different timbral combinations. One was Ferde Grofé, who worked first with Hickman in California and after 1919 as an arranger and pianist with Whiteman. Grofé helped Whiteman develop a concept of symphonic jazz through changes in orchestration. He added strings and double-reed instruments (oboe and bassoon) to the standard brass, single-reed (saxophone and clarinet), and rhythm sections, and borrowed themes from the classical repertory—such as Rimsky-Korsakov's "Song on the Indian Guest" (Vic., 1921) from his opera *Sadko*—to produce dance music that evoked the "high art" of the concert hall (*see* SWEET DANCE MUSIC and CONCERT JAZZ). In Chicago, Isham Jones was another prominent white bandleader who by the late 1910s was fronting an ensemble made up of three distinct sections (brass, reeds, and rhythm instruments) with the addition of violin, which later disappeared from the standard dance-band ensemble. Jones's arrangements often featured "hot" sections, such as the cornetist Louis Panico's muted, growling statement on "Never Again" (Bruns., 1924), that emphasized syncopation and improvising soloists.

By the early 1920s, then, jazz and jazz-like music could be heard on recordings made by such small ensembles as the Original Dixieland Jazz Band, the New Orleans Rhythm Kings, and Ory's group; by medium-sized dance bands, including those of Hickman and Jones; and by larger ensembles, notably Europe's society orchestra and Whiteman's concert orchestra. Yet another recording outlet for jazz musicians came in the form of small pick-up groups accompanying female blues singers. Beginning with the recordings that Mamie Smith made in 1920 with her promoter Perry Bradford and continuing with the flood of "blues craze" singers that followed, it was customary for producers to hire two to five instrumentalists to accompany vocalists for recording dates, especially those made for race labels in Chicago and New York. Often these hired musicians had experience playing jazz in dance bands and displayed their skills as improvisers in their studio work. In 1920 the New York trumpeter Johnny Dunn and a small band with rotating personnel took part in a number of sessions with the singer Edith Wilson. The loose ensemble work on such recordings as "Nervous Blues" and "Vampin' Liza Jane" (Col., 1921)—with clarinet, trombone, and trumpet sometimes doubling, embellishing, or playing around the melody—hints at the kind of informal accompanying conventions players were using in clubs and theaters. At times the interweaving polyphonic strands suggest the New Orleans small-group model, but Dunn's style is both busier and more clipped rhythmically than that of such Crescent City lead cornetists as King Oliver and Tommy Ladnier. Other musicians with jazz credentials turn up on these blues recordings from the early 1920s, including the

Wynton Marsalis, 2004. (Lloyd Wolf/Lebrecht Music & Arts)

trumpeter Bubber Miley and the clarinetist Buster Bailey with Mamie Smith (1921), the trumpeter Joe Smith and the pianist Fletcher Henderson with Ethel Waters (1922), and the pianist Fats Waller with Sara Martin (1922).

In 1923, six years after the Original Dixieland Jazz Band recorded its first sides, African American jazz musicians started getting more opportunities to distribute their work via recordings. That year companies in Chicago and Richmond, Indiana, issued the first recordings of such noted New Orleans figures as Oliver and Jelly Roll Morton. In New York, Henderson and his orchestra began recording regularly for various labels, and Bessie Smith cut her first sides accompanied by jazz instrumentalists. In St. Louis Bennie Moten's Kansas City Orchestra made its first recordings. From this time on, recordings offered a more accurate and representative sampling of jazz activity in the United States.

The recordings made in 1923 by Oliver's Creole Jazz Band reveal the cohesive, relaxed yet hard-driving rhythmic style of a band of mostly New Orleanians working regularly on Chicago's South Side. Although slightly larger than the Original Dixieland Jazz Band or Ory's band, Oliver's group featured a similar two-part configuration: a front line of melody-playing instruments made up of clarinet, trombone, and two cornets (played by Oliver and the young Louis Armstrong) and a rhythm section of piano, banjo, drums, and occasionally bass. Oliver's repertory combined older, ragtime-based strain forms ("Froggie Moore," Gen., 1923) with current pop songs ("I ain't gonna tell nobody," OK, 1923) and blues ("Jazzin' Babies Blues," OK, 1923). Blues lyricism was central to their brand of jazz and was epitomized in Oliver's muted solos—notably his celebrated one on "Dipper Mouth Blues" (Gen., 1923)—which later trumpeters emulated and embellished. The fuller, more dynamic rhythm section in Oliver's band (compared to

those of Ory and the Original Dixieland Jazz Band earlier) reflected the group's experience playing for dancers, a point that might have been more audibly obvious had the drummer Baby Dodds been able to use his entire drum kit instead of being restricted largely to wood blocks. The group's mode of interplay, which gave each individual a voice in a harmoniously working unit, was a model of ensemble coordination positioned midway between the loosely improvised accompaniments of Johnny Dunn and his Jazz Hounds and the precisely notated arrangements of Whiteman. For these reasons and by virtue of their exuberance and rhythmic momentum, Oliver's recordings of 1923 made a powerful statement about the expressive potential of New Orleans jazz that resonated loudly for decades to follow.

A contrasting strain of African American jazz in about 1923 is found on recordings made in New York by Henderson's orchestra. For its leader "hot jazz" did not circumscribe his group's identity, as it did Oliver's in Chicago; alongside "sweet" popular songs, novelty numbers, and waltzes, hot music constituted but one of the idioms the group provided for dancers. It was in part Henderson's versatility, as Jeffrey Magee (G2005, pp. 33–8) noted, that helped him succeed as a black bandleader competing with other white and black ensembles for jobs in New York, including a long-term engagement he secured at the Roseland Ballroom in Manhattan (1924). On recordings, Henderson and his musicians at times appear to be following commercially published stock arrangements ("Oh! Sister, ain't that hot?," Emerson, 1924); at other times they play arrangements by Don Redman, a member of the band's reed section. In general the reliance on notation and the three-section configuration (brass, reeds, and rhythm) of Henderson's group placed it more in the dance-band tradition of Hickman and Whiteman than in the New Orleans mold of Oliver, Ory, and the Original Dixieland Jazz Band.

Joe "King" Oliver (standing with trumpet) leads the Creole Jazz Band from New Orleans, including Louis Armstrong (kneeling with trumpet), 1923. (Lebrecht Music & Arts)

Nevertheless, traces of the New Orleans polyphonic weave show up occasionally, notably in the final chorus of "When you walked out someone else walked right in" (Puritan, 1923), an arrangement by Redman of an Irving Berlin song. Together with the active sectional interplay and set melodic variations dictated by arrangements, Henderson's band also featured "hot" improvised (or improvised-sounding) solos by such players as Coleman Hawkins ("Dicty Blues," Voc., 1923), the trombonist Charlie Green ("Shanghai Shuffle," Pathé, 1924), and Armstrong ("Copenhagen," Voc., 1924).

4. THE JAZZ AGE (1920–30). "Jazzin', everybody's jazzin' now," sang Trixie Smith in "The world's jazz crazy and so am I" (Para., 1925). The song attested to the fever generated by jazz during the 1920s as it spread throughout North America and to Europe, Latin America, and distant parts of the globe. This expansion occurred in two concurrent phases. First, American jazz was exported overseas in the form of recordings, published sheet music, and written arrangements and by traveling ensembles. As early as 1918–19 Louis Mitchell and his Jazz Kings performed in Paris, and the Original Dixieland Jazz Band undertook a long residency in England. They were followed in the 1920s by Benny Peyton, Arthur Briggs, Sidney Bechet (who returned

after his first trip in 1919), and other American musicians scattered throughout Europe. Europeans could also hear jazz interpreted by orchestras touring with such black musical revues as *From Dover to Dixie* (1923), *Plantation Days* (1923), and *Chocolate Kiddies* (1925–6). The market for jazz extended beyond Western Europe: Sam Wooding's orchestra appeared in Hungary, Russia, and Argentina, and the pianist Teddy Weatherford traveled with Jack Carter's orchestra to East Asia in the late 1920s.

At the same time as American jazz reached new listeners abroad, those living in different parts of the world began to perform, record, and write about the new music. Local jazz bands sprang up everywhere, from those led by Bernard Etté in Germany and Fred Elizalde in England to those of Dajos Bela in Hungary and Eduardo Andreozzi in Brazil. A number of these ensembles recorded for such major labels as Columbia, Decca, Odeon, and Victor. Jazz also made an impact on European composers of concert music, just as ragtime had done earlier. Attempts to incorporate (or parody) the rhythmic patterns, harmonic vocabulary, and sonorities of jazz were undertaken in France by Milhaud (*La Création du Monde*, 1923) and in Germany by Hindemith (*Suite "1922,"* 1922) and Krenek (*Jonny spielt auf*, 1925). During the same period writings on jazz began to proliferate in newspapers, periodicals, and literary magazines. The German periodical *Der Querschnitt* published articles on jazz in 1922–3, and in Leipzig Alfred Baresel turned out pedagogical materials and *Das Jazz-Buch* (1925), which Bradford Robinson called the first comprehensive textbook on jazz in any language.

Public reaction to jazz varied widely in the United States during the 1920s. Early on, some commentators, with concert music as a point of reference and with race and class as subtexts, condemned the music as improper, even immoral. Jazz "excite[s] the baser instincts," said John Philip Sousa (Ogren, E1989, p. 56). It "offends people with musical taste already formed," charged an editorial in the *New York Times* (8 October 1924), "and it prevents the formation of musical taste by others." Among those oriented toward the concert hall, however, jazz also had supporters. Carl Engel, head of the Music Division of the Library of Congress, noted that "jazz finds its last and supreme glory in the skill for improvisation exhibited by its performers ... [Good jazz is] music that is recklessly fantastic and joyously grotesque" (G1922, p. 187). For some, jazz symbolized the spirit and temper of contemporary American life, whether it was F. Scott Fitzgerald in *Tales of the Jazz Age* (1923) describing the rebellious hedonism of the younger generation or the music critic W.J. Henderson claiming in 1925 that jazz expressed "ebulliency, our carefree optimism, our nervous energy, and our extravagant humor" (*New York Times Book Review*, 8 February 1925). Not everyone linked jazz exclusively with the United States. For the American cultural critic Waldo Frank, jazz was emblematic of the "Machine" and symbolized the diseased condition of industrialized society, describing it as "the music of a revolt that fails" (*In the American Jungle* (*1925–1936*), New York, 1937, p. 119). In 1921, the English critic Clive Bell equated jazz with artistic modernism, identifying such figures as Picasso, Stravinsky, T.S. Eliot, and Woolf with the "jazz movement," finding in their work an underlying quality of "impudence in quite natural and legitimate revolt against Nobility and Beauty" ("Plus de Jazz," *The New Republic*, 21 September 1921).

The varied reactions that jazz occasioned in the 1920s notwithstanding, the music itself served two primary functions. First and foremost it accompanied dancing, as jazz bands supplied lively music that inspired people to dance; recordings issued by jazz groups often identified on their labels the particular dance step for which the music was suitable: Oliver's "Chattanooga Stomp" (Col., 1923) was a "shimmy one step," Ellington's "East St. Louis Toodle-oo" (Voc., 1926) a "fox trot." James P. Johnson's "Charleston," written in 1923 for the show *Runnin' Wild*, inspired a popular craze for this dance, and its characteristic rhythmic motive (related to the *tresillo*; Ex.2) turned up in individual solos and arrangements played by jazz orchestras. Many jazz instrumentals referred to specific dances or implied dance movement in their titles, among them "Doin' the New Low Down," "St. Louis Shuffle," "Birmingham Breakdown," "Hop Off," "18th Street Strut," and "Moten Stomp." Jazz musi-

cians accompanied not just social dancers but professional dance acts in vaudeville and musical theater. When Coleman Hawkins performed during the period 1921–2 as one of Mamie Smith's Jazz Hounds, he and other band members accompanied both the singer and various dancers appearing on the same bill. Similarly, Count Basie joined the vaudeville act of Gonzelle White (1926) in which fellow band members danced and performed stunts onstage. The drummer Freddy Crump, Basie recalled, "used to come dancing back in from the wings and hit the drum as he slid into a split. He used to grab the curtain and ride up with it, bowing and waving at the audience applauding" (Basie and Murray, F1985, p. 86).

Ex.2

Basie's recollection of Crump points up the second main function of jazz in the 1920s: to provide entertainment that often had a comedic flair or novelty component. Jazz bands were often visually stimulating, with players throwing objects such as hats and drumsticks in the air, striking dramatic positions while performing and taking part in stage business, and theaters were a common venue for presenting musicians on bills with other performers. As a result, audiences often judged a jazz band by the quality of its visual presentation or act, on one hand, and its ability to play racially prescribed roles, on the other. Duke Ellington's band once performed a routine at a Harlem theater in which the set resembled a backwoods church and Bubber Miley dressed as a preacher to deliver a musical sermon on his trumpet. Louis Armstrong had a similar preacher's act, calling himself Reverend Satchelmouth, when he played in New York with Fletcher Henderson's orchestra and in Chicago with Erskine Tate and the Vendome orchestra. Audiences from varying backgrounds could find humor in such performances. In some cases, though, the routines expected by "slummers" or "racial tourists" seeking exotic entertainment were haunted by the specter of minstrelsy in plantation and jungle scenarios in which black musicians and dancers—performing in venues located in transitional areas known as vice districts—catered to the "night-life fantasies cherished by white customers" (Ogren, E1989, pp. 42–3, 74–5; Kenney, E1993, pp. 15–16, 24–5). Some of the less racially demeaning theatrical aspects of performance were continued by Cab Calloway and Jimmie Lunceford in the 1930s, avoided by most after World War II, and revived in the 1960s by Sun Ra and his Arkestra, the Art Ensemble of Chicago, and Cecil Taylor.

A concert staged by Paul Whiteman at New York's Aeolian Hall on 12 February 1924 crystallized conflicting views of jazz in the 1920s. Entitled "An Experiment in Modern Music," Whiteman's event sought, among other things, to suggest that the old "discordant jazz" (the New Orleans small-group style identified with the

Original Dixieland Jazz Band) was being replaced by "the really melodious music of today," which he called "modern jazz." George Gershwin's *Rhapsody in Blue*, arranged by Grofé and first performed on this occasion, was described in the press as a "jazz rhapsody." For Whiteman and others, then, jazz was a form of American popular music, not necessarily racially marked, suitable for polite dancing by urban sophisticates, and adaptable by composers for use in the concert hall. This perspective on jazz also dominated Henry O. Osgood's *So this is Jazz* (Boston, 1926), the first book-length study of the subject in English. The main figures profiled by Osgood were all successful white bandleaders or composers, among them Whiteman, Gershwin, Berlin, and Ted Lewis.

Jazz in the 1920s was a fluid, unstable construct. Depending on who used the term, it could refer to Jelly Roll Morton, Vincent Lopez and his Hotel Pennsylvania orchestra, T.S. Eliot's *The Waste Land*, or Gershwin's *Rhapsody in Blue*. The breadth of its semantic range is demonstrated by the film *The Jazz Singer* (1927), in which the lead character, played by Al Jolson, is a white Jewish singer who performs in blackface, employs jerky body movement, and does trick whistling. Jolson's taut delivery and histrionic mode of "jazz" singing contrasted sharply with the work of other contemporary musicians, such as the stark tonal portrait sketched by Ellington and his orchestra in "Black and Tan Fantasy" (Bruns., 1927) and the jubilant strains of Armstrong and his Hot Five in "Struttin' with Some Barbecue" (OK, 1927). Armstrong's landmark recordings with this group and his Hot Seven during this period also signaled the growing importance of the virtuoso soloist to jazz practices that developed further in subsequent decades.

5. SWING AND BIG BANDS (1930–45). If Paul Whiteman programmed his Aeolian Hall concert in 1924 to suggest what type of jazz would prevail in the years to come, his prediction was completely wrong. It was not his symphonic jazz that captured the public imagination. Instead, it was the rhythmically charged jazz of black bands like McKinney's Cotton Pickers and the orchestras of Fletcher Henderson, Duke Ellington, and Bennie Moten along with that of such white bands as the Casa Loma Orchestra that set the tempo for developments in the 1930s and 1940s. Unlike Whiteman's 20-piece orchestra, these ensembles, each numbering roughly a dozen players around 1930, were sleeker and usually comprised three trumpets, two trombones, three reeds (including one saxophonist doubling on clarinet), and four in the rhythm section. By the early 1930s the tuba had been replaced by a string bass and the banjo by a guitar, yielding a leaner sound overall. Arrangers for these bands, including Benny Carter, John Nesbitt, Eddie Durham, Don Redman, Horace and Fletcher Henderson, and Gene Gifford, discovered ways to translate the freedom and flexibility of improvising soloists into the parts they wrote. Sometimes they played the reeds off against the brass, as in the final "shout" chorus of Fletcher Henderson's "New King Porter Stomp" (OK, 1932); this was based on an antiphonal call-and-response figure that reached back to such older African American musical forms as the work song and spiritual. They also devised short, repeated melodic-rhythmic cells called riffs that could accompany solos or serve a primary melodic function, as in "Casa Loma Stomp" (OK, 1930) by the Casa Loma Orchestra and the last chorus of "Moten Swing" (Vic., 1932) by Moten's orchestra. In addition, they lightened textures by reduc-

The Benny Goodman Quartet: Lionel Hampton, vibraphone; Teddy Wilson, piano; Benny Goodman, clarinet; and Gene Krupa, drums; in Busby Berkeley's 1937 film, Hollywood Hotel. *(MaxJazz/Lebrecht Music & Arts)*

ing the number of doubled parts and streamlining harmonies. Such techniques gave large-ensemble jazz speed and grace and made the rhythm buoyant and propulsive. The term for this rhythmic quality—taken from the vocabulary of black musicians— was "Swing," and it soon became a stylistic designation synonymous with jazz and a rallying cry for a new generation of listeners, dancers, and critics.

Benny Goodman played a major role in popularizing the latter two senses of "swing" in the mid-1930s. Like Whiteman earlier and Elvis Presley a few decades later, Goodman was a white musician who could successfully mediate between an African American musical tradition and the large base of white listeners making up the majority of the American population. Wearing glasses and conservative suits—"looking like a high school science teacher," according to one observer (Stowe, E1994, p. 45)—Goodman appeared to be an ordinary, respectable white American. Musically he was anything but ordinary: a virtuoso clarinetist, a skilled improviser who could solo "hot" on up-tempo numbers and "sweet" on ballads, and a disciplined bandleader who demanded excellence from his players. With these combined personal and musical attributes, he built a following through radio network programs ("Let's Dance," 1934–5, and "The Camel Caravan," 1936–9), recordings made for the Victor label (from 1935), and live performances nationwide. Jazz historians have often used the date of one of these appearances (21 August 1935, when his orchestra broadcast live from the Palomar Ballroom in Los Angeles) to mark the beginning of the swing era, a period stretching into the late 1940s during which the large-ensemble jazz purveyed by Goodman and other bandleaders was the popular music of choice for many in the United States. Significantly, the pieces that galvanized listeners most during the Palomar performance were hot jazz numbers from Goodman's repertory that had been arranged by an African American musician, Fletcher Henderson.

In some ways Goodman practiced a racial politics that was more inclusive than that of his predecessors, although he was not the first prominent white bandleader to perform music written by African Americans: Whiteman, for example, had commissioned arrangements from William Grant Still in the late 1920s. Besides featuring the work of such black arrangers as Fletcher and Horace Henderson, Jimmy Mundy, Edgar Sampson, and Mary Lou Williams, Goodman formed small groups that brought white musicians together on the bandstand and in the recording studio with such notable black players as Lionel Hampton, Teddy Wilson, Charlie Christian, and Cootie Williams. During a concert he gave at Carnegie Hall on 16 January 1938, members of his band jammed onstage with musicians from Count Basie's orchestra. Color lines were also crossed when black musicians were hired as featured soloists with white bands, such as Billie Holiday with Artie Shaw (1938) and Roy Eldridge with Gene Krupa (1941–3). Despite these short-term examples of integration, black musicians still faced systemic segregation and discrimination during the swing era, often hired to perform in venues where they would not be admitted as patrons. While they thus profited economically from the vogue for swing, an idiom their predecessors had largely invented in the late 1920s and early 1930s, most black musicians were unable to realize the level of commercial success and media visibility enjoyed by the bands of Goodman, Tommy and Jimmy Dorsey, Glenn Miller, Harry James, and Shaw.

In the guise of swing, jazz appeared domesticated in the 1930s. Earlier, it had been associated with gin mills and smoky cabarets, illegal substances (alcohol and drugs), and illicit sex. Swing generally enjoyed a more wholesome reputation, although some preached of the dangers it posed to the morals of young people. This exuberant, extroverted music, performed by well dressed musicians and their clean-cut leaders, entered middle-class households through everyday appliances like the living room Victrola and the kitchen radio. It reached a wider populace as musicians transported it from large urban centers into small towns and rural areas. Criss-crossing North America by bus, car, and train, big bands played single-night engagements in dance halls, ballrooms, theaters, hotels, nightclubs, country clubs, military bases, and outdoor pavilions. They attracted hordes of teenagers who came to hear the popular songs of the day and dance the jitterbug, lindy hop, and Susie Q. The strenuous touring schedule of big bands was far from glamorous. Nevertheless, musicians who played in these ensembles could symbolize achievement and prove inspirational, as the writer Ralph Ellison recalled from his early years growing up in Oklahoma City (H1986, p. 220):

> And then Ellington and the great orchestra came to town; came with their uniforms, their sophistication, their skills; their golden horns, their flights of controlled and disciplined fantasy; came with their art, their special sound; came with Ivie Anderson and Ethel Waters singing and dazzling the eye with their high-brown beauty and with the richness and bright feminine flair of their costumes, their promising manners. They were news from the great wide world, an example and a goal.

In less densely populated areas of the United States, bands might be based in one location but travel regularly within a circumscribed area covering two or more states. These so-called territory bands were especially active in the Midwestern and south-central parts of the country (see Territory band and Southwest jazz). Among the better-known leaders of black territory bands were Don Albert and Alphonso Trent (based in Dallas), Troy Floyd (San Antonio), Jesse Stone (Dallas and Kansas City), Walter Page (Oklahoma City), and Moten and Andy Kirk (Kansas City, Missouri). Although territory bands enjoyed modest financial success and made relatively few recordings (with the exception of those led by Moten and Kirk), they provided black musicians with important professional opportunities and fused together the vocal expressivity of the blues with the rhythmic drive of dance music and the spontaneity of improvised solos and ensemble riffs.

These latter stylistic traits became hallmarks of the Kansas City-based orchestra led by Basie from 1935. Basie had earlier worked the Southwest territory circuit

Ella Fitzgerald. (RA/Lebrecht Music & Arts)

with Walter Page's Blue Devils (1928–9) and Moten (1929–35). After Moten died, he formed his own band and drew upon the local blues- and riff-oriented ensemble style to create a dynamic version of swing that had gained national exposure by the late 1930s. His orchestra featured a rhythm section renowned for its smoothly interlocking parts and relaxed teamwork, reed and brass sections capable of explosive accents and muscular phrasing, compelling improvising soloists such as the saxophonist Lester Young, the trumpeter Buck Clayton, and the trombonist Dicky Wells, and the warm, expressive vocals of Helen Humes and Jimmy Rushing. The heat and excitement generated by the Basie band comes across especially on recordings of live radio broadcasts from this period, but can also be heard on such studio issues as "Doggin' around" (Decca, 1938), "Jumpin' at the Woodside" (Decca, 1938), and "Oh, Lady, Be Good" (Voc., 1936).

The big bands of the swing era were entertaining for both listeners and dancers and instructive for the musicians who played with them. Although there were various means of informal, school-based, and on-the-job tuition for musicians (Chevan, H 1997, pp. 31–49), formal education specifically oriented toward jazz was scarce before the 1950s; in particular, racial discrimination often blocked access to music conservatories for black musicians. Working and travelling with big bands, however, young musicians learned how to blend and balance their playing within an ensemble, how to construct terse, shapely solos, how to set background riffs, and how to coordinate with rhythm sections; older musicians offered technical tips and help in interpreting written arrangements. Players also learned the non-musical values of presentation and appearance, managing finances, and maintaining disciplined habits.

These groups, then, represented both self-contained social units as well as systems of apprenticeship. Most of the leading jazz instrumentalists who emerged in the 1940s and 1950s had spent time in big bands.

Big bands also provided a training and proving ground for vocalists. Ensembles usually carried with them at least one solo singer; some had both male and female singers as well as small vocal groups, and these expanded the timbral palette of big bands as arrangers used harmonized voices to deliver melody lines as well as to supply background harmonies. (The Boswell Sisters had begun exploring this vocal jazz territory in the early 1930s.) In 1929 Whiteman became one of the first major bandleaders to feature singers regularly with his ensemble; these included the soloist Mildred Bailey and a vocal trio, the Rhythm Boys (Bing Crosby, Harry Barris, and Al Rinker). The practice became standard in the 1930s and 1940s, with the roster of distinguished big band vocalists including Ivie Anderson with Ellington, Ella Fitzgerald with Chick Webb, Billie Holiday with Basie and Shaw, Peggy Lee with Goodman, Anita O'Day with Krupa, Frank Sinatra with Harry James and Tommy Dorsey, and Sarah Vaughan and Billy Eckstine with Earl Hines. The exposure and experience these singers received from big bands helped them launch successful solo careers: performing each night with 15-piece orchestras, they absorbed important lessons about rhythm and phrasing and learned how to use limited space (a 32-bar vocal chorus inserted in the middle of a three-minute instrumental arrangement) to maximum advantage. Singers were also presented as featured soloists who received accompanying support from big bands; a number of Fitzgerald's recordings with Webb's band, such as "A-tisket, A-tasket" (Decca, 1938), "Bei mir bist du schön" (Decca, 1938), and "Undecided" (Decca, 1939), placed her at the center of attention, dominating the arrangements.

For those aspiring to compose and arrange in the jazz idiom, big bands offered a ready-made outlet. New pieces were constantly needed, whether original works or fresh arrangements of older ones; many bands hired staff arrangers to fill the demand. Commercially published arrangements were also widely used, but it was the specials (distinctive arrangements owned by individual ensembles and often not circulated) that helped give bands a unique sound, setting them apart from their competitors. Ellington's orchestra was identified by its signature muted brass sonorities, its thick polyphonic textures, and its high level of dissonance, all of which characterized such compositions as "East St. Louis Toodle-oo" (Voc., 1926), "Ko-Ko" (Vic., 1940), and "Blue Serge" (Vic., 1941). Showmanship, novelty vocals, and razor-sharp precision contributed to the musical persona of Jimmie Lunceford's orchestra, as did the polished, economical arrangements of his staff arranger, Sy Oliver. Shaw's big band was distinguished by the leader's clarinet as well as its employment of a string section, effectively used by William Grant Still in his arrangement for Shaw of "Frenesi" (Vic., 1940).

Some composers approached writing for big bands not only as a practical assignment but also as an opportunity for musical experimentation. Eddie Sauter stretched conventional harmonic practice in arrangements for Red Norvo and Goodman, raising dissonance to a level higher than was customary in popular dance music. In this he was joined by Don Redman in "Chant of the Weed" (Bruns., 1931), Coleman Hawkins in "Queer Notions" (Voc., 1933), Lunceford in "Stratosphere" (Decca, 1935), and Claude Thornhill in "Portrait of a Guinea Farm" (OK, 1941). Efforts to stretch the length of big-band compositions beyond the usual three-minute limit of 78 r.p.m. recordings were made by Ellington in "Reminiscing in Tempo" (Bruns., 1935) and "Diminuendo in Blue/Crescendo in Blue" (Bruns., 1937). Ellington, Sauter, Shaw, and Mel Powell invoked the classical concerto tradition when they wrote vehicles for soloists with big bands, although they did so without directly borrowing formal procedures and compositional techniques. Another example of swing-classical hybridity surfaced in arrangements for big bands of pieces from the concert-music repertory, as in Still's version of Edward MacDowell's "A Deserted Plantation" (Vic., 1940) for Shaw's band.

By the late 1930s there were signs that jazz was gaining cultural and institutional respect as a musical tradition in the United States. It began to be heard more often in Carnegie Hall (where James Reese Europe's Clef Club Orchestra had performed several times before 1920), notably during Goodman's first concert there (1938), John Hammond's Spirituals to Swing evenings (1938–9), and Ellington's annual series of programs there (from 1943). Winthrop Sargeant's book *Jazz, Hot and Hybrid* (New York, 1938, 3/1976) treated the music as a subject fit for musicological inquiry, analyzing rhythmic, melodic, and harmonic features in close detail. Interest in reconstructing jazz history was evident in Frederic Ramsey Jr. and Charles Edward Smith's *Jazzmen* (New York, 1939/R), which explored the origins of jazz in late 19th-century New Orleans and traced the later evolution of hot jazz and blues in Chicago and New York.

Serious interest in jazz also developed in Europe during the 1930s. Such visiting American musicians as Armstrong, Ellington, and Hawkins gave jazz lovers in England and on the continent first-hand opportunities to hear major artists whose careers they had been following on recordings. Some European writers sought to define what they called authentic or real jazz in order to distinguish it from the more commercialized forms offered up by Tin Pan Alley songwriters and white "sweet" orchestras. This was the critical agenda set by the Belgian writer Robert Goffin in *Aux frontières du jazz* (Paris, 1932) and the Frenchman Hugues Panassié in *Le jazz hot* (Paris, 1934) and *The Real Jazz* (New York, 1942/R). Panassié's passion for traditional and hot jazz led him to help found the Hot Club de France in 1932 and edit its magazine *Jazz hot* for a number of years. Another member of this group of French enthusiasts was Charles Delaunay, who published one of the

first comprehensive reference guides to jazz recordings, *Hot Discography* (Paris, 1936), and started the French jazz record label Swing. Also affiliated with this group was the Quintette du Hot Club de France, featuring the guitarist Django Reinhardt and the violinist Stephane Grappelli. The recordings of this ensemble provided a showcase for the nimble technique and inventive soloing of Reinhardt and Grappelli and established the quintet as one of the first major jazz groups to emerge from Europe.

The vogue for swing and jazz was widespread in the late 1930s. In Holland the Ramblers (a big band formed in 1926) made recordings on its own and accompanied Coleman Hawkins and Benny Carter. In England the BBC initiated the program *Radio Rhythm Club* (1940) that featured jazz on a regular basis. Political authorities in some nations (Germany and the Soviet Union) perceived jazz as a threat, branding it as unwholesome and decadent; the Nazis termed it *entartete Musik* and attempted to put forward their own sanitized forms of popular dance music allegedly purged of unwanted "black" and "Jewish" characteristics. Despite this crackdown, which in some cases resulted in the persecution of musicians, jazz continued to circulate in Nazi Germany and in the USSR under Stalin. As the historian S. Frederick Starr noted (E1983, p. 175), "Jazz everywhere proved far easier to denounce than eradicate."

6. SMALL GROUPS AND SOLOISTS OF THE SWING ERA. While big bands offered many musicians steady employment and professional training during the 1930s and 1940s, smaller groups were also prevalent. They approached the problem of balancing composition and improvisation in different ways, ranging along a continuum from the highly controlled to the loosely coordinated. The Raymond Scott Quintette and John Kirby Sextet were like miniature big bands, specializing in precisely executed and, at times, intricate arrangements that displayed the talents of arrangers as much as performers. Other small groups were less rigorously scripted, relying more on head arrangements (memorized riffs and harmonized parts scattered throughout a given piece) or using composed sections to start pieces followed by improvised solos and ad-lib final choruses for the full ensemble. This latter approach, which shifted the balance away from writers and arrangers toward improvising instrumentalists, can be heard on recordings by the Kansas City Six (made up of members of Count Basie's big band) and the various Ellington and Goodman small-band units of the late 1930s. Looser still, on the opposite end of the spectrum from Scott and Kirby, were groups that adopted an informal, jam session approach. Musicians in these settings depended little or not at all on preplanned parts, relying instead on familiar performing conventions and a common musical vocabulary to play a repertory drawn largely from the 12-bar blues and familiar popular songs such as "I got rhythm," "Sweet Georgia Brown," and "Oh, Lady, Be Good." Such ensembles could be heard in many situations: in nightclubs when the regular evening's entertainment

was over; on recordings, such as those made for Milt Gabler's Commodore label, that assembled skilled improvisers in the studio and let them generate performances with minimal rehearsal; on the soundtrack to Gjon Mili's film *Jammin' the Blues* (1944), which recreated a late-night session using such players as the saxophonists Lester Young and Illinois Jacquet, the trumpeter Harry Edison, and the drummers Sid Catlett and Jo Jones; and in the series of Jazz at the Philharmonic concerts launched by the impresario and record producer Norman Granz (1944) which, like the Commodore recordings and Mili's film, set up controlled performing contexts within which jazz musicians were expected to play with freedom and spontaneity.

Small groups were particularly valuable for soloists honing their skills. Such ensembles gave individual players more time to develop their ideas than was customary or practical in big-band arrangements. (The pianist Sammy Price recalled stopping in a Kansas City club one night when a jam session was underway, going home, then returning more than three hours later to find the same piece still being played.) In competitive "cutting contests," musicians took turns building long, virtuosic solos designed to impress or outdo opposing players. Small-group recordings did not permit such extended excursions, but they could still let soloists luxuriate in the spotlight. The several sides made for Commodore in 1940 by the Chocolate Dandies (featuring the trumpeter Roy Eldridge, the tenor saxophonist Coleman Hawkins, and the alto saxophonist Benny Carter) emphasized individual statements over ensemble playing. On the ballad "I surrender dear," Hawkins states the theme in the first chorus, Eldridge solos in the second chorus, then Hawkins returns for the third; all the while the rhythm section sustains behind them a steady, secondary accompaniment. This practice of placing a higher value on creative soloing than on sectional interplay and group collaboration differed markedly from that of the big bands of the swing era (as well as the New Orleans and Chicago groups of the 1920s), which strove for more parity between soloing and ensemble playing.

The emphasis on solos in small-group jazz of the 1930s and 1940s raised prevailing standards of virtuosity and instrumental proficiency. Hawkins inspired other saxophonists who wished to learn some of the advanced ideas he applied to the changes (chord progressions) of popular songs; trumpeters admired Eldridge's control of the upper register and daring construction of phrases. The pianist Art Tatum, who performed both as soloist and with his trio at the Onyx on 52nd Street, brought to jazz a new combination of harmonic savvy, playful wit, and transcendent technique: what he did seemed so impossible that it helped raise the ceiling for what other musicians might accomplish. The guitarist Charlie Christian, with his fluent, horn-like phrasing and clean articulation, demonstrated how his instrument could assume a leading soloistic role in jazz, and Jimmy Blanton performed a similar function for the bass through his work with Ellington's orchestra (1939–41).

The rise of virtuosity in jazz was due not solely to exceptionally talented individuals, however. In the United States opportunities for instrumental instruction in high schools and colleges helped improve the general level of musicianship. Such African American teacher-bandleaders as N. Clark Smith and Walter Dyett in Chicago fostered the development of many young black musicians—among them Lionel Hampton, Nat "King" Cole, Milt Hinton, and Ray Nance—who later moved into the world of big bands and instrumental jazz. Jimmie Lunceford's popular orchestra grew out of the student group the Chickasaw Syncopators, which he had formed at a high school in Memphis. Another band that emerged from an institutional program was the all-female group the International Sweethearts of Rhythm, formed in 1939 at the Piney Woods Country Life School in Mississippi. By the early 1940s the general technical ability of jazz players was significantly higher than it had been a decade or two earlier: recordings of both small groups and big bands would soon provide convincing demonstrations of the improvement.

7. TRADITIONAL AND MODERN JAZZ IN THE 1940s. The swing era reached its apogee in the early 1940s, with the bands of Ellington, Basie, Goodman, Shaw, Dorsey, Miller, and many others enjoying unprecedented popularity and commercial success. They faced difficulties nonetheless: wartime conscription thinned the ranks of big bands; record manufacturing was slowed by a shortage of shellac used in the war effort; shortages of rubber made it difficult for bands to tour using automobiles or buses; and the musicians' union called for a ban on commercial recording which limited distribution of the music between 1942 and 1944 (DeVeaux, E1997). Generally, however, swing remained the popular music of choice throughout World War II, in tandem with a craze for the blues-based, ostinato-driven style of boogie-woogie.

Meanwhile other forms of jazz during the 1940s presented alternatives to the swing offered by big bands. A resurgence of interest in older, pre-swing jazz led to what some critics later called a New Orleans or Dixieland revival. The musicians identified with this movement came from different places and backgrounds. Some were older black players from Louisiana such as the clarinetist George Lewis and the cornetist Bunk Johnson, both of whom had performed mainly in and around New Orleans until they began receiving national recognition through recordings and live performances in the 1940s. Johnson in particular was hailed as a living link to an older, "authentic" jazz tradition, since he had figured prominently among New Orleans musicians in the early 1900s. Louis Armstrong praised Johnson's playing from that period, comparing it favorably to that of his then-contemporaries Buddy Bolden and King Oliver. Yet Johnson's recordings, made between 1942 and 1947, when he was in his 60s and perhaps past his prime, do not convincingly present him as the accomplished musician Armstrong remembered. Other exponents of earlier jazz during this period were white northerners who drew upon their experience playing

New Orleans and Chicago small-group styles in the 1920s, among them the cornetists Wild Bill Davison and Muggsy Spanier, the clarinetist Mezz Mezzrow, and the guitarist Eddie Condon (see CHICAGO JAZZ). Davison's version of "Eccentric" (Cir., 1947), a piece the New Orleans Rhythm Kings had recorded 25 years earlier, combined the instrumentation and interweaving polyphonic textures of older New Orleans ensembles with the smoother rhythmic flow of swing. Another group of musicians participating in this revival of interest in early jazz were white players on the West Coast such as the cornetist Lu Watters and the trombonist Turk Murphy, who attempted more self-consciously to recreate the styles of such celebrated early jazz bands as Oliver's Creole Jazz Band. Altogether, the New Orleans revival made its impact through recordings, through performances at such venues as Condon's and the Stuyvesant Casino in New York and Earthquake McGoon's in San Francisco, and through articles in the jazz press, often polemical in tone, in which critics championed early jazz as more expressive and "authentic" than what they considered to be the vitiated commercial product presented by big bands. In effect, these writers, labeled as "moldy figs" because of their conservative tastes, carried on the work begun by Robert Goffin and Hugues Panassié during the previous decade, waging a similar battle with only the terrain and the opposing factions being changed.

While some musicians and fans assumed a retrospective stance in the 1940s, seeking to reclaim the roots of jazz tradition, others began to construct a musical vocabulary that would set them apart from both the traditional and swing camps. If the New Orleans revival was a nationwide phenomenon, the impetus to forge a modern jazz idiom was centered in New York, initially in Harlem, and came from a younger generation of African American musicians born between 1913 and 1925. Major figures involved in the effort included Kenny Clarke (b 1914), Dizzy Gillespie (b 1917), Thelonious Monk (b 1917), Charlie Parker (b 1920), Bud Powell (b 1924), and Max Roach (b 1924). These players did not deliberately set out to create a new jazz idiom, but the work they did with like-minded musicians resulted in one. During informal and after-hours jam sessions held in small nightclubs and musicians' apartments, a process of collaborative discovery unfolded in which new ideas about harmonic substitutions, rhythmic vocabulary, and melodic construction were worked out, shared, and tested on the bandstand.

Among the primary sites for this activity were the Harlem clubs Minton's Playhouse, Clark Monroe's Uptown House, and Dan Wall's Chili Shack, although what occurred in them is difficult to ascertain. Musicians who performed in such spaces give conflicting accounts about what happened. Gillespie, for example, recalled some of the advance preparation he did for informal Monday night jams at Minton's: "On afternoons before a session, Thelonious Monk and I began to work out some complex variations on chords and the like, and we used them at night to scare away the no-talent guys" (Shapiro and Hentoff, E1955, p. 337). Monk,

however, told Nat Hentoff in 1956 that the atmosphere was both more ordinary and supportive: "I was playing a gig, tryin' to play music. While I was at Minton's, anybody sat in who would come up there if he could play, I never bothered anybody. It was just a job" (Kelley, F2009, p. 67). In addition, journalists and historians have at times exaggerated and embellished data for dramatic effect. In one famous account, Parker, who first visited New York in 1939, is quoted directly describing how he spontaneously made harmonic discoveries while jamming in a Harlem "chili house." Having grown weary of conventional pitch choices when improvising, he described a moment of revelation: "I was working over [the popular song] 'Cherokee,' and as I did, I found that by using the higher intervals of a chord as a melody line and backing them with appropriately related changes, I could play the thing I'd been hearing. I came alive" (Shapiro and Hentoff, E1955, p. 354). According to a recent biography, however, most of the quoted material comes from a passage in an article by Michael Levin and John S. Wilson published in 1949, in which Parker's only reported speech is "I kept thinking there's bound to be something else...I could hear it, but I couldn't play it" (Woideck, F1996, pp. 16–17). In any event, evidence of Parker's "Cherokee" experimentation can be heard in a private recording made in early 1942 at Monroe's Uptown House. This document points toward Parker's magisterial treatment of the "Cherokee" chord progression a few years later on his commercial recording "Koko" (Savoy, 1945).

Recordings from the early 1940s can provide only limited evidence of the emergence of "modern jazz," or BOP and bebop as it was onomatopoeically dubbed by critics. The recording ban of 1942–4 was partly to blame, but as Scott DeVeaux noted, even without the recording ban it is doubtful that companies would have found bop to be an appealing, marketable commodity, characterized as it was by "a loose, improvisatory format and an eclectic repertory of standards studded with harmonic obstacles" (DeVeaux, E1997, p. 298). There are examples in such recordings, though, of modern techniques being introduced in conventional swing contexts. Live recordings of sessions at Minton's in 1941, when Monk and Kenny Clarke were members of the house band, contain the pianist's dissonant, chromatically inflected harmonies and the drummer's explosive accents, the latter of which later dominated the rhythmic topography of bop. Similarly, a few of Parker's solos with the Jay McShann band hint at imminent departures from swing conventions, as in the saxophonist's asymmetrical phrasing on "Moten Swing" and double-time lines on "Body and Soul" (both from the 1940 Wichita transcriptions).

More dramatic evidence of modern jazz practice, however, turns up in recordings from the period 1944–5, by which time the experimentation described by musicians had presumably been going on for several years. The use of chromatically altered pitches within a diatonic harmonic context (e.g. flattened 5th and 9th, sharp 9th, flat 13th) can be heard in some of Gillespie's solos recorded with Hawkins and his orchestra in

February 1944, and the trumpeter's trademark double-time phrasing can be heard toward the end of the ballad "I stay in the mood for you" (Deluxe, 1944), recorded with the Billy Eckstine orchestra. The dissonant syntax, whole-tone runs, and off-kilter rhythmic patterns of Monk contrast with the longer, spun-out phrases of Hawkins on the latter's recordings of "On the Bean" (Joe Davis, 1944) and "Flyin' Hawk" (Joe Davis, 1944). Differences between the older swing style and the newer bop idiom are vividly illustrated by instrumentalists on Sarah Vaughan's recording of "Mean to me" (Contl, 1945), in which the relaxed, flowing solo of the tenor saxophonist Flip Phillips is followed by the darting, agitated lines of Parker and Gillespie.

A stylistically cohesive example of bop can be heard in "Shaw' Nuff," recorded by Gillespie and his All Star Quintette (Guild, 1945). The ominous tone of the introduction comes from the flattened 5ths played in the bass register of the piano by Al Haig, shadowed by Sid Catlett on tom-toms. The dissonant tritone also figures in the rapidly moving melody, or "head," played in unison by Gillespie and Parker, and returns at the end with the repeat of the introduction and the final D♭ to G fillip in the piano. The rapid tempo, irregular phrase groups (in both head and solos), sudden, sharp drum accents, chromatically altered notes, spare piano accompaniment, and the enigmatic introduction and coda are all aspects that point to the development of a modernist, "artistic" aesthetic that stood in marked contrast to the entertainment trajectory of swing and the apparent folkloric echoes of traditional jazz.

Although bop was primarily a small-group style of jazz, performed usually with two or three lead instruments (most often trumpet and saxophone) and three or four in the rhythm section, some big bands played a role in promoting this music. Earl Hines and Billy Eckstine both directed ensembles that featured young modernists in their ranks, among them Gillespie, Parker, Vaughan, and Fats Navarro. Gillespie himself led a big band in the second half of the 1940s; his recording of Gil Fuller's "Things to Come" (also known as "Bebop," Musi., 1946), with its breakneck tempo, seemingly frenetic phrasing, and ubiquitous flattened 5ths, is an attempt to make bop effective in a large-ensemble format. The big band of Boyd Raeburn in the mid-1940s was known for its provocatively dissonant harmonies and unusual timbral combinations. Even such an avid exponent of entertaining swing as Hampton recalled wanting "some of that bebop sound in [his] performances" and he hired Betty Carter (Lorraine Carter at that time) for that purpose in 1948. Other bands, such as those led by Woody Herman, Artie Shaw, Claude Thornhill, and Duke Ellington, featured bop-flavored arrangements in their repertory without necessarily championing the cause of modern jazz.

In addition to drawing upon the newly minted expressive resources of the bop idiom, some modern groups in the 1940s began incorporating features from Afro-Latin musics. To be sure, sonic elements from the Caribbean and Latin America had been part of jazz from early on, as in Jelly Roll Morton's "Spanish tinge" pieces

and in the presence of dance forms like the Argentine tango and Cuban rhumba in the repertories of jazz orchestras in the 1920s and 1930s. Latin stylistic features had also been introduced to American dance orchestras by musicians who had come to the United States from Caribbean nations, such as Ellington's trombonist Juan Tizol (Puerto Rico), the flutist and reed player Alberto Soccarras (Cuba), and the trumpeter Mario Bauzá (Cuba). In the 1940s some musicians from the United States, continuing the "Atlantic world" traffic in sounds and commodities that helped give birth to jazz in New Orleans, heard new possibilities for their work through the work of Frank "Machito" Grillo and his Afro-Cubans and the contributions made by the Cuban percussionist Chano Pozo to Dizzy Gillespie's orchestra in the period 1947–8. Gillespie showcased Pozo's talents in such compositions as "Manteca" (Vic., 1947) and the two-part "Cubana Be/Cubana Bop" (Vic., 1947), composed by Gillespie with George Russell, which fused together forward-looking, dissonant harmonies with Afro-Cuban conga patterns and vocal chanting led by Pozo. Similar features are heard in Pete Rugolo's "Cuban Carnival," recorded by Stan Kenton's orchestra (Cap., 1947). The impact of Afro-Cuban rhythmic practices on small-group jazz performance can be heard in Max Roach's playing with the Bud Powell trio on Powell's composition "Un poco loco" (BN, 1951) and Gillespie's "A Night in Tunisia" (BN, 1951). While inspired, these acts of incorporation were mostly superficial: rhythmic patterns extracted from much larger complexes of interlocking lines were grafted onto existing jazz formal structures without significantly altering the phrasing of soloists. Nonetheless, they were another manifestation of the exploratory leanings of some musicians.

In seeking to understand the development of "modern jazz" in the 1940s, historians have tended to stress either its affinities with swing and earlier jazz (bop as an incremental advance beyond the harmonic sophistication and virtuosity cultivated in the 1930s) or its radical, self-conscious break with tradition (bop as a revolt against the watered-down, commodified form of jazz presented by big bands). Other writers, among them DeVeaux and David Stowe, described bop as a de facto response to the contingencies of professional music-making and the economic structures of the music industry. These two scholars depicted the emergence and reception of modern jazz as a complex, socially mediated process, not merely as an artistic decision to replace a prominent older style with an innovative new one. Another way of viewing bop is as a response to social and political conditions that African Americans faced in the 1940s. Claiming that swing was not "expressive of the emotional life of most young Negroes after the war," Amiri Baraka (LeRoi Jones) argued that the "willfully harsh, *anti-assimilationist* sound of bebop" reflected the anger and alienation of those who felt themselves to be "outside the mainstream of American culture" (Baraka, H1967, pp. 81–2). Eric Lott, similarly, called bop "intimately if indirectly related to the militancy of its moment" (Gabbard, H1995, p. 246). These interpretations are not mutually exclusive, and none of them takes precedence over any other; all prove useful in understanding a dynamic musical movement that fundamentally changed the way that musicians played jazz and that they and their audiences perceived it.

8. POST-BOP DEVELOPMENTS IN THE 1950s. Enthusiasm for big-band swing gradually waned after World War II: the postwar generation preferred to dance and listen to other kinds of music. The popularity of rhythm and blues in the late 1940s signaled a shift in taste towards non-Tin Pan Alley songs, especially those featuring a strong, shuffling backbeat. In the emerging styles, the rich, orchestrated textures of big bands gave way to a leaner, more streamlined sound emphasizing vocals, one or two horns, electric guitar, bass, and drums. Figures formerly associated with instrumental jazz, such as the pianist Nat "King" Cole and the saxophonist Louis Jordan, highlighted their vocal talents as they moved into the more commercially driven fields of contemporary pop and rhythm-and-blues, respectively. Singers who had launched careers with big bands, such as Frank Sinatra, Ella Fitzgerald, and Sarah Vaughan, found success as soloists in the later 1940s and 1950s, often recording pop songs with orchestral accompaniment in settings removed from the jazz sphere. The appeal of solo singers and close-harmony vocal groups, and the rise of rhythm and blues and early rock and roll, brought the swing era to a definitive close and created problems for many jazz musicians whose skills and/or predilections limited them to working with big bands. While a few of the most successful big bands survived this period and continued as they were, others were forced to reduce their numbers or broke up altogether. Count Basie led smaller units in the period 1950–51, then reconstituted a big band that gained popularity with slow, melodious, gently swinging pieces such as Frank Foster's "Shiny Stockings" (Verve, 1956) and Neal Hefti's "Lil' Darlin'" (Roul., 1957) and riff-driven blues numbers with a heavier backbeat ("Every day I have the blues," Clef, 1955, and "Blues in Hoss' Flat," Roul., 1959). To survive economically, big bands had to be conversant with current popular tastes or, in the case of Ellington's and Kenton's, assemble a repertory so distinctive and players so accomplished that they could still command a public following.

With big bands becoming increasingly risky ventures, small-group activity picked up during the 1950s. But if jazz lost popularity and commercial currency, those musicians who could afford to continue performing gained the creative freedom to try new approaches. For some this meant finding fresh ways to integrate composition and improvisation, while for others it meant tapping into the rich vein of African American vernacular idioms—blending jazz with rhythm-and-blues, blues, and gospel—and, for musicians like Milt Hinton, working as session players on rhythm-and-blues recordings. This was a time of synthesis and consolidation, in which techniques from both swing and bop were freely mixed together. Bop initially may have been, as Baraka noted, "harsh" and "anti-assimilationist," but during the 1950s

its profile changed: as a metaphoric musical language, it seemed more moderate as it was absorbed into the everyday speech of newer generations of jazz performers and cultural institutions in the United States.

The work of Miles Davis and like-minded musicians shows the processes of synthesis and consolidation in action. Although Davis had been a member of Charlie Parker's band (1945–8), his own playing differed from the brilliant virtuoso style of Gillespie: Davis was a slower, sparer, and softer—more lyrical—performer. During the period 1949–50 he collaborated with such arrangers as Gil Evans, Gerry Mulligan, and John Lewis and assembled a nine-piece band to record a group of compositions which were later reissued as a long-playing album entitled *Birth of the Cool* (Cap., 1957). These recordings combined the harmonic language and gestural vocabulary of bop with the ensemble precision of big-band swing; all the musicians had experience playing with big bands, and Evans's arranging for the orchestra of Claude Thornhill made a direct impact on the sound and style of the Davis nonet, particularly in his use of tuba and french horn in the ensemble and in such slow, atmospheric numbers as "Moon Dreams." Throughout *Birth of the Cool* a sense of relaxation prevails quite different from the constant motion and whirling turbulence of bop. At the same time, the basic idiom on such pieces as "Move" and "Boplicity" displays features recognizable from the work of Parker, Gillespie, Powell, and other bop pioneers. Beyond transforming—and to an extent subduing—the language of bop, the Davis nonet sought in these performances to find a more flexible model for integrating solo improvisation with group ensemble passages. Improvised and written lines often intertwine symbiotically, departing from the conventional big-band practice of having soloists play only with a rhythm section or accompanying riffs.

Some of the same qualities manifest on Davis's nonet sides (relaxed pacing, understated expression, softer-edged tone) were evident in the work of other jazz musicians of the 1950s, leading critics to describe their collective output as COOL JAZZ. The Modern Jazz Quartet drew upon players formerly in Gillespie's big band: the pianist John Lewis, the vibraphonist Milt Jackson, the bass player Ray Brown (later Percy Heath), and the drummer Kenny Clarke (later Connie Kay). They specialized in classical music-tinged, small-group swing that was presented with an air of formality reminiscent of the concert hall. Like the Davis nonet, the Modern Jazz Quartet sought creative solutions to the problem of combining written parts with improvisation, with Lewis composing many of the vehicles used for such exploration. The group also introduced new formal models for jazz, not simply with extended works or suites made up of shorter movements (as Ellington had been doing since the 1940s) but with different structures used for soloing, as in the 32-bar chorus form for "Django" (1954, Prst.), organized *A* (6 bars) *A* (6) *B* (8) *A'* (4) *C* (8). Another composer-driven small group of the same period that became identified with cool jazz was the Dave Brubeck Quartet (featuring the alto saxophonist Paul Desmond). They enjoyed great success with such albums as *Jazz Goes to College* (Col., 1954) and *Time Out* (Col., 1959). The latter of those albums featured pieces whose thematic statements used time signatures unusual for jazz (5/4 for "Take Five," 9/8 for "Blue Rondo a la Turk"), but whose improvised passages did not appreciably depart from standard practice: only Desmond soloed in the conventional sense on "Take Five," and the solos for "Blue Rondo…" were restricted to phrases and sections in 4/4. More experimental and less popular than either Brubeck or the Modern Jazz Quartet were New York-based groups led by the pianist and teacher Lennie Tristano. Two early recordings by his sextet minus the drummer Denzil Best, "Intuition" and "Digression" (Cap., 1949), were perhaps the first jazz recordings to include improvisations not governed by song forms or pre-set harmonic schemes, although Tristano did provide instructions to the musicians regarding, for example, when to enter and in what order (Shim, F2007, pp. 178–9). The pianist's most celebrated ensembles featured two of his students, the saxophonists Lee Konitz and Warne Marsh, whose playing, more austere and restrained than that of Charlie Parker, also departed from bebop precedents. Historians have tended to view Konitz and Marsh, as well as Desmond, Stan Getz, Zoot Sims and, in California, Chet Baker, Bud Shank, and Jimmy Giuffre—the so-called cool school of playing in the 1950s and 1960s—as having been more profoundly influenced by the tenor saxophonist Lester Young than by Charlie Parker. Young, though, played an important role in Parker's musical development, and Parker himself (according to Gerry Mulligan, recalling the *Birth of the Cool* period) was the "no.1 influence on us all." So the critically convenient opposition of 1940s bop and 1950s cool jazz belies underlying lines of musical kinship (*see* WEST COAST JAZZ).

As the decade proceeded, Davis did not confine himself to the cool aesthetic mapped out by the nonet. Drawing inspiration from the Ahmad Jamal trio's use of space, choice of material, and style of arrangement, Davis led a quintet in the years 1955–7 with the tenor saxophonist John Coltrane, the pianist Red Garland, the bass player Paul Chambers, and the drummer Philly Joe Jones, which delivered a mixed repertory of up-tempo bop ("Oleo," Prst., 1955), medium-tempo blues ("Blues by Five," Prst., 1956), and haunting ballads ("My Funny Valentine," Prst., 1956). Beginning in 1957 he made a series of albums in collaboration with Evans, in which he held forth as a lead soloist against a lush orchestral backdrop in album-length suites that resembled extended jazz concertos. (One piece, in fact, was Evans's arrangement of a movement from Rodrigo's *Concierto de Aranjuez*, included on *Sketches of Spain*, Col., 1960). Concurrent with these Evans collaborations, Davis toured and recorded in a sextet format that contrasted his aphoristic style with the more effusive phrasing of the saxophonists Coltrane and Cannonball Adderley. Whatever cool aspects might have formed part of Davis's musical persona were effectively complemented (or countered) by fellow group members, especially the propulsive playing of the drummer Jimmy Cobb. Nevertheless, on the album *Kind of Blue* (Col., 1959), the Davis sextet reprised the nonet's cool affect from a decade earlier via subdued tone poems like "Flamenco Sketches" and "Blue in Green" that, in contrast, relied mostly on individual solos rather than on pre-arranged parts. Each of the album's selections, moreover, presented players with specific modes (other than major or minor) to guide their pitch choices rather than a series of goal-directed harmonies. In a interview with Nat Hentoff in 1958, Davis explained his approach as part of a general movement in jazz "away from the conventional string of chords, and a return to emphasis on melodic rather than harmonic variation" (Williams, G1962, p. 167) and cited J.J. Johnson and George Russell as musicians with similar ideas. Davis's modal experiments on *Kind of Blue* opened up liberating possibilities that his groups and others would explore more extensively in the 1960s (*see* MODAL JAZZ).

During the 1950s, though, jazz musicians discovered many other ways of assimilating and transforming the bop idiom that had seemed so experimental and self-contained in the previous decade. Among the younger players who absorbed the lessons of their "modern jazz" elders but struck out in their own directions was the trumpeter Clifford Brown, who joined with Max Roach to form a quintet in the mid-1950s that extended the reach of bop while making it more accessible. Adapting musical vocabularies from the work of Parker and Gillespie, the Brown–Roach quintet offered renditions of popular songs and bop standards that were often inventively arranged. As the quintet approached it, the idiom of "modern jazz" was less a statement of their difference or being part of an artistic vanguard, as had been the case for the first generation of boppers, than it was an effective and familiar set of guidelines for group coordination and individual expression. The intense rhythmic drive and powerful articulation of their performances—as well as their difference from "cool" ensembles like Brubeck's—may have been what led some critics to label them as a HARD BOP group. This designation, implying a stylistic variant of 1940s bop, was also applied to the work of the drummer Art Blakey and his Jazz Messengers, Horace Silver (a pianist who co-founded the Jazz Messengers before leaving Blakey in the mid-1950s), Sonny Rollins (who worked with the Brown–Roach quintet and Davis, before leading his own groups), and Davis's mid-1950s quintet, among others.

Although such journalist-coined labels as hard bop and bop tend to restrict jazz to uncomfortably narrow categories, there were some significant departures in the small-group modern jazz of Blakey, Silver, and others from the work of those who preceded them. Tempos tended to be more moderate, allowing drummers and bass players to articulate a more elastic rhythmic groove. Melodies were smoother and simpler; the jagged intricacies of Parker's "Donna Lee" and Gillespie's "Be-bop" gave way to sectional, riff-based tunes such as Silver's "Doodlin'" and Bobby Timmons's "Moanin'" (BN, 1958). The blues presence became stronger in hard bop, and rhythms and harmonies evoking those used in (Southern) African American churches helped anchor the music solidly in the vernacular, as in the instrumental "amen" responsorial figures in "Moanin'" and the folksy melody of Silver's "The Preacher" (BN, 1955). Even the titles of pieces became friendlier, more familiar: in place of Parker's "Klactoveedsedstene" and Monk's "Epistrophy," there were Davis's "Walkin'," Brown's "Swingin'," and Silver's "Señor Blues." As a result, then, when recordings like the latter three were issued as 45-r.p.m., 7-inch singles, they sold moderately well, especially to jukebox vendors serving African American communities, and often helped to drive their parent albums' initial sales to more than twice the point (2500 units) where a label would start to realize a profit (Rosenthal, E1992, pp. 62–8). If the end of the swing era meant that jazz had ceased to be the popular music of the United States, these figures indicate that it remained a popular music in some quarters.

There were many other signs which, taken together, indicate that jazz remained viable and was continuing to gain respectability in other segments of society as well. Although New York-based jazz and dance ensembles had been entertaining audiences on a circuit of summer resort towns in the northeastern United States since the mid-1920s (Tucker, F1991, pp. 183–6) and had occasionally graced the stages of concert halls, the 1950s saw jazz musicians in general performing in other prestigious settings. Using a model that had already proved successful in extra-urban classical music festivals like those established at Ravinia Park, outside Chicago, in 1915, at Tanglewood in Lenox, Massachsetts, in 1937, and in Aspen, Colorado, in 1949, George Wein mounted the First American Jazz Festival (which later became the Newport Jazz Festival) in Rhode Island in 1954. The invited musicians for the first evening— Eddie Condon, Gillespie, the Modern Jazz Quartet, and Konitz—represented the already broad sweep of jazz-related styles and, according to a *New York Times* article published on 19 July 1954, drew an audience of 7000. Despite inclement weather, the second, final night drew an additional 4000, and the festival received enough national press coverage to encourage its organizers to repeat and expand it in subsequent years (Wein, F2003, pp. 133–40). Although Newport had been preceded by an international festival in Nice, France in February 1948, it received more attention: the Duke Ellington orchestra's appearance in 1956, for example, made it the subject of a *Time* magazine cover story, and the festival of 1958 was the focus of Bert Stern and Aram Avakian's documentary *Jazz on a Summer's Day* (1959). This attention was perhaps the impetus for others to organize their own festivals, such as the one established in Monterey, California, in 1958. In addition, thanks in part to a generation of writers who came of age before rock and roll became a soundtrack for adolescent white middle-class rebellion, discussions of jazz appeared more frequently in mass market, literary, and lifestyle publications in the 1950s, and the musicians themselves enjoyed more opportunities to appear on relatively high-profile programs on the still relatively new medium of television (Gennari, H2006, pp. 172–3). "The Sound of Jazz," an episode of the CBS television series *The Seven Lively*

Arts, was broadcast to a national audience on a Sunday evening in December 1957 and, as had been the case at Newport, such featured musicians as Count Basie, Jimmy Giuffre, Jim Hall, Billie Holiday, Thelonious Monk, Gerry Mulligan, Pee Wee Russell, and Lester Young who not only came from different generations, but had divergent stylistic orientations.

9. MAINSTREAM, THIRD STREAM, AND THE EMERGING AVANT GARDE. Thus, with the fundamentals of 1940s bop having become part of daily practice, forming a common foundation for many younger musicians to follow, what was once "outside the mainstream," in LeRoi Jones's phrase, moved to the center. A broader, more inclusive conception of jazz began to take hold that folded bop or "modern jazz" in with other styles that made up a "jazz tradition." This consolidating process can be seen in the jazz literature of the time, such as M.W. Stearns's *The Story of Jazz* (New York, 1956), Shapiro and Hentoff's oral-history anthology, *Hear me Talkin' to Ya* (New York, 1955) and the *Jazz Review* (1958–61), a journal that gave serious consideration to jazz from all eras.

The perception of a common practice within the multi-layered jazz tradition led to the use of the adjective "mainstream" as a descriptive label during the 1950s (*see* MAINSTREAM JAZZ). The British-born critic Stanley Dance, often credited with introducing the term, issued a series of albums under the rubric "mainstream jazz," featuring artists who had emerged on the scene in the 1930s and 1940s, among them Coleman Hawkins, Earl Hines, the trombonist Dicky Wells, and the cornetist Rex Stewart. Dance used "mainstream" as a delimiter, referring to musicians whose work fell both chronologically and stylistically between the "traditional" and "modern" categories. By the early 1960s, though, bop had become old and familiar enough to join the jazz mainstream that now was bounded on one side by New Orleans jazz, or TRADITIONAL JAZZ, and on the other by the experimentation associated with an emergent avantgarde. From this time on, "mainstream" has remained a popular signifier to imply such paradigmatic traits as improvised solos over cyclical, repeating chorus forms; the use of popular songs, blues, and short original compositions as basic units of structure; a pervasive rhythmic feeling of swing; a reliance on functional harmony within a tonal system; and a greater weight placed on improvisation than on the playing of pre-set or composed material.

Consensus about a jazz mainstream was also reflected in the term "THIRD STREAM," coined by Gunther Schuller (1957), which described music that drew upon jazz techniques as well as aspects of the European art-music tradition. Schuller was particularly interested in finding ways to juxtapose composed and improvised parts and to integrate post-Schoenberg tonal practice into the active vocabulary of jazz musicians. These aspirations are apparent in his composition "Transformation" (on the collection *The Birth of the Third Stream*, Col., 1957), which was recorded by an 11-piece ensemble including the trombonist Jimmy Knepper and the pianist Bill Evans and consisted of an improvised middle section flanked by a pre-composed introduction and coda evoking Webern's spare textures and *Klangfarbenmelodie*. Similar blends and juxtapositions of jazz with European art music (from the Baroque to the post-tonal) can be heard in compositions from this time by John Lewis of the Modern Jazz Quartet ("Vendome," "La Ronde Suite," "Concorde," and "Piazza Navona"), George Russell ("Concerto for Billy the Kid," written for Bill Evans, and "All about Rosie"), and Charles Mingus ("Gregarian Chant" and "Revelations"). Much of this repertory was presented not in the nightclub venues customary for jazz but in concert halls, school settings (for example, at the Brandeis Jazz Festival and the Lenox School of Jazz), and art museums. If one result of modern jazz in the 1940s had been the introduction of a musical vocabulary that later formed the basis of mainstream practice, third stream represented an ambivalent extension of its legacy, embodying, on one hand, deep knowledge and appreciation of western European art music and, on the other, anxiety that jazz could become a serious form of artistic expression only via borrowings from it.

There were other paths that musicians followed in search of fresh modes of jazz expression in the 1950s. In New York, Mingus adopted a workshop format in which players collaborated in rehearsals and public performances to produce music that grew out of a process of group composition and improvisation. Such works as "Pithecanthropus erectus" (Atl., 1956), "Haitian Fight Song" (Atl., 1957), and "Ecclusiastics" (Atl., 1961) contained thematic material supplied by Mingus, but their fluidity and sense of collective creation reflected the workshop ideals he fostered. At the same time, while some of Mingus's work showed the forceful impact made upon him by early 20th-century European musical modernism, his pieces often drew deeply upon the African American vernacular, particularly blues and gospel, as in the 12/8 meter and plagal harmonies of "Better get hit in your soul" (Col., 1959), which displays a soulfulness and exuberance associated more with hard bop than with third stream. Indeed, even hard bop musicians were experimenting with form and harmony. Horace Silver's "The Outlaw" (BN, 1958) featured an unusual structure which was maintained for solos, wherein two *A* sections (13 measures, divided into 7- and 6-bar units) were followed by a *B* section (10 measures), a *C* section (16 measures), and a break (2 measures) with shifts in feel from section to section and even within them. Likewise, Wayne Shorter's "Simply Diana" (BN, 1960) was a 30-measure theme, structured *AA′A″B* and divided into 10-, 8-, 4-, and 8-bar units that only ambiguously favor a single tonal center (Julien, G2003, pp. 151–75).

The saxophonist John Coltrane was another musician searching for challenges and new means of expression in the late 1950s. Moving at first further into the realm of density and building upon the expanded harmonic vocabulary of bop, he employed techniques of chord substitution and superimposition to loosen his improvised lines from their tonal moorings. Original pieces such as "Giant Steps" and "Countdown" (both Atl., 1959) used unconventional chord movement, for example, root motion by 3rds replacing cycles of 5ths, and chromaticism to create rich harmonic environments. Like Miles Davis, his former bandleader, Coltrane gravitated toward the combination of modal melodies with stable harmonic fields. He based "Impressions" (from the album *Impressions*, Imp., 1961–3) on the two-mode framework (D and E♭ Dorian) of Davis's "So What" and used pedal points in "My Favorite Things" (Atl., 1960) and "A Love Supreme" (Imp., 1964) to provide tonal reference points while permitting melodic excursions to go even further afield. Coltrane's virtuosity and lyricism enhanced the appeal of his musical experimentation, and his personal conception of the tenor saxophone proved greatly influential for several generations of players in the following decades.

Beyond third-stream blends, structural experiments, and the modal techniques taken up by Coltrane and Davis, other means were adopted by musicians seeking to expand the tonal vocabulary of jazz. Thelonious Monk brought a high level of dissonance (for jazz, at least) in his piano solos and compositions, and his interest in chromatically rich chord progressions can be traced back to compositions written in the early 1940s, such as "Epistrophy" and "Well, You Needn't." As an accompanist, he often stopped playing while a horn player improvised, thus allowing soloists greater harmonic freedom as they continued with just drums and bass. (Gerry Mulligan also explored the idea of a pianoless quartet in the 1950s.) Examples of that freedom can be heard in recordings made by Monk with Coltrane (1957) and in live recordings featuring both artists when they played together at the Five Spot Café (1957). Monk's interest in raising the dissonance threshold and rewriting the rules of functional harmony were later taken up by fellow pianist-composers Herbie Nichols, Cecil Taylor, and Andrew Hill (notably the last's "New Monastery," BN, 1964). Lennie Tristano had displayed a similar penchant for dissonance, although in his case it was often linear and contrapuntally derived rather than introduced through vertical harmonies. In contrast to these figures, Bill Evans treated dissonance as a coloristic device, using minor 2nds in voicings, for example, to lend an edge of tension to rich chords built upon extended triads or occasionally 4ths. Evans also pursued a piano sound ideal that was radically different from that of Monk, Taylor, and Tristano, and was distinguished by a singing, rounded tone, a legato touch, and especially on ballads a liberal use of the damper pedal, all features that pointed in the direction of 19th- and early 20th-century European composers (Chopin, Brahms, and Ravel) whose works Evans knew and admired.

In addition to developing new technical resources in the late 1950s and early 1960s, some artists showed a concern with addressing social and political issues through their music. Jazz had perhaps always implicitly modeled how individuals might exercise personal freedom within the constraints imposed by society, but it had rarely been overtly political: Billie Holiday's performance of the anti-lynching song "Strange Fruit" (Com., 1939),

Duke Ellington's satirical treatment of racial inequities in the musical *Jump for Joy* (1941), and Louis Armstrong's condemnation of segregationist Arkansas governor Orval Faubus and President Dwight D. Eisenhower in September 1957 (Giddins, F2001, pp. 127–8) were unusual statements for jazz musicians to make. As already noted, however, some commentators believed that bop embodied the protest of young African Americans who felt marginalized and oppressed by Jim Crow racial strictures in the United States. And it was partly the space opened by Parker and Gillespie as well as Holiday, Ellington, and Armstrong that enabled a young musician like Mingus to comment directly on current political events and social conditions, as when he indicted the same Arkansas governor as Armstrong in "Original Faubus Fables" (Cand., 1960) or protested against the unequal treatment of African Americans in "Freedom" (UA, 1962). During this period, as the civil rights movement was gathering momentum and black nationalism was emerging as a powerful political force, other jazz musicians spoke out as well. The liner notes of Sonny Rollins' album *The Freedom Suite* (Riv., 1958) contained a statement by the saxophonist decrying the fact that "the Negro, who more than any other people can claim America's culture as his own, is being persecuted and repressed…[and] is being rewarded with inhumanity." Max Roach collaborated with the singer and songwriter Oscar Brown Jr. on *We Insist! Freedom Now Suite* (Can., 1960), which featured sections entitled "Driva' Man" and "Tears for Johannesburg"; the album implicitly connected the brutality of American slavery in the former with the Sharpeville Massacre in South Africa (1960) in the latter. The pianist Randy Weston, in collaboration with the poet Langston Hughes and the arranger Melba Liston, celebrated the cultural and spiritual homeland of African Americans in *Uhuru Afrika!* (Roul., 1960). Abbey Lincoln, similarly, affirmed pride in her black heritage through the songs "When Malindy Sings" and Weston's "African Lady" on her album *Straight Ahead* (Can., 1961). Critics, however, did not always respond positively to such efforts. Ira Gitler, in a now infamous review of Lincoln's album in *Down Beat,* complained that the work was more propaganda than art and accused Lincoln of being a "professional Negro." The ensuing controversy led the magazine's editors in March 1962 to publish the edited transcript of a heated conversation between critics and musicians, including Gitler and Lincoln, discussing the issues raised by the review under the heading "Racial Prejudice in Jazz."

Critics and musicians also engaged in contentious debates about the saxophonist Ornette Coleman, a musician who perhaps personified the searching spirit of progressive jazz in the late 1950s and early 1960s more than anyone else. Although steeped in the bop of Parker and the hard-edged blues of his home state of Texas, Coleman ventured far beyond this musical territory in the company of several musicians he met in Los Angeles in the mid-1950s: the cornetist Don Cherry, the bass player Charlie Haden, and the drummer Billy Higgins. Coleman's pianoless quartet came to New York in 1959 and drew considerable critical attention performing at the Five Spot Café. Although Coleman's compositions had discernible formal contours and although his tunes and solo lines frequently implied an underlying tonality and relied on gestures derived from the blues, the group's collective effect suggested to some an abandonment of set chord changes, known forms, and conventional instrumental functions. Haden and Higgins proved to be not just supportive accompanists but assertive participants in a four-way conversation. Harmonic activity was unpredictable, phrase lengths were flexible, and functional tonality at times erased. "Blues Connotation" (from *This is our Music*, Atl., 1960) begins with saxophone and trumpet stating an aggressive theme—not quite in 12-bar blues form—that almost sounds typical of the Silver–Blakey school of hard bop. As Coleman delves into his solo, however, the structure opens up and dissolves, and the established tonality flickers in and out of focus. The blues is no longer a formal principle but a point of reference, as Coleman explained (N. Hentoff: disc notes, *The Best of Ornette Coleman*, Atl., 1970): "[The piece] is played in the blues tradition, which makes it sound like a blues, but as you listen throughout you hear that the minor 3rds do not dominate but act as a basis for the melody." Coleman, like Davis around the same time, thus demonstrated an interest in "melodic rather than harmonic variation," jettisoning the bopper's chord-driven engine in order to increase the melodic options for improvised lines.

The titles of Coleman's albums sought to reflect the spirit of innovation driving his activity: *Tomorrow is the Question! The New Music of Ornette Coleman* (Cont., 1959), *The Shape of Jazz to Come* (Atl., 1959), and especially *Free Jazz* (Atl., 1960), in which a double quartet collectively improvises, at times producing dense textures, jarring dissonance, and agitated rhythmic activity. While some hailed *Free Jazz* as a liberating manifesto, opening a new world of possibilities for adventurous musicians working in jazz, others saw it as a violent, even destructive act: the *Down Beat* reviewer John A. Tynan wrote:

> This witches' brew is the logical end product of a bankrupt philosophy of ultraindividualism in music…These eight nihilists were collected together in one studio at one time and with one common cause: to destroy the music that gave them birth.

10. Free jazz, fusion, and beyond (1960–79). In the 1960s the bold challenges to mainstream jazz posed by such figures as Ornette Coleman and John Coltrane appealed to younger musicians seeking to find their voices. A movement formed within the jazz community, analogous in some ways to the ideological formation of the bop school 20 years earlier, in which proponents of what some called Free jazz (or "the new thing") distanced themselves from the mainstream that had gradually taken shape during the 1950s. These musicians, most of them in their early to mid-20s, sought challenges beyond the constraints of chord progressions, pre-composed melodies, swing, the Tin Pan Alley songbook, and predictable roles for ensemble players. They gave priority to music that pressed against boundaries,

formal and interactive, some favoring a more literal brand of collective improvisation. In contrast to what preceded it, their music seemed to such critics as John A. Tynan fierce, angry, passionate, chaotic, discordant, and uncompromising.

Prominent figures in this group were the saxophonists Archie Shepp, Pharoah Sanders, Albert Ayler, Marion Brown, and John Tchicai, the trombonists Grachan Moncur III and Roswell Rudd, the cornetist Don Cherry, the trumpeter Bill Dixon, the pianist Cecil Taylor, the bass players Gary Peacock and Buell Neidlinger, and the drummers Ed Blackwell, Andrew Cyrille, and Sunny Murray. They found outlets for their music in artists' lofts, galleries, and small concert halls. Recording studios also formed part of the free jazz scene. Coltrane's historic recording session for *Ascension* (Imp., 1965) brought together members of his own quartet with seven young players based in New York. The issued disc contained a 40-minute performance that had some elements of pre-planning (melodic motifs and mode choices) but relied primarily on spontaneous collaboration. "The emphasis was on textures rather than the making of an organizational entity," said Shepp, one of the participants. "There is no casual approach to be taken to this record," warned A.B. Spellman in the liner notes, observing that the group formed "a plexus of voices, all of different kinds, but most belonging to that generation which grew up on Charles Mingus, Thelonious Monk, [Cecil] Taylor, [Jackie] McLean, Coleman, Coltrane, the human rights struggle, and nuclear weapons." Impulse, a label which had already built an iconic visual identity with its black and orange album spines, established its sonic identity in the latter half of the 1960s beginning with *Ascension*. It cemented for itself a vanguardist reputation by issuing recordings by young experimental musicians under the rubric "the new wave in jazz." Impulse's activities were complemented by scattered album releases from Blue Note and Atlantic and much more concentrated efforts by such independent labels as ESP-disk. Typical among such efforts—musically, politically, and culturally—were pieces like Shepp's "Rufus (swung his face at last to the wind, then his neck snapped)" (Imp., 1964) and Albert Ayler's "Ghosts: Second Variation" (ESP-disk, 1965). Both recordings showcase fluid group dynamics: bass players and drummers perform free from their conventional time-keeping roles, while horn players, liberated from having to relate their pitch choices to repeating harmonic progressions, explored a much broader range of melodic possibilities. Like other experimental musicians of the era, moreover, all of the musicians involved exploited the timbral capabilities of their instruments more extensively than their predecessors, spending more time in precincts that some listeners might have labeled "noise."

The styles cultivated by the free jazz players perhaps limited their music's appeal, especially for conventional audiences, just at the point when the always volatile financial world of performing venues became even more unstable. As America's post-World War II manufacturing and export boom subsided, the surpluses that provided even African Americans with disposable income to buy recordings and support the bars and clubs where many musicians plied their trade gradually diminished. In addition, municipalities in the United States had since the 1950s been mounting a number of urban regeneration projects which disproportionately affected poor and African American communities and forced venues that served them to close or relocate (Lewis, E2008, pp. 85–7; Isoardi, E2006, pp. 40–47). Partially in response to such conditions, a number of musicians formed collectives to help them present their own performances and connect with sympathetic audiences. These collectives functioned partially as self-help groups, helping musicians establish firmer economic bases for their activities, but their members also evinced a concern with the future through their teaching young musicians in their communities, often at no cost. One such organization, the Underground Musicians Association, later the Union of God's Musicians and Artists Ascension, was formed in Los Angeles in late 1961 by Horace Tapscott and became a significant force in politically oriented arts activities and in nurturing the careers of the saxophonist Arthur Blythe, the cornetist Butch Morris, and the drummer (and later critic) Stanley Crouch, among others. In Chicago, a similar group was the Association for the Advancement of Creative Musicians, founded (1965) by the composer and pianist Muhal Richard Abrams, out of which emerged the Art Ensemble of Chicago (1969) and the trio Air (1975). The Black Artists Group took shape in St. Louis (1968), serving as a meeting ground for Julius Hemphill, Hamiet Bluiett, and Oliver Lake, who later formed the World Saxophone Quartet with David Murray (1976).

Other important music collectives supporting experimental jazz improvisation and composition included the Jazz Composers Guild and the Jazz Composers' Orchestra Association in New York, the Creative Arts Collective in Detroit, the Instant Composers Pool in Amsterdam, and New Artists Guild (later Free Music Production) in Germany. The mystic, pianist, composer, and bandleader Sun Ra perhaps took those tendencies the furthest in fostering communal structures for AVANT-GARDE JAZZ. He lived together with members of his Arkestra first in Chicago, later in New York and Philadelphia, rehearsing and touring with the group while issuing recordings on small independent labels such as ESP-disk and Saturn. Sun Ra and his Arkestra, like the Art Ensemble of Chicago after them, used theatrical elements and costumes drawn from an eclectic range of sources to present performance as ritualized event and cultural critique.

Because of their novelty and innovative edge, free jazz players of the 1960s have received considerable attention from historians writing about that period. But they represented only one of many currents in jazz flourishing by this time. Mainstream or "straightahead" jazz continued to be the dominant style heard around the world. This category now subsumed both the work of bop and post-bop musicians like Gillespie, Monk, Sarah Vaughan, Bill Evans, Sonny Rollins, and Art Blakey, as well as older musicians still active, including

Earl Hines, Coleman Hawkins, and Roy Eldridge. Some among them sought to reach wider audiences by performing popular material: Louis Armstrong with "Hello, Dolly!," Ella Fitzgerald with the country-and-western album *Misty Blue*, and Duke Ellington and the guitarist Wes Montgomery with songs by the Beatles. Others drew upon African American vernacular idioms like blues, rhythm and blues, and soul to bring their music closer to prevailing popular music styles. Horace Silver incorporated rock and urban Latin American boogaloo beats in "The Jody Grind" (BN, 1966) and "Psychedelic Sally" (BN, 1968), as did Les McCann and Eddie Harris on their hit "Compared to What?" (Atl., 1969). Cannonball Adderley also achieved commercial success with his rendition of Joe Zawinul's "Mercy, Mercy, Mercy" (Cap., 1966). Some of the most inventive small-group jazz by younger players who did not exclusively embrace the free jazz aesthetic can be sampled in the series of albums Blue Note issued featuring such artists as Lee Morgan, Donald Byrd, Freddie Hubbard, Woody Shaw, Joe Henderson, Andrew Hill, Larry Young, Hank Mobley, Tony Williams, Wayne Shorter, and Herbie Hancock.

Vital life signs in the field of big-band jazz were also present during the 1960s. Ellington produced some of the most memorable music of his career during this period on such albums as *Afro Bossa* (Rep., 1963) and *The Far East Suite* (RCA, 1966). He also turned to composing concerts of sacred music requiring the combined forces of orchestra, solo singers, choir, and dancers; these works, didactic in tone and devout in character, were performed in cathedrals and churches in the United States and Europe. Meanwhile, he and his orchestra kept touring steadily and performing for both listeners and dancers, as did other swing era survivors such as Count Basie, Benny Goodman, and Woody Herman. Joining these veterans on the scene were newly formed ensembles, including the Kenny Clarke–Francy Boland Big Band in Germany, the Thad Jones–Mel Lewis Orchestra in New York, and the Don Ellis Orchestra in Los Angeles. These groups attested to the continued appeal of the big-band sound while seeking to attract younger listeners by incorporating features drawn from other idioms, as in the funky rhythm and blues groove in the Jones–Lewis orchestra's version of "Central Park North" (Solid States Records, 1969).

An important stream of jazz activity during the 1960s flowed from Brazil. The popularity of Brazilian samba and bossa nova first reached American jazz musicians through recordings by Antonio Carlos Jobim, João Gilberto, and Laurindo Almeida. In the early 1960s the guitarist Charlie Byrd introduced Stan Getz to bossa nova this way, and both went on to perform pieces from this repertory together and with Brazilian musicians on such albums as *Jazz Samba* (Verve, 1962) and *Getz/Gilberto* (Verve, 1963). The latter featured Jobim's "Girl from Ipanema" performed by João and Astrud Gilberto; its nearly whispered vocals, gently plucked guitar rhythms, and cool affect occupied vastly different aesthetic terrain from the free jazz emerging at the same time. The use of Brazilian elements in jazz grew stronger in the decades to follow, from artistic collaborations between musicians (Shorter and Milton Nascimento on *Native Dancer*, Col., 1974) to the series of important Brazilian performers who contributed to the jazz scene, among them the percussionists Airto Moreira and Alphonse Mouzon, the singer Flora Purim, and the pianist Eliane Elias.

Japan was another country that began to figure more prominently on the world jazz scene in the 1960s and 1970s. Beyond developing a significant base of jazz fans that would draw American musicians to cities like Tokyo and Osaka and for a time support festivals like the one at Mount Fuji, Japan produced musicians who launched successful international careers as performers and recording artists, among them the pianist and bandleader Toshiko Akiyoshi, the saxophonist and flutist Sadao Watanabe, the trumpeter Terumasa Hino, and the pianist Yosuke Yamashita. Record companies in Japan also issued music by American artists that featured both a higher quality of sound and at times material that had not been released in the United States and Europe.

Just as Miles Davis in the 1950s had been among those inspiring jazz musicians to embrace a "cool" aesthetic and to explore modal options, so in the 1960s and 1970s he trod a path others found attractive. The quintet he led from 1965 to 1968 featured Shorter (saxophone), Hancock (piano), Ron Carter (bass), and Tony Williams (drums) and specialized in richly textured compositions written by its members. It perfected a free and fluid performance style that nevertheless remained tonally anchored, although often modally inflected, and used cyclical harmonic structures derived from earlier jazz practice. Davis was also increasingly drawn to using static harmonic fields as a basis for lengthy group jams, and this tendency, together with the adoption of a solid backbeat, even eighth-note rhythmic motion, and amplified instruments (such as bass guitar and keyboards), brought his music closely in line with rock and funk on such albums as *In a Silent Way* (Col., 1969) and *Bitches Brew* (Col., 1969). Both albums featured "compositions" that were as much a product of Davis and the producer Teo Macero's post-hoc tape editing as they were of performances by the assembled musicians. This JAZZ-ROCK and JAZZ-FUNK admixture came to be called fusion by the critics, some of whom considered the music no longer part of the jazz tradition. Davis continued undeterred and later wrote of this time: "I wanted to change course, *had* to change course for me to continue to believe in and love what I was playing" (Davis, with Troupe, F1989, p. 298). He also observed that fewer black musicians were playing jazz in the 1960s because it was "becoming the music of the museum."

A number of young musicians who played with Davis in the late 1960s followed their former leader's example in creating fusions that combined elements of jazz, rock, funk, and soul, as well as those from non-western musical traditions. In 1970 Shorter and the keyboard player Joe Zawinul co-founded Weather Report, a group that combined the improvisatory freedom of jazz with a rhythmic vocabulary derived from rock and Latin American and Afro-Caribbean traditions. Weather Report could produce elastic, floating textures that resembled those of Davis's mid-1960s quintet but was also adept at harder-driving rock grooves, as on "Teen Town" from the album *Heavy Weather* (Col., 1976). Chick Corea, another Davis alumnus, formed a jazz-rock unit, Return to Forever, that reached its peak of popularity in the mid-1970s. Hancock similarly extended his style through bringing experimentation with synthesizers and the possibilities of the recording studio into contact with elements of funk and soul on the albums *Head Hunters* (Col., 1973) and *Man-Child* (Col., 1975). In 1971 the English guitarist John McLaughlin, who had performed with Davis on *In a Silent Way* and *Bitches Brew*, formed his own high-energy, high-decibel electric band, the Mahavishnu Orchestra, which took jazz-rock fusion further into the acid-rock mode of the period, also incorporating hypnotic ostinatos and modal melodies derived from Indian music. Also in the 1970s McLaughlin pursued a different kind of fusion with the acoustic trio Shakti, in which he collaborated with the Indian musicians Lakshminarayana Shankar and Zakir Hussein. Virtually alone among these gifted Davis alumni in the 1970s, Keith Jarrett rejected the electrified rock, funk, and fusion options, preferring instead to appear before the public as a solo acoustic pianist, spinning out lengthy, discursive improvisations, as on *The Köln Concert* (ECM, 1975), that at times took on the aura of religious ritual.

While many musicians in the 1970s were intrigued by the possibilities of mingling jazz with rock, funk, and non-western influences—some of them enjoying commercial success in the process—others continued to pursue the adventurous artistic agenda set by free jazz exponents in the 1960s. Interest in free jazz was especially high in Europe. Among the important musicians there contributing to a robust alternative jazz scene against the backdrop of mainstream and traditional jazz were the guitarist Derek Bailey, the drummer Eddie Prévost, and the saxophonists John Surman and Evan Parker in Britain; the trombonist Albert Mangelsdorff, the vibraphone player Gunter Hampel, and the pianist Alex Schlippenbach in Germany; the drummer Han Bennink, the pianist Misha Mengelberg, and the reed player Willem Breuker in the Netherlands; and the Ganelin Trio and Sergey Kuryokhin in the USSR. Large ensembles also emerged from this activity, notably Schlippenbach's Globe Unity Orchestra (founded in 1966), the Breuker Collective (1974), Mathias Rüegg's Vienna Art Orchestra (1977), and Pierre Dørge and the New Jungle Orchestra (1980). These aggregations tended to be highly eclectic in style and drawn to open-ended forms and spontaneous compositional procedures. Jazz constituted only part of their musical identities, which also included folk songs, rock, 20th-century art-music techniques, and liberal doses of satire and Dadaesque humor. The European avant garde also proved nurturing for American musicians touring or living abroad, such as Don Cherry, Steve Lacy, and Anthony Braxton.

Stylistic pluralism also characterized approaches to avant-garde jazz in the United States during the 1970s. Two important centers of activity were New York and Chicago. In Lower Manhattan a vibrant scene developed in lofts and other non-commercial performing spaces that featured artists who sought alternative venues as well as those whom club owners and concert promoters might have been reluctant to book. At Sam Rivers's Studio Rivbea in New York's SoHo, a series of recordings made over ten days in May 1976 documented some of what occurred in such spaces; released under the title *Wildflowers*, the five resultant albums featured the saxophonists Kalaparusha Maurice McIntyre, Byard Lancaster, Marion Brown, Anthony Braxton, and David Murray, the drummers Sunny Murray and Andrew Cyrille, and the trumpeters Olu Dara and Leo Smith, among others. For these figures, as for their European contemporaries, playing "free" was more a performing option than a mandate. Although Lancaster and Murray took considerable harmonic and rhythmic liberties with the Harold Arlen song "Over the Rainbow" (Douglas, 1977), the original melody was still there for listeners; in McIntyre's "Jays" (Douglas, 1977), similarly, the saxophonist's free and probing solo unfolds over a bass ostinato that serves a binding rhythmic function throughout. The *Wildflowers* selections, like the recordings on Anthony Braxton's two *In the Tradition* albums (Inner City, 1974), perhaps signaled a change in emphasis for some experimental musicians. Having established their work as an addition to the family of jazz, it mattered less whether they continued to imagine themselves as a literal avant-garde, eschewing what came before, than it did that they explored their relationships to the various mainstreams and traditions that preceded them. As the 1980s approached, in fact, musicians' stances on such relationships became central to jazz's development and public debates about it.

11. IN THE TRADITION? ECLECTICISM, CANONICITY, AND CONSERVATISM (1979–2001). A number of recordings released in 1979 stake out direct and dynamic positions on the idea of tradition in their selection of material as well as their approaches to it. Ornette Coleman's progenitive role in establishing free jazz looms over the work of Old and New Dreams, a quartet consisting of Don Cherry, Charlie Haden, Ed Blackwell, and the saxophonist Dewey Redman, all of whom performed on Coleman's 1960s recordings. The group's second eponymous release (1979, ECM) provides an expansive view of tradition, one that reaches back in time with Coleman's "Lonely Woman," through space with the West African timeline patterns in "Togo," and even across species barriers with "Song for the Whales." In a narrower but no less profound sense, the instrumentation of the trio Air—consisting of Henry Threadgill (saxophone), Fred Hopkins (bass), and Steve McCall (drums)—presented its musicians both challenges and opportunities on *Air Lore* (Arista) as they revisited nascent manifestations of jazz: compositions by Scott Joplin and Jelly Roll Morton. While the group's two pitched instruments could only with difficulty reproduce all the inner voices of materials originally composed with piano or larger ensembles in mind, that seeming limitation facilitated a wider-ranging exploration of pieces like Joplin's "Ragtime

Dance." Rather than replicate the piece's notated version or a recording of it made from a piano roll, the group treated tempo, form, melody, and timbre as well as accompaniment patterns and instrumental roles elastically and perhaps blurred any distinction between looking forward and looking back. Arthur Blythe's quartet had a similar approach on *In the Tradition* (Col.), an album comprising four tunes drawn from the jazz past alongside two compositions by Blythe. The quartet, which included Hopkins and McCall, treated Juan Tizól's "Caravan" and Fats Waller's "Jitterbug Waltz," for example, in the same open-ended, exploratory manner as they did the 12-bar blues on the new composition "Hip Dripper."

With the exception of Blythe's recordings and those issued by Elektra/Musician, such work appeared mostly on independent labels based in Western Europe, notably ECM and Black Saint, and their US counterparts, Inner City and India Navigation, among others. In contrast, the recording industry's largest companies, such as Warner Brothers and A&M, steered a less adventurous course, devoting their resources to the kinds of pop and R&B fusions exemplified in recordings by George Benson, Herb Alpert, and Bob James. In either case, on the cusp of the 1980s, the diverse and multifaceted character of recorded jazz, given concrete form on the first edition of the *Smithsonian Collection of Classic Jazz* (1973), was striking. Nearly all the major styles from the past—New Orleans, big-band swing, bop, mainstream, free jazz, and fusion—were still being performed and freely mixed by contemporary musicians, their longevity calling into question familiar unilinear, evolutionary models of music history.

While not always sharing in a spirit of exploration, the jazz festivals of the era were likewise celebrations of the music's diversity. Following the establishment of festivals in Montreux (1967) and New Orleans (Jazz and Heritage, 1970), a number of cities and regions turned to such events as one strategy among many to encourage tourism and promote (or invent) their contributions to jazz's development. Like the theater and film festivals which proliferated during those years, jazz festivals made good economic sense to some civic and corporate leaders in response to such changes in global economies as currency devaluation, fuel shortages, and the decreasing viability of manufacturing as a generator of tax income. The longest-running events, in addition to those already mentioned, took place annually in Umbria (from 1973), The Hague then Rotterdam (North Sea, 1976), Chicago (1978), Detroit (1980), Montreal (1980), Lisbon (Jazz em Agosto, 1983), and Guelph (1994), in some cases consolidating disparate events under a single rubric. Many short-lived festivals emerged in other locations, often with corporate sponsorship or other private underwriting, showing the continued commercial and public relations potential of jazz performances, especially those by the music's most senior and least controversial practitioners. Nonetheless, definitional questions frequently came to the fore when presenters included such musicians as Roberta Flack (Newport Jazz Festival

New York, 1972) and Van Morrison (Montreux, 1974) on event rosters.

During the 1980s and 1990s many musicians continued to regard all previous jazz styles as well as other forms of music as potential inputs for individualized hybrids. Among those with experimental backgrounds, some took a synthetic tack, creating musics neither reducible to stylistic constituents as varied as hymns, samba, rhythm and blues, and jazz standards nor to sonorities associated with Hollywood film music or New Orleans brass bands. One can hear such hybrids on releases by the World Saxophone Quartet (*Revue*, BS, 1980, and *Dances and Ballads*, Nonesuch, 1987), the Henry Threadgill Sextet (*Just the Facts and Pass the Bucket*, About Time, 1983), and Steve Lacy (*The Door*, Novus, 1988). On such recordings, performers perhaps highlighted the importance of authorial voice (or brand) while downplaying stylistic cohesion, at least in a conventional sense. Some of their counterparts, while maintaining an emphasis on authorial integrity, opted for something more stochastic and collage-like. John Zorn's *Naked City* (Nonesuch, 1989), for example, features such compositions as "Snagglepuss," which present wildly divergent styles sequentially, sometimes in bursts lasting only long enough for them to register for attentive listeners.

During those same years, however, there were perhaps equal numbers of musicians whose hybrids had a deliberately more narrow range. On *Still Life (Talking)* (Geffen, 1987), the Pat Metheny Group used the harmonic, rhythmic, and timbral elements of a variety of musics from Brazil as its point of departure, while Latin American musical traditions, particularly those of Cuba and Puerto Rico, were the focus of recordings by Jane Bunnett, Roy Hargrove, Marc Ribot, and David Sánchez, among others. These recordings were part of a broad reinvigoration of LATIN JAZZ in the 1990s, although such groups as Manny Oquendo y Libre and the Fort Apache Band had been mining that vein since the 1970s. Among the most inventive collections to emerge from attempts to fuse jazz and Latin styles were Danilo Pérez's *Pana-Monk* (Imp., 1996) and Conrad Herwig's *The Latin Side of John Coltrane* (Astor Place, 1996). In trio and big band settings, respectively, the bandleaders highlighted what they regarded as seldom explored rhythmic, melodic, and structural potentials in compositions by or associated with canonic musicians. A similar focus on musical reimagining characterized the collaboration between Cassandra Wilson and the producer Craig Street that resulted in *Blue Light 'til Dawn* (BN, c1993) and *New Moon Daughter* (BN, c1995). On those albums, songs by such performers and songwriters from the United States and Canada as Robert Johnson, Joni Mitchell, Thom Creed, Linda Bell, Hank Williams, and Neil Young appeared alongside jazz standards and original material in arrangements that evoked southern US United States acoustic and African diaspora musical traditions more clearly than did mainstream jazz.

While all those musicians had more-or-less explicit imperatives in making those recordings, it is nonetheless difficult to escape the impression that, as had been the case at the dawn of jazz recording, concerns in addition to artistic ones governed the selection and treatment of material. This seemed particularly true of recordings that functioned as homage: the saxophonist Antonio Hart's *For Cannonball and Woody* (Novus, 1993), honoring Cannonball Adderley and Woody Shaw; the pianist Jessica Williams's *In the Key of Monk* (Jazz Focus, 1999); the trumpeter and composer Dave Douglas's tribute to Wayne Shorter, *Stargazer* (Arabesque, 1997); and the saxophonist Joe Henderson's series of discs devoted to the music of Billy Strayhorn, Miles Davis, and Antonio Carlos Jobim. Like Wilson on her mid-1990s work, musicians undertaking such concept albums usually sought to capture distinctive traits of the artists being honored while retaining their respective individual voices and perhaps reaching audiences more familiar with their chosen subjects.

In at least one case, a recording label clearly acknowledged its role in molding a product it hoped would interest youthful, non-jazz audiences in its catalog material. Seeing commercial potential in ACID JAZZ—a style of electronic dance music in which producers and DJs fused the sounds of such 1960s and 1970s SOUL JAZZ and jazz-funk artists as the Blackbyrds, Tom Scott, Bobbi Humphrey, and Roy Ayers with the rhythms, rapping, and textures of hip-hop—officials at Capitol Records gave the British duo Us3 full access to its archives and released the group's debut album *Hand on the Torch* in 1993. The album's major hit "Cantaloop (Flip Fantasia)" employed backing tracks that were sampled from Herbie Hancock's "Cantaloupe Island" (from *Empyrean Isles*, BN, 1964) and Pee Wee Marquette's introduction of Art Blakey and the Jazz Messengers from the live recording *At the Jazz Corner of the World* (BN, 1959), and like other acid jazz recordings it comprised rapping over short, riff-like phrases, layered, digitally processed sound effects, and collage-like construction. Another recording by the Jazz Messengers, James Williams's "Stretchin'" from *Reflections in Blue* (Timeless, 1979), furnished the primary samples for another commercially successful fusion of jazz and hip-hop, Digable Planets' "Rebirth of Slick (Cool like dat)" (Pendulum, 1993). This process of rearranging and updating is traditional for jazz musicians. Hancock himself had done it with "Cantaloupe Island" on his album *Secrets* (Col., 1976). Earlier, bop musicians had supplied new melodies for familiar harmonic structures: for example, Miles Davis based "Donna Lee" on the harmonies of "(Back Home Again in) Indiana." And arrangers had revised older pieces from the repertory, for example, Don Redman's transformation of King Oliver's "Dippermouth Blues" into "Sugar Foot Stomp" for Fletcher Henderson's orchestra. While the methods of production used for acid jazz have led some to question whether it qualifies as jazz, the music is part of the jazz family, no further removed from paradigmatic work, in some ways, than the third-stream experiments of the 1950s or the free jazz of the 1960s. Questions of definition and the sales of some acid jazz releases notwithstanding, the style's impact on the practices of improvising musicians, who were rarely featured as live performers

on its most representative recordings, was minimal, and the vogue for the style was brief.

Even in those cases where jazz musicians engaged stylistically with hip-hop performers, the former were more likely to be inspired by the work of such hip-hop producers as Ali Shaheed Muhammad (of A Tribe Called Quest), DJ Premier (of Gang Starr), and Pete Rock, with whom they shared an interest in lesser-known funk and rock recordings. The saxophonists Greg Osby and Steve Coleman, both members of Brooklyn's M-BASE Collective, were among the musicians associated with jazz to produce album-length collaborations with rappers, the former with *3-D Lifestyles* (BN, 1993) and the latter with *A Tale of 3 Cities* (Novus, 1995). Each recording had moments pointing toward something greater than the sum of its parts, but the fluid group dynamics and harmonic and metric complexity that characterized the leaders' other projects assumed less prominence in these final mixes than their ability to provide backgrounds for the vocalists' work. In other words, even when skilled performers attempted such fusions, they found themselves subordinate to partners who might not have been able to follow them down more adventurous paths.

Other musicians in the 1990s incorporated aspects of popular, classical, and non-western traditions on a more limited basis. On *Wish* (WB, 1993), Joshua Redman performed his own compositions, standards from the swing and bop eras, and songs by Stevie Wonder, Eric Clapton, and Pat Metheny. With his group Masada, the composer and saxophonist John Zorn filtered traditional Jewish musical materials through the lens of contemporary jazz practice and chamber music performance; in other settings he explored music from films and cartoons. The pianist Uri Caine released a series of discs exploring the music of Gustav Mahler, Bach, and Schumann, and the saxophonist Jane Ira Bloom integrated movement and live electronics into her performances. Fred Ho, Jon Jang, Francis Wong, and Tatsu Aoki drew upon East Asian musical resources in works conceived for their ensembles, while Hafez Modirzadeh incorporated Persian modal practices into his compositions and improvisational work. Among all those players, the clarinetist Don Byron has proven remarkably versatile, exploring post-bop mainstream styles, free jazz, klezmer music, small-group swing, and jazz-funk fusion inspired by Funkadelic and Mandrill on a series of albums for Nonesuch and Blue Note.

Simultaneous with these hybridizing projects were those of musicians participating in the jazz repertory movement who viewed the past and the world around them in more curatorial terms. Their ensembles, typically big bands affiliated with universities, conservatories, or large cultural institutions—the Lincoln Center Jazz Orchestra or Smithsonian Jazz Masterworks Orchestra, for example—attempted to revive the sounds of earlier well-known ensembles, such as those of Ellington, Basie, and Goodman, often playing from transcriptions of recordings and reproducing solos as well as ensemble and rhythm section parts. If the transformative recycling of acid jazz reflected African American traditions extending back for centuries, the re-creative impulse behind jazz repertory groups derived from the model of European art music, interpreting finished "works" (scores generated from recordings) and striving for "authenticity" through historically informed performing practice.

The jazz repertory movement was but one symptom of the larger process of institutionalization that jazz underwent in the 1980s and 1990s. As the Congressional Resolution of 1987 indicates (see JAZZ, §1), jazz in the 1980s started receiving a level of economic support and recognition previously reserved for classical music. Private foundations, government arts agencies, museums, and major corporations became important sources of funding, underwriting special events and media projects and sponsoring fellowships, awards, and competitions for jazz musicians. Institutions of higher learning established jazz degree programs and hired seasoned professionals to serve as teachers. Those institutions, in part, helped to spur renewed interest in big bands, not as repertory units, but as outlets for new creative work from such artists as Jason Lindner and Maria Schneider. The literature on jazz expanded greatly in the form of textbooks, scholarly monographs, popular biographies and histories, and pedagogical materials, some following broader intellectual currents and taking a critical view of jazz historiography and processes of canon formation. Recordings of jazz became more readily available as record labels, spurred by the arrival of the compact-disc format, undertook extensive campaigns of reissues. And when in 1997 a Pulitzer Prize committee gave its composition award to Wynton Marsalis—after a previous board had controversially overruled a jury's decision to honor Duke Ellington in 1965—it was evident that jazz had covered vast cultural distance over the relatively short course of its history.

Marsalis, a trumpeter, composer, bandleader, and educator from New Orleans, received such recognition partly because of the crucial role he had played in popularizing and promoting jazz. After emerging in the early 1980s as a fiery soloist with Art Blakey and the Jazz Messengers, he was signed to Columbia Records, which heavily promoted the recordings he made with groups featuring his older brother Branford on saxophone. After Wynton had won two Grammy Awards in 1984, some critics considered his work a harbinger of a jazz rebirth (following its presumed death from experimentation and fusion in the 1970s), and younger musicians who might have gone in other directions drew inspiration from albums like *Black Codes (From the Underground)* (Col., 1985), which highlighted Marsalis's interest as a bandleader in exploring the rhythmic freedom, expressive vocabulary, and formal play of Miles Davis's mid-1960s quintet and John Coltrane's quartet (Elie, G1990, pp. 272–4). He sharply changed direction at the end of the 1980s, when he both spent more time investigating pre-bop jazz styles and became the founding artistic director of the jazz program at Lincoln Center, New York's prestigious and powerful sponsor of European-derived performing arts (opera, ballet, and symphony and chamber music). By that point, however,

his celebrity had already encouraged other record labels, large and small, to invest more money in recording and promoting mainstream jazz styles. In other words, Marsalis had helped to bring jazz solidly within the embrace of America's cultural establishment. He increased visibility for the music through his concerts and recordings, television and radio programs, and book and video projects; he commissioned new works and sponsored high-school band competitions; he toured widely with the Lincoln Center Jazz Orchestra and appeared regularly as clinician and lecturer in schools throughout the country. At the same time, he sparked controversy by articulating views some considered to be unduly rigid and conservative, particularly through insisting that certain musical features—swing, the blues, and call and response—must be present in order for music to qualify as jazz. Others criticized his programming at Lincoln Center, claiming that it excluded members of the jazz avant garde or that it did not adequately highlight contributions of white and female musicians.

Those criticisms, perhaps, mattered little to the millions of people who watched the Ken Burns documentary *Jazz*, a ten-part television series which aired on American public stations in January 2001. Along with Stanley Crouch and Albert Murray—two of his advisors as well as fellow board members of Jazz at Lincoln Center—Marsalis was a star of the documentary, an on-camera personality who in charming but sometimes hyperbolic fashion extolled the artistry of such figures as Louis Armstrong and Duke Ellington over all others. Viewers without other historical knowledge, upon hearing the condemnations some commentators offered of 1960s experimentalism, may have come away unaware that anything of lasting significance, besides Marsalis's emergence, happened after 1960. As a cultural event, despite the brief boost it gave to jazz record sales, "Jazz" perhaps represented the end of the era in which projects addressed the question of tradition head on.

12. JAZZ IN THE NEW CENTURY. Of course, the end of "Jazz" was not the end of jazz. Although Columbia Records and other major labels had released most jazz artists, including Marsalis, from their contracts by 2003 and some independents in the parlance of the time "diversified" their rosters to include more popular musics at the beginning of the 21st century, those actions were not necessarily indicative of any specific trouble for jazz as a set of musical styles. Although the novelty of compact discs was fading and recording and distribution became more strictly regulated by a few multinational conglomerates, record sales started declining in the second half of the 1990s, forcing all divisions of major recording corporations to implement accounting changes and show quarterly profits (Negus, H1999). Such expectations ironically caused Sony's classical division to sign the trumpeter Terence Blanchard, who had previously been under contract to Sony Jazz, and the rock singer-songwriter Joe Jackson, and Blue Note to release recordings by Al Green and Anita Baker, among others.

As in the past, though, independent labels like ECM, Criss Cross, and Enja released recordings that represented the variety of approaches that still characterized jazz and related styles. Their work was complemented by and in many ways surpassed that of newer labels. New York's Pi Recordings and AUM Fidelity emerged as specialists in experimental musics, presenting recordings by such established performers as Muhal Richard Abrams, the Art Ensemble of Chicago, and William Parker as well as the work of newer artists including the drummer Susie Ibarra, the pianist Vijay Iyer (a former sideman of Steve Coleman), the saxophonist Steve Lehman (some of whose work adapts Tristan Murail's ideas about spectral harmony), and the drummer Tyshawn Sorey; the last three played together in the collaborative trio Fieldwork. The St. Louis-based label Maxjazz gave such mainstream performers as the guitarist Russell Malone, the pianist Mulgrew Miller, and the trumpeter Jeremy Pelt continued exposure through instrumental and vocal series presented in visually distinctive packages. Detroit's Mack Avenue took a slightly more varied course, including post-Marsalis straightahead artists like the saxophonists Kenny Garrett and Ron Blake and the bass player Christian McBride on a roster that also features the Gerald Wilson Orchestra and the guitarist Stanley Jordan.

Jazz venues and festivals also experienced changes that were signs less of a decline than they were of a return to the leaner state of affairs preceding what in retrospect can be seen a boom time for jazz. The most famous and best-capitalized clubs, including the Village Vanguard in New York and Yoshi's in Oakland, California, continued doing business as they had before, although perhaps with fewer tourists and casual spectators in their audiences. The proprietors of many other venues—particularly such non-profit arts spaces that had been supportive of jazz musicians as the Jazz Bakery in Los Angeles, the Hot House in Chicago, and the Painted Bride Art Center in Philadelphia—were forced to become concert presenters without a fixed location or to alter the balance of jazz in their programming. The organizers of festivals faced similar issues, and their responses were often to scale down their offerings and to focus less on variety and more on targeting specific segments (demographics) of the jazz audience. Ironically, perhaps, the Vision Festival, first presented in 1996, might have furnished a model for organizers attempting to succeed in difficult financial times. Just as experimental musicians had formed collectives in the 1960s to help them and sympathetic audiences to find one another, a number of Lower East Side musicians and their supporters worked together to create this festival which, although originally ignored by major press outlets, quickly became a critical and financial success precisely because of its small scale and focus on experimentation rather than the whole of jazz performance (Currie, H2009, pp. 189–97).

Strategies like those employed by Vision's organizers seemed even more necessary at a time when public radio stations—the last major outlets for presenting jazz recordings on radio and promoting performances by jazz artists—were becoming increasingly dependent on grants and listener donations and acted on the advice of marketing consultants in replacing jazz (and classical music) with news and lifestyle programming. Festival organizers and program directors were responding to demographic changes in their audiences. Indeed, the Survey of Public Participation in the Arts published by the NEA in 2008 indicated that jazz audiences were not only aging but declining for the first time since 1982. However, far from auguring the imminent death of jazz, which had been proclaimed several times since the 1970s, the report suggested that jazz was again one of many areas with which a broader public seemed less engaged.

Partly because of their own desires for challenges, but also in response to such market realities, jazz musicians continued adapting to new technologies and styles of performance as well as revisiting older formats. Uri Caine's trio Bedrock experimented with electronics and the textures of the dance music subgenre drum 'n' bass (*Shelf-life*, Winter and Winter, 2005), and the drummer Karriem Riggins excelled as a straightahead performer while also producing album tracks for the hip-hop and R&B artists Erykah Badu, Common, and the Roots. The bass players Dave Holland and Ron Carter, the pianist Orrin Evans, and the guitarist Kurt Rosenwinkel undertook big band projects that were far from nostalgic, and the drummer Brian Blade, in addition to long-term collaborations with the rock producer Daniel Lanois, led the Fellowship Band, an ensemble that explored the same range of musics as Cassandra Wilson had in the 1990s, although in new compositions that were both more expansive and meditative. Blade also held the drum chair in a quartet formed by the saxophonist Wayne Shorter in 2000 which featured the pianist Danilo Pérez and the bass player John Patitucci as well. Revisiting material from each of the manifestations of Shorter's career—including his time with Weather Report in the 1970s and with Miles Davis and Art Blakey in the 1960s—the quartet nonetheless seemed to bring together both a reverence for what had gone before and a desire for the in-the-moment invention that had characterized jazz practice through much of the music's first century.

During that period, Mary Lou Williams, Duke Ellington, and Art Blakey, among others, likened jazz to a tree, and with that metaphor suggested that the music had roots extending deep into African American, African, and European musical traditions. Since its emergence, jazz has grown upward and outward, its branches and limbs representing varied styles all joined to a sturdy trunk that keeps alive connections to a rich musical past. Music scholars have also described jazz as a family of styles, each containing enough traits in common with its counterparts to resemble them while remaining distinctive. However jazz performers have been perceived—as branches on a tree or members of a global extended family—and wherever they have performed—in nightclubs, concert halls or festival stages, street parades, or high school jazz programs—they have been able to trace their work back to late 19th-century

New Orleans, a time and place equally alive with mixtures and creative collaborations and fraught with questions of inequality. They and their audiences have been drawn one and all to a resilient musical tradition that beckons with a promise of self-discovery and preserves the hope of freedom.

BIBLIOGRAPHY

A: GENERAL REFERENCE

GroveJ

L. Feather: *The Encyclopedia of Jazz* (New York, 1955, suppl. 1956; enlarged 2/1960/R)

L. Feather: *The Encyclopedia of Jazz in the Sixties* (New York, 1966)

J. Chilton: *Who's Who of Jazz: Storyville to Swing Street* (London, 1970, 4/1985)

R. Kinkle: *The Complete Encyclopedia of Popular Music and Jazz, 1900–1950* (New Rochelle, NY, 1974)

L.G. Feather and I. Gitler: *The Encyclopedia of Jazz in the Seventies* (New York, 1976)

I. Carr, D. Fairweather, and B. Priestley: *Jazz: the Essential Companion* (London, 1987)

I. Carr and others: *Jazz: the Rough Guide* (London, 1995)

B. Kirchner, ed.: *The Oxford Companion to Jazz* (New York, 2000)

J.F. Szwed: *Jazz 101: a Complete Guide to Learning and Loving Jazz* (New York, 2000)

M. Cooke and D. Horn, eds: *The Cambridge Companion to Jazz* (Cambridge, 2002)

B: DISCOGRAPHIES

C. Delaunay: *Hot Discography* (Paris, 1936, 4/1943, enlarged 1948 by W.E. Schaap and G. Avakian as *New Hot Discography*)

C.E. Smith: *The Jazz Record Book* (New York, 1942)

B. Rust: *Jazz Records, A–Z* (London, 1961–5, enlarged 5/1983 as *Jazz Records, 1897–1942*)

J.G. Jepsen: *Jazz Records, 1942–[1969]* (Holte and Copenhagen, 1963–71)

W. Bruyninckx: *50 Years of Recorded Jazz (1917–1967)* (Mechelen, 1968–75, enlarged 6/2007 as *90 Years of Recorded Jazz (1917–2007)*)

M. Ruppli: *Prestige Jazz Records, 1949–1971* (Copenhagen, 1972)

M. Cabanowski and H. Choliâski: *Polskie Dyskografia Jazzowa, 1955–1972* (Warsaw, 1974)

M. Harrison and others: *Modern Jazz: the Essential Records, 1945–1970* (London, 1975)

M. Ruppli: *Atlantic Records* (Westport, CT, 1979)

H. Nicolausson: *Swedish Jazz Discography* (Stockholm, 1983)

J. Leder: *Women in Jazz: a Discography of Instrumentalists, 1913–1968* (Westport, CT, 1985)

G.G. Simon: *Magyar Jazzmelek 1912–1984* (Pecs, 1985)

M. Ruppli and B. Porter: *The Clef/Verve Labels* (New York, 1987)

M. Cuscuna and M. Ruppli: *The Blue Note Label* (New York, 1988)

J. Mitchell: *Australian Jazz on Record, 1925–80* (Canberra, 1988)

T. Lord: *The Jazz Discography* (West Vancouver, BC, 1992–)

E. Raben and O.J. Nielsen: *Jazz Records, 1942–80* (Copenhagen, 1995)

C: BIBLIOGRAPHIES

A.P. Merriam and R.J. Benford: *A Bibliography of Jazz* (Philadelphia, 1954/R)

R. Reisner: *The Literature of Jazz: a Preliminary Bibliography* (New York, 1954, enlarged 2/1959 as *The Literature of Jazz: a Selective Bibliography*)

C.G. Herzog zu Mecklenburg: *International Jazz Bibliography: Jazz Books from 1919 to 1968* (Strasbourg, 1969, 2/1975)

D. Kennington: *The Literature of Jazz: a Critical Guide* (London, 1970, rev. 2/1980 by D. Kennington and D.L. Read)

B. Hefele: *Jazz Bibliography* (Munich, 1981)

E.S. Meadows: *Jazz Research and Performance Materials: a Select Annotated Bibliography* (New York, 1981, 2/1995)

D.-R. De Lerma: *Bibliography of Black Music* (Westport, CT, 1984)

W.H. Kenney: "Jazz: a Bibliographical Essay," *American Studies International*, xxv/1 (1987), 3–27

G. Carner: *Jazz Performers: an Annotated Bibliography of Biographical Materials* (New York, 1990)

J. Gray: *Fire Music: a Bibliography of the New Jazz, 1959–1990* (New York, 1991)

D: PERIODICALS

Australia: Australian Jazz Quarterly (1946–57); *Jazz* (1981–); *Jazz Australia* (1976–)

Austria: Jazzforschung (1969–); *Jazz Forum* (1967–)

Belgium: Jazz Hot (1945–)

Canada: Coda (1958–2008), *Critical Studies in Improvisation* (2004–)

England: Crescendo (1962–1990); *Jazz Journal* (1974–7); *Jazz Journal International* (1977–2009); *Jazz Monthly* (1955–71); *Jazz Perspectives* (2007–); *Jazz Research Journal* (2007–); *Music Mirror* (1954–8); *The Wire* (1982–)

Finland: Rytmi (1934–7, 1949–)

France: Cahiers du jazz (1959–); *Jazz-hot* (1935–9); *Jazz magazine* (1954–); *Revue du Jazz* (1948–)

Germany: Jazz Revue (1950–54)

Japan: Swing Journal (1947–)

Netherlands: Jazz Wereld (1965–73)

USA: American Music (1983–2008); *Annual Review of Jazz Studies* (1982–2009); *Black Music Research Journal* (1980–); *Black Perspective in Music* (1973–90); *Cadence* (1976–); *Clef* (1946); *Down Beat* (1934–); *Hot Record Society Rag* (1938–41); *Jazz* (1962–7); *Jazz: a Quarterly of American Music* (1958–60); *Jazz Review* (1958–61); *Journal of Jazz Studies* (1973–81, 2010–); *Journal of the Society for American Music* (2007–); *Metronome* (1885–1961); *Record Changer* (1942–58); *Record Research* (1955–); *Signal to Noise* (1998–); *Tempo* (1933–40)

E: HISTORIES

A. Baresel: *Das Jazz-Buch* (Leipzig, 1925)

R. Goffin: *Aux frontières du jazz* (Paris, 1932)

W. Hobson: *American Jazz Music* (New York, 1939/R)

F. Ramsey Jr and C. Smith, eds.: *Jazzmen* (New York, 1939/R)

R. Goffin: *Jazz: from the Congo to the Metropolitan* (Garden City, NY, 1944, 2/1948 as *Nouvelle histoire du jazz: du Congo au bebop*; Eng. trans., 1975)

B. Ulanov: *A History of Jazz in America* (New York, 1952)

N. Shapiro and N. Hentoff: *Hear me Talkin' to ya: the Story of Jazz as Told by the Men who Made it* (New York, 1955, 2/1966)

M. Stearns: *The Story of Jazz* (New York, 1956, 3/1970)

N. Hentoff and A.J. McCarthy, eds.: *Jazz: New Perspectives on the History of Jazz by Twelve of the World's Foremost Jazz Critics and Scholars* (New York, 1959)

S.B. Charters and L. Kunstadt: *Jazz: a History of the New York Scene* (Garden City, NY, 1962)

J. Goldberg: *Jazz Masters of the Fifties* (New York, 1965/R)

R. Hadlock: *Jazz Masters of the Twenties* (London, 1965/R)

I. Gitler: *Jazz Masters of the Forties* (New York, 1966/R)

H.A. Kmen: *Music in New Orleans: the Formative Years, 1791–1841* (Baton Rouge, 1966)

M. Williams: *Jazz Masters of New Orleans* (New York, 1967)

D.H. Kraner and K. Schulz: *Jazz in Austria: a Brief History and a Discography of all Jazz and Jazz-Like Recordings Made in Austria* (Graz, 1969/R1972 as *Jazz in Austria: Historische Entwicklungund Diskographie des Jazz in Osterreich*)

F. Kofsky: *Black Nationalism and the Revolution in Music* (New York, 1970, 2/1998 as *John Coltrane and the Jazz Revolution of the 1960s*)

M. Williams: *Jazz Masters in Transition 1957–69* (New York, 1970)

R. Russell: *Jazz Style in Kansas City and the Southwest* (Berkeley, 1971)

A. Shaw: *The Street that never Slept: New York's Fabled 52nd Street* (New York, 1971/R1977 as *52nd Street: the Street of Jazz*)

E. Southern: *The Music of Black Americans: a History* (New York, 1971, 3/1997)

R. Stewart: *Jazz Masters of the Thirties* (New York, 1972)

I. Carr: *Music Outside: Contemporary Jazz in Britain* (London, 1973)

D. Morgenstern: *The Jazz Story: an Outline History of Jazz* (New York, 1973)

L.W. Levine: *Black Culture and Black Consciousness: Afro-American Folk thought from Slavery to Freedom* (New York, 1977)

F. Tirro: *Jazz: a History* (New York, 1977, 2/1993)

V. Wilmer: *As Serious as your Life: the Story of the New Jazz* (London, 1977, 2/1980)

J.L. Collier: *The Making of Jazz: a Comprehensive History* (Boston, 1978)

A. Bisset: *Black Roots, White Flowers: a History of Jazz in Australia* (Sydney, 1979, 2/1987)

C. Nanry and E. Berger: *The Jazz Text* (New York, 1979)

E.A. Berlin: *Ragtime: a Musical and Cultural Study* (Berkeley, 1980)

F. Driggs and L. Harris: *Black Beauty, White Heat: a Pictorial History of Classic Jazz, 1920–1950* (New York, 1982)

M. Miller: *Jazz in Canada: Fourteen Lives* (Toronto, 1982)

S. Placksin: *American Women in Jazz, 1900 to the Present: their Words, Lives, and Music* (New York, 1982)

S.F. Starr: *Red and Hot: the Fate of Jazz in the Soviet Union, 1917–1980* (New York, 1983, 2/1994 as *Red and Hot: the Fate of Jazz in the Soviet Union, 1917–1991*)

L. Dahl: *Stormy Weather: the Music and Lives of a Century of Jazz-women* (New York, 1984)

J. Godbolt: *A History of Jazz in Britain, 1919–50* (London, 1984)

J. Litweiler: *The Freedom Principle: Jazz after 1958* (New York, 1984)

S. DeVeaux: *Jazz in Transition: Coleman Hawkins and Howard McGhee, 1935–1945* (diss., U. of California, Berkeley, 1985)

L. Feigin: *Russian Jazz: New Identity* (London, 1985)

I. Gitler: *Swing to Bop: an Oral History of the Transition in Jazz in the 1940s* (New York, 1985)

R. Gordon: *Jazz West Coast: the Los Angeles Jazz Scene of the 1950s* (London, 1986)

A. Medvedev and O. Medvedeva: *Sovetskiy dzhaz: problemï, sobïtiya, mastera* (Moscow, 1987)

W. Schworer: *Jazzscene Frankfurt: eine musiksoziologische Untersuchungen zur Situation anfangs derachtziger Jahre* (diss., Giessen U., 1987)

C. Small: *Music of the Common Tongue: Survival and Celebration in Afro-American Music* (New York, 1987)

J.L. Collier: *The Reception of Jazz in America: a New View* (Brooklyn, NY, 1988)

D.D. Harrison: *Black Pearls: Blues Queens of the 1920s* (New Brunswick, NJ, 1988)

L.A. Erenberg: "Things to Come: Swing Bands, Bebop, and the Rise of a Postwar Jazz Scene," *Recasting America: Culture and Politics in the Age of Cold War*, ed. L. May (Chicago, 1989), 221–45

J. Godbolt: *A History of Jazz in Britain, 1950–70* (London, 1989)

K.J. Ogren: *The Jazz Revolution: Twenties America and the Meaning of Jazz* (New York, 1989)

P.J. Broome and C. Tucker: *The Other Music City: the Dance Bands and Jazz Musicians of Nashville, 1920 to 1970* (Nashville, 1990)

S. Nicholson: *Jazz: the Modern Resurgence* (London, 1990)

T. Gioia: *West Coast Jazz: Modern Jazz in California, 1945–1960* (New York, 1992)

M.H. Kater: *Different Drummers: Jazz in the Culture of Nazi Germany* (New York, 1992)

B.W. Peretti: *The Creation of Jazz: Music, Race and Culture in Urban America* (Urbana, IL, 1992)

D.H. Rosenthal: *Hard Bop: Jazz and Black Music, 1955–1965* (New York, 1992)

C. Ballantine: *Marabi Nights: Early South African Jazz and Vaudeville* (Johannesburg, 1993)

P. De Barros: *Jackson Street after Hours: the Roots of Jazz in Seattle* (Seattle, 1993)

W.H. Kenney: *Chicago Jazz: a Cultural History, 1904–1930* (New York, 1993)

C.E. Kinzer: *The Tio Family: Four Generations of New Orleans Musicians, 1814–1933* (diss., Louisiana State U., 1993)

B. Moody: *The Jazz Exiles: American Musicians Abroad* (Reno, NV, 1993)

L. Porter and M. Ullman: *Jazz: from its Origins to the Present* (Englewood Cliffs, NJ, 1993)

D.G. Such: *Avant-garde Jazz Musicians: Performing "Out There"* (Iowa City, IA, 1993)

T.J. Hennessey: *From Jazz to Swing: African-American Jazz Musicians and their Music, 1890–1935* (Detroit, 1994)

W. Knauer, ed.: *Jazz in Europa* (Hofhenn, 1994)

D.W. Stowe: *Swing Changes: Big-Band Jazz in New Deal America* (Cambridge, MA, 1994)

L. Gourse: *Madame Jazz: Contemporary Women Instrumentalists* (New York, 1995)

E. Kolleritsch: *Jazz in Graz: von den Anfängen nach dem Zweiten Weltkrieg bis zu seiner akademischen Etablierung* (Graz, 1995)

H.H. Lange: *Jazz in Deutschland: die Deutsch Jazz-Chronik bis 1960* (Hildesheim, 1996)

S. DeVeaux: *The Birth of Bebop: a Social and Musical History* (Berkeley, 1997)

T. Gioia: *The History of Jazz* (New York, 1997)

M. Miller: *Such Melodious Racket: the Lost History of Jazz in Canada, 1914–1949* (Toronto, 1997)

L. Porter: *Jazz: a Century of Change* (New York, 1997)

S. Nicholson: *Jazz Rock: a History* (New York, 1998)

K. Whitehead: *New Dutch Swing* (New York, 1998)

R.M. Sudhalter: *Lost Chords: White Musicians and their Contribution to Jazz, 1915–1945* (New York, 1999)

L. Tournés: *New Orleans sur Seine: histoire du jazz in France* (Paris, 1999)

S. Tucker: *Swing Shift: "All-Girl" Bands of the 1940s* (Durham, NC, 2000)

E.T. Atkins: *Blue Nippon: Authenticating Jazz in Japan* (Durham, NC, 2001)

L. Björn and J. Gallert: *Before Motown: a History of Jazz in Detroit, 1920–60* (Ann Arbor, 2001)

A.F. Jones: *Yellow Music: Media Culture and Colonial Modernity in the Chinese Jazz Age* (Durham, NC, 2001)

B. Looker: *Point from which Creation Begins: the Black Artists' Group of St. Louis* (St. Louis, 2004)

M. Heffley: *Northern Sun, Southern Moon: Europe's Reinvention of Jazz* (New Haven, 2005)

S.L. Isoardi: *The Dark Tree: Jazz and the Community Arts in Los Angeles* (Berkeley, 2006)

G.E. Lewis: *A Power Stronger than itself: the AACM and American Experimental Music* (Chicago, 2008)

F: BIOGRAPHIES

L. Armstrong: *Swing that Music* (New York, 1936)

M. Mezzrow and B. Wolfe: *Really the Blues* (New York, 1946)

L. Armstrong: *Satchmo: my Life in New Orleans* (New York, 1954)

S. Bechet: *Treat it Gentle: an Autobiography* (London, 1960)

W. Smith: *Music on my Mind: the Memoirs of an American Pianist* (Garden City, NY, 1964)

A.B. Spellman: *Four Lives in the Bebop Business* (New York, 1966/R2004 as *Four Jazz Lives*)

S. Dance: *The World of Duke Ellington* (New York, 1970)

C. Mingus: *Beneath the Underdog: his World as Composed by Mingus* (New York, 1971)

C. Albertson: *Bessie* (New York, 1972)

D. Ellington: *Music is my Mistress* (Garden City, NY, 1973)

B. Holiday: *Lady Sings the Blues* (New York, 1973)

A. Lomax: *Mister Jelly Roll: the Fortunes of Jelly Roll Morton, New Orleans Creole and Inventor of Jazz* (Berkeley, 1973)

S. Dance: *The World of Swing* (New York, 1974)

H. Hawes and D. Asher: *Raise up off me* (New York, 1974)

R.M. Sudhalter, P.R. Evans, and W. Dean-Myatt: *Bix, Man and Legend* (New York, 1974)

J.C. Thomas: *Chasin' the Trane: the Music and Mystique of John Coltrane* (Garden City, NY, 1975)

C. Calloway and B. Rollins: *Of Minnie the Moocher & Me* (New York, 1976)

S. Dance: *The World of Earl Hines* (New York, 1977)

M. Waller and A. Calabrese: *Fats Waller* (New York, 1977)

D. Gillespie and A. Fraser: *To be, or not…to Bop: Memoirs* (Garden City, NY, 1979)

A. Pepper and L. Pepper: *Straight Life: the Story of Art Pepper* (New York, 1979, 2/1994)

S. Dance: *The World of Count Basie* (New York, 1980)

A. O'Day and G. Eells: *High Times, Hard Times* (New York, 1981/R1989 with updated discography)

I. Carr: *Miles Davis: a Critical Biography* (London, 1982, 2/1998 as *Miles Davis: the Definitive Biography*) [incl. discography by B. Priestley]

B. Priestley: *Mingus: a Critical Biography* (London, 1982)

J. Chambers: *Milestones, i: The Music and Times of Miles Davis to 1960* (Toronto, 1983); ii: *The Music and Times of Miles Davis since 1960* (Toronto, 1985); complete edn (1989)

D. Travis: *An Autobiography of Black Jazz* (Chicago, 1983)

W. Basie and A. Murray: *Good Morning Blues: the Autobiography of Count Basie* (New York, 1985)

D. Barker: *A Life in Jazz* (London, 1986)

J. Chilton: *Sidney Bechet: the Wizard of Jazz* (Basingstoke, 1987)

T. Fitterling: *Thelonious Monk: sein Leben, seine Musik, seine Schallplatten* (Waakirchen, 1987; Eng. trans., 1997, as *Thelonious Monk: his Life and Music*)

G. Giddins: *Celebrating Bird: the Triumph of Charlie Parker* (New York, 1987)

G. Bushell: *Jazz from the Beginning* (Ann Arbor, 1988)

G. Giddins: *Satchmo* (New York, 1988, 2/2001)

M. Hinton: *Bass Line: the Stories and Photographs of Milt Hinton* (Philadelphia, 1988)

J.L. Collier: *Benny Goodman and the Swing Era* (New York, 1989)

M. Davis (with Q. Troupe): *Miles: the Autobiography* (New York, 1989)

J. Chilton: *The Song of the Hawk: the Life and Recordings of Coleman Hawkins* (London, 1990)

R. O'Meally: *Lady Day: the Many Faces of Billie Holiday* (New York, 1991)

D. Rosenberg: *Fascinating Rhythm: the Collaboration of George and Ira Gershwin* (New York, 1991)

R. Stewart: *Boy Meets Horn* (Ann Arbor, 1991)

M. Tucker: *Ellington: the Early Years* (Urbana, IL, 1991)

J. Litweiler: *Ornette Coleman: a Harmolodic Life* (London, 1992)

L. Wright and E. Anderson: *"Fats" in Fact* (Chigwell, Essex, 1992)

S. Nicholson: *Ella Fitzgerald* (London, 1993)

R.M. Radano: *New Musical Figurations: Anthony Braxton's Cultural Critique* (Chicago, 1993)

E.A. Berlin: *King of Ragtime: Scott Joplin and his Era* (New York, 1994)

W.D. Clancy: *Woody Herman: Chronicles of the Herds* (New York, 1995)

G. Lees: *Leader of the Band: the Life of Woody Herman* (New York, 1995)

S. Nicholson: *Billie Holiday* (London, 1995)

D. Hajdu: *Lush Life: a Biography of Billy Strayhorn* (New York, 1996)

F.M. Hall: *It's about Time: the Dave Brubeck Story* (Fayetteville, AR, 1996)

D.L. Maggin: *Stan Getz: a Life in Jazz* (New York, 1996)

C. Woideck: *Charlie Parker: his Music and Life* (Ann Arbor, 1996)

J.F. Szwed: *Space is the Place: the Lives and Times of Sun Ra* (New York, 1997)

L. Porter: *John Coltrane: his Life and Music* (Ann Arbor, 1998)

S. Nicholson: *Reminiscing in Tempo: a Portrait of Duke Ellington* (Boston, 1999)

A. Shipton: *Groovin' High: the Life of Dizzy Gillespie* (New York, 1999)

G. Wein and N. Chinen: *Myself among Others: a Life in Music* (Cambridge, MA, 2003)

E. Determeyer: *Rhythm is our Business: Jimmie Lunceford and the Harlem Express* (Ann Arbor, 2006)

H. Silver: *Let's Get to the Nitty Gritty: the Autobiography of Horace Silver*, ed P. Pastras (Berkeley, 2006)

E. Shim: *Lennie Tristano: his Life in Music* (Ann Arbor, 2007)

R.D.G. Kelley: *Thelonious Monk: the Life and Times of an American Original* (New York, 2009)

G: THEORY, ANALYSIS, AND CRITICISM

SchullerEJ

C. Engel: "Jazz: a Musical Discussion," *Atlantic Monthly*, cxxx (1922), 182–9

H.O. Osgood: *So this is Jazz* (Boston, 1926/R)

H. Panassié: *The Real Jazz* (New York, 1942/R)

R. de Toledano, ed.: *Frontiers of Jazz* (New York, 1947, 3/1994)

A. Hodeir: *Hommes et problèmes du jazz* (Paris, 1954; Eng. trans., enlarged, 1956/R, 2/1979 as *Jazz: its Evolution and Essence*)

J.F. Mehegan: *Jazz Improvisation* (New York, 1958–65)

E.J. Hobsbawn: *The Jazz Scene* (London, 1959, 2/1993)

L. Ostransky: *The Anatomy of Jazz* (Seattle, 1960)

B. Green: *The Reluctant Art* (London, 1962, enlarged 2/1991)

A. Hodeir: *Toward Jazz* (New York, 1962/R)

M. Williams, ed.: *Jazz Panorama: from the Pages of the Jazz Review* (New York, 1962/R)

F. Tirro: "The Silent Theme Tradition in Jazz," *MQ*, liii (1967), 313–34

W. Russo: *Jazz Composition and Orchestration* (Chicago, 1968)

M. Williams: *The Jazz Tradition* (New York, 1970, 3/1993)

M.L. Stewart: *Structural Development in the Jazz Improvisational Technique of Clifford Brown* (diss., U. of Michigan, 1973)

R. Wang: "Jazz circa 1945: a Confluence of Styles," *MQ*, lix (1973), 531–46

N.T. Davis: *The Early Life and Music of Charlie Parker* (diss., Wesleyan U., 1974)

E. Jost: *Free Jazz* (Graz, 1974)

T. Owens: *Charlie Parker: Techniques of Improvisation* (diss., UCLA, 1974)

F. Tirro: "Constructive Elements in Jazz Improvisation," *JAMS*, xxvii (1974), 285–305

R. Byrnside: "The Performer as Creator: Jazz Improvisation," *Contemporary Music and Music Cultures*, ed. B. Nettl and others (Englewood Cliffs, NJ, 1975), 233–51

W.E. Taylor: *The History and Development of Jazz Piano: a New Perspective for Educators* (diss., U. of Massachusetts, 1975)

T.D. Brown: *A History and Analysis of Jazz Drumming to 1942* (diss., U. of Michigan, 1976)

M. Harrison: *A Jazz Retrospect* (Newton Abbot, 1976, 2/1991)

C.C. Blancq: *Melodic Improvisation in American Jazz: the Style of Theodore "Sonny" Rollins, 1951–1962* (diss., Tulane U., 1977)

L. Gushee: disc notes, *Steppin' on the Gas: Rags to Jazz, 1913–1927*, New World NW 269 (1977)

L. Gushee: "Lester Young's 'Shoeshine Boy'," *IMSCR XII: Berkeley 1977*, 151–69

R.L. Stein: *The Jazz Trumpet: Development of Styles and an Analysis of Selected Solos from 1924 to 1961* (diss., U. of Miami, 1977)

M.J. Budds: *Jazz in the Sixties: the Expansion of Musical Resources and Techniques* (Iowa City, IA, 1978, 2/1990)

J. Coker: *Listening to Jazz* (Englewood Cliffs, NJ, 1978)

M.C. Gridley: *Jazz Styles* (Englewood Cliffs, NJ, 1978, 7/1997)

D. Bailey: *Improvisation: its Nature and Practice in Music* (Ashbourne, 1980)

G. Giddins: *Riding on a Blue Note* (New York, 1981)

B. Kernfeld: *Adderley, Coltrane, and Davis at the Twilight of Bebop: the Search for Melodic Coherence (1958–59)* (diss., Cornell U., 1981)

O. Perguson: *The Otis Ferguson Reader* (Highland Park, IL, 1982/R1997 as *In the Spirit of Jazz: the Otis Ferguson Reader*)

A. Jaffe: *Jazz Theory* (Dubuque, IA, 1983)

G.F. Smith: *Homer, Gregory, and Bill Evans? The Theory of Formulaic Composition in the Context of Jazz Piano Improvisation* (diss., Harvard U., 1983)

P. Alperson: "On Musical Improvisation," *Journal of Aesthetics and Art Criticism*, xxxxiii (1984), 17–29

G. Giddins: *Rhythm-a-ning: Jazz Tradition and Innovation in the '80s* (New York, 1985)

H. Martin: *Enjoying Jazz* (New York, 1985)

L. Porter: *Lester Young* (Boston, 1985)

M. Williams: *Jazz Heritage* (New York, 1985)

W. Balliett: *American Musicians: Fifty Six Portraits in Jazz* (New York, 1986, 2/1996 as *American Musicians II: Seventy-Two Portraits in Jazz*)

F. Davis: *In the Moment: Jazz in the 1980s* (New York, 1986)

G. Schuller: *Musings: the Musical Worlds of Gunther Schuller* (New York, 1986)

C. Suhor: "Jazz Improvisation and Language Performance: Parallel Competencies," *Etc.*, xxxxiii (1986), 133–40

S. Larson: *Schenkerian Analysis of Modern Jazz* (diss., U. of Michigan, 1987)

O. Keepnews: *The View from Within: Jazz Writings, 1948–1987* (New York, 1988)

J. Pressing: "Improvisation: Methods and Models," *Generative Processes in Music: the Psychology of Performance, Improvisation, and Composition*, ed. J.A. Sloboda (New York, 1988), 129–78

E.S. Meadows: "Africa and the Blues Scale: a Selected Review of the Literature," *African Musicology…a Festschrift presented to J.H. Kwabena Nketia*, ed. J.C. Djedje and W.G. Carter (Los Angeles, 1989–92), 263–76

R.F. Rose: *An Analysis of Timing in Jazz Rhythm Section Performance* (diss., U. of Texas, Austin, 1989)

G. Schuller: *The Swing Era: the Development of Jazz, 1930–1945* (New York, 1989)

D. Baker, ed.: *New Perspectives on Jazz* (Washington, DC, 1990)

A. Beeson: "'Quoting Tunes': Narrative Features in Jazz," *Collectanea*, i (1990), 1–15

F. Davis: *Outcats: Jazz Composers, Instrumentalists, and Singers* (New York, 1990)

L.E. Elie: "An Interview with Wynton Marsalis," *Callaloo*, xiii (1990), 271–90

W. Friedwald: *Jazz Singing: America's Great Voices from Bessie Smith to Bebop* (New York, 1990)

W. Knauer: *Zwischen Bebop und Free Jazz: Komposition und Improvisation des Modern Jazz Quartet* (Mainz, 1990)

G. Potter: "Analyzing Improvised Jazz," *College Music Symposium*, xxx/1 (1990), 64–74

S. DeVeaux: "Constructing the Jazz Tradition: Jazz Historiography," *Black American Literature Forum*, xxv (1991), 525–60

J. Gennari: "Jazz Criticism: its Development and Ideologies," *Black American Literature Forum*, xxv (1991), 449–523

R.T. Dean: *New Structures in Jazz and Improvised Music since 1960* (Philadelphia, 1992)

J. Taylor: *Earl Hines and Black Jazz Piano in Chicago, 1923–1928* (diss., U. of Michigan, 1993)

M. Tucker, ed.: *The Duke Ellington Reader* (New York, 1993)

P.F. Berliner: *Thinking in Jazz: the Infinite Art of Improvisation* (Chicago, 1994)

G.P. Ramsey Jr.: *The Art of Bebop: Earl "Bud" Powell and the Emergence of Modern Jazz* (diss., U. of Michigan, 1994)

N. Hentoff: *Listen to the Stories: Nat Hentoff on Jazz and Country* (New York, 1995)

B. Kernfeld: *What to Listen for in Jazz* (New Haven, CT, 1995)

J.A. Prögler: "Searching for Swing: Participatory Discrepancies in the Jazz Rhythm Section," *EthM*, xxxix (1995), 21–54

G. Carner: *The Miles Davis Companion* (New York, 1996)

H. Martin: *Charlie Parker and Thematic Improvisation* (Newark, NJ, 1996)

I. Monson: *Saying Something: Jazz Improvisation and Interaction* (Chicago, 1996)

T.F. Coolman: *The Miles Davis Quintet of the Mid-1960s: Synthesis of Improvisational and Compositional Elements* (diss., New York U., 1997)

J. King: *What Jazz is: an Insider's Guide to Understanding and Listening to Jazz* (New York, 1997)

P. Julien: *The Structural Function of Harmonic Relations in Wayne Shorter's Early Compositions: 1959–1963* (diss., U. of Maryland, College Park, 2003)

J. Magee: *The Uncrowned King of Swing: Fletcher Henderson and Big Band Jazz* (New York, 2005)

T.A. Jackson: *Blowin' the Blues Away: Performance and Meaning on the New York Jazz Scene* (Berkeley, 2012)

H: OTHER STUDIES

M. Berger: "Jazz: Resistance to the Diffusion of a Culture Pattern," *Journal of Negro History*, xxxii (1947), 461–94

S. Finkelstein: *Jazz: a People's Music* (New York, 1948)

H.S. Becker: "The Professional Dance Musician and his Audience," *American Journal of Sociology*, lvii (1951), 136–44

R.A. Waterman: "African Influence on the Music of the Americas," *Acculturation in the Americas:…XXIXth International Congress of Americanists: New York 1949*, ed. S. Tax (Chicago, 1952), 207–18

J. Berendt: *Das Jazzbuch: Entwicklung und Bedeutung der Jazzmusik* (Frankfurt, 1953, 6/1992 as *The Jazz Book: from Ragtime to Fusion and Beyond*)

W.B. Cameron: "Sociological Notes on the Jam Session," *Social Forces*, xxxiii (1954), 174–82

A.P. Merriam and R.S. Mack: "The Jazz Community," *Social Forces*, xxxviii (1960), 211–22

P. Oliver: *Blues Fell this Morning: the Meaning of the Blues* (London, 1960, 2/1990)

N. Hentoff: *The Jazz Life* (New York, 1961/R)

N. Leonard: *Jazz and the White Americans: the Acceptance of a New Art Form* (Chicago, 1962)

A. Baraka [L. Jones]: *Blues People: Negro Music in White America* (New York, 1963)

R. Ellison: *Shadow and Act* (New York, 1964)

R.S. Gold: *A Jazz Lexicon* (New York, 1964/R1975 as *Jazz Talk*)

A. Baraka [L. Jones]: *Black Music* (New York, 1967)

A.P. Merriam and F.H. Garner: "Jazz: the Word," *EthM*, xii (1968), 373–96

M. Stearns and J. Stearns: *Jazz Dance: the Story of American Vernacular Dance* (New York, 1968, rev. 2/1994 by B. Buffalino)

R.A. Stebbins: "A Theory of the Jazz Community," *Sociological Quarterly*, ix (1968), 318–31

C.A. Nanry: *The Occupational Subculture of the Jazz Musician: Myth and Reality* (diss., Rutgers U., 1970)

W.C. Allen, ed.: *Studies in Jazz Discography* (Newark, NJ, 1972)

D. Meeker: *Jazz in the Movies* (London, 1972, 3/1981)

G. Stevenson: "Discography: Scientific, Analytical, Historical, and Systematic," *Library Trends*, xxi (1972), 101–35

J. Buerkle and D. Barker: *Bourbon Street Black: the New Orleans Black Jazzman* (New York, 1973)

A. Murray: *Stomping the Blues* (New York, 1976)

Z. Knauss: *Conversations with Jazz Musicians* (Detroit, 1977)

F. Kofsky: "The State of Jazz," *BPM*, v (1977), 44–68

A. Taylor: *Notes and Tones: Musician-to-Musician Interviews* (Liège, 1977)

L. Ostransky: *Jazz City: the Impact of our Cities on the Development of Jazz* (Englewood Cliffs, NJ, 1978)

D. Sudnow: *Ways of the Hand: the Organization of Improvised Conduct* (Cambridge, MA, 1978)

J.S. Roberts: *The Latin Tinge: the Impact of Latin American Music on the United States* (New York, 1979, 2/1999)

M. Gordon: *Live at the Village Vanguard* (New York, 1980)

L.A. Erenberg: *Steppin' Out: New York Nightlife and the Transformation of American Culture, 1890–1930* (Chicago, 1984)

B. Rusch: *Jazztalk: the Cadence Interviews* (Secaucus, NJ, 1984)

G. Sales: *Jazz: America's Classical Music* (Englewood Cliffs, NJ, 1984)

K. Bilby: "Caribbean Crucible," *Repercussions: a Celebration of African American Music*, ed. G. Haydon and D. Marks (London, 1985), 128–51

U.B. Davis: *Paris without Regret: James Baldwin, Kenny Clarke, Chester Himes, and Donald Byrd* (Iowa City, IA, 1986)

R. Ellison: *Going to the Territory* (New York, 1986)

A. Baraka and A. Baraka: *The Music: Reflections on Jazz and Blues* (New York, 1987)

D.J. Elliott: "Structure and Feeling in Jazz: Rethinking Philosophical Foundations," *Bulletin of the Council for Research in Music Education*, no.95 (1987), 13–38

N. Leonard: *Jazz: Myth and Religion* (New York, 1987)

E.S. Meadows: "Ethnomusicology and Jazz Research: a Selective Viewpoint," *Bulletin of the Council for Research in Music Education*, no.95 (1987), 61–70

S. DeVeaux: "Bebop and the Recording Industry: the 1942 AMF Recording Ban Reconsidered," *JAMS*, lxi (1988), 126–165

T. Gioia: *The Imperfect Art: Reflections on Jazz and Modern Culture* (New York, 1988)

H. Gray: *Producing Jazz: the Experience of an Independent Record Company* (Philadelphia, 1988)

F.A. Salamone: "The Ritual of Jazz Performance," *Play and Culture*, i (1988), 85–104

G. Early: *Tuxedo Junction: Essays on American Culture* (New York, 1989)

M. Gridley and others: "Three Approaches to Defining Jazz," *MQ*, lxxiii (1989), 513–31

R.J. Powell, ed.: *The Blues Aesthetic: Black Culture and Modernism* (Washington DC, 1989)

R.T. Buckner and S. Weiland, eds.: *Jazz in Mind: Essays on the History and Meanings of Jazz* (Detroit, 1991)

P. Chevigny: *Gigs: Jazz and the Cabaret Laws in New York City* (New York, 1991)

G. Tomlinson: "Cultural Dialogics and Jazz: a White Historian Signifies," *BMRJ*, xi (1991), 229–64

R. Crawford: "Notes on Jazz Standards by Black Authors and Composers, 1899–1942," *New Perspectives on Music: Essays in Honor of Eileen Southern*, ed. J. Wright and S.A. Floyd (Warren, MI, 1992), 245–87

R. Crawford and J. Magee: *Jazz Standards on Record, 1900–1942: a Core Repertory* (Chicago, 1992)

Y. Hayashi and others: *Tokyo Shitamachi Jazzdori* (Tokyo, 1992)

K. Stratemann: *Duke Ellington, Day by Day and Film by Film* (Copenhagen, 1992)

P.L. Sunderland: *Cultural Meanings and Identity: Women of the African American Art World of Jazz* (diss., U. of Vermont, 1992)

J.L. Collier: *Jazz: the American Theme Song* (New York, 1993)

B. Johnson: "Hear me Talkin' to Ya: Problems of Jazz Discourse," *Popular Music*, xii (1993), 1–12

D. Meltzer, ed.: *Reading Jazz* (San Francisco, 1993)

G.L. Starks Jr: "Jazz Literature and the African American Aesthetic," *The African Aesthetic: Keeper of the Traditions*, ed. K. Welsh-Asante (Westport, CT, 1993), 143–57

C. Keil and S. Feld, eds.: *Music Grooves: Essays and Dialogues* (Chicago, 1994)

W. Marsalis and F. Stewart: *Sweet Swing Blues on the Road* (New York, 1994)

S. DeVeaux: *Jazz in America: Who's Listening* (Carson, CA, 1995)

S.A. Floyd Jr: *The Power of Black Music: Interpreting its History from Africa to the United States* (New York, 1995)

K. Gabbard, ed.: *Jazz among the Discourses* (Durham, NC, 1995)

K. Gabbard, ed.: *Representing Jazz* (Durham, NC, 1995)

W. Minor: *Unzipped Souls: a Jazz Journey through the Soviet Union* (Philadelphia, 1995)

T. Owens: *Bebop: the Music and the Players* (New York, 1995)

K. Gabbard: *Jammin' at the Margins: Jazz and the American Cinema* (Chicago, 1996)

R. Gottlieb, ed.: *Reading Jazz: a Gathering of Autobiography, Reportage, and Criticism from 1919 to Now* (New York, 1996)

D. Chevan: *Written Music in Early Jazz* (diss., City U. of New York, 1997)

R.G. O'Meally, ed: *The Jazz Cadence of American Culture* (New York, 1998)

K. Negus: *Music Genres and Corporate Cultures* (London, 1999)

R. Walser, ed.: *Keeping Time: Readings in Jazz History* (New York, 1999) [incl. E. Ansermet: *"A 'Serious' Musician Takes Jazz Seriously,"* 9–11]

J. Gennari: *Blowin' Hot and Cool: Jazz and its Critics* (Chicago, 2006)

A.S. Currie: *Sound Visions: an Ethnographic Study of Avant-Garde Jazz in New York City* (diss., New York U., 2009)

D. Ake, C.H. Garrett, and D. Goldmark, eds.: *Jazz/Not Jazz: the Music and its Boundaries* (Berkeley, 2012)

MARK TUCKER/TRAVIS A. JACKSON (1–10),
TRAVIS A. JACKSON (11–12, BIBLIOGRAPHY)

Jazz at Lincoln Center [JALC]. Jazz division of Lincoln Center for the Performing Arts in New York. In 1987 Lincoln Center launched Classical Jazz, its first concert series devoted solely to jazz. In 1996 JALC became an autonomous jazz division with WYNTON MARSALIS at the helm. Marsalis has continued to work as the artistic director of JALC and the music director of the Jazz at Lincoln Center Orchestra. This ensemble maintains an extensive repertoire of classic jazz works while continuing to commission and premiere new pieces. It tours extensively, frequently collaborating with guest artists, and participates in JALC programs, such as the annual Essentially Ellington High School Jazz Band Competition & Festival. JALC also maintains a busy schedule of concerts by visiting artists, lectures, and jazz education initiatives.

The construction of Frederick P. Rose Hall in 2004 expanded the educational and broadcasting resources available to the organization, including a fully equipped recording studio, the Nesuhi Ertegun Jazz Hall of Fame, and the Irene Diamond Education Center. Products of these new developments include *Jazz at Lincoln Center Radio with Wendell Pierce*, an award-winning, nationally distributed radio series, and American Music Abroad, a program run in collaboration with the US Department of State Bureau of Educational and Cultural Affairs which aims to promote cross-cultural understanding through music and by 2012 had taken 118 musicians to 97 countries since its launch in 2005.

SARAH E. SUHADOLNIK

Jazz at the Philharmonic. International jazz concert series founded in Los Angeles by NORMAN GRANZ.

Jazz choir. *See* VOCAL JAZZ ENSEMBLE.

Jazz Composer's Orchestra Association [JCOA]. A collective organization for the promotion of avant-garde jazz, co-founded in 1966 by CARLA BLEY.

Jazz dance. An American art form that grew up alongside and in direct relationship with jazz music. Emerging primarily from the influence of the West African aesthetic in the Americas that began with the trans-Atlantic slave trade, it became a physical expression of both the complexity and exuberance of American culture and history.

As with jazz music, jazz dance incorporates improvisation and reflects the power of community supporting the individual creative voice in a non-literal expression of storytelling and connection to the human experience. Its many manifestations include SOCIAL DANCE, TAP DANCE, theatrical dance, concert dance, and film performance. These manifestations have produced a variety of styles called jazz dance that embrace to various degrees fundamental qualities associated with jazz expression.

1. History. 2. Components.

1. HISTORY. The early forms that gave rise to jazz dance are described as African American vernacular dance. These dances retained the West African tradition of dance and music as conversational partners and the featuring of individual dancers. They included ring shouts, JUBA, and dances such as the buzzard lope and the CAKEWALK. An earlier dance, the cakewalk was performed to the syncopated rhythms of ragtime music and served as an incubator for inventive new steps in minstrel shows and vaudeville.

The heart and soul of jazz dance crystallized between the 1920s and 1940s. As jazz music exploded in popularity, a number of vernacular dance crazes emerged, the most significant being the LINDY HOP. The essence of jazz dance is contained in these vernacular dances that made their way on to vaudeville stages across the country. They were performed by such groups as Whitey's Lindy Hoppers, which polished their skills at the Savoy Ballroom in New York. Many of these dances were either introduced or popularized in Broadway shows. *Shuffle Along*, a successful all-black musical that opened on Broadway in 1921, set a new standard for stage dancing and choreography. Tap dance also emerged on the national scene during this era with such performers as Bill Robinson appearing in venues from vaudeville to Broadway to film. Katherine Dunham contributed jazz choreography to such films as *Stormy Weather*. In the late 1940s the Russian-born dancer Mura Dehn, known for filming and documenting these early dances, established the Academy of Jazz for training dancers in classic vernacular jazz dance forms.

The 1950s and 1960s were a major transitional era in jazz dance. Jazz as a formal and teachable style of dance was relatively new. Influenced by the swing era and the emerging popularity of jazz dance as a theatrical dance style, teachers and choreographers embraced the form from their own aesthetic perspective resulting in diverse approaches to the creation, performance, and teaching of jazz dance. Pepsi Bethel began his Authentic Jazz Dance Theatre maintaining roots to the vernacular forms. Modern jazz dance began to be taught in dance studios primarily as a style of theatrical dance that was becoming popular on Broadway and in film through the works of such choreographers as Jack Cole and Jerome Robbins. Over time modern jazz dance drew upon a diversity of popular music styles. It significantly influenced MUSICAL THEATER DANCE which saw further developments by such choreographers as Bob Fosse. Concurrently, Broadway musicals such as *Black and Blue* and *Sophisticated Ladies* maintained the connection to jazz music for performance.

2. COMPONENTS. Within the complexity of the jazz dance genre in the early 21st century, there are core physical components identified as integral and traceable back to their West African roots. These components include a weighted release into gravity, rhythmic complexity, call and response, and attention to syncopation and musicality, all of which are fundamental to the concept of swing. Additional core qualities include improvisation, movement isolations, challenging physical coordination, explosive energetics, and a stylistic relationship to the vernacular roots.

The many styles of jazz dance that have emerged since its inception have been named in a variety of ways, including: vernacular, classic, afro, theatrical, concert, lyrical, modern, hip-hop, and music-based. Descriptions of these various styles vary depending upon the point of view and approach of the individual teacher or choreographer. In general, the styles reflect an emphasis to one degree or another on the various integral components. Many styles also incorporate other dance forms such as ballet and modern. Some of the important jazz dancers who developed their own signature teaching techniques include Bethel, Matt Mattox, Frank Hatchett, Luigi, Lynn Simonson, and Billy Siegenfeld. The Broadway and film choreographers Cole and Fosse are among those who contributed their own style to the jazz dance lexicon. Dance companies that have committed to the jazz dance idiom in performance include Pepsi Bethel's Authentic Jazz Dance Company, Decidedly Jazz Danceworks, Jump Rhythm Jazz Project, Giordano Dance Chicago, and the Danny Buraczeski's Jazzdance. Other companies and dancers who are known for performing and choreographing to jazz music or working with a jazz influence include Donald McKayle, Talley Beatty, Daniel Nagrin, Dianne McIntyre, and Hubbard Street Dance Chicago.

BIBLIOGRAPHY
M. Stearns and J. Stearns: *Jazz Dance: the Story of American Vernacular Dance* (New York, 1979)

L.F. Emery: *Black Dance in the United States from 1619 to Today* (Pennington, NJ, 2/1989)
K. Hazzard-Gordon: *Jookin' the Rise of Social Dance Formations in African-American Culture* (Philadelphia, 1990)
J.F. Crosby: *Will the Real Jazz Dance Please Stand Up: a Critical Examination of the Roots and Essence of Jazz Dance with Implications for Education* (diss., Teachers College, Columbia U., 1995)
B.D. Gottschild: *Digging the Africanist Presence in American Performance: Dance and Other Contexts* (Westport, CT, 1996)
J. Malone: *Steppin on the Blues: the Visible Rhythms of African American Dance* (Urbana, IL, 1996)

JILL FLANDERS CROSBY, KATHERINE KRAMER

Jazz education. A subdivision and subculture within music education that focuses on the pedagogy of jazz, including style, improvisation, technique, composing, and arranging. Jazz education began as a means of sharing knowledge about jazz performance technique and improvisation in informal settings among musicians in cities and geographical areas where jazz developed. Early jazz musicians learned to play the style and improvise jazz by imitating others. This required direct observation of performers in typical venues such as dance halls, nightclubs, and bordellos. Aspiring musicians also participated in jam sessions to acquire, share, and hone their jazz performance skills.

The first audio recordings of jazz performances were made in 1917. Since then recordings have facilitated the dissemination of exemplary compositions, improvisations, and stylistic performances without limits of distance or time. Through careful study of recorded performances one may still learn to play like Louis Armstrong from "Satchmo" himself. The educational role of listening to and imitating jazz recordings cannot be overstated.

In subsequent decades private studio instruction was offered in metropolitan areas where jazz flourished. Printed instructional materials appeared as the education of jazz musicians became more formalized. Norbert Bleihoof first attempted to explain jazz improvisation and arranging in a 1935 publication entitled *Modern Arranging and Orchestration*. Professional musicians wrote method books, some with accompanying play-along records. *DownBeat* magazine published transcribed solos and pedagogical articles. In 1941 Joseph Schillinger published *The Schillinger System of Musical Composition*, a widely used text based on his own system of jazz arranging. George Russell wrote a text entitled *The Lydian Chromatic Concept* in 1953, promoting the idea that jazz chords have corresponding scales that may be used for improvisation.

Since the late 1960s, Jamey Aebersold has produced an ever-expanding library of play-along recordings to facilitate the development of jazz improvisation skills. The recordings feature accompaniments performed by professional rhythm sections without melody or soloist, which allows another musician to assume the role of soloist. Today, numerous play-along series focus on chord/scale relationships, common chord progressions, and standard repertoire. Important texts on improvisation that appeared in the 1960s include Jerry Coker's *Improvising Jazz* (1964), David Baker's *Jazz Improvisation: A Comprehensive Method of Study for All Players*

(1969), and John LaPorta's *A Guide to Improvisation* (1968).

An early notable figure in jazz education was Len Bowden. He was associated with many colleges in the South during the 1920s, including Tuskegee Institute (now Tuskegee University), Georgia State College (now Savannah State University), and Alabama State Normal College (now Alabama State University). During World War II, Bowden directed the training of musicians at the US Naval Training Station Great Lakes, where he worked with more than 5000 men (1942–5).

Historically, jazz bands and combos have been the primary vehicles for teaching jazz in academic settings. Jazz bands in secondary schools and colleges typically emerged as extracurricular auxiliary ensembles, derived from larger concert or marching bands. The earliest college jazz bands were not offered for academic credit and were usually organized and led by students. Secondary school bands experienced a period of growth following World War I and jazz bands experienced a period of growth after World War II. Musicians' return from military service in World War II coincided with the decline in popularity of big bands. Finding fewer performing opportunities, many became band directors. Secondary school jazz bands were frequently called "stage bands" to avoid the negative connotations of the term "jazz." The influx of skilled jazz musicians into the music education field had positive effects on the quantity and quality of jazz offerings in secondary school settings.

Early high school jazz bands performed selections arranged by their directors or simplified versions of professional arrangements produced by music publishers. Although repertoire composed and arranged for professional jazz ensembles is often available commercially, graded repertoire composed by individuals who write specifically for school jazz ensembles has become the norm. Notable composer/arrangers whose works were performed widely by high school jazz ensembles include Sammy Nestico, Neal Hefti, and Lennie Niehaus.

Extracurricular, generally student-led ensembles also preceded formal instruction in colleges and universities. Aside from performance-based instruction, Leonard Feather and Robert Goffin taught one of the first jazz history courses at the New School for Social Research in Manhattan in 1941. Later important developments in post-secondary education occurred in Boston and in Denton, Texas.

Lawrence Berk opened a music school in Boston in 1945 that offered course work emphasizing jazz composing and arranging based on Joseph Schillinger's system. The school, known as the Schillinger House, offered a two-year curriculum and awarded an artist diploma. Eventually the name was changed to Berklee School of Music; after becoming accredited to award bachelor degrees, it became the Berklee College of Music (1973).

The first college degree in jazz (BM with emphasis in "Dance Band") was offered in 1947 at North Texas State Teachers College in Denton, now the University of North Texas. M.E. "Gene" Hall, who had written a master's thesis there in which he outlined a proposed college-level jazz curriculum, became the first faculty member in the new program. Central to Hall's curriculum was an arranging class for which a laboratory ensemble performed student arrangements and compositions. That ensemble became the world-renowned One O'Clock Lab Band.

Performing arts high schools experienced a growth period during the 1980s and 1990s. They offered a pre-conservatory, professional music curriculum that often included a jazz track. One of the first of these, the High School of Music and Art in New York City (now the Fiorello H. LaGuardia High School of Music & Art and Performing Arts), continues to feature a fully credited jazz curriculum for secondary students. Other notable performing arts magnet schools with a jazz emphasis include Booker T. Washington High School for the Performing Arts in Dallas and the High School for the Performing and Visual Arts in Houston. Model public school curricula and programs include those of New Trier High School in Winnetka, Illinois, and a curriculum originally published jointly by the International Association of Jazz Education (IAJE) and MENC: The National Association for Music Education (MENC).

Common components of jazz curricula include theory and analysis, improvisation, arranging/composing, history, keyboard, and pedagogy, all specifically within the realm of jazz. Performance experiences include large ensembles and small combos. These components are common in secondary and post-secondary curricula that offer jazz studies.

Following the success of school jazz ensembles, Waldo King, Hal Malcolm, and John Moawad sought to develop a vocal counterpart to instrumental ensembles in the Pacific Northwest during the 1960s. The movement spread, and by the late 1970s and early 1980s workshops, clinics, and festivals devoted to vocal jazz and vocal jazz arrangements had become available, including a well-known vocal jazz program at the University of Miami (1981).

Once maligned by educators as music of low value antithetical to the goals of music education, jazz steadily gained acceptance within the profession. In the 1940s some music education leaders spoke and wrote disparagingly about the music, but great strides toward acceptance and inclusion occurred during the 1960s. The MENC conventions of 1958 and 1960 included panel discussions on jazz. The Yale Seminar of 1963 recommended a broader repertoire in public school music education, with specific mention of jazz. The Tanglewood Symposium of 1967 declared that music of all periods, styles, forms, and cultures belong in the curriculum. Over the course of the decade the number of jazz ensembles in public high schools doubled to approximately 10,000, and the number of colleges and universities with jazz ensembles for which academic credit was awarded doubled to approximately 100. It was in the late 1960s that jazz rose to a level of acceptance that would allow it to proliferate within the world of music education in the 1970s and 1980s.

The National Association of Jazz Educators (NAJE) was founded in 1968 after a group of educators had begun meeting during MENC conferences earlier in the decade. The group broke away from MENC, held the first NAJE convention in 1973, and became the International Association of Jazz Educators (IAJE) in 1989. The purposes of the organization were to foster and promote the understanding, appreciation, and artistic performance of jazz and popular music, to lend assistance and guidance in developing jazz curricula, to disseminate professional and educational news, and to assist in the organization of clinics, festivals, and symposia. However, the organization began to struggle financially, filed for bankruptcy in 2008, and officially dissolved in 2009. Former IAJE and MENC president Willie Hill then worked to establish a subsidiary group within MENC, the Society for Jazz Education (2008), and served as its first chair. Another group that emerged to fill the void created by the demise of the IAJE, The Jazz Education Network, was founded in Chicago in June 2008 by Mary Jo Papich, Lou Fischer, and 40 other jazz educators, businessmen, and professionals.

Many factors contributed to the acceptance and proliferation of jazz in music education. The music itself changed during the 1940s, when jazz combos began to replace big bands. More emphasis was placed on improvisation, and performances served less for dancing and more for concert-type listening for audiences. Some critics who were skeptical of the integrity of the music were silenced as the music evolved into the more complex and virtuosic performances of the bebop era. While the evolution of the art form itself contributed to its eventual acceptance, the perception of jazz as a threat to society was slowly displaced during the 1950s and 1960s by other manifestations of changing culture and a rising counterculture, such as rock and roll music, the civil rights movement, anti-war protests, illegal drugs, and various alternative lifestyles.

Some have argued that the integration of jazz into academia has distanced the music from African American culture, and that the academic setting has stifled the art form. Nevertheless, jazz educators have promoted the art form as an authentic, indigenous fusion of musical influences that embodies the diversity of the American experience, something to be performed and appreciated by all, regardless of race or gender.

Jazz artists at the highest levels have taken active roles in promoting and participating in jazz education. Consequently, the educational enterprise has remained closely tethered to the professional practice of jazz since its inception. Jazz education events—including festivals, conventions, and summer clinics and workshops—have allowed student musicians to interact with jazz masters to learn about performance practice and improvisation in educational settings. Master classes and clinics in which students interact with professionals are well-established traditions in jazz education.

Not all educational experiences occur in classrooms and rehearsal halls. Collegiate jazz festivals provide regional and national venues that historically have functioned to elevate the performance level and validity of college jazz ensembles and combos. Summer jazz camps provide opportunities for jazz musicians to hone their performance and improvisation skills. The Lenox School of Jazz in Massachusetts operated as an annual summer program from 1957 through 1960. Ken Morris, a jazz promoter, wanted to develop a summer program similar to the Tanglewood Institute and the Aspen Music Festival and School, which would allow students and educators to study and perform with top professional jazz performers and arrangers such as members of the Stan Kenton Orchestra. Consequently, the first National Stage Band Camp was held in 1959 at Indiana University. In 1973, Morris started the Jazz Combo/Improvisation Clinics held in the summers at various locations under the direction of Jamey Aebersold.

Jazz at Lincoln Center and the Thelonious Monk Institute of Jazz are two exceptional examples of organizations that promote the performance and appreciation of jazz. The Jazz at Lincoln Center Orchestra under the artistic direction of Wynton Marsalis produces concerts, programs, and tours, and hosts high school jazz band competitions and festivals and a jazz band director academy. The Thelonious Monk Institute of Jazz promotes jazz education through solo competitions and performance programs that place promising young jazz musicians with jazz masters. The institute presents a multitude of educational programs and performances, primarily in public schools.

Contemporary concerns in jazz education include the emphasis on the large ensemble over the small combo in educational settings, the need to include jazz pedagogy in the preparatory curriculum of music educators, the extent to which vocal jazz has established itself within music education and distanced itself from the "show choir," and the organizational void at the national level since the demise of the IAJE.

BIBLIOGRAPHY

F. Ferriano: "A Study of the School Jazz Ensemble in American Music Education," *NAJE Educator*, vii/3 (1975), 4–6, 18
C. Suber: "Jazz Education," *The Encyclopedia of Jazz in the Seventies*, ed. L. Feather and I. Gitler (New York, 1976), 366–81
R.W. Miller: *The North Texas State University Jazz Degree: A History and Study of Its Significance* (PhD diss., Michigan State U., 1979)
G. Aitken: "What Is Vocal Jazz?" *NAJE Educator*, xiii/1 (1980), 9–10
C. Suber: "The Summer Jazz Clinics: A Memoir and a Salute," *Jazz Educators Journal*, xiv/4 (1982), 17–21
W. Carter: "Jazz Pedagogy: A History Still in the Making," *Jazz Educators Journal*, xviii/3 (1986), 10–3, 49–50
M. Williams and D. Richards: "Jazz Classics: The Missing Essential in Jazz Education," *Bulletin of the Council for Research in Music Education*, no. 96 (1988), 1–6
R. Witmer and J. Robbins: "A Historical and Critical Survey of Recent Pedagogical Materials for the Teaching and Learning of Jazz," *Bulletin of the Council for Research in Music Education*, 96 (1988), 7–9
E.M. Pisciotta: *The History of Jazz Choir in the United States* (DMA diss., U. of Missouri-Kansas City, 1992)
J.B. Dyas: "Jazz Education in Performing Arts High Schools," *Jazz Educators Journal*, xxvii/1 (1994), 32–4
D. Murphy: "Jazz Studies in American Schools and Colleges: A Brief History," *Jazz Educators Journal*, xxvi/3 (1994), 34–8
L. Bash: "Reminiscences: The Founding of NAJE/IAJE," *Jazz Educators Journal*, xxviii/1 (1995), 45–9
M.L. Small: "Berklee: Looking toward the Next Millennium," *Jazz Educators Journal*, xxviii/3 (1995), 20–6

D. Joyner: "Fifty Years of Jazz Education at North Texas," *Jazz Educators Journal*, xxx/2 (1997), 53–62

D. Phillips: "Jazz Studies, Objectives, Rationales, Activities, and Evaluation: The New Trier High School Model," *Jazz Educators Journal*, xxx/5 (1998), 32–43

R.L. Snyder: *College Jazz Education during the 1960s: Its Development and Acceptance* (DMA diss., U. of Houston, 1999)

K.E. Prouty: "The History of Jazz Education: A Critical Reassessment," *Journal of Historical Research in Music Education*, xxvi/2 (2005), 79–100

T. Whyton: "Birth of the School: Discursive Methodologies in Jazz Education," *Music Education Research*, viii/1 (2006), 65–81

MICHAEL D. WORTHY

Jazz-funk. Occasionally an alternative term for fusion or JAZZ-ROCK, the term generally describes a musical style in which JAZZ and FUNK elements interpenetrate. Arising in the United States in the late 1960s and flowering throughout the 1970s, jazz-funk later gathered additional meaning as it spread internationally. Originally associated closely with jazz musicians incorporating funk elements—but also including other concurrent influences, themselves hybrid, such as boogaloo and New Orleans-style rhythm-and-blues—the later developments have become less firmly attached to a jazz identity, as its practitioners have come from more dispersed musical backgrounds, locales, and audiences.

Initially jazz-funk was dominated by young African American jazz musicians, such as Herbie Hancock, George Duke, George Benson, and the Blackbyrds (mostly former students of the trumpeter Donald Byrd), who became attracted to the funk style developed by James Brown, among others. Stylistically, it embraced funk's dance orientation, especially in the rhythm section's straight (as opposed to swung) eighth-note metrical underpinning; a highly percussive slap and pop electric bass-guitar style (Louis Johnson and Paul Jackson); a drum technique emphasizing intricate interaction between bass drum, snare drum, and hi-hat cymbals (Mike Clark and Ndugu Chancler); and the distribution of a dance groove across the entire band, exemplified in the opening groove of Hancock's "Chameleon" (from the album *Head Hunters*, Col., 1973), the early style's most emblematic recording. Distinctions between jazz-funk and funk itself include jazz-funk's relative absence of vocals, its jazz-oriented emphasis on extended improvisational solos, and its prominent inclusion of analog synthesizers.

By 1980 and through the next two decades, jazz-funk's popularity spawned international practitioners, notably the drummer Vladimer Vasilov (USSR), Asymuth (Brazil), T-Square (Japan), and the Brand New Heavies and Jamiroquoi (both UK and both of which featured vocals prominently). Concurrently, DJs and record producers, especially in the UK, began incorporating earlier jazz-funk samples in acid jazz and neo soul recordings, along with disco and its offshoot electronic dance music styles, leading to a somewhat blended stylistic identity.

STEVEN F. POND

Jazz Messengers. Jazz ensemble co-founded and led by ART BLAKEY.

Jazz-rock. A term used to describe an approach to jazz that pointedly includes elements from other idioms; it is also used to refer to a broad style of music that emerged in the mid-1960s and gained importance in the 1970s. Jazz-rock initially incorporated musical and cultural elements of jazz and the youth-oriented popular music of the time, which was itself dominated by rock, soul, and funk. "Jazz-rock" is closely associated with the term "fusion," the two frequently mentioned as a compound term ("jazz-rock fusion"), although "fusion" has overtaken "jazz-rock" in usage. Rather than a singular style, fusion emerged as (and has continued to be) an approach to music making, in which jazz musicians adapted jazz's recent stylistic past and adopted practices—and attracted participants and audiences—from outside jazz's mainstream.

To some musicians and observers, fusion's rise represented a conscious move away from jazz's bop and post-bop conventions and toward a youth-oriented, pop sensibility. To others, fusion reflected eclectic exposure to myriad musical styles, aided in part by expanding international record production and distribution; another interpretation is that fusion's rise in the 1960s represents a spike in jazz's established penchant for stylistic hybridization and adaptation. Because of fusion's breadth, all of these interpretations pertain. A definition of fusion, then, is first: the music resulting from musicians' attempts to extend jazz's traditional aesthetics of adventure and improvisation, borrowing from a range of other musics; and second: the drawing together of jazz constituencies with others formerly beyond jazz's scope.

1. Style. 2. History.

1. STYLE. By the early 1960s several post-bebop trends had emerged within jazz, including hard bop, cool jazz, and free improvisation. Although often considered to be competing styles, these trends shared some procedures, aesthetic predilections, and personnel. Overall, musicians associated with these movements sought to distinguish their playing from bebop conventions largely through avenues of sound, harmony, rhythm, and form. Fusion extended these explorations through the lenses of rock music (hence, "jazz-rock"), R&B-derived forms (soul and funk), and non-Western traditional musics, particularly those of the Iberian Peninsula, India, West Africa, and the Caribbean. Nevertheless, jazz musicians have drawn significant influence from all of these sources for decades. From this perspective, although it is possible to describe the 1970s through the 1980s as a "fusion era," meaning a period of heightened interest in these engagements, fusing is a long-term factor in jazz.

Although creative manipulations of timbre and texture are long-standing aspects of jazz practice, these took on renewed importance with the post-bebop stylists. Raspy and other "voice-like" timbral inflections, *altissimo* squeals on saxophone, and aggressive, soloistic drumming (notably in hard bop and free improvisation) as well as restrained, chamber-like tones (cool jazz) became key stylistic markers. Trumpet-muting devices gained renewed emphasis, especially through Miles Davis's use of the Harmon mute. At the same time, pop musicians, especially in rock, soul, and funk, expanded those technologies and techniques of amplification and sound distortion which had begun in the 1940s and 1950s with such blues guitarists as Muddy Waters and John Lee Hooker. By the late 1960s the advent of affordable modular synthesizers, such as the Minimoog, ushered in a range of synthesized sounds that were available to avant-garde jazz musicians and in due course to fusion players. Especially as jazz-rock gained broad recognition in the early 1970s, loud amplification, electric guitars with such sound distortion devices as wah-wah pedals, fuzz boxes, and echo effects, and electronic keyboards became regarded as sine qua non. Similar distortion devices could be used on acoustic instruments; Davis made notable use of them on trumpet. In jazz as well as in rock and funk the role of percussion expanded; drum kits grew in complexity and the hand percussionist became a common addition to the rhythm section. These pop-inflected performing technologies complemented recording techniques such as splice tape-editing and overdubbing which dislodged jazz musicians' normal recording routine of capturing a live performance on tape.

Mirroring developments in free jazz and the modalism trend in post-bebop jazz—as well as in the Western art-music canon and the academic avant-garde—fusion initially gestured away from functional harmony. This did not amount to a rejection of harmony per se, but fusion musicians, like those performing other idioms, sought pathways out of harmonic predictability. Surface harmonies favored tone clusters, extreme dissonance, and gestural figures, often over short, cyclic vamps or modal (non-diatonic) harmonic foundations. Other harmonies borrowed from non-Western melodic note-groupings, such as Indian raga and Arabian *maqām*.

Fusion players also looked beyond jazz's normal, swing-based, rhythmic approach. They tended to favor straight eighth-note (duple) beat subdivisions that were common to rock, soul, and funk; these beat subdivisions were also common in various Afro-Caribbean musics, which contributed directly and indirectly to fusion. By the early 1960s asymmetrical meters had entered the jazz mainstream, with such recordings as Dave Brubeck's "Take Five" (from *Time Out*, Col., 1959); some fusion artists, notably the Mahavishnu Orchestra, embraced these, as well as more extended, additive metric patterns.

Fusion improvisers exploited the timbral possibilities of sound distortion, incorporating sound gestures as well as melodic and harmonic figures into their expressive palettes. Especially in the early to mid-1970s fusion soloists tended to emphasize extremely fast, complex figures. This approach dovetailed with aesthetics borrowed from other idioms and mirrored similar developments in the progressive rock and heavy metal idioms within rock music, as well as traditional aesthetics of Spanish flamenco and Indian raga.

Whether derived from modal jazz's radically slowed harmonic rhythm, Afro-Cuban–derived music's extended

montuno sections, James Brown's funk, or a combination of these, many fusion songs featured extended or even song-length sections of densely textured backgrounds, often made up of a matrix of short, interactive figures spread throughout the band, over which a soloist played.

As the fusion movement solidified, musicians largely adopted the rock model of a self-contained band with a relatively stable set of musicians. This stability added impetus to a later trend within the fusion movement that favored intricate compositions rather than the bebop-derived structure of playing the song form as written, followed by a sequence of solo choruses over a popular song's chord progression, and finally a restatement of the song form, or a coda (head–solos–out-chorus). However, this is not to suggest a standardization of form; compositions ranged from head–solos–out-chorus forms to multi-section forms of great variety.

2. HISTORY. Since fusion so completely resists a standardized understanding, or even nomenclature, much of its recognizability relies on music industry marketing, critical reception, and public perception. Before 1970 jazz record sales had been charted as pop or R&B; there was no jazz chart as such. As the 1960s drew to a close, *Billboard* instituted a Top Jazz Albums record sales chart, and *Down Beat*, the dominant jazz industry periodical in the United States, added news and criticism about rock and soul. Jazz-rock also began to appear in newspaper criticism at this time. Critics tended either to enthuse about fusion's emphasis on virtuosity or to deride its seeming pandering to youth. Permeability in perceived categorical borders between jazz and other musics was further aided by the advent of free format (free-form) FM radio, a precursor to college radio stations, in which independently minded DJs pointedly avoided pop radio's narrow playlists, purveying instead a broad assortment of jazz, folk, non-Western, rock, funk, and spoken-word recordings to a young adult audience. Joining in the era's celebration of eclecticism (while simultaneously building youth-oriented pop to unprecedented sales levels), record stores and labels cross-marketed the same music to several divergent audiences at once (fans of album-oriented rock, funk, soul, blues, or jazz as distinct from each other)—and to all these audiences as newly homogeneous (youth, generally). The rise of jazz-rock or fusion must be understood in the context in which jazz aesthetics, technologies, and public perceptions refocused on contemporaneous, youth-oriented projections of style and sophistication.

Mainstream attention accrued to jazz-rock with Miles Davis's late 1960s recordings, especially *Bitches Brew* (Col., 1969), which was released in 1970. Although that album demonstrated fusion's potential to dwarf other jazz styles in record sales, several jazz-rock projects had already been recorded, beginning around 1966. Among them were small-group jazz players exploring rock and funk sensibilities; these included Larry Coryell's group Free Spirits (*Out of Sight and Sound*, Sunbeam, 1966) and the vibraphonist Gary Burton's *Duster* (RCA, 1967), with Coryell (guitar), Steve Swallow (bass), and Roy Haynes (drums), although the acoustic bass, clean guitar sound, and relative absence of bass drum in the sound mix undermine the rock side of the equation.

Several typical formations arose from the mid-1960s through the early 1970s: small-group jazz players attracted to rock and funk (for example, Davis and Burton); rock groups expanded by (often jazz-oriented) horn sections (Blood, Sweat, and Tears, Electric Flag, Ten Wheel Drive, and the Chicago Transit Authority, later renamed Chicago); avant-garde jazz players incorporating rock, funk, or soul elements (Ornette Coleman's Prime Time); small groups with jazz-affiliated members joining those from rock or funk backgrounds (Tony Williams's Lifetime and Return to Forever); soul, funk, or R&B musicians whose style grew out of earlier soul-jazz fusions of post-bebop and R&B styles (the pianist Les McCann, the guitarist George Benson, and the Crusaders); rock-affiliated groups whose influences leaned toward jazz (the Jimi Hendrix Experience and King Crimson); groups and headliners whose membership and musical elements leaned heavily on non-Western traditional and popular musics contributing to a "world fusion" movement (Oregon, the Brazilian singer and guitarist Milton Nascimento, the steel drummer Andy Narell, and the oud player Rabih Abou-Khalil); and artists whose eclectic interests pointedly eschewed categorization (the Mahavishnu Orchestra). The varied work of such key performers as the keyboard players Herbie Hancock and Chick Corea and the guitarist John McLaughlin exemplified all of these formations.

Fusion cemented its market importance in the mid-1970s with the rise of several super-groups. Some of these featured Davis alumni—Hancock, whose Headhunters sidemen also included the saxophonist Bennie Maupin); Chick Corea's Return to Forever, Tony Williams's Lifetime (with McLaughlin); McLaughlin's Mahavishnu Orchestra; and Weather Report (led by the keyboard player Joe Zawinul and the saxophonist Wayne Shorter)—although several such personnel constellations held sway. These groups and their like emphasized virtuosic improvisation and often performed at blazing tempos, which at times drew critical ire as "empty" display. Fans, on the other hand, valorized in heroic terms the emphasis on speed, intricacy, and clear articulation.

In the mid-1970s a counter trend arose featuring a coterie of sidemen and leaders associated with Creed Taylor International and Dave Grusin and Larry Rosen's GRP Records. These musicians became closely identified with R&B-inflected arrangements and Afro-Brazilian and Afro-Caribbean rhythms and phrasing, which emphasized dance grooves and understated improvisation. Some of these artists—notably, the saxophonist Grover Washington Jr., the keyboard player Bob James, the saxophonist David Sanborn, the flutist Hubert Laws, and the guitarist Earl Klugh—appeared frequently on each other's recordings; their work drew criticism for a certain homogeneity and was christened SMOOTH JAZZ in the 1980s. The most conspicuous sales success, even as critics gnashed their teeth, was achieved by the saxophonist Kenny G.

Another fusion trend, ACID JAZZ, appeared in the early 1990s. Hip-hop artists such as US3 and Digable Planets used hard-bop and other historical jazz recordings as source material to create an acid-jazz movement in which they blended digitized snippets (samples) of these recordings with a funk-oriented drum and electric bass underlay as a basis for MC rapping.

Fusion's eclectic personnel, contexts, and influences cultivated a variety of interpretive stances. For example, the guitarist Pat Metheny, who has worked frequently with the keyboard player Lyle Mays, claimed several influences, including country music, Afro-Brazilian samba-based musics, the Beatles, and folk-revivalists and singer-songwriters, as well as various jazz streams. These combined factors, along with such album titles as *New Chautauqua* (ECM, 1979), *American Garage* (Geffen, 1979), and *Still Life (Talking)* (Geffen, 1987), evoked a nostalgic, introspective Americana. McLaughlin, who was originally attracted to the music of John Coltrane, Thelonious Monk, and Django Reinhardt as well as to flamenco and blues, embraced Indian classical music. He incorporated its harmonic and rhythmic structures into his electric guitar style in the Mahavishnu Orchestra, before forming an acoustic ensemble, Shakti (1975–1977), with Carnatic and Hindustani instrumentalists, and an acoustic flamenco guitar trio with Al Di Meola and Paco de Lucia. Michael (saxophone) and Randy (trumpet) Brecker, both as featured soloists and as bandleaders, drew influence from Coltrane, rock, and R&B in equal measure. Michael Brecker was particularly prolific as a soloist and sideman, appearing on around 700 albums by such varied artists as Frank Sinatra, Paul Simon, Parliament/Funkadelic, and Aerosmith. He played for several years in Steps Ahead, led by the vibraphonist Mike Manieri, during which there were several personnel and style changes including a fusion style played on acoustic jazz instruments and another which owed much of its sound to synthesizer processing. Brecker frequently played the EWI (electronic woodwind instrument) synthesizer in the latter context. However, Brecker never abandoned his acoustic horn nor did he constrain himself to any single style. Similarly, the saxophonist John Zorn's frenetic stylistic unpredictability has carried him from klezmer to punk, hip-hop, and avant-garde influences. The musician most visibly resistant to style containment, Hancock has since the 1970s recorded landmark projects in a variety of styles: synthesizer-enhanced free improvisation (*Mwandishi*, WB, 1970); jazz-funk (*Head Hunters*, Col., 1973); post-bebop reminiscent of Miles Davis's second quintet (*V.S.O.P.: the Quintet*, Col., 1977); electronic dance music (*Future Shock*, Col., 1983); hip-hop (*Dis is da Drum*, Mer., c1992–4), a stylistically kaleidoscopic take on George Gershwin (*Gershwin's World*, Verve, 1998), and reinterpretations of the singer-songwriter Joni Mitchell's songs (*River: the Joni Letters*, Verve, 2007).

Despite a stylistic reaction against fusion known as neo-bop which began in the mid-1970s, fusion's many manifestations have continued to develop, but also to interact, further blurring genre and sub-genre distinctions. For example, Steps Ahead's initial acoustic orientation, described above, could be understood to further post-bebop trends of the mid-1960s, but the group's attraction to dance-friendly grooves, emphasis on virtuosic soloing, and ready, if intermittent, embrace of electronics also suggest fusion. Likewise, Hancock's openness to a variety of orchestral, electronic, and pianistic effects, along with his use of West African drummers, hip-hop DJs, and operatic singers, can also be perceived in the work of the pianist Jason Moran (*Artist in Residence*, BN, 2006), whose reputation has adhered more closely to a youthful but mainstream jazz identity.

Under its various names (jazz-rock and jazz-rock fusion) and sub-trends (jazz-funk, acid jazz, world fusion, and acoustic fusion), fusion has continually encountered heated rejection by musicians and critics intent on reasserting jazz's post-bebop pedigree. The fusion era has waxed and waned since its heyday in the late 20th century; nevertheless, as an expansive approach to jazz music-making, fusion has continued to adapt to changes in tastes and technologies.

BIBLIOGRAPHY

J.-E. Berendt: *Das Jazzbuch: Entwicklung und Bedeutung der Jazzmusik* (Frankfurt, 1953, 2/1959, Eng. trans., 1962; rev. and enlarged 6/1989 by G. Huesmann as *Das Jazzbuch*, Eng. trans., 1992)

E. Jost: "Zur Ökonomie und Ideologie der sogenannten Fusion Music," *Jf*, ix (1977), 9

J. Coryell and L. Friedman: *Jazz-rock Fusion* (New York, 1978)

G. Reynard: *Encyclopédie jazz hot: fusion* (Paris, 1990)

S. Crouch: "Play the Right Thing," *The New Republic* (12 Feb 1990), 30–7; repr. in *The Miles Davis Reader: Four Decades of Commentary*, ed. G. Carner (New York, 1996), 21–40

S. Nicholson: *Jazz-Rock: a History* (Edinburgh, 1998)

S. Pond: *Head Hunters: the Making of Jazz's First Platinum Album* (Ann Arbor, MI, 2005)

D. Ake: "The Emergence of the Rural American Ideal in Jazz: Keith Jarrett and Pat Metheny on ECM Records," *Jazz Perspectives*, i/1 (2007), 29–59

J. Smith: "Sell it Black: Race and Marketing in Miles Davis's Early Fusion Jazz," *Jazz Perspectives*, iv/1 (2010), 7–33

K. Fellezs: *Birds of Fire: Jazz, Rock, Funk, and the Creation of Fusion* (Chapel Hill, NC, 2011)

STEVEN F. POND

J.B.'s, the [JB's, the; Fred Wesley and the JBs; Maceo and the Macks]. Instrumental funk group and backing band to JAMES BROWN. Formed in 1970, they made a number of recordings over the next five years. Their varied personnel included Fred Wesley (trombone and director), Maceo Parker (alto saxophone), Brown (keyboards), and Bootsy Collins (bass guitar). The lineup featured up to six horns, two guitars, organ, bass guitar, one or two drummers, and percussion. Their sound was essentially an extension of Brown's (most of the material was written by Brown and arranged by Wesley) and featured Wesley and Parker's unique improvisations. "Gimme some more," "Pass the peas," and "Cross the track (We better go back)" are typical: a repetitive groove on a 9th or minor 7th chord, created from a number of short riffs and vamps, underpins the horns' riff-based melodies which are interspersed with collective vocals made up of singing, raps, random chatter, and background noise. Like much of Brown's music, the bridge, on the subdominant or dominant, varies the groove and typically lasts eight bars. In their solos, Wesley and Parker employ simple blues riffs and create an exciting rhythmic impetus by varied attack and lengths of notes.

While Brown is rightly credited with an enormous influence over a range of musical styles since the early 1970s, his rhythm section created the most subtle, distinctive, and danceable grooves, on which his reputation rests. In Britain the J.B.'s had a significant impact on the acid jazz scene of the late 1980s and early 1990s, when groups such as the James Taylor Quartet resurrected the jazz-funk instrumental. As instrumentalists Wesley and Parker created significant alternatives to jazz and rhythm and blues styles.

CHARLIE FURNISS/R

J Dilla [Yancey, James DeWitt; Jay Dee] (*b* Detroit, MI, 7 Feb 1974; *d* Los Angeles, CA, 10 Feb 2006). Hip-hop producer and MC. He grew up the oldest of four children in a musical household in Detroit, Michigan. In his late teens he honed his music production abilities in the Detroit studio of Parliament Funkadelic veteran Amp Fiddler. J Dilla's embrace of tonal and rhythmic complexity, openness to diverse source material, and imaginative use of sampling was showcased in the mid-1990s on *Fantastic vol. 1*, the unofficially released first album of his own trio Slum Village. This work garnered the attention of many prominent hip-hop artists including Q-Tip, formerly of A Tribe Called Quest, who was instrumental in expanding Dilla's exposure. By the early 2000s Dilla had produced tracks for Janet Jackson, Busta Rhymes, De La Soul, Erykah Badu, Common, and other hip-hop notables.

J Dilla's ability to explore the avant-garde while maintaining an accessible core hip-hop identity—best demonstrated on his solo projects (*Welcome 2 Detroit*, 2001; and *Ruff Draft*, 2003) and collaboration with fellow hip-hop eccentric Madlib (*Champion Sound*, 2003)—made him one of the most respected and sought-after producers in the mid-2000s. Sadly, a rare blood disease with which he had struggled for years claimed his life just days after his 32nd birthday and the concomitant release of his album *Donuts* (2006). Ever prolific, Dilla left behind a vast body of work, some of which has reached his fans through various official and unofficial posthumous releases.

WILL BOONE

Jeanty, Occide [Occilius] (*b* Port-au-Prince, Haiti, 18 March 1860; *d* Port-au-Prince, Haiti, 28 Jan 1936). Haitian composer and military band director. He received musical training with his father, Occilius Jeanty, who was the director of both the Ecole Centrale de Musique in Port-au-Prince and the Musique du Palais, the Haitian presidential band. He studied cornet with Jean-Baptiste Arban at the Paris Conservatory on a scholarship awarded him by the Haitian government in 1881. With his father he published a music theory textbook titled *Petite grammaire musicale* in Paris in 1882. After his father's death in 1892, Jeanty assumed the directorship of the Musique du Palais. Most of his output was written specifically for the presidential band, including many waltzes, polkas, quadrilles, marches, and *méringues*. During the United States occupation of Haiti between 1915 and 1934, Jeanty was known to Haitian audiences as an outspoken Haitian nationalist. He was dismissed from his post by President Philippe Sudre Dartiguenave in 1916, then reinstated by Louis Borno in 1922, and subsequently remained director of the presidential band until 1934. Jeanty's most famous work, "1804," was written to commemorate Haitian independence, but became associated with Haitian resistance to the presence of United States Marines during the occupation. Haitian audiences frequently demonstrated during performances of the work which led the United States occupation forces to ban Jeanty from conducting "1804."

BIBLIOGRAPHY
E.C.E.M. Dumervé: *Histoire de la musique en Haïti* (Port-au-Prince, 1968)
M. Largey: *Vodou Nation: Haitian Art Music and Cultural Nationalism* (Chicago, 2006)

MICHAEL LARGEY

Jeffers, Ronald (Harrison) (*b* Springfield, IL, 25 March 1943). Composer and conductor. He studied composition with ROSS LEE FINNEY at the University of Michigan (BM 1966, MA 1968) and with ROBERT ERICKSON, KENNETH GABURO, PAULINE OLIVEROS, and ROGER REYNOLDS at the University of California, San Diego (1970–72). He also studied choral conducting with HOWARD SWAN at Occidental College in Los Angeles (1968–70). During the academic year 1973–4 he served as director of choral activities at SUNY, Stony Brook, and then accepted a similar position at Oregon State University and conducted the Oregon State University Choir with which he made extensive European tours in 1978 and 1982. Jeffers subsequently retired from teaching and performing and concentrated instead on publishing translations of choral texts. As a conductor he participated in two major American premieres, of Lajos Bárdos's *A nyúl éneke* and Paul Patterson's *Kyrie*. Jeffers' major works are vocal compositions (for either chorus or solo voice), many of which are settings of his own texts. His music exhibits ingenious interplays of timbre and texture and an intuitive mastery of rhythm and pitch.

WORKS
Prayer of St. Francis, 1v, 1965; Missa concrete, 3 choruses, 1969, rev. 1973; In memoriam, chbr ens, 1973; Time Passes (D. Thomas, T.S. Eliot), Mez, 4-track tape, chimes, gongs, 2 dancers, 1974–81; Sanctus, SATB, 1975; Transitory (trad.), SATB, 4-track tape, 1980; Transitory III (R. Jeffers), female vv, 1981; Arise, my love! (Jeffers), 12 vv, chimes, gongs, 1981; Crabs (R. Weaver), tape, 1981; several other works, mainly vocal

Principal publisher: Earthsongs

WRITINGS
Translations and Annotations of Choral Repertoire, i: *Sacred Latin Texts* (Corvallis, OR, 1988)
R. Jeffers and G. Paine: *Translations and Annotations of Choral Repertoire*, ii: *German Texts* (Corvallis, OR, 2000)
Reincarnations (Corvallis, OR, 2003)

DAVID COPE/ROBERT PAUL KOLT

Jefferson, (Blind) Lemon [Lemmon] **(Henry)** (*b* Couchman, TX, 24 Sept 1893; *d* Chicago, IL, 19 Dec 1929). Blues singer and guitarist. His sight deteriorated in early childhood, and as a teenager he made a living by singing in the streets of various Texas towns. In 1917 he moved to Dallas, where he sang with Leadbelly. After traveling in various southern states in the early 1920s, he went to Chicago (1925), where he began a series of recordings of exceptional importance. Jefferson was the most influential of all African American folk-blues singers and one of the greatest performers in his idiom. His voice was not strident, but high enough to carry above street noises and attract attention from some distance. At times he sang in a low, moaning fashion, which he complemented by the use of bent notes on the guitar; "Long Lonesome Blues" and "Shuckin' Sugar Blues" (both Para., 1926) are representative of his haunting, melancholy style. Although he rarely used a slide, an exception being on the blues-ballad "Jack O'Diamond Blues" (Para., 1926), he produced cries or imitative passages on the strings, most characteristically on his two best recorded songs, "Black Snake Moan" and "Match Box Blues" (both OK, 1927). His compositions, which often imply that he had at least partial sight, were frequently autobiographical, as in "Pneumonia Blues" (Para., 1929); others showed a concern for the fate of prison inmates, such as "Hangman's Blues" and "Blind Lemon's Penitentiary Blues" (both Para., 1928). Jefferson's songs were recorded in many versions by other blues singers, but his unique guitar playing was rarely successfully imitated.

BIBLIOGRAPHY
P. Oliver: "Match Box Blues: Blind Lemon Jefferson," *The Jazz Review* (Aug 1959), 9–12
R. Groom: "The Legacy of Blind Lemon," *Blues World*, nos.18–40 (1968–71)
J.T. Titon: *Early Downhome Blues: a Musical and Cultural Analysis* (Urbana, IL, 1977)
A. Governar: "Blind Lemon Jefferson," *Bluesland*, ed. T. Byron and P. Welding (New York, 1991), 16–37
D. Evans: "Musical Innovation in the Blues of Blind Lemon Jefferson," *Black Music Research Journal*, xx/1 (Spring 2000), 83–116
A.B. Govenar: "Blind Lemon Jefferson: the Myth and the Man," *Black Music Research Journal*, xx/1 (Spring 2000), 7–21
C. Lornell: "Blind Lemon Meets Leadbelly," *Black Music Research Journal*, xx/1 (Spring 2000), 23–33
L. Monge: "The Language of Blind Lemon Jefferson: the Covert Theme of Blindness," *Black Music Research Journal*, xx/1 (Spring 2000), 35–81
R.L. Uzzel: *Blind Lemon Jefferson: his Life, his Death, and his Legacy* (Austin, TX, 2002)
L. Monge and D. Evans: "New Songs of Blind Lemon Jefferson," *The Journal of Texas Music History*, iii/2 (Fall 2003), 8–28
T. Rowden: *The Songs of Blind Folk: African American Musicians and the Cultures of Blindness* (Ann Arbor, MI, 2009), 40–2, 53–8

PAUL OLIVER/R

Jefferson, Eddie [Edgar] (*b* Pittsburgh, PA, 3 Aug 1918; *d* Detroit, MI, 9 May 1979). Jazz singer, lyricist, and dancer. For many years he worked primarily as a tap dancer. In the late 1940s he created what came to be called (misleadingly) jazz "vocalese" (*see* VOCALESE) by setting lyrics to various improvisations, including the famous take on "Body and Soul" by the tenor saxophonist

Coleman Hawkins. A decade later this type of piece became an important element in the success of the singing group Lambert, Hendricks, and Ross. From 1952, following King Pleasure's popular recording of Jefferson's "Moody's Mood for Love" (based on a saxophone solo by James Moody), Jefferson was able to record his own gritty-voiced "vocalese." For two decades he sang with and managed Moody's bop combo (1953–73); later he joined Roy Brooks (1974–5) and Richie Cole (1975–9), and had just begun to receive critical recognition for his work when he was murdered in Detroit.

BIBLIOGRAPHY

GroveJ2

C. Crawford: "Woodshed: Eddie Jefferson, Vocalese Giant," *Jazz Magazine*, iii/1 (1978), 46

Obituary, *New York Times* (10 May 1979)

Obituary, *DB*, xlvi/12 (1979), 15

K. Silsbee: "An Interview with Eddie Jefferson," *Coda*, no.174 (1980), 10

G.V. Johnson Jr.: "Eddie Jefferson the Innovator," *Jazz Spotlite News*, ii/3 (1981), 46

BARRY KERNFELD/R

Jefferson, Marshall (*b* Chicago, IL, 19 Sept 1959). House music producer, musician, and DJ. He was first attracted to dance music in 1983 at Chicago's Music Box on hearing early influential DJs such as Ron Hardy and the ground-breaking house music of Jesse Saunders. Using the most basic of instrumentation, he recorded classic tracks of early Chicago house music; his debut, "Go Wild Rhythm Trax" (1985), paved the way for "Move your body," acknowledged as one of house music's most important works. He then produced "Acid Trax" (1988) for Phuture which, in using the sound of the Roland TB-303 synthesizer, created the acid house genre; both the track and genre spawned more imitators than developers of the sound, something which drove Jefferson back underground to record the sweeping, less TB-303-oriented "Open your eyes." This attempt to recreate his early feelings for Chicago house led to "deep house." He also put together and produced the vocal dance group Ten City throughout the late 1980s and early 1990s. He spent the mid-1990s working as a DJ, primarily in London, then resumed his recording and producing career in the United States. His defining work centers on the intensely creative and inspiring period in the late 1980s.

IAN PEEL/R

Jefferson Airplane. Rock group. It was formed in San Francisco in 1965 by Marty Balin (Martyn Jerel Buchwald; *b* Cincinnati, OH, 30 Jan 1943; vocals) and Paul (Lorin) Kantner (*b* San Francisco, CA, 17 March 1941; guitar and vocals) and was among the most important rock groups to emerge from the Haight-Ashbury psychedelic scene of 1966–9. The band's second album, *Surrealistic Pillow* (RCA, 1967), contained two hit singles, "Somebody to Love" and "White Rabbit," and featured Balin, Kantner, Jorma Kaukonen (*b* Washington, DC, 23 Dec 1940; guitar), Jack Casady (*b* Washington, DC, 13 April 1944; bass), Spencer Dryden (*b* New York, NY, 7 April 1943; *d* Petaluma, CA, 11 Jan 2005; drums), and the charismatic Grace Slick (Grace Barnett Wing; *b* Chicago, IL, 30 Oct 1939; vocals). This lineup subsequently recorded a series of successful and often innovative albums, including *After Bathing at Baxter's* (RCA, 1967), *Crown of Creation* (RCA, 1968), and the politically inspired *Volunteers* (RCA, 1969), all of which became staples of progressive FM radio in the late 1960s. The group's early influences were primarily American folk and blues, but elements of modal jazz and Indian music can be found throughout their music, especially in the sometimes extended instrumental solos. After the band's last studio album, *Long John Silver* (RCA, 1972), Slick and Kantner reformed the group into Jefferson Starship, which, while much less adventurous musically, enjoyed tremendous commercial success in the 1970s and 1980s with numerous hit singles, including "Miracles" (1975, featuring Balin) and "Jane" (1979), and hit albums. Starship, through various changes in personnel, has continued touring and performing into the 2010s. The late-1960s lineup (without Dryden) reunited briefly in 1989, releasing *Jefferson Airplane*.

BIBLIOGRAPHY

"Jefferson Airplane Loves You," *Look*, xxxi (1967), 58–62

R. Gleason: *The Jefferson Airplane and the San Francisco Sound* (New York, 1969)

B. Fong-Torres: "Jefferson Airplane Grunts: 'Gotta Evolution'," *Rolling Stone*, xcii (1971), 1, 28–30

G. Slick: *Somebody to Love? A Rock-and-Roll Memoir* (New York, 1998)

J. Tamarkin: *Got a Revolution!: the Turbulent Flight of Jefferson Airplane* (London, 2003)

JOHN COVACH/R

Jeffries, Herb [Herbert; Jeffrey, Herbert; Balentino, Umberto; the Bronze Buckaroo] (*b* Detroit, MI, 24 Sept 1916). Jazz vocalist and actor. He began his professional singing career at 14 and then worked with such well-known jazz musicians as Erskine Tate, Earl Hines, and Blanche Calloway. In the late 1930s he made five films as America's first black singing cowboy starting with *Harlem on the Prairie* (1937). He conceived the idea of making the movie himself in a conscious effort to create a character that could be a model for brown-skinned children. Jeffries, who identified his mother as Irish and his father as mixed-race Sicilian, was almost denied the role because his physical features were considered by some not to be African American enough, although he proudly identified himself as black in both professional and social terms. He successfully fought for the role, which earned him the nickname the Bronze Buckaroo, and his films appealed to a more widespread audience than expected. Jeffries worked with the Duke Ellington Orchestra from 1940 through 1942, during which time he recorded his most famous hit, "Flamingo." After moving to Los Angeles he opened a nightclub called the Black Flamingo. He has continued to perform jazz and cowboy songs.

BIBLIOGRAPHY

L. McClellan: *The Swing Era, 1942 to 1955* (Westport, CT, 2004)

C. Clark: "A Driving Force to be a Hero," *American Legacy*, xv/2 (2009) 38–44

E. RON HORTON

Jehin-Prume, Frantz [Jehin, François-Henri] (*b* Spa, Belgium, 18 April 1839; *d* Montreal, PQ, 29 May 1899). Canadian violinist, composer, and teacher of Belgian birth. He was a student of Nicholas Servais and of his uncle François Prume at the Liège Conservatoire. After the latter's death in 1849, Jehin added "Prume" to his own name and continued his studies at the Brussels Conservatoire with Hubert Léonard; he graduated with *premier prix* from the class of Johann Christoph Lauterbach in 1852. From about 1855 he performed throughout Europe and in 1864 was invited to perform for the imperial court in Mexico City. In the spring and summer of 1865 he gave numerous concerts in Canada and in December made his debut with the New York Philharmonic performing the Mendelssohn Violin Concerto in E minor. He returned to Canada the following summer to marry the Montreal-based soprano Rosita del Vecchio. Together, they traveled extensively, setting off that fall on the first of several US tours organized by Max Strakosch. In the years 1869–70, as part of a concert company that included Carlotta Patti-Strakosch and the pianist Theodore Ritter, they performed in 59 towns and cities. In 1875 Jehin-Prume established a teaching studio in Montreal and in later years devoted most of his time to instruction. Among his students were François Boucher and Alfred De Sève. He wrote two violin concertos and numerous transcriptions; only a few works, published in Belgium, Canada, and France or preserved in manuscript at the National Library of Canada, survive.

BIBLIOGRAPHY

DCB (H. Kallmann)

C. Huot: "Musiciens belges au Québec," *Les Cahiers canadiens de musique*, viii/Spring–Summer (1974), 69–71

J.-A. Houle: "Frantz Jehin-Prume (1839–99): son apport culturel au milieu Québecois," *Les Cahiers canadiens de musique*, xxii/April (1990), 48–53

J.-A. Houle and C. Huot: "Frantz Jehin-Prume," *Encyclopedia of Music in Canada* (Toronto, 2007)

BRIAN C. THOMPSON

Jellison, Judith A(nne) (*b* Homestead, PA, 3 April 1940). Music educator and music therapist. She holds degrees in music education from Indiana University of Pennsylvania (BS 1962, MEd 1964) and Florida State University (PhD 1972), in music history from the University of Missouri, Columbia (MA 1967), and she completed therapy course work at Florida State University. She taught public school music in Murrysville and Munhall, Pennsylvania and Prairie Home, Missouri (1962–5) and was a music therapist at the Tallahassee Developmental Center (1971–2). She was the founding director of the music therapy degree program at the University of Minnesota (1972–83). Since 1983 Jellison has taught at the University of Texas at Austin, where she is the Mary D. Bold Regents Professor in Music and Human Learning and a University Distinguished Teaching Professor. She is a recipient of the Senior Researcher Award from the Music Educators National Conference (2004) and a Publication Award from the American Music Therapy Association (2001). She has served on editorial boards for

both organizations and was chair of the MENC Music Education Research Council (1990–92). Her publications focus on changes in educational practices to increase adult music participation and facilitate music learning in inclusive classrooms and rehearsals.

JERE T. HUMPHREYS

Jemez. Native Americans belonging to the Towa subgroup of the EASTERN PUEBLO.

Jenkins, Edmund Thornton (*b* Charleston, SC, 9 April 1894; *d* Paris, France, 12 Sept 1926). Composer. He studied the clarinet, the piano, and the violin at Atlanta Baptist College (now Morehouse College) where his teachers included KEMPER HARRELD. In 1914 he performed with his father's ensemble, the Jenkins Orphanage Band, at the Anglo-American Exposition in London. He later enrolled at the RAM, where he studied the clarinet, piano, and singing, and had composition lessons with Corder. His awards included an orchestral scholarship (1915–17), medals for singing, and clarinet and piano playing, and the Ross Scholarship (1919–21). He became an Associate of the RAM in 1921.

After working in British theater orchestras and dance bands, employment that resulted in a number of recordings (1921), he moved to Paris. He continued performing and composing, and established the Anglo-Continental-American Music Press. Among his published works are songs, compositions for solo piano, and orchestral works. Black musical culture is particularly evident in his jazz phrasing, for instance in the *Folk Rhapsody* for orchestra. Retitled *Charlestonia*, the *Folk Rhapsody* was issued on *Got the Saint Louis Blues: Classical Music in the Jazz Age* (2004, Clarion CLR907CD). His involvement with the Pan-African congresses of 1921 and 1923 was also influential. In 1923 he embarked on what was to be a disillusioning tour of America, an experience that introduced black theatrical elements into his compositional style. His manuscripts are held at the Center for Black Music, Columbia College, Chicago.

BIBLIOGRAPHY

J. Green: *Edmund Thornton Jenkins: the Life and Times of an American Black Composer, 1894–1926* (Westport, CT, 1982)

J. Green: "Roland Hayes in London, 1921," *BPiM*, x/1 (1982), 29–42

B. Hillmon: "In Retrospect: Edmund Thornton Jenkins," *BPiM*, xiv/2 (1986), 143–80

J. Green: "The Negro Renaissance and England," *Black Music in the Harlem Renaissance*, ed. S. Floyd (Knoxville, TN, 1993), 151–71

M. Berresford, H. Rye and E. Walker: "The Versatile Four: Ambassadors of Syncopation," *VJM's Jazz and Blues Mart*, no.98 (1995), 8–14

H. Rye and J. Green: "Black Musical Internationalism in England in the 1920s," *Black Music Research Journal*, xv (1995), 93–107

JEFFREY GREEN

Jenkins, Ella (*b* St. Louis, IL, 6 Aug 1924). Singer of children's songs. Known as the First Lady of Children's Music, she is one the most important children's entertainers of the late 20th and early 21st centuries. She has spent most of her life in Chicago. While working for the YWCA in 1952, she began to host a television show called *This is Rhythm*. In 1957 she released her first album for the New York-based label Folkways Records. By 2010 she had released more than 30 albums for Folkways and its successor, Smithsonian Folkways Records. For most of the history of Folkways, Jenkins has been its top-selling artist.

Many generations of students have grown up with her music; it is not uncommon to have grandmothers, mothers, and their children in the same audience. Jenkins has played numerous instruments and sung in many languages using songs to teach world music. She has often employed a call-and-response technique to encourage audience interaction. She was a champion of multicultural education long before the term was in common usage.

Jenkins has appeared on most of the major children's television shows in the United States including *Mister Rogers' Neighborhood*, *Barney & Friends*, and *Sesame Street*. She has performed internationally. In 2004 she was awarded the prestigious Grammy Lifetime Achievement Award.

BIBLIOGRAPHY
P.D. Goldsmith: *Making People's Music: Moe Asch and Folkways Records* (Washington, DC, 2000)
R. Carlin: *Worlds of Sound: the Story of Smithsonian Folkways* (Washington, DC, 2008)

JEFF PLACE

Jenkins, Florence Foster [née Foster, Nascina Florence] (*b* Wilkes-Barre, PA, 19 July 1868; *d* New York, NY, 26 Nov 1944). Amateur soprano. Born Nascina Florence Foster, she was married briefly to a doctor, Frank Thornton Jenkins. A significant inheritance following her father's death allowed Jenkins to pursue her musical

Florence Foster Jenkins as the Angel of Inspiration.
(NYPL Performing Arts/Lebrecht Music & Arts)

ambitions, which had been discouraged by her family. An eccentric New York socialite, Jenkins was involved in a number of New York clubs, musical and otherwise, including the Euterpe Club and the Verdi Club, the latter of which she founded in 1917. Jenkins achieved renown, however, for the vocal recitals she began to present annually from the 1930s in New York and the surrounding area. These immensely popular invitation-only events featured multiple elaborate costumes, semi-staging, and a program of art songs and opera arias drawn from the coloratura and dramatic soprano repertoires. In 1941 she recorded a number of arias and songs with Melotone Studios; RCA Victor later collected and released these recordings as albums. Much of her fame rests with these recordings, the best known of which is the Queen of the Night's "Der Hölle Rache" from Mozart's *Die Zauberflöte*. Her other well-known arias include the Bell Song from Delibes's *Lakmé* and Adele's Laughing Song from Strauss's *Die Fledermaus*. Jenkins's recordings reveal a thin coloratura voice with pervasive inconsistencies of tone and pitch. By all accounts, however, she remained unaware of her vocal limitations, which likely contributed to her appeal. On 25 October 1944 she presented a sold-out recital at Carnegie Hall, accompanied by her regular pianist Cosme McMoon. Although the concert was thoroughly excoriated by critics, her popularity remained undiminished.

RYAN EBRIGHT

Jenkins, Gordon (*b* Webster Groves, MO, 12 May 1910; *d* Malibu, CA, 24 April 1984). Arranger, composer, and conductor. He played cinema organ and piano before joining a radio station in St. Louis. He began arranging for Isham Jones's dance orchestra (1936) and then composed and arranged for Benny Goodman, Woody Herman, Lennie Hayton, and André Kostelanetz. After a brief spell conducting on Broadway he moved to California (1936) to work for Paramount and later was a music director and performer for NBC's Hollywood network (1938–44). He returned to New York in 1949. He is best known for his light orchestral music such as the mood suites *Seven Dreams* and *Manhattan Tower*, and conducted his own light orchestra from the mid-1940s to the early 1950s. In 1950 he launched the recording career of the Weavers when he took them to Decca Records to record their first single "Goodnight Irene." He arranged for many other popular singers, including Frank Sinatra (the song "It was a very good year," for which he won a Grammy Award in 1965, and the albums *Where are you?* (Cap., 1957) and *No One Cares* (Cap., 1959). He composed the music for the "Future" section of Sinatra's ambitious three record set *Trilogy: Past Present Future* (Rep., 1980). He also recorded with Nat "King" Cole, Louis Armstrong, and Peggy Lee.

BIBLIOGRAPHY
C. Granata: *Sessions with Sinatra: Frank Sinatra and the Art of Recording* (Chicago, 1999)
B. Jenkins: *Goodbye: in Search of Gordon Jenkins* (Berkeley, CA, 2005)

TIM SMOLKO

Jenkins, Leroy (*b* Chicago, IL, 11 March 1932; *d* New York, NY, 24 Feb 2007). Jazz violinist, composer, and bandleader. He was influenced by the violinists Jascha Heifetz, Eddie South, and Bruce Hayden, as well as the saxophonists Charlie Parker, Ornette Coleman, and John Coltrane. From 1965 to 1969 he played in Chicago with the Association for the Advancement of Creative Musicians and the Creative Construction Company, becoming the leading violinist in the free jazz style. He then helped to organize the Revolutionary Ensemble (1971) and led his own trio (1977–9) and quintet (1982–3). In addition to collaborating with such musicians as Cecil Taylor, Joseph Jarman, and Myra Melford, he also contributed to the new music scene by serving on the board of directors of the Composer's Forum. In his later career, he turned to creating theatrical productions, including the operas *Mother of Three Sons* (collaborating with Bill T. Jones, 1990) and *Fresh Faust* (libretto by Greg Tate, 1994). Jenkins was known for expanding the vocabulary of sounds associated with the violin in jazz and for integrating free-form and composed approaches in small-combo performance. He performed extensively in Europe, wrote works for solo performer, small combo, 20-piece big band, and orchestra, and presented numerous collective improvisations.

BIBLIOGRAPHY

B. Primack: "Leroy Jenkins: Gut-plucking Revolutionary," *DB*, xlv/19 (1978), 23

B. Blumenthal: "Leroy Jenkins: Violinist of the New Music," *DB*, xlix/3 (1982), 20

L. Birnbaum: "Leroy Jenkins: Space Minds, New Worlds, Survival of America," *Ear*, xiv/9 (1989–90), 34–9

C.E. Baugher: "Leroy Jenkins: Violin Visionary," *Fable Bulletin: Violin Improvisation Studies*, iii/10 (1998), 29

B. Bang: "Farewells: Leroy Jenkins," *JT*, xxxviii/2 (2008), 42–3

MARK C. GRIDLEY/R

Jenks, Alden (*b* Harbor Beach, MI, 10 Aug 1940). Composer and performer. He began playing piano as a child and later studied with ROBERT HELPS and Barbara Shearer. He attended the Aspen Institute in 1956, studying with DARIUS MILHAUD, and Yale University (BA, music theory, 1962), where his principal teachers were MEL POWELL, LAWRENCE K. MOSS, and DONALD MARTINO. Jenks worked with Karlheinz Stockhausen at the University of California, Davis, and performed in Stockhausen's work *Ensemble* at Darmstadt in 1967. He also studied composition with ANDREW IMBRIE and SEYMOUR SHIFRIN at the University of California, Berkeley (MA 1968).

Jenks became interested in electronic music through the San Francisco Tape Music Center, run by Pauline Oliveros and Ramón Sender, and thereafter associated with David Tudor and Anthony Gnazzo at Mills College. He created the performing group Deus ex Machina in collaboration with Martin Bartlett and built a large digital synthesizer called the Grand WebUrl Ensemble. Since the late 1960s much of his work has been electroacoustic. Jenks designed, contributed to, and edited *Bagazine* (1969)—a collection of musical scores, poems, and graphic works, with contributions by Bartlett, Philip Glass, Patrick Gleason, Gnazzo, and Steve Reich published by the Mills Tape Music Center and distrib-

uted free in large white paper bags. His work *Videom 1* (1971) included acoustic instruments, color TV/oscilloscope, and TV monitors with video modulation. From 1972 he has been professor of composition and director of the E.L. Wiegand Electronic Composition Studio at San Francisco Conservatory, where John Adams cited his influence and credited Jenks with introducing him to Wagner. His work of the late 1970s includes *The Confines of Symmetry* (1977), which marries woodwinds, brass, and percussion to a computer-generated symmetrical rhythmic process. The two-piano work *Marrying Music* won the Viotti–Valsesia International Music Competition (1978) and his tape piece *Nagasaki* (1983) was a prizewinner at the Bourges International Electronic Music Competition. Through the years he has continued to be active as a performer, including appearing on synthesizer in the 25th-anniversary concert of Terry Riley's *In C* in 1989; a recording of this performance was released on New Albion (1995). Jenks's interest in poetry has led to an increasing number of acoustic vocal pieces in the 1990s and the first decade of the 2000s, in an eclectic style quite distinct from his electronic work.

WORKS

El-ac: At it's, tape, 1968; Chez elle, tape, 1968; Lapis, tape, 1968; Namo, tape, 1971; Seeing in the Dark, male v or male actor/dancer, 1972; Space, acoustic insts, tape, 1972; Mummermusic (P. Kors), mime, synth, tape, 1975; Waving (B. Pyland, E. Lipkin), tape, elec images, 1975; Those Long Canadian Winters, actor, synth, 2 tapes, slide projections, 1976; Ohio, tape, 1980; And the Winner is…(dance drama), dancers, tape, 1983; Nagasaki, tape, 1983; Sneak Preview or Houses of Mud and Rock (soundtrack for video drama), 1987; West Meets East (soundtrack for instructional video), 1989; Calcululations, tape, 1990; Menage, synth, pf, perc, 1994; The Candle a Saint (W. Stevens), narr., gui, tape, 1994/5

Inst: Videom I, 1971; The Confines of Symmetry, ww, brass, perc, 1977; Femme Fatale: the Invention of Personality (dance drama, F. Farabough), cl, str qt, pf, perc, 1981; Martin Put that Gun Away, 2000; Sour Music, 12 insts, elecs, 2002; Ognaggio al'anzzonio, 2003

Kbd: Marrying Music, 2 pf, 1978; Four Piano Ballads, pf, 1988; Ansichtskarte an Johann, 2 pf, 1989/94; Prelude for Organ, 2003

Vocal: Two Rimbaud Songs, Bar, pf, 1964; Three Stafford Songs (W. Stafford), T, fl, cl, va, 1988; Explorers (C. Simic), v, tape, synth, perc, cptr, 1994/5; Letter from Linda, S, actress, pf, 1998–9; Ghost Songs (C. Simic: Night Picnic, Ghosts, Shadow Publishing Company), S, pf, 2004; Time Suite (J. Harrison), Bar, pf, 2005; Five California Songs (R. Brautigan, L. Nathan, R. Hass, P. Whalen), T, vc, pf, 2006

BIBLIOGRAPHY

J. Kramer: "Karlheinz in California," *PNM*, xxxvi (1998), 247–61

MARK ALBURGER

Jenks, Stephen (*b* Glocester, RI, 17 March 1772; *d* Thompson, OH, 5 June 1856). Composer and tunebook compiler. The son of John Jenks and Lydia Bucklin, he was born in Rhode Island, but grew up in Ellington, Connecticut. He taught singing-schools in Connecticut, Massachusetts, and New York state, primarily in rural areas, and cultivated a network of pupils and fellow teachers whose compositions he published. He was a prolific exponent of the American idiom developed by Daniel Read and other Connecticut composers in the 1780s and 1790s and contributed 127 pieces to the ten collections of psalmody he issued, alone and with others, from *The New-England Harmonist* (Danbury,

CT, 1799) to *The Harmony of Zion, or Union Compiler* (Dedham, MA, 1818); he also published two books of secular songs. He was one of the few prolific 19th-century composers of fuging-tunes. While taking most of his texts from Isaac Watts and other English evangelical poets, Jenks showed considerable interest in patriotic, commemorative, and elegiac verse. His "Mount Vernon" is perhaps the best known of the many American pieces mourning the death of George Washington; "Sorrow's Tear" (1804) may be the earliest American setting of a poem by Thomas Moore.

In 1829 Jenks moved to Geauga County, Ohio, where he lived out his life in obscurity, farming and reportedly making percussion instruments, although he continued to compose until 1850. His manuscript copybook, which is held in the Newberry Library, Chicago, includes settings of popular camp-meeting and revival hymns in a contemporary style incorporating folk elements. A few of his late pieces appeared in William Batchelder Bradbury's *The Shawm* (1853). Although Jenks's music was long neglected in the North, several of his tunes, including "Liberty," "Evening Shade," and "North Salem," have been regularly performed as part of the Sacred Harp and related shape-note traditions.

BIBLIOGRAPHY
S.P. Cheney: *The American Singing Book* (Boston, MA, 1879/R), 182
Pioneer and General History of Geauga County (Chardon, OH, 1880), 806–8, 815
N.H. Allen: "Music in a New England State" (MS, Trinity Col., Hartford, 1922), 78
F.J. Metcalf: *American Writers and Compilers of Sacred Music* (New York, 1925/R)
D.W. Steel, ed.: *Stephen Jenks: Collected Works* (Madison, WI, 1995)
D.W. Steel (with R.H. Hulan): *The Makers of the Sacred Harp* (Urbana, IL, 2010)

DAVID WARREN STEEL

Jennings, Joseph (Howell) (*b* Augusta, GA, 1 Jan 1954). Conductor, arranger, and composer. Jennings earned a bachelor's degree in music education from Case Western Reserve University and a master's degree in conducting from Colorado State University. Jennings served as artistic director of CHANTICLEER from 1984 until his retirement in 2008. He began singing as a countertenor with the group in 1983. After assuming the role of artistic director, he helped shape the group by introducing and arranging a broader variety of repertoire including spirituals, gospel, and jazz standards. Under his direction Chanticleer released 25 recordings. Jennings served as Musical Adviser to Chanticleer in 2008–9. In May 2008 he was recognized as one of ASCAP's four Concert Music Honorees.

Jennings also has taught at the College of the Siskiyous in Weed, the University of California at Berkeley, and has served as guest conductor for the San Francisco Girls Chorus and the Estonia Philharmonic Chamber Choir. As a composer and arranger Jennings has been commissioned by the Palo Alto High School Chorus, the San Francisco Girls Chorus, the Plymouth Music Series, the GALA V Festival Chorus, the New York City Gay Men's Chorus, the Dale Warland Singers, the Phoenix Bach Choir, and the Los Angeles Vocal and Instrumental Ensemble. His compositions and arrangements are published by Oxford University Press, Hinshaw Music Company of Chapel Hill, North Carolina, and Yelton Rhodes Music.

BIBLIOGRAPHY
R. Dyer: "The Rise of Chanticleer: America's Only Full-time Chorus Offers Something Unique," *Boston Globe* (2 Feb 1994)

MICHAEL HIX

Jennings, Terry (*b* Eagle Rock, CA, 19 July 1940; *d* San Pablo, CA, 11 Dec 1981). Composer and performer. He had a background in jazz, playing piano, clarinet, and alto and soprano saxophones. In 1953 he met La Monte Young in Los Angeles, where they played jazz together. Jennings first came to musical prominence in the late 1950s when he began to compose in the style of Young's influential early works involving sustained tones and expanded time concepts. He was introduced to the New York avant garde in 1960, when Young opened his series of concerts at Yoko Ono's loft with two programs of Jennings's music. Jennings participated in many concerts of new music in the 1960s, both as composer and performer, giving the first performance of, among other works, Richard Maxfield's *Wind* for tape and saxophone, which was composed as a musical portrait of him. He worked with the James Waring Dance Company (1962) and performed and recorded with Young's Theatre of Eternal Music. Jennings's Piano Piece (June 1960) and String Quartet (1960) were published in *An Anthology* (edited by Young, 1963), which led to their performance in England by Cornelius Cardew and others. Two concerts of Jennings's music were presented at Steinway Hall, New York, in Ben Patterson's series of avant-garde music, "January to June." With Young and Terry Riley, Jennings was involved in the earliest developments of drone-inspired, modal, repetitive music. He is best known for two piano works of 1965, *Winter Trees* and *Winter Sun*, both of which exemplify the repetitive, non-virtuoso keyboard style he was among the first to employ; sets of phrases are played quietly in a specified order but repeated at will, in relatively free rhythm, and with liberal use of the sustaining pedal, creating a meditative mood and an understated lyricism. Jennings had a decisive influence on such composers as Harold Budd, Peter Garland, and Howard Skempton, who were among the few musicians to perform his works. In later years Jennings composed works in a neo-romantic style, including the song cycle *The Seasons* (1975).

BIBLIOGRAPHY
L. Young: "Lecture 1960," *Tulane Drama Review*, x/2 (1965), 73–83; repr. in L. Young and M. Zazeela: *Selected Writings* (Munich, 1969) [unpaginated]
B. Patterson: "Terry Jennings: Making of a Musician, 1968," *Village Voice* (11 Jan 1968)
M. Nyman: *Experimental Music: Cage and Beyond* (London, 1974)

PETER GARLAND, LA MONTE YOUNG/R

Jennings, Waylon [Wayland Arnold] (*b* Littlefield, TX, 15 June 1937; *d* Chandler, AZ, 13 Feb 2002). Country singer-songwriter. Born into a family of itinerant farm laborers, he showed an early interest in music, learning to play guitar from his parents and becoming a fan of the cowboy actor Lash LaRue and the *Grand Ole Opry*. At the age of 12 he began entering talent contests in the Texas Panhandle, performing on radio and television broadcasts and in theaters in the region. After achieving regional success as a guitarist and singer, Jennings dropped out of high school in the tenth grade to pursue a career in music. From 1955 he worked as a disc jockey on several stations around Lubbock, where he befriended local rock musicians Buddy Holly and Roy Orbison. In late 1958 Jennings became the bass guitarist in Holly's band, the Crickets, but returned to Lubbock following Holly's death in 1959.

Jennings then began to focus on his songwriting and formed a road band to play clubs throughout the Texas Panhandle, New Mexico, and Arizona, including a particularly successful stint at J.D.'s in Phoenix (1964–5). His first single, "Jole Blon" (Bruns., 1958), had been produced by Holly, but it was not until the mid-1960s that he began to record in earnest. By then he had settled in Nashville, where he worked with the producer Chet Atkins to develop a folk-country style. Jennings played the role of a Nashville rebel both professionally and personally, negotiating a contract with RCA Victor in 1972 that allowed him to record with his own band, the Waylors, at Tompall Glaser's Hillbilly Central studio in Nashville. Jennings's recordings in the period between 1972 and 1977 are characterized by their sparc textures, ragged grooves, and intensely emotional repertory, particularly on such albums as *Honky Tonk Heroes* (RCA Victor, 1973), *Ramblin' Man* (RCA Victor, 1974), and *Ol' Waylon* (RCA Victor, 1977). In 1976 RCA Victor released a compilation album featuring Jennings, Willie Nelson, Glaser, and Jennings's wife Jessi Colter titled *Wanted! The Outlaws* in an effort to capitalize on increasing youth interest in country-rock crossovers. Drug addiction affected Jennings's career in the late 1970s and early 1980s. However, by the mid-1980s his health had recovered, and from 1985 to 1995 he recorded and toured with the country supergroup the Highwaymen, which included Nelson, Johnny Cash, and Kris Kristofferson.

BIBLIOGRAPHY

M. Bane: *The Outlaws: Revolution in Country Music* (New York, 1978)
R. Serge Denisoff: *Waylon: a Biography* (Knoxville, TN, 1983)
W. Jennings (with L. Kaye): *Waylon: an Autobiography* (New York, 1996)

LIZ THOMSON/TRAVIS D. STIMELING

Jensen, Ingrid (*b* Vancouver, BC, 12 Jan 1966). Canadian trumpeter and flugelhorn player. A graduate of the Berklee College of Music (BM 1989), she has worked in both big band and small group settings. She has played in the Grammy-winning Maria Schneider Orchestra, the DIVA Big Band, and her sister's Juno Award-winning group, the Christine Jensen Orchestra. She has also worked in smaller ensembles, including the Mosaic Project (with the pianist Geri Allen, the drummer Terri Lyne Carrington, and the bass player Esperanza Spalding), and performed and recorded with Clark Terry, Marc Copeland, Bob Berg, Jeff "Tain" Watts, Global Noize (featuring DJ Logic and Jason Miles), Virginia Mayhew, and the Bill Cosby All-Stars. Jensen has collaborated on a wide range of projects, including performances with the soul singer Corrine Bailey Rae and Tribute to Billie Holiday featuring the vocalist Madeleine Peyroux, the bass player Ron Carter, and the pianist Mulgrew Miller. As an educator, she has served on the faculty of the Bruckner Conservatory of Music in Austria and as an artist-in-residence at the University of Michigan, Ann Arbor. She has recorded numerous albums as a leader and also with the small group Nordic Connect. As a player capable of producing breath-defying phrases, Jensen is known for her inventive lyricism and technical dexterity; her style, while often engagingly compositional in arc, can also channel the directness of the trumpeters Woody Shaw and Freddie Hubbard. She is a Canadian Juno Award winner (for her album *Vernal Fields*, 1995) and a two-time Jazz Journalist Award nominee for Best Trumpet Player.

JEFFREY HOLMES

Jensen, Wilma Hoyle (*b* Bushnell, IL, 8 March 1929). Organist and teacher. She began the study of organ at an early age and at age 12 was publicized as the "Youngest Organist in Methodism." She studied organ at Eastman School of Music, studying with both Harold Gleason and Catharine Crozier, receiving a degree in Organ Performance with distinction (BM 1951) and in Music Literature and Organ (MM 1953). During that time she received the highly coveted Performer's Certificate in Organ. She received an Honorary Doctorate from Piedmont College, Demorest, Georgia, in May 2004. Jensen devoted her career to teaching, church music, and performing. She was Professor of Organ at Indiana University (1977–81), and she also taught at Oklahoma City University, Scarritt Graduate School, and the Blair School of Music at Vanderbilt University. She was Choirmaster/Organist at St George's Episcopal Church, Nashville, Tennessee (1982–2002). Jensen's extensive concert career as a recitalist has taken her throughout the United States and Europe. Her long and active music career also includes choral workshops, church music workshops, and organ masterclasses. She has made two solo recordings on the Arkay and Pro Organo labels, and two recordings conducting the St George's Choir on the Pro Organo label.

SARAH L. MARTIN

Jenson [Lockington], **Dylana (Ruth)** (*b* Los Angeles, CA, 14 May 1961). Violinist and violin teacher. She received her first violin lessons from her mother in 1963 and began formal study with Eunice Wennermark at six and Manuel Compinsky at age seven. As a child she played for JASCHA HEIFETZ and at the ages of 16 and 17 she studied with JOSEF GINGOLD. At the age of seven she performed as soloist in Bach's Violin Concerto in A minor under the direction of Compinsky. She made her professional debut in 1973, performing Mendelssohn's Concerto with the New York PO under André Kostelanetz. In 1975 she made her European debut with the

Tonhalle Orchestra in Zurich, where she attended master classes given by NATHAN MILSTEIN in the years 1974–6. She won second prize in the International Tchaikovsky Competition in Moscow in 1978, the youngest woman ever to do so. Jenson is an honorary citizen of Costa Rica and was appointed Distinguished Professor of Music at Grand Valley State University's Pew Campus in Grand Rapids, Michigan. She has performed extensively with major orchestras in the United States and undertaken tours of Europe, Australia, Japan, the Soviet Union, and Latin America. One of the finest violinists of her generation, she has made recordings of the Sibelius Violin Concerto with Eugene Ormandy and the Philadelphia Orchestra and of two Brahms sonatas. In 2008 Jenson recorded the Shostakovich Violin Concerto op.99 no.1 and the Samuel Barber Violin Concerto with the London SO. Instruments she has played include a Montagnana, a "del Gesù" Guarneri, and a contemporary violin by the Brooklyn-based luthier Samuel Zygmuntowicz.

BIBLIOGRAPHY
B. Schwarz: *Great Masters of the Violin* (New York, 1983)
L. Niles: "Interview with Dylana Jenson," <http://www.violinist.com/blog/laurie/20102/10956/> (2013)
SORAB MODI/SARAH EYERLY

Jepson, Benjamin (*b* 1832; *d* 1914). Music educator and editor. The son of an oratorio singer, he studied with Gustav Stoeckel and directed children's choruses. After serving in the Union Army during the Civil War, he introduced music instruction in the New Haven, Connecticut public schools, where he taught for more than 40 years. In the "rote versus note" controversy in music education, he promoted sight-reading. At an MMTA conference in 1887, he presented a paper on "The Science of Music vs. Rote Practice in Public Schools" in which he emphasized that "the object of public school instruction is to make readers of music, not singers." He published *The Elementary Music Reader: a Progressive Series of Lessons* (New York, 1871, 1873; revised as *The Standard Music Reader* (New York, 1888); *The New Standard Music Reader* (New Haven, CT, 1904); and *Dictation in Music* (New Haven, CT, 1894).

He received an honorary MA degree in 1912 from Yale University, and the School Board of New Haven opened the Benjamin Jepson Elementary School in his honor. His son, Harry Benjamin Jepson (1870–1952), an organist, choir director, and composer, was on the faculty at Yale University.

BIBLIOGRAPHY
A.L. Rich: *Lowell Mason* (Chapel Hill, NC, 1946)
E.B. Birge: *History of Public School Music in the United States* (Washington, DC, 1966)
M.L. Mark and C.L. Gary: *A History of American Music Education* (New York, 1992)
SONDRA WIELAND HOWE

Jepson, Harry Benjamin (*b* New Haven, CT, 16 Aug 1870; *d* Noank, CT, 23 Aug 1952). Organist and composer. The son of a music supervisor in the New Haven public schools, Jepson graduated from Yale University in 1893; the following year, after further studies in piano, organ, and composition, he was awarded the BM degree, and in 1895 he became Yale University organist. Between 1899 and 1909 he made five trips to Paris to study with Widor and Vierne. His career centered around Yale University, where he remained until his retirement in 1939. He was first a composition pupil and then a faculty colleague of HORATIO PARKER. He directed the Yale Chapel choir in Battell Chapel and presided over the enormous Woolsey Hall organ, which by 1929 had four manuals and 230 stops. Jepson toured extensively in his early years. His published organ compositions were much admired when they appeared: *Pantomime* and *Toccata*, both published in 1919, became especially popular though they were technically demanding.

VERNON GOTWALS/JUDI CALDWELL

Jeritza, Maria [Mizzi] [Jedlitzka, Marie] (*b* Brno, Czech Republic, 6 Oct 1887; *d* Orange, NJ, 10 July 1982). Moravian soprano, active in Austria and the United States. After studies in Brno and Prague, she made her debut at Olmütz in 1910 as Elsa; she then joined the Vienna Volksoper and in 1912 appeared at the Hofoper. She quickly became an immense favorite in Vienna, where she sang regularly for over two decades; she was especially admired as Tosca, Minnie, and Turandot, and in many roles in Richard Strauss's operas. She was the first Ariadne in both versions of *Ariadne auf Naxos* (1912, Stuttgart; 1916, Vienna) and the first Empress in *Die Frau ohne Schatten* (1919, Vienna). Her Salome was a remarkably vivid assumption. Having sung Marietta in the first Vienna performance of Erich Wolfgang Korngold's *Die tote Stadt*, she repeated this role for her Metropolitan debut later in the same year (19 November 1921). Of greater musical significance was her Jenůfa in both the first Viennese (1918) and first New York (1924) performances of Leoš Janáček's opera. During the next 12 years she became recognized as the Metropolitan's most glamorous star since the days of Geraldine Farrar, and appropriately introduced to New York both Giacomo Puccini's *Turandot* and Strauss's *Die ägyptische Helena*. Her Covent Garden performances were confined to seven roles during 1925 and 1926, whereas at the Metropolitan she sang 290 performances in 20 roles. After World War II she made isolated appearances in Vienna and New York (having become a naturalized American). Though endowed with an ample and lustrous voice, Jeritza belonged to the category of artist known as a "singing actress," freely yielding both dramatically and vocally to impulses that were sometimes more flamboyant than refined. In her numerous recordings, faults of taste and technique coexist with genuine vocal achievements. Archival material from the Vienna Staatsoper in the 1930s testifies to the magnetic effect she had on audiences.

BIBLIOGRAPHY
GV (L. Riemens and R. Celletti; S. Smolian)
M. Jeritza: *Sunlight and Song: a Singer's Life* (New York, 1924/*R*)
R. Werba: *Maria Jeritza: Primadonna des Verismo* (Vienna, 1981)
DESMOND SHAWE-TAYLOR/R

Jerome, William (1865–1932). Lyricist who collaborated with JEAN SCHWARTZ.

Jessye, Eva (Alberta) (*b* Coffeyville, KS, 20 Jan 1895; *d* Ann Arbor, MI, 21 Feb 1992). Choral director, composer, and arranger. She graduated in 1914 from Western University, Kansas, and earned a BA and teaching certification at Langston University, Oklahoma. For several years she taught in public and private schools in Oklahoma, before leaving in 1919 to serve briefly as director of music at Morgan College, Baltimore. A year after joining the staff at the *Baltimore Afro-American* in 1925, she moved to New York to study composition with WILL MARION COOK and PERCY GOETSCHIUS. By 1930 her Original Dixie Jubilee Singers (later the Eva Jessye Choir) was popular on both stage and radio. It performed spirituals, work songs, mountain ballads, ragtime jazz, and light opera and appeared regularly on "Major Bowes Amateur Hour" and "The General Motors Hour." The first black woman to win international distinction as a choral director, Jessye performed with her choir throughout the world and in numerous Broadway shows and motion pictures, the first being King Vidor's *Hallelujah* (1929). In 1934 she was the choral director of the first production of Gertrude Stein and Virgil Thomson's *Four Saints in Three Acts*, and in 1935 she was asked by George Gershwin to direct the chorus for *Porgy and Bess*; she continued to serve in the latter capacity for productions into the 1960s. In 1963 her choir was designated the official chorus of the March on Washington for Jobs and Freedom led by Martin Luther King Jr. After formally disbanding her choir in 1970, she remained active as a guest conductor, lecturer, and artist-in-residence at a variety of schools, including the University of Michigan, Ann Arbor, and Pittsburg State University in Kansas. She established major collections of African American music history at these two universities in 1974 and 1977, respectively. Her arrangements include *My Spirituals* (1927), a collection of 16 spirituals for solo voice and piano, and three unpublished oratorios based on spirituals, *The Life of Christ in Negro Spirituals* (1931), *Paradise Lost and Regained* (1934), and *The Chronicle of Job* (1936). She received many honorary doctorates and was a member of ASCAP and the Negro Actors Guild.

BIBLIOGRAPHY

SouthernB

D.F. Black: *The Life and Work of Eva Jessye and her Contributions to American Music* (diss., U. of Michigan, Ann Arbor, 1986)

B. Lanke: *I Dream a World: Portraits of Black Women who Changed America* (New York, 1989)

D.L.J. Wilson: *Eva Jessye: Afro-American Choral Director* (diss., Washington U., 1989)

H. Walker-Hill: "Western University at Quindaro, Kansas (1865–1943) and its Legacy of Pioneering Musical Women," *Black Music Research Journal*, xxvi/1 (2006), 7–37

J. Weisenfeld: "'Truths that Liberate the Soul': Eva Jessye and the Politics of Religious Performance," *Women and Religion in the African Diaspora: Knowledge, Power, and Performance*, ed. R.M. Griffith and B.D. Savage (Baltimore, 2006), 222–44

JAMES STANDIFER/GWYNNE KUHNER BROWN

Jeter, Claude (*b* Montgomery, AL, 1919; *d* New York, NY, 6 Jan 2009). Gospel singer. After leaving high school he took a job in the coal mines of West Virginia and in 1938 organized a gospel quartet, the Four Harmony Kings, with his brother and two miners. When the group became established its members were Jeter (first tenor and lead), Solomon Womack (second lead), John Myles (baritone), and Henry Bossard (bass). They performed in the traditional barbershop style, in which Jeter's light and lyrical voice, as well as his extraordinary falsetto, contrasted well with Womack's heavier, energetic tenor. The group moved to Knoxville, Tennessee, and worked as full-time professional singers, broadcasting five days a week on WNOX. In order to advertise the bakery that sponsored their broadcasts, they changed their name to the SWAN SILVERTONES. Under this title they made their first recordings, *All Alone* (1947) and *My Rock* (1950). The group moved again in 1948 and settled in Pittsburgh. With a new membership consisting of Jeter, Louis Johnson (second lead), Paul Owens (alternate lead and second tenor), Myles, and William "Pete" Connor (bass), they recorded their biggest hit, "Mary, don't you weep" (1959). Jeter left the group in the mid-1960s to enter the ministry, but continued to record as a soloist (including "Lord, I've tried," 1972) and appear in concert throughout the rest of his life. His last solo project was an album, *Yesterday and Today* (Shanachie, 1991), which included "Careless Soul" and "Motherless Child." Jerry Lawson's song "The Man in Room 1009" (2009) addresses Jeter's contributions to gospel.

BIBLIOGRAPHY

T. Heilbut: *The Gospel Sound: Good News and Bad Times* (New York, 1971/*R*)

K.L. Rubman: *From Jubilee to Gospel in Black Male Quartet Singing* (diss., U. of North Carolina, 1980)

S. Jarrett: "Rev. Claude Jeter: a Legend Rediscovered," *Living Blues*, xxxvi/1 (2005), 72–9

Obituary: *New York Times* (10 Jan 2009)

HORACE CLARENCE BOYER/JONAS WESTOVER

Jett [Larkin], Joan (Marie) (*b* Wynnewood, PA, 22 Sept 1958). Rock singer, songwriter, producer, and guitarist. She spent several years in Rockville, Maryland, after which her family relocated to West Covina, California, when she was in her early teens. As an habitué of Rodney Bingenheimer's English Disco, she was exposed to glam rock music and musicians, notably Suzi Quatro, an early and profound influence. It was here, in 1975, that she met the producer Kim Fowley, as well as Sandy West and Cherie Currie, both of whom subsequently worked with Jett as members of the all-girl glam rock band THE RUNAWAYS. The band's other original members were Lita Ford and Jackie Fox. The group was signed to Mercury Records in 1976, and their first album, *The Runaways*, was released soon thereafter. They released three more albums, including *Queens of Noise* (1977), on that label. The group severed ties with Fowley in 1978 and disbanded in 1979.

Jett began her solo career as the producer of the Germs' only album, *GI*, in 1979. She also recorded three songs with the Sex Pistols' Paul Cook and Steve Jones in London in 1979. She then began working with the songwriter and producer Kenny Laguna, who later became her manager and business partner. According to Laguna and Jett, 23 record labels rejected her first album, so they created Blackheart Records and released it as *Joan Jett* (1980) in Europe. Boardwalk Records then signed her and re-released the album as *Bad Reputation* (1981); its propulsive title track performed well. She formed a backup group, the Blackhearts, with whom she released *I Love Rock and Roll* (1981), an album that has sold more than ten million copies. The title track debuted in the American Top 40 and stayed at number one for seven weeks; "Crimson and Clover" also charted. Although she has only occasionally achieved subsequent chart success, with songs such as "I hate myself for loving you" (1988), Jett has remained active, releasing new material and touring internationally. She is known as a powerful and pioneering performer, who also helped to carve space for succeeding generations of women in rock.

BIBLIOGRAPHY

S. Reynolds: *The Sex Revolts: Gender Rebellion and Rock 'n' Roll* (Cambridge, MA, 1995)

D. Frost: "Garageland," *Trouble Girls: the Rolling Stone Book of Women in Rock*, ed. B. O'Dair (New York, 1997), 415–25

K. Kennedy: "Results of a Misspent Youth: Joan Jett's Performance of Female Masculinity," *Women's History Review*, xi/1 (2002), 89–114

S. Waksman: *This Ain't the Summer of Love: Conflict and Crossover in Heavy Metal and Punk* (Berkeley, CA, 2009)

C. Currie: *Neon Angel: Memoir of a Runaway* (New York, 2010)

LISA L. RHODES

Jewel [Kilcher, Jewel] (*b* Payson, UT, 23 May 1974). Singer-songwriter. She grew up in Homer, Arkansas, where she and her father, a cowboy singer-songwriter, performed together. She went solo at 15 and won a scholarship to Interlochen Arts Academy High School in Michigan the following year. After graduation she moved to San Diego, where she lived in her van while trying to make a living as a singer-songwriter. She was discovered by an Atlantic Records executive while performing at the Inner Change Café. Her debut album, *Pieces of You* (1995), and hit single, "Who will Save your Soul," illustrate Jewel's sensitive songwriting and expressive vocals. After extensive marketing and touring *Pieces of You* became one of the best-selling debuts of all time. Jewel won an American Music Award and an MTV Video Music Award for another single from the same album, "You were meant for me." In 1998 she released her second album, *Spirit*, a collection of inspirational ballads. A remixed version of "Serve the Ego" from the album *This Way* (2001) topped the American dance club charts in 2002, suggesting a new direction for Jewel. Her next album, *0304* (2003), was full of dance beats, synthesizers, and layered vocal overdubs. She returned to her earlier style in 2006 with *Goodbye Alice in Wonderland* and then capitalized on her rustic upbringing to recreate herself as a country singer for *Perfectly Clear* (2008). After this album went to number one on the Billboard country chart, Jewel released another country album, *Sweet and Wild* (2010). In addition to her own recordings, Jewel has contributed music to films such as *Clueless* (1995) and *Sweet Home Alabama* (2002).

COLETTE SIMONOT

Jewell, Fred(erick Alton) (*b* Worthington, IN, 28 May 1875; *d* Worthington, IN, 11 Feb 1936). Composer, bandmaster, publisher, and teacher. He studied baritone horn as a child, and joined the Gentry Brothers Dog and Pony Show when he was 16, remaining there until 1902 when he joined the Ringling Brothers Band. In 1905 he joined the Otto-Floto Circus, which became the Sells-Floto Circus in 1906; in that year he assumed leadership of its band. In 1907 he joined the Ringling Brothers Circus, and from 1908–10 was bandmaster of the Barnum & Bailey Circus. In 1916 he became director of the Hagenbeck-Wallace Circus Band, but two years later went to Oskaloosa, Iowa, to succeed C.L. Barnhouse, a friend and publisher, as director of the Iowa Brigade Band. He started his own music publishing business in 1920. In 1923 he returned to Worthington, directed the Murat Temple Band in nearby Indianapolis, and taught music in local schools. Jewell composed over 130 works, some of which were published under the pseudonym J.E. Wells. A number of his works are recorded in Robert Hoe's *Heritage of the March* series (3, B, C, I, N, P, LL, ZZ, and EEEE).

WORKS
(all for band)

104 marches, incl.: Battle Royal; Cavaletta; Circusdom; Crawley's; E pluribus unum; Gentry's Triumphal; High and Mighty; Old Circus Band; Pageant of Progress; Pride and Glory; Quality-plus; Screamer; Shrine of Liberty; Supreme Triumph; Trooping of the Colors; 5 galops, incl.: Go; Whirlwind; Skidoo; 6 waltzes, incl.: Crimson Petal; Myrtle; Roses of Memory; 8 ovs.; 5 serenades; 10 novelties, incl.: Pumpkin Center Cornet Band; Rosemary Cuban Dance; Trombone Blues; Trombone Smiles

Principal publishers: Barnhouse, Jewell

BIBLIOGRAPHY

R. Hoe, Jr., ed.: "Brief Biographies of Famous March Composers," *Journal of Band Research*, xiv/2 (1979), 52 only

W.H. Rehrig: *The Heritage Encyclopedia of Band Music* (Westerville, OH, 1991, suppl. 1996); CD-ROM (Oskaloosa, IA, 2005) [includes selective list of works]

C.P. Conrad: *Fred Jewell (1875–1936): His Life as Composer of Circus and Band Music, Bandmaster and Publisher* (diss., Ball St. U. 1994)

N.E. Smith: *Program Notes for Band* (Lake Charles, LA, 2000), 329–30

CHARLES CONRAD

Jewish music. The search for a satisfactory understanding of Jewish music in America has inspired numerous competing ideas both within and outside of Jewish populations. Music has played a key role in debates about Jews' personal identities, communal concerns, and spiritual affinities in performance, ritual, and creative production. The involvement of Jewish Americans with music in the public sphere, meanwhile, has contributed to larger conversations about the ways subpopulations have influenced American sound. As both model minorities and classic outsiders, Jews have consequently figured in numerous musical worldviews that changed with changing populations and political conditions.

The variable aspects of Jewish identity, whether cultural, national, religious, ethnic, or racial, reveal the complications involved in defining music's relationship with Judaism. Answers to the often-asked question "What is Jewish music?" highlight the different parameters used to define Jewish American sounds: from the use of particular intervals, timbres, or instruments, to the encoding of music with variously defined ethnic essences, to self-definition along a range of historical narratives, to the manifestation of anti-Semitic stereotypes, to the belief in music's power to revive flagging traditions, spur interest in spiritual pursuits, or reinforce moral positions. These parameters have in turn supported a variety of activities that assist the creation of Jewish genres, ideologies, and cultural groupings.

Scholarship on this topic has developed largely in dialogue with Jewish communal activity. Researchers' attempts to categorize Jewish musical expression along "sacred," "folk," and "popular" lines, for example, reflect a combination of academic, political, and religious influences, as well as patterns of support by Jewish-interest institutions and foundations. Debates over the influence of popular culture in sacred music, consequently, rely on both academic and moral arguments; and similar concerns surround discussions about the ways Jewish sacred sounds have entered American popular music—exemplified by the plot of the 1927 film *The Jazz Singer*—and of how the promotion of folk music in Jewish liturgy addresses contemporary needs. Individual assessments of music's quality tend further to reflect perceived comparisons between the "Jewish" world and the "outside" world. Engaged with contemporary discourses about Jewish identity, the complex nature of American Jewish music scholarship thus can be best understood.

1. The colonial period and the early republic (1630s–1840s). 2. The age of Eastern European migration (1880–1924). 3. Growth and threat (1924–45). 4. Postwar (1946–64). 5. Exploration and revival (1964–80). 6. Late 20th and early 21st century (1981–2011).

1. THE COLONIAL PERIOD AND THE EARLY REPUBLIC (1630s–1840s). We know little about the musical practices of the first Jews who arrived in North America around the mid-17th century. Mostly descended from populations in Spain and Portugal that had been sent underground during the Inquisition, these Sephardic Jews eventually reestablished communities in such cities as London, Hamburg, and Amsterdam, and traveled along their parent countries' trade routes to the northern coast of South America, the Caribbean, and several North American cities. These small communities likely drew heavily on the vocal music and chant style of their European parent communities during religious gatherings, while enjoying and participating in local musical events outside of the synagogue. In the 18th century, a few people assumed the title of "Hazzan" or "Haham" in America and performed specialized leadership roles in religious services: Gershon Mendes Seixas, for example, was appointed *hazzan* at New York's congregation Shearith Israel in 1768. While communities generally recognized these figures' liturgical knowledge, their level of formal religious training did not reach that of European rabbis, and their exact musical functions varied from place to place. By 1800 these leaders helped administer to approximately 2500 Jews in congregations at most major seaports, including Newport, New York, Philadelphia, Charleston, Savannah, and New Orleans.

Around the same time, widespread European governmental emancipation and religious reform began to facilitate significant changes to the European synagogue service ritual. Sephardic congregations and pockets of Ashkenazic Jews in Central Europe began to formalize their music programs and revise the liturgy in an effort to present greater continuity with broader society. Attempts to maintain a more orderly appearance, institute multipart male choirs, and employ organs in worship often accompanied movements for change, becoming key points of tension in disputes between self-identified groups of "reformers" and "orthodox" congregants. Among American congregations, the best-documented controversy of this sort surrounded the decision to install an organ in the Sephardic synagogue in Charleston, South Carolina. This issue caused a portion of the membership to secede between 1828 and 1840.

During the next several decades, the United States received a growing number of progressive religious leaders and musical publications that would help a liberal form of Jewish observance take root in America. The arrival of about 400,000 Jews between 1820 and 1880, most Ashkenazim from central Europe, remade the sociomusical landscape of Jewish America. Large congregations grew up in New York, Chicago, Mobile, Baltimore, Cincinnati, San Francisco, and elsewhere, and several hired personnel that championed the style of the Viennese cantor Salomon Sulzer (1804–90). Some, such as Reform Judaism's founding father Isaac Mayer Wise, effected these changes through Sulzer's 1839 publication *Schir Zion* (a second, equally influential volume would appear in 1865). Starting in 1849, Sulzer's students began to take leadership positions as cantors in the United States. Figures such as Leon Sternberger (1819–97; arrived 1849, served in New York), Alois Kaiser (1840–1908; arrived 1865, served in Baltimore), and Samuel Welsch (1835–1901; arrived 1865, served in New York) brought a kind of celebrity to the role, implementing Sulzerian reforms while raising the stature of the cantor as a musical authority. Combined with a rising generation of mostly non-Jewish organists, these cantors worked with their rabbinical colleagues to develop new forms of American Jewish liturgy, with choirs and hymn singing gaining popularity among both progressive and conservative congregations of means. Increasingly frequent want ads for cantors from congregations around the country—often combining musical, communal, and educational responsibilities—appeared in Jewish periodicals, reinforcing the significance of these changes to American Jewish life.

These developments also spurred Jewish liturgical music publication in America. As American rabbis promoted their liturgical innovations through new prayerbooks, so their musical collaborators accompanied the revised liturgies with new or rearranged compositions.

The Klezmer Conservatory Band on the cover of their first album, Yiddishe Renaissance, *1981. (Vanguard Records, A Welk Music Group Company)*

Local compilations began to appear in the 1850s and 1860s. A national initiative spearheaded by Alois Kaiser, Samuel Welsch, Moritz Goldstein, and Isaac L. Rice came to fruition in *Zimrath Yah* (1871–86), a four-volume series of settings for the American Jewish liturgical year. The vision of the *Zimrath Yah* editors coincided with the founding of key institutions in American Jewish life, including the Hebrew Union College in 1873 and the Union of American Hebrew Congregations (UAHC, later the Union for Reform Judaism) in 1875. Their publication, in turn, became influential in helping to define the American Jewish Reform movement; and Kaiser was tapped to produce the movement's first hymnal (1897).

The growth of formal American synagogue music complemented efforts among Jews to join the main stream of American society. Cantors sometimes assisted in these efforts, using their formal musical training as a bridge to the musical world outside of the synagogue. When not officiating at services, some cantors performed alongside dance orchestras and other popular entertainments at formal banquets sponsored by Jewish communities. Jews also set up their own musical societies, such as New York's Cecelia Club, which sponsored regular performances showcasing the community's young talent. Jewish-interest newspapers reported on these evenings, while including additional articles on performances by Jewish opera singers, composers, and others in the concert world. Advertisements for local voice, instrumental, and piano lessons in these same papers also reflected the desirability of musical literacy among Jewish populations of the time.

2. THE AGE OF EASTERN EUROPEAN MIGRATION (1880–1924). With the Central European Jewish population

firmly established and an American Jewish movement centered in Cincinnati, the publication of Jewish musical materials increased substantially. These works brought new music to the American synagogue, while simultaneously embracing new perspectives on Jewish music and its historical trajectories. New York-based cantor William Sparger (1860–c1903) collaborated with Kaiser in 1893, for example, to create "A collection of the principal melodies of the synagogue from the earliest time to the present" as a celebrated souvenir program for the Jewish Women's Congress at Chicago's Columbian Exhibition. Likewise the printing of the *Union Hymnal* in 1897 helped consolidate a variety of musical practices employed by the UAHC's member synagogues.

As the Reform movement stabilized, however, a new cultural paradigm began to establish itself in the United States. Roughly 2.3 million Eastern European Jews, driven by political instability in their homelands and opportunity in America, arrived between 1880 and 1924 and quickly became the dominant demographic of Jewish America. Existing Jewish populations viewed the arrivals as both boon and cultural threat. In response, the cantors' network that had developed since the mid-19th century expressed growing concern that the Eastern European Jews' musical prayer leaders would lower the quality of liturgical music, and consequently created the Society of American Cantors as a means of preserving musical standards. The Society of American Cantors held occasional concerts, including a celebration of Salomon Sulzer's centennial in 1904, and sought to create its own training programs. Ultimately, however, the group's efforts largely succumbed to the musical worlds the new arrivals created as they settled in America.

Eastern European cantors gained fame in their own regard, redefining the Jewish liturgical singer's image and creating what has since been described as a "Golden Age" of the cantorate. Figures such as YOSSELE ROSENBLATT (1882–1933), Mordecai Hershman (1888–1940), Berele Chagy (1892–1954), and Gershon Sirota (1874–1943) emerged from a culture of musical apprenticeship and mastery rooted in the Russian Pale of Settlement and sang in a style celebrated for its unvarnished emotionality, improvisatory flair, and religious devotion. Sometimes lured from Europe with highly lucrative salaries, Eastern European cantors administered to a growing number of synagogues and became subjects of attention, admiration, and intrigue. In addition to thrilling congregations with their solo singing, they generated broad followings through recordings and, for the best-known cantors, global concert tours. The synagogue, the recording studio, and the concert stage invited different types of performance: in religious settings cantors often led male a cappella choirs, while on recordings and in concerts the choirs eventually gave way to instruments, mirroring the recording standards of the day. These cantors also served as symbols of ethnic pride, with the best compared to top opera singers (more than one received the label "The Jewish Caruso"), and occasionally actually crossing over into opera or vaudeville performance.

Matisyahu performing at the Coachella Valley Music Festival, Indio, California, 2006. (AP Photo/Matt Sayles)

Wedding musicians ("klezmorim") constituted another important part of Eastern European Jewish musical life in America. Transforming practices from their lands of origin, klezmorim formed unions and established themselves as a soundtrack for American Jewish celebrations. (*See* KLEZMER.) With the clarinet taking precedence over the violin, which was more common in Eastern Europe, star players such as Dave Tarras (1897–1989) and Naftule Brandwein (1884–1963) joined others in accompanying lifecycle events, playing for gatherings of Jewish Landsmanschaftn (homeland societies), and touring Jewish resort hotels emerging in the Catskill and Pocono mountains. As with other musicians serving ethnic communities, klezmorim often became proficient in more than one cultural style and played alongside Greek, Italian, Romanian, and Arab musicians both at live events and on recordings.

Eastern European Jews also established their own forms of theatrical entertainment, with numerous Yiddish-language theaters opening up on Manhattan's Second Avenue to perform plays and musicals. Drawing from a format first popularized in Eastern Europe by Avraham Goldfaden, numerous musical theater works addressed such themes as classical romance, adapting to America, and nostalgia for the "Old World." Actors such as Aaron Lebedeff (1873–1960), MOLLY PICON (1898–1992), and Pesakhke Burstein (1896–1986) gained fame on the stage, as did composers Abraham Ellstein (1907–63), Alex-

ander Olshanetsky (1892–1946), JOSEPH RUMSHINSKY (1881–1956), and Sholom Secunda (1894–1974). The success of the theater scene translated into swift sales of sheet music and recordings, to be played on the pianos and gramophones that appeared with increasing frequency in Jewish homes.

Many Jews also brought their music into the emerging American art music and popular music realms. Songwriters such as Irving Berlin and Jerome Kern, performers such as Al Jolson, Benny Goodman, and Belle Baker, and composer-performers such as George Gershwin ventured into a scene that sought sounds that could capture the American imagination. Often having to balance their "Jewish" public identities with their writing, these figures became icons of Americanism, whether as ambassadors of jazz, new forms of musical theater, or the emergence of an American style of art music.

The influx of Eastern European Jews also deeply affected perceptions of music in new and existing Jewish religious communities. Reform Judaism, for example, rethought its musical paradigms during this era and began to seek a new approach to Jewish sound in its synagogues' religious rituals. Abraham Z. Idelsohn (1882–1938) came to the United States in 1922 and became a key player in this conversation. Born in Latvia, trained in both Eastern and Central Europe, and leaving behind 14 years of activity in pre-State Palestine, Idelsohn took a position at Cincinnati's Hebrew Union College and set about recasting Jewish music as a unique, Middle East-derived expression of the Jewish spirit. His book *Jewish Music in Its Historical Development* (1929) and his ten-volume *Thesaurus of Hebrew Oriental Melodies* (1914–32) became signal works that served as the basis for future research and musical composition; and, in parallel with Israel Goldfarb at New York's Jewish Theological Seminary, he transmitted these ideas to American rabbis in training. In New York City, Abraham Wolf Binder (1895–1966) created a music department at the 92nd Street YMHA in 1917 and inaugurated a music school there two years later, allowing Jews to develop Western music skills within the context of a Jewish institution. Amateur Jewish choral societies, associated with both religious and secular Jewish institutions across the country, performed concerts for Jewish and non-Jewish audiences alike. And the orthodox Young Israel movement introduced Jews to newly composed congregational melodies in the hope of preventing religious attenuation among young adults and families. These initiatives recast music as a central mode for maintaining Jewish communal vitality in a pluralistic environment.

3. GROWTH AND THREAT (1924–1945). As Jewish immigration to the United States dwindled after restrictive laws were implemented in 1924, the previously mentioned modes of musical expression and other new directions would help succeeding generations adapt as Jews and as Americans. Alongside these developments, however, came a wave of Jewish exclusion in America born of rising xenophobia. Competing ideas about the nature

of new art music in America split the International Composers Guild, for example, with most self-identified Jews leaving to help create the League of Composers in 1923, perhaps in partial response to anti-Semitic remarks by some Guild members. Occasional harangues about "Jewish jazz" in media outlets propagated stereotypes about the Jewish influence in popular culture. These views, which saddled Jews with the perceived responsibility for degrading American life through music, complemented broader attempts to exclude Judaism as foreign to the American experience.

Through the 1930s, as Eastern European-born Jewish populations settled into their new home, their musical activities became increasingly diverse. Some composers and performers continued to populate a Yiddish-language music, theater, film and concert scene that thrived on both sides of the Atlantic. Others became part of the emerging commercial jazz, swing, and film music industries as both performers and producers. Jews and African Americans in particular found ways to interact, with black performers such as Paul Robeson and Cab Calloway including Yiddish songs in their repertoires, Jewish songwriters such as Harold Arlen writing for Harlem nightclubs, and Jewish and black musicians regularly collaborating in both the performance and presentation of jazz events.

Jews also had a strong presence in Socialist and Labor Zionist groups that used recently composed folksongs to reinforce solidarity and group identity: Socialist groups used Yiddish songs to organize workers and promote the common cause of collective labor, while Zionist organizations distributed the most current Hebrew songs to promote a Hebrew-speaking culture in a future state of Israel. By the 1920s both of these groups disseminated their repertoires in local gatherings and at youth summer camps (such as Camp Kinderland and the Cejwin Camps), where organizers buttressed each movement's ideals by introducing songbooks and singing for the youth at mealtimes and around campfires.

The 1930s also produced a number of significant American presentations of Jewishness in music. Several members of the St. Petersburg Jewish Folk Music Society, recently arrived in the United States, helped create *Mailamm* (the America-Palestine Institute of Musical Sciences), a New York-based organization that held art music concerts, promoted collaboration with musical initiatives in Palestine, and cosponsored a short-lived periodical; it was succeeded in spirit by the Jewish Music Forum (most active 1939–1945). The giant pageants *The Romance of a People* (1933, Chicago, music by Isaac van Grove) and *The Eternal Road* (1938, New York, music by Kurt Weill) presented elaborately staged synopses of Jewish history for general audiences, with each narrative pointing the way toward a hoped-for Zionistic redemption. Swiss composer Ernest Bloch's *Sacred Service/Avodath HaKodesh* received accolades as a breakthrough in American Jewish music after its 1934 Carnegie Hall premiere and later was performed in concert and synagogue settings. The 1932 Yiddish theater song "Bei Mir Bist du Shein," reissued by the

Andrews Sisters with English lyrics by Sammy Cahn and Saul Chaplin in 1937, became a massive hit. These events exemplified an era of negotiation between Jews and mainstream society while presaging the closing of the European Jewish theater under a rising Nazi threat.

World War II largely extinguished musical relations between Jews in America and Europe, while making the United States a gathering place for the refugees who could escape the scourge before and afterward. Hebrew Union College hired the Jewish music scholar Eric Werner in 1938 to replace the recently deceased Idelsohn. The opera singer Fritz Lechner immigrated in 1936, eventually securing a position as cantor at New York's Central Synagogue. Members of various Hasidic sects regrouped in the United States, bringing with them their *nigunim* (holy melodies). As the war progressed and the Nazis began implementing their Final Solution, meanwhile, music became one means of alerting the American public to the tragedy of European Jewry through such productions as Ben Hecht and Kurt Weill's 1943 pageant *We Will Never Die*.

4. POSTWAR (1946–1964). The end of the war and the decimation of European Jewry shifted the center of Jewish life to the United States. Many American Jews, faced with the destruction of a site that represented a source of Jewish authenticity, began to embark upon projects of reclamation that would either establish a Jewish homeland in Israel or reconstruct key Jewish traditions on American soil. Consequently, in the cultural and economic boom of the late 1940s and 1950s, American Jews commenced an era of remarkable musical productivity.

Hasidic groups began to gather their *nigunim* in published collections and recordings. Exemplified by Chabad Lubavitch's *Nichoach* project—an acronym for *Nigunei Chasidei Chabad* (The Melodies of the Chabad Hasidim), published in three volumes between 1948 and 1965—these efforts allowed uprooted religious dynasties to preserve and "purify" their musical heritage as part of a general regrouping to face a new life in the United States. The introduction of the long-playing record in 1948 assisted in this process by allowing groups to complement their collections with recordings.

With the help of Eric Werner (1911–1988) and the New York-based Society for the Advancement of Jewish Liturgical Music, efforts to preserve the cantorial cultures of Eastern Europe bore fruit in the creation of American cantorial schools. The Reform movement established its School of Sacred Music in 1948; the Conservative movement's Cantors Institute opened in 1952, and the Modern Orthodox movement started the Cantorial Training Institute (later the Belz School of Jewish Music) at Yeshiva University in 1954. Modeled on central European cantorial training curricula, which themselves aspired to maintain an Eastern European aesthetic, these schools reprinted 19th- and early 20th-century synagogue music collections, commissioned recognized cantorial authorities to notate and publish their chant melodies (*nusach*), and hired other recognized cantors to train incoming students. These schools also promoted the cantorial role to each movement's constituent synagogues in the hope of preserving and renewing the profession.

Many klezmorim continued to sustain viable careers in the years after World War II, but their audiences began to splinter generationally. Those who remained aesthetically tied to Eastern Europe were aging; their children found these sounds increasingly archaic, particularly as Israeli culture gained primacy over Yiddish culture among young people. With the players and their main supporters dwindling, the scene slowly began to shift away from the urban centers and toward sites of nostalgia.

Younger generations, meanwhile, began to explore American Jewish identity by engaging with the emerging folksong revival. As liberal religious movements opened a network of summer camps starting in the late 1940s, for example, the rabbi-staffers used communal singing, sometimes accompanied by piano, banjo, mandolin, or guitar, to enact and communicate specific Jewish theologies. Other adults and cantors eventually contributed songs to these scenes, as did song leaders brought over from Israel. Young people consequently came to relate the unique repertoire they experienced at camp with the intense Jewish social and religious experiences they had there, and took this aesthetic back to their home communities.

Composers of art music increasingly chose Jewish topics in the postwar period, perhaps in part because of the increasing mythification of Eastern European Jewish culture. Arnold Schoenberg's 1947 *A Survivor from Warsaw* offered an early reflection on the experiences of Jews during the Holocaust (in this case the Warsaw Ghetto uprising), as did Alfred Newman's score for the 1959 film *The Diary of Anne Frank*. American companies premiered European operatic works on Jewish biblical themes such as Schoenberg's *Moses und Aron* (premiered 1954), as well as new American works on various aspects of Jewish culture (including operatic settings of the Golem legend by Lazar Weiner [1958] and Abraham Ellstein [1962]). Collaborations between composers and modern dancers resulted in Jewish-themed works such as Pearl Lang's 1949 *Song of Deborah* (music by Richard Winslow) and Sophie Maslow's 1950 *The Village I Knew* (music by Samuel Matlowsky). Leonard Bernstein's emergence as a public figure, meanwhile, opened widespread conversations about musical Jewishness: in the eyes of many Bernstein became a model of American-Jewish achievement, unapologetically integrating his identity into his compositions, musical activities, and political philosophy.

The desire for greater musical and artistic prestige also extended to synagogues, which continued to hire musical directors and present new compositions that could garner respect outside of Jewish circles. Temple Israel in Lawrence, New York, had engaged the composer Isadore Freed since the 1930s, and the Free Synagogue in Flushing, New York, engaged the composer Frederick Piket as its musical director in the early 1950s. Commissioning programs also flourished during this

time. For example, David Putterman, cantor at New York City's Park Street Synagogue, ultimately commissioned more than seventy composers between 1943 and 1975 to write new liturgical music for his annual Sabbath Evening Liturgical Service of New Music. These projects exemplified broader efforts by which American Jews sought to achieve respect and recognition in the mainstream of American culture without compromising their identity.

5. EXPLORATION AND REVIVAL (1964–1980). Synagogues, Jewish community institutions, and civic arts organizations continued to support musical explorations of Judaism in the 1960s. Jerry Bock and Sheldon Harnick's 1964 musical *Fiddler on the Roof*, for example, opened the door for a re-ethnicization of American Jewish musical expression, while the Hebrew Union College School of Sacred Music's decision to admit female cantorial students in the mid-1970s marked a turning point in the presentation of liturgical music. These activities involved mainly adults; young people, in contrast, had largely remained outside of the conversation, limited to reproducing materials that adults created for them. This situation changed drastically as young people began to exercise their political strength en masse, youth culture became an increasingly powerful part of the American economy, and Jewish institutions expressed rising anxiety about the youth's continuing commitment to Jewish life and culture.

Shlomo Carlebach (1925–1994) became one of the first people to use music to speak directly to young people. In the 1950s Carlebach began a guitar-based ministry through Chabad Lubavitch, which had begun to target college-aged youth. Through his melodies and unadorned strumming technique, he built up a following while becoming a fixture in folk music circles. After leaving Chabad, he set up centers in San Francisco (the House of Love and Prayer), Israel (Moshav Mevo Modi'im), and New York (the Carlebach Shul), composing nearly five thousand tunes along the way. Carlebach's activity, which looked to general musical trends among young people, inspired others. Among Orthodox Jews, musicians and musical groups such as the Rabbis' Sons, D'veykus, Mordecai Ben David, Avraham Fried, and The Diaspora Yeshiva Band began to set devotional texts to contemporary musical styles, providing young religious Jews a way to enjoy their own contemporary music.

In liberal settings, meanwhile, Carlebach's popularity combined with a regular influx of popular music from Israel—including popular music settings of devotional texts from the annual Hasidic Song Festival—to inspire young people to create their own guitar-based liturgical music. By the 1970s, liturgical settings created by Reform Jewish song leaders such as Debbie Friedman, Loui Dobin, Jeffrey Klepper, and Daniel Freelander had begun to compete with settings used in adult services, and they would continue to gain popularity as these young people grew into positions of leadership.

Camp Massad, a Zionist organization in the Poconos, served as the basis for a revival of the Jewish choral scene, incubating a group that became known as the Zamir Chorale. Over the following decades, alumni of the group started their own ensembles for adults (including the Zamir Chorale of Boston) and children (the *HaZamir* choirs) across the country. Drawing their repertoire from defunct Eastern European Jewish choral ensembles, new Israeli choral music, and American works, these high-level amateur ensembles developed a devoted network of singers, many of whom also participated in a broad range of Jewish communal activities.

Other young musicians followed paths of discovery to Jewish musical styles through the jazz/folk and early music movements of the 1960s and 1970s. Musicians such as Hankus Netsky, Walter Z. Feldman, Joel Rubin, Alan Bern, Michael Alpert, and Henry Sapoznik came to see Yiddish music as a means for expressing personal, and sometimes family-based, identity. Judith Wachs (founder of Voice of the Turtle) discovered the Sephardic Romancero while working in Boston with Marleen Montgomery. Noah Greenberg's New York Pro Musica and Joel Cohen's Boston Camerata researched and performed medieval and Renaissance Jewish music. Others came to the repertoire through folk music channels. In many cases, artists devoted themselves to the music through acts of ethnographic reclamation: interviewing old practitioners, analyzing recordings, seeking out published collections, and visiting archives to obtain a deep knowledge about the people and conditions that produced the music. Their efforts often became a means for performers to explain their own Jewish identities.

These changes also led to shifts in Jewish music scholarship. During the 1960s, musical research agendas had been heavily supported by Jewish institutions and consequently tended to promote Jewish self-assurance and continuity, distill Jewish qualities in religious chants, or identify Jewish elements in the lives and works of composers such as Schoenberg, Felix Mendelssohn, and Aaron Copland. By the 1970s the discipline of ethnomusicology, combined with the opening of collegiate area studies programs, brought new approaches and methods to the field that contextualized Jews within a global model of music making. Music scholars such as Kay Shelemay, Mark Slobin, Philip Bohlman, Ellen Koskoff, and Edwin Seroussi secured positions at secular universities; capable of producing their own doctoral students, they mediated between the needs of Jewish communal institutions and the demands of academic rigor to take the field in new directions.

6. Late 20th and early 21st century (1980s–2011). The end of the 20th century and the start of the 21st century saw continued crossing and convergence between scholarship, performance, and communal activity. Those specializing in Jewish music continued to perform locally but found particular success at regional Jewish conferences and conventions—some (such as Klez-Kamp or the North American Jewish Choral Festival) devoted to a particular type of music, others (such as

LIMMUD, a Jewish education conference) serving as important artist showcases. The wide array of Jewish music festivals that arose after the Berkeley Jewish Music Festival in 1986 opened the way for careers devoted to Jewish music. And since the 1990s, mega-concerts in venues such as Madison Square Garden and Avery Fisher Hall have become mainstays for orthodox Jewish artists and audiences.

New genres of Jewish music developed in the 1980s and 1990s, including the avant-garde jazz-based "Radical Jewish Culture" movement spearheaded by John Zorn and centered in lower Manhattan, an a cappella scene that originated with Columbia University's Pizmon in 1986 and quickly spread across the collegiate world, and a Jewish hip-hop culture that gained a foothold among both liberal and orthodox Jewish communities. These and many other forms of "Jewish" music exemplified young Jews' desire to assert their identity in ways that reflected their particular life experiences.

Scholarship accompanied this expansion as a legitimizing—and to some extent unifying—entity. Several klezmer and Yiddish musicians, for example, completed doctorates (often in ethnomusicology) to supplement their performing careers, and in turn became the authorities for the next generation of performers. The academic field of Jewish music itself, meanwhile, continued to involve a broad mediation between disinterested scholarship and interested practitioners. For the most part, this mediation led to mutual benefit: festivals began to call on scholars to supplement their offerings, and communal organizations could call on a wider array of speakers and published materials. Scholarly organizations such as the American Society for Jewish Music (which revived the Jewish Music Forum in 2006) provided opportunities for researchers to exchange their ideas, and publications such as *Musica Judaica*, the *Journal of Synagogue Music*, and the *Journal of Jewish Music and Liturgy* sought to increase their scholarly rigor while still catering to a relatively broad Jewish readership that included clergy and interested laypeople. By 2011 Jewish music interest groups had formed in the American Musicological Society, the Society for Ethnomusicology, the Society for American Music, and (informally) the Association for Jewish Studies. These endeavors, combined with the rise of a new generation of scholars of music and Judaism, sought new paradigms for engaging with intellectual discourses on music, while maintaining fruitful relationships with Jewish populations and foundations that comprised an important part of their audience.

Measures to consolidate a kind of Jewish music industry received support from Jewish community organizations and venture philanthropy outlets around the turn of the 21st century under the premise that culture could be equated with communal commitment among Jewish youth and young adults. Though economically unsustainable, these initiatives resulted in the founding of the labels JDub (2002–11), Jewish Music Group (2006–8), Modular Moods/Shemspeed (*c*2003), and Reboot Stereophonic/Idelsohn Society for Musical Preservation (2005), along with festivals (including the

OyHoo! Festival) and efforts to create a systemic award system, including several failed attempts to create a Jewish Grammy award. On the surface these and other endeavors appeared to flame out quickly. Yet they also brought many of their participants into Jewish communal networks and subsequent long-term commitments to Jewish life. Meanwhile, some performers, such as alternative rock/reggae/hip-hop musician Matisyahu, managed to achieve success as self-consciously Jewish artists who could make it in the music industry on their own merits.

In early 2011 the American Reform movement's cantorial school was renamed in memory of songleader Debbie Friedman, spiritually merging two musical styles that had been at odds for the previous 40 years. This act in some ways exemplified the continued experiences of Jews and music in America, highlighting the tensions inherent in musical self-representation and the multiple, complex identities that accompany the American idea of Jewish music.

BIBLIOGRAPHY

GMO (Bohlman, "Jewish music")

A. Idelsohn: *Jewish Music in its Historical Development* (New York, 1929)

J. Reider: "Jewish Music in Pennsylvania in the Eighteenth Century," *Church Music and Musical Life in Pennsylvania*, ed. Pennsylvania Society of the Colonial Dames of America, iii (Philadelphia, 1947), 331

A. Sendrey: *Bibliography of Jewish Music* (New York, 1951)

S. Rosowsky: *The Cantillation of the Bible* (New York, 1957)

I. Freed: *Harmonizing the Jewish Modes* (New York, 1958)

A.W. Binder: *Biblical Chant* (New York, 1959)

E. Werner: *Mendelssohn: a New Image of the Composer and His Age* (Glencoe, 1963)

E. Werner: *From Generation to Generation* (New York, 1968)

A. Weisser: *Bibliography of Publications and other Resources on Jewish Music* (New York, 1969)

I. Heskes, ed.: *Studies in Jewish Music: Collected Writings of A. W. Binder* (New York, 1971)

I.J. Katz: "A Musical Survey of the Judeo-Spanish *Romancero*," *Judeo-Spanish Traditional Ballads from Jerusalem: an Ethnomusicological Study*, i (New York, 1972), 20–124

E.G. Mlotek, ed.: *Mir trogn a gezang* (New York, 1974) [annotated anthology]

M. Nulman: *Concise Encyclopedia of Jewish Music* (New York, 1975)

E. Werner: *A Voice Still Heard…: the Sacred Songs of the Ashkenazic Jews* (University Park, PA, 1976)

R. Rubin: *Voices of a People: The Story of Yiddish Folksong* (Philadelphia, 1979)

M. Slobin: *Tenement Songs: the Popular Music of the Jewish Immigrants* (Urbana, IL, 1982)

J. Levine: *Synagogue Song in America* (Crown Point, IN, 1989)

R. Liberles: "Conflict Over Reforms: The Case of Congregation Beth Elohim, Charleston, South Carolina," *The American Synagogue: A Sanctuary Transformed*, ed. J. Wertheimer (Hanover, NH, 1995), 274–96

K. Shelemay: "Music in the American Synagogue: A Case Study from Houston," *The American Synagogue: A Sanctuary Transformed*, ed. J. Wertheimer (Hanover, NH, 1995), 395–415

M. Kligman: "On the Creators and Consumers of Orthodox Popular Music in Brooklyn," *YIVO Annual*, xxiii (1996), 259–94

N. Levin: "Music at JTS," *Tradition Renewed: A History of the Jewish Theological Seminary of America*, ed. J. Wertheimer (New York, NY, 1997), vol.1, 717–792

J. Melnick: *A Right to Sing the Blues: African Americans, Jews, and American Popular Song* (Cambridge, MA, 1999)

E. Koskoff: *Music in Lubavitcher Life* (Urbana, 2000)

J. Summit: *The Lord's Song in a Strange Land: Music and Identity in Contemporary Jewish Worship* (New York, 2000)

M. Kligman: "Contemporary Jewish Music in America," *American Jewish Year Book*, ci (2001), 88–141

K. Shelemay: "Toward an Ethnomusicology of the Early Music Movement: Thoughts on Bridging Disciplines and Musical Worlds," *Ethnomusicology*, xlv (2001), 1–29

M. Slobin, ed.: *American Klezmer: It Roots and Offshoots* (Berkeley, CA, 2001)

Various, *The Milken Archive of American Music*. 50 CDs (New York, NAXOS, 2002–2006);

J. Sarna: "The Question of Music in American Judaism: Reflections at 350 Years," *American Jewish History*, xci (2003), 195–203

D. Schiller: *Bloch, Schoenberg, Bernstein: Assimilating Jewish Music* (New York, 2003)

M. Slobin: *Fiddler on the Move: Exploring the Klezmer World* (New York, 2003)

A. Most: *Making Americans: Jews and the Broadway Musical* (Cambridge, MA, 2004)

J. Cohen: "Singing Out for Judaism: a History of Songleaders and Songleading at Olin-Sang-Ruby Union Institute," *A Place of Our Own: The Beginnings of Reform Jewish Camping in* America, ed. G. Zola and M. Lorge (Tuscaloosa, AL, 2006), 173–208

A. Wood: "The Multiple Voices of American Klezmer," *JSAM*, i (2007), 367–92

J. Cohen: "Whither Jewish Music?: Jewish Studies, Music Scholarship, and the Tilt Between Seminary and University," *AJS Review*, xxxii (2008), 29–48

M. Kligman: *Maqam and Liturgy: Ritual, Music and Aesthetics of Syrian Jews in Brooklyn* (Detroit, 2008)

J. Cohen: "Hip-hop Judaica: The Politics of Representin' Heebster Heritage," *Popular Music*, xxviii (2009), 1–18

J. Cohen: *The Making of a Reform Jewish Cantor: Musical Authority, Cultural Investment* (Bloomington, IN, 2009)

D. Lehman: *A Fine Romance: Jewish Songwriters, American Songs* (New York, 2009)

J. Cohen: "Rewriting the Grand Narrative of Jewish Music: A.Z. Idelsohn in the United States," *Jewish Quarterly Review*, c (2010), 417–53

"Milken Archive of Jewish Music: The American Experience," <www.milkenarchive.org> (2010)

J. Pinnolis: "'Cantor Soprano' Julie Rosewald: The Musical Career of a Jewish American 'New Woman,'" *American Jewish Archives Journal*, lxii, 2 (2010), 1–53

J. Cohen: *Sounding Jewish Tradition: The Music of Central Synagogue* (New York, 2011)

JUDAH M. COHEN

Jewish Music Forum. *See* AMERICAN SOCIETY FOR JEWISH MUSIC.

Jicarilla. APACHE Indian group of the Southwest.

Jim and Jesse. Country and bluegrass music duo. It comprised the brothers James McReynolds (*b* Coeburn, VA, 13 Feb 1927; *d* Gallatin, TN, 31 Dec 2002) and Jesse McReynolds (*b* Coeburn, VA, 9 July 1929), grandsons of the fiddle player Charles McReynolds, who recorded with the Bull Mountain Moonshiners for Victor's Bristol Sessions in 1927. Their professional career began in 1947 on the radio station WNVA in Norton, Virginia, where they were billed as the McReynolds Brothers and the Cumberland Mountain Boys. During the late 1940s and 1950s they broadcast for several radio stations in the South and Midwest, and in 1951 they made their first recordings for the Kentucky label in Cincinnati. A distinctive and consistently professional sound emerged: Jim played guitar and sang high tenor with effortless clarity, and Jesse sang baritone and played mandolin in a unique cross-picking style (also called McReynolds style) that resembles three-finger banjo figuration. In 1952 Ken Nelson took the pair to Capitol Records; they changed their name to Jim and Jesse and the Virginia Boys and released songs including "Are you missing me" (1952) and "Just wondering why" (1953).

Jim and Jesse's Virginia Boys were one of the premiere bluegrass bands of the mid-1950s and early 1960s. During this period its members included Curly Seckler, Tommy Jackson, Bobby Thompson, Vassar Clements, Allen Shelton, and Jim Buchanan. Local television became Jim and Jesse's principal medium during the late 1950s. Although bluegrass was overshadowed by rock and roll, the duo returned to recording and issued material on Starday (1959) and Columbia (1961). They moved to Epic in 1962 and released albums including *Bluegrass Special* (1963) and *Diesel on my Tail* (1967). They made their first guest appearance on the Grand Ole Opry in 1961 and became regular cast members in 1964. They also played at the Newport Folk Festival from 1963 to 1966. As the folk revival declined, Jim and Jesse's style became closer to that of mainstream country music. In 1967 they began a syndicated television series, *Country Carousel*, followed by *The Jim and Jesse Show* in 1970. They returned briefly to Capitol in 1971 to record the popular album *Freight Train*, and in early 1973 they founded their own label, Old Dominion Records. During the next three decades they recorded for a variety of labels and maintained an active career as bluegrass artists. Jesse has continued to perform after his brother's death in 2002.

BIBLIOGRAPHY

J. Tottle: "The Grass Is Greener in the Mountains," *Muleskinner News*, v/March (1974), 6–10

R.K. Oermann: "Jim & Jesse: Testing the Boundaries of Bluegrass Music," *Bluegrass Unlimited*, xxvii/Sept (1982), 18–24

S. Hambly: "Jim and Jesse: Reprising their 'Epic' Best," *Bluegrass Unlimited*, xxi/Aug (1986), 8–22

RONNIE PUGH/JOTI ROCKWELL

Jiménez, Flaco [Leonardo] (*b* San Antonio, TX, 11 March 1939). Accordionist and songwriter. He inherited his nickname Flaco ("skinny") from his accordionist father, SANTIAGO JIMÉNEZ. Like many Texas-Mexican musicians of his generation, he was born into a musical family—his grandfather Patricio played the accordion, as does his younger brother Santiago Jr.—and has played the three-row, diatonic Hohner button accordion; his father played the two-row model. He began performing in his father's conjunto band at the age of seven, accompanying him on the *bajo sexto*. By age 16 he was playing accordion and had his own conjunto band, Los Caporales. This was during the early rock-and-roll years when such artists as Elvis Presley and Buddy Holly made a lasting impression on him. In 1973 he recorded with Doug Sahm, a founding member of 1960s San Antonio's rock pioneers Sir Douglas Quintet. Jiménez developed a syncopated and lively modern accordion sound by ornamenting and extending simple folk melodies and using fermatas. He has continued to mine blues, country, R&B, and pop music to update his style and as a result has collaborated with Bob Dylan, Ry Cooder, Dr. John,

and Los Super Seven, among others. He has received an NEA National Heritage Fellowship and multiple Grammy Awards.

CATHY RAGLAND

Jiménez, José Julián (*b* Trinidad, Cuba, 9 Jan 1823; *d* Havana, Cuba, 1880). Afro-Cuban violinist and pianist. The son of an orchestral conductor, Jiménez was part of a vibrant class of free black and *mulato* musicians who marked Cuba's musical life in the 19th century. In 1849, he moved to Havana, where he studied with Italian violinist and composer Luigi Arditi. In 1849 Jiménez founded a dance band in Havana and composed many *danzas* and *guarachas* for the ensemble. At the end of that year he moved to Germany and entered the Leipzig Conservatorium, where he studied violin with Ferdinand David, piano with Ignaz Moscheles, and harmony with Alexander Ritter. In Leipzig he performed professionally as a member of the Gewandhaus Orchestra. Upon his graduation from the conservatory, Jiménez returned to Cuba. In 1869, he returned to Leipzig with his sons, Nicasio and José Manuel (Lico) Jiménez-Berroa, where he continued to perform with the Gewandhaus Orchestra, as a recitalist, and, from 1871–5, in the "*Negertrio* Jiménez" with his sons. The trio concertized across Europe arousing a mix of enthusiasm and curiosity from the press. In 1879 Jiménez returned to Cuba and died shortly thereafter.

BIBLIOGRAPHY

J. Wright: "'*Das Negertrio*' Jiménez in Europe," *The Black Perspective in Music*, ix/2 (1981), 161–76

A. Carpentier: *Music in Cuba*, ed. T. Brennan (Minneapolis, 2001)

SUSAN THOMAS

Jiménez, Santiago (*b* San Antonio, TX, 25 April 1913; *d* San Antonio, 18 Dec 1984). Accordionist, songwriter, and composer, father of the accordionists FLACO JIMÉNEZ and Santiago Jiménez Jr. He is known as a pioneering accordionist and composer of many classic polkas. With encouragement from his accordion-playing father Patricio Jiménez, he began playing at age eight. Although he released his first recording, "Dices pescao" (Decca), in 1936, he was best known for weekly live performances on a Spanish-language radio program, *La hora anáhuac*, which aired in the 1940s on San Antonio's KCOR. He recorded two popular polkas, "Viva Seguin" and "La piedrera," in 1942 for the Mexican Victor label, the latter written while he worked in a quarry. They were his most popular and have been widely performed and recorded by musicians since. Compared with that of Narciso Martínez, his main rival, Jiménez's playing style was smoother with less syncopation and fewer 16th notes; he never graduated to the three-row button accordion. However, his precision and rich musicality has remained unmatched. Like Martínez, Jiménez could not make a living from music, and in the 1960s he moved to Dallas and worked as a janitor. He returned to San Antonio in 1977, where he played in local restaurants and bars and at festivals.

CATHY RAGLAND

Jiménez-Berroa, José Manuel (Lico) (*b* Trinidad, Cuba, 7 Dec 1855; *d* Hamburg, Germany, 15 Jan 1917). Afro-Cuban pianist and composer. The son of violinist José Julián Jiménez, Jiménez-Berroa moved to Leipzig, Germany at the age of 14. At the Leipzig Conservatorium he studied piano with Ignaz Moscheles and composition with Carl Reinicke, eventually receiving first prize in piano. From 1871–5, he played in the family "*Ne-gertrio* Jiménez," concertizing across Europe. In 1875, following the trio's successful Parisian debut, he began study with Antoine François Marmontel at the Paris Conservatory, where he won first prize in piano. He met Wagner and Liszt, who both praised his piano playing. He returned to Cuba in 1879 and is credited with bringing the music of German composers, especially that of Beethoven, to Cuban audiences. His compositions show a greater German influence, particularly of the music of Schumann and Liszt, than they do of an attempt to create a Cuban national style. He is considered to be the first Cuban composer to compose lieder, and his *Elegía* won the composition prize at the Matanzas Exhibition in 1881. Unable to surpass the racist barriers in Cuban society, Jiménez returned to Germany in 1879, where he taught in the Hamburg Conservatory until his death.

BIBLIOGRAPHY

J. Wright: "'*Das Negertrio* Jiménez' in Europe," *The Black Perspective in Music* ix/2 (1981), 161–76

A. Carpentier: *Music in Cuba*, ed. T. Brennan (Minneapolis, 2001)

SUSAN THOMAS

Jimmy Jam and Terry Lewis. Songwriting and production duo. Jimmy Jam (James Samuel Harris; *b* Minneapolis, MN, 6 June 1959) and Terry [Steven] Lewis (*b* Omaha, NE, 24 Nov 1956) have helped to reshape African American popular music since the 1980s with edgy, street-smart productions and sophisticated song lyrics that appealed to a broad audience. Their hits also popularized new jack swing, a style of youth-oriented dance music closely related to hip-hop and R&B. Harris and Lewis began working together in the Minneapolis-based R&B band Flyte Tyme. After Prince recruited them in 1981 and took over as their primary writer and producer, they became the Time, with Morris Day as lead vocalist. The pair were dismissed from the group before its appearance in Prince's film *Purple Rain* (1984).

Harris and Lewis formed the production company Flyte Tyme to develop material for other artists, including the SOS Band, Cheryl Lynn, Klymaxx, and Alexander O'Neal, with Harris writing the music and Lewis contributing lyrics. Their first top ten pop hit came with "Tender Love" (recorded by the Force M.D.'s, 1985) which was an early fusion of R&B with hip-hop beats using the Roland TR-808 electronic drum machine. In 1986 Harris and Lewis collaborated on Janet Jackson's *Control*, producing the album and co-writing seven of its nine tracks including "Control," "Nasty," and "What have you done for me lately." The album, which also mixed R&B with electronic drum machine sounds, was a critical and commercial success and elevated Jackson to superstardom. It also won Harris and Lewis a Grammy Award as producers of the year. Over the next two decades they produced Jackson's albums *Rhythm Nation 1814* (1989), *Janet* (1993), *The Velvet Rope* (1997), *All for You* (2001), *Damita Jo* (2004), and *20 Y.O.* (2006).

Harris and Lewis have written and produced for a diverse range of artists including Boyz II Men, Vanessa Williams, Mariah Carey, New Edition, Usher, the Human League, Rod Stewart, Robert Palmer, George Michael, Gwen Stefani, Chaka Khan, Mary J. Blige, and Prince. By the early 2010s they had produced more than 40 pop and R&B number one hit singles and more than 100 albums that achieved gold certification status. Based in Minneapolis for most of their partnership, they moved in 2005 to a new recording studio, Flyte Tyme West, in Santa Monica, where they have also produced film soundtracks. Harris has also held the position of Chairman Emeritus of the National Academy of Recording Arts and Sciences.

MILES WHITE

Jin [Au-Yeung, Jin] (*b* Miami, FL, 4 June 1982). Rapper. He came to prominence in 2001, winning seven consecutive Freestyle Friday competitions on BET's *106 & Park*. This success led him to become the first Asian American rapper signed to a major record label, with New York-based Ruff Ryders Entertainment. His Ruff Ryders debut album, *The Rest is History*, was released in 2004. The album was originally scheduled for release in 2003, but was delayed for more than a year due to internal label politics. It was commercially disappointing, peaking at number 54 on the Billboard charts. In 2005 Jin took part in a popular battle with his fellow rapper Serius Jones that was eventually featured on the DVD *Fight Klub*. His second album *100 Grand Jin* was released in 2006, and in 2008 he signed with Universal Music Group Hong Kong. He subsequently moved to Hong Kong. Jin has also embraced Christianity and was baptized in 2008. He has continued to release albums including *ABC* (2007), whose name is a colloquial acronym short for "American-born Chinese." *ABC* was recorded in his parent's native language Cantonese.

JARED PAULEY

Jingle. A short, catchy song used in ADVERTISING. Jingles arose first in verse without music in the second half of the 19th century. In early radio in the 1920s there were countless local and regional instances, but the first nationally known jingle did not appear until 1926: "Have you tried Wheaties" was based on the chorus of a 1919 song, arranged for barbershop quartet. Despite its success, jingles were not seen as truly effective sales devices until the 1940s, following the massive success of a jingle, "Pepsi-Cola hits the spot," by Austen Croom-Johnson and Alan Bradley Kent. Commercial music production companies sprang up throughout the 1940s and 1950s. The jingle became the workhorse of the advertising music industry for decades. Jingles lasted until baby boomers came to power in the advertising industry in the 1980s, who viewed jingles as trite and wanted to employ music of their youth in commercials, a trend that has continued into the early 21st century, along with the use of contemporary popular music. Jingles have continued to be used in local and regional markets, and some famous nationally broadcast jingles from the past are still occasionally heard.

BIBLIOGRAPHY

T.D. Taylor: *The Sounds of Capitalism: Advertising, Music, and the Conquest of Culture* (Chicago, 2012)

TIMOTHY D. TAYLOR

Jitterbug. A strenuous social dance for couples, performed to quick-tempo jazz or swing music. The name is used primarily to identify the modified version of the LINDY HOP that was widespread from about 1935 to the end of World War II. The recording of Cab Calloway's "Call of the Jitter Bug" (1934) and the short film *Cab Calloway's Jitterbug Party* (1935), which features a performance of the song by Calloway and his orchestra, introduced the term into popular culture. Calloway originally used "jitter bug" not as the name of a dance but to indicate a person who had drunk from a jug with "whiskey, wine, and gin within" and was suffering a severe case of the jitters as a result. In the film, as Calloway sings, party guests dance a lively foxtrot before forming a line, side by side, and keeping time to the up-tempo beat by prancing in place with rapid shifts of weight from foot to foot. Their movements bear no resemblance to the swing dance that soon became known as jitterbug. It is said that when Calloway saw dancers doing a frenetic Lindy hop at the Savoy Ballroom in Harlem he remarked that they "looked like a bunch of jitter bugs." Thus, the name came to be applied to the fast, acrobatic type of Lindy invented in the early 1930s by Frankie Manning at the Savoy; by the early 1940s, it was being used to identify the more sedate form of the Lindy that had become popular throughout the country. It was also used generally to refer to almost all kinds of dance to swing music. Besides its various meanings in relation to dance, "jitterbug" can signify a jazz musician, a devotee of jazz, or, in its most general senses, an alarmist or a nervous or jittery person.

BIBLIOGRAPHY

C. Calloway and B. Rollins: *Of Minnie the Moocher and Me* (New York, 1976)

M. Stearns and J. Stearns: *Jazz Dance: the Story of American Vernacular Dance* (New York, 1983)

F. Manning and C.R. Millman: *Frankie Manning: Ambassador of Lindy Hop* (Philadelphia, 2007)

A. Shipton: *Hi-De-Ho: the Life of Cab Calloway* (New York, 2010)

CLAUDE CONYERS

Jive (i). African American urban popular music of the 1940s. The word has many meanings in African American usage and may derive from the Wolof word *jev*, meaning "to talk disparagingly," a usage it retains in the United States. It is also applied to witty or deceitful speech, to a form of stylized jitterbugging or athletic dancing, and to marijuana. It was especially applied to the lightweight, rhythmic form of hokum blues popular in the 1940s during the swing era. Although the words of jive songs were often insinuating, witty, sophisticated, or sly, the music was associated with "good

times." Its principal exponent was the much recorded singer and alto saxophonist Louis Jordan, whose "You run your mouth and I'll run my business" (Decca, 1940), "The chick's too young to fry" (Decca, 1945), "Let the good times roll" (Decca, 1945), and "Saturday Night Fish Fry" (Bruns., 1949) show a typically extroverted style. Other jive artists included Phil Moore, whose "I'm gonna see my baby" (Vict., 1944) is a patriotic wartime piece, and the white pianist Harry "the Hipster" Gibson, who made a number of outrageous songs, including "Who put the benzedrine in Mrs. Murphy's Ovaltine?" (Musicraft, 1944). Although jive as such declined, it survived as a vein in the rhythm-and-blues idiom, particularly through the recordings of Wynonie Harris, for example "Grandma plays the numbers" (King, 1948) and "Bloodshot Eyes" (King, 1951).

BIBLIOGRAPHY

D. Burley: *Dan Burley's Original Handbook of Harlem Jive* (New York, 1944)

C. Calloway: *The New Cab Calloway's Hepsters Dictionary* (New York, 1944); repr. in *Riffs & Choruses: a New Jazz Anthology*, ed. A. Clark (New York, 2001), 351–6

L. Shelly: *Hepcats: Jive Talk Dictionary* (Derby, CT, 1945)

B.M. Tyler: "Black Jive and White Repression," *Journal of Ethnic Studies*, xvi/4 (Winter 1989), 31–66

R.R. Jerving: *Hep: Jazz Modernisms* (diss., U. of Illinois, Urbana-Champaign, 2000)

B. Milkowski: *Swing It!: an Annotated History of Jive* (New York, 2001)

PAUL OLIVER/R

Jive (ii). An American social dance of the 20th century. Rooted in the Swing dances of the 1940s, jive is classified in the International Latin division of competitive Ballroom dance. It is the fastest of the Latin dances, characterized by quick kicks, flicks of the feet, and twirling of the female partner. A joyful, boppy dance that seems uninhibited, it does, in fact, require tight technical control.

CLAUDE CONYERS

João Grande [Mestre João Grande; dos Santos, João Olivera] (*b* Itají, Bahia, Brazil, 15 Jan 1933). Brazilian teacher and master practitioner of capoeira angola. After migrating from rural Bahia to Salvador, he learned capoeira in the Centro Esportivo de Capoeira Angola under the legendary *mestre* Vicente Ferreira Pastinha. Influenced also by such veteran practitioners as Cobrinha Verde and Barbosa, he became a widely respected *capoeirista*, adept at the art's movements, songs, and instrumental music, especially that of the *berimbau*, a musical bow. João Grande and three other students accompanied Pastinha to Senegal for the first World Festival of Black Arts in 1966. He later joined Viva Bahia, a folk dance troupe directed by Emília Biancardi, touring Europe in 1976 and was publicly recognized as a successor by Pastinha. In 1990 he moved to New York, where he established the Capoeira Angola Center of João Grande. He has received a medal from the Brazilian ministry of sports (1990), an honorary doctorate from Upsala College (1995), and a National Heritage Fellowship from the NEA (2001). His acrobatic, ornamented movement style, traditionalist singing, and instrumental prowess helped to revive interest in capoeira angola in the 1980s when more sport-oriented styles of capoeira overshadowed its cultural and musical traditions.

BIBLIOGRAPHY

C.D. Dawson: *Capoeira Angola and Mestre Joao Grande: the Saga of a Tradition; the Development of a Master* (New York, 1993)

GREG DOWNEY

Jobim, Antônio Carlos [Tom] **(Brasileiro de Almeida)** (*b* Rio de Janeiro, Brazil, 25 Jan 1927; *d* New York, NY, 8 Dec 1994). Brazilian composer, pianist, guitarist, and arranger. In his early teens he took piano lessons from Koellreutter and later from Branco and Tomás Terán, and also studied orchestration, harmony, and composition. In the mid-1940s he began to work as a pianist in the bars and nightclubs of Rio's beach areas of Copacabana and Ipanema. In 1952 he worked as an arranger for the recording firm Continental and his first recorded pieces appeared in the following year. He became the artistic director for the Odeon label in 1956 and began a lifelong association with the poet Vinicius de Morais, composing and conducting the music for the play *Orfeu da Conceição*.

In 1959 the aesthetic manifesto of the BOSSA NOVA was famously presented on João Gilberto's album *Chega de Saudade*, which included Jobim's song "Desafinado," with lyrics by Newton Mendonça, and Jobim's "Samba de uma nota só" was included on Gilberto's second album, *O amor, o sorriso e a flor* (1960). Among the many Vincius-Jobim collaborations, however, none won more international popularity than "Garota de Ipanema" ("The Girl from Ipanema") (1962). With Stan Getz and Charlie Byrd's instrumental version of "Desafinado" the American bossa nova craze took hold: Audio Fidelity promoted a concert of bossa nova music at Carnegie Hall in November 1962, and in 1963 *The Composer of Desafinado Plays* was issued, Jobim's first solo recording. From 1964 onwards his success in the United States grew rapidly, with various Grammy awards, several LP releases including *Francis Albert Sinatra and Antonio Carlos Jobim* (1967), and television and film soundtrack contracts. By the late 1960s his music had become part of the repertory of leading international pop and jazz artists.

During the last 25 years of his life the worldwide recognition of his talents was unprecedented for a Brazilian popular musician: his music was recorded in the best studios of New York and Los Angeles and released on the largest multinational labels. He toured with his Banda Nova on several continents and received many awards and honors, including several further Grammy awards and honorary doctorates from Brazilian and Portuguese universities. Most important were his collaborations with other Brazilian musicians, including João Gilberto, Chico Buarque, Edu Lobo, Caetano Veloso, and Milton Nascimento. Several biographies, songbooks, and monographs on his work were published. His output, which numbers some 250 titles, reveals his talents as a profoundly creative composer whose innovative and inspiring melodies, harmonies, rhythms, and inventive orchestration always expressed his passionate love for his native city and its people with simplicity and honest emotion.

BIBLIOGRAPHY

A. de Campos, ed.: *Balanço da Bossa: antologia crítica da moderna música popular brasileira* (São Paulo, 1968, 2/1974)

G. Béhague: "Bossa and Bossas: Recent Changes in Brazilian Urban Popular Music," *EthM*, xvii/2 (1973), 209–33

A.R. de Sant'Anna: *Música popular e moderna poesia brasileira* (Petrópolis, Brazil, 1978, 3/1986)

A.C. Jobim: *A vida de Tom Jobim: depoimento* (Rio de Janeiro, 1982)

M. Martins and P.R. Abrantes, eds.: *3 Antônios & 1 Jobim* (Rio de Janeiro, 1993)

M. Cezimbra, T. Callado, and T. de Souza: *Tons sobre Tom* (Rio de Janeiro, 1995)

J.L. Sánchez: *Tom Jobim: a simplicidade do gênio* (Rio de Janeiro, 1995)

H. Jobim: *Antônio Carlos Jobim: Um Homem Iluminado* (Rio de Janeiro, 1996)

S.A. Reily: "Tom Jobim and the Bossa Nova Era," *Popular Music*, xv/1 (Jan 1996), 1–16

S. Cabral: *Antônio Carlos Jobim: Uma Biografia* (Rio de Janeiro, 1997)

P. Freeman: "Antonio Carlos Jobim: Eclecticism in Popular Music," *Music Research: New Directions for a New Century*, eds. M. Ewans, R. Halton, and J.A. Phillips (London, 2004), 263–75

GERARD BÉHAGUE/R

Jobin, Sara (Elisabeth) (*b* Norwood, MA, 26 Oct 1970). Conductor and lecturer. A precocious talent, she began piano and viola lessons at eight and attended the Boston University Tanglewood Institute as a pianist at 15. She graduated from Harvard and Radcliffe Colleges (AB in women's studies and music, 1991) as a Leonard Bernstein Music Scholar with a senior thesis focused on female orchestral conductors. She then studied conducting with Charles Bruck (1911–95) at the Pierre Monteux School in Maine as a John Knowles Paine Traveling Fellow.

Jobin received the first JoAnn Falletta Conducting Award from the Women's Philharmonic in recognition of her outstanding promise and joined the staff of the San Francisco Opera (SFO) in 1999. On 7 November 2004 she became the first woman to conduct a main stage production with the SFO in a performance of *Tosca*. Performances of *The Flying Dutchman*, *Norma*, and Philip Glass's *Appomattox* preceded her appointment to lead a joint production of Rachel Portman's *The Little Prince* by the SFO and Cal Performances in 2008.

As a freelance conductor she has worked with myriad organizations across the country and gave her first performances in Europe during the 2009–10 season with the San Francisco Contemporary Music Players at the Musiques Actuelles Nice Côte D'Azur festival in Nice, France, and with the Bochumer Symphoniker in Germany. In addition to traditional romantic fare, she has conducted works by John Harbison, Morton Feldman, Edmund Campion, Ken Ueno, Donnacha Dennehy, and Philippe Leroux, and she presented the world premiere of Glass's Greek play, *The Bacchae*, with the New York Shakespeare Festival. Her recording of John Musto's comic opera *Volpone* with the Wolf Trap Opera Company earned a Grammy nomination for Best Opera Recording in 2010.

GARY GALVÁN

Jocelin [Jocelyn], **Simeon** (*b* Branford, CT, 22 Oct 1746; *d* New Haven, CT, 5 June 1823). Tunebook compiler, composer, clock maker, and engraver. An influential compiler of tunebooks in the 1780s and 1790s, he included established English and American favorites in his books and introduced the works of such new American composers as Lewis Edson and Daniel Read. His significant compilations are *The Chorister's Companion* (1782/*R*), which was issued in collaboration with the publisher Amos Doolittle; a 48-page supplement to *The Chorister's Companion* entitled "Part Third" (1783); *A Collection of Favorite Psalm Tunes* (1787); *The Federal Harmony* (1793); and *The New Haven Collection of Sacred Music* (1818). Jocelin helped to create a distinctive New England idiom which is representative of early American psalmody; his publications are counted among the important early American tunebooks. Details about his life remain scarce. However, Eli Whitney served as his partner in the manufacture of clocks, and his sons Simeon Jr. and Nathaniel, an aspiring portrait painter and active abolitionist, bought several firms in 1858 and formed the American Bank Note Company, which sold their ink patent to the US government.

BIBLIOGRAPHY

R.F. Goldman and R. Smith: *Landmarks of Early American Music, 1760–1800* (New York, 1943/*R*)

R. Crawford: "Connecticut Sacred Music Imprints, 1778–1810," *Notes*, xxvii (1971), no.3, pp.445–52; no.4, pp.671–79

S.E. Murray: "Timothy Swan and Yankee Psalmody," *MQ*, lxi (1975), 433–63

A.P. Britton, I. Lowens, and R. Crawford: *American Sacred Music Imprints, 1698–1810: a Bibliography* (Worcester, MA, 1990)

R. Crawford: *The American Landscape* (Berkeley, CA, 1993), 141–7, 307

D.C. O'Brien: *Amos Doolittle: Engraver of the New Republic* (New Castel, DE, 2007), 5, 11

KIMBERLY GREENE

Joe Cuba [Calderón, Gilberto Miguel] (*b* New York, NY, 22 April 1931; *d* New York, NY, 15 Feb 2009). Bandleader and percussionist. As a member of the Nuyorican community, he became known as the father of Latin boogaloo for his pioneering blend of various Afro-Caribbean styles with R&B and soul, along with lyrics that alternated between English and Spanish. In 1954 he founded the José Calderón Sextet, which later became known as the Joe Cuba Sextet. This group featured timbale and vibraphone (reminiscent of Tito Puente's mambo style), conga drums, piano, and bass, as well as the singer Cheo Feliciano. Their release of "To be with you" in 1962 predated the emergence of slow-paced Latin soul, whereas "El pito" (1965) heralded the Latin boogaloo era with its 1-2-3-4 clappings, cha-cha-cha-related rhythms, blues-related keyboard riffs, ostinato whistles evoking street noises together with the code switching between English and Spanish common among Nuyoricans. This musical framework was considerably enriched and developed in "Bang Bang" (1966), a seemingly spontaneous recording said to mark the beginning of the Latin boogaloo craze and the sextet's crossover to US mainstream and international audiences. Alongside these stylistic landmarks, Cuba is often said to have contributed the salsa industry's first great hit, "El ratón," and helped spawn a series of salsa compositions directly addressing life in el Barrio (Spanish Harlem).

BIBLIOGRAPHY

C.M. Rondón: *El libro de la salsa* (Caracas, 1980)

J. Flores: *From Bomba to Hip-hop: Puerto Rican Culture and Latino Identity* (New York, 2000)

EDGARDO DIAZ DIAZ

Joel, Billy [William Martin] (*b* Bronx, NY, 9 May 1949). Songwriter, pianist, and singer. In the early 1950s he moved with his family to Hicksville, NY, where he began classical piano lessons at the age of four. His parents were musical and exposed him to many genres, particularly classical and theater music. Between 1964 and 1971 he played in several Long Island bar bands, performing both covers and original songs. He went solo in 1971 and moved to Los Angeles, where he lived until 1974. There he performed in piano bars and cocktail lounges; the experience inspired his well-known song "Piano Man," as well as much of the album *Streetlife Serenade* (Col., 1974). His first major commercial success was *The Stranger* (Col., 1977), which went multi-platinum and won two Grammy awards. His next album, *52nd Street* (Col., 1978), was his first to reach number one. *Nylon Curtain* (Col., 1982) contains his most heavily Beatles-influenced songs and includes the working-class anthem "Allentown." *An Innocent Man* (Col., 1983) was a tribute to the early rock-and-roll styles that also influenced his songwriting. In 1987 he was one of the first major American rock stars to perform in the Soviet Union. He maintained his popular appeal into the late 1980s and 1990s with the albums *Storm Front* (Col., 1989) and *River of Dreams* (Col., 1993), both of which reached number one in the United States. In 1994 Joel performed the first of many concert tours with his English counterpart Elton John. In 1999 he was inducted into the Rock and Roll Hall of Fame by one of his idols, Ray Charles. He turned to classical composition in 2001 and released the album *Fantasies and Delusions* (Sony Classical, 2001), a collection of solo piano works performed by the pianist Richard Joo. These works invoke a romantic sensibility and exhibit a command of melodic writing similar to that found in Joel's rock songs. In 2002 *Movin' Out*, a jukebox musical based on Joel's songs and classical works and choreographed by Twyla Tharp, premiered on Broadway to critical acclaim, leading to a Tony award for Joel's orchestration.

Joel's oeuvre consists of carefully crafted melody-oriented songs that demonstrate a command of counterpoint and formal structure, a manifestation of his diverse influences from Beethoven and Chopin to 1960s popular music, notably that of the Beatles. Although he has had an international following, Joel has been particularly beloved in his native New York and the surrounding region, where he has been an icon for generations of fans. Many of his songs, which have become local anthems, contain references to specific places and landmarks in New York and Long Island, including "New York State of Mind," "Miami 2017 (I've seen the lights go out on Broadway)," "Scenes from an Italian Restaurant," "Captain Jack," and "Downeaster Alexa."

BIBLIOGRAPHY

J. Tamarkin: *Billy Joel: from Hicksville to Hitsville* (Port Chester, NY, 1984)

B. DeMain: "Interview with Billy Joel," *The Performing Songwriter*, 3/16 (1996)

W. Everett: "The Learned vs. the Vernacular in the Works of Billy Joel," *Contemporary Music Review*, xviii/4 (2000), 105–29

H. Bordowitz: *Billy Joel: the Life & Times of an Angry Young Man* (New York, 2005)

M. Bego: *Billy Joel: the Biography* (New York, 2007)

S. Radlmaier: *Die Joel-Story: Billy Joel und seine deutsch-jüdische Familiengeschichte* (München, 2009)

HEATHER LAUREL

Joffrey [Khan], **Robert** [Anver, Abdullah Jaffa Anver Bey] (*b* Seattle, WA, 24 Dec 1930; *d* New York, NY, 25 March 1988). Dancer, choreographer, teacher, and ballet company director. After early studies in ballet, he presented his first choreography in his native Seattle in 1948. He continued training in New York at the School of American Ballet, and studied modern dance with May O'Donnell and Gertrude Shurr. He performed with Roland Petit's Ballets de Paris and O'Donnell's modern dance company. In 1953 he established the American Ballet Center, which became the official school of his company. His first dance group, Robert Joffrey Ballet Concert, was founded in 1954; two years later he began a new company, the Robert Joffrey Ballet. With Gerald Arpino as chief choreographer, Joffrey molded the company (subsequently known as City Center Joffrey Ballet and, beginning in 1977, simply as the Joffrey Ballet) into a purveyor of dynamic, youth-oriented ballets with wide appeal. *Astarte* (1967), his best-known ballet, conveyed the psychedelic imagery of the counterculture through live action, film, and the music of the rock band Crome Syrcus. He commissioned works from young, cutting-edge ballet and modern dance choreographers, among them Twyla Tharp, Jiri Kylian, Mark Morris, and William Forsythe. He also began to acquire revivals of significant ballets from the recent past, most notably Vaslav Nijinsky's *Le sacre du printemps* (music, Igor Stravinsky), reconstructed by Millicent Hodson and Kenneth Archer in 1987. These revivals served to educate American audiences as well as to recapture something of the fleeting history of the dance. In the 1950s and 1960s Joffrey was also active outside his own company, creating dances for musicals, television, and opera, and serving as resident choreographer for New York City Opera. He will be best remembered, however, as a visionary artistic director who shaped his ballet company into a force to be reckoned with in American dance.

BIBLIOGRAPHY

International Dictionary of Ballet (Detroit, 1993)

S. Anawalt: *The Joffrey Ballet: Robert Joffrey and the Making of an American Dance Company* (New York, 1996)

International Encyclopedia of Dance (New York, 1998)

SUSAN AU

Johannesen, Grant (*b* Salt Lake City, UT, 30 July 1921; *d* Berlin, Germany, 27 March 2005). Pianist. He studied the piano with Robert Casadesus at Princeton University and EGON PETRI at Cornell University, and theory with ROGER SESSIONS and NADIA BOULANGER. He made his debut at Times Hall, New York, in 1944. In 1949 he won first prize at the Concours International at Ostend and also undertook his first international tour. In 1956 and 1957 he toured Europe with the New York PO and Mitropoulos. He made an extensive tour of the USSR and Europe with the Cleveland Orchestra and George Szell in 1968, and solo tours of the USSR in 1962 and 1970; he also appeared regularly at the leading festivals in the United States and Europe. He was on the faculty of the Aspen Music School (1960–66) and in 1973 became music consultant and advisor to the Cleveland Institute of Music of which he was later music director (from 1974) and president (from 1977); he announced his resignation in 1984. His honors include the Harriet Cohen International Award (1960) and doctorates from the University of Utah (1968) and the Cleveland Institute of Music (1975). An intelligent, sensitive, restrained player over a broad repertory, Johannesen was best known for his performances of French music. He championed the piano music of Gabriel Fauré, which he recorded complete, and celebrated the 150th anniversary of the composer's birth in 1995 with an all-Fauré recital in London. He recorded, too, such unusual material as the Variations by Paul Dukas and works by Albert Roussel and Déodat De Séverac. His compositions include *Improvisations over a Mormon Hymn* as well as cadenzas to Classical concertos. From 1963 to 1973 he was married to cellist Zara Nelsova, with whom he often appeared in concerts and made recordings.

MICHAEL STEINBERG/R

Johansen, Gunnar (*b* Copenhagen, Denmark, 21 Jan 1906; *d* Blue Mounds, WI, 25 May 1991). Pianist and composer of Danish birth. From the age of ten he received lessons in piano and theory from his violinist and conductor father, and at 12 he made his first public appearance, inspired by the example of Ignaz Friedman, whom he had heard the previous year. After studies with Victor Schiøler Johansen moved to Berlin and worked briefly with Frederic Lamond (1921) and then most significantly with EGON PETRI at the Hochschule für Musik (1922–4). The studies with Petri not only enabled Johansen to refine his technical command of the instrument, but they also formed the basis of many of his subsequent musical and aesthetic values. Johansen also studied composition with Paul Juon, which gave him a firm grounding in late-Romantic technique. During this period he moved among the Busoni circle, and in July 1923 gave the premiere of Busoni's *Zehn Variationen über ein Präludium von Chopin*. Between 1924 and 1929 he toured Europe before moving to San Francisco, where he made weekly radio broadcasts for the West Coast on NBC (1930–35) in addition to championing recent works such as Ravel's G major Concerto and Rachmaninoff's Fourth Concerto. In 1935 he first presented a cycle of 12 historical recitals with music ranging from Frescobaldi to Stravinsky, in San Francisco and Berkeley, which he repeated in Chicago, New York, Stockholm, and Madison. Over his career Johansen appeared with numerous conductors (including Pierre Monteux, Artur Rodzinski, Frederick Stock, Ernst Bacon, Hans Schmidt-Isserstedt, and Eugene Ormandy), performed chamber music extensively under the auspices of Elizabeth Sprague Coolidge and with the Pro-Arte Quartet (complete Beethoven and Brahms chamber music), Rudolf Kolisch, the Paganini Quartet, and Kathleen Parlow. In 1939 Johansen was appointed the first Artist-in-Residence in Music at any school in the United States by the University of Wisconsin-Madison, a position he held until his retirement in 1976. In the earlier part of his tenure (1945–53) he presented broadcast series in which he performed the complete piano works of Beethoven, Mozart, Schubert, Chopin, and Bach, as well as a cycle devoted to the development of the piano sonata. He also became involved in the technical possibilities of recording offered by magnetic tape, and from his private studio (and company "Artist Direct") he issued a series devoted to the complete keyboard works of Bach; one to the complete mature works of Busoni; another to the piano music of Ignaz Friedman; and, most notably, one that featured a large selection of Liszt's original compositions and many of his transcriptions. He also recorded many works by Chopin, Edward Collins, Godowsky, Grieg, Carl Nielsen, Reger, and himself. His own compositions, including over 100 notated works and some 560 Sonatas and *Psalms of David* improvised directly onto tape, reveal a remarkable assimilation of diverse styles yet with a distinctively personal voice. All these performances are notable for Johansen's technical mastery and questing intellect, an intellect not only directed towards music (including his early and significant support of Harry Partch) but also to a wide-ranging field of scholarship and interdisciplinary activity through his own Leonardo Academy.

WORKS
(selective list)

Orch: 3 Piano Concs. (1930, 1947, 1969–71); Variations, Disguises and Fugue on a Merry Theme of Cyrus McCormick (1937)
Piano: Sonatas 1–31 (1940–51), toccatas, suites, many shorter works; transcriptions, cadenzas, embellishments, elaborations of works by a number of composers.
Chamber music: 3 vn sonatas (1930, 1933, 1935), str qt (1937), Triptych (1984) for cello and piano
Vocal: East-West Cantata (1943) pf, choir, small ens; songs on texts by Wilde, Longfellow and others; Vocalise (1975)
Improvisations: Improvised Sonatas 32–551 (1953–90); Improvisations after the Psalms of David (1–41)

BIBLIOGRAPHY

F. Cooper: "Gunnar Johansen Talks to Clavier," *Clavier* (Apr 1969), 15–16
A. Corleonis, "Ferruccio Busoni: historia abscondita," *Fanfare* (Jan 1984), 90–116
A. Corleonis: xA Birthday Greeting to Gunnar Johansen on His 80th," *Fanfare* (Jan/Feb 1986), 89–96
J. Wagner: "Gunnar Johansen: Renaissance Man," *Clavier* (Dec 1987), 8–13
G. Rumson: "Gunnar Johansen: the Trajectory of a Life," *Journal of the American Liszt Society*, xxxvii (Jan–June 1995), 26–45
C. Hopkins, "A Danish phenomenon," *International Piano Quarterly*, ii/6 (Winter 1999), 60–65
S. Pierce: *Gunnar Johansen: A Critical Consideration of and Perspective on his Legacy as 20th Century Pianist and Composer* (diss., University of Minnesota, 2001)
J. Gunnar: The Gunnar and Lorraine Johansen Charitable Trust, James P. Colias, Trustee <http://www.gunnarjohansen.org/>

CHARLES HOPKINS/GORDON RUMSON

John, Sir Elton (Hercules) [Dwight, Reginald Kenneth] (*b* Pinner, England, 25 March 1947). English singer, songwriter, and pianist. Although much of his music was written in England, his importance to American culture cannot be understated; according to *Billboard*, he is the most successful solo male musician on its *Hot 100 Top All-Time Artists* chart. Known for his own compositions and his many collaborations with the lyricist Bernie Taupin, John is also a performer whose flamboyant costumes and style has garnered significant attention. Among his singles to reach number one on the charts in the United States are "Crocodile Rock" (1972), "Bennie and the Jets" (1974), "Philadelphia Freedom" (1975), "Don't go breaking my heart" (1976), and "Candle in the Wind 1997." Many of his other singles and albums have reached gold and platinum status. In the 1990s John turned to scoring Hollywood films, most prominently the soundtrack for Disney's *The Lion King* (1994), which generated the hits "Can you feel the love tonight" and "The Circle of Life." As Disney branched onto the Broadway stage, John made the move as well, contributing music to *The Lion King* (1997), *Billy Elliot: the Musical* (2005), and *Lestat: the Musical* (2006). As one of the world's most famous openly gay men, he has used his fame to champion AIDS awareness and the search for a cure through the Elton John AIDS Foundation among many other initiatives.

JONAS WESTOVER

Johns, Clayton (*b* New Castle, DE, 24 Nov 1857; *d* Boston, MA, 5 March 1932). Composer, pianist, and teacher. After studying architecture with Theophilus P. Chanler in Philadelphia (1875–9), he went to Boston to enter the Institute of Technology but, after hearing the Boston SO, decided to study music instead. As a special student at Harvard he studied composition with JOHN KNOWLES PAINE (1879–81) and piano with WILLIAM H. SHERWOOD (1879–82). He met Joseph Joachim in Berlin in 1882 and on his advice studied counterpoint and composition with Friedrich Kiel and piano with Friedrich Grabau and Oskar Raif, all faculty at the Berlin Hochschule für Musik. A letter of introduction from Joachim made it possible for him to attend Liszt's master class at Weimar in July 1883. He returned to Boston in June 1884, and established himself as a composer and teacher of piano and composition. On 25 April 1885 he gave the first of more than 20 annual recitals of his own compositions. In the summer of 1895 he spent six weeks in London where he accompanied Melba, Eames, Bispham, and others in public and private performances of his songs. From 1912 to 1928 he taught piano at the New England Conservatory. In addition to his autobiography, *Reminiscences of a Musician* (1929), Johns published three books, *The Essentials of Pianoforte Playing* (1909), *From Bach to Chopin* (1911), and *Do You Know That—?*

(1926). He is best known for his more than 100 songs and his Introduction and Fugue for piano (1899), a favorite of Josef Hofmann.

WORKS
(selective list)

Stage: The Mystery Play (incidental music for a miracle play), vv, insts, perf. Boston, 1905, *NYp*

Inst: Introduction and Fugue, e, pf 1899; Berceuse and Scherzino, str, Boston, 22 March 1894; 2 Mazurkas, G, pf; Impromptu Capriccietto, pf; Melody, Berceuse, Intermezzo, Romance, Scherzino, vn, pf; several other pf pieces

Vocal: over 100 songs, for 1v, pf, incl. Farmer's Daughter (J. Boit) 1880, 7 Songs (L. Uhland: *Wanderlieder*) 1885, Song of Four Seasons (A. Dobson) 1885, The Rose and the Gardener (A. Dobson) 1886, Marie (R. von Gottschall) 1886, Two Songs: No Lotus Flower on Ganges Borne (A. Bates), Deep in a Rose's Glowing Heart (M. Deland) 1888, Four Songs (A. Christen) 1888, Were I a Prince Egyptian (A. Bates) 1888, Thou Art So Like a Flower (H. Heine) 1888, Scythe Song (A. Lang) 1890, *I Love, and the World Is Mine* (F.E. Coates) 1891, Songs of Sleep 1892, English Songs 1894, French Songs (S. Prudhomme) 1894, Wonder Songs, op. 19 (O. Herford) 1895, I Cannot Help Loving Thee (Anon.) 1895, Album of Songs 1896, A Cycle of German Songs (J. Ambrosius) 1898, Forever and a Day (T. B. Aldrich) 1898, Barefoot Boy with Cheek of Tan (J.G. Whittier) 1901, Two Songs (P. Verlaine) 1904, Malindy (P.F. Camp) 1905, If Love Were Not (F.E. Coates) 1914; 4 partsongs, mixed/female vv

Principal publishers: Birchard, Boston Music, Church, Ditson, G. Schirmer, Schmidt

BIBLIOGRAPHY

DAB (J.T. Howard)

R. Hughes and A. Elson: *American Composers* (Boston, 1914)

Obituaries: *Boston Evening Transcript*, 5 Mar 1932; *New York Times*, 6 Mar 1932; Musical *Courier*, civ (12 Mar 1932); *New England Conservatory of Music Bulletin*, xiv/3 (1932)

R.P. Locke: "Johns, Clayton," *American National Biography Online* (2000)

MARGERY MORGAN LOWENS/JOHN C. SCHMIDT

Johns, Paul Emile (*b* Kraków, Poland, *c*1798; *d* Paris, France, 10 Aug 1860). Pianist, composer, and publisher of Polish birth. He was in New Orleans by 25 November 1818, when he performed in a concert at Salle d'Orléans conducted by M. Desforges; ten days later he performed Dussek's Military Concerto and a set of his own variations. He frequently played the piano, as soloist and accompanist, until 1830. He is credited with the first performance in the United States of a piano concerto by Beethoven, on 10 February 1819. In 1824 he composed *A Warlike Symphony*, *Grand Military March*, and a comic opera, *The Military Stay*, all now lost. He became a music dealer in 1826 and opened his own store in New Orleans in 1830, but sold it in 1846 to W.T. Mayo (who sold it in turn in 1854 to P.P. Werlein). In the early 1830s Johns published jointly with Pleyel in Paris his *Album louisianais*, an elegant collection of six romances for voice accompanied by piano or harp, and a waltz and a polonaise for piano solo; this is the first music known to have been written and published in New Orleans. Each composition is dedicated to a lady of Louisiana. A few pieces of sheet music also survive. He went to Paris in 1832 and met Chopin, who subsequently dedicated his Mazurkas op.7 to Johns. Johns was organist at St. Louis Cathedral in 1843–4. A cotton magnate in later life, he served as Russian consul in New Orleans from 1848 to 1860.

BIBLIOGRAPHY

J.H. Baron: "Paul Emile Johns of New Orleans: Tycoon, Musician, and Friend of Chopin," *IMSCR XI: Copenhagen 1972*, 246–50

A. Janta: *A History of Nineteenth-Century American-Polish Music* (New York, 1982)

A.E. Lemmon: "Footnotes to History: Emile Johns," *Historic New Orleans Collection Quarterly*, x/3 (1992), 5

JOHN H. BARON

Johnson, A(rtemas) N(ixon) (*b* Middlebury, VT, 22 June 1817; *d* New Milford, CT, 1 Jan 1892). Music educator, editor, and composer. After study in Boston with GEORGE JAMES WEBB and Lowell Mason, Johnson taught for the Musical Education Society (1837–41), Boston Public Schools (1839–54), and Boston Academy of Music (1844–9). He was choir leader and organist for the Park Street Church (1840–*c*1856). Among his early private students were GEORGE FREDERICK ROOT and ISAAC BAKER WOODBURY. After studying in Frankfurt under the composer-theorist Xaver Schnyder von Wartensee, Johnson published *Instructions in Thorough Base* in 1844. It established him as the nation's first professional music theorist. He subsequently founded the (Boston) *Musical Gazette* (1846–50), a music book publishing business favoring works by Americans (1851–6), and with B.F. Baker, the *Boston Musical Journal* (1853–4), which in 1855 Johnson reestablished as the *Massachusetts Musical Journal*, making his protégé Eben Tourjée editor and publisher.

Johnson invented a learning-by-doing approach to music teaching. Nationally known as "Johnson's System," its choral version rivaled Mason's European-based "Pestalozzian" system. Ultimately, Johnson's American bias led to his rejection by the nation's European-influenced musical establishment. Undaunted, he found acceptance outside East Coast cities. As president of the Allegany Academy of Music in Friendship, New York (*c*1863–70), he employed the conservatory system, as also later when establishing nine music schools in New York, Ohio, Indiana, and Pennsylvania (1870–88). With Johnson's encouragement, THEODORE PRESSER, a former student and instructor at Johnson's Miami Conservatory of Music in Xenia, Ohio, founded the Music Teachers National Association, assisted by another former pupil of Johnson's, WILLIAM HENRY DANA.

Johnson produced 36 music books, two pasticcio cantatas, and about 500 compositions, mostly tunes, anthems, and gospel music.

BIBLIOGRAPHY

J.W. Moore: "A.N. Johnson," "Complete Encyclopaedia of Music," ii, appended to *Moore's Musical Record*, i/May (1867), 25–6

G.F. Root: *The Story of a Musical Life* (Cincinnati, OH, 1891)

J.B. Stopp: "A.N. Johnson, Out of Oblivion," *American Music*, iii/2 (1985), 152–70

J.B. Stopp: "Historical Introduction," *American Church Organ Voluntaries* [by H.C. Cutler and A.N. Johnson] (New York, 1987), ii–xiv [facs. of 1852 edn]

J.B. Stopp: "Johnson versus Mason: Musical Politics, 1843 Style," *Quarterly Journal of Music Teaching and Learning*, iii/Fall (1992), 54–60

JACKLIN BOLTON STOPP

Johnson, Billy [William Francis] (*b* Charleston, SC, *c*1858; *d* Chicago, IL, 12 Sept 1916). Minstrel performer. He joined J.W. Hyatt's Colored Minstrels in 1881 and later performed with various companies, including Lew Johnson's Black Baby Boy Minstrels (1884), the Hicks and Sawyer Refined Colored Minstrels (1887), Sam T. Jack's Creole Company (1890s), and John Isham's Octoroons Company (*c*1895). While with Black Patti's Troubadours (1896–7) he met BOB COLE, and the two men left to form their own company. In 1898 they presented in New York the first musical to be written, produced, and staged by African American artists, *A Trip to Coontown*, which stimulated a series of similar productions over the next decade; the show went on tour for four years, after which Johnson and Cole disbanded their company. Johnson then performed a solo act on the vaudeville circuit before settling in Chicago. He formed a new company there with Tom Brown in 1914.

BIBLIOGRAPHY

SouthernB

DOMINIQUE-RENÉ DE LERMA

Johnson, (Blind) Willie (*b* Brenham, TX, 22 Jan 1897; *d* Beaumont, TX, 18 Sept 1945). Gospel singer and guitarist. Blinded at the age of seven, he learned to play guitar and accompanied himself when singing at Baptist Association meetings and in country churches around Hearne, Texas. He was married at the age of 25, and thereafter was led by his wife Angeline, who accompanied him on several recordings made on location between 1927 and 1930. Johnson possessed a remarkably deep voice, melodious yet with a pronounced rasp, as exemplified in his extraordinary narrative of Samson and Delilah, "If I had my way I'd tear that building down" (Col. 14343, 1927). His guitar playing was unique, with a pronounced emphasis on rhythm on the majority of his 30 recordings; he also had a sensitive slide technique, as in the "spiritual moaning" on "Dark was the night, cold was the ground" (Col. 14303, 1927) and "Bye and bye I'm going to see the King" (Col. 14504, 1929). Angeline Johnson sang antiphonally to his leads on several recordings, including "The rain don't fall on me" (Col. 14537, 1930) and "Church I'm fully saved today" (Col. 14582, 1930). Johnson's recordings were of exceptionally high quality and exercised a strong influence on other African American gospel singers. After the Depression he did not record again but continued to beg as a street singer, dying of pneumonia contracted after a house fire.

BIBLIOGRAPHY

S.B. Charters: *Blind Willie Johnson*, FW 3585 (1959) [liner notes]

B. Basiuk: "The Guitar Style of Blind Willie Johnson," *Blues Magazine*, iii/5 (Oct 1977), 35–47 [incl. guitar tablature]

P. Oliver: *Songsters and Saints: Vocal Traditions on Race Records* (Cambridge, England, 1984)

J. Obrecht: "Can't Nobody Hide from God: the Steel-String Evangelism of Blind Willie Johnson," *Guitar Player*, xxxii/6 (June 1998), 57–62

J.A. Brisbin: "Willie Johnson," *Rollin' and Tumblin': the Postwar Blues Guitarists*, ed. J. Obrecht (San Francisco, CA, 2000), 193–203

M. Corcoran: "The Soul of Blind Willie Johnson," *Da capo Best Music Writing 2004*, ed. M. Hart and P. Bresnick (Cambridge, MA, 2004), 60–67

PAUL OLIVER/R

Johnson, Bunk [Willie Gary] (*b* New Orleans, LA, 27 Dec ?1879; *d* New Iberia, LA, 7 July 1949). Jazz trumpeter, cornetist, and bandleader. He claimed to have been born in 1879 and, despite research suggesting that it might have been ten years later, the evidence of contemporary musicians suggests that the earlier date is true. He was probably active as a musician before 1900, and it is likely that he was a casual member of one of Buddy Bolden's bands. He also worked with the Eagle and Superior Bands and paraded with Henry Allen's Brass Band. However, the majority of his career was spent outside New Orleans touring with theater, minstrel, and circus bands. He moved to New Iberia, Louisiana, in 1931 and joined the Banner Band, but gave up playing in 1935 after his teeth decayed. In 1938 Johnson was rediscovered by BILL RUSSELL; equipped with a new set of teeth and trumpet, he recorded in New Orleans in June 1942 with George Lewis and Jim Robinson. During the period 1943–4 he performed with members of Lu Watters's Yerba Buena Band in San Francisco. In New Orleans he recorded for the American Music label in 1944 and worked with Sidney Bechet at the Savoy Café in Boston the following year. After further American Music sessions in New Orleans, his band opened at the Stuyvesant Casino in New York (1945–6). He recorded with Don Ewell in 1946 and toured with him in the spring of 1947. Having moved to New York in October, he appeared at the Caravan Ballroom and recorded in December. Returning to New Iberia he occasionally played with local bands, but suffered two strokes in November 1948 and died the following July.

Johnson was remembered for his beautiful tone and relaxed delivery. While some of this is evident in his later work, alcoholism caused much of his output to be uneven. His first recording (Good Time Jazz, 1942) was probably his most exciting, showing zest and enthusiasm for his comeback. But by 1944 his lip had improved and "Tiger Rag," "Panama," and "There's Yes, Yes in your Eyes" (all AM) show him at his most inventive. However, he had to wait until his last session (Del., 1947) to record some of Joplin's rags as he had always wanted.

BIBLIOGRAPHY

GroveJ (J.R. Taylor)

F. Ramsey and C.E. Smith, ed.: *Jazzmen* (New York, 1939/*R*)

F. Ramsey: "We Shall Walk through the Streets of the City," *Record Changer* (Dec 1945); repr. in *The PL Year Book of Jazz*, ed. A. McCarthy (London, 1946), 17–25

V. Thompson: *The Musical Scene* (New York, 1945)

M. Williams: *Jazz Masters of New Orleans* (New York, 1967/*R*), 222–50

D.M. Marquis: *In Search of Buddy Bolden, First Man of Jazz* (Baton Rouge, LA, 1978)

M. Hazeldine: *Bill Russell's American Music* (New Orleans, 1993)

MIKE HAZELDINE

Johnson, Charles L(eslie) (*b* Kansas City, KS, 3 Dec 1876; *d* Kansas City, MO, 28 Dec 1950). Ragtime pianist and composer. He studied the piano, harmony, and theory in the public schools and taught himself to play the banjo, guitar, mandolin, and violin. For about 20 years he worked as a pianist in orchestras, hotels, and theaters in Kansas City before obtaining employment as a song and piano demonstrator for J.W. Jenkins' Sons Music Company in about 1899. He also worked for the music publisher Carl Hoffman for several years. He founded his own publishing company in about 1907 and published his own works as well as the music of several local songwriters.

Johnson wrote 32 piano rags, beginning with *Scandalous Thompson* in 1899; most consist of three simple themes voiced in thin textures. His most popular piece was *Dill Pickles* (1906), which is built around a catchy three-note motif. It became one of the most successful ragtime compositions, appearing 31 times on 78 r.p.m. recordings alone, and entered the aural tradition of country, string-band, and bluegrass music. His *Iola* (1906) helped create a fashion for "Indian intermezzi"— piano pieces that supposedly evoked Native American culture; words were later added, and the piece eventually sold more than 1.2 million copies. Several of Johnson's rags became popular during the ragtime revival of the 1970s and 1980s. In 1919 he wrote the successful song, "Sweet and Low," but by the 1920s he devoted most of his time to arranging the works of other composers. He issued most of his compositions under his own name, but also used the pseudonyms Raymond Birch, Ethel Earnist, Herbert Leslie, and Fannie B. Woods.

WORKS
(selective list)

Pf: Doc Brown's Cake Walk, 1899; Scandalous Thompson, 1899; A Black Smoke, 1902; A Whispered Thought, 1904; Dill Pickles, 1906; Iola, 1906; Powder Rag, 1908; Porcupine Rag, 1909; Tobasco Rag Time Waltz, 1909; Cum Bac Rag, 1911; Tar Babies Rag, 1911; Crazy Bone Rag, 1913; Blue Goose Rag, 1916; Snookums Rag, Chicago, 1918

Songs: It takes a coon to do the rag time dance (R. Penick), 1899; Iola (J. O'Dea), 1906; If I only had a sweetheart (R. Spencer), 1909; I'm goin', goodbye, I'm gone (Johnson), 1912; Sweet and Low (J.S. Royce), 1919

Principal publishers: Johnson, Remick, Rossiter

BIBLIOGRAPHY

GroveA (J.E. Hasse)

"Charles L. Johnson," *American Musician and Art Journal* (11 June 1909)

R. Blesh and H. Janis: *They All Played Ragtime* (New York, 1950, 4/1971)

D.A. Jasen and T.J. Tichenor: *Rags and Ragtime: a Musical History* (New York, 1978) Sheet music and manuscripts in *KC* and material relating to life and work in the Public Library, Kansas City, MO

JOHN EDWARD HASSE

Johnson, Craig Hella (*b* Brainerd, MN, 15 June 1962). Conductor, pianist, singer, composer, and arranger. As the son of a Lutheran minister, he became a church organist at an early age and also studied piano and trumpet. In addition to music degrees from St. Olaf College (BA, piano, 1984), the University of Illinois (MM, choral conducting, 1985), and Yale University (MMA 1990, DMA, choral conducting, 1994), Johnson studied piano at Aspen Music School (1982) and the Juilliard School (1985) and conducting with HELMUTH RILLING at the International Bach Academy in Stuttgart, Germany, as a recipient of a National Arts Fellowship. While director of

choral activities at the University of Texas, Austin (1990–2001), he took a leave to serve as artistic director of Chanticleer (1998), but soon returned to focus on his conducting. As founder and artistic director of the critically acclaimed Conspirare (known as the New Texas Festival, 1991–4, and New Texas Music Works, 1994–7), Johnson has developed a professional ensemble of skilled singers from across North America. Under his creative and inspired leadership, Conspirare—meaning "to breathe together" in Latin and implying "to unite"— has received five Grammy nominations, an Edison Award (the Dutch equivalent of a Grammy, for *Requiem*, 2010), and Chorus America awards, and represented the United States at the World Symposium on Choral Music in Copenhagen (2008); it has also performed as part of Carnegie Hall's Weill Music Institute, including two Community Sing events (2011). Johnson's programming is imaginative and wide ranging, traversing common musical divides, notably sacred–secular and popular–classical. Even more impressive than the technical precision of his performances are his passionate commitment to communicating through music, the chorus's vibrant and warm tone, and his nuanced musicality. Johnson has been featured, sometimes with Conspirare, at many national and regional conventions of the American Choral Directors Association, including an especially memorable peace-themed collage in Oklahoma City (2009) in tribute to all affected by the bombing there in 1995. Johnson has served as artistic director of the annual Victoria Bach Festival in Texas (from 1992) and music director of the Houston Masterworks Chorus (2001–4) and held guest teaching residencies at Beloit College (1999), Southeastern Oklahoma State University (2004, 2008), Westminster College (2005), and St. Olaf College (2007). He has acted as guest conductor with the Austin, San Antonio, and Santa Fe symphony orchestras, as well as Chicago's Music of the Baroque, the Berkshire Choral Festival, and the Taipei Male Choir. In 2009 he released his first solo album, *Thorns on the Rose* (Booker Music), of original and favorite songs. Johnson has also published choral compositions and arrangements.

WORKS

Hard Times, arr. of S. Foster, mixed chorus divisi, 2005; Lo, How a Rose/The Rose, arr. of Praetorius and A. McBroom, T, mixed chorus, pf, 2005; Motherless Child, arr. of spiritual, solo v, mixed chorus, 2005; Requiem, arr. of E. Gilkyson, mixed chorus, 2005; Will there really be a morning? (E. Dickinson), 2-part treble chorus, pf, 2006; Light of a Clear Blue Morning, arr. of D. Parton, S, mixed chorus, 2008

BIBLIOGRAPHY

R. Beegle: "Through the Green Fuse," *Fanfare*, xxviii/5 (2005), 249–50

S. Ratcliffe: "Dynamic Direction," *Choir & Organ*, xvi/6 (2008), 43–6

R. Faires: "A Choral Welcome to the New Year that Opened One up to All Time and All Creation: A New Year's Conspirare Classic," *Austin Chronicle* (15 Jan 2010)

J. MICHELE EDWARDS

Johnson, David (Carl) (*b* Batavia, NY, 30 Jan 1940). Composer and flutist. He studied composition with WALTER F. ANDERSON, DONALD KEATS, and DAVID M EPSTEIN at Antioch College (BA 1962) and with LEON KIRCHNER and BILLY JIM LAYTON at Harvard University (MA 1964), before traveling to Paris for studies with EMILE BOULANGER (1964–5). He then moved to Cologne, where he studied (1965–6) and taught at the Rheinische Musikschule in the Cologne Courses for New Music (1966–7). He collaborated with Stockhausen (on *Hymnen*) and others in the electronic studio of West German Radio (1966–7) and was a member of the Stockhausen ensemble that for six months gave performances of that composer's music at the Osaka World's Fair (1970). With Rolf Gehlhaar and Johannes Fritsch, he cofounded Feedback Studio, a music publishing house and concert space near Cologne (1970); he also studied electronics and circuitry at the Institut voor Sonologie, Utrecht (1971). He directed the electronic music studio at the Music Academy in Basel from 1975 to 1985.

Johnson's early works are serial. In 1967, he began working extensively with electronic music and in 1969 became interested in sound-environment works (e.g., *Music Makers*) that involved cybernetic sound objects (objects that by means of electronics can vary sounds in response to an audience). He collaborated with Gehlhaar on *Cybernet* (1972), for which a large room was transformed into an acoustic feedback environment by means of microphones, loudspeakers, circuits, resonating wires, and sound objects; the piece was repeated at the 1972 Munich Olympics. Later works such as *Calls in Search 1, 2* (1981) are meditative and use long drones of electronic sounds; some also involve cybernetics. Johnson has published several articles in the series Feed-back Papers.

WORKS

Stage: Jedermann (incidental music, H. von Hofmannsthal), elec, 1980; Bach: Encounter of the Third Kind, actor, 2 spkrs, cptr, lights, 1981

Chamber and inst: 5 Movts, fl, 1962; Bells, fl, gui, vc, 1964; Pf Pieces 1, 2, 1964; Thesis, str qt, 1964; Recitative, Aria, Choral, fl, 1965; 3 Pieces, str qt, 1966; Pf Piece 1a, 1966; Envelope 1: the Little Cantus Firmus, pf, 1966; other works

Elec: Ton-Antiton, tape, 1968; TeleFun, tape, unspecified insts ad lib, 1968; Process of Music, tapes, insts, collab. R. Gehlhaar, 1970; Proganica, speaker, 2 elec org, 1973; Triangles, 3 insts, 3 ring modulators, 1975; Arbeitslied, tape, collab. P. Eötvös, Gehlhaar, M. Maiguashca, 1975; Audioliven, fl, live elec, 1976; Ars Subtilior Electrica, tape, 1977; In memoriam Uschi, tape, 3 insts, 1977; Tempata, tape, 3 insts, 1978; Calls in Search 1, 2, tape, 1981

Sound-environment works: Music Makers, 1969; Gyromes mit & für Elise, 1970; Cybernet, collab. Gehlhaar, 1972; Organica I–IV, 1973–4; Klangkoffer, 1974

Principal publisher: Feedback Studio (Cologne)

BIBLIOGRAPHY

M. Morawska-Büngeler: *Schwingende Elektonen: eine Dokumentation über das Studio für Elektronische Musik des Westdeutschen Rundfunks in Köln 1951–1986* (Köln, 1988)

STEPHEN MONTAGUE/KATIE BUEHNER

Johnson, Edward [Di Giovanni, Edoardo]   (*b* Guelph, ON, 22 Aug 1878; *d* Guelph, ON, 20 April 1959). Canadian tenor and impresario. His father hoped he would become a lawyer, but in 1899 he took his savings and went to New York to study music. In 1902 he was the hero in Reginald De Koven's *Maid Marian* in Boston, and he starred on Broadway (1908) in

Oscar Straus's *A Waltz Dream*. On Enrico Caruso's advice he went to Florence (1909) to work with Vincenzo Lombardi. As Edoardo di Giovanni he made his operatic debut in Padua (1912) in *Andrea Chénier*, and sang in many Italian premieres, including *Parsifal* in Italian (his La Scala debut, 1914), Giacomo Puccini's *Il tabarro* and *Gianni Schicchi* (1919, Rome), and works by Ildebrando Pizzetti and Franco Alfano.

Johnson left Italy to become the leading tenor of the Chicago Opera (1919–22) and the Metropolitan Opera (1922–35) where he was a favorite as Pelléas, Romeo, and Peter Ibbetson, a role he created in the Deems Taylor opera. Also in his repertory were Siegfried and Faust (1923, Covent Garden). His musicianship, romantic appearance, and ability to project a character were coupled with a lyric voice of good quality and range, a sound technique, and a seldom-used but easy high E. He followed Herbert Witherspoon, Giulio Gatti-Casazza's successor, as general manager of the Metropolitan (1935–50), instituted the Auditions of the Air and successfully guided the Metropolitan through the war period. On retirement (1950) Johnson moved to Guelph but remained chairman of the board of Toronto's Royal Conservatory of Music. He held honors from many countries, but was especially proud that a Guelph school and a music foundation bore his name.

BIBLIOGRAPHY

J. Bauer: "Edward Johnson," *Canadian Review and Musical Art*, iii/7–8 (1944), 14–6

H.P. Court: "Edward Johnson," *Record News* [Toronto], ii (1957–8), 193–202 [with discography]

N.A. Benson: "Edward Johnson," *Canadian Music Journal*, ii (1958), 28–34

R. Mercer: *The Tenor of his Time: Edward Johnson of the Met* (Toronto, 1976)

RUBY MERCER

Johnson, (Francis) Hall (*b* Athens, GA, 12 March 1888; *d* New York, NY, 30 April 1970). Choral director and composer. He received his first music degree from the University of Pennsylvania in 1910 and studied further at the Juilliard School and the University of Southern California. In 1934 he received an honorary DMus from the Philadelphia Music Academy. Johnson began his career as a violinist and violist, but turned to choral conducting in 1925 and organized the Hall Johnson Choir, which became famous. The most notable appearances of the choir were in the stage and film productions of *The Green Pastures*, in the film *Lost Horizon*, and at the 1951 International Festival of Fine Arts in Berlin.

Johnson's principal works are the folk drama *Run Little Chillun* (1933), the cantata *Son of Man* (1946), the operetta *Fi-Yer*, several art songs, and many spirituals arranged for solo voice or chorus.

BIBLIOGRAPHY

E. Southern: *The Music of Black Americans: a History* (New York, 1971, 2/1983), 429–32, 434, 439

E. Southern, ed.: *Readings in Black American Music* (New York, 1971, 2/1983), 268–75

M.G. Carter: "The 'New Negro' Choral Legacy of Hall Johnson," *Chorus and Community*, ed. K. Ahlquist (Urbana, IL, 2006), 185–201

E.T. Simpson: *Hall Johnson: his Life, his Spirit, and his Music* (Lanham, MD, 2008)

EILEEN SOUTHERN/R

Johnson, Frank [Francis B.] (*b* Philadelphia, PA, 16 June 1792; *d* Philadelphia, PA, 6 April 1844). Violinist, Kent-bugle player, bandmaster, and composer. His early musical influences were probably from black musicians active during his adolescence and later with RICHARD WILLIS. Johnson first gained public fame for his publications in 1818. He had been engaged in early militia affairs around 1815, and in 1821 he led the official band of the Philadelphia State Fencibles in their military excursions and dance affairs. He was sought after by the leading dance masters of his day, including Victor Guillou and A. Bonnafon, both of whom had French connections. Johnson usually supplied music for the annual birthday celebrations of George Washington. In 1824 his band provided music for the reception of General Lafayette, and in 1825 for the Haitian leader Jean Pierre Boyer. Throughout the 1820s, he joined with other musicians in New York and Philadelphia performing for church-related events.

During the 1820s Johnson and his band achieved an enviable fame by performing at important affairs—militia, marriages, dances, etc.—including activities at the spas of Brandywine, Chalybeate Springs, White Sulphur Springs (West Virginia), Congress Springs, Cape May, and Bedford Springs, which brought him in contact with wealthy citizens of other states. He earned his sustenance from the insatiable appetite of Philadelphians for new novelties.

Already familiar with contemporary music in America, Johnson desired more knowledge and sought new material in London and Paris. Although present at the time of the coronation of Queen Victoria, he did not play at that event. After the coronation, he did perform for Her Majesty, who awarded him a silver bugle. After his return Johnson performed the latest music in cities from New York to Toronto. He also participated in presidential events between Martin Van Buren and Henry Clay at Saratoga Springs.

Johnson experienced discrimination in several cities — New York, Providence, and St. Louis. On the whole he and his band were well received elsewhere, especially in Louisville (Kentucky), where he was aided by his friend Guillou, and in Cincinnati. Johnson's activities in Philadelphia from about 1839 to 1844 included performing music for firemen's dances, and for temperance, literary, and philanthropic societies. His contribution to the sacred music of black churches provided another opportunity to show off the versatility of his band in classic music of the period.

A summary of Johnson's musical achievements as America's premier bandsman was such that he is easily labeled the Sousa of the period. His publications resulted in other black musicians finding music publishers. Johnson's novelty was to turn a current melody into a danceable form. He often used tunes from current operas.

WORKS

Editions: *Selected Works of Francis Johnson Bicentennial Edition*, ed. A.R. LaBrew (Detroit, 1977)

A Choice Collection of the Works of Francis Johnson, eds. C.K. Jones and L.K. Greenwich II (New York, 1983)

Captain Francis Johnson (1792–1844), Great American Black Bandsman: Life and Works, i–ii, ed. A.R. LaBrew (Detroit, 2009)

BIBLIOGRAPHY

T. Lanard: *One Hundred Years with the State Fencibles* (Philadelphia, 1913)

Philadelphia Public Ledger (1936–44)

R.J. Wolfe: *Secular Music in America, 1801–25: a Bibliography* (New York, 1964)

E. Southern, ed.: *Readings in Black American Music* (New York, 1971, 2/1983)

J.W. Cromwell: "Frank Johnson's Military Band," *BPM*, iv/2 (1976), 208–12

A.R. LaBrew: *Francis Johnson (1792–1844)* (Detroit, 1977)

"Black Music Precursors: the Writings of Arthur Randolph LaBrew," *Inter-American Music Review*, i/2 (1979), 229

C. Jones: *Francis Johnson (1792–1844): Chronicle of a Black Musician in Early Nineteenth Century Philadelphia* (Bethlehem, PA, 2006)

ARTHUR R. LABREW

Johnson, George W. (*b* ?Wheatland, VA, Oct 1846; *d* New York, NY, 23 Jan 1914). Singer. He was the first widely popular African American recording artist. Born a slave in Virginia, he was raised by a white family, the Moores. He migrated in the 1870s to New York, where he became a street entertainer performing for coins. In 1890 he was recruited by one of the newly established phonograph companies to make cylinder recordings of his most popular songs, "The Laughing Song" (in which he laughed in time to the music) and "The Whistling Coon" (in which he whistled). These became two of the best-selling recordings of the 1890s. In 1894 he joined the white producer Len Spencer in a series of minstrel show recordings which were also highly successful. Because of the limited technology of the time, best sellers had to be continuously re-recorded and he was steadily employed. In 1899 he was arrested on a dubious charge of murder, but white friends rallied to his side and the case was dropped. Johnson's repertoire was limited and his career went into severe decline in the early 1900s when the recording companies developed means to mass-produce original recordings, without paying royalties. He died alone and penniless.

BIBLIOGRAPHY

T. Brooks: *Lost Sounds: Blacks and the Birth of the Recording Industry, 1890–1919* (Urbana, IL, 2004)

TIM BROOKS

Johnson, H(arold) Earle (*b* Connecticut, May 1908; *d* Williamsburg, VA, 24 Oct 1988). Writer on music. He studied at Yale University (BM 1933, MM 1935) and Boston University (BM 1935); he continued graduate study at Harvard (1937–8). With a break for military service, he was on the faculty at Clark University (1936–42, 1946–53). He continued his writing and research in New England until 1975, when he became professor in the Eminent Scholars Program at the College of William and Mary (1975–83). Johnson served as music critic for the *New Haven Register* (1936–42, 1945–8) and the *Virginia Gazette* (1981–2). He was a founder of the Sonneck Society and was made an honorary member of the Society in 1987 (*see* SOCIETY FOR AMERICAN MUSIC). His writings address the history of American music, particularly music in New England.

WRITINGS

Musical Interludes in Boston, 1795–1830 (New York, 1943/R)
Symphony Hall, Boston (Boston, 1950/R)
"The Adams Family and Good Listening," *JAMS*, xi/2 (1958), 165–76
Operas on American Subjects (New York, 1964)
Hallelujah, Amen! The Story of the Handel and Haydn Society of Boston (Boston, 1965/R)
"The John Rowe Parker Letters," *MQ*, lxii/1 (1976), 72–86
First Performances in America to 1900: Works with Orchestra (Detroit, 1979)
"The Folio of White, Smith and Company," *American Music*, ii/1 (1984), 88–104
"Music Publishing in New England," *Richard S. Hill: Tributes*, ed. C.J. Bradley and J.B. Coover (Detroit, MI, 1987), 199–210
"Longfellow and Music," *American Music Research Center Journal*, vii (1997), 1–99

PAULA MORGAN/R

Johnson, Howard (Lewis) (*b* Montgomery, AL, 7 Aug 1941). Jazz tuba player, baritone saxophonist, and bandleader. Largely self-taught, he first learned baritone saxophone, then tuba. In 1963 he moved to New York, where he quickly established himself as a leading jazz tuba player and performed with Charles Mingus, Archie Shepp, and, notably, Gil Evans. He played with Evans's orchestra from 1966 until the leader's death in 1988. He also worked with Charlie Haden, Jack DeJohnette, Chet Baker, and McCoy Tyner and spent several years with the Norddeutscher Rundfunk orchestra. From 1975 to 1980 he was a member of the house band for "Saturday Night Live," serving as bandleader from 1979 to 1980.

Although Johnson has been recognized for his work on baritone saxophone, he is best known for his tuba playing and for his work with tuba ensembles. In 1968 he formed the first jazz tuba ensemble, Substructure. Although this group never recorded, Johnson subsequently formed Gravity, an ensemble with six tubas, in the 1970s; it released *Gravity!!!* (Verve, *c*1995) and *Right Now!* (Verve, 1996), with Taj Mahal. Johnson has continued to tour and record as a soloist and with Gravity.

BIBLIOGRAPHY

C. Kleinsteuber: "An Interview with Howard Johnson," *T.U.B.A. Journal*, xi/1 (1983), 6–11
R.W. Morris and E.R. Goldstein, eds.: *The Tuba Source Book* (Bloomington, IN, 1996)

RICHARD H. PERRY

Johnson, Hunter (*b* Benson, NC, 14 April 1906; *d* Smithfield, NC, 27 Aug 1998). Composer and teacher. He studied at the University of North Carolina (1924–6) and at the Eastman School (1929). Appointments followed as a teacher of composition at the University of Michigan (1929–33), the University of Manitoba (1944–7), Cornell University (1948–53), the University of Illinois (1959–65), and the University of Texas (1966–71). His honors included a Rome Prize (1933), Guggenheim Fellowships (1941, 1954), an award from the National Institute of Arts and Letters, and the Fine Arts Award of North Carolina (1965). As a composer Johnson used established materials in an individual way, integrating elements of jazz into his style. His musical language is closely related to that of Charles Ives and Aaron Copland, but there is an intensity in his best works that creates a very individual style, evident in *Letter to the World*, a ballet commissioned by Martha Graham, and in the Piano Sonata, which has found a lasting place in the repertory. *The Scarlet Letter*, written in 1975, was the result of another Graham commission.

WORKS

Orch: Prelude, 1930; Sym. no.1, 1931; Conc., pf, chbr orch, 1935–6; For an Unknown Soldier, fl, str, 1938; Letter to the World (ballet), 1940, suite, chbr orch, 1952, full orch version, 1959; Deaths and Entrances (ballet), 1943; Music for Str Orch, 1949–54; North State, 1963; Past the Evening Sun, 1964; The Scarlet Letter (ballet), 1975
Chbr and solo inst: Scherzo from the South, pf, 1928; Pf Sonata, 1933–4, rev. 1936 and 1947–8; Elegy for Hart Crane, cl qnt, 1936; Serenade, fl, cl, 1937; In Time of Armament (ballet), 2 pf, 1939; Trio, fl, ob, pf, 1954
Songs: 2 Songs, 1932; 3 Songs (E. Dickinson), 1956–9
MSS in *GRB*
Principal publishers: Galaxy, Presser, Valley

BIBLIOGRAPHY

P. Rosenfeld: "The Newest American Composers," *MM*, xv (1937–8), 153–9
J. Bloch: "Some American Piano Sonatas," *Juilliard Review*, iii (1956), 9–14
R.A. Monaco: *The Music of Hunter Johnson* (diss., Cornell U., 1960)
W. Black: "New Music Corner: Hunter Johnson," *Keyboard Classics*, viii/1 (1988), 24–7

RICHARD A. MONACO/MICHAEL MECKNA

Johnson, James P(rice) (*b* New Brunswick, NJ, 1 Feb 1894; *d* Queens, NY, 17 Nov 1955). Ragtime and jazz pianist and composer. He was one of the most influential pianists of his generation, with his solo work giving valuable insight into the transition from ragtime to jazz piano. Especially since the 1940s, he has been frequently referred to as the Father of Stride Piano, even though this latter term was not used to describe a specific early style of jazz piano until his later years. (In a famous interview in 1953 with Tom Davin, Johnson did not use the term "stride" and instead referred to his style as "orchestral piano.") More recently, with the re-examination of many of his scores and manuscripts, he has also claimed a position as one of America's foremost composers, of works that range from piano solos and popular songs to symphonic works and opera.

Johnson maintained vivid memories of his childhood years, when he heard local brass bands perform, was exposed to church music, and perhaps most importantly witnessed social events organized by his Virginia-born mother. At these gatherings many of the guests were from South Carolina and Georgia, and the Southern-style country and set dances he saw influenced many of his later compositions. Like Louis Armstrong, he made his first public performances as a singer, and he remained an active vocalist through his teenage years.

Johnson's first important exposure to ragtime came after his family moved to Jersey City in 1902. He recalled that dozens of ragtime piano players (or "ticklers," as they were known at the time) from the South and Midwest ended up there, many of them escaping the law in their hometowns. Thus Johnson was exposed to a variety of regional piano styles. In 1908 the family moved to New York, where Johnson's musical education began in earnest. He listened to a host of piano players, many of whom never left a written or sound record of their playing, and are thus lost to modern ears; these included such "ticklers" as Charlie Cherry, Alberta Simmons, and Raymond "Lippy" Boyette as well as a few only remembered by their nicknames, like Abba Labba and a hard-drinking club owner named Souser. Johnson also heard more famous artists like Luckey Roberts, Jelly Roll Morton, and Eubie Blake, as well as many classical pianists who were active in the city. He also attended orchestral concerts of music by Mozart, Wagner, Beethoven, and others, heard light classical music by such composers as Victor Herbert and Rudolph Antonín Friml, and even sang in the chorus for a performance of Haydn's *Creation*, under Frank Damrosch.

The year 1917 was a pivotal period for Johnson. He began making piano rolls of his own compositions (meeting George Gershwin in the process) and started publishing what eventually became a catalog of some 200 popular songs. He quickly became a major player in New York's black entertainment industry of the 1920s. He scored a variety of productions, notably *Runnin' Wild* (1923); this included the iconic hit "Charleston," which became associated with the dance craze of the time. Johnson also published a host of tunes that have become popular standards, including "Old Fashioned Love" (also from *Runnin' Wild*) and "If I could be with you one hour tonight." He recorded sensitive accompaniments with a variety of singers, including Bessie Smith. His piano rolls and recordings have inspired legions of pianists, including Duke Ellington, who at a young age learned Johnson's "Carolina Shout" by watching how the keys were depressed during a player piano performance. Johnson also personally mentored some of his most important contemporaries, notably Fats Waller.

Johnson's debut recordings, which he made in 1921, are often considered the first examples of jazz piano playing, although they remain firmly rooted in the ragtime with which he grew up. As his artistry developed in the 1920s, however, his playing incorporated stronger elements of the blues, which he married to a breathtaking technique and a mastery of brief melodic and rhythmic devices ("tricks") that the "ticklers" shared with white novelty players such as Zez Confrey and Roy F. Bargy. Even after the super-human fireworks of Art Tatum's style had seemed to overshadow his artistry in the 1930s, Johnson's influence could still be keenly felt in the work of Thelonious Monk as well as a host of pianists, such as Dick Wellstood, Ralph Sutton, and Don Ewell, who consciously evoked his style.

The musicologist John Howland has speculated that Johnson's interest in extended orchestral composition may date from his arrangements of "Charleston" in the early 1920s. He also outlines the complicated performance and recording history of Johnson's *Yamekraw: a Negro Rhapsody*, first published in a piano arrangement in 1927. After 1930 Johnson turned primarily to the creation of concert music, largely leaving behind his successful entertainment career. With *Harlem Symphony* (1932), *Concerto Jazz a Mine* (1934) and various other pieces, some incomplete and some lost, Johnson built a repertory of works that celebrated the diversity of the composer's musical background. Perhaps inspired by Gershwin's *Porgy and Bess* (1935), he also composed two one-act operas in the late 1930s, *The Dreamy Kid* (based on a play by Eugene O'Neill from 1918) and *De Organizer* (with a libretto by Langston Hughes). Unfortunately, the performance and recording history of all these concert and operatic works was checkered, and they were not widely heard nor appreciated during Johnson's lifetime.

The record producer John Hammond promoted recordings and live performances by Johnson in the late 1930s and early 1940s, including two events entitled Spirituals to Swing at Carnegie Hall. However, Johnson suffered a stroke in 1940 and never fully recovered. A second stroke in 1951 left him bed-ridden for the remainder of his life.

As a pianist, Johnson has always been celebrated as one of jazz and ragtime's greatest artists. But modern interest in his orchestral works was spurred by a recording made in 1994 of *Harlem Symphony*, *Concerto Jazz a Mine*, and several other works conducted by Marin Alsop. In 2003 Johnson's grandson Barry Glover donated a vast archive of materials, including scores of orchestral works, to the Institute of Jazz Studies at Rutgers University; these manuscripts have served as the basis for new performances. In 2006 the University of Michigan staged Johnson's two single-act operas, in reconstructions by the jazz scholar and pianist James Dapogny. And in 2011 Naxos issued the first complete orchestral performance of *Yamecraw*, with Richard Rosenberg conducting. Johnson seems poised now to take his place as a significant American composer of the first half of the 20th century.

SELECTED RECORDINGS

James P. Johnson: Harlem Stride Piano 1921–1929 (EPM, 1992); *Victory Stride: the Symphonic Music of James P. Johnson* (Musical Heritage Society, 1994); *The Original James P. Johnson* (Smithsonian, 1996); *James P. Johnson: Parlor Piano Solos from Rare Piano Rolls* (Biography, 1997); *Father of the Stride Piano* (Sony, 2000)

BIBLIOGRAPHY

R. Blesh and H. Janis: *They all Played Ragtime* (New York, 1950, 4/1971)

R.S. Schiff, ed.: *Jazz, Blues, Boogie & Swing for Piano* (New York, 1977/R)

E.A. Berlin: *Ragtime: a Musical and Cultural History* (Berkeley, CA, 1980)

S.E. Brown: *A Case of Mistaken Identity: the Life and Music of James P. Johnson* (Metuchen, NJ, 1984)

J.E. Hasse, ed.: *Ragtime: its History, Composers, and Music* (New York, 1985)

T. Davin: "Conversations with James P. Johnson," *Musica oggi*, xxiii (2003–04)

H. Martin: "Balancing Composition and Improvisation in James P. Johnson's 'Carolina Shout,'" *Journal of Music Theory*, xlix/2 (2005), 277–99

J. Taylor: "American Opera: an Evening with James P. Johnson," *ISAM Newsletter*, xxxv/2 (2006), 10

J. Howland: *Ellington Uptown: Duke Ellington, James P. Johnson, and the Birth of Concert Jazz* (Ann Arbor, MI, 2009)

JEFFREY TAYLOR

Johnson, James Weldon [William] (*b* Jacksonville, FL, 17 June 1871; *d* Wiscasset, ME, 26 June 1938). Lyricist, poet, novelist, anthologist, civil rights leader, and international diplomat. He began his professional life as an educator and lawyer in Florida (one of the early African Americans admitted to the Florida Bar), but in the summer of 1899 he and his brother, composer J. Rosamond Johnson, went to New York with hopes of finding a producer for their operetta. Although they were unsuccessful in this endeavor, they gained entrance to the musical-theater circles of New York; they formed a collaborative relationship with Bob Cole and became one of the outstanding songwriting teams of the early 1900s. Many of their approximately 200 songs were interpolated in musical comedies; among the most successful were "Nobody's lookin' but de owl and de moon" (*The Sleeping Beauty and the Beast*, 1901), "Under the Bamboo Tree" (*Sally In Our Alley*, 1902), and "The Congo Love Song" (*Nancy Brown*, 1903). In 1907 their own all-black musical *The Shoo-fly Regiment* appeared on Broadway. This was Johnson's last major work as a lyricist, for in 1906 he embarked on a career with the US diplomatic service, first as consul in Venezuela, then, from 1909–13, in Nicaragua.

In 1912 Johnson published *The Autobiography of an Ex-Colored Man*, a short novel which, because of its vivid and faithful descriptions of ragtime and the society and aesthetic climate in which it existed, has become an important document on the time and the music. In 1914 he became a contributing editor of the black newspaper the *New York Age*. In 1915, he translated the libretto for Enrique Granados's opera *Goyescas* into English; the translation was sold at the New York premiere performance by the Metropolitan Opera the following year. In 1916 he joined the NAACP as Field Secretary, later becoming Executive Secretary. At the same time, in the 1920s, he became a leading figure in the Harlem Renaissance. Concerned with the preservation of black culture, Johnson compiled *The Book of American Negro Poetry* (1922), two collections of Negro Spirituals (1925 and 1926), with introductions by himself and arrangements by his brother, and wrote *Black Manhattan* (1930), a history of black theater and musical theater in New York.

In addition to his popular-song lyrics, Johnson wrote much of his poetry with music in mind, and some of these poems have been used by composers. Aside from the many settings by his brother (among which *Lift Every Voice and Sing*, 1901, became known as the "Negro National Anthem"), Johnson's texts have been set by Harry T. Burleigh (*Passionale*, 1915), Louis Gruenberg (*The Creation: a Negro Sermon*, 1926), Otto Mortensen (*Sence You Went Away*, 1945), and Wolfgang Fortner (*The Creation*, 1957).

WRITINGS

Johnson's writings are on deposit at NHub

The Autobiography of an Ex-colored Man (Boston, 1912; repr. in *James Weldon Johnson: Writings*, New York, 2004)

Introductions to *The Book of American Negro Spirituals* (New York, 1925) and *The Second Book of American Negro Spirituals* (New York, 1926); repr. together as *The Books of American Negro Spirituals* (New York, 1969)

Black Manhattan (New York, 1930; repr. in *James Weldon Johnson: Writings*, New York, 2004)

Along This Way (New York, 1933; repr. in *James Weldon Johnson: Writings*, New York, 2004) [autobiography]

BIBLIOGRAPHY

E. Levy: *James Weldon Johnson: Black Leader, Black Voice* (Chicago, 1973)

R.E. Fleming: *James Weldon Johnson* (Boston, 1987)

K.M. Price and L.J. Oliver, eds.: *Critical Essays on James Weldon Johnson* (New York, 1997)

EDWARD A. BERLIN

Johnson, J.J. [James Louis] (*b* Indianapolis, IN, 22 Jan 1924; *d* Indianapolis, IN, 4 Feb 2001). Jazz trombonist and composer. Between the ages of nine and 11 he studied the piano with a church organist, and took up the trombone when he was 14. In 1941–2 he toured with bands led by Clarence Love and Isaac "Snookum" Russell, whose trumpeter Fats Navarro had a strong impact on Johnson's playing. He then began an important engagement with Benny Carter's orchestra (1942–5), touring the United States, writing a few arrangements and making numerous radio broadcasts and transcriptions. His earliest recorded solo was on "Love for Sale" (Cap., 1943), and he appeared at the first Jazz at the Philharmonic concert (1944).

By May 1945 Johnson was working with the Count Basie Orchestra, mostly in New York. He moved permanently to New York in mid-1946, and for the next few years played small-group jazz at various clubs with Bud Powell, Max Roach, Miles Davis, Navarro, Charlie Parker, Dizzy Gillespie, and others, becoming increasingly absorbed in the new bop style. In 1949–50 he participated with Davis in the sessions that became known as "the Birth of the Cool." In 1951 he toured Korea, Japan, and the South Pacific for the United Service Organizations in a band under Oscar Pettiford, and during 1952 he toured with an all-star group that included Davis. However, his worsening financial situation forced him to retire from music in August 1952; he worked as a blueprint inspector at the Sperry Gyroscope Company, and performed only sporadically.

Then, in August 1954, Johnson formed a highly successful trombone duo with Kai Winding. Their group, called Jay and Kai, remained intact until 1956, bringing Johnson's work to a larger audience and establishing his reputation as the leading jazz trombonist. His *Poem for Brass* (also known as *Jazz Suite for Brass*), recorded for Columbia in 1956, drew attention to his talents as a composer: many of his skillfully orchestrated works employ fugal passages and out-of-tempo chorales as well as more conventional jazz swing sections.

After disbanding Jay and Kai, Johnson led his own quintet until summer 1960, touring Europe and composing large-scale works such as *El camino real* and *Sketch for Trombone and Band*, which were first performed at the Monterey Jazz Festival in 1959. He taught at the Lenox School of Jazz in summer 1960 and in the following year wrote a new major work, *Perceptions*, for Gillespie.

Johnson continued to combine careers as a performer and composer throughout the 1960s. He played with Davis's group (1961–2), formed a new quartet of his own (1963), and led a sextet, which included Clark Terry and Sonny Stitt, on a tour of Japan (1964). By 1967 he was staff composer and conductor for MBA Music in New York. From 1970, when he moved to Los Angeles, he primarily wrote scores for television and films; his infrequent recordings and performances, however, invariably reestablished his preeminence among jazz trombonists. In 1987 he returned to Indianapolis and became more active as a player.

Johnson was the most important postwar jazz trombonist and a major influence on all players of the instrument. His earliest recorded solos up to 1945 reveal a thick tone, aggressive manner, and impressive mobility. They are not yet far removed, though, from the solos of his early influences—Lester Young, Roy Eldridge, and the trombonist Fred Beckett, who emphasized the linear qualities of the instrument rather than the effects of the slide.

During the 1940s Johnson developed such an astounding technical facility that some record reviewers insisted, erroneously, that he played a valve trombone; the speed of his playing and the clarity and accuracy he achieved at fast tempos have never been surpassed. In 1947 he began to play with a lighter tone (occasionally enhanced by a felt mute) and reserved vibrato for special effects. The result was a rather dry but attractive sound resembling that of a French horn. Johnson also worked diligently at this period to adapt bop patterns to the trombone, and his solos suffer from an emphasis on speed and an overreliance on memorized formulas incorporating such bop trademarks as the flattened 5th. His performances on both versions of "Crazeology" with Charlie Parker (Dial, 1947) begin with the same phrase and contain other whole phrases in common. The same is true of the two renditions of Johnson's celebrated solo on "Blue Mode" (NewJ, 1949), despite their very different tempos.

During the late 1950s Johnson's playing matured: he relied less on formulas and speed, and more on a scalar approach and motivic development. Recordings of live performances dating from this time provide examples of brilliant developmental sequences that were delivered with powerful emotion. The features of Johnson's mature style are well illustrated in ex.1 (from "Mack the Knife," Col., 1961), where the opening phrase is a rhythmicized version of Kurt Weill's theme and the rest of the chorus is built in the modal manner from a single scale, connecting without a break to the next chorus.

Ex.1 First chorus of Johnson's solo on "Mack the Knife" (1961, Col.); transcr. L. Porter

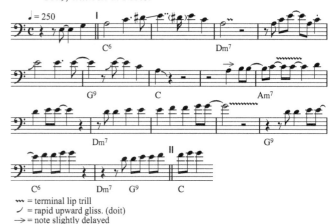

$\mathbf{w}$ = terminal lip trill
$\diagup$ = rapid upward gliss. (doit)
$\longrightarrow$ = note slightly delayed
$\diagdown$ = fall off (fall)

WORKS
(selective list)

Orch: Scenario, trbn, orch; Rondeau, jazz qt, orch; Diversions, 6 trbn, orch

Other inst: Poem for Brass, 1956; El Camino real, 1959; Sketch for Trbn and Band, 1959; Perceptions, 1961; Euro-Suite, 1966

Many jazz charts, incl. Aquarius, Azure, Ballade, Blue, Blue Nun, Blues for Trombones, Boneology, Coffee Pot, Concepts in Blue, Enigma, Euro, In walked Horace, Kelo, Lament, Little Dave, Mad Bebop, Mohawk, Nermus, Say When, Short Cake, Sidewinder, Space, Splashes, Walk, Turnpike

Many film and television scores

BIBLIOGRAPHY

Oral history material in *DSI (JOHP)*

M. Harrison: "Some Early J.J. Johnson Recordings," *Jazz Journal*, xii/10 (1959), 6, 10 only

I. Gitler: "The Remarkable J.J. Johnson," *DB*, xxviii/10 (1961), 17–9

G. Schuller: *J.J. Johnson: a List of Compositions Licensed by B.M.I.* (New York, 1961)

M. Harrison: "'Perceptions' and a Question of Unity," *JazzM*, viii/5 (1962), 25 only

G. Hoefer: "Early J.J.," *DB*, xxxii/2 (1965), 16, 33 only

J. Burns: "J.J. Johnson: the Formative Years," *Jazz Journal*, xxviii/8 (1975), 4–7

D. Baker: *J.J. Johnson, Trombone* (New York, 1979) [transcrs.; incl. discography and list of works]

M. Hennessey: "The Return of J.J. Johnson," *JJI*, xxxiii/5 (1980), 6–7

L.G. Bourgois III: *Jazz Trombonist J.J. Johnson: a Comprehensive Discography and Study of the Early Evolution of his Style* (diss., Ohio State U., 1986)

G. Kalbacher: "J.J. Johnson: Bringing it all back Home," *DB*, lv/3 (1988), 16–9 [incl. discography]

J. Berrett and L. Bourgois: *The Musical World of J.J. Johnson* (Lanham, MD, 1999)

Obituary, B. Ratliff, *New York Times* (6 Feb 2001)

K. Mathieson: *Cookin': Hard Bop and Soul Jazz, 1954–65* (Edinburgh, 2002)

LEWIS PORTER/R

Johnson, J(ohn) Rosamond (*b* Jacksonville, FL, 11 Aug 1873; *d* New York, NY, 11 Nov 1954). Composer, lyricist, vocalist, actor, theatrical director, and educator, brother of JAMES WELDON JOHNSON. He was born to James Johnson, a freeman from Virginia, and Helen Louise [née Dillett] Johnson, born free in Nassau, the Bahamas. His mother, a trained singer and educator, began teaching Johnson piano when he was four. From 1890 to 1896 Johnson studied music at the New England Conservatory. He then performed in John W. Isham's *Oriental America*, which whetted his appetite for theater. After returning to Jacksonville (spring 1897), he taught music privately and was supervisor of music for Jacksonville public schools (1896–9). He was also choirmaster and organist at a large Baptist church and taught music at the Baptist Academy. Johnson's earliest compositions, with his brother as lyricist, date from this time.

In summer 1899 the Johnson brothers went to New York hoping to get their operetta *Toloso* produced. Their lack of success was mitigated by encouragement from major theatrical figures: Isidore Witmark, Harry B. Smith, Reginald De Koven, Oscar Hammerstein I, Bert Williams and George Walker, Ernest Hogan, Will Marion Cook, Henry T. Burleigh, and BOB COLE. Cole and the Johnson brothers wrote their first song together, "Louisiana Lize," and sold the singing rights to May Irwin. The pair returned to Jacksonville in the fall, where Johnson composed the music to his brother's poem "Lift Every Voice and Sing." Since its initial performance by 500 schoolchildren on Lincoln's Birthday (12 February) in 1900, it has become known as the black national anthem.

In summer 1900 the brothers returned to New York and formed an official partnership with Cole. Between 1900 and 1905 their songs were interpolated into at least 16 white shows and sung by prominent stars, among them Irwin ("Ma Mississippi Bell," 1900), Anna Held ("The Maiden with the Dreamy Eyes," 1901), Marie Cahill ("Congo Love Song," 1903), and Lillian Russell ("The Flowers of Dixie Land," 1903). It was common for one song to appear in several shows; for example, the team's hit song "Under the Bamboo Tree," written for *Toloso*, was performed in *Sally in our Alley* (1902), *Nancy Brown* (1903), and *The Red Moon* (1907). Cole and the Johnson brothers signed a three-year contract with the production team Klaw & Erlanger to write the lyrics and music for white musical comedies, including a revival of *Humpty Dumpty* (1904) and the burlesque *In Newport* (1904). Although their creative roles were fluid, Johnson was primarily responsible for the music; the partners shared their earnings equally. Cole was musically illiterate; where music is credited to him in published songs, it is usually marked "arr. J.R. Johnson." Johnson wrote around 200 songs during his career, some uncredited or under pseudonyms.

In 1902 Johnson and Cole created a headlining vaudeville act that toured the United States and appeared in London. Dressed in evening clothes, Cole sang the team's own compositions, with Johnson providing supporting vocals and piano accompaniment. The duo began writing, directing, producing, and starring in their own musicals. *The Shoo-Fly Regiment* (1906) tells the story of a Tuskegee graduate who wants to sacrifice his teaching job in order to fight in the Spanish–American War, against his girlfriend's wishes. The plot of *The Red Moon* (1908–9) draws on relations between Native Americans and African Americans at industrial schools like Hampton Institute. Black audiences appreciated the topicality of these plays and especially the love scenes, which were the first serious depictions of romance between blacks on stage. Despite almost universal praise for the singing, dancing, and artistic quality of the syncopated melodies, many white reviewers found the productions too "refined" and unrepresentative of black life. Unable to turn a profit with these touring productions, Cole and Johnson returned to vaudeville before Cole's death in 1911.

Johnson subsequently served up revues as music director of Hammerstein's theater the London Opera House (1912–13); directed the Music School Settlement for Colored People in Harlem (1914–19); and toured with his own vocal ensembles. His later stage roles included Lawyer Frazier in *Porgy and Bess* (1935), Rev. Quintus Whaley in *Mamba's Daughters* (1939–41), and Prof. Arnold Harmon in *A Young American* (1946). His J. Rosamond Johnson Singers were featured in the films *Jazz* (1929) and *Cabin in the Sky* (1941, in which he portrayed Brother Green). Johnson also wrote the vocal arrangements for *The Emperor Jones* (1933).

Johnson's songs typically blended the syncopated rhythms of early 20th-century Tin Pan Alley with stylistic elements of light classical music (particularly contrapuntal piano accompaniment), as demonstrated by "My Castle on the Nile" (1901, sung by Bert Williams in *In Dahomey*) and *Under the Bamboo Tree*. Other, larger works, such as the musical suite *The Evolution of Ragtime* (1903) and *The Red Moon*, show stronger evidence of his classical training, particularly in their harmonic adventurousness. Johnson's songs were an important departure from the prevailing caricatures of crap-shooting, razor-wielding African Americans.

Of the few piano solos he published, Johnson was proudest of *African Drum Dance no.1* (1928, later scored for orchestra). He created piano and vocal arrangements for more than 150 spirituals, which were published in *The Book of American Negro Spirituals* (1925) and *The Second Book of American Negro Spirituals* (1926), compiled with his brother, and subsequently in *Shout Songs* (1936), *Rolling Along in Song: a Chronological Survey of American Negro Music* (1937), *Sixteen New Negro Spirituals* (1939), and *The Album of Negro Spirituals* (1940).

Throughout his career Johnson was dedicated to advancing the dignity of African American artists. He was a founding officer of the Frogs (1908, named after Aristophanes's comedy), a professional organization for black artists and businesspeople, as well as a charter member of ASCAP (1914) and a founding member of the Negro Actors Guild of America (1939). In recognition of the dignified representation of American Indians in *The Red Moon*, Johnson was made a sub-chief of the Iroquois (Caughawaga, Quebec) in 1921.

His papers are housed at the Irving S. Gilmore Music Library, Yale University.

WORKS
(selective list)
(some music composed in collaboration with Cole;
some productions also contain songs by other composers;
authors shown as lyricist; librettist)

Stage: The Shoo-Fly Regiment (J.W. Johnson; B. Cole), Cumberland, MD, 6 Aug 1907; *The Red Moon* (J.W. Johnson; Cole), Wilmington, DE, 31 Aug 1908; Mr. Lode of Koal, New York, 1 Nov 1909, collab. A. Rogers, J.A. Shipp, B. Williams; Hello Paris (musical revue), New York, 19 Aug 1911; Come over Here (musical revue), London Opera House, 1913

BIBLIOGRAPHY
J.W. Johnson: *Black Manhattan* (New York, 1930)
J.W. Johnson: *Along This Way* (New York, 1933)
J. Lovell Jr: "Johnson, J[ohn] Rosamond," *Dictionary of American Negro Biography*, ed. R.W. Logan and M.R. Winston (New York, 1982)
A.L. Woll: *Black Musical Theatre: from Coontown to Dreamgirls* (Baton Rouge, LA, 1989)
E. Southern: *The Music of Black Americans: a History* (New York, 3/1997)
K. Sotiropoulos: *Staging Race: Black Performers in Turn of the Century America* (Cambridge, MA, 2006)
L. Abbott and D. Seroff: *Ragged but Right: Black Traveling Shows, "Coon Songs," and the Dark Pathway to Blues and Jazz* (Jackson, MS, 2007)
P.M. Seniors: *Beyond Lift Every Voice and Sing: the Culture of Uplift Identity and Politics in Black Musical Theater* (Columbus, 2009)
SANDRA JEAN GRAHAM

Johnson, Lew (*b* Chicago, IL, *c*1840; *d* Grand Forks, BC, 27 Feb 1910). Minstrel show manager. He organized his first successful minstrel company in St. Louis around 1869, after which he managed various groups, including the Plantation Minstrels (early 1870s), the Original Jubilee Singers (mid-1870s), Lew Johnson's Tennessee Jubilee Singers (late 1870s), the Black Baby Boy Minstrels (1890s), and Uncle Tom's Cabin Company. Johnson was one of the most successful African American minstrel managers of the period; among the performers who worked with him were Sam Lucas, George Walker, and Bert Williams. In about 1898 he moved to British Columbia, where he became manager of the Grand Forks Opera House.

BIBLIOGRAPHY
SouthernB
DOMINIQUE-RENÉ DE LERMA

Johnson, Lockrem (*b* Davenport, IA, 15 March 1924; *d* Seattle, WA, 5 March 1977). Composer, music publisher, and pianist. He studied composition with GEORGE FREDERICK MCKAY at the University of Washington (1938–42) and after military service joined the faculty there to teach piano and theory (1947–9). He was music director of the Eleanor King Dance Company (1947–50) and the pianist of the Seattle SO (1948–51); during these years he performed extensively throughout the Pacific Northwest in chamber ensembles and as a soloist.

In 1951 Johnson moved to New York, where he worked in the music publishing business as education director for Mercury Music (1951–4), head of the orchestral department at C.F. Peters (1954–8), and president of Dow Publishers (1957–62). After returning to Seattle, he served at the helm of the Cornish School of Music (1962–9) and in 1970 founded Puget Music Publications, a firm devoted to the publication of works by composers of the Pacific Northwest.

An active composer throughout his career, Johnson wrote chiefly chamber and piano compositions in a lyrical and dramatic style. A number of his works were quite successful during his lifetime; his one-act chamber opera *A Letter to Emily*, based on an incident in the life of Emily Dickinson, was staged nearly 50 times during the decade following its composition (1951). He received numerous commissions, a Guggenheim Fellowship (1952), and two MacDowell Colony Fellowships (1956, 1965). He contributed many articles to the *Piano Quarterly*, the *American Composers Alliance Bulletin*, and other periodicals.

WORKS
Stage: She (ballet), op.28, 1948, rev. 1950; A Letter to Emily (chbr op, 1, Johnson, after R. Hupton), op.37, 1951; King Lear (incid music, W. Shakespeare)
Orch: Lyric Prelude, op.30, 1948, rev. 1949; Sym. no.1, op.46, 1966
Chbr and solo inst: Sonata no.1, op.14, vn, pf, 1942; Pf Sonata no.1, op.24, 1947, rev. 1983; Sonata no.2, op.26, vn, pf, 1948, rev. 1949, 1953; Chaconne, op.29, pf; Sonata no.1, op.33, vc, pf, 1949; Pf Sonata no.2, op.34, 1949; Sonatina, op.35, tpt, pf, 1950; Sonata no.3, op.38, vn, pf, 1952; Sonata no.2, op.42, vc, pf, 1953; Pf Sonata no.3, op.43, 1954; 24 Preludes, op.50, pf; Gui Sonata; 7 Gui Preludes; smaller chbr pieces; other pf pieces
Vocal: 2 Songs to a Child (L. Carroll, M. Twain), op.47, 1948; Songs in the Wind (R. McDonald), song cycle, op.32, 1949; 4 Songs, op.44, 1950–57; Songs on Leaving Winter (Ps xxiii), op.25, low v, pf, vc ad lib, 1951; Suite of Noels, cant., op.40, SATB, kbd, 1954; Lament and Mourning Dance, op.39, SSA, chbr orch, 1953
Many early works, withdrawn

Principal publishers: ACA, Dow, Mercury, G. Schirmer

BIBLIOGRAPHY
A. Freed: "Lockrem Johnson: Conservative Rebel," *American Composers Alliance Bulletin*, viii/4 (1959), 12–7
KATHERINE K. PRESTON/MICHAEL MECKNA

Johnson, Lonnie [Alonzo] (*b* New Orleans, LA, 8 Feb 1894; *d* Toronto, ON, 16 June 1970). Blues and jazz guitarist and singer. Research indicates that Johnson was born in 1894 (Alger). He was influenced by the musical activities of his family and the rich musical environment in New Orleans of the early 1900s, including the early blues, jazz, and the lyrically expressive French and Spanish music traditions. He began playing violin, developed excellent guitar skill, and by the 1920s was also recording on piano, banjo, mandolin, and harmonium.

Johnson performed on violin with Charlie Creath's band on the Mississippi riverboat *St. Paul*, and after winning a blues singing contest in St. Louis, he began his recording career with OKeh Records. His first recording featured "Mr. Johnson's Blues" and "Falling Rain Blues" (OK, 1925) and was a two-sided hit. From 1925 through 1932 he made more recordings than any other bluesman. In late 1927 he played guitar on three of Louis Armstrong's landmark Hot Five recordings; in 1928 he recorded four tunes as a guest guitarist with Duke Ellington's band, including "The Mooche," which has since become known as an early classic. He was equally comfortable performing blues, jazz, and other popular genres.

In February 1928 Johnson recorded four brilliant solo guitar instrumentals, notably "Away Down in the Alley Blues." In November 1928 and in 1929 he recorded ten highly acclaimed guitar duets with Eddie Lang, including

"Hot Fingers." More than any other early popular musician, Johnson demonstrated the full expressive potential of the guitar, notably on the dazzling "Uncle Ned" (1931), and he pioneered the virtuoso lead guitar role that subsequently shaped jazz, blues, and rock. His playing influenced Robert Johnson, T-Bone Walker, Chuck Berry, Buddy Holly, Chet Atkins, Eric Clapton, and B.B. King, among others.

In addition to his solo recordings Johnson also served as an accompanist on recordings by Texas Alexander (e.g., "No More Women Blues") and Clara Smith, among others, and toured with Bessie Smith during the period 1929–1930. Although less recognized as such, he was an excellent songwriter and wrote striking lyrics that told coherent, compelling stories (through "Mr. Blues Walks" in 1965). He also possessed a superb voice, which he used to powerful effect on blues numbers. In the early 1940s Johnson turned to rhythm and blues and adopted the electric guitar, after which he achieved his biggest hit with "Tomorrow Night" (King, 1948). In the 1960s he made another comeback, recording several albums for Prestige/Bluesville, Columbia, and Folkways.

SELECTED RECORDINGS

As leader: *Blues by Lonnie Johnson* (Prst./Bluesville, 1984); *Steppin' on the Blues* (Col., 1990); with E. Lang: *Blue Guitars*, i–ii (Beat Goes On, 1997); *The Rhythm and Blues Years*, ii: *1947–1952* (EPM Musique-Blues, 2003)

BIBLIOGRAPHY

J. Sallis: *The Guitar Players* (Lincoln, NE, 1994)

T. Russell: "The Guitar Breaks Through," *Masters of Jazz Guitar*, ed. C. Alexander (London, 1999), 4–9

D. Alger: *The Original Guitar Hero and the Power of Music: The Legendary Lonnie Johnson, B.B. King, and Louis Armstrong: Music and Civil Rights* (forthcoming)

DEAN ALGER

Johnson, Pete(r) [Holden, Kermit] (*b* Kansas City, MO, 25 March 1904; *d* Buffalo, NY, 23 Mar 1967). Pianist, singer, and composer. Born into a poor family, he dropped out of school and played drums for some years before studying piano with his uncle, Charles "Smash" Johnson, from 1922 to 1926. He worked in town with small bands and singers, notably Joe Turner. In 1936 the producer John Hammond persuaded him and Turner to move to New York. Together with the pianists Meade Lux Lewis and Albert Ammons, they performed at the Carnegie Hall concert entitled From Spirituals to Swing (1938), which launched boogie woogie as a public craze. Shortly thereafter these pianists were in great demand, and they recorded copiously, alone and together, for years. "Roll 'em Pete" (Voc., 1938), by Johnson and Turner, is considered a progenitor of rock and roll. In 1950 Johnson moved to Buffalo and turned to extra-musical jobs, with rare exceptions. In 1958, after touring with Jazz at the Philharmonic, a stroke left him half paralyzed; he died in poverty. Basically a blues musician, Johnson displayed relentless rhythmic drive and a clear-cut touch. He was an effective accompanist for singers, his embellishments being brilliant yet unobtrusive.

BIBLIOGRAPHY

P. Silvester: *A Left Hand like God: a History of Boogie-Woogie Piano* (New York, 1989, 2/2009 as *The Story of Boogie-Woogie: a Left Hand like God*)

T. Russell: *The Blues: from Robert Johnson to Robert Cray* (New York, 1997)

MARCELLO PIRAS

Johnson [Dodds; Spencer], **Robert** [Little Robert Dusty] (*b* Hazlehurst, MS, 8 May 1911; *d* Greenwood, MS, 16 Aug 1938). Blues singer and guitarist. Born out of wedlock to Julia Dodds and Noah Johnson, he relocated frequently within the Mississippi Delta including stints in Memphis, Tennessee, and Lucas Township, Arkansas, before he and his mother settled in Robinsonville, Mississippi, around the time he was seven years old. Johnson played the jaw harp, harmonica, and the diddley bow (a makeshift string instrument played with a slide) before acquiring a guitar sometime around 1927. In his teenage years he intently studied performances of older bluesmen including Son House and Willie Brown. He was married in 1929 but his wife died in childbirth the following year. Shortly thereafter he left Robinsonville, remarried, and took lessons from the Alabama-born guitarist Ike Zinneman. Between 1931 and his apparent murder by poison in 1938, he worked as a professional traveling musician, performing as far afield as Chicago and New York, and using Helena, Arkansas, as his home base. He made a number of excellent and highly influential recordings in San Antonio (November 1936) and Dallas (June 1937) that indicate a mastery of numerous blues styles. Many of the sides characterize Mississippi blues of the mid-1930s and stand as the link between this tradition and modern Chicago blues. His work was influenced by Son House and clearly shows an awareness of Skip James and Hambone Willie Newbern, whose themes he adapted in "32·20 Blues" (1936) and "If I had possession over Judgment Day" (1936). From recordings of other blues singers, many outside the Delta sphere of influence, Johnson picked up many stylistic and thematic tropes: "From Four till Late" (1936) and "Last Fair Deal Gone Down" (1937) are reminiscent of eastern blues by the likes of Blind Blake; "Malted Milk" and "Drunken Hearted Man" (both 1937) show the influence of the urban blues of Lonnie Johnson; and "Love in Vain" (1937) is a reworking of Leroy Carr's "When the Sun Goes Down."

Johnson's voice was taut and often strained, and he frequently used falsetto effectively, as on "Kind Hearted Woman" (1936). His guitar playing combined dramatic, often irregular rhythms with agitated whining effects produced by a bottleneck slide. The persistent walking bass rhythm in "I believe I'll dust my broom," "Sweet Home Chicago," and "Ramblin' on my Mind" (all 1936) profoundly influenced both the postwar generation of blues singers—including Elmore James, his one-time companion Johnny Shines, and his stepson Robert Lockwood Jr.—and the blues revivalists of the 1960s. Alternate takes of his performances show that they were well rehearsed. He was also known to perform popular songs, learning many Bing Crosby and Jimmie Rodgers hits from recordings and radio.

Contrary to his widely acknowledged, posthumous reputation as the king of the Delta blues, Johnson was little more than an aspiring musician during his lifetime. Reported sales figures indicate that prior to his passing Johnson records sold no more than 5000 copies. Only one, "Terraplane Blues" (1936), was a regional Delta hit. His canonization began only months after his death. John Hammond invited Johnson to take part in the first From Spirituals to Swing concert, on 23 December 1938. After learning of Johnson's death Hammond elected to play two of his recordings, "Walkin' Blues" and "Preachin' Blues" (both 1936), from the stage of Carnegie Hall in tribute. In 1961 Columbia released an album of 17 tracks recorded by Johnson under the title *King of the Delta Blues Singers*, a record that became a cult favorite among blues aficionados including those involved in the British blues-rock boom of the 1960s such as Eric Clapton, Jimmy Page, and John Mayall. For white blues enthusiasts Robert Johnson epitomized the quintessential African American blues artist. His life and work have become the stuff of romantic legend. Central to his image as the rambling, hard drinking, womanizing, tragic bluesman is the myth that Johnson sold his soul to the devil at a crossroads in exchange for mastery of the blues. When his complete recordings were reissued as two albums in 1990, the set rapidly sold 500,000 copies; it became the most successful blues issue to that date and has since been certified platinum.

BIBLIOGRAPHY

P. Welding: "Hell Hound on his Trail," *DB Yearbook* (1966)

J. Shines: "The Robert Johnson I Knew, " *American Folk Music Occasional*, ii (1970), 30–33

S.B. Charters: *Robert Johnson* (New York, 1973)

B. Groom: "Standing at the Crossroads: Robert Johnson's Recordings," *Blues Unlimited* (1976), no.118, pp.17–20; no.119, pp.11–14; no.120, pp.15–17; no.121, pp.20–21

R. Palmer: *Deep Blues* (New York, 1981/*R*)

J. Obrecht: "Robert Johnson Revisited," *Guitar Player*, xxiv/9 (1990), 60–66, 69–72

P. Guralnick: *Searching for Robert Johnson* (New York, 1992)

G. Lipsitz: "Remembering Robert Johnson: Romance and Reality," *Popular Music and Society*, xxi/4 (1997), 39–50

E. Wald: *Escaping the Delta: Robert Johnson and the Invention of the Blues* (New York, 2004)

E. Rothenbuhler: "For-the-Record Aesthetics and Robert Johnson's Blues Style as a Product of Recorded Culture," *Popular Music*, xxvi/1 (2007), 65–81

S. LaVere: "Robert Johnson's Census Records," *Living Blues*, xl/5 (2009), 72–5

PAUL OLIVER/SEAN LORRE

Johnson, Scott (Richard) (*b* Madison, WI, 12 May 1952). Composer and electric guitarist. He studied music and the visual arts at the University of Wisconsin (BS 1974). In 1975 he moved to New York, where he became active in the downtown music scene. He was first brought to wider attention in 1982 with his composition *John Somebody*, a long and exhilarating piece for sampled speaking voices and electric guitar. With this work, he became one of the first composers to incorporate elements of rock music into classical composition and the first to forge musical motifs from sampled speech. Continuing his efforts to unite the American vernacular

with techniques of classical composition, he formed the amplified Scott Johnson Ensemble, a group consisting of three saxophonists, two electric guitarists, an electric bass guitarist, and two percussionists. One of his works from this period, *Simple Engines* (1986), expands a six-note riff from a James Brown song into a 12-note row that is then used as a melodic device. Later works include *Rock/Paper/Scissors* and *How It Happens*, commissioned by the Kronos Quartet. The latter of these returns to sampling techniques: the first half is built around the recorded voice of the American political commentator I.F. Stone, while the second half uses synthesizers to create a dense, Latin-influenced reminiscence of life on New York's Lower East Side. He has also completed a film score (*Patty Hearst*) and commissions from the London Contemporary Dance Theatre and Boston Ballet. He received a Guggenheim Fellowship in 2006 and has received multiple grants and fellowships from the New York State Council on the Arts and the National Endowment for the Arts.

WORKS
(selective list)

John Somebody, elec gui, tape, 1982; Before Winter I–II, s sax + bar sax, a sax + fl, t sax + b cl, 2 elec gui, 2 perc, 1984–5; Bird in the Domes, str qt, 1986; Simple Engines, s sax + bar sax, a sax + fl, t sax + b cl, 2 elec gui, elec b gui, 2 perc, 1986; Patty Hearst (film score), vn, vc, synth, elec gui, 1988, arr. as suite; Confetti of Flesh (J. Cortez), S, va, elec gui, pf/synth, perc, 1990; Rock/Paper/Scissors, vn, vc, synth, elec gui, 1991–4; How It Happens, str qt, tape, 1993; Rent Party, vn, vc, 1994; Convertible Debts, vols.1–2, vn, vc, elec gui, pf, tape, 1995–8; Jet Lag Lounge, pf, 1998; The Value of People and Things, vn, vc, elec gui, pf, sampled speech, 1997–9; The Pietist and the Hedonist, fl, cl/b cl, vn, vc, pf, perc, 2000–2; The Illusion of Guidance, cl, vc, db, elec gui, pf, mar/perc, 2002; Americans, cl/b cl, s/t sax, va, elec gui, elec b gui, pf, drumset, sampled speech, 2003; Gone, gui, 2004; Bowery Haunt, 2 elec gui, 2005; Up and Back, shamisen, elec gui, vc, pf, 2005; Pact, vc, elec gui, pf, db/elec b gui, sampled speech, 2006; Stalking Horse, elec gui, chbr orch, 2007

Principal recording companies: Nonesuch/Tzadik

BIBLIOGRAPHY
G. Sandow: "Vernacular Roots," *Village Voice* (27 Apr 1982)

GREGORY SANDOW/HILARY BAKER

Johnson, Tom (*b* Greeley, CO, 18 Nov 1939). Composer and critic. He was educated at Yale University (BA 1961, MM 1967) and studied composition privately with MORTON FELDMAN in New York during the late 1960s, while he worked as a dance accompanist. In 1971 he was hired by the *Village Voice* to report on experimental music, and during his tenure became one of the most influential critics in the United States, writing on the music of Reich, Glass, Ashley, and other important composers. Active as a composer of experimental works in a variety of media, he has received commissions from the St. Paul Chamber Orchestra and the American Dance Festival and in 1978 was awarded an NEA grant. Premieres of his works have been performed by Richard Stoltzman, Ursula Oppens, and the St. Paul Chamber Orchestra, among others. In *The Four-note Opera* (1972), one of his most successful works, only four pitches are employed; the text consists of the singers' description of the music they sing and of the delights and frustrations of their roles. In *Nine Bells* (1979), which Johnson has himself presented in the United States and in Europe, the performer, by walking rhythmically through a labyrinth of nine fire-alarm bells hung from the ceiling, creates both visual patterns and, as he strikes the bells, evocative and varied music. In 1983 he resigned his position at the *Village Voice* and moved to Paris.

Johnson is the author of three books, including *Imaginary Music* (New York 1974), a collection of cartoons (some of which resemble conceptual scores) drawn with elements of musical notation. A collection of his writings from the *Village Voice*, titled *The Voice of New Music*, appeared in 1989. His book *Self-Similar Melodies* (1996) reveals his techniques for translating mathematical patterns into audible phenomena. Consequently, he claims that much of his music is "found" music: his *Chord Catalogue* (1986) was the first work he regarded as such. The *Chord Catalogue* is a taxonomy of the 8178 possible chords in an octave. Of his *Rational Melodies* (1982), he writes: "After a few bars, the sequence had begun, the rules were clear, and the rest of the piece was inevitable" ("I Want to Find the Music," 4).

Since 1984, Johnson has written several pieces intended for radio. Some of these works have been produced as scores; others exist as recordings. Among the more well known are *Bedtime Stories* (1986), *Music for 88* (1988), *Music and Questions* (1989), and *Die Melodiemaschinen* (1996). His largest work to date is an oratorio based on the texts of the German theologian Dietrich Bonhoeffer. The *Bonhoeffer Oratorium* was composed between 1988 and 1992. The two-and-a-half hour work is modeled on the traditional German oratorio, but features elements of jazz and American gospel music as well. It was premiered by the Dutch Radio Orchestra and Chorus in 1996.

Mathematical notions of tiling, combinatorics, and permutations form the basis of his works from the early 2000s. The *Tileworks* project, composed in 2002, includes a series of 14 works for different solo instruments. These solo works were followed by *Tileworks for Five Conductors and One Drummer*, *Tileworks for Piano*, and *Tileworks for String Quartet* in 2003. His piece *Kientzy Loops* (2000) earned him the Victoires de la Musique Prize in 2001.

WORKS
(selective list)

Opera: The Four-note Opera (Johnson, R. Kushner), 1972; The Masque of Clouds (Johnson, R. Kushner), 1975; 5 Shaggy-dog Operas (Johnson), 1978; Reservé aux sopranes (Johnson), 1984; Riemannoper (Riemann), 1988

Orch: The Secret of the River, 1966; Dragons in A, 1979; Loops for Orchestra, 1999; 360 Chords, 2005

Inst: Transitory Circumlocutions, trbn, 1973; Failing, db, 1975; Verses for A Fl, Hn, and Harp, 1975; Verses for Perc, 1975; 60-note Fanfares for 4 Antiphonal Tpts, 1975; Monologue, tuba, 1976; Scrawls, bn, pf, 1976; Verses for Va, 1976; Risks for Unrehearsed Performers, any inst(s), 1977–; Doublings, db, 1980; Movts, wind qnt, 1980; Counting to 8, vn, va/cl, fl, 1981; Symmetries, 8 va, 1981, arr. pf 4 hands, 1981; Elegy, str qt, 1982; Rational Melodies, any inst, 1982; The Towers of Hanoi, gamelan, 1982; Harpiano, harp, pf, 1983; Formulas for string quartet, str qt, 1994; Kientzy Loops, sax(s), 2000; Tilework, various solo inst, 2003

Kbd: Scenes, pf, tape, 1969; Spaces, pf, 1969; An Hour for Pf, 1971; Septapede, pf, 1973; Far Rockaway, pf, 1975; Private Pieces: Pf Music for Self-entertainment, 1976; Triple Threat for Pf, 1979; Counting Keys, pf, 1982; Fives, org, 1982; Voicings, 4 pf, 1984; Music for 88, pf, 1988; Same or Different, pf, 2004

Vocal: Hank and Mary, 1v, gui, 1975; Trinity, SATB, 1978; Wesley's Challenge, SATB, 1982; Bonhoeffer Oratorium, SATB, soloists, orch, 1996; 1 2 3, speakers, 2002

Other: Lectures with Audience Participation, ?1970; Running Out of Breath, dancer, 1976; Secret Songs, speaker, 1977; 9 Bells, fire-alarm bells, 1979; Blocks, theater piece, 1982; Counting Duets, 2 speakers, 1982; Counting Languages, speaker, 1982–; Self-portrait, actor/box mover, inst ens, 1983; Music and Questions, bells, speaker, 1988; Narayana's Cows, inst ens, speaker, 1989

BIBLIOGRAPHY

C. Stone: "Patterns in Sound and Motion," *Artweek* (2 Feb 1980), 15

G. Sandow: "Three Cheers for Nine Bells," *Village Voice* (10 June 1981)

D. Burge: "Theater Pieces of the '60s," *Keyboard*, viii/1 (1982), 69

P. Robinson: "Tom Johnson in Paris," *Contact*, no.29 (1985), 35

T. Johnson: *Self-Similar Melodies* (Paris, 1996)

T. Johnson: "I Want to Find the Music, Not to Compose It," <http://www.editions75.com/Articles/I%20WANT%20TO%20FIND%20THE%20MUSIC.pdf>

GREGORY SANDOW/MICHAEL BERRY

Johnson, Tommy (i) (*b* Terry, MS, *c*1896; *d* Crystal Springs, MS, 1 Nov 1956). Blues singer and guitarist. He moved to Crystal Springs as a child, and worked there mainly as a field hand and farmer. He was taught to play guitar by his brother, and performed at local functions and occasionally with traveling shows. Before World War I he was influenced by Charley Patton and his circle in Drew, Mississippi. He developed a beautiful and moving performing style exemplified on his first recording, "Cool Drink of Water Blues" (Vic. 21279, 1928), which was taken slowly with falsetto phrases and accompanied by a complementary line in mandolin style by the guitarist Charlie McCoy. His "Big Road Blues" (Vic. 21279, 1928) consisted of traditional verses forcefully sung against a compelling accompaniment of ascending steps. Johnson was addicted to alcohol, and sang about it on "Canned Heat Blues" (Vic. 38535, 1928), a performance of great beauty with elements related to the aforementioned songs. In 1930 he recorded some exceptionally rare titles, of which "Lonesome Home Blues" (Para. 13000, 1930) is unusual in being sung in a low and brooding voice set against a deceptively economical guitar accompaniment. Although his qualities as a blues singer and musician are known only by a handful of recordings, Johnson was arguably the finest, and certainly the most influential, of all the Mississippi bluesmen. He shared his recording sessions with another Mississippi singer, Ishmon Bracey (*b* Byram, MS, 9 Jan 1901; *d* Jackson, MS, 12 Feb 1970), whose performances were scarcely less remarkable. Many singers have recorded versions of Johnson's "Big Road Blues," and the guitar part has become a blues standard.

BIBLIOGRAPHY

SouthernB

D. Evans: *Tommy Johnson* (London, 1971)

S. Harris: *Blues Who's Who* (New Rochelle, NY, 1979), 290 only

D. Evans: *Big Road Blues* (Berkeley, CA, 1982)

PAUL OLIVER

Johnson, Tommy [John Thomas] **(ii)** (*b* Los Angeles, CA, 7 Jan 1935; *d* Los Angeles, CA, 16 Oct 2006). Tuba player and educator. He attended the University of Southern California (BM 1956), where he studied with Robert Marsteller. In 1958 he began a recording career that eventually included more than 2000 film soundtracks, notably those for *The Godfather, Jaws, Titanic, The Matrix,* and the Indiana Jones and Star Trek movies, and hundreds of television shows. During his lifetime Johnson was thought to be the most heard tuba player in the United States. He received the National Academy of Recording Arts and Sciences Most Valuable Player award for tuba for six years in a row from 1974 to 1980; the following year he was designated Emeritus Most Valuable Tuba Player, making him ineligible to win the award again. Johnson also was a member of the Glendale SO and the Los Angeles Tuba Quartet, and he appeared with the Los Angeles Philharmonic, the Pasadena Symphony, and the LA Pops Orchestra.

In addition to his recording activity, Johnson was an active music educator. He taught music at the junior high level in the Los Angeles Unified School District for more than 20 years and served on the faculties of the University of Southern California and the University of California, Los Angeles, from 1972 until his death. He was one of the most influential teachers on his instrument, and several of his students have occupied prominent orchestral chairs in the United States.

BIBLIOGRAPHY

R.W. Morris and E.R. Goldstein, eds.: *The Tuba Source Book* (Bloomington, IN, 1996)

G. Pokorny: "2006 ITEA Lifetime Achievement Awards: Tommy Johnson," *ITEA Journal,* xxxiii/4 (2006), 21–2

RICHARD H. PERRY

Johnson, Thor (Martin) (*b* Wisconsin Rapids, WI, 10 June 1913; *d* Nashville, TN, 16 Jan 1975). Conductor. While studying at the University of North Carolina, he became president of the Phi Mu Alpha Sinfonia fraternity. While still a student, he became associate conductor of the North Carolina State SO. At the University of Michigan (where he received the MA in 1935) he founded the Little SO, which he conducted (1934–6, 1938–42) and led on tours in the United States. He continued his studies at the Salzburg Mozarteum (1936–7) and at the conservatories of Leipzig and Prague with BRUNO WALTER, NIKOLAI MALKO, Felix Weingartner, and Hermann Abendroth. On his return to the United States he became an assistant professor at the University of Michigan and conducted the WPA Orchestra in Asheville, North Carolina. He studied with SERGE KOUSSEVITZKY at the first Berkshire Music Center courses (1940 and 1941), and from 1940 to 1942 was conductor of the Grand Rapids SO. During service in the US Army (1942–6) he conducted the First Army SO in Fort Myers, Virginia, and was given leave to conduct in New York, Cleveland, Boston, Philadelphia, and Chicago. His first postwar performances with the New York PO led to the conductorship of the Juilliard School orchestra, which he left in 1947 to become music director of the Cincinnati SO, a position he held until 1958. As one of the first native conductors to direct a major American orchestra, Johnson helped to pave the way for the next generation of American conductors. During his tenure at Cincinnati he performed large-scale and little-known works, including a much praised *Gurrelieder* as early as 1953. In the same year, he made several important stereophonic recordings for Remington Records. He also organized festivals in Ohio, Wisconsin, and Ojai, California. He was a professor and head of orchestral activities at Northwestern University (1958–64) and director of the Interlochen Arts Academy (1964–7). From 1967 to 1975 he directed the Nashville SO. Johnson's broad-spanned conducting was best heard in the large works of the late 19th and early 20th centuries. His authority and energy, as well as his organizational abilities, were widely acknowledged in the United States, though he was little known elsewhere. He was also a key voice for his religious faith, the Moravian church, and he supported the wide-ranging dissemination of music from this group.

BIBLIOGRAPHY

L. Nicholas: *Thor Johnson: American Conductor* (Ephraim, WI, 1982)

RICHARD BERNAS/DENNIS K. MCINTIRE/
JONAS WESTOVER

Johnson, William Allen (*b* Nassau, NY, 27 Oct 1816; *d* Westfield, MA, 20 Jan 1901). Organ builder. His father, a millwright, moved to Westfield when he was a child, and as a youth he worked in local factories and apprenticed to a mason, eventually setting himself up as a contractor. In 1843, while doing masonry work on a newly built Methodist church in Westfield, he was recruited to help in the installation of the church's E. & G.G. Hook organ, and in the following winter he successfully essayed the building of a small parlor organ. During the next two winters he built others, which he succeeded in selling, and eventually established a small workshop where his first church organ was built for Grace Church in nearby Chicopee in 1848. The following year he produced his first two-manual organ for the First Congregational Church in Westfield. As his business grew, he was able to attract skilled workmen such as Edwin Hedges, a pipemaker who worked for him from around 1852 until the closing of the firm in 1898. In 1854, at which time he was employing about 20 men, Johnson built his first three-manual organ for South Church in Hartford, Connecticut. By the 1860s business was flourishing; larger organs included those in Fourth Presbyterian Church in Albany (1866) and St. Paul's Church, Burlington, Vermont (1867).

In 1871 Johnson's son William H. (1840–1921) joined the firm, and in the same year the factory was destroyed by fire. A larger factory was built, and in 1875 the name of the firm was changed to Johnson & Son. Much of Johnson's clientele up to the mid-1860s had been concentrated in western New England and eastern New York, but the building of the Hoosick Canal and railroads made Westfield an ideal location for shipping to the growing cities to the west, particularly Chicago in the years following the great fire of 1871, where a large organ was built in 1875 for St. James's Church, and

Buffalo, where an organ of similar size was built for Delaware Avenue Methodist Church the following year. In that same year Johnson replaced the small Hook organ that had first stirred his interest in organs with a large instrument for the Methodist Church of Westfield. What would be the firm's largest organ was built in 1877 for St. Mary's Church in Boston, and 1880 was marked by an organ for the Central Music Hall in Chicago. During the 1890s William H. Johnson assumed the management of the firm, but he was too conservative for a period in which many changes were occurring, and, after completing one last organ for a Chicago church, the firm closed its doors in 1898, selling the factory to a former employee, Emmons Howard.

BIBLIOGRAPHY

H.D. Blanchard: "Johnson's 860 Organs Present a Challenge to Designers Today," *The Diapason*, xxxvi (1945), no.5, pp.20–21; no.6, p.14

K.F. Simmons: *The Johnson Organ Company* (thesis, Union Theological Seminary, 1949)

B. Owen: *The Organ in New England* (Raleigh, NC, 1979)

J.V.V. Elsworth: *The Johnson Organs* (Harrisville, NH, 1984)

W.T. Van Pelt: "The Johnson Organ Company," *The American Organist*, xxi/5 (May 1987), 48

BARBARA OWEN

Johnson, William H(enry) (*b* Westfield, MA, 30 June 1841; *d* Westfield, MA, 20 April 1922). Organ builder. He was the son of WILLIAM A. JOHNSON and worked at his father's firm from age 16. He also performed as an organist. In 1875 the firm's name was changed to Johnson & Son, and a decade later the growing popularity of Johnson organs and a disastrous fire necessitated a larger factory. After this the factory failed to achieve the high output of the earlier years, never again completing more than 28 organs a year. When William A. retired in 1890 his son became head of the firm. Johnson's impatience and stubborn refusal to accommodate new organ technologies such as pneumatic or electric types of action caused the business to falter and the firm closed in 1898. Johnson then became a salesman of stocks and bonds, which had always held more appeal to him.

BIBLIOGRAPHY

O. Ochse: *The History of the Organ in the United States* (Bloomington, IN, 1975)

B. Owen: *The Organ in New England* (Raleigh, 1979)

J.V. Elsworth: *The Johnson Organ* (Harrisville, NH, 1984)

N. LEE ORR

Johnson (Severns), Theodate (*b* Cleveland, OH, 13 Aug 1907; *d* New York, NY, 13 March 2002). Soprano, music publisher, and concert manager. She studied singing with Ruth Thayer Burnham while attending Abbot Academy, Andover, and later at Wellesley College (BA 1929). After two years as an actress at the Cleveland Playhouse, she sang in Gabriel Pierné's *La croisade des enfants* with the Cleveland Orchestra (1932). She was then coached by EVA GAUTHIER in New York and made her debut there in 1934 at Town Hall in the North American premiere of Handel's solo cantata *La Lucrezia*. Three years later she sang Butterfly and Tosca with the Royal Flemish Opera in Antwerp. After meeting Sibelius in Finland, she returned to the United States and introduced a number of his songs in concert (1938). During World War II Johnson escorted a convoy of refugees from Paris to Spain and as a result of the ordeal lost her voice. She joined the staff of *Musical America* in 1954 and was its owner-publisher from 1959 to 1964. Later she became a concert manager and a board member of a number of musical institutions, including the Musicians Club of New York.

NADIA TURBIDE/R

Johnston, Ben(jamin Burwell, Jr.) (*b* Macon, GA, 15 March 1926). Composer, theorist, and educator. His music was first performed in public when he was 16, and his interest in "more nearly perfect" tuning is documented as early as 1944. After serving in the US Navy, he played piano in dance bands and then completed the BFA at William and Mary College, Williamsburg (1949). In 1950 he abandoned composition studies with Mary Leighton at the Cincinnati Conservatory to work with HARRY PARTCH in Gualala, California; he also enrolled at Mills College and studied with DARIUS MILHAUD (MFA 1952). In 1951 he was appointed to a combined dance and music position at the University of Illinois; he was granted tenure there in 1959, became a professor in 1967, and retired as professor emeritus in 1983. In addition to composition and teaching, he organized the premiere of Partch's *The Bewitched* with Alwin Nikolais's choreography (Urbana, 1957), chaired the university's influential Festival of Contemporary Arts (1962–5), held guest professorships and lectured widely on microtonality and other subjects. He also sought performers willing to learn his music, made more challenging by a microtonal notation based on actual pitch (rather than the tablature found in Partch's music).

He has received many honors, including a Guggenheim Fellowship (1959), the Deems Taylor Award (2007), a grant from the National Council on the Arts and the Humanities (1966), and two commissions from the Smithsonian Institute. The American Academy of Arts and Letters honored him in 2007, and his *Quintet for Groups* was awarded the SWR Orchestra prize at the 2008 Donaueschinger Musiktage.

Johnston's reputation has rested primarily on his work in microtonality. However, his earlier music was in equal temperament, with a tendency towards neoclassicism (*Septet*, the early piano pieces), theater music, and sensitive song-settings. Beginning with sections of *Gambit*, he explored serial techniques, later incorporating metric modulation and proportional relationships. Humor found its way into his work through quotation and pun (*Ivesberg Revisited, Newcastle Troppo*) and popular eclecticism (*Gertrude, or Would She Be Pleased to Receive It?*). He also experimented with indeterminacy (influenced by his teacher and friend Cage) and improvisation, especially in a performance-theater context (*Five Do-It-Yourself Pieces*).

With *Five Fragments* (1960), Johnston began using just intonation. While Partch's theory was profoundly influential on him, his more comfortable relationship to

Western art music and lack of instrument-building skills led him to compose primarily for traditional instruments and genres, especially the string quartet. In many works he has synthesized just intonation, proportions, and serialism, where ratios might determine duration or metric modulation (*Knocking Piece*) or a row exist in microtonal as well as transposed forms. He employs two structuralist approaches to just intonation: scalar (e.g. *Suite* for Microtonal Piano), where the 12 repeating pitch classes per octave range as far as the 27th partial; and three-dimensional "lattice-work," starting from C and evolving according to the partials chosen; this develops Partch's theory of expanded consonance beyond the 11th-partial limit while increasing greatly the potential for modulation, a frequent device in the quartets.

Despite his commitment to just intonation, Johnston has never been dogmatic about compositional choices. The majority of his pieces are tonal; many works or movements are in ternary or variation form. He has often composed for amateur ensembles, although many have found these works difficult. While he has composed relatively little theatrical music since the 1950s, *Carmilla* (written with Wilford Leach) and the tour de force *Calamity Jane to Her Daughter* have proven two of his most popular works.

The 1960s were years of personal crisis, and this is reflected in a pervasive use of almost violent contrasts and personality changes (*Sonata/Grindlemusic* for microtonal piano, with 81 different pitch-classes spread among the 88 keys). In *Crossings*, the conflict of Quartet no.3 ("Vergings") is followed by a period of silence, and then resolution in Quartet no.4 ("Ascent"), a variation set also known as *Amazing Grace*. Johnston's subsequent conversion to Catholicism is felt more in the spirit of later works than in specific borrowings; their tone is more American vernacular than religious.

The string quartets figure centrally in Johnston's output, and, though Johnston and the Kronos Quartet often discussed their recording the complete quartets, negotiations with Nonesuch have not come to fruition. With a 2006 release of quartets 2, 3, 4, and 9, the Kepler Quartet embarked on a recording of all ten quartets. In 2011 they released a second installment of the project with recordings of quartets 1, 5, and 10 on New World Records.

See also NOTATION *and* TUNING SYSTEMS.

WORKS

DRAMATIC

Stage: St Joan (ballet), pf, 1955; Gertrude, or Would She be Pleased to Receive It? (chbr op, 2, W. Leach), 1956; Gambit (ballet, choreog. M. Cunningham), 1959, arr. as Ludes, 12 insts; Carmilla (chbr op, Leach), 1970; 5 Do-It-Youself Pieces (indeterminate theater pieces), nos.1–4, 1969, no.5, 1981; Calamity Jane to Her Daughter, S, vn, synth, drums, 1989

Incid music: The Wooden Bird (Leach), 1950, collab. H. Partch; Fire (A. Gregor), 1952; The Zodiac of Memphis Street (Leach), 1954; Ring Round the Moon (J. Anouilh), 1954; The Taming of the Shrew (W. Shakespeare), 1961

VOCAL

Choral: Night (cant. R. Jeffers), Bar, female chorus, ens, 1955; Prayer, SSA, 1996; Ci-Gît Satie (S. Johnston), chorus, db, drums, 1967; Rose (Johnston), SATB, 1971; Mass, SATB, 8 trbn, perc, 1972; I'm Goin' Away, SATB, 1973; Vigil (Amerindian), improvising vv, 1976; Since Adam, STB/SAB, 1977, lost; Sonnets of Desolation (G.M. Hopkins), double SATB, 1980; On Love (Bible), chorus, orch (1986), Mantram and Raga, SATB, 1993; Secret (R. Bly), SATB, 1994

Solo vocal: Somewhere I have never travelled (E.E. Cummings), T, 1949; Le Gout de Néant (C. Baudelaire: *Les Fleurs du Mal*), Bar, pf, 1950; A Nocturnal upon St. Lucie's Day (J. Donne), Bar/A, pf, 1951; 3 Chin. Lyrics (Rihaku, trans. E. Pound), S, 2 vn, 1955; 5 Fragments (H. Thoreau: *Walden*), A, ob, vc, bn, 1960; A Sea Dirge (Shakespeare), Mez, fl, ob, vn, 1962; Songs of Innocence (W. Blake), S, ens, 1975; 2 Sonnets of Shakespeare, B-Bar/Ct, ens, 1978; Songs of Loss (Donne), T, str ens, 1986; Journeys, A, chorus, orch (1986); M'amie qui danse (Inouye), S, microtonal pf, 1990; A man and a woman sit near each other (Bly), Bar, cl, hn, 1993; Quietness (Rumi, trans. Barks), speaking B, str qt, 1996; Invocation (Attar, trans. Nott), S, ens, 1997; The Tavern (Rumi, trans. Barks), vox, microtonal gui, 1999

INSTRUMENTAL

Orch: Korybas, 1949, withdrawn; Ivesberg Revisited, Newcastle Troppo, jazz band, 1960; Passacaglia and Epilogue from St Joan, 1960; Qnt for Groups, 1966; Sym., A, 1987; Chbr Sym., 1990

10 Str qts: no.1 (9 Variations), 1959; no.2, 1964; no.3 "Vergings," 1966–73; no.4 "Ascent" (Amazing Grace), 1973 [nos.3 and 4 combined as Crossings]; no.5, 1979; no.6, 1980; no.7, 1984; no.8, 1986; no.9, 1989; no.10, 1996

Other chbr: Conc., brass ens, 1951, arr. for pf 4-hand; Conc., perc ens. 1952; Septet, wind qnt, vc, db, 1956–8; Sonata for 2, vn, vc, 1960; Knocking Piece, 2 perc, 1962; Duo, fl, db, 1963; Diversions for 4, jazz qt, 1963–83, withdrawn; Lament, wind/str ens, 1966; One Man, trbn, perc, 1967; 2 Ob and 2 Tablas and 2 Banyas, 1969–70, lost; Duo, 2 vn, 1978; Diversion, 11 insts, 1979; 12 Partials, fl, microtonal pf, 1980; Trio, cl, vn, vc, 1981; The Demon Lover's Doubles, tpt, microtonal pf, 1985; Pursuit, bn, tuba, 1992; Trio Variations, fl, cl, db, 1994; Sleep and Waking, perc ens, 1994, collab. R. George; Nightreach, sax qt, 1999; O Waly Waly Variations, sax qt, 1999; Octet, fl, cl, bsn, str qt, db, 2000

Solo inst (for pf unless otherwise stated): Etude-Toccata, 1949; Satires, 1953, lost; Celebration, 1953; Portrait, 1953, lost; Variations, lost, 1954; Aubade, 1959, lost; Sonata/Grindlemusic, microtonal pf, 1965; Suite, microtonal pf, 1978; Toccata, vc, 1984; Ponder Nothing, cl, 1989; Progression, db, 1993; Alap, db, 1996

ELECTRO-ACOUSTIC

Auto Mobile, exhibition music, tape, 1968–9; Museum Piece, film score, tape, 1968–9, collab. J. Spek; Kindergartenlieder, 2-track tape, 1969; Knocking Piece Collage, tape, 1969; In Memory, str/perc ens, tape, slides, 1975, rev. as In Memory, S, str, perc, tape, 1976: 1 Visions and Spels [realization of vocal work Vigil, 1976], 2 At the Strong Point; Strata, tape, 1978, collab. B. Mazurek

Principal publishers: Foster, J. Marx, MEDIA, Orchesis, Smith

WRITINGS

VintonD ("Microtonality," "Partch, Harry")

"Letter from Urbana," *PNM*, ii/1 (1963–4), 137–41

"Scalar Order as a Compositional Resource," *PNM*, ii/2 (1963–4), 56–76

"Proportionality and Expanded Music Pitch Relations," *PNM*, v/1 (1966–7), 112–20

"Three Attacks on a Problem," *Proceedings of the American Society of University Composers*, ii (1967), 89–98

"A.S.U.C. Keynote Address," *PNM*, xxvi (1968), 236–42

"On Context," *Proceedings of the American Society of University Composers*, iii (1968), 32–6; repr. in *Source*, ii/2 (1968), 44–5

"How to Cook an Albatross," *Arts in Society*, vii/1 (1970), 33–8; repr. in *Source*, iv/1 (1970), 63–5

with E. Kobrin: "Phase la," *Source*, iv/1 (1970), 27–45

"Art and Survival," *Composer* [Hamilton, OH], iii (1971–2), 9–16

"Tonality Regained," *Proceedings of the American Society of University Composers*, vi (1971), 113–19

"The Corporealism of Harry Partch," *PNM*, xiii/2 (1974–5), 85–97

"Rational Structure in Music," *Proceedings of the American Society of University Composers*, xi–xii (1976–77), 102–18

"Harry Partch—John Cage," *New World Records,* 214 (1978) [disc notes]

"The Genesis of *Knocking Piece,*" *Percussive Notes,* xxii/3 (1983), 25–31

"Extended Just Intonation: a Position Paper," *PNM,* xxv (1987), 517–19

Recorded interviews in *NHoh*

BIBLIOGRAPHY

EwenD; VintonD

B. Childs: "Ben Johnston's Quintet for Groups," *PNM,* vii/1 (1968–9), 110–21

R. Shinn: "Ben Johnston's Fourth String Quartet," *PNM,* xv/2 (1976–7), 145–73

W. Zimmermann: "Ben Johnston about Partch," *Desert Plants: Conversations with 23 American Musicians* (Vancouver, 1976), 347–65

C. Gagne and T. Caras: *Soundpieces: Interviews with American Composers* (Metuchen, 1982)

H. Von Gunden: *The Music of Ben Johnston* (Metuchen, 1986)

J.J. Gibbens: "Design in Ben Johnston's Sonata for Microtonal Piano," *Interface,* xviii (1989), 161–94

R. Carl: "Six Case Studies in New American Music: a Postmodern Portrait Gallery," *College Music Symposium,* xxx/1 (1990), 45–63

S. Elster: "A Harmonic and Serial Analysis of Ben Johnston's Quartet no.6," *PNM,* xxix/2 (1991), 138–65

J. Fonville: "Ben Johnston's Extended Just Intonation: a Guide for Interpreters," *PNM,* xxix/2 (1991), 106–37

D. Keislar: "Six Composers on Non-Standard Tunings," *PNM,* xxix/1 (1991), 176–211

P. Rapport: "Just Inton(ot)ation," *1/1,* vii/1 (1991), 1, 12–14

W. Duckworth: *Talking Music: Conversations with John Cage, Philip Glass, Laurie Anderson, and Five Generations of American Experimental Composers* (New York, 1995)

B. Johnston: *"Maximum Clarity" and Other Writings on Music,* ed. B. Gilmore (Urbana, IL, 2006)

B. Johnston and S. Smith: *Who Am I? Why Am I Here?: Ben Johnston Reflects on His Life in Music* (Baltimore, MD, 2006)

RICHARD KASSEL/ALAN SHOCKLEY

Johnston, Daniel (*b* Sacramento, CA, 22 Jan 1961). Singer, songwriter, and artist. His idiosyncratic musical approach means that his music does not fit easily into an established genre and is often described as outsider music. His difficulties with bipolar disorder have shaped his artistic output and his unconventional career path. He began to record his own music in the late 1970s. He attracted attention in Austin, Texas, after moving there in 1983, including national coverage when he appeared on an episode of MTV's *Cutting Edge* that featured members of Austin's new-sincerity music scene. In 1988 he made his first studio recording, producing the album *1900* in New York, and in the early 1990s his work was championed by Kurt Cobain, among others. Johnston signed with Atlantic Records in 1994, resulting in his first widely distributed album, *Fun,* which was produced by fan and musician Paul Leary. He also contributed two songs to soundtrack for the film *Kids* (1995). *The Late Great Daniel Johnston: Discovered Covered* (Gammon, 2004) featured a wide range of covers of his songs by such well-known indie musicians as Eels, Beck, and Death Cab for Cutie. He is the subject of a documentary, *The Devil and Daniel Johnston* (2006), and has continued to record and tour into the 2010s.

BIBLIOGRAPHY

T. Yazdani and D. Goede: *The Life, Art, and Music of Daniel Johnston* (San Francisco, 2006)

JONAS WESTOVER

Johnston, Thomas (*b* Boston, MA, 1708; *d* Boston, MA, 8 May 1767). Organ builder, musician, and artist. A man of many skills, Johnston was the first to engage professionally in organ building in Boston, although interleaving this with his other work as a copperplate engraver, japanner, and woodworker. His training in the craft derived largely from his study of the imported English organs in the area that he is recorded as having tuned and repaired. His earliest instruments were small chamber organs, one of which he kept in his own home, and others that he sold or loaned. His first church organ was probably that built for St. Peter's Church, Salem, in 1754. The 1756 Richard Bridge organ in Boston's King's Chapel, where he sang in a choir, seems clearly to have been the inspiration for a larger organ built in 1759 for nearby Christ Church ("Old North"), the handsome casework of which survives. At around the same time he built an organ for Deblois's Concert Hall in Boston, and in 1760 an organ for St. John's Church in Portsmouth, New Hampshire. At the time of his death he left an unfinished chamber organ, but the exact number of organs he built is unknown. As well as being a singer and a player of keyboard instruments, Johnston's musical accomplishments also include the engraving of a set of psalm tunes to accompany the 1755 edition of Tate and Brady's *Psalms of David* and plates for a 1764 revision of Thomas Walter's *Grounds and Rules of Musick Explained.* His son Benjamin (1742–1818) was also a musician and is believed to have been the engraver of William Billings's *Music in Miniature.* Another son, William (1732–1772), was the organist of Christ Church, Boston, from 1750 to 1753.

BIBLIOGRAPHY

F.W. Coburn: "The Johnstons of Boston," *Art in America,* xxi/1 (Dec 1932), 27-36; xxi/4 (Oct 1933), 132–138

M.K.D. Babcock: *Christ Church, Salem Street, Boston* (Boston, 1947)

J. Fesperman: "Music and Organs at 'The Old North'," *Organ Institute Quarterly,* x/3 (1963), 15

S. Hitchings: "Thomas Johnston," *Boston Prints and Printmakers* (Boston, 1973)

B. Owen: *The Organ in New England* (Raleigh, NC, 1979)

S. Hitchings: "The Musical Pursuits of William Price and Thomas Johnston," *Music in Colonial Massachusetts* (Boston, 1985)

BARBARA OWEN

Jolas, Betsy (*b* Paris, France, 5 Aug 1926). French composer. She was brought up in an artistic and literary milieu, which included visits from writers such as Joyce, Stein, or Breton, who were all published in the literary journal *Transition* that her parents founded and edited (1937–47). After her American-born parents moved from Paris to New York in 1940 she studied at the Lycée Français and then at Bennington College (1945–6), where in addition to her formal studies she gained a thorough acquaintance with the 16th-century polyphonists and especially Orlande de Lassus and Josquin des Prez ("when I became a contrapontist rather than a harmonist"). She sang and accompanied the Dessoff choir. Returning to France in 1948, she married Gabriel Illouz the following year; they had three children. Meanwhile Jolas continued her studies at the Paris Conservatoire, where her teachers included OLIVIER MESSIAEN and DARIUS MILHAUD. She first heard Webern's *Fünf Stücke* op.10 in the early 1950s, a discovery which struck her like "a lightning bolt," and soon, despite Milhaud's misgivings, she became familiar with the music of avant-garde contemporaries such as Boulez and Karlheinz Stockhausen.

With their rigorously contrapuntal conception of musical form and their enthusiasm for unusual timbres and previously unexplored means of sound-production, from voices and instruments alike, these composers provided a source for much that was to become characteristic of Jolas's own emerging style. But there were important differences in her outlook, not least her passion for the voice and its expressive qualities. The confrontation of this essentially lyrical impulse with vocal writing, which embraces the full gamut of avant-garde fragmentation, timbral experimentation, and virtuosity gives her vocal works a special intensity. In her *Plupart du temps II* (1989) she creates a dialogue of voice, tenor saxophone, and cello in which, in her words, "The instruments are made to do what the voice does in daily life, but whereby the instruments are stylized, laughing, weeping, calling out." The work represents a main genre of her work related to the Conservatoire de Paris, that of the *morceau de concours*, in this case for saxophone.

Stemming from Jolas's vocality, the deliberate exploitation of the confusions and complexities of contrapuntal text-setting occupies her in *Mots* (1963), or the later *Sonate à 12* (1970), a tour-de-force of vocal invention and wordless drama. In *Quatuor II*, for soprano and string trio (1964), the textless voice sometimes opposes the strings, sometimes combines with them in more homogenous textures, but is always treated as fully equal to the other three parts in flexibility and sophistication, pursuing a kaleidoscopic and restless stream of invention. The work was commissioned and first performed by the Domaine Musical, and marked a breakthrough in public recognition for Jolas. *D'un opéra de voyage* (1967) brings about a complementary transformation, as the instrumental parts are treated like voices. This urge to celebrate the dramatic and expressive qualities of individual musical lines, whether instrumental or vocal, suggests parallels with the music of Berio.

Another distinctive feature of Jolas's music that crystallized during the 1960s was her approach to rhythm and meter. Already she had been moved by sources as varied as Modest Musorgsky in *Boris Godunov*, Lassus, and Léo Delibes in the "Bell Song" from *Lakmé*. Debussy in *Pelléas et Mélisande* also suggested a prosody that reframes the pulse, whereby Jolas alters the tempo of the beat places notes in unsuspected groupings within the beat, creating her characteristic wave rhythm. *J.D.E.* (1966) presents one of the first in a long line of inventive and economical solutions to the problem of writing polyphonic music, which loosens the ties of conventional rhythmic coordination without sacrificing the contrapuntal relation of the parts by allowing freely unsynchronized playing. This fluidity is also apparent in her melodic contours, which frequently involve portamento and glissando, and in the textures and larger formal sections of a work, which are often seamlessly transformed one into another.

While continuing to compose for non-standard ensembles (as in *D'un opéra de poupée* and *Points d'or*, both 1982), she began in the 1970s to write for full orchestra, often with a solo instrument. Several of these concerto-style pieces are cast in the form of a wordless song-cycle, beginning with the lyrical *11 Lieder* for trumpet and orchestra (1977). At the same time she began to make use of the traditional ensembles of chamber music, beginning with the string quartet in *Quatuor III* (1973), an especially concentrated work cast as a succession of short études each exploring a specific kind of musical material or relationship between the four parts. Given her view of music as "sung" melodic expression, it was inevitable that this reconsideration of the ensembles and institutions of the past would culminate in an opera. Two chamber operas seek in different ways to recreate the immediacy of popular (and ancient) theatrical forms: in the second of these, *Le Cyclope* (1986), which sets a satyr-play by Euripides word for word (in French), she succeeds in creating a particularly fluid, conversational kind of word-setting. The piece was written as a respite from work on her grand opera *Schliemann* (1983–93), an epic work on the theme of a lifelong quest that includes much play with different languages and musical cultures. While working on the score Jolas studied some of the operas she most admires, from *Don Giovanni* to *Wozzeck*, and occasionally acknowledged her debt in the music: she has no desire to reject the past, and feels able to take inspiration from earlier composers without compromising the integrity of her own, fully contemporary language. Thus she has described the organ piece *Musique de jour* (1976) as "a sort of four-voice fugue" and an "homage to Monteverdi and Bach," yet these models have been wholly absorbed into the work's own highly individual means of expression. Since about 1990 she has increasingly turned to chamber music as in *Quatuor V* (1995), that for solo instruments, such as *Come follow* for viola and bassoon (2001), and aesthetically if not literally historicizing works such as *Jean Sébastien Bach-Contrapunctus IV* for chamber orchestra (2001, and vocal quartet).

Since 1953, Jolas has accrued a host of prestigious awards and honors. She has also had a distinguished career as a teacher. She has taught at Harvard, Yale, and the University of Michigan, to name a few, and at Tanglewood and Mills College, occupying as a guest professor the Chair of her former teacher Milhaud. She also assisted and then succeeded Messiaen as professor of analysis (1975) and professor of composition (1978) at the Paris Conservatoire.

WORKS

STAGE

Le pavillon au bord de la rivière (chbr op, 4, M. Raoul-Davis, after Kuan HanChin), 1975; Avignon, 4 Aug 1975; Le Cyclope (op, 1, after Euripides: *Cyclops*), 1986; Avignon, 27 July 1986; Schliemann (op, 3, B. Bayen and B. Jolas, after Bayen), 1987; concert perf., Paris, Bastille,

4 Apr 1990, stage perf., Lyon, Opéra, 3 May 1995; Well Met 04, 2004, Nice 2006, dir. Laurent Cuniot; stage C. Gangneron; L'ascension du Mont Ventoux, S, insts, 2004, Mulhouse, Ensemble Accrochenote, Cie Houdart-Heuclin

VOCAL AND CHORAL

With orch: 5 poèmes de Jacques Dupin, S, pf, orch, 1959; L'oeil égare dans les plis d'obéissance du vent (V. Hugo), radiophonic cant., S, A, Bar, chorus, orch, 1961; Dans la chaleur vacante (A. du Bouchet), radiophonic cant., solo vv, chorus, orch, 1963; Motet II (J. Dupin), chorus 36vv, chbr orch, 1965; Liring ballade (E. Jolas), Bar, orch, 1980; Sigrancia Ballade (du Bouchet), Bar, orch, 1995; Lovaby, S, chbr orch, 2000

With inst ens or pf: Plupart du temps (P. Reverdy), Mez, pf, 1949; Chansons pour Paule, S, pf, 1951; Everyone Sings, female double chorus, brass, 1955; Mots (B. Jolas), S, Mez, C, T, B, 8 insts, 1963; Quatuor II, S, str trio, 1964; Plupart du temps II (Reverdy), T, t sax, vc, 1989; Titivillus, Mez, fl, pf, 2000; Concerto-Fantaisie: "O Night, Oh…," chorus, pf, 2001; Motet IV "Ventosum Vocant," S, insts, 2002

Unacc.: Arbres, 1954; Enfantillages, female chorus, 1954; Et le reste à l'avenant, 1954; Pantagruel, 1954; Orca, 1955; Diurnes, chorus 12–72vv, 1970; Sonate à 12, 12 solo vv, 1970; Voix premières, radiophonic work, 1974; Caprice à 1 voix, male or female v, 1975; Caprice à 2 voix, S, Ct/C, 1978; Perriault le déluné (F. Illouz), 12vv, 1993; Für Cecilia Affettuoso, 6vv, 1998; Enfantillages, female and children's choruses, 2000, 2001

ORCHESTRAL AND CHAMBER

9 or more insts: Figures, 9 insts, 1956–65; J.D.E., 14 insts, 1966; D'un opéra de voyage, 22 insts, 1967; Points d'aube, solo va, 13 wind insts, 1967, rev. 1969; 4 plages, str orch, 1968; Lassus ricercare, 10 insts, 1970; 3 rencontres, str trio, orch, 1970–72; Musique d'hiver, org, small orch, 1971; Well Met, 12 str, 1973; 11 Lieder, tpt, chbr orch, 1977; Tales of a Summer Sea, orch, 1977; Stances, pf, orch, 1978; D'un opéra de poupée en 7 musiques, 11 insts, 1982; 5 pièces pour Boulogne, small orch, 1982; Points d'or, sax, 15 insts, 1982; Préludes-Fanfares-Interludes-Sonneries, wind, perc, 1983; Frauenleben, 9 lieder, va, orch, 1992; Lumor, 7 lieder spirituels, sax, orch, 1996; 4 psaumes de Schütz, small orch, 1996; Petite Symphonie Concertante, vn, orch, 1997; Wanderlied, vc solo, 15 insts, 2003; B Day 2006

1–8 insts: Episode no.1, fl, 1964; Tranche, hp, 1967; Etats, vn, 6 perc, 1969; Fusain, pic, b fl, 1971; Remember, eng hn/va, vc, 1971; How Now, 8 insts, 1973; Quatuor III, 9 études, str qt, 1973; Scion, vc, 1973; O Wall, wind qnt, 1976; Episode no.2 "Ohne Worte," fl, 1977; 4 duos, va, pf, 1979; Episode no.3, tpt, 1982; 3 duos, tuba, pf, 1983; Episode no.4, t sax, 1983; Episode no.5, v, 1983; 4 pièces en marge, vc, pf, 1983; Episode no.6, va, 1984; Episode no.7, elec gui, 1984; Episode no.8, db, 1984; Trio, pf, vn, vc, 1988; Music for Joan, vib, pf, 1989; Quatuor IV "Menus propos," str qt, 1989; E.A., petite suite variée, tpt, vib, 1990; Episode no.9 "Forte magnum coloratum," cl, 1990; Trio "Les heures," str trio, 1990; Etudes aperçues, vib, 5 cowbells, 1992; Musique pour Delphine, vn, vc, 1992; Musique pour Xavier, cl, t sax, vn, 1992; Lettere amorosi, tpt, str qt, 1993; Quoth the Raven…cl, pf, 1993; Music for here, bn, va, vc, 1994; Quatuor V, str qt, 1994; Music to go, va, vc, 1995; Quatuor VI, cl, vn, va, vc, 1997; Sonata à 8, 8 vc, 1997; Trio sopra "et sola facta," cl, vn, pf, 1998; Come follow, va, bn, 2002; Lovemusic, fl, b cl, 2005; Suite: Puer apud magistros exercentur, 2 a sax, 2007; Ah! Haydn, pf, vn, vc, 2007

KEYBOARD

Pf: Chanson d'approche, 1972; B for Sonata, 1973; Mon ami, ariette variée, pf + female or child v, 1974; Pièce pour St Germain, 1981; Calling E.C., 1982; Une journée de Gadad, 1983; Petite suite sérieuse pour concert de famille, 1983; Tango si, 1984; Signets: hommage à Maurice Ravel, 1987; Pièce pour, 1997; Ô Bach!, 2007; Teletalks, 2 pf, 2008;

Other kbd: Autour, hpd, 1972; Musique de jour, org, 1976; Auprès, hpd, 1980; 3 études campanaires, kbd carillon/pf, 1980; Leçons du petit jour, org, 2007

Also incid and film music

Principal publishers: Billaudot, B.J., Editions Françaises de Musique, Heugel, Leduc, Ricordi, Salabert

BIBLIOGRAPHY

CC1 (V. Perlis)

B. Jolas: "Il fallait voter sériel même si…," *Preuves*, no.178 (1965), 40–42

M.J. Chauvin: "Entretien avec Betsy Jolas," *Courrier musical de France*, no.27 (1969), 163–73

B. Jolas: "Voix et musique," *Bulletin de la Société française de philosophie*, lxvi/2 (1972) [whole issue]

I. Krastewa: "Betsy Jolas," *SMz*, cxiv (1974), 342–9

D. Henahan: "Betsy Jolas Winning Recognition in the USA," *New York Times* (30 Aug 1976)

J.W. LePage: "Betsy Jolas," *Women Composers, Conductors, and Musicians of the Twentieth Century*, i (Metuchen, NJ, 1981), 103–15

B. Massin: "Betsy Jolas: Roland de Lassus me fascine," *Panorama-musiques*, no.41 (1981) [interview]

"Voir la musique," *L'âne*, no.10 (1983) [interview]

J.-P. Derrien, ed.: *20ème siècle: images de la musique française* (Paris, 1985), 143–5 [interview]

V. Perlis: "Recordings in Review: Betsy Jolas," *Yale Review* (1995), 179–85

J. Briscoe: "Betsy Jolas: Plupart du Temps II," *Contemporary Anthology of Music by Women* (Bloomington and Indianapolis, IN,1997)

B. Jolas: *Molto espressivo* (Paris, 1999) [collected writings]

JEREMY THURLOW/JAMES R. BRISCOE

Jolley, David (*b* Los Angeles, CA, 1948). Horn player. He moved from Los Angeles to New York, where he attended the Juilliard School (BM 1971, MM 1972). He was a founding member of the Orpheus Chamber Orchestra, with which he had made more than two dozen recordings by the early 2010s, at which time he was an emeritus member. In 1994 he organized the wind quintet Windscape. Other chamber groups with which Jolley has worked include the Guarneri Quartet, the Areopagitica Brass Trio, the American String Quartet, and the Beaux Arts Trio. Jolley's solo recordings include *Mozart: Horn Concertos* (Arabesque, 2004); *Strauss: Horn Concertos nos. 1 & 2* (Arabesque, 2006); *Villanelle: French Masterworks for Horn* (Arabesque, 2006); *Music for Horn* (Arabesque, 2008) featuring the work of Alec Wilder; and *Adagio & Allegro: German Romantic Works for Horn* (Arabesque, 2008). Recognition for Jolley's performing skills include the Concert Artists Guild award and the Top Prize at the Heldenleben International Horn Competition. Several composers have written works specifically for him, including Ellen Taaffe Zwilich (Concerto for Horn and String Orchestra), John Harbison (*Twilight Music*), and George Perle (Duo for Horn and String Quartet). He has served on the faculties of the Colburn School, the Hartt School, Manhattan School, Queens College–CUNY, the North Carolina School for the Arts, and Mannes College (from 1985).

PATRICK RICHARDS

Jolson, Al [Yoelson, Asa] (*b* Srednice [now Seredzius], Lithuania, ?26 May ?1886; *d* San Francisco, CA, 23 Oct 1950). Popular singer of Lithuanian birth. Jolson's father, Moshe, was a rabbi and cantor who immigrated to Washington, DC, in 1890. His family arrived in 1894;

soon after, young Al began appearing in burlesques and vaudeville in various partnerships that often included his older brother Harry (1882–1953). By 1906 he was performing as a vaudeville "single" and in 1908 he joined Lew Dockstader's Minstrels.

Since 1904 Jolson's act had included the performance of "coon songs" and comedic banter in blackface. These were incorporated into his first Broadway appearance in *La Belle Paree* (1911), a revue produced by the Shubert Brothers at their newly opened Winter Garden theater. Jolson would make the Winter Garden his Broadway home until 1925; by then, he had been billed as "the world's greatest entertainer" for almost ten years, a sobriquet earned through countless national tours and concert appearances. In *The Whirl of Society* (1912), he introduced his trademark blackfaced stage persona, "Gus," a good-hearted, mischievous servant or butler who deflates the pretensions of the society around him through wit and ingenuity. This show also incorporated a runway built from the back of the theater extending across the center of the Winter Garden auditorium; Jolson used this device to achieve an intense, almost erotic intimacy with audience members, who would often be led in singalongs or included in comedy routines.

His other Broadway shows included *Vera Violetta* (1911), *The Honeymoon Express* (1913), *Dancing Around* (1914), *Robinson Crusoe, Jr.* (1916), *Sinbad* (1918), *Bombo* (1921), and *Big Boy* (1925). All were loose-limbed extravaganzas that left plenty of room for comedic improvisation and interpolated songs. Among these were "Waiting for the Robert E. Lee," "You Made Me Love You" (the first song he performed on bent knee, a subsequent Jolson "bit"), "Rock-a-Bye Your Baby with a Dixie Melody," "Swanee," "Avalon," "My Mammy," "April Showers," "Toot, Toot, Tootsie," and "California, Here I Come." Critics were constantly awed by his ability to raise trivial songs and stale jokes to the level of folk myth. His recordings from this period as well exerted an enormous influence on subsequent generations of popular singers.

Jolson's appearances in two part-sound, part-silent films, *The Jazz Singer* (1927) and *The Singing Fool* (1928), marked the pinnacle of his career. "Sonny Boy," from the latter, was one of the first recordings to sell over a million copies. Subsequent films such as *Hallelujah, I'm a Bum* (1933), *Go into Your Dance* (1935), as well as two returns to Broadway in *Wonder Bar* (1931) and *Hold on to Your Hats*, were not nearly as successful as two film biographies made near the end of Jolson's life, *The Jolson Story* (1946), and *Jolson Sings Again* (1949), in which actor Larry Parks portrayed Jolson. These films featured Jolson's voice on the soundtrack and were the culmination of a renewed interest in his career engendered by his numerous performances for American servicemen during World War II. From 1947 to 1949 he hosted NBC's *Kraft Music Hall*, his only real success in series radio.

Jolson's infectious energy and childlike innocence were part of a melting pot of vocal characteristics he absorbed from a variety of theatrical traditions. He would glide as easily between singing, declamation, and speaking, within the course of a song, as he would shift between the mixed register production of an operatic tenor and the growling baritonal shouting of a blues singer. He made liberal use of *portamento, appoggiaturas*, and mordents, while his rhythmic and melodic inventiveness matched that of any "jazz" singer, as a comparison between the printed score and any of his recordings of a given song will demonstrate. Finally, his diction featured the nasal vowels, word-pulling ("belew" for blue), and aspirated attacks ("a-you") of the stereotypical Irish tenor. His best performances were recorded before his style became mannered in the 1920s.

For many, Jolson's role in *The Jazz Singer*, where he played a cantor's son who temporarily abandons the tradition of his ancestors to become a popular singer, embodied the paradox of the American immigrant who must negotiate a fine line between assimilation and authenticity. Contemporary scholars argue over whether Jolson's use of blackface—a trait shared with other entertainers of his era, both white (Eddie Cantor) and black (Bert Williams)—represented sincere empathy with another prominent group of American outsiders or was rather an attempt at appropriating "whiteness" by participating in a time-honored form of American entertainment. Nevertheless, many black performers and audiences appreciated his well-documented efforts to combat discrimination in the entertainment industry as well as his popularization of ragtime, jazz, and blues.

BIBLIOGRAPHY

H. Jolson: *Mistah Jolson* (Hollywood, 1951)
P. Sieben: *The Immortal Jolson: His Life and Times* (New York, 1962)
H.G. Goldman: *Jolson: the Legend Comes to Life* (New York, 1988)
L.F. Kiner: *Al Jolson: a Bio-Discography* (Metuchen, NJ, 1992)
J. Fisher: *Al Jolson: a Bio-Bibliography* (Bio-Bibliographies in the Performing Arts, no.48) (Westport, CT, 1994)
M. Alexander: *Jazz Age Jews* (Princeton, 2001)

HOWARD GOLDSTEIN

Jones. Family of jazz musicians.

1. HANK [HENRY] JONES (*b* Vicksburg, MS, 31 Aug 1918; *d* Bronx, NY, 16 May 2010). Jazz pianist. He grew up in Pontiac, Michigan, where he studied piano at an early age and came under the influence of Earl Hines, Fats Waller, Teddy Wilson, and Art Tatum. By the age of 13 he was performing locally in Michigan and Ohio. While playing with territory bands in Grand Rapids and Lansing he met the tenor saxophonist Lucky Thompson, who invited him to New York in 1944 to work at the Onyx Club with the trumpeter Hot Lips Page.

In New York Jones regularly listened to leading bop musicians and was inspired to master the new style. While practicing and studying the music he worked with John Kirby, Howard McGhee, Coleman Hawkins, Andy Kirk, and Billy Eckstine. In autumn 1947 he began touring in Norman Granz's Jazz at the Philharmonic concerts. From 1948 to 1953 he was accompanist for Ella Fitzgerald, developing a harmonic facility of extraordinary taste and sophistication. During this period he also made several historically important recordings with Charlie Parker for Verve.

After several years as a freelance player, which included engagements with Artie Shaw and Benny Goodman, and recordings with such artists as Lester Young, Milt Jackson, and Cannonball Adderley, in 1959 Jones joined the staff of CBS, where he stayed until the staff was disbanded 17 years later. He worked mostly with big bands such as the Ray Block Orchestra on the *Ed Sullivan Show*, but continued touring and recording with leading jazz groups. With his rare combination of talents as a strong soloist, sensitive accompanist, and adept sight-reader, Jones was always in great demand for recording sessions of all kinds and may be heard on thousands of albums. In the late 1970s his involvement as a pianist and conductor with the Broadway musical *Ain't Misbehavin'* (based on the music of Fats Waller) informed a wider audience of his unique qualities as a musician. Over the last several decades of his career, Jones achieved even greater renown as a thoughtful and elegant stylist, performing, recording, and touring internationally into his final years.

BIBLIOGRAPHY
GroveJ2
A.J. Smith: "The Impeccable Hank Jones," *DB*, xliii/11 (1976), 14
"Great Jazz Piano," *Swing Journal*, xxxi/7 (1977), 288 [discography]
L. Feather: "Piano Giants of Jazz: Hank Jones," *Contemporary Keyboard*, iv/2 (1978), 63
B. Primack and R. Dubin: "Detroit's Triple Gift to the Jazz Piano World," *Contemporary Keyboard*, v/12 (1979), 12
J. Réda: "Transparence de Hank Jones," *L'improviste* (Paris, 1980), 173
A. Sussman: "Hank Jones: Indefatigable Elegance," *DB*, xlviii/5 (1981), 23
S.-I. Iwamato: *Have you Met Mister Jones* (Tokyo, 1987) [discography]
D. Heckman: Obituary, *JT*, xxxix/1 (2010), 58–62
P. Keepnews: Obituary, *New York Times* (18 May 2010)

2. THAD(DEUS JOSEPH) JONES (*b* Pontiac, MI, 28 March 1923; *d* Copenhagen, Denmark, 20 Aug 1986). Jazz cornetist, flugelhorn player, composer, and bandleader. He taught himself trumpet from about the age of 13, and by the time he was 16 was playing professionally with his older brother, the pianist Hank Jones (*see* JONES family, (1)), and in summer jobs with Sonny Stitt. During the 1940s he played in midwestern dance and show bands, and in USO shows. From 1950 to 1953 he appeared with his younger brother, the drummer Elvin Jones (*see* JONES family, (3)), in Billy Mitchell's jazz quintet in Detroit. Thereafter he had important engagements in Charles Mingus's Jazz Composers' Workshop (1954–5) and the Count Basie Orchestra (1954–63).

In December 1965 Jones and the drummer Mel Lewis (*b* Buffalo, NY, 10 May 1929; *d* New York, NY, 2 Feb 1990) organized an outstanding 18-piece band which from February 1966 played regularly on Monday nights at the Village Vanguard, New York. This arrangement lasted for more than a decade and gave Jones ample opportunity to display his gifts as a conductor, composer, arranger, and flugelhorn soloist. Later the group also appeared in extended nightclub engagements and collegiate and festival concerts, and undertook tours to Japan, the USSR, and Europe. In 1979, after injuring his lip, Jones took up valve trombone. In that same year he ended his partnership with Lewis and moved to Denmark, where he established a new big band, the Thad Jones Eclipse, and led the Danish Radio Orchestra. He returned to the United States in 1985 to assume leadership of the Count Basie Orchestra, a position he held until February 1986.

Jones played cornet in the bop style with a compact, crisp tone, his improvised melodies often elaborating sequences with striking dissonances. With the Thad Jones–Mel Lewis Orchestra he concentrated on playing sustained, lyrical melodies on flugelhorn. His compositions provided substantial, flexible opportunities for the band's excellent soloists and have become a staple in the repertory of school stage bands. They cover a wide range of styles, exploring waltz rhythms, boogaloo, and ballad combinations, swing with traditional riffs or unpredictable melodies, bossa nova, bop, and jazz-rock. Dozens of them have been published by D'Accord Music, and his scores are held by the George P. Vanier Library of Concordia University, Montreal.

BIBLIOGRAPHY
GroveJ2
N. Hentoff: "They're all Talking about the Jones Boy," *DB*, xxii/23 (1955), 9
B. Coss: "Thad Jones: Horn of Plenty," *DB*, xxx/11 (1963), 16
D. Morgenstern: "The Big Bands: in New York...Signs of Life," *DB*, xxxiii/8 (1966), 19
I. Gitler: "Thad's Things," *DB*, xxxv/4 (1968), 18
L. Tompkins: "The Thad Jones Story," *CI*, x (1972), no.10, p.20; no.11, p.14
A. Smith: "Thad Jones Conducts an Interview," *DB*, xli/20 (1974), 14
"Thad Jones Discography," *Swing Journal*, xxviii/2 (1974), 262
C. Sheridan: "Greetings and Salutations," *JJI*, xxxi/6 (1978), 6 [Jones–Lewis discography]
M. Gordon: *Live at the Village Vanguard* (New York, 1980/*R*)
W.R. Stokes: "Thad Jones: at the Helm of the Basie Band," *JT* (1985), 10
O. Curth: "Untersuchungen zu Big Band Arrangements von Thad Jones für das Thad Jones–Mel Lewis Jazz Orchestra," *Jazzforschung*, xxii (1990), 53
L.T. Petruzzi: *Lead Trumpet Performance in the Thad Jones–Mel Lewis Jazz Orchestra: an Analysis of Style and Performance Practices* (diss., New York U., 1993)
L. Gourse, "In the Heyday of the Studio Musician, Thad Jones and Mel Lewis start a big band at the Village Vanguard," *Massachusetts Review*, xxxix/4 (1998), 585–95

3. ELVIN (RAY) JONES (*b* Pontiac, MI, 9 Sept 1927; *d* Englewood, NJ, 18 May 2004). Jazz drummer. He began his professional career playing in local bands in Pontiac and Detroit. From 1946 to 1949 he was a member of the US Army and played in military bands. After returning to Michigan he resumed his professional career and performed with various bands in the area, including some organized by his brother Thad Jones (*see* JONES family, (2)), and occasionally toured. In 1956 he moved to New York, where he began to establish a reputation as a dynamic drummer in the tradition of Art Blakey. Among the most notable groups and individuals with whom he recorded or performed during this period were the J.J. Johnson Quintet, the Donald Byrd Quintet, Harry Edison, Bud Powell, Sonny Rollins, and Stan Getz.

In 1960 Jones joined the John Coltrane Quartet, beginning a five-year association that became one of the most significant in jazz history. The innovative performances and recordings of this group, led by Coltrane at the height of his powers, established the standard for excellence in the modal, open-form style of this period. During his years with Coltrane, Jones emerged as the premier jazz drummer of the 1960s and brought his unique style to a state of maturity which irrevocably altered the nature of jazz drumming.

After leaving Coltrane, Jones formed several trios, quartets, and sextets, occasionally in conjunction with Coltrane's former bass player Jimmy Garrison. These groups usually dispensed with a pianist and characteristically consisted of one and often two saxophonists, a strong bass player, and Jones on drums. Among the musicians who frequently played and recorded with Jones's groups were the saxophonists Joe Farrell, Frank Foster, and George Coleman, and the bass players Garrison, Bill Wood, Wilbur Little, and Gene Perla. Jones's groups appeared throughout the United States and Europe and conducted major tours of South America and Asia. In 1970 Jones appeared in the film *Zachariah*. He continued to pursue an active performing and recording career in his later years, often recording and performing with his own group, Elvin Jones Jazz Machine, which included such players as Ravi Coltrane and Sonny Fortune; he also taught regularly and gave frequent drum clinics.

Jones's style was a logical extension of the bop approach established by Kenny Clarke and Max Roach and modified by Art Blakey. In bop drumming a repeated rhythmic pattern is maintained only on the ride and hi-hat cymbals, the remaining instruments being used to mark the main structural divisions of the performance, to articulate the solo improvisation, and to interject counter-rhythmic motifs against the prevailing regular pulse. Blakey, while adhering to this general style, altered it by increasing the level of activity of the accompanying drums and utilizing a greater number of cross rhythms in his interjected patterns. Jones built on Blakey's techniques and added new ones to the extent that the fundamental role of the drummer changed from that of an accompanist to one of an equal collaborative improviser. Jones played several metrically contrasting rhythms simultaneously, each of which was characterized by irregularly shifting accents that were independent of the basic pulse. Of particular note was Jones's ingenious mixture of playing irregularly accented half-, quarter-, eighth-, and 16th-note triplet subdivisions over an extended period as a means of generating a wide array of poly-rhythms. An excellent example of this technique can be heard on "Nuttin' Out Jones," recorded by the Jones–Garrison Sextet (from the album *Illumination*, Imp., 1963). In addition Jones shaped the background counter-rhythmic motifs associated with bop drumming into extended coherent musical statements with a logical internal development of their own (a classic example may be heard in "Part I: Acknowledgement" on Coltrane's *A Love Supreme*, Imp., 1964).

Jones's techniques resulted in dense percussive textures characterized by greater diversity of timbre, heightened polyrhythmic activity, and increased intensity and volume. Moreover, as the richness of these composite textures made it difficult to discern the basic pulse, they contributed to the development of a new style of "free improvisation" which underplayed or dispensed with regular pulse altogether (as on Coltrane's *Ascension*, Imp., 1965). The salient aspects of Jones's style were adopted by many avant-garde drummers of the late 1960s and 1970s. Ultimately Jones's innovations gave the drummer a broader role in ensemble playing, as a collaborative improviser and as the principal architect of large-scale, organically evolving percussive textures, while removing the emphasis on timekeeping.

BIBLIOGRAPHY

GroveJ2
M. Hennessey: "The Emancipation of Elvin Jones," *DB*, xxxiii/6 (1966), 23–5
R. Kettle: "Re: Elvin Jones: a Technical Analysis of the Poll-winning Drummer's Recorded Solos," *DB*, xxxiii/16 (1966), 17
I. Gitler: "Playing the Truth: Elvin Jones," *DB*, xxxvi/20 (1969), 12
B. Mintz: *Different Drummers* (New York, 1975)
B. Cole: *John Coltrane* (New York, 1976)
"Elvin Jones," *SJ*, xxx/1 (1976), 280; xxxii/4 (1978), 290 [discography]
F. Kofsky: "Elvin Jones: Rhythmic Displacement in the Art of Elvin Jones," *JJS*, iv (1977), 11–32
R. Mattingly: "Elvin," *Modern Drummer*, vi/9 (1982), 8–13, 42–51
R. Mattingly: "Elvin Jones: Once More, with Feeling," *Modern Drummer*, xvi/5 (1992), 22–7, 53–66
A. Kahn: "Elvin Jones: at this Point in Time," *JT*, xxxii/9 (2002), 40–47
K. Micallef: "Elvin Jones: the Legend Only Grows," *Modern Drummer*, xxvi/7 (2002), 52–8, 60–66

BILL DOBBINS/R (1), BARRY KERNFELD/R (2), OLLY WILSON/R (3)

Jones, Alton (*b* Fairfield, NE, 3 Aug 1899; *d* New York, NY, 2 Jan 1971). Pianist and teacher. After studying piano with Paul van Katwijk and composition with WALLINGFORD RIEGGER at Drake University (BM 1919) he attended the Institute of Musical Art, New York, where he studied piano with EDWIN HUGHES and RICHARD BUHLIG (diploma 1921). He made his orchestral début playing Liszt's Concerto in E♭ with the American Orchestral Society in New York in 1924, and his recital debut the following year at Aeolian Hall (New York). He performed frequently with orchestras in Europe and the United States, including the New York PO in 1949, and gave 25 recitals at Town Hall (New York) between 1925 and 1955. His repertory, chiefly of 19th- and 20th-century compositions, included works by MacDowell and Riegger. An important teacher, he taught at Columbia University (summers, 1929–41) and at the Juilliard School from 1921 until his death.

R. ALLEN LOTT

Jones, Bessie (*b* Smithville, GA, 8 Feb 1902; *d* Brunswick, GA, 4 Sept 1984). Folksinger. She spent her childhood in Dawson, Georgia, where she was brought up by her grandparents; they had been slaves, and she learned a large repertory of traditional African American songs from them. In 1933 she moved to St. Simons Island, Georgia, where many African traditions have survived;

she joined a local group, the GEORGIA SEA ISLAND SINGERS, which made several recordings. In the 1950s and 1960s she toured both with the singers and independently, performing at the Newport Folk Festival, the Smithsonian Institution's Festival of American Folklife, and Expo 67 in Montreal. She appeared in several documentary films on African American folk subjects, and her vast repertory of children's game songs was recorded on videotape by the Smithsonian; some of these are included in her book *Step it Down: Games, Plays, Songs, and Stories from the Afro-American Heritage* (New York, 1972), written with Bess Lomax Hawes. In 1976 Jones taught a course on African American folk traditions at Yale University. She was awarded a National Heritage Fellowship by the NEA in 1982.

BIBLIOGRAPHY
M.J. Sanna: In Retrospect: Bessie Jones, Singing for the Ancestors, *BPM*, xiii/1 (1995), 91–114

DANIEL SHEEHY/R

Jones, Bill T. [William Tass Jones] (*b* Bunnell, FL, 15 Feb 1952). Dancer, choreographer, designer, author, and company director. He did not begin his dance training until his freshman year in college, at the State University of New York at Binghamton. There he met Arnie Zane (1948–88), who became his companion and collaborator for seventeen years. After creating their first dance together, *Pas de Deux for Two* (1973; music by Benny Goodman), they founded American Dance Asylum in 1974, for which they created both individual and collaborative choreographies. Prior to founding the Bill T. Jones/Arnie Zane Dance Company in 1982, Jones choreographed and performed nationally and internationally as a soloist and as a duo with Zane. In addition to making more than fifty works for his own company, he has created dances for numerous American and European ballet, modern dance, and opera companies. Many of his works are set to music by American composers or to audio collages of music and spoken text. Characteristic of his early work with Zane are *Monkey Run Road* (1979; music by Helen Thorington, text by Jones, set and costumes by Jones and Zane) and *Intuitive Momentum* (1983; music by Max Roach and Connie Crothers). Notable among his later works are *Last Supper at Uncle Tom's Cabin/The Promised Land* (1990; music by Julius Hemphill, text by various authors) and *Fondly Do We Hope…Fervently Do We Pray* (2009), an evening-length, multi-disciplinary work exploring the legacy of Abraham Lincoln.

BIBLIOGRAPHY
E. Zimmer and S. Quasha, eds.: *Body against Body: The Dance and Other Collaborations of Bill T. Jones and Arnie Zane* (New York, 1989)
B.T. Jones with P. Gillespie: *Last Night on Earth* (New York, 1995)
A. Rasminsky: "Tackling the Future: Bill T. Jones's Company at 25," *Dance Magazine* (1 Feb 2009)

CLAUDE CONYERS

Jones, Bobby (*b* Henry, TN, 18 Sept 1938). Gospel music television and radio host, singer, choir director, and media executive. He began singing publicly in the Methodist church as a child, although his first exposure to gospel music came in sanctified churches. His involvement with gospel music deepened in Nashville when he served as keyboard player, singer, and director for church and civic choirs while studying at Tennessee State University. In 1978 Jones recorded the first of many albums with his small ensemble, the New Life Singers, whose aesthetic leaned more toward contemporary Christian music than black gospel. Around this time he began hosting children's and gospel music shows on Nashville television stations. In 1980 Black Entertainment Television began broadcasting one of these programs, *Bobby Jones Gospel*. The popular program has featured performances by Jones's ensembles, established gospel stars, and up-and-coming gospel artists. Firmly within the gospel entrepreneurial tradition, Jones's other enterprises include music festivals, workshops, radio shows, the gospel opera *Make a Joyful Noise* (which Jones wrote and performed in for PBS in 1982), inspirational and autobiographical books, and film appearances. His many honors include Dove, Grammy, and Stellar awards. Interested in preserving gospel music history, Jones has donated his television archives to Tennessee State University and has served on the board of directors for a gospel museum in Florida. Although his recording career has spanned four decades, his primary impact on the gospel music industry has been as a television personality. His willingness to embrace non-religious venues and media spaces may have contributed to his massive popularity.

BIBLIOGRAPHY
B. Jones and L. Sussman: *Make a Joyful Noise: My 25 Years in Gospel Music* (New York, 2000)
"Bobby Jones: Gospel Music on the Rise," <http://www.npr.org/templates/story/story.php?storyId=4984337> (2013) [audio archive and transcript of radio program first broadcast in 2005]
C. Waldron: "Dr. Bobby Jones: Ambassador of Gospel Celebrates 30 Years of TV, Music Success," *JET* (11 Aug 2008)

CARRIE ALLEN TIPTON

Jones, Charles (*b* Tamworth, ON, 21 June 1910; *d* New York, NY, 6 June 1997). Composer. He studied violin at the Institute of Musical Art in New York (1928–32) and composition under BERNARD WAGENAAR at the Juilliard School (diploma 1939). He taught at Mills College (1939–44), the Music Academy of the West, Santa Barbara (1949–54), the Aspen Music School (from 1951), the Juilliard School (1954–60, 1973), and the Mannes College of Music (from 1972), where he became chairman of the composition department in 1973. Jones was a prolific composer. The diatonic and neoclassical tendencies of his early works, dating from the 1930s and 1940s, gave way to an increased complexity and chromaticism. All his music is marked by a keen lyrical sense and a prevalence of long melodic lines. Of his more significant compositions, the oratorio *Piers the Plowman* (1963) was commissioned and first performed by the Interracial Chorus of New York. The Second Symphony was written to fulfill the Copley Award of 1956 and, like several others of his pieces, was introduced at the Aspen Festival. A recording of the Sixth

Quartet with the Sonatina for violin and piano was sponsored by the Ford Foundation.

WORKS

Orch: Suite, str orch, 1937; Suite, small orch, 1937; Sym. no.1, 1939; Portrait of the Park, band, 1957; Suite after a Notebook of 1762, chbr orch, 1957; Sym. no.2, 1957; Sym. no.3, 1962; Conc., 4 vn, orch, 1963; Sym. no.4, 1965; Allegory, divided orch, 1970; other orch works

Chbr and inst: 6 str qts, 1936, 1944, 1951, 1954, 1961, 1970; Serenade, fl, vn, vc, hpd, 1973; Triptychon, vn, va, pf, 1975; Str Qt no.7, 1978; Pf Trio, 1982; Meditation, b cl, pf, 1982; Str Qt no.8, 1984; other chbr works

Kbd: Sonata no.1, pf, 1946; Sonata, 2 pf, 1947; Sonata no.2, pf, 1950; Kbd Book, hpd, 1953; Sonata, pf 4 hands, 1984; other pf works

Vocal: Piers the Plowman (W. Langland), T, chorus, orch, 1963; other vocal and choral works

Principal publisher: Peters

BIBLIOGRAPHY

EwenD

STEVEN E. GILBERT

Jones, Dolly [Doli; Doll; Hutchinson, Dolly; Armenra, Dolly; Armena, Doli] (*b* Chicago, IL, *c*1906; *d* ?Philadelphia, PA). Trumpeter and cornetist. Little is known about certain details of her life, except that she was the daughter of the female trumpeter Diyah [Diyer] Jones. She began her career as a member of the family band, which recruited Josephine Baker to dance with them around 1919. She was one of the first female jazz trumpeters to be heard on record. She recorded "When"/"That Creole Band" (1926, OK) as a soloist and a member of Al Wynn's Creole Jazz Band; it may have been her only release. She spent much of her life in Chicago, where she played with Ma Rainey's group in the mid-1920s. After marrying Jimmy Hutchinson she began to use his surname; later she returned to "Dolly Jones" and also used the surname Armenra, sometimes with variant spellings. By the middle of the next decade, she was performing regularly with Lil Armstrong's band. She made a notable appearance in Oscar Micheaux's all-black short film, *Swing!* (1938). She also worked with Mezz Mezzrow, Sammy Price, and Eddie Durham. She eventually moved to Philadelphia, where she played locally into the 1970s. Her playing was known for its sweetness and nuance. Scholars, contemporaries, and discographers point to her lack of showmanship as one of the reasons she did not become more well known, but Jones's struggle to gain acceptance in the male-dominated world of jazz appears a more likely explanation.

BIBLIOGRAPHY

GroveJ

L. Dahl: *Stormy Weather: the Music and Lives of a Century of Jazz-women* (New York, 1984)

S. Tucker: "Beyond the Brass Ceiling: Dolly Jones Trumpets Modernity in Oscar Micheaux's *Swing!*" *Jazz Perspectives*, iii/1 (2009), 3–34

JONAS WESTOVER

Jones, Edwin Arthur (*b* Stoughton, MA, 28 June 1853; *d* Stoughton, MA, 9 Jan 1911). Composer, teacher, and violinist. After studying violin, organ, and harmony at the New England Conservatory he attended Dartmouth College, where he was organist for the Handel Society, concertmaster of the orchestra, and director of the glee club. His first major composition, *The Farewell Waltzes*, was published in Baltimore in 1874 in an arrangement for piano; in 1880 his First String Quartet was given its première at the Peabody Institute, where it was well received.

The following year Jones returned to Stoughton, where he spent the remainder of his life teaching music, playing violin in his own orchestra, and composing. He wrote more than 40 works, including orchestral overtures and marches, string quartets, string trios, some songs and short choral works, the cantata *Song of our Savior* (1881), and an oratorio, *Easter Concert* (1890). An ardent admirer of Handel's music, Jones wrote in a style that is an unusual mixture of Baroque and Classical models.

WORKS
(selective list)

Vocal: Supposing, op.11, 1v, pf, 1878; Song of our Savior (cant.), op.14, solo vv, chorus, org, orch, 1881 [rev. of The Nativity Hymn, 1879]; Wake, Maiden, Wake (K. Sanborn), op.16, male chorus, pf (Northampton, MA, 1881); Old Stoughton, op.18 4 vv (Boston, 1886); Up the Hillside, op.20, 4vv (Boston, 1886); Love Hailed a Little Maid, op.26, 1v, pf, 1888; Snowflakes, op.27, 1v, pf, 1888; Easter Concert (orat.), op.28, solo vv, chorus, pf (Boston, 1890) [rev. of Easter Anthem, 1887]; Hail, Smiling Morn!, op.33, B, chbr ens, inc.

Orch: Dedication March, op.15, 1881; Suite ancienne, op.17, 1886; Invocations and Benediction, op.35; Lochinvar, ov., op.38

Chamber: Duo, op.1, 2 vn, 1871; 2 trios, op.2, pf, vn, db, 1871; The Farewell Waltzes, op.8, pf (Baltimore, 1874) [rev. of version for chamber ensemble, 1871–2]; 2 str trios, op.12, 1878; Str Qt no.1, op.13, 1880; Str Qt no.2, op.22, 1887; Lament, op.24, str qt, 1888; Minuet and Trio, op.39, str trio

MSS *in Old Stoughton Musical Society, Stoughton, MA*

BIBLIOGRAPHY

L.W. Standish, ed.: *The Old Stoughton Musical Society* (Stoughton, MA, 1929)

M. Jones and F.W. Reynolds: *History of the Musical Society in Stoughton* (Stoughton, 1970)

R.L. Hall: *E. A. Jones: his Life and Music* (Stoughton, 1984)

ROGER L. HALL

Jones, George (Glenn) (*b* Saratoga, TX, 12 Sept 1931; *d* Nashville, TN, 26 April 2013). Country music singer and songwriter. Growing up near Beaumont, Texas, he drew his earliest inspiration from church music and such country-music singers as Lefty Frizzell, Roy Acuff, and Hank Williams. After a stint in the marine corps, Jones was signed to Starday Records in 1954 and began an association with the producer and manager Pappy Daily which lasted through 1968. During that period he developed a distinctive and much admired vocal style exploiting extreme contrasts in register and dynamics and often singing with his teeth clenched and throat constricted to maximize the emotional effect of his songs. With the success of his recordings for Starday, Mercury-Starday, Mercury, United Artists, and Musicor, Jones became a champion for traditional hard-core country music. In 1969 he married the country-music singer TAMMY WYNETTE and their recordings for Epic, produced by Billy Sherrill, molded the pair into one of the most successful country-music duos until their divorce in 1975. Throughout the 1960s and 1970s, however, drug, alcohol, and marital problems took their toll, causing Jones to cancel hundreds of shows, earning him the nickname No-Show Jones. In 1983 Jones married Nancy Sepulvada and began his detoxification and rehabilitation. He was elected to the Country Music Hall of Fame in 1992. Despite living out the difficulties he often portrayed in song, he survived his addictions and in 1999 published his autobiography, *I Lived to Tell it All*. He was widely respected by fellow performers and often regarded as the greatest country-music singer.

SELECTED RECORDINGS
As leader: Why Baby Why? (Starday, 1955); White Lightning (Mer., 1958); The Window up Above (Mer., 1960); She thinks I still care (UA, 1962); Things have gone to pieces (Musicor, 1965); with T. Wynette: We're gonna hold on (Epic, 1973); He stopped loving her today (Epic, 1980); The One I Loved Back Then (The Corvette Song) (Epic, 1985); I am what I am (Epic, 1980)

BIBLIOGRAPHY
B. Allen: *George Jones: the Saga of an American Singer* (Garden City, NY, 1984)
D. Carlisle: *Ragged but Right: the Life and Times of George Jones* (Chicago, 1984)
G. Jones: *I Lived to Tell it All* (New York, 1997)
N. Gibson: *The Starday Story: the House that Country Music Built* (Jackson, 2011)
BILL C. MALONE/NATHAN D. GIBSON

Jones, Grace [Mendoza, Grace] (*b* Spanish Town, Jamaica, 19 May?1952). Singer, model, and actress of Jamaican birth. Jones and her siblings were raised in Jamaica by strict Pentecostal grandparents. At the age of 12, she joined her parents in Syracuse, New York, later studying theater and drama at Syracuse University. She signed with Island Records in 1977 and released three critically acclaimed disco albums, *Portfolio*, *Fame*, and *Muse*. Jones then moved in more exploratory directions with *Warm Leatherette* and *Nightclubbing*, which contained one of her biggest hits, "Pull Up to the Bumper." Both albums were collaborations with Sly Dunbar and Robbie Shakespeare, with whom she again worked on *Hurricane* (2008) alongside Brian Eno and Tricky. Jones's performance practice has consistently involved collaborations with visual artists, including Andy Warhol, Jean-Paul Goude, and Keith Haring, and her earlier studies in theater and extensive training as a fashion model have ensured spectacularly visual concert performances characterized by multilayered explorations and subversions of gender, sexual, and racial stereotypes.

BIBLIOGRAPHY
L. Norment: "The Outrageous Grace Jones," *Ebony* (July 1979), 84–94
M. Kershaw: "Postcolonialism and Androgyny: the Performance Art of Grace Jones," *Art Journal*, lvi/4 (1997), 19–25
M.J. Gutzman: *Grace Jones in "One Man Show": Music and Culture* (diss., Ohio U., 2007)
LISA MACKINNEY

Jones, Grandpa [Louis Marshall] (*b* Niagra, KY, 20 Oct 1913; *d* Nashville, TN, 19 Feb 1998). Country music singer, guitarist, and banjoist. During a professional career lasting almost 70 years, Grandpa Jones remained an energetic and popular country musician who self-consciously practiced older, traditional country and gospel music and country comedy. The son of a Kentucky sharecropper, he began his professional singing career in Akron, Ohio in 1929, performing with a number of local groups that appealed to the area's transplanted southerners. In the 1930s, he gained the nickname "Grandpa," owing to his high-pitched, peevish on-air voice, and began wearing spectacles and a false mustache, in keeping with a tradition of country performers purposely donning rustic costumes and adopting personaes to match their music.

In the 1940s, at Cincinnati radio station WLW, he met Merle Travis and the Delmore Brothers; together, they formed one of country music's most popular gospel quartets, the Brown's Ferry Four. Travis and Jones became the first singers to record for Cincinnati's King label in 1943, and two of Jones's recordings, "Eight More Miles to Louisville" (1946) and "Old Rattler" (1947), propelled him to nationwide fame. With "Mountain Dew" (1947), his success as a banjo-playing comedian was confirmed. In 1946, Jones married Ramona Riggins, a fiddler and mandolinist, and the two began working together. They moved to Nashville in 1952 and became regular members of the *"Grand Ole Opry,"* which Jones had first appeared upon in the late 1940s.

Jones and Wiggins continued to focus their attention on traditional country music, tapping into the folk music revival of the 1960s by recording a series of brilliant albums produced by Fred Foster for the Monument label. In 1969, he became a central figure on the long-running national television show HEE HAW, where he frequently collaborated with fellow country comedienne Minnie Pearl. With Buck Owens, Kenny Price, and Roy Clark, he formed the Hee Haw Gospel Quartet, modeled on the Brown's Ferry Four, and the new group became one of the most commercially successful country-gospel groups of the 1970s. In the mid-1970s, concerned about the shifting musical identity of country music, Jones became active in the Association of Country Entertainers, the aim of which was to counter modernizing influences on the genre. Jones continued to perform on television shows and in concert until his death, suffering a stroke after performing twice in one day on the *"Grand Ole Opry"* in 1998. He was elected to the Country Music Hall of Fame in 1978.

BIBLIOGRAPHY
C. Wolfe: "The Music of Grandpa Jones," *Journal of Country Music*, viii/3 (1981), 47
L.M. Jones and C. Wolfe: *Everybody's Grandpa: Fifty Years Behind the Mike* (Knoxville, TN, 1984)
J. Aylesworth: *The Corn Was Green: the Inside Story of Hee Haw* (Jefferson, NC, 2010)
CHARLES K. WOLFE/CLAY MOTLEY

Jones, Dame Gwyneth (*b* Pontnewynydd, Wales, 7 November 1936). Welsh soprano. She studied at the Royal College of Music in London, with A. Smith and Ruth Packer, and at Accademia Musicale Chigiana in Siena and the International Opera Studio in Zurich with

Maria Carpi. She made her debut in Zurich as a mezzo-soprano in Gluck's *Orfeo ed Eurydice* (1962). She then sang Lady Macbeth (1963) and Leonore in *Fidelio* (1964) for the Welsh National Opera and was a member of the Royal Opera from 1963, singing both Lady Macbeth and Oktavian (*Der Rosenkavalier*) on tour and making her Covent Garden debut substituting for Leontyne Price in Verdi's *Il trovatore*. From 1977 she made frequent appearances in Vienna, Rome, Munich, Milan, San Francisco, and Chicago. She made her New York debut in a concert performance of Cherubini's *Médée* in 1966 and first performed at the Metropolitan Opera in 1972, as Sieglinde in *Die Walküre*. Jones appeared frequently at the Bayreuth Festival, making her debut in 1966, also as Sieglinde. Her roles at Bayreuth included Eva in *Die Meistersinger*, Kundry in *Parsifal*, Elizabeth/Venus in *Tannhäuser*, Senta in *Der Fliegende Holländer*, and Brünnhilde in the centenary production of the *Ring* (1976).

In 2000 Jones turned to directing, in which capacity she made her debut with *Der fliegende Holländer* in Weimar in 2003. She has been active as a teacher and has led frequent master classes; she has also served as an adjudicator. She has continued to add roles to her repertory, concentrating on new productions of contemporary works, as well as Strauss operas, and has performed frequently in concert and on the stage in Europe. She has expanded her range as well, exploring mezzo and contralto roles. She was awarded the CBE in 1976 and a knighthood in 1986. She has received numerous additional awards and honorary degrees.

KAREN M. BRYAN

Jones, Irving (*b* c1874; *d* c1932). Stage performer and composer. He appeared on stage as a comic performer throughout his adult life, touring mainstream vaudeville and minstrel show circuits. His breakout performance occurred in 1890 during his tenure with Sam T. Jack's Creole Burlesque Company. He later toured with such high-profile groups as the Black Patti Troubadours (1900) and the Famous Georgia Minstrels (1925). Jones's early compositions, such as "Possumala Dance" (1894), emerged before the height of the COON SONG craze on Tin Pan Alley and are notable for their use of ragtime's rhythmic elements. "Home ain't nothing like this" (1902) was also popular and was adopted by other well-known African American performers such as Ernest Hogan. Other songs including "My money never gives out" and "The Ragtime Millionaire" evoked the caricature of the black dandy common in the minstrel show; "The Ragtime Millionaire" was also one of the first to evoke "the blues," linking Jones to the later style. Jones did not appear to take issue with the negative associations of the coon song. He occasionally used the genre to address political issues, as in "I want a Filipino man" (1899), which offered satirical commentary about the US acquisition of the Philippines. Jones's musical production waned with the decline of the coon song, but he remained a popular and active performer until his death.

BIBLIOGRAPHY

SouthernB

D. Janson and G. Jones: *Spreadin' Rhythm Around: Black Popular Songwriters, 1880–1930* (New York, 1998)

L. Abbott and D. Seroff: *Ragged but Right: Black Traveling Shows, "Coon Songs" and the Dark Pathway to Blues and Jazz* (Jackson, MI, 2007)

BRANDI A. NEAL

Jones, Jo(nathan David Samuel) (*b* Chicago, IL, 7 Oct 1911; *d* New York, NY, 3 Sept 1985). Jazz drummer. He grew up in Alabama and toured as an instrumentalist and tap-dancer with various carnival shows. In 1934 he began his long association with COUNT BASIE. He left Basie briefly in 1936 to join Walter Page in the Jeter-Pillars Orchestra in St. Louis, but by the end of the year both musicians had returned to Basie's group. When guitarist Freddie Green replaced Claude Williams in 1937, Basie's celebrated four-member rhythm section was complete and soon became the most outstanding and influential of its time. Jones appeared in the film *Jammin' the Blues* in 1944. Apart from a period in the army (1944–6), he remained with Basie until 1948, when he began a varied and active freelance career with many mainstream jazz musicians, revealing an uncommon mastery of swing and modern drumming styles. In 1947 he made the first of several tours with Jazz at the Philharmonic; the organization took him to Europe a number of times and led to his recording with such musicians as Billie Holiday, Teddy Wilson, Duke Ellington, Johnny Hodges, Lester Young, Art Tatum, and Benny Goodman. Later he performed and recorded on many occasions in groups modeled on Basie's "Kansas City" ensembles.

Jones is generally credited with transferring the basic pulse in jazz from the bass drum to the hi-hat, which he left slightly open to produce a light, continuous sound unlike the staccato ideal of earlier jazz drumming. This novel technique, which was fully developed by the time he made his first recordings with Basie in 1936, including "Shoe Shine Boy" (Voc.), completely revolutionized the timbre of the jazz rhythm section, making it more subtle and responsive to solo improvisation than had earlier been the case. Recordings with Basie, notably "Swingin' the Blues" (Decca, 1938), also show that he had conceived of the jazz pulse as four evenly stressed beats in a bar, thus helping to establish the four-beat jazz that characterized the later swing period; late in life he recorded the double album *The Drums* (Jazz Odyssey, 1973), giving a uniquely detailed demonstration of swing percussion techniques. By concentrating the pulse in the hi-hat, Jones freed his other instruments for irregular accents such as the rim-shots and bass drum bombs for which he became famous (ex. 1). He was also among the first jazz drummers to realize the full potential of the brushes, which he used with remarkable facility. Though not given to long solos in the manner of his contemporaries Chick Webb, Gene Krupa, and Cozy Cole, Jones was an expert soloist; his varied phrase lengths, free handling of the bass drum, and avoidance of auxiliary instruments such as woodblocks and cowbells foreshadowed future developments in jazz drumming. As adapted by Kenny Clarke and other drummers of the bop school, Jones's innovations became an integral part of modern jazz.

Ex.1

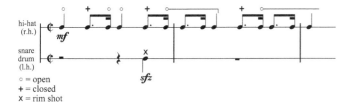

hi-hat (r.h.)
mf
snare drum (l.h.)
sfz
○ = open
+ = closed
x = rim shot

BIBLIOGRAPHY

GroveJ2 (J.B. Robinson and B. Kernfeld)

W. Balliett: "Jo Jones, Dms.," *Dinosaurs in the Morning* (Philadelphia, 1962/*R*), 61–7

T.D. Brown: *A History and Analysis of Jazz Drumming to 1942* (diss., U. of Michigan, 1976)

S. Dance: "Jo Jones," *The World of Count Basie* (New York, 1980), 47–59

C. Stern: "Papa Jo," Modern Drummer, viii/1 (1984), 8–13

Obituary, J. Pareles, *New York Times* (5 Sept 1985)

G. Schuller: The Swing Era: the Development of Jazz, 1930–1945 (New York, 1989)

B. Korall: Drummin' Men: the Heartbeat of Jazz: the Swing Years (New York, 1990)

"Jo Jones," *JazzTimes*, xxv/9 (Nov 1995), 56–9

Oral history material in *NEij* and *NH*

J. BRADFORD ROBINSON/R

Jones, Joe (*b* New York, NY, 19 June 1934; *d* Wiesbaden, Germany, 9 Feb 1993). Composer, artist, and instrument builder. Brought up in Brooklyn, he attended the Hartnett School of Music in Manhattan and studied composition with EARLE BROWN. In the late 1950s he was a student in JOHN CAGE's experimental music class at the New School for Social Research. Associated with Fluxus, an international avant-garde art movement, he became famous for his kinetic sculptures, which range from single instruments to mechanical orchestras.

Jones built his first automatic mechanical musical instruments in 1962. *Fluxorchestra* consisted of self-playing whistles, reeds, horns, violins, bells, gongs, and other instruments; *Mechanical Violin* (1968) used both traditional instruments, and toys and other suspended objects driven by electric motors. Several of Jones's smaller instruments were included in "Fluxus Yearboxes," mass-produced collections of Fluxus art, music, and other materials. These sometimes contained short filmstrips called "Fluxfilms" that could by seen through eye viewers. Several films by artists such as Jones, Yoko Ono, and Mieko (Chieko) Shomi are minimalist, slow-motion depictions of everyday activities. In *Smoking* (Fluxfilm no.18), for example, Jones exhales smoke from a cigarette. In 1969 Jones opened the Music Store in Manhattan, a shop in which his self-playing mechanical instruments could be activated by visitors or passersby. Several Fluxus events featuring John Lennon and Yoko Ono took place in this venue. Jones left New York in 1972, eventually settling in Wiesbaden. A retrospective exhibition of his work was held at the DAAD Galerie, Berlin in 1990.

BIBLIOGRAPHY

Grovel (H. Davies)

Joe Jones: Music Machines from the Sixties until Now (Berlin, 1990)

R. van Peer: *Interviews with Sound Artists: Taking Part in the Festival Echo, the Images of Sound II* (Eindhoven, 1993), 9–22

D. Senn: "Systems for Nonlinear Instruments and Notation," *Journal of New Music Research*, xxiii/3 (1994), 209–34

F. Gertich: "Real erklingender Mechanismus," *NZM*, clvi/2 (1995), 4–13

T. Kellein: *Fluxus* (London, 1995)

DAVID W. BERNSTEIN/R

Jones, Mason (*b* Hamilton, NY, 16 June 1919; *d* Wynnewood, PA, 19 Feb 2009). Horn player. He attended the Curtis Institute (1936–8), where he was a pupil of MARCEL TABUTEAU and FRITZ REINER, and joined the Philadelphia Orchestra at Eugene Ormandy's invitation in 1938. He was its principal horn from 1940 until he retired in 1978. He also worked as its personnel manager (1963–86) and conductor of its in-school concerts. Jones appeared as a soloist and made recordings with the orchestra, as well as with the Philadelphia Woodwind Quintet and the Philadelphia Brass Ensemble. His publications include editions of solos and orchestral studies for horn. In 1946 he was appointed to the faculty of the Curtis Institute, where he served as professor of horn for 49 years. Jones's playing is characterized by great warmth and naturalness and by a rare cantabile quality. A total control of the dynamic possibilities of his instrument enabled him to achieve a particularly expressive sound.

BIBLIOGRAPHY

J. Kirschen: "A Profile of Mason Jones," *The Horn Call*, xxvi/2 (1996), 27–30

MARTHA WOODWARD/R

Jones (Shankar), (Geethali) Norah (*b* Brooklyn, NY, 30 March 1979). Singer-songwriter and musician, daughter of the concert producer Sue Jones and the Indian sitar player RAVI SHANKAR. She grew up in New York and Texas. She won several DownBeat Student Music Awards in high school and furthered her jazz training at the University of North Texas. In 1999 she signed with Blue Note Records and moved to New York. Her debut album, *First Sessions*, was released in 2001, but she did not gain critical acclaim until *Come away with me* (BN, 2002), which sold more than 20 million copies and earned five Grammy Awards (2003). Although Jones's subsequent solo albums have not matched this success, they have been well received by critics. Jones is noted for her eclectic mix of styles. *Come away with me* features a blend of mellow, acoustic pop with soul and jazz, while *Feels like Home* (BN, 2004) has a distinct country influence, which is also heard in her recordings with the Little Willies. Jones changed direction again in 2007 with the release of an album with the rock band El Madmo. *Featuring* (BN, 2010) is a compilation of collaborations with musicians such as Willie Nelson, Outkast, Dolly Parton, and Herbie Hancock.

COLETTE SIMONOT

Jones, Philly Joe [Joseph Rudolph] (*b* Philadelphia, PA, 15 July 1923; *d* Philadelphia, PA, 30 Aug 1985). Drummer.

He acquired the nickname "Philly" from the clarinetist Tony Scott while working at Minton's Playhouse in New York in 1953. Scott used the nickname, which refers the city of Philadelphia where Jones had grown up, to distinguish him from famous and influential jazz drummer Jo Jones who rose to fame in Count Basie's big band and was 22 years Philly Joe's senior. Best known for his drumming, Philly Joe Jones was also an able pianist, tap dancer, and composer who enjoyed playing tenor saxophone and double bass and singing.

Jones studied drums with James "Coatsville" Harris and worked with local bands in Philadelphia at the Roseland and Downbeat clubs, where he began playing professionally with Benny Golson. In 1947 he moved to New York, where he studied for three years with COZY COLE. While the house drummer at Café Society and a frequenter of other clubs, he played with the bebop pioneers Dizzy Gillespie, Dexter Gordon, Fats Navarro, and Charlie Parker. He also played in a band led by Joe Morris and Johnny Griffin with Tiny Grimes and Lionel Hampton. From 1955 to 1958 he played with Miles Davis in the trumpeter's celebrated first quintet, alongside John Coltrane, Red Garland, and Paul Chambers. During much of this time Jones, like many of his contemporaries on the jazz scene, was beleaguered by an addiction to heroin; he earned the nickname "Crazy Joe" and took many years to shake the lifestyle and image. Jones was for several years Davis's favorite drummer, and after he left Davis berated his successor in the band, Jimmy Cobb, for not playing the "Philly lick" that he had come to expect. Davis claimed that Jones had an uncanny knack for anticipating what the trumpeter was going to play.

During the 1950s and 1960s Jones worked with Chet Baker, Tadd Dameron, Bill Evans, Gil Evans, Abbey Lincoln, Wes Montgomery, Ben Webster, and Joe Zawinul, among others. From 1967 to 1969 he lived in London, where he collaborated with such musicians as Peter King and Kenny Wheeler. After living in Paris between 1969 and 1972, he returned to Philadelphia in 1972 to form the jazz-rock band Le Grand Prix. In the 1980s he formed the band Dameronia, an ensemble dedicated to performing Tadd Dameron's music. Jones wrote one of the enduring tutor books on playing drum set with brushes, *Brush Artistry* (Leicester, 1968), and holds a position as one of the quintessential bebop, hard-bop, and cool-jazz drummers. He strived to incorporate the drumming rudiments into his playing vocabulary. A deft and subtle accompanist, he was also capable of aggressively driving a band and noted for his hard swinging style, brush technique, delicate work on the cymbals, and mastery of cross-rhythms.

BIBLIOGRAPHY

K. Larcombe "The Great Jazz Masters, Part III: Kenny Clarke," *Modern Drummer*, iv/4 (1980), 23–25, 79–80

M. Davis (with Q. Troupe): *Miles: the Autobiography* (New York, 1989)

B. Korall: *Drummin' Men the Heartbeat of Jazz: the Bebop Years* (New York, 2002)

A. Budofsky, ed.: *The Drummer: 100 Years of Rhythmic Power and Invention* (Cedar Grove, 2006)

GARETH DYLAN SMITH

Jones, Quincy (Delight) [Q] (*b* Chicago, IL, 14 March 1933). Producer, composer, arranger, and musician. Epitomizing a fusion of record production excellence and astute artistic sensibility, he is best known for his success with Michael Jackson. However, he also has remarkable credentials for his creative and commercial consistency with other artists, for his work as a record label executive, and for his own composing and performing career. Few producers have been as well regarded within the music industry or have had such recognition beyond it, and his solo releases have incorporated every major aspect of the African American popular music experience, including hip-hop. By the early 2010s he had won the greatest number of Grammy Awards for a non-classical artist. He has worked with key creative figures spanning generations in the music business.

Jones grew up in Seattle, where he played with the young Ray Charles as a teenager before taking up a scholarship at Boston's Schillinger House (now the Berklee School of Music) in 1950; he earned money for his education by playing strip-joint gigs at night. With an appetite for jazz fueled by work with Count Basie, Jones played trumpet with Lionel Hampton, touring internationally for several years from 1951, and later became an arranger in Dizzy Gillespie's band; he has described Gillespie and Miles Davis as his creative essence. Having spent much of the 1950s on the road, toward the end of the decade he opted to remain in Paris, where he studied composition with the renowned pedagogue NADIA BOULANGER and arranged music for the French record label Barclay.

A disastrous experience managing an 18-piece big band based in Europe between 1959 and 1960 saddled Jones with debt for several years after the event. His efforts to combine composing with band management resulted in the sale of his publishing companies, but heightened his awareness of the industry's business aspects. After returning to the United States, he became the first black A&R executive at Mercury Records and served as its vice president from 1961 to 1968. Lesley Gore's "It's my party" was an early success and other hits followed while he remained creatively active in freelance production and arranging, notably with Charles and Frank Sinatra.

After paying off his European debts, Jones freed himself from the restrictive record executive role. Instead, he followed his artistic temperament: he began a career in film and television soundtrack composition with Sidney Lumet's *The Pawnbroker* (1964) and raised his profile with other cinema hits such as *In the Heat of the Night* (1967) and the TV drama *Ironside*. By 1969 he was a solo artist with A&M Records, generating albums, such as *Walking in Space* (A&M, 1969), that combined orchestral, jazz-oriented arrangements and funky, groove-driven rhythms; *Walking in Space* was recorded in three days and won a Grammy Award for Best Instrumental Jazz Performance. Jones's dramatic music for the television series *Roots* (1977) garnered acclaim and his second gold album after *Body Heat* (A&M, 1974).

A simultaneous spell in pop production began inauspiciously, with the chart failure of Aretha Franklin's album *Hey Now Hey (The Other Side of the Sky)* (Atlantic, 1973). However, there were major commercial results in the second half of the decade with the Brothers Johnson, Rufus & Chaka Khan, and Jackson, whose album *Off the Wall* (Epic, 1979) foreshadowed future success. Despite his developing strong pop and R&B credentials, Jones was perceived as an unusual choice for Jackson because of his extensive jazz credentials. However, *Off the Wall* revealed that Jones's creative instincts were as sharp as ever.

Jones achieved greater solo success with *The Dude* (A&M, 1981). It is worth noting that he never sang on his own records; instead he hired vocalists and concentrated on playing to his production and arranging strengths. These found full form on Jackson's album *Thriller* (Epic, 1982), which had become the best-selling album of all time by 1984, though its sales have since been surpassed. In 1980, Jones had also established his own record label imprint, Qwest, and gained major hits including George Benson's platinum album *Give me the Night* (Warner Bros.,1980) and Patti Austin and James Ingram's duet "Baby, Come to Me" (Qwest, 1982).

In a decade of major successes in the 1980s, Jones produced the multi-million-selling humanitarian single "We are the World," for which he steered the superstar talents of several eras and consolidated his impeccable industry status. After scoring the soundtrack and serving as co-producer for the hit movie *The Color Purple* (1986), producing Jackson's follow-up to *Thriller*, *Bad* (Epic, 1987), and his own platinum Grammy Award-winning album *Back on the Block* (Qwest, 1989), Jones was less visibly active in the pop world. However, with his platinum release *Q's Jook Joint* (Qwest, 1995), Jones continued extending the scope of his creative activities. In the early 21st century he became known as the consummate artistic mentor, philosopher, humanitarian, and entrepreneur, in which roles he shared the benefits of his experiences and ambitions.

BIBLIOGRAPHY

M. Clifford, ed.: *The Illustrated Encyclopedia of Black Music* (New York, 1982)
R. Horricks and T. Middleton: *Quincy Jones* (New York, 1985)
C.S. Ross: *Listen Up: the Lives of Quincy Jones* (New York, 1990)
D. Seay: "Quincy Jones, Record-Making Executive." *Billboard*, 16 Dec. 1995: 36
E. Olsen, P. Verna, C. Wolff, eds.: *The Encyclopedia of Record Producers* (New York, 1999)
Q. Jones: *Q: the Autobiography of Quincy Jones* (New York, 2001)

MIKE ALLEYNE

Jones, Rickie Lee (Chicago, IL, 8 Nov 1954). Singer, songwriter, and producer. She began her career as a musician with the band Easy Money, which with she performed throughout the Los Angeles area. She signed with Warner Bros and began singing at clubs across the country. Her early music drew on jazz, R&B, and rock, but she moved towards mainstream pop music as she became more well known, although she still included some jazz standards in her repertoire. Her romantic relationship with Tom Waits in the late 1970s also influenced her musically. Songs from her first, self-titled album in 1979 include "Young Blood," "Night Train," "Coolsville," and the jazz-inflected hit single "Chuck E.'s in Love." The recording brought her a Grammy Award for Best New Artist. Jones's second album, *Pirates* (Warner Bros., 1981), also spawned popular singles including "Lucky Guy" and "Woody and Dutch on the Slow Train to Peking." Jones also became known for her distinctive fashion, which often featured a beret, long gloves, and skin-tight pantsuits. Although her subsequent work did not garner the same level of success, she continued to sing and record throughout the 1980s and 1990s, sometimes touring with her longtime collaborator Rob Wasserman. In 1997 she released an album entitled *Ghostyhead* (Warner Bros.), which drew on electronica. She has continued to tour extensively and has begun producing music.

BIBLIOGRAPHY

R.L. Jones: *The Best of Rickie Lee Jones* (New York, 2006)

JONAS WESTOVER

Jones, Robert Edmond (*b* Milton, NH, 12 Dec 1887; *d* Milton, NH, 26 Nov 1954). Designer. He graduated from Harvard University (1910), where he remained for two years as an instructor. On a trip to Europe (1913–4), he was much influenced by Max Reinhardt in Berlin, Jacques Coupeau in Paris, and by the work of Adolph Appia and Jaques-Dalcroze at Hellarau. He returned to Europe in 1922 with Kenneth Macgowan; they recorded their impressions in *Continental Stagecraft* (New York, 1923). With Lee Simonson (1888–1967) and Norman Bel Geddes, Jones was responsible for introducing a "new stagecraft" to America: the fusion of acting, lighting, and setting into a dramatic whole. His output over 25 years was prodigious and wide ranging. His designs for *The Man Who Married a Dumb Wife* (1915) for Harley Granville-Barker are said to be the first important, indigenous expression of the new stagecraft and his *Macbeth* (1921) for Arthur Hopkins created a sensation for its use of expressionism.

Jones designed the first American productions of Schoenberg's *Die glückliche Hand* (1930), Alban Berg's *Wozzeck* (1931), and Igor Stravinsky's *Oedipus Rex* (1931), all in Philadelphia, and the premiere of Douglas Moore's *The Devil and Daniel Webster* (1938, New York). Designs for his last production, *Der fliegende Holländer* (1950), were realized by Charles Elson at the Metropolitan on the occasion of Hans Hotter's debut as the Dutchman. Jones's unity of craft elements with a unique style was never a formula but a constant endeavor to realize the rhythm of each production. A simplified realism and poetic use of light were his trademarks. "When I go to the theatre, I want to get an eyeful," he wrote.

BIBLIOGRAPHY

R.E. Jones: *The Dramatic Imagination* (New York, 1941)
R. Pendleton: *The Theatre of Robert Edmond Jones* (Middleton, CT, 1958)
A.B. Feinsod: "Stage Designs of a Single Gesture: the Early Work of Robert Edmond Jones," *The Drama Review*, xxviii/2 (1984), 102–20

D.S. McDermott: "Creativity in the Theatre: Robert Edmond Jones and C.G. Jung," *Theatre Journal*, xxxvi/2 (1984), 212–30

DAVID J. HOUGH/R

Jones, Samuel (*b* Inverness, MS, 2 June 1935). Composer and conductor. Receiving his undergraduate degree at Millsaps College, Jones earned his MA and PhD in composition at the Eastman School of Music, studying under HOWARD HANSON. After graduating, he conducted several small orchestras before being appointed to the conducting staff of the Rochester PO (1965–72). Jones was selected by Rice University in 1973 to become the founding dean of Rice's Shepherd School of Music, where he also taught composition and conducting until his retirement in 1997. Subsequently named the Seattle Symphony's composer in residence, he served at this post until 2011, one of the longest such tenures on record.

Jones has won numerous awards for his compositions including the Ford Foundation Recording and Publication Award, several awards from the Mississippi Institute of Arts and Letters and ASCAP awards, as well as grants, including NEA Grants and a Martha Baird Rockefeller Grant. Much of his work has been orchestral, though he has also composed an opera, *A Christmas Memory*, an oratorio, *The Temptation of Jesus*, and other choral and chamber works. His works contain tonal references and centers, and often alternate lyrical sections with periods of kinetic energy. The Americanist quality of his work can be seen in his quotation of American hymns and folk songs, as in his work *Let us now praise famous men* and *Listen Now My Children*, and evocation of landscapes in the texts or programs of his work, for example, Symphony No. 3 (Palo Duro Canyon). Additionally, his work often features American literature, as in *Eudora's Fable: the Shoe Bird*, the recording of which received a Grammy nomination in 2002. From 2005–10 he composed and premiered an acclaimed series of concertos for solo instruments and orchestra.

WORKS
(selected list)

ORCHESTRAL WORKS
Symphony No. 1, 1960; Elegy, 1963, str orch; Festival Fanfare [short], 1964; Overture for A City, 1964; Let us now praise famous men, 1972; Fanfare and Celebration, 1980; A Symphonic Requiem (Variations on a theme of Howard Hanson), 1983; Listen Now, My Children, 1985; Symphony No. 3 (Palo Duro Canyon), 1992; Janus, chbr orch, 1998; Roundings: Musings and meditations on Texas New Deal Murals, 2000; Chorale-Overture for Organ and Orchestra, 2003; Concerto for Tuba and Orchestra, 2005; Benediction, chbr orch, 2006; Concerto for Horn and Orchestra, 2008; Concerto for Trombone and Orchestra, 2009; Concerto for Cello and Orchestra, 2010; Reflections: Songs of Fathers and Daughters, 2011; Other orchestral works

CHORAL AND VOCAL WORKS
Four Haiku (J. Stone), Mez, pf, 1961; A Christmas Memory (T. Capote), op, 1966; Canticles of Time (Symphony No. 2) (Stone), 1990; The Trumpet of the Swan (E. Welty), chorus, orch, 1985; Eudora's Fable: the Shoe Bird (Welty), children's chorus, orch, 2002; The Seas of God (W. Whitman), chorus, orch, 1992; The Temptation of Jesus (Bible, T. Merton), B, orat, chorus, children's chorus, orch, 1995; Meditations, chorus, 2010

SOLO AND CHAMBER WORKS
Piano Sonata, 1963; *Spaces*,vc, nar, 1974; Two Movements for Harpsichord, 1990; Sonata for Cello and Piano, 1996; Organ Benediction, org, str(s), 2010; Other chamber works

Primary publishers: Carl Fischer, Campanile Music Press
Primary record labels: Naxos, CRI

BIBLIOGRAPHY
C. Wilkinson-Thompson: *The Significance of Borrowing Sacred Material in Three Twentieth-Century American Works for Orchestra* (diss., U. of Iowa, 1993)
J.H. Tucker and C.R. McCord, eds.: *Growing Up in Mississippi* (Jackson, MS, 2008)
J. Smolko: *Reshaping American Music: the Quotation of Shape-Note Hymns by Twentieth-Century Composers* (diss., U. of Pittsburgh, 2009)

JOANNA R. SMOLKO

Jones, Shirley (*b* Charleroi, PA, 31 March 1934). Actress and singer. Her career as a singing actress on film and television began with starring roles in two Rodgers and Hammerstein film adaptations: Laurie Williams in *Oklahoma!* (1955) and Julie Jordan in *Carousel* (1956). Subsequent films included *April Love* (1957), *Never Steal Anything Small* (1959), *Elmer Gantry* (1960), and *Two Rode Together* (1961). She won an Academy Award as best supporting actress for her portrayal of a prostitute in *Elmer Gantry*, but it was the wholesome "girl next door" that was the typical Jones character. In 1962 she played the prim and proper librarian, Marian, in *The Music Man* opposite Robert Preston. From 1970 to 1974 she costarred in the television series *The Partridge Family* with her stepson, singer and actor David Cassidy, in which she portrayed the widowed mother of a singing family, thus having the weekly opportunity to showcase her vocal abilities, albeit in a soft rock idiom somewhat distinctive from the Broadway style in which established her career. She has continued to perform into the 2010s and has remained in great demand.

Jones has possessed a well-trained, versatile voice that she has been able to adapt to any of the roles and personas she has pursued throughout her career. With a technique verging on the operatic, she has demonstrated an amazing ability to avoid the pitfalls of oversinging and so is able to effectively portray the type of character adored by Americans.

WILLIAM A. EVERETT, LEE SNOOK

Jones [née Joyner], **(Matilda) Sissieretta** [Black Patti] (*b* Portsmouth, VA, 5 Jan 1868; *d* Providence, RI, 24 June 1933). Soprano. From the age of 15 she studied singing in Providence, Rhode Island, and later studied privately in Boston at the New England Conservatory, and with Louise Cappiani and a Mme Scongia in London. On 5 April 1888 she made her debut, at Steinway Hall, New York, in a Bergen Star Concert. From 1888 to 1895 she toured the United States, Canada, Europe, and the West Indies as a soloist, attracting national attention with her well-publicized appearances at the Grand Negro Jubilee at Madison Square Garden, Carnegie Hall, and the 1892 Pittsburgh Exposition. She sang in the Women's Pavilion at the World's Columbian Exposition in Chicago on 25 September 1893 but did not perform in the Colored Americans Day concert on

25 August 1893, as originally announced. She was invited to sing at the White House by Benjamin Harrison in 1892 and subsequently performed for Grover Cleveland, William McKinley, and Theodore Roosevelt. From 1896 to 1915 she was the leading soloist of Black Patti's Troubadours, a vaudeville company managed by Rudolf Voelckel and James Nolan; she toured internationally with this company, performing staged "kaleidoscopes" of arias and choruses from grand opera. Her repertory also included art songs and sentimental ballads. Jones was greatly admired for the richness and power of her voice as well as her musicality and technique. Like Elizabeth Taylor Greenfield, Marie Selika, and Flora Batson, she was an African American who specialized in European repertoire and vocal techniques. Her career was an anomaly in the United States in the 19th century and served as a harbinger for the pathbreaking accomplishments of Marian Anderson in the 20th century. Collections of memorabilia concerning Jones are held in the library of Howard University, Washington, DC, and the Schomburg Center for Research in Black Culture at the New York Public Library.

BIBLIOGRAPHY
SouthernB
E. Southern: *The Music of Black Americans: a History* (New York, 1971, 3/1997)
E. Southern and J. Wright: "Sissieretta Jones," *BPM*, iv (1976), 191–201 [special issue]
T. Riis: *Just before Jazz: Black Musical Theater in New York, 1890–1915* (Washington, DC, 1989)
J. Graziano: "The Early Life and Career of the 'Black Patti': the Odyssey of an African American Singer in the Late Nineteenth Century," *JAMS*, liii (2000), 543–96
W.E. Daughtry: *Vision and Reality: the Story of "Black Patti" Matilda Sissieretta Joyner Jones* (Pittsburgh, 2002)
E. Gardner: "Jones, Sissieretta" <http://www.anb.org/articles/18/18-03740.html> (2013)

JOSEPHINE WRIGHT/R

Jones, Spike [Lindley Armstrong] (*b* Long Beach, CA, 14 Dec 1911; *d* Los Angeles, CA, 1 May 1965). Musical satirist, bandleader, and drummer. Billed for most of his career as Spike due to his thin build, he was also known as the King of Corn for his stage antics and ruthless parodies of popular artists, television shows, and classical music. Jones organized a band, Spike Jones and his Five Tacks, for performances on local radio stations in California. During the 1930s he played drums in studio bands for radio shows, working with Al Jolson and Bing Crosby, among others, and was soon known for adding quirky sounds—e.g., gunshots, fire bells, washboards, and automobile horns—in performances for comedic effect.

Jones reorganized a band he had helped to start with Del Porter in the 1930s and began promoting it as Spike Jones and his City Slickers in 1942. In the same year, due in large part to Jones's tireless self-promotion, he and his group were catapulted to celebrity status with their rendition of the song "Der Fuehrer's Face." Written for a Donald Duck cartoon, it featured a raspberry, or Bronx cheer, at every iteration of "heil." During the 1940s Jones and his band toured throughout the United States, including appearances at war bond rallies and

army hospitals, and eventually traveled to Europe to perform for Allied troops in 1944. By 1945 the City Slickers had begun escalating their performances to manic levels of excitement and wearing outrageous costumes. Jones became known for his characteristically vibrant checkered suits. His skill at developing routines, delegating managerial duties, and negotiating opportunities for promotion were integral to the band's success; on occasion, however, he could be cruel in his treatment of band members. Often he would serve as a master of ceremonies for concerts, leaving the actual performances of comic numbers to others.

In 1946 Jones and the City Slickers began touring with their *Musical Depreciation Revue*. In these numbers, slapstick comedy was wed to standard pieces of classical music, often to the point of absurdity. These performances commonly involved swords, dwarfs, pigeons, bottles of seltzer waters, and men dressed as women or children. Sometimes Jones would perform on his own instrumental creations, such as the "latrinophone" harp, which was made of wire strung across a toilet seat, or conduct with a plunger.

The band made their television debut on *The Colgate Comedy Hour* in 1951, and Jones was eventually given his own show, *The Spike Jones Show*, which ran in several versions on NBC and CBS through 1961. Spike Jones and his City Slickers appeared in a number of films, including *Fireman, Save my Child* (1954), and sometimes in short music videos parodying popular tunes like "Cocktails for Two." He may be seen performing in the DVD *The Best of Spike Jones: the Funniest Show on Earth* (2009).

SELECTED RECORDINGS
Spike Jones is Murdering the Classics (RCA Red Seal, 1971); *Dinner Music for People who aren't very Hungry* (Rhino, 1988); *The Jones Laughing Record* (Avid, 1998); *Spike Jones Greatest Hits* (RCA, 1999); *The Classic Songs of Spike Jones and his City Slickers* (Varèse Sarabande, 2007)

BIBLIOGRAPHY
Obituary, *New York Times* (2 May 1965)
J.R. Young: *Spike Jones and his City Slickers: an Illustrated Biography* (Beverly Hills, CA, 1984, rev. 3/2004 as *Spike Jones off the Record: the Man who Murdered Music*)
J. Mirtle, ed.: *Thank You Music Lovers: a Biodiscography of Spike Jones and his City Slickers, 1941 to 1965* (Santa Barbara, CA, 1986)

JOHN MACINNIS

Jones, Tom (*b* Littlefield, TX, 17 Feb 1928). Lyricist and composer. He has often worked with the composer HARVEY SCHMIDT, and the duo bear the distinction of writing *The Fantasticks*, which in the early 2010s was the longest-running off-Broadway musical of all time. It opened on 3 May 1960 and ran 17,162 performances before closing on 13 January 2002. It received a Special Tony Award in 1992 for its staying power and status as a musical theater icon, and a film version was released in 1995. Jones and Schmidt had met at the University of Texas, Austin, and collaborated on a few projects, but were mired in a complicated, overly large project based on an Edmond Rostand play (a spoof of *Romeo and Juliet*) when they got the offer to create the musical one-act that became their signature piece. They kept their play's basic concept but jettisoned all of their material except the song "Try to Remember," and the result was *The Fantasticks* (eventually slightly expanded). Two Broadway musicals by the duo followed: *110 in the Shade* (1963), and *I Do! I Do!* (1966); the former ran just under a year and the latter a year and a half, and Schmidt and Jones were nominated for Tony Awards for both scores. Jones struck out on his own for *Celebration* (1969), for which he provided the book, music, lyrics, and direction. His style is deceptively simple, with lyrics abounding in vivid imagery and character revelations without sounding overly worked or complicated.

BIBLIOGRAPHY

S. Suskin: *Show Tunes: the Songs, Shows, and Careers of Broadway's Major Composers* (New York, 1986, enlarged 3/2000)

R. Viagas and D.C. Farber: *The Amazing Story of "The Fantasticks": America's Longest-Running Play* (New York, 1991, 2/1995 as *The Fantasticks: America's Longest Running Play*)

T. Jones and H. Schmidt: *The Fantasticks: the Complete Illustrated Text plus the Official Fantasticks Scrapbook and History of the Musical* (New York, 2000)

JESSICA STERNFELD

Joplin, Janis (Lyn) (*b* Port Arthur, TX, 19 Jan 1943; *d* Hollywood, CA, 4 Oct 1970). Blues and rock singer. After a middle-class upbringing in Port Arthur, where she became thoroughly absorbed in the blues, folk music, and the arts, she ran away from home at the age of 17, hitchhiking with a friend, Chet Helms. She returned to Texas and attended the University of Texas at Austin for a year, during which time she performed with bar bands in Texas until she moved in 1966 to San Francisco, where Helms recruited her to join the recently formed group Big Brother and the Holding Company. Her demonic, trance-like performances were best suited to extended, semi-improvised blues songs, which she sang in a vocal style that mixed howls and whispers with a hoarse alto. The Big Brother musicians—Peter Albin, Sam Andrews, James Gurley, and David Getz—specialized in such blues, and although technically rough, their playing was often intense and inspired. Joplin was only an occasional songwriter, but her interpretations were so radical and personal that she reshaped the songs of other writers into something of her own. The group's appearance at the Monterey Pop Festival in June 1967 surprised the audience, garnered critical acclaim, and gained them contracts with the manager Albert Grossman and with Columbia Records. The group's first album for the label was *Cheap Thrills* (they had already recorded the fairly successful *Big Brother and the Holding Company*, Mainstream, 1967); it went to number one on the chart in 1968. The album yielded a top 20 single, "Piece of my Heart," originally recorded by the R&B singer Erma Franklin, as well as a version of George Gershwin's "Summertime."

By this time Joplin had been persuaded that Big Brother was insufficiently professional, and she and Andrews left to form the Kozmic Blues Band. Joplin's first solo album, *I got dem ol' Kozmic Blues again Mama!*, reached number five in 1969. Joplin was, by now, pursuing a punishing round of concert appearances, while her private life was marked by a series of personal upheavals and reliance on alcohol and drugs. In 1970 she formed yet another new group, the Full Tilt Boogie Band, whose album *Pearl* not only yielded a single that reached number one on the chart—Joplin's version of Kris Kristofferson's "Me and Bobby McGee"—but itself rose to number one, after Joplin's death. Joplin performed several blues standards and her own songs at the Woodstock festival in August 1969, including "Work me, Lord," a riveting, improvisational version captured in Michael Wadleigh's documentary film. In the early summer of 1970 Joplin was a headlining act for the Festival Express, a traveling festival that made its way across Canada by train. In August 1970 Joplin purchased a headstone for Bessie Smith's unmarked grave as a tribute to one of her foundational influences.

Joplin was found dead from an overdose of heroin at the Landmark Hotel in Hollywood on 4 October 1970. A live album, *Joplin in Concert* (no.4, 1972), was a posthumous success, as was a film, *The Rose* (1979), based on Joplin's life, with Bette Midler in the principal role. In 1987 an unreleased recording of a Joplin concert from 1962 surfaced; it included Carter Family and Leadbelly covers, as well as Joplin originals. Joplin was inducted into the Rock and Roll Hall of Fame in 1995. A musical about her life, *Love, Janis*, opened in 2001.

Joplin's appeal was largely based on two primary elements of her performance: her unique, at times shocking voice and her rejection of typically feminine characteristics. Basing her musical style on past blues, soul, and R&B artists such as Smith and Big Mama Thornton, Joplin developed a shouting, howling, growling style of singing that often featured multiphonics. She was instrumental in resurrecting Thornton's career in the late 1960s, although her own music did not cross over to the R&B charts despite the fact that she released numerous blues standards and soul covers as singles. Her singing style also reflected internal and personal struggles stemming from a childhood in which she was tormented by peers and continuing psychological and addiction problems in her adult life. Nevertheless, during her brief career, Joplin came to embody the burgeoning feminist movement through her unbridled onstage performances, her ability to lead a band of male musicians with clear direction and purpose, and the general challenges her achievements presented to stereotypical notions of gender roles. She was often noted for the contradictorily quiet and introverted behavior that she exhibited offstage.

Joplin was the most powerful white exponent of the exuberant musical styles and unbridled countercultural sexuality of the late 1960s. Her performance at Monterey in 1967 became widely influential through the documentary film released the following year and helped to persuade the recording industry to focus its resources on rock music and the youth market. Like most pop stars of the period she came to represent a certain ideology—in her case the communal spirit of the hippie movement in San Francisco and unconventional feminine self-assertion. Her death was seen by many as one of the events that marked the end of 1960s popular culture. Remembered as one of the central female singers of her time, Joplin has influenced many other artists ranging from her contemporary, Grace Slick, to subsequent artists such as Melissa Etheridge, Joss Stone, and Crystal Bowersox.

SELECTED RECORDINGS
Big Brother and the Holding Company (Mainstream, 1967); *Cheap Thrills* (Col., 1968); *I got dem ol' Kozmic Blues again Mama!* (Col., 1969); *Pearl* (Col., 1971); *Joplin in Concert* (Col., 1972); *Janis* (Col., 1993)

BIBLIOGRAPHY
"Joplin, Janis," *CBY 1970*
"Janis Joplin," *Rolling Stone*, no.69 (1970)
M. Terry: "Joplin, Janis Lyn," *Notable American Women*, eds., E.T. James, J.W. James, and P.S. Bowyer (Cambridge, MA, 1971; suppl., 1980)
M. Friedman: *Buried Alive: the Biography of Janis Joplin* (New York, 1973)
E. Willis: "Janis Joplin," *Beginning to See the Light: Pieces of a Decade* (New York, 1981, rev. 2/1992 as *Beginning to See the Light: Sex, Hope and Rock-and-Roll*)
D. Dalton: *Piece of my Heart: the Life, Times, and Legend of Janis Joplin* (New York, 1985)
L. Starr, C. Waterman, and J. Hodgson: *Rock: a Canadian Perspective* (Don Mills, ON, 2009)

JOHN ROCKWELL, GILLIAN TURNBULL

Joplin, Scott (*b* northeast TX, between 19 July 1867 and mid-Jan 1868; *d* New York, NY, 1 Apr 1917). Composer. He is regarded as ragtime's greatest exponent. Census records of 1870 and 1880 and Joplin's death certificate establish that the frequently cited birth date of 24 November 1868 is incorrect.

1. Life. 2. Works.

1. LIFE. Joplin was the child of a former slave and a free-born black woman and grew up in the town of Texarkana on the Texas–Arkansas border. His mother took an active interest in his musical education, and most members of his family played musical instruments; a German immigrant musician (perhaps Julius Weiss) who taught the young Joplin also seems to have played a significant role in the formation of his artistic aspirations.

His activities during the 1880s are not documented, but anecdotal evidence suggests that he lived for a while in Sedalia, Missouri, a town later linked to his early fame. He also worked as a travelling musician and became a close associate of the ragtime pioneer Tom Turpin in St. Louis. In 1891 he was back in Texarkana, performing with a minstrel company. He toured with his vocal group the Texas Medley Quartette during most of 1893–94, traveling widely between Omaha and Boston and stopping in Chicago during the World's Columbian Exposition (open from May through October, 1893). His first two publications, the songs "Please say you will" and "A Picture of her face," both issued in Syracuse in 1895, were one result of the tour.

After returning to Sedalia in 1894, he joined the Queen City Cornet Band, a 12-piece ensemble of Afri-

can American musicians in which he played lead cornet, and also formed his own dance band. In 1895 he traveled to Texas, where he apparently witnessed the staged Crush Collision between two locomotives, and wrote "The Crush Collision March" to commemorate the event. This piece, along with his "Harmony Club Waltz" and "Combination March" were published in Temple, Texas, that year. Joplin attended music classes at the George R. Smith College in Sedalia and taught piano and composition to several younger ragtime composers, including Arthur Marshall and Scott Hayden (with whom he composed collaborative rags). In 1898 and 1899 he performed as a pianist at the Maple Leaf Club (made famous by his "Maple Leaf Rag") and the Black 400 Club, and formed a fruitful relationship with the publisher John Stark, who published about one-third of Joplin's known works.

Early in 1899 Joplin issued his first piano rag, "Original Rags." Dissatisfied with the usual arrangement whereby publishers purchased popular music outright for $25 or less, Joplin then obtained the services of a lawyer before publishing again. This was a wise decision, for his next publication, "Maple Leaf Rag," on which he had a royalty contract paying one cent per copy, was an extraordinary success. Its success was not immediate—only 400 copies were sold in the first year—but it had sold half a million copies by 1909, thereby providing Joplin with a steady, albeit small, income. The most famous of all piano rags, "Maple Leaf Rag" formed the basis of Joplin's renown and justified his title, the King of Ragtime Writers.

In 1901 Joplin moved to St. Louis with Belle, his new wife, and devoted his time to composition and teaching, relegating performance to a minor part of his activities. Adding to his fame through the next few years were such outstanding rags as "Sunflower Slow Drag" (1901, with Scott Hayden), "The Easy Winners" (1901), "The Entertainer" (1902), and "The Strenuous Life" (1902); the last of these was a tribute to President Theodore Roosevelt and was probably named in response to the president's White House dinner with the black leader Booker T. Washington on 16 October 1901.

Despite his success as a ragtime composer, his ambition was to write for the lyric theater. His first effort in this direction was *The Ragtime Dance*, a ballet for dancers and a singer–narrator that depicts an African American ball such as those held at Sedalia's Black 400 Club. It was first staged on 24 November 1899 at Wood's Opera House in Sedalia, although it was not published until 1902. His next stage work was *A Guest of Honor*, an opera that dramatizes Washington's dinner with Roosevelt. Joplin applied for a copyright in February 1903 and took the opera on tour with his company of 30 the end of August 1903. Early in the tour the receipts were stolen and the company disbanded. The score was never published and has been lost.

A notable rag of 1904 was "The Cascades," named after the attraction at the St. Louis World's Fair, where it was performed (for the photograph used on the sheet music see illustration). Another was "The Chrysanthemum," which was dedicated to Freddie Alexander,

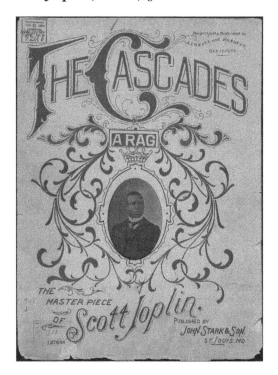

Portrait of Scott Joplin on the cover of sheet music for "The Cascades." (Library of Congress, Music Division)

whom Joplin married in June 1904. She died the following September.

In 1907, by which time he had published almost 40 works, mostly rags, Joplin moved to New York with the intention of finding a publisher for his second opera, *Treemonisha*, on which he was still working. Within his first year in New York he befriended, helped, and encouraged Joseph F. Lamb, a young white man who became one of ragtime's greatest composers. Joplin left his longtime publisher Stark and tried several New York firms before finally settling with Seminary Music, with which he published such piano pieces as "Wall Street Rag" (which includes a descriptive narrative of events in the famed financial district), "Paragon Rag" (dedicated to the Colored Vaudeville Benevolent Association, of which he was a member), "Solace," and "Pine Apple Rag." Seminary Music was linked to and shared an office with Ted Snyder Music, where Irving Berlin was employed at the beginning of his long career. It was through this connection, Joplin maintained, that Berlin had access to the score of *Treemonisha*, from which he supposedly stole a theme for the verse of his hit song "Alexander's Ragtime Band."

Joplin completed *Treemonisha* in 1910, and after failing to find a publisher willing to issue the score of some 250 pages he published it himself in May 1911. It received a very favorable review in the *American Musician and Art Journal* in June 1911, and soon afterwards Joplin announced several stagings, but none reached fruition. The only known performances during his lifetime were an informal run-through without scenery or orchestra in 1911, a staging of only the final

number in Bayonne, New Jersey, in 1913, and an orchestral performance in 1915 of the ballet from act 2, "Frolic of the Bears." Joplin wrote the libretto, which presents his view that his racial peers could find a better life through education. The opera seems to have both textual and musical autobiographical references and is set in the month and year of his late wife Freddie's birth.

The last work Joplin saw in print was "Magnetic Rag" (1914), which he issued with his own publishing company, formed with Lottie Stokes, his third wife. He continued composing almost to the end of his life, including more stage works and orchestral music, but the manuscripts remained unpublished. Joplin reportedly destroyed some of these before his death; those that remained, including his orchestration for *Treemonisha,* were apparently discarded in 1961.

Joplin's music was mostly forgotten in the 1920s and 1930s, the main exception being "Maple Leaf Rag," which was absorbed into the jazz repertory. A renewed interest in his music began in the early 1940s, with the advent of such traditional jazz groups as Lu Watters' Yerba Buena Jazz Band, which sought to return to a pre-swing style of jazz. The book *They all Played Ragtime* (1950), by Rudi Blesh and Harriet Janis, added to this interest, which continued to grow through the next two decades. With the 1970s came a succession of events that brought to Joplin an astonishing amount of popular and scholarly attention. The first was a recording by Joshua Rifkin, *Piano Rags by Scott Joplin* (issued on the classical music label Nonesuch, 1970), with the music performed mostly as written, in other words, in a classical style, instead of the jazz or "honky-tonk" renditions common for ragtime performances in the 1950s-60s; this meant that instead of viewing Joplin's music as a vehicle for improvisation, Rifkin presented it as Joplin had crafted it, with its interesting harmonies, inner voices, and bass lines. The recording became a best-seller and led to many more performances of Joplin's music by classical artists. The following year, the New York Public Library published the two-volume *The Collected Works of Scott Joplin* (1971; reissued with three additional rags in 1981 as *The Complete Works of Scott Joplin*), making the music widely available to performers and scholars. The most momentous development was the use of Joplin's music as a soundtrack in the award-winning film *The Sting* (1973). The film brought Joplin to the attention of the widest possible audience, which made his music—especially his rag "The Entertainer" (1902)—popular again. It was performed and recorded widely, reaching the top positions in the sales charts. Joplin's music was played more widely than ever before and not just on piano; there were performances and recordings for orchestra, band, string quartet, duos (piano and violin, and piano and flute), organ, guitar, and a variety of other ensembles. Never before had a popular music from decades earlier been the focus of such a revival. Along with the acclaim came three different productions of *Treemonisha*. The first was given by the Morehouse College Afro-American Workshop on 28 January 1972 at the Atlanta Memorial Arts Center, with orchestration by T.J. Anderson and staging by Katherine Dunham. The second took place from 10 to 14 August 1972 at Wolf Trap outside Washington, DC, with orchestration by William Bolcom. The third was performed by the Houston Opera and featured orchestration by Gunther Schuller; its premiere took place in Houston on 23 May 1975, and it reached Broadway on 20 October that year, where it remained for a six-week run. Official recognition came in the form of a special Pulitzer Prize in 1976 and a commemorative postage stamp in 1983.

Although the enthusiasm generated by the Joplin revival in the 1970s subsequently faded, Joplin's music has not again been forgotten. In the early 2010s it was still heard frequently in the United States on radio and television commercials, in background scores, and ringing from neighborhood ice cream trucks. It was also programmed regularly for recordings and concerts and was a favorite in ballet. In addition, it has been featured at annual ragtime music festivals in the United States, Canada, and Europe. Joplin's life has inspired novels and plays. He has remained a presence in American life.

2. Works. Joplin's pre-ragtime works of 1895–6, a waltz, two songs, and two marches, are competent but do not foreshadow the greatness that was to come. That was first revealed in the two rags he published in 1899, "Original Rags" and especially "Maple Leaf Rag." The latter became the most imitated rag of the period, and Joplin himself used it as a model for several others: "The Cascades" (1904), "Leola" (1905), "Gladiolus Rag" (1907), and "Sugar Cane" (1908). While these derivative works are apparent attempts to recapture the unprecedented success of "Maple Leaf Rag," they are recompositions rather than imitations, with that rag's harmonic pattern serving as a foundation for elaborate new melodies.

Along with some 40 rags, Joplin continued composing songs, marches, and waltzes, some of the waltzes being syncopated. "Solace" (1909), subtitled "A Mexican Serenade," uses a syncopated, habanera rhythm in a non-rag setting and seems to have been based on Will Etter's "Whoa! Maude" (1905).The two pieces are possibly based on a common source. However, Joplin's working of the material is clearly superior.

Joplin was the pre-eminent composer of piano ragtime. Working primarily in a popular idiom, he strove for a "classical" excellence in his music and recognition as a composer of artistic merit, rather than one simply of popular acclaim. Although he lavished much of his creative efforts on extended works, it was with his piano rags—miniatures rarely exceeding 72 measures of music (ignoring repeats)—that he attained greatness. Both he and Stark referred to these pieces as "classic rags," comparing their artistic merit to that of European classics. The comparison is not unwarranted, for Joplin clearly sought to transcend the indifferent and commonplace quality of most ragtime. This aim is evident in his comments regarding his music, in his plea for faithful renderings of his scores and—most of all—in

the care and skill with which he crafted his compositions. Joplin's rags, unlike those of most of his contemporaries, are notable for their melodically interesting inner voices, consistent and logical voice-leading, subtle structural relationships, and rich chromatic harmonies supported by strongly directed bass lines. Throughout his music Joplin reveals himself as a composer of substance.

BIBLIOGRAPHY

"A Musical Novelty," *American Musician and Art Journal*, xxvii/12 (1911), 7 [review of vocal score of *Treemonisha*]

R. Blesh and H. Janis: *They all Played Ragtime* (New York, 1950, 4/1971)

A. Reed: *The Life and Works of Scott Joplin* (diss., U. of North Carolina, 1973)

J. Haskins and K. Benson: *Scott Joplin* (Garden City, NY, 1978)

T. Albrecht: "Julius Weiss: Scott Joplin's First Piano Teacher," *College Music Symposium*, xix/2 (1979), 89–105

E.A. Berlin: *Ragtime: a Musical and Cultural History* (Berkeley, CA, 1980/R1984 with addenda)

E.A. Berlin: "On the Trail of *A Guest of Honor*: in Search of Scott Joplin's Lost Opera," *A Celebration of American Music: Words and Music in Honor of H. Wiley Hitchcock*, ed. R. Crawford and others (Ann Arbor, MI, 1990), 51–65

E.A. Berlin: *King of Ragtime: Scott Joplin and his Era* (New York, 1994)

J. Keene: "Joplin in New York: a Post-Mortem Walking Tour," *Ragtime Ephemeralist*, no.3 (2002), 216–25

D. Pash: "The White-Backed Book: the Joplin String Arrangements," *Ragtime Ephemeralist*, no.3 (2002), 84–99

T. Samuelson: "Scott Joplin Slept Here: Some Notes on the King of Ragtime's Chicago Residences," *Ragtime Ephemeralist*, no.3 (2002), 210–15

F.J. Spenser: *Jazz and Death: Medical Profiles of Jazz Greats* (Jackson, MS, 2002), 170–80

T. Albrecht: "African, Autobiographical, and Earlier Operatic Elements in Scott Joplin's *Treemonisha*," *African Perspectives: Pre-colonial History, Anthropology, and Ethnomusicology*, eds. R. Allgayer-Kaufmann and M. Weber (Frankfurt, 2008), 215–40

M. Piras: "*Treemonisha*, or *Der Freischütz* Upside Down," *Current Research in Jazz*, IV (2012), <http://www.crj-online.org/v4/CRJ-Treemonisha.php>

A. Sears: "Political Currents and Black Culture in Scott Joplin's *Treemonisha*," *Blackness in Opera*, eds. N. André, K. M. Bryan, and E. Saylor (Urbana, IL, 2012), 101–15

EDWARD A. BERLIN

Jorda [Jordá], **Enrique** (*b* San Sebastián, Spain, 24 March 1911; *d* Brussels, Belgium, 18 March 1996). Conductor of Spanish birth. After studies at San Sebastián and Madrid University, he went to the Sorbonne in Paris, initially to study medicine, but soon changed to music and studied harmony and composition with Paul Le Flem, organ with Marcel Dupré, and conducting with François Rühlmann, making his debut as a conductor in Paris in 1938. He returned to Spain and became conductor of the Madrid SO (1940–5), then of the Cape Town SO (1948–54), and the San Francisco SO (1954–63), a posting that was marred by controversy. He later served as conductor of the Antwerp PO (1970–6), and the Euskadi SO of San Sebastián (1982–4). Jorda also toured widely as a guest conductor, appearing with the BBC SO and the LSO, as well as in Central and South America and in Australia. He gave the first performances of symphonies by Darius Milhaud (nos.8 and 12) and Roy Harris (no.8), Andrew Imbrie's *Legend* (1959), and of Joaquín Rodrigo's *Fantasía para un gentilhombre* (1954) with Andrés Segovia. His recordings, mostly issued during the 1950s, include the finest early LP version of Manuel de Falla's *Noches en los jardines de España* with Clifford Curzon. He received the Spanish honor of Comendador del Orden de Alfonso el Sabio and wrote a book, *El director de orquesta ante la partitura* (Madrid, 1969).

NOËL GOODWIN/CHARLES BARBER

Jordan, Clifford [Cliff] **(Laconia)** (*b* Chicago, IL, 2 Sept 1931; *d* New York, NY, 27 March 1993). Tenor saxophonist and bandleader. He was one of several notable jazz musicians to come out of DuSable High School on Chicago's South Side, where his contemporaries included the tenor saxophonists Johnny Griffin and John Gilmore and the bass player Richard Davis. During his early years in Chicago he played with Max Roach and Sonny Stitt and a variety of rhythm-and-blues bands. In 1957 he moved to New York and recorded his first album, *Blowing in from Chicago* (BN) with the hard-bop pioneers Horace Silver on piano and Art Blakey on drums. In the years that followed Jordan performed and recorded prolifically, appearing with groups led by Silver and J.J. Johnson, as a sideman on recordings by Lee Morgan, among others, and co-leading a group with Kenny Dorham. In 1964 he toured Europe with the Charles Mingus Sextet playing alongside Eric Dolphy.

In the late 1960s Jordan toured West Africa and the Middle East with Randy Weston for the US State Department. He moved his family to Belgium for a time, but returned to the United States to produce some ambitious albums for Strata East, notably *Clifford Jordan in the World* (Strata East, 1972), which features Jordan's own compositions and a host of musicians including Don Cherry, Julian Priester, Wilbur Ware, and Wynton Kelly. He then toured and recorded throughout Europe with the Magic Triangle, a group that included Cedar Walton, Sam Jones, and Billy Higgins. During the 1980s and 1990s Jordan continued to record and lead his own groups, notably a big band that was a mainstay at Condon's in New York.

SELECTED RECORDINGS

As leader: with J. Gilmore: *Blowing in from Chicago* (1957, BN); *In the World* (1972, SE); *Glass Bead Games* (1973, SE); *Night of the Mark VII* (1975, Muse); *Dr. Chicago* (1985, BH); *Down through the Years: Live at Condon's, New York* (1991, Mlst.)

As sideman: L. Morgan: *Expoobident* (1960, VJ); M. Roach: *It's Time* (1962, Imp.); A. Farmer: *You make me smile* (1985, SN); A. Hill: *Shades* (1987, SN)

BIBLIOGRAPHY

L. Lewis: "Clifford Jordan," *Cadence*, xvi/9 (1990), 5–12
B. Shoemaker: "Clifford Jordan: Toast of the Town," *JT*, xxii/5 (1992), 34 only
M. Gardner: "Clifford Jordan," *JJI* (2002), 36 only

RUTH ROSENBERG

Jordan, Joe (*b* Cincinnati, OH, 11 Feb 1882; *d* Tacoma, WA, 11 Sept 1971). Pianist, arranger, and songwriter. He grew up in St. Louis, where he was inspired by the rag-time pianist Tom Turpin. He then studied music at the Lincoln Institute in Jefferson, Missouri, learning to play violin and drums as well as piano. With Ernest Hogan he wrote the score for the musical *Rufus Rastus*, which was performed in New York in 1902. In 1905 he helped organize and wrote music for the Memphis Students, a 17-member ensemble of African American singers, dancers, and instrumentalists, who under his direction appeared in concerts throughout Europe. James Weldon Johnson recalled that this group was the first jazz band ever heard on a New York stage.

In 1906 Jordan became music director of the Pekin Theater, the first all-black theater in Chicago, for which he wrote and arranged more than 600 pieces. He also published five rags between 1902 and 1910 which contain many original ideas while incorporating stylistic elements common to St. Louis and folk ragtime. His most popular piece, *That Teasin' Rag*, was issued in 1909. Eight years later it appeared, uncredited, recorded by the Original Dixieland Jazz Band as part of "The Original Dixieland One-step," but after a long legal battle Jordan eventually received a sizable settlement. Also in 1909 he worked with Bob Cole and J. Rosamond Johnson on their innovative musical *The Red Moon*.

Jordan became recognized not only for his music, but also for his speed, efficiency, and organizational skills at the Pekin Theater. In a span of 16 months during the period 1906–7, he composed, arranged, and conducted 15 musical comedies. Another of his well-known songs, "Lovie Joe," was written for and made famous by the singer Fanny Brice. Being African American, Jordan had to stand on the sidewalk outside the Jardin de Paris, where the song received its Broadway premiere, while Brice was cheered inside. In the 1920s and 1930s Jordan continued to compose, arrange, and conduct for musical revues, and after World War II taught at the Modern Institute of Music in Tacoma while continuing to compose. By the end of his career he had written more than 2000 songs.

WORKS
(selective list)

Songs: Oh! Say wouldn't it be a dream (E.C. Jones) (New York, 1905); Sweetie Dear (Chicago, 1906); I'm going to exit (New York, 1907); That Teasin' Rag (New York, 1909); Lovie Joe (W.M. Cook) (New York, 1910); Dat's ma honey sho's yo' born (Chicago, 1912); Corsica (1915); Morocco Blues (C. Williams) (1926)

Pf rags: Double Fudge: Ragtime Two Step (St. Louis, 1902); Nappy Lee: a Slow Drag (Des Moines, 1903); Pekin Rag: Intermezzo (Chicago, 1904); J.J.J. Rag (Chicago, 1905); The Darkey Todalo: a Raggedy Rag (New York, 1910); Whippoorwill Rag

BIBLIOGRAPHY

R. Blesh and H. Janis: *They all Played Ragtime* (New York, 1950, 4/1971)
D. Zimmerman: "A Visit with Joe Jordan," *Rag Times*, ii/3 (1968), 6 only
D.A. Jasen and T.J. Tichenor: *Rags and Ragtime: a Musical History* (New York, 1978)
L.C. Johnson: "The Remarkable Joe Jordan," *Mississippi Rag*, v/8 (1978), 1 only
R. Benjamin: disc notes, *From Barrelhouse to Broadway: the Musical Odyssey of Joe Jordan* (New World Records, 80649-2, 2006)

RICHARD ZIMMERMAN/TIM SMOLKO

Jordan, Jules (*b* Willimantic, CT, 10 Nov 1850; *d*,Providence, RI, 5 March 1927). Conductor, composer, teacher, and tenor. Jordan moved to Providence in 1870 to work as a telegraph operator. Intending to study cornet, he instead became a chorister at Grace Church, where he would later direct the choir. Jordan studied voice with GEORGE OSGOOD; he later studied with William Shakespeare in London and Giovanni Sbriglia in Paris. For the first American performance of Berlioz's *The Damnation of Faust* (New York, 14 February 1880), Jordan sang the title role (in English) under Leopold Damrosch. From 1881 to 1921, he conducted the Arion Club, a Providence singing society that presented oratorios and operas (in concert), for which famous singers (e.g., Nellie Melba, Lillian Nordica, Italo Campanini) were engaged. Brown University awarded Jordan a DMus *honoris causa* in 1895.

Known for his songs and choral music, Jordan also wrote for the stage, producing two school operettas, several one-act operas and operettas, music for vaudeville sketches, and two full-length operas: *Rip Van Winkle* (Providence, RI, 25 May 1897), a three-act romantic comic opera, and *Nisida*, an unpublished three-act grand opera. As one might expect of a choral conductor and singer, his works exhibit a gift for melody and a thorough knowledge of the voice.

BIBLIOGRAPHY

J. Jordan and G.T. Bulling: *Jordan's New Method of Sight-Singing* (New York and Chicago, 1883)

J. Jordan: *The Happenings of a Musical Life* (Providence, RI, 1922)

E.E. Hipsher: *American Opera and Its Composers* (Philadelphia, 1934), 280–81

A. Basse: *The Songs and Larger Choral Works of Jules Jordan* (thesis, Brown U., 1959)

SCOTT ALAN SOUTHARD

Jordan, Louis (Thomas) (*b* Brinkley, AR, 8 July 1908; *d* Los Angeles, CA, 4 Feb 1975). Saxophonist, bandleader, and singer. He began studying clarinet at age seven and quickly moved to saxophone. As a teenager he toured with the Rabbit Foot Minstrels, a group led by his father, who was a music teacher. After graduating from high school he went to Arkansas Baptist College where he majored in music and played with the Imperial Serenaders led by Jimmy Pryor. By 1930 he had moved to Philadelphia, where he worked with Charlie Gaines's orchestra and Jim Winters's band. In 1936 he was hired by Chick Webb in New York and recorded "Gee, but you're swell," a song that established Jordan as a singer and front man.

Jordan left Webb's ensemble in 1938 to form his own small band. Billing himself early on as "the modern Bert Williams," Jordan led his group in Harlem where it became the resident band at the club Elk's Rendezvous.

Louis Jordan and his Tympany Five in the film Caldonia, *1942. (JazzSign/Lebrecht Music & Arts)*

Between 1938 and 1942 the band, which adopted the name Louis Jordan and the Tympany Five, played at the Capitol Theater in Chicago and the Fox Head Tavern in Cedar Rapids, Iowa. Jordan's skills as a singer and showman developed and the band's repertoire grew with skilled arrangements provided by Wild Bill Davis and Bill Doggett, among others. By the mid-1940s the band was touring successfully throughout the United States to well established nightclubs and theaters such as the Oriental Theatre in Chicago, the Apollo in Harlem, and the Paradise Theatre in Detroit.

Jordan's Tympany Five signed with Decca in 1938 and released "Knock me a Kiss" and "I'm gonna move to the outskirts of town." Frequent recording eventually led to "Is you is, or is you ain't (my baby?)" (1944), the first of a string of million-selling singles that included "Caldonia (What makes your big head so hard?)" (1945) and "Beware, Brother, Beware" and "Choo Choo Ch'boogie" (both 1946). Soon enough the charts belonged to Jordan, who scored 54 singles that made the R&B charts and 18 that went to number one. Influenced by the dance beat of swing and the sound of big bands, Jordan's music exemplified what has become known as jump blues; Jordan recalled: "With my little band, I did everything they did with a big band. I made the blues jump." Known as the King of the Juke Boxes, he also recorded during World War II for the Armed Forces Radio Service and the V-Disc program, and starred in short musical films known as soundies. His recording "Saturday Night Fish Fry" (1949) held the number one position for 12 weeks and is often cited as a strong candidate for the first rock-and-roll record.

Dubbed the Father of Rhythm and Blues and the Grandfather of Rock and Roll by the Rock and Roll Hall of Fame, which inducted him in 1987, Jordan delivered a unique blend of big band swing, blues, novelty, and up-tempo dance music—all serving as a bridge between the swing of the 1930s and the rock and roll of the 1950s.

SELECTED RECORDINGS

V-Disc Recordings (Collector's Choice, 1998); *Swingsation* (Verve, 1999); *At the Swing Cat's Ball* (MCA Import, 1999); *Louis Jordan and his Tympany Five* (JSP, 2001); *G.I. Jive* (Double Pleasure, 2004); *Five Guys Named Mo* (PID, 2008); *Reet Petite & Gone* (Unforgettable, 2008)

BIBLIOGRAPHY
J. Chilton: *Let the Good Times Roll: the Story of Louis Jordan and his Music* (Ann Arbor, MI, 1997)
D. Ake: *Jazz Cultures* (Berkeley, CA, 2002)
RANDOLPH LOVE

Jordan [née Dawson], **Sheila (Jeanette)** (*b* Detroit, MI, 18 Nov 1928). Jazz singer and songwriter. Raised in Summerhill, PA, she returned to Detroit in the early 1940s and eventually formed a vocal trio, Skeeter, Mitch, and Jean (after her middle name), which performed versions of Charlie Parker arrangements and improvisations. In 1951 she moved to New York and in the following year she married Duke Jordan, Parker's pianist; they divorced in 1956. Around this time she studied jazz

theory with Lennie Tristano and Charles Mingus. In the 1960s she performed regularly at the Page Three Club in Greenwich Village and recorded with Peter Ind. George Russell asked her to record his inventive arrangement of "You are my sunshine" (a song she sang as a child) on his album *The Outer View* (Riv., 1962). In 1962 she recorded *Portrait of Sheila* with the guitarist Barry Galbraith for Blue Note; it was one of the few vocal recordings released by the label around this time. She became artist in residence at the City College of New York in 1974 and continued to teach there for the next several decades. Her singing often employs surprising glissandi and she seems equally comfortable in bebop and free improvisation.

BIBLIOGRAPHY
H. Cutler: "Sheila Jordan," *Cadence*, xiii/11 (1987), 5
W.P. Hinely: "Sheila Jordan: Calling her own Tune," *JT*, xxvi/6 (1991), 30
CHADWICK JENKINS

Jordanaires, the. Gospel vocal quartet. It was formed by the brothers Bill (tenor; 1948–51) and Monty (baritone; 1948–52) Matthews as the Melodizing Matthews in 1948 in Springfield, Missouri, but the group has subsequently seen a number of personnel changes. Longtime members include Gordon Stoker (first tenor, manager, from 1950), Hoyt Hawkins (second tenor, baritone, 1952–82), Neal Matthews Jr. (second tenor, 1953–2000), Ray Walker (bass, from 1958), and Duane West (baritone, 1982–99). The white gospel group's recording career began in the early 1950s with Decca covering black gospel songs and spirituals; they later worked for RCA Victor and Capitol. Their reputation grew when they began to back such country singers as Red Foley ("Just a Closer Walk with Thee") and made television appearances on *The Eddy Arnold Show* and NBC's *The Grand Ole Opry*. The group reportedly met Elvis Presley in Memphis while touring with Eddy Arnold in 1955. Presley invited them to participate on his first RCA session in January 1956, and they provided backup vocals on some of his biggest hits, including "Don't be cruel," "Are you lonesome tonight," and "It's now or never." Over their long career, the group has recorded with many top pop and country stars including Jimmy Dean ("Big Bad John"), Loretta Lynn ("Coal Miner's Daughter"), Patsy Cline ("Crazy"), and Conway Twitty ("It's only make believe"). The group's many honors include induction into the Gospel Music Hall of Fame (1998), the Country Music Hall of Fame (1998), and the Christian Music Hall of Fame (2002).

RANDOLPH LOVE

Jorgensen, Estelle R(uth) (*b* Melbourne, Australia, 28 May 1945). Music educator and scholar of Australian birth. She received degrees from the University of Newcastle, NSW, Australia (BAHons 1967, DipEd 1968), Andrews University, Michigan (MMus 1970), and the University of Calgary, Alberta (PhD 1976). She taught in public secondary schools in Australia (1968) and Canada (1968–9, 1971–6), and at Andrews University (1970–71), Notre Dame University in Nelson, British Columbia

(1976–7), McGill University, Montreal (1977–86), and Indiana University (1986–). She was founding chair of the Philosophy Special Research Interest Group of the Music Educators National Conference (1988–94), and founding co-chair of the International Society for the Philosophy of Music Education (2003–5). She is editor of *Philosophy of Music Education Review* (from 1993) and *The Philosopher, Teacher, Musician: Perspectives on Music Education* (1993); general editor of *Counterpoints: Music and Education* series; author of *In Search of Music Education* (Urbana, 1997), *Transforming Music Education* (Bloomington, 2003), and *The Art of Teaching Music* (Bloomington, 2008); and a frequent contributor of articles on the philosophy of music education. She has lectured in Australia, Britain, Canada, Finland, Japan, Sweden, and the United States, is a Fellow of the Philosophy of Education Society (2000), and holds an honorary doctorate in music from Andrews University (1995).

JERE T. HUMPHREYS

Joseffy, Rafael (*b* Hunfalu, Hungary, 3 July 1852; *d* New York, NY, 25 June 1915). Hungarian pianist and editor, naturalized American. He studied with Liszt during the summers of 1869 and 1870, but felt that he learned more from Carl Tausig at the Berlin Conservatory from 1866 to 1869. His American debut took place on 13 October 1879 at Chickering Hall in New York on a piano designed and constructed by C. Frank Chickering. He also used pianos by Bösendorfer, Blüthner, and Erard, but ultimately became a Steinway artist. His playing changed after his move to America, the tone generally becoming bigger. He held that practice should be either for perfection (slow and accurate) or endurance (continuous without rest or repair of errors). Immediately hailed by critics, he almost vanished from the stage within ten years. W.J. Henderson attributed this to performance anxiety; however, the issue is complex. Despite Steinway's having engaged Joseffy for the 1891 season at $125 for each of 30 concerts, William Steinway agreed in that same season to guarantee Ignacy Jan Paderewski $366 for each of 80 concerts. Joseffy taught from 1888 to 1906 at the National Conservatory in New York. By December 1893 Steinway calculated that Joseffy had borrowed $18,000 with neither a performance nor an endorsement of Steinway pianos within the previous four years. From 1894 until his death Joseffy produced noteworthy editions of works by Chopin and Liszt, among others, for G. Schirmer. In 1902 that firm published his book *School of Advanced Piano Playing*. He lived in North Tarrytown, NY, but the manuscripts and scores in his library were destroyed by a fire in his house in April 1895. Fingering, he felt, was the basis of fine tone; he admired the fingerings in editions by Karl Klindworth and Karol Mikuli.

BIBLIOGRAPHY

GMO
"Joseffy's House Said to be Burned," *New York Times* (23 April 1895)
C. Adler and B. Lewinson: "Joseffy, Rafael," *The Jewish Encyclopedia* (New York, 1901–6)

W.J. Henderson: "Musical Topics of the Week: a Wave of Editions of Music," *New York Times* (13 April 1902)
The Spokesman-Review Spokane. Washington (Sunday Morning, 11 January 1903) p. 11, col. 1
A. Dolge: *Pianos and their Makers* (Covina, CA, 1911)
E. Hughes: "Rafael Joseffy's Contributions to Piano Technic," *MQ*, ii (1916), 349–64
D.W. Fostle: *The Steinway Saga* (New York, 1995)

MARK RADICE

Josefowicz, Leila Bronia (*b* Toronto, ON, 20 Oct 1977). Violinist of Canadian birth. She spent her early childhood in California, where she began to study Suzuki violin at the age of three and started formal lessons at five. From the age of eight she studied with Robert Lipsett. Early performances included an appearance at the age of ten on an NBC television tribute to Bob Hope. From 1991 to 1994 she studied at the Curtis Institute in Philadelphia, where her teachers were JAIME LAREDO, JOSEPH GINGOLD, FELIX GALIMIR, and JASCHA BRODSKY. She made her Carnegie Hall debut, playing the Tchaikovsky Concerto, in 1994, and the same year recorded the Tchaikovsky and Sibelius concertos.

Josefowicz first toured Japan in 1995, and by 1997, the year of her successful Proms debut, she had played with many of the leading orchestras in the United States and Europe. She has been a keen advocate of contemporary music and has collaborated regularly with John Adams and Oliver Knussen. She has premiered concertos written for her by Esa-Pekka Salonen, Steven Mackey, and Colin Matthews and also gave the premiere of Thomas Adès's concerto *Concentric Paths*. Among her recordings are the Mendelssohn and Prokofiev concertos, powerfully intense readings of Shostakovich's Violin Sonata and First Violin Concerto, Adams's *Road Movies* and Violin Concerto, and an American program that includes jazz arrangements and a ragtime tune specially written for her by her long-standing accompanist John Novacek. In 2007 Josefowicz was awarded a United States Artists Cummings Fellowship and in 2008 a MacArthur Foundation Fellowship.

RICHARD WIGMORE/MICHAEL BERRY

Josephson, Kim (*b* Akron, OH, 10 Nov 1954). Baritone and teacher. He received his vocal training at the University of Houston where he earned bachelor's and master's degrees in music. His teachers included Franco Corelli, Jean Preston, LOUIS QUILICO, and Michael Trimble. He made his debut at the Metropolitan Opera in 1991 and has subsequently sung numerous roles there, including Germont (*La traviata*), Enrico (*Lucia di Lammermoor*), and Rigoletto (*Rigoletto*). In 2009 he appeared in the premiere of André Previn's opera *Brief Encounter* with Houston Grand Opera and in 2010 the premiere of Stephen Schwartz's *Séance on a Wet Afternoon* with Opera Santa Barbara. In 2011 he performed William Bolcom's *A View from the Bridge* with the Rome Opera Theater. He has been recognized with awards from the William Sullivan–George London Foundation, the Loren L. Zachary Society, the Licia Albanese–Puccini Foundation, and the Bagby Foundation, and has also received a Bruce Yarnell Scholarship and a career grant from the Richard Tucker Foundation. He has also worked as associate professor of voice at the University of Oklahoma.

ANYA LAURENCE

Josten, Werner (Erich) (*b* Elberfeld, Wuppertal, Germany, 12 June 1885; *d* New York, NY, 6 Feb 1963). Composer and conductor of German birth; naturalized American. After five years in commerce he turned to music, studying with Rudolf Siegel (harmony and counterpoint) in Munich and with Emile Jaques-Dalcroze in Geneva. He then lived in Paris (1912–4), returned to Munich at the outbreak of World War I, and in 1918 was appointed assistant conductor of the Munich Opera. In 1920 he visited the United States to tour as a composer-accompanist for song recitals, and he remained there as professor of counterpoint and composition at Smith College, Northampton, Massachusetts (1923–49), taking American citizenship in 1933. He was conductor of the Amherst and Smith College Orchestra and of the Northampton Opera Festival Orchestra, guest conductor of the Lewisohn Stadium Concerts, New York, and director of the Pioneer Valley Orchestra in Greenfield, Massachusetts (1947–50). While at Smith he conducted the first American productions of Claudio Monteverdi's *Orfeo*, *Il combattimento di Tancredi e Clorinda*, and *L'incoronazione di Poppea*, George Frideric Handel's *Apollo e Dafne*, *Giulio Cesare*, *Rodelinda*, and *Serse*, and Johann Joseph Fux's *Costanza e fortezza*. The honors he received included two Juilliard Music Foundation publication awards (1931, 1938).

Josten's music came to wide attention in 1929 with the first performances of the *Ode for St Cecilia's Day* (1925) and of *Jungle* (1928) (given by the Boston SO under Serge Koussevitzky). During the next decade his works were played by leading orchestras; Leopold Stokowski concluded his opening concert of the 1932–3 season with *Jungle*, in defiance of the Philadelphia Orchestra's directors' wishes. The Violin Sonata (1936) was performed at the 1938 ISCM Festival, and in the same year the Composers' Forum Laboratory gave a concert of Josten's works in New York; a second followed at the New York World's Fair (1939). Josten's early orchestral pieces are harmonically expansive and often betray medieval, non-Western, or modern French influences. After 1936 he concentrated on chamber works in concise Classical forms and with a mildly dissonant, sometimes bitonal harmony.

WORKS

Ballets: Batouala, 1930–31; Joseph and his Brethren, 1932; Endymion, 1933

Orch: Conc. sacro I–II, 1925; Jungle, 1928; Serenade, small orch, 1934; Sym., str, 1935; Sym., F, 1936; Rhapsody, vn, orch, 1959

Choral: Crucifixion (W. von der Vogelweide), 1916; Hymnus to the Quene of Paradys (old Eng. and Lat.), 1922; Ode for St Cecilia's Day (J. Dryden), 1925; Fragments from the Brome Play "Abraham and Isaac" (anon., 15th century), solo vv, chorus, orch, 1926

Chbr and solo inst: Str Qt, 1934; Sonata, vn, pf, 1936; Pf Sonata, 1937; Sonata, vn, vc, pf, 1938; Sonata, vc, pf, 1938; Concertante, 4 bn, 1939, arr. 4 vc, 1941; Canzona seria, low str, 1940; Sonatina, vn, pf, 1940; Trio, fl, cl, bn, 1941; Sonata, hn, pf, 1952; Canzona seria (A Hamlet Monologue), fl, ob, cl, bn, pf, 1957; other pf works; Str Trio [unpubd]

Other: over 40 songs, incl. 3 Songs (C. Baudelaire, P.B. Shelley), T, orch, 1918–29

MSS in *Wc*, *NYp*, *Nsc*, and *PHff*

Principal publishers: Associated, Ditson, Elkan-Vogel, G. Schirmer, Universal

BIBLIOGRAPHY

EwenD
P. Keppler: "Baroque Beachhead: Recollections of a Bold Venture," *ON*, xxiii/5 (1958), 30
Werner Josten 1885–1963: a Summary of his Compositions with Press Reviews (New York, 1964)
Baroque Opera at Smith College, 1926–1931 (New York, 1966)

LESTER D. BROTHERS

Journey. Rock group. Formed in San Francisco in 1973, the group initially comprised performers of the city's psychedelic rock scene, including Neal Schon (*b* Oklahoma City, OK, 27 Feb 1954; lead guitar) and Gregg Rolie (*b* Seattle, WA, 17 June 1947; keyboards) of the band Santana and Ross Valory (*b* San Francisco, CA, 2 Feb 1949; bass) of Frumious Bandersnatch. Its first three albums with Columbia Records exhibit a progressive jazz-fusion influence and were coolly received. At Columbia's instigation Journey espoused a more harmonious vocal style in combination with keyboards, energetic guitar riffs, and a distinct pop orientation. The hiring of the vocalist Steve Perry (*b* Hanford, CA, 22 Jan 1949) in 1977 capped this decisive turning point. Steve Smith quietly became the drummer in 1978.

The group achieved international notoriety between 1978 and 1980 with a string of memorable singles written before and after Perry joined ("Wheel in the Sky" and "Any Way You Want It"). Helping to define arena rock, the group toured assiduously across North America. The album *Escape* (1981) includes Journey's best known material, marks the apex of its commercial influence and promotional success, and offers a deft melange of anthemic rock and lighter ballads ("Open Arms" and "Who's Crying Now"). "Don't Stop Believing" has been endlessly recontextualized: on Broadway, with professional sports, and in US presidential campaigns, video games, and countless movies and television programs. Solo projects, disbandment, personnel reconfigurations, and reunion followed. Among the voices of its several lead singers, Perry's high tessitura is generally considered definitive. The group was inducted into the Hollywood Walk of Fame in 2005.

BIBLIOGRAPHY

R. Flans: "Recording Notes: Journey's 'Don't Stop Believin'," *Mix*, xxxi/6 (2007), 114–15
A. Greene: "R&R: Sad 'Journey' for New Singer," *Rolling Stone*, mlxii (2008)

MICHAEL ETHEN

Jovanovich, Brandon (*b* Billings, MT, 5 Oct 1970). Tenor. His wide-ranging repertory includes leading roles in *Tosca*, *Madama Butterfly*, and *Il tabarro*; Macduff in *Macbeth* and Alfredo in *La traviata*; Don José in *Carmen*; the title role in *Les Contes d'Hoffmann* and Paris in *La belle Hélène*; the title role in *Werther* and Jean Gaussin in *Sapho*; Narraboth in *Salome*, Bacchus in *Ariadne auf Naxos* and Baron Lummar in *Intermezzo*; Boris in *Katya Kabanova* and Steva in *Jenůfa*;

Ladislov in *Two Widows*; Sergei in *Lady Macbeth of Mtsensk*; the Earl of Essex in *Gloriana*, Prologue and Peter Quint in *The Turn of the Screw*, and the title role in *Peter Grimes*; Sam Kaplan in *Street Scene*; the title role in *Candide*; and Sam in *Susannah*. He has appeared in the world premieres of David Carlson's *Anna Karenina*, Craig Bohmler's *The Tale of the Nutcracker*, and Marco Tutino's *Senso*, as well as the American premieres of Lowell Liebermann's *The Picture of Dorian Gray* and Jonathan Dove's *Flight*. Jovanovich's ringing tone and arresting stage presence have led to engagements at companies across the United States, as well as the opera houses of Antwerp, Barcelona, Beijing, Bregenz, Bordeaux, Lille, Milan, Munich, Naples, Palermo, Stuttgart, Toulouse, and Trieste. His recordings include *Sapho*, Sir Richard Rodney Bennett's *The Mines of Sulphur*, Dvorak's *Rusalka*, and Sigmund Romberg's *The New Moon* as well as a DVD of Walter Braunfels's *Die Vogel*.

BIBLIOGRAPHY
E. Myers: "Sound Bites: Brandon Jovanovich," *ON*, lxiii/12 (2004), 16–17
M. Gurewitsch: "Brandon Jovanovich: Finding his Voice, the Slow, Steady Way," *New York Times* (29 Oct 2010)

KELLEY ROURKE

J-Pop. A form of popular music that has been dominant in Japan and features catchy melodies with Japanese lyrics sung over Western-pop accompaniments. The term was coined by foreign-owned record chains such as Tower Records in the 1980s and was picked up in 1988 by the radio station J-Wave; it came into general parlance in the 1990s. The genre was partly the product of the mainstreaming of rock and the blending of that style with *kayōkyoku* (Japanese-language pop music in Western style). Musical tracks may draw from a number of styles, including pop, rock, R&B, hip-hop, and Okinawan music, and "world music" catchy melodies that can be used as hooks for jingles or sung in a karaoke bar are highly prized. Notable artists include the female pop idols Ayumi Hamasaki, Utada Hikaru, and Koda Kumi; boy bands, such as SMAP and Arashi, from the artist management company Johnny's; and rock bands such as the B'z.

J-Pop is often marketed in the form of theme songs for television commercials, drama series, anime, and video games (e.g., Utada Hikaru's songs feature in the game *Kingdom Hearts* and the Nintendo DS commercial); consequently, the last two have served as the conduit through which many American fans have discovered J-Pop. In addition, the female pop duo Puffy AmiYumi was featured in the Cartoon Network animated series *Hi Hi Puffy AmiYumi* (2004–06). J-Pop is thus part of a larger package of Japanese culture in the American imagination, alongside toy and video game franchises such as Pokémon and icons such as Hello Kitty.

Nonetheless, J-Pop artists have generally failed to win over the American mainstream. Neither of Utada Hikaru's two English-language albums has sold well, nor did Seiko Matsuda's before her. Japanese musicians who have found a fan base in the United States have often been seen as more alternative than strictly J-Pop. Japanese experimental rock and noise groups (e.g., Boredoms), punk-influenced bands (Shonen Knife), glam-rock inspired *visual-kei* bands (X Japan), and DJs (DJ Krush) are among those to have found a wider following in the United States.

BIBLIOGRAPHY
J. Stanlaw: "Open your File, Open your Mind: Women, English, and the Changing Roles and Voices of Japanese Pop Music," *Japan Pop! Inside the World of Japanese Popular Culture* (Armonk, NY, 2000), 75–100
H. Aoyagi: *Island of Eight Million Smiles: Idol Performance and Symbolic Production in Contemporary Japan* (Cambridge, MA, 2005)
R. Kelts: *Japanamerica: how Japanese Pop Culture has Invaded the U.S.* (New York, 2006)
C. Stevens: *Japanese Popular Music: Culture, Authenticity and Power* (New York, 2007)
A. Allison: "The Attractions of the J-Wave for American Youth," *Soft Power Superpowers: Cultural and National Assets of Japan and the United States* (Armonk, NY, 2008), 131–42

NORIKO MANABE

Juba. An elaborate form of handclapping and body slapping practiced by African Americans as the rhythmic accompaniment to improvised dance, usually creating complex cross-rhythms with the fall of the feet. The juba routine may be performed by the dancer himself or by onlookers and is sometimes accompanied by a rhymed chant. In a typical juba the performer strikes the hands on the knees, then strikes the hands together, then strikes the right shoulder with one hand, and the left with the other; the rhymes used while "patting juba" are of this type:

> Juba jump, Juba sing,
> Juba cut that pigeon wing.
> Juba kick off this old shoe,
> Juba dance that Jubilo.
> Juba whirl them feet about,
> Juba blow the candle out.
> Juba swing, undo the latch.
> Juba do that long dog scratch.

The earliest known reference to the practice (Bibb) dates it from the 1820s in the United States; it is thought to have its roots in African music and it is possible that its development in the United States was the result of the prohibition of the use of drums among the slaves. Lafcadio Hearn described it as it was known on the Cincinnati levees, and Mark Twain refers to it in *Life on the Mississippi* (1883). In the 1890s the white blackface performers Golden and Grayton performed "patting rabbit hash" to the tune "Turkey in the Straw."

The term is also applied to the spectacular dance (sometimes accompanied by banjo) that uses the routine; one such dance is the Hambone. In the 19th century dancers who performed juba were often referred to by the same name. Among the most famous of these was William Henry Lane (*c*1825–1853), born a free man, who gained his fame on the American stage in the 1840s; in 1844, in a series of challenge dances with John Diamond, he earned the title "King of all Dancers."

548 Jubilee Singers

BIBLIOGRAPHY

H. Bibb: *The Narrative of the Life and Adventures of Henry Bibb, an American Slave, Written by Himself* (New York, 1849)

L. Hearn: "Levee Life," *Cincinnati Commercial* (17 March 1849)

S. Northup: *Twelve Years a Slave* (Auburn, NY, 1853)

T.W. Talley: *Negro Folk Rhymes* (New York, 1922)

H. Courlander: *Haiti Singing* (Chapel Hill, NC, 1939/R)

H. Courlander: *Negro Folk Music, USA* (New York, 1963)

L.F. Emery: *Black Dance in the United States from 1619 to 1970* (Palo Alto, CA, 1972, 2/1980)

D.J. Epstein: *Sinful Tunes and Spirituals: Black Folk Music to the Civil War* (Urbana, IL, 1977)

W.K. McNEIL/R

Jubilee Singers [Fisk Jubilee Singers]. Choral group that introduced Negro spirituals in concert. The original troupe of ten students consisted of six women and four men and began touring the northern United States on 6 October 1871 to raise funds for the indigent Fisk University at Nashville, Tennessee, a college for freed slaves established in 1866 by the American Missionary Association. They disbanded in June 1878. The number of singers varied over the years as members left the troupe and new ones joined.

George L. White (1838–95), the school's white treasurer and music teacher, trained the singers in a repertory of patriotic tunes, hymns, and popular songs of the day, assisted by student Ella Sheppard (1851–1914), who served as soprano and pianist. The singers' tour initially followed the route of the Underground Railroad in Ohio, with the aim of finding sympathetic audiences. Their early concerts failed to provoke interest until White changed the repertory to spirituals and christened the group (which until then had had no official name) the Jubilee Singers after the Old Testament's year of jubilee (Leviticus xxv), when slaves were freed. In December 1871 Henry Ward Beecher, the nationally celebrated minister of Plymouth Congregational Church in Brooklyn, endorsed the group and used his influence to arrange engagements in the northeast. From early 1872 they enjoyed consistent success, singing for both white and black audiences.

The Singers performed their concert spirituals a cappella, in SATB harmony or as solo or unison songs. The students taught the spirituals to each other, and White (most likely assisted by Sheppard) arranged them, musically translating folk songs into dramatic presentational miniatures through strategic variation of dynamics, tempo, and articulation. The singers were initially reluctant to sing the spirituals in public, both because the songs were sacred and because they were painful reminders of the degradations of slavery. White and other teachers at Fisk eventually persuaded them.

In 1872 Theodore F. Seward (1835–1902), a church musician, was hired to transcribe 23 spirituals, with the help of Sheppard. These were published in booklet form and sold at concerts that March. The publication was so popular that a new edition with 61 songs was produced that same year. In 1873 Gustavus D. Pike of the American Missionary Association wrote a narrative of the Jubilee Singers, to which the spirituals were appended. The narrative was later updated by J.B.T. Marsh

The Fisk Jubilee Singers, 1871. (NYPL Performing Arts/Lebrecht Music & Arts)

and Frederick J. Loudin, and also translated into Dutch. At least 35 editions of the narrative were published through 1903, with regular infusions of new spirituals.

The Jubilee Singers ignited intense public interest in spirituals, and rival groups began forming almost immediately. Some were affiliated with educational institutions (e.g., Hampton Institute) and others were independent (e.g., the Hyers Sisters). The Fisk singers returned to Nashville in June 1872 having earned $20,000. During the course of their career they raised $150,000 and funded the construction of Jubilee Hall, which was dedicated in January 1876 and is still standing in the early 21st century.

Despite public acclaim and having sung for President Ulysses S. Grant and other high-ranking politicians, the Jubilee Singers were routinely barred from US hotels and railcars because of their color. On their tour of the British Isles (1873–4) under the patronage of the Earl of Shaftesbury they encountered a much more accepting racial atmosphere, which encouraged them to spend most of the remainder of their career in Europe. Their final tour (1875–8) took them to the British Isles, the Netherlands, Switzerland, and Germany.

After the original troupe disbanded, White formed an independent troupe of Fisk Jubilee Singers that included original members Sheppard and Frederick Loudin (c1840–1904); Fisk allowed use of the name even though the singers were not affiliated with the university. White's group toured from 1879 to 1882 in support of the Civil Rights Act of 1875. In 1882 Loudin organized his own independent troupe, also called the Fisk Jubilee Singers; they toured Europe, Australasia, East Asia, and India, where they sang three spirituals in the Taj Mahal. Loudin's troupe disbanded in 1902.

A second generation of jubilee singers emerged when Ella Sheppard Moore (who married in 1882) returned to Fisk as a vocal coach in the 1890s. Among them was John W. Work II (1873–1925), who went on to lead several famous male jubilee quartets. His groups were the first Fisk Jubilee Singers to make sound recordings, starting in 1909; Archeophone restored these early recordings and made them commercially available with critical notes in 2010 (*There Breathes a Hope*).

The jubilee tradition is a hallowed one at Fisk University that has endured for more than a century and is still going strong. The university commemorates the original Jubilee Singers every 6 October with a convocation and school holiday, and the name "Jubilee Singers" has become a registered trademark of the university. The original singers' heavy touring schedule prevented all but one of them from graduating; in 1978 their college degrees were conferred posthumously. In 2008 President George W. Bush awarded the Fisk Jubilee Singers the National Medal of Arts, the nation's highest honor for artists and patrons. Important documents concerning the singers are held in the Special Collections of Fisk University Library, and in the American Missionary Archives at the Amistad Research Center, New Orleans.

BIBLIOGRAPHY

[T.F. Seward:] *Jubilee Songs: as Sung by the Jubilee Singers of Fisk University* (New York, 1872)

G.D. Pike: *The Jubilee Singers and their Campaign for Twenty Thousand Dollars* (Boston, 1873)

J.B.T. Marsh: *The Story of the Jubilee Singers; with their Songs* (London, 1875)

C.S.A. van Scheltema: *De geschiednis van de Jubilee-Zangers: met hunne liederen* (Amsterdam, 1877)

J.B.T. Marsh: *The Story of the Jubilee Singers by J.B.T. Marsh, with Supplement Containing an Account of the Six Years' Tour around the World, and Many New Songs, by F.J. Loudin* (Cleveland, 1892)

J.M. Richardson: *A History of Fisk University, 1865–1946* (Tuscaloosa, 1980)

D.J. Epstein: "The Story of the Jubilee Singers: an Introduction to its Bibliographic History," *Essays in Honor of Eileen Southern*, ed. J. Wright and S.A. Floyd Jr (Warren, MI, 1992)

A. Ward: *Dark Midnight when I Rise: the Story of the Jubilee Singers who Introduced the World to the Music of Black America* (New York, 2000)

D. Seroff: "A Voice in the Wilderness: the Fisk Jubilee Singers' Civil Rights Tours of 1879–1882," *Popular Music and Society*, xv/1–2 (2001), 131–78

L. Abbott and D. Seroff: *Out of Sight: the Rise of African American Popular Music, 1889–1895* (Jackson, MS, 2002)

T. Brooks, "The Fisk Jubilee Singers and the Popularization of Negro Spirituals," *Lost Sounds: Blacks and the Birth of the Recording Industry, 1890–1919* (Urbana, IL, 2004), 192–214

S. Graham: "On the Road to Freedom: the Contracts of the Fisk Jubilee Singers," *American Music*, 24/1 (2006), 1–29

T.P. Anderson: *"Tell them we are Singing for Jesus": the Original Fisk Jubilee Singers and Christian Reconstruction, 1871–1878* (Macon, GA, 2010)

D. Seroff: disc notes, *There Breathes a Hope: the Legacy of John Work II and his Fisk Jubilee Quartet, 1909–1916*, Archeophone 5020 (2010)

SANDRA JEAN GRAHAM

Juch, Emma (Antonia Joanna) (*b* Vienna, Austria, 4 July 1863; *d* New York, NY, 6 March 1939). Soprano and impresario of Austrian birth. Born of naturalized American parents, she grew up in New York, where she studied with her father and with Adeline Murio-Celli. Her concert debut (1881) at Chickering Hall attracted the attention of James Henry Mapleson, who signed her for three seasons at Her Majesty's Theatre, London, where she made her operatic debut in June 1881 as Philine in Thomas's *Mignon*; she sang the same role in her American debut with the Mapleson Company at the New York Academy of Music (October 1881). In 1884 she toured the United States with a troupe of Wagnerian artists under Theodore Thomas, and in 1886 became a principal (under Thomas) with the ill-fated American (later the National) Opera Company. In 1889 Juch formed her own opera troupe, which traveled and performed throughout North America for two years; its all-English repertory included French, Italian, German, and English operas. Between 1891 and 1894 (when she retired from the stage) Juch appeared in numerous concerts, recitals, and music festivals. She was a champion of opera in English, and her refined diction (in English, French, German, and Italian) was considered a model. She had a voice of exceptional purity and wide compass, and was a skilled actress. She was recorded by the Victor Talking Machine Company (some of these recordings can be found in research libraries in the United States).

BIBLIOGRAPHY
O. Thompson: *The American Singer* (New York, 1937/*R*), 119
Obituary, *New York Times* (7 March 1939)
Obituary, *Musical America* (10 March 1939)
N.S. Putnam: "Juch, Emma Johanna Antonia," *Notable American Women*, ed. E.T. James, J.W. James, and P.S. Boyer (Cambridge, MA, 1971)

KATHERINE K. PRESTON

Judas Priest. English heavy metal band. It was a bluesy psychedelic outfit until its second album *Sad Wings of Destiny* (Gull, 1976), which provided a blueprint for the young genre of heavy metal: a powerful singer, guitar virtuosity, a bass-heavy sound, and lyrics that reference chaos if not cosmic doom. Priest's signature sound remained basically unchanged into the early 2010s: the multi-octave operatic shrieks and growls of the vocalist Rob Halford (*b* Birmingham, England, 25 Aug 1951); the riff-heavy playing of the lead guitarists K.K. Downing (*b* West Midlands, England, 27 Oct 1951) and Glenn Tipton (*b* West Midlands, England, 25 Oct 1948); and the steady bass of Ian Hill (*b* West Midlands, England, 20 Jan 1952). The group also initiated heavy metal's studded black-leather, biker-from-hell look.

Judas Priest's songs, such as "Breaking the Law" (Columbia, 1980) and "Beyond the Realms of Death" (Columbia, 1978), often address injustice. The latter song brought the band to court in Reno, Nevada, where they were accused of provoking the suicide of two young men; *Stained Class* (Columbia, 1978), the record on which the song appeared, was on their phonograph the day they shot themselves. Originally the suit claimed that it was the lyrics to the song that caused the deaths, but when the complainants learned that lyrics were protected free speech, they called in engineers to find subliminal messages on the album. A message of sorts was found—"Do it"—but since it was made by chance—audible breathing by the singer and a guitar strum—the case against the band was thrown out.

The band recruited a new young drummer Scott Travis (*b* Norfolk, VA, 6 Sept 1971) and released one of its strongest albums, *Painkiller* (Columbia), in 1990. But Halford left the band in 1992 and was replaced by a singer who had imitated him in a Priest tribute band. In 2003 Halford, then publicly out of the closet, returned to the fold, and the band continued on its path, retaining its popularity.

DEENA WEINSTEIN

Judd, William M(orton) (*b* Newton, MA, 8 Aug 1916; *d* Southampton, NY, 12 Jan 1987). Concert manager. His father, George E. Judd, was manager of the Boston SO, and his brother George E. Judd Jr. managing director of the New York PO. While studying at Harvard University he worked as the first Tanglewood guide at the Berkshire Music Festival. In 1940 he went to New York to do press liaison work for the Columbia Concerts Corporation (later Columbia Artists Management, Inc.; CAMI) and the New York PO. By 1947 he was a partner in Judson, O'Neill and Judd (later Judd, Ries and Dahlgren), a division of CAMI which specialized in representing conductors and instrumentalists. At Columbia he initiated such large-scale events as Columbia Festivals, a series of arena concerts (1960), and also booked the Heifetz–Piatigorsky Concerts and Music from Marlboro into large auditoriums, where they encouraged the growth of interest in chamber music during the 1970s. Rudolf Serkin, Claudio Arrau, Van Cliburn, William Kapell, Jascha Heifetz, George London, Richard Tucker, and André Watts were among the artists he managed for Columbia. In 1969 Judd left to form the Judd Concert Artist Bureau (from 1975, the Judd Concert Bureau), which continued to represent Serkin and Watts. His unexpected move, along with Harold Shaw's departure from Hurok Concerts the same year, reintroduced diversity to concert management after the mergers of the 1930s.

BIBLIOGRAPHY
S. Chapin: *Musical Chairs* (New York, 1977)
W. Crutchfield: Obituary, *New York Times* (13 Jan 1987)

DAVID WRIGHT/R

Judds, the. Country music duo. Comprising Naomi [Diana Ellen] Judd (*b* Ashland, KY, 1 Jan 1946) and her daughter Wynonna Judd (née Christina Claire Ciminella; *b* Ashland, KY, 30 May 1964), they made their major label debut with *Wynonna and Naomi* (RCA) in 1983 and quickly became the most celebrated duo of the decade, winning the Country Music Association's Horizon Award (1984) and awards for Vocal Group of the Year (1985–7) and Vocal Duo of the Year (1988–91). Naomi, a divorced mother of two who had left Kentucky for California in 1972 and had supported her children through various jobs including nursing, moved to the Nashville area in 1979 with her two daughters, Ashley—who later became a well-known Hollywood film actor—and Wynonna. Naomi and Wynonna entered the commercial music industry performing semi-regularly on Ralph Emery's morning Nashville television show in the early 1980s. Following the success of their debut album and their first number-one hit, "Mama he's Crazy" (1984), the Judds followed suit with a string of hit records, including *Why not me* (Curb, 1984), *Rockin' with the Rhythm* (Curb, 1985), *Heartland* (Curb, 1987), and *The Greatest Hits* (Curb, 1988), that collectively added 13 more number ones to their credit, such as "Rockin' with the Rhythm of the Rain" (1985), "Have Mercy" (1985), "Grandpa (Tell me 'bout the good old days)" (1985), "Maybe your Baby's Got the Blues" (1987), "Turn it Loose" (1987), "Change of Heart" (1988), and "Young Love (Strong Love)" (1989). By 1991 the duo had sold more than ten million albums, accumulated six Grammy awards, and earned the Academy of Country Music award for Top Vocal Duet seven times (1984–90), just before Naomi announced her retirement from the concert stage due to a chronic hepatitis infection. Wynonna continued to perform, forging a successful solo career throughout the 1990s and into the new millennium, as well as reuniting briefly in 1999 with Naomi, with whom she has subsequently toured occasionally.

DAVID B. PRUETT

Judson, Arthur (*b* Dayton, OH, 17 Feb 1881; *d* Rye, NY, 29 Jan 1975). Orchestra manager, artist manager, and writer. He was a powerful figure in concert music with a career that spanned six decades and included an array of musical interests, all of which related in some way to the American orchestra. As a young man he was a promising violinist. He performed in local orchestras and studied violin in New York with MAX BENDIX and Leopold Lichtenberg. In 1900 Denison University in Granville, Ohio, hired Judson, at age 19, to form an orchestra for its new conservatory. Within four years Judson was conservatory dean, conductor of several ensembles, author of a music history text, and founder of a large annual music festival. He also continued to perform. In 1903 he gave one of the first American performances of Strauss's Violin Sonata op.18. In the summers he was concertmaster of a prominent summer musical retreat at Ocean Grove, New Jersey. In 1907 Judson left Denison for New York to pursue a solo career. He struggled as a violinist and supported himself writing articles for *Musical America*. He eventually became a staff writer and columnist and wrote more than 200 articles for the publication between 1908 and 1915. He also served as its advertising manager from 1911 to 1915.

Judson was hired to manage the Philadelphia Orchestra in 1915. He formed a close partnership with its young leader, Leopold Stokowski, and in the late 1910s and 1920s this ensemble became the premier orchestra in the United States. He also ventured into other forms of management, including chamber music and solo artist representation. In 1918 he formed Concert Management Arthur Judson (CMAJ). His success in Philadelphia brought offers from New York, first from the Stadium Concerts summer series and then from the New York Philharmonic. He managed these three prominent organizations concurrently for many years (Philadelphia Orchestra, 1915–35; Stadium Concerts, 1920–43; New York Philharmonic, 1922–56). Meanwhile he was part of two pioneering national booking networks: the Associated Musical Bureaus (1923) and Community Concerts (1927). He also embraced new technology, creating in 1926 a radio network, United Independent Broadcasters (UIB), to rival NBC. UIB was soon purchased by the Columbia Gramophone Company and later became CBS. In 1930, in the grip of the Depression, Judson and William S. Paley formed a coalition of independent managers called Columbia Concerts Corporation (later renamed CAMI), which became the dominant concert management firm of the mid-20th century. Judson presided over CAMI until 1947, and remained with the company until 1962. His CAMI division (CMAJ and later Judson, O'Neill and Judd) managed numerous artists, but Judson focused particularly on conductors. In the 1940s and 1950s he represented most of the major conductors working in the United States.

Judson resigned as New York Philharmonic manager in 1956, and thereafter his prominence waned. In 1962 he left CAMI, at age 81, to form Judson, O'Neill, Beall and Steinway; the name changed to Arthur Judson Management in 1969 and to Harry Beall Management, Inc., following Judson's retirement in 1972.

BIBLIOGRAPHY

P. Hart: "Arthur Judson: Manager," *Orpheus in the New World: the Symphony Orchestra as an American Cultural Institution* (New York, 1973), 71–95

Obituary, *New York Times* (29 Jan 1975)

J. Doering: *The Great Orchestrator: Arthur Judson and American Arts Management* (Urbana, 2013)

JAMES M. DOERING

Judson Dance Theater. A loosely organized collective of avant-garde choreographers, formed in Greenwich Village, New York, in 1962. It began as an extension of a choreography class taught by Robert Dunn at the Merce Cunningham studio and was active as a performing organization from 1962 to 1964; after that time the group continued to promote avant-garde dance until the late 1960s. The Judson Dance Theater brought together artists from several disciplines: while many of its members were trained dancers, others were visual artists, filmmakers, writers, and composers (Malcolm Goldstein, Philip Corner, James Tenney, John Herbert McDowell). Ideas and structures from the various arts were exchanged as the members of the group questioned the traditional aesthetics and production of dance. They advocated the use of "natural" or ordinary movements, the repudiation of training and professional technique, methods that metaphorically stood for freedom and democracy (chance, improvisation, spontaneous determination), attention to choreographic process, stress on formal structure, and dances about dancing, all of which not only reflected the cultural milieu of the United States in the 1960s but also laid the groundwork for the postmodern movement in dance.

BIBLIOGRAPHY

S. Banes: *Judson Dance Theater: Democracy's Body 1962–1964* (Ann Arbor, MI, 1983)

SALLY BANES

Jug band. An instrumental ensemble style developed by African Americans from the urban South in the 1920s and 1930s as a popular novelty entertainment. The eponymous jug was a bass instrument into which a player made buzzing sounds with the lips so that the jug could act as a resonator. Louisville produced some of the earliest jug bands to record, including the Dixieland Jug Blowers, which employed two jugs on "Skip Skat Doodle Do" (1926), and Clifford Hayes' Louisville Stompers. Despite some jazz connections through Johnny Dodds and Clarence Williams, the jug is mainly associated with blues groups. Will Shade's Memphis Jug Band and Gus Cannon's Jug Stompers were pre-eminent among Memphis jug bands. The former's "K.C. Moan" and the latter's "Going to Germany," minor masterpieces of the genre from 1929, feature an interplay of harmonica or kazoo against strings and jug. Cannon is perhaps the best known of the banjo players who seemed essential to the Mississippi Valley jug bands of the 1920s. The style of Jack Kelly's South Memphis Jug Band was more primitive, as is demonstrated by "Highway no.61 Blues"

(1933). Jug bands even backed up religious singers such as Elder Bryant and the Holy Ghost Sanctified Singers. Similar jug bands existed in other states, including the Birmingham Jug Band from Alabama, which recorded a fine version of "Gettin' Ready for Trial" (1930), and the Cincinnati Jug Band, which was led by the guitarist Bob Coleman on "Newport Blues" (1929). White musicians also took to the jug. In 1928, with fellow millhands in Gastonia, North Carolina, Dave McCarn joined a jug band called the Yellow Jackets that played old-time tunes and current hits at house parties and on radio. Bill Gatins led his white jug band on Atlanta radio and Columbia Records during the 1930s.

During the folk revival of the 1960s jug bands were reintroduced by white performers, notably the Even Dozen and Jim Kweskin jug bands. The Rooftop Singers earned a number one pop single with a version of Cannon's "Walk Right In." Early in the 21st century young African American musicians involved in the black banjo revival, particularly the Carolina Chocolate Drops and the Ebony Hillbillies, adopted the jug and jug-band styles and repertoire. Younger musicians in New York and on the West Coast have formed often experimental jug bands, and jug band festivals have emerged since the release of the documentary film *Chasin' Gus' Ghost* in 2007.

BIBLIOGRAPHY

S.B. Charters: *The Country Blues* (New York, 1959)
P. Oliver: *Conversation with the Blues* (New York, 1965)
B. Olsson: *Memphis Blues and Jug Bands* (London, 1970)
P. Oliver: *Songsters and Saints: Vocal Traditions on Race Records* (Cambridge, 1984)
W. Daniel: *Pickin' on Peachtree: a History of Country Music in Atlanta, Georgia* (Champaign, 1990)
P. Huber: *Linthead Stomp: the Creation of Country Music in the Piedmont South* (Chapel Hill, 2008)

PAUL OLIVER/ART MENIUS

Juilliard, Augustus D. (*b* 19 April 1836; *d* New York, NY, 25 April 1919). Music patron. The son of Huguenot refugees, he was born on board a ship bound for the United States, after which his family settled in Ohio. Juilliard moved to New York at a young age, and eventually became an enormously successful textile merchant. A lifelong lover of the arts, Juilliard was a trustee of the Metropolitan Opera House. His will left approximately $12 million for the advancement of music in the United States; he stipulated that the fund be used to support the Metropolitan Opera, finance concerts, and assist deserving students. The trustees of his estate established the Juilliard Musical Foundation in 1920 and the Juilliard Graduate School in 1924. The latter merged with the Institute of Musical Art in 1946 to become the Juilliard School of Music.

BIBLIOGRAPHY

DAB (W.B. Shaw)
Obituary, *New York Times* (26 April 1919)
"Gives $5,000,000 to Advance Music: Will of A.D. Juilliard Provides Aid for Worthy Students," *New York Times* (27 June 1919)
"To the Glory of Music: a Fund for the Art Bequeathed by Augustus D. Juilliard," *The Baton*, xi/3–5 (1932)
A. Olmstead: *Juilliard: a History* (Urbana, 1999)

ROBERT STEVENSON/JANE GOTTLIEB

Juilliard School, the. Conservatory formed in New York in 1946 by the amalgamation of the Institute of Musical Art (founded by Walter Damrosch in 1905) with the Juilliard Graduate School (opened in 1924 with money from the Juilliard Musical Foundation).

See NEW YORK *and* LIBRARIES AND COLLECTIONS.

Juilliard String Quartet. String quartet founded in 1946 by WILLIAM SCHUMAN, then president of the Juilliard School. In the early 2010s its members were Joseph Lin (*b* United States, 1978), who had studied at Harvard and become a faculty member at Cornell University in 2007 and at Juilliard in 2011; Ronald Copes (*b* Arkansas, 1950), who had studied at Oberlin Conservatory and the University of Michigan, taught at the University of California, Santa Barbara, and been a member of the Dunsmuir and the Los Angeles piano quartets as well as appearing as a soloist; Samuel Rhodes (*b* Long Beach, NY, 1941), who had studied viola with Sydney Beck and Walter Trampler and composition with Earl Kim and Roger Sessions, before working in the Galimir Quartet (1961–9) and as a professor at Juilliard; and Joel Krosnick (*b* New Haven, CT, 1941), who had studied with William D'Amato, Luigi Silva, Jens Nygaard, and Claus Adam, been a member of the New York Chamber Soloists, and given the premieres of György Ligeti's Cello Concerto and Gerhard Samuel's *Three Hymns to Apollo*. At its founding the quartet was lead by Robert Mann (*b* Portland, OR, 1920), who studied violin with Edouard Déthier and composition at Juilliard and appeared frequently as a soloist; he was replaced by Joel Smirnoff (1997–2009), Nick Eanet (2009–11), and Lin (from 2011). The original second violinist was Robert Koff, who was succeeded by Isidore Cohen (1958–66), Earl Carlyss (1966–86), Joel Smirnoff (1986–97), and Ronald Copes (from 1997). Rhodes replaced the group's original viola player, Raphael Hillyer, in 1969. Its original cellist, Arthur Winograd, was succeeded by Adam in 1955 and by Krosnick in 1974.

The Juilliard String Quartet has been the quartet-in-residence at Juilliard, the Library of Congress (from 1962), and Michigan State University (from 1977). Although it has usually been identified as specializing in 20th-century music (its repertory of nearly 600 works includes more than 150 by 20th-century composers), it has devoted an equal amount of time to the standard repertory, notably the Beethoven quartets, of which it has presented numerous complete cycles and which it has recorded. Its efforts on behalf of American composers are noteworthy; its many dozens of first performances of American works include Elliott Carter's second and third quartets and Leon Kirchner's first quartet, as well as works by Schuman, Sessions, Walter Piston, Aaron Copland, Milton Babbitt, Foss, Mennin, and Diamond, among others. Its recordings include the complete chamber music for strings of Schoenberg, Webern, and Carter, Bach's *Art of Fugue*, and the quartets of Debussy, Ravel, and Henri Dutilleux. The group has commissioned a wide range of works by international and, especially, American composers; in 2006 they performed Ezequiel Viñao's Quartet no.2, *The Loss and the Silence*, for

Juilliard's centennial. It has appeared throughout the world and at most of the international music festivals and in 1961 was the first American quartet to visit the USSR. Since Mann's retirement the ensemble sound—once aggressive, impetuous, and described as "contemporary, urban-American"—has become sweeter in tone and more elegant in execution. The group has won numerous major awards, including four Grammys, and in 2011 it received the Lifetime Achievement Grammy Award. It has also been inducted into the National Academy of Recording Arts and Sciences Hall of Fame for its extraordinary efforts on behalf of classical music. It is frequently lauded as the most important string quartet in modern American music history.

BIBLIOGRAPHY
H. Gay: *The Juilliard String Quartet* (New York, 1974)

HERBERT GLASS/JONAS WESTOVER

Jukebox. Coin-operated phonograph. In 1889 a cylinder phonograph in San Francisco was equipped with four ear-tubes and a coin apparatus that accepted a nickel. The success of this and later devices revived interest in the phonograph, which had enjoyed only a brief success as a novelty and had failed as an office machine for use in the dictation of correspondence. Coin-operated phonographs of this era reproduced recordings acoustically, usually offered only one piece of music, and employed primitive coin mechanisms. They were installed in "phonograph parlors" and penny arcades. By 1908 they had been superseded by the louder player piano and the motion-picture nickelodeon.

Use of coin-operated phonographs grew with the development of machines offering multiple selections and, after their electrification in 1927, amplified music. Although official figures do not exist, it is reported that 25,000 machines were in use in 1933. The repeal of Prohibition in that year marked the beginning of a "golden age" of jukeboxes, and by 1939 over 300,000 were in use in America. They also served the record industry by providing a showcase for new releases and a barometer of a recording's commercial potential. The major manufacturers of the eye-catching, multicolored, and streamlined machines were Wurlitzer, Rock-Ola, AMI, and Seeburg.

In the 1950s the jukebox industry in America was the subject of congressional investigations into the influence of organized crime on machine and record distributors. Competition from other electronic entertainment devices and the diminishing interest in singles contributed to the decline of the jukebox in the early 1980s. The advent of the compact disc and digitized audio players has led to increasingly smaller machines able to offer vastly greater selections of music.

BIBLIOGRAPHY
J. Krivine: *Juke Box Saturday Night* (London, 1977)
V. Lynch: *Jukebox: the Golden Age* (Berkeley, CA, 1981/*R*)
K. Terry: "Jukebox Biz Is in a Fatal Decline," *Variety* (2 Dec 1981)
V. Lynch: *American Jukebox, 1939–1948: the Classic Years* (San Francisco, CA, 1990)
W. Bunch: *Jukebox America* (New York, 1994)

SAMUEL S. BRYLAWSKI/R

Jullien, Louis (George Maurice Adolphe Roch Albert Abel Antonio Alexandre Noé Jean Lucien Daniel Eugène Joseph-le-brun Joseph-Barême Thomas Thomas Thomas-Thomas Pierre Arbon Pierre-Maurel Barthélemi Artus Alphonse Bertrand Dieudonné Emanuel Josué Vincent Luc Michel Jules-de-la-plane Jules-Bazin Julio César) (*b* Sisteron, France, 23 April 1812; *d* Paris, France, 14 March 1860). French conductor and composer. He was educated at the Paris Conservatoire and in 1836 started conducting dance music at the Jardin Turc. He moved to England in 1838 and began a spectacular career, conducting promenade concerts, balls, and festivals in London and regularly taking his orchestra on provincial tours. In August 1853 he traveled to New York with 27 European instrumental soloists, to which he added more than 60 local musicians. His nightly concerts began at Castle Garden on 29 August; after 48 performances there and at Metropolitan Hall, Jullien took his now-famous orchestra to cities on the East Coast, where its reception was similarly enthusiastic. After an additional month of performances in New York in December, he took a pared-down orchestra, including most of the soloists, on an extended tour as far south as New Orleans and north to Cleveland, Buffalo, Rochester, and Boston. The ensemble returned to New York in May and June for a final series of concerts, culminating in what was called the Grand Musical Congress, in which 1500 performers took part. In total Jullien mounted more than 200 concerts during his visit to the United States.

Jullien was an extraordinary showman who paid careful attention to his attire and the trappings of his concerts: he conducted Beethoven, for example, with a jeweled baton. But he was also a virtuoso conductor, and his orchestra was the best that Americans had ever heard. Although some critics decried his "humbug," even the skeptics were won over by its excellence; praise for Jullien's orchestra was undiminished throughout its entire ten-month visit. Because his goal was to educate and to entertain, his repertory was a mixture of lighter works—dances and semi-narrative compositions like the deliberately patriotic *American Quadrille*—alongside compositions by such composers as Beethoven and Mendelssohn. Thousands of Americans attracted to his concerts had never before attended an orchestra concert, and many performances of European works were local premieres. Jullien's repertory mixture became a model later in the century for ensembles conducted by Patrick Sarsfield Gilmore, John Philip Sousa, and Theodore Thomas, and American musicians who played under him—including George Frederick Bristow and Thomas—learned much from the experience. Some of the instrumentalists Jullien brought with him remained in the United States, and their presence helped to elevate musical standards.

Jullien was also an important champion of American composers, in particular William Henry Fry and George Frederick Bristow. He commissioned and performed works by them not only in America, but also in England when he returned. His strong support for American musicians was in marked contrast to the perception growing at the time that the Philharmonic Society deliberately neglected American composition, and his activities were probably the catalyst for the journalistic Musical Battle of the Century that erupted in January 1854 between Fry and Bristow and the critic Richard Storrs Willis, the basis of which was the perceived anti-Americanism of the Philharmonic.

Jullien was surprised at his American reception and pleased that he had achieved his goal "to popularize music; first in France, then in England, [and] lastly in America" (*New York Times*, 27 June 1854). He intended to return, but setbacks in London—and his subsequent breakdown—prevented this.

BIBLIOGRAPHY

GMO

A. Carse: *The Life of Jullien* (Cambridge, 1951)

J. Graziano. "Jullien and his *Music for the Millions*," R. Crawford, R.A. Lott, and C.J. Oja, *A Celebration of American Music* (Ann Arbor, MI, 1990), 192–215

J. Spitzer: "The Entrepreneur-conductors and their Orchestras," *Nineteenth-Century Music Review*, v/1 (2008), 3–24

K.K. Preston: "Introduction," *George F. Bristow's Symphony no.2 ("Jullien"): a Critical Edition* (Madison, WI, 2010), xv–cvi.

K.K. Preston: "'A Concentration of Talent on our Musical Horizon': the 1853–54 American Tour by Jullien's Extraordinary Orchestra," J. Spitzer, American Orchestras in the Nineteenth Century (Chicago, 2012), 321–347.

KATHERINE K. PRESTON

Jungle Brothers. Rap group. Its members were Afrika Baby Bam (Nathanial Hall; *b* Brooklyn, NY), Mike Gee (Michael Small; *b* Harlem, NY), and, until 1997, DJ Sammy B (Samuel Burrell; *b* Harlem, NY). They were members of the Native Tongues, a collective of likeminded Afrocentric rappers that included De La Soul, A Tribe Called Quest, and Queen Latifah. Their early music was produced by DJ Red Alert, and they were affiliated with Afrika Bambaataa, from whom the rapper Afrika Baby Bam drew his pseudonym. After making "The Promo" (1988) for Red Alert's WBLS radio show, the group recorded their first album, *Straight out the Jungle* (Warlock, 1988). The album represented a new style in hip-hop, with its mellow, Afrocentric lyrics, jazz samples, and moody textures; it was a critical influence in the development of "alternative rap" styles. It also featured the first hip-house recording, "I'll House You."

The group's second album, *Done by the Forces of Nature* (Warner Bros., 1990), continued their affiliation with the Native Tongues' De La Soul and A Tribe Called Quest, as well as their interest in club music ("What U Waitin' 4"). Later albums *J Beez wit the Remedy* (Warner Bros., 1993) and *V.I.P.* (Gee Street, 2000) were less successful with hip-hop audiences, as the Jungle Brothers struggled to maintain their identity after the dissolution of the Native Tongues. However, the group's interest in club music gained them popularity with techno producers and led to genre-crossing work with the Stereo MCs, the Propellerheads, and Aphrodite.

WILL FULTON

Jurassic 5. Rap group formed in 1993 after meeting at the Good Life Health Food Centre's open mic nights in Los Angeles. Two rappers from the Rebels of Rhythm, Akil (Dante Givens; *b* Los Angeles, CA, 1971) and Zaakir (Courtenay Henderson; *b* 1971), joined with three members of the Unity Committee, the rappers Chali 2na (Charles Stewart Jr.; *b* Chicago, IL, 1971) and Mark 7even (Marc Stuart; *b* Paterson, NJ) and DJ Cut Chemist (Lucas Macfadden; *b* Los Angeles, CA, 1973). Shortly after, they added a second DJ, Nu-Mark (Mark Potsic; *b* Los Angeles, CA, 1971). Their characteristic style features group arrangements that showcase the distinctive vocal timbres, wordplay, and rhythmic versatility of each rapper. Backing tracks consist of inventive loops and edits of little-known samples as well as drum machine beats. The group is noted for revitalizing an older style of hip-hop, for their political and social activism, and for providing an alternative to gangsta rap. They released four major albums, including *Jurassic 5* (Interscope, 1998), *Quality Control* (Interscope, 2000), *Power in Numbers* (Interscope, 2002), and *Feedback* (Interscope, 2006), which was recorded without Cut Chemist, who left the group before the album's release. DJs Nu-Mark and Cut Chemist are largely responsible for the production on every album except for *Feedback*, on which a number of producers collaborated. Jurassic 5 songs have been featured in several video games and on various compilations, and the group has toured extensively in Europe and the United States. They disbanded in 2007, but several members have remained active as solo artists.

BIBLIOGRAPHY

D. Diallo: "From Electro-Rap to G-Funk: a Social History of Rap Music in Los Angeles and Compton, California," *Hip Hop in America: a Regional Guide*, ed. M. Hess (Santa Barbara, CA, 2010), 225–55

ELIZABETH SURLES

Jurmann, Walter (*b* Vienna, Austria, 12 Oct 1903; *d* Budapest, Hungary, 17 June 1971). Austrian composer naturalized American. After abandoning medical studies at Vienna University in 1927, he moved to Berlin where he worked as a bar pianist, composer, and crooner. He teamed up with Fritz Rotter (1900–84), one of the most successful lyricists of his time, and their first collaboration resulted in the big hit "Was weisst denn du, wie ich verliebt bin." Jurmann wrote various hit songs that were interpreted by the leading singers of the day.

A successful transition into sound movies followed when Rotter introduced him to Bronislaw Kaper. For the next 12 years the partnership of Jurmann and Kaper proved to be one of the most successful and long lasting of its kind. For the music for some 24 films made in Germany, France, and the United States, Jurmann provided the melodies, while Kaper produced the arrangements and orchestrations. Among their most popular musical collaborations are the films *A Night at the Opera* (1935), *Mutiny on the Bounty* (1935), *San Francisco* (1936), *A Day at the Races* (1937), and *Nice Girl?* (1941). In 1938 he was awarded the honorary citizenship of San Francisco for "San Francisco," while the song itself was proclaimed the official city song by popular demand in 1984.

WORKS
(selective list)
Film: Escapade, 1935 [incl. You're all I need]; Kind Lady, 1935; Last of the Pagans, 1935; Mutiny on the Bounty, 1935 [incl. Love Song of Tahiti]; A Night at the Opera, 1935 [incl. Cosi, Cosa]; The Perfect Gentleman, 1935; San Francisco, 1936 [incl. San Francisco]; Three Smart Girls, 1936 [incl. My heart is singing]; A Day at the Races, 1937 [incl. All God's chillun got rhythm]; Maytime, 1937; Everybody Sing, 1938 [incl. The One I Love]; The Adventures of Huckleberry Finn, 1939; Miracle on Main Street, 1939; Nice Girl?, 1941 [incl. Thank you, America]; Seven Sweethearts, 1941; His Butler's Sister, 1942; Presenting Lily Mars, 1943; Thousands Cheer, 1943 [incl. Three Letters in the Mail Box]

BIBLIOGRAPHY
J. Brand, ed.: *Walter Jurmann: Catalogue of Works* (Munich, 1995)
W. Pass, G. Scheit, and W. Swoboda: *Orpheus im Exil: die Vertreibung der österreichischen Musik von 1938 bis 1945* (Vienna, 1995)
THOMAS L. GAYDA/R

Just Intonation Network. United States-based collective founded in 1984 by David Doty, Henry Rosenthal, and Carola Anderson. The Just Intonation Network's membership has attracted a wide-ranging group of musicians including composers, theorists, performers, and instrument designers and builders as well as hobbyists whose work is primarily focused on just intonation. Dealing with the physical properties of sound, just intonation is an expandable tuning system in which pitches are derived from the overtone series of a specific fundamental pitch and are expressed in relation to said fundamental. As a collective, the group has served as a forum for just intonation on an international scale.

In addition to providing a meeting ground for musicians, the Just Intonation Network has published several works including Doty's *The Just Intonation Primer* (San Francisco: 1993, 1994, 2002) and has made available three compilation recordings of members' compositions: *Tellus 14: Just Intonation* (1986, a volume of the Tellus audio cassette magazine), *Rational Music for an Irrational World* (Just Intonation Network, 1989), and *Numbers Racket* (JIN, 1992). The collective established a resource center for obtaining rare and hard-to-find recordings and texts related to just intonation. As an active composer and founding member, Doty also served as a guiding force by editing and contributing to the group's periodical *1/1: the Journal of the Just Intonation Network*.

Published between the years 1984 and 2007, *1/1* primarily comprises articles dealing with the subjects of compositional practice and theoretical research regarding just intonation, along with additional historical articles, composer interviews, reviews, scores, and occasional recordings. Notable contributors to *1/1* are Ben Johnston, Lou Harrison, La Monte Young, John Schneider, and Dean Drummond. After Doty's resignation as editor of *1/1* in 2006, the Just Intonation Network ceased publishing new works and newsletters although it has continued to remain a loosely connected collective.

See also TUNING SYSTEMS.

PAUL R. WEST

Just Tunings. *See* TUNING SYSTEMS.

K

Ka'ai [Kaai], **Ernest (Kaleihoku)** (*b* Honolulu, Hawaii, 7 Jan 1881; *d* Miami, FL, 1962). Hawaiian ukulele, slide guitar, and mandolin player, singer, writer, teacher, and manufacturer. Active in a wide variety of musical roles, he was the most influential Hawaiian musician of the early 20th century. An accomplished performer and recording artist, he played in and organized many ensembles as the century opened, and was said to have established Honolulu's first modern dance band, fostering a number of talented musicians including Johnny Noble. From 1909 to 1917 he manufactured ukuleles through the Kaai Ukulele Manufacturing Company and initiated the role of the ukulele as a featured instrument of the Hawaiian orchestra (*see* UKULELE). He

Ernest Ka'ai with mandolin. (Bishop Museum)

subsequently introduced and popularized Hawaiian music through his music schools in Honolulu, Detroit, and San Francisco, and on ensemble tours of Australasia, Southeast Asia, Japan, and India between 1911 and 1937.

He wrote the earliest known ukulele method (*The Ukulele, A Hawaiian Guitar and How to Play It*, 1906), which was published with chord frames and basic tablature. He later produced an improved method for the ukulele (*The Ukulele and How Its* [*sic*] *Played*, 1916) as well as other instructional manuals and songbooks. He was also an accomplished arranger and composer best known for the compositions "Across the Sea," cowritten with Ray Kinney and Johnny Noble, and "Pu'uwa'awa'a" with Mary E. Low. Based in Sri Lanka from the late 1920s, he returned to Hawaii briefly in the late 1930s before moving to New York and in 1941 to Miami, where he opened a music studio and continued to teach and perform.

BIBLIOGRAPHY

G. Kanahele, ed.: *Hawaii Music and Musicians: an Illustrated History* (Honolulu, HI, 1979)

L. Ruymar: *The Hawaiian Steel Guitar and its Great Hawaiian Musicians* (Anaheim Hills, CA, 1996)

J. King and J. Tranquada: "A New History of the Origins and Development of the 'Ukulele, 1838–1915," *The Hawaiian Journal of History*, xxxvii (2003), 1–32

ANDREA LOW

Kagen, Sergius (*b* St. Petersburg, Russia, 9/22 Aug 1909; *d* New York, NY, 1 March 1964). Teacher, composer, and pianist of Russian birth; naturalized American. In 1921 he went to Berlin, where he studied with Leonid Kreutzer and Paul Juon at the Hochschule für Musik. After immigrating in 1925 to the United States, he attended the Juilliard School, studying with Carl Friedberg, RUBIN GOLDMARK, and MARCELLA SEMBRICH (diploma 1934). He taught singing and vocal literature at Juilliard from 1940 to 1964 and at the Union Theological Seminary from 1957 until his death. Through his teaching, writings, and editions of a wide variety of vocal works he was an influential vocal pedagogue. As a pianist, he specialized in accompanying singers. His compositions include more than 50 songs written in a chromatic idiom with careful attention to text declamation. His three-act opera *Hamlet*, in a lyrical style ranging from tonal to 12-tone, was first performed in Baltimore on 9 November 1962. A second opera, *The Suitor* (based on Molière's *Monsieur de Pourceaugnac*), was never completed. He became an American citizen in 1930.

WRITINGS
Music for the Voice (New York, 1949, 2/1968)
On Studying Singing (New York, 1950/R)

BIBLIOGRAPHY
R. Starer: "A Tribute to Sergius Kagen," *Juilliard Review Annual 1963–1964*, 52–3
J. Collins: "Quotations from a Great Teacher," *Juilliard Review Annual 1967–1968*, 30–4
B.J. Woods: *Sergius Kagen: his Life and Works* (diss., George Peabody College for Teachers, 1969)
B.J. Woods: "The Songs of Sergius Kagen," *NATS Bulletin*, xxvii/3 (1970–1), 24–5, 51 [incl. complete list of songs]
R.C. Friedberg: *American Art Song and American Poetry*, ii (Metuchen, NJ, 1984), 167–81

R. ALLEN LOTT

Kahane, Jeffrey (Alan) (*b* Los Angeles, CA, 12 Sept 1956). Pianist and conductor. He studied at the San Francisco Conservatory, from which he graduated in 1977, and at the Juilliard School. He won second prize in the Clara Haskil Competition in 1977 (he was the only American to enter that year), fourth prize in the Van Cliburn Competition in 1981, and first prize in the Arthur Rubinstein International Piano Master Competition in 1983. Kahane has performed at the Mostly Mozart Festival, New York, and under Leonard Bernstein at the Hollywood Bowl, and has appeared with the San Francisco, Pittsburgh, and Oregon symphony orchestras, the Philadelphia and Leipzig Gewandhaus orchestras, and the Rochester, Los Angeles, and Israel philharmonic orchestras. Kahane made his conducting debut in 1988 at the Oregon Bach Festival. In 1997 he became Music Director of the Los Angeles Chamber Orchestra, and in 2005 he assumed the post of Music Director of the Colorado Symphony Orchestra, which he held until 2010. He frequently performs as conductor-pianist, leading concertos from the keyboard. The orchestras he has led as guest conductor include the Los Angeles and New York philharmonic orchestras, the San Francisco and Chicago symphonies, and the Philadelphia Orchestra.

ALLAN ULRICH/ELIZABETH N. MORGAN

Kahn, Erich Itor (*b* Rimbach, Germany, 23 July 1905; *d* New York, NY, 5 March 1956). Pianist and composer of German birth. He studied at the Hoch Conservatory in Frankfurt and was co-director of the state radio there from 1928 to 1933. Touring extensively both as a soloist and in ensemble, he was influential in introducing contemporary music. After moving to Paris in 1933, he became active mostly in chamber music and was one of the founders of the Schubert Society. He toured Europe and North Africa with Pablo Casals in 1938–9 and settled in New York in 1941, performing thereafter with such artists as Jennie Tourel, Zino Francescatti, Samuel Dushkin, and Roland Hayes. With Alexander Schneider and Benar Heifetz he formed the Albeneri Trio in 1944 (the name was derived from the first names of the members). In 1948 he was awarded the Coolidge Medal for eminent service to chamber music. Three years later he joined the Bach Aria Group as a pianist. As a composer he inventively used both traditional and serial techniques. He employed the latter freely, with clear tonal implications, as in the *Ciaccona* (1943), and strictly, as in the String Quartet (1954).

WORKS
(selective list)
Präludien zur Nacht, suite, chbr orch, 1927; Suite, va, pf, 1937, rev. as Suite concertante, vn, orch, 1937, orchestration completed by R. Leibowitz, 1964; 3 chansons populaires (J. Leibowitz), Mez, pf, 1938; Les symphonies bretonnes, orch, 1940; 3 caprices de Paganini, vn, pf, 1942; Ciaccona dei tempi di guerra, pf, 1943; Actus tragicus, 9 insts, 1946; 4 Nocturnes (T. Corbière, J.P. Worlet, V. Hugo, P.B. Shelley), S, pf, 1954; Str Qt, 1954

MSS in *NYp*

BIBLIOGRAPHY
Obituary: *International Herald Tribune* (6 March 1956); *New York Times* (6 March 1956)
D. Newlin: "In Memoriam: Erich Itor Kahn, Retrospect and Prospect," *ACAB*, vi/3 (1957), 16–8
R. Leibowitz and K. Wolff: *Erich Itor Kahn: un grand représentant de la musique contemporaine* (Paris, 1958)
F. Kahn: *Generation in Turmoil* (Great Neck, NY, 1960)
W. Black: "New Music Corner," *Keyboard Classics*, vii/1 (1988), 24–7
J. Allende-Blin: *Erich Itor Kahn*, Musik-Konzepte 85 (1994) [incl. complete list of works]

PHILIP L. MILLER/MICHAEL MECKNA

Kahn, Gus(tav Gerson) (*b* Koblenz, Germany, 6 Nov 1886; *d* Los Angeles, CA, 8 Oct 1941). Lyricist of German birth. He immigrated with his family to the United States in 1891 and settled in Chicago, where he showed an early talent for writing and the use of rhyme despite having learned English as a second language. After graduating from high school, he worked various nonmusical jobs from driving a horse-drawn truck to working as a clerk in a mail-order company, all the while writing over 200 songs as a hobby. A chance meeting with a Remick employee (and his future wife) resulted in Kahn's first hit, "I Wish I Had a Girl" (1909).

Kahn continued to work in Chicago, and began collaborating with Walter Donaldson in 1921 throughout the decade on hits including "Carolina in the Morning" (1932), "Yes Sir, That's My Baby" (1925), and "Makin' Whoopee" (1928). Other standards from this period include "Toot Toot Tootsie" (1922), "Ain't We Got Fun?" (1921), and "Liza" (1929), as well as "It Had to Be You" (1924). Other prominent collaborators included Egbert Van Alstyne, George Gershwin, Isham Jones, Jimmy McHugh, Sigmund Romberg, Harry Warren, and Vincent Youmans.

In 1932 Kahn moved to Hollywood to work as a lyricist for RKO and MGM on films including *Flying Down to Rio*, *The Girl of the Golden West*, and the Marx Brothers' *A Day at the Races*, with songs including "Carioca"

(1933) and "You Stepped Out of a Dream" (1940). After a career spanning 32 years and over 800 compositions, Kahn died in Los Angeles in 1941. His life story became the subject of the 1951 movie *I'll See You in My Dreams*.

MICHAEL J. BUDDS/MARISTELLA FEUSTLE

Kahn, Otto (Hermann) (*b* Mannheim, Germany, 21 Feb 1867; *d* New York, NY, 29 March 1934). Banker and music patron of German birth. Unlike his brother, Robert Kahn, who became a concert pianist, composer, and professor at the Berlin Hochschule für Musik, Otto Kahn found his niche in the more lucrative profession of finance. After working in London from 1888 to 1893, he came to New York City (1893) and became a partner in the firm Kuhn, Loeb & Co. His most important contribution to music was his work as a member of the board of the Metropolitan Opera Company from 1903 until his death in 1934. In 1908 when the Met suffered economically, Kahn was one of 14 subscribers to raise $150,000 to bring the Met out of its crisis. He served as the board's president for seven years (starting in 1924), during which time he campaigned for a new opera house to no avail. Kahn was also the vice president for a time of the New York Philharmonic board, and was an honorary director of Covent Garden and the Boston Opera.

As a prominent person in New York society, Kahn gave numerous speeches to various civic and professional organizations, many of which were on topics germane to the arts. Among his published speeches were: *Art and the People* (1916), *Some Observations of Art in America* (1918), *Our Economic and Other Problems: a Financier's Point of View* (1920), *The Value of Art to the People* (1924), *Art and America* (1924), *The American Stage: Reflections of an Amateur* (1925), and *The Problem of Leisure* (1928). His musical publications include: *The Metropolitan Opera: a Statement* (1925), and *George Gershwin and American Youth: an Appreciation* (1929).

BIBLIOGRAPHY

N. Slonimsky: *Baker's Biographical Dictionary of Musicians* (New York, 1900, 8/1992), 878

D. Ewen: *The New Encyclopedia of the Opera* (New York, 1971)

J. Kobler: *Otto, the Magnificent: the Life of Otto Kahn* (New York, 1988)

T.M. Collins: *Otto Kahn: Art, Money & Modern Time* (Chapel Hill, NC, 2002)

DANIEL JAY GRIMMINGER

Khan, Steve [Cahn, Steven Harris] (*b* Los Angeles, CA, 28 April 1947). Jazz guitarist, composer, and arranger. The son of the famous lyricist SAMMY CAHN, he was a drummer in his teens before switching to guitar at age 19. After graduating from UCLA in 1969, he moved to New York, where in 1974 he performed guitar duos with Larry Coryell. He also played in the Brecker Brothers, whose personnel contributed to his first three Columbia releases as a leader: *Tightrope*, *The Blue Man*, and *Arrows*. The acoustic guitar album *Evidence* (1980, AN) showcased his prowess interpreting the music of

Thelonious Monk, after which he formed a new quartet, Eyewitness. This group recorded three more albums and toured with Joe Zawinul's group Weather Report. Khan's duo album with Rob Mounsey, *Local Color* (1987, Ari.), was nominated for a Grammy award, after which he undertook straight-ahead jazz trio projects featuring Ron Carter and Al Foster in 1991 and 1992. Possessing an eclectic musical palate of playing styles, Kahn made two recordings with the re-formed Caribbean Jazz Project, which also featured Dave Samuels and Dave Valentin, in 2000 and 2001. He had a Grammy-nominated recording *Borrowed Time* in 2007 with Jack DeJohnette and John Patitucci. Recordings with Miles Davis, James Brown, Steely Dan, Freddie Hubbard, Gil Evans, and Steps Ahead, four acclaimed guitar books, and a surfeit of guitar-solo transcriptions give further testimony to the multi-faceted talents of this performer and teacher.

SELECTED RECORDINGS

As unaccompanied soloist: *Evidence* (1980, AN)

As leader: *Public Access* (1989, GRP); *Collection* (1994, Sony); *Got my Mental* (1996, Tokuma [Jap.]); *Borrowed Time* (2007, Tone Center); *The Suitcase: Live in Koln '94* (2008, Tone Center); *Parting Shot* (2011, Tone Center)

JEFFREY HOLMES

Kahumoku. Family of Hawaiian musicians. Often described as a Hawaiian renaissance man, George Kahumoku, Jr. (*b* 1951) is a slack key guitarist, singer, sculptor, teacher, farmer, author, and music promoter. He was raised in a musical family with legacies in both hula and slack key. His first teacher was his great-grandfather, Willie, whose father, George Kalua Mahikoa Kahumoku, received a guitar from the *paniolo* (Mexican cowboys) who introduced the instrument to Hawaii's ranches in the 1830s. His great-grandmother Lottie Koko'o, who raised him, and father, George Sr., also influenced him deeply.

George favors the 12-string guitar and often introduces his songs with narratives that draw on autobiography and establish the cultural contexts. He made his public debut at 11 at the Forbidden City nightclub after being invited inside by Ku'i Lee to play a song. At Kamehameha Schools in Honolulu, he performed with fellow students and, after graduating in 1969, joined his brother Moses as The Kahumoku Brothers.

Moses Kahumoku (*b* 1953), a nylon string guitarist known for his improvisational skills, began performing around age five. His distinctive style incorporates fast picking, flamenco-like effects, tempo changes, and extensive use of the thumb for arpeggios. His ballads are also highly regarded, especially the original "Pohakuloa." He and George performed together intermittently for 20 years, recording four albums and accompanying Aunty Edith Kanaka'ole on her celebrated *Hi'ipoi I Ka 'Aina Aloha* (Cherish the Beloved Land) album in 1978.

In 1990 George began performing solo or in duets with his son, Keoki (*b* 1970), who has become an accomplished musician, teacher, and recording artist. In 2005 Keoki created the Hawaiian Music and Lifestyle Workshop in Ka'u, which complements the Annual

Maui ʻUkulele and Slack Key Guitar Workshop his father runs on Maui. Keoki made his recording debut in 1995 on *Hooʻoilina-The Legacy*, an album of family songs released on George's Kealia Farms label. That same year Moses released a solo album, *Hoʻokupu* (The Gift) on Dancing Cat Records. In 1997 George also began recording with Dancing Cat.

In 1999 George began working with musician and producer Daniel Ho, recording both solo and duet albums including two Na Hoku Hanohano (Hawaiian music award) winning CDs: *Hymns of Hawaii*, volumes 1 and 2. In 2003 George began a weekly Masters of Hawaiian Music concert series on Maui. Compilation recordings produced from these performances received four Grammy Awards for Best Hawaiian Music Album.

J.W. JUNKER

Kaibab. Native American group of the Great Basin area, belonging to the PAIUTE.

Kainah [Blood]. Native American tribe of Montana, and Alberta, Canada; *see* BLACKFOOT (i).

Kaiser, Henry (John) (*b* Oakland, CA, 19 Sept 1952). Guitarist, synthesizer player, and producer. He studied economics at Harvard University (BA 1976) and began performing in improvisational contexts in 1974. In 1979 he became involved in experimental rock and has since performed extensively in the United States and abroad. He has worked with, among others, Derek Bailey, David Lindley, Fred Frith, Herbie Hancock, Jerry Garcia, Bill Laswell, Eugene Chadbourne, Michael Stipe, Diamanda Galás, John Zorn, Richard Thompson, and John Oswald; he has also played with the Rova Saxophone Quartet and many free-music groups in the San Francisco Bay area, where he has been based. In both solo and ensemble performance he characteristically aims for some type of fusion of rock, jazz, non-Western, and avant-garde classical styles and focuses on "language elements of attack, articulation, pitch bend trajectory, and velocity." His use of elastic rhythms, non-tempered scales, and widely varied timbres shows the influence of Southeast Asian and Indian musics and the blues. His extended solo improvisations (such as "The Shadow Line" on the album *Aloha*) draw on a wide range of contemporary and older instrumental styles. His interest in various jazz styles infuses *Yo Miles!* (1989, Shanachie), a collaborative series of tributes to the music of Miles Davis, performed with Wadada Leo Smith. He has made more than 140 recordings, which mix his own compositions, cover interpretations, and free improvisations. In addition to his musical explorations, Kaiser is a renowned underwater photographer; his footage has been used in films by Werner Herzog and he worked for 15 years as a senior instructor in underwater scientific research at the University of California at Berkeley.

STEPHEN RUPPENTHAL/R

Kaiser, Michael (*b* New York, NY, 27 Oct 1953). Arts manager and consultant. In addition to pursuing vocal studies, he earned degrees in economics from Brandeis University, where he wrote a senior thesis exploring the economics of opera production, and in management from the Massachusetts Institute of Technology. After starting his own consulting firm in 1981, Kaiser transitioned into arts management, first working as general manager of the Kansas City Ballet (1985–90) and then as executive director of the Alvin Ailey American Dance Theater (1991–5). In 1995 he moved to the American Ballet Theatre, where his unexpected success led to his nickname "the turnaround king," a title coined by the *Chicago Tribune* and later solidified by the *Guardian* and the *New York Times*. In 1998 he was appointed general manager of the Royal Opera House in London, where he repaired its waning reputation by erasing deficits and establishing an endowment.

In 2001 Kaiser was named president of the Kennedy Center for the Performing Arts in Washington, DC, where he also runs the DeVos Institute of Arts Management and serves as a cultural ambassador for the US State Department. His tenure at the Kennedy Center has been marked by several visionary projects, including the Arts in Crisis Initiative, which provides free arts management consultation for selected nonprofits, and the Any Given Child Project, a national program supporting arts education in public schools. His controversial and often expensive approach to mending struggling arts organizations—invest in programming and marketing to increase an organization's value and reputation—is detailed in his book, *The Art of the Turnaround: Creating and Maintaining Healthy Arts Organizations* (Waltham, MA, 2008).

BIBLIOGRAPHY
J. Allison: "An American in London: Michael Kaiser Talks to John Allison," *Opera*, l (1999), 1388–95

MICHAEL MAUSKAPF

Kalanduyan, Danongan (Sibay) (*b* Datu Piang, Philippines, 1 May 1947). Master musician and teacher of *kulintang*, of Filipino birth. Kalanduyan is a respected artistic figure in Filipino communities around the United States and Canada for promoting KULINTANG, an indigenous musical heritage predating Spanish and American colonization of the Philippines. Before settling in San Francisco, California, he was raised in the fishing village of Datu Piang, the artistic center of the Maguindanao people on the island of Mindanao, Philippines. As a young man, he won island-wide competitions on the *gandingan* (set of four large hanging knobbed gongs). As an undergraduate at Mindanao State University–Marawi, he toured the Far East with the Darangen Cultural Troupe. He was an artist-in-residence at the University of Washington (UW) in Seattle under a Rockefeller Foundation grant in 1976, and graduated from UW with a MA in ethnomusicology in 1984. In 1995 Kalanduyan became the first artist of Filipino descent to be awarded a National Heritage Fellowship by the National Endowment for the Arts. Kalanduyan has taught and performed with nearly all of the *kulintang* ensembles in the United States including the Mindanao Kulintang

Ensemble, World Kulintang Ensemble, and the Pakaraguian Kulintang Ensemble. From 2003–9, Kalanduyan taught *kulintang* as an artist-in-residence at San Francisco State University. He continues to perform internationally with his group, the Palabuniyan Kulintang Ensemble. In 2009 the United States Artists Organization awarded him a Broad Fellow to recognize the caliber and impact of his work.

MARY TALUSAN

Kalapana. Rock group. Kalapana are Hawaii's longest-active rock group, with loyal audiences in Hawaii and Japan. Their instrumentation and lyrics are not specific to Hawaii but their image and overall feeling effectively reflect the zeitgeist of island life. In many regards, the group represents Hawaii's response to the singer-songwriter and R&B fads of the 1970s. Formed in 1973, Kalapana perform mostly original material full of catchy melodies, strong bass lines, well-crafted bridges, rock-inflected solos, and self-reflexive lyrics or instrumental jams. Founding members were D.J. Pratt (guitar/percussion/vocals), Malani Bilyeu (guitar/bass/vocals), Mackey Feary (guitar/piano/bass/vocals), and Kirk Thompson (keyboards, bass, vocals), joined frequently by Michael Paulo (sax/flute) and Alvin Fejarang (drums). Feary and Bilyeu served as the main songwriters and singers. Early shows at The Toppe Ada Shoppe led to their opening for Cecilio & Kapono and visiting artists. Their self-titled debut album in 1975 was a local sensation, including hits such as "The Hurt," "Nightbird," and "Naturally."

In 1976 Kalapana released *Kalapana II*, and headlined a three-night stand at the Waikiki Shell that attracted then-record crowds. Shortly after, Feary departed. New members were recruited, including Kimo Cornwell (keyboards). Mainland tours did not prove as successful as hoped, although trips to Japan led to concert and recording opportunities that continue to the present. In 1979 the group began to dissolve but reformed with various members as projects arose. In 1986 Feary returned and a second period of popularity commenced, particularly in Japan. He died in 1999. Current members are Pratt, Bilyeu, Gaylord Holomalia (keyboards), and Japanese-born bassist Kenji Sano.

J.W. JUNKER

Kalichstein, Joseph (*b* Tel-Aviv, Israel, 15 Jan 1946). Pianist of Israeli birth. He studied in Israel with Joshua Shor, and then he immigrated to the United States in 1962 and studied with EDWARD STEUERMANN and Ilona Kabos at Juilliard (master's degree 1969). In 1967 he won the Young Concert Artists' Award and made his New York recital debut. The next year, in a nationally televised performance on CBS, he performed Beethoven's Piano Concerto no.4 in his first appearance with Leonard Bernstein and the New York Philharmonic Orchestra. He won first prize in the Leventritt Competition in 1969, and made his European debut with André Previn and the London Symphony Orchestra in 1970. Among the music festivals in which he has participated are Tanglewood, Verbier, Salzburg, and the

Aspen Music Festival, which, in 2008, marked his twenty-fifth consecutive appearance. Kalichstein has performed with orchestras in the United States, Israel, Japan, Australia, and Europe; among the many conductors with whom he has worked are Daniel Barenboim, Pierre Boulez, Zubin Mehta, Erich Leinsdorf, and George Szell. An avid chamber music player, Kalichstein performs regularly with the Guarneri and Emerson String Quartets. He is also a founding member of the KLR Trio, which is named for Kalichstein and its other two members, the violinist Jaime Laredo and the cellist Sharon Robinson. In 1997 Kalichstein was appointed Artistic Advisor for Chamber Music and Artistic Director of the Fortas Chamber Music Concerts at the Kennedy Center for the Performing Arts. In 1983 Kalichstein joined the faculty of Juilliard, and in 2003 he was appointed to the first Edwin S. and Nancy A. Marks Chair in Chamber Music Studies.

Kalichstein's style is distinguished by his sparkling technique, the rich tones he generates from the instrument, and his unique, pulsating energy that brings every piece to life. His repertoire ranges from Mozart and Brahms to Prokofiev, Zwilich, and Kirchner.

JAMES WIERZBICKI/REBECCA SCHWARTZ-BISHIR

Kalish, Gilbert (*b* Brooklyn, NY, 2 July 1935). Pianist and teacher. A graduate of Columbia University (1956–8), he studied with LEONARD SHURE, Julius Hereford, and ISABELLE VENGEROVA. In 1962 he gave his New York debut (Carnegie Recital Hall, programming J.S. Bach and Arnold Schoenberg), and appeared for the first time in Europe (Wigmore Hall, London, playing Ludwig van Beethoven, Franz Schubert, and Frederic Chopin). A founder-member of the Contemporary Chamber Ensemble (active in New York during the 1960s and 70s), he has been the pianist of the Boston Symphony Chamber Players since 1969. Artist-in-residence at Rutgers, the State University of New Jersey (1965–7), and Swarthmore College, Pennsylvania (1966–72), Kalish was for many years an influential faculty member of the Berkshire Music Center, Tanglewood (1968–97, chairman 1985–97). He has also appeared at the Banff Center and Steans Institute, Ravinia. In 1970 he was appointed professor at SUNY, Stony Brook, where he later became head of performing studies. With a discography of around 100 recordings (ranging from landmark Joseph Haydn sonatas to reference versions of Charles Ives, Bela Bartók, Elliott Carter, and George Crumb), Kalish is an admired modernist. He presented the world premieres of works by Ernst Bacon, Aaron Copland, Ives, Leon Kirchner, George Perle, Ralph Shapey, and Stanley Walden, among others, as well as giving the first performance of works written for him by such composers as Carter, Crumb, Roger Reynolds, and Meyer Kupferman. His 30-year partnership with the mezzo-soprano JAN DEGAETANI (with whom he recorded Ives songs), and his more recent collaboration with the soprano Dawn Upshaw both drew particular critical acclaim. His consistent work with cellists Timothy Eddy and Joel Krosnick, respectively, has also been well received. Kalish has performed throughout the United States and

Europe, as well as in Japan and South America. In 1995 the University of Chicago presented him with the Paul Fromm Award for distinguished service to the music of our time.

ATEŞ ORGA/MEGAN E. HILL

Kallir, Lilian (*b* Prague, Czechoslovakia, 6 May 1931; *d* New York, NY, 25 Oct 2004). Pianist of Czechoslovakian birth, naturalized American. Brought to the United States at an early age, she studied privately with ISABELLE VENGEROVA and at the Mannes College of Music with Herman de Grab (1946–9). She also studied composition, theory, and harmony with HUGO KAUDER, whose music she would later perform in recital. When she was 16 she won the National Music League Award and the American Artists Award of the Brooklyn Institute of Arts and Sciences. She subsequently appeared as an orchestral soloist and recitalist throughout the United States, Europe, Israel, and South America, and performed regularly at major music festivals, including frequent appearances at the Mostly Mozart Festival and 12 summers in residence at the Marlboro Music Festival. In 1959 she married pianist CLAUDE FRANK, with whom she would perform frequently as a piano-duo, recording Brahms's *Liebeslieder* waltzes in 1966. She concentrated on Classical and Romantic repertory and was acclaimed for her elegant delivery of Mozart's music, as well as her renditions of Chopin. She performed chamber music with members of the Guarneri, Juilliard, Cleveland, Tokyo, and Emerson quartets, the violinist Pinchas Zuckerman, cellist Yo-Yo Ma, and clarinetist Richard Stolzman, and she toured with Music from Marlboro. She also performed with her daughter, violinist PAMELA FRANK. In 1975 she joined the faculty of the Mannes College of Music; she also taught and performed at the Aspen Music School and the Berkshire Music Center.

KAREN MONSON/ELIZABETH N. MORGAN

Kallman, Chester (*b* Brooklyn, NY, 7 Jan 1921; *d* Athens, Greece, 18 Jan 1975). Poet, librettist, and translator. W.H. Auden said Kallman "was the person responsible for arousing my interest in opera, about which previously…I knew little or nothing." Their collaborative works are discussed under W.H. AUDEN. Independently, Kallman—a witty, resourceful, and most "musical" poet and an operatic erudite—wrote a libretto for Carlos Chávez, *The Tuscan Players*, and made singing translations of, among other operas, Claudio Monteverdi's *L'incoronazione di Poppea*, Giuseppe Verdi's *Falstaff*, and Bela Bartók's *Bluebeard's* Castle.

ANDREW PORTER/R

Kalmar, Bert (*b* New York, NY, 10 Feb 1884; *d* Los Angeles, CA, 18 Sept 1947). Lyricist who formed a songwriting partnership with HARRY RUBY.

Kalmus, Edwin F. (*b* Vienna, Austria, 15 Dec 1893; *d* New York, NY, 30 April 1989). Music publisher. He founded his firm in New York in 1926. With his son-in-law, Lawrence Galison, who became the vice president and manager in 1961 and later chairman of the board, the firm began printing its own music, established an art and camera department, and later added a complete bindery; it is one of the largest self-contained publishing houses in the United States. Kalmus publishes orchestral music, as well as music for piano, organ, and solo instruments, and reprints of standard classics. With the exception of its orchestral department, Kalmus was purchased by Belwin-Mills in 1976. The company's headquarters in Boca Raton, Florida, continues to handle orchestral music and offers a rental service.

W. THOMAS MARROCCO, MARK JACOBS/R

Kalvos & Damian [K&D]. Radio show and cybercast devoted to new music. Hosted by composers Dennis Báthory-Kitsz ("Kalvos") and David Gunn ("Damian"), the show aired weekly from 1995 to 2005 on the WGDR-FM 91.1 station at Goddard College in Plainfield, Vermont. Since 2005, new K&D shows have been made available online, albeit on an occasional and irregular basis. *Kalvos & Damian's New Music Sesquihour* started on 27 May 1995 as a 90-minute weekly summer radio show. That September they expanded to a permanent two-hour slot, retitled *Kalvos & Damian's New Music Bazaar*, and introduced a website (<www.kalvos.org>) that offered live online streaming and, eventually, archived broadcasts, which reached a much wider audience. In 2000 K&D was recognized as "a music website of singular excellence" and its hosts were awarded an ASCAP-Deems Taylor Internet Award.

K&D shows are characterized by a humorous, quirky, playful, and unpretentious tone. Their opening segment consists of a ten-minute "introductory essay," an often zany, Dadaist narrative written and read by Damian, accompanied by sound effects and banter from Kalvos. The main portion of the show is devoted to interviews and recordings of new music. Over the years, K&D has interviewed a vast range of contemporary composers: experimental and mainstream, symphonic and electronic, prominent and emerging, Vermont natives and overseas figures. K&D also ran online mentoring programs for junior high and high school students and organized the Ought-One Festival of Non-Pop in Montpelier, Vermont. After Báthory-Kitsz and Gunn decided to pursue new projects, the final radio broadcast of K&D aired on 17 September 2005. In addition to occasional K&D shows, the website now also hosts N&K, a light-hearted online show also featuring composer interviews and new music, hosted by Manhattan-based composers Gene Pritsker ("Noizepunk") and Charles Coleman ("Das Krooner").

K&D pioneered the use of streaming audio internet technology to promote new music by a very wide variety of composers and to make it accessible to a worldwide audience. The show's audio archive contains thousands of pieces that continue to be freely available, making the K&D website an invaluable resource for new music at the turn of the 21st century.

BIBLIOGRAPHY
B. Moon: "The End of the Bazaar: Kalvos & Damian Cease Broadcasting New Music after a Decade," *NewMusicBox* (14 Sept 2005),

<http://www.newmusicbox.org/articles/the-end-of-the-bazaar-kalvos-damian-cease-broadcasting-new-music-after-a-decade/>

FRANCIS KAYALI

Kam, Dennis (Koon Ming) (*b* Honolulu, HI, 8 May 1942). Composer. He studied composition at Oberlin College (1960–4), at the East-West Center at University of Hawaii (1964–6), and at University of Illinois (1966–74) with SALVATORE MARTIRANO. He also attended the Mozarteum in Salzburg and the Toho Gakuen in Tokyo. Kam is a prolific composer whose music exhibits an organic sense of time and unusually effective orchestration. His compositions from the 1960s were influenced by post-Webern atonality and experimentalism, as evidenced in *Sections* (1963) and in *String Quartet no.1* (1966), both of which won BMI awards. The work *Ad Hoc* (1971), composed as Ford Foundation/MENC Composer-in-Residence for the State of Hawaii, would mark a turning point in his compositional practice: a departure from clustered sonorities and angular gestures toward consonant "sound objects" and transparent harmonic voicings.

In 1974 both his doctoral dissertation, *Repetition and the Drift towards Constant Focus in the Pattern-Pulse Works of Terry Riley and Steve Reich*, and his work *Ditto Varianti* for orchestra reflected an interest in new conceptions of tonal and formal structures. Resulting explorations of diachronic and synchronic facets of music led to a novel approach to layering and juxtaposition; these techniques would flourish in his compositions of later decades. During the 1980s, he incorporated minimalist techniques—including interest in repetition, rhythmic regularity, and simple/direct musical statements—in *Fantasy Variations* (1980) for flute and piano, *The Epistemology of Delicate Time in Blue Three* (1982) for two pianos, and in *String Quartet no.2* (1984). Kam's compositions from the 1990s to the present illustrate further refinement and synthesis of style. *Sonata no.1* for piano (2002), *Sonata for Clarinet and Piano* (2004), and *Sonata Ibis* for clarinet, cello, and piano (2005), are works based on his unique method of layering: these three works contain identical piano parts, while the latter two contain identical clarinet parts; the result is a trilogy that explores changes in musical perception, contexts, and foci. Similarly, his ten-minute *Opera 101* (2009) and *Now…with Dashes of Prelude no.4* (2008) for two pianos, explore familiar gestures and materials with disparate continuities, resulting in the altered perception of musical ideas unfolding within dissimilar contexts.

Kam has been one of the most influential pedagogues in the United States. In 1974 he began teaching at the University of Miami School of Music in Coral Gables, Florida, where he remains today. His students include Charles Mason, Dorothy Hindman, Daniel Adams, Robin Cox, and ORLANDO JACINTO GARCÍA, among many others. He served as President of the Southern Chapter and as National Board Member for Composition within the College Music Society, and as a member of the Executive and National Councils within the Society of Composers, Inc. Kam's music has been published by Kalmus, Smith Publications, Media Press, and Belwin-Mills, and can be heard on Capstone Records, TNC, Albany Records, and Living Artist Recordings.

BIBLIOGRAPHY

D. Kam: *Repetition and the Drift Towards Constant Focus in the Pattern-Pulse Works of Terry Riley and Steve Reich* (diss., U. of Illinois, Urbana-Champaign, 1974)

B. Milovanovic: *A Study and Performance Guide to Dennis Kam's Sonata Ibis for Clarinet, Violin, Cello and Piano and a Performance Comparison to Four Earlier Versions of the Work* (diss., U. of Miami, 2008)

JUAN R. CHATTAH

Kamae, Eddie [Edward] **(Leilani)** (*b* Honolulu, Hawaii, 4 Aug 1927). Hawaiian musician, bandleader, songwriter, and researcher. A leading figure in the late 20th century revival of Hawaiian culture, Kamae has led the seminal Sons of Hawaii band for over 50 years. He has reintroduced a large number of classic Hawaiian songs from earlier eras, composed several standards, and has documented important Hawaiian topics on over 1000 hours of film.

He began his career in 1948 performing light classics and pop with Shoi Ikemi as The Ukulele Rascals. Self taught, Kamae developed chord voicings and plucking techniques that expanded the instrument's reach. In 1959 Kamae met Gabby Pahinui and formed Sons of Hawaii. He radically transformed his style for the group, moving between rhythmic accompaniment and *pa'ani* (soloing) in a fluid give and take. He also began singing in a distinctive voice full of Hawaiian vocal inflections. With mentoring from scholar Mary Kawena Pukui and others, Kamae began researching older Hawaiian repertoire and composing. His arrangement of waltzes, such as "Sanoe," and other songs of the 19th century introduced a classical elegance into the group. At the same time The Sons performed downhome party favorites, like "'Ama 'Ama."

Despite enormous success, The Sons did not work steadily and side projects were frequent. In 1975 Kamae was one of the first Hawaiian artists to take total control of his business affairs. At that time the group reemerged as a vital force performing more originals, including Kamae's popular "E Ku'u Morning Dew." In 1988 Kamae and his wife Myrna began producing documentaries on Hawaiian music and culture. A biography, *Hawaiian Son: the Life and Music of Eddie Kamae* ('Ai Pohaku Press), appeared in 2004. In 2007 he received an NEA National Heritage Fellowship.

J.W. JUNKER

Kamakahi, Dennis (David Kahekilimamaoikalanikeha) (*b* Honolulu, Hawaii, 31 March 1953). Hawaiian singer, songwriter, and slack key guitarist. One of Hawaii's most prolific songwriters, Reverend Dennis Kamakahi is responsible for Hawaiian-language standards such as "Koke'e" and "Wahine Ilikea" and English songs like "Golden Stallion" and "Maui Mountain Morning." He composes in a poetic style inspired by earlier masters of the Hawaiian form such as Queen Lili'uokalani and Sam Li'a Kalainaina. Traces of country and folk can be heard in the melodies. He is also a warm, evocative singer and a *ki ho'alu* (slack key guitar) master.

Kamakahi was raised in Honolulu, though his family has close ties to the island of Moloka'i. He first learned slack key from his grandfather at age ten but cites popular artists such as Gabby Pahinui and others as main influences. During high school at Kamehameha Schools, Kamakahi formed a trio with Aaron Mahi and Kalena Silva. They received valuable mentoring from older artists such as Kahauanu Lake and The Sons of Hawaii. In 1974 Eddie Kamae asked Dennis to join The Sons to fill the spot vacated by Gabby Pahinui. He began to develop his songwriting with help from noted Hawaiian language scholar Mary Kawena Pukui and has composed approximately 500 songs. He was ordained a minister in 1977 and established Ka Leo Mana O Ke Akua Mission. From 1974 to 1995 Kamakahi recorded seven albums with The Sons. In 1996 he released his first solo album, *Pua'ena* (Glow Brightly) for George Winston's Dancing Cat label. In 1998 he began performing with his son, ukulele player David Kamakahi (*b* 1980) and others. In 2009 he was inducted into the Hawaiian Music Hall of Fame.

J.W. JUNKER

Kamakawiwo'ole, Israel (Ka'ano'i) [Iz] (*b* Honolulu, HI, 20 May 1959; *d* Honolulu, HI, 26 June 1997). Hawaiian singer and musician. Israel Kamakawiwo'ole is the best-selling Hawaiian singer of the modern era. His music has achieved global success while resonating deeply throughout the Hawaiian community. Six feet two inches tall and over 700 pounds, Kamakawiwo'ole sang in a smooth, full bodied tenor that worked well for harmony or lead vocals. He accompanied himself on ukulele, a common approach in Hawaii. His core repertoire consisted of Hawaiian standards and songs in English associated with Hawaii, but he was no purist. He also performed pop ballads as well as some Latin and early Jawaiian music. His sound was bright and positive with subtle undertones of plaintiveness. Some of his later recordings incorporated strings, electronics, and even a few special effects, but for the most part Kamakawiwo'ole played acoustic music in a traditional Hawaiian string band setting.

He was born into a musical family with roots on the tiny, isolated island of Ni'ihau. His uncle, Moe Keale, was a popular solo artist and former member of The Sons of Hawaii. His older sister Lydia was a *kumu hula* (hula teacher). In 1975 Israel helped found The Makaha Sons of Ni'ihau, which included his older brother Skippy. They recorded four popular albums together and performed throughout the islands. When Skippy died in 1982, Israel took over as onstage spokesperson and became a local celebrity, known for his spontaneous wit and devil-may-care attitude as well as his angelic voice. In 1990 he released a solo album, *Ka 'Ano'i*, on the small Discos Tropical label. He left the Makaha Sons of Ni'ihau after the album *Ho'oluana* in 1991. A period of retrenchment followed, when he recorded several songs with The Hawaiian Style Band, then signed with the locally powerful Mountain Apple label. Working with label owner Jon de Mello, Kamakawiwo'ole released his second solo album, *Facing Future*, in 1993. The first Hawaiian album to be certified platinum, *Facing Future* mixes Hawaiian classics with romantic English language ballads, reggae-flavored pop, cover tunes and what for Hawaiian music is an unusually personal two-part revision of "Hawaii 78," a protest song originally recorded with the Makaha Sons of Ni'ihau. *Facing Future* also features a solo reworking of "Somewhere Over the Rainbow/What a Wonderful World," a medley that first appeared on *Ka 'Ano'i*. Though recorded as a rough sketch without a lyric sheet, it perfectly captures Kamakawiwo'ole's artistry and de Mello was wise to release it. It has become a worldwide phenomenon frequently heard in soundtracks and commercials.

Kamakawiwo'ole and de Mello maintained the same winning formula on *E Ala E* (1995), and *In Dis Life* (1996). Respiratory problems began to limit Kamakawiwo'ole's live performances by this time and his public demeanor grew more serious. In many ways he assumed a role similar to Bob Marley in reggae as a respected cultural icon and popular entertainer. When he died, Kamakawiwo'ole's casket was laid in state at the capitol rotunda in Honolulu, the first musician to be so honored. Several posthumous releases have since appeared and his recordings remain popular. His name (shortened to Iz) can still be seen around the Hawaiian Islands on bumper stickers. Fans widely circulate his music and image on the Internet.

J.W. JUNKER

Kamen, Michael (*b* New York, NY, 15 April 1948; *d* London, UK, 18 Nov 2003). Film composer, orchestral arranger, conductor, oboist, hornist, and keyboardist. Son of a dentist and a teacher, Kamen attended the High School of Music & Art with classmates singer-songwriter Janis Ian and fellow future film composer Mark Snow (*b* Martin Fulterman). He then attended the Juilliard School alongside Leonard Slatkin and played the oboe under Jean Morel. With Fulterman and cellist-composer Dorian Rudnytsky he formed the rock/classical fusion band the New York Roll & Roll Ensemble, which performed in 1967 as Janis Ian's backing ensemble, played in 1969 in Leonard Bernstein's Young People's Concerts with the New York PO at Lincoln Center, and made a series of albums from 1968 to 1972.

Kamen's early combination of orchestral music with rock firmly established the direction of his career. He composed orchestral works, including several dozen film and TV scores, ballets (beginning with *Rodin mis en vie* for the Harkness Ballet, 1973), saxophone (1990) and guitar concertos, and the symphonic poem *The New Moon in the Old Moon's Arms* (2000). His work in popular music continued during the 1970s with contributions on horn, oboe, and synthesizer to the soundtrack for *Godspell* and to albums by Jim Croce, Tim Curry, and others; he also served as music director and performer on David Bowie's tour for *Diamond Dogs* (1974). He contributed orchestral arrangements for such British artists as Pink Floyd (especially *The Wall*,

1979, but also including solo projects by David Gilmour and Roger Waters), Eurythmics, Queen, the Who, and Kate Bush. In addition, he worked with the Irish band the Cranberries, Canadian artists Liona Boyd, Bryan Adams, and Rush (*Counterparts*, 1993), and such US artists as Indigo Girls, Queensrÿche, and Metallica (*S&M*, 1999).

Kamen's earliest film scores were for little-known shorts and TV and feature films from 1976 onward. His reputation brought him more prominent scoring assignments in the early 1980s, and he became particularly associated with action-adventure films, working at least twice with directors Terry Gilliam, Richard Donner, and John McTiernan.

In 1996 Kamen created the Mr. Holland's Opus Foundation (named for the popular 1995 film about a music teacher) in order to support music education; he arranged and conducted *Diana, Princess of Wales: Tribute* (1997), and he similarly arranged and conducted the string orchestra for the 2002 memorial "Concert for George [Harrison]." The music for *Edge of Darkness* won a British Academy of Film and Television Arts Award for best original television music; *Robin Hood: Prince of Thieves* won a Grammy for best pop instrumental performance, and its theme song, "(Everything I Do) I Do It for You," likewise won a Grammy; "An American Symphony" from *Mr. Holland's Opus* won a Grammy for Best Instrumental Arrangement; and the *S&M* version of Metallica's "The Call of Ktulu" won the 2000 Grammy for Best Rock Instrumental Performance. Kamen was diagnosed with multiple sclerosis in 1997 and died of heart attack in 2003.

WORKS

FILM AND TV SCORES
The Next Man (1976); Polyester (1981); The Dead Zone (1983); Brazil (1985); Edge of Darkness (1985); Amazing Stories (1986); Highlander (1986); Mona Lisa (1986); Shoot for the Sun (TV, 1986); Adventures in Babysitting (1987); Lethal Weapon (1987); Someone to Watch Over Me (1987); Suspect (1987); Crusoe (1988); Die Hard (1988), The Adventures of Baron Munchausen (1988); Road House (1989); Licence to Kill (1989); Lethal Weapon 2 (1989); Die Hard 2 (1990), The Krays (1990); Robin Hood: Prince of Thieves (1991); Hudson Hawk (1991); The Last Boy Scout (1991); Lethal Weapon 3 (1992); Tales from the Crypt (1992–93); Splitting Heirs (1993); Last Action Hero (1993); The Three Musketeers (1993); Don Juan DeMarco (1994); Die Hard: With a Vengeance (1995); Mr. Holland's Opus (1995); 101 Dalmatians (1996); Event Horizon (1997); The Winter Guest (1997); From the Earth to the Moon (1998); Jerry Seinfeld: "I'm Telling You for the Last Time" (1998); Lethal Weapon 4 (1998); The Iron Giant (1999); X-Men (2000); Band of Brothers (2001); Mr. Dreyfuss Goes to Washington (2001); Open Range (2003)

ORCHESTRA
Rodin mis en vie ballet, 1973; Sax Conc., 1990; The New Moon in the Old Moon's Arms, 2000

WRITINGS
"Rock: Can the Atomic Oboe Be Far Behind?" *New York Times* (2 Jan 1972)

BIBLIOGRAPHY
F. Groult: "Mr. Kamen's Opus," *Underscores: le magazine de la musique de film* (3 July 2008) [in French, interview made in 2001]

DURRELL BOWMAN

Kamensek, Karen (*b* Chicago, IL, 2 Jan 1970). Conductor. Growing up in a family that included three choral conductors, including her mother, Kamensek sought to conduct from age 11. She studied piano at Indiana University (BM 1991), playing in opera studios and in the string studios of Josef Gingold and Janos Starker, who offered career support. After she developed tendinitis in her arm from overuse, she studied conducting at Indiana U (MM 1996) with Imre Palló, Thomas Baldner, Jan Harrington, and Robert Porco. She first established herself in Europe. While assisting conductor Dennis Russell Davies (1991–6), she was involved in two recording projects: music by Philip Glass and a CD including works by Lou Harrison and Peggy Glanville-Hicks. She conducted two world premieres of music-theater pieces by Philip Glass: *Orphée* in her European debut at a Festival in Weikersheim, Germany, with the Jeunesses Musicales (1993), and *Les Enfants Terribles* at the 1996 Spoleto Festival resulting in a live recording issued by Orange Mountain Music. Her persistence over four years to assist conductor Simone Young finally earned Kamensek an opportunity at the Bergen Philharmonic Orchestra (1999–2000) and marked a turning point in her career. Since then, Kamensek has held a series of conducting posts in Europe: Kapellmeisterin, Vienna Volksoper (2000–2); Music Director, Freiburg Theatre (2003–6); interim Chief Conductor, Slovenian National Theatre in Maribor, Slovenia, the homeland of her parents (2007–8 season); Deputy Music Director, Hamburg State Opera (2008–9 season); and Music Director, Hannover State Opera (appointed in March 2010, beginning with the 2011–12 season). In addition to opera, Kamensek conducts a broad spectrum of symphonic repertoire, classic to modern music, including film music and crossover projects in jazz and has made appearances as guest conductor with orchestras in Europe, the United States, and Asia.

BIBLIOGRAPHY
F. Hoffmann and E. Rieger, eds: *Europäischer Dirigentinnenreader*, Schriftenreihe Frau und Musik, Internationaler Arbeitskreis e.V., Bd. 4 (Kassel, 2002), 79
K. Liese: "'Sie suchen eine Assistentin, das bin ich': Karen Kamensek im Interview mit Kirsten Liese (You Look for an Assistant, I Am It)," *VivaVoce*, lxiv (spring 2003)
H. Peters: "Die Frau an ihrer Seite (The Woman at her Side)," *Welt Online* (5 Jan 2009)
R. Wagner: "Karen Kamensek wird Musikdirektorin an Oper Hannover," *Hannoversche Allgemeine* (2 March 2010)

J. MICHELE EDWARDS

Kaminsky, Laura (*b* New York, NY, 28 Sept 1956). Composer and performer. She attended Oberlin College and the City College of New York, where she studied composition (MA 1980). She has received commissions from a number of organizations, including the New York State Council on the Arts and the 92nd Street Y Chorale, and has been awarded grants from Meet the Composer (1983–92) and a fellowship from the Tuch Foundation (1978–80). She co-founded the contemporary music ensemble Musicians' Accord (1980) and from 1988 to 1992 was artistic director of Town Hall, New York. She was a visiting lecturer at the National Academy of Music in Winneba, Ghana (1992–3), and served as director of the European Mozart Academy in Poland in 1996–7. She was chair of the music department at the Cornish College of the Arts in Seattle (1999–2004) and Dean of the Conservatory of Music at Purchase College, SUNY (2004–8). As of 2012 she was serving as the associate artistic director at New York's Symphony Space and was on the board of Chamber Music America. Kaminsky's compositions consist mainly of intimate chamber works that are characterized by luminous textures and an understated sensuality.

WORKS
(selective list)

Orch: Untitled, 1992; Spiritlines, str orch, pf, 2006; Terra Terribilis: Concerto for Three Percussionists and Orchestra, 2008

Chbr, inst: Str Qt no.1, 1977; Enkomios, fl, pf, 1980; In memoriam Eleazer, tpt, 2 hn, trbn, 1980; Duo, fl, perc, 1982; Five for Three, fl, vc, pf, 1982; Remembering August, vn, va, vc, 1983; Still Life for the End of the Day, fl + a fl, ob, cl + b cl, vc, hp, 1984; A Dream Revisited, fl, perc, 1985; Juderla, vn, 1987; Just Here, Sitting Now, cl, pf, 1987; Proverbs of Hell, S, mar, pf, 1989; Whence It Comes, vc, perc, 1989; It Comes and It Goes, fl, gui, 1990; Triftmusik, pf, 1991; And Trouble Came: an African AIDS Diary, nar, va, vc, pf, 1993; Transformations, str qt, 2000; Transformations II, str qt, 2002; Monotypes, str qt, 2005; American Nocturne, str qt, 2009; Wave Hill, vn, pf, 2009; Cadmium Yellow, str qt, 2010;

Vocal: 13 Ways of Looking at a Blackbird, chorus, fl, 1977; 2 Songs of Emily Dickinson, S, fl, 1980; Para mi corazon, high v, fl, s sax/cl, vc, vib, pf, 1982; Sonnet Lines, Mez/S, fl, vib, pf, 1982; Sonnet Lines no. 2, S, pf, 1982; Twilight Settings, S, str qt, perc, 1985, rev. 1988; There is a Season, chorus, cl, vc, perc, pf, 1986; Whitman Songs, Bar, pf, 1992

Dance scores: Steepletop Dances, dancer, ob, perc, 1984; Phaethon, dancer, perc, 1987

LISA B. ROBINSON/JONAS WESTOVER

Kampela, Arthur (*b* Rio de Janeiro, Brazil, 6 Feb 1960). Brazilian composer, guitarist, and singer. He studied composition at Escola de Música da Universidade do Rio de Janeiro, Manhattan School of Music, and Columbia University, where he earned a DMA in 1998, working with MARIO DAVIDOVSKY and FRED LERDAHL. He also received private instruction from Brian Ferneyhough. His music reflects the aesthetics of New Complexity, exploring extended techniques for acoustic instruments as exemplified in works such as *Percussion Study III* for guitar solo (1997), *Exoskeleton* for viola alla chitarra (2003), and *Naked Singularity* for tuba solo (2004). Of particular significance is his treatment of rhythm, which explores the connection between nonequivalent metric figures through micrometric modulations—an elaboration on the theoretical work of Henry Cowell and the music of Elliott Carter. Kampela also applies contemporary compositional techniques to music of the popular and vernacular traditions, as in *Epopéia* (1988) and *Valsa do assassino* (1988). He won the International Guitar Composition Competition in Caracas, Venezuela (1995), and the Lamarque Pons Guitar Composition Competition in Montevideo, Uruguay (1988). He has received fellowships from the Brazilian government and Columbia University and has received commissions from the Fromm and Koussevitzky Foundations and the New York PO, among others.

BIBLIOGRAPHY
A. Kampela: "A Knife All Blade: Deciding Which Side Not to Take," *CMc*, lxvii–lxviii (1999), 167–93
G. Bortz: *Rhythm in the Music of Brian Ferneyhough, Michael Finnissy, and Arthur Kampela: a Guide for Performers* (diss., CUNY, 2003)

SILVIO J. DOS SANTOS

Kampuchean American music. *See* ASIAN AMERICAN MUSIC.

Kanahele, George (Hu'eu Sanford) (*b* Kahuku, Hawaii, 17 Oct 1930; *d* Guam, 15 Sept 2000). Scholar and activist. Kanahele graduated from Kamehameha Schools in 1948 and then became a missionary for the Church of Jesus Christ of Latter-Day Saints, working mainly in Japan. During the 1960s, he attended Brigham Young University–Hawaii, earning both bachelor's and master's degrees in political science. Kanahele then studied Government and Southeast Asian Affairs at Cornell University (PhD 1967), with a dissertation on the relationship between Japan and Indonesia. Over the following decade, he became immersed in Hawaiian cultural issues. His groundbreaking book, *Hawaiian Music and Musicians: An Illustrated History* (Honolulu, 1979/*R* 1986), offered an extensive history of Hawaiian music, ranging from traditional styles to contemporary developments. Continuing to contribute to what became known as the Hawaiian Renaissance, which saw renewed local interest in traditional island culture, he also wrote several other books about the culture of the islands. Kanahele sought to translate scholarship into action, which included helping indigenous peoples create sustainable businesses and supporting other local causes that benefited the Islands.

JONAS WESTOVER

Kanahele, Pualani Kanaka'ole and Nalani Kanaka'ole Sisters Pualani Kanaka'ole Kanahele (*b* Keaukaha, HI, 14 Sept 1937), writer, teacher, and producer, and Nalani Kanaka'ole Kanahele (*b* Hawaii, 19 March 1946), choreographer and teacher, are the daughters of Edith Kanaka'ole, famed chanter and *kumu hula* (master teacher) of Hilo, Hawaii. After Edith's death in 1979, they inherited her hula school, Halau o Kekuhi, and became respected elders and teachers in their own right. The sisters continue the legacy of their mother by preserving ancient practices while incorporating innovations into their hula presentations. They codirected and coproduced the hula drama, *Holo Mai Pele*, the epic tale of the goddess of fire, Pele, and Hi'iaka, the patron goddess of hula dancers. The production blends traditional hula and oli (chant) with narration and modern stagecraft into a theatrical performance. Pualani and Nalani have created other experimental hula performances that utilize new or non-Hawaiian influences, while maintaining a strong classical hula tradition.

Pualani teaches Hawaiian studies at the University of Hawaii. She also serves as the President of Edith Kanaka'ole Foundation, which supports various cultural preservation and education projects. Nalani is the Artistic Director of the Foundation. Both sisters are leaders in local and worldwide efforts to protect native cultures. They received a National Heritage Fellowship Award from the National Endowment for the Arts in 1993. The Hawaiian Academy of Recording Arts presented them with the Na Hoku Hanohano Award for Haku Mele, an award for the composition of a song or chant primarily in the Hawaiian language, for their song "Eo Mai 'O Ka'uku" (1999), and Best Hawaiian Language Performance of the Year for the album *Uwolani*, produced by their hula school (1998).

WRITINGS
(selected)
P.K. Kanahele and D.K. Wise: *Ka Honua Ola (The Living Earth): an Introduction to Pele and Hi'iaka with Annotated Bibliography* (Honolulu, 1989)
P.K. Kanahele: *Holo Mai Pele*, trans. K. Higashi, ed. D.M. Dudoit (Honolulu, 2001)

PAULA J. BISHOP

Kander, John (Harrold) (*b* Kansas City, MO, 18 March 1927). Composer. He studied music at Oberlin College, where he composed songs with James Goldman (a childhood friend) and at Columbia University, where he studied with composers JACK BEESON, OTTO LUENING, and DOUGLAS S. MOORE, while working as a vocal accompanist. After serving as the dance music arranger for *Gypsy* (1959) and *Irma La Douce* (1960), Kander was given the opportunity to compose *A Family Affair* (1962) for Broadway with James Goldman and his brother William. Publisher Tommy Valendo introduced him to Fred Ebb (*b* New York, 8 April 1928; *d* New York, 11 Sept 2004) in 1962, and the new team immediately produced two hits, "My Coloring Book" and "I Don't Care Much," both recorded by Barbra Streisand. From 1965 to 1997 Kander and Ebb produced 11 musicals on Broadway (two additional musicals begun with Ebb appeared since Ebb's death), including the Tony Award-winning *Cabaret* (1966; revived 1987 and 1998), concerning the moral decline of Germany in 1929–30 as reflected in a cabaret, and *Kiss of the Spider Woman* (1993), about an unlikely friendship between cell mates and escaping reality through film in a South American dictatorship, and at least two other major successes, *Zorbá* (1968; revived 1983), based on Nikos Kazantzakis's novel *Zorbá the Greek*, and *Chicago* (1975; revived 1996), a story of two glamorous, unapologetic, and celebrity-seeking murderesses in 1920s Chicago. They also created numerous song hits in films, "Mein Herr," "Maybe this Time," and "Money, Money" (*Cabaret*, 1972), "How Lucky Can You Get?" (*Funny Lady*, 1975), "But the World Goes Round," and "New York, New York" (*New York, New York*, 1977).

The careers of several major female stars were greatly aided by Kander and Ebb's special material and star turns, in particular Liza Minnelli, who received a Tony Award in her debut at the age of 19 in the title role of their first Broadway show, *Flora, The Red Menace* (1965), an Emmy for her one-woman television broadcast, *Liza with a Z* (1972), and an Oscar for her portrayal of Sally Bowles in the film version of *Cabaret* (1972). She played the starring roles in their shows *Chicago* (in the role originally created for Gwen Verdon), *The Act* (1977), and *The Rink* (1984). Other featured female stars cultivated

by Kander and Ebb included Chita Rivera (*Chicago*, *The Rink*, *Kiss of the Spider Woman*), Lauren Bacall (*Woman of the Year*), and, in film, Streisand (*Funny Lady*).

Despite several commercial failures (*Flora*, *70, Girls, 70*, and *The Rink*), Kander is almost invariably praised for his tuneful scores, his professionalism, and his ability to compose music that serves the show at hand. His impressive mastery of styles range from Weill pastiches (*Cabaret*), Greek bouzouki music (*Zorbá*), and popular styles of the 1920s and 30s (*Flora*, *Chicago*, and *Steel Pier*) to the glittery musical spectacles of Las Vegas floor shows (*The Act*). In 1991 about 30 Kander and Ebb songs formed the centerpiece of a popular Broadway revue, *And the World Goes 'Round*; the following year another revue anthology of Kander and Ebb songs appeared in London, *Sing Happy*.

The revival *Cabaret* of 1998 enjoyed one of the longest runs of any Broadway musical, first-run, or revival, and the still-running revival of *Chicago* is the longest-running Broadway revival and the fifth-longest running book musical of all time. The film adaptation of *Chicago* (2002) was the first film musical to win the Academy Award for Best Picture in 34 years. Kander's singular collaboration with one partner (they worked almost every day for 42 years, usually composing together in the same room) surpassed Richard Rodgers's 40-year creative serial monogamy with Lorenz Hart and Oscar Hammerstein II. At the time of Ebb's death, the pair had made significant progress on four musicals. Two of these works appeared on Broadway over the next six years, *Curtains* (2007), a light-hearted backstage murder mystery spoof begun in the 1980s, and *The Scottsboro Boys* (2010), a serious musicalization of the infamous Scottsboro trial of the 1930s and a powerful indictment of racism told as a minstrel show by a nearly all-black cast for which Kander wrote the lyrics for several planned songs, including "That's Not the Way We Do Things."

WORKS

MUSICALS
(selective list. Unless otherwise indicated, all are musicals, and dates are those of first New York performances. Librettists and lyricists are listed in that order in parentheses.)
A Family Affair (J. and W. Goldman), orchd. R. Ginzler, 27 Jan 1962
Never Too Late (incidental music to play by S.A. Long), 27 Nov 1962
Flora, The Red Menace (G. Abbott and R. Russell, F. Ebb, after L. Atwell: *Love Is Just Around the Corner*), orchd. D. Walker, 11 May 1965 (incl. "A Quiet Thing" and "Sing Happy")
Cabaret (J. Masteroff, Ebb, after J.V. Druten: *I Am a Camera* and stories by C. Isherwood), orchd. Walker, 20 Nov 1966 (incl. "Wilkommen," "If You Could See Her," and "Cabaret"); film 1972 (incl. "Mein Herr," "Maybe this Time," and "The Money Song")
The Happy Time (N.R. Nash, Ebb, after novel by R.L. Fontaine), orchd. Walker, 18 Jan 1968 (incl. "The Happy Time" and "I Don't Remember You")
Zorbá (J. Stein, Ebb, after N. Kazantzakis: *Zorbá the Greek*), orchd. Walker, 17 Nov 1968 (incl. "Life Is")
70, Girls, 70 (Ebb, N.L. Martin, Ebb, after Masteroff: *Make Mine Mink*), orchd. Walker, 15 April 1971 (incl. "Yes")
Chicago (Ebb and B. Fosse, Ebb, after play by M.D. Watkins), orchd. R. Burns, 3 June 1975 (incl. "All That Jazz," "Cell Block Tango," "Mister Cellophane," and "Razzle Dazzle"); film 2002 ("I Move On")
The Act (G. Furth, Ebb), orchd. Burns, 29 Oct 1977 (incl. "City Lights")

Madwoman of Central Park West (P. Newman, A. Laurents) (one song
with Ebb)

Woman of the Year (P. Stone, Ebb, after screenplay by R. Lardner and
M. Kanin), orchd. M. Gibson, 29 March 1981 (incl. "The Grass Is
Always Greener")

The Rink (T. McNally, Ebb), orchd. Gibson, 9 Feb 1984 (incl. "Colored Lights")

Kiss of the Spider Woman (McNally, Ebb, after novel by M. Puig),
orchd. Gibson, 20 Oct 1992 (London); 3 May 1993 (incl. "I Do Miracles" and "Kiss of the Spider Woman")

Steel Pier (D. Thompson, Ebb), orchd. Gibson, 24 April 1997

All About Us (originally Over and Over) (J. Stein, Ebb, after play *The
Skin of Our Teeth* by T. Wilder), orchd. Gibson, Brohn, 6 Jan 1999
(Arlington, VA); 10 April 2007 (Westport, CT)

Curtains (R. Holmes, Ebb, Kander, Holmes, after an original book and
concept by P. Stone), orchd. Brohn, 22 March 2007 (incl. "Thinking
of Him," "Show People," and "I Miss the Music")

The Visit (McNally, Ebb, after play by F. Dürrenmatt), orchd. Gibson, 1
Oct 2001 (Chicago); 27 May 2008 (Arlington, VA)

The Scottsboro Boys (originally Minstrel Show) (Thompson, Ebb,
Kander), orchd. L. Hochman, 31 Oct 2010 (incl. "Shout!" and "Go
Back Home")

FILMS, TELEVISION, AND AUDIO
(selective list)

Films: Something for Everyone (1970); Cabaret (with Ebb) (1972);
Funny Lady (with Ebb), Lucky Lady (with Ebb) (1975); A Matter of
Time (1976); New York, New York (with Ebb) (1977); French Post-
cards (with Ebb) (1979); Kramer vs. Kramer (1979); The Still of the
Night (1982); Blue Skies Again (1983); Places in the Heart (1984);
I Want to Go Home (1989); Stepping Out (1991)

Television: Liza with a Z (with Ebb) (1972); An Early Frost (1985)

Album: An Evening with John Kander & Fred Ebb (with John Kander
at the piano), DRG (1973)

BIBLIOGRAPHY

S. Green: *The World of Musical Comedy* (New York, 1960, 4/ 1980)

A. Kasha and J. Hirschhorn: *Notes on Broadway: Conversations with
the Great Songwriters* (Chicago, 1985)

K. Mandelbaum: *Not Since "Carrie": Forty Years of Broadway Musical
Flops* (New York, 1991)

S. Suskin: *Show Tunes: The Songs, Shows, and Careers of Broadway's
Major Composers* (New York, 1992; 4/2010)

J. Kander and F. Ebb (as told to Greg Lawrence): *Colored Lights: Forty
Years of Words and Music, Show Biz, Collaboration, and All That
Jazz* (New York, 2003)

J.R. Bryer and R.A. Davison, ed.: *The Art of the American Musical:
Conversations with the Creators* (New Brunswick, NJ, 2005)

J. Leve: *Kander and Ebb* (New Haven, 2009)

GEOFFREY BLOCK

Kane, Raymond (Kaleoalohapoinaʻoleohelemanu)
(*b* Koloa, Kauai, HI, 2 Oct 1925; *d* Honolulu, HI, 27 Feb
2008). Hawaiian slack key guitarist and singer. Kane
was one of the first masters of Hawaiian slack key guitar
to give solo concerts, tour extensively, and teach students from around the world. He was an effective ambassador for the style, with simple but deeply emotive
material and an extroverted personality.

He was born into a large musical family though his
mother and adoptive father did not perform. In 1934
Albert Kawelo taught him the rudiments of slack key in
exchange for fish. Kane was never a virtuoso in the
same sense as Gabby Pahinui and others. He tuned to
his voice and did not improvise except within strict parameters. His repertoire consisted of original compositions and arrangements. He normally picked with only
thumb and index finger, but his sound was rich, flowing, and smooth as on his signature tune "Punahele."
He sang with a distinctive low-pitched growl.

Kane recorded several tracks in 1958 for the
Tradewinds label and his first full album in 1975. By
then he was concertizing for the newly created Hawaiian Music Foundation and teaching *ki hoʻalu* (slack key
guitar), though his main job was welding. In 1987 he
received a National Endowment for the Arts Heritage
Fellowship and began touring outside Hawaii. At that
same time he began an extensive recording project for
George Winston's Dancing Cat label. He also recorded
for Hula, Rounder, and Respect Records of Japan. Kane
died in 2008, two days after his cousin, Genoa Keawe.
He translated his middle name into English as "the
voice of love that comes and goes like a bird and will
never be forgotten."

J.W. JUNKER

Kanengiser, William (James) (*b* Orange, NJ, 22 July
1959). Classical guitarist. He studied guitar first at the
Mannes Conservatory Preparatory School and then at
the University of Southern California (BM, 1981; MM,
1983) with Pepe Romero. He has recorded and performed since 1980 with the Los ANGELES GUITAR QUARTET of
which he was an original member. As a soloist, he
began his career with first prizes in the Toronto Guitar
Competition (1981) and the Concert Artists Guild New
York Competition (1987), and has recorded several solo
CDs, including *Rondo Alla Turka* (1991) and *Classical
Cool* (2003). *Classic Mancini* (1991), with guitarist
Gregg Nestor and several other instrumentalists, is an
album featuring chamber music settings of Mancini's
film scores. Kanengiser has published arrangements
and transcriptions for solo guitar, including pieces by
Gottschalk, Mozart, and Handel, and guitar quartet arrangements of Bizet's *Carmen* suite and Liszt's *Hungarian Rhapsody no.2*. Many of these arrangements have
been recorded either by Kanengiser as a soloist or by
the LAGQ. The Quartet has also recorded original
Kanengiser compositions such as *Air and Ground* (on
the recording of the same name, 1999), *Turn to the Sea*
(on *Spin*, 2006), and *African Suite: "Mbira"* (on *L.A.G.Q.*,
1998). Kanengiser has taught at the University of Southern California since 1983, and was Artist-in-Residence
at Whittier College from 1990 to 1994. He has made two
instructional DVDs: *Effortless Classical Guitar* and *Classical Guitar Mastery*.

BIBLIOGRAPHY

M. Summerfield: *The Classical Guitar: its Evolution, Players and Personalities since 1800* (Blaydon on Tyne, England, 1982, 5/2002)

J. Ferguson: "Classical Artist: William Kanengiser," *Guitar Player*, xxi/5
(1987), 84–88

D. Bell: "A Conversation with William Kanengiser," *Soundboard*, xx/2
(1993), 31–36

LARS HELGERT

Kanitz, Ernest [Ernst] (*b* Vienna, Austria, 9 April 1894;
d Menlo Park, CA, 7 April 1978). Composer of Austrian
birth. He studied law at the University of Vienna (doctorate 1918) and was a composition pupil of Franz
Schreker (1914–20). Kanitz became a lecturer at the
Neues Konservatorium (1922–38) and in 1930 founded
the Vienna Women's Chamber Choir. After immigrating

to the United States in 1938, he was appointed professor at Winthrop College, Rockhill (1938–41); he later served as director of the music department at Erskine College (1941–4) and professor at the University of Southern California, Los Angeles (1945–59), and Marymount College (1960–3). After early works reflecting the colorful chromaticism of the Schreker school, his style assumed a neo-classical simplicity. From the 1950s he also employed 12-tone techniques within his principally free-tonal compositions. His honors included the Austrian State Prize for composition (1936). He is the author of *A Counterpoint Manual* (Boston, 1948).

WORKS

Ops: Der Wunder-Wilan (prol, 3, Kanitz), 1923–9, rev. 1930; Room #12 (1, R. Thompson), 1956; Royal Auction (1, S. Shrager and A. Chorney), 1957; The Lucky Dollar (chbr op, 2 scenes, A. Stanford), 1959; Perpetual (chbr op, 1, E. Terry), 1960, rev. 1963, 1971

Vocal: Das Hohelied (Bible), solo vv, chorus, orch, 1920; 4 Gesänge (R. Tagore, P. Louÿs), S, orch, 1922; Abendfeier, S, orch, 1930; Zeitmusik (Kanitz), solo female vv, Bar, chorus, chbr orch, 1932; Gotthelf Schlicht (Das Lebenslied eines einfachen Menschen) (W. Alt), solo vv, chorus, orch, 1936; songs, other choral works

Orch: Heitere Ov., 1916–8; Intermezzo, chbr orch, 1917; Ballett-Musik, female vv, chbr orch, 1929; Bläserspiel (Serenade), wind, pf, perc, 1930; Concertino, theremin, orch, 1938; Motion Picture, 1944; Concerto grosso, 1945; Intermezzo concertante, a sax, sym. band, 1948; Concert Piece, tpt, orch, 1950; Conc., chbr orch, 1955; Bn Conc., 1962; Sinfonia seria (Sym. no.1), 1963; Moods, chbr orch, 1965; Sym. no.2, 1965; Sinfonia concertante (Sym. no.3), vn, vc, orch, 1967

Chbr music and solo inst works

MSS in *LAusc*

Principal publishers: Schlesingersche, Universal, Artisan, Associated, C.C. Birchard, Carl Fischer, Hall & McCreary, Mills, Theodore Presser, Valley Music

REINHARD KAPP

Kanno, Yōko (*b* Miyagi, Japan, 19 March 1964). Japanese pianist, arranger, and composer. Since 1988 she has composed and arranged select studio tracks for a wide range of mostly female Japanese pop artists. Her longest musical relationship has been with the singer Maaya Sakamoto, with whom she collaborated on eight albums between 1997 and 2009. Her initial forays into film music were for Japanese video games. Combining her pop studio work and game scoring, she developed a typically Japanese approach to film scoring based on polyglot styles, studio ensemble production, and embellished orchestral arrangements. Her first distinctive work accompanied a range of anime (Japanese animation) titles, mostly based on shojo manga (girls' comics), which included theme music for *Please Save my Earth* (1994) and *The Vision of Escaflowne* (1996). Their floral vocal harmonies and swirling mix of real and synthesized instrumentation aptly interpret the baroque richness of shojo manga. Kanno's break-out score was for the television series *Cowboy BeBop* (1998), which employed a range of jazz idioms to color the series' characters with an emotional complexity unexpected for anime at the time. Successive anime series established her creative power in molding character through musical portraiture: *Earth Girl Arjuna* (1998), *Brain Powerd* (1998), *Ghost in the Shell: Stand Alone Complex* (2002–2005), and *Darker than Black* (2007). Her feature film

scores for live action titles, most of which have been screened at international film festivals, evidence her most delicate orchestrations and arrangements: *Woman of Water* (2002), *Tokyo.Sora* (2002), *Kamikaze Girls* (2004), *Ashura* (2005), *Su-ki-da* (2005), and *Honey and Clover* (2006).

PHILIP BROPHY

Kansas. Rock group. It was formed in Topeka, Kansas, by Phil Ehart (*b* Coffeyville, KS, 4 Feb 1950; drums), Dave Hope (*b* 7 Oct 1949; bass guitar), Robby Steinhardt (*b* 25 May 1950; vocals, violin, viola, cello), Steve Walsh (*b* St. Louis, MO, 15 June 1951; vocals, keyboards, synthesizers, percussion), guitarist Rich Williams (*b* Topeka, KS, 1 Feb 1950), and Kerry Livgren (*b* Topeka, KS, 18 Sept 1949; guitar and keyboards). Their albums characteristically alternate between guitar-driven boogie-rock tracks and complex symphonic arrangements featuring mercurial time signatures.

Kansas was America's unlikely answer to British progressive rock. They were perceived as wan rehashing of a genuine article by British devotees, to whom it appeared incongruous that rock-and-blues midwesterners would aspire to more elaborate forms. Early iconography respected the contentious place of slavery in antebellum Kansas, and corresponding lyrics foregrounded notions of freedom, which appealed particularly to young male fans preferring imaginative quests over empty idolization. A cult following blossomed into mainstream success as *Leftoverture* (1976) and *Point of Know Return* (1977) introduced "Carry on wayward son" and "Dust in the Wind," respectively, the band's top singles which have enjoyed a second life complementing Hollywood soundtracks. Both albums went quadruple platinum, and the group's subsequent releases fared well into the early 1980s. The group was overhauled as Walsh, Steinhardt, Livgren, and Hope all departed; this second instantiation fared less well than the third, formed in 1986, with the addition of bassist Billy Greer and guitar virtuoso Steve Morse (*b* Hamilton, OH, 28 July 1954).

BIBLIOGRAPHY

E. Macan: *Rocking the Classics: English Progressive Rock and the Counterculture* (New York, 1997)

M. Morris: "Kansas and the Prophetic Tone," *AM*, xviii/1 (2000), 1–38

MICHAEL ETHEN

Kansas, University of. State-supported university founded in Lawrence in 1866. A Department of Music was established within the School of Fine Arts in 1884. Dance was part of the department from 1985 until 2009, when a free-standing School of Music was formed. In the fall of 2009, the School of Music had 300 undergraduates, 220 graduate students, and nearly 60 full- and part-time instructors. It offers the bachelor's, master's, and doctoral degrees in performance, theory, composition, music education, musicology, and music therapy, and a combined BFA degree in theatre and vocal music. The Department of Music founded the long-standing Midwestern Music Camp in the summer of 1936. It also offered the nation's first graduate program in music therapy (1948). Notable facilities include the World War II Memorial Campanile and Carillon (1951), and the Bales Organ Recital Hall (1996) with its Hellmuth Wolff tracker organ. The Thomas Gorton Music and Dance Library boasts an outstanding collection with over 100,000 books, bound journals, and scores, 15,000 LPs, over 10,000 CDs, and 2000 videos. Other notable resources include the Richard M. Wright Jazz Archive and Seaver Opera Collection in the Archive of Recorded Sound.

BIBLIOGRAPHY

J.B. Clark: *Music & Dance at KU: A History of Two Performing Arts at the University of Kansas*, revised and updated by P.R. Laird (Lawrence, 2007)

PAUL R. LAIRD

Kansas City. City in Missouri (pop. 459,787; metropolitan area: 2,035,334; 2010 US Census). Although in Missouri, about half of the inhabitants of the metropolitan area live across the state line in Kansas. The city was incorporated in 1850 and there are records of musical activity from that time onwards. With the opening of the Coates Opera House in 1870, touring opera companies began visiting. During the first half of the 20th century, the city's position as a communication center for the southwestern and midwestern states, combined with four decades of lenient government under the political machine of the Pendergast brothers, gave it an extraordinarily active night life, providing ideal conditions for the development of ragtime and jazz. The opening of the Kauffman Center for the Performing Arts in fall 2011 provides new homes for the Kansas City Symphony Orchestra, the Lyric Opera of Kansas City, and the Kansas City Ballet.

1. Classical music. 2. Jazz. 3. Popular and ethnic music.

1. CLASSICAL MUSIC. In the latter part of the 19th century, numerous opera companies, orchestras, and soloists included Kansas City on their tours. Emma Abbott and her company played 15 times at the Coates Opera House between 1879 and 1889. The National Opera Company gave a series of performances in late fall 1887, and Theodore Thomas led the Chicago SO in April 1895.

Two men contributed significantly to the development of orchestral music in Kansas City in the late 19th century. John Behr, who had been a violinist with the Boston SO, arrived in Kansas City in 1885. He conducted the orchestra of the Beethoven Club (established 1890) and later founded and conducted the Kansas City SO (active 1895–1904). He also directed the Willis Wood Theatre Orchestra, considered one of the finest in the area. Ultimately more influential than Behr was the conductor, composer, and teacher CARL BUSCH (1862–1943). Born in Denmark, Busch and three friends formed a string quartet and arrived in Kansas City in 1887. In 1895 Busch founded the short-lived Philharmonic Orchestra of Kansas City. He subsequently inaugurated a new Kansas City Symphony (active 1911–18) that gave Saturday afternoon pops concerts attended by 40,000 people and offered the first young people's con-

certs in Kansas City. In fall 1927 Busch joined the faculty at the Horner Institute–Kansas City Conservatory, and in fall 1933, became the orchestra conductor at the newly established University of Kansas City. Also a composer, Busch wrote his *Liberty Memorial Ode* for the dedication of the Liberty Memorial, now home to the National World War I Museum, in 1921. Busch received knighthoods from the kings of both Denmark and Norway for his contributions to music.

In 1897 W.H. Leib organized the Oratorio Society, which continued until 1917 under Busch; at its peak it had about 1000 members. Other choral groups have included the Apollo Club (founded 1899), the Schubert Club (1912), the Haydn Male Chorus (1925), and Choral Arts (1982). Active choral ensembles today include the Kansas City Symphony Chorus (which originated as the Mendelssohn Choir in 1960 and became the Civic Chorus before taking its present name in 1988), the Fine Arts Chorale (1972), and the Grammy Award–winning Kansas City Chorale (1981).

Early concert venues in Kansas City included the Grand Opera House (1891, converted into a parking garage in 1926), Butler Standard Theater (from 1900), the Gillis Opera House (1902–17), the Shubert Theatre (1906–35), and the Convention Hall (1899–1935, rebuilt after a fire in 1900 to seat 15,000).

Professional orchestral music in Kansas City continued when Karl Krueger founded the Kansas City PO in 1934 and conducted it until 1943. He was followed by Efrem Kurtz (1943–8), Hans Schwieger (1948–71), Jorge Mester (1971–4), and Maurice Peress (1974–80). It was dissolved in 1982; a new Kansas City SO was founded months later by R. Crosby Kemper, Jr., under the aegis of the Lyric Opera of Kansas City, whose director Russell Patterson conducted the orchestra until 1986, followed by William McGlaughlin (1986–97), Anne Manson (1998–2003), and Michael Stern (since 2005).

The Kansas City Chamber Orchestra (established 1987) performs under its founding conductor, Bruce Sorrell. Community orchestras include the Kansas City Civic Orchestra (1959), the Medical Arts Symphony, and the Philharmonia of Greater Kansas City.

The Lyric Opera of Kansas City was founded in 1958 to present opera in English. Along with the standard repertory, the company has given first or early performances of many American operas including works by Samuel Barber, Carlisle Floyd, Lee Hoiby, Jake Heggie, Henry Mollicone, and Kirke Mechem. In 1998 the company began performing in original languages with English supertitles. Prior to the establishment of the Lyric Opera, the Performing Arts Foundation sponsored performances of operas by Handel and Purcell in 1965–6.

Other professional music ensembles based in Kansas City include the contemporary music ensemble newEar (founded 1994) and the Bach Aria Soloists (1999). Summerfest (1991) offers an annual series of summer chamber music concerts.

Grace and Holy Trinity Cathedral (consecrated 1898) has long had an active music program. The world headquarters of the Community of Christ (formerly known as the Reorganized Church of Jesus Christ of Latter Day

Kauffman Center for the Performing Arts. (Photo by Timothy Hursley courtesy of Kauffman Center for the Performing Arts)

Saints), in nearby Independence, has two large and outstanding organs, by Aeolian-Skinner (1959, in the auditorium) and Casavant (1993, in the temple). Handel's *Messiah* has been performed in its auditorium annually since 1916.

Other musical organizations include the Kansas City Athenaeum (established 1894), the Kansas City Musical Club (1899), and the Kansas City Chapter of Young Audiences (1961). The Harriman-Jewell Series (1965) and the Friends of Chamber Music (1975) bring world-class soloists and ensembles to Kansas City. Concert series are also given at Johnson County Community College in Overland Park, KS, and at the University of Kansas in Lawrence.

The Kansas City Conservatory of Music was founded in 1906 and the Horner Institute of Fine Arts in 1914; the two were joined in 1926, and in 1959 they merged with the music department of the University of Kansas City. The latter became a unit of the University of Missouri in 1963.

In 2003 Van Cliburn Award winner Stanislav Ioudenitch founded Park University's International Center for Music.

Formal concert venues include the 1600-seat Lyric Theatre, a former Masonic temple built in the 1920s, the 1100-seat Folly Theater (originally the Standard, restored 1981), the 2400-seat Music Hall (1936), and the 1300-seat Yardley Hall and 400-seat Polsky Theater, both at Johnson County Community College's Carlsen Center (1990). The 285,000-square-foot Kauffman Center for the Performing Arts opened in fall 2011 with two performance venues, the 1800-seat Muriel Kauffman Theater and the 1600-seat Helzberg Hall.

2. JAZZ. Kansas City along with New Orleans, Chicago, and New York served as a cradle of jazz. Geographically isolated from the other jazz centers, Kansas City developed a distinctive hard swinging style of jazz distinguished by 4/4 rhythm and virtuoso solos accentuated with riffing sections.

The Coon-Sanders Original Night Hawk Orchestra (1919–32) was the most successful and influential of the early bands to come out of Kansas City. A white jazz band, led by Carleton Coon and Joe Sanders, the Night Hawks first achieved national recognition from their late night radio broadcasts over WDAF, a clear channel station. These pioneering broadcasts first established Kansas City as a beacon of jazz across North America. The success of the Night Hawks inspired a number of African American bands from Kansas City's 18th and Vine area. During the time of racial segregation, the 18th and Vine district was the center for commerce and social activities for the African American community. In the early 1920s, 18th and Vine fostered a number of notable bands including BENNIE MOTEN's Kansas City Orchestra (1919–35) and George E. Lee's Novelty Singing Orchestra (1919–36). These early orchestras favored a rhythmic western stomp-down style that employed simple head arrangements, so-called because they were played from memory, and collective improvisation.

During the Great Depression, musicians from the territorial bands flocked to Kansas City where work was plentiful. The Blue Devils, Blues Serenaders, ANDY KIRK and the Twelve Clouds of Joy, and other bands based in Texas and Oklahoma were called territorial bands for the vast swaths of territory they staked out across the Western United States. (*See* TERRITORY BAND.) Once established in Kansas City, veterans of the territorial tradition joined the African American Local No. 627 of the American Federation of Musicians. These new arrivals brought a tradition of arranging and solo excellence to the Kansas City style.

Bennie Moten hired COUNT BASIE, arranger Eddie Durham, and other members of the Blue Devil to modernize his band. Basie and Durham created a distinct style of jazz that employed a driving 4/4 rhythm, riffing sections, and solos. The riff, which is a short melodic phrase stated in forceful terms, became the signature of the Golden Age of Kansas City style. After Moten died in 1935, Count Basie formed a band at the Reno Club with former members of the Blue Devils and the Moten Band. Late night broadcasts from the Reno over radio station W9XBY caught the attention of John Hammond, a record producer and impresario. In 1936 Hammond helped Count Basie move his band to New York.

In the early 1940s, the Jay McShann band featuring CHARLIE PARKER ("Bird") followed the Basie band to national success. Originally from Kansas City, Kansas, Parker grew up in Kansas City, Missouri. He cut his musical teeth during late night jam sessions in the nightclubs lining 12th Street. As a star soloist with the McShann band, Parker honed his mastery of harmonic changes and quicksilver execution that led to the creation of bebop. Settling down in New York, Parker along with Dizzy Gillespie, Bud Powell, Thelonious Monk, and other modernists created bebop—a revolution in music. (See BOP.) Parker became one of the most influential musicians of all time, revered by legions of fans, musicians, writers, and artists.

Since then, Kansas City has produced a host of great jazz musicians including Bob Brookmeyer, Chris Connor, Curtis Counce, Big John Patton, Pat Metheny, Kevin Mahogany, Bobby Watson, Eldar, and Karrin Allyson. Today, Kansas City has a thriving jazz scene with a new generation of musicians keeping the Kansas City beat going strong in the Phoenix, the Blue Room, and other clubs located throughout the city. Kansas City also supports thriving jazz series at the Folly and Gem Theaters.

See also SOUTHWEST JAZZ.

3. POPULAR AND ETHNIC MUSIC. Much popular music in the Kansas City area, like its more storied jazz tradition, has roots in the blues. Boogie-woogie pianist Pete Johnson and blues shouter Big Joe Turner teamed up in Kansas City in the late 1920s, but New York was where they recorded "Roll 'Em Pete" (1938)—often cited as an important precursor to rock 'n' roll. This pattern of Kansas-city-bred musicians moving elsewhere to find their fortunes (e.g., Gene Clark, Bloodstone, Oleta Adams, Janelle Monae) was reversed for a short time in the rock era when the former jazz venue El Torreon Ballroom (founded in 1927) reopened as Cowtown Ballroom (1971–4). With impresario Stanley Plesser heading both the ballroom and artist-management company Good Karma Productions, Cowtown played host to top national touring acts and became home base for folk-rock performers Brewer and Shipley, Danny Cox, and Ozark Mountain Daredevils. Roots-rockers The Rainmakers flirted with international success in the 1980s.

Blues have attracted local crowds since the postwar days of the Orchid Room at the fabled corner of 12th and Vine streets. It has been fostered since 1980 by the Kansas City Blues Society and by club owners Roger Naber (Grand Emporium, 1985–2004), Lindsay Shannon (BB's Lawnside BBQ, 1990–present), and Frank Hicks (Knuckleheads, 2004–present). Author and archivist Chuck Haddix has hosted the "Fish Fry" program every Friday and Saturday night (1985–present) on public radio station KCUR-FM. Local blues performers of note include singer-guitarists Millage Gilbert and Sonny Kenner (1933–2001), harmonica player Provine "Little" Hatch (1921–2003), and the group Trampled Under Foot, founded in 2002 by siblings Danielle, Nicholas, and Kristopher Schnebelen.

Soul and gospel influences can be heard in the work of Kansas City vocalists Marva Whitney and Ida McBeth, as well in the music of The Blue Riddim Band, which received a 1986 Grammy nomination for its reggae album, *Alive in Jamaica* (1984). Relying heavily on internet distribution, local artist Tech N9ne (Aaron Dontez Yates) claims to have become the world's best-selling independent rapper, selling more than one million copies of twelve studio albums on his homegrown Strange Music label since 1999.

The community also supports a wide variety of traditional musicians. Since the 1950s accordionist Don Lipovac has combined the sounds of his own Slovenian heritage with that of the neighboring Croatian community in Kansas City, Kansas, performing polkas and other dances for local and national audiences. Lipovac has often been featured at the annual Slavic Festival in suburban Sugar Creek, Missouri. In 1998, a group of longtime rock musicians joined to back Irish-born vocalist Ian Byrne as The Elders. Their amped-up Celtic music has made them the toast of KC's Irish American community, including regular appearances at the Kansas City Irish Fest (2002–present). Music, dance, and food from around the world have been featured each summer since 1980 at the city's annual Ethnic Enrichment Festival in Swope Park.

BIBLIOGRAPHY

C.W. Whitney: *Kansas City, Missouri: its History and its People, 1808–1908* (Chicago, 1908)
E.C. Krohn: *Missouri Music* (New York, 1924/R1971)
F. Driggs: "Kansas City and the Southwest," *Jazz*, ed. N. Hentoff and A.J. McCarthy (New York, 1959/R1974), 189–230
J.M. Crabb: *A History of Music in Kansas City, 1900–1965* (diss., U. of Missouri, Kansas City, 1967)
G. Schuller: *Early Jazz: Its Roots and Musical Development* (New York, 1968), 279–319
R. Russell: *Jazz Style in Kansas City and the Southwest* (Berkeley, CA, 1971, 2/1973)
L. Ostransky: *Jazz City: the Impact of Our Cities on the Development of Jazz* (Englewood Cliffs, NJ, 1978), chaps. 7–8
M. Williams: "Jazz: What Happened in Kansas City?," *AM*, iii/2 (1985), 171–79
N.W. Pearson: *Goin' to Kansas City* (Urbana, IL, 1987)
P.A. Munstedt, "Kansas City music publishing: the First Fifty Years," *AM*, ix/4 (1991), 353–83
H. Jennings: "The Early Days of Grand Opera in Kansas City, Missouri, 1860–1879," *OQ*, xv/4 (1999), 677–96
M. Rice: "Dances, Frolics, and Orchestra Wars: The Territory Bands and Ballrooms of Kansas City, Missouri, 1925–1935," *Perspectives on American Music 1900–1950*, ed. M. Saffle (New York, 2000), 137–70

F. Driggs and C. Haddix: *Kansas City Jazz: From Ragtime to Bebop—A History* (New York, 2005)

H. Jennings: "Her Majesty's Opera Company in Kansas City," *OQ*, xxi/2 (2005), 227–41

A.R. Clifford: *Queering the Inferno: Space, Identity, and Kansas City's Jazz Scene* (diss., University of Kansas, 2007)

JACK L. RALSTON/SCOTT CANTRELL, J. BRADFORD ROBINSON/WILLIAM EVERETT (1); CHUCK HADDIX (2); RICK HELLMAN (3)

Kansas City jazz. *See* SOUTHWEST JAZZ.

Kapayou, Everett (*b* Tama, IA, 13 May 1933; *d* Ames, IA, 16 Aug 2006). Native American (Meskwaki) singer, drummer, and flute player. Kapayou was born on the Meskwaki Indian Settlement in Tama, Iowa, where his mother Lucille, a flute player, taught him sacred and secular repertoires of Meskwaki music. While serving in the Army and working in construction, Kapayou retained his commitment to these traditions. He received a National Heritage Fellowship from the NEA in 1993 for his knowledge of and commitment to Meskwaki music, especially the genre of love songs, which reflect intimate aspects of that tribal heritage. Kapayou performed at the Smithsonian Festival of American Folklife in 1996, and his singing and drumming may be heard on the companion recording entitled *Iowa State Fare: Music from the Heartland* (Smithsonian Folkways, 1996/2010).

JOHN-CARLOS PEREA

Kapell, William (*b* New York, NY, 20 Sept 1922; *d* King's Mountain, CA, 29 Oct 1953). Pianist. He studied with Dorothea Anderson La Follette in New York, then with OLGA SAMAROFF in Philadelphia and at the Juilliard School. In 1941 he won the Philadelphia Orchestra's youth competition and the Naumberg Award; the Naumberg Foundation then sponsored his New York debut on 28 October the same year, which brought him the Town Hall Award for the year's outstanding concert by a musician under 30. He achieved fame in the next few years not least by his championship of the Piano Concerto of Aram Khachaturian, at that time a name new to the United States, and proceeded to an international career which was cut short by his death in a plane crash on the way back from Australia.

There was some tendency to typecast Kapell as a performer of flashy repertory; his technique was exceptional, but he was a versatile pianist and could also give memorably graceful performances of Wolfgang Amadeus Mozart and Fryderyk Chopin, as well as championing the works of contemporary composers such as Aaron Copland, sometimes against the advice of managers and promoters. Copland wrote of him: "I cannot conceive of his ever having given a dull performance—an erratic one, perhaps, a misguided or stylistically incongruous one maybe, but invariably one that was electric and alive." During the 1990s Kapell's recordings of works by Chopin, Serge Rachmaninoff, Khachaturian, and others were reissued and achieved something of a cult following.

MICHAEL STEINBERG/R

Kaper, Bronislaw [Bronislau] (*b* Warsaw, Poland, 5 Feb 1902; *d* Los Angeles, CA, 26 April 1983). Composer of Polish birth. He was educated at the Warsaw Conservatory and was active as composer and pianist in Warsaw, Berlin, Vienna, London, and Paris before settling in Hollywood and joining the staff of MGM in 1940. He was one of a number of versatile musicians of European origin and orientation who helped to create Hollywood music. He composed a number of popular songs besides his articulate and closely knit film scores. His best work dates from the 1960s: *Mutiny on the Bounty* (1962) and *Lord Jim* (1965) reveal a pronounced flair for musical depiction of the sea and tropical landscapes. Kaper's theme from *Green Dolphin Street* (1947) became popularized when recorded in a jazz idiom by Miles Davis; his theme for *Invitation* (1952) was also widely recorded. Kaper's dramatic score for the science fiction film *Them!* (1954) is largely regarded as one of the classics of horror movie music of the period; regrettably, a "Fugue for Ants" that Kaper wrote for the film was ultimately deleted from the final soundtrack. After 28 years and more than 100 scores for MGM, Kaper, like many Hollywood composers in the mid-1960s, found film work declining as pop music became more prevalent. As a result he turned to composing for television.

Kaper's style, which was securely rooted in late European Romanticism, has fluency, melodic charm, and fine, elegant craftsmanship; like many Hollywood composers he established a useful rapport between popular and symphonic music (e.g., from his Oscar-winning score, the song "Hi-lili, Hi-lo" in *Lili*, 1953, and the use of extended ballet in *The Glass Slipper*, 1955). While his music is warm, colorful, and melodically appealing, it is rarely meretricious and, within the confines of its idiom, achieves a certain individuality of voice. Other notable scores of his include *Gaslight* (1944), *The Naked Spur* (1952), *The FBI* (television theme, 1965), *Tobruk* (1967), and *The Way West* (1967).

BIBLIOGRAPHY

T. Thomas: *Music for the Movies* (Los Angeles, 1973, expanded and updated 2/1997), 103–13

W.F. Krasnoborski: "A Conversation with B. Kaper," *Soundtrack Collector's Newsletter*, no.2 (1975), 13; no.3 (1976), 3; repr. in *Motion Picture Music*, ed. L. Van de Ven (Mechelen, Belgium, 1980), 122

E. Bernstein: "Interview with Bronislau Kaper," *Film Music Notebook*, iv/2 (1978), 12–28

T. Thomas: *Film Score: the View from the Podium* (South Brunswick, NJ, and New York, 1979), 115–25

V.J. Francillon, ed.: *Film Composers Guide* (Los Angeles, 1990, 3/1996), 223–4

CHRISTOPHER PALMER/RANDALL D. LARSON

Kaplan, Abraham (*b* Tel-Aviv, Israel, 5 May 1931). Conductor of Israeli birth. After graduation from the Israeli Academy in Jerusalem (1954), he moved to New York to attend the Juilliard School (1955, post-graduate diploma 1957). He studied conducting with WILLIAM STEINBERG, Eleazar De Carvalho, HUGH ROSS, and FREDERIK PRAUSNITZ, and composition with DARIUS MILHAUD. Kaplan was awarded the Frank Damrosch Prize in Conducting (1956) and a Koussevitzky Scholarship to the Berkshire Music Center (1956). While still a student, he made his American professional debut. A third-generation choral conductor, Kaplan directed the Kol Israel Chorus for two seasons (1953–4, 1958–9) and served as conductor of the Haifa Oratorio Society (1958–9) before returning to the United States in 1960 to found the Camerata Singers. As director of choral music at the Juilliard School (1961–77) and of the Symphonic Choral Society of New York (1968–77), Kaplan led choruses that made numerous appearances and recordings with the New York Philharmonic. In addition to serving as musical director of the Collegiate Chorale in New York (1961–73), in 1968 Kaplan became director of choral activities for New York's Park Avenue Synagogue, a position he held for more than 30 years. He has also appeared as guest conductor of many orchestras in the United States and Israel, and until 1977 conducted the Camerata SO, which he had founded in 1968. Through the course of his career, Kaplan has collaborated with several prominent composers and musicians, including Igor Stravinsky, Loren Maazel, Seiji Ozawa, and Frank Sinatra. Kaplan also worked with Leonard Bernstein for more than 13 years.

He has taught at the Berkshire Music Center, Boston University, and the School of Sacred Music at Union Theological Seminary, New York (1961–73). In 1976 he was appointed director of the School of Choral Studies at Chautauqua, New York, and in 1977 he became Professor of Music at the University of Washington, Seattle. Kaplan has also served as associate director for choral activities of the Seattle Symphony (1995–2000). As of 2013 he was directing the Choral Studies Department at the University of Washington. He has composed a *Sanctification Symphony* and various works for chorus and orchestra; Kaplan's recorded compositions include *Glorious: A collection of Psalms and Biblical songs, Arvit Leshabat, The K'dusha Symphony, Crystal Cathedral Psalms*, and *Psalms of Abraham*. Kaplan has also edited choral music and written a college textbook on choral conducting (New York, 1985). Kaplan's musical memoir, *Splendid Encounters*, was published by iUniverse in 2009.

RICHARD BERNAS/ELIZABETH PERTEN

Kappa Kappa Psi. Wind-band society, founded in 1919; *see* Fraternities and sororities.

Karaoke. The term karaoke derives from a Japanese portmanteau that translates loosely as "empty orchestra," and refers to the practice of removing a song's vocal tracks, thus allowing amateur singers to sing the song themselves. Once dismissed by Americans as a last-call refuge for drunkards and hacks, karaoke underwent a radical cultural transformation in the early 2000s, becoming not only more popular but also quasi-respectable, with karaoke machines popping up everywhere from church picnics to shopping malls. While most participants remained decidedly nonprofessional, a growing number of wannabe-stars came to view karaoke not as a lark but as a legitimate way to hone their craft.

Perhaps fittingly, karaoke was invented by a man who could barely sing a note: Daisuke Inoue, an Osaka-born jazz drummer whose stalled career prompted him to get into band management. While working the club scene in the port city of Kobe, Inoue noticed that, whenever a pianist performed at a local bar, the customers would get up and sing along. Reasoning that it would be easier and cheaper to simply replace the pianist with a machine, Inoue designed the Juke-8, a crate-sized 8-track player equipped with a microphone and a coin slot. Introduced in 1971, the Juke-8 allowed users to sing over instrumental tracks, using a binder full of printed-out lyric sheets as their guide.

Over the course of the next decade, Inoue improved on his invention, hustling karaoke machines around Japan, city by city. His success was due in part to Japan's long-held cultural emphasis on education and discipline, as many singers would spend hours perfecting one song, which they would perform for friends or coworkers. By the early 1980s karaoke had spread throughout Asia. But it proved to be a tricky export, particularly to America, where notions of modesty and good taste—not to mention a limited English-language song selection—discouraged all but the most soused bar patrons from getting up to perform. Still, a few brazen business owners gave it a go: In Los Angeles, a karaoke bar called Dimples opened in 1982, making it the first in the country; three years later, two brothers in Charlotte, North Carolina, opened Sound Choice, a karaoke-track company that employed professional musicians to record accurate-sounding instrumentals (the company ultimately produced more than 18,000 rerecorded songs). Meanwhile, electronics giant Pioneer gambled that karaoke could boost sales of its Laserdisc players, producing lavish, expensive, and patently absurd karaoke videos that displayed the lyrics on-screen.

Yet despite the enthusiasm of these early adopters, most Americans did not hear about karaoke until the late 1980s, when the booming Japanese economy made cities like Osaka and Tokyo a prime business-trip destination for Western dealmakers. For many Japanese, a trip to the local karaoke bar was an ideal way to cap off a meeting, and soon, US executives were introduced to the goofy kicks of a tipsy sing-along; some even brought machines back stateside. Although karaoke had become popular in some Asian American communities, most Americans still considered it to be, at best, a guilty pleasure.

In the late 1990s, however, a new generation of American music fans—weaned on teen-pop, and blessed with disposable income—took up karaoke as a hobby, aided by the introduction of cheap at-home machines that allowed them to circumvent bars altogether. Unlike their parents, these young singers had few hang-ups about being the center of attention; to them, karaoke was just another form of self-expression. Their passion soon trickled back into the popular culture: When *American Idol* premiered in 2002, the show's producers had a bumper-crop of young singers to choose from, some of whom had been all but raised on karaoke; in turn, the show's success prompted countless other teens (and no shortage of adults) to take up the habit.

By the end of the first decade of the 2000s, karaoke accompaniment was available on a variety of platforms—from sing-along websites to smartphone applications to 24-hour cable channels—and it also had mutated into hands-on, immersive video games such as *Rock Band* and *Guitar Hero*. Meanwhile, artists who once would have rolled their eyes at karaoke now record instrumental tracks for their fans to sing. After decades of scorn or derision, karaoke has become a staple of American nightlife.

BIBLIOGRAPHY

D. Wong: "'I want the microphone': Mass Mediation and Agency in Asian American Popular Music," *TDR*, xxxviii/3 (1994), 152–67

C.M.K. Long: *In Search of a Voice: Karaoke and the Construction of Identity in Chinese America* (Mahwah, NJ, 1996)

B. Raftery: *Don't Stop Believin': How Karaoke Conquered the World and Changed my Life* (New York, 2008)

K.P. Brown: *'My Way': Karaoke and the Performance of Gender, Ethnicity, and Class* (diss., U. of Colorado, Boulder, 2009)

BRIAN RAFTERY

Karayanis, Plato (*b* Pittsburgh, PA, 26 Dec 1928). Baritone and impresario. He studied voice at the Curtis Institute of Music and moved to Europe in 1958, performing with opera companies in Switzerland and Germany. He returned to the United States in 1964 and held administrative positions at San Francisco Opera, Metropolitan Opera, and Affiliate Artists before taking the helm of The Dallas Opera in 1977. He felt strongly about a general director's role as "curator of the art form" and brought an expanded artistic vision to a company once known as "La Scala West." While maintaining The Dallas Opera's commitment to standard opera repertory, he commissioned Dominick Argento's *The Aspern Papers* and Tobias Picker's *Thérèse Raquin*. He also programmed, for the first time in the company's history, works by Igor Stravinsky, George Gershwin, Virgil Thomson, Benjamin Britten, Manuel de Falla, Samuel Barber, and Leoš Janáček, as well as Wagner's Ring Cycle. Under his leadership The Dallas Opera more than doubled its number of performances and became a leader in community programming with nationally recognized initiatives in education and adult minority partnerships. Karayanis served as president and chairman of OPERA America, the national service organization for opera, from 1993–7. In 1998 The Dallas Opera opened a $3 million rehearsal/production center, which was later named in honor of Karayanis and his wife, Dorothy. Throughout his tenure, Karayanis worked to build support for a proper opera house in Dallas, a vision that was realized in 2009, nine years after his retirement.

BIBLIOGRAPHY

W. Albright: "Southwest Passage: Dallas Opera Celebrates its Fortieth Anniversary," *ON*, lxi/5 (Nov 1996), 36–8

S. Cantrell: "And That Spells Dallas," *ON*, lxxi/5 (Nov 2006), 28–31

KELLEY ROURKE

Karchin, Louis (Samuel) (*b* Philadelphia, PA, 8 Sept 1951). Composer and conductor. He attended the East-man School of Music (BM 1973) and Harvard University (MA 1975, PhD 1978), where he studied with SAMUEL ADLER, JOSEPH SCHWANTNER, FRED LERDAHL, and EARL KIM. He cofounded the Harvard Group for New Music and later studied conducting with LEON BARZIN in Paris (1978–9). In 1979 he joined the composition department at New York University. He has served as president and chair of the US section of ISCM (1981–5), codirector of the Washington Square Contemporary Music Society, and he cofounded the ISCM chamber players. He has been active as a conductor of the Chamber Players of the League-ISCM, the Washington Square Ensemble, and the Orchestra of the League of Composers. Among his honors are the Koussevitzky Tanglewood Award, the Bearns Prize, and grants from the American Academy of Arts and Letters, the ACA, the New Music Consort, and the Fromm Foundation. His work has been commissioned or performed by the Group for Contemporary Music, the New York New Music Ensemble, the Da Capo Chamber Players, the Delta Ensemble of Amsterdam, Holland, and the Louisville Orchestra, among others.

An advocate of the American modernist tradition, Karchin follows in the tradition of Stefan Wolpe, Luigi Dallapiccola, and late Igor Stravinsky. His music is characterized by intense, angular, rhythmically active surfaces, as in the *Capriccio* (1977), but it is also distinguished by a lyricism and formal clarity that suggests a classical influence. The *Songs of John Keats* (1984) and *Songs of Distance and Light* (1988) feature consonant, even overtly tonal gestures. The first movement of the Cello Sonata (1990) articulates a sonata form through long-range tonal centers and the *Sonata da Camera* (1995), crafted around widely voiced motifs, suggests a Beethovenian rhetoric.

WORKS
(selective list)

Op: Romulus (A. Dumas, trans. B. Shaw), S, T, Bar, B, fl, cl, hn, pf, perc, str, 1990, rev. 2006; Orpheus (S. Kunitz), Bar, fl/picc, cl/b cl, vn, vc, pf, perc, hp, dancers, 2003

Vocal: Songs of John Keats, S, fl, cl, perc, pf, vn, vc, 1984 [arr. chbr orch]; 5 Songs (S. Standing), S, orch, 1985 [arr. S, pf, 1985]; Songs of Distance and Light (E. Bishop, J. Rose), S, fl/picc, ob, b cl, perc, pf, vn, va, vc, 1988; A Way Separate…(R. Whitman, H. Senesh), S, fl/picc, cl, vn, vc, pf, 1992; 2 Songs (Y. Yevtushenko), Bar, fl/picc, cl/b cl, perc, pf, vn, vc, 1999; Four Songs, S, pf, 2001–3; Gods of Winter (D. Gioia), Bar, fl/picc, cl, hn, 2 vn, vc, perc, pf, 2006 (also arr. orch) American Visions: Two Songs on Poems of Yevgeny Yevtushenko, Bar, orch, 2011

Inst ens: Capriccio, solo vn, fl, ob, b cl, perc, pf, va, db, 1977; Duo, vn, vc, 1981; Viola Variations, va, pf, 1981; Orch Variations, 1982; Canonic Mosaics II, fl, cl, bn, perc, pf, vn, va, vc, 1986; Sonata, vc, pf, 1990; Str Qt, 1991; Galactic Folds, fl + pic, cl, vn, vc, pf, 1992; Str Qt no.2, 1995; Rustic Dances, vn, cl, mar, 1995; Sonata da Camera, vn, pf, 1995; Rhapsody, orch, 1996; Chesapeake Festival Overture, orch, 2006

Solo inst: Attuned to the Times, vn, 1978; Soliloquy, fl, 1982; 3 Miniatures, pf, 1983; Caprice, pf, 1984; Canzona and Elegy, vn, 1988; Pf Sonata, 1988; Soliloquy II "Chimerical Images," fl, 1988; Ricercare, vn, 1992; Summer Songs, cl, 1994; Cascades, pf, 1997; Fanfare/Pavane, fl, 2000; Quartet, perc, 2000; Voyages, alto sax, pf, 2001; Three Epigrams, pf, 2008

Principal publisher: C.F. Peters

Principal recording companies: New World, CRI, Albany Records

BIBLIOGRAPHY
R. Carl: "Three Points on the Spectrum: The Music of Louis Karchin, Lois V. Vierk and Paul Dresher," *CMR*, x/1 (1994), 11–31
ROBERT CARL/BENJAMIN PIEKUT

Karis, Aleck (*b* Washington, DC, 21 Jan 1954). Pianist. He studied composition at the Manhattan School (BM 1976) with LUDMILA ULEHLA and CHARLES WUORINEN and piano at the Juilliard School (MM 1979) with BEVERIDGE WEBSTER; he also studied piano with ARTUR BALSAM and William Daghlian. Among his awards are the special prize for performance of American music in the Rockefeller Foundation International Competition (1978), two Fromm Foundation grants ("in recognition of his commitment to the music of our time"), and an NEH fellowship (1984). In 1983 he became an associate professor in music performance at Columbia University. In 1990 he joined the faculty at the University of California, San Diego, where he is currently Professor of Music.

Although Karis has performed concerti by Mozart and recorded Schumann and late Chopin solo works, he has become known for his performances of contemporary music. At his Latin American debut in 1981 in São Paulo, Brazil, he played a Chopin program; for his formal New York debut on 15 October 1984 at Merkin Concert Hall, he performed works by Chopin, Carter, Stravinsky, and Schumann. His premiere performances include works by Davidovsky, Subotnick, and Babbitt. He has recorded solo music by Carter, Cage, Davidovsky, Babbitt, Glass, Primosch, Allen Anderson, and Yuasa, as well as chamber music by Crumb, Babbitt, Feldman, Wolpe, Martino, Steiger, Cowell, Karchin, Moę, and Hyla. He became a member of Speculum Musicae in 1983 and has appeared regularly with various New York ensembles, including the Group for Contemporary Music, the Contemporary Chamber Ensemble, and St. Luke's Chamber Ensemble, and in concerts organized by the Guild of Composers and the League-ISCM. He has been featured at the Warsaw Autumn Festival and the New York Philharmonic's Horizons Festival, as well as other international music festivals in Bath, Geneva, Sao Paulo, Los Angeles, and Miami.

MICHAEL CANICK/ALAN SHOCKLEY

Karl, Tom (*b* Dublin, Ireland, 19 Jan 1846; *d* Rochester, NY, 19 March 1916). Tenor of Irish birth. After studying with Henry Phillips in England he moved to Italy. He made his New York debut in 1871 with the Parepa-Rosa English Opera Company, and in the mid-1870s moved permanently to the United States as a singer of opera, light opera, and oratorio. He was a founding member of the Boston Ideal Opera Company (1887). During the next ten years he became one of the most popular tenors in the country, celebrated for a number of Gilbert and Sullivan roles and for the title role in De Koven's *Robin Hood*. He retired in 1896 and taught in New York, then lived briefly in California before settling in Rochester about 1912. Karl possessed a light, lyric voice and considerable personal charm; his integrity and prestige contributed significantly to the popularization of light opera in the United States.

BIBLIOGRAPHY
W.S.B. Mathews, ed.: *A Hundred Years of Music in America* (Chicago, 1889/*R*1970)
Obituary, *Union and Advertiser* (Rochester, 20 March 1916)
WILLIAM BROOKS

Karlin, Fred(erick James) (*b* Chicago, IL, 16 June 1936; *d* Culver City, CA, 26 March 2004). Composer and arranger. As a teenager in Chicago he began playing trumpet. After graduating from Amherst College in 1956, he returned to Chicago and played at the Jazz Limited Club. After moving to New York, he wrote stage band arrangements, conducted recordings, and assisted Rayburn Wright at Eastman School's summer Arrangers' Laboratory-Institute and at Radio City Music Hall. In addition to Wright, he studied privately with WILLIAM RUSSO and TIBOR SERLY. His first feature film score was for *Up the Down Staircase* (1967). After writing "Come Saturday Morning" his career took a new direction with his Academy Award for "For All we Know" from *Lovers and Other Strangers* (1970). On other film songs he collaborated with his wife, Meg Welles Karlin, sometimes credited as Tylwyth Kymry, her adopted Welsh name. The couple, who met in New York when he became music director for her jazz quintet, relocated to Los Angeles in 1969. He collected American music in all forms, and his own music reflected his knowledge and interest in folk, jazz, Dixieland, and Civil War and minstrel songs. After the success of his music for *The Autobiography of Miss Jane Pittman* in 1974, he went on to score nearly 100 television movies. He founded and led the Fred Karlin Film Scoring Workshop at ASCAP from 1988 to 1996. In the 1990s he concentrated on writing and teaching, produced a documentary on Jerry Goldsmith, and made jazz arrangements of film themes for recordings. *On the Track*, cowritten with Wright, became the authoritative manual on contemporary film scoring.

WORKS
(*selective list*)
FILM SCORES
The Last Man, 1965; Up the Down Staircase, 1967; Yours, Mine, and Ours, 1968; The Sterile Cuckoo, 1969; The Baby Maker, 1970; Lovers and Other Strangers, 1970; The Little Ark, 1972; Westworld, 1973; Futureworld, 1976; Leadbelly, 1976; Greased Lightning, 1977; Loving Couples, 1980; Strawberry Road, 1991

FILM SONGS
(*names of lyricists are given in parentheses*)
"Come Saturday Morning" (D. Previn) from The Sterile Cuckoo; song score, including "People Come, People Go" (T. Kymry) from The Baby Maker; "For All we Know" (R. Royer, J. Griffin) from Lovers and Other Strangers; "Come Follow, Follow Me" (M. Karlin) from The Little Ark

TELEVISION MUSIC
The Autobiography of Miss Jane Pittman, 1974; Minstrel Man, 1977; Jacqueline Susann's Valley of the Dolls, 1981; Dream West, 1985; Robert Kennedy and his Times, 1985

CONCERT MUSIC
Reflections, 1993; The Peace Seeker (C. Hai), orch, folk-rock band, vocalists, boys choir, 3 actors, 1998

MSS in American Heritage Center, University of Wyoming

WRITINGS

On the Track: a Guide to Contemporary Film Scoring (New York, 1990, rev. 2004)

Listening to Movies: the Film Lover's Guide to Film Music (New York, 1994)

BIBLIOGRAPHY

ASCAP Biographical Dictionary (New York, 4/1980), 261

D. Mangodt: "Music Is my Life: an Interview with Fred Karlin," *Soundtrack!* xiii/52 (Dec 1994), 19–21

Obituaries: *Los Angeles Times*, 4 May 2004; *Variety*, weekly ed., 10 May 2004

WARREN M. SHERK

Karlins, M(artin) William (*b* New York, NY, 25 Feb 1932; *d* Northbrook, IL, 11 May 2005). Composer. He studied privately with Frederick Piket (1954–7), at the Manhattan School with VITTORIO GIANNINI (BM and MM 1961), and at the University of Iowa (PhD 1965), where his principal teachers were RICHARD B. HERVIG and PHILIP BEZANSON. After teaching at Western Illinois University (1965–7), he joined the faculty of Northwestern University (Evanston, IL) in 1967, where he taught for the remainder of his career. His notable students include AUGUSTA READ THOMAS, MAGGI PAYNE, and David Gaines. At the time of his death, he was the Harry N. and Ruth F. Wyatt Professor of Music Theory and Composition Emeritus. Among his honors were grants from the Mac-Dowell Colony (1977), the NEA (1979), and the Meet the Composer program (1980); he received many commissions, including those from Western Illinois University (his second woodwind quintet, "And all our world is dew"), the American Chamber SO (Symphony no.1), WFMT-Chicago (Fanfare with Fugato), and the Fox Valley SO (Catena III). A prolific composer with a taut and highly disciplined musical idiom, Karlins concentrated on instrumental works, including many for wind instruments, in particular the saxophone. His saxophone music has been widely performed, both in the United States and abroad. His music is generally lyrical, highly chromatic, and linear. His works have been recorded on many labels, including CRI, Opus One, and Arktos.

WORKS
(selective list)

Orch: Concert Music no.1, 1959, no.2, chorus orch, 1960, no.3, ww, brass, pf, perc, 1963–4, no.4, 1964, no.5, 1972–3; Lamentations—In memoriam, speaker, 3 fl + pic, 3 tpt, 3 trb, tb, hp, perc, org, 1968; Passacaglia and Rounds, band, 1970; Reflux, conc., db, winds, 1971–2; Sym. no.1, 1979–80; Catena, cl, small orch, 1980–1, arr. chbr orch; Conc., a sax, orch, 1981–2; Catena III, conc., hn, orch, 1983

Other inst: Conc. grosso no.1, 10 insts, 1959–60, no.2, 7 insts, 1961–2; 3 pf sonatas, 1959, 1962, 1965; Str Qt, S, str qt, 1960; Outgrowths-Variations, pf, 1961; Birthday Music no.1, fl, b cl/cl, db, 1962, no.2, fl, db, 1963; Solo Piece with Passacaglia, cl, 1964; Variations on "Obiter dictum," vc, pf, perc, 1965; 2 sax qts, 1966–7, 1975; Music for Vc Alone, no.1, 1966, no.2, with mobiles, 1969; Music for t sax, pf, 1969; 2 ww qnts, no.1, 1970, no.2 "And all our world is dew," 1977–8; Qnt, a sax, str qt, 1973–4; Fanfare with Fugato, amp vc, 2 tpt, 2 trbn, 1981; Catena II, s sax, brass qnt, 1982; Seasons, sax, 1987; Nostalgie, sax ens., 1994; Yesterday's Memories, s sax, pf, 1999; several other works for various ens, pieces for solo org, cl, vc, fl

Vocal: 3 unacc. choral works; Song, S, a fl, vc, 1963; Looking out my Window, Tr chorus, va, 1990; several other works for various vocal ens

Principal publishers: C. Fischer, Media, Seesaw, Southern, Tritone

BIBLIOGRAPHY

EwenD

KAREN MONSON/ANDERS TOBIASON

Karok. Native American group of California. Their music shared some characteristics with that of the SHASTA and the YUROK.

Karpeles, Maud (*b* London, England, 12 Nov 1885; *d* London, England, 1 Oct 1976). English folk-music scholar. In 1909 she met CECIL SHARP; this was the beginning of an association that lasted till Sharp's death in 1924 and led to a lifetime of collecting and studying Anglo-American folk music and serving in national and international organizations. With her sister Helen she became a key figure in the English Folk Dance Society (founded by Sharp in 1911). From 1916 to 1918 she served as Sharp's assistant during three trips to the United States, where they studied the folk music of the Appalachian Mountains and, in 46 weeks spent among scattered and almost inaccessible communities, collected 1612 tunes representing some 500 different songs. Some of these were published by Sharp with his own piano accompaniments; two volumes of tunes and texts were later edited by Karpeles and published as *English Folk Songs from the Southern Appalachians* (1932/*R*1973, 3/1960). The efforts of Sharp and Karpeles gave impetus to folk-music collecting in the United States, especially by universities. In 1929 and 1930 Karpeles visited Newfoundland and collected 191 songs, of which she selected 30 for setting with piano accompaniments by Vaughan Williams and others (*Folk Songs from Newfoundland*, 1932, 2/1971). In 1935 she organized an international folk-dance festival in London, and in 1947 was the chief agent in establishing a more permanent international organization, the International Folk Music Council, which she served as secretary for 15 years, and of which she was honorary president from 1963 until her death. She was also the founding editor, in 1949, of the *Yearbook of the International Folk Music Council*.

BIBLIOGRAPHY

Obituaries: *MT*, cxvii (1976), 932; *YIFMC*, viii (1976), 9–11; *Folk Music Journal*, iii/3 (1977), 292–94

FRANK HOWES

Karpman, Laura (*b* La Jolla, CA, 1 March 1959). Composer for film, television, and the concert stage. She began composing at age seven, later studying with NADIA BOULANGER and completing a PhD in composition at the Juilliard School under MILTON BABBITT. After moving to Los Angeles in 1989, she established herself as a film and television composer. She scored 21 episodes of the documentary series *The Living Edens* (1997–2002), for which she received four Emmys. She then composed the music for Steven Spielberg's miniseries *Taken* (2002), and worked on other series, including *Odyssey 5*, *In Justice*, *Masters of Science Fiction*, and *Craft in America*. Since 2004 she has also composed extensively for video games, producing a symphonic score for *EverQuest II*, among others. Her multimedia opera *Ask your Mama*, based on a text by Langston Hughes and created in collaboration with Jessye Norman, received its premiere on 16 March 2009 in Carnegie Hall, and her concert music has been performed at Lincoln Center and the Tanglewood Music Festival. She has received the Ives Fellowship from the American Academy of Arts and Letters and two ASCAP Foundation grants, and has participated in residencies at Tanglewood, the MacDowell Colony, and the Sundance Institute. As of 2012 she was teaching in the UCLA School of Theater, Film, and Television.

BIBLIOGRAPHY

L. Hunter: "Exploring the Concert Saxophone Repertoire: Laura Karpman's 'Matisse and Jazz'," *Saxophone Journal*, xiii (1989), 32–7

J. Bond: "'Taken' with her Music (Interview with Laura Karpman)," *Film Score Monthly*, viii/6 (2003), 30–31

M. Carlsson: "Women in Film Music, or How Hollywood Learned to Hire Female Composers for (at Least) Some of their Movies," *IAWM Journal*, xi/2 (2005), 16–9

JAMES DEAVILLE

Karr, Gary (Michael) (*b* Los Angeles, CA, 20 Nov 1941). Double bass player. Born into a family of double bass players he studied with Herman Reinshagen, Warren Benfield, and Stuart Sankey. In 1962 he appeared as a soloist with the New York PO under Leonard Bernstein and gave his recital debut at Town Hall, New York. He toured Europe in 1964, making his London debut at the Wigmore Hall. In 1967 he founded the International Institute for the String Bass (later the International Society of Bassists), which published 17 issues of the *Bass Sound Post*, at the time the only journal devoted to the instrument.

One of the most influential players of his generation, Karr has enjoyed a successful international solo career, has recorded extensively, and has pioneered new and individual playing techniques. His repertory of concertos, several commissioned by him or written specially for him, includes works by Hans Werner Henze (1967), Gunther Schuller (1968), Wilfred Josephs (1980), John Downey (1985), and others. In 1971 he formed a duo with the pianist Harmon Lewis, with whom he gave over 50 premieres. He has held teaching posts at Yale University, the Juilliard School, and other American and Canadian universities, and has written double bass methods. His often humorous approach to the instrument made him a popular figure at summer schools and double bass gatherings, as well as with television audiences worldwide.

In 1984 Karr set up a charitable foundation to lend instruments to promising young bassists. Retiring from the concert platform in June 2001 at the International Society of Bassists' Indianapolis Convention, he was awarded the ISB's Distinguished Teacher Award after his final public recital. The Karr-Koussevitzky double bass, once believed to have been an Amati and given to him by Koussevitzky's widow Olga in 1961, was gifted to the ISB in 2005. He lives in Victoria, British Columbia.

RODNEY SLATFORD

Kashkashian, Kim (*b* Detroit, MI, 31 Aug 1952). Viola player and teacher of Armenian descent. She studied at the Peabody Conservatory in Baltimore with WALTER TRAMPLER (1969–70) and Karen Tuttle (1970–75), and won both the Lionel Tertis and the ARD (Munich) competitions. Her career developed rapidly both as a soloist and chamber music player, and also as a teacher. She was a faculty member at the New School of Music in Philadelphia (1981–6), the Mannes College in New York (1983–6), and the Indiana University School of Music in Bloomington (1985–7), and teaches regularly at the Lausanne Conservatoire. She has also taught at the Hochschule für Musik in Freiburg since 1989 and teaches regularly at festivals such as Marlboro, Spoleto, and Lockenhaus. A fine chamber music player, she has played with the Beaux Arts Trio and the Guarneri, Parker, Galimir, and Tokyo string quartets. In 1984 she discovered two unpublished sonatas for viola by Paul Hindemith which she subsequently recorded. Kashkashian has collaborated with many contemporary composers who have written works for her; these include Arvo Pärt, Krzysztof Penderecki, Paul Chihara, Linda Bouchard, Giya Kancheli, György Kurtág, Sofiya Gubaydulina, Peter Eötvös, Betty Olivero, Alfred Schnittke, Betsy Jolas, Alvin Brehm, and Meyer Kupferman. She has made a sustained effort to advocate for Armenian composer Tigran Mansurian, who has written pieces for her. She also took part in the first performances of Kolb's *Related Characters* (1982) and Penderecki's Quartet for clarinet and strings (1993). Her 2007 release *Astrurian* with pianist Robert Levin, a frequent collaborator, presents arrangements of Spanish and Argentine art songs. Her interest in a variety of musical traditions prompted Kashkashian to release *Neharót* (2009), a collection of pieces based on traditional laments of the Near East, Armenian chants, and Hasidic melodies.

MARGARET CAMPBELL/MEGAN E. HILL

Kastle, Leonard (Gregory) (*b* New York, NY, 11 Feb 1929; *d* Westerlo, NY, 18 May 2011). Composer, screenplay writer, and director. Kastle attended the Juilliard School (1939–40), the Mannes College for Music, where he studied piano with Frank Sheridan and composition with GEORGE SZELL (1940–42), and the Curtis Institute of Music, Philadelphia (BA 1950), where he studied composition with ROSARIO SCALERO, GIAN CARLO MENOTTI, and SAMUEL BARBER, and piano with ISABELLE VENGEROVA. He also studied piano with PAUL WITTGENSTEIN (1942–52), attended Columbia University (1947–50), and studied conducting with Carl Bamberger in New York (1950–52). Kastle was music director for Broadway revivals of Menotti's *The Medium* and *The Telephone* (1950) and for Kurt Weill's *Lady in the Dark* (1951). He wrote a number of screenplays, most notably *The Honeymoon Killers*, which he also directed (1970). Kastle received numerous prizes, grants, awards, and commissions including first prize in the Leschetizky Piano Competition (1948), a commission from the Deerfield Foundation for his opera *The Pariahs* (1961–6), a Baxter Prize for choral composition (*Three Songs from Moby Dick*, 1963), a grant from the NEA (1974), and two Meet-the-Composer grants (1981, 1985). In 1978 Kastle became a visiting professor of composition at the State University of New York, Albany, retired in 1989, and then stayed on as an adjunct professor. As a composer, Kastle is known mostly for vocal compositions that make liberal use of modern harmonies yet retain a sense of melodic and lyrical Romanticism. His papers are held by the State University of New York, Albany.

WORKS

Stage: The Swing (op, 1), 1954; Deseret (op, 3, A.H. Bailey), 1960, rev. solo vv, pf, org, 1978; The Pariahs (op, 3, Kastle), 1962–70; The Birdwatchers (play with music, Kastle), 1980–81; The Calling of Mother Ann (op), 1985; The Journey of Mother Ann, 1987; Professor Lookalike and the Children (children's op, 1), 1988

Vocal: From a Whitman Reader, 1v, orch, 1954; 3 Walt Whitman Songs (W. Whitman), chorus, 1956; Three Songs from Moby Dick (H. Melville), chorus, 1963; Pontoosuc (H. Melville), Bar, orch, 1974–5; Mass, chorus, org, pf, 1977–8; Weeping Pleiades, song cycle, 1v, pf, 1979

Other: Pf Sonata, 1950; Pf Suite, 1957; Pf Conc., 1981

Principal publisher: Ricordi

BIBLIOGRAPHY

Obituary, *New York Times* (21 May 2011)

KATHERINE K. PRESTON/ROBERT PAUL KOLT

Kastner, Alfred (*b* Vienna, Austria, 10 March 1870; *d* Hollywood, CA, 24 May 1948). Harpist, teacher, and composer of Austrian birth. He studied the harp under Antonio Zamara at the Vienna Conservatory (1882–8). His first important position was in 1890 as first harpist with the Polish National Opera in Warsaw. From 1893 he played with the Royal Hungarian Opera under Arthur Nikisch, then played in Zurich with the Municipal Orchestra, and gave concerts in Switzerland. During 1901–2 and 1903–4 he came to the United States as first harpist with the Philadelphia Orchestra. Between seasons he rejoined his family in Warsaw (his wife was Polish) and gave concerts in Poland, Russia, Finland, and Sweden. In 1904 he joined the Queen's Hall Orchestra, London. He played in the London premieres of Claude Debussy's *Danse sacrée et danse profane* and Maurice Ravel's *Introduction et allegro*, and taught at the Royal Academy of Music (1909–13) and the Guildhall School of Music. At the outbreak of World War I he returned to the United States to play with the New York Philharmonic, and in September 1919 he became principal harpist on the founding of the Los Angeles PO, from which he retired in 1936. Kastner was the founder of the Southern California Chapter of the National Association of Harpists (1923). He was a highly regarded teacher during the period of intensive growth in the film industry and may be regarded as the first harpist to gain prominence on the West Coast. His compositions, which are all for harp, include *50 leichte Übungen*, op.11 (?1901), *Richard Wagner-Orchesterstudien* (n.d.), and about 20 other works.

BIBLIOGRAPHY

M.H. Cambern: "Alfred Kastner, Man, Musician, Pedagogue," *Harp News*, i/10 (1954), 6

A.M. Stockton: "Alfred Kastner," *American Harp Journal*, i/4 (1968), 5

ALICE LAWSON ABER-COUNT

Katchen, Julius (*b* Long Branch, NJ, 15 Aug 1926; *d* Paris, France, 29 April 1969). Pianist. The son of a pianist and a violinist, he was educated privately. He played Wolfgang Amadeus Mozart's D minor Concerto K466 in public at the age of ten and repeated it the following year with the Philadelphia Orchestra under Eugene Ormandy. Shortly afterwards he played with the New York Philharmonic and at the age of 12 gave his first New York recital. However, his parents then withdrew him from concert life, and he subsequently entered Haverford College, Pennsylvania, where he specialized in English literature and philosophy. Later he claimed that such breadth of education was vital to his musical thinking. Subsequently awarded a French government fellowship, Katchen left for France in 1946 and settled in Paris, which became his home for the rest of his life. An ambitious 20-year-old with a powerful musical intelligence and a virtuoso technique, he quickly became a major figure on the international music scene and signed an exclusive recording contract with Decca. He included Benjamin Britten's left-hand Diversions (which he recorded with the composer) and Ned Rorem's Second Sonata in his repertory; but the composer with whom he was most closely associated was Johannes Brahms. His cycle of the complete solo piano music was given in Berlin, London, New York, Amsterdam, and Vienna, a formidable undertaking complemented by frequent performances of both the piano concertos and much of the chamber music of Brahms. He recorded all these works for Decca, along with a vast range of other music; his recording of Brahms's Piano Sonata in F minor op.5 was purportedly the first solo piano LP record. Katchen gave regular tours, covering all six continents, often giving more than 100 concerts per season. It has been said that as a young player his technique was flawless, striving for speed, though often at the expense of musicality. Later in his career, however, he was noticed more for his gift of interpretation. His musical potential was cut short in 1969 when he died of cancer at the age of 42.

BIBLIOGRAPHY

R. Minshull: "Julius Katchen," *Gramophone*, xlvii (1969), 21 only

BRYCE MORRISON/MEGAN E. HILL

Kates, Stephen (Edward) (*b* New York, NY, 7 May 1943; *d* Baltimore, MD, 18 Jan 2003). Cellist. Following studies with LEONARD ROSE and CLAUS ADAM at the Juilliard School (1961–8) and participation in GREGOR PIATIGORSKY's master classes at the University of Southern California, Los Angeles (1964–7), Kates won a silver medal in the Tchaikovsky Competition in Moscow (1966). He made his New York recital debut in 1963 while still a student at Juilliard, and appeared as a soloist with most of the major American orchestras, as well as in Europe. He was equally involved with chamber music and performed with the Chamber Music Society of Lincoln Center, the Aspen Festival, and the Spoleto Festival, among many others. In 1983 he formed the chamber music ensemble Musica Camerit with Carol Wincenc, Joseph Swenson, Masao Kawasaki, and Samuel Sanders. He recorded concertos by Frank Martin and Claus Adam (he commissioned the latter through the Ford

Foundation's Program for Concert Artists in 1971) with the Louisville Orchestra under Jorge Mester. He taught at Ohio State University, Brooklyn College, CUNY, and the Peabody Institute, where he served for 28 years.

KAREN MONSON/R

Katims, Milton (*b* New York, NY, 24 June 1909; *d* Shoreline, WA, 27 Feb 2006). Conductor and violist. After attending Columbia University, where he studied violin with Herbert Dittler, he changed to the viola and developed an interest in conducting. In both these activities his mentor was LEON BARZIN, who at the time conducted the National Orchestral Association in New York. Katims was a violist and assistant conductor for the WOR radio station from 1935 to 1943, when he joined the NBC SO under Arturo Toscanini as first-desk viola, later becoming principal guest conductor (1947–54). During his time with the NBC SO he gave a master class for violists at the Juilliard School, was a member of the New York Piano Quartet, and was guest violist with the Budapest String Quartet. From 1954 to 1975 he was music director and conductor of the Seattle SO; he also conducted the New York Philharmonic, the Philadelphia Orchestra, the Boston SO, the London PO, the Israel PO, and other orchestras, and conducted premieres of works including *Visions of Poets* (1962) and *Spectrum* (1964), both by Benjamin Lees, Leon Kirchner's Piano Concerto no.2 (1964) and Roger Reynolds's *Graffiti* (1966); as a violist he gave the premiere of Morton Gould's Viola Concerto (1952). Katims was a member of the music panel of the US Information Service (1960–67) and of the first Washington State Arts Commission (1961); he became a member of the US State Department Music Panel for Cultural Presentations in 1967. He was artistic director of the School of Music, University of Houston, Texas, from 1976 to 1984. He received many awards, including the Columbia University Medal of Excellence (1954), the Alice M. Ditson Award (1965), and several honorary degrees, including one from Seattle University (1971).

GEORGE GELLES/JACOB HOSLER/R

Katz, Erich (*b* Posen [now Poznań], Poland, 31 July 1900; *d* Santa Barbara, CA, 30 July 1973). German composer and music educator; naturalized American. He studied at the Berlin Hochschule für Musik and the University of Berlin (1918–21) and completed the PhD in musicology at the University of Freiburg (1922–6). Co-founder (1928) and co-director of the Freiburger Kurse für Musiktheorie (later the Freiburg Music Seminary), he was also a choral conductor, organist, and music critic, and the editor of *Das neue Chorbuch* (Mainz, 1931). In 1939 he fled to England, where he taught at the Bunce Court School. He moved to the United States in 1943 and became head of the composition department at the New York College of Music (later New York University) and the New School for Social Research. He also served as director of the American Recorder Society, which he helped to reorganize in 1947, and the Musicians' Workshop, a performing group specializing in early and contemporary works. Influenced by *Gebrauchsmusik*, Katz composed for recorders, other instruments, and voices and made numerous transcriptions and editions of early music. After retiring to California in 1959, he taught at the Santa Barbara City College and directed a Collegium Musicum.

MSS in *BO*

BIBLIOGRAPHY

B.R. Atwater: "Erich Katz: Teacher-Composer, 1900–1973," *American Recorder*, xiv/4 (1973), 115–35 [incl. work-list]

C. Primus: "Erich Katz: the Pied Piper Comes to America," *American Music Research Center Journal*, i (1991), 1–19

M. Davenport: "Carl Orff: the Katz Connection," *American Recorder*, xxxvi/4 (1995), 7–15, 34–9

CONSTANCE M. PRIMUS

Katz, Martin (*b* Los Angeles, CA, 27 Nov 1945). Pianist. He began piano lessons at the age of five. As a scholarship student at the University of Southern California, he studied accompanying with Gwendolyn Koldofsky, and while still a student accompanied the masterclasses of LOTTE LEHMANN, JASCHA HEIFETZ, Pierre Bernac, and GREGORY PIATIGORSKY; after graduation, he served as pianist for the US Army chorus in Washington (1966–9). Katz has been in constant demand as an accompanist and has worked with such artists as Marilyn Horne, Nicolai Gedda, Frederica von Stade, Kiri Te Kanawa, Teresa Berganza, Judith Blegen, Tatiana Troyanos, and José Carreras in concert tours that have spanned five continents. His numerous collaborative recordings, with luminaries such as Von Stade, Horne, Carreras, David Daniels, and Karita Mattila, have been issued by CBS Masterworks, Ondine, RCA Victor, Sony Classical, and Decca. Mainly through his association with Horne, he has become a specialist in the music of the Baroque and in bel canto. His editions of Rossini operas have been used by the Houston Grand Opera and at the 1982–3 Rossini Festival in New York, and his version of Handel's *Rinaldo*, made for the Ottawa Festival in 1982, was adopted for the production at the Metropolitan Opera in 1984. He has led opera productions for San Francisco Opera's Merola program, the British Broadcasting Corporation, and Tokyo's NHK Broadcast Center. Katz has taught at the University of Maryland and the Westminster Choir College. Since 1983, he has been on the faculty at the University of Michigan, where he serves as Artur Schnabel Collegiate Professor of Music and is the head of the program in collaborative piano. He was honored as "Accompanist of the Year" in 1998 by Musical America.

BIBLIOGRAPHY

A. Ulrich: "The Diva Doctor Is In," *San Francisco Chronicle* (8 July 2007)

M. Katz: *The Complete Collaborator: the Pianist as Partner* (New York, 2009)

PHILIP LIESON MILLER/MICHAEL HIX

Kauder, Hugo (*b* Tobitschau, Moravia [now Tovačov, Czech Republic], 9 June 1888; *d* Bussum, Netherlands, 22 July 1972). Austrian composer, violinist, and writer on music. His formal musical training consisted of violin lessons in his home town. He moved to Vienna, where he played in the orchestra of the Konzertverein (1910–19). He was a self-taught composer whose works, contrapuntal in texture and harmonically conservative, include five symphonies, nine concertos, 19 string quartets, other chamber works, choral music, and songs. He settled in New York in 1940. His honors include the City of Vienna composition prize (1928) for his First Symphony and a Fromm Foundation Award (1953). Kauder wrote many essays on music and two books, *Entwurf einer neuen Melodie- und Harmonielehre* (1932) and *Counterpoint: an Introduction to Polyphonic Composition* (1960/R).

BIBLIOGRAPHY

GMO

O. Kauder: *Hugo Kauder: Biografie und Wersverzeichnis* (New York, 1975)

THOMAS L. GAYDA/R

Kaufman, Fredrick (*b* Brooklyn, NY, 24 March 1936). Composer. He studied trumpet with WILLIAM VACCHIANO, composition with VITTORIO GIANNINI, and jazz performance and arranging with JOHN LEWIS and John La Porte at the Manhattan School (BMus 1959, MMus 1960). He also studied composition with VINCENT PERSICHETTI at the Juilliard School, and took private trumpet lessons with Harry Glantz. He performed as a trumpeter in the New York City Ballet Orchestra, the Goldman Band (now the Guggenheim Band), the Woody Herman Band, and the Sauter-Finnegan Band, as well as in various Broadway shows. Kaufman became composer-in-residence at the University of Wisconsin in 1969. That same year his Violin Concerto was performed by Avigdor Zamir and the Pittsburgh SO under William Steinberg, and his Symphony no.1 was presented by the St. Paul Chamber Orchestra under Leopold Sipe.

In 1971 Kaufman moved to Israel, where he served as director of music for the city of Haifa (1971–2) and taught at the Rubin Academy in Jerusalem. His music was performed by the Israel PO, the Jerusalem SO, and the Batsheva Dance Company, among others. A television documentary, *Fredrick Kaufman: Life of a Composer* (1976), was made about his life and work in Israel. He returned to the United States in 1976 and served as chairman of the music department of Eastern Montana College (1977–82); dean, director, and professor of composition at the Philadelphia College of the Performing Arts/University of the Arts (1982–93); and Director (1993–2003), Professor/Composer-in-Residence (2003–8), and Professor Emeritus (from 2008) at the School of Music, Florida International University.

Kaufman's works show the influence of jazz in their rhythmic intensity and harmonic language, which is based on tone-clusters and the massed sonorities of unrelated chords played simultaneously, as in *When the Twain Meet* (1981). His interest in jazz and its origins led him to travel in 1973 to West Africa, which informed his book *The African Roots of Jazz* (1979).

WORKS

Dramatic: A Children's Opera (Kaufman), 1967; The Nothing Ballet, 1971; The Changling (Drama), elec tape, rhythm & blues band, con-

crete sounds, 1971; And the World Goes On (theater piece), perc, t sax, bar sax, elec gui, elec tape, pf, 1971; Birds (ballet), elec tape, 1974; The Cage (ballet), elec tape, 1976; MASADA (op, 3), 1989–91; Regal Fanfare, brass, chorus, band, orch, 1996; Silver Fanfare, chorus, orch, 1997

Film Scores: Scenes in Ein Hod, inst, 1973; San Francisco Bay, insts, elec, 1977; Arabs in America, inst, 1979

Orch and choral: Conc., vn, str, 1968; Sym. no.1, str, 1968; Sym. for Winds, 1969; Sym. no.2, wind orch, 1970; 5 Psalms, 1973; The Journey, orch, 1974; 3 Cants. (Pss.), chorus, org, 1975; Triple Conc., pf, t sax, jazz band, orch, 1975; Ballet Music, orch, 1976; Echoes (Kaufman), chorus, fl, cl, perc, 1978; Sym., str, perc, 1976; When the Twain Meet, orch, 1981; Southeast Fantasy, sym. wind ens, 1982; Stars and Distances, spoken sounds and words, chorus, 1982; Masada (Eisendrath), chorus, cl, perc, 1985; Mother of Exiles, chorus, str, 1986; Seascape, str, cel, hp, perc, 1987; Kaddish Conc., vc, str orch, 1987; Conc., cl, str, "The Arronson," 1988; Sym. no.5 "The American," orch, 1987, arr. for band, 1988; Prayer, chorus, cl, perc, 1988; The Dance of Death, orch, 1990; The Dance of Death II, orch, 1997; Conc., trbn, str, 1998; Catalan Concertante, orch, 2000; Conc., "The Guernica," pf, orch, 2011

Chbr: 3 Poems by W.E. Henley, voice, pf, 1968; Str Qt no.1, 1969 [based on Sym. no.1]; Gigue, pf/hpd, 1969; Ww Trio, fl, cl, bn, 1969; Sonata, vn, pf, 1969; Interiors, vn, pf, 1971; And the World Goes On, perc, elec gui, elec tape, pf, bar sax, t sax, 1971; Str Qt, 1972, withdrawn; Yom Kippur War Piece, shofar, drum, elec tape, 1974; Introduction & Dance, cl, vn, vc, pf, 1975; 5 Moods, ob, 1975; Perc Trio, 1975; Str Qt no.2, 1978; 5 Fragrances of Winter, cl, hp, perc, 1980; Str Qt no.3, 1980; Gigue, 2 vn, 1980; Gigue no.2, pf/hpd, 1980; Gigue, hpd, 1980; Duo, vn, gui, 1980; Metamorphosis, pf, 1981; Time and Space, pf, 1981; Meditation for a Lonely Flute, 1983; Str Qt no.4, 1984; A/V Slide Show, trbn, 1984–5; Mobile Str Qt, 1985; A Bud for Bloom, fl, ob, pf, 1988; Aaronson Clarinet Qnt, 1988; Echoes, Mez, ob, vn, va, 1990; Fanfare, ob, 1990; Nodus I, cl, pf, 1991; Catalan Concertante, gui qt, 1991; Fanfare, a sax, 1991; Catalan Concertante, str qt, 1992; Fanfare, cbn, 1996; Nodus II, cl, pf, 1997; Catalan Concertante II, str qt, 1998; Sudon, cl, pf, 1999; Echoes II, T, ob, va, 2002; Wild Wind, cl, 2002; Kaminarimon, flam dance, taiko dr, 2002; Wild Wind II, b cl, 2003; The Dynamic Duo, 2 va, 2003; Yin & Yang: A Dialogue Between Two Grand Pianos, 2003; Inner Sanctum II, b cl, 2003; Asturias, gui qt, 2003; Coda, cl, va, pf, 2003; Str Qt no.6, "The Urban," 2006; Echoes…The Beat Poets, T, ob, va, 2009

Electronic: 11 works conceived 1971–83 on Moog, Arp, & Buchla synthesizers

Incidental Music: 12 miscellaneous incid chbr and solo works for stage productions

DOUGLAS TOWNSEND/GREG A STEINKE

Kaufman, George S(imon) (*b* Pittsburgh, PA, 16 Nov 1889; *d* New York, NY, 2 June 1961). Librettist and director. He first worked as a journalist, serving for a time as head of the drama desk at the *New York Times*, but resigned in order to write his own plays. His first libretto, produced in collaboration with Marc Connelly, was for *Helen of Troy, New York* (1923; music by B. Kalmar and H. Ruby) and established his reputation for witty and satirical writing. He then created two important shows for the Marx Brothers, *The Cocoanuts* (1925; I. Berlin) and, with Morrie Ryskind, *Animal Crackers* (1928; Kalmar and Ruby), and also collaborated with Ryskind on the libretto for the highly successful *Of Thee I Sing* (1931; G. Gershwin), the first musical to be awarded a Pulitzer Prize for drama, and *Let 'Em Eat Cake* (1933; Gershwin). Kaufman contributed both libretto and lyrics for *Hollywood Pinafore* (1945; based on Arthur Sullivan's *H.M.S. Pinafore*), which includes some of his drollest work, and provided sketches for several revues, including *The 49ers* (1922), *Music Box Revue* (1923), *The Band Wagon* (1931; A. Schwartz), and *Sing Out the News* (1938; H. Rome). He served as director for many of his own shows as well as for such productions as Berlin's *Face the Music* (1932) and Loesser's *Guys and Dolls* (1950).

BIBLIOGRAPHY

H. Teichmann: *George S. Kaufman* (New York, 1972)

S. Meredith: *George S. Kaufman and his Friends* (Garden City, NY, 1974)

M. Goldstein: *George S. Kaufman: his Life, his Theatre* (New York, 1979)

J.W. Combe: *The Aesthetics of Collaboration: Adaptation and Creation in the Musical and Film* Guys and Dolls (diss., U. of California, Riverside, 1998)

GERALD BORDMAN/R

Kaufman, Louis (*b* Portland, OR, 10 May 1905; *d* Los Angeles, CA, 9 Feb 1994). Violinist and viola player. He studied with Henry Bettman and then FRANZ KNEISEL at the Institute of Musical Art in New York, graduating in 1926 with the Loeb Award. In 1927 he won the Naumburg Award, which resulted in a New York recital in 1928. He played the viola in the Musical Art Quartet from 1926 to 1933 but left to pursue a career as a solo violinist. In 1933 he married pianist Annette Leibole, and together they appeared in concerts and made recordings for over 50 years. He was then engaged by MGM and subsequently played solos in some 400 film scores. He gave many premieres of modern works, including Anthony Collins's Violin Concerto and Leighton Lucas's *Concert champêtre*. Kaufman possessed a faultless technique but sought above all else beauty of sound, perpetuating the school of Mischa Elman, Fritz Kreisler, and Jascha Heifetz. He owned both the "exZimbalist" Guadagnini (1775) and the "ex-Barrère" Stradivari (1727).

BIBLIOGRAPHY

H. Roth: "Louis Kaufman," *The Strad*, xcviii (1983), 98–101

A. Mell: "An Interview with the Violinist Louis Kaufman," *Journal of the Violin Society of America*, vii/4 (1986), 3–38

M. Campbell: Obituary, *The Independent* (14 Feb 1994)

A. Mell: "Louis Kaufman (1905–1994)," *Journal of the Violin Society of America*, xiii/2 (1994), 215–8

L. Kaufman and A. Kaufman: *A Fiddler's Tale: How Hollywood and Vivaldi Discovered Me* (Madison, 2003) [memoir with afterword by A. Kaufman]

MARGARET CAMPBELL/R

Kaufman, Sarah (*b* Austin, TX, 16 May 1963). Dance critic. She studied ballet while growing up before earning a bachelor's degree in English from the University of Maryland and a master's degree in journalism from Northwestern University. Early in her career she worked for the *Buffalo News*, the *Daily Herald* in Arlington Heights, Illinois, and for English-language journals in Munich, Germany. She freelanced for the *Washington Post* until 1996, when she succeeded Alan Kriegsman, the *Post*'s long-time writer and the first dance critic to win a Pulitzer Prize.

Kaufman's writing about dance has earned her notice, including the Missouri Lifestyle Journalism Award for Arts and Entertainment Reporting (2001), and the Pulitzer Prize for Criticism (2010). She has covered such diverse subjects as George Balanchine and Michael Jackson, and she has examined dance in ballets, film, popular culture, and everyday life. In July 2000 she broke the story that works by Martha Graham may not have copyright protection. Kaufman's style blends acute description and historical savvy with fearless wit. She explains the hard truths and beautiful meanings of the art of movement.

REBECCA SCHWARTZ-BISHIR

Kaun, Bernhard Theodor Ludwig (*b* Milwaukee, WI, 5 April 1899; *d* Baden-Baden, Germany, 3 Jan 1980). German composer of American birth, son of Hugo Kaun. Largely self-taught as a composer, he was tutored by his father, and studied violin and piano while attending Gymnasium in Berlin. During World War I he served in the German army, playing clarinet in a military band. After the war he arranged and conducted for RCA Victor in Berlin for several years. In 1924 he moved to the United States, where he worked as a music copyist in New York, conducted at the Alhambra Theater, Milwaukee (1924), and taught at the Eastman School of Music (1925–8). Recognized particularly for his orchestrations, he arranged music from Richard Wagner's music dramas for the New York release of Fritz Lang's film *Siegfried* and orchestrated Howard Hanson's *Legend of Beowulf* and Organ Concerto.

In 1930 Kaun was invited to Hollywood by Heinz Roemheld, music director of Universal Studios. Over the following decade he worked for both Warner Bros. and Paramount, composing music for over 170 films; his first assignments included the first full-length score for a sound film (*Heaven on Earth*, 1931) and music for *Frankenstein* (1931). Highly sought after as an orchestrator, he orchestrated now classic film scores for Max Steiner (*King Kong*, 1933; *Gone with the Wind*, 1939), Erich Wolfgang Korngold, Ernst Toch (*Peter Ibbetson*, 1935), Dimitri Tiomkin (*Lost Horizon*, 1937) and Charlie Chaplin, as well as orchestrating his own scores. His eclectic, coloristic style, influenced by the music of Richard Strauss, Jean Sibelius, Maurice Ravel, and early Arnold Schoenberg, was praised by Igor Stravinsky. In 1941 Kaun left Hollywood for New York, where he devoted himself to composing concert music. He returned to Germany in 1953, where he conducted the Graunke Orchestra (Munich) until 1963.

WORKS
(selective list)

Film scores: Frankenstein, 1931; Heaven on Earth, 1931; Doctor X, 1932; I am a Fugitive of a Chain Gang, 1932; The Mystery of the Wax Museum, 1932; 20,000 Years at Sing Sing, 1932; A Farewell to Arms, 1933, collab. W.F. Harling and others; Luxury Liner, 1933; Death Takes a Holiday, 1934, collab. M. Roder and others; The Firebird, 1934 [after Stravinsky]; The Scarlet Empress, 1934, collab. J. Leipold and others; Oil for the Lamps of China, 1935, collab. H. Roemheld; She, 1935, collab. M. Steiner; The Black Legion, 1936; The Petrified Forest, 1936; Story of Louis Pasteur, 1936, collab. Roemheld; The Walking Dead, 1936; The Patient in Room 18, 1937; The Return of Doctor X, 1939; Forest Murmurs, 1947; Special Delivery, 1955; Alle Wege führen heim, 1957; Lassie (TV series), 1958–9

Other works: Entice Italienne; Zeitstimmung, female vv; Sketches, suite, orch, 1927; Nederländisches Volkslied, 1v, pf, 1929–30; Romantic Sym., C, 1930s, rev. 1960s; Qnt, ob, str, 1940; Sinfonia concertante, hn, orch, 1940; The Vagabond, suite, orch, 1956 [based on film and TV scores]; 20 pf pieces

BIBLIOGRAPHY

W.H. Rosar: "Music for the Monsters: Universal Pictures' Horror Film Scores of the Thirties," *Quarterly Journal of the Library of Congress*, xl (1983), 390–421

C. McCarty: *Film Composers in America: a Filmography 1911–1970* (Oxford, 2000)

WILLIAM ROSAR

Kavafian, Ani (*b* Istanbul, Turkey, 10 May 1948). Violinist, sister of IDA KAVAFIAN. She immigrated to the United States with her Armenian family in 1956 and began violin studies in Detroit with Ara Zerounian (1957–62) and MISHA MISCHAKOFF (1962–6). At the Juilliard School of Music from 1966 (MA 1972), she studied violin with IVAN GALAMIAN and chamber music with FELIX GALIMIR and the Juilliard Quartet. In 1969 she made her debut at Carnegie Recital Hall. Her European debut was at the Salle Gaveau in Paris (1973). After winning the Avery Fisher Prize (1976), she performed with the New York Philharmonic (1977), when she played Ludwig van Beethoven's Violin Concerto under the direction of Erich Leinsdorf. She has appeared with many other major orchestras.

Kavafian has balanced her career as a solo artist with that of a chamber musician. She toured with Music from Marlboro (1971–2) and in 1972 began playing with the Chamber Music Society of Lincoln Center, of which she became an artist-member in 1980; in 1978 she made her first appearance with the Santa Fe Chamber Music Festival. Her premieres include works by Karel Husa, Ned Rorem, Tison Street, and Tōru Takemitsu, and she has made several chamber music recordings. She has performed regularly with her sister, and they celebrated the 25th anniversary of their first Carnegie Hall concert with another in 2008. She combines technical virtuosity with sensitive musicianship, and her warm and rich tone is complemented by her violin, the "Muir Mackenzie" Stradivari of 1736. Professor of violin at the Mannes College from 1982, she was appointed in 1983 to the same position at the Manhattan School and Queens College, CUNY. As of 2012 Kavafian was also a member of the da Salo String Trio.

K. ROBERT SCHWARZ/JONAS WESTOVER

Kavafian, Ida (*b* Istanbul, Turkey, 29 Oct 1952). Violinist, sister of ANI KAVAFIAN. She immigrated to the United States with her Armenian family in 1956 and began violin studies in Detroit at the age of six with Ara Zerounian; later she studied with MISHA MISCHAKOFF and (from 1969) at the Juilliard School (MA 1975) with OSCAR SHUMSKY and IVAN GALAMIAN. In 1973 she won the Vianna da Motta International Violin Competition in Lisbon, and in the same year was one of the founding members of the chamber ensemble TASHI; her recordings and engagements with the group demonstrated a devotion to chamber music, and especially new music. She joined the Beaux Arts Trio in 1992.

Kavafian made her New York recital debut in 1978, accompanied by Peter Serkin. Her European debut was in 1982 at the Queen Elizabeth Hall in London. She has appeared as a soloist with many orchestras, and as a chamber musician with the Guarneri String Quartet and at several festivals, including Spoleto (United States and Italy), the Berkshire Music Festival, the Santa Fe Chamber Music Festival, and the Chamber Music Society of Lincoln Center. Active as both violinist and violist, she performed with her sister Ani Kavafian at a duo recital in Carnegie Hall (1983), and gave an anniversary concert there in 2008. She has given premieres of works by Tōru Takemitsu, Charles Wuorinen, Peter Lieberson, and Ruth Crawford, and joined Chick Corea and Gary Burton for an international jazz tour (1983–4). Her playing is fiery and uninhibited, and her sensuous tone is enhanced by her instrument, a J.B. Guadagnini of 1751. Kavafian has been the director of Music from Angel Fire since 1990, has a small ensemble called Opus One, and founded the Bravo! Vail Valley Music Festival.

K. ROBERT SCHWARZ/JONAS WESTOVER

Kavanaugh [Kavanagh], **Joseph H.** (*fl* 1840s–60s). Singer and composer. Throughout the 1840s he appeared frequently in New York in vocal concerts, often in the company of Frank Lynch, George Holman, and Nelson Kneass. Kavanaugh also sang in the chorus for several operas, including Ferdinand Herold's *Zampa* in 1841 and Michael William Balfe's *The Bohemian Girl* in 1844. Early in 1845 Kavanaugh appeared with Kneass's Ethiopian Troupe of Burlesquers at Palmo's Opera House, again with Holman and Lynch. This troupe performed burlesques of opera in blackface. By the early 1850s Kavanaugh's name appeared more frequently in advertisements for minstrel troupes than for the vocal concerts and operatic performances that characterized his early career. In 1849 he composed "Virginia Rose Bud," a popular sentimental song. The refrain parodies the overture to Daniel Auber's opera *Le cheval de bronze*. "Virginia Rose Bud," which was performed both in and out of blackface, constitutes a fitting representative of Kavanaugh's career: he was able to remain active for decades by moving between legitimate genres and minstrelsy.

The name Thomas Kavanagh also appears in theatrical records. Because primary sources frequently list only the last name, it is difficult to know whether such references are to Thomas or Joseph. To further complicate matters, "Virginia Rose Bud" was published by Lee and Walker as "composed and sung by F.H. Kavanaugh," and this apparent error was repeated on later editions. The present identification of Joseph H. Kavanaugh is based on Odell's and Mahar's records, which place J.H. Kavanaugh as the performer who appeared repeatedly with Lynch, Holman, and Kneass.

BIBLIOGRAPHY

G.C.D. Odell: *Annals of the New York Stage* (New York, 1927/R1970)

C. Hamm: *Yesterdays: Popular Song in America* (New York, 1983)

W. Mahar: *Behind the Burnt Cork Mask: Early Blackface Minstrelsy and Antebellum American Popular Culture* (Urbana, IL, 1999)

RENEE LAPP NORRIS

Kay. Manufacturer of fretted stringed instruments. The Kay Musical Instrument Company began as the Andrew Groehsl (*b* Austria, 1859; *d* Chicago, IL, 1952) company in 1890 or later in Chicago, Illinois, primarily manufacturing mandolins. Groehsl built Mayflower-brand mandolins for Harry Flower (*b* Poland, 1862), some labeled Flower & Groehsl. Groehsl's interests were purchased by Charles G. Stromberg (*b* Sweden, 1873), Frank C. Voisinet (*b* Ohio, 1877), and Henry Kuhrmeyer (*b* St. Paul, MN, 1895; *d* Chicago, IL, 1956) at the beginning of 1922, becoming the Stromberg-Voisinet Company. Stromberg-Voisinet produced instruments for the low to middle range of the market.

In 1922 Stromberg-Voisinet debuted its distinctive "Venetian" head guitars and asymmetrical double-pointed mandolins. In 1924 Stromberg-Voisinet introduced new laminating techniques that were used on some tops and bodies. In 1927 Stromberg-Voisinet applied the "Venetian" shape to its Stromberg guitars, which would become KayKraft-brand in 1931. In 1928 Stromberg introduced the first documented electric guitar and amplifier, the Electro. By 1930, Henry Kuhrmeyer had become president of Stromberg-Voisinet and on 1 July 1931, the company became the Kay Manufacturing Company, sometimes called the Kay Musical Instrument Company.

The company introduced its first archtop Arch Kraft guitars in 1933 and Kaywood Amplifying (resonator) guitars in 1933. Kay made many guitars bearing other companies' brands. In 1936 Kay produced its first archtop Electric Amplifying Guitar for catalog retailer Montgomery Ward and began using steel-reinforced necks. Use of the Kay brand began in around 1937.

Kay electric guitars became more prominent following World War II. The semi-hollow cutaway Thin Twin electric and Kay's first solid-body (K125) appeared in 1952. Upon retirement in 1955, Kuhrmeyer was succeeded by Sidney M. Katz. In 1965 Kay was sold to Louis J. Nicastro's Seeburg Corporation, with Robert Keyworth heading Kay. In 1967 Seeburg sold Kay to Valco, maker of National and Supro guitars. The combined Valco/Kay company closed in bankruptcy in 1968, with assets auctioned off in 1969. The brand name was purchased by Tony "Blair" Ruzbasan (*b* East Chicago, IN, 31 March 1947), moved to Fishers, Indiana, and has been used on electric and acoustic "copy" guitars made in Asia to the present day. In 2000 Kay moved to Irvine, California, and in 2007 introduced two series of vintage reissues of 1950s Kay designs, some made in Asia, some built by Roger E. Fritz (*b* Pittsburgh, PA, 15 July 1951) in Albion, California.

BIBLIOGRAPHY

The Music Trade Reivew (New York City, NY)
The Music Trades Magazine (Englewood, NJ)
T. Wheeler: *American Guitars* (New York, 1982/R1992)
M. Wright: *Electric Guitars, the Illustrated Encyclopedia* (San Diego, CA, 2000)
M. Wright: *Acoustic Guitars, the Illustrated Encyclopedia* (San Diego, CA, 2003)

MICHAEL WRIGHT

Kay, Connie [Conrad] **(Henry Kirnon)** (*b* Tuckahoe, NY, 27 April 1927; *d* New York, NY, 30 Nov 1994). Jazz drummer. Kay, who had piano lessons from age six, but was mostly self-taught on drums, began his professional career in 1939. He played at *Minton's Playhouse* in New York in 1944–5 with Sir Charles Thompson and Miles Davis, and toured in a rhythm-and-blues show throughout the late 1940s. In the early 1950s Kay worked as a studio musician, recording and performing with Cat Anderson, Milt Jackson, Miles Davis, Ray Charles, and especially Lester Young. He also played in small groups led by Beryl Booker, Stan Getz, Coleman Hawkins, and Charlie Parker. In February 1955 he replaced Kenny Clarke in the MODERN JAZZ QUARTET and stayed until it formally broke up in 1974, also participating in subsequent re-formations of the MJQ after 1981. Kay was influenced by drummers such as Gene Krupa, Buddy Rich, Chick Webb, and Big Sid Catlett, but he did not favor drum solos; in the MJQ he served as a fully integrated part of the quartet's concept. During the MJQ's annual summer breaks from performance Kay recorded with Randy Weston, Chet Baker, Paul Desmond, Cannonball Adderley, and many others. After the MJQ disbanded Kay played with Benny Goodman as well as the group *Soprano Summit*, and was house drummer at the New York club Eddie Condon's (1975–84). After a stroke in 1992 he shortly returned to playing in spring 1993.

BIBLIOGRAPHY

K. Mohr: "Connie Kay," *Jazz Hot*, no.117 (1957), 17
J. Potter: "Connie Kay: Sophisticated Swing," *Modern Drummer*, xi/2 (1987), 22–5
W. Knauer: *Zwischen Bebop und Free Jazz: Komposition und Improvisation des Modern Jazz Quartet* (Mainz, 1990)

WOLFRAM KNAUER

Kay, Hershy (*b* Philadelphia, PA, 17 Nov 1919; *d* Danbury, CT, 2 Dec 1981). Composer and arranger. He studied at the Curtis Institute (1936–40), where his teachers included RANDALL THOMPSON (composition). Self-taught as an orchestrator, he began a successful career orchestrating musicals and ballets in New York. His first professional project was to orchestrate several Brazilian songs for soprano Elsie Houston's nightclub act in the Rainbow Room. Beginning with Leonard Bernstein's *On the Town* in 1944, Kay became one of the most sought after orchestrators on Broadway. His credits include later works by Bernstein, Marc Blitzstein, Harvey Schmidt, Cy Coleman, Andrew Lloyd Webber, and others. He created ballet scores for George Balanchine and the New York City Ballet, the Joffrey Ballet, the Royal Ballet, and the Royal Danish Ballet. He also arranged film and television scores, and nightclub acts. He completed the orchestration of Robert Kurka's opera *The Good Soldier Schweik* after the composer's death. His last arrangement was of Bernstein's *Olympic Hymn*, first performed at the opening of the Olympic Congress in Baden-Baden (1981).

Kay's original compositions draw on a wide range of styles, including serialism (*The Clowns*, 1968). His ballets show the influence of a variety of sources, from folk music and British music hall ditties to John Philip

Sousa, Noël Coward, Francis Poulenc, Jacques Offenbach, and others. His reconstruction for Eugene List of Louis Moreau Gottschalk's *Grande tarantelle* for piano and orchestra, later choreographed by Balanchine as *Tarantella*, led to a revival of interest in Gottschalk's music. A modest, self-effacing man, Kay claimed he could teach all he knew about orchestration "in twenty minutes"; he was widely admired for his skills and his ability to work well under pressure. He was a strong advocate for paying royalties to arrangers, rather than a set fee per page of completed work. He taught orchestration for a year (1972) at Columbia University.

WORKS
(selective list)

Ballets: The Thief who Loved a Ghost, 1950 [after C.M. von Weber]; Cakewalk, 1951 [after L.M. Gottschalk]; Western Sym., 1954 [based on Amer. folksongs]; The Concert, 1956 [after F. Chopin]; Stars and Stripes, 1958 [after J.P. Sousa]; Tarantella, pf, orch, 1961 [after Gottschalk]; L'inconnue, 1963 [after F. Poulenc]; The Clowns, 1968; Cortège burlesque, 1969; Meadowlark, 1969; Who Cares?, 1970 [after G. Gershwin]; Grand Tour, 1971 [after N. Coward]; Winter's Court, 1972 [based on Renaissance dances]; Union Jack, 1976 [based on British folksongs]

Orchestrations (musicals, unless otherwise stated): L. Bernstein: On the Town, 1944; K. Weill: A Flag is Born (pageant), 1946; Bernstein: Peter Pan, 1950; J. Moross: The Golden Apple (op), 1954; E. Robinson: Sandhog, 1954; M. Blitzstein: Reuben, Reuben, 1955; Bernstein: Candide, 1956, rev. 1974; J. Urbont: Livin' the Life, 1957; R. Kurka: The Good Soldier Schweik (op), 1958 [completed by Kay]; Mother Goose Rhymes, 1958 [background music for C. Ritchard recording]; Blitzstein: Juno, 1959; M. Rodgers: Once Upon a Mattress, 1959; The Happiest Girl in the World, 1961 [after J. Offenbach]; J. Herman: Milk and Honey, 1961; H. Schmidt: 110 in the Shade, 1963; M. Charlap: Kelly, 1965; M. Schafer: Drat! The Cat!, 1965; A. Previn: Coco, 1969; Bernstein: Mass (theater piece), 1971; M. Hamlisch: A Chorus Line, 1975; Bernstein: 1600 Pennsylvania Avenue, 1976; J. Ross: Music Is, 1976; C. Coleman: On the Twentieth Century, 1978; B. Lane: Carmelina 1979; A. Lloyd Webber: Evita, 1979; Coleman: Barnum, 1980

Orchestrations (film scores): A. North: Man with the Gun, 1955; North: The King and Four Queens, 1956; North: South Seas Adventure, 1958; S. Kaplan: Girl of the Night, 1960; T.Z. Shepard: Such Good Friends, 1971; North: Bite the Bullet, 1975

Other works: Gottschalk: Grande tarantelle, pf, orch, 1961 [reconstruction]; wind music; music for TV, radio, night club acts

Principal publisher: Boosey & Hawkes, Presser

BIBLIOGRAPHY

R. Landry: "Says Arrangers Rate Royalties: Hershy Kay Argues that Orchestrating in Modern Sense is Comparatively New Profession," *Variety*, no.224 (1961), 79 only

M. Sonino: "Hershy Kay," *MusAm*, lxxxi/10 (1961), 10–11, 56–7

"Hershy Kay, Arranger, Dies: Did Shows, Ballets and Films," *New York Times* (4 Dec 1981)

WAYNE J. SCHNEIDER

Kay, Ulysses (Simpson) (*b* Tucson, AZ, 7 Jan 1917; *d* Englewood, NJ, 20 May 1995). Composer. He was the nephew of African American jazz cornetist and bandleader Joe "King" Oliver. After studying piano, violin, and saxophone from a young age, Kay enrolled at the University of Arizona as a liberal arts student but soon changed his focus to school music. Several meetings with WILLIAM GRANT STILL helped encourage his growing interest in composition, leading him to pursue an MA in composition at the Eastman School, where he studied with BERNARD ROGERS and HOWARD HANSON. A particularly important mentor was PAUL HINDEMITH, who taught Kay

at the Berkshire Music Center and Yale University. After military service, during which Kay played in the US Navy Band and in the dance orchestra at Quonset Point, Rhode Island, he studied with OTTO LUENING at Columbia University on a Rosenwald Fellowship. Between 1949 and 1952 Kay lived in Italy, both as a Fulbright Scholar and as the first African American recipient of the Rome Prize, which he received twice. On his return he was appointed editorial advisor (1953) and later music consultant for Broadcast Music, Inc., New York, a position he held until 1968. After serving briefly as visiting professor at Boston University and UCLA, he was appointed professor at Herbert H. Lehman College, CUNY (1968). He was named a distinguished professor in 1972, serving until his retirement in 1988. During his career he accrued numerous honors, including a Guggenheim Fellowship (1964) and six honorary doctorates. In 1958 he was selected by the US State Department to tour Russia with a delegation of American composers as part of a cultural exchange. He was elected to the American Academy and Institute of Arts and Letters in 1979.

Kay's musical language is tonal, though extensively chromatic, with many neo-classical features. Lyrical melodies, rich harmonies, and polyphonic textures are also characteristic. His orchestration reflects a creative understanding of the timbral possibilities of orchestral instruments. *Sinfonia in E* (1950) is based on classical ideals, while *Six American Dances for String Orchestra* (1954) embodies a distinctly American spirit. Imitative counterpoint is employed in *How Stands the Glass Around?* (1954) and techniques such as *Klangfarbenmelodie* are explored in *Markings* (1966), a work that Howard Klein (*New York Times*) praised as "a masterpiece of conservative modern orchestral writing."

For most of his life Kay showed no interest in employing race-related subject matter. This changed, however, with two late operas, *Jubilee* (1976) and *Frederick Douglass* (1985), in which he and librettist Donald Dorr examined issues surrounding American slavery.

WORKS
DRAMATIC

Ops: Danse Calinda (ballet, after R. Torrence), 1941, Rochester, NY, 23 April 1941, arr. orch, 1947; The Boor (op, 1, U. Kay, after A. Chekhov), 1955, Lexington, KY, 2 April 1968; The Juggler of Our Lady (op, 1, A. King), 1956, New Orleans, 23 Feb 1962; The Capitoline Venus (op, 1, J. Dvorkin, after M. Twain), 1969, Urbana, IL, 12 March 1971; Jubilee (op, 3, D. Dorr, after M. Walker), 1976, Jackson, MS, 20 Nov 1976; Frederick Douglass (op, 3, Dorr), 1985, Newark, NJ, 14 April 1991

Film scores: The Quiet One, 1948, arr. orch, 1948; The Lion, the Griffin and the Kangaroo, 1951; Going Home, 1962; Nosotros, 1962; A Thing of Beauty, 1966

TV scores: FDR: From Third Term to Pearl Harbor, 1958; New York: City of Magic, 1958; The Fall of China, 1959; Submarine!, 1959; Admiral Byrd, 1960; The Shape of Things, 1960; The Three Musketeers, 1960; The Land, 1962; Essay on Death, 1964.

ORCHESTRAL

Orch: Qnt, fl, str orch, 1943; Evocation, band, 1944; Of New Horizons, ov., 1944; Suite, 1945; A Short Ov., 1946; Brief Elegy, ob, str, 1946; Ancient Saga, pf, str, 1947; Suite, str, 1947; Conc. for Orch, 1948; Portrait Suite, 1948; Pietà, eng hn, str, 1950; Sinfonia, E, 1950; Short Suite, band, 1950; Solemn Prelude, band, 1950; 6 American Dances, str, 1954; Serenade no.1, 1954; Trigon, ww orch, 1961; Forever Free, band, 1962; Fantasy Variations, 1963; Umbrian Scene, 1963; Reverie and Rondo, 1964; Concert Sketches, band, 1965; Presidential Suite, 1965; Markings, 1966; Aulos, fl, 2 hn, perc, str, 1967; Sym., 1967; Scherzi musicali, chbr orch, 1968; Theater Set, 1968; Four Silhouettes, band, 1972; Harlem Children's Suite, 1973; Qnt Conc., 5 brass, orch, 1974; Southern Harmony, 1975; The Western Paradise (D. Dorr), nar, orch, 1975; Prologue and Parade, band, 1977; Chariots: Orch Rhapsody, 1978; Str Triptych, str orch, 1987.

VOCAL

Choral with insts: Song of Jeremiah (cant., J. Moffatt, after Bible), B-Bar, SATB, orch, 1945, rev. 1947; Song of Ahab (cant.), Bar, 10 insts, 1950 [withdrawn]; Phoebus, Arise (cant., Kay, T. Hood, Lord Herbert of Cherbury, W. Drummond, T. Middleton, W. Rowley, A. Cowley), S, B, SATB, orch, 1959; Choral Triptych (cant., Pss v, xiii, Bible: *Alleluia*), SATB, str/org, 1962; Inscriptions from Whitman (cant., W. Whitman), SATB, orch, 1964; Stephen Crane Set (cant., S. Crane), SATB, 13 insts, 1967; Once There was a Man (A Covenant for our Time) (R. Caudill), nar, SATB, orch, 1969; Parables (anon.), SATB, chbr orch, 1969

Choral with kbd: Grace to You, and Peace (T. Melnechuk, after Bible), SATB, org, 1955; Hymn-Anthem on "Hanover" (O worship the King) (R. Grant), SATB, org/pf, 1959; To Light that Shines (S. Johnson), SAB, pf/org, 1962; Emily Dickinson Set (E. Dickinson), SSA, pf, 1964; 4 Hymn-Anthems (J. Keble, Bible: *Psalms*, H.W. Longfellow, C. Wesley, Lat. antiphon), SATB, org, 1965; The Birds (P. Bailey, J. Hogg, W. Cowper, A. Tennyson, S. Taylor), SA, pf, 1966; Epigrams and Hymn (J. Whittier, J. Murray, S. Longfellow), SATB, org, 1975; Festival Pss (Bible), Bar, SATB, pf, 1983–4.

Unacc. choral: 4 Pieces (C. Sandburg, W. Shakespeare, A.E. Housman, W. Cather), TTBB, 1941; As Joseph was A-Walking (anon.), SATB, 1943; Christmas Carol (S. Teasdale), SSA, 1943; Come Away, Come Away Death (Shakespeare), TTB, 1944; A Lincoln Letter (A. Lincoln), B, SATB, 1953; Triumvirate (R.W. Emerson, H.W. Longfellow, H. Melville), TTBB, 1953; A Wreath of Waits (anon.), SATB, 1954; How Stands the Glass Around? (J. Wolfe), SSATB, 1954; A New Song (Pss cxlix, ciii, cxvii), SATB, 1955; What's in a Name? (H.F. More), SSATB, 1956; Flowers in the Valley (anon.), SATB, 1961; 2 Dunbar Lyrics, SATB, 1965; Triple Set (M. Bruce, R. Sheridan), TBB, 1971; Pentagraph, SSSAAA, 1972; 2 Folksong Settings, SATB, 1975.

Solo: 3 Pieces after Blake, S, orch, 1952 [arr. as Triptych on Texts of Blake, S, pf trio, 1962]; Jersey Hours (Triptych) (D. Dorr), 1v, 3 hp, 1978; 10 other songs for 1v and pf.

CHAMBER

3 or more insts: Pf Qnt, 1949; Brass Qt, 1950; Str Qt no.2, 1956; Serenade no.2, 4 hn, 1957; Serenade no.3, str qt, 1960; Str Qt no.3, 1961; Heralds I, 4 tpt, 4 trbn, 1968; Facets, ww qnt, pf, 1971; Heralds II, 3 tpt, 1974; 5 Winds, ww qnt, 1984

1–2 insts: 10 Short Essays, pf, 1939; Duo, fl, ob, 1943; Prelude, fl, 1943, rev. 1975; 4 Inventions, pf, 1946; 2 Meditations, org, 1950; Partita, A, vn, pf, 1950; 2 Short Pieces, pf 4 hands, 1957; Org Suite no.1, 1958; 5 Portraits, vn, pf, 1972; Guitarra, gui, 1973, rev. 1985; Nocturne no.1, pf, 1973; Visions, pf, 1974–5; 2 Impromptus, pf, 1986; Pantomime, cl, 1986; 5 other works for brass insts.

Principal publishers: Associated, Duchess, Carl Fischer, Peer, Peters

BIBLIOGRAPHY

EwenD; *SouthernB*

N. Slonimsky: "Ulysses Kay," *American Composers Alliance Bulletin*, vii/1 (1957), 3–11

D. Baker, L.B. Baker, and H. Hudson, eds.: *The Black Composer Speaks* (Metuchen, NJ, 1978) [incl. interview, work-list, and discography]

C.T. Hobson and D.A. Richardson: *Ulysses Kay: a Bio-Bibliography* (Westport, CT, 1994)

S.A. Floyd Jr., ed.: *The International Dictionary of Black Composers* (Chicago, 1999)

LUCIUS R. WYATT/EMILY ABRAMS ANSARI

Kaye, Carol (*b* Everett, WA, 24 March 1935). Electric bass guitarist and guitarist. The daughter of professional musicians, she began playing and teaching guitar in her teens. She played jazz guitar professionally in Los Angeles in the 1950s before beginning her studio recording career with Sam Cooke in 1957. After filling in for a bassist who missed a recording in 1963 at Capitol Records, she became a first-call session bassist. Although the exact extent of her discography is disputed, some have estimated that she worked on more than 10,000 recordings as a session musician, including pop music tracks, film, and television. She appeared on numerous top hits including "Good Vibrations," "California Girls," and other numbers by the Beach Boys. She performed as a guitarist and more frequently as a bassist, both independently and as a member of THE WRECKING CREW, a group of session musicians favored by Phil Spector and other Los Angeles producers.

As one of the few female session musicians of her time, her exceptional skills as a sight-reader and creative improviser, combined with the versatility as both a bassist and guitarist, secured her continued employment until the mid-1970s, when she retired from studio work due to arthritis. She later returned to play in the studio, perform live, and teach in a career that spanned more than 50 years. She authored the popular method book *How to Play the Electric Bass* (New York, 1969), the success of which helped popularize the generic term over the proprietary term "Fender bass."

LUKAS PEARSE

Kaye, Danny [Kaminski, David Daniel] (*b* Brooklyn, NY, 18 Jan 1913; *d* Los Angeles, CA, 3 March 1987). Singer, dancer, and actor. Kaminski began his career as an entertainer by traveling widely and working nonmusical day jobs. He was first billed as Danny Kaye in 1933 while working with the dancing act of David Harvey and Kathleen Young. Kaye specialized in singing with non-English accents punctuated with spurts of double-talk, tongue twisters, face contortions, and dancing. He met his wife, pianist and songwriter Sylvia Fine, while working variety shows in New York, and, with her assistance, developed some of his most famous numbers, including "Stanislavsky," "Anatole of Paris," and "Melody in Four F." In 1939 Kaye appeared in Broadway in his *Straw Hat Revue* and again in 1941 in Cole Porter's *Let's Face It*.

Kaye's film career began in 1944 with the RKO film *Up in Arms*. Other musical comedy films in which he starred included *The Secret Life of Walter Mitty* (1947), for which Sylvia Fine wrote the songs, *White Christmas* (1954), *Knock on Wood* (1954), and *The Court Jester* (1956). Another film, *Hans Christian Andersen* (1952), was relished internationally, and many of its songs by Frank Loesser were successful apart from the movie, such as "The Ugly Duckling" and "The Inch Worm." Throughout his life Kaye was also featured on radio shows (he had his own program with CBS in 1945) and on television singing humorous songs and dancing. From 1963 to 1967 he hosted *The Danny Kaye Show*, a variety television show on CBS. During the 1970s and 80s he appeared on TV shows such as *What's my Line?*, *The Muppet Show*, and *The Twilight Zone*. In 1970 Kaye starred as Noah in Richard Rodgers's and Martin

Charnin's Broadway musical *Two by Two*. Even though he injured his leg in the course of the production, he continued to appear on stage in a wheelchair and cast.

Throughout his career, Kaye toured widely and was especially well received in the UK where his shows were attended even by the Royal Family. Although he was unable to enlist in the US forces in World War II, Kaye performed for soldiers and sold war bonds. Beginning in 1953 and until his death, Kaye spent much time and energy crossing the globe as an unofficial advocate for the United Nations Children's Fund (UNICEF). The United Nations honored him with a special ceremony in 1987. Kaye also adapted his skills as an entertainer while conducting symphony orchestras around the world to raise money for musicians' pension funds. On one occasion, while conducting the Cleveland Symphony, Kaye led "Flight of the Bumblebee" with a flyswatter. In 1982 Kaye received an award from the Academy of Motion Picture Arts and Sciences for his humanitarian activities, and in 1984 Kaye received a Kennedy Center Honor.

BIBLIOGRAPHY
M. Freedland: *The Secret Life of Danny Kaye* (New York, 1985)
Obituary, *Washington Post*, 4 March 1987
P. Lewis: "U.N. Praises Danny Kaye at Tribute," *New York Times* (22 Oct 1987), C28
M. Gottfried: *Nobody's Fool: the Lives of Danny Kaye* (New York, 1994)
K. Marcus: "The Seriousness of Comedy: the Benefit Concerts of Jack Benny and Danny Kaye," *American Music*, xxv/2 (2007), 137–68
JOHN MACINNIS

Kazee, Buell (Hilton) (*b* Magoffin Co., KY, 29 Aug 1900; *d* Winchester, KY, 31 Aug 1976). Folksinger. He learned traditional ballads and hymns from his parents, and accompanied himself on banjo. While preparing for the Missionary Baptist ministry at Georgetown College, he took singing lessons, developed a polished vocal style in place of his mountain tenor, and began to give folksong recitals and lectures. Between 1927 and 1929 he recorded nearly 60 songs for Brunswick; these included traditional, religious, and pop material. After a period of comparative obscurity, he was rediscovered in the 1960s and performed at schools and folk festivals; in these appearances he combined his singing and banjo picking with enlightened commentary on Appalachian music and culture.

BIBLIOGRAPHY
L. Jones: "Buell Kazee," *JEMF Quarterly*, xiv/50 (1978), 57–67
L. Jones: *Buell Kazee* (June Appal 009, 1978) [liner notes]
C.K. Wolfe: *Kentucky Country: Folk and Country Music of Kentucky* (Lexington, KY, 1982), 32
JUDITH McCULLOH

Kazoo. A type of tube mirliton of African American origin, first manufactured in the United States around 1850. It amplifies and distorts the voice, creating a nasal, buzzing quality when the player hums, sings, or talks into the instrument. It differs from other types of mirliton in having on top a turret or trumpet which acts as a collection chamber for the external vibrations of a resonating membrane, thereby enriching the overtones considerably.

The kazoo generally consists of a metal or plastic tubular body open at both ends, with a large elliptical mouth-hole at one end and a smaller round aperture at the other. The turret contains a resonating skin, made of animal membrane, wax paper, or plastic, which is often referred to as a diaphragm or vibrator. The tubular body is slightly larger directly below the turret to allow maximum rebound and interchange of the vibrations from the membrane. The flange of the turret is usually removable to allow easy replacement of a worn or broken membrane.

The kazoo is often viewed primarily as a toy, particularly in Europe. In the United States, however, it played an important role in early African American music, country string-band music, early jazz, and occasionally later popular music. The best-known American kazoo group is Kazoophony, a professional comedy ensemble that performs a satirical, choreographed program of "symphonic kazoo music." In 2007 the Kazoo Museum was established in Seattle, Washington; it has since moved to Beaufort, South Carolina, where it is part of the Kazoobie Kazoos factory, which produces hundreds of thousands of kazoos each year.

BIBLIOGRAPHY
GMO
B. Hopkin: "Mirlitons: Kazoos and Beyond," *Experimental Musical Instruments*, v/1 (1989), 4–8
B. Stewart: *The Complete How to Kazoo* (New York, 2006)
BARBARA D. STEWART/R

KC and the Sunshine Band. Disco group. It was formed by Harry (Wayne) Casey (KC; *b* Opa-locka, FL, 31 Jan 1951), songwriter, singer, and keyboard player. An avid record collector, he began his professional career in 1973, when he started writing songs and recording with the double bass player and recording engineer Richard Finch. Together they devised a rich, brassy, percussive style of funk and rhythm-and-blues with a Caribbean flavor, which they called "the sunshine sound." In this style they wrote and produced for George McCrae the song "Rock your baby" (1974), which reached no.1 on the pop and soul charts. In 1973 Casey and Finch formed the Sunshine Band (originally called the Sunshine Junkanoo Band, after a Bahamian popular style), with seven African American studio musicians from Miami; of the nine players six played wind and percussion instruments. KC and the Sunshine Band produced a series of recordings that each sold a million copies. Of their 14 songs that appeared on the pop chart in the 1970s five reached the no.1 position: "Get down tonight" (1975), "That's the way (I like it)" (1975), "(Shake, shake, shake) shake your booty" (1976), "I'm your boogie man" (1977), and, in a mellower, slower style, "Please don't go" (1979); "Keep it comin' love" (1977), reached no.2. The energetic, funky "sunshine sound" proved irresistible to disco fans in the 1970s, and it continued to make hit recordings into the 1980s: "Give it up" reached no.18 in 1984. Since the mid-1980s the band has broken up and reformed a few times, releasing a number of compilations and making occasional live appearances.

GARY THEROUX/R

Keane, James (*b* 7 Feb 1948, Dublin, Ireland). Button accordion player of Irish birth; naturalized American. Hailing from Dublin's Drimnagh neighborhood, both of his parents and much of his extended family were musicians. He took up accordion when he was six years old. By the time he was ten, he was well known in Dublin's traditional music scene and performed frequently with notables such as Séamus Ennis, Leo Rowsome, and others. In 1962 Keane cofounded the influential Castle Céilí Band with his brother Séan (fiddle) and their friend Mick O'Connor (flute). In 1963 he was the under-18 All-Ireland accordion champion at the Mullingar Fleadh, and won the Dundalk open All-Ireland fleadh in 1964, 1965, and 1966. In 1968 he immigrated to the United States.

Keane played throughout New York City the 1970s. In 1979 he moved to Nova Scotia to join the group Ryan's Fancy. He returned to New York in 1983 and established himself as a stalwart of the city's traditional music scene. He has recorded several albums and toured extensively both as a solo performer and as a member of the groups Green Fields of America and Fingal. He was inducted into the Comhaltas Ceoltóirí Éireann's Mid-Atlantic Region Hall of Fame in 2004.

SELECTED RECORDINGS

As member: with Ryan's Fancy: *The Sea People* (Boot Records, 1979); with Fingal: *Fingal* (New Folk, 2008)

As leader: *Roll away the Reel World* (Green Linnet, 1980); *That's the Spirit* (Green Linnet, 1994); *With Friends Like These* (Shanachie, 1998); *Sweeter As the Years Roll By* (Shanachie, 1999)

DANIEL NEELY

Keats, Donald (Howard) (*b* New York, NY, 27 May 1929). Composer. He studied at Yale University with QUINCY PORTER and PAUL HINDEMITH (MusB 1949) and at Columbia University with Otto Luening and HENRY COWELL (MA 1951); as a Fulbright Scholar he attended the Staatliche Hochschule für Musik in Hamburg (1954–6) for studies with Philipp Jarnach. He received the PhD (1961) at the University of Minnesota, where his teachers included Dominick Argento and Paul Fetler. In 1957 he joined the faculty of Antioch College, becoming full professor in 1967. In 1975 he became a faculty member of the Lamont School of Music at the University of Denver, where he held the Lawrence C. Phipps Chair in the Humanities (1982–5). His awards include two Guggenheim Fellowships (1964, 1972) and an NEA grant (1975).

Keats's early works, while making use of dissonance, are often based on clearly articulated tonal centers. With the String Quartet no.2 (1964–5) he moved away from tonality; instead, short motivic ideas and sonorities became increasingly important (as in his use of quarter-tone "bends" in the Puerto Rican song cycle *Tierras del alma*, 1979). A sparing use of systematic techniques (such as serialism in the Piano Sonata), subtle metric-rhythmic relationships (as in the String Quartet no.1) and lyricism (*An Elegiac Symphony*) are of particular importance to Keats, as are occasional fast, driving, scherzo-like movements.

WORKS

Orch: Concert Piece, 1952; Sym. no.1, 1955–7; An Elegiac Sym., 1960–62, rev. 1973; The New Work, ballet, 1967; Branchings, 1976; Pf Conc., 1981–5; Elegy, 1993

Chbr and solo inst: 2 str qts, 1951, 1964–5; Theme and Variations, pf, 1954–5; Pf Sonata, 1960–61; Polarities, vn, pf, 1970; Dialogue, pf, winds, 1973; Diptych, vc, pf, 1973–4; Epithalamium, pf trio, 1977; Musica Instrumentalis I, 10 insts, 1980; Revisitations, pf trio, 1992; several other early works

Vocal: The Hollow Men (T.S. Eliot), SATB, (cl, 3 trbn, pf)/pf, 1952; A Love Triptych (W.B. Yeats), S, pf, 1973; Tierras del alma (Poemas de amor) (C.A.C. de Ruibal), song cycle, S, fl, gui, 1979; other songs and choruses

Principal publisher: Boosey & Hawkes

JEROME ROSEN/MICHAEL MECKNA

Keaulumoku (*b* Kohala, Hawaii, 1716; *d* Kauhola, Hawaii, 1784). Hawaiian poet and chanter. He served as a poet to several Hawaiian chiefs, including Kalani'opu'u, chief of the leeward side of the island of Hawaii. During a period of unrest and rivalry among island chiefs, Keaulomuku was able to travel among the warring factions because of his reputation as a gifted and important composer of chants. He was fluent in many forms of chant, including genealogical, war, praise, and love chants, but achieved much of his fame for his prophetic chants, particularly those involving the warrior Kamehameha. The chant "Haui Ka Lani," probably composed in 1782, describes the civil war among the chiefs and islands and foretells of Kamehameha's victory over the warring factions. In "Au'a 'Ia," composed shortly before his death in 1784, Keaulumoku predicts Kamehameha's conquest and unification of the islands, but he also foretells of the early decline of the dynasty and the gradual extinction of the Hawaiian people.

Keaulumoku's verses were well constructed, incorporating numerous rhetorical and poetic innovations. He employed vivid metaphors and double meanings throughout his works. King David Kalakaua in 1888 described his voice as tremulous and wild. A number of Keaulumoku's chants have survived to modern times and have continued to be performed. In 1995 the Hawaiian Music Hall of Fame inducted Keaulumoku, the first chanter to be honored.

BIBLIOGRAPHY

D. Kalakaua: "The Prophecies of Keaulumoku," *The Legends and Myths of Hawaii: the Fables and Folk-lore of a Strange People* (New York, 1888), 351–67

J. Charlot: *The Hawaiian Poetry of Religion and Politics: Some Religio-Political Concepts in Postcontact Literature* (La'ie, HI, 1985)

J. Charlot: "Prophet of the Earth Overturned: Ke'aulumoku on Early Contact in Hawai'i," *Rongorongo Studies*, xiii/1 (2003), 20–36

PAULA J. BISHOP

Keawe(-Aiko), Genoa (Leilani Adolpho) (*b* Honolulu, HI, 31 Oct 1918; *d* Honolulu, HI, 25 Feb 2008). Hawaiian singer and musician. She was a prominent, influential Hawaiian singer for more than six decades. Affectionately known as Aunty Genoa, she recorded prolifically and her versions of many songs are considered definitive. Her vocal style combined important Hawaiian vocal techniques such as *ha'i* (accented break between registers) with discreet elements of pop music, and appealed to both traditionalists and general audiences. She was a master of correct pronunciation, dynamics, and breath control as in her signature song "Alika," where she held notes for as long as two minutes. A strong advocate of hula, she recorded several albums without *pa'ani* (instrumental breaks) specifically for dancers. She accompanied herself on six-string ukulele augmented by steel guitar, acoustic guitar, and stand-up bass.

The Mormon Church provided Keawe's earliest musical training, and she always described her voice as a gift from God. She began her career in the early 1940s. Her mother-in-law, who taught her Hawaiian, and composers John K. Almeida and Alice Namakelua were important mentors. In 1946 she made her first recordings for the 49th State label. Through the 1950s she was a regular on local radio and performed in the lively nightclub scene as well as at numerous community events. In the 1960s Keawe led an all-star band with Vickie I'i Rodrigues, Benny Rogers, and others, recording classic albums such as *Party Hulas* (1963). In 1966 she founded Genoa Keawe Records, one of the first labels owned by a female artist.

Keawe was a prime mover in the Hawaiian cultural renaissance of the 1970s, performing, mentoring, and raising funds for important causes. In the mid-1980s she retired briefly but then spent two more decades concertizing throughout the islands and abroad, often with longtime bassist Violet Liliko`i. Her live appearances combined the polish of professional entertainment with the high spirits of a family party and the solemnity of a religious service. She dedicated songs to audience members, called visiting performers onstage, joked, cried, and ended with a group sing-along of the popular himeni (hymn) "Hawaii Aloha." Many singers perpetuate Aunty Genoa's legacy, such as her granddaughter, Pomaika'i Keawe Lyman, falsetto master Richard Ho'opi'i, and Amy Hanaiali'i.

J.W. JUNKER

Keb' Mo' [Moore, Kevin] (*b* Los Angeles, CA, 3 Oct 1951). Blues singer and guitarist. He was an accomplished musician by the time he was a teenager and showed an early appreciation for blues and gospel music. He began his musical career playing in a variety of blues bands throughout the 1970s. During this time, he also began to record with Jefferson Airplane and violinist Papa John Creach. In 1980 he recorded his first solo album *Rainmaker* under his birth name Kevin Moore, but would later become known as "Keb' Mo'," a shortened version of his name that reflected his blues orientation. His distinctive sound encompasses a variety of musical styles, including pop, rock, folk and jazz. He has worked as a staff writer for A&M Records, played with the Whodunit Band, and performed with Albert Collins and Big Joe Turner. In 1994, he released his first eponymous album as "Keb' Mo'," which featured two Robert Johnson covers, "Come On In My Kitchen" and "Kind Hearted Woman Blues." His second album, *Just Like You*, won a Grammy Award for Best Contemporary Blues Album in 1997, and featured guest appearances from Jackson

Browne and Bonnie Raitt. He also won Grammy Awards in 1999 for *Slow Down* and 2005 for *Keep It Simple* in the same category. Throughout the 1990s, he appeared in a variety of film projects, including a title role in a documentary film on Robert Johnson and acting appearances in the television dramas *Touched by an Angel* and *West Wing*. In 2009, Keb' Mo' released the live album *Live & Mo'*.

DINA M. BENNETT

Keel, Howard [Leek, Harold Clifford] (*b* Gillespie, IL, 13 April 1917; *d* Palm Desert, CA, 7 Nov 2004). Singer and actor. Known primarily for his starring roles in MGM musicals from the 1950s, he began his career as a singer on Broadway and in the West End. His Broadway debut was as Billy Bigelow in *Carousel*, succeeding John Raitt in the role. He subsequently played Curly McLain in *Oklahoma!* in both New York and London. Other stage roles included Clint Maroon in *Saratoga* and David Jordan in *No Strings*. His film debut was in the English motion picture *The Small Voice* (1948), and it was his performance in *Annie Get Your Gun* (1950) that established his career in Hollywood. Subsequent credits included *Pagan Love Song* (1950), *Show Boat* (1951), *Lovely to Look At* (1952), *Calamity Jane* (1953), *Kiss me, Kate* (1953), *Deep in my Heart* (1954), *Rose-Marie* (1954), *Seven Brides for Seven Brothers* (1954), *Jupiter's Darling* (1955), and *Kismet* (1955).

Keel's robust and intensely masculine baritone necessitated his performing strong lead characters, and he was known for his excellent technique, wide range, and commanding tone quality. He continued to give concerts into the 1990s, particularly in the UK, where he remained especially popular.

WILLIAM A. EVERETT, LEE SNOOK

Keeler, Ruby [Ethel Hilda] (*b* Halifax, NS, 25 Aug 1910; *d* Rancho Mirage, CA, 28 Feb 1993). Dancer, singer, and actress. Born in Canada, she moved in 1912 with her family to New York, where she studied tap. She made her Broadway debut in 1923 and continued to work in musical theater before marrying Broadway star Al Jolson in 1928. In 1933 Daryl Zanuck cast her in *42nd Street*, the first of a successful series of "backstage" musicals that Keeler made with choreographer BUSBY BERKELEY for Warner Bros.—*Gold Diggers of 1933* (1933), *Footlight Parade* (1933), and *Dames* (1934)—and for which she is best known. While Keeler herself remarked that she had limited talent, she possessed a charm and wide-eyed sincerity that, along with her energetic dancing, appealed to Depression-era audiences. After Keeler and Jolson divorced, she remarried in 1941 and retired from performing. Thirty years later Keeler returned to the Broadway stage for the successful revival of the musical *No, No, Nanette* (1971).

BIBLIOGRAPHY

S. Holden: "Ruby Keeler, Tap-Dancing Actress, Is Dead at 82," *New York Times*, 1 March 1983
D. Bubbeo: *The Women of Warner Brothers: the Lives and Careers of 15 Leading Ladies* (Jefferson, NC, 2002)

F. Miller: *Leading Couples: the Most Unforgettable Screen Romances of the Studio Era* (San Francisco, 2008)

GORDON HARAMAKI

Keeling, Richard H(amilton) (*b* Oakland, CA, 7 June 1945). Ethnomusicologist and Native Americanist scholar. As a PhD student at the University of California, Los Angeles, his 1982 dissertation fieldwork focused on the study of oral expressive magic of the Hupa, Karok, and Yurok tribes in northwestern California. Keeling's continuing study of historical relationships between the vocal style, healing practices, spirituality, gender roles, and cultural survival among California tribes has resulted in numerous publications, including a published collection of music research sources, a guide to early field recordings, and the book *Cry for Luck* (1992), which was based on song and spoken narrative collections from the first half of the 20th century. In 1991 he received a Fulbright scholarship to conduct field research among the indigenous Ainu in Japan, and to date he has continued to build upon his historical approach through the publication of overviews and guides to Native North American recorded and written sources.

WRITINGS

"Contrast of Song Performance Style as a Function of Sex Role Polarity in the Hupa Brush Dance," *EthM*, xxix (1985), 185–212

"Sources for Research Concerning Music among Indians of the California Region," *California's Musical Wealth: Sources for the Study of Music in California* (ed. Stephen Fry; Los Angeles, 1988), 76–89

ed.: "Musical Evidence of Female Spiritual Life Among the Yurok," *Women in North American Indian Music: Six Essays* (Ann Arbor, 1989), 66–78

Cry for Luck: Sacred Song and Speech among the Yurok, Hupa, and Karok Indians of Northwestern California (Berkeley and Los Angeles, 1992)

ed.: "The Sources of Indian Music: an Introduction and Overview," *Music and Spiritual Power Among the Indians of North America*, xxxiv/2 (1992), 3–22

North American Indian Music: a Guide to Published Sources and Selected Recordings (New York, 1997)

"California," *The Garland Encyclopedia of World Music*, iii (USA and Canada, 2001), 412–19

JAMES E. CUNNINGHAM

Keen. Record company. Based in Los Angeles, Keen was an independent record company that specialized in popular music performed by African American artists. It was formed in 1957 by artist and producer Bob Keane, businessman John Siamas, producer and songwriter Robert "Bumps" Blackwell, along with performer and songwriter Sam Cooke. Keen is perhaps best known as the record company that released Cooke's first mainstream hit, "You Send Me" in 1957. Keen also released recordings on the Ensign and Andex labels. A major factor in the success of Keen and Cooke was the production of Blackwell, who worked on the majority of Cooke's Keen recordings. Cooke left in 1959 to join RCA; the company soon ceased its operations. Between 1957 and 1959 Keen also released the music of Johnny "Guitar" Watson, including the first recorded version of his song "Gangster of Love."

BIBLIOGRAPHY

B. Keane: *The Oracle of Del-Fi* (Los Angeles, 2005)

ANDREW FLORY

Keen, Robert Earl (*b* Houston, TX, 11 Jan 1956). Singer-songwriter. The son of an oil executive father and an attorney mother, he graduated from Texas A&M in 1978 after developing a friendship with Lyle Lovett, a friendship that led to a signature song for both men, "This Old Porch." *No Kinda Dancer* (Philo, 1984) was Keen's first album, self-financed in Austin. After a short stint in Nashville he returned to Texas, and *West Textures* (Sugar Hill, 1989) contained one of Keen's signature songs, "The Road Goes on Forever." *Gringo Honeymoon* (Sugar Hill, 1994) blended his stories with the guitar licks of Gurf Morlix, who also produced albums for Lucinda Williams. Keen moved in the direction of alternative country with *Picnic* (Arista, 1997). *Gravitional Forces* (Lost Highway, 2001) became a stepping-stone for more touring and recording. He has been a leading figure among Texas songwriters, touring up to 200 days each year and writing songs based on vivid settings, small-time losers, the common person, memory, and good stories. From his first recording to the Lloyd Maines-produced album *Ready for Confetti* (Lost Highway, 2011), Keen has been opening up space for a new wave of independent spirit in Texas music. Keen's literary interests include Cormac McCarthy, and his songwriting carries a strong emphasis on narrative. As of 2012 he was residing in Kerrville, Texas, home of the Kerrville Folk Festival, where he was awarded a New Folk Songwriters award in 1983.

KATHLEEN HUDSON

Keenan, Paddy (*b* Trim, Co. Meath, Ireland, 30 Jan 1950). Traditional musician, uilleann piper, and low whistle player of Irish birth. Born into a musical family of Irish Travelers, he began playing whistle at the age of six and switched to the pipes at ten, learning the "open" style of legato fingering (often associated with Traveler pipers, such as Johnny Doran) from his father. By 14 he was active in Dublin's folk scene.

He moved to London when he was 17 and joined the counterculture. There he took up the guitar and busked until he rediscovered piping and moved back to Ireland to become more involved with traditional music. He released his first (eponymous) solo album in 1974 and later that year he became part of the Bothy Band (1974–8), a hugely influential group that featured Keenan's improvisational playing style.

Keenan recorded an important album, *Doublin'*, with fiddler Paddy Glackin in 1978 and an acclaimed solo album (*Poirt An Phiobaire*, 1983), but his career was sidetracked for much of the 1980s. He relocated to the United States in 1991 and contributed to several recording projects highlighted by a third solo album (*Ná Keen Affair*, 1997). In 2001 he recorded with guitarist Tommy O'Sullivan (*The Long Grazing Acre*) and in 2002 was named TG4's Traditional Musician of the Year. Since 2009 has been a member of the group Shelta.

BIBLIOGRAPHY

B. Ring: *Travelling Style: the Uilleann Piping of Paddy Keenan* (thesis, U. College Cork, 1992)

DANIEL NEELY

Keene, Christopher (*b* Berkeley, CA, 21 Dec 1946; *d* New York, NY, 8 Oct 1995). Conductor. He studied the piano and the cello, conducted several ensembles at high school, attended the University of California at Berkeley, and made his opera debut in a 1965 production of Benjamin Britten's *Rape of Lucretia* at Berkeley. In 1966 he served as assistant conductor at the San Francisco Opera, and a year later held the same position in San Diego. At the Spoleto Festival in 1968 he conducted, at Gian Carlo Menotti's invitation, *The Saint of Bleecker Street*. In 1969 he received the first Julius Rudel Award, and was appointed music director to the American Ballet Company, a position he held for one year. From 1971 to 1976 Keene served in various positions at Spoleto, and from 1977 to 1980 was music director of Spoleto USA. In this period Keene gained his early reputation as a champion of new and American music. He directed the Syracuse SO (1975–84), the New York Artpark summer festival (1978–89), and founded and conducted the Long Island PO (1979–90). As guest conductor, Keene appeared at the Metropolitan Opera, Covent Garden, the Deutsche Oper in Berlin, the Lyric Opera of Chicago, and the Vienna Volksoper. He also conducted the Chicago SO and the New York PO. Keene's greatest influence was at the New York City Opera. After his 1970 debut there in Alberto Ginastera's *Don Rodrigo*, he conducted some 300 performances of more than 50 operas. Early success led to his appointment as music director of New York City Opera (1982–6), and subsequently as general director (1989–95). His tenure was riddled with difficulties, including problems with finance, a musicians' strike, administrative conflicts, and Keene's own battles with alcoholism and AIDS lymphoma. He was a steadfast advocate for the music of Menotti, Hans Werner Henze, Toshirō Mayuzumi, Paul Hindemith, Aribert Reimann, Thomas Pasatieri, Roger Sessions, Carlisle Floyd, Keith Jarrett, John Corigliano, Jody Diamond, and Philip Glass, and conducted numerous premieres, including Menotti's *The Hero* (Philadelphia, 1976) and Floyd's Bilby's *Doll* (Houston, 1976). However, some of his NYCO repertory failed to attract audiences, and in 1993 its board relieved Keene of his administrative duties. Nevertheless, he remained a constant supporter of contemporary music. He was also a composer and librettist, and his considerable library is housed at Indiana University.

CHARLES BARBER, JOSÉ A. BOWEN

Keenlyside, Simon (*b* London, England, 3 Aug 1959). English baritone. He studied with John Cameron at the Royal Northern College of Music (Manchester), where he sang Lescaut in *Manon* (1987). His professional stage debut was as Count Almaviva (*Le nozze di Figaro*) in 1988 at Hamburg. He then joined the roster of the Scottish Opera (1989–94), where he sang Billy Budd, Rossini's Figaro, Marcello, Danilo (*Die lustige Witwe*), Belcore, and Papageno, the last-named hailed as a virtuoso performance. He made his Covent Garden debut, as Silvio, in 1989, followed by Guglielmo, which was also the role of his admired Glyndebourne debut in 1995. His debut at La Scala in 1995 was Papageno (with

Muti), and he returned to the house for Count Almaviva and Ubalde (Gluck's *Armide*) in 1999. He made his first Metropolitan appearance, as Belcore, in 1996, the year in which he scored a notable success as Thomas's Hamlet at Geneva, catching all the role's inwardness. This was followed in 1997 by an ardent Pelléas at San Francisco and a mercurial Don Giovanni at Ferrara with Abbado. Keenlyside's interpretation of the title part in Monteverdi's *Orfeo*, in which he toured with René Jacobs in 1998–9, was notable for its single-minded intensity; and he revealed his comic gifts as Rossini's Figaro at the Berlin Staatsoper, and as Dandini at the Paris Opéra (both 1998), where he also sang Yeletsky in 1999. In 2000 he was a compelling, athletic Billy Budd at Covent Garden, conveying the character's goodness with no hint of insipidity. Keenlyside created the role of Winston for the world premiere of Maazel's *1984* at Covent Garden in 2005. He returned to the Metropolitan Opera in 2010 to sing the title role in Thomas' *Hamlet*. His operatic recordings include Don Giovanni (with Abbado) Ned Keene (*Peter Grimes*), Count Almaviva in *Le nozze di Figaro* (with Jacobs) and Prospero in the recording of Thomas Adès's *The Tempest*. He was awarded a Grammy for his recording of Count Almaviva and a Gramophone Award for his recording of *The Tempest*. He is also an accomplished interpreter of lieder (as revealed on his Hyperion recordings of Schubert and Schumann) and French *mélodie*. All his performances are distinguished by his mellow yet incisive tone and high intelligence as an interpreter.

BIBLIOGRAPHY
R. Milnes: "Simon Keenlyside," *Opera*, xlviii (1997), 1284–90
W.R. Braun: "A Prince Apart," *ON* lxxiv/9 (March 2010), 12–17

ALAN BLYTH/MICHAEL HIX

Keil, Charles (*b* Norwalk, CT, 12 Aug 1939). Ethnomusicologist. He was educated in American studies at Yale University (BA 1961) and in anthropology at the University of Chicago (MA 1964, PhD 1979 with a dissertation on the Tiv song) with Leonard Meyer, David Schneide, and Clifford Geertz. He became affiliated with the State University of New York, Buffalo in 1968, was made professor in 1983, and retired in 2000. He has held visiting appointments at Trent University, Ontario (1982, 1983) and at the University of Natal (1993), and has received numerous grants, including a Guggenheim fellowship (1979–80) and a Rockefeller Foundation Research Grant (1975). In 1990 he became president of Musicians United for Superior Education and has served on the board of directors. The main areas of his work have been African American blues, Polish American polka music in everyday life, and the creation of grooves in all musics of the world, with a focus on African and African diaspora musics.

WRITINGS
Urban Blues (Chicago, 1966/*R*)
Tiv Song: The Sociology of Art in a Classless Society (diss., U. of Chicago, 1979; Chicago, 1979/*R*)
"Slovenian Style in Milwaukee," *Folk Music and Modern Sound*, ed. W. Ferris and M.L. Hart (Jackson, MS, 1982), 32–59

"The Dyna-Tones: a Buffalo Polka Bank in Performance, in Rehearsal, and on Record," *New York Folklore*, x/3–4 (1984), 117–34

"Paideia con Salsa: Ancient Greek Music Education for Active Citizenship and the Role of Latin Dance-Music in Our Schools," *Becoming Human through Music: Middletown, CT, 1984* (Middletown, CT, and Reston, VA, 1985), 87–94

"People's Music Comparatively: Style and Stereotype, Class and Hegemony," *Dialectical Anthropology*, x (1985), 119–30

"Sociomusicology: a Participatory Approach," *Echology*, ii (1988), 125–32

"Culture, Music and Collaborative Learning," *Dialectical Anthropology: Essays in Honor of Stanley Diamond*, ed. C.W. Gailey (Gainesville, FL, 1992), 327–33

with A. Keil and R. Blau: *Polka Happiness* (Philadelphia, 1992)

ed., with S. Crafts and D. Cavicchi: *My Music* (Hanover, NH, 1993)

"Ritual Happiness: Music and Human Rites," *Music in Southern Africa: Symposium on Ethnomusicology XI*, ed. C.A. Muller (Durban, South Africa, 1993), 66–73

with S. Feld: *Music Grooves: Essays and Dialogues* (Chicago, 1994/R)

"The Theory of Participatory Discrepancies: a Progress Report," *EthM*, xxxix/1 (1995), 1–19

"Applied Sociomusicology and Performance Studies," *EthM*, xlii/2 (1998), 303–12

with A. Keil: *Bright Balkan Morning: Romani Lives and the Power of Music in Greek Macedonia* (Middletown, CT, 2002)

GREGORY F. BARZ

Keïta, Mamady (*b* Balandugu, Guinea, West Africa, 1950). Drummer, director, and teacher of Guinean birth. Mamady Keïta began his official apprenticeship with the village *djembéfola* at the age of eight. By his late teens, he was lead drummer of Ballet D'Joliba. By 22 he became the company's first drummer to act as artistic director. Upon his retirement from the ballet in 1986, Keïta played briefly for the national ballet in *Côte D'Ivoire* before settling in Belgium where he founded an international *djembé* school called Tam Tam Mandingue.

Keïta came to live in the United States in 2004. At his first official workshop as an American resident, Keïta announced: "I spent fifteen years cleaning up the *djembé* drumming in Europe. Now it is time to do the same in America." Despite the growing popularity of the *djembé*, Keïta was surprised by the lack of understanding about its history and music within American drum circles. Keïta, together with six other *djembé* masters from West Africa, signed a statement expressing their commitment to DRTM (*Djembé Rhythm Mandingue Traditional*). Keïta also created a certification program for Tam Tam Mandingue professors and drum schools. Drummers must pass rigorous testing (which includes technique as well as memorization of traditional rhythms, solos, and their history and cultural context) to use his official TTM logo; drum schools must also meet certain standards. Keïta and TTM USA are based in San Diego.

BIBLIOGRAPHY

U. Billmeier and M. Keïta: *Mamady Keïta: a Life for the Djembé* (Kirchhasel-Uhlstädt, Germany, 1999)

V.H. Flaig: *The Politics of Representation and Transmission in the Globalization of Guinea's Djembé* (diss., U. of Michigan, 2010)

VERA H. FLAIG

Keith, B(enjamin) F(ranklin) (*b* Hillsborough Bridge, NH, 26 Jan 1846; *d* Palm Beach, FL, 26 March 1914). Theater owner, producer, and manager. Although his family did not have theatrical connections, Keith appears to have been attracted to the itinerant life of the circus world, and ran away with a circus at age 17. He worked with P.T. Barnum and Forepaugh's Circus for the following 13 years, working primarily as a grifter selling gadgets and other novelties. Keith married Mary Catherine Branley in 1873. In 1880 he left the circus world and settled in his wife's hometown, Providence, RI, where he manufactured and sold brooms. In 1883 Keith was lured back into the theatrical profession when he opened a small museum that presented oddities and circus-style acts in Boston. In 1884 Keith became a partner in Boston's Gaiety Theater, where he met Edward Franklin Albee, with whom he later built a theatrical empire.

Keith acquired the lease on the Bijou Theatre in Boston in 1885 and installed Albee as the manager. Keith made his first experiments here in presenting a clean, respectable variety entertainment to Boston audiences, which had traditionally been less receptive to variety than others on the east coast. Keith later claimed to have invented vaudeville, which was somewhat of an exaggeration. While regional variety managers had been using the term vaudeville as early as the mid-1870s, Keith did so in ways that drew firmer lines between his set shows as opposed to the more freewheeling and improvisational variety.

In 1896 Keith and Albee moved to Manhattan and leased the Union Square Theater, where they were the first managers to exhibit moving pictures. Keith retired in 1909, leaving his son Andrew to manage his interests in his partnership with Albee.

BIBLIOGRAPHY

R. Snyder: *The Voice of the* City: *Vaudeville and Popular Culture in New York* (Chicago, 1989/R2000)

C.W. Carey, Jr.: "Keith, B.F. and E.F. Albee," *American Inventors, Entrepreneurs, and Business Visionaries* (New York, 2002), 218–19

GILLIAN M. RODGER

Keith and Albee. Vaudeville organization that grew out of the partnership between Benjamin Franklin Keith (1846–1914) and Edward Franklin Albee II (1857–1930). In 1885 Keith hired Albee to manage his Gaiety Theater in Boston and together the two worked to shape the development of variety entertainment in order to make it suitable for the conservative Boston audience. In the following decade, Keith continued to refine his business model, forming agreements with rivals to eliminate competition. The B.F. Keith Corporation gained interests in theaters throughout New England as well as in New York and Philadelphia. Keith and Albee partnered with F.F. Proctor, extending their theatrical circuit into the Midwest in 1906, and their agreements with early film studios for the right to exhibit their films made them the first theater to consistently show moving pictures. They also formed a centralized booking office, the United Booking Office, which eliminated the need for agents and negotiation in the booking process for their theaters, as well as for other vaudeville houses. This enabled the Corporation to benefit financially from every vaudeville booking made through the office, and also to tightly regulate the wages paid to vaudeville performers. Keith and Albee also introduced a tiered system of contracts that institutionalized the great difference between the "stars" and the regular vaudeville performers who provided the majority of bill. Their industrial efficiencies came to be a standard part of the entertainment world in the 20th century.

BIBLIOGRAPHY

R. Snyder: *The Voice of the City: Vaudeville and Popular Culture in New York* (Chicago, 1989/*R*2000)

C.W. Carey, Jr.: "Keith, B.F. and E.F. Albee," *American Inventors, Entrepreneurs, and Business Visionaries* (New York, 2002), 218–19

GILLIAN M. RODGER

Kekuku, Joseph [Apuakehau, Jr., Joseph Kekuku'upenak ana'iapuniokamehameha] (*b* La'ie, Oahu, Hawaii, 1874; *d* Dover, NJ, 16 Jan 1932). Steel guitarist, teacher, and inventor. The Hawaiian steel guitar's invention is largely credited to Joseph Kekuku. Joseph and his cousin, Samuel Kalanahelu Nainoa (1877–1950) were raised in the rural village of La'ie, Oahu. By the age of 11, the close companions had become skilled musicians under the tutelage of the elders of La'ie. Prior to the creation of the Hawaiian steel guitar, Hawaiian musical combos featured primarily violin, flute, "Spanish" guitar, and 'ukulele performances. Sam played the violin, while Joseph spent much of his time trying to make his guitar sound like Sam's violin.

Joseph's first experiments involved running various implements across the strings of a conventional gut-string guitar, including a steel bolt, a penknife, a pocket comb, a dull straight razor blade, and a tumbler, with the guitar laying across his lap. When the cousins enrolled as boarding students at Kamehameha School for Boys in the fall of 1889, Joseph created a slender four-inch steel cylinder bar in the school's machine shop. Switching to steel strings, he also raised the strings off of the guitar frets to allow the bar to slide noiselessly across them. As others learned to play the new instrument, contoured metal finger and thumb picks were crafted to grip the individual strings more securely than previously possible with only the fingers or fingernails. In 1904 Joseph shortened his lengthy Hawaiian name to Kekuku, and left the Territory of Hawaii for the United States mainland, touring as a performing steel guitarist and an instructor. In 1919 Kekuku left for an eight-year tour of Europe. He returned to the United States in 1927 and settled in Chicago, where he opened a music school.

BIBLIOGRAPHY

D.D. Mitchell: *Kika Kila: the Story of the Steel Guitar* (Honolulu, 1973)

T. Todaro: *The Golden Years of Hawaiian Entertainment, 1874–1974* (Honolulu, 1974)

G.S. Kanahele: *Hawaiian Music and Musicians: an Illustrated History* (Honolulu, 1979)

L. Ruymar: *The Hawaiian Steel Guitar and its Great Hawaiian Musicians* (Anaheim Hills, CA, 1996)

Sol Ho'opi'i: King of the Hawaiian Steel Guitar (Hana Ola A682617, 2006) [incl. liner notes by H.B Soria, Jr.]

HARRY B. SORIA JR.

Kell, Reginald (Clifford) (*b* York, England, 8 June 1906; *d* Frankfort, KY, 5 Aug 1981). Clarinetist and teacher of English birth. Kell studied with noted virtuoso Haydn Draper at the Royal Academy of Music from 1929 to 1932. He later taught there (1935–9 and 1957–9) and was made a Fellow in 1941. In 1932, along with acclaimed oboist Léon Goossens, he was appointed to the woodwind section of Sir Thomas Beecham's newly formed London PO. Kell enjoyed a distinguished orchestral career, playing principal clarinet in the Royal Philharmonic (1931–2), Royal Opera House (1932–6), London SO (1936–9), Lucerne Festival Orchestra (1939), Liverpool Philharmonic (1942–5), and Philharmonia (1945–8). He immigrated to the United States in 1948 and toured as a soloist throughout much of North America. Kell was trustee and professor at the Aspen Music School in Colorado from 1951 to 1957. His many recordings include a notable account of the Brahms Clarinet Quintet with the Busch Quartet (1937). He published the *Kell Method* (New York, 1968) and a collection of studies, and was director of the Boosey & Hawkes band instrument division from 1959 to 1966. Kell is known to have given lessons in technique to jazz musician Benny Goodman. Much influenced by Goossens, Kell distinguished himself from celebrated contemporary Fredrick Thurston with a consistent vibrato and liberal use of rubato. His open and naturally expressive manner was much admired.

BIBLIOGRAPHY

R. Gelatt: *Music Makers* (New York, 1953)

Obituary, *The Clarinet*, ix/2 (1982), 6–11

P. Weston: *Clarinet Virtuosi of Today* (London, 1989), 12–13

S. Pitfield: "Clarinet and Piano Music—Performance Practice 1880 to 1945," *The Clarinet*, xxix/3 (June 2002), 54–59

PAMELA WESTON/JONATHAN HOLDEN

Keller, Kate [Kitty] **Van Winkle** (*b* Providence, RI, 28 April 1937). Scholar of American dance and dance music. After studies at the Hartford Conservatory of Music, she was awarded the BA in music from Vassar College in 1959, the same year she married Robert Monteith Keller (*b* 1934). Keller's interest in colonial-era dance began during the time of the Bicentennial celebrations in the mid-1970s. She and her family were living in a former tavern in Coventry, Connecticut—built in 1801—that had a 42-foot ballroom on the second floor, which was open to the public during the Bicentennial festivities in the town. Curious about what kind of dances had been held there, she and her husband began a quest to bring early American dance back to life. (Her husband has aided her in her research since that time, especially in the area of data management.)

Keller was the first scholar to thoroughly and systematically investigate American dance music of the colonial era and early Republic. She compiled a comprehensive database of dance tunes of American (and many foreign) sources from the 18th century, with Carolyn Rabson, which resulted in the *National Tune Index* (1980). This NEH-supported project, originally published in microfilm, is now expanded as *Early American Secular Music and Its European Sources, 1589–1839: An*

Index (available at <http://www.colonialdancing.org/Easmes/index.html>). With Mary Jane Corry and Robert M. Keller, she created *The Performing Arts in Colonial American Newspapers, 1690–1783* (1997), an NEH-funded index and abstract on CD-ROM of newspaper references to music, song lyrics, dance, and theater in American newspapers issued in English, French, and German (available at <http://www.colonialdancing.org/PacanNew/Index.htm>).

Keller and her husband are expert dancers in a wide variety of period styles; as such, she served as choreographer for the film *The Last of the Mohicans* (1992). In addition to her significant contribution to indexing dance music, Keller has published numerous interpretive studies and collections of early American dance music, and other secular music, both for scholarly and general readerships. Her largest work is the magisterial *Dance and Its Music in America, 1528–1789* (2007), which gives a comprehensive view of dance and dance music throughout British, French, and Spanish North America in the territories that form the present-day United States. Her forthcoming *Songs in Vogue in 1814: The Isaiah Thomas Broadside Ballad Collection* (with the late Arthur F. Schrader) is a facsimile edition and study of ballads and their song lyrics collected by Isaiah Thomas, printer and founder of the American Antiquarian Society.

Keller served as Curator of the Library and Archives of the Country Dance and Song Society from 1985 to 1992, and was named Honorary Member in 2004. The same year she was elected to membership in the American Antiquarian Society. She served on the board and then as Executive Director of the Society for American Music (formerly the Sonneck Society for American Music) from 1977 to 2000. The Society awarded her its Distinguished Service Citation in 1995 and Lifetime Achievement Award in 2011.

WRITINGS
(selected list)

Giles Gibbs, Jr., His Book for the Fife (Hartford, CT, 1974)
with C. Rabson: *National Tune Index: 18th-Century Secular Music* (New York, 1980)
with R. Wilson: *Connecticut's Music in the Revolutionary Era* (Hartford, CT, 1980)
Popular Secular Music in America through 1800: a Preliminary Checklist of Manuscripts in North American Collections (Philadelphia, 1981)
"Selected American Country Dances and their English Sources," *Music in Colonial Massachusetts, 1630–1820. 1. Music in Public Places*, ed. B. Lambert (Boston, MA, 1981), 2–73
"*Upon a Summer's Day* to *The Federal March*: Indexing British-American Melody, 1651–1800," *English Dance and Song*, xlvi/1 (1984), 18–21
"John Griffiths, 18th-century Itinerant Dancing Master and His Influence on Traditional Social Dance in New England," *Itinerancy in New England and New York*, ed. P. Benes, Dublin Seminar for New England Folklife, Annual Proceedings, 1984 (Boston, MA, 1986), 90–111
"A Bibliography of Eighteenth-Century American Social Dance," *Country Dance and Song*, xviii (1988), 9–22
"James Alexander's Collection of Dances, New York, 1730," *Libraries, History, Diplomacy, and the Performing Arts: Essays in Honor of Carleton Sprague Smith*, ed. I.J. Katz (Stuyvesant, NY, 1991), 353–69
Fife Tunes from the American Revolution (Sandy Hook, CT, 1997)

"The Eighteenth-Century Ballroom: a Mirror of Social Change," *New England Music: the Public Sphere, 1600–1900*, ed. P. Benes, Dublin Seminar for New England Folklife, Annual Proceedings, 1996 (Boston, MA, 1998), 16–29
with J. Koegel: "Secular Music to 1800," *Cambridge History of American Music*, ed. D. Nicholls (Cambridge, 1998), 49–77
"Hezekiah Cantelo, 18th-century Dance Collector in Occupied New York," *Vistas of American Music: Essays and Compositions in Honor of William K. Kearns*, ed. S.L. Porter and J. Graziano (Warren, MI, 1999), 19–38
"Flute Music from Eighteenth-Century Lancaster: John Hoff's Collection," *Journal of the Lancaster County Historical Society*, ciii/1 (2001), 28–47
with G.A. Fogg: *Social Dances from 18th-Century Virginia: the Richmond Assemblies* (Annapolis, MD, 2003)
with G. Anderson and others: "Forgery in the Music Library: a Cautionary Tale," *Notes*, lx/4 (June 2004), 865–92
Dance and Its Music in America, 1528–1789 (Hillsdale, NY, 2007)
"Purveyor to the Peddlers: Nathaniel Coverly Jr., Printer of Songs for the Streets of Boston," *Life on the Streets and Commons, 1600 to the Present*, ed. P. Benes, Dublin Seminar for New England Folklife, Annual Proceedings, 2005 (Boston, MA, 2007), 11–26
with D. Hildebrand: *Music of the War of 1812 in America* (Annapolis, MD, 2011)
with A.F. Schrader: *Songs in Vogue in 1814: the Isaiah Thomas Broadside Ballad Collection* (Worcester, MA, forthcoming)

JOHN KOEGEL

Kelley, Edgar Stillman [Stillman-Kelley, Edgar] (*b* Sparta, WI, 14 April 1857; *d* New York, NY, 12 Nov 1944). Organist, composer, and writer on music. He began piano lessons with his mother, then studied with F.W. Merriam (1870–4) before going to Chicago, where he continued his piano studies with N. Ledochowski and took harmony and counterpoint lessons with CLARENCE EDDY. In 1876 he went to Stuttgart and studied under Max Seifritz (composition and orchestration), Wilhelm Krüger and Wilhelm Speidel (piano), and Friedrich Finck (organ). Here, Kelley befriended Edward MacDowell, a friendship that would last for many years, eventually leading to Kelley's teaching at the MacDowell Colony. While in Europe he also had his first experience of performing with orchestras. Kelley returned to the United States in 1880 and settled in San Francisco. For six years he taught, composed, and gave piano and organ recitals; he also studied the music of the Chinese community, which resulted in the suite *Aladdin* for orchestra (1887–93). His incidental music for *Macbeth* brought him critical attention while in the West.

Kelley spent the years 1886 to 1892 in New York, conducting light opera, arranging music, composing, and teaching theory and piano. In 1891 he married Jessie Gregg (1865–1949), a pianist and teacher, who was later prominent in the National Federation of Music Clubs; her promotional and managerial efforts greatly enhanced her husband's career. In 1892 Kelley returned to the West Coast to become music critic of the *San Francisco Examiner*, but he moved back to New York four years later. He taught at New York University and the New York College of Music. In 1898 he was elected to the National Institute of Arts and Letters. For the academic year 1901–2 he was acting professor of music at Yale.

From 1902 to 1910 Kelley lived in Berlin, where he taught piano and composition; WALLINGFORD RIEGGER was one of his pupils. He returned to the United States in 1910 to teach at Western College for Women at Oxford, Ohio; the following year the college granted him a permanent fellowship in composition. He also accepted an appointment at the Cincinnati College of Music to teach theory and composition (1911–34), where one of his students was future faculty member C. Hugo Grimm. During this period he published two books, *Chopin the Composer* (1913) and *Musical Instruments* (1925). Kelley received honorary degrees from Miami University, Oxford, Ohio (DLitt 1916), and the University of Cincinnati (LLD 1916). From the 1920s he and his wife traveled widely, often performing.

Kelley's music shows the influence of his training in the Germanic tradition; harmony is tempered by a sure instinct for thematic development and a sense of symmetry. His works, predominantly programmatic, are characterized by clear writing, free experimentation with tonal color, and the use of whimsical details that enliven otherwise conventional methods. In his liking for circumspect musical innovation, extra-musical depiction, and humor he bears an affinity with the Boston composer, George Whitefield Chadwick. His theater works, particularly the incidental music to *Ben Hur*, foreshadow the film music of the next several decades, and in fact Kelley wrote one film score, though the film, *Corianton*, apparently was never released.

Typical compositional traits are revealed in his Chinese suite *Aladdin*, whose four movements depict a wedding, palace garden, flight of a genie, and "Feast of Lanterns." The music is filled with pentatonic melodies and instrumental sounds, and displays picturesque orchestration. In sharp contrast, his Symphony no.2 ("New England") reflects his New England ancestry, which is steeped in Puritan history. Its four movements are cast in typical symphonic structures. The music, less obviously programmatic than in the suite, is grave and reflective, as the composer ponders the experiences of the Pilgrims who settled in Plymouth in 1620. The third movement makes moving use of Timothy Swan's New England hymn "Why do we mourn departing friends." Almost all of Kelley's compositions adhere either to the colorfulness of the suite or the solemn expressivity of the symphony.

Kelley had strong ideas about nationalism in music and the position of American composers, which he expressed in numerous articles. He was avowedly an American composer and his works embody the spirit and sentiment of American life. Although many of Kelley's stage works and symphonic pieces achieved success when first performed, little of his music has continued to be performed. Kelley and his wife's musical manuscripts and papers are held at the Western Collection of Miami University. Very few of Kelley's works have been put on compact disc, with only a collection of piano music devoted to the composer's pieces available on the Albany label. The performer Brian Kovach has also published an edition of Kelley's piano works.

WORKS

Stage: Music to Macbeth (incid music, W. Shakespeare), op.7, 1882–4, rev. as orch suite; Gaelic March, arr. pf 4 hands (1886); Pompeiian Picnic (operetta, A.C. Gunter), op.9, 1887; Prometheus Bound (incid music, Aeschylus), op.16, 1891; Puritania (operetta, C.M.S. McLellan), op.11, 1892; Ben Hur (incid music, L. Wallace), op.17, 1899; The Pilgrim's Progress (musical miracle play, after J. Bunyan), op.37 (Boston, 1917); other incid music

Orch: Confluentia, op.2 no.2, str, 1882 [arr. of no.2 of 3 Pieces, pf]; Aladdin: a Chinese Suite, op.10, 1887–93; Sym. no.1 '"Gulliver: his Voyage to Lilliput," after J. Swift, op.15, 1900; Sym. no.2 "New England," op.33, 1913; Alice in Wonderland, suite, 1919; The Pit and the Pendulum, suite after E.A. Poe (New York, 1930); Corianton, film score, c1930

Vocal: A Wedding Ode, op.4, male chorus, orch, 1882; Phases of Love, 6 songs, op.6, S, pf, no.6 pubd (1888); 2 Songs, op.8 (1901); O Captain! My Captain! (W. Whitman), op.19, chorus, orch (Boston, n.d.); A California Idyll, op.38, S, orch, 1918; America's Creed, op.40, chorus, orch (Boston, 1919); other choral pieces, songs

Chbr and solo inst: Theme and Variations, op.1, str qt, c1880, rev. as op.25; 3 Pieces, op.2, pf (1891), no.2 Confluentia arr. str orch; Lyric Opera Sketches, pf (1894); Pf Qnt, op.20, 1898–1901; Str Qt, op.25 (New York, 1907); other pieces, arrs., pf

MSS in OX

Principal publishers: G. Schirmer, Stillman-Kelley Publication Society, Birchard, Ditson

BIBLIOGRAPHY

EwenD; *Grove*, Amer. suppl; *GroveA*

R. Hughes: "Edgar Stillman Kelley," *Music*, x (1896), 279–87

A. Shepherd: "Stillman-Kelley, Edgar," *Cobbett's Cyclopedic Survey of Chamber Music*, ed. W.W. Cobbett (London, 1929–30, 2/1963)

M.R. King: *Edgar Stillman Kelley: American Composer, Teacher, and Author* (diss., Florida State U., 1970)

L.L. Rivenburg: "Edgar Stillman Kelley and the American Musical Theatre," *Musical Theatre in America*, ed. F. Loney (Westport, CT, 1984), 111–22

N.E. Tawa: *Mainstream Music of Early Twentieth Century America* (Westport, CT, 1992)

F.K. Meyers: *America's Musical Pioneers and the Cornish Colony* (Melrose, FL, 2005)

KATHERINE K. PRESTON/NICHOLAS E. TAWA/
JONAS WESTOVER

Kelley, Norman (*b* Eddington, ME, 27 Aug 1911; *d* Rockland, MA, 4 Sept 2006). Tenor. He attended the New England Conservatory of Music, Pasadena College (now Point Loma Nazarene University), and Eastman School of Music before serving in the US military during World War II. He performed many roles for New York City Opera, including Pandarus in William Walton's *Troilus and Cressida* (1956), the narrator in Carl Orff's *Der Mond* (1956), Count Mancini in Ward's *He Who Gets Slapped* (1959), Mr. Scratch in Douglas Stuart Moore's *The Devil and Daniel Webster* (1959), and Méphistophélès in Prokofiev's *The Fiery Angel* (1965). He made his Metropolitan Opera debut as Mime in a 1957 production of Wagner's Ring Cycle and developed a reputation as a character role specialist. He was featured in 34 performances with the Metropolitan Opera between 1957 and 1961. His notable roles with this company included Herod in *Salome*, Don Basilio in *Le nozze di Figaro*, and Alcindoro in *La bohème*. Kelley was also recognized as an interpreter of contemporary operas, creating four leading roles including: Joseph Schweik in Robert Kurka's *The Good Soldier Schweik* (1958), Samuel Parris in Robert Ward's *The Crucible* (1961, released on CD by Albany Music in 1989), Lord Mark in Douglas Moore's *Wings of the Dove* (1962), and Ely Pratt in Carlisle Floyd's *Passion of Jonathan Wade* (1962). He was a featured soloist on several recordings of Gian

Carlo Menotti's theatrical works including *Maria Golovin* (recorded on RCA Victor in 1958), and *The Consul* (recorded on RCA Victor in 1962). In addition to his operatic ventures, he was a regular performer with the City Center Gilbert and Sullivan Company. His English translation of Humperdinck's *Hansel and Gretel* was first performed in 1967 and has since entered the standard repertoire.

MATTHEW ALAN THOMAS

Kellogg, Clara Louise (*b* Sumterville [now Sumter], SC, 9 July 1842; *d* New Hartford, CT, 13 May 1916). Soprano and impresario. She learned music from her parents and started studying the piano at the age of five. In 1857 her family moved to New York, where she studied with ACHILLE ERRANI, Emanuele Muzio, and others. After a modest concert tour (1860), she made her debut as Gilda at the Academy of Music (27 February 1861) and subsequently sang opera in New York and Boston. During the Civil War she toured, performing opera from Boston to Chicago and giving operatic concerts. Her first notable triumph was as Marguerite in the New York premiere of Gounod's *Faust* (Academy of Music, 25 November 1863). Although she became closely identified with the role, she described Marguerite in her memoirs as "a little fool" and preferred Aida and Carmen.

Kellogg's London debut, also as Marguerite, was at Her Majesty's Theatre (2 November 1867); she subsequently performed at Drury Lane, at the 1868 Handel Festival, and regularly in opera and concerts from 1868 to 1873. In 1872 she joined Pauline Lucca in the United States in an opera troupe managed by Maretzek, and in 1873 organized the Kellogg Grand English Opera Company, for which she was prima donna and artistic director. Kellogg's desire to establish English-language opera in America built on the successful English companies of Caroline Richings and Euphrosyne Parepa-Rosa from the late 1860s and early 70s. It was also an extension of a similar vernacular mid-century English opera movement in the UK; her troupe used the advertising slogan "opera for the people." She was widely touted as the "first American prima donna" and for four years her company enjoyed extraordinary success. She disbanded her English company after the 1876 season to resume performances of opera in Italian. She continued to sing in the United States and Europe until she retired in 1887 shortly after marrying her manager Carl Strakosch, nephew of Max Strakosch.

Kellogg had a pure, sweet soprano voice of large range and penetrating quality; she was also a good actress. She sang more than 40 roles (in Italian, English, and French) and had immense energy and stamina: during the 1874–5 season alone she gave 125 performances. She was well-known in the United States as a native-born opera star, and was one of the first American prima donnas to achieve a solid European reputation.

BIBLIOGRAPHY

DAB (F.H. Martens); *NAW* (W. Lichtenwanger); *DNB* (K.K. Preston)
"Miss Kellogg and English Opera," *New York Times* (20 Feb 1874)
P. Hanaford: *Women of the Century* (Boston, 1877)

F.E. Willard and M.A.R. Livermore: "Kellogg, Clara Louise," *A Woman of the Century* (New York, 1893), 432
C. Lahee: *Famous Singers of Today and Yesterday* (Boston, 1898)
T. Hopkins: *The Kelloggs in the Old World and the New* (San Francisco, 1903)
C.L. Kellogg: *Memoirs of an American Prima Donna* (New York/London, 1913/R)
E.E. Hipsher: *American Opera and Its Composers* (Philadelphia, 1927/R1934)
O. Thompson: *The American Singer* (New York, 1937/R)
K.K. Preston: *Opera on the Road: Traveling Opera Troupes in the United States, 1825-1860* (Urbana, IL, 1993/R)
Scrapbook and personal letters, Metropolitan Opera Archives, NYC

H. WILEY HITCHCOCK/KATHERINE K. PRESTON

Kellogg, Paul (*b* Hollywood, CA, 11 March 1937). Impresario. Educated in comparative literature and French, he joined the faculty, in 1961, of the Allen-Stevenson School in New York, where he became Head of the Lower School. Kellogg moved to rural Cooperstown, New York, in 1975, the year Glimmerglass Opera staged its first performances in a local high school, and volunteered to source props for the fledgling company. In 1979 he was appointed its general director. Kellogg presided over the 1987 construction of the 900-seat Alice Busch Opera Theater, designed by Hugh Hardy, which signaled the company's evolution from a community organization to a major international festival. By its seventh season in the new theater, Glimmerglass Opera had established a two-month rotating repertory season of four new productions each summer. Kellogg's 26-year tenure saw productions of rarities by composers ranging from Francesco Cavalli to John Philip Sousa, as well as innovative approaches to standard repertory led by directors including Martha Clarke, Mark Lamos, Jonathan Miller, and Christopher Alden. In 1996 Kellogg became the general director of New York City Opera and initiated a practice of sharing productions between New York City Opera and Glimmerglass Opera, where he retained the position of artistic director. Kellogg brought more than 60 new productions to New York City Opera's repertory, about half of which originated in Cooperstown. In 1999 he inaugurated an annual series of new opera readings with the New York City Opera Orchestra. Kellogg retired from Glimmerglass Opera in 2006 and New York City Opera in 2007.

BIBLIOGRAPHY

A. Tommasini: "The New Kid on the Opera World's Toughest Block," *New York Times* (15 Sept 1996)
P.J. Smith: "Under New Management," *ON*, lxi/12 (8 March 1997), 10–16
A. Tommasini: "At City Opera, an Innovator Bows Out," *New York Times* (6 May 2007)

KELLEY ROURKE

Kelly, Gene [Curran, Eugene] (*b* Pittsburgh, PA, 23 Aug 1912; *d* Beverly Hills, CA, 2 Feb 1996). Dancer, actor, choreographer, and film director. Kelly started out in Pittsburgh, running a family-owned dance studio and performing regionally. Turning down an opportunity to join the Ballet Russe de Monte Carlo touring company, he graduated from the University of Pittsburgh in 1933 and briefly attended law school before going to New York

Gene Kelly, right, with Frank Sinatra in the 1945 film Anchors Aweigh. *(Reuters/Landov)*

in 1937. On Broadway, Kelly quickly went from chorus boy (*Leave It to Me*, 1938) to leading man (*Pal Joey*, 1940) and soon departed for Hollywood, making his film debut opposite Judy Garland in *For Me and My Gal* (1942). Under contract with MGM, Kelly first made his mark in a loan out to Columbia (*Cover Girl*, 1944); the innovative "Alter Ego" solo in the film initiated Kelly's interest in both directing and integrating musical numbers into the plot. He is among very few studio-era stars to cross over into directing. Most of his director credits were shared with Stanley Donen, including *On the Town* (1949), *Singin' in the Rain* (1952), and *It's Always Fair Weather* (1955). *Anchors Aweigh* (1945) displayed Kelly's innovative use of special effects—he danced with animated characters—and *An American in Paris* (1951), directed by Vincente Minnelli, won multiple Oscars. Box office failures like *The Pirate* (1948) and *Invitation to the Dance* (released 1956) expressed Kelly's character-driven mix of ballet and modern dance, but were neither commercially savvy nor critically well received. Kelly also played leading roles in nonmusical films throughout his years at MGM and most all his film roles reinforced his screen persona as an energetic, athletic common man. After the closing of the musical production units, Kelly created a live television show exploring dance and masculinity (*Dancing: A Man's Game*, 1958) and directed the Broadway show *Flower Drum Song* (1958). Appearing in a handful of film musicals in the 1960s, Kelly ended his film-musical directing career with the disappointing *Hello, Dolly!* (1969).

BIBLIOGRAPHY
C. Hirschhorn: *Gene Kelly: a Biography* (Chicago, 1975, 2/1984)
H. Fordin: *MGM's Greatest Musicals: the Arthur Freed Unit* (New York, 1996)
A. Yudkoff: *Gene Kelly: a Life of Dance and Dreams* (New York, 1999)

TODD DECKER

Kelly, R(obert Sylvester) (*b* Chicago, IL, 8 Jan 1967). R&B singer, writer, producer, and arranger. Kelly was born on the South side of Chicago. Raised, with his three siblings, by a single mother, he was encouraged to pursue a musical career by his high school music teacher and mentor, Lena McLin, who was the chair of the music department at the Kenwood Academy and the niece of the legendary gospel music composer Thomas Dorsey. In high school Kelly formed the group MGM (Musically Gifted Men), which won a $100,000 grand prize on the television talent show *Big Break*, hosted by Natalie Cole. The group eventually signed with Jive Records, though after creative and financial tensions, three of the members were replaced and the group renamed R. Kelly and Public Announcement. After a moderately successful debut that produced the hit singles "She's Got That Vibe" and "Honey Love," Kelly left the group in early 1993 to embark upon a solo career.

Kelly's debut solo recording *12 Play* (1993) immediately established him as an influential figure in contemporary R&B, not only as a performer, but as a producer and arranger. On the strength of the album and its follow-up *R. Kelly* (1995), Kelly worked with artists such as Changing Faces, Aaliyah, Toni Braxton, Michael Jackson, and Ronald Isley. Kelly contributed the song "I Believe I Can Fly," which has become a modern standard, to the soundtrack of the animated film *Space Jam*; it was also included on his 1998 double-disc recording *R*. Through the first decade of the 21st century, Kelly's career was dogged with charges of statutory rape, though he was eventually acquitted of all charges in June 2008. Kelly broke new ground in 2005 with the single, "Trapped in the Closet" which became the foundation for a 33-episode telenovela that was broadcast on The Independent Film Channel (IFC).

MARK ANTHONY NEAL

Kelly, Wynton (*b* Jamaica, 2 Dec 1931; *d* Toronto, ON, 12 April 1971). Jazz pianist. His family moved to the United States when he was four years old and settled in Brooklyn. As a youth he played professionally in rhythm-and-blues bands. By fusing earthy blues elements with those of the bop style as exemplified by Bud Powell, he developed a highly accessible and personal approach to jazz piano playing which influenced many subsequent performers. After working with the saxophonist Eddie "Lockjaw" Davis and the singer Dinah Washington, Kelly gained attention as a soloist while performing with Lester Young and Dizzy Gillespie. He continued to work for Washington and Gillespie in the mid-1950s and also played with Benny Carter and Charles Mingus. Although he frequently led his own trio from 1957 until his death, he was best known as a member of Miles Davis's sextets and quintets from 1959. A consistent and sometimes brilliant improviser, he had exceptional skill as an accompanist, although this often overshadowed his rhythmically infectious solo style. His influence can be heard in the early work of Victor Feldman, Herbie Hancock, McCoy Tyner, and other pianists who emerged the 1960s.

SELECTED RECORDINGS

As leader: *Kelly Blue* (1959, Riv.); *Smokin' at the Half Note* (1965, Verve); *Full View* (1967, Mlst.)

As sideman with M. Davis: *Someday my Prince will Come* (1961, Col.); *At Carnegie Hall* (1961, Col.); *In Person: Friday and Saturday Nights at the Blackhawk* (1961, Col.)

BIBLIOGRAPHY

V. Wilmer: *Jazz People* (New York, 1970/R)

L. Feather and J. Levin: "Wynton Kelly," *Jazz Magazine*, no.189 (1971), 30

P. Moon: "Wynton Kelly Discography," *Discographical Forum*, nos. 32–41 (1973–8)

C. Schlouch: *Wynton Kelly: a Discography* (Marseilles, 1992, 2/1993)

BILL DOBBINS/R

Kelly and Leon's Minstrels. Minstrel troupe starring tenor, interlocutor, actor Edwin Kelly (*b* Dublin, Ireland, 1835; *d* Adelaide, Australia, 24 Dec 1898) and female impersonator, singer, and dancer Patrick Francis "Leon" Glassey (*b* New York, NY, 21 Nov *c*1840; *d* unknown). Kelly immigrated to the United States after completing medical studies in London. Leon sang as a child in the St. Stephen's Church choir, New York, and graduated from the Jesuit College Fordham. Both entered minstrelsy in the 1850s, Kelly with Ordway's Aeolians and Leon with Wood's Minstrels. They seem to have met as members of George Christy's Minstrels in 1860. They established their own troupe in Chicago *c*1863 and in 1866 moved to New York, where they played for three years.

Leon's sensitive female impersonations contrasted with the farcical wench roles that had dominated minstrelsy until then. Eschewing "costumes," he wore women's clothing onstage and kept a wardrobe of some 300 dresses. His voice (a soprano that remained with him throughout adulthood), balletic dancing, and delicate mannerisms furthered the impression that he was a real woman. Leon and Kelly's lavish, full-length opera burlesques blurred the line between legitimate performance and parody. They specialized in Offenbach, offering *The Grand Dutch S* (featuring "The Cheese Knife of My Pa," a parody of "Le Sabre de mon père"), *Barber Blu*, and *La Bell-L.N.* Leon declared himself "the only Leon" because of his many imitators. After 1868 Kelly and Leon traveled with other minstrel companies in England, the United States, and Australia, where they dissolved their partnership around 1880. Leon remained active in minstrelsy and vaudeville, retiring in *c*1903.

BIBLIOGRAPHY

"Were Stage Favorites in Days Long Gone By," *Brooklyn Times*, 7 March 1903

E.L. Rice: *Monarchs of Minstrelsy, from "Daddy" Rice to Date* (New York, 1911)

R. Toll: *Blacking Up: the Minstrel Show in Nineteenth-Century America* (New York, 1974)

SANDRA JEAN GRAHAM

Kelpius, Johannes (*b* nr Schässburg [now Sighişoara, Romania], 1667; *d* Germantown, PA, 1708). German theologian, mystic, composer, musician, writer, and hymnbook compiler. Three friends of his father (a pastor in Transylvania who died in 1685) sent him to the University of Altdorf, near Nuremberg, where in 1689 he obtained a master's degree in theology and published his thesis, *Theologiae Naturalis*. He published two additional works in 1690, *Scylla Theologica* and *Inquisitio, an Ethicus Ethnicus*, in collaboration with Johannes Fabricius. After Kelpius and 40 celibate followers sojourned for six months in England, securing close connections with the Philadelphian Society, they immigrated to America in preparation for the imminently expected millennium. He is credited as the founder of the Rosicrucian movement in America.

On 22 June 1694 the group disembarked at Bohemia Landing, Maryland, proceeding to Germantown, Pennsylvania, where they settled on a wooded ridge overlooking Wissahickon Creek. Kelpius, a psractical musician, compiled a 70-page hymnal, entitled *The Lamenting Voice of the Hidden Love* (1705), which, with the English translation of his disciple Christopher Witt (*c*1675–1765), is probably the earliest extant musical manuscript compiled in the 13 British colonies (Philadelphia, Historical Society of Pennsylvania, Ac. 189). Four of the ten melodies copied for the singing of his perfervid poetry come from Christian Knorr von Rosenroth's *Neuer Helicon* (1684), and another four derive from German sources dated 1690 and later. The rich harmonies in the seven melodies with basses are realized for keyboard, not four voices, and show musical skill far beyond anything known among 18th-century English-speaking colonists.

BIBLIOGRAPHY

DAB ("Kelpius, Johann"; G.H. Genzmer)

J.F. Watson: "Notes of the Early History of Germantown," *Hazard's Register of Pennsylvania*, i (Philadelphia, PA, 1828), Jan–July, 281

J.F. Sachse: *The German Pietists of Provincial Pennsylvania, 1694–1708* (Philadelphia, PA, 1895), 219–49

J.F. Sachse, ed.: "The Diarium of Magister Johannes Kelpius," *Proceedings and Addresses of the Pennsylvania-German Society*, xxv/2 (1917), 5–100

"Johannes Kelpius: Pennsylvania's Earliest Hymnologist and Musician," "Hymn Book of Magester Johannes Kelpius," *Church Music and Musical Life in Pennsylvania in the Eighteenth Century*, ed. Pennsylvania Society of the Colonial Dames of America, i (Philadelphia, PA, 1926), 1–165

E.G. Alderfer: Introduction to Kelpius: *a Method of Prayer* (New York, 1951) [Eng. trans. of Ger. orig.]

A.G. Hess: "Observations on 'The Lamenting Voice of the Hidden Love'," *JAMS*, v/3 (1952), 211–23

E. Wolf: *Germantown and the Germans* (Philadelphia, PA, 1983)

S.E. Fullenwieder: *Johannes Kelpiuş* (n.p., 1993)

E. Reichmann, L.J. Rippley, and J. Nagler: *Emigration and Settlement Patterns of German Communities in North America* (Indianapolis, IN, 1995), 31–54

A. Versluis: *Wisdom's Children: a Christian Esoteric Tradition* (Albany, NY, 1999), 89–112

ROBERT STEVENSON/R

Kementzides, Ilias (*b* Nikolinka, Kazakhstan, 2 April 1926; *d* Norwalk, CT, 11 Nov 2006). Lyra player of Kazakhstani birth. Born to Pontic Greek parents, he began at age eight playing the lyra (a bottle-shaped violin with three strings), taking lessons from his uncle. In 1940 his family moved to Greece, where he became a professional musician, mainly performing at social clubs and theatres. In 1974 Kementzides immigrated to the United States with his wife and children. They lived in Norwalk, Connecticut, where he worked in an electronics factory. He continued to play lyra as a soloist—a distinctive break from the traditional three-piece ensemble—and made his own instruments. He was also recognized for his compelling, expressive voice. Performing from memory, he typically sang in the Pontic dialect but was also fluent in Greek, Turkish, and Russian. In addition to performing at dances, weddings, community gatherings, and religious occasions in Connecticut and New York, he participated in cultural festivals and national Greek music tours. In 1989 he received the National Heritage Fellowship from the National Endowment for the Arts.

CATHERINE WOJTANOWSKI

Kemp, Father (Robert J.) (*b* Wellfleet, MA, 6 June 1821; *d* Boston, MA, 15 May 1897). Showman and conductor. He was a shoe merchant and an amateur musician, who devised a highly successful format for the type of entertainment known as the OLD-FOLKS CONCERT. Father Kemp's Old Folks Concert Troupe added theatrical devices to the basic musical repertory of 18th-century psalmody: performers, appearing in period costume, gave impersonations of figures from the Revolution, and parodies in appropriate dialect of old-fashioned theatrical acts. Kemp's first troupe was formed from his Opera Class Chorus in Reading, Massachusetts; its début was on 6 December 1855, and its first Boston concert on 13 March 1856. Regular concerts were given in New York, Philadelphia, Washington, and Boston between 1856 and 1866, and the troupe went on a tour of the West in the 1858–9 season. The climax of Kemp's career was his tour of England in 1861. *Father Kemp's Old Folks' Concert Tunes*, a compilation of New England psalmody and a few popular songs and patriotic pieces, was published in 1860.

BIBLIOGRAPHY
R.J. Kemp: *Father Kemp and his Old Folks* (Boston, 1868/*R*)
G.C.D. Odell: *Annals of the New York Stage*, i–vii (New York, 1927–31/*R*)
J.T. Steinberg: "Old Folks Concerts and the Revival of New England Psalmody," *MQ*, lix (1973), 602

JUDITH TICK

Kemp, Mark (*b* Asheboro, NC, 10 April 1960). Author and journalist. Kemp's career was founded on his journalistic work and, in more recent years, his publications on popular music topics. A graduate of East Carolina University, Kemp began as a newspaper reporter but then, during the late 1980s, secured work with the alternative music title *Option* and, by 1991, had risen to editor. He caught the eye of *Rolling Stone* and became music editor of the magazine during the early 1990s. His tenure coincided with the rise of a number of key acts from the period from Pearl Jam to Beck. Later he became vice president of the music editorial division for the music video network MTV. In 1997 he earned a Grammy nomination for his liner notes to a retrospective

of protest singer Phil Ochs, *Farewells and Fantasies*. Departing MTV in 2000, he concentrated on writing his memoir of Southern life, *Dixie Lullaby: a Story of Music, Race, and New Beginnings in a New South* (New York, 2004), which attracted widespread praise. Returning to his home state in 2002, Kemp has since edited the Charlotte edition of the alternative newsweekly *Creative Loafing*.

SIMON WARNER

Kendall, Edward [Ned] (*b* Newport, RI, 20/21 March 1808; *d* Boston, MA, 26 Oct 1861). Bandmaster and keyed bugle player. After studying fife, drum, and clarinet, he became a noted performer on the keyed bugle, which was rapidly becoming popular. He made his professional début as a bugler in Boston about 1825, and appeared as a soloist with the Tremont Theatre Orchestra and the Boston Brigade Band, both conducted by his brother James Kendall (1803–c1874), a well-known clarinetist and trombonist. In 1835 Edward formed the Boston Brass Band, one of the earliest ensembles in the American brass band movement, which flourished until the late 1880s. He became leader of the Boston Brigade Band in 1849, and was also a well-known circus bandsman and soloist with touring companies such as Spalding & Rogers and Nixon's Great American Circus. Like other American keyed-bugle soloists, Kendall played a high E♭ instrument, equipped with extra left-hand keys for fine tuning and to extend the instrument's range. He was a formidable player, greatly admired for elaborate versions of showpieces such as Joseph Holloway's *Wood Up Quick Step*. The solo style of Kendall and other American buglers foreshadowed an era of cornet solo playing that was to remain immensely popular well into the 20th century.

BIBLIOGRAPHY
H.W. Schwartz: *Bands of America* (New York, 1957)
R.E. Eliason: *Keyed Bugles in the United States* (Washington, DC, 1972)
R. Kitchen: "Edward Kendall: America's First Circus Bandmaster," *Bandwagon*, xxi/4 (1977), 25
R. Dudgeon: *The Keyed Bugle: its History, Literature and Technique* (diss., U. of California, San Diego, 1980)

R.E. SHELDON

Kennan, Kent (Wheeler) (*b* Milwaukee, WI, 18 April 1913; *d* Austin, TX, 1 Nov 2003). Composer and teacher. After private piano, flute, and organ studies he attended the University of Michigan (1930–2) and then studied composition with HOWARD HANSON at the Eastman School (BM 1934, MM 1936). The award of the Prix de Rome took him to the Italian capital for three years, and there he studied for a short period with Ildebrando Pizzetti. Returning to the United States in 1939, he was appointed to teach at Kent State University; a professorship at the University of Texas, Austin, was interrupted by service as an army bandmaster, after which he taught at Ohio State University (1947–9) before returning to his position as professor of composition at the University of Texas. After retiring in 1983, Kennan discontinued composition, working mainly on educational material.

He won the highest honor bestowed by the University of Texas, the E. William Doty Award, in 2001. His earlier music shows Romantic, Impressionist, and some jazz influences, but from the 1940s his style was mainly neo-Classical. Several of his works have been released on compact disc on the Mercury label. Of special importance is his *Sonata for Trumpet and Piano* (1956), which has become a standard part of the repertory for trumpet students.

WORKS
(selective list)

Night Soliloquy, (fl, str, pf)/(fl, wind)/(fl, pf), 1936; Il campo dei fiori, tpt, orch, 1937; Noctorno "From a Rome Diary," va, orch, 1937; Dance Divertimento, orch, 1938, rev. 1988; arr. 2 pf; Promenade, orch, 1938; Sym., orch, 1938; Blessed Are They That Mourn (Bible), chorus, orch, 1939; Elegy, ob, orch, 1939; 3 Preludes, pf, 1939; Retrospectives, 12 pieces, pf, 1939–60, rev. 1988; Sea Sonata, vn, pf, 1939; The Unknown Warrior Speaks, male chorus, 1944; Sonatina, pf, 1945; Concertino, pf, orch, 1946, arr. pf, wind, 1963; A Clear Midnight (W. Whitman), 1v, pf, 1947, arr. SATB, pf, 1989; Scherzo, Aria, and Fugato, ob, pf, 1948; 2 Preludes, pf, 1951; Variations on a Quiet Theme, org, 1952; Sonata, tpt, pf, 1956; Threnody, fl/vn, pf, 1994; other kbd pieces, orch works, songs

Principal publishers: Remick, G. Schirmer, C. Fischer

WRITINGS

The Technique of Orchestration (Englewood Cliffs, NJ, 1952, 3/1983 with D. Grantham, 5/1997)
Counterpoint: Based on Eighteenth-Century Practice (Englewood Cliffs, 1959, 4/1999)

BIBLIOGRAPHY
EwenD
J.A. Wyss: *The Art Songs of Kent Kennan* (diss., U. of Texas, Austin, 1981)

W. THOMAS MARROCCO/JONAS WESTOVER

Kennedy, John (*b* Alberta Lee, MN, 7 April 1959). Composer, conductor, and percussionist. He attended Oberlin College and Northwestern University where he studied percussion. He then moved to New York, where he began to focus on conducting and composition; he also began an association with John Cage and the Merce Cunningham Dance Company. In 1988 he also founded and for 13 years conducted the ensemble Essential Music, which performed experimental American music and other avant-garde works. In 1990 he began his affiliation with the Spoleto Festival USA in Charleston, South Carolina, directing its contemporary music series, then working as Artistic Associate. He currently serves as the festival's resident conductor and Director of Orchestral Activities. In 2000 he founded Santa Fe New Music, a concert series committed to new classical music. He has also served as an advocate for new music through his role as President of the Board of the American Music Center (2002–5). Kennedy's experience as a percussionist and conductor has influenced his compositional style. *First Deconstruction (in Plastic)* (2007), for example, draws on the history of found-object percussion music and the series of *Constructions* made by John Cage. His works have been performed worldwide and featured at major international festivals. He has been commissioned by the Other Minds Festival, Sarasota Opera (*The Language of Birds*, 2004), the Santa Fe Opera (*Trinity*, 2007), and many others. From operas to symphonic pieces to chamber works, his music has been praised for its lyricism, luminous sound, and accessibility within experimental constructs.

ELIOT GATTEGNO

Kennedy Center for the Performing Arts, John F. Arts complex in Washington, DC, inaugurated in 1971; *see* WASHINGTON, D.C.

Kenny G [Gorelick, Kenneth] (*b* Seattle, WA, 5 June 1956). Smooth jazz saxophonist. He is one of the most popular instrumentalists of the late 20th and early 21st centuries, when he sold more than 75 million albums. He began playing saxophone at the age of ten. During his formative years he was influenced by the tone and improvisational approach of Grover Washington Jr. In 1973 he landed his first professional engagement, as a sideman for Barry White's Love Unlimited Orchestra. This led to further opportunities touring with such artists as the Spinners and Liberace. In 1979 he began performing and recording with the Jeff Lorber Fusion. Lorber's group was polished, experienced, and had ties to Arista Records. After taking part in two albums Gorelick left Lorber's group and made his debut recording, *Kenny G* (1982, Arista).

Although Kenny G's subsequent albums *G Force* (1982, Arista) and *Gravity* (1985, Arista) were successful, *Duotones* (1986, Arista) was even more popular, and its sales eclipsed those of previous recordings. Propelled by the single "Songbird," it sold more than five million copies in the United States. Gorelick's phenomenal album sales continued with *Silhouette* (1988, Arista) and *Breathless* (1992, Arista). The latter sold more than 12 million copies in the United States, and its track "Forever in Love" won a Grammy Award for Best Instrumental Composition. Kenny G's tremendous popularity can be attributed to his timely entry into the growing adult contemporary and smooth jazz radio market. During the 1980s and 90s he took advantage of this expanding audience with a strong work ethic and tireless touring schedule. *Miracles: the Holiday Album* (1994, Arista), featuring his rhythm-and-blues influenced variations on Christmas classics, was perfectly tailored to this mature and affluent audience. After selling more than eight million copies, it became one of the best-selling Christmas albums of all time. By the mid-2000s the popularity of smooth jazz and Kenny G had waned. Although he has continued to release new albums roughly every two years, he has not duplicated the sales numbers of the 1980s and 90s.

Kenny G's style is predicated on tone and ornamentation. His tone, especially on soprano saxophone, features a brilliance and clarity that can often serve as a satisfying substitution for a vocalist. With respect to improvisation, Gorelick does not rely on an approach built around scalar passages; instead, he engages with the melody through a repeating series of ornamentations. This style of improvisation is antithetical to conventional jazz improvisational approaches and has frequently been the target of criticism from jazz critics and performers.

BIBLIOGRAPHY
S. Stein: "Kenny G: Songbird in Full Flight," *DB*, lv/1 (1988), 16–18, 48
H. Bordowitz: "Songbird Syndrome: the Triple Platinum Dilemma of Kenny G," *Jazziz*, vi/1 (1989), 52–4, 85–6
C.A. Olson: "Kenny G: the Billboard Interview," *Billboard* (14 Sept 2002)
R. Walser: "Ten Apothegms and Four Instances," *Analyzing Popular Music*, ed. A.F. Moore (Cambridge, 2003), 36–7
C. Washburne: "Does Kenny G Play Bad Jazz?" *Bad Music: the Music we Love to Hate*, ed. C. Washburne and M. Derno (New York, 2004), 123–47
A.J. West: *Caught between Jazz and Pop: the Contested Origins, Criticism, Performance Practice, and Reception of Smooth Jazz* (diss., U. of North Texas, 2008), 132–65

AARON J. WEST

Kent bugle. One of several alternate names for the KEYED BUGLE, patented in 1810. The first method book for keyed bugle was dedicated to the Duke of Kent, and early versions of the instrument were labeled "Royal Kent Bugle."

Kenton, Stan(ley Newcomb) (*b* Wichita, KS, 15 Dec 1911; *d* Los Angeles, CA, 25 Aug 1979). Bandleader, pianist, and composer. He worked as a pianist and arranger for the swing bands of Everett Hoagland, Gus Arnheim, and Johnny Davis before starting his own ensemble, the Artistry in Rhythm Orchestra, in the early 1940s. Although he was steeped in the big band dance tradition, Kenton soon pursued more complex arrangements with an expanded instrumentation that swelled to five trumpets, five trombones, five saxophones, and at times a full complement of Latin percussionists. Indebted to modernist trailblazers such as his fellow Arnheim sideman Woody Herman and Boyd Raeburn (who discovered Kenton's first important female vocalist, June Christy), he quickly became the face of a new wave of big band leaders steadily attracting copious young, talented personnel, and, by the 1950s, had assumed unchallenged dominance over the movement. His first band reached a sizeable audience as part of Bob Hope's radio program in 1943, but regular touring and prolific recording thereafter inspired legions of devotees, due in no small part to Kenton's tireless self-promotion. At the core of this successful campaign lay an ambitious, if self-serving, "neophonic" philosophy that asserted the primacy of symphonic jazz over other modern forms of popular music such as bebop, hard bop, and even rock.

Despite a commanding reception during his opening night at the Rendezvous Ballroom in Balboa, California, in June 1941, Kenton began to explore music that steadily veered away from the exclusivity of dance. By 1947 he had coined the term PROGRESSIVE JAZZ to market his new direction—a style he once tellingly called "free swing"—and left Decca for the newly established Capitol Records. New compositions integrated elements of concert music and downplayed the role of solo improvisation. While a host of arrangers filtered through the band from its inception, no single collaborator embodied the new musical territory Kenton had prospected more than PETE RUGOLO. Designated Kenton's chief arranger by 1946, Rugolo represented the height of ingenuity during this stage in the group's development and much of this pioneering work remains strikingly fresh. The stylistic range encompassing both the severe timbral odyssey "Impressionism" and the contemplative "This is my theme" (1947, Cap.) epitomizes the unique approach that informed Rugolo's inventive charts. All but free of swing, the former tune suggests a strong link to serialist trends in European art music.

These efforts paved the way for Kenton's seminal recording, *New Concepts of Artistry in Rhythm* (1952, Cap.), which represented a natural culmination of this early adventurous period and a harbinger of his later career's mounting expressive extremes. Other notable efforts involved Afro-Cuban, or cubop, collaborations with Frank "Machito" Grillo; Kenton's 43-member Innovations in Modern Music Orchestra, which employed a string section in bop-inspired arrangements by Shorty Rogers; and Bob Graettinger's explorations beyond conventional harmony (*City of Glass*, 1951, Cap.). In the early 1960s Kenton's ensemble, New Era in Modern American Music, featured mellophoniums, while later groups in the 1970s flirted with fusion under his independent record label, Creative World.

For the jazz cognoscenti, Kenton's extraordinary popular success proved a liability. Many have considered his bombastic, strident music to lack true artistic merit—its pretentious statement the misguided, if entertaining, byproduct of an eccentric, self-important showman. Although there is no denying the caliber of musicians who both contributed to and benefited from his success, this stigma continues to overshadow serious evaluation of Kenton's output. The most flattering sources tend to fetishize the intoxicating skill of his sidemen or merely to note the demanding nature of his catalog. A clear benefit of the latter penchant, however, has proven its stimulation of numerous devoted discographies that track each and every recording detail through his long career. Inundated with fanatical supporters and steadfast detractors alike, Kenton has seemed to escape controversy only through his educational legacy. Owing to the prominence and high technical standards of his players, Kenton's frequent contributions at instructional jazz clinics and camps spawned generations of healthy big band programs still active in high schools and colleges across the United States.

SELECTED RECORDINGS
As leader: Artistry in Rhythm (1941, Cap.); Eager Beaver (1943, Cap.); And her tears flowed like wine (1944, Cap.); Tampico (1945, Cap.); The Peanut Vendor (1947, Cap.); Impressionism (1947, Cap.); This is my theme (1947, Cap.); How High the Moon (1947, Cap.); Jolly Rogers (1950, Cap.); *City of Glass* (1951, Cap.); *New Concepts of Artistry in Rhythm* (1952, Cap.); *A Merry Christmas* (1961, Cap.); *West Side Story* (1961, Cap.); *Live at Brigham Young University* (1971, Creative World)
As sideman: with G. Arnheim: The image of you (1937, Br)

BIBLIOGRAPHY
J. McKinney: "The Kenton Story: the Rise and Achievements of the Most Controversial Figure in the History of Jazz," *Crescendo*, iv (1965–6), no.3, pp. 20–23; no.4, pp. 17–19; no.5, pp. 32–3; no.6, pp. 24–6; no.7, pp. 12–14
P. Newman: "Stan Kenton 'Speaks Out'," *DB*, xl/21 (1973), 19, 39–40.

W.F. Lee: *Stan Kenton: Artistry in Rhythm*, ed. A. Coke (Los Angeles, 1980)

A.J. Agostinelli: *Stan Kenton: the Many Musical Moods of his Orchestras* (Providence, RI, 1986) [bio-discography]

L. Arganian: *Stan Kenton: the Man and his Music* (East Lansing, MI, 1989)

T. Gioia: *West Coast Jazz: Modern Jazz in California 1945–1960* (New York, 1992)

M. Sparke, P. Venudor, and J. Hartley: *Kenton on Capitol and Creative World: a Discography* (Lake Geneva, WI, 1994)

R. Jones: "'Free Swing' and the Emergent Neophonic: Forging Progressive Jazz with Stan Kenton in the 1947 Dance Hall," *Jazz Research Journal*, ii/1 (2008), 29–54

RYAN PATRICK JONES

Keppard, Freddie (*b* New Orleans, LA, 27 Feb 1890; *d* Chicago, IL, 15 July 1933). Jazz cornetist and bandleader. He studied mandolin, violin, and accordion, and was active professionally as a cornetist from about 1907 with his own group, the Olympia Orchestra, and other New Orleans ensembles of black musicians. In 1914 he moved to Los Angeles to join the Original Creole Band. After touring in vaudeville and performing in Chicago and New York with this group, he settled in Chicago; he was prominent there throughout the 1920s with his own bands, including the Jazz Cardinals (1926), and those of Doc Cook, Erskine Tate, Ollie Powers, and Charlie Elgar.

Among the leading New Orleans trumpeters who left recordings of their work, Keppard is notable for a brusque and staccato style that comes closest to ragtime. Few of the recordings definitely identified as his substantiate either the esteem accorded him by other jazz musicians or his considerable popularity; but he seldom recorded before 1926, by which time his health was failing. Although his stature may never be fully assessed, he was one of the first musicians to lead a New Orleans jazz ensemble in the northern and western United States.

BIBLIOGRAPHY

O. Spencer: "Trumpeter Freddie Keppard Walked out on Al Capone!," *Music and Rhythm*, ii/6 (1941), 13–7

W.C. Allen: "Trumpet Giants, 3: Freddie Keppard," *Hot Notes*, ii/3 (1947), 2–5 [incl. discography]

N. Shapiro and N. Hentoff, eds.: *Hear me Talkin' to ya: the Story of Jazz by the Men who Made it* (New York, 1955/R)

S.B. Charters and L. Kunstadt: *Jazz: a History of the New York Scene* (Garden City, NY, 1962/R)

L. Gushee: "How the Creole Band Came to Be," *Black Music Research Journal*, viii (1988), 83–100

L. Gushee: *Pioneers of Jazz: the Story of the Creole Band* (New York, 2005/R)

J.R. TAYLOR/R

Kerker, Gustave A(dolph) (*b* Herford, Germany, 28 Feb 1857; *d* New York, NY, 29 June 1923). Composer and conductor of German birth. Kerker came from a musical family and studied the cello as a child. His family immigrated to the United States in 1867; they settled in Louisville, Kentucky, where Kerker continued to play the cello and began directing several theatre orchestras.

His first stage work, *The Cadets*, was performed by the Herman Grau English Opera Company on a four-month tour of the South in 1879. Kerker moved to New York the following year to conduct orchestras at the H.V.B. Mann Opera Company (1800), the Thalia Theatre (1883), and the Bijou Opera House (1884) before becoming music director at the Casino Theatre (1888). He also conducted on tour with the Alfa Norman Opera Company, performing Balfe's *The Enchantress* (1885).

Kerker increasingly interpolated his own music into the scores he conducted. *The Skating Rink* (1887), a vehicle for vaudevillian Nat C. Goodwin that had already played Chicago and New York, opened under Kerker's baton at the Bijou Theater; he was credited for the music and it ran for 24 performances. For *The Pearl of Pekin* (1888), Kerker used a libretto by Charles Alfred Byrne to revamp Charles Lecocq's *La fleur de thé* with his own interpolations. Following its success, Kerker worked again with Byrne to produce *Castles in the Air* (1890), borrowing heavily from Offenbach's *Les Bavards*. *Little Christopher Columbus* (1894) did particularly well on Broadway and on tour after Ivan Caryll's original had been modified to suit American taste; eight additional Kerker songs were among the alterations.

Several similar reworkings ensued before Kerker composed *The Belle of New York* (1897) to a libretto by Hugh Morton (pseudonym for C.M.S. McLellan), with whom he had previously collaborated. In addition to its title song, the score includes "The Purity Brigade," "Teach Me How to Kiss, Dear," and "They All Follow Me." Although it had an unexceptional New York run of almost 60 performances, *The Belle of New York* became the work by which Kerker is best remembered. With almost 700 performances in London, it was the first American work to run for over a year on the West End, where it starred Edna May and a chorus line of vivacious American beauties. Other Kerker works transplanted to London include *An American Beauty* (1896) and *The Girl from Up There* (1901), starring Edna May.

Building on the success of *The Belle of New York* in London, Paris, and Vienna, Kerker briefly attempted to establish himself as a European composer. In 1909 there were Berlin productions of *The Upper Ten Thousand* and *The Social Whirl*, and *Schneeglöckchen* (*Snowdrops*) premiered in Vienna the following year.

Kerker was married twice, first to Rose Leighton, a prominent comic-opera contralto, and subsequently to Mattie Rivenberg, a showgirl considerably his junior who had appeared in *The Social Whirl*. He was a member of the Lambs and Green Room Clubs, and for 35 years belonged to the St. Cecile Lodge #568 of the Free and Associated Masons. Kerker's works list contains more than two dozen titles.

BIBLIOGRAPHY

"Gustave A. Kerker, Composer, Dead." *New York Times*, (30 June 1923), 11

R. Traubner: *Operetta: a Theatrical History* (New York, 1983/R2003)

ORLY LEAH KRASNER

Kern, Jerome (David) (*b* New York, NY, 27 Jan 1885; *d* New York, NY, 11 Nov 1945). Composer. A seminal and prolific figure in the development of 20th-century American musical theater and popular song, he scored some 40 complete musicals, contributed to dozens more, and wrote over 1200 songs. As a musical dramatist, Kern's reputation rests primarily upon his contributions to the development of the book musical, in which songs and music play an integral role in the dramatic narrative. As a songwriter, he is best remembered for the superior craftsmanship he brought to American popular music. In both respects he was enormously influential. His career spanned four decades, and his successes bridged immense changes in musical style and theatrical genre.

1. Life. 2. Works.

1. LIFE. Born into a middle-class Jewish family in Manhattan, Kern's musical education began with his mother, an amateur but skilled pianist, who gave him his first piano lessons. At Newark High School (the family moved to New Jersey in 1897) he served as pianist and organist for school functions, and, when a junior, contributed at least one song to a school minstrel show, *The Melodious Menu*. An amateur effort at a complete musical came in 1902, when he wrote music for a Newark Yacht Club parody of *Uncle Tom's Cabin*. Kern's more formal musical studies took place at the New York College of Music, where he studied counterpoint with Austin Pierce, piano with Albert von Doenhoff, and possibly harmony and composition with Paolo Gallico and Alexander Lambert. Kern spoke of "some European training in a small town outside of Heidelberg," but the details and extent of this study have never been determined.

A family connection facilitated Kern's introduction to the music publisher Edward B. Marks, who offered Kern a clerk's position in his firm, Lyceum, which ultimately published Kern's first composition, a short piano work entitled "At the Casino" (1902). Like many would-be songwriters, Kern also worked as a song-plugger, demonstrating sheet music for Lyceum at Wanamaker's Department store. Greater opportunity lured Kern to the publishing firm of T.B. Harms, headed by Max Dreyfus, who had an ear for talent and later attracted the likes of George Gershwin, Cole Porter, and Richard Rodgers. Dreyfus saw that Kern's first songs were interpolated into musicals, mostly into British imports, including *An English Daisy* (1904) and *Mr. Wix of Wickham* (1904). Kern's work as a rehearsal pianist also placed him in an opportune position to plug his own songs and to provide new material as needed. By 1905 an inheritance, probably from his grandfather, allowed Kern to become a partner in T.B. Harms, which not only allowed him greater opportunity to place his songs in shows, but also provided a valuable apprenticeship to the business aspects of the trade.

As an envoy for Harms, in 1905, Kern made the first of several trips to London, where he tended to the firm's agreements with English publishers Francis, Day, and Hunter, and Ascherberg, Hopwood, and Crew. For Kern, who remained a lifelong Anglophile, these trips were formative professionally and personally. In London he made the acquaintance of Seymour Hicks and George Edwardes, both purveyors of a brand of British musical comedy associated with the Gaiety Theatre, and whom Kern credited as his early mentors in the musical comedy business. He also met his lifelong partner, Eva Leale, an Englishwoman, whom he married in 1910.

Between 1905 and 1915, Kern worked mainly as an interpolator, writing songs that were inserted into other composers' musical scores. He worked for three of the major theatrical producers of the day, the Shubert brothers, Charles Frohman, and Seymour Hicks. The Shuberts purchased performing rights to Kern's first hit "How'd You Like to Spoon with Me?" which appeared in the American production of the British musical comedy *The Earl and the Girl* (1905). Its success established Kern as a bankable commodity, and Frohman (with Hicks) contracted Kern to write 12 songs a year, mostly for New York productions of British musical comedy and German operetta. Before book-oriented musicals became the norm, it was common practice for producers to replace or augment the scores of principal composers with song interpolations. Thus it was Kern's job to replace weak numbers, to write for particular talents, and sometimes to Americanize these scores. Although his contributions often went uncredited, the experience was invaluable. Kern wrote music of varying styles for a variety of different theatrical genres—operetta, musical comedy, revue, and vaudeville—all of which he would employ in his full scores to great dramatic effect. By 1916 Kern had contributed over 100 songs to at least 62 productions.

In 1912 the Shuberts gave Kern his first professional opportunity to compose a full score, *The Red Petticoat*, whose novel setting took place in a Nevada mining camp. Although not a success, Kern's score showed many of the organizational and integrating techniques of his later work, particularly his juxtaposition of diverse musical idioms—melodrama, operetta, musical comedy, and vaudeville—to develop character, advance plot, and enhance narrative setting. It was also Kern's first handling of a subject rich in Americana, a theme he would return to in later works, including *Show Boat* (1927), *Sweet Adeline* (1929), and the western film musical *Can't Help Singing* (1944). For the time being, however, Kern's biggest successes came from interpolations, particularly those catering to the modern dancing craze. "You're Here and I'm Here" was a syncopated one-step that first appeared in *The Laughing Husband* (1914) and remained Kern's best-selling piece of sheet music into the 1920s. A second interpolation, "They Didn't Believe Me," was sung by Julia Sanderson and Donald Brian in *The Girl from Utah* (1914). A romantic show ballad in duple time, it set the lyrical melodies usually associated with the waltz to the 4/4 (later alla breve) pace of the foxtrot. Such foxtrot ballads eventually supplanted the waltz as the dominant musical symbol of theatrical romance. "They Didn't Believe in Me" was the earliest of Kern's songs to become a popular standard, and he followed its formula in later songs of melancholic optimism, including "Till the Clouds Roll By" (1917) and "Look for the Silver Lining" (1920).

In 1915 theatrical agent Elisabeth Marbury and theater manager F. Ray Comstock engaged Kern and British

Jerome Kern, piano, with Oscar Hammerstein II. (Rodgers & Hammerstein Organization/Lebrecht Music & Arts)

author Guy Bolton to write the first of a series of musical comedies for the small Princess Theatre. The shows were aimed toward a more cosmopolitan, smarter set (Dorothy Parker was a big fan), and relied less on spectacle and more on an intimate approach dictated in part by the venue (just 299 seats). The shows' contemporary, farcical plots were topical and more everyday, and, for the genre of musical comedy, they featured a closer integration of songs and plot. The size of the chorus was curtailed, and the orchestra was reduced, too, limited to the 11 or so musicians that could fit in the tiny pit. Kern's orchestrator, Frank Saddler, contributed to the successful sound of the shows; his transparent arrangements, with many novel effects, were exemplary. Although Kern's musical style still owed much to British musical comedy (as did Bolton's books), the syncopated trots and one-steps gave the scores a distinctly American sound, particularly in *Nobody Home* (1915) and *Very Good Eddie* (1915). P.G. Wodehouse, whose witty lyrics provided an ideal complement to Kern's rhythmic numbers, joined Bolton and Kern for *Oh, Boy!* (1917) and *Oh, Lady! Lady!* (1918). Together these collaborations established a new model for American musical comedy, which made an indelible impression on George Gershwin and Richard Rodgers, who both spoke of the shows' influence on their own work.

Kern's shows in the 1920s were often star vehicles whose books involved Cinderella stories of the showbiz variety. These were the specialty of mega-producers like Florenz Ziegfeld, for whom Kern wrote *Sally* (1920), featuring Marilyn Miller. The show's 570-performance

run made it one of the top successes of the 1920s, and it contained one of Kern's most enduring early standards, "Look for the Silver Lining." Kern wrote a follow-up for Miller in *Sunny* (1925), which also marked Kern's first work with author and lyricist Oscar Hammerstein II.

Kern's biggest artistic and commercial triumph came with *Show Boat* (1927), produced by Florenz Ziegfeld. It was Kern's idea to set Edna Ferber's novel as a musical, and he persuaded Hammerstein to write the book and lyrics. *Show Boat*'s treatment of important social issues—single motherhood, miscegenation, and race relations in the post–Civil War South—marked a significant broadening of the dramatic possibilities represented on the popular stage and thus established an important precedent for the musical plays of Rodgers and Hammerstein. The generational span of the narrative allowed Kern to draw upon a variety of historical and popular styles for his score, each bringing rich affective associations. Kern also interpolated period pieces by other composers to enhance the historic narrative and engender nostalgia. An unusual number of songs in *Show Boat* became popular standards, including "Ol' Man River," "Can't Help Lovin' Dat Man," "You are Love," "Bill," and "Make Believe." *Show Boat* was Kern's most frequently revived work and spawned three film versions.

In the 1930s, like other theatrical composers, Kern turned toward Hollywood for work in film. After the failure of the stage musical *Three Sisters* (1934), he spent increasing amounts of time in Los Angeles, and the city became his primary residence in 1937. Although he had written music for silent film in the teens, including instrumental selections for a serial called *Gloria's Romance*, starring Billie Burke, his first original film musical was *Men of the Sky* (1931), with lyricist Otto Harbach. Kern also continued to write for the stage, and with Harbach, conceived the innovative stage musical *The Cat and the Fiddle* (1931; film, 1934). Featuring a romance between a Romanian classical composer and a popular songwriter, the plot provided the diegetic opportunities for one of Kern's most musically adventurous scores, juxtaposing jazz and classical styles in kaleidoscopic fashion. Another Harbach collaboration, *Roberta* (1933; film, 1935), featured two perennial songs, "Smoke Gets in Your Eyes" and "Yesterdays." With lyricist Dorothy Fields, Kern wrote some of his most successful music for film, including *Swing Time* (1936), starring Ginger Rogers and Fred Astaire. Astaire sang "The Way You Look Tonight," which won an Academy Award for best song. Kern's last stage musical was *Very Warm for May* (1939). Although a flop, it contained one of Kern's most celebrated songs, "All the Things You Are."

Kern died in 1945, aged 60, of a cerebral hemorrhage. His health had been precarious since suffering a heart attack shortly after his move to Los Angeles. Unfinished projects included a revival of *Show Boat* and a musical on the life of Annie Oakley, which later became *Annie Get Your Gun*, with music by Irving Berlin. An MGM musical biography of Kern's life, *Till the Clouds Roll By*, was already in production and was released the following year. Like most biopics, it is more fiction than fact.

2. WORKS. Kern once called himself "a musical clothier," a descriptor that captures his approach to assembling scores. Rather than a wholly organic approach, Kern preferred to tailor the right song to the right occasion, freely recycling older tunes and melodic material to meet new theatrical contexts. One famous example is "Bill," which first appeared in *Oh, Lady! Lady!* (1918), with a lyric by P.G. Wodehouse, and was later revised by Hammerstein for use in *Show Boat*. Kern's music for overtures, act finales, and connecting material was typically culled from songs within the shows, with newly composed music used to bridge the gaps. Such practices afforded a simple structural unity, but were more importantly indicative of business aspects of the trade, wherein repetition assured that audience members would remember the tunes and subsequently purchase recordings and sheet music. Later in his career, particularly with *Show Boat*, Kern made greater and more sophisticated use of leitmotif-like devices, most notably in the *Cat and the Fiddle* and *Music in the Air* (1932). Kern enjoyed close collaborations with his two principal orchestrators, Frank Saddler and Robert Russell Bennett. While Kern provided detailed instructions for arrangement and orchestration, both orchestrators contributed their own innovations and added immeasurably to the sound of Kern's music on stage and film.

Kern's approach to song construction assured memorable melodies, the best of which rely on carefully crafted melodic sequences which delay resolution to tonic and trace strong dramatic arcs. Stephen Sondheim used the adjective "cigar-shaped" to describe these fastidiously constructed melodies, with a clear sense of development, peak, and resolution—a dramatic narrative in miniature that Kern once referred to as "musical plot." In form, Kern used the older ABAC chorus types more frequently than his younger contemporaries but also freely exploited the AABA form after it became the norm in the 1920s. Kern often varied phrases upon repetition, sometimes repeating phrases at a different interval, or varying harmony and accompaniment figures for dramatic effect. The building blocks of his craft, however, are best revealed in shorter melodic units within the eight-bar phrase, which illuminate tightly conceived substructures (see, for example, "They Didn't Believe Me"). Although Kern spoke of composing at the keyboard as a potential hindrance to innovation, he often auditioned his tunes melodically at the piano, making sure that the tunes made linear sense without harmonic support. Kern might use an unusual twist of intervals in the first measures of a chorus, but the way the melodic idea progressed—often sequentially, with a few punctuated surprises—could seem almost inevitable, as in "Smoke Gets in Your Eyes" and "All the Things You Are." Both songs also illustrate Kern's harmonic gifts, featuring the enharmonic modulations for which he was well-known. The expansive harmonic sequences of "All the Things You Are," modulating with each phrase, made it a favorite improvisatory vehicle for

bebop musicians, who used its novel chord changes for new compositions, including "Bird of Paradise" by Charlie Parker.

Kern collaborated with numerous fine lyricists, including P.G. Wodehouse, Oscar Hammerstein II, Otto Harbach, Ira Gershwin, Johnny Mercer, Dorothy Fields, and E.Y. Harburg. Early in his career, he occasionally wrote his own words. Kern preferred to write the music first, often to a dummy lyric, before the lyricist set the final text. The most famous exception is "The Last Time I Saw Paris," which Kern set to Hammerstein's already finished lyric. Although Kern's famous reluctance to change even minor rhythms to accommodate a lyric frustrated some wordsmiths, others enjoyed the challenge. In his maturity Kern preferred to exert creative control in all areas of collaboration and was often involved in the initial development of his musicals for stage and film. In adapting stories for musicals, Kern spoke early on of the necessity of "an atmosphere which lends itself to music." Kern followed this credo throughout his career, scoring many shows revolving around music and show business, including *Show Boat*, of course, but also *Nobody Home*, *Sweet Adeline*, *Sally*, *Sunny*, and *Swing Time*, among others. In the case of *The Cat and the Fiddle* and *Music in the Air*, the craft of composition itself was a central conceit.

A songwriter of Kern's abilities might have been less successful had his talent not been paired with an excellent business instinct. Kern's father, Henry, a successful businessman himself, probably first instilled this quality, but it was honed in Kern's partnership and responsibilities with T.B. Harms. In 1914, with Victor Herbert, Irving Berlin, and others, he was a founding member of the American Society of Composers, Authors and Publishers (ASCAP), which sought to protect musical copyrights. Kern's pecuniary sense was also reflected in his investments in rare books. Upon auction in 1929, his collection earned $1.75 million just in time to beat the Great Depression.

WORKS

COLLECTIONS
Jerome Kern: Collected Songs (Boca Raton, FL, 1992)
Jerome Kern Rediscovered (Miami, FL, 2000)

STAGE
(The following shows have full scores by Kern, or featured significant contributions. Authors and lyricists are in parentheses. Dates are New York premieres, unless otherwise stated.)
Mr. Wix of Wickham, principal comp. H. Darnley, 19 Sept 1904
The Earl and the Girl, principal comp. Ivan Caryll, 4 Nov 1905 [incl. How'd You Like to Spoon with Me (E. Laska)]
The Rich Mr. Hoggenheimer, principal comp. L. Englander, 22 Oct 1906
Fascinating Flora, principal comp. G. Kerker, 20 May 1907
The Dairymaids, principal comps. P. Rubens and F. Tours, 26 Aug 1907
Fluffy Ruffles, principal comp. W.T. Francis, 7 Sept 1908
The King of Cadonia, principal comp. S. Jones, 10 Jan 1910
La Belle Paree (E. Smith; E. Madden), collab. Tours, 20 March 1911
The Red Petticoat (R.J. Young; P. West), 13 Nov 1912
Oh, I Say! (S. Blow and D. Hoare, after H. Keroul and A. Barré; H.B. Smith), 30 Oct 1913
The Doll Girl, principal comp. Leo Fall, 25 Aug 1913

The Laughing Husband, principal comp. E. Eysler, 2 Feb 1914 [incl. You're Here and I'm Here (H. Smith)]

The Girl from Utah (J. Tanner/Rubens; A. Ross/P. Greenback), principal comps. Rubens and S. Jones, 24 Aug 1914 [incl. They Didn't Believe Me (H. Reynolds)]

Ninety in the Shade (G. Bolton), 25 Jan 1915

Nobody Home (Bolton, Rubens), 20 April 1915

Cousin Lucy (C. Klein; S. Green), 27 Aug 1915

Miss Information (P. Dickey, C.W. Goddard), 5 Oct 1915 [incl. Some Sort of Somebody (E. Janis)]

Very Good Eddie (P. Bartholomae, Bolton; Green), 23 Dec 1915 [incl. Babes in the Wood]

Ziegfeld Follies of 1916 (revue, various collaborators), 12 June 1916

Theodore and Co. (H. Harwood, G. Grossmith; A. Ross, C. Grey), principal comp. Ivor Novello, London, 19 Sept 1916.

Have a Heart (Bolton; P.G. Wodehouse), 11 Jan 1917

Love o' Mike (T. Sydney; H.B. Smith), 15 Jan 1917

Oh, Boy (Bolton, after G. Ade; Wodehouse), 20 Feb 1917

Miss 1917 (revue, Bolton; Wodehouse), collab. V. Herbert, 5 Nov 1917

Oh Lady! Lady!! (Bolton; Wodehouse), 1 Feb 1918

Toot-Toot! (E.A. Woolf, after R. Hughes; B. Braley), 11 March 1918

Rock-a-Bye Baby (Woolf, M. Mayo; H. Reynolds), 22 May 1918

Head over Heels (Woolf, after N. Bartley), 29 Aug 1918

She's a Good Fellow (A. Caldwell), 5 May 1919

Zip, Goes a Million (Bolton; B.G. DeSylva), Worcester, MA, 8 Dec 1919

The Night Boat (Caldwell, after A. Bisson), 2 Feb 1920 [incl. Whose Baby Are You?]

Hitchy Koo: 1920 (revue, G. MacDonough, Caldwell), 19 Oct 1920

Sally (Bolton; C. Grey), ballet music by Herbert, 21 Dec 1920 [incl. Look for the Silver Lining (B. DeSylva), Whip-poor-Will (DeSylva), Wild Rose, Sally]; film, 1929

Good Morning, Dearie (Caldwell), 1 Nov 1921 [incl. Kailua]

The Cabaret Girl (G. Grossmith, Wodehouse), London, 19 Sept 1922

The Bunch and Judy (Caldwell, H. Ford; Caldwell), 28 Nov 1922

The Beauty Prize (Grossmith, Wodehouse), London, 5 Sept 1923

Stepping Stones (Caldwell, R.H. Burnside; Caldwell) 6 Nov 1923

Sitting Pretty (Bolton; Wodehouse), 8 April 1924

Dear Sir (E. Selwyn; H. Dietz), 23 Sept 1924

Sunny (O. Harbach, O. Hammerstein II), 22 Sept 1925 [incl. Who?, D'ye Love Me?, Sunny, Two Little Birds]; films, 1930, 1941

The City Chap (J. Montgomery, after W. Smith; Caldwell), 26 Oct 1925

Criss Cross (Caldwell, Harbach), 12 Oct 1926

Lucky (Harbach, B. Kalmar), collab. H. Ruby, 22 March 1927

Show Boat (Hammerstein, after E. Ferber), 27 Dec 1927 [incl. Ol' Man River, Make Believe, Bill (Wodehouse, Hammerstein), Can't Help Lovin' Dat Man, Why Do I Love You?, You Are Love]; films, 1929, 1936 [incl. Ah Still Suits Me], 1951

Blue Eyes (Bolton, G. John), London, 27 April 1928

Sweet Adeline (musl romance, Hammerstein), 3 Sept 1929 [incl. Why Was I Born?, Don't Ever Leave Me]; film, 1934

The Cat and the Fiddle (Harbach), 15 Oct 1931 [incl. She Didn't Say Yes]; film, 1934

Music in the Air (Hammerstein), 8 Nov 1932 [incl. The Song is You, I've Told Ev'ry Little Star]; film, 1934

Roberta (Harbach, after A.D. Miller), 18 Nov 1933 [incl. Smoke Gets in Your Eyes]; films, 1935 [incl. I Won't Dance (Hammerstein, D. Fields), Lovely to Look At (Fields)], 1952

Three Sisters (Hammerstein), London, 9 April 1934

Gentlemen Unafraid (Hammerstein, Harbach, after E. Boykin), St. Louis, MO, 3 June 1938

Very Warm for May (Hammerstein), 17 Nov 1939 [incl. All the Things You Are]

OTHER WORKS

Film: Gloria's Romance, 1916; I Dream Too Much (D. Fields), 1935; Swing Time (Fields), 1936 [incl. The Way You Look Tonight, A Fine Romance, Pick Yourself Up]; High, Wide, and Handsome (Hammerstein), 1937 [incl. The Folks Who Live on the Hill, Can I Forget You?]; When You're in Love (Fields), 1937; Joy of Living (Fields), 1938 [incl. You Couldn't Be Cuter]; One Night in the Tropics (Fields), 1940; You Were Never Lovelier (J. Mercer), 1942 [incl. Dearly Beloved, I'm Old Fashioned, You Were Never Lovelier]; Cover Girl (I. Gershwin), 1944 [incl. Long Ago and Far Away]; Can't Help Singing (E.Y. Harburg), 1944 [incl. Can't Help Singing]; Centennial Summer (L. Robin, Hammerstein, Harburg), 1946 [incl. All Through the Day]

Inst: At the Casino, pf (New York, 1902); In a Shady Bungalow, pf (New York, 1902); Scenario, orch, 1941 [on themes from Show Boat]; Mark Twain Suite, orch, 1942

BIBLIOGRAPHY

"The Music of the Moment. How Leading Revue Composers Write Their Melodies," *Strand Magazine*, (Feb 1916), 54–60

L. Reid: "Composing While You Wait," *The Dramatic Mirror* (2 June 1917), 5

C.R.: "Three Makers of Popular Music," *Musical Courier*, lxxvi/8 (1918), 6–7

R. Simon: "Jerome Kern," *Modern Music*, vi/2 (Jan–Feb 1929), 20–25

K. List: "Jerome Kern and American Operetta," *Commentary*, iii (1947), 433–41

D. Ewen: *The Story of Jerome Kern* (New York, 1953)

P.G. Wodehouse and G. Bolton: *Bring on the Girls* (New York, 1953)

"The Story of Jerome Kern," *Music Journal*, xiii/1 (Jan 1955), 31–33

S. Sondheim: Liner notes, *The CBS Album of Jerome Kern: Paul Weston and His Orchestra* (Columbia C2L-2, 1957)

D. Ewen: *The World of Jerome Kern* (New York, 1960)

A. Wilder: *American Popular Song* (New York, 1972)

M. Wilk: *They're Playing Our Song* (New York, 1973/R1991)

H. Fordin: *Jerome Kern: the Man and his Music* (Santa Monica, CA, 1975)

M. Kreuger: *Show Boat: the Story of a Classic American Musical* (New York, 1977)

M. Freedland: *Jerome Kern: a Biography* (London, 1978)

R. Olin: "A History and Interpretation of the Princess Theatre Musical Plays: 1915–1919" (diss, New York U., 1979)

G. Bordman: *Jerome Kern: his Life and Music* (New York, 1980)

A. Lamb: *Jerome Kern in Edwardian London* (Littlehampton, UK, 1981, 2/1985)

M. Babbitt: "All the Things They Are," *I.S.A.M. Newsletter*, xiv/2 (May 1985), 8–9

G. Bordman: "Jerome David Kern, Innovator/Traditionalist," *MQ* lxxi/4 (1985), 468–73

G. Mast: *Can't Help Singin': the American Musical on Stage and Screen* (Woodstock, NY, 1987)

S. Suskin: *Berlin, Kern, Rodgers, Hart, and Hammerstein: a Complete Song Catalogue* (Jefferson, NC, 1990)

J. Swain: *The Broadway Musical: a Critical and Musical Survey* (New York, 1990)

L. Davis: *Bolton and Wodehouse and Kern: the Men who Made Musical Comedy* (New York, 1993)

P. Martin: "Development and Interpretation of the Elements of Integration in the Princess Theatre Musicals" (diss., U. of Utah, 1993)

R. Breon: "*Show Boat*: The Revival, the Racism," *Drama Review*, xxxix/2 (1995), 86–105

A. Forte: *The American Popular Ballad of the Golden Era* (Princeton, NJ, 1995)

G. Block: *Enchanted Evenings: the Broadway Musical from Show Boat to Sondheim* (New York, 1997)

G. Ferencz, ed.: *"The Broadway Sound": the Autobiography and Selected Essays of Robert Russell Bennett* (Rochester, NY, 1999)

J. Randall: "Becoming Jerome Kern: the Early Songs and Shows" (diss., U. of Illinois, Urbana-Champaign, 2004)

S. Banfield: "Scholarship and the Musical: Reclaiming Jerome Kern," *Proceedings of the British Academy*, cxxv (2005), 183–210

S. Banfield: *Jerome Kern* (New Haven, CT, 2006)

T. Decker. "Black/white Encounters on the American Musical Stage and Screen (1924–2005)" (diss., U. of Michigan, 2007)

K. Axtell. "Maiden Voyage: the Genesis and Reception of *Show Boat*, 1926–1932" (diss., Eastman School of Music, 2009)

L. Botkin. "Jerome Kern's Musical Style from 'Oh, Boy!' (1917) to 'Show Boat' (1927): an Analysis of Musical and Integrative Techniques" (diss., U. of Colorado, Boulder, 2010)

JAMES RANDALL

Kerner, Leighton (*b* Somerville, MA, 11 Jan 1927; *d* New York, NY, 29 April 2006). Music critic. Kerner studied chemical engineering at Tufts University (1949) and earned a master's in journalism at Boston College (1951). At the outset of his career, he served as a free-lance theater critic, but increasingly turned to music. Kerner's reviews brought serious consideration for classical music to *The Village Voice*, for which he served as a staff writer from 1961–98 and contributed articles from 1957 to his death. He also wrote for *Opera News*, *Musical America*, and *Travel & Leisure*. Though a classical music critic by trade, Kerner was known for his voracious enthusiasm for New York's diverse music scene, which he shared in his criticism through encyclopedic references to past concerts. This vigor infected his energetically optimistic writing style, in which he maintained a witty tone unencumbered by condescension. Kerner's belief in the vital future of classical music performance and composition in America stood out in late 20th-century musical discourse. In recognition of his contribution to American musical writing and culture, he received two ASCAP Deems Taylor Awards and a Letter of Distinction from the American Music Center.

ANDREA F. BOHLMAN

Kernis, Aaron Jay (*b* Philadelphia, PA, 15 Jan 1960). Composer. He studied at the San Francisco Conservatory, the Manhattan School (BM 1981), and Yale University. His composition teachers included JOHN ADAMS, JACOB DRUCKMAN, MORTON SUBOTNICK, and CHARLES WUORINEN. He received national recognition when his first orchestral work, *dream of the morning sky* (1982–3), was given its premiere by the New York PO in 1983. Kernis has served as composer-in-residence for the St. Paul Chamber Orchestra, Minnesota Public Radio, and American Composers Forum (1993–1996); for the Minnesota Orchestra he was new music advisor (1998–2009) and is founder-director of their annual Composer Institute. He won the Pulitzer Prize in 1998 for his second string quartet and the Grawemeyer Award in 2002 for the cello version of *Colored Field*. In 2011 Kernis was elected to the American Academy of Arts and Letters. He has taught composition at Yale since 2003.

Kernis's eclectic musical language draws upon and juxtaposes a variety of styles, including American popular and vernacular music; however, his *oeuvre*, which preserves melody and lyricism as key compositional elements, remains rooted in the classical tradition. He incorporates historical structural forms into pieces exploring the musical past: a passacaglia governs *musica celestis*, which recalls Hildegard's soaring melodies; String Quartet no.2, inspired by the Fitzwilliam Virginal Book and J.S. Bach's keyboard suites, sets Renaissance and Baroque dance forms including sarabande and gigue; *Concerto in Echoes* uses the contrapuntal spirit and orchestration of Brandenburg Concerto no.6 as catalyst.Kernis's works often exude an exhilaration spiced with wry musical humor or evoke profound emotion by pitting moments of consonance and beauty against passages of drama and darkness. Poetic and visual imagery abound in his compositions; bright, bell-like timbres, ascending melodic lines, and high registers are frequently employed.

Kernis's oeuvre can be divided into three main style periods. His early "process" works draw upon rigorous precompositional structures. *Morningsongs* (1982–3), for example, employs a limited number of pitches at any given time; groups of tones change to delineate formal sections. After 1983 Kernis embraced a more intuitive approach, formulating only the large-scale structure of a work before composing. The form of *Love Scenes* (1986–7) mirrors the decline of a relationship; increasingly angular, dissonant music is sporadically interrupted by fragmented lyrical motives. The colors and complex patterns of Ravenna's Byzantine mosaics are reflected in the rapidly unfolding musical material of his *Invisible Mosaic* triptych (1986–8); sonic fragments coalesce into coherent patterns, in a musical analogy of the mosaics' gradual disclosure of underlying shape and line. From 1988 Kernis sought greater continuity, simplicity, and emotional directness. He began to embrace traditional forms such as the symphony and string quartet, albeit in untraditional ways. Unity is projected in the *Symphony in Waves* (1989) through the abstract depiction of wave motion in melodic, dynamic, textural, and timbral domains. The cycle of works consisting of the Second Symphony (1991), *Still Movement with Hymn* (1993), *Colored Field* (1994), and *Lament and Prayer* (1996) reflects the horror of war and suffering as well as the composer's sensitivity to loss and other political and social issues. *Le quattro stagioni dalla cucina futurismo* (1991), a manifesto on food preparation, *New Era Dance* (1992), an evocation of contemporary urban life, and *Goblin Market* (1995), an erotic theatrical setting of Rossetti's Victorian tale, display Kernis's extravagant imagination.

Kernis's most recent compositions reveal a consolidation and mastery of musical materials, with expression achieved through economical means. Throughout his career Kernis has explored philosophical questions with an instinctive understanding remarkable for his youth. In the mid-2000s, however, major events in his personal life—fatherhood and the death of his parents—allowed him to address life's meaning now from the perspective of a lived experience, not merely an intellectual concept. Among Kernis's works in this area: *Newly Drawn Sky* (2005) (on children, color in the natural world, constancy of change), *Two Awakenings and a Double Lullaby* (2006) (meaning of existence, children's discovery of the world), and *Symphony of Meditations* (2009), an introspective memorial tribute to his parents (religious faith, the passing of time, interconnectedness of death and life).

WORKS
(selective list)
STAGE

Goblin Market (C. Rossetti), nar, pic + fl + a fl, ob + eng hn, cl + E♭ cl + b cl, bn, hn, tpt, pf + synth, perc, str, 1995

VOCAL

Choral: Stein Times Seven (G. Stein), SSATB, pf, 1980; How God Answers the Soul (Mechthild of Magdeburg), SSAATTBB, 1996; Ecstatic Meditations, chorus, 1998; Dorma, Ador, Mez, SATB, opt. handbells,

2000; The Wheel of Time, the Dance, SATB, 2003; Two Meditations, SATB, org, 2006

Solo: 6 Fragments of Gertrude Stein, S, pic + fl + a fl, 1979; dream of the morning sky (Cycle V, Part I) (N.S. Momaday), S, orch, 1982–3; Nocturne (Bible: *Song of Songs*), S, tpt, 2 glock, 2 pf, 1982; Morningsongs (J. Anderson), Bar, pic + fl + a fl, 2 cl + b cl, bn, hn, perc, hp, vn, va, vc, 1982–3; America(n) (Day)dreams (M. Swenson), Mez, pic + fl, cl + b cl, hn, tpt, perc, hp, str, 1984; Love Scenes (A. Swir, trans. M.L. Nathan), S, vc, 1986–7; Songs of Innocents I (anon. Sanskrit text, trans. W.S. Merwin, R.L. Stevenson, M. Swenson, W. Ramal), S, pf, 1989; Brilliant Sky, Infinite Sky (J. Joubert, trans. D. Levertov, G. du Maurier, J. Ash, C. Milosz), Bar, vn, perc, pf, 1990; Le quattro stagioni dalla cucina futurismo (F.T. Marinetti), nar, vn, vc, pf, 1991; Simple Songs (Hildegard of Bingen, Pss, Rumi, Ryokan), S/T, chbr orch, 1991; Songs of Innocents II (C.H. Ross, J. Keats, Swenson, anon.), S, pf, 1991; Garden of Light (misc. Eng texts), Boy S, Mez., T, Bar, SATB, children's chorus, orch., 1999; Valentines, S, orch, 2000; Two Awakenings and a Double Lullaby (T. Traherne, C. Duffy, trad.), S, vn, opt. gui, pf, 2006; da L'Arte Della Danssar (from The Art of the Dance), 15th c. Ital. texts, trans. A. William Smith and A.S. Kline, S, fl + pic, va, hp, perc, 2011

INSTRUMENTAL

Orch: Invisible Mosaic III, 1986–8; Sym. in Waves, 1989; Musica celestis, str, 1990 [arr. 2nd movt of Str Qt]; Sym. no.2, 1991; New Era Dance, 1992; Colored Field, conc., eng hn, orch, 1994, arr. vc, orch, 2000; Air, vn, orch, 1995, arr. vc, orch, 2000; Lament and Prayer, vn, orch, 1996; Too Hot Toccata, 1996; Double Conc., vn, gui, orch, 1997; Concierto de "Dance Hits," gui, str, 1999; Ov. in Feet and Meters, 2000; Color Wheel, 2001; Toy Piano Conc., pf + amp toy pf, orch, 2002; Sarabanda in Memoriam, str orch, 2004; Newly Drawn Sky, 2005; Symphony of Meditations (Symphony no.3), Hebrew text S.I. Gabirol, trans. P. Cole, S, B-Bar, SATB, orch, 2009; Concerto with Echoes, chbr orch (no vn), 2009; a Voice, a Messenger, tpt, orch (or wind ens), 2009

Chbr and solo inst: Music for Trio (Cycle IV), pic + fl + a fl, vc, pf, 1982; Invisible Mosaic I, cl, vn, vc, pf, 1987; Phantom Polka, accdn, 1987; Invisible Mosaic II, pic + fl, ob, cl + b cl, bn, hn, tpt, trbn, tuba, 2 perc, hp, pf + cel, str qt, db, 1988; Before Sleep and Dreams, pf, 1990; Str Qt "Musica celestis," 1990; Mozart en Route "A Little Traveling Music," vn, va, vc, 1991; Superstar Etude no.1, pf, 1992; 100 Greatest Dance Hits, gui, str qt, 1993; Still Movement with Hymn, vn, va, vc, pf, 1993; Air, vn, pf, 1995; Str Qt no.2, 1997; Trio in Red, cl, vc, pf, 2001; Ballad, vc, 7 recorded vc, 2004; Playing Monster, pf, 2006; Two Movements (with Bells), vn, pf, 2007; Ballad(e) out of the Blues— Superstar Etude no.3, pf, 2008

Recorded interviews in *NHoh*

Principal publishers: AJK Music, Associated

BIBLIOGRAPHY

K.R. Schwarz: "A Young Musician and his Dilemma," *New York Times* (27 June 1993)

J. Adams: "An Interview with Aaron Kernis," *Conjunctions*, xix (1994), 174–90

M. Gustavson: "Conversation in New York," *Contemporary Music Review*, x (1994), 121–32

M. Swed: *Aaron Jay Kernis* (New York, 1995) [Associated catalog]

J. Kosman: "String Players' Choice," *Strings*, xiv (1999), 32–7

MARY LOU HUMPHREY

Kerns, Robert (*b* Detroit, MI, 8 June 1933; *d* Vienna, Austria, 15 Feb 1989). Baritone. He studied at the University of Michigan and made his debut in 1955 at Toledo, Ohio, as Sharpless. After a year with the New York City Opera, in 1960 he was engaged at Zürich. From 1963 he sang in Vienna and in 1964 made his Covent Garden debut as Billy Budd. He sang at the Spoleto, Aix-en-Provence, and Salzburg festivals, at the Paris Opéra, San Francisco, and the Deutsche Oper, Berlin, where from 1973 he was a permanent guest. His earlier repertory included Mozart's Count Almaviva, Don Giovanni, Papageno, and Guglielmo, as well as Rossini's Figaro and Donizetti's

Belcore. Later he took on heavier roles, Verdi's Germont, Posa, Guy de Montfort, Ford, and Falstaff, and also Yevgeny Onegin, Scarpia, and Marcello. His Wagner roles included Donner, Amfortas, and Wolfram. A stylish singer with a firmly placed though not very large voice, he excelled in parts such as the Barber in Strauss's *Die schweigsame Frau* where acting ability is paramount.

ELIZABETH FORBES

Kerr, Harrison (*b* Cleveland, OH, 13 Oct 1897; *d* Norman, OK, 15 Aug 1978). Composer and educator. His principal studies were with JAMES H. ROGERS in Cleveland and with NADIA BOULANGER in Paris (1921). He returned to the United States in 1921 to begin a long career as a teacher and administrator: first in Cleveland, then briefly at Greenbrier College, West Virginia, and subsequently at the Chase School, Brooklyn, where he remained from 1928 until after World War II. It was there that he became active in several interrelated organizations, among them the ACA and the AMC. He served as executive secretary for both of these as well as serving on the editorial boards of the New Music Edition and New Music Quarterly Recordings. During the immediate postwar years he spent much time abroad as chief of the Music, Art, and Exhibits Section of the Army Civil Affairs Division; he was then also a member of the music panel for UNESCO. From 1949 until his retirement in 1968 he was professor of music and composer-in-residence at the University of Oklahoma; he was also dean of the university's College of Fine Arts until 1959. Despite these many activities he composed a wide variety of scores, chiefly during the periods 1935–40 and after 1950. His most extensive work is an opera, *The Tower of Kel* (1958–60), from which he extracted material for several smaller compositions. In general, Kerr's musical language combines linear chromaticism, vertical dissonances built largely from triads and perfect intervals, and strong rhythms with a feeling for classical form and gesture.

WORKS

Stage: Dance Sonata (ballet), 2 pf, perc, 1938, Bennington, 1938; The Tower of Kel (op, 4, Kerr), 1958–60

Orch: 3 syms., 1927–9, rev. 1938, 1943–5, 1953–4; Movt, str orch, 1936; Dance Suite, 1939–40; Vn Conc., 1950–51, rev. 1956; Variations on a Ground Bass, 1966; Sinfonietta, 1967–8; Episodes from The Tower of Kel, 1971–2

Vocal: 3 Songs (E. St.Vincent Millay), 1v, pf/chbr orch, 1924–8; 6 Songs (A. Crapsey), 1924–8; Notations on a Sensitized Plate (C. Ross), high/medium v, cl, pf, str qt, 1935; Wink of Eternity (H. Crane), chorus, orch, 1937; In Cabin'd Ships at Sea (W. Whitman), chorus, orch, 1971; The Friar's Sermon (Kerr), Bar, pf, 1973 [arr. from The Tower of Kel]; 2 other song cycles, 5 songs, 1919–52

Chbr and solo inst: Poem, pf, 1929; Sonata no.1, pf, 1929; Str qt no.1, 1935; Trio, cl, vc, pf, 1936; Str Qt no.2, 1937; Study, vc, 1937; Pf Trio, 1938; Suite, fl, pf, 1940–1; Ov., Arioso and Finale, vc, pf, 1941–51, arr. vc, orch, 1966–7; 4 Preludes, pf, 1943; Sonata no.2, pf, 1943; Sonata, vn solo, 1954; Frontier Day, pf, 1956; Sonata, vn, pf, 1956; Variations on a Theme from the Tower of Kel, gui, 1971; other pf works

MSS in *NYamc*

Principal publishers: Berben, Boosey & Hawkes, Marks, Presser

BIBLIOGRAPHY

G. Chase: *America's Music* (New York, 1955, 3/1987)

A. Ringer: "Harrison Kerr: Composer and Educator," *ACAB*, viii/2 (1959), 10–6

R. Mead: *Henry Cowell's New Music 1925–1936* (diss., CUNY, 1981)

R.B. Kohlenberg: *Harrison Kerr: Portrait of a Twentieth-Century American Composer* (Metuchen, NJ, 1997)

STEVEN E. GILBERT

Kersands, Billy [William] (*b* Baton Rouge, LA, ?1842; *d* Artesia, NM, 30 June 1915). Comedian, singer, and dancer. He began performing with the minstrel troupes managed by Charles Hicks in the early 1860s, soon winning a reputation as a comic song-and-dance man. After a European tour in 1870, he played with most of the major black minstrel troupes in America, and in 1885 he formed his own company, which became well known for its marching band. He was the most popular and the best paid African American comedian of his day, renowned for his comic routines involving his large mouth, which he could contort in odd ways or stretch to accommodate a variety of unlikely objects. He was also proficient at dancing, singing, acrobatics, and drumming. As a dancer, his specialty was the Virginia essence, a flat-footed, smoothly gliding dance style that accommodated his comic antics. Among his signature songs, "Old Aunt Jemima" (1875), his own composition, presented a stereotypical image of the black mammy but also incorporated elements of African American folklore that audiences, both black and white, found appealing. Another specialty song, James E. Stewart's "Mary's Gone with a Coon" (*c*1880), reinforced the stereotype of the dim-witted black man, which was his comic stage persona. In more than 50 years of performing, Kersands never made the transition to the vaudeville circuit, preferring the tradition of blackface Minstrelsy he knew best.

BIBLIOGRAPHY

R.C. Toll: *Blacking Up: the Minstrel Show in Nineteenth-Century America* (New York 1974)

B.L. Peterson Jr: *Profiles of African American Stage Performers and Theater People, 1816–1960* (Westport, CT, 2001)

CLAUDE CONYERS

Kershaw, Doug(las James) (*b* Tiel Ridge, LA, 24 Jan 1936). Cajun and country fiddler, singer, and songwriter. Raised in a musical family in the Cajun culture of Louisiana, Kershaw began playing the fiddle at age five, learning from a variety of local and itinerant fiddlers. His family moved to Lake Arthur, Louisiana, when he was seven, and he began working as a shoeshine boy and entertaining customers with his fiddling. In 1953 he formed the Continental Playboys with his younger brothers Rusty (Russell Lee) and Pee Wee (Nelson); the string band performed in bars around Lake Arthur and on KPLC-TV (Lake Charles, LA). In 1955 Rusty and Doug recorded as a duo for Feature Records and soon moved to Hickory Records in Nashville. That year, they joined KWKH's *Louisiana Hayride* and appeared on WWVA's *World's Original Jamboree*, and, in 1958, they became members of the *Grand Ole Opry*. After army service, Rusty and Doug Kershaw had their biggest hit with "Louisiana Man" (Hickory, 1961), the song that became Doug Kershaw's theme song and, during the *Apollo 12* mission in November 1969, was the first song

to be broadcast from space. A series of releases on Hickory, Mercury, RCA Victor, and Princess followed, but the duo disbanded in 1964. Doug Kershaw subsequently achieved considerable prominence as a solo artist with an uninhibited, gymnastic fiddling style that channeled Cajun, bluegrass, and old-time influences, most notably in his albums *The Cajun Way* (Warner Bros., 1969) and *Spanish Moss* (Warner Bros., 1970). In 1969 he began appearing on ABC-TV's *The Johnny Cash Show*, and, in the mid-1970s, he was a fixture in the progressive country music scene that flourished around Austin, Texas. Inducted into the Louisiana Music Hall of Fame in 2009, Kershaw continues to perform throughout Louisiana and Texas.

RONNIE PUGH/TRAVIS D. STIMELING

Kessel, Barney (*b* Muskogee, OK, 17 Oct 1923; *d* San Diego, CA, 6 May 2004). Jazz guitarist. He played with Chico Marx (1943) and performed in the short film *Jammin' the Blues* (1944) before attracting attention in several big bands, including Artie Shaw's (1945). Later he became a freelance studio guitarist in Los Angeles, although he interrupted this work for a lengthy tour with Oscar Peterson's trio (1952–3), various recordings for the Verve and Contemporary labels, and club engagements with his own combos (early 1960s). In 1969, following a successful European tour, he shifted his focus away from studio work. From the early 1970s until he suffered a stroke in 1992 he performed in clubs and concerts, often with the jazz guitarists Charlie Byrd and Herb Ellis in the group Great Guitars. He also led workshops, made jazz recordings, and toured internationally. Although Kessel possessed the smooth tone and immaculate technique required of a studio musician, he improvised swinging, infectious jazz melodies. He published instruction manuals, including *The Guitar: a Tutor* (1967, 4/1975).

BIBLIOGRAPHY

G. Lees: "Barney Kessel: Why he Went Back on the Road," *DB*, xxviii/1 (1961), 21

H. Siders: "Kessel '66," *DB*, xxxiii/14 (1966), 28

M. Joyce and J. DeMuth: "Barney Kessel: Interview," *Cadence*, iii/11–12 (1978), 10

"Barney Kessel," *Swing Journal*, xxxvi/7 (1982), 240 [discography]

E. Benson, ed.: *Barney Kessel* (Atlanta, 1997) [incl. discography]

M.J. Summerfield: *Barney Kessel: a Jazz legend* (Newcastle upon Tyne, 2008)

BARRY KERNFELD/R

Kessner, Daniel (*b* Los Angeles, CA, 3 June 1946). Composer, conductor, flutist, and lecturer. Kessner studied composition with HENRI LAZAROF at UCLA where he earned a PhD with Distinction in 1971. He taught music composition and theory at California State University, Northridge, from 1970 to 2006. Kessner has composed more than 100 works: orchestral (14), choir and stage (9), symphonic band (8), and various chamber music settings (80). His music is performed worldwide and has been recorded commercially. His compositional style evolved into centric harmony with explorations in microtonality and free rhythmic associations. While at California State University, he founded and directed

The Discovery Players, a contemporary music performance group. He has served as guest conductor for several regional orchestras in the United States and for the Black Sea Philharmonic of Constanta, Romania. With his wife and pianist Dolly Eugenio Kessner, he created the Duo Kessner, which primarily performs contemporary flute literature. Since 1983 he has been a regular contributor to the Los Angeles Philharmonic's preconcert lecture series "Upbeat Live." Since 2010 he has been conducting and performing with the ensemble TEMPO (The Epicenter Music Performance Organization). He currently serves as president of the NACUSA (National Association of Composers USA), based in Los Angeles.

DANILO MEZZADRI

Keyed bugle [key bugle, Kent bugle, Royal Kent bugle, Kent horn]. A conical military bugle with tone-holes controlled by keys similar to those found on woodwind instruments. The instrument was the first fully chromatic soprano brass voice in bands in Europe and the United States. The first keyed bugles had five keys; seven keys made the instrument fully chromatic. Extra keys on later instruments increased alternate fingerings and extended the low range. American keyed bugles were commonly pitched in C, with a crook to B♭, and provided the alto and soprano voices in brass bands, with the bandleader often playing a high E♭ model. Elaborate keyed bugles with up to 12 keys were presented to outstanding bandmasters and soloists. Keyed bugles were normally made of copper with brass or German silver keys and fittings, but some were made of solid silver, gold, and tortoise-shell.

George Astor of London announced a bugle horn with finger holes and keys in 1800, but an Irish bandmaster, Joseph Haliday, patented the instrument in 1810. Haliday signed over manufacturing rights to Smolett Holden of Dublin. Holden approached the Duke of Kent about naming the new instrument after him and subcontracted production to Matthew Pace of Dublin. In 1813 John Bernhard Logier dedicated the first method book for the keyed bugle to the Duke of Kent and began, with an array of makers, to sell instruments, labeled "Royal Kent Bugle." By the occupation of Paris in 1815, the instrument was popular in military bands and theater orchestras and was soon copied or modified by firms in France and Saxony.

In 1817 Richard Willis, who had emigrated from Ireland to New York the year before, became the first director of the US Military Academy band at West Point and popularized the keyed bugle as a solo instrument. FRANK JOHNSON, an African American bandleader and composer, pioneered the use of the high E♭ bugle as a solo instrument with his own band in Philadelphia. Bands featuring keyed bugles played for dances, concerts, circuses, summer resorts, and political events from the 1830s to 1860s. New England was a center, but keyed bugles were played as far west as Minnesota and as far south as New Orleans. EDWARD KENDALL, founder of the Boston Brass Band, was the leading keyed bugle virtuoso for three decades. His death in 1861 marked the end of the keyed bugle era in the United States, though other players continued as bandmasters and soloists into the 1870s.

American keyed bugles developed from English models. NATHAN ADAMS (Lowell, Massachusetts, c1825) made the earliest American instrument. Makers who may have also imported keyed bugles include Klemm & Brother(s) of Philadelphia and Firth, Hall, & Pond of New York, while Henry Sibley (Boston) made keyed bugles comparable to the best imports. In 1845 George W. Shaw (Thompson, CT) patented a tortoise-shell keyed bugle. Notable makers include E.G. WRIGHT (Boston), known for his fine E♭ presentation keyed bugles; THOMAS D. PAINE (Woonsocket, Rhode Island), who produced keyed bugles in the style of Wright; and J. Lathrop Allen (Boston), associated with Wright. James Keat left England in the mid-1830s to partner with Graves & Co. (Winchester, New Hampshire, and Boston) and set a high standard for brass instrument construction in the United States. Samuel W. Richardson worked with Graves from 1832 to 1845 and established his firm in Rochester in 1847. Beginning in the late 20th century, Los Angeles maker Robb Stewart has made keyed bugle reproductions based on originals of Graves and Wright.

American keyed-bugle repertoire is found in manuscript and published band music. The bulk of the repertoire consists of quicksteps, waltzes, themes and variations, and arrangements of popular operatic airs; keyed-bugle obbligatos to vocal selections were popular. Encore pieces like Joseph Holloway's *Wood Up Quick Step* (1835) were American contributions to the instrument's literature. Anthony Philip Heinrich's *Concerto for Kent Bugle or Klappenflügel* (1834) is the largest American work for the keyed bugle, but was not performed until 1987, when Ralph Dudgeon and the Sudetendeutsche Orchestra (Regensburg, Germany) gave its world premiere.

A keyed bugle revival began in the 1970s. The Chestnut Brass Company, featuring Bruce Barrie on keyed bugle, recorded the music of Frank Johnson and other 19th-century American composers. Henry Meredith appeared as a keyed bugle soloist with the Yankee Brass Band (NH) and the Detroit-based Dodworth's Saxhorn Reserve Band. Stephen K. Charpié performed the music of F. Johnson with the late Joe Utley. Kenneth Hufford was a regular keyed bugle soloist with the Yankee Brass Band. Jeff Stockham is the leader and keyed bugle soloist for the Excelsior Cornet Band (NY), and Bruno J. Pino, Jr., uses keyed brasses in his reenactment ensemble, The Indiana Brass Band (PA). A new concerto for the keyed bugle and orchestra was written by the English composer Simon Proctor in 1991 and saw its first performance by Ralph Dudgeon and the Richmond (Virginia) Philharmonic in 1994. Dudgeon appears as a keyed bugle soloist and with orchestras and bands in the United States, Europe, and China.

BIBLIOGRAPHY

GMO

J.B. Logier: *Introduction to the Art of Playing on the Royal Kent Bugle* (Dublin, 1813, 2/1823)

J. Hyde: *A New and Complete Preceptor for the Royal Kent or Keyed Bugle* (London, c1818)

E. Goodale: *The Instrumental Director* (Hallowell, ME, 3/1829) [only this edition has keyed bugle instructions, which are taken from Logier]

H. Prentiss: *Complete Preceptor, for the Cornopean, Bugle Horn, and Key'd Bugle…* (Boston, c1840/R1980)

B.A. Burditt: *The Complete Preceptor for the Bugle* (Boston, c1850)

A. Dodworth: *Dodworth's Brass Band School* (New York, 1853)

R.E. Eliason: *Keyed Bugles in the United States* (Washington, DC, 1972)

R.T. Dudgeon: "Joseph Haliday, Inventor of the Keyed Bugle," *JAMIS*, ix (1983), 53–67

R.T. Dudgeon: "Ned Kendall, American Virtuoso," *International Trumpet Guild Journal*, viii/1 (1983), 16

R.T. Dudgeon: *The Keyed Bugle* (Metuchen, NJ, 1993, 2/2004)

D. Lasocki: "New Light on the Early History of the Keyed Bugle, Part 1: The Astor Advertisement and Collins V. Green," *Historic Brass Society Journal*, xxi (2009), 11–50; "Part II: More on England and Ireland; The United States," *Historic Brass Society Journal*, xxii (2010), 19–54

RALPH T. DUDGEON

Keys [Cook], **Alicia (Augello)** (*b* New York, NY, 25 Jan 1981). Singer, songwriter, and pianist. She began piano studies at age seven and has been a songwriter since her teenage years, when she attended the Professional Performing Arts School in Manhattan. Discovered by an agent at 14, her rise to fame was meteoric. She adopted the stage name Alicia Keys and eventually found an artistic match with Clive Davis's J Records in 2000, working with producer Kerry "Krucial" Brothers. Here Keys found a team dedicated to cultivating her individual sound, a fusion of hip-hop, rhythm-and-blues, soul, and jazz.

Keys' sound is essential to her success, and her individuality as a songstress and writer has proven an advantage, placing her in the ranks of female musical artists such as Beyoncé Knowles and Missy Elliott, with whom she toured in 2004. *Songs in A Minor* (2001) earned her five Grammy awards in 2002. The album's lead single, "Fallin" (2001), topped the *Billboard* Hot 100 chart for six weeks, and demonstrated her leanings toward the acoustic piano, introspective lyrics, and the combination of gospel blues and smooth contemporary R&B. Her following albums, *The Diary of Alicia Keys* (2003), *Unplugged* (live album, 2005), *As I Am* (2007), and *The Element of Freedom* (2009), also achieved success, with *Diary* earning her four more Grammys. She has received a total of 14 Grammy awards to date, and has been presented with many other high-profile honors, including an array of awards from BET, *Billboard*, and MTV.

In addition to her work as a musical artist, Keys has found success as a writer, with the *New York Times* bestseller *Tears for Water: Songbook of Poems & Lyrics* (2004). She is also well-known as an actress, appearing in such movies as *The Nanny Diaries* (2007) and *The Secret Life of Bees* (2008). She directed a segment of the television film *Five* (2011), and her philanthropic efforts include work with "Keep a Child Alive (KCA)" and other humanitarian charities involving HIV/AIDS support and youth development.

BIBLIOGRAPHY

G. Horn: *Alicia Keys* (Milwaukee, WI, 2006)

JESSICA L. GETMAN

Keys, Will (Allison) (*b* Washington County, TN, 4 Oct 1923; *d* Gray, TN, 4 Nov 2005.) Old-time banjo player. Keys was born in rural Washington County in northeast Tennessee. When he was eight years old, he began to play an old banjo his brother, Jay, had strung up with wire pulled from a screen door. Keys attended high school in Sulphur Springs and joined the US Marines in 1941. After the war, he returned home to East Tennessee. In 1950 he married Lola Hobbs and settled down in Gray, Tennessee, home of old time fiddler Charlie Bowman. During the 42 years he worked for the Tennessee Eastman chemical company in Kingsport, Tennessee, Keys kept playing his banjo after coming home from work.

Keys experimented with three-finger bluegrass banjo for a while but switched back to the East Tennessee two-finger up-picking style when he decided to enter the old time banjo division of the Old Time Fiddlers Contest in Galax, Virginia. His reputation spread as he traveled to festivals and fiddle contests across the Southeast. In 1978 he won first place in the old-time banjo division at Galax. Keys retired in 1984 and began playing music as a full-time hobby. He appeared at the Festival of Fiddle Tunes in Port Townsend, Washington, performed at two Smithsonian Folklife Festivals, and also traveled with The National Council for The Traditional Arts' Masters of The Banjo tour in 1994. In 1996 Keys was awarded a National Heritage Fellowship from the National Endowment for the Arts.

RICHARD BLAUSTEIN

Khan, Ali Akbar (*b* Shivpur, East Bengal [now Bangladesh], 14 April 1922; *d* San Anselmo, CA, 18 June 2009). Indian *sarod* player. The global expansion of the classical music of North India in the late 20th century is associated with two pioneering artists: the *sarod* player Ali Akbar Khan and his brother-in-law, the *sitār* player Ravi Shankar. While neither was the first Indian artist to tour the West, their touring and teaching was of premier importance in popularizing Hindustani classical music among Western musicians.

Ali Akbar Khan is the son of Allauddin Khan, the early 20th-century master of many instruments, who was widely respected for his fusion of many separate regional styles into a modern concert style that influenced many instrumentalists and established instrumental music on a par with long-respected vocal traditions. Allauddin Khan taught this style to several musicians including his son Ali Akbar, Ravi Shankar, the flautist Pannalal Ghosh, and the *sitār* player Nikhil Banerjee.

When Ali Akbar was born, his father was court musician to the Maharaja of Madhya Pradesh. The family home, the Madina Bhavan, was an ashram for music. Ali Akbar was taught the traditional literature of *rāga* and *tāla* in Hindustani style and was expected to practice for several hours every day. During his teens he studied side by side with Ravi Shankar, and when they emerged as young artists in the 1940s they astounded their audiences with the brilliance of their technique as well as the depth of their knowledge. After a short period as a music director of All-India Radio in Lucknow, Ali Akbar became court musician to the Maharaja of Jodhpur. Following the dissolution of the court system, Ali Akbar moved to Bombay and was music director for several films, winning awards for the scores of *The Hungry Stones* and *Devi*.

The development of his classical concert career was assisted by his recording of the rāga *Chandranandan*, which he composed in the recording studio, "and then I had to get the recording to learn how the rāga went," as he describes the creation of one of his signature rāgas. He decided to concentrate on the classical music of his training, and in 1955 he founded the Ali Akbar College of Music in Calcutta to pass on the teachings of his father. Later that year Yehudi Menuhin invited him to come to the United States to record and appear on television. The recording was the first long-playing recording of Indian classical music and convinced Ali Akbar that there was interest in the West for Hindustani classical music. After several tours, he began to teach near San Francisco in 1965. Word of his teaching spread rapidly after the beginning of the Beatles' association with the music of Ravi Shankar, and in 1968 he founded the Ali Akbar College of Music in Berkeley (later in San Rafael). He taught a new generation of musicians including his sons Ashish, Alam and the late Dhyanesh Khan and the Western students George Ruckert, Ken Zuckerman, James Pomerantz, Bruce Hamm, Daisy Paradis, Peter van Gelder, and Richard Harrington; the *sarod* player Zuckerman has opened a branch of the Ali Akbar College in Basle.

Ali Akbar Khan was awarded many titles and honors including the Padma Bhushan, which he received in 1988. Other awards included the McArthur Fellowship, the Shiromani Hall of Fame Award and a fellowship from the NEA. He received honorary doctoral degrees from Rabindra Bharati University and the California Institute of the Arts.

Up until the final days of his life he continued to record, perform, and teach from his base at the Ali Akbar College in California. His tradition is carried on by his sons, and his College is the site of a large library of recordings and music manuscripts of his and his father's legacy.

DISCOGRAPHY

Rags Pilu and Shri, perf. A.A. Khan, *Angel 35283*, (1955) *Ustad Ali Akbar Khan, Master Musician of India* [rāgas *Chandranandan* and *Gauri Manjari*], (Connoisseur Society CS 462 (1966) *The Forty Minute Raga: Rag Marwa*, perf. A.A. Khan and M. Misra, Connoisseur Society CS 2008 (1968)
Journey, perf. A.A. Khan and others, Triloka 184–2 (1990)
Passing on the Tradition, *AMMP CD9608* (1996)

BIBLIOGRAPHY

R. Shankar: *My Music, My Life* (New York, 1968)
W. van der Meer: *Hindustani Music in the 20th Century* (The Hague, 1980)
A.A. Khan and G. Ruckert: *Introduction to the Music of North India* (St. Louis, 1991)
A.J. Miner: *Hindustani Instrumental Music in the Early Modern Period* (New Delhi, 1996)

GEORGE RUCKERT

Khan, Chaka [Stevens, Yvette Marie] (*b* Chicago, IL, 23 March 1953). Funk and soul singer. A product of the South Side of Chicago, she was the oldest of five children. Raised as a devout Roman Catholic, she was exposed to jazz music by her grandmother. She sang in several girl groups as a teen including the Shades of Black. In 1971 she was asked to replace vocalist Paulette McWilliams in the funk group Ask Rufus. The group shortened its name to Rufus and signed to ABC records in 1972. Khan recorded three albums with them before the band's name was changed to Rufus and Chaka Khan to reflect Khan's increasing influence on the group's sound. After recording four more albums with Rufus throughout the end of the 1970s, Khan recorded her first solo recording *Chaka* in 1978, which featured her signature tune "I'm Every Woman."

Throughout the 1980s, Khan established herself as the heir apparent to 1970s fixtures such as Diana Ross and Natalie Cole, reaching the pinnacle of pop success with her cover of Prince's "I Feel for You," which featured Stevie Wonder on harmonica and one of the first rap cameos on an R&B recording, performed by Melle Mel. In 1982 Khan broadened her appeal to jazz audiences with a collection of jazz and fusion standards, *Echoes of an Era*, recorded with Joe Henderson, Chick Corea, Freddie Hubbard, Lenny White, and Stanley Clarke. Throughout her career jazz artists such as Herbie Hancock and Miles Davis would appear on her recordings. Khan continued to record throughout the 1990s and early 21st century, though with less frequency. Her cover of Bruce Hornsby's "Love Me Still" was included on the soundtrack to Spike Lee's film *Clockers* (1995). Khan has directly influenced contemporary singers such as Mary J. Blige, Fantasia Barrino, and Jennifer Hudson.

MARK ANTHONY NEAL

Kidd, Michael [Greenwald, Milton] (*b* New York, NY, 12 Aug 1915; *d* Los Angeles, CA, 23 Dec 2007). Dancer and choreographer for stage and film. After winning a scholarship to the School of American Ballet in 1937, he decided to pursue a career in dance. He danced on Broadway and with several ballet companies before joining Ballet Theatre in 1942. During his five years as a soloist with that company, he choreographed his only ballet, *On Stage*, to music by Norman Dello Joio, in 1945. This led to a commission to create dances for the Broadway musical *Finian's Rainbow* (1947; music by Burton Lane), for which he won the first of five Tony awards for his choreography. He won the award again for *Guys and Dolls* (1950; music by Frank Loesser), *Can-Can* (1953; music by Cole Porter), *Li'l Abner* (1956; music by Gene de Paul), and *Destry Rides Again* (1959; music by Harold Rome).

Kidd was also active in Hollywood, staging dances for numerous films. He won particular acclaim for the numbers he staged for *The Band Wagon* (1953) and *Seven Brides for Seven Brothers* (1954). *The Band Wagon*, with songs by Howard Dietz and Arthur Schwartz, starred Fred Astaire and Cyd Charisse and included the now-famous "Girl Hunt Ballet," a spoof of hard-boiled detective stories, and the lyrical "Dancing in the Dark." *Seven Brides for Seven Brothers*, with music by Gene de Paul, includes rousing, rollicking group dances that show Kidd at the top of his form. In 1997 he received a special Academy Award "in recognition of his services to the art of dance in the art of the screen."

BIBLIOGRAPHY

E. Coleman: "The Dance Man Leaps to the Top," *New York Times Magazine* (19 April 1959)
L. Billman: *Film Choreographers and Dance Directors* (Jefferson, NC, 1997)
E. Mordden: *Coming Up Roses: the Broadway Musical in the 1950s* (New York, 1998)
Obituary, *New York Times* (25 Dec 2007)

CLAUDE CONYERS

Kid Rock [Ritchie, Robert James] (*b* Romeo, MI, 17 Jan 1971). Popular musician. Raised in Romeo, Michigan, he relocated to New York City in 1990, where he released his debut album, *Grits Sandwiches for Breakfast* (Jive Records), which failed to garner wide praise. Through the mid-1990s, Kid Rock struggled to market his stylistic combination of blues, southern rock, heavy metal, and rap, and sales of his next three albums—*The Polyfuze Method* (Continuum, 1993), *Fire It Up* (Continuum, 1993), and *Early Mornin' Stoned Pimp* (Top Dog, 1996)—were poor. However, amid the growing popularity of rap-metal and nu-metal acts in the 1990s, Kid Rock attracted the attention of Atlantic Records, which, in 1998, signed him to a recording contract and released *Devil Without a Cause*, a nationwide hit that reached number three on *Billboard*'s catalog album chart and sold over 11 million copies by 2003. Kid Rock released five albums in the first decade of the new millennium, three of which—*Cocky* (2001), *Kid Rock* (2003), and *Rock and Roll Jesus* (2007)—were certified platinum or better. Independent of his music career, Kid Rock garnered significant public attention for his six-year relationship with actress Pamela Anderson, roles in the feature films *Joe Dirt* (2001) and *Larry the Cable Guy: Health Inspector* (2006), and frequently publicized court cases. Since 2001 Kid Rock has been increasingly accepted by country music audiences, in large part due to his studio and concert collaborations with such artists as Hank Williams, Jr., Gretchen Wilson, and Sheryl Crow, as well as a contemporaneous resurgence of hardcore country music.

DAVID B. PRUETT

Kieffer, Aldine S(illman) (*b* Saline Co., MO, 1 Aug 1840; *d* Dayton, VA, 30 Nov 1904). Music publisher and tunebook compiler. His father died shortly after he was born, and he grew up in Singer's Glen, Virginia, under the influence of his grandfather, JOSEPH FUNK. In 1865 he and William S. Rohr revived Funk's periodical the *Southern Musical Advocate and Singer's Friend*, but it was discontinued in 1869. The following year he began (with others, as the Patent Note Publishing Co.) to issue the *Musical Million and Fireside Friend*, a monthly periodical edited by Kieffer, which was a primary instrument for the promotion of shape-note gospel hymnody in the South. In 1872 Kieffer formed a new company, Ruebush, Kieffer & Co. (later the Ruebush-Kieffer Co.) with his brother-in-law, singing-school teacher Ephraim Ruebush, and John W. Howe, to publish the *Musical Million*, which continued to appear regularly until 1914. Kieffer was also a poet and composer, his most popular works being "My Mountain Home," "Grave on the Green Hillside," "Twilight is Falling," and "To my Blanket." With his associates he published 18 songbooks between 1868 and 1898.

See also SHAPE-NOTE HYMNODY.

BIBLIOGRAPHY

G.P. Jackson: *White Spirituals in the Southern Uplands* (Chapel Hill, NC, 1933/R)
P.M. Hall: *The 'Musical Million': a Study and Analysis of the Periodical Promoting Music Reading through Shape-Notes in North America from 1870 to 1914* (diss., Catholic U. of America, 1970)
G.I. Showalter: *The Music Books of Ruebush & Kieffer, 1866–1942: a Bibliography* (Charlottesville, VA, 1975)
C.E. Morrison: *Aldine S. Kieffer and Ephraim Ruebush: Ideals Reflected in Post–Civil War Ruebush-Kieffer Company Publications* (diss., Arizona State U., 1992)

HARRY ESKEW

Kienzle, Rich[ard] (*b* Greensburg, PA, 1 March 1951). Country music critic and historian. An occasionally controversial journalist and tough critic, Kienzle's work challenges notions of genre that are often used to separate country, jazz, pop, and rock into discrete categories, instead arguing for a holistic approach that is more representative of the diverse musical interests of recording artists. After graduating from the University of Pittsburgh (BA, English, 1973), he sold his first reviews to *Country Music Magazine* and, over the next 25 years, served as a columnist, critic, and contributing editor for the publication. His contributions to *Guitar Player* and *Vintage Guitar* have documented the lives and careers of numerous country and jazz guitarists, while his reviews and articles for *No Depression* helped to shape the alternative country movement's view of country music history. To date, he has contributed liner notes for more than 370 CD reissues of country, pop, and jazz records, including several notable releases for Sony Legacy and Bear Family Records. In 2003 he published *Southwest Shuffle: Pioneers of Honky Tonk, Western Swing, and Country Jazz* (New York), which uses more than a dozen biographical studies to explore the intersections of jazz and country music. Since 2008 he has contributed to the "Believe Your Ears" podcast for the *Pittsburgh Post-Gazette*.

TRAVIS D. STIMELING

Kilenyi, Edward (*b* Békésszentandrás, Hungary, 25 Jan 1884; *d* Tallahassee, FL, 15 Aug 1968). Composer and violinist of Hungarian birth. He was the father of pianist Edward Kilenyi (1910–2000). The elder Edward received his general education principally in Budapest and Szarvas, receiving the BA in 1902 at the State College, Hungary, and then studied briefly at the Scuola Nazionale Musicale in Rome with Pietro Mascagni and at the Cologne Conservatory (1902–7). At Columbia University, where he was a Mosenthal Fellow, he studied with Daniel Gregory Mason and received the MA (1915) and the PhD. Kilenyi is best remembered as a teacher of GEORGE GERSHWIN, whom from 1919 to 1921 he instructed in theory and advanced harmony while also providing advice on orchestration and conducting. He published accounts of Gershwin's study with him as well as a number of articles on music, including a study of Hungarian music (*MQ*, v, 1919, 20–39); he also edited *Folksongs from Mexico and South America* (with Eleanor Hague, 1914). Kilenyi was associated with the motion picture industry for over 30 years as music director for various early sound films, including *Abie's Irish Rose* (1928) and *Tillie's Punctured Romance* (1939).

Though few of his original works are available in print or have been recorded, a vocal score of his opera *The Cry of the Wolf* is held at the Library of Congress, and the film *The Adventures of Chico* (1937), for which he wrote the music, has been preserved at several libraries in the United States.

WORKS

Str Qt, 1912; Ov. (incid music, Kleist), 1913; Modern Variations on an Old English Tune, vn, pf, 1915; The Cry of the Wolf (op, 1, C.E. Parker), 1916; Str Qnt; other works for vn; songs

BIBLIOGRAPHY

E. Kilenyi: *Gershwiniana: Recollections and Reminiscences of Times Spent with my Student George Gershwin* (n.p., 1963)
Obituary, *Variety*, no.252 (21 Aug 1968)
S.R. Tilford: *The Musical Legacy of Edward Kilenyi* (diss., Florida State U., 1999)

ALLAN B. HO/R

Kiley, Richard (*b* Chicago, IL, 31 March 1922; *d* Warwick, NY, 5 March 1999). Actor and singer. Kiley attended Loyola University and acting school in Chicago before serving in the US Navy from 1943 to 1946. He began his acting career in radio and eventually settled in New York. Kiley toured in the play *A Streetcar Named Desire* before embarking on several television projects in the early 1950s. His Broadway debut was in the play *Misalliance* (1953). Later that year he played the Caliph in the musical *Kismet*, singing "Stranger in Paradise." The play *Time Limit!* (1956) and work in Hollywood preceded his appearance in the musical *Redhead* (1959) opposite Gwen Verdon, for which he won his first Tony Award. Kiley continued his musical career as Diahann Carroll's lover in *No Strings* (1962), the substitute male lead in *Here's Love* (1963), and Stan the Shpieler in *I Had a Ball* (1964). Kiley won his second Tony for his portrayal of Cervantes/Don Quixote in *Man of La Mancha* (1965), the role with which he is most identified. His dramatic Broadway performance of "The Impossible Dream" with his striking baritone voice became iconic. His final appearance in a new musical was in the unsuccessful *Her First Roman* (1968); in 1972 and 1977 he reprised his quintessential role in Broadway revivals of *Man of La Mancha*. Kiley brought his virile, nuanced acting presence to many films and television shows, but seldom to film musicals, a prominent exception being the unsuccessful *The Little Prince* (1974) with a score by Lerner and Loewe.

BIBLIOGRAPHY

Obituaries: *New York Times* (6 March 1999); *The Independent* (11 March 1999)

PAUL R. LAIRD

Kilgen. Organ building firm. It was founded by George Kilgen (*b* Durlach, Germany, 19 March 1821; *d* St. Louis, MO, 6 Dec 1902), who apprenticed with Louis Voit and immigrated to New York in 1848, where he worked for the Jardine firm before opening his own workshop in 1851. In 1873 he moved to St. Louis, and his son Charles Christian (1859–1932) became his partner in 1886 under the firm name of George Kilgen & Son. Most of the firm's earlier organs had been relatively small, many of them built for Catholic churches in the Midwest. After 1902 Charles Christian Kilgen became president, and under his leadership the company grew, producing instruments for large churches such as St. Patrick's Cathedral in New York (1930) and St. Agnes's Church in Louisville, Kentucky (1934). A number of theater organs were also built. After Charles's death, the firm foundered during the Depression, and was split into two entities by dissension among his sons George, Charles, and Eugene. One branch closed in 1939, another in 1943, although some members continued to build organs on a small scale until 1960.

BIBLIOGRAPHY

"American Organ Builders of Today: George Kilgen & Son," *The Diapason*, xv/12 (Nov 1924)
P. Eversden: "The Kilgen Family," *The American Organist*, xii/5 (May 1929)
Seven Generations in the Building of Pipe Organs (Kilgen Organ Co., 1951)
O. Ochse: *The History of the Organ in the United States* (Bloomington, IN, 1975)
E.T. Schmitt: "George Kilgen—the New York Years," *The Tracker*, xliv/3 (2000), 26-31

BARBARA OWEN

Killebrew, Gwendolyn (*b* Philadelphia, PA, 26 Aug 1939). Mezzo-soprano and contralto. After obtaining a degree in music education at Temple University she studied voice at the Juilliard School and the Metropolitan Opera Studio, making her debut in 1967 as Waltraute in *Die Walküre*. In 1973 Killebrew sang Baba the Turk in *The Rake's Progress* at Washington, DC, and in the world premiere of Carl Orff's *De Temporum fine Comoedia* at Salzburg with Herbert von Karajan conducting. In the same year, she made her San Francisco debut as Léonor in *La favorite* and Marina in *Boris Godunov*. A respected African American singer, Killebrew appeared at Santa Fe as Carmen in 1975, and her interpretation created a demand for her to perform at the Metropolitan. In 1976 she became a member of the Deutsche Oper am Rhein, Düsseldorf, where her roles included Gluck's Orpheus, Isabella in *L'italiana in Algeri*, Azucena, Preziosilla, and Frau Leimberger in Klebe's *Der jüngste Tag* (1988). Her powerful rich-toned voice made her an ideal interpreter of Amneris and Mistress Quickly, which she sang in Amsterdam (1980) and Zürich (1981). She performed Wagnerian roles, including Fricka and Waltraute in *Götterdämmerung*, in which she made her Bayreuth debut in 1978. Killebrew has continued to teach and offer master classes in the United States and in Germany.

ELIZABETH FORBES/MEREDITH ELIASSEN

Killoran, Paddy [Patrick] (*b* Emlagation, Co. Sligo, Ireland, 1904; *d* New York, NY, 1965). Fiddle player of Irish birth, naturalized American. Born into a musical family (his mother played concertina and his father played flute), he immigrated to New York in 1925, where he took several fiddle lessons with JAMES MORRISON and recorded with fiddler Paddy Sweeney, another emigrant from Sligo. Killoran worked as an elevator operator and later opened a bar in the Bronx, but he is best known for his 78 rpm recordings and for playing in the Irish dance halls that were especially popular in New York in the 1930s. His Pride of Erin Orchestra played both Irish and popular tunes, served as the house band at the Pride of Erin Ballroom in Brooklyn, and performed live on Brooklyn's WBBC. Over the next several decades, Killoran and his ensembles remained active in New York and performed on passenger ships to and from Ireland. In an era most often associated with fiddler Michael Coleman's ornate style, Killoran's bowed triplets and danceable rhythms distinguish his playing. He recorded extensively in the 1930s for the Crown and Decca labels, and recorded half of an LP for Colonial in the 1950s.

BIBLIOGRAPHY

B. O'Neill: Liner notes, *Paddy Killoran's Back In Town* (Shanachie 33003, 1977)

G. Ó hAllmhuráin: *A Pocket History of Irish Traditional Music* (Dublin, 1998)

TES SLOMINSKI

Kill Rock Stars. Record company. Based in Portland, Oregon, and Olympia, Washington, Kill Rock Stars (KRS) was started by Slim Moon in 1991. Moon ran the label until 2006, when his wife, Portia Sabin, took over as president. KRS primarily promotes music by local artists and has remained unaffiliated with a major label. The label describes itself as "queer-positive, feminist and artist friendly." KRS and many of its artists have been closely associated with RIOT GRRRL, an underground feminist punk movement.

KRS's first release was a spoken word split single entitled KRS-101 (1991), featuring Moon and Kathleen Hanna, lead vocalist of the band Bikini Kill. Later that year, KRS released a compilation album featuring Olympia-area bands including Bikini Kill, Bratmobile, and The Melvins. Singles, compilations, and LPs by riot grrrl bands such as Bikini Kill, Huggy Bear, and Team Dresch were released by KRS throughout the early 1990s. Subsequent artists of note included Sleater-Kinney and The Gossip. In 1997 KRS formed a spin-off label for experimental rock music called 5 Rue Christine (5RC). While independent rock music remains its focus, KRS has also released albums by singer-songwriters such as Mary Lou Lord, Linda Perry, and Elliot Smith, as well as spoken word albums by Kathy Acker and Juliana Lueking.

BROOKE BRYANT

Kim, Earl [Eul] (*b* Dinuba, CA, 6 Jan 1920; *d* Cambridge, MA, 19 Nov 1998). Composer. Of Korean descent, he began piano lessons at age nine, and was a pupil of Homer Grun for seven years. In 1939 he studied composition and theory with ARNOLD SCHOENBERG at UCLA; in 1940 he transferred to the University of California, Berkeley, where he studied with ERNEST BLOCH, but his education was interrupted by a stint in the US Army Intelligence Service during World War II. He returned to Berkeley after the war and studied with ROGER SESSIONS (MM 1952). He served on the faculty at Princeton University from 1952 to 1967, and from 1967 taught at Harvard University, where he was James Edward Ditson Professor of Music. He retired in 1990 and continued to live in Cambridge until his death in 1998. Throughout his career he was active as a conductor, performer, and ensemble pianist. Kim served terms as Composer-in-Residence at the Princeton Seminar in Advanced Musical Studies and at the Marlboro, Dartmouth, Tanglewood, Cape and Islands, and Aspen Music Festivals. Among his awards were those from the National Institute of Arts and Letters; the Ingram Merrill, Fromm, Guggenheim, Koussevitzky, and Naumburg foundations; Brandeis Creative Arts Medal; and Mark Horbitt Award of the Boston Symphony. Kim was active in politics, particularly in the 1980s, co-founding Musicians Against Nuclear Arms in 1981 and serving as its president for four years.

Kim's compositional aesthetic crystallized during the early 1960s, in response to such diverse influences as the texts of Samuel Beckett and Kim's apprehension of the structure of a Japanese stone garden. Describing the latter, Kim said: "It summed up my theory of composing: discrete images not taken in by the eye or ear at once, but seen or heard consecutively. At the end there is a whole that is somehow synthesized from all these separate pieces. Multiplicity becomes unity…transitions take place by means of silences. Statements are being made when nothing is being said." In "Thither" (from *Now & Then*, 1981) and in much of Kim's other music, segments of various sizes, from individual tones to large-scale sections, are often framed by silence. The segments often recur, largely unaltered, after the presentation of a contrasting section as in the Violin Concerto. Kim's writing for voice demonstrates a sensitive response to the rhythms and intonations of spoken language, whether the speech patterns are dramatically intensified (as in *Lines*, 1975), spoken with only rhythms and dynamics specified (as in *Melodrama*, 1975), or sung. The instrumental accompaniments are often in rhythmic unison with the voice, sometimes doubling the vocal lines or following the contours of the spoken text. Though its harmonic materials and dramatic contexts are diverse, Kim's music is economic in means, delicate, and subtle in its inflections. His 12-tone sets and procedures are occasionally used but pitch structures are not derived from such sets.

Violinist Itzhak Perlman, for whom Earl composed two of his major works, remembered him in the *New York Times* as a "composer, devoted teacher, musician extraordinaire. Earl brought to music colors we only dreamed existed but had never before heard. Creative and imaginative, he was truly inspired."

WORKS
(texts by Beckett unless otherwise stated)
Footfalls (opera, 1), 1981
Vocal: Letters found near a Suicide (F. Horne), S, pf, 1954; Exercises en route: Dead Calm, Rattling on, Gooseberries, she said, They are far out, S, fl, ob, cl, vn, vc, perc, actors, dancers, film, 1961–71; Narratives: Monologues, Melodrama 1, Lines, Eh Joe, Melodrama 2, Duet, Earthlight, actress/female nar, actor, S, 2 tpt, trbn, 2 vn, 2 vc, pf, television, lights, 1973–9; Now & then: On the Meadow (Chekhov), Thither, Roundelay, S, fl, harp, va, 1981; Where Grief Slumbers (Apollinaire, Rimbaud), 7 songs, S, harp, str orch, 1982; Cornet for Narrator and Orchestra, 1982; The 7th Dream for Soprano, Bar, vn, vc, and pf, 1986; The 11th Dream for Soprano, Baritone, Violin, Cello, and Piano, 1988; 3 Poems in French for Soprano and String Quartet, 1989; 4 Lines from Mallarmé for Voice, Flute, Vibraphone, and Percussion, 1989; Some Thoughts on Keats and Coleridge, "In Memoriam Roger Sessions," for Chorus, 1990; The 26th Dream for Baritone, Chorus, and Strong Orchestra, 1991–92; Dear Linda for Woman's Voice, Flute or Piccolo, Piano, Marimba, Percussion, and Cello, 1992
Inst: 2 Bagatelles, pf, 1952; Dialogues, pf, orch, 1959; Vn Conc., 1979; 12 Caprices, vn, 1980; Scenes from Childhood for Brass Quintet, 1984; The White Hour for Chamber Orchestra, 1998
3 early works, withdrawn

Principal publishers: Composers Collaborative and Theodore Presser
Principal record labels: Albany, Bis, Naxos, New World, and Nonesuch

BIBLIOGRAPHY
E. Barkin: "Earl Kim: Earthlight," *PNM*, xix/1–2 (1981), 269
G.L. Jeffers: *Non-narrative Drama: Settings by Virgil Thomson, Ned Rorem and Earl Kim of Plays by Gertrude Stein and Samuel Beckett* (diss., UCLA, 1983)
J. Tassell: "Golden Silences: the Flowering of Earl Kim," *Boston Globe Magazine* (27 Feb 1983), 10
M.E. Jeon: "I am Concerned with What is Good," *Sonus*, vii/11 (1987), 1–9 [interview]
Obituary, *New York Times* (26 Nov 1998)
A. Brandt: Liner notes, *Earl Kim* (New World Records, 2001)
MARTIN BRODY/GREG A STEINKE

Kim, Hi Kyung (*b* Seoul, South Korea, 15 March 1954). Composer of Korean birth. She studied at Seoul National University with Sung-Jae Lee and at the University of California, Berkeley (MA, 1985; PhD, 1993), with ANDREW IMBRIE and OLLY W. WILSON, JR. At Berkeley, she received the George C. Ladd *Prix de Paris*, which enabled her to pursue advanced studies at the Institut de Récherche et Coordination Acoustique Musique (IRCAM) and the École Normale Supérieure in Paris (1988–90) as a student of Gérard Grisey. Kim is currently a faculty member at the University of California, Santa Cruz, where she founded the Pacific Rim Music Festival in 1996. Her honors include the Walter Hinrichsen Award from the American Academy and Institute of Arts and Letters, and fellowships from the Tanglewood Music Center, the MacDowell Colony, the Djerassi Foundation, the Korea Foundation, and the Asian Cultural Council. She was a Fulbright scholar to Korea, and has received commissions from the Serge Koussevitzky Music Foundation at the Library of Congress, the Fromm Music Foundation at Harvard University, Meet the Composer/Commissioning USA, and Arts Council Korea.

Her research on the music of Elliott Carter and on traditional Korean music is reflected in her compositions.

Rhythmic complexity and formal intricacy underlie even her most accessible works, and many of her structural and timbral ideas owe something to Korean music. Her piece *Intrigues* (1985) for clarinet and prepared piano is an exploration of timbre and explores the development of intricate rhythms in the phrase structure. As a composer, she is noted for her creative unification of contemporary Western and traditional Korean musical vocabulary, philosophy, art forms, and performers, including collaborations with a number of Korean master performers, and her use of Korean musical instruments, such as gayageum (12-string zither), daegeum (bamboo flute), and ajaeng (bowed zither). *At the Edge of the Ocean* (2001, chamber ensemble) was written for the Hún Qiáo project of the Chamber Music Society of Minnesota, and featured cellist Yo-Yo Ma. In this work she uses elements of Korean folk songs, with four different *Arirangs* (regional variations of the popular Korean folksong *Arirang*) in one long movement. Her three major multi-disciplinary works, *Rituel I, II, and III* (2001–5), require improvisation and employ Korean and Western ensembles and dancers. As artistic director of the Pacific Rim Music Festival, Kim has presented works from composers around the world that embody this idea of cultural synthesis. She was invited to address her ideas on cross-cultural synthesis and development in a keynote speech at the UNESCO Second World Conference on Arts Education (Seoul, 2010).

WORKS
Pathway, pf, 1973; Romance, pf, 1973; Dialogue, vn, pf, 1974; Crash, str qt, 1975; Fugue, pf, 1975; Resistance, S, pf, 1975; Sonata no.1, pf, 1975; Conversation, orch, 1976; Harmony, wind qnt, 1976; Looking at New Heaven and Earth, cho, pf, 1976; Satisfaction, chbr ens, 1977; A-Ri, S, str qt, 1983; Intrigues, cl, prep pf, 1985; Reflection, cl, 1985; Encounter, cl, b cl, bn, vc, 5 perc, 1986; Short Dance, str qt, 1987; Step, cptr, 1988; What are Years?, S, fl, cl, vn, db, gui, 1988; Dance, str qt, 1990; When you Rush, chbr ens, 1991; Islands in the Bay, perc, orch, 1993; Unknown Lives, chbr ens, 1995; Breaking the Silence, pf trio, 1996; After the Fall, cl, b cl, 1998; Primitive Dance, str qt, 1999; Instant Breath, fl, 1999; At the Edge of the Ocean, fl, cl, vn, va, vc, perc, 2001; Orange Pastel, 2 perc, 2001; Rituel for Korean Dance/Percussion and Violin, Cello, Clarinet, and Percussion, dance, clar, vn, vc, perc, 2001; Rituel II, Korean Zen dance, piri, yangkeum, clar, vn, vc, perc, 2002 (rev 2002); Trio Sori, daekeum, clar, vc, 2002; Crystal Drops, 2 pf, 2003; Rituel III, Korean dance, changgo, daegeum, clar, vc, perc, multi-media, 2004 (rev 2005); A Story, gayageum, 2006; Two Years with the Seine, clar, vc, 2007; The Poet/KIM SAT GAT, daegeum, 2007; Secret Wine, 2008, perc; A Piece for Gayageum Solo, gayageum, 2009; Clarinet Quintet (completion of an unfinished work by Andrew Imbrie), 2009; When He Was Six-Hundred Years Old, ajaeng, 2010; Isle of Eeo, str qt, perc, 2011; Blue-White Oysters, str qt, 2011

Principal publishers: Edition C. F. Peters, Soo Moon Dang Publishing (Korea)
Principal record labels: Albany, Centaur, Capstone
JOSHUA KOSMAN/SARAH EYERLY

Kim, Jin Hi (*b* Incheon, South Korea, 6 Feb 1958). Composer and komungo performer of South Korean birth. She is internationally recognized as an innovative virtuoso on the komungo (a Korean fourth-century fretted-board zither) as well as for her cross-cultural compositions. She learned to play piano as a child, but followed her father's encouragement to study Korean music. She was in the first class of students to be accepted to Korea's National High School for Korean Traditional Music, and chose to pursue komungo, traditionally associated with male performers. She subsequently earned a bachelor's degree in music at Seoul National University. After immigrating to the United States, she attended Mills College (MFA 1985). Her teachers have included JOHN ADAMS, LOU HARRISON, TERRY RILEY, and DAVID ROSENBOOM.

An invitation in 1987 to improvise on komungo with avant-garde guitarist Henry Kaiser led to a decade of creative activity with the world's leading jazz and avant-garde improvisers, including William Parker, Oliver Lake, Reggie Workman, Elliott Sharp, Derek Bailey, Eugene Chadbourne, James Newton, Joelle Leandre, Mark Dresser, Jane Ira Bloom, and Evan Parker. She designed the world's first electric komungo and currently uses a model built by Joseph Yanuziello in 1998. Almost as large as a traditional komungo, and able to produce a lush sound, the instrument is manipulated by a computer system, and a foot pedal offers the capability to blend acoustic and processed sounds. She also uses it in interactive pieces using MIDI triggers generated by the electric komungo.

She typically integrates the komungo (either acoustic or electric) into compositions for chamber ensemble and orchestra, mixed ensembles, and avant-garde jazz improvisations. In collaboration with Alex Noyes, Kim has created live interactive pieces that were premiered at the Smithsonian Institution's Freer Gallery in Washington, DC, and at the Asia Society in New York City. Through the use of improvisation, Kim conveys Korean court music's meditative energy and sense of time, as well as folk music's vigorous energy. During her career she has developed the concept of "Living Tones," the central premise of which is that each tone is alive, embodying its own individual shape, sound, and sub-text deeply rooted in Korean traditional music. The philosophy derives from Buddhism's reverence for life coupled with a Shamanistic expression of color and nuance.

Kim's works have been presented at premiere venues, including Carnegie Hall, Lincoln Center for the Performing Arts, John F. Kennedy Center for the Performing Arts, Brooklyn Academy of Music, and Royal Festival Hall (London), and festivals such as Musique Action Festival (France), the Asian Pacific Festival (New Zealand), Nazuca Music Festival (Peru), Moers New Jazz Festival (Germany), and the Vancouver International Jazz Festival (Canada). In 2001 Kim received the Award for Music Composition from the Foundation For Contemporary Performance Art. In 2010 she received a Guggenheim fellowship and served as Composer-In-Residence with the New Haven Symphony Orchestra. She published her autobiography, *Komungo Tango,* in 2007 (Seoul).

WORKS
(selective list)

Linking (1986), str qt; Nong Rock (1992), str qt and komungo; Voices of Sigimse (1996), komungo and chbr orch; Dragon Bond Rite (1997), cross-cultural mask dance drama; Agate Slice (1998), chbr ens; One Sky (1998), str chbr orch; "Dong Dong" Touching the Moons (2000), elec komungo, Indian table, Korean kagok singer,

Indian kathak dancer with computer-controlled MIDI, sensors and digital animation; Eternal Rock (2001), orch and komungo; Eternal Rock II (2006), orch and Korean barrel drums; Monk Dance (2007), orch and Korean barrel drums; NORI III (2009), perc qt and elec komungo; Tribal Greetings (2010), fl, cb, perc, and komungo

ELDONNA L. MAY

Kim, Young Uck (*b* Seoul, Korea, 1 Sept 1947). Violinist of Korean birth. After leaving Korea, he made his way to the United States along with his sister, Duck Ju Kim, a pianist; the two played for Rudolf Serkin, who suggested they study at the Curtis Institute. Kim studied there with IVAN GALAMIAN from 1961 to 1969 and made his orchestral debut in 1963 with the Philadelphia Orchestra under Eugene Ormandy in a concert broadcast on national television. In 1966 he made his New York recital debut, and from this time his solo career rapidly reached international status. In 1992 he gave the premiere of Gunther Schuller's Violin Concerto at Carnegie Hall, New York, and the European premiere with the Rotterdam PO. In 1980 he formed a piano trio with Emanuel Ax and Yo-Yo Ma, which has successfully toured internationally; their recording of Antonín Dvořák's trios won an award in 1988. He was a member of the Beaux Arts Trio from 1998 to 2002. He has also taught and in 1988 was appointed professor of string studies at the Hochschule für Musik in Detmold. By 2010 he was the artistic director of the Seoul Arts Center and taught at Seoul National University. Kim's solo recordings have been highly acclaimed, especially those of Wolfgang Amadeus Mozart's complete concertos. Kim's playing is innately musical with a sweet tone, yet also very personal in approach. He has played the "Cessole" Stradivarius dating from 1716 (D. Rooney: "Prodigy Matured," *The Strad,* xcix, 1988, 308–11).

MARGARET CAMPBELL/JONAS WESTOVER

Kimball. Piano, reed organ, and pipe organ manufacturer. Founded in Chicago by William Wallace Kimball (*b* Rumford, ME, 22 March 1828; *d* Chicago, IL, 16 Dec 1904). In 1857 Kimball, who had been an insurance agent in Decorah, Iowa, moved to Chicago, where a chance purchase of a consignment of pianos at an auction launched his career as a dealer in pianos and reed organs under the name of W.W. Kimball Co., at first purchasing its stock from eastern manufacturers. In 1865 he married Evalyne M. Cone, whose brother Alfred (*d* 1900) soon entered his firm and eventually became its treasurer. Kimball's flourishing store was destroyed in the great Chicago fire of 1871, but the setback was only temporary. In 1880 he opened his first factory, for the manufacture of reed organs; in 1882 his firm was incorporated with Kimball, Cone, and Edwin S. Conway as principals, and in 1887 piano manufacture was begun. Kimball's business credo stressed volume, reasonable price, and quality construction. He encouraged his staff to develop improvements, and over time many patents were granted for innovations in reed organ and piano design; these factors doubtless contributed to the high awards Kimball instruments received at the 1893 World's Columbian Exposition.

Some skilled immigrants helped to keep the firm abreast of European developments, and included Peter Tapper from Bechstein's Berlin piano factory, and Frederic W. Hedgeland, trained in his family's British organ works, who in 1890 superintended Kimball's new pipe organ department. Beginning with his ingenious design of a small "portable" organ of two manuals with a reed stop in the pedal, production soon expanded to standard "catalog" designs and much larger instruments, including those for Washington Hebrew Congregation, Washington, DC (1900); Mormon Tabernacle, Salt Lake City (1901); First Baptist Congregational Church, Chicago (1927); Minneapolis Auditorium (1928); First Congregational Church, Columbus, Ohio (1931); Memorial Auditorium, Worcester, Massachusetts (1933); and Municipal Auditorium, Pretoria, South Africa (1935). Self-playing organs were introduced in 1896, followed by player pianos in 1901. In 1883 Kimball's nephew, Wallace W. Lufkin (d 1945), joined the firm, eventually becoming president, as did another nephew, Curtis N. Kimball (d 1936). From 1901 to 1925 Kimball manufactured a gramophone invented by Albert A. Huseby, a Norwegian who superintended the piano factory, and in 1931 Kimball took over the assets of the Welte-Tripp firm. The reed organ branch closed in 1922, having produced 403,390 instruments, while the pipe organ branch continued until 1942, with a total output of 7326.

Curtis N. Kimball had become president upon his uncle's death, and was succeeded by W.W. Lufkin, who in turn was succeeded by the founder's grandnephew W.W. Kimball in 1945. After this time the firm concentrated on piano manufacture, moving production in 1955 to a new factory in Melrose Park, Illinois. In 1959 Kimball became part of the larger Jasper Corporation, moving to Jasper, Indiana, in 1961, taking over Bösendorfer of Vienna in 1966 and incorporating Bösendorfer features into Kimball pianos. In 1961 the firm also began manufacture of several models of electronic "spinet" organs with two manuals and one octave of pedal keys, the sound being derived from 12 oscillators, and featuring a rhythm section and automatic bass. During this period the firm was known as Kimball Piano and Organ Co., but in 1974 Jasper and its several subsidiaries consolidated as Kimball International, and ceased making pianos in 1996. The electronic instrument division became a subsidiary called Kimball Electronics Group and ceased making musical instruments in the 1980s, operating subsequently only as a supplier of electronic components to other industries.

BIBLIOGRAPHY

Musical Instruments at the World's Columbian Exposition (Chicago, 1895)
A. Dolge: *Pianos and their Makers* (Covina, CA, 1911/*R*1972)
"American Organ Builders of Today: W.W. Kimball Co." *The Diapason*, xvi/3 (Feb 1925)
V.A. Bradley: *Music for the Millions: the Kimball Piano and Organ Story* (Chicago, 1957).
O. Ochse: *History of the Organ in the United States* (Bloomington, IN, 1975)
B. Owen: *The Mormon Tabernacle Organ* (Salt Lake City, 1990)

BARBARA OWEN

Kimball, Jacob (*b* Topsfield, MA, 15 Feb 1761; *d* Topsfield, 24 July 1826). Composer and tunebook compiler. His father, also named Jacob, was a blacksmith by trade and was chosen in 1764 to help lead singing in the Topsfield meetinghouse. The younger Jacob played fife and drum in the local militia at the battles of Lexington and Bunker Hill in 1775. The next year he entered Harvard College, from which he graduated in 1780. He was a schoolmaster in Ipswich from 1781 to 1783 and at various times between 1792 and 1814 in Topsfield. He also studied law and was reportedly admitted to the bar in Strafford County, New Hampshire (1795), though he seems to have practiced only briefly.

Kimball was active in sacred music making during much of his adult life. He is known to have taught singing-schools in Marblehead in the early 1790s and at Danvers in 1800, and had a reputation as a good singer. References to performances in which he participated in northern Massachusetts cover at least three decades and begin as early as 1787. He joined the Essex Musical Association around 1798. He made his chief mark, however, as a composer. Among his more than 120 published compositions, many were introduced in the two tunebooks he compiled: *The Rural Harmony* (Boston, 1793), devoted entirely to his own music, and *The Essex Harmony* (Exeter, NH, 1800), containing 44 pieces by Kimball and two by Samuel Holyoke; a few more appeared in *The Village Harmony* (Exeter, 4/1798 and later editions). Kimball's compositional style shows that he had a grasp of European theoretical principles exceeding that of many of his American contemporaries. His harmonies, consistently full triads, connect mostly in orthodox fashion. Few of his pieces won wide circulation, perhaps because most were introduced in copyrighted collections. But a piece reprinted in many 18th- and 19th-century American tunebooks, the smoothly harmonized "Invitation," reveals that, contrary to some contemporary opinion, fuging-tunes did not have to be compositional exercises in musical crudeness.

Kimball is reputed to have been a heavy drinker who died in poverty. The Essex Institute in Salem owns a manuscript collection of more than 60 of his unpublished pieces, which is dated 26 May 1808, at Malden, Massachusetts.

BIBLIOGRAPHY

S.P. Cheney: *The American Singing Book* (Boston, 1879/*R*1980), 177
F.J. Metcalf: *American Writers and Compilers of Sacred Music* (New York, 1925/*R*1967)
G.C. Wilcox: *Jacob Kimball, Jr. (1761–1826): his Life and Works* (diss., U. of Southern California, 1957)
G.C. Wilcox: "Jacob Kimball, a Pioneer American Musician," *Essex Institute Historical Collections*, xciv (1958), 356–78
A.P. Britton, I. Lowens, and R. Crawford: *American Sacred Music Imprints, 1698–1810: a Bibliography* (Worcester, MA, 1990)
H. Eskew and K. Kroeger: *Selected Works of Samuel Holyoke and Jacob Kimball* (New York, 1998)
M.J. Hatchett: *A Companion to the New Harp of Columbia* (Knoxville, TN, 2003)

RICHARD CRAWFORD/R

Kimbrough, Junior [David] (*b* Hudsonville, MS, 28 July 1930; *d* Holly Springs, MS, 17 Jan 1998). Bluesman, bandleader, and juke joint owner. He began playing guitar as a youth in northern Mississippi and developed a fiercely independent playing style marked by constant droning bass notes articulated by the thumb, leaving the other fingers free to play melodies in the middle and upper ranges. His music is characterized by its hypnotic and droning quality and seldom adheres to traditional harmonic frameworks. A lack of recognizable harmonic direction and the use of a limited melodic vocabulary give Kimbrough's music a modal character, and the prominent use of syncopation and polyrhythm firmly root it in the African American tradition.

Kimbrough recorded only sporadically throughout the majority of his career. In 1992, Fat Possum Records released his debut album *All Night Long* and around the same time he opened his juke joint "Junior's Place" in Chulahoma, Mississippi, where he would play regularly with his band the Soul Blue Boys. Following the success of *All Night Long* and his venue, Kimbrough continued to record for Fat Possum Records until his death in 1998. The label released a number of posthumous albums, tributes, and greatest hits packages as interest in Kimbrough's music continued to grow. He has inspired modern rock acts such as the Black Keys who, as well as covering his songs on numerous albums, released the 2006 EP *Chulahoma* that consists entirely of Kimbrough compositions.

RYAN KIRK

Kimmel, John J. (*b* Brooklyn, NY, 13 Dec 1866; *d* Brooklyn, NY, 18 Sept 1942). Accordion and melodeon player and pioneer recording artist. Kimmel is something of an enigma. He was the child of German immigrant parents but was known for playing traditional Irish dance music—jigs, reels, and hornpipes—on the button accordion (and most often on a one-row melodeon). This earned him the nickname: "The Irish Dutchman." His many recordings, which also included non-Irish material, show him to have been a virtuoso of the first order, with a firm grasp of Irish traditional musical style, but because he recorded so early—Kimmel made his first records in 1904 or 1905—and because there is little documentation of the accordion in Irish music before this era, the question of who his stylistic models might have been remains unanswered. Also, in spite of the fact that Kimmel recorded extensively over a period of 25 years, and his records seem to have sold well, he apparently was relatively unknown in the Irish American musical community that flourished in New York in the 1920s. His records were very influential among Quebecois musicians, but much less so among Irish players. This was likely due to the fact that his records generally were not marketed in the specialized series aimed specifically at the Irish audience. Nevertheless, reissues of some of Kimmel's recordings have brought his music to the attention of modern audiences, and present-day Irish accordion players such as Paul Brock and Jackie Daly stand in awe of his playing.

RECORDINGS
(selective list)
Early Recordings of Irish Traditional Dance Music (Leader Records, 1977)

BIBLIOGRAPHY
J. Walsh: "John H. [*sic*] Kimmel, 'The Irish Scotchman [*sic*]'," *Hobbies, the Magazine for Collectors*, lxii/12 (1958), 30–5

PAUL F. WELLS

Kincaid, Bradley (*b* Point Leavell, KY, 13 July 1895; *d* Springfield, OH, 23 Sept 1989). Country and folk music performer. Raised in Garrard County, Kentucky, Kincaid absorbed the religious music and ballad traditions of his family. He learned to play on a guitar his father reputedly acquired from trading a dog, and his "hound dawg" guitar became his trademark throughout his career. Kincaid dropped out of school after fifth grade and later resumed his education at Berea College Academy, completing high school at age 26. At Berea, Kincaid began to systematically collect ballads and other forms of traditional music. After graduation, he married his music teacher, a graduate of Oberlin Conservatory. Kincaid relocated to Chicago to attend the YMCA College and there auditioned with a college quartet at WLS, a local radio station. Kincaid, "the Kentucky Mountain Boy," soon became a hit with his clear tenor and his rendition of traditional ballads such as "Barbara Allen." By the early 1930s, Kincaid was one of the most popular radio performers nationally, and he augmented his radio salary with songbook sales and live performances. He also he recorded prolifically for Gennett, Brunswick, ARC, Decca, RCA, and others. He worked at radio stations in Pittsburgh, New York, Boston, Cincinnati, and Wheeling with his partner "GRANDPA" JONES. From 1942 until 1947, he performed in Nashville on WSM as a member of the Grand Ole Opry. In the late 1940s, Kincaid semi-retired to Springfield, Ohio, where he ran a radio station and a music store and continued to issue commercial records and perform at folk festivals though the final decades of his life. Although he was one of the early stars of country music and his repertoire ran the gamut from traditional to popular songs, Kincaid viewed himself as a collector and performer of folk, rather than "hillbilly," music, and his career exemplifies the relative lack of distinction made between these genres in the early decades of commercial country music.

BIBLIOGRAPHY
D.K. Wilgus: "Bradley Kincaid," *Stars of Country Music*, ed. B.C. Malone and J. McCulloh (Urbana, IL, 1975), 86
L. Jones: *Radio's Kentucky Mountain Boy. Bradley Kincaid* (Berea, KY, 1980)
C.K. Wolfe: *Kentucky Country* (Lexington, KY, 1982)

CHARLES K. WOLFE/MICHAEL ANN WILLIAMS

Kincaid, William (*b* Minneapolis, MN, 26 April 1895; *d* Philadelphia, PA, 27 March 1967). Flutist. He began to play flute at the age of eight. In 1911 he moved to New York, where he entered the Institute of Musical Art, studying theory and composition and becoming the prize flute pupil of GEORGES BARRÈRE. From 1913 to 1918 he played in the New York SO under Walter Damrosch. Following war service in the US Navy he played from 1918 to 1921 with the New York Chamber Music Society. In 1921 Leopold Stokowski invited him to join the Philadelphia Orchestra as solo flutist, a post he held until his retirement in 1960. His appearances as soloist with the orchestra on more than 150 occasions did much to establish public acceptance of the flute as a solo instrument. He made many recordings, both as a soloist and as a member of the Philadelphia Woodwind Quintet, with which he played from 1952 to 1957. He taught at the Curtis Institute from its foundation in 1924 until 1967, and numbered many eminent American flutists among his pupils. From 1939 until his death he played on a platinum flute made by Verne Q. Powell of Boston.

BIBLIOGRAPHY

J. Krell: *Kincaidiana: a Flute Player's Notebook* (Culver City, CA, 1973/*R*)

PHILIP BATE/JOHN SOLUM

King. Record company. It was formally established in Cincinnati by Syd Nathan in August 1944, though issues began in November the previous year; at first the catalog consisted solely of country music including recordings by Moon Mullican and the Delamore Brothers. "Country boogie," the precursor to rockabilly, was also regularly recorded by King. A companion race label, Queen, was established in 1945. Recordings by several small groups from Lucky Millinder's band were among the company's first releases. Recordings were also acquired from 20th Century and from J. Mayo Williams's labels Southern and Harlem. Blues artists represented included Lonnie Johnson, Memphis Slim, and Wynonie Harris.

In July 1947 the company began issuing recordings by Earl Bostic on Queen, but discontinued the label the following month. Thereafter King itself became the race label, though Queen's numerical series was continued and the country series remained separate. In 1948 King acquired De Luxe, which it operated until 1949 as a separate subsidiary. In 1950 the company established another label, Federal, to which James Brown was signed in 1956; this label continued until the mid-1960s. Throughout the 1950s, King also sold and distributed portable record players.

In 1961 King acquired Bethlehem and its highly regarded material by Duke Ellington and much important swing, hard bop, and West Coast jazz. Following Nathan's death in 1968, King was purchased by Starday, which remained the owner until 1971 and instigated a program of reissues; this has been continued by the company Gusto, which purchased the King catalog in 1975.

BIBLIOGRAPHY

A. Rotante, ed.: "The 'King' of R & B Labels," *Record Research* (1959), no.22, 9–10; no.24, 11 only; no.25, 14 only
A. Shaw: *Honkers and Shouters: the Golden Years of Rhythm and Blues* (New York, 1978), 275
B. Daniels: "Queen Records," *Whiskey, Women, and...*, no.11 (1983), 12–4
M. Ruppli and B. Daniels: *The King Labels: a Discography* (Westport, CT, and London, 1985)
T. Burke: "Syd Nathan and the King Records Story," *Blues & Rhythm: the Gospel Truth*, no.113 (1996), 10
J.H. Fox: *Queen of the King City: The Story of King Records* (Urbana, 2009)

HOWARD RYE/JONAS WESTOVER

King, Albert (*b* Indianola, MS, 25 April 1923; *d* Memphis, TN, 21 Dec 1992). Blues guitarist and singer. He began his musical career singing with a family gospel group before becoming a blues musician. A self-taught guitarist, he played left-handed and held his Gibson Flying V electric guitar upside-down with the strings set for a right-handed player. He concentrated on tone and intensity and was known for bending his strings to produce a distinct blues sound. He had his first major hit in 1961 with the release of "Don't Throw Your Love on Me So Strong," but did not become a big blues star until he signed with Stax Records in 1966. There he created a blues sound with Memphis soul underpinnings which gave him crossover appeal with rock fans through records such as "Born Under a Bad Sign" (1967), with Stax's house band Booker T. & the MG's. He was the first blues artist to play the San Francisco rock venue the Fillmore West and the first bluesman to record with a symphony orchestra when he performed with the St. Louis Symphony in 1969. During the 1970s he worked with The Bar-Kays and added strong funk elements to his music. His 1972 hit "I'll Play the Blues for You" showcases this collaboration. In the 1980s, he continued to tour and played many festivals and concerts, often with B.B. King. He was inducted into the Blues Foundation's Hall of Fame in 1983.

BIBLIOGRAPHY

L. Cohn: *Nothing but the Blues* (New York, 1993)
J. Rolf, ed.: *The Definitive Illustrated Encyclopedia of Jazz & Blues* (London, 2008)

DINA M. BENNETT

King, B.B. [Riley B.] (*b* Itta Bena, MS, 16 Sept 1925). Blues singer and guitarist. He grew up on a tenant farm in the Mississippi Delta and taught himself guitar. Taking the name Blues Boy (later abbreviated to B.B.), he appeared as a blues singer, guitarist, and disc jockey for the WDIA radio station in Memphis. His recording of *"Three O'Clock Blues"* (1952, RPM) brought him some success, but his international breakthrough came in the early 1960s when, as the idol of British rock musicians, he influenced such figures as John Mayall, Eric Clapton, and Mick Jagger. Since then he has been a leading figure on the blues scene.

King has occupied a commanding position among contemporary blues singers, analogous to that of Bessie Smith in the 1920s. Even his early recordings reveal a distinctive mixture of jazz, swing, gospel, and rhythm-and-blues styles, which he synthesized without stylistic inconsistency or incongruity. Although not notably original, his guitar playing is both distinctive and characteristic, and owes something to the earlier jazz guitarists Django Reinhardt and Charlie Christian, as well as his blues predecessors T-Bone Walker and

Muddy Waters. He has had the finest voice among blues singers—a high tenor which, when he was younger, easily reached *c″* and *d″*, with an upward extension to *f″* in falsetto. Although he has also be able to sustain a melody successfully, he has been most convincing when performing blues in the declamatory tradition, with its fusion of speech and song. The blues gained stature in the 1960s and 70s largely on account of the eloquence of King's singing and his charming and benign personality both on and off the stage; throughout these decades he enjoyed considerable commercial success, many of his recordings appearing on the rhythm-and-blues chart. His album *There Must Be a Better World Somewhere* (1981, MCA) earned one of his 15 Grammy Awards in 1981, but perhaps his finest recorded work is *Live at the Cook County Jail* (1970, ABC). He was inducted into both the Blues Hall of Fame and the Rock and Roll Hall of Fame, received a Grammy Lifetime Achievement Award, and was awarded the National Medal of Arts, the Kennedy Center Honors, and the Presidential Medal of Freedom. Although he no longer toured regularly, King continued to perform on special occasions into the 2010s.

BIBLIOGRAPHY
SouthernB
C. Keil: *Urban Blues* (Chicago, 1966/*R*)
P. Garland: "King of Blues," *The Sound of Soul* (Chicago, 1969), 98
C. Gillett: *The Sound of the City: the Rise of Rock and Roll* (New York, 1970, enlarged 2/1983, 3/1996)
K. Mohr: "B.B. King," *Soul Bag*, no.32 (1973), 19; no.47 (1975), 1 [discography]
C. Sawyer: *The Arrival of B.B. King: the Authorized Biography* (Poole, England, 1980)
J.S. Richardson: *The Blues Guitar Style of B.B. King* (diss., U. of Memphis, 1987)
J. Richardson and R. Bourman: "Conversation with B.B. King: 'King of the Blues'," *BPM*, xvii (1989), 135–52
B. Gibbons and J. Obrecht: "B.B. & Billy: Memphis and the Early Years," *Guitar Player*, xxv/7 (1991), 24–35
D. Erlewine: "B.B. King: Talking about Lucille," *Guitar Player*, xxvi/6 (1992), 78–86
B.B. King with D. Ritz: *Blues All Around Me: the Autobiography of B.B. King* (New York, 1996)

HENRY PLEASANTS/R

King, Ben E. [Nelson, Benjamin Earl] (*b* Henderson, NC, 28 Sept 1938). Popular singer. He was the principal vocalist with the Five Crowns and the Drifters, recording with the latter the hit songs "There Goes My Baby" and "Save the Last Dance for Me." He began a solo career in 1961 with recordings including Otis Blackwell's "Brace Yourself" and a duet with LaVern Baker, "How Often." In the early 1960s he made three highly successful recordings in association with leading New York composer-producers: "Spanish Harlem" with Phil Spector included Latin rhythms and percussion, "Don't Play that Song" was composed by King and Ahmet Ertegun, while "Stand by Me" was co-written by King with Leiber and Stoller. The stark arrangement of the last song made it a classic of the emerging soul music genre and King's recording had a new lease of life when it was used in a 1986 film named after the song. King's later

recordings of the 1960s showed his versatility but were less memorable. He sang a version of the show ballad "I (Who Have Nothing)" before shifting in 1964 to the more declamatory style associated with Solomon Burke for "It's All Over" and "Seven Letters." His final hit came in 1975 with the disco-styled "Supernatural Thang" but he continued to perform in concert into the 2010s.

DAVE LAING/R

King, Carole [Klein, Carol] (*b* Brooklyn, NY, 9 Feb 1942). Singer-songwriter, and pianist. Carole King co-wrote numerous hit singles with husband GERRY GOFFIN and other writers throughout the 1960s, before reinventing herself as a singer-songwriter with albums such as *Tapestry* (1971), which propelled her to a successful solo career.

At age four, her mother began instructing her in piano, and she was writing music by the time she was a teenager, when she also adopted her professional name. A childhood friend, Neil Sedaka, introduced her into the music industry, finding her jobs playing piano, singing backup, and arranging studio sessions while she attended Queens College. There she met Gerry Goffin, and the two began a personal and professional relationship. By 1960, she and Goffin worked at Aldon Music in New York's Brill Building. The next year they wrote the million-seller, "Will you love me tomorrow?" recorded by the Shirelles. Written after King and Goffin had married following an unexpected pregnancy, the song spoke directly to its teenage audience.

The pair enjoyed hits throughout the 1960s, including songs written, arranged, and produced for Bobby Vee, the Drifters, Little Eva, and the Cookies. For babysitter Little Eva, King wrote "The Loco-Motion" based on movements the singer made. In 1962, King released her own recording, "It might as well rain until September," but her solo career did not take off. The Cookies recorded the duo's "Chains" in 1962, which was covered by The Beatles. The writing pair composed over 100 songs in the 1960s, which were recorded by various girl groups as well as other acts such as the Byrds, Dusty Springfield, the Animals, Herman's Hermits, the Monkees, and Aretha Franklin.

Goffin and King attempted to launch their own label, Tomorrow Records, in 1967, but the venture was a failure, and their marriage and writing partnership also disintegrated. King moved to Los Angeles and started a recording career, forming The City with guitarist Danny Kortchmar and bassist Charles Lackey, who later became her second husband. The band released only one album, presciently titled *Now That Everything's Been Said*. Encouraged by fellow singer-songwriter James Taylor, King started a solo career and released *Tapestry* in 1971. The remarkably successful and influential album drew on King's musicianship while Taylor accompanied on acoustic guitar. The duo marked the emergence of a new type of singer-songwriter, writing songs that reflected awareness of the environment, politics, religion, and the dynamics of personal relationships. *Tapestry* reached number one, won four Grammy Awards, and since its release has sold over 25 million copies worldwide.

Follow-up albums explored similar terrain, but never approached *Tapestry*'s broad impact. *Music* (1972) and *Wrap around Joy* (1973) both hit number one in the album charts and earned gold status. In 1980, she released *Pearls*, comprised of her versions of Goffin/King hits from the early 1960s. King became involved in environmental affairs in the 1980s, and restricted her live performances to charity concerts. In 1993, *Tapestry* was adapted into a theatrical show, and a tribute album followed in 1995. She collaborated with Céline Dion on an internationally popular single, "The Reason" (1997), and released *The Living Room Tour* (2005), a live album that became her highest-charting release since the late 1970s. In 2010, she released *The Essential Carole King*, containing songs from her solo career and material written for other musicians. She and James Taylor reunited in 2007 for the Troubadour Reunion Tour, which led to the release *Live at the Troubadour* in 2010.

RECORDINGS
(selective list)

Albums: *Writer* (1970); *Tapestry* (1971); *Music* (1972); *Rhymes and Reasons* (1972); *Wrap around Joy* (1973); *Thoroughbred* (1976); *Her Greatest Hits* (1978); *Pearls: the Songs of Goffin and King* (1980); *One to One* (1982); *The Living Room Tour* (2005); *Live at the Troubadour* with James Taylor (2010);*The Essential Carole King* (2010)

BIBLIOGRAPHY

M. Walker: *Laurel Canyon: the Inside Story of Rock-and-Roll's Legendary Neighborhood* (New York, 2006)

J. Warwick: *Girl Groups, Girl Culture: Popular Music and Identity in the 1960s* (New York, 2007), 109–17

S. Weller: *Girls Like Us: Carole, King, Joni Mitchell, and Carly Simon—And the Journey of a Generation* (New York, 2008)

RICHARD D. DRIVER

King, Charles E(dward) (*b* Honolulu, HI, 29 Jan 1874; *d* Elmhurst, NY, 27 Feb 1950). Composer, arranger, band-leader, and teacher. King was influenced by the classic compositions of members of the Hawaiian royalty from the 19th century, and his compositions reflected his understanding of Hawaiian culture. King influenced the direction of Hawaiian music in the 20th century through his work as a composer, arranger, publisher, lecturer, teacher, and radio host.

Born in Honolulu, King graduated from Kamehameha Schools in 1891 and the Pratt Institute in 1900. He soon returned to Kamehameha Schools as a teacher. His success as a composer of Hawaiian music began in 1915 with "Na Lei O Hawaii" (Song of the Islands). King published numerous song sheets and songbooks, featuring both his work and that of other Hawaiian composers, and also wrote the Hawaiian operetta, *The Prince of Hawaii* (1925). He hosted a popular weekly Hawaiian radio show that featured live performances. King served as the bandmaster of the Royal Hawaiian Band in 1932–34 and 1939–40. In 1942, he moved to New York, where he became more involved in publishing and distribution, and assisted with the earliest presentation of Hawaiian music on television. Among his most famous compositions are "Na Lei O Hawaii," "Ke Kali Nei Au," "Imi Au Ia Oe," "Kamehameha Waltz," "Ku'u I'ini," "Mi

Nei," "Uheuhene," "Imua Kamehameha," and "Pidgin English Hula." His best known publications are *King's Book of Hawaiian Melodies* and *King's Songs of Hawaii*.

BIBLIOGRAPHY

T. Todaro: *The Golden Years of Hawaiian Entertainment, 1874–1974* (Honolulu, 1974)

G.S. Kanahele: *Hawaiian Music And Musicians: an Illustrated History* (Honolulu, 1979)

HARRY B. SORIA JR.

King, E(lisha) J. (*b* Wilkinson Co., GA, *c*1821; *d* nr Talbotton, GA, 31 Aug 1844). Composer and singing-school teacher. In collaboration with B.F. White he compiled *The Sacred Harp* (published in Hamilton, GA, printed in Philadelphia, 1844, 3/1859/*R*, 4/1869), a collection of folk hymns, revival spirituals, fuging-tunes, odes, and anthems, which became the most widely used tune book in four-shape notation. It went through numerous editions and revisions in the late 19th and early 20th century and has remained in use at numerous singings and weekend conventions in the southern states (*see* SHAPE-NOTE HYMNODY). The number of songs attributed to King in the first edition is larger than that by any other composer; they include the tunes of the hymns "The Child of Grace," "Bound for Canaan," and "Gospel Trumpet." Two of his brothers, Joel King and Elias L. King, also made contributions to the volume. Other tune books containing King's works are William Hauser's *Hesperian Harp* (1848), John McCurry's *Social Harp* (1853), and William Walker's *Southern Harmony* (later editions) and *Christian Harmony* (1867). King also achieved some prominence as a singing-school teacher.

BIBLIOGRAPHY

B.E. Cobb: *The Sacred Harp: a Tradition and its Music* (Athens, GA, 1978, 2/1989)

BUELL E. COBB, HARRY ESKEW

King, James (Ambros) (*b* Dodge City, KS, 22 May 1925; *d* Naples, FL, 20 Nov 2005). Tenor. King, who originally thought himself a baritone, studied music at Louisiana State University and University of Kansas City–Missouri. He taught voice at UMKC for many years before training in New York with MARTIAL SINGHER in the late 1950s. He briefly served as resident tenor for the Saint Louis Municipal Opera before winning the 1961 American Opera Auditions in Cincinnati, a feat that sent him to Europe, where he made his professional debut in Florence as Cavaradossi. He held a resident appointment with the Deutsche Oper, Berlin (1962), and engagements followed at Salzburg (1962), Vienna (1963), Bayreuth (1965), and La Scala (1968). Some of King's performances in the United States included his 1961 debut as Don José in San Francisco and his appearance as Florestan at the Metropolitan in 1966. He sang the Emperor in both the Metropolitan and Covent Garden premieres of *Die Frau ohne Schatten*. King's bright, incisive tone, easy top voice and remarkable stamina made him particularly successful in the more lyrical

Wagnerian roles such as Walther von Stolzing, Parsifal (recorded under Boulez at Bayreuth) and Lohengrin, and as Bacchus in *Ariadne auf Naxos*, which he recorded with Kempe. His repertory also included Otello; Siegmund (which can be heard in both Solti's and Böhm's Bayreuth recordings of the *Ring*); the title role in Pfitzner's *Palestrina*, Aegisthus, which he sang at Salzburg in 1989; and the Drum-Major (Metropolitan, 1990). King was also a sterling soloist in works such as Beethoven's Ninth Symphony, Verdi's Requiem, and Mahler's *Das Lied von der Erde*, all of which he recorded. King taught voice at Indiana University from 1984 to 2002.

MARTIN BERNHEIMER/ALAN BLYTH/ANNE SHELLEY

King, Karl L(awrence) (*b* Paintersville, OH, 21 Feb 1891; *d* Fort Dodge, IA, 31 March 1971). Bandmaster and composer. After appearing as a baritone player in several town and circus bands, he became bandmaster for Sells Floto-Buffalo Bill (1914–6) and Barnum & Bailey's Greatest Show on Earth (1917–8), with which he made experimental recordings. In 1920 he became leader of the Fort Dodge Military Band, and held the position for 38 years. The band operated in the manner of the earlier Sousa, Gilmore, and Pryor bands, by touring, playing at fairs, and training many capable musicians. King was one of the founders of the American Bandmasters Association (1930), of which he was named honorary life president in 1967.

King's most famous composition is the march *Barnum & Bailey's Favorite*; among others written for circuses are *Robinson's Grand Entry*, *Sells Floto Triumphal*, *The Big Cage,* and *Circus Days*. He also wrote marches and fight songs for many American universities, and much tuneful, engaging music designed for the burgeoning school band movement. He published 11 volumes of music including *Marching to Victory Band Book* (1942) and *The Uncle Sam A-Strut Book* (1943); in contrast to the simpler works, these contain the massive "triumphals" and "grand entries" that have challenged the capabilities of top circus bands.

WORKS
(selective list; all for band)

13 galops, including Excelsior, 1910; Homestretch, 1912; Emporia, 1913; Eclipse, 1917; Majestic, 1919; Royal Hippodrome, 1928; Prestissimo, 1931; The Big Cage Circus, 1934; Rough Riders, 1943; Circus Days, 1944 29 waltzes, including Venetian Beauties, 1909; Moonlight on the Nile, 1909; American Beauty, 1910; Desdemona, 1910; Love's Way, 1910; My Lady, 1910; Southern Roses, 1910; The Siren, 1910; Over the Stars, 1910; Water Lilies, 1910; Belle Isle, 1912; Roses and Orchids, 1912; Spirit of Springtime, 1912; Persian Moonlight, 1915; Alpine Sunset, 1916; In Old Portugal, 1917; Enchanted Night, 1919; June Twilight, 1921; Glory of Egypt, 1923; The Silver Fountain, 1923; Dreamy Dawn, 1931; Mystic Night, 1931; Morning Glory, 1932; Vision of Cleopatra, 1934

10 serenades, including Evening Shadows, 1910; Fond Hearts, 1912; A Night in June, 1912; Nightfall, 1914; Eventide, 1914; An Autumn Romance, 1920; Twilight, 1934

7 intermezzi, including Wyoming Days, 1914; On The Warpath, 1915; Arabian Nights, 1915; Spanish Romance, 1917; Ung-Kung-Foy-Ya, 1919; In A Moonlit Garden, 1924

22 overtures, including The Conqueror, 1910; The Iron Count, 1911; Royal Emblem, 1912; The Royalist, 1912; Princess of India, 1912; Gypsy Queen, 1914; Royal Palm, 1914; The Baronet, 1914; Invincible, 1915; The Altar of Genius, 1916; The Golden Dragon, 1917;

Fountain of Youth, 1924; The Wanderer, 1926; The Magic Garden, 1928; National Glory, 1931; Old Vienna, 1938; The Voyager, 1944; Golden Days, 1951

25 misc., including 3 dirges: Our Last Farewell, 1909; Westlawn, 1910; Remembrance, 1912; Dance of the Imps, 1910; Ragged Rozey, 1913; Georgia Girl, 1914; Wood-Nymphs, 1914; Passing of the Red Man, 1916; Kentucky Sunrise, 1919; Broadway One Step, 1919; The Walking Frog, 1919; Abdallah, 1920

MSS in *Cp*
Principal publishers: Barnhouse, Kalmus, King

BIBLIOGRAPHY
J.L. Gerardi: *Karl L. King* (diss., U. of Colorado, 1973)
T.J. Hatton: *Karl L. King: an American Bandmaster* (Evanston, IL, 1975) [incl. complete list of works]
B.E. Kopetz: "Karl L. King: a Biographical Sketch of the Early Years (1891–1920)," *Journal of Band Research*, xxv/2 (1990), 47–63

TOM PARKINSON/CHARLES CONRAD

King, Pee Wee [Kuczynski, Julius Frank Anthony] (*b* Milwaukee, WI, 18 Feb 1914; *d* Louisville, KY, 7 March 2000). Country music accordionist, bandleader, songwriter, and vocalist. His musical career was inspired by his father, John, a Polish American who led a local polka band. At 15, he began learning accordion and, in 1930, met popular bandleader Wayne King who suggested the youth take the surname "King" in the interest of simplicity. His first band, the King's Jesters, played both country music and polkas. In 1934, the group filled in for Gene Autry's band when Autry, then a star of WLS's *National Barn Dance*, toured Wisconsin. King joined Autry (who dubbed him "Pee Wee") in Louisville until the singer left to launch his Hollywood film career. He briefly led a Louisville band known as the Log Cabin Boys, then in 1937 organized the Golden West Cowboys, who joined the *Grand Ole Opry* with a distinctive, progressive repertoire blending country, pop, polkas, waltzes, and western swing. From 1938 to 1943, Eddy Arnold was their vocalist. Fiddler Redd Stewart, who joined in 1940, later doubled as vocalist. In 1947, inspired by Bill Monroe's hit recording "Kentucky Waltz," King and Stewart added lyrics to "No-Name Waltz," the Cowboys' instrumental theme song, to create "Tennessee Waltz." Three hit versions appeared in 1948: by King (RCA), Cowboy Copas (King), and Roy Acuff (Columbia). It became a 1950 pop hit for Patti Page and Tennessee's official state song. King and Stewart co-wrote "Slow Poke," the band's only number one country hit (RCA, 1951), and, with amateur songwriter Chilton Price, wrote the pop ballad "You belong to me." In 1947, King and the band left the *Opry* to host a weekly television show at WAVE in Louisville and, in the 1950s, simultaneously hosted similar local shows in Cleveland, Cincinnati, and Chicago in addition to touring. King disbanded the Golden West Cowboys in 1969, but continued performing occasionally with Stewart into the 1990s. Inducted into the Country Music Hall of Fame in 1974, he died of a heart attack in 2000.

BIBLIOGRAPHY
W. Hall: *Hell-Bent for Music: the Life of Pee Wee King* (Lexington, KY, 1996)

RICH KIENZLE

King Biscuit Time. Blues radio program. On 21 November 1941, King Biscuit Time premiered on Helena, Arkansas' KFFA 1360 AM. Initially sponsored by Interstate Grocer as a marketing promotion for King Biscuit Flour, the show featured musicians Sonny Boy Williamson and Robert Lockwood Jr., collectively known as the King Biscuit Entertainers. Later band members included Dudlow Taylor, James Peck Curtis, Pinetop Perkins, Willie Love, Robert Nighthawk, and Houston Stackhouse. In 1951, Sunshine Sunny (John William) Payne became the program's host. The show could be heard across the Mississippi/Arkansas Delta region and was among the earliest radio programs in the country to feature live blues. In 1992, KFFA and King Biscuit Time were recognized with a George Peabody Award for outstanding achievement in broadcast journalism. As of 2011, King Biscuit Time and Sunshine Sunny Payne are still on the air, broadcasting daily from the Arkansas Delta Cultural Center in Helena, Arkansas.

The long history of King Biscuit Time has helped established Helena, Arkansas as an important center for blues tourism. Since 1986, the city has hosted the King Biscuit Blues Festival, known from 2005 to 2010 as the Arkansas Blues and Heritage Festival, which features traditional and contemporary blues and annually attracts thousands of blues aficionados.

BIBLIOGRAPHY
D.S. Rotenstein: "The Helena Blues: Cultural Tourism and African American Folk Music," *Southern Folklore*, xl/2 (1992), 135–45
R. Fry: *We Are the Blues: Independent and Communal Performances of the King B Biscuit Tradition* (diss., Florida State U., 2010)
ROBERT WEBB FRY II

King Curtis [Ousley, Curtis] (*b* Fort Worth, TX, 7 Feb 1934; *d* New York, NY, 13 Aug 1971). Tenor saxophonist and bandleader. As one of the most versatile studio saxophonists of the 1950s and 60s in New York, he appeared on countless recordings as a session musician, mostly for Atlantic Records. He worked with artists as diverse as the post-doo-wop Coasters (notably "Yakety Yak") and the rockabilly singer Buddy Holly ("Reminiscing," which he co-wrote). In addition, King Curtis recorded successfully under his own name (1962–70). These recordings capitalized on the popularity of soul jazz, using blues-derived harmonic progressions, open-ended vamps and syncopated riffs. In the late 1960s he became the musical director for Aretha Franklin and was working on John Lennon's album *Imagine* at the time of his death in 1971. King Curtis was inspired by such saxophonists as Louis Jordan, Illinois Jacquet, Earl Bostic, and Gene Ammons. Although he was influenced by the rhythm and blues "honkin'" style of the 1940s and 50s, his playing reveals a debt to jazz as well. With a searing edge to his sound resembling gospel vocal tones, his style frequently featured a staccato, stuttering technique, combined with melodic mobility and a variety of slurs, bends, and use of the instrument's harmonic register.

BIBLIOGRAPHY
A. Shaw: *Honkers and Shouters: the Golden Years of Rhythm and Blues* (New York, 1978)
C. Escott: liner notes, *Instant Soul: the Legendary King Curtis*, (Razor & Tie Music 852 and 853, 1994)
DAVID BRACKETT

King Musical Instruments. Firm of instrument makers. It was founded as the H.N. White Company (Cleveland) in 1893 by Henderson Nelson White (1873–1940), an instrument repairman, amateur musician, and businessman. White created the company's first instrument, a trombone, in consultation with trombonist Thomas H. King (1868–1926), after whom the King line was named. The company was renamed King Musical Instruments in 1966.

Foster A. Reynolds (1884–1960) managed White's factory and a full line of band instruments from 1903 to 1935. A department of acoustical research was established in 1909 in a new factory at 5225 Superior Avenue. Saxophone manufacture began in 1916, followed by the invention of the King saxello (1924; a straight soprano sax with a curved neck and half-turned bell) and the pioneering introduction of sterling silver bells on cornets, trumpets, and trombones. White purchased the Cleveland Musical Instrument Company (1925), added stringed instruments to his line (1934), and introduced the trombonium (1938; an upright valved tenor instrument).

Edna Richert White (1895–1969) became company president in 1941, upon the death of her husband. Her daughter, Cathryn (Kay) Colbert White Ludwig Sylvester (1920–2005) became vice president in 1945. Edna sold the company to Nate Dolin Associates in 1965, after which it merged with The Seeburg Corporation (1966), moved to Eastlake, Ohio, and was renamed King Musical Instruments. The company was later bought by C.G. CONN owner, Daniel J. Henkin (1983), then sold to Swedish conglomerate Skåne Gripen AB (1985), under which King became a division of United Musical Instruments. An investment group headed by Bernhard Muskantor purchased UMI in 1989 and sold it to Steinway Musical Instruments, Inc. (2000), which created Conn-Selmer, Inc. (2002), of which King Musical Instruments is a division.

MARTIN KRIVIN/MARGARET DOWNIE BANKS

Kingsmen, the. Rock and roll group. Formed in Portland, Oregon, in 1959, this cover band is chiefly known for its recording of "Louie, Louie," which gave rise to hundreds of other recorded versions of the song. The band members at that session were Jack Ely, vocalist and rhythm guitarist; Lynn Easton, drummer; Mike Mitchell, lead guitarist; Don Galluci, keyboard player; and Bob Nordby, bass guitarist. "Louie, Louie" was written by Richard Berry, an African American rhythm and blues singer from Los Angeles, who drew on the Latin tune "El Loco Cha Cha Cha" for the song's rhythm, and on the standard "One More for My Baby" for its lyrics; his rather dull recording, made in 1956, was moderately successful but swiftly forgotten. Five years later an aspiring white singer, Rockin' Robin Roberts, recorded the song with the Wailers of Tacoma (Washington); their version inspired the Kingsmen, who incorporated "Louie, Louie" into the repertory they performed nightly in dance halls and recorded it in 1963. Although the Kingsmen's version was raucous, brutal, and clumsy, and the lyrics unintelligible, their release became enormously successful. Prompted by rumors that the song was obscene, the government investigated and pronounced it "indecipherable at any speed." The song was performed by thousands of amateur bands, and recorded by such diverse artists as Julie London and the punk group Black Flag. In 1983 radio station KFJC of Los Altos, California, broadcast over 700 versions of the song. With some breaks as well as a number of personnel changes, the group has spent more than four decades presenting concerts featuring "Louie, Louie."

BIBLIOGRAPHY

D. Marsh: *Louie Louie: the History and Mythology of the World's Most Famous Rock 'n' roll Song* (New York, 1993)

GREIL MARCUS/R

King's Singers, the. British vocal ensemble. The group is one of the oldest and most successful choral ensembles in the world. The ensemble was formed in 1965 at King's College in Cambridge, England. The King's Singers' distinctive approach is inspired by the English choral tradition, as well as American barber-shop quartet style. The ensemble's popularity is largely due to its wide variety of repertoire ranging from Renaissance works to popular music, sung in exquisitely tuned, often humorous performances. Since the 1970s, the group has frequently toured the United States, in addition to collaborating with many American artists and organizations. They have recorded over 60 albums with BMG Classics and RCA Victor, including performances with American ensembles such as the Boston Pops, Cincinnati Pops, and the Mormon Tabernacle Choir. The King's Singers has commissioned new choral works from several American composers, including Libby Larson's *A Lover's Journey*, Ned Rorem's *Pilgrim Strangers*, and Eric Whitacre's *The Stolen Child*.

RECORDINGS

Gesualdo: Tenebrae Responses for Maundy Thursday (Signum UK, SIGCD048, 2004)
Rejoice and be Merry! (Intellectual Reserve CFN 0815-2, 2008)

BIBLIOGRAPHY

N. Perrin and others: *The King's Singers: a Self Portrait* (London, 1980)
L. Kandell: "Music; A Cappella Distinction from a New Generation," *New York Times* (21 Feb 1999)

MICHAEL HIX

Kingston, Richard (Joseph) (*b* Philadelphia, PA, June 1947). Harpsichord maker. As a child he lived in France, and dates his interest in musical instruments from a post horn he found and repaired. He attended Temple University in Philadelphia, Pennsylvania, Lamar University in Beaumont, Texas, and the University of Texas at Arlington. At age 23 he made a harpsichord from a Zuckermann Kit. Convinced that he would rather be a builder than a CPA, he left school to set up shop in Dallas, Texas. In 1979 he moved to North Carolina, where he had studios in Marshall, Asheville, and Mooresboro, before moving to Fort Mill, South Carolina.

Kingston has made more than 300 harpsichords in Italian and northern European styles. While he never served an apprenticeship, he counts Boston builder William Dowd as a strong influence on his building. In 1991 he received the Spivey award for Excellence in Harpsichord Building. His 333rd harpsichord, a large, powerful double-manual instrument in the northern European tradition completed in 2009, was commissioned by performer Elaine Funaro (an advocate for new music for harpsichord) and decorated in a strikingly contemporary manner by painter Lisa Creed. Kingston is known for the reliability and high quality of his instruments, which are refined in both sound and finish.

EDWARD L. KOTTICK

Kingston Trio, the. Folk group. It was formed in 1957 in San Francisco, California by Dave Guard (*b* 19 Oct 1934; *d* 22 March 1991; guitar, banjo), Bob Shane (*b* 1 Feb 1934; vocals, guitar), and Nick Reynolds (*b* 27 July 1933; *d* 1 Oct 2008; guitar, bongos). Each member self-taught, the Trio enjoyed immense popularity and success between 1958–61. They are credited with sparking THE FOLK REVIVAL of the late 1950s and making the singer-songwriter viable in the music industry.

Guard and Shane grew up in Hawaii and played together in high school, later meeting Reynolds in California, where they had both moved for college. After briefly returning to Hawaii to pursue a solo career, Shane formed the Kingston Trio with Guard and Reynolds. In July 1957, the group became the headline act at San Francisco's Purple Onion Club. Capitol Records signed the group and the Trio released their self-titled debut album in June 1958. The album was influenced by other folk musicians Woody Guthrie and the Weavers, and included the Top Ten single "Tom Dooley." Subsequent albums expanded the group's sound, including live performances and vocal overdubs. Guard, Shane, and Reynolds represented an alternative to fears related to rock and rollers in the 1950s: all three married and committed to their home structures, but were still young, energetic, and creative.

The group's first six albums were each certified gold, but Capitol's insistence that the Trio release three albums a year depleted their stock of material quickly. The group's popularity declined through the 1960s, following the departure of the three founders by 1967 and attempts to include protest songs as part of their repertoire. Shane re-formed the group as the New Kingston Trio in the mid-1970s with Roger Gamble and George Grove. Different line-ups continued to tour and record through the 1980s into the 2000s; Guard died from cancer in 1991, and Reynolds retired in 1999.

BIBLIOGRAPHY

H. George-Warren and P. Romanowski, eds.: *The Rolling Stone Encyclopedia of Rock & Roll* (New York, 1983, rev. 3/2001), 531
R. Cohen: *Rainbow Quest: the Folk Music Revival and American Society, 1940–1970* (Amherst, MA, 2002), 125–156

RICHARD D. DRIVER

Kinkeldey, Otto (*b* New York, NY, 27 Nov 1878; *d* Orange, NJ, 19 Sept 1966). Musicologist, teacher, and librarian. He studied at the College of the City of New York (AB 1898), English and philosophy at the New York University (MA 1900), and music with EDWARD MACDOWELL at Columbia University (1900–02); concurrently he was organist and choirmaster at the Chapel of the Incarnation (1898–1902) and taught in New York schools. He continued his study of music, literature, and philosophy (1902–9), with Robert Radecke at the Königliches Akademisches Institut für Kirchenmusik and with Oskar Fleischer, Max Friedländer, Hermann Kretzschmar, and Johannes Wolf at the Universität zu Berlin, taking the doctorate (a rare achievement for an American in a German university at the time) in 1909 with a dissertation on 16th-century organ and keyboard music. He was also organist and choirmaster of the American Church in Berlin (1903–5) and was sent by the Prussian government on a tour of the central German states (1906–7) to catalog the music and music literature in church, ducal, and civic libraries. In 1909 he was offered the posts of librarian at the Breslau Königliches Institut für Kirchenmusik and instructor in music theory and the organ at Breslau University, where he subsequently became lecturer in music history with the honorary title of professor (1912–14). He was also appointed to the board of directors of the Breslau Opera. Despite the university's offer to create an extraordinary chair for him, the outbreak and continuation of war prompted him to return to New York, where he became head of the New York Public Library's Music Division (1915–23) and organist of All Souls Universalist Church in Brooklyn. After the war (during which he served as a training officer, 1917–19) he travelled in France, Spain, Germany, and Italy making purchases for the library. After a period as head of the music department at Cornell University (1923–7) he returned to the New York Public Library (1927–30) and continued to make buying trips to Europe for this and other libraries. He was drawn back to Cornell by the offer of the first American chair of musicology in 1930, created especially for him; he was also made university librarian, a post he held until 1946. Before his retirement from the Music Department in 1958 (because of increasing difficulties in hearing) he also taught at Harvard, Princeton, Texas, Illinois, Berkeley, Boston, and Washington State. In 1942 he was elected a Fellow of the American Academy of Arts and Sciences, and in 1947 awarded the Litt. D. (*honoris causa*) from Princeton University.

Kinkeldey was the founder of American musicology, even though he was an inheritor of European methods. It was owing to him more than to any other individual that musicology, after a long struggle for recognition as a serious discipline, became an accepted subject in the curriculum of American universities. It was chiefly to him that subsequent American music scholars, directly and indirectly, owed (and often acknowledged) their livelihood. In establishing the subject he drew on his experience of German music scholarship, and throughout his work he maintained that intellectual breadth, exacting standards, and close adherence to the music

itself are essential in an approach to any topic. His ability as a performing musician informed his interpretation of musical texts and history, while his wide range of interests in the humanities and comprehensive grasp of the current state of research, as well as an uncanny power of defining the essential issues with clarity, force, and common sense, made him an outstanding teacher. He was a founder and president of the American Musicological Society (1935–37; 1941–43) and a leading member of its predecessor, the Music Teachers National Association. In his research he was similarly a pioneer: he was one of the first investigators of early keyboard music and Renaissance dance, and his *Orgel und Klavier in der Musik des 16. Jahrhunderts* (1910), combining his characteristic attributes of breadth and thoroughness, remains a fundamental exploration.

He was also a founder of American music librarianship, and was the Music Library Association's first president (1931–35). He made the first statement on the essentials of practitioners' training (1937), still the model for research librarians. His demanding concept of the librarian's role was evident in his statement that it necessitates knowledge of archaeology, paleography, art history, acoustics, economics, education, and literature. His early calls for cooperative efforts in music collection development and cataloging standards were visionary, as was his understanding of the dependency of music librarians upon their colleagues. He was among the first to be awarded the Music Library Association's highest honor (Citation and Honorary Membership) in 1965.

WRITINGS

"Music in the Universities of Europe and America," *MTNA: Proceedings*, x (1915), 79–91; see also xxix (1934), 20–28

"The New York Public Library, and Its Music Division," *Library Journal* [Music number] 40 (1915), 589–92

"Music Education and Public Libraries," *National Education Association of the United States. Journal of Proceedings and Addresses* (s.l., 1916), 596–600; repr. *The Music Bulletin*, 3 (Sept 1916), 11–14

"Beginnings of Beethoven in America," *MQ*, xiii (1927), 217–48

"American Scholarship in Music since 1876," *MTNA: Proceedings*, xxiii (1928), 244–56

"Musicology in American Colleges and Universities," *Yearbook of the Music Educators National Conference 1934*, 125

"The Preparation of the College Student for Graduate Study," *MTNA: Proceedings*, xxix (1934), 165–70

"Research Librarian," *ALA Bulletin* 29 (Sept 1935), 598–9

"Changing Relations within the Field of Musicology," *PAMS* (1936), 42–57; also in *Music Teachers National Association: Proceedings*, xxxi (1936), 246–61

"Training for Music Librarianship: Aims and Opportunities," *ALA Bulletin* xxxi (1937), 459–63; repr. C. J. Bradley, *Reader in Music Librarianship* (Washington, DC, 1973), 299–302

"The Artist and the Scholar," *PAMS* (1940), 126–36; also in *MTNA: Proceedings*, xxxv (1940), 67–79

"Waldo Selden Pratt," *MQ*, xxvi (1940), 162–74

"Palm Leaf Books," *William Warner Bishop: a Tribute*, ed. H.M. Lydenburg and A. Keogh (New Haven, CT, 1941), 88–115

What We Know about Music (Ann Arbor, MI, 1946)

"Musical Scholarship and the University," *JRBM*, i (1946–7), 10–18

"The Music Teacher and the Library," *MTNA: Proceedings*, xlii (1948), 81–6

"To Alfred Einstein: 30 Dec 1950," *Notes*, viii (1950), 33–9

"Oscar George Theodore Sonneck," *Notes*, xi (1953–4), 25–32

"Consequences of the Recorded Performance," in *Music and Criticism: A Symposium*, ed. R.L. French (Port Washington, NY, 1969), 115–36

BIBLIOGRAPHY

GMO

E.J. Dent: "Otto Kinkeldey," *MQ* xxiv (1938), 405–11

G.S. Dickinson: "Otto Kinkeldey: an Appreciation," *MQ* xxiv (1938), 412–18

R. Angell: "Otto Kinkeldey," *College & Research Libraries* vii (1946), 262–3

"Otto Kinkeldey in Honor of his Seventieth Birthday, November 27, 1948," *Notes*, vi (1948) [incl. C. Sprague Smith: "Otto Kinkeldey," 27–37]

E.T. Ferand: "Otto Kinkeldey zum 80. Geburtstag am 27. November 1958," *Mf* xii (1959), 3–4

P.H. Lang: "Editorial," *MQ*, xlv (1959), 85–7

C. Seeger: "Otto Kinkeldey," *AcM*, xxxi (1959), 7–8

"A Musicological Offering to Otto Kinkeldey upon the Occasion of his Eightieth Birthday," *JAMS*, xiii (1960) [papers presented at the Cornell Club, New York City, 28 Nov 1958]

R. Benton: "Early Musical Scholarship in the United States," *FAM*, xi (1964), 12–21

Obituaries: G. Reese, *JAMS*, xix (1966), 433–4; D.J. Grout, *AcM*, xxxix (1967), 1–2; P.H. Lang, *MQ*, liii (1967), 77–9; J. LaRue, *Mf*, xx (1967), 121–2

P.L. Miller and F.C. Campbell: "How the Music Division of the New York Public Library Grew," *Notes*, xxxv (1978–9), 537–55

K.W. Geck: *Otto Kinkeldey (1878 bis 1966): ein amerikanischer Musikwissenschaftler und Musikbibliothekar im Spiegel der Fachliteratur* (thesis, Fachhochschule für Bibliotheks- und Dokumentationswesen, Köln, 1987)

C.E. Steinzor: *American Musicologists, c.1890–1945: a Bio-Bibliographical Sourcebook ot the Formative Period* (New York, 1989), 125–33

C.J. Bradley, "Otto Kinkeldey (1878–1966)," *American Music Librarianship: a Biographical and Historical Survey* (Westport, CT, 1990), 9–20

Papers, 1902–1966. Division of Rare and Manuscript Collections, Cornell University Library

Papers, 1908–1962. Research Division, *NYp*

DONALD JAY GROUT/MARY WALLACE DAVIDSON

Kinney, Ray(mond Leimona) (*b* Kaumana, HI, 26 Sept 1901; *d* Honolulu, HI, 1 Feb 1972). Singer, musician, bandleader, composer, and recording artist. Kinney's career stretched over 57 years, and he achieved the greatest popularity of any Hawaiian singer-musician during his era. Sent to school in Utah, Kinney and his brothers toured as a Hawaiian band. In 1920, his mother died, and he was summoned home to Hawaii, where he continued to hone his musical skills as an accomplished tenor balladeer with exceptional diction and clarity. In 1925, he toured California as a member of Charles E. King's "Prince of Hawaii" cast. Returning home to Hawaii, he joined the David Burrows Trio and was named the most popular male singer in Hawaii at that time. For the rest of his life, he alternated between touring the continental United States and performing in Hawaii. He was engaged for four years at The Hawaiian Room at Hotel Lexington in New York City. In a 1938 New York popularity poll of American singers, Kinney scored higher than Rudy Vallee or Guy Lombardo.

As a recording artist, Kinney appears to be the most prolific of all Hawaiian singers with over 598 recordings, beginning in 1928 on the Brunswick label, and continuing on to Decca, Victor, and countless other labels. Among his most famous recordings are "Hapa Haole Hula Girl," "Ke Kali Nei Au," "Waipi'o," "Uhehene," "Hawaii Calls," "Sweet Lei Lehua," "Hawaiian Hospitality," and his signature tune, "Across the Sea." Among his most famous compositions are "Across the Sea," "Hawaiian Hospitality," and "Not Pau." Ray Kinney, the consummate entertainer, made his final recordings at the age of 65.

BIBLIOGRAPHY

T. Todaro: *The Golden Years of Hawaiian Entertainment, 1874–1974* (Honolulu, 1974)

G.S. Kanahele: *Hawaiian Music and Musicians: an Illustrated History* (Honolulu, 1979)

HARRY B. SORIA JR.

Kinscella, Hazel Gertrude (*b* Nora Springs, IA, 27 April 1893; *d* Seattle, WA, 14 July 1960). Music educator. She was a piano pupil of RAFAEL JOSEFFY (1912–3) and studied at the University of Nebraska (BM 1916, BFA 1928, BA 1931), Columbia University (MA 1934), and the University of Washington (PhD 1941). After teaching at the University of Nebraska (1918–38), she served on the faculty of the University of Washington (1942–58, professor from 1947). In 1919 she began a series of state school piano classes in Lincoln, Nebraska; this was one of the first American experiments in state school piano teaching and led to the publication of a series of piano books, *First[–Sixth] Steps for the Young Pianist* (1919–26). Kinscella was the author of several anecdotal books for music appreciation classes, including *History Sings*, which deals with music in the United States (Lincoln, Nebraska, 1940, 3/1957). She also wrote *Music on the Air* (New York, 1934), a reference book for radio listeners, and, with Elizabeth M. Tierney, two books on music education, *Music in the Small School* (Lincoln, Nebraska, 1939), and *The Child and His Music* (Lincoln, Nebraska, 1953).

WAYNE D. SHIRLEY/R

Kiowa. Native American tribe of the southern Plains. During the 18th century the Kiowa migrated from western Montana to what is now Oklahoma; they adopted a nomadic existence typical of Plains dwellers. In the 2010s the Kiowa tribe had more than 12,000 members, the largest number living near Carnegie, Oklahoma.

During pre-reservation days the Kiowa economy was based largely on the buffalo hunt and the horse raid. The horse became the standard of wealth and a means of achieving social rank and status. Equally important were honors gained in warfare, which led to the development of warrior societies, each having its own set of rituals, dances, and songs. Music and dance also supported the institutions of raiding and warfare. Before leaving camp, for example, war parties performed the Buffalo Dance and addressed songs to the Buffalo Guardian spirit, a symbol of power and courage. On the return of a successful war party, the women performed the Scalp Dance in its honor. If any warrior did not return, the women performed the Mourning Dance instead. Kiowa servicemen are still honored on Veterans Day with a modern version of the Scalp Dance.

Of the six original warrior societies, three remain active: the Black Leggings, the Tiah-pah (both revived in the 1950s), and the Ohoma Lodge (revived in the 1970s). "Ohoma" is a corruption of "Omaha," the tribal source. Distinguishing symbols of the Black Leggings society are their black-painted legs, the black strong shawl worn at the waist, the red cape draped over the shoulders, and the decorated lance. The Tiah-pah ("red berries") society developed the Gourd Dance, which consists of an elaborate set of rituals, dances, and songs relating to historical acts of bravery. The Gourd Dance ceremony, held on Independence Day as a substitute for the extinct Sun Dance (K'aw-tow), includes Tiah-pah warrior songs recounting historical events, Give-away and Honoring songs, the Brush Dance (formerly part of the preparation for the Sun Dance), and finally the Gourd Dance itself. The Kiowa, specifically the Tiah-pah society, and other southern Plains tribes are responsible for the development of an intertribal form of the Gourd Dance that has become an important pan-Indian expression (Howard, 1976). The Ohoma Dance was traditionally performed after successful war expeditions. An extensive ceremony, it is made up of many dances and songs: a slow, dignified Opening Song, a Feast or Kettle song, a Charging Song, and a Tail Feather (or Ritual) Song, in which the two chief dancers perform in the "fancy" War Dance style typical of the southern Plains. The ceremony continues with Give-away dances, Mourning songs, Battle Story songs (in which a dancer may sing personal songs recounting family history or heroic deeds), and a Closing Song. Both the Black Leggings and Ohoma have annual summer dances.

Social dances performed by the Kiowa at pan-Indian powwows include the War Dance, the Round (or Circle) Dance, the Forty-niner, the Oklahoma Two-step, and the Stomp Dance. Each of these has its own repertory of songs. The Kiowa are leaders in the southern style of singing and dancing the "fancy" War Dance. The Sun Dance, last held in 1887, was the central religious ceremony of the Kiowa. It conformed to the general Plains pattern of several days' preparation followed by four days of dancing. After the government ban on the Sun Dance, the Kiowa participated in the Ghost dance movement, performing their variant, the Feather Dance, until 1916. Many Kiowa follow the Peyote religion; others follow the Christian faith, for which they have created a body of original Christian hymns.

Some traditional Kiowa songs were composed (and therefore owned) by individuals; some were received in visions, dreams, or trances. Songs for many important ceremonies (such as the Gourd Dance) are thought to have been given to the Kiowa by supernatural beings (usually in the form of animals); others, such as the Ghost Dance songs, were simply borrowed. Since the Kiowa believed that the spirit forces around them were influenced by music, they have songs for every element and sought harmony with nature by using them. The instrument used most often in Kiowa ceremonies is the double-headed big drum, around which five to eight singers may be seated. It is regarded as the "voice of thunder" and held in reverence. Formerly the drum was a stiff, dried buffalo hide without a frame, held by a circle of singers and beaten with sticks. To accompany solo singing, a small, single-headed frame drum is used. Spherical rawhide rattles, gourd rattles, and modern substitutes made of baking powder tins or aluminum salt shakers are associated with the Gourd Dance. During the Feather Dance, cluster rattles of deer hooves were shaken. Another Kiowa instrument, the wooden flute, was traditionally used by young men during courtship.

Kiowa music has stylistic features common to many Plains tribes; these include a tense, pulsating singing style, a forceful attack, and a high tessitura. Melodies, based principally on pentatonic scales using major seconds and minor thirds, descend in terrace fashion over the range of an octave or more. The most common song form is *AABCBC*, in which the opening phrase (*A*) is sung by the leader and repeated by the group; the remaining sections (*BC*) are then sung by the ensemble and repeated. Most songs contain only vocables; those with meaningful texts are often personal songs from warrior societies. Drum accompaniment is common, the beats typically occurring either just before or after the pulse of the song.

Archival recordings of traditional Kiowa music are housed in the Archive of Folk Culture at the Library of Congress; the American Indian Studies Research Institute at Indiana University; the Kiowa Historical and Research Society, Lawton, Oklahoma; and the Kiowa Tribal Museum, Carnegie, Oklahoma.

During the latter portion of the 20th century, a number of Kiowa musicians infused traditional Kiowa music with a more contemporary sound. Notable figures include the composer James Anquoe, the singer and flutist Cornel Pewawardy, and the flutist and record label owner Tom Mauchahty-Ware. Prominent contemporary powwow drum groups led by Kiowa members include the Cozad Singers, the Bad Medicine Singers, the Zotigh Singers, and the Thunder Hill Singers. Each of these groups has won the Gathering of Nations Southern Challenge, held annually in Albuquerque, New Mexico.

See also Powwow.

RECORDINGS
(selective list)

Kiowa: Music of the American Indian (Library of Congress, 1954); *War Dance Songs of the Kiowa* (IH, 1976); *Flute Songs of the Kiowa and Comanche* (IH, 1978); *Spirit Journey* (Soar, 1993); *Flute Songs of Kiowa* (Allegro, 1995); *Kiowa Gourd Dance* (IH, 1996); *Kiowa: Traditional Kiowa Songs* (Canyon, 1998); *Dancing Buffalo: Dances & Flute Songs of the Southern Plains* (Music of the World, 1999)

BIBLIOGRAPHY
J. Howard: "The Plains Gourd Dance as a Revitalization Movement," *American Ethnologist*, iii/2 (1976), 243–59
M. Boyd: *Kiowa Voices: Ceremonial Dance, Ritual and Song* (Fort Worth, 1981)
L. Lassiter: *Power of Kiowa Song* (Tucson, 1998)
L. Lassiter: *The Jesus Road: Kiowas, Christianity, and Indian Hymns* (Lincoln, 2002)
C. Ellis: *A Dancing People: Powwow Culture on the Southern Plains* (Lawrence, KS, 2003)
C. Ellis, L. Lassiter, and G. Dunham, eds.: *Powwow* (Lincoln, 2005)

MARY RIEMER-WELLER/ANN McFARLAND

Kiowa-Apache. Apache Indian group of the Southwest.

Kiowa-Tanoan. Native American language family; *see* PICURIS; TAOS; TEWA.

Kipnis, Alexander (*b* Zhitomir, Ukraine, *c*13 Feb 1891; *d* Westport, CT, 14 May 1978). Bass of Ukrainian birth, naturalized American. After studying conducting at the Warsaw Conservatory and singing in Berlin (with Ernst Grenzebach), he sang with the Hamburg Opera (1915–17) and in Wiesbaden (1917–22). In 1919 he joined the Berlin Charlottenburg Opera (later the Städtische Oper) where he became leading bass (1922–30); during these years he made his American debut in Baltimore as Pogner in *Die Meistersinger* with the visiting German Opera Company (31 Jan 1923). After 1930 he was associated with the Berlin Staatsoper (1930–35) and the Vienna Staatsoper (1935–8).

Long before Kipnis became a US citizen in 1934, he had established himself as an outstanding bass specializing in Wagner and Mozart as well as a distinguished interpreter of Italian and Russian roles. He appeared at the Bayreuth (1927, 1930, 1933) and Salzburg (1937) Festivals, and in the leading opera houses of the world. But his career took him increasingly to both North and South America. He was particularly appreciated in Chicago, where he was a regular member of the company (1923–32); his 30 roles included as many in Italian and French operas as in German. Between 1926 and 1936 he took part in six seasons at the Teatro Colón, Buenos Aires. After a surprisingly late debut at the Metropolitan Opera (on 5 January 1940 as Gurnemanz) he remained in New York until his retirement in 1946, singing his first Boris Godunov there in 1943. Pogner, King Marke, Ochs, and Verdi's Philip II were among his other most successful roles. With a voice of wide range and variety of color, as well as of unusual refinement and flexibility for a bass, he also made his mark as a lieder singer, contributing extensively and valuably to the albums of the Hugo Wolf and Brahms Song Societies. The best of his many opera records are those made in Berlin in the early 1930s, especially Osmin's first song from *Die Entführung* and "Il lacerato spirito" from *Simon Boccanegra*. His son, IGOR KIPNIS, was a noted harpsichordist and critic. Kipnis's papers are in the Mugar Memorial Library, Boston University.

BIBLIOGRAPHY
L. Riemens: "Kipnis, Alexander," *Le grandi voci*, ed. R. Celletti (Rome, 1964) [with discography]
A. Frankenstein, E. Arnosi, and J. Dennis: "Alexander Kipnis," *Record Collector*, xxii (1974–5), 53 [with discography]
DESMOND SHAW-TAYLOR/R

Kipnis, Igor (*b* Berlin, Germany, 27 Sept 1930; *d* Redding, CT, 23 Jan 2002). Harpsichordist, fortepianist, and critic, son of ALEXANDER KIPNIS. After studying at the Westport School of Music, Connecticut, and at Harvard, he worked as art and editorial director of Westminster Records (1955–9), as director of recorded music for a chain of radio stations based in New York (1959–61) and as a music critic (from 1955). In the meantime he took up the harpsichord professionally. Although essentially self-taught, he was guided and encouraged by

a number of musicians, notably Thurston Dart. He made his debut in a radio broadcast in New York in 1959 and gave his first recital there in 1962. He performed widely as a soloist with leading orchestras and as a recitalist, touring Europe, Israel, South America, Australia, the Soviet Union, and East Asia. His teaching career began in 1964 at the Berkshire Music Center, where he taught Baroque performance practice, and continued at Fairfield University, Connecticut, where he was associate professor of fine arts (1971–5) and artist-in-residence (1975–7). In 1982 he was appointed visiting tutor at the RNCM, Manchester. He also edited harpsichord music and was a frequent contributor to periodicals.

Kipnis's enormous repertory included a large selection of harpsichord music of every national school, as well as many contemporary and jazz works. His playing, while founded on a solid technique, stressed the expressive and stylistic features of the music rather than its purely instrumental qualities. His performances of 17th- and 18th-century music were noteworthy for their bold and imaginative free ornamentation. He made numerous recordings, some of which have received awards in Europe and the United States.

BIBLIOGRAPHY
E. Blau: Obituary, *New York Times* (25 Jan 2002)
HOWARD SCHOTT/DENNIS K. McINTIRE

Kirby, John (*b* Baltimore, MD, 31 Dec 1908; *d* Hollywood, CA, 14 June 1952). Jazz double bass player and bandleader. Originally a trombonist, he played tuba and double bass with Fletcher Henderson (1930–34, 1935–6) and Chick Webb (1934–5), attracting attention with his strong pulse and walking bass lines. In 1937 he established his own small group at the Onyx Club, New York, with the trumpeter Frankie Newton and the alto saxophonist Pete Brown. The following year the band's personnel stabilized into a sextet: Charlie Shavers (trumpet), Russell Procope (alto saxophone), Buster Bailey (clarinet), Billy Kyle (piano), O'Neill Spencer (drums), and Kirby, with the frequent addition of the singer Maxine Sullivan (Kirby's wife). From 1938 to 1942 this group was perhaps the leading small jazz ensemble in the swing style and gained a nationwide from its many recordings and network radio broadcasts. The group concentrated on a chamber jazz style with intricate arrangements (many of them by Shavers), a subdued dynamic level, light swing, and extremely precise ensemble playing. In this way they presaged many cool jazz groups of the late 1940s and early 1950s, particularly those of Lennie Tristano. From 1942 Kirby's group lost its stability as its members were drafted; it disbanded in 1946 and, despite several attempts to reconstitute his sextet, Kirby gradually fell into obscurity.

BIBLIOGRAPHY
GroveJ2
L. Feather: Obituary, *DB*, xix/15 (1952), 17
R. Stewart: "Flow Gently, Sweet Kirby," *Jazz Masters of the Thirties* (New York, 1972/*R*), 151
D. Bakker: "John Kirby, 1938–42," *Micrography*, no.29 (1973), 3; no.30 (1974), 1

C. Garrod: *John Kirby and his Orchestra; Andy Kirk and his Orchestra* (Zephyrhills, FL, 1991)

A. Williams: *Fall from Grace: the John Kirby Story* (Pensacola, FL, 1993)

J. BRADFORD ROBINSON/R

Kirchner, Leon (*b* Brooklyn, NY, 24 Jan 1919; *d* New York, NY, 17 Sept 2009). Composer, pianist, and conductor. When he was nine years old his family moved to Los Angeles, where he was raised and educated at a time when the city's intellectual and artistic life was undergoing fundamental changes, due in large part to the influx of leading figures fleeing Adolf Hitler's Europe. He thus enjoyed the early encouragement of ERNST TOCH, who, impressed with his musicality and creative potential, recommended him to ARNOLD SCHOENBERG, who became his principal mentor and the determining force, aesthetically and ethically, of all his subsequent work. Although Kirchner eschewed strictly dodecaphonic techniques, his music owes much of its characteristic forward drive to the Viennese tradition as represented by Schoenberg and to a certain extent Alban Berg. Kirchner's work ranges from agonizing ruminations over the human condition to the liberating interplay of rhythmically energized pitches and timbres. Invariably it is governed by the same distinctive sense of structural discipline that underlies his ever insightful and imaginative renditions of a wide range of music, whether as a pianist in a concerto by W.A. Mozart or as a conductor in a symphony by Anton Bruckner. These qualities, reflective of a profoundly humane individual, have distinguished him no less as a teacher at Harvard, from where he retired in 1989.

Kirchner's own studies were primarily with ERNEST BLOCH at the University of California at Berkeley, where in 1942 he was awarded the George Ladd Prix de Paris. By then, however, study in France was out of the question, and Kirchner settled in New York to work with ROGER SESSIONS, himself a one-time Bloch pupil. After four years of military service Kirchner returned to Berkeley for further study with Sessions. Although he later disavowed much of the creative result, it brought him the early recognition of a Guggenheim Fellowship in 1948–9, after which he obtained an appointment at the University of Southern California, rising from assistant to full professor in four years. In 1954 he became Luther Brusie Marchant Professor at Mills College, Oakland, a position he occupied until moving to Harvard in 1961, where in 1966 he succeeded Walter Piston as Walter Bigelow Roser Professor of Music. Having already distinguished himself as a performer at Mills College, Kirchner initiated at Harvard a novel course that combined musical analysis with performance; this in turn gave birth to the Harvard Chamber Orchestra.

In the footsteps of Schoenberg, Kirchner remained consistently individual, unimpressed by changing fashion where "idea, the precious ore of art, is lost in the jungle of graphs, prepared tapes, feedbacks and cold stylistic minutiae." His music unfolds freely, unencumbered by technical straightjackets, imaginatively responding only to the underlying idea, Schoenberg's *Gedanke*, though with due regard to instrumental possibilities and limitations. His effectively written concertos offer every opportunity for virtuosity in display, but never at the expense of an unfailing seriousness of purpose. One critic's assessment of the Second Piano Concerto (1963) as "occasionally difficult to follow, always interesting, and charged with a sense of urgency and power" (R.F. Goldman, 1975) may stand for Kirchner's output as a whole. The poetic, emotionally demanding "duo-drama" *Of Things Exactly as They Are* for two singers, chorus and orchestra (1997) exhibits a similar compelling force.

Kirchner's powerful strain of musical communication led to recognition and awards from such institutions as the Guggenheim Foundation, the American Academy of Arts and Letters (1962), the American Academy of Arts and Sciences (1963), and the Center for Advanced Study of Behavioral Sciences (1974). The New York Critics Circle honored him twice with its annual award (for the First and Second String Quartets); his First Piano Concerto led to a Naumburg Award and the Third Quartet to the Pulitzer Prize (1967).

Aaron Copland observed in the 1950s that there were moments in Kirchner's music that seemed nearly "out-of-control." However, in the course of time such youthful ardor—especially evident in the Piano Trio of 1954—inevitably yielded to more reflective manifestations of "inner necessity." Thus, the Second Piano Trio (1993) evokes, rather, some particularly passionate episodes in late Romantic music, Gustav Mahler certainly inspiring the closing portion of this single-movement work, which ends almost demonstratively in C-sharp minor. Nor is Mahler's unmistakable stamp missing from certain parts of the later "duo-drama." But even direct allusions to *Das Lied von der Erde*, its probable model, assume entirely new meanings in this very individual context.

By and large, Kirchner favored compact structures based on a minimal number of motifs. Ever new intervallic combinations of, in particular, characteristically Schoenbergian 2nds and 3rds, generate abundant energy for an expressive flow of ideas, due in no small part to judicious meter and tempo changes. Such "rhapsodic" traits are discernible not only in a purely melodic composition like *Triptych* for solo violin and cello but also in the second of two works entitled Music for Orchestra (1989). By the same token, though, in *Lily*, Kirchner's only opera, a measure of tension between the very fertility of his musical imagination and certain strictly literary aspects of his textual choice (Saul Bellow's *Henderson, the Rain King*), appears to persist at times. Fortunately, some of its finest musical moments have been recaptured in an identically titled chamber work as well as in the separately published solo piece *Flutings for Paula* (1977).

WORKS

Op: Lily (3, Kirchner, after S. Bellow: *Henderson, the Rain King*), 1973–6; New York, 14 April 1977, arr. S, tape, chbr ens, 1973

Orch: Piece, pf, orch, 1946, unpubd; Sinfonia, 1951; Pf Conc. no.1, 1953; Toccata, str, wind, perc, 1955; Conc., vn, vc, 10 wind, perc, 1960; Pf Conc. no.2, 1963; Music for Orch, 1969; Music for Fl and Orch, 1978; Music for Orch II, 1989; Music for Vc and Orch, 1992

Kirk, Roland   631

Chbr and solo inst: Duo, vn, pf, 1947; Pf Sonata, 1948; Little Suite, pf, 1949; Str Qt no.1, 1949; Sonata concertante, vn, pf, 1952; Trio, vn, vc, pf, 1954; Str Qt no.2, 1958; Fanfare for Brass Trio, 1965; Str Qt no.3, 1966; Flutings for Paula, fl, 1973 [from op Lily], version for fl, opt. perc, 1977; A Moment for Roger, pf, 1978; 5 Pieces, pf, 1984; Fanfare, 7 brass, 1985; Music for Twelve, 1985; Illuminations, brass ens, 1986; Vc Solo, 1986; 5 Pieces, pf, 1987; Vn Solo, 1987; 2 Duos, vn, vc, 1988; Triptych, vn, vc, 1988 [consists of Vc Solo, 1986 and 2 Duos, 1988]; Vn Solo II, 1988; Interlude, pf, 1989; Trio, vn, vc, pf, 1993; For the Left Hand, pf, 1995; Interlude II, pf, 2003; Str Qt no.4, 2006

Vocal: Letter (S. Alexander), S, pf, 1943, unpubd; The Times are Nightfall (G. Hopkins), S, pf, 1943, unpubd; Dawn (F. García Lorca), chorus, org, 1943–6, unpubd; Of Obedience (W. Whitman), S, pf, 1950, unpubd; The Runner (Whitman), S, pf, 1950, unpubd; Words from Wordsworth, chorus, 1968; Lily (S. Bellow), S, chbr ens, tape, 1973 [arr. of op]; The Twilight Stood (E. Dickinson), song cycle, S, pf, 1983; Of Things Exactly as They Are, S, Bar, chorus, orch, 1997

Recorded interviews in *NHoh*
Principal publishers: Associated

WRITINGS

with A. Copland: "The Composer as Conductor and Performer," *The American Symphony Orchestra*, ed. H. Swoboda (New York, 1967), 75–89
"A Boo for the Boos of Boulez," *New York Times* (22 June 1969)
"Notes on Understanding," *Daedalus: Proceedings of the American Academy of Arts and Sciences*, xcviii/3 (1969), 739–46

BIBLIOGRAPHY

CBY 1967; *EwenD*
A.L. Ringer: "Current Chronicle: San Francisco", *MQ*, xlii (1956), 244–7
A.L. Ringer: "Leon Kirchner," *MQ*, xliii (1957), 1–20
R.F. Goldman: "Current Chronicle: New York," *MQ*, xlvi (1960), 71–6; xlviii (1962), 93–9; li (1965), 399–406
N. True: *A Style Analysis of the Published Solo Piano Music of Leon Kirchner* (diss., Peabody Conservatory of Music, 1976)
R. Riggs: *Leon Kirchner: Composer, Performer, and Teacher* (Rochester, NY, 2010)

ALEXANDER L. RINGER/R

Kirk, Andy [Andrew Dewey] (*b* Newport, KY, 28 May 1898; *d* New York, NY, 11 Dec 1992). Jazz saxophonist and bandleader. He spent his childhood in Denver, where he studied piano, singing, alto saxophone, and music theory with Paul Whiteman's father, Wilberforce Whiteman, among others. In 1918 he joined George Morrison's orchestra as a bass saxophonist and tuba player. Around 1927 he moved to Dallas, where he joined Terrence Holder's Dark Clouds of Joy orchestra; he assumed its leadership in 1929. In that year he transferred the band to Kansas City, Missouri, where it was known as the Clouds of Joy (among other related titles), rivaled Bennie Moten's band, and made its first recordings (1929–30). From 1930 he made several nationwide tours, although the band continued to be based primarily in Kansas City. The success of "Until the Real Thing Comes along" (1936, Decca) established the band's lasting popularity. Until the group disbanded in 1949 it was regularly on tour and made many recordings; thereafter Kirk occasionally led ad hoc orchestras.

Kirk was not a soloist and rarely played ensemble parts after the early 1930s, but he made an important contribution to jazz through his leadership of the Clouds of Joy. His was the only Kansas City group with a strong reputation both as a jazz orchestra and commercial "sweet" band. Its style was largely determined by the compositions and arrangements of MARY LOU WILLIAMS,

the band's pianist from 1929 to 1942; although vigorous, her pieces were more subtly orchestrated than those of most other midwestern bands of the period and less dependent on riffs. Kirk's outstanding soloists included Williams and the pianist Kenny Kersey, the tenor saxophonists Dick Wilson and Don Byas, the trumpeters Shorty Baker, Howard McGhee, and Fats Navarro, and for a brief period the alto saxophonist Charlie Parker.

BIBLIOGRAPHY

R. Russell: "Andy Kirk and the Clouds of Joy," *Jazz Style in Kansas City and the Southwest* (Berkeley, CA, 1971, 2/1973/R), 163
A. Kirk (with A. Lee): *Twenty Years on Wheels* (Ann Arbor, MI, 1989)
F. Driggs: *Kansas City Jazz, from Ragtime to Bebop: a History* (New York, 2005)

J.R. TAYLOR/R

Kirk, Colleen (Jean) *b* Champaign IL, 7, Sept 1918; *d* Paxton, IL, 5 March 2004). Teacher, author, and conductor. She received degrees from the University of Illinois at Urbana-Champaign (BME 1940, MM 1945) and Teachers College, Columbia University (EdD 1953). She began her career teaching band, chorus, and general music in the public schools of Danvers, Illinois (1940–44). Although her teaching career in public schools and universities spanned over 50 years, she developed her skills and expertise for choral music through church involvement, primarily at the Wesley United Methodist Church in Champaign, Illinois. She eventually received a Minister of Music Certificate from the United Methodist Church (1945). In 1949 Kirk joined the music education faculty at the University of Illinois, where she taught music education courses, supervised student teachers, and became known for her great care and devoted mentoring of students. In 1970 she joined the choral music education faculty at Florida State University, retiring in 1990. Recognized for programming quality literature and her communication skills, Kirk was influential in shaping the development of the American Choral Directors Association, in part through her membership on committees for repertoire and standards and for publications.

BIBLIOGRAPHY

D.L. Chandler: *Colleen Jean Kirk (1918–2004): Her Life, Career and Her Influence on American Choral Music Education* (diss., Florida State U., 2004)

STEVEN N. KELLY

Kirk, (Rahsaan) Roland [Ronald Theodore] (*b* Columbus, OH, 7 Aug 1935; *d* Bloomington, IN, 5 Dec 1977). Tenor saxophonist, flutist, and multi-instrumentalist. Blind from the age of two, he took up saxophone and clarinet at the Ohio State School for the Blind in 1948. By 1951 he was performing on tenor saxophone professionally in several local rhythm-and-blues bands. In the second half of the 1950s he worked in Louisville, Nashville, Cincinnati, and Indianapolis, before moving in 1960 to Chicago, where he recorded his first jazz album under his own name, *Introducing Roland Kirk* (1960, Argo). In 1961 he moved to New York, was part of the Charles Mingus Workshop for three months, and toured Germany in April and California in December. In 1963 he began a residency at Ronnie Scott's club in London, an engagement which he repeated nearly every year during the 1960s. Until his death, Kirk led his own group, the Vibration Society. With this band he toured North America, Europe, Australia, and New Zealand performing in a multitude of jazz styles. In the early 1970s he was the leader of the Jazz and People's Movement, an organization for the promotion of black music. In November 1975 he suffered from a stroke which paralyzed his right side. Strong-minded, he developed a technique that allowed him to play his tenor saxophone with one hand and he performed again from 1976, notably at Newport. He died following a second stroke in December 1977.

Kirk belonged to a group of multi-reed players who began to emerge during the latter half of the 1950s. In comparison with Eric Dolphy, Yusef Lateef, James Moody, and Sam Most, Kirk was arguably the most eccentric and radical in terms of his aesthetic beliefs. He developed a technique that enabled him simultaneously to play the manzello (a variant of the soprano saxophone) and a stritch (a modified alto saxophone) together with a tenor saxophone (e.g., on the album *Triple Threat*, 1956, King). From 1960 he expanded his instrumental assortment with a siren whistle, clavietta (a type of melodica), piccolo, flute, and a series of homemade creations (trumpophone, slidesophone, rokon whistle, mystery pipes). He performed these instruments on several albums recorded for Mercury between 1962 and 1964, which are some of the finest and most overlooked jazz of the time. Later Kirk experimented with such avant-garde techniques as quartertones and nasal timbres. Furthermore, he perfected the circular breathing technique that allowed him to sustain a single note for an extended period of time. Finally, a series of recordings he made for Atlantic (1965–76) revealed John Coltrane's influence on Kirk, notably the former's approach to soprano saxophone.

BIBLIOGRAPHY
H. Böhm: "Aspekte zur Entwicklung des Flötenspiels im Jazz zwischen 1950 und 1980," *Jf*, xx (1988), 9–54
M.C. Cole: *The Life and Music of Rahsaan Roland Kirk* (diss., U. of Cincinnati, 1998)
M. Jouan: *Notoriété et légitimation en jazz: l'exemple de Rahsaan Roland Kirk* (Paris, 1999)
J. Kurth: *Bright Moments: the Life and Legacy of Rahsaan Roland Kirk* (New York, 2000)
D.P. Brown: *Noise Orders: Jazz, Improvisation, and Architecture* (Minneapolis, 2006)
G. Cosson: *Rahsaan Roland Kirk* (Paris, 2006)
T. Rowden: *The Songs of Blind Folk: African American Musicians and the Cultures of Blindness* (Ann Arbor, MI, 2009)
MICHAEL BAUMGARTNER

Kirkpatrick, John (*b* New York, NY, 18 March 1905; *d* Ithaca, NY, 8 Nov 1991). Pianist, editor, and music scholar. After attending Princeton University he continued his musical studies with NADIA BOULANGER at Fontainebleau during the summers from 1925 to 1928 and at the Ecole Normale de Musique in 1926 and 1927. From 1925 to 1928 he studied piano with ISIDORE PHILIPP;

from 1928 to 1931 he studied with Louta Nouneberg. In 1942 he became chairman of the music department at Monticello College. He then taught at Mount Holyoke College from 1943 until 1946, when he was appointed to the music faculty of Cornell University. He served as chairman of the department at Cornell from 1949 to 1953 and as director of the chapel choir from 1953 to 1957. In 1968 he became curator of the Ives Collection at Yale University (Professor Emeritus from 1973). From 1973 to 1985 he served as Executive Editor of the Charles Ives Society.

Kirkpatrick championed a range of American music, working with composers including Aaron Copland, Virgil Thomson, Roy Harris, Elliott Carter, and others. He is most well known for giving the first full performance of Charles Ives's *Concord Sonata* in 1939. He recorded that work twice for Columbia, and with Helen Boatwright issued the first recordings of numerous Ives songs. Kirkpatrick's other recordings feature works by Carl Ruggles, Robert Palmer, Edward MacDowell, and Louis Moreau Gottschalk.

Following Ives's death, Kirkpatrick cataloged the composer's manuscripts; this resulted in a temporary catalog issued by Yale in 1960. He edited Ives's memoranda, with additional notes and appendixes, and numerous works by Ives. Additionally, Kirkpatrick served as the musical executor for Ruggles.

MSS in *NH*

WRITINGS
"On Copland's Music," *Fontainebleau Alumni Bulletin*, i (May 1928), 1–6
"Aaron Copland's Piano Sonata," *MM*, xix (1941–2), 246–50
A Temporary Mimeographed Catalogue of the Music Manuscripts and Related Materials of Charles Edward Ives (New Haven, CT, 1960)
"The Evolution of Carl Ruggles: a Chronicle Largely in his Own Words," *PNM*, vi/2 (1967–8), 146–66
ed.: *Memos* (New York, 1972)

RECORDINGS
A. Copland: Concerto for Piano and Orchestra (Cos Cob, 1929; Two piano (four-hand) arrangement)
E. Carter: *Voyage* (South Hadley, 1945)
A. Farwell: *Navajo War Dance, No. 2 for Piano, Op. 29* (New York, 1947)
R.L. Finney: Piano Sonata no. 4 in E Major (New York, 1947)
H. Johnson: Piano Sonata (New York, 1948)
C. Ruggles: *Evocations: Four Chants for Piano* (Revision of 1954) (New York, 1956)
C. Ives: *Sunrise: for Voice, Violin, and Piano* (New York, 1977)

BIBLIOGRAPHY
V. Perlis: "Aaron Copland and John Kirkpatrick: 'Dear John, Can You Help Me Out?,'" *Copland Connotations*, ed. Peter Dickinson (Woodbridge, UK, 2002), 57–65
C. Bruhn, "The Transitive Multiverse of Charles Ives's 'Concord' Sonata, *Journal of Musicology* 28, no. 2 (2011), 166–94.
D. Massey, *John Kirkpatrick, American Music, and the Printed Page* (Rochester, NY: University of Rochester Press, 2013).
PAULA MORGAN/DREW MASSEY

Kirkpatrick, Ralph (Leonard) (*b* Leominster, MA, 10 June 1911; *d* Guilford, CT, 13 April 1984). Harpsichordist, clavichordist, and pianist. After studying piano from the age of six he began to play harpsichord in 1930 while an undergraduate at Harvard, where he took the

AB in fine arts (1931) and was awarded a Paine Traveling Scholarship to study in Europe. In the years 1931–2 he did research at the Bibliothèque Nationale in Paris and studied harpsichord with WANDA LANDOWSKA and Paul Brunold and theory with NADIA BOULANGER. He later studied briefly with ARNOLD DOLMETSCH, Heinz Tiessen, and Günther Ramin.

Kirkpatrick first performed publicly as a harpsichordist in 1930 in Cambridge, Massachusetts, and as a clavichordist in a radio broadcast from New York in 1946. At his European debut (Berlin, 1933) he played J.S. Bach's Goldberg Variations with great success. He subsequently toured extensively in North America and Europe, first performing in Britain in 1947. His extensive repertory included all of Bach's keyboard music, a great many sonatas of Domenico Scarlatti, the 18th-century French school, and some virginal music. He was also well known as an interpreter of much late 18th-century keyboard music, particularly W.A. Mozart's, on the fortepiano. His many recordings included Bach's complete keyboard works played on the harpsichord and clavichord, and the set of 60 of Scarlatti's sonatas, which he also edited. His playing was characterized by rhythmic vitality, stylistic authority, and, where appropriate, great bravura. Perhaps in reaction to the romantic excesses of the oldest generation of modern harpsichordists, he sometimes allowed a certain academic dryness to blunt his natural expressiveness.

Although in great demand as a solo harpsichordist and chamber musician Kirkpatrick continued his scholarly work. In 1937 he received a Guggenheim Fellowship for research into 17th- and 18th-century performing practice in chamber music, and began to gather material for his monumental study *Domenico Scarlatti* (Princeton and London, 1953). His editions included Bach's Goldberg Variations and, in addition to a selection of 60 sonatas, the complete keyboard sonatas of Domenico Scarlatti in facsimile. His teaching career began in the years 1933–4, when he held a post at the Salzburg Mozarteum. In 1940 he joined the staff of Yale University, and was professor of music, 1965–76. In 1964 he served as first Ernest Bloch Professor of Music at the University of California, Berkeley. He received honorary degrees from Yale and Rochester universities and Oberlin College.

WRITINGS

Interpreting Bach's Well-Tempered Clavier: a Performer's Discourse of Method (New Haven, CT, and London, 1984)
Early Years (New York, 1985)

BIBLIOGRAPHY
"On Concert Halls: Conversations with Ralph Kirkpatrick," *Perspecta*, xvii (1983), 92–9
L. Palmer: *Harpsichord in America: a Twentieth-Century Revival* (Bloomington, IN, 1989), 95–105

HOWARD SCHOTT/R

Kirkpatrick, William J(ames) (*b* Duncannon, PA, 27 Feb 1838; *d* Germantown, PA, 20 Sept 1921). Compiler of Sunday-school and gospel songbooks, gospel song composer, and music teacher. He studied music with Pasquale Rondinella, LEOPOLD MEIGNEN, and T. Bishop and worked as a music teacher in the Philadelphia area, where he led music at a number of Methodist Episcopal churches including Wharton Street, Ebenezer, and Grace. In the 1870s he became associated with GEORGE FREDERICK ROOT, first as a student and then as a teacher at his National Normal Institute for training music teachers.

Although his first songs were transcriptions of melodies heard at camp meetings near Philadelphia, his own musical style reflected the developing gospel hymn, which he helped to establish and popularize. His earliest collaboration was with A.S. Jenks who employed him as editor for the hymn and tunebook *Heart and Voice*. In 1878 he joined forces with gospel songwriter John R. Sweney to form the Praise Publishing Company. The two compiled about 50 songbooks and collections with sales running into the millions. The name "Sweney and Kirkpatrick" became almost a trademark as they collaborated with the leading poets of gospel hymnody, publishing nearly 1000 of Fanny Crosby's hymns alone. Kirkpatrick's collections—he produced about 50 further items after Sweney's death—were used in revivals and camp meetings, such as the Methodist gatherings at Ocean Grove, New Jersey, and many of his more animated tunes, such as "Jesus Saves" (1882), reflect brass band influences. His other popular tunes were set to "Redeemed, how I love to proclaim it" (1882), "'Tis so sweet to trust in Jesus" (1882)," A wonderful savior is Jesus, my Lord" ("He hideth my soul," 1890), "I've wandered far away from God" ("Lord, I'm coming home," words and music,1892), and "King of my life, I crown Thee now" (1921).

BIBLIOGRAPHY
J.H. Hall: *Biography of Gospel Song and Hymn Writers* (New York, 1914/R 1971)
M.R. Wilhoit: *A Guide to the Principal Authors and Composers of Gospel Song of the Nineteenth Century* (diss., Southern Baptist Theological Seminary, 1982)
W.K. McNeil: "Kirkpatrick, William James" *Encyclopedia of American Gospel Music*, ed. W.K. McNeil (New York, 2005), 220

MEL R. WILHOIT

Kirshbaum, Ralph (Henry) (*b* Denton, TX, 4 March 1946). Cellist. He studied with Lev Aronson in Dallas (1962–4) and made his professional debut with the Dallas SO at 13. He completed his studies with ALDO PARISOT at Yale University (1964–8), and after two years in Paris won both the International Cassadó Competition in Florence (1969) and the International Tchaikovsky Competition in Moscow (1970). He then embarked upon an international solo career, making his London debut at the Wigmore Hall in 1970 and his British orchestral debut playing Tchaikovsky's Variations on a Rococo Theme in 1972. His New York recital debut was in 1976. In 1970 Kirshbaum joined Peter Frankl and György Pauk to form a piano trio which has gained an international reputation; he has also long been associated with Pinchas Zukerman in performances of chamber music. During the 1980 Proms, Kirshbaum, Pauk, and Nobuko Imai gave the world premiere of Tippett's Triple Concerto, of which they subsequently made an award-winning recording. Kirshbaum's repertory ranges from the Bach Suites to contemporary works. In 1988 he founded and served as artistic director of the RNCM Manchester International Cello Festival, which staged its ninth and final festival in 2007. Kirshbaum began to teach at the RNCM in 1976 and has conducted master classes throughout the world. In 2008, he assumed the Gregor Piatgorsky Endowed Chair in Violoncello at the University of Southern California's Thornton School of Music. His playing is admired for its beauty of tone and conviction of interpretation. He plays a cello by Montagnana dated 1729, the "ex-Piatti."

BIBLIOGRAPHY
CampbellGC
F. Shelton: "Promise Fulfilled," *The Strad*, xcviii (1987), 188–90
MARGARET CAMPBELL/R

Kirshner, Don(ald) (*b* Bronx, NY, 17 April 1934; *d* Boca Raton, FL, 17 Jan 2011). Publisher, promoter, and producer. He was known as "The Man with the Golden Ear" for possessing a remarkable ability to identify music that would sell. After attending Upsala College in East Orange, New Jersey, he gravitated immediately to the music industry, finding success at the Brill Building with Aldon Music Publishing. He and his partner, Al Nevins, contracted a wide variety of top-selling songwriters and performers including Neil Sedaka, Carole King, Jack Keller, and Gerry Goffin, among others. A big part of his success involved pairing writers with appropriate singers. Sedaka credited his opportunity to become a performer largely to Kirshner's promotion; Neil Diamond, Kansas, Connie Francis, and Bobby Darin also profited from his work as a producer. Kirshner branched into recording, becoming involved with three separate labels: Chairman, Calendar, and Kirshner. One of his biggest successes came with the creation of the Monkees; he was responsible for providing the corporate-formed group with songs for their television program and spin-off albums. He also managed the studio musicians who performed on their records. Kirshner returned to this strategy with The Archies, the late 1960s band of bubblegum pop fame. From 1973 to 1981, he produced "Don Kirshner's Rock Concert," a television show that featured some of the biggest names in pop music, including the Rolling Stones, ABBA, and the Eagles. He was inducted into the Songwriters Hall of Fame in 2007.

JONAS WESTOVER

Kirstein, Lincoln [Lincoln Edward] (*b* Rochester, NY, 4 May 1907; *d* New York, NY, 5 Jan 1996). Impresario, arts patron, writer, editor, and ballet company director. He was the embodiment of a 20th-century Renaissance man, blessed not only with many diverse talents and interests but also with the financial resources and connections to realize his visions. His achievements spanned the arts of dance, theater, painting, sculpture, photography, film, and literature, but he is perhaps best known for his decades-long association with choreographer GEORGE BALANCHINE and the school and ballet company they founded together.

He was educated at Harvard, earning Bachelor's (1929) and Master's (1930) degrees. Although he first saw Anna Pavlova dance in Boston when he was thirteen, his passion for dance did not take fire until he saw Diaghilev's Ballets Russes in Europe. Among Diaghilev's dancers and choreographers was Balanchine, whom he first met in 1933. Balanchine came to the United States at his invitation, and opened the School of American Ballet in New York City in 1934. Kirstein became its first director, a post he held until his retirement in 1989. Together the two men founded four ballet companies in succession: the American Ballet (1935–8), American Ballet Caravan (1941), Ballet Society (1946–8), and the New York City Ballet (1948–). Kirstein served the New York City Ballet as its general director until 1989. He also formed Ballet Caravan (1936–41), an ensemble dedicated to producing new ballets on American themes, with American talent. He wrote libretti for several of its ballets, most notably Eugene Loring's *Billy the Kid* (1938; Aaron Copland). A prolific writer since his days at Harvard, he penned poetry, novels, art, film, and literary criticism, and many works on dance. His book *Dance: a Short History of Classical Theatrical Dancing* (New York, 1935) presented a richly detailed survey of the history of dance, a then neglected subject. He founded and edited the periodicals *Hound and Horn* (1927–34) and *Dance Index* (1942–8). Active also as a collector, he established the Dance Archives at the Museum of Modern Art in 1940; this material was later incorporated into the Dance Collection of the New York Public Library. His interest in the visual arts, which had led him to found the Harvard Society for Contemporary Art in 1928, was never eclipsed by his love for dance. He served the Museum of Modern Art as curator, consultant, and cataloger, contributing to exhibitions on Gaston Lachaise, Elie Nadelman, Walker Evans, Pavel Tchelitchew, and others. Captivated by the art and culture of Japan, where he lived periodically, in 1959–60 he took part in arranging the US appearances of Gagaku, the musicians and dancers of the Japanese Imperial Household, and the Grand Kabuki.

WRITINGS
Dance: a Short History of Classic Theatrical Dancing (New York, 1935)
Movement and Metaphor: Four Centuries of Ballet (New York, 1970)
The New York City Ballet (New York, 1973, expanded 2/1978 as *Thirty Years*)
Nijinsky Dancing (New York, 1975)
Ballet, Bias and Belief: *Three Pamphlets Collected and Other Dance Writings of Lincoln Kirstein* (New York, 1983)
Quarry: a Collection in Lieu of Memoirs (Pasadena, CA, 1986)
The Poems of Lincoln Kirstein (New York, 1987)
By With To & From: a Lincoln Kirstein Reader, ed. N. Jenkins (New York, 1991)
Mosaic: Memoirs (New York, 1994)

BIBLIOGRAPHY
H. Simmonds, L. H. Silverstein, and N. Lassalle: *Lincoln Kirstein, the Published Writings, 1922–1977: a First Bibliography* (New Haven, CT, 1978)
International Encyclopedia of Dance (New York, 1998)
M. Duberman: *The Worlds of Lincoln Kirstein* (New York, 2007)
N. Reynolds, ed.: *Remembering Lincoln* (New York, 2007)
SUSAN AU

Kirsten, Dorothy (*b* Montclair, NJ, 6 July 1910; *d* Los Angeles, CA, 18 Nov 1992). Soprano. She studied at the Juilliard School of Music, then in Italy, and made her debut in 1940 as Pousette in *Manon* with the Chicago Opera Company, where she also sang Musetta to Grace Moore's Mimi. She co-hosted a weekly radio program, *Keepsakes* (1943–4), with baritone Mack Harrell. She made her debut at the New York City Opera as Violetta (1944), and at the Metropolitan as Mimi the following year; she sang at the Metropolitan intermittently for 30 years, making her formal farewell as Tosca in 1975. Her roles with the company included Violetta, Louise (which she had studied with Charpentier), Marguerite, Gounod's Juliet, Manon Lescaut (her favorite role), Minnie, and Fiora (*L'amore dei tre re*). She performed regularly at the San Francisco Opera, where she sang Blanche in Poulenc's *Dialogues des Carmélites* and undertook Cressida in the American premiere of Walton's opera (1955). She also appeared in the film *The Great Caruso* (1951). Kirsten recorded extracts from several of her roles (most notably her feisty Minnie), which reveal her gleaming, if not particularly beguiling, *lirico spinto* soprano and her unfailingly secure technique. She published an autobiography, *A Time to Sing* (1982).

BIBLIOGRAPHY
A. Blyth: Obituary, *Opera*, xliv (1993), 163–4
B. Burroughs: "Golden Girl of the West," *Opera News*, lxviii/1 (2003), 40–5

MAX DE SCHAUENSEE/KATIE BUEHNER

Kirtan. *See* BUDDHISM.

KISS [Kiss]. Rock group. Its foundational lineup comprised bassist Gene Simmons (*b* Chaim Witz, Haifa, Israel, 25 Aug 1949), guitarist Paul Stanley (*b* Stanley Harvey Eisen, New York, NY, 20 Jan 1952), drummer Peter Criss (*b* Peter George John Criscuola, New York, NY, 20 Dec 1945), and lead guitarist Ace Frehley (*b* Paul Daniel Frehley, New York, NY, 27 April 1951). Core members Simmons and Stanley founded the group in 1972, and embraced Criss and Frehley by early 1973. It is difficult to discount their attempts to shock audiences with grotesquerie, studded black leather, platform boots, and individualized *Kabuki-like* facial makeup. Their concerts showcased pyrotechnics and hydraulics, theatricalized gore, and wooden choreography in contrast with their appealing, well-crafted power pop sound. Supported by loyal fans ("the KISS Army"), the band endured despite a tortuous personnel record of firings, re-hirings, and willful departures.

Neither of their first two albums with the upstart Casablanca record label was commercially viable. KISS broke through in 1975 with the anthem "Rock and Roll all Nite," and a live double LP (*Alive!*). Softer material of the mid-1970s ("Beth") was equally ironic and incommensurate with their "evil incarnate" appearance. Their unrivaled merchandising enterprise and popular success peaked in the late 1970s; personnel upheavals followed: Criss and Frehley were replaced by Eric Carr (*b*Paul Caravello, New York, NY, 12 July 1950; *d* New York,

Guitarist Gene Simmons of Kiss, 1979. (Commercial Appeal/Dave Darnell /Landov)

24 Nov 1991) and Vinnie Vincent [Vincent John Cusano] (*b* 6 Aug 1952). Sans distinctive makeup, KISS released *Lick it Up* (1983), revealing the kinship between KISS and the hair metal bands they had come to resemble. After submerging, they resurfaced with the ballad "Forever" (1989) and performances with *MTV Unplugged* (1995) and the 2002 Olympic Games. Instrumental in the formation of arena rock, KISS was rewarded with a Lifetime Achievement Grammy Award in 2006. The proliferation of tribute bands makes clear their lasting, carnivalesque allure.

MICHAEL ETHEN

Kissin, Yevgeny (*b* Moscow, Russia, 10 Oct 1971). Russian pianist. He has studied exclusively with Anna Pavlovna Kantor, beginning in 1977, at Moscow's Gnesin State Institute for Musical Education; he made his orchestral debut at age ten and gave his first Moscow recital the following year. However, it was the masterly performances he gave with the Moscow State Philharmonic of both Chopin Concertos in 1984, at age 12, that fully alerted the world to his extraordinary gifts. Since that time Kissin has played in all the major musical centers and established a reputation as one of the most formidable pianists of his generation. He made his Japanese debut in 1986, subsequently returning there regularly, and in 1988–9 performed with Karajan and the Berlin PO. His wide-ranging discography includes several recitals recorded live (among them his 1990 Carnegie Hall debut which contains a performance of Prokofiev's Third Etude) and Concertos by Bach, Mozart, Beethoven, Chopin (taken from that

1984 concert), Schumann, Tchaikovsky, Prokofiev, Rachmaninoff, and Shostakovich. Kissin's other recordings include such works as Schumann's *Fantasie* and *Carnaval*, Schubert's *Wandererfantasie* and Sonata in B-flat, Chopin's B minor Sonata, Brahms's Paganini Variations, Scriabin's Sonata No.3 and 5 Preludes, Medtner's Sonata Reminiscenza, three movements from Stravinsky's Pétrouchka, and Mussorgsky's *Pictures at an Exhibition*. His 2009 recording of Prokofiev's Piano Concertos Nos.2 and 3, with the Philharmonia Orchestra conducted by Ashkenazy, earned a Grammy Award. A documentary film about the pianist, *Evgeny Kissin: The Gift of Music*, directed by Christopher Nupen, was released in 2000. In 2003 Kissin received the Shostakovich Award, and in 2005 was awarded honorary membership of the RAM in London. Beyond classical music, in 2010, he released a recording of Russian and Yiddish poetry.

BRYCE MORRISON/RICHARD WIGMORE/
MEGAN E. HILL

Kitkahahki. Native American tribe of the PAWNEE Confederacy.

Kitt, Eartha [Keith, Mae Eartha] (*b* North, SC, 17 Jan 1927; Weston, CT, 25 Dec 2008). Singer, actress, and dancer. Kitt came from a poor family, but managed to make her way into show business. Her first break came in 1943 when she was hired by the Katherine Dunham Company as a dancer, and she remained with that organization until 1948. Given the opportunity to perform throughout Europe, Kitt learned French and incorporated it into her vocal performances at cabarets. Kitt began to record in the early 1950s, and her distinctive voice—somewhat deep, purposefully raspy, and openly seductive—made her an African American sex symbol. Her early hits include a cover of "Let's Do It" by Cole Porter, "C'est si bon," "Love for Sale," "Je cherche un homme," and "Mink, Schmink." Kitt's breakout Broadway appearance came when she appeared in the revue, *New Faces of 1952*, singing "Monotonous," which she revived for a 1954 film called simply *New Faces*. Kitt is perhaps best remembered as a singer for her 1953 Christmas hit, "Santa Baby." Throughout the 1950s, she appeared as a dramatic actress in films such as *The Mark of the Hawk* (1957) and *Anna Lucasta* (1959). As her singing career dwindled, she resumed her role as a sex kitten by playing Catwoman on the television series *Batman*. An anti-war remark made in the presence of Lady Bird Johnson left Kitt blackballed by the entertainment industry, and she moved to Europe, not returning to the United States until the 1970s. She starred in the 1978 Broadway musical *Timbuktu!* and later released a disco hit "Where is my man?" (1984). In 2000, she received a Tony Award for Best Actress for her role in *The Wild Party* and continued to perform in cabarets in New York until her death.

BIBLIOGRAPHY
E. Kitt: *I'm Still Here: Confessions of a Sex Kitten* (New York, 1993) [autobiography]

JONAS WESTOVER

Kittredge, Walter (*b* Reed's Ferry, NH, 8 Oct 1834; *d* Reed's Ferry, NH, 8 July 1905). Vocalist and songwriter. Born to a prosperous farmer and brickyard owner, Kittredge learned the family business, attending school and teaching himself music as his work schedule permitted. His first choice of career was the theater, but his family opposed it. At age 21 he became a wandering minstrel, traveling through New England villages in a wagon and accompanying himself on melodeon. Around 1856 he met the HUTCHINSON family, and performed with them (especially with Joshua Hutchinson) intermittently over the next 20 years. Gradually Kittredge began to compose and sing his own songs, which were first published in his *Union Song Book* (1862).

Believing his abolitionist songs and lectures to be the greater weapon, Kittredge did not enlist in the army, but was drafted and then excused because of a previous case of rheumatic fever. In 1863 he wrote "Tenting on the Old Camp Ground," which would become one of the best-loved songs of the Civil War. Asa Hutchinson helped popularize it in concert and arranged for its publication by Ditson in 1864. It sold 10,000 copies within three months, and as late as 1897 its royalties rivaled the highest of preceding years. It became a staple of community sings, patriotic ceremonies, and home performance, its message of peace embraced equally by North and South. Most of Kittredge's compositions were never published. Although popular in their day, none achieved the same success as "Tenting."

BIBLIOGRAPHY
G.H. Gerould: "'Tenting on the Old Camp Ground,' and its Composer," *New England Magazine* xx/6 (1899), 723–31
G.C. Carter: *Walter Kittredge, Minstrel of Merrimack* (Manchester, NH, 1953)

SANDRA JEAN GRAHAM

Kitziger, Frederick E. (*b* Altenburg, Germany, 25 Jan 1844; *d* New Orleans, 3 Feb 1903). Composer of German birth. He studied in Germany, and in 1865 moved to New Orleans, where he performed in marching bands as a brass player. In the 1870s he led his section in the English, then French opera orchestras; he also served as organist and choir director at St. Alphonse's Church (1877) and St. Louis Cathedral (1880–86). From 1881 to 1903 he was organist and music director of Touro Synagogue. He occasionally conducted choirs in public concerts, and on 14 April 1879 at Grunewald Hall performed in a Haydn quartet. Although he was a Christian, he wrote hundreds of synagogue compositions for all occasions in German, English, and Hebrew, and arranged works by Beethoven, Mendelssohn, and others for Jewish liturgical use. By the 1890s these works had wide distribution in the United States and abroad. He also wrote Catholic church music, including *Venez Dirin Messie*, performed at St. Louis Cathedral on 17 April 1886. His secular compositions include piano pieces published by Ditson and Blackmar & Finney, and several operas and symphonies (now lost); copies of his manuscripts are held at Howard-Tilton Memorial Library, Tulane University.

BIBLIOGRAPHY

A.Z. Idelson: *Jewish Music* (New York, 1929), 327 only

J.H. Baron: "Frederick Emil Kitziger of New Orleans," *Musica Judaica*, v (1982), 20–33

JOHN H. BARON

Kízh kízh díhí. *See* Tsli'edo'a'tl.

Kjelson, Lee R(ichard) (*b* Stromsburg, NE, 27 Aug 1926; *d* Coral Gables, FL, 4 May 2009). Choral director, teacher, composer, and writer. He earned degrees from the University of Nebraska (BME 1948, MM 1951) and University of Iowa (PhD 1957). He taught music in the public schools of Valentine, Nebraska (1948–52) and Shenandoah, Iowa (1952–5), and at Western State College in Gunnison, Colorado (1957–60), and California State University, Hayward (1960–67). He was director of choral activities at the University of Miami (1967–93), where he led the UM Singers on 21 international concert tours and in numerous other performances, including appearances at Carnegie Hall, the Kennedy Center for the Performing Arts, and national conventions of professional organizations. Kjelson also conducted honor choirs in 40 states, and founded and conducted the Civic Chorale of Greater Miami (1970–2006). He was inducted into the Florida Music Educators Association Hall of Fame (1990), and received the Hugoboom Service Award from the Florida Chapter of American Choral Directors Association (1990) and an outstanding alumnus award from the University of Nebraska (1997). He composed over 150 choral works and wrote several textbooks. During retirement, he founded the Kjelson Visiting Choral Scholars Residency program at the University of Nebraska and the Russian American Choral Institute at Moscow Conservatory.

STEPHEN F. ZDZINSKI

Klauser, Karl (*b* St Petersburg, 24 Aug 1823; *d* Farmington, CT, 9 Jan 1905). Swiss-German music educator and editor. He immigrated to the United States in 1850, joined Miss Porter's School in Farmington, Connecticut, as music teacher in 1855, and remained with them until retirement in 1883.

Klauser's reputation as a teacher, concert promoter, writer, and arranger-editor of music (chiefly for the home) brought him into contact with many eminent musicians, among them Franz Liszt, Hans von Bülow, Anton Rubinstein, and Leopold Damrosch.

In 1891 he collaborated with John Knowles Paine and Theodore Thomas to publish the anthology *Famous Composers and their Works* (Boston; two volumes of text, one of music). It included essays by some of the finest living writers on music, such as Philipp Spitta and W.S. Rockstro, and illustrated the best principles of music excerpting and arranging. Most of the 120 pieces were meant for the piano.

Three years later Klauser alone edited the monumental collection *Half Hours with the Best Composers* (Boston, 1894–5; thirty parts in four volumes). Whereas *Famous Composers* had excluded them, the later collection included 30 American composers, each one heading a part. The 419 musical selections are all for the piano.

BIBLIOGRAPHY

L. Damrosch: "Karl Klauser. Musical Sketch," *Dwight's Journal of Music*, xxxi (1872), 203–4

E. Johnson: "A Musician's Reminiscences: Told by Karl Klauser," *The Farmington Magazine*, i/Nov (1900), 4–6

ZOLTAN ROMAN

Kleber, Henry (*b* Darmstadt, Germany, 4 May 1816; *d* Pittsburgh, PA, 20 Feb 1897). Composer, conductor, performer, merchant, impresario, and teacher of German birth. Kleber immigrated with his family to Pittsburgh around 1832 from Darmstadt, where he was trained in piano and voice. Three years later he launched his long career in Pittsburgh as music "professor" by becoming an instructor at Western Collegiate Institute for Young Ladies. In 1839 he organized a brass band, first known as the Kleber Band, then The Pittsburgh Band, described as the first brass band west of the Alleghenies. That year also marked his entry into the music business with a piano salesroom under the name "Ye Golden Harp." By 1850 he was operating a growing business in pianos, organs, instruments, and sheet music. The store was a gathering place for the city's musicians, including Stephen Foster, for whom Kleber served as a mentor.

Fluent in German, French, and Italian as well as English, Kleber acted as an impresario throughout much of his career, serving as a local manager for many European touring artists who were a mainstay of the American concert stage. He also organized concerts for local musicians, featuring himself variously as conductor, pianist, and singer. Considered by some to be brash, aggressive, self-promoting, and combative, he and Augustus, his brother and business partner, gained notoriety as well as a $100 fine each in March 1850 after they horsewhipped a local music critic who had written an unfavorable review of Kleber's singing.

Kleber composed more than 120 works consisting principally of pieces issued as piano sheet music aimed at the home market. Most were in dance form: march, quick step, galop, polka, schottisch, waltz, mazurka, or varsovienne. Some works achieved national popularity— *Rainbow Schottisch*, *Signal March*, *Coral Schottisch*, and *Spirit March*—and appear in several anthologies, including Stephen Foster's *Social Orchestra*.

BIBLIOGRAPHY

A.M. Foerster: "Outlines of Musical History in Pittsburgh," *Musical Forecast* (Feb 1923), 2

H. Gaul: "Henry Kleber, Pioneer in Music," *The Musical Forecast*, (July 1936), 7–14

E.G. Baynham: "Henry Kleber, Early Pittsburgh Musician," *Western Pennsylvania Historical Magazine*, xxv (1942), 115–8

E.F. Morneweck: *Chronicles of Stephen Foster's Family* (Pittsburgh, PA, 1944)

J.T. Howard: *Stephen Foster, America's Troubadour* (New York, 1953)

E.G. Baynham: *History of Pittsburgh Music* 2 volumes (unpublished typescript, Pittsburgh, PA, 1970)

J. Thomas: "Bullwhips and Bad Reviews: the Colorful Career of Music Man Henry Kleber," *Pittsburgh History*, lxxxi/3 (Fall 1998), 108–17

JEAN W. THOMAS

Klein, Bruno Oscar (*b* Osnabrück, Hanover, Germany, 6 June 1856; *d* New York, NY, 22 June 1911). Organist, pianist, and composer of German birth. He studied music with his father, organist at the cathedral in Osnabrück, and graduated from the Gymnasium Carolinum. He attended the Munich Conservatorium, studying counterpoint with Josef Rheinberger, score-reading with Franz Wüllner, and piano with Carl Baermann. At age 17 he published some compositions that prompted an encouraging letter from Liszt. Klein traveled to Philadelphia in 1878 to visit a brother, returning to Germany in 1880. He moved permanently to the United States in 1881, becoming organist for the College and Church of St. Francis Xavier in New York and head of the piano area at the Manhattanville Academy of the Sacred Heart. He was professor of counterpoint and composition at the National Conservatory (1887–92). His works include an opera, *Kenilworth* (produced in Hamburg, 1895), orchestral works, concertos for piano and violin, concert arias with orchestra, five Masses, many sacred motets, partsongs, over 75 solo songs, many piano pieces, and two sonatas for violin and piano.

BIBLIOGRAPHY

"Klein, Bruno Oscar," *Cyclopedia of Music and Musicians*, ii, ed. J.D. Champlin, Jr. (New York, 1888), 374 only

"Klein, Bruno Oscar," *The American History and Encyclopedia of Music: Musical Biographies*, i, ed. W.L. Hubbard (Toledo, 1908), 435–6

Obituary, *New York Times* (23 June 1911)

JOHN C. SCHMIDT

Klein, Judy [Judith] (*b* Chicago, IL, 14 April 1943). Composer. She took the BA at the University of California, Berkeley (1967), a diploma at the conservatory in Basle (1977), and the MA at New York University (1987). Her principal teachers were REYNOLD WEIDENAAR, Kessler, Dodge, Lilli Friedemann, and RUTH ANDERSON. She has been an instructor and director at the computer music studios of New York University and created the Electro-Acoustic Music Archive at the New York Public Library for the Performing Arts. She has been guest composer and artist-in-residence at Dartmouth College, at the Brooklyn College Center for Computer Music, and at the Studio for Electronic Music in Basle, and a guest lecturer at Columbia University, Brooklyn College, and New York University. She has been a contributing editor to *The Open Space Magazine* since 2006. Her works are mostly for the electronic medium and include sound installations, music for theater and collaborations with visual artists. In 1988 she was awarded special honors at the Bourges international electro-acoustic music competition for *From the Journals of Felix Bosonnet* and her *railcar* has received *recording* recognition from the Society for Electro-Acoustic Music in the United States (SEAMUS). She received a commission by the International Electroacoustic Music Institute in Bourges, France (IMEB) in 2007 and has served as an adjudicator and curator for IMEB.

WORKS
(selective list)

Dead End, tape, 1979; Little Piece, tape, 1979; Dream/Song, tape, 1980; Journeys, tape, 1982 [for art installation, collab. B. Nathan]; God Bites, tape, 1983; The Mines of Falun, pt 1, tape, 1983; The Tell-Tale Heart (film score, dir. H. Marti), 1983; From the Journals of Felix

Bosonnet, tape, 1987; Elements 1.1., tape, 1992; 88" for Nick, tape, 1992; Elements 1.2., sound installation, 1993 [collab. C. Furukawa and N. Yatsuyanagi]; The Wolves of Bays Mountain, tape, 1998; railcar, tape, 2008

Incid music (elec), incl. Family Play, Unheile DreifaltigkeitProductions: Eine Reise in Unbekannte, Klein—Felix Bosonnet, 1998

Principal recording companies: Open Space CDs, Cuneiform, International Computer Music Association, SEAMUS

BIBLIOGRAPHY

C. Dodge and T.A. Jerse: Computer Music: Synthesis, Composition and Performance (New York, 1985, 2/1997)

C. Cox: Listening to Acousmatic Music (diss., Columbia University, 2006)

E. Hinkle-Turner: Crossing the Line: Women Composers and Music Technology in the United States (Burlington, VT, 2006)

ELIZABETH HINKLE-TURNER

Klein, Kenneth (*b* Los Angeles, CA, 5 Sept 1939). Conductor. He studied violin with Vera Barstow and Eudice Shapiro at the University of Southern California, conducting with Fritz Zweig (1959–79) and Richard Lert in Los Angeles and with NADIA BOULANGER in Paris. Klein led a string quartet that was coached by Gregor Piatigorsky and William Primrose. After organizing and conducting the Westside SO in Los Angeles (1963–7), he was music director of the Guadalajara SO (1967–78); his tenure was distinguished by an expansion of repertory and a significant increase both in attendance and in the number of concerts each season. These years culminated in the recordings *Music from Mexico* (1979, 1993). He made his European debut in 1970 as guest conductor of the Nuremberg SO and has subsequently appeared with many major European orchestras. Klein has had a long association with Puerto Rico, first conducting there at the invitation of Pablo Casals (1973). From 1981 to 1985 he served as music director of the Santa Cruz (California) SO, and in 1982 he became music director of the New York Virtuosi Chamber Symphony, which he founded. Klein has also appeared as a guest conductor with numerous American orchestras, including the New York City Ballet in 1994. A champion of the music of the Americas (for which he has received two ASCAP awards), he is equally well versed in the Classical and Romantic repertory. His recordings for Angel/EMI Classics have been widely hailed as impressive accomplishments, especially his release of Morton Gould orchestral repertoire and John Alden Carpenter's *Skyscrapers*.

BIBLIOGRAPHY

J. Rockwell: "L.A. Conductor Gives Music in Mexico a Lift," *Los Angeles Times* (27 Jan 1970)

R. Brown: "An Interview with Kenneth Klein," *Fanfare*, xvi/2 (1992–3), 157–62

JUDITH ROSEN/JONAS WESTOVER

Kleinsinger, George (*b* San Bernardino, CA, 13 Feb 1914; *d* New York, NY, 28 July 1982). Composer. He attended New York University (BA 1937), where he studied with MARION BAUER, CHARLES HAUBIEL, and PHILIP JAMES; as a scholarship student at the Juilliard School (1938–40) he was a pupil of FREDERICK JACOBI and BERNARD WAGENAAR. During World War II he served as music supervisor of the

Second Service Command and worked mainly in army hospitals. His first success came with the cantata *I Hear America Singing* (1940), based on poems of Walt Whitman. This was followed by a series of extremely popular melodramas including *Tubby the Tuba* (1942), in which narrator and orchestra tell the story of a hapless tuba who ultimately achieves his desire to play melodies instead of nothing but "oompahs"; the work sold over half a million records and was made into a film by Paramount, earning Kleinsinger an Oscar nomination. His chamber opera *Shinbone Alley* (1954), based on Don Marquis's *Archy and Mehitabel*, also enjoyed a popular success. Kleinsinger's music is characterized by simple melody, direct rhythm, and a colorful instrumental style.

WORKS

Melodramas, unless otherwise stated: Farewell to a Hero (W. Whitman), 1941; Tubby the Tuba (P. Tripp), 1942; Peewee the Piccolo (Tripp), 1945; Pan the Piper (P. Wing), 1946; The Story of Celeste (Tripp), 1947; Shinbone Alley (chbr op, J. Darion, after D. Marquis: *Archy and Mehitabel*), 1954; The Tree that Found Christmas (Darion, after C. Morley), 1955; 3 other melodramas

Orch: Sym., 1942; 3 concs., vc, 1946, harmonica, 1947, vn, 1953; other works

Chbr and solo inst: Str Qt, 1940; Cl Qnt, 1949; Trio, cl, vc, pf, 1955; Dance Portraits, pf, 1956; other works

Choral: I Hear America Singing (Whitman), cant., 1940; Brooklyn Baseball Cant. (M. Stratton), 1942

Songs, incl. Christmas is a Feeling in your Heart (Darion), 1953

Film scores, incl. Greece, the Golden Age, 1963; incid music for TV

Principal publishers: Chappell, E.B. Marks

BIBLIOGRAPHY

Baker8

C. Reis: *Composers in America: Biographical Sketches* (New York, 4/1947/*R*, enlarged edn of *American Composers*)

D. Ewen: *American Composers Today* (New York, 1949)

B. Cummings: "'Tubby's' Great Complaint," *International Tuba and Euphonium Association*, xxxiv/1 (Fall 2006), 113–6

MICHAEL MECKNA

Klemm [Clemm, Clem], **Johann Gottlob** (*b* nr Dresden, Germany, 12 May 1690; *d* nr Bethlehem, PA, 5 May 1762). Instrument maker of German birth. The son of a schoolmaster and organist who is said to have also been engaged in instrument making, young Klemm initially studied theology in Freiberg and Leipzig but returned to Dresden, working for an unknown organ builder there. During this period he met Count Zinzendorf, founder of the *Unitas Fratrum* (or Moravian) sect, and moved with his family to their settlement in nearby Herrnhut in 1726. In 1733 the Klemm family immigrated to Philadelphia, where Johann established a workshop for making keyed stringed instruments and organs. A spinet made by Klemm is in the instrument collection of the Metropolitan Museum of Art in New York, dated 1739, and in the same year he is recorded as having built a small organ for the Gloria Dei ("Old Swedes'") Church in Philadelphia. In 1741 he completed what was undoubtedly his largest organ, for Trinity Church in New York, but other organs attributed to him were small, including one made for the Moravian Church in Bethlehem, Pennsylvania, in 1746. In 1757 he moved to Bethlehem, reconnecting with the

Moravians there, continuing to make clavichords and small organs, and soon taking on a young apprentice, David Tannenberg. In 1758, with Tannenberg's assistance, Klemm built an organ for the Moravian Church in Nazareth, and the two built a few other organs together until Klemm's death four years later, after which Tannenberg succeeded his mentor.

BIBLIOGRAPHY

W.H. Armstrong: *Organs for America* (Philadelphia, 1967)

L. Libin: "New Facts and Speculations on John Clemm," *The Tracker*, xxxi/2 (1987), 19–23

R.J. Brunner: "*That Ingenious Business*": *Pennsylvania German Organ Builders* (Birdsboro, PA, 1990)

B. Owen: "Brother Klemm, Organ Builder," *Moravian Music Journal*, xl/1 (1995), 3–13

L. Libin: "The *Personalia* of John Clemm," *The Tracker*, li/3 (Summer 2007), 8–16

BARBARA OWEN

Klemm & Brother(s). German and American firm of instrument importers and dealers, also manufacturers and publishers. The family was known in Neukirchen (now Markneukirchen), Saxony, in 1710, when Johann Klemm, a wind instrument maker, joined the violin makers' guild. They were associated with other local firms, notably the Schusters and the Meinels, to whom they were related by marriage. Frederick Augustus Klemm (*b* Neukirchen, Germany, 20 Nov 1797; *d* Philadelphia, PA, 6 July 1876) immigrated to the United States in 1816 and, with his brother John George (*b* Neukirchen, Germany, 18 June 1795; *d* after 1833) imported instruments from Germany, probably mainly from their relations Georg and August Klemm in Neukirchen, and sold them in Philadelphia. Together they formed the firm of Klemm & Brothers; in 1833 it became known as Klemm & Brother. From 1860 the firm also included two sons of F.A. Klemm, John George (1838–93) and Edward Meinel (1839–1909). The firm supplied large numbers of bugles, military trumpets, fifes, and drums to the Philadelphia arsenal, and brass instruments by the firm were used by both the Federal and Confederate troops during the Civil War. Most of their instruments were imported, but there is evidence that some were of local origin. In 1825, when the firm had premises in the main piano-making district of Philadephia, it was associated with Alpheus Babcock of Boston, the inventor of cast-iron piano frames. For many years the firm was pre-eminent among suppliers of instruments in the United States; the instruments they supplied included boxwood flutes with four, six, or eight keys, clarinets with five, and rotary-valve saxhorns and bugles with six or eight keys.

The firm was also involved in publishing, though chiefly in the reprinting of material from plates used by other publishers, notably Allyn & Bacon. Among Klemm's own publications is the earliest instruction book for a valved brass instrument printed in America, F. Rasche's *New and Complete Method for Cornet à Pistons* (Philadelphia, 1844).

After the civil war, the Klemms' dominant position was challenged by the rise of American manufacturers. The firm does not seem to have functioned after 1879.

Their wind instruments can be found in major American collections; a piano made by Babcock for Klemm is at the Smithsonian Institution.

BIBLIOGRAPHY

Waterhouse-LangwillI; *GroveA*

R.J. Wolfe: *Early American Music Engraving and Printing* (Urbana, IL, 1980)

C.L. Venable: *Philadelphia Biedermeier: Germanic-American Craftsmen and Design in Philadelphia, 1820 to 1850* (thesis, U. of Delaware, 1986)

LLOYD P. FARRAR/R

Klemperer, Otto (*b* Breslau [now Wrocław], Poland, 14 May 1885; *d* Zurich, Switzerland, 6 July 1973). German conductor and composer. He studied piano with James Kwast and composition and conducting with Hans Pfitzner in Berlin. On Mahler's recommendation he was appointed chorus master (1907) and later conductor at the Deutsches Landestheater in Prague. After 1918 he rapidly emerged as one of the leading German conductors of his generation. He was chosen as director when, in 1927, the Prussian Ministry of Culture set up a branch of the Berlin Staatsoper, whose special task it was to perform new works and repertory works in a non-traditional manner; this Staatsoper am Platz der Republik played in the Kroll Theater and became known as the Kroll Opera.

In April 1933 Klemperer left Germany, coming to the United States (where he had made his debut in 1927). Klemperer's best known American association occurred when he assumed directorship of the Los Angeles PO (1933–9). Although the American orchestra's comparatively strenuous performance schedule and summer Hollywood Bowl engagements taxed him, he contributed to the financial security and artistic achievement of the ensemble. Klemperer became particularly well known for his introduction of new repertoire and interpretation of Beethoven. During the mid-1930s Klemperer guest-conducted the New York PO and the Philadelphia Orchestra, and in 1937–8 played a part in the reorganization of the Pittsburgh SO. Despite seeming the presumptive successor to these posts, Klemperer was not selected in New York or Philadelphia. In 1939 he underwent an operation for a brain tumor and did little conducting for some years thereafter. Klemperer began exhibiting increased manic-depressive behavior that led to the end of his tenure with the Los Angeles PO and damaged his relationship with numerous other American ensembles. His next regular engagement was at the Budapest Opera (1947–50). In 1959 he was appointed principal conductor of the Philharmonia Orchestra of London, where he remained until his retirement from public concert life in 1972.

Klemperer's performances were notable for their power and intensity, but above all for their heroic dimensions and architectural clarity. In Beethoven, a composer central to his vision, he achieved an uncontested authority; his interpretations of Brahms emphasized what was Beethovenian in the music, and few conductors have equaled the monumental grandeur he brought to Bruckner's symphonies. His outstanding achievement, however, was to reveal the full extent of Mahler's genius by rescuing his music from the rather sentimental style of interpretation that had been widely accepted.

Klemperer studied composition with ARNOLD SCHOENBERG in the mid-1930s in Los Angeles and was a prolific, if intermittently active, composer. Despite periods of strain in his relationship with Schoenberg, Klemperer periodically advocated the composer's music and was instrumental in Schoenberg's appointment at UCLA. Klemperer's output includes an opera, a considerable number of songs, and nine string quartets, as well as six symphonies in a post-Mahlerian style. His book *Erinnerungen an Gustav Mahler* (1960) was published in an enlarged English translation, as *Minor Recollections*, in 1964.

BIBLIOGRAPHY

"Klemperer, Otto," *CBY* 1965

R. Crichton: Obituary, *MT*, cxiv (1973), 933

P. Heyworth, ed.: *Conversations with Klemperer* (London, 1973) [with discography by M. Walker]

H. Curjel: *Experiment Krolloper*, ed. E. Kruttge (Munich, 1975)

O. Klemperer, *Klemperer on Music: Shavings from a Musician's Workbench*, ed. M. Anderson (Exeter, 1986)

P. Heyworth, *Otto Klemperer: his Life and Times*, 2 vols. (Cambridge, 1996)

PETER HEYWORTH/PAUL LUONGO

Klezmer. From the Hebrew-Aramaic words *kley* ("instrument") and *zemer* ("song"), the Yiddishized contraction refers to a musician while the Americanized usage ("klezmer music") refers to a genre of Jewish music with roots in Yiddish folk traditions.

Like the Yiddish language, klezmer music was a key cultural component of the Ashkenazi civilization dating from its inception in the 9th century. Its musical dynamics reflect the Jewish soundscape, featuring the modes, scales, and articulations of cantorial (synagogue) music as a foundation upon which other forms (gypsy, peasant, and art music) were joined. With weddings making up the core outlet for the music, the instrumentation reflected local and regional availability, including fiddles, cello, bass, flute, *baraban* (bass drum), and *tats* (cymbal). Certain instruments, such as the *tsimbl* (hammered dulcimer), were most closely identified with Jews, and it was Jews who were most responsible for their wide European dissemination. By the end of the 19th century, string-based ensembles had been joined (and often surpassed) by louder brass and reed instruments such as clarinet, trumpet, trombone, and tuba.

The late 19th century also saw the large scale emigration of Jews from Eastern Europe to the United States, where the music underwent new transformations. Thanks to a growing Yiddish theater (with its ancillary arm of sheet music publishing), the dual mass outlets of recording and radio, and the continued availability of live performance venues such as weddings, concerts, and Catskill hotel engagements, this music was able to survive and thrive in the early 20th century. Between 1895 and 1942 nearly a thousand klezmer 78s were released on labels such as Victor and Columbia, making recording artists such as fiddler Abe Schwartz and

Klezmer musicians march through the Lower East Side of New York as part of a celebration of Eastern European culture, 2007. (AP Photo/Mary Altafer)

clarinetists Naftule Brandwein and Dave Tarras into a new breed of musical stars.

Acculturation was inevitable, and most Jewish musicians and composers chose to cross over to mainstream American music. The destruction of East European Jewry and the rise of Israel and its attendant Hebrew-language culture after World War II also spelled the decline of this Yiddish-based music. In the 1970s a rediscovery of the classic klezmer 78s of the 1920s fed a grassroots movement to reclaim the music among young American Jews. Such performers as Andy Statman and Israeli clarinetist Giora Feidman, and bands such as the Klezmorim, Kapelye and the Klezmer Conservatory Band, led what was soon to be a worldwide revival. The establishment of KlezKamp: the Yiddish Folk Arts Program in 1985 established a standard platform for the recontextualization and updated transmission of the music. Soon, veteran players like Dave Tarras, Sid Beckerman, and Paul Pincus were roused from retirement to greet a new generation of appreciative fans and students. Other programs modeled after KlezKamp soon followed in countries around the world.

By the 1980s such groups as the Klezmatics and Brave Old World, solo performers including David Krakauer, and even a brief foray into klezmer by renowned classical violinist Itzhak Perlman, helped the music find even wider audiences. Today there are untold thousands of klezmer bands around the world, from pre-industrial, 19th-century-style klezmer bands with period instruments, to edgy, avant-garde fusion ensembles mixing klezmer with punk, funk, techno, jazz, and rap.

BIBLIOGRAPHY

H. Sapoznik and P. Sokolow: *The Compleat Klezmer* (New York, 1987)

H. Sapoznik: *Klezmer! Jewish Music From Old World to Our World* (New York, 1999)

M. Slobin, ed.: *Old Jewish Folk Music: the Collections and Writings of Moshe Beregovskii* (Syracuse, NY, 2000)

J. Horowitz: *The Ultimate Klezmer* (New York, 2001)

HENRY SAPOZNIK

Klohr, John Nicholas (*b* Cincinnati, OH, 27 July 1869; *d* Cincinnati, OH, 17 Feb 1956). Composer and arranger. After graduating from the Cincinnati public schools, he worked as a vaudeville and band trombonist and an editor for the John Church Company. Klohr began his professional life near the high point of the American amateur-band tradition: his first known publication is the *Y.M.I. March* (1895), and in the years before World War I he published not only marches but a number of band arrangements, medleys, and novelties like *Ma Mobile Babe* (1899). By the end of his career he was supplying music mostly for school bands, notably the *Apex March Book* (1938), a collection of sixteen new marches ordered from the easiest to the most difficult. Around fifty of his compositions survive; the trio of his circus march *The Billboard* (1901), his only work still in the standard repertory, is one of the best-known tunes in the band literature.

BIBLIOGRAPHY

W.H. Rehrig: *The Heritage Encyclopedia of Band Music* (Westerville, OH, 1991, suppl. 1996); CD-ROM (Oskaloosa, IA, 2005) [includes list of works]

N.E. Smith: *Program Notes for Band* (Lake Charles, LA, 2000), 349 only

KENNETH KREITNER

Klotman, Robert H(oward) (*b* Cleveland, OH, 22 Nov 1918). Music educator. He received degrees in music education from Ohio Northern University (BS 1940), Western Reserve University (MA 1951), and Teachers College, Columbia University (EdD 1956). He was supervisor/director of music in the public schools of Dola (1940–2) and Akron (1959–63), Ohio and Detroit (1963–69); he also taught instrumental music in Euclid (1942, 1946, interrupted by military service in World War II) and Cleveland Heights (1946–59), Ohio. He taught at Indiana University (1969–89, chair of music education 1969–84). He was president of the American String Teachers Association (1962–4), the North Central Division of the Music Educators National Conference (MENC) (1972–4), and the national MENC (1976–8). In 1964 he (with John Kendall and Clifford Cook) brought Suzuki to the MENC convention in Philadelphia. He was also a conductor or clinician for numerous professional, community, and school orchestras, including 30 all-state orchestras.

Klotman published several articles and books, including (with Harold F. Abeles and Charles R. Hoffer) *Foundations of Music Education* (1984, 2/1994). He received awards from the MidWest Band and Orchestra Clinic (1984), the Indiana Music Educators Association (1986), and the governor of Indiana (1991). He received an honorary doctorate in music from Ohio Northern University (1984), and was inducted into the Music Educators Hall of Fame (2004).

BIBLIOGRAPHY

R.A. Ritsema: *A History of the American String Teachers Association: The First Twenty-Five Years* (Ed.D. diss., U. of Michigan, 1971), 100–12

"Change, Progress, and an Appreciation for Music," *Teaching Music* xii (2004), 18

JERE T. HUMPHREYS

Klucevsek, Guy (*b* New York, NY, 26 Feb 1947). Composer and accordion player. He grew up on the outskirts of Pittsburgh, where playing the accordion was a part of the local Polish American culture. He attended Indiana University of Pennsylvania (BA 1969), the University of Pittsburgh (MA 1971), and the California Institute of the Arts, studying with Robert Bernat, MORTON SUBOTNICK, GERALD SHAPIRO, JAMES TENNEY (acoustics), and HAROLD BUDD (jazz). From 1972 to 1976 he taught at Glassboro State College, Philadelphia; though he later moved to Manhattan, he became known for his performances with Philadelphia's Relache Ensemble (1980–90).

Inspired by Steve Reich and Terry Riley, Klucevsek's early music exhibits strict minimalist tendencies and a concern for psychoacoustic phenomena. Contact with John Zorn (from 1985) and other New York musicians who were freely mixing jazz and vernacular influences in their work, however, led Klucevsek back to his Polish background, a style clearly in evidence in the accordion polka "The grass, it is blue" (1986). Starting with *Scenes from a Mirage* (1987) he began to incorporate different styles within single works; theme and variations became the formal basis of many subsequent compositions. As a virtuoso performer he commissioned a series of polkas from avant-garde composers in 1987. Called *Polka from the Fringe*, the set includes works by William Duckworth, Lois V. Vierk, Anthony Coleman, and Mary Ellen Childs.

Despite Klucevsek's involvement in the Downtown Manhattan improvisation scene, his own music remained lyrical and sometimes charmingly simple. Works such as *Flying Vegetables of the Apocalypse* (1988) and *Transylvanian Software* (1991) refer to Eastern European traditions and jazz; *Viavy Rose Variations* (1989) is a set of poignant variations on melodies from Madagascar. In *Stolen Memories* and *Tesknota* (both 1993) he returned to quasi-minimalist processes. His extended works, such as *Chinoiserie* (1995) for the performance artist Ping Chong, are mostly theater and dance scores. He founded an international accordion ensemble called Accordion Tribe in 1996; they toured internationally and became the subject of a documentary by Stefan Schwietert, *Accordion Tribe: Music Travels*. In 2010 Klucevsek received a United States Artists Collins Fellowship.

WORKS

Dramatic: The Palatine Light (Y. Mintzer), S, vn + va, pf, accdn, 1985; Fallen Shadows (Mintzer and B. Rosenstein), S, vn, pf, accdn, 1993; Chinoiserie, 4vv, 3 insts, 1995 [for Ping Chong]; Cover Up (dance film, dir. V. Marks and M. Whiting), 1995; Bits and Pieces of Hard Coal, vv, vn, 1999; A Guy Called Dan and Dave, 2 accdn, sax, vv, 2000; The Heart of the Andes, accdn, 2000; Obon: Tales of Rain and Moonlight, chbr ens, 2002

Accdn: Mounted on the Fairground's Magic Horses, 1982; The grass, it is blue (Ain't nothin' but a polka), 1986; Samba d'hiccup, 1986; And then there were none, 1987; Awakening, 1987; Dining in the Rough in the Buff, 1987; Loosening up the Queen, 1987; Old Woman who Dances with the Sea, 1987; Scenes from a Mirage, 1987; An Air of Gathering Pipers, 1988; Perusal, 1988; Viavy Rose Variations, 1989; 3 Microids, 1991; Transylvanian Software, 1991; Bandoneons, Basil and Bay Leaves, 1992; Altered Landscapes, 1994; Accdn Misdemeanors, 1996; Festina Tarde, 1999; Return of the Microids, 2001; The Well-Tampered Accordion, 2002; Four Portraits, 2003; The Return of Lasse, 2005; Waltz for Sandy, 2005; Soft Landing, 2006; Dancing on the Volcano, 2006; Grooved Shoulders, 2006; My Walk with Ligeti, 2006; Meet me on the midway, 2008; The Man with the Rubber Head, 2008; Lars Song, 2009; The C&M Waltz, 2009; Breathless and Bewildered, 2009; Ratatatatouille, 2009; Ice Flowers, 2009

Accdn ens: The Flying Pipe Org, 1985; The Gunks, 1995; Wave Hill, 1995; Three of a Kind, 1997

Accdn, vn, vc, db: Urban Rite, 1986; Flying Vegetables of the Apocalypse, 1988; Waltzing above Ground, 1988; Citrus, my Love, 1990; Passage North, 1990; Patience and Thyme, 1991; Stolen Memories, 1993; The Gunks, 1995; Regunkitation, 1995; Rumbling, 1995; Skating on Thin Air, 1995; Wave Hill, 1995; Donut Ask, Donut Tell, with vv, 1996; Life, Liberty and the Prosciutto Happiness, 1998; Mr. Glime-Glide, 1998; Chalk Dust, 2001; Swither, 2001; Tangocide, 2001; Spinning Jennie, 2001; March of the Wild Turkey Hens, 2 accdn; Plain and Fancy, 2005; Any Day Now, 2008

Other chbr and solo inst: Oscillation no.2, pf, 1980; Blue Window, a sax, accdn, 1985; The Flying Pipe Org of Xian, 5–12 insts, 1985; The grass, it is blue, accdn, elec gui, db, drums, 1986; Some of that "Old Time Soul," polka, accdn, elec gui, db, drums, 1986; Fez Up, cl, s, sax, accdn, elec gui, db, drums, 1988; Reprieve, 2 vn, vc, accdn., 1988; Union Hall, accdn, cl + sax, db, 1989; The Singing Sands, vn, hp, accdn, 1991; Tesknota, 4–8 melody insts, 1993; Wave Hill, 2 pf,

1995; Cameos, 2 pf, 1996; Sweet Chinoiserie, toy pf, 1996; Mug Shots, 2 accdn or tr, accdn, 1997; Astor Place, accdn, pf, 1998; Bar Talk, accdn, pf, 1998; The Gift, s sax, accdn, 2000; A Goyish Kind of Blue, s sax, accdn, 2000; No More Mr. Nice Guy, s sax, accdn, 2000; A Pear for Satie, s sax, accdn, 2000; Spin Cycle, s sax, accdn, 2000; Tulips are better than one, s sax, accdn, 2000; Still Life with Canon, chbr ens, 2002; Wing/Prayer, chbr ens, 2002; Don't let the boogieman get you, pf, 2005; Notefalls, a Musical Day Book, melodica, 2 accdn, pf, kbd, 2006; March of the Lazy Prognosticators, cl, accdn, 2006; Closer by Far, s sax, 2006; Bone Dance, s sax, accdn, 2007; Night Traveler, cl, accdn, drums, bs, 2007; Gimme a minute, please (My sequins are showing), chorus, accdn, 2007; Haywire Rag, vn, pf or pf or toy pf, 2010; Industrious Angels, vn, pf, accdn, 2010; Three Hymnopedies, any inst, 2010

BIBLIOGRAPHY

K. Gann: "Music Notes: Guy Klucevsek plays polkas for weird people," *Chicago Reader* (24 March 1989)

L. Polak: "Guy Klucevsek: he doesn't do weddings," *Philadelphia Inquirer* (26 Feb 1989)

L. Kelp: "Putting the Squeeze on the Avant-Garde," *Piano & Keyboard*, no.162 (1993), 38–41

KYLE GANN

K'naan [Warsame, Keinan Abdi] (*b* Mogadishu, Somalia, 1 Feb 1978). Somali-Canadian hip hop artist, singer, and songwriter. K'naan ("traveler") was born in the midst of Somalia's civil war. His grandfather Haji Mohamed was a famous poet, and his aunt Magool a well-known singer. As a child he became interested in rap recordings sent from the United States by his father. In 1991 he left as a refugee with his mother and sister, moving to New York and then Toronto. By 1993 he had learned English, left school, and was performing professionally. In 2001 he sang at the 50th anniversary of the United Nations High Commission for Refugees. His full-length debut album, *The Dusty Foot Philosopher* (2005), won a Juno Award for Rap Recording of the Year and was nominated for the Polaris Music Prize. In 2005, he performed at the Live 8 concert in Barrie, Canada. His second album, *Troubadour* (2009), included high-profile American guests such as Damian Marley, Adam Levine, and Mos Def. In 2010 K'naan won Juno Awards for Canada's Artist of the Year and Songwriter of the Year. His renown increased when his song "Waving Flag" was chosen as the FIFA 2010 World Cup anthem. It originally appeared on *Troubadour* with lyrics about poverty and war in Somalia; the World Cup version presents a more positive view of his homeland and adds identifiably African musical elements such as drums and chorus. The song was then recorded by Young Artists for Haiti, a group composed of more than 50 Canadian musicians, as a benefit project for Haitian earthquake relief.

STEPHANIE CONN

Knabe. Firm of piano makers. In 1837 William Knabe (*b* Kreuzburg, Berlin, 3 June 1803; *d* Baltimore, MD, 21 May 1864) established the firm in Baltimore in partnership with Henry Gaehle after training as a piano maker in Germany and immigrating to Baltimore in 1833. The firm Knabe & Gaehle advertised "pianos of quality for genteel people of means." When Gaehle withdrew from the company in 1854, Knabe continued the business under the title Knabe and Co. Knabe controlled the piano market in the majority of the southern states by 1860, but the Civil War had a disastrous effect on the firm because its market was so dependent on the South.

After Knabe's death, his sons Ernest Knabe (1837–94) and William Knabe (1841–89) re-established the firm's position as one of the leading piano makers in the United States. Ernest toured to arrange new agencies for the sale of Knabe pianos in the northern and western states, and a direct agency was founded in New York in 1864. He also designed new string scales for their concert grands and upright pianos. The firm became one of the most important American piano makers, and by the turn of the century they were building about 2000 pianos annually. The Japanese government selected Knabe in 1879 to supply pianos for use in Japanese schools. The firm continued to prosper as a family concern until Ernest and William died, when it became a public company. Like other well-known American piano manufacturers, Knabe was purchased by the American Piano Co. in 1908. (Ernest's two sons left the American Piano Co. in 1911 to establish their own firm, Knabe Brothers Co., which lasted until 1914.) The firm continued to flourish, and in 1926 its pianos were officially chosen to be used at the Metropolitan Opera. In 1929 the firm moved to East Rochester, New York, and from 1932 it formed part of the Aeolian American Corporation there. (*See* AEOLIAN.) Following the bankruptcy of the Aeolian Corporation in 1985, the Knabe name, patterns, equipment, and unfinished pianos were sold to Sohmer & Co. Other changes in ownership ensued until 1996, when brothers Kirk and Gary Burgett, owners of Music Systems Research/ PianoDisc, bought the conglomerate and resumed production of the Knabe piano line, engaging the Korean piano manufacturer Young Chang. In 2001 the Samick company of South Korea and Indonesia acquired the Wm. Knabe name. They produce Knabe pianos in Indonesia, but ship them to the United States for inspecting, tuning, regulating, and voicing before they are sent to dealers.

BIBLIOGRAPHY

D. Spillane: *History of the American Pianoforte, its Technical Development, and the Trade* (New York, 1890/R)

A. Dolge: *Pianos and Their Makers* (Covina, CA, 1911–13/R)

MARGARET CRANMER/R

Knaebel, Simon (*b* Baden, Germany, 1812; *d* Ossining, NY, *c*1880). Composer, arranger, horn player, violinist, cellist, and pianist of German birth. He immigrated to the United States in the mid-1830s and took up residence in Boston, where he became well known as an arranger for Ned Kendall's Boston Brass Band. The noted African American composer Justin Holland studied with Knaebel in the late 1830s. After a brief trip to Germany in 1840, Knaebel relocated to Brooklyn, New York, where he remained for most of his life. He joined the New York Philharmonic in 1842 as a charter member and violinist and occasionally performed french horn solos with the orchestra. His descriptive symphony commemorating the 75th anniversary of the

Battle of Bunker Hill, scored for two dueling orchestras, solidified his reputation as a serious local composer at its first performance in 1851. While touring the United States in 1854, the London-based French conductor Louis-Antoine Jullien refused to program the symphony due to its anti-British sentiment; Knaebel nevertheless played french horn in Jullien's orchestra. During the Civil War, Knaebel conducted army band concerts in Brooklyn and directed the Brooklyn Amateur Musical Society. Throughout his career, he composed and arranged lighter works such as quick steps and waltzes.

BIBLIOGRAPHY
V.B. Lawrence, ed.: *Strong on Music: the New York Music Scene in the Days of George Templeton Strong*, ii (Chicago, 1995)

DOUGLES W. SHADLE

Knapp, Phoebe [Phebe] **Palmer** (*b* New York, NY, 8 March 1839; *d* Poland Springs, ME, 10 July 1909). Philanthropist, activist, composer, and hymnal compiler. She was the daughter of lay Methodist evangelists Phoebe Palmer (1807–74), considered the founder of the American Holiness movement, and medical doctor Walter Palmer. The younger Phoebe began composing hymns and songs as a child; two of her earliest tunes, set to hymn texts by her mother, were published in Joseph Hillman's revival song collection, *The Revivalist* (1868). At 16 she married Joseph F. Knapp, later founder of the Metropolitan Life Insurance Company of New York. As a wealthy society woman in New York, she entertained dignitaries, including four American presidents, at evening musicales held regularly in her home; a trained singer, she often performed at these events. She also hosted religious leaders, social reformers including Harriet Beecher Stowe, and female gospel hymn writers such as Fanny Crosby, with whom she formed a close friendship. In the late 1860s, Knapp wrote her most successful piece, the tune "Assurance," to Crosby's text "Blessed assurance, Jesus is mine." It was circulated internationally after Ira D. Sankey included it in *Gospel Hymns No.5* (1887) and later editions of *Sacred Songs and Solos*. She devoted great energy and finances to philanthropic pursuits and to mission rescue work in New York slums, particularly the Five Points Mission, where she and Crosby volunteered for years and which her mother had helped to found. Knapp's son Joseph Palmer Knapp (who eventually became head of Crowell-Collier publishers) published much of her music and her two collections, *Notes of Joy for the Sabbath School* (1869) and *Bible School Songs* (1873). The composer of over 500 gospel hymn and Sunday school tunes, anthems, parlor songs, and a cantata, Palmer holds a unique place in the history of the gospel hymn movement due to her social status, and her family's roles in holiness revivalism and music publishing. Knapp was accorded 14 pieces in Eva Munson Smith's pioneering anthology *Woman in Sacred Song* (1885).

BIBLIOGRAPHY
F.E. Willard and M.A. Livermore: *American Women* (New York, 1897/R1973)
E.H. Rothenbusch [Crookshank], "'The Joyful Sound': Women in the Nineteenth-Century United States Hymnody Tradition," *Women and Music in Cross-Cultural Perspective*, ed. E. Koskoff (New York, 1987), 177–94
C.E. White: "Holiness Fire-Starter," *Christian History & Biography*, lxxxii (2004), 16–21

PAUL C. ECHOLS/ESTHER R. CROOKSHANK

Kneass, Nelson (*b* 1823, in Lancaster or Philadelphia, PA; *d* Chillicothe, MO, 10 Sept 1868). Composer, manager, arranger, singer, and pianist. Of German ancestry, Kneass began his career as a child, appearing in 1828 in Philadelphia. By the early 1840s, he was performing vocal concerts in New York with a group that included Mrs. Eliza Sharpe (whom he may have married), George Holman, and Joseph H. Kavanagh. In the autumn of 1844, Kneass, Holman, and Kavanagh sang in the chorus for the American premiere of Michael William Balfe's opera *The Bohemian Girl*. In the spring of 1845, Kneass directed and performed as a blackface minstrel with the Ethiopian Troupe of Burlesquers, which also included Sharpe, Holman, and Kavanagh. They performed opera parody skits at Palmo's Opera House in New York City, including *The Virginian Girl*, a parody of *The Bohemian Girl*. During the next several years, Kneass performed with the New Orleans Serenaders, a troupe known for its opera parodies, and managed the Sable Harmonists, which toured the American South and the British Isles. In 1848 Kneass published his best-known composition, "Ben Bolt," a nostalgic parlor song. His other compositions include dances, sentimental songs, and minstrel show songs. He appeared as Aunt Chloe in George Christy and Wood's Minstrels' parody of *Uncle Tom's Cabin* in 1854. From the late 1850s until his death, Kneass appeared in minstrel shows, plays, and vocal concerts, often with his family, and often with touring theatrical troupes.

BIBLIOGRAPHY
E. Krohn: "Nelson Kneass: Minstrel Singer and Composer," *Yearbook for Inter-American Musical Research* vii (1971), 17–41
W. Mahar: *Behind the Burnt Cork Mask: Early Blackface Minstrelsy and Antebellum American Popular Culture* (Urbana, IL, 1999)
R.L. Norris: "Opera and the Mainstreaming of Blackface Minstrelsy," *Journal of the Society for American Music* i/3 (2007): 341–65

RENEE LAPP NORRIS

Kneisel, Franz (*b* Bucharest, Romania, 26 Jan 1865; *d* New York, NY, 26 March 1926). Violinist and teacher of Romanian birth. The son of a bandmaster, he learned to play the flute, clarinet, and trumpet as well as violin. After graduating from the Bucharest Conservatory in 1879, he went to Vienna, where he continued his studies with Jakob Grün and Joseph Hellmesberger until 1882; he made his solo debut in Vienna at the end of the year. The next season he became concertmaster at the Hoftheater and in 1884 went to Berlin to fill the same position in the Bilsesche Kapelle. In October 1885, though only 20 years old, he was engaged by Wilhelm Gericke as concertmaster of the Boston SO. For the next 20 years he was concertmaster and assistant conductor; he appeared as soloist in many violin concertos and gave the first American performances of the concertos by Brahms and Karl Goldmark, as well as the premiere of the First Violin Concerto of Gustav Strube. As assistant conductor, he led the Boston SO performances at the Columbian Exposition in Chicago in 1893. Shortly after his arrival in Boston, Kneisel formed the KNEISEL QUARTET from among the members of the orchestra, at the instigation of its founder Henry Lee Higginson; all four players (Kneisel was the leader) later resigned their positions in the Boston SO to devote themselves to the ensemble, which did much to raise standards of chamber playing in the United States. The quartet also toured abroad; it was disbanded in 1917.

Kneisel was for many years associated with the Worcester Festival in Massachusetts, first as concertmaster and assistant conductor (1885–96) and then as conductor (1897–1909). In 1905 he moved to New York to become the first head of the violin department of the newly established Institute of Musical Art, where he remained until his death. He also established a summer school of violin and chamber-music playing at his home in Blue Hill, Maine, which he led from 1902 until his death. The school was reopened by his daughter in 1953. He was a demanding teacher, requiring much in both technical ability and expressive insight; in addition, he expected his pupils to become familiar with literature and history as well as other subjects. At the time of his death, his renown as a teacher caused him to be ranked with Leopold Auer. He was awarded honorary doctorates by Yale and Princeton universities (1911, 1915).

Kneisel played a leading role in American music as a soloist and ensemble performer, both for the range and variety of his programs and for his dedication to the highest performance standards. Many Boston composers wrote works for him personally or for the quartet that bore his name, and these formed a substantial part of his repertory. He composed a Grand Concert Etude for violin and also published a number of technical studies. There are collections of Kneisel memorabilia at Blue Hill and at the Chapin Library of Williams College, Williamstown, Massachusetts.

BIBLIOGRAPHY
L. Maas: "Franz Kneisel," *The Musical Courier*, xiii/17 (27 Oct 1886), 260; repr. *Brainard's Biographies of American Musicians*, ed. E.D. Bomberger (Westport, CT, 1999), 159–61
M.A.D. Howe: *The Boston Symphony Orchestra: an Historical Sketch* (Boston, 1914, rev. and enlarged 2/1931/R1978)
M.D.H. Norton: "Franz Kneisel," *The Violinist*, xxxviii (1926), 154
R. Aldrich: "Franz Kneisel," *Musical Discourse* (New York, 1928), 226
A. Foote: *An Autobiography* (Norwood, MA, 1946/R1979)
V.B. Danek: *A Historical Study of the Kneisel Quartet* (DMEd diss., Indiana U., 1962)
B. Schwarz: *Great Masters of the Violin* (New York, 1983)
L. Forsyth: "Cradle of Chamber Music Teaching in America—Kneisel Hall: Franz Kneisel's Living Legacy," *Chamber Music*, ix/1 (1992), 15–7
P. Deitz: "Toting Chamber Music to Some Unexpected Chambers," *New York Times* (18 Aug 1998), 2
Kneisel Hall Chamber Music School and Festival, <http://www.kneisel.org/history1.html>
STEVEN LEDBETTER/E. DOUGLAS BOMBERGER

Kneisel Quartet. String quartet. It was formed in 1885 by FRANZ KNEISEL, concertmaster of the Boston SO, at the instigation of the orchestra's founder, HENRY LEE HIGGINSON. The other members were Emanuel Fiedler (second violin; later replaced by Otto Roth (1887–99), Karl Ondříček (1899–1902), Julius Theodorowicz (1902–7), Julius Roentgen (1907–12), and Hans Letz (1912–17); Louis Svečenski (viola, who, like Kneisel, remained a member throughout the quartet's existence); and Fritz Giese (cello; later replaced by Anton Hekking (1889–91), Alwin Schroeder (1891–1907), and Willem Willeke (1907–17). The quartet gave its first concert on 28 December 1885. The members were all principal players in the Boston SO, but in 1903 they resigned from the orchestra to perform only as a string quartet. In 1905 they moved to New York and became affiliated with the newly founded Institute of Musical Art, later the Juilliard School.

The Kneisel Quartet built an audience for chamber music all over the country. It gave an annual concert series in Boston and New York, and performed in nearly 170 other places, setting new standards of performance in the United States; it was particularly noted for its precise ensemble playing and evenness of tone. Guest performers often joined the group to play chamber works other than string quartets. The musicians set out to educate their audiences by performing the complete quartets of Haydn, Mozart, and Beethoven (including his then little-known late quartets), and they introduced many new European compositions, among them works by Brahms, Debussy, Franck, Dvořák, Bruckner, Wolf, Smetana, Enescu, Ravel, Glazunov, Kodály, and Schoenberg (*Verklärte Nacht*). They also played many works by American composers, several of which were written for and dedicated to the quartet; their repertory included works by Chadwick, Foote, Loeffler, Amy Beach, Arthur Whiting, Paine, Frederick S. Converse, Huss, Horatio Parker, D.G. Mason, and Henry Hadley.

Though it prospered in Boston from its inception, the Kneisel Quartet was not immediately successful on tour, and had at times to restrict its programs to the lighter quartet literature. Eventually, however, it did achieve a genuine popularity; and by the time it was disbanded in 1917, its chamber music concerts were well established. Programs, scrapbooks, photographs, and obituaries of the Kneisel Quartet are at Kneisel Hall, Blue Hill, Maine, and in the Willem Willeke Collection in the Chapin Library, Williams College, Williamstown, Massachusetts.

BIBLIOGRAPHY
M.A.D. Howe: *The Boston Symphony Orchestra: an Historical Sketch* (Boston, 1914, rev. and enlarged 2/1931/R1978)
F.H. Martens: "Franz Kneisel: the Perfect String Ensemble" in *Violin Mastery: Interviews with Heifetz, Auer, Kreisler, and Others* (New York, 1919/R 2006)
D.G. Mason: *Music in My Time, and Other Reminiscences* (New York, 1938)
A. Foote: *An Autobiography* (Norwood, MA, 1946/R1979)
V.B. Danek: *A Historical Study of the Kneisel Quartet* (DMEd diss., Indiana U., 1962)
Kneisel Hall Chamber Music School and Festival, <http://www.kneisel.org/history1.html>
STEVEN LEDBETTER/R

Knight, Gladys. *See* GLADYS KNIGHT AND THE PIPS.

Knowles, Beyoncé (Giselle) [Beyoncé] (*b* Houston, TX, 4 Sept 1981). R&B singer and actress. She was given the name Beyoncé, her mother's maiden name, as a tribute to her Creole heritage. Knowles began performing semi-professionally at the age of eight, in a group called Girl's Tyme, which also featured Kelly Rowland and LaTavia Roberson. The group formed in 1990 and appeared on the television show *Star Search* in 1993. Beyoncé's father, Matthew Knowles, renamed the group Destiny's Child, adding Letoya Luckett to round out the quartet. The group signed with Columbia Records in 1997 and released their debut *Destiny's Child* in 1998. The group's follow-up recordings *The Writing's on the Wall* (1999), *Survivor* (2001), and *Destiny Fulfilled* (2004) established the group as one of the most popular acts in recent years and Beyoncé, often known simply by her first name, as one of the most recognizable performers in the world.

Knowles took a hiatus from Destiny's Child in 2003 to record her debut solo project *Dangerously in Love*, which spawned the hits, "Crazy in Love," with future husband Shawn Carter (Jay-z), and "Baby Boy" with dancehall artist Sean Paul. Her follow-up album *B'Day* (2006) featured cover-art that gestured to her family heritage in Gulf Coast region. The recording was released the same year as the film *Dreamgirls*, the cinematic adaptation of the Tony Award Winning musical (1981); Knowles starred as Deana Jones, a character loosely based on Diana Ross. Knowles's song "Listen," from the film, was nominated for a Golden Globe Award. Months after her marriage to Carter, she released the double-disc recording *I Am . . . Sasha Fierce* (2008), which earned six Grammy Awards and featured the international hit "Single Ladies (Put A Ring on It)." The music video for the song became a popular Internet download and inspired several parodies, most famously from the cast of *Saturday Night Live*. In 2011, she released her fourth solo album, simply titled *4*.

MARK ANTHONY NEAL

Knoxville. City in Tennessee (pop. 178,874; metropolitan area 698,030; 2010 US Census). Founded as a territorial capital in 1791, Knoxville became Tennessee's first state capital, a distinction it held until 1819. Remote from new networks of steam transportation, Knoxville languished until after the arrival of railroads in 1855 and recovery from the Civil War, whereupon it re-emerged as an industrial city. In 1879, Knoxville's regional college became the University of Tennessee; by the mid-20th century, UT was a major cultural presence.

A rare early association with music comes by way of a traveler's 1798 account of Knoxville townspeople dancing to African American banjoists. Despite its obscure provenance, the description has been cited as unusual early evidence of whites responding to the African banjo. In its earliest days, Knoxville found use for a "ballroom," presumably a venue for dances and musical performances, years before the construction of the city's first church building; after 1816, churches became centers for sacred music. *The Knoxville Harmony*

of Music Made Easy (1838), a shape-note hymnbook, became a well-known text in sacred-harp singing.

By the 1860s, Knoxville supported orchestral groups, some led by talented German immigrants. Gustavus Knabe (1817–1906), of Leipzig, a veteran of Mendelssohn's orchestra, was a prominent teacher and conductor. In 1872, Swiss immigrant Peter Staub built Knoxville's "opera house," a grandiose structure with three balconies. By the early 1880s, Knoxville was throwing springtime Music Festivals featuring opera stars from the Northeast and Europe. By 1883, first in reaction to an opera festival, local fiddlers began gathering in Knoxville for public performances of old-time folk tunes, decades prior to the flowering of country music as a popular form.

Around 1903 noted Cincinnati-trained violinist Bertha Roth (later Bertha Walburn Clark, 1882–1972), became a popular performer among local audiences. By 1918 she was organizing small-symphony ensembles. In 1935 she founded the permanent Knoxville Symphony Orchestra (KSO), which has performed a subscriber-based program each year since. Clark herself was the KSO's conductor for its first 11 years. Conductor-composer David Van Vactor led the KSO from 1947 to 1972. Other conductors have included Lamar Stringfield, Arpad Joo, Zoltan Rosnyai, Kirk Trevor, and Grammy laureate Lucas Richman.

In 1947, Samuel Barber wrote his famous soprano piece, "Knoxville: Summer of 1915," based on native James Agee's 1935 poetic essay.

In its early years the KSO played most often at the 1909 Bijou Theater, a former vaudeville venue hailed for its acoustics. The Bijou still thrives as an intimate and critically praised venue for chamber music, folk music, and pop. Another historic theater, the 1600-seat Tennessee Theatre (1928), was elaborately restored, expanded, and acoustically improved in 2005. Both landmarks, two blocks apart, frequently host musical events.

Country music continued to develop alongside symphonic music, occasionally sharing players, especially violinists and bassists. Knoxville street performers like singer-guitarists Charlie Oaks and George Reneau made early "hillbilly" recordings. By 1924 Knoxville's Sterchi Brothers Furniture, a major regional Victrola retailer, sponsored some discs recorded in New York.

In 1929, Richard Voynow, a former pianist-bandleader for Bix Beiderbecke's Wolverines, organized a musical expedition remembered as the St. James (Hotel) Sessions: dozens of performers recorded about half country music with an eclectic sampling of jazz, blues, and novelty music. Several St. James recordings, by jazz bandleader Maynard Baird, blues-gospel singer Leola Manning, and country act the Tennessee Ramblers, have appeared on latter-day CD compilations.

In the 1930s and 1940s, Knoxville radio stations WNOX and WROL became famous for introducing new talent, notably fiddler Roy Acuff and innovative guitarist Chet Atkins, longtime Knoxville-area performers whose influence on Nashville, onstage and off, would be profound. Nominated as the Cradle of Country Music,

Knoxville has bred numerous stars, among them Dolly Parton, songwriter Don Gibson, and the Everly Brothers. Flatt & Scruggs were based in Knoxville for a time in the 1940s, as were the Louvin Brothers, whose cover of the traditional murder ballad "Knoxville Girl" became a country hit.

Blues and jazz have also been part of Knoxville's musical fabric. Several blues musicians, including brothers Brownie McGhee and Stick McGhee, as well as Howard Armstrong and his partner Carl Martin, lived in Knoxville, performing first as street musicians. Martin, Bogan, and Armstrong, then known as the Tennessee Chocolate Drops, made their first recordings at the St. James sessions. The local jazz scene has been energized lately by the University of Tennessee's vigorous jazz program, led by composer-keyboardist Donald Brown. The Knoxville Jazz Orchestra, an independent 17-piece ensemble conducted by trumpeter Vance Thompson, has made several recordings, some of which have earned critical praise.

The Knoxville Opera was founded in 1978, led first by Edward Zambara, followed by Robert Lyall, Francis Graffeo, and Brian Salesky. The KO's annual opera-themed Rossini Festival, launched in 2002, has become one of the city's most popular springtime events. Sopranos Grace Moore and Mary Costa grew up in or near Knoxville; later, sopranos Cheryl Studer and Delores Ziegler came through UT's music program and have performed worldwide. UT's School of Music enrolls several hundred students and sustains the 70-piece UT Symphony Orchestra, UT Chamber Orchestra, UT Opera Theater, and a large choral ensemble, and has risen to acclaim in public performances under conductor James Fellenbaum.

In the 21st century, former public-radio announcer Ashley Capps, co-founder of mammoth music festival Bonnaroo, has become a major influence through his music-promotion company AC Entertainment. In addition to booking both the city's renovated historic theaters and some nightclubs, AC launched the widely hailed Big Ears Festival in 2008, a three-day international festival devoted to music that resists mainstream formats.

With the help of vigorous roots music public radio station WDVX, which sponsors a daily live-broadcast folk and country performances in a public downtown studio, Knoxville has attempted to position itself as a national center for Americana music.

BIBLIOGRAPHY

L. Deaderick, ed.: *Heart of the Valley* (Knoxville, TN, 1976)
C.K. Wolfe: *Tennessee Strings: The Story of Country Music in Tennessee* Knoxville, TN, 1977)
J. Stokely and J. Johnson, eds.: *an Encyclopedia of East Tennessee* (Oak Ridge, TN, 1982)
C. Van West, ed.: *The Tennessee Encyclopedia of History and Culture* (Knoxville, TN, 1998)
J. Neely: *A History of Knoxville's Market Square: the Most Democratic Place on Earth* (Knoxville, TN, 2009)

JACK NEELY

Knuckles, Frankie (Warren, Jr.) (*b* New York, NY, 18 Jan 1955). DJ, producer, and remixer. He has made major contributions to the development of disco and house music. A regular dancer at David Mancuso's Loft, Knuckles worked at Nicky Siano's Gallery before his close friend Larry Levan invited him to share the turntables at the Continental Baths. Knuckles took over the position when Levan moved on and subsequently relocated to Chicago when Robert Williams invited him to work at the Warehouse. DJing at the Warehouse from its 1977 opening to its 1983 closing, Knuckles helped dance culture survive the backlash against disco, which peaked in Chicago in the summer of 1979. Knuckles went on to become the resident DJ at the Power Plant, where he became one of the first DJs to play house music. Often described as the "Godfather of House," Knuckles was in fact less open to the sound's initially raw aesthetic than Ron Hardy, who DJed at the Music Box, Williams' post-Warehouse venue.

Knuckles made his studio debut with a B-side remix of First Choice's "Let No Man Put Asunder"—Shep Pettibone's version of the same song appeared on the A-side—and he went on to work on groundbreaking house tracks such as Jamie Principle's "Baby Wants to Ride" and "Waiting On My Angel." Knuckles left Chicago under acrimonious circumstances in 1987 and played at Delirium in London for two months before returning to New York at the beginning of 1988. He went on to hold notable residencies at the World, the Sound Factory, and the Sound Factory Bar before he switched his focus to making international appearances. Cultivating a sensibility that highlights lush instrumentation and vocals, Knuckles has also enjoyed a successful studio career that has seen him release two albums under his own name and numerous remixes, including Satoshi Tomiie's "Tears." In 1998 he was named remixer of the year at the 40th Grammy Awards.

BIBLIOGRAPHY

B. Brewster and F. Broughton: *Last Night a DJ Saved my Life: The History of the Disc Jockey* (London, 1999)
T. Lawrence: *Love Saves the Day: a History of American Dance Music Culture, 1970–79* (Durham, NC, 2004)

TIM LAWRENCE

Knutsen, Chris [Cammon, Johan Christian] (*b* Leikanger, Sogn og Fjordane, Norway, 24 June 1862; *d* Los Angeles, CA, 6 Nov 1930). Maker of fretted stringed instruments of Norwegian birth. Knutsen, born Johan Christian Cammon, is best known for the harp guitars and Hawaiian-style instruments he designed and built between 1895 and his death in 1930. The early part of his career began in Port Townsend, Washington, where he received two patents for harp guitars with an auxiliary, hollow "arm" on the bass side of the sound box, extending to the peghead of the instrument. The second of these harp guitar patents shows two extended, sub-bass strings mounted on the arm in addition to the standard six strings of the guitar. Surviving instruments made from this patent design have between zero and five sub-bass strings. Knutsen harp guitars produced after 1898 most frequently have five sub-bass strings.

Knutsen expanded his production while living in Tacoma (1898–1906) and Seattle (1906–14). During his residence in Tacoma, Knutsen began to refer to his instruments as Symphony Harp Guitars on the interior labels, and established a licensing agreement with W.J. Dyer & Co., St. Paul, Minnesota, for the production of instruments bearing that name. Knutsen began offering a new type of Hawaiian-style guitar around 1907, likely prompted by the Hawaiian musicians touring the West Coast at that time. He unsuccessfully applied for a patent for guitars with sloped shoulders and convertible neck brackets, which allowed players to change the neck angles for Spanish- or Hawaiian-style playing. These early continental-made Hawaiian guitars were the models for the Kona instruments marketed by Charles S. DeLano, a student of the Hawaiian guitar master Joseph Kekuku. Between 1914 and 1916, Knutsen moved to Los Angeles, where DeLano's operation was based. Knutsen appeared to halt production of harp guitars following his move to California, and focused his attention on what he dubbed his New Hawaiian Family. Knutsen's unique Hawaiian-influenced inventions included harp steel guitars, or Hawaiian-style, sloped-shouldered guitars with sub-bass strings such as the harp guitar, and ukuleles with bass-side body arms extending to the pegheads.

BIBLIOGRAPHY
G. Noe and D. Most: *Chris J. Knutsen: From Harp Guitars to the New Hawaiian Family: History and Development of the Hawaiian Steel Guitar* (Everett, WA, 1999)

ARIAN SHEETS

Kobbé, Gustav (*b* New York, NY, 4 March 1857; *d* Babylon, NY, 27 July 1918). Writer on music. After studies in Wiesbaden and New York he attended Columbia University, graduating from the School of Arts in 1877 and the School of Law in 1879. From 1879 to 1880 he was editor of the *Musical Review*. Beginning in 1880 he was music critic for a series of New York papers, *The Sun*, *The World*, the *Mail and Express*, and *The Herald*; he was music and art critic for *The Herald* at the time of his death. In 1883 Kobbé was sent to Bayreuth by *The World* to report on the first performance of *Parsifal*.

A prolific writer, he is chiefly known for his *Complete Opera Book* (1919), a collection of opera plots and analyses, which has become a standard work of reference; he also published books on Richard Wagner and other composers, opera singers, and works on the pianola and the Aeolian pipe organ.

WRITINGS
Wagner's Life and Works (New York, 1890, 2/1896)
Opera Singers (New York, 1901, 6/1913)
ed.: *Wagner and his Isolde* (New York, 1905)
Famous American Songs (New York, 1906)
How to Appreciate Music (New York, 1906, 3/1912)
Kobbé's Complete Opera Book (New York, 1919; ed. and rev. 9/1976 by the Earl of Harewood as *The New Kobbé's Complete Opera Book*, 11/1997 as *The New Kobbé's Opera Book*)
Kobbé's Illustrated Opera Book, ed. Earl of Harewood (London, 1989, enlarged 2/1991)

PAULA MORGAN

Koch, Caspar (Petrus) (*b* Karnap, Germany, 25 Nov 1872; *d* Pittsburgh, PA, 3 April 1970). Organist of German birth. His parents immigrated to the United States in 1881 and settled near Alton, Illinois. Koch had to struggle for a musical education but managed to graduate from St Francis College, Joliet, Illinois. He later studied in Berlin with Heinrich Reimann, Franz Kullak, and others, and at the Kirchenmusikschule in Regensburg. He was for 33 years organist at Holy Trinity Catholic Church in Pittsburgh and served as a faculty member at Carnegie Institute of Technology from 1914 to 1941. He wrote the authoritative *Book of Scales for the Organ* (New York, 1918) and the *Organ Student's Gradus ad Parnassum* (1945), an interesting, informed, and sensible performance-practice book that became well known. "It deals in *detail* with the art of organ playing, which outside France and Germany has seemed to lack definition," wrote Virgil Fox (*Notes*, iii, 1945–6, 47). Koch played the first local organ broadcast in Pittsburgh, a city that pioneered in radio broadcasting. He was city organist there for 50 years (1904–54) and played more than 2000 recitals in North Side Carnegie Hall, where there is a large four-manual Skinner organ. He was succeeded in this post by his son Paul.

VERNON GOTWALS/JUDI CALDWELL

Kodály, Zoltán (*b* Kecskemét, Hungary, 16 Dec 1882; *d* Budapest, Hungary, 6 March 1967). Hungarian composer, music educator, and ethnomusicologist. Kodály studied modern languages at the University of Budapest beginning in 1900. During the same period he studied music and completed a PhD in philosophy and linguistics at the Franz Liszt Academy of Music (1906), also in Budapest. He collected and recorded Hungarian folk songs beginning in 1905, and after 1906 collaborated in the venture with Béla Bartók (1881–1945). Though his compositions met with success, Kodály's main contributions were in music education. He began composing pieces for children's choruses in the 1920s, many drawing upon his experience with Hungarian folk songs. Along with Jeno Adam (1898–1982) and other students and colleagues, he developed a concept of music education with singing as its essence and folk songs of the culture as the repertoire. Kodály considered solfège the best tool for developing the inner ear, and expected that music reading and writing would be taught sequentially using the highest quality music. Kodaly's method came to the United States in the 1950s and 1960s when music teachers emigrated to escape the communist regime in Hungary. At the invitation of the Ford Foundation, Kodály visited the United States in 1965 to observe methodology in universities. In 1966 he lectured at American universities and spoke at the International Society for Music Education conference in Interlochen, Michigan. The International Kodály Society is the umbrella organization and the Kodály Institute in Kecskemét is active in training teachers in the Kodály method.

BIBLIOGRAPHY
GMO
M. Houlahan and P. Tacka: *Zoltán Kodály: a Guide to Research* (New York, 1998)

ALAN L. SPURGEON

Koehler, Ted (L.) (*b* Washington, DC, 14 July 1894; *d* Santa Monica, CA, 17 Dec 1973). Popular song lyricist and pianist. Koehler began a career as a photo-engraver, but soon found work in movie theaters as a pianist and song plugger. This led to producing nightclub floorshows and songwriting. His first major collaboration was "When the Lights Are Low," (1923) with Gus Kahn and Ted Fio Rito. Teaming with Harold Arlen in 1930 at Harlem's Cotton Club, the two composed for starring performers, including Ethel Waters, Cab Calloway, and Lena Horne. Many of their songs from 1930 to 1934 became standards, including "Get Happy," "Between the Devil and the Deep Blue Sea," and "Stormy Weather." Koehler was particularly suited to writing lyrics for blues and jazz performers, with a remarkable ability for alliteration and phrasing. Arlen and Koehler also wrote for Broadway productions such as Earl Carroll's *Vanities* (1932), and Hollywood films, including *Let's Fall in Love* (1933).

After 1934 Koehler moved to Hollywood, continuing to write film music, sporadically with Arlen, but also with others. From the mid-1930s through the 1940s he co-wrote songs for dozens of films, including *Curly Top* (1935), *Springtime in the Rockies* (1942), and *Hollywood Canteen* (1944), teaming with composers such as Jimmy McHugh ("Lovely Lady"), Rube Bloom ("Don't worry 'bout me"), and Burton Lane ("What are you doing the rest of your life").

BIBLIOGRAPHY
P. Furia: *The Poets of Tin Pan Alley: a History of America's Great Lyricists* (New York, 1990)

JEFFERY WANSER

Koehnken & Grimm. Organ building firm. It was established by Johann Heinrich (John Henry) Koehnken (1819–97), a native of Altenbühlstedt near Hanover, Germany, who, with his brother Johann, immigrated to the United States in 1837. Trained as a cabinetmaker, he found employment the following year with Cincinnati's major organbuilder, Matthias Schwab (1808–62), a native of Switzerland who had apprenticed there, and who established a workshop in Cincinnati shortly after his arrival in 1831. Koehnken quickly learned the trade of organ building, and soon was assuming major responsibilities under Schwab, including the installation of some of Schwab's larger organs, such as that built in 1859 for St. Joseph's Church in Covington, Kentucky. Upon Schwab's retirement in 1860, Koehnken took over his workshop, establishing his own business under the name of Koehnken & Company. Among his workmen was Gallus Grimm (1827–97), a native of Württemberg who had apprenticed with Martin Braun of Spaichingen. He had immigrated to Cincinnati in 1853 and initially found employment with Schwab, staying on when Koehnken took over the business, and eventually becoming his partner around 1870 under the name of Koehnken & Grimm. In the time before the railroads reached Cincinnati, Koehnken & Grimm, like Schwab before them, built a number of organs in the city, as well as for locations up and down the Ohio and Mississippi rivers. Among the firm's larger organs were the

three-manual instruments for the Plum Street Temple in Cincinnati (1866; restored 2005) and Mother of God Church in Covington, Kentucky (1876), and a large two-manual organ for St. Paul's Episcopal Church in Cincinnati (1861). Koehnken and Grimm both died within a short time of each other in 1897, and the business was carried on for a short time by Grimm's son, Edward, but by this time its work consisted largely of rebuilding and maintenance, and it was closed in 1907.

BIBLIOGRAPHY
H.S. Humphreys: "The Koehnken Orgelbau—a Casualty to Progress," *Music, the AGO/RCCO Magazine*, iv/9 (1970), 23–24
K.W. Hart: "Cincinnati Organ Builders of the Nineteenth Century," *The Tracker*, xx/4 (1976), 5–12; xxi/1 (1976), 4–10
F. Noack: "Koehnken's Magnum Opus Restored," *The Tracker*, l/2 (2006), 8–21; reprinted in *ISO Journal*, no.26 (2007)
B. Owen: "Schwab, Koehnken, Grimm," *The Tracker*, l/3–4 (2006), 6–21

BARBARA OWEN

Kohn, Karl (George) (*b* Vienna, Austria, 1 Aug 1926). Composer, pianist, conductor, and teacher of Austrian birth; naturalized American. He immigrated to the United States in 1939 and studied at the New York College of Music (1940–4). He became a naturalized American in 1945. Following service in the US Army during World War II, he attended Harvard University, studying composition with WALTER PISTON, EDWARD BALLANTINE, IRVING FINE, and RANDALL THOMPSON (BA 1950, MA 1955). In 1950 he was appointed to Pomona College and Claremont Graduate School, where he became Thatcher Professor of Music. For three years he was on the faculty of the Berkshire Music Center. He has received two Wig Distinguished Professorship awards from Pomona College (1968, 1975), a Fulbright scholarship (1955–6), and a Guggenheim Fellowship (1961–2), and has had works commissioned by Coleman Concerts, the American Conference of Cantors, and the Claremont Music Festival. With his wife, Margaret, Kohn performs music for two pianos with a repertory emphasizing 20th-century music, giving concerts in the United States and abroad. As a choral conductor he has concentrated on Medieval, Renaissance, and 20th-century works; he conducts performances of his own music; he has also served for two decades on the board of directors of the Monday Evening Concerts. Kohn is now W.M. Keck Distinguished Service Professor Emeritus at Pomona and remains active as a composer and pianist.

Kohn's early works were couched in harmonic idioms derived from Bartók and Hindemith. From the mid-1950s until the early 1960s, his music was derived from serial procedures; this practice culminated in the *Concerto mutabile* (1962). Since then, his music has been remarkable for its chromatic and athematic character combined with chords, figurations, and textures evocative of earlier musics. Often these reminiscences are direct parodies or reworkings of materials borrowed from the past; *Introductions and Parodies* (1967), for example, modifies fragments from Mendelssohn's Violin Concerto within its own chromatic context. The resulting pitch contexts for both melodic and harmonic succession are flexible, generating powerful musical structures. Kohn's choral and vocal compositions form a substantial part of his output. Between 1963 and 1966 he contributed several of the "Current Chronicle" columns to *Musical Quarterly*.

WORKS

Orch: Sinfonia concertante, pf, orch, 1951; Ov., str, 1953; Castles and Kings, suite for children, orch/pf 4 hands, 1958; Scenes, 1960; Concerto mutabile, pf, orch, 1962; Episodes, pf, orch, 1964, arr. 2 pf, 1966; Interludes, 1964; Interlude I, fl, str, 1969; Interlude II, pf, str, 1969; Centone, 1973; Hn Conc., hn, small orch/pf, 1974; Innocent Psaltery, wind band, perc, 1975; Serenade II, concert band, 1977; Waldmusik, conc., cl, orch/pf, 1979, arr. cl, pf, wind ens, 1983; Wind Chamber, concert band, 1981; Time Irretrievable, 1983; Return, brass, str, perc, 1990; Ode for Str Orch, 1993; Memory and Hope: Essay for Str Orch, 1996

Chbr: Str Trio, 1950; Concert Music, 12 wind, 1956; Song, vn/cl, pf, 1956; Vn Sonata, 1956, Capriccios, fl, cl, vc, hp, bn, 1962; Kaleidoscope, str qt, 1964; Encounters I–VI, various solo insts, pf, 1965–77; Introductions and Parodies, cl, hn, bn, str qt, pf, 1967; Rhapsodies, perc, 1968; Impromptus, 8 wind, 1969; Trio, vn, hn, pf, 1972; Paronyms, fl, pf, 1974; The Prophet Bird, chbr ens, 1976; Son of Prophet Bird, hp, 1977; Paronyms II, sax, pf, 1978; Prophet Bird II, pf, chbr ens, 1980; Recreations II, 2 gui, 1980; Capriccios II, chbr ens, 1983; An Amiable Piece, 2 pf, wind, perc, 1987; Reconnaissance, chbr ens, 1995; More Reflections, cl, pf, 1997; Capriccio, vn, s sax, a sax, pf, 1998; Toccata and Virelais, accdn, hp, 1998

Kbd: Rhapsodie no.1, pf, 1960; Recreations, pf 4 hands, 1968; Prelude and Fantasia, org, 1968; Rhapsody no.2, pf, 1971; Rhapsody no.3, pf, 1977; Shadow Play, 2 pf, 1981; Dream Pieces, 2 pf, 1983; Neofantasy, org, 1990; Little Pieces, pf, 1993; Metasuite, pf, 1994; Adagio for Dancing, 2 pf, 1995; Allegro for Dancing, 2 pf, 1996; Number Play, 2 pf, 1999; Again, Again, 2 pf, 2000

Vocal: 3 Songs (T. Carew, J. Lyly, F. Beaumont), Tr vv, 1956; 3 Descants (Bible: *Ecclesiastes*), chorus, brass, 1957; Sensus spei (Bible: *Lamentations*), chorus, pf, 1961; Leisure (A. Lowell), Bar, chbr ens, 1965; Madrigal (R. Chester), chorus, pf, 1966; Esdras: Anthems and Interludes, chorus, fl, pf, orch, 1970, arr. chorus, pf, 1975; Only the Hopeful (Heb.), male v, chorus, 1971; What Heaven Confers (Chin.), chorus, vib/pf, 1981; Alleluia (Militant Praise), mixed vv, brass/pf, 1982; The Resplendent Air, 5 songs, high v, pf, 1985; Lions on a Banner (Sufi texts), S, chorus, orch, 1988

MSS in Central Library, Claremont, CA; Honrold Library, Claremont, CA
Principal publishers: C. Fischer, GunMar, Edition Contemp Art

BIBLIOGRAPHY

L. Morton: "Current Chronicle," *MQ*, xlix (1963), 229–35
P. Oliveros: "Karl Kohn: *Concerto mutabile*," *PNM*, ii/2 (1963), 873–99
H. Pollack: *Harvard Composers: Walter Piston and his Students, from Elliott Carter to Frederic Rzewski* (Metuchen, NJ, 1992), 228ff
N. Slonimsky: *Baker's Biographical Dictionary of Twentieth-Century Classical Musicians* (New York, 1997, ed. L. Kuhn, assoc ed. D. McIntire)

RICHARD SWIFT/GREG A STEINKE

Kohs, Ellis (Bonoff) (*b* Chicago, IL, 12 May 1916; *d* Los Angeles, CA, 17 May 2000). Composer and teacher. He studied at the San Francisco Conservatory, at the Institute of Musical Art (NYC), at the University of Chicago with Carl Bricken (1933–8, MA 1938), at the Juilliard School with BERNARD WAGENAAR (1938–9), and at Harvard University with WALTER PISTON, Willi Apel, and Hugo Leichtentritt (1939–41). After war service as a bandmaster in the US Army Air Force (Fort Benning, Georgia; St. Joseph, Missouri; and Nashville, Tennessee) he taught at the Kansas City Conservatory (summers of 1946, 1947), Wesleyan University, Connecticut (composition, 1946–8), the College of the Pacific (1948–50), Stanford

University (1950), and the University of Southern California (from 1950), where he served as chairman of the music theory department until 1973 and professor of music. His textbook *Music Theory* (1961) has been widely used; it was followed by *Musical Form* (1976) and *Musical Composition* (1980). He published many articles on music. His compositions show an imaginative use of variation technique. While he used newer techniques in his later works, including 12-note serialism, he never departed from established Classical forms, and employed melodic and rhythmic unifying techniques. One of his more humorous works is "The Automatic Pistol," in which he set the text of an army weapons manual for male a cappella chorus. He composed in a range of genres: opera, ballet, incidental music, symphonies, concertos, chamber music, vocal works, and keyboard works. Among the awards he received were the Alice M. Ditson Award (1946) and the BMI Publication Award (1948); he also received commissions from Pierre Monteux (for Symphony no.1) and the Fromm Foundation (Symphony no.2). His papers are deposited at the New York Public Library for the Performing Arts.

WORKS

Stage: Amerika (op, Kohs, after F. Kafka), 1966–9; Macbeth (incid music, after Shakespeare), 1947; Lohiau and Hiiaka (incid music, after a Hawaiian legend), 1987

Orch: Conc. for Orch, 1942; Legend, ob, str, 1946; Vc Conc., 1947; Sym. no.1, 1950; Sym. no.2, chorus, orch, 1956; Vn Conc., 1980

Choral: Ps xxv, SATB, org/orch, 1947; Lord of the Ascendant (D. Allen, after Epic of Gilgamesh), 7 solo vv, chorus, orch, 8 dancers, 1955; Ps xxiii, 4 solo vv, chorus, 1957; 3 Songs from the Navajo, 1957; unacc. choruses

Chbr and solo inst: Str Qt no.1, 1940; Night Watch, fl, hn, timp, 1944; Sonatina, bn, pf, 1944; Passacaglia, org, str, 1946; Sonatine, vn, pf, 1948; Str Qt no.2 "A Short Concert," 1948; Chbr Conc., va, 9 str, 1949; Sonata, vc, pf, 1951; Studies in Variation: I, wind qnt, II, pf qt, III, pf (Pf Sonata no.2), IV, vn (Sonata), 1962; Sonata, snare drum, pf, 1966; Duo after Kafka's "Amerika," vn, vc, 1970

Kbd: Pf Variations, 1946; Variations on "L'homme armé", pf, 1947; Capriccio, org, 1948; Toccata, hpd/pf, 1948; 3 Chorale Variations on Hebrew Hymns, org, 1952; Suite, 2 pf, 1980; Etude-Variations after a Theme by Johannes Brahms, pf RH, 1985; 2 pf sonatas, other shorter pieces

Songs, incl. Fatal Interview (E. St. Vincent Millay), low v, pf, 1951; Epitaph (E. Santayana), T, pf, 1959; 4 Orch Songs (A. Lotterhos, Santayana), 1v, orch, 1959

Principal publishers: ACA, Associated, BMI, Merrymount, Presser; Recording: Composers Recordings, Inc.

BIBLIOGRAPHY

EwenD; *VintonD*
E.B. Kohs: "Thoughts from the Workbench," *American Composers Alliance Bulletin*, vi/1 (1956), 3–5
Compositores de América/Composers of the Americas, ed. Pan American Union, xv (Washington, DC, 1969) [incl. list of works]
Unpubd essays in *NYp*

BARBARA A. RENTON

Kolb, Barbara (*b* Hartford, CT, 10 Feb 1939). Composer and clarinetist. A clarinetist, she studied composition with ARNOLD FRANCHETTI at Hartt College of Music (BM 1961, MM 1964); she also studied with LUKAS FOSS and GUNTHER SCHULLER at the Berkshire Music Center (1964, 1968). From 1960 to 1966 she was a clarinetist in the Hartford SO. She was the first American woman to receive the Prix de Rome (1969–71); enabling her to study in Vienna and Paris and at Mills College (electronic music). She has received numerous awards including a Fulbright scholarship, three Tanglewood fellowships, four MacDowell Colony fellowships, and two Guggenheim fellowships. During 1983 until 1984, Kolb spent nine months at IRCAM and produced her memorable *Millefoglie*, a one-movement work for chamber ensemble and tape, which subsequently won the Kennedy Center Friedheim Award (1987). *Trobar Clus* (1970), commissioned by the Berkshire Music Center and the Fromm Foundation, was based on the medieval form "trobar clus" and dedicated to Lukas Foss. Her *Soundings* (1972) for the Koussevitzky Foundation, was premiered by Pierre Boulez conducting the New York PO in 1975. In 1983, she ventured into film scores, writing the music for *Cantico*. Subsequent commissions include *The Enchanted Loom* (1989) for the Atlanta SO, *Voyants* (1991) for Radio France (dedicated to Aaron Copland), and *All in Good Time* (1993) for the 150th anniversary of New York PO. Bassoonist Stefano Canuti commissioned her *Sidebars* (1996) for bassoon and piano.

Kolb was composer-in-residence at the Marlboro Music Festival (1973), the American Academy in Rome (1975), and IRCAM (1983–4), and held teaching positions in theory and composition at Brooklyn College, CUNY, Temple University, and the Eastman School of Music. Between 1982 and 1986 she developed a music theory course, sponsored by the Library of Congress, for the blind and physically disabled.

Kolb's music is highly eclectic, assimilating diverse styles and exploring different media; various idioms, ranging from serialism to jazz, are uniquely synthesized. Many of her works also respond to a variety of extra-musical sources, including the visual arts (*Grisaille*) and poetry (*Appello* and *Spring River Flowers Moon Night*). Jazz elements are incorporated most notably in *Chromatic Fantasy* and *Homage to Keith Jarrett and Gary Burton*. Besides fusing different styles, Kolb has combined electronic and acoustic media. In *Millefoglie* a computer-generated tape and a chamber orchestra blend diverse colors and interweave contrasting layers of sound. Many of her pieces, in addition to *Millefoglie*, explore the superimposition of multiple harmonic and rhythmic layers. *Soundings*, her best-known work, is based on the technique of depth-measurement and cast in a tripartite, quasi-palindromic form. One of the piece's more interesting characteristics involves Kolb's use of the same musical elements played at different speeds by contrasting sections of the orchestra. The opening of *Soundings* "descends" through successive layers to a climax, and the last section "ascends" to the surface with rhythmic acceleration. In the central section the texture dissipates, as motivic patterns from the opening are isolated and developed.

WORKS
(selective list)

Orch: Crosswinds, wind, perc, 1968; Trobar Clus, chbr orch, 1970; Soundings, chbr orch, tape, 1971–2, rev. 1975, 1978; Grisaille, 1978–9; Millefoglie, chbr orch, cptr-generated tape, 1984–5; Yet that Things go Round, chbr orch, 1986–7, rev. 1988; The Enchanted Loom, 1988–9, rev. 1992; Voyants, pf, chbr orch, 1991; All in Good Time, 1993; Criss Cross, perc, orch, 2000; Aubade, mandolin orchestra, 2003

Chbr and solo inst: Rebuttal, 2 cl, 1965; Figments, fl, pf, 1967, rev. 1969; 3 Place Settings (I. Diamond, C., R. and B. Brown, R. Costa), nar, cl, perc, vn, db, 1968; Solitaire, pf, tape, 1971; Toccata, hpd, tape, 1971; Spring River Flowers Moon Night, 2 pf, perc, tape, 1974–5; Looking for Claudio, gui, tape, 1975; Appello, pf, 1976; Homage to Keith Jarrett and Gary Burton, fl, vib, 1976; Musique pour un vernissage, fl, gui, vn, va, 1977 [withdrawn]; Chromatic Fantasy (H. Stern), amp nar, amp a fl, ob, s sax, tpt, el gui, vib, 1979; 3 Lullabies, gui, 1980; Related Characters, tpt/cl/a sax/va, pf, 1980; Cantico, film score, tape, 1982; Cavatina, vn/va, 1983, rev. 1985; Time…and Again, ob, str qt, tape, 1985; Umbrian Colors, vn, gui, 1986; Broken Slurs, gui, 1988, rev. 1992, 2001; Extremes, fl, vc, 1989; Cloudspin, org, tape, 1991, rev. 2007; Introduction and Allegro, gui, 1992 [replaces Molto Allegro, 1988]; Monticello Trio, vn, vc, pf, 1992; In Memory of David Huntley, str qt, 1994; Turnabout, fl, pf, 1994; New York Moonglow, fl + s sax, cl + s sax, tpt, vib + perc, va, vc, 1995; Sidebars, bn, pf, 1995–6; Antoine's Tango, pf, 2001; The Web Spinner, chamber orch, 2003

Vocal: [7] Chansons bas (S. Mallarmé), S, hp, perc, 1966; [5] Songs before an Adieu (R. Pinsky, e.e. cummings, Stern, V. Popa, G. Apollinaire), S, fl, gui, 1976–9; Poem, chorus, 1980; The Point that Divides the Wind (Franciscan and Gregorian chant), 3 solo male vv, org, perc, 1982; The Sundays of my Life, jazz song, 1982; Virgo mater creatrix (S. Mesmer), chorus, 1998

Principal publishers: Boosey & Hawkes, C. Fischer, Peters

BIBLIOGRAPHY

CC (B. Weir); *GroveW* (D. Metzer and L. Starr) [incl. further bibliography]

C. Gange and T. Caras: "Barbara Kolb," *Soundpieces: Interviews with American Composers* (Metuchen, NJ, 1982), 269–79

D. Wright: "Looking for Barbara Kolb," *MT*, cxxxiv (1993), 9–13

J. Peyser: *The Music of my Time* (New York, 1995), 221–32

E. Perconti: "Three Keyboard Pieces by Barbara Kolb," *Women of Note Quarterly*, iv/2 (1996), 20–6

J. Lochhead: "Texture and Timbre in Barbara Kolb's *Millefoglie*," *Engaging Music: Essays in Music Analysis* (New York, 2005), 253–72

DAVID METZER, LAWRENCE STARR/ALYSON PAYNE

Koldofsky, Adolph (*b* London, England, 13 Sept 1905; *d* Los Angeles, CA, 8 April 1951). Canadian violinist and conductor. In 1912 he moved to Toronto, where he studied the violin with Harry Adaskin, Luigi von Kunits, and Geza de Kresz. He also studied with EUGÈNE YSAŸE in Brussels (1925–8) and with Otakar Ševčík in Czechoslovakia (1929–30). In Toronto he was important in musical life as chamber player, soloist, and conductor, and from 1938 to 1942 he played in the Hart House Quartet. He became leader of the Vancouver SO in 1944, and in 1946 he moved to Los Angeles, where his interest in contemporary music brought him into close association with Ernst Krenek and Arnold Schoenberg; the latter composed his *Phantasy* op.47 for him. As a scholar Koldofsky was notable for bringing to light several harpsichord concertos (now in *BEm*) by C.P.E. Bach, performances of which he conducted for the CBC with Wanda Landowska as soloist in 1943. In 1934, he married the Canadian pianist Gwendolyn Williams (*b* Bowmanville, Ontario, 1 Nov 1906; *d* Santa Barbara, CA, 12 Nov 1998), with whom he gave many concerts. Gwendolyn Williams Koldofsky initiated the accompanying program at the University of Southern California in 1947 and remained there until retirement in 1988. She was also closely associated with the Music Academy of the West in Santa Barbara and appeared frequently in recital with outstanding singers.

CARL MOREY

Kolisch, Rudolf (*b* Klamm am Semmering, Austria, 20 July 1896; *d* Watertown, MA, 1 Aug 1978). Violinist of Austrian birth. An injury to his left hand in childhood, after he had begun violin lessons, compelled him to hold the violin with his right hand and the bow with his left. He studied at the Vienna Music Academy and Vienna University (where he attended Guido Adler's musicology lectures), and after graduating in 1913 continued to study violin with Otakar Ševčík and theory and composition with Franz Schreker and ARNOLD SCHOENBERG (who married Kolisch's sister Gertrud in 1924). Kolisch began his career as a conductor and violin virtuoso, and from 1919 to 1921 played a leading role in Schoenberg's Verein für Musikalische Privataufführungen. In 1922 he formed the Kolisch Quartet, which became internationally known. Its membership changed in the early years but by 1927 consisted of Kolisch, Felix Khuner, Jenö (Eugene) Lehner, and Benar Heifetz. This quartet toured in Europe, Africa, South America, and the United States, where the members settled in 1935.

The Kolisch Quartet was the first to insist on playing the standard repertory from memory and made a still stronger impression as the champion of new music, particularly of works by Schoenberg, Alban Berg, and Anton Webern. Among its important premieres were Schoenberg's String Quartets nos.3 and 4 and Quartet Concerto (after G.F. Handel), Berg's Lyric Suite in its original form, Webern's String Trio and String Quartet, and Béla Bartók's Quartet no.6. Schoenberg dedicated his Fourth Quartet jointly to Elizabeth Sprague Coolidge (who commissioned it) and to "its ideal interpreters, the Kolisch Quartet," and wrote to the former that they were "the best string quartet I ever heard," praising "their virtuosity, their sonority, their understanding, their style." Tonal richness was helped by their instruments: Kolisch played a Stradivari violin, Lehner a viola by Gasparo da Salò, Heifetz an Amati cello. They disbanded in 1939 after a reorganization of membership proved ineffective. Kolisch was leader of the Pro Arte Quartet from 1942, and from 1953 again appeared in Germany, most often at the Darmstadt summer courses. He taught violin and chamber music at the University of Wisconsin, 1944–67, and was artist-in-residence and head of the chamber music department at the New England Conservatory of Music, Boston.

BIBLIOGRAPHY

E. Stein, ed.: *Arnold Schoenberg: Ausgewählte Briefe* (Mainz, 1958; Eng. trans., enlarged, 1964)

A. Mell: "In memoriam: Rudolf Kolisch (1896–1978)," *Journal of the Violin Society of America*, iv/1 (1977–8), 142–5

M. Steinberg: "Rudolf Kolisch (1896–1978): Encomium," *Journal of the Arnold Schoenberg Institute*, iv (1980), 7–11

Rudolf Kolisch zur Theorie der Aufführungen: ein Gespräch mit Berthold Türcke, Musik-Konzepte, nos.29–30 (1983)

D. Satz: *Rudolf Kolisch als Lehrer* (Vienna, 1986)

M. Grassl and R. Kapp, eds.: *Die Lehre von der musikalischen Aufführung in der Wiener Schule* (Vienna, 2002)

A.C. Shreffler and D. Trippett, eds.: *Musiktheorie: Zeitschrift für Musikwissenschaft*, xxiv/3 (2009) [Rudolf Kolisch in Amerika: Aufsätze und Dokumente]

BERNARD JACOBSON/R

Kolodin, Irving (*b* New York, NY, 21/22 Feb 1908; *d* New York, NY, 29 April 1988). Music critic. He studied harmony and theory at the Institute of Musical Art in New York (1930–1) and was music critic of the *New York Sun* (1932–50) and the *Saturday Review* (1947–82). He also wrote program notes for the New York Philharmonic (1953–8) and taught music criticism at the Juilliard School of Music (1968–1986). Because of his affiliation with the *Saturday Review*, Kolodin was one of the most widely read and influential classical music critics in the United States. He published books prolifically and the wide-ranging musical subjects of his writings matched his diverse interests. His monographs engaged in the politics of the music business, colorfully assessed the current state of musical culture with programming suggestions (*The Musical Life*, 1958), and also discussed aesthetics (*The Interior Beethoven*, 1965). Kolodin's monographs were popular in the United Kingdom, where they brought British audiences in contact with American musical life. As an editor Kolodin brought composers' and musicians' voices to the general public, writing portions of Benny Goodman's autobiography (*The Kingdom of Swing*, 1939) and collecting composers' writings on their peers throughout history (*The Composer as Listener*, 1969). As an unofficial historian of the Metropolitan Opera, he chronicled the institution in a volume that underwent four revisions during the 20th century. Kolodin's criticism responded to the increasing presence and influence of the recording industry. He was one of the first American critics to give extensive reviews devoted to phonograph records: his first record guide appeared in 1941. In the 1950s he curated albums for RCA Victor that brought together recent outstanding recordings. In his writing, Kolodin drew attention to performances' specifics while casting a dramatic picture of the musical event to engage non-specialist readers. He drew in readers unfamiliar with music through his attention to performers' personalities and casual reference to insiders' anecdotes.

PATRICK J. SMITH/ANDREA F. BOHLMAN

Konitz, Lee (*b* Chicago, IL, 13 Oct 1927). Jazz alto saxophonist of Austrian and Russian Jewish parentage. He has been one of the most original and distinctive alto saxophonists in jazz and master improviser of the bebop generation. His apprenticeship to bebop was indirect, however, and he has carved out an uncompromising solo career guided by a singular artistic vision. He has been a highly self-critical, reflective musician who plays intuitively, with an intensely emotional sensibility, ingeniously creating novel contexts for the theme-and-variations approach on standard material.

He received classical lessons on clarinet from age 11 before switching to tenor and then alto saxophone. In 1943 he met his decisive personal and musical influence, the teacher and pianist LENNIE TRISTANO, through whom he thoroughly assimilated the heritage of Charlie Parker and Lester Young. Konitz's partnership with Tristano, and with his fellow pupil Warne Marsh, were defining ones of his career. His earliest commercially recorded solos, with Claude Thornhill's orchestra (1947), show a developing individual style, with a tonal purity often mistakenly regarded as vibrato-less and "classical," when in fact it was a genuine jazz sound.

As a member of Miles Davis's nonet (1948–50), which was later known as the Birth of the Cool band, Konitz is generally regarded, with Tristano and Davis, as an architect of the cool jazz style. An excellent early solo is "Subconscious-Lee" (1949, Prst.), an original line on the changes to "What is this thing called love?" Konitz recorded as a leader with Marsh in 1949 and 1955, and worked with Tristano's quartet from 1954 to 1955.

Playing in Stan Kenton's band (1952–3) extended his range of playing contexts, and he has since periodically returned to larger ensembles. But his most original and challenging work has been in smaller groups. Konitz is the spontaneous improviser par excellence, constantly finding inspiration in jazz standards. Throughout his career he has composed, often but not always based on the chords of standards.

Konitz's career was at its lowest ebb commercially in the early 1960s, but in 1961 he recorded one of his most renowned albums, *Motion*, with John Coltrane's drummer Elvin Jones. In 1967 he recorded *Duets*, a series of duos with Joe Henderson, Richie Kamuca, Jim Hall, Ray Nance, and Jones, among others. In the 1970s he sometimes worked with Marsh, and in 1975 he returned to the nonet format which was compared, not totally accurately, with the Birth of the Cool band.

For much of the time since the mid-1960s, Konitz has lived and worked in Europe and Japan. He recorded with Dave Brubeck and Anthony Braxton, with Andrew Hill, and with Marsh and Bill Evans (1977). He has subsequently worked with such younger players as Matt Wilson and Dan Tepfer, as well as enjoying reunions with players closer to his own generation such as Charlie Haden and Paul Motian.

RECORDINGS
(selective list)
Duos with D. Tepfer: *Duos with Lee* (Sunnyside, 2009)
As leader: *Lee Konitz* (1949, Prst.); *Lee Konitz with Warne Marsh* (1955, Atl.)
with L. Tristano and W. Marsh: *The Complete Atlantic Recordings* (1955–8, Mosaic)
Motion (1961, Verve); *The Lee Konitz Duets* (Mlst., 1967); *Jazz à Juan* (1974, Steeplechase); with G. Evans: *Heroes* (1980, Verve); *Thingin'* (1995, Hatology)

BIBLIOGRAPHY
M. Harrison and M. James: "Lee Konitz: a Dialogue," *Jazz Review*, iii/6 (1960), 10–2
M. James: "Lee Konitz," *Ten Modern Jazzmen* (London, 1960), 49–64
W. Balliett: "Jazz: Ten Levels," *New Yorker* (16 Aug 1982)
M. Frohne: *Subconscious-Lee: 35 Years of Records and Tapes: the Lee Konitz Discography, 1947–1982* (Freiburg, 1983)
W. Enstice and P. Rubin: "Lee Konitz," *Jazz Spoken Here: Conversations with Twenty-two Musicians* (Baton Rouge, LA, 1992), 197–211
A. Hamilton: *Lee Konitz: Conversations on the Improviser's Art* (Ann Arbor, MI, 2007)

ANDY HAMILTON

Konkow. Native American group belonging to the Maidu.

Konomihu. Native American group of California, belonging to the Shasta.

Konpa. A popular dance music genre that rose to prominence in Haiti during the mid-1950s and which remains at the forefront of the Haitian music scene, both in Haiti and in the Haitian diaspora. There are two conflicting theories of the genre's origins. Some scholars explain that konpa was adapted from the *merengue típico* from the Cibão region of the Dominican Republic. Others locate its roots in the Haitian folkloric music that includes the *contredanse, quadrille,* and *menuet* of European origin, in addition to the *rada, kongo* (also, *congo*), and *petwo* (also, *pétro*) rhythms that have provenance in Africa.

Early ensembles typically comprised vocals, saxophones, accordion, acoustic guitar, string bass, drum set, and various percussion instruments. From the 1960s, band composition decreased in size and shifted to include more electronic instruments (guitar, bass, and synthesizers). During the 1970s, konpa bands began widely incorporating trumpets, trombones, and congas or *tambou* (a drum similar to the conga) and reflected the popular sounds of jazz, funk, and soul. Konpa music today often bears the influence of hip-hop, reggae, ragga, and R&B. Many of today's most profitable bands, such as Gabel, Nu-Look, Carimi, Zenglen, Zin, and T-Vice, are based in the North American diaspora but regularly perform in Haiti. Konpa Kreyol, Djakout #1, Tropicana, and Septentrional are popular Haiti-based bands. The lyrical content of konpa, from the time of the genre's inception to the present, has ranged broadly from themes of love to political and social critique.

BIBLIOGRAPHY
G. Averill: *A Day for the Hunter, a Day for the Prey: Popular Music and Power in Haiti* (Chicago, 1997)
E.R. Sainvill: *Tambours Frappés, Haitiens Campés: La fabuleuse histoire de la musique haitienne* (Port-au-Prince, nouvelle edition, 2001)
T. Louis-Charles: *Le compas direct: La vraie musique entraînante haïtienne de tous les temps* (Port-au-Prince, 2003)

REBECCA DIRKSEN

Kool & the Gang. Soul and funk group. Its members included Robert "Kool" Bell (*b* Youngstown, OH, 8 Oct 1950; bass guitar), Ronald (Nathan) Bell (*b* Youngstown, OH, 1 Nov 1951; tenor saxophone), Dennis "Dee Tee" (Ronald) Thomas (*b* Orlando, FL, 9 Feb 1951; saxophone, flute), Claydes (Eugene) Smith (*b* Jersey City, NJ, 6 Sept 1948; *d* Maplewood, NJ, 20 June 2006; guitar), Robert "Spike" Mickens (*b* Jersey City, NJ, 1951; trumpet), Rickey Westfield (*b* Jersey City, NJ; *d* 1985; keyboards), and George "Funky" Brown (*b* Jersey City, NJ, 5 Jan 1949; drums). Originally formed in Jersey City in 1964 as the Jazziacs, by 1969 the group had changed its name to Kool & the Gang and the style from jazz to funk. Released on the band's own De-Lite Records, *Kool and the Gang* (1969) established the sound that characterized their recordings during the mid-1970s. The bass and guitar play hyperactive, syncopated parts, while the drums maintain a steady pattern, with prominently recorded congas adding to the excitement. The horns contribute staccato riffs and fills, and a party atmosphere is created by voices talking, shouting, and laughing.

Kool & the Gang enjoyed a string of hits during the period 1973–4, including "Funky Stuff," "Jungle Boogie," and "Hollywood Swinging," which featured chanted group vocals in the choruses and complex forms not easily described by the usual verse–chorus–bridge terminology. In the late 1970s the band's popularity declined, but adding the smooth soul-influenced lead singer James "J.T." Taylor and the producer Eumir Deodato, the group reached new heights, notably with their number-one hit "Celebration" (1980), which has remained widely popular decades later. In addition to the disco-funk of this record they explored calypso-influenced rhythms in "Let's go dancin' (Ooh La, La, La)" (1982), middle-of-the-road ballads in "Joanna" (1983) and "Cherish" (1985), and hard rock on "Misled" (1984). Although they have not duplicated their earlier chart success, the group has remained active in performance and in the studio into the 2010s.

BIBLIOGRAPHY

L. Hildebrand: *Stars of Soul and Rhythm and Blues* (New York, 1994)
R. Vincent: *Funk: the Music, the People, and the Rhythm of "The One"* (New York, 1996)

DAVID BRACKETT/R

Kool Herc [Campbell, Clive; DJ Kool Herc; Kool DJ Herc] (*b* Kingston, Jamaica, 16 April 1955). DJ and hip hop pioneer of Jamaican birth. As a boy in West Kingston, he became well-versed with Jamaican sound systems, whose mobile crews held dances during which selectors played reggae records over public address systems, and DJs toasted improvised percussive rhymes over the instrumental sections of these records. Campbell was familiar with American music due to his father's extensive record collection, which included music by James Brown, Nina Simone, and other American artists. In the winter of 1967, his family moved to the Bronx, New York, into a recently completed apartment building at 1520 Sedgwick Avenue.

Campbell, nicknamed "Herc" (from Hercules) by his friends, began playing records to entertain friends and neighbors. He found his audience resistant to Jamaican music and culture, but enthusiastic about James Brown, American R&B, and Latin jazz. Using his father's public address system, Campbell began DJing at parties held in the recreation room of his Sedgwick Avenue building. The first party was held on 11 August 1973 in honor of his sister Cindy's birthday, and this event is sometimes described as the birth date of hip hop. Drawing influences from the sound system "toasting" style, while using the slang of the New York streets, Herc talked to the crowd on the microphone. He enlisted a friend Coke [Coco] La Rock (*b* 24 April 1955), to make announcements and improvise rhymes over the records.

Herc found the dancers at his parties were most excited by the percussion-heavy instrumental "vocal-breaks," or "breaks," on certain soul and jazz records. He developed a technique called the "Merry-Go-Round," in which he could turn relatively brief breaks into repeating ostinatos. Using two copies of the same record on different turntables, he would find the "break" and repeat it as many times as he wished. This technique also allowed Herc to transition from break to break without stopping the music or playing undesired portions of these recordings. The Merry-Go-Round prefigured later musical practices in hip hop, particularly the digital sampling techniques of "looping" common to rap music since the mid-1980s. While Herc repeated instrumental breaks, La Rock and others improvised rhymes, establishing the musical model for rap's musical style. Records with notable breaks that were mainstays of Herc's DJ set included Michael Viner's Incredible Bongo Band's "Apache" and "Bongo Rock" (from *Bongo Rock*, 1973) and James Brown's "Give It Up, Turn It Loose" (People, 1970).

DJ Kool Herc is widely considered the first hip hop DJ, and Coke La Rock the first hip hop rapper/emcee. Kool Herc continued to deejay throughout and beyond the 1970s with fellow DJs Grandmaster Flash, Afrika Bambaataa, and Jazzy Jay, who are commonly described as the principal innovators of hip hop music. Neither he nor Coke La Rock ever made commercial recordings.

BIBLIOGRAPHY

M. Forman & M.A. Neal: *That's the Joint!: the Hip-Hop Studies Reader* (New York, 2004)
J. Chang: *Can't Stop Won't Stop: a History of the Hip-Hop Generation* (New York, 2005)

WILL FULTON

Koonce, Paul (*b* Aurora, IL, 5 July 1956). Composer and pianist. He studied at the University of Illinois with HERBERT BRÜN (MM 1983) and at the University of California, San Diego (PhD 1989), working with ROGER REYNOLDS and acquiring software programming skills to process musical sounds. He subsequently produced programs designed to analyze and synthesize audio signals. He has taught at Princeton University and, since 2002, at the University of Florida.

Koonce is a distinguished pianist who has performed demanding contemporary pieces by Boulez, Subotnick, and Xenakis. His reputation, however, rests primarily on his use of technology within his compositions. He has realized many pieces for fixed media (both tape music and digital media), which places him among the community of electroacoustic music composers especially popular in Europe and Asia. (Many US composers tend to prefer using electronic sources mixed with live instruments.) Koonce has composed instrumental pieces as well as compositions which integrate digital media.

His music draws on the tradition of musique concrète and often involves transforming and montaging a variety of sound sources. The diversity and contrast of these sound sources produces a distinctive liveness uncommon in electroacoustic music. For Koonce, each sound conveys a sense of rhythm, texture, and color. His compositional strategy weaves tension and energy rather than merely juxtaposing diverse sounds. Koonce's music increases one's awareness of the sounds that surround us and to their unexpected and beautiful structures.

Among his many achievements are honorable mention awards at the Prix Ars Electronica (1994), the Luigi Russolo International Competition for Composers of Electronic Music (1988), and ASCAP Awards (1999–2003), and the Euphonies d'Or Award (2004). His music is widely performed in North America as well as in Europe and Asia.

WORKS
(selective list)

Inst.: Escape Tone, fl, 1985; Ritornello, str orch, 1990; On the Bias, fl, pf, 1993; Afterglow, ens, tape, 2002
Elec: Pins, 1992; The Flywheel Dream, 1994; Hothouse, 1996; Walkabout, 1998; Breath and the Machine, 1999; Anacrusis, 2000; Out of Breath, 2000; Midnight Oil, 2001; Infant Aulos, 2004; Adolescent Aulos, 2005; Hair of the Bow, 2006; Träumerei Machine, 2007; Clockwork, 2008

MARC BATTIER

Korean American music. *See* ASIAN AMERICAN MUSIC.

Korn [née Gerlach], **Clara Anna** (*b* Berlin, Germany, 30 Jan 1866; *d* New York, NY, 14 July 1940). Pianist, composer, and teacher of German birth. She arrived in the United States at the age of three and later studied with William G. Vogt. After a brief career as a concert pianist she received a letter from Pyotr Il'yich Tchaikovsky, who had seen some of her compositions in manuscript while visiting New York. He urged her to devote her time to composing, and in late 1891 she won a scholarship to the National Conservatory in New York, where she studied with ANTONÍN DVOŘÁK, HORATIO PARKER, and BRUNO OSCAR KLEIN. From 1893 until 1898 she taught theory at the conservatory. She was a founder of the National Federation of Music Clubs, the Women's Philharmonic Society, and the Manuscript Society of New York. In 1899 she settled in Brooklyn, where she taught the piano privately.

Korn wrote for several music journals. She spoke out regarding the difficulty women faced in obtaining orchestral performances and encouraged women composers not to isolate themselves or retreat to club work. Her compositions are varied and numerous, including an opera, *Their Last War*, orchestral works, chamber music, piano works, and songs. Few were published. Korn's style varies by genre and medium but is generally characterized by short, lyrical phrases, a conservative yet effective harmonic language, and careful part-writing.

WORKS
(selective list)

Stage: Their Last War (op, Korn) (Boston, 1932)
Orch: Sym., c; Morpheus, sym. poem; 2 suites: Ancient Dances, Rural Snapshots; Pf Conc.; Vn Conc.
Other inst: Suite, vn, vc, pf; Pf Sonata (Nautical), op.14 (East Orange, NJ, 1911); Gymnasium March, pf (Philadelphia, n.d.); Swinging (Philadelphia, n.d.); Ov. solennelle (arr. of Tchaikovsky: 1812 Ov.), 2 pf (n.d.); pieces for vn, pf
Solo vocal: 9 Songs, S/T, pf (New York, 1903)

BIBLIOGRAPHY
S.R. Crothers: "Woman Composers of America: Clara A. Korn," *MusAm*, x/4 (1909), 4–26

PAMELA FOX

Korn, Peter Jona (*b* Berlin, Germany, 30 March 1922; *d* Munich, Germany, 12 Jan 1998). Composer of German birth; naturalized American. He studied at the Palestine Conservatory, Jerusalem (from 1936), where his teachers included STEFAN WOLPE and Hermann Scherchen. After immigrating to the United States in 1941, he studied with ARNOLD SCHOENBERG and later at the University of Southern California with ERNST TOCH, HANNS EISLER, MIKLÓS RÓZSA, and Lilian Steuber, among others. He took American citizenship in 1944. In 1948 he founded the New Orchestra of Los Angeles. His teaching appointments included positions at the Trapp Conservatory, Munich (1960–1), and the University of California (1961–4). An active participant in German musical life after his return in 1965, he served as director of the Richard Strauss Conservatory (1967–87), chair of the Association of Munich Musicians (1974–8), vice president of the German Composers' Association, and co-founder of the Richard Strauss Society.

Korn described himself as an eclectic who reformed divergent styles into his own musical language. His book *Musikalische Umweltverschmutzung* (Wiesbaden, 1975) objects to the politics of controlled music and to the demands for absolutism within certain schools of composition, pleading instead for a more liberal approach. His honors include the Munich music prize (1968) and the distinguished service cross of Bavaria (1984).

WORKS
(selective list)

Op: Heidi in Frankfurt (3, Korn, after J. Spyri), op.35, 1961–3, Saarbrücken, 28 Nov 1978
Orch: Romantic Ov., op.1, 1943, rev. 1983; Sym. no.1, op.3, 1946, rev. 1977; Tom Paine Ov., op.9, 1950, rev. 1985; Sym. no.2, op.13, 1951, rev. 1983; Hn Conc., op.15, 1952; Adagietto, op.23, small orch, 1954, rev. 1986; Variations on a Tune from Beggar's Op, op.26, 1955; Sax Conc., op.31, 1956, rev. 1982; Sym. no.3, op.30, 1956, rev. 1969; Berolinasuite, op.34, 1959; Vn Conc., op.39, 1965; Exorcism of a Liszt Frag., op.44, 1968; Beckmesser Variations, op.64, 1977; Tpt Conc., op.67, 1979; Sym. "Salute to the Lone Wolves," op.69, wind, 1980; Romanza concertante, op.84, ob, orch, 1987; Conc. classico, hpd, orch, 1988; Eine kleine Festmusik, op.92, str, 1991; 10 other orch works
Vocal: Yes and No (P. Bargman, Korn), op.8, S, pf, 1951; 2 Nocturnes (P.B. Shelley), op.20, S, A-cl, hp/pf, 1953; Der Pfarrer von Cleversulzbach (E. Mörike), op.24, Bar, pf, 1954; Von Krieg und Frieden (M. Claudius), op.48, low v, pf, 1971; Eine kleine deutsche Stadt (cant., R. Kunze), op.71, T, hpd, orch, 1981; Der Psalm vom Mut (cant., L. Feuchtwanger), op.75, Bar, orch, 1983; Wir sind die letzten (H. Sahl), op.98, Bar, pf; many other vocal pieces, incl. choral works
Chbr (3 or more insts): Str Qt no.1, op.10, 1950; Aloysia-Serenade, op.19, fl, va, vc, 1953; Fantasy, op.28, hn, vn, vc, pf, 1955; Serenade, op.33, 4 hn, 1957 [arr. 4 trbn, 1997]; Str Qt no.2, op.36, 1963; Wind Qnt, op.40, 1966; Serenade, op.45, 12 str, 1968; Pf Trio, op.56, 1975; Wind Octet, op.58, 1976; Bei Nacht im Dorf der Wächter rief, op.63, ob, hn, pf, 1977 [arr. ob, hn, str qt, 1988]; Goya, op.72/3a, 12 vc, 1982, rev. 1987; Pavane nocturne, op.74, fl, vn, vc, pf, 1983; Divertimento, op.97, vn, va, vc, 1992; 7 other chbr works
Chbr (1–2 insts): Sonata, op.6, vc, pf, 1949; Sonata, op.7, ob, pf, 1949; Sonata, op.18, hn, pf, 1952; Duo, op.66, va, pf, 1978, rev. 1986; 3 intermezzi, op.73, fl, pf, 1982; ...ruft uns die Stimme, op.81, trbn,

org; Sonata, op.83, vn, pf, 1986; Gavotte für Felix, op.95, vn, pf, 1992; solo works for pf, org; 5 other works

Principal publishers: Leukart, Peters, J. Schuberth & Co., Simrock, Zinneberg

BIBLIOGRAPHY
A. Ott: "Mentor liberaler Musikpolitik," *Neue Musikzeitung*, xxi/2 (1972)

N. Düchtel, ed.: *Peter Jona Korn* (Tutzing, Germany, 1989) [incl. selection of writings]

H. Müller: "Zum Tode Peter Jona Korns," *Cellesche Zeitung* (20 Jan 1998)

HARALD MÜLLER

Korngold, Erich Wolfgang (*b* Brno, Moravia [now Czech Republic], 29 May 1897; *d* Hollywood, CA, 29 Nov 1957). Austrian composer. The second son of the eminent music critic Julius Korngold (1860–1945), he was a remarkable child prodigy composer. In 1906 he played his cantata *Gold* to Gustav Mahler, who pronounced him a genius and recommended that he be sent to Zemlinsky for tuition. At age 11 he composed the ballet *Der Schneemann*, a sensation when it was first performed at the Vienna Court Opera (1910); he followed this with a Piano Trio and a Piano Sonata in E that so impressed Artur Schnabel that he championed the work all over Europe. Richard Strauss remarked: "One's first reaction that these compositions are by a child are those of awe and concern that so precocious a genius should follow its normal development….This assurance of style, this mastery of form, this characteristic expressiveness, this bold harmony, are truly astonishing!" Giacomo Puccini, Jean Sibelius, Bruno Walter, Arthur Nikisch, Engelbert Humperdinck, Karl Goldmark, and many others were similarly impressed.

Korngold was 14 when he wrote his first orchestral work, the *Schauspiel Ouvertüre*; his *Sinfonietta* appeared the following year. His first operas, *Der Ring des Polykrates* and *Violanta*, were completed in 1914. With the appearance of the opera *Die tote Stadt*, completed when he was 23 and acclaimed internationally after its dual premiere in Hamburg and Cologne (1920), his early fame reached its height, and he briefly outstripped Richard Strauss as the most performed composer from German-speaking countries. After completing the first Left Hand Piano Concerto, commissioned by Wittgenstein in 1923, he began his fourth and arguably greatest opera, *Das Wunder der Heliane* (1927), and started arranging and conducting classic operettas by Johann Strauss and others. He also began teaching opera and composition at the Vienna Staatsakademie and was awarded the title Professor *honoris causa* by the president of Austria.

Max Reinhardt, with whom Korngold had collaborated on versions of *Die Fledermaus* and *La belle Hélène*, invited him to Hollywood in 1934 to work on his celebrated film of Shakespeare's *A Midsummer Night's Dream*. Over the next four years, Korngold pioneered a new art form, the symphonic film score, in such classics as *Captain Blood*, *The Prince and the Pauper*, and *Anthony Adverse* (for which he won the first of two Academy Awards). The Anschluss prevented him from staging his fifth opera, *Die Kathrin*, and he remained in Hollywood composing some of the finest music written for the cinema. *The Adventures of Robin Hood* (1938, winner of his second Academy Award), *The Sea Hawk* (1940), and *Kings Row* (1941) are his greatest works in the genre. Treating each film as an "opera without singing" (each character has his or her own leitmotif), he created intensely romantic, richly melodic, and contrapuntally intricate scores, the best of which are a cinematic paradigm for the tone poems of Richard Strauss and Franz Liszt. He intended that, when divorced from the moving image, these scores could stand alone in the concert hall. His style exerted a profound influence on modern film music.

After the war Korngold returned to absolute music, composing, among other works, a Violin Concerto (1937, rev. 1945) first performed by Heifetz, a Cello Concerto (1946), a Symphonic Serenade for String Orchestra (1947) given its premiere by Furtwängler, and the Symphony in F♯ (1947–52). His late-Romantic style, however, was completely out of step with the postwar era and when he died at the age of 60, he believed himself forgotten. After decades of neglect, a gradual reawakening of interest in his music occurred. At the time of his centenary (1997) his works were becoming increasingly popular, appearing on major recordings and concert programs around the world. By 2010, his Violin Concerto and the opera *Die tote Stadt* had become repertoire works again, and all of his works had been recorded.

WORKS
(selective list)

DRAMATIC

Ops: Der Ring des Polykrates (1, J. Korngold and L. Feld, after H. Teweles), op.7, 1913, Munich, 28 March 1916; Violanta (1, H. Müller), op.8, 1914, Munich, 28 March 1916; Die tote Stadt (3, P. Schott [E.W. and J. Korngold], after G. Rodenbach: *Bruges la morte*), op.12, 1916–20, Hamburg and Cologne, 4 Dec 1920; Das Wunder der Heliane (3, Müller, after H. Kalneker), op.20, 1921–27, Hamburg, 7 Oct 1927; Die Kathrin (3, E. Decsey), op.28, 1932–37, Stockholm, 7 Oct 1939

Film scores: A Midsummer Night's Dream (dir. M. Reinhardt), 1934 [arr. of Mendelssohn]; Captain Blood (dir. M. Curtiz), 1935; Anthony Adverse (dir. M. Le Roy), 1936; Give Us This Night (dir. A. Hall), 1936; The Green Pastures (dir. W. Keighley), 1936 [orch sequences]; Rose of the Rancho, 1936 [one song]; Another Dawn (dir. W. Dieterle), 1937; The Prince and the Pauper (dir. Keighley), 1937; The Adventures of Robin Hood (dir. Curtiz and Keighley), 1938; Juarez (dir. Dieterle), 1939; The Private Lives of Elizabeth and Essex (dir. Curtiz), 1939; The Sea Hawk (dir. Curtiz), 1940; Kings Row (dir. S. Wood), 1941; The Sea Wolf (dir. Curtiz), 1941; The Constant Nymph (dir. E. Goulding), 1942; Between Two Worlds (dir. E.A. Blatt), 1944; Devotion (dir. C. Bernhardt), 1943; Of Human Bondage (dir. Goulding), 1944; Deception (dir. I. Rapper), 1946; Escape Me Never (dir. P. Godfrey), 1946; Magic Fire (dir. Dieterle), 1954 [arr. of Wagner]

Other: Gold (cant.), solo vv, pf, 1906, lost; Der Schneemann (ballet pantomime, E.W. Korngold), 1908–9, Vienna, 4 Oct 1910 [orchd Zemlinsky, rev. Korngold 1913]; Much Ado about Nothing (incid music, W. Shakespeare), op.11, 1918–19, 6 May 1920; The Silent Serenade (stage comedy, E.W. Korngold, B. Reisfeld and W. Okie), op.36, 1946, Vienna, 26 March 1951

ORCHESTRAL

Schauspiel Ouvertüre, op.4, 1911; Sinfonietta, op.5, 1912; Sursum corda, sym. ov., op.13, 1919; Pf Conc., C♯, op.17, pf left hand, orch, 1923; Baby Serenade, op.24, small orch, 1928–9; Vn Conc., D, op.35, 1937, rev. 1945; Tomorrow, sym. poem, op.33, Mez, chorus, orch,

1942; Vc Conc., C, op.37, 1946; Sym., F♯, op.40, 1947–52; Sym. Serenade, B♭, str, op.39, 1947; Theme and Variations, op.42, school orch, 1953

CHAMBER AND KEYBOARD

Don Quixote, pf, pieces, 1907–8; Pf Sonata no.1, d, 1908; Pf Trio, D, op.1, 1909; Pf Sonata no.2, E, op.2, 1910; Märchenbilder, 7 pf pieces, op.3, 1910; Sonata, D, op.6, vn, pf, 1912; Str Sextet, D, op.10, 1914–16; Pf Qnt, E, op.15, 1921; Str Qt no.1, A, op.16, 1920–3; 4 Little Caricatures, op.19, pf, 1926; Tales of Strauss, op.21, pf, 1927; Suite, op.23, pf left hand, str, 1928–30; Pf Sonata no.3, C, op.25, 1931; Str Qt no.2, E♭, op.26, 1933; Str Qt no.3, D, op.34, 1944–5; Romance impromptu, vc, pf, op. posth., 1946

SONGS

6 einfache Lieder (J.F. von Eichendorff, E. Honold, H. Kipper, S. Trebitsch), op.9, 1911–13; [4] Abschiedslieder (C. Rosetti, A. Kerr, E. Ronsperger, E. Lothar), op.14, A, pf/orch, 1920–21; 3 Lieder (H. Kaltneker), op.18, 1924; 3 Lieder (K. Kobald, E. van der Straten), op.22, 1928–9; The Eternal (E. van der Straten), song cycle, op.27, 1933; 4 Lieder (Shakespeare: *Othello, As You Like It*), op.31, 1937; Songs of the Clown (W. Shakespeare: *Twelfth Night*), op.29, 1937; 5 Lieder (R. Dehmel, Eichendorff, H. Koch, Shakespeare), op.38, medium v, pf, 1948; Sonett für Wien (Kaltneker), op.41, Mez, pf, 1953

MSS in *Wc*
Principal publisher: Schott

BIBLIOGRAPHY

KdG (S. Rode-Breymann)
E. Newman: "The Problem of Erich Korngold," *The Nation* (24 Aug 1912)
R.S. Hoffmann: *Erich Wolfgang Korngold* (Vienna, 1922)
E.W. Korngold: "Some Experiences in Film Music," *Music and Dance in California*, ed. J. Rodríguez (Hollywood, 1940), 137–9
R. Behlmer: "Erich Wolfgang Korngold – Established Some of the Film Music Basics Film Composers Now Ignore," *Films in Review*, no.182 (1967), 86–100
L. Korngold: *Erich Wolfgang Korngold* (Vienna, 1967)
J. Korngold: *Die Korngolds in Wien* (Zürich, 1991)
S. Blickensdorfer: *Erich Wolfgang Korngold: Opern und Filmmusik* (diss., U. of Vienna, 1993)
R. van der Lek, trans. M. Swithinbank: "Concert Music as Reused Film Music," *AcM*, lxvi (1994), 8–112
B.G. Carroll: *The Last Prodigy* (Portland, OR, 1997)
G. Wagner: *Korngold "Musik ist Musik"* (Berlin, 2008)
A. Stollberg, ed: *Erich Wolfgang Korngold—Wunderkind der Moderne oder Letzter Romantiker* (Munich, 2009)

BRENDAN G. CARROLL

Korte, Karl (Richard) (*b* Ossining, NY, 25 Aug 1928). Composer. He studied at the Juilliard School (BS 1952, MS 1956) with AARON COPLAND, OTTO LUENING, PETER MENNIN, VINCENT PERSICHETTI, and Gofredo Petrassi. After teaching at Arizona State University (1963–4) and at SUNY, Binghamton (1964–70), he was appointed professor of music at the University of Texas, Austin (1971–97). His awards include two Guggenheim Fellowships (1960, 1970), the Gershwin Memorial Award (1957), the gold medal in the 1969 Queen Elisabeth International Competition, Belgium, and two NEA grants (1975, 1978). His Concerto for Piano and Winds was commissioned for the centennial of the Music Teachers National Association (1976). In 2002 his *Four Songs of Experience* (Blake; SSA, pf) won "Top Honors" in the international Waging Peace through Singing competition held at the University of Oregon, Eugene.

A prolific composer, Korte has written in virtually every genre of music except opera and has explored the major compositional techniques of the 20th century, including serialism, neotonality, electronic music, and computer-generated music. In the Piano Trio (1977, rev. 1982) and subsequent works, he has sought ways of achieving a simpler style in a basically tonal language.

WORKS

Orch: Concertato on a Choral Theme, 1955; For a Young Audience, 1959; Sym. no.2, 1961; Southwest, 1963; Sym. no.3, 1968
Band: Ceremonial Prelude and Passacaglia, 1962; Nocturne and March, 1962; Prairie Song, tpt, band, 1963; Gestures, wind ens, perc, pf, amp db, 1970; I think you would have understood, tpt, band, tape, 1971; Fibers, 1977; Texarkana, 1991
Chbr and solo inst: Str Qt no.2, 1966; Matrix, wind qnt, sax, perc, pf, 1968; Remembrances, fl, tape, 1971; Conc., pf, wind, 1977; Pf Trio, 1977, rev. 1982; Concertino, b trbn, wind, perc, 1981; Double Conc., fl, db, tape, 1983; Te Maori, vc, 1987; Evocation and Dance, b trbn, tape, 1988; other works, incl. pf pieces
Vocal and choral: 4 Blake Songs, female vv, pf, 1961; Mass for Youth, SSA, orch, 1963; Aspects of Love (Bible: *Song of Solomon*, R.L. Stevenson, R.W. Emerson, Li Po, L. Hunt, W. Blake), SATB, 1968; May the sun bless us (R. Tagore), male vv, brass, perc, 1968; Ps xiii, SATB, tape, 1970; Pale is this good prince (orat, Egyptian), solo and choral vv, 2 pf, 4 perc, 1973; Songs of Wen I-to, high v, pf, 1973; Of Time and Season (various texts), solo vv, SATB, pf, mar, 1975; The Whistling Wind (Wang Xiaoni), Mez, tape, 1982; 5 New Zealand Songs, v, pf, 1989; Christmas music, other choral works
Tape: Hill Country Birds, tape, slides, 1982

Principal publishers: Elkan-Vogel, Galaxy, E.C. Schirmer, Seesaw, Presser

BIBLIOGRAPHY

R.E. Faust: "Composer Profile: Karl Korte," *National Association of College Wind and Percussion Instructors Journal*, xxxix/4 (1991), 45–7
B.D. Sanchez: *An Investigation and Analysis of Selected Choral Works by Karl Korte* (diss., U. of Texas, 1998)

JEROME ROSEN/MICHAEL MECKNA

Kortschak, Hugo (*b* Graz, Austria, 24 Feb 1884; *d* Honolulu, HI, 20 Sept 1957). Violinist and conductor. He studied violin with Otakar Ševčík at the Prague Conservatory and, after immigrating to the United States in the early 1900s, toured as a concert violinist and conductor, and served as director of a number of American and European music festivals. He headed the violin department at Yale University for 28 years. Having organized his own string quartet in Chicago (1913) and participated in the founding of the Coolidge Chamber Music Festival in Pittsfield, Massachusetts (1918), he was awarded the Coolidge Medal for distinguished service to chamber music in 1938. After retiring from Yale in 1952, he played in the violin section of the Honolulu Symphony as "honorary concertmaster" until his death. One of his early students was the comedian JACK BENNY, whose attempts to play the violin were a regular part of his routine for many years.

ROBERT FINN

k-os [Brereton, Kevin] (*b* Toronto, ON, 20 Feb 1972). Canadian rapper, songwriter, singer, and record producer. k-os (pronounced chaos) is an internationally known Canadian musical artist whose music fuses rap, rock, reggae, and pop, among other genres. He is a self-proclaimed "rap and roller" whose music transcends musical boundaries while drawing upon his Trinidadian roots. A prolific singer/songwriter, he has produced and written the majority of the songs on his four studio albums. His debut album, *Exit* (Astralwerks, 2002), garnered multiple accolades including a Source Award for Best International Hip Hop artist in 2003. His follow-up album, *Joyful Rebellion* (EMI/Virgin, 2004), was certified platinum. Its debut single, "B-Boy Stance," won two awards from the Canadian Urban Music Association. His third album, *Atlantis: Hymns for Disco* (EMI/Virgin, 2006), also certified platinum, marked a lyrical departure from the social commentary emphasized in his first two albums and further showcased k-os' versatility as a musician. For example, the single "Sunday Morning" is a melodic, pop-infused song which showcases his singing abilities. In 2006, k-os collaborated with the Canadian Broadcasting Corporation (CBC) radio orchestra to compose "Burn to Shine." The same year he also released a version of John Legend's "Jealous Guy" for Amnesty International. His fourth studio album, *Yes!* (EMI/Virgin, 2009), continues to challenge conceptions of what is and is not considered hip hop.

ATHENA ELAFROS

Koskoff, Ellen (Gilbert) (*b* Pittsburgh, PA, 8 Dec 1943). Ethnomusicologist. She received her PhD from the University of Pittsburgh in 1976 with a dissertation titled *The Effect of Mysticism on the Nigunim of the Lubavitcher Hasidim*. She has continued to work extensively on the Lubavitcher sect (Brooklyn, NY) of the Hasidic community, particularly from the perspective of gender in the music. Koskoff is Professor of Ethnomusicology and the Director of the World Music Certificate and Ethnomusicology Diploma Program at the Eastman School of Music, where she also directs the Eastman School's Balinese Gamelan Lila Muni. She has been a visiting professor at Syracuse University, UCLA, and New York University, and has served as the President for the Society for Ethnomusicology. She was the ethnomusicology advisor for the second edition of *The New Grove Dictionary of American Music* and an editor and contributor to *The Garland Encyclopedia of World Music, iii, United States and Canada,* and *Women and Music in Cross-Cultural Perspective*. Her work has been published in *Ethnomusicology, Selected Reports in Ethnomusicology,* and *Women & Music*, among others. Koskoff is also the radio host for the program, "What in the World is Music?" on WXXI-FM (NPR), which is broadcast weekly. The program offers a range of music, from "yodels of a Bulgarian shepherd" to a "Balinese fisherman wailing song about entrails." She was the recipient of the ASCAP-Deems Taylor Award for Excellence in Music Scholarship for *Music in Lubavitcher Life* in 2002.

WRITINGS

The Effect of Mysticism on the Nigunim of the Lubavitcher Hasidim (diss., U. of Pittsburgh, 1976)

ed.: *Women and Music in Cross Cultural Perspective* (Urbana, 2/1988)

"Miriam Sings Her Song: the Self and Other in Anthropological Discourse," *Musicology and Difference*, ed. R. Solie (Berkeley, 1993), 149–63

Music in Lubavitcher Life (Urbana, IL, 2001)

"(Left Out in) Left (the Field): the Effects of Post-Postmodern Scholarship on Feminist and Gender Studies in Musicology and Ethnomusicology, 1990–2000," *Women and Music*, ix (2005), 90–98

Music Cultures in the United States (New York, 2005)

KENDRA PRESTON LEONARD

Kosman, Joshua (*b* Boston, MA, 27 Oct 1959). Music critic. Kosman has worked as the classical music critic for the *San Francisco Chronicle* since 1988. He received a BA in music from Yale College and an MA from the University of California, Berkeley. At the *Chronicle*, Kosman has championed modern American composers including John Adams, Aaron Jay Kernis, Michael Gordon, Chen Yi, and Lisa Bielawa; he writes about field-wide issues, including orchestra management, the development of contemporary repertoire, and the brief public fascination with the pianist David Helfgott, with a congenial, probing tone that blends a reporter's instincts with a critic's acumen. A 2006 recipient of the ASCAP-Deems Taylor Award for music criticism, he is a contributor to the *New Grove Dictionary of Music & Musicians,* 2nd Edition, and the *New Grove Dictionary of Opera*, and his writing has appeared in *Gramophone, Opernwelt, Bookforum, Smithsonian, Piano & Keyboard, Symphony,* the *Journal of Musicology*, and other publications. He blogs about music at <http://www.pacificaisle.blogspot.com>.

JAYSON GREENE

Kostelanetz, André (*b* St. Petersburg, Russia, 22 Dec 1901; *d* Port-au-Prince, Haiti, 13 Jan 1980). Conductor and arranger of Russian birth, naturalized American. He studied at the conservatory in Petrograd (now St. Petersburg) from 1920 to 1922, when he went to the United States; he became an American citizen in 1928. In 1930 he was engaged as a conductor for the CBS radio network, beginning an association with broadcasting and film work, and with the popularizing of classical music, for which he principally became known, in performances of lively and robust style. During World War II he conducted many concerts for the US armed forces. Also a successful guest conductor elsewhere, and principal conductor of the New York PO's promenade concerts, he made a valuable contribution to musical life by commissioning works by Copland (*Lincoln Portrait*), Schuman, Hovhaness, and other contemporary composers. He is the dedicatee of Walton's *Capriccio burlesco*, of which he conducted the premiere by the New York PO in 1968. Kostelanetz's successful arrangements of light music, using densely concentrated instrumental sonorities and rich, saturated harmonies, influenced film music of the time. Together with G. Hammond he wrote *Echoes: Memoirs of André Kostelanetz* (New York, 1981).

BERNARD JACOBSON

Koster, John (*b* Gloversville, NY, 4 June 1950). Organologist and conservator. He was educated at Harvard College and studied harpsichord building under HUGH GOUGH. Since 1991 Koster has been on the faculty of the University of South Dakota and the National Music

Museum, where he holds the title of Conservator and Professor of Music. He is a leading authority on the history and development of early keyboard instruments, a topic on which he has extensively published. Between 1975 and 1991, Koster served as a technician and conservator to the Museum of Fine Arts, Boston. In 1994 he published a monumental catalog of that museum's collection of keyboard instruments, *Keyboard Musical Instruments in the Museum of Fine Arts, Boston* (Boston, 1994), which was awarded the American Musical Instrument Society's Bessaraboff Prize in 1997. In addition to his work in the area of historic keyboard instruments, Koster has undertaken research on the choralcelo, an early electronic instrument developed during the first years of the 20th century.

EDMOND T. JOHNSON

Kosugi, Takehisa (*b* Tokyo, Japan, 24 March 1938). Japanese composer. He studied musicology at the National University of Fine Arts and Music in Tokyo, graduating in 1962; with the foundation in 1960 of Group Ongaku, he began his work in group improvisation and event music. Works such as *South II* (1964) and *Instrumental Music* (1965) were performed by avant-garde Fluxus artists during his stay in the United States, mainly in New York, from 1965 to 1967. He established the electro-acoustic group Taj Mahal Travellers in 1969 and performed music for mixed media with them until 1975. After immigrating to the United States in 1977 he was active as a composer and performer with the Merce Cunningham Dance Company, along with Cage and David Tudor; he has served as the company's musical director since 1995. The many exhibitions and festivals at which he presented sound installations include Für Augen und Ohren, held in Berlin in 1980. In 1994 he won the John Cage Award for Music from the Foundation for Contemporary Performance Arts. His compositional interests lie in Messiaen's rhythmic modes and in jazz, rock, and folk music; his performances on the electric violin and on electronic modulation devices are informed by Asian sonic gestures. He continues to push musical boundaries in recent collaborations across genres with musicians such as post-punk band Sonic Youth.

WORKS
(composed in the United States)

Events: South III "Malika," v/action, 1965; Film & Film IV, paper screen, 1965; Piano, object floating on pond, 1966; South VIII, mixed-media, 1979; Cycles for 7 Sounds, multi-space performing event, 1981; Walking, 1983; + –, multi-purpose event, 1987; Metal Interspersion, sound object, 1992

Sound installations: Interspersion for 54 Sounds, 1980; Melodies, mixed-media, 1984; Loops I, II, 1988; Modulation, 1991; Islands, 1991; Streams, 1993; Zoom, 1993; Imitated Summer, 1996; Illuminated Summer, 1996

Mixed-media performance: Tender Music, 1965; Instrumental Music, 1965; Music G, 1966; Eclipse, 1967; Module, audio-visual music, 1990

El-ac:Interspersion, 1979; Assemblage, 1986; Rhapsody, el-ac, v, 1987; Spectra, 1989

Live elecs: Catch-Wave "Mano-Dharma," 1967; Heterodyne, 1972; Untitled Piece, 1980; Cycles, 1981; Spacing, 1984; Streams, 1991;

Reflections, 1992; Transfiguration, 1993; Streams II, 1994; Tetrafeed, 1997; Wave-Code A–Z, 1997

Other elec: The Fly, tape, 1982; Intersection, pf, elecs, 1983

Principal publisher: Lovely Music

YOKO NARAZAKI/R

Kotani, Ozzie (*b* Honolulu, HI, 12 April 1956). Hawaiian slack-key guitarist, arranger, and composer. He first became interested in *ki ho'alu*, or slack-key guitar, after hearing a recording of renowned player Keola Beamer. He learned to play slack key by listening to recordings of Beamer, and later studied with Peter Medeiros at the University of Hawai'i and privately with SONNY CHILLINGWORTH. He performs on both nylon and steel-string guitars and typically uses a four-finger picking method. He incorporates Spanish, Brazilian, American folk, Japanese, and other non-Hawaiian influences into his compositions and style. His playing technique is notable for the alternating bass in imitation of the double bass typical of a Hawaiian band, and for arpeggiations played evenly with the thumb and three fingers; he is known for producing a balanced and artistic sound. He often expands the standard slack-key tonic-dominant-subdominant harmonic language with added chord tones.

Kotani has released five unaccompanied solo albums. His choice of material includes original compositions and interpretations of slack key and Hawaiian standards. He is a featured artist on several slack key compilation albums, two of which won Grammy Awards (2006, 2007), and has collaborated with and accompanied others. In 2004, the Hawai'i Academy of Recording Arts awarded Kotani a Lifetime Achievement Award for Ki Ho'alu. Since 1986 Kotani has taught slack key at the University of Hawai'i at Manoa. He also teaches master classes and workshops and performs internationally. In 2000, he released his first instruction book, later followed by two instructional DVDs.

RECORDINGS
(selective list)

Classical Slack (Pacific Sound Design 1001, 1988); *Kani Ki Ho'Alu* (Dancing Cat Records 38013, 1995); *To Honor a Queen: the Music of Lili'uokalani* (Dancing Cat Records 38018, 2001); *Paka Ua (Raindrops)* (Daniel Ho Creations 16, 2005); *Ho'ihi (Respect)* (2008)

PAULA J. BISHOP

Kotík, Petr (*b* Prague, Czechoslovakia [now Czech Republic], 27 Jan 1942). Composer and conductor of Czech birth. He studied the flute in Prague with František Čech and composition with Jan Rychlík; while at the Vienna Music Academy Kotík studied composition with Karl Schieske, Jelinek, and Cerha (1963–66), and flute with Hans Reznicek. In Prague, Kotík founded and directed two experimental music ensembles: Musica Viva Pragensis (1961–4) and the QUAX Ensemble (1966–9), performing his own and other Czech compositions, as well as music by Boulez, Cage, Cardew, Feldman, Nono, Schwertsik, Stockhausen, Webern, and others.

In 1969 Kotík moved to the United States as a member of the Center of the Creative and Performing Arts at SUNY Buffalo (1969–73). In 1970 he founded the SEM Ensemble, which toured the United States, Europe, and

South America. In 1992 he created the Orchestra of the SEM Ensemble, one of America's leading large-scale new music groups. Kotík is the recipient of several grants and commissions including a prestigious award from the Foundation for Contemporary Arts (1996). In 2001 Kotík established the biennial summer institute and festival Ostrava Days (Ostrava, Czech Republic), where he currently serves as artistic director.

Kotík's compositional method is based on indeterminacy as well as conscientiously controlled decisions. Since the early 1960s he has worked with graphic material to determine parameters in the compositional process. Kotík's compositions between 1970 and 1983 contain independent sections which can, by overlapping, form various ensembles. A common pulse serves as a unifying element for the diverse parts which can be performed either as a solo or simultaneously with any number of other parts. During the 1980s Kotík's compositions became more fixed, his latest scores being precisely notated. Even though his recent pieces involve complex harmonies, the basic structure of the chords is still based on 5ths, 4ths, and octaves.

WORKS
(selective list)
Alley, variable ens, 1960–70; Congo, 7 insts, 1962; Kontrapunkt II, a fl, eng hn, cl, bn, va, vc, 1962–3; Music for Three, va, vc, db, 1964; Spontano, pf, 10 insts, 1964; 6 Plums, orch, 1965–8; Kontrabandt, elecs, 2–6 pfmrs, 1967; There is Singularly Nothing (G. Stein), 10vv, 12 insts, 1995; If I Told Him (Stein), insts, 1971–3, rev. 1995; John Mary (Stein), 2vv, fl, ob, trbn, perc, 1974; Many, Many Women (Stein), 6vv, 6 insts, 1975, rev. 1978; Adagio, orch, 1977; Drums, 2 perc, 1977–81; Explorations in the Geometry of Thinking (R. Buckminster Fuller), 2vv, 1981; Commencement (Fuller), 2vv, 1981; Aug/Oct, va, ens, 1981, rev. as Apparent Orbit, a fl, ens, 1984–5; Music for Winds, variable ens, 1981–2; Solos and Incidental Harmonies, fl, vn, 2 perc, 1983, rev. 1984; Integrated Solos, fl, tambourine, tpt, elec, 1986–8; Wilsie Bridge, 2 fl, 2 tpt, 2 synth, 8 perc, 1986–7; Letters to Olga (V. Havel), 5 spkrs, 7 insts, 1989–91; Quiescent Form, orch, 1994–96; Music in Two Movements, timp, 2 vib, str, 1998–2003; For ZS, 2 ten sax, 2 elec gui, 2 perc, 2004; Spheres & Attraction (Fuller), 2 vv, str qt, 2 perc, 2006

Principal publishers: Srajer, Universal

IVAN POLEDŇÁK/ELIZABETH PERTEN

Kotzschmar, (Johann Carl) Hermann (*b* Finsterwalde, Germany, 4 July 1829; *d* Portland, ME, 12 April 1909). Composer, conductor, and teacher of German birth. From age three Kotzschmar was taught how to play the piano, organ, violin, flute, and horn by his father, the *Stadtmusiker*, or City Musician, of Finsterwalde. At age 14 he was sent to Dresden to study with Julius Otto, cantor of the Kreuzkirche. Five years later he and others formed the 20-man Saxonia Band. The ensemble sought its fortunes in this country and worked with William Henry Fry's Italian Opera troupe for several months in New York, Philadelphia, and Boston, where the enterprise failed and the Saxonians disbanded. Kotzschmar moved to Portland, Maine, to assume a temporary job as a theater musician.

Kotzschmar initially led a four-man band at the Union Street Theater, but in 1851 became organist of the Portland Sacred Music Society (until 1857) and also of First Parish Church, a position he was to hold for 47 years

before resigning because of budget cuts to his program; he then served State Street Congregational Church for five years. He taught through his Kotzschmar Piano School, the most notable of the myriad of his pupils being JOHN KNOWLES PAINE (whose oratorio, *St. Peter*, was performed in Portland under the mentor's direction on 3 June 1873 with the assistance of the Harvard Orchestra of Boston). The preeminent musical figure in Portland for more than a half century, Kotzschmar won particular attention as conductor of a re-organized Haydn Society for 30 years, beginning in March 1869. Beginning with their namesake's *The Creation* (presented with a chorus of 300 voices and the 30 instrumentalists of the Germania Orchestra of Boston), the group performed not only standard literature such as Handel's *Solomon* and *Joshua* or Mendelssohn's *Elijah*, but also works like Frederic H. Cowen's *Ruth* and (in English) Schumann's *Pilgrimage of the Rose*, op.112, Louis Spohr's *Fall of Babylon*, and Buck's *The Light of Asia*, often with the support of only a piano. For a tribute on 30 June 1899, a Kotzschmar Jubilee Chorus of 250 voices was joined by Emil Mollenhauer's Boston Festival Orchestra and guest soloists for an evening that involved portions of Haydn's *The Creation*, as well as other varied literature, including Kotzschmar's *Intermezzo* for orchestra and his *Te Deum*, sung by the "Quartette Choirs of the City." He also left pieces for the piano, solo and partsongs, other sacred music, and a handful of more substantial works. Materials relating to Kotzschmar may be found in the collections of the Portland Public Library and Maine Historical Society. Selected items are available on <http://www.MaineMemory. net and VintageMaineImages.com>.

BIBLIOGRAPHY
G.T. Edwards: *Music and Musicians of Maine* (Portland, 1928/*R*) [incl. list of works, 168–9]

WILLIAM OSBORNE

Koussevitzky (née Naumoff), Olga (*b* Samara [known as Kuybyshev between 1935 and 1990], Russia, 2 July 1901; *d* New York, NY, 5 Jan 1978). Philanthropist of Russian birth. Her father, a government minister under Czar Nicolas II until 1916, fled Russia prior to the Bolshevik takeover. She was the niece of Serge Koussevitzky's second wife, Nathalie (née Ushkov), and moved from Nice to Mendou (near Paris) to become the conductor's personal secretary. Olga moved to Boston and took up residence with the Koussevitzkys in 1929. She was a constant travel companion of the couple on trans-Atlantic voyages, and together the three became naturalized citizens of the United States on 16 April 1941. In August 1947, five and a half years after Nathalie's death, Olga and SERGE KOUSSEVITZKY married in a secret ceremony witnessed by the Boston Symphony Orchestra concertmaster Richard Burgin and wife, Ruth.

When Serge died in 1951, Olga continued his legacy as a board member of the Koussevitzky Music Foundation, and as president of the American International Music Fund (*see* KOUSSEVITZKY FOUNDATIONS). As a member, and later President (1962–1975), of the New York

Musicians Club, she established the annual Olga Koussevitzky Young Artists Competition and Koussevitzky International Recording Award (now the Olga Koussevitzky International Recording Award). She also aided organizations such as the MacDowell Colony, the American-Israel Cultural Foundation, and the Harlem School of the Arts. For her philanthropic endeavors, Koussevitzky was awarded the National Arts Club Medal of Honor, the Jewish Forum Foundation Louis D. Brandeis Gold Medal, and was honored by the Friends of Music at Tanglewood.

Kossevitzky revealed a talent for caricatures and created many images of famed musicians. She provided illustrations for Samuel Chotzinoff's volume of interviews with seven musical icons, and a collection of her caricatures appeared in an exhibit at the Hammond Museum in North Salem, New York, in 1971. Upon her death, the Boston Symphony Orchestra purchased Seranak, her estate in Lenox, Massachusetts.

BIBLIOGRAPHY

A. Hughes: "Olga Koussevitzky, Widow of Conductor," *New York Times* (7 Jan 1978)

M. Mender: *Extraordinary Women in Support of Music* (Lanham, MD, 1997)

GARY GALVÁN

Koussevitzky [Kusevitsky], **Serge (Alexandrovich)** (*b* Vishny-Volotchok, Tver [now Kalinin], Russia, 26 July 1874; *d* Boston, MA, 4 June 1951). Conductor of Russian birth; naturalized American. He was one of three glamorous iconic maestros who dominated American symphonic culture after World War I. Though he never attained the national renown of Arturo Toscanini or Leopold Stokowski, he far surpassed both as an influential advocate of American music. And neither Toscanini nor Stokowski left as tangible a legacy as Koussevitzky's Tanglewood. Having entered the Moscow Philharmonic Music School at 14, he chose the double bass as one of three instruments for which open scholarships were available. He joined the double basses of the Bolshoi Theatre Orchestra six years later, and began touring as a double bass virtuoso two years after that. His 1905 marriage to Natalie Uškov made him wealthy. Having acquired some knowledge of conducting, he engaged the Berlin PO for his public podium debut in 1908, and led the London SO the same year. In 1909, he founded a publishing house and formed his own orchestra. Among those whose works he both published and performed were Medtner, Prokofiev, Rachmaninoff, Scriabin, and Stravinsky. After the 1917 Revolution he left the USSR for Berlin, Rome, and ultimately Paris, where his Concerts Koussevitzky—again with an orchestra of his own—championed contemporary French and Russian repertoire.

Koussevitzky came to the United States in 1924 to succeed Pierre Monteux as conductor of the Boston SO—a great orchestra in transition: the embattled wartime departure of Karl Muck ensured that its established Germanic identity could not be sustained. Koussevitzky's first Boston program, on 10 October 1924—a Vivaldi concerto grosso, Berlioz's *Roman Carnival Overture*, Brahms's *Haydn Variations*, Honegger's *Pacific*

231, and Scriabin's *Poem of Ecstasy*—was a statement and a challenge. It signaled Koussevitzky's preoccupation with French and Russian repertoire, and with the music of his time. In 25 Boston seasons, the 20th-century composers he favored included Martinů, Prokofiev, Shostakovich, Sibelius, and Stravinsky. Important Koussevitzky commissions (via the Boston SO or the Koussevitzky Music Foundation) included Bartók's Concerto for Orchestra, Hindemith's Konzertmusik for Strings and Brass, Stravinsky's Symphony of Psalms, and Britten's *Peter Grimes*. The long list of significant American or world premieres during his Boston tenure includes Falla's *El amor brujo* and Harpsichord Concerto; Harris's Third Symphony; Mahler's Ninth Symphony; the Mussorgsky/Ravel *Pictures at an Exhibition,* Prokofiev's two violin concertos, Fifth Symphony, and *Peter and the Wolf*; Ravel's Piano Concerto for the Left Hand; Strauss's *Metamorphosen*; and Stravinsky's Concerto for Piano and Winds, *Oedipus Rex,* and Violin Concerto. Most of all, however, Koussevitzky made American music a cause.

He conducted 11 works by Aaron Copland (including five premieres); his concertmaster and assistant, Richard Burgin, led another two. This act of advocacy was singularly thorough. Copland himself commented in 1944: "To Dr. Koussevitzky each untried composition is a fresh adventure…the composer is present, of course, for morning rehearsals; these are generally followed by evening discussions….The conductor walks to the podium with a full sense of his responsibility to the composer and to the work. No wonder other premieres seem perfunctory by comparison." The other Americans Koussevitzky championed most often included Samuel Barber, Howard Hanson, Roy Harris, Edward Burlingame Hill, Walter Piston, and William Schuman. He twice brought to Carnegie Hall two all-American programs in the course of a single season. His omissions were also significant. Chadwick and other important turn-of-the-century Bostonians were not for him. Neither were "ultra-moderns" like Varèse or Antheil. He programmed American premieres of Webern's Five Pieces (Op. 10) and of Berg's Violin Concerto and *Lulu Suite*—and nothing more by either composer.

When Koussevitzky acquired American citizenship in 1941, he led an outdoor "I am an American day" concert. His voice shaking with emotion, he told an audience of more than 10,000: "I believe there is no other country today like America, where freedom of life, that vital factor for the happiness of humanity, is preserved." The program opened with "God Bless America." His concurrent writings and speeches (typically typed in capital letters with stresses and pronunciation fastidiously marked) argued that the New World was the place to democratize "serious music."

The capstone of Koussevitzky's mission was the Berkshire Music Center at Tanglewood. The Boston SO gave summer concerts in the Berkshires beginning in 1936. The 5000-seat "shed" was inaugurated in 1938, the Tanglewood Festival School in 1940. Koussevitzky's conducting students included Leonard Bernstein and Lukas Foss, both of whom he treated as surrogate sons; the composition faculty included Copland. An opera division was led by Hebert Graf. When in 1942 the trustees voted to cancel the festival and school during wartime, Koussevitzky unforgettably responded: "I consider it an act of vandalism....It bespeaks....a profound misunderstanding of the fundamental duties and aims of a musical institution.....I cannot participate in a premeditated destruction of cultural and artistic values or even remain as a passive witness of such an act." He proceeded to subsidize the festival himself via the foundation he established in memory of Natalie (who died in 1942). His politically charged performances that season included Shostakovich's "Leningrad" Symphony. When Tanglewood fully resumed in 1946, *Time* magazine reported Koussevitzky's response when visitors called it "an American Salzburg": "Salzburg....is the most commercialized thing you can imagine. Most people who come to Salzburg are snobs who come to say they have been in Salzburg....Why not a Tanglewood, U.S.A.? We play here something that is more perfect than ever a performance in Salzburg."

His fractured English and sartorial elegance—he was partial to capes—were Koussevitzky signatures. His podium presence was magisterial. In rehearsals, he was a martinet. Harry Ellis Dickson, one of his violinists, called him "the greatest conductor who ever lived." Dickson also testified: "Almost every rehearsal was a nightmare, every concert a thrilling experience." Koussevitzky paternally shepherded his musicians, and—in Dickson's words—awakened in them "a sense of individualism and self-respect." When in 1942 the Boston SO became the last major American orchestra to become a union shop, Koussevitzky personally negotiated the agreement with American Federation of Musicians President James Caesar Petrillo.

That Koussevitzky was virtually self-taught as a conductor was no secret. He employed a pianist to help him read scores. He had difficulty beating complex rhythms. In rehearsal, his favorite prescriptions included "dolce" and "varm." Like most conductors, he is less vividly represented by studio recordings than by live broadcasts. An 9 October 1943, performance of the Mussorgky/Ravel *Pictures at an Exhibition* (which he had commissioned and premiered in Paris) documents the fabled Koussevitzky electricity; the "Great Gate of Kiev" ends on a high plateau of elation. The genesis of Bartók's Concerto for Orchestra encapsulates Koussevitzky's significance. He tenaciously commissioned the work in a Manhattan hospital, overcoming Bartók's insistence that he was too ill to fulfill a major request. In rehearsal, he proclaimed the Concerto the "greatest since Beethoven"—and also, in his dressing room, disdained every suggestion volunteered by the assiduous composer. Following the first performances, on 1 and 2 December 1944, Koussevitzky scheduled further performances on 29 and 30 December. The latter, preserved as the broadcast premiere, remains a marvel of sustained ardor, underlined by the sheen and fullness of the Boston strings.

Late in life, Koussevitzky said of Tanglewood, "It is my blood and tears. I will never give it up." He designated Bernstein his successor, and outlined a three-year plan to gradually implant him. But the Boston SO board in 1949 chose Charles Munch as the orchestra's new conductor, including jurisdiction over Tanglewood as of 1951. Bernstein thrived elsewhere as Koussevitzky's most important protégé, fired by his mentor's pedagogical idealism.

There is no adequate Koussevitzky biography available in English. Moses Smith's otherwise unmemorable *Koussevitzky* (1947) portrays Koussevitzky's Boston musicians resorting to a system of signals to maintain ensemble in complex music "out of sheer self-protection." Koussevitzky responded with a ludicrous and futile lawsuit. As a composer, Koussevitzky contributed a Double Bass Concerto (assisted by Glière), a *Humoresque, Valse miniature, Chanson triste,* and similar pieces for double bass, as well as a Passacaglia on a Russian Theme (1934) for orchestra. Besides receiving many honorary degrees from the leading American universities, he was appointed a Chevalier of the Légion d'honneur and received the Finnish Order of the White Rose. Many of Koussevitzky's papers are held in the Serge Koussevitzky Archive at the Library of Congress.

See also KOUSSEVITZKY FOUNDATIONS and OLGA KOUSSEVITZKY.

BIBLIOGRAPHY
M.A.D. Howe: *The Boston Symphony Orchestra* (Boston, 1914, rev. and enlarged 2/1931/*R*1978)
A. Lourié: *S.A. Koussevitzky and his Epoch* (New York, 1931/*R*1969)
"Koussevitzky, Serge," *CBY* 1940
A. Copland: "Serge Koussevitzky and the American Composer," *MQ,* xxx (1944), 255
A. Lourié: "A Tribute to Koussevitzky," *MQ,* xxx (1944), 270
M.A.D. Howe: *The Tale of Tanglewood* (Boston, 1946)
H. Leichtentritt: *Serge Koussevitzky, the Boston Symphony Orchestra and the New American Music* (Cambridge, MA, 1946)
M. Smith: *Koussevitzky* (New York, 1947)
Catalog of Works Commissioned by the Koussevitzky Music Foundation (Lenox, MA, 1958)
The Koussevitzky Music Foundation in the Library of Congress, Washington, D.C. (New York, 1958)
H.C. Schonberg: *The Great Conductors* (New York, 1968), 300ff
D. Wooldridge: *A Conductor's World* (London, 1970), 137ff [with partial discography]
"Koussevitzky's Grandchildren," *HiFi,* xxviii/10 (1978), 88
J.L. Holmes: *Conductors on Record* (Westport, CT, 1982), 360
R.S. Morgan: *Critical Reaction to Serge Koussevitzky's Programming of Contemporary Music with the Boston Symphony Orchestra, 1924–1929* (MA thesis, North Texas State U., 1982)
V. Yuzefovich: *Serge Koussevitzky.* Volume One: *Russian Years* (Moscow, 2004)
J. Horowitz: *Classical Music in America: A History* (New York, 2005)
G.N. Humphrey: *Becoming a Musician* (Philadelphia, 2007)
P. Daniel: *Tanglewood: A Group Memoir* (New York, 2008)
J. Horowitz: *Artists in Exile: How Refugees from Twentieth Century War and Revolution Transformed the American Performing Arts* (New York, 2008)

JOSEPH HOROWITZ

Koussevitzky Foundations. Two American funding organizations established by SERGE KOUSSEVITZKY "to encourage contemporary composers and provide them with opportunities to create new works." The first, the Koussevitzky Music Foundation, Inc. (founded 1942), was established by the conductor in memory of his first wife. During World War II it funded the Berkshire Music Center in Lenox, Massachusetts, which had been established by Koussevitzky in 1940. The foundation continued to pursue a variety of activities, sponsoring concerts of new music and awarding scholarships and prizes at the Berkshire center and the festival associated with it. The Serge Koussevitzky Music Foundation in the Library of Congress is a permanent endowment established by the original foundation in December 1950; it assumed responsibility for commissioning new works from composers and has continued to encourage the dissemination of this music through performance and other means. Since its inception, the foundation has served as one of the oldest and foremost commissioning initiatives, inspiring other organizations such as the Louisville Orchestra and the Rockefeller Foundation to support newly composed music. Koussevitzky himself was an ardent proponent and mentor of young composers, both in America and Europe. Through his search for the "Great American Symphony" and his role as music director of the Boston Symphony Orchestra, with which the foundations were closely aligned until the conductor's death in 1951, Koussevitzky influenced a generation of American symphonic music.

Although many of the early commissions were of a conservative nature, the foundation has since supported a wide variety of styles and genres. As of 2010, a small number of grants ranging from $12,500 for chamber works and a minimum of $30,000 for orchestral compositions are conferred each year. Nominations are submitted on behalf of the composer by a performing arts organization, which jointly sponsors the commission with the Koussevitzky foundations and commits to performing the composition's world première. Sponsoring organizations have included most major orchestras, as well as chamber music organizations such as eighth blackbird and the New York New Music Ensemble. Some of the best known commissions include Béla Bartók's Concerto for Orchestra, Benjamin Britten's *Peter Grimes*, and Aaron Copland's Third Symphony. Both foundations are administered jointly from New York and assisted by the Aaron Copland Fund and the Library of Congress, where the original manuscripts of all commissioned works are deposited.

LIST. The following is a list of completed works commissioned by the Koussevitzky Foundations, arranged by date of commission.

1942: S. Barber, *Prayers of Kierkegaard*, vv, orch; N. Berezowsky, Sym. no.4; B. Britten, *Peter Grimes* (op); B. Martinů, Sym. no.1

1943: B. Bartók, Conc. for Orch; W. Bergsma, Str Qt no.2; R. Palmer, Str Qt no.2; W. Schuman, Sym. for Str; I. Stravinsky, *Ode*, orch

1944: A. Copland, Sym. no.3; N. Lopatnikoff, Concertino; D. Milhaud, Sym. no.2; B. Phillips, *Tom Paine*, orch

1945: D. Diamond, Sym. no.4; L. Foss, *Capriccio*, vc, pf; A. Haieff, *Eclogue*, vc, pf; H. Hanson, Conc., pf, orch; O. Messiaen, *Turangalîla-Symphonie*; N. Nabokov, *The Return of Pushkin*, S, orch; H. Shapero, Sym. for Classical Orch; H. Villa-Lobos, *Madona*, orch

1946: G.F. Malipiero, Sym. no.4, "In Memoriam"; W. Piston, Sym. no.3

1947: B. Galindo, Sonata, vc, pf; E. George, Arioso, vc, pf; R. Harris, Sym. no.7; A. Schoenberg, *A Survivor from Warsaw*, nar, vv, orch

1948: A. Honegger, Sym. no.5, "di tre re"; R. Thompson, *A Trip to Nahant*, orch

1949: I. Fine, Str Qt; T. Kassern, *The Anointed* (op); A. Lourié, *The Blackamoor of Peter the Great* (op); P. Mennin, Str Qt no.2; V. Thomson, *Lord Byron* (op)

1950: L. Dallapiccola, *Tartiniana*, vn, orch; J. Fitelberg, *Concertino de Camera*, vn, pf; M.C. Guarnieri, *Brasiliana*, orch; J. Ibert, *Caprilena*, vn, *Ghirlarzana*, vc, *Impromptu*, tpt, pf; L. Mennini, Sonatina (formerly *Three Short Pieces*), vc, pf

1951: L. Bernstein, *Serenade (Symposium after Plato)*, vn, str, perc; I. Hamilton, Sym. no.2; L. Kirchner, Conc., pf, orch; D. Milhaud, *David* (op, A. Lunel; L. Smit, Sym. no. 1; A. Tcherepnin, Sym. no.4

1952: P. Ben-Haim, *The Sweet Psalmist of Israel*, vv, orch; C. Chávez, Sinfonia no.5, str; R. Chevreuille, *Short Symphony* [Sym. no.4]; E. B. Hill, Prelude, orch; W. Riegger, Sextet, wind qnt, pf; B. Rogers, Trio, vn, va, vc

1953: A. Avshalomov, Sym. no.3; W. S. Hartley, Chbr Sym.; A. Imbrie, Conc., vn, orch; U. Kay, *The Boor* (op); D. Moore, *The Ballad of Baby Doe* (op); H. Saeverud, Conc., vn, orch

1954: S. Barber, *Die Natali*, orch; L. Bernstein, Sym. no.3 "Kaddish"; A. Copland, Sym. Ode [rev.]; H. Dutilleux, Conc. for Two Orch (Sym. no.2); G. von Einem, Sym. Scenes; H. Hanson, *Elegy to the Memory of My Friend, Serge Koussevitzky*, orch; J. Ibert, Symphonic Movt [First movt of Sym. no.2]; C. McPhee, *Transitions*, orch; D. Milhaud, Sym. no.6; R. Moevs, Fourteen Variations, orch; H. Overton, Sym. for Str; V. Persichetti, Quintet, pf, str; G. Petrassi, *Quinto Concerto*, orch; W. Piston, Sym. no.6; W. Schuman, Sym. no.7; R. Sessions, Sym. no.3; E. Toch, *Peter Pan*, orch; H. Villa-Lobos, Sinfonia no.11

1956: L. Foss, Sym. of Chorales

1957: I. Dahl, Trio; K.A. Hartmann, Sym. no.7; A. Hovhaness, Magnificant, vv, orch; S. Martirano, Octet; J. Orbón, Conc. Grosso, str qt, orch; G. Rochberg, *Dialogues*, cl, pf; M. Tippett, *King Priam* (op)

1958: E. Blackwood, Str Qt no.2; M. Blitzstein, *Regina* (op); R. L. Finney, Sym. no.2; A. Ginastera, Concierto, pf, orch; M. Powell, Quintet; W. Russo, Sym. no.2, "Titans"; H. Somers, *Lyric*, orch; H. Tosar Errecart,Te Deum, brass, vv, orch; E. Varèse, *Notturno*, vv, orch; W. Walton, *The Bear* (op); Y. Wyner, *Intermedio*, S, str

1959: H. Cowell, Sym. no.14; K. Gaburo, *Subito (Theater for Four Instruments)*, 1v, tpt, va, db; R. Gerhard, *Collages*, orch, tape; F. Poulenc, *Gloria*, s, vv, orch; A.A. Saygun, Symphonie no.3; L. Talma, *All the Days of My Life*, T, chbr ens

1960: J. Orrego-Salas, *Concerto a Tre* (Conc. Grosso), vn, vc, pf, orch

1961: L. Berio, *Traces* (op, E. Sanguinetti); R. Cordero, *Concierto*, vn, orch; A. Franchetti, Conc. in Do, orch; H.W. Henze, *Being Beauteous*, S, hp, 4 vc; Y. Matsudaira, Suite, chbr ens; H. Weisgall, *Lyrical Interval*, B, pf; Stefan Wolpe, Chbr Piece no.1

1962: C. Garrido-Lecca, Cuarteto no.1, str; Y. Irino, *Wandlungen*, orch; G. Klebe, Missa "Misere Nobis"; E. Krenek, *Fivefold Enfoldment*, orch; L. Nono, *Canciónes á Guiomar*, S, chbr ens; G. Schuller, Conc., db, chbr orch; S. Shifrin, Str Qt no.3

1963: L. Trimble, Sym. no.2

1964: M. Babbitt, *Relata I*, orch; G. Crumb, Three Madrigals, Books I, II; M. Davidovsky, *Synchronisms no.7*, orch, elecs; P.M. Davies, *Offenbarung und Untergang* [Revelation and Fall], S, chbr ens; V.S. Frohne, Str Qt; A. Haieff, *Éloge*, chbr ens; G. Ligeti, *Ramifications*, str; K. Stockhausen, *Mixtur*, orch, elecs; C. Wuorinen, Chbr Conc., ob, chbr ens; I. Xenakis, *Akrata*, chbr ens

1965: G.B. Schmidt, *Alturas de Macchu Picchu* (orat.); R.R. Bennett, Woodwind Quintet; A. Berger, Septet; J. Cage, *Cheap Imitation*, orch; C. Halffter, *Symposion*, Bar, vv, orch; R. Lombardo, *Dialogues of Lovers*, chbr ens; N. Rorem, *Paris Journal*, "Letters from Paris", vv, chbr orch; R. Shapey, Partita-Fantasia, vc, chbr ens; T. Takemitsu, *Dorian, the Horizon*, str

1966: G. Arrigo, *Petit Requiem pour une Troisième Possibilité*, chbr ens; N. Castiglioni, *Carmina* [later *Masques*], chbr ens; D. Del Tredici,

Syzgy, S, chbr orch; H. Partch, *Delusion of the Fury*, orch; K. Penderecki, Conc., vc, orch; H. Pousseur, *Couleurs croisées*, orch; D. Reck, *Number 3—MeteMusic*, chbr ens; V. Silvestrov, *Eschatophony*, orch; H. Sollberger, *Flutes and Drums*, chbr ens; W. Sydeman, Texture Study no.2, orch; A. Vieru, *Steps of Silence*, str qt, perc

1968: T. Baird, Sym. no.3; L. Bassett, Sextet, str, pf; F. Donatoni, *Orts (Souvenir no.2)*, chbr ens; E. Miller, Orchestral Fantasies; G. Perle, Serenade no.2, chbr ens; R.M. Schafer, *Sapho*, chbr ens; N. Sheriff, Str Qt

1969: C. Dodge, *Changes*, tape; J. Druckman, *Windows*, orch; J. Eaton, Mass; A. Goehr, Conc., pf, orch; M. Keleman, *Floreal*, orch; E. Kim, *Earthlight*, S, vn, pf, lights

1971: F. Cerha, *Curriculum*, chbr ens; K. Husa, Sonata, vn, pf; B. Kolb, *Soundings*, chbr ens; T. Olah, *The Time of Memory*, chbr ens; S. Silverman, *Crepuscule*, orch

1972: T. Antoniou, *Fluxus*, orch; E. Brown, *Cross Sections and Color Fields*, orch; Z. Durkó, Chbr Music, 2 pf, str; F. Miroglio, *Eclipses*, str; T. Musgrave, *Space Play*, chbr ens; E. O'Brien, *Dédales*, S, chbr orch; J. Yuasa, *Time of Orchestral Time*

1973: G. Amy, *Echos XIII*, chbr ens; E. Dugger, *Matsukaze*, S, chbr orch; J. Harbison, *Di tima*, orch; L. Harrison, *Elegiac Symphony*; C. Ung, *Mohori*, Mez, chbr ens

1974: H. Birtwistle, *Silbury Air*, chbr ens; W. Bolcom, Pf Qt; B. Jolas, *O Wall*, chbr ens; O. Knussen, *Ophelia Dances I*, chbr orch; F. Lerdahl, *Eros*, Mez, chbr ens

1975: M. Feldman, *Instruments II*, chbr ens; T. Street, *Variations on a Ground*, orch; I. Taxin, *Timpani in Solo and Ensemble*

1976: D. Martino, *Fantasies and Impromptus*, pf; T. Scherchen-Hsiao, *Lo*, trbn, str

1977: S. Balassa, *Glarusi ének* [Chant of Glarnerland], orch; H. Dutilleux, *Ainsi la nuit*, str qt; D. Harris, *Prelude to a Concert in Connecticut*, orch; R.H. Lewis, Str Qt no.3

1981: M.-A. Consoli, *Afterimages*, orch; M. Davidovsky, Divertimento, vc, orch; G. Edwards, *Moneta's Mourn*, orch; P. Lansky, *As It Grew Dark*, tape; A. Panufnik, *Arbor Cosmica*, str; S. Reich, *Three Movements*, orch; N. Thorne, *From the Dying Earth, Books 2 and 3*, chbr ens; R. Zupko, *Canti Terrae*, orch

1982: R. Holloway, Dbl Conc., cl, sax, 2 chbr orch; N. Osborne, *Zansa*, orch; D. Stock, *Parallel Worlds*, chbr ens; J. Tower, *Music*, vc, orch

1983: S. Adler, Sym. no.6; B. Fennelly, Fantasy Variations, orch; T. Machover, *Nature's Breath*, chbr ens; W.T. McKinley, Sym. no.3; T. Murail, *De Terre et de Ciel*, orch; B. Rands, Suite no. 2, "Le Tambourin," orch; R. Selig, Conc., 2 pf; E. Sims, Str Qt no. 4

1984: J. Adams, *Eros Piano*, pf, orch; T. Brief, *Idols*, chbr ens; V. Fine, *Poetic Fires*, pf, orch; H.K. Gruber, Vc Conc.; E. Laderman, Duo, vc, pf; T.O. Lee, *Waltzes*, chbr ens; R. Lister, *Where I Say Hours*, cl, str; M. Shinohara, *Cooperation*, chbr ens; O. Wilson, *Expansions II*, orch; C. Wuorinen, Concertino

1985: M. Boykan, Sym.; J. Harvey, *Timepieces*, orch; L. Hyla, *The Dream of Innocent III*, amp. vc, pf, perc; H. Wood, Trio, hn, vn, pf

1986: M. Bresnick, *Pontoosuc*, chbr orch; S. Mackey, *Moebius Band*, S, chbr ens; M. Torke, *Chalk*, str qt; S. Wheeler, *Northern Lights*, orch

1987: A. Anderson, Str Qt; D. Asia, Pf Qt; T. Diesendruck, *Such Stuff*, str qt; K. Ince, *Waves of Talya*, chbr ens; E. Moe, *Up and At 'Em*, chbr ens; D. Olan, Str Qt no.2; J. Primosch, *Five Meditations*, orch; F. Thorne, Rhapsodic Variations no.5, vn, pf; G. Tsontakis, *Winter Lightning*, orch; I. Yun, *Konzert*, ob, orch

1988: L. Dobbins, *Tres Recuerdos del Cielo*, S, chbr ens; J. Fontyn, *Rêverie et Turbulence*, pf, orch; M. Gustavson, Qt, str qt; A.J. Kernis, *Song of Innocents, Book I*, S, pf; S. Lindroth, Duo, 2 vn; U. Mamlok, *Girasol*, chbr ens; G. Walker, Sinfonia no.2

1990: L. Bassett, Conc. for Orch; M. Gandolfi, *Caution to the Wind*, fl, chbr ens; A. Goehr, *Colossos or Panic*, orch; G. Levinson, Sym. no.2; N. Maw, Trio; W. Peterson, *Diptych*, chbr ens; J. Wolfe, *Four Marys*, str qt

1991: M. Babbitt, *Septet, But Equal*; A. Jarvinen, *The Modulus of Elasticity*, va, chbr ens; A. Korf, Cant.; G. Perle, Conc. no.2, pf, orch; T. Riley, *June Buddhas*, "The Mexico City Blues," vv, orch; D. soley, *"de camara…,"* chbr ens; S. Stucky, *Four Poems of A.R. Ammons*, Bar, chbr ens

1992: W. Bolcom, *Lyric Conc.*, fl, orch; D. Drummond, *Dance of the Seven Veils*, chbr ens; D. Felder, *Inner Sky*, chbr ens; S. Hartke, Conc., vn, orch; L. Kirchner, *Of Things Exactly as They Are*, orch; W. Kraft, *Encounters X*, vn, marimba; F. Rzewski, *Histories*, sax qt; Y. Wyner, *Second Madrigal: Voices of Women*, S, chbr ens

1993: L. Andriessen, *Zilver*, chbr ens; K. Husa, Five Poems, wind quintet; D. Sheinfeld, *Dear Theo*, Bar, chbr ens; T. Takemitsu, *Fantasma/Cantos II*, trbn, orch; C. Ung, *Sprial VII*, chbr ens; Zhou Long, *The Ineffable*, chbr ens

1994: R. Bauer, *Halcyon Birds*, chbr orch; S. Currier, *Broken Consort*, chbr ens; D. Erb, Str Qt no.3; R. Greenberg, *Among Friends* (Str Qt no.3); P. Lieberson, Hn Conc.; B. Rands, Canzoni, orch; P. Ruders, Sym. no.2, "Symphony and Transformation"

1995: H. Brant, *Plowshares and Swords*, orch; D. Froom, *Emerson Songs*, S, chbr ens; M. Tenzer, *Sources of Current*, orch

1996: F. Donatoni, *Esa*, orch; D. Martino, *Serenata Concertante*, octet; D. Rakowski, *Sesso e Violenza*, chbr ens; S. Reich, *Cello Counterpoint*; M. Rosenzweig, Str Qt; C. Rouse, *Compline*, chbr ens; B. Sheng, *Tibetan Swing*, orch; R. Wernick, Trio; R. Wilson, Triple Conc., hn, b cl, marimba, orch; C. Wuorinen, *Sym. Six*

1997: P. Alexander, *Ferrafunx*, drum set, brass qnt; D. Chaitken, Trio; J. Dashow, *Far Sounds, Broken Cries*, chbr ens; R. Festinger, *Tapestries*, vn, vc, pf; J. Harvey, *Tranquil Abiding*, chbr orch; R. Helps, Pf Qt; C. Yi, *Chinese Folk Dance Suite*, vn, orch; E. London, *Federico's Follies*, chbr ens; H. Sollberger, *Obsessions*, fl, cl, vn, vc, pf; L. Spratlan, *Sojourner*, chbr ens; D. Vayo, *Signals*, chbr orch

1998: D. Godfrey, Str Qt no.3; A. Krieger, *Unlimited Partnerships*, chbr ens; W. Marsalis, *All Rise*, vv, sym. orch, jazz orch; K. Rohde, *Minerva's Pool*, str; A.R. Thomas, *…Dawn Dream Dazzle Landscapes at twilight…*, str qt; J.M. Viera, *Ricercare*, orch; G. Walker, *Wind Set*, wind qnt

1999: J. Eckhardt, *Tongues*, S, chbr ens; R. Felciano, *An American Decameron: Songs from the Interviews of Studs Terkel*, S, chbr ens; B. Fennelly, Arias and Interludes (Str Qt no.2); P. Furman, *Vox Chordae*, chbr orch; L. Hyla, Violin Concerto; S. Mackey, *Ars Moriendi*, str qt; P. Ortiz, *Raya en el Mar*, chbr ens; S. Ran, *Under the Sun's Gaze*, chbr ens; R. Sierra, *Concerto para Orquesta*

2000: Chen Qigang, *Iris Dévoilée*, orch, vv, Chin. inst; D. Del Tredici, *Wondrous the Merge*, bar, str qt; L. Foss, Str Qt no.5; T. Leon, *Desde*, orch; T. Musgrave, *The Mocking-Bird*, chbr ens; B. Olivero, Str Qt no.2; A. Rindfleisch, *The Light Fantastic*, wind

2001: M. Bates, *Mercury Soul*, cl, pf; J. Dawe, *Lieber de Arte Contrapuncti 1477/2001*, str qt; R. Dick, *A New Prehistory*, chbr ens; Kui Dong, *Fantasia: A Dialogue with Wind*, chbr ens; A. Goehr, *Marching to Carcassonne*, pf, inst; J. Kramer, *Imagined Ancestors*, chbr ens; J. Mobberley, *Vox Inhumana*, S, chbr ens; L. Schwendinger, *Celestial City*, chbr ens; M. Wagner, *Whirl's End*, chbr ens

2002: C. Baker, *Märchenbilder*, orch; G. D'Alessio, Sym.; N. Hyo-Shin, *Cycle of Sixty*, str, perc, komungo; M. Lindberg, *Sculpture*, orch; W. Peterson, *A Three Piece Suite*, orch; A. Singleton, *When Given a Choice*, orch; S. Wheeler, *Wakefield Doubles*, str

2003: W. Kraft, *Vintage Renaissance and Beyond*, chbr ens; P. Leroux, *De la Texture*, chbr ens; N. Maw, Cor Anglais Conc.; T. Street, *Sym. V: Colonial Scenes*; D. Taddie, *Amazonia II*, pf, hp, perc, orch; B. White, *Enough Rope*, S, fl

2004: M. Chuaqui, *Desde el Límite (From the Border)*, chbr ens; J. Fontyn, *Tree of Life*, perc qt; D. Sanford, *Scherzo Grosso*, vc, big band; M.-A. Turnage, *Chicago Remains*, orch; Zhou Long, *Five Elements*, conc., fl, orch

2005: R. Chasalow, Flute Conc.; W. Chou, *Twilight Colors*, double trio for wind, str; S. Hartke, *A Brandenburg Autumn*, chbr orch; B. Rands, *"Now Again" Fragments from Sappho*, Mez, chbr ens; R. Reynolds,

Illusion, chbr ens, vv, elec; C. Sanchez-Guiterrez, *...[and of course Henry the Horse] Dances the ...*, 2 pf, perc, str qt; C. Ung, *Spiral X "In Memoriam"*, amp. str qt

2006: B. Current, Conc. for Accdn and Orch; J. Harbison, The Seven Ages, S, chbr ens; D. Rakowski, Pf Conc.; P. Ruders, Sym. no.3, "Dreamcatcher"

2007: C. Biscardi: Sailors and Dreams, v, chbr ens; M. Greenbaum, *Es ist zum Lachen*, chbr ens; J. Keren, *On the Bridge of Words*, chbr orch, cl, pf, nar; T. Lancino, Requiem; D. Yuhas, *Collissions*, chbr ens

2008: D. Bermel, *A Shout, a Whisper, and a Trace*, chbr orch; Y. Chang: At the Brink of the Chill, chbr ens

BIBLIOGRAPHY

H. Leichtentritt: *Serge Koussevitzky: the Boston Symphony Orchestra and the New American Music* (Cambridge, MA, 1946)

J. Horowitz: *Classical Music in America: a History of its Rise and Fall* (New York and London, 2005), 302–4

JANE GOTTLIEB/MICHAEL MAUSKAPF

Koutzen, Boris (*b* Uman, nr Kiev, Russia [now Ukraine], 1 April 1901; *d* Mount Kisco, NY, 10 Dec 1966). Violinist and composer of Russian birth. He studied violin with his father. In 1918 he entered the Moscow Conservatory, where he studied violin with Leo Zetlin and composition with Reinhold Glière. At age 17 he was named first violinist of the State Opera House Orchestra in Moscow and joined the Moscow SO under Koussevitzky. In 1923 he came to the United States and became a member of the Philadelphia Orchestra. He was head of the violin department of the Philadelphia Conservatory (1925–62), and from 1944 to 1966 taught and was conductor at Vassar College, Poughkeepsie, New York. He was also a member of the NBC SO, under Toscanini, from 1937 to 1945.

Koutzen began composing as a child; he was six when he produced his first work. His earliest symphonic composition, *Solitude*, was given its first performance by the Philadelphia Orchestra in 1927, with the composer conducting. Koutzen's style is almost exclusively contrapuntal and often highly chromatic. Though the ethos of his music is Romantic, he was deeply interested in new musical trends. In 1944 he received publication awards from the Juilliard Foundation for *Valley Forge*, and the Society for the Publication of American Music for the Second String Quartet. He also won first prize in the ACA-BMI competition with his Serenade. Most of Koutzen's manuscripts, papers, clippings, programs, and other memorabilia are held at the Library of Congress, while others are kept at the George Sherman Dickson Music Library at Vassar College.

WORKS

Stage: The Fatal Oath (opera, 1, after Balzac). *c*1938–54; You Never Know (comic opera, 1, Koutzen), 1962

Orch: Solitude, 1926; Sym. Movt, vn. orch, 1928–9; Valley Forge, sym. poem, 1931; Conc., fl, cl, bn, hn, vc, str orch, 1934; Sym. in C, 1939; From the American Folklore, 1943; Vn Conc., 1946; Sinfonietta, 1947; Va Conc., 1949; Morning Music, fl, str orch, 1950; Divertimento, 1956; Concertino, pf, str orch, 1959; Rhapsody, sym. band, 1959; Elegiac Rhapsody, 1961; Fanfare, Prayer and March, 1961; Concertante, 2 fl, orch, 1965; Conc., chorus, orch, 1966, inc.

Inst: 3 str qts, 1921, 1936, 1944; Legende, vn, pf, 1928; 2 vn sonatas, 1929, 1951; Nocturne, vn, pf, 1930; Trio, fl, vc, harp, 1933; Concert Piece, vc, str orch/str qt/pf, 1940; Holiday Mood, vn, pf, 1943; Serenade, sax, bn, vc, 1943; Duo concertante, vn, pf, 1944; Pf Trio, 1948;

Sonata, vn, vc, 1952; Landscape and Dance, wind qnt, 1953; Poem, vn, str qt, 1963; Music for Vn Alone, 1966

Kbd: Feuille d'album, pf, 1924; Enigma, pf, 1929; Sonatina, pf, 1931; Sonatina, 2 pf, 1944; Sonnet, org, 1946; Eidolons, pf, 1953

Vocal: An Invocation (J. A. Symonds), female vv, orch, 1948; Lethe (E. St. V. Millay), medium v, *c*1955; Words of Cheer for Zion (Bible), 1962; Dreamland (Poe), Mez, pf, 1965

Other: teaching pieces, arrs., several cadenzas

Principal publishers: Elkan Vogel, Mercury, Sirène Musicale

JONAS WESTOVER

Kovacevich [Bishop], **Stephen** (*b* San Pedro, CA, 17 Oct 1940). Pianist. He studied with Lev Schorr (a student of Anna Essipoff), made his debut at the age of 11, playing Jean Françaix's Concertino, and gave a solo recital in the same year. Three years later he played Maurice Ravel's G major Concerto and Robert Schumann's Concerto with the San Francisco SO. In 1959 he moved to London to study with Myra Hess, who rekindled his early love of Ludwig van Beethoven's late works. His Wigmore Hall debut in 1961 was notable for an outstanding performance of the "Diabelli" Variations, a triumph later repeated at the Royal Festival Hall (he subsequently made a memorable recording of the work). He made a strong impression with his 1967 New York debut, as well. His repertory was, however, already eclectic, and his many recordings include works by Edvard Grieg, Schumann, Frydryk Chopin, Béla Bartók, and Richard Rodney Bennett (whose Piano Concerto is dedicated to him), as well as Johann Sebastian Bach, Wolfgang Amadeus Mozart, Beethoven, and Johannes Brahms. His series of the sonatas of Beethoven and of Franz Schubert (begun in the 1990s) are notable for their uncompromising strength, articulateness, and acuity, and his noble, searching reading of Brahms's D minor Concerto with Wolfgang Sawallisch won a Gramophone Award. He has been nominated for numerous Grammys during his career, often for works from the Classical era. His recorded set of the complete sonatas of Beethoven was completed in 2003. He has performed all Mozart's piano concertos and has made something of a specialty of Michael Tippett's Piano Concerto, while his recordings with Jacqueline du Pré and Martha Argerich are also justly celebrated. He has been a highly sought after chamber musician, having worked with Nigel Kennedy, Sarah Chang, and Lynn Harrell, among others. In 1984 Kovacevich embarked on a second career as a conductor, working frequently with the Australian Chamber Orchestra and, subsequently, the Irish Chamber Orchestra. At times, he conducts from the podium, but just as often, his direction comes from the piano. In the 2003–4 season alone, he conducted the London Mozart Players, the Royal Liverpool SO, and the Vancouver SO. He went on to lead Mozart's *Cosi fan tutte* with the Geneva Opera the following year.

BIBLIOGRAPHY

R. Wigmore: "Second Time Around," *Gramophone*, lxxii/Oct (1994), 14–7

BRYCE MORRISON/JONAS WESTOVER

Koykkar, Joseph (Noel) (*b* Milwaukee, WI, 1951). Composer, teacher, keyboardist and sound designer. Koykkar's principal composition teachers have been JOHN C. EATON, DENNIS KAM and JOHN DOWNEY. He spent two years as composer-in-residence with the Artists-in Schools Program in Virginia (1978–80) and studied at the University of Miami (DMA 1983). He has received grants and awards from, among others, ASCAP, Truman State University, Meet the Composer, the American Music Center, the National Endowment for the Arts, and the Pew Charitable Trust for Music. He has held visiting fellowships at various festivals, seminars, and institutes in the United States and Europe. He has also served as president of the Wisconsin Alliance for Composers (1990–3).

Koykkar's works have been performed in Europe and the Americas by ensembles such as the New York New Music Ensemble, California EAR Unit, Relache, Compagnia Brasileira De Music, and Slovak Radio Symphony, among many others. His musical syntax seeks to produce musical gestures that can be perceived as outgrowths of preceding ones, gradually transforming over time. In works that range from music for dance and film-video to computer and electronic music, Koykkar tends to achieve perceptual clarity and economy of musical materials in such a way that popular and cultivated traditions both find their place as sources of inspiration. As a faculty member at the University of Wisconsin–Madison since 1987, he currently teaches courses in electroacoustic music and sound design for the Interarts & Technology Program and serves as Music Director for the UW-Madison Dance Program.

WORKS
(selective list)
Chamber Symphony (1975), chbr orch; Sonata for Violin (1978), vn, pf; Divertimento (Octet) (1980), 7 winds & perc.; Evocations (1981), orch; String Quartet (1981); Circumstance (1983), vn, cl, pf, perc.; Modus Operandum (1984), ob, cl, bn, vn, va, pf, perc.; A Three-Point Perspective (1987), ob, cl, bn, vn, pf; The Other Side Show (1988); Lost Pieces from a Night Puzzle (1989), digital sampler; She Thought She Knew (1990), sampler/synthesizers; Shiftings (1991), sampler/synthesizers; Touchings: A Love Story (1991), Interactive Music/Video Composition; The Front Lines (1994), fl, cl & tape; With Wood, Wire, Hammers and Mallets (1995), fl, ob, cl, bn, va, db, pf, perc.; Composite for Concert Band (1996); Interfacing (1997), piano and computer technology; High Strung (1999), vc & technology; Keyboard Dances (1998), piano duo; Tour De Force (2000), percussion & technology; Panache (2001), fl, ob, cl, bn, va, db, pf, perc.; Music For Three (2002), ob, vc, pf; In Celebration (2004), fl, ob, cl, hn, vn, db, pf; Suite: Cosmic Code (2005), chbr orch; Double Take for 18 Instr. (2006), chbr wind ens; Beyond Circumstance (2007), orch; Inside Out (2009), sax qt

Principal publisher: JNK Music

DANIELE BUCCIO

Koz, Dave (*b* Encino, CA, 27 March 1963). Jazz saxophonist. A smooth jazz artist, he is best known for playing soprano and alto saxophone but has performed on tenor and baritone as well. His professional career began in 1986 when he joined the vocalist Bobby Caldwell on tour. This initial success propelled him to work as a sideman throughout the late 1980s with the keyboard player Jeff Lorber and the vocalist Richard Marx. In 1990 Koz recorded his self-titled debut album. Most of his subsequent albums, including *Lucky Man*

(1993, Capitol), *Off the Beaten Path* (1996, Capitol), *The Dance* (1999, Capitol), *At the Movies* (2006, Capitol), and *Hello Tomorrow* (2010, Concord) have achieved commercial success. His work typically features a blend of rhythm-and-blues and pop music melodicism.

Koz has also maintained a presence in other areas of the entertainment industry. In 1995 he began hosting a radio program, "Personal Notes," which later became "The Dave Koz Show." He founded Rendezvous Entertainment in 2006 with fellow smooth jazz luminaries Frank Cody and Hyman Katz. In addition he has promoted a series of smooth jazz-based cruises, called Dave Koz and Friends Jazz Cruises.

Koz's style is indebted to Tower of Power, Stevie Wonder, and David Sanborn. Sanborn's brilliant and broad tone has been an obvious influence, and although his sound may recall Sanborn's, Koz has proven to be a distinctive instrumentalist whose versatility has led similarly to commercial success.

BIBLIOGRAPHY
K. Richmond: "Dave Koz," *Saxophone Journal*, xviii/Jan–Feb (1994), 17
D. Kasrel: "Dave Koz: True Colors," *JT*, xxvi/10 (1996), 80
T. Erdmann: "Dave Koz," *Saxophone Journal*, xxvi/July–Aug (2002), 4 [incl. discography]
G. Mitchell: "Koz and Effect," *Billboard* (16 Oct 2010)

AARON J. WEST

Kraft, Edwin Arthur (*b* New Haven, CT, 8 Jan 1883; *d* Cleveland, OH, 15 July 1962). Organist and editor. His older brother William, a professional organist and musician in New York City, was his first teacher. He studied at Yale with HORATIO PARKER and HARRY JEPSON and in Paris with Alexandre Guilmant and Charles-Marie Widor. Following appointments as organist at St Thomas' Church in Brooklyn (1901–4) and St Matthew's in Wheeling, West Virginia (1905–7), he became organist and choirmaster of Trinity Cathedral in Cleveland in 1907 and remained there until 1959 (except for two years when he served as municipal organist in Atlanta, 1914–16). His recitals in Cleveland in his early days were popular events and he toured widely in the United States. In 1933 he became director of music for Lake Erie College in Painesville, Ohio, retiring in 1951; he was also head of the organ department of the Cleveland Institute of Music. Besides playing and teaching, he edited an impressive amount of organ, piano, vocal, and choral music.

VERNON GOTWALS/JUDI CALDWELL

Kraft, Leo (Abraham) (*b* Brooklyn, NY, 24 July 1922). Composer, teacher, conductor, and writer on music. He studied composition with KAROL RATHAUS at Queens College, CUNY (BA 1945), with RANDALL THOMPSON at Princeton University (MFA 1947) and with NADIA BOULANGER in Paris on a Fulbright Scholarship (1954–5). From 1947 to 1989 he taught at Queens College. He has held important posts in the College Music Society (CMS), the American Society of University Composers, the Society for Music Theory, the American section of ISCM, and AMC (president, 1976–8). From 1989 to 1992, he was Distinguished Composer-in-Residence at New York University.

Kraft's numerous music theory and ear-training texts and his active role in CMS attest to his involvement in university teaching. As a conductor, he led the New Repertory Ensemble beginning in 1978. His pedagogical approach has been influenced by Boulanger's emphasis on practical musical skills and by Heinrich Schenker's theories as exposed in Salzer's *Structural Hearing* (New York, 1952, 2/1962). His early music reflects the neo-classical attitudes of his teachers, together with the diatonicism of Hindemith and Copland. With his Second String Quartet (1959) he began to develop a more chromatic and intense musical language. During the 1980s, however, his style returned to its diatonic roots and developed greater lyricism, though harmonic tension can still be heard in *Omaggio* (1993). Later works, such as *Cloud Studies* (1989) and *From the Hudson Valley* (1997), reflect his lifelong love of nature. His rhythms draw upon diverse sources that range from the Baroque to jazz. (*EwenD*)

WORKS

Orch: Conc. no.1, fl, cl, tpt, str, 1951; Larghetto in Memory of Karl Rathaus, str, timp, 1955; Variations, 1958; 3 Pieces, 1963; Conc. no.2, 13 insts, 1966, rev. 1972; Toccata, band, 1967; Conc. no.3, vc, wind qnt, perc, 1969; Conc. no.4, pf, 14 insts, 1979, rev. 1982; Chbr Sym. no.1, 1980; A New Ricercare, str, 1983; Conc. no.6, cl, orch, 1986; Pacific Bridges, cl, str, 1989; Sym. Prelude, 1993; Chbr Sym. no.2, 1996; From the Hudson Valley, fl, hp, str, 1997 (rev. 1999); Symphonic Prelude, 1998; Overture to Spring, 1999; Jacob Wrestles With the Angels, 2002;Clarinet Concerto, cl, orch, 2006

Choral: Festival Song, SATB, 1951; Let me Laugh, 3vv, pf, 1954; Ps xviii, SA, pf, 1954; A Proverb of Solomon, SATB, orch, 1957; Thanksgiving, SATB, 1958; Pss xl, lxxxix, TB, 1963–8; When Israel came Forth (Ps cxiv), SATB, 1963; Fyre and Yse, SATB, tape, 1966; 8 Choral Songs (Moses Ibn Ezra), SATB, 1974; 3 3-Part Songs, SSA/TTB, 1975; Set me as a Seal, SATB, vc, hp, 1993; The Vision of Isaiah, SATB, orch, 1998; other choral songs

Solo vocal: Pastorale, 1v, pf, 1949; 3 Songs from the Hebrew, 1v, vn, cl, pf, 1949; 4 English Lovesongs, 1v, pf, 1961; Spring in the Harbor (S. Stepanchev), S, fl, vc, pf, 1970; 4 Songs from the Chinese, S, fl, perc, 1990; Cummingsong, T, fl, ob, vn, va, vc, 1995

Chbr: Suite, brass, 1947; Str Qt [no.1], 1950; Short Suite, fl, cl, bn, 1951; Sextet, cl, str qt, pf, 1952–3; Sonata, vc, pf, 1954; Sonata, vn, pf, 1956; Wind Qnt, 1956; Two's Company, 2 cl, 1957; Str Qt [no.2], 1959; Partita no.2, vn, vc, 1961; 5 Pieces, cl, pf, 1962; Ballad, cl, pf, 1963; Fantasy no.1, fl, pf, 1963; Partita no.3, wind qnt, 1964; Trios and Interludes, fl, va, pf, 1965; Str Qt [no.3], 1966; Dialogues, fl, tape, 1968; Dualities, 2 tpt, 1970; Pentagram, a sax, 1971; Line Drawings, fl, perc, 1972; Diaphonies, ob, pf, 1975; Partita no.4, fl, cl, vn, db, pf, 1975; Conductus novus, 4 trbn, 1979; Strata, 8 insts, 1979, rev. 1984; Fantasy no.2, fl, pf, 1980, rev. 1997; O Primvera, fl, ob, cl, 1983; Inventions and Airs, cl, vn, pf, 1984, rev. 1997; Cloud Studies, 12 fl, 1989; 5 Fantasies, vn, vc, 1990; Washington Square, 12 players, 1990; 6 Pieces, vn, pf, 1991; Cape Cod Sketches, fl, vn, va, vc, 1992; Omaggio, fl, cl, vn, va, vc, 1993; Duettini, 2 tpt, 1996; 5 Short Pieces, ww qt, 1997; Inventions and Airs, jazz ens, 1998; Ten Tuneful Airs, non-keyboard solo inst, 1998; Six Bagatelles for Clarinet in Bb, cl, perc, pno, 1999

Kbd (pf, unless otherwise stated): Scherzo, 1949; Variations, 1951; Sonata, 1956; Allegro giocoso, 1957; Partita no.1, 1958; Statements and Commentaries, 1965, rev. 1996; Short Sonata no.1, hpd, 1969; Antiphonies, 4 hands, tape, 1970; Sestina, 1974; 10 Short Pieces, 1977; 5 Short Pieces and a Reprise, 1981; Venetian Reflections, 1988; The Garden of Memory, 1998

Other works, withdrawn

Principal publishers: Seesaw, Presser

WRITINGS

with S. Berkowitz and G. Fontrier: *A New Approach to Sight Singing* (New York, 1960, rev. 2/1997)

A New Approach to Ear Training (New York, 1967, rev. 2/1999)

Gradus: an Integrated Approach to Harmony, Counterpoint and Analysis (New York, 1976, rev. 2/1988)

with A. Brings and others: *A New Approach to Keyboard Harmony* (New York, 1979)

BRUCE SAYLOR/R

Kraft, William (*b* Chicago, IL, 6 Sept 1923). Composer, conductor, timpanist, and percussionist. He studied at Columbia University (BA 1951, MA 1954), where his teachers included JACK BEESON, HENRY COWELL, OTTO LUENING, and VLADIMIR USSACHEVSKY. He also studied privately with Morris Goldenberg and Saul Goodman at the Juilliard School of Music. In addition to performing as percussionist (1955–61) and principal timpanist (1962–81) with the Los Angeles PO, Kraft served as the orchestra's assistant conductor (1969–72) and composer-in-residence and founder/director of LAPO New Music Group (1981–5). He has also acted as composer-in-residence for the Cheltenham New Music Festival (1986). His honors include fellowships from the Guggenheim Foundation and the Norlin/MacDowell Colony, residencies at the Rockefeller Foundation Center in Bellagio (1975, 1996), and awards from the Kennedy Center, the American Academy and Institute of Arts and Letters, the ACA, the Australia Symphony, Vienna Modern Masters, and other organizations. He retired as chair of the composition department at University of California, Santa Barbara, in 2002, but has remained active in Los Angeles's musical life. In 2009 he received the Forte Award for his contribution to contemporary music in Los Angeles.

Most of Kraft's music from the 1960s and 70s is serial. He also experimented with electronic music. During the 1980s rhythmic elements derived from jazz and Impressionistic harmonies were absorbed into his style. Although he is particularly known for his percussion works, from 1996 to 1998 he devoted his compositional energies exclusively to his first opera, *Red Azalea*.

Kraft's contribution to the percussion literature is among the most significant of any American composer. His extensive chamber series of *Encounters*, analogous to Berio's *Sequenzas,* spans nearly four decades. All but one involve percussion, sometimes solo, but most often as an instrumental duet with another orchestral instrument. Even when he combines percussion with a conventional chamber ensemble such as a wind quintet, it is the specific timbres of the ensemble's component members that seem to fire his imagination, rather than the massed sound of the ensemble. These chamber works show him at his best, exploring the infinite variety of timbres and effects available both within the percussion family and especially in combination with other pitched instruments. He has an ear for color and mood, creating dramatic tension even in hypnotic passages with the most subtle gradations of dynamics, attack, and rhythmic nuance. He has expanded his horizons as the world of percussion has expanded, embracing instruments and modes of expression from the Far East, Middle East, Africa, and the Americas, and employing new techniques for marimba and other mallet percussion. Many of the *Encounters* have extramusical subtexts, and several are tributes to composers whose music has influenced Kraft, including Scriabin (*Encounters* V), the jazz drummer Joe Jones (*Encounters XIII*), and Debussy and Ravel (*Encounters* XV). Kraft's Concerto No. 2 for timpani "The Grand Encounter" is, in a sense, the culmination of the series, entailing piccolo timpani in addition to a full set of kettledrums, and a large supporting complement of orchestral percussion. This and Kraft's Concerto no.1 are arguably the most important concerted works for timpani since Poulenc's Concerto for Organ, Timpani, and Strings.

WORKS
(selective list)

Dramatic: Red Azalea (op, 2, C. Hawes), 1996–8; rev.2002–8, London, April 1999; film, TV and radio scores

Orch: A Simple Introduction to the Orch, 1958; Contextures I: Riots—Decade 1960, 1967; Pf Conc., 1972; Dream Tunnel, 1976; Double Play, vn, pf, chbr orch, 1982; Interplay, vc, orch, 1982, rev. 1984; Of Ceremonies, Pageants and Celebrations, 1986, rev. 1987; A Kennedy Portrait, nar, orch, 1988; Veils and Variations, hn, orch, 1988; Vintage Renaissance, 1989; Fanfare Vintage 90–91, 1990; Gossamer Glances, 1993; Sym. of Sorrows, 1995; In Memoriam Toru Takemitsu, str, opt. EH, perc, hp, 1999; EH Conc, 2002;Vintage Renaissance and Beyond, wind sym (also chbr ens), 2005

Vocal: Silent Boughs (E. St Vincent Millay), Mez, str, 1963; The Sublime and the Beautiful (F.M. Dostoyevsky, A. Rimbaud), T, fl, cl, vn, vc, pf, perc, 1979; Contextures II: the Final Beast (Virgil, H.W. Longfellow, W. Owen, others) S, T, chorus, chbr ens, 1985, orchd 1986; Settings from Pierrot lunaire (after A. Giraud), S, chbr ens, 1987–90; Songs of Flowers, Bells and Death (K. Issa, M. Bashō, W. Owen, others), SATB, perc, 1991

Perc: Theme and Variations, perc qt, 1956; 3 Miniatures, perc, orch, 1958; Momentum, 8 perc, 1958; Suite, 4 perc, 1958; French Suite, 1962; Corrente II Triangles, conc., perc, 10 insts, 1965–8; Conc., 4 perc, orch, 1966; Des imagistes (E. Pound, e.e. cummings, others), 2 nar, perc ens, 1974; Soliloquy: Encounters I: Soliloquy, perc, tape, 1975; Encounters III, perc, tpt, 1971; Encounters IV, perc, tbn, 1972; Encounters V: In the Morning of the Winter Sea (Homage to Scriabin), perc, vc, 1975; Encounters VI, rototoms, perc quartet, 1976; Encounters VII: Blessed are the Peacemakers, for they shall be called the Children of God, 2 perc, 1977; Images, perc solo, 1978; Timp Conc., 1983; Perc Qt, 1988; Conc., perc, chbr ens, 1993; Encounters VIII: Divinations, solo perc, 1995; Encounters IX, alto sax, perc, 1998; Encounters X, mar, vn, 1992; Encounters XI: The Demise of Suriyodhaya, perc, EH, 1998; Encounters XII: The Gabrielic Foray, perc, hp, 2003; Perc Conc. no.2, "The Grand Encounter," 2004, rev. 2006; Encounters XIII, Concertino for perc & ww qnt, 2008; Encounters XIV (Concerto a tre), vn, perc, pf, 2005; Encounters XV, perc, guit, 2008; Encounters XVI, perc, fl, 2011; Encounters XVII, perc, cl, 2011

Other chbr and solo inst: Nonet, brass, perc, 1958; Double Trio, tuba, perc, pf, prep pf, amp gui, 1966; Encounters II, tuba, 1966; Games: Collage no.1, brass, 1969; Requiescat for Rhodes Elec Pf, 1975; Translucences, pf, 1977; Gallery '83, fl, cl, vn, vc, pf, perc, 1983; Gallery 4–5, cl, vn, va, vc, pf, 1985; Melange, fl, cl, vn, vc, pf, cel, perc, 1985; Episodes, vn, pf, 1987; Qt for the Love of Time, cl, pf trio, 1987; Suite from "Cascando," fl, cl, vn, vc, pf, 1988; Cadeau, fl, pf, 1992; Music for Str Qt and Perc, 1993; Vintage Renaissance and Beyond, fl, cl, pf, vn, va, vc (also wind sym), 2005

El-ac music, cptr installations incl. Sky's the Limit, O'Hare Airport, Chicago

BIBLIOGRAPHY

A. Rich, "A Different Drummer," *California Magazine,* Sept 1983

W.G. Harbinson: "Analysis: William Kraft's Dialogues and Entertainments," *Journal of Band Research,* xix/2 (1983–4), 16–25

P. Wilson: "William Kraft on Conducting, Performance and New Music," *Symphony,* xxxvii/6 (1986), 18–20, 69, 71

E. Hendricks, "A Chat with David Herbert," *Percussive Notes,* xlvii/3 (2009), 50–1

LAURIE SHULMAN

Kraftwerk. Electronic popular music group. It formed in Düsseldorf, (West) Germany in 1970. Ralf Hütter (*b* Krefeld, Germany, 20 Aug 1946) and Florian Schneider-Esleben (*b* Düsseldorf, Germany, 7 April 1947) were the band's core until Schneider-Esleben's departure in 2008, though there have been many musical and technical collaborators. They emerged from the experimental West German rock scene that fused psychedelic rock, free jazz, and academic electronic music. Early albums used sound processed oscillators, tape recordings, flute, violin, keyboards, electric guitar, and acoustic and electronic drums. Synthesizers and vocoders were later added to the mix. Kraftwerk initially achieved only moderate success at home and abroad. However, *Autobahn* (1974) proved an unexpected commercial breakthrough. A 3:27 version of the 22:43 title track "Autobahn" reached no.25 on the *Billboard* Singles chart in 1975, and similar success followed elsewhere.

The success of "Autobahn" convinced Kraftwerk to pursue a fully electronic sound in the context of multilingual, idiosyncratic songs and trance-like instrumentals. They pioneered the use of synthesizers, drum machines, sequencers, vocoders, and speech synthesis, and released three albums, *Trans-Europe Express* (1977), *The Man-Machine* (1978), and *Computer World* (1981), that were central to later developments in synthpop, post-punk/new wave, electro/hip-hop in New York, and techno in Detroit. This neatly dovetails with the fact they looked to US soul and funk for musical inspiration, though they also counted The Velvet Underground, MC5, and Iggy and the Stooges among their influences. Though the band continues to perform, their earlier work remains their key legacy.

BIBLIOGRAPHY

GMO

P. Bussy: *Kraftwerk: Man, Machine and Music*, 3rd ed. (London, 2005)

S. Albiez and D. Pattie, eds.: *Kraftwerk: Music Non Stop* (New York/London, 2011)

SEAN ALBIEZ

Krainis, Bernard (*b* New Brunswick, NJ, 28 Dec 1924; *d* Great Barrington, MA, 18 Aug 2000). Recorder player. Originally a trombonist, he started to play recorder only at age 21. He studied music at Denver University (1946–8) and musicology with Gustave Reese at New York University (1948–50). In 1952, with NOAH GREENBERG, Krainis founded the NEW YORK PRO MUSICA ANTIQUA, and he remained with the group until 1959; in the 1960s he organized and toured extensively with the Krainis Baroque Ensemble, the Krainis Baroque Trio, and the Krainis Consort, a recorder ensemble. He gave up touring in 1970, but continued to perform occasionally as a soloist and has made a number of recordings of 17th- and 18th-century music such as *The Virtuoso Recorder from Folk Dances to Blues* (1965). Krainis sought to promote recorder music composed throughout music history, as evidenced by his recording *Sweet Pipes: Five Centuries of Recorder Music* (1963). His playing is characterized by superb technique and warm, vibrant tone-color. Past President of the American Recorder Society,

Krainis also held teaching positions at Kirkland College (1969–71), the Eastman School (1976), and Smith College (1977–81); he joined the faculty of the Aston Magna Festival in 1973 and, in 1980, that of the Mannes College. In 1985, Krainis retired as a performer, yet continued his role as a board member and teacher at Aston Magna until his death.

JAMES WIERZBICKI/ELIZABETH PERTEN

Krall, Diana (Jean) (*b* Nanaimo, BC, 16 Nov 1964). Canadian vocalist, pianist, and composer. She started playing piano when she was four years old. When she was 17 she moved to Boston to attend the Berklee College of Music, where she studied piano with Ray Santisi. Later she relocated to Los Angeles and was mentored by local jazz musicians Jeff Hamilton, RAY BROWN, and JIMMY ROWLES. During this time she began to pursue her singing more seriously, while continuing to accompany herself on piano. Krall formed a jazz trio in 1990 and moved to New York. A small Canadian label released her first album, in 1993, and by the mid-1990s she was recording for Impulse!; she later recorded with Verve. *Love Scenes* (1997, Imp.), which featured an intimate-sounding trio of piano, bass, and guitar accompanying Krall's vocals, was her first platinum release, and featured renditions of such jazz standards as "All or Nothing at All." Later albums, such as *When I Look in your Eyes* (1998, Imp.) and *The Look of Love* (2001, Verve), featured more fully orchestrated arrangements of jazz standards. The former was extremely successful in mainstream markets and was the first jazz record in a quarter century to be nominated for the Grammy Album of the Year. In 2003 Krall married the English singer-songwriter Elvis Costello, and in 2004 she released *The Girl in the Other Room*, which departed from her previously traditional choice of material by including six new songs co-written by the pair. She has also worked for television and film, contributing to soundtracks and appearing in films such as *De-lovely* (2004). Krall sings in a strong, low alto voice and focuses on lyrical interpretation rather than overt vocal virtuosity. Her primarily melodic-oriented and at times minimalist piano solos complement her vocal style.

RECORDINGS
(selective list)
Stepping Out (1992, Justin Time); *Only Trust your Heart* (1994, GRP); *All for you: a Dedication to the Nat King Cole Trio* (1995, Imp.); *Love Scenes* (1997, Imp.); *When I Look in your Eyes* (1998, Imp.); *The Look of Love* (2001, Verve); *The Girl in the other Room* (2003, Verve); *From this Moment On* (2006, Verve); *Quiet Nights* (2008, Verve), *Glad Rag Doll* (2012, Verve).

HILARY BAKER

Kramer, A(rthur) Walter (*b* New York, NY, 23 Sept 1890; *d* New York, NY, 8 April 1969). Publisher, editor, critic, and composer. He studied violin with his father, Maximilian Kramer, and with Carl Hauser and Richard Arnold. After studying at the College of the City of New York he joined the staff of the magazine *Musical America* (1910–22) and then spent several years studying, writing, and composing in Europe; for a time he worked with Gian Francesco Malipiero. In 1927 he became music supervisor for the CBS Radio Network, and then returned as editor-in-chief to *Musical America* (1929–36); subsequently he became managing director of the music publishers Galaxy Music Corporation (1936–56), and after his retirement he continued to write and compose. He helped to found the Society for Publication of American Music (1919) and served as its president (1934–40) and on the board of directors of the ASCAP (1941–56). In addition to many articles and reviews in music periodicals, Kramer published over 300

Diana Krall, 2007. (Photo by Paul Drinkwater/NBCU Photo Bank via AP Images)

compositions, including works for full orchestra, string orchestra, string quartet, voice, chorus, piano, violin, cello, and organ, as well as numerous instrumental and choral transcriptions. His compositions, which are fairly conservative, are marked by much technical refinement and understanding of the instrumental or vocal medium used.

WRITINGS

Discussion of contemporary Italian composers in *The Art of Music*, iii: *Modern Music*, ed. E.B. Hill and E. Newman (New York, 1915), iii, 366–403

"The Things we Set to Music," *MQ*, vii (1921), 309–13

"Three Italian Modernists: Malipiero, Pizzetti, Respighi," *The Chesterian*, xiii (1931–2), 68–74

"Berg's *Wozzeck* has U.S. Premiere in Philadelphia," *MusAm*, li/6 (1931), 3, 13

BIBLIOGRAPHY

J.T. Howard: *A. Walter Kramer* (New York, 1926) [comprehensive bio-bibliography; part of biography repr. as "A. Walter Kramer: the Early Years," *MJ*, xxx/3 (1972), 30–1]

W.T. Upton: *Art-Song in America* (Boston and Chicago, 1930/*R*, suppl. 1938/*R*), 225ff

GUSTAVE REESE/RAMONA H. MATTHEWS

Kramer, Jonathan D. (*b* Hartford, CT, 7 Dec 1942; *d* New York, NY, 3 June 2004). Composer and theorist. He was a pupil of LEON KIRCHNER and BILLY JIM LAYTON at Harvard (BA 1965) and did postgraduate work at the University of California, Berkeley (MA 1967, PhD 1969), where his teachers in composition included SEYMOUR SHIFRIN, ANDREW IMBRIE, ROGER SESSIONS, and RICHARD FELCIANO. He also studied with Stockhausen at the University of California, Davis (1966–7), and with JOHN M. CHOWNING at Stanford (computer music, 1967–8). He served on the faculties of the University of California, Berkeley (1969–70), Oberlin (1970–1), Yale (1971–8), the Cincinnati College-Conservatory (1978–90), and Columbia University (1988–2004). From 1980 he was program annotator for the Cincinnati SO, a position he also held with the San Francisco SO (1967–70) and the National SO (1989–92). He received grants from the Martha Baird Rockefeller Fund, the NEA, the MC, and Meet the Composer, among others. His *Renascence* (1974, rev. 1977, 1985, 1997) was one of three American works performed at the 1980 World Music Days in Israel. *Music for Piano V* (1980) won the International Rostrum of Composers competition in 1983 and was programmed at the 1985 World Music Days in the Netherlands. *Musica Pro Musica* (1986–7), commissioned by the NEA, was performed by the Warsaw PO in the 1992 World Music Days in Poland.

Much of Kramer's music is highly eclectic, particularly his early works, which include conceptual pieces (*For Broken Piano, Truck, Shaving Cream, Fruit Salad, Toilet, Wife, San Francisco, Color TV, and*, 1969–70), as well as highly structured compositions (Music for Piano, nos.2–3). From the mid-1970s he worked toward the reconciliation of these divergent compositional approaches. Later works employ a limited array of pitches (six was his preferred number), but also allow for influences such as jazz. The propulsive rhythms associated with minimalism are employed in *Atlanta Licks* (1984). Works from the mid-1980s, including *Musica Pro* *Musica* and *Notta Sonata* (1992–3), revel in conflict and contradiction. As a theorist, Kramer frequently wrote and lectured on musical time and postmodernism.

WORKS
(selective list)

Stage and multimedia: For Broken Pf, Truck, Shaving Cream, Fruit Salad, Toilet, Wife, San Francisco, Color TV, and, tape, slide projections, 1969–70; An Imaginary Dance, tape, slide projections, 1970–73; Blue Music, actor, tape, 1970–72; Higher Education, teacher, office, 1971; You, Too, Can Be a Composer, music theory class, teacher, 1971; Fanfare, actors, tape, 1973–6; En noir et blanc, dancer, 2 pf, 1988

Orch: Requiem for the Innocent, 1970; Moments In and Out of Time, 1983; Musica Pro Musica, 1986–7; About Face, 1989, rev. 1991; Cincy in C, 1994; Remembrance of a People (text by Roger Goodman), spkr, pf, str orch, 1996; Rewind: a Semi-Suite, 2000, rev. 2003

Symphonic Band: Variations, 1969; Obsessions, 2001

Chbr: Septet, fl, ob, bn, vn, va, vc, hp, 1968; One for Five in Seven, Mostly, ww qnt, 1971; The Canons of Blackearth, perc qt, tape, 1972–3; Renascence, cl, tape delay, tape, 1974, rev. cl, tape, 1977, 1985, rev. cl, cptr, 1997; Moving Music, 13 cl, 1975–6; 5 Studies on Six Notes, perc trio, 1976–80; Licks, 3 db/(db, tape), 1980–81; Atlanta Licks, fl, cl, vn, va, vc, pf, 1984; A Game, vc, pf, 1988–92; Another Sunrise, fl, ob, bn, va, vc, perc, pf, 1990; Notta Sonata, 2 pf, perc, 1993; Serbelloni Serenade, cl, vn, pf, 1995; Remembrance of a People, str qnt, pf, 1996; Surreality Check, vn, vc, pf, 1998; Imbrication, fl, cl, vn, va, vc, 2000; Imagined Ancestors, cl, vn, vc, pf 4 hds, 2002–3

Solo inst: 3 Pieces, cl, 1965–6; Music for Pf nos.1–6, 1966–97; 5 Tunes, pf, 1970–78; One More Piece, cl, 1972; 5 Studies on Six Notes, hpd, 1976–7, arr. gui, 1978, arr. perc trio, 1980; The Sunrise Sonata, hpd, 1984–5

Vocal: No Beginning, No End, SATB, orch, 1982–3; Into the Labyrinth, SATB, pf, 1985–6; Another Anniversary, spkr, cl, 1989

Principal publishers: MMB, G. Schirmer

WRITINGS

"The Row as Structural Background and Audible Foreground: the First Movement of Webern's First Cantata," *JMT*, xv (1971), 158–81

"The Fibonacci Series in Twentieth-Century Music," *JMT*, xvii (1973), 110–48

"Multiple and Nonlinear Time in Beethoven's Opus 135," *PNM*, xi/2 (1973), 122–45

"Moment Form in Twentieth Century Music," *MQ*, lxiv/2 (1978), 177–95; repr. in *Breaking the Sound Barrier*, ed. G. Battcock (New York, 1981)

"New Temporalities in Music," *Critical Inquiry*, vii (1981), 539–56

"The Impact of Technology on Music Time," *Percussive Notes*, xxii/3 (1984), 16

"Studies of Time and Music: a Bibliography," *Music Theory Spectrum*, vii (1985), 72–106

"Temporal Linearity and Nonlinearity in Music," *The Study of Time V*, ed. J.T. Fraser, N. Lawrence and F.C. Haber (Amherst, MA, 1986)

"Discontinuity and Proportion in the Music of Stravinsky," *Confronting Stravinsky*, ed. J. Pasler (Berkeley, 1986), 174–94

Listen to the Music (New York, 1988); repr. as *Listening to Music* (London, 1991); Sp. trans. as *Invitacion a la musica* (Buenos Aires, 1993)

The Time of Music (New York, 1988)

ed.: *Time in Contemporary Musical Thought* (London, 1993)

"Beyond Unity: Toward an Understanding of Postmodernism in Music and Music Theory," *Concert Music, Rock and Jazz since 1945*, ed. E. West Marvin and R. Hermann (Rochester, NY, 1995)

"Postmodern Concepts of Musical Time," *Indiana Theory Review*, xvii/2 (1997), 21

"The Nature and Origins of Musical Postmodernism," *Postmodern Music/Postmodern Thought*, ed. J. Lochhead and J. Auner (New York, 2002), 13–26

BIBLIOGRAPHY

K. Gann: "Shaken, Not Stirred: Jonathan Kramer mixes musical styles that don't belong together," *Village Voice* (26 March 2002), <http://www.villagevoice.com/2002-03-26/music/shaken-not-stirred/1/>

K. Gann: Obituary, *Village Voice* (8 June 2004)

M.D. Johnson: "Classical Currents: An Interview with Jonathan D. Kramer," *The Partial Observer*, 9 Jan 2004, <http://www.partialobserver.com/article.cfm?id=964>

JAMES CHUTE

Krasner, Louis (*b* Cherkassy, Ukraine, 21 June 1903; *d* Boston, MA, 4 May 1995). Violinist of Ukrainian birth. He was brought to Providence, Rhode Island, at age five and graduated in 1923 from the New England Conservatory, where he studied the violin with Eugene Gruenberg and composition with FREDERICK SHEPHERD CONVERSE. Further studies in Europe, under C. Flesch, Lucien Capet, and O. Ševčík, led to an active concert career there and in the United States. Krasner became leader of the Minneapolis SO under Mitropoulos (1944–9), and moved to Syracuse University in 1949, where he taught the violin and chamber music until 1972. He became a visiting professor at the New England Conservatory in 1976 and taught at the Berkshire Music Center in Tanglewood.

Krasner became closely identified with 20th-century music. He gave the European premiere of Achron's concerto in Vienna and the American premiere of A. Casella's in Boston, both in 1928. In 1934, he commissioned Berg's concerto, believing that the cause of serial music would be helped by an effective virtuoso work in Berg's impassioned melodic style. He gave its premiere at the 1936 ISCM Festival in Barcelona under Hermann Scherchen. As a request of the composer, he premiered Schoenberg's concerto in Philadelphia under Stokowski in 1940, attracting a rare testament of approval from Schoenberg after the premiere (letter, 17 December 1940) (SchwarzGM). Krasner also recorded both Berg's (under A. Webern in 1936) and Schoenberg's (under Mitropoulos, 1952) concertos for the first time. Later he played the first performance of Sessions's concerto (1946, Minneapolis), as well as shorter works by Cowell and Harris.

MSS. at Harvard University, Cambridge, Massachusetts.

BIBLIOGRAPHY

J. Davidoff: "An Interview with L. Krasner," *Journal of the Violin Society of America*, viii/2 (1987), 4–30

B. Schwarz: *Great Masters of the Violin* (New York, 1987), 517–9

A. Mell: "Louis Krasner," *Journal of the Violin Society of America*, xiv/2 (1995), special edition

MICHAEL STEINBERG/MICHAEL BAUMGARTNER

Kraus, Lili (*b* Budapest, Hungary, 4 March 1903; *d* Asheville, NC, 6 Nov 1986). New Zealand pianist of Hungarian birth, active in the United States. She took her first piano lessons at the age of six, and two years later entered the Royal Academy of Music, Budapest, where her teachers included ZOLTÁN KODÁLY and BÉLA BARTÓK. In 1922 she graduated with a first-class degree, and traveled to Vienna to study with CLARA STEUERMANN and ARTUR SCHNABEL at the Vienna Conservatory, where she was appointed a full professor in 1925 at the age of 22. After teaching there for six years, she embarked on a world concert tour, and rapidly established herself during the 1930s as a successful soloist. About this time a number of valuable recordings of Mozart, Haydn, and Beethoven, both solos and chamber music, did much to spread her fame as an exceptionally clear and musicianly interpreter of the Classics. In 1942 at the start of another tour she was taken prisoner by the Japanese in Java, and for three years was interned. After the war she toured Australia and New Zealand, and for her "unrelenting efforts in the aid of countries in need" was granted New Zealand citizenship. She returned to the international circuit in 1948 and then travelled widely, giving recitals and playing with leading orchestras. A pianist of considerable virtuosity and stamina, she played 25 Mozart concertos in a single series in New York in 1966–7; and the next season she gave there the complete Mozart sonatas. In 1968 she was named artist-in-residence at Texas Christian University in Fort Worth, Texas, where she remained until her retirement in 1983. A public concert artist until 1982, Kraus was also a regular juror at the Van Cliburn International Piano Competition. The Austrian government recognized Kraus with the Cross of Honor for Science and Art in 1978.

DOMINIC GILL/ELIZABETH PERTEN

Krauss, Alison (Maria) (*b* Decatur, IL, 23 July 1971). Country and bluegrass recording artist. The most celebrated woman in bluegrass music during the 1990s, Alison Krauss was named Female Vocalist of the Year four times by the International Bluegrass Music Association (1990–91, 1993, and 1995) and once by the Country Music Association (CMA) (1995). Krauss's stylistic combination of mainstream country and bluegrass, her career 26 Grammy awards—more than any other woman—and considerable solo album sales in excess of 6.5 million units distinguish her, albeit with some controversy, among traditional bluegrass artists. While growing up in Champaign, Illinois, Krauss was exposed to a wide variety of music, learning classical violin from the age of five before settling on country and bluegrass. By age eight, she was competing in local talent shows.

Alison Krauss, 2008. (AP Photo/Dave Martin)

In 1983, Krauss won the Illinois State Fiddle Championship, and the Society for the Preservation of Bluegrass in American honored her with the title of Most Promising Fiddler in the Midwest. In 1985, she signed with Rounder Records, which released her critically-acclaimed debut album, *Too Late to Cry*, in 1987. Her follow-up, *Two Highways* (Rounder, 1989), defined her signature style and that of her band Union Station: a combination of her intimate soprano sensitivity with pop country-inspired melodic lines and string band accompaniment. In 1990, Krauss won her first Grammy for Best Bluegrass Album with *I've Got That Old Feeling*, and in 1993, she joined the *Grand Ole Opry*. Two years later, she made bluegrass sales history with the album *Now That I've Found You: a Collection* (Rounder, 1995), which was eventually certified double platinum and earned four CMA awards, including Single of the Year for "When You Say Nothing at All." Krauss's popularity continued into the new millennium through her contributions to the soundtrack of the Coen Brothers' film *O Brother, Where Art Thou?* (Touchstone, 2000). The soundtrack's success equaled or surpassed that of the movie, eventually selling over eight million copies and inspiring a concert tour and the film *Down from the Mountain* (Mike Zoss Productions, 2000), a documentary performance of the *O Brother* soundtrack at Nashville's historic Ryman Auditorium. In addition to her work with Union Station, Krauss collaborated with numerous artists throughout the millennium, including duets with Sting ("You will be my ain true love," 2003), Brad Paisley ("Whisky Lullaby," 2003), James Taylor ("How's the world treating you?," 2003), and Robert Plant, which whom she recorded the platinum-selling album *Raising Sand* (Rounder, 2007).

DAVID B. PRUETT

Kraut, Harry (John) (*b* Brooklyn, NY, 11 April 1933; *d* Key West, FL, 11 Dec 2007). Music administrator. He was educated at Harvard College and Harvard Business School, where he was student manager of the Harvard Glee Club. In 1958 he joined the administrative staff of the Boston SO, and during his time there managed a pioneering system of syndicating concert tapes to radio and television broadcasters, in addition to other duties. He also served as assistant and then principal (from 1963) administrator of the Berkshire Music Center, the orchestra's summer school at Tanglewood. In 1971 he became the administrative head of LEONARD BERNSTEIN's firm, Amberson Enterprises, and executive producer of all the Bernstein television programs; he was also involved as business manager with Bernstein's recordings, concerts, and publications. Kraut was trustee of the Peabody Institute of Johns Hopkins University, and served as president of the Brooklyn Boys' Choir School, the Cambridge (Massachusetts) Society for Early Music, and the Harvard Glee Club Foundation.

LEONARD BURKAT/R

Krehbiel, Henry (Edward) (*b* Ann Arbor, MI, 10 March 1854; *d* New York, NY, 20 March 1923). Critic and writer on music. He studied law in Cincinnati, Ohio, but became a reporter and critic for the *Cincinnati Gazette*. He was self-taught in music. His long memory, pontifical tone, and vast learning made him the acknowledged dean of New York music critics as critic of the *New York Tribune* from 1880 to 1923. By birth (both his parents were German-born) and intellectual orientation, he was a Germanophile who honored the Classical symphonists with a purist's integrity.

Krehbiel completed the first English-language edition of Thayer's *Life of Ludwig van Beethoven*—the monumental task of his last years—and wrote a dozen books. He also translated operas from French and German, composed exercises for the violin and edited collections of songs and arias. *How to Listen to Music* (1896) was reprinted 30 times. *Chapters of Opera* (1908) and *More Chapters of Opera* (1919) are a two-volume history of opera in New York that has not been superseded. An industrious student of music and ethnicity, he believed that musical expression relied upon "dialects and idioms which are national or racial in origin and structure." *Afro-American Folksongs* (1914) espoused the music of the black slave as the "most beautiful and most vital in our folk song." Dvořák's similar viewpoint reflected frequent contact with Krehbiel, who influentially championed the former's "New World" Symphony. Krehbiel's closest friends included the conductor Anton Seidl, the key figure in an American Wagner movement, of which Krehbiel was the central chronicler. He was also prominent as a lecturer and program annotator.

After the turn of the 20th century, Krehbiel's taste became increasingly conservative. His insistence that art serve a moral purpose was at odds with the new modernism; he chafed at the Caruso cult and other harbingers of a less élitist artistic climate. In a notorious obituary documenting his fierce admiration for the *fin-de-siècle* achievements of Seidl and Dvořák, Krehbiel denounced Gustav Mahler, whose New York career he had followed, for rescoring Beethoven, composing polyglot symphonies, and underestimating the sophistication of New York's concert and operatic culture. His review of the American première of Strauss's *Salome* (in *Chapters of Opera*) is a masterpiece of shrewd opprobrium. No subsequent New York music critic has played so influential a role within the city's community of artists.

Krehbiel embodied an activist American school of criticism. He considered himself a newspaperman— "proud of journalism as a liberal profession," "incessantly jealous of its honor and high standing," according to Richard Aldrich, whom Krehbiel mentored at the *Tribune*. Krehbiel also wrote: "The power of the press will…work for good." Krehbiel's German contemporaries pondered musical affairs from a height Krehbiel, who swiftly composed his characteristically dense sentences and long paragraphs, was a messenger of daily events. An empiricist, he visited synagogues to research cantorial chant; to research *Die Meistersinger* he visited Nuremberg. When the Met claimed that Wagner no longer made money, he tabulated box office receipts to prove otherwise.

Krehbiel equally expected activist listening. His *How to Listen to Music: Hints and Suggestions to Untaught Lovers of the Art* was a central source of instruction for generations of American music-lovers. Its 350 pages enshrine a proud definition of the critic's role—"the first, if not the sole, office of the critic should be to guide public judgment. It is not for him to instruct the musician in his art....He labors to steady and dignify public opinion." To fulfill this "great mission," a "vast responsibility," the critic should be "catholic in taste, outspoken in judgment, unalterable in allegiance to his ideas, unwavering in integrity"—a mentor, that is, in equal measure pragmatic and moral. Central to Krehbiel's sense of high calling as a newsman was his sense of responsibility as a public educator. An ethically endowed criterion of beauty buoyed his notions of musical enjoyment.

Krehbiel believed that the special intensities of American life—"a mad scramble for material things"—demanded compensatory guidance. At the same time, he bristled when Europeans characterized American musical life as underdeveloped. He took a special pride in the American choral tradition, and claimed that "amateur choir-singing is no older anywhere than in the United States" because "the want of professional musicians in America compelled the people to enlist amateurs at a time when in Europe choral activity rested on the church, theatre, and institute choristers, who were practically professionals." Though his eagerness to educate new listeners was egalitarian, he packed his pedagogy with recondite asides. Like so many aspects of his writing and personality, this duality in Krehbiel suggestively defines him as a late 19th-century "German-American." As with so many others so defined, the Great War made Krehbiel an unhyphenated American. He called the Kaiser's war effort "the most monstrous crime of a millennium." Though its ban on Wagner seemed philistine to him, when the Metropolitan Opera returned to Wagner in February 1920, a new *Parsifal* translation by Krehbiel appointed English the language of redemption.

WRITINGS

Notes on the Cultivation of Choral Music and the Oratorio Society of New York (New York, 1884)
Review of the New York Musical Season, i–v (New York, 1886–90)
Studies in the Wagnerian Drama (New York, 1891, 2/1893)
The Philharmonic Society of New York: a Memorial published on the Occasion of the Fiftieth Anniversary of the Founding of the Philharmonic Society (New York, 1892)
How to Listen to Music (New York, 1896/R)
Music and Manners in the Classical Period (New York, 1898, 3/1899)
Chapters of Opera (New York, 1908, 3/1911)
A Book of Operas: their Histories, their Plots, and their Music (New York, 1909)
The Pianoforte and its Music (New York, 1911)
Afro-American Folksongs: a Study in Racial and National Music (New York, 1914)
A Second Book of Operas (New York, 1917)
More Chapters of Opera (New York, 1919)
editor of A.W. Thayer: *The Life of Ludwig van Beethoven* (New York, 1921, rev. 2/1964 by E. Forbes)

BIBLIOGRAPHY

R. Aldrich: "Henry Edward Krehbiel," *ML*, iv (1923), 266–8 [obituary]
J. Horowitz: *Understanding Toscanini* (New York, 1987)
M. Beckerman: "Henry Krehbiel, Antonín Dvořák, and the Symphony 'From the New World'," *Notes*, xlix (1992–3), 447–73
J. Horowitz: *Wagner Nights: an American History* (Berkeley, CA, 1994)
M.N. Grant: *Maestros of the Pen: a History of Classical Music Criticism in America* (Boston, 1998)
D. Bomberger, *"A Tidal Wave of Encouragement": American Composers Concerts in the Gilded Age* (Westport, CT, 2002)
J. Horowitz, *Classical Music in America: a History* (New York, 2005)
H.-L. de La Grange, *Gustav Mahler*, Volume 4: *A New Life Cut Short (1907–1911)* (Oxford, 2008)

JOSEPH HOROWITZ

Kreisler, Fritz (*b* Vienna, Austria, 2 Feb 1875; *d* New York, NY, 29 Jan 1962). Violinist and composer of Austrian birth; naturalized American. He began to learn violin at the age of four with his father, a doctor and enthusiastic amateur violinist. After lessons with Jacques Auber, he gained admission to the Musikverein Konservatorium at the age of seven—the youngest child ever to enter. For three years he studied violin with Joseph Hellmesberger Jr. and theory with Anton Bruckner. He gave his first performance there when he was nine and won the gold medal when he was ten—an unprecedented distinction. He then studied at the Paris Conservatoire under J.L. Massart, who had taught Henryk Wieniawski. Kreisler left the Conservatoire in 1887, sharing the *premier prix* with four other violinists, all some ten years older. From the age of 12 he had no further violin instruction.

From 1889 to 1890 Kreisler toured the United States as assisting artist to Moriz Rosenthal but with only moderate success. He returned to Vienna: two years at the Gymnasium and two as a pre-medical student were followed by military service. All this time, Kreisler barely touched the violin. However, once he decided on a musical career, he quickly regained his technique. In 1896 he applied to join the orchestra of the Vienna Hofoper but failed, allegedly because of poor sight-reading. Two years later he had the satisfaction of scoring a notable success with the Vienna PO, actually the same ensemble that had denied him a place. A year later, in December 1899, his debut with the Berlin Philharmonic under Arthur Nikisch marked the beginning of an international career. He reappeared in the United States during the 1900–1 season, then made his London debut at a Philharmonic concert under Hans Richter on 12 May 1902. In 1904 he was presented with the Philharmonic Society's gold medal. Edward Elgar composed his Violin Concerto for Kreisler, who gave its premiere on 10 November 1910 at Queen's Hall, with Elgar conducting.

At the outbreak of World War I Kreisler joined the Austrian Army. He was medically discharged after being wounded and embarked for the United States (his wife's native country) in November 1914. However, anti-German feelings ran so high that he withdrew from the platform, reappearing in New York on 27 October 1919. From 1924 to 1934 he lived in Berlin. When Austria was annexed by the Nazis, the French government offered him citizenship. In 1939 he returned for good to the United States, and he became an American citizen in 1943. A traffic accident in 1941 impaired his hearing and eyesight; nevertheless, he resumed his career. He made his last Carnegie Hall appearance on 1 November 1947, though he broadcast during the 1949–50 season. After that, his interest in the violin waned; he sold his collection of instruments and kept only an 1860 Vuillaume.

Kreisler was unique. Without exertion (he practiced little) he achieved a seemingly effortless perfection. There was never any conscious technical display. The elegance of his bowing, the grace and charm of his phrasing, the vitality and boldness of his rhythm, and above all his tone of indescribable sweetness and expressiveness were marveled at. Though not very large, his tone had unequaled carrying power because his bow applied just enough pressure without suppressing the natural vibrations of the strings. The matchless color was achieved by vibrato in the style of Wieniawski, who (in Kreisler's words) "intensified the vibrato and brought it to heights never before achieved, so that it became known as the 'French vibrato.'" However, Kreisler applied vibrato not only on sustained notes but also in faster passages, which lost all dryness under his magic touch. His methods of bowing and fingering were equally personal. In fact his individual style was, as Carl Flesch said, ahead of his time, and may explain his comparatively slow rise to fame. Yet there is hardly a violinist in the 20th century who has not acknowledged admiration of and indebtedness to Kreisler.

Kreisler was also a gifted composer. Among his original works are a string quartet, an operetta, *Apple Blossoms* (with Viktor Jacobi, 1919), cadenzas to Ludwig van Beethoven's and to Johannes Brahms's concertos, and numerous short pieces (*Tambourin chinois, Caprice viennois*, etc.). He made many transcriptions and editions. In addition, he composed dozens of pieces in the "olden style," which he ascribed to various 18th-century composers, such as Gaetano Pugnani, François Francoeur, and Padre Martini. When Kreisler admitted in 1935 that these pieces were a hoax, many critics (including Ernest Newman) were indignant while others accepted it as a joke. It is strange indeed that so many experts were misled by Kreisler's impersonations; at any rate, these charming pieces have continued to enrich the violin repertory.

WRITINGS
Four Weeks in the Trenches (Boston and New York, 1915)

BIBLIOGRAPHY
CampbellGV; SchwarzGM
L.P. Lochner: *Fritz Kreisler* (New York, 1950/*R*) [with discography and repr. of the controversy with Newman]
F. Bonavia: "Fritz Kreisler," *MT*, ciii (1962), 179
J.W. Hartnack: *Grosse Geiger unserer Zeit* (Munich, 1967, 4/1993)
J. Creighton: *Discopaedia of the Violin, 1889–1971* (Toronto, 1974)
I. Yampol'sky: *Frits Kreysler: zhizn´ i tvorchestvo* (Moscow, 1975)
The Strad, xcviii (1987) [Kreisler edition]
A.C. Bell: *Fritz Kreisler Remembered: a Tribute* (Braunton, 1992)
H. Adamson: "Forgotten Treasure," *The Strad*, cvii (1996), 692–3
A. Biancolli: *Fritz Kreisler: Love's Sorrow, Love's Joy* (Portland, OR, 1998)
C.R. Scheidemantle: *The Violin of Fritz Kreisler: an Analysis and Performance Guide* (diss., New York U., 1999)

BORIS SCHWARZ/R

Kreisler, Georg Franz (*b* Vienna, Austria, 18 July 1922; *d* Salzburg, Austria, 22 Nov 2011). Composer, cabaret performer, singer, and author. Born into a Jewish middle-class family, Kreisler immigrated after the Austrian Anschluss in 1938, becoming an American citizen in 1943. He served in the US Army during World War II, mainly as a translator and troop entertainer. Here and during years in New York (1946–1955), many of Kreisler's later characteristics as an artist developed: he was professionally trained as a singer/pianist for night clubs and cabarets, toured widely, wrote and recorded his first satiric songs, and composed several musicals.

Kreisler returned to Vienna in 1955 and immediately became a star lyricist, composer, and performer of cabaret style songs (now with German texts) such as "Tauben vergiften im Park." Written for one female singer/actress with piano accompaniment and additional voice tracks, his musical *Heute Abend: Lola Blau* (1971) has been one of the most performed works of popular musical theater in German-speaking Europe for the past four decades. Kreisler wrote dozens of songs, almost 30 works of musical theater, including two operas (premiered 2000 and 2009), a Piano Concerto, a Piano Sonata, and several books of fiction, poetry, and autobiographical stories.

He performed and recorded widely, partly in the 1960s and early 1970s with his third wife, Topsy Küppers, for whom he also wrote *Heute Abend: Lola Blau*, and subsequently with his fourth wife, Barbara Peters. Although he stopped his signature performances as a cabaret style singer/pianist in 2001, Kreisler remained active in his late years as an author of poetry, literature, and musical theater, and took part in stagings and public readings of his work. His personal archive is held by the Academy of Arts in Berlin.

WORKS
(selective list)
Orchestral: Piano Concerto, *c*1954
Keyboard: Piano Sonata, *c*1952
Songs (Lyrics by Kreisler): Das Mädchen mit den drei blauen Augen, 1955; Opernboogie, 1956; Tauben vergiften im Park, 1956; Der Bluntschli, 1957; Telefonbuchpolka, 1960; Max auf der Rax, 1957; Der Musikkritiker, 1959; Zwei alte Tanten tanzen Tango, 1957; Unheilbar gesund, 1959; Zu leise für mich, 1968
Stage (Lyrics by Kreisler): *Heute Abend: Lola Blau* (Musical for one actress, P.: Vienna 1971); *Du sollst nicht lieben* (Musical for two actors, P.: Cologne 1999); *Der Aufstand der Schmetterlinge* (Opera, P.: Vienna 2000); *Adam Schaf hat Angst* (Musical for one actor, P.: Berlin 2002); *Das Aquarium oder Die Stimme der Vernunft* (Opera, P.: Rostock 2009)

RECORDINGS
(selective list)
Vienna Midnight Cabaret (1956, Amadeo AVRS 8012); *Die Georg Kreisler Platte* (1962, Preiser Records 93032); *Unheilbar gesund* (1964, Preiser Records 93040); *Nichtarische Arien* (1966, Preiser Records 93121); *Heute Abend: Lola Blau* (with Kreisler and Topsy Küppers, 1971, Preiser Records 90044); *Der Aufstand der Schmetterlinge* (2000, Kip Records 6021); *Adam Schaf hat Angst* (with Tim Fischer, 2007, Sony 9680571)

BIBLIOGRAPHY
H.J. Fink and M. Seufert: *Georg Kreisler gibt es gar nicht: Die Biographie* (Munich, 2005)

A. Riethmüller and M. Custodis, ed.: *Georg Kreisler, Grenzgänger* (Freiburg, 2009)

F. Döhl: "Georg Kreisler," *KdG*, (Munich, 2013) [with full list of works, discography and bibliography]

FRÉDÉRIC DÖHL

Kreizberg, Yakov (*b* Leningrad, USSR [St. Petersburg, Russia], 15 June 1959). Conductor of Russian birth, brother of SEMYON BYCHKOV. He began to take piano lessons at the age of five, and in his early teens he studied conducting privately with Ilya Musin. In 1976 he immigrated to the United States, where he won conducting fellowships at Tanglewood (with Leonard Bernstein, Seiji Ozawa, and Erich Leinsdorf) and at the Los Angeles Institute. In 1985 he was appointed music director of the Mannes College Orchestra, New York, and the following year he won first prize in the Leopold Stokowski conducting competition. After moving to Europe, he was music director of the Krefeld–Mönchengladbach Opera from 1988 to 1994, and of the Komische Oper, Berlin, from 1994 to 2001. In Berlin he conducted an enterprisingly wide repertory, ranging from Wolfgang Amadeus Mozart to rare 20th-century works such as Berthold Goldschmidt's *Der gewaltige Hahnrei* and Hans Werner Henze's *König Hirsch*.

In 1995 Kreizberg became music director of the Bournemouth SO, a post he held until 2001. Meanwhile he had made his Proms debut, with the BBC SO, in 1993, and was in increasing demand as a guest conductor, both in the concert hall, with major orchestras in Europe and the United States, and in the opera house. His first appearance at Glyndebourne in 1992, conducting notably impassioned performances of *Jenůfa*, was hailed by the *Sunday Times* as "one of the most sensational debuts here within living memory." He made an equally successful ENO debut, with *Der Rosenkavalier*, in 1994, and returned to Glyndebourne in 1995 (*Don Giovanni*) and 1998 (*Kátá Kabanová*). Other highlights in his operatic career include Kurt Weill's *Der Protagonist* and *Royal Palace* at Bregenz in 2004, and his Covent Garden debut, conducting *Macbeth*, in 2006. In 2003 Kreizberg became principal conductor of the Netherlands PO and the Netherlands Chamber Orchestra; in 2009, he became director of the Monte Carlo PO. Among his recordings are Franz Schmidt's Symphony no.4, violin concertos by Sergey Prokofiev, Aram Khachaturian, and Aleksander Glazunov (with Julia Fischer), and Anton Bruckner's Symphony no.7 with the Vienna SO, of which he has been principal guest conductor.

RICHARD WIGMORE/R

Krell, William H(enry) (*b* Tamaqua, PA, May 1868; *d* Miami, FL, 30 Sept 1933). Bandleader and composer. Born to a German immigrant cigar maker and his American-born wife, Krell began musical training as a child, studying both brass instruments and piano. In his teens he led local bands, writing arrangements for them. He moved to Chicago sometime around 1890, where he married and began leading a touring band professionally. His first published composition, "Our Carter: A Beautiful Ballad" (with Silas Leachman), appeared in 1893, dedicated to the recently assassinated Chicago mayor, Carter Harrison Sr. In the seven years that followed, Krell published an additional 16 pieces, mostly waltzes, marches, or cakewalks. He is best remembered for his "Mississippi Rag," copyrighted 27 January 1897, which is the earliest copyrighted piece designated "Rag" in the title. The piece does not follow the classic AAB-BACCDD piano rag form, but like many early so-called rags, it strings together several lightly syncopated melodic strains in imitation of a "cakewalk patrol." Krell evokes the sound of a passing parade band, beginning with a quiet, repetitive opening motive that crescendos to a boisterous middle section, concluding with a return to the opening motive that decrescendos to a quiet finish. Although Krell originally conceived of the piece for band, it became famous through a piano reduction arrangement. Although Krell published no new pieces after 1901, he continued to lead a band in Chicago until the late 1910s when he left the music business for a brief career as a traveling salesman. In the early 1920s he moved to Miami, Florida, working in the real estate business as president of the Republic Securities Corporation until his death.

BRYAN S. WRIGHT

Kremenliev, Boris (*b* Razlog, Bulgaria, 23 May 1911; *d* Los Angeles, CA, 25 April 1988). Composer and ethnomusicologist. He came to the United States in 1929 and studied at DePaul University, Chicago (BM 1936, MM 1938), at the Eastman School (PhD 1942), with HOWARD HANSON and Harris (composition) and Altschuler (conducting). During 1945 to 1946 he was music director of the South German radio network; later he was appointed professor of composition at UCLA, from which he retired in 1978. He experimented with electronics and other new compositional resources, but then returned to a simpler style, colorful, rhythmically intense, terse, and texturally unconventional; a shared cultural background led to some similarity with the music of Bartók. As an ethnomusicologist he concentrated on the folk music of Bulgaria and on Slavic music in general. He wrote a book, *Bulgarian-Macedonian Folk Music* (Berkeley, 1952), and many articles including several on 20th-century music. Kremenliev received grants from the American Philosophical Society (1955), the Ford Foundation (1962), the Creative Arts Institute (1966–7), and the Bulgarian Academy of Arts and Sciences (1979).

WORKS
(selective list)

Op: The Bridge (3, E. Kremenliev), 1966–85

Orch: Sym. no.1 (Song Sym.), A, orch, 1940–41; The Odyssey of Runyon Jones (N. Corwin), 1946; 3 Village Sketches, band, 1949; Bulgarian Rhapsody, 1952; Elegy: 5 June 1968, 1968–9; Peasant Dance, 1984

Chbr and solo inst: 6 Miniatures, pf, 1952; Pf Sonata no.1, 1954; Str Qt no.1, 1954; Pf Sonata no.2, 1959; Str Qt no.2, 1965; Sonata, db, pf, 1966–7; Divertimento, vn, vc, 1967; Overtones, brass, 1983–4

Vocal: Song for Parting (E. Kremenliev), female vv, eng hn, str, 1949; Grapes (A.S. Pushkin), female vv, str qt, 1951; Facing West from California's Shores (W. Whitman), mixed vv, band, 1954; KOAN no.77 (E. Kremenliev), A, fl, cl, pf, perc, 1979; The Children (D. Dugau), S, pf, mand/vn, 1982

Crucifixion (film score), 1952 [on paintings of Rico Lebrun]; other incid music for stage, film, radio, TV

Principal publishers: *Bruzzichelli, Foster, Leeds, Ocorr, Clayton Summy*

W. THOMAS MARROCCO/R

Kremer, Gidon [Krēmers, Gidons] (*b* Riga, Latvia, 27 Feb 1947). Latvian violinist and conductor. He began studying the violin at age four with his parents and grandfather, who were professional string players. At age seven, he entered Riga Music School. At 16 he was awarded the first Prize of the Latvian Republic and two years later he began his studies with David Oistrakh at the Moscow Conservatory. He won awards at a number of prestigious competitions, including first place at both the Paganini Competition (1969) and the International Tchaikovsky Competition in Moscow (1970). His first appearance outside of the Soviet Union occurred in Germany in 1975, and was followed by performances at the Salzburg Festival in 1976 and in New York City in 1977.

Kremer has performed with nearly every major orchestra in North America and Europe. He is acclaimed for his ability to play virtually any style of music from Baroque compositions to the latest contemporary pieces. He has championed the music of Alfred Schnittke, Arvo Pärt, Giya Kancheli, Sofia Gubaidulina, Valentin Silvestrov, Luigi Nono, Aribert Reimann, Peteris Vasks, John Adams, and Astor Piazzolla.

In 1981 Mr. Kremer founded the Lockenhaus Chamber Music Festival in Austria. In 1997, he founded the Kremerata Baltica Chamber Ensemble to promote outstanding young musicians from the Baltic States. The ensemble's world tours with Kremer have included several visits to the United States, and its performances have consistently received high praise. He has made more than 100 albums, many of which garnered international awards and prizes in recognition of his exceptional and individualistic interpretative power. The ensemble has released a number of CDs for Teldec, Nonesuch, ECM, and Deutsche Grammophon. In 2002, he and the Kremerata Baltica received a Grammy Award for Best Small Ensemble Performance for the Nonesuch recording *After Mozart*. From 2002 until 2006, Kremer was the artistic leader of a new festival in Basel, Switzerland, "Les muséiques."

Kremer plays a "Nicola Amati," dated from 1641, and is the author of four books, published in German, which reflect his artistic pursuits.

BIBLIOGRAPHY

D. Felsenfeld: "Gentle sovereign," *Strings*, xvii/5 (Jan 2003), 54–9

G. Kremer: *Ceļa* (Riga, 2007)

JAMES BASH

Krenek [Křenek], **Ernst** (*b* Vienna, Austria, 23 Aug 1900; *d* Palm Springs, CA, 22 Dec 1991). Composer and writer of Austrian origin, naturalized American in 1945. One of the most prolific composers of the 20th century, he wrote in a wide variety of contemporary idioms.

Krenek began piano lessons at age six and was soon writing short piano pieces. In 1916 he began composition study with Franz Schreker. Conscripted into the Austrian Army during World War I, Krenek was posted to Vienna where he was able to continue his studies. In 1920 he followed Schreker to Berlin, where his mature compositional voice emerged. The stark dissonances and vigorous Bartókian rhythms of the First String Quartet (1921) inspired more than 50 reviews, gaining Krenek a reputation that produced a contract with

Ernst Krenek, 1970. (Horst Tappe/Lebrecht Music & Arts)

Universal Edition. Krenek's radicalism also made him notorious; his atonal Second Symphony (1923) caused an uproar. In late 1922 Krenek was invited to join the board of the newly created ISCM. During the next three years many of his works were performed at ISCM concerts.

In early 1925 Krenek traveled to Paris, where he met Les Six. Deciding that his music should become more accessible, he began sketching ideas for an opera. The completion of *Jonny spielt auf* (1925) marked a return to tonality and the beginning of what Krenek called his neo-Romantic period, influenced in part by his study of Schubert. The opera's premiere in early 1927 soon had Krenek riding a wave of success. After a second trip to Paris, during which he met Antheil, he settled in Vienna. *Leben des Orest* (1928–9), a grand opera, and *Reisebuch aus den österreichischen Alpen* (1929), a cycle of 20 songs extolling the Austrian countryside, date from this period.

On his return to Vienna, Krenek became good friends with Berg and Webern. Although he studied their scores, he did not discuss their music with them. He did engage in discussions with Theodor Adorno, however, with whom he had become friends in 1924. After both were appointed to the board of *Anbruch* in 1928, a debate between them over artistic responsibility appeared in print. Adorno argued that artists had a sociological responsibility to the conditions of the time, while Krenek maintained that artists were responsible only to a personal standard of merit. When Krenek received a commission from the Vienna Staatsoper in 1929, however, he decided to write a work based on the life of Emperor Charles V, reflecting the disintegration of society, extolling Austrian nationalism and employing the new 12-note compositional technique. A meeting with Karl Kraus in 1930 motivated two sets of songs on Kraus's texts (1931) that experiment with 12-note writing. *Karl V*, the first 12-note opera, was completed in 1933. Although political events cancelled its Viennese production, it was performed in Prague in 1938.

After regularly contributing to the arts page of the *Frankfurter Zeitung* from 1930 to 1933, Krenek could no longer write for the German press. The growing Nazi movement branded him a radical artist and banned his music and writings. In 1932 Krenek, Berg, Rudolph Ploderer, and Willi Reich founded *23 (Dreiundzwandzig)*, a satirical magazine they continued to publish until 1937. In 1936 Krenek was also asked to prepare an edition of Monteverdi's *L'incoronazione di Poppea* for the Salzburg Opera Guild's American tour. He traveled to the United States with the company in 1937, presenting lecture recitals and recording his impressions and experiences for the *Wiener Zeitung*. It was on this trip that he first visited Los Angeles and became enamored with the American West.

Shortly after his return to Europe the Nazis annexed Austria and Krenek subsequently immigrated to America, where he became a naturalized citizen. He taught at the Malkin Conservatory, Boston (1938–9), where Schoenberg had begun his American career, the University of Michigan summer school (1939), where his

students included GEORGE PERLE and ROBERT ERICKSON, and Vassar College (1939–42). *Lamentatio Jeremiae prophetae* (1941–2), written after a careful study of Ockeghem editions in the Vassar library, anticipated the serial techniques of Boulez and Stockhausen. In 1942 Krenek accepted a position at Hamline University, St Paul, Minnesota, where he taught until 1947. During the summers he taught at the universities of Michigan and Wisconsin. His close friendship with Mitropoulos and Krasner led to the foundation of the Minneapolis chapter of ISCM. Compositions from the Hamline years include the impassioned *Cantata for Wartime* (1943), the Seventh String Quartet (1943–4), *Santa Fe Timetable* (1945), the lighthearted chamber opera *What Price Confidence?* (1945), the gravely lyrical *Symphonic Elegy* (1946), dedicated to the memory of Webern, and the Fourth Symphony (1947).

In 1947, at the encouragement of Antheil, Krenek moved to Los Angeles, where he hoped to support himself through composition. When he found this to be impossible, he taught at small schools for a number of years. In 1949 he was appointed to a position at the Chicago Musical College (1949), but left Chicago in December due to the cold weather. He returned to Europe in 1950 and 1951 to teach at the Darmstadt summer courses, where he learned about developments in electronic music and heard serial and aleatory works. After an absence of two years (1952–3), however, he found his influence waning in the ascent of Boulez and Stockhausen. Many of his important works were commissioned during this period, among them the chamber operas *Dark Waters* (1950) and *The Bell Tower* (1955–6), the fifth and sixth piano sonatas (1950, 1951), *Eleven Transparencies* (1954), for soprano and orchestra, and *Pallas Athene weint* (1952–5), a parable on the downfall of democracy dedicated to Adlai Stevenson.

In 1955 Krenek was invited by Eimert to work in his electronic music studio. This experience proved pivotal to Krenek's compositional style, resulting in *Spiritus intelligentiae, sanctus* (1955–6), a work for two voices and tape. The electronic medium motivated Krenek to develop a serial idiom; he became interested in the dialectic of predetermination and chance, as well as in the significance of time. As the Christian Gauss lecturer at Princeton University in the spring of 1957, Krenek learned of the medieval poetic form Sestina, which seemed compatible with his serial ideas. In his composition *Sestina* (1957) he combined note row rotations with the medieval form. Many works composed in the following decade continued to employ serial techniques. In 1958 a renewed friendship with Stravinsky after years of estrangement, owing to a satirical remark made by Krenek about 12-note music at the 1925 Congress for Aesthetics, created many opportunities for the discussion of 12-note and serial procedures. He returned to Princeton in 1959 to lecture at the Seminars in Advanced Musical Studies.

In 1960 Krenek received several honors including the Silver Medal of Austria; the Gold Medal of Vienna; and memberships in the Berlin Academy of Arts, the Austrian State Academy of Music, Vienna, and the National

Institute of Arts and Letters, New York. He moved to Palm Springs in 1966, where he served as an adviser in the formation of the music department at the University of California, San Diego (UCSD). During this time, collections of his essays and opera librettos were published. He also composed eight significant orchestral works, five major works for soprano and ensemble, two electronic works (along with several others including electronic music) and two television operas concerning chance and order (*Ausgerechnet und verspielt*, 1961; *Der Zauberspiegel*, 1963–6). He received commissions from the Hamburg State Opera for *Der goldene Bock* (1962–3), a work including elements of surrealism and the absurd, and *Sardakai, oder Das kommt davon* (1967–9), which makes use of ironic elements from the *Così fan tutte* story. His interest in serialism and time were often reflected in the titles of his instrumental music, such as *Quaestio temporis* (1959), *From Three Make Seven* (1960–61), and *Instant Remembered* (1967–8). Some of these works use timbres structurally, as do *Horizon Circled* (1967) and *Statisch und ekstatisch* (1971–2), while others leave a number of parameters open to performer manipulation, or offer performers various ways to combine composed elements.

In 1970 Krenek was appointed to the post of Regent's Lecturer at UCSD. He was awarded the Cross of Austria and a Berlin Festival commission (*Feiertags-Kantate*) in 1975. During the last years of his life his compositional style became more relaxed, though he continued to use elements of 12-note and serial systems. Both his writings and his compositions, such as *Spätlese* (1972) for Fischer-Dieskau, became more introspective and biographical. The last works include the humorous television opera *Flaschenpost vom Paradies* (1972–3), vocal compositions such as *They Knew What they Wanted* (1977), and *The Dissembler* (1978), and three major orchestral compositions, most notably the autobiographical *Arc of Life* (1981). He summarized his compositional career in the Eighth String Quartet (1980–81), a work that quotes from his other quartets. The oratorio *Opus sine nomine* (1980–88) was his final large work. In 1982 he was appointed an honorary citizen of Vienna. He spent his remaining summers at the Arnold Schoenberg House in Mödling. In 1986 the first annual Krenek Prize for composition was established in Vienna.

WORKS
only those works composed since 1938 are listed below

OPERAS
librettos by the composer unless otherwise stated

Tarquin (chbr op, 2, Eng. text by E. Lavery, Ger. text by M.-C. Schulte-Strahaus and P. Funk), op.90, 1940, Poughkeepsie, NY, Vassar College, 13 May 1941; What Price Confidence? [Vertrauenssache] (chbr op, 9 scenes), op.111, 1945, Saarbrücken, Stadt, 23 May 1962

Dark Waters [Dunkle Wasser] (1, after H. Melville: *The Confidence Man*), op.125, 1950, Los Angeles, U. of Southern California, 2 May 1951

Pallas Athene weint (3), op.144, 1952–5, Hamburg, Staatsoper, 17 Oct 1955

The Bell Tower [Der Glockenturm] (1, after Melville), op.153, 1955–6, Urbana, IL, U. of Illinois, 17 March 1957

Ausgerechnet und verspielt (TV op, 1), op.179, 1961, Österreichisches Fernsehen, 25 July 1962

Der goldene Bock [Chrysomallos] (4), op.179, 1962–3, Hamburg, Staatsoper, 16 June 1964

Der Zauberspiegel (TV op, 14 scenes), op.192, 1963–6, Bayerischer Fernsehen, 6 September 1967

Sardakai, oder Das kommt davon (Wenn Sardakai auf Reisen geht) (11 scenes), op.206, 1967–9, Hamburg, Staatsoper, 27 June 1970

Flaschenpost von Paradies, oder Der englische Ausflug (TV op), op.217, 1972–3, Österreichisches Fernsehen, 8 March 1974

OTHER STAGE
Ballets: Eight Column Line, op.85, 1939; Jest of Cards, op.162a, 1962 [arr. from Marginal Sounds, op.162]; Alpbach Qnt (choreog. Y. Georgi), op.180a, wind qnt, perc, 1962

Incid music: König Oedipus, op.188 (Sophocles), 1964

ORCHESTRAL
Syms.: Little Conc., op.88, pf, org, chbr orch, 1939–40; Pf Conc. no.3, op.107, 1946; Conc., op.124, vn, pf, chbr orch, 1950; Pf Conc. no.4, op.123, 1950; Conc., op.126, hp, chbr orch, 1951; 2 Pf Conc., op.127, 1951; Vc Conc. no.1, op.133, 1953; Vn Conc. no.2, op.140, 1953–4; Suite, op.147a, fl, str, 1954; Capriccio, op.145, vc, small orch, 1955; Suite, op.148a, cl, str, 1955; Kitharaulos, op.213, ob, hp, small orch, 1971; Conc., op.230, org, str, 1979; Org Conc., op.235, 1982; Vc Conc. no.2, op.236, 1982

Other: Sym. Piece, op.86, str, 1939; I Wonder as I Wander, op.94, 1942 [variations on North Carolina folksong]; Tricks and Trifles, op.101, 1945 [arr. of Hurricane Variations]; Sym. elegy, op.105, str, 1946; Brazilian Sinfonietta, op.131, str, 1952; Scenes from the West, op.134, school orch, 1952–3; 7 Easy Pieces, op.146, str, 1955; Kette, Kreis und Spiegel, op.160, 1956–7; Hexaedron, op.167, chbr orch, 1958; Quaestio temporis, op.170, small orch, 1959; From Three Make Seven, op.177, 1960–61; Nach wie von der Reihe nach, op.182, 2 spkrs, orch, 1962; 6 Profiles, op.203, 1965–8; Exercises of a Late Hour, op.200, small orch, tape, 1967; Horizon Circled, op.196, 1967; Instant Remembered, S, spkr, orch, tape, 1967–8; Perspectives, op.199, 1967; Fivefold Enfoldment, op.205, 1969; Statisch und ekstatisch, op.214, 1971–2; Auf- und Ablehnung, op.220, 1974; Von vorn herein, op.219, small orch, pf, cel, 1974; Dream Sequence, op.224, wind, 1975; Im Tal der Zeit, op.232, 1979; Arc of Life, op.234, chbr orch, 1981

CHORAL
Mixed vv: Symeon der Stylit (orat), 1935–7, rev. 1987; Lamentatio Jeremiae prophetae, op.93, 1941–2; Santa Fe Timetable, op.102, 1945; O Would I Were, canon, op.109, 1946; 4 Choruses, op.138, mixed vv, org, 1953; Motette zur Opferung, op.141, 3vv, 1954; Ich singe wieder wenn es tagt (W. von der Vogelweide), op.151, mixed vv, str, 1955–6; Proprium missae in domenica III in quadragesima, op.143, 3vv, 1955; Psalmenverse zur Kommunion, op.149, 2–4vv, 1955; Guten Morgen, Amerika (C. Sandburg), op.159, 1956; Missa duodecim tonorum, op.165, mixed vv, org, 1957–8; 6 Motets (F. Kafka), op.169, 4vv, 1959; 3 Madrigals, 3 Motets, op.174, children's vv, 1960; Canon for Stravinsky's 80th Birthday (Krenek), op.181, 2vv, 1962; O Holy Ghost (J. Donne), op.186a, 1964; Glauben und wissen, op.186a, mixed vv, orch, 1966; Deutsche Messe, op.204, mixed vv, insts, 1968; 3 Lessons (Krenek), op.210, 1971; Settings of Poems by William Blake, op.226, 1976; Opus sine nomine (orat), op.238, 1980–88; For Myself, at Eightyfive, canon, op.238a, 4vv, ?1985

Female vv: 2 Choruses on Jacobean Poems (W.H. Drummond, W. Raleigh), op.87, 1939; Proprium missae in festo SS Innocentium martyrum, op.89, 1940; Cant. for Wartime (H. Melville), op.95, female vv, orch, 1943; Aegrotarit Ezechias, motet, op.103, 1944; 5 Prayers (Donne), op.97, 1944; In paradisum, motet, op.106, 1946; Remember Now, motet, op.115a, female vv, pf, 1947

With solo vv: Proprium missae Trinitatis, op.195, S, mixed vv, insts, 1966–7; Messe "Gib uns den Frieden," op.208, solo vv, mixed vv, insts, 1970; Feiertags-Kantate (Krenek), op.221, Mez, Bar, spkr, chorus, orch, 1974–5

SOLO VOCAL
With orch: Medea (dramatic monologue, R. Jeffers, after Euripides), op.129, Mez, orch, 1951; 11 Transparencies, op.142, S, orch, 1954; The Dissembler (monologue, Krenek), op.229, Bar, chbr orch, 1978

With inst(s): The Ballad of the Railroads (Krenek), op.98, 1944; 4 Songs (G.M. Hopkins), op.112, 1946–7; 2 Sacred Songs, op.132, 1952; The Flea (Donne), op.175, 1960; Wechselrahmen (E. Barth), op.189, 1965; 3 Songs (L. von Sauter), op.216, 1972; Spätlese (Krenek), op.218, 1972; Two Silent Watchers (M. Rudulph), op.222, 1975; Albumblatt (Krenek), op.228, 1977

With tape: Spiritus intelligentiae, sanctus, op.152, 2 solo vv, tape, 1955–6; Quintina (Krenek), op.191, S, 6 insts, tape, 1965; They Knew What they Wanted (Krenek), op.227, nar, ob, pf, perc, tape, 1977

Unacc.: Étude, op.104, coloratura S, A, 1945

CHAMBER

3 or more insts: Trio, op.108, vn, cl, pf, 1946; 5 Short Pieces, op.116; Str Qt, 1948; Str Trio, op.118, 1948–9; Parvula corona musicalis ad honorem Johannes Sebastiani Bach, op.122, str trio, 1950; Wind Qnt, op.130, 1952; Marginal Sounds, op.162, vn, pf, perc, 1957; Pentagram, op.163, wind qnt, 1957; Flötenstück neunphasig, op.171, fl, 6 pf, 1959; Hausmusik, op.172, various insts, 1959; Fibonacci mobile, op.187, str qt, pf 4 hands, 1964; Str Qt no.8, op.233, 1980–81; Streichtrio in 12 Stationen, op.235, str trio, 1985; Akrostichon, op.237a, 6 vc, 1987

1–2 insts: Suite, op.84, vc, 1939; Sonata, op.92/3, va, 1942; Sonatina, op.92/2a, fl, va, 1942 [arr. op.92/2b, fl, cl, 1942]; Sonata, op.99, vn, pf, 1944–5; Sonata, op.115, vn, 1948; Sonata, op.117, va, pf, 1948; Phantasiestück, op.135, vc, pf, 1953; Suite, op.147, fl, pf, 1954; Sonata, op.150, hp, 1955; Suite, op.164, gui, 1957; Studien, op.184, vc, 1963; 4 Pieces, op.193, ob, pf, 1966; 5 Pieces, op.198, trbn, pf, 1967; Op.231, vn, org, 1979; Dyophonie, op.241, 2 vc, 1988; Op.239, hn, org, 1988; Suite, op.242, mand, gui, 1989

El-ac: San Fernando Sequence, op.185, tape, 1963; Quintona, op.190, tape, 1965; Doppelt beflügeltes Band, op.207, 2 pf, tape, 1969–70; Duo, op.209, fl, db, tape, 1970; Orga-nastro, op.212, org, tape, 1971

KEYBOARD

Pf: 12 Short Pieces, op.83, 1938; Sonata no.3, op.92/4, 1943; Hurricane Variations, op.100, 1944; 8 Pieces, op.110, 1946; Sonata no.4, op.114, 1948; George Washington Variations, op.120, 1950; Sonata no.5, op.121, 1950; Sonata no.6, op.128, 1951; 20 Miniatures, op.139, 1953–4; Echoes from Austria, op.166, 1958 [arr. Austrian folksongs]; 6 Vermessene, op.168, 1958; Basler Massarbeit, op.173, 2 pf, 1960; Piece, op.197, 1967; Sonata no.7, op.240, 1988

Other: Sonata, op.92/1, org, 1941; Organologia, op.180.5, org, 1962; Toccata, op.183, accdn, 1962; 10 Choral vorspiele, op.211, org, 1971; Acco-muuic, op.225, accdn, 1976; Four Winds, op.223, org, 1979

MSS in A-Wn, Wst, SPma, Wc, U. of California, San Diego
Principal publishers: Bärenreiter, Schott, Universal

WRITINGS
(selective list)

Über neue Musik: sechs Vorlesungen zur Einführung in die theoretischen Grundlagen (Vienna, 1937/R; Eng. trans., rev. 1939/R as *Music Here and Now*)

Studies in Counterpoint, Based on the Twelvetone Technique (New York, 1940; Ger. trans., 1952)

Selbstdarstellung (Zürich, 1948) [rev. and enlarged as "Self Analysis," *New Mexico Quarterly*, xxiii (1953), 5–57]

Musik im goldenen Westen, ed. F. Saathen (Vienna, 1949)

Johannes Okeghem (New York, 1953)

Zur Sprache gebracht (Munich, 1958; Eng. trans. 1966 as *Exploring Music*) [essays]

Tonal Counterpoint in the Style of the 18th Century (New York, 1958)

Gedanken unterwegs, ed. F. Saathen (Munich, 1959) [essays]

Modal Counterpoint in the Style of the 16th Century (New York, 1959)

"Extents and Limits of Serial Techniques," *MQ*, xlvi (1960), pp. 210–32

Komponist und Hörer (Kassel, Germany, 1964)

Prosa, Drama, Verse (Munich, 1965)

Briefwechsel: Theodor W. Adorno und Ernst Krenek (Frankfurt, 1974)

Horizons Circled: Reflections on my Music (Berkeley, 1974)

Das musikdramatische Werk (Vienna, 1974–90) [librettos]

Im Zweifelsfalle (Vienna, 1984) [essays]

Die amerikanischen Tagebücher, 1937–1942 (Vienna, 1992)

ed. S. Schulte: *Im Atem der Zeit: Erinnerungen an die Moderne* (Hamburg, 1998)

Many articles in *Anbruch, Frankfurter Zeitung, Hamline University Bulletin, Measure* [Chicago], *Melos, Musica, Musical America, MQ,*

PNM, Prisma [Stockholm], *University of New Mexico Quarterly*; recorded interviews in *NHoh*

BIBLIOGRAPHY
GMO

R. Erickson: "Křenek's Later Music," *MR*, ix (1948), 29–44

W. Grandi: *Il sistema tonale ed il sontrappunto dodecafonia di Ernst Krenek* (Rome, 1954)

M.J. Colucci: *A Comparative Study of Contemporary Musical Theories in Selected Writings of Piston, Křenek and Hindemith* (diss., U. of Pennsylvania, 1957)

T.W. Adorno: "Zur Physiognomik Ernst Kreneks," *Moments musicaux* (Frankfurt am Main, Germany, 1964)

L. Knessl: *Ernst Krenek*, Österreichische Komponisten des XX. Jahrhunderts, xii (Vienna, 1967)

W. Rogge: *Ernst Kreneks Opern* (Wolfenbüttel, 1970)

J. Hughes: "Ernst Krenek Festival Concerts," *MQ*, lxi (1975), 464–70

O.J. Bailey: *The Influence of Ernst Krenek on the Musical Culture of the Twin Cities* (diss., U. of Minnesota, 1980)

C. Maurer Zenck: *Ernst Krenek, ein Komponist im Exil* (Vienna, 1980)

H.K. Metzger and R. Riehn, eds.: *Ernst Krenek*, Musik-Konzepte, xxxiv/xxxx (1984)

G.H. Bowles: *Ernst Krenek: a Bio-Bibliography* (New York, 1989)

M. Staehle-Laburda: *Ernst Krenek and the 12-Tone Technique* (diss., U. of California, San Diego, 1989)

Newsletter of the Ernst Krenek Archive (La Jolla, CA, 1990)

J.L. Stewart: *Ernst Krenek: the Man and his Music* (Berkeley, 1991)

P.J. Tregear: *Ernst Krenek and the politics of musical style* (diss., Univ. of Cambridge, 1999)

C. Taggatz: *Gesang des Greises: Ernst Krenek und die historische Notwendigkeit des Serialismus* (diss., Universität Münster, 2006)

GARRETT BOWLES/R

Kretszchmar, Florence (*b* Detroit, MI, 22 June 1909; *d* Trenton, MI, 25 Dec 1992). Librarian and publisher. She received a degree in Library and Information Science from Simmons College (BS 1935). She was founder and editor-in-chief of Information Coordinators, Inc., best known as the publisher of *The Music Index*, the first comprehensive index to music periodicals. Under Kretzschmar's guidance the company also published monographs in three series: *Detroit Studies in Music Bibliography, Detroit Monographs in Musicology,* and *Bibliographies of American Music.*

Kretzschmar spent most of her early career at the Detroit Public Library, working in various positions, including in the War Information Center from 1943 to 1945, that gave her experience in technology, business, and commerce. In recognizing the need for an index to music periodical literature, she obtained support from the Music Library Association in 1948, and by 1949, with the help of MLA members Dorothy Tilly and Kurtz Myers, she published the first issue of *The Music Index*. She retired in 1987 and sold Information Coordinators, Inc. but continued to serve as an informal consultant. In August 1987, Information Coordinators changed its name to Harmonie Park Press. Kretzschmar received MLA's Citation for lifetime achievement in 1982.

BIBLIOGRAPHY
"Notes for Notes," *Notes*, xxxvi (1979), 347–9 [interview]

DEBORAH CAMPANA

Kreutz, Arthur (Rudolph) (*b* La Crosse, WI, 25 July 1906; *d* Oxford, MS, 11 March 1991). Composer, conductor, and violinist. He attended the University of Wisconsin

(BS 1930, chemical engineering; BM 1938), the Royal Conservatory in Ghent, Belgium (diploma in violin, 1933), and Teachers College, Columbia University (MA 1940, music education). He also studied composition with CECIL BURLEIGH and ROY HARRIS. He was awarded the Rome Prize by the American Academy in Rome (1940), but remained in New York due to World War II. He taught at the University of Texas at Austin (1942–4), Columbia University (1946–52), and the University of Mississippi (1952–72). During the 1970s he was music director of the Tupelo SO (Mississippi).

The compositions in his Rome Prize entry represent Kreutz's two main styles: light treatments of vernacular music, in the *Paul Bunyan Suite* (1939), and serious concert music, in *Music for Symphony Orchestra* (Symphony no.1, 1940). For many light works, such as *Variations on a Pop Tune* (1945–6) and *Dixieland Concerto* (1949), he drew from his experiences in early jazz bands and the recordings of the violinist Joe Venuti. With his second wife, Zoe Lund Schiller, Kreutz created several stage works for college groups, including *Acres of Sky* (1950), *The University Greys* (1954), and *Sourwood Mountain* (1958). His most accomplished music may be found in his works for featured soloist, particularly *Jazzonata no.1* (1961) for violin and piano, his Violin Concerto no.2 (1965), and Piano Concerto (1970). His papers are housed at the John D. Williams Library at the University of Mississippi.

BIBLIOGRAPHY

D. Ewen: *American Composers: a Biographical Dictionary* (New York, 1982)

E. Komara and L. McNeill [Aldana]: *Arthur Kreutz: a Classified List of Works (Preliminary Version)* (Jackson, 1996)

EDWARD KOMARA

Krick, George C. (*b* Germany, 1872; *d* St. Louis, MO, 3 April 1962). Guitarist, music collector, and teacher. He immigrated to the United States at age 15 and settled in St. Louis. He played banjo and mandolin as well as guitar, and was largely self-taught, although the guitarist WILLIAM FODEN, whom he met in 1904, was his teacher before becoming his duet partner. Krick moved to Philadelphia in 1906, where he founded the Germantown Conservatory and was its director until the early 1940s. While there he edited a column on fretted instruments for *The Etude* magazine, and led the Mandoliers, a fretted-instrument quartet. The last two decades of his life were spent in St. Louis, where he taught privately. Krick met the Spanish guitarist Andrés Segovia when both were on concert tours of Germany in 1924, and was influential in arranging Segovia's first tour of the United States in 1928. He imported much European guitar and mandolin music, building one of the world's richest private collections of guitar music. The collection was left partly to the Gaylord Music Library, Washington University, St. Louis, and partly to the Krick Guitar Guild of St. Louis, which was formed in his honor in 1963.

BIBLIOGRAPHY

D.B. Bowes: "Gentle Champion of Classic Guitar," *St. Louis Post Dispatch* (15 Dec 1961)

"George C. Crick," *Guitar News*, no. 64 (1962), 3

Obituary, *Guitar News*, no. 65 (1962), 15

J. Dallman: *Guitar Teaching in the United States: the Life and Work of Sophocles Papas* (Washington, DC, 1978) [interviews with Papas, pubd by the Washington Guitar Society, containing reminiscences of Krick]

T.F. Heck: *Guitar Music in the Archive of the Guitar Foundation of America and at Cooperating Collections: a Computerized Catalog* (Columbus, OH, 1981) [index to the Krick collection at Washington University]

L.S. Powers: *George C. Krick—American Guitarist: 1871–1962* (diss., U. of Memphis, 2008)

THOMAS F. HECK/R

Kriegsman, Alan M(ortimer) (*b* Brooklyn, NY, 28 Feb 1928). Critic of dance, theater, film, and television. Kriegsman served as critic for the *Washington Post* from 1966 until 1996, when he retired and was named critic emeritus. From 1974 he was the paper's first full-time dance critic, and in 1976 he received the first Pulitzer Prize in criticism to be awarded for dance writing. Initially a physics major at MIT, he received both a BA and an MA in music from Columbia University. Kriegsman has taught at Columbia, Barnard, Harvard, Juilliard, Temple, and George Washington University and has served on the board of the Merce Cunningham Dance Foundation, the Dance Institute of Washington, and the Choo-San Goh & H. Robert Magee Foundation. In 2002 he received a special Metro DC Award for distinguished service in dance. In 2004 he was awarded a special recognition from Dance/USA for "his unique and significant contributions to dance journalism and American dance, spanning the last third of the 20th century." His archives are held by Wc.

BIBLIOGRAPHY

H.-D. Fischer and E.J. Fischer: *The Pulitzer Prize Archive*, vol. 6, *Cultural Criticism, 1969–1990* (Munich, 1992)

ELIZABETH ALDRICH

Krigbaum, Charles Russell (*b* Seattle, WA, 31 March 1929). Organist. He studied with Margaret Maass (piano) in Livingston, New Jersey, and with Margaret McPherson Dubocq (organ) in New York City before entering Princeton (BA 1950, MFA 1952), where he was a pupil of CARL WEINRICH. From 1956 to 1958 he studied on a Fulbright grant with Helmut Walcha at the Hochschule für Musik, Frankfurt am Main, and worked privately with André Marchal. He then joined the faculty of Yale University, where he became university organist in 1965 and professor in 1974. He contributed "A Description of *The Ochsenhausen Manuscript* (1735)" to *Bach-stunden: Festschrift für Helmut Walcha* (1978). Active as a recitalist and recording artist, Krigbaum has displayed a special interest in the organ works of Messiaen. His influence has been most widely felt through his organ students at Yale.

VERNON GOTWALS

Krips, Josef (*b* Vienna, Austria, 8 April 1902; *d* Geneva, Switzerland, 13 Oct 1974). Austrian conductor, brother of the conductor/composer Henry Krips (1912–87).

A student of the Vienna Academy of Music with Eusebius Mandyczewski and Felix Weingartner, he made his concert and opera conducting debut in 1921. He held posts with several Austrian and German opera companies before becoming a resident conductor at the Vienna Staatsoper (1933) and a professor at the Vienna Academy (1935), but lost both positions after the Nazi annexation of Austria in 1938. After World War II he played a leading part in reorganizing musical life in Vienna. He was appointed principal conductor of the London SO (1950–54) and much improved its musical standing. After making his American debut in 1953 with the Buffalo PO (he had been invited to conduct the Chicago SO in 1950 but was refused admittance to the United States by immigration authorities), he became the orchestra's music director (1954–63). He held similar appointments with the Cincinnati May Festival (1954–60) and the San Francisco SO from 1963 to 1970, when he was made conductor emeritus. During Bernstein's sabbatical from the New York PO in the 1964–5 season, Krips led the orchestra for ten weeks, giving a cycle of the Bruckner symphonies. From 1966 he was a guest conductor at the Metropolitan Opera, and from 1970 at the Deutsche Oper, Berlin. His repertory was broad, including the Viennese Classics (Mozart above all) but also music by Stravinsky, Bartók, Hindemith, Janáček, and Shostakovich, and French and Italian opera. Frequent tours with leading orchestras in Europe, North America, and Asia, as well as many recordings, enhanced his reputation. His unaffected interpretations and warmth of expressive feeling served as ideal introductions to the Viennese Classics for a postwar generation of concert-goers.

BIBLIOGRAPHY
H. Stoddard: "Josef Krips," *Symphony Conductors of the U.S.A.* (New York, 1957)
J. Holmes: *Conductors on Record* (Westport, CT, 1982), 366
D. Sheinfeld: *The San Francisco Symphony: Music, Maestros, and Musicians* (Novato, CA, 1983)
J.L. Holmes: *Conductors: a Record Collector's Guide* (London, 1988), 152–5

NOËL GOODWIN/R

Kristofferson [Carson], Kris (*b* Brownsville, TX, 22 June 1936). Country-music singer-songwriter and actor. He studied at Pomona College and attended Oxford University on a Rhodes scholarship. A captain in the U.S. Army, Kristofferson was hired to teach English at the United States Military Academy at West Point in 1965, but he decided instead to move to Nashville to begin a songwriting career. After a brief stint as a helicopter pilot in the Gulf Coast oilfields, he became a janitor at Columbia Records' Nashville studio, where he met many of the city's leading session musicians, recording artists, producers, and songwriters. His first hit songs were "Me and Bobby McGee" (1969, recorded by Roger Miller and later by Janis Joplin), and "Sunday Morning Coming Down" (1970), which earned the 1970 Country Music Association Song of the Year. He also recorded several albums for Fred Foster's Monument Records, including the gold-certified *The Silver-Tongued Devil and I* (1971), and *Jesus Was a Capricorn* (1972), which yielded the chart-topping single "Why Me?" in 1973.

From 1973 to 1979, he was married to the singer Rita Coolidge, with whom he frequently recorded and toured. Kristofferson enjoyed a successful film career in the 1970s and 1980s, earning critical acclaim for his lead roles in Martin Scorsese's *Alice Doesn't Live Here Anymore* (1974) and, with Barbra Streisand, in *A Star Is Born* (1976). In 1985, he joined Willie Nelson, Waylon Jennings, and Johnny Cash to form the country super group, The Highwaymen. In the late 1980s and early 1990s, his songs became increasingly critical of the United States' foreign policy in Latin America, most notably those in his album *Third World Warrior* (1990). He is a member of the Nashville Songwriters' Hall of Fame (1977), the Songwriters' Hall of Fame (1985), and the Country Music Hall of Fame (2004).

BIBLIOGRAPHY
B. Friskics-Warren: "To Beat the Devil: Intimations of Immortality," *No Depression* 62 (March–April 2006)
M. Chapman: *They Came to Nashville* (Nashville, TN, 2010)

STEPHEN HOLDEN/TRAVIS D. STIMELING

Kroeger, Ernest Richard (*b* St Louis, MO, 10 Aug 1862; *d* St Louis, MO, 7 April 1934). Organist, composer, and teacher. He studied piano with his father and with CHARLES KUNKEL. He served as organist at various churches in St Louis, including Trinity Episcopal (1878–85) and the Church of the Messiah (1885–1921). He was one of the founders of the American Guild of Organists in 1896. In 1904 he served as the Master of Musical Programs for the Louisiana Purchase Exposition. In 1915 he was elected to the National Institute of Arts and Letters. He taught and lectured at schools in St. Louis and elsewhere, and contributed articles to various periodicals, including *Kunkel's Musical Review*. Among his numerous compositions are the symphonic poem *Mississippi, Father of Waters* (first performed on 19 February 1926), a String Quartet, and several chamber works with piano, as well as some 175 piano pieces and 80 songs.

JAMES M. BURK

Kroeger, Karl (*b* Louisville, KY, 13 April 1932). Musicologist, music editor, composer, and bibliographer. He studied composition with Claude Almand and GEORGE PERLE at the University of Louisville (BM 1954, MM 1959), composition with GORDON BINKERD and musicology with Dragan Plamenac at the University of Illinois (MS 1961), and musicology with Janet Knapp at Brown University (PhD 1976). From 1962 until 1964 he was curator of the Americana Collection in the Music Division of the New York Public Library and from 1964 to 1967 composer-in-residence with the Eugene (Oregon) public school system as a Ford Foundation Fellow. He taught at Ohio University (1967–8), Moorhead (Minnesota) State College (1971–2), and Wake Forest University at Winston-Salem (North Carolina), where he also served as director of the Moravian Music Foundation from 1972 until 1980. As a Leverhulme Fellow he taught at the University of Keele, UK (1980–81), before becoming associate professor and music librarian at the

University of Colorado, Boulder (1982). He was appointed full professor in 1990 and professor emeritus in 1994, retiring from active teaching at Colorado in 1999. He has won several awards, including the American Bandmasters Association Ostwald Award (1971) and two NEH Senior Research Fellowships (1981, 1989).

Kroeger has made his strongest impact through meticulous and voluminous scholarly editing of well over 1000 individual works, chiefly anthems, hymns, and psalm settings, composed before 1820. His editions include extensive historical commentary, and he has written numerous articles and reviews on Moravian music and other musical subjects in colonial and early Federal period America. He has edited three of the four volumes of *The Complete Works of William Billings*, a volume of American fuging-tunes, the works of Daniel Read, and 15 volumes in the series *Music of the New American Nation*, which include the works of 23 composers active before 1820. He also cataloged the musical works of William Billings and American fuging-tunes from 1770 to 1820. With Marie Kroeger, he prepared *Index of Anglo-American Psalmody in Modern Critical Editions* (Madison, WI, 2001).

Kroeger's own music, which has been performed in the United States, South America, and Europe, is tonal, rhythmically varied, and in traditional forms. His compositions include a symphony (1965, rev. 2002), two suites for orchestra (2002, 2003), two suites for wind band (1958, 1982), and 15 other works for large instrumental ensembles; 18 chamber works, including 3 string quartets and 4 canzonas for brass; 12 pieces for keyboard; and 25 works for solo and choral voices, some with instruments. His principal publishers are Boosey & Hawkes, Brodt, Broude, CMP, Carl Fischer, Tenuto, Merion Music, Joseph Boonin, Tritone, and Lawson-Gould.

EDITIONS

A Moravian Music Sampler (Winston-Salem, NC, 1974)
The Complete Works of William Billings, i, iii, iv (Charlotteville, VA, 1981, 1986, 1990)
Pelissier's Columbian Melodies: Music for the New York and Philadelphia Theaters, RRAM, xiii–xiv (Madison, WI, 1984)
The Collected Works of Daniel Read, MUSA, iv (Madison, WI, 1995)
Music of the New American Nation (New York, 1995–9)
D. Read: *Musica Ecclesia*, i, ii, iii [with M. Kroeger] (Madison, WI, 2005)
D. Moritz Michael: *Der 103te Psalm* (Madison, WI, 2008)
Anthems and several separate works in folio editions of two dozen other composers.

KATHERINE K. PRESTON/THOMAS L. RIIS

Kroll, William (*b* New York, NY, 30 Jan 1901; *d* Boston, MA, 10 March 1980). Violinist. He studied at the Berlin Hochschule with Henri Marteau (1911–4), made his debut in New York in 1915, and continued his studies with violinist FRANZ KNEISEL and theorist PERCY GOETSCHIUS at the Institute of Musical Art, New York (1917–22). As a soloist, and chamber music player with groups such as the Elshuco Trio (1922–9), the Coolidge Quartet (1936–44), and the Kroll Quartet (1944–69), he toured extensively in the United States, Mexico, Canada, and Europe. In the years 1958–9 he played sonatas with Arthur Balsam, mainly in Europe. In 1942 he was awarded the Coolidge Medal for services to chamber music.

Kroll taught at the Institute of Musical Art (1922–38), at the Peabody Conservatory (1947–65), and at the Cleveland Institute (1964–7). In 1943 he joined the staff of the Mannes College, New York, and in 1949 he began teaching at Tanglewood. In 1969 he was appointed professor of the violin at Queens College, New York. He published works for string quartet, chamber orchestra, and solo violin. Kroll's playing combined vigor and elegance, and he was at his best in chamber music. He played the "ex-Ernst" Stradivari of 1709.

BORIS SCHWARZ/MARGARET CAMPBELL

Kronos Quartet. String quartet formed in Seattle in 1973. It was founded by violinists David Harrington and James Shaellenberger, violist Tim Kilian, and cellist Walter Gray. It served a two-year residency at SUNY, Geneseo (1975–7) and underwent several personnel changes—Shaellenberger being replaced in turn by Roy Lewis (1975–7) and Ella Gray (1977–8), and Kilian being succeeded by Michael Jones (1976–7) and Hank Dutt—before relocating to San Francisco in 1978. At that point John Sherba came in as second violinist and Joan Dutcher Jeanrenaud as cellist to join Harrington and Dutt. For a time the group was based at Mills College, Oakland, but since 1982 it has been in residence at the University of Southern California. In 1999 Jeanrenaud left the ensemble and was replaced by Jennifer Culp. Culp left in 2005 and was replaced by Jeffrey Ziegler. Despite its changes of personnel, the quartet has retained its distinctive aggressiveness as it responds to the challenge of the most formidable scores with fervor and vitality.

Since making its New York debut in 1984, the quartet typically spends five months of each year on tour, appearing in concert halls, clubs, and festivals around the world. From the beginning, the ensemble has concentrated on new music and has commissioned more than 700 works and arrangements. Among its numerous notable premieres are Hamza El Din's *Escalay: The Water Wheel* (1992), Henryk Górecki's *Already it is dusk* (1988), Sofia Gubaidulina's *Fourth Quartet*, Thomas Oboe Lee's *Third String Quartet...Child of Uranus, Father of Zeus* (1982), Terry Riley's *Salome Dances for Peace* (1989) and *The Cusp of Magic* (2005), John Zorn's *The Dead Man*, Paul Dresher's *Casa Vecchia* (1982), John Cage's *30 Pieces for String Quartet* (1983), and Pauline Oliveros's *The Wheel of Time* (1983). Morton Feldman wrote his four-hour Second Quartet and 80-minute Piano Quintet for the group, which has also collaborated extensively with Philip Glass, recording his complete string quartets and many film scores. Its enterprising recitals and its 45 recordings (to date) range widely, including new music (Aleksandra Vrebalov, John Adams, and Alfred Schnittke), 20th-century classics (Ives, Nancarrow, Schoenberg, Webern, Berg, Bartók, and Shostakovich), and stylized interpretations of jazz and rock (Charles Mingus, Thelonious Monk, and Jimi Hendrix). Of special note are its recordings of

George Crumb's *Black Angels* and Steve Reich's *Different Trains*, a haunting work dedicated to the ensemble. It has received many awards, including a Grammy for Best Chamber Music Performance (2004) and "Musicians of the Year" (2003) from Musical America. The quartet has mentored young professional performers, and in 2007 it led its first masterclass as part of the Weill Music Institute at Carnegie Hall.

BIBLIOGRAPHY

D. Richardson: "Portrait of a Quartet," *Strings*, xiii/5 (1999), 48–57

D. Headlam: "Re-drawing Boundaries: the Kronos Quartet," *CMR*, xix/1 (2000), 113–40

J. McCalla: *Twentieth-Century Chamber Music* (New York, 2003)

D. Bennett: "Postmodern Eclecticism and the World Music Debate: The Politics of the Kronos Quartet," *Context: a Journal of Music Research*, xxix–xxx (2005), 5–15

MICHAEL WALSH/JAMES BASH

Krosnick, Joel (*b* New Haven, CT, 3 April 1941). Cellist. He studied with William D'Amato, LUIGI SILVA, Jens Nygaard, and CLAUS ADAM. In 1962 he cofounded and directed the Group for Contemporary Music at Columbia University, where he also studied. From 1963 to 1966 he was a professor at the University of Iowa and cellist of the university string quartet. He held a similar position at the University of Massachusetts (1966–70), while performing with the New York Chamber Soloists and touring as a soloist to London, Berlin, Amsterdam, Hamburg, and Belgrade; he made his New York solo debut in 1970. From 1970 to 1974 he taught at the California Institute of the Arts and then joined the JUILLIARD STRING QUARTET, succeeding his teacher Claus Adam. He is a well-known exponent of modern scores, and has given the premieres of works by Ligeti, Samuel, Shapey, Babbitt, Karlins, and Subotnick. Krosnick has worked extensively with pianist Gilbert Kalisch since 1976 and the two of them have performed the sonata repertory throughout the world, often featuring new music on their programs. He also holds honorary doctorates from many institutions, including the San Francisco Conservatory of Music. His recording of Carter's Cello Sonata reveals an intensely focused though not large tone, and a degree of rhythmic agility not usually found in players of low string instruments. Krosnick has twice received Grammy Awards and has been nominated for several more.

RICHARD BERNAS/JONAS WESTOVER

KRS-One [Parker, Lawrence "Krisna"] (*b* Brooklyn, NY, 20 Aug 1965). Rapper and activist. Parker grew up in the Park Slope area of Brooklyn. By age 13 he was homeless and drifted among shelters and libraries where he read voraciously. At one shelter, he met a social worker, Scott Sterling, who also DJ'ed in the evenings under the name Scott La Rock. Parker adapted his graffiti tag, KRS-One, as his stage name, and the duo called themselves BDP (Boogie Down Productions). They released their first single, "Crack Attack," on B-Boy Records in 1986. In 1987, their debut album, *Criminal Minded* appeared; later that year, La Rock was shot to death. KRS-One decided to forge ahead with a new lineup for BDP and released *By All Means Necessary* in 1988.

At a 1988 concert featuring BDP, a fan was killed in a fight. KRS-One launched the "Stop the Violence" movement in response to the tragedy. This initiative raised KRS-One's profile and made him an in-demand commentator on hip hop culture. He lectured at universities all around the country and wrote op-ed pieces for the *New York Times*. He was honored at the 2008 BET Awards with a Lifetime Achievement Award for his devotion to this cause.

KRS-One's style often features a reggae-influenced delivery. His material is wide-ranging: he is credited with laying the foundation for both gangsta rap and socially conscious rap. He saw himself as a teacher, believing that a lack of education was the biggest problem facing urban youth. He occasionally adopted the moniker "The Teacher," and even stated that KRS-One stood for "Knowledge Reigns Supreme Over Nearly Everyone."

BDP released two more albums, *Edutainment* (1990) and *Sex and Violence* (1992) before disbanding. KRS-One launched his solo career in 1993 with *Return of the Boom-Bap*. Three albums followed during the period from 1995 until 1997. In 1996, KRS-One founded the Temple of Hiphop, an organization whose mission is "to promote, preserve, and protect Hip hop as a strategy toward health, love, awareness, and wealth for all who declare 'hip hop' their lifestyle" (the word "hip hop" is not hyphenated to signify the unity among members of the hip hop community).

KRS-One returned to recording in 2001 and released a string of albums at the rate of roughly one per year; none of these has received the acclaim of his early work with BDP.

MICHAEL BERRY

Krueger, Karl (Adelbert) (*b* Atchison, KS, 19 Jan 1894; *d* Elgin, IL, 21 July 1979). Conductor. As a youth he learned cello and organ, then studied at Midland College in Atchison, Kansas (BA 1913), the New England Conservatory with GEORGE WHITEFIELD CHADWICK and WALLACE GOODRICH (1914–5), and the University of Kansas (MA 1916). After serving as organist and choirmaster of St. Ann's Episcopal Church, New York (1916–20), he toured Brazil as an organist (1920), then went to Vienna to continue his musical studies with Robert Fuchs and Franz Schalk (1920–2). He also studied economics at the universities of Vienna and Heidelberg before returning to the United States late in 1922. Krueger's conducting career included positions as assistant to the conductor of the Vienna Staatsoper (1920–2) and conductor of the Seattle SO (1925–32), the Kansas City PO (1933–43), and the Detroit Orchestra (1943–9); he also appeared as a guest conductor in the United States and abroad. In each of these positions, his powerful direction led to a leap in the prestige of the organization, especially in Seattle. His work was strong enough that his tenure in Kansas City was as the founding conductor of that institution. In 1950 he organized the American Arts Orchestra for radio broadcasts in New York;

the programs lasted one season. In 1958 he founded the Society for the Preservation of the American Musical Heritage, for which he made a number of recordings in England with the Royal PO. He was the first American-born conductor to become music director of an important American orchestra. He wrote two books, *The Way of the Conductor: His Origins, Purpose and Procedures* (1958) and *The Musical Heritage of the United States: The Unknown Portion* (1973).

MARTHA D. MINOR/R

Krummel, D(onald) W(illiam) (*b* Sioux City, IA, 12 July 1929). Music librarian, bibliographer, and educator. He received the BMus (1951), the MMus (1953), and the MA (1954) and PhD (1958) in library science, all from the University of Michigan. He taught at the University of Michigan from 1952 to 1956; from 1956 to 1961 he was a reference librarian in the music division of the Library of Congress. In 1962 he joined the Newberry Library in Chicago, first as head of the reference department, then as associate librarian. In 1970 he was appointed professor of library science and music at the University of Illinois. He held a Guggenheim Fellowship in 1976–7, and was director of the pioneering project Resources of American Music History, funded by the National Endowment for the Humanities, from 1976 to 1979. His accolades include the G.K. Hall Award for Library Literature in 1987 and the Lowens Award from the Society for American Music in 1989.

Krummel's principal fields of research are music printing and publishing, and early American music. In his dissertation and subsequent writings, he has been concerned with the dating of music publications, particularly those issued by American publishers; he has employed both cultural and bibliographical evidence, including graphic analysis, to the study of the printed musical page. As a commentator on libraries and their central role in the development of intellectual endeavor, Krummel has been a tireless advocate. As an educator of music librarians and bibliographers Krummel has greatly influenced a generation of scholar-librarians.

Krummel has been an active member of the Music Library Association (serving as president 1981–3) and the International Association of Music Libraries, Archives, and Documentation. He also compiled the quarterly book list for the *Musical Quarterly* (1957–60) and has been an enthusiastic reviewer throughout his career. Following his official retirement in 1997, Krummel has continued to teach at the University of Illinois and at the Rare Books School held each summer at the University of Virginia (and previously at Columbia University).

WRITINGS

Philadelphia Music Engraving and Publishing, 1800–1820: a Study in Bibliography and Cultural History (diss., U. of Michigan, 1958)
"Graphic Analysis: its Application to Early American Engraved Music," *Notes*, xvi (1958–9), 213–33
with J.B. Coover: "Current National Bibliographies: their Music Coverage," *Notes*, xvii (1959–60), 375–84
"Late 18th Century French Music Publishers' Catalogs in the Library of Congress," *FAM*, vii (1960), 61–4
"Twenty Years of *Notes*: a Retrospect," *Notes*, xxi (1963–64), 56–82

"The Newberry Library, Chicago," *FAM*, xvi (1969), 119–24
Bibliotheca Bolduaniana: a Renaissance Music Bibliography (Detroit, 1972)
Guide for Dating Early Published Music (Hackensack, NJ, 1974)
English Music Printing, 1553–1700 (London, 1975)
"Musical Functions and Bibliographical Forms," *The Library*, 5th ser., xxi (1976), 327–50
ed.: *Bibliographical Inventory to the Early Music in the Newberry Library, Chicago, Illinois* (Boston, 1977)
"Little RAMH, Who Made Thee? Observations on an American Music Census," *Notes*, xxxvii (1980), 227–38
Resources of American Music History: a Directory of Source Materials from Colonial Times to World War II (Urbana, IL, 1981)
with R. Crawford: "Early American Music Printing and Publishing," *Printing and Society in Early America*, ed. W.L. Joyce (Worcester, MA, 1983), 186–227
Bibliographies: their Aims and Methods (London, 1984)
"The Second Twenty Years of *Notes*: a Retrospective Re-Cast," *Notes*, xli (1984), 7–25
"The Origins of Modern Music Classification," *Festschrift Albi Rosenthal*, ed. R. Elvers (Tutzing, 1984), 181–98
"Early German Partbook Type Faces," *Gutenburg Jb*, lx (1985), 80–98
"Citing the Score: Descriptive Bibliography and Printed Music," *The Library* 6th ser., ix (1987), 329–46
"The Beginnings of Current National Bibliography for German Music," *Richard S. Hill: Tributes*, ed. C.J. Bradley and J.B. Coover (Detroit, 1987), 307–29
Bibliographical Handbook of American Music (Urbana, IL, 1987)
The Memory of Sound: Observations on the History of Music on Paper (Washington DC, 1988)
"The Presence of the Note: Modern Music Publishing," *Modern Music Librarianship: Essays in Honor of Ruth Watanabe*, ed. A. Mann (Stuyvesant, NY, 1989), 41–58
"Accustomed to the Interface: Observations on the Bibliography of American Music," *A Celebration of American Music: Words and Music in Honor of H. Wiley Hitchcock*, ed. R.A. Crawford, R.A. Lott and C.J. Oja (Ann Arbor, 1990), 427–38
"Searching and Sorting on the Slippery Slope: Periodical Publications of Victorian Music," *Notes*, xlvi (1990), 593–608
with Stanley Sadie, *Music Printing and Publishing* (London, 1990)
"Singing the Body Eclectic: Immigrant Cultural Resources in America's Music Libraries," *Harvard Library Bulletin* new ser., ii (1991), 77–84
The Literature of Music Bibliography: an Account of the Writings on the History of Music Printing & Publishing (Berkeley, 1992)
"The Varieties and Uses of Music Bibliography," *Music Reference Services Quarterly*, ii (1993), 1–25
"The Bay Psalm Book Tercentenary, 1698–1998," *Notes*, lv (1998), 281–86
"On Digressive Music Bibliography," *Notes* lvi (2000), 867–78
"Petruccio's Predicament and the Taming of the Muse," *Inte Bara Katalogregler: Festskrift till Anders Lönn*, ed. V. Heintz (Stockholm, 2003), 49–58
"*Notes*: A Sixtieth Birthday Retrospective," *Notes*, lxi (2004), 9–23
"Early American Imprint Bibliography and its Stories: An Introductory Course in Bibliographical Civics," *Libraries & Culture*, xl (2005), 239–50

BIBLIOGRAPHY

D. Hunter, ed.: *Music Publishing & Collecting: Essays in Honor of Donald W. Krummel* (Urbana, IL, 1994) [incl. list of writings]

PAULA MORGAN/DAVID HUNTER

Krupa, Gene [Eugene Bertram] (*b* Chicago, IL, 15 Jan 1909; *d* Yonkers, NY, 16 Oct 1973). Jazz drummer. Although he consciously modeled his drumming style on that of his idols, Chick Webb and Baby Dodds, he became the first superstar of drumming, bringing great showmanship and charisma to the role of the drummer. He was the first to draw a large audience's attention to the drummer's role in a band being more than that of just a timekeeper. He was the first true drum soloist, introducing the idea and practice of the extended drum solo into jazz ensemble performances, most famously with Benny Goodman's "Sing Sing Sing" (1937, Vic.). Krupa is also credited with having persuaded the drum manufacturer Slingerland to produce tunable tom-toms, in 1936; before this only the bass and snare drums of the kit had adjustable tuning. Drummers ever since have been able to personalize the sound of their instruments through how they pitch their drums.

In 1927, during a recording session with Eddie Condon, Krupa became the first drummer to have his bass drum recorded, after insisting that the recording engineers find a way to prevent the needle from jumping. Krupa rose to prominence in Benny Goodman's band. Goodman shared Krupa's passion for playing hot jazz rather than the dance music usually required of big bands in the mid-1930s. The two shared a working relationship that Krupa described as "magical…a deeply musical experience." Krupa led his own big band from 1938 into the 1950s and was among the first bandleaders to introduce bebop to the big band format. Throughout the 1950s and 60s he also led the Gene Krupa Trio and played in the Benny Goodman Quartet. Krupa provided the drumming for the soundtrack to *The Gene Krupa Story* (1959), in which his character was played by Sal Mineo.

Much was made of the supposed rivalry between Krupa and his friend and protégé Buddy Rich. However, the two men admired one another's playing, and Rich acknowledged that without Krupa he would not have earned the fame and respect that he did. Krupa was responsible for making drummers worthy of note as legitimate musicians. From 1941 he ran an annual drumming contest, which was won in the first year by Louie Bellson. With fellow drummer Cozy Cole he opened the Krupa–Cole Drum School in New York, which ran from March 1954 until Krupa's death in 1973.

RECORDINGS
(selective list)
As leader: with B. Rich: *Krupa and Rich* (1955, Clef), *The Drum Battle: Gene Krupa and Buddy Rich at JATP* (1952 Polygram); *The Gene Krupa Story* (1999, Proper Box)
As sideman with B. Goodman: *The Famous 1938 Jazz Concert* (1938, Col.)

BIBLIOGRAPHY
K. Larcombe: "Gene Krupa: 1909–1973," *Modern Drummer*, iii/5 (1979), 12–4
B. Korall: *Drumming Men the Heartbeat of Jazz: the Swing Years* (New York, 1990)
R. Spagnardi: *The Great Jazz Drummers* (Cedar Grove, 1992)
A. Budofsky: *The Drummer: 100 Years of Rhythmic Power and Invention* (Cedar Grove, 2006)

GARETH DYLAN SMITH

Kryl, Bohumir (*b* nr Prague, Bohemia, 2 May 1875; *d* Wilmington, NY, 7 Aug 1961). Cornetist and conductor of Bohemian birth. He began studying violin when he was ten, but ran away from home the following year to join a circus as a tumbler and trapeze artist. At 14 he earned his passage to the United States by playing violin and cornet in a ship's orchestra. He settled in Indianapolis, where he joined the When (Clothing Company) Band, and built a reputation as a cornetist. In 1898 he joined Sousa's Band, but left it to play for two seasons with T.P. Brooke's Band; he then joined Innes's Band as a soloist, and in 1901 became its assistant conductor. In 1906 he formed the Bohemian Band, which for the next 25 years played at fairs, expositions, and on the Chautauqua circuit. He later formed a women's symphony orchestra, with which he appeared as conductor and soloist. As a cornetist, he was noted for his brilliant technique, rich velvet tone, and deep pedal tones. Continuing to play cornet into his late 60s, he once remarked that he had played over 12,000 solos in his lifetime and had traveled over 1,000,000 miles.

BIBLIOGRAPHY
H.W. Schwartz: *Bands of America* (Garden City, NY, 1957)
N.H. Quayle: "The Cornet's Sole Survivor," *MJ*, xix/6 (1961), 44, 97
G.D. Bridges: *Pioneers in Brass* (Detroit, 1972); CD-ROM (Coupeville, WA, 2000)
W.H. Rehrig: *The Heritage Encyclopedia of Band Music* (Westerville, OH, 1991, suppl. 1996); CD-ROM (Oskaloosa, IA, 2005)

RAOUL F. CAMUS

Kubera, Joseph (*b* Buffalo, NY, 25 May 1949). Pianist. He is best known for his performances of contemporary music. He studied piano with Warren Case at the Community Music School in Buffalo, with LEO SMIT at SUNY, Buffalo (BFA 1969), and with Walter Hautzig at the Peabody Conservatory (MA 1970). From 1974 until1976 he held a fellowship from the Center for the Creative and Performing Arts at SUNY, Buffalo. He has also received grants through the NEA Solo Recitalist Program and the Foundation for Contemporary Performance Arts. He is well known as an interpreter of the music of John Cage, having recorded the complete *Music of Changes* and the Concert for Piano and Orchestra, and having toured with the Merce Cunningham Dance Company at Cage's invitation. Composers who have written for him include Larry Austin, Anthony Coleman, Alvin Lucier, Roscoe Mitchell, and "Blue" Gene Tyranny. He is a core member of S.E.M. Ensemble and Orchestra and the Downtown Ensemble. He formed a duo-team with pianist Sarah Cahill, for whom Terry Riley and Ingram Marshall have written, and tours with baritone Thomas Buckner. He has performed as soloist at such festivals as the Berlin Inventionen, the Warsaw Autumn and Prague Spring, Miami's Subtropics Festival and Berkeley's Edgefest. He has recorded for New World, New Albion, Albany, and Opus One labels, among others.

STEPHEN RUPPENTHAL/ELIZABETH N. MORGAN

Kubik, Gail (Thompson) (*b* South Coffeyville, OK, 5 Sept 1914; *d* West Covina, CA, 20 July 1984). Composer. At the age of 15 he won a full scholarship to the Eastman School, where he studied violin with Samuel Belov and composition with BERNARD ROGERS and Edward Royce (1930–34). He then joined the faculty of Monmouth College (Illinois) and continued his compositional studies with WALTER PISTON and NADIA BOULANGER at Harvard University (1937–8). After serving as staff composer and program adviser for NBC radio in New York (1940–41), he became music consultant to the Office of War Information film bureau

(1942–3) and composed superlative scores to a number of documentary films, after which he joined the First Motion Picture Unit of the US Army Air Corps as a staff composer scoring documentary films, the most famous of which is *The Memphis Belle*. He served in the army until 1946, gaining a reputation as one of the foremost composers for wartime documentaries. After leaving military service, he taught briefly at the University of Southern California and composed for the CBS radio network, in Hollywood, before moving to New York City. There, he arranged a number of very successful pieces of Americana for Robert Shaw's vocal ensemble and returned to film scoring with Joseph Lerner's *C-Man*. This imaginative and carefully wrought film score received immediate critical and scholarly attention and later became the basis for his Pulitzer Prize–winning composition, Symphony Concertante. He returned to Hollywood briefly to score two innovative cartoons for John Hubley and United Productions of America, *Gerald McBoing Boing*, which won the Academy Award (1951), and *The Miner's Daughter*. 1950 marked his receipt of the Rome Prize and inaugurated the first of two long periods spent in Europe (1950–5, 1959–67). In 1955, Kubik returned to Hollywood to score William Wyler's film, *The Desperate Hours*, and his trenchant music pushed the boundaries of traditional Hollywood film scores. Back in New York, Kubik provided noteworthy scores for two television programs, "Hiroshima" and "The Silent Sentinel," for the CBS series *The Twentieth Century*. From 1970 until his retirement in 1980 he was composer-in-residence at Scripps College in Claremont, California. His awards include the Jascha Heifetz prize for his violin concerto (1940–41), two Guggenheim Fellowships (1944, 1965), and the Pulitzer Prize, which, as its youngest recipient to that date, he won for Symphony Concertante (1952). His Second and Third Symphonies were commissioned respectively by the Louisville Orchestra and the New York PO. Kubik's music, though often dissonant and angular, remains tonal, notable for its rhythmic vitality and virtuosity as well as its fine craftsmanship and orchestration. Equally adept at writing for the concert hall as for broadcast media, he derived many of his concert works from his scores for film, radio, and television. In this regard, he was exceptional. For much of his career he was considered a modernist: the forceful idiom of his music for William Wyler's film *The Desperate Hours* led the studio, Paramount, to cut much of it and, in a surprising and unprecedented gesture, return the musical rights to him. In later life, he felt ill at ease with changing musical styles, and he composed little between 1959 and 1967. He returned to composing in 1968 and, for the next decade, wrote a number of choral and chamber pieces, as well as music for a radio documentary. His finest work is to be found in his film scores, vocal and choral compositions, and chamber music. His symphonies and violin concerto, though not often heard, contain well-crafted and compelling music.

WORKS
(selective list)

Dramatic: Puck: a Legend of Bethlehem (radio score), 1940; Men and Ships (film score), 1940; They Walk Alone (incid music, play), 1941; The World at War (film score), 1942; Paratroops (film score), 1942; Dover (film score), 1943; Earthquakers (film score), 1943; The Memphis Belle (film score), 1944; Thunderbolt (film score), 1945; A Mirror for the Sky (folk op), 1946; Frankie and Johnnie (ballet seq), 1946; C-Man (film score), 1949; Gerald McBoing-Boing (animated film score), 1950, concert version for nar, 9 insts, perc, 1950; The Miner's Daughter (animated film score), 1950; Two Gals and a Guy (film score), 1951; Transatlantic: a Shortcut through History (animated film score), 1952; The Desperate Hours (film score), 1955; Hiroshima (TV score), 1958; The Silent Sentinel (TV score), 1958; Down to Earth (animated film), 1959; The Eisenhower Years (radio score), 1970

Orch: American Caprice, pf, orch, 1932, rev. 1936; Lyric Piece, vn, orch, 1934, rev. 1936; Variations on a 13th-Century Troubadour Song, 1935, rev. 1937; Vn Conc., 1939–40, rev. 1941; Scherzo, 1941; Folk Song Suite, 1941–4; The Erie Canal, 1944; Memphis Belle, spkr, orch, 1944; Toccata, org, str, 1946; Spring Valley Overture, 1947, rev. 1969–73 as Pastorale and Spring Valley Ov.; Sym. no.1, Eb, 1947–9; Sym. Concertante, pf, va, tpt, orch, 1951, rev. 1953; Bennie the Beaver: a Children's Story for nar, solo perc, and chbr orch, 1952; 54–40 or Fight: Centennial March, 1952; A Mirror for the Sky, Ov., 1946–52; Thunderbolt Ov., 1953; Sym. no.2, F, 1954–6; Scenario for Orch, 1955–57; A Festival Opening, 1957; Sym. no. 3, 1956; Scenes for Orch, (music composed for the film "I thank a fool"), 1964; Prayer and Toccata, org, chbr orch, 1969

Band: Stewball, 1942; Fanfare and March, 1945; Fanfare for One World, 1947; Fanfare for the Century, 3 tpt, 3 trbn, 1968

Vocal: In Praise of Johnny Appleseed (V. Lindsay), B-Bar, chorus, orch, 1938, rev. 1961; Litany and Prayer, male chorus, brass, perc, 1943–5; A Mirror for the Sky, folk op in two acts, 1946–47; Boston Baked Beans: a New England Fable, S, Bar, cl, tpt, pf, db, 1950; Fables in Song (T. Roethke), Mez/Bar, pf, 1950–69; A Christmas Set (medieval), chbr chorus, chbr orch, 1968; A Record of our Time (cant.), nar, chorus, orch, 1970; Scholastica, unacc., 1972; Magic, Magic, Magic!, A, chbr chorus, chbr orch, 1973–6

Chbr and solo inst: Two Sketches for String Quartet, 1931, rev. 1936; Trivialities, fl, hn, str qt, 1934–6; Pf Trio, a, 1934; Serenade for Violoncello and Piano, 1936; Celebrations and Epilogue, pf, 1938–50; Suite for Three Recorders, 1941, also arranged as Little Suite for Flute and Two Clarinets, 1948; Nocturne for Flute and Piano, 1947; Soliloquy and Dance, vn, pf, 1948; Song and Scherzo, 2 pf, 1940, rev. 1961; Pf Sonatina, 1941; Sonatina, vn, pf, 1941; Sonata, vn, pf, 1947; Celebrations for Ww Qnt, 1958; Divertimento no.1, 13 players, 1958; Divertimento no.2, 8 players, 1958; Sonatina, cl, pf, 1959; Intermezzo: Music for Cleveland, pf, 1967; Five Birthday Pieces for recorders or fl, cl, 1968–74; Music for Bells, handbells, 1969; A Kansas Idyll, vn, vc, pf, 1970; 5 Theatrical Sketches (Divertimento no.3), pf trio, 1970–1; Sym., Eb, 2 pf, 1979 (based on Sym. no.1)

Principal publishers: Boosey & Hawkes, Chappell, Colombo, MCA, Paramount, Ricordi, G. Schirmer, Southern

Most of Kubik's music is held at Kansas State University and the Library of Congress.

BIBLIOGRAPHY

F.W. Sternfeld: "Gail Kubik's Score for *C-Man*," *Hollywood Quarterly*, iv/4 (Summer 1950), 360–9

E. Helm: "Gail Kubik's Score for *C-Man*: the Sequel," *Quarterly of Film Radio and Television*, ix/3 (Spring 1955), 263–82

I. Bazelon: *Knowing the Score: Notes on Film Music* (New York, 1973), 287–97

M.D. Lyall: *The Piano Music of Gail Kubik* (DMA diss., Peabody Institute, Johns Hopkins U., 1980)

A. Cochran: "Kubik, Gail T.," *American National Biography*, ed. J.A. Garraty and M.C. Carnes (New York, 1998)

A. Cochran: "The Functional Music of Gail Kubik: Catalyst for the Concert Hall," *Indiana Theory Review*, xix (Spring-Fall 1998), 1–11

A. Cochran: "Cinema Music of Distinction: Virgil Thomson, Aaron Copland, and Gail Kubik," *Perspectives on American Music, 1900–1950*, ed. Michael Saffle (New York: Garland, 2000), 323–48

A. Cochran: "The Documentary Film Scores of Gail Kubik," *Film Music: Critical Approaches*, ed. K.J. Donnelly (New York, 2001), 117–28

A. Cochran: "Works of Distinction: the Functional Music of Gail Kubik," *Film Music 2: History, Theory, Practice*, ed. C. Gorbman, W. Sherk (Sherman Oaks, CA, 2004)

ALFRED W. COCHRAN

Kuchar, Theodore (*b* New York, NY, 31 May 1960). Conductor and violist. A graduate of the Cleveland Institute of Music, he is known for extensive recordings on Naxos, Brilliant Classics, and Marco Polo. In 1992, Kuchar was appointed Principal Guest Conductor of the Ukrainian State Symphony Orchestra, and later Artistic Director and Principal Conductor of the renamed (1994) National Symphony Orchestra of Ukraine (NSOU). His recordings of the complete symphonies of Boris Lyatoshynsky for Marco Polo (1993, 1994) marked the first time a significant Ukrainian composer was featured on a major international recording label. This was followed by over 80 CDs with that orchestra for Naxos of the cycle of the complete orchestral works of Prokofiev, and works by Tchaikovsky, Borodin, Mussorgsky, Khachaturian as well as several early entries in the noted Naxos "American Classics" series, including works by Piston, Antheil, Lees, Harris, and Gould. In 2004 he was appointed Conductor Laureate for Life of the NSOU. In 2005 he became Artistic Director and Principal Conductor of the Janacek Philharmonic Orchestra (in the Czech Republic) with which he has recorded the complete symphonies of Nielsen, and orchestral works of Smetana and Dvořák for Brilliant Classics.

Kuchar divides his time between international and American activities. He is currently Music Director and Principal Conductor of both the Fresno Philharmonic and the Reno Chamber Orchestra. He serves as Resident Conductor of the Kent/Blossom Music Festival and Artistic Director of the Nevada Chamber Music Festival (since 2005), and was Artistic Director of the Australian Festival of Chamber Music (1990–2006). In 2011, he began leading the Orquesta Sinfonica de Venezuela (National Symphony Orchestra of Venezuela).

DENIS HLYNKA

Kuerti, Anton (*b* Vienna, Austria, 21 July 1938). Pianist, teacher, and composer of Austrian birth, naturalized Canadian. He studied piano at the Longy School of Music in Cambridge, Massachusetts, with Erwin Brodky and Gregory Tucker, at the Cleveland Institute of Music with ARTHUR LOESSER, and at the Curtis Institute in Philadelphia with MIECZYSŁAW HORSZOWSKI and RUDOLF SERKIN. At age 11 he performed Grieg's Piano Concerto with Arthur Fiedler and the Boston Pops Orchestra. In 1957 Kuerti appeared with the New York Philharmonic and the Cleveland Orchestra, and since the early 1960s he has performed regularly with the Toronto SO and the Montreal SO. He has collaborated with nearly every major orchestra in North America and Canada. At the University of Toronto, Kuerti served as a pianist-in-residence (1965–8) and an associate professor (1968–72).

Kuerti specializes in music of the German romantics, especially Beethoven, but he has also championed Canadian composers and premiered Oskar Morawetz's Piano Concerto (1963) and Suite (1968) as well as Sophie C. Eckhardt-Gramatté's Piano Concerto (1967). His recorded legacy includes Beethoven's complete piano sonatas, Schubert's complete sonatas, Mendelssohn's piano

concertos, and Carl Czerny's solo piano works. Kuerti's own compositions include the *Linden Suite* for piano (1971), *Magog* for cello and piano (1972), two string quartets (1954, 1972), a symphony, *Epomeo* (1973), a violin sonata (1973), a piano concerto (1985), *Piano Man Suite* (1986), a clarinet trio (1989), and a concertino for piano, violin, and flute (1996). Kuerti performs at festivals worldwide, directs the Mooredale Youth Orchestra in Toronto, and founded the Marlboro Trio and Festival of Sound. His many awards include the Leventritt Award (1957), Juno Award (1976), Opus Award (1998), Office of the Order of Canada (1998), the Robert Schumann Prize (2007), the Banff Centre National Arts Award (2007), and the Canadian Governor General's Performing Arts Award for Lifetime Artistic Achievement (2008).

BIBLIOGRAPHY

F. Bowers: "Anton Kuerti: a Pianistic Supernova," *New York Times* (27 Feb 1972)
U. Colgrass: *For the Love of Music* (Toronto and New York, 1988)
M. Dineen: "The Thinking Person's Pianist," *Ottawa Citizen* (23 May 1998)

T. BROWN/JESSICA DUCHEN/LINCOLN BALLARD

Kuhlmann, Kathleen (*b* San Francisco, CA, 7 Dec 1950). Mezzo-soprano. After attending the Lyric Opera Center for American Artists in Chicago, she made her debut in 1979 as Maddalena (*Rigoletto*) with the Lyric Opera, with which she also sang Bersi (*Andrea Chénier*) and Princess Clarice (*The Love for Three Oranges*). She made her European debut in 1980 at Cologne as Preziosilla (*La forza del destino*), followed by Rosina and Nancy (*Martha*). In 1982 she made her debuts at La Scala as Meg Page and at Covent Garden as Ino/Juno (*Semele*), returning to Covent Garden as Carmen and, in 1992, as Bradamante (*Alcina*). Kuhlmann's other roles include Monteverdi's Octavia and Penelope, Gluck's Orpheus, Cenerentola (the role of her Glyndebourne debut in 1983), Dorabella, Nicklausse, and Charlotte (*Werther*), which she sang for her Metropolitan debut in 1989. She has a rich, vibrant tone, an agile florid technique and an exciting dramatic temperament. She has frequently given concert performances, including with the Amsterdam Bach Soloists (with whom she has recorded), the Berlin Symphony, and the Radio Symphony Orchestra Leipzig. She has been engaged by the Santa Fe Opera and the San Francisco Opera. One of her most well-known recordings is with William Christie and Les Arts Florissants in *Alcina* (2000). She can be seen in several filmed operas, including Verdi's *Rigoletto* (1991, Vienna) and Vivaldi's *Orlando Furioso* (2000, San Francisco).

ELIZABETH FORBES/JONAS WESTOVER

Kuhlmann, Rosemary (*b* New York, NY, 30 Jan 1922). Mezzo-soprano. Kulhmann is best known for creating the role of the Mother in Menotti's *Amahl and the Night Visitors*. After the start of World War II, Kuhlmann joined WAVES (Women Accepted for Volunteer Emergency Services), where she learned Morse Code to send messages to ships at sea. Her musical talent was recognized after she performed on radio programs promoting WAVES and soon had her own weekly show, *Navy Serenade*, where she sang popular songs of the period.

After the war, Kulhmann attended Juilliard on a full scholarship through the G.I. Bill, received her degree in 1950, and sang with Robert Shaw's professional chorus. She then auditioned for Menotti's *The Consul*, and earned the role of the Secretary. After performing in a revival of *Music in the Air* directed by Oscar Hammerstein, Kuhlmann landed the role of the Mother in *Amahl*, which premiered 24 December 1951 on live television. Kulhmann continued to appear in *Amahl* for the next eight Christmas Eves, her broadcast performances reaching nearly 200 million viewers.

She then toured Europe as the secretary in *The Consul* with Mennoti and sang for New York City Opera between 1952 and 1955, which included her portrayal of Magda in *The Consul*, Carmen, Meg Page in *Falstaff*, Angelina in *La cenerentola*, and Nicklauss in *Hoffmann*. Kuhlmann was also a frequent soloist with symphony orchestras and in 1957 gave two memorable NBC Opera performances in *The Saint of Bleecker Street* and *Dialogues of the Carmelites*. Her final performance was the 1961 NBC opera telecast of Leonard Kastle's *Deseret*.

BIBLIOGRAPHY

K. Whaschin: *Gian Carlo Menotti on Screen* (Jefferson, NC, 1999)

R. Paller: "Reunion: Rosemary Kuhlmann," *ON*, 71/7 (2007), 12–5

TRUDI ANN WRIGHT

Kuhn, Judy (*b* New York, NY, 20 May 1958). Singer and actor. A graduate of Oberlin Conservatory, Judy Kuhn made her Broadway acting debut in *The Mystery of Edwin Drood* (1985). She was nominated for a Drama Desk Award for her performance as Bella Cohen in the four-performance run of *Rags* (1986). Tony and Drama Desk nominations followed for her portrayal of Cosette in *Les Misérables* (1987) as well as of Florence in *Chess* (1988). She received a Tony nomination for Amalia Balash in the *She Loves Me* (1993) revival, performed as Michal in *King David* (1997) and as a replacement for Fantine in the 2006 revival of *Les Misérables*. Other non-Broadway musical theater credits include an Olivier Award-nominated turn as Maria/Futura in *Metropolis* (London, 1989), Betty Schaefer in *Sunset Boulevard* (Los Angeles, 1994), and Fosca in *Passion* (Kennedy Center's Sondheim Celebration, 2001). In addition to many nonsinging roles on stage, television and film, Kuhn provided the title character's singing voice in Disney's *Pocahontas* (1995) and its sequel.

Kuhn's performance presence is characterized by appealing vulnerability, but she is most notable for her well-trained lyric soprano voice. She sings with tremendous control and wide expressive range in both legitimate and belt styles.

BIBLIOGRAPHY

T.S. Hischak: "Judy Kuhn," *The Oxford Companion to the Musical: Theatre, Film and Television* (Oxford, 2008), 407

SHARON O'CONNELL CAMPBELL

Kuhn, Steve [Stephen Lewis] (*b* New York, NY, 24 March 1938). Jazz pianist and composer. A pianist with a distinctive voice, he started classical piano lessons at five and at 17 began studies with Madame Chaloff in Boston, where he led a trio and accompanied such visiting greats as Coleman Hawkins, Chet Baker, and Vic Dickenson. After graduating from Harvard University in 1959, he returned to New York where he worked with Kenny Dorham, John Coltrane (in the saxophonist's first quartet), Stan Getz (alongside the bass player Scott LaFaro, who influenced his playing significantly), and Charles Lloyd. He then worked in Art Farmer's quartet with Steve Swallow and Pete La Roca, appearing on the trumpeter's album *Sing Me Softly of the Blues* (1965, Atlantic). The rhythm section also recorded together on La Roca's album *Basra* (1965, BN, with the saxophonist Joe Henderson) and on Kuhn's first trio date as a leader, *Three Waves* (1966, Contact). After moving to Stockholm in 1967, Kuhn returned to the United States in 1971 and recorded *Live in New York* the following year. A series of albums for ECM showcased the pianist's unusual compositions; his group often featured Sheila Jordan, with whom he has continued to collaborate. After working as a commercial pianist in the early 1980s he returned to the jazz scene with an expanded musical palette and frequently led an all-star trio featuring Ron Carter and Al Foster. In 2009 he recorded *Mostly Coltrane* with Joe Lovano and began performing regularly in a quartet with the saxophonist as well as with his own trio.

BIBLIOGRAPHY

Feather-Gitler BEJ

L. Lyons: "Steve Kuhn," *The Great Jazz Pianists: Speaking of their Lives and Music* (New York, 1983)

RUSS MUSTO

Kuinova, Fatima (*b* Samakand, Tajikstan [Uzbekistan], 28 Dec 1920). Bukharan Jewish singer. From an early age, she immersed herself in Bukharan Jewish traditions, first under the influence of her father, a cantor, who died when she was six. Her original surname was changed to Kuinova in an attempt to avoid anti-Semitic persecution by the Soviet government. She began vocal lessons at the age of 14, performing first in her school choir and on Soviet radio. Renowned for her expertise in traditional music, she toured the Soviet Union widely, performed for foreign dignitaries and at state functions, and earned the award of Honored Artist of the Soviet Union. Kuinova also became an expert in shashmaqam, a traditional music of Central Asia which features texts that date from 15th century. In 1980, she immigrated to the United States, settling in Queens, New York, becoming an active member of the Bukharan Jewish musical community, and participating in the Soviet Jewish Community Cultural Initiative. She has performed in a variety of settings, often supported by two or three instrumentalists. In 1986, her shashmaqam ensemble performed in the Salute to Immigrant Cultures at the Statue of Liberty Centennial. In 1992, the NEA awarded Kuinova the National Heritage Fellowship.

CATHERINE WOJTANOWSKI

Kuivila, Ron(ald J.) (*b* Boston, MA, 19 Dec 1955). Composer. He studied at Wesleyan University (BA 1977) with ALVIN LUCIER and Richard Winslow, among others, and at Mills College (MFA 1979), where his teachers included ROBERT ASHLEY and DAVID BEHRMAN. He joined the music department at Wesleyan in 1982. Kuivila's style developed from the disjuncture between Cage's antipathy to recording and Walter Benjamin's belief in the potential for technical reproduction to liberate perception. While his structures generally derive from technical processes, his realized compositions resemble spontaneous improvisations. His first work, *The Essential Conservatism of Feedback* (1974), established a process of audible self-correction. His interest in motion-sensing spatial fields resulted in *Comparing Habits* (1978) and *Sailing Ship/Flying Machine* (1983), both of which function either as concert works or sound installations. In the 1980s he explored compositional algorithms (*Loose Canons*, 1986–90), high voltage phenomena (*Parallel Lines*, 1989; *Radial Arcs*, 1989; *Spark Harp*, 1989) and speech synthesis (*The Linear Predictive Zoo*, 1989). Much of his work since the 1990s took the form of site-specific, interactive multimedia installations. In *Il giardino de Babele* (1990) a virtual "performer" reacts to musical choices made by visitors as they walk over floor tiles that trigger musical pitches; in *ShadowPlay* (1996) voices in an ongoing composition are changed as visitors cast shadows over light sources. In *Sparks on Paper* (2000–5), pairs of steel wires strung around the exhibition space are highly electrified, and touches from brave visitors trigger crackling noises and rhythms. He also has composed music for dance, collaborating on several works with Susan Foster in the 1980s, and with Merce Cunningham in the 1980s and 1990s.

WRITINGS
"Sound Installations," *Words and Spaces*, ed. T. DeLio (Lanham, MD, 1989), 209–29

"VR on $5 a Day," *Immersed In Technology*, ed. M.A. Moser and D. Macleod (Cambridge, MA, 1996), 291–7

"Composing with Shifting Sand: A Conversation between Ron Kuivila and David Behrman on Electronic Music and the Ephemerality of Technology," *Leonardo Music Journal* 8 (1998), 13–6

"Open Sources: Words, circuits and the notation-realization relation in the music of David Tudor," *Leonardo music journal* 14 (2004), 17–23

WORKS
(selective list)

Chorus: The Essential Conservatism of Feedback (1974)

Concert works (all live elecs): Sketch, 1980; In Appreciation, 1982; Alphabet, 1983; Household Object, 1983; Minute Differences/Closely Observed, 1985; A Kbd Study, 1986; Loose Canons, 1986–90; The Linear Predictive Zoo, 1989; Pythagorean Puppet Theater, 1989; Fine Muck and His Good Fellows, 1990; Second Surface, 1991; Jocular State, 1992; Fugue States, 1995; Parsable, 1995; Elec Wind (for BH), 1996; Technoirama (obsessive/compulsive), 2001; An Outgoing Message, 2002; The Sophisticated Filters (collab. E. Tomney), 2002–6; Architectonirama, 2005–6

Music for dance: Studio Events (choreog. M. Cunningham), 1978–81; The Smell of Fact (choreog. S. Foster), 1985; Engrams (choreog. S. Foster), 1988; Events (choreog. M. Cunningham), 1993; Tune in/Spin Out (choreog. M. Cunningham), 1996

Installations: Comparing Habits, performance and installation, 1978; Sailing Ship/Flying Machine, 1983; Parallel Lines, 1989; Radical Arcs, 1989; Spark Harp, 1989; Il giardino de Babele, 1990; Dolci mura (Athabasca), 1992; The Factory of Light, 1993; Killeroki, 1994; VR on

$5 a Day, 1994; Spark Armonica, 1996; ShadowPlay, 1996; Broken Lines, 1997; Visitations, 1999; Sparks on Paper, 2000–5; Impulsive Arcs, 2000–2; Open Shadows, 2003; Skewed Lines, 2007–8

Recorded interviews in *NHoh*

STEVAN KEY/BENJAMIN PIEKUT

Kulintang [kolintang] The *kulintang* is a gong and drum ensemble of the southern Philippines. Although the ensemble takes various forms, Filipino Americans most commonly study and perform the traditional music of the Maguindano and Maranao people of Mindanao. Many Filipino Americans rely on recordings of folkloric troupes from the Philippines to accompany dance presentations; however, influential artists such as Danongan Kalanduyan and Usopay Cadar, both ethnomusicologists, have propagated music in the United States considered to be closer to their home traditions.

The instruments of the *kulintang* ensemble include the *kulintang*, a set of eight knobbed pot gongs on a horizontal wooden frame that plays the melodic line. The gongs ascend in pitch from the player's left to right, and they are struck with a pair of soft-wooden sticks. The *dabakan* is a standing goblet drum played with bamboo strips. The *agung* (also *agong*) is a set of two medium-sized hanging knobbed gongs of different pitches played with rubber-headed mallets. The Maguindano people also use the "talking gongs" known as *gandingan*, a set of four hanging gongs of different pitches that play rhythmic ostinatos and secondary melodic lines. The *babandil* (also *babendil*, *babendir*) is a small hanging gong used as a timekeeper.

Kulintang has gained popularity among Filipino Americans due to a number of factors, including its perceived authenticity as a pre-Hispanic and pre-colonial expression, the prominence of its teachers, and the ability to learn the fundamentals of playing through imitation and simplified notation. More advanced students often develop individualized relationships with their teachers, through which they can learn more complex pieces, how to differentiate musical genres, and sometimes how to improvise appropriately and add stylized movements to their playing. The *kulintang* is also used in nontraditional music, such as that by ELEANOR ACADEMIA.

BIBLIOGRAPHY
GMO ("Kulintang") [includes further bibliography]

U. Cadar: "The Role of Kolintang Music in Maranao Society," *Asian Music*, xxvii/2 (1996), 81–104

D. Kalanduyan: "Instruments, Instrumentation, and Social Context of Maguindanaon Kulintang Music," *Asian Music*, xxvii/2 (1996), 3–18

K. Benitez: *The Maguindanaon Kulintang: Musical Innovation, Transformation and the Concept of Binalig* (diss., U. of Michigan, 2005)

CHRISTI-ANNE CASTRO

Kullman, Charles (*b* New Haven, CT, 13 Jan 1903; *d* New Haven, CT, 8 Feb 1983). Tenor. He studied at Yale University and the Juilliard School of Music. After making his debut with the American Opera Company as Pinkerton in 1929, he went to Europe and sang the same role with the Kroll Oper in Berlin in 1931. He later appeared at the Berlin Staatsoper and Covent Garden, and in

Vienna and Salzburg. He made his Metropolitan debut in 1935 in Charles Gounod's *Faust*. For 25 seasons he sang with the company while still making guest appearances elsewhere. Kullman was one of the most versatile tenors ever to sing with the Metropolitan. He was able to adapt his lyric voice to heavy roles, and his repertory ranged from Tamino and Rinuccio to Tannhäuser and Parsifal. He had an appealing vocal quality and a pleasing stage personality. He was also an admired concert singer and sang in the famous 25th anniversary performance in Vienna of *Das Lied von der Erde* under Bruno Walter in 1936. The recording of the occasion offers a fine souvenir of Kullman's voice and artistry. He taught at Indiana University from 1956 to 1971.

BIBLIOGRAPHY

C.I. Morgan: "Charles Kullman," *Record Collector*, xx (1972), 243–58

P. Jackson: *Saturday Afternoons at the Old Met* (New York, 1992)

ALAN BLYTH/R

Kumbia Kings. Mexican American music group based in Corpus Christi, Texas. The group performed *cumbias* in a style mixed with hip-hop, rhythm and blues, and various Caribbean styles. Their contemporary Tejano sound prominently featured the electric keyboard, but silky vocals—predominantly in Spanish—were the centerpiece. The group was created in 1999 by A.B. Quintanilla (born Abraham Isaac Quintanilla III), brother of the Tejano singer Selena, as well as bassist, bandleader, and producer of her act. Quintanilla led the Kumbia Kings with Cruz Martínez, but their combination faltered and Quintanilla left the group in 2006. Martínez carried on with a remnant as Los Super Reyes. Quintanilla founded the Kumbia All Starz (or A.B. Quintanilla's All Starz).

The Kumbia Kings represented a new direction for the Tejano style, which had slowly been losing popularity since the death of Selena in 1995. Their music also offered an urban Tejano response to the popularity of international Latin pop at the turn of the 21st century.

BIBLIOGRAPHY

G. San Miguel, Jr.: *Tejano Proud: Tex-Mex Music in the Twentieth Century* (College Station, TX, 2002)

ESTEVAN CÉSAR AZCONA

Kunkel, Charles (*b* Sipperfeld, Rheinland-Pfalz, Germany, 22 July 1840; *d* St. Louis, MO, 3 Dec 1923). Pianist, publisher, and composer of German origin. He came to the United States with his father and brother, Jacob (1846–82), in 1848, and settled in Cincinnati. He studied with SIGISMOND THALBERG and LOUIS MOREAU GOTTSCHALK, and played duets with Gottschalk in the latter's recitals; he also played duets with his brother. In 1868 the Kunkel brothers moved to St. Louis, where they established a music store, publishing business, and the periodical, *Kunkel's Music Review* (1878–1906), which included articles and sheet music. Kunkel founded the St. Louis Conservatory of Music in 1872 and Kunkel's Popular Concerts (1884–1900). He also wrote piano works, including *Alpine Storm*, songs, and a comic opera, *A Welsh Rarebit* (1901).

BIBLIOGRAPHY

E.C. Krohn: "Charles Kunkel and Louis Moreau Gottschalk," *Bulletin of the Missouri Historical Society*, xxi (1965), 284

JAMES M. BURK

Kunzel, Erich (*b* New York, NY, 21 March 1935; *d* Bar Harbor, ME, 1 Sept 2009). Conductor. He attended Dartmouth College (BMus 1957) and undertook postgraduate studies at Harvard and Brown Universities; from 1963 until1964 he worked as assistant to PIERRE MONTEUX. From 1958 to 1965 he taught and was director of choral music at Brown University and also conducted the Rhode Island PO from 1960 to 1965, when he was appointed assistant to Max Rudolf, the conductor of the Cincinnati SO. He became that orchestra's associate conductor in 1967 and was its resident conductor from 1969 to 1974. Kunzel made his operatic debut in 1957 with the Santa Fe Opera Company in Pergolesi's *La serva padrona*, and conducted the American premiere of Dmitri Shostakovich's *The Nose* in 1965.

He was conductor of the Cincinnati Opera (1966) and the Cincinnati Ballet (1966–8) and served as conductor of the Cincinnati Pops Orchestra from 1965 until 2009. The *Chicago Tribune* gave him the title, "Prince of Pops." The Cincinnati Symphony Orchestra posthumously named him Founder and Conductor Emeritus of the Pops. He also worked extensively in the area of jazz and was especially noted for his long-standing collaboration with jazz pianist and composer Dave Brubeck. He gave the premiere of Brubeck's *The Light in the Wilderness* (1968, which he also recorded), *The Gates of Justice* (1969), and *The Truth is Fallen* (1971). He also collaborated with Duke Ellington, Ella Fitzgerald, Benny Goodman, Chet Atkins, George Shearing, and Sarah Vaughan.

SORAB MODI/ANYA LAURENCE

Kupferman, Meyer (*b* New York, NY, 3 July 1926; *d* nr Rhinebeck, NY, 26 Nov 2003). Composer and clarinetist. He was educated at the High School of Music and Art, New York City, and at Queens College, CUNY, but was self-taught as a composer. In 1951 he joined the music faculty of Sarah Lawrence College, where he later became professor of composition and chamber music, served five terms as department chair, and retired in 1994. He received a composition prize and recording grant from the American Academy and Institute of Arts and Letters (1981), a Guggenheim Fellowship (1975), and many other awards, grants, and commissions. A virtuoso clarinetist, Kupferman gave numerous concerts at Carnegie Recital Hall and elsewhere on the East Coast in which he played many first performances of his own and others' music. He was a prolific composer whose output encompassed a variety of forms and styles. His aesthetic is demonstrated by his *Cycle of Infinities*, a group of over 30 chamber pieces that he began in 1961. The entire group, scored for a wide range of ensembles, is based on a single 12-note set and combines serial procedures, the popular appeal and rhythmic propulsion of jazz, and aleatory elements. Thus *Infinities I* is an entire concert for solo flute; *Infinities 5* is a concert for solo cello, including pieces for cello and bass voice, cello and tape, and a concerto for cello and jazz band; and *Infinities 6* is a cantata for unaccompanied chorus. *Superflute* (1972, commissioned by Samuel Baron) was the first of many works that Kupferman called "Gestalt forms"; these include works using mirror tape, polylingual cantatas, and new theatrical and improvisational forms. Among his major "Gestalt" works are *Celestial City*, *Angel Footprints*, and *Fantasy Concerto* (all 1973). An amateur painter, he was inspired by visual artists in works such as *Motherwell Fantasy* and *Images of Chagall*. His dramatically effective film music ranges widely from the satirical German march in *Goldstein* to sentimental folksong-like material in Truman Capote's *Trilogy*. Kupferman also composed scores for ballet and opera, and arranged and orchestrated two musicals by Harold Rome. Symphony no.10 "FDR" (1981) was commissioned and given its premiere by Imre Palló and the Hudson Valley PO. He was the author of *Atonal Jazz* (Medfield, MA, 1992).

WORKS

Stage: In a Garden (op, 1, G. Stein), 1948; The Judgment (Infinities 18) (op, 3, P. Freeman, after Bible: *Genesis*), vv, taped chorus, 1966; Persephone (ballet, P. Lang), 1968; Prometheus Condemned (op, 5 scenes, Kupferman, after J.W. v. Goethe), 1975; The Proscenium:…on the Demise of Gertrude (op, 1, Kupferman, after G. Stein), 1991; stage works, incl. 4 other ops, 8 other ballets

11 syms., 1950–83, incl. no.6, Yin-Yang Sym., 1972, no.10, FDR, 1981

Other orch: Pf Conc. no.1, 1948; Libretto, 1948; Moonchild and the Doomsday Trombone, ob, insts, jazz ens, 1968; Sculptures, 1971; Conc., vc, orch, tape, 1974; Atto, 1975; Pf Conc. no.2, 1978; Phantom Rhapsody, gui, orch, 1980; Challenger, 1983; Cl Conc., 1984; Quasar Infinities, 1984; Wings of the Highest Tower, 1988; Savage Landscape, 1989; Double Conc., 2 cl, orch, 1991; Hexagon Skies, gui, orch, 1994; A Faust Conc., hn, orch, 1996; Conc. Brevis, fl, orch, 1997; over 25 other works

Cycle of Infinities 1–34, 1961–83, incl. no.1, Line Fantasy, fl, 1961, no.4 (A. Rimbaud), S, 1962, no.5, vc, B, tape, jazz band, 1962, no.6 (cant., Rimbaud), unacc. chorus, 1962, no.34, org, 1983

Str Qts, incl. no.3, 1949, no.4, 1959, no.5, 1959–60, no.6, Jazz Str Qt, 1964, no.7, 1980

c200 other chbr and solo inst works, incl. Variations, pf, 1948

Chbr Conc., fl, pf, str qt, 1955; Sonata on Jazz Elements, pf, 1958; 3 Ideas, tpt, pf, 1967; Mask of Electra, S, ob, elec hpd, 1968; Brass Qnt, 1970; Madrigal, brass qt, 1970; Superflute, taped a fl, taped pic, 1972; Angel Footprints, vn, tape, 1973; Celestial City, pf, tape, 1973; Fantasy Conc., vc, pf, tape, 1973; Premeditation, cl, gui, 1975; Abracadabra, pf, str trio, 1976; Icarus, gui, va, vc, 1976; Sound Phantoms 2, fl, va, db, 8 gui, 1979; Poems, fl, vn, vc, hp, 1984; Moonflowers, Baby!, cl, opt. perc, 1986; Images of Chagall, cl, bn, tpt, trbn, vn, db, perc, 1987; Motherwell Fantasy, cl, 1991; Chaconne Sonata, fl, 1994; Poor Little Buddha's Gate, cl, 1994; Serenade, cl, gui, 1994; improvisation and tape pieces

Vocal: A Nietzsche Cycle, S, hn, pf, 1979; Dem unbekannten Gott (cant., F. Nietzsche), S, 7 insts, 1982; Torchwine (R. Kelley), S, bassethn, pf, 1983; 2 other cants., choral works, songs

17 film scores, incl. Blast of Silence, 1961; Black Like Me, 1964; Goldstein, 1964; Trilogy, 1969; Zamzok, 1982

MSS in *Wc*

Principal publishers: Chappell, EMI, General, Mercury, Presser, Soundspells

Principal recording companies: CRI, Crystal, Louisville, Serenus, Soundspells, Vanguard, Vox

BIBLIOGRAPHY

EwenD; *GroveO*
C. Di Santo: "Perpetual Licorice: an Interview with Meyer Kupferman," *The Clarinet*, xxiv/2 (1997), 38–47
C. Vassiliades: "Infinities Odyssey: a Conversation with Meyer Kupferman," vi/2 (Feb 1999), 1–12
D. Denton: "A 75th Birthday Present: an Interview with Meyer Kupferman," *Fanfare*, xxiv/5 (May–June 2001), 87–8, 90–2

JEROME ROSEN/MICHAEL MECKNA

Kurath, Gertrude Prokosch (Tula) (*b* Chicago, IL, 19 Aug 1903; *d* Ann Arbor, MI, 1 Aug 1992). Ethnomusicologist. She studied at Bryn Mawr College (BA 1922, MA in art history 1928), concurrently receiving training in music and dance in Berlin, Philadelphia, New York, and Providence, Rhode Island (1922–8); she then attended the Yale School of Drama (1929–30). Later she was employed as a field research worker by the Wenner-Gren Foundation (1949–73), the American Philosophical Society (1951–65), and the National Museum of Canada (1962–5, 1969–70). Her main areas of interest were ethnomusicology and dance ethnology, and she made particularly substantial contributions to the study of Amerindian dance, and to dance theory and notation. She also taught dance and lectured on dance history. From 1958 to January 1972 she was dance editor for the journal *Ethnomusicology*. Her other scholarly interests included the fields of folk liturgy and rock music.

WRITINGS

"The Tutelo Harvest Rite: a Musical and Choreographic Analysis," *Scientific Monthly*, no.76 (1953), 153–62
"Chippewa Sacred Songs in Religious Metamorphosis," *Scientific Monthly*, no.79 (1954), 312–7
"The Tutelo Fourth Night Spirit Release Singing," *Midwest Folklore*, iv (1954), 87–105
Songs of the Wigwam (Delaware, OH, 1955)
"Antiphonal Songs of Eastern Woodland Indians," *MQ*, xlii (1956), 520–6
"Dance Relatives of Mid-Europe and Middle America," *Journal of American Folklore*, lxix (1956), 286–98
"Catholic Hymns of Michigan Indians," *Anthropological Quarterly*, xxx/2 (1957), 31–44
"Cochiti Choreographies and Songs," in C.H. Lange: *Cochiti* (Austin, 1959/R), 539–56
"Menomini Indian Dance Songs in a Changing Culture," *Midwest Folklore*, ix (1959), 31–8
"Panorama of Dance Ethnology," *Current Anthropology*, i (1960), 233–54; repr. in *History, Definitions, and Scope of Ethnomusicology*, ed. K.K. Schelemay (New York, 1992), 71–92
with S. Martí: *Dances of Anáhuac: the Choreography and Music of Precortesian Dances* (Chicago, 1964)
Iroquois Music and Dance: Ceremonial Arts of Two Seneca Longhouses (Washington DC, 1964/R)
"Dogrib Choreography and Music," *The Dogrib Hand Game*, ed. J. Helm and N.O. Lurie (Ottawa, 1966), 13–28
"The Kinetic Ecology of Yaqui Dance Instrumentation," *EthM*, x (1966), 28–42
Michigan Indian Festivals (Ann Arbor, 1966)
"Dance, Drama, and Music," *Handbook of Middle American Indians*, vi: *Social Anthropology*, ed. M. Nash (Austin, 1967), 158–90
Dance and Song Rituals of Six Nations Reserve, Ontario (Ottawa, 1968)
with A. Garcia: *Music and Dance of the Tewa Pueblos* (Santa Fe, 1970)
"Space Rock: Music and Dance of the Electronic Era," *The Performing Arts: Music and Dance: Chicago 1973*, 319–30
Tutelo Rituals on Six Nations Reserve, Ontario (Ann Arbor, 1981)

BIBLIOGRAPHY

J.W. Kealiinohomoku and F.J. Gillis: "Special Bibliography: Gertrude Prokosch Kurath," *EthM*, xiv (1970), 114–28 [incl. complete list of pubns to 1970]

DORIS J. DYEN

Kurka, Robert (Frank) (*b* Cicero, IL, 22 Dec 1921; *d* New York, NY, 12 Dec 1957). Composer. He studied briefly with OTTO LUENING and DARIUS MILHAUD but was principally self-taught. He was a faculty member at Queens College, CUNY, and, briefly, at Dartmouth College. He received a Guggenheim Fellowship (1951–2), an award from the National Institute of Arts and Letters (1952), and a Creative Arts Award from Brandeis University (1957).

Kurka is best known for his orchestral suite *The Good Soldier Schweik* (1956), which he later expanded into a two-act opera. *Schweik* is often compared with Kurt Weill's *Kleine Dreigroschenmusik*; not only are its instrumentation and tonal language similar, but both combine references to popular musical idioms (dances, marches, the ballad style) with pungent dissonances and brittle rhythms for ironic effect.

Neo-classical in style and influenced by the folk music of former Czechoslovakia (his parents' birthplace), Kurka's work is most particularly characterized by its use of repeated melodic and rhythmic motifs, the appearance of dissonant elements within a tonal structure, and an energetic rhythmic drive (notably in the Symphony no.2 and the Serenade).

WORKS
Opera: The Good Soldier Schweik (2, L. Allen, after J. Hašek), 1957, NY City Op, 23 April 1958 [completed by H. Kay]

Orch: Serenade (after W. Whitman), op.25, small orch, perf. 1954; Chbr Sym., op.3; Sym., brass, str, op.7; Conc., vn, chbr orch, op.8; Music for Orch, op.11; 3 Pieces, op.15; Sym. no.1, op.17; The Good Soldier Schweik, op.22, suite, fl, pic, ob, eng hn, cl, b cl, cbbn, perc, 1956; Sym. no.2, op.24, perf. 1958; John Henry, op.27, orch; Julius Caesar, sym. epilogue (after W. Shakespeare), op.28; Conc., op.31, 2 pf, str, tpt; Mar Conc., op.34, perf. 1958; Ballad, op.36, hn, str; Chbr Sinfonietta, op.39

Vocal: Who shall Speak for the People (C. Sandburg), TTBB; Song of the Broadaxe, TTBB; several choral pieces and songs

Chbr and solo inst: Sonata, op.5, vn; Pf Sonatina, op.6; Str Qt no.4, op.12, perf. 1950; For the Piano, op.13, pf; Music for cl, hn, tpt, vn, db, op.14; Pf Trio, op.16; Pf Sonata, op.20; Sonatina, vc, op.21; Sonata no.3, vn, pf, op.23, perf. 1953; Dance Suite, op.29, pf 4 hands; Sonatina for Young Persons, op.40, pf; 7 Moravian Folksongs, fl, ob, cl, bn; Notes from Nature, pf; Ballad, hn; 4 other str qts; 3 other vn sonatas; pf pieces

Principal publisher: Weintraub

BIBLIOGRAPHY
J.W. Freeman: "Robert Kurka," *ON*, xxiii/2 (1958), 8 only
K. Kastner: "Creston, Milhaud and Kurka," *Percussive Notes*, xxxii/4 (1994), 83–7

JAMES WIERZBICKI/R

Kuronen, Darcy (*b* Deadwood, SD, 9 Nov 1955). Curator and organologist. He studied cabinet making at Western Dakota Vocational–Technical Institute (1978) and harpsichord (BM 1982) and the history of musical instruments (MM 1986) at the University of South Dakota. While an undergraduate, he served as research assistant at the National Music Museum. Since 1986 he has worked at the Museum of Fine Arts, Boston, as assistant curator (1986–1995) and subsequently curator of musical instruments (from 1995); in 2010 he was named the first Pappalardo Curator of Music Instruments. His tenure has included the exhibitions "Dangerous Curves: Art of the Guitar" (2000), and "Sounds of the Silk Road: Musical Instruments of Asia" (2005). Kuronen's research on the history of musical instrument manufacturing in the United States has focused particularly on pianos, violins, guitars, and free reeds. He has also created an inventory of musical instruments in museums and historical societies throughout New England. His article "The Musical Instruments of Benjamin Crehore" was awarded the Frances Densmore Prize in 1992 by the American Musical Instrument Society. Kuronen has served as vice president and board member of the American Musical Instrument Society, on the board of directors of the Midwest Historical Keyboard Society, and as volunteer curator for the Boston SO's collection of historical instruments.

WRITINGS
"The Musical Instruments of Benjamin Crehore," *The Journal of the Museum of Fine Arts, Boston*, iv (1992), 52–79
Dangerous Curves: the Art of the Guitar (Boston, 2000)
"Early Violin Making in New England," *JAMIS*, xxviii (2002), 5–62
MFA Highlights: Musical Instruments (Boston, 2004)
"An Organized Piano by Alpheus Babcock," *Organ Restoration Reconsidered: Proceedings of a Colloquium*, ed. John R. Watson (Warren, MI, 2005), 159–69
"James A. Bazin and the Development of Free-Reed Instruments in America," *JAMIS*, xxxi (2005), 133–82

SARAH ADAMS HOOVER

Kurzweil, Raymond (*b* Queens, NY, 1948). Manufacturer of digital synthesizers, computer scientist, author, and inventor. In 1965, he built a computer that composed original melodies using pattern recognition; it analyzed patterns in musical compositions and then created original melodies based on these patterns. This invention won him First Prize at the International Science Fair and national attention. He founded Kurzweil Computer Products in 1974. The company created the first omni-font (any font) Optical Character Recognition (OCR) technology, the first CCD flat-bed scanner, and the first full text-to-speech synthesizer. The three technologies were combined to create the Kurzweil Reading Machine, which was announced on 13 January 1976. This led to a collaboration with the musician Stevie Wonder, who purchased the first production unit. On 1 July 1982, Kurzweil founded Kurzweil Music Systems, with Wonder as musical advisor. The company set out to invent electronic instruments that could capture and recreate the true sounds and musical responses of acoustic musical instruments. Kurzweil created the K250 keyboard synthesizer (originally designed in late 1982, exhibited in June 1983 with production beginning in 1984). The keyboard had a 12-track sequencer, sound layering capabilities, and extensive sound modification facilities, and is considered the first electronic musical instrument to successfully reproduce the sounds of acoustic instruments. The K250 was followed by the K1000 series. Kurzweil Music Systems was sold to Young Chang in 1990, with Ray Kurzweil as a consultant through 1994. Since 1994, Kurzweil has created numerous noninstrument-related companies and inventions.

BIBLIOGRAPHY

D. Byrd and C. Yavelow, "The Kurzweil 250 Digital Synthesizer," *Computer Music Journal*, x/1 (Spring, 1986): 64–86

R. Kurzweil, *The Age of Intelligent Machines* (Cambridge, MA, 1990), 278–81

SARAH DETERS RICHARDSON

Kuss, Malena (*b* Córdoba, Argentina, 11 Aug 1940). Musicologist of Argentine birth. She studied composition with Alberto Ginastera in Buenos Aires before coming to the United States, where she studied piano under ROSINA LHÉVINNE (1961–3), GYÖRGY SÁNDOR, and Alexander Uninsky at Southern Methodist University (MMus 1964). She subsequently received the PhD in musicology (1976) at the University of California, Los Angeles under ROBERT M. STEVENSON. In Los Angeles, she also studied analysis of 20th-century music with Leonard Stein. In 1973 she received a Fulbright-Hays doctoral dissertation fellowship for research on operas by Argentine composers. She taught musicology with specialization in 20th-century music at the University of North Texas, Denton from 1976 until her retirement in 1999; she became Professor Emeritus in 2000. Between 2008 and 2010 she served as Consulting Curator for Latin America and the Caribbean at the Musical Instrument Museum, (Phoenix, Arizona). As a specialist in Latin America, she has published two books and over 60 articles on music historiography, compositional approaches to the incorporation of folk elements in operas, pitch organization in works by Ginastera, and musical traditions in comparative cultural contexts. Her collaborative history of performing traditions in Latin America and the Caribbean (2004 and 2007) gathered contributions by over 100 scholars in 36 countries and introduced the work of many musicologists in English translation, thereby disseminating their perspectives in the Anglophone sphere of influence. She has received numerous awards, most notably the Platinum Konex Award for long-term achievements in the arts (Buenos Aires, 2009), and has been active in many scholarly societies, including serving as Vice President (2009–12) of the International Musicological Society, and on the Advisory Panel of Grove Music Online.

WRITINGS
(selective list)

Latin American Music: an Annotated Bibliography of Reference Sources and Research Materials (Paris, 1984)

"Current State of Bibliographic Research in Latin American Music," *Fontes artis musicae*, xxxiv/4 (1984), 20–39

Alberto Ginastera: Musikmanuskripte (Inventare der Paul Sacher Stiftung, No.8) (Winterthur, Switzerland 1990)

"The Structural Role of Folk Elements in 20th-Century Art Music," *Proceedings of the XIVth Congress, International Musicological Society: Transmission and Reception of Musical Culture*, ed. L. Bianconi, et. al (Torino, 1990), vol. iii, 99–120

"Identity and Change: Nativism in Operas from Argentina, Brazil, and Mexico," *Musical Repercussions of 1492: Encounters in Text and Performance*, ed. C.E. Robertson (Washington, DC, 1992), 299–335

"The 'Invention' of America: Encounter Settings on the Latin American Lyric Stage," *Proceedings of the XVth Congress, International Musicological Society* (Madrid, 1992), *Revista de Musicología*, xvi/1 (1993), 185–204

"La certidumbre de la utopía: Estrategias interpretativas para una historia musical americana,"*Música* (La Habana, Boletín de Casa de las Américas), Nueva Época, iv (2000), 4–24

"'Si quieres saber de mí, te lo dirán unas piedras': Alberto Ginastera, autor de *Bomarzo*," *Ópera en España e Hispanoamérica*, ed. E.C. Rodicio and Á. Torrente (Madrid, 2002), vol. ii, 393–411

ed.: *Music in Latin America and the Caribbean*, vol. 1: *Performing Beliefs: Indigenous Peoples of South America, Central America, and Mexico* (Austin, 2004)

"Il pensiero occidentale da un punto di vista transculturale (la decolonizzazione dell'America latina)"/"Western thought from a transcultural perspective: Decolonizing Latin America," *Enciclopedia della musica: L'unità della musica*, vol. 5, ed. J.-J. Nattiez (Torino, 2005), 32–64

ed.: *Music in Latin America and the Caribbean*, vol. 2: *Performing the Caribbean Experience* (Austin, 2007)

MARK McKNIGHT

Kwalwasser, Jacob (*b* New York, NY, 27 Feb 1894; *d* Pittsburgh, PA, 7 Aug 1977). Educator. He studied at the University of Pittsburgh (BA, BEd 1917) and the University of Iowa (MA 1923, PhD 1925); during his residence at Iowa he served as head of the music education department and was elected president of the Iowa State Music Teachers Association. His principal position was at Syracuse University, where he taught for 28 years and was head of music education (1926–50) and of research in music education (1951–4). He also taught at Columbia University, the Juilliard School, the Chicago Musical College, and the universities of Texas, Minnesota, Idaho, and Arkansas. Best known for his work in musical testing and measurement, Kwalwasser developed tests of both music achievement and music aptitude, and, in addition to numerous publications in music and psychology journals, wrote *Tests and Measurements in Music* (New York, 1927), *Problems in Music Education* (New York, 1932), and *Exploring the Musical Mind* (New York, 1955). He was inducted into the Music Educators Hall of Fame in 2006.

ALICE-ANN DARROW/R

Kwan, Leonard (Keala) (*b* Honolulu, HI, 1931; *d* Honolulu, HI, 13 Aug 2000). Hawaiian slack key guitarist. Best known for his recordings and innovative use of amplification, Kwan was the first slack key guitarist to enjoy a hit with an original composition, "Opihi Moemoe." His style has exerted enormous influence on younger musicians. It is very *nahenahe* (sweet) with subtle use of passing tones, modulations and idiomatic bass runs. Kwan favored *wahine* (Major 7th) tunings, especially (C-G-D-G-B-D) often called Leonard's C, and Leonard's F (C-F-C-G-C-E).

Kwan's uncle Joseph "Pete" Hauoli taught him slack key in the 1940s. He also played bass and alto saxophone. As a bassist he turned professional in 1947 with dance bands and Hawaiian musicians such as Sonny Chillingworth. He began recording in 1957 for Island Recording Sound. He wrote and first recorded "Opihi Moemoe" for Tradewinds in 1960. It quickly became a standard. Offers for studio work at Tradewinds followed and he appeared on about 60 recordings with other artists. In 1974, he released *The Old Way* album, the first slack key album to list the tunings used. With guitarist/librarian Dennis Ladd, Kwan also compiled a slack key instruction book. He retired from active performance due to medical problems just as the audience for slack key was building. In the late 1980s Kwan began an extensive documentation project with George Winston for the Dancing Cat label. He also gave several concerts with his sons Keala and Kevin. In 1993, Kwan received the Bank of Hawai'i Ki Ho'alu Award from the Hawai'i Academy of Recording Arts. In 1994, he was named a Living Treasure by the City and County of Honolulu.

J.W. JUNKER

Kyr, Robert (*b* 1952). Composer and educator. He received his BA from Yale University (1974) and attended the Royal College of Music, London, and the Dartington Summer School for the Arts, where he studied with Sir Peter Maxwell Davies (1974–6). After returning to the United States, Kyr studied with GEORGE ROCHBERG and GEORGE CRUMB at the University of Pennsylvania (MA 1980) and with DONALD MARTINO and EARL KIM at Harvard University (PhD 1989). Kyr has held teaching positions in composition and theory at the Aspen Music School, the Hartt School of Music, the Justus-Liebig-Universität Giessen, the Longy School of Music (Cambridge, MA), UCLA, Yale University, and since 1990, at the University of Oregon where he is the Philip H. Knight Professor of Composition and Theory, and chair of the composition department. He also serves as director of the Oregon Bach Festival Composers Symposium, the University of Oregon Composers Forum, the Music Today Festival, the Vanguard Concert and Workshop Series, and the Pacific Rim Gamelan. Kyr has received awards and commissions from, among others, the Canada Council, Chamber Music America, the Massachusetts Council for the Arts and Humanities, Meet the Composer, the National Endowment for the Arts, the New England Foundation for the Arts, the Oregon Regional Arts and Culture Council, the Paul Allen Foundation, the Scottish Arts Council, and Telarc International. His music has been performed around the world by a variety of ensembles including the Back Bay Chorale (Boston), Cappella Nova (Scotland), the Moscow State Chamber Choir, the New England Philharmonic, the Oregon Symphony, the San Francisco Symphony Chorus, and the Yale Symphony Orchestra, among others.

An activist for world peace and environmentalism, Kyr has been involved with a number of projects that bring together musicians from diverse cultures. The concepts and titles of many of Kyr's works reveal spiritual, environmental, or metaphysical themes, including Violin Concerto no.1 *(On the Nature of Love)*, *The Passion According to Four Evangelists*, *In Praise of Music*, *A Time for Life*, *Songs of the Shining Wind*, and *White Tigers*. He also has created numerous large-scale projects that focus on peace and reconciliation. He envisioned and implemented "Waging Peace through Singing" (2000–2), a global initiative that encouraged the creation of an international repertoire of choral music based on peace-related texts. Similarly, as the composer-in-residence of the Oregon Repertory Singers (2000–4), Kyr created an extensive repertoire of music on peace-related themes such as *Alleluia for*

Peace, Eight Steps for Peace, Into the Hour of New Life, O Jerusalem, and *On the Nature of Creation*, a large-scale motet cycle. For most of these works, he either wrote or created composite texts from diverse sources that are elegantly crafted so that each word is clearly audible. His compositions are stylistically diverse and he considers himself to be a "21st-century composer"; yet, while much of his choral music is distinguished by a compelling lyricism and contrapuntal mastery that arises from his fondness for early music, he categorizes himself as neither a modernist nor neo-Romantic. Although his music is intensely melodic, essentially consonant, and often harmonically and rhythmically complex, Kyr's works are often luminous and sometimes ecstatic—a consequence that derives from the synthesis of both modern and ancient harmonic practices, as well as Western and Asian musical traditions.

WORKS

Piano: Surfacing (1979); White Tigers (1987); Transcendental Nocturnes (1992)

Chamber: Three Rounds, 6 vlc (1986); Marimolin Variations, marim, vn (1990); Millennium Dreamscape, fl, clar, vn, vlc, perc, pf (1999); Pure Silver, fl solo, 5 fl (2005); Riverbend, trpts (2007)

Symphonic: Voyage, ch orc (1974); The Aleph (1980); Symphony No. 1, "Book of the Hours," sop, cntr ten, orch (1988); Symphony No. 5, "Voice of the Rainbow" (1990); Violin Concerto No. 1, "On the Nature of Love," vn, str orc (1996); Symphony No. 10, "Ah, Nagasaki: Ashes into Light," 4 soloists, 2 youth soloists, double chor, Noh chanter, taiko ens, orc (2005)

Vocal: Songs of the Shining Wind, sop, cntr ten, ten, lute, vielle (1991); The Passion According to Four Evangelists, 4 soloists, chor, orc (1995); On the Nature of Creation, mixed chor (2000); Into the Hour of New Life, mixed chor (2001); O Jerusalem (2002); Eight Steps for Peace, treble chor (2003); Alleluia for Peace (2005); In Praise of Music, mixed chor (2006); A Time for Life, 3 soloists, mixed chor, strngs (2007); numerous other works in all categories

Principal recording companies: New Albion, Telarc

ROBERT PAUL KOLT

Kyser, Kay [James King Kern] (*b* Rocky Mount, NC, 18 June 1905; *d* Chapel Hill, NC, 23 July 1985). Bandleader, actor, humanitarian, and religious leader. Sometimes known as "The Ol' Professor of Swing," Kyser climbed to the heights of pop success from 1935 to 1950 with an orchestra that played novelty songs as well as swing and ballads. Though he couldn't read music or play an instrument, he was a brilliant businessman and front man, chalking up 35 top ten records and 11 number ones.

Kyser attended and graduated from UNC Chapel Hill (business degree, 1928), where he produced plays, organized a band (1926), and began to use "Kay" (derived from his middle initial) as his stage name. They recorded six songs for the Victor label between 1928 and 1929, but didn't record commercially again until 1935. They broke into the big time in Chicago in 1937 with a quiz and music radio show called *Kay's Klass* (later *Kay Kyser's College of Musical Knowledge*). He played against type with much silliness, swing dancing with contestants and making faces. He also further perfected a routine called "singing song titles," where the title is sung at the start of each arrangement. This was used on many Kyser records for Brunswick, which signed them in 1935, and later on Columbia. "Three Little Fishies," "Jingle Jangle, Jingle," "Praise the Lord and pass the ammunition," and "On a Slow Boat to China" are among the popular Kyser titles. During the war years, Kyser's also band played the Hollywood Canteen and entertained the troops tirelessly, performing in excess of 1800 camp shows in the United States and the Pacific region. He also appeared in seven feature films, many of which were hits with the teen set. After *College of Musical Knowledge* ended its run on radio in 1949 and a short-run on television the next year, Kyser, who battled health issues (from which he later recovered),

decided to retire permanently. He moved to Chapel Hill and became a practitioner, teacher, and lecturer of Christian Science. Toward the end of his life, he almost always refused to discuss his big band days at length, preferring to "live in the present."

BIBLIOGRAPHY

G.T. Simon: *The Big Bands* (New York, 1967)

R. Palmer: Obituary, *New York Times* (24 July 1985)

S. Beasley: *Kay Kyser—The Ol' Professor of Swing! America's Forgotten Superstar* (Northridge, CA, 2009)

STEVEN BEASLEY